Ounces	9 x 12 envelope, 9 x 12 SASE number of pages	9 x 12 SASE (for return trips) number of pages	First Class ** Postage	Third Class ** Postage	Postage from U.S. to Canada **
under 2	...	1 to 2	$.39*	$.39*	$.63*
2	1 to 4	3 to 8	.52	.52	.73
3	5 to 10	9 to 12	.75	.75	.86
4	11 to 16	13 to 19	.98	.98	1.09
5	17 to 21	20 to 25	1.21	1.21	1.32
6	22 to 27	26 to 30	1.44	1.21	1.55
7	28 to 32	31 to 35	1.67	1.33	1.78
8	33 to 38	36 to 41	1.90	1.33	2.01
9	39 to 44	42 to 46	2.13	1.44	2.24
10	45 to 49	47 to 52	2.36	1.44	2.47
11	50 to 55	53 to 57	2.59	1.56	2.70
12-32	56 to 99	58 to 101	2.90	1.56	2.80

* This cost includes a 10¢ assessment for oversized mail that is light in weight.

** A postage increase proposed for 1995 will likely raise the cost of a first-class stamp to 32¢. All other postal rates will increase accordingly—to about higher than current rates. Check with your local post office for exact rates.

1995
Writer's
Market

Where & how
to sell what you write

Editor: Mark Garvey

Assistant Editor: Kirsten Holm

WRITER'S DIGEST BOOKS
Cincinnati, Ohio

Distributed in Canada by
McGraw-Hill Ryerson
300 Water St.
Whitby, Ontario L1N 9B6

Distributed in Australia by
Kirby Book Co.
Private Bag No. 19
Alexandria NSW 2015

Managing Editor, Market Books Department:
Constance J. Achabal
Production Editor: Richard D. Muskopf

This edition of Writer's Market features a "self-jacket" that eliminates the need for a separate dust jacket. It provides sturdy protection for your book while it saves paper, trees and energy.

Library of Congress Catalog Number
31-20772
International Standard Serial Number
0084-2729
International Standard Book Number
0-89879-673-3

Cover photo: Guildhaus Photographics
U.S. Postage by the Page by Carolyn Lieberg
Canadian Postage by the Page by Barbara Murrin

Contents

Getting Published

Before Your First Sale *5*

Whether you're new to the writing business or you'd like to brush up on the fundamentals of selling your writing, this section is for you. Author Scott Smith discusses his first novel's path to publication. Magazine writer Kathleen Heins shares advice on establishing your freelance career.

Current Trends in Publishing, by Kirsten Holm *22*

This analysis of recent trends in the world of book and magazine publishing will clue you in to what's hot, what's not and what's on the horizon.

The Business of Writing

Minding the Details *28*

From contracts to rights, copyright, money and taxes, this section will help you negotiate and secure fair agreements, keep track of your rights, and handle earnings responsibly and legally. Book publishing executive Brandon Toropov and magazine editor Pamela O'Brien offer valuable tips for writers hoping to break in.

A Writer's Guide to Money, by Gary Provost *37*

Provost, a successful writer and teacher, sets the record straight about where the money is in publishing and how to get your fair share.

How Much Should I Charge? *42*

Setting your freelance writing fees can be a real headache. Our suggestions for determining your fees — along with our list of hundreds of freelance jobs and typical fees — will help take some of the guesswork out of it.

The Markets

Book Publishers 56

Hundreds of places to sell your book ideas. The introduction to this section includes tips on approaching publishers and interviews with Bantam VP Nita Taublit and nonfiction author Tom Ogden.

Canadian and International Book Publishers 213

Subsidy/Royalty Book Publishers 232

Small Presses 254

Book Producers 270

Consumer Magazines 280

Over a thousand magazines in dozens of subject categories. The introduction features tips on selling your article ideas to magazine editors as well as an interview with USA Weekend managing editor, Amy Eisman.

Trade, Technical and Professional Journals *670*

The magazines in this section serve a wide variety of trades and professions. The introduction tells how to break in and establish yourself in the trades. Agricultural freelancer Linda Leake tells how she has succeeded in her trade niche.

Resources

From the Editors

Writers are a fortunate lot. What other business allows and even encourages such shameless whim-following as does the business of freelance writing? One writer makes the rounds with a New York City exterminator for the sake of a story. Another navigates the Amazon in a dugout canoe—again, for the story. Still another prefers to gather his facts in a less exotic locale—the stacks of his local library. And for some, of course, the journey is not in the real world at all, but along a path through the imagination. The appeal of being a writer is obvious: Writers enjoy the luxury of pursuing their interests.

When a writer's interests match the interests of an editor and the editor's audience, publication generally follows. Luckily, for the thousands of writers pursuing their own ideas, there are outlets for nearly every kind of writing (always excepting, of course, *bad* writing). There is a magazine published to match almost every special interest imaginable, and you would be hard-pressed to think of a topic that has not been the subject of a book.

Learning about the broad range of publishing opportunities available to writers is one of the most interesting and encouraging aspects of working on *Writer's Market*. We are always gratified to see each year's deluge of new *Writer's Market* listings funneling into our offices, a sure sign that, while individual publishers and periodicals may come and go, the market for freelance writing remains vibrant. And with the explosion of electronic publishing, multimedia and interactive media gathering steam, writers can expect an even wider market for their work in the future.

We are pleased to offer again this year thousands of markets (including more than 700 new ones) for writing of every description. Every listing in the book reflects the most current information available about the market at press time. Whether you're writing mainstream how-to books or searching out obscure corners of your world for article ideas, you'll find book publishers and magazines in this year's *Writer's Market* that publish on subjects you want to write about. And we'll give you plenty of tips on how to contact the listed publishers and improve your chances of making sales.

In order to make room for the increased number of book and magazine publishers' listings in this year's *Writer's Market*, we have temporarily removed the Literary and "Little" section of Consumer Magazines. For information on literary magazine markets, check *Novel & Short Story Writer's Market*, published every spring, and *Poet's Market*, published every fall.

As always, we provide a wealth of added features that will help you understand the publishing industry and approach it professionally. The articles in the first section of the book are designed to teach you the ins and outs of the writing business. In Getting Published, you'll learn all the basics, including how to target likely markets for your ideas, how to grab an editor's interest with queries and book proposals, how to format your manuscripts for submission and much more. Current Trends in Publishing clues you in to the state of the book and magazine publishing industries. The Business of Writing offers advanced information for writers who know the basics and would like to brush up on topics—including copyright, contracts, finances and taxes—that are typically of concern to writers who are already selling their work. Our updated How Much Should I Charge? feature returns, with pages of specific figures and advice to help you set your freelance fees. In "A Writer's Guide to Money," successful freelancer Gary Provost talks frankly about the money you can expect to make as a writer and how you might make more.

Along the way, you'll read interviews with editors and successful writers offering tips that will help you get published. Our interview subjects this year include a first-time novelist, book publishing executives from small and large presses, a first-time nonfiction book author, successful magazine freelancers, magazine editors and a film director. These experienced voices offer useful insights into the expectations and realities of today's publishing marketplace.

Whatever direction your writing takes you, *Writer's Market* is here to help you find a market and an audience for your work. We wish you success in reaching your writing goals in 1995.

Mark Garvey
Editor

Kirsten Holm
Assistant Editor

How to Get the Most Out of *Writer's Market*

Writer's Market is here to assist you in deciding where and how to submit your writing to appropriate markets. Each individual listing contains information about the editorial focus of the market, how they prefer material to be submitted, payment information and other helpful tips.

Where to start

A quick look at the Table of Contents will familiarize you with the arrangement of *Writer's Market*. The three largest sections of the book are the market listings of Book Publishers; Consumer Magazines; and Trade, Technical and Professional Journals. You will also find sections for scriptwriting markets, syndicates and greeting card publishers. Be sure to read the introduction for each section before you turn to the listings. The section introductions contain specific information about trends, submission methods and other helpful resources for the material included in that section.

Narrowing your search

After you've identified the market categories you're interested in, you can begin researching specific markets within each section.

Publishers listed in the Book Publishers section are categorized, in the Book Publishers Subject Index, according to types of books they are interested in. If, for example, you plan to write a book on a religious topic, simply turn to the Book Publishers Subject Index and look under the Religion subhead in Nonfiction for the names and page numbers of companies that publish such books.

Consumer Magazines and Trade, Technical and Professional Journals are categorized by subject to make it easier for you to identify markets for your work. If you want to publish an article dealing with some aspect of retirement, you could look under the Retirement category of Consumer Magazines to find an appropriate market. You would want to keep in mind, however, that magazines in other categories might also be open to your article (for example, women's magazines publish such material as well). Keep your antennae up while studying the markets: less obvious markets often offer the best opportunities.

Interpreting the markets

Once you've identified companies or publications that cover the subjects you're interested in, you can begin evaluating specific listings to pinpoint the markets most receptive to your work and most beneficial to you.

In evaluating an individual listing, first check the location of the company, the types of material it is interested in seeing, submission requirements, and rights and payment policies. Depending upon your personal concerns, any of these items could be a deciding factor as you determine which markets you plan to approach. In addition to this information, many listings also include a reporting time. This lets you know how long it will typically take for the publisher to respond to your initial query or submission. (We suggest that you allow an additional month for a response, just in case your submission is under further review or the publisher is backlogged.)

Check the Glossary at the back of the book for unfamiliar words. Specific symbols and abbreviations are explained in the table on page 54. The most important abbreviation is SASE—self-addressed, stamped envelope. Always enclose one when you send unsolicited queries, proposals or manuscripts. This requirement is not included in most of the individual market listings because it is a "given" that you must follow if you expect to receive a reply.

A careful reading of the listings will reveal many editors are very specific about their needs. Your chances of success increase if you follow directions to the letter. Often companies do not accept unsolicited manuscripts and return them unread. Read each listing closely, heed the tips given, and follow the instructions. Work presented professionally will normally be given more serious consideration.

Whenever possible, obtain writer's guidelines before submitting material. You can usually obtain them by sending a SASE to the address in the listing. You should also familiarize yourself with the company's publications. Many of the listings contain instructions on how to obtain sample copies, catalogs or market lists. The more research you do upfront, the better your chances of acceptance, publication and payment.

Additional help

This year's book contains articles on making money with your writing, current trends in book and magazine publishing and much more. "Insider Reports"—interviews with writers, editors and publishers—offer advice and an inside look at publishing. Some listings contain editorial comments, indicated by a bullet (●), that provide additional information about the listings discovered during our compilation of this year's *Writer's Market*.

Minding the Details offers valuable information about rights, taxes and other practical matters. New or unpublished writers should also read Before Your First Sale. There is also a helpful section titled How Much Should I Charge? that offers guidance for setting your freelance writing fees.

Getting Published

Before Your First Sale

Many writers new to the craft feel that achieving publication—and getting paid for their work—is an accomplishment so shrouded in mystery and magic that there can be little hope it will ever happen to *them*. Of course, that's nonsense. All writers were newcomers once. Getting paid for your writing is not a matter of learning a bit of privileged information or being handed the one "key" to success by an insider. There's not even a secret handshake.

Making money from your writing will require three things of you:
- Good writing;
- Knowledge of writing markets (magazines and book publishers) and how to approach them professionally;
- Persistence.

Good writing without marketing know-how and persistence might be art, but who's going to know if it never sells? A knowledge of markets without writing ability or persistence is pointless. And persistence without talent and at least a hint of professionalism is simply irksome. But a writer who can combine the above-mentioned virtues stands a good chance of not only selling a piece occasionally, but enjoying a long and successful writing career.

You may think a previously unpublished writer has a difficult time breaking into the field. As with any profession, experience is valued, but that doesn't mean publishers are closed to new writers. While it is true some editors are partial to working with certain writers, most are open to professional submissions and good ideas from any writer, and quite a few magazine editors like to feature different styles and "voices" in their publications.

In nonfiction book publishing, experience in writing or in a particular subject area is valued by editors as an indicator of the author's ability and expertise in the subject. Again, as with magazines, the idea is paramount, and new authors break in every year with good, timely ideas.

As you work in the writing field, you may read articles or talk to writers and editors who give conflicting advice. There are some norms in the business, but they are few. You'll probably hear as many different routes to publication as writers you talk to. You could easily drive yourself crazy trying to do, or not do, everything you're told.

The following information on submissions has worked for many writers, but it's not the *only* method you can follow. It's easy to get wrapped up in the specifics of submitting (should my name go at the top left or right of the manuscript?) and fail to consider weightier matters (is this idea appropriate for this market?). Let common sense and courtesy be your guides as you work with editors, and eventually you'll develop your own most effective submission methods.

Targeting your ideas

Writers often think of an interesting story, complete the manuscript and then begin to look for a suitable publisher or magazine. While this approach is common for fiction, poetry and screenwriting, it reduces your chances of success in many other writing areas. Instead, try choosing categories that interest you and study those sections in *Writer's Market*. Select several listings that you consider good prospects for your type of writing. Sometimes the individual listings will even help you generate ideas.

Next, make a list of the potential markets for each idea. Make the initial contact with markets using the method stated in the market listings. If you exhaust your list of possibilities, don't give up. Reevaluate the idea, revise it or try another angle. Continue developing ideas and approaching markets with them. Identify and rank potential markets for an idea and continue the process.

As you submit to the various periodicals listed in *Writer's Market*, it's important to remember that every magazine is published with a particular slant and audience in mind. Probably the number one complaint we hear from editors is that writers often send material and ideas that are completely wrong for their magazines. The first mark of professionalism is to know your market well. That knowledge starts here in *Writer's Market*, but you should supplement that by searching out back issues of the magazines you wish to write for and learning what specific subjects they have published in past issues and how those subjects have been handled.

Prepare for rejection and the sometimes lengthy wait. When a submission is returned, check your file folder of potential markets for that idea. Cross off the market that rejected the idea and immediately mail an appropriate submission to the next market on your list. If the editor has given you suggestions or reasons as to why the manuscript was not accepted, you might want to incorporate these when revising your manuscript.

About rejection. Rejection is a way of life in the publishing world. It's inevitable in a business that deals with such an overwhelming number of applicants for a limited number of positions. Anyone who has published has lived through many rejections, and writers with thin skin are at a distinct disadvantage. The key to surviving rejection is to remember that it is not a personal attack—it's merely a judgment about the appropriateness of your work for that particular market at that particular time. Writers who let rejection dissuade them from pursuing their dream or who react to each editor's "No" with indignation or fury do themselves a disservice. Writers who let rejection stop them do not publish. Resign yourself to facing rejection now. You will live through it, and you will eventually overcome it.

Query and cover letters

A query letter is a brief but detailed letter written to interest an editor in your manuscript. It is a tool for selling both magazine articles and nonfiction books. With a magazine query you are attempting to interest an editor in your writing an article for her periodical. A book query's job is to get an editor interested enough to ask you to send in either a full proposal or the entire manuscript. [Note: Some book editors accept proposals on first contact. Refer to individual listings for contact guidelines.] Some beginners are hesitant to query, thinking an editor can more fairly judge an idea by seeing the entire manuscript. Actually, most editors of nonfiction prefer to be queried.

SAMPLE MAGAZINE QUERY

Walter J. Fehn
523 S. Willow Rd.
Newton, OH
45267

June 7, 1995

Donald Clement
Ohio Outdoors Today
9289 Wabash Ave.
Cincinnati, OH
45212

Dear Mr. Clement:

When you think of the Ohio River, what comes to mind? Tug boats and coal barges? Steamboats? Pearl diving?

Pearl diving?

Yes. In 1981, oyster beds totalling more than 700 tons were relocated from the mid-Atlantic coast to a twenty-mile stretch of the Ohio River east of Cincinnati. Under the watchful eye of the Ohio Department of Fisheries, the oyster population has flourished, and this quirky transplant to the Midwest is now a booming mini-industry. The oysters are harvested—for food and for pearls—by a group of highly-paid seasonal workers who have come to the region from as far away as the South Pacific to ply their traditional trade.

The divers who risk their lives harvesting the oysters are a fascinating study, and I would like to write about them for *Ohio Outdoors Today*. Thousands of miles from home, they spend up to five hours a day on the floor of the river. Dressed only in swim trunks, and with canvas bags slung across their shoulders, the divers scour the riverbed for mature oysters, dodging debris and groping their way through the often murky water. They are paid well for their trouble—up to $40,000 a year. Yet they miss their homes.

I am a freelance writer who has covered the Ohio outdoor scene for local and regional publications. I would like to tell your readers about the Ohio pearl divers, their exotic occupation and their fascinating lives. I can deliver the completed article, at any desired length from 1,000 to 3,000 words, two months after assignment. Photos can be included if you wish. I look forward to hearing from you.

Sincerely,

Walter J. Fehn

There is no query formula that guarantees success, but there are some points to consider when you begin. Queries should:
- Be limited to one page, single-spaced, and address the editor by name (Mr. or Ms. and the surname).
- Grab the editor's interest with a strong opening. Some magazine queries begin with a paragraph meant to approximate the lead of the intended article.
- Indicate how you intend to develop the article or book. Give the editor some idea of the work's structure and contents.
- Let the editor know if you have photos available to accompany your magazine article (never send original photos—send duplicates).
- Mention any expertise or training that qualifies you to write the article or book. If you've published before, mention it; if not, don't.
- End with a direct request to write the article (or, if you're pitching a book, ask for the go-ahead to send in a full proposal or the entire manuscript). Give the editor an idea of the expected length and possible delivery date of your manuscript.

Fiction is sometimes queried, but most fiction editors don't like to make a final decision until they see the complete manuscript. Most editors will want to see a synopsis and sample chapters for a book, and a complete manuscript of a short story. If a fiction editor does request a query, briefly describe the main theme and story line, including the conflict and resolution of your story.

Some writers state politely in their query letters that after a specified date (slightly beyond the listed reporting time), they will assume the editor is not currently interested in their topic and will submit the query elsewhere. It's a good idea to do this only if your topic is a timely one that will suffer if not considered quickly.

For more information about writing query letters, read *How to Write Irresistible Query Letters*, by Lisa Collier Cool (Writer's Digest Books).

A brief single-spaced cover letter enclosed with your manuscript is helpful in personalizing a submission. If you have previously queried the editor on the article or book, the cover letter should be a brief reminder, not a sales pitch. "Here is the piece on digital recording technology, which we discussed previously. I look forward to hearing from you at your earliest convenience."

If you are submitting to a market that considers unsolicited complete manuscripts, your cover letter should tell the editor something about your manuscript and about you—your publishing history and any particular qualifications you have for writing the enclosed manuscript.

Once your manuscript has been accepted, you may offer to get involved in the editing process, but policy on this will vary from magazine to magazine. Most magazine editors don't send galleys to authors before publication, but if they do, you should return the galleys as promptly as possible after you've reviewed them. Book publishers will normally involve you in rewrites whether you like it or not.

Book proposals

Most nonfiction books are sold by book proposal, a package of materials that details what your book is about, who its intended audience is, and how you intend to write it. Most fiction is sold either by complete manuscript, especially for first-time authors, or by two or three sample chapters.

The nonfiction book proposal includes some combination of a cover or query letter, an overview, an outline, author's information sheet and sample chapters. Editors also want to see information about the audience for your book and about titles that compete with your proposed book.

Take a look at individual listings to see what submission method editors prefer. If

Scott Smith's simple publishing plan: storytelling, hard work and good fortune

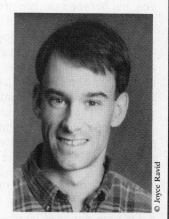

Scott Smith

Hank, Jacob and Lou, the three main characters in Scott Smith's first novel, *A Simple Plan* (Alfred A. Knopf, 1993), stumble across the wreckage of a small plane in a secluded Ohio woods. Inside the plane are a dead pilot and over $4 million in cash. In the time it takes to entertain a second thought, the trio discard a notion to turn the money in to authorities. Hank devises a "simple plan" that will allow the three to split the money and avoid detection. Needless to say, things don't proceed according to plan. The rest of the book is a study in expedient morality, paranoia, and Sam Peckinpah-style bloodshed. *A Simple Plan* is a startling and skillfully constructed debut novel.

What could be better than finding a few unmissed millions lying around for the taking? Most writers would agree that one thing better than such a windfall would be publishing their first novel to critical and popular acclaim, making a lucrative sale of the movie rights to the story, and then being offered a contract for a second book. Scott Smith has walked into the woods of book publishing and emerged with just such a prize under his arm.

Like most successful first novels, Smith's achievement is due to a potent combination of hard work, luck, and a flair for the kind of plotting and storytelling that make readers willingly forgo meals and stay up later than they ought to. Smith studied for an MFA in Columbia University's writing program. It was there, in a screenwriting class, that he wrote a scene that became the germ for *A Simple Plan*. "I was interested in film noir; I knew I wanted to write something in that vein, something very dark. I thought of what eventually became chapter six in the book—a series of killings at an isolated farmhouse. It was just an opening to a movie, killings that you see enacted and then covered up. I didn't really know the story around the killings." Smith did not finish the screenplay during the course, and he put the scene away for about a year. He came back to it later when he had decided to write a novel. "I looked at different ideas that I had, and I came back to that scene. I came up with the money and the plane as a way to explain those killings."

The publication of Smith's novel was preceded by the publication of a short story, titled "The Empty House," in *The New Yorker*. His success in placing that story, and the subsequent sale of *A Simple Plan* are due largely to Smith's willingness to cheerfully accept criticism from editors and agents and act on their advice.

"I had heard of Alice Quinn [fiction editor at *The New Yorker*]; she had taught at Columbia. I hadn't taken her course, but I knew of her. I sent her two stories before the one she published, both without cover letters, just addressed to her. The first one I got a rejection slip back, the second one she wrote a nice note, and the third one she ended up taking." Why no cover letter? "I guess I figured that, since I didn't know her, anything she might assume would be better than the fact that I had just overheard her name." Smith's writing got Quinn's attention, but between the two of them, they edited "The Empty House" for about a year before it was finished.

Smith eventually mentioned to Quinn that he was writing a novel, and she offered to read it. She thought enough of it to pass it along to an agent. The agent had reservations about the book, but agreed to represent it if Smith addressed her concerns. "I spent about three months working on those changes and I sent it back to the agent, at which point she took it and sent it to an editor at Knopf." The editor accepted the manuscript, but with a request for further changes. "She had me continue along the path that my agent had already set me out on." That path involved fleshing out the character of Hank, the protagonist, and making him a more sympathetic character than he had been in early drafts. Smith rewrote the book again from March to October of 1992. It was published in September of 1993.

Smith is now at work on the screenplay adaptation of *A Simple Plan* (film rights were optioned by director Mike Nichols), and his second novel is also underway. Smith's path to publication clearly involved a lot of hard work, but he is the first to admit that good fortune also played a role. "I feel incredibly fortunate – to the point that I keep expecting bad things to happen," he says. "There's a passage in the book where Hank goes through all this stuff that has happened and thinks about his good luck; it gives him a panicky feeling because he thinks something bad is going to happen. Well, that's exactly how I feel."

they have not specified, send as much of the following information as you can.
- The cover or query letter should be a short introduction to the material you include in the proposal.
- An overview is a brief summary of your book. For nonfiction, it should detail your book's subject and give an idea of how that subject will be developed. If you're sending a synopsis of a novel, cover the basic plot.
- An outline covers your book chapter by chapter. The outline should include all major points covered in each chapter. Some outlines are done in traditional outline form, but most are written in paragraph form.
- An author's information sheet should – as succinctly and clearly as possible – acquaint the editor with your writing background and convince her of your qualifications to write about the subject.
- Many editors like to see sample chapters, especially for a first book. In fiction it's

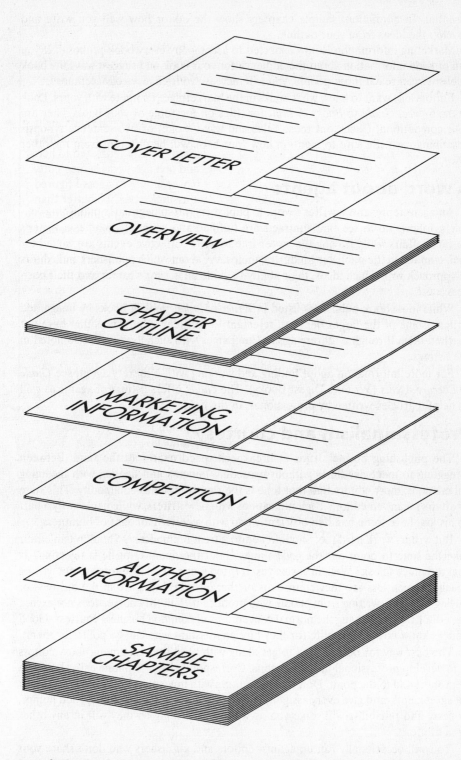

A nonfiction book proposal will usually consist of the elements illustrated above.
Their order is less important than the fact that you have addressed each component.

essential. In nonfiction, sample chapters show the editor how well you write and develop the ideas from your outline.

● Marketing information is now expected to accompany every book proposal. If you can provide information about the audience for your book and suggest ways the book publisher can reach those people, you will increase your chances of acceptance.

Editors also want to know what books in the marketplace compete with yours. Look in the *Subject Guide* to *Books in Print* for titles on the topic of your book. They are your competition. Check out those titles and write a one- or two-sentence synopsis describing each. Be sure to mention how your book will be different from the other titles.

A word about agents

An agent represents a writer's work to publishers, often negotiates publishing contracts, follows up to see that contracts are fulfilled and generally handles a writer's business affairs while leaving the writer free to write. Effective agents are valued for their contacts in the publishing industry, their savvy about which publishers and editors to approach with which ideas, their ability to guide an author's career and their business sense.

While most book publishers listed in *Writer's Market* publish books by unagented writers, some of the larger ones are reluctant to consider submissions that have not reached them through a literary agent. Companies with such a policy are so noted in the listings.

For more information about finding and working with a literary agent, see *Guide to Literary Agents* (Writer's Digest Books). The *Guide* offers listings of agents as well as helpful articles written by professionals in the field.

Professionalism and courtesy

The publishing business runs at breakneck speed nearly all the time. Between struggling to meet deadlines without exceeding budgets and dealing with incoming submissions, most editors find that time is their most precious commodity. This state of affairs means an editor's communications with new writers, while necessarily a part of his job, have to be handled efficiently and with a certain amount of bluntness.

But writers work hard too. Shouldn't editors treat them nicely? Shouldn't an editor take the time to point out the *good* things about the manuscript he is rejecting? Is that too much to ask? Well, in a way, yes. It *is* too much to ask. Editors are not writing coaches; much less are they counselors or therapists. Editors are in the business of buying workable writing from people who produce it. This, of course, does not excuse the editor from observing the normal conventions of common business courtesy. Good editors know how to be polite (or they hire an assistant who can be polite for them).

The best way for busy writers to get along with (and flourish among) busy editors is to develop professional business habits. Correspondence and phone calls should be kept short and to the point. Don't hound editors with unwanted calls or letters. Honor all agreements, and give every assignment your best effort. Pleasantness, good humor, honesty and reliability will serve you as well in publishing as they will in any other area of life.

You will occasionally run up against editors and publishers who don't share your standard of business etiquette. It is easy enough to withdraw your submissions from such people and avoid them in the future.

The outline

The outline included in your proposal package should most often be the kind known as a "chapter outline." A "formal outline," the kind with Roman and Arabic numerals and upper and lower case letters that we all learned in high school, may be useful for your own purposes when you sit down to write the book, but the chapter outline will be more effective at quickly giving an editor a sense of the scope of your material and how you plan to develop it.

In a chapter outline, you simply describe in clear prose, as succinctly and lucidly as possible, the content and thrust of each chapter—forgoing the formal outline's hierarchical arrangement of subheads. If you like, you can devote one page of your chapter outline to each chapter.

Writing tools

Typewriters and computers. For many years, *the* tool of the writer's trade was the typewriter. While many writers do continue to produce perfectly acceptable material on their manual or electric typewriters, more and more writers are discovering the benefits of writing on a computer. Editors, too, have benefited from the change; documents produced on a computer are less likely to present to the editor such distractions as typos, eraser marks or globs of white correction fluid. That's because writing composed on a computer is generally corrected before it is printed out.

If you think computers are not for you, you should reconsider. A desktop computer, running a good word processing program, can be the greatest boon to your writing career since the dictionary. For ease of manipulating text, formatting pages and correcting spelling errors, the computer handily outperforms the typewriter. Many word processing programs will count words for you, offer synonyms from a thesaurus, construct an index and give you a choice of typefaces to print out your material. Some will even correct your grammar (if you want them to). When you consider that the personal computer is also a great way of tracking your submissions and staying on top of all the other business details of a writing career—and a handy way to do research if you have a modem—it's hard to imagine how we ever got along without them.

Many people considering working with a computer for the first time are under the mistaken impression that they face an insurmountable learning curve. That's no longer true. While learning computer skills may once have been a daunting undertaking, today's personal computers are specifically designed to be usable by beginners. They are much more user-friendly than they once were.

Whether you're writing on a computer or typewriter, your goal should be to produce pages of clean, error-free copy. Stick to standard typefaces, avoiding such unusual styles as script or italic. Your work should reflect a professional approach and consideration for your reader. If you are printing from a computer, avoid sending material printed from a low-quality dot-matrix printer, with hard-to-read, poorly shaped characters. Many editors are unwilling to read these manuscripts. New dot-matrix and ink jet printers, however, produce "near letter-quality" pages that *are* acceptable to editors. Readability is the key.

Electronic submissions. Many publishers are accepting or even requesting that final manuscript submissions be made on computer disk. This saves the magazine or book publisher the expense of having your manuscript typeset, and can be helpful in the editing stage. The publisher will simply download your finished manuscript into the computer system they use to produce their product. If a listing in *Writer's Market* specifies "Query for electronic submissions," you should inquire about what computer format they use and how they would like to receive your material. Most will prefer a 3.5″ diskette.

Some publishers who accept submissions on disk also will accept electronic submissions by modem. Modems are computer components that can use your phone line to send computerized files to other computers with modems. It is an extremely fast way to get your manuscript to the publisher. You'll need to work out submission information with the editor before you send something via modem.

About electronic submissions

Publishers that accept submissions by disk or modem have this phrase in their listings: Query for electronic submissions. We give the information this way because you'll need to speak with someone before you send anything by these methods. Also, many magazines and publishers change system requirements as equipment and software are updated. Instead of listing information that you may find is outdated when you begin to send the submission, we have put general information in the listing.

Be prepared when you discuss your submission to note the operating system and software you used. Most publishers can work with DOS or Macintosh files, but it will expedite matters to get this clear up front.

Fax machines and boards. We have included publishers' facsimile machine numbers in the listings. Fax machines transmit copy across phone lines. Those publishers who wanted to list their facsimile machine numbers have done so.

Between businesses, the fax has come into standard daily use for materials that have to be sent quickly. In addition, some public fax machines are being installed in airports, hotels, libraries and even grocery stores.

The fax information we have included in listings is not to be used to transmit queries or entire manscripts to editors, unless they specifically request it. Although some machines transmit on regular bond paper, most still use a cheaper grade that is difficult to write on, making it unsuitable for editing. In most cases, this paper also fades with time, an undesirable characteristic for a manuscript. Writers should continue to use traditional means for sending manuscripts and queries and use the fax number we list only when an editor asks to receive correspondence by this method.

Some computer owners also have fax boards installed to allow transmissions to their computer screens or computer printers. Unless the fax board can operate independently from the computer's main processor, an incoming fax forces the user to halt whatever work is in process until the transmission ends. You should never send anything by this method without calling or arranging with the editor for this type of transmission.

Letters and manuscripts sent to an editor for consideration should be presented in a neat, clean and legible format. That means typed (or computer-printed), double spaced, on 8½ × 11 inch paper. Handwritten materials will most often not be considered at all. The typing paper should be at least 16 lb. bond (20 lb. is preferred). Very thin papers and erasable bond papers are not recommended for manuscripts. Paper with a 25% cotton fiber content will provide a crisp, sharp surface for your typewritten words and will stand up to the frequent handling many manuscripts receive. The first impression an editor has of your work is its appearance on the page. Why take the chance of blowing that impression with a manuscript or letter that's not as appealing as it could be?

You don't need fancy letterhead for your correspondence with editors. Plain bond paper is fine. Just type your name, address, phone number and the date at the top of the page—centered or in the right-hand corner. If you want letterhead, make it as simple and businesslike as possible. Many quick print shops have standard typefaces and can supply letterhead stationery at a relatively low cost. Never use letterhead for typing your manuscripts. Only the first page of queries, cover letters and other correspondence should be typed on letterhead.

Manuscript format

When submitting a manuscript for possible publication, you can increase its chances of making a favorable impression by adhering to some fairly standard matters of physical format. Many professional writers use the format described here. Of course, there are no "rules" about what a manuscript must look like. These are just guidelines— some based on common sense, others more a matter of convention—that are meant to help writers display their work to best advantage. Strive for easy readability in whatever method you choose and adapt your style to your own personal tastes and those of the editors to whom you submit. Complete information on formats for books, articles, scripts, proposals and cover letters, with illustrated examples, is available in *The Writer's Digest Guide to Manuscript Formats*, by Dian Dincin Buchman and Seli Groves (Writer's Digest Books).

Most manuscripts do not use a cover sheet or title page. Use a binder only if you are submitting a play or a television or movie script. Use a paper clip to hold pages together, not staples. This allows editors to separate the pages easily for editing.

The upper corners of the first page of an article manuscript contain important information about you and your manuscript. This information should be single-spaced. In the upper *left* corner list your name, address, phone number and Social Security number (publishers must have this to file accurate payment records with the government). If you are using a pseudonym for your byline, your legal name still must appear in this space. In the upper *right* corner, indicate the approximate word count of the manuscript, the rights you are offering for sale and your copyright notice (© 1995 Patrick Jones). A handwritten copyright symbol is acceptable. [For more information about rights and copyright, see Minding the Details on page 28.] For a book manuscript include the same information with the exception of rights. Do not number the first page of your manuscript.

Center the title in capital letters one-third of the way down the page. Set your typewriter to double-space. Type "by" centered one double-space under your title, and type your name or pseudonym centered one double-space beneath that.

After the title and byline, drop down two double-spaces, paragraph indent, and begin the body of your manuscript. Always double-space your manuscript and use standard paragraph indentations of five spaces. Margins should be about 1½ inches on all sides of each full page of typewritten manuscript.

On every page after the first, type your last name, a dash and the page number in either the upper left or right corner. The title of your manuscript may, but need not, be typed on this line or beneath it. Page number two would read: Jones—2. Follow this format throughout your manuscript.

If you are submitting novel chapters, leave the top one-third of the first page of each chapter blank before typing the chapter title. Subsequent pages should include the author's last name, the page number, and a shortened form of the book's title: Jones—2—Skating. (In a variation on this, some authors place the title before the name on the left side and put the page number on the right-hand margin.)

When submitting poetry, the poems should be typed single-spaced (double-space between stanzas), one poem per page. For a long poem requiring more than one page, paper clip the pages together. You may want to write "continued" at the bottom of the page, so if the pages are separated, editors, typesetters and proofreaders won't assume your poem ends at the bottom of the first page.

Estimating word count

Many computers will provide you with a word count of your manuscript. Don't be surprised if your editor does another count after editing the manuscript. While your computer is counting characters, an editor or production editor is more concerned with the amount of space the text will occupy on a page. If you have several small headlines, or subheads, for instance, they will be counted the same by your computer as any other word of text. An editor may count them differently to be sure enough space has been estimated for larger type.

For short manuscripts, it's often quickest to count each word on a representative page and multiply by the number of pages. You can get a very rough count by multiplying the number of pages in your manuscript by 250 (the average number of words on a double-spaced typewritten page). Do not count words for a poetry manuscript or put the word count at the top of the manuscript.

To get a more precise count, add the number of characters and spaces in an average line and divide by six for the average words per line. Then count the number of lines of type on a representative page. Multiply the words per line by the lines per page to find out the average number of words per page. Then count the number of manuscript pages (fractions should be counted as fractions, except in book manuscript chapter headings, which are counted as a full page). Multiply the number of pages by the number of words per page you already determined. This will give you the approximate number of words in the manuscript.

Photographs and slides

The availability of good quality photos can be a deciding factor when an editor is considering a manuscript. Many publications also offer additional pay for photos accepted with a manuscript. When submitting black-and-white prints, editors usually want to see 8 × 10 glossy photos, unless they indicate another preference in the listing. The universally accepted format for transparencies is 35mm; few buyers will look at color prints. Don't send any transparencies or prints with a query; wait until an editor indicates interest in seeing your photos.

On all your photos and slides, you should stamp or print your copyright notice and "Return to:" followed by your name, address and phone number. Rubber stamps are preferred for labeling photos since they are less likely to cause damage. You can order them from many stationery or office supply stores. If you use a pen to write this information on the back of your photos, be careful not to damage the print by pressing too hard or by allowing ink to bleed through the paper. A felt tip pen is best, but you should take care not to put photos or copy together before the ink dries.

Captions can be typed on a sheet of paper and taped to the back of the prints. Some writers, when submitting several transparencies or photos, number the photos and type captions (numbered accordingly) on a separate 8½ × 11 sheet of paper.

Submit prints rather than negatives or consider having duplicates made of your slides or transparencies. Don't risk having your original negative or slide lost or damaged when you submit it.

Photocopies

Make copies of your manuscripts and correspondence before putting them in the mail. Don't learn the hard way, as many writers have, that manuscripts get lost in the mail and that publishers sometimes go out of business without returning submissions. You might want to make several copies of your manuscript while it is still clean. Some writers keep their original manuscript as a file copy and submit good quality photocopies.

Some writers include a self-addressed postcard with a photocopied submission and suggest in the cover letter that if the editor is not interested in the manuscript, it may be tossed out and a reply returned on the postcard. This practice is recommended when dealing with international markets. If you find that your personal computer generates copies more cheaply than you can pay to have them returned, you might choose to send disposable manuscripts. Submitting a disposable manuscript costs the writer some photocopy or computer printer expense, but it can save on large postage bills.

Mailing submissions

No matter what size manuscript you're mailing, always include sufficient return postage and a self-addressed envelope large enough to contain your manuscript if it is returned.

A manuscript of fewer than six pages may be folded in thirds and mailed as if it were a letter using a #10 (business-size) envelope. The enclosed SASE can be a #10 folded in thirds or a #9 envelope which will slip into the mailing envelope without being folded. Some editors also appreciate the convenience of having a manuscript folded into halves in a 6 × 9 envelope.

For manuscripts of six pages or longer, use 9 × 12 envelopes for both mailing and return. The return SASE may be folded in half.

A book manuscript should be mailed in a sturdy, well-wrapped box. Enclose a self-addressed mailing label and paper clip your return postage stamps or International Reply Coupons to the label.

Always mail photos and slides First Class. The rougher handling received by Fourth Class mail could damage them. If you are concerned about losing prints or slides, send them certified or registered mail. For any photo submission that is mailed separately from a manuscript, enclose a short cover letter of explanation, separate self-addressed label, adequate return postage and an envelope. Never submit photos or slides mounted in glass.

To mail up to 20 prints, you can buy photo mailers that are stamped "Photos—Do Not Bend" and contain two cardboard inserts to sandwich your prints. Or use a 9 × 12 manila envelope, write "Photos—Do Not Bend" and make your own cardboard inserts. Some photography supply shops also carry heavy cardboard envelopes that are reusable.

When mailing a number of prints, say 25-50 for a book with illustrations, pack them in a sturdy cardboard box. A box for typing paper or photo paper is an adequate mailer. If, after packing both manuscript and photos, there's empty space in the box,

INSIDER REPORT

Making it as a fulltime freelancer

"When my friends who are writers say they're hesitant to send their ideas to national publications, I always want to ask them, 'What are you waiting for?'" says freelance writer Kathleen Heins. "When I send a proposal off and it comes back, I just turn around and send it to the next person on the list. That way I make a negative into a positive." Rejection, she says, is part of the business of writing.

Russell D. Stevens III

Kathleen M. Heins

This attitude has served Heins well. Her work has been published in numerous national, regional and local publications, including *USA Weekend*, *New Woman*, *American Health* and *Runner's World*. In 1982 she sold her first piece to a suburban New York publication, one of a group of magazines called Spotlight Publications.

"At the time I didn't know what 'on spec' meant, but since I was unpublished, I told the editor the idea for a story I had in mind and said if she didn't like it, she didn't have to pay me. I remember her asking what made me think I was a writer. I told her I had always had a compulsion to write and had been doing so since I was a teenager. I really don't think you need to be published to be considered a writer. It was a hard sell, but she agreed."

A few days after her conversation with the editor, Heins got a call. "I hadn't even finished the article, my 'test,' when the editor called and asked me to put it on hold and write something else she needed right away. From then on she kept me as busy as I wanted to be. I didn't get paid much but I didn't care. I was thrilled to see my name in print and I was building a great portfolio and clips file. As soon as I had three clips from her I used them to take off."

Heins has been writing and publishing ever since, switching to a fulltime freelance career a few years ago. Yet, she warns writers, it can be a difficult move. "I don't recommend fulltime freelancing unless you have a list of steady clients that you know are going to pay you regularly. Even after I decided to go fulltime, I ended up working about 20 hours a week writing and producing material for a television newsroom to supplement my freelance income for a while."

One way Heins keeps the work coming in is by being open to a variety of writing assignments. In addition to articles for consumer and trade publications on both a local and national level, she also writes for newspapers, businesses and hospitals. In fact, her specialties are health, fitness and medicine.

Heins found her writing niche after she started writing for *American Health* magazine. She had also worked for a time in hospital public relations. "I think if you become known for writing about certain subjects, you have a better chance of getting those assignments than other people. One thing I recommend to writers interested in developing a specialty is to find ways to enhance their marketability. For example, I recently took a course in medical terminology and also became licensed as an emergency medical technician. Look for ways to stand above the competition."

Asked if there was a danger of getting "pegged" or locked into writing only about certain subjects, Heins says she hasn't had much trouble with it. She says writing about health and fitness keeps her busy and she's comfortable with it. "I have done some nutrition and some relationship pieces which are not my specialty, so I don't think having a specialty has kept me from working in other areas. I think what really speaks for you anyway is your writing credits."

Because Heins is the mother of a toddler, she says making time to write is a juggling act. "I usually try to wake up a few hours before my daughter does and use that time for writing and organizing for the day. That way I'm free to spend most of the day with her. In the afternoon I may have a teenager come over to babysit while I do interviews or research. Then, after my daughter goes to sleep for the night, I do some more writing."

A new laptop computer will make things easier, says Heins, who plans to write while her daughter is playing outside or finger painting at the kitchen table. She advises all serious freelancers to invest in a computer — most editors ask if she has an IBM compatible. A fax machine is also becoming an essential. "Editors don't ask if you have access to a fax anymore. Now they just ask 'What's your fax number?'

"I also think every writer should have a portfolio. When you send an editor your bio and clips you can offer to stop by and show a portfolio. It gives you an in and gives the editor an opportunity to get to know you in person."

Keeping up with paper work is a necessity when operating a freelance business, although, Heins admits, it's not her favorite part. She tries to set aside time each week to write invoices, make queries and search for possible reprint markets. "I really hate to do phone expenses, but that's one thing you have to keep track of. Not all your calls are going to be your sources. Sometimes you make a call that leads to a source and it's easy to forget that one. I've started recording all my long distance calls and who I made them to on a special calendar just for phone expenses."

Heins writes two to three major pieces a month. "Although I do look through newspapers to get ideas from their features, I find I have the best luck drawing on my personal experiences or those of my friends and family." As far as the actual writing goes, she may edit a piece dozens of times before she has a final draft.

"If a piece isn't going the way you'd like," she advises, "get all the basics down so you at least have a skeleton of the article and then do something else for awhile. Sometimes a short break is all you need to get your writing back in gear. At the same time you should also act on moments of inspiration even if they don't come at the most convenient times. Sometimes I do my best work while the rest of the neighborhood is asleep."

—Robin Gee

slip in enough cardboard inserts to fill the box. Wrap the box securely.

To mail transparencies, first slip them into protective vinyl sleeves, then mail as you would prints. If you're mailing a number of sheets, use a cardboard box as for photos.

Types of mail service

● First Class is the most expensive way to mail a manuscript, but many writers prefer it. First Class mail generally receives better handling and is delivered more quickly. Mail sent First Class is also forwarded for one year if the addressee has moved, and is returned automatically if it is undeliverable.

● Fourth Class rates are available for packages, but be sure to pack your materials carefully because they will be handled roughly. To make sure your package will be returned to you if it is undeliverable, print "Return Postage Guaranteed" under your address.

● Certified Mail must be signed for when it reaches its destination. If requested, a signed receipt is returned to the sender. There is a $1 charge for this service, in addition to the required postage, and a $1 charge for a return receipt.

● Registered Mail is a high-security method of mailing. The package is signed in and out of every office it passes through, and a receipt is returned to the sender when the package reaches its destination. This service begins at $4.40 in addition to the postage required for the item. If you obtain insurance for the package, the cost begins at $4.50.

● United Parcel Service may be slightly cheaper than First Class postage if you drop the package off at UPS yourself. UPS cannot legally carry First Class mail, so your cover letter needs to be mailed separately. Check with UPS in your area for current rates. The cost depends on the weight of your package and the distance to its destination.

● If you're in a hurry to get your material to your editor, you have a lot of choices these days. In addition to fax and modem technologies mentioned earlier, overnight and two-day mail services are provided by both the U.S. Postal Service and several private firms. More information on next day service is available from the U.S. Post Office in your area, or check your Yellow Pages under "Delivery Services."

Other correspondence details

Use money orders if you are ordering sample copies or supplies and do not have checking services. You'll have a receipt, and money orders are traceable. Money orders for up to $35 can be purchased from the U.S. Postal Service for a 75¢ service charge; the cost is $1 for a maximum $700 order. Banks, savings and loans, and some commercial businesses also carry money orders; their fees vary. *Never* send cash through the mail for sample copies.

Insurance is available for items handled by the U.S. Postal Service but is payable only on typing fees or the tangible value of the item in the package—such as typing paper—so your best insurance when mailing manuscripts is to keep a copy of what you send. Insurance is 75¢ for $50 or less and goes up to a $5 maximum charge.

When corresponding with publications and publishers in other countries, International Reply Coupons (IRCs) must be used for return postage. Surface rates in other countries differ from those in the U.S., and U.S. postage stamps are of use only within the U.S. Currently, one IRC costs 95¢ and is sufficient for one ounce traveling at surface rate; two must be used for airmail return. Canadian writers pay $1.50 for an IRC.

Because some post offices don't carry IRCs (or because of the added expense), many writers dealing with international mail send photocopies and tell the publisher

to dispose of them if the manuscript is not appropriate. When you use this m
it's best to set a deadline for withdrawing your manuscript from consideration, so yo
can market it elsewhere.

International money orders are also available from the post office for a $3 charge.
See U.S. and Canadian Postage by the Page on the inside covers for specific mailing
costs. All charges were current at press time but are subject to change during the year.

Recording submissions

Once you've begun submitting manuscripts, you'll need to manage your writing
business by keeping copies of all manuscripts and correspondence, and by recording
the dates of submissions.

One way to keep track of your manuscripts is to use a record of submissions that
includes the date sent, title, market, editor and enclosures (such as photos). You
should also note the date of the editor's response, any rewrites that were done, and,
if the manuscript was accepted, the publication date and payment information. You
might want to keep a similar record just for queries.

Also remember to keep a separate file for each manuscript or idea along with its
list of potential markets. You may want to keep track of expected reporting times on
a calendar, too. Then you'll know if a market has been slow to respond and you can
follow up on your query or submission. It will also also provide you with a detailed
look at your sales over time.

Current Trends in Publishing

by Kirsten Holm

Book publishing

Trade book publishing has been undergoing massive changes. Houses being bought, editors leaving, imprints closing, company names changing (and changing back!) all paint a picture of an industry in flux, but, as the numbers show, not in crisis. Last year trade book sales were up 7.2% overall, although some in the industry feel that is due more to higher prices than to increased numbers of books sold. Adult hardcover and juvenile paperback sales, up 14.9% and 15.7% respectively, carried adult paperbacks, up only 1.7%, and compensated for the 8% drop in juvenile hardcover. The Commerce Department predicted an 8.5% sales increase for 1994, and forsaw the addition of 1,000 jobs, primarily in the editorial, marketing and administrative areas.

It's important to note that most of the cutbacks and closures have been in the trade book sector, which accounts for approximately 25% of the industry. Professional, scholarly and academic publishing remain relatively unaffected. In fact, the elhi and professional segments increased in 1993 by 10.9% and 9.5%, respectively.

Within the large conglomerate publishers that control much of the marketplace, expectations of profit and return on investments are higher than ever. Seven companies accounted for over 80% of the bestseller entries last year. Publishing executives place increasing emphasis on marketability, and with so much money at stake are less willing to take chances. Publishers must have a sense of marketing, finance and media relations in addition to an idea of what makes a good read. While the larger houses are still interested in first novels, this bottom-line awareness often means that it is extremely difficult to do a second or third book if the previous efforts didn't meet financial expectations.

The emerging small press

Recent acquisitions and mergers have created seven giant communications conglomerates at the expense of the moderate to large size publishers. While the large New York publishing concerns are restructuring, scaling back and generally becoming more conservative, small independent and university presses have stepped up to the plate. The small press is responsible for books existing that otherwise might not be published and provide avenues for midlist and new authors to reach their audiences. As larger publishing houses in New York have gotten bigger, small presses have developed strong grass roots. A few nonprofit literary presses are now paying modest advances and marketing on a national level, with impressive results. Many small presses report their best year ever. *New York Newsday* has even launched a column devoted to reviewing hardcover fiction from small and independent presses. Some of the larger small presses may be poised to move up in size in the coming years.

Electronic publishing

A current topic at many conferences and seminars is electronic publishing. This can take the form of books on disk or may encompass video and computer technology in an interactive or multimedia format. Currently, books on disk lend themselves more readily to reference works or computer-related topics. Many in the industry see the strongest competition for potential readers' attention coming not from other publishers but from entertainment companies. Multimedia or interactive products feature the intertwining of computer and television or video technologies with traditional publishing content. This leads to alliances such as Random House and Broderbund or Simon & Schuster and Davidson & Associates to jointly develop, publish and distribute multimedia products for the consumer, education, business and reference markets. See the *Insider Report* featuring Kirby Timmons of CRM Films in the Scriptwriting section for a discussion of multimedia and its uses.

An issue of especial concern for writers in this area is electronic rights. The Author's Guild, American Society of Journalists and Authors, National Writers Union and Assocation of Authors Representatives have all published position papers outlining suggested guidelines. The NWU and Author's Guild/ASJA papers call for a revision of standard royalty rates and new definitions of "out of print" in a medium that can print on demand. The Author's Guild/ASJA also would bar the use of a work without the author's approval of media, form and content, and recommends that where rights are licensed from another party, such as the print publisher, the licensor be compensated on the traditional basis of a literary agent's commission, with the writer receiving 85-90%. The controversy over Random House's boilerplate contract language that assigns rights to the publisher for media "yet to be invented" has yet to be resolved.

More and more, successful book publishing is a combination of good marketing and good content. One way to put yourself above the crowd is to stay abreast of what types of books are popular now. We will be focusing primarily on nonfiction; for a more thorough discussion of directions in fiction, see "Commercial Fiction Trends Report" in *Novel & Short Story Writer's Market*.

Nonfiction currents

It is difficult to say "This is out. This is in." There will always be exceptions. In general, our listings report that hot topics currently include health care, multicultural issues, gift books and aging. Topics that may have peaked are recovery, biography and cookbooks. However, the success of the self-help books of Susan Powter, or the "Oprah cookbook" of Rosie O'Daley, testify to the powerful marketing tools of infommercials and personal TV appearances on a popular talk show.

Due in part, perhaps, to the continuing growth of superstores and their need to fill the increased shelf space, there is a strong movement to identify small niche markets and create titles to meet their needs. In the area of business, the "Great Jobs" series for English, Foreign Language, History and Psychology majors exists alongside the "Careers for" series, which includes animal lovers, film buffs, and kids at heart. Résumé books and career guides continue to sell, with specialization, as evidenced by such titles as *Electronic Résumé Revolution, The Minority Career Guide* and *The Smart Woman's Guide to Interviewing and Salary Negotiation*.

Baby boomers

Another popular wave introduces a mixture of self-help, recovery, religion and Eastern philosophy known generally as "spirituality." The works of Thomas Moore, Marianne Williamson, Lawrence Kushner and others deal with different facets of the search for meaning, a topic that seems to resonate with many baby boomers. New titles include women's spiritual issues, overcoming addictions, personal growth, and general care and feeding of the soul. Other popular related areas are examining and developing values, the "kindness movement" and inspiration/affirmation books.

Angels continue to do well, with an "Oprah" show and NBC specials fueling demand for books on this topic.

Physical health, as well as spiritual health, is also a popular subject. Baby boomers again form the core buyers of diet, health and fitness books, but now these books focus on personal choices and abilities to effect change. The popularity of Deepak Chopra, Susan Powter and the myriad of low-fat high-taste cookbooks testify to current concerns in making healthy lifestyle choices and the connection between the mind, body and spirit.

The subjects of women's issues and women's studies is also a strong trend. The number of feminist bookstores increased 27% over last year, despite competition from larger chain stores and a weak economy. The market for gay and lesbian fiction and nonfiction continues to grow as well, largely through small presses. Some credit the gay/lesbian rights ballot initiatives with sparking more activity and interest in the community as a whole.

. . . and the baby boomlet

Children's books have not enjoyed the same level of growth as in recent years. Juvenile hardcover sales are down, but juvenile paperbacks are doing well. This may be due to the fact that the children of baby boomers are reaching adolescence, when reading is often replaced with other activities. *Publishers Weekly* reports that of the 48 frontlist juvenile hardcovers that sold more than 75,000 copies last year, ten were connected to movies and another ten were based on TV shows. Middle-grade horror continues to run strongly, with R.L. Stine and Christopher Pike heading the list, and series such as the Babysitters Club and Sweet Valley High also remain popular.

Computer products for children, however, are exploding, with sales of educational software growing 77% in the first six months of 1993, faster than any other category. Since many schools feature computer classes and up to a third of American households include a child who uses the PC for schoolwork, school-age children are computer-literate and media-savvy. Publishers are forging alliances to enter this potentially lucrative market. Multilingual interactive storybooks on CD-ROM with accompanying book have been created jointly by Random House and Broderbund, for example. From Sesame Street on CD-ROM to electronic math and science textbooks, publishers and software companies alike recognize the great potential that exists in this market.

The largest growth in U.S. population is coming not from births but from immigration. Hispanic and Asian populations are growing, and are often ill-served by traditional books. Multicultural approaches in social studies curricula, combined with the whole language approach to reading, increases the need for children's works that encompass and embrace different peoples and cultures.

The cross-pollination of trends continues unabated. Women's issues and spirituality? Marianne Williamson's *Measure of a Woman*. Business and self-help? *Superself*, by Charles Givens. Low-fat cooking and multimedia? *Betty Crocker's New Choices*. It seems there are any number of combinations and permutations of current trends. To differentiate your proposal from what has already been published and others being suggested, you must be able to show a prospective publisher why *your* book is special.

Gathering market information

Many of the publishers this year have stressed inclusion of marketing information in book proposals. How many other books are being published on this topic? What makes your take on the subject different (and better) than these others? Who *will* buy (not who *ought* to buy) this book? Publishers must answer these questions before they offer you a contract. By answering these questions for them upfront you give yourself an edge. But this edge takes research.

To keep up with trends in book publishing you can turn to several sources. One invaluable reference is your local bookseller, who is keenly aware of which subjects are running hot or cold. *Publishers Weekly*, *Library Journal* and *The American Bookseller* feature up-to-date news on publishing and bookselling, as well as chart book sales and trends. *Book Industry Trends* published by the Book Industry Study Group predicts how the industry will perform in the years ahead. Almost all writers' organizations offer newsletters with markets information. Check into the writers' organizations in your area, or contact national groups such as the National Writers' Association which have regional chapters. These all can offer invaluable market direction insights that help present your book proposal in its most favorable light.

Consumer magazines

The magazine market is definitely looking up. After several years of downturn, ad revenues are up and ad pages are increasing. While newsstand sales are down for a variety of reasons, subscription circulation is increasing.

Last year was a record year for consumer magazine startups, 789 as opposed to 679 for the previous year, according to *Samir Husni's Guide to New Consumer Magazines*. Forecasts predicted fewer acquisitions of established magazines and increased start-ups for 1994. The life expectancy of these magazines, however, is a consideration. Half of all new magazines will be operating after one year, and only three out of ten will be in business after four years. All in all, though, the consumer magazine market is the best it has been in 13 years.

Many magazines listed in *Writer's Market* this year have increased the number of issues per year, and we've been happily surprised by the large number of magazines that, after an absence of a year or two, have asked to be listed again. Business is better in most categories, with the possible exception of juvenile magazines, which report a drop in subscriptions.

Most of the trends we will be examining are specific to the consumer magazine market. For more information on trade journals see the introduction to that section. Trade journals tend to be more stable and less susceptible to trends, since they exist to serve a specific industry or profession. While there may be less prestige in the trade and professional market, it is definitely a way to build your portfolio of clips and perhaps a career. Many writers with a particular professional expertise parlay that knowledge into a successful career writing for trade magazines, as in the case of Linda Leake, a featured *Insider Report* in the Trade Journal section.

The future is now

Just as electronic publishing is a hot topic in book publishing circles, electronic media is the new wave in magazines as well. Many major magazine companies, including Time Inc., Hearst, Condé Nast and Times Mirror are establishing divisions and executive positions to deal with multimedia development. The lure of capturing new markets with the treasure trove of content these companies possess is compelling.

Some companies are developing programs for niche cable markets based on the content of their magazines. Times Mirror, for example, is planning the Outdoor Life Channel, a 24-hour network that will draw on outdoor and sporting titles such as *Outdoor Life*, *Salt Water Sportsman*, *Field & Stream* and *Yachting*.

Most entering this arena, however, are eyeing online services and CD-ROM as the most potentially lucrative area. A few magazine groups are launching their own online services. Ziff-Davis planned to launch the Interchange Online Network (ION) in the fall of 1994, drawing on content from their many computer magazines even though ZiffNet is currently found on CompuServe. Although initially directed towards computer professionals, plans are for the new service to expand and cover various general consumer subjects as well. Other magazines, such as *Writer's Digest, Spin, Atlantic Monthly* and *Kiplinger's Personal Finance* are participating in already existing services such as eWorld, America Online and Prodigy.

Other magazines are exploring the potential of CD-ROM technology. One major newsmagazine has already produced several quarterly CD-ROM issues, incorporating multimedia elements not included in the print version. *Money Magazine* has produced "Money in the 90s," a compilation of monthly issues from January 1990 to December 1993, which includes full-motion video and full-text search capabilities.

And some companies are combining all these into one package. Hearst plans to launch HomeNet in late 1994, an interactive multimedia online, television and CD-ROM service that will draw on the content of their many magazines, such as *Good Housekeeping* and *Popular Mechanics*, as well as Hearst books, newspapers and television programming. HomeNet will treat every aspect of the home, from design, construction and decorating to maintenance, repair and gardening.

While these magazines and others have already started down the electronic path, many more companies are hanging back watchfully, ready to jump in when they feel the time is right.

Keeping up with the trends

Thirty-one computer magazines debuted last year, a testament to the exciting changes ahead in this industry. In the annual *Folio:500* review, of the top 100 magazines by revenue 12 were computer titles, more than any other category, and computer-oriented magazines comprised the top 5 in volume of advertising pages. While many of the new magazines are aimed primarily at readers with technical backgrounds, quite a few target the consumer audience. There is even a new interactive CD-ROM magazine about the people, politics and issues surrounding creation and production of CD-ROM products.

Health and fitness is a hot topic, with an emphasis on holistic well-being and strength. A number of new magazines have been created to fit the needs of specific demographic groups. The health needs of men, women, African-American women and children, among others, are the focus of magazines that debuted this past year. *TravelFit*, for example, focuses on fitness while on the road. This trend is complimented by an emphasis on natural foods, healthy cooking and added interest in vegetarianism. *Eating Well* grew 30% in circulation last year, and 28% in advertising pages.

Baby boomers' muscle is felt in consumer magazines as well. The interests of this age group are reflected in personal finance, lifestyle and travel offerings, among others. Magazines such as *Kiplinger's Personal Finance* (formerly *Changing Times*), *Family Life* and *Condé Nast Traveler* serve affluent middle-aged Americans, answering their needs with a service edge. These publications provide information and knowledge to an upscale audience who may not be interested in the least expensive options, but rather the *smartest* way to spend money.

Magazines emphasizing child care and parental guidance are doing well, with new publications such as the self-explanatory *Biracial Child* and *Divorced Parents X-Change* aimed at individuals whose particular concerns are addressed in their own forum. Magazines for children themselves are suffering a drop in circulation, which parallels the downturn in juvenile hardcover books. On the other hand, a corollary to the increased sales in middle grade paperbacks is an upsurge of glossy magazines aimed at the teenage market.

Know your markets

With magazines starting up and shutting down so rapidly, it's important for writers to stay on top of changes not only in the industry but also in the specific markets they target. Libraries, bookstores and newsstands are good sources for field research. Trade magazines such as *Folio*, *Advertising Age* and *Writer's Digest* offer information and analysis of trends in subject matter as well as the economics of advertising and circulation.

Perhaps the most important step in building a career in magazine writing is magazine reading. Check your local library's holdings or order a few sample copies for a market in which you are particularly interested. Peruse a few issues to get the flavor and perspective of a magazine, and gather a list of article ideas they might be interested in. Request a copy of the writer's guidelines and editorial calendar. Study the listing information closely and construct your query letter with care. Make your query letter impress the editor with your knowledge of the magazine and understanding of its editorial mission. Presenting an editor with well-written, appropriately targeted material is the unchanging key to success in this changeable business.

The Business of Writing

Minding the Details

Writers who have had some success in placing their work know that the effort to publish requires an entirely different set of skills than does the act of writing. Whether it's a question of left brain vs. right brain or art vs. commerce, a definite shift in perspective is required when you move from creating your work to selling it. Like it or not, successful writers — *career* writers — have to keep the business side of the writing business in mind as they work.

Each of the following sections discusses a writing business topic that affects anyone selling his writing. We'll take a look at contracts and agreements — the documents that license a publisher to use your work. We'll consider your rights as a writer and sort out some potentially confusing terminology. We'll cover the basics of copyright protection — a topic of perennial concern for writers. And for those of you who are already making money with your writing, we'll offer some tips for keeping track of financial matters and staying on top of your tax liabilities.

Our treatment of the business topics that follow is necessarily limited. Look for complete information on each subject at your local bookstore or library — both in books (some of which are mentioned below) and periodicals aimed at writers. Information is also available from the federal government, as indicated later in this article.

Contracts and agreements

If you've been freelancing even a short time, you know that contracts and agreements vary considerably from one publisher to another. Some magazine editors work only by verbal agreement; others have elaborate documents you must sign in triplicate and return before you begin the assignment. As you evaluate any contract or agreement, consider carefully what you stand to gain and lose by signing. Did you have another sale in mind that selling all rights the first time will negate? Does the agreement provide the publisher with a number of add-ons (advertising rights, reprint rights, etc.) for which they won't have to pay you again?

In contract negotiations, the writer is usually interested in licensing the work for a particular use but limiting the publisher's ability to make other uses of the work in the future. It's in the publisher's best interest, however, to secure rights to use the work in as many ways as possible, both now and later on. Those are the basic positions of each party. The negotiation is a process of compromise and capitulation on questions relating to those basic points — and the amount of compensation to be given the writer for his work.

A contract is rarely a take-it-or-leave-it proposition. If an editor tells you that his company will allow *no* changes on the contract, you will then have to decide how important the assignment is to you. But most editors are open to negotiation, and you should learn to compromise on points that don't matter to you while maintaining your stand on things that do.

When it's not specified, most writers assume that a magazine publisher is buying one-time rights. Some writers' groups can supply you with a sample magazine contract to use when the publisher doesn't supply one, so you can document your agreement in writing. Members of The Authors Guild are given a sample book contract and information about negotiating when they join. For more information about contracts and agreements, see *Business and Legal Forms for Authors & Self-Publishers*, by Tad Crawford (Allworth Press, 1990); *From Printout to Published*, by Michael Seidman (Carroll & Graf, 1992) or *The Writer's Guide to Contract Negotiations*, by Richard Balkin (Writer's Digest Books, 1985), which is out of print but should be available in libraries.

Rights and the writer

A creative work can be used in many different ways. As the originator of written works, you enjoy full control over how those works are used; you are in charge of the rights that your creative works are "born" with. When you agree to have your work published, you are giving the publisher the right to use your work in one or more ways. Whether that right is simply to publish the work for the first time in a periodical or to publish it as many times as he likes and in whatever form he likes is up to you—it all depends on the terms of the contract or agreement the two of you arrive at. As a general rule, the more rights you license away, the less control you have over your work and the more money you should be paid for the license. We find that writers and editors sometimes define rights in different ways. For a classification of terms, read Types of Rights, below.

Sometimes editors don't take the time to specify the rights they are buying. If you sense that an editor is interested in getting stories but doesn't seem to know what his and the writer's responsibilities are regarding rights, be wary. In such a case, you'll want to explain what rights you're offering (preferably one-time or first serial rights only) and that you expect additional payment for subsequent use of your work.

You should strive to keep as many rights to your work as you can from the outset, otherwise, your attempts to resell your writing may be seriously hampered.

The Copyright Law that went into effect January 1, 1978, said writers were primarily selling one-time rights to their work unless they—and the publisher—agreed otherwise in writing. Book rights are covered fully by the contract between the writer and the book publisher.

Types of rights

• First Serial Rights—First serial rights means the writer offers the newspaper or magazine the right to publish the article, story or poem for the first time in any periodical. All other rights to the material belong to the writer. The qualifier "North American" is often added to this phrase to specify a geographical limit to the license.

When material is excerpted from a book scheduled to be published and it appears in a magazine or newspaper prior to book publication, this is also called first serial rights.

• One-Time Rights—A periodical that licenses one-time rights to a work (also known as simultaneous rights) buys the *nonexclusive* right to publish the work once. That is, there is nothing to stop the author from selling the work to other publications at the same time. Simultaneous sales would typically be to periodicals without overlapping

Nonfiction publisher looks for authors who can solve problems

Bob Adams, Inc., is known as a successful publisher of how-to and self-help titles. Brandon Toropov, vice president of editorial, says the thing that distinguishes Bob Adams titles is that they solve problems for readers—whether the problem is selling your home, writing your own wedding vows or finding a job in Phoenix. "The ideal author, for us, is not necessarily somebody who's been published before," says Toropov, "but it does need to be somebody who has a solution to a problem. Obviously there are a lot of other types of publishing where that's not the issue, but for the types of books I acquire, that's one of the big yardsticks."

In addition to the problem-solving angle, Toropov has strong feelings about how writers can improve their chances of constructing a proposal that will make it past the first cut. "The thing I'm looking for is someone who, in the first paragraph of the cover letter, can prove that they've got both a hook and a compelling way of expressing that hook. The author's experience or background should support the hook they've established, and they should have some writing skills." One of the first indications of a writer's facility with words (or lack of it) is the cover letter, Toropov says. "One of the ways I answer the question of whether or not a person can write is to see how they handle their first encounter with a reader, which is me. If they take forever to get to the point in the cover letter or give me a lot of information that doesn't have anything to do with the book, that's an indication that they're probably going to treat other readers after me the same way."

Toropov makes the point that, in their proposals, writers should attempt to focus on the publisher's perspective; that means taking the time to study the market for your book and realistically assessing your book's chances. "I can't tell you the number of times I've seen bits of market research done by authors in which they'll say, 'There's *absolutely* no book out there that does this type of thing!' That tends to sound a little flat after a while; you just don't believe it when you read it anymore. What's more persuasive is a line by line analysis of the whole category, what's been done recently, what's hit a bestseller list and for how long, that kind of thing. The question we've got to answer is, 'What are retailers, for better or for worse, going to compare this to?' " Toropov says the fact that nothing's been published on your topic before is not necessarily a good sign. "Actually," he says, "that kind of short-circuits the proposal because, even if it's true (which I tend to doubt), that means there's nothing to compare it to in the marketplace. It might also mean that there is no market for it."

The preferred first submission to Bob Adams, Inc., is a brief cover letter and a two-page query. Toropov warns against a tendency to send too much material in your initial submission. Writers tend to think there's less chance to gain some-one's attention with a small package, but actually, according to Toropov, it works just the opposite. "I'm much more likely to look through a brief, compelling summary in two or three pages than I am to wade through an entire manuscript."

audiences.

- Second Serial (Reprint) Rights—This gives a newspaper or magazine the opportunity to print an article, poem or story after it has already appeared in another newspaper or magazine. Second serial rights are nonexclusive—that is, they can be licensed to more than one market.
- All Rights—This is just what it sounds like. If you license away all rights to your work, you forfeit the right to ever use it again.

If you think you want to use the material later, you must avoid submitting to such markets or refuse payment and withdraw your material. Ask the editor whether he is willing to buy first rights instead of all rights before you agree to an assignment or sale. Some editors will reassign rights to a writer after a given period, such as one year. It's worth an inquiry in writing.

- Subsidiary Rights—These are the rights, other than book publication rights, that should be covered in a book contract. These may include various serial rights; movie, television, audiotape and other electronic rights; translation rights, etc. The book contract should specify who controls these rights (author or publisher) and what percentage of sales from the licensing of these sub rights goes to the author. Remember, though, that just because a publishing company wants control of all sub rights does not mean they are actually going to use them. If you think you or your agent would be more effective at seeking out subsidiary uses of your work, you should strive to retain as many of these rights as your can.
- Dramatic, Television and Motion Picture Rights—This means the writer is selling his material for use on the stage, in television or in the movies. Often a one-year option to buy such rights is offered (generally for 10% of the total price). The interested party then tries to sell the idea to other people—actors, directors, studios or television networks, etc. Some properties are optioned over and over again, but most fail to become dramatic productions. In such cases, the writer can sell his rights again and again—as long as there is interest in the material. Though dramatic, TV and motion picture rights are more important to the fiction writer than the nonfiction writer, producers today are increasingly interested in nonfiction material; many biographies, topical books and true stories are being dramatized.

Copyright

Copyright law exists to protect creators of original works. It is engineered to encourage creative expression and aid in the progress of the arts and sciences by ensuring that artists and authors hold the rights by which they can profit from their labors.

Copyright protects your writing, unequivocally recognizes you (its creator) as its owner, and grants you all the rights, benefits and privileges that come with ownership. The moment you finish a piece of writing—whether it is a short story, article, novel or poem—the law recognizes that only you can decide how it is to be used.

The basics of copyright law are discussed here. More detailed information can be obtained from the Copyright Office and in the books mentioned at the end of this section.

Copyright law gives you the right to make and distribute copies of your written works, the right to prepare derivative works (dramatizations, translations, musical arrangements, etc. – any work based on the original) and the right to perform or publicly display your work. With very few exceptions, anything you write today will enjoy copyright protection for your lifetime plus 50 years. Copyright protects "original works of authorship" that are fixed in a tangible form of expression. Titles, ideas and facts can *not* be copyrighted.

Some people are under the mistaken impression that copyright is something they have to send away for, and that their writing is not properly protected until they have "received" their copyright from the government. The fact is, you don't have to register your work with the Copyright Office in order for your work to be copyrighted; any piece of writing is copyrighted the moment it is put to paper. Registration of your work does, however, offer some additional protection (specifically, the possibility of recovering punitive damages in an infringement suit) as well as legal proof of the date of copyright.

Registration is a matter of filling out a form (for writers, that's generally form TX) and sending the completed form, a copy of the work in question and a check for $20 to the Register of Copyrights, Library of Congress, Washington DC 20559. If the thought of paying $20 each to register every piece you write does not appeal to you, you can cut costs by registering a group of your works with one form, under one title for one $20 fee.

Most magazines are registered with the Copyright Office as single collective entities themselves; that is, the individual works that make up the magazine are *not* copyrighted individually in the names of the authors. You'll need to register your article yourself if you wish to have the additional protection of copyright registration. It's always a good idea to ask that your notice of copyright (your name, the year of first publication, and the copyright symbol ©) be appended to any published version of your work. You may use the copyright notice regardless of whether or not your work has been registered.

While it is a good idea to have your notice of copyright appear with any published version of your work, it is not necessary to put it on unpublished submissions you send in for consideration to periodicals and publishing companies. They *know* your work is copyrighted simply by virtue of the fact that it exists. Writers who insist on displaying the copyright notice on manuscripts risk appearing amateurish and distrustful.

One thing writers need to be wary of is "work for hire" arrangements. If you sign an agreement stipulating that your writing will be done as work for hire, you will not control the copyright of the completed work – the person or organization who hired you will be the copyright owner. Work for hire arrangements and transfers of exclusive rights must be in writing to be legal, but it's a good idea to get every publishing agreement in writing before the sale.

You can obtain more information about copyright from the Copyright Office, Library of Congress, Washington DC 20559. To get answers to specific questions about copyright, call the Copyright Public Information Office at (202)707-3000 weekdays between 8:30 a.m. and 5 p.m. eastern standard time. To order copyright forms by phone, call (202)707-9100. A thorough (and thoroughly enjoyable) discussion of the subject of copyright law as it applies to writers can be found in Stephen Fishman's *The Copyright Handbook: How to Protect and Use Written Works* (Nolo Press, 1994). A shorter but no less enlightening treatment is Ellen Kozak's *Every Writer's Guide to Copyright & Publishing Law* (Henry Holt, 1990).

Finances and taxes

As your writing business grows, so will your obligation to keep track of your writing-related finances and taxes. Keeping a close eye on these details will help you pay as little tax as possible and keep you apprised of the state of your freelance business. A writing business with no systematic way of tracking expenses and income will soon be no writing business at all. If you dislike handling finance-related tasks, you can always hire someone else to handle them for a fee. If you do employ a professional, you must still keep the original records with an eye to providing the professional with the appropriate information.

If you decide to handle these tasks yourself—or if you just want to know what to expect of the person you employ—consider these tips:

Accurate records are essential, and the easiest way to keep them is to separate your writing income and expenses from your personal ones. Most professionals find that separate checking accounts and credit cards help them provide the best and easiest records.

Get in the habit of recording every transaction (both expenses and earnings) related to your writing. You can start at any time; you don't need to begin on January 1. Because you're likely to have expenses before you have income, start keeping your records whenever you make your first purchase related to writing—such as this copy of *Writer's Market.*

Any system of tracking expenses and income will suffice, but the more detailed it is, the better. Be sure to describe each transaction clearly—including the date; the source of the income (or the vendor of your purchase); a description of what was sold or bought; whether the payment was by cash, check or credit card; and the amount of the transaction.

The other necessary component of your financial record-keeping system is an orderly way to store receipts related to your writing. Check stubs, receipts for cash purchases, credit card receipts and similar paperwork should all be kept as well as recorded in your ledger. Any good book about accounting for small business will offer specific suggestions for ways to track your finances.

Freelance writers, artists and photographers have a variety of concerns about taxes that employees don't have, including deductions, self-employment tax and home office credits. Many freelance expenses can be deducted in the year in which they are incurred (rather than having to be capitalized, or depreciated, over a period of years). For details, consult the IRS publications mentioned below. Keep in mind that to be considered a business (and not a hobby) by the IRS you need to show a profit in three of the past five years. Hobby losses are deductible only to the extent of income produced by the activity.

There also is a home office deduction that can be claimed if an area in your home is used *exclusively* and *regularly* for business. Contact the IRS for information on requirements and limitations for this deduction. If your freelance income exceeds your expenses, regardless of the amount, you must declare that profit. If you make $400 or more after deductions, you must pay Social Security tax and file Schedule SE, a self-employment form, along with your Form 1040 and Schedule C tax forms.

While we cannot offer you tax advice or interpretations, we can suggest several sources for the most current information.

- Call your local IRS office. Look in the white pages of the telephone directory under U.S. Government—Internal Revenue Service. Someone will be able to respond to your request for IRS publications and tax forms or other information. Ask about the IRS Tele-tax service, a series of recorded messages you can hear by dialing on a

Careful Research Grabs an Editor's Attention

Having recently celebrated her ninth anniversary at *Ladies' Home Journal*, Features Editor Pamela Guthrie O'Brien has become an expert at unearthing the talent buried beneath the slush pile. It's no easy endeavor. On a typical day, O'Brien receives a stack of queries several feet high.

What makes a writer, even the beginner, stand out from the rest? "It really comes across when someone has taken the time to read the magazine and do his research," says O'Brien. "You think if they put that much effort into their query they're going to put a lot of work into any article they write for you." O'Brien says that two of her contributing editors were discovered in her slush pile.

Pamela O'Brien

Kathleen M. Heins

"They both sent in terrific queries and you could tell they had really researched their ideas and our magazine," says O'Brien. "I can't emphasize enough the importance of reading at least a year of back issues before sending us a proposal."

Any response outside of the standard rejection letter, says O'Brien, should not be taken lightly. "When an editor tells you, 'Your idea isn't right for us but we'd like to hear more from you,' you should really take them up on that offer because they're not just saying it to be nice, they really mean it." O'Brien also recommends getting out some additional proposals fairly quickly after such a response while you're still fresh on the editor's mind.

What's the best way for a writer to break into *Ladies' Home Journal*? O'Brien says your best bet is to submit stories to their columns known as "A Woman Today" and "Woman to Woman". Although the magazine typically prefers queries over manuscripts, these two columns are an exception.

"A Woman Today" (mail to Box WT at the magazine) is a first-person, true-story column which runs 1,500 words. "These are stories of women who have overcome some terrible obstacles in life," says O'Brien. "They are pieces that make you think and you may not always agree with them but they're very provocative and sometimes controversial," she adds. "The person who reads them should be inspired and learn something from them."

"Woman to Woman" (mail to box WW), which runs 1,000 words, are stories that you would only tell your best friend. These are true stories about an experience that changed your life and that you would only share with a close female friend. All writers are kept anonymous upon request.

Getting published in one of these columns puts you in a better position to approach editors for bigger assignments. "Once you show you can do the job you develop a relationship with editors at the magazine," says O'Brien. "It's like anything else. Once you have a foot in the door it's always easier."

The average response time at *Ladies' Home Journal* runs anywhere from one to three months "at the absolute latest." For columns such as "A Woman Today" and "Woman to Woman," writers need to be particularly patient regarding response time because of the abundance of submissions the magazine receives.

If you haven't received a response in a few months and you've included a SASE, O'Brien recommends sending a note along with another copy of the proposal. "Sometimes things do get lost in the mail; no system is perfect," says O'Brien, "but we ask people not to call us because a lot of time we're not going to remember their query off the top of our heads." Every query letter is carefully reviewed and everyone who sends in a SASE can expect a response.

When submitting proposals to *Ladies' Home Journal*, keep in mind their readership. Basically, they're 30 to 49 years old, married, have children and are balancing work with family. "Time is of an essence to our readers because they have a lot to do," says O'Brien.

Any proposal or manuscript should be accompanied by four or five clips and a SASE. "The more recent the clips the better," says O'Brien. "If someone sends me a clip from 1980, I wonder what they've been doing from 1980 until now. A résumé or bio sheet including a list of credits is also helpful."

One of the most common mistakes writers make in submitting ideas is proposing stories that have appeared in the magazine during the past year or even the previous month. O'Brien says it's also important writers check the masthead. "Don't send me stuff for the health editor and be sure to check the spelling of an editor's name before sending your query." Seasonal material should also be sent four to six months in advance.

Queries should be as specific as possible. "Really think it through, give me an example of the lead and tell me how you're going to research the piece and the angle you're going to take and keep it to two pages tops," says O'Brien. "You really need to be clear about what you're going to do," she adds. "If you're talking about a big subject such as breast cancer, the angle is particularly important because we've done this subject numerous times."

What would she like to see more of? *Ladies' Home Journal* is currently looking for psychology pieces, particularly those with a news hook. They're also interested in relationship ideas including situations that may arise between siblings or friends. O'Brien also suggests looking at your own life for ideas. "If there's something that's happend to you and a lot of your friends, chances are it's something that other women want to hear about too. Lately the magazine is also buying more inspirational, happy ending types of pieces."

Writers in other parts of the country, says O'Brien, may actually have an advantage over their New York City area counterparts in submitting proposals. "Sometimes you may read about a great story in a small newspaper that we may never hear of in New York."

O'Brien says that writers who believe in their abilities should not get discouraged. "If you've done all your homework don't give up," she says. "If you write a good proposal, even if it isn't right at the time, you're going to get some encouragement from an editor. Sometimes it takes a while to get in. Like anything else, you have to work at it."

—*Kathleen M. Heins*

touch-tone phone. If you need answers to complicated questions, ask to speak with a Taxpayer Service Specialist.

• Obtain the basic IRS publications. You can order them by phone or mail from any IRS office; most are available at libraries and some post offices. Start with *Your Federal Income Tax* (Publication 17) and *Tax Guide for Small Business* (Publication 334). These are both comprehensive, detailed guides—you'll need to find the regulations that apply to you and ignore the rest. There are many IRS publications relating to self-employment and taxes; Publication 334 lists many of these publications—such as *Business Use of Your Home* (Publication 587) and *Self-Employment Tax* (Publication 533).

• Consider other information sources. Many public libraries have detailed tax instructions available on tape. Some colleges and universities offer free assistance in preparing tax returns. And if you decide to consult a professional tax preparer, the fee is a deductible business expense on your tax return.

A Writer's Guide to Money

By Gary Provost

A friend of mine, who I'll call Rocky, spent 15 years writing a very good 500-page novel. When he sold his novel to a major hardcover publisher he received an advance of $3,000, which he probably spent on therapy. The novel got a small first printing and good reviews. Soon after that all existing copies of the book were sucked into an enormous black hole, never to be seen again. Rocky's novel was not reprinted in paperback; no producer bought a movie option; no magazine published excerpts; nobody asked for Rocky's autograph. In short, Rocky's book met the fate of most literary first novels: no advertising, no publicity, few sales, a short life. Almost certainly, that $3,000 is all the money Rocky will ever receive for his 15 years of work.

On the other hand, Robert James Waller required only a few weeks to write *The Bridges of Madison County*. The book took up almost permanent residence on the bestseller list (96 weeks and counting as I write). In 1993 *The Bridges of Madison County* sold more copies than the top ten best selling books of 1983 combined. Waller's follow-up book, *Slow Waltz in Cedar Bend*, which some have seen as a thinly disguised rewrite of *Bridges*, also went directly to the bestseller list without passing go. Waller, a singer before he was a writer, has parlayed his fame into a successful CD. Steven Spielberg has bought film rights to *Bridges*. And Waller, I'm sure, now gets hundreds of letters from beautiful women offering to have his baby. All of this has brought to Waller a paycheck well into the multi millions of dollars, putting him in the same tax bracket as Shaquille O'Neal.

Hardly seems fair, does it?

Of course not. Rule number one about writing and money is that fair has nothing to do with it. Nobody is going to buy your book, short story or magazine article just because you worked really hard. "A fair day's pay for a fair day's work" doesn't apply to writing for a living.

If you want to understand how writers make money you must first lose a lifetime of assumptions about work and money. Specifically, you must delete these three ideas from your mind:

- My pay is related to the number of hours I work (the hourly wage);
- My pay is related to the number of items I produce (piecemeal);
- My pay is related to the quality of my work (merit).

Look at my example above. Waller worked fewer hours, wrote fewer pages and created a work of, some might argue, lesser quality. But his paycheck was thousands of times greater than Rocky's.

Certainly the hours put in, the volume of work turned out and the quality of your writing will contribute to the overall financial success of your writing career. But the number one determiner of your paycheck on any given project is not hours, volume or quality. It is the market. Who bought it? And who did they sell it to?

In the case of my friend Rocky, he sold his product to a book publisher and they in turn sold it to the small number of people who were willing to spend $22 for a

Gary Provost *is the author of 23 books, the most recent of which is* High Stakes: Inside the New Las Vegas *(Dutton, 1994).*

hardcover literary novel by an unknown writer. In the case of Waller, he sold his product to a big publisher, Warner Books, but for various reasons, Warner was able to sell *The Bridges of Madison County* to millions of people who had heard about the book.

Your short stories and magazine articles are also 'resold,' as part of the periodical in which they appear. The market for your article on how to frame your own photos can be the small town newspaper that in turn 'sells' it to their 5,000 subscribers, or the regional magazine that sells it to their 70,000 subscribers, or the big national magazine that sells it to their 3 million subscribers.

The editors of all these publications have two things in common: One, they are looking for well written material that will interest their readers, and two, they're not particularly concerned about how hard you worked to come up with the material. Did you make 30 phone calls trying to get that interview with Tommy Lee Jones, or did Tommy talk to you right away because he went to school with your cousin? They don't care. Did you walk into the library and find what you needed right away, or did you spend hours there because some sophomore was using the computer for his science project? They don't care. Did you use your research material in three other articles, thus making your time more cost effective, or is this article the only one you will write on the subject? They don't care. You are going to get paid what your work is worth to the editor, not what it is worth to you. In the case of Rocky that is bad news. In the case of Waller that is good news. So the question is not, "What's fair?" The question is what can you do to be more like a Waller than a Rocky.

Periodical pay rates

You can begin by understanding the writer's market. Let us start with magazines and newspapers. We can generalize and say that a magazine or newspaper makes money by selling advertising space. If a magazine has a big circulation it can charge advertisers more money, then it will have more money to spend on writers. That means that if you write a 750-word column about how to have fun with a fax machine and sell it to a small town newspaper you might get $30 for it. If you were to sell the same column to a newspaper in a mid-sized city, you might get $80-100 for it, and if you sold the column to a big city newspaper you might get $200-300 for it. If you write a 2,000-word article on tax revolt for a city magazine, like *Atlantic City Magazine*, you might get $300. Sell the same piece to a regional magazine like *Yankee* and maybe you'll get $900. Sell it to a big circulation national like *Reader's Digest* and maybe you'll get $2,000 or even $3,000. Same article, different markets.

This generalization is useful, but not absolute. There are, for example, magazines that don't need a lot of advertising money in order to pay you well, because they are not trying to make a profit. Magazines such as *Modern Maturity* exist not to make money on their own, but to serve the members of an organization, in this case the American Association of Retired Persons. In this year's *Writer's Market* you will find that *Modern Maturity* pays up to $3,000 for nonfiction articles. And there are hundreds of magazines which have low circulation but high ad rates because they are able to reach a very select audience. There are also magazines, like the *New Yorker*, that make a lot of money because they are able to reach the desirable upscale readers who can afford the sports cars and expensive evening wear advertised in their pages.

So you can see that the writer's market is sometimes as complex as the stock market and if you want to make money from your writing you must study this *Writer's Market*, and the publishers listed in it. Remember, better writing without better marketing won't earn you a dime more. The lifestyle editor of the local newspaper is not going to pay you *Redbook* wages just because your piece on the history of spoons is of *Redbook* quality.

Efficient writing

However, as important as the market is, there are many things you can do as a writer to make money flow to you more often and in greater amounts. (Notice that I didn't say faster. Money moves very slowly toward writers. More about that later.)

While time, volume and quality are not directly responsible for the size of your paycheck, they will in the long run combine to make you solvent or lead you into bankruptcy. The freelance magazine and newspaper writers who are making a good living are the ones who have created an effective equation of marketing, quality and speed. The quality of your writing is what will help you compete with top writers for the best paying markets. And the speed of your writing will help you turn out a lot of material, even if it happens to be for lower-paying markets.

When you combine all of these—market awareness, good writing and speed—you have efficient writing. Efficient writing means not just studying the market and writing well, but thinking about how you can squeeze the most dollars from each hour spent on your writing and research. You will learn your own money-making tricks as you move through your career. But here are a few basics.

1. Use research time wisely. This means when you research a subject for an article, learn enough for two or three or more articles on the subject. This goes for books, too. If, like me, you write fiction and nonfiction, so much the better. I wrote a nonfiction book called *High Stakes: Inside the New Las Vegas*. Now I am working on a mystery that takes place in Las Vegas. The research is paying off twice.

2. Reslant your article for another magazine. Let's say you've written an article for *Inside Detective* on people who took the law into their own hands. Maybe one of your most interesting anecdotes concerns a Boston man who foiled a pet shop holdup. He might get three paragraphs in your piece for *Inside Detective*, but maybe you could write a complete article about his case for *Boston Magazine* or the Sunday supplements of the *Boston Herald* or *Boston Globe*.

When you can't use all of the research, use part of it. Maybe in your research you found that most of these people used handguns. You could use your stories as a taking off point in another article either for or against gun control.

3. Think about added value. To the writer added value means giving the customer a little bit more and getting paid for it. Once you've agreed to write an article on ceramic banks for, say $400, there are a few things you can do to fatten the paycheck. Artwork, meaning photos or illustrations, is usually paid for separately, and often brings in more money than the article itself, so be creative in coming up with ways to illustrate your article. Another source of revenue is sidebars. A sidebar is a small article, perhaps 200 words, that runs in a box beside or below the main article. For your article on ceramic banks, you could write a sidebar explaining how the pig came to be the model for piggy banks. (And by the way, the reason I thought of that example is that I came upon the answer while researching another article.)

4. Resell your article or story. As you thumb through your *Writer's Market* you will see that many magazines buy "reprint" rights or "second serial rights." That means they will pay you money for the right to publish a story or article that you have already published elsewhere. Maybe you spent ten hours on your piece about backyard swimming pools and you got $500. That's $50 an hour. Now you sell it again for $200. You've just raised your hourly rate to $70 an hour. Just be sure that you sold the previous publisher "first rights" only.

Another way to get more money for your magazine article or short story is to make it part of a book. For example, I once wrote an article called "The Seven Beacons of

Good Writing" for *Writer's Digest* magazine. I have sold reprint rights to that article to six different writing anthologies, for a total of $2,000.

Another possibility: Give a talk at the library or the Rotary Club on the subject you have written about.

Books and money

While the principles of efficient magazine writing also apply to book writing, there are important differences regarding money in book writing.

The money you get for writing a book comes from two sources: the royalties and advance, and the subsidiary rights.

Advance and royalties

Author royalties vary, but not by much. There are standards in the industry: ten percent of the cover price on a hardcover book, six to eight percent on a paperback. Usually there is an "escalator," an increase in the royalty rate after the book has sold a certain number of copies.

The advance is an amount of money you will get before the book is published, usually one half when you sign a book contract and one half when you deliver the completed manuscript. It is an advance against royalties and your royalty statements will arrive without a check until that advance has been earned back. I can give you some examples of advances, but I can't promise that they will be useful. Two women I know recently sold their first true crime books as paperback originals. One got $10,000, the other got $12,000. One of my students recently sold her first novel, a paperback original, for $8,000. Another sold his in hardcover for $4,000 and still another sold his in paperback for $3,000. I have another friend, very well established, who gets $300,000 advances for his hardcover novels. I have a friend who sold her first novel for a $7,000 advance, gradually worked her way up to $50,000 per paperback novel, and is now writing novels for about $30,000. My own advances for true crime books have been in the $50,000-70,000 range, but I only got $40,000 for a business book last year, $10,000 for a book about writing, and when I write a children's book I'm lucky to get $7,000. I know of one author who was offered a $15,000 advance for his novel by one publisher, and $400,000 by another.

As you can see, when it comes to money, book publishing is a very crazy business. Certainly the great majority of advances fall between $4,000 and $50,000, but there are many superstars like Stephen King and Jackie Collins, who get millions. Robert Waller probably got a small advance for *The Bridges of Madison County* because nobody had ever heard of him, but he probably got a zillion dollars for the next book because by then everybody had heard of him.

The reason for all this diversity is that the advance is based on perceptions, not realities. A publisher bases his advance on what he thinks the first print run of the book will be. That number is based on what he thinks will be the advance orders for the book. That guess, in turn, is based on how enthusiastic he thinks the sales force will be about selling the book. That guess could be based on what he thinks the finished manuscript will look like. And so forth. It is all guesswork fueled by such varied things as the fact that a similar book did well last year; the author has a good track record; Madonna has agreed to write a quote for the front jacket; Stephen Spielberg is interested in making a movie of it; or the author's agent has a reputation for discovering great new talents. Of course, it is not as much of a crapshoot as it seems, because these beliefs tend to be self-fulfilling. When you pay a million dollar advance to an author, you automatically print a lot of books and spend a lot of money on promotion and advertising.

Subsidiary rights

The other source of money for the book author comes from subsidiary rights. That is, all the rights he hasn't sold to the publisher. Subsidiary rights include audio rights, foreign rights, movie rights, electronic rights, serialization (in a magazine) rights, and in some cases the right to base a T-shirt, towel or desk calendar on your book. The best way to wring the most money out of these rights is to get a good literary agent before you sign the book contract.

Bad and good news

Certainly, there is some good news about writing and money. But first, two bits of bad news.

One, publishers do not look at you as a partner, they look at you as a supplier. This fact saddens me more than anything I have learned in 25 years of professional writing and I take no joy in breaking the news to you, but it's best that you know now. Publishers are not your friends. All of the horror stories you've heard are, unfortunately, true.

Literary agent, Richard Curtis, in his book *How to Be Your Own Literary Agent*, writes, "Publishers have always cheated authors. I believe that publishers are still cheating authors. There is little question that many authors are being taken for a ride totaling millions of dollars.

"Publishers kill authors by creative bookkeeping. By depriving authors of vital information about book sales, delaying disbursements interminably, obscuring the meaning of figures, manipulating collection dates of subsidiary income, and withholding excessive royalties as a cushion against returns, many publishers figuratively strangle writers and literally poison their good will."

The other bit of bad news is that Alaskan glaciers move much faster than does money in the publishing industry. My advance checks arrive two to four months after I sign the book contract. I've published 22 books and I have never seen a royalty statement arrive on time, and I don't know of any author who has. Most magazines pay for stories and articles 'on publication,' which means you could wait years for your check. Many pay 'on acceptance,' but that just means they begin the payment process when your piece is accepted. You still have months to wait. I know of at least one book publisher that requires five people in two cities to approve a check of any size before payment can be made. Everything about the payment process is designed to keep the money in the publisher's bank and out of your hands as long as possible.

So, if you are going to write for a living you simply have to accept the fact that what you do today as a writer will have no effect on your ability to pay your bills this month or next month or even the month after. You always have to be thinking six months ahead.

Did I say there was good news? Yes. The good news is that after all the small checks and the slow checks and the frustrations that come with this profession, we writers have something that sane people do not. We all have it in us to write that next bestseller that brings the six figure royalty checks, the movie deal, the book club offer, the huge paperback reprint, the letters from adoring fans. We won't all be Robert James Waller. In fact very few of us will be. But all of us can wake up each morning, knowing that we are part of a profession that makes that dream at least possible.

How Much
Should I Charge?

Most freelance writers take on a variety of different types of writing work. Knowing what to charge for each job is a difficult task, as there are many factors involved in the decision. The size and scope of the job is a primary concern, but other variables such as your level of experience, the size of your client, the nature of your client's business and even where you and your client are located can affect how much you feel comfortable charging. All these considerations must be weighed carefully to come up with terms satisfying to both you and your client.

The information supplied in this section will help you get an idea of what other writers across the country are charging for different tasks. Yet, you will notice some of the ranges given are quite broad, taking location and other factors into account. To find out exactly what the market will bear in your area, networking with other writers is essential. Not only can contacts with others in your area give you an idea of what to charge, but you will also learn who uses freelance help and who the best clients are.

You'll want to make sure you aren't selling yourself short, of course, but you'll want to avoid pricing yourself out of the market. In preparing for a bid, look at the range of fees listed for that particular service. Then, using what you've learned from other writers in your area, try to assess how much you think the client is willing to pay. If you are unsure, ask them what they have budgeted for the project and start from there.

Location has had a strong influence on fees in the past and it is still true that you can charge higher fees in larger metropolitan areas. It used to be that you could charge more on the East or West Coasts, but larger cities in other areas such as Chicago or Houston are catching up.

The nature of your client's business can also affect how much you may want to charge. For example, work for business clients tends to bring higher fees than editorial work for magazines and newspapers. Nonprofit organizations do not generally pay rates as high as those paid by corporations. Smaller circulation publications tend to pay less than larger ones.

Your familiarity and experience with a particular type of work will also affect what you will charge. If you will be working in an area new to you, you may want to begin by charging an hourly rate rather than a flat fee.

One way to figure an hourly fee is to determine how much a company might pay per hour for someone on staff to do the same job. If, for example, you think a buyer would have to pay a staff person $26,000 per year, divide that by 2,000 (approximately 40 hours per week for 50 weeks) and you arrive at $13 per hour.

Next, add another 33% to cover the cost of fringe benefits that an employer normally pays (but that you must now absorb) in Social Security, unemployment insurance, hospitalization, retirement funds, etc. This figure varies from employer to employer, but the U.S. Chamber of Commerce reports that the U.S. average paid by employers is 37.6% of an employee's salary.

Then add another dollars-per-hour figure to cover your actual overhead expense for office space, equipment, supplies; plus time spent on professional meetings, researching and writing unsuccessful proposals. (To get this figure, add one year's expenses and divide by the number of hours per year you have been freelancing.) In the beginning—when you may have large one-time expenses, such as a computer—you may have to adjust this figure to avoid pricing yourself out of the market. Finally, you may wish to figure in a profit percentage to be used for capital investments or future growth.

Here's an example:

$26,000 (salary) ÷ 2,000 (hours) = **$13.00** per hour
+ **4.29** (33% to cover fringe benefits, taxes, etc.)
+ **2.50** (overhead based on annual expenses of $5,000)
+ **1.30** (10% profit margin)
_____
$21.09 per hour charge

We present this formula to help you determine what to charge based on what a client might expect to pay a staff person on a per-hour basis. Keep in mind, however, that few "fulltime" freelancers bill 2,000 hours per year. Most who consider themselves fulltime end up billing for about half that many hours. Using this formula, therefore, will probably not bring in the same amount of money as a fulltime staff position. Some experienced freelancers keep this in mind when setting rates and adjust their hourly charge upward to compensate. Again, this depends on the client's budget, your experience and what that particular market will bear.

Once you have worked repeatedly for a particular client or have established a specific area of expertise, you will get a feel for the time and effort involved. Then you may feel more comfortable charging a flat fee for projects rather than an hourly rate. Businesses are sometimes more likely to agree to flat fees because they like to know ahead of time how much a project will cost.

Reservations about hourly rates can be alleviated through effective communication. Be sure to get a letter of agreement signed by both parties covering the work to be done and the fee or rate to be paid. If there is any question about how long the project will take, be sure the agreement indicates that you are estimating the time and that your project fee is based on a certain number of hours. If you quote a flat fee, you should stipulate in your agreement that a higher rate might be charged for overtime hours or late changes in the project.

If you find that the project will take more time, be sure to let the client know right away and be certain the client understands and approves of the additional time and charges. Be sure to have any renegotiated fees put in writing. Some freelancers require a partial payment as parts of the job are completed, so both you and the client have a better idea of the time involved.

Sometimes it is worth working for lower rates if it means gaining valuable experience or establishing yourself in a certain field. You may also agree to a low-paying assignment if it supports a cause that you believe in.

This year we have some rates charged by freelancers in Canada. Whenever this information is available, we indicate it within the categories. The figures given for Canadian rates are in Canadian dollars.

The rates given are generally for "average" projects within a field. For translation, for example, translations from exotic languages into English or English into another language or translations of highly technical material will bring higher rates than the range listed. Whenever a project requires you to draw on your expertise in a technical area, you will be able to charge fees on the higher end of the range.

In markets where payment methods vary, both kinds of rates—hourly and per-project—are given so you have as many pricing options as possible. Please note that the categories often encompass a wide range due to responses from various locations and from writers at varying levels of experience.

Advertising, Copywriting & PR

Advertising copywriting: Advertising agencies and the advertising departments of large companies need part-time help in rush seasons. Newspapers, radio and TV stations also need copywriters for their small business customers who do not have agencies. Depending on the client, the locale and the job, the following rates could apply: $20-100 per hour, $250 and up per day, $500 and up per week, $1,000-2,000 as a monthly retainer. Flat-fee-per-ad rates could range from $100 and up per page depending upon size and kind of client. In Canada rates range from $40-80 per hour.

Book jacket copywriting: From $100-600 for front cover jacket plus flaps and back jacket copy summarizing content and tone of the book.

Brochures: $20-600 per published page or $100-7,500 and up per project depending on client (small nonprofit organization to large corporation), length and complexity of job.

Consultation for communications: *See Business & Technical Writing.*

Copyediting for advertising: $25 per hour.

Copywriting for book club catalogs: $85-200.

Direct-mail catalog copy: $75-200 per item; $150-1,000 per page.

Direct-mail packages: Copywriting direct mail letter, response card, etc., $500-30,000 depending on writer's skill, reputation and the client.

Direct response card on a product: $250-500.

Events promotion: $20-30 per hour. *See also Shopping mall promotion (this section).*

Fliers for tourist attractions, small museums, art shows: $50 and up for writing a brief bio, history, etc.

Fundraising campaign brochure: $5,000 for 20 hours' research and 30 hours to write a major capital campaign brochure, get it approved, lay out and produce with a printer. For a standard fundraising brochure, many fund-raising executives hire copywriters for $50-75 an hour to do research which takes 10-15 hours and 20-30 hours to write/produce.

New product release: $300-500 plus expenses.

News release: *See Press release (this section).*

Picture editing: *See Editorial/Design Packages.*

Political writing: *See Public relations and Speechwriting (this section).*

Press background on a company: $500-1,200 for 4-8 pages.

Press kits: $500-3,000.

Press release: 1-3 pages, $25-500.

Print advertisement: $200 per project. In Canada, $100-200 per concept.

Product literature: Usually paid per hour or day: $60 per hour; $400 per day. Per page, $100-300.

Promotional materials: *See Brochures (this section).*

Proofreading corporate publications and documents: $15-25 per hour.

Public relations for business: $250-600 per day plus expenses; up to $1,750 for large corporations.

Public relations for conventions: $500-2,500 flat fee.

Public relations for libraries: Small libraries, $5-10 per hour; larger cities, $35 per hour and up.

Public relations for nonprofit or proprietary organizations: Small towns, $100-500 monthly retainers.

Public relations for politicians: Small town, state campaigns, $10-50 per hour; incumbents, congressional, gubernatorial, and other national campaigns, $25-100 per hour; up to 10% of campaign budget.

Public relations for schools: $15-20 per hour and up in small districts; larger districts have full-time staff personnel.

Radio advertising copy: $20-100 per script; $200-225 per week for a four- to six-hour day; larger cities, $250-400 per week.

Recruiting brochure: 8-12 pages, $500-2,500.

Rewriting: Copy for a local client, $25-100 per hour, depending on the size of the project.

Sales brochure: 12-16 pages, $750-3,000. Up to $500 per page.

Sales letter for business or industry: $350-1,000 for one or two pages.

Services brochure: 12-18 pages, $1,250-2,000.

Shopping mall promotion: $500-1,000 monthly retainer up to 15% of promotion budget for the mall.

Speech, editing and evaluation: $18 per hour and up.

Speech for government official: $4,000 for 20 minutes plus up to $1,000 travel and miscellaneous expenses.

Speech for local political candidate: $250 for 15 minutes; for statewide candidate, $375-500.

Speech for national congressional candidate: $1,000 and up.

Speech for owner of a small business: $100 for 6 minutes.

Speech for owners of larger businesses: $500-3,000 for 10-30 minutes.

Speech for statewide candidate: $500-800.

Speechwriting (general): $20-75 per hour. In Canada, $70-125 per hour or $70-100 per minute of speech.

Trade journal ad copywriting: $250-500.

TV commercial: $60-375 per finished minute; $10-2,000 per finished project. In Canada, $3 per second of script.

TV home shopping: Local ad copy: $6 per hour. Writing, miscellaneous freelance: $15-85 per hour; 50¢-$1 per word.

Audiovisuals & Electronic Communications

Audiocassette scripts: $10-50 per scripted minute, assuming written from existing client materials, with no additional research or meetings; otherwise $75-100 per minute, $750 minimum.

Audiovisuals: For writing, $250-350 per requested scripted minute; includes rough draft, editing conference with client, and final shooting script. For consulting, research, producing, directing, soundtrack oversight, etc., $400-600 per day plus travel and expenses. Writing fee is sometimes 10% of gross production price as billed to client. Some charge flat fee of 1,500-2,100 per package.

Book summaries for film producers: $50-100 per book. *Note: You must live in the area where the business is located to get this kind of work.*

Copyediting audiovisuals: $20 per hour.

Industrial product film: $125-150 per minute; $500 minimum flat fee.

Novel synopsis for film producer: $150 for 5-10 pages typed, single-spaced.

Radio advertising copy: *See Advertising, Copywriting & PR.*

Radio continuity writing: $5 per page to $150 per week, part-time. In Canada, $40-80 per minute of script; $640 per show for a multi-part series.

Radio copywriting: *See Advertising, Copywriting & PR.*

Radio documentaries: $258 for 60 minutes, local station.

Radio editorials: $10-30 for 90-second to two-minute spots.

Radio interviews: For National Public Radio, up to 3 minutes, $25; 3-10 minutes, $40-75; 10-60 minutes, $125 to negotiable fees. Small radio stations would pay approximately 50% of the NPR rate; large stations, double the NPR rate.

Script synopsis for business: $40 per hour.

Script synopsis for agent or film producer: $75 for 2-3 typed pages, single-spaced.

Scripts for nontheatrical films for education, business, industry: Prices vary among producers, clients, and sponsors and there is no standardization of rates in the field. Fees include $75-120 per minute for one reel (10 minutes) and corresponding increases with each successive reel; approximately 10% of the production cost of films that cost the producer more than $1,500 per release minute.

Screenwriting: $6,000 and up per project.

Slide presentation: Including visual formats plus audio, $150-600 for 10-15 minutes.

Slide/single image photos: $75 flat fee.

Slide/tape script: $75-100 per minute, $750 minimum.

TV commercial: *See Advertising, Copywriting & PR.*

TV copywriting: *See Advertising, Copywriting & PR.*

TV documentary: 30-minute 5-6 page proposal outline, $1,839 and up; 15-17 page treatment, $1,839 and up; less in smaller cities. In Canada research for a documentary runs about $6,500.

TV editorials: $35 and up for 1-minute, 45 seconds (250-300 words).

TV home shopping, local ad copy: *See Advertising, Copywriting & PR.*

TV information scripts: Short 5- to 10-minute scripts for local cable TV stations, $10-15 per hour.

TV instruction taping: *See Educational & Literary Services.*

TV news film still photo: $3-6 flat fee.

TV news story: $16-25 flat fee.

TV filmed news and features: From $10-20 per clip for 30-second spot; $15-25 for 60-second clip; more for special events.

TV, national and local public stations: $35-100 per minute down to a flat fee of $5,186 and up for a 30- to 60-minute script.

TV scripts: (Teleplay only), 60 minutes; network prime time, Writers Guild rates: $14,048; 30 minutes, $10,414. In Canada, $60-130 per minute of script.

Books

Abstracting and abridging: Up to $75/hour for nonfiction; $30/hour for reference material and professional journals.

Anthology editing: Variable advance plus 3-15% of royalties. Advance should cover reprint fees or fees handled by publisher. Flat-fee-per-manuscript rates could range from $500-5,000 or more if it consists of complex, technical material.

Book proposal consultation: $20-75 per hour, or flat rate, $100-250.

Book proposal writing: $175-3,000 depending on length and whether client provides full information or writer must do some research, and whether sample chapter is required. Also up to $150 per page.

Book query critique: $50 for letter to publisher and outline.

Book summaries for book clubs: $50-100 per book.

Consultant to publishers: $25-75 per hour.

Content editing: $15-50 per hour; $600-5,000 per manuscript, based on size and complexity of the project. *See also Manuscript criticism (this section).*

Copyediting: $10-35 per hour, $6 per 1,000 words or $2 per page. Rates generally on lower end of scale for juvenile books, mid-range for adult trade, and higher for reference material.

Ghostwriting a religious book: $6,000-15,000. 50% of flat fee in advance and 50% upon completion of accepted ms.

Ghostwriting, as told to: Author gets full advance and 50% of royalties; subject gets 50%. Hourly rate for subjects who are self-publishing ($25-50 per hour). In Canada, author also gets full advance and 50% of royalties or $10,000-20,000 plus research time (for a 200-300 page book).

Ghostwriting without as-told-to credit: For clients who are either self-publishing or have no royalty publisher lined up, $5,000 to $35,000 (plus expenses) with one-fourth down payment, one-fourth when book half finished, one-fourth at three quarters mark and last fourth of payment when manuscript completed; or chapter by chapter; or $100 per page.

Ghostwriting a corporate book: *See Business & Technical Writing.*

Indexing: $15-40 per hour; charge higher hourly rate if using computer indexing software programs that take fewer hours; $1.50-6 per printed book page; 40-70¢ per line of index; or flat fee of $250-500, depending on length.

Jacket copywriting: *See Advertising, Copywriting & PR.*

Manuscript criticism: $160 for outline and first 20,000 words; $300-500 for up to 100,000 words. Also $15-35 per hour for trade books, slightly lower for nonprofit. Some writers charge on a per-page basis of $1.25-2 per page.

Movie novelization: $3,500-15,000, depending on writer's reputation, amount of work to be done, and amount of time writer is given.

Novel synopsis for literary agent: $150 for 5-10 pages typed, single-spaced.

Packaging consultation: $75 per hour.

Picture editing: *See Editorial/Design Packages.*

Production editing: $22-30 per hour; for reference/professional books, up to $50 per hour.

Proofreading: $12-25 per hour and up; sometimes $1.50-3 per page.

Research for writers or book publishers: $15-40 an hour and up; $15-200 per day and all expenses. Some quote a flat fee of $300-500 for a complete and complicated job.

Rewriting: $18-50 per hour; sometimes $5 per page. Some writers have combination ghostwriting and rewriting short-term jobs for which the pay could be $350 per day and up. Some participate in royalties on book rewrites.

Science writing, textbook: *See Business & Technical Writing.*

Science writing, encyclopedias: *See Business & Technical Writing.*

Textbook copyediting: $15-20 per hour, depending on whether el-hi, college, technical or non-technical.

Textbook editing: $15-30 per hour.

Textbook proofreading: $13-20 per hour.

Textbook writing: $15-50 per hour.

Translation, literary: $25 per hour; also $95-125 per 1,000 English words.

Business & Technical Writing

Annual reports: A brief report with some economic information and an explanation of figures, $25-50 per hour; 12-page report, $600-1,500; a report that must meet Securities and Exchange Commission (SEC) standards and reports that use legal language could bill at $40-75 per hour. Some writers who provide copywriting and editing services charge flat fees ranging from $5,000-10,000.

Associations: Miscellaneous writing projects, small associations, $15-25 per hour; larger groups, up to $50 per hour; or a flat fee per project, such as $550-1,000 for 2,000-word magazine articles, or $1,200-1,800 for a 10-page booklet.

Audiovisuals/audiocassette scripts: *See Audiovisuals & Electronic Communications.*

Book, ghostwritten, as told to: *See Books.*

Book summaries for business people: 4-8 printed pages, $400.

Brochures: *See Advertising, Copywriting & PR.*

Business booklets, announcement folders: Writing and editing, $100-1,000 depending on size, research, etc.

Business content editing: $20-35 per hour.

Business facilities brochure: 12-16 pages, $1,000-4,000.

Business letters: Such as those designed to be used as form letters to improve customer relations, $100 per letter for small businesses; $500 and up per form letter for corporations.

Business meeting guide and brochure: 4 pages, $200; 8-12 pages, $400. *See also Advertising, Copywriting & PR.*

Business plan: $1 per word; $200 per manuscript page; or $100-1,500 per project.

Business writing: On the local or national level, this may be advertising copy, collateral materials, speechwriting, films, public relations or other jobs—see individual entries on these subjects for details. General business writing rates could range from $25-60 per hour; $100-200 per day, plus expenses. In Canada, $1-2 per word or $50-100 per hour.

Business writing seminars: $250 for a half-day seminar, plus travel expenses. *See also Educational & Literary Services.*

Catalogs for business: $25-40 per hour or $25-600 per printed page; more if many tables or charts must be reworked for readability and consistency. *See also Advertising, Copywriting & PR.*

Collateral materials for business: *See Catalogs for business (this section).*

Commercial reports for businesses, insurance companies, credit agencies: $6-10 per page; $5-20 per report on short reports.

Company newsletters and inhouse publications: Writing and editing 2-4 pages, $200-500; 4-8 pages, $500-1,000; 12-48 pages, $1,000-2,500. Writing, $20-100 per hour; editing, $15-40 per hour. *See also Editorial/Design Packages.*

Consultation on communications: $250 per day plus expenses for nonprofit, social service and religious organizations; $500 per day to others.

Consultation to business: On writing, PR, $25-60 per hour.

Consumer complaint letters: $25 each.

Copyediting for business: $20-50 per manuscript page or $15-25 per hour; up to $40 per hour for business proposals.

Copyediting for nonprofit organizations: $15-30 per hour.

Corporate comedy: Half-hour show, $300-800.

Corporate history: $1,000-20,000, depending on length, complexity and client resources.

Corporate periodicals, editing: $50-60 per hour.

Corporate periodicals, writing: $25-100 per hour, depending on size and nature of corporation. Also $1 per word. In Canada, $1-2 per word or $40-90 per hour.

Corporate profile: Up to 3,000 words, $1,250-2,500.

Editing/manuscript evaluation for trade journals: $20-25 per hour.

Executive biography: Based on a résumé, but in narrative form, $100.

Financial presentation for a corporation: 20-30 minutes, $1,500-4,500.

Fundraising campaign brochure: *See Advertising, Copywriting & PR.*

Ghostwriting, general: $25-100 per hour; $200 per day plus expenses.

Ghostwriting article for a physician: $2,500-3,000.

Ghostwriting a corporate book: 6 months' work, $20,000-40,000.

Government public information officer: Part-time, with local governments, $25 per hour; or a retainer for so many hours per period.

Government research: $35 per hour.

Government writing: In Canada $50-80 per hour.

Grant appeals for local non-profit organizations: $50 per hour or flat fee.

Grant proposals: $40-100 per hour. Also $500-1,000 each.

Handbooks: $50-100 per hour; $25 per hour for nonprofit.

Indexing for professional journals: $15-40 per hour.

Industrial manual: $50-100 per manuscript page or $4,000 per 50 pages.

Industrial product film: *See Audiovisuals & Electronic Communications.*

Industrial promotions: $15-40 per hour.

Job application letters: $20-40.

Manuals/documentation: $25-60 per hour.

Market research survey reports: $15-30 per hour; writing results of studies or reports, $500-1,200 per day; also $500-2,000 per project.

Medical editing: $25-65 per hour.

Medical proofreading: $12-30 per hour.

Medical writing: $25-100 per hour; manuscript for pharmaceutical company submitted to research journal, $4,500-5,000.

Newsletters, abstracting: $30 per hour.

Newsletters, editing: $50-500 per issue (up to $850 per issue if includes writing); also $25-150 per published page. Some writers who do this charge regularly on a monthly basis. *See also Company newsletters (this section) and Desktop publishing (Editorial/ Design Packages).*

Newsletter writing: $10-800 per published page (depending on type of client); also $500-5,000 per issue. Also $250-400 per article. In Canada, $45-70 per hour. *See also Company newsletters and Retail business newsletters (this section) and Desktop publishing (Editorial/Design Packages).*

Opinion research interviewing: $4-6 per hour or $15-25 per completed interview.

Picture editing: *See Editorial/Design Packages.*

Production editing: $15-35 per hour.

Programmed instruction consultant fees: *See Educational & Literary Services.*

Programmed instruction materials for business: *See Educational & Literary Services.*

Proofreading: $15-50 per hour; $20 per hour limit for nonprofit.

Public relations for business: *See Advertising, Copywriting & PR.*

Résumé writing: $25-500 per résumé.

Retail business newsletters for customers: $175-300 for writing 4-page publications. Also $100 per page. Some writers work with a local printer and handle production details as well, billing the client for the total package. Some writers also do their own photography. *See also Editorial/Design Packages.*

Sales letter for business or industry: *See Advertising, Copywriting & PR.*

Science writing: For newspapers $150-600; magazines $2,000-5,000; encyclopedias $1 per line; textbook editing $40 per hour; professional publications $500-1,500 for 1,500-3,000 words.

Scripts for nontheatrical films for business & industry: *See Audiovisuals & Electronic Communications.*

Services brochure: *See Advertising, Copywriting & PR.*

Software manual writing: $35-50 per hour for research and writing.

Special news article for trade publication: *See Magazines & Trade Journals.*

Speech for business owner: *See Advertising, Copywriting & PR.*

Teaching business writing to company employees: *See Educational & Literary Services.*

Technical editing: $15-60 per hour.

Technical typing: $1-5 per double-spaced page.

Technical writing: $35 per ms page or $35-75 per hour, depending on degree of complexity and type of audience.

Translation, commercial: Final draft from one of the common European languages, $115-120 per 1,000 words.

Translation for government agencies: Up to $125 per 1,000 foreign words into English.

Translation through translation agencies: Agencies pay 33⅓% (average) less than end-user clients and mark up tranlators' prices as much as 100% or more.

Translation, technical: $125 per 1,000 words.

Editorial/Design Packages

Business catalogs: *See Business & Technical Writing.*

Demo software: $70 per hour.

Desktop publishing: For 1,000 dots-per-inch type, $10-15 per camera-ready page of straight type; $30 per camera-ready page with illustrations, maps, tables, charts, photos; $100-150 per camera-ready page for oversize pages with art. Also $20-40 per hour depending on graphics, number of photos, and amount of copy to be typeset. Packages often include writing, layout/design, and typesetting services.

Fundraising campaign brochure: *See Advertising, Copywriting & PR.*

Greeting cards ideas (with art included): Anywhere from $30-300, depending on size of company.

Newsletters: *See Desktop Publishing (this section) and Newsletters (Business & Technical Writing).*

Picture editing: $20-35.

Photo brochures: $700-15,000 flat fee for photos and writing.

Photo research: $12-25 per hour.

Photography: $5-150 per b&w photo; $10-300 per color photo; also $800 per day.

Printers' camera-ready typeset copy: Usually negotiated with individual printers. *See also Manuscript typing (Miscellaneous).*

Educational & Literary Services

Business writing seminars: *See Business & Technical Writing.*

Copyediting for theses/dissertations: $15-20 per hour.

Educational consulting and educational grant and proposal writing: $250-750 per day or $25-75 per hour.

English teachers, lay reading for: $6 per hour.

Lectures at national conventions by well-known authors: $2,500-20,000 and up, plus expenses; less for panel discussions.

Lectures at regional writers' conferences: $300 and up, plus expenses.

Lectures to local librarians or teachers: $50-100.

Lectures to school classes: $25-75; $150 per day; $250 per day if farther than 100 miles.

Indexing for scholarly journals: $12 per hour.

Manuscript evaluation for scholarly journals: $15 per hour.

Manuscript evaluation for theses/dissertations: $15-30 per hour.

Programmed instruction consultant fees: $300-700 per day; $50 per hour.

Programmed instruction materials for business: $50 per hour for inhouse writing and editing; $500-700 per day plus expenses for outside research and writing. Alternate method: $2,000-5,000 per hour of programmed training provided, depending on technicality of subject.

Public relations for schools: *See Advertising, Copywriting & PR.*

Readings by poets, fiction writers: $25-600 depending on the author.

Scripts for nontheatrical films for education: *See Audiovisuals & Electronic Communications.*

Short story manuscript critique: 3,000 words, $40-60.

Teaching adult education course: $10-60 per class hour; fee usually set by school, not negotiated by teachers.

Teaching adult seminar: $350 plus mileage and per diem for a 6- or 7-hour day; plus 40% of the tuition fee beyond the sponsor's break-even point. In Canada, $35-50 per hour.

Teaching business writing to company employees: $60 per hour.

Teaching college course or seminar: $15-70 per class hour.

Teaching creative writing in school: $15-70 per hour of instruction, or $1,500-2,000 per 12-15 week semester; less in recessionary times.

Teaching elementary and middle school teachers how to teach writing to students: $75-120 for a 1-1½ hour session.

Teaching home-bound students: $5-15 per hour.

Teaching journalism in high school: Proportionate to salary scale for full-time teacher in the same school district.

Tutoring: $25 per 1-1½ hour private session.

TV instruction taping: $150 per 30-minute tape; $25 residual each time tape is sold.

Writer-in-schools: Arts council program, $130 per day; $650 per week. Personal charges plus expenses vary from $25 per day to $100 per hour depending on school's ability to pay.

Writer's workshop: Lecturing and seminar conducting, $50-150 per hour to $750 per day plus expenses; local classes, $35-50 per student for 10 sessions.

Writing for scholarly journals: $75 per hour.

Magazines & Trade Journals

Abstracting: $20-30 per hour for trade and professional journals; $8 per hour for scholarly journals.

Article manuscript critique: 3,000 words, $40.

Arts reviewing: Regional arts events summaries for national trade magazines, $35-100.

Book reviews: $50-300.

Consultation on magazine editorial: $1,000-1,500 per day plus expenses.

Copyediting: $13-30 per hour.

Editing: General, $25-500 per day or $250-2,000 per issue; Religious publications, $200-500 per month or $15-30 per hour.

Fact checking: $17-25 per hour.

Feature articles: Anywhere from 20¢ to $4 per word; or $200-2,000 per 2,000 word article, depending on size (circulation) and reputation of magazine.

Feature article for an association: *See Business & Technical Writing.*

Ghostwriting articles (general): Up to $2 per word; or $300-3,000 per project.

Ghostwritten professional and trade journal articles under someone else's byline: $400-4,000.

Ghostwriting article for physician: $2,500-3,000.

Indexing: $15-40 per hour.

Magazine, city, calendar of events column: $150.

Magazine column: 200 words, $40; 800 words, $400. Also $1 per word. Larger circulation publications pay fees related to their regular word rate.

Manuscript consultation: $25-50 per hour.

Manuscript criticism: $40-60 per article or short story of up to 3,000 words. Also $20-25 per hour.

Picture editing: *See Editorial/Design Packages.*

Permission fees to publishers to reprint article or story: $75-500; 10-15 per word; less for charitable organizations.

Production editing: $15-25 per hour.

Proofreading: $12-20 per hour.

Poetry criticism: $25 per 16-line poem.

Research: $12-20 per hour.

Rewriting: Up to $80 per manuscript page; also $100 per published page.

Science writing for magazines: $2,000-5,000 per article. *See also Business & Technical Writing.*

Short story manuscript critique: 3,000 words, $40-60; $1.25 and up per page.

Special news article: For a business's submission to trade publication, $250-500 for 1,000 words. In Canada, 25-45¢ per word.

Stringing: 20¢-$1 per word based on circulation. Daily rate: $150-250 plus expenses; weekly rate: $900 plus expenses. Also $10-35 per hour plus expenses; $1 per column inch.

Trade journal ad copywriting: *See Advertising, Copywriting & PR.*

Trade journal feature article: For business client, $400-1,000. Also $1 per word.

Translation: $17 per hour.

Newspapers

Ads for small business: $25 for a small, one-column ad, or $10 per hour and up. *See also Advertising, Copywriting & PR.*

Arts reviewing: For weekly newspapers, $15-35; for dailies, $45 and up; for Sunday supplements, $100-400.

Book reviews: For small newspapers, byline and the book only; for larger publications, $35-200.

Column, local: $10-20 for a weekly; $15-30 for dailies of 4,000-6,000 circulation; $30-50 for 7,000-10,000 dailies; $40-75 for 11,000-25,000 dailies; and $100 and up for larger dailies.

Copyediting: $10-30 per hour; up to $40 per hour for large daily paper.

Copywriting: *See Advertising, Copywriting & PR.*

Dance criticism: $25-400 per article.

Drama criticism: Local, newspaper rates; non-local, $50 and up per review.

Editing/manuscript evaluation: $25 per hour.

Fact checking: *See Magazines & Trade Journals.*

Feature: $25-35 per article plus mileage for a weekly; $40-500 for a daily (depending on size of paper). Also 10-20¢ per word. In Canada $15-40 per word, but rates vary widely.

Feature writing, part-time: $2,000 a month for an 18-hour week.

Obituary copy: Where local newspapers permit lengthier than normal notices paid for by the funeral home (and charged to the family), $15-20. Writers are engaged by funeral homes.

Picture editing: *See Editorial/Design Packages.*

Proofreading: $20 per hour.

Science writing for newspapers: *See Business & Technical Writing.*

Stringing: Sometimes flat rate of $20-35 to cover meeting and write article; sometimes additional mileage payment.

Syndicated column, self-promoted: $5-10 each for weeklies; $10-25 per week for dailies, based on circulation.

Miscellaneous

Church history: $200-1,000 for writing 15 to 50 pages.

College/university history: $35 per hour for research through final ms.

Comedy writing for night club entertainers: Gags only, $5-25 each. Routines, $100-1,000 per minute. Some new comics may try to get a 5-minute routine for $150; others will pay $2,500 for a 5-minute bit from a top writer.

Comics writing: $35-50 per page and up for established comics writers.

Contest judging: Short manuscripts, $5 per entry; with one-page critique, $15-25. Overall contest judging: $100-500.

Copyediting and content editing for other writers: $10-50 per hour or $2-5 per page.

Craft ideas with instructions: $50-200 per project.

Encyclopedia articles: Entries in some reference books, such as biographical encyclopedias, 500-2,000 words; pay ranges from $60-80 per 1,000 words. Specialists' fees vary.

Greeting card verse: Anywhere from $25 up to $300 per sentiment, depending on the size of the company. Rates generally run higher for humorous material than for traditional. *See also Editorial/Design Packages.*

Genealogical research: $25 per hour.

Histories, family: Fees depend on whether the writer edits already prepared notes or does extensive research and writing; and the length of the work, $500-15,000.

Histories, local: Centennial history of a local church, $25 per hour for research through final manuscript for printer.

Manuscript criticism, poetry: $25 per 16 line poem.

Manuscript typing: Depending on ms length and delivery schedule, $1.25-2 per page with one copy; $15 per hour.

Party toasts, limericks, place card verses: $1.50 per line.

Research for individuals: $5-30 per hour, depending on experience, geographic area and nature of the work.

Restaurant guide features: Short article on restaurant, owner, special attractions, $20; interior, exterior photos, $25.

Special occasion booklet: Family keepsake of a wedding, anniversary, Bar Mitzvah, etc., $120 and up.

Writing for individual clients: $15-100 per hour for books; $15-20 per hour for thesis or dissertation.

Important Listing Information

- *Listings are based on editorial questionnaires and interviews. They are not advertisements; publishers do not pay for their listings. The markets are not endorsed by* Writer's Market *editors.*
- *All listings have been verified before publication of this book. If a listing has not changed from last year, then the editor told us the market's needs have not changed and the previous listing continues to accurately reflect its policies. We require documentation in our files for each listing and never run a listing without its editorial office's approval.*
- Writer's Market *reserves the right to exclude any listing.*
- *When looking for a specific market, check the index. A market may not be listed for one of these reasons.*
    1. *It doesn't solicit freelance material.*
    2. *It doesn't pay for material.*
    3. *It has gone out of business.*
    4. *It has failed to verify or update its listing for the 1995 edition.*
    5. *It was in the middle of being sold at press time, and rather than disclose premature details, we chose not to list it.*
    6. *It hasn't answered* Writer's Market *inquiries satisfactorily. (To the best of our ability, and with our readers' help, we try to screen out fraudulent listings.)*
    7. *It buys few manuscripts, thereby constituting a very small market for freelancers.*
- *See the lists of changes at the end of each major section for specific information on individual markets not listed.*

Key to Symbols and Abbreviations

●*—Editorial comment offering additional market information from the editors of* Writer's Market

‡*—New listing in all sections*

**—Subsidy book publisher in Small Press section*

□*—Cable TV market in Scriptwriting section*

ms*—manuscript;* **mss***-manuscripts*

b&w*—black and white (photo)*

SASE*—self-addressed, stamped envelope*

SAE*—self-addressed envelope*

IRC*—International Reply Coupon, for use on reply mail in countries other than your own.*

See Glossary for definitions of words and expressions used in writing/publishing.

The Markets

Book Publishers 56

Book Publishers

The path to publication

The book business, for the most part, runs on hunches. Whether the idea for a book comes from a writer, an agent or the imagination of an acquiring editor, it is generally expressed in these terms: "This is a book that I *think* people will like. People will *probably* want to buy it." The decision to publish is mainly a matter of the right person, or persons, agreeing that those hunches are sound.

Ideas reach editors in a variety of ways. They arrive unsolicited every day through the mail. They come by phone, sometimes from writers but most often from agents. They arise in the editor's mind because of his daily traffic with the culture in which he lives. The acquiring editor, so named because he is responsible for securing manuscripts for his company to publish, sifts through the deluge of possibilities, waiting for a book idea to strike him as extraordinary, inevitable, profitable.

In some companies, usually very large ones or very small ones, acquiring editors possess the authority required to say, "Yes, we will publish this book." In most publishing houses, though, the acquiring editor must prepare and present the idea to a proposal committee made up of marketing and administrative personnel. Proposal committees are usually less interested in questions of extraordinariness and inevitability than they are in profitability. The editor has to convince them that it makes good business sense to publish this book.

Once a contract is signed, several different wheels are set in motion. The author, of course, writes the book if he hasn't done so already. While the editor is helping to assure that the author is making the book the best it can be, promotion and publicity people are planning mailings of review copies to influential newspapers and review periodicals, writing catalog copy that will help sales representatives push the book to bookstores, and plotting a multitude of other promotional efforts (including interview tours and bookstore signings by the author) designed to dangle the book attractively before the reading public's eye.

When the book is published, it usually receives a concerted promotional push for a month or two. After that, the fate of the book—whether it will "grow legs" and set sales records or sit untouched on bookstore shelves—rests in the hands of the public. Publishers have to compete with all of the other entertainment industries vying for the consumer's money and limited leisure time. Successful books are reprinted to meet the demand. Unsuccessful books are returned from bookstores to publishers and are sold off cheaply as "remainders" or are otherwise disposed of.

The state of the business

If you've been reading the publishing industry trade magazines for the past year or so, you know that there has been some commotion at the large publishing houses. Somewhat large publishing companies are being bought up by larger publishing companies, who are in turn looking for ways to combine interests with giant companies in other areas of the entertainment industry. The fallout is—as it has always been when large companies seek first to become larger—an intense focus on the corporate bottom line. In the case of publishing, that translates to a "bestseller" mentality that tends to push all other concerns aside.

Publishers, like many other businesses these days, have been streamlining their operations in an effort to cut expenses and raise profits. Some imprints have been shut down altogether, and staffs have been cut. Many publishers talk about "trimming" their lists, publishing fewer books, in the coming seasons. That means fewer slots for new writers and an even more intense scrutiny paid to a book's marketability before a contract is offered.

Another effect of the recent mergers and staff cuts is that there are fewer people available in the publishing houses with the time or inclination to cull through the slush pile (the mass of unsolicited submissions that flows—slowly—through a publisher's editorial offices). Some houses refuse to consider unsolicited material of any kind, choosing instead to return it unopened or destroy it. Those who will look at unsolicited proposals are sometimes glacially slow to respond.

What all this means is that it is probably tougher now than it's ever been to break through at the large publishing houses. What this also means is that writers should consider channeling their efforts in other directions—toward the many medium and small publishers listed here. It is not our intention to discourage writers from trying their luck with the conglomerate publishers; if you are writing blockbuster commercial fiction or high-profile nonfiction (e.g., you are a celebrity or your subject is of intense interest to many people), they may be thrilled to hear from you. If not, you should consider concentrating your efforts on courting smaller, more specialized publishers.

What's hot

The bestseller lists of the past year indicate a continuing interest in several popular subjects. In nonfiction these include health care, relations between men and women, business and management advice, spiritual and psychological topics, dieting, and just about anything with a multicultural slant. Fiction bestsellers of the past year included love stories (led by the phenomenally successful *Bridges of Madison County*), still more legal thrillers (by now a genre in its own right), and an eclectic mix of more atypical fare such as *Pigs in Heaven*, *Like Water for Chocolate* and *Griffin & Sabine*. It's hard— and perhaps foolish—to predict what the hot topics will be in the coming year. One general bit of accepted wisdom is to pay close attention to the needs and interests of the "baby boom" generation. As they grow older, raise their families and head toward middle age and beyond, certain subjects will appeal to them, and they will often turn to books to solve a problem, learn a skill or entertain themselves.

How to publish your book

The markets in this year's Book Publishers section offer opportunities in nearly every area of publishing. Large, commercial houses are here as are their smaller counterparts; large and small "literary" houses are represented as well. In addition, you'll find university presses, industry-related publishers, textbook houses and more.

The Book Publishers Subject Index is the place to start. You'll find it before the General Index. Subject areas for both fiction and nonfiction are broken out for the more than 900 total book publisher listings. Not all of them buy the kind of book you've written, but this Index will tell you which ones do.

When you have compiled a list of publishers interested in books in your subject area, read the detailed listings. Pare down your list by cross-referencing two or three subject areas and eliminating the listings only marginally suited to your book. When you have a good list, send for those publishers' catalogs and any writer's guidelines available. You want to make sure your book idea is not a duplicate of something they've already published. Visit bookstores and libraries to see if their books are well represented. When you find a couple of books they have published that are similar to

INSIDER REPORT

Bantam VP on change and growth in publishing

As vice president and deputy publisher of Bantam Books, Nita Taublit is responsible for overseeing the publication of over 350 books each year. She is responsible for all aspects of the Bantam adult hardcover, trade and mass market paperback publishing program—from acquisition to scheduling to packaging and production.

We asked Taublit how recent upheavals (mergers, acquisitions, staff cuts, etc.) in the New York publishing world will affect writers hoping to publish with one of the big houses. "It's tough," she says. "I think the reason it's tough is because everybody is trimming down their list, not looking for fillers anymore." In today's economy, the time-honored publishing practice of allowing books not sold to be returned from the bookstores to the pub-

Nita Taublit

lisher is a source of financial strain and has caused publishers to publish and distribute somewhat more conservatively than in the past. "The number of titles published will continue to diminish," Taublit predicts. "It's not economically viable to publish things that have a limited distribution—to push out hundreds of thousands of books that you later eat. Every publishing company I can think of has trimmed its list."

While the current emphasis is on producing a taut and prosperous frontlist and keeping midlist publishing to a minimum, Taublit says most publishers are still interested in publishing good first-time novelists and nonfiction writers. "We have always published first-time writers, and we will continue to do so. They've just got to write a great book. One of the greatest pleasures I have is finding new writers and working with new writers who have talent."

If the opportunities in traditional book publishing are tightening up, there is one growth area that Taublit advises writers to keep an eye on—electronic media. "Book publishing as we know it in the next 10 or 15 years is going to change, with all the electronic publishing and the new media, the CD-ROM. But no matter what format it's in, we have got to have the talent; we have got to have the creative drive from the writers." Taublit sees the electronic horizon as offering not only opportunities for writers, but great benefits for the public, as well. "I'd like to think it will open up publishing, or reading, to people who perhaps don't traditionally read. Especially for younger children, I'm hoping that some of the things we're planning and that other publishers are planning that merge electronic publishing and traditional book publishing will bring those readers to publishing."

yours, write or call the company to find out who edited these books. This last, extra bit of research could be the key to getting your proposal to precisely the right editor.

Publishers prefer different kinds of submission on first contact. Most like to see a one-page query with SASE, especially for nonfiction. Others will accept a brief proposal package that might include an outline and/or a sample chapter. Some publishers will accept submissions from agents only. Virtually no publisher wants to see a complete manuscript on initial contact, and sending one when they prefer another method will signal to the publisher "this is an amateur's submission." Editors do not have the time to read an entire manuscript, even editors at small presses who receive fewer submissions. Perhaps the only exceptions to this rule are children's book manuscripts and poetry manuscripts, which take only as much time to read as an outline and sample chapter anyway.

In your one-page query, give an overview of your book, mention the intended audience, the competition (check *Books in Print* and local bookstore shelves), and what sets your book apart. Detail any previous publishing experience or special training relevant to the subject of your book. All of this information will help your cause; it is the professional approach.

Only one in a thousand writers will sell a book to the first publisher they query, especially if the book is the writer's first effort. Make a list of a dozen or so publishers that might be interested in your book. Try to learn as much about the books they publish and their editors as you can. Research, knowing the specifics of your subject area, and a professional approach are often the difference between acceptance and rejection. You are likely to receive at least a few rejections, however, and when that happens, don't give up. Rejection is as much a part of publishing, if not more, than signing royalty checks. Send your query to the next publisher on your list. You may be able to speed up the process at this early stage by sending simultaneous queries, but do so only to publishers who state they accept them.

Personalize your queries by addressing them individually and mentioning what you know about a company from its catalog or books you've seen. Never send a form letter as a query. Envelopes addressed to "Editor" or "Editorial Department" end up in the dreaded slush pile.

If a publisher offers you a contract, you may want to seek advice before signing and returning it. An author's agent will very likely take 15% if you employ one, but you could be making 85% of a larger amount. For more information on literary agents, contact the Association of Author's Representatives, 3rd Floor, 10 Astor Place, New York NY 10003, (212)353-3709. Also check the current edition of *Guide to Literary Agents* (Writer's Digest Books). Attorneys will only be able to tell you if everything is legal, not if you are getting a good deal, unless they have prior experience with literary contracts. If you have a legal problem, you might consider contacting Volunteer Lawyers for the Arts, 6th Floor, 1 E. 53rd St., New York NY 10022, (212)319-2787.

Special notice about subsidy publishing

Following the listings of Canadian and International Book Publishers, you'll find listings of Subsidy/Royalty Publishers.

Subsidy publishing involves paying money to a publishing house to publish a book. The source of the money could be a government, foundation or university grant, or it could be the author of the book. When a book publisher has informed us that it considers author-subsidy arrangements, we have placed that publisher in the Subsidy/Royalty section. For more information on subsidy publishing, see the introduction to Subsidy/Royalty Book Publishers on page 232.

Writer's Market is primarily a reference tool to help you sell your writing, and we

First-time author breaks in with reference work

Tom Ogden's first book is a reference volume on the history of the circus. *Two Hundred Years of the American Circus: From Aba-Daba to the Zoppe-Zavatta Troupe* was published in 1993 by Facts on File, Inc., a New York-based publisher of reference works and other "informational" nonfiction trade books. The book, an encyclopedia, is a 400-page hardbound collection of fascinating circus facts and photographs. It also represents three years of Ogden's life and labor.

Ogden is a professional magician and motivational speaker. His background includes stints with several circuses. He called on that background and his abiding interest in circuses when a writer friend, Michael Kurland, suggested that Facts on File might be interested in an encyclopedia of the

Tom Ogden

circus. "So I put together a proposal package," says Ogden, "which consisted of a three- or four-page introductory letter saying what I proposed to do, why the book was needed, why I was the person who should write it and who I thought would buy it." The proposal also contained several sample entries of various lengths to give the editors an idea of his writing ability and his vision for the book. After the publisher expressed enthusiasm about the project, Ogden contacted an agent who agreed to represent him in negotiating the contract. The proposal committee at Facts on File agreed to publish the book, and it took "three or four months" for the agent and publisher to work out the contract.

Ogden began his research in earnest after the contract was signed. "I amassed a huge library about the circus. I joined all the fraternal and historical circus societies to get their literature, their magazines, and to get contacts of people I could call. And I did a lot of interviewing. To find birth and death dates, I spent weeks at the library going through obituaries. I wanted this to be the most complete and accurate reference book ever written on the circus." Typical of many book projects, in light of ever-shifting editorial personnel in the publishing industry, Ogden's circus book was overseen by three different editors throughout the period when he was researching and writing.

After the first draft was completed, Ogden's editor dove into the manuscript. "Three months later, I got my edited manuscript back. I found some little style corrections, things they didn't like, which I started arguing about. Well, I discovered very quickly that you compromise on a lot of things so that you can save your ammunition for the fights you really want to win." Ogden chose to relent on most of the publisher's stylistic preferences but stood firm on some of the larger content decisions he found questionable. When the book was finally printed, Ogden says he found the arrival of the finished books anticlimactic. "What was exciting was not the finished book—the proof pages were what I found exciting, because that was when I first saw the words typeset. At that point I knew it was going to be a book."

Two Hundred Years of the American Circus has done well. It was named Best Reference Book of 1993 by the American Library Association. And Facts on File has paid Ogden the highest compliment an author can hope for from a publisher: They've signed a contract for his second book.

encourage you to work with publishers that pay a royalty. If one of the publishers in the Book Publishers section offers you an author-subsidy arrangement (sometimes called "cooperative publishing" or "co-publishing") or asks you to pay for all or part of the cost of any aspect of publishing (printing, advertising, etc.) or asks you to guarantee the purchase of any number of the books yourself, we would like you to let us know about that company immediately.

Publishers are offering more author-subsidy arrangements than ever before. Some publishers feel they must seek them to expand their lists beyond the capabilities of their limited resources. While this may be true, and you may be willing to agree to it, we would like to keep subsidy publishers and royalty publishers separate, so that you will be able to choose more easily between them.

Publishers that publish fewer than four books per year, but not more than 50% of them on an author-subsidy basis, are still listed in Small Presses with an asterisk (*). Author-subsidy publishers in Canada are also denoted with an asterisk (*), and are listed in Canadian and International Book Publishers.

For a list of publishers according to their subjects of interest, see the nonfiction and fiction sections of the Book Publishers Subject Index. Information on some book publishers and producers not included in this edition of *Writer's Market* can be found in Book Publishers and Producers/Changes '94-'95.

A.R.E. PRESS, 68th St. and Atlantic Ave., P.O. Box 656, Virginia Beach VA 23451-0656. Fax: (804)422-6921. Editor-in-Chief: Jon Robertson. Publishes hardcover and trade paperback originals. Publishes 14 titles/year. Receives 400 proposals and mss/year. 75% of books from first-time authors; 95% from unagented writers. Pays 10-15% royalty on net receipts after returns and discounts. Offers $2,000 maximum advance. Publishes book approximately 18 months after acceptance of ms. Reports in 2 months on queries. No unsolicited mss. Book catalog and author's guidelines for #10 SASE.

Nonfiction: "While we market books to the general public, proposals must have a connection to the Edgar Cayce psychic material. We seek proposals for topical books that show how to apply the Cayce spiritual principles, and also strong stories of people who have applied them successfully in their lives. Mistakes are made when writers do not follow our Author Guidelines, and are not familiar with the thrust of the Cayce material." Query or submit chapter outline with 3 sample chapters, including cover letter and brief synopsis.

Recent Nonfiction Title: *A Physician's Diary* by Dana Myatt, N.D.; *Facing Myself: Reflections from Past Lives, Dreams, and Psychic Readings* by Jennifer Borchers; *Spiritual Secrets of Learning to Love* by Lin Cochran; *Money and Spirit* by Frederick S. Brown.

Fiction: "We consider spiritual and metaphysical fiction that has an uplifting slant and is compatible with the Cayce philosophy. We are especially interested in novels that treat the topics of reincarnation and psychic phenomena. We reject anything that could be considered 'dark' or 'occult'." Query first.

Tips: "Our audience is comprised of people of all ages, races and religious persuasions who are seeking deeper insights into themselves, their spirituality, and their connection to God. Keep your queries and proposals brief and to the point. Please don't send superfluous material with your proposal. Always send SASE."

ABBOTT, LANGER & ASSOCIATES, 548 First St., Crete IL 60417-2199. (708)672-4200. President: Dr. Steven Langer. Estab. 1967. Publishes trade paperback originals and loose-leaf books. Averages 18 titles/year. Receives 25 submissions annually. 15% of books from first-time authors; 100% of books from unagented writers. Pays 10-15% royalty. Publishes book an average of 18 months after acceptance. Query for electronic submissions. Book catalog for 6×9 SAE with 2 first-class stamps. Reports in 1 month on queries; 3 months on mss.
Nonfiction: How-to, reference, technical on some phase of personnel administration, industrial relations, sales management, etc. Especially needs "a very limited number (3-5) of books dealing with very specialized topics in the field of personnel management, wage and salary administration, sales compensation, recruitment, selection, etc." Publishes for personnel directors, wage and salary administrators, sales/marketing managers, security directors, etc. Query with outline. Reviews artwork/photos.
Tips: "A writer has the best chance selling our firm a how-to book in personnel management, sales/marketing management or security management."

ABC-CLIO, INC., Suite 805, 50 S. Steele St., Denver CO 80209-2813. (303)333-3003. Fax: (303)333-4037. Subsidiaries include Cliop Press, Ltd. and ABC-CLIO Int'l. President: Heather Cameron. Estab. 1955. Publishes hardcover originals. Firm averages 35 titles/year. Receives 500 submissions/year. 20% of books from first-time authors; 95% from unagented writers. Pays royalty on net receipts. Publishes ms an average of 10 months after acceptance. Query for electronic submissions. Reports in 2 months on queries. Free book catalog and ms guidelines.
Nonfiction: Reference. Subjects include art/architecture, education, government/politics, history, multicultural studies, literary studies, mythology, science, environmental issues, women's issues/studies. "Looking for reference books on current world issues, women's issues, and for subjects compatible with high school curriculum. No monographs or textbooks." Query or submit outline and sample chapters.
Recent Nonfiction Title: *Dictionary of Native American Mythology.*

‡THE ABERDEEN GROUP, 426 S. Westgate St., Addison IL 60101. (708)543-0870. Special Projects Editor: Kari Moosmann. Publishes trade paperback originals. Publishes 6 titles/year. Receives 3 queries and 3 mss/year. 10% of books from first-time authors; 100% from unagented writers. Pays 6-18% royalty on retail price. Offers $1,000-3,000 advance. Publishes book 6 months after acceptance of ms. Accepts simultaneous submissions. Query for electronic submissions. Reports in 1 month on queries and proposals; 2 months on mss. Book catalog free on request.
Nonfiction: How-to, technical. Subjects include architecture, construction, general engineering and construction business. Query with outline, 2-3 sample chapters and definition of topic, features, market.
Recent Nonfiction Title: *Excavation Safety,* by Suprenant/Basham (how-to/technical).

ABINGDON PRESS, Imprint of The United Methodist Publishing House, P.O. Box 801, Nashville TN 37202-0801. (615)749-6301. Fax: (615)748-6512. President & Publisher: Robert K. Feaster. Editorial Director: Neil M. Alexander. Managing Editor/Assistant Editorial Director: Michael E. Lawrence. Senior Editor General Interest Books & Resources Books: Mary Catherine Dean. Senior Editor Academic Books: Rex Mathews. Senior Editor United Methodist Book & Resources: J. Richard Peck. Editor Professional Books: Paul Franklyn. Editor Reference Books: Jack Keller. Estab. 1789. Publishes hardcover and paperback originals and reprints; church supplies. Average 100 titles/year. Receives approximately 2,500 submissions annually. Few books from first-time authors; 90-95% of books from unagented writers. Average print order for a writer's first book is 4,000-5,000. Pays royalty. Publishes book an average of 3 months after acceptance. Query for electronic submissions. Manuscript guidelines for SASE. Reports in 3 months.
Nonfiction: Religious-lay and professional, children's religious books, academic texts. Length: 32-300 pages. Query with outline and samples only.

ACADEMY CHICAGO, 363 W. Erie, Chicago IL 60610-3125. (312)751-7300. Fax: (312)751-7306. Editorial Director/Senior Editor: Anita Miller. Estab. 1975. Publishes hardcover and paperback originals and reprints. Averages 20 titles/year. Receives approximately 2,000 submissions annually. Average print order for a writer's first book is 1,500-5,000. Pays 7-10% royalty; modest advances. Publishes book an average of 18 months after acceptance. Book catalog for 9×12 SAE with 3 first-class stamps. Manuscript guidelines for #10 SASE. Submit cover letter with first 4 chapters. Reports in 2 months.
• The editor reports this press is cutting back on publishing fiction.
Nonfiction: Adult, travel, true crime, historical. No how-to, cookbooks, self-help, etc. Query and submit first 4 consecutive chapters.
Recent Nonfiction Title: *A Gathering of Heroes,* by Gregory Alan-Williams.
Fiction: "Mysteries, mainstream novels." No "romantic," children's, young adult, religious or sexist fiction; nothing avant-garde.
Recent Fiction Title: *Celibacy of Felix Greenspan,* by Lionel Abrahams.
Tips: "At the moment, we are looking for good nonfiction; we certainly want excellent original fiction, but we are swamped."

ACCELERATED DEVELOPMENT INC., 3808 Kilgore Ave., Muncie IN 47304-4896. (317)284-7511. Fax: (317)284-2535. President: Dr. Joseph W. Hollis. Executive Vice President: Marcella Hollis. Estab. 1973. Publishes textbooks, paperback originals and tapes. Averages 10-15 titles/year. Receives 170 submissions annually. 50% of books from first-time authors; 100% of books from unagented writers. Query for electronic submissions. Pays 6-15% royalty on net price. Publishes book an average of 1 year after acceptance. Reports in 3 months. Book catalog for 6½ × 9½ SAE with 3 first-class stamps.
Nonfiction: Reference books and textbooks on psychology, counseling, guidance and counseling, teacher education, death education. "Especially needs psychologically-based textbook or reference materials, death education material, theories of counseling psychology, techniques of counseling, and gerontological counseling." Publishes for professors, counselors, teachers, college and secondary students, psychologists, death educators, psychological therapists, and other health-service providers. "Write for the graduate level student and at elementary and secondary school level in the affective domain." Submit outline, 2 sample chapters, prospectus and author's résumé. Reviews artwork/photos.
Tips: "Freelance writers should be aware of American Psychological Association style of preparing manuscripts."

‡ACCENT ON LIVING, Subsidiary of Cheever Publishing, Inc., P.O. Box 700, Bloomington IL 61702. (309)378-2961. Editor: Betty Garee. Publishes 4 titles/year. Receives 300 queries and 150 mss/year. 70% of books from first-time authors; 100% from unagented writers. Pays 6% royalty or makes outright purchase. Publishes book 3 months after acceptance of ms. Accepts simultaneous submissions. Query for electronic submissions. Reports on queries in 1 month. Book catalog for 8 × 10 SAE with 2 first-class stamps. Manuscript guidelines for #10 SASE.
Nonfiction: How-to. Anything pertaining to physically disabled. Query. Reviews artwork/photos as part of ms package. Writers should send snapshots or slides.
Recent Nonfiction Title: *Ideas for Easy Traveling*, by Wrights.

ACCENT PUBLICATIONS, P.O. Box 15337, Denver CO 80215. (303)988-5300. Managing Editor: Mary B. Nelson. Estab. 1947. Publishes evangelical Christian education and church resource products. Manuscript guidelines for #10 SASE. 100% of books from unagented writers. Pays royalty on cover price or purchases outright. Publishes book an average of 1 year after acceptance. Query or submit 3 sample chapters with brief synopsis and chapter outline. Do not submit full ms unless requested. No phone calls, please. Reports in 8 months. Book catalog for 9 × 12 SAE with 6 first-class stamps.
 • No longer considers fiction.
Nonfiction: "We are currently soliciting only nonfiction proposals in the areas of Christian education and Church Resources. C.E. products are teaching tools designed for the volunteer or professional Christian leadership to use in the church's education process. Church Resources are products that can be used in any aspect of the local church ministry. We would consider Bible studies, study guides, teacher helps, ministry aids, and other C.E. products. We do not consider fiction for children, youth, or adults. We do not consider devotionals, poetry, biographies, autobiographies, personal experience stories, mss. with a charismatic emphasis, or general Christian living books."

ACCORD COMMUNICATIONS, LTD., Suite B, 18002 15th Ave. NE, Seattle WA 98155. Managing Editor: Karen Duncan. Imprints are Evergreen Pacific Publishing, Larry Reynolds, Managing Editor; A.K.A./Seattle Books, Karen Duncan, Managing Editor. Publishes hardcover originals and trade paperback originals and reprints. Publishes 7 titles/year. Receives 200 queries, 350 mss/year. 80% of books from first-time authors; 100% from unagented writers. Pays royalty on wholesale price. Publishes ms 1 year after acceptance. Accepts simultaneous submissions. Reports in 3 months on proposals.
Nonfiction: How-to (marine-related), reference, atlases and guides, hobbies, recreation, mystery criticism and history. Query. Reviews artwork/photos as part of freelance ms package. Writers should send photocopies.
Recent Nonfiction Title: *Cruising Guide to the West Coast of Vancouver Island*, by Don Watmough (text, photos and charts for boaters).
Fiction: Mystery. Submit synopsis with 3 sample chapters. "We plan to publish traditional detective/amateur sleuth mysteries, preferably with series characters."
Recent Fiction Title: *In Blacker Moments*, by S.E. Schenkel.

ACE SCIENCE FICTION, Imprint of The Berkley Publishing Group, 200 Madison Ave., New York NY 10016. (212)686-9820. Associate Editor: Laura Anne Gilman. Estab. 1953. Publishes paperback originals and reprints. Averages 96 titles/year. Reports in 3-6 months. Manuscript guidelines for #10 SASE.
Fiction: Science fiction and fantasy. Query with synopsis and first 3 chapters.
Recent Fiction Title: *Spindoc*, by Steve Perry.

ACTA PUBLICATIONS, 4848 N. Clark St., Chicago IL 60640-4711. Co-Publisher: Gregory F. Augustine Pierce. Estab. 1958. Publishes trade paperback originals. Publishes 10 titles/year. Receives 50 queries and 15 mss/year. 50% of mss from first-time authors; 90% from unagented writers. Pays 7½-12½% royalty on wholesale

price. Publishes book 1 year after acceptance of ms. No simultaneous submissions. Reports in 2 months on proposals. Book catalog and author guidelines for SASE.
Nonfiction: Religion. "We publish non-academic, practical books aimed at the mainline religious market." Submit outline and 1 sample chapter. Reviews artwork/photos as part of freelance ms package. Writers should send photocopies.
Tips: "Don't send a submission unless you have read our catalog or one of our books."

‡ACTIVE PARENTING PUBLISHERS, INC., 810-B Franklin Court, Marietta GA 30067. Editorial Manager: Suzanne De Galan. Publishes 4 titles/year. Receives 16 queries and 8 mss/year. 100% of books from unagented writers. Pays 6-10% royalty on retail price. Publishes book 1 year after acceptance of ms. Accepts simultaneous submissions. Query for electronic submissions. Reports in 2 months on proposals. Book catalog for 8½×11 SAE with 4 first-class stamps.
Nonfiction: Self-help, textbook, educational. Subjects include child guidance/parenting, psychology, loss, self-esteem. Nonfiction work; mainly parent education and family issues. Submit outline and 2 sample chapters.
Recent Nonfiction Title: *Active Teaching Leader's Guide*, by Michael H. Popkin, Ph.D. (textbook).

‡BOB ADAMS, INC., 260 Center St., Holbrook MA 02343. (617)767-8100. Managing Editor: Brandon Toropov. Estab. 1980. Publishes hardcover and trade paperback originals. Averages 50 titles/year. Receives 1,000 submissions/year. 25% of books from first-time authors; 25% of books from unagented writers. Variable royalty "determined on case-by-case basis." Publishes book an average of 12-18 months after acceptance. Reports in 6-8 weeks "if interested. We accept no responsibility for unsolicited manuscripts." Book catalog for 9×12 SAE with 10 first-class stamps.
Nonfiction: Reference books on careers, self-help, business. Query with SASE.
Recent Nonfiction Title: *The Everything Wedding Book*, by Michelle Bruilacqua.

‡ADAMS-BLAKE PUBLISHING, 8041 Sierra St., Fair Oaks CA 95628. (916)962-9296. Vice President: Paul Raymond. Publishes trade paperback originals and reprints. Publishes 8-12 titles/year. Receives 50 queries and 40 mss/year. 90% of books from first-time authors; 90% from unagented writers. Pays 8% royalty on wholesale price. Offers $500-1,000 advance. Publishes book 5 months after acceptance of ms. Simultaneous submissions OK. Reports in 1 month mss.
Nonfiction: How-to, technical. Subjects include business and economics, computers and electronics, health/medicine, money/finance, software. "We are looking for business, technology and finance titles that can be targeted to older or retired members of the workforce." Query with sample chapters or complete ms. Reviews artwork/photos as part of freelance ms package. Writers should send photocopies.
Recent Nonfiction Title: *Computer Money*, by A. Canton (business); *Tears And Rage*, by J. Schweitzer (medicine); *The PC Consultant's Secrets*, by B. Cowen (computer).
Tips: "We will take a chance on material the big houses reject. Since we sell the majority of our material directly, we can publish material for a very select market."

‡ADVANCE CORPORATION, P.O. Box 292700, Cooper City FL 33329. Contact: Albert Kadoch. Publishes trade and mass market paperback originals. Publishes 40-50 titles/year. Each imprint publishes 30 titles/year. Receives 200 queries and 100-200 mss/year. 80% of books from first-time authors; 50% from unagented writers. Makes outright purchase of $350-2,500. Publishes book 3-6 months after acceptance of ms. Simultaneous submissions OK. Query for electronic submissions. Reports in 2 months on queries, 1 month on proposals, 1 month on mss. Manuscript guidelines for #10 SASE.
Nonfiction: How-to, illustrated book, children's/juvenile, reference, self-help. Subjects include agriculture/horticulture, animals, child guidance/parenting, computers and electronics, education, money/finance, translation. Submit outline. Reviews artwork/photos as part of freelance ms package. Writers should send photocopies.
Fiction: Adventure, juvenile. Submit synopsis.

‡ADVOCACY PRESS, Division of Girls Incorporated of Greater Santa Barbara, P.O. Box 236, Santa Barbara CA 93102. (805)962-2728. Contact: Editor. Estab. 1983. Publishes hardcover children's illustrated books and trade paperback texts and workbooks for teens and young adults. All books have an equity/self-esteem focus. Does not publish young adult fiction. Children's books must focus on specific concepts, e.g. leadership, self-reliance, etc. Publishes 3-4 titles/year. Receives 150 submissions/year. Most from first-time authors; 100% from unagented writers. Accepts simultaneous submissions if so noted. Reports in 6 weeks.

The double dagger before a listing indicates that the listing is new in this edition. New markets are often more receptive to freelance submissions.

Nonfiction: Texts, journal workbooks featuring self-awareness, personal planning for maximizing potential, gender equity. New series planned to feature job preparation and job analysis for specific industry (i.e., *Foodwork: Jobs in the Food Industry and How to Get Them*).
Recent Nonfiction Title: *Making Choices: Life Skills for Adolescents.*
Recent Fiction Title: *Shadow and the Ready Time*, by Sheehan and Maeno. Illustrated children's book based on wolf pack behavorial habits.

‡**AEGEAN PARK PRESS**, P.O. Box 2837, Laguna Hills CA 92654. (714)586-8811. President: Wayne G. Barker. Publishes trade paperback originals and reprints. Publishes 15 titles/year. Receives 30 queries and 10 mss/year. Makes outright purchase of $200-500. Offers $200 advance. Publishes book 6 months after acceptance of ms. Simultaneous submissions OK. No unsolicited mss. Book catalog free on request.
Nonfiction: Technical. Subjects include anthropology/archaeology, computers and electronics, history, military/war, espionage, communications, cryptology. "We want nonfiction books dealing with 'high-tech' communications, cryptology, espionage." Query.

‡**AFCOM PUBLISHING**, P.O. Box H, Harbor City CA 90710-0330. (213)544-2314. Manager: Greg Cook. Estab. 1988. Publishes mass market paperback originals and reprints. 80% of books are originals; 20% are reprints. Firm averages 5 titles/year. Receives 200 submissions/year. 50% of books from first-time authors; 100% from unagented writers. Pays 5-15% royalty on wholesale price. Publishes book an average of 9 months after acceptance. Simultaneous submissions OK. Reports in 2 months on queries; 3 months on mss.
Nonfiction: How-to, reference, self-help, textbook. Subjects include business, education, hobbies, recreation, sports, total quality management, sex and sex education. "We are looking for how-to books, total quality management, business textbooks, and books on sex." Submit detailed explanation of how you could reach your market along with the complete ms including artwork/photos.
Recent Nonfiction Title: *Sex is Like a Hot Fudge Sundae.*
Fiction: Humor, juvenile.
Recent Fiction Title: *The 12 Powers of Animals*, by Eloise Dickis (juvenile).
Tips: "Writers have the best chance selling us how-to books with an easily reachable market and any books related to total quality management including books on quality function deployment, design of experiments, statistical process controls, cycle-time management, value engineering, benchmarking and/or team building. If I were a writer trying to market a book today, I would concentrate on books that have an easily reached target market or books that would interest libraries."

‡**AFRICAN AMERICAN IMAGES**, 1909 W. 95th St., Chicago IL 60643. (312)445-0322. Publisher: Dr. Jawanza Kunjufu. Publishes trade paperback originals. Publishes 10 titles/year. Receives 520 queries and 520 mss/year. 90% of books from first-time authors; 95% from unagented writers. Pays 10% royalty on wholesale price. Publishes book 6 months after acceptance of ms. Simultaneous submissions OK. Reports in 1 month on queries, 2 months on mss. Book catalog and ms guidelines free on request.
Nonfiction: Children's/juvenile. Subjects include education, ethnic, history, psychology. Submit complete ms.
Fiction: Juvenile.

ALASKA NORTHWEST BOOKS, Imprint of Graphic Arts Center Publishing. Editorial offices: Suite 300, 2208 NW Market St., Seattle WA 98107. (206)784-5071. Fax: (206)784-5316. Contact: Acquisitions Editor. Estab. 1959. Publishes hardcover and trade paperback originals and reprints. Firm averages 15 titles/year. Receives hundreds of submissions/year. 30% of books from first-time authors; 80% from unagented writers. Pays 10-15% royalty on wholesale price. Buys mss outright (rarely). Offers advance. Publishes book an average of 1 year after acceptance. Simultaneous submissions OK. Reports in 6 months on queries. Book catalog and ms guidelines for 9×12 SAE with 6 first-class stamps.
  • Editor reports this house is initiating more of their own projects and publishing fewer unsolicited manuscripts.
Nonfiction: "All written for a general readership, not for experts in the subject." Subjects include nature and environment, travel, cookbooks, Native American culture, adventure, outdoor recreation and sports, the arts, children's books. "Our book needs are as follows: one-quarter Alaskan focus, one-quarter Northwest, one-quarter Pacific coast, one-quarter national (looking for logical extensions of current subjects)." Submit outline/synopsis and sample chapters.
Recent Nonfiction Title: *The Last Light Breaking: Living Among Alaska's Inupiat Eskimos*, by Nick Jans.
Tips: "Book proposals that are professionally written and polished, with a clear market receive our most careful consideration. We are looking for originality. We publish a wide range of books for a wide audience. Some of our books are clearly for travelers, others for those interested in outdoor recreation or various regional subjects. If I were a writer trying to market a book today, I would research the competition (existing books) for what I have in mind, and clearly (and concisely) express why my idea is different and better. I would describe the bookbuyers (and readers) —where they are, how many of them are there, how they can be reached (organizations, publications), why they would want or need my book."

THE ALBAN INSTITUTE, Suite 433 North, 4550 Montgomery Ave., Bethesda MD 20814-3341. (301)718-4407. Fax: (301)718-1958. Editor-in-Chief: Celia A. Hahn. Publishes trade paperback originals. Averages 9 titles/ year. Receives 100 submissions annually. 100% of books from unagented writers. Pays 7-10% royalty on books; $50-100 on publication for 450-3,600 word articles relevant to congregational life — practical — ecumenical. Publishes book an average of 1 year after acceptance. Reports in 2 months. Proposals must be submitted. No unsolicited mss. Book catalog and ms guidelines for 9 × 12 SAE with 3 first-class stamps.
Nonfiction: Religious — focus on local congregation — ecumenical. Must be accessible to general reader. Research preferred. Needs mss on the task of the ordained leader in the congregation, the career path of the ordained leader in the congregation, problems and opportunities in congregational life, and ministry of the laity in the world and in the church. No sermons, devotional, children's titles, inspirational or prayers. Query for guidelines.
Tips: "Our audience is comprised of intelligent, probably liberal mainline Protestant and Catholic clergy and lay leaders, executives and seminary administration/faculty — people who are concerned with the local church at a practical level and new approaches to its ministry. We are looking for titles on Problems and Opportunities in Congregational Life, The Clergy Role and Career, and The Ministry of the Laity in the Church and in the World."

ALLEN PUBLISHING CO., 7324 Reseda Blvd., Reseda CA 91335. (818)344-6788. Owner/Publisher: Michael Wiener. Estab. 1979. Publishes mass market paperback originals. Firm averages 4 titles/year. Receives 50-100 submissions/year. 50% of books from first-time authors; 90% from unagented writers. Buys mss outright for negotiable sum. Publishes book an average of 6 months after acceptance. Simultaneous submissions OK. Reports in 2 weeks. *Writer's Market* recommends allowing 2 months for reply. Book catalog and writer guidelines for #10 SASE.
● This publisher reports having received many manuscripts outside its area of interest. Writers are encouraged to follow the publisher's subject matter guidelines.
Nonfiction: How-to, self-help. Subjects include how to start various businesses and how to improve your financial condition. "We want self-help material, 25,000 words approximately, aimed at wealth-builders, opportunity seekers, aspiring entrepreneurs. We specialize in material for people who are relatively inexperienced in the world of business and have little or no capital to invest. Material must be original and authoritative, not rehashed from other sources. All our books are marketed exclusively by mail, in soft-cover, 8½ × 11 format. We are a specialty publisher and will not consider anything that does not exactly meet our needs." Query. Reviews artwork/photos as part of ms package.
Recent Nonfiction Title: *How To Find The One Opportunity Offer That Can Make You Rich.*
Tips: "We are a specialty publisher, as noted above. If your subject does not match our specialty, do not waste your time and ours by submitting a query we cannot possibly consider."

ALLWORTH PRESS, 10 E. 23rd St., New York NY 10010-4402. Editor: Ted Gachot. Estab. 1989. Publisher: Tad Crawford. Publishes trade paperback originals. Publishes 10 titles/year. Pays 6-7½% royalty (for paperback) on retail price. Reports in 1 month on queries and proposals. Book catalog and ms guidelines free on request.
Nonfiction: How-to, reference. Subjects include the business aspects of art, design, photography, writing, as well as legal guides for the public. "We are trying to give ordinary people advice to better themselves in practical ways — as well as helping creative people in the fine and commercial arts." Query.

ALMAR PRESS, 4105 Marietta Dr., Vestal NY 13850-4032. (607)722-0265. Fax: (607)722-0265. Editor-in-Chief: A.N. Weiner. Managing Editor: M.F. Weiner. Estab. 1977. Publishes hardcover and paperback originals and reprints. Averages 8 titles/year. Receives 200 submissions annually. 75% of books from first-time authors; 100% from unagented writers. Average print order for a first book is 2,000. Pays 10% royalty, no advance. Publishes book an average of 6 months after acceptance. Prefers exclusive submissions; however, accepts simultaneous submissions (if so indicated). Query for electronic submissions. Reports in 2 months. Book catalog for #10 SAE with 2 first-class stamps. *"Submissions must include SASE for reply."*
Nonfiction: Publishes business, technical, regional, consumer books and reports. "These main subjects include general business, financial, travel, career, technology, personal help, Northeast regional, hobbies, general medical, general legal, how-to. *Almar Reports* are business and technology subjects published for management use and prepared in 8½ × 11 book format. Reprint publications represent a new aspect of our business." Submit outline and sample chapters. Reviews artwork/photos as part of ms package.
Tips: "We're adding a new series of postcard books for various topics where the picture postcards are illustrated and the captions describe the scene on the postcard and the history related to it. Approximately 225 illustrations per book. We are open to any suggested topic. This type of book will be important to us. We look for timely subjects. The type of book the writer has the best chance of selling to our firm is something different or unusual — *no* poetry or fiction, also *no* first-person travel or family history. The book must be complete and of good quality."

‡ALYSON PUBLICATIONS, INC., 40 Plympton St., Boston MA 02118-2425. (617)542-5679. Publisher: Sasha Alyson. Estab. 1979. Imprints are Lace, Alyson Wonderland, and Perineum Press. Publishes trade paperback originals and reprints. Averages 20 titles/year. Receives 500 submissions annually. 30% of books from first-time authors; 80% from unagented writers. Average print order for a first book is 6,000. Pays 8-15% royalty on net price. Offers $1,000-3,000 advance. Publishes book an average of 15 months after acceptance. Reports in 1 month. *Writer's Market* recommends allowing 2 months for reply. Book catalog and ms guidelines for 6×9 SAE with 3 first-class stamps.

Nonfiction: Gay/lesbian subjects. "We are especially interested in nonfiction providing a positive approach to gay/lesbian issues." Accepts nonfiction translations. Submit 2-page outline. Reviews artwork/photos as part of ms package. Include SASE.

Recent Nonfiction Title: *Members of the Tribe*, by Michael Willhoite.

Fiction: Gay novels. Accepts fiction translations. Submit 1-2 page synopsis. Include SASE.

Recent Fiction Title: *Captain Swing*, by Larry Duplechan.

Tips: "We publish many books by new authors. The writer has the best chance of selling to our firm well-researched, popularly-written nonfiction on a subject (e.g., some aspect of gay history) that has not yet been written about much. With fiction, create a strong storyline that makes the reader want to find out what happens. With nonfiction, write in a popular style for a non-academic audience. Actively soliciting manuscripts aimed at kids of lesbian and gay parents."

AMACOM BOOKS, Imprint of American Management Association, 135 W. 50th, New York NY 10020-1201. (212)903-8081. Director: Weldon P. Rackley. Estab. 1923. Publishes hardcover and trade paperback originals and trade paperback reprints. Averages 68 titles/year. Receives 200 submissions/year. 50% of books from first-time authors; 90% from unagented writers. Pays 10-15% royalty on net receipts by the publisher. Publishes book an average of 9 months after acceptance. Query for electronic submissions. Reports in 2 months. Free book catalog and proposal guidelines.

Nonfiction: Publishes business books of all types, including management, marketing, technology (computers), career, professional skills, small business. Retail, direct mail, college, corporate markets. Query. Submit outline/synopsis, sample chapters, résumé/vita.

Tips: "Our audience consists of people in the business sector looking for practical books on business issues, strategies, and tasks."

‡AMADEUS PRESS, Timber Press, Inc., Suite 450, 133 SW Second Ave., Portland OR 97204. General Editor: Dr. Reinhard Pauly. Publishes hardcover originals and reprints and trade paperback originals. Publishes 8-10 titles/year. Receives 150 queries and 25 mss/year. 50% of books from first-time authors; 95% from unagented writers. Pays 10% royalty on net billings. Rarely offers advance. Accepts simultaneous submissions, if informed. Query for electronic submissions. Reports in 2 months on proposals. Book catalog and ms guidelines for #10 SASE.

Nonfiction: Biography, reference. Subjects include music, classical music, opera. Submit outline, 2 sample chapters and sample illustrations. Reviews artwork/photos as part of freelance ms package if appropriate. Writers should send photocopies.

Recent Nonfiction Title: *Saturday Afternoons at the Old Met*, by Paul Jackson (music history and criticism); *Adelina Patti: Queen of Hearts*, by John Cone (opera biography); *Olivier Messiaen: Music and Color*, by Claude Samuel (conversations with composer).

Tips: "Our audience is discerning music lovers, opera and concert goers, amateur and professional musicians, music teachers, music scholars. We demand much of our authors—we expect them to make editorial changes on computer disks to supply and pay for permissions, illustrations, music examples and index, and to proofread. In return we supply excellent editorial and pre-production support, and publish beautiful books."

AMERICA WEST PUBLISHERS, P.O. Box 3300, Bozeman MT 59772-3300. (406)585-0700. Fax: (406)585-0703. Review Editor: George Green. Estab. 1985. Publishes hardcover and trade paperback originals and reprints. Averages 20 titles/year. Receives 50 submissions/year. 30% of books from first-time authors; 90% from unagented writers. Pays 10% on wholesale price. Offers $300 average advance. Publishes book an average of 6 months after acceptance. Simultaneous submissions OK. Reports in 1 month. Free book catalog and ms guidelines.

Nonfiction: UFO—metaphysical. Subject includes health/medicine (holistic self-help), political (including cover-up), economic. Submit outline/synopsis and sample chapters. Reviews artwork/photos as part of ms package.

Recent Nonfiction Title: *Committee of 300*, by John Coleman.

Tips: "We currently have materials in all bookstores that have areas of UFO's and also political and economic nonfiction."

‡AMERICAN ASSOCIATES, PUBLISHING, 4500 Skyline Court, NE, Albuquerque NM 87111-3001. (505)293-9349. CEO: H.J. Hsia. Publishes hardcover, trade and mass market paperback originals. Publishes 8-10 titles/year. Pays 15-20% royalty on wholesale price or makes outright purchase of $500-5,000. Simultaneous submissions OK. Query for electronic submissions. Reports in 2 weeks on queries, 1 month on mss.

Nonfiction: Reference, technical, textbook. Subjects include ethnic, history, philosophy, regional, sociology, women's issues/studies. "Particularly interested in ethnic Americans (Italian-Americans, Polish-Americans,

Russian-Americans, etc.), their migration, personalities, achievements, culture, arts and struggles. Prefer a series to a book." Submit complete ms.

Recent Nonfiction Title: *The Fair Sex in China* (history, women); *Philosophical and Religious Thought in China* (history, religion, philosophy); *The East is East and The West is West (East-West relations); Harmony and Conflict in Chinese Society and Family* (culture, family, sociology); *Chinese Culture in a Kaleidoscope* (history, culture, history) all by Hsia.

AMERICAN ASSOCIATION FOR STATE AND LOCAL HISTORY, Suite 600, 530 Church St., Nashville TN 37219-2325. (615)255-2971. Fax: (615)255-2979. Estab. 1940. Publishes paperback originals. Averages approximately 6 titles/year. Receives 20-30 submissions annually. 50% of books from first-time authors; 100% from unagented writers. Query for royalty rates. Publishes book an average of 1 year after acceptance. Reports in 3 months on submissions. Free book catalog.

Nonfiction: How-to, reference, collections, preservation, textbook. "We publish books, mostly technical, that help people do effective work in historical societies, sites and museums, or do research in, or teach, history. No manuscripts on history itself—that is, on the history of specific places, events, people." Write for ms guidelines.

Recent Nonfiction Title: *Boats: A Manual for Their Documentation*, edited by Paul Lipke and Peter Spectre.

Tips: "The American Association for State and Local History provides leadership for and service to those who practice and support history in North America: historical societies, museums, historic sites, parks, libraries, archives, historic preservation organizations, schools, colleges, and other educational organizations."

AMERICAN ASTRONAUTICAL SOCIETY, Univelt, Inc., Publisher, P.O. Box 28130, San Diego CA 92198. (619)746-4005. Fax: (619)746-3139. Editorial Director: Robert H. Jacobs. Estab. 1970. Publishes hardcover originals. Averages 8 titles/year. Receives 12-15 submissions annually. 5% of books from first-time authors; 5% from unagented writers. Average print order for a first book is 600-2,000. Pays 10% royalty on actual sales. Publishes book an average of 4 months after acceptance. Simultaneous submissions OK. Reports in 1 month. *Writer's Market* recommends allowing 2 months for reply. Book catalog and ms guidelines for 9 × 12 SAE with 3 first-class stamps.

Nonfiction: Proceedings or monographs in the field of astronautics, including applications of aerospace technology to Earth's problems. "Our books must be space-oriented or space-related. They are meant for technical libraries, research establishments and the aerospace industry worldwide." Submit outline and 1-2 sample chapters. Reviews artwork/photos as part of ms package.

Recent Nonfiction Title: *Space Business Opportunities*, edited by Wayne J. Essen and Don K. Tomajan.

‡AMERICAN ATHEIST PRESS, P.O. Box 2117, Austin TX 78768-2117. (512)458-1244. Editor: R. Murray-O'Hair. Estab. 1959. Imprints include Gusttav Broukal Press. Publishes trade paperback originals and reprints. Publishes 12 titles/year. Receives 200 submissions annually. 40-50% of books from first-time authors; 100% from unagented writers. Pays 5-10% royalty on retail price. Publishes book an average of 2 years after acceptance. Simultaneous submissions OK. Reports in 4 months on queries. Book catalog for 6½ × 9½ SAE. Writer's guidelines for 9 × 12 SAE.

Nonfiction: Biography, humor, reference, general. Subjects include history (of religion and Atheism, of the effects of religion historically); philosophy and religion (from an Atheist perspective, particularly criticism of religion); politics (separation of state and church, religion and politics); Atheism (particularly the lifestyle of Atheism; the history of Atheism; applications of Atheism). "We are interested in hard-hitting and original books expounding the lifestyle of Atheism and criticizing religion. We would like to see more submissions dealing with the histories of specific religious sects, such as the L.D.S., the Worldwide Church of God, etc. We are generally not interested in biblical criticism." Submit outline and sample chapters. Reviews artwork/photos.

Recent Nonfiction Title: *Manual of a Perfect Atheist*, by Rios.

Fiction: Humor (satire of religion or of current religious leaders); anything of particular interest to Atheists. "We rarely publish any fiction. But we have occasionally released a humorous book. No mainstream. For our press to consider fiction, it would have to tie in with the general focus of our press, which is the promotion of Atheism and free thought." Submit outline/synopsis and sample chapters.

Tips: We will need more how-to types of material—how to argue with creationists, how to fight for state/church separation, etc. We have an urgent need for literature for young Atheists."

AMERICAN BAR ASSOCIATION, PUBLICATIONS PLANNING & MARKETING, 750 N. Lake Shore Dr., Chicago IL 60611. (312)988-6104. Fax: (312)988-6281. Manager, Book Development: Susan Yessne. Publishes hardcover and trade paperback originals and trade paperback reprints. Publishes 50 titles/year. Receives 100 queries/year. Pays royalties; "varies a great deal." Publishes book 6 months after acceptance of ms. Simultaneous submissions OK. Query for electronic submission: prefers disk; WordPerfect or Microsoft Word software. Reports in 2 months on queries and proposals, 3 months on mss. Manuscript guidelines free on request.

Nonfiction: Law. Subjects include law practice. "All proposals should be for books that will help lawyers practice law better—no treatises, no memoirs, no philosophical meanderings. Writers should avoid not thinking of the audience; not meeting the needs of the reader; not writing well about practical matters." Query with outline and 1 sample chapter.

Tips: "We mainly serve lawyers. The best authors for us have an idea of what the law is about and, in fact, are probably practicing or teaching law."

‡AMERICAN CHEMICAL SOCIETY, 1155 16th St., NW, Washington DC 20036. (202)872-4564. Acquisitions: Cheryl Shanks. Publishes hardcover originals. Publishes 50 titles/year. Pays royalty. Publishes book 9-20 months after acceptance of ms. Simultaneous submissions OK. Query for electronic submissions. Submissions not returned. Reports in 6 weeks on proposals. Book catalog free on request.

Nonfiction: Technical. Subjects include science. "Emphasis is on professional reference books (e.g., dictionaries,, data books, handbooks)." Submit outline with 2 sample chapters.

Recent Nonfiction Title: *Laboratory Waste Management: A Guidebook.*

AMERICAN CORRECTIONAL ASSOCIATION, 8025 Laurel Lakes Court, Laurel MD 20707-5075. (301)206-5100. Fax: (301)206-5061. Managing Editor: Marianna Nunan. Estab. 1870. Publishes hardcover and trade paperback originals. Averages 18 titles/year. Receives 40 submissions/year. 90% of books from first-time authors; 100% from unagented writers. Pays 10% royalty on net sales. Publishes book an average of 9 months after acceptance. Query for electronic submissions. Reports in 3 months. Free book catalog and ms guidelines.
- This publisher advises out-of-town freelance editors and proofreaders to refrain from requesting work from them.

Nonfiction: How-to, reference, technical, textbook, correspondence courses. "We are looking for practical, how-to texts or training materials written for the corrections profession. No true-life accounts by current or former inmates or correctional officers, theses, or dissertations." Query. Reviews artwork/photos as part of ms package.

Tips: "People in the field want practical information, as do academics to a certain extent. Our audience is made up of criminal justice students and corrections professionals. If I were a writer trying to market a book today, I would contact publishers while developing my manuscript to get a better idea of the publishers' needs."

AMERICAN EAGLE PUBLICATIONS INC., P.O. Box 41401, Tuscon AZ 85717-1401. (602)888-4957. Publisher: Mark Ludwig. Estab. 1988. Publishes hardcover and trade paperback originals and reprints. Averages 8 titles/year. 50% of mss from first-time authors; 100% from unagented writers. Pays 5-12% royalty on retail price. Offers $1,000 average advance. Publishes book 6 months after acceptance of ms. Simultaneous submissions OK. Query for electronic submissions. Reports in 2 months. Catalog for #10 SASE.
- Publisher reports no interest in seeing military or other *auto*-biographies.

Nonfiction: Historical biography, technical. Subjects include computers and electronics (security), military/war and science (computers and artificial intelligence). "We are highly specialized in nonfiction. Writers should call and discuss what they have first." Query. Reviews artwork/photos as part of freelance ms package. Writers should send photocopies.

Recent Nonfiction Title: *Paul Schneider: The Witness of Buchenwald,* by Rudolf Wentorz.

Tips: Audience is "scholarly, university profs, (some used as textbooks) very technical programmers and researchers, military, very international."

‡AMERICAN EDUCATION PUBLISHING, Suite 145, 150 E. Wilson Bridge Rd., Columbus OH 43085. Contact: Diane Mangan. Imprint is Creative Editions. Publishes hardcover and trade paperback originals and trade paperback reprints. Publishes 25 titles/year. Imprint publishes 10 titles/year. Receives 200 queries and 700 mss/year. 15% of books from first-time authors; 20% unagented writers. Pays 4-10% royalty on retail price or makes outright purchase of $2,000-10,000. Offers $5,000-15,000 advance. Publishes book 9 months after acceptance of ms. Simultaneous submissions OK. Query for electronic submissions. Reports in 3-4 months on mss. Manuscript guidelines for #10 SASE.

Nonfiction: Children's/juvenile. Subjects include animals, education, nature/environment. "Looking for beginning readers nonfiction with educational value for retail, *not* textbook publishing." Submit outline and 2 sample chapters.

Recent Nonfiction Title: *Poe,* by Nancy Loewen; *Images Series,* by Michael George; *My First Nature Books Series,* by Kitty Benedict.

Fiction: Juvenile, picture books. "Particularly interested in manuscripts for children's picture story books. We are launching a mid-priced hardcover line." Submit synopsis and 3 sample chapters.

Recent Fiction Title: *A Number of Animals,* by Christopher Wormell; *Rip Van Winkle,* by Gary Kelley, illustrator; *Mouse Book Series,* by Monique Felix.

A bullet introduces comments by the editor of Writer's Market ***indicating special information about the listing.***

‡**AMERICAN FEDERATION OF ASTROLOGERS,** P.O. Box 22040, Tempe AZ 85285. Publications Manager: Kris Brandt Riske. Publishes trade paperback originals and reprints. Publishes 15-20 titles/year. Receives 10 queries and 20 mss/year. 30% of books from first-time authors; 100% from unagented writers. Pays 10% royalty. Publishes book 10 months after acceptance of ms. Simultaneous submissions OK. Query for electronic submissions. Reports in 3-6 months on mss. Book catalog for $2. Manuscript guidelines free on request.
Nonfiction: Astrology. Submit complete ms.
Recent Nonfiction Title: *Modern Horary Astrology,* by Doris Chase Doane; *Astrology Drawn to Life,* by Jairy Willingham-French; *Understanding Planetary Placements,* by Sophia Mason.

AMERICAN HOSPITAL PUBLISHING, INC., American Hospital Association, 737 N. Michigan Ave., Chicago IL 60611-2615. (312)440-6800. Fax: (312)951-8491. Vice President, Books: Brian Schenk. Estab. 1979. Publishes trade paperback originals. Averages 20-30 titles/year. Receives 75-100 submissions/year. 20% of books from first-time authors; 100% from unagented writers. Pays 10-12% royalty on retail price. Offers $1,000 average advance. Publishes book an average of 1 year after acceptance. Reports in 2-3 months. Book catalog and ms guidelines for 9×12 SAE with 7 first-class stamps.
Nonfiction: Reference, technical, textbook. Subjects include business and economics (specific to health care institutions); health/medicine (never consumer oriented). Need field-based, reality-tested responses to changes in the health care field directed to hospital CEO's, planners, boards of directors, or other senior management. No personal histories, untested health care programs or clinical texts. Query.
Tips: "The successful proposal demonstrates a clear understanding of the needs of the market and the writer's ability to succinctly present practical knowledge of demonstrable benefit that comes from genuine experience that readers will recognize, trust and accept. The audience is senior and middle management of health care institutions. These days we're a little more cautious in what we choose to publish."

AMERICAN LIBRARY ASSOCIATION, 50 E. Huron St., Chicago IL 60611-2795. (312)944-6780. Fax: (312)280-3255. Senior Editor-Acquisitions: Herbert Bloom. Estab. 1896. Publishes hardcover and paperback originals for use by librarians. Averages 35 titles/year. Pays royalty. Book catalog and ms guidelines free.
Nonfiction: Reference and library science. Curriculum material based on library resources. Query.
Recent Nonfiction Title: *Musicals!,* by R.C. Lynch.

AMERICAN PRESS, 520 Commonwealth Ave., Boston MA 02215-2605. Editor: Marcy Taylor. Publishes college textbooks. Publishes 25 titles/year. Receives 350 queries and 100 mss/year. 50% of books from first-time authors; 90% from unagented writers. Pays 5-15% royalty on wholesale price. Publishes book 9 months after acceptance of ms. Reports in 3 months. Book catalog free on request.
Nonfiction: Technical, textbook. Subjects include agriculture/horticulture, anthropology/archaeology, art/architecture, business and economics, education, government/politics, health/medicine, history, music/dance, psychology, science, sociology, sports. "We prefer that our authors actually teach courses for which the manuscripts are designed." Do not send complete ms. Query or submit outline with tentative table of contents.

THE AMERICAN PSYCHIATRIC PRESS, INC., 1400 K St. NW, Washington DC 20005. (202)682-6268. Editor-in-Chief: Carol C. Nadelson, M.D. Estab. 1981. Publishes hardcover and trade paperback originals. Averages 50 titles/year, 2-4 trade books/year. Receives about 300 submissions annually. 10% of books from first-time authors; 95% from unagented writers. Pays 10% minimum royalty based on all money actually received, maximum varies. Offers $3,000-5,000 average advance. Publishes book an average of 9 months after acceptance. Simultaneous submissions OK (if made clear in cover letter). Query for electronic submissions. Reports in 6 weeks "in regard to an *initial* decision regarding our interest. A *final* decision requires more time." Author questionnaire and proposal guidelines available for SASE.
Nonfiction: Reference, technical, textbook, general nonfiction. Subjects include psychiatry and related subjects. Authors must be well qualified in their subject area. No first-person accounts of mental illness or anything not clearly related to psychiatry. Query with outline and sample chapters.
Tips: "Because we are a specialty publishing company, books written by or in collaboration with a psychiatrist have the best chance of acceptance. Make it authoritative and professional."

AMERICAN SOCIETY OF CIVIL ENGINEERS, ASCE Press, 345 E. 47th St., New York NY 10017-2398. (212)705-7689. Book Acquisitions Editor: Joy Chan. Estab. 1988. Imprint averages 5-10 titles/year. 80% of books from first-time authors; 100% from unagented writers. Pays 10% royalty. No advances available. Simultaneous submissions OK. Query for electronic submissions. Reports in 2 months.
Nonfiction: Civil engineering. "We are looking for topics that are useful and instructive to the engineering practitioner." Query with outline and sample chapters.
Tips: "ASCE is a not-for-profit organization, so we've always been cost conscious. The recession has made us *more* conscious and much more cautious about our spending habits."

AMHERST MEDIA, INC., 418 Homecrest Dr., Amherst NY 14226-1219. (716)874-4450. Fax: (716)874-4508. Publisher: Craig Alesse. Estab. 1974. Publishes hardcover and trade paperback originals and reprints. Averages 7 titles/year. Receives 20 submissions/year. 80% of books from first-time authors; 100% from unagented writers. Pays 5-8% royalty. Publishes book an average of 6 months after acceptance. Simultaneous submissions OK. Reports in 2 months. Book catalog for #10 SAE with 3 first-class stamps. Manuscript guidelines free on request.

Nonfiction: How-to. Subjects include photography, business, sales, marketing, astronomy, video. We are looking for well-written and illustrated photo, video and astronomy books. Query. Reviews artwork/photos as part of ms package.

Tips: "Our audience is made up of beginning to advanced photographers and videographers. If I were a writer trying to market a book today, I would fill the need of a specific audience and self-edit in a tight manner."

ANCESTRY INCORPORATED, P.O. Box 476, Salt Lake City UT 84110-0476. (801)531-1790. Fax: (801)531-1798. Managing Editor: Anne Lemmon. Estab. 1983. Publishes hardcover, trade and paperback originals. Averages 6-8 titles/year. Receives over 100 submissions annually. 70% of books from first-time authors; 100% from unagented writers. Pays 8-12% royalty or purchases mss outright. Advances discouraged. Publishes book an average of 1 year after acceptance. Simultaneous submissions OK. Reports in 2 months. Book catalog for 9×12 SAE with 2 first-class stamps.

Nonfiction: How-to, reference, genealogy. Subjects include Americana; historical methodology, genealogical research techniques. "Our publications are aimed exclusively at the genealogist. We consider everything from short monographs to book length works on immigration, migration, record collections and heraldic topics." No mss that are not genealogical or historical. Query, or submit outline/synopsis and sample chapters. Reviews artwork/photos.

Recent Nonfiction Title: *U.S. Miltary Records*, by James C. Neagles.

Tips: "Genealogical reference, how-to, and descriptions of source collections have the best chance of selling to our firm. Be precise in your description. Please, no family histories or genealogies."

ANCHORAGE PRESS, INC., P.O. Box 8067, New Orleans LA 70182-8067. (504)283-8868. Fax: (504)866-0502. Editor: Orlin Corey. Publishes hardcover originals. Estab. 1935. Firm averages 10 titles/year. Receives 450-900 submissions/year. 50% of books from first-time authors; 80% from unagented writers. Pays 10-15% royalty on retail price. Playwrights also receive 50-75% royalties. Publishes book an average of 1 year after acceptance. Reports in 1 month on queries; 4 months on mss. Free book catalog and ms guidelines.

Nonfiction: Textbooks, plays. Subjects include education, language/literature, plays. "We are looking for play anthologies; and texts for teachers of drama/theater (middle school and high school.)" Query. Reviews artwork/photos as part of ms package.

Recent Nonfiction Title: *Short Plays of Theatre Classics*, selected and edited by Aurand Harris (12 beloved plays from the Middle Ages to the 20th Century for students and readers).

Fiction: Plays of juvenile/young people's interest. Query.

AND BOOKS, 702 S. Michigan, South Bend IN 46601. (219)232-3134. Editor: Janos Szebedinsky. Estab. 1980. Publishes trade paperback originals. Averages 10 titles/year. Receives 1,000 submissions/year. 50% of books from first-time authors; 90% from unagented writers. Pays 6-10% royalty on retail price. Simultaneous submissions OK. Publishes books an average of 1 year after acceptance. Query for electronic submissions. Reports in up to 3 months. Book catalog for #10 SASE.

Nonfiction: Subjects include computers (consumer-level), current affairs, social justice, psychology, religion, music: jazz, blues, classical. Especially needs books on computers and electronic publishing. No biography, humor or diet books.

Tips: "Attempt to get an intro or foreword by a respected authority on your subject. Include comments by others who have reviewed your material. Research the potential market and include the results with your proposal. In other words, make every effort to communicate your knowledge of the publishing process. A little preliminary legwork and market investigation can go a long way to influence a potential publisher. No longer interested in books on sports or law."

ANDREWS AND McMEEL, 4900 Main St., Kansas City MO 64112. Editorial Director: Donna Martin. Publishes hardcover and paperback originals. Averages 30 titles/year. Pays royalty on retail price. "Query only. No unsolicited manuscripts. Areas of specialization include humor, how-to, and consumer reference books, such as *The Universal Almanac*, edited by John W. Wright." Reports in 2 months.

‡APPALACHIAN MOUNTAIN CLUB BOOKS, 5 Joy St., Boston MA 02108. Editor: Gordon Hardy. Publishes trade paperback originals. Averages 6-10 titles/year. Receives 200 submissions annually. Receives 200 queries and 20 mss/year. 30% of books from first-time authors; 90% from unagented writers. Pays 6-12% royalty on retail price. Offers $1,000-4,000 advance. Publishes book an average of 10 months after acceptable of ms. Simultaneous submissions OK. Query for electronic submissions. ASCII text format; DOS or Apple Mac. Reports in 2-3 months on proposals. Book catalog for 8½×11 SAE with 4 first-class stamps. Manuscript guidelines for #10 SASE.

Nonfiction: How-to, guidebooks. Subjects include history (mountains, Northeast), nature/environment, recreation, regional (Northeast outdoor recreation). "We publish hiking guides, water-recreation guides (non-motorized), nature, conservation and mountain-subject guides for America's Northeast. Writers should avoid submitting: proposals on Appalachia (rural southern mountains); not enough market research; too much personal experience — autobiography." Query. Reviews artwork/photos as part of freelance ms package. Writers should send photocopies and transparencies "at your own risk."

Recent Nonfiction Title: *Quiet Water Canoe Guide: MA/CT/RI*, by Alex Wilson (family canoe guidebook); *AMC Guide to Mt. Desert Island and Acadia Nat'l Park*, by Chris Efriny et. al. (hiking guidebook); *Nature Walks in Eastern Massachusetts*, by Michael Tougias (country walks guidebook).

Tips: "Our audience is outdoor recreationalists, conservation — minded hikers and canoeists, family outdoor lovers, armchair enthusiasts. Always connect recreation with conservation — all our guidebooks have a strong conservation message."

APPLAUSE BOOKS, 211 W. 71st St., New York NY 10023. Managing Editor: Andrew Pontious. Publishes hardcover and trade paperback originals and trade paperback reprints. Publishes 25 titles/year. Receives 500 queries and 400 ms/year. Pays royalty. Publishes book 8 months after acceptance of ms. Reports in 1 months on queries, 2 months on proposals, 3 months on mss. Book catalog free on request.

Nonfiction: All unsolicited mss are returned unopened.

Recent Nonfiction Title: *Acting in Film*, by Michael Caine; *JFK: Book of the Film*, by Oliver Stone; *Actor & The Text*, by Cicely Berry.

APPLEZABA PRESS, P.O. Box 4134, Long Beach CA 90804. (213)591-0015. Publisher: D.H. Lloyd. Estab. 1977. Publishes hardcover and trade paperback originals. Averages 4 titles/year. Receives 1,000 submissions/year. 5% of books from first-time authors; 95% from unagented writers. Pays 8-15% royalty on retail price. Publishes book average of 3 years after acceptance. Simultaneous submissions OK. Reports in 2 months. Book catalog and ms guidelines for #10 SASE.

Nonfiction: Query. Reviews artwork/photos as part of ms package.

Fiction: Literary and short story collections. Query or submit outline/synopsis and sample chapters.

‡AQUA QUEST PUBLICATIONS, INC., P.O. Box 700, Locust Valley NY 11560-0700. (516)759-0476. Fax: (516)759-4519. President: Anthony A. Bliss, Jr. Estab. 1989. Publishes trade paperback originals and reprints. Publishes 4-6 titles/year. Receives 40 queries and 12 mss/year. 60% of books from first-time authors; 100% from unagented writers. Pays royalty on wholesale price. Offers $700-1,500 advance. Publishes books 1-2 years after acceptance of ms. Simultaneous submissions OK. Query for electronic submissions. SASE. Reports in 1 month on queries, 6 months on proposals, 1-6 months on mss. Book catalog free on request.

Nonfiction: How-to, reference, technical. Subjects include nature/environment, photography, recreation, sports, travel, marine-related (scuba diving/marine life/shipwrecks). Query. Reviews artwork/photos after query approval — sample acct, outline & chapter.

Fiction: Adventure, historical, mainstream/contemporary and suspense. Submit 3 sample chapters.

ARCADE PUBLISHING, 141 Fifth Ave., New York NY 10010. (212)475-2633. Publisher: Richard Seaver. Publishes hardcover originals and trade paperback reprints. Publishes 40 titles/year. 5% of books from first-time authors. Pays royalty on retail price. Offers $3,000-100,000 advance. Publishes book 12-18 months after acceptance of ms. Simultaneous submissions OK. Query for electronic submissions: "via disk — but only if accompanied by a printout." Prefers Mac compatible. Reports in 2-3 months on queries.

Nonfiction: Biography, cookbook, general nonfiction. Subjects include cooking, foods & nutrition, government/politics, history, nature/environment and travel. Query. Reviews artwork/photos as part of freelance ms package. Writers should send photocopies.

Recent Nonfiction Title: *Images: My Life in Film*, by Ingmar Bergman (autobiography).

Fiction: Ethnic, historical, humor, literary, mainstream/contemporary, mystery, short story collections, suspense. Query. Agented submissions only.

Recent Fiction Title: *Dreams of Fair to Middling Women*, by Samuel Beckett.

Poetry: "We do not publish poetry as rule; in our three-and-half years we have published only one volume of poetry." Query.

ARCHITECTURAL BOOK PUBLISHING CO., INC, 268 Dogwood Lane, Stamford CT 06903. (203)322-1460. Editor: Walter Frese. Estab. 1891. Averages 10 titles/year. Receives 400 submissions annually. 80% of books from first-time authors; 95% from unagented writers. Average print order for a first book is 5,000. Royalty is percentage of retail price. Publishes book an average of 10 months after acceptance. Prefers queries, outlines and 2 sample chapters with number of illustrations. Reports in 2 weeks. *Writer's Market* recommends allowing 2 months for reply.

Nonfiction: Publishes architecture, decoration, and reference books on city planning and industrial arts. Accepts nonfiction translations. Also interested in history, biography, and science of architecture and decoration. Query with outline and 2 sample chapters. Enclose SASE for return of materials.

ARCHIVES PUBLICATIONS, 334 State St., Los Altos CA 94022. Contact: Phil Wycliff. Imprints are Archives Press. Contact: Phil Wycliff; Epona Media, Contact: Hazel Pethig; Book Processor, Contact: Donna Maria Cordoba. Publishes hardcover and trade paperback originals and reprints. Publishes 15 titles/year. Each imprint publishes 2/year. Receives 2,000 queries/year. 70% of books from first-time authors, 100% from unagented writers. Pays 7½-10% royalty on retail price or make outright purchase (negotiable). Offers $500-5,000 advance. Publishes book 16 months after acceptance of ms. No simultaneous submissions. Query for electronic submission. Reports in 4 months. Book catalog and ms guidelines free on request.

● Archives Publications does not wish to see any unsolicited manuscripts without an initial query letter. If a full manuscript is requested, Archives requires a $25 reading and shipping fee at the time you send your manuscript. Contracts are only offered on completed manuscripts.

Nonfiction: Biography, cookbook, how-to, children's/juvenile, reference. Subjects include anthropology/archaeology, art/architecture, cooking, foods and nutrition, history (Irish only), music/dance, psychology, astronomy, literary. "We are deeply committed to excellence in literature, both fiction and nonfiction. If you're not a deep thinker don't bother us." Query by mail only. No response unless queried first. Do not send anything registered or certified mail.

Fiction: Historical, literary, occult, religious (no New Age), equestrian. "We take a serious look at all well presented manuscripts *after* query." Query by mail only. All unsolicited mss are returned unread.

Tips: "All prospective authors should subscribe to our newsletter, *The Independent Publisher,* which gives guidelines, changes, new titles and important tidbits on our style and publications philosophy. The newsletter comes out three times a year and costs $5. We can fax it to you if you prefer. Do not send a SASE. Send loose stamps and a 3×5 card or a check or money order for $3 for each submission. This defrays the cost of reading it and sending it back. Stick to the topics. We publish equestrian, rock and roll, archaeology, astronomy, anthropology and Celtica. No New Age. We emphasize Irish topics. No explicit sex or UFO's."

ARCHWAY PAPERBACKS/MINSTREL BOOKS, Imprint of Pocket Books, 1230 Avenue of the Americas, New York NY 10020. (212)698-7268. Editorial Director: Patricia MacDonald. Send all submissions Attn: Manuscript Proposals. Publishes mass market paperback originals and reprints. Averages 80 titles/year. Receives over 1,000 submissions/year. Pays royalty. Publishes book an average of 2 years after acceptance. Reports in 3 months. SASE for all material necessary or query not answered.

Nonfiction: Middle grade, young adult. Subjects include current popular subjects or people, sports. Query with SASE. Submit outline/synopsis and 2 sample chapters. Reviews artwork/photos as part of ms package.

Fiction: Middle grade, young adult. Suspense thrillers and soap-opera romances for YA; mysteries, school stories, funny/scary stories, animal stories for middle grade readers. No picture books. Query with SASE. Submit outline/synopsis and sample chapters.

Recent Fiction Title: *Aliens Ate My Homework,* by Bruce Coville (Minstrel); *Fear Street: Silent Night 2,* by R.L. Stine (Archway).

‡ARDEN PRESS INC., P.O. Box 418, Denver CO 80201-0418. (303)697-6766. Publisher: Susan Conley. Estab. 1980. Publishes hardcover and trade paperback originals and reprints. 95% of books are originals; 5% are reprints. Averages 4-6 titles/year. Receives 600 submissions/year. 20% of books from first-time authors. 80% from unagented writers. Pays 8-15% royalty on wholesale price. Offers $2,000 average advance. Publishes book an average of 6 months after acceptance. Simultaneous submissions OK. Query for electronic submissions. Reports in 1 month on queries. Manuscript guidelines free on request.

Nonfiction: Biography, reference, textbooks. Subjects include women's issues/studies (history, biography, practical guides.) Query. Submit outline/synopsis and sample chapters.

Tips: "Writers have the best chance selling us nonfiction on women's subjects. We sell to general and women's bookstores and public and academic libraries. Many of our titles are adopted as texts for college courses. If I were a writer trying to market a book today, I would learn as much as I could about publishers' profiles *then* contact those who publish similar works."

JASON ARONSON, INC., 230 Livingston St., Northvale NJ 07647-1726. (201)767-4093. Fax: (201)767-4330. Vice President: Arthur Kurzweil. Estab. 1967. Publishes hardcover originals and reprints. 80% of books are originals; 20% are reprints. Averages 100 titles/year. 50% of books from first-time authors; 95% from unagented writers. Pays 10-15% royalty on retail price. Publishes book an average of 1 year after acceptance. Reports in 1 month on queries. *Writer's Market* recommends allowing 2 months for reply. Free book catalog.

Nonfiction: How-to, reference, technical. Subjects include psychology, religion. "We publish in two fields: psychotherapy and Judaica. We are looking for high quality books in both fields." Query. Reviews artwork/photos as part of ms package.

ART DIRECTION BOOK COMPANY, 6th Floor, 10 E. 39th St., New York NY 10016. (212)889-6500. Editorial Director: Dan Barron. Senior Editor: Loren Bliss. Imprint is Infosource Publications. Publishes hardcover and paperback originals. Publishes 12 titles/year. Pays 10% royalty on retail price. Offers average $1,000 advance. Publishes book an average of 1 year after acceptance. Reports in 3 months. Book catalog for 6×9 SASE.

Nonfiction: Commercial art, ad art how-to and textbooks. "We are interested in books for the professional advertising art field—books for art directors, designers, etc.; also entry level books for commercial and advertising art students in such fields as typography, photography, paste-up, illustration, clip-art, design, layout and graphic arts." Query with outline and 1 sample chapter. Reviews artwork/photos as part of ms package.

ASIAN HUMANITIES PRESS, P.O. Box 3523, Fremont CA 94539. (510)659-8272. Fax: (510)659-0501. Editor: Lew Lancaster. Other imprint is Jain Publishing Co. (for non-Asian subjects). Estab. 1976. Publishes hardcover and trade paperback originals and reprints. Averages 10 titles/year. Receives 200 submissions/year. 90% of books from unagented authors. Pays up to 6-10% royalty on net sale. Publishes book an average of 1 year after acceptance. Query for electronic submissions. Reports on queries in 1 month. Book catalog for 6×9 SAE with 2 first-class stamps.
- Publisher reports an increased emphasis on undergraduate level textbooks and culture-related books.

Nonfiction: Reference, textbooks, general trade books. Subjects include Asian classics (fiction and nonfiction), language/literature/poetry (Asian), philosophy/religion (Asian and East-West), psychology/spirituality (Asian and East-West), art/culture (Asian and East-West). Submit proposal package, including vita and a list of prior publications with SASE. Reviews artwork/photos as part of ms package. Writers should send photocopies.

‡ASQC, Imprint of ASQC Quality Press, 611 E. Wisconsin Ave., P.O. Box 3005, Milwaukee WI 53201-3005. (414)272-8575. Acquisitions Editor: Susan Westergarde. Publishes hardcover and paperback originals. Publishes 30 titles/year. Receives 300 queries and 120 mss/year. 65% of books from first-time authors; 100% from unagented writers. Pays 10% royalty on wholesale price. Publishes book 9 months after acceptance of ms. No simultaneous submissions. Reports in 2 months on proposals. Book catalog and ms guidelines free on request.
Nonfiction: Technical and business/manufacturing how-to. Subjects include business, education, government, health care, finance, software—all topics are dealt with only as they relate to quality. "Our primary focus is on quality in manufacturing, education, government, health care and finance." Submit proposal package, including outline, sample chapters, résumé, market analysis. Reviews artwork/photos as part of ms package. Writers should send photocopies.
Recent Nonfiction Title: *Reengineering the Organization,* by Jeffrey N. Lowenthal (professional/technical).

ASTRO COMMUNICATIONS SERVICES, INC., P.O. Box 34487, San Diego CA 92163-4487. (619)297-9203. Editorial Director: Maritha Pottenger. Estab. 1973. Publishes trade paperback originals and reprints. Averages 4-6 titles/year. Receives 400 submissions annually. 50% of books from first-time authors; 95% from unagented writers. Average print order for a first book is 3,000. Pays 10-15% royalty "on monies received through wholesale and retail sales." No advance. Publishes book an average of 1 year after acceptance. Query for electronic submissions. Reports in 3 months. Book catalog and ms guidelines for 9×12 SAE with 2 first-class stamps.
Nonfiction: Astrology. "Our market is astrology. We are seeking pragmatic, useful, immediate applicable contributions to field; prefer psychological approach. Specific ideas and topics should enhance people's lives. Research also valued. No determinism ('Saturn made me do it.'). No autobiographies. No airy-fairy 'space cadet' philosophizing. Keep it grounded, useful, opening options (not closing doors) for readers." Query or submit outline and 3 sample chapters.
Tips: "The most common mistake writers make when trying to get their work published is to send works to inappropriate publishers. We get too many submissions outside our field or contrary to our world view."

ATHENEUM BOOKS FOR YOUNG READERS, Imprint of Simon & Schuster, 866 Third Ave., New York NY 10022-6299. (212)702-7894. Vice President/Editorial Director: Jonathan J. Lanman. Editors: Marcia Marshall, Ana Curro and Jean Karl. Estab. 1960. Publishes hardcover originals. Averages 60 titles/year. Receives 9,000-10,000 submissions annually. 8-12% of books from first-time authors; 50% from unagented writers. Pays 10% royalty on retail price. Offers average $2,000-3,000 advance. Publishes book an average of 18 months after acceptance. Reports in up to 3 months on outline and sample chapters. Manuscript guidelines for legal SASE.
Nonfiction: Biography, how-to, humor, illustrated book, juvenile (pre-school through young adult), self-help, all for juveniles. Subjects include: Americana, animals, art, business and economics, cooking and foods, health, history, hobbies, music, nature, philosophy, photography, politics, psychology, recreation, religion, sociology, sports, travel, all for young readers. "Do remember, most publishers plan their lists as much as two years in advance. So if a topic is 'hot' right now, it may be 'old hat' by the time we could bring it out. It's better to steer clear of fads. Some writers assume juvenile books are for 'practice' until you get good enough to write adult books. Not so. Books for young readers demand just as much 'professionalism' in writing as adult books. So save those 'practice' manuscripts for class, or polish them before sending them." Query with outline and sample chapters.

Fiction: Adventure, ethnic, experimental, fantasy, gothic, historical, horror, humor, mainstream, mystery, romance, science fiction, suspense, western, all in juvenile versions. "We have few specific needs except for books that are fresh, interesting and well written. Again, fad topics are dangerous, as are works you haven't polished to the best of your ability. (The competition is fierce.) We've been inundated with dragon stories (misunderstood dragon befriends understanding child), unicorn stories (misunderstood child befriends understanding unicorn), and variations of 'Ignatz the Egg' (Everyone laughs at Ignatz the egg [giraffe/airplane/accountant] because he's square [short/purple/stupid] until he saves them from the eggbeater [lion/storm/I.R.S. man] and becomes a hero). Other things we don't need at this time are safety pamphlets, ABC books, and rhymed narratives. In writing picture book texts, avoid the coy and 'cutesy.'" Query with outline/synopsis and sample chapters for novels; complete ms for picture books. Do not send illustrations.
Recent Fiction Title: *Harper and Moon*, by Ramon Ross.
Poetry: "At this time there is a growing market for children's poetry. However, we don't anticipate needing any for the next year or two, especially rhymed narratives."
Tips: "Our books are aimed at children from pre-school age, up through high school. We no longer publish Argo Books."

‡**AUDIO ENTERTAINMENT, INC.,** P.O. Box 461059, Aurora CO 80046-1059. (303)680-6020. President: Judy Prager. Imprint is Love Everlasting. Publishes original audio stories (90 minutes). Publishes 14 titles/year. Receives 200 mss/year. 50% of books from first-time authors; 85% from unagented writers. Pays royalty on wholesale price or makes outright purchase $500-1,500. Publishes book 8 months after acceptance of ms. Simultaneous submissions OK. Reports in 3 months on proposals. Book catalog and ms guidelines free on request.
Fiction: Romance—all genres. "These are audio stories—language must be conducive to hearing the story come alive." Submit complete ms, approximately 16,000 words.
Recent Fiction Title: *Star of Kashmir*, by Laura Hayden (contemporary romance); *Puzzle Mansion*, by Colleen Edwards (romantic mystery); *Gold is the Game*, by Ray Muir (historical romance).

‡**AUGSBURG BOOKS,** Imprint of Augsburg Fortress, Publishers, 426 S. Fifth St., P.O. Box 1209, Minneapolis MN 55440. Publishes hardcover originals and trade and mass market paperback originals and reprints. Publishes 40 titles/year. Receives 5,000 queries/year. 2-3% of books from first-time authors. Pays royalty. Publishes book 18 months after acceptance of ms. Accepts simultaneous submissions. Query for electronic submissions. Reports in 2 months. Book catalog for 8½×11 SAE with 65¢ first-class postage. Manuscript guidelines for #10 SASE.
Nonfiction: Children's/juvenile, self-help. Subjects include religion. "We publish for the mainline Christian market." Submit outline and 1-2 sample chapters.
Fiction: Historical, juvenile, young adult. Submit synopsis and 1-2 sample chapters.

‡**AUSTIN & WINFIELD, PUBLISHERS INC.,** P.O. Box 2590, San Francisco CA 94126. (415)981-5144. Publisher: Robert West. Publishes hardcover and trade paperback originals. Publishes 40 titles/year. Receives 350 queries and 250 mss/year. 50% of books from first-time authors; 100% from unagented writers. Pays 8% royalty on wholesale price. Publishes book 1 year after acceptance of ms. Accepts simultaneous submissions. Reports in 1 month on queries and proposals, 3 months on mss. Book catalog and ms guidelines free on request.
Nonfiction: Biography, reference, textbook, monographs. Subjects include anthropology/archaeology, art/architecture, business and economics, education, government/politics, history, language/literature, law, philosophy, psychology, religion, sociology, women's issues/studies. Submit proposal package, including table of contents, precis, introduction and 2-3 chapters. Reviews artwork/photos as part of ms package. Writer should send photocopies.
Recent Nonfiction Title: *Challenges of a Changing America*, by Ernest Myers.

AVALON BOOKS, Imprint of Thomas Bouregy & Co., Inc., 401 Lafayette St., New York NY 10003-7014. Vice President and Publisher: Marcia Markland. Estab. 1950. Publishes 60 titles/year. Reports in 3-6 months.
Fiction: "We publish wholesome romances, mysteries, westerns. Our books are read by adults as well as teenagers, and their characters are all adults. All the romances and mysteries are contemporary; all the westerns are historical." Length: 40,000-50,000 words. Submit first chapter and a brief, but complete summary of the book. Enclose sufficient SASE.
Tips: "We are looking for love stories, heroines who have interesting professions, and we are actively seeking ethnic fiction. We do accept unagented mss, and we do publish first novels. Right now we are concentrating on finding talented new mystery and romantic suspense writers."

AVANYU PUBLISHING INC., P.O. Box 27134, Albuquerque NM 87125. (505)266-6128. Fax: (505)821-8864. President: J. Brent Ricks. Estab. 1984. Publishes hardcover and trade paperback originals and reprints. Averages 4 titles/year. Receives 40 submissions/year. 30% of books from first-time authors; 90% from unagented writers. Pays 8% maximum royalty on wholesale price. No advance. Publishes book an average of 1 year after acceptance. Query for electronic submissions. Reports in 6 weeks. *Writer's Market* recommends allowing 2 months for reply. Book catalog for #10 SASE.

Nonfiction: Biography, illustrated book, reference, Southwest Americana. Subjects include Americana, anthropology/archaeology, art/architecture, ethnic, history, photography, regional, sociology. Query. Reviews artwork/photos as part of ms package.

Fiction: Adventure, historical, Western. Query.

Tips: "Writers have the best chance selling us history oriented books with lots of pictures, or contemporary Indian/Western art. Our audience consists of libraries, art collectors and history students."

AVERY PUBLISHING GROUP, 120 Old Broadway, Garden City Park NY 11040. (516)741-2155. Fax: (516)742-1892. Contact: Managing Editor. Estab. 1976. Publishes hardcover and trade paperback originals. Averages 40 titles/year. Receives 200-300 submissions/year. 90% of books from first-time authors; 95% from unagented writers. Pays 10% royalty on wholesale price. Publishes book an average of 1 year after acceptance. Simultaneous submissions OK. Reports in 1 week. *Writer's Market* recommends allowing 2 months for reply. Book catalog free on request.

Nonfiction: Cookbook, how-to, reference, textbook. Subjects include business and economics, child guidance/parenting, cooking, foods and nutrition, health/medicine, history, military/war, nature/environment, childbirth, alternative health. Query.

AVON BOOKS, Division of the Hearst Corp., 1350 Avenue of the Americas, New York NY 10019. (212)261-6800. Fax: (212)532-2172. Vice President/Editor-in-Chief: Robert Mecoy. Estab. 1941. Publishes trade and mass market paperback originals and reprints. Averages 400 titles/year. Pay and advance are negotiable. Publishes ms an average of 2 years after acceptance. Simultaneous submissions OK. Reports in 2 months. Book catalog for SASE.

Nonfiction: How-to, popular psychology, self-help, health, history, war, sports, business/economics, biography, politics. No textbooks. Query only.

Recent Nonfiction Title: *Don't Know Much About Geography* (trade).

Fiction: Romance (contemporary), historical romance, science fiction, fantasy, men's adventure, suspense/thriller, mystery, western. Submit query letter only.

Recent Fiction Title: *List of 7*, by Mark Frost.

AVON FLARE BOOKS, Young Adult Imprint of Avon Books, Division of the Hearst Corp., 1350 Avenue of the Americas, New York NY 10019. (212)261-6817. Fax: (212)261-6895. Editorial Director: Ellen Krieger. Publishes mass market paperback originals and reprints. Imprint publishes 20-24 new titles annually. 25% of books from first-time authors; 15% from unagented writers. Pays 6-8% royalty. Offers minimum $2,500 advance. Publishes book an average of 15 months after acceptance. Simultaneous submissions OK. Reports in 4 months. Book catalog and ms guidelines for 8 × 10 SAE with 5 first-class stamps.

Nonfiction: General. Submit outline/synopsis and sample chapters. "*Very* selective with young adult nonfiction."

Fiction: Adventure, ethnic, humor, mainstream, mystery, romance, suspense, contemporary. "Very selective with mystery." Manuscripts appropriate to ages 12-18. Query with sample chapters and synopsis.

Recent Fiction Title: *Out of Control*, by Norma Fox Nazer.

Tips: "The YA market is not as strong as it was five years ago. We are very selective with young adult fiction. Avon does not publish picture books, nor do we use freelance readers."

AZTEX CORP., P.O. 50046, Tucson AZ 85703-1046. (608)882-4656. Estab. 1976. Publishes hardcover and paperback originals. Averages 10 titles/year. Receives 250 submissions annually. 100% of books from unagented writers. Average print order for a first book is 3,500. Pays 10% royalty. Publishes book an average of 18 months after acceptance. Query for electronic submissions. Reports in 3 months. "Queries without return envelopes or postage are not responded to."

Nonfiction: "We specialize in transportation subjects (how-to and history)." Accepts nonfiction translations. Submit outline and 2 sample chapters. Reviews artwork/photos as part of ms package.

Recent Nonfiction Title: *Tire Wars: Racing with Goodyear*, by William Neely.

Tips: "We look for accuracy, thoroughness and interesting presentation."

BACKCOUNTRY PUBLICATIONS, Imprint of The Countryman Press, Inc., P.O. Box 175, Woodstock VT 05091-0175. (802)457-4826. Fax: (802)457-3250. Managing Editor: Helen Whybrow. Estab. 1973. Publishes trade paperback originals. Averages 12 titles/year. 50% of books from first-time authors; 95% from unagented writers. Pays 7-10% royalty on retail price. Offers $750 average advance. Publishes book average of 9 months after acceptance. Simultaneous submissions OK. Reports in 2 months. Book catalog free.

● Publisher reports more emphasis on books about fishing—particularly fly fishing.

Nonfiction: Reference. Subjects include recreation. "We're looking for regional guides to hiking, walking, bicycling, cross-country skiing, canoeing, and fishing for all parts of the country." Submit outline and sample chapters. Reviews artwork/photos as part of ms package.

Recent Nonfiction Title: *Michigan Trout Streams*, by Bob Linsehman and Steve Nevels.
Tips: "No unsolicited manuscripts please! No material is returned without SASE."

BAEN PUBLISHING ENTERPRISES, Distributed by Simon & Schuster, P.O. Box 1403, Riverdale NY 10471-0671. (718)548-3100. Editor-in-Chief: Jim Baen. Executive Editor: Toni Weisskopf. Consulting Editor: Josepha Sherman. Estab. 1983. Publishes mass market paperback originals and reprints. Averages 80-100 titles/year. Receives 6,000 submissions annually. 10% of books from first-time authors; 25% from unagented writers. Pays 6-8% royalty on cover price. Reports in 2 weeks on partials, 1-4 months on complete mss. Queries not necessary. Manuscript guidelines for #10 SASE.
Fiction: Fantasy, science fiction. Submit outline/synopsis and sample chapters or (preferred) synopsis and complete ms.
Recent Fiction Title: *The Ship Who Won*, by Anne McCaffrey and Jody Lynn Nye.
Tips: "Our audience includes those who are interested in *hard* science fiction and quality fantasy pieces that engage the mind as well as entertain."

BAKER BOOK HOUSE COMPANY, P.O. Box 6287, Grand Rapids MI 49516-6287. Director of Publications: Allan Fisher. Assistant to the Director of Publications: Jane Dekker. Estab. 1939. Publishes hardcover and trade paperback originals. Averages 120 titles/year. 10% of books from first-time authors; 85% from unagented writers. Queries and proposals only. No unsolicited mss. Pays 14% royalty on net receipts. Publishes book within 1 year after acceptance. Simultaneous submissions (if so identified) OK. Reports in 2-3 months. Book catalog for 9 × 12 SAE with 6 first-class stamps.
Nonfiction: Contemporary issues, women's concerns, parenting, singleness, seniors' concerns, self-help, children's books, Bible study, Christian doctrine, reference books, books for pastors and church leaders, textbooks for Christian colleges and seminaries. Query with proposal.
Fiction: Novels focusing on women's concerns, mysteries. Query.
Tips: "Most of our authors and readers are evangelical Christians, and our books are purchased from Christian bookstores, mail-order retailers, and school bookstores."

BALE BOOKS, Division of Bale Publications, P.O. Box 2727, New Orleans LA 70176. Editor-in-Chief: Don Bale, Jr. Estab. 1963. Publishes hardcover and paperback originals and reprints. Averages 10 titles/year. Receives 25 submissions annually. 50% of books from first-time authors; 90% from unagented writers. Average print order for a first book is 1,000. Offers standard 10-12½-15% royalty contract on wholesale or retail price; sometimes purchases outright for $500. No advance. Publishes book an average of 3 years after acceptance. Reports in 3 months. Book catalog for #10 SAE with 2 first-class stamps.
Nonfiction: Numismatics. "Our specialties are coin and stock market investment books; especially coin investment books and coin price guides. Most of our books are sold through publicity and ads in the coin newspapers. We are open to any new ideas in the area of numismatics. The writer should write for a teenage through adult level. Lead the reader by the hand like a teacher, building chapter by chapter. Our books sometimes have a light, humorous treatment, but not necessarily. We look for good English, construction and content, and sales potential." Submit outline and 3 sample chapters.

‡BALLANTINE BOOKS, Imprint of Random House, Inc., 201 E. 50th St., New York NY 10022. (212)572-2149. Assistant Editor: Betsy Flagler.
Nonfiction: How-to, humor, illustrated book (cartoons), reference, self-help. Subjects include animals, child guidance/parenting, cooking, foods and nutrition, health/medicine. Submit proposal and 100 ms pages. Reviews artwork/photos as part of the freelance ms package. Writers should send photocopies.
Recent Nonfiction Title: *Bride's Organizer*, by Hudak (reference).
  • Also see the listing for Random House, Inc.

BANDANNA BOOKS, 319-B Anacapa St., Santa Barbara CA 93101. (805)962-9915. Fax: (805)504-3278. Publisher: Sasha Newborn. Ms Editor: Joan Blake. Publishes trade paperback originals and reprints. Publishes 3 titles/year. Receives 100 queries and 40 mss/year. 50% of books from first-time authors; 100% from unagented writers. Pays 5-10% royalty on retail price (a few books gratis). Offers $50-200 advance. Publishes book 9 months after acceptance. Simultaneous submissions OK. Query for electronic submissions. Reports in 2 months on proposals.
Nonfiction: Illustrated book, textbook. Subjects include history, language/literature, translation, women's issues/studies. "Bandanna Books seeks to humanize the classics and language-learning materials in nonsexist, modernized translations and plain-English texts, suitable for advanced high-school and college classes." Submit outline and 1 or 2 sample chapters. Reviews artwork/photos. Writers should send photocopies.
Tips: "Our readers are age 16-22, high school or college age, liberal arts orientation. A well-thought-out proposal is important, even if unconventional."

B&B PUBLISHING, INC., P.O. Box 393, Fontana WI 53125-0393. Fax: (414)275-9530. Contact: Lisa Turner. Publishes hardcover and trade paperback originals. Publishes 5-10 titles/year. Receives 200 queries, 100 mss/

year. 10% of books from first-time authors; 100% from unagented writers. Pays 2½-5% royalty on net receipts or makes outright purchase for $2,000-5,000. Offers $2,000 advance. Publishes book 1 year after acceptance. Simultaneous submissions OK. Query for electronic submissions; disk only. Prefers Macintosh or PC in Microsoft Word. SASE. Reports in 1 month on queries and proposals, 3 months on mss. Book catalog and ms guidelines free on request.

• Publisher would like to hear from journalists interested in writing/researching state trivia almanacs.

Nonfiction: Children's/juvenile, reference, Americana, trivia. "We are seeking innovative supplementary educational materials for grades K-12." Query. Reviews artwork/photos as part of ms package. Writers should send photocopies.

Recent Nonfiction Title: *Serengeti Plain*, by Terri Wills.

Tips: Audience is general trade schools and public library.

BANKS-BALDWIN LAW PUBLISHING CO., 1904 Ansel Rd., Cleveland OH 44106. (216)721-7373. Fax: (216)721-8055. Editor-in-Chief: P.J. Lucier. Acquisitions Supervisor: Fred K. Gordon. Estab. 1804. Publishes law books and services in a variety of formats. Averages 10 new titles/year. Receives 10-15 submissions annually. 5% of books from first-time authors; 90% from unagented writers. "Most titles include material submitted by outside authors." Pays 8-16% on net revenue, or fee. Offers advance not to exceed 25% of anticipated royalty or fee. Publishes book an average of 18 months after acceptance, 3 months after receipt of ms. Query for electronic submissions. Reports in 3 weeks on queries. *Writer's Market* recommends allowing 2 months for reply. Book catalog and ms guidelines for SASE.

Nonfiction: Reference, law/legal. Query.

Tips: "We publish books for attorneys, government officials and professionals in allied fields. Trends in our field include more interest in handbooks, less in costly multi-volume sets; electronic publishing. A writer has the best chance of selling us a book on a hot new topic of law. Check citations and quotations carefully."

BANTAM BOOKS, Subsidiary of Bantam Doubleday Dell, 1540 Broadway, New York NY 10036. (212)354-6500. Imprints are Spectra, Crime Lane, New Age, New Science, Domain, Fanfair, Bantam Classics, Bantam Wisdom Editions, Loveswept. Publishes hardcover, trade paperback and mass market paperback originals, trade paperback, mass market paperback reprints and audio. Publishes 350 titles/year. Publishes book an average of 8 months after ms is accepted. Simultaneous submissions from agents OK.

Nonfiction: Biography, how-to, cookbook, humor, illustrated book, self-help. Subjects include Americana, business/economics, child care/parenting, diet/fitness, education, cooking, foods and nutrition, gay/lesbian, government/politics, health/medicine, history, language/literature, military/war, mysticism/astrology, nature, philosophy/mythology, psychology, religion/inspiration, science, sociology, spirituality, sports, true crime, women's studies.

Fiction: Adventure, fantasy, feminist, gay/lesbian, historical, horror, juvenile, literary, mainstream/contemporary, mystery, romance, science fiction, suspense, western. Query or submit outline/synopsis. All unsolicited mss returned unopened.

BANTAM DOUBLEDAY DELL, 1540 Broadway, New York NY 10036.

• See separate listings from Bantam Books, Doubleday and Dell Publishing.

‡BARBOUR AND COMPANY, INC., P.O. Box 719, Uhrichsville OH 44683. Vice President Editorial: Stephen Reginald. Imprints are Barbour Books and Heartsong Presents (fiction). Publishes hardcover, trade paperback and mass market paperback originals and reprints. Publishes 75 titles/year. Receives 300 queries and 150 mss/year. 40% of books from first-time authors; 99% from unagented writers. Subsidy publishes .5% of books. Pays royalty on wholesale price or outright purchase of $1,000-2,500. Offers $250-500 advance. Publishes book 6 months after acceptance of ms. Simultaneous submissions OK. Query for electronic submissions. Reports in 1 month on queries, 3 months on proposals, 3 months on mss. Book catalog for $2. Manuscript guidelines for #10 SASE.

Nonfiction: Biography, humor, children's/juvenile. Subjects include religion. "We're a Christian evangelical publisher." Query.

Fiction: Historical, religious, romance. "All these elements combined. We publish four inspirational romance titles per month. Two historical and two contemporary romances." Submit synopsis and 3 sample chapters.

Tips: "Having a great agent won't help here. A great idea or book will catch our attention."

‡BARRICADE BOOKS INC., 61 Fourth Ave., New York NY 10003. Publisher: Carole Stuart. Publishes hardcover and trade paperback originals and trade paperback reprints. Publishes 30 titles/year. Receives 200 queries and 100 mss/year. 80% of books from first-time authors; 50% from unagented writers. Pays 10-12% royalty on retail price for hardcover. Advance varies. Publishes book 18 months after acceptance of ms. Simultaneous submissions not encouraged. Reports in 1 month on queries. Book catalog for $1.

Nonfiction: Biography, how-to, reference, self-help. Subjects include business and economics, child guidance/parenting, ethnic, gay/lesbian, government/politics, health/medicine, history, nature/environment, psychology, sociology, women's issues/studies. Query with outline and 1-2 sample chapters. Reviews artwork/photos as part of ms package. Writers should send photocopies.

Recent Nonfiction Title: *The Secret Life of Bob Hope*, by Arthur Marx (biography).
Tips: "Do your homework. Visit bookshops to find publishers who are doing the kinds of books you want to write. Always submit to a *person* — not just 'editor.' Always enclose SASE."

BARRON'S EDUCATIONAL SERIES, INC., 250 Wireless Blvd., Hauppauge NY 11788. Fax: (516)434-3723. Director of Acquisitions: Grace Freedson. Publishes hardcover and paperback originals and software. Publishes 170 titles/year. 10% of books from first-time authors; 90% from unagented writers. Pays royalty, based on both wholesale and retail price. Publishes book an average of 1 year after acceptance. Simultaneous submissions OK. Reports in 6-8 months. Book catalog free.
Nonfiction: Adult education, art, business, cookbooks, crafts, foreign language, review books, guidance, pet books, travel, literary guides, parenting, health, juvenile, young adult sports, test preparation materials and textbooks. Reviews artwork/photos as part of ms package. Query or submit outline/synopsis and 2-3 sample chapters. Accepts nonfiction translations.
Recent Nonfiction Title: *Spanish for Health Care Professionals*, by William C. Harvey.
Tips: "The writer has the best chance of selling us a book that will fit into one of our series."

BAYWOOD PUBLISHING CO., INC., 26 Austin Ave., Amityville NY 11701. (516)691-1270. Fax: (516)691-1770. Publishes 25 titles/year. Pays 7-15% royalty on retail price. Publishes book within 1 year after acceptance of ms. Book list and ms guidelines free on request.
Nonfiction: Technical, scholarly. Subjects include anthropology/archaeology, computers and electronics, gerontology, imagery, labor relations, education, death and dying, drug, nature/environment, psychology, public health/medicine, sociology, technical communications, women's issues/studies. Submit outline/synopsis and sample chapters.

BEACON HILL PRESS OF KANSAS CITY, Book Division of Nazarene Publishing House, 6401 The Paseo, Kansas City MO 64131. Fax: (816)333-1748. Coordinator: Bonnie Perry. Estab. 1912. Publishes hardcover and paperback originals. Averages 50 titles/year. Standard contract is 12% on net sales for first 10,000 copies and 14% on subsequent copies. (Sometimes flat rate purchase.) Publishes book within 1 year after acceptance. Reports within 4 months. Accent on holy living; encouragement in daily Christian life. Query or proposal preferred. Average ms length: 30,000-60,000 words.
Nonfiction: Inspirational, Bible-based. Doctrinally must conform to the evangelical, Wesleyan tradition. No autobiography, poetry, short stories or children's picture books. Contemporary issues acceptable.
Fiction: Wholesome, inspirational. Will consider historical and Biblical fiction, Christian romance, but no teen or children's.

BEACON PRESS, 25 Beacon St., Boston MA 02108-2892. (617)742-2110. Fax: (617)723-3097. Director: Wendy J. Strothman. Estab. 1854. Publishes hardcover originals and paperback reprints. Averages 50 titles/year; receives 4,000 submissions annually. 10% of books from first-time authors; 70% from unagented writers. Average print order for a first book is 3,000. Offers royalty on net retail price. Advance varies. Publishes book an average of 1 year after acceptance. Simultaneous submissions OK. Include SASE for return of materials. Reports in 3 months.
Nonfiction: General nonfiction including works of original scholarship, religion, women's studies, philosophy, current affairs, anthropology, environmental concerns, African-American studies, gay and lesbian studies. Query or submit outline/synopsis and sample chapters.
Recent Nonfiction Title: *Life Work*, Donald Hall.
Tips: "We probably accept only one or two manuscripts from an unpublished pool of 4,000 submissions per year. No fiction, children's book, or poetry submissions invited. Authors should have academic affiliation."

BEAR AND CO., INC., P.O. Box 2860, Santa Fe NM 87504-2860. (505)983-5968. Vice President, Editorial: Barbara Clow. Estab. 1978. Publishes trade paperback originals. Averages 12 titles/year. Receives 6,000 submissions/year. 20% of books from first-time authors; 90% from unagented writers. Pays 10% royalty on net. Publishes book an average of 18 months after acceptance. Query for electronic submissions. Reports in 1 month on queries. *Writer's Market* recommends allowing 2 months for reply. "No response without SASE." Book catalog for 9 × 12 SAE with 3 first-class stamps.
Nonfiction: Illustrated books, science, theology, mysticism, religion, ecology. "We publish books to 'heal and celebrate the earth.' Our interest is in New Age, western mystics, new science, ecology. We are not interested in how-to, self-help, etc. Our readers are people who are open to new ways of looking at the world. They are spiritually oriented but not necessarily religious; interested in healing of the earth, peace issues, and receptive to New Age ideas." Query or submit outline and sample chapters. Reviews artwork/photos as part of ms package.
Tips: "We have continued to publish 12 titles/year, instead of going to 15-20 at this point. We have *increased* publicity and marketing work, and our sales have not dropped."

BEHRMAN HOUSE INC., 235 Watchung Ave., West Orange NJ 07052-9827. (201)669-0447. Fax: (201)669-9769. Projects Editor: Adam Siegel. Managing Editor: Adam Bengal. Estab. 1921. Publishes Jewish nonfic-

tion-history, Bible, philosophy, holidays, ethics—for children and adults. Averages 20 titles/year. Receives 200 submissions/year. 20% of books from first-time authors; 95% from unagented writers. Pays 2-10% on wholesale price or retail price. Buys some mss outright for $500-10,000. Offers $1,000 average advance. Publishes book an average of 18 months after acceptance. Simultaneous submissions OK. Reports in 2 months. Free book catalog.
Nonfiction: Juvenile (1-18), reference, textbook. Subjects include religion. "We want Jewish textbooks for the El-Hi market." Query with outline and sample chapters.

FREDERIC C. BEIL, PUBLISHER, INC., 609 Whitaker St., Savannah GA 31401. (912)233-2446. Editor: Mary Ann Bowman. Publishes hardcover originals and reprints. Publishes 11 titles/year. Receives 200 queries and 9 mss/year. 15% of books from first-time authors; 100% from unagented writers. Pays 7½% royalty on retail price. Publishes book 20 months after acceptance. Simultaneous submissions OK. Query for electronic submissions. Reports in 1 month on queries. Book catalog free on request.
Nonfiction: Biography, illustrated book, general trade, reference. Subjects include art/architecture, history, language/literature, book arts, regional, religion. Query. Reviews artwork/photos as part of freelance ms package. Writers should send photocopies.
Fiction: Historical and literary. Query.

ROBERT BENTLEY, INC., Automotive Publishers, 1000 Massachusetts Ave., Cambridge MA 02138. (617)547-4170. Publisher: Michael Bentley. Estab. 1949. Publishes hardcover and trade paperback originals and reprints. Publishes 15-20 titles/year. 20% of books are from first-time authors; 95% from unagented writers. Pays 10-15% royalty on net price, or makes outright purchase. Advance negotiable. Publishes book an average of 1 year after acceptance. Query for electronic submissions. Reports in 3-6 weeks. Book catalog and ms guidelines for 8½×11 SAE with 4 first-class stamps.
Nonfiction: How-to, technical, theory of operation, coffee table. Automotive subjects only; this includes motor sports. Query or submit outline and sample chapters. Reviews artwork/photos as part of ms package.
Tips: "We are excited about the possibilities and growth in the automobile enthusiast book market. Our audience is composed of serious and intelligent automobile, sports car, or racing enthusiasts, automotive technicians and high performance tuners."

THE BERKLEY PUBLISHING GROUP, Publishers of Berkley/Berkley Trade Paperbacks/Jove/Diamond/Pacer/Ace Science Fiction, Division of the Putnam Berkley Group, 200 Madison Ave., New York NY 10016. (212)951-8800. Editor-in-Chief: Leslie Gelbman. Publishes paperback originals and reprints. Publishes approximately 800 titles/year. Pays 4-10% royalty on retail price. Offers advance. Publishes book an average of 2 years after acceptance.
Nonfiction: How-to, family life, business, health, nutrition, true crime.
Fiction: Mystery, historical, mainstream, suspense, western, romance, science fiction. Submit outline/synopsis and first 3 chapters for Ace Science Fiction *only*. No other unagented mss accepted.
Tips: "No longer seeking adventure or occult fiction. Does not publish memoirs or personal stories."

BERKSHIRE HOUSE PUBLISHERS, INC., P.O. Box 297, Stockbridge MA 01262-0297. Fax: (413)298-5323. . President: Jean J. Rousseau. Estab. 1989. Publishes 12-15 titles/year. Receives 100 queries and 6 mss/year. 50% of books from first-time authors; 100% from unagented writers. Pays 5-10% royalty on retail price. Offers $500-5,000 advance. Publishes book 6-12 months after acceptance. Simultaneous submissions OK. Query for electronic submissions. Reports in 1 month on proposals. Book catalog free on request.
Nonfiction: Biography, cookbook. Subjects include Americana, history, nature/environment, recreation (outdoors), wood crafts, regional. "All our books have a strong Berkshires or New England orientation—no others, please. To a great extent, we choose our topics then commission the authors, but we don't discourage speculative submissions. We just don't accept many. Don't overdo it; a well-written outline proposal is more useable than a full manuscript. Also, include a c.v. with other writing credits." Submit outline proposal and c.v. with writing credits.
Tips: "Our readers are literate, active, prosperous, interested in travel, especially in selected 'Great Destinations' areas and outdoor activities and cooking."

‡BERWICK PUBLISHING, Alan Sutton, Inc., P.O. Box 275, Dover NH 03820. (603)742-5184. Senior Editor: Kirsty Sutton. Publishes trade paperback originals. Publishes 50 titles/year. Receives 70 queries/year. 70% of books from first-time authors. Pays royalty. Publishes book 9 months after acceptance of ms. Accepts simultaneous submissions. Query for electronic submissions. Reports in 3 months.
Nonfiction: Coffee table book. Subjects include Americana, history, photography, regional. "Heavy concentration on regional old photograph collections." Query. Reviews artwork/photos as part of ms package.
Recent Nonfiction Title: *York Beach, Maine in Old Photos*, by John Bardwall.

BETHEL PUBLISHING, Subsidiary of Missionary Church, Inc., 1819 S. Main St., Elkhart IN 46516-4299. (219)293-8585. Fax: (800)230-8271. Executive Director: Rev. Richard Oltz. Estab. 1903. Publishes trade paperback originals and reprints. Averages 5 titles/year. Receives 250 submissions/year. 80% of books from first-time authors; 90% from unagented writers. Pays 5-10% royalties. Publishes book an average of 1 year after acceptance. Simultaneous submissions OK. Reports in 2 months. Book catalog for 9×12 SAE with 3 first-class stamps.

Nonfiction: Reference. Subjects include religion. Reviews artwork/photos as part of ms package. Query.

Fiction: Adventure, religious, suspense, young adult. Books must be evangelical in approach. No occult, gay/lesbian or erotica. Query.

Tips: "Our audience is made up of Christian families with children. If I were a writer trying to market a book today, I would find out what publisher specializes in the type of book I have written."

BETTER HOMES AND GARDENS BOOKS, Division of the Meredith Corporation, 1716 Locust St., Des Moines IA 50309-3023. Editorial Director and Vice President: Elizabeth P. Rice. Estab. 1930. Publishes hardcover and trade paperback originals. Averages 40 titles/year. "Although many of our books are produced by on-staff editors, we often buy book-length manuscripts from outside authors. We also use freelance writers on assignment for sections or chapters of books already in progress." Reports in 6 weeks.

Nonfiction: "We publish nonfiction in many family and home-service categories, including gardening, decorating and remodeling, crafts, money management, handyman's topics, cooking and nutrition, Christmas activities, and other subjects of home-service value. Emphasis is on how-to and on stimulating people to action. We require concise, factual writing. Audience is comprised of readers with home and family as their main center of interest. Style should be informative and lively with a straightforward approach. Stress the positive. Emphasis is entirely on reader service. Because most of our books are produced by on-staff editors, we're less interested in book-length manuscripts than in hearing from freelance writers with solid expertise in gardening, do-it-yourself, health/fitness, and home decorating. We have no need at present for cookbooks or craft books. The Executive Editor recommends careful study of specific Better Homes and Gardens Books titles before submitting material." Prefers outline and sample chapters. *"Please include SASE with appropriate return postage."*

Tips: "Writers often fail to familiarize themselves with the catalog/backlist of the publishers to whom they are submitting. We expect heavier emphasis on health/fitness, gardening and do-it-yourself titles. But, again, we're most interested in hearing from freelance writers with subject expertise in these areas or in receiving queries for book-length manuscripts. Queries/mss may be routed to the Executive Editor in the publishing group."

BETTERWAY BOOKS, Imprint of F&W Publications, 1507 Dana Ave., Cincinnati OH 45207. (513)531-2690. Editors: David Lewis, William Brohaugh. Estab. 1982. Publishes hardcover and trade paperback originals, and trade paperback reprints. Averages 30 titles/year. Pays 10% royalty on net receipts. Simultaneous submissions OK (if so advised). Publishes book an average of 12-18 months after acceptance. Reports in 2 months. Book catalog for 9×12 SAE with 6 first-class stamps.

Nonfiction: How-to, illustrated book, reference and self-help in eight categories. Direct queries for these categories to David Lewis: home building and remodeling, woodworking, small business and personal finance, hobbies and collectibles. Direct queries for these categories to William Brohaugh: sports and recreation, reference books and handbooks (including genealogy), lifestyle (including home organization), theater and the performing arts. "Betterway books are instructional books that are to be *used*. We like specific step-by-step advice, charts, illustrations, and clear explanations of the activities and projects the books describe. We are interested mostly in original material, but we will consider republishing self-published nonfiction books and good instructional or reference books that have gone out of print before their time. Send a sample copy, sales information, and reviews, if available. If you have a good idea for a reference book that can be updated annually, try us. We're willing to consider freelance compilers of such works." No cookbooks, diet/exercise, psychology self-help, health or parenting books. Query or submit outline and sample chapters. Reviews artwork/photos as part of ms package.

Recent Nonfiction Title: *Kids, Money & Values,* by Patricia Schiff Estess and Irving Barocas.

Tips: "Keep the imprint name well in mind when submitting ideas to us. What is the 'better way' you're proposing? How will readers benefit *immediately* from the instruction and information you're giving them?"

BICYCLE BOOKS, INC., P.O. Box 2038, Mill Valley CA 94942-2038. (415)381-2515. Fax: (415)381-6912. Editor: Rob van der Plas. Estab. 1985. Publishes hardcover and trade paperback originals. Firm averages 6 titles/year. Receives 20 submissions/year. 20% of books from first-time authors; 50% from unagented writers. Pays 15% of net royalty. Publishes book an average of 1 year after acceptance. Simultaneous submissions OK. Query for electronic submissions. Reports in 2 months. Book catalog free on request.

Nonfiction: How-to, technical. Subjects include bicycle-related titles only. "Bicycle travel manuscripts must include route descriptions and maps. Please, do not send anything outside the practical how-to field." Submit complete ms. Artwork/photos essential as part of the freelance ms package.

Tips: "Writers have a good chance selling us books with better and more illustrations and a systematic treatment of the subject. Our audience: sports/health/fitness conscious adults; cyclists and others interested in technical aspects. If I were a writer trying to market a book today, I would first check what is on the market and ask myself whether I am writing something that is not yet available and wanted."

BLACK SPARROW PRESS, 24 10th St., Santa Rosa CA 95401. (707)579-4011. Assistant to Publisher: Michele Filshie. Estab. 1966. Publishes hardcover and trade paperback originals and reprints. Averages 12 titles/year. 15% of books from first-time authors; 75% from unagented writers. Pays 5-10% royalty on retail price. Publishes book an average of 1 year after acceptance. Simultaneous submissions OK. Reports in 1 month on queries; 2 months on mss. Book catalog free on request.
Nonfiction: Subjects include language/literature. No how-to, cookbook, juvenile, self-help. Query.
Recent Nonfiction Title: *Time and Western Man*, by Wyndham Lewis.
Fiction: Literary, feminist, gay/lesbian, short story collections. We generally solicit from authors we are interested in. "We only publish 12 new books a year so our schedule is quickly filled." No genre such as romance, westerns, mystery, etc. Query.
Recent Fiction Title: *Pulp*, by Charles Bukowski.
Poetry: "We generally solicit from authors we are interested in." No light verse, nonsense verse, limmerick, traditional rhymed verse. Submit 5 samples.
Recent Poetry Title: "According to Her Contours," by Nancy Boutilier.

‡BLACKBIRCH PRESS, INC., 1 Bradley Rd., Woodbridge CT 06525. Editorial Director: Bruce Glassman. Publishes hardcover and trade paperback originals. Publishes 30 titles/year. Receives 400 queries and 75 mss/year. 100% of books unagented writers. Pays 4-8% royalty on wholesale price or makes outright purchase. Offers $1,000-5,000 advance. Publishes book 1 year after acceptance of ms. Simultaneous submissions OK. Reports in 2 months.
Nonfiction: Biography, illustrated books, children's/juvenile, reference. Subjects include animals, anthropology/archeology, health/medicine, history, nature/environment, science, sports, women's issues/studies. Does not accept unsolicited mss or proposals. Cover letters and résumés are useful for identifying new authors. Query. Reviews artwork/photos as part of freelance ms package. Writers should send photocopies.

JOHN F. BLAIR, PUBLISHER, 1406 Plaza Dr., Winston-Salem NC 27103-1470. (919)768-1374. Fax: (919)768-9194. Editor: Carolyn Sakowski. Estab. 1954. Publishes hardcover originals and trade paperbacks. Receives 2,000 submissions annually. 20-30% of books from first-time authors; 90% from unagented writers. Average print order for a first book is 3,500-5,000. Royalty negotiable. Publishes book an average of 12-18 months after acceptance. Query for electronic submissions. Reports in 3 months. Book catalog and ms guidelines for 9×12 SAE with 5 first-class stamps.
Nonfiction: Especially interested in travel guides dealing with the Southeastern United States. Also interested in civil war, outdoors, travel and Americana; query on other nonfiction topics. Looks for utility and significance. Submit outline and first 3 chapters. Reviews artwork/photos as part of ms package.
Fiction: "We are interested only in material related to the Southeastern United States." No category fiction, juvenile fiction, picture books or poetry.

BLUE BIRD PUBLISHING, #306, 1739 E. Broadway, Tempe AZ 85282. (602)968-4088. Fax: (602)831-1829. Publisher: Cheryl Gorder. Estab. 1985. Publishes trade paperback originals. Averages 6 titles/year. 50% of books from first-time authors; 100% from unagented writers. Pays 10% royalty on wholesale price; 15% on retail price. Publishes book an average of 9 months after acceptance. Simultaneous submissions OK. Reports in 3 months. Book catalog and ms guidelines for #10 SASE.
Nonfiction: How-to, reference. Subjects include child guidance/parenting, education (especially home education), sociology (current social issues). "The homeschooling population in the US is exploding. We have a strong market for anything that can be targeted to this group: home education manuscripts, parenting guides, curriculum ideas. We would also like to see complete nonfiction manuscripts in current issues, how-to topics." Submit complete ms. Reviews artwork/photos as part of ms package.
Recent Nonfiction Title: *Expanding Your Child's Horizons*.
Tips: "We are interested if we see a complete manuscript that is aimed toward a general adult nonfiction audience. We are impressed if the writer has really done his homework and the manuscript includes photos, artwork, graphs, charts, and other graphics." Please do not send fiction or short stories.

BLUE DOLPHIN PUBLISHING, INC., P.O. Box 1920, Nevada City CA 95959-1920. (916)265-6925. Fax: (916)265-0787. Imprint is Pelican Pond Publishing (health and ecology titles). Publisher: Paul M. Clemens. Estab. 1985. Publishes hardcover and trade paperback originals. Publishes 12-15 titles/year. Receives over 2,500 submissions/year. 75% of books from first-time authors; 90% from unagented writers. Pays 10% royalty on wholesale price. Publishes book an average of 4-8 months after acceptance. Simultaneous submissions OK. Query for electronic submissions. Reports in 1 month on queries; "longer with books we're considering more closely." Please send SASE with query. Book catalog free.
• The publisher reports that sales have doubled in the past year.
Nonfiction: Biography, cookbook, how-to, humor, self-help. Subjects include anthropology/archaeology, cooking, foods and nutrition, ecology, education, health/medicine, psychology, comparative religion. "We are interested primarily in self-help psychology, health and the environment, comparative spiritual traditions, including translations." Submit outline and sample chapters with SASE. Reviews artwork as part of package.

Recent Nonfiction Title: *Messages to Our Family*, by Annie and Bryan Kirkwood.
Poetry: "We will only consider previously published authors of some merit or translations of noted works." Submit complete ms.
Tips: "Our audience is the concerned person interested in self-growth and awareness for oneself and the planet."

BLUE HERON PUBLISHING, 24450 NW Hansen Rd., Hillsboro OR 97124. (503)621-3911. President: Dennis Stovall. Vice President: Linny Stovall. Estab. 1985. Publishes trade paperback originals and reprints. Firm averages 6 titles/year. Reports in 6 weeks. Book catalog for #10 SASE.
Fiction: Juvenile, young adult. "We are doing reprints of well known Northwest authors." Query with SASE.
Tips: "We publish Northwest writers *only*."

‡BLUE MOON BOOKS, INC., North Star Line, Rosset & Co., 61 Fourth Ave., New York NY 10003. Publisher/Editor: Barney Rosset. Publishes trade paperback and mass market paperback originals. Publishes 24-40 titles/year. Receives 700 queries and 500 mss/year. Pays 7½-10% royalty on retail price. Offers $500 and up advance. Publishes book 6-12 months after acceptance of ms. Simultaneous submissions OK. Query for electronic submissions. Reports in 1-2 months. Book catalog free on request. Ms guidelines for #10 SASE.
Nonfiction: Query with outline and 3-6 sample chapters. Reviews artwork/photos as part of freelance ms package if part of story. Color photocopies are best but not necessary.
Recent Nonfiction Title: *Two Dogs & Freedom*, by The Open School at Soweto, South Africa (essays by children on apartheid).
Fiction: Erotica. Query or submit synopsis and 3-6 sample chapters.

BLUE POPPY PRESS, 1775 Linden Ave., Boulder CO 80304-1537. (303)442-0796. Fax: (303)447-0740. Editor-in-Chief: Bob Flaws. Publishes trade paperback originals. Publishes 8-10 titles/year. Receives 6-10 queries and 5-8 mss/year. 10-15% of books from first-time authors; 100% from unagented writers. Pays 10-15% royalty "of sales price at all discount levels." Publishes book 6-10 months after acceptance. Simultaneous submissions OK. Query for electronic submissions. Prefers WordPerfect 3.5″ disks. Reports in 1 month. Book catalog and ms guidelines for #10 SASE.
Nonfiction: Self-help, technical, textbook, health/medicine, women's issues/studies. "Books must be related to Chinese/Oriental medicine, philosophy, history, culture, etc." Submit outline and 1 sample chapter. Reviews artwork/photos as part of ms package "if part of the whole, or necessary to an understanding of the overall project."
Tips: Audience is "people interested in alternatives in healthcare, preventive medicine, Chinese philosophy and medicine."

BNA BOOKS, Division of The Bureau of National Affairs, Inc., 1250 23rd St. NW, Washington DC 20037-1165. (202)833-7470. Fax: (202)833-7490. Contact: Acquisitions Manager. Estab. 1929. Publishes hardcover and softcover originals. Averages 35 titles/year. Receives 200 submissions/year. 20% of books from first-time authors; 95% from unagented writers. Pays 5-15% royalty on net cash receipts. Offers $500 average advance. Simultaneous submissions OK. Publishes book an average of 1 year after acceptance. Reports in 3 months on queries. Free book catalog and ms guidelines.
Nonfiction: Reference, professional/scholarly. Subjects include business law and regulation, environment and safety, legal practice, labor relations and human resource management. No biographies, bibliographies, cookbooks, religion books, humor or trade books. Submit detailed table of contents or outline.
Tips: "Our audience is made up of practicing lawyers and business executives; managers, federal, state, and local government administrators; unions; and libraries. We look for authoritative and comprehensive works on subjects of interest to executives, professionals, and managers, that relate to the interaction of government and business."

THE BOLD STRUMMER LTD., 20 Turkey Hill Circle, P.O. Box 2037, Westport CT 06880-2037. (203)259-3021. Fax: (203)259-7369. Contact: Nicholas Clarke. Publishes hardcover and trade paperback originals and reprints. Publishes 6-8 titles/year. Receives 5 queries and 2 mss/year. 50% of books from first-time authors; 100% from unagented writers. Pays 10% royalty on retail price. Publishes book 9-12 months after acceptance of ms. Query for electronic submissions. Book catalog and ms guidelines free on request.
Nonfiction: Music with an emphasis on guitar and piano-related books. Query. Writers should send photocopies.
Tips: "The Bold Strummer Ltd, or our associate publisher Pro/Am Music resources, publishes most good quality work that is offered in our field(s). BSL publishes guitar and related instrument books (guitar, violin,

drums). Bold Strummer has also become a leading source of books about Flamenco. Pro/AM specializes in piano books, composer biography, etc. Very narrow niche publishers."

BONUS BOOKS, INC., 160 E. Illinois St., Chicago IL 60611. (312)467-0580. Associate Editor: Anne Barthel. Estab. 1985. Publishes hardcover and trade paperback originals and reprints. Averages 30 titles/year. Receives 400-500 submissions/year. 40% of books from first-time authors; 60% from unagented writers. Royalties vary. Advances are not frequent. Publishes book an average of 8 months after acceptance. Simultaneous submissions OK "if informed they are such." Query for electronic submissions. Reports in 2 months on queries. Book catalog free on request. All submissions and queries must include SASE.
Nonfiction: Biography, coffee table book, how-to. Subjects include business and economics, foods and nutrition, government/politics, health/medicine, money/finance, recreation, true crime, sports, women's issues/studies. Query with outline and sample chapters. Reviews artwork/photos as part of ms package.

BOOKCRAFT, INC., 1848 W. 2300 S., Salt Lake City UT 84119. (801)972-6180. Editorial Manager: Cory H. Maxwell. Estab. 1942. Publishes mainly hardcover originals and reprints. Pays standard 7½-10-12½-15% royalty on retail price. Rarely gives advance. Averages 40-45 titles/year. Receives 500-600 submissions annually. 20% of books from first-time authors; virtually 100% from unagented writers. Publishes book an average of 6 months after acceptance. Reports in about 3 months. Will send general information to prospective authors on request; ms guidelines for #10 SASE.
Nonfiction: "We publish for members of The Church of Jesus Christ of Latter-Day Saints (Mormons) and do not distribute to the national market. All our books are closely oriented to the faith and practices of the LDS church, and we will be glad to review such mss. Those which have merely a general religious appeal are not acceptable. Ideal book lengths range from about 100 to 300 pages or so, depending on subject, presentation, and age level. We look for a fresh approach—rehashes of well-known concepts or doctrines not acceptable. Manuscripts should be anecdotal unless truly scholarly or on a specialized subject. We do not publish anti-Mormon works. We also publish short and moderate length books for children and young adults, and fiction as well as nonfiction. These reflect LDS principles without being 'preachy'; must be motivational. 30,000-45,000 words is about the right length, though good, longer mss are not ruled out. We publish only 5 or 6 new juvenile titles annually. No poetry, plays, personal philosophizings, or family histories." Query. "Include contents page with manuscript."
Fiction: Should be oriented to LDS faith and practices.
Tips: "The competition in the area of fiction is much more intense than it has ever been before. We receive two or three times as many quality fiction manuscripts as we did even as recently as five years ago."

BOWLING GREEN STATE UNIVERSITY POPULAR PRESS, Bowling Green State University, Bowling Green OH 43403-1000. (419)372-7866. Fax: (419)372-8095. Editor: Ms. Pat Browne. Estab. 1967. Publishes hardcover originals and trade paperback originals and reprints. Averages 25 titles/year. Receives 400 submissions/year. 50% of books from first-time authors; 100% from unagented writers. Pays 5-12% royalty on wholesale price or buys mss outright. Publishes book an average of 9 months after acceptance. Reports in 3 months. Book catalog and ms guidelines free on request.
Nonfiction: Biography, reference, textbook. Subjects include Americana, art/architecture, ethnic, history, language/literature, regional, sports, women's issues/studies. Submit outline and 3 sample chapters.
Recent Nonfiction Titles: *Steven King's America*, by Jonathan Davis; *Alice & Eleanor*, by Sandra Curtis.
Tips: "Our audience includes university professors, students, and libraries."

BOYD & FRASER PUBLISHING COMPANY, Division of South-Western Publishing Company, One Corporate Place, Ferncroft Village, Danvers MA 01923-4001. (508)777-9069. Executive Editor: James H. Edwards. Publishes hardcover and paperback originals primarily for the college textbook market; some trade sales of selected titles. Averages 40-50 titles/year. Receives 100 submissions/year. 50% of books from first-time authors; 100% from unagented writers. Pays 15% royalty on wholesale price. Advance negotiated individually. Publishes book an average of 1 year after acceptance. Simultaneous submissions OK. Query for electronic submissions. Reports in 1 month on queries, 2 months on mss. Book catalog and ms guidelines free on request.
Nonfiction: Textbook. Subjects include computer information systems and application software. Query or submit outline/synopsis first; unsolicited mss not invited. Reviews artwork/photos as part of ms package.

Market conditions are constantly changing! If this is 1996 or later, buy the newest edition of Writer's Market *at your favorite bookstore or order directly from* Writer's Digest Books.

Tips: "Writers have the best chance sending us proposals for college-level textbooks in computer education. Our audience consists of students enrolled in business-oriented courses on computers or computer application topics."

BOYDS MILLS PRESS, Subsidiary of *Highlights for Children*, 815 Church St., Honesdale PA 18431-1895. (717)253-1164. Imprint is Wordsong—publishes works of poetry. Manuscript Coordinator: Beth Troop. Estab. 1990. Publishes hardcover originals. Publishes 70 titles/year. Receives 10,000 queries and mss/year. 20% of books are from first-time authors; 75% from unagented writers. Pays varying royalty on retail price. Offers varying advance. Simultaneous submissions OK. Reports in 1 month. *Writer's Market* recommends allowing 2 months for reply. Free book catalog and ms guidelines.
Nonfiction: Juvenile on all subjects. "Boyds Mills Press is not interested in manuscripts depicting violence, explicit sexuality, racism of any kind or which promotes hatred. We also are not the right market for self-help books." Submit outline and sample chapters. Reviews artwork/photos as part of ms package.
Recent Nonfiction Title: *Extra Cheese, Please!* by Cris Peterson.
Fiction: Juvenile—picture book, middle grade, young adult, poetry. Submit outline/synopsis and sample chapters or complete ms.
Recent Fiction Title: *Elliot Fry's Good-Bye*, by Larry Dane Brimner.
Tips: "Our audience is pre-school to young adult. Concentrate first on your writing. Polish it. Then—and only then—select a market." Needs primarily picture book material.

BRANDEN PUBLISHING CO., INC., 17 Station St., Box 843, Brookline Village MA 02147. Editor: Adolph Caso. Estab. 1965. Subsidiaries include International Pocket Library and Popular Technology, Four Seas and Brashear. Publishes hardcover and trade paperback originals, reprints and software. Averages 15 titles/year. Receives 1,000 submissions annually. 80% of books from first-time authors; 90% from unagented writers. Average print order for a first book is 3,000. Pays 5-10% royalty on net. Offers $1,000 maximum advance. Publishes book an average of 10 months after acceptance. Query for electronic submissions. Reports in 1 month. *Writer's Market* recommends allowing 2 months for reply.
Nonfiction: Biography, illustrated book, juvenile, reference, technical, textbook. Subjects include Americana, art, computers, health, history, music, photography, politics, sociology, software, classics. Especially looking for "about 10 manuscripts on national and international subjects, including biographies of well-known individuals." No religion or philosophy. Prefers paragraph query with author's vita and SASE; no unsolicited mss. No telephone inquiries. Reviews artwork/photos as part of ms package.
Recent Nonfiction Title: *Mary Dyer—Biography of a Rebel Quaker.*
Fiction: Ethnic (histories, integration); religious (historical-reconstructive). No science, mystery or pornography. Paragraph query with author's vita and SASE; no unsolicited mss. No telephone inquiries!
Tips: "Branden publishes only manuscripts determined to have a significant impact on modern society. Our audience is a well-read general public, professionals, college students, and some high school students. If I were a writer trying to market a book today, I would thoroughly investigate the number of potential readers interested in the content of my book. We like books by or about women."

BRASSEY'S INC., Division of Brassey's Ltd. (London), 1st Floor, 8000 Westpark Dr., McLean VA 22102-3101. (703)442-4535. Fax: (703)790-9063. Associate Director of Publishing: Don McKeon. Publishes hardcover and trade paperback originals and reprints. Publishes 30 titles/year. Receives at least 600 queries/year. 30% of books from first-time authors; 80% from unagented writers. Pays 6-12% royalty on wholesale price. Offers $50,000 maximum advance. Publishes book 8½ months after acceptance of ms. Simultaneous submissions OK. SASE required. Query for electronic submissions. Reports in 2 months on proposals. Book catalog and ms guidelines free on request.
Nonfiction: Biography, coffee-table book, reference, textbook. Subjects include government/politics, national and international affairs, history, military/war and intelligence studies. "We are seeking to build our biography, military history and national affairs lists." When submitting nonfiction, be sure to include sufficient biographical information (e.g., track records of previous publications), and "make clear in proposal how your work might differ from other such works already published and with which yours might compete." Submit proposal package, including outline and 1 sample chapter, biographical information, analysis of book's competition and return postage. Reviews artwork/photos as part of freelance ms package. Send photocopies.
Fiction: "Submissions must be related to history, military, or intelligence topics, and authors must have been previously published or have some special qualifications relevant to the topic." Submit synopsis and 1 sample chapter.
Tips: "Our audience consists of military personnel, government policymakers, and general readers with an interest in military history, biography, national and international affairs, defense issues and intelligence studies."

BREVET PRESS, INC., P.O. Box 1404, Sioux Falls SD 57101. Publisher: Donald P. Mackintosh. Managing Editor: Peter E. Reid. Estab. 1972. Publishes hardcover and paperback originals and reprints. Receives 40 submissions annually. 50% of books from first-time authors; 100% from unagented writers. Average print order for a first book is 5,000. Pays 5% royalty. Advance averages $1,000. Publishes book an average of 1 year after acceptance. Simultaneous submissions OK. Reports in 2 months. Free book catalog.

Nonfiction: Specializes in business management, history, place names, and historical marker series. Americana (A. Melton, editor); business (D.P. Mackintosh, editor); history (B. Mackintosh, editor); technical books (Peter Reid, editor). Query; "after query, detailed instructions will follow if we are interested." Reviews artwork/photos. Writers should send copies.

Tips: "Write with market potential and literary excellence. Keep sexism out of the manuscripts."

‡**BREWERS PUBLICATIONS**, Division of Association of Brewers, 736 Pearl St., Boulder CO 80302. (303)447-0816. Publisher: Elizabeth Gold. Publishes trade paperback and mass market paperback originals. Publishes 8-10 titles/year. Receives 50 queries and 6 mss/year. 25% of books from first-time authors; 100% from unagented writers. Pays 2-20% royalty on net receipt. Offers $500 maximum advance. Publishes book 9-24 months after acceptance of ms. Simultaneous submissions OK. Reports in 3 months. Book catalog free on request.

Nonfiction: "We only publish books about beer and brewing—for professional brewers, homebrewers and beer enthusiasts." Query first then submit outline if requested. Reviews artwork/photos only after a ms is accepted.

Recent Nonfiction Title: *Great American Beer Cookbook*, by Candy Schermerhorn (cookbook); *Evaluating Beer*, compiled articles (technical); *Scotch Ale*, by Greg Noonan (history, recipes of beer style).

BRICK HOUSE PUBLISHING CO., #4 Limbo Ln., P.O. Box 266, Amherst NH 03031. (603)672-5112. President/Publisher: Robert Runck. Estab. 1976. Publishes hardcover and trade paperback originals. Averages 8 titles/year. Receives 200 submissions annually. 20% of books from first-time authors; 100% of books from unagented writers. Pays 10% royalty on wholesale price. Publishes book an average of 6-12 months after acceptance. Simultaneous submissions OK. Query for electronic submissions. Reports in 3-4 months on queries. *Writer's Market* recommends allowing 2 months for reply. Book catalog and ms guidelines for 9×12 SAE with 4 first-class stamps.

Nonfiction: How-to, reference, technical, textbook. "Subjects we are concentrating on now are renewable energy, energy conservation and environmental concerns. Other subjects include Northeast regional, business, self-help and sane public policy, but these are not being focused on as much."

Tips: "Authors should address the following questions in their query/proposals: What are my qualifications for writing this book? What distinguishes it from other books on the same topic. What can I do to promote the book?"

BRIGHTON PUBLICATIONS, INC., P.O. Box 120706, St. Paul MN 55112-0706. (612)636-2220. Editor: Sharon E. Dlugosch. Publishes trade paperback originals. Publishes 4 titles/year. Receives 20 queries and 4 mss/year. 50% of books from first-time authors; 100% from unagented writers. Pays 10% royalty on wholesale price. Publishes book 6 months after acceptance. Simultaneous submissions OK. Query for electronic submissions. Reports in 3 months. Book catalog and ms guidelines for #10 SASE.

Nonfiction: How-to, business, tabletop, party themes, home making. "We're interested in topics telling how to live any part of life well. Specifically, we're developing business how-to, celebration themes, and time crunch solutions." Query. Submit outline and 2 sample chapters.

BRISTOL PUBLISHING ENTERPRISES, INC., P.O. Box 1737, San Leandro CA 94577. (415)895-4461. Imprints include Nitty Gritty Cookbooks. Chairman: Patricia J. Hall. President: Brian Hall. Estab. 1988. Publishes 12-14 titles/year. Receives 750 proposals/year. 10% of books from first-time authors; 100% from unagented writers. Pays 6% royalty on wholesale price. Average advance $500. Publishes within 1 year of acceptance. Reports in 3-4 months. Book catalog for SAE with 2 first-class stamps.

Nonfiction: Cookbooks. Submit theme, outline and author's background.

BRITISH AMERICAN PUBLISHING, 19B British American Blvd., Latham NY 12110-1420. (518)786-6000. Contact: Jane Conners. Estab. 1987. Imprint is The Paris Review Editions. Publishes hardcover and trade paperback originals and hardcover reprints. Averages 15 titles/year. Receives 1,000 submissions/year. 10% of books from first-time authors; 10% from unagented writers. Pays royalties. Publishes book an average of 1 year after acceptance. Simultaneous submissions OK. Reports in 2 months. Manuscript guidelines for #10 SASE.

Nonfiction: Biography, humor, self-help, how-to. Subjects include business and economics, child guidance/parenting, cooking, foods and nutrition, education, government/politics, history, language/literature, psychology, recreation, regional, sports, travel. Submit complete ms, competitive title information, and SASE. *Writer's Market* recommends query with SASE first.

Recent Nonfiction Title: *Just Let Me Play*, by Charlie Sifford.

Fiction: Adventure, confession, experimental, fantasy, feminist, historical, horror, humor, literary, mainstream/contemporary, mystery, religious, romance, short story collections, suspense. Submit complete ms and SASE. *Writer's Market* recommends query with SASE first.

Poetry: Submit complete ms.

Tips: "We have more interest in nonfiction this year than last."

BROADWAY PRESS, P.O. Box 1037, Shelter Island NY 11964-1037. (516)749-3266. Fax: (516)749-3267. Publisher: David Rodger. Estab. 1985. Publishes trade paperback originals. Averages 2-3 titles/year. Receives 50-75 submissions annually. 50% of books from first-time authors; 75% from unagented writers. Pays negotiable royalty. Publishes book an average of 18 months after acceptance. Simultaneous submissions OK. Reports in 3 months on queries.
Nonfiction: Reference, technical. Subjects include theatre, film, television, performing arts. "We're looking for professionally-oriented and authored books." Submit outline and sample chapters.
Tips: "Our readers are primarily professionals in the entertainment industries. Submissions that really grab our attention are aimed at that market."

‡BROOKINGS INSTITUTION, 1775 Massachusetts Ave. NW, Washington DC 20036. (202)797-6260. Acquisitions Editor: Nancy D. Davidson. Publishes hardcover and trade paperback originals. Publishes 35-40 titles/year. Receives 50 queries and 30 mss/year. 100% of books from unagented writers. Pays royalty on net receipts. Publishes book 9 months after acceptance of ms. Accepts simultaneous submissions. Query for electronic submissions. Reports in 1 month on queries. Book catalog and ms guidelines free on request.
Nonfiction: Business and economics, education, government/politics, money/finance, political, science, foreign affairs. "We focus on *current* public policy issues. Our acquisitions program is a small part of our total list; we primarily publish the work of our own scholars." Query.
Recent Nonfiction Title: *Beyond the Wall: Germany's Road to Unification*, by Elizabeth Pond (foreign policy).

‡BUCKNELL UNIVERSITY PRESS, Lewisburg PA 17837. (717)524-3674. Fax: (717)524-3760. Director: Mills F. Edgerton, Jr. Estab. 1969. Publishes hardcover originals. Averages 25 titles/year; receives 150 submissions annually. 20% of books from first-time authors; 99% from unagented writers. Pays royalty. Publishes book an average of 2 years after acceptance. Query for electronic submissions. Reports in 1 month on queries. *Writer's Market* recommends allowing 2 months for reply. Free book catalog.
Nonfiction: Subjects include scholarly art, history, literary criticism, music, philosophy, politics, psychology, religion, sociology. "In all fields, our criterion is scholarly presentation; manuscripts must be addressed to the scholarly community." Query.
Tips: "An original work of high-quality scholarship has the best chance with us. We publish for the scholarly community."

‡BULL PUBLISHING CO., 110 Gilbert, Menlo Park CA 94025-2833. (415)332-2855. Fax: (415)327-3300. Publisher: David Bull. Estab. 1974. Publishes hardcover and trade paperback originals. Averages 2-4 titles/year. Receives 100 submissions/year. 40-50% of books from first-time authors; 99% from unagented writers. Pays 14-16% royalty on wholesale price (net to publisher). Publishes ms an average of 6 months after acceptance. Simultaneous submissions OK. Query for electronic submissions. Reports in 2 months. Book catalog free on request.
Nonfiction: How-to, self-help. Subjects include foods and nutrition, fitness, child health and nutrition, health education, sports medicine. "We look for books that fit our area of strength: responsible books on health that fill a substantial public need, and that we can market primarily through professionals." Submit outline and sample chapters. Reviews artwork/photos as part of ms package.
Recent Nonfiction Title: *Living A Healthy Life With Chronic Conditions: Self-Management of Heart Disease, Arthritis, Stroke, Diabetes, Asthma, Bronchitis, Emphysema & others* by Kate Lorig, RN DrPH et al.

‡BURNING GATE PRESS, Suite 123, 18401 Burbank Blvd., Tarzana CA 91356. (818)776-8836. Publisher: Mark Kelly. Publishes hardcover originals and trade paperback originals and reprints. Publishes 4 titles/year. Receives 400 queries and 150 mss/year. 25% of books from first-time authors; 50% from unagented writers. Pays 18% royalty on net of distributor's fees or on publisher's net sales. Publishes book 1 year after acceptance of ms. Accepts simultaneous submissions. Query for electronic submissions. Reports in 3 months on mss. Manuscript guidelines free on request.
Nonfiction: Biography, how-to, illustrated book, self-help, technical. Subjects include art/architecture, business and economics, history, military/war, travel, women's issues/studies. Query with outline and 3 sample chapters.
Recent Nonfiction Title: *Sisters on the Bridge of Fire*, by Debra Denker (travel/women).
Fiction: Adventure, literary, mainstream/contemporary. "We have published World War II fiction. We are *not* anxious to publish much more of it unless it is *brilliant*. We are interested in contemporary issues." Submit synopsis and 3 sample chapters.
Recent Fiction Title: *Seven Six One*, by G. F. Borden (WWII).
Tips: "If you are uncertain about your work, take a class at a nearby college. Take a workshop. Don't ask us for advice. If you want us to take your efforts seriously, please read your work for glaring problems before you send it in. Check the grammar, check the spelling, check everything. If you let a typo slip by in the cover letter, I won't read any further."

‡BUSINESS & LEGAL REPORTS, INC., 39 Academy St., Madison CT 06443-1513. (203)245-7448. Fax: (203)245-2559. Editor-in-Chief: Stephen D. Bruce, Ph.D. Estab. 1978. Publishes loose leaf and soft cover originals. Averages 20 titles/year. Receives 100 submissions/year. Pays 2½-5% royalty on retail price; or makes outright purchase for $1,000-5,000. Offers $3,000 average advance. Publishes book an average of 6 months after acceptance. Simultaneous submissions OK. Query for electronic submissions. Book catalog free on request.

Nonfiction: Reference. Subjects include human resources, management, human resources, safety, environmental management. Query.

● Publisher reports a special interest in "how-to" compliance guides.

‡**BUSINESS McGRAW-HILL**, McGraw Hill Inc., 11 W. 19th St., New York NY 10011. (212)337-4098. Publisher: Philip Ruppel. Publishes hardcover and trade paperback originals. Publishes 100 titles/year. Receives 1,200 queries and 1,200 mss/year. 30% of books from first-time authors; 60% from unagented writers. Pays 5-17% royalty on net price. Offers $1,000-100,000 advance. Publishes book 6 months after acceptance of ms. Simultaneous submissions OK. Query for electronic submissions. Reports in 2-3 months. Book catalog and ms guidelines free on request.

Nonfiction: How-to, reference, self-help, technical. Subjects include business and economics, government/politics, money/finance. "Current, up to date ideas, original ideas are needed. Good self promotion is key. We publish in a broad area of business." Submit outline and proposal package, including t-o-c, concept.

Recent Nonfiction Title: *Buying Stock without a Broker*, by C. Carlson (investing); *Beyond Maximarketing*, by S. Rapp (marketing); *The Trust Factor*, by J.Whitney (management).

C Q INC., Imprint of Congressional Quarterly, Inc., 1414 22nd St. NW, Washington DC 20037. (202)887-8642 or 8645. Acquisitions Editors: Jeanne Ferris, Shana Wagger. Publishes 30-40 hardcover and paperback titles/year. 95% of books from unagented writers. Pays royalties on net receipts. Sometimes offers advance. Publishes book an average of 6-12 months after acceptance. Simultaneous submissions OK. Reports in 3 months. Free book catalog.

Nonfiction: Reference books, information directories and monographs on federal and state governments, national elections, politics and governmental issues. Public affairs paperbacks on developing issues and events. Submit prospectus, writing sample and curriculum vitae.

Tips: "Our books present important information on American government and politics, and related issues, with careful attention to accuracy, thoroughness and readability."

C Q PRESS, Imprint of Congressional Quarterly, Inc., 1414 22nd St. NW, Washington DC 20037. (202)887-8641. Acquisitions Editor: Brenda Carter. Publishes 20-30 hardcover and paperback original titles annually. 95% of books from unagented writers. Pays standard college royalty on wholesale price; offers college text advance. Publishes book an average of 6 months after acceptance of final ms. Simultaneous submissions OK. Reports in 3 months. Free book catalog.

Nonfiction: All levels of college political science texts. "We are interested in areas of American government, public administration, comparative government, and international relations." Submit proposal, outline and author biography.

CADDO GAP PRESS, Suite 275, 3145 Geary Blvd., San Francisco CA 94118-3300. (415)750-9978. Publisher: Alan H. Jones. Estab. 1989. Publishes trade paperback originals and educational journals and newsletters. Publishes 4 titles/year. Receives 20 queries and 10 mss/year. 50% of books from first-time authors; 100% from unagented writers. Pays 10% royalty on wholesale price. Publishes book 1 year after acceptance of ms. Simultaneous submissions OK. Query for electronic submissions. Reports in 2 months on proposals.

Nonfiction: Subjects limited to California education only. Query.

Recent Nonfiction Titles: *The Los Angeles School Board vs. Frances Eisenberg*, by Martha Kransdorf.

CAMBRIDGE EDUCATIONAL, P.O. Box 2153, Charleston WV 25328-2153. (800)468-4227. Fax: (304)744-9351. Subsidiaries include: Cambridge Parenting and Cambridge Job Search. President: Edward T. Gardner, Ph.D. Estab. 1980. Publishes hardcover and trade paperback originals. Averages 12 titles/year. Receives 200 submissions/year. 20% of books from first-time authors; 90% from unagented writers. Makes $1,500-4,000 outright purchase. Occasional royalty arrangement. Publishes book an average of 8 months after acceptance. Simultaneous submissions OK. "No report unless interested." Free book catalog and ms guidelines.

Nonfiction: How-to, young adult (13-24), self-help. Subjects include child guidance/parenting, cooking, foods and nutrition, education, health/medicine, money/finance, recreation, sports. "We need high quality books written for young adults (13 to 24 years old) on job search, career guidance, educational guidance, personal guidance, home economics, physical education, coaching, recreation, health, personal development, substance abuse. We are looking for scriptwriters in the same subject area and age group. We only publish books written for young adults and primarily sold to libraries, schools, etc. We do not seek books targeted to adults or written at high readability levels." Query or submit outline/synopsis and sample chapters or send complete ms. Reviews artwork/photos as part of ms package.

● Publisher reports a greater focus on parenting and job search issues.

Tips: "We encourage the submission of high-quality books on timely topics written for young adult audiences at moderate to low readibility levels. Call and request a copy of all our current catalogs, talk to the management about what is timely in the areas you wish to write on, thoroughly research the topic, and write a manuscript that will be read by young adults without being overly technical. Low to moderate readibility yet entertaining, informative and accurate."

CAMBRIDGE UNIVERSITY PRESS, 40 W. 20th St., New York NY 10011-4211. Editorial Director: Sidney Landau. Estab. 1534. Publishes hardcover and paperback originals. Publishes 1,300 titles/year. Receives 1,000 submissions annually. 50% of books from first-time authors; 99% from unagented writers. Subsidy publishes (nonauthor) 8% of books. Pays 10% royalty on receipts; 8% on paperbacks. Publishes book an average of 1 year after acceptance. Query for electronic submissions. Reports in 4 months.
Nonfiction: Anthropology, archeology, economics, life sciences, medicine, mathematics, psychology, physics, art history, upper-level textbooks, academic trade, scholarly monographs, biography, history, and music. Looking for academic excellence in all work submitted. Department Editors: Frank Smith (history, social sciences); Mary Vaughn (English as second language); Deborah Goldblatt (English as a second language); Sidney Landau (reference); Lauren Cowles (mathematics, computer science); Scott Parris (economics); Julia Hough (developmental and social psychology, cognitive science); Alex Holzman (politics, history of science); Beatrice Rehl (fine arts, film studies); Richard Barling (medicine); Robin Smith (life sciences); Catherine Flack (earth sciences); Alan Harvey, (applied mathematics); Florence Padgett, (engineering, materials science); Terence Moore (philosophy); Susan Chang (American literature, Latin American literature); Elizabeth Neal (sociology, East Asian studies). Query. Reviews artwork/photos.

CAMDEN HOUSE, INC., P.O. 2025, Columbia SC 29202. (803)788-8689. Editor: J. Bruno. Estab. 1981. Publishes hardcover originals and reprints. Publishes 25-30 titles/year. 75% of books from first-time authors. Pays 5-10% royalties on retail price. Publishes ms an average of 10 months after acceptance. Query for electronic submissions. Reports in 1 month on queries. "No phone calls, please."
Nonfiction: "Reference works, especially local history published under the aegies of civic organizations." Query. SASE a necessity. Reviews artwork/photos as part of ms package.
• The editor does not want to see any fiction or poetry submissions.

CAMELOT BOOKS, Children's Book Imprint of Avon Books, Division of the Hearst Corp., Dept. WM, 1350 Avenue of the Americas, New York NY 10019. (212)261-6817. Fax: (212)261-6895. Editorial Director: Ellen Krieger. Publishes paperback originals and reprints. Averages 60-70 titles/year. Receives 1,000-1,500 submissions annually. 10-15% of books from first-time authors; 50% from unagented writers. Pays 6-8% royalty on retail price. Offers minimum advance of $2,000. Publishes book an average of 2 years after acceptance. Simultaneous submissions OK. Reports in 10 weeks. Book catalog and ms guidelines for 8×10 SAE with 5 first-class stamps.
Fiction: Subjects include adventure, fantasy, humor, juvenile (Camelot, 8-12 and Young Camelot, 7-10) mainstream, mystery, ("very selective with mystery and fantasy") and suspense. Avon does not publish picture books. Submit entire ms or 3 sample chapters and a brief "general summary of the story, chapter by chapter."
Recent Fiction Title: *Crossroads*, by Charles Pitts.

CAMINO BOOKS, INC., P.O. Box 59026, Philadelphia PA 19102. (215)732-2491. Publisher: E. Jutkowitz. Estab. 1987. Publishes hardcover and trade paperback originals. Averages 5 titles/year. Receives 500 submissions/year. 20% of books from first-time authors. Pays 6-12% royalty on net price. Offers $1,000 average advance. Publishes book an average of 1 year after acceptance. Reports in 2 weeks on queries. *Writer's Market* recommends allowing 2 months for reply.
Nonfiction: Biography, cookbook, how-to, juvenile. Subjects include agriculture/horticulture, Americana, art/architecture, child guidance/parenting, cooking, foods and nutrition, ethnic, gardening, government/politics, history, regional, travel. Query or submit outline/synopsis and sample chapters. Include SASE.
Tips: "The books must be of interest to readers in the Middle Atlantic states, or they should have a clearly defiend niche, such as cookbooks."

C&T PUBLISHING, #1, 5021 Blum Rd., Martinez CA 94553. (510)370-9600. Fax: (510)370-1576. Editorial Directors: Diane Pedersen, Liz Aneloski. Estab. 1983. Publishes hardcover and trade paperback originals. Publishes 10-12 titles/year. Receives 48 submissions/year. 10% of books from first-time authors; 100% from unagented writers. Pays 5-10% royalty on retail price. Offers $1,000 average advance. Publishes book an average of 9 months after acceptance. Simultaneous submissions OK. Reports in 1 month. *Writer's Market* recommends allowing 2 months for reply. Free book catalog and ms guidelines.
Nonfiction: Quilting books, primarily how-to, occasional quilt picture books, children's books relating to quilting, quilt-related crafts, wearable art, other books relating to fabric crafting. "Please submit ms with color photos of your work."
Recent Nonfiction Title: *Christmas Traditions From The Heart Volume Two*, by Margaret Peters.
Tips: "In our industry, we find that how-to books have the longest selling life. The art quilt is coming into its own as an expression by women. Quiltmakers, sewing enthusiasts and fiber artists are our audience."

CAPRA PRESS, P.O. Box 2068, Santa Barbara CA 93120. (805)966-4590. Contact: Noel Young. Estab. 1970. Publishes hardcover and trade paperback originals. Averages 15 titles/year. Receives 4,000 submissions/year. 1% of books from first-time authors. 20% from unagented writers. Pays 10-15% royalty on wholesale price. Offers $1,000 average advance. Publishes book an average of 18 months after acceptance. Simultaneous submissions OK. Query for electronic submissions. Reports in 2 months. Book catalog for 6×9 SAE with 2 first-class stamps.
Nonfiction: Biography, how-to, self-help, natural history. Subjects include animals, art/architecture, gardening, language/literature, nature/environment, recreation, regional, sociology. "We are looking for general trade titles with focus on the West." No juvenile books, code books or poetry. Query or submit outline and sample chapters. Reviews artwork/photos as part of ms package.
Recent Nonfiction Title: *The Sudden Disappearance of Japan*, by J.D. Brown.
Fiction: Historical (western states), literary (from established authors), mainstream/contemporary, short story collections (only if stories have been in periodicals previously). No experimentals, fantasy, or genre fiction. Submit complete ms.
Recent Fiction Title: *Learning to Love It*, by Thomas Farber.
Tips: "Writers have the best chance selling us nonfiction relating to architecture, natural history (birds, animals) or environmental subjects."

CAPSTONE PRESS, INC., 2440 Fernbrook Lane, Minneapolis MN 55447. (507)387-4492. Contact: Acquisitions Editor. Publishes hardcover originals. Averages 24 titles titles/year. Makes outright purchase. Publishes book an average of 6 months after acceptance. Reports in 2 weeks. *Writer's Market* recommends allowing 2 months for reply. Book catalog free on request.
Nonfiction: Juvenile nonfiction only. Subjects include vehicles, racing, animals, sports. "We are not accepting unsolicited manuscripts at this time."

CARADIUM PUBLISHING, # 435, 2503 Del Prado Blvd S., Cape Coral FL 33904. Product Evaluation: Troy Dunn. Estab. 1989. Publishes hardcover originals and trade and mass market paperback originals. Publishes 15-20 titles/year. Receives 300 queries and 250 mss/year. 50% of books from first-time authors; 90% from unagented writers. Pays 15-20% royalty on retail price or makes outright purchase, $100 minimum. Offers $0-5,000 advance. Publishes book 3 months after acceptance of ms. Simultaneous submissions OK. Does not return submissions. Books remain on file or destroyed. Reports on queries in 2 months.
Nonfiction: Business related: how-to, reference, self-help. Subjects include business and economics (motivation and how-to), money/finance. "We specialize in infomercials for our products." Query with outline and 3 sample chapters. Reviews artwork/photos as part of freelance ms package. Writers should send photocopies.
Tips: "Know the market you want to reach statistically and be creative in your submissions."

CARDOZA PUBLISHING, 132 Hastings St., Brooklyn NY 11235. (718)743-5229. Acquisitions Editor: Rose Swann. Imprints are Gambling Research Institute and Word Reference Library. Publishes trade paperback originals and reprints and mass market paperback originals. Publishes 10 titles/year. Receives 50 queries and 12 mss/year. 50% of books from first-time authors; 100% from unagented writers. Pays 5% royalty on retail price. Offers $500-2,000 advance. Publishes book 6 months after acceptance of ms. Simultaneous submissions OK. Reports in 2 months on queries.
Nonfiction: How-to, reference. Subjects include recreation, gaming, golf, travel. "The presentation should be typed and professional looking. Sample writing a must. Our specialties are reference (words), gambling (games)." Submit outline with 1 or 2 sample chapters.

‡THE CAREER PRESS INC., P.O. Box 34, Hawthorne NJ 07507-0034. (201)427-0229. Fax: (201)427-2037. President: Ron Fry. Editor-in-Chief: Betsy Sheldon. Estab. 1985. Publishes hardcover, trade paperback and mass market paperback originals and reprints. Approximately 4-6 hardcover originals in 1994. Averages 50 titles in 1994. Receives 500 submissions/year. 50% of books from first-time authors; 50% from unagented writers. Pays 8-15% royalty on net. Offers $2,000-5,000 advance. Publishes book an average of 1 year after acceptance. Simultaneous submissions OK. Reports in up to 3-6 months. Book catalog and ms guidelines free.
Nonfiction: How-to, reference, self-help. Subjects include business and economics, reference, education, money/finance, career/job search/résumé. Submit 2-3 sample chapters, author bio and marketing information. Reviews artwork/photos as part of ms package.
Recent Nonfiction Title: *For Entrepreneurs Only By Wilson Harrell*, (former publisher of *Inc.* magazine).

CAREER PUBLISHING, INC., P.O. Box 5486, Orange CA 92613-5486. (714)771-5155. Fax: (714)532-0180. Editor-in-Chief: Marilyn M. Martin. Publishes paperback originals and software. Averages 6-20 titles/year. Receives 300 submissions annually. 80% of books from first-time authors; 90% from unagented writers. Average print order for a writer's first book is 3,000-10,000. Pays 10% royalty on actual amount received; no advance. Publishes book an average of 1 year after acceptance. Simultaneous submissions OK (if so informed with names of others to whom submissions have been sent). Query for electronic submissions. Reports in 2 months. Book catalog and ms guidelines for 9×12 SAE with 2 first-class stamps.

Nonfiction: Microcomputer material, educational software, work experience, allied health and medical, and transportation (trucking) business, etc. "Textbooks should provide core upon which class curriculum can be based: textbook, workbook or kit with 'hands-on' activities and exercises, and teacher's guide. Should incorporate modern and effective teaching techniques. Should lead to a job objective. We also publish support materials for existing courses and are open to unique, marketable ideas with schools (secondary and post secondary) in mind. Reading level should be controlled appropriately—usually 7th-10th grade equivalent for vocational school and community college level courses. Any sign of sexism or racism will disqualify the work. No career awareness masquerading as career training." Submit outline, 2 sample chapters and table of contents. Reviews artwork/photos as part of ms package. If material is to be returned, enclose SAE and return postage.

Recent Nonfiction Title: *IBM Linkway*, by Annette Lamb.

Tips: "Authors should be aware of vocational/career areas with inadequate or no training textbooks and submit ideas and samples to fill the gap. Trends in book publishing that freelance writers should be aware of include education—especially for microcomputers."

CAROL PUBLISHING, 600 Madison Ave., New York NY 10022. (212)486-2200. Publisher: Steven Schragis. Imprints include Lyle Stuart, Birch Lane Press, Citadel Press and University Books. Publishes hardcover originals, and trade paperback originals and reprints. Averages 125 titles/year. Receives 1,000 submissions/year. 5% of books from first-time authors; 5% from unagented writers. Pays 10-15% royalty on retail price. Publishes book an average of 1 year after acceptance. Simultaneous submissions OK. Reports in 2 months.
Nonfiction: Biography, how-to, humor, illustrated book, self-help. Subjects include Americana, animals, art/architecture, business and economics, child guidance/parenting, computers and electronics, cooking, foods and nutrition, ethnic, gay/lesbian, health/medicine, history, hobbies, money/finance, music/dance, nature/environment, philosophy, psychology, recreation, regional, science, sports, travel, women's issues/studies. Submit outline/synopsis and sample chapters.
Recent Nonfiction Title: *Her Name is Barbra*, by Randall Reise.
Fiction: Very infrequently.
Recent Fiction Title: *All Kinds of Love*, by Carol Reicher.

CAROLRHODA BOOKS, INC., 241 First Ave. N., Minneapolis MN 55401. (612)332-3344. Submissions Editor: Rebecca Poole. Estab. 1969. Publishes hardcover originals. Averages 50-60 titles/year. Receives 1,500 submissions/year. 15% of books from first-time authors; 95% from unagented writers. Pays 4-6% royalty on wholesale price, makes outright purchase, or negotiates cents per printed copy. Publishes book an average of 18 months after acceptance. Simultaneous submissions OK. Must send SASE with all submissions for return of mss. Book catalog and ms guidelines for 9 × 12 SASE with 4 first-class stamps. No phone calls please.
• Publisher reports a need for more multicultural stories, fewer issue-related stories, for now.
Nonfiction: Publishes only children's books. Subjects include biography, animals, art, history, music, nature. Needs "biographies in story form on truly creative individuals—25 manuscript pages in length." Send full ms. Reviews artwork/photos separate from ms. Send color copies. No originals, please.
Recent Nonfiction Title: *Say It With Music: A Story About Irving Berlin*, by Tom Streissguth, illustrated by Jennifer Hagerman.
Fiction: Children's historical. No anthropomorphized animal stories. Submit complete ms.
Recent Fiction Title: *Jennifer Jean, the Cross-Eyed Queen*, by Phyllis Reynolds Naylor, illustrated by Jennifer Hagerman.
Tips: "Our audience consists of children ages four to eleven. We publish very few picture books. Nonfiction science topics, particularly nature, do well for us, as do biographies, photo essays, and easy readers. We prefer manuscripts that can fit into one of our series. Spend time developing your idea in a unique way or from a unique angle; avoid trite, hackneyed plots and ideas."

CARSTENS PUBLICATIONS, INC., Hobby Book Division, P.O. Box 700, Newton NJ 07860-0700. (201)383-3355. Publisher: Harold H. Carstens. Estab. 1933. Publishes paperback originals. Averages 8 titles/year. 100% of books from unagented writers. Pays 10% royalty on retail price. Offers advance. Publishes book an average of 1 year after acceptance. Query for electronic submissions. *Writer's Market* recommends allowing 2 months for reply. Book catalog for SASE.
Nonfiction: Model railroading, toy trains, model aviation, railroads and model hobbies. "We have scheduled or planned titles on several railroads as well as model railroad and model airplane books. Authors must know their field intimately because our readers are active modelers. Our railroad books presently are primarily photographic essays on specific railroads. Writers cannot write about somebody else's hobby with authority. If they do, we can't use them." Query. Reviews artwork/photos as part of ms package.
Tips: "No fiction. We need lots of good b&w photos. Material must be in model, hobby, railroad and transportation field only."

CASSANDRA PRESS, P.O. Box 868, San Rafael CA 94915. (415)382-8507. Fax: (415)382-7758. President: Gurudas. Estab. 1985. Publishes trade paperback originals. Averages 6 titles/year. Receives 200 submissions/year. 50% of books from first-time authors; 50% from unagented writers. Pays 6-8% maximum royalty on retail price. Advance rarely offered.Publishes book an average of 1 year after acceptance. Simultaneous submissions OK. Reports in 3 weeks on queries, 2-3 months on mss. Free book catalog and ms guidelines.

Nonfiction: New Age, cookbook, how-to, self-help. Subjects include cooking, foods and nutrition, health/medicine (holistic health), philosophy, psychology, religion (New Age), metaphysical. "We like to do around six titles a year in the general New Age, metaphysical and holistic health fields so we continue to look for good material. No children's books." Submit outline and sample chapters. Reviews artwork/photos as part of ms package.

Tips: "Not accepting fiction or children's book submissions."

CATBIRD PRESS, 16 Windsor Rd., North Haven CT 06473-3015. (203)230-2391. Fax: (203)230-8029. Publisher: Robert Wechsler. Estab. 1987. Publishes hardcover and trade paperback originals and trade paperback reprints. Averages 5-6 titles/year. Receives 1,000 submissions/year. 10% of books from first-time authors; 100% from unagented writers. Pays 2½-10% royalty on retail price. Offers $1,500 average advance. Publishes book an average of 1 year after acceptance. Simultaneous submissions OK, if so notified. Reports in 1 month on nonfiction queries if SASE is included. *Writer's Market* recommends allowing 2 months for reply. Book catalog free on request. Manuscript guidelines for #10 SASE.

Nonfiction: Humor, reference. "We are looking for up-market humor and legal humor books. No New Age or joke books." Submit outline and sample chapters.

Fiction: Humor, literary. "We are looking for well-written literature with a comic vision or style that takes a fresh approach. No genre, wacky, or derivative mainstream fiction." Submit outline/synopsis and sample chapter.

Tips: "Our audience is generally up-market. If I were a writer trying to market a book today, I would learn about the publishing industry just as a musician learns about night clubs. If you play jazz, you should know the jazz clubs. If you write children's books, you should learn the children's book publishers. Writing is just as much an art and a business as jazz."

CATHOLIC UNIVERSITY OF AMERICA PRESS, 620 Michigan Ave. NE, Washington DC 20064. (202)319-5052. Fax: (202)319-5802. Director: Dr. David J. McGonagle. Estab. 1939. Marketing Manager: Val Poletto. Averages 15-20 titles/year. Receives 100 submissions annually. 50% of books from first-time authors; 100% from unagented writers. Average print order for a first book is 750. Pays variable royalty on net receipts. Publishes book an average of 1 year after acceptance. Query for electronic submissions. Reports in 3 months. Book catalog for SASE.

Nonfiction: Publishes history, biography, languages and literature, philosophy, religion, church-state relations, political theory. No unrevised doctoral dissertations. Length: 80,000-200,000 words. Query with sample chapter plus outline of entire work, along with curriculum vitae and list of previous publications.

Tips: "Freelancer has best chance of selling us scholarly monographs and works suitable for adoption as supplementary reading material in courses."

CATO INSTITUTE, 1000 Massachusetts Ave. NW, Washington DC 20001. (202)842-0200. Executive Vice President: David Boaz. Senior Editor: Sheldon Richman. Estab. 1977. Publishes hardcover originals, trade paperback originals and reprints. Averages 12 titles/year. Receives 50 submissions/year. 25% of books from first-time authors; 90% from unagented writers. Makes outright purchase for $1,000-10,000. Publishes book an average of 9 months after acceptance. Simultaneous submissions OK. Reports in 3 months. Book catalog free on request.

Nonfiction: Public policy *only*. Subjects include foreign policy, economics, education, government/politics, health/medicine, monetary policy, sociology. "We want books on public policy issues from a free-market or libertarian perspective." Query.

CAVE BOOKS, 756 Harvard Ave., St. Louis MO 63130-3134. (314)862-7646. Editor: Richard Watson. Estab. 1980. Publishes hardcover and trade paperback originals and reprints. Publishes 4 titles/year. Receives 20 queries and 10 mss/year. 75% of books from first-time authors; 100% from unagented writers. Pays 10% royalty on retail price. Publishes book 18 months after acceptance. Simultaneous submissions OK. Reports in 3 months on mss. Book catalog free on request.

Nonfiction: Biography, technical (science), adventure. Subjects are Americana, animals, anthropology/archaeology, history, nature/environment, photography, recreation, regional, science, sports (cave exploration), travel. "We publish only books on caves, karst, and speleology." Send complete ms. Reviews artwork/photos as part of freelance ms package. Writers should send photocopies of illustrations.

Fiction: Adventure, historical, literary, mystery. "All must be realistic and related to cave exploration." "No gothic, science fiction, fantasy, romance, or novels having nothing to do with caves. The cave and action in the cave must be central, authentic, and realistic." Send complete ms.

Tips: "Our readers are interested only in caves, karst, and speleology. Please do not send manuscripts on other subjects. Query with outline first."

THE CAXTON PRINTERS, LTD., 312 Main St., Caldwell ID 83605-3299. (208)459-7421. Fax: (208)459-7450. President: Gordon Gipson. General Editor: Pam Hardenbrook. Estab. 1895. Publishes hardcover and trade paperback originals. Averages 6-10 titles/year. Receives 250 submissions annually. 50% of books from first-time authors; 60% from unagented writers. Pays royalty. Offers advance of $500-2,000. Publishes book an average of 18 months after acceptance. Simultaneous submissions OK. Reports in 3 months. Book catalog for 9×12 SASE.

Nonfiction: Coffee table, Americana and Western Americana. "We need good Western Americana, especially the Northwest, preferably copiously illustrated with unpublished photos." Query. Reviews artwork/photos as part of ms package.

Tips: "Audience includes Westerners, students, historians and researchers."

CCC PUBLICATIONS, 21630 Lassen St., Chatsworth CA 91311-6044. (818)407-1661. Contact: Editorial Director: Cliff Carle. Estab. 1983. Publishes trade paperback and mass market paperback originals. Averages 15-20 titles/year. Receives 400-600 mss/year. 50% of books from first-time authors; 50% from unagented writers. Pays 7-12% royalty on wholesale price. Publishes book an average of 6 months after acceptance. Simultaneous submissions OK. Reports in 3 months. Catalog for 10×13 SAE with 2 first-class stamps.

• CCC Publications is looking for shorter, punchier pieces with *lots* of cartoon illustrations.

Nonfiction: Humorous how-to/self-help. "We are looking for *original, clever* and *current* humor that is not too limited in audience appeal or that will have a limited shelf life. All of our titles are as marketable five years from now as they are today. No rip-offs of previously published books, or too special interest manuscripts." Query first with SASE. Reviews artwork/photos as part of ms package.

Tips: "Humor—we specialize in the subject and have a good reputation with retailers and wholesalers for publishing super-impulse titles. SASE is a must!"

CENTER PRESS, Box 16452, Encino CA 91416-6452. Managing Editor: Jana Cain. Publishes hardcover and trade paperback originals. Publishes 4-6 titles/year. Receives 600 queries and 300 mss/year. "We are no longer accepting unsolicited manuscripts. Only manuscripts received from agents, direct solicitation and through our sponsored literary contest will be read through 01/01/96."

CENTERING CORPORATION, 1531 N. Saddle Creek Rd., Omaha NE 68104. (402)553-1200. Director: Joy Johnson. Publishes trade paperback originals. Publishes 12 titles/year. Receives 90 queries/year. 98% of books from first-time authors; 100% from unagented writers. Pays 8% royalty on wholesale price. Publishes book 6 months after acceptance of ms. Reports in 2 months. Book catalog free on request.

• This press is not interested in seeing novels or personal stories.

Nonfiction: Children's/juvenile, self-help. Subjects include bereavement. "We accept only manuscripts dealing with grief." Submit complete ms. *Writer's Market* recommends query with SASE first.

Fiction: Grief. Submit complete ms.

CENTERSTREAM PUBLICATIONS, P.O. Box 5450, Fullerton CA 92635. (714)779-9390. Owner: Ron Middlebrook. Estab. 1980. Publishes hardcover and mass market paperback originals and trade paperback and mass market paperback reprints. Publishes 12 titles/year. Receives 15 queries and 15 mss/year. 80% of books from first-time authors; 100% from unagented writers. Pays royalty on wholesale price. Offers $300-3,000 advance. Publishes book 8 months after acceptance of ms. Simultaneous submissions OK. Query for electronic submissions. Reports in 3 months on queries. Book catalog free on request.

Nonfiction: Currently only publishing music history.

‡CHAMPION BOOKS INC., P.O. Box 636, Lemont IL 60439. (800)230-1135. Contact: Rebecca Rush. Imprint is New Shoes Series. Publishes trade paperback originals. Publishes 5 titles/year. 100% of books from first-time authors; 100% from unagented writers. Pays 8-10% royalty on retail price. Publishes book 3-5 months after acceptance of ms. Simultaneous submissions OK. Reports in 4 months on mss. Book catalog and ms guidelines free on request.

Fiction: Ethnic, feminist, gay/lesbian, literary, short story collections, poetry. Any finished/unfinished fiction works will be considered.

CHARLESBRIDGE PUBLISHING, 85 Main St., Watertown MA 02172. (617)926-0329. Managing Editor: Elena Dworkin Wright. Estab. 1980. Publishes school programs and hardcover and trade paperback originals. Receives 1,000 submissions/year. 10% of books from first-time authors; 100% from unagented writers. Publishes books an average of 1 year after acceptance. Reports in 2 months.

Nonfiction: Picture books. "We look for nature/science books that teach about the world from a perspective that is relevant to a young child." Submit complete mss with written description proposing art.

Fiction: Multicultural picture books.

Tips: "Markets through schools, book stores and specialty stores at museums, science centers, etc."

CHELSEA GREEN, P.O. Box 130, Post Mills VT 05058-0130. (802)333-9073. Editor: Jim Schley. Estab. 1984. Publishes hardcover and paperback trade originals. Averages 6 titles/year. Reports in 2 months.

• No longer considering fiction, poetry, art or history books. Query only and include SASE.

Nonfiction: Biography, nature, politics, travel, environmental issues and sustainable lifestyle.
Tips: "We do not accept unsolicited mss and we are reviewing very few submissions." Looking for authors with a background in writing published articles/books; also likes advance sale contacts from author.

CHESS ENTERPRISES, 107 Crosstree Rd., Caraopolis PA 15108-2607. Fax: (412)262-2138. Owner: Bob Dudley. Estab. 1981. Publishes trade paperback originals. Publishes 10 titles/year. Receives 35 queries and 14 mss/year. 20% of books from first-time authors; 100% from unagented writers. Makes outright purchase—dependent upon author and subject. Offers 50% advance. Publishes book 4 months after acceptance of ms. Simultaneous submissions OK. Query for electronic submissions. Reports in 1 month on queries. *Writer's Market* recommends allowing 2 months for reply. Book catalog free on request.
Nonfiction: Game of chess only. Query.
Tips: "Books are targeted to chess tournament players, book collectors."

CHICAGO REVIEW PRESS, 814 N. Franklin, Chicago IL 60610-3109. (312)337-0747. Editorial Director: Amy Teschner. Estab. 1973. Imprints are A Capella Books and Ziggurat Books. Publishes hardcover and trade paperback originals. Averages 15 titles/year. Receives 500 submissions annually. 50% of books from first-time authors; 75% from unagented writers. Pays 7½-12½% royalty. Offers average $1,000 advance. Publishes book an average of 15 months after acceptance. Simultaneous submissions OK. Query for electronic submissions. Reports in 2 months on queries. Book catalog for 9 × 12 SAE with 10 first-class stamps.
Nonfiction: How-to, guidebooks, architecture, specialty cookbooks, popular science, adoption, Midwest gardening, urban issues, feminism, recreation, regional titles. Needs regional Chicago and the Midwest material and how-to, popular science, and nonfiction project books in the arts and sciences for ages 10 and up. Query or submit outline and sample chapters. Reviews artwork/photos.
Recent Nonfiction Title: *The Mole People: Life in the Tunnels Beneath New York City,* by Jennifer Toth.
Tips: "The audience we envision for our books is comprised of adults and young people 15 and older, educated readers with special interests, do-it-yourselfers. Right now, we also are very excited about our series called Ziggurat Books, hands-on books for kids 10 and up on subjects such as astronomy, architecture and photography."

CHILD WELFARE LEAGUE OF AMERICA, Suite 310, 440 First St. NW, Washington DC 20001. (202)638-2952. Director, Publications: Susan Brite. Publishes hardcover and trade paperback originals. Publishes 10-12 titles/year. Receives 60-100 submissions/year. 95% of books from unagented writers. 50% of books are nonauthor-subsidy published. Pays 0-10% royalty on net domestic sales. Publishes book an average of 1 year after acceptance. Query for electronic submissions. Reports on queries in 3 months. Free book catalog and ms guidelines.
Nonfiction: Child welfare. Subjects include child guidance/parenting, sociology. Submit outline and sample chapters.
Tips: "Our audience is child welfare workers, administrators, agency executives, parents, etc. We also publish training curricula, including videos."

CHINA BOOKS & PERIODICALS, INC., 2929 24th St., San Francisco CA 94110-4126. (415)282-2994. Fax: (415)282-0994. Senior Editor: Wendy K. Lee. Estab. 1960. Publishes hardcover and trade paperback originals. Averages 5 titles/year. Receives 300 submissions/year. 10% of books from first-time authors; 95% from unagented writers. Pays 8-10% royalty on net receipts. Offers $1,000 average advance. Publishes book an average of 1 year after acceptance. Simultaneous submissions OK. Query for electronic submissions. Reports in 1 month on queries. *Writer's Market* recommends allowing 2 months for reply. Book catalog free on request. Manuscript guidelines for #10 SASE.
Nonfiction: "*Important:* All books *must* be on topics related to China or East Asia, or Chinese-Americans. Books on China's history, politics, environment, women, art, architecture; language textbooks, acupuncture and folklore." Biography, coffee table book, cookbook, how-to, juvenile, self-help, textbook. Subjects include agriculture/horticulture, art/architecture, business and economics, cooking, foods and nutrition, ethnic, gardening, government/politics, history, language/literature, nature/environment, religion, sociology, translation, travel, women's issues studies. Query with outline and sample chapters. Reviews artwork/photos as part of ms package.
Fiction: Ethnic, experimental, historical, literary. "*Must* have Chinese, Chinese-American or East Asian theme. We are looking for high-quality fiction with a Chinese or East Asian theme or translated from Chinese that makes a genuine literary breakthrough and seriously treats life in contemporary China or Chinese-Americans. No fiction that is too conventional in style or treats hackneyed subjects. No fiction without Chinese or Chinese-American or East Asian themes, please." Query with outline/synopsis and sample chapters.
Recent Fiction Title: *The Beijinger in New York,* by Glen Cao.
Tips: "We have a very much stronger need for writers and illustrators to work in children's nonfiction with a Chinese theme. We look for a well-researched, well-written book on China or East Asia that contains fresh insights and appeals to the intelligent reader. Our audience consists of educated and curious readers of trade books, academics, students, travelers, government officials, business people and journalists. I would also

make sure to submit queries to the *smaller* publishers, especially those in your home region, because they will treat your work more seriously."

CHOSEN BOOKS PUBLISHING CO., LTD., Division of Baker Book House Company, 3985 Bradwater St., Fairfax VA 22031-3702. (703)764-8250. Fax: (703)764-3995. Editor: Jane Campbell. Estab. 1971. Publishes hardcover and trade paperback originals. Averages 6-8 titles/year. Receives 600 submissions annually. 15% of books from first-time authors; 99% from unagented writers. Pays royalty on net receipts. Publishes book an average of 1-2 years after acceptance. Simultaneous submissions OK. Reports in 2-3 months. Manuscript guidelines for #10 SASE.

Nonfiction: How-to, self-help, and a very limited number of first-person narratives. "We publish books reflecting the current acts of the Holy Spirit in the world, books with a charismatic Christian orientation." No New Age, poetry, fiction, academic or children's books. Submit synopsis, chapter outline, two sample chapters and SASE. No complete mss. No response without SASE.

Tips: "In expositional books we look for solid, practical advice for the growing and maturing Christian from authors with professional or personal experience platforms. Narratives must have a strong theme and reader benefits. No conversion accounts or chronicling of life events, please. State the topic or theme of your book clearly in your cover letter."

‡CHRISTIAN EDUCATION PUBLISHERS, P.O. Box 261129, San Diego CA 92196. (619)578-4700. Managing Editor: Carol Rogers. Publishes curriculum paperback originals. Publishes 64 titles/year. Receives 100 queries/year. 25% of books from first-time authors; 100% from unagented writers. Makes outright purchase of 2-3¢/word. Publishes book 1 year after acceptance of ms. Simultaneous submissions OK. Query for electronic submissions. Reports in 1 month on queries. Book catalog for 9 × 12 SAE with 2 first-class stamps. Manuscript guidelines for #10 SASE.

Nonfiction: Curriculum, Bible studies, take-home papers. Subjects include curriculum for preschool-high school. "All writing is done on assignment. Writers should send a letter with the age level they'd like to write for (preschool-high school), and their qualifications." Query. "Freelance illustrators should send query and photocopies of artwork samples."

Recent Nonfiction Title: *Honeybees Leader's Program Plans*, by Wanda Pelfrey (2-3 year-old curriculum); *Whirlybirds Leader's Program Plans*, by Ellen Humbert (primary curriculum); *Space Cubs Leader's Program Plans*, by Loretta Henson (4-5 year-old curriculum).

Fiction: Juvenile, religious. "We publish juvenile fiction for take-home papers. All writing is on assignment and should be age appropriate—preschool through 6th grade." Query with age level preferred and qualifications.

‡CHRISTIAN PUBLICATIONS, INC., 3825 Hartzdale Dr., Camp Hill PA 17011. (717)761-7044. Associate Editor: David E. Fessenden. Imprints are Christian Publications, Inc., Horizon Books. Publishes hardcover originals and trade paperback originals and reprints. Publishes 30 titles/year (about 50% are reprints of classic authors). Receives 100 queries and 400 mss/year. 25% of books from first-time authors; 80% from unagented writers. Pays variable royalty or makes outright purchase. Publishes book 15 months after acceptance of ms. Accepts simultaneous submissions. Query for electronic submissions. Book catalog free on request. Manuscript guidelines for #10 SASE.

Nonfiction: Biography (missions-related *only*), how-to, reference (reprints *only*), self-help. Subjects include religion (Evangelical Christian perspective). "We are owned by the Christian and Missionary Alliance denomination; while we welcome and publish authors from various denominations, their theological perspective must be compatible with the Christian and Missionary Alliance. We are especially interested in fresh approaches to sanctification and the deeper life." Submit proposal package, including chapter synopsis, 2 sample chapters (including chapter 1), audience and market ideas, author's biography.

Recent Nonfiction Title: *The Basics: Nailing Down What Builds You Up*, by Mark Littleton (youth devotional/ Christian growth).

Fiction: Juvenile (missions-related *only*), religious. "Must have a clear but subtle Christian message. Stories about the good Christian girl who is attracted to the bad guy, who gets saved at the end, are completely unacceptable. We publish very little fiction; what we do publish must integrate the writer's faith." Submit synopsis and 2 sample chapters (include chapter 1).

Recent Fiction Title: *Vanishing Lights*, by Mark Weinrich (preteen Christian mystery novel).

Tips: "Take time with your proposal—make it thorough, concise, complete. You *must* do your homework to see the general trend of the books we publish. Also remember that if we publish a book on a particular topic, we probably don't want to see manuscripts on that same narrow topic for years."

CHRONICLE BOOKS, Chronicle Publishing Co., 275 Fifth St., San Francisco CA 94103. (415)777-7240. Fax: (415)777-8887. Associate Publishers: Nion McEvoy, Caroline Herter, Victoria Rock. Editor, fiction: Jay Schaefer. Editor, cookbooks: Bill LeBlond. Editor, children's: Victoria Rock. Publishes hardcover and trade paperback originals. Averages 200 titles/year. Receives 2,500 submissions annually. 20% of books from first-time authors; 15% from unagented writers. Publishes book an average of 18 months after acceptance. Simultaneous submissions OK. Reports in 3 months on queries. Book catalog for 11×14 SAE with 5 first-class stamps.

● See the Insider Report on Nick Bantock, author/illustrator of the *Griffin & Sabine* books, published by Chronicle Books, in the 1995 *Artist's & Graphic Designer's Market.*

Nonfiction: Coffee table book, cookbook, regional California, architecture, art, design, gardening, health, nature, nostalgia, photography, recreation, travel. Query or submit outline/synopsis and sample chapters.

Fiction: Juvenile, picture books, novels, novellas, short story collections. Query or submit outline/synopsis and sample chapters. Picture books, submit ms, no query; middle grade, query first.

CHRONIMED PUBLISHING, Suite 250, 13911 Ridgedale Dr., Minneapolis MN 55305. (612)541-0239. Fax: (612)541-4969. Associate Publisher: David Wexler. Estab. 1986. Publishes hardcover and trade paperback originals. Publishes 20-25 titles/year. Receives 600 submissions/year. 30% of books are from first-time authors; 60% from unagented writers. Pays 8-12% royalties on net price. Publishes ms an average of 6 months after acceptance. Simultaneous submissions OK. Query for electronic submissions. Reports in up to 3 months. Book catalog and ms guidelines free.

Nonfiction: Cookbook, self-help. Subjects include cooking, foods and nutrition, health/medicine, psychology. "We are seeking anything relating to health, from fitness to family psychology from authoritative sources. No New Age material." Submit outline and sample chapters.

Recent Nonfiction Title: *The Business Travelers Guide to Good Health On the Road*, by Dr. Karl Neuman and Maury Rosenbaum.

CIRCLET PRESS INC., P.O. Box 15143, Boston MA 02215-0143. Publisher/Editor: Cecilia Tan. Publishes hardcover and trade paperback originals. Publishes 6-10 titles/year. Receives 50-100 queries and 200-300 mss/year. 50% of books from first-time authors; 90% from unagented writers. Pays 4-12% royalty on retail price or outright purchase (depending on rights); also pays in books if author prefers. Publishes book 3-12 months after acceptance. Simultaneous submissions OK. Query for electronic submissions. Prefers Macintosh DD disk 3.5, queries via e-mail to "ctan@world.std.com." Reports in 1 month on queries. Book catalog for #10 SASE. Manuscript guidelines for #10 SASE.

Fiction: Erotic science fiction and fantasy short stories only. "Fiction must combine both the erotic and the fantastic. The erotic content needs to be an integral part of a science fiction story, and vice versa. Writers should not assume that any sex is the same as erotica." Submit full short stories up to 10,000 words. Queries only via e-mail to "ctan@world.std.com."

Recent Fiction Title: *Techno Sex Anthology.*

Tips: "Our audience is adults who enjoy science fiction and fantasy, especially the works of Anne Rice, Storm Constantine, Samuel Delany, who enjoy vivid storytelling and erotic content. Seize your most vivid fantasy, your deepest dream and set it free onto paper. That is at the heart of all good speculative fiction. Then if it has an erotic theme as well as a science fictional one, send it to me. No horror, rape, death or multilation! I want to see stories that *celebrate* sex and sexuality in a positive manner."

CITADEL PRESS, Imprint of Carol Publishing Group, 120 Enterprise, Secaucus NJ 07094. Fax: (201)866-8159. Editorial Director: Allan J. Wilson. Estab. 1945. Other imprints are Lyle Stuart, Birch Lane Press and University Books. Publishes hardcover originals and paperback reprints. Averages 60-80 titles/year. Receives 800-1,000 submissions annually. 7% of books from first-time authors; 50% from unagented writers. Average print order for a first book is 5,000. Pays 10% royalty on hardcover, 5-7% on paperback. Offers average $10,000 advance. Publishes book an average of 1 year after acceptance. Simultaneous submissions OK. Reports in 2 months. Book catalog for $1.

● Citadel Press also publishes books in conjunction with the Learning Annex, a popular adult education and self-improvement school in New York City. Recently published examples include *Starting Your Own Import-Export Business* and *Driving Your Woman Wild in Bed.*

Nonfiction and Fiction: Biography, film, psychology, humor, history. Also seeks "off-beat material, but no poetry, religion, politics." Accepts nonfiction and fiction translations. Query or submit outline/synopsis and 3 sample chapters. Reviews artwork/photos as part of ms package.

Tips: "We concentrate on biography, popular interest, and film, with limited fiction (no romance, religion, poetry, music)."

CLARION BOOKS, Imprint of Houghton Mifflin Company, 215 Park Ave. S., New York NY 10003. Editor and Publisher: Dorothy Briley. Executive Editor: Dinah Stevenson. Senior Editor: Nina Ignatowicz. Estab.

A bullet introduces comments by the editor of Writer's Market *indicating special information about the listing.*

1965. Publishes hardcover originals. Averages 50 titles/year. Pays 5-10% royalty on retail price. Advances from $2,500, depending on whether project is a picture book or a longer work for older children. Prefers no multiple submissions. Reports in 2 months. Publishes book an average of 2 years after acceptance. Manuscript guidelines for #10 SASE.

Nonfiction: Americana, biography, history, holiday, humor, nature, photo essays, word play. Prefers books for younger children. Reviews artwork/photos as part of ms package. Query.

Fiction: Adventure, humor, mystery, strong character studies, suspense. "We would like to see more distinguished short fiction for readers seven to ten." Accepts fiction translations. Send complete ms. Looks for "freshness, enthusiasm—in short, life" (fiction and nonfiction).

CLARKSON POTTER, Imprint of The Crown Publishing Group, Division of Random House, 201 E. 50th St., New York NY 10022. Editorial Director: Lauren Shakely. Publishes hardcover and trade paperback originals. Averages 55 titles/year. 5% of books from first-time authors. Responds in 2-3 months on queries and proposals.

Nonfiction: Art/architecture, biography, child guidance/parenting, cooking and foods, crafts, decorating, design, gardening, how-to, humor, juvenile, photography, popular psychology. Query or submit outline and one sample chapter with tearsheets from magazines and artwork copies (e.g.—color photocopies or duplicate transparencies).

CLEAR LIGHT PUBLISHERS, 823 Don Diego, Santa Fe NM 87501-4224. (505)989-9590. Publisher: Harmon Houghton. Estab. 1981. Publishes hardcover and trade paperback originals. Publishes 12 titles/year. Receives 100 queries/year. 10% of books from first-time authors; 50% from unagented writers. Pays 10% royalty on wholesale price. Offers advance: 50% of gross potential. Publishes book 1 year after acceptance of ms. Simultaneous submissions OK. Query for electronic submissions. Reports in 3 months on queries. Book catalog free on request.

Nonfiction: Biography, coffee table book, cookbook, humor. Subjects include Americana, anthropology/archaelogy, art/architecture, cooking, foods and nutrition, ethnic, history, nature/environment, philosophy, photography, regional (Southwest). Query. Reviews artwork/photos as part of freelance ms package. Send photocopies.

CLEIS PRESS, P.O. Box 14684, San Francisco CA 94114-0684. Fax: (415)864-3385. Acquisitions Coordinator: Frederique Delacoste. Estab. 1980. Publishes trade paperback originals and reprints. Publishes 10 titles/year. 20% of books are from first-time authors; 75% from unagented writers. Royalties vary on retail price. Publishes book an average of 1 year after acceptance. Simultaneous submissions OK "only if accompanied by an original letter stating where and when ms was sent." No electronic submissions. Reports in 2 months. Book catalog for #10 SAE with 2 first-class stamps.

Nonfiction: Subjects include feminist, gay/lesbian, queer human rights. "We are interested in books that: will sell in feminist and progressive bookstores, and will sell in Europe (translation rights). We are interested in books by and about women in Latin America; on lesbian and gay rights; on sexuality; and other feminist topics which have not already been widely documented. We do not want religious/spiritual tracts; we are not interested in books on topics which have been documented over and over, unless the author is approaching the topic from a new viewpoint." Query or submit outline and sample chapters.

Recent Nonfiction Title: *The Good Vibrations Guide to Sex,* ed. Anne Semens and Cathy Winks.

Fiction: Feminist, gay/lesbian, literary. "We are looking for high quality fiction by women. We are especially interested in translations of Latin American women's fiction. No romances!" Submit complete ms.

Recent Fiction Title: *We Came All the Way from Cuba for You to Dress Like This,* by Achy Obejas.

Tips: "If I were trying to market a book today, I would become very familiar with the presses serving my market. More than reading publishers' catalogs, I think an author should spend time in a bookstore whose clientele closely resembles her intended audience; be absolutely aware of her audience; have researched potential market; present fresh new ways of looking at her topic; avoid 'PR' language in query letter."

CLEVELAND STATE UNIVERSITY POETRY CENTER, R.T. 1815, Cleveland State University, Cleveland OH 44115. (216)687-3986. Fax: (216)687-9366. Editor: Leonard M. Trawick. Estab. 1962. Publishes trade paperback and hardcover originals. Averages 3 titles/year. Receives 400 queries and 900 mss/year. 60% of books from first-time authors; 100% from unagented writers. 30% of titles subsidized by CSU, 30% by government subsidy. CSU poetry series pays one-time, lump-sum royalty of $200-400 plus 50 copies; Cleveland Poetry Series (Ohio poets only) pays 100 copies. $1,000 prize for best ms each year. No advance. Publishes book an average of 1 year after acceptance. Simultaneous submissions OK. Reports in 2 weeks on queries; 6-8 months on mss. Book catalog for 6×9 SAE with 2 first-class stamps. Ms guidelines for SASE.

Poetry: No light verse, "inspirational," or greeting card verse. ("This does not mean that we do not consider poetry with humor or philosophical/religious import.") Query—ask for guidelines. Submit only December-February. Reviews artwork/photos if applicable (e.g., concrete poetry).

Tips: "Our books are for serious readers of poetry, i.e. poets, critics, academics, students, people who read *Poetry, Field, American Poetry Review, Antaeus*, etc. Trends include movement away from 'confessional' poetry; greater attention to form and craftsmanship. Try to project an interesting, coherent personality; link poems so as to make coherent unity, not just a miscellaneous collection. Especially needs poems with *mystery*, i.e., poems that suggest much, but do not tell all."

CLIFFS NOTES, INC., P.O. Box 80728, Lincoln NE 68501. (402)423-5050. General Editor: Michele Spence. Notes Editor: Gary Carey. Studyware Editor: Chrissie Frye. Imprint is Centennial Press. Estab. 1958. Publishes trade paperback originals and educational software. Averages 20 titles/year. 100% of books from unagented writers. Pays royalty on wholesale price. Buys majority of mss outright; "full payment on acceptance of ms." Publishes book an average of 1 year after acceptance. Reports in 1 month. *Writer's Market* recommends allowing 2 months for reply. "We provide specific guidelines when a project is assigned."

Nonfiction: Self-help, textbook. "We publish self-help study aids directed to junior high through graduate school audience. Publications include *Cliffs Notes, Cliffs Test Preparation Guides, Cliffs StudyWare*, and other study guides. Most authors are experienced teachers, usually with advanced degrees. Some books also appeal to a general lay audience. Query.

Recent Nonfiction Title: Cliffs *Quick Review Chemistry*.

‡CLINE/FAY INSTITUTE, INC., The Love and Logic Press, Inc., 2207 Jackson St., Golden CO 80401. (303)278-7552. Executive Vice President/Publisher: Nancy M. Lozano. Publishes hardcover and trade paperback originals. Publishes 18 titles/year. Pays 5-7.5% royalty. Offers $500-5,000 advance against royalties. Publishes book 1 year after acceptance of ms. Accepts simultaneous submissions. Query for electronic submissions. Reports in 2 months on queries; 3 months on proposals; 4 months on mss. Book catalog free on request.

Nonfiction: Self-help. Subjects include child guidance/parenting, education, health/medicine, psychology, sociology, current social issue trends. "We will consider any queries/proposals falling into the above categories (with the exception of parenting) but especially psychology/sociology and current social issues and trends." Query. Reviews artwork/photos as part of ms package. Writers should send photocopies.

Recent Nonfiction Title: *Grandparenting with Love and Logic*, by Jim Fay and Foster W. Cline.

COBBLEHILL BOOKS, Affiliate of Dutton Children's Books, 375 Hudson St., New York NY 10014. (212)366-2000. Editorial Director: Joe Ann Daly. Executive Editor: Rosanne Lauer. Pays royalty. Publishes fiction and nonfiction for young readers, middle readers and young adults, and picture books. Query for mss longer than picture book length; submit complete ms for picture books. Reports in 1 month. Simultaneous submissions OK if so noted.

COFFEE HOUSE PRESS, Suite 400, 27 N. Fourth St., Minneapolis MN 55401. Editorial Assistant: David F. Caligiuri. Estab. 1984. Publishes trade paperback originals. Publishes 10 titles/year. Receives 3,000 queries and mss/year. 95% of books are from unagented writers. Pays 8% royalty on retail price. Offers average $500 advance. Publishes book an average of 18 months after acceptance. Reports in 2 months on queries, 6 months on mss. Book catalog and ms guidelines for #10 SAE with 2 first-class stamps.

● Coffee House Press received two nominations for the 1993 National Book Critics Circle Awards.

Fiction: Literary novels, short story collections. No genre. Looking for prose by women and writers of color. Query first with SASE and samples.

Tips: Look for our books at stores and libraries to get a feel for what we like to publish. Please, no phone calls or faxes.

THE COLLEGE BOARD, Imprint of College Entrance Examination Board, 45 Columbus Ave., New York NY 10023-6992. (212)713-8000. Director of Publications: Carolyn Trager. Publishes trade paperback originals. Firm publishes 30 titles/year; imprint publishes 12 titles/year. Receives 50-60 submissions/year. 25% of books from first-time authors; 50% from unagented writers. Pays royalty on retail price of books sold through bookstores. Offers advance based on anticipated first year's earnings. Publishes book an average of 9 months after acceptance. Reports in 1 month on queries. *Writer's Market* recommends allowing 2 months for reply. Book catalog free on request.

Nonfiction: Education-related how-to, reference, self-help. Subjects include college guidance, education, language/literature, science. "We want books to help students make a successful transition from high school to college." Query or send outline and sample chapters. Reviews artwork/photos as part of ms package.

Tips: "Our audience consists of college-bound high school students, beginning college students and/or their parents."

COMPASS AMERICAN GUIDES INC., Imprint of Fodor's/Random House, 6051 Margarido Dr., Oakland CA 94618. Managing Editor: Kit Duane. Editor: Christopher Burt. Publishes hardcover and trade paperback originals. Publishes 10 titles/year. Receives 50 queries and 5 mss/year. 50% of books from first-time authors; 90% from unagented writers. Makes outright purchase of $5,000-10,000. Offers $1,500-3,000 advance. Publishes book an average of 8 months after acceptance of ms. Simultaneous submissions OK. Query for electronic submissions. Reports in 6 months. Book catalog for $1.

● Query this publisher about their suggested format.

Nonfiction: Travel guides. "We publish guides to US and Canadian states, provinces or cities." Reviews artwork/photo as part of ms package. Writers should send duplicate slides. "We cannot guarantee the return of any submissions."

COMPUTE BOOKS, General Media Company, 324 W. Wendover Ave., Greensboro NC 27408. (919)275-9809. Editor-in-Chief: Stephen Levy. Estab. 1979. Publishes trade paperback originals. Averages 16 titles/year. Pays royalties based on gross wholesale receipts. Simultaneous submissions OK if noted in cover letter. Publishes ms an average of 8 months after acceptance. Query for electronic submissions. Reports in 4 months.

Nonfiction: Books on computers. "We publish books for the home and business computer user and are always looking for PC and video game books. We are also interested in entertainment programs, educational programs and Nintendo and Sega Genesis related books. Submit outline and synopsis with sample chapters. "Writers who are known to us through articles in *Compute Magazine* already have our trust—we know they can come through with the right material—but we have often bought from writers we did not know, and from writers who had never published anything before."

Tips: "If I were trying to create a marketable computer book today, I would become intimately familiar with one computer, then define a specific area to explain to less-familiar computer users, and write a clear, concise outline of the book I meant to write, along with a sample chapter from the working section of the book (not the introduction). Then send that proposal to a publisher whose books you believe are excellent and who targets the same audience you are aiming at. Once the proposal was in the mail, I'd forget about it. Keep learning more about the computer and develop another book proposal. *Don't write a book without a go-ahead from a publisher.* The chances are too great that you will spend six months writing a book, only to discover that there are nine on the market with the same concept by the time your manuscript is ready to send out."

‡COMPUTER TECHNOLOGY RESEARCH CORP., 6 N. Atlantic Wharf, Charleston SC 29401. (803)853-6460. Editor: Brian J. Lindgren. Publishes trade paperback originals. Publishes 12-15 titles/year. Receives 16-20 queries and 12-15 mss/year. 100% of books from unagented writers. Makes outright purchase of $2,500-8,000 or pays per-page. Offers $500-1,000 advance. Publishes book 3 months after acceptance of ms. Accepts simultaneous submissions. Query for electronic submissions. Reports in 1 month on proposals. Manuscript guidelines free on request.

Nonfiction: Reference, technical. Subjects include business and economics, computers and electronics, software. Query with outline. Reviews artwork/photos as part of ms package. Writers should send photocopies and sketches/line art.

Recent Nonfiction Title: *Client/Server Networking Protocols,* by Jerry Cashin (computer network strategies).

Tips: "Audience is executives who are considering new directions for their organizations' information systems and need unbiased technical information to help them decide. Since our books are read globally but not translated, write in strict third-person, no contractions, formal 'vanilla' English with as little slang or jargon as possible. Call first to discuss topic, then submit an outline."

CONARI PRESS, Suite B, 1144 65th St., Emeryville CA 94608. (510)596-4040. Executive Editor: Mary Jane Ryan. Estab. 1987. Publishes hardcover and trade paperback originals. Averages 12 titles/year. Receives 200 submissions/year. 50% of books from first-time authors; 50% from unagented writers. Pays 8-12% royalty on list price. Offers $1,500 average advance. Publishes book an average of 1 year after acceptance. Simultaneous submissions OK. Query for electronic submissions. Reports in 3 months. Manuscript guidelines for #10 SASE.

Nonfiction: Psychology/self-help, spirituality, women's issues. Submit outline and sample chapters. Reviews artwork/photos as part of ms package.

Tips: "Writers should send us well-targeted, specific and focused manuscripts. No recovery issues."

‡CONFLUENCE PRESS, INC., Lewis-Clark State College, 500 Eighth Ave., Lewiston ID 83501-1698. (208)799-2336. Publisher/Director: James R. Hepworth. Publishes hardcover originals and trade paperback originals and reprints. Publishes 4-5 titles/year. Receives 500 queries and 150 mss/year. 50% of books from first-time authors; 50% from unagented writers. Pays 10-15% royalty on net sales price. Offers $100-2,000 advance. Publishes book 18 months after acceptance of ms. Accepts simultaneous submissions. Reports in 2 months on queries; 1 month on proposals; 3 months on mss. Book catalog and ms guidelines free on request.

Nonfiction: Reference, bibliographies. Subjects include Americana, ethnic, history, language/literature, nature/environment, regional, translation. Query.

Recent Nonfiction Title: *Norman MacLean*, edited by Ron McFarland and Hugh Nichols (literary criticism).
Fiction: Ethnic, literary, mainstream/contemporary, short story collections. Query.
Recent Fiction Title: *Gifts and Other Stories*, by Charlotte Holmes (short stories).
Poetry: Submit 6 sample poems.
Recent Poetry Title: *My Name Is William Tell*, by William Stafford.

THE CONSULTANT PRESS, #201, 163 Amsterdam Ave., New York NY 10023-5001. (212)838-8640. Fax: (212)873-7065. Publisher: Bob Persky. Imprint is The Photographic Arts Center. Estab. 1980. Publishes trade paperback originals. Averages 7 titles/year. Receives 25 submissions/year. 20% of books from first-time authors. 75% from unagented writers. Pays 7-12% royalty on receipts. Offers $500 average advance. Publishes book an average of 6 months after acceptance. Simultaneous submissions OK. Reports in 3 weeks. Free book catalog.
Nonfiction: How-to, reference, art/architecture, business and economics, photography. "Our prime areas of interest are books on the business of art and photography. Writers should check *Books In Print* for competing titles." Submit outline and 2 sample chapters.
Tips: "Artists, photographers, galleries, museums, curators and art consultants are our audience."

CONSUMER REPORTS BOOKS, Subsidiary of Consumers Union, 101 Truman Ave., Yonkers NY 10703-1057. Fax: (914)378-2902. Contact: Mark Hoffman. Estab. 1936. Publishes trade hardcover and paperback originals and reprints. Averages 15-20 titles/year. Receives 500 submissions annually. Pays variable royalty on retail price; buys some mss outright. Publishes book an average of 18 months after acceptance. Simultaneous submissions OK. Reports in 6 weeks on queries; 2 months on mss. Free catalog on request.
Nonfiction: How-to, reference, self-help, automotive. Subjects include health and medicine, automotive, consumer guidance, home owners reference, money and finance. Submit outline/synopsis and 1-2 sample chapters.

CONTEMPORARY BOOKS, INC., 180 N. Michigan Ave., Chicago IL 60601. (312)782-9182. Editorial Director: Nancy J. Crossman. Estab. 1947. Publishes hardcover originals and trade paperback originals and reprints. Averages 65 titles/year. Receives 2,500 submissions annually. 10% of books from first-time authors; 25% of books from unagented writers. Pays 6-15% royalty on retail price. Publishes book an average of 10 months after acceptance. Query for electronic submissions. Simultaneous submissions OK. Reports in 3 weeks. *Writer's Market* recommends allowing 2 months for reply. Manuscript guidelines for SASE.
Nonfiction: Biography, cookbook, how-to, humor, reference, self-help. Subjects include business, finance, cooking, health, fitness, psychology, sports, real estate, nutrition, popular culture, women's studies. Submit outline and sample chapters. Reviews artwork/photos as part of ms package.
Tips: "The New Age market has become saturated. Also, competition in cookbooks mean we need professional, accomplished cooks instead of amateurs to write them."

COOL HAND COMMUNICATIONS, INC., #1, 1098 NW Second Ave., Boca Raton FL 33432-2616. (407)750-9826. Fax: (407)750-9869. Publisher: Chris K. Hedrick. Editor: Susan L. Carr. Publishes hardcover and trade paperback. Publishes 15-20 titles/year. Receives 1,000 queries/year. 40% of books from first-time authors; 80% from unagented writers. Pays 6-15% royalty on wholesale price. Advance varies. Publishes book 12-18 months after acceptance. Simultaneous submissions OK. Query for electronic submissions. Reports in 6 weeks on queries, 3 months on mss. Catalog and ms guidelines for 9 × 12 SAE with 4 first-class stamps.
Nonfiction: Biography, cookbook, how-to, humor, self-help, books on important issues, cooking, foods and nutrition, health/medicine, travel, true crime. "We're looking for books that can make a positive difference in the lives of readers and society as a whole – novel, innovative approaches to the important issues of our times – the environment, poverty, race relations, animal and human abuse, drugs, crime, etc. We don't want to see anything so specialized that the subject matter limits the size of the potential audience. Nothing too esoteric – we prefer practical, useful information and material that offers concrete solutions to difficult problems. We seek positive, uplifting books that educate and entertain. We don't want lists of questions – we want answers." Query. Reviews artwork/photos as part of ms package.
Recent Nonfiction Title: *How to Figure Out A Man/Woman*, by Joella Cain (humor).
Fiction: Horror, maintream/contemporary, mystery. "We're in the market for fiction with great story lines and strong characters. Subject matter isn't nearly as important as the quality of the writing and whether the work has soul – it has to make the reader feel as well as think. And if the book succeeds in communicating a positive message, so much the better. No science fiction or fantasy, and we're not big for historical romance or *anything* with salacious sex, unwarranted violence or material intended to shock simply for shock's sake. The chance of our accepting a fiction manuscript is very slim – we've published one novel in two years. The writing must be of *superior* quality before we will even consider it."

CORNELL MARITIME PRESS, INC., P.O. Box 456, Centreville MD 21617-0456. (410)758-1075. Fax: (410)758-2478. Managing Editor: Charlotte Kurst. Estab. 1938. Publishes hardcover originals and quality paperbacks for professional mariners and yachtsmen. Averages 7-9 titles/year. Receives 150 submissions annually. 41% of books from first-time authors; 99% from unagented writers. Payment is negotiable but royalties do not exceed 10% for first 5,000 copies, 12½% for second 5,000 copies, 15% on all additional. Royalties for original paperbacks are invariably lower. Revised editions revert to original royalty schedule. Publishes book an average of 1 year after acceptance. Query for electronic submissions. Send queries first, accompanied by writing samples and outlines of book ideas. Reports in 2 months. Book catalog for 10 × 13 SAE with 5 first-class stamps.

Nonfiction: Marine subjects (highly technical), manuals, how-to books on maritime subjects. Tidewater imprint publishes books on regional history, folklore and wildlife of the Chesapeake Bay and the Delmarva Peninsula.

Recent Nonfiction Title: *Survival Guide for the Mariner*, Robert J. Meurn.

CORWIN PRESS, INC., 2455 Teller Rd., Thousand Oaks CA 91320. (805)499-9734. Project Development Editor: Ann McMartin. Publishes hardcover and paperback originals. Publishes 40 titles/year. Pays 10% royalty on net sales. Publishes book 7 months after acceptance of ms. Simultaneous submissions OK. Reports on queries in 1 month. *Writer's Market* recommends allowing 2 months for reply. Book catalog and ms guidelines for #10 SASE.

Nonfiction: Professional-level publications. Subjects include educational policy, educational administration, educational evaluation primarily in K-12. Query.

COTTONWOOD PRESS, INC., Suite 398, 305 W. Magnolia, Fort Collins CO 80521. Editor: Cheryl Thurston. Publishes trade paperback originals. Publishes 2-8 titles/year. Receives 50 queries and 400 mss/year. 50% of books from first-time authors; 100% from unagented writers. Pays 10-12% royalty on net sales. Publishes book 1 year after acceptance. Simultaneous submissions OK (if notified). Reports in 1 month on queries and proposals, 3 months on mss. Book catalog for 6 × 9 SAE with 2 first-class stamps. Manuscript guidelines for #10 SASE.

Nonfiction: Textbook. Subjects include education, language/literature. "We publish *only* supplemental textbooks for English/language arts teachers, grades 5-12, with an emphasis upon middle school and junior high materials. Don't assume we publish educational materials for all subject areas. We do not. Never submit anything to us before looking at our catalog. We have a very narrow focus and a distinctive style. Writers who don't understand that are wasting their time." Query with outline and 1-3 sample chapters.

COUNCIL FOR INDIAN EDUCATION, 2032 Woody Dr., Billings MT 59102-2228. (406)252-7451. Editor: Hap Gilliland. Estab. 1963. Publishes hardcover and trade paperback originals. Publishes 6 titles/year. Receives 200 queries/year. 75% of books from first-time authors; 100% from unagented writers. Pays 10% (book mss) on wholesale price or makes outright purchase of short stories. Publishes book 1 year after acceptance of ms. Simultaneous submissions OK. Reports in 3 months on queries. Book catalog and ms guidelines for #10 SASE.

Nonfiction: Biography, how-to, humor, illustrated book, children's/juvenile. Subjects include anthropology/archaeology, education, ethnic, history, hobbies, nature/environment, recreation related to Indian life. Query. Reviews artwork/photos as part of the freelance ms package. Writers should send photocopies.

Fiction: Adventure, ethnic, historical, humor, juvenile, mystery, picture books, short story collections, Western. All must be Indian related. Submit synopsis or complete mss.

Poetry: "We publish one poetry book per year—all poems related to Indian life must be upbeat, positive—no complaining." Submit individual poems or submit complete ms.

Tips: "Our books are for students, kindergarten through high school. Many are American Indian. We buy *only* books related to Native American Life and culture, suitable for use in schools (all levels). We accept no manuscripts June thru September."

THE COUNTRYMAN PRESS, INC., P.O. Box 175, Woodstock VT 05091-0175. (802)457-1049. Managing Editor: Helen Whybrow. Estab. 1973. Imprints include Foul Play Press and Backcountry Publications. Publishes hardcover and trade paperback originals and paperback reprints. Publishes 20-25 titles/year. Receives 2,500 submissions/year. 50% of books from first-time authors; 75% from unagented writers. Pays 5-10% royalty on retail price. Offers $750 average advance. Publishes book an average of 1 year after acceptance. Simultaneous submissions OK. Reports in 2 months. "No material returned w/o SASE; no unsolicited manuscripts *please!*" Free book catalog.

Nonfiction: Cookbook, how-to, travel guides. Subjects include cooking, foods and nutrition, adult fitness, history, nature/environment, recreation, fishing, regional (New England, especially Vermont), travel. "We want good 'how-to' books, especially those related to rural life; also nature/environmental issues." Submit outline and sample chapters. Reviews artwork/photos as part of ms package.

Fiction: Mystery. Submit inquiries, or outline, sample chapter and SASE. No unsolicited mss *please!*

CRAFTSMAN BOOK COMPANY, 6058 Corte Del Cedro, Carlsbad CA 92009-9974. (619)438-7828 or (800)829-8123. Fax: (619)438-0398. Editorial Manager: Laurence D. Jacobs. Estab. 1957. Publishes paperback originals. Averages 12 titles/year. Receives 50 submissions/year. 85% of books from first-time authors; 98% from unagented writers. Pays 7½-12½% royalty on wholesale price or retail price. Publishes book an average of 18 months after acceptance. Simultaneous submissions OK. Query for electronic submissions.

Reports in 1 month on queries. *Writer's Market* recommends allowing 2 months for reply. Free book catalog and ms guidelines.

Nonfiction: How-to, technical. All titles are related to construction for professional builders. Query. Reviews artwork/photos as part of ms package.

Tips: "The book should be loaded with step-by-step instructions, illustrations, charts, reference data, forms, samples, cost estimates, rules of thumb, and examples that solve actual problems in the builder's office and in the field. The book must cover the subject completely, become the owner's primary reference on the subject, have a high utility-to-cost ratio, and help the owner make a better living in his chosen field."

‡**CREATION HOUSE**, Strang Communications, 190 N. Westmonte Dr., Altamonte Springs FL 32701. (407)862-7565. Submissions Coordinator: Barb Dycus. Publishes hardcover and trade paperback originals. Publishes 18 titles/year. Receives 100 queries and 400 mss/year. 2% of books from first-time authors; 95% from unagented writers. Pays 5-20% royalty on wholesale price. Offers $500-3,000 advance. Publishes book 6-9 months after acceptance of ms. Simultaneous submissions OK. Reports in 2 months on proposals. Manuscript guidelines for #10 SASE.

Nonfiction: Christian. "Our target market is Pentecostal/charismatic Christians." Submit outline, 3 sample chapters and author bio. Reviews artwork/photos as part of freelance ms package. Writers should send photocopies.

Recent Nonfiction Title: *Kids Are a Plus: The Bible and Parenting*, by Ray Mossholder.

CREATIVE PUBLISHING CO., The Early West, Box 9292, College Station TX 77842-0292. (409)775-6047. Contact: Theresa Earle. Estab. 1978. Publishes hardcover originals. Receives 20-40 submissions/year. 50% of books from first-time authors; 100% from unagented writers. Royalty varies on wholesale price. Publishes book an average of 8 months after acceptance. *Writer's Market* recommends allowing 2 months for reply. Free book catalog.

Nonfiction: Biography. Subjects include Americana (western), history. No mss other than 19th century Western America. Query. Reviews artwork/photos as part of ms package.

CROSS CULTURAL PUBLICATIONS, INC., P.O. Box 506, Notre Dame IN 46556. Fax: (219)273-5973. General Editor: Cyriac Pullapilly. Publishes hardcover and software originals. Publishes 15-20 titles/year. Receives 1,000 queries and 600 mss/year. 25% of books from first-time authors; 99% from unagented writers. Pays 10% royalty on wholesale price. Publishes book 6 months after acceptance of ms. Simultaneous submissions OK. Reports in 1 month on queries. *Writer's Market* recommends allowing 2 months for reply. Book catalog free on request.

Nonfiction: Biography. Subjects include government/politics, history, philosophy, religion, sociology, scholarly. "We publish scholarly books that deal with intercultural topics—regardless of discipline. Books pushing into new horizons are welcome, but they have to be intellually sound and balanced in judgement." Query.

THE CROSSING PRESS, 97 Hanger Way, Watsonville CA 95019. Co-Publishers: Elaine Goldman Gill, John Gill. Publishes hardcover and trade paperback originals. Averages 40 titles/year. Receives 1,600 submissions annually. 10% of books from first-time authors; 75% from unagented writers. Pays royalty. Publishes book an average of 18 months after acceptance. Simultaneous submissions OK. Reports in 6 weeks on queries. *Writer's Market* recommends allowing 2 months for reply. Free book catalog.

Nonfiction: Cookbook, how-to, men's studies, literary, feminist. Subjects include cooking, health, gays, mysteries, sci-fi. Submissions to be considered for the feminist series must be written by women. Submit outline and sample chapter.

Recent Nonfiction Title: *Natural Remedy Book for Women*, by Diane Stein (health).

Fiction: Good literary material. Submit outline and sample chapter.

Recent Fiction Title: *When Warhol Was Alive*, by Margaret McMullen.

Tips: "Simple intelligent query letters do best. No come-ons, no cutes. It helps if there are credentials. Authors should research the press first to see what sort of books it publishes."

CROSSWAY BOOKS, Imprint of Good News Publishers, 1300 Crescent St., Wheaton IL 60187-5800. Fax: (708)682-4785. Editorial Director/Editor-in-Chief: Leonard G. Goss. Estab. 1938. Publishes hardcover and trade paperback originals. Averages 50 titles/year. Receives 3,000 submissions annually. 5% of books from first-time authors; 90% from unagented writers. Average print order for a first book is 5,000-10,000. Pays negotiable royalty. Offers negotiable advance. Publishes book an average of 1 year after acceptance. No phone queries! Reports in up to 9 months. Book catalog and ms guidelines for 9 × 12 SAE with 6 first-class stamps.

Nonfiction: Subjects include issues on Christianity in contemporary culture, Christian doctrine, church history. "All books must be written out of Christian perspective or world view." Query with outline.

Fiction: Contemporary, science fiction, fantasy (genuinely creative in the tradition of C.S. Lewis, J.R.R. Tolkien and Madeleine L'Engle), juvenile (10-14; 13-16). No formula romance, short stories, poetry, true stories, children's illustrated. Also, no horror novels of "Issue" novels. Query with synopsis. "All fiction must be written from a genuine Christian perspective."

Tips: "The writer has the best chance of selling our firm a book which, through fiction or nonfiction, shows the practical relevance of biblical doctrine to contemporary issues and life."

‡**DA CAPO PRESS**, Plenum Publishing, 233 Spring St., New York NY 10013. Senior Editor: Yuval Taylor. Publishes trade paperback reprints. Publishes 60 titles/year. 10% of books from unagented writers. Pays 6% royalty on wholesale price. Offers $1,500-2,000 advance. Publishes book 6 months after acceptance of ms. Accepts simultaneous submissions. Reports in 3 months on queries. Book catalog free on request.
Nonfiction: Biography, history. Subjects include art/architecture, gay/lesbian, government/politics, military/war, music/dance, psychology, science, sports. Query.
Recent Nonfiction Title: *The Collapse of the Third Republic*, by William L. Shirer (history).

‡**DAN RIVER PRESS**, Imprint of The Conservatory of American Letters, P.O. Box 298, Thomaston ME 04861. (207)354-0998. Editor: Robert W. Olmsted. Imprints are Dan River Press and Northwoods Press. Publishes hardcover and trade paperback originals. Publishes 6-7 titles/year. Receives 600 queries and 200 mss/year. 100% of books from unagented writers. Pays 10-15% royalty on amount received by us. Offers $250-500 advance. Publishes book 1 year after acceptance of ms. Simultaneous submissions OK if so stated. Query for electronic submissions. Reports in 2 months on mss. Book catalog for 6×9 SAE with 2 first-class stamps. Manuscript guidelines for #10 SASE.
Nonfiction: Biography. "We don't do much nonfiction." Query. Reviews artwork/photos as part of ms package. Writers should send photocopies.
Fiction: Adventure, confession, erotica, experimental, fantasy, gothic, historical, horror, humor, literary, mainstream/contemporary, mystery, occult, plays, romance, science fiction, short story collections, suspense, western. Submit entire ms after reading guidelines and a book or two.
Recent Fiction Title: *The Secret War*, by R. Jack Smith (spy).
Poetry: Submit complete ms.

DANCE HORIZONS, Imprint of Princeton Book Co., Publishers, P.O. Box 57, 12 W. Delaware Ave., Pennington NJ 08534. (609)737-8177. Fax: (609)737-1869. Managing Editor: Debi Elfenbein. Estab. 1976. Publishes hardcover and paperback originals and paperback reprints on dance only. Averages 10 titles/year. Receives 25-30 submissions annually. 50% of books from first-time authors; 98% of books from unagented writers. Pays 10% royalty on net receipts; offers no advance. Publishes book an average of 10 months after acceptance. Simultaneous submissions OK. Reports in 3 months. Free book catalog.
Nonfiction: Dance-related subjects only. Query first. Reviews artwork/photos.
Recent Nonfiction Title: *Inside Ballet Technique*, by Valerie Grig.
Tips: "We're very careful about the projects we take on. They have to be, at the outset, polished, original and cross-marketable."

JOHN DANIEL AND COMPANY, PUBLISHERS, Imprint of Daniel & Daniel, Publishers Inc., P.O. Box 21922, Santa Barbara CA 93121-1922. (805)962-1780. Publisher: John Daniel. Estab. 1985. Publishes trade paperback originals. Averages 4 titles/year. Receives 1,500-4,000 submissions annually. 50% of books from first-time authors; 100% from unagented writers. Pays 10% royalty on wholesale price. Publishes book an average of 1 year after acceptance. Simultaneous submissions OK. Query for electronic submissions. No telephone or fax submissions, please. Reports in 2 months. Book catalog and ms guidelines for #10 SASE.
Nonfiction: Autobiography, biography, literary memoir, essays. "We'll look at anything, but are particularly interested in books in which literary merit is foremost—as opposed to books that simply supply information. No libelous, obscene, poorly written or unintelligent manuscripts." Query or submit outline and sample chapters.
Recent Nonfiction Title: *Tiger Bridge: Nine Days on a Bend of the Nauranata*, by Barbara Curtis Horton (memoir).
Fiction: Novels, short story collections. "We do best with books by authors who have demonstrated a clear, honest, elegant style. No libelous, obscene, poorly written, or boring submissions." Query or submit synopsis and sample chapters.
Recent Fiction Title: *Heaven Lies About*, by Maclin Bocock (stories).
Poetry: "We're open to anything, but we're very cautious. Poetry's hard to sell." Submit complete ms.
Tips: "If fame and fortune are what you're after, you should aim for the major leagues, the big time publishers, and I wish you luck. But in the meantime, remember there is a friendlier, smaller, more approachable market among small press magazines and book publishers. The small press has been around since Gutenberg, and is still alive and well. It has given us the first works of Herman Melville, Mark Twain, James Joyce, Virginia Woolf, Anais Nin, Raymond Chandler, and a host of other stars that light up the literary heavens."

DANTE UNIVERSITY OF AMERICA PRESS, INC., P.O. Box 843, Brookline Village MA 02147-0843. President: Adolph Caso. Estab. 1975. Publishes hardcover and trade paperback originals and reprints. Averages 5 titles/year. Receives 50 submissions annually. 50% of books from first-time authors; 50% from unagented writers. Average print order for a first book is 3,000. Pays royalty. Offers negotiable advance. Publishes book an average of 10 months after acceptance. No simultaneous submissions. Query for electronic submissions. Reports in 2 months.

Nonfiction: Biography, reference, reprints, translations from Italian and Latin. Subjects include general scholarly nonfiction, Renaissance thought and letter, Italian language and linguistics, Italian-American history and culture, bilingual education. Query first with SASE. Reviews artwork/photos as part of ms package.

Fiction: Translations from Italian and Latin. Query first with SASE.

Poetry: "There is a chance that we would use Renaissance poetry translations."

MAY DAVENPORT, PUBLISHERS, 26313 Purissima Rd., Los Altos Hills CA 94022. (415)948-6499. Editor/Publisher: May Davenport. Estab. 1976. Imprint is md Books (nonfiction and fiction). Publishes hardcover and trade paperback originals. Averages 4 titles/year. Receives 1,000-2,000 submissions annually. 95% of books from first-time authors; 5% from professional writers. Pays 15% royalty on retail price. No advance. Publishes book an average of 1-3 years after acceptance. Reports in 1 month. *Writer's Market* recommends allowing 2 months for reply. Manuscript guidelines for #10 SASE.

Nonfiction: Juvenile (13-17). Contemporary literature (40,000-60,000 words) to interest ages 13-17. "Our readers are students in elementary and secondary public school districts, as well as correctional institutes of learning, etc. No hack writing." Query.

Recent Nonfiction Title: *Blow Away Seaweeds! (Memoir of an Artist)*, by May Davenport.

Fiction: Adventure, Americana. "We're overstocked with picture books and first readers; prefer literature for TV-oriented teenagers. Be entertaining while informing." No sex or violence. Query with SASE.

Recent Fiction Title: *A Fine Line*, by Constance D.Casserly.

Tips: "Imagine yourself a teen narrator in today's complex computer world with problems and solutions teens face uninhibitedly, so other teens will laugh and read your tale. . . .if you can't, forget it."

JONATHAN DAVID PUBLISHERS, INC., 68-22 Eliot Ave., Middle Village NY 11379-1194. Fax: (718)894-2818. Editor-in-Chief: Alfred J. Kolatch. Estab. 1948. Publishes hardcover and trade paperback originals and reprints. Publishes 20-25 titles/year. 50% of books from first-time authors; 90% from unagented writers. Pays royalty or makes outright purchase. Offers $1,000-5,000 advance. Publishes book 18 months after acceptance of ms. Reports in 2 months on queries. Book catalog for 6×9 SAE with 4 first-class stamps.

• Publisher has expressed an interest in seeing more projects geared toward children.

Nonfiction: Cookbook, how-to, reference, self-help. "We specialize in Judaica." Submit outline and 1 sample chapter with SASE.

HARLAN DAVIDSON, INC., 773 Glenn Ave., Wheeling IL 60090-6000. (708)541-9720. Fax: (708)541-9830. Editor-in-Chief: Maureen G. Hewitt. Estab. 1972. Additional Imprint is Forum Press, Inc. Publishes college texts, both hardcover and paperback. Publishes 15 titles/year. Receives 200 queries and 25 mss/year. 100% of books from unagented writers. Manuscripts contracted as work for hire. Pays royalty on net. Publishes book 10 months after acceptance of ms. Simultaneous submissions OK. Query for electronic submissions. Reports in 3 months on proposals. Book catalog free on request.

Nonfiction: Subjects include business, education, government, history (main list), biographical history, literature, philosophy, regional state histories, sociology, ethnic history, women's issues/studies. "Because we are a college textbook publisher, academic credentials are extremely important. We usually find our own authors for a need in the field that we identify, but we are also receptive to ideas brought to us by qualified professionals, in history, especially." Submit proposal package, including outline, brief description of proposed book and its market and competition, and a recent vita.

DAVIS PUBLICATIONS, INC., 50 Portland St., Worcester MA 01608. (508)754-7201. Fax: (508)753-3834. Managing Editor: Wyatt Wade. Acquisitions Editors: Claire M. Golding, Helen Ronan. Estab. 1901. Averages 5-10 titles/year. Pays 10-12% royalty. Publishes book an average of 1 year after acceptance. Book catalog for 9×12 SAE with 2 first-class stamps. Write for copy of guidelines for authors.

Nonfiction: Publishes technique-oriented art, design and craft books for the educational market. Accepts nonfiction translations. "Keep in mind the intended audience. Our readers are visually oriented. All illustrations should be collated separately from the text, but keyed to the text. Photos should be good quality transparencies and black and white photographs. Well-selected illustrations should explain, amplify, and enhance the text. We average 2-4 photos/page. We like to see technique photos as well as illustrations of finished artwork, by a variety of artists, including students. Recent books have been on printmaking, clay sculpture, design, jewelry, drawing and watercolor painting." Submit outline, sample chapters and illustrations. Reviews artwork/photos as part of ms package.

Recent Nonfiction Title: *Brown Bag Ideas from Many Cultures*, by Irene Tejada; *Pictures and Poetry*, by Stephanie Briggs and Janis Bunchman.

‡DAW BOOKS, INC., 3rd Floor, 375 Hudson St., New York NY 10014-3658. Submissions Editor: Peter Stampfel. Estab. 1971. Publishes science fiction and fantasy hardcover and paperback originals and reprints. Publishes 60-80 titles/year. Pays in royalties with an advance negotiable on a book-by-book basis. Sends galleys to author. Simultaneous submissions "returned unread at once, unless prior arrangements are made

by agent." Reports in 6 weeks "or longer, if a second reading is required." Free book catalog.
Fiction: "We are interested in science fiction and fantasy novels only. We do not publish any other category of fiction. We accept both agented and unagented ms. We are not seeking collections of short stories or ideas for anthologies. We do not want any nonfiction manuscripts." Submit complete ms.

W.S. DAWSON CO., P.O. Box 62823, Virginia Beach VA 23466. (804)499-6271. Fax: (804)490-0922. Publisher: C.W. Tazewell. Publishes hardcover and trade paperback originals. Publishes 10 titles/year. Receives 16 queries and 6 mss/year. Pays negotiated royalty. Publishes book 6 months after acceptance of ms. Simultaneous submissions OK. Query for electronic submissions. Reports in 1 month on queries. *Writer's Market* recommends allowing 2 months for reply. Book catalog free on request.
Nonfiction: Biography and humor. Subjects include history, regional. "Most publications are Virginia local history, genealogy and biography, and in particular Eastern Virginia. Advance approval is requested before sending mss, etc." Query. Reviews artwork/photos as part of ms package. Writers should send photocopies.
Recent Nonfiction Title: *Bricks and Mortar: What's New in Old Princess Ann County and New Virginia Beach.*

DEACONESS PRESS, 2450 Riverside Ave. South, Minneapolis MN 55454. (612)672-4180. Senior Editor: Jack Caravela. Publishes hardcover and trade paperback originals. Averages 10 titles/year. 30% of books from first-time authors; 50% from unagented writers. Pays 6-15% royalty on wholesale price. Offers $1,000-2,500 advance. Publishes book 6 months after acceptance of ms. Simultaneous submissions OK. Query for electronic submissions. Reports in 2 months on proposals. Book catalog free on request.
Nonfiction: Self-help, social issues. Subjects include child guidance/parenting, health/medicine, psychology, sociology, young adult self-help. "We publish nonfiction titles which promote healthy living for teens and adults, with an emphasis on how physical health, mental health, and relationship issues affect the family." Query, or submit proposal package, including outline, sample chapters (2-3), marketing information, rationale, and information on competitive titles.
Tips: Audience is "individuals and families facing physical health issues, mental health issues, and other stresses and changes in their lives. Learn about titles competitive to your work and be prepared to tell us how your manuscript is different and/or better than what has already been written about the subject."

DEARBORN FINANCIAL PUBLISHING, INC., 520 N. Dearborn St., Chicago IL 60610-4354. (312)836-4400. Fax: (312)836-1021. Senior Vice President: Anita Constant. Estab. 1959. Imprints are Dearborn/R&R Newkirk (contact: Anne Shropshire), Enterprise/Dearborn (contact: Kathleen A. Welton) and Real Estate Education Co. (contact: Carol Luitjens). Publishes hardcover and paperback originals. Averages 200 titles/year. Receives 200 submissions/year. 50% of books from first-time authors; 50% from unagented writers. Pays 1-15% on wholesale price. Publishes book an average of 6 months after acceptance. Simultaneous submissions OK. Query for electronic submissions. Reports in 1 month. *Writer's Market* recommends allowing 2 months for reply. Free book catalog and ms guidelines.
Nonfiction: How-to, reference, textbooks. Subjects include small business, real estate, insurance, banking, securities, money/finance. Query.
Tips: "People seeking real estate, insurance, broker's licenses are our audience; also business professionals interested in information on managing their finances, and people starting and running a small business."

IVAN R. DEE, INC., 1332 N. Halsted St., Chicago IL 60622-2632. (312)787-6262. Fax: (312)787-6269. President: Ivan R. Dee. Estab. 1988. Imprint is Elephant Paperbacks. Publishes hardcover originals and trade paperback originals and reprints. Averages 25 titles/year. 10% of books from first-time authors; 75% from unagented writers. Pays royalty. Publishes book an average of 9 months after acceptance. Reports in 1 month on queries. *Writer's Market* recommends allowing 2 months for reply. Book catalog free on request.
Nonfiction: History, literature and letters, biography, politics, contemporary affairs, theater. Submit outline and sample chapters. Reviews artwork/photos as part of ms package.
Recent Nonfiction Title: *Molotov Remembers*, edited by Felix Chuev and Albert Resis.
Tips: "We publish for an intelligent lay audience and college course adoptions."

DEL REY BOOKS, Imprint of Ballantine Books, Division of Random House, 201 E. 50th St., New York NY 10022-7703. (212)572-2677. Executive Editor: Shelly Shapiro. Senior Editor: Veronica Chapman. Estab. 1977. Publishes hardcover, trade paperback, and mass market originals and mass market paperback reprints. Averages 60 titles/year. Receives 1,900 submissions annually. 10% of books from first-time authors; 40% from unagented writers. Pays royalty on retail price. Offers competitive advance. Publishes book an average of 1 year after acceptance. Reporting time 1-6 months, occasionally longer. Writer's guidelines for #10 SASE.
Fiction: Fantasy ("should have the practice of magic as an essential element of the plot"), science fiction ("well-plotted novels with good characterization, exotic locales, and detailed alien cultures"). Submit complete ms or outline and first 3 chapters.
Recent Fiction Title: *The Tangle Box*, by Terry Brooks.
Tips: "Del Rey is a reader's house. Our audience is anyone who wants to be pleased by a good, entertaining novel. Pay particular attention to plotting and a satisfactory conclusion. It must be/feel believable. That's what the readers like."

DELACORTE PRESS, Imprint of Dell Publishers, Division of Bantam Doubleday Dell, 1540 Broadway, New York NY 10036. (212)354-6500. Editor-in-Chief: Leslie Schnur. Publishes hardcover originals. Publishes 36 titles/year. Royalty and advance vary. Publishes book an average of 2 years after acceptance, but varies. Simultaneous submissions OK. Reports in 2 months. Book catalog and guidelines for 9 × 12 SASE.
Nonfiction and Fiction: *Query, outline, first 3 chapters or brief proposal.* No mss for children's or young adult books accepted in this division.

DELL PUBLISHERS, division of Bantam Doubleday Dell, Inc., 1540 Broadway, New York NY 10036. Imprints include Delacorte, Delta Books and Laurel Books. General interest publisher of both fiction and nonfiction. This company did not respond to our request for information. Query before submitting.

DELPHI PRESS, INC., P.O. Box 1538, Oak Park IL 60304-1538. (708)524-7900. Fax: (708)524-7902. Publisher: Karen Jackson. Estab. 1989. Publishes trade paperback originals and reprints. Publishes 10-12 titles/year. Receives 50-100 queries and 20-30 mss/year. 95% of books from first-time authors; 95% from unagented writers. Pays 7½-12% royalty on wholesale price. Publishes book within 1 year after acceptance of ms. Simultaneous submissions OK. Reports in 1-2 months on proposals. *Writer's Market* recommends allowing 2 months for reply. Book catalog and ms guidelines free on request.
Nonfiction: Delphi Press focuses on women's spirituality, men's mysteries; Wicca, witchcraft and pagan practice; ritual, healing, divination and magick; nature/earth religions and deep ecology; sacred psychology and inner development especially utilizing magick or psychic techniques. Submit complete ms or outline and 3 sample chapters.
Tips: "Audience is educated-up-scale 30+ adults interested in alternative spirituality and personal power."

THE DENALI PRESS, P.O. Box 021535, Juneau AK 99802-1535. (907)586-6014. Fax: (907)463-6780. Editorial Director: Alan Schorr. Editorial Associate: Sally Silvas-Ottumwa. Estab. 1986. Publishes trade paperback originals. Averages 5 titles/year. Receives 120 submissions/year. 50% of books from first-time authors; 80% from unagented writers. Pays 10% royalty on wholesale price; buys some mss by outright purchase. Publishes book an average of 9-12 months after acceptance. Simultaneous submissions OK. Query for electronic submissions. Reports in 2 months. Author must contact prior to sending mss. Prefer letter of inquiry. Book catalog free on request.
Nonfiction: Reference. Subjects include Americana, Alaskana, anthropology, ethnic, government/politics, history, recreation. "We need reference books – ethnic, refugee and minority concerns." Query with outline and sample chapters; all unsolicited mss are tossed.
Recent Nonfiction Title: *Building a New South*, edited by Wilkinson, Stoltz, Richards and Cox.
Tips: "We are looking for reference works suitable for the educational, professional and library market."

T.S. DENISON & CO., INC., 9601 Newton Ave. S., Minneapolis MN 55431-2590. (612)888-3831. Fax: (612)888-9641. Editor-in-Chief: Sherrill B. Flora. Acquisitions Editor: Baxter Brings. Estab. 1876. Publishes teacher aid materials. Receives 500 submissions annually. 90% of books from first-time authors; 100% from unagented writers. Average print order for a first book is 3,000. Royalty varies. No advance. Publishes book an average of 1-2 years after acceptance. Reports in 2 months. Book catalog and ms guidelines for 9 × 12 SAE with 3 first-class stamps.
Nonfiction: Specializes in early childhood and elementary school teaching aids. Send prints if photos are to accompany ms. Submit complete ms. *Writer's Market* recommends query with SASE first. Reviews artwork/photos as part of ms package.

DEVYN PRESS, Subsidiary of Baron Barclay Bridge Supplies, Suite 230, 3600 Chamberlain Lane, Louisville KY 40241. (502)426-0410. President: Randy Baron. Publishes hardcover and trade paperback originals and reprints. Publishes 10 titles/year. Receives 40 queries and 20 mss/year. 50% of books from first-time authors; 90% from unagented writers. Pays 5-10% royalty on wholesale price. Offers $500-1,000 advance. Publishes book 6 months after acceptance of ms. Simultaneous submissions OK. Query for electronic submissions. Reports in 2 months on queries. Book catalog and ms guidelines free on request.
Nonfiction: How-to, self-help. Subjects include sports and games/bridge. "We are the world's largest publisher of books on the game of bridge." Query. Reviews artwork/photos as part of freelance ms package. Writers should send photocopies.

‡DIAL BOOKS FOR YOUNG READERS, Division of Penguin USA Inc., 3rd Floor, 375 Hudson St., New York NY 10014. (212)366-2800. Imprints include Dial Easy-to-Read Books, Dial Very First Books. No unsolicited mss. Publishes hardcover originals. Averages 80 titles/year. Receives 8,000 submissions annually. 10% of books from first-time authors. Pays variable royalty and advance. Simultaneous submissions OK, but not preferred. Reports in 4 months. Book catalog and ms guidelines for 9 × 12 SASE and 4 first-class stamps.
Nonfiction: Juvenile picture books, young adult books. Especially looking for "quality picture books and well-researched young adult and middle-reader mss." Not interested in alphabet books, riddle and game books, and early concept books. Query with outline/synopsis and sample chapters. Reviews artwork/photos.

Fiction: Juvenile picture books, young adult books. Adventure, fantasy, historical, humor, mystery, romance (appropriate for young adults), suspense. Especially looking for "lively and well written novels for middle grade and young adult children involving a convincing plot and believable characters. The subject matter or theme should not already be overworked in previously published books. The approach must not be demeaning to any minority group, nor should the roles of female characters (or others) be stereotyped, though we don't think books should be didactic, or in any way message-y. No topics inappropriate for the juvenile, young adult, and middle grade audiences. No plays." Submit complete ms. Also publishes Pied Piper Book (paperback Dial reprints) and Pied Piper Giants (1½ feet tall reprints).
Tips: "Our readers are anywhere from preschool age to teenage. Picture books must have strong plots, lots of action, unusual premises, or universal themes treated with freshness and originality. Humor works well in these books. A very well thought out and intelligently presented book has the best chance of being taken on. Genre isn't as much of a factor as presentation."

DISCIPLESHIP RESOURCES, 1908 Grand Ave., Box 840, Nashville TN 37202-0840. (615)340-7068. Fax: (615)340-7006. Editor: Craig B. Gallaway. Publishes trade paperback originals and reprints. Publishes 30 titles/year. Receives 300 queries and 150 mss/year. 20% of books from first-time authors; 40% from unagented writers. Pays 5-10% royalty on retail price or makes outright purchase of $250-1,500. Offers $250 advance. Publishes book 6 months after acceptance of ms. Query for electronic submissions. Reports in 2 months on queries. Book catalog free on request. Manuscript guidelines for #10 SASE.
Nonfiction: Subjects include theology of ministry, evangelism, worship, stewardship, ministry of laity, family ministry, Christian education, ethnic (church), history (Methodist/church), music/dance (religious), nature/environment (ecology), recreation (leisure ministry), Christian biography (ecclesiastical). "Materials must be focused on specific ministries of the church, in particular the United Methodist Church, but we also work with ecumenical resources." Query or submit proposal package, including outline, sample chapter, description of audience! Reviews artwork/photos as part of freelance mss package. Writers should send photocopies.
Tips: "Focus on ministry, write simply, and do more research."

‡DISTINCTIVE PUBLISHING CORPORATION, P.O. Box 17868, Plantation FL 33318-7868. (305)975-2413. Editor: D.P. Brown. Contact: C. Pierson. Estab. 1986. Publishes hardcover and trade paperback originals and trade paperback reprints. Publishes 25 titles/year. Receives 1,200 submissions/year. 60% of books from first-time authors; 80% from unagented writers. Pays 6-10% royalty on retail price. Publishes book an average of 1 year after acceptance. Simultaneous submissions OK. Reports in up to 2 months on queries. Book catalog and ms guidelines free on request.
Nonfiction: How-to, humor, reference, self-help, technical, textbook. Subjects include art/architecture, child guidance/parenting, education, health/medicine, music/dance, psychology, regional, sociology. Submit complete ms. Reviews artwork/photos as part of ms package.

DOUBLEDAY, division of Bantam Doubleday Dell, Inc., 1540 Broadway, New York NY 10036. (212)354-6500. Imprints are Anchor Books, Nan A. Talese, Image, Currency Books, Perfect Crime, Main Street Books, DD Western, Loveswept and Perfect Crime. General interest publisher of both fiction and nonfiction. This publisher did not respond to our request for information. Query before submitting.

DOWN EAST BOOKS, Division of Down East Enterprise, Inc., P.O. Box 679, Camden ME 04843-0679. Managing Editor: Karin Womer. Estab. 1954. Publishes hardcover and trade paperback originals and trade paperback reprints. Averages 10-14 titles/year. Receives 300 submissions annually. 50% of books from first-time authors; 90% from unagented writers. Average print order for a first book is 3,000. Pays 10-15% on receipts. Offers average $200 advance. Publishes book an average of 1 year after acceptance. Simultaneous submissions OK. Reports in 2 months. Manuscript guidelines for 9×12 SAE with 3 first-class stamps.
Nonfiction: Books about the New England region, Maine in particular. Subjects include Americana, history, nature, guide books, crafts, recreation. "All of our books must have a Maine or New England emphasis." Query. Reviews artwork/photos as part of ms package.
Fiction: "We generally publish no fiction except for an occasional juvenile title (average 1/year) but are now keeping alert for good general-audience novels—same regional criteria apply."

DRAMA BOOK PUBLISHERS, 260 Fifth Ave., New York NY 10001. (212)725-5377. Fax: (212)725-8506. Managing Editor: Judith Durant. Estab. 1967. Publishes hardcover and paperback originals and reprints. Averages 4-15 titles/year. Receives 420 submissions annually. 70% of books from first-time authors; 90%

For information on book publishers' areas of interest, see the nonfiction and fiction sections in the Book Publishers Subject Index.

from unagented writers. Royalty varies. Advance varies; negotiable. Publishes book an average of 18 months after acceptance. Reports in 2 months.

Nonfiction: Texts, guides, manuals, directories, reference—for and about performing arts theory and practice: acting, directing; voice, speech, movement, music, dance, mime; makeup, masks, wigs; costumes, sets, lighting, sound; design and execution; technical theatre, stagecraft, equipment; stage management; producing; arts management, all varieties; business and legal aspects; film, radio, television, cable, video; theory, criticism, reference; playwriting; theatre and performance history. Accepts nonfiction, drama and technical works in translations also. *Query;* accepts 1-3 sample chapters; no complete mss. Reviews artwork/photos as part of ms package.

DUQUESNE UNIVERSITY PRESS, 600 Forbes Ave., Pittsburgh PA 15282-0101. (412)396-6610. Fax: (412)434-5780. Contact: Acquisitions Editor. Estab. 1927. Averages 9 titles/year. Receives 400 submissions annually. 25% of books from first-time authors; 100% from unagented writers. Average print order for a first book is 1,000. Subsidy publishes (nonauthor) 20% of books. Pays 10% royalty on net sales. No advance. Publishes book an average of 1 year after acceptance. Query for electronic submissions. Query. Reports in 3 months. Book catalog for 9×12 SAE with 2 first-class stamps.

Nonfiction: Scholarly books in the humanities, social sciences for academics, libraries, college bookstores and educated laypersons. Looks for scholarship. No unsolicited mss. Query.

DUSTBOOKS, Box 100, Paradise CA 95967. (916)877-6110. Publisher: Len Fulton. Publishes hardcover and paperback originals. Averages 7 titles/year. Offers 15% royalty. Simultaneous submissions OK if so informed. Reports in 2 months. Book catalog free. Writer's guidelines for #10 SASE.

Nonfiction: "Our specialty is directories of small presses, poetry publishers, and two monthly newsletters on small publishers (*Small Press Review* and *Small Magazine Review*)." Publishes annual *International Directory of Little Magazines & Small Presses.*"

DUTTON, (formerly N.A.L. Dutton), Imprint of Penguin USA, 375 Hudson St., New York NY 10014. (212)366-2000. Publisher: Elaine Koster. Estab. 1852. Publishes hardcover originals. Firm averages 90 titles/year. Does not read unsolicited mss.

Nonfiction: Biography, self-help, serious nonfiction, politics, psychology, science.

Fiction: Mainstream/contemporary. "We don't publish genre romances or westerns."

EAGLE'S VIEW PUBLISHING, 6756 N. Fork Rd., Liberty UT 84310. Editor-in-Chief: Denise Knight. Estab. 1982. Publishes trade paperback originals. Publishes 4-6 titles/year. Receives 40 queries and 20 mss/year. 90% of books from first-time authors; 100% from unagented writers. Pays 8-10% royalty on wholesale price. Publishes book 1 year or more after acceptance of ms. Simultaneous submissions OK. Query for electronic submissions. Reports on proposals in 4-6 months. Book catalog and ms guidelines for $1.50.

Nonfiction: How-to, Indian and mountain man and American frontier (history and craft). Subjects include anthropology/archaeology (native American crafts), ethnic (native American), history (American frontier), hobbies (crafts, especially beadwork, earrings). "We are expanding from our Indian craft base to more general crafts." Submit outline and 1 or 2 sample chapters. Reviews artwork/photos as part of freelance ms package. Writers should send photocopies or sample illustrations. "We prefer to do photography in house."

EAST COAST PUBLISHING, P.O. Box 2829, Poughkeepsie NY 12603-0888. (800)327-4212. Vice President: K.K. Makris. Estab. 1987. Publishes hardcover and trade paperback originals. Publishes 5 titles/year. Receives more than 100 submissions/year. 50% of books from first-time authors; 100% from unagented writers. Pays 10% on wholesale price or makes outright purchase of $1,000. Publishes book an average of 1 year after acceptance. Simultaneous submissions OK. Query for electronic submissions. Reports in 2 months on queries. Book catalog for 9×12 SAE and 3 first-class stamps. Manuscript guidelines for #10 SASE.

Nonfiction: How-to, reference, technical. Subjects include business and economics, government/politics and law. "The publisher is interested in reviewing manuscripts which deal with technical legal and business areas, including banking, in a manner which withstands the scrutiny of the industry, but appeals to the lay person reader. No biographies, autobiographies, cookbooks, art-related books, juvenile, alternative/New Age, religion, self-help psychology or humor books please." Reviews artwork/photos as part of ms package.

Tips: "When considering a manuscript, the most essential element evaluated is the ability of the writer to impart the information in clear, concise language, creating an elegant delivery of the subject matter. Our audience consists of both the professional and general public communities. If I were a writer trying to market a book today, I would allow my editor to prevail in implementing revisions which will ultimately result in a better ms. Unless the editing is fatal to the originally intended thought, the writer should allow the editor to polish and fine tune the ms."

‡THE ECCO PRESS, 100 W. Broad St., Hopewell NJ 08525. (609)466-4748. Editor-in-Chief: Daniel Halpern. Publishes hardcover and mass market paperback originals and reprints and trade paperback reprints. Publishes 20 titles/year. Receives 1,200 queries/year. Pays 7½-12% royalty. Offers $250-1,000 advance. Publishes book 1 year after acceptance of ms. No simultaneous submissions. Reports in 2 months on queries. Book catalog and ms guidelines free on request.

Nonfiction: Biography, coffee table book, cookbook. Subjects include Americana, art/architecture, cooking, foods and nutrition, government/politics, history, language/literature, music/dance, regional, translation, travel. Query. Reviews artwork/photos as part of ms package. Writers should send transparencies.

Recent Nonfiction Title: *On Water*, by Thomas Ferber (short essays).

Fiction: Ethnic, historical, literary, plays and short story collections.

Recent Fiction Title: *The American Story*, edited by Michael Rea (short story anthology).

Poetry: Submit 10 sample poems.

Recent Poetry Title: *Essential Haiku*, edited by Robert Hass (haiku anthology).

THE EDUCATION CENTER, INC., Product Development Division, 1607 Battleground Ave., Greensboro NC 27408. Development Manager: Charlotte Perkins. Estab. 1973. Publishes supplementary resource books for elementary teachers: preschool/grade 6. Publishes 25 titles/year. Receives 100 queries and 50 mss/year. Less than 5% of books from first-time authors; 100% from unagented writers. Pays 2-6% royalty on wholesale price (on books sold through dealers); 2-6% royalty on retail price (on books sold through direct mail). "Payment schedule and amount negotiated when contract signed." Publishes book 2-12 months after acceptance of ms (depending on condition of ms). Query for electronic submissions. Prefers Macintosh. Reports in 2 months on proposals. Book catalog and ms guidelines for 9 × 12 SASE.

Nonfiction: Teacher resource/supplementary materials. Subjects include education P/K-6, language/literature. "We place a strong emphasis on materials that teach the basic language arts and math skills. We are also seeking materials for teaching science and geography, literature-based activities for the whole language classroom, cooperative learning ideas and multicultural materials. Technical, complex or comprehensive manuscripts (such as textbooks) are not accepted." Submit outline with 1 sample chapter.

Recent Nonfiction Title: *Creative Crafts for Year-Round Fun*, by Jennifer Gverend.

ELLIOTT & CLARK PUBLISHING, INC., Suite 21, 1638 R Street NW, Washington DC 20009. Fax: (202)483-0355. Publisher: Carolyn M. Clark. Publishes hardcover and trade paperback originals. Publishes 7 titles/year. 50% of books from first-time authors; 90% from unagented writers. Pays royalty on wholesale price. Offers $1,000-7,500 advance. Publishes book 15 months after acceptance. Simultaneous submissions OK. Reports in 2 months on proposals. Book catalog and ms guidelines free on request.

Nonfiction: Biography, coffee table book, self-help. Subjects include Americana, art/architecture, gardening, history, nature/environment, photography. "We specialize in illustrated histories — need to think of possible photography/illustration sources to accompany manuscript. Submit an analysis of audience or a discussion of possible sales avenues beyond traditional book stores (such as interest groups, magazines, associations, etc.)." Submit proposal package, including possible illustrations (if applicable), outline, sales avenues. Reviews artwork/photos as part of freelance ms package. Writers should send transparencies.

Recent Nonfiction Titles: *Mapping For Stonewall*, William J. Miller (Civil War history/biography hardcover).

Tips: "We prefer proactive authors who are interested in providing marketing and the rights leads."

ELYSIUM GROWTH PRESS, 5436 Fernwood Ave., Los Angeles CA 90027. (310)455-1000. Fax: (310)455-2007. Publishes hardcover and paperback originals and reprints. Averages 4 titles/year. Receives 20 submissions/year. 20% of books from first-time authors; 100% from unagented writers. Pays $3,000 average advance. Publishes book an average of 18 months after acceptance. Query for electronic submissions. Reports in 1-2 months on queries; 2 months on submissions. Book catalog free on request.

Nonfiction: Illustrated book, self-help, textbook. Subjects include health, nature, philosophy, photography, psychology, recreation, sociology, travel. A nudist, naturist, special niche publisher. Needs books on "body self-image, body self-appreciation, world travel and subjects depicting the clothing-optional lifestyle." Query. All unsolicited mss are returned unopened. Reviews artwork/photos as part of ms package.

ENSLOW PUBLISHERS INC., Bloy St. and Ramsey Ave., P.O. Box 777, Hillside NJ 07205. (908)964-4116. Editor: Brian D. Enslow. Estab. 1977. Publishes hardcover and paperback originals. Averages 80 titles/year. 30% require freelance illustration. Pays royalty on net price. Offers advance. Publishes book an average of 8 months after acceptance. Reports in 2 weeks. *Writer's Market* recommends allowing 2 months for reply. Book catalog for $2 check and 9 × 12 SAE with 3 first-class stamps.

Nonfiction: Interested in mss for young adults and children. Some areas of special interest are science, social issues, biography, reference topics, recreation. Query with information on competing titles and writer's résumé.

 • This publisher is especially interested in ideas for series.

‡EPICENTER PRESS INC., Box 82368, Kenmore Station, Seattle WA 98028. Publisher: Kent Sturgis. Imprint is Umbrella Books. Publishes hardcover and trade paperback originals. Publishes 6-8 titles/year. Imprint publishes 2-3 titles/year. Receives 50 queries and 75 mss/year. 25% of books from first-time authors; 100% from unagented writers. Pays 10-16% royalty on net price. Offers $0-5,000 advance. Publishes book 1 year after acceptance of ms. No simultaneous submissions. Reports in 6 months on mss. Book catalog and ms guidelines free on request.

Nonfiction: Biography, coffee table book, humor, illustrated books. Subjects include animals, history, nature/environment, photography, recreation, regional, travel. "Our focus is the Pacific Northwest and Alaska." Submit proposal package, including ms, marketing ideas and a discussion of competing titles if any. Reviews artwork/photos as part of freelance ms package. Writers should send photocopies.

Recent Nonfiction Title: *Two Old Women*, by Velma Wallis (creative nonfiction); *Tales of Alaska's Bush Rat Governor*, by Jay Hammond (autobiography); *Cheating Death: Amazing Survival Stories from Alaska*, by Larry Kaniut (general adult nonfiction).

PAUL S. ERIKSSON, PUBLISHER, P.O. Box 62, Forest Dale VT 05745-4210. (802)247-8415. Publisher/Editor: Paul S. Eriksson. Associate Publisher/Co-Editor: Peggy Eriksson. Estab. 1960. Publishes hardcover and paperback trade originals and paperback trade reprints. Averages 5 titles/year. Receives 1,500 submissions annually. 25% of books from first-time authors; 95% from unagented writers. Average print order for a first book is 3,000-5,000. Pays 10-15% royalty on retail price. Offers advance if necessary. Publishes book an average of 6 months after acceptance. *Writer's Market* recommends allowing 2 months for reply. Catalog for #10 SASE.

Nonfiction: Americana, birds (ornithology), art, biography, business/economics, cookbooks/cooking/foods, health, history, hobbies, how-to, humor, nature, politics, psychology, recreation, self-help, sociology, sports, travel. Query with SASE.

Fiction: Serious, literary. Query with SASE. No simultaneous submissions.

Tips: "We look for intelligence, excitement and saleability—serious, literary fiction, not mainstream fiction."

ETC PUBLICATIONS, 700 E. Vereda Sur, Palm Springs CA 92262-4816. (619)325-5352. Editorial Director: LeeOna S. Hostrop. Senior Editor: Dr. Richard W. Hostrop. Estab. 1972. Publishes hardcover and paperback originals. Averages 6-12 titles/year. Receives 100 submissions annually. 75% of books from first-time authors; 90% from unagented writers. Average print order for a first book is 2,500. Offers 5-15% royalty, based on wholesale and retail price. No advance. Publishes book an average of 9 months after acceptance. *Writer's Market* recommends allowing 2 months for reply.

Nonfiction: Educational management, gifted education, futuristics, textbooks. Accepts nonfiction translations in above areas. Submit complete ms with SASE. *Writer's Market* recommends query first with SASE. Reviews artwork/photos as part of ms package.

Tips: "ETC will seriously consider textbook manuscripts in any knowledge area in which the author can guarantee a first-year adoption of not less than 500 copies. Special consideration is given to those authors who are capable and willing to submit their completed work in camera-ready, typeset form."

M. EVANS AND CO., INC., 216 E. 49 St., New York NY 10017-1502. Fax: (212)486-4544. Editor-in-Chief: George C. deKay. Estab. 1960. Publishes hardcover originals. Royalty schedule to be negotiated. Averages 30-40 titles/year. 5% of books from unagented writers. Publishes book an average of 8 months after acceptance. "No manuscript should be sent unsolicited. A letter of inquiry is essential." Reports in 2 months. Book catalog for 9 × 12 SAE with 3 first-class stamps.

Nonfiction and Fiction: "We publish a general trade list of adult fiction and nonfiction, cookbooks and semi-reference works. The emphasis is on selectivity because we publish only 30 titles a year. Our general fiction list, which is very small, represents an attempt to combine quality with commercial potential. We also publish westerns. Our most successful nonfiction titles have been related to health and the behavioral sciences. No limitation on subject. A writer should clearly indicate what his book is all about, frequently the task the writer performs least well. His credentials, although important, mean less than his ability to convince this company that he understands his subject and that he has the ability to communicate a message worth hearing." Reviews artwork/photos.

Tips: "Writers should review our book catalog or the *Publishers Trade List Annual* before making submissions."

‡EXPLORER'S GUIDE PUBLISHING, 4843 Apperson Dr., Rhinelander WI 54501. (715)362-6029. Managing Editor: Gary Kulibert. Publishes trade paperback originals. Publishes 4 titles/year. Receives 3 queries and 3 mss/year. 50% of books from first-time authors; 100% from unagented writers. Pays 6-12% royalty on wholesale price. Publishes book 9 months after acceptance of ms. Accepts simultaneous submissions. Query for electronic submissions. Reports in 2 months on queries. Book catalog free on request.

Nonfiction: Cookbook, children's/juvenile, guide books. Subjects include cooking, foods and nutrition, nature/environment, recreation, regional, travel. Query. Reviews artwork/photos as part of ms package. Writers should send photocopies.

FABER & FABER, INC., Division of Faber & Faber, Ltd., London, England; 50 Cross St., Winchester MA 01890. (617)721-1427. Fax: (617)729-2783. Contact: Publishing Assistant. Estab. 1976. Publishes hardcover and trade paperback originals and trade paperback reprints. Averages 30 titles/year. Receives 1,200 submissions annually. 10% of books from first-time authors; 25% from unagented writers. Pays 10% royalty on wholesale or retail price. Advance varies. Publishes book an average of 1 year after acceptance. Simultaneous submissions OK. Reports in 3 months on queries. Book catalog for 9 × 12 SAE with 4 first-class stamps. Writer's guidelines for #10 SASE.

Nonfiction: Anthologies, biography, contemporary culture, film and screenplays, history and natural history. Subjects include Americana, animals, pop/rock music, New England, sociology. Query with synopsis and outline with SASE. Reviews artwork/photos as part of ms package.

Recent Nonfiction Title: *Battlefield: Farming A Civil War Battleground*, by Peter Svenson.

Fiction: Collections, ethnic, experimental and regional. No historical/family sagas or mysteries, no children's, juvenile or poetry. Query with synopsis and outline with SASE.

Recent Fiction Title: *The Museum of Happiness*, by Jesse Le Kercheval.

Tips: "Subjects that have consistently done well for us include popular culture; serious, intelligent rock and roll books; anthologies; and literary, somewhat quirky fiction. Please do not send entire manuscript; include SASE for reply."

FACTS ON FILE, INC., 460 Park Ave. S., New York NY 10016-7382. (212)683-2244. Editorial Director: Susan Schwartz. Estab. 1941. Publishes hardcover originals and reprints. Averages 135 titles/year. Receives approximately 2,000 submissions annually. 25% of books from unagented writers. Pays 10-15% royalty on retail price. Offers average $10,000 advance. Simultaneous submissions OK. Query for electronic submissions. No submissions returned without SASE. Reports in 2 months on queries. Free book catalog.

Nonfiction: Reference, other informational books on economics, cooking and foods (no cookbooks), health, history, entertainment, natural history, philosophy, psychology, recreation, religion, language, sports, multicultural studies, science, popular culture. "We need serious, informational books for a targeted audience. All our books must have strong library interest, but we also distribute books effectively to the book trade." No computer books, technical books, cookbooks, biographies (except YA), pop psychology, humor, do-it-yourself crafts, fiction or poetry. Query or submit outline and a sample chapter.

Tips: "Our audience is school and public libraries for our more reference-oriented books and libraries, schools and bookstores for our less reference-oriented informational titles."

FAIRLEIGH DICKINSON UNIVERSITY PRESS, 285 Madison Ave., Madison NJ 07940. (201)593-8564. Fax: (201)593-8543. Director: Harry Keyishian. Estab. 1967. Publishes hardcover originals. Averages 30 titles/year. Receives 300 submissions annually. 33% of books from first-time authors; 100% from unagented writers. Average print order for a first book is 1,000. "Contract is arranged through Associated University Presses of Cranbury, New Jersey. We are a *selection* committee only." Subsidy publishes (nonauthor) 2% of books. Publishes book an average of 1 year after acceptance. Reports in 2 weeks on queries. *Writer's Market* recommends allowing 2 months for reply.

Nonfiction: Reference, scholarly books. Subjects include art, business and economics, Civil War, film, history, Jewish studies, literary criticism, music, philosophy, politics, psychology, sociology, women's studies. Looking for scholarly books in all fields. No nonscholarly books. Query with outline and sample chapters. Reviews artwork/photos as part of ms package.

Tips: "Research must be up to date. Poor reviews result when authors' bibliographies and notes don't reflect current research. We follow *Chicago Manual of Style* style in scholarly citations."

THE FAMILY ALBUM, Rt. 1, Box 42, Glen Rock PA 17327. (717)235-2134. Fax: (717)235-8042. Contact: Ron Lieberman. Estab. 1969. Publishes hardcover originals and reprints and software. Averages 2 titles/year. Receives 150 submissions annually. 30% from first-time authors; 100% from unagented writers. Average print order for a first book is 1,000. Pays royalty on wholesale price. Publishes book an average of 10 months after acceptance. Simultaneous submissions OK. Query for electronic submissions. Reports in 2 months.

Nonfiction: "Significant works in the field of (nonfiction) bibliography. Worthy submissions in the field of Pennsylvania history, biography, folk art and lore. We are also seeking materials relating to books, literacy, and national development. Special emphasis on Third World countries, and the role of printing in international development." No religious material. Submit outline and sample chapters.

FARRAR, STRAUS AND GIROUX, INC., 19 Union Square W., New York NY 10003. Imprints are Noonday Press, Hill and Wang, Sunburst Books, Mirasol and North Point Press. Editor-in-Chief, Books for Young Readers: Margaret Ferguson. Publishes hardcover originals. Receives 5,000 submissions annually. Pays royalty. Offers advance. Publishes book an average of 18 months after acceptance. Reports in 3 months. Catalog for 9 × 12 SAE with 3 first-class stamps.

Nonfiction and Fiction: "We are primarily interested in fiction picture books and novels for children and middle readers, but do some nonfiction—both picture book and longer formats." Submit outline/synopsis and sample chapters. Reviews copies of artwork/photos as part of ms package.

Recent Nonfiction Title: *Making Sense*, by Bruce Brooks.

Recent Fiction Title: *Tell Me Everything*, by Carolyn Coman.

Recent Picture Book Title: *Carl Goes to Daycare*, by Alexandra Day.

Tips: "Study our style and our list."

FAWCETT JUNIPER, Imprint of Ballantine/Del Rey/Fawcett/Ivy, Division of Random House, 201 E. 50th St., New York NY 10022. (212)751-2600. Editor-in-Chief, Vice President: Leona Nevler. Publishes 24 titles/year. Pays royalty. Publishes book an average of 1 year after acceptance. Simultaneous submissions OK. Reports in 2 months on queries.

Nonfiction: Adult books.

Recent Nonfiction Title: *My Life: Magic Johnson,* by Magic Johnson.

Fiction: Mainstream/contemporary, young adult (12-18). No children's books. Query.

Recent Fiction Title: *The Secret History,* by Donna Tartt.

THE FEMINIST PRESS AT THE CITY UNIVERSITY OF NEW YORK, 2nd Floor, 311 E. 94th St., New York NY 10128. (212)360-5790. Senior Editor: Susannah Driver. Estab. 1970. Publishes hardcover and trade paperback originals and reprints. Publishes 8-10 titles/year. Receives 500 queries/mss/year. 20% of books from first-time authors; 90% from unagented writers. Pays royalty on net price. Offers $100 average advance. Simultaneous submissions OK. Query for electronic submissions. Reports in 4 months on proposals. Book catalog and ms guidelines free on request.

Nonfiction: "The Feminist Press's primary mission is to publish works committed to the eradication of gender-role stereotyping that are multicultural in focus. Persons should write for our guidelines for submission and catalog; note that we generally publish for the college classroom." Children's (ages 10 and up)/ juvenile, primary materials for the humanities and social science classroom and general readers. Subjects include ethnic, gay/lesbian, government/politics, health/medicine, history, language/literature, music, sociology, translation, women's issues/studies and peace, memoir, international. Send proposal package, including materials requested in our guidelines. Reviews artwork/photos as part of freelance ms package. Writers should send photocopies and SASE.

Recent Nonfiction Title: *The Answer/La Respuesta,* by Sor Juana Inés de la Cruz. Edited and translated by Electa Avenal and Amanda Powell.

Fiction: "The Feminist Press publishes fiction reprints only. No original fiction is considered."

Tips: "Our audience consists of college students, professors, general readers."

J.G. FERGUSON PUBLISHING COMPANY, Suite 300, 200 W. Madison, Chicago IL 60606. Editorial Director: C.J. Summerfield. Estab. 1940. Publishes hardcover originals. Publishes 4-8 titles/year. Pays by project. Reports in 3 months on queries.

Nonfiction: Reference. "We publish work specifically for the high school/college library reference market. Nothing is a single-author project. They are encyclopedic in nature. We mainly publish medical and career encyclopedias. No mass market, scholarly, or juvenile books, please." Query or submit outline and one sample chapter.

DONALD I. FINE, INC., 19 W. 21st St., New York NY 10010. (212)727-3270. Fax: (212)727-3277. Imprints include Primus Library of Contemporary Americana. Publishes hardcover originals and trade paperback originals and reprints. Averages 45-60 titles/year. Receives 1,000 submissions/year. 30% of books from first-time authors. Pays royalty on retail price. Advance varies. Publishes book an average of 1 year after acceptance. Book catalog for 6×9 SASE.

Nonfiction: Biography, cookbook, humor, self-help. Subjects include history, military/war, sports. All unsolicited mss are returned unopened. Reviews artwork/photos as part of ms package.

Recent Nonfiction Title: *The Man Who Framed The Beatles,* by Andrew Yule.

Fiction: Adventure, ethnic, historical, horror, humor, literary, mainstream/contemporary, mystery, suspense, western. All unsolicited mss returned unopened.

Recent Fiction Title: *The Conquering Heroes,* by Peter Gent.

‡FIRE ENGINEERING BOOKS & VIDEOS, Division of Penn Well Publishing Co., Park 80 W., Plaza 2, Saddle Brook NJ 07662. (201)845-0800. Director, Book Publishing: Joanne Ezersky. Publishes hardcover originals. Publishes 10 titles/year. Receives 24 queries/year. 50% of books from first-time authors; 100% from unagented writers. Pays 7-15% royalty on net sales. Publishes book 6 months after acceptance of ms. No simultaneous submissions. Query for electronic submissions. Reports in 3 months on proposals. Book catalog free on request.

Nonfiction: Reference, technical, textbook. Subjects include firefighter training, public safety. Submit outline and 2 sample chapters.

Recent Nonfiction Title: *Fire Department Water Supply Handbook,* by Eckman (text).

FIREBRAND BOOKS, 141 The Commons, Ithaca NY 14850. (607)272-0000. Publisher: Nancy K. Bereano. Estab. 1985. Publishes hardcover and trade paperback originals. Averages 8-10 titles/year. Receives 300-400 submissions annually. 50% of books from first-time authors; 90% from unagented writers. Pays 7-9% royalty on retail price, or makes outright purchase. Publishes book an average of 18 months after acceptance. Simultaneous submissions OK "with notification." Reports in 1 month on queries. *Writer's Market* recommends allowing 2 months for reply. Free book catalog.

Nonfiction: Personal narratives, essays. Subjects include feminism, lesbianism. Submit complete ms.
Fiction: Will consider all types of feminist and lesbian fiction.
Tips: "Our audience includes feminists, lesbians, ethnic audiences, and other progressive people."

FISHER BOOKS, 4239 W. Ina Road, Tucson AZ 85741. (602)744-6110. Fax: (602)744-0944. Contact: Editorial Submissions Director. Estab. 1987. Publishes trade paperback originals and reprints. Averages 8 titles/year. 25% of books from first-time authors; 75% from unagented writers. Pays 10-15% royalty on wholesale price. Simultaneous submissions OK. Reports in 2 months. Book catalog for SAE with 3 first-class stamps.
Nonfiction: Subjects include cooking, automotive, foods and nutrition, regional gardening, family health, self-help/parenting. Submit outline and sample chapters, not complete ms. Include return postage.

J. FLORES PUBLICATIONS, P.O. Box 830131, Miami FL 33283-0131. Editor: Eli Flores. Estab. 1982. Publishes trade paperback originals and reprints. Averages 10 titles/year. 99% of books from unagented writers. Pays 10-15% royalty on net sales. No advance. Publishes book an average of 1 year after acceptance. Simultaneous submissions OK. Reports in 1 month on queries. *Writer's Market* recommends allowing 2 months for reply. Book catalog for 9×12 SAE with 2 first-class stamps.
Nonfiction: How-to, illustrated book, self-help. "We need original nonfiction manuscripts on outdoor adventure, military science, weaponry, current events, self-defense, personal finance/careers. How-to manuscripts are given priority." Query with outline and 2-3 sample chapters. Reviews artwork/photos. "Photos are accepted as part of the manuscript package and are strongly encouraged."
  • Publisher reports a special need for manuscripts on careers, starting your own business and credit and consumer matters. Previously published books will also be considered.
Recent Nonfiction Title: *How To Be Your Own Detective,* by Kevin Sherlock.
Tips: "Trends include illustrated how-to books on a specific subject. Be thoroughly informed on your subject and technically accurate."

FOCAL PRESS, Subsidiary of Butterworth Heinemann, Division of Reed Elsevier (USA) Inc., 313 Washington St., Newton MA 02158-1630. (617)928-2600. Publishing Director: Karen M. Speerstra. Estab. US, 1981; UK, 1938. Imprint publishes hardcover and paperback originals and reprints. Averages 30-35 UK-US titles/year; entire firm averages 100 titles/year. Receives 500-700 submissions annually. 25% of books from first-time authors; 90% from unagented writers. Pays 10-12% royalty on wholesale price. Offers $1,500 average advance. Publishes book an average of 1 year after acceptance. Simultaneous submissions OK. Reports in 2 months. Book catalog and ms guidelines free.
Nonfiction: How-to, reference, technical and textbooks in media arts: photography, film and cinematography, broadcasting, theater and performing arts. High-level scientific/technical monographs are also considered. "We do not publish collections of photographs or books composed primarily of photographs. Our books are text-oriented, with artwork serving to illustrate and expand on points in the text." Query preferred, or submit outline and sample chapters. Reviews artwork/photos as part of ms package.
Recent Nonfiction Title: *Programming for TV, Radio and Cable,* by Gross/Vane.
Tips: "We are publishing fewer photography books. Our advances and royalties are more carefully determined with an eye toward greater profitability for all our publications."

FOCUS ON THE FAMILY BOOK PUBLISHING, 8605 Explorer Dr., Colorado Springs CO 80920. Managing Editor: Gwen Weising. Publishes hardcover and trade paperback originals. Publishes 15-20 titles/year. Receives 1200 mss/year. 25% of books from first-time authors; 25% from unagented writers. Pays royalty. Offers advance. Publishes book 1 year after acceptance of ms. Simultaneous submissions OK. Query for electronic submissions. Reports in 1 month on queries, 2 months on proposals. Book catalog free on request. Manuscript guidelines for #10 SASE.
Nonfiction: How-to, juvenile, self-help. Subjects include child guidance/parenting, money/finance, women's issues/studies. "We are the publishing arm of Focus on the Family, an evangelical Christian organization. Authors need to be aware that our book publishing is closely related to the focus of the organization, which is the strengthening and preservation of family and marriages." Query.
Tips: Our audience is "families and the people who make up families. Know what we publish before submitting query."

‡FOGHORN PRESS, #220, 555 De Haro St., San Francisco CA 94107. (415)255-9550. Acquisitions Editor: Judith Pynn. Publishes trade paperback originals and reprints. Publishes 20 titles/year. Receives 500 queries and 200 mss/year. 50% of books from first-time authors; 98% from unagented writers. Pays 12% royalty on wholesale price; occasional work for hire. Publishes book 1 year after acceptance of ms. Accepts simultaneous submissions. Query for electronic submissions. Reports in 1 month on queries; 2 months on proposals; 3 months on mss. Book catalog and ms guidelines free on request.
Nonfiction: Guidebooks. Subjects include nature/environment, recreation, regional, sports, travel, outdoors, leisure. Submit proposal package, including outline or chapter headings, 2 or more sample chapters, marketing plan.
Recent Nonfiction Title: *California Hiking,* by Michael Hodgson and Tom Stienstra (hiking guidebook).

‡FORUM PUBLISHING COMPANY, 383 E. Main St., Centerport NY 11721. (516) 754-5000. Contact: Martin Stevens. Publishes trade paperback originals. Publishes 12 titles/year. Receives 200 queries and 25 mss/year. 75% of books from first-time authors; 75% from unagented writers. Makes outright purchase of $250-750. Publishes book 4 months after acceptance of ms. Accepts simultaneous submissions. Reports in 1 month on mss. Book catalog free on request.

Nonfiction: Subjects include business and economics, money/finance. "We only publish business titles." Submit outline. Reviews artwork/photos as part of ms package. Writers should send photocopies.

Recent Nonfiction Title: *Selling Information By Mail*, by Glen Gilcrest.

FOUR WALLS EIGHT WINDOWS, Room 503, 39 W. 14th St., New York NY 10011. Estab. 1987. Publishes hardcover and trade paperback originals and trade paperback reprints. Averages 16 titles/year. Receives 2,000 submissions/year. 15% of books from first-time authors; 70% from unagented writers. Pays royalty (depends—negotiated contract) on retail price. Offers $1,5000 average advance. Publishes book an average of 12 months after acceptance. Reports in 2 months on queries. Book catalog for 6 × 9 SAE with 3 first-class stamps.

● Publisher reports this house is concentrating more on quality nonfiction.

Nonfiction: Political, investigative. Subjects include art/architecture, cooking, foods and nutrition, government/politics, history, language/literature, nature/environment, science, travel. "We do not want New Age works." Query first. Submit outline with SASE. All sent without SASE discarded.

Recent Nonfiction Title: *Censored: The News That Didn't Make the News and Why*, by Carl Jensen and Project Censored, with introduction by Jessica Mitford and cartoons by Tom Tomorrow.

Fiction: Ethnic, experimental, feminist, literary, mystery. "No romance, popular." Query first. Submit outline/synopsis with SASE.

Tips: "Send us something original, unusual, off-beat, possibly 'alternative.' "

‡FOX CHAPEL PUBLISHING, P.O. Box 7948, Lancaster PA 17604. Acquisitions: John Alan. Publishes hardcover and trade paperback originals and trade paperback reprints. Publishes 8 titles/year. Receives 50 queries and 12 mss/year. 80% of books from first-time authors; 100% from unagented writers. Pays royalty or makes outright purchase. Offers $200-1,000 advance. Publishes book 6 months after acceptance of ms. Accepts simultaneous submissions. Query for electronic submissions. Reports in 1 month on queries. Book catalog for #10 SASE.

Nonfiction: Cookbook, how-to, technical. Subjects include Americana, art/architecture, cooking, foods & nutrition, hobbies. Query. Reviews artwork/photos as part of ms package. Writers should send photocopies.

Recent Nonfiction Title: *Afternoon Teas* (illustrated gift book).

Tips: "We're looking for knowledgeable artists, woodworkers first, writers second in our how-to line. For cookbooks we expect a more sophisticated author."

FPMI COMMUNICATIONS, INC., 707 Fiber St., NW, Huntsville AL 35801-5833. (205)539-1850. Fax: (205)539-0911. President: Ralph Smith. Estab. 1985. Publishes trade paperback originals. Averages 4-6 titles/year. Receives 4-5 submissions/year. 60% of books from first-time authors; 100% from unagented writers. Pays 15% on retail price. Publishes book an average of 1 year after acceptance. Simultaneous submissions OK. Query for electronic submissions. Reports in 3 weeks on queries, 2 months on mss. Free book catalog.

Nonfiction: Technical. Subjects include government/politics, labor relations, personnel issues. "We will be publishing books for government and business on topics such as sexual harassment, drug testing, and how to deal with leave abuse by employees. Our books are practical, how-to books for a supervisor or manager. Scholarly theoretical works do not interest our audience." Submit outline/synopsis and sample chapters or send complete ms.

Tips: "We are interested in books that are practical, easy-to-read and less than 150 pages. Primary audience is federal managers and supervisors—particularly first and second level. If I were a writer trying to market a book today, I would emphasize practical topics with plenty of examples in succinct, concrete language."

‡SAMUEL FRENCH, INC., 45 W. 25th St., New York NY 10010. (212)206-8990. Fax: (212)206-1429. Editor: Lawrence Harbison. Estab. 1830. Subsidiaries include Samuel French Ltd. (London); Samuel French (Canada) Ltd. (Toronto); Samuel French, Inc. (Hollywood); and Baker's Plays (Boston). Publishes paperback acting editions of plays. Averages 50-70 titles/year. Receives 1,500 submissions annually, mostly from unagented playwrights. About 10% of publications are from first-time authors; 20% from unagented writers. Pays 10% book royalty on retail price. Publishes book an average of 6 months after acceptance. Simultaneous submissions OK. *Writer's Market* recommends allowing 2 months for reply. 1994 basic catalog $1.50. Manuscript submission guidelines $4.

Nonfiction: Acting editions of plays.

Tips: "Broadway and Off-Broadway hit plays, light comedies and mysteries have the best chance of selling to our firm. Our market is comprised of theater producers—both professional and amateur—actors and students. Read as many plays as possible of recent vintage to keep apprised of today's market; write plays with good female roles; and be one hundred percent professional in approaching publishers and producers (see Guidelines)."

FRIENDS UNITED PRESS, 101 Quaker Hill, Richmond IN 47374. (317)962-7573. Fax: (317)966-1293. Editor/Manager: Ardith Talbot. Estab. 1968. Publishes 12 titles/year. Receives 100 queries and 80 mss/year. 50% of mss from first-time authors; 99% from unagented authors. Pays 7½% royalty. Publishes ms 1 year after acceptance of ms. Simultaneous submissions OK. Query for electronic submissions. Reports in 12-16 months. Book catalog and ms guidelines free on request.
Nonfiction: Biography, humor, children's/juvenile, reference, textbook. Subjects include religion. "Authors should be Quaker and should be familiar with Quaker history, spirituality and doctrine." Submit proposal package. Reviews artwork/photos as part of ms package. Writers should send photocopies.
Fiction: Historical, juvenile, religious. "Must be Quaker-related." Query.
Tips: "Spirituality mss must be in agreement with Quaker spirituality."

GALLAUDET UNIVERSITY PRESS, 800 Florida Ave. NE, Washington DC 20002. (202)651-5488. Imprints include Kendall Green Publications, Clerc Books and Gallaudet University Press. Managing Editor: Ivey Pittle Wallace. Estab. 1980. Publishes hardcover and paperback originals and reprints. Averages 15 titles/year. Pays 10-15% royalty on wholesale price (net). Simultaneous submissions OK. Query for electronic submissions. Reports in 3 months. Free ms guidelines.
Nonfiction: Scholarly and serious books on deafness and hearing loss. Topics include audiology, biography, education, health/medicine, history, linguistics, literature, parenting, psychology, sign language, sociology, sports. Submit outline/synopsis and sample chapters or complete ms. Reviews artwork/photos as part of ms. package.
Recent Nonfiction Title: *All of Us Together*, by Jeri Banks.
Tips: "Individuals in our audience come from many walks of life and include every age group. The common denominator among them is an interest and/or openness to learn more about deafness."

‡GARLAND PUBLISHING, INC., 717 Fifth Ave., New York NY 10022. (212)751-7447. Vice Presidents: Leo Balk, Gary Muris. Estab. 1969. Publishes hardcover originals. Averages 250 titles/year. 100% from unagented writers. Pays 15% royalty on wholesale price. "Depending on marketability, authors may prepare camera-ready copy." Publishes book an average of 1 year after acceptance. Reports in 2 months. Free book catalog. Ms guidelines for SASE.
Nonfiction: Scholarly and reference books for libraries. Subjects include humanities, social sciences. Accepts nonfiction translations. "We're interested in scholarly books—encyclopedias, essay collections, textbooks, anthologies, sourcebooks, etc.—in all fields." Submit outline and 1-2 sample chapters. Reviews artwork/photos as part of ms package.
Recent Nonfiction Title: *Encyclopedia of Ethics*, ed. by Lawrence Becker.

GARRETT PARK PRESS, P.O. Box 190, Garret Park MD 20896. Publisher: Robert Calvert. Estab. 1967. Publishes trade paperback originals. Publishes 6 titles/year. Receives 80 submissions/year. 20% of books from first-time authors; 100% from unagented writers. Pays 10-15% royalty on wholesale or retail price. Publishes book an average of 8 months after acceptance. Reports in 1 month on queries. *Writer's Market* recommends allowing 2 months for reply. Free book catalog.
Nonfiction: Reference. Subjects include employment, education, ethnic. Query.
Tips: "We publish books on careers only."

‡GASLIGHT PUBLICATIONS, 626 N. College Ave., Bloomington IN 47404. (812)332-5169. Publisher: Jack Tracy. Estab. 1979. Imprints include McGuffin Books. Publishes hardcover and paperback originals. Publishes 6 titles/year. Receives 15-20 submissions/year. 75% of books from first-time authors; 90% from unagented writers. Pays 10% royalty. Publishes book an average of 1 year after acceptance. Simultaneous submissions OK. Reports in 1 month. Free book catalog.
Nonfiction: "We publish specialized studies of the mystery genre and related fields: biography, criticism, analysis, reference, film, true crime. Submissions should be serious, well-researched, not necessarily for the scholar, but for readers who are already experts in their own right. 12,000 words minimum." Query with outline/synopsis and sample chapters or send complete ms. Reviews artwork/photos as part of ms package. "Please—we do *not* publish unsolicited fiction."
Recent Nonfiction Title: *Myth and Modern Man in Sherlock Holmes: Sir Arthur Conan Doyle and the Uses of Nostalgia*.
Tips: "Our purchasers tend to be public libraries and knowledgeable mystery aficionados."

GAY SUNSHINE PRESS and LEYLAND PUBLICATIONS, P.O. Box 410690, San Francisco CA 94141-0690. (707)996-6082. Editor: Winston Leyland. Estab. 1970. Publishes hardcover and trade paperback originals and trade paperback reprints. Averages 6-8 titles/year. Pays royalty or makes outright purchase. Reports in 6 weeks on queries. Book catalog for $1.
Nonfiction: How-to and gay lifestyle topics. "We're interested in innovative literary nonfiction which deals with gay lifestyles." No long personal accounts, academic or overly formal titles. Query. "After query is returned by us, submit outline and sample chapters. Enclose SASE. All unsolicited manuscripts are returned unopened."

Fiction: Erotica, ethnic, experimental, historical, mystery, science fiction, gay fiction in translation. "Interested in well-written novels on gay themes; also short story collections. We have a high literary standard for fiction." Query. "After query is returned by us, submit outline/synopsis and sample chapters. Enclose SASE. All unsolicited manuscripts are returned unopened."

GEM GUIDES BOOK COMPANY, Suite F, 315 Cloverleaf Dr., Baldwin Park CA 91706-6510. (818)855-1611. Fax: (818)855-1610. Imprints include Gembooks. Editor: Robin Shepherd. Publishes trade paperback originals. Averages 6-8 titles/year. Receives 40 submissions/year. 30% of books from first-time authors; 100% from unagented writers. Pays 6-10% royalty on wholesale price. Offers $1,000 average advance. Publishes book an average of 4 months after acceptance. Simultaneous submissions OK. Reports in 1 month. *Writer's Market* recommends allowing 2 months for reply.
Nonfiction: Regional books for the Western US. Subjects include hobbies, nature/environment, recreation, travel. We are looking for books on earth sciences, nature books, also travel/local interest titles for the Western US. Query. Submit outline/synopsis and sample chapters. Reviews artwork/photos as part of ms package.
Recent Nonfiction Title: *The Old West Trivia Book*, by Don Bullis.
Tips: "Authors have the best chance selling us books about rocks, minerals, and recreational opportunities in the Western US. We have a general audience of people interested in recreational activities. Publishers plan and have specific books lines in which they specialize. Learn about the publisher and submit materials compatible with that publisher's product line."

‡THE C.R. GIBSON COMPANY, 32 Knight St., Norwalk CT 06856. (203)847-4543. Editor: Julie Mitchell. Publishes hardcover originals. Publishes 15 titles/year. Receives 300 queries and 400 mss/year. 20% of books from first-time authors; 80% from unagented writers. Pays 6% royalty on wholesale price or makes outright purchase $100-3,000. Offers $500-5,000 advance. Publishes book 18 months after acceptance of ms. Simultaneous submissions OK. Query for electronic submissions. Reports in 4 months on mss. Manuscript guidelines free on request.
Nonfiction: Children's/juvenile, gift book. Subjects include religion, wedding, sympathy, friendship, Christmas. Submit sample chapter.
Recent Nonfiction Title: *The Shelter of His Wings*, by Joan Winmill Brown (inspirational); *All Things Bright & Beautiful*, by Laura Lanier (inspirational).
Fiction: Humor, picture books, religious, short story collections. Submit sample chapters.
Recent Fiction Title: *I Climbed a Rainbow Once*, by Christopher Lane; *I Saw an Angel Yesterday*, by Christopher Lane; *What Does the Tooth Fairy Do with All Those Teeth?*, by George Kelly.
Poetry: Submit complete ms.
Recent Poetry Title: *A Gift of Time*, by Susan Florence; *Come to the Garden*, by JoAnna O'Keefe.

GIFTED EDUCATION PRESS, The Reading Tutorium, 10201 Yuma Ct., P.O. Box 1586, Manassas VA 22110. (703)369-5017. Publisher: Maurice D. Fisher. Estab. 1981. Publishes paperback originals for school districts and libraries. Averages 5 titles/year. Receives 50 submissions annually. 100% of books from first-time authors; 100% from unagented writers. Pays royalty of $1 per book. Publishes book an average of 6 months after acceptance. Simultaneous submissions OK. Reports in 4 months. Book catalog for #10 SAE with 2 first-class stamps. Send letter of inquiry first. No unsolicited mss.
Nonfiction: How-to. Subjects include philosophy, psychology, education of the gifted, the humanities, science and technology; how to teach adults to read. "Need books on how to educate gifted children—both theory and practice, and adult literacy. Also, we are searching for books on using computers with the gifted, and teaching the sciences to the gifted. Need rigorous books on procedures, methods, and specific curriculum for the gifted. We need individuals to write brief book reviews and 'blurbs' for our Gifted Ed. News Page. *Send letter of inquiry only.* Do not send manuscripts or parts of manuscripts. Unsolicited manuscripts will be promptly returned without being read!"
Tips: "If I were a writer trying to market a book today, I would develop a detailed outline based upon intensive study of my field of interest. Present creative ideas in a rigorous fashion. Be knowledgeable about and comfortable with ideas. We are looking for books on using computers with gifted students; books on science and humanities education for the gifted; and books on how to teach adults to read."

GLENBRIDGE PUBLISHING LTD., 6010 W. Jewell Ave., Denver CO 80232-7106. Fax: (303)987-9037. Editor: James A. Keene. Estab. 1986. Publishes hardcover originals and reprints, and trade paperback originals. Publishes 6 titles/year. Pays 10% royalty. Publishes book an average of 1 year after acceptance. Simultaneous submissions OK. Reports in 2 months on queries. Book catalog for 6×9 SASE. Manuscript guidelines for #10 SASE.
Nonfiction: General. Subjects include Americana, business and economics, history, music, philosophy, politics, psychology, sociology. Query or submit outline/synopsis and sample chapters. Include SASE.

‡GLOBAL PROFESSIONAL PUBLICATIONS, Global Engineering Documents/IHS Group, 15 Inverness Way E., Englewood CO 80112. Publisher: Eugene M. Falken. Imprints are Global Professional Publications,

Global Engineering Documents. Publishes hardcover and trade paperback originals and reprints. Firm publishes 20 titles/year; imprint publishes 10 titles/year. Receives 20 queries and 5 mss/year. 5% of books from first-time authors; 100% from unagented writers. Pays 10-15% royalty on wholesale price or makes outright purchase of $1,100-2,000. Publishes book 6 months after acceptance of ms. Simultaneous submissions OK. Reports in 2 months on mss. Book catalog free on request.

Nonfiction: Reference, technical, textbook. Subjects include agriculture/horticulture, business and economics, computers and electronics, health/medicine, science, software. Query. Reviews artwork/photos as part of freelance ms package. Writers should send photocopies.

Recent Nonfiction Title: *Software Engineering Standards*, by Magee (technical); *Questions & Answers on Quality*, by Breitenberg (technical); *Building Air Quality*, by NIOSH (technical).

THE GLOBE PEQUOT PRESS, INC., P.O. Box 833, Old Saybrook CT 06475-0833. (203)395-0440. Fax: (203)395-0312. Managing Editor: Bruce Markot. Assistant Editor: Melissa Holcombe. Estab. 1947. Imprints are Voyager Books and East Woods Books. Publishes hardcover and paperback originals and paperback reprints. Averages 80 titles/year. Receives 1,500 submissions annually. 30% of books from first-time authors; 60% from unagented writers. Average print order for a first book is 4,000-7,500. Offers 7½-10% royalty on net price. Offers advance. Publishes book an average of 1 year after acceptance of ms. Simultaneous submissions OK. Reports in 3 months. Book catalog for 9×12 SASE.

Nonfiction: Travel guidebooks (regional OK), natural history, outdoor recreation, business, careers, gardening, carpentry, how-to, Americana, cookbooks. No doctoral theses, fiction, genealogies, memoirs, poetry or textbooks. Submit outline, table of contents, sample chapter and résumé/vita. Reviews artwork/photos.

DAVID R. GODINE, PUBLISHER, INC., Horticultural Hall, 300 Massachusetts Ave., Boston MA 02115. President: David Godine. Editorial Director: Mark Polizzotti. Estab. 1970. Publishes hardcover and trade paperback originals and reprints. Publishes 30 titles/year. Pays royalty on retail price. Publishes book 3 years after acceptance of ms. Reports in 3 months on queries. Book catalog for 5×8 SAE with 75¢ postage.

Nonfiction: Biography, coffee table book, cookbook, illustrated book, children's/juvenile. Subjects include Americana, art/architecture, gardening, nature/environment, photography, literary criticism, current affairs. Query (2-page maximum) with SASE. No original artwork.

Fiction: Literary, mystery, short story collection, young adult. "We are not currently considering unsolicited manuscripts."

Recent Fiction Title: *Sherlock in Love*, by Gena Nashund.

Poetry: "Our poetry list is filled through 1996."

Recent Poetry Title: *My Brother Running*, by Wesley McNain.

GOLDEN WEST BOOKS, Box 80250, San Marino CA 91118. (818)458-8148. Editor-in-Chief: Donald Duke. Managing Editor: Vernice Dagosta. Publishes hardcover and paperback originals. Averages 4 titles/year. Receives 50 submissions annually. 50% of books from first-time authors; 100% from unagented writers. Pays 10% royalty contract. No advance. Publishes book an average of 3 months after acceptance. Simultaneous submissions OK. Reports in 1 month.

Nonfiction: Publishes selected Western transportation Americana. Query or submit complete ms. "Illustrations and photographs will be examined if we like manuscript."

‡GOLDEN WEST PUBLISHERS, 4113 N. Longview, Phoenix AZ 85014. (602)265-4392. Editor: Hal Mitchell. Estab. 1973. Publishes trade paperback originals. Averages 5-6 titles/year. Receives 200 submissions annually. 50% of books from first-time authors; 100% from unagented writers. Average print order for a first book is 5,000. Prefers mss on "work for hire" basis. No advance. Publishes book an average of 6 months after acceptance. Simultaneous submissions OK. Query for electronic submissions. Reports in 4 weeks on queries, 2 months on mss.

Nonfiction: Cookbooks, books on the Southwest and West. Subjects include cooking and foods, southwest history and outdoors, travel. Query or submit outline/synopsis and sample chapters. Prefers query letter first. Reviews artwork/photos as part of ms package.

Tips: "We are interested in Arizona and Southwest material and cookbooks, and welcome material in these areas."

‡GOLD'N' HONEY BOOKS, Questar Publishers, Inc., P.O. Box 1720, Sisters OR 97759. Writer/Editor: Thomas Womack. Publishes hardcover and trade paperback originals and reprints. Firm publishes 60 titles/year; imprint publishes 20 titles/year. Receives 300 queries and 200 mss/year. 5% of books from first-time authors; 100% from unagented writers. Pays 5-18% royalty on wholesale price. Publishes book 10 months after acceptance of ms. No simultaneous submissions. Reports in 2 months on queries. Book catalog for $2.

Nonfiction: Illustrated book, children's/juvenile. Subjects include religion. "Must reflect evangelical Christian world-view and values." Query.

Recent Nonfiction Title: *The First Step Bible*, by Mack Thomas (children's Bible); *Someday Heaven*, by Larry Libby; *Teach Me about Jesus*, by L.J. Sattgast.

Fiction: Picture books, religious. Query.
Recent Fiction Title: *In His Hands, What Would Jesus Do?, Let's Make Jesus Happy,* all by Mack Thomas.

GOVERNMENT INSTITUTES, INC., Suite 200, 4 Research Place, Rockville MD 20850-3226. (301)921-2355. Director of Acquisitions: Roland W. Schumann III. Estab. 1973. Publishes hardcover and softcover originals and CD-ROM/disk products. Averages 45 titles/year. Receives 20 submissions annually. 50% of books from first-time authors; 100% from unagented writers. Pays royalty or fee. No advance. Publishes book an average of 2 months after acceptance. Simultaneous submissions OK with notification. Reports in 1 month on queries. *Writer's Market* recommends allowing 2 months for reply. Book catalog available on request.
Nonfiction: Reference, technical. Subjects include environmental law, employment law, FDA matters, industrial hygiene and safety, real estate with an environmental slant. Needs professional-level titles in those areas. Also looking for international environmental topics. Submit outline and at least one sample chapter.
Recent Nonfiction Title: *Eco-Data: Using Your PC To Obtain Free Environmental Information,* edited by Roland Schumann
Tips: "We also conduct courses. Authors are frequently invited serve as instructors."

GRAPEVINE PUBLICATIONS, INC., P.O. Box 2449, Corvallis OR 97339-2449. (503)754-0583. Fax: (503)754-6508. Managing Editor: Christopher M. Coffin. Estab. 1983. Publishes trade paperback originals. Averages 2-4 titles/year. Receives 200-300 submissions/year. 20% of books from first-time authors; 100% from unagented writers. Pays 6-9% royalty on net sales. Publishes book an average of 6 months after acceptance. Simultaneous submissions OK. Due to volume, responds only if interested.
Nonfiction: Tutorials on technical subjects written for the layperson, innovative curricula or resources for math and science teachers. Subjects include math, science, computers, calculators, software, video, audio and other technical tools. Submit complete ms.
Recent Nonfiction Title: *Algebra/Precalculus on the HP48G/GX.*
Fiction: Children's picture books and juvenile fiction.

GRAPHIC ARTS CENTER PUBLISHING CO., 3019 NW Yeon Ave., P.O. Box 10306, Portland OR 97210-1519. (503)226-2402. Fax: (503)223-1410. General Manager: Douglas Pfeiffer. Managing Editor: Jean Andrews. Imprint is Alaska Northwest Books. Estab. 1968. Publishes hardcover originals. Makes outright purchase, averaging $3,000. Reports in 6 months. Book catalog for 9 × 12 SAE with 3 first-class stamps.
Nonfiction: "All titles are pictorials with text. Text usually runs separately from the pictorial treatment. Authors must be previously published and are selected to complement the pictorial essay." Query.
Recent Nonfiction Title: *Rock Art,* by Scott Thybony.
Tips: "Our subject areas include international, national, regional and state subjects. Working in conjunction with an established professional photographer to submit an idea is an excellent approach."

GREAT NORTHWEST PUBLISHING AND DISTRIBUTING COMPANY, INC., P.O. Box 21-2383, Anchorage AK 99521-2383. (907)373-0122. President: Marvin H. Clark Jr. Estab. 1979. Imprint is Alaska Outdoor Books. Publishes hardcover and trade paperback originals. Averages 5 titles/year. Receives 22-25 submissions annually. 30% of books from first-time authors; 100% of books from unagented writers. Pays 10% royalty. Publishes book an average of 1 year after acceptance. Simultaneous submissions OK. Query for electronic submissions. Reports in 2 weeks on queries. *Writer's Market* recommends allowing 2 months for reply. Free book catalog.
Nonfiction: Biography, how-to. Subjects include Alaska and hunting. "Alaskana and hunting books by very knowledgable hunters and residents of the Far North interest our firm." Query.
Tips: "Pick a target audience first, subject second. Provide crisp, clear journalistic prose."

‡GREAT QUOTATIONS PUBLISHING, 1967 Quincy Ct., Glendale Heights IL 60139. (708)582-2800. Editor/Publisher: Ringo Suek. Publishes 40 titles/year. Receives 400 queries and 300 mss/year. 50% of books from first-time authors; 80% from unagented writers. Pays 3-10% royalty on net sales or makes outright purchase of $300-3,000. Offers $200-1,200 advance. Publishes book 6 months after acceptance of ms. Simultaneous submissions OK. Query for electronic submissions. "Usually we return them, but we do not guarantee 100% that they will be returned." Reports in 2 months. Book catalog for $1.50. Manuscript guidelines for #10 SASE.
Nonfiction: Humor, illustrated book, children's/juvenile, self-help, quotes. Subjects include business and economics, child guidance/parenting, nature/environment, relition, sports, women's issues/studies. "We look for subjects with identifiable markets, appeal to the general public." Submit outline with 2 sample chapters. Reviews artwork/photos as part of freelance ms package. Writers should send photocopies, transparencies.
Recent Nonfiction Title: *As A Cat Thinketh,* by Jim Proimos (humorous illustrated); *Motivation Magic,* by Great Quotations/inhouse (quotes); *Cheatnotes on Life,* by Donna Blaurock (self-help).
Fiction: Juvenile, literary, mainstream/contemporary, mystery, picture books, young adult. "Presently, we are making the transition from gift books to a more mainstream publisher. We are open to consider all subjects as we begin to expand our product line." Submit 2 sample chapters.

Poetry: "Presently, we would be most interested in upbeat and juvenile poetry."
Tips: "Be prepared to submit final manuscript on computer disk, according to our specifications. necessary to try and format the typesetting of your manuscript to look like a finished book.)"

GREENHAVEN PRESS, INC., P.O. Box 289009, San Diego CA 92198-9009. Managing Editor: Katie de Koster. Estab. 1970. Publishes hard and softcover educational supplementary materials and (nontrade) juvenile nonfiction. Averages 10 juvenile mss published/year; all are works for hire. Receives 100 submissions/year. 50% of juvenile books from first-time authors; 100% of juvenile books from unagented writers. Makes outright purchase of $1,000-3,000. Publishes ms an average of 1 year after acceptance. Does not accept unsolicited mss. Book catalog for 9×12 SAE with 3 first-class stamps.
Nonfiction: Juvenile. "We produce tightly formatted books for young people grades 5-8. Each series has specific requirements. Potential writers should familiarize themselves with our catalog and senior high material. No unsolicited mss."

‡GREENLAWN PRESS, 107 S. Greenlawn Ave., South Bend IN 46617. (219)234-5088. Publishes trade paperback originals and reprints. Publishes 4 titles/year. Receives 10 queries and 5 mss/year. 50% of books from first-time authors; 100% from unagented writers. Pays royalty. Reports in 1 month on queries, 3 months on proposals, 2 months on mss. Book catalog free on request.
Nonfiction: Christian. "We publish Christian books only, including books on prayer, personal relationships, family life, testimonies." Submit outline.
Recent Nonfiction Title: *Fathers, Come Home*, by Bill Swindell (family).

GROSSET & DUNLAP PUBLISHERS, Imprint of the Putnam Berkley Publishing Group, 200 Madison Ave., New York NY 10016. Publisher/Vice President: Craig Walker. Estab. 1898. Imprints are Tuffy Books and Platt & Munk. Publishes hardcover and paperback originals. Averages 75 titles/year. Receives more than 3,000 submissions annually. Publishes book an average of 18 months after acceptance. Simultaneous submissions OK. Reports in 2 months.
Nonfiction: Juveniles. Submit proposal or query first. Nature and science are of interest. Looks for new ways of looking at the world of a child.
Fiction: Juveniles, picture books for 3-7 age group and some higher. Submit proposal or query first.
Tips: "Nonfiction that is particularly topical or of wide interest in the mass market; new concepts for novelty format for preschoolers; and very well-written easy readers on topics that appeal to primary graders have the best chance of selling to our firm."

‡GROUP PUBLISHING, INC., 2890 N. Monroe Ave., Box 481, Loveland CO 80538. Book Acquisitions Editor: Mike Nappa. Publishes trade paperback originals. Publishes 20-30 titles/year. Receives 200-400 queries and 300-500 mss/year. 30% of books from first-time authors; 100% from unagented writers. Pays up to 10% royalty on wholesale price or variable outright purchase. Offers up to $1,000 advance. Publishes book 12-18 months after acceptance of ms. Simultaneous submissions OK. Reports in 1-2 months on queries, 3-6 months on proposals. Book catalog for 9×12 SAE with 2 first-class stamps. Manuscript guidelines for #10 SASE.
Nonfiction: How-to, youth and children's ministry resources. Subjects include education, religion and any subjects pertinent to youth or children's ministry in a church setting. "We're an interdenominational publisher of resource materials for people who work with youth or children in a Christian church setting. We don't publish materials for use directly by youth or children (such as devotional books, workbooks or stories). Everything we do is based on concepts of active and interactive learning as described in *Why Nobody Learns Much of Anything at Church: And How to Fix It* by Thom and Joani Schultz. We need new, practical, hands-on, innovative, out-of-the-box ideas—things that no one's doing . . . yet." Submit outline and 2 sample chapters, proposal package, including introduction to the book (written as if the reader will read it), and sample activities if appropriate.
Recent Nonfiction Title: *Why Nobody Learns Much of Anything at Church: And How to Fix It*, by Thom and Joani Schultz (foundational); *Low Cost, No Cost Ideas for Youth Ministry*, (programming); *Fun Group Devotions for Children's Ministry*, (programming).

‡GROUP'S HANDS-ON™ BIBLE CURRICULUM, Group Publishing, Inc., 2890 N. Monroe Ave., Box 481, Loveland CO 80538. Book Acquisitions Editor: Mike Nappa. Publishes trade paperback originals. Publishes 24 titles/year. Receives 100-200 queries/year. 40% of books from first-time authors; 100% from unagented writers. Pays outright purchase. Publishes book 12-18 months after acceptance of ms. Simultaneous submissions OK. Reports in 3-6 months on on trial assignment submissions. Book catalog and trial assignment guidelines for 9×12 SAE with 2 first-class stamps.
Nonfiction: Preschool and elementary Sunday School curriculum based on principles of active and interactive learning. Subjects include curriculum for pre-schoolers, 1st-2nd, 3rd-4th and 5th-6th graders. "Hands-On™ Bible Curriculum is an innovative, interdenominational approach to teaching children about God. It's based on the concepts of active and interactive learning. If you're not sure what that means, read *Why Nobody Learns Much of Anything at Church: And How to Fix It* by Thom and Joani Schultz, and study a teachers guide for any Hands-On™ Bible Curriculum age group. Don't approach us without knowing who Group is and

what Hands-on™ Bible Curriculum is!" Query requesting a trial assignment.

Recent Nonfiction Title: *Why Nobody Learns Much of Anything at Church: And How to Fix It,* by Thom and Joani Schultz (foundational); *Hands-On™ Bible Curriculum (any age group),* by various (Sunday School curriculum for kids).

GROVE/ATLANTIC, INC., 841 Broadway, New York NY 10003. General interest publisher of both fiction and nonfiction. This company did not respond to our request for information. Query before submitting.

GRYPHON PUBLICATIONS, P.O. Box 209, Brooklyn NY 11228. Owner/Publisher: Gary Lovisi. Imprints are: Paperback Parade Magazine; Hardboiled Magazine; Other Worlds Magazine; Gryphon Books & Gryphon Doubles. Publishes hardcover and trade paperback originals and reprints. Publishes 10 titles/year. Receives 500 queries and 1,000 mss/year. 60% of books from first-time authors; 90% from unagented writers. Makes outright purchase by contract, price varies. Publishes book 12-18 months after acceptance of ms. Query for electronic submissions. Reports in 2 weeks on queries. *Writer's Market* recommends allowing 2 months for reply. Book catalog and ms guidelines for #10 SASE.

Nonfiction: Reference, bibliography. Subjects include hobbies, literature and book collecting. "We need well-written, well-researched articles, but query first on topic and length. Mistakes writers often make when submitting nonfiction are submitting not fully developed/researched material." Query. Reviews artwork/photos as part of freelance ms package. Writers should send photocopies (slides, transparencies may be necessary later).

Fiction: Mystery, science fiction, suspense, urban horror, hardboiled fiction. "We want cutting-edge fiction, under 3,000 words with impact!" Query or submit complete ms.

Tips: "We are very particular about novels and book-length work. A first-timer has a better chance with a short story or article. On anything over 6,000 words *do not* send manuscript, send *only* query letter about the piece with SASE."

GYLANTIC PUBLISHING COMPANY, P.O. Box 2792, Littleton CO 80161-2792. Fax: (303)727-4279. Editor: Julie Baker. Estab. 1991. Publishes hardcover and trade paperback originals. Publishes 5 titles/year. Receives 600 queries and mss/year. 50% of books from first-time authors; 100% from unagented writers. Pays 7½-12½% royalty on retail price. Publishes book 1 year after acceptance of ms. Simultaneous submissions OK. Reports in 2 months. No unsolicited mss. Manuscript guidelines for #10 SASE.

Nonfiction: Subjects include child guidance/parenting, gay/lesbian, health, women's and men's issues/studies. "We are looking for self-help and information books concerning young adults, aging America, men's issues, women's issues and minorities. No 'slice of life,' autobiographical, New Age, mystical, technically scientific, religious, art or music." Query.

● Publisher reports needs have narrowed. Concentrating on nonfiction parenting, young adult, men's and women's issues.

Tips: "If I were a writer trying to market a book today, I would learn how to write a good proposal, have my work professionally edited, select an appropriate publisher for my subject, and study the market of my subject."

HALF HALT PRESS, INC., 6416 Burkittsville Rd., Middletown MD 21769-7006. (301)371-9110. Fax: (301)371-9211. Publisher: Elizabeth Carnes. Estab. 1986. Publishes hardcover and trade paperback originals and reprints (90% originals, 10% reprints). Averages 15 titles/year. Receives 50+ submissions/year. 50% of books from first-time authors; 50% from unagented authors. Pays 10-12½% royalty on retail price. Offers advance by agreement. Publishes book an average of 1 year after acceptance. Reports in 1 month on queries. *Writer's Market* recommends allowing 2 months for reply. Book catalog for 6×9 SAE with 2 first-class stamps.

Nonfiction: Instructional: Horse and equestrian related subjects only. "We need serious instructional works by authorities in the field on horse-related topics, broadly defined." Query. Reviews artwork/photos as part of ms package.

Tips: "Writers have the best chance selling us well written, unique works that teach serious horse people how to do something better. If I were a writer trying to market a book today, I would offer a straightforward presentation, letting work speak for itself, without hype or hard sell. Allow publisher to contact writer, without frequent calling to check status. They haven't forgotten the writer but may have many different proposals at hand; frequent calls to 'touch base,' multiplied by the number of submissions, become an annoyance. As the publisher/author relationship becomes close and is based on working well together, early impressions may be important, even to the point of being a consideration in acceptance for publication."

ALEXANDER HAMILTON INSTITUTE, 70 Hilltop Rd., Ramsey NJ 07446-1119. (201)825-3377. Fax: (201)825-8696. Editor-in-Chief: Brian L.P. Zevnik. Estab. 1909. Publishes 3-ring binder and paperback originals. Averages 12 titles/year. Receives 150 submissions annually. 40% of books from first-time authors; 90% from unagented writers. "We pay advance against negotiated royalty or straight fee (no royalty)." Offers average $3,000 advance. Publishes book an average of 10 months after acceptance. Simultaneous submissions OK. Reports in 1 month on queries, 2 months on mss.

Nonfiction: Executive/management books for 2 audiences. The first is overseas, upper-level manager. "We need how-to and skills building books. *No* traditional management texts or academic treatises." The second audience is US personnel executives and high-level management. Subject is legal personnel matters. "These books combine court case research and practical application of defensible programs." Query or submit outline or synopsis. Preferred form is outline, 3 paragraphs on each chapter, examples of lists, graphics, cases.

Tips: "We sell exclusively by direct mail to managers and executives around the world. A writer must know his/her field and be able to communicate practical systems and programs."

HANCOCK HOUSE PUBLISHERS LTD., 1431 Harrison Ave., Box 1, Blaine WA 98231-0959. (604)538-1114. Fax: (604)538-2262. Publisher: David Hancock. Estab. 1971. Publishes hardcover and trade paperback originals and reprints. Averages 12 titles/year. Receives 400 submissions annually. 50% of books from first-time authors; 100% from unagented writers. Pays 10% maximum royalty on wholesale price. Simultaneous submissions OK. Publishes book an average of 6 months after acceptance. Reports in 6 months. Book catalog free on request.

Nonfiction: Pacific Northwest history and biography, nature guides, native culture, natural history.

HARCOURT BRACE & COMPANY, 6277 Sea Harbor Dr., Orlando FL 32887. Divisions include Harcourt Brace Children's Books Division and Holt, Rinehart & Winston. "The trade division of Harcourt Brace & Company does *not* accept any unsolicited manuscripts."

HARCOURT BRACE & COMPANY, Children's Books Division, 1250 Sixth Ave., San Diego CA 92101. (619) 699-6810. Contact: Manuscript Submissions. Imprints include Harcourt Brace Children's Books, Gulliver Books, Browndeer Press, Voyager and Odyssey Paperbacks, and Jane Yolen Books. Publishes hardcover originals and trade paperback reprints. Considers only query letters and agented mss.

HARPER SAN FRANCISCO, Division of HarperCollins, 3rd floor, 1160 Battery St., San Francisco CA 94111-1213. (415)477-4400. Fax: (415)477-4444. Publisher: Thomas Grady. Estab. 1817. Publishes hardcover and trade paperback originals and trade paperback reprints. Publishes 180 titles/year. Receives about 10,000 submissions/year. 5% of books from first-time authors; 50% from unagented writers. Pays royalty. Publishes book an average of 18 months after acceptance. Simultaneous (if notified) submissions OK. Reports in 2 months on queries. Free book catalog and ms guidelines.

Nonfiction: Biography, how-to, reference, self-help. Subjects include addiction/recovery, philosophy, psychology, religion, women's issues/studies, theology, New Consciousness, anthropology, spirituality, gay and lesbian studies, new science. Query or submit outline and sample chapters.

Recent Nonfiction Title: *Men and the Water of Life*, by Michael Meade.

HARPERCOLLINS PUBLISHERS, 10 E. 53rd St., New York NY 10022. (212)207-7000. Executive Managing Editor: Tracy Behar. Imprints include Harper Adult Trade; Harper San Francisco (religious books only); Harper Perennial; Harper Reference; Basic Books; Harper Business; Harper Torchbooks; Harper Paperbacks; Harper Audio. Publishes hardcover and paperback originals and paperback reprints. Trade publishes more than 500 titles/year. Pays standard royalties. Advance negotiable. *No unsolicited queries or mss.* Reports on solicited queries in 6 weeks. *Writer's Market* recommends allowing 2 months for reply.

● HarperCollins will be releasing its first CD-ROM product, *The American Sign Language Dictionary*, in September 1994.

Nonfiction: Americana, animals, art, biography, business/economics, current affairs, cookbooks, health, history, how-to, humor, music, nature, philosophy, politics, psychology, reference, religion, science, self-help, sociology, sports, travel.

Recent Nonfiction Title: *Reengineering the Corporation*.

Fiction: Adventure, fantasy, gothic, historical, mystery, science fiction, suspense, western, literary. "We look for a strong story line and exceptional literary talent."

Recent Fiction Title: *Downtown*.

Tips: "We do not accept any unsolicited material."

HARTLEY & MARKS, P.O. Box 147, Point Roberts WA 98281. (206)945-2017. Editorial Director: Sue Tauber. Estab. 1973. Publishes hardcover and trade paperback originals. Averages 8-10 titles/year. Receives 700 submissions/year. 80% of books from first-time authors; 95% from unagented writers. Pays 7-10% royalty on retail price. Reports in 2 months. Book catalog for SASE.

Nonfiction: How-to, self-help, technical. Subjects include agriculture/gardening (organic), building, healthy lifestyles, preventive and holistic medicine, useful crafts, nature/environment (practical how-to), psychology self-help, typography, translations of aforementioned subjects. No metaphysical books, autobiography or recipe books. Query by letter or submit outline and sample chapters.

THE HARVARD COMMON PRESS, 535 Albany St., Boston MA 02118-2500. (617)423-5803. Fax: (617)695-9794. President: Bruce P. Shaw. Managing Editor: Dan Rosenberg. Imprint is Gambit Books. Estab. 1976.

Publishes hardcover and trade paperback originals and reprints. Averages 8 titles/year. Receives 1,000 submissions annually. 50% of books from first-time authors; 75% of books from unagented writers. Average print order for a first book is 7,500. Pays royalty. Offers average $2,000 advance. Publishes book an average of 9 months after acceptance. Simultaneous submissions OK. Reports in 2 months. Book catalog for 9 × 12 SAE with 3 first-class stamps. Manuscript guidelines for SASE.
● Harvard Common Press has changed subject focus from family matters to childcare.
Nonfiction: Travel, cookbook, how-to, health, reference and self-help. Emphasis on travel, childcare and cooking. "We want strong, practical books that help people gain control over a particular area of their lives, whether it's family matters, business or financial matters, health, careers, food or travel. An increasing percentage of our list is made up of books about family matters; in this area we are looking for authors who are knowledgeable, if not experts, and who can offer a different approach to the subject. We are open to good nonfiction proposals that show evidence of strong organization and writing, and clearly demonstrate a need in the marketplace. First-time authors are welcome." Accepts nonfiction translations. Submit outline and 1-3 sample chapters. Reviews artwork/photos.
Recent Nonfiction Title: *Texas Home Cooking*, by Cheryl and Bill Jamison.

HARVEST HOUSE PUBLISHERS, 1075 Arrowsmith, Eugene OR 97402-9197. (503)343-0123. Fax: (503)342-6410. Vice President of Editorial: Eileen L. Mason. Manuscript Coordinator: LaRae Weikert. Estab. 1974. Publishes hardcover, trade paperback and mass market originals and reprints. Averages 70-80 titles/year. Receives 3,500 submissions annually. 10% of books from first-time authors; 90% from unagented writers. Pays 14-18% royalty on wholesale price. Publishes book an average of 1 year after acceptance. Simultaneous submissions OK. Reports in 10 weeks. Book catalog for 9 × 12 SAE with 2 first-class stamps. Manuscript guidelines for SASE.
● Harvest House is no longer interested in seeing manuscripts dealing with counseling.
Nonfiction: Juvenile (picture books ages 2-8; ages 9-12), self-help, current issues, women's and family on Evangelical Christian religion. No cookbooks, theses, dissertations, music, or poetry. Query or submit outline and sample chapters.
Recent Nonfiction Title: *Embracing God*, by David Swartz.
Fiction: Historical, mystery, religious. No short stories. Query or submit outline/synopsis and sample chapters.
Recent Fiction Title: *The Reckoning*, by James Byron Huggins.
Tips: "Audience is primarily women ages 25-40 — evangelical Christians of all denominations."

HASTINGS HOUSE, Eagle Publishing Corp., 141 Halstead Ave., Mamaroneck NY 10543-2652. (914)835-4005. Fax: (914)835-1037. Editor/Publisher: Hy Steirman. Publishes hardcover and trade paperback originals and reprints. Publishes 12 titles/year. Receives 350 queries and 125 mss/year. 5% of books from first-time authors; 40% from unagented writers. Pays 8-10% royalty on retail price. Offers $1,000-10,000 advance. Publishes book 10 months after acceptance of ms. Reports in 1 month. *Writer's Market* recommends allowing 2 months for reply. Book catalog for SAE with 3 first-class stamps.
● Hastings House is putting less emphasis on children's titles.
Nonfiction: Biography, coffee table book, cookbook, how-to, humor, children's/juvenile, reference, self-help, consumer. Subjects include business and economics, cooking, foods and nutrition, health/medicine, psychology, travel, writing. "We are looking for books that address consumer needs." Query or submit outline.
Recent Nonfiction Title: *Do Black Women Hate Black Men?*, by A.L. Reynolds III.

THE HAWORTH PRESS, INC., 10 Alice St., Binghampton NY 13904-1580. (607)722-5857. Managing Editor: Bill Palmer. Estab. 1973. Imprints are Harrington Park Press; Food Products Press; Pharmaceutical Products Press; International Business Press; The Haworth Medical Press; The Haworth Pastoral Press. Publishes hardcover and trade paperback originals. Firm publishes 75 titles/year; each imprint publishes 5-10 titles/year. Receives 110 queries and 46 mss/year. 20% of books from first-time authors, 98% from unagented writers. Pays 7 1/2-12% royalty on wholesale price. Publishes book 16 months after acceptance of ms. Reports in 3 months on mss. Book catalog and ms guidelines free on request.
Nonfiction: Reference, textbook, popular trade. Subjects include agriculture/horticulture, business and economics, cooking/foods/nutrition, gay/lesbian, health/medicine, psychology, religion, sociology, women's issues/studies, pharmacy. Submit outline and 3 sample chapters. Reviews artwork/photos as part of freelance ms package. Writers should send camera-ready artwork, b&w photos.

HAY HOUSE, INC., P.O. Box 6204, Carson CA 90749-6204. (310)605-0601. Editorial Director: Jill Kramer. Estab. 1985. Imprint is Lulu's Library (children's division). Publishes hardcover and trade paperback originals, and trade paperback reprints. Firm publishes 10 titles/year; imprint averages 10 titles/year. Receives approximately 350 submissions/year. 20% of books are from first-time authors; 25% from unagented writers. Pays 8-12% royalty. Offers $0-5,000 average advance. Publishes book an average of 8-15 months after acceptance. Simultaneous submissions OK. Reports in 2 months. Free book catalog.
Nonfiction: Biography, how-to, humor, juvenile, reference, self-help. Subjects include ecology, healing power of pets, business and economics/self-help, cooking, foods and nutrition, education/self-help, gardening/

environment, gay/lesbian, health/medicine, money/finance/self-help, nature/environment/ecology, philoso-phy/New Age, psychology/self-help, recreation, religion, science/self-help, sociology/self-help, women's is-sues/studies. "Hay House is interested in a variety of subjects so long as they have a positive self-help/metaphysical slant to them. No poetry or negative concepts that are not conducive to helping/healing our-selves or our planet." Query or submit outline and sample chapters with SASE. Reviews artwork/photos as part of ms package if duplicate.

Tips: "Our audience is concerned with ecology, our planet, the healing properties of love, self-help, and teaching children loving principles. Hay House has noticed that our reader is interested in taking more control of his/her life. A writer has a good chance of selling us a book with a unique, positive, and healing message. If I were a writer trying to market a book today, I would research the market thoroughly to make sure that there weren't already too many books on the subject I was interested in writing about. Then I would make sure that I had a unique slant on my idea."

‡HEALTH PRESS, P.O. Box 1388, Santa Fe NM 87504. (505)982-9373. Editor: Corie Conwell. Publishes hardcover and trade paperback originals. Publishes 4 titles/year. Receives 80 queries and 20 mss/year. 90% of books from first-time authors; 90% from unagented writers. Pays 10-12½% royalty on wholesale price. Publishes book 1 year after acceptance of ms. Accepts simultaneous submissions. Reports in 2 weeks on proposals. *Writer's Market* recommends allowing 2 months for reply. Book catalog and ms guidelines free on request.
Nonfiction: Subjects include health/medicine, patient education. "We want books by health care profession-als on cutting-edge patient education topics." Submit proposal package, including résumé, outline and 3 complete chapters. Reviews artwork/photos as part of ms package. Writers should send photocopies.
Recent Nonfiction Title: *Beautiful Again: Restoring Your Image & Enhancing Body Changes,* by Jan Willis.

HENDRICK-LONG PUBLISHING CO., INC., P.O. Box 25123, Dallas TX 75225-1123. (214)358-4677. Contact: Joann Long. Estab. 1969. Publishes hardcover and trade paperback originals and hardcover reprints. Aver-ages 8 titles/year. Receives 500 submissions/year. 90% of books from unagented writers. Pays royalty on selling price. Publishes book an average of 18 months after acceptance. Reports in 1 month on queries, 2 months if more than query sent. *Writer's Market* recommends allowing 2 months for reply. Book catalog for 9 × 12 SAE with 4 first-class stamps. Manuscript guidelines for #10 SASE.
Nonfiction: Biography, juvenile. Subject mainly Texas focused material for children and young adults. Query or submit outline and 2 sample chapters. Reviews artwork/photos as part of ms package; copies of material are acceptable. Do not send original art.
Recent Nonfiction Title: *Hats Are For Watering Horses: Why the Cowboy Dressed That Way,* by Mary Blount Christian.
Fiction: Adventure, historical, mystery, western (all Texas juvenile). Query or submit outline/synopsis and 2 sample chapters.
Recent Fiction Title: *New Medicine,* by Jeanne Williams.

HENDRICKSON PUBLISHERS, INC., 137 Summit St., P.O. Box 3473, Peabody MA 01961-3473. Acquisitions Editor: Phil Anderson. Estab. 1983. Publishes hardcover and trade paperback originals and reprints. Aver-ages 8-12 titles/year. Receives 100-125 submissions annually. 3% of books from first-time authors; 100% from unagented writers. Publishes book an average of 8 months after acceptance. Simultaneous submissions OK (if so notified). Reports in 2 months. Book catalog and ms guidelines for SASE.
Nonfiction: Religious, principally academic. "We will consider any quality manuscript within the area of religion specifically related to biblical studies and related fields. Popularly written manuscripts, poetry, plays or fiction are not acceptable." Submit outline and sample chapters.

VIRGIL W. HENSLEY, INC., 6116 E. 32nd St., Tulsa OK 74135-5494. (918)664-8520. Editor: Terri Kalfas. Estab. 1965. Publishes hardcover and paperback originals. Publishes 5-10 titles/year. Receives 600 submis-sions/year. 50% of books from first-time authors; 50% from unagented writers. Pays 5% minimum royalty on gross sales or makes outright purchase of $250 minimum for study aids. Publishes ms an average of 18 months after acceptance. Reports in 2 months on queries. Manuscript guidelines for #10 SASE.
Nonfiction: Bible study curriculum. Subjects include child guidance/parenting, money/finance, religion, women's issues/studies. "We look for subjects that lend themselves to long-term Bible studies—prayer, proph-ecy, family, faith, etc. We do not want to see anything non-Christian." Actively seeking nonfiction other than Bible studies. No new age, poetry, plays, sermon collections. Query with synopsis and sample chapters.
Recent Nonfiction Title: *Dear Christian Friends,* by Daisy Tweeddale.
Fiction: Christianity must be germane to the plot without sermonizing.
Tips: "Submit something that crosses denominational lines directed toward the large Christian market, not small specialized groups. We serve an interdenominational market—all Christian persuasions. No new age."

HERALD PRESS, Imprint of Mennonite Publishing House, 616 Walnut Ave., Scottdale PA 15683-1999. (412)887-8500. Fax: (412)887-3111. Book Editor: David Garber. Estab. 1908. Publishes hardcover and trade paperback originals and reprints. Averages 30 titles/year. Receives 1,000 submissions annually. 15% of books from first-time authors; 95% from unagented writers. Pays royalty of 10-12% retail. Advance seldom given. Publishes book an average of 1 year after acceptance. Query for electronic submissions. Reports in 3 months. Book catalog for 50¢.

Nonfiction: Christian inspiration, Bible study, current issues, missions and evangelism, peace and justice, family life, Christian ethics and theology, ethnic (Amish, Mennonite), self-help, juvenile (mostly ages 8-14). No drama or poetry. Query or submit outline and 2 sample chapters. Reviews artwork/photos as part of ms package.

Recent Nonfiction Title: *Cherish the Earth*, by Janice E. and Donald R. Kirk.

Fiction: Religious. Needs some fiction for youth and adults reflecting themes similar to those listed in nonfiction, also "compelling stories that treat social and Christian issues in a believable manner." No fantasy. Query or submit outline/synopsis and sample chapters.

Recent Fiction Title: *Deborah*, by James R. Shott.

Tips: "We currently have a surplus of juvenile book proposals. We have been more selective to make sure of market for proposed book."

HERALD PUBLISHING HOUSE, Division of Reorganized Church of Jesus Christ of Latter Day Saints, 3225 South Noland Rd., P.O. Box 1770, Independence MO 64055. (816)252-5010. Fax: (816)252-3976. Editorial Director: Roger Yarrington. Estab. 1860. Imprints include Independence Press and Graceland Park Press. Estab. 1860. Publishes hardcover and trade paperback originals and reprints. Averages 30 titles/year. Receives 70 submissions annually. 20% from first-time authors; 100% of books from unagented writers. Pays 5% maximum royalty on retail price. Offers average $400 advance. Publishes book an average of 14 months after acceptance. Reports in 3 weeks on queries, 2 months on mss. Book catalog for 9 × 12 SASE.

Nonfiction: Self-help, religious (RLDS Church). Subjects include Americana, history, religion. Herald House focus: history and doctrine of RLDS Church. Independence Press focus: regional studies (Midwest, Missouri). No submissions unrelated to RLDS Church (Herald House) or to Midwest regional studies (Independence Press). Query. Use *Chicago Manual of Style*. Reviews artwork/photos as part of ms package.

Tips: "The audience for Herald Publishing House is members of the Reorganized Church of Jesus Christ of Latter Day Saints; for Independence Press, persons living in the Midwest or interested in the Midwest; for Graceland Park Press, readers interested in academic and exploratory studies on religious topics."

HERITAGE BOOKS, INC., 1540-E Pointer Ridge Place, Bowie MD 20716-1859. (301)390-7708. Fax: (301)390-7193. Editorial Director: Elaine Fiehrer. Estab. 1978. Publishes hardcover and paperback originals and reprints. Averages 100 titles/year. Receives 300 submissions annually. 25% of books from first-time authors; 100% from unagented writers. Pays 10% royalty on retail price. No advance. Publishes book an average of 6 months after acceptance. Simultaneous submissions OK. Reports in 1 month. *Writer's Market* recommends allowing 2 months for reply. Book catalog for SAE.

Nonfiction: "We particularly desire nonfiction titles dealing with history and genealogy including how-to and reference works, as well as conventional histories and genealogies. Ancestries of contemporary people are not of interest. The titles should be either of general interest or restricted to Eastern US and Midwest. Material dealing with the present century is usually not of interest. We prefer writers to query or submit an outline." Reviews artwork/photos.

Tips: "The quality of the book is of prime importance; next is its relevance to our fields of interest."

HEYDAY BOOKS, Box 9145, Berkeley CA 94709-9145. (415)549-3564. Publisher: Malcolm Margolin. Estab. 1974. Publishes hardcover and trade paperback originals, trade paperback reprints. Averages 4-6 titles/year. Receives 200 submissions annually. 50% of books from first-time authors; 75% from unagented writers. Pays 8-15% royalty on net price. Publishes book an average of 8 months after acceptance. Reports in 1 week on queries, up to 5 weeks on mss. Book catalog for 7 × 9 SAE with 2 first-class stamps.

Nonfiction: Books about California only: how-to, reference. Subjects include Americana, history, nature, travel. "We publish books about native Americans, natural history, history, and recreation, with a strong California focus." Query with outline and synopsis. Reviews artwork/photos.

Tips: "Give good value, and avoid gimmicks. We are accepting *only* nonfiction books with a California focus."

HIGH PLAINS PRESS, P.O. Box 123, 539 Cassa Rd., Glendo WY 82213. Publisher: Nancy Curtis. Publishes hardcover and trade paperback originals. Publishes 4 titles/year. Receives 300 queries and 200 mss/year. 80% of books from first-time authors; 95% from unagented writers. Pays 10-15% royalty on wholesale price. Offers $100-300 advance. Publishes book 2 years after acceptance. Simultaneous submissions OK. Query for electronic submissions. Prefers Mac Word. Reports in 1 month on queries, 1 month on proposals, 3 months on mss. Book catalog and ms guidelines for #10 SASE.

Nonfiction: Biography, Western Americana, Americana, art/architecture, history, nature/environment, regional, travel. "We plan to focus on books of the American West, particularly history." Submit outline. Reviews artwork/photos as part of freelance ms package. Writer should send photocopies.

Recent Nonfiction Title: *The Wyoming Lynching of Cattle Kate, 1889*, by George W. Hufsmith.

Poetry: "We only seek poetry closely tied to the Rockies. Poets should not submit single poems." Query; submit complete ms.

Recent Poetry Title: *No Roof But Sky*, by Jane Candia Coleman (Western, free verse).

‡**HIGHSMITH PRESS**, P.O. Box 800, Ft. Atkinson WI 53538-0800. (414)863-9571. Publisher: Donald J. Sager. Publishes hardcover originals. Publishes 18-20 titles/year. Receives 500-600 queries and 400-500 mss/year. 20% of books from first-time authors; 100% from unagented writers. Pays 6-12% royalty on wholesale price. Offers $250-2,000 advance. Publishes book 6 months after acceptance of ms. Accepts simultaneous submissions. Query for electronic submissions. Reports in 1 month on queries, 2 months on proposals, 3 months on mss. Book catalog and ms guidelines free on request.
Nonfiction: Children's/juvenile, reference. Subjects include education, language/literature, multicultural, professional (library science), teacher activity. "We are primarily interested in reference and library professional books, multicultural resources for youth, and curricular and activity books for teachers and others who work with preschool through high school youth." Query with outline and 1-2 sample chapters. Reviews artwork/photos as part of ms package. Writers should send transparencies.
Recent Nonfiction Title: *Guide to Multicultural Resources*, edited by Charles Taylor (reference).
Fiction: Picture books. "Prefer children's fiction with illustrations—strong emphasis on African, Hispanic, Asian and Native American authors, illustrators and topics." Query with entire ms and art for picture books; synopsis and 2 chapters for young adult fiction.
Recent Fiction Title: *Women Working A to Z*, by Maria Kunstadter.

HIPPOCRENE BOOKS INC., 171 Madison Ave., New York NY 10016. (212)685-4371. President: George Blagowidow. Estab. 1971. Publishes hardcover and trade paperback originals. Averages 100 titles/year. Receives 250 submissions annually. 10% of books from first-time authors; 95% from unagented writers. Pays 6-10% royalty on retail price. Offers $2,000 advance. Publishes book an average of 16 months after acceptance. Simultaneous submissions OK. Reports in 2 months. Book catalog for 9×12 SAE with 5 first-class stamps. Manuscript guidelines for #10 SASE.
Nonfiction: Reference. Subjects include foreign language, ethnic travel, military history, dictionaries. Submit outline and 2 sample chapters.
Recent Nonfiction Titles: *Terrible Innocence*, by Mark Coburn.
Tips: "Our recent successes in publishing general books considered midlist by larger publishers is making us more of a general trade publisher. We continue to do well with reference books like dictionaries, atlases and language studies. We ask for proposal, sample chapter, and table of contents. We then ask for material if we are interested."

HOLMES & MEIER PUBLISHERS, INC., East Building, 160 Broadway, New York NY 10038. (212)374-0100. Fax: (212)374-1313. Publisher: Miriam H. Holmes. Editor: Sheila Friedling. Executive Editor: Katharine Turok. Estab. 1969. Imprint is Africana Publishing Co. Publishes hardcover and paperback originals. Publishes 30 titles/year. Pays royalty. Publishes book an average of 18 months after acceptance. Reports in up to 6 months. Send SASE. Free book catalog.
Nonfiction: Africana, art, biography, business/economics, history, Judaica, Latin American studies, literary criticism, politics, reference, women's studies. Accepts translations. "We are noted as an academic publishing house and are pleased with our reputation of excellence in the field. However, we are also expanding our list to include books of more general interest." Query first and submit outline, sample chapters, curriculum vitae and idea of intended market/audience.

HENRY HOLT & COMPANY, INC., 115 W. 18th St., New York NY 10011. Imprints include Owl Books, MIS: Press Inc. and Twenty-First Century Books. General interest publisher of both fiction and nonfiction. This company did not respond to our request for information. Query before submitting.

HOME EDUCATION PRESS, P.O. Box 1083, Tonasket WA 98855. (509)486-1351. Publisher: Helen Hegener. Publishes trade paperback originals. Publishes 6-8 titles/year. Receives 20-40 queries and 10-12 mss/year. 95% of books from first-time authors; 95% from unagented writers. Pays 10% royalty on retail price. Publishes book 1 year after acceptance of ms. Query for electronic submissions. Reports in 1 month on queries. *Writer's Market* recommends allowing 2 months for reply. Book catalog free on request. Manuscript guidelines for #10 SASE.
Nonfiction: How-to, education; specifically homeschooling. Subjects include child guidance/parenting, education and homeschooling. Query. Reviews artwork/photos as part of freelance ms package as appropriate. Writers should send photocopies.
Tips: "We are not interested in any books not directly relating to homeschooling." Mistake writers often make when submitting nonfiction is "submitting curriculum or 'how to teach. . .' books. We are *not* interested in new ideas for teaching kids to read or write. We're more interested in real life experiences than academic expertise."

HOUGHTON MIFFLIN CO., Adult Trade Division, 222 Berkeley St., Boston MA 02116-3764. General interest publisher of both fiction and nonfiction. This division of Houghton Mifflin did not respond to our request for information. Query before submitting.

HOUGHTON MIFFLIN CO., Children's Trade Books, 222 Berkeley St., Boston MA 02116-3764. Submissions Coordinator: Michele Ganter. Estab. 1864. Publishes hardcover originals and trade paperback reprints (picture books and novels). Averages 60 titles/year. Pays standard royalty. Offers advance. Reports in 2 months. Enclose SASE.
Nonfiction: Submit outline/synopsis and sample chapters. No dot-matrix print-outs. Reviews artwork/photos as part of ms package.
Recent Nonfiction Title: *Shaker Home*, by Raymond Bial.
Fiction: Submit complete ms.
Recent Fiction Title: *The Giver*, by Lois Lowry.

HOWELL PRESS, INC., Suite 2, 1147 River Rd., Charlottesville VA 22901-4172. (804)977-4006. President: Ross A. Howell Jr. Estab. 1985. Firm averages 6 titles/year. Receives 500 submissions/year. 10% of books from first-time authors; 80% from unagented writers. Pays 5-7% on net retail price. "We generally offer an advance, but amount differs with each project and is generally negotiated with authors on a case-by-case basis." Publishes book an average of 18 months after acceptance. Reports in 2 months. Book catalog for 9 × 12 SAE with 4 first-class stamps.
Nonfiction: Illustrated books, historical texts. Subjects include aviation, military history, cooking, maritime history, motorsports, gardening. "Generally open to most ideas, as long as writing is accessible to average adult reader. Our line is targeted, so it would be advisable to look over our catalog before querying to better understand what Howell Press does." Query. Submit outline and sample chapters. Reviews artwork/photos as part of ms package. Manuscripts submitted without return postage will not be returned.
Tips: "Focus of our program has been illustrated books, but we will also consider nonfiction manuscripts that would not be illustrated. Selections limited to history, transportation, cooking and gardening."

HOWELLS HOUSE, Box 9546, Washington DC 20016-9546. (202)333-2182. Publisher: W.D. Howells. Estab. 1988. Imprints are The Compass Press; Whalesback Books. Publishes hardcover and trade paperback originals and reprints. Firm publishes 4 titles/year; each imprint publishes 2-3 titles/year. Receives 2,000 queries and 300 mss/year. 50% of books from first-time authors; 60% from unagented writers. Pays 15-20% net royalty or makes outright purchase. May offer advance. Publishes book 8 months after ms development completed. Reports in 2 months on proposals.
 • Howells House no longer publishes coffee table books or humorous fiction.
Nonfiction: Biography, illustrated book, textbook. Subjects include Americana, anthropology/archaeology, art/architecture, business and economics, education, government/politics, history, military/war, photography, science, sociology, translation. Query.
Fiction: Historical, literary and mainstream/contemporary. Query.
Tips: "Our interests will focus on institutions and institutional change."

HRD PRESS, INC., 22 Amherst Rd., Amherst MA 01002. (413)253-3488. Fax: (413)253-3490. Publisher: Robert W. Carkhuff. Estab. 1970. Publishes hardcover and trade paperback originals. Averages 15-20 titles/year. Receives 300-400 submissions/year. 25% of books from first-time authors; 100% from unagented writers. Pays 10-15% royalty on wholesale price. Offers $1,000 average advance. Publishes book an average of 6 months after acceptance. Simultaneous submissions OK. Reports in 1 month on queries. *Writer's Market* recommends allowing 2 months for reply. Book catalog and ms guidelines free.
Nonfiction: Reference, software, technical. Subjects include business. "We are looking for mostly business oriented titles, training and the development of human resources. Submit outline and samples chapters.
Tips: "We are no longer seeking juvenile nonfiction or psychology titles."

HUDSON HILLS PRESS, INC., Suite 1308, 230 Fifth Ave., New York NY 10001-7704. (212)889-3090. Fax: (212)889-3091. President/Editorial Director: Paul Anbinder. Estab. 1978. Publishes hardcover and paperback originals. Averages 10 titles/year. Receives 50-100 submissions annually. 15% of books from first-time authors; 90% from unagented writers. Average print order for a first book is 3,000. Offers royalties of 4-6% on retail price. Average advance: $3,500. Publishes book an average of 1 year after acceptance. Simultaneous submissions OK. Reports in 2 months. Book catalog for 6 × 9 SAE with 2 first-class stamps.
Nonfiction: Art, photography. "We are only interested in publishing books about art and photography, including monographs." Query first, then submit outline and sample chapters. Reviews artwork/photos as part of ms package.

HUMAN SERVICES INSTITUTE, INC., Apt. 7-H, 165 W. 91st St, New York NY 10024-1357. (212)769-9738. Senior Editor: Dr. Lee Marvin Joiner. Estab. 1988. Publishes hardcover and trade paperback originals. Averages 10-12 titles/year. Receives 100 submissions/year. 95% of books are from first-time authors; 100% from unagented writers. Pays 7-15% royalty on wholesale price. Publishes book an average of 9 months after acceptance. Query for electronic submissions. Reports in 1 month on queries, 2 months on mss. Book catalog and ms guidelines free.
Nonfiction: Self-help. Subjects include child guidance/parenting, psychology, women's issues/studies. "We are looking for books on divorce, cocaine, cults, sexual victimization, alternative medicine, mental health,

secular recovery and violence. No autobiographical accounts." Query or submit outline/synopsis and sample chapters.

Tips: "Our audience is made up of clinics, hospitals, prisons, mental health centers, human service professionals and general readers."

HUMDINGER BOOKS, #115, 1889 Preston White Dr., Reston VA 22091. (703)620-1100. Publisher: Jennifer Kuchta. Publishes hardcover, trade paperback and mass market paperback originals. Publishes 6-10 titles/year. Payment "negotiated profit sharing—case-by-case." Publishes book 3-6 months after acceptance of ms. Simultaneous submissions OK. Query for electronic submissions. Reports in 1 month.
Nonfiction: Personal development, self-help, small business and entrepreneurialism. "We are looking for unique works with a niche appeal." Query. All unsolicited mss returned unopened.
Recent Nonfiction Title: *The Power of Your Actions*, by James R. Ball.

HUNTER PUBLISHING, INC., 300 Raritan Center Pkwy., Edison NJ 08818. President: Michael Hunter. Editor: Kim Antre. Estab. 1985. Averages 100 titles/year. Receives 300 submissions annually. 10% of books from first-time authors; 75% from unagented writers. Pays royalty. Offers $0-2,000 average advance. Publishes book on average 5 months after acceptance. Simultaneous submissions OK. Query for electronic submissions. Prefers final text submission on IBM disk. Reports in 3 weeks on queries, 1 month on ms. *Writer's Market* recommends allowing 2 months for reply. Book catalog for #10 SAE with 4 first-class stamps.
Nonfiction: Reference. Subjects include travel. "We need travel guides to areas covered by few competitors: Caribbean Islands, South and Central America, Mexico, regional US from an active 'adventure' perspective." No personal travel stories or books not directed to travelers. Query or submit outline/synopsis and sample chapters. Reviews artwork/photos as part of ms package.
Tips: "Study what's out there, pick some successful models, and identify ways they can be made more appealing. We need active adventure-oriented guides and more specialized guides for travelers in search of the unusual."

HUNTINGTON HOUSE PUBLISHERS, P.O. Box 53788, Lafayette LA 70505-3788.(318)237-7049. Editor-in-Chief: Mark Anthony. Estab. 1982. Publishes hardcover, trade paperback and mass market paperback originals, trade paperback reprints. Averages 25-30 titles/year. Receives 1,500 submissions annually. 25% of books from first-time authors; 90% from unagented writers. Average print order for a first book is 5,000-10,000. Pays up to 10% royalty on sale price. Publishes book an average of 1 year after acceptance. Simultaneous submissions OK. Query for electronic submissions. Reports in 4 months. Free book catalog and ms guidelines.
Nonfiction: Current social and political issues, biographies, self-help, inspirational, children's books. Query with descriptive outline.
Tips: "Write clear, crisp and exciting manuscripts that grab the reader. The company's goal is to educate and keep readers abreast of critical current events. Published authors should expect a heavy publicity schedule."

HYPERION, division of Disney Book Publishing, Inc., 114 Fifth Ave., New York NY 10011. General interest publisher of both fiction and nonfiction. This company did not respond to our request for information. Query before submitting.

ICS PUBLICATIONS, Institute of Carmelite Studies, 2131 Lincoln Rd. NE, Washington DC 20002. (202)832-8489. Editorial Director: Steven Payne, O.C.D. Publishes hardcover and trade paperback originals and reprints. Publishes 8 titles/year. Receives 10-20 queries and 10 mss/year. 10% of books from first-time authors; 90-100% from unagented writers. Pays 2-6% royalty on retail price or makes outright purchase. Offers $500 advance. Publishes book an average of 1-2 years after acceptance. Accepts simultaneous submissions if so noted. Query for electronic submissions. Reports in 2 months on proposals. Book catalog for 7×10 SAE and 2 first-class stamps; writer's guidelines for #10 SASE.
Nonfiction: Religious (should relate to Carmelite spirituality and prayer). "We are looking for significant works on Carmelite history, spirituality, and main figures (Saints Theresa, John of the Cross, Therese of Lisieux, etc.). Also open to more general works on prayer, spiritual direction, etc. Too often we receive proposals for works that merely repeat what has already been done, or are too technical for a general audience, or have little to do with the Carmelite tradition and spirit." Query or submit outline with 1 sample chapter.
Tips: "Our audience consists of those interested in the Carmelite tradition or in developing their life of prayer and spirituality."

‡**IDE HOUSE PUBLISHERS**, 4631 Harvey Dr., Mesquite TX 75150. (214)686-5332. Senior Executive Vice President: Ryan Idol. Publishes hardcover and trade paperback originals. Publishes 10 titles/year. Receives 300 queries and 500 mss/year. 70% of books from first-time authors; 100% from unagented writers. Pays 1-7% royalty on retail price. Publishes book 4 months after acceptance of ms. No simultaneous submissions. Query for electronic submissions. Reports in 1 month on queries and proposals; 4 months on mss. Book catalog for 6×9 SAE with 5 first-class stamps. Manuscript guidelines for #10 SASE.

Nonfiction: Women's history. Subjects include gay/lesbian, government/politics (liberal only), history, women's issues/studies. "We accept only nonsexist/nonhomophobic scholarly works." Query with outline and 2 sample chapters. All unsolicited mss are returned unopened.
Recent Nonfiction Title: *Politics of Women's Health*, by Karen Levy (women and politics).

‡IDEALS CHILDREN'S BOOKS, Imprint of Hambleton-Hill Publishing, Inc., 1501 County Hospital Rd., Nashville TN 37218. Contact: Copy Editor. Publishes hardcover and trade paperback originals. Publishes 30 titles/year. Receives 200 queries and 800-1,000 mss/year. 10% of books from first-time authors; 50% from unagented writers. Pay determined by individual contract. Publishes book 1 year after acceptance of ms. Accepts simultaneous submissions. Reports in 2 months on queries; 6 months on proposals and mss. Book catalog for 9 × 12 SAE with 5 first-class stamps. Manuscript guidelines for #10 SASE.
Nonfiction: Children's/juvenile. Subjects include Americana, animals, art/architecture, nature/environment, science, sports. Submit proposal package; prefers to see entire ms. Reviews artwork/photos as part of ms package. Writers should send photocopies.
Recent Nonfiction Title: *Children's Atlas of the World*, by Stephen Attmore.
Fiction: Prefers to see entire ms.
Recent Fiction Title: *Don't Forget to Write*, by Martina Selway (children's picture book).
Poetry: Submit complete ms.
Recent Poetry Title: *A Rainbow of Friends*, by P.K. Hallinan (children's picture book).
Tips: Audience is children in the toddler to ten-year-old range.

IDEALS PUBLICATIONS INC., (formerly Ideals Publishing Corp.), Suite 800, 565 Marriott Dr., Nashville TN 37214-8000. (615)321-6740. Publisher: Patricia Pingry. Editor: Lisa Thomspon. Estab. 1944. Publishes highly illustrated seasonal and nostalgic hardbound books. Uses short prose and poetry. Also publishes *Ideals* magazine. Publishes 4 hardbound books, 8 *Ideals*, 1-2 other titles/year. Payment varies. Simultaneous submissions OK. Accepts previously published material. Send information about when and where the article previously appeared. Reports in 2 months. Manuscript guidelines free on request.
   • No longer publishing children's titles.
Nonfiction: Coffee table book. Query. Reviews artwork/photos as part of ms package.

ILR PRESS, Division of the School of Industrial and Labor Relations, Cornell University, Ithaca NY 14853-3901. (607)255-3061. Fax: (607)255-2750. Director: E. Benson. Estab. 1945. Publishes hardcover and trade paperback originals and reprints. Averages 5-10 titles/year. Pays royalty. Reports in 2 months on queries. Book catalog free.
Nonfiction: All titles relate to industrial and labor relations, including relevant work in the fields of history, sociology, political science, economics, human resources, and organizational behavior. Needs for the next year include "manuscripts on workplace problems, employment policy, women and work, personnel issues, current history, and dispute resolution that will interest academics and practitioners." Query or submit outline and sample chapters.
Recent Nonfiction Title: *Gender and Racial Inequaity at Work*, by Donald Tomaskouk-Devy.
Tips: "We are interested in manuscripts that address topical issues in industrial and labor relations that concern both academics and the general public. These must be well documented to pass our editorial evaluation, which includes review by academics in the industrial and labor relations field."

IMAGINE, INC., P.O. Box 9674, Pittsburgh PA 15226. (412)921-8777. Fax: (412)921-8777. President: Bob Michelucci. Managing Editor: J. Russo. Estab. 1982. Publishes trade paperback originals. Averages 3-5 titles/year. Receives 50 submissions annually. 50% of books from first-time authors; 75% from unagented writers. Pays 6-10% royalty on retail price. Offers average $500 advance. Publishes book an average of 1 year after acceptance. Reports in up to 3 months. SASE a *must* for all replies.
   • Imagine did not publish any new writers last year.
Nonfiction: Coffee table book, how-to, illustrated book, reference. Subjects include films, science fiction, fantasy and horror films. Submit outline and sample chapters with illustrations and/or photos.
Tips: "If I were a writer trying to market a book today, I would research my subject matter completely before sending a manuscript. Our audience is between ages 18-45 and interested in film, science fiction, fantasy and the horror genre. We do not solicit nor publish fiction *novels*, please don't submit fiction manuscripts."

INCENTIVE PUBLICATIONS, INC., 3835 Cleghorn Ave., Nashville TN 37215-2532. (615)385-2934. Editor: Leslie Britt. Estab. 1970. Publishes paperback originals. Averages 25-30 titles/year. Receives 350 submissions annually. 25% of books from first-time authors; 95% from unagented writers. Pays royalty or makes outright purchase. Publishes book an average of 1 year after acceptance. Reports in 1 month on queries. *Writer's Market* recommends allowing 2 months for reply. Book catalog and ms guidelines for SAE with 3 first-class stamps.
Nonfiction: Teacher resources and books on educational areas relating to children. Query with synopsis and detailed outline.

Recent Nonfiction Title: *The Definitive Middle School Guide* (comprehensive guidebook to establishing and running a successful middle school).

‡**INDEX PUBLISHING GROUP, INC.**, Suite 273, 3368 Governor Dr., San Diego CA 92122.(619)281-2957. Fax: (619)281-0547. Publisher: Linton M. Vandiver. Publishes hardcover and trade paperback originals. Published 12 titles for 1994; will publish 20 for 1995. Receives 100 queries and 40 mss/year. 40% of books from first-time authors; 100% from unagented writers. Pays 6-20% royalty on wholesale price. Publishes book 4 months after acceptance of ms. Accepts simultaneous submissions. Query for electronic submissions. Reports in 1 week on queries; 2 weeks on proposals. Book catalog and ms guidelines free on request.
Nonfiction: Reference, technical, trade nonfiction. Subjects include computers and electronics, hobbies (consumer electronics: ham radio, scanners), electronic crime: cellular telephones, computer hacking, etc. "Index Publishing specializes in trade nonfiction (paper and hardcover) in two areas: (1) communication electronics, especially ham radio, scanning and radio monitoring, cellular telephones, computer hacking, etc.; (2) controversial topics such as eavesdropping, cable and satellite TV signal piracy, identity changes, electonic crime prevention." Query.
Recent Nonfiction Title: *The Television Gray Market*, by Henry L. Eisenson (exposé of electronic piracy of cable TV, satellite, and videotape programming).

INDIANA UNIVERSITY PRESS, 601 N. Morton St., Bloomington IN 47404-3797. (812)337-4203. Fax: (812)855-7931. Director: John Gallman. Estab. 1951. Publishes hardcover and paperback originals and paperback reprints. Averages 175 titles/year. 30% of books from first-time authors; 98% from unagented writers. Average print order for a first book varies depending on subject. Subsidy publishes (nonauthor) 9% of books. Pays maximum 10% royalty on retail price; offers occasional advance. Publishes book an average of 1 year after acceptance. Reports in 2 months. Free book catalog and ms guidelines.
Nonfiction: Scholarly books on humanities, history, philosophy, religion, Jewish studies, Black studies, criminal justice, translations, semiotics, public policy, film, music, philanthropy, social sciences, regional materials, African studies, Russian studies, women's studies, and serious nonfiction for the general reader. Also interested in textbooks and works with course appeal in designated subject areas. Query or submit outline and sample chapters. "Queries should include as much descriptive material as is necessary to convey scope and market appeal to us." Reviews artwork/photos.
Recent Nonfiction Title: *Charles Sanders Peirce: A Life*, by Joseph Brent.
Tips: "We have been a bit more cautious about specialized monographs."

INDUSTRIAL PRESS INC., 200 Madison Ave., New York NY 10016-4078. (212)889-6330. Fax: (212)545-8327. Editorial Director: Woodrow Chapman. Estab. 1884. Publishes hardcover originals. Averages 12 titles/year. Receives 25 submissions annually. 2% of books from first-time authors; 100% of books from unagented writers. Publishes book an average of 1 year after acceptance of finished ms. Query for electronic submissions. Reports in 1 month. *Writer's Market* recommends allowing 2 months for reply. Free book catalog.
Nonfiction: Reference, technical. Subjects include business and economics, science, engineering. "We envision professional engineers, plant managers, on-line industrial professionals responsible for equipment operation, professors teaching manufacturing, engineering, technology related courses as our audience." Especially looking for material on manufacturing technologies and titles on specific areas in manufacturing and industry. Computers in manufacturing are a priority. No energy-related books or how-to books. Query.

INFORMATION RESOURCES PRESS, Division of Herner and Company, Suite 550, 1110 N. Glebe Rd., Arlington VA 22201. (703)558-8270. Fax: (703)558-4979. Managing Editor: Roberta Gorinson. Estab. 1970. Publishes hardcover originals. Averages 6 titles/year. Receives 25 submissions annually. 80% of books from first-time authors; 100% from unagented writers. Pays 10-15% royalty on net cash receipts after returns and discounts. Publishes book an average of 1 year after acceptance. Simultaneous submissions OK. Query for electronic submissions. Reports in 2 months. Free book catalog available.
Nonfiction: Reference, technical, textbook. Subjects include health, library and information science. Needs basic or introductory books on information science, library science, and health planning that lend themselves for use as textbooks. Preferably, the mss will have been developed from course notes. No works on narrow research topics (nonbasic or introductory works). Submit outline and sample chapters.
Tips: "Our audience includes libraries (public, special, college and university); librarians, information scientists, college-level faculty; schools of library and information science; health planners, graduate-level students of health planning, and administrators; economists. Our marketing program is slanted toward library and

The double dagger before a listing indicates that the listing is new in this edition. New markets are often more receptive to freelance submissions.

information science and health planning, and we can do a better job of marketing in these areas."

INNER TRADITIONS INTERNATIONAL, P.O. Box 388, 1 Park St., Rochester VT 05767. (802)767-3174. Fax: (802)767-3726. Acquisitions Editor: (Ms.) Robin Dutcher-Bayer. Estab. 1975. Imprints are Inner Traditions, Destiny Books, Healing Arts Press, Park Street Press. Publishes hardcover and trade paperback originals and reprints. Averages 40 titles/year. Receives 2,000 submissions/year. 5% of books from first-time authors; 5% from unagented writers. Pays 8-10% royalty on net receipts. Offers $1,000 average advance. Publishes book an average of 1 year after acceptance. Reports in 3 months on queries, 3-6 months on mss. Book catalog and ms guidelines free.
Nonfiction: Subjects include anthropology/archaeology, natural foods, cooking, nutrition, health/alternative medicine, history and mythology, indigenous cultures, music/dance, nature/environment, esoteric philosophy, psychology, world religions, women's issues/studies, New Age. Query or submit outline and sample chapters with return postage. Manuscripts without postage will not be returned. Reviews artwork/photos as part of ms package.
Tips: "We are interested in the spiritual and transformative aspects of the above subjects, especially as they relate to world cultures. We are not interested in autobiographical stories of self-transformation."

INSIGHT BOOKS, Imprint of Plenum Publishing Corp., 233 Spring St., New York NY 10013-1578. (212)620-8000. Fax: (212)463-0742. Editor: Frank K. Darmstadt. Estab. 1946. Publishes trade hardcover and paperback originals. Averages 12 titles/year. Receives 1,000 submissions/year. 50% of books from first-time authors; 75% from unagented writers. Pays royalty. Advance varies. Publishes book an average of 1½-2 years after acceptance. Simultaneous submissions OK. Query for electronic submissions. Reports in 2 months. Book catalog free.
Nonfiction: Self-help, how-to, treatises, essays, biography. Subjects include anthropology/archaeology, art/ architecture, business and economics, child rearing and development, education, ethnic, gay and lesbian studies, government/politics, health/medicine, language/literature, money/finance, nature/environment, psychology, parenting, science, sociology, women's issues/studies. Submit outline and sample chapters.
Recent Nonfiction Title: *The Danger From Strangers: Confronting the Threat of Assault,* by James D. Brewer.
Tips: "Writers have the best chance selling authoritative, quality, well-written, serious information in areas of health, mental health, social sciences, education and child-rearing and development. Our audience consists of informed general readers as well as professionals and students in human, life and social sciences. If I were a writer trying to market a book today, I would say something interesting, important and useful, and say it well."

INTERLINK PUBLISHING GROUP, INC., 99 Seventh Ave., Brooklyn NY 11215. (718)797-4292. Fax: (718)855-7329. Publisher: Michel Moushabeck. Imprints are Interlink Books, Crocodile Books, USA, Olive Branch Press. Publishes hardcover and trade paperback originals. Averages 30 titles/year. Receives 200 submissions/ year. 30% of books from first-time authors; 50% from unagented writers. Pays 5-7% royalty on retail price. Publishes book an average of 18 months after acceptance. Simultaneous submissions OK. Reports in 1 month on queries. *Writer's Market* recommends allowing 2 months for reply. Book catalog and ms guidelines free.
Nonfiction: Coffee table book, cookbook, how-to, illustrated book, juvenile. Subjects include art/architecture, child guidance/parenting, cooking, foods and nutrition, ethnic, gardening, government/politics, history, nature/environment, religion, travel, women's issues/studies and third world literature, criticism. Submit outline and sample chapters for adult nonfiction; complete ms for juvenile titles. Reviews artwork/photos as part of ms package.
Fiction: Ethnic, feminist, juvenile, picture books, short story collections (only third world). "Adult fiction— We are looking for translated works relating to the Middle East, Africa or Latin America. Juvenile/Picture Books—Our list is full for the next two years." No science fiction, romance, plays, erotica, fantasy, horror. Submit outline/synopsis and sample chapters.
Tips: "Any submissions that fit well in our International Folktale Series series will receive careful attention."

INTERNATIONAL FOUNDATION OF EMPLOYEE BENEFIT PLANS, P.O. Box 69, Brookfield WI 53008-0069. (414)786-6700. Fax: (414)786-2990. Director of Publications: Dee Birschel. Estab. 1954. Publishes hardcover and trade paperback originals. Averages 10 titles/year. Receives 20 submissions annually. 15% of books from first-time authors; 80% from unagented writers. Pays 5-15% royalty on wholesale and retail price. Publishes book an average of 1 year after acceptance. Reports in 3 months on queries. Book catalog free on request. Manuscript guidelines for SASE.
Nonfiction: Reference, technical, consumer information, textbook. Subjects include health care, pensions, retirement planning, business and employee benefits. "We publish general and technical monographs on all aspects of employee benefits—pension plans, health insurance, etc." Query with outline.
Tips: "Be aware of interests of employers and the marketplace in benefits topics, for example, how AIDS affects employers, health care cost containment."

INTERNATIONAL INFORMATION ASSOCIATES, INC., P.O. Box 773, Morrisville PA 19067-0773. (215)493-9214. Vice President/Publisher: Richard Bradley. Publishes trade paperback originals. Publishes 4-6 titles/

year. Receives 25 queries and 6 mss/year. 98% of books from first-time authors; 100% from unagented writers. Pays 10-12% royalty on retail price. Publishes book 12-14 months after acceptance. Simultaneous submissions OK. Query for electronic submissions. Prefers "any major MS-DOS or ASCII." Reports in 3 weeks on queries. Book catalog free on request. Manuscript guidelines for #10 SASE.

• International Information Associates no longer publishes self-help titles and did not publish any new titles in 1994 nor will they in the first half of 1995.

Nonfiction: How-to, reference, technical, textbook. Subjects include business and economics, health/medicine, money/finance, psychology, science. "Writers should be qualified in some way to write the text, if not by academic background then by experience." Query. Reviews artwork/photos as part of freelance ms package. Writers should send photocopies.

Tips: "Our audience is the professional at work in a particular field—on an international basis. Please remember that *anything* you write us will be used to judge *how* you write. Whether an author can write is as important as the topic."

INTERNATIONAL MARINE PUBLISHING CO., Division of TAB Books, Inc., McGraw-Hill Company, P.O. Box 220, Camden ME 04843-0220. Fax: (207)236-6314. Imprints are Seven Seas and Ragged Mountain Press. Acquisitions Editor: James R. Babb. Vice President, Editorial: Jonathan Eaton. Estab. 1971. Publishes hardcover and paperback originals. Averages 40 titles/year. Receives 500-700 mss/year. 30% of books from first-time authors; 80% from unagented writers. Pays standard royalties, based on net price, with advances. Publishes book an average of 1 year after acceptance. Reports in 2 months. Book catalog and ms guidelines for SASE.

Nonfiction: "Marine nonfiction. A wide range of subjects include: boatbuilding, boat design, yachting, seamanship, boat maintenance, maritime history, etc." All books are illustrated. "Material in all stages welcome. We prefer queries first with outline and two to three sample chapters." Reviews artwork/photos as part of ms package.

Tips: "Freelance writers should be aware of the need for clarity, accuracy and interest. Many progress too far in the actual writing, with an unsaleable topic."

INTERNATIONAL MEDICAL PUBLISHING, 404 Second St., Alexandria VA 22314. (703)519-0807. Fax: (703)519-0806. Editor: Thomas Masterson, MD. Publishes mass market paperback originals. Publishes 11 titles/year. Receives 5 queries and 2 mss/year. 100% of books from first-time authors; 100% from unagented writers. Pays royalty on retail price. Publishes book 8 months after acceptance. Query for electronic submissions. Prefers disk. Reports in 2 months on queries. Book catalog free on request.

Nonfiction: Reference, textbook. Subjects include health/medicine. "We distribute only through medical and scientific bookstores. Look at our books. Think about practical material for doctors-in-training. We are interested in handbooks. Writers should avoid lack of clarity in writing. Keep prose simple when dealing with very technical subjects." Query with outline. Writers should send photocopies.

Tips: Audience is medical students and physicians.

INTERNATIONAL PUBLISHERS CO., INC., P.O. Box 3042, New York NY 10116-3042. (212)366-9816. Fax: (212)366-9820. President: Betty Smith. Estab. 1924. Publishes hardcover and trade paperback originals and trade paperback reprints. Averages 10-15 titles/year. Receives 50-100 mss/year. 10% of books from first-time authors. Pays 5-7½% royalty on paperbacks; 10% royalty on cloth. No advance. Publishes book an average of 6 months after acceptance. Simultaneous submissions OK. Reports in 1 month on queries (send SASE), 6 months on mss. Book catalog and ms guidelines for SAE with 2 first-class stamps.

Nonfiction: Biography, reference, textbook. Subjects include Americana, economics, history, philosophy, politics, social sciences, Marxist-Leninist classics. "Books on labor, black studies and women's studies based on Marxist science have high priority." Query or submit outline and sample chapters. Reviews artwork/photos as part of ms package.

Recent Nonfiction Title: *Marxism, A Living Science*, by Kenneth Neill Cameron.

Tips: No fiction or poetry.

INTERNATIONAL WEALTH SUCCESS, P.O. Box 186, Merrick NY 11570-1310. (516)766-5850. Editor: Tyler G. Hicks. Estab. 1967. Averages 10 titles/year. Receives 100 submissions annually. 100% of books from first-time authors; 100% from unagented writers. Average print order for a first book "varies from 500 and up, depending on the book." Pays 10% royalty on wholesale or retail price. Buys all rights. Usual advance is $1,000, but this varies, depending on author's reputation and nature of book. Publishes book 4 months after acceptance. Query for electronic submissions. Reports in 1 month. Book catalog and ms guidelines for 9 × 12 SAE with 3 first-class stamps.

Nonfiction: Self-help, how-to. "Techniques, methods, sources for building wealth. Highly personal, how-to-do-it with plenty of case histories. Books are aimed at the wealth builder and are highly sympathetic to his and her problems." Financing, business success, venture capital, etc. Length: 60,000-70,000 words. Query. Reviews artwork/photos as part of ms package.

Tips: "With the mass layoffs in large and medium-size companies there is an increasing interest in owning your own business. So we will focus on more how-to hands-on material on owning—and becoming successful in—one's own business of any kind. Our market is the BWB—Beginning Wealth Builder. This person has so little money that financial planning is something they never think of. Instead, they want to know what kind of a business they can get into to make some money without a large investment. Write for this market and you have millions of potential readers. Remember—there are a lot more people *without* money than *with* money."

INTERWEAVE PRESS, 201 E. Fourth St., Loveland CO 80537. (303)669-7672. Book Coordinator: Barbara Liebler. Estab. 1975. Publishes hardcover and trade paperback originals. Publishes 8 titles/year. Receives 50 submissions/year. 60% of books from first-time authors; 98% from unagented writers. Pays 10% royalty on net receipts. Offers $500 average advance. Publishes book an average of 1 year after acceptance. Simultaneous (if clearly identified) submissions OK. Query for electronic submissions. Reports in 2 months. Book catalog and ms guidelines free.
Nonfiction: How-to, technical. Subjects limited to fiber arts—basketry, spinning, knitting, dyeing and weaving. Submit outline/synopsis and sample chapters. Reviews artwork/photos as part of ms package.
Tips: "We are looking for very clear, informally written, technically correct manuscripts, generally of a how-to nature, in our specific fiber fields only. Our audience includes a variety of creative self-starters who like fibers and appreciate inspiration and clear instruction. They are often well educated and skillful in many areas."

IOWA STATE UNIVERSITY PRESS, 2121 S. State Ave., Ames IA 50010-8300. (515)292-0140. Fax: (515)292-3348. Acquisitions Editor: Gretchen Van Houten. Editor-in-Chief: Bill Silag. Estab. 1924. Hardcover and paperback originals. Averages 55 titles/year. Receives 450 submissions annually. 98% of books from un-agented writers. Average print order for a first book is 1,200. Subsidy publishes (nonauthor) some titles, based on sales potential of book and contribution to scholarship on trade books. Pays 10% royalty for trade books on wholesale price. No advance. Publishes book an average of 1 year after acceptance. Simultaneous submissions OK, if advised. Query for electronic submissions. Reports in up to 6 months. Book catalog free. Manuscript guidelines for SASE.
 • Iowa State University Press now publishes books with environmental themes.
Nonfiction: Publishes agriculture, environmental, engineering, history, scientific/technical textbooks, food and nutrition, economics, aviation, journalism, veterinary sciences. Accepts nonfiction translations. Submit outline and several sample chapters, preferably not in sequence; must be double-spaced throughout. Looks for "unique approach to subject; clear, concise narrative; and effective integration of scholarly apparatus." Send contrasting b&w glossy prints to illustrate ms.

ISHIYAKU EUROAMERICA, INC., (IEA Publishers), 716 Hanley Industrial Court, St. Louis MO 63144-1904. (314)644-4322 or (800)633-1921. Fax: (314)644-9532. Estab. 1983. Reports in 2 months. Free book catalog. Manuscript guidelines for SASE.
Nonfiction: Reference and textbooks in the field of dental science and translation rights.
Tips: "Dental authors have a tendency to overstress facts, thereby requiring considerable editing."

ITALICA PRESS, Suite 605, 595 Main St., New York NY 10044-0047. (212)935-4230. Fax: (212)838-7812. Publisher: Eileen Gardiner. Estab. 1985. Publishes trade paperback originals. Receives 75 queries and 20 mss/year. 50% of books from first-time authors; 100% from unagented writers. Pays 7-15% royalty on wholesale price. Publishes book 1 year after acceptance of ms. Simultaneous submissions OK. Query for electronic submissions. Reports in 1 month on queries. *Writer's Market* recommends allowing 2 months for reply. Book catalog free.
Nonfiction: "We publish *only* English translations of medieval and Renaissance source materials and English translations of modern Italian fiction." Query. Reviews artwork/photos as part of freelance ms package. Writers should send photocopies.
Tips: "We are interested in considering a wide variety of medieval and Renaissance topics (not historical fiction), and for modern works we are only interested in translations from Italian fiction."

‡JACOBS PUBLISHING, LTD., 13929 Castle Blvd., #24, Silver Spring MD 20904-4995 (202)388-9742. Publisher: Todd A. Jacobs. Publishes electronic originals and reprints. Pays 5-20% royalty. Publishes book 2-4 months after acceptance of ms. Simultaneous submissions OK. Query for electronic submissions. Reports in 1 month on queries, 3 months on mss. Manuscript guidelines for #10 SASE or e-mail to info@epub.com.
Nonfiction: Coffee table book, cookbook, how-to, humor, illustrated book, children's/juvenile, self-help, technical, textbook. Subjects include animals, anthropology/archaeology, business and economics, computers and electronics, cooking foods & nutrition, government/politics, money/finance, psychology, recreation, science. "Fact-filled doesn't mean dull. Entertain as well as enlighten." Query with outline and sample chapter. Reviews artwork/photos as part of freelance ms package. Writers should send photocopies.
Fiction: Adventure, erotica, entertainment, fantasy, horror, humor, juvenile, mystery, picture books, plays, romance, science fiction, short story collections, suspense, young adult. Query with synopsis and 1 sample chapter.

Poetry: Query or submit complete ms.

Tips: "Know something about computers and electronic publishing. We appreciate authors who understand how to write for this modern medium."

JAIN PUBLISHING CO., P.O. Box 3523, Fremont CA 94539. (510)659-8272. Fax: (510)659-0501. Editor-in-chief: M.K. Jain. Estab. 1987. Imprint is Asian Humanities Press. Publishes hardcover and trade paperback originals and reprints. Publishes 10 titles/year. Receives 500 queries/year. 20% of books from first-time authors; 100% from unagented writers. Pays 6-10% royalty on net sales or makes outright purchase of $500-2,000. Offers occasional $1,000-2,000 advance. Publishes book approximately 1 year after acceptance. Query for electronic submissions. Reports in 3 months on mss. Book catalog for 6 × 9 SAE with 2 first-class stamps. Manuscript guidelines for #10 SASE.

● Jain is putting more emphasis on travel, gift and reference books and less emphasis on nature/environment. Also, they are increasing focus on undergraduate textbooks.

Nonfiction: Self-help (motivational/inspirational), how-to, cooking, foods and nutrition (vegetarian), health/medicine (holistic/alternative), gift books, guides and handbooks, personal and organizational development, money and personal finance, computer books (general purpose), business/management, travel, multi-cultural, reference, textbooks. "Manuscripts should be related to our subjects and written in an 'easy to read' and understandable format. Preferably between 40,000-80,000 words." Submit proposal package, including curriculum vitae and list of prior publications with SASE. Reviews artwork/photos as part of freelance package. Writers should send photocopies.

Tips: "We're interested more in user-oriented books than general treatises."

JIST WORKS, INC., 720 N. Park Ave., Indianapolis IN 46202-3431. (317)264-3709. Fax: (317)264-3709. Acquisitions Editor: Sara Adams. Estab. 1981. Publishes trade paperback originals and reprints. Receives 300 submissions/year. 60% of books from first time authors; 100% from unagented writers. Pays 5-12% royalty on wholesale price or makes outright purchase (negotiable). Publishes ms an average of 6-12 months after acceptance. Simultaneous submissions OK. Query for electronic submissions. Reports in 3 months on queries. Book catalog and ms guidelines for 9 × 12 SAE with 4 first-class stamps.

● JIST Works has adopted a new imprint, Park Avenue Publications, to enable them to publish business and self-help manuscripts that fall outside of the JIST topical parameters.

Nonfiction: How-to, career, reference, self-help, software, textbook. Specializes in job search, self-help and career related topics. "We want text/workbook formats that would be useful in a school or other institutional setting. We also publish trade titles. All reading levels. Will consider books for professional staff and educators, appropriate software and videos." *Writer's Market* recommends query with SASE first. Reviews artwork/photos as part of ms package.

Tips: "Institutions and staff who work with people of all reading and academic skills, making career and life decisions or who are looking for jobs are our primary audience, but we're focusing more on business and trade topics for consumers."

JOHNSON BOOKS, Johnson Publishing Co., 1880 S. 57th Court, Boulder CO 80301. (303)443-9766. Fax: (303)443-1679. Managing Editor: Walter R. Bornemen. Estab. 1979. Imprints are Spring Creek Press and Cordillera Press. Publishes hardcover and paperback originals and reprints. Publishes 10-12 titles/year. Receives 500 submissions annually. 30% of books from first-time authors; 90% from unagented writers. Average print order for a first book is 5,000. Royalties vary. Publishes book an average of 1 year after acceptance. Reports in 2 months. Book catalog and ms guidelines for 9 × 12 SAE with 5 first-class stamps.

Nonfiction: General nonfiction, books on the West, environmental subjects, natural history, paleontology, geology, archaeology, travel, guidebooks, outdoor recreation. Accepts nonfiction translations. "We are primarily interested in books for the informed popular market, though we will consider vividly written scholarly works. As a small publisher, we are able to give every submission close personal attention." Query first or call. Submit outline/synopsis and 3 sample chapters. Looks for "good writing, thorough research, professional presentation and appropriate style. Marketing suggestions from writers are helpful." Reviews artwork/photos.

Tips: "We are looking for nature titles with broad national, not just regional, appeal. We are trying to include more outdoor recreation books in addition to our other areas listed."

BOB JONES UNIVERSITY PRESS, Greenville SC 29614-0001. Acquisitions Editor: Ms. Gloria Repp. Estab. 1974. Publishes trade paperback originals and reprints. Publishes 10 titles/year. Receives 50 queries and 300 mss/year. 40% of books from first-time authors; 100% from unagented writers. Makes outright purchase of $500-1,250. Publishes book 1 year after acceptance. Simultaneous submissions OK. Query for electronic submissions. Reports in 2 months on mss. Book catalog and ms guidelines free on request.

For information on setting your freelance fees, see How Much Should I Charge?

Nonfiction: Biography (for teens), children's/juvenile. Subjects include animals, gardening, health/medicine, history, nature/environment, sports. "We're looking for concept books on almost any subject suitable for children. We also like biographies." Submit outline and 3 sample chapters.

Fiction: Juvenile, young adult. "We're looking for well-rounded characters and plots with plenty of action." Submit synopsis and 5 sample chapters or complete ms.

Tips: "Our readers are children ages two and up, teens and young adults. We're looking for high-quality writing that reflects a Christian perspective and features well-developed characters in a convincing plot. Most open to: first chapter books; adventure; biography."

JUDSON PRESS, P.O. Box 851, Valley Forge PA 19482-0851. (610)768-2118. Fax: (610)768-2056. Publisher: Harold W. Rast. Managing Editor: Mary Nicol. Estab. 1824. Publishes hardcover and paperback originals. Averages 15-20 titles/year. Receives 750 queries annually. Average print order for a first book is 5,000. Pays royalty or flat fee. Publishes book an average of 15 months after acceptance. Simultaneous submissions acceptable. Reports in 6 months. Enclose return postage. Book catalog for 9 × 12 SAE with 4 first-class stamps. Manuscript guidelines for #10 SASE.

 • Judson Press has expanded its line from 10-15 titles/year to 15-20 titles/year.

Nonfiction: Adult religious nonfiction of 30,000-80,000 words. "Our audience is mostly church members who seek to have a more fulfilling personal spiritual life and want to serve Christ in their churches and other relationships." Query with outline and 1 sample chapter.

Tips: "Writers have the best chance selling us practical books assisting clergy or laypersons in their ministry and personal lives. Our audience consists of Protestant church leaders and members. Be sensitive to our workload and adapt to the market's needs. Books on multicultural issues are very welcome."

‡JUSTICE SYSTEMS PRESS, P.O. Box 2852, Port Angeles WA 98362. (206)457-0590. President: Barbara J. Birkland. Publishes trade paperback originals. Publishes 6 titles/year. Receives 15 queries and 2 mss/year. 20% of books from unagented writers. Pays 5-12% royalty on retail price. Publishes book 1 year after acceptance of ms. Accepts simultaneous submissions. Query for electronic submissions. Reports in 2 months on queries and proposals, 4 months on mss. Book catalog free on request.

Nonfiction: Textbook. Subjects include government/politics, law, military/war. "Justice Systems Press publishes only for the criminal justice audience. Specific topics include police management, supervision, legal references, and the investigation of crimes." Submit outline and 3 sample chapters. Reviews artwork/photos as part of ms package. Writers should send photocopies or transparencies.

Recent Nonfiction Title: *Military Police Guide to the Federal Criminal Code*, by Birkland and Kernes.

‡K.I.P. CHILDREN'S BOOKS, Imprint of Kasan Imprints, Suite 3, 1239 Nile Dr., Corpus Christi TX 78412. (512)992-6611. Publication Director: Toni Annable. Publishes trade paperback originals. Publishes 6 titles/year. Receives 30 queries and 100 mss/year. 20% of books from first-time authors; 100% from unagented writers. Pays 5-10% royalty on wholesale price after the first 2,500; or makes variable outright purchase. Publishes book 1 year after acceptance of ms. Simultaneous submissions OK if noted. Reports in 1 month on queries; 2 months on mss. Book catalog free on request. Manuscript guidelines for #10 SASE.

Nonfiction: Children's/juvenile and adult literacy. Subjects include animals, education, ethnic, health/medicine, history, language/literature, science. "Our nonfiction is teaching-oriented for grades K-8." Submit outline and 2 sample chapters; full ms if short. Reviews artwork/photos as part of ms package. Writers should send photocopies.

Recent Nonfiction Title: *Columbus*, by Biji Surber (coloring workbook).

Fiction: Adventure, ethnic, fantasy, juvenile, mystery, adult literacy, multicultural. "We publish fiction as language learning tools, English, Spanish or French. Our adult literacy is nonviolent, clean. Send for guidelines for adult literacy." Submit synopsis and 2 sample chapters; complete ms if short.

Recent Fiction Title: *The Doorman and the Case of the Gold Shoes*, by T.C. Bell (mystery, adult literacy).

KALMBACH PUBLISHING CO., 21027 Crossroads Circle, P.O. Box 1612, Waukesha WI 53187-1612. Fax: (414)796-1142. Senior Acquisitions Editor: Terry Spohn. Estab. 1934. Publishes hardcover and paperback originals and paperback reprints. Averages 15-20 titles/year. Receives 100 submissions annually. 85% of books from first-time authors; 100% from unagented writers. Offers 8-10% royalty on net. Average advance is $1,000. Publishes book an average of 18 months after acceptance. Reports in 2 months.

Nonfiction: Hobbies, how-to, amateur astronomy, railroading. "Our book publishing effort is in amateur astronomy, railroading and hobby how-to-do-it titles *only*." Query first. "I welcome telephone inquiries. They save me a lot of time, and they can save an author a lot of misconceptions and wasted work." In written query, wants to see "a detailed outline of two or three pages and a complete sample chapter with photos, drawings, and how-to text." Reviews artwork/photos as part of ms package.

Recent Nonfiction Title: *The Guide to North American Steam Locomotives*, by George Drury.

Tips: "Our books are about half text and half illustrations. Any author who wants to publish with us must be able to furnish good photographs and rough drawings before we'll consider contracting for his book."

KAR-BEN COPIES INC., 6800 Tildenwood Lane, Rockville MD 20852-4371. (301)984-8733 or 1-800-4KAR-BEN. Fax: (301)881-9195. President: Judye Groner. Contact: Madeline Wikler. Estab. 1975. Publishes hardcover and trade paperback originals. Averages 8-10 titles/year. Receives 150 submissions annually. 25% of books from first-time authors; 100% from unagented writers. Average print order for a first book is 5,000. Pays 6-8% royalty on net receipts or makes negotiable outright purchase. Offers average $1,000 advance. Publishes book an average of 1 year after acceptance. Reports in 2 months. Book catalog and ms guidelines for 9 × 12 SAE with 2 first-class stamps.
Nonfiction: Jewish juvenile (ages 1-12). Especially looking for books on Jewish life-cycle, holidays, and customs for children—"early childhood and elementary." Send only mss with Jewish content. Query with outline and sample chapters. Reviews artwork/photos as part of ms package.
Fiction: Adventure, fantasy, historical, religious (all Jewish juvenile). Especially looking for Jewish holiday and history-related fiction for young children. Submit outline/synopsis and sample chapters or complete ms.
Tips: "We envision Jewish children and their families, and juveniles interested in learning about Jewish subjects, as our audience."

KENT STATE UNIVERSITY PRESS, P.O. Box 5190, Kent OH 44242-0001. (216)672-7913. Fax: (216)672-3104. Director: John T. Hubbell. Senior Editor: Julia Morton. Estab. 1965. Publishes hardcover and paperback originals and some reprints. Averages 20-25 titles/year. Subsidy publishes (nonauthor) 20% of books. Standard minimum book contract on net sales. Rarely offers advance. "Always write a letter of inquiry before submitting manuscripts. We can publish only a limited number of titles each year and can frequently tell in advance whether or not we would be interested in a particular manuscript. This practice saves both our time and that of the author, not to mention postage costs. If interested we will ask for complete manuscript. Decisions based on inhouse readings and two by outside scholars in the field of study." Reports in 3 months. Enclose return postage. Book catalog free.
Nonfiction: Especially interested in "scholarly works in history and literary studies of high quality, any titles of regional interest for Ohio, scholarly biographies, archaeological research, the arts, and general nonfiction."
Tips: "We are cautious about publishing heavily illustrated manuscripts."

MICHAEL KESEND PUBLISHING, LTD., 1025 Fifth Ave., New York NY 10028. (212)249-5150. Director: Michael Kesend. Editor: Judy Wilder. Estab. 1979. Publishes hardcover and trade paperback originals and reprints. Averages 4-6 titles/year. Receives 150 submissions annually. 50% of books from first-time authors; 50% from unagented writers. Pays 3-12½% royalty on wholesale price or retail price, or makes outright purchase for $500 minimum. Advance varies. Publishes book an average of 18 months after acceptance. Reports in 2 months on queries. Guidelines for #10 SASE.
Nonfiction: Biography, how-to, illustrated book, self-help, sports. Subjects include animals, health, history, hobbies, nature, sports, travel, the environment, guides to several subjects. Needs sports, health self-help and environmental awareness guides. No photography mss. Submit outline and sample chapters. Reviews artwork/photos as part of ms package.
Fiction: No science fiction or romance. No simultaneous submissions. Submit outline/synopsis and 2-3 sample chapters.
Tips: "We are now more interested in nature-related topics, national guides, outdoor travel guides and sports nonfiction. Very little fiction is being published by us."

KINSEEKER PUBLICATIONS, P.O. Box 184, Grawn MI 49637-0184. (616)276-6745. Editor: Victoria Wilson. Estab. 1986. Publishes trade paperback originals. Averages 6 titles/year. 100% of books from unagented writers. Pays 10-25% royalty on retail price. Publishes book an average of 8 months after acceptance. Simultaneous submissions OK. Reports in 3 months. Book catalog and ms guidelines for #10 SASE.
Nonfiction: Reference books. Subjects are local history and genealogy. Query or submit outline and sample chapters. Reviews artwork/photos as part of ms package.

ALFRED A. KNOPF, INC., Division of Random House, 201 E. 50th St., New York NY 10022. (212)751-2600. Submit mss to Senior Editor or Children's Book Editor. Publishes hardcover and paperback originals. Averages 200 titles/year. 15% of books from first-time authors; 30% from unagented writers. Royalty and advance vary. Publishes book an average of 1 year after acceptance. Simultaneous submissions OK (if so informed). Reports in 3 months. Book catalog for 7½ × 10½ SAE with 5 first-class stamps.
   • Alfred A. Knopf received three nominations for the 1993 National Book Critics Circle Awards.
Nonfiction: Book-length nonfiction, including books of scholarly merit. Preferred length: 50,000-150,000 words. "A good nonfiction writer should be able to follow the latest scholarship in any field of human knowledge, and fill in the abstractions of scholarship for the benefit of the general reader by means of good, concrete, sensory reporting." Query. Reviews artwork/photos as part of ms package.
Recent Nonfiction Title: *How We Die*, by Sherwin Nuland (medicine).
Fiction: Publishes book-length fiction of literary merit by known or unknown writers. Length: 40,000-150,000 words. *Writer's Market* recommends writers query with sample chapters.
Recent Fiction Title: *A Lesson Before Dying*, by Ernest T. Gaines.

KNOWLEDGE BOOK PUBLISHERS, Suite 100, 3863 SW Loop 820, Fort Worth TX 76133-2063. (817)292-4270. Fax: (817)294-2893. Editor/Publisher: Dr. O.A. Battista. Estab. 1976. Publishes hardcover, trade paperback and mass market paperback originals. Publishes 4-6 titles/year. Receives 50-100 submissions/year. 75% of books from first-time authors. 0% from unagented writers. Pays 10-15% royalty on wholesale price. Advance varies. Publishes book an average of 1 year after acceptance. Query for electronic submissions. Reports in 1 month on queries. *Writer's Market* recommends allowing 2 months for reply. Book catalog and ms guidelines for $5.
Nonfiction: How-to, humor, juvenile, technical. Subjects include Americana, health/medicine, science. Submit through agent only.
Fiction: Juvenile. Submit through agent only.
Tips: "Our audience is a general audience interested in *new* knowledge useful in everyday life. If I were a writer trying to market a book today, I would do intense research on a new knowledge data that the general public can use to their *personal* benefit in everyday life."

KNOWLEDGE INDUSTRY PUBLICATIONS, INC., 701 Westchester Ave., White Plains NY 10604. (914)328-9157. Fax: (914)328-9093. Senior Vice President: Janet Moore. Publishes hardcover and paperback originals. Averages 10 titles/year. Receives 30 submissions annually. 25% of books from first-time authors; 100% from unagented writers. Average print order for a first book is 2,500. Offers negotiable advance. Publishes book an average of 1 year after acceptance. Query for electronic submissions. Reports in 3 months. Book catalog free. Manuscript guidelines for SASE.
Nonfiction: Corporate, industrial video, interactive video, computer graphics. Especially needs TV and video. Query first, then submit outline and sample chapters. Reviews artwork/photos as part of ms package.

KODANSHA AMERICA, INC., 114 Fifth Ave., New York NY 10011. (212)727-6460. Contact: Editorial Department. Estab. 1989 (in US). Publishes hardcover and trade paperback originals (50%); trade paperback originals and reprints in Kodansha Globe series (50%). Averages 35-40 titles/year. Receives 3,000 submissions/year. 10% of books from first-time authors; 30% from unagented writers. Pays 6-15% royalty on retail price. Offers $2,000 (reprints), $5,000 (original) average advances. Publishes book an average of 9 months after acceptance. Simultaneous submissions OK. Reports in up to 3 months. Book catalog for 9×12 SAE with 6 first-class stamps.
  • Kodansha America published the extremely successful book, *Having Our Say,* by the Delany sisters, which spent 16 weeks on national bestseller lists, with 310,000 copies in print. *The Delany Sisters' Book of Wisdom* is scheduled to be published in the fall of 1994.
Nonfiction: Biography, anthropology/archaeology, business and economics, cooking, ethnic, gardening, history, craft, language, nature/environment, philosophy, psychology, religion, science, sociology, translation, travel, Asian subjects. We are looking for distinguished critical books on international subjects. No pop psychology, how-to, true crime, regional. Query with sample. SASE. Reviews artwork/photos as part of ms package.
Recent Nonfiction Title: *Having Our Say: The Delany Sisters' First 100 Years.*
Tips: "Our focus is on nonfiction titles of an international and cross-cultural nature, well-researched, written with authority, bringing something of a world view to the general reading public. We are especially interested in titles with staying power, which will sell as well in five years' time as now. Potential authors should be aware of what comparable titles are on the market, and from whom."

‡KREGEL PUBICATIONS, Kregel, Inc., P.O. Box 2607, Grand Rapids MI 49501. Senior Editor: Dennis R. Hillman. Imprints are Kregel Publications, Kregel Resources, Kregel Classics. Publishes hardcover and trade paperback originals and reprints. Publishes 50 titles/year. Receives 100 queries and 30 mss/year. 5% of books from first-time authors; 100% from unagented writers. Pays 8-14% royalty on wholesale price or makes outright purchase of $500-1,000. Offers $1,000-2,000 advance. Publishes book 9 months after acceptance of ms. Simultaneous submissions OK. Query for electronic submissions. Reports in 1 month on queries and proposals, 3 months on mss. Book catalog for 9×12 SAE with 3 first-class stamps. Manuscript guidelines for #10 SASE.
Nonfiction: Biography (Christian), reference, textbook. Subjects include religion. "We serve evangelical Christian readers and those in career Christian service." Query with outline and 2 sample chapters, bio and market comparison.
Recent Nonfiction Title: *Create & Celebrate,* by Harold Westing (text); *Strength of Soul,* by Phillip Keller (devotional); *God's Best Secrets,* by Andrew Murray (devotional).

KRIEGER PUBLISHING CO., P.O. Box 9542, Melbourne FL 32902-9542. (407)724-9542. Fax: (407)951-3671. Production Manager: Marie Bowles. Imprints are Orbit Series, Anvil Series and Public History. Publishes hardcover and paperback originals and reprints. Averages 120 titles/year. Receives 50-60 submissions/year. 30% of books from first-time authors; 100% from unagented writers. Pays royalty on net realized price. Publishes book an average of 8 months after acceptance. Reports in 1 month. *Writer's Market* recommends allowing 2 months for reply. Book catalog free.

Nonfiction: College reference, technical, textbook. Subjects include history, music, philosophy, psychology, space science herpetology, chemistry, physics, engineering, medical. Query. Reviews artwork/photos as part of ms package.

Recent Nonfiction Title: *The Dream Machines: An Illustrated History of the Spaceship in Art, Science, and Literature*, by Ron Miller.

‡**LAKE VIEW PRESS**, P.O. Box 578279, Chicago IL 60657. Director: Paul Elitzik. Publishes hardcover and trade paperback originals. Publishes 5 titles/year. Receives 100 queries and 10 mss/year. 100% of books from unagented writers. Pays 6-10% royalty on wholesale price. Publishes book 1 year after acceptance of ms. No simultaneous submissions. Query for electronic submissions. Reports in 1 month on queries. Book catalog for #10 SASE.

Nonfiction: Biography, reference, technical. Subjects include government/politics, history, language/literature, sociology, women's issues/studies. "We are interested mainly in scholarly nonfiction which is written in a manner accessible to a nonprofessional reader." Query.

Recent Nonfiction Title: *Political Companion to American Film*, by Gary Crowdus (encyclopedia/film).

‡**LANGENSCHEIDT PUBLISHING GROUP**, 46-35 54th Rd., Maspeth NY 11378. (800)432-MAPS. Sales Director: Susan Pohja. Imprints are Hagstrom Map, American Map, Trakker Map, Arrow Map, Creative Sales. Publishes hardcover, trade paperback and mass market paperback originals. Publishes over 100 titles/year; each imprint publishes 20 titles/year. Receives 5 queries and 5 mss/year. 100% of books from unagented writers. Pays royalty or makes outright purchase; each situation is different. Offers advance of a percentage of the retail price/cost of the project. Publishes book 6 months after acceptance of ms. Accepts simultaneous submissions. Reports in 2 months on proposals. Book catalog free on request.

Nonfiction: Reference. Subjects include foreign language. "Any foreign language that fills a gap in our line is welcome." Submit outline and 2 sample chapters.

Recent Nonfiction Title: *Picture Dictionary Spanish*, by Renyi (juvenile reference).

LARK BOOKS, Altamont Press, 50 College St., Asheville NC 28801. Publisher: Rob Pulleyn. Estab. 1976. Imprints are: Lark Books; Sterling/Lark Books. Publishes hardcover and trade paperback originals and reprints. Publishes 35 titles/year. Sterling publishes 25; Lark publishes 10. Receives 100 queries and 50 mss/year. 80% of books from first-time authors; 100% from unagented writers. Pays 5-20% royalty on gross income or makes outright purchase. Offers up to $2,500 advance. Publishes book 1 year after acceptance of ms. Simultaneous submissions OK. Query for electronic submissions. Reports in 2 months.

Nonfiction: Coffee table book, cookbook, how-to, illustrated book, children's/juvenile. Subjects include cooking, foods and nutrition, gardening, hobbies, nature/environment, crafts. "We publish high quality, highly illustrated books, primarily in the crafts/leisure markets. We work closely with bookclubs. Our books are either how-to, 'gallery' or combination books." Submit outline and 1 sample chapter or proposal package, including sample projects, table of contents. Reviews artwork/photos as part of the freelance ms package. Writers should send transparencies if possible.

MERLOYD LAWRENCE BOOKS, Imprint of Addison Wesley, 102 Chestnut St., Boston MA 02108. President: Merloyd Lawrence. Estab. 1982. Publishes hardcover and trade paperback originals. Averages 7-8 titles/year. Receives 400 submissions/year. 25% of books from first-time authors; 20% from unagented writers. Pays royalty on retail price. Publishes book an average of 1 year after acceptance. Simultaneous submissions OK. Reports in 3 weeks on queries; no unsolicited ms read. All queries with SASE read and answered. Book catalog available from Addison Wesley.

Nonfiction: Biography. Subjects include child development/parenting, health/medicine, nature/environment, psychology. Query with SASE.

SEYMOUR LAWRENCE INC., Houghton Mifflin Co., 215 Park Ave. South, New York NY 10003. (212)420-5825.

• Seymour Lawrence died early in 1994 and Houghton Mifflin has closed the imprint.

LAWYERS & JUDGES PUBLISHING CO., P.O. Box 30040, Tucson AZ 85751-0040. (602)751-1500. Fax: (602)751-1202. President: Steve Weintraub. Publishes professional hardback originals. Publishes 15 titles/year. Receives 200 queries and 10 mss/year. 5% of books from first-time authors; 100% from unagented writers. Pays 7-10% royalty on retail price. Publishes book 5 months after acceptance of ms. Simultaneous submissions OK. Query for electronic submissions. Reports in 2 months. Book catalog free.

Nonfiction: Reference. Subjects include legal/insurance. "We are a highly specific publishing company, reaching the legal and insurance fields and accident reconstruction. Unless a writer is an expert in these areas, we are not interested." Submit proposal package, including full or *very* representative ms. *Writer's Market* recommends query with SASE first.

Recent Nonfiction Title: *Bicycle Accident Reconstruction, 3rd Edition*, by James Green.

LEADERSHIP PUBLISHERS, INC., Talented and Gifted Education, P.O. Box 8358, Des Moines IA 50301-8358. (515)278-4765. Editorial Director: Lois F. Roets. Estab. 1982. Publishes trade paperback originals. Publishes 5 titles/year. Receives 25 queries and 10 mss/year. Pays 10% royalty of sales. Publishes book 1 year after acceptance of ms. Reports in 3 months. Book catalog and ms guidelines for 9×12 SAE with 3 first-class stamps.
Nonfiction: Textbook. Subject is education. "We publish enrichment/supplementary educational programs and teacher reference books; our specialty is education of the talented and gifted." Submit outline and 2 sample chapters. Reviews artwork/photos as part of ms package. Writers should send photocopies.

LEHIGH UNIVERSITY PRESS, Linderman Library, 30 Library Dr., Lehigh University, Bethlehem PA 18015-3067. (610)758-3933. Fax: (610)974-2823. Director: Philip A. Metzger. Estab. 1985. Publishes hardcover originals. Publishes 10 titles/year. Receives 30 queries and 25 mss/year. 70% of books from first-time authors; 100% from unagented writers. Pays royalty. Publishes book 18 months after acceptance of ms. Simultaneous submissions OK. Reports in 3 months. Book catalog and ms guidelines free.
Nonfiction: Biography, reference, academic. Subjects include Americana, art/architecture, history, language/literature, science. "We are an academic press publishing scholarly monographs. We are especially interested in works on 18th century studies and the history of technology, but consider works of quality on a variety of subjects." Submit 1 sample chapter and proposal package.

LEISURE BOOKS, Division of Dorchester Publishing Co., Inc., Suite 1008, 276 Fifth Ave., New York NY 10001-0112. (212)725-8811. Editorial Assistant: Kim Mattson. Estab. 1970. Publishes mass market paperback originals and reprints. Averages 160 titles/year. Receives thousands of submissions/year. 20% of books from first-time authors; 20% from unagented writers. Pays royalty on retail price. Advance negotiable. Publishes book an average of 18 months after acceptance. Reports in 1 month on queries. *Writer's Market* recommends allowing 2 months for reply. Book catalog and ms guidelines for #10 SASE.
• Love Spell, an imprint, publishes only romance titles.
Nonfiction: "Our needs are minimal as we publish perhaps two nonfiction titles a year." Query.
Fiction: Historical romance (115,000 words); time-travel romance (90,000 words); futuristic romance (90,000 words). "We are strongly backing historical romance. No sweet romance, gothic, science fiction, western, erotica, contemporary women's fiction, mainstream or male adventure." Query or submit outline/synopsis and sample chapters. "No material will be returned without SASE."
Tips: "Historical romance is our strongest category. We are also seeking time-travel and futuristic romances."

LERNER PUBLICATIONS COMPANY, 241 First Ave. N., Minneapolis MN 55401. (612)332-3344. Submissions Editor: Jennifer Martin. Estab. 1959. Imprints are Runestone Press, First Avenue Editions. Publishes hardcover originals. Averages 75-100 titles/year. Receives 1,000 queries and 300 mss/year. 50% of books from first-time authors; 90% from unagented writers. Royalty or outright purchase negotiable. Offers $200-1,000 advance. Publishes book 18-24 months after acceptance of ms. Simultaneous submissions OK. Query for electronic submissions. Reports in 2 months on proposals. Catalog for 9×12 SAE with 6 first-class stamps. Manuscript guidelines for #10 SAE.
Nonfiction: Children's/juvenile. Subjects include animals, anthropology/archaeology, art/architecture, business and economics, computers and electronics, cooking/foods/nutrition, ethnic, government/politics, health/medicine, history, language/literature, money/finance, multicultural, music/dance, nature/environment, recreation, science, sports, biography and geography. "We are interested in multicultural work by authors of the focus ethnic groups. Picture books or any work clearly intended for adults (parents and teachers) are not of interest to us. We also do not publish video or audio cassettes. Our main audience consists of children in grades 3 through 9." Submit proposal package, including introductory letter, outline, 1-2 sample chapters, résumé, SASE.
Fiction: Young adult and middle grade. "We publish very little fiction—usually only one or two titles per year—mainly in the mystery and/or multicultural issues areas. We do not publish adult fiction, picture books, 'Babysitters Club'-type series." Query.
Recent Fiction Title: *Ransom for a River Dolphin*, by Sarita Kendall (multicultural juvenile).

LEXIKOS, P.O. Box 296, Lagunitas CA 94938. (415)488-0401. Editor: Mike Witter. Estab. 1981. Imprint is Don't Call It Frisco Press. Publishes hardcover and trade paperback originals and trade paperback reprints. Averages 8 titles/year. Receives 200 submissions annually. 50% of books from first-time authors; 90% from unagented writers. Average print order for a first book is 5,000. Royalties vary from 8-12½% according to books sold. "Authors asked to accept lower royalty on high discount (50% plus) sales." Offers average $1,000 advance. Publishes book an average of 10 months after acceptance. Simultaneous submissions OK. Reports in 1 month. Book catalog and ms guidelines for 6×9 SAE with 2 first-class stamps.
Nonfiction: Coffee table book, illustrated book. Subjects include regional, outdoors, oral histories, Americana, history, nature. Especially looking for 50,000-word "city and regional histories, anecdotal in style for a general audience; books of regional interest about *places*; adventure and wilderness books; annotated reprints of books of Americana; Americana in general." No health, sex, European travel, diet, broad humor,

fiction, quickie books (we stress backlist vitality), religion, children's or nutrition. Submit outline and sample chapters. Reviews artwork/photos as part of ms package.

Recent Nonfiction Title: *A River Went Out Of Eden*, by Chana Cox.

Tips: "A regional interest or history book has the best chance of selling to Lexikos. Submit a short, cogent proposal; follow up with letter queries. Give the publisher reason to believe you will help him *sell* the book (identify the market, point out the availability of mailing lists, distinguish your book from the competition). Avoid grandiose claims."

‡LEXINGTON BOOKS, Imprint of The Free Press, Division of Simon & Schuster, 866 Third Ave., New York NY 10022. (212)702-3130. Senior Editor: Beth Anderson. Publishes hardcover originals. Imprint publishes 40 titles/year. Receives 500 queries and 100 mss/year. 50% of books from first-time authors; 70% from unagented writers. Pays 10-15% royalty on wholesale or retail price. Publishes book 1-2 years after acceptance of ms. Accepts simultaneous submissions. Reports in 2 months on proposals. Book catalog and ms guidelines free on request.

Nonfiction: Reference, trade. Subjects include business and economics, child guidance/parenting, gay/lesbian, money/finance, psychology, sociology, women's issues/studies, criminology. "We publish practical books." Query.

‡THE LIBERAL PRESS, P.O. Box 140361, Las Colinas TX 75014. (214)686-5332. Executive Vice President: Rick Donovon. Publishes trade paperback originals. Publishes 4 titles/year. Receives 50 queries and 100 mss/year. 50% of books from first-time authors; 100% from unagented writers. Pays 2% royalty on retail price. Publishes book 4 months after acceptance of ms. No simultaneous submissions. Query for electronic submissions. Reports in 1 month on queries; 4 months on mss. Book catalog for 6×9 SAE with 5 first-class stamps. Manuscript guidelines for #10 SASE.

Nonfiction: Textbook. Subjects include gay/lesbian, government/politics (liberal only), history, women's issues/studies. "Work must be gender-free nonsexist, historical/factual with necessary bibliographic material (footnote/bibliography)." Query with outline and 2 sample chapters. All unsolicited mss are returned unopened.

Recent Nonfiction Title: *An Ambitious Sort of Grief*, by Marion Cohen (neo-natal loss).

LIBRARIES UNLIMITED, P.O. Box 6633, Englewood CO 80155-6633. Fax: (303)220-8843. Editor-in-Chief: Bohdan S. Wynar. Estab. 1964. Imprints are Teacher Ideas Press, Ukranian Academic Press. Publishes hardcover and paperback originals. Averages 70 titles/year. Receives 100-200 submissions/year. 10-20% of books from first-time authors. Average print order for a first book is 2,000. 10% royalty on net sales. Publishes book an average of 1 year after acceptance. Reports in 2 months. Book catalog and ms guidelines free.

Nonfiction: Publishes reference and library science textbooks, teacher resource and activity books, also software. Looks for professional experience. Query or submit outline and sample chapters; state availability of photos/illustrations with submission. All prospective authors are required to fill out an author questionnaire.

LIFETIME BOOKS, INC., 2131 Hollywood Blvd., Hollywood FL 33020. (305)925-5242. Senior Editor: H. Allen Etling. Imprints are Fell Publishers, Compact Books, Blockbuster Periodicals. Publishes hardcover and trade paperback originals and reprints. Publishes 25 titles/year. Receives 3,500 queries and 2,500 mss/year. 90% of books from first-time authors; 90% from unagented writers. Pays 6-15% royalty on retail price. Offers advance of $500-5,000. Publishes book an average of 6-12 months after acceptance. Simultaneous submissions OK. Reports in 6 months on mss. Book catalog and ms guidelines for 9×12 SAE with 5 first-class stamps.

Nonfiction: Cookbook, how-to, self-help. Subjects include business and economics, child guidance/parenting, cooking, foods and nutrition, education, history, hobbies, money/finance, true crime. "We are interested in material on business, finance, health and fitness, self-improvement and medicine. We will not consider topics that only appeal to a small, select audience." Submit outline and 2 sample chapters. Reviews artwork as part of ms package. Writers should send photocopies.

Recent Nonfiction Title: *A Matter of Judgment*, by Joseph A. Varon, Esq. (true crime); *Cholesterol Cure Made Easy*, by Sylvan R. Lewis, M.D. (health and diet).

Fiction: "We are currently publishing very little fiction." Submit outline/synopsis and sample chapters.

Tips: "We are most interested in well-written, timely nonfiction with strong sales potential. Our audience is very general. Learn markets and be prepared to help with sales and promotion."

‡LIGOURI PUBLICATIONS, One Liguori Dr., Liguori MO 63057. (314)464-2500. Publisher: Thomas M. Santa, C.SS.R. Imprint is Triumph™ Books (contact Patricia Kossman, Executive Editor). Publishes hardcover and trade paperback originals and trade paperback reprints. Publishes 50 titles/year; each imprint publishes 15 titles/year. Pays 9% royalty on retail price or makes outright purchase of $400. Advance varies. Publishes book 2 years after acceptance of ms. No simultaneous submissions. Query for electronic submissions. Reports in 2 months on queries and proposals, 3 months on mss. Book catalog and ms guidelines free on request.

Nonfiction: Children's/juvenile, self-help, devotional. Subjects include religion. Query with outline and 3 sample chapters.

‡LIMELIGHT EDITIONS, Imprint of Proscenium Publishers Inc., 118 E. 30th St., New York NY 10016. President: Melvyn B. Zerman. Publishes hardcover and trade paperback originals and trade paperback reprints. Publishes 14 titles/year. Receives 150 queries and 40 mss/year. 15% of books from first-time authors; 20% from unagented writers. Pays 7½-10% royalty on retail price. Offers $500-2,000 advance. Publishes book 10 months after acceptance of ms. No simultaneous submissions. Query for electronic submissions. Reports in 1 month on queries and proposals, 3 months on mss. Book catalog and ms guidelines free on request.
Nonfiction: Biography, humor, illustrated book, music/dance, self-help, theater/film. "All books are on the performing arts *exclusively*." Query with proposal package, including 2-3 sample chapters and outline. Reviews artwork/photos as part of ms package. Writers should send photocopies.
Recent Nonfiction Title: *Free Admissions*, by Jonathan Kalb (theater criticism).

‡LITERARY WORKS PUBLISHERS, The Writers' Guild, 214-21 Hillside Ave., Queens Village NY 11427. (800)647-4286. Managing Editor: Michael Morales. Imprints are The Writers' Guild and The Literary Guild. Publishes hardcover, trade paperback and mass market paperback originals. Publishes 15 titles/year. Receives 1,500 queries and 2,500 mss/year. 60% of books from first-time authors; 75% from unagented writers. Pays 10-15¼% royalty on retail price or makes outright purchase of $10,000-25,000. Offers $5,000-10,000 advance. Publishes book 10 months after acceptance of ms. Simultaneous submissions OK. Reports in 1 month on queries and proposals, 2 months on mss. Book catalog and ms guidelines for #10 SASE.
Nonfiction: How-to, humor, children's/juvenile, reference, self-help. Subjects include anthropology/archaeology, art/architecture, computers and electronics, cooking, foods & nutrition, education, ethnic, gardening, gay/lesbian, government/politics, history, hobbies, language/literature, nature/environment, philosophy, recreation, regional, science, software, translation, travel, women's issues/studies. Submit outline with 2 sample chapters. Reviews artwork/photos as part of freelance ms package. Writers should send transparencies.
Fiction: Adventure, ethnic, experimental, fantasy, feminist, gay/lesbian, historical, humor, juvenile, literary, mainstream/contemporary, picture books, plays, religious, short story collections, poetry. Submit complete ms.
Recent Fiction Title: *Blacken Rose*, by Kate Kowalski (women's mainstream); *Beauty's Flower*, by Misha (short story/collection).
Poetry: "We plan to pubilsh more poetry because there is a market for it and none of the big houses will even look at it." Query or submit 5 sample poems. Submit complete ms.
Recent Poetry Title: *Beauty and Her Rose*, by Misha (Stunnins).
Tips: Do not get an agent. It is more trouble than it is worth. You can do a better job yourself by looking for a small press than can accomodate you and your book.

LITTLE, BROWN AND CO., INC., Division of Time Warner Inc., 1271 Avenue of the Americas, New York NY 10020. (212)522-8700. Contact: Editorial Department, Trade Division. Estab. 1837. Imprint is Bullfinch Press. Publishes hardcover and paperback originals and paperback reprints. Averages 100 titles/year. "Royalty and advance agreements vary from book to book and are discussed with the author at the time an offer is made. Submissions *only* from authors who have had a book published or have been published in professional or literary journals, newspapers or magazines."
Nonfiction: "Some how-to books, distinctive cookbooks, biographies, history, popular science and nature, and sports." Query *only*. Will not accept unsolicited mss or proposals.
Recent Nonfiction Title: *The Cat and the Curmudgeon*, by Cleveland Amory.
Fiction: Contemporary popular fiction as well as fiction of literary distinction. Query *only*. Will not accept unsolicited mss or proposals.
Recent Fiction Title: *The Last Voyage of Somebody the Sailor*, by John Barth.

LITTLE, BROWN AND COMPANY, CHILDREN'S BOOK DIVISION, 34 Beacon St., Boston MA 02108. (617)227-0730. Editorial Assistant: Erica Lombard. Publishes hardcover originals. Only accepting submissions through literary agents and from previously published authors. Pays royalty on retail price. Offers advance to be negotiated individually. Publishes book 2 years after acceptance of ms. Simultaneous submissions OK "if indicated as such." Reports in 1 month on queries, 3 months on proposals and mss. Book catalog for 8 × 10 SAE with 3 first-class stamps. Manuscript guidelines free on request.
Nonfiction: Children's/juvenile. Subjects include animals, art/architecture, cooking/foods/nutrition, ethnic, gay/lesbian, history, hobbies, nature/environment, recreation, science, sports. "We have published and will continue to publish books on a wide variety of nonfiction topics which may be of interest to children and are looking for strong writing and presentation, but no predetermined topics." Writers should avoid "looking for the 'issue' they think publishers want to see, choosing instead topics they know best and are most enthusiastic about/inspired by." Submit outline and 3 sample chapters "including first and last if possible" or proposal package, including "most complete outline, possible samples and background info (if project is not complete due to necessary research)." Reviews artwork/photos as part of freelance package. Writers should include photocopies (color if possible).
Recent Nonfiction Title: *Voices From the Fields: Children of Migrant Farmworkers Tell Their Stories*, by S. Beth Atkin (middle grade photo essay).

Fiction: All juvenile/young adult. Categories include adventure, ethnic, fantasy, feminist, gay/lesbian, historical, humor, mystery, picture books, science fiction, short story collections and suspense. "We are looking for strong fiction for children of all ages in any area, including multicultural. We always prefer full manuscripts for fiction."

Recent Fiction Title: *Kinda Blue*, by Ann Grifalconi (picture book).

Tips: "Our audience is children of all ages, from preschool through young adult. We are looking for quality material that will work in hardcover—send us your best."

LLEWELLYN PUBLICATIONS, Subsidiary of Llewellyn Worldwide, Ltd., P.O. Box 64383, St. Paul MN 55164-0383. (612)291-1970. Fax: (612)291-1908. Acquisitions Manager: Nancy J. Mostad. Estab. 1901. Publishes trade and mass market paperback originals. Averages 60 titles/year. Receives 500 submissions/year. 30% of books from first-time authors; 90% from unagented writers. Pays 10% royalty on moneys received both wholesale and retail. Publishes book an average of 16 months after acceptance. Simultaneous submissions OK. Query for electronic submissions. Reports in 3 months. Book catalog for 9 × 12 SAE with 4 first-class stamps. Manuscript guidelines for SASE.

  • Llewellyn has had a 20% growth rate each year for the past five years.

Nonfiction: How-to, self-help. Subjects include nature/environment, health and nutrition, metaphysical/magic, psychology, women's issues/studies. Submit outline and sample chapters. Reviews artwork/photos as part of ms package.

Recent Nonfiction Title: *Maiden, Mother, Crone*, by D.J. Conway.

Fiction: Metaphysical/occult, which is authentic, yet entertaining.

LOCUST HILL PRESS, P.O. Box 260, West Cornwall CT 06796-0260. (203)672-0060. Fax: (203)672-4968. Publisher: Thomas C. Bechtle. Publishes hardcover originals. Publishes 12 titles/year. Receives 150 queries and 20 mss/year. 100% of books from unagented writers. Pays 12-18% royalty on retail price. Publishes book 6 months after acceptance of ms. Simultaneous submissions OK. Query for electronic submissions. Reports in 1 month on queries. Book catalog free.

  • Locust Hill's sales plummeted from early 1991 to late 1992, but have come back stronger than ever since January of 1993.

Nonfiction: Reference. Subjects include art/architecture, business and economics, ethnic, language/literature, music/dance, philosophy, psychology, religion, science, women's issues/studies. "Since our audience is exclusively college and university libraries (and the occasional specialist), we are less inclined to accept manuscripts in 'popular' (i.e., public library) fields. While bibliography has been and will continue to be a specialty, our Locust Hill Literary Studies is gaining popularity as a series of essay collections and monographs in a wide variety of literary topics." Query.

Tips: "Remember that this is a small, very specialized academic publisher with no distribution network other than mail contact with most academic libraries worldwide. Please shape your expectations accordingly. If your aim is to reach the world's scholarly community by way of its libraries, we are the correct firm to contact. But *please*: no fiction, poetry, popular religion, or personal memoirs."

LODESTAR BOOKS, Affiliate of Dutton Children's Books, division of Penguin Books USA, 375 Hudson St., New York NY 10014. (212)366-2627. Editorial Director: Virginia Buckley. Senior Editor: Rosemary Brosnan. Publishes hardcover originals. Publishes juveniles, young adults, fiction, nonfiction and picture books. Averages 25-30 titles/year. Receives 1,000 submissions annually. 10-20% of books from first-time authors; 25-30% from unagented writers. Average print order for a first novel or nonfiction is 4,000-5,000; picture book print runs are higher. Pays royalty on invoice list price. Offers advance. Publishes book an average of 18 months after acceptance. Reports in 3 months. Manuscript guidelines for SASE.

  • Lodestar now only accepts queries (previously it would review chapters or complete mss) enabling it to cut reporting time from four months to three months.

Nonfiction: Query letters only. State availability of photos and/or illustrations. Reviews artwork/photos as part of ms package.

Recent Nonfiction Title: *The Other Side*, by Kathleen Krull; photographs by David Hautzig.

Fiction: Publishes for young adults (middle grade) and juveniles (ages 5-17). Subjects include multicultural, adventure, fantasy, historical, humorous, contemporary, mystery, science fiction, suspense, western books, also picture books. Submit query letters only.

Recent Fiction Title: *Celebrating the Hero*, by Lyll Becerra de Jenkins.

Tips: "A young adult or middle-grade novel that is literary, fast-paced, well-constructed (as opposed to a commercial novel); well-written nonfiction on contemporary issues, photographic essays, and nonfiction picture books have been our staples. We do only a select number of picture books, which are very carefully chosen."

LONE EAGLE PUBLISHING CO., Suite 9, 2337 Roscomare Rd., Los Angeles CA 90077-1851. (310)471-8066. Fax: (310)471-4969. Toll Free: 1-800-FILMBKS. President: Joan V. Singleton. VP/Editorial: Beth Ann Wetzel. Estab. 1982. Publishes perfect bound and trade paperback originals. Averages 8 titles/year. Receives 20-30 submissions/year. 95% of books from unagented writers. Pays 10% royalty minimum on net income wholesale and retail. Offers $250-500 average advance. Publishes a book an average of 1 year after acceptance. Simultaneous submissions OK. Query for electronic submissions. Reports quarterly on queries. Book catalog for #10 SAE with 2 first-class stamps.

Nonfiction: Technical, how-to, reference. Subjects include films and television. "We are looking for technical books in film and television. No unrelated topics or biographies." Submit outline and sample chapters. Reviews artwork/photos as part of ms package.

Tips: "A well-written, well-thought-out book on some technical aspect of the motion picture (or video) industry has the best chance: for example, script supervising, editing, special effects, costume design, production design. Pick a subject that has not been done to death, make sure you know what you're talking about, get someone well-known in that area to endorse the book and prepare to spend a lot of time publicizing the book."

LONELY PLANET PUBLICATIONS, Suite 251, 155 Filbert St., Oakland CA 94607-2538. Publishing Manager: Sue Mitra. Estab. 1973. Publishes trade paperback originals. Publishes 30 titles/year. Receives 500 queries and 100 mss/year. 5% of books from first-time authors; 50% from unagented writers. Makes outright purchase or negotiated fee — ⅓ on contract, ⅓ on submission, ⅓ on approval. Publishes book 1-2 years after acceptance of ms. Simultaneous submissions OK. Query for electronic submissions. Reports in 3 months on queries. Book catalog free.

Nonfiction: Travel guides and travel phrasebooks exclusively. "Writers should request our catalog first to make sure we don't already have a book similar to what they have written or would like to write. Also they should call and see if a similar book is on our production schedule. Lonely Planet publishes travel guides and phrasebooks, period." Submit outline or proposal package. Reviews artwork/photos as part of ms package. Writers should send photocopies. "Don't send unsolicited transparencies!"

LONGMAN PUBLISHING GROUP, 10 Bank St., White Plains NY 10606-1951. (914)993-5000. Fax: (914)997-8115. Contact: Barbara McIntosh. Estab. 1974. Publishes hardcover and paperback originals. Publishes 200 titles/year. Pays variable royalty. Offers variable advance. Reports in 2 months.

Nonfiction: Textbooks only (elementary/high school, college and professional): history, political science, economics, communications, social sciences, social work, education, English, Latin, foreign languages, English as a second language. No trade, art or juvenile.

LONGSTREET PRESS, INC., Suite 118, 2140 Newmarket Parkway, Marietta GA 30144-30067. (404)980-1488. Fax: (404)859-9894. Associate Editor: Suzanne Bell. Estab. 1988. Publishes hardcover and trade paperback originals. Averages 40 titles/year. Receives 2,500 submissions/year. 25-30% of books from first-time authors. Pays royalty. Publishes book an average of 1 year after acceptance. Simultaneous submissions OK. Reports in 3 months. Book catalog for 9×12 SAE with 4 first-class stamps. Manuscript guidelines for #10 SASE.

Nonfiction: Biography, coffee table book, cookbook, humor, illustrated book, reference. Subjects include Americana, cooking, foods and nutrition, gardening, history, language/literature, nature/environment, photography, regional, sports, women's issues/studies. "We want serious journalism-oriented nonfiction on subjects appealing to a broad, various audience. No poetry, how-to, religious or inspirational, scientific or highly technical, textbooks of any kind, erotica." Query or submit outline and sample chapters. Reviews artwork as part of ms package.

Fiction: Literary, mainstream/contemporary. Agented fiction only. "We are not interested in formula/genre novels, but we're open to popular fiction that's exceptionally well done."

  ● Longstreet now accepts only agented fiction.

Tips: "Midlist books have a harder time making it. The nonfiction book, serious or humorous, with a clearly defined audience has the best chance. The audience for our books has a strong sense of intellectual curiosity and a functioning sense of humor. If I were a writer trying to market a book today, I would do thorough, professional work aimed at a clearly defined and reachable audience."

LOOMPANICS UNLIMITED, P.O. Box 1197, Port Townsend WA 98368-0997. President: Michael Hoy. Editorial Director: Steve O'Keefe. Estab. 1975. Publishes trade paperback originals. Publishes 15 titles/year. Receives 500 submissions/year. 40% of books from first-time authors; 100% from unagented writers. Average print order for a first book is 2,000. Pays 10-15% royalty on wholesale or retail price or makes outright purchase of $100-1,200. Offers average $500 advance. Publishes book an average of 1 year after acceptance. Simultaneous submissions OK. Reports in 2 months. Free author guidelines. Book catalog for $5, postpaid.

  ● Loompanics is doing fewer books, (down from 20 to 15/year) but is putting more work into them and says their business is very, very good.

Nonfiction: How-to, reference, self-help. Subjects include the underground economy, crime, drugs, privacy, self-sufficiency, anarchism and "beat the system" books. "We are looking for how-to books in the fields of espionage, investigation, the underground economy, police methods, how to beat the system, crime and criminal techniques. No cookbooks, inspirational, travel, management or cutesy-wutesy stuff." Query or submit outline/synopsis and sample chapters. Reviews artwork/photos.

Tips: "Our audience is young males looking for hard-to-find information on alternatives to 'The System.' Your chances for success are greatly improved if you can show us how your proposal fits in with our catalog."

LOTHROP, LEE & SHEPARD BOOKS, Imprint of William Morrow & Company, 1350 Avenue of the Americas, New York NY 10019. (212)261-6500. Fax: (212)261-6648. Editor-in-Chief: Susan Pearson. Estab. 1859. Other children's imprints are Morrow Junior Books, Greenwillow Books and Tambourine Books. Publishes hardcover original children's books only. Royalty and advance vary according to type of book. Averages 60 titles/ year. Fewer than 2% of books from first-time authors; 25% of books from unagented writers. Average print order for a first book is 6,000. Publishes book an average of 2 years after acceptance. Does *not* accept unsolicited mss. Reports in 3 months.

Fiction and Nonfiction: Publishes picture books, general nonfiction, and novels. Juvenile fiction emphasis is on novels for the 8-12 age group. Looks for "organization, clarity, creativity, literary style." Query *only*. Does *not* read unsolicited mss.

Recent Nonfiction Title: *Kangaroos: On Location*, by Kathy Darling; photos by Tara Darling.

LOUISIANA STATE UNIVERSITY PRESS, Baton Rouge LA 70894-5053. (504)388-6294. Editor-in-Chief: Margaret Fisher Dalrymple. Estab. 1935. Publishes hardcover originals and hardcover and trade paperback reprints. Averages 60-70 titles/year. Receives 500 submissions/year. 33% of books from first-time authors. 90% from unagented writers. Pays royalty on wholesale price. Publishes book an average of 1 year after acceptance. Reports in 3 weeks on queries. *Writer's Market* recommends allowing 2 months for reply. Free book catalog and ms guidelines.

● This university press no longer publishes any fiction.

Nonfiction: Biography and literary poetry collections. Subjects include anthropology/archaeology, art/architecture, ethnic, government/politics, history, language/literature, military/war, music/dance, philosophy, photography, regional, sociology, women's issues/studies. Query or submit outline and sample chapters/poems.

Tips: "Our audience includes scholars, intelligent laymen, general audience."

LOVE CHILD PUBLISHING, P.O. Box 7374, Culver City CA 90233-7374. (213)960-3991. Publisher/Editor: Tanya-Monique Kersey. Estab. 1990. Publishes trade paperback originals. Publishes 5-7 titles/year. Receives 20 queries and 5 mss/year. 90% of books from first-time authors; 75% from unagented writers. Pays 5-12% royalty. Terms are negotiable. Advance varies. Publishes book 1 year after acceptance. Simultaneous submissions OK. Reports in 3 months on queries. Book catalog and ms guidelines for #10 SASE.

Nonfiction: How-to, reference, performing arts, entertainment. "We publish career publications (books, guides, directories, monologue/scene books) for African-Americans in the entertainment industry. We also publish some career publications that are not specifically for minorities." Submit outline with 1-2 sample chapters.

Recent Nonfiction Title: *The Black Actor's Book of Original Scenes & Monologues*, by ToniAnn Johnson, Leslie Lee, Cheryl Lane-Lewis and Zelda Patterson.

Tips: "Know the entertainment industry!"

LOYOLA UNIVERSITY PRESS, 3441 N. Ashland Ave., Chicago IL 60657-1397. (312)281-1818. Fax: (312)281-0555. Editorial Director: Rev. Joseph F. Downey. Estab. 1912. Imprints are Campion Books, Values & Ethics. Publishes hardcover and trade paperback originals and reprints. Averages 12 titles/year. Receives 150 submissions annually. 60% of books from first-time authors; 95% from unagented writers. Pays 10% royalty on net price, retail and wholesale. No advance. Publishes book an average of 1 year after acceptance. Simultaneous submissions OK. Query for electronic submissions. Reports in 2 months. Book catalog for 6×9 SASE.

Nonfiction: Biography, textbook. Subjects include art (religious); history (church); religion. The four subject areas of Campion Books include Jesuitica (Jesuit history, biography and spirituality); Literature-Theology interface (books dealing with theological or religious aspects of literary works or authors); contemporary Christian concerns (books on morality, spirituality, family life, pastoral ministry, prayer, worship, etc.); Chicago/art (books dealing with the city of Chicago from historical, artistic, architectural, or ethnic perspectives, but with religious emphases). Values & Ethics Series favors mss of a more scholarly and interdisciplinary bent. Query before submitting ms. Reviews artwork/photos.

Recent Nonfiction Titles: *The Catholic Tradition*, by Timothy G. McCarthy.

Tips: "Our audience is principally the college-educated reader with a religious, theological interest."

LUCENT BOOKS, P.O. Box 289011, San Diego CA 92198-9011. (619)485-7424. Managing Editor: Bonnie Szumski. Publishes hardcover originals and reprints. Publishes 50 titles/year. 50% of books from first-time authors; 90% from unagented writers. No unsolicited mss. *Writing by assignment only*. Makes outright purchase of $2,000-3,000. Offers average advance of 1/3 of total fee. Publishes book an average of 9 months after acceptance. Book catalog and ms guidelines for 9×12 SAE with 3 first-class stamps.

Nonfiction: Juvenile. Subjects include controversial issues, discoveries and inventions, anthropology/archaeology, business and economics, computers and electronics, government/politics, history, military/war, nature/ environment, science, sports, women's issues/studies, biographies, histories. All on the juvenile level. Absolutely publishes *no* fiction or *anything* resembling fiction. All unsolicited mss returned unopened.

Tips: "Please do not send material inappropriate to a company's list. In our case, no unsolicited manuscripts are accepted and no fiction is published. When writers send inappropriate material, they can make a lifetime enemy of the publisher."

LURAMEDIA, P.O. Box 261668, San Diego CA 92196-1668. (619)578-1948. Fax: (619)578-7560. Editorial Director: Lura Jane Geiger, Ph.D. Estab. 1982. Publishes trade paperback originals. Averages 6-8 titles/year. Receives 250 submissions annually. 60% of books from first-time authors; 90% from unagented writers. Pays 10% royalty on wholesale price. Publishes book an average of 15 months after acceptance. Proposals only; no unsolicited mss. Reports in 3 months. Book catalog and ms guidelines for 9 × 12 SAE with 2 first-class stamps.
Nonfiction: "Books for Healing & Hope, Balance & Justice. We publish books that contribute to spiritual, emotional and physical renewal. Our subjects include health of body and mind, woman's issues, relationships, prayer/meditation, creativity, journaling, relational group work, creative biblical education, values for children/family, aging, justice, alternative life-styles, ecology, experience of minorities, social issues. We especially favor approaches that utilize self disclosure, personal reflection, journal writing, stories/fables/parables, essays, meditations, sermons and prayers. We are looking for books that are well-thought out, books that encourage creative thinking rather than giving all the answers."
Tips: "Our audience includes people who want to grow and change; who want to get in touch with their spiritual side; who want to relax; who are creative and want creative ways to live."

LYONS & BURFORD, PUBLISHERS, INC., 31 W. 21 St., New York NY 10010. (212)620-9580. Fax: (212)929-1836. Publisher: Peter Burford. Estab. 1984. Publishes hardcover and trade paperback originals and reprints. Averages 40-50 titles/year. 50% of books from first-time authors; 75% from unagented writers. Pays varied royalty on retail price. Publishes book an average of 1 year after acceptance. Simultaneous submissions OK. Reports in 2 weeks on queries. *Writer's Market* recommends allowing 2 months for reply. Book catalog free.
Nonfiction: Subjects include agriculture/horticulture, Americana, animals, art/architecture, cooking, foods and nutrition, gardening, hobbies, nature/environment, science, sports, travel. Query.
Recent Nonfiction Title: *The Habit of Rivers,* by Ted Leeson.
Tips: "We want practical, well-written books on any aspect of the outdoors."

McDONALD & WOODWARD PUBLISHING CO., P.O. Box 10308, Blacksburg VA 24062-0308. (703)951-9465. Fax: (703)552-0210. Managing Partner: Jerry N. McDonald. Estab. 1986. Publishes hardcover and trade paperback originals. Publishes 5 titles/year. Receives 30 queries and 10 mss/year. 50% of books from first-time authors; 100% from unagented writers. Pays 10% royalty on net receipts. Publishes book 1 year after acceptance of ms. Simultaneous submissions OK. Query for electronic submissions. Reports in 2 months. Book catalog free.
Nonfiction: Biography, coffee table book, how-to, illustrated book, self-help. Subjects include Americana, animals, anthropology, ethnic, history, nature/environment, science, travel. "We are especially interested in additional titles in our 'Guides to the American Landscape' series. Should consult titles in print for guidance. We want well organized, clearly written, substantive material." Query or submit outline and sample chapters. Reviews artwork/photos as part of freelance ms package. Writers should send photocopies.

MARGARET K. McELDERRY BOOKS, Imprint of Simon & Schuster Children's Publishing and New Media, Division of Simon & Schuster, 866 Third Ave., New York NY 10022. Fax: (212)605-3045. Editor: Margaret K. McElderry. Associate Editor: Emma D. Drydon. Estab. 1971. Publishes hardcover originals. Publishes about 25 titles/year. Receives 4,000 submissions annually. 8% of books from first-time authors; 50% from unagented writers. Average print order is 6,000-7,500 for a first teen book; 10,000-15,000 for a first picture book. Pays royalty on retail price. Publishes book an average of 18 months after acceptance. Reports in 3 months. Catalog for 9 × 12 SAE with 4 first-class stamps. Manuscript guidelines for #10 SASE.
  • Margaret K. McElderry was named the 1993 recipient of the Association of American Publishers' Curtis Benjamin Award for Creative Publishing.
Nonfiction and Fiction: Quality material for preschoolers to 16-year-olds, but publishes only a few YAs. Looks for "originality of ideas, clarity and felicity of expression, well-organized plot and strong characterization (fiction) or clear exposition (nonfiction); quality." *Writer's Market* recommends query with SASE first. Reviews artwork/photos as part of ms package, but prefers to review texts only.
Recent Title: *The Boggart,* by Susan Cooper.
Tips: "There is not a particular 'type' of book that we are interested in above others, though we always look for humor. Rather, we look for superior quality in both writing and illustration. Freelance writers should be aware of the swing away from teen-age novels to books for younger readers and of the growing need for beginning chapter books for children just learning to read on their own."

McFARLAND & COMPANY, INC., PUBLISHERS, P.O. Box 611, Jefferson NC 28640. (919)246-4460. Fax: (919)246-5018. President and Editor-in-Chief: Robert Franklin. Vice President: Rhonda Herman. Editors: Lisa Camp, Steve Wilson. Estab. 1979. Publishes mostly hardcover and a few "quality" paperback originals; a non-"trade" publisher. Averages 115 titles/year. Receives 1,000 submissions annually. 70% of books from first-time authors; 95% from unagented writers. Average print order for a first book is 1,000. Pays 10-12½% royalty on net receipts. No advance. Publishes book an average of 9 months after acceptance. Reports in 2 weeks. *Writer's Market* recommends allowing 2 months for reply.

Nonfiction: Reference books and scholarly, technical and professional monographs. Subjects include Americana, art, business, chess, drama/theatre, cinema/radio/TV (very strong), health, history, librarianship (very strong), music, sociology, sports/recreation (very strong) women's studies (very strong), world affairs (very strong). "We will consider *any* scholarly book—with authorial maturity and competent grasp of subject." Reference books are particularly wanted—fresh material (i.e., not in head-to-head competition with an established title). "We don't like manuscripts of fewer than 200 pages. Our market consists mainly of libraries." No New Age material, memoirs, poetry, children's books, devotional/inspirational works or personal essays. Query or submit outline and sample chapters. Reviews artwork/photos as part of ms package.

Recent Nonfiction Title: *African Placenames: Origins and Meanings of the Names for Over 2000 Natural Features, Towns, Cities, Provinces and Countries*, by Adrian Room.

Tips: "We do *not* accept novels or fiction of any kind or personal Bible studies. What we want is well-organized *knowledge* of an area in which there is not good information coverage at present, plus reliability so we don't feel we have to check absolutely everything."

McGRAW-HILL INC., 1221 Avenue of the Americas, New York NY 10020. Divisions include McGraw-Hill Ryerson (Canada), Osborne/McGraw-Hill, and TAB Books. General interest publisher of both fiction and nonfiction. This company did not respond to our request for information. Query before submitting.

MCGUINN & MCGUIRE PUBLISHING INC., P.O. Box 20603, Bradenton FL 34203-0603. Managing Editor: Christopher Carroll. Estab. 1991. Publishes hardcover and trade paperback originals. Publishes 6 titles/year. Receives 500 queries and 75 mss/year. 50% of books from first-time authors; 100% from unagented writers. Pays 10-15% royalty on net receipts. Offers $250 advance. Publishes book 1 year after acceptance of ms. Simultaneous submissions OK. Query for electronic submissions. Reports in 1 month on queries and proposals, 2 months on mss. Book catalog and ms guidelines for #10 SASE. "Will not return submissions without SASE."

Nonfiction: Biography, technical. Subjects include business and economics, history. "We are not interested in religious materials, memoirs, books relating a personal philosophy, diet books, or investment books. Author should be able to demonstrate how his/her book fills a void in the market." Query or submit outline and 3 sample chapters. Reviews artwork/photos as part of the freelance ms package. Writers should send photocopies.

Recent Nonfiction Title: *The Making of a Manager*, by Donald A. Wellman (business/management).

Tips: "Always include a word count with queries and proposals. We will only consider books which are at least 50,000 words. Our audience consists of college-educated adults who look for books written by experts in their field. We are particularly interested in reviewing business books which help managers improve their business skills."

MADISON BOOKS, 4720 Boston Way, Lanham MD 20706. (301)459-3366. Fax: (301)459-2118. Publisher: James E. Lyons. Managing Editor: Julie Kirsch. Estab. 1984. Publishes hardcover originals and trade paperback originals and reprints. Averages 40 titles/year. Receives 1,200 submissions/year. 15% of books from first-time authors; 50% from unagented writers. Pays 10-15% royalty on net price. Publishes ms an average of 1 year after acceptance. *Writer's Market* recommends allowing 2 months for reply. Book catalog and manuscript guidelines for 9 × 12 SAE and 4 first-class stamps.

Nonfiction: History, biography, contemporary affairs, popular culture, trade reference. Query or submit outline and sample chapter. No complete mss.

‡MAGNA PUBLICATIONS, 2718 Dryden Dr., Madison WI 53704. (608)246-3580. Editor: Linda Babler. Publishes trade paperback originals. Publishes 4-6 titles/year. Receives 50 queries/year. 100% of books from unagented writers. Pays 10-12% royalty on actual sales. Publishes book 8-10 months after acceptance of ms. Simultaneous submissions OK. Query for electronic submissions. Reports in 2 months on queries. Book catalog and ms guidelines free.

Nonfiction: Subjects include education. Query with outline and 3 sample chapters.

Recent Nonfiction Title: *The Quality Professor: Implementing TQM in the Classroom*, by Robert Cornesky; *Charting Your Course: How to Prepare to Teach More Effectively*, by Richard Prégent.

‡M&T BOOKS, division of MIS: Press, subsidiary of Henry Holt, 115 W. 18th St., New York NY 10011. (212)886-9355. Fax: (212)807-6654. Publisher: Steven Berkowitz. Publishes trader paperback computer books for the higher level user. Publishes 40 titles/year. Receives 200 queries/year. 20% of books from first-time authors. Royalties 5-15% of net receipts. Offers average advance $8,000. Publishes book an average of 4 months after contract.

Nonfiction: Networking, programming, databases, operating systems.

MARKETSCOPE BOOKS, 119 Richard Court, Aptos CA 95003. (408)688-7535. Editor-in-Chief: Ken Albert. Estab. 1985. Publishes hardcover and trade paperback originals. Averages 10 titles/year. 50% of books from first-time authors; 50% from unagented writers. Pays 10-15% royalty on wholesale price. Publishes book an average of 6-12 months after acceptance. Simultaneous submissions OK. Reports in 1 week on queries. *Writer's Market* recommends allowing 2 weeks for reply.
Nonfiction: Biography, how-to, humor, self-help. Subjects include anthropology/archaeology, child guidance/parenting, sexuality, health/medicine, hobbies, money/finance, nature/environment, recreation, regional, religion, sociology. Submit query letter. Reviews artwork/photos as part of the freelance ms package.

‡MARKOWSKI INTERNATIONAL PUBLISHERS, 1 Oakglade Circle, Hummelstown PA 17036-9525. (717)566-0468. Fax: (717)566-6423. Editor: Marjorie A. Markowski. Estab. 1981. Publishes hardcover and trade paperback originals. Averages 6 titles/year. Receives 50 submissions/year. 50% of books from first-time authors; 100% from unagented writers. Average print order for a first book is 5,000. Pays 10-15% royalty on wholesale price; buys some mss outright. Offers average $1,000-1,500 advance. Publishes book an average of 1 year after acceptance. Simultaneous submissions OK. Reports in 2 months. Book catalog and ms guidelines for #10 SAE with 2 first-class stamps.
  ● Markowski is really focusing on the "people," success, motivation and self-help areas.
Nonfiction: Primary focus on popular health and fitness, marriage and human relations, human development, self-help, personal growth, sales and marketing, leadership training, network marketing, motivation and success. Also publishes books on various aviation and model aviation topics. We are interested in howto, motivational and instructionl books of short to medium length that will serve recognized and emerging needs of society." Query or submit outline and 3 sample chapters. Reviews artwork/photos as part of ms package.
Recent Nonfiction Title: *Dreams Do Come True,* by Markowski (successful people).
Tips: "We're very interested in publishing bestsellers."

MARLOR PRESS, INC., 4304 Brigadoon Dr., St. Paul MN 55126. (612)484-4600. Publisher: Marlin Bree. Estab. 1981. Publishes trade paperback originals. Averages 6 titles/year. Receives 100 queries and 25 mss/year. Pays 10% royalty on wholesale price. Publishes book an average of 8 months after final acceptance. Reports in 2 months on queries and proposals, 3 months on mss. Book catalog for 6×9 SAE with 2 first-class stamps. Manuscript guidelines for #10 SASE.
Nonfiction: General nonfiction, children's books. Subjects include boating, child guidance/parenting, travel. Please query first, and submit outline with sample chapters only when requested. Do not send full ms. Reviews artwork/photos as part of ms package.
Recent Nonfiction Title: *London for the Independent Traveler,* by Ruth Numlekev; *Kid's Book to Welcome a New Baby,* by Barbara J. Collman.

‡MASQUERADE BOOKS, 801 Second Ave., New York NY 10017. Publisher: Richard Kasak. Imprints are Bad Boy, Rosebud, Rhinoceros, Richard Kasak Books. Publishes trade and mass market paperback originals and reprints. Publishes 132 titles/year; each imprint publishes 30 or more titles/year. Pays royalty on retail price. Offers $1,500 advance. No simultaneous submissions. Query for electronic submissions. Reports in 1 month on queries.
Nonfiction: Subjects include gay/lesbian. Submit outline and 1 sample chapter.
Recent Nonfiction Title: *Motion of Light in Water,* by Samuel R. Delany (autobiography).
Fiction: Erotica, gay/lesbian, literary. Submit synopsis and 2 sample chapters.
Recent Fiction Title: *American Prelude,* by Lars Eiginer (short stories).

MASTERS PRESS, division of Howard W. Sams & Co., Suite 300, 2647 Waterfront Pkwy. E. Dr., Indianapolis IN 46214-2041. (317)298-5706. Fax: (317)298-5604. Managing Editor: Mark Montieth. Estab. 1986. Imprint is Spalding Sports Library. Publishes trade paperback originals and reprints. Firm publishes 30-40 titles/year; imprint publishes 20 titles/year. Receives 60 queries and 30 mss/year. 50% of books from first-time authors; 100% from unagented writers. Pays 7½-15% royalty. Publishes book 6-12 months after acceptance. Simultaneous submissions OK. Query for electronic submission: prefers WordPerfect 5.1 or ASCII DOS. Reports in 2 months on proposals. Book catalog free on request.
Nonfiction: Sports. Submit proposal package, including outline, 3-4 sample chapters, author information and marketing ideas.
Recent Nonfiction Title: *Tourney Time—It's Awesome Baby,* by Dick Vitale and Mike Douchant.
Tips: "Our audience is athletes, coaches, fans and participants of various sports."

The double dagger before a listing indicates that the listing is new in this edition. New markets are often more receptive to freelance submissions.

MAVERICK PUBLICATIONS, P.O. Box 5007, Bend OR 97708. (503)382-6978. Fax: (503)382-4831. Publisher: Gary Asher. Estab. 1968. Publishes trade paperback originals and reprints. Averages 10 titles/year. Receives 100 submissions annually. Pays 15% royalty on wholesale price. Publishes book an average of 1 year after acceptance. Simultaneous submissions OK. Reports 2 months.
Nonfiction: Pacific Northwest only: aviation, cooking, history, hobby, how-to, marine, native American, nature and environment, recreation, reference, sports, travel. Submit proposal.

‡MAYFIELD PUBLISHING COMPANY, 1280 Villa St., Mountain View CA 94041. President: Richard Greenberg. Publishes 40-50 titles/year. Simultaneous submissions OK. Reports in 2 months. Manuscript guidelines free on request.
Nonfiction: Textbook (college only). Subjects include anthropology/archaeology, art/architecture, child guidance/parenting, ethnic, health/medicine, language/literature, music/dance, philosophy, psychology, religion, sociology. Submit proposal package including outline, table of contents, sample chapter and description of proposed market.

MEADOWBROOK PRESS, 18318 Minnetonka Blvd., Deephaven MN 55391. (612)473-5400. Fax: (612)475-0736. Contact: Submissions Editor. Estab. 1975. Publishes trade paperback originals and reprints. Averages 12 titles/year. Receives 500 queries/year. 25% of books from first-time authors; 75% from unagented writers. Pays 5-7½% royalty. Offers $2,000 average advance. Publishes book an average of 1 year after acceptance. Simultaneous submissions OK. Reports in 3 months on queries. Book catalog and ms guidelines for #10 SASE.
 • Meadowbrook has a greater need for children's poems and poetry in general, but no longer does travel or cookbook titles.
Nonfiction: How-to, humor, juvenile, illustrated book, reference. Subjects include baby and childcare, senior citizen's, children's activities, relationships. No academic, autobiography, semi-autobiography or fiction. Query with outline and sample chapters. "We prefer a query first; then we will request an outline and/or sample material."
Recent Nonfiction Title: *The Joy of Marriage*, by Monica and Bill Dodds.
Tips: "We like how-to books in a simple, accessible format and any new advice on parenting. We look for a fresh approach to overcoming traditional problems (e.g. potty training)."

MEDIA FORUM INTERNATIONAL, LTD., RFD 1, P.O. Box 107, W. Danville VT 05873. (802)592-3444. Or P.O. Box 265, Peacham VT 05862-0265. (802)592-3310. Managing Director: D.K. Bognár. Estab. 1969. Imprints are Media Forum Books, Division, Ha' Penny Gourmet. Publishes hardcover and trade paperback originals. Averages 4 titles/year. Pays 10% minimum royalty.
Nonfiction: Biography, humor, reference. Subjects include ethnic, broadcast/film and drama. *"All mss are assigned."*

MEDIA PUBLISHING/MIDGARD PRESS, Division of Westport Publishers, Inc., #310, 4050 Pennsylvania Ave., Kansas City MO 64111-3024. (816)756-1490. President: Paul C. Temme. Publishes hardcover originals and trade paperback originals and reprints. Averages 4 titles/year. Receives 125 submissions/year. 60% of books from first-time writers; 95% from unagented writers. Pays royalty based on net sales. "Midgard Press provides publishing on a contract basis. Media Publishing is trade publishing." Publishes book an average of 6 months after acceptance. Simultaneous submissions OK. Reports in 2 months. Submit query or ms with SASE.
Nonfiction: Biography, reference, self-help. Subjects include Americana, history, regional studies. Query or submit outline and sample chapters. Reviews artwork/photos as part of ms package.
Recent Nonfiction Title: *Guns Gold and Glory*, by Larry Underwood.

‡MEDICAL PHYSICS PUBLISHING, 732 N. Midvale Blvd., Madison WI 53705. (608)262-4021. Acquisitions Editor: John Cameron. Imprint is Cogito Books. Publishes hardcover and trade paperback originals and reprints. Publishes 10 titles/year; imprint publishes 3-5 titles/year. Receives 10-20 queries/year. 100% of books from unagented writers. Pays 10-20% royalty on wholesale price. Publishes book 2 months after acceptance of ms. Accepts simultaneous submissions. Reports in 2 months on mss. Book catalog free on request.
Nonfiction: Children's/juvenile (limited to science themes), technical, textbook. Subjects include health/medicine, environment, science. "We are developing a 'Focus on Health' and 'Focus on Science' series under our Cogito Books imprint. We need writers who are experts in general health and science fields to write books on issues such as AIDS, radon in the home, radiation, environmental policy, etc. with the public in mind." Submit entire ms. Reviews artwork/photos as part of ms package. Writers should send photocopies.

‡MERCURY HOUSE, INC., Suite 400, 201 Filbert St., San Francisco CA 94133. (415)433-7042. Assistant Editor: K. Janene-Nelson. Publishes hardcover originals and trade paperback originals and reprints. Averages 10 titles/year. Receives 1,500 queries and 800 mss/year. 3-4% from first-time authors. 50% from unagented writers. Pays 10-20% royalty on retail price. Offers $3,000-6,000 advance. Publishes book 12 months after acceptance of ms. Query for electronic submissions. Reports in 1-2 months on queries, 2-3 months on proposals and manuscripts. Catalog for 52¢ (postage). Writers guidelines for #10 SASE. "No submissions accepted between June 1 and September 1. Manuscripts received during this period will be returned."

Nonfiction: Biography, essays, memoirs. Subjects include anthropology/archaeology, ethnic, gay/lesbian, politics/current affairs, history, language/literature, literary current affairs, music/dance, nature/environment, philosophy, translation, travel, women's issues/studies, human rights/indigenous peoples. "Within the subjects we publish, we are above all a literary publisher looking for a high quality of writing and innovative approach to book structure, research approach, etc." Query with outline, 1-2 sample chapters and SASE.

Recent Nonfiction Title: *Temporary Homelands*, by Deming (nature essays).

Fiction: Ethnic, experimental, feminist, gay/lesbian, gothic, historical, literary, short story collections, literature in translation. "Very limited spots. We prefer sample chapters to determine writing style. It's very important to submit only if the subject is appropriate (as listed), though we do enjoy mutations/blending of genres (high quality, thoughtful work!). We do not publish mainstream, thrillers, sexy books. We look for a well-written cover letter and dynamic writing that stands out from the first page on." Query with synopsis, 1-2 sample chapters and SASE.

Recent Fiction Title: *In the Mountains of America*, by Willis.

Tips: "Our reader is a person who is discriminating about his/her reading material, someone who appreciates the extra care we devote to design, paper, cover, and exterior excellence to go along with the high quality of the writing itself. Be patient with us concerning responses: it's easier to reject the manuscript of a nagging author than it is to decide upon it. The manner in which an author deals with us (via letter of phone) gives us a sense of how it would be to work with this person for a whole project; good books with troublesome authors are to be avoided."

MERIWETHER PUBLISHING LTD., 885 Elkton Dr., Colorado Springs CO 80907-3557. (303)594-4422. Editors: Arthur or Theodore Zapel. Estab. 1969. Publishes hardcover and trade paperback originals and reprints. Publishes 45-60 books/year; 35-50 plays/year. Receives 1,200 submissions/year. 50% of books from first-time authors; 90% from unagented writers. Pays 10% royalty on retail price or makes outright purchase. Publishes book an average of 6 months after acceptance. Simultaneous submissions OK. Reports in 2 months. Book catalog and ms guidelines for $2.

• Meriwether is looking for more books of short scenes and textbooks on directing, staging, make-up, lighting etc.

Nonfiction: How-to, reference, educational, humor, inspirational. Also textbooks. Subjects include art/theatre/drama, music/dance, recreation, religion. "We're looking for unusual textbooks or trade books related to the communication or performing arts and "how-to" books on staging, costuming, lighting, etc. We are not interested in religious titles with fundamentalist themes or approaches—we prefer mainstream religion titles." Query or submit outline/synopsis and sample chapters.

Fiction: Plays. "Plays only—humorous, mainstream, mystery, religious, suspense."

Tips: "Our educational books are sold to teachers and students at college and high school levels. Our religious books are sold to youth activity directors, pastors and choir directors. Our trade books are directed at the public with a sense of humor. Another group of buyers is the professional theatre, radio and TV category. We will focus more on books of plays and theater texts."

METAMORPHOUS PRESS, P.O. Box 10616, Portland OR 92710-0616. . (503)228-4972. Fax: (503)223-9117. Publisher: David Balding. Acquisitions Editor: Nancy Wyatt-Kelsey. Estab. 1982. Publishes trade paperback originals and reprints. Averages 4-5 titles/year. Receives 2,500 submissions annually. 90% of books from first-time authors; 90% from unagented writers. Average print order for a first book is 2,000-5,000. Pays minimum 10% profit split on wholesale prices. No advance. Publishes book an average of 1 year after acceptance. Simultaneous submissions OK. Query for ms and electronic submissions. Reports in 3 months. Book catalog and ms guidelines for 9×12 SAE with 3 first-class stamps.

Nonfiction: How-to, illustrated book, reference, self-help, technical, textbook—all related to behavioral science and personal growth. Subjects include business and sales, health, psychology, sociology, education, science and new ideas in behavioral science. "We are interested in any well-proven new idea or philosophy in the behavioral science areas. Our primary editorial screen is 'will this book further define, explain or support the concept that we are responsible for our reality or assist people in gaining control of their lives.' " Submit idea, outline, and table of contents only. Reviews artwork/photos as part of ms package.

METEOR PUBLISHING CORPORATION, 3369 Progress Dr., Bensalem PA 19020. (215)245-1489. Senior Editor: Catherine Carpenter. Estab. 1989. Publishes mass market paperback originals. Publishes 72 titles/year. Receives 700 queries and 1,500 mss/year. 40% of books from first-time authors; 60% from unagented writers. Offers advance (negotiable). Simultaneous submissions OK. Reports in 3 months on mss. Manuscript guidelines for #10 SASE.

Fiction: Romance. "We publish category, contemporary series romance." If unpublished in contemporary romance, submit complete ms; published authors may submit partials.

Recent Fiction Title: *Midnight Sun*, by Vella Munn (contemporary romance).

Tips: Audience is readers of romance fiction.

MICHIGAN STATE UNIVERSITY PRESS, Room 25, 1405 S. Harrison Rd., East Lansing MI 48823-5202. (517)355-9543. Fax: (800)678-2120; local/international (517)336-2611. Director: Fred Bohm. Editor-in-Chief: Julie Loehr. Contact: Acquisitions Editor. Estab. 1947. Publishes hardcover and softcover originals. Averages 20 titles/year. Receives 400 submissions/year. 75% of books from first-time writers; 100% from unagented writers. Pays 10% royalty on net sales. Publishes ms an average of 9 months after acceptance. Query for electronic submissions. Reports in 2 months. Book catalog and ms guidelines for 9 × 12 SASE.
Nonfiction: Reference, technical, scholarly. Subjects include African Studies, agriculture, American Studies, business and economics, Canadian Studies, Civil War history, literature, philosophy, politics, world religion. Looking for "scholarship that addresses the social and political concerns of the late 20th century." Query with outline and sample chapters. Reviews artwork/photos.
Recent Nonfiction Title: *The Wounded River: The Civil War Letters of John Vance Lauderdale, M.D.*, Peter Josyph, Editor.

MILKWEED EDITIONS, Suite 400, 430 First Ave. N, Minneapolis MN 55401-1743. (612)332-3192. Editor: Emilie Buchwald. Estab. 1980. Publishes hardcover originals and paperback originals and reprints. Averages 12-14 titles/year. Receives 1,560 submissions/year. 30% of books from first-time authors; 70% from unagented writers. Pays 7.5% royalty on list price. Advance varies. Publishes work an average of 1 year after acceptance. Simultaneous submissions OK. Reports in 1-6 months. Book catalog for 2 first-class stamps. Manuscript guidelines for SASE.
Nonfiction: Literary. Subjects include government/politics, history, language/literature, nature/environment, women's issues/studies, education. Query.
Recent Nonfiction Title: *Transforming a Rape Culture*, edited by Emilie Buchwald, Pamela Fletcher and Martha Roth.
Fiction: Literary. Query.
Recent Fiction Title: *Montana 1948*, by Larry Watson.
Children's: Novels and biographies for readers aged 8-14. High literary quality.
Tips: "We are looking for excellent writing in fiction, nonfiction, poetry and children's novels. Write for our national fiction or children's literature contest guidelines. Fourteen books will be chosen for our 1995 list."

THE MILLBROOK PRESS INC., 2 Old New Milford Rd., Brookfield CT 06804. Manuscript Coordinator: Tricia Bauer. Estab. 1989. Publishes hardcover and paperback originals. Publishes 120 titles/year. Pays varying royalty on wholesale price or makes outright purchase. Advance varies. Publishes book 1 year after acceptance of ms. Reports on queries and proposals in 1 month. Book catalog for 9 × 12 SAE with 4 first-class stamps. Manuscript guidelines for #10 SASE.
Nonfiction: Children's/juvenile. Subjects include animals, anthropology/archaeology, government/politics, ethnic, health/medicine, history, hobbies, nature/environment, science, sports. "We publish curriculum-related nonfiction for the school/library market. Mistakes writers most often make when submitting nonfiction are failure to research competing titles and failure to research school curriculum." Query or submit outline with 1 sample chapter.

MILLS & SANDERSON, PUBLISHERS, Suite 201, 41 North Rd., Bedford MA 01730-1021. (617)275-1410. Fax: (617)275-1713. Publisher: Jan H. Anthony. Estab. 1986. Publishes trade paperback originals. Publishes 6-8 titles/year. Receives 500 submissions/year. 50% of books from first-time authors; 80% from unagented writers. Pays 12½% royalty on net price. Offers standard $1,000 advance. Publishes book 1 year after acceptance. Simultaneous submissions OK. Reports in 2-4 months. Manuscript guidelines for #10 SASE.
● Mills & Sanderson is making extra certain books can be "sold" before contracting. Not looking at anything "experimental."
Nonfiction: Family problem solving. No religion or travel. Query first.
Recent Nonfiction Title: *Surviving Your Crises, Reviving Your Dreams*, by Donald E. Watson, M.D.
Tips: "We are currently publishing **only** nonfiction titles dealing with widely-shared, specific problems faced by today's families. Manuscript must cover an interesting subject with broad appeal, be written by an author whose credentials indicate he/she knows a lot about the subject. There must be a certain uniqueness about it."

MINNESOTA HISTORICAL SOCIETY PRESS, Minnesota Historical Society, 345 Kellogg Blvd. W., St. Paul MN 55102-1906. (612)296-2264. Managing Editor: Ann Regan. Imprint is Borealis Books (reprints only). Firm publishes hardcover and trade paperback originals and trade paperback reprints. Averages 10 titles/ year (4 for each imprint). Receives 50 queries and 25 mss/year. 8% of books from first-time authors; 100% from unagented writers. Pays 5% royalty on net income. Publishes book 14 months after acceptance. Query for electronic submissions. Reports in 1 month on queries. *Writer's Market* recommends allowing 2 months for reply. Book catalog free on request.
● Minnesota Historical Society Press is getting many inappropriate submissions from their listing. A regional connection is required.
Nonfiction: Regional works only: biography, coffee table book, cookbook, illustrated book, reference, anthropology/archaeology, art/architecture, history, photography, regional, women's issues/studies, Native

American studies. Query with proposal package including letter, outline, vita, and sample chapter. Reviews artwork/photos as part of freelance ms package. Writer should send photocopies.

Recent Nonfiction Title: *African-American Music in Minnesota from Spirituals to Rap*, by Judy M. Henderson (recording with booklet).

MIS PRESS, subsidiary of Henry Holt & Co., 115 W. 18th St., New York NY 10011. (212)886-9210. Fax: (212)807-6654. Publisher: Steven Berkowitz. Publishes trade paperback originals. Publishes 60 titles/year. Receives 250 queries/year. 20% of books from first-time authors; 50% from unagented writers. Pays 5-15% royalty on net price received (receipts), or makes outright purchase of $5,000-20,000. Offers $7,000 advance. Publishes book an average of 4 months after acceptance. Simultaneous submissions OK. Query for electronic submissions. Book catalog and ms guidelines free on request.

Nonfiction: Technical, computer, electronic. "Submissions should be about or related to computer software or hardware." Submit outline and proposal package.

MODERN LANGUAGE ASSOCIATION OF AMERICA, Dept. WM, 10 Astor Pl., New York NY 10003. (212)475-9500. Fax: (212)477-9863. Director of Book Acquisitions and Development: Joseph Gibaldi. Director of MLA Book Publications: Martha Evans. Estab. 1883. Publishes hardcover and paperback originals. Averages 15 titles/year. Receives 125 submissions annually. 100% of books from unagented writers. Pays 5-10% royalty on net proceeds. Publishes book an average of 1 year after acceptance. Query for electronic submissions. Reports in 3 weeks on mss. Book catalog free on request.

Nonfiction: Scholarly, professional. Subjects include language and literature. Publishes mss on current issues in literary and linguistic research and teaching of language and literature at postsecondary level. No critical monographs. Query or submit outline/synopsis and sample chapters.

MONITOR BOOK CO., Box 9078, Palm Springs CA 92263. (619)323-2270. Editor-in-Chief: Alan F. Pater. Publishes hardcover originals. "We generate our own titles by inhouse staff. We do not encourage outside manuscripts, but will consider when subject matter warrants."

Nonfiction: Scholarly reference works, current events, directories.

‡MONUMENT PRESS, P.O. Box 140361, Las Colinas TX. 75014-0361. (214)686-5332. Contact: Mary Markal. Publishes trade paperback originals. Publishes 15 titles/year. Receives 100 queries and 50 mss/year. 100% of books from first-time authors; 100% from unagented writers. Pays 1% and up royalty on retail price. Publishes book 4 months after acceptance of ms. No simultaneous submissions. Query for electronic submissions. Reports in 1 month. Book catalog for 6×9 SAE with 6 first-class stamps. Manuscript guidelines for #10 SASE.

Nonfiction: Textbook. Subjects include gay/lesbian, government/politics, health/medicine, military/war, religion, women's issues/studies. Query with outline and 3 sample chapters. All unsolicited mss returned unopened.

Recent Nonfiction Title: *Military Secret*, by Robert Graham (homosexuality in Navy).

MOON PUBLICATIONS, INC., P.O. Box 3040, Chico CA 95927-3040. (916)345-3778. Fax: (916)345-6751. Executive Editor: Taran March. Estab. 1973. Publishes trade paperback originals. Publishes average of 15 titles/year. Receives 100-200 submissions/year. 50% from first-time authors; 95% from unagented writers. Pays royalty on wholesale price. Offers advance of up to $10,000. Publishes book an average of 9 months after acceptance. Simultaneous submissions OK. Query for electronic submissions. Reports in 2 months. Book catalog and proposal guidelines for 7½×10½ SAE with 2 first-class stamps.

• Moon is putting increased emphasis on acquiring writers who are experts in a given destination and demonstrate above-average writing ability.

Nonfiction: "We specialize in travel guides to Asia and the Pacific Basin, the United States, Canada, the Caribbean, Latin America and South America, but are open to new ideas. Our guides include in-depth cultural and historical background, as well as recreational and practical travel information. We prefer comprehensive guides to entire countries, states, and regions over more narrowly defined areas such as cities, museums, etc. Writers should write first for a copy of our guidelines. Query with outline, table of contents, and writing sample. Author should also be prepared to provide photos, artwork and base maps. No fictional or strictly narrative travel writing; no how-to guides." Reviews artwork/photos as part of ms package.

Recent Nonfiction Title: *Costa Rica Handbook*, by Christopher Baker.

Tips: "Moon Travel Handbooks are designed by and for independent travelers seeking the most rewarding travel experience possible. Our Handbooks appeal to all travelers because they are the most comprehensive and honest guides available."

MOREHOUSE PUBLISHING CO., 871 Ethan Allen Hwy., Ridgefield CT 06877-2801. Fax: (203)431-3964. Publisher: E. Allen Kelley. Senior Editor: Deborah Grahame-Smith. Estab. 1884. Publishes hardcover and paperback originals. Averages 20 titles/year. Receives 500 submissions annually. 40% of books from first-time authors; 75% from unagented writers. Pays 6-10% royalty on retail price. Publishes book an average of

8 months after acceptance. Reports in 1-4 months, "depending on material submitted." Book catalog for 9×12 SAE with 5 first-class stamps.

Nonfiction: Specializes in Christian publishing (with an Anglican emphasis). Theology, spirituality, ethics, church history, pastoral counseling, liturgy, religious education activity and gift books, children's books (preschool-teen). No poetry or drama. Accepts outline/synopsis and 1-2 sample chapters. Reviews artwork/photos as part of ms package.

Recent Nonfiction Title: *Journeying With Julian*, by Hugh Hildesley

WILLIAM MORROW AND CO., 1350 Avenue of the Americas, New York NY 10019. (212)261-6500. Fax: (212)261-6595. Editorial Director: Adrian Zackheim. Managing Editor: Debbie Mercer-Sullivan. Imprints include Beech Tree Books (juvenile), Amy Cohn, editor-in-chief. Greenwillow Books (juvenile), Susan Hirschman, editor-in-chief. Hearst Books (trade), Ann Bramson, editorial director. Hearst Marine Books (nautical), Ann Bramson, editor. Lothrop, Lee & Shepard (juvenile), Susan Pearson, editor-in-chief. Morrow Junior Books (juvenile), David Reuther, editor-in-chief. Mulberry Books (juvenile), Paulette Kaufmann, editor-in-chief. Quill Trade Paperbacks, Andrew Dutter, editor. Tambourine Books (juvenile), Amy Cohn, editor-in-chief. Estab. 1926. Publishes 200 titles/year. Receives 10,000 submissions/year. 30% of books from first-time authors; 5% from unagented writers. Payment is on standard royalty basis on retail price. Advance varies. Publishes book an average of 1-2 years after acceptance. Reports in 3 months. Query letter on all books. *No unsolicited mss or proposals.*

Nonfiction and Fiction: Publishes adult fiction, nonfiction, history, biography, arts, religion, poetry, how-to books, cookbooks. Length: 50,000-100,000 words. Query only; mss and proposals should be submitted only through an agent.

MORROW JUNIOR BOOKS, Division of William Morrow and Co., 1350 Avenue of the Americas, New York NY 10019. (212)261-6691. Editor-in-Chief: David L. Reuther. Executive Editor: Meredith Charpentier. Senior Editor: Andrea Curley. Publishes hardcover originals. Publishes 50 titles/year. All contracts negotiated separately. Offers variable advance. Book catalog and guidelines for 9×12 SAE with 2 first-class stamps.

Nonfiction: Juveniles (trade books). No textbooks.

Fiction: Juveniles (trade books).

Tips: "We are no longer accepting unsolicited manuscripts."

MOTORBOOKS INTERNATIONAL, 275 S. Third St., Stillwater MN 55082. Fax: (612)439-5627. Editor-in-Chief: Michael Dregni. Estab. 1973. Hardcover and paperback originals. Averages 100 titles/year. 95% of books from unagented writers. Pays 12% royalty on net receipts. Offers $3,000 average advance. Publishes book an average of 1 year after acceptance. Simultaneous submissions OK. Query for electronic submissions. Reports in 3 months. Free book catalog. Manuscript guidelines for #10 SASE.

Nonfiction: Biography, history, how-to, photography (as they relate to cars, trucks, motorcycles, motor sports, aviation—domestic, foreign and military). Accepts nonfiction translations. Submit outline, 1-2 sample chapters and sample of illustrations. "State qualifications for doing book." Reviews artwork/photos as part of ms package.

Recent Nonfiction Title: *The American Gas Station*, by Witzel.

MOUNTAIN PRESS PUBLISHING COMPANY, P.O. Box 2399, Missoula MT 59806-2399. (406)728-1900. Fax: (406)728-1635. History Editor: Daniel Greer. Natural History Editor: Kathleen Ort. Estab. 1948. Imprints are Roadside Geology Series, Roadside History Series, Classics of the Fur Trade. Publishes hardcover and trade paperback originals. Averages 15 titles/year. Receives 250 submissions/year. 50% of books from first-time authors; 90% from unagented writers. Pays 7-15% on wholesale price. Publishes book an average of 1 year after acceptance. Query for electronic submissions. Reports in 1 month on queries. *Writer's Market* recommends allowing 2 months for reply. Free book catalog.

Nonfiction: Western history, Americana, nature/environment, regional, earth science, travel. "We are expanding our Roadside Geology and Roadside History series (done on a state by state basis). We are interested in how-to books (about horses) and well-written regional outdoor guides—plants, flowers and birds. No personal histories or journals." Query or submit outline and sample chapters. Reviews artwork/photos as part of ms package.

Tips: "It is obvious that small- to medium-size publishers are becoming more important, while the giants are becoming harder and less accessible. If I were a writer trying to market a book today, I would find out what kind of books a publisher was interested in and tailor my writing to them. Research markets and target my audience. Research other books, on the same subjects. Make yours different. Don't present your manuscript to a publisher—*sell* it to him. Give him the information he needs to make a decision on a title."

THE MOUNTAINEERS BOOKS, Suite 107, 1011 SW Klickitat Way, Seattle WA 98134-1162. (206)223-6303. Director: Donna DeShazo. Acquisitions Manager: Margaret Foster. Estab. 1961. Publishes hardcover and trade paperback originals (95%) and reprints (5%). Averages 35 titles/year. Receives 150-250 submissions/year. 25% of books from first-time authors; 98% from unagented writers. Average print order for a first book is 5,000-7,000. Offers royalty based on net sales. Offers advance on occasion. Publishes book an average of 1 year after acceptance. Reports in 2 months. Book catalog and ms guidelines for 9×12 SAE with 3 first-class stamps.

● Mountaineers Books is looking for manuscripts with more emphasis on regional conservation and natural history.

Nonfiction: Guidebooks for adventure travel, recreation, natural history, conservation/environment, non-competitive self-propelled sports, and outdoor how-to books. "We specialize in books dealing with mountaineering, hiking, backpacking, skiing, snowshoeing, canoeing, bicycling, etc. These can be either how-to-do-it or where-to-do-it (guidebooks)." Does *not* want to see "anything dealing with hunting, fishing or motorized travel." Submit author bio, outline and minimum of 2 sample chapters. Accepts nonfiction translations. Looks for "expert knowledge, good organization." Also interested in nonfiction adventure narratives. Ongoing award—The Barbara Savage/"Miles from Nowhere" Memorial Award for outstanding adventure narratives is offered.

Fiction: "We might consider an exceptionally well-done book-length manuscript on mountaineering." Does *not* want poetry or mystery. Query first.

Tips: "The type of book the writer has the best chance of selling our firm is an authoritative guidebook (*in our field*) to a specific area not otherwise covered; or a how-to that is better than existing competition (again, *in our field*)."

MUSEUM OF NORTHERN ARIZONA PRESS, Rt. 4, Box 720, Flagstaff AZ 86001. (602)774-5213. Fax: (602)779-1527. Publisher: Diana Clark Lubick. Editorial Assistant: D.A. Boyd. Estab. 1926. Publishes hardcover and trade paperback originals, and quarterly magazine. Averages 10-12 titles/year. Receives 35 submissions/year. 10% of books from first-time authors; 100% from unagented writers. Subsidy publishes (nonauthor) 15% of books. Pays one-time fee on acceptance of ms. No advance. Publishes book an average of 1 year after acceptance. Queries only. Query for electronic submissions. Reports in 2 months. Book catalog for 9×12 SAE. Manuscript guidelines for #10 SASE.

Nonfiction: Coffee table book, reference, technical. Subjects include Southwest, art, nature, science. "Especially needs manuscripts on the Colorado Plateau that are written for a well-educated general audience." Query or submit outline and 3-4 sample chapters. Reviews artwork/photos as part of ms package.

Recent Nonfiction Title: *Canyon Country*, by Wayne Ranney.

MUSTANG PUBLISHING CO., P.O. Box 3004, Memphis TN 38173-0004. (901)521-1406. President: Rollin Riggs. Estab. 1983. Publishes nonfiction hardcover and trade paperback originals. Averages 10 titles/year. Receives 1,000 submissions/year. 50% of books from first-time authors; 90% from unagented writers. Pays 6-8% royalty on retail price. Publishes book an average of 1 year after acceptance. Simultaneous submissions OK. Address proposals to Rollin Riggs. No electronic submissions. No phone calls, please. Reports in 1 month. *Writer's Market* recommends allowing 2 months for reply. SASE a must. Book catalog for $1 and #10 SASE.

Nonfiction: How-to, humor, self-help. Subjects include Americana, hobbies, recreation, sports, travel. "Our needs are very general—humor, travel, how-to, etc.—for the 18-to 40-year-old market." Query or submit outline and sample chapters.

Recent Nonfiction Title: *The Complete Book of Beer Drinking Games*, by Andy Griscom, Ben Rand and Scott Johnston.

Tips: "From the proposals we receive, it seems that many writers never go to bookstores and have no idea what sells. Before you waste a lot of time on a nonfiction book idea, ask yourself, 'How often have my friends and I actually *bought* a book like this?' Know the market, and know the audience you're trying to reach."

THE MYSTERIOUS PRESS, Subsidiary of Warner Books, 1271 Avenue of the Americas, New York NY 10020. (212)522-5144. Fax: (212)522-7990. Editor-in-Chief: William Malloy. Editorial Assistant: Amye Dyer. Estab. 1976. Publishes hardcover originals, trade paperback and mass market paperback reprints. Averages 70-90 titles/year. Receives 750 submissions annually. 10% of books from first-time authors. *Accepts no unagented mss.* Pays standard, but negotiable, royalty on retail price. Amount of advance varies widely. Publishes book an average of 1 year after acceptance. Reports in 2 months.

Nonfiction: Reference books on criticism, biography, history of crime fiction. Submit complete ms. *Writer's Market* recommends query with SASE first. Reviews artwork/photos as part of ms package.

Recent Nonfiction Title: *Had She But Known: A Biography of Mary Roberts Rinehart*, by Charlotte MacLeod.

Fiction: Mystery, suspense, espionage. "We will consider publishing any outstanding crime/espionage/suspense/detective novel that comes our way. No short stories." Submit complete mss. *Writer's Market* recommends query with SASE first.

Recent Fiction Title: *The Mexican Tree Duck*, by James Crumley.

Tips: "We do not read unagented material. Agents only, please."

THE NAIAD PRESS, INC., P.O. Box 10543, Tallahassee FL 32302. (904)539-5965. Fax: (904)539-9731. Editorial Director: Barbara Grier. Estab. 1973. Publishes paperback originals. Averages 24 titles/year. Receives over 1,000 submissions annually. 20% of books from first-time authors; 99% from unagented writers. Average print order for a first book is 12,000. Pays 15% royalty on wholesale or retail price. No advance. Publishes book an average of 2 years after acceptance. Reports in 4 months. Book catalog and ms guidelines for 6×9 SAE and $1.50 postage and handling

• Due to movie tie-in, and good marketing, Naiad Press has rebounded strongly from a 1992-low.

Fiction: "We publish lesbian fiction, preferably lesbian/feminist fiction. We are not impressed with the 'oh woe' school and prefer realistic (i.e., happy) novels. We emphasize fiction and are now heavily reading manuscripts in that area. We are working in a lot of genre fiction—mysteries, short stories, fantasy—all with lesbian themes, of course. We have instituted an inhouse anthology series, featuring short stories only by our own authors (i.e. authors who have published full length fiction with us or those signed to do so)." Query.

Tips: "There is tremendous world-wide demand for lesbian mysteries from lesbian authors published by lesbian presses, and we are doing several such series. We are no longer seeking science fiction. Manuscripts under 60,000 words have twice as good a chance as over 60,000."

NASW PRESS, a division of National Association of Social Workers, Suite 700, 750 First St., NE, Washington DC 20002-4241. Fax: (202)336-8312. Executive Editor: Linda Beebe. Estab. 1956. Averages 8-10 titles/year. Receives 100 submissions annually. 20% of books from first-time authors; 100% from unagented writers. Pays 10-15% royalty on net prices. Publishes book an average of 8 months after acceptance of completed ms. Reports in 4 months on submissions. Free book catalog and ms guidelines.

• NASW is a growing company. They will be putting more emphasis on publishing health policy books.

Nonfiction: Textbooks of interest to professional social workers. "We're looking for books on social work in health care, mental health, multi-cultural competence and substance abuse. Books must be directed to the professional social worker and build on the current literature." Submit outline and sample chapters. Rarely reviews artwork/photos as part of ms package.

Tips: "Our audience includes social work practitioners, educators, students and policy makers. They are looking for practice-related books that are well grounded in theory. The books that do well are those that have direct application to the work our audience does. New technology, AIDS, welfare reform and health policy will be of increasing interest to our readers. We are particularly interested in manuscripts for fact-based practice manuals that will be very user-friendly."

NATIONAL PRESS BOOKS, INC., Suite 212, 7200 Wisconsin Ave., Bethesda MD 20814. (301)657-1616. Editorial Director: G. Edward Smith. Estab. 1984. Publishes hardcover and trade paperback originals. Publishes 23 titles/year. Receives 1,500 submissions/year. 40% of books are from first-time authors; 80% from unagented writers. Pays 5-10% royalty on wholesale or retail price or makes outright purchases. Offers flexible average advance. Publishes book an average of 8 months after acceptance. Simultaneous submissions OK. Reports in 4 months. Book catalog and ms guidelines for 7½×10½ SAE with 4 first-class stamps.

Nonfiction: Biography, cookbook, self-help. Subjects include business and economics, child guidance/parenting, cooking, foods and nutrition, government/politics, history, money/finance, psychology, regional, sports. Query or submit outline and sample chapters. Reviews artwork/photos as part of ms package.

NATIONAL TEXTBOOK CO., Imprint of NTC Publishing Group, 4255 W. Touhy Ave., Lincolnwood IL 60646. (708)679-5500. Fax: (708)679-2494. Vice President/Business Manager: Mark R. Pattis. Publishes originals for education and trade market, and software. Averages 100-150 titles/year. Receives 200 submissions annually. 10% of books from first-time authors. 80% from unagented writers. Manuscripts purchased on either royalty or buy-out basis. Publishes book an average of 1 year after acceptance. Reports in 4 months. Book catalog and ms guidelines for 6×9 SAE and 2 first-class stamps.

Nonfiction: Textbooks. Major emphasis being given to foreign language and language arts classroom texts, especially secondary level material, and business and career subjects (marketing, advertising, sales, etc.). John T. Nolan, Language Arts Executive Editor; N. Keith Fry, Executive Editor/Foreign Language and ESL; Anne Knudsen, Executive Editor/NTC Business Books and VGM Career Horizons, and Daniel Spinella, Associate Editor/Passport Books. Send sample chapter and outline or table of contents.

Recent Nonfiction Title: *The Career Book*, by Joyce Lain Kennedy.

THE NAUTICAL & AVIATION PUBLISHING CO., 8 W. Madison St., Baltimore MD 21201. (410)659-0220. Fax: (410)539-8832. President/Publisher: Jan Snouck-Hurgronje. Editor: Robert Bischoff. Estab. 1979. Publishes hardcover originals and reprints. Averages 10-12 titles/year. Receives 20-25 submissions/year. Pays 10-15% royalty on net selling price. Rarely offers advance. Simultaneous submissions OK. *Writer's Market* recommends allowing 1 month for reply. Free book catalog.

Nonfiction: Reference. Subjects include history, military/war. Submit synopsis and cover letter, or a maximum of 3 chapters. Reviews artwork/photo as part of package.

Recent Nonfiction Title: *Southern Campaigns of the American Revolution*, by Dan Morrill.

Fiction: Historical. Submit outline/synopsis and sample chapters.

Recent Fiction Title: *Straits of Messina*, by William P. Mack.

Tips: "Please note that we are publishers of *military* history only—our name is misleading, and we often get inquiries on general nautical or aviation books. We generally do not publish fiction titles. We are primarily and increasingly a nonfiction publishing house."

NAVAL INSTITUTE PRESS, Imprint of U.S. Naval Institute, 118 Maryland Ave., Annapolis MD 21402-5035. Executive Editor: Paul Wilderson. Press Director: Ronald Chambers. Contact: Anne Collier, acquisitions editor. Estab. 1873. Averages 50 titles/year. Receives 400-500 submissions annually. 60% of books from first-time authors; 75% from unagented writers. Average print order for a first book is 3,000. Pays 6-10% royalty based on net sales. Pays advance. Publishes book an average of 1 year after acceptance. Query letter strongly recommended. *Writer's Market* recommends allowing 2 months for reply. Free book catalog. Manuscript guidelines for SASE.

Nonfiction: "We are interested in naval and maritime subjects and in broad military topics, including government policy and funding. Specific subjects include: tactics, strategy, navigation, military history, biographies, aviation and others."

Fiction: Limited fiction on military and naval themes.

NEAL-SCHUMAN PUBLISHERS, INC., 100 Varick St., New York NY 10013. (212)925-8650. Editorial Director: Margo Hart. Publishes hardcover originals. Publishes 30 titles/year. Receives 80 submissions/year. 75% of books from first-time authors; 80% from unagented writers. Pays 10% royalty on net sales. Publishes book an average of 9-12 months after acceptance. Query for electronic submissions. Reports in 1 month on proposals. *Writer's Market* recommends allowing 2 months for reply. Book catalog and ms guidelines free.

Nonfiction: How-to, reference, software, technical, textbook, texts and professional books in library and information science. Subjects include business and economics, child guidance/parenting, computers and electronics, education, gay/lesbian, government/politics, health/medicine, language/literature, money/finance, recreation, software, travel. "We are looking for reference books in business and health-related sciences." Submit proposal package, including vita, outline, preface and sample chapters.

Recent Nonfiction Title: *A CD/ROM Primer,* by Cheryl LaGuardia.

THOMAS NELSON PUBLISHERS, Nelson Place at Elm Hill Pike, P.O. Box 141000, Nashville TN 37214-1000. (615)889-9000. Contact: Submissions Editor. Estab. 1798. Imprints are Oliver-Nelson, Janet Thoma, Jan Dennis Books. Publishes hardcover and paperback originals and reprints. Averages 250 titles/year. Pays royalty or makes outright purchase. Publishes book an average of 1 year after acceptance. Send proposal to Book Editorial. Reports in 2 months. SASE must accompany submissions or unable to return proposals.

Nonfiction: Adult inspirational/motivational Christian trade books and reference books on the Bible and Christianity. Accepts outline/synopsis and 3 sample chapters.

Fiction: Seeking high quality novels with Christian themes for adults and teens.

THE NEW ENGLAND PRESS, INC., P.O. Box 575, Shelburne VT 05482. (802)863-2520. Fax: (802)863-1510. President: Alfred Rosa. Managing Editor: Mark Wanner. Estab. 1978. Publishes hardcover and trade paperback originals and trade paperback reprints. Averages 6-12 titles/year. Receives 200 submissions annually. 25% of books from first-time authors; 75% from unagented writers. Publishes ms an average of 1 year after acceptance. Reports in 3 months. Catalog for 6×9 SAE and 4 first-class stamps.

Nonfiction: Biography, how-to, nature, illustrated book. Subjects include Vermontiana and Northern New England topics; history (New England orientation); essays (New England orientation). No juvenile or psychology. Query or submit outline and sample chapters. Reviews artwork/photos.

Fiction: Historical (New England orientation). No novels. Query.

‡NEW HOPE, Woman's Missionary Union, P.O. Box 12065, Birmingham AL 34202-2065. Contact: Cindy McClain. Publishes 25 titles/year. Receives 25 queries and 60 mss/year. 50% of books from first-time authors; 100% from unagented writers. Pays 7-10% royalty on retail price or makes outright purchase. Publishes book 12-18 months after acceptance of ms. No simultaneous submissions. Reports in 6 months on mss. Book catalog for 9×12 SAE with 3 first-class stamps. Manuscript guidelines for #10 SASE.

Nonfiction: How-to, children's/juvenile (religion), personal growth, first person experience. Subjects include child guidance/parenting (from Christian perspective), education (Christian church), religion (Christian faith—must relate to missions work, culture, Christian concerns, Christian ethical issues, spiritual growth, etc.), women's issues/studies from Christian perspective. "We publish Christian education materials that focus on missions work or educational work in some way. Teaching helps, spiritual growth material, ideas for working with different audiences in a church, etc.—missions work overseas or church work in the US, women's spiritual issues, guiding children in Christian faith." Submit outline and 3 sample chapters for review. Submit complete ms for acceptance decision.

NEW LEAF PRESS, INC., P.O. Box 311, Green Forest AR 72638-0311. Fax: (501)438-5120. Contact: Editorial Board. Estab. 1975. Publishes hardcover and paperback originals. Publishes 15-20 titles/year. Receives 400 submissions annually. 15% of books from first-time authors; 90% from unagented writers. Average print order for a first book is 10,000. Pays 10% royalty on first 10,000 copies, paid once per year. No advance. Send photos and illustrations to accompany ms. Publishes book an average of 10 months after acceptance. Simultaneous submissions OK. Reports in 3 months. Book catalog and ms guidelines for 9×12 SAE with 5 first-class stamps.

Nonfiction: How to live the Christian life, humor, self-help. Length: 100-400 pages. Submit complete ms. Reviews artwork/photos as part of ms package.

Tips: "Self-help and Christian living guides, devotionals, relevant nonfiction and humor are areas our firm is looking at. Quality Christian writing is still the measuring stick, so writers should submit accordingly."

NEW READERS PRESS, Publishing Division of Laubach Literacy International, P.O. Box 131, Syracuse NY 13210-0131. Fax: (315)422-6369. Editorial Director: Marianne Ralbovsky. Estab. 1959. Publishes paperback originals. Averages 70 titles/year. Receives 500 submissions/year. 40% of books by first-time authors; 95% by unagented writers. Average print order for a first book is 5,000. "Most of our sales are adult basic education programs, volunteer literacy programs, private human services agencies, prisons, and libraries with literacy outreach programs." Pays royalty on retail price, or by outright purchase. Rate varies according to type of publication and length of ms. Advance is "different in each case, but does not exceed projected royalty for first year." Publishes book an average of 1 year after acceptance. Query for electronic submissions. Reports in 3 months. Free book catalog and authors' brochure.

Nonfiction: "Our audience is adults with limited reading skills (12th grade level and below). We publish basic education and ESL literacy materials in reading and writing, math, social studies, health, science, and English as a second language. We are particularly interested in materials that fulfill curriculum requirements in these areas. Manuscripts must be not only easy to read (0 to 6th grade level) but mature in tone and concepts. We are not interested in anything at all written for children or teenagers." Write for guidelines or submit outline and 1-3 sample chapters.

Fiction: Short novels (7,500-10,000 words) at 3rd-5th grade reading level on themes of interest to adults and older teenagers. Write for guidelines or submit synopsis.

Tips: "We have a structured library of fiction and nonfiction titles for pleasure reading that need to follow specific guidelines."

NEW RIVERS PRESS, Ste. 910, 420 N. 5th St., Minneapolis MN 55401. Managing Editor: Michelle. Publishes trade paperback originals. Publishes 8-10 titles/year. Receives 500 queries and 450 mss/year. 95% of books from first-time authors; 99.9% from unagented writers. Pays royalty or makes outright purchase. Publishes book 14 months after acceptance of ms. Please query first with a synopsis of proposal. Reports in 6 months. Book catalog free on request. Manuscript guidelines for #10 SASE.

Nonfiction: Creative prose. "We publish memoirs, essay collections, and other forms of creative nonfiction." Query. Reviews artwork/photos as part of freelance ms package, but not usually.

Fiction: Literary and short story collections. Query or submit synopsis and 2 sample chapters.

Poetry: Query or submit 10-15 sample poems.

NEW VICTORIA PUBLISHERS, P.O. Box 27, Norwich VT 05055-0027. (802)649-5297. Editor: Claudia Lamperti. Estab. 1976. Publishes trade paperback originals. Averages 5-6 titles/year. 50% of books from first-time authors; most books from unagented writers. Pays 10% royalty on wholesale price. Publishes book an average of 1 year after acceptance. Reports on queries in 1 month. *Writer's Market* recommends allowing 2 months for reply. Book catalog free.

Nonfiction: History. "We are interested in feminist history or biography and interviews with or topics relating to lesbians. No poetry." Submit outline and sample chapters.

Fiction: Adventure, erotica, fantasy, historical, humor, mystery, romance, science fiction, western. "We will consider most anything if it is well written and appeals to lesbian/feminist audience." Submit outline/synopsis and sample chapters.

Tips: "Try to appeal to a specific audience and not write for the general market."

NEW YORK ZOETROPE, INC., 838 Broadway, New York NY 10003. (212)420-0590. Fax: (212)529-3330. Contact: Olenthia Nelson. Publishes hardcover and trade paperback originals, reprints and software. Averages 10 titles/year. Receives 100 submissions annually. 25% of books from first-time authors; 75% from unagented writers. Subsidy publishes (nonauthor) 3% of books. Pays 10-20% royalty on wholesale prices or makes outright purchase of $500-1,000. Offers average $1,000 advance. Publishes book an average of 9 months after acceptance. Simultaneous submissions OK. Query for electronic submissions. Reports in 2 months. Book catalog and guidelines for 6×9 SAE.

Nonfiction: Reference, technical, textbook. Subjects include film, TV, entertainment industry, media. Interested especially in film and television. No fiction. Query with synopsis and outline.

Tips: "Film- or media-oriented (academic and popular) subjects have the best chance of selling to our firm. Media books (reference) are our strongest line."

THE NOBLE PRESS, INC., Suite 508, 213 W. Institute Place, Chicago IL 60610. (312)642-1168. Executive Editor: Douglas Seibold. Estab. 1988. Publishes hardcover and trade paperback originals. Publishes 8-12 titles/year. Receives 1,500 submissions/year. 50% of books from first-time authors; 50% from unagented writers. Pays 5-15% royalty on retail price. Advance varies. Publishes book an average of 8 months after acceptance. Simultaneous submissions OK. Reports in 10 weeks. Manuscript guidelines for SASE.

● This publisher has launched a book club aimed at African-American readers called Noble Literary

Society. It will feature commercial titles but also focus on new writers, first novelists, works on race relations, art books and children's books as well as Caribbean and African history.

Nonfiction: Subjects include education, ethnic, government/politics, history, nature/environment, philosophy, sociology, women's issues/studies. No cookbooks, technical manuals, or texts in full. Query or submit outline and 1 sample chapter.

Recent Nonfiction Title: *Volunteer Slavery*, by Jill Nelson.

Tips: "The writer has the best chance of selling us a nonfiction book that addresses contemporary issues of importance to our society. Many of our books take subjects often explored in academic arenas, and we translate them in such a way that mainstream readers can understand and become involved in them."

NORTH LIGHT BOOKS, Imprint of F&W Publications, 1507 Dana Ave., Cincinnati OH 45207. Editorial Director: David Lewis. Publishes hardcover and trade paperback originals. Averages 30-35 titles/year. Pays 10% royalty on net receipts. Offers $4,000 advance. Simultaneous submissions OK. Reports in 2 months. Book catalog for 9 × 12 SAE with 6 first-class stamps.

Nonfiction: Art and graphic design instruction books. Interested in books on watercolor painting, oil painting, pastel, basic drawing, pen and ink, airbrush, markers, basic design, computer graphics, desktop design, layout and typography. Do not submit coffee table art books without how-to art instruction. Query or submit outline and examples of artwork (transparencies and photographs OK).

Recent Nonfiction Titles: *Timeless Techniques for Better Oil Paintings*.

NORTHERN ILLINOIS UNIVERSITY PRESS, DeKalb IL 60115-2854. (815)753-1826/753-1075. Fax: (815)753-1845. Director: Mary L. Lincoln (history). Acquisitions Editor: Dan Coran (literature, political science). Estab. 1965. Pays 10-15% royalty on wholesale price. Book catalog free.

Nonfiction: "The NIU Press publishes mainly history, political science, social sciences, philosophy, literary criticism and regional studies. We do not consider collections of previously published articles, essays, etc., nor do we consider unsolicited poetry." Accepts nonfiction translations. Query with outline and 1-3 sample chapters.

NORTHLAND PUBLISHING CO., INC., P.O. Box 1389, Flagstaff AZ 86002-1389. (602)774-5251. Fax: (602)774-0592. Editor: Erin Murphy. Estab. 1958. Publishes hardcover and trade paperback originals. Averages 25 titles/year. Receives 4,000 submissions/year. 30% of books from first-time authors; 95% from unagented writers. Pays 8-12% royalty (on net receipts), depending upon terms. Offers $1,000-3,000 average advance. Publishes book an average of 1-2 years after acceptance. Simultaneous submissions OK. Reports in 1 month on queries, 2 months on mss. Book catalog and ms guidelines free.

● Northland has temporarily ceased publishing coffee table books.

Nonfiction: Subjects include animals, anthropology/archaeology, art/architecture, cooking, history, nature/environment, photography and regional (American West/Southwest). "We are seeking authoritative, well-written manuscripts on natural history subjects. We do not want to see poetry; general fiction; mainstream, or New Age or science fiction material." Query or submit outline/synopsis and sample chapters. Reviews artwork/photos as part of ms package.

Recent Nonfiction Title: *Survivors in the Shadows: Threatened and Endangered Mammals of the American West*, by Gary Turbak.

Fiction: Unique children's stories, especially those with Southwest/West regional theme; Native American folktales (retold by Native Americans only, please); natural history subjects. Manuscripts should be no shorter than 350 words, no longer than 1,500. We do not want to see chapter books or "mainstream" stories.

Recent Fiction Title: *Monster Birds: A Navajo Folktale*, retold by Vee Brown.

Tips: "Our audience is composed of general interest readers and those interested in specialty subjects such as Native American culture and crafts. It is not necessarily a scholarly market, but is sophisticated."

NORTHWORD PRESS, INC., P.O. Box 1360, Minocqua WI 54548. (715)356-9800. Editorial Dept: Attn: Donna F. Lebrecht. Imprint: Heartland Press. Publishes hardcover and trade paperback originals. Estab. 1984. Firm averages 20 titles/year; imprint averages 5 titles/year. Receives 500 submissions/year. 50% of books are from first time authors; 90% are from unagented writers. Pays 10-15% royalty on wholesale price. Offers $2,000-20,000 advance. Publishes book an average of 9 months after acceptance. Simultaneous submissions OK. Query for electronic submissions. Reports in 6 weeks on queries. Book catalog for 9 × 12 SAE with 2 first-class stamps. Manuscript guidelines for SASE.

● The editor reports rapid growth for this company.

Nonfiction: Coffee table book, how-to, illustrated book, juvenile. Subjects include nature/environment (exclusive). "We are seeking nature topics only with special attention to wildlife. Environmental issue (green

A bullet introduces comments by the editor of Writer's Market **indicating special information about the listing.**

books) a new area of interest." Submit outline and sample chapters. Reviews artwork/photos as part of ms package.
Recent Nonfiction Title: *Brother Wolf*, by Jim Brandenburg (nature photographs and text).
Tips: "Think nature and wildlife. That's exclusively what we publish."

W.W. NORTON CO., INC., 500 Fifth Ave., New York NY 10110. General interest publisher of both fiction and nonfiction, educational and professional books. This company did not respond to our request for information. Query before submitting.
• Norton published the winner of the 1993 National Book Award for poetry, A.R. Ammons' *Garbage*.

‡NOVA SCIENCE PUBLISHERS INC., Suite 207, 6080 Jericho Turnpike, Commack NY 11725. (516)499-3103. Editor-in-Chief: Frank Columbus. Publishes hardcover originals. Publishes 100 titles/year. Receives 150 queries/year. Pays royalty. Publishes book 6 months after acceptance of ms. Accepts simultaneous submissions. Query for electronic submissions. Reports in 1 month. Book catalog and ms guidelines free on request.
Nonfiction: Biography, cookbook, self-help, technical, textbook. Subjects include Americana, business and economics, computers and electronics, cooking, foods and nutrition, education, government/politics, health/medicine, money/finance, nature/environment, philosophy, psychology, science, sociology, software, sports. Query. Reviews artwork/photos as part of ms package. Writers should send photocopies.
Recent Nonfiction Title: *Understanding Suicide*, by D. Lester.

NOYES DATA CORP., 120 Mill Rd., Park Ridge NJ 07656. Fax: (201)391-6833. Estab. 1959. Publishes hardcover originals. Averages 40 titles/year. Pays 10%-12% royalty on retail price. Advance varies, depending on author's reputation and nature of book. Reports in 2 weeks. Book catalog free.
Nonfiction: Noyes Publications and Noyes Data Corp. publish technical books on practical industrial processing, science, economic books pertaining to chemistry, chemical engineering, food, textiles, energy, electronics, pollution control—primarily of interest to the business executive. Length: 50,000-250,000 words. Query the Editorial Department.

NTC PUBLISHING GROUP, 4255 W. Touhy Ave., Lincolnwood IL 60646-1975. (708)679-5500. Fax: (708)679-2494. Imprints include National Textbook Company, Passport Books, NTC Business Books, VGM Career Books. Foreign Language and English as a Second Language Executive Editor: Keith Fry. Language Arts Executive Editor: John Nolan. Passport Books Editor: Dan Spinella. NTC Business Books and VGM Career Books Executive Editor: Anne Knudsen. Director of Dictionaries: Richard Spears. Estab. 1960. Publishes hardcover and trade paperback originals and reprints. Averages 150 titles/year. Receives 800 submissions/year. 98% of books from unagented writers. Pays royalty or makes outright purchase. Offers varying advance. Publishes book an average of 8 months after acceptance. Simultaneous submissions OK. Query for electronic submissions. Reports in 2 months. Book catalog free on request.
Nonfiction: Textbook, travel, foreign language, reference, advertising and marketing business books. Subjects include business, education, language/literature, photography, travel. Query. Reviews artwork/photos as part of ms package.
Recent Nonfiction Title: *English Communication Skills for Professionals*.

‡OAK KNOLL PRESS, 616 Delaware St., New Castle DE 19720. (302)328-7232. Publishing Manager: Paul Wakeman. Publishes hardcover and trade paperback originals and reprints. Publishes 12 titles/year. Receives 25 queries and 5 mss/year. 5% of books from first-time authors; 100% from unagented writers. Pays 7-10% royalty on income. Publishes book 18 months after acceptance of ms. Accepts simultaneous submissions. Query for electronic submissions. Reports in less than 1 month on queries. Book catalog free on request.
Nonfiction: Book arts. Subjects include printing, papermaking, bookbinding, book collecting, etc. "We only specialize in books about books." Query. Reviews artwork/photos as part of ms package. Writers should send photocopies.
Recent Nonfiction Title: *American Metal Typefaces of the Twentieth Century*, by Mac McGrew (typography/printing history).

‡OCEANA PUBLICATIONS, INC., 75 Main St., Dobbs Ferry NY 10522. (914)693-5956. Senior Editor: M.C. Susan De Maio. Publishes 200 looseleaf and clothbound titles/year. Receives 250 queries and 150 mss/year. 85% of books from first-time authors; 100% from unagented writers. Pays 10-15% royalty. Publishes book 3 months after acceptance of ms. Accepts simultaneous submissions. Query for electronic submissions. Reports in 1 month. Book catalog and ms guidelines free on request.
Nonfiction: Reference. Subjects include international law, business. "Most of Oceana's titles are looseleaf in format and should be structured accordingly." Query with outline, table of contents and 2 sample chapters.

OCTAMERON ASSOCIATES, 1900 Mt. Vernon Ave., Alexandria VA 22301. (703)836-5480. Editorial Director: Karen Stokstad. Estab. 1976. Publishes trade paperback originals. Averages 15 titles/year. Receives 100 submissions annually. 10% of books from first-time authors; 100% from unagented writers. Average print order for a first book is 8,000-10,000. Pays 7½% royalty on retail price. Publishes book an average of 6 months after acceptance. Simultaneous submissions OK. Query for electronic submissions. Reports in 2 months. Book catalog for #10 SAE with 2 first-class stamps.

Nonfiction: Reference, career, post-secondary education subjects. Especially interested in "paying-for-college and college admission guides." Query or submit outline and 2 sample chapters. Reviews artwork/photos as part of ms package.

‡**ONE ON ONE COMPUTER TRAINING**, Subsidiary of Mosaic Media, Suite 100, 2055 Army Trail Rd., Addison IL 60101. Manager Product Development: N.B. Young. Imprints are Flip Track Learning Systems, One On One Computer Training, Math House. Publishes 5-10 titles/year. 100% of books from unagented writers. Makes outright purchase of $2,000-12,000. Advance depends on purchase contract. Publishes book 6 months after acceptance of ms. Accepts simultaneous submissions. Query for electronic submissions. Reports in 2 months on proposals. Book catalog free on request.

Nonfiction: How-to, self-help, technical. Subjects include computers, software. Query. All unsolicited mss returned unopened.

Recent Nonfiction Title: *How to Use PowerPoint 3.*

OPEN COURT PUBLISHING COMPANY, Carus Publishing, Suite 2000, 332 S. Michigan Ave., Chicago IL 60604-9968. Editorial Director: David Ramsay Steele. Assistant Editor: Edward Roberts. Estab. 1887. Publishes hardcover and trade paperback originals. Publishes 15 titles/year. Receives 400 queries and 200 mss/year. 20% of books from first-time authors; 85% from unagented writers. Pays royalty on wholesale price. Offers $1,000-2,000 advance. Publishes book 1-3 years after acceptance of ms. Reports in 6 months. Book catalog free on request.

Nonfiction: Textbook and academic philosophy. Subjects include education, philosophy, psychology, religion, women's issues/studies, Eastern thought. "We market to academic and intelligent lay readers. We are interested in manuscripts on social issues, cosmology, feminist thought, cognition, Eastern thought, comparative religion, Jungian psychology, academic philosophy, education and psychotherapy. When submitting nonfiction, writers often fail to specify the market for their books. It is not enough to list all the groups of people who *should* be interested." Submit outline and 2 sample chapters or proposal package, including prospectus, sample chapters, vita. Reviews artwork/photos as part of the freelance ms package. Writers should send photocopies.

‡**OPEN ROAD PUBLISHING**, P.O. Box 11249, Cleveland Park Station, Washington DC 20008. Contact: B. Borden. Publishes trade and mass market paperback originals. Publishes 15-17 titles/year. Receives 80 queries and 60 mss/year. 40% of books from first-time authors; 95% from agented writers. Pays 5-6% royalty on retail price. Offers $500-2,000 advance. Publishes book 3 months after acceptance of ms. Accepts simultaneous submissions. Query for electronic submissions. Reports in 1 month on proposals. Book catalog free on request. Manuscript guidelines for #10 SASE.

Nonfiction: Guides. Subjects include sports, travel. "We're looking for opinionated, selective travel guides that appeal to mainstream travelers in their mid-20s to early 50s. Our guides are fun, literate, and have a sense of adventure, offering readers solid cultural background and the opportunity to experience the country or city—not just visit it." Submit cover letter, outline and 2 sample chapters.

Recent Nonfiction Title: *China Guide*, by Ruth Lor Malloy.

‡**ORBIS BOOKS**, P.O. Box 308, Maryknoll NY 10545-0308. (914)941-7590. Editor-in-Chief: Robert Ellsberg. Publishes hardcover and trade paperback originals. Publishes 50-55 titles/year. Receives 1,500 queries and 700 mss/year. 2% of books from first-time authors; 99% from unagented writers. Subsidy publishes 0-2% of books, depending on the year. Pays 10-15% royalty on wholesale price net. Offers $500-3,000 advance. Publishes book 15 months after acceptance of ms. Query for electronic submissions. Reports in 2 months on proposals. Book catalog and ms guidelines free on request.

Nonfiction: Reference. Subjects include religion. "Seeking books illuminating religious and social situation of Third World Christians and the lessons of Third World for the North." Submit proposal package, including outline, summary, 10-20 page chapter of intro."

Recent Nonfiction Title: *Is the Bible True?: Understanding the Bible Today*, by David Ord and Robert Coote.

‡**ORCHARD BOOKS**, Subsidiary of Grolier Inc., 95 Madison Ave., New York NY 10016. Contact: Submissions Committee. Imprints are Orchard Books, Richard Jackson Books, Melanie Kroupa Books. Publishes hardcover originals and trade paperback reprints. Publishes 60 titles/year. Receives 3,000 mss/year. 5-10% of books from first-time authors; 50% from unagented writers. Pays royalty within trade hardcover norms for children's publishers on retail price. Publishes book 1 year after acceptance of ms, longer for picture books. Reports in 1 month on mss, longer for novels. Book catalog for 8 × 10 SAE with 4 first-class stamps. Manuscript guidelines for #10 SASE.

Nonfiction: Children's/juvenile. "We publish very little nonfiction. Writers should review our list before submitting. Although we have done photo-illustrated nonfiction, we are moving away from it." Submit proposal package, including entire ms if picture-book length. Reviews artwork/photos as part of ms package. Writers should send photocopies.

Recent Nonfiction Title: *The Life and Times of the Apple*, by Charles Mizucci (picture book).
Fiction: All within children's category: adventure, ethnic, experimental, fantasy, feminist, gay/lesbian, gothic, historical, horror, humor, literary, mainstream/contemporary, mystery, picture books, romance, science fiction, suspense, young adult. "We publish a distinguished fiction list. There's room for variety within it, but writers should think about their submissions—an *unusual* genre novel may work for us—*not* a standard one." Submit entire ms.
Recent Fiction Title: *Toning the Sweep*, by Angela Johnson (middle grade fiction).
Poetry: "We publish very little. Poetry collections for children need a theme." Submit complete ms.
Recent Poetry Title: *Stardust Otel*, by Paul Janeczko

ORCHISES PRESS. P.O. Box 20602, Alexandria VA 22320-1602. (703)683-1243. Editor-in-Chief: Roger Lathbury. Estab. 1983. Publishes hardcover and trade paperback originals and reprints. Publishes 4-5 titles/year. Receives 200 queries and 100 mss/year. 1% of books from first-time authors; 95% from unagented writers. Pays 36% of receipts after Orchises has recouped its costs. Publishes book 1 year after acceptance of ms. Simultaneous submissions OK. Query for electronic submissions. Reports in 3 months. Book catalog for #10 SASE.
Nonfiction: Biography, how-to, humor, reference, technical, textbook. No real restrictions on subject matter. Query. Reviews artwork/photos as part of the freelance ms package. Writers should send photocopies.
Poetry: Poetry must have been published in respected literary journals. Although we publish free verse, have strong formalist preferences. Query or submit 5 sample poems.
Recent Poetry Title: *Patterns of Descent*, by Richard Foerster.
Tips: "Audience is professional, literate and academic. Show some evidence of appealing to a wider audience than simply people you know."

OREGON HISTORICAL SOCIETY PRESS, Oregon Historical Society, 1200 SW Park, Portland OR 97205-2483. (503)222-1741. Fax: (503)221-2035. Director—Publications & Special Projects: Bruce Taylor Hamilton. Estab. 1873. Publishes hardcover originals, trade paperback originals and reprints and a quarterly historical journal, *Oregon Historical Quarterly*. Publishes 2-4 titles/year. Receives 150 submissions/year. 75% of books from first-time authors; 100% from unagented writers. Pays royalty on wholesale price or makes outright purchase. Publishes book an average of 18 months after acceptance. Simultaneous submissions OK. Query for electronic submissions. Reports in 3 months. Book catalog free. Manuscript guidelines for #10 SASE.
Nonfiction: Subjects include Americana, art/architecture, biography, business history, ethnic, government/politics, history, nature/environment, North Pacific Studies, photography, reference, regional juvenile, women's. Query or submit outline/synopsis and sample chapters or submit complete ms. Reviews artwork/photos as part of ms package.
Recent Nonfiction Title: *Hail, Columbia: Robert Gray, John Kendrick and the Pacific Fur Trade*, by John Scofield.

OREGON STATE UNIVERSITY PRESS, 101 Waldo Hall, Corvallis OR 97331-6407. (503)737-3166. Fax: (503)737-3170. Managing Editor: Jo Alexander. Estab. 1965. Publishes hardcover and paperback originals. Averages 6 titles/year. Receives 100 submissions annually. 75% of books from first-time authors; 100% of books from unagented writers. Average print order for a first book is 1,500. Pays royalty on net receipts. No advance. Publishes book an average of 1 year after acceptance. Query for electronic submissions. Reports in 3 months. Book catalog for 6×9 SAE with 2 first-class stamps.
Nonfiction: Publishes scholarly books in history, biography, geography, literature, life sciences and natural resource management, with strong emphasis on Pacific or Northwestern topics. Submit outline and sample chapters.

O'REILLY & ASSOCIATES, 103 Morris St., Sebastopol CA 95472. (707)829-0515. Publisher: Tim O'Reilly. Managing Editor: Frank Willison. Publishes hardcover and trade paperback originals. Publishes 30 titles/year. Receives 200 queries and 30 mss/year. Pays 10% royalty on net. Offers $3,000-5,000 advance. Publishes book 6 months after acceptance. *Writer's Market* recommends allowing 2 months for reply. Simultaneous submissions OK. Query for electronic submissions. Prefers modem. Reports in 1 month. Book catalog and ms guidelines free on request.
Nonfiction: Technical. Subjects include chiefly computers and electronics. "We publish books that interest our editors. They tend to be books that are useful as opposed to theoretical, 'state of the art' technology,

For information on book publishers' areas of interest, see the nonfiction and fiction sections in the Book Publishers Subject Index.

can become the definitive work on a topic." Query with 1 sample chapter and proposal package, including your credentials. Reviews artwork/photos as part of freelance ms package.

ORYX PRESS, Suite 700, 4041 N. Central Ave., Phoenix AZ 85012. (602)265-2651. President: Phyllis B. Steckler. Acquisitions Editor: Tracy Moore. Estab. 1975. Publishes hardcover and paperback originals, disk and CD-ROM format. Averages 55 titles/year. Receives 300 submissions annually. 40% of books from first-time authors; 90% from unagented writers. Average print order for a first book is 1,500. Pays 10% royalty on net receipts. No advance. Publishes book an average of 9 months after acceptance. Query for electronic submissions. Reports in 3 months. Free book catalog and ms guidelines.
Nonfiction: Directories, general reference, library and information science, education, business reference, health care, gerontology, automation. Publishes nonfiction for public, college and university, junior college, school and special libraries; agriculture specialists, health care deliverers; managers and technical writers. Query or submit outline/synopsis and 1 sample chapter. Queries/mss may be routed to other editors in the publishing group.
Recent Nonfiction Title: *Business Information: How to Find It, How to Use It*, 2nd ed., by Michael R. Lavin.

OUR SUNDAY VISITOR, INC., 200 Noll Plaza, Huntington IN 46750-4303. (219)356-8400. Fax: (219)356-8472. President/Publisher: Robert Lockwood. Editor-in-Chief: Greg Erlandson. Acquisitions Editor: Jacquelyn Murphy. Estab. 1912. Publishes paperback and hardbound originals. Averages 20-30 titles a year. Receives over 100 submissions annually. 10% of books from first-time authors; 90% from unagented writers. Pays variable royalty on net receipts. Offers average $1,000 advance. Publishes book an average of 1 year after acceptance. Query for electronic submissions. Reports in 3 months on most queries and submissions. Author's guide and catalog for SASE.
  • Our Sunday Visitor has decreased the number of titles being released.
Nonfiction: Catholic viewpoints on current issues, reference and guidance, Bibles and devotional books, and Catholic heritage books. Prefers to see well-developed proposals as first submission with "annotated outline, three sample chapters, and definition of intended market." Reviews artwork/photos as part of ms package.
Tips: "Solid devotional books that are not first person, well-researched church histories or lives of the saints and catechetical books have the best chance of selling to our firm. Make it solidly Catholic, unique, without pious platitudes."

THE OVERLOOK PRESS, Distributed by Viking/Penguin, 149 Wooster St., New York NY 10012. Contact: Editorial Department. Imprint is Tusk Books. Publishes hardcover and trade paperback originals and hardcover reprints. Averages 40 titles/year. Receives 300 submissions annually. Pays 3-15% royalty on wholesale or retail price. Submissions accepted only through literary agents. Reports in 5 months. Book catalog free.
Nonfiction: Art, architecture, design, film, history, biography, current events, popular culture, New York State regional. No pornography.
Fiction: Literary fiction, fantasy, foreign literature in translation. "We tend not to publish commercial fiction."

‡RICHARD C. OWEN PUBLISHERS INC., P.O. Box 585, Katonah NY 10536. Editor/Art Director: Janice Boland. Publishes hardcover and trade paperback originals. Publishes 12 titles/year. Receives 50 queries and 1,000 mss/year. 95% of books from first-time authors; 100% from unagented writers. Pays 8% royalty on wholesale price. Publishes book 2 years after acceptance of ms. Accepts simultaneous submissions. Reports in 4 months on mss. Manuscript guidelines for #10 SASE.
Nonfiction: Illustrated book and children's/juvenile. Subjects include animals, education, folktales, legends, multicultural, contemporary storybook. Submit full ms.
Fiction: Juvenile (5, 6, 7 year olds), picture books, legends and folktales. "Brief, strong story line, real characters, natural language, exciting—child-appealing stories with a twist." Submit full ms.
Poetry: Poems that excite children, fun, humorous, fresh. Submit complete ms.
Tips: "Look at the best children's literature that is being published today—then write your story in your own voice—but from a child's point of view."

PACIFIC BOOKS, PUBLISHERS, P.O. Box 558, Palo Alto CA 94302-0558. (415)965-1980. Editor: Henry Ponleithner. Estab. 1945. Averages 6-12 titles/year. Royalty schedule varies with book. No advance. Send complete ms. Reports in 1 month. Book catalog and guidelines for 9×12 SASE.
Nonfiction: General interest, professional, technical and scholarly nonfiction trade books. Specialties include western Americana and Hawaiiana. Looks for "well-written, documented material of interest to a significant audience." Also considers text and reference books for high school and college. Accepts artwork/photos and translations.

PACIFIC PRESS PUBLISHING ASSOCIATION, Book Division, Seventh-day Adventist Church, P.O. Box 7000, Boise ID 83707-7000. (208)465-2595. Fax: (208)465-2531. Vice President for Editorial Development: B. Russell Holt. Acquisitions Editor: Marvin Moore. Estab. 1874. Publishes hardcover and trade paperback originals and reprints. Averages 35 titles/year. Receives 600 submissions and proposals annually. Up to 35% of books from first-time authors; 100% from unagented writers. Pays 8-16% royalty on wholesale price. Offers average $300-500 advance depending on length. Publishes books an average of 6-10 months after acceptance. Query for electronic submissions. Reports in 3 months. Manuscript guidelines for #10 SASE.

Nonfiction: Biography, cookbook (vegetarian), how-to, juvenile, self-help, textbook. Subjects include cooking and foods (vegetarian only), health, nature, religion, family living. "We are an exclusively religious publisher. We are looking for practical, how-to oriented manuscripts on religion, health, and family life that speak to human needs, interests and problems from a Biblical perspective. We can't use anything totally secular or written from other than a Christian perspective." Query or submit outline and sample chapters. Reviews artwork/photos as part of ms package.

Tips: "Our primary audiences are members of our own denomination (Seventh-day Adventist), the general Christian reading market, and the secular or nonreligious reader. Books that are doing well for us are those that relate the Biblical message to practical human concerns and those that focus more on the experiential rather than theoretical aspects of Christianity. We are assigning more titles, using less unsolicited material—although we still publish manuscripts from freelance and proposals."

PALADIN PRESS, P.O. Box 1307, Boulder CO 80306-1307. (303)443-7250. Fax: (303)442-8741. President/Publisher: Peder C. Lund. Editorial Director: Jon Ford. Estab. 1970. Publishes hardcover and paperback originals and paperback reprints. Averages 36 titles/year. 50% of books from first-time authors; 100% from unagented writers. Pays 10-12-15% royalty on net sales. Publishes book an average of 1 year after acceptance. Simultaneous submissions OK. Reports in 2 months. Book catalog free.

Nonfiction: "Paladin Press primarily publishes original manuscripts on military science, weaponry, self-defense, personal privacy, espionage, police science, action careers, guerrilla warfare, fieldcraft and 'creative revenge' humor. How-to manuscripts are given priority. Manuals on building weapons, when technically accurate and clearly presented, are encouraged. If applicable, send sample photographs and line drawings with complete outline and sample chapters." Query or submit outline and sample chapters.

Tips: "We need lucid, instructive material aimed at our market and accompanied by sharp, relevant illustrations and photos. As we are primarily a publisher of 'how-to' books, a manuscript that has step-by-step instructions, written in a clear and concise manner (but not strictly outline form) is desirable. No fiction, first-person accounts, children's, religious or joke books. We are also interested in serious, professional videos."

PANDEMIC INTERNATIONAL PUBLISHERS INC., P.O. Box 61849, Vancouver WA 98666-1849. (503)281-0339. Editor: Jeff Cart. Estab. 1990. Publishes hardcover and trade paperback originals. Publishes 12 titles/year. Receives 20 queries and 5 mss/year. 50% of books from first-time authors; 50% from unagented writers. Pays 6-10% royalty on retail price. Publishes book 3 months after acceptance of ms. Simultaneous submissions OK. Query for electronic submissions. Reports in 3 months. Book catalog free on request. Manuscript guidelines for #10 SASE.

Nonfiction: Reference, foreign language. Subjects include travel and phrase books (foreign language). Query.

Recent Nonfiction Title: *Business Travel Made Easy*, by David Trost.

Tips: Our readers are "travelers who seek independent vacations, away from the usual tourist areas. Those who wish to improve their language skills. Travel guides should be based on *your* experience. Most important of all, how will your guide help others have a better and easier trip? Unusual locations are the key and language information will improve your chances."

‡P&R PUBLISHING, P.O. Box 817, Marble Hill Rd., Phillipsburg NJ 08865. (908)454-0505. Editor: Thom Notaro. Acquisitions: Barbara Lerch. Publishes hardcover originals and trade paperback originals and reprints. Publishes 8 titles/year. Receives 200 queries and 80 mss/year. 20% of books from first-time authors; 100% from unagented writers. Pays 10-14% royalty. Publishes book 1 year after acceptance of ms. Accepts simultaneous submissions. Query for electronic submissions. Reports in 1 month on queries; 2 months on proposals and mss. Book catalog free on request. Manuscript guidelines for #10 SASE.

Nonfiction: Religious (Reformed view). "Semi-popular and popular material for laypersons, pastors, seminarians. Strong use of Scripture, irenic tone, personal application and Reformed perspective." Query with outline and 2 sample chapters.

Recent Nonfiction Title: *The Kingdom and the Power*, by Peter Leithart (challenge to church).

‡PARABLE BOOKS, 2123 S. 22nd St., Philadelphia PA 19145. (215)463-0972. Editor-in-Chief: Elizabeth B. Weatherford. Publishes hardcover, trade paperback and mass market paperback originals. Publishes 12 or more titles/year. Receives 275 queries and 115 mss/year. 20% of books from first-time authors; 10% from unagented writer. Pays 8-12% royalty on retail price. Offers $1,500-3,000 advance. Publishes book 1 year after acceptance of ms. Accepts simultaneous submissions. Reports in 1-3 months. Book catalog and ms guidelines for #10 SASE.

Nonfiction: Self-help. Subjects include health/medicine, music/dance, psychology, religion. Query with outline and 2 sample chapters.

Recent Nonfiction Title: *Life Skills Self-Helpapedia*, by Steve Mensing (self-help/psychology).

‡PARADIGM PUBLISHING INC., Subsidiary of EMC Publishing Corporation, 280 Case St., St. Paul MN 55101. (612)771-1555. Publisher: Mel Hecker. Publishes 50 titles/year. Receives 40 queries and 20 mss/year. 20% of books from first-time authors; 100% from unagented writers. Pays 6-10% royalty on net. Offers $1,000-2,500 advance. Publishes book 1 year after acceptance of ms. Accepts simultaneous submissions. Query for electronic submissions. Reports in 2 months on proposals. Book catalog for 8 × 12 SAE with 4 first-class stamps. Manuscript guidelines free on request.
Nonfiction: Textbook. Subjects include business and economics, communications, computers and electronics, psychology and software. "We focus on textbooks for business and office education marketed to proprietary business schools and community colleges." Submit outline and 2 sample chapters.
Recent Nonfiction Title: *WordPerfect 6.0 for Windows*, by Nita Rutkosky.

PARENTING PRESS, P.O.Box 75267, Seattle WA 98125. Submissions: John Shoemaker. Estab. 1979. Publishes hardcover and trade paperback originals. Averages 6-8 titles/year. Receives 150 queries and 300 mss/year. 75% of books from first-time authors; 100% from unagented writers. Pays royalty on wholesale price. Publishes book 18 months after acceptance of ms. Simultaneous submissions OK. Reports in 3 months. Catalog and ms guidelines free on request.
Nonfiction: Children's/juvenile, parenting. Subjects include child guidance/parenting. "We do not publish 'complete' parenting books. We look for books that offer choices to different parenting topics. We are interested in nonfiction books that build competence in parents, children and those who work with them." Query, submit outline with 1 sample chapter, or proposal package, including marketing info. Reviews artwork/photos as part of freelance ms package. Writers should send photocopies.
Tips: "Request submission guidelines first."

PASSPORT PRESS, P.O. Box 1346, Champlain NY 12919-1346. Publisher: Jack Levesque. Estab. 1975. Publishes trade paperback originals. Averages 4 titles/year. 25% of books from first-time authors; 100% from unagented writers. Pays 6% royalty on retail price. Publishes book an average of 9 months after acceptance. *Send 1-page query only. Unsolicited mss or samples and non-travel material will not be returned even if accompanied by postage.*
Nonfiction: Travel books only, not travelogues. Especially looking for mss on practical travel subjects and travel guides on specific countries. Query. Reviews artwork/photos as part of ms package.

PAULIST PRESS, 997 Macarthur Blvd., Mahwah NJ 07430. (201)825-7300. Fax: (201)825-8345. Editor: Rev. Kevin A. Lynch. Managing Editor: Donald Brophy. Estab. 1865. Publishes hardcover and paperback originals and paperback reprints. Averages 90-100 titles/year. Receives 500 submissions annually. 5-8% of books from first-time authors; 95% from unagented writers. Subsidy publishes (nonauthor) 1-2% of books. Pays royalty on retail price. Usually offers advance. Publishes book an average of 10 months after acceptance. Reports in 2 months. Query for electronic submissions.
Nonfiction: Philosophy, religion, self-help, textbooks (religious). Accepts nonfiction translations from German, French and Spanish. "We would like to see theology (Catholic and ecumenical Christian), popular spirituality, liturgy, and religious education texts." Submit outline and 2 sample chapters. Reviews artwork/photos as part of ms package.
Recent Nonfiction Title: *Paul VI: The First Modern Pope*, by Peter Hebblethwaite.

PBC INTERNATIONAL INC., 1 School St., Glen Cove NY 11542. (516)676-2727. Fax: (516)676-2738. Publisher: Mark Serchuck. Managing Editor: Susan Kapsis. Estab. 1980. Imprints are Library of Applied Design (nonfiction), Architecture & Interior Design Library (nonfiction), Great Graphics Series (nonfiction) and Design In Motion Series (nonfiction), and Showcase Edition (nonfiction). Publishes hardcover and paperback originals. Averages 18 titles/year. Receives 100-200 submissions annually. Most of books from first-time authors and unagented writers done on assignment. Pays royalty and/or flat fees. Simultaneous submissions OK. Reports in 2 months. Book catalog for 9 × 12 SASE.
Nonfiction: Subjects include design, graphic art, architecture/interior design, packaging design, marketing design, product design. No submissions not covered in the above listed topics. Query with outline and sample chapters. Reviews artwork/photos as part of ms package.
Recent Nonfiction Title: *Rooms with a View: Two Decades of Outstanding American Interior Design from the Kips Bay Decorator Show Houses.*
Tips: "PBC International is the publisher of full-color visual idea books for the design, marketing and graphic arts professional."

PEACHPIT PRESS, 2414 Sixth St., Berkeley CA 94710. (510)548-4393. Estab. 1986. Publishes trade paperback originals. Publishes over 30 titles/year. Receives 250 queries and 6 mss/year. 10% of books from first-time authors; 80% from unagented writers. Pays 12-20% royalty on wholesale price. Offers $3,000-10,000 advance. Publishes book 6 months after acceptance of ms. Simultaneous submissions OK. Query for electronic submissions. Reports in 3 months on proposals. Book catalog free on request.

Nonfiction: How-to, reference, technical. Subjects include computers and electronics. "We prefer no phone calls." Submit short, 1-page proposal (preferred) or outline. Reviews artwork/photos as part of the freelance ms package. Writers should send photocopies.
Recent Nonfiction Title: *The Little PC Book*, by Larry Magid (advice for computer novices).

PEACHTREE PUBLISHERS, LTD., 494 Armour Circle NE, Atlanta GA 30324-4888. (404)876-8761. Contact: Managing Editor. Estab. 1977. Publishes hardcover and trade paperback originals. Averages 15-20 titles/year. Receives up to 18,000 submissions annually. 25% of books from first-time authors; 75% from unagented writers. Average print order for a first book is 5,000-10,000. Publishes book 1-2 years after acceptance. Reports in 6 months on queries. Book catalog for 9 × 12 SAE with 3 first-class stamps.
Nonfiction: General and humor. Subjects include juvenile, cooking and foods, history, self-help, gardening, biography, general gift, recreation. No technical, reference or animals. Submit outline and sample chapters. Reviews artwork/photos as part of ms package. No originals, please.
Recent Nonfiction Title: *Margaret Mitchell & John Marsh: The Love Story Behind Gone with the Wind*, by Marianne Walker (biography).
Fiction: Literary, juvenile, mainstream. "We are particularly interested in fiction with a Southern feel." No fantasy, science fiction or romance. Submit sample chapters.
Recent Fiction Title: *Jessie and Jesus and Cousin Claire*, by Raymond Andrews (fiction).
Tips: "We're looking for mainstream nonfiction and fiction of general interest. Although our books are sold throughout North America, we consider ourselves the national publisher with a Southern voice."

PELICAN PUBLISHING COMPANY, 1101 Monroe St., P.O. Box 3110, Gretna LA 70053. (504)368-1175. Editor: Nina Kooij. Estab. 1926. Publishes hardcover, trade paperback and mass market paperback originals and reprints. Averages 40 titles/year. Receives 5,500 submissions annually. 5% of books from first-time authors; 60% from unagented writers. Pays royalty on publisher's actual receipts. Publishes book an average of 18 months after acceptance. Reports in 1 month on queries. *Writer's Market* recommends allowing 2 months for reply. Writer's guidelines for SASE.
   • Pelican continues to reduce the number of freelance projects it pursues, but their submissions are growing.
Nonfiction: Travel, biography, coffee table book (limited), cookbook, how-to, humor, illustrated book, juvenile, self-help, motivational, inspirational, Scottish. Subjects include Americana (especially Southern regional, Ozarks, Texas and Florida); business and economics (popular how-to and motivational, if author is a speaker); cooking and food; health; history; music (American artforms: jazz, blues, Cajun, R&B); politics (special interest in conservative viewpoint); recreation; religion (for popular audience mostly, but will consider others); travel. *Travel*: Regional and international (especially areas in Pacific). *Motivational*: with business slant. *Inspirational*: author must be someone with potential for large audience. *Cookbooks*: "We look for authors with strong connection to restaurant industry or cooking circles, i.e. someone who can promote successfully." Query. "We require that a query be made first. This greatly expedites the review process and can save the writer additional postage expenses." Does not consider multiple queries or submissions. Reviews artwork/photos as part of ms package; absolutely no art originals—copies only.
Recent Nonfiction Title: *The California Farm Cookbook*, by Kitty Morse.
Fiction: Historical, humor, Southern, juvenile. "We publish maybe one novel a year, ususally by an author we already have. Almost all proposals are returned. We are most interested in Southern novels." No young adult, romance, science fiction, fantasy, gothic, mystery, erotica, confession, horror, sex or violence. Submit outline/synopsis and 2 sample chapters.
Recent Fiction Title: *Toby Belfer's Seder: A Passover Story Retold*, by Gloria Teles Pushker.
Tips: "We do extremely well with cookbooks, travel and popular histories. We will continue to build in these areas. The writer must have a clear sense of the market and this includes knowledge of the competition. A query letter should describe the project briefly, give the author's writing and professional credentials, and promotional ideas. Include a SASE."

PENDAYA PUBLICATIONS, INC., 510 Woodvine Ave., Metairie LA 70005. (504)834-8151. Manager: Earl J. Mathes. Estab. 1986. Publishes hardcover originals. Publishes 1 or 2 titles/year. Receives 6-8 queries and 3-4 mss/year. 100% of mss from unagented writers. Pays 4-8% royalty on retail price (varies). Offers $500-3,000 advance. Publishes book 9 months after acceptance. Reports in 6 months on mss.
Nonfiction: Coffee table book, illustrated book. Subjects include anthropology/archaeology, art/architecture, photography, travel, design. Submit proposal package. Writers should send transparencies.

PENGUIN USA, 375 Hudson St., New York NY 10014. Imprints include Dial Books for Young Readers, NAL/Dutton, Penguin, Plume, Signet, Topaz and Viking. General interest publisher of both fiction and nonfiction. The company did not respond to our request for information. Query before submitting.

PENNSYLVANIA HISTORICAL AND MUSEUM COMMISSION, Imprint of the Commonwealth of Pennsylvania, P.O. Box 1026, Harrisburg PA 17108-1026. (717)787-8099. Fax: (717)787-8312. Chief, Publications and Sales Division: Diane B. Reed. Estab. 1913. Publishes hardcover and paperback originals and reprints.

Averages 6-8 titles/year. Receives 25 submissions annually. Pays 5-10% royalty on retail price. May make outright purchase of mss; sometimes makes special assignments. Publishes book an average of 18 months after acceptance. Simultaneous submissions OK. Query for electronic submissions. Reports in 4 months. Manuscripts prepared according to the *Chicago Manual of Style*.

Nonfiction: All books must be related to Pennsylvania, its history or culture: biography, coffee table, how-to, illustrated book, cookbook, reference, technical, visitor attractions and historic travel guidebooks. "The Commission seeks manuscripts on Pennsylvania in general, but more specifically on archaeology, history, art (decorative and fine), politics, travel, photography, nature, sports history and cooking." Query or submit outline and sample chapters. Guidelines and proposal forms available.

Recent Nonfiction Title: *Canoeing on the Juniata*, by Henry K. Landes.

Tips: "Our audience is diverse—students, specialists and generalists—all of them interested in one or more aspects of Pennsylvania's history and culture. Manuscripts must be well researched and documented (footnotes not necessarily required depending on the nature of the manuscript) and interestingly written. Because of the expertise of our reviewers, manuscripts must be factually accurate, but in being so, writers must not sacrifice style. We have a tradition of publishing scholarly and reference works, as well as more popularly styled books that reach an even broader audience."

‡PENNWELL BOOKS, PennWell Publishing, P.O. Box 1260, 1421 S. Sheridan Rd., Tulsa OK 74101-6619. Editor: Sue Rhodes Sesso. Estab. 1910. Publishes hardcover originals. Publishes 20 titles/year. Receives 200 queries and 75 mss/year. 50% of books from first-time authors; 99% from unagented writers. Pays 5-15% royalty on net receipts. Publishes book 6-9 months after acceptance of ms. "IBM or Mac-compatible; must have two hard copies of manuscript too." SASE, "but we expect all authors to keep their originals and cannot be held responsible for any submissions." Reports in 6 months on proposals. Book catalog free on request. "Must call 1-800-752-9764."

Nonfiction: Technical. Subjects include petroleum, dental, environmental, power. "Texts must have practical application for professionals in the markets we serve. Study our catalog first before submitting anything. Your expertise as a practitioner within the specific industry is an essential component. We do not publish theory or philosophy, nor do we publish texts for the general public. We do publish practical, how-to, reference-type books ONLY for the industries we serve." Submit proposal package, including table of contents, chapter-by-chapter synopsis, résumé and sample chapter(s). Reviews artwork/photos as part of freelance ms package. Writers should send photocopies.

Recent Nonfiction Title: *Where's the Shortage? A Nontechnical Guide to Petroleum Economics*, by Bob Tippee.

Tips: Audiences include: Petroleum—engineers, geologists, chemists, geophysicists, economists, managers. Environmental—petroleum industry people needing information on hazardous materials, safety and crisis management. Power—professionals in utility industry. Dental—practicing dentists and their staffs.

‡PENNYWHISTLE PRESS, P.O. Box 734, Teseque NM 87574. (505)982-0066. Managing Editor: Jeanie C. Williams. Publishes 6-12 titles/year. Receives 250 queries and 125 mss/year. 50% of books from first-time authors; 100% from unagented writers. Pays $100, chapbook plus 50 copies of book to author. Publishes book 9-12 months after acceptance of ms. Simultaneous submissions OK. Query for electronic submissions. Reports in 1 month on queries, 2 months on proposals, 3 months on mss. Book catalog for 9×12 SAE with 98¢ postage. Manuscript guidelines free on request.

● Pennywhistle publishes only poetry chapbooks.

Poetry: Submit 30 sample poems.

THE PERMANENT PRESS/SECOND CHANCE PRESS, 4170 Noyac Rd., Sag Harbor NY 11963. (516)725-1101. Fax: (516)725-1101. Editor: Judith Shepard. Estab. 1978. Publishes hardcover originals and reprints. Permanent Press publishes literary fiction. Second Chance Press devotes itself exclusively to re-publishing fine books that are out of print and deserve continued recognition. Averages 12 titles/year. Receives 5,000 submissions annually. 35% of books from first-time authors; 75% from unagented writers. Average print order for a first book is 2,000. Pays 10% royalty on wholesale price. Offers $1,000 advance for Permanent Press books and royalty only on Second Chance Press titles. Publishes book an average of 18 months after acceptance. Simultaneous submissions OK. Reports in 4 months on queries. Book catalog for 7 first-class stamps.

● Permanent Press does not employ readers and the number of submissions it receives has grown (3,000 to 5,000) so much response time has had to increase (3 to 4 months). If the writer sends a query or manuscript that the press is not interested in, they may hear in two or three weeks. But if there is interest, it may take 3 to 6 months.

Nonfiction: Biography, autobiography, historical. No scientific and technical material or academic studies. Query.

Fiction: Adventure, ethnic, historical, humor, mainstream, mystery, suspense. Especially looking for high line literary fiction, "original and arresting." No mass market romance. Query.

Recent Fiction Title: *Littlejohn*, by Howard Owen.
Tips: "We are no longer looking for the following types of fiction: confession, experimental, science fiction and fantasy."

PERSPECTIVES PRESS, P.O. Box 90318, Indianapolis IN 46290-0318. (317)872-3055. Publisher: Pat Johnston. Estab. 1982. Publishes hardcover and trade paperback originals. Averages 4 titles/year. Receives 200 queries annually. 95% of books from first-time authors; 95% from unagented writers. Pays 5-15% royalty on net sales. Publishes book an average of 1 year after acceptance. Simultaneous submissions OK. Reports in 1 month on queries. *Writer's Market* recommends allowing 2 months for reply. Book catalog and writer's guidelines for #10 SAE with 2 first-class stamps.
Nonfiction: How-to, juvenile and self-help books on health, psychology and sociology—all related to adoption or infertility. Query.
Fiction: Query.
Tips: "For adults we are seeking infertility and adoption decision-making materials, books dealing with adoptive or foster parenting issues, books to use with children, books to share with others to help explain infertility or adoption or foster care, special programming or training manuals, etc. For children we will consider adoption or foster care related fiction manuscripts that are appropriate for preschoolers and for early elementary children. We do not consider YA. Nonfiction manuscripts are considered for all ages. No autobiography or adult fiction. While we would consider a manuscript from a writer who was not personally or professionally involved in these issues, we would be more inclined to accept a manuscript submitted by an infertile person, an adoptee, a birthparent, an adoptive parent, a professional working with any of these."

PETER PAUPER PRESS, INC., 202 Mamaroneck Ave., White Plains NY 10601-5376. (914)681-0144. Fax: (914)681-0389. Co-Publisher: Nick Beilenson. Estab. 1928. Publishes hardcover originals. Averages 24 titles/year. Receives 200 submissions annually. Buys some mss outright for $1,000. Offers no advance. Publishes ms an average of 9 months after acceptance. Simultaneous submissions OK. Reports in 1 month. *Writer's Market* recommends allowing 2 months for reply. Book catalog for #10 SAE with 2 first-class stamps.
Nonfiction: Subjects include compilations of quotes, Americana, humor, holidays, inspirational. *No* cookbooks, religion, fiction, or children's books. Submit complete ms. *Writer's Market* recommends query with SASE first. Reviews artwork as part of ms package.
Tips: "We are looking especially for collections of quotes."

PETERSON'S, P.O. Box 2123, Princeton NJ 08543-2123. (800)338-3282. President: Peter W. Hegener. Publisher: Carole Cushmore. Editor-in-Chief: Jim Gish. Estab. 1966. Publishes trade and reference books. Averages 55-75 titles/year. Receives 200-250 submissions annually. 30% of books from first-time authors; 90% from unagented writers. Average print order for a first book is 10,000-15,000. Pays 10-12% royalty on net sales. Offers advance. Publishes book an average of 1 year after acceptance. Reports in 2 months. Catalog free.
Nonfiction: Parenting, family and business books, as well as educational and career directories. Submit complete ms or detailed outline and sample chapters. *Writer's Market* recommends query with SASE first. Looks for "appropriateness of contents to our market, accuracy of information, author's credentials, and writing style suitable for audience." Reviews artwork/photos as part of ms package.
Recent Nonfiction Title: *The Working Parent's Help Book*.

PFEIFFER & COMPANY, 8517 Production Ave., San Diego CA 92121. (619)578-5900. Fax: (619)578-2042. President: J. William Pfeiffer. Estab. 1968. Publishes paperback and hardback originals and reprints. Averages 80 titles/year. Specializes in practical materials for human resource development, consultants and general management. Pays average 10% royalty. No advance. Publishes book an average of 6 months after acceptance. Markets books by direct mail and through bookstores. Simultaneous submissions OK. Reports in 3 months. Book catalog and guidelines for SASE.
Nonfiction: HRD mss to: Richard Roe, Vice President, Publications. Management mss to: Leslie S. Smith, Senior Vice President. Publishes (in order of preference) human resource development and group-oriented material, management education, personal growth, business. No materials for grammar school or high school classroom teachers. Use *American Psychological Association Style Manual*. Query. Send prints or completed art or rough sketches to accompany ms.

‡PHB PUBLISHERS, 83 Washington St., Dover NH 03820. (603)743-4266. Senior Editor: P.H. Burr. Publishes 25 titles/year. Receives 50 queries/year. 50% of books from first-time authors. Pays royalty. Publishes book 6 months after acceptance of ms. Accepts simultaneous submissions. Query for electronic submissions. Reports in 3 months.
Nonfiction: Subjects include Americana, history, photography.

‡PHI DELTA KAPPA EDUCATIONAL FOUNDATION, P.O. Box 789, Bloomington IN 47402. (812)339-1156. Editor of Special Publications: Donovan R. Walling. Publishes hardcover and trade paperback originals. Publishes 24-30 titles/year. Receives 100 queries and 50-60 mss/year. 50% of books from first-time authors;

100% from unagented writers. Pays honorarium of $500-5,000. Publishes book 6-9 months after acceptance of ms. No simultaneous submissions. Query for electronic submissions. Reports in 1-3 months on proposals. Book catalog and ms guidelines free on request.

Nonfiction: How-to, reference, essay collections. Subjects include child guidance/parenting, education, and legal issues. "We publish books for educators — K-12 and higher ed. Our professional books are often used in college courses but are never specifically designed as textbooks." Query or submit with outline and 1 sample chapter. Reviews artwork/photos as part of freelance ms package.

Recent Nonfiction Title: *The State of the Nation's Public Schools*, edited by Elam (essay collection); *Twelve Schools That Succeed*, by Horenstein (educational analysis); *Women in Cross-Cultural Transitions*, edited by Bysdyzienski and Resnik.

PHILOMEL BOOKS, Division of The Putnam Publishing Group, 200 Madison Ave., New York NY 10016. (212)951-8700. Editor-in-Chief: Paula Wiseman. Editorial Director: Patricia Lee Gauch. Editorial Assistant: Laura Walsh. Estab. 1980. Publishes hardcover originals. Publishes 25-30 titles/year. Receives 2,600 submissions annually. 15% of books from first-time authors; 30% from unagented writers. Pays standard royalty. Advance negotiable. Publishes book an average of 1-2 years after acceptance. Reports in 1 month on queries, 3 months on unsolicited mss. Book catalog for 9×12 SAE with 4 first-class stamps. Request book catalog from marketing department of Putnam Publishing Group.

Nonfiction: Young adult and children's picture books (ages 2-17). No series or activity books. Query first. Always include SASE. Looks for quality writing, unique ideas, suitability to our market.

Fiction: Young adult and children's books (ages 2-17) on any topic. Particularly interested in fine regional fiction and quality picture books. Query to department.

Tips: "We prefer a very brief synopsis that states the basic premise of the story. This will help us determine whether or not the manuscript is suited to our list. If applicable, we'd be interested in knowing the author's writing experience or background knowledge. We are always looking for beautifully written manuscripts with stories that engage. We try to be less influenced by the swings of the market than in the power, value, essence of the manuscript itself."

PICCADILLY BOOKS, P.O. Box 25203, Colorado Springs CO 80936-5203. (719)548-1844. Publisher: Bruce Fife. Estab. 1985. Publishes hardcover and trade paperback originals and trade paperback reprints. Publishes 3-8 titles/year. Receives 120 submissions/year. 70% of books from first-time authors; 95% from unagented writers. Pays 5-10% royalty on retail price. Offers $250 average advance. Publishes book an average of 9 months after acceptance. Simultaneous submissions OK. Responds only if interested. Manuscript guidelines for #10 SASE.

• Picadilly is no longer interested in any fiction or children's plays.

Nonfiction: How-to, humor, performing arts, business. "We are looking for how-to books on entertainment, humor, performing arts, small and /or home-based businesses and careers. We have a strong interest in subjects on clowning, magic, puppetry and related arts, including comedy skits and dialogs." Query with sample chapters.

Recent Nonfiction Title: *Clown Magic*.

THE PICKERING PRESS, P.O. Box 331531, Miami FL 33233-1531. (305)444-8784. Fax: (305)444-8784. President: Brenda Beck. Estab. 1986. Publishes hardcover and trade paperback originals and trade paperback reprints. Publishes 1-2 titles/year. Receives 25 submissions/year. 10% of books from first-time authors; 100% from unagented writers. Pays 6-15% on wholesale price. Buys mss outright for $2,500. Publishes book an average of 9 months after acceptance. Query for electronic submissions. Reports in 2 months on queries. Book catalog free.

Nonfiction: How-to, illustrated book, self-help. Subjects include art/architecture, history, regional. Looking for regional/Florida history ms. No regional books outside of Florida. Submit query or outline and sample chapters. Reviews artwork/photos as part of ms package.

Tips: "Nonfiction and regional history have the best chance of being sold to our firm. If I were a writer trying to market a book today, I would clearly define the market for my book prior to approaching publishers, and be prepared to offer non-book trade suggestions in addition to traditional techniques."

‡PICTON PRESS, Imprint of Picton Corporation, P.O. Box 250, Rockport ME 04856-0250. (207)236-6565. Imprints are Picton Press (contact Cindy Gustavson), Penobscot Press (contact Lew Rohrbach), Cricketfield Press (contact Lew Rohrbach). Publishes hardcover and mass market paperback originals and reprints. Publishes 30 titles/year. Receives 30 queries and 15 mss/year. 50% of books from first-time authors; 100% from unagented writers. Pays 0-10% royalty on wholesale price or makes outright purchase of $1,000 minimum. Offers $1,000-3,000 advance. Publishes book 6 months after acceptance of ms. No simultaneous submissions. Reports in 2 months on queries and proposals, 3 months on mss. Book catalog free on request.

Nonfiction: Reference, textbook. Subjects include Americana, genealogy, history, military/war, religion. Query with outline.

Recent Nonfiction Title: *Puritan in the Wilderness*, by Fitch.

Fiction: Historical. Query with synopsis.

THE PILGRIM PRESS, United Church Board for Homeland Ministries, 700 Prospect Ave. E., Cleveland OH 44115-1100. (216)736-3703. Editorial Director: Richard E. Brown. Publishes hardcover and trade paperback originals. Averages 30 titles/year. 40% of books from first-time authors; 100% from unagented writers. Pays standard royalties and advances where appropriate. Publishes book an average of 18 months after acceptance. Reports in 6 months on queries. Book catalog and ms guidelines free on request.
Nonfiction: Ethics, social issues with a strong commitment to justice—addressing such topics as public policy, sexuality and gender, economics, medicine, gay and lesbian concerns, human rights, minority liberation and the environment—primarily in a Christian context, but not exclusively. Also, publishes books on American religious history.
Tips: "We are concentrating more on academic/scholarly submissions. Writers should send books about contemporary social issues in a Christian context. Our audience is liberal, open-minded, socially aware, feminist, educated lay church members and clergy, teachers and seminary professors."

PILOT BOOKS, 103 Cooper St., Babylon NY 11702-2319. (516)422-2225. Fax: (516)422-2227. President: Sam Small. Estab. 1959. Publishes paperback originals. Averages 20-30 titles/year. Receives 100-200 submissions annually. 20% of books from first-time authors; 90% from unagented writers. Average print order for a first book is 3,000. Offers standard royalty contract based on wholesale or retail price. Usual advance is $250, but this varies, depending on author's reputation and nature of book. Publishes book an average of 8 months after acceptance. Reports in 1 month. *Writer's Market* recommends allowing 2 months for reply. Book catalog and guidelines for #10 SASE.
Nonfiction: Financial, business, travel, career, personal guides and training manuals. "Our training manuals are utilized by America's major corporations as well as the government. Directories and books on travel and moneymaking opportunities. Wants clear, concise treatment of subject matter." Length: 8,000-30,000 words. Send outline. Reviews artwork/photos as part of ms package.
Recent Nonfiction Title: *Home-Based Business Ideas For Women*, by Priscilla Y. Huff.

PINEAPPLE PRESS, INC., P.O. Box 16008, Southside Station, Sarasota FL 34239. (813)952-1085. Editor: June Cussen. Estab. 1982. Publishes hardcover and trade paperback originals. Averages 14 titles/year. Receives 1,500 submissions annually. 20% of books from first-time authors; 80% from unagented writers. Pays 6½-15% royalty on retail price. Seldom offers advance. Publishes book an average of 1 year after acceptance. Simultaneous submissions OK. Reports in 3 months. Book catalog for 9 × 12 SAE with $1.05 postage.
Nonfiction: Biography, how-to, reference, nature. Subjects include animals, history, gardening, nature. "We will consider most nonfiction topics. We are seeking quality nonfiction on diverse topics for the library and book trade markets." No pop psychology or autobiographies. Query or submit outline/brief synopsis and sample chapters with SASE.
Recent Nonfiction Title: *Spanish Treasure Fleets*, by Timothy Walton.
Fiction: Literary, historical, mainstream. No romance, science fiction, children's. Submit outline/brief synopsis and sample chapters.
Recent Fiction Title: *Thunder on the St. Johns*, by Lee Gramling.
Tips: "If I were a writer trying to market a book today, I would learn everything I could about book publishing and book publicity and agree to actively participate in promoting my book. A query on a novel without a brief sample seems useless."

PIPPIN PRESS, 229 E. 85th St., P.O. Box 1347, Gracie Station, New York NY 10028. (212)288-4920. Fax: (212)563-5703. Publisher/President: Barbara Francis. Estab. 1987. Publishes hardcover originals. Publishes 4-6 titles/year. Receives 4,500 queries/year. 80% of queries from unagented writers. Pays royalty. Publishes book an average of 18-24 months after acceptance. Reports in 3 weeks on queries. Do *not* send mss. "We do not accept unsolicited manuscripts, but we welcome queries (with SASE)." *Writer's Market* recommends allowing 2 months for reply. Book catalog for 6 × 9 SASE. Manuscript guidelines for #10 SASE.
Nonfiction: Children's books: biography, humor, picture books. Animals, history, language/literature, nature, science. General nonfiction for children ages 4-10. Query only. Reviews copies of artwork/photos as part of ms package.
Fiction: Adventure, fantasy, historical, humor, mystery, picture books, suspense. "We're looking for small chapter books with animal-fantasy themes, stories for 7-11 year olds, by people of many cultures." Wants humorous fiction for ages 7-11. Query only.
Recent Fiction Title: *The Sounds of Summer*, by David Updike.
Tips: "Read as many of the best children's books published in the last five years as you can. We are looking for multi-ethnic fiction and nonfiction for ages 7-10, as well as general fiction for this age group. I would pay particular attention to children's books favorably reviewed in *School Library Journal, The Booklist, The New York Times Book Review*, and *Publishers Weekly*."

PLAYERS PRESS, INC., P.O. Box 1132, Studio City CA 91614-0132. (818)789-4980. Vice President, Editorial: Robert W. Gordon. Estab. 1965. Publishes hardcover and trade paperback originals, and trade paperback reprints. Averages 25-35 titles/year. Receives 200-1,000 submissions annually. 10% of books from first-time authors; 80% from unagented writers. Pays royalty on wholesale price. Publishes book an average of 20 months after acceptance. Reports on queries in 1 month, up to 1 year on mss. Book catalog and guidelines for 9×12 SAE with 4 first-class stamps.

Nonfiction: Juvenile and theatrical drama/entertainment industry. Subjects include the performing arts, costume, theater and film crafts. Needs quality plays and musicals, adult or juvenile. Query. Reviews artwork/photos as part of package.

Fiction: Subject matter of plays include adventure, confession, ethnic, experimental, fantasy, historical, horror, humor, mainstream, mystery, religious, romance, science fiction, suspense, western. Submit complete ms for theatrical plays only. "No novels or story books are accepted. We publish plays, musicals and books on theatre, film and television, only."

Tips: "Plays, entertainment industry texts, theater, film and television books have the only chances of selling to our firm."

‡PLEASANT COMPANY PUBLICATIONS, Imprint of American Girls Collection®. 8400 Fairway Pl., Middleton WI 53562. Book Editor: Roberta Johnson. Publishes hardcover and trade paperback originals. Publishes 3-25 title/year. Receives 100 queries and 75 mss/year. 50% of books from unagented writers. Pays royalty. Advance varies. Accepts simultaneous submissions. Reports in 2 months. Book catalog free on request.

Nonfiction: Children's/juvenile. Subjects include Americana. "Our audience is girls ages 7-12. We also publish for the education market." Query.

Recent Nonfiction Title: *America at School* (curriculum unit for grades 3-5).

Fiction: Juvenile. Query.

Recent Fiction Title: *Meet Addy*, by Connie Porter (juvenile fiction).

PLENUM PUBLISHING, 233 Spring St., New York NY 10013-1578. (212)620-8000. Senior Editor, Trade Books: Linda Greenspan Regan. Estab. 1946. Publishes hardcover originals. Averages 350 titles/year. Plenum Trade publishes 12. Receives 250 submissions annually. 25% of books from first-time authors; 20% from unagented writers. Publishes book an average of 8-16 months after acceptance. Simultaneous submissions OK. Query for electronic submissions. Reports in 6 months.

Nonfiction: Subjects include trade science, criminology, sociology, psychology, health. "We are seeking high quality, popular books in the sciences and social sciences." Query only.

Tips: "Our audience consists of intelligent laymen and professionals. Authors should be experts on subject matter of book. They must compare their books with competitive works, explain how theirs differs, and define the market for their books."

PLEXUS PUBLISHING, INC., 143 Old Marlton Pike, Medford NJ 08055-8750. (609)654-6500. Fax: (609)654-4309. Editorial Director: Thomas Hogan. Estab. 1977. Publishes hardcover and paperback originals. Averages 4-5 titles/year. Receives 10-20 submissions annually. 70% of books from first-time authors; 90% from unagented writers. Pays 10-20% royalty on wholesale price; buys some booklets outright for $250-1,000. Offers $500-1,000 advance. Simultaneous submissions OK. Reports in 3 months. Book catalog and guidelines for 10×13 SAE with 4 first-class stamps.

Nonfiction: Biography (of naturalists), reference. Subjects include plants, animals, nature, life sciences. "We will consider any book on a nature/biology subject, particularly those of a reference (permanent) nature that would be of lasting value to high school and college audiences, and/or the general reading public (ages 14 and up). Authors should have authentic qualifications in their subject area, but qualifications may be by experience as well as academic training." No gardening, philosophy or psychology; generally not interested in travel but will consider travel that gives sound ecological information. Also interested in mss of about 20-40 pages in length for feature articles in *Biology Digest* (guidelines available with SASE). Query. Reviews artwork/photos as part of ms package.

Tips: "We will give serious consideration to well-written manuscripts that deal even indirectly with biology/nature subjects. For example, *Exploring Underwater Photography* (a how-to for divers) and *The Literature of Nature* (an anthology of nature writings for college curriculum) were accepted for publication."

POCKET BOOKS, Division of Simon & Schuster, Dept. WM, 1230 Avenue of the Americas, New York NY 10020. Imprints include Pocket Star Books, Washington Square Press (high-quality mass market), Archway and Minstrel (juvenile/YA imprints), Folger Shakespeare Library, Star Trek. Publishes paperback originals and reprints, mass market and trade paperbacks and hardcovers. Averages 450 titles/year. Receives 5,000 submissions annually. 15% of books from first-time authors; 100% from agented writers. Pays royalty on retail price. Publishes book an average of 1 year after acceptance. *No unsolicited mss or queries.* "All submissions must go through a literary agent."

Nonfiction: History, biography, reference and general nonfiction, cookbooks, humor, calendars.

Fiction: Adult (mysteries, thriller, psychological suspense, Star Trek ® novels, romance, westerns).

POGO PRESS, INCORPORATED, 4 Cardinal Lane, St. Paul MN 55127-6406. Vice President: Leo J. Harris. Publishes trade paperback originals. Publishes 3 titles/year. Receives 20 queries and 20 mss/year. 100% of books from unagented writers. Pays royalty on wholesale price. Publishes book 6 months after acceptance. Query for electronic submissions; "negotiable." Reports in 2 months. Book catalog free on request.

Nonfiction: "We limit our publishing to Breweriana, history, art and popular culture. Our books are heavily illustrated." Query. Reviews artwork/photos as part of freelance ms package. Writers should send photocopies.

Recent Nonfiction Title: *Ponce de Leon*, by Douglas T. Peck.

‡**POLICY STUDIES ORGANIZATION**, 702 S. Wright St., Urbana IL 61801. (217)359-8541. Publications Coordinator: Stuart Nagel. Publishes trade paperback originals. Publishes 10 titles/year. Pays 10% royalty. Book catalog and ms guidelines free on request.

Nonfiction: Reference, technical, textbook. Subjects include business and economics, computers and electronics, education, ethnic, government/politics, money/finance, nature/environment, philosophy, science, sociology. Query.

‡**POLYCHROME PUBLISHING CORPORATION**, 4509 N. Francisco, Chicago IL 60625. (312)478-4455. Vice President: Brian Witkowski. Publishes hardcover originals and reprints. Publishes 6 titles/year. Receives 250 queries and 850 mss/year. 50% of books from first-time authors; 100% from unagented writers. Pays royalty, "usually a combination of fee plus royalties." Advance "depends upon amount of editorial work necessary." Publishes book 10 months after acceptance of ms. Accepts simultaneous submissions. Query for electronic submissions. Reports in 3 months on mss. Book catalog and ms guidelines for #10 SASE.

Nonfiction: Children's/juvenile. Subjects include ethnic. Submit outline and 3 sample chapters. Reviews artwork/photos as part of ms package, but not necessary. Writers should send photocopies.

Fiction: Ethnic, juvenile, picture books, young adult. "We do not publish fables, folktales, fairytales or anthropomorphic animal stories." Submit synopsis and 3 sample chapters; picture books, whole ms.

Recent Fiction Title: *One Small Girl*, by Jennifer L. Chan (picture book).

PRAKKEN PUBLICATIONS, INC., P.O. Box 8623, Ann Arbor MI 48107-8623. (313)769-1211. Fax: (313)769-8383. Publisher: George Kennedy. Estab. 1934. Publishes educational hardcover and paperback originals as well as educational magazines. Averages 4 book titles/year. Receives 50 submissions annually. 20% of books from first-time authors; 95% from unagented writers. Pays 10% royalty on net price of book (negotiable, with production costs). Publishes book an average of 6 months after acceptance. Simultaneous submissions OK. Reports in 2 months if reply requested and SASE furnished. *Writer's Market* recommends allowing 2 months for reply. Book catalog for #10 SASE.

Nonfiction: Industrial, vocational and technology education and related areas, general educational reference. "We are interested in manuscripts with broad appeal in any of the specific subject areas of industrial arts, vocational-technical education, and reference for the general education field." Submit outline and sample chapters. Reviews artwork/photos as part of ms package.

Recent Nonfiction Title: *High School to Employment Transition: Contemporary Issues*.

Tips: "We have a continuing interest in magazine and book manuscripts which reflect emerging issues and trends in education, especially vocational, industrial, and technical education."

PRECEPT PRESS, Subsidiary of Bonus Books, 160 E. Illinois St., Chicago IL 60611. (312)467-0424. Associate Editor: Anne Barthel. Publishes hardcover and trade paperback originals. Publishes 20 titles/year. Receives 300 queries and 100 mss/year. 25% of books from first-time authors; 90% from unagented writers. Pays royalty. Publishes book 8 months after acceptance. Simultaneous submissions OK if informed. Query for electronic submissions. Reports in 3 months on proposals. All submissions and queries must include SASE. Manuscript guidelines for #10 SASE.

Nonfiction: Reference, technical, textbook. Subjects include business and economics, health/medicine, science. Query.

THE PRESERVATION PRESS, Imprint of the National Trust for Historic Preservation, 1785 Massachusetts Ave. NW, Washington DC 20036-2117. Fax: (202)673-4172. Director: Buckley C. Jeppson. Estab. 1975. Publishes nonfiction books on historic preservation (saving and reusing the "built environment"). Averages 14 titles/year. Receives 150 submissions annually. 20% of books from first-time authors; 50% from unagented writers. Books are often commissioned by the publisher. Publishes book an average of 1 year after acceptance. Query for electronic submissions. *Writer's Market* recommends allowing 3 months for reply. Book catalog for 9 × 12 SASE.

● Preservation Press reduced its number of titles from 20 to 14.

Nonfiction: Subject matter encompasses architecture and architectural history, building restoration and historic preservation, architectural and historical guide books. No local history. Looks for "relevance to national history-aware audience; educational or instructional value; depth; uniqueness; need in field." Query. Reviews artwork/photos as part of ms package.

Tips: "The writer has the best chance of selling our press a book clearly related to our mission—historic preservation—that covers new ideas and is unique and practical. If it fills a clear need, we will know immediately. Currently looking especially for juvenile books."

PRESIDIO PRESS, Suite 300, 505B San Marin Dr., Novato CA 94945-1340. (415)898-1081, ext. 125. Fax: (415)898-0383. Editor-in-Chief: Dale Wilson. Estab. 1974. Imprint is Lyford Books. Publishes hardcover originals and reprints. Averages 25 titles/year. Receives 1,000 submissions/year. 35% of books from first-time authors; 65% from unagented writers. Pays 15-20% royalty on net receipts. Advances vary. Publishes book an average of 12-18 months after acceptance. Reports within 1 month on queries. Book catalog and ms guidelines for 7½ × 10½ SAE with 4 first-class stamps.

Nonfiction: Subjects include military history and military affairs. Query. Reviews artwork/photos as part of ms package. "Prefer photocopies with initial submission, not originals."

Recent Nonfiction Title: *A Life in a Year*, by James R. Ebert.

Fiction: Men's action-adventure, thriller, mystery, military, historical. Query.

Recent Fiction Title: *Synbat*, by Bob Mayer.

Tips: "Our audience consists of readers interested in military history and military affairs as well as general fiction. If I were a writer trying to market a book today, I would study the market. Find out what publishers are publishing, what they say they want and so forth. Then write what the market seems to be asking for, but with some unique angle that differentiates the work from others on the same subject. We feel that readers of hardcover fiction are looking for works of no less than 100,000 words."

PRICE STERN SLOAN, INC., (a member of the Putnam & Berkley Group, New York), 11150 Olympic Blvd., Los Angeles CA 90064-1823. Juvenile submissions to Associate Editor: Cindy Chang. Adult trade/humor/calendars submissions to Editor: Bob Lovka. Estab. 1963. Imprint is Troubador Press. Publishes trade paperback originals. Averages 80 titles (90% children's) a year. Receives 3,000 submissions annually. 20% of books from first-time authors; 20% from unagented writers. Pays royalty and advance on wholesale prices or makes outright purchase. Publishes book an average of 1 year after acceptance. Reports in 3 months. Catalog for 9 × 12 SAE with 5 first-class stamps. Manuscript guidelines for SASE.

● Price Stern Sloan currently has smaller print runs and fewer titles per list.

Nonfiction: Subjects include humor, calendars and satire (limited). Juveniles (all ages). Query *only*, please. Reviews artwork/photos as part of ms package. Please do not send *original* artwork or ms. "Most titles are unique in concept as well as execution."

PRIMA PUBLISHING, P.O. Box 1260, Rocklin CA 95677-1260. (916)768-0426. Publisher: Ben Dominitz. Senior Editor: Jennifer Basye. Imprint is Prima Computer Books (contact: Roger Stewart). Estab. 1984. Publishes hardcover and trade paperback originals and trade paperback reprints. Publishes 150 titles/year. Receives 750 queries/year. 10% of books from first-time authors; 30% from unagented writers. Pays 15-20% royalty on wholesale price. Advance varies. Publishes books an average of 6-9 months after acceptance. Simultaneous submissions OK. Query for electronic submissions. Reports in 3 months. Catalog for 9 × 12 SAE with 8 first-class stamps. Writer's guidelines for #10 SASE.

Nonfiction: Biography, cookbook, how-to, self-help, travel. Subjects include business and economics, cooking and foods, health, music, politics, psychology. "We want books with originality, written by highly qualified individuals. No fiction at this time." Query.

Tips: "Prima strives to reach the primary and secondary markets for each of its books. We are known for promoting our books aggressively. Books that genuinely solve problems for people will always do well if properly promoted. Try to picture the intended audience while writing the book. Too many books are written to an audience that doesn't exist."

PRINCETON BOOK COMPANY, PUBLISHERS, P.O. Box 57, Pennington NJ 08534. (609)737-8177. President: Charles H. Woodford. Estab. 1976. Imprint is Dance Horizons. Publishes hardcover originals, trade paperback originals and reprints. Averages 10 titles/year. Receives 100 submissions/year. 25% of books from first-time authors; 100% from unagented writers. Pays 10% royalty on wholesale price. Publishes book an average of 10 months after acceptance. Simultaneous submissions OK. Reports in 1 month. *Writer's Market* recommends allowing 2 months for reply. Book catalog free.

Nonfiction: How-to, reference, self-help, textbook. Subjects include dance. Query or submit outline and sample chapters. Reviews artwork/photos as part of manuscript package.

Tips: "Books that have appeal to both trade and text markets are of most interest to us. Our audience is made up of dance professors, students and professionals. If I were a writer trying to market a book today, I would write with a clear notion of the market in mind. Don't produce a manuscript without first considering what is needed in your field."

‡PRO/AM MUSIC RESOURCES, INC., 63 Prospect St., White Plains NY 10606. (914)948-7436. Publisher: Thomas P. Lewis. Publishes hardcover and trade paperback originals and reprints. Publishes 10 titles/year. Receives 50 mss/year. 50% of books from first-time authors; 90% from unagented writers. Pays royalty on retail price. Publishes book 18 months after acceptance of ms. Accepts simultaneous submissions. Query for electronic submissions. Reports in 3 months. Book catalog free on request.

Nonfiction: Music subjects only.

PROBUS PUBLISHING CO., 1925 N. Clybourn St., Chicago IL 60614. (312)868-1100. Fax: (312)868-6250. VP/Editorial Director: James M. McNeil. Director, Production Services: Kevin Thorton. Estab. 1983. Imprints are Probus/Healthcare Financial Management Association. Publishes hardcover and paperback originals and trade paperback reprints. Averages 140 titles/year. Receives 250 submissions annually. 60% of books from first-time authors; 95% from unagented writers. Pays 10-15% royalty on net receipts. Advance varies. Publishes book an average of 5 months after acceptance. Simultaneous submissions OK. *Writer's Market* recommends allowing 2 months for reply. Book catalog free. Manuscript guidelines for SASE.

Nonfiction: How-to, technical. Subjects include banking, investment, corporate finance, small business, marketing, healthcare administration and finance, futures/options trading. Query or submit outline and sample chapters.

PROFESSIONAL PUBLICATIONS, INC., 1250 Fifth Ave., Belmont CA 94002-3863. (415)593-9119. Fax: (415)592-4519. Acquisitions Editors: Gerald Galbo, Liz Fisher. Estab. 1975. Publishes hardcover and paperback originals. Averages 12 titles/year. Receives 100-200 submissions annually. Publishes book an average of 6-18 months after acceptance. Simultaneous submissions OK. Query for electronic submissions. Reports in 2 weeks on queries. *Writer's Market* recommends allowing 2 months for reply. Book catalog and ms guidelines free.

● Professional Publications wants only professionals practicing in the field to submit material.

Nonfiction: Reference, technical, textbook. Subjects include mathematics, engineering, architecture, interior design, contracting and building. Especially needs "review books for all professional licensing examinations." Query or submit outline and sample chapters. Reviews artwork/photos as part of ms package.

Tips: "We specialize in books for working professionals: engineers, architects, contractors, interior designing, etc. The more technically complex the manuscript is the happier we are. We love equations, tables of data, complex illustrations, mathematics, etc. In technical/professional book publishing, it isn't always obvious to us if a market exists. We can judge the quality of a manuscript, but the author should make some effort to convince us that a market exists. Facts, figures, and estimates about the market—and marketing ideas from the author—will help sell us on the work. Besides our interest in highly technical materials, we will be trying to broaden our range of titles in each discipline. Specifically, we will be looking for career guides for interior designers and architects, as well as for engineers."

‡PROFESSIONAL RESOURCE PRESS, Imprint of Professional Resource Exchange, Inc., Suite 215, 2033 Wood St., Sarasota FL 34237. (813)366-7913. Managing Editor: Debra Fink. Publishes trade paperback originals. Publishes 15 titles/year. Receives 100 queries and 80 mss/year. 50% of books from first-time authors; 100% from unagented writers. Pays 6-10% royalty on wholesale price. Publishes book 1 year after acceptance of ms. No simultaneous submissions. Query for electronic submissions. Reports in 6 months. Book catalog and ms guidelines free on request.

Nonfiction: Reference, textbook; books for mental health professionals. "Authors must be mental health professionals and works must be highly applied and focused." Submit outline and 2-4 sample chapters.

Recent Nonfiction Title: *Writing Psychological Reports: A Guide for Clinicians*, by Greg J. Wolber and William F. Carne.

PROLINGUA ASSOCIATES, 15 Elm St., Brattleboro VT 05301. (802)207-7779. Senior Editor: Raymond C. Clark. Publisher: Arthur A. Burrows. Estab. 1980. Publishes paperback originals. Averages 6 titles/year. Receives 30-50 submissions annually. 25% of books from first-time authors; 100% from unagented writers. Pays 5-10% royalty on wholesale price. Offers $200 average advance. Publishes book an average of 1 year after acceptance. Simultaneous submissions OK. Reports in 2 weeks on queries. *Writer's Market* recommends allowing 2 months for reply. Book catalog for 9×12 SAE with 4 first-class stamps.

Nonfiction: Reference, textbook. Subjects include English as a second language, French and Spanish. "We are always willing to consider innovative language texts and language teacher resources which fit with our approach to language teaching. Also interested in intercultural training." Query or submit outline and sample chapters.

Tips: "Get a catalog of our books, take a couple of books by ProLingua out of the library or from a nearby language department, ask about ProLingua, and in general try to determine whether your book would fit into ProLingua's list."

PRUETT PUBLISHING, 2928 Pearl St., Boulder CO 80301. (303)449-4919. Publisher: Jim Pruett. Editor: Dianne Russell. Estab. 1959. Publishes hardcover originals and trade paperback originals and reprints. Averages 10-12 titles/year. 60% of books are from first-time authors; 100% from unagented writers. Pays 10-12% royalty on net income. Publishes book an average of 18 months after acceptance. Simultaneous submissions OK. Reports in 2 months on queries. Book catalog and ms guidelines free.

Nonfiction: Biography, illustrated book, textbook. Subjects include agriculture/horticulture (western), Americana (western), animals (western), archaeology (Native American), cooking, foods and nutrition, ethnic (Native American), gardening (western), history, nature/environment, recreation (outdoor), regional, travel, sports (cycling, hiking, flyfishing). *No longer seeking coffee table books, child guidance/parenting books* *or railroad histories.* "We are looking for nonfiction manuscripts and guides that focus on the rocky Mountain West." Reviews artwork/photos as part of ms package.

Tips: "There has been a movement away from large publisher's mass market books and towards small publisher's regional interest books, and in turn distributors and retail outlets are more interested in small publishers. Author's don't need to have a big-name to have a good publisher. Look for similar books that you feel are well produced — consider design, editing, overall quality and contact those publishers. Get to know several publishers, and find the one that feels right — trust your instincts."

PSI RESEARCH, 300 N. Valley Dr., Grants Pass OR 97526. (503)479-9464. Fax: (503)476-1479. Contact: Acquisitions Editor. Estab. 1975. Imprint is Oasis Press. Publishes hardcover, trade paperback and binder originals. Publishes 20-30 books/year. Receives 90 submissions/year. 60% of books from first-time authors; 90% from unagented writers. Pays royalty. Publishes ms an average of 6-12 months after acceptance. Simultaneous submissions OK. Reports in 2 months (initial feedback) on queries. Book catalog and ms guidelines free.

Nonfiction: How-to, reference, textbook. Subjects include business and economics, computers, education, money/finance, retirement, exporting, franchise, finance, marketing and public relations, relocations, environment, taxes, business start up and operation. Needs information-heavy, readable mss written by professionals in their subject fields. Interactive where appropriate. Authorship credentials less important than hands-on experience qualifications. Must relate to either small business or to individuals who are entrepreneurs, owners or managers of small business (1-300 employees). Query for unwritten material or to check current interest in topic and orientation. Submit outline/synopsis and sample chapters. Reviews artwork/photos as part of freelance ms package.

Recent Nonfiction Title: *Power Marketing*, by Jody Hornor; *The Business Environmental Handbook*, by Martin Westerman; *Top Tax Saving Ideas for Today's Small Business*, by Thomas J. Stemmy.

Tips: "Best chance is with practical, step-by-step manuals for operating a business, with worksheets, checklists. The audience is made up of entrepreneurs of all types: small businesses and those who would like to be; attorneys, accountants and consultants who work with small businesses; college students; dreamers. Make sure your information is valid and timely for its audience, also that by virtue of either its content quality or viewpoint, it distinguishes itself from other books on the market."

PUBLISHERS ASSOCIATES, P.O. Box 140361, Las Colinas TX 75014-0361. (214)686-5332. Senior Editor: Belinda Buxjom. Manuscript Coordinator: Mary Markal. Estab. 1974. Imprints are Hercules Press, The Liberal Press, Liberal Arts Press, Minuteman Press, Monument Press, Nichole Graphics, Scholars Books, Tagelwüld. Publishes trade paperback originals. Receives 1,500 submissions/year. 60% of books from first-time authors; 100% from unagented writers. Pays 4% and up royalty on retail price. Publishes book an average of 4 months after acceptance. Reports in up to 4 months. Book catalog for 6×9 SAE with 4 first-class stamps. Manuscript guidelines for #10 SAE with 2 first-class stamps.

Nonfiction: Textbook (scholarly). Subjects include gay/lesbian, government politics (liberal), history, religion (liberation/liberal), women's issues/studies. "We are looking for gay/lesbian history, pro-choice/feminist studies and liberal politics. Quality researched gay/lesbian history will have beginning royalty of 7% and up. Academics are encouraged to submit. No biographies, evangelical fundamentalism/bible, conservative politics, New Age studies or homophobic. No fiction or poetry." Query. Reviews artwork/photos as part of ms package.

Tips: "Writers have the best chance with gender-free/nonsexist, liberal academic studies. We sell primarily to libraries and to scholars. Our audience is highly educated, politically and socially liberal, if religious they are liberational. If I were a writer trying to market a book today, I would compare my manuscript with books already published by the press I am seeking to submit to."

PURDUE UNIVERSITY PRESS, 1532 South Campus Courts, Bldg. B, West Lafayette IN 47907-1532. (317)494-2038. Director: David Sanders. Managing Editor: Margaret Hunt. Estab. 1960. Publishes hardcover and trade paperback originals and trade paperback reprints. Averages 12 titles/year. Receives 150 submissions annually. Royalties vary. No advance. Publishes book an average of 15 months after acceptance. Reports in 2 months. Book catalog and ms guidelines for 9×12 SASE.

Nonfiction: Biography, scholarly, regional. Subjects include Americana (especially Indiana), scholarly studies in history, philosophy, politics, religion, sociology, theories of biology and literary criticism. "The writer must present good credentials, demonstrate good writing skills, and above all explain how his/her work will make a significant contribution to scholarship/regional studies. Our purpose is to publish scholarly and regional books. We are looking for manuscripts on these subjects: theory of biography, Balkan and Danubian studies, interdisciplinary, regional (Midwest) interest, horticulture, history, literature, history of philosophy, criticism, and effects of science and technology on society. No cookbooks, nonbooks, textbooks, theses/dissertations, manuals/pamphlets, fiction, or books on how-to, fitness/exercise or fads. Submit prospectus."

Recent Nonfiction Title: *The Vienna Coffeehouse Wits, 1890-1938*, by Harold B. Segel.

THE PUTNAM BERKLEY GROUP, 200 Madison Ave., New York NY 10016. Divisions and imprints include the Berkley Publishing Group (including Ace Science Fiction & Fantasy), G.P. Putnam's Sons, Perigee

Books, Grosset & Dunlap, Philomel Books and Price Stern Sloan. Putnam did not respond to our request for information. Query before submitting.

RAGGED MOUNTAIN PRESS, Imprint of International Marine/McGraw-Hill, P.O. Box 220, Camden ME 04843-0220. (207)236-4837. Fax: (207)236-6314. Acquisitions Editor: James R. Babb. Estab. 1971. Publishes hardcover and trade paperback originals and reprints. Publishes 40 titles/year. Imprint publishes 12 (Ragged Mountain), remainder are International Marine. Receives 200 queries and 100 mss/year. 30% of books from first-time authors; 90% from unagented writers. Pays 10-15% royalty on wholesale price. Offers advances. Publishes book 1 year after acceptance of ms. Simultaneous submissions OK. Query for electronic submissions. Reports in 1 month on queries. *Writer's Market* recommends allowing 2 months for reply. Book catalog for 9×12 SAE with 10 first-class stamps. Manuscript guidelines for #10 SASE.
Nonfiction: Outdoor-related biography, cookbook, how-to, humor, essays. Subjects include animals, outdoor cooking, fishing, camping, climbing and kayaking. "Ragged Mountain publishes nonconsumptive outdoor and environmental issues books of literary merit or unique appeal. Be familiar with the existing literature. Find a subject that hasn't been done, or has been done poorly, then explore it in detail and from all angles." Query or submit outline with 3 sample chapters. Reviews artwork/photos as part of freelance ms package. Writers should send photocopies.
Recent Nonfiction Title: *The Essential Touring Cyclist*, by Richard A. Lovett.

RAINBOW BOOKS, P.O. Box 430, Highland City FL 33846-0430. Phone/Fax: (813)648-4420. Editorial Director: B. A. Lampe. Estab. 1979. Publishes hardcover, trade paperback originals, video (VHS) and audio tapes and does book packaging. Averages 20-25 titles/year. Receives 600 submissions annually. 70% of books from first-time authors; 90% from unagented writers. Publishes book an average of 8 months after acceptance. Reports in 2 weeks on queries. Reports in 2 months on mss. Book catalog for 6×9 SAE with 75¢ postage. Manuscript guidelines for #10 SASE.
Nonfiction: Self-help, how-to, travel, business, science, resource books etc. a broad category of nonfiction books. Require query first on all books. Does not accept proposals. Interested in all nonfiction books.
Recent Nonfiction Title: *Discovering Life's Trails*, by Tom Dennard.
Tips: "No SASE, no response. We do not accept proposals."

‡RAINBOW PUBLISHERS, P.O. Box 261129, San Diego CA 92196. (619)578-4700. Managing Editor: Carol Rogers. Publishes 8-12 titles/year. Receives 100 queries and 50 mss/year. 50% of books from first-time authors. Makes outright purchase of $500 maximum. Publishes book 12-18 months after acceptance of ms. Simultaneous submissions OK. Query for electronic submissions. Reports in 3 months on queries and proposals, 3-6 months on mss. Book catalog for 9×12 SAE with 2 first-class stamps. Manuscript guidelines for #10 SASE.
Nonfiction: How-to, textbook. Subjects include religion and reproducible activity books for Sunday school teachers. "We publish 64-page reproducible activity books for teachers to use in teaching the Bible to children ages 2-12." Query with outline, sample pages, age leve, introduction. "We do use freelance artists. Send a query and photocopies of art samples."
Recent Nonfiction Title: *52 Ways to Teach Children to Share the Gospel*, by Barbara Hibschman; *Bible Crafts on a Shoestring Budget, Gr. 1&2*, by Ellen Humbert; *Bible Heroes, Ages 4&5*, by Nancy Sanders; *Bible Stories About Jesus, Ages 2-3*, by Darlen Hoffa (all reproducible activity books).

RANDOM HOUSE, INC., Subsidary of Advance Publications, 11th Floor, 201 E. 50th St., New York NY 10022. (212)751-2600. Random House Trade Division publishes 120 titles/year. Receives 3,000 submissions annually. Imprints include Random House, Alfred A. Knopf, Ballantine, Crown, Del Rey, Fawcett, Harmony, Modern Library, Pantheon, Clarkson N. Potter, Villard, and Vintage. Pays royalty on retail price. Simultaneous submissions OK. Reports in 2 months. Free book catalog. Manuscript guidelines for #10 SASE.
● Fodor's Travel Publications Inc., a division of Random House Inc., will be publishing and distributing the Mobil Travel Guides, formerly marketed by Prentice Hall, beginning in 1995.
Nonfiction: Biography, cookbook, humor, illustrated book, self-help. Subjects include Americana, art, business and economics, classics, cooking and foods, health, history, music, nature, politics, psychology, religion, sociology and sports. No juveniles or textbooks (separate division). Query with outline and at least 3 sample chapters.
● Random House published the winner of the 1993 National Book Award for nonfiction, Gore Vidal's *United States: Essays 1952-1992.*
Fiction: Adventure, confession, experimental, fantasy, historical, horror, humor, mainstream, mystery, and suspense. Submit outline/synopsis and at least 3 sample chapters.
Tips: "Enclose SASE for reply or return of materials."

REFERENCE SERVICE PRESS, Suite 9, 1100 Industrial Rd., San Carlos CA 94070-4131. (415)594-0743. Fax: (415)594-0411. Acquisitions Editor: Stuart Hauser. Estab. 1977. Publishes hardcover originals. Publishes 5 titles/year. 100% of books from unagented writers. Pays 10% or higher royalty. Publishes book an average of 3-6 months after acceptance. Simultaneous submissions OK. Query for electronic submissions. Reports in 2 months. Book catalog for #10 SASE.

Nonfiction: Reference. Subjects include education, ethnic, military/war, women's issues/studies, disabled. "We are interested only in directories and monographs dealing with financial aid." Submit outline and sample chapters.

Tips: "Our audience consists of librarians, counselors, researchers, students, reentry women, scholars and other fundseekers."

‡REGNERY PUBLISHING, INC., (formerly Regnery/Gateway, Inc.), Suite 300, 422 First St. SE, Washington DC 20003. Editor: Kaari Reierson. Estab. 1947. Imprints are Gateway Editions and Tumbleweed Press. Publishes hardcover and paperback originals and paperback reprints. Averages 30 titles/year. Pays 8-15% royalty on retail price. Offers $0-50,000 advance. Publishes book 9-12 months after acceptance of ms. Simultaneous submissions OK. Reports in 6-9 months on proposals. Book catalog and ms guidelines free on request. "Responds only to submissions in which we have interest."

Nonfiction: Biography. Subjects include business and economics, education, government/politics, health/medicine, history, military/war, nature/environment, philosophy, religion, science, sociology. Submit outline, 2-3 sample chapters and cover letter, etc. Reviews artwork/photos as part of freelance ms package. Writers should send photocopies.

Recent Nonfiction Title: *Environmental Overkill*, by Dixie Lee Ray w/ Guzzo; *Presumed Guilty: The Tragedy of the Rodney King Affair*, by Stacey Koon; *Solzhenitsyn and the Modern World*, by Ed Erickson.

RENAISSANCE HOUSE PUBLISHERS, Subsidiary of Jende-Hagan, Inc., 541 Oak St., P.O. Box 177, Frederick CO 80530-0177. (303)833-2030. Fax: (303)833-2030. Editor: Eleanor Ayer. Publishes an ongoing series of 48-page guidebooks of travel-related interest. Averages 8 titles/year. Receives 125 submissions annually. 60% of books from first-time authors; 75% of books from unagented writers. Pays 8-10% royalty on net receipts. Offers average advance of 10% of anticipated first printing royalties. May consider work for hire by experts in specific fields of interest. Publishes book an average of 18 months after acceptance. Query for electronic submissions. Reports in 1 month on queries. *Writer's Market* recommends allowing 2 months for reply.

Nonfiction: Subjects include regional guidebooks. No fiction, personal reminiscences, general traditional philosophy, books on topics totally unrelated to subject areas specified above. "Please — no inquiries outside the topic of regional guidebooks! We publish to a very specific formula." *Writer's Market* recommends query with SASE first.

Tips: "We rely exclusively on in-house generation of book concepts and then find authors who will write for hire to our specifications. We are continually adding to our American Traveler Guidebooks series."

‡REPUBLIC OF TEXAS PRESS, Imprint of Wordware Publishing, Inc., 1506 Capitol Ave., Plano TX 75074. (214)423-0090. Acquisitions Editor: Mary Goldman. Publishes trade and mass market paperback originals. Publishes 50-70 titles/year; imprint publishes 12-15 titles/year. Receives 40-60 queries and 20-30 mss/year. 95% of books from unagented writers. Pays 8-12% royalty on wholesale price. Publishes book 6 months after acceptance of ms. Accepts simultaneous submissions. Query for electronic submissions. Reports in 1 month. Book catalog and ms guidelines free on request.

Nonfiction: Humor, general interest. Subjects include animals, cooking, foods and nutrition, government/politics, history, recreation, regional. Submit table of contents, 2 sample chapters, target audience; list any competing books.

Fiction: Historical, western. Submit synopsis and 2 sample chapters.

Recent Fiction Title: *Just Passing Through*, by Beth Beggs (novel).

‡RESURRECTION PRESS, LTD., P.O. Box 248, Williston Park NY 11596. (516)742-5686. Publisher: Emilie Cerar. Imprint is Spirit Life Series. Publishes trade paperback originals and reprints. Firm publishes 10-12 titles/year; imprint publishes 6 titles/year. Receives 70 queries and 60 mss/year. 50% of books from first-time authors; 100% from unagented writers. Pays 5-10% royalty on retail price. Offers $250-2,000 advance. Publishes book 1 year after acceptance of ms. Simultaneous submissions OK. Query for electronic submissions. Reports in 1 month on queries and proposals, 2 months on mss. Book catalog and ms guidelines free on request.

Nonfiction: Self-help. Subjects include religion. Wants mss of no more than 150 double-spaced typewritten pages. Query with outline and 2 sample chapters. Reviews artwork/photos as part of freelance ms package. Writers should send photocopies.

‡FLEMING H. REVELL PUBLISHING, Subsidiary of Baker Book House, P.O. Box 6287, Grand Rapids MI 49516. Editorial Director: William J. Petersen. Imprint is Spire Books. Publishes hardcover, trade paperback and mass market paperback originals and reprints. Publishes 50 titles/year; imprint publishes 10 titles/year. Receives 750 queries and 1,000 mss/year. 10% of books from first-time authors; 90% from unagented writers. Pays royalty on wholesale price. Publishes book 1 year after acceptance of ms. Accepts simultaneous submissions. Query for electronic submissions. Reports in 2 months. Manuscript guidelines for #10 SASE.

Nonfiction: Biography, coffee table book, how-to, self-help. Subjects include child guidance/parenting, religion. Query with outline and 2 sample chapters.
Recent Nonfiction Title: *Bible Power for Successful Living*, by Norman Vincent Peale (inspirational).
Fiction: Religious. Submit synopsis and 2 sample chapters.
Recent Fiction Title: *The Quality of Mercy*, by Gilbert Morris (religious/detective).

‡**REVISIONIST PRESS**, GPO Box 2009, Brooklyn Heights NY 11202. Editor: B. Chaim. Imprints are The Martin Buber Press, The Mutualist Press. Publishes hardcover originals and reprints. Publishes 14 titles/year; each imprint publishes 4 titles/year. Receives 20 queries and 12 mss/year. 80% of books from first-time authors; 100% from unagented writers. Pays 10% royalty on retail price. Publishes book 10 months after acceptance of ms. Accepts simultaneous submissions. Reports in 1 month. Book catalog and ms guidelines for #10 SASE.
Nonfiction: Bibliography, biography, cookbook, how-to, reference, self-help, technical, textbook. Subjects include agriculture/horticulture, Americana, anthropology/archaeology, art/architecture, business and economics, computers and electronics, cooking, foods and nutrition, education, ethnic, gardening, government/politics, health/medicine, history, language/literature, military/war, money/finance, music/dance, nature/environment, philosophy, psychology, recreation, regional, religion, science, sociology, software, translation, travel, women's issues/studies. Query with outline. Reviews artwork/photos as part of ms package. Writers should send photocopies.
Recent Nonfiction Title: *The Eclectic Anarchism of Erich Muhsam*, by Lawrence Baron (biography).

RICHBORO PRESS, P.O. Box 947, Southampton PA 18966-0947. (215)364-2212. Fax: (215)364-2212. Editor: George Moore. Estab. 1979. Publishes hardcover, trade paperback originals and software. Publishes 4 titles/year. Receives 500 submissions annually. 90% of books from unagented writers. Pays 10% royalty on retail price. Publishes book an average of 1 year after acceptance. Electronic submissions preferred. Reports in 2 months on queries. Free book catalog. Manuscript guidelines for $1 and #10 SASE.
Nonfiction: Cookbook, how-to, gardening. Subjects include cooking and foods. Query.

RISING TIDE PRESS, 5 Kivy St., Huntington Station NY 11746-2020. (516)427-1289. Editor/Publisher: Lee Boojamra. Senior Editor: Alice Frier. Estab. 1991. Publishes trade paperback originals. Publishes 10-20 titles/year. Receives 500 queries and 150 mss/year. 75% of books from first-time authors, 100% from unagented writers. Pays 10-15% royalty on wholesale price. Publishes book 12-15 months after acceptance. Query for electronic submissions: prefers any major IBM compatible WP program on 5¼" or 3½" disk. Reports in 1 week on queries, 1 months on proposals, 2 months on mss. Book catalog for $1. Writer's guidelines for #10 SASE.
Nonfiction: Lesbian nonfiction. Subjects include gay/lesbian. Submit outline. Query with proposal including entire ms with *large* SASE. Reviews artwork/photos as part of freelance ms package. Writers should include photocopies.
Fiction: "Lesbian fiction only." Adventure, erotica, fantasy, historical, horror, humor, literary, mainstream/contemporary, mystery, occult, romance, science fiction, suspense, mixed genres. "Major characters must be lesbian. Primary plot must have lesbian focus and sensibility." Query with synopsis or submit entire ms.
Tips: "Our books are for, by and about lesbian lives. We welcome unpublished authors. We do *not* consider agented authors. Any material submitted should be proofed."

ROCKY TOP PUBLICATIONS, P.O. Box 5256, Albany NY 12205. President/Publisher: Joseph D. Jennings. Contact: Emerson Bach. Estab. 1982. Publishes hardcover and paperback originals. Averages 4-6 titles/year. 70% of books from first-time authors; 95% from unagented writers. Pays 4-10% royalty (may vary) on wholesale price. Publishes book an average of 6 months after acceptance. Reports in up to 6 months.
Nonfiction: How-to, reference, self-help, technical. Subjects include animal health, health, hobbies (crafts), medical, nature, philosophy (Thoreau or environmental only), science. No autobiographies, biographies, business "get rich quick" or fad books. Query.
Tips: "No unsolicited manuscripts."

‡**THE ROSEN PUBLISHING GROUP**, 29 E. 21st St., New York NY 10010. (212)777-3017. Editor: Gina Strazzabosco. Publishes hardcover and trade paperback originals. Publishes 100 titles/year. Receives 150 queries and 75 mss/year. 10% of books from first-time authors; 95% from unagented writers. Pays 6-10% royalty on retail price or makes outright purchase of $300-1,000. Offers $500-1,000 advance. Publishes books 9 months

Market conditions are constantly changing! If this is 1996 or later, buy the newest edition of Writer's Market at your favorite bookstore or order directly from Writer's Digest Books.

after acceptance of ms. Reports in 2 months on proposals. Book catalog and ms guidelines free on request.
Nonfiction: Children's/juvenile, self-help. Submit outline and 1 sample chapter.

• The Rosen Publishing Group publishes young adult titles for sale to schools and libraries. Each book is aimed at teenage readers and addresses them directly. Books should be written to 4.0-9.0 grade reading level. Areas of particular interest include careers, coping with social and personal problems, values and ethical behavior, drug abuse prevention, self-esteem and social activism.

Recent Nonfiction Title: *Coping with Interracial Dating*, by Renea Nash.
Tips: "The writer has the best chance of selling our firm a book on vocational guidance or personal social adjustment, or high-interest, low reading level material for teens."

‡**ROSS BOOKS**, P.O. Box 4340, Berkeley CA 94704. Fax: (415)841-2695. President: Franz Ross. Estab. 1979. Publishes hardcover and paperback originals, paperback reprints, and software. Averages 4-6 titles/year. Receives 200 submissions annually. 90% of books from first-time authors; 99% from unagented writers. Average print order for a first book is 5,000-10,000. Offers 8-12% royalty on net price. Offers average advance of 2% of the first print run. Publishes book an average of 1 year after acceptance. Simultaneous submissions OK. Query for electronic submissions. Reports in 1 month. Book catalog for 6 × 9 SAE with 2 first-class stamps.
Nonfiction: Popular how-to on science, business, general how-to. No political, religious or children's books. Accepts nonfiction translations. Submit outline or synopsis of no more than 3 pages and 1 sample chapter with SASE. Reviews artwork/photos as part of ms package.
Recent Nonfiction Title: *Holography Marketplace 4th Ed.*, edited by F. Ross and E. Kluepfer
Tips: "We are looking for books on holography and computers."

ROXBURY PUBLISHING CO., P.O. Box 491044, Los Angeles CA 90049. (213)653-1068. Executive Editor: Claude Teweles. Publishes hardcover and paperback originals and reprints. Averages 10 titles/year. Pays royalty. Simultaneous submissions OK. Reports in 2 months.
Nonfiction: College-level textbooks only. Subjects include business and economics, humanities, speech, English, developmental studies, social sciences, sociology. Query, submit outline/synopsis and sample chapters, or submit complete ms.

RUNNING PRESS, 125 South 22nd St., Philadelphia PA 19103. General interest nonfiction publisher. This company did not respond to our request for information. Query before submitting.

RUTGERS UNIVERSITY PRESS, 109 Church St., New Brunswick NJ 08901. (908)932-7762. Acting Editor-in-Chief: Leslie Mitchner. Publishes hardcover and trade paperback originals and trade paperback reprints. Publishes 70 titles/year. Receives up to 1,500 queries and up to 300 books/year. Up to 30% of books from first-time authors; 70% from unagented writers. Pays 7½-15% royalty on retail price. Offers $1,000-10,000 advance. Publishes book 1 year after acceptance of ms. Simultaneous submissions OK if so noted. Query for electronic submissions. Reports in 1 month on proposals. Book catalog free on request.
Nonfiction: Biography, textbook and books for use in undergraduate courses. Subjects include Americana, anthropology, Black studies, education, gay/lesbian, government/politics, health/medicine, history, language/literature, multicultural studies, nature/environment, regional, science, sociology, translation, women's issues/studies. "Our press aims to reach audiences beyond the academic community. Writing should be accessible." Submit outline and 2-3 sample chapters. Reviews artwork/photos as part of the freelance ms package. Writers should send photocopies.
Recent Nonfiction Title: *Frauen: German Women Recall the Third Reich*, by Alison Owings.
Tips: Both academic and general audiences. "Many of our books have potential for undergraduate course use. We are more trade-oriented than most university presses. We are looking for intelligent, well-written and accessible books. Avoid overly narrow topics."

RUTLEDGE HILL PRESS, 211 Seventh Ave. N., Nashville TN 37219-1823. (615)244-2700. Fax: (615)244-2978. President: Lawrence Stone. Vice President: Ron Pitkin. Estab. 1982. Publishes hardcover and trade paperback originals and reprints. Averages 35 titles/year. Receives 600 submissions annually. 40% of books from first-time authors; 90% from unagented writers. Pays 10-20% royalty on wholesale price. Publishes book an average of 1 year after acceptance. Reports in 3 months. Book catalog for 9 × 12 SAE with 4 first-class stamps.
Nonfiction: Biography, cookbook, humor, reference, self-help. "The book must have an identifiable market, preferably one that is geographically limited." Submit outline and sample chapters. Reviews artwork/photos as part of ms package.

ST. ANTHONY MESSENGER PRESS, 1615 Republic St., Cincinnati OH 45210-1298. (513)241-5615. Fax: (513)241-0399. Editor-in-Chief: The Rev. Norman Perry, O.F.M. Managing Editor: Lisa Biedenbach. Estab. 1970. Publishes paperback originals. Averages 14 titles/year. Receives 250 submissions annually. 10% of books from first-time authors; 100% from unagented writers. Pays 10-12% royalty on net receipts of sales. Offers $600 average advance. Publishes book an average of 1 year after acceptance. Books are sold in bulk to groups (study clubs, high school or college classes, and parishes) and in bookstores. No simultaneous submissions. Query for electronic submissions. Reports in 2 months. Book catalog and ms guidelines for 9×12 SAE with 2 first-class stamps.

Nonfiction: Religion. "We try to reach the Catholic market with topics near the heart of the ordinary Catholic's belief. We want to offer insight and inspiration and thus give people support in living a Christian life in a pluralistic society. We are not interested in an academic or abstract approach. Our emphasis is on popular writing with examples, specifics, color and anecdotes." Length: 25,000-40,000 words. Query or submit outline and 2 sample chapters. Reviews artwork/photos as part of ms package.

Recent Nonfiction Title: *Images of Jesus: Ten Invitations to Intimacy*, by Alfred McBride, O. Praem.

Tips: "We are looking for aids to parish ministry, prayer, spirituality, scripture, liturgy and the sacraments. Also, we are seeking manuscripts that deal with Catholic identity — explaining it, identifying it, understanding it. The book cannot be the place for the author to think through a subject. The author has to think through the subject first and then tell the reader what is important to know. Style uses anecdotes, examples, illustrations, human interest, 'colorful' quotes, fiction techniques of suspense, dialogue, characterization, etc. Address practical problems, deal in concrete situations, free of technical terms and professional jargon. We do not publish fiction, poetry, autobiography, personal reflections, academic studies, art or coffee-table books."

ST. BEDE'S PUBLICATIONS, Subsidiary of St. Scholastica Priory, P.O. Box 545, Petersham MA 01366-0545. (508)724-3407. Fax: (508)724-3574. Editorial Director: Sr. Scholastica Crilly, OSB. Estab. 1978. Publishes hardcover originals, trade paperback originals and reprints. Averages 8-12 titles/year. Receives 100 submissions annually. 30-40% of books from first-time authors; 90% from unagented writers. Subsidy publishes (nonauthor) 10% of books. Pays 5-10% royalty on wholesale price or retail price. No advance. Publishes book an average of 2 years after acceptance. Simultaneous submissions OK. Query for electronic submissions. Unsolicited mss are not returned unless accompanied by sufficient return postage. Reports in 2 months. Book catalog and ms guidelines for 9×12 SAE and 2 first-class stamps.

Nonfiction: Textbook (theology), religion, prayer, spirituality, hagiography, theology, philosophy, church history, related lives of saints. "We are always looking for excellent books on prayer, spirituality, liturgy, church or monastic history. Theology and philosophy are important also. We publish English translations of foreign works in these fields if we think they are excellent and worth translating." No submissions unrelated to religion, theology, spirituality, etc. Query or submit outline and sample chapters.

Tips: "There seems to be a growing interest in monasticism among lay people and we will be publishing more books in this area. For our theology/philosophy titles our audience is scholars, colleges and universities, seminaries, etc. For our other titles (i.e. prayer, spirituality, lives of saints, etc.) the audience is above-average readers interested in furthering their knowledge in these areas."

ST. MARTIN'S PRESS, 175 Fifth Ave., New York NY 10010. Imprints include Bedford Books and Tor Books. General interest publisher of both fiction and nonfiction. The company did not respond to our request for information. Query before submitting.

ST. PAUL BOOKS & MEDIA, Daughters of St. Paul, 50 St. Paul's Ave., Boston MA 02130. (617)522-8911. Fax: (617)541-9805. Director, Editorial Department: Sister Mary Mark, FSP. Estab. 1948. Publishes hardcover and trade paperback originals and reprints. Average 35 titles/year. Receives approximately 900 proposals/year. Pays authors 9-12% royalty on net sales. Publishes ms an average of 1-2 years after acceptance. Reports in 3 months. Book catalog for 9×12 SAE with 4 first-class stamps.

Nonfiction: Biography, juvenile, spiritual growth and development. Subjects include child guidance/parenting, psychology, religion. "No strictly secular manuscripts." Query only. No unsolicited mss without prior query.

Recent Nonfiction Title: *Midwife for Souls: Spiritual Care for the Dying*, by Kathy Kalina.

Fiction: Juvenile. Query only. No unsolicited mss, without prior query.

Tips: "We are more interested in books concerning faith and moral values, as well as in works on spiritual growth and development. Always interested in books of Christian formation for families. No New Age books or poetry please."

SAN FRANCISCO PRESS, INC., P.O. Box 42680, San Francisco CA 94142-6800. (510)524-1000. President: Terry Gabriel. Founded 1959. Publishes hardcover originals and trade paperback originals and reprints. Averages 5-10 titles/year. Receives over 100 submissions/year. 50% of books from first-time authors; 90% from unagented writers. Pays 10-15% on wholesale price. Publishes book an average of 6 months after acceptance. Simultaneous submissions OK. Reports in 1 month on queries. *Writer's Market* recommends allowing 2 months for reply. Book catalog for #10 SAE with 1 first-class stamp.

Nonfiction: Technical, college textbook. Subjects include computers and electronics, biotechnology, public health, history of technology, musicology, science. Submit outline and sample chapters.

● This press has been overwhelmed with music book manuscripts when their need is for musicology.

Tips: "Our books are aimed at specialized audiences; we do not publish works intended for the general public."

SANDHILL CRANE PRESS, PUBLISHERS, (formerly Sandhill Crane Nature Books), 2406 NW 47th Terrace, Gainesville FL 32606-6583. (904)371-9858. Fax: (904)371-0962. Publisher: Dr. Ross H. Arnett, Jr. Estab. 1947. Imprint is Flora & Fauna Publications. Publishes hardcover and trade paperback originals. Publishes 10-12 titles/year. Receives 70 submissions annually. 50% of books from first-time authors; 100% from unagented writers. Average print order for a first book is 1,500. Pays 10% royalty on list price. Advance negotiable. Publishes book an average of 1 year after acceptance. Query for electronic submissions. Reports in 2 months on queries.
Nonfiction: Reference, technical, textbook, directories. Subjects include plants and animals (for amateur and professional biologists), natural history and environment. Looking for "books dealing with kinds of plants and animals; nature guide series. No nature stories or 'Oh My' nature books." Query with outline and 2 sample chapters. Reviews artwork/photos as part of ms package.
Tips: "Well-documented books, especially those that fit into one of our series, have the best chance of selling to our firm—biology, natural history, environment, usually no garden books."

SANDLAPPER PUBLISHING, INC., P.O. Box 730, Orangeburg SC 29116-0730. (803)531-1658. Fax: (803)534-5223. Acquisitions: Frank N. Handal. Estab. 1982. Publishes hardcover and trade paperback originals and reprints. Averages 6 titles/year. Receives 200 submissions annually. 80% of books from first-time authors; 95% from unagented writers. Pays 15% maximum royalty on net receipts. Publishes book on average of 20 months after acceptance. Simultaneous submissions OK if informed. Reports in 3 months. Book catalog and ms guidelines for 9×12 SAE with 4 first-class stamps.
 • Sandlapper has extended its reporting time from 2 to 3 months.
Nonfiction: History, biography, illustrated books, humor, cookbook, juvenile (ages 9-14), reference, textbook. Subjects are limited to history, culture and cuisine of the Southeast and especially South Carolina. "We are looking for manuscripts that reveal under-appreciated or undiscovered facets of the rich heritage of our region. If a manuscript doesn't deal with South Carolina or the Southeast, the work is probably not appropriate for us. We don't do self-help books, children's books about divorce, kidnapping, etc., and absolutely no religious manuscripts." Query or submit outline and sample chapters "if you're not sure it's what we're looking for, otherwise complete ms." *Writer's Market* recommends query with SASE first. Reviews artwork/photos as part of ms package.
Fiction: We do not need fiction submissions at present, "and will not consider any horror, romance or religious fiction." Query or submit outline/synopsis and sample chapters. "Do check with us on books dealing with regional nature, science and outdoor subjects."
Tips: "Our readers are South Carolinians, visitors to the region's tourist spots, and friends and family that live out-of-state. We are striving to be a leading regional publisher for South Carolina. We will be looking for more history and biography."

‡SARPEDON PUBLISHERS, 166 Fifth Ave., New York NY 10010. Contact: Steven Smith. Publishes hardcover originals and trade paperback reprints. Publishes 6 titles/year. Receives 24 queries/year. 15% of books from first-time authors; 50% from unagented writers. Pays royalty. Offers $500-2,000 advance. Publishes book 6 months after acceptance of ms. Simultaneous submissions OK. Reports in 1 months on queries, 2 months on proposals, 3 months on mss. Book catalog and ms guidelines for #10 SASE.
Nonfiction: Biography. Subjects include Americana, government, history, military/war. "We specialize in military history." Submit outline and 2 sample chapters and synopsis. Reviews artwork/photos as part of freelance ms package. Writers should send photocopies.
Recent Nonfiction Title: *Night of Fire*, by Rox; *Citadel: The Battle of Kursk*, by Cross; *Or Go Down in Flame*, by Wood.

SAS INSTITUTE INC., SAS Campus Dr., Cary NC 27513-2414. (919)677-8000. Fax: (916)677-8166. Acquisitions Editor: David D. Baggett. Estab. 1976. Publishes hardcover and trade paperback originals. Averages 40 titles/year. Receives 10 submissions/year. 50% of books from first-time authors; 100% from unagented writers. Payment negotiable. Offers negotiable advance. Query for electronic submissions. Reports in 2 weeks on queries. *Writer's Market* recommends allowing 2 months for reply. Book catalog and ms guidelines free.
Nonfiction: Software, technical, textbook, statistics. "SAS Institute's Publications Division publishes books developed and written inhouse. Through the Books by Users program, we also publish books by SAS users on a variety of topics relating to SAS software. We want to provide our users with additional titles to supplement our primary documentation and to enhance the users' ability to use the SAS System effectively. We're interested in publishing manuscripts that describe or illustrate using any of SAS Institute's software products. Books must be aimed at SAS software users, either new or experienced. Tutorials are particularly attractive, as are descriptions of user-written applications for solving real-life business, industry, or academic problems. Books on programming techniques using the SAS language are also desirable. Manuscripts must reflect current or upcoming software releases, and the author's writing should indicate an understanding of the SAS System and the technical aspects covered in the manuscript." Query. Submit outline/synopsis and sample chapters. Reviews artwork/photos as part of ms package.
Recent Nonfiction Titles: *Beyond the Obvious with SAS Screen Control Language*, by Don Stanley; *SAS Software Roadmaps: Your Guide to Discovering the SAS System*, by Laurie Burch and SherriJoyce King.

Tips: "Our readers are SAS software users, both new and experienced. If I were a writer trying to market a book today, I would concentrate on developing a manuscript that teaches or illustrates a specific concept or application that SAS software users will find beneficial in their own environments or can adapt to their own needs."

SASQUATCH BOOKS, #300, 1008 Western Ave., Seattle WA 98104. (206)467-4300. Fax: (206)467-4338. Contact: Acquisitions Editor. Estab. 1975. Publishes regional hardcover and trade paperback originals. Averages 10-15 titles/year. 25% of books from first-time authors; 95% from unagented writers. Pays authors royalty on cover price. Offers wide range of advances. Publishes ms an average of 6 months after acceptance. No simultaneous submissions. Query first. Reports in 2 months. Book catalog for 9 × 12 SAE with 2 first-class stamps.
Nonfiction: Subjects include regional art/architecture, children's books, cooking, foods, gardening, history, nature/environment, recreation, sports, travel. "We are seeking quality nonfiction works about the Pacific Northwest and West Coast regions. In this sense we are a regional publisher, but we do distribute our books nationally." Submit outline and sample chapters.
Recent Nonfiction Title: *Carla Emery's Encyclopedia of Country Living.*
Tips: "We sell books through a range of channels in addition to the book trade. Our audience consists of active, literate residents of the Pacific Northwest."

‡SAURIE ISLAND PRESS, P.O. Box 751, Beaverton OR 97075. Editor: Susan Roberts. Publishes hardcover, trade paperback and mass market paperback originals. Publishes 12 titles/year. Receives 108 queries and 12 mss/year. 85% of books from first-time authors; 100% from unagented writers. Pays 20-40% royalty on retail price. Publishes book 1 year after acceptance of ms. Accepts simultaneous submissions. Query for electronic submissions. Reports in 3 months on queries. Manuscript guidelines for $2.
Nonfiction: How-to, self-help, technical. Subjects include New Age/occult. "Query first. Submit electronically." Reviews artwork/photos as part of ms package. Writers should send electronic copy.
Fiction: Adventure, erotica, fantasy, historical, horror, literary, mystery, occult, romance, science fiction, short story collections, suspense. Query or electronic to 1:105/290.3 or SIP@EPUB.RAIN.COM or NWLC BBS (503)644-8223.
Recent Fiction Title: *Witness to Death*, by Derek Sanzhiel (mass paperback).
Poetry: "No religious subjects." Submit complete ms in electronic format only; PC-compatible 3.5" disk, WordPerfect 5.25 or ASCII.

SCARECROW PRESS, INC., Division of Grolier, 52 Liberty St., P.O. Box 4167, Metuchen NJ 08840-1279. Fax: (908)548-5767. President: Albert W. Daub. Vice President, Editorial: Norman Horrocks. Estab. 1950. Publishes hardcover originals. Averages 110 titles/year. Receives 600-700 submissions annually. 70% of books from first-time authors; 100% from unagented writers. Average print order for a first book is 1,000. Pays 10% royalty on net of first 1,000 copies; 15% of net price thereafter. 15% initial royalty on camera-ready copy. Offers no advance. Publishes book 6-18 months after receipt of ms. Query for electronic submissions. Reports in 1 month. *Writer's Market* recommends allowing 2 months for reply. Book catalog for 9 × 12 SAE and 4 first-class stamps.
Nonfiction: Needs reference books and meticulously prepared annotated bibliographies, indexes and books on women's studies, music, movies and stage. Query. Occasionally reviews artwork/photos as part of ms package.
Tips: "Essentially we consider any scholarly title likely to appeal to libraries. Emphasis is on reference material, but this can be interpreted broadly, provided author is knowledgeable in the subject field."

SCHIFFER PUBLISHING LTD., 77 Lower Valley Rd., Atglen PA 19310. (610)593-1777. Fax: (610)593-2002. President: Peter Schiffer. Estab. 1972. Imprint is Whitford Press. Publishes hardcover and trade paperback originals and reprints. Firm averages 100 titles/year; imprint averages 40 titles/year. Receives 500 submissions/year. 90% of books from first-time authors; 95% from unagented writers. Pays royalty on wholesale price. Publishes book an average of 6 months after acceptance. Simultaneous submissions OK. Reports in 1 month. Book catalog free.
Nonfiction: Coffee table book, how-to, illustrated book, reference, textbook. Subjects include Americana, art/architecture, aviation, history, hobbies, military/war, regional. "We want books on collecting, hobby carving, military, architecture, aeronautic history and natural history." Query with SASE. Submit outline and sample chapters. Reviews artwork/photos as part of ms package.

SCHIRMER BOOKS, Imprint of Simon & Schuster, 866 Third Ave., New York NY 10022. Fax: (212)605-9368. Editor-in-Chief: Richard Carlin. Editor: Jonathan Wiener. Assistant Editor: Christine Gibbs. Publishes hardcover and paperback originals, related audio recordings, paperback reprints and some software. Averages 20 books/year; receives 250 submissions annually. 25% of books from first-time authors; 75% of books from unagented writers. Submit photos and/or illustrations only "if central to the book, not if decorative or tangential." Publishes book an average of 1 year after acceptance. Query for electronic submissions. Reports in 4 months. Book catalog and ms guidelines for SASE.

Nonfiction: Publishes college texts, biographies, scholarly, reference, and trade on the performing arts specializing in music, film and theatre. Submit outline/synopsis and sample chapters and current vita. Reviews artwork/photos as part of ms package.

Recent Nonfiction Title: *Black and Blue: The Life and Lyrics of Andy Razof*, by Barry Singer.

Tips: "The writer has the best chance of selling our firm a music book with a clearly defined, reachable audience, either scholarly or trade. Must be an exceptionally well-written work of original scholarship prepared by an expert in the field who has a thorough understanding of correct manuscript style and attention to detail (see the *Chicago Manual of Style*)."

SCHOLASTIC, INC., 555 Broadway, New York NY 10012. (212)343-6100. Editorial Director: Bonnie Verburg. Estab. 1920. Publishes trade paperback originals and hardcovers. Pays royalty on retail price. Reports in 3 months. Manuscript guidelines for #10 SASE.

Nonfiction: Publishes general nonfiction. Query.

Recent Nonfiction Title: *Sojourner Truth: Ain't I a Woman*, by Patricia C. and Frederick McKissack.

Fiction: Family stories, mysteries, school, friendships for ages 8-12, 35,000 words. YA fiction, romance, family and mystery for ages 12-15, 40,000-45,000 words for average to good readers. Query. Not accepting unsolicited mss at this time.

Tips: Queries may be routed to other editors in the publishing group.

SCHOLASTIC PROFESSIONAL BOOKS, 411 Lafayette, New York NY 10003. Publishing Director: Claudia Cohl. Editor-in-Chief: Terry Cooper. Editorial Coordinator: Shawn Richardson. Buys 45-50 mss/year from published or unpublished writers. "Writer should have background working in the classroom with elementary or middle school children teaching pre-service students and developing quality, appropriate, and innovative learning experiences and/or solid background in developing supplementary educational materials for these markets." Offers standard contract. Reports in 2 months. Book catalog for 9×12 SAE.

Nonfiction: Elementary and middle-school level enrichment—all subject areas, whole language, theme units, integrated materials, writing process, management techniques, teaching strategies based on personal/professional experience in the classroom. Production is limited to printed matter: resource and activity books, professional development materials, reference titles. Length: 6,000-12,000 words. Query should include table of contents.

‡SEASIDE PRESS, Imprint of Wordware Publishing, Inc., 1506 Capitol Ave., Plano TX 75074. (214)423-0090. President: Russell A. Stultz. Publishes trade paperback originals and reprints and mass market paperback originals. Publishes 50-70 titles/year. Receives 50-60 queries and 10-15 mss/year. 40% of books from first-time authors; 95% from unagented writers. Pays 8-12% royalty on wholesale price. Publishes book 6 months after acceptance of ms. Accepts simultaneous submissions. Query for electronic submissions. Reports in 1 month. Book catalog and ms guidelines free on request.

Nonfiction: How-to, children's/juvenile, self-help. Subjects include history, philosophy, religion. Submit proposal package, including table of contents, 2 sample chapters, target audience summation, competing products.

Recent Nonfiction Title: *The Bible for Busy People*, by Mark Berrier (religious).

‡SERENDIPITY SYSTEMS, P.O. Box 140, San Simeon CA 93452. (805)927-5259. Internet e-mail: j.galuszka@genie.geis.com. Publisher: John Galuszka. Imprints are Books-on-Disks, Eco-Books. Publishes electronic books for IBM-PC compatible computers. Publishes 4-6 titles/year; each imprint publishes 0-6 titles/year. Receives 52 queries and 12 mss/year. 100% of books from unagented writers. Pays 25-33% royalty on wholesale price or on retail price, depending on how the book goes out. Publishes book 1 month after acceptance of ms. Accepts simultaneous submissions. Electronic submissions required. Reports in 1 month on mss. Book catalog free on request to writers. Manuscript guidelines for #10 SASE.

Nonfiction: Reference on literature, writing, publishing. Subjects include computers and electronics, language/literature, software. "We only publish nonfiction books on literature, writing and electronic publishing." Submit entire ms on disk in ASCII files.

Recent Nonfiction Title: *Electronic Books in Print - 1994* (reference).

Fiction: Adventure, erotica, ethnic, experimental, feminist, gay/lesbian, historical, horror, humor, juvenile, literary, mainstream/contemporary, mystery, plays, science fiction, short story collections, suspense, western, young adult, hypertext, multimedia and interactive fiction. Submit entire ms on disk in ASCII files.

Recent Fiction Title: *Force of Habit*, by M. Allen (science fiction novel).

SERVANT PUBLICATIONS, 840 Airport Blvd., P.O. Box 8617, Ann Arbor MI 48107. (313)761-8505. Editorial Director: Ann Spangler. Estab. 1972. Imprints are Vine Books, "especially for evanglical Protestant readers"; and Charis Books, "especially for Roman Catholic readers." Publishes hardcover, trade and mass market paperback originals and trade paperback reprints. Averages 40 titles/year. 5% of books from first-time authors; 85% from unagented writers. Publishes book an average of 1 year after acceptance. Reports in 2 months. Book catalog for 9×12 SASE.

Nonfiction: "We're looking for practical Christian teaching, self-help, scripture, current problems facing the Christian church, and inspiration." No heterodox or non-Christian approaches. Query or submit brief outline/synopsis and 1 sample chapter. All unsolicited queries and mss are returned unopened. Only accept queries from agents or from published authors.

Fiction: Historical fiction; will accept unsolicited queries. Submit brief outline/synopsis and 1 sample chapter.

Recent Fiction Title: *Bloodlines*, by John Jenkins and Mark Weaver.

HAROLD SHAW PUBLISHERS, 388 Gundersen Dr., P.O. Box 567, Wheaton IL 60189. (708)665-6700. Director of Editorial Services: Ramona Cramer Tucker. Estab. 1967. Publishes mostly trade paperback originals and reprints. Averages 32 titles/year. Receives 4,000 submissions annually. 10% of books from first-time authors; 90% from unagented writers. Offers 5-10% royalty on retail price. Sometimes makes outright purchase for $1,000-2,500. Publishes book an average of 12-15 months after acceptance. Reports in 1 month on queries. *Writer's Market* recommends allowing 2 months for reply. Book catalog and ms guidelines for 9 × 12 SAE with 5 first-class stamps.

Nonfiction: Subjects include marriage, family and parenting, self-help and spiritual growth and Bible study. "We are looking for general nonfiction, with different twists—self-help manuscripts on issues and topics such as marriage, parenting and family with fresh insight and colorful, vibrant writing style. No autobiographies or biographies accepted. Must have an evangelical Christian perspective for us even to review the manuscript." Query. Reviews artwork/photos as part of ms package.

Tips: "Get an editor who is not a friend or a spouse who will tell you honestly whether your book is marketable. It will save a lot of your time and money and effort. Then do an honest evaluation. Who would actually read the book other than yourself? If it won't sell at least 5,000 copies, it's not very marketable and most publishers wouldn't be interested."

‡THE SHEEP MEADOW PRESS, P.O. Box 1345, Riverdale-on-Hudson NY 10471-2825. (212)548-5547. Publisher/Editor: Stanley Moss. Associate Publisher: Deborah Baker. Estab. 1978. Publishes hardbound and trade paperback originals. Averages 10-12 titles/year. Receives 1,000 submissions/year. 75% of books from first-time authors; 90% from unagented writers. Pays royalty. Reports in 1 month. Book catalog for 6 × 9 SASE.

Poetry: Query before submitting.

Recent Poetry Title: *The Landscape Is Behind the Door*, by Pierre Martory, translated by John Ashbery.

‡THE SIDRAN PRESS, Imprint of The Sidran Foundation, Suite 15, 2328 W. Joppa Rd., Lutherville MD 21093. (410)825-8888. President: Esther Giller. Publishes hardcover originals and trade paperback originals and reprints. Publishes 5-6 titles/year. Receives 75 queries and 40 mss/year. 40% of books from first-time authors; 95% from unagented writers. Pays 8-10% royalty on wholesale price. Publishes book 1 year after acceptance of ms. No simultaneous submissions. Query for electronic submissions. Reports in 1 month on queries, 3 months on proposals, 6 months on mss. Book catalog and ms guidelines free on request.

Nonfiction: Reference, self-help, textbook, professional. Subjects include child guidance/parenting, health/medicine, psychology, women's issues/studies. Specializes in trauma/abuse/domestic violence and mental health issues. Query with proposal package including outline, 2-3 sample chapters, introduction, competing titles, market information.

Recent Nonfiction Title: *My Mom is Different*, by Deborah Sessions (children's).

SIERRA CLUB BOOKS, Dept. WM, 100 Bush St., San Francisco CA 94104. (415)291-1600. Fax: (415)291-1602. Senior Editor: James Cohee. Estab. 1962. Publishes hardcover and paperback originals and reprints. Averages 30 titles/year. Receives 1,000 submissions annually. 50% of books from unagented writers. Royalties vary by project. Offers average $3,000-15,000 advance. Publishes book an average of 12-18 months after acceptance. Reports in 2 months. Book catalog free.

• Sierra Club Books looks for literary nonfiction.

Nonfiction: Animals; health; history (natural); how-to (outdoors); juveniles; nature; philosophy; photography; recreation (outdoors, nonmechanical); science; sports (outdoors); travel (by foot or bicycle). "The Sierra Club was founded to help people to explore, enjoy and preserve the nation's forests, waters, wildlife and wilderness. The books program looks to publish quality trade books about the outdoors and the protection of natural resources. Specifically, we are interested in literary natural history, environmental issues such as nuclear power, self-sufficiency, politics and travel, and juvenile books with an ecological theme." Does *not* want "proposals for large color photographic books without substantial text; how-to books on building things outdoors; books on motorized travel; or any but the most professional studies of animals." Query first, submit outline and sample chapters. Reviews artwork/photos ("duplicates, not originals") as part of ms package.

Fiction: Adventure, historical, mainstream and ecological fiction. "We do very little fiction, but will consider a fiction manuscript if its theme fits our philosophical aims: the enjoyment and protection of the environment. Does *not* want any manuscript with animals or plants that talk; apocalyptic plots." Query first, submit outline/synopsis and sample chapters.

SIGNATURE BOOKS, 564 West 400 North, Salt Lake City UT 84116-3411. (801)531-1483. Fax: (801)531-1488. Publisher: Gary Bergera. Estab. 1981. Publishes hardcover, trade and mass market paperback originals. Publishes 12 titles/year. Receives 100 queries and 100 mss/year. 10% of books from first-time authors, 100% from unagented writers. Pays royalty. Publishes book 1 year after acceptance of ms. Simultaneous submissions OK. Query for electronic submissions. Reports in 6 months on proposals. Book catalog and ms guidelines free on request.
Nonfiction: Biography, humor, essays. Subjects under Western Americana heading include gay/lesbian, history, religion (predominantly Mormon), women's issues/studies. "We prefer manuscripts in Utah/western studies. Familiarize yourself with our backlist before submitting a proposal." Submit proposal package, including 2-3 sample chapters. Reviews artwork/photos as part of freelance ms package. Writers should send photocopies.
Fiction: Western Americana: historical, humor, religious. Query or submit synopsis.
Poetry: Submit complete ms.
Tips: "We have a general adult audience that is somewhat Mormon-oriented."

SILHOUETTE BOOKS, 300 E. 42nd St., New York NY 10017. (212)682-6080. Fax: (212)682-4539. Editorial Director, Silhouette Books, Harlequin historicals: Isabel Swift. Estab. 1979. Publishes mass market paperback originals. Averages 350 titles/year. Receives 4,000 submissions annually. 10% of books from first-time authors; 25% from unagented writers. Pays royalty. Publishes book an average of 1 year after acceptance. No unsolicited mss. Send query letter, 2 page synopsis and SASE to head of imprint. Manuscript guidelines for #10 SASE.
Imprints: Silhouette Romances (contemporary adult romances), Anne Canadeo, Senior Editor; 53,000-58,000 words. Silhouette Special Editions (contemporary adult romances), Tara Gavin, Senior Editor; 75,000-80,000 words. Silhouette Desires (contemporary adult romances), Lucia Macro, Senior Editor; 55,000-60,000 words. Silhouette Intimate Moments (contemporary adult romances), Silhouette Shadows (contemporary adult gothic romances), Leslie Wainger, Senior Editor and Editorial Coordinator; 80,000-85,000 words. Harlequin Historicals (adult historical romances), Tracy Farrell, Senior Editor; 95,000-105,000 words.
Fiction: Romance (contemporary and historical romance for adults). "We are interested in seeing submissions for all our lines. No manuscripts other than the types outlined above. Manuscript should follow our general format, yet have an individuality and life of its own that will make it stand out in the readers' minds."
Recent Fiction Title: *Night Smoke*, by Nora Roberts.
Tips: "The romance market is constantly changing, so when you read for research, read the latest books and those that have been recommended to you by people knowledgeable in the genre. We are actively seeking new authors for all our lines, contemporary and historical."

SIMON & SCHUSTER, 1230 Avenue of the Americas, New York NY 10020. Imprints include Fireside, Touchstone, Simon & Schuster, Lisa Drew, Scribners, Otto Penzler Books, Free Press and Pocketbooks. Simon & Schuster Children's Publishing and New Media Division includes these imprints: Atheneum Books for Young Readers, Macmillan Books for Young Readers, Margaret K. McElderry Books. Simon & Schuster Books for Young Readers, Aladdin Paperbacks and Little Simon. General interest publisher of both fiction and nonfiction.The company did not respond to our request for information. Query before submitting.

‡SINGER MEDIA CORP., Unit 106, 1030 Calle Cordillera, San Clemente CA 92673. (714)498-7227. Editor: Janis Hawkridge. Imprints are Non Fiction Series, Fiction Series, Target-Horror, Puzzles and Games Series. Publishes hardcover, trade paperback and mass market paperback reprints. Publishes 100 titles/year. Receives 2,000 queries and 600 mss/year. 3% of books from first-time authors; 6% from unagented writers. Pays 5-15% royalty on retail price. Offers $500-10,000 advance. Publishes book 12-18 months after acceptance of ms. Accepts simultaneous submissions. Reports in 1 month. Book catalog and ms guidelines for $2.
Nonfiction: Biography, coffee table book, how-to, illustrated book, children's/juvenile, reference, self-help, horror, puzzles. Subjects include business and economics, child guidance/parenting, computers and electronics, health/medicine, money/finance, psychology, recreation, software, sports, women's issues/studies. "Must be for a global market." Query. Reviews artwork/photos as part of ms package. Writers should send no original pictures; dupes only.
Recent Nonfiction Title: *Home Medical Dictionary*, by Janis Hawkridge (health, medical reference).
Fiction: Erotica, fantasy, horror, juvenile, mainstream/contemporary, mystery, occult, picture books, romance, suspense, young adult. "We have a worldwide readership, not just the USA." Query.
Recent Fiction Title: *Drifthaven*, by Clarissa Ross (gothic romance).

‡SJL PUBLISHING COMPANY, P.O. Box 152, Hanna IN 46340. (219)324-9678. Publisher/Editor: Sandra J. Cassady. Publishes hardcover and trade paperback originals. Publishes 8-10 titles/year. Receives 100 queries and 50 mss/year. 40% of books from first-time authors; 100% from unagented writers. Pays 10% royalty or makes outright purchase. Publishes book 1 year after acceptance of ms. Accepts simultaneous submissions. Reports in 1 month on queries and proposals; 2 months on mss. Manuscript guidelines for #10 SASE.
Nonfiction: Cookbook, children's/juvenile, reference, self-help, technical. Subjects include business and economics, computers and electronics, cooking, foods and nutrition, gardening, government/politics, science,

sports. "Looking for good scientific publications." Submit outline and proposal package. Reviews artwork/ photos as part of ms package. Writers should send photocopies.
Recent Nonfiction Title: *A Short Course in Permanent Magnet Materials*, by Wm. A. Cassady (reference/ science).
Fiction: Humor, juvenile, science fiction. Submit synopsis and complete ms.

SKY PUBLISHING CORP., 49 Bay State Rd., Cambridge MA 02138-9111. (617)864-7360. Fax: (617)864-6117. Director, Books & Products Division: Susan Cummings. Estab. 1941. Publishes hardcover and trade paperback originals. Publishes 6 titles/year. Receives 25 queries and 12 mss/year. 20% of books from first-time authors; 95% from unagented writers. Pays 10-15% royalty on retail price. Publishes book 6 months after acceptance of ms. Query for electronic submissions. Reports in 2 months on proposals. Book catalog free on request.
Nonfiction: Biography, how-to, illustrated books, reference, technical, textbook. Subjects include hobbies (amateur astronomy), nature/environment, astrophotography, science (astronomy/space). "Sky Publishing specializes in books on astronomy and earth science, for all ages and levels of experience. Writers should have a clear idea of the audience or market for the book." Submit marketing analysis, outline of chapters, brief description of book, sample chapter, résumé and art/illustration plan.

GIBBS SMITH, PUBLISHER, Dept. WM, P.O. Box 667, Layton UT 84041. (801)544-9800. Editorial Director: Madge Baird. Estab. 1969. Imprint is Peregrine Smith Books. Publishes hardcover and paperback originals and reprints. Averages 40 titles/year. Receives 2,000 submissions annually. 20% of books from first-time authors; 50% from unagented writers. Average print order for a first book is 3,000-4,000. Starts at 8% royalty on wholesale price. Offers average $1,000 advance. Publishes book an average of 18 months after acceptance. Reports in 2 months. Book catalog for 6×9 SAE with 3 first-class stamps. Manuscript guidelines for #10 SASE.
Nonfiction: Subjects include cowboy western, natural history, architecture, fine arts decorating, humor and gardening. "We are interested in manuscripts for a popular audience for all of the above. "We consider biographical, historical, and descriptive studies in all of the above. Emphasis is also placed on pictorial content." Query. Reviews artwork/photos as part of ms package.
Recent Nonfiction Title: *Don't Squat With Your Spurs On*, by Texas Bix Bender.
Tips: "We are interested in work with a broad general appeal or a strong regional western interest: We want to publish books that have strong gift appeal."

THE SMITH, The Generalist Association, Inc., 69 Joralemon St., Brooklyn NY 11201-4003. (718)834-1212. Publisher: Harry Smith. Estab. 1964. Publishes hardcover and trade paperback originals. Averages 5 titles/ year. Receives 2,500 queries/year. 50% of books from first-time authors; more than 90% from unagented writers. Pays royalty. Offers $500-1,000 advance. Publishes book 9 months after acceptance. Simultaneous submissions OK. Reports in 3 months. Book catalog and guidelines free on request.
Nonfiction: Literary essays, language and literature. "The 'how' is as important as the 'what' to us. Don't bother to send anything if the prose is not outstanding itself. We don't publish anything about how to fix your car or your soul." Query or submit proposal package including outline and sample chapter. Reviews artwork/photos as part of freelance ms package. Artists should send photocopies.
Fiction: Experimental, fantasy, feminist, literary, science fiction. "Emphasis is always on artistic quality. A synopsis of almost any novel sounds stupid." Query or submit 1 sample chapter.
Poetry: "No greeting card sentiments, no casual jottings. Do not send complete ms." Submit 7-10 sample poems.

SOCIAL SCIENCE EDUCATION CONSORTIUM, Suite 240, 3300 Mitchell Lane, Boulder CO 80301-2296. (303)492-8154. Fax: (303)449-3925. Managing Editor: Laurel R. Singleton. Estab. 1963. Publishes trade paperback originals. Publishes 8 titles/year. 25% of books from first-time authors; 100% from unagented writers. Pays 8-12% royalty, net sales (retail price minus average discount). Publishes book 6 months after acceptance of ms. Simultaneous submissions OK. Query for electronic submissions. Reports in 1 month on proposals. *Writer's Market* recommends allowing 2 months for reply.
Nonfiction: Teacher resources. Subjects include education, government/politics, history. "We publish titles of interest to social studies teachers particularly; we do not generally publish on such broad educational topics as discipline, unless there is a specific relationship to the social studies/social sciences." Submit outline and 1-2 sample chapters.

‡SOCIETY PUBLISHING, P.O. Box 66271, Auburndale Branch, Boston MA 02165. (617)965-7129. Contact: Editor. Publishes hardcover and trade paperback originals. Publishes 4 titles/year. Receives 6 queries/year. 50% of books from first-time authors; 100% from unagented writers. Pays on contract basis. Offers $500-1,500 advance. Publishes book 1 year after acceptance of ms. No simultaneous submissions. Query for electronic submissions. Reports in 2 months on queries.
Nonfiction: Self-help. Subjects include health/medicine, psychology. Query.

SOHO PRESS, INC., 853 Broadway, New York NY 10003. (212)260-1900. Editor-in-Chief: Juris Jurjevics. Estab. 1986. Publishes hardcover and trade paperback originals. Averages 25 titles/year. Receives 5,000 submissions/year. 75% of books from first-time authors; 50% from unagented writers. Pays 10-15% on retail price. Publishes book an average of 1 year after acceptance. Simultaneous submissions OK. Reports in 1 month. Book catalog for 6×9 SAE with 2 first-class stamps.

Nonfiction: Biography. "We want literary nonfiction: travel, autobiography, biography, etc. No self-help." Submit outline and sample chapters.

Recent Nonfiction Title: *Red Flower of China*, by Zhai Zhenhua.

Fiction: Adventure, ethnic, feminist, historical, literary, mainstream/contemporary, mystery, suspense. Submit complete ms with SASE. *Writer's Market* recommends query with SASE first.

Recent Fiction Title: *The Sixteen Pleasures*, by Robert Hellenga.

SOUNDPRINTS, Division of Trudy Management Corporation, P.O. Box 679, Norwalk CT 06856. Assistant Editor: Dana M. Rau. Publishes hardcover originals. Publishes 9-12 titles/year. Receives 50 queries and unsolicited ms/year. 90% of books from unagented writers. Makes outright purchase or pays royalty on wholesale price. Publishes book 1-2 years after acceptance of ms. Simultaneous submissions OK. Reports on queries in 1 month. *Writer's Market* recommends allowing 2 months for reply. Book catalog for 9×12 SAE. Manuscript guidelines for #10 SASE.

• This publisher creates multimedia sets for the Smithsonian Wild Heritage Collection. Sets include a book, read-a-long audiotape and realistic stuffed animal, combining facts about North American wildlife with stories about each animal's habits and habitats.

Nonfiction: Children's/juvenile, animals. "We focus on North American wildlife and ecology. Subject animals must be portrayed realistically and must not be anthropomorphic. Meticulous research is required." Query. Reviews artwork/photos as part of freelance ms package, although we usually contract with a separate illustrator. (All of our books are now being illustrated in full color.)

Recent Nonfiction Title: *Puffin's Homecoming: The Story of an Atlantic Puffin*, by Darice Bailer (winner of the 1993 Parent's Choice Award).

Fiction: Juvenile. "When we publish juvenile fiction, it will be about wildlife and all information in the book *must* be accurate." Query.

Tips: "Our books are written for children from ages 4-8. Our most successful authors can craft a wonderful story which is derived from authentic wildlife facts. First inquiry to us should ask about our interest in publishing a book about a specific animal or habitat."

SOURCEBOOKS, INC., P.O. Box 313, Naperville IL 60566. (312)961-3900. Fax: (312)961-2168. Publisher: Dominique Raccah. Associate Editor: John Santucci. Estab. 1987. Publishes hardcover and trade paperback originals. Averages 20 titles/year. 50% of books from first-time authors; 100% from unagented writers. Pays 5-15% royalty on wholesale price, or buys mss outright. Publishes book an average of 6 months after acceptance. Simultaneous submissions OK. Query for electronic submissions. Reports in 3 months on queries. "We do not want to see complete mss." Book catalog and ms guidelines for 8×10 SASE.

Nonfiction: *Small Business Sourcebooks:* books for small business owners, entrepreneurs and students. "A key to submitting books to us is to explain *how* your book helps the reader, *why* it is different from the books already out there (please do your homework) and the *author's credentials* for writing this book." *Financial Sourcebooks:* economics, finance, banking and insurance, directories and reference materials for financial executives. *Sourcebook Trade:* gift books, self-help and how to. "Books likely to succeed with us are self-help, New Age, psychology, women's issues, how-to, house and home, gift books or books with strong artwork." Query or submit outline and sample chapters (2-3 chapters, not the first). Reviews artwork/photos as part of ms package.

Recent Nonfiction Title: *Soft Sell: The New Art of Selling, Self-Empowerment and Persuasion.*

Tips: "We love to develop books in new areas or develop strong titles in areas that are already well developed. Our goal is to provide customers with terrific innovative books at reasonable price."

SOUTH END PRESS, 116 Saint Botolph St., Boston MA 02115. (617)266-0629. Fax: (617)266-1595. Contact: Dionne Brooks. Publishes hardcover and trade paperback originals and reprints. Publishes 15 titles/year. Receives 400 queries and 100 mss/year. 50% of books from first-time authors; 95% from unagented writers. Pays 10% royalty on wholesale price. Occasionally offers $500-2,500 advance. Publishes book 9 months after acceptance of ms. Simultaneous submissions OK. Query for electronic submissions. Reports in up to 3 months on queries and proposals. Book catalog and ms guidelines free on request.

Nonfiction: Subjects include economics, education, ethnic, gay/lesbian, government/politics, health/medicine, history, military/war, music/dance, nature/environment, philosophy, science, sociology, women's issues/studies, political. "We publish books with a new left/feminist multi-cultural perspective." Query or submit 2 sample chapters including intro or conclusion. Reviews artwork/photos as part of the freelance ms package. Writers should send photocopies.

Recent Nonfiction Title: *Year 501*, by Noam Chomsky (political).

SOUTHERN ILLINOIS UNIVERSITY PRESS, P.O. Box 3697, Carbondale IL 62901-3697. (618)453-2281. Fax: (618)453-1221. Director: John F. (Rick) Stetter. Editorial Director: Curtis Clark. Estab. 1956. Averages 60 titles/year. Receives 500 submissions annually. 50% of books from first-time authors; 99% from unagented writers. Publishes book an average of 1 year after acceptance. Reports in 2 months. Book catalog free.
Nonfiction: "We are interested in scholarly nonfiction on the humanities, social sciences and contemporary affairs. No dissertations or collections of previously published articles." Accepts nonfiction translations from French, German, Scandinavian and Hebrew. Query.
Recent Nonfiction Title: *Paul Bowles: Romantic Savage.*

SOUTHERN METHODIST UNIVERSITY PRESS, P.O. Box 415, Dallas TX 75275. Fax: (214)768-1428. Senior Editor: Kathryn Lang. Establ. 1937. Publishes hardcover and trade paperback originals and reprints. Publishes 10-15 titles/year. Receives 500 queries and 500 mss/year. 75% of books from first-time authors; 95% from unagented writers. Pays up to 10% royalty on wholesale price. Offers $500 advance. Publishes book 1 year after acceptance of ms. Query for electronic submissions. Reports in 1 month on queries and proposals, 6 months on mss.
● Southern Methodist University Press has been accepting fewer mss.
Nonfiction: Subjects include medical ethics/human values and history (regional). "We are seeking works on the following areas: theology; film/theater; medical ethics/human values." Query with outline, 3 sample chapters and table of contents. Reviews artwork/photos as part of the freelance ms package. Writers should send photocopies.
Fiction: Literary novels and short story collections. Query.
Tips: Audience is general educated readers of quality fiction and nonfiction.

SOUTHPARK PUBLISHING GROUP, INC., Suite 156-359, 4041 W. Wheatland Rd., Dallas TX 75237-9991. (214)296-5657. Managing Editor: Ms. Susan Watson. Publishes trade paperback originals. Publishes 6 titles/year. Receives 50 queries/year and 10 mss/year. 25% of books from first-time authors; 100% from unagented writers. Pays 10-15% royalty on retail price. Publishes book 9 months after acceptance. Simultaneous submissions OK. Reports on queries in 2 months. Book catalog and ms guidelines for #10 SASE.
Nonfiction: How-to, self-help, travel guides. Subjects include hobbies, recreation, travel for and by disabled people. "Our intent is to publish a series of domestic and international travel, how-to and self-help guidebooks." Query. Reviews artwork/photos as part of freelance ms package (upon request).
Tips: "Our audience is the general public."

SOUTHWEST PUBLISHING COMPANY OF ARIZONA, #194, 9666 E. Riggs Rd., Sun Lakes AZ 85248. (602)895-7995. Editor: Barbara DeBolt. Publishes trade and mass market paperback originals. Publishes 10-12 titles/year. Receives 500 queries and 400-500 mss/year. 99% of books from first-time authors; 100% from unagented writers. Pays 10% royalty on wholesale or retail price. Reports in 1 month on queries, 2 months on proposals, 4-6 months on mss. Book catalog free on request. Manuscript guidelines for #10 SASE.
Nonfiction: Subjects include philosophy, ufology, religion (metaphysical). Reviews artwork/photos as part of the freelance ms package. Writers should send photocopies.
Recent Nonfiction Title: *We Have Watched You . . .*, by Anonymous, (extraterrestrial); *Homecoming of the Alien Heart*, by B. Lambert.
Fiction: Fantasy, religious (metaphysical), UFO's "As a small press, we are doing everything possible for our authors with regard to distribution, etc. Some authors come to us knowing we are small yet expect celebrity results." Query or submit synopsis and the first 3 chapters.
Recent Fiction Title: *Mortal Choices*, by James Coppola (mainstream); *Turn a Blind Eye*, by Donna B. Harper (mystery); *Remember Me With Love*, by Mary Ann Artrip (romance suspense); *Crazy Horse, The Boy*, by Edward Heisel (Native American); *Brothers of the Pine*, by Tim Simmons (Native American).
Tips: "Know our no-advance policy beforehand and know our guidelines. No response ever without a SASE. Absolutely no phone queries. We have temporarily restricted our needs to those manuscripts whose focus is metaphysical, ufology, time travel and Native American. Query to see if this restriction has been lifted before submitting other material."

‡SPECTRUM PRESS INC., #109, 3023 N. Clark St., Chicago IL 60657. (312)281-1419. Editor-in-Chief: Dan Agin. Publishes floppy disk books. Publishes 50 titles/year. Receives 300 queries and 100 mss/year. 75% of books from first-time authors; 90% from unagented writers. Pays 10-15% royalty on retail price. Publishes book 3 months after acceptance of ms. Simultaneous submissions OK. Query for electronic submissions. Reports in 1 month on mss. Book catalog and ms guidelines for #10 SASE.
Nonfiction: Biography, reference. Subjects include Americana, anthropology/archaeology, art/architecture, ethnic, gay/lesbian, government/politics, history, language/literature, philosophy, sociology, translation, women's issues/studies. Query.
Fiction: Erotica, ethnic, experimental, feminist, gay/lesbian, literary, mainstream/contemporary, plays, short story collections. Submit synopsis and 3 sample chapters.
Recent Fiction Title: *Tell Me In Darkness*, by Julian Dacanay (contemporary novel); *Performance Poetry and Other Essays*, by Gloria Klein (literary criticism); *Rainy Season*, by Barbara Sheen (short stories).

Poetry: "Interested in new strong poetry." Submit 10 sample poems or complete ms.
Recent Poetry Title: *Song of the Sixties*, by Howard Rawlinson; *Poetry School*, by Mark Spitzer.

THE SPEECH BIN, INC., 1965 25th Ave., Vero Beach FL 32960-3062. (407)770-0007. Senior Editor: Jan Binney. Estab. 1984. Publishes trade paperback originals. Publishes 10-20 titles/year. Receives 500 mss per year. 50% of books from first-time authors; 90% from unagented writers. Pays negotiable royalty on wholesale price. Publishes ms average of 6 months after acceptance. Query for electronic submissions. Do NOT fax mss. Reports in up to 3 months. Book catalog for 9 × 12 SASE and $1.21 postage.
● The Speech Bin is increasing the number of books published per year and is especially interested in reviewing treatment materials for adults and adolescents.

Nonfiction: How-to, illustrated book, juvenile (preschool-teen), reference, textbook, educational material and games for both children and adults. Subjects include health, communication disorders and education for handicapped persons. Query or submit outline and sample chapters. Reviews artwork/photos as part of ms package. Do not send original artwork; photocopies only, please.
Recent Nonfiction Title: *Exercise Your Voice to Health*, by Sally Stefanini.
Fiction: "Booklets or books for children and adults about handicapped persons, especially with communication disorders." Query or submit outline/synopsis and sample chapters. "This is a potentially new market for The Speech Bin."
Tips: "Our audience is made up of special educators, speech-language pathologists and audiologists, parents, caregivers, and teachers of children and adults with developmental and post-trauma disabilities. Books and materials must be research-based, clearly presented, well written, competently illustrated, and unique. We'll be adding books and materials for use by occupational and physical therapists and other allied health professionals. We are also looking for more materials for use in treating adults and very young children with communication disorders. Please do not fax manuscripts to us."

SPINSTERS INK, P.O. Box 300170, Minneapolis MN 55403-0170. (612)377-0287. Editor: Kelly Kager. Estab. 1978. Publishes trade paperback originals and reprints. Averages 6 titles/year. Receives 200 submissions annually. 50% of books from first-time authors; 95% from unagented writers. Pays 7-11% royalty on retail price. Publishes book an average of 18 months after acceptance. Reports in 4 months. Book catalog free. Manuscript guidelines for SASE.
● Spinsters Ink has a smaller staff and they are taking longer to respond. They have changed their reporting time from 3 months to 4 months.

Nonfiction: Self-help and feminist analysis for positive change. Subjects include women's issues. "We are interested in books that not only name the crucial issues in women's lives, but show and encourage change and growth. We do not want to see work by men, or anything that is not specific to women's lives (humor, children's books, etc.)." Query. Reviews artwork/photos as part of ms package.
Fiction: Ethnic, women's, lesbian. We do not publish poetry or short fiction. We are interested in fiction that challenges women's language that is feminist, stories that treat lifestyles with the diversity and complexity they deserve. We are also interested in genre fiction, especially mysteries. Submit outline/synopsis and sample chapters.
Recent Fiction Title: *Trees Call for What They Need*, by Melissa Kwasney (novel).

STACKPOLE BOOKS, 5067 Ritter Rd., Mechanicsburg PA 17055. Fax: (717)796-0412. Editorial Director: Judith Schnell. Estab. 1935. Publishes hardcover and paperback originals. Publishes 70 titles/year. Publishes book an average of 1 year after acceptance. Reports in 1 month. *Writer's Market* recommends allowing 2 months for reply.
Nonfiction: Outdoor-related subject areas—fishing, hunting, wildlife, adventure, outdoor skills, gardening, decoy carving/woodcarving, outdoor sports, crafts, military guides, history. Submit proposal. Reviews artwork/photos as part of ms package.
Recent Nonfiction Title: *Basic Fly Fishing*, by Dave Hughes.
Tips: "Stackpole seeks well-written, authoritative manuscripts for specialized and general trade markets. Proposals should include chapter outline, sample chapter and illustrations and author's credentials."

STANDARD PUBLISHING, Division of Standex International Corp., 8121 Hamilton Ave., Cincinnati OH 45231. (513)931-4050. Publisher/Vice President: Eugene H. Wiggington. Estab. 1866. Publishes hardcover and paperback originals and reprints. Specializes in religious books for children. Publishes book an average of 18 months after acceptance. Reports in 3 months. Manuscript guidelines for #10 SASE; send request to Acquisitions Coordinator.
Nonfiction: Publishes crafts (to be used in Christian education), juveniles, Christian education (teacher training, working with volunteers), quiz, puzzle. All mss must pertain to religion. Query.
Recent Nonfiction Title: *Volunteer Ministries*, by Margie Morris.
Tips: "Children's books (picture books, ages 4-7), Christian education, activity books, and helps for Christian parents and church leaders are the types of books writers have the best chance of selling to our firm."

STANFORD UNIVERSITY PRESS, Stanford CA 94305-2235. (415)723-9598. Editor-in-Chief: Norris Pope. Estab. 1925. Averages 75 titles/year. Receives 1,500 submissions annually. 40% of books from first-time authors; 95% from unagented writers. Subsidy publishes (nonauthor) 65% of books. Pays up to 15% royalty ("typically 10%, often none"); sometimes offers advance. Publishes book an average of 1 year after receipt of final manuscript. Query for electronic submissions. Reports in 6 weeks. Free book catalog.
Nonfiction: Scholarly books in the humanities, social sciences, and natural sciences: history and culture of China, Japan, and Latin America; European history; biology, natural history, and taxonomy; anthropology, linguistics, and psychology; literature, criticism, and literary theory; political science and sociology; archaeology and geology; and medieval and classical studies. Also high-level textbooks and books for a more general audience. Query. "We like to see a prospectus and an outline." Reviews artwork/photos as part of ms package.
Tips: "The writer's best chance is a work of original scholarship with an argument of some importance."

STAR BOOKS INC., 408 Pearson St., Wilson NC 27893-1850. (919)237-1591. President: Allen W. Harrell. Estab. 1982. Averages 9-15 titles/year. 90% of books from first-time authors; 100% from unagented writers. Pays 10-15% royalty on retail price. No advance. Publishes book an average of 1 year after acceptance. Reports in 4 months.
• No book-length manuscripts for now.
Nonfiction: Biography, humor, juvenile, self-help. Subjects include abortion, alcoholism, biography, Christian testimony, cartoons (Christian), devotionals, divorce, personal experiences (specifically Christian), prayer (devotional books), rape. "We are looking for first-person accounts (testimonies) by persons who have found God's answers for the difficult problems of life. No third-person, impersonal, researched material." Submit complete ms. *Writer's Market* recommends query with SASE first. Reviews artwork/photos (b&w only) as part of ms package.
Fiction: Adventure, confession, ethnic, fantasy, humor, juvenile, picture books (b&w only), poetry (with Christian focus), novels (biblical or contemporary Christian), short stories (Christian), religious, romance, short story collections, young adult. All must have strong Christian focus. "We don't want to see anything that is not specifically Christian or is too esoteric." Submit complete ms. *Writer's Market* recommends query with SASE first. No simultaneous submissions.

‡STAR SONG PUBLISHING GROUP, Star Song Distribution Group, 2325 Crestmoore, Nashville TN 37215. Vice President: Matthew Price. Imprints are Abbott-Marthyn Press (contact Robert Webber), Contemporary Classics (contact Kay Moser), Squeaky Sneaker Books (contact Kay Moser). Publishes hardcover, trade paperback and mass market paperback originals and reprints. Publishes 40 titles/year. Receives 250 queries and 50 mss/year. 10% of books from first-time authors; 90% from unagented writers. Pays 15-20% royalty on wholesale price. Publishes book 1 year after acceptance of ms. Simultaneous submissions OK. Reports in 4 months on queries. Book catalog and ms guidelines free on request.
Nonfiction: Biography, coffee table book, children's/juvenile, reference, textbook. Subjects include relition. "Star Song is an evangelical, non-denominational Christian publishing house." Query.
Recent Nonfiction Title: *George MacDonald: Victorian Myth Maker*, by Roland Hein (biography).
Fiction: Adventure, ethnic, experimental, feminist, historical, humor, juvenile, literary, mainstream/contemporary, religious, young adult. Query.
Recent Fiction Title: *Celebration*, by Kay Moser (contemporary drama).
Poetry: "Must reflect evangelical Christian viewpoint." Query.
Recent Poetry Title: *Between 2 Thieves*, by Kevin Smith (experimental).

STARBURST PUBLISHERS, P.O. Box 4123, Lancaster PA 17604. (717)293-0939. Editorial Director: Ellen Hake. Estab. 1982. Publishes hardcover and trade paperback originals and trade paperback reprints. Averages 10-15 titles/year. Receives 1,000 submissions/year. 60% of books by first-time authors; 90% from unagented writers. Pays 6-15% royalty on net price to retailer. Publishes book an average of 1 year after acceptance. Reports in 1 month on queries. Book catalog for 9 × 12 SAE with 4 first-class stamps. Manuscript guidelines for #10 SASE.
Nonfiction: General nonfiction, how-to, self-help, Christian. Subjects include business/economics, child guidance/parenting, cooking/foods/nutrition, counseling/career guidance, educational, gardening, health/medicine, juvenile (Bible-based teaching picture books), money/finance, nature and environment, psychology, real estate, recreation, religion. No poetry. "We are looking for contemporary issues facing Christians and today's average American." Submit outline, 3 sample chapters, bio, photo and SASE. Reviews artwork/photos as part of freelance ms package.
Recent Nonfiction Title: *Stay Well Without Going Broke*, by Dr. John Renner et al. (health medicine).
Fiction: Adventure, fantasy, historical, mainstream/contemporary, romance, western. "We are looking for good, wholesome Christian fiction." Submit outline/synopsis, 3 sample chapters, bio, photo and SASE.
Recent Fiction Title: *Beyond The River*, by Gilbert Morris (historical/fantasy).
Tips: "50% of our line goes into the Christian marketplace; 50% into the general marketplace. We are one of the few publishers that has *direct sales representation* into both the Christian and general marketplace (bookstore, library, health and gift). Write on an issue that slots you on talk shows and thus establish your name as an expert and writer."

STERLING PUBLISHING, 387 Park Ave. S., New York NY 10016. (212)532-7160. Acquisitions Manager: Sheila Anne Barry. Estab. 1949. Publishes hardcover and paperback originals and reprints. Averages 200 titles/year. Pays royalty. Offers advance. Publishes book an average of 8 months after acceptance. Reports in 2 months. Guidelines for SASE.

Nonfiction: Alternative lifestyle, fiber arts, games and puzzles, health, how-to, business, hobbies, children's humor, children's science, nature and activities, militaria, pets, recreation, reference, sports, technical, wine, gardening, art, home decorating, dolls and puppets, ghosts, woodworking, crafts, history, medieval, Celtic subjects. No longer seeking New Age. Query or submit complete chapter list, detailed outline and 2 sample chapters with photos if applicable. Reviews artwork/photos as part of ms package.

Recent Nonfiction Title: *Nature Crafts with a Microwave*, by Dawn Cusick.

STILL WATERS PRESS, 112 W. Duerer St., Galloway NJ 08201-9402. (609)652-1790. Editor: Shirley Warren. Estab. 1989. Publishes trade paperback originals. Publishes 7 titles/year. Receives 300 queries and 500 mss/year. 75% of books from first-time authors; 100% from unagented writers. Pays 10% royalty on wholesale and retail price, or pays in copies—initial press run 10%; subsequent runs 10%. Author receives 50% discount purchasing her own books. Publishes book 4 months after acceptance of ms. Simultaneous submissions OK. Reports in 1 month on queries. *Writer's Market* recommends allowing 2 months for reply. Book catalog and ms guidelines for #10 SASE.

• Still Waters Press no longer looks at uninvited nonfiction.

Fiction: Short-short fiction. "Mistakes writers most often make when submitting fiction: Not compelling, characters boring, descriptions nondescript, storyline too soft." Submit short-short only; maximum 10 typewritten double-spaced pages.

Poetry: Length: Maximum 28 pages. No "abused childhood" works or poems about writing or teaching poetry. Prefers American settings and single-spaced poetry. "Mistakes poets most often make when submitting poetry: Spelling errors, patriarchal attitude, twisted syntax to achieve weak rhyme, lines way too long for our format, poems about dead poets, settings in the past rather than present." Submit 5 sample poems.

Recent Poetry Title: *The Marigold Poems*, by Margaret Renkl.

Tips: "Read other poets, both contemporary and traditional; attend some workshops, establish rapport with your local peers, attend readings. We prefer to publish people who are actively engaged in the literary life of their own community—writers' groups, readings, arts festivals, etc. Keep your best work in circulation—someone out there is looking for you."

STILLPOINT PUBLISHING, Division of Stillpoint International, Inc., P.O. Box 640, Walpole NH 03608. (603)756-9281. Fax: (603)756-9282. Senior Editor: Dorothy Seymour. Publishes hardcover originals and trade paperback originals and reprints. Averages 8-10 titles/year. Receives 500 submissions/year. 50% of books from first-time authors; 90% from unagented writers. Pays royalty. Publishes book an average of 9-15 months after acceptance. Simultaneous submissions OK. Reports in 6-8 weeks. Manuscript guidelines for SASE.

Nonfiction: Topics include personal growth and spiritual development; holistic health and healing for individual and global well-being; sacred ecology and eco-spirituality; earth-sustainable economics; social responsibility, justice and ethics in business and society.

Tips: "We are looking for manuscripts with unique, clearly-stated theme supported by persuasive arguments and evidence. We publish nonfiction that offers a new perspective gained from life experience and/or research that addresses the spiritual foundations of a current aspect of personal, social or global change. The work needs to be insightful and practical, and to reflect a level of spiritual values. Stillpoint specializes in books that approach personal and planetary issues from their spiritual core. We are looking for manuscripts that apply spiritual values—expressed in mainstream, non-denominational terms—to the development of personal and global well-being. Query, with statement of theme, or submit outline and sample chapters."

STIPES PUBLISHING CO., 10-12 Chester St., Champaign IL 61824-9933. (217)356-8391. Contact: Robert Watts. Estab. 1925. Publishes hardcover and paperback originals. Averages 15-30 titles/year. Receives 150 submissions annually. 50% of books from first-time authors; 100% from unagented writers. Pays 15% maximum royalty on retail price. Publishes book an average of 4 months after acceptance. Reports in 2 months.

Nonfiction: Technical (some areas), textbooks on business and economics, music, chemistry, agriculture/horticulture, environmental education, and recreation and physical education. "All of our books in the trade area are books that also have a college text market. No books unrelated to educational fields taught at the college level." Submit outline and 1 sample chapter.

STOEGER PUBLISHING COMPANY, 55 Ruta Court, S. Hackensack NJ 07606-1799. (201)440-2700. Fax: (201)440-2707. Publisher: Robert E. Weise. Estab. 1925. Publishes trade paperback originals. Averages 12-15 titles/year. Royalty varies, depending on ms. Simultaneous submissions OK. Reports in 1 month on queries. *Writer's Market* recommends allowing 2 months for reply. Book catalog for #10 SAE with 2 first-class stamps.

Nonfiction: Specializing in reference and how-to books that pertain to hunting, fishing and appeal to gun enthusiasts. Submit outline and sample chapters.

Recent Nonfiction Title: *Modern Beretta Firearms*, by Gene Gangarosa.

STONEYDALE PRESS, 205 Main St., Stevensville MT 59870. (406)777-2729. Publisher: Dale A. Burk. Estab. 1976. Publishes hardcover and trade paperback originals. Publishes 4-6 titles/year. Receives 40-50 queries and 6-8 mss/year. 90% of books from unagented writers. Pays 12-15% royalty. Publishes book 18 months after acceptance of ms. Reports in 2 months. *Writer's Market* recommends allowing 2 months for reply. Book catalog available.
Nonfiction: How-to hunting books. "We are interested only in hunting books." Query.

STOREY COMMUNICATIONS/GARDEN WAY PUBLISHING, Schoolhouse Rd., Pownal VT 05261. (802)823-5200. Fax: (802)823-5819. Senior Editor/Director of Acquisitions: Gwen Steege. Estab. 1983. Publishes hardcover and trade paperback originals and reprints. Publishes 25 titles/year. Receives 300 queries and 150 mss/year. 30% of books from first-time authors; 80% from unagented writers. Pays royalty or makes outright purchase. Publishes book 2 years after acceptance of ms. Simultaneous submissions OK. Query for electronic submissions. Reports in 1 month on queries, 3 months on proposals and mss. Book catalog and ms guidelines free on request.
Nonfiction: Cookbook, how-to, children's/juvenile. Subjects include agriculture/horticulture, animals, building, cooking/foods/nutrition, crafts, gardening, hobbies, nature/environment. Submit proposal package, including outline, sample chapter, competitive books, author résumé. "Occasionally" reviews artwork/photos as part of the freelance ms package.

SUCCESS PUBLISHING, P.O. Box 30965, Palm Beach Gardens FL 33420. (407)626-4643. Fax: (407)775-1693. President: Allan H. Smith. Submission Manager: Robin Garretson. Estab. 1982. Publishes trade paperback originals. Averages 6 titles/year. Receives 200 submissions annually. 75% of books from first-time authors; 100% from unagented writers. Pays 7% royalty. Publishes book an average of 3 months after acceptance. Simultaneous submissions OK. Reports in 2 months on queries. Book catalog and ms guidelines for #10 SAE with 2 first-class stamps.
Nonfiction: How-to, humor, self-help. Business and economics, hobbies, money/finance. "We are looking for books on how-to subjects such as home business and sewing." Query.
• Success Publishing is looking for ghostwriters.
Recent Nonfiction Title: *How To Write A "How To" Book*, by Smith (how-to).
Tips: "Our audience is made up of housewives, hobbyists and owners of home-based businesses. If I were a writer trying to market a book today, I would read books about how to market a self-written book."

‡SULZBURGER & GRAHAM PUBLISHING, LTD., 165 W. 91st St., New York NY 10024. Publisher: Neil Blond. Imprints are Human Services Institute, Blond's Law Guides, Carroll Press. Publishes hardcover and trade paperback originals and reprints. Publishes 35 titles/year. Publishes 10-15 imprint titles/year. Receives 400 queries and 100 mss/year. 80% of books from first-time authors; 95% from unagented writers. Pays 0-15% royalty on wholesale price. Offers $100-2,000 advance. Publishes book 6 months after acceptance of ms. Simultaneous submissions OK. Query for electronic submissions. Reports in 2 months on queries and proposals, 4 months on mss. Book catalog for 8×11 SAE with 4 first-class stamps. Manuscript guidelines for #10 SASE.
Nonfiction: How-to, reference, self-help, technical, textbook. Subjects include business and economics, child guidance/parenting, computers and electronics, education, health/medicine, hobbies, money/finance, psychology, recreation, science, software, travel, women's issues/studies. Query with outline and 1 sample chapter. Reviews artwork/photos as part of freelance ms package. Writers should send photocopies.
Recent Nonfiction Title: *Gross Anatomy*, by John Tesoriero, Ph.D. (study guide); *Single Fatherhood*, by Chuck Gregg, Ph.D. (self-help); *From Contact to Contract: A Teacher's Employment Guide*, by Anthony and Roe (self-help).

SUNBELT MEDIA, INC., P.O. Box 90159, Austin TX 78709-0159. (512)288-1771. Fax: (512)288-1813. Imprints are Eakin Press and Nortex Press. Editorial Director: Edwin M. Eakin. Estab. 1978. Publishes hardcover and paperback originals and reprints. Averages 35 titles/year. Receives 500 submissions annually. 50% of books from first-time authors; 90% from unagented writers. Average print order for a first book is 2,000-5,000. Pays 10-12-15% on net sales as royalty. Publishes book an average of 12-18 months after acceptance. Simultaneous submissions OK. Query for electronic submissions. Reports in 3 months. Book catalog and ms guidelines for #10 SAE with 4 first-class stamps.
Nonfiction: Adult nonfiction categories include Western Americana, African American studies, business, sports, biographies, Civil War, cookbooks, regional Texas history. Juvenile nonfiction includes biographies

---

For information on book publishers' areas of interest, see the nonfiction and fiction sections in the Book Publishers Subject Index.

of historic personalities, prefer with Texas or regional interest, or nature studies. Easy read illustrated books for grades 1-3. *Writer's Market* recommends query with SASE first.
Recent Nonfiction Title: *Talk That Talk Some More*, by Marian Barnes.
Fiction: No longer publishes adult fiction. Juvenile fiction for grades four through seven, preferably relating to Texas and the southwest or contemporary. Query or submit outline/synopsis and sample chapters.

SUNSTONE PRESS, Imprint of Sunstone Corporation. P.O. Box 2321, Santa Fe NM 87504-2321. (505)988-4418. President: James C. Smith Jr. Estab. 1971. Other imprint is Sundial Publications. Publishes paperback originals; few hardcover originals. Averages 20 titles/year. Receives 400 submissions annually. 70% of books from first-time authors; 100% from unagented writers. Average print order for a first book is 2,000-5,000. Pays royalty on wholesale price. Publishes book an average of 1 year after acceptance. Reports in 1 month. Book catalog for 9×12 SAE with 3 first-class stamps.
  ● The focus of this publisher is still Southwestern US but it receives many, many submissions outside this subject, unfortunately.
Nonfiction: How-to series craft books. Books on the history and architecture of the Southwest. "Looks for strong regional appeal (Southwestern)." *Writer's Market* recommends query with SASE first. Reviews artwork/photos as part of ms package.
Recent Nonfiction Title: *Kachina Tales from the Indian Pueblos*, by Gene Hodge.
Fiction: Publishes material with Southwestern theme. *Writer's Market* recommends query with SASE first.
Recent Fiction Title: *Tubar*, by John Tilley.

‡SWAN-RAVEN & CO., Imprint of Blue Water Publishing, Inc., P.O. Box 726, Newberg OR 97132. (503)538-0264. President: Pam Meyer. Publishes trade paperback originals. Publishes 6 titles/year. Receives 25 queries and 15 mss/year. 80% of books from first-time authors; 90% from unagented writers. Pays 5-12% royalty on wholesale price. Publishes book 7-16 months after acceptance of ms. Accepts simultaneous submissions. Query for electronic submissions. Reports in 1 month on mss. Book catalog free on request. Manuscript guidelines for #10 SASE.
Nonfiction: UFO. Subjects include health, philosophy, software, women's issues/studies, spiritual, future speculation. Query with outline. Reviews artwork/photos as part of ms package. Writers should send photocopies.
Recent Nonfiction Title: *Ritual: Power, Healing and Community*, by Malidema Somé.
Fiction: Juvenile.

SYBEX, INC., 2021 Challenger Dr., Alameda CA 94501. (510)523-8233. Fax: (510)523-2373. Editor-in-Chief: Dr. Rudolph S. Langer. Acquisitions Editor and Manager: Joanne Cuthbertson. Estab. 1976. Publishes paperback originals. Averages 120 titles/year. Royalty rates vary. Offers average $3,000 advance. Publishes book an average of 3 months after acceptance. Simultaneous submissions OK. Query for electronic submissions. Reports in up to 6 months. Free book catalog.
Nonfiction: Computers, computer software. "Manuscripts most publishable in the field of personal computers, desktop computer business applications, hardware, programming languages, and telecommunications." Submit outline and 2-3 sample chapters. Looks for "clear writing; technical accuracy; logical presentation of material; and good selection of material, such that the most important aspects of the subject matter are thoroughly covered; well-focused subject matter; and well-thought-out organization that helps the reader understand the material." Reviews artwork/photos as part of ms package.
Tips: Queries/mss may be routed to other editors in the publishing group.

SYRACUSE UNIVERSITY PRESS, 1600 Jamesville Ave., Syracuse NY 13244-5160. (315)443-5534. Fax: (315)443-5545. Executive Editor: Cynthia Maude-Gembler. Estab. 1943. Averages 30 titles/year. Receives 400 submissions annually. 40% of books from first-time authors; 95% from unagented writers. Subsidy publishes (nonauthor) 20% of books. Pays royalty on net sales. Publishes book an average of 15 months after acceptance. Simultaneous submissions discouraged. Reports in 2 months. Book catalog and ms guidelines for 9×12 SAE with 3 first-class stamps.
Nonfiction: "Special opportunity in our nonfiction program for freelance writers of books on New York state. We have published regional books by people with limited formal education, but authors were thoroughly acquainted with their subjects, and they wrote simply and directly about them. Provide precise descriptions about subjects, along with background description of project. The author must make a case for the importance of his or her subject." Query. Accepts outline and at least 2 sample chapters. Reviews artwork/photos as part of ms package.

TAB BOOKS, Imprint of McGraw-Hill, Inc., Blue Ridge, Summit PA 17294-0850. (717)794-2191. Fax: (717)794-5344. Editorial Director: Ron Powers. Estab. 1964. Imprint is Windcrest computer books (Contact: Brad Schepp). Publishes hardcover and paperback originals and reprints. Publishes 275 titles/year. Receives 600 submissions annually. 50% of books from first-time authors; 85% from unagented writers. Average print order for a first book is 10,000. Pays variable royalty; buys some mss outright for a negotiable fee. Offers advance. Query for electronic submissions. Reports in 3 months. Write for free book catalog and ms guidelines.

Nonfiction: TAB publishes titles in such fields as computer hardware, computer software, business, startup guides, with marine line, aviation, automotive, construction and mechanical trades, science, juvenile science, education, electronics, electrical and electronics repair, amateur radio, shortwave listening, calculators, robotics, telephones, TV servicing, audio, recording, hi-fi and stereo, electronic music, electric motors, electrical wiring, electronic test equipment, video programming, CATV, MATV and CCTV, broadcasting, appliance servicing and repair, license study guides, mathematics, reference books, schematics and manuals, small gasoline engines, two-way radio and CB. Accepts unsolicited proposals. Query with outline. Reviews artwork/photos as part of ms package.

Tips: "Many writers believe that a cover letter alone will describe their proposed book sufficiently; it rarely does. The more details we receive, the better the chances are that the writer will get published by us. We expect a writer to tell us what the book is about, but many writers actually fail to do just that."

TAMBOURINE BOOKS, Imprint of William Morrow & Co., Inc., 1350 Avenue of the Americas, New York NY 10019. (212)261-6500. Estab. 1989. Publishes hardcover originals. Publishes 50 titles/year. Receives 300 queries and 3,000 mss/year. Simultaneous submissions OK. Reports in 3 months on queries. Book catalog for 9×12 SASE. Manuscript guidelines for #10 SASE.

Nonfiction and Fiction: Children's trade books, preschool through young adult. Primary emphasis on picture books and fiction. Reviews artwork/photos as part of freelance ms package. Writers should send photocopies (color copies).

Recent Nonfiction Title: *Puppy Care and Critters, Too*, by Bill Fleming and Judy Petersen-Fleming.
Recent Fiction Title: *No Milk*, by Jennifer Ericsson.

TAYLOR PUBLISHING COMPANY, 1550 W. Mockingbird Lane, Dallas TX 75235. (214)819-8100. Contact: Editorial Assistant, Trade Books Division. Estab. 1981. Publishes hardcover and softcover originals. Averages 30 titles/year. Receives 1,000 submissions annually. 25% of books from first-time authors; 25% from unagented writers. Buys some mss outright. Publishes book 18 months after acceptance. Simultaneous submissions OK. Reports in 2 months. Book catalog and ms guidelines for 9×12 SASE.

Nonfiction: Gardening, nature/outdoors, sports, popular culture, parenting, health, home improvement, popular biography, history, miscellaneous nonfiction. Submit outline and sample chapters. Also submit author bio as it pertains to the proposed subject matter. Reviews artwork/photos as part of ms package.

• No longer seeking true crime, cookbooks, humor, self-help or trivia.
Recent Nonfiction Title: *How I Played the Game*, by Byron Nelson.

TEACHERS COLLEGE PRESS, 1234 Amsterdam Ave., New York NY 10027. (212)678-3929. Fax: (212)678-4149. Director: Carole P. Saltz. Executive Acquisitions Editor: Sarah Biondello. Estab. 1904. Publishes hardcover and paperback originals and reprints. Averages 40 titles/year. Pays royalty. Publishes book an average of 1 year after acceptance. Reports in 2 months. Book catalog free.

Nonfiction: "This university press concentrates on books in the field of education in the broadest sense, from early childhood to higher education: good classroom practices, teacher training, special education, innovative trends and issues, administration and supervision, film, continuing and adult education, all areas of the curriculum, computers, guidance and counseling and the politics, economics, philosophy, sociology and history of education. We have recently added women's studies to our list. The Press also issues classroom materials for students at all levels, with a strong emphasis on reading and writing and social studies." Submit outline and sample chapters.

TEMPLE UNIVERSITY PRESS, Broad and Oxford Sts., Philadelphia PA 19122. (215)204-8787. Fax: (215)204-4719. Editor-in-Chief: Michael Ames. Publishes 70 titles/year. Pays royalty of up to 10% on wholesale price. Publishes book an average of 1 year after acceptance. Query for electronic submissions. Reports in 2 months. Book catalog free.

Nonfiction: American history, sociology, women's studies, health care, ethics, labor studies, photography, urban studies, law, Latin American studies, Afro-American studies, Asian-American studies, public policy and regional (Philadelphia area). "No memoirs, fiction or poetry." Uses *Chicago Manual of Style*. Reviews artwork/photos as part of ms package. Query.

TEN SPEED PRESS, P.O. Box 7123, Berkeley CA 94707. (510)559-1600. Acquisitions Editor: Eva Horning. Estab. 1971. Imprints are Celestial Arts and TriCycle Press. Publishes trade paperback originals and reprints. Firm publishes 60 titles/year. Imprint averages 20 titles/year. 25% of books from first-time authors; 50% from unagented writers. Pays 8-12% royalty on retail price. Offers $2,500 average advance. Publishes book an average of 1 year after acceptance. Simultaneous submissions OK. Reports in 2-3 months on queries. Book catalog for 9×12 SAE with 6 first-class stamps. Manuscript guidelines for #10 SASE.

Nonfiction: Cookbook, how-to, reference, self-help. Subjects include business and career, child guidance/parenting, cooking, foods and nutrition, gardening, health/medicine, money/finance, nature/environment, recreation, science. "We mainly publish innovative how-to books. We are always looking for cookbooks from proven, tested sources—successful restaurants, etc. *Not* 'grandma's favorite recipes.' Books about the 'new science' interest us. No biographies or autobiographies, first-person travel narratives, fiction or humorous treatments of just about anything." Query or submit outline and sample chapters.

Recent Nonfiction Title: *Running a One-Person Business*, by Claude Whitmyer, Salli Raspberry and Michael Phillips (business/career).

Tips: "We like books from people who really know their subject, rather than people who think they've spotted a trend to capitalize on. We like books that will sell for a long time, rather than nine-day wonders. Our audience consists of a well-educated, slightly weird group of people who like food, the outdoors and take a light but serious approach to business and careers. If I were a writer trying to market a book today, I would really study the backlist of each publisher I was submitting to, and tailor my proposal to what I perceive as their needs. Nothing gets a publisher's attention like someone who knows what he or she is talking about, and nothing falls flat like someone who obviously has no idea who he or she is submitting to."

TEXAS A&M UNIVERSITY PRESS, Drawer C, College Station TX 77843-4354. (409)845-1436. Fax: (409)847-8752. Editor-in-Chief: Noel Parsons. Editorial Assistant: Diana Vance. Estab. 1974. Publishes 30 titles/year. Subsidy publishes (nonauthor) 25% of books. Pays in royalties. Publishes book an average of 1 year after acceptance. Query for electronic submissions. Reports in 1 month on queries. Book catalog free.

Nonfiction: Natural history, American history, environmental history, military history, women's studies, economics, regional studies. *Writer's Market* recommends query with SASE first.

Recent Nonfiction Title: *The Meaning of Nolan Ryan*, by Nick Trujillo.

TEXAS CHRISTIAN UNIVERSITY PRESS, P.O. Box 30783, TCU, Fort Worth TX 76129-0783. (817)921-7822. Director: Judy Alter. Editor: A.T. Row. Estab. 1966. Publishes hardcover originals, some reprints. Averages 8 titles/year. Receives 100 submissions annually. 10% of books from first-time authors; 75% from unagented writers. Subsidy publishes (nonauthor) 10% of books. Pays royalty. Publishes book an average of 16 months after acceptance. Reports in 3 months on queries.

Nonfiction: American studies, juvenile (Chaparral Books, 10 and up), Texana, literature and criticism. "We are looking for good scholarly monographs, other serious scholarly work and regional titles of significance." Query. Reviews artwork/photos as part of ms package.

Fiction: Adult and young adult regional fiction. Query.

Tips: "Regional and/or Texana nonfiction or fiction have best chance of breaking into our firm."

‡**TEXAS STATE HISTORICAL ASSOCIATION**, 2.306 Richardson Hall, University Station, Austin TX 78712. (512)471-1525. Assistant Director: George Ward. Publishes hardcover and trade paperback originals and reprints. Publishes 8 titles/year. Receives 50 queries and 50 mss/year. 10% of books from first-time authors; 95% from unagented writers. Pays 10% royalty of net cash proceeds. Publishes book 6-12 months after acceptance of ms. No simultaneous submissions. Query for electronic submissions. Reports in 2 months on mss. Book catalog and ms guidelines free on request.

Nonfiction: Biography, coffee table book, illustrated book, reference. Subjects include history. "We are interested primarily in scholarly historical articles and books." Query. Reviews artwork/photos as part of ms package. Writers should send photocopies.

Recent Nonfiction Title: *Art for History's Sake*, by Cecelia Steinfeldt (art history).

TEXAS TECH UNIVERSITY PRESS, Mail Stop 41037, Lubbock TX 79409-1037. (800)832-4042. Fax: (806)742-2979. Managing Editor: Carole Young. Publishes hardcover and trade paperback originals and reprints. Publishes 20 titles/year. Receives 200 queries and mss/year. 10% of books from first-time authors; 80% from unagented writers. Subsidy publishes 50% of books. Decision to subsidy publish is based upon size of the market and cost of production. Pays 5-20% royalty on wholesale price. Publishes book 18 months after acceptance of ms. No multiple submissions. Photocopied submissions OK. Query for electronic submissions. Reports in 1 month on queries, 6 months on mss. Book catalog free on request.

Nonfiction: "Coffee table" book, illustrated book, technical, memoirs, scholarly works; medical books. Subjects include Americana, animals, art/architecture, ethnic, health/medicine, history, language/literature, music/dance, nature/environment, regional (Texas/New Mexico), science. "We will consider all manuscripts that meet our requirements. Competition is stiff, however, and we suggest that authors present well-researched, amply documented, well-written manuscripts. No philosophy, psychology, or business and economics." Query with outline/synopsis and sample chapters or complete ms. Reviews artwork/photos as part of freelance ms package.

Recent Nonfiction Title: *Pumping Granite and Other Portraits of People at Play*, by Mike D'Orso (trade sports & recreation).

Poetry: "We only consider submissions that were finalists or winners in one of the national poetry contests. We also host an invitation-only poetry contest for first book authors." Submit complete ms.

Recent Poetry Title: "The Andrew Poems," by Shelly Wagner (contemporary).

Tips: "Our trade books are for general audiences. Our scholarly books are directed toward specific disciplines."

TEXAS WESTERN PRESS, Imprint of The University of Texas at El Paso, El Paso TX 79968-0633. (915)747-5688. Fax: (915)747-5111. Director: John Bristol. Estab. 1952. Imprint is Southwestern Studies. Publishes hardcover and paperback originals. Publishes 7-8 titles/year. "This is a university press, 41 years old; we offer a standard 10% royalty contract on our hardcover books and on some of our paperbacks as well. We try to treat our authors professionally, produce handsome, long-lived books and aim for quality, rather than quantity of titles carrying our imprint." Reports in 2 months. Book catalog and ms guidelines free.

Nonfiction: Scholarly books. Historic and cultural accounts of the Southwest (West Texas, New Mexico, northern Mexico and Arizona). Occasional technical titles. "Our *Southwestern Studies* use manuscripts of up to 30,000 words. Our hardback books range from 30,000 words up. The writer should use good exposition in his work. Most of our work requires documentation. We favor a scholarly, but not overly pedantic, style. We specialize in superior book design." Query with outline. Follow *Chicago Manual of Style*.

Tips: "Texas Western Press is interested in books relating to the history of Hispanics in the US, will experiment with photo-documentary books, and is interested in seeing more 'popular' history and books on Southwestern culture/life."

THE THEOSOPHICAL PUBLISHING HOUSE, Subsidiary of The Theosophical Society in America, 306 W. Geneva Rd., Wheaton IL 60187-0270. (708)665-0130. Fax: (708)665-8791. Senior Editor: Brenda Rosen. Estab. 1968. Imprint is Quest Books. Publishes cloth and trade paperback originals. Averages 12 titles/year. Receives 750-1,000 submissions annually. 20% of books from first-time authors; 80% from unagented writers. Average print order for a first book is 5,000. Pays 12½% royalty on net price. Offers average $3,000 advance. Publishes book an average of 18 months after acceptance. Simultaneous submissions OK. Reports in 2 months. Book catalog free. Manuscript guidelines for SASE.

- Quest gives preference to writers with established reputations/successful publications. Manuscript required on disk if accepted for publication.

Nonfiction: Subjects include self-development, self-help, philosophy (holistic), psychology (transpersonal), Eastern and Western religions, theosophy, comparative religion, men's and women's spirituality, Native American spirituality, holistic implications in science, health and healing, yoga, meditation, astrology. "TPH seeks works that are compatible with the theosophical philosophy. Our audience includes the 'New Age' community, seekers in all religions, general public, professors, and health professionals. No submissions that do not fit the needs outlined above." Accepts nonfiction translations. Query or submit outline and sample chapters. Reviews artwork/photos as part of ms package.

Recent Nonfiction Title: *Celebrate the Solstice: Honoring the Earth's Seasonal Rhythms through Festival and Ceremony*, by Richard Heinberg.

Tips: "The writer has the best chance of selling our firm a book that illustrates a connection between spiritually-oriented philosophy or viewpoint and some field of current interest."

‡THIRD WORLD PRESS, P.O. Box 19730, Chicago IL 60619. (312)651-0700. Publisher: Haki R. Madhubuti. Senior Editor: Bakari Kitwana. Publishes hardcover and trade paperback originals and reprints. Publishes 10 titles/year. Receives 200-300 queries and 200 mss/year. 20% of books from first-time authors; 80% from unagented writers. Pays 7% royalty on retail price. Publishes book 18 months after acceptance of ms. Accepts simultaneous submissions. Query for electronic submissions. Reports in 6 months. Book catalog and ms guidelines free on request.

Nonfiction: Illustrated book, children's/juvenile, reference, self-help, textbook. Subjects include anthropology/archaeology, Black studies, education, ethnic, government/politics, health/medicine, history, language/literature, literary criticism, philosophy, psychology, regional, religion, sociology, women's issues/studies. Query with outline and 5 sample chapters. Reviews artwork/photos as part of ms package. Writers should send photocopies.

Recent Nonfiction Title: *The Rebirth of African Civilization*.

Fiction: Ethnic, feminist, historical, juvenile, literary, mainstream/contemporary, picture books, plays, short story collections, young adult. Query with synopsis and 5 sample chapters.

Recent Fiction Title: *The Sweetest Berry On The Bush*.

Poetry: Submit complete ms.

Recent Poetry Title: *Mis Taken Brilliance*.

THOMAS INVESTIGATIVE PUBLICATIONS, INC., Box 142226, Austin TX 78714. (512)928-8190. Contact: Ralph D. Thomas. Publishes trade paperback originals and reprints. Averages 8-10 titles/year. Receives 20-30 submissions annually. 90% of books from first-time authors; 90% from unagented writers. Pays 10-15% royalty on wholesale or retail price, or makes outright purchase of $500-2,000. Publishes book an average of 1 year after acceptance. Simultaneous submissions OK. Reports in 2 weeks on queries; 1 month on mss. Book catalog for $5.

Nonfiction: How-to, reference, textbook. Subjects include sociology, investigation and investigative techniques. "We are looking for hardcore investigative methods books, manuals on how to make more dollars in private investigation, private investigative marketing techniques, and specialties in the investigative professions." Query or submit outline/synopsis and sample chapters. Reviews artwork/photos as part of ms package.

Tips: "Our audience includes private investigators, those wanting to break into investigation, related trades such as auto repossessors, private process servers, news reporters, and related security trades."

THREE CONTINENTS PRESS, P.O. Box 38009, Colorado Springs CO 80937-8009. Fax: (719)576-4689. Publisher/Editor-in-Chief: Donald E. Herdeck. General Editor: Harold Ames, Jr. Estab. 1973. Publishes hardcover and paperback originals and reprints. Averages 20-30 titles/year. Receives 200 submissions annually. 15% of books from first-time authors; 99% from unagented writers. Average print order for a first book is 1,000. Subsidy publishes (nonauthor) 5% of books. Pays 10% royalty; advance "only on delivery of complete manuscript which is found acceptable; usually $300." Simultaneous submissions OK. State availability of photos/illustrations. Reports in 2 months.
Nonfiction and Fiction: Specializes in African, Caribbean, Middle Eastern (Arabic and Persian) and Asian-Pacific literature, criticism and translation, Third World literature and history. Scholarly, well-prepared mss; creative writing. Fiction, poetry, criticism, history and translations of creative writing. "We search for books that will make clear the complexity and value of non-Western literature and culture, including bilingual texts (Arabic language/English translations). We are always interested in genuine contributions to understanding non-Western culture." Length: 50,000-125,000 words. Query. "Please do not submit manuscript unless we ask for it. We prefer an outline, and an annotated table of contents, for works of nonfiction; and a synopsis, a plot summary (one to three pages), for fiction. For poetry, five to ten sample poems." Reviews artwork/photos as part of ms package.
Recent Nonfiction Title: *Tangier And All That,* by Hugh A. Harter.
Recent Poetry Title: *I Was A Point, I Was A Circle,* (Arabic-English texts), by Houda Naamani.
Tips: "We need a *polished* translation, or original prose or poetry by non-Western authors *only.*"

THUNDER'S MOUTH PRESS, 7th Floor, 632 Broadway, New York NY 10012. (212)226-0277. Publisher: Neil Ortenberg. Estab. 1982. Publishes hardcover and trade paperback originals and reprints, almost exclusively nonfiction. Averages 15-20 titles/year. Receives 1,000 submissions annually. 10% of books from unagented writers. Average print order for a first book is 7,500. Pays 5-10% royalty on retail price. Offers average $15,000 advance. Publishes book an average of 8 months after acceptance. Reports in 3 months on queries. No unsolicited mss.
Nonfiction: Biography, politics, popular culture. *Writer's Market* recommends query with SASE first.
Fiction: Query only.

‡TIA CHUCHA PRESS, A Project of The Guild Complex, P.O. Box 476969, Chicago IL 60647. (312)252-5321. Director: Luis Rodriguez. Publishes trade paperback originals. Publishes 4-6 titles/year. Receives 60-70 queries and 25-30 mss/year. 100% of books from first-time authors; 100% from unagented writers. Pays 10% royalty on wholesale price. Publishes book 6 months after acceptance of ms. No simultaneous submissions. Query for electronic submissions. Reports in 3 months on mss. Book catalog and ms guidelines free on request.
Poetry: "We are a cross-cultural poetry press—not limited to style." Submit complete manuscript.
Recent Poetry Title: *Crossing with Light,* by Dwight Okita.
Tips: Audience is "those interested in strong, multicultural, urban poetry—the best of bar-cafe poetry."

TIARE PUBLICATIONS, P.O. Box 493, Lake Geneva WI 53147-0493. President: Gerry L. Dexter. Estab. 1986. Imprints are Limelight Books and Balboa Books. Publishes trade paperback originals. Publishes 6-12 titles/year. Receives 25 queries and 10 mss/year. 40% of books from first-time authors; 100% from unagented writers. Pays 15% royalty on retail/wholesale price. Publishes book 3 months after acceptance of ms. Query for electronic submission. Reports in 1 month on queries. Book catalog for $1.
Nonfiction: Technical, general nonfiction, mostly "how-to," (Limelight); jazz/big bands (Balboa). "We are always looking for new ideas in the areas of amateur radio, shortwave listening, scanner radio monitoring, monitoring satellite transmissions—how to, equipment, techniques, etc." Query.
Recent Nonfiction Title: *Citizens Guide to Scanning,* by Laura E. Quarantello.

TIDEWATER PUBLISHERS, Imprint of Cornell Maritime Press, Inc., P.O. Box 456, Centreville MD 21617-0456. (410)758-1075. Fax: (410)758-2478. Managing Editor: Charlotte Kurst. Estab. 1938. Publishes hardcover and paperback originals. Imprint averages 7-9 titles/year. Receives 150 submissions/year. 41% of books from first-time authors; 99% from unagented writers. Pays 7½-15% royalty on retail price. Publishes book an average of 1 year after acceptance. Query for electronic submissions. Reports in 2 months. Book catalog for 10×13 SAE with 5 first-class stamps.
Nonfiction: Cookbook, history, illustrated book, juvenile, reference. Subjects are all regional. Query or submit outline and sample chapters. Reviews artwork/photos as part of ms package.
Recent Nonfiction Title: *Chesapeake Bay Skipjacks,* by Pat Vojtech.
Fiction: Regional juvenile fiction only. Query or submit outline/synopsis and sample chapters.
Recent Fiction Title: *Chadwick Forever,* by Priscilla Cummings; illustrated by A.R. Cohen.
Tips: "Our audience is made up of readers interested in works that are specific to the Chesapeake Bay and Delmarva Peninsula area."

TIMBER PRESS, INC., Suite 450, 133 SW Second Ave., Portland OR 97204-3527. (503)227-2878. Fax: (503)227-3070. Publisher: Robert B. Conklin. Neal Maillet, acquisitions in horticulture and botany. Dr. Reinhard Pauly, acquisitions in music. Estab. 1976. Imprints are Timber Press (horticulture), Dioscorides Press (botany), Amadeus Press (music). Publishes hardcover and paperback originals. Publishes 40 titles/year. Receives 300-400 submissions annually. 75% of books from first-time authors; 95% of books from unagented writers. Pays 10% royalty. Sometimes offers advance to cover costs of artwork and final ms completion. Publishes book an average of 2 years after acceptance. Query for electronic submissions. Reports in 2 months. Book catalogs for 9 × 12 SAE with 5 first-class stamps.
Nonfiction: Horticulture, botany, plant sciences, natural history, Northwest regional material, classical and traditional music. Accepts nonfiction translations from all languages. Query or submit outline and 3-4 sample chapters. Reviews artwork/photos as part of ms package.
Recent Nonfiction Title: *Plant Propagation Made Easy,* by Alan Toogood.
Tips: "The writer has the best chance of selling our firm good books on botany, plant science, horticulture, or serious music."

‡TIME-LIFE BOOKS INC., Division of Time Warner Inc., 777 Duke St., Alexandria VA 22314. (703)838-7000. Fax: (703)838-7042. Managing Editor: Bobbie Conlan. Estab. 1960. Publishes hardcover originals. Averages 40 titles/year. Books are almost entirely staff-generated and staff-produced, and distribution is primarily through mail order sale. Query to Managing Editor. Reports in 2 weeks.
  • Time-Life is always interested in narrative and how-to writers.
Nonfiction: "General interest books. Most books tend to be heavily illustrated (by staff), with text written by assigned non-staff authors. We almost never accept manuscripts or book ideas submitted from outside our staff."
Recent Nonfiction Title: *Journey through the Mind and Body* (series).

TIMES BOOKS, Imprint of Random House, Inc., 201 E. 50 St., New York NY 10022. (212)872-8110. Vice President and Publisher: Peter Osnos. Editorial Director: Steve Wasserman. Publishes hardcover and paperback originals and reprints. Publishes 50-60 titles/year. Pays royalty. Offers average advance. Publishes book an average of 1 year after acceptance. *Writer's Market* recommends allowing 2 months for reply.
Nonfiction: Business/economics, science and medicine, history, biography, women's issues, the family, cookbooks, current affairs. Accepts only solicited mss. *Writer's Market* recommends query with SASE first. Reviews artwork/photos as part of ms package.
Recent Nonfiction Title: *Somebody Somewhere: Breaking Free From The World of Autism,* by Donna Williams.

TOR BOOKS, Subsidiary of St. Martin's Press, 14th Floor, 175 Fifth Ave., New York NY 10010. (212)388-0100. Fax: (212)388-0191. Publisher: Tom Doherty. Editor-in-Chief: Robert Gleason. Estab. 1980. Publishes mass market, hardcover and trade paperback originals and reprints. Averages 250 books/year. Pays 6-8% royalty. Offers negotiable advance. Reports in 4 months. Book catalog for 9 × 12 SAE with 2 first-class stamps.
  • TOR publishes selected nonfiction. Query first.
Fiction: Science fiction, fantasy, horror, techno-thrillers, "women's" suspense, American historicals. "We prefer an extensive chapter-by-chapter synopsis and the first three chapters complete." Prefers agented mss or proposals.
Recent Fiction Title: *Zero Coupon,* by Paul Erdman.
Tips: "We're never short of good sci fi or fantasy, but we're always open to solid, technologically knowledgeable hard science fiction or thrillers by writers with solid expertise."

‡TRANSNATIONAL PUBLISHERS, INC., One Bridge St., Irvington NY 10533. (914)591-4288. Editor: Marc Fenton. Publishes hardcover and trade paperback originals. Publishes 10 titles/year. Receives 60 queries and 30 mss/year. Pays 10% minimum royalty on wholesale or retail price; depends on contract. Publishes book 3-6 months after acceptance of ms. Accepts simultaneous submissions. Query for electronic submissions. Reports in 2 weeks on queries. Book catalog and ms guidelines free on request.
Nonfiction: Textbooks, law books. Subjects include law, environment, women's rights, human rights. Query with outline and 1 sample chapter.

TRANSPORTATION TRAILS, Imprint of National Bus Trader, Inc., 9698 W. Judson Rd., Polo IL 61064-9015. (815)946-2341. Fax: (815)946-2347. Editor: Larry Plachno. Estab. 1977. Publishes hardcover, trade paperback and mass market paperback originals. Publishes 8 titles/year. Receives 10 submissions/year. 50% of books from first-time authors; 100% from unagented writers. Pays 10-15% on retail price. Publishes book an average of 1 year after acceptance. Simultaneous submissions OK. Reports in 1 month. *Writer's Market* recommends allowing 2 months for reply. Free book catalog and ms guidelines.
Nonfiction: "We are interested in transportation history—prefer electric interurban railroads or trolley lines but will consider steam locomotives, horsecars, buses, aviation and maritime." Query. Reviews artwork/photos as part of ms package.
  • This publisher is also interested in books on family cohesion and the need for Christian values in America.

Tips: "We are not interested in travel nonfiction."

TREND BOOK DIVISION, P.O. Box 611, St. Petersburg FL 33731-0611. (813)821-5800. Fax: (813)822-5083. Chairman: Andrew Barnes. President: Andrew Corty. Publisher: Lynda Keever. Contact: Jerry Cascy. Estab. 1958. Publishes paperback originals and reprints. Specializes in books on Florida—all categories. Pays royalty. No advance. Books are marketed through *Florida Trend* magazine. Publishes book an average of 8 months after acceptance. Reports in 1 month.
Nonfiction: Business, economics, history, law, politics, reference, textbooks, travel. "All books pertain to Florida." Query. Reviews artwork/photos as part of ms package.
Tips: "We are shifting to more emphasis on books of a Florida business/economics nature."

TSR, INC., P.O. Box 756, Lake Geneva WI 53147. (414)248-3625. Estab. 1975. Executive Editor: Brian Thomsen. Imprints are TSR™ Books, Dungeons & Dragons Books, Dragonlance® Books, Forgotten Realms™ Books, Ravenloft™ Books, and Dark Sun™ Books. Publishes hardcover and trade paperback originals and trade paperback reprints. Publishes 40-50 titles/year. Receives 600 queries and 300 mss/year. 10% of books from first-time authors; 20% from unagented authors. Pays 4-8% royalty on retail price. Offers $4,000-10,000 average advance. Publishes book an average of 6-12 months after acceptance. Simultaneous submissions OK. Query for electronic submissions. Send to submissions editor. Reports in 2 months on queries.
Nonfiction: "All of our nonfiction books are generated inhouse."
Fiction: Fantasy, gothic, humor, science fiction short story collections, young adult. "We have a very small market for good science fiction and fantasy for the TSR Book line, but also need samples from writers willing to do work-for-hire for our other lines. No excessively violent or gory fantasy or science fiction." Query with outline/synopsis and 3 sample chapters.
Recent Fiction Title: *Elfsong*, by Elaine Cunningham; *Hederick the Theocrat*, by Ellen Dodge Severson.
Tips: "Our audience is comprised of highly imaginative 12-40 year-old males."

‡TWAYNE PUBLISHERS, Imprint of Simon & Schuster, 866 Third Ave., New York NY 10022. (212)702-2000. Publishes hardcover and paperback originals. Publishes 100 titles/year. Receives 1,000 submissions annually. 5% of books from first-time authors; 90% from unagented writers. Pays royalty. Reports in 4 months on queries.
Nonfiction: Publishes scholarly books and volumes in series for the general and academic reader. Literary criticism, biography, history, women's studies, film studies, current affairs, social science. Query only.
Recent Nonfiction Title: *Jane Austen*, by John Lauber; *Garrison Keillor*, by Peter A. Scholl.
Tips: "Queries may be routed to other editors in the publishing group. Unsolicited manuscripts will not be read."

TWIN PEAKS PRESS, P.O. Box 129, Vancouver WA 98666-0129. (206)694-2462. President: Helen Hecker. Estab. 1984. Publishes hardcover and trade paperback originals and reprints. Averages 7-10 titles/year. Receives 1,000 submissions/year. 25% of books from first-time authors; 100% from unagented writers. Payment varies by individual agreement. Publishes book an average of 6 months after acceptance. Simultaneous submissions OK. *Does not report unless interested.* Do *not* send unsolicited mss.
Nonfiction: General nonfiction.
Fiction: All topics.

TYNDALE HOUSE PUBLISHERS, INC., 351 Executive Dr., P.O. Box 80, Wheaton IL 60189-0080. (708)668-8300. Vice President, Editorial: Ronald Beers. Contact: Marilyn Dellorto. Estab. 1962. Publishes hardcover and trade paperback originals and mass paperback reprints. Averages 100 titles/year. 5-10% of books from first-time authors. Average first print order for a first book is 5,000-10,000. Royalty and advance negotiable. Publishes book an average of 12-18 months after acceptance. Send query and synopsis, not whole ms. Reviews solicited mss only. Reports in up to 3 months. Book catalog and ms guidelines for 9×12 SAE with 9 first-class stamps.
Nonfiction: "Practical, user-friendly Christian books: home and family, Christian growth/self-help, devotional/inspirational, theology/Bible doctrine, children's nonfiction, contemporary/critical issues." Query.
Fiction: "Biblical, historical and other Christian themes. No short story collections. Youth books: character building stories with Christian perspective. Especially interested in ages 10-14." Query.

‡ULI, THE URBAN LAND INSTITUTE, 625 Indiana Ave. NW, Washington DC 20004-2930. (202)289-8500. Fax: (202)624-7140. Vice President/Publisher: Frank H. Spink, Jr. Estab. 1936. Publishes hardcover and trade paperback originals. Averages 15-20 titles/year. Receives 20 submissions annually. 0% from first-time authors; 100% from unagented writers. Pays 10% royalty on gross sales. Offers advance of $1,500-2,000. Publishes book an average of 6 months after acceptance. Query for electronic submissions. Book catalog and ms guidelines for 9×12 SAE.
Nonfiction: Technical books on real estate development and land planning. "The majority of manuscripts are created in-house by research staff. We acquire two or three outside authors to fill schedule and subject

areas where our list has gaps. We are not interested in real estate sales, brokerages, appraisal, making money in real estate, opinion, personal point of view, or mss negative toward growth and development." Query. Reviews artwork/photos as part of ms package.

Recent Nonfiction Title: *Golf Course Development and Real Estate*, by Guy Rondo and Desmond Muirhead.

ULYSSES PRESS, Suite 1, 3286 Adeline St., Berkeley CA 94703. (510)601-8301. Editorial Director: Leslie Henriques. Estab. 1982. Publishes trade paperback originals. Averages 15 titles/year. 25% of books from first-time authors; 75% from unagented writers. Pays 12-16% royalty on wholesale price. Offers $2,000-8,000 advance. Publishes book 6 months after acceptance. Simultaneous submissions OK. Query for electronic submissions. Reports in 2 months on proposals. Book catalog free on request.

● Ulysses is rapidly expanding its line of health books and is very interested in looking at proposals in this area.

Nonfiction: Travel, health. Submit proposal package including outline, 2 sample chapters, and market analysis. Reviews artwork/photos as part of freelance ms package. Writers should send photocopies.

Recent Nonfiction Title: Publishes three series of travel guidebooks—*Hidden, Ultimate* and the *The New Key to* . . . .

UMBRELLA BOOKS, Imprint of Epicenter Press Inc., Box 82368, Kenmore Station, Seattle WA 98028-0368. (206)485-6822. President: Kent Sturgis. Estab. 1988. Publishes 4-6 titles/year. Pays royalty on net price. Publishes book an average of 1 year after acceptance. Query for electronic submissions. Reports in 3 months on queries. Manuscript guidelines for #10 SASE.

● Umbrella welcomes marketing and promotion ideas.

Nonfiction: Travel (West Coast and Alaska). Query; do *not* send photos.

‡UNITY BOOKS, Unity School of Christianity, Unity Village MO 64065. (816)524-3550 x3190. Associate Editor: Gayle Revelle. Publishes hardcover and trade paperback originals and reprints. Publishes 14 titles/year. Receives 25 queries and 100-120 mss/year. 30% of books from first-time authors; 95% from unagented writers. Pays 10-11.5% royalty on retail price. Offers $250 advance. Publishes book 11 months after acceptance of ms. Accepts simultaneous submissions. Query for electronic submissions. Reports in 1 month on queries and proposals; 2 months on mss. Book catalog and ms guidelines free on request.

Nonfiction: Children's/juvenile, reference (spiritual/metaphysical), self-help. Subjects include health/medicine (nutrition/holistic), philosophy (perennial/new thought), psychology (transpersonal), religion (spiritual/metaphysical Bible interpretation/modern Biblical studies). "Writers should be familiar with principles of metaphysical Christianity but not feel bound by them. We are interested in works in the related fields of holistic health, spiritual psychology as well as the philosophy of other world religions." Query with outline and 3 sample chapters. Reviews artwork/photos as part of ms package. Writers should send photocopies.

Recent Nonfiction Title: *Spiritual Economics*, by Eric Butterworth (spiritual approach to prosperity).

Fiction: Picture books (spiritual/inspirational), religious, metaphysical. Query with synopsis and 3 sample chapters.

Recent Fiction Title: *Ted Bear's Magic Swing*, by Dianne Baker (picture book).

UNIVELT, INC., P.O. Box 28130, San Diego CA 92198. (619)746-4005. Fax: (619)746-3139. Publisher: Robert H. Jacobs. Estab. 1970. Imprints are American Astronautical Society, National Space Society, Lunar & Planetary Institute. Publishes hardcover originals. Averages 8 titles/year. Receives 20 submissions annually. 5% of books from first-time authors; 5% from unagented writers. Subsidy publishes (nonauthor) 10% of books. Average print order for a first book is 1,000-2,000. Pays 10% royalty on actual sales. No advance. Publishes book an average of 4 months after acceptance. Reports in 1 month. *Writer's Market* recommends allowing 2 months for reply. Book catalog and ms guidelines for SASE.

Nonfiction: Publishes in the field of aerospace, especially astronautics and technical communications, but including application of aerospace technology to Earth's problems, also astronomy. Submit outline and 1-2 sample chapters. Reviews artwork/photos as part of ms package.

Tips: "Writers have the best chance of selling manuscripts on the history of astronautics (we have a history series) and astronautics/spaceflight subjects. We publish for the American Astronautical Society. Queries may be routed to other editors in the publishing group."

UNIVERSITY OF ALABAMA PRESS, P.O. Box 870380, Tuscaloosa AL 35487-0380. Fax: (205)348-9201. Director: Malcolm MacDonald. Estab. 1945. Publishes hardcover originals. Averages 40 titles/year. Receives 200 submissions annually. 80% of books from first-time authors; 100% from unagented writers. "Pays maximum 10% royalty on wholesale price. No advance." Publishes book an average of 16 months after acceptance. Free book catalog. Manuscript guidelines for SASE.

● University of Alabama Press responds to an author immediately upon receiving the manuscript. If they think it is unsuitable for Alabama's program, they tell the author at once. If the manuscript warrants it, they begin the peer-review process, which may take two to four months to complete. During that process, they keep the author fully informed.

Nonfiction: Biography, history, politics, religion, literature, archaeology. Considers upon merit almost any subject of scholarly interest, but specializes in speech communication, political science and public administration, literary criticism and biography, and history. Accepts nonfiction translations. Reviews artwork/photos as part of ms package.

Tips: "The University Press does not commission projects with freelance writers. Some who submit their manuscripts to us are independent scholars who have written on speculation, but they are not freelancers in the commonly accepted meaning of that word."

UNIVERSITY OF ALASKA PRESS, P.O. Box 756240, 1st Floor Gruening Bldg., UAF, Fairbanks AK 99775-6240. (907)474-6389. Fax: (907)474-5502. Manager: Debbie Van Stone. Acquisitions: Pam Odom. Estab. 1967. Imprints are Ramuson Library Historical Translation Series, Lanternlight Library, Oral Biographies, and Classic Reprints. Publishes hardcover originals and trade paperback originals and reprints. Averages 5-10 titles/year. Receives 100 submissions/year. 0% of books from first-time authors; 100% from unagented writers. Pays 7½-10% royalty on net sales. Publishes book an average of 2 years after acceptance. Query for electronic submissions. Reports in 2 months. Book catalog free on request.

Nonfiction: Biography, reference, technical, textbook, scholarly nonfiction relating to Alaska-circumpolar regions. Subjects include agriculture/horticulture, Americana (Alaskana), animals, anthropology/archaeology, art/architecture, education, ethnic, government/politics, health/medicine, history, language, military/war, nature/environment, regional, science, translation. Nothing that isn't northern or circumpolar. Query or submit outline. Reviews copies of artwork/photos as part of ms package.

Tips: "Writers have the best chance with scholarly nonfiction relating to Alaska, the circumpolar regions and North Pacific Rim. Our audience is made up of scholars, historians, students, libraries, universities, individuals."

UNIVERSITY OF ARIZONA PRESS, #102, 1230 N. Park Ave., Tucson AZ 85719-4140. (602)621-1441. Fax: (602)621-8899. Director: Stephen Cox. Senior Editor: Joanne O'Hare. Estab. 1956. Publishes hardcover and paperback originals and reprints. Averages 50 titles/year. Receives 300-400 submissions annually. 30% of books from first-time authors; 95% from unagented writers. Average print order is 1,500. Royalty terms vary; usual starting point for scholarly monograph is after sale of first 1,000 copies. Publishes book an average of 1 year after acceptance. Query for electronic submissions. Reports in 3 months. Book catalog for 9 × 12 SAE. Manuscript guidelines for #10 SASE.

Nonfiction: Scholarly books about anthropology, Arizona, American West, archaeology, environmental science, global change, Latin America, Native Americans, natural history, space sciences and women's studies. Query and submit outline, list of illustrations and sample chapters. Reviews artwork/photos as part of ms package.

Tips: "Perhaps the most common mistake a writer might make is to offer a book manuscript or proposal to a house whose list he or she has not studied carefully. Editors rejoice in receiving material that is clearly targeted to the house's list, 'I have approached your firm because my books complement your past publications in . . . ,' presented in a straightforward, businesslike manner."

THE UNIVERSITY OF ARKANSAS PRESS, 201 Ozark Ave., Fayetteville AR 72701-1201. (501)575-3246. Fax: (501)575-6044. Director: Miller Williams. Acquisitions Editor: Scot Danforth. Estab. 1980. Publishes hardcover and trade paperback originals and reprints. Averages 36 titles/year. Receives 4,000 submissions annually. 30% of books from first-time authors; 90% from unagented writers. Pays 10% royalty on net receipts from hardcover; 6% on paper. Publishes book an average of 1 year after acceptance. Simultaneous submissions OK (if so informed). Manuscript OK at submission stage but disk must follow on acceptance. Reports in up to 3 months. Book catalog for 9 × 12 SAE with 5 first-class stamps. Manuscript guidelines for #10 SAE with 2 first-class stamps.

Nonfiction: Americana, history, humanities, nature, general politics and history of politics, sociology. "Our current needs include literary criticism, history and biography. We won't consider manuscripts for texts, juvenile or religious studies, or anything requiring a specialized or exotic vocabulary." Query or submit outline and sample chapters.

Recent Nonfiction Title: *Pres: The Story of Lester Young*, by Luc Delannoy.

Fiction: "Works of high literary merit; short stories; rarely novels. No genre fiction." Query.

Recent Fiction Title: *Overgrown with Love*, short stories by Scott Ely.

Poetry: "Because of small list, query first." Arkansas Poetry Award offered for publication of first book. Write for contest rules.

Recent Poetry Title: *In the Dreaming*, by William Dickey.

UNIVERSITY OF CALIFORNIA PRESS, 2120 Berkeley Way, Berkeley CA 94720. Director: James H. Clark. Associate Director: Lynne E. Withey. Estab. 1893. Los Angeles office: 405 Hilgard Ave., Los Angeles CA 90024-1373. New York office: Room 513, 50 E. 42 St., New York NY 10017. UK office: University Presses of California, Columbia, and Princeton, 1 Odlands Way, Bognor Regis, W. Sussex PO22 9SA England. Publishes hardcover and paperback originals and reprints. "On books likely to do more than return their costs, a standard royalty contract beginning at 7% on net receipts is paid; on paperbacks it is less." Publishes

180 titles/year. Queries are always advisable, accompanied by outlines or sample material. Accepts nonfiction translations. Send to Berkeley address. Reports vary, depending on the subject. *Writer's Market* recommends allowing 2 months for reply. Enclose return postage.
Nonfiction: "Most of our publications are hardcover nonfiction written by scholars." Publishes scholarly books including history, art, literary studies, social sciences, natural sciences and some high-level populariza-tions. No length preferences. *Writer's Market* recommends query with SASE first.
Fiction and Poetry: Publishes fiction and poetry only in translation.

UNIVERSITY OF IDAHO PRESS, 16 Brink Hall, Moscow ID 83844-1107. (208)885-5939. Fax: (208)885-9059. Imprints are: Northwest Folklife; Idaho Yesterdays; Northwest Naturalist Books. Director: Peggy Pace. Estab. 1972. Publishes hardcover and trade paperback originals and reprints. Publishes 8-10 titles/year. Receives 150-250 queries and 25-50 mss/year. 100% of books from unagented writers. Pays up to 10% royalty on net sales. Publishes book 1 year after acceptance of ms. Query for electronic submissions. Reports in 6 months. Book catalog and ms guidelines free on request.
Nonfiction: Biography, reference, technical, textbook. Subjects include agriculture/horticulture, Americana, anthropology/archaeology, ethnic, folklore, history, language/literature, nature/environment, recreation, re-gional, women's issues/studies. "Writers should contact us to discuss projects in advance and refer to our catalog to become familiar with the types of projects the press publishes. Avoid being unaware of the con-straints of scholarly publishing, and avoid submitting queries and manuscripts in areas we don't publish in." Query or submit proposal package, including sample chapter, contents, vita. Reviews artwork/photos as part of the freelance ms package. Writers should send photocopies.
Tips: Audience is educated readers, scholars.

UNIVERSITY OF ILLINOIS PRESS, 1325 S. Oak St., Champaign IL 61820-6903. (217)333-0950. Fax: (217)244-8082. Director/Editor-in-Chief: Richard L. Wentworth. Contact: Janice Roney. Estab. 1918. Publishes hard-cover and trade paperback originals and reprints. Averages 100-110 titles/year. 50% of books from first-time authors; 95% from unagented writers. Subsidy publishes (nonauthor) 20% of books. Pays 0-10% royalty on net sales; offers average $1,000-1,500 advance (rarely). Publishes book an average of 1 year after acceptance. Query for electronic submissions. Reports in 1 month. *Writer's Market* recommends allowing 2 months for reply. Book catalog for 9×12 SAE and 2 first-class stamps.
Nonfiction: Biography, reference, scholarly books. Subjects include Americana, history (especially American history), music (especially American music), politics, sociology, philosophy, sports, literature. Always looking for "solid scholarly books in American history, especially social history; books on American popular music, and books in the broad area of American studies." Query with outline.
Recent Nonfiction Title: *Thunder Below! The USS Barb Revolutionizes Submarine Warfare in World War II,* by Admiral Eugene B. Fluckey.
Fiction: Ethnic, experimental, mainstream. "We are not presently looking at unsolicited collections of stories. We do not publish novels." Query.
Recent Fiction Title: *Middle Murphy,* by Mark Costello (stories).
Tips: "Serious scholarly books that are broad enough and well-written enough to appeal to non-specialists are doing well for us in today's market."

UNIVERSITY OF IOWA PRESS, 119 W. Park Rd., Iowa City IA 52242-1000. (319)335-2000. Fax: (319)335-2055. Director: Paul Zimmer. Estab. 1969. Publishes hardcover and paperback originals. Averages 35 titles/ year. Receives 300-400 submissions annually. 30% of books from first-time authors; 95% from unagented writers. Average print order for a first book is 1,000-1,200. Pays 7-10% royalty on net price. "We market mostly by direct mailing of fliers to groups with special interests in our titles and by advertising in trade and scholarly publications." Publishes book an average of 1 year after acceptance. Query for electronic submis-sions. Reports within 4 months. Book catalog and ms guidelines free.
Nonfiction: Publishes anthropology, archaeology, British and American literary studies, history (Victorian, US, regional Latin American), jazz studies, history of photography and natural history. Looks for evidence of original research; reliable sources; clarity of organization, complete development of theme with documen-tation and supportive footnotes and/or bibliography; and a substantive contribution to knowledge in the field treated. Query or submit outline. Use *Chicago Manual of Style.* Reviews artwork/photos as part of ms package.
Recent Nonfiction Title: *The Art of the Autochrome,* by John Wood.
Fiction and Poetry: Currently publishes the Iowa Short Fiction Award selections and winners of the Iowa Poetry Prize Competition. Please query regarding poetry or fiction before sending manuscript.
Tips: "Now seeking regional history instead of German and medieval history."

UNIVERSITY OF MASSACHUSETTS PRESS, P.O. Box 429, Amherst MA 01004-0429. (413)545-2217. Fax: (413)545-1226. Director: Bruce Wilcox. Editoral Assistant: Chris Hammel. Estab. 1963. Publishes hardcover and paperback originals, reprints and imports. Averages 30 titles/year. Receives 600 submissions annually. 20% of books from first-time authors; 90% from unagented writers. Average print order for a first book is 1,500. Royalties generally 10% of net income. Advance rarely offered. No author subsidies accepted. Pub-lishes book an average of 1 year after acceptance. Query for electronic submissions. Preliminary report in 1

month. *Writer's Market* recommends allowing 2 months for reply. Book catalog free.
Nonfiction: Publishes African-American studies, art and architecture, biography, criticism, history, natural history, philosophy, poetry, public policy, sociology and women's studies in original and reprint editions. Accepts nonfiction translations. Submit outline and 1-2 sample chapters. Reviews artwork/photos as part of ms package.
Recent Nonfiction Title: *Black Legacy: America's Hidden Heritage*, by William D. Piersen.

UNIVERSITY OF MISSOURI PRESS, 2910 LeMone Blvd., Columbia MO 65201. (314)882-7641. Director: Beverly Jarrett. Publishes hardcover and paperback originals and paperback reprints. Averages 50 titles/ year. Receives 500 submissions annually. 25-30% of books from first-time authors; 90% from unagented writers. Average print order for a first book is 1,000-1,500. Pays up to 10% royalty on net receipts. No advance. Publishes book an average of 1 year after acceptance. Query for electronic submissions. Reports in 6 months. Book catalog free. Manuscript guidelines for SASE.
Nonfiction: Scholarly publisher interested in history, literary criticism, political science, social science, some art history. Also regional books about Missouri and the Midwest. No mathematics or hard sciences. Query or submit outline and sample chapters. Consult *Chicago Manual of Style*.
Fiction: "Collections of short fiction are considered throughout the year; the press does not publish novels. Inquiries should be directed to Clair Willcox, Editor, and should include a table of contents and a brief description of the ms that notes its length."

UNIVERSITY OF NEBRASKA PRESS, Dept. WM, 312 N. 14th St., P.O. Box 880484, Lincoln NE 68588-0484. (402)472-3581. Editor-in-Chief: Daniel J.J. Ross. Estab. 1941. Publishes hardcover and paperback originals and reprints. Specializes in scholarly nonfiction, some regional books; reprints of Western Americana; natural history. Averages 50 new titles, 50 paperback reprints (*Bison Books*)/year. Receives more than 1,000 submissions annually. 25% of books from first-time authors; 95% from unagented writers. Average print order for a first book is 1,000. Royalty is usually graduated from 10% on wholesale price for original books; no advance. Reports in 4 months. Book catalog and guidelines for 9×12 SAE with 5 first-class stamps.
Nonfiction: Publishes Americana, biography, history, nature, photography, psychology, sports, literature, agriculture, American Indian themes. Accepts nonfiction and fiction translations but no original fiction. Query. Accepts outline/synopsis, 2 sample chapters and introduction. Looks for "an indication that the author knows his/her subject thoroughly and interprets it intelligently." Reviews artwork/photos as part of ms package.
Recent Nonfiction Title: *Billy the Kid*, by Robert Utley.
Recent Fiction Title: *Mad Love*, by André Breton (translation).

UNIVERSITY OF NEVADA PRESS, Reno NV 89557-0076. (702)784-6573. Fax: (702)784-6200. Director: Thomas R. Radko. Editor-in-Chief: Nick Cady. Estab. 1961. Publishes hardcover and paperback originals and reprints. Averages 22 titles/year. 20% of books from first-time authors; 99% from unagented writers. Average print order for a first book is 2,000. Pays average of 10% royalty on net price. Publishes book an average of 1 year after acceptance. Preliminary report in 2 months. Book catalog and ms guidelines free.
Nonfiction: Specifically needs regional history and natural history, literature, current affairs, ethnonationalism, gambling and gaming, anthropology, biographies, Basque studies. "We are the first university press to sustain a sound series on Basque studies—New World and Old World." No juvenile books. Submit complete ms. *Writer's Market* recommends query with SASE first. Reviews photocopies of artwork/photos as part of ms package.
Recent Nonfiction Title: *Neon Nevada*, by Sheila Swan and Peter Laufer.

UNIVERSITY OF NEW MEXICO PRESS, 1720 Lomas Blvd. NE, Albuquerque NM 87131-1591. (505)277-2346. Contact: Editor. Estab. 1929. Publishes hardcover originals and trade paperback originals and reprints. Averages 50 titles/year. Receives 500 submissions/year. 12% of books from first-time authors; 90% from unagented writers. Pays up to 15% royalty on wholesale price. Publishes book an average of 1 year after acceptance. Reports in 2 weeks on queries. *Writer's Market* recommends allowing 2 months for reply. Free book catalog.
Nonfiction: Biography, illustrated book, scholarly books. Subjects include anthropology/archaeology, art/ architecture, ethnic, history, photography. "No how-to, humor, juvenile, self-help, software, technical or textbooks." Query. Reviews artwork/photos as part of ms package. Prefers to see photocopies first.
Tips: "Most of our authors are academics. A scholarly monograph by an academic has a better chance than anything else. Our audience is a combination of academics and interested lay readers."

THE UNIVERSITY OF NORTH CAROLINA PRESS, P.O. Box 2288, Chapel Hill NC 27515-2288. (919)966-3561. Director: Kate Douglas Torrey. Publishes hardcover and paperback originals and occasionally, paperback reprints. Specializes in scholarly books and regional trade books. Averages 65 titles/year. 70% of books from first-time scholarly authors; 90% from unagented writers. Royalty schedule "varies." Occasional advances. Query for electronic submissions. Publishes book an average of 1 year after acceptance. Reports in 5 months. Free book catalog; ms guidelines for SASE.

Nonfiction: "Our major fields are American history, American studies and Southern studies." Also, scholarly books in legal history, Civil War history, literary studies, classics, gender studies, oral history, folklore, political science, religious studies, historical sociology, Latin American studies. In European studies, focus is on history of the Third Reich, 20th-century Europe, and Holocaust history. Special focus on general interest books on the lore, crafts, cooking, gardening and natural history of the Southeast. Submit outline/synopsis and sample chapters; must follow *Chicago Manual of Style*. Looks for "intellectual excellence and clear writing. We do *not* publish poetry or original fiction." Reviews artwork/photos as part of ms package.
Recent Nonfiction Title: *Walking the Blue Ridge: A Guide to the Trails of the Blue Ridge Parkway,* by Leonard M. Adkins.

UNIVERSITY OF NORTH TEXAS PRESS, P.O. Box 13856, Denton TX 76203-3856. Fax: (817)565-4590. Director: Frances B. Vick. Editor: Charlotte Wright. Estab. 1987. Publishes hardcover and trade paperback originals and reprints. Publishes 15 titles/year. Receives 300 queries and mss/year. 99% of books from unagented writers. Pays 7½-10% royalty of net. Publishes book 1 year after acceptance of ms. Query for electronic submissions. Reports in 2 months on queries. Book catalog free on request.
Nonfiction: Biography, reference. Subjects include agriculture/horticulture, Americana, computers and electronics, ethnic, government/politics, history, language/literature, military/war, nature/environment, regional. "We have a series called War and the Southwest; Environmental Philosophy Series; Texas Folklore Society Publications series, the Western Life Series. Poetry series—Texas poets; literary biographies of Texas writers series." Query. Reviews artwork/photos as part of freelance ms package. Writers should send photocopies.
Fiction: Literary and short story collections. Submit sample chapters.
Poetry: The Vassar Miller Prize in Poetry is an annual, national competition resulting in the publication of a winning manuscript each fall. Submissions should be sent to Scott Cairns, editor of poetry mss.

UNIVERSITY OF OKLAHOMA PRESS, 1005 Asp Ave., Norman OK 73019-0445. (405)325-5111. Fax: (405)325-4000. Editor-in-Chief: John Drayton. Estab. 1928. Imprint is Oklahoma Paperbacks. Publishes hardcover and paperback originals and reprints. Averages 80 titles/year. Pays royalty comparable to those paid by other publishers for comparable books. Publishes book an average of 12-18 months after acceptance. Query for electronic submissions. Reports in 3 months. Book catalog for $1 and 9 × 12 SAE with 6 first-class stamps.
Nonfiction: Publishes American Indian studies, Western US history, literary theory, natural history, women's studies, classical studies. No unsolicited poetry and fiction. Query, including outline, 1-2 sample chapters and author résumé. Use *Chicago Manual of Style* for ms guidelines. Reviews artwork/photos as part of ms package.

UNIVERSITY OF PENNSYLVANIA PRESS, 418 Service Dr., Philadelphia PA 19104-6097. (215)898-6261. Fax: (215)898-0404. Editorial Director: Timothy Clancy. Estab. 1860. Publishes hardcover and paperback originals and reprints. Averages 70 titles/year. Receives 650 submissions annually. 10-20% of books from first-time authors; 99% from unagented writers. Subsidy publishes (nonauthor) 4% of books. Subsidy publishing is determined by evaluation obtained by the press from outside specialists; approval by Faculty Editorial Committee and funding organization. Royalty determined on book-by-book basis. Publishes book an average of 10 months after delivery of final ms. Query for electronic submissions. Reports in 3 months or less. Book catalog for 9 × 12 SAE with 6 first-class stamps. No unsolicited mss.
Nonfiction: Publishes Americana, literature, women's studies, cultural studies, business, economics, history, medicine, biological sciences, law, anthropology, folklore, art history, architecture. "Serious books that serve the scholar and the professional." Follow the *Chicago Manual of Style*. Query with outline and letter describing project, state availability of photos and/or illustrations to accompany ms, with copies of illustrations. Do not send ms with query. Include résumé or vita.
Recent Nonfiction Title: *Emancipation: The Making of the Black Lawyer, 1844-1944,* by J. Clay Smith, Jr.
Tips: "Queries/manuscripts may be routed to other editors in the publishing group."

UNIVERSITY OF PITTSBURGH PRESS, Dept. WM, 127 N. Bellefield Ave., Pittsburgh PA 15260. (412)624-4110. Fax: (412)624-7380. Editor-in-Chief: Catherine Marshall. Estab. 1936. Publishes hardcover and trade paperback originals and reprints. Averages 55 titles/year. 5% of books from first-time authors; 99% from unagented writers. Pays royalties on net sales (per contract). Publishes books an average of 1 year after acceptance. Query for electronic submissions. Reports in 2 months. Book catalog free on request. Manuscript guidelines for contests for #10 SASE.
Nonfiction: Biography, reference, textbook, scholarly monographs. Subjects include anthropology/archaeology, art/architecture, business and economics, ethnic, government/politics, health/medicine, history, language/literature, music/dance, philosophy, regional, Latin American studies, Russian and East European studies, social and labor history, Milton studies. Query. Reviews artwork/photos as part of ms package.
Recent Nonfiction Title: *Sport in Cuba: The Diamond in the Rough,* by Paula J. Pettavino and Geralyn Pye.
Fiction: Literary. "One title per year, winner of the Drue Heinz Literature Prize." No novels; short fiction (stories) only. Submit complete ms via contest; send SASE for rules.

Recent Fiction Title: *In the Walled City*, by Stewart O'Nan.
Poetry: Seven titles/year; one from previously unpublished author. Submit complete ms via contest; send SASE for rules; authors with previous books send direct to press in September and October.
Recent Poetry Title: *Late Empire*, by David Wojahn.

UNIVERSITY OF SCRANTON PRESS, University of Scranton, Scranton PA 18510-4660. (717)941-7449. Fax: (717)941-4309. Director: Richard Rousseau. Estab. 1981. Imprint is Ridge Row Press. Publishes hardcover originals. Publishes 4 titles/year. Receives 200 queries and 45 mss/year. 60% of books from first-time authors; 100% from unagented writers. Pays 10% royalty. Publishes book 1 year after acceptance of ms. Query for electronic submissions. Reports in 1 month on queries. *Writer's Market* recommends allowing 2 months for reply. Book catalog and ms guidelines free on request.
Nonfiction: Scholarly monographs. Subjects include art/architecture, language/literature, philosophy, religion and sociology. Looking for clear editorial focus: Theology/religious studies; philosophy/philosophy of religion; scholarly treatments; the culture of northeastern Pennsylvania. Query or submit outline and 2 sample chapters.
Poetry: Only poetry related to northeastern Pennsylvania.

THE UNIVERSITY OF TENNESSEE PRESS, 293 Communications Bldg., Knoxville TN 37996-0325. Fax: (615)974-3724. Acquisitions Editor: Meredith Morris-Babb. Estab. 1940. Averages 30 titles/year. Receives 300 submissions annually. 50% of books from first-time authors; 99% from unagented writers. Average print order for a first book is 1,000. Subsidy publishes (nonauthor) 10% of books. Pays negotiable royalty on net receipts. Publishes book an average of 1 year after acceptance. Reports in 2 months. Book catalog for 12×16 SAE with 2 first-class stamps. Manuscript guidelines for SASE.
Nonfiction: American history, cultural studies, religious studies, vernacular architecture and material culture, literary criticism, African-American studies, women's studies, Caribbean, anthropology, folklore and regional studies. Prefers "scholarly treatment and a readable style. Authors usually have Ph.D.s." Submit outline, author vita, and 2 sample chapters. No fiction, poetry or plays. Reviews artwork/photos as part of ms package.
Recent Nonfiction Title: *American Home Life, 1880-1930: A Social History of Spaces and Services*, edited by Jessica H. Foy and Thomas J. Schlereth.
Tips: "Our market is in several groups: scholars; educated readers with special interests in given scholarly subjects; and the general educated public interested in Tennessee, Appalachia and the South. Not all our books appeal to all these groups, of course, but any given book must appeal to at least one of them."

UNIVERSITY OF TEXAS PRESS, P.O. Box 7819, Austin TX 78713-7819. Fax: (512)320-0668. Executive Editor: Theresa May. Estab. 1952. Averages 80 titles/year. Receives 1,000 submissions annually. 50% of books from first-time authors; 99% from unagented writers. Average print order for a first book is 1,000. Pays royalty usually based on net income. Offers advance occasionally. Publishes book an average of 18 months after acceptance. Query for electronic submissions. Reports in up to 3 months. Book catalog and ms guidelines free.
Nonfiction: General scholarly subjects: natural history, American, Latin American and Middle Eastern studies, native Americans, classics, films, biology, contemporary architecture, archeology, anthropology, geography, ornithology, ecology, Chicano studies, linguistics, 20th-century and women's literature. Also uses specialty titles related to Texas and the Southwest, national trade titles, and regional trade titles. Accepts nonfiction and fiction translations (Middle Eastern or Latin American fiction). Query or submit outline and 2 sample chapters. Reviews artwork/photos as part of ms package.
Tips: "It's difficult to make a manuscript over 400 double-spaced pages into a feasible book. Authors should take special care to edit out extraneous material. Looks for sharply focused, in-depth treatments of important topics."

UNIVERSITY PRESS OF COLORADO, P.O. Box 849, Niwot CO 80544-0849. (303)530-5337. Fax: (303)530-5306. Director: Luther Wilson. Estab. 1965. Publishes hardcover and paperback originals. Averages 30 titles/year. Receives 500 submissions annually. 50% of books from first-time authors; 99% from unagented writers. Average print order for a first book is 1,500-2,000. Pays 10-12½-15% royalty contract on net price. No advance. Publishes book an average of 10 months after acceptance. Electronic submissions mandatory. Reports in 3 months. Book catalog free.
Nonfiction: Scholarly, regional and environmental subjects. Length: 250-500 pages. Query first with table of contents, preface or opening chapter. Reviews artwork/photos as part of ms package.
Recent Nonfiction Title: *Rocky Times in Rocky Mountain National Park*, by Karl Hess, Jr.
Tips: "Books should be solidly researched and from a reputable scholar, because we are a university press. We have new series on world resources and environmental issues, and on Mesoamerican worlds."

UNIVERSITY PRESS OF KENTUCKY, 663 S. Limestone, Lexington KY 40508-4008. (606)257-2951. Fax: (606)257-2984. Editor-in-Chief: Nancy Grayson Holmes. Estab. 1951. Publishes hardcover and paperback originals and reprints. Averages 45 titles/year. Payment varies. No advance. Publishes ms an average of 1 year after acceptance. Reports in 2 months on queries. Book catalog free.

Nonfiction: Biography, reference, monographs. "We are a scholarly publisher, publishing chiefly for an academic and professional audience. Strong areas are history, literature, political science, international studies, folklore and sociology. No textbooks, genealogical material, lightweight popular treatments, how-to books or books unrelated to our major areas of interest." Query. Reviews artwork/photos, but generally does not publish books with extensive number of photos.

Recent Nonfiction Title: *Ailing, Aging, Addicted: Studies of Compromised Leadership,* by Bert E. Park, M.D.

Tips: "Most of our authors are drawn from our primary academic and professional audience. We are probably not a good market for the usual freelance writer."

UNIVERSITY PRESS OF MISSISSIPPI, 3825 Ridgewood Rd., Jackson MS 39211-6492. (601)982-6205. Fax: (601)982-6217. Director: Richard Abel. Associate Director and Editor-in-Chief: Seetha Srinivasan. Estab. 1970. Imprint is Muscadine Books (regional trade). Publishes hardcover and paperback originals and reprints. Averages 50 titles/year. Receives 500 submissions annually. 20% of books from first-time authors; 95% from unagented writers. "Competitive royalties and terms." Publishes book an average of 1 year after acceptance. Reports in up to 3 months. Book catalog for 9 × 12 SAE with 3 first-class stamps.

Nonfiction: Americana, biography, history, politics, folklife, literary criticism, ethnic/minority studies, natural sciences, popular culture with scholarly emphasis. Interested in southern regional studies and literary studies. Submit outline and sample chapters and curriculum vita to Acquisitions Editor. "We prefer a proposal that describes the significance of the work and a chapter outline." Reviews artwork/photos as part of ms package.

Fiction: Commissioned trade editions by prominent writers.

UNIVERSITY PRESS OF NEW ENGLAND, (Includes Wesleyan University Press), 23 S. Main St., Hanover NH 03755-2048. (603)643-7100. Fax: (603)643-1540. Director: Thomas L. McFarland. Editor: David Caffry. Estab. 1970. "University Press of New England is a consortium of university presses. Some books — those published for one of the consortium members — carry the joint imprint of New England and the member: Wesleyan, Dartmouth, Brandeis, Brown, Tufts, Universities of Connecticut, New Hampshire, Vermont, Rhode Island and Middlebury. Associate member: Salzburg seminar." Publishes hardcover and trade paperback originals and trade paperback reprints. Averages 60 titles/year. Subsidy publishes (nonauthor) 80% of books. Pays standard royalty. Offers advance occasionally. Query for electronic submissions. Reports in 2 months. Book catalog and guidelines for 9 × 12 SAE with 5 first-class stamps.

Nonfiction: Americana (New England), art, biography, history, music, nature, politics, psychology, reference, science, sociology, regional (New England). No festschriften, memoirs, unrevised doctoral dissertations, or symposium collections. Submit outline and 1-2 sample chapters.

Fiction: Regional (New England) novels and reprints.

UTAH STATE UNIVERSITY PRESS, Logan UT 84322-7800. (801)750-1362. Fax: (801)750-1541. Director: Michael Spooner. Estab. 1972. Publishes hardcover and trade paperback originals and reprints. Averages 6 titles/year. Receives 170 submissions annually. 8% of books from first-time authors. Average print order for a first book is 1,000. Subsidy publishes (nonauthor) 45% of books. Pays royalty on net price. No advance. Publishes book an average of 18 months after acceptance. Query for electronic submissions. Reports in 2 weeks on queries. *Writer's Market* recommends allowing 2 months for reply. Book catalog free. Manuscript guidelines for SASE.

• Utah State University Press is especially interested in supporting Native American writers with scholarly or creative manuscripts.

Nonfiction: Biography, reference and textbook on folklore, Americana (history and politics). "Particularly interested in book-length scholarly manuscripts dealing with folklore, Western history, Western literature. All manuscript submissions must have a scholarly focus." Submit complete ms. *Writer's Market* recommends query with SASE first. Reviews artwork/photos as part of ms package.

Poetry: "Accepting very few creative works at present. Recommend a query before sending manuscript."

Tips: "Marketability of work is more important than ever."

VANDAMERE PRESS, Subsidiary of AB Associates, P.O. Box 5243, Arlington VA 22205. Acquisitions Editor: Jerry Frank. Publishes hardcover and trade paperback originals and reprints. Publishes 8 titles/year. Receives 750 queries and 2,000 mss/year. 50% of books from first-time authors; 90% from unagented writers. Pays royalty on revenues generated. Publishes book 6-24 months after acceptance of ms. Simultaneous submissions OK. Reports in 3 months.

For explanation of symbols, see the Key to Symbols and Abbreviations. For unfamiliar words, see the Glossary.

Nonfiction: Subjects include Americana, biography, child guidance/parenting, education, gardening, history, military/war, recreation, regional, career guide. Submit outline and 1 or 2 sample chapters. Reviews artwork/photos as part of the freelance ms package. Writers should send photocopies.

Fiction: General fiction including adventure, erotica, humor, mystery, suspense. Submit synopsis and 5-10 sample chapters.

Tips: "Authors who can provide endorsements from significant published writers, celebrities, etc. will *always* be given serious consideration. Clean, easy-to-read, *dark* copy is essential. Patience in waiting for replies is essential. All unsolicited work is looked at but at certain times of the year our review schedule will stop." No response without SASE.

‡VENTURE PUBLISHING, INC., 1999 Cato Ave., State College PA 16801. Publishes hardcover originals and reprints. Publishes 6-8 titles/year. Receives 50 queries and 20 mss/year. 40% of books from first-time authors; 100% from unagented writers. Pays royalty on wholesale price. Offers $1,000 advance. Publishes book 9 months after acceptance of ms. Reports in 1 month on queries; 2 months on proposals and mss. Book catalog and ms guidelines free on request.

Nonfiction: Textbook, college academic, professional. Subjects include nature/environment (outdoor recreation management and leadership texts), recreation, sociology (leisure studies), long-term care nursing homes, therapeutic recreation. "Textbooks and books for recreation activity leaders high priority." Submit outline and 1 sample chapter.

THE VESTAL PRESS, LTD., P.O. Box 97, Vestal NY 13851-0097. (607)797-4872. Fax: (607)797-4898. Publisher: Grace L. Houghton. Editor: Karen Bernardo. Estab. 1961. Publishes hardcover and trade paperback originals and reprints. Averages 6-8 titles/year. Receives 50-75 submissions annually. 20% of books from first-time writers; 95% from unagented authors. Pays 10% maximum royalty on net sales. Publishes books an average of 1 year after acceptance. Simultaneous submissions OK. Reports in up to 6 months. Book catalog for $2 and 6×9 SAE with 2 first-class stamps.

Nonfiction: Technical antiquarian hobby topics in antique radio, mechanical music (player pianos, music boxes, etc.), reed organs, carousels, antique phonographs, early cinema history, regional history based on postcard collections. Also publishes titles in woodcarving. Query or submit outline and sample chapters.

Recent Nonfiction Title: *Lon Chaney: The Man Behind the Thousand Faces,* by Michael F. Blake.

VGM CAREER HORIZONS, Imprint of NTC Publishing Group, 4255 W. Touhy Ave., Lincolnwood IL 60646-1975. (708)679-5500. Fax: (708)679-2494. Executive Editor: Anne Knudsen. Editor: Sarah Kennedy. Estab. 1963. Publishes hardcover and paperback originals. Averages 50-55 titles/year. Receives 200-250 submissions annually. 15% of books from first-time authors; 95% from unagented writers. Pays royalty or makes outright purchase. Advance varies. Publishes book an average of 1 year after acceptance. Simultaneous submissions OK. Query for electronic submissions. Reports in 3 months. Book catalog and ms guidelines for 9×12 SAE with 5 first-class stamps.

● VGM is looking for more revision authors to handle rewrites and new editions of existing titles.

Nonfiction: Textbook and general trade on careers in medicine, business, environment, etc. Query or submit outline and sample chapters. Reviews artwork/photos as part of ms package.

Tips: "Our audience is made up of job seekers, career planners, job changers, and students and adults in education and trade markets. Study our existing line of books before sending proposals."

VICTOR BOOKS, Division of Scripture Press Publications, Inc. 1825 College Ave., Wheaton IL 60187-4498. Fax: (708)668-3806. Contact: Acquisitions Editor. Estab. 1934. Publishes hardcover and trade paperback originals. Averages 110-120 titles/year. Receives 1,500-2,000 submissions/year. Royalty on all books, advances on some. Simultaneous submissions OK if specified. Reports in 1 month on queries. *Writer's Market* recommends allowing 2 months for reply. Manuscripts guidelines for #10 SASE; specify general, children's adult novels or academic (BridgePoint). Catalog and guidelines for 4 first-class stamps.

Tips: "All books must in some way be Bible-related by authors who themselves are evangelical Christians. Victor, therefore, is not a publisher for everybody. Only a small fraction of the mss received can be seriously considered for publication. Most books result from contacts that acquisitions editors make with qualified authors, though from time to time an unsolicited proposal triggers enough excitement to result in a contract. A writer has the best chance of selling Victor a well-conceived and imaginative manuscript that helps the reader apply Christianity to his/her life in practical ways. Christians active in the local church and their children are our audience."

VILLARD BOOKS, Random House, 201 E. 50th St., New York NY 10022. (212)572-2720. Publisher and Editor-in-Chief: Diane Reverand. Contact: Melanie Cecka. Estab. 1983. Publishes hardcover and trade paperback originals. Averages 55-60 titles/year. 95% of books are agented submissions. Pays varying advances and royalties; negotiated separately. Simultaneous submissions OK. Query for electronic submissions. *Writer's Market* recommends allowing 2 months for reply.

Nonfiction and Fiction: Looks for commercial nonfiction and fiction. Submit outline/synopsis and up to 50 pages in sample chapters. No unsolicited submissions.

VOYAGEUR PRESS, 123 N. Second St., Stillwater MN 55082. (612)430-2210. Acquisitions Editor: Tom Lebovsky. Publishes hardcover and trade paperback originals. Publishes 20 titles/year. Receives 1,200 queries and 500 mss/year. 10% of books from first-time authors; 90% from unagented writers. Pays royalty. Publishes book 1 year after acceptance of ms. Simultaneous submissions OK. Reports in 3 months. Book catalog and ms guidelines free on request.
Nonfiction: Coffee table book (and smaller format photographic essay books), cookbook, how-to (photography), children's/juvenile. Subjects include natural history, nature/environment, photography, outdoor recreation, regional, travel. Query or submit outline and proposal package. Reviews artwork/photos as part of the freelance ms package. Photographers should send transparencies—duplicates only please and tearsheets.
Tips: "Our audience includes readers interested in wildlife biology and natural history and tourists wishing to learn more about wilderness or urban areas. Please present as focused an idea as possible in a brief submission (1 page cover letter; 2 page outline or proposal). Note your credentials for writing the book. Tell all you know about the market niche and marketing possibilities for proposed book."

WAITE GROUP PRESS, 200 Tamal Plaza, Corte Madera CA 94925. Editor-in-Chief: Scott Calamar. Publishes trade paperback originals. Publishes 30 titles/year. Receives 50 queries and 35 mss/year. 50% of mss from first-time authors; 100% from unagented writers. Pays royalty on wholesale price or makes outright purchase. Publishes book 4 months after acceptance of ms. Query for electronic submissions. Reports in 2 months. Book catalog free on request.
Nonfiction: How-to, reference, self-help, technical. Subjects include computers and software. "We specialize in computer language and computer graphics." Query or submit outline.
Recent Nonfiction Title: *Visual Basic How-to*, by Zane Thomas.
Tips: Audience is "those interested in having fun and learning about their PC's and Macintoshes. We emphasize new technologies and graphics. Agents are not necessary or preferable. Know your subject and please be patient!"

‡WAKE FOREST UNIVERSITY PRESS, P.O. Box 7333, Winston-Salem NC 27109. (910)759-5448. Director: Dillon Johnston. Manager: Candide Jones. Estab. 1976. Publishes hardcover and trade paperback originals. Averages 5 titles/year. Receives 80 submissions/year. Pays 10% on retail price. Offers $500 average advance. Publishes book an average of 6 months after acceptance. Reports in 2 months on queries. Book catalog free.
Nonfiction: Subjects include language/literature. "We publish exclusively poetry and criticism of the poetry of Ireland and bilingual editions of contemporary French poetry." Query.
Recent Nonfiction Title: *First Language*, by Ciaran Carson.
Tips: "Readers of contemporary poetry and of books of Irish interest or French interest are our audience. We are no longer considering books on or about photography."

J. WESTON WALCH, PUBLISHER, P.O. Box 658, Portland ME 04104-0658. (207)772-2846. Fax: (207)772-3105. Editor-in-Chief: Richard S. Kimball. Editor: Jane Coe. Math/Science Editor: Tom Cohn. Computer Editor: Robert Crepeau. Assistant Editor: Kate O'Halloran. Estab. 1927. Publishes paperback originals and software. Averages 75 titles/year. Receives 300 submissions annually. 10% of books from first-time authors; 95% from unagented writers. Average print order for a first book is 700. Offers 10-15% royalty on gross receipts; buys some titles by outright purchase for $100-2,500. No advance. Publishes book an average of 18 months after acceptance. Query for electronic submissions. Reports in 4 months. Book catalog for 9 × 12 SAE with 5 first-class stamps. Manuscript guidelines for #10 SASE.
Nonfiction: Subjects include art, business, computer education, economics, English, foreign language, geography, government, health, history, literacy, mathematics, middle school, music, psychology, science, social studies, sociology, special education. "We publish only supplementary educational material for grades six to twelve in the US and Canada. Formats include books, posters, blackline masters, card sets, cassettes, microcomputer courseware, video and mixed packages. Most titles are assigned by us, though we occasionally accept an author's unsolicited submission. We have a great need for author/artist teams and for authors who can write at third- to tenth-grade levels. We do *not* want basic texts, anthologies or industrial arts titles. Most of our authors—but not all—have secondary teaching experience. *Query first.* Looks for sense of organization, writing ability, knowledge of subject, skill of communicating with intended audience." Reviews artwork/photos as part of ms package.
Recent Nonfiction Title: *The Walch Workplace Skills Series*, by William Webb Sprague.

WALKER AND CO., Division of Walker Publishing Co., 435 Hudson St., New York NY 10014. Fax: (212)727-0984. Contact: Submissions Editor. Estab. 1959. Publishes hardcover and trade paperback originals and reprints of British books. Averages 100 titles/year. Receives 4,500 submissions annually. 50% of books from first-time authors; 50% from unagented writers. Pays varying royalty or makes outright purchase. Advance averages from $1,000-3,000 "but could be higher or lower." Do not telephone submissions editors. Material without SASE will not be returned. *Writer's Market* recommends allowing 3 months for reply. Book catalog and guidelines for 9 × 12 SAE with 3 first-class stamps.

Nonfiction: Biography, business, histories, science and natural history, health, music, nature and environment, parenting, reference, popular science, and self-help books. Query or submit outline and sample chapter. Reviews photos as part of ms package. Do not send originals.
Fiction: Mystery/suspense, juvenile (ages 5 and up), western.
Tips: "We also need preschool to young adult nonfiction, science fiction, historical novels, biographies and middle-grade novels. Query."

WARD HILL PRESS, P.O. Box 04-0424, Staten Island NY 10304-0008. (718)816-9449. Editorial Director: Elizabeth Davis. Estab. 1989. Publishes trade paperback originals. Publishes 4-6 titles/year. Receives 50 or more queries and 25 mss/year. 75% of books from first-time authors; 90% from unagented writers. Pays 6-12% royalty on retail price. Offers $800-1,600 advance. Publishes book 6-12 months after acceptance. Query for electronic submissions. Prefers disk. Reports in 2 months on queries. Book catalog and ms guidelines free on request.
 • Ward Hill Press has narrowed its focus to young adult fiction and nonfiction only.
Nonfiction: Young adult, biography and multicultural fiction and nonfiction for the same age group. Query. Reviews artwork/photos as part of freelance ms package. "Query first." Writers should send photocopies. "No phone calls please."

WARNER BOOKS, Warner Publishing Inc., Time & Life Bldg., 1271 Avenue of the Americas, New York NY 10020. Does not accept unsolicited manuscripts or proposals.

WARREN PUBLISHING HOUSE, INC., P.O. Box 2250, Everett WA 98203-0250. (206)353-3100. Managing Editor: Kathleen Cubley. Estab. 1975. Publishes educational paperback originals. Publishes 12-14 titles/year. Receives 200 queries and 1,000 activity ideas/year. 50% of books from first-time authors; 100% from unagented writers. Makes outright purchase plus copy of book/newsletter author's material appears in. Simultaneous submissions OK. Reports in 2 months. Book catalog and ms guidelines free on request.
 • Warren is no longer accepting picture book manuscripts or any manuscripts at all for children's books, but is still looking for activity book ideas.
Nonfiction: Cookbook, illustrated activity book, children's/juvenile, textbook. Subjects include agriculture/horticulture, animals, art/architecture, child guidance/parenting, cooking, foods & nutrition, education, ethnic, gardening, health/medicine, history, hobbies, language/literature, music/dance, nature/environment, science. "We consider activity ideas that are appropriate for people (teacher/parents) who work with children two to six years old." Query.
Tips: "Our audience is teachers and parents who work with children ages two to six. Write for submission requirements."

WASHINGTON STATE UNIVERSITY PRESS, Pullman WA 99164-5910. (800)354-7360. Fax: (509)335-8568. Director: Thomas H. Sanders. Editors: Glen Lindeman and Keith Peterson. Estab. 1928. Publishes hardcover originals, trade paperback originals and reprints. Averages 10 titles/year. Receives 75-150 submissions annually. 50% of books from first-time writers; 100% from unagented authors. Subsidy publishes 40% of books. "The nature of the manuscript and the potential market for the manuscript determine whether it should be subsidy published." Pay starts at 5% royalty and graduates according to sales. Publishes book an average of 18 months after acceptance. Query for electronic submissions. Reports on queries in 1 month. *Writer's Market* recommends allowing 2 months for reply.
Nonfiction: Biography, academic and scholarly. Subjects include Americana, art, economics, ethnic studies history (especially of the American West and the Pacific Northwest), nature, politics, sociology. "Needs for the next year are quality manuscripts that focus on the development of the Pacific Northwest as a region, and on the social and economic changes that have taken place and continue to take place as the region enters the 21st century. No romance novels, historical fiction, how-to books, gardening books, or books specifically written as classroom texts." Submit outline and sample chapters. Reviews artwork/photos as part of ms package.
Tips: "Our audience consists of scholars, specialists and informed general readers who are interested in well-documented research presented in an attractive format. Writers have the best chance of selling to our press completed manuscripts on regional history. We have developed our marketing in the direction of regional and local history and have attempted to use this as the base around which we hope to expand our publishing program. In regional history, the secret is to write a good narrative – a good story – that is substantiated factually. It should be told in an imaginative, clever way. Have visuals (photos, maps, etc) available to help the reader envision what has happened. Tell the local or regional history story in a way that ties it to larger, national, and even international events. Weave it into the large pattern of history."

FRANKLIN WATTS, INC., Division of Grolier, Inc., 95 Madison Ave., New York NY 10016. (212)686-7070. Editorial Director: John Selfridge. Publishes both hardcover and softcover originals for middle schoolers and young adults. Entire firm publishes 150 titles/year. 10% of books from first-time authors; 80% from unagented writers. Simultaneous queries OK. Reports in 3 months on queries, "if SASE included." Book catalog free.

Nonfiction: History, science, social issues, biography. Subjects include American and world history, politics, natural and physical sciences. Multicultural, curriculum-based lists published twice a year. Strong also in the area of contemporary problems and issues facing young people. No humor, coffee table books, cookbooks or gardening books. Query. No calls or unsolicited mss.

WAYFINDER PRESS, P.O. Box 217, Ridgway CO 81432-0217. (303)626-5452. Owner: Marcus E. Wilson. Estab. 1980. Publishes trade paperback originals. Publishes 3 titles/year. Receives 80 submissions/year. 30% of books are from first-time authors; 90% from unagented writers. Pays 8-12% royalty on retail price. Publishes book an average of 6 months after acceptance. Simultaneous submissions OK. Reports in 2 weeks on queries. Return postage must be included.
Nonfiction: Biography, illustrated book, reference. Subjects include Americana, government/politics, history, nature/environment, photography, recreation, regional, sociology, travel. "We are looking for books on western Colorado: history, sociology, nature, recreation, photo, and travel. No books on subjects outside our geographical area of specialization." Query or submit outline/synopsis and sample chapters. Reviews artwork/photos as part of ms package.
Fiction: Adventure, historical, humor, mystery, picture books. "We are looking for fiction with a specific Colorado perspective." Query or submit outline/synopsis and sample chapters.
Tips: "Writers have the best chance selling us tourist oriented books. The local population and tourists comprise our audience."

‡WEIDNER & SONS, PUBLISHING, P.O. Box 2178, Riverton NJ 08077. (609)486-1755. President: James H. Weidner. Estab. 1967. Publishes hardcover and trade paperback originals and reprints. Imprints are Hazlaw Books, Medlaw Books, Bird Sci Books, Delaware Estuary Press, Tycooly Publishing USA and Pulse Publications. Firm publishes 10-20 titles/year; imprint publishes 10 titles/year. Receives 50 queries and 3 mss/year. 100% of books from first-time authors; 100% from unagented writers. Pays 10% maximum royalty on wholesale price. Average time between acceptance and publication varies with subject matter. Simultaneous submissions OK. Query for electronc submissions. Reports in 1 month on queries. *Writer's Market* recommends allowing 2 months for reply. Book catalog for $1 ("refundable with order").
Nonfiction: Reference, technical, textbook. Subjects include agriculture/horticulture, animals, business and economics, child guidance/parenting, computers and electronics, education, gardening, health/medicine, hobbies (electronic), language/literature, nature/environment, psychology, science and ecology/environment. "We are primarily science, text and reference books. Rarely fiction; never poetry. No topics in the 'pseudosciences': occult, astrology, new age and metaphysics, etc." Query or submit outline and sample chapters. Reviews artwork/photos as part of the freelance ms package. Writers should send photocopies.
Recent Nonfiction Title: *At-Risk: The Vo-Tech Student in Suburban Society.*
Tips: "Our audience consists of scholars, college students and researchers."

SAMUEL WEISER, INC., P.O. Box 612, York Beach ME 03910-0612. (207)363-4393. Fax: (207)363-5799. Editor: Eliot Stearns. Estab. 1956. Publishes hardcover originals and trade paperback originals and reprints. Publishes 18-20 titles/year. Receives 200 submissions annually. 50% of books from first-time authors; 98% from unagented writers. Pays 10% royalty on wholesale or retail price. Offers average $500 advance. Publishes book an average of 18 months after acceptance. Query for electronic submissions. Reports in 3 months. Book catalog free.
Nonfiction: How-to, self-help. Subjects include health, music, philosophy, psychology, religion. "We look for strong books in our specialty field—written by teachers and people who know the subject. Don't want a writer's rehash of all the astrology books in the library, only texts written by people with strong background in field. No poetry or novels." Submit complete ms. *Writer's Market* recommends query with SASE first. Reviews artwork/photos as part of ms package.
Recent Nonfiction Title: *Mysticism*, by Bruno Borchert.
Tips: "Most new authors do not check permissions, nor do they provide proper footnotes. If they did, it would help. We specialize in oriental philosophy, metaphysics, esoterica of all kinds (tarot, astrology, qabalah, magic, etc.). We look at all manuscripts submitted to us. We are interested in seeing freelance art for book covers."

WESCOTT COVE PUBLISHING CO., P.O. Box 130, Stamford CT 06904-0130. President: Julius M. Wilensky. Estab. 1968. Publishes trade paperback originals and reprints. Publishes 4 titles/year. Receives 20 queries and 8 mss/year. 50% of books from first-time authors; 100% from unagented writers. Pays 5-10% royalty on retail price, depending on complexity. Offers $1,500 advance. Publishes book 8 months after acceptance of ms. Simultaneous submissions OK. Reports in 1 month on queries. *Writer's Market* recommends allowing 2 months for reply. Book catalog free on request.
Nonfiction: Cruising guides, nautical books. "Our authors must be longtime expert sailors, familiar with the area they write about." Query with outline and 1 or 2 sample chapters.

WESTPORT PUBLISHERS, INC., #310, 4050 Pennsylvania, Kansas City MO 64111-3051. (816)756-1490. Fax: (816)756-0159. Publisher: Paul Temme. Estab. 1982. Subsidiaries include Media Publishing, Midgard Press (author-subsidy division), Media Periodicals. Publishes hardcover and trade paperback originals. Averages 5-6 titles/year. Receives 125 submissions/year. 50% of books from first-time authors; 100% from unagented writers. Pays royalty. Publishes book an average of 1 year after acceptance. Reports in 2 months on queries. Send SASE with queries and mss.

Nonfiction: Subjects include child guidance/parenting, foods and nutrition, wellness and psychology. Submit query letter and outline with SASE. Reviews artwork/photos as part of ms package.

Recent Nonfiction Title: *Hugs from the Refrigerator*, by James McClearnan, Ed. D.

Tips: "Books with a well-defined audience have the best chance of succeeding. An author must have demonstrated expertise in the topic on which he or she is writing."

‡**WHITE PINE PRESS**, 10 Village Square, Fredonia NY 14063. (716)672-5743. Director: Dennis Maloney. Imprint is Springhouse Editions. Publishes hardcover and trade paperback originals. Publishes 10 titles/year. Receives 200 queries and 150 mss/year. 20% of books from first-time authors; 99% from unagented writers. Pays 5-10% royalty on wholesale price. Offers $250 and up advance. Publishes book 18 months after acceptance of ms. Accepts simultaneous submissions. Query for electronic submissions. Reports in 2 months on queries. Book catalog free on request.

Nonfiction: Textbook. Subjects include ethnic, language/literature, translation, women's issues/studies. Query.

Recent Nonfiction Title: *Surviving Beyond Fear*, edited by Agosin (human rights).

Fiction: Ethnic, literary, short story collections. Query with synopsis and 2 sample chapters.

Recent Fiction Title: *Pleasure in the Word*, edited by Olmos and Gebert (anthology-Latin American literature).

Poetry: "We do a large amount of poetry in translation. We will be starting a poetry contest for US writers this year." Query.

Recent Poetry Title: *Anxious Moments*, by Debeljak (translation/Slovenian).

‡**WHITFORD PRESS**, Imprint of Schiffer Publishing, Ltd., 77 Lower Valley Rd., Atglen PA 19310. (610)593-1777. Managing Editor: Ellen Taylor. Estab. 1985. Publishes trade paperback originals. Averages 3-4 titles/year. Receives 400-500 submissions annually. 50% of books from first-time authors; 90% from unagented writers. Pays royalty on wholesale price; no advances. Publishes on an average of 9-12 months after acceptance and receipt of complete ms. Simultaneous submissions OK. Reports within 3 months. Book catalog free. Manuscript guidelines for SASE.

Nonfiction: How-to, self-help, reference. Subjects include astrology, metaphysics, New Age topics. "We are looking for well written, well-organized, originals books on all metaphysical subjects (except channeling and past lives). Books that empower the reader or show him/her ways to develop personal skills are preferred. New approaches, techniques, or concepts are best. No personal accounts unless they directly relate to a general audience. No moralistic, fatalistic, sexist or strictly philosophical books. Query first or send outline. Enclose SASE large enough to hold your submission if you want it returned.

Tips: "Our audience is knowledgeable in metaphysical fields, well-read and progressive in thinking. Please check bookstores to see if your subject has already been covered thoroughly. Expertise in the field is not enough; your book must be clean, well written and well organized. A specific and unique marketing angle is a plus. No Sun-sign material; we prefer more advanced work. Please don't send entire manuscript unless we request it, and be sure to include SASE. Let us know if the book is available on computer diskette and what type of hardware/software. Manuscripts should be between 60,000 and 110,000 words."

ALBERT WHITMAN AND CO., 6340 Oakton St., Morton Grove IL 60053-2723. (708)581-0033. Editor-in-Chief: Kathleen Tucker. Estab. 1919. Publishes hardcover originals and paperback reprints. Averages 30 titles/year. Receives 5,000 submissions/year. 20% of books from first-time authors; 70% from unagented writers. Pays 10% royalty. Publishes book an average of 18 months after acceptance. Simultaneous submissions OK. Reports in 5 months. Book catalog for 8 × 10 SAE and 2 first-class stamps. Manuscript guidelines for #10 SASE.

Nonfiction: "All books are for ages 2-12." Biography and concept books which are about special problems children have. "We are looking for picture books for young children. No adult subjects, please." Submit complete ms (picture books).

Fiction: "All books are for ages 2-12." Adventure, ethnic, fantasy, historical, humor, mystery, picture books and concept books (to help children deal with problems and concerns). "We need historical fiction and picture books. No young adult and adult books." Submit outline/synopsis and sample chapters (novels) and complete ms (picture books).

Recent Fiction Title: *Two of Everything*, by Lily Toy Hong (folktale).

Tips: "There is a trend toward highly visual books. The writer can most easily sell us a strong picture book text that has good illustration possibilities. We sell mostly to libraries, but our bookstore sales are growing. If I were a writer trying to market a book today, I would study published picture books."

THE WHITSTON PUBLISHING CO., P.O. Box 958, Troy NY 12181-0958. (518)283-4363. Fax: (518)283-4363. Editorial Director: Jean Goode. Estab. 1969. Publishes hardcover originals. Averages 20 titles/year. Receives

100 submissions annually. 50% of books from first-time authors; 100% from unagented writers. Pays 10% royalty on price of book (wholesale or retail) after sale of 500 copies. Publishes book an average of 30 months after acceptance. Reports in up to 6 months. Catalog for $1.

Nonfiction: "We publish scholarly and critical books in the arts, humanities and some of the social sciences. We also publish bibliographies and indexes. We will consider author bibliographies. We are interested in scholarly monographs and collections of essays." Query. Reviews artwork/photos as part of ms package.

‡**WILD FLOWER PRESS**, Imprint of Blue Water Publishing, P.O. Box 726, Newberg OR 97132. (503)538-0264. President: Pam Meyer. Publishes hardcover originals and trade paperback originals and reprints. Publishes 6 titles/year. Receives 50 queries and 45 mss/year. 80% of books from first-time authors; 90% from unagented writers. Pays royalty. Publishes book 6-16 months after acceptance of ms. Accepts simultaneous submissions. Query for electronic submissions. Reports in 2 months on mss. Book catalog and ms guidelines free on request.

Nonfiction: U.F.O. Submit outline. Reviews artwork/photos as part of ms package. Writers should send photocopies.

Recent Nonfiction Title: *Close Extraterrestrial Encounters*, by Richard J. Boylan.

Fiction: Juvenile.

WILDERNESS ADVENTURE BOOKS, P.O. Box 217, Davisburg MI 48350-0217. Fax: (810)634-0946. Editor: Erin Sims Howarth. Estab. 1983. Publishes hardcover and trade paperback originals and reprints. Publishes 6 titles/year. Receives 250 submissions/year. 90% of books from first-time authors; 90% from unagented writers. Pays 5-10% royalty on retail price. Offers $100 average advance. Publishes book an average of 16 months after acceptance. Simultaneous submissions OK. Reports in 2 months.

Nonfiction: Biography, how-to, illustrated book. Subjects include Americana, animals, history, nature/environment, regional, non-competitive sports, travel. Query. Reviews artwork/photos as part of ms package.

WILDERNESS PRESS, 2440 Bancroft Way, Berkeley CA 94704-1676. (510)843-8080. Fax: (510)548-1355. Editorial Director: Thomas Winnett. Estab. 1967. Publishes paperback originals. Averages 5 titles/year. Receives 150 submissions annually. 20% of books from first-time authors; 95% from unagented writers. Average print order for a first book is 5,000. Pays 8-10% royalty on retail price. Offers average $1,000 advance. Publishes book an average of 8 months after acceptance. Reports in 1 month. *Writer's Market* recommends allowing 2 months for reply. Book catalog for 9×12 SASE.

Nonfiction: "We publish books about the outdoors. Most of our books are trail guides for hikers and backpackers, but we also publish how-to books about the outdoors. The manuscript must be accurate. The author must thoroughly research an area in person. If he is writing a trail guide, he must walk all the trails in the area his book is about. The outlook must be strongly conservationist. The style must be appropriate for a highly literate audience." Query or submit outline and sample chapters demonstrating "accuracy, literacy, and popularity of subject area." Reviews artwork/photos as part of ms package.

Recent Nonfiction Title: *California County Summits*, by Gary Seattle.

‡**JOHN WILEY & SONS, INC.**, 605 Third Ave., New York NY 10158. Associate Publisher/Editor-in-Chief: Carole Hall. Publishes hardcover originals and trade paperback originals and reprints. Publishes 250 titles/year. Pays 10% royalty on wholesale price. Publishes book 1 year after acceptance of ms. Accepts simultaneous submissions. Query for electronic submissions. Book catalog free on request.

Nonfiction: Biography, how-to, children's/juvenile, reference, self-help, technical, textbook. Subjects include business and economics, child guidance/parenting, computers and electronics, gay/lesbian, government/politics, health/medicine, history, language/literature, military/war, psychology, science, sociology, software, women's issues/studies. Query.

Recent Nonfiction Title: *Janet Reno: Doing the Right Thing*, by Paul Anderson (biography).

WILLIAMSON PUBLISHING CO., P.O. Box 185, Church Hill Rd., Charlotte VT 05445. (802)425-2102. Editorial Director: Susan Williamson. Estab. 1983. Publishes trade paperback originals. Averages 12 titles/year. Receives 1,000 submissions annually. 50% of books from first-time authors; 80% from unagented writers. Average print order for a first book is 20,000. Pays 10% royalty on sales dollars received. Advance negotiable. Publishes book an average of 1 year after acceptance. Simultaneous submissions OK. Reports in 3 months on queries with SASE. Book catalog for 8×10 SAE with 4 first-class stamps.

● Williamson's biggest success is their *Kids Can!* series with books like *The Kids' Nature Book* and *Kids Create. The Kids' Multicultural Art Book* won the Parents' Choice Gold Award.

Nonfiction: Subjects include children's activity, nonfiction, science, math and history books; education; gardening; careers; psychology; home crafts; parenting; building; animals; cooking and foods; nature; landscaping; children. "Our areas of concentration are children's interactive and project books, family fun and learning books, psychology books, women's issues, cookbooks, gardening, family housing (all aspects), health and education." No children's fiction books, no picture books, photography, politics, religion, diet books, history, art or biography. Query with outline and sample chapters.

Recent Nonfiction Title: *The Kids' Multicultural Art Book*, by Alexandra M. Terzian.
Tips: "We're most interested in authors who are experts in their fields—doers, not researchers. Give us a good, solid manuscript with original ideas and we'll work with you to refine the writing. We also have a highly skilled staff to develop the high quality graphics and design of our books."

WILLOWISP PRESS, INC., Division of Pages, Inc., 801 94th Ave. N., St. Petersburg FL 33702-2426. (813)578-7600. Contact: Acquisitions Editor. Publishes trade paperback originals. 10% of books are from first-time authors; 80% from unagented writers. Pays royalty or buys by outright purchase. Offers varying average advance. Publishes book an average of 9-18 months after acceptance. Simultaneous submissions OK. Electronic submissions "only upon request." Reports in 5 weeks on queries; 2 months on mss. Book catalog for 9 × 12 SAE with 5 first-class stamps. Manuscript guidelines for #10 SASE.
• Willowisp plans to develop a line of pre-school books and welcomes submissions from qualified writers. Also they would like to see strong, tightly-written suspense titles for kids 10-13.
Nonfiction: Illustrated book, juvenile. Subjects include animals, science, sports, environmental, etc. Query with outline. Reviews artwork/photos as part of ms package "rarely."
Recent Nonfiction Title: *10 Women: Political Pioneers*, by Carol J. Perry.
Fiction: (Pre-k through Middle School only). Adventure, humor, juvenile, literary, contemporary, mystery, picture books, romance, science fiction, short story collections, suspense and young adult. "Three to six grade level a prime market for both fiction and nonfiction. Nothing directed at high school; no poetry or religious orientation."
Recent Fiction Titles: *The Congressman's Daughter*, by Patricia Markum.

WILSHIRE BOOK CO., 12015 Sherman Rd., N. Hollywood CA 91605-3781. (818)765-8579. Publisher: Melvin Powers. Senior Editor: Marcia Grad. Estab. 1947. Publishes trade paperback originals and reprints. Publishes 50 titles/year. Receives 5,000 submissions annually. 80% of books from first-time authors; 75% from un-agented writers. Average print order for a first book is 5,000. Pays standard royalty. Offers variable advance. Publishes book an average of 9 months after acceptance. Reports in 2 months.
Nonfiction: Self-help, motivation, inspiration, psychology, recovery, how-to, entrepreneurship, mail order, horsemanship. "We are always looking for books such as *Psycho-Cybernetics, The Magic of Thinking Big, Guide to Rational Living* and *Think and Grow Rich*. We also need manuscripts teaching mail order and entrepreneur techniques. All we need is the concept of the book to determine if project is viable. I welcome phone calls to discuss manuscripts or book ideas with authors." Synopsis or detailed chapter outline, 3 chapters and SASE required. Reviews artwork/photos as part of ms package.
Fiction: Adult fables that teach principles of psychological growth or offer guidance in living.
Tips: "We are looking for such books as *Illusions, The Little Prince, The Greatest Salesman in the World* and *The Knight in Rusty Armor*."

WINDSOR BOOKS, Subisidary of Windsor Marketing Corp., P.O. Box 280, Brightwaters NY 11718-0280. (516)321-7830. Managing Editor: Stephen Schmidt. Estab. 1968. Publishes hardcover and trade paperback originals, reprints, and very specific software. Averages 8 titles/year. Receives approximately 40 submissions annually. 60% of books from first-time authors; 90% from unagented writers. Pays 10% royalty on retail price; 5% on wholesale price (50% of total cost). Offers variable advance. Publishes book an average of 6 months after acceptance. Simultaneous submissions OK. Reports in 2 weeks on queries. *Writer's Market* recommends allowing 2 months for reply. Book catalog and ms guidelines free.
Nonfiction: How-to, technical. Subjects include business and economics (investing in stocks and commodities). Interested in books on strategies, methods for investing in the stock market options market and commodity markets. Query or submit outline and sample chapters. Reviews artwork/photos as part of ms package.
Tips: "Our books are for serious investors; we sell through direct mail to our mailing list and other financial lists. Writers must keep their work original; this market tends to have a great deal of information overlap among publications."

WINDWARD PUBLISHING, INC., P.O. Box 371005, Miami FL 33137-1005. (305)576-6232. Vice President: Jack Zinzow. Estab. 1973. Publishes trade paperback originals. Publishes 6 titles/year. Receives 50 queries and 10 mss/year. 35% of books from first-time authors; 100% from unagented writers. Pays 10-15% royalty on wholesale price. Publishes book 14 months after acceptance of ms. Simultaneous submissions OK. Query for electronic submissions. Reports in 2 weeks on queries. *Writer's Market* recommends allowing 2 months for reply. Book catalog for SASE.
Nonfiction: How-to, illustrated book, children's/juvenile, handbooks. Subjects include agriculture/horticulture, animals, gardening, nature/environment, recreation (fishing, boating, diving, camping), science. Query. Reviews artwork/photos as part of the freelance ms package.
Recent Nonfiction Title: *Florida Mammals*, by Larry Brown.

WINE APPRECIATION GUILD LTD., 155 Connecticut St., San Francisco CA 94107-2414. (415)864-1202. Fax: (415)864-0377. Director: Maurice Sullivan. Estab. 1973. Imprints are Vintage Image, Wine Advisory Board (nonfiction). Publishes hardcover and trade paperback originals, trade paperback reprints, and software.

Averages 12 titles/year. Receives 30-40 submissions annually. 30% of books from first-time authors; 100% from unagented writers. Pays 5-15% royalty on wholesale price or makes outright purchase. Publishes book an average of 18 months after acceptance. Simultaneous submissions OK. Query for electronic submissions. Reports in 3 months. Book catalog for $2.

Nonfiction: Cookbook and how-to—wine related. Subjects include wine, cooking and foods, travel—all wine-related. Submit outline/synopsis and sample chapters. Reviews artwork/photos as part of ms package.

Tips: "Our books are read by wine enthusiasts—from neophytes to professionals, and wine industry and food industry people. We are interested in anything of a topical and timely nature connected with wine, *by a knowledgeable author*. We do not deal with agents of any type. We prefer to get to know the author as a person and to work closely with him/her."

‡WISDOM PUBLICATIONS, 4th Floor, 361 Newbury St., Boston MA 02115. (617)536-3358. Editorial Project Manager: Constance Miller. Publishes hardcover originals and trade paperback originals and reprints. Publishes 8-10 titles/year. Receives 150 queries and 50 mss/year. 50% of books from first-time authors; 95% from unagented writers. Pays 6-10% royalty on wholesale price (net). Publishes book 2 years after acceptance. Query for electronic submissions. Reports in 6 months on mss. Catalog and ms guidelines free on request.

Nonfiction: Reference, self-help, textbook. Subjects include philosophy (Buddhist or Comparative Buddhist/ Western), East-West, Buddhism, Buddhist texts and Tibet. Submit proposal package, including hard copy of ms. Reviews artwork/photos as part of ms package. Writers should send photocopies.

WOODBINE HOUSE, 6510 Bells Mill Rd., Bethesda MD 20817. Editor: Susan Stokes. Estab. 1985. Publishes hardcover and trade paperback books. 80% of books from unagented writers. Pays royalty. Publishes book an average of 18 months after acceptance. Simultaneous submissions OK. Query for electronic submissions. Reports in 2 months. Book catalog and ms guidelines for 6×9 SAE with 3 first-class stamps.

 • Woodbine is less likely to publish illustrated children's books than other children's publishers.

Nonfiction: Primarily publishes books for and about children with disabilities, but will consider other nonfiction books that would appeal to a clearly defined audience. No personal accounts or general parenting guides. Submit outline and sample chapters. Reviews artwork/photos as part of ms package.

Recent Nonfiction Title: *Communication Skills in Children with Down Syndrome,* by Libby Kumin.

Tips: "Before querying, familiarize yourself with the types of books we publish and put some thought into how your book could be marketed (aside from in bookstores). Keep cover letters concise and to the point; if it's a subject that interests us, we'll ask to see more."

WOODBRIDGE PRESS, P.O. Box 209, Santa Barbara CA 93102. (805)965-7039. Editor: Howard Weeks. Estab. 1971. Publishes hardcover and trade paperback originals. Publishes 4-5 titles/year. Receives 500 submissions/year. 60% of books from first-time authors; 80% from unagented writers. Pays 10-15% on wholesale price. Publishes book an average of 8 months after acceptance. Simultaneous submissions OK. Reports as expeditiously as possible with SASE. *Writer's Market* recommends allowing 2 months for reply. Book catalog free.

Nonfiction: Cookbook (vegetarian), self-help. Subjects include agriculture/horticulture, cooking, foods and nutrition, gardening, health, psychology (popular). Query. Reviews artwork/photos as part of ms package.

Recent Nonfiction Title: *Muffin Magic . . . and More,* by Kathleen Mayes.

‡WORDWARE PUBLISHING, INC., 1506 Capitol Ave., Plano TX 75074. (214)423-0090. President: Russell A. Stultz. Publishes trade paperback and mass market paperback originals. Publishes 50-70 titles/year. Receives 100-150 queries and 50-75 mss/year. 40% of books from first-time authors; 95% from unagented writers. Pays 8-12% royalty on wholesale price. Publishes book 6 months after acceptance of ms. Accepts simultaneous submissions. Electronic submissions mandatory; IBM/PC compatible word processing. Reports in 1 month. Book catalog and ms guidelines free on request.

Nonfiction: Reference, technical, textbook. Subjects include computers, electronics. Submit proposal package, including table of contents, 2 sample chapters, target audience summation, competing books.

WRITER'S DIGEST BOOKS, Imprint of F&W Publications, 1507 Dana Ave., Cincinnati OH 45207. Editorial Director: William Brohaugh. Estab. 1920. Publishes hardcover and paperback originals. Averages 16 titles/ year. Pays 10% royalty on net receipts. Simultaneous submissions OK (if so advised). Publishes book an average of 12-18 months after acceptance. Enclose return postage. *Writer's Market* recommends allowing 2 months for reply. Book catalog for 9×12 SAE with 6 first-class stamps.

Nonfiction: Instructional and reference books for writers. "Our instruction books stress results and how very specifically to achieve them. Should be well-researched, yet lively and readable. Our books concentrate on writing techniques over marketing techniques. We do *not* want to see books telling readers how to crack specific nonfiction markets: *Writing for the Computer Market* or *Writing for Trade Publications,* for instance. Concentrate on broader writing topics. In the offices here we refer to a manuscript's 4T value—manuscripts must have information writers can Take To The Typewriter. We are continuing to grow our line of reference books for writers, such as *Private Eyes* and *Police Procedural* in our Howdunit series, and *A Writer's Guide to Everyday Life in the 1800s*. References must be usable, accessible, and, of course, accurate. Query or submit

outline and sample chapters. Be prepared to explain how the proposed book differs from existing books on the subject." No fiction or poetry. "Writer's Digest Books also publishes instructional books for photographers and songwriters but the main thrust is on writing books. The same philosophy applies to songwriting and photography books: they must instruct about the creative craft, as opposed to instructing about marketing."
Recent Nonfiction Title: *Writing the Short Story: A Hands-on Program*, by Jack M. Bickham.

WRS PUBLISHING, 701 N. New Rd., Waco TX 76710. (817)776-6461. Fax: (817)757-1454. Acquisitions Director: Ann Page. Estab. 1967. Publishes hardcover, trade and mass market paperback originals. Publishes 30-35 titles/year. Receives 600 submissions/year. 20% of books from first-time authors; 50% from unagented writers. Pays 15% royalty on wholesale price. Advance negotiable. Publishes book an average of 1 year after acceptance. Simultaneous submissions OK if so stated. Query for electronic submissions. Reports in 1 month on queries. Book catalog and ms guidelines for SASE.
Nonfiction: Subjects include "inspirational stories of ordinary people with extraordinary potential. We are looking for stories which have received extensive, spontaneous publicity on TV, radio and in newspapers. Ideally, subjects of these books should be active on the speaking circuit after the book is published." Query or submit outline and sample chapters. Submit artwork/photos as part of ms package with SASE.
Recent Nonfiction Title: *Chains to Roses*, by Joseph Cicippio.
Tips: "We are primarily interested in inspiring stories and health-related subjects which fit the bookstore market and library needs. Our books appeal primarily to educated persons with an interest in improving their general lifestyle."

ZEBRA and PINNACLE BOOKS, 850 Third Ave., New York NY 10022. (212)407-1500. Publisher: Lynn Brown. Publishes hardcover, trade paperback and mass market paperback originals, trade paperback and mass market paperback reprints. Zebra publishes 360 titles/year; Pinnacle publishes 120 titles/year. Pays royalty. "Rarely" makes outright purchase. Publishes book 2 years after acceptance of ms. Simultaneous submissions OK. Reports in 3 months on proposals. Manuscript guidelines for #10 SASE.
Nonfiction: Biography, how-to, humor, self-help. Subjects include business and economics, health/medicine, military/war, money/finance. Submit outline with 3-5 sample chapters.
Fiction: Adventure, erotica, fantasy, gothic, historical, horror, humor, literary, mainstream/contemporary, mystery, occult, romance, short story collections, suspense, western, young adult. Submit synopsis with 3-5 sample chapters.

ZOLAND BOOKS, INC., 384 Huron Ave., Cambridge MA 02138-6828. (617)864-6252. Fax: (617)661-4998. Publisher/Editor: Roland Pease, Jr. Managing Editor: Ann McArdle. Marketing Director: Christine Alaimo. Estab. 1987. Publishes hardcover and trade paperback originals. Averages 8-15 titles/year. Receives 400 + submissions/year. 15% of books from first-time authors. 60% from unagented writers. Pays 7% royalty on retail price. Publishes book an average of 1½ years after acceptance. Reports in 6 months. Book catalog for 6½ × 9½ SAE with 2 first-class stamps.
Nonfiction: Biography, coffee table book. Subjects include art/architecture, language/literature, nature/environment, photography, regional, translation, travel, women's issues/studies. Query. Reviews artwork/photos as part of ms package.
Fiction: Literary and short story collections. Submit complete ms. *Writer's Market* recommends query with SASE first.
Recent Fiction Title: *Whistling and Other Stories*, by Myra Goldberg.
Tips: "We are most likely to publish books which provide original, thought-provoking ideas, books which will captivate the reader, and are evocative."

ZONDERVAN PUBLISHING HOUSE, 5300 Patterson Ave. SE, Grand Rapids MI 49530-0002. (616)698-6900. Contact: Editorial Coordinator. Estab. 1931. Publishes hardcover and trade paperback originals and reprints. Averages 130 titles/year. Receives 3,000 submissions annually. 20% of books from first-time authors; 80% from unagented writers. Average print order for a first book is 5,000. Pays royalty of 14% of the net amount received on sales of cloth and softcover trade editions and 12% of net amount received on sales of mass market paperbacks. Offers variable advance. Reports in 3 months on proposals. SASE required. Recommend ms guidelines for #10 SASE. To receive a recording about submission call (616)698-3447.
Nonfiction and Fiction: Biography, autobiography, self-help, devotional, contemporary issues, Christian living, Bible study resources, references for lay audience; some adult fiction; youth and children's ministry, teens and children. Academic and Professional Books: college and seminary textbooks (biblical studies, theology, church history, the humanities); preaching, counseling, discipleship, worship, and church renewal for pastors, professionals, and lay leaders in ministry; theological and biblical reference books. All from religious perspective (evangelical). Immediate needs listed in guidelines. Submit outline/synopsis, 1 sample chapter, and SASE for return of materials.
Recent Nonfiction Title: *False Assumptions*, by Dr. Henry Cloud and Dr. John Townsend.
Recent Fiction Title: *McKinney High, 1946*, by Ken Gire.

Canadian and International Book Publishers

This section lists book publishers whose addresses of principal contact lie outside the United States. Some of the publishers listed in this section also have offices in the U.S. A few of the publishers listed in the previous section have offices worldwide, and are certainly "international" in the subjects of the books they publish and distribute.

The Canadian and International Book Publishers section is intended for writers whose ideas and books are better suited for the Canadian or international marketplace. Writers should be aware that the requirements of these publishers are quite different from those of their U.S. counterparts. Some publishers listed here concentrate solely on subjects and authors from their own countries (or landed immigrants) and do not accept queries, proposals or manuscripts from American writers.

There is more government support of book publishing in Canada than in the U.S. A number of national and provincial arts councils subsidize book publishing. Most subsidy arrangements with Canadian publishers involve such an agency, not the author, as the source of the subsidy. However, there are a few author-subsidy publishers in Canada and writers should proceed with caution when they are made this offer. We have denoted partial author-subsidy publishers with an asterisk (*).

Despite a healthy book publishing industry, Canada is still dominated by publishers from the United States. Two out of every three books found in Canadian bookstores are published in the U.S. These odds have made some Canadian publishers even more determined to concentrate on Canadian authors and subjects. Writers interested in additional Canadian book publishing markets should consult *Literary Market Place* (R.R. Bowker & Co.), *The Canadian Writer's Guide* (Fitzhenry & Whiteside) and *The Canadian Writer's Market* (McClelland & Stewart).

International mail

Whatever your nation of residence may be, enclose International Reply Coupons (IRCs) with all correspondence to publishers outside your country. Postage stamps from your country are not valid on letters and parcels originating elsewhere. Publishers receiving SASEs and manuscripts with stamps from other countries are not likely to return or respond to the material, as international mailing costs are a considerable expense.

To defer a portion of this expense otherwise paid by you, consider sending disposable (photocopies or computer generated) outlines, synopses, sample chapters or manuscripts. This eliminates the cost of having an entire manuscript package returned to you. One IRC will cover the cost of the publisher's reply. They are available at post offices all over the world and can be redeemed for stamps of any country. Please note that the cost for items such as catalogs is expressed in the currency of the country in which the publisher is located.

For a list of publishers according to their subjects of interest, see the nonfiction and fiction sections of the Book Publishers Subject Index. Information on some book pub-

lishers and producers not included in this edition of *Writer's Market* can be found in Book Publishers and Producers/Changes '94-'95.

‡**ANAYA PUBLISHERS LTD.**, 3rd Floor, 50 Osnaburgh St., London NW1 3ND United Kingdom. (44)0-71-383-2997. Managing Director: Colin Ancliffe. Publishes hardcover and trade paperback originals. Publishes 40 titles/year. Receives 200 queries and 40 mss/year. 65% of books from first-time authors; 90% from unagented writers. Pays 2.5%-7.5% royalty on retail price or makes outright purchase of $6,000-12,000. Offers 20-30% of first year's earnings. Publishes books 9 months after acceptance of ms. No simultaneous submissions. Query for electronic submissions. Reports in 2 months on proposals.
Nonfiction: Coffee table book, how-to, illustrated book. Subjects include art/architecture, gardening, hobbies (especially crafts). "*Anaya* offers "up-market," international, full colour, co-editions with a strong "how to" flavour and very high production/quality standards." Query. Reviews artwork/photos as part of the freelance ms package. Writers should send photocopies.
Recent Nonfiction Title: *Classic English Interiors* by Henrietta Spencer-Churchill (interior style); *Fishermen's Sweaters*, by Alice Starmore (designer knitwear); *A Treasury of Handmade Gifts*, by Anaya staff ('how-to' present album).

ARSENAL PULP PRESS, 100-1062 Homer St., Vancouver British Columbia V6B 2W9 Canada. (604)687-4233. Editor: Linda Field. Estab. 1980. Imprint is Tillacum Library. Publishes hardcover and trade paperback originals. Publishes 12-15 titles/year. Receives 400 queries and 200 mss/year. 25% of books from first-time authors; 100% from unagented writers. Pays 15% royalty on wholesale price. Advance varies. Publishes book 1 year after acceptance of ms. Simultaneous submissions OK. Query for electronic submissions. Reports in 3-4 months on queries, with exceptions. Book catalog and ms guidelines free on request.
Nonfiction: Humor. Subjects include ethnic (Canadian, aboriginal issues), gay/lesbian, history (cultural), literature, regional (British Columbia), women's issues/studies. "We focus on Canadian or British Columbia issues." Submit outline and 2-3 sample chapters.
Recent Nonfiction Title: *Imaging Ourselves: An Anthology of Canadian Non-fiction*, edited by D. Francis (anthology).
Fiction: Experimental, feminist, gay/lesbian, literary and short story collections. "We only publish Canadian authors." Submit synopsis and 2-3 sample chapters.
Recent Fiction Title: *Lovely in Her Bones*, by J. Jill Robinson (short stories).

BEACH HOLME PUBLISHERS LTD., 4252 Commerce Circle, Victoria, British Columbia V8Z 4M2 Canada. (604)727-6514. Managing Editor: Guy Chadsey. Editor: Antonia Banyard. Estab. 1971. Publishes trade paperback originals. Averages 12 titles/year. Receives 300 submissions annually. "Accepting Canadian submissions." 40% of books from first-time authors; 70% from unagented writers. Pays 10% royalty on retail price. Offers $600 average advance. Publishes ms an average of 18 months after acceptance. Simultaneous submissions OK (if so advised). Reports in 4 months.
Nonfiction: Wicca (no occult, but "white" witchcraft). "Interested in serious, well-written, marketable work, not sensationalism." Submit outline and sample chapters.
Recent Nonfiction Title: *The Witch's Book of Days*, by Jean Kozocari.
Fiction: Experimental, young adult (pref. historical/regional). "Interested in excellent quality, imaginative writing."
Recent Fiction Title: *White Jade Tiger* (young adult fiction) by Julie Lawson.
Tips: "Make sure the manuscript is well written. We see so many that only the unique and excellent can't be put down."

‡**BLIZZARD PUBLISHING**, 301-89 Princess St., Winnipeg, Manitoba R3B 1K6 Canada. (204)949-0511. Editorial Assistant: Anna Synenko. Imprint is Bain & Cox, Publishers. Publishes hardcover and trade paperback originals. Averages 8 titles/year. Imprint publishes 6 titles/year. Receives 100 queries and 50 mss/year. 50% of books from first-time authors; 60% from unagented writers. Pays 10-12% royalty on retail price. Offers $200-500 advance. Publishes book 7 months after acceptance of ms. Query for electronic submissions. No simultaneous submissions. Reports in 6 months on queries; 5 months on proposals; 4 months on mss. Book catalog and ms guidelines free on request.
Nonfiction: Coffee table book, cookbook, how-to, children's/juvenile. Subjects include anthropology/archaeology, art/architecture, cooking, foods and nutrition, ethnic, gardening, gay/lesbian, government/politics, history, hobbies, language/literature, music/dance. "Bain & Cox, Publishers is a new imprint looking for exciting new books." Query with outline, 2 sample chapters and synopsis. Reviews artwork/photos as part of ms package. Writers should send photocopies.
Fiction: Adventure, ethnic, experimental, fantasy, feminist, gay/lesbian, juvenile, literary, mainstream/contemporary, mystery, picture books, plays, science fiction, short story collections, young adult. Query with synopsis and 2 sample chapters.
Recent Fiction Title: *Of Two Minds*, by C. Matas (YA, science fiction).
Poetry: "We like poets who work at getting published in small journals." Query with 5 sample poems.

BOREALIS PRESS, LTD., 9 Ashburn Dr., Nepean, Ontario K2E 6N4 Canada. Editorial Director: Frank Tierney. Senior Editor: Glenn Clever. Estab. 1972. Publishes hardcover and paperback originals. Averages 4 titles/year. Receives 400-500 submissions annually. 80% of books from first-time authors; 95% from unagented writers. Pays 10% royalty on retail price. No advance. Publishes book an average of 18 months after acceptance. "No multiple submissions or electronic printouts on paper more than 8½ inches wide." Reports in 2 months. Book catalog for $2 and SAE with IRCs.
Nonfiction: "Only material Canadian in content." Query. Reviews artwork/photos as part of freelance ms package. Looks for "style in tone and language, reader interest, and maturity of outlook."
Recent Nonfiction Title: *New Canadian Drama-6: Two Feminist Plays*, ed. Rita Much.
Fiction: "Only material Canadian in content and dealing with significant aspects of the human situation." Query.
Recent Fiction Title: *Margin of Error*, by Lesley Chayce.
Tips: "Ensure that creative writing deals with consequential human affairs, not just action, sensation, or cutesy stuff."

THE BOSTON MILLS PRESS, 132 Main St., Erin, Ontario N0B 1T0 Canada. (519)833-2407. Fax: (519)833-2195. President: John Denison. Estab. 1974. Publishes hardcover and trade paperback originals. Averages 16 titles/year. Receives 100 submissions annually. 75% of books from first-time authors; 90% from unagented writers. Pays 10% royalty on retail price. Small advance. Publishes book an average of 8 months after acceptance. Simultaneous submissions OK. Query for electronic submissions. Reports in 2 months. Book catalog free.
Nonfiction: Illustrated book. Subjects include history. "We're interested in anything to do with Canadian or American history—especially transportation. We like books with a small, strong market." No autobiographies. Query. Reviews artwork/photos as part of freelance ms package.
Recent Nonfiction Title: *Heartland*, by Greg McDonnell.
Tips: "We can't compete with the big boys so we stay with short-run specific market books that bigger firms can't handle. We've done well this way so we'll continue in the same vein."

BROADVIEW PRESS LTD., P.O. Box 1243, Peterborough, Ontario K9J 7H5 Canada. (705)743-8990. Fax: (705)743-8353. Senior Editor: Don LePan. Estab. 1985. Publishes hardcover and trade paperback originals and academic texts. Firm averages 16-18 titles/year. Receives 250 submissions/year. 40% of books from first-time authors; 100% from unagented writers. Royalty varies and negotiable. Publishes book 6-18 months after acceptance. Simultaneous submissions OK. Query for electronic submissions. Reports in 4 months. Book catalog free.
Nonfiction: Biography, reference, self-help, textbook, general nonfiction. Subjects include anthropology/archaeology, art/architecture, business and economics, government/politics, health/medicine, history, language/literature, money/finance, nature/environment, philosophy, psychology, sports, travel, women's issues/studies. "We specialize in university/college supplementary textbooks which often have both a trade and academic market. Nothing in the form of a nonfiction novel." Submit outline and sample chapters. Sometimes reviews artwork/photos as part of freelance ms package.
Recent Nonfiction Title: *Being Changed By Cross-Cultural Encounters: The Anghropology of Extraordinary Experience*.
Tips: "Publishing has become more concentrated in specific areas, with small print runs and more cost effective production. The days of large advances and long runs are over."

‡CACANADADADA PRESS, 3350 W. 21st Ave., Vancouver, British Columbia V6S 1G7 Canada. Director: Ronald B. Hatch. Publishes trade paperback originals. Publishes 6 titles/year. Receives 100 queries and 80 mss/year. 60% of books from first time authors; 100% from unagented writers. Pays 10% royalty on retail price. Publishes book 6 months after acceptance of ms. Simultaneous submissions OK. Query for electronic submissions. Reports in 1 week on queries, 1 month on proposals, 3 months on mss. Book catalog for #10 SASE. Writers *must* be Canadian citizens or landed immigrants.
Nonfiction: Biography, children's/juvenile. Subjects include history, language/literature, nature/environment, regional. Query. Reviews artwork/photos as part of freelance ms package. Writers should send photocopies.
Fiction: Experimental, novels, short story collections. Query with 2 sample chapters.
Poetry: "Poets should have published some poems in magazines/journals." Submit complete ms.

ALWAYS submit unsolicited manuscripts or queries with a self-addressed, stamped envelope (SASE) within your country or a self-addressed envelope with International Reply Coupons (IRC) purchased from the post office for other countries.

THE CAITLIN PRESS, P.O. Box 2387 Station B, Prince George, British Columbia V2N 2S6 Canada. (604)964-4953. Contact: Cynthia Wilson. Estab. 1978. Publishes trade paperback and soft cover originals. Publishes 4-5 titles/year. Receives 105-120 queries and 50 mss/year. 100% of books from unagented writers. Pays 15% royalty on wholesale price. Publishes book 18 months after acceptance of ms. Simultaneous submissions OK. Reports in 3 months on queries. Book catalog for #10 SASE.

Nonfiction: Biography, cookbook. Subjects include history, photography, regional. "We publish books about the British Columbia interior or by people from the interior. We are not interested in manuscripts that do not reflect a British Columbia influence." Submit outline and proposal package. Reviews artwork/photos as part of freelance ms package. Writers should send photocopies.

Fiction: Adventure, historical, humor, mainstream/contemporary, short story collections, young adult. Submit ms only. *Writer's Market* recommends query with SASE first.

Poetry: Submit sample poems or complete ms.

Tips: "Our area of interest is British Columbia and northern Canada. Submitted manuscripts should reflect our interest area."

CAMDEN HOUSE PUBLISHING, Telemedia Communications Inc., 7 Queen Victoria Rd., Camden East, Ontario K0K 1J0 Canada. (613)378-6661. Fax: (613)378-6123. Imprint is Old Bridge Press. Editor: Tracy Read. Estab. 1976. Publishes hardcover originals and reprints. Averages 4-8 titles/year. Receives 75-100 submissions annually. 20% of books from first-time authors; 90% from unagented writers. Pays 7-10% royalty on retail price. Offers average $5,000 advance. Publishes book an average of 18 months after acceptance. Reports in up to 2 months. Book catalog free.

Nonfiction: Cookbooks, how-to, juvenile, reference. Subjects include agriculture/horticulture, animals, natural history, cooking, foods and nutrition, gardening, hobbies, nature/environment, photography, recreation, travel. No New Age material. Submit outline and sample chapters. Reviews artwork/photos as part of freelance ms package.

Tips: "Old Bridge copublishes books with American publishers seeking access to the Canadian marketplace. We will arrange for distribution and commit to a print run. Same categories of interest as Camden House."

‡CANADIAN INSTITUTE OF UKRAINIAN STUDIES PRESS, CIUS Toronto Publications Office, University of Toronto, Dept. of Slavic Languages and Literatures, 21 Sussex Ave., Toronto, Ontario M5S 1A1 Canada. (416)978-8240. Fax: (416)978-2672. Director: Maxim Tarnawsky. Estab. 1976. Publishes hardcover and trade paperback originals and reprints. Publishes 10-15 titles/year. Receives 10 submissions/year. Subsidy publishes 20-30% of books. (Subsidies from granting agencies, not authors.) Pays 0-2% on retail price. Publishes book an average of 2 years after acceptance. Query for electronic submissions. Reports in 1 month on queries; 3 months on mss. Book catalog and ms guidelines free.

Nonfiction: Scholarly. Subjects include education, ethnic, government/politics, history, language/literature, religion, sociology, translation. "We publish scholarly works in the humanities and social sciences dealing with the Ukraine or Ukrainians in Canada." Query or submit complete ms. Reviews artwork/photos as part of ms package.

Recent Nonfiction Title: *Ukraine And Russis in Their Historical Encounter*, edited by Peter J. Potichay; Marc Raeff, Jaroslaw Pelenski, Cleb Žekulin.

Fiction: Ukrainian literary works. We do not publish fiction that have scholarly value.

Recent Fiction Title: *Yellow Boots*, by Vera Lysenko.

Tips: "We are a scholarly press and do not normally pay our authors. Our audience consists of University students and teachers; general public interested in Ukrainian and Ukrainian-Canadian affairs."

CANADIAN PLAINS RESEARCH CENTER, University of Regina, Regina, Saskatchewan S4S 0A2 Canada. (306)585-4795. Fax: (306)585-4699. Coordinator: Brian Mlazgar. Estab. 1973. Publishes scholarly paperback originals and some casebound originals. Averages 5-6 titles/year. Receives 10-15 submissions annually. 35% of books from first-time authors. Subsidy publishes 80% (nonauthor) of books. Publishes book an average of 2 years after acceptance. Query for electronic submissions. Reports in 2 months. Book catalog and ms guidelines free. Also publishes *Prairie Forum*, a scholarly journal.

Nonfiction: Biography, coffee table book, illustrated book, technical, textbook, scholarly. Subjects include animals, business and economics, history, nature, politics, sociology. "The Canadian Plains Research Center publishes the results of research on topics relating to the Canadian Plains region, although manuscripts relating to the Great Plains region will be considered. Material *must* be scholarly. Do not submit health, self-help, hobbies, music, sports, psychology, recreation or cookbooks unless they have a scholarly approach. For example, we would be interested in acquiring a pioneer manuscript cookbook, with modern ingredient equivalents, if the material relates to the Canadian Plains/Great Plains region." Submit complete ms. *Writer's Market* recommends query with SASE first. Reviews artwork/photos as part of freelance ms package.

Recent Nonfiction Title: *The Records of the Department of the Interior and Research Concerning Canada's Western Frontier of Settlement*, by Irene M.Spry and Bennett McCardle.

Tips: "Pay great attention to manuscript preparation and accurate footnoting, according to the *Chicago Manual of Style*."

COACH HOUSE PRESS, Suite 107, 50 Prince Arthur St., Toronto, Ontario M5R 1B5 Canada. (416)921-3910. Fax: (416)921-4403. Publisher: Margaret McClintock. Estab. 1964. Publishes trade paperback originals. Averages 16 titles/year. Pays 10-15% royalty on retail price. Publishes book an average of 1 year after acceptance. Book catalog free.

• Coach House no longer accepts unsolicited manuscripts.

Nonfiction: Illustrated book, criticism and essays. Subjects include art, social commentary, language/literature. *Submit ms through agent only.*

Fiction: Drama, poetry, experimental, feminist, gay/lesbian, literary, short story collections.

COTEAU BOOKS, Suite 401, 2206 Dewdney Ave., Regina, Saskatchewan S4R 1H3 Canada. (306)777-0170. Fax: (306)522-5152. Managing Editor: Shelley Sopher. Estab. 1975. Publishes hardcover, trade paperback and mass market paperback originals. Publishes 11 titles/year. Receives approximately 1,000 queries and mss/year. 10% of books from first-time authors; 95% from unagented writers. Pays 10% royalty on retail price or makes outright purchase of $50-200 for anthology contributors. Publishes book an average of 18 months after acceptance. Reports in 2 months on queries, 4 months on mss. Book catalog free with SASE or IRC.

Nonfiction: Reference, desk calendars. Subjects include language/literature, regional studies. "We publish only Canadian authors; **we will consider NO American manuscripts.**"

Recent Nonfiction Title: *On Air: Radio in Saskatchewan*, by Wayne Schmalz.

Fiction: Ethnic, feminist, humor, juvenile, literary, mainstream/contemporary, plays, short story collections. "No popular, mass market sort of stuff. We are a literary press." Submit complete ms. **We only publish fiction and poetry from Canadian authors.**

Recent Fiction Title: *The Crew*, by Don Dickinson.

Tips: "We are not publishing children's picture books, but are still interested in juvenile and YA fiction from Canadian authors."

HARRY CUFF PUBLICATIONS LIMITED, 94 LeMarchant Rd., St. John's, Newfoundland, Labrador A1C 2H2 Canada. (709)726-6590. Fax: (709)726-0902. Publisher: Harry Cuff. Managing Editor: Robert Cuff. Estab. 1980. Publishes hardcover and trade paperback originals. Averages 10 titles/year. Receives 50 submissions annually. 50% of books from first-time authors; 100% from unagented writers. Pays 10% royalty on retail price. No advance. Publishes book an average of 8 months after acceptance. Reports in 6 months on mss. Book catalog for 6×9 SASE.

Nonfiction: Biography, humor, reference, technical, textbook, all dealing with Newfoundland, Labrador. Subjects include history, photography, politics, sociology. Query.

Recent Nonfiction Title: *Coastal Cruising Newfoundland* by Rob Mills.

Fiction: Ethnic, historical, humor, mainstream. Needs fiction by Newfoundlanders or about Newfoundland, Labrador. Submit complete ms. *Writer's Market* recommends query with SASE first.

Recent Fiction Title: *The Burned Baby's Arm*, by Randy Lieb.

Tips: "We are currently dedicated to publishing books about Newfoundland, Labrador, but we will accept other subjects by Newfoundland, Labrador, authors. We will return 'mainstream' manuscripts from the US unread."

DUNDURN PRESS LTD., 2181 Queen St. E., Toronto, Ontario M4E 1E5 Canada. (416)698-0454. Fax: (416)698-1102. Publisher: Kirk Howard. Senior Editor: Judith Turnball. Estab. 1972. Publishes hardcover and trade paperback originals and reprints. Averages 20 titles/year. Receives 500 submissions annually. 45% of books from first-time authors; 90% from unagented writers. Average print order for a first book is 2,000. Pays 10% royalty on retail price; 8% royalty on some paperback children's books. Publishes book an average of 1 year after acceptance. Query for electronic submissions. Reports in 3 months.

Nonfiction: Biography, coffee table books, juvenile (12 and up), literary, reference. Subjects include Canadiana, art, history, hobbies, Canadian history, literary criticism. Especially looking for Canadian biographies. No religious or soft science topics. Query with outline and sample chapters. Reviews artwork/photos as part of ms package.

Tips: "Publishers want more books written in better prose styles. If I were a writer trying to market a book today, I would visit bookstores and watch what readers buy and what company publishes that type of book 'close' to my manuscript."

‡ECRITS DES FORGES, C.P. 335, 1497 Laviolette, Trois-Rivières, Quebec G9A 5G4 Canada. (819)379-9813. President: Gaston Bellemare. Publishes hardcover originals. Publishes 40 titles/year. Receives 30 queries and 1,000 mss/year. 10% of books from first-time authors; 90% from unagented writers. Pays 10-30% royalty. Offers 50% advance. Publishes book 6-9 months after acceptance of ms. Accepts simultaneous submissions. Query for electronic submissions. Reports in 6-9 months. Book catalog free on request.

Poetry: Poetry only and written in *French*. Submit 20 sample poems.

Recent Poetry Title: *Phoenix Intégral*, by Paul Chamberland.

2nd Floor, 1980 Queen St. E., Toronto, Ontario M4L 1J2 Canada. (416)694-3348. Fax: (416)698-...nt: Jack David. Estab. 1979. Publishes hardcover and trade paperback originals. Publishes 30-... Receives 120 submissions annually. 50% of books from first-time authors; 80% from unagented writers. Subsidy publishes (nonauthor) up to 5% of books. Pays 10% royalty on retail price. Simultaneous submissions OK. Query for electronic submissions. Reports in 2 months. Free book catalog.
Nonfiction: Biography, directories, reference, Canadian literary criticism. "ECW is particularly interested in popular biography and all Canadian literary criticism aimed at the undergraduate and graduate university market." Query. Reviews artwork/photos as part of freelance ms package.
Tips: "The writer has the best chance of selling reference works, biography, or literary criticism to our firm. ECW does not publish fiction or poetry."

‡ÉDITIONS LA LIBERTÉ INC., 3020 Chemin Ste-Foy, Ste-Foy, Quebec G1X 3V6 Canada. (418)658-3763. Director of Operations: Pierre Reid. Publishes trade paperback originals. Publishes 4-5 titles/year. Receives 125 queries and 100 mss/year. 75% of books from first-time authors; 90% from unagented writers. Pays 10% royalty on retail price. Publishes book 4 months after acceptance of ms. Accepts simultaneous submissions. Reports in 1 month on queries; 2 months on proposals; 3 months on mss. Book catalog free on request.
Nonfiction: Biography, children's/juvenile. Subjects include Americana, animals, anthropology/archaeology, child guidance/parenting, cooking, foods and nutrition, education, government/politics, history, hobbies, language/literature, music/dance, nature/environment, psychology, science, sociology. Submit proposal package, including complete ms.
Recent Nonfiction Title: *Cahiers Des Dix #48*, collective (history).
Fiction: Historical, juvenile, literary, mainstream/contemporary, short story collections, young adult. Query with synopsis.
Recent Fiction Title: *Le Chant de Les Brises . . . Orleans*, by Vaillancourt (novels).

‡EKSTASIS EDITIONS, P.O. Box 8474, Main Post Office, Victoria, British Columbia V8W 3S1 Canada. Phone/fax: (604)385-3378. Publisher: Richard Olafson. Publishes hardcover and trade paperback originals and reprints. Publishes 8-12 titles/year. Receives 85 queries and 100 mss/year. 65% of books from first-time authors; 100% from unagented writers. Pays 10% royalty on wholesale price. Publishes book 6 months after acceptance of ms. Accepts simultaneous submissions. Query for electronic submissions. Reports in 5 months on mss. Book catalog free on request.
Nonfiction: Biography. Subjects include government/politics, nature/environment, psychology, translation. Query. Reviews artwork/photos as part of ms package. Writers should send photocopies.
Recent Nonfiction Title: *Eternal Lake O'Hara*, by Carol Ann Sokoloff (history).
Fiction: Erotica, experimental, gothic, juvenile, literary, mainstream/contemporary, plays, science fiction, short story collections. Query with synopsis and 3 sample chapters.
Recent Fiction Title: *Bread of the Birds*, by André Carpentier (short story collection).
Poetry: "Ekstasis is a literary press, and is interested in the best of modern poetry." Submit 20 sample poems.
Recent Poetry Title: *From the Mouths of Angels*, by Richard Stevenson (lyric poetry).

FITZHENRY & WHITESIDE, LTD., 195 Allstate Parkway, Markham, Ontario L3R, 4T8 Canada. (905)477-9700. Fax: (905)477-9179. Senior Vice President: Robert Read. Estab. 1966. Publishes hardcover and paperback originals and reprints. Publishes 25 titles/year, text and trade. Royalty contract varies. Advance negotiable. Reports in 3 months. Enclose return postage.
Nonfiction: "Especially interested in topics of interest to Canadians, and by Canadians." Textbooks for elementary and secondary schools, also biography, history, health, fine arts, Native studies, and children's books. Submit outline and 1 sample chapter. Length: open.
Recent Title: *Art for Enlightenment*.

‡FORMAC PUBLISHING, 5502 Atlantic St., Halifax, Nova Scotia B3H 1G4 Canada. (902)421-7022. Contact: Carolyn MacGregor. Imprint is Goodread Biographies. Publishes hardcover originals and trade paperback and mass market paperback originals and reprints. Publishes 10 titles/year. 30% of books from first-time authors; 100% from unagented writers. Pays royalty. Publishes book 1 year after acceptance of ms. Accepts simultaneous submissions. Query for electronic submissions. Book catalog free on request.
Nonfiction: Biography, coffee table book, cookbook, illustrated book, children's/juvenile, reference, textbook. Subjects include business and economics, cooking, foods and nutrition, ethnic, government/politics, nature/environment, regional, sociology, travel, women's issues/studies. Canadian content required. Query with résumé.

GOOSE LANE EDITIONS, 469 King St., Fredericton, New Brunswick E3B 1E5 Canada. Acquisitions Editor: Laurel Boone. Estab. 1956. Firm averages 12-14 titles/year. Receives 350 submissions/year. 20% of books from first-time authors; 75-100% from unagented writers. Pays royalty on retail price. Reports in 4 months. Book catalog and ms guidelines free with SASE. Please use Canadian stamps or IRCs.

Nonfiction: Biography, illustrated book, literary history (Canadian). Subjects include art/architecture, history, language/literature, nature/environment, photography, translation, women's issues/studies. No how-to books. Query first.

Fiction: Experimental, feminist, historical, literary, short story collections. "Our needs in fiction never change: substantial, character-centred literary fiction (either as novel or collection of short stories) which shows more interest in the craft of writing (i.e. use of language, credible but clever plotting, shrewd characterization) than in cleaving to tired, mainstream genre-conventions. No children's, YA, mainstream, mass market, genre, mystery, thriller, confessional or sci-fi fiction." Query or submit complete ms.

Tips: "Trends we have noticed are continuing cutbacks, close-downs, belt-tightening, and drying-up of funds and government support for the arts. Writers should send us books that show a very well-read author who has thought long and deeply about the art of writing and, in either fiction or nonfiction, has something of Canadian relevance to offer. We almost never publish books by non-Canadian authors. Our audience is literate, thoughtful, well-read, non-mainstream. If I were a writer trying to market a book today, I would contact the targeted publisher with a query letter and synopsis, and request a book catalog and ms guidelines. Purchase a recent book from the publisher in a relevant area, if possible. Never send a complete manuscript blindly to a publisher. **Never** send a manuscript or sample without IRC's or sufficient return postage in Canadian stamps."

GUERNICA EDITIONS, Box 117, Station P, Toronto, Ontario M5S 2S6 Canada. Fax: (416)657-8885. Editor/Publisher: Antonio D'Alfonso. Estab. 1978. Publishes trade paperback originals, reprints and software. Averages 20 titles/year. Receives 1,000 submissions annually. 5% of books from first-time authors. Average print order for a first book is 1,000. Subsidy publishes (nonauthor) 50% of titles. "Subsidy in Canada is received only when the author is established, Canadian-born and active in the country's cultural world. The others we subsidize ourselves." Pays 3-10% royalty on retail price or makes outright purchase of $200-5,000. Offers 10¢/word advance for translators. IRCs required. "American stamps are of no use to us in Canada." Reports in 3 months. Book catalog for SASE.

Nonfiction: Biography, art, film, history, music, philosophy, politics, psychology, religion, literary criticism, ethnic history, multicultural comparative literature.

Fiction: Ethnic, translations. "We wish to open up into the fiction world and focus less on poetry. Also specialize in European, especially Italian, translations." Query.

Poetry: "We wish to have writers in translation. Any writer who has translated Italian poetry is welcomed. Full books only. Not single poems by different authors, unless modern, and used as an anthology. First books will have no place in the next couple of years." Submit samples.

Recent Poetry Title: *Songs And Ballads*, by Federico Garcia Lorca, translated by Robin Skelton.

Tips: "We are seeking less poetry, more prose, essays, novels, and translations into English or French."

HERALD PRESS CANADA, Subsidiary of Mennonite Publishing House, 490 Dutton Dr., Waterloo, Ontario N2L 6H7 Canada. (412)887-8500. Fax: (412)887-3111. Book Editor: S. David Garber. Estab. 1908. Firm publishes hardcover and trade paperback originals and reprints. Publishes 30 titles/year. Receives 1,000 submissions/year. 15% of books are from first-time authors; 98% from unagented writers. Subsidy publishes 5% of books, "only for a church agency." Pays 10-12% royalty on retail price. Publishes book an average of 1 year after acceptance. Accepts electronic submissions only with hard copy. SASE. Reports in 1 month on queries. *Writer's Market* recommends allowing 2 months for reply. Book catalog 60¢. Manuscript guidelines free on request.

Nonfiction: Coffee table book, cookbook, illustrated book, juvenile, reference, self-help, textbook. Subjects include child guidance/parenting, cooking, foods and nutrition, education, Christian, ethnic, Mennonite, Amish, history, language/literature, money/finance, stewardship, nature/environment, psychology, counseling, self-help, recreation, lifestyle, missions, justice, peace. "We will be seeking books on Christian inspiration, medium-level Bible study, current issues of peace and justice, family life, Christian ethics and lifestyle, and earth stewardship." Does not want to see war, politics, or scare predictions. Query or submit outline and sample chapters. Reviews artwork/photos as part of freelance ms package.

Recent Nonfiction Title: *Paul and the Roman House Churches*, by Reta Halteman Finger.

Fiction: Ethnic (Mennonite/Amish), historical (Mennonite/Amish), humor, juvenile (Christian orientation), literary, picture books, religious, romance (Christian orientation), short story collections, young adult. Does not want to see war, gangsters, drugs, explicit sex, or cops and robbers. Query or submit outline/synopsis and sample chapters.

Recent Fiction Title: *Polly*, by Mary Christner Borntrager.

HMS PRESS, P.O. Box 340, Station B, London, Ontario H6A 4W1 Canada. (519)660-8976. E-mail: wayne.ray@onlinesys.com. President: Wayne Ray. Publishes books on disk only. Publishes 4-10 titles/year. Receives 30 queries and 10 mss/year. Pays 10% royalty on retail price and $100 in kind. Publishes book 1 month after acceptance of ms. Simultaneous submissions OK. Query for electronic submissions. Reports in 1 month on mss. Book catalog free on request.

Nonfiction: Biography, how-to, humor, children's/juvenile, reference, self-help, textbook. Subjects include agriculture/horticulture, Americana, animals, anthropology/archaeology, art/architecture, business and economics, child guidance/parenting, computers and electronics, cooking, foods & nutrition, education, ethnic, gardening, gay/lesbian, government/politics, health/medicine, history, hobbies, lanuage/literature, military/war, money/finance, music/dance, nature/environment, philosophy, photography, psychology, recreation, regional, religion, science, sociology, software, sports, translation, travel, women's issues/studies. Submit complete ms on diskette only.

Recent Nonfiction Title: *Incest: Review of the Literature*, by Sue Ray, M.Sc.N. (nursing); *Winter of Dishonor*, by Bruce Micari (Korean War); *The Rock: US Military in Newfoundland*, by Wayne Ray (Canadian History).

Fiction: Adventure, erotica, fantasy, feminist, gay/lesbian, historical, horror, humor, juvenile, literary, mainstream/contemporary, mystery, plays, religious, romance, science fiction, short story collections, suspense, young adult. Submit complete ms on diskette only.

Recent Fiction Title: *Desert*, by Robert McKay (science fiction); *The Embezzler*, by LeRoy Hicks (mystery); *Tiger Tracks*, by Eric VonGris (Vietnam).

Poetry: Well written, nothing maudlin, little to no rhyme. Submit all poems on diskette.

Recent Poetry Title: *Blowing Holes through the Everyday*, by Sheila Dalton (personal and life); *A Star Struck Night*, by Berry Stewart (presonal and life); *Subterfuge*, by Leanne Ray and Lisa Nickole (teenage themes).

‡**HORSDAL & SCHUBART PUBLISHERS LTD.**, 623-425 Simcoe St., Victoria, British Columbia V8V 4T3 Canada. (604)360-0829. Editor: Marlyn Horsdal. Publishes hardcover originals and trade paperback originals and reprints. Publishes 8-10 titles/year. 50% of books from first-time authors; 100% from unagented writers. Pays 15% royalty on wholesale price. Negotiates advance. Publishes books 6 months after acceptance of ms. Accepts simultaneous submissions. Query for electronic submissions. Reports in 1 month on queries. Book catalog free on request.

Nonfiction: Biography, humor. Subjects include anthropology/archaeology, art/architecture, government/politics, history, nature/environment, recreation, regional, sports, travel. Query with outline and 2-3 sample chapters. Reviews artwork/photos as part of ms package. Writers should send photocopies.

Recent Nonfiction Title: *Forgive Me My Press Passes*, by Jim Taylor (sports/humor).

HOUNSLOW PRESS, Subsidiary of Dundurn Press Limited, Suite 301, 2181 Queen St., Toronto, Ontario M4E 1E5 Canada. Fax: (416)698-1102. General Manager: Tony Hawke. Estab. 1972. Publishes hardcover and trade paperback originals. Averages 8 titles/year. Receives 250 submissions/year. 10% of books from first-time authors; 95% from unagented writers. Pays 10-12½% royalty on retail price. Offers $500 average advance. Publishes book an average of 1 year after acceptance. Reports in 2 months on queries. Book catalog free.

Nonfiction: Biography, coffee-table book, cookbook, how-to, humor, illustrated book, self-help. Subjects include animals, art/architecture, business and economics, child guidance/parenting, cooking, foods and nutrition, health/medicine, history, money/finance, photography, translation, travel. "We are looking for controversial manuscripts and business books." Query.

Fiction: Literary and suspense. "We really don't need any fiction for the next year or so." Query.

Tips: "If I were a writer trying to market a book today, I would try to get a good literary agent to handle it."

‡**HYPERION PRESS, LTD.**,, 300 Wales Ave., Winnipeg, Manitoba R2M 2S9 Canada. (204)256-9204. Publishes hardcover and trade paperback originals and reprints. Publishes 10 titles/year. Receives 500 queries and 1,000 mss/year. 30% of books from first-time authors; 100% from unagented writers. Pays royalty. Publishes book 6-12 months after acceptance of ms. Simultaneous submissions OK. Query for electronic submissions. Reports in 3-6 months on mss. Book catalog free on request.

Nonfiction: How-to, children's/juvenile. Subjects include ethnic. Reviews artwork/photos as part of freelance ms package. Writers should send photocopies.

Recent Nonfiction Title: *A Dozen Silk Diapers*, by Melissa Kajpust (children's picture); *The Singing Snake*, by Stefan Czernecki & Timothy Rhodes (children's picture); and *Super Toys & Games From Paper*, by Virginia Walter (craft-how-to).

‡**INSTITUTE OF PSYCHOLOGICAL RESEARCH, INC./INSTITUT DE RECHERCHES PSYCHOLOGIQUES, INC.**, 34 Fleury St. W., Montréal, Québec H3L 1S9 Canada. (514)382-3000. Fax: (514)382-3007. President and General Director: Jean-Marc Chevrier. Estab. 1958. Publishes hardcover and trade paperback originals and reprints. Averages 12 titles/year. Receives 15 submissions/year. 10% of books from first-time authors, 100% from unagented writers. Pays 10-12% royalty. Publishes book an average of 6 months after acceptance. Reports in 2 months.

Nonfiction: Textbooks, psychological tests. Subjects include philosophy, psychology, science, translation. "We are looking for psychological tests in French or English." Submit complete ms. *Writer's Market* recommends query with SASE first.

Recent Nonfiction Title: *Épreuve individuelle d'habileté mentale*, by Jean-Marc Chevrier (intelligence test).

Tips: "Psychologists, guidance counsellors, professionals. Schools, school boards, hospitals, teachers, government agencies and industries comprise our audience."

‡**KEY PORTER BOOKS LTD.**, 70 The Esplanade, Toronto, Ontario M5E 1R2 Canada. (416)862-7777. Editor-in-Chief: Susan Renoux. Publishes hardcover originals and trade paperback originals and reprints. Publishes 50-60 titles/year. Receives 1,000 queries and 600 mss/year. 10% of books are from first-time authors; 5% from unagented writers. Pays 4-15% royalty on retail price. Offers $1,000-10,000 advance. Publishes book 1 year after acceptance of ms. Accepts simultaneous submissions. Reports in 2 months on proposals. Book catalog and ms guidelines free on request.
Nonfiction: Biography, coffee table book, cookbook, humor, illustrated book, children's/juvenile, self-help. Subjects include agriculture/horticulture, animals, business and economics, cooking, food and nutrition, government/politics, health/medicine, military/war, money/finance, nature/environment, photography, sports, women's issues/studies. Submit outline and 2 sample chapters. Reviews artwork/photos as part of ms package. Writers should send transparencies.
Recent Nonfiction Title: *A Life In Progress*, by Conrad Black (autobiography).
Fiction: Humor, mainstream/contemporary, picture books. Submit synopsis and 2 sample chapters.
Recent Fiction Title: *Daughters of Capt. Cook*, by Linda Spalding (contemporary).

‡**LES EDITIONS LA LIGNÉE**, 140 Brunelle, Beloeil, Quebec J3H 2Z1 Canada. (514)467-6641. Contact: Michel Paquin. Publishes hardcover originals and reprints. Publishes 3-4 titles/year. Receives 8 mss/year. 50% of books from first-time authors; 100% from unagented writers. Pays 10-15% royalty. Offers variable advance. Publishes book 30 months afer acceptance of ms. Accepts simultaneous submissions. Query for electronic submissions. Reports in 1 month. Book catalog free on request.
Nonfiction: Textbook. Subjects include lanuage/literature. "Our publications concern post-secondary studies—French teaching." Submit 1 sample chapter.

LONE PINE PUBLISHING, #206 10426 81st Ave., Edmonton, Alberta T6E 1X5 Canada. (403)433-9333. Editor-in-Chief: Glenn Rollans. Estab. 1980. Imprints are Lone Pine, Home World, Pine Candle and Pine Cone. Publishes hardcover and trade paperback originals and reprints. Averages 12-20 titles/year. Receives 200 submissions/year. 45% of books from first-time authors; 95% from unagented writers. Pays royalty. Simultaneous submissions OK. Reports in 2 months on queries. Book catalog free.
Nonfiction: Biography, how-to, juvenile, nature/recreation guide books. Subjects include animals, anthropology/archaeology, art/architecture, business and economics, gardening, government/politics, history, nature/environment ("this is where most of our books fall"), photography, sports, travel ("another major category for us"). We publish recreational and natural history titles, and some historical biographies. Most of our list is set for the next year and a half, but we are interested in seeing new material." Submit outline and sample chapters. Reviews artwork/photos as part of ms package.
Recent Nonfiction Title: *Plants of Coastal British Columbia including Washington Oregon and Alaska*, by Pojar & Mackinnon.
Tips: "Writers have their best chance with recreational or nature guidebooks and popular history. Most of our books are strongly regional in nature. We are mostly interested in books for Western Canada and Ontario, with some limited interest in the US Pacific Northwest. If I were a writer trying to market a book today, I would query first, to save time and money, and contact prospective publishers before the book is completed. Always send material with SASE (Canadian postage) or IRC's, and make the manuscript clean and easy to read."

‡**JAMES LORIMER & CO., PUBLISHERS**, 35 Britain St., Toronto, Ontario M5A 1R7 Canada. (416)362-4762. Publishing Assistant: Melinda Tate. Publishes trade paperback originals. Publishes 20 titles/year. Receives 150 queries and 50 mss/year. 10% of books from first-time authors; 100% from unagented writers. Pays 5-10% royalty on retail price. Publishes book 6 months after acceptance of ms. Query for electronic submissions. Reports in 4 months on proposals. Book catalog and ms guidelines for #10 SASE.
Nonfiction: Children's/juvenile. Subjects include business and economics, government/politics, history, sociology, women's issues/studies. "We publish Canadian authors only and Canadian issues/topics only." Submit outline, 2 sample chapters and résumé.
Recent Nonfiction Title: *Canadian Women's Issues*, by R. Pierson et al (college/university); *Canada and the Global Economy*, by R. Chodos et al (trade-economics); *Rise & Fall of a Middle Power*, by A. Andrew (trade-foreign policy).
Fiction: Juvenile, young adult. "No fantasy, science fiction, talking animals; realistic themes only. Currently seeking chapter books for ages 7-11 and sports novels for ages 9-13 (Canadian writers only)." Submit synopsis and 2 sample chapters.
Recent Fiction Title: *Gallop for Gold*, by S. Siamon (chapter book-adventure); *Curve Ball*, by J. Danakas (YA novel); *Maya*, by K. Ellis (YA novel based on TV series).

‡**McCLELLAND & STEWART INC.**, Suite 900, 481 University Ave., Toronto, Ontario M4P 2C4 Canada. (416)598-1114. Imprints are McClelland & Stewart, Stewart House, New Canadian Library. Publishes hardcover, trade paperback and mass market paperback originals and reprints. Publishes 80 titles/year. Receives thousands of queries/year; does not accept unsolicited mss. 10% of books from first-time authors; 30% from unagented writers. Pays 10-15% royalty on wholesale price (hardcover rates). Publishes book 1 year after

acceptance of ms. No simultaneous submissions. Query for electronic submissions. Reports in 2 months on proposals. Book catalog for $5.

Nonfiction: Biography, coffee table book, how-to, humor, illustrated book, children's/juvenile, reference, self-help, textbook. Subjects include agriculture/horticulture, animals, art/architecture, business and economics, Canadiana, child guidance/parenting, cooking, foods and nutrition, education, gardening, gay/lesbian, government/politics, health/medicine, history, hobbies, language/literature, military/war, money/finance, music/dance, nature/environment, philosophy, photography, psychology, recreation, religion, science, sociology, sports, translation, travel, women's issues/studies. "We publish books by Canadian authors or on Canadian subjects." Submit outline; all unsolicited mss returned unopened.

Recent Nonfiction Title: *Memoirs*, by Pierre Trudeau (political memoirs).

Fiction: Experimental, historical, humor, juvenile, literary, mainstream/contemporary, mystery, short story collections, young adult. "We publish quality fiction by prize-winning authors." Query; all unsolicited mss returned unopened.

Recent Fiction Title: *The Robber Bride*, by Margaret Atwood (novel).

Poetry: "Only Canadian poets should apply. We publish only 4 titles each year." Query.

Recent Poetry Title: *Stranger Music*, by Leonard Cohen.

‡**MACMILLAN CANADA**, Division of Canada Publishing Corporation, 29 Birch Ave., Toronto, Ontario M4V 1E2 Canada. (416)963-8830. Vice President & Publisher: Denise Schon. Publishes hardcover and trade paperback originals. Publishes 30-35 titles/year. Receives 100-200 queries/year. 30% of books from first-time authors; 90% from unagented writers. Pays royalty. Publishes book 1 year after acceptance of ms. Accepts simultaneous submissions. Query for electronic submissions. Reports in 2 months. Book catalog free on request.

Nonfiction: Biography, cookbook, humor, reference, self-help. Subjects include business and economics, Canadiana, cooking, foods and nutrition, health/medicine, history, military/war, money/finance, recreation, sports. Submit outline with 1-3 sample chapters, author biography and letter explaining rationale for book. Reviews artwork/photos as part of ms package. Writers should send photocopies.

‡**MARCUS BOOKS**, P.O. Box 327, Queensville, Ontario L0G 1R0 Canada. (905)478-2208. President: Tom Rieder. Publishes trade paperback originals and reprints. Publishes 3-4 titles/year. Receives 12 queries and 6 mss/year. 90% of books from first-time authors; 100% from unagented writers. Pays 10% royalty on retail price. Publishes book 6 months after acceptance of ms. No simultaneous submissions. Query for electronic submissions. Reports in 4 months on mss. Book catalog for $1.

Nonfiction: "Interested in alternative health and esoteric topics." Submit outline and 3 sample chapters.

THE MERCURY PRESS, Imprint of Aya Press, 137 Birmingham St., Stratford, Ontario N5A 2T1 Canada. Editor: Beverley Daurio. Estab. 1978. Publishes trade paperback originals and reprints. Averages 10 titles/year. Receives 200 submissions/year. 10% of books from first-time authors; 99% from unagented writers. Pays 10% royalty on retail price. Publishes book an average of 1 year after acceptance. Query for electronic submissions. Reports in 2 months. Book catalog free. "We publish *only* Canadian writers."

Nonfiction: Biography. Subjects include art/architecture, government/politics, history, language/literature, music/dance, sociology, women's issues/studies. Query.

Recent Nonfiction Title: *Frontiers: Essays on Race and Culture*, by Marlene Nourbese Philip.

Fiction: Feminist, literary, mainstream/contemporary, short story collections. No genre fiction except Canadian murder mysteries, published under the Midnight Originals imprint. Submit complete ms with SASE.

Poetry: No unsolicited mss until 1997. No traditional, rhyme, confessional.

Tips: "If I were a writer trying to publish a book today, I would study markets objectively, listen to feedback, present manuscripts professionally."

‡**NETHERLANDIC PRESS**, Box 396, Station A, Windsor Ontario N9A 6L7 Canada. (519)944-2171. Editor: Hendrika Ruger. Publishes trade paperback originals 60-100 pages in length. Publishes 4 title/year. Receives 60 queries and 40 mss/year. 2% of books from first-time authors; 100% from unagented writers. Pays 10% royalty on retail price. Publishes books 3 months after acceptance of ms. Simultaneous submissions OK. Query for electronic submissions. Reports in 1 month on queries and proposals, 3 months on mss. Book catalog and ms guidelines free on request.

Nonfiction: Subjects include ethnic, history, language/literature. "Netherlandic Press publishes works with Netherlandic (Dutch, Belgian—(Flemish) content or influences (circa 100 printed pages). Query.

Recent Nonfiction Title: *100 years Ago*, by Jan Kryff (pioneer history); *The Sack of Veracruz*, by David F. Marley (pirates).

Fiction: Literary and short story collections. "Should have Netherlandic aspect." Query.

Poetry: Query.

NEWEST PUBLISHERS LTD., #310, 10359 Whyte Ave., Edmonton, Alberta T6E 1Z9 Canada. (403)432-9427. Fax: (403)432-9429. General Manager: Liz Grieve. Editorial Coordinator: Eva Radford. Estab. 1977. Publishes trade paperback originals. Averages 8 titles/year. Receives 100 submissions/year. 40% of books from first-time authors; 90% from unagented writers. Pays 10% royalty. Publishes book an average of 2 years after acceptance. Simultaneous submissions OK. Reports in 3 weeks on queries. *Writer's Market* recommends allowing 2 months for reply. Book catalog for 9 × 12 SAE with 4 first-class Canadian stamps or US postal forms.

Nonfiction: Literary/essays. Subjects include ethnic, government/politics (Western Canada), history (Western Canada), Canadiana. Query.

Fiction: Literary and short story collections. "We are looking for Western Canadian authors." Submit outline/synopsis and sample chapters.

Recent Fiction Title: *Boundless Alberta,* edited by Aritha van Herk.

Tips: "Our audience consists of people interested in the west and north of Canada; teachers, professors. Trend is towards more nonfiction submissions. Would like to see more full-length literary fiction."

ORCA BOOK PUBLISHERS LTD., P.O. Box 5626 Station B., Victoria, British Columbia V8R 6S4 Canada. (604)380-1229. Publisher: R. Tyrrell. Children's Book Editor: Ann Featherstone. Estab. 1984. Publishes hardcover and trade paperback originals. Publishes 15-20 titles/year. Receives 500-600 submissions/year. 50% of books from first-time authors; 80% from unagented writers. Pays 10-12½% royalty on retail price. Offers average $1,000 advance. Publishes ms an average of 9-12 months after acceptance. Reports in 3 weeks on queries. *Writer's Market* recommends allowing 2 months for reply. Book catalog for 9 × 12 SAE and $1 (Canadian) postage. Manuscript guidelines for SASE or IRCs.

Nonfiction: Biography, illustrated book, travel guides, children's. Subjects include history, nature/environment, recreation, sports, travel. Needs history (*west coast Canadian*) and young children's book. Query or submit outline and sample chapters. All unsolicited mss are returned unopened. Reviews artwork/photos as part of ms package. *Publishes Canadian material only.*

Fiction: Juvenile, literary, mainstream/contemporary. Needs west coast Canadian contemporary fiction; illustrated children's books, 4-8-year-old range older juvenile and YA. Query or submit outline/synopsis and sample chapters. All unsolicited mss are returned unopened.

Recent Fiction Title: *Belle's Journey,* by Marilyn Reynolds.

OUTCROP, THE NORTHERN PUBLISHERS, Box 1350, Yellowknife, Northwest Territories X1A 2N9 Canada. (403)920-4652. Publisher: Ronne Heming. Publishes trade paperback originals. Publishes 4 titles/year. Receives 20 queries and 10 mss/year. 90% of books from first-time authors; 100% from unagented writers. Pays 8-10% on retail price. Publishes book 10 months after acceptance of ms. Reports in 3 months on queries and proposals. Book catalog free on request.

Nonfiction: Biography, cookbook, reference. Subjects include anthropology/archaelogy, business and economics, ethnic, government/politics, history, nature/environment, science, travel. Looking for books with "specific Northwest Territories/Yukon focus." Query or submit outline and 3 sample chapters. Reviews artwork/photos as part of freelance package. Writers should send photocopies.

Recent Nonfiction Title: *Barrenland Beauties,* by Page Burt.

‡PACIFIC EDUCATIONAL PRESS, Faculty of Education, University of British Columbia, Vancouver, British Columbia V6T 1Z4 Canada. Director: Catherine Edwards. Publishes trade paperback originals. Publishes 6-8 titles/year. Receives 200 submissions/year. 15% of books from first-time authors; 100% from unagented writers. Pays 6-12% royalty on wholesale price. Publishes book 1 year after acceptance of ms. Simultaneous submissions OK if so informed. Query for electronic submissions. Reports in 3-6 months on mss. Book catalog free on request.

Nonfiction: Children's/juvenile, reference for teacher, textbook. Subjects for children: animals, Canadiana, history, language/literature. Subjects for children and teachers: art/architecture, education, ethnic (for children or professional resources for teachers), music/dance, nature/environment, regional (Pacific Northwest), science. "Our books often straddle the trade/educational line, but we make our selections based on educational potential (in classrooms or school libraries)." Submit outline and 3 sample chapters. Reviews artwork/photos as part of ms package. Writers should send photocopies (in color, if possible).

Recent Nonfiction Title: *On the Write Track!,* by Margriet Ruurs (teacher resource and activity guide).

Fiction: For children: ethnic, historical, juvenile, mystery, science fiction, young adult. For children or teachers: plays. "We select fiction based on its potential for use in language arts classes as well as its literary merit." Submit synopsis and 5 sample chapters; whole ms is best.

Recent Fiction Title: *A Sea Lion Called Salena,* by Dayle Gaets (juvenile novel with an environmental theme).

PANDORA PRESS, Imprint of HarperCollins, 77-85 Fulham Palace Rd., Hammersmith, London W6 8JB England. Fax: 081-307-4440. Publishing Director: Eileen Campbell. Commissioning Editor: Belinda Budge. Publishes hardcover and paperback originals. Publishes 20 titles/year. Pays 7½-10% royalty. Reports in 2 months. Book catalog free.

• No longer publishes fiction.

Nonfiction: Wide-ranging list of feminist writing includes subjects on culture and media, health, lifestyle and sexuality, biography and reference, and women's issues/studies.

PEGUIS PUBLISHERS LIMITED, 318 McDermot Ave., Winnipeg, Manitoba R3A OA2 Canada. (204)956-1486. Fax: (204)947-0080. Acquisitions, Managing Editor: Annalee Greenberg. Estab. 1967. Educational paperback originals. Averages 8 titles/year. Receives 150 submissions/year. 50% of books from first-time authors; 100% from unagented writers. Pays 10% average royalty on educational net (trade less 20%). Publishes book an average of 1-2 years after acceptance. Simultaneous submissions OK. Reports in 3 months on queries; 1 month on mss if quick rejection, up to 1 year if serious consideration. Book catalog free.
Nonfiction: Educational (focusing on teachers' resource material for primary education, integrated whole language). Submit outline/synopsis and sample chapters or complete ms.
Recent Nonfiction Title: *Looking, Listening & Learning: Observing and Assessing Young Readers*, by Carl Braun.
Fiction: None.
Tips: "Writers have the best chance selling us quality professional materials for teachers that help them turn new research and findings into classroom practice.

‡PINTER PUBLISHERS LTD.,, 25 Floral St., London WC2E 9D5 England. (71)240-9233. Managing Director: Frances Pinter. Publishes hardcover originals. Publishes 100 titles/year. Receives 1,000 queries and 100 mss/year. 10% of books from first-time authors; 99% from unagented writers. Pays 0-10% royalty. Publishes books 6 months after acceptance of ms. No simultaneous submissions. Reports in 1 month on proposals. Book catalog and ms guidelines free on request.
Nonfiction: Reference, technical, textbook. Subjects include anthropology/archaeology, business and economics, government/politics, history, sociology, linguistics. Submit outline.

PLAYWRIGHTS CANADA PRESS, Imprint of Playwrights Union of Canada, 54 Wolseley St., 2nd floor, Toronto, Ontario M5T 1A5 Canada. (416)947-0201. Fax: (416)947-0159. Managing Editor: Tony Hamill. Estab. 1972. Publishes paperback originals and reprints of plays by Canadian citizens or landed immigrants, whose plays have been professionally produced on stage. Receives 100 member submissions/year. 50% of plays from first-time authors; 50% from unagented authors. Pays 10% royalty on list price. Publishes about 1 year after acceptance. Simultaneous submissions OK. Reports in up to 1 year. Play catalog and ms guidelines free. Non-members should query. Accepts children's plays.

PRENTICE-HALL CANADA, INC., Trade Division, Subsidiary of Paramount Publishing, 1870 Birchmount Rd., Scarborough, Ontario M1P 2J7 Canada. (416)293-3621. Editorial Director: Herb Hilderley. Estab. 1960. Publishes hardcover and trade paperback originals. Averages about 15 titles/year. Receives 750-900 submissions annually. 30% of books from first-time authors; 40% from unagented writers. Negotiates royalty and advance. Publishes book an average of 9 months after acceptance. Query for electronic submissions. Reports in 3 months. Manuscript guidelines for #10 SAE and 1 IRC.
Nonfiction: Subjects of Canadian and international interest: politics and current affairs, business, health and food. Send outline and sample chapters. Reviews artwork/photos as part of freelance ms package.
Recent Nonfiction Title: *Balancing Act: A Canadian Women's Financial Survival Guide*, by Joanne Thomas Yaccato.
Tips: "Present a clear, concise thesis, well-argued with a thorough knowledge of existing works with strong Canadian orientation. Needs general interest nonfiction books on topical subjects."

PRODUCTIVE PUBLICATIONS, P.O. Box 7200 Station A, Toronto, Ontario M5W 1X8 Canada. Owner: Iain Williamson. Estab. 1985. Publishes trade paperback originals. Publishes 21 titles/year. Receives 30 queries and 20 mss/year. 80% of books from first-time authors; 100% from unagented writers. Pays 5-25% royalty on wholesale price. Publishes book 3 months after acceptance of ms. Query for electronic submissions. Reports in 1 month on queries and proposals, 3 months on mss. Book catalog free on request.
• Productive Publications is also interested in books on investment, stock market and mutual funds, etc.
Nonfiction: How-to, reference, self-help, technical. Subjects include business and economics, health/medicine, hobbies, software (business). "We are interested in small business/entrepreneurship/employment/self-help (business)/how-to/health and wellness – 100 pages." Submit outline. Reviews artwork/photos as part of the freelance ms package. Writers should send photocopies.
Recent Nonfiction Title: *Your Guide to Starting & Self-Financing Your Own Business in Canada*, by Iain Williamson (business).
Tips: "We are looking for books written by *knowledgeable, experienced experts* who can express their ideas *clearly* and *simply*."

‡RANDOM HOUSE OF CANADA, Subsidiary of Random House, Inc., Suite 210, 33 Yonge St., Toronto, Ontario M5E 1G4 Canada. Imprint is Vintage Canada. Publishes hardcover and trade paperback originals. Publishes 50 titles/year. Receives 600 queries and 300 mss/year. 10% of books from first-time authors. Pays royalty. Publishes book 1 year after acceptance of ms. No simultaneous submissions. Reports on proposals in 3 months. No unsolicited mss.

Nonfiction: Biography, cookbook. Subjects include cooking, foods and nutrition, gardening, history, military/war, women's issues/studies. Agented submissions only.

Fiction: Literary. Agented submissions only; all unsolicited mss are returned unopened.

Tips: "We are NOT a mass market publisher, i.e., no historical romances, epics, Grisham-types, or thrillers of any kind."

REIDMORE BOOKS, INC., 1200 Energy Square, 10109-106 Street, Edmonton, Alberta T5J 3L7 Canada. (403)424-4420. Fax: (403)441-9919. Director of Sales: Janet Mayfield. Director of Marketing: Cathie Crooks. Estab. 1979. Publishes hardcover originals, modular materials for elementary mathematics (grades 4, 5, 6), and high interest, low vocabulary novels for boys in grades 6, 7, and 8. Publishes 10-12 titles/year. Receives 18-20 submissions/year. 60% of books from first-time authors; 100% from unagented writers. Subsidy publishes 5% of books. Pays royalty. Offers $1,500 average advance. Publishes book an average of 8 months after acceptance. Query for electronic submissions. Reports in 1-3 months on queries. Book catalog free.

Nonfiction: Textbook. Subjects include ethnic, government/politics, history, elementary mathematics. Query. All unsolicited mss are returned unopened. Reviews artwork/photos as part of ms package.

‡ROCKY MOUNTAIN BOOKS, #4 Spruce Centre SW, Calgary, Alberta T3C 3B3 Canada. Publisher: Tony Daffern. Publishes trade paperback originals. Publishes 5 titles/year. Receives 30 queries/year. 75% of books from first-time authors; 100% from unagented writers. Pays 10% royalty. Offers $1,000-2,000 advance. Publishes books 1 year after acceptance of ms. No simultaneous submissions. Query for electronic submissions. Reports in 1 month on queries. Manuscript guidelines free on request.

Nonfiction: How-to. Subjects include nature/environment, recreation, travel. "Our main area of publishing is outdoor recreation guides to western and northern Canada." Query.

Recent Nonfiction Title: *Backcountry Biking in the Canadian Rockies*, by Eastcott & Lepp (outdoor recreation paperback); *Nahanni The River Guide*, by Jowett (outdoor recreation paperback).

‡ROUSSAN PUBLISHERS INC., Division of Roussan Editeur Inc., 175 Sherbrooke St. W., Montreal, Quebec H2X 1X5 Canada. (514)284-2832. Editor: Kathryn Rhoades. Publishes trade paperback originals. Publishes 12 titles/year; each division publishes 6 titles/year. Receives 75 queries and 75 mss/year. 40% of books from first-time authors; 100% from unagented writers. Pays 8% royalty on retail price. Publishes book 6-8 months after acceptance of ms. Accepts simultaneous submissions. Query for electronic submissions. Reports in 3 months on proposals.

Fiction: Young adult and junior readers only—adventure, fantasy, feminist, historical, juvenile, mystery, science fiction. No picture books. Submit synopsis and 3 sample chapters.

Recent Fiction Title: *Summer of the Hand*, by Ishbel Moore (mystery/time travel).

SELF-COUNSEL PRESS, 1481 Charlotte Rd., North Vancouver, British Columbia V7J 1H1 Canada. (604)986-3366. Also 1704 N. State Street, Bellingham, WA 98225. (206)676-4530. Managing Editor: Ruth Wilson. Estab. 1970. Publishes trade paperback originals. Averages 15-20 titles/year. Receives 1,000 submissions/year. 80% of books from first-time authors; 95% from unagented writers. Average print run for first book is 6,000. Pays 10% royalty on net receipts. Publishes book an average of 9 months after acceptance. Simultaneous submissions OK. Query for electronic submissions. Reports in 2 months. Book catalog and ms guidelines for 9×12 SAE.

Nonfiction: How-to, self-help. Subjects include business, law, psychology, reference. Query or submit outline and sample chapters.

Recent Nonfiction Title: *Start and Run a Profitable Catering Business* (self-help business).

Tips: "The self-counsel author is an expert in his or her field and capable of conveying practical, specific information to those who are not. We look for manuscripts full of useful information that will allow readers to take the solution to their needs or problems into their own hands and succeed. We do not want personal self-help accounts, however."

‡SEVERN HOUSE PUBLISHERS, 9-15 High St., Sutton, Surrey SM1 1DF United Kingdom. (081)770-3930. Editorial Assistant: Samantha Brown. Publishes hardcover and trade paperback originals and reprints. Publishes 120 titles/year. Receives 250 queries and 50 mss/year. 0.5% of books from first-time authors; 0.5% from unagented writers. Pays 7½-15% royalty on retail price. Offers $750-2,500. Simultaneous submissions OK. Query for electronic submissions. Reports in 3 months on proposals. Book catalog free on request.

Fiction: Adventure, fantasy, historical, horror, mainstream/contemporary, mystery, romance, science fiction, short story collections, suspense. Submit synopsis and 3 sample chapters or agented submissions only.

Recent Fiction Title: *Cinders To Satin*, by Fern Michaels (historical romance); *Earth Song*, by Catherine Coulter (historical romance); *The Love Talker*, by Elizabeth Peters (crime and mystery).

‡SHOESTRING PRESS, Edmonton Central Post Office, Box 1223, Edmonton, Alberta T5J 2J1 Canada. Fax: (403)426-0853. Editor: A. Mardon. Publishes hardcover and trade paperback originals and reprints. Averages 12 titles/year. Receives 98 submissions/year. 50% of books from first-time authors; 100% from unagented writers. Subsidy publishes 10% of books. Pays 3-15% royalty. Publishes book an average of 9 months after acceptance. Simultaneous submissions OK. Reports in 7 months.

Nonfiction: Biography, illustrated book, juvenile, reference, technical. Subjects include Canadiana/Americana, anthropology/archaeology, cooking, foods and nutrition, ethnic, government/politics (of Canada), history (of Alberta), military/war (theory and history), nature/environment, regional (Alberta, Western Canada and Western USA), science (for broad market), travel (accounts), Native Canadian. "We are interested in native American stories." Query. Submit outline with appropriate SASE with Canadian stamps or IRCs.

Fiction: Adventure, experimental, fantasy, historical, juvenile, literary, picture books (native American), religious, science fiction. Submit outline/synopsis and sample chapters with appropriate SASE or IRCs.

Tips: "We are interested in non-clichéd storylines of some complexity that are well written and accounts of personal experiences including international niche oriented books. Our audience includes intelligent people of all ages in the Canadian and international markets."

SIMON & PIERRE PUBLISHING CO. LTD., A Subsidiary of Dundurn Press, Suite 301, 2181 Queen St. E., Toronto, Ontario M4E 1E5 Canada. (416)463-0313. Director of Operations: Jean Paton. Estab. 1972. Publishes hardcover and trade paperback originals and reprints. Averages 6-8 titles/year. Receives 300 submissions/year. 50% of books are from first-time authors; 85% from unagented writers. Trade book royalty 10-15% on retail price. Education royalty 8% of net. Offers $500 average advance. Publishes book an average of 1 year after acceptance. Simultaneous submissions OK. Reports in 3 weeks on queries. *Writer's Market* recommends allowing 3 months for reply. Free ms guidelines.

 • Simon & Pierre no longer publishes any children's or young adult books.

Nonfiction: *Canadian authors only.* Biography, reference, language/literature, music/dance (drama), Sherlockian literature and criticism. "We are looking for Canadian drama and drama related books." Query or submit outline and sample chapters. Sometimes reviews artwork/photos as part of ms package.

Fiction: Adventure, literary, mainstream/contemporary, mystery, plays (Canadian, must have had professional production). "No romance, sci-fi or experimental." Query or submit outline/synopsis and sample chapters.

Recent Fiction Title: *Found: A Body*, by Betsy Struthers (novel).

Tips: "We are looking for Canadian themes by Canadian authors. Special interest in drama and drama related topics; also Sherlockian. If I were a writer trying to market a book today, I would check carefully the types of books published by a publisher before submitting manuscript; books can be examined in bookstores, libraries, etc.; should look for a publisher publishing the type of book being marketed. Clean manuscripts essential; if work is on computer disk, give the publisher that information. Send information on markets for the book, and writer's résumé, or at least why the writer is an expert in the field. Covering letter is important first impression."

SONO NIS PRESS, 1745 Blanshard St., Victoria, British Columbia V8W 2J8 Canada. Editor: Angela Addison. Estab. 1976. Publishes hardcover and trade paperback originals and reprints. Receives hundreds of queries/year. 5-10% of books from first-time authors; 100% from unagented writers. Pays 10-12 royalty on retail price. Publishes book 8 months after acceptance of ms. Simultaneous submissions OK. Query for electronic submissions. Reports in 2 months on queries. Book catalog for 9×12 SAE with 3 IRCs.

 • Sono Nis Press is expanding its criteria for history to include areas outside British Columbia — national and international.

Nonfiction: Biography, reference. Subjects include history (British Columbia), hobbies (trains), regional (British Columbia), maritime (British Columbia), transportation (western Canada). Query or submit outline and 3 sample chapters. Reviews artwork/photos as part of the freelance ms package. Writers should send photocopies.

Recent Nonfiction Title: *Journey Back to Peshawar*, by Rona Murray.

Poetry: Query.

Recent Poetry Title: *Briefly Singing*, by Robin Skelton.

THISTLEDOWN PRESS, 633 Main St., Saskatoon, Saskatchewan S7H 0J8 Canada. (306)244-1722. Editor-in-Chief: Patrick O' Rourke. Estab. 1975. Publishes trade paperback originals by resident Canadian authors *only*. Averages 10-12 titles/year; receives 350 submissions annually. 10% of books from first-time authors; 90% from unagented writers. Average print order for a first poetry book is 500; fiction is 1,000. Pays standard royalty on retail price. Publishes book an average of 18-24 months after acceptance. Reports in 2 months. Book catalog and guidelines for #10 SASE.

 • Thistledown is publishing less poetry and fewer titles in general.

Some Canadian publishers will consider book proposals by Canadian authors only. Please check each listing carefully for this restriction.

Fiction: Juvenile (ages 8 and up), literary. Interested in fiction mss from resident Canadian authors only. Minimum of 30,000 words. Accepts no unsolicited work. Query first.

Recent Fiction Title: *It's A HardCow*, by Terry Jordan (short fiction).

Poetry: "The author should make him/herself familiar with our publishing program before deciding whether or not his/her work is appropriate." No poetry by people *not* citizens and residents of Canada. Prefers poetry mss that have had some previous exposure in literary magazines. Accepts no unsolicited work. Query first.

Recent Poetry Title: *Angel Wings All Over*, by Anne Cample.

Tips: "We prefer to receive a query letter first before a submission. We're looking for quality, well-written literary fiction—for children and young adults and for our adult fiction list as well. Increased emphasis on fiction (short stories and novels) for young adults, aged 12-18 years."

‡THOMPSON EDUCATIONAL PUBLISHING INC., Suite 105, 14 Ripley Ave., Toronto, Ontario M6S 3N9 Canada. (416)766-2763. President: Keith Thompson. Publishes trade paperback originals. Publishes 10 titles/year. Receives 15 queries and 10 mss/year. 80% of books from first-time authors; 100% from unagented writers. Pays 10% royalty on wholesale price. Publishes book 1 year after acceptance of ms. Query for electronic submissions. Reports in 1 month on proposals. Book catalog free on request.

Nonfiction: Textbook. Subjects include business and economics, education, government/politics, sociology, women's issues/studies. Submit outline and 1 sample chapter.

‡TITAN BOOKS LTD., 42-44 Dolben St., London SE1 OUP England. Editor: D. Barraclongh. Publishes trade and mass market paperback originals and reprints. Publishes 30-60 titles/year. Receives 1,000 queries and 500 mss/year. Less than 1% of books from first-time authors; 10% from unagented writers. Pays royalty of 6-10% on retail price. Advance varies. Publishes books 1 year after acceptance of ms. Simultaneous submissions OK. Query for electronic submissions. Reports in 1 month on queries; 3 months on proposals; 6 months on mss. Manuscript guidelines for IRCs.

Nonfiction: Biography, how-to, humor, illustrated book. Subjects include music, film and TV, true crime, comics. Query. Reviews artwork/photos as part of freelance ms package. Writers should send photocopies.

Recent Nonfiction Title: *Anime*, by Helen McCarthy (animation); *Illustrated Vampire Movie Guide*, by Stephen Jones (cinema); *Don't Panic*, by Neil Galman (biography).

Recent Fiction Title: *Star Trek: Galactic Whirlpool*, by Gerrold (SF); *Star Trek Next Generation: Here There Be Dragons*, by Peel (SF); *Return of Superman*, by various authors (comic).

TUNDRA BOOKS INC., Suite 604, 345 Victoria Ave., Montreal, Quebec H3Z 2N2 Canada. (514)932-5434. Associate Editor: Arjun Basu. Estab. 1967. Publishes hardcover and trade paperback originals. Publishes 12-15 titles/year. Receives 100 queries and 250-300 mss/year. 10% of books from first-time authors; 100% from unagented writers. Pays 3½-10% royalty on wholesale price. Offers $1,500-3,000 advance. Publishes book 15 months after acceptance of ms. Simultaneous submissions OK. Reports in 6 months. Manuscript guidelines free on request.

• Tundra is not accepting unsolicited manuscripts until December 1995.

Fiction: Juvenile, picture book, young adult. "Look at our books. We are not a trendy company. We work with artists primarily. Our motto is: Children's books as works of art." Query.

Tips: "*Always* query. Our audience consists of kids and their parents."

TURNSTONE PRESS, 607-100 Arthur St., Winnipeg, Manitoba R3B 1H3 Canada. (204)947-1555. Managing Editor: James Hutchinson. Estab. 1971. Publishes trade paperback originals. Publishes 8 titles/year. Receives 600-800 mss/year. 25% of books from first-time authors; 75% from unagented writers. Pays 10% royalty on retail price. Offers $100-500 advance. Publishes book 1 year after acceptance of ms. Query for electronic submissions. Reports in 4 months. Book catalog free on request.

• Turnstone Press accepts manuscripts from Canadians and permanent residents only. They do not publish works by US writers.

Fiction: Adventure, ethnic, experimental, feminist, humor, literary, mainstream/contemporary, mystery, short story collections. Submit full ms. *Writer's Market* recommends query with SASE (Canadian postage) first.

Recent Fiction Title: *Some Great Thing*, by Lawrence Hill.

Poetry: Submit complete ms.

Recent Poetry Title: *Jiggers*, by Todd Bruce.

Tips: "We also publish one literary critical study per year and one general interest nonfiction book per year. Would like to see more ethnic writing, women's writing, gay and lesbian writing."

‡UMBRELLA PRESS, 56 Rivercourt Blvd., Toronto, Ontario M4J 3A4 Canada. Publisher: Ken Pearson. Publishes hardcover originals. Publishes 6 titles/year. Receives 10 queries and 5 mss/year. 75% of books from first-time authors; 100% from unagented writers. Pays 10-15% royalty on wholesale price for education, on retail price for trade. Offers $250-500 advance. Publishes book 18 months after acceptance of ms. Accepts simultaneous submissions. Reports in 1 month on queries; 2 months on proposals; 3 months on mss. Book catalog and ms guidelines free on request.

Nonfiction: Biography, reference, library/education supplement. Subjects include education, history, women's issues/studies, multiculturalism. Submit outline with 2 sample chapters.
Recent Nonfiction Title: *Trials & Triumphs: Blacks in Canada*, by L. Hill (reference).

‡**THE UNITED CHURCH PUBLISHING HOUSE (UCPH)**, 85 St. Clair Ave. E., Toronto, Ontario M4T 1M8 Canada. (416)925-4850. Managing Editor: Elizabeth Phinney. Publishes hardcover and trade paperback originals. Publishes 13 titles/year. Receives 30 queries and 20 mss/year. 80% of books from first-time authors; 99% from unagented writers. Pays 8-10% royalty on retail price. Offers $100-300 advance. Publishes books 4-6 months after acceptance of ms. No simultaneous submissions. Query for electronic submissions. Reports in 2 months on proposals. Book catalog and ms guidelines free on request.
Nonfiction: Biography, reference, self-help. Subjects include history, religion, sociology, women's issues/ studies, theology and biblical studies. Submit outline and 1 sample chapter.

THE UNIVERSITY OF ALBERTA PRESS, 141 Athabasca Hall, Edmonton, Alberta T6G 2E8 Canada. (403)492-3662. Fax: (403)492-0719. Director: Norma Gutteridge. Editor: Mary Mahoney-Robson. Estab. 1969. Subsidiary/imprint is Pica Pica Press. Publishes hardcover and trade paperback originals and trade paperback reprints. Averages 10 titles/year. Receives 100-200 submissions annually. 60% of books from first-time authors; majority from unagented writers. Average print order for a first book is 1,000. Pays 10% royalty on retail price. Publishes book an average of 1 year after acceptance. Query for electronic submissions. Reports in on queries; 3 months on mss. Free book catalog and ms guidelines.
  • University of Alberta Press is looking for shorter works with minimum illustration.
Nonfiction: Biography, how-to, reference, technical, textbook, scholarly. Subjects include art, history, nature, philosophy, politics, sociology. Especially looking for "biographies of Canadians in public life, and works analyzing Canada's political history and public policy, particularly in international affairs. No pioneer reminiscences, literary criticism (unless in Canadian literature), reports of narrowly focused studies, unrevised theses." Submit complete ms. Reviews artwork/photos as part of freelance ms package.
Tips: "We are interested in original research making a significant contribution to knowledge in the subject."

‡**UNIVERSITY OF BRITISH COLUMBIA PRESS**, 6344 Memorial Rd., Vancouver, British Columbia V6T 1Z2 Canada. (604)822-4161. Senior Editor: Jean Wilson. Publishes hardcover and trade paperback originals and reprints. Publishes 25 titles/year. Receives 400 queries and 240 mss/year. Pays 0-10% royalty on net. Simultaneous submissions OK. Query for electronic submissions. Reports in 1 month on proposals. Book catalog and ms guidelines free on request.
Nonfiction: Reference, scholarly, technical, textbook. Subjects include anthropology/archaeology, business and economics, government/politics, history, military/war, nature/environment, regional, science, sociology. Query. Reviews artwork/photos as part of the freelance ms package. Writers should send photocopies.

UNIVERSITY OF MANITOBA PRESS, 244-106 Curry Place, Winnipeg, Manitoba R3T 2N2 Canada. Director: Patricia Dowdall. Estab. 1967. Publishes hardcover and trade paperback originals. Publishes 4-6 titles/year. Pays 5-15% royalty on wholesale price. Reports in 3 months.
Nonfiction: Scholarly. Subjects include history, regional, religion, women's issues/studies, native. Query.

THE UNIVERSITY OF OTTAWA PRESS, 542 King Edward, Ottawa, Ontario K1N 6N5 Canada. (613)564-2270. Fax: (613)564-9284. Editor, English Publications: Suzanne Bossé. Estab. 1936. Publishes 25 titles/year; 12 titles/year in English. Receives 100 submissions/year. 20% of books from first-time authors; 95% from unagented writers. Determines subsidy by preliminary budget. Pays 5-10% royalty on net price. Publishes book an average of 1 year after acceptance. Reports in 2 months on queries; 4 months on mss. Book catalog and ms guidelines free.
Nonfiction: Reference, textbook, scholarly. Subjects include education, Canadian government/politics, Canadian history, language/literature, nature/environment, philosophy, religion, sociology, translation, women's issues/studies. "We are looking for scholarly manuscripts by academic authors resident in Canada." No trade books. Submit outline/synopsis and sample chapters.
Recent Nonfiction Title: *Home-Based Care, the Elderly, the Family, and the Welfare State: an International Comparison*, by Frédéric Lesemann and Claude Martin.
Tips: "Envision audience of academic specialists and (for some books) educated public."

VANWELL PUBLISHING LIMITED, 1 Northrup Crescent, P.O. Box 2131, St. Catharines, Ontario L2M 6P5 Canada. (905)937-3100. Fax: (905)937-1760. General Editor: Ms. Lynn J. Hunt. Estab. 1983. Publishes trade originals and reprints. Averages 5-7 titles/year. Receives 100 submissions/year. 85% of books from first-time authors; 100% from unagented writers. Pays 8-15% royalty on wholesale price. Offers $200 average advance. Publishes book an average of 1 year after acceptance. Query for electronic submissions. Reports in 1 month on queries. *Writer's Market* recommends allowing 2 months for reply. Book catalog free.
Nonfiction: Biography. Subjects include military/war. All military/history related. *Writer's Market* recommends query with SASE first. Reviews artwork/photos as part of freelance ms package.

Tips: "The writer has the best chance of selling a manuscript to our firm which is in keeping with our publishing program, well written and organized. Our audience: older male, history buff, war veteran; regional tourist; students. Military/aviation and Canadian military/history have the best chance with us."

VEHICULE PRESS, Box 125, Place du Parc Station, Montreal, Quebec H2W 2M9 Canada. (514)844-6073. Fax: (514)844-7543. President/Publisher: Simon Dardick. Estab. 1973. Imprints include Signal Editions (poetry) and Dossier Quebec (history, memoirs). Publishes trade paperback originals by Canadian authors *only*. Averages 13 titles/year. Receives 250 submissions annually. 20% of books from first-time authors; 95% from unagented writers. Pays 10-15% royalty on retail price. Offers $200-500 advance. Publishes book an average of 1 year after acceptance. Query for electronic submissions. Reports in 4 months on queries. Book catalog for 9 × 12 SAE with IRCs.
Nonfiction: Biography, memoir. Subjects include Canadiana, feminism, history, politics, social history, literature. Especially looking for Canadian social history. Query. Reviews artwork/photos as part of freelance ms package.
Recent Nonfiction Title: *Foxspirit A Woman in Mao's China*, by Zhimei Zhang.
Poetry: Contact Michael Harris, editor. Looking for Canadian authors *only*. Submit complete ms.
Recent Poetry Title: *The Signal Anthology*, edited by Michael Harris.
Tips: "We are only interested in Canadian authors."

‡VERSO, 6 Meard St., London W1V 3HR England. Fax: (71)734-0059. Commisioning Editor: Malcolm Imrie. Estab. 1970. Publishes hardcover and tradepaper originals. Publishes 60 titles/year. Receives 500 submissions/year. 15% of books from first-time authors; 80% from unagented writers. Pays 7-10% royalty on retail price. Offers $1,000 average advance. Publishes book an average of 15 months after acceptance. Reports in 2 months.
Nonfiction: Academic and general. Subjects include economics, education, government/politics/social sciences, language/literature, nature/environment, philosophy, science, cultural and media studies, sociology, travel, women's issues/studies. Submit outline and sample chapters. Unsolicited mss not accepted.
Recent Nonfiction Title: *Deterring Democracy*, by Noam Chomsky (hardback).

VESTA PUBLICATIONS, LTD., Box 1641, Cornwall, Ontario K6H 5V6 Canada. (613)932-2135. Fax: (613)932-7735. President: Ajay Gill. Editor: Stephen Gill. Estab. 1976. Publishes trade paperback and mass market paperback originals. Pays 10% minimum royalty on wholesale price. Subsidy publishes 5% of books. "We ask a writer to subsidize a part of the cost of printing; normally, it is 50%. We do so when we find that the book does not have a wide market, as in the case of university theses and the author's first collection of poems. The writer gets 25 free copies and 10% royalty on paperback editions." No advance. Publishes 4 titles/year. Receives 350 submissions annually. 100% of books from unagented writers. Simultaneous submissions OK if so informed. Query for electronic submissions. Reports in 1 month. *Writer's Market* recommends allowing 2 months for reply. "Phone us before submission and save time." Send SAE with IRCs. Book catalog for SASE with IRC.
Nonfiction: Publishes Americana, biography, ethnic, government/politics, philosophy, language/literature, money/finance, reference, religious books. Accepts nonfiction translations. Query. Looks for knowledge of the language and subject. State availability of photos and/or illustrations to accompany ms.
Fiction: Ethnic, literary. Query.
Poetry: Submit 5-6 samples.

WALL & EMERSON, INC., 6 O'Connor Dr., Toronto, Ontario M4K 2K1 Canada. (416)467-8685. Fax: (416)696-2460. President: Byron E. Wall. Vice President: Martha Wall. Estab. 1987. Imprints are Wall & Thompson and Wall & Emerson. Publishes hardcover and trade paperback originals and reprints. Publishes 5 titles/year. 50% of books from first-time authors; 100% from unagented writers. Subsidy publishes 10% of books. Only subsidies provided by external granting agencies accepted. Generally these are for scholarly books with a small market. Pays royalty of 8-15% on wholesale price. Publishes book an average of 1 year after acceptance. Simultaneous submissions OK. Prefers electronic submissions. Reports in 2 months on queries.
Nonfiction: Reference, textbook. Subjects include adult education, health/medicine, philosophy, psychology, science, mathematics. "We are looking for any undergraduate college text that meets the needs of a well-defined course in colleges in the US and Canada." Submit outline and sample chapters.
Recent Nonfiction Title: *Calculus: The Analysis of Functions*, by Peter D. Taylor.
Tips: "We are most interested in textbooks for college courses; books that meet well defined needs and are targeted to their audiences are best. Our audience consists of college undergraduate students and college libraries. If I were a writer trying to market a book today, I would identify the audience for the book and write directly to the audience throughout the book. I would then approach a publisher that publishes books specifically for that audience."

WEIGL EDUCATIONAL PUBLISHERS LTD., 1900A 11th St. SE, Calgary, Alberta T2G 3G2 Canada. (403)233-7747. Fax: (403)233-7769. Publisher: Linda Weigl. Estab. 1979. Publishes hardcover originals and reprints.

Publishes 6-7 titles/year. Receives 50-100 submissions/year. 30% of books from first-time authors; 100% from unagented writers. Pays 5-12% royalty on retail price. Publishes book an average of 2 years after acceptance. Query for electronic submissions. Reports in up to 4 months. Book catalog free.
Nonfiction: K-12 student and teacher materials: social studies, language arts, science/environmental studies, life skills, multicultural texts: Canadian focus. Submit outline and sample chapters with SASE or IRCs. Reviews artwork/photos as part of freelance ms package.
Recent Nonfiction Title: *Alberta, It's People in History.*
Fiction: Juvenile educational: multicultural and environmental.
Tips: "Audience is school students and teachers. Curriculum fit is very important."

WHITECAP BOOKS LTD., 1086 W. Third St., North Vancouver, British Columbia V7P 3J6 Canada. (604)980-9852. Fax: (604)980-8197. Editorial Director: Pat Crowe. Publishes hardcover and trade paperback originals. Publishes 24 titles/year. Receives 150 queries and 50 mss/year. 20% of books from first-time authors; 90% from unagented writers. Pays 10% royalty on retail price. Offers $500-2,000 advance. Publishes book 8 months after acceptance of ms. Simultaneous submissions OK. Query for electronic submissions. Reports in 2 months on proposals.
Nonfiction: Biography, coffee table book, cookbook, children's/juvenile. Subjects include animals, gardening, history, nature/environment, recreation, regional, travel. "We require an annotated outline. Writers should also take the time to research our list through our catalogue." Submit outline, 2 sample chapters, table of contents. Reviews artwork/photos as part of the freelance ms package. Writers should send photocopies, transparencies, relevant material.
Recent Nonfiction Title: *Guardians of the Whales*, by Bruce Obee (natural history).
Tips: "Our readership is a general audience."

‡WINDFLOWER COMMUNICATIONS, 67 Flett Ave., Winnipeg, Manitoba R2K 3N3 Canada. (204)668-7475. Editorial Director: Susan Braun Bramdt. Publishes hardcover and trade paperback originals. Publishes 5 titles/year. Receives 250 queries and 125 mss/year. 85% of books from first-time authors; 100% from unagented writers. Subsidy publishes 30% of books. Pays 15% royalty on wholesale price. Publishes book 9 months after acceptance. Simultaneous submissions OK. Query for electronic submissions. Reports in 1 month on queries, 3 months on proposals, 6 months on mss. Book catalog and ms guidelines free on request.
Nonfiction: Biography, children's juvenile, self-help. Subjects include ethnic, history, religion, sociology, women's issues/studies, Canadiana. "Must be family value-oriented; and be very carefully researched as to uniqueness for market. Often writers have not checked market, competition or have not been careful about sources." Submit proposal package, including outline, 4-6 chapters. Reviews artwork/photos as part of the freelance ms package. Writers should send photocopies.
Fiction: Adventure, fantasy, historical, juvenile, religious, Canadiana. "We are promoting Canadiana (Canadian historical fiction) and religious fiction of quality. Common mistakes are poor editing and re-writing. Submit synopsis with 4-6 sample chapters.
Poetry: Submit complete ms.
Tips: "Audience is family oriented people; religious (Christian) bent."

WOLSAK AND WYNN PUBLISHERS LTD., P.O. Box 316, Don Mills, Ontario M3C 2S7 Canada. President: Heather Cadsby. Secretary/Treasurer: Maria Jacobs. Estab. 1982. Publishes trade paperback originals. Publishes 5 titles/year. Receives 100 queries/year. Pays 10% royalty on retail price. Publishes book 1 year after acceptance of ms. Query for electronic submissions. Reports in 6 months on queries. Book catalog and ms guidelines free on request.
Poetry: Submit 10 sample poems. Include SAE with IRC's.

‡WOMEN'S PRESS, #233-517 College St., Toronto, Ontario M6G 4A2 Canada. Co-Managing Editors: Ann Decter, Martha Ayim. Publishes trade paperback originals. Publishes 10 titles/year. Receives 150 queries/year. 50% of books from first-time authors; 100% from unagented writers. Pays 10-15% royalty on retail price. Offers $300 advance. Publishes books 6 months after acceptance of ms. Simultaneous submissions OK if notified. Reports in 3 months on queries; 6 months on proposals; 1 year on mss. Book catalog and ms guidelines free on request.
Nonfiction: "Only women authors." Biography, children's/juvenile. Subjects include education, ethnic, gay/lesbian, government/politics, health/medicine, history, language/literature, philosophy, sociology, sports, women's issues/studies. "Must be feminist and anti-racist looking for mostly Canadian material." Query.
Recent Nonfiction Title: *And Still We Rise*, by Linda Carty (anthology-politics); *Private Lives, Public Policy*, by Jane Ursel (sociology); *Petticoats & Prejudice*, by Constance Backhouse (legal history).
Fiction: Erotica, feminist, lesbian, short story collections, young adult. Wants work that is "overtly feminist." Query.
Recent Fiction Title: *Tahuri*, by Ngahuia Te Aweletulcer (short stories); *Division of Surgery*, by Donna McFarlane (novel); *Throw It To The River*, by Nice Rodriguez (short stories).
Poetry: Wants poetry that is feminist/political/lesbian. Query.
Recent Poetry Title: *Women Do This Every Day*, by Lillian Allen.

YORK PRESS LTD., P.O. Box 1172, Fredericton, New Brunswick E3B 5C8 Canada. (506)458-8748. General Manager/Editor: Dr. S. Elkhadem. Estab. 1975. Publishes trade paperback originals. Averages 10 titles/year. Receives 50 submissions annually. 10% of books from first-time authors; 100% from unagented writers. Pays 10-20% royalty on wholesale price. Publishes book an average of 6 months after acceptance. Reports in 2 weeks. *Writer's Market* recommends allowing 2 months for reply. Book catalog free. Manuscript guidelines for $2.50.

Nonfiction and Fiction: Reference, textbook, scholarly. Especially needs literary criticism, comparative literature and linguistics and fiction of an experimental nature by well-established writers. Query.

Recent Nonfiction Title: *Tennessee Williams: Life, Work and Criticism,* by F. Londré.

Recent Fiction Title: *Red White & Blue,* by Ben Stoltzfus.

Tips: "If I were a writer trying to market a book today, I would spend a considerable amount of time examining the needs of a publisher *before* sending my manuscript to him. Scholarly books and creative writing of an experimental nature are the only kinds we publish. The writer must adhere to our style manual and follow our guidelines exactly."

Subsidy/Royalty Book Publishers

In this section you'll find listings for U.S. book publishers that publish even a small percentage of their books on an author-subsidy basis.

Also known as "vanity presses," "co-publishers" or "cooperative publishers," they offer services ranging from editing and printing your book to distributing and promoting it. They are called "subsidy" publishers because they ask you, the author, to subsidize (pay for) all or part of the cost of publishing your book. Their prices can run as high as $25,000.

Letters making subsidy offers sometimes are the first and only encouraging correspondence writers receive about their book proposals. You should read with a grain of salt how much a publisher loves your book if they are asking you to pay for its production, marketing and/or distribution. Other letters express how much a publisher would like to publish a writer's book, if only they had sufficient funds. They ask if you, the author, would consider investing in a portion of the cost of the book's publication. These letters are often persuasive, and perhaps you will decide that co-publishing may be the route you want to take. Just be certain you know what you're getting into.

Full subsidy publishers often argue that the current economic climate necessitates authors paying the costs of publishing. Because subsidy publishers make a profit on simply producing 1,000 or so bound books, they don't have a stake in marketing the books they publish. Royalty publishers, on the other hand, must sell books to make money because they pay the publishing costs.

Before agreeing to a subsidy contract, ask yourself some questions. What would you do with 1,000 or even 500 copies of your book, if the distribution were left to you? How many do you realistically think you could sell? Few bookstores deal with individuals selling single books. Talk to a local bookstore owner before you sign a contract to see if they stock any titles by the publisher who wants to print your book.

In a co-publishing arrangement, the publisher will usually market its co-published books because it has paid part of the production cost, but writers have other concerns. How do you know the 50% you are paying is truly 50% of the total cost? If you are unsure, call a printer in your area and ask for an estimated cost of printing the type and number of books the publisher has proposed to you. If the printer's quote is significantly lower than the original figure you received, contact the publisher to discuss the matter.

Also at issue is your royalty arrangement. Often a writer is asked for up to half the cost to publish a book, and yet offered a royalty of less than 15%. Authors eager to have their books published find themselves adding up the number of sales they would need to break even. They forget that bookstores take 40-50% of the cover price for each copy they sell, and there are other charges: distributors, shippers and wholesalers all must be paid as well. Be realistic about what you think you could make back, and proceed cautiously.

Don't bow to pressure from any subsidy publisher who claims you must "act now" or the offer to publish may be withdrawn. Don't confuse subsidy publishers with royalty publishers. Unlike the relationship you might have with a royalty publisher, in which

you attempt to earn their favor, you are a subsidy publisher's *customer*, not a suppli-
cant. And as a customer, you should approach the relationship as you would when
considering the purchase of any other service—with a dose of skepticism and clear
ideas about the contractual assurances you want to see. It is recommended that you
consult with an attorney before signing any publishing contract.

If you are truly committed to your book and think there is a market for it, consider
self-publishing as an option. It generally costs less than subsidy publishing for essentially the same services, and you have much more control over what is done with your
book. For more information on self-publishing, take a look at *The Complete Guide to
Self-Publishing*, by Tom and Marilyn Ross (Writer's Digest Books) or *The Publish It
Yourself Handbook*, by Bill Henderson (Pushcart Press). In any case, proceed with
caution any time a publisher is asking you to finance all or part of the cost of publication.

While we encourage writers to sell their work to royalty publishers, we have listed
other book publishing options here. Publishers with the longer listings publish at least
50% of their books on a royalty basis. The shorter listings at the end of this section
are the names and addresses of publishers producing more than 50% of their books
on an author-subsidy basis.

**For a list of publishers according to their subjects of interest, see the nonfiction and
fiction sections of the Book Publishers Subject Index. Information on some book publishers and producers not included in this edition of *Writer's Market* can be found in
Book Publishers and Producers/Changes '94-'95.**

‡A CAPPELLA BOOKS, Subsidiary of Chicago Review Press, Inc., 814 N. Franklin St., Chicago IL 60201.
(312)337-0747. Fax: (312)5985. Editor: Linda Matthews. Estab. 1990. Publishes hardcover originals and trade
paperback originals and reprints. Publishes 4 titles/year. Receives 30 queries and 25 mss/year. 25% of books
from first-time authors; 80% from unagented writers. Subsidy publishes 10% of books. Pays 10-15% royalty.
Offers $500-1,000 advance. Publishes book 8 months after acceptance of ms. Simultaneous submissions OK.
Query for electronic submissions. Reports in 2 months on proposals. Book catalog free on request.
Nonfiction: Biography, how-to, reference, technical, textbook. Subjects include art/architecture, music/
dance, travel. "We publish books on dance and music, primarily, but also theater and the arts. We do not
publish academic books, but rather books aimed at a general audience. Do not submit manuscripts before
they are ready; i.e. in a very rough form." Submit outline and 1 sample chapter. Reviews artwork/photos as
part of freelance ms package. Writers should send photocopies.
Tips: "Our audience consists of general trade, libraries and students at high school or college level. Send a
sample chapter, a descriptive outline, and a résumé with sample photos (if applicable). In your cover letter,
tell us what the market for your book is, what the competition is, and how your idea/book is different."

‡AARDVARK PUBLISHING COMPANY, P.O. Box 951, Lake Worth FL 33460-0951. (407)586-0483. Fax:
(407)547-9677. President: Meyer L. Abrams, M.D. Editor: Rhoda S. Abrams. Estab. 1993. Publishes hardcover originals and reprints. Publishes 4 titles/year. 90% of books from first-time authors; 100% from unagented writers. Pays 5-10% royalty. Estab. 1993. Publishes books 4 months after acceptance of ms. Simultaneous submissions OK. "Prefer: 1) Camera-ready copy of manuscript or 2) diskette (Word for Windows)."
Reports in 2 months on mss.
Nonfiction: Biography, coffee table book, humor, illustrated book, children's/juvenile. Subjects include
Americana, history. Query with outline and 3-4 sample chapters. Submit proposal package, including "What
do you see as your market? Are you willing to participate in marketing?". Writers should send actual artwork
or color photos.
Fiction: Adventure, confession, historical, horror, humor, juvenile, literary, mainstream/contemporary, mys-
tery, romance, science fiction, short story collections, suspense, young adult. Query or submit synopsis and
3-4 sample chapters.
   • This publisher no longer accepts poetry..
Tips: Publishes books for libraries, as well as the general adult market and children's books.

ALPINE PUBLICATIONS, INC., 225 S. Madison Ave., Loveland CO 80537-6514. (303)667-9317. Publisher: B.J.
McKinney. Estab. 1975. Publishes hardcover and trade paperback originals. Averages 6 titles/year. Subsidy
publishes 2% of books when "book fits into our line but has a market so limited (e.g., rare dog breed) that
we would not accept it on royalty terms." Occasional advances. Pays 7-15% royalty. Publishes book an average

of 18 months after acceptance. Reports in 3-4 months. Writer's guidelines for #10 SAE with 2 first-class stamps.
Nonfiction: How-to books about companion animals. "We need comprehensive breed books on the more popular AKC breeds, books on showing, breeding, genetics, gait, care, new training methods, and cat and horse books. No fiction or fictionalized stories of real animals; no books on reptiles; no personal experience stories except in case of well-known professional in field." Submit outline and sample chapters. Reviews artwork/photos as part of ms package.

AMERICAN MEDIA, P.O. Box 4646, Westlake Village CA 91359. (805)496-1649. President: G. Edward Griffin. Publishes hardcover, trade paperback and mass market paperback originals. Publishes 2 titles/year. Receives 60 queries and 10 mss/year. 75% of books from first-time authors; 100% from unagented writers. Subsidy publishes 10% of books. "Marketability determines whether author should be subsidy published." Pays 5-15% royalty on retail price. Publishes book 4 months after acceptance of ms. Simultaneous submissions OK. SASE. Reports in 1 month. Book catalog free on request.
Nonfiction: Biography, coffee table book, cookbook, reference, documentaries. Subjects include anthropology/archaeology, business and economics, cooking, foods & nutrition, education, government/politics, health/medicine, history, military/war, money/finance. Query with outline and 1 sample chapter. Reviews artwork/photos as part of ms package. Writers should send photocopies.

ASHGATE PUBLISHING COMPANY, Old Post Rd., Brookfield VT 05036. (802)276-3162. Fax: (802)276-3837. President: James W. Gerard. Estab. 1978. Imprints include Ashgate, Avebury, Avebury Technical, Scolar, Varorium. Publishes hardcover originals and reprints and trade paperback originals. Averages 250 titles/year. Receives 100 submissions/year. 25% of books from first-time authors; 100% from unagented writers. Subsidy publishes 10% of books. Pays royalty on retail price or buys mss outright. Publishes book an average of 3 months after acceptance. Simultaneous submissions OK. Query for electronic submissions. Reports in 2 months.
Nonfiction: Reference, technical, textbook. Subjects include art/architecture, business and economics, government/politics, money/finance, philosophy, sociology. Submit outline and sample chapters.

ASYLUM ARTS PUBLISHING, P.O. Box 6203, Santa Maria CA 93456-6203. Publisher: Greg Boyd. Publishes hardcover and trade paperback originals. Publishes 6-10 titles/year. Receives 200 queries and 25 mss/year. 10% of books from first-time authors; 100% from unagented writers. Subsidy publishes 20% of books. Subsidized projects must be of the same literary quality as other titles and must "fit" our list—subsidized books are usually in difficult to sell genres, i.e. poetry, drama. Pays 7-10% royalty on wholesale price. Publishes book 18 months after acceptance of ms. Query for electronic submissions. Reports in 2 months on mss. Book catalog free on request.
  • Asylum Arts expects to cut back the number of new titles. Aso, their list is already 75% complete for 1995, which means extremely tough competition for writers. The editor strongly discourages most potential authors from considering Aslyum Arts at this time.
Fiction: Erotica, experimental, literary, plays, short story collections. "Writers should be able to recognize our preferences by familiarizing themselves with the kind of work published in *Asylum Annual* magazine. We lean toward post-modern fiction and translations of 19th century French texts, as well as translations of contemporary authors." Query.
Poetry: "Writers and poets should be familiar with our books and with the contents of *Asylum Annual* magazine. Poets should be forewarned that we can afford to publish very few poetry titles. We do not consider chapbook-length manuscripts." Query.
Tips: Audience is libraries, college students and faculty, sophisticated readers of contemporary literature. "Writers should always query before sending a manuscript that may be totally inappropriate for our list."

BEAVER POND PUBLISHING & PRINTING, P.O. Box 224, Greenville PA 16125. (412)588-3492. Owner: Richard E. Faler, Jr. Estab. 1989. Publishes 95% mass market paperback originals, 5% reprints. Averages 5 titles/year. Receives 20 submissions/year. 20% of books from first-time authors; 20% from unagented writers. Subsidy publishes 10% of books. Determines subsidy "if we don't wish to take on the book as publisher, but the author still wants us to print it." Pays 8-10% royalty on net sales or makes outright purchase for $100-1,000 on booklets. Publishes book an average of 11 months after acceptance. Simultaneous submissions OK. Reports in 2 months. Manuscript guidelines for #10 SASE.
  • Beaver Pond wants to concentrate on 20-40 page booklets with outdoor photography or sporting

focus. They must be very specific. Also, they have begun a co-publishing division under the imprint of Fire Heart.

Nonfiction: How-to. Subjects include animals, natural history of wildlife, nature/environment, photography especially of wildlife, recreation, hunting, fishing. "We want to see manuscripts suitable for 24 page booklets through 200 page books that are written with authority on very specific topics and that are how-to. Example: "Photographing Birds in Flight." Query. Submit outline/synopsis and sample chapters and complete ms. Reviews artwork/photos as part of ms package.

Tips: "We're looking for very specific topics in both consumptive and non-consumptive animal use that are too specific for larger publishers. There are experts out there with valuable information. We want to make that information available. Our primary audiences are hunters, fishermen and photographers. If I were a writer trying to market a book today, I would look for a niche, fill that niche, and attempt to fill it with a work that would be difficult, if not impossible, for someone to duplicate or do better. We are particularly interested in 3,000-7,000 word booklet manuscripts at this time."

‡BENJAMIN PUBLISHING CO., INC., 1862 Akron-Peninsula Rd., Akron OH 44313.(216)928-3674. President: Barry Benjamin. Publishes hardcover originals. Publishes 1 title/year. Receives 7-10 queries and 4-5 mss/ year. 100% of books from first-time authors; 90% from unagented writers. Subsidy publishes 20% of books. Pays 7-10% royalty on retail price. Offers $500 advance. Publishes book 3 months after acceptance. No simultaneous submissions. Query for electronic submissions. Reports in 1 month on queries. Book catalog and ms guidelines for #10 SASE.

Nonfiction: Coffee table book, cookbook, children's/juvenile. Subjects include ethnic, photography, travel. "Have a plan developed with a target market of buyers of your book. Do your research before submitting manuscripts. Develop possible size and number of pages, photos, illustrations." Query with outline and 1-2 sample chapters. Reviews artwork/photos as part of ms package. Writers should send whatever is available, but no originals.

Recent Nonfiction Title: *So, You Want To Be A Veterinarian*, by Melvin S. Wolfman.

BERGH PUBLISHING, INC., subsidiary of Bergh & Bergh Verlagsanstalt GmbH, Switzerland, Suite 715E, 20 E. 53rd St., New York NY 10022. (212)593-1040. Fax: (212)593-4638. Contact: Sven-Erik Bergh. Publishes hardcover originals and reprints. Publishes 10-15 titles/year. Receives 74 submissions/year. 40% of books from first-time authors; 60% from unagented writers. Subsidy publishes 2% of books. Pays 10-15% on whole-sale price. Preliminary letter with SASE required.

Nonfiction: Biography, cookbook, illustrated book, juvenile. Subjects include animals, cooking, foods and nutrition, government/politics. Query.

Recent Nonfiction Title: *Bergh's International Annual Digest of Gastronomy*.

BINFORD & MORT PUBLISHING, 1202 NW 17th Ave., Portland OR 97209-2405. (503)221-0866. Publisher: James Gardenier. Editor: James Roberts. Estab. 1891. Publishes hardcover and paperback originals and reprints. Publishes about 10-12 titles/year. Receives 500 submissions annually. 60% of books from first-time authors; 90% from unagented writers. Average print order for a first book is 5,000. Pays 10% royalty on retail price. Offers variable advance (to established authors). Occasionally does some subsidy publishing (10%), at author's request. Publishes book an average of 1 year after acceptance. Reports in 4 months.

Nonfiction: Books about the Pacific Coast and the Northwest. Subjects include Western Americana, biography, history, nature, maritime, recreation, reference, travel. Query with sample chapters and SASE. Reviews artwork/photos as part of ms package.

Recent Nonfiction Title: *Aurora, Their Last Utopia: Oregon's Christian Commune, 1856-1883*, by Eugene Edmund Snyder.

BLACK HAT PRESS, Box 12, Goodhue MN 55027. (612)923-4590. Editor/Publisher: Beverly Voldseth. Estab. 1989. Publishes poetry. Is "open to any good writing." Reports in 2 months. Also publishes *Rag Mag*, a semiannual literary magazine.

BLUE HORIZON PRESS, #206, 21301 Powerline Rd., Boca Raton FL 33433-2388. (407)487-8823. Director: Clint Nangle. Estab. 1992. Subsidiary of Gulfstream Equity Management, Inc.

Tips: "Looking for top recognized experts, particularly in recovery subjects and international investing and finance. We are looking for premium information that will sell for a premium price."

‡DON BOSCO MULTIMEDIA, 475 N. Ave., Box T, New Rochelle NY 10802. (914)576-0122. Publisher: James Hurley. Subsidiaries include Salesiana Publishers. Publishes hardcover and trade paperback originals. Averages 10-20 titles/year. Receives 50 submissions annually. 15% of books from first-time authors; 100% from unagented writers. Average print order for a first book is 2,500. Subsidy publishes 10% of books. Subsidy publishes (nonauthor) 30% of books. "We judge the content of the manuscript and quality to be sure it fits the description of our house. We subsidy publish for nonprofit and religious societies." Pays 5-10% royalty on retail price; offers average $100 advance. Publishes book an average of 10 months after acceptance. Reports in 6 weeks on queries, 3 months on mss. Book catalog free.

Nonfiction: Biography, juvenile, textbook on Roman Catholic religion. "Biographies of outstanding Christian men and women of today. We are a new publisher with wide experience in school marketing, especially in religious education field." Accepts nonfiction translations from Italian and Spanish. Query or submit outline/synopsis and 2 sample chapters. Occasionally reviews artwork/photos as part of ms package.
Tips: Queries/mss may be routed to other editors in the publishing group.

THE BOXWOOD PRESS, 183 Ocean View Blvd., Pacific Grove CA 93950. (408)375-9110. Editor: Dr. Ralph Buchsbaum. Imprints include Viewpoint Books, Free Spirit Books. Publishes hardcover and trade paperback originals. Averages 5 titles/year. Receives 25 submissions/year. Subsidy publishes 25% of books. Determines subsidy by high merit; low market. Pays 10% royalty. Publishes book an average of 10 months after acceptance. Query for electronic submissions. Reports in 6 weeks on queries; 2 months on mss. Book catalog free on request.
Nonfiction: Biography, technical, textbook. Subjects include biology (plants and animals), health/medicine, history, nature/environment, philosophy, psychology, regional or area studies and other science. Submit complete ms. Reviews artwork/photos as part of ms package.
Tips: "Writers have the best chance selling us sound science and natural history books. Our audience is high school and college, general and educated. If I were a writer trying to market a book today, I would know my subject, readership and do my clearest writing."

BRIARCLIFF PRESS PUBLISHERS, 11 Wimbledon Ct., Jericho NY 11753. Editorial Director: Trudy Settel. Senior Editor: J. Frieman. Estab. 1977. Publishes hardcover and paperback originals. Averages 5-7 titles/year. Receives 250 submissions annually. 10% of books from first-time authors; 60% from unagented writers. Average print order for a first book is 5,000. Subsidy publishes 20% of books. Pays $4,000-5,000 for outright purchase. Offers average $1,000 advance. Publishes book an average of 6 months after acceptance. Reports in 3 months. Catalog for 9×12 SAE with 3 first-class stamps.
Nonfiction: How-to, cookbooks, sports, travel, fitness/health, business and finance, diet, gardening, crafts. "We want our books to be designed to meet the needs of specific businesses." Accepts nonfiction translations from French, German and Italian. Query or submit outline and 2 sample chapters. Reviews artwork/photos as part of ms package.
Tips: "We do not use unsolicited manuscripts. Ours are custom books prepared for businesses, and assignments are initiated by us."

‡BRIDGE PUBLISHING, 2500 Hamilton Blvd., South Plainfield NJ 07080. (908)754-0745. Editor: Catherine J. Barrier. Imprints are Bridge, Logos, Haven, Open Scroll. Publishes hardcover, trade paperback and mass market paperback originals and reprints. Publishes 50 titles/year; imprint publishes 12 titles/year. Receives 1,000 queries and 300 mss/year. 50% of books from first-time authors; 80% from unagented writers. Subsidy publishes 20% of books. Pays 10-20% royalty on wholesale price. Offers $1,000-25,000 advance. Publishes book 4 months after acceptance of ms. Simultaneous submissions OK. Query for electronic submissions. Reports in 3 months on proposals. Book catalog and ms guidelines free on request.
Nonfiction: Biography, coffee table books, children's/juvenile, self-help, textbook. Subjects include religion. "We are a flexible, dedicated Christian publisher. We are particularly interested in materials for Christian evangelism, spiritual growth, education and self-help." Query with brief synopsis (500-600 words), detailed and concise chapter by chapter outline, author bio information (including ministry involvements), any marketing ideas and 3 sample chapters. Reviews artwork/photos as part of freelance ms package. Writers should send photocopies.
Recent Nonfiction Title: *God Doesn't Believe In Atheists*, by Ray Comfort (apologetics); *365 Ways to Love Your Wife*, by Glenn Egli (self help/coffee table); *This Thousand Years*, by L.B. Brooks (history).
Fiction: Religious. Query or submit synopsis and 3 sample chapters.

*BUDDHA ROSE PUBLICATIONS, P.O. Box 548, Hermosa Beach CA 90254. Eidtor-in-Chief: Scott Shaw. Publishes hardcover and trade paperback originals. Publishes 25 titles/year. Pays 15% royalty on wholesale price. Offers $100-10,000 advance. Publishes book 6 months after acceptance of ms.
● Buddha Rose is now accepting only agented submissions.
Nonfiction: Reference, self-help, textbook. Subjects include anthropology/archaeology, art/architecture, ethnic, government/politics, history, nature/environment, philosophy, psychology, religion, science, sociology, travel.
Fiction: Experimental, literary. Submit entire ms.
Poetry: "Make your poetry scream of experience—forget boring rhymes." Submit 5 sample poems.
Tips: "Live what you write; be it fiction, poetry or cultural, for this is the only place where knowledge is born."

‡ARISTIDE D. CARATZAS, PUBLISHER, Box 210/30 Church St., New Rochelle NY 10801. (914)632-8487. Fax: (914)636-3650. Managing Editor: John Emerich. Estab. 1975. Publishes hardcover originals and reprints. Averages 20 titles/year. Receives 100 submissions annually. 35% of books from first-time authors; 80% from unagented writers. Subsidy publishes 25% of books. "We seek grants/subsidies for limited run scholarly books; granting organizations are generally institutions or foundations." Pays royalty. Offers $1,500 average advance. Publishes book an average of 18 months after acceptance. Simultaneous submissions OK. Query for electronic submissions. Reports in 1 month on queries. *Writer's Market* recommends allowing 2 months for reply. Book catalog free.

Nonfiction: Reference, technical, textbook. Subjects include art, history (ancient, European, Russian), politics, religion, travel, classical languages (Greek and Latin), archaeology and mythology. Nonfiction book ms needs for the next year include "scholarly books in archaeology, mythology, ancient and medieval history, and art history." Query or submit outline and sample chapters. Reviews artwork/photos as part of ms package.

‡THE CENTER FOR WESTERN STUDIES, Augustana College, Box 727, Sioux Falls SD 57197. (605)336-4007. Managing Editor: Harry F. Thompson. Publishes hardcover and trade paperback originals and reprints. Publishes 2-3 titles/year. Receives 25-30 queries and 10-12 mss/year. 50% of books from first-time authors; 90% from unagented writers. Subsidy publishes 25% of books. Pays 7-10% royalty on wholesale price and copies of publication for resale. Publishes book 8 months after acceptance. Accepts simultaneous submissions. Reports in 2 months on queries; 4 months on proposals; 6-12 months on mss. Book catalog free on request.

Nonfiction: Biography, coffee table book, reference, textbook. Subjects include anthropology/archaeology, art/architecture, ethnic, history, regional, translation. "We are a small house, a program closely connected with the other activities of the Center for Western Studies, such as museum interpretation, archives, and Northern Plains/Western cultures. Most of our titles have foundation or commercial backing." Query with outline and 2 sample chapters.

Recent Nonfiction Title: *The Northern Pacific Railroad and the Selling of the West*, by Sig Mickelson (history).

Fiction: Historical, short story collections, western. "We are not especially interested in fiction, but would consider fiction that relates directly to the Northern Plains region." Query with synopsis and 3 sample chapters.

Recent Fiction Title: *The Wind is in the South and Other Short Stories*, by Ole E. Rolvaag.

THE CHARLES PRESS, PUBLISHERS., P.O. Box 15715, Philadelphia PA 19103. (215)545-8933 or 545-8934. Fax: (215)545-8937. Also 1238 Callowhill St., Philadelphia PA 19123. Editor-in-Chief: Lauren Meltzer. Estab. 1983. Publishes hardcover and trade paperback originals and reprints. Publishes 12-15 titles/year. Receives 300 queries and 100 mss/year. 20% of books from first-time authors; 100% from unagented writers. Subsidy publishes 1% of books "but we plan to increase this. If the project is for one reason or another, very high risk, then we would consider this." Pays 10-12% royalty on retail price. Publishes book 3-8 months after acceptance of ms. Simultaneous submissions OK. Query for electronic submission: prefers IBM-compatible – WordPerfect/MicroSoft Word, WordPerfect or Word for Window. Reports in 3 months on proposals.

Nonfiction: How-to, coping. Subjects include health/medicine, psychology of illness, grief. Query.

Recent Nonfiction Title: *Now I Lay Me Down: Suicide in the Elderly*, by David Lester.

‡CHRISTIAN CLASSICS, INC., P.O. Box 30, Westminster MD 21158-0930. (410)848-3065. President: John J. McHale. Imprint is Wakefield Editions. Publishes hardcover and trade paperback originals and reprints. Publishes 8-15 titles/year. Receives 100 queries and 50 mss/year. 10% of books from first-time authors; 100% from unagented writers. Subsidy publishes 5% of books. Pays 10-12½% royalty on net received. Offers $750 advance. Publishes book 3 months after acceptance of ms. No simultaneous submissions. Query for electronic submissions. Reports in 1 month on queries. Book catalog free on request.

Nonfiction: Biography, reference, textbook. Subjects include history, philosophy, religion, theology, hagiography. "We are known for classical works of secondary level. Modern works must fit the classical category." Query with outline and 1-2 sample chapters.

Recent Nonfiction Title: *Dunwoodie*, by Shelley (history); *What Are The Theologians Saying Now*, by Hellwig (theology); *Summa Theologiae* (St. Thomas Aquinas), translated by McDermott (philosophy).

THE CHRISTOPHER PUBLISHING HOUSE, 24 Rockland St., Commerce Green, Hanover MA 02339-0024. (617)826-7474. Fax: (617)826-5556. Managing Editor: Nancy Lucas. Estab. 1910. Publishes hardcover and trade paperback originals. Averages 10-20 titles/year. Receives 400-500 submissions annually. 30% of books from first-time authors; 100% from unagented writers. Subsidy publishes 15% of books. Pays 5-30% royalty on net proceeds. No advance. Publishes book an average of 12-15 months after acceptance. Simultaneous submissions OK. Query for electronic submissions. Reports in 2 months. Book catalog for #10 SAE with 2 first-class stamps. Manuscript guidelines for SASE.

Nonfiction: Biography, how-to, reference, self-help, textbook. Subjects include Americana, animals, art, business and economics, cooking and foods (nutrition), health, history, philosophy, politics, psychology, religion, sociology, travel. "We will be glad to review all nonfiction manuscripts, particularly college textbook and religious-oriented." Submit complete ms. *Writer's Market* recommends query with SASE first. Reviews artwork/photos as part of ms package.

Poetry: "We will review all forms of poetry." Submit complete ms.

Recent Poetry Title: *The Sea Cries Over My Shoulder*, by Jonathan Russell.

Tips: "Our books are for a general audience, slanted toward college-educated readers. There are specific books targeted toward specific audiences when appropriate."

ARTHUR H. CLARK CO. , P.O. Box 14707, Spokane WA 99214. (509)928-9540. Fax: (509)928-4364. Editorial Director: Robert A. Clark. Estab. 1902. Publishes hardcover originals. Averages 8 titles/year. Receives 40 submissions annually. 40% of books from first-time authors; 100% from unagented writers. Subsidy publishes 15% of books based on whether they are "high-risk sales." Subsidy publishes (nonauthor) 5% of books. Pays 10% minimum royalty on wholesale price. Publishes book an average of 9 months after acceptance. Reports in 2 months. Book catalog for 6×9 SASE.
Nonfiction: Biography, reference, historical nonfiction. Subjects include Americana, history. "We're looking for documentary source material in Western American history." Query or submit outline/synopsis with SASE. Looks for "content, form, style." Reviews artwork/photos as part of ms package.
Tips: "Western Americana (nonfiction) has the best chance of being sold to our firm."

CLEANING CONSULTANT SERVICES, INC., P.O. Box 1273, Seattle WA 98111. (206)682-9748. President: William R. Griffin. Publishes trade paperback originals and reprints. Averages 4-6 titles/year. Receives 15 submissions annually. 75% of books from first-time authors; 100% from unagented writers. Subsidy publishes 5% of books. "If they (authors) won't sell it and won't accept royalty contract, we offer our publishing services and often sell the book along with our books." Pays 5-15% royalty on retail price or makes outright purchase, $100-2,500, depending on negotiated agreement. Publishes book an average of 6-12 months after acceptance. Reports in 6 weeks on queries. *Writer's Market* recommends allowing 2 months for reply. Book catalog free. Manuscript guidelines for SASE.
Nonfiction: How-to, illustrated book, reference, self-help, technical, textbook, directories. Subjects include business, health, cleaning and maintenance. Needs books on anything related to cleaning, maintenance, self-employment or entrepreneurship. Query or submit outline and sample chapters. Reviews artwork/photos as part of ms package.
Tips: "Our audience includes those involved in cleaning and maintenance service trades, opportunity seekers, schools, property managers, libraries — anyone who needs information on cleaning and maintenance. How-to and self-employment guides are doing well for us in today's market. We are now seeking books on fire damage restoration and also technical articles for *Cleaning Business Magazine*, a quarterly. We are also interested in video or audio tapes, software and games that are specific to the cleaning industry."

COLLEGE PRESS PUBLISHING CO., INC., P.O. Box 1132, Joplin MO 64802-1132. (417)623-6280. Fax: (417)623-8250. Contact: John M. Hunter. Estab. 1958. Publishes hardcover and trade paperback originals and reprints. Publishes 25 titles/year. Receives 400 submissions/year. 25% of books from first-time authors; 100% from unagented writers. Subsidy publishes 5% of books. Subsidy considered "if we really want to publish a book, but don't have room in schedule at this time or funds available." Pays 10% royalty on net receipts. Publishes book an average of 1 year after acceptance. Simultaneous submissions OK. Reports on queries in 2 months. Book catalog for 9×12 SAE with 5 first-class stamps.
Nonfiction: Bible commentaries, topical Bible studies. (Christian church, Church of Christ.) Query.
Recent Nonfiction Title: *Gender Roles and the Bible: Creation, the Fall and Redemption*, by Jack Cottrell.
Fiction: Religious. No poetry. Query.
Tips: "Topical Bible study books have the best chance of being sold to our firm. Our audience consists of Christians interested in reading and studying Bible-based material."

CONSORTIUM PUBLISHING, 640 Weaver Hill Rd., West Greenwich RI 02817-2261. Chief of Publications: John Carlevale. Estab. 1990. Publishes 10-12 titles/year. Receives 30 queries and 25 mss/year. 50% of books from first-time authors; 90% from unagented writers. Subsidy publishes 5% of books. Pays royalty. Publishes book 2-3 months after acceptance. Simultaneous submissions OK. Query for electronic submissions. Reports in 1 month on queries, 1-2 months on proposals or mss. Book catalog and ms guidelines free on request.
Nonfiction: Biography, self-help, technical, textbook. Subjects include child guidance/parenting, education, health/medicine, language/literature, music/dance, psychology, science, sociology. Query. Writers should send photocopies.
Fiction: Juvenile. Query.

CREATIVE ARTS BOOK COMPANY, 833 Bancroft Way, Berkeley CA 94710. (415)848-4777. Fax: (510)848-4844. Publisher: Donald S. Ellis. Senior Editor: George Samsa. Estab. 1976. Publishes hardcover and paperback originals and paperback reprints. Averages 20 titles/year. Receives 800-1,000 submissions annually. 10% from first-time authors; 20% from unagented writers. Subsidy publishes 5% of books. Pays 5-15% royalty on retail price. Offers minimum $500 advance. Publishes book an average of 12-18 months after acceptance. Simultaneous submissions OK. Reports in 2 months. Book catalog free.
Nonfiction: Biographies, essays. Especially interested in music, works on California and minorities (African-Americans, Chicanos and Asians). *Writer's Market* recommends query with SASE first.
Recent Nonfiction Title: *Mingus/Mingus*, by Janet Coleman and Al Young (memoir).
Fiction: "Looking for serious literary fiction of broad appeal," especially books by and/or about women, crime and Western fiction. *Writer's Market* recommends query with SASE first.
Recent Fiction Title: *Samurai of Gold Hill*, by Yoshiko Uchida (Japanese short stories).

CSS PUBLISHING COMPANY, P.O. Box 4503, Lima OH 45802-4503. (419)227-1818. Editorial Director: Fred Steiner. Estab. 1970. Publishes trade paperback originals. Publishes 50 titles/year. Receives 300 mss/year. 65% of books from first-time authors; 100% from unagented writers. Subsidy publishes 20%. "If books have limited market appeal and/or deal with basically same subject matter as title already on list, we will consider subsidy option." Pays outright purchase of $25-400. Publishes book 1-2 years after acceptance. Simultaneous submissions OK. Query for electronic submissions. Reports on mss in 3 months. Book catalog free on request. Manuscript guidelines for #10 envelope and stamp.

Nonfiction: "We are looking for innovative Christian resources for mainline Protestant denominations; some Catholic resources. We are interested in worship resources, preaching illustrations, collections of short stories based on modern adaptations of scripture, Advent-Christmas dramas for congregations, Lent-Easter season dramas for congregations."

Recent Nonfiction Title: *In Other Words*, by Merle Franke.

Tips: "Books that sell well for us are seasonal sermon and worship resources; books aimed at clergy on professional growth and survival; also books of children's object lessons; seasonal plays (Christmas/Lent/Easter etc.). Our primary market is the clergy in all mainline denominations; others include church leaders, education directors, Sunday school teachers, women's groups, youth leaders; to a certain extent we publish for the Christian layperson. Write something that makes Christianity applicable to the contemporary world, something useful to the struggling, searching Christian. The treatment might be humorous, certainly unique. We have published a few titles that other houses would not touch—with some degree of success. We are open to new ideas and would be pleased to see anything new, different, creative, and well-written that fits our traditional markets."

DELTA SALES PUBLISHING CO., Suite 520, 4195 Chino Hills Pkwy, Chino Hills CA 91709-5232. (909)393-9737. President: Dick Bathurst. Estab. 1991. Publishes hardcover and trade and mass market paperback originals. 100% of books are original. Firm averages 5 titles/year. Receives 20 submissions/year. 25% from first-time authors; 100% from unagented writers. Subsidy publishes 25% of books. Determines subsidy on case by case basis. Pays 10-15% royalty on wholesale price. Publishes book an average of 6 months after acceptance. Simultaneous submissions OK. Reports in 2 months. Catalog for 9×12 SAE.

Nonfiction: How-to, humor, self-help, leadership. Subjects include business and economics, money/finance, psychology. "We are looking for books on creativity, self-help and success-oriented topics. No sex-related material." Query or submit outline and sample chapters. Reviews artwork/photos as part of ms package.

Fiction: Fantasy, humor, mystery, science fiction. Query or submit synopsis and sample chapters.

Tips: "We would like to see self-help material that is geared toward 21-45-year-old people. Our audience consists of students and entry-level and middle level managers. If I were a writer trying to market a book today, I would focus on books that have 'catchy' titles and wide-spread appeal."

DISCOVERY ENTERPRISES, LTD., Suite 210, 134 Middle St., Lowell MA 01852-1815. (508)459-1720. Executive Director: JoAnne B. Weisman. Estab. 1989. Publishes hardcover and trade paperback originals. Publishes 6-8 titles/year. Receives 500 queries and 100 mss/year. 25% of books from first-time authors; 100% from unagented writers. Subsidy publishes 10% of books. Pays 6-10% royalty. Offers $400-1,500 advance. Publishes book 6 months after acceptance. Simultaneous submissions OK. Reports in 6 months. Book catalog and ms guidelines for #10 SASE.

Nonfiction: Biography (illustrated biographies for ages 10-15), illustrated book, children's/juvenile, textbook and educational manuals, classroom plays for grades 3-6 (historical only). Subjects include education (teachers curriculum guides in social studies), history (American history series, including primary and secondary source materials—ages 10-18), global studies classroom materials for ages 8-12. "We're interested in biographies which are sophisticated—reading level for kids ages 10-15; 10-12,000 words, well-documented. Do not provide illustrations other than photos, as we hire illustrators independently. Include documentation of research. Do not "write down to children. Include a curriculum vitae or résumé with submission." Query with outline and 2 sample chapters. Writers should send photocopies.

Tips: "Query first, and then if asked, send sample chapters. Work must be neat, double-spaced, and must have a post-paid return envelope."

‡EASTWIND PUBLISHING, P.O. Box 1861, Dubuque IA 52004-1861. (319)557-9077. Marketing/Acquisitions: Marty Lange. Publishes trade paperback originals. Publishes 5-8 titles/year. Receives 60 queries and 25 mss/year. 50% of books from first-time authors; 100% from unagented writers. Subsidy publishes 20% of books. Pays 10-20% royalty on retail price. Publishes book 4-6 months after acceptance of ms. Simultaneous submissions OK. Query for electronic submissions. Reports in 2 months on mss. Book catalog and ms guidelines free on request.

Nonfiction: How-to, reference, technical, college textbook. Subjects include business and economics, heatlh/medicine, philosophy, religion, science, software. "Submit something unique. Choose a niche market in which text will be a supplement or 'one-of-a-kind' usage. College target markets preferred, but not a prerequisite for publication." Submit outline, 3-5 sample chapters and proposal package, including target market, product appeal, general marketability. Reviews artwork/photos as part of freelance ms package. Writers should send photocopies or transparencies.

EDICIONES UNIVERSAL, P.O. Box 450353, Miami FL 33245-0353. (305)642-3355. Fax: (305)642-7978. Director: Juan M. Salvat. General Manager: Martha Salvat-Golik. Estab. 1965. Publishes trade paperback originals in Spanish. Publishes 50 titles/year. Receives 150 submissions/year. 40% of books from first-time authors; 90% from unagented writers. Subsidy publishes 10% of books. Pays 5-10% royalty on retail price. Publishes book an average of 9 months after acceptance. Simultaneous submissions OK. Reports in 1 month on queries. *Writer's Market* recommends allowing 2 months for reply. Book catalog free on request.

Nonfiction: Biography, cookbook, humor, reference. Subjects include cooking and foods, philosophy, politics, psychology, sociology. "We specialize in Cuban topics." All mss must be in Spanish. Submit outline and sample chapters. Reviews artwork/photos as part of freelance ms package.

Fiction: "We will consider everything as long as it is written in Spanish." Submit synopsis and sample chapters.

Poetry: "We will consider any Spanish-language poetry." Submit 3 or more poems.

Tips: "Our audience is composed entirely of Spanish-language readers. This is a very limited market. Books on Cuban or Latin American topics have the best chance of selling to our firm."

WILLIAM B. EERDMANS PUBLISHING CO., 255 Jefferson Ave. SE, Grand Rapids MI 49503. (616)459-4591. Fax: (616)459-6540. Editor-in-Chief: Jon Pott. Assistant to the Editor: Anne Salsich. Managing Editor: Charles Van Hof. Children's Book Editor: Amy Eerdmans. Estab. 1911. Publishes hardcover and paperback originals and reprints. Averages 65-70 titles/year. Receives 3,000-4,000 submissions annually. 25% from first-time authors; 95% from unagented writers. Average print order for a first book is 4,000. Subsidy publishes 1% of books. Pays 7½-10% royalty on retail price. No advance usually. Publishes book an average of 1 year after acceptance. Simultaneous submissions OK if noted. Reports in 3 weeks for queries. *Writer's Market* recommends allowing 2 months for reply. Book catalog free.

Nonfiction: Religious, reference, textbooks, monographs, children's books. Subjects include children's religious literature, history, philosophy, psychology, religion, sociology, regional history, geography. "Approximately 80% of our publications are religious—specifically Protestant—and largely of the more academic or theological variety (as opposed to the devotional, inspirational or celebrity-conversion books). Our history and social studies titles aim, similarly, at an academic audience; some of them are documentary histories. We prefer that writers take the time to notice if we have published anything at all in the same category as their manuscript before sending it to us." Accepts nonfiction translations. Query. Include SASE for return of ms. Accepts outline and 2-3 sample chapters. Reviews artwork/photos.

Recent Nonfiction Title: *Bill McKibben, The Comforting Whirlwind*.

Tips: "We look for quality and relevance."

FALCON PRESS PUBLISHING CO., INC., P.O. Box 1718, Helena MT 59624. (406)442-6597. Fax: (406)442-2995. Publisher: Bill Schneider. Publishing Director: Chris Cauble. Estab. 1979. Imprint is Skyhouse Publications (subsidy publisher; contact: Rick Newby). Publishes hardcover and trade paperback originals. Averages 50-60 titles/year. Subsidy publishes 20% of books. Pays 8-15% royalty on net price or pays flat fee. Publishes book an average of 6 months after ms is in final form. Reports in 2 months on queries. *Writer's Market* recommends allowing 2 months for reply. Book catalog free.

Nonfiction: "We're primarily interested in ideas for recreational guidebooks and books on regional outdoor subjects for either adults or children. We can only respond to submissions that fit these categories." No fiction or poetry. Query only; do not send ms.

Recent Nonfiction Title: *The Traveler's Guide to the Oregon Trail*.

Tips: "We are concentrating even more on seeking people with outdoor recreational writing experience to write our guidebooks for fishing, hiking, scenic driving, rockclimbing wildlife watching and birding. Especially interested in rockclimbing guides to western states, and hiking guides to eastern and southern states."

FILTER PRESS, P.O. Box 5, Palmer Lake CO 80133-0005. (719)481-2523. President: Gilbert L. Campbell. Estab. 1956. Publishes trade paperback originals and reprints. Publishes 2-3 titles/year. Receives 100 mss/year. 25% of books are from first-time authors; 100% from unagented writers. Subsidy publishes 10% of books, "if the book has merit, but it is not one we would commission." Pays 6-10% royalties on wholesale price. Publishes ms an average of 6-8 months after acceptance. SASE. Reports in 3 months.

Nonfiction: Cookbook, how-to. Subjects include Americana, anthropology/archaeology, cooking, foods and nutrition, ethnic, hobbies, regional, travel. "We will consider some Western Americana, up to 72 pages. We do not want family diaries. Most of our works are reprints of 19th century published things on Indians, Gold rushes, western exploration, etc. Very rarely do we use unsolicited material. I dream up a project, find an author in 90% of them." Query. Reviews artwork/photos as part of ms package.

Tips: "We are cutting back to 2-3 new titles, and *none* over 72 pages."

‡GARDNER PRESS, INC., #104, 6801 Lake Worth Rd., Lake Worth FL 33467. (407)964-9700. Publisher: G. Spungin. Imprint is Gatto Associates Press. Publishes hardcover and trade paperback originals and reprints. Publishes 15 titles/year. Imprint publishes 3 titles/year. Receives 300 queries and 200 mss/year. 15% of books from first-time authors; 95% from unagented writers. Subsidy publishes 5% of books. Pays 6-15% royalty on wholesale price. Publishes book 8 months after acceptance. Accepts simultaneous submissions. Reports in 1 month on queries. Book catalog free. Manuscript guidelines for $5.

Nonfiction: Reference, self-help, technical, textbook. Subjects include child guidance/parenting, education, health/medicine, psychology, sociology, women's issues/studies. Query.

Recent Nonfiction Title: *Women & Alcohol*, by Stammer (self-help).

‡**GENEALOGICAL PUBLISHING CO., INC.**, 1001 N. Calvert St., Baltimore MD 21202-3897. (410)837-8271. Fax: (410)752-8492. Editor-in-Chief: Michael H. Tepper, Ph.D. Estab. 1959. Imprint is Clearfield Co. Estab. 1959. Publishes hardcover originals and reprints. Subsidy publishes 10% of books. Averages 80 titles/year. Receives 400 submissions annually. 50% of books from first-time authors; 100% from unagented writers. Average print order for a first book is 2,000-3,000. Offers straight 10% royalty on retail price. Publishes book an average of 6 months after acceptance. Reports in 3 months. Enclose SAE and return postage.

Nonfiction: Reference, genealogy, immigration records. "Our requirements are unusual, so we usually treat each author and his subject in a way particularly appropriate to his special skills and subject matter. Guidelines are flexible, but it is expected that an author will consult with us in depth. Most, though not all, of our original publications are offset from camera-ready typescript. Since most genealogical reference works are compilations of vital records and similar data, tabular formats are common. We hope to receive more manuscript material covering vital records and ships' passenger lists. We want family history compendia, basic methodology in genealogy, heraldry, and immigration records." Prefers query first, but will look at outline and sample chapter. Reviews artwork/photos as part of ms package.

‡**GOLDEN EAGLE PRESS**, Subsidiary of Golden Eagle International Group, Inc., 9700 Topanga Canyon Blvd., Chatsworth CA 91311. (818)727-9284. Publisher: David Wolf. Publishes trade paperback originals and reprints. Publishes 5 titles/year. Receives 120 queries and 20 mss/year. 80% of books from first-time authors; 100% from unagented writers. Subsidy publishes 35% of books "depending on how closely the work matches our specific objectives." Pays 10-20% royalty on wholesale price; subsidy royalties based on percentage of author investment. Publishes book 9 months after acceptance of ms. No simultaneous submissions. Query for electronic submissions. Reports in 1 month on queries; 2 months on proposals and mss. Manuscript guidelines for #10 SASE.

Nonfiction: How-to, reference. Subjects include business and economics, computers and electronics, government/politics, military/war, money/finance. "We focus exclusively on issues of interest to Western business people looking to understand the Chinese business environment, or to Chinese executives seeking to understand the Western markets." Query. Reviews artwork/photos as part of ms package. Writers should send photocopies.

Recent Nonfiction Title: *Partners in Profit*, by David Wolf.

THE GRADUATE GROUP, 86 Norwood Rd., West Hartford CT 06117-2236. (203)232-3100. President: Mara Whitman. Estab. 1964. Publishes 25 titles/year. Receives 10 queries/year. Subsidy publishes 5% of books. Reports in 1 month. Flyers free on request.

Nonfiction: Reference, career/internships. Subjects include career/internship. Query.

Tips: "Our audience is career planning offices and college and law school libraries. We are a small publishing company that specializes in career planning and internship-related publications. Reference books that help students with their career."

‡**WARREN H. GREEN, INC.**, 8356 Olive Blvd., St. Louis MO 63132. (314)991-1335. Fax: (314)997-1788. Editor: Warren H. Green. Estab. 1966. Imprints are Pioneer Press, Epoch Press, Fireside Books. Publishes hardcover, trade paperback and mass market originals. Offers "10-20% sliding scale of royalties based on quantity distributed. All books are short run, highly specialized, with no advance." Subsidy publishes 5% of books. Determines subsidy by subject matter vs. market. Averages 60 titles/year. Receives 200 submissions annually. 90% of books from first-time authors; 100% from unagented writers. Publishes book an average of 10 months after acceptance. Simultaneous submissions OK. Reports in 2 months. Manuscript guidelines free on request.

Nonfiction: Health/medicine, medical, philosophy, psychology, sociology, technical. Submit outline and author vita. Reviews artwork/photos as part of ms package. Send photocopies.

Tips: "We are looking for books from dedicated doctors."

HAMPTON ROADS PUBLISHING COMPANY, INC., 891 Norfolk Sq., Norfolk VA 23502-3209. (804)459-2453. Fax: (804)455-8907. Publisher: Robert S. Friedman. Vice President: Frank DeMarco. Estab.1989. Publishes hardcover and trade paperback originals and reprints. Publishes 20 titles/year. Receives 400 queries and 325 mss/year. 25% of books from first-time authors; 50% from unagented writers. Determined by market risk. Pays 8-15% royalty on wholesale/retail price. Offers advance. Publishes book 3-6 months after acceptance of ms. Simultaneous submissions OK. Query for electronic submissions. Does not return submissions without SASE. Reports in 3 months on queries. Book catalog for 9×12 SAE with 2 first-class stamps.

Nonfiction: Concentration on "self-help metaphysics," alternative medicine, nutrition and health, New Age and spiritual subjects in general. Query first. Reviews artwork/photos as part of freelance ms package. Writers should send photocopies.
Recent Nonfiction Title: *Ancient Echoes,* by Mary Summer Rain (inspirational).
Fiction: Literary, mainstream, metaphysical. Submit synopsis and 3 sample chapters.

HARMONY HOUSE PUBLISHERS, 1008 Kent Rd., Goshen KY 40026. (502)228-4446. Fax: (502)228-2010. Contact: William Strode. Estab. 1980. Publishes hardcover originals. Publishes 20 titles/year. Subsidy publishes 8% of books. Pays royalty. Offers advance. Publishes book 18 months after acceptance of ms. Simultaneous submissions OK. Query for electronic submissions. Reports in 2 months on proposals.
Nonfiction: Coffee table book, cookbook, illustrated book. Subjects include animals, education, military/war, nature/environment, photography, sports. Query. Reviews artwork/photos as part of ms package. Writers should send photocopies or transparencies.

HAWKES PUBLISHING, INC., 5947 South 350 West, Murray UT 84107. (801)266-5555. President/Editor: John Hawkes. Estab. 1965. Publishes mostly trade paperback originals. Averages 24 titles/year. Receives 200 submissions annually. 70% of books from first-time authors; 90% from unagented writers. Subsidy publishes 25-50% of books/year based on "how promising they are." Pays varying royalty of 10% on retail price to 10% on wholesale. No advance. Publishes book an average of 6 months after acceptance. Submit complete ms. Reports in 9 months on queries. Book catalog free.
Nonfiction: Cookbook, how-to, self-help. Subjects include cooking and foods, health, history, hobbies, psychology. Query or submit outline and sample chapters. Reviews artwork/photos.

HEART OF THE LAKES PUBLISHING, P.O. Box 299, Interlaken NY 14847-0299. (607)532-4997. Fax: (607)532-4684. Contact: Walter Steesy. Estab. 1976. Imprints include Empire State Books, Windswept Press. Publishes hardcover and trade paperback originals and reprints. Averages 20-25 titles/year. Receives 20 submissions annually. 100% of books from unagented writers. Average print order for a first book is 500-1,000. Subsidy publishes 10% of books, "depending on type of material and potential sales." 15% author subsidized; 35% nonauthor subsidized. Payment is "worked out individually." Publishes book an average of 1-2 years after acceptance. Simultaneous submissions OK. Query for electronic submissions. Reports in 1 month. *Writer's Market* recommends allowing 2 months for reply. Current books flier for #10 SAE with 2 first-class stamps.
Nonfiction: New York state and regional, history, genealogy source materials. Query. Reviews artwork/photos.
Fiction: Done only at author's expense.

HOPE PUBLISHING HOUSE, P.O. Box 60008, Pasadena CA 91116. Publisher: Faith A. Sand. Imprint is New Paradigm Books. Assistant Editor: Susan L. Parry. Marketing Director: Albert G. Cohen. Publishes trade paperback originals, hardcover originals and reprints. Publishes 6 titles/year. Imprints publish 4 (Hope); 2 (New Paradigm). Receives 120 queries and 30 mss/year. 20% of books from first-time authors; 100% from unagented writers. Subsidy publishes 20% of books (by foundations or church organizations wanting us to publish a certain work for their use). Pays 10% royalty on net. Publishes book 9 months after acceptance. Query for electronic submissions. Reports in 2 months on queries. Book catalog and ms guidelines for #10 SASE.
Nonfiction: Biography, how-to, children's/juvenile, reference, technical, textbook. Subjects include Americana, anthropology/archaeology, child guidance/parenting, education, ethnic, government/politics, heath/medicine, language/literature, military/war, nature/environment, philosophy, psychology, religion, sociology, translation, travel, women's issues/studies. "We are a nonprofit program unit of the Southern California Ecumenical Council dedicated to publishing books that are of service to the faith community on religious and current social issues." Query. Reviews artwork/photos as part of freelance ms package. Writers should send photocopies.
Recent Nonfiction Title: *The Elephant in the Bedroom: Automobile Dependence and Denial* (the economy and the environment).
Poetry: "Needs to be of interest to religious community."
Tips: "Our readers are part of the faith community and are interested in current social issues."

HUNTER HOUSE INC., PUBLISHERS, P.O. Box 2914, Alameda CA 94501-2914. Fax: (510)865-4295. Publisher: K.S. Rana. Editor: Lisa E. Lee. Estab. 1978. Publishes trade paperback and hardcover originals. Averages 12 titles/year. Receives 200 submissions annually. 60% of books from first-time authors; 60% from unagented writers. "We will consider whether an author should be subsidy published based upon subject matter, quality of the work, and if a subsidy is available." Pays 12-15% royalty on net price. Offers modest

---

For explanation of symbols, see the Key to Symbols and Abbreviations. For unfamiliar words, see the Glossary.

advance. Publishes book an average of 1-2 years after acceptance and receipt of final ms. Simultaneous submissions OK. Reports in 3-4 months. Book catalog and ms guidelines for 9 × 12 SAE with 2 first-class stamps.

Nonfiction: Health, social issues, young adult nonfiction, self-help. Subjects include family, health, women's health, self-help, psychology, spiritual. Needs mss on new health, care and treatment older people and intergenerational concerns. No evangelical, overly political, Americana, esoteric or erotica. Looking specifically for titles concerning natural healing, violence, and teens. Query or submit outline and sample chapters. Reviews artwork/photos. "Please enclose return postage for material you wish returned."

Tips: "Manuscripts on family, health, psychology and social/women's issues for an *aware* public do well for us. Write simply, with established credentials and imagination. Submit queries with an overview, outline, sample chapters, foreword, testimonies from people in the field, marketing information, competition and anything unique about your work. We respect writers and do not mistreat them. We ask for the same consideration."

‡ICAN PRESS BOOK PUBLISHERS, INC., Ican Press Building, 616 Third Ave., Chula Vista CA 91910. (619)425-8945. Senior Editor: Josette Rice. Publishes hardcover and trade paperback originals. Publishes 30 titles/year. Receives 3,000 queries and 900 mss/year. 85% of books from first-time authors; 90% from unagented writers. Subsidy publishes 40% of books. Pays 25-50% royalty after cost, based on gross sales, net %. Publishes book 6 months after acceptance of ms. Simultaneous submissions OK. Reports in 1 month on queries and on proposals, 6 weeks on mss. Book catalog and ms guidelines free on request.

Nonfiction: Biography, cookbook, how-to, humor, children's/juvenile, self-help, technical, textbook. Subjects include business and economics, computers and electronics, cooking, foods and nutrition, education, ethnic, government/politics, health/medicine, history, military/war, psychology, religion, sociology, travel. Query with outline and 3 sample chapters (first, middle and last). Reviews artwork/photos as part of freelance ms package. Writers should send photocopies.

Recent Nonfiction Title: *Split Second Decision Making*, by Dr. Burdette Hansen (management); *Fine-Tuning The Human Machine*, by Dr. Harold Elrick (health); *Common Sense Leadership*, by Dr. Warren Knox (management).

Fiction: Adventure, ethnic, fantasy, gothic, historical, humor, juvenile, literary, mainstream/contemporary, military/war, mystery, plays, religious, romance, science fiction, short story collections, suspense, western, young adult. Query with synopsis and 3 sample chapters (first, middle and last).

Recent Fiction Title: *The Cruise of the Dancer*, by Phil Young and Bill McCarty (historical); *Knights of the White Camelia*, by James Hester (suspense); *A Panzer Called Iron Maiden*, by Warren Knox (war).

IEEE PRESS, Subsidiary of The Institute of Electrical and Electronics Engineers, P.O. Box 1331, Piscataway NJ 08855-1331. (908)562-3967. Fax: (908)981-8062. Director of Book Publishing: Dudley R. Kay. Senior Acquisitions Editor: Russ Hall. Estab. 1971. Publishes hardcover and softcover originals and reprints. Averages 45-50 titles/year. Receives 100-120 submissions/year. 50% of books from first-time authors; 90% from unagented writers. Subsidy publishes 10% of books. Pays 10-18% royalty on wholesale price. Publishes book an average of 7-9 months after acceptance. Simultaneous submissions OK. Query for electronic submissions. Reports in 2 months. Book catalog and ms guidelines free.

Nonfiction: Technical reference, textbooks. Subjects include computers, electronics. "We need advanced texts and references in electrical engineering but we're also recently interested in more accessible "understanding technology" books for the non-specialist, as well as historical aspects of electro-technology. No trade/consumer orientation books in electronics and computers. We publish for the professional, engineering and science and advanced student." Query. Submit outline and sample chapters.

Tips: "Professional reference books have flourished due to changing technologies and need to keep current. However, technical writers are few. Engineers and scientists should consider trained technical writers as co-authors. We are now more open to 'entry-level' overviews of a technical specialty. Our audience consists of engineers—largely at management and project leader levels. If I were a writer trying to market a book today, I would work with a good agent or other experienced writer with contacts and knowledge of the 'system.' Authors expend too much energy, and endure unnecessary frustration, because they don't know how to match a good idea and respectable proposal with the *appropriate* publishers."

INTERSTATE PUBLISHERS, INC., 510 N. Vermilion St., P.O. Box 50, Danville IL 61834-0050. (217)446-0050. Fax: (217)446-9706. Acquisitions/Vice President-Editorial: Ronald L. McDaniel. Estab. 1914. Hardcover and paperback originals and software. Publishes about 30 titles/year. 50% of books from first-time authors; 100% from unagented writers. Usual royalty 10%. No advance. Markets books by mail and exhibits. Publishes book an average of 9-12 months after acceptance. Reports in 4 months. Book catalog for 9 × 12 SAE with 4 first-class stamps. "Our guidelines booklet is provided only to persons who have submitted proposals for works in which we believe we might be interested. If the booklet is sent, no self-addressed envelope or postage from the author is necessary."

• Interstate's interest at this time is in high school agricultural materials into which science has been integrated: agriscience.

Nonfiction: Publishes high school and undergraduate college-level texts and related materials in agricultural education (production agriculture, agriscience and technology, agribusiness, agrimarketing, horticulture). "We wish to expand our line of *AgriScience* textbooks and related materials for grades 9-12." Also publishes items in correctional education (books for professional training and development and works for use by and with incarcerated individuals in correctional facilities). "We favor, but do not limit ourselves to, works that are designed for class-quantity rather than single-copy sale." Query or submit outline and 2-3 sample chapters. Reviews artwork/photos as part of freelance ms package.
Recent Nonfiction Title: *Biological Science Applications in Agriculture*, by Edward W. Osborne.
Tips: "Freelance writers should be aware of strict adherence to the use of nonsexist language; fair and balanced representation of the sexes and of minorities in both text and illustrations; and discussion of computer applications and career opportunities wherever applicable. Writers commonly fail to identify publishers who specialize in the subject areas in which they are writing. For example, a publisher of textbooks isn't interested in novels, or one that specializes in elementary education materials isn't going to want a book on auto mechanics."

JORDAN ENTERPRISES PUBLISHING CO., Subidiary of ScoJtia, Publishing Co., P.O. Box 15111, St. Louis MO 63110. Managing Editor: Patrique Quintahlen. Publishes hardcover and trade paperback originals and reprints. Publishes 3 titles/year. Receives 3,000 queries and 2,000 mss/year. 50% of books from first-time authors; 5% from unagented writers. Subsidy publishes 1% of books. "We subsidy publish books of poetry: subjects family, love, philosophy." Pays 10-15% royalty on retail price or makes outright purchase of $200-5,000. Offers $500-5,000 advance. Publishes book 1 year after acceptance. Simultaneous submissions OK. Query for electronic submissions. Prefers Macintosh compatible. Reports in 2 months on queries and proposals, 6-12 months on mss. Manuscript guidelines for #10 SASE.
Nonfiction: Biography, how-to, humor, illustrated book, children's/juvenile, reference, self-help, technical, textbook. Subjects include animals, art/architecture, child guidance/parenting, cooking, foods & nutrition, education, ethnic, gardening, health/medicine, history, hobbies, language/literature, money/finance, music/dance, nature/environment, philosophy, photography, psychology, recreation, regional, religion, science, sociology, sport, translation, travel, women's issues/studies. "We plan to publish more biographies and how-to, self-help books for children in upcoming seasons. Writers should send nonfiction submissions to Scojtia division of our company." Query with outline and 3 sample chapters. Writers should send photocopies. "Tearsheets are preferred, kept on file."
Recent Nonfiction Title: *The Guide to Self Mastery of Adolescence In Group Homes*.
Fiction: Adventure, fantasy, juvenile, literary, mainstream/contemporary, mystery, picture books, romance, science fiction, suspense and young adult. "We plan to publish picture book fantasies, and juvenile and young adult fantasy novels from new unpublished writers." Submit synopsis and 3 sample chapters.
Recent Fiction Title: *Thinking Cap* (picture book).
Poetry: "We plan to publish more poetry for the hew American Family. Writers must submit fifty poems to be considered for publication." Query. Submit complete ms.
Tips: "We publish books for children around the globe, who look to books for joy and inspiration between fun times at play."

KUMARIAN PRESS, INC., Suite 119, 630 Oakwood Ave., W. Hartford CT 06110-1529. (203)953-0214. Fax: (203)953-8579. Editor: Trish Reynolds. Imprints are Kumarian Press Books for a World that Works and Kumarian Press Library of Management for Development. Estab. 1977. Publishes hardcover and paperback originals and paperback reprints. Averages 8-12 titles/year. Receives 100-150 submissions/year. 10% of books from first-time authors; 100% from unagented writers. Pays 0-10% royalty on net. Publishes book an average of 9 months after acceptance. Query for electronic submissions. Reports in 2 months. Book catalog and ms guidelines free.
Nonfiction: "Kumarian Press Books for aWorld that Works are global in focus and appeal to the reader who is interested in world affairs, but who does not want an academic read. Subjects of interest include: global issues, environment, women, community development and travel. Kumarian Press Library of Management for Development is the professional, academic line. This line targets readers interested in international development and management. Subject areas include: nongovernmental organizations, people-centered development, women in development, international public administration, democratization, microenterprise, health and the environment."
Tips: "Please do not send a complete manuscript. Call and ask for a free copy of our writer's guidelines. The guidelines show you how to submit your book proposal for possible publication."

PETER LANG PUBLISHING, Subsidiary of Verlag Peter Lang AG, Bern, Switzerland, 62 W. 45th St., New York NY 10036-4208. (212)302-6740. Fax: (212)302-7574. Managing Director: Christopher S. Myers; Senior Acquisitions Editor: Michael Flamini. Estab. 1952. Publishes mostly hardcover originals. Averages 200 titles/year. 75% of books from first-time authors; 98% from unagented writers. Subsidy publishes 25% of books. All subsidies are guaranteed repayment plus profit (if edition sells out) in contract. Subsidy published if ms is highly specialized and author relatively unknown. All subsidized wroks must pass complete internal and external peer review process. Pays 10-20% royalty on net price. Translators get flat fee plus percentage of royalties. No advance. Publishes book an average of 1 year after acceptance. Reports in 2 months. Book catalog free.

Nonfiction: General nonfiction, reference works, scholarly monographs. Subjects include literary criticism, Germanic and Romance languages, art history, business and economics, American and European political science, history, music, philosophy, psychology, religion, sociology, biography. All books are scholarly monographs, textbooks, reference books, reprints of historic texts, critical editions or translations. No mss shorter than 200 pages. Submit complete ms. *Writer's Market* recommends query with SASE first. Fully refereed review process.

Fiction and Poetry: "We do not publish original fiction or poetry. We seek scholarly and critical editions only. Submit complete manuscript."

Tips: "Besides our commitment to specialist academic monographs, we are one of the few US publishers who publish books in most of the modern languages. A major advantage for Lang authors is international marketing and distribution of all titles. Translation rights sold for many titles."

‡LARKSDALE, P.O. Box 70456, Houston TX 77270-0456. Assistant to Publisher: Charlotte St. John. Imprints are Lindahl Books, The Linolead Press, Better Life Books, Post Oak Press. Publishes hardcover and trade paperback originals and hardcover reprints. Publishes 52 titles/year; each imprint publishes 4-10 titles/year. Receives 800 queries and 200 mss/year. 50% of books from first-time authors; 100% from unagented writers. Pays 10-15% royalty on wholesale price. Publishes book 6 months after acceptance of ms. Accepts simultaneous submissions. Electronic submissions required after acceptance. Reports in 1 month on queries and proposals, 3 months on mss.

Nonfiction: Coffee table book, cookbook, how-to, self-help. Subjects include business management, cooking, foods and nutrition, health/medicine, history, military/war (Civil War, WWII), money/finance. "Look in Waldenbooks, B. Dalton. Do your marketing homework. We don't want any book that sells less than 10,000 copies. Don't kid yourself or us about the marketability." Query with proposal package, including complete letter of transmittal, synopsis/outline, table of contents, author background, market analysis and 3 sample chapters.

Recent Nonfiction Title: *Birth Mother Search*, by E. B. McDonald (adoption search how-to).

Fiction: "As of May 31, 1994, we only accept fiction on subsidy basis. We will co-publish and share the cost with the author or investor."

Poetry: As of May 31, 1994, all poetry is subsidy published.

LIBRA PUBLISHERS, INC., Suite 383, 3089C Clairemont Dr., San Diego CA 92117-6892. (619)571-1414. Contact: William Kroll. Estab. 1960. Publishes hardcover and paperback originals. Specializes in the behavioral sciences. Averages 15 titles/year. Receives 300 submissions annually. 60% of books from first-time authors; 85% from unagented writers. 10-15% royalty on retail price. No advance. "In addition, we will also offer our services to authors who wish to publish their own works. The services include editing, proofreading, production, artwork, copyrighting, and assistance in promotion and distribution." Publishes book an average of 8 months after acceptance. Reports in 2 weeks. *Writer's Market* recommends allowing 2 months for reply. Book catalog free. Writer's guidelines for #10 SASE.

Nonfiction: Manuscripts in all subject areas will be given consideration, but main interest is in the behavioral sciences. Prefers complete ms but will consider outline and 3 sample chapters. Reviews artwork/photos as part of freelance ms package.

LIBRARY RESEARCH ASSOCIATES, INC., RD #6, Box 41, Dunderberg Rd., Monroe NY 10950-3703. (914)783-1144. President: Matilda A. Gocek. Editor: Dianne D. McKinstrie. Estab. 1968. Publishes hardcover and trade paperback originals. Averages 4 titles/year. Receives about 300 submissions annually. 100% of books from first-time authors; 100% from unagented writers. Pays 10% maximum royalty on sales. Offers 20 copies of the book as advance. Publishes book an average of 11 months after acceptance. Reports in 3 months. Book catalog free on request.

Nonfiction: Biography, how-to, reference, technical, American history. Subjects include Americana, business and economics, history, politics. "Our nonfiction book manuscript needs for the next year or two will include books about historical research of some facet of American history, and definitive works about current or past economics or politics." No astrology, occult, sex, adult humor or gay rights. Submit outline and sample chapters.

Recent Nonfiction Title: *Maxwell Anderson, European Stage 1929-1992.*

Tips: "Our audience is adult, over age 30, literate and knowledgeable in business or professions. The writer has the best chance of selling our firm historical nonfiction texts. Fiction has been eliminated from our lists. We now consider American historical and political works and legal manuscript."

LONGSTREET HOUSE, P.O. Box 730, Hightstown NJ 08520-0730. (609)448-1501. Editor: Dr. David Martin. Estab. 1985. Publishes hardcover and trade paperback originals and reprints. Publishes 5 titles/year. Receives 30 queries and 20 mss/year. 40% of books from first-time authors; 100% from unagented writers. Subsidy publishes 25% of books. Pays 8-12% royalty on retail price. Publishes book 18 months after acceptance of ms. Simultaneous submissions OK. Reports in 2 months on proposals. Book catalog free on request.

Nonfiction: Biography, history. Subjects include history, military/war (Civil War), regional. Submit outline. Reviews artwork/photos as part of freelance ms package. Writers should send photocopies.
Recent Nonfiction Title: *Three Rousing Cheers*, by Bilby (Civil War history).

‡**MAGICIMAGE FILMBOOKS**, Subsidiary of MagicImage Productions, Inc., 740 S. Sixth Ave., Absecon NJ 08201. (609)652-6500. President: Michael Stein. Publishes hardcover and trade paperback originals. Publishes 6 titles/year. Receives 20 queries and 10 mss/year. 10% of books from first-time authors; 80% from unagented writers. Subsidy publishes 20% of books. Pays 8-10% royalty on retail price. Publishes book 6 months after acceptance. Accepts simultaneous submissions. Query for electronic submissions. Reports in 1 month. Book catalog free on request.
Nonfiction: Biography, coffee table book. Subjects include entertainment, motion picture and Hollywood history. "Looking for Hollywood biographies and film history." Submit outline with 3 sample chapters. Reviews artwork/photos as part of ms package. Writers should send photocopies.
Recent Nonfiction Title: *Phantom of the Opera*, by Riley (film history).

‡**MANCORP PUBLISHING INC.**, P.O. Box 21492, Tampa FL 33622. (813)837-8888. Publisher: M.N. Manougian. Publishes hardcover, trade paperback and mass market paperback originals. Publishes 12-20 titles/year. Receives 50-75 queries and 40-50 mss/year. 60% of books from first-time authors; 90% from unagented writers. Subsidy publishes 10% of books. Pays 10-15% royalty on wholesale price. Publishes book 9 months after acceptance. Accepts simultaneous submissions. Reports in 1 month.
Nonfiction: Cookbook, how-to, reference, self-help, technical, textbook. Subjects include business and economics, cooking, foods and nutrition, education, government/politics, health/medicine, language/literature, music/dance, psychology, regional, travel. Submit proposal package.
Fiction: Adventure, humor, literary, mainstream/contemporary, religious, romance. Submit synopsis.

‡**MAUPIN HOUSE**, P.O. Box 90148, Gainesville FL 32607. Contact: Julie. Publishes hardcover and trade paperback originals. Publishes 5 titles/year. Receives 20 queries/year. 50% of books from first-time authors; 100% from unagented writers. Subsidy publishes 10% of books. Pays 5-10% royalty on retail price. Publishes book 9 months after acceptance. Accepts simultaneous submissions. Query for electronic submissions. Reports in 6 weeks. No unsolicited mss. Book catalog for #10 SASE.
Nonfiction: Teacher resource. Subjects include agriculture/horticulture, education, regional, sports. "We are looking for teachers with good classroom-proven ideas." Query.

‡**MAYHAVEN PUBLISHING**, P.O. Box 557, Mahomet IL 61853. Contact: Doris R. Wenzel. Publishes hardcover, trade paperback and mass market paperback originals and reprints. Publishes 4-11 titles/year. Receives 150 queries and 100 mss/year. 60% of books from first-time authors; 98% from unagented writers. Subsidy publishes 5% of books. Pays 6-12% royalty on wholesale price or retail price; subsidy author gets 40% of net sales. Offers $100-250 advance. Publishes book 1½ years after acceptance. No simultaneous submissions. Query for electronic submissions. Reports in 6 months on queries and proposals, 9 months on mss. Book catalog for $1. Manuscript guidelines for #10 SASE.
Nonfiction: Coffee table book, cookbook, humor, illustrated book, children's/juvenile, reference, railroad history. Subjects include agriculture/horticulture, Americana, animals, anthropology/archaeology, art/architecture, computers and electronics, cooking, foods and nutrition, history, hobbies, nature/environment, regional. "We are seeking nonfiction (history, natural history, cookbooks, hobbies/reference)." Submit 3 sample chapters.
Recent Nonfiction Title: *America's Rural Hub*, by Stanley A. Changnon (railroading).
Fiction: Adventure, ethnic, gothic, historical, humor, juvenile, mainstream/contemporary, mystery, picture books, romance, science fiction, short story collections, suspense, western, young adult. "Seeking more humor, mystery and young adult." Submit 3 sample chapters.
Recent Fiction Title: *Murder at the Strawberry Festival*, by Warren Carrier (mystery).

‡**MOUNT OLIVE COLLEGE PRESS**, 634 Henderson St., Mount Olive NC 28365. (919)658-2502. Editor: Dr. Pepper Worthington. Publishes trade paperback originals. Averages 5 titles/year. Receives 500 queries/year. 60% of books from first-time authors; 100% from unagented writers. Subsidy publishes 35% of books. Publishes book 2 years after acceptance of ms. No simultaneous submissions. Reports in 6 months. Book catalog and ms guidelines free on request.
Nonfiction: Biography, coffee table book, cookbook, how-to, children's/juvenile. Subjects include cooking, foods and nutrition, education, language/literature, religion, travel. Submit outline and 1 sample chapter. Reviews artwork/photos as part of ms package. Writers should send photocopies.
Fiction: Literary, mainstream/contemporary, plays, religious. Submit synopsis and 1 sample chapter.
Poetry: Submit 6 sample poems.

NEW FALCON PUBLICATIONS, Subsidiary of J.W. Brown, Inc., 655 E. Thunderbird, Phoenix AZ 85022. Editor: Frank Martin. Estab. 1980. Publishes hardcover and trade paperback originals and reprints. Publishes 25 titles/year. Receives 200 queries and 50 mss/year. 20% of books from first-time authors; 20% from unagented writers. Subsidy publishes 8% of books. Pays 6-12% royalty on retail price; on subsidy—by agreement. Offers $0-5,000 advance. Publishes book 18 months after acceptance. Simultaneous submissions OK. Query for electronic submissions. SASE. Reports in 2 months on queries and proposals, 3 months on mss. Book catalog free on request.

Nonfiction: Biography, how-to, self-help, textbook. Subjects include anthropology/archaeology, education, gay/lesbian, health/medicine, philosophy, psychology, religion, sociology, occult, metaphysical. Submit outline and 3 sample chapters.

Recent Nonfiction Title: *The Game of Life*, by Timothy Leary (psychology).

Fiction: Erotica, experimental, fantasy, gay/lesbian, horror, occult, religious, science fiction. Submit 3 sample chapters.

Recent Fiction Title: *The Tree of Life*, by J. Marvin Speigelman (psychology).

Tips: "Be polite, be timely, have patience, be neat. Include short résumé."

NORTH COUNTRY BOOKS, INC., 18 Irving Place, Utica NY 13501-5618. Phone/fax: (315)738-4342. Publisher: Sheila Orlin. Imprints are Pine Tree Press, North Country Books. Publishes hardcover and trade paperback originals and reprints. Publishes 6-20 titles/year. Receives 300-500 queries and 200-300 mss/year. 80% of books from first-time authors; 99% from unagented writers. Pays 8-10% royalty on retail price. Publishes book 1-2 years after acceptance. Simultaneous submissions OK. Reports in 6-9 months on mss. Book catalog free on request.

Nonfiction: New York State regional history, biography, field guides, stories, coffee table, children's, etc. Submit proposal package including completed ms, number of photos/artwork, any pertinent information. Photocopies of photos/artwork helpful, but not imperative. An outline with 2-3 sample chapters would be read, but complete ms preferred.

Recent Nonfiction Title: *Adirondack Archive*, by Nan Hudnut Clarkson (family history).

Fiction: Seldom publishes fiction. Adventure, mystery, romance, suspense. Submit synopsis and 2-3 sample chapters (completed ms preferred).

Tips: "We are a New York State regional publisher appealing to a general trade market of people interested in NY State."

‡O'DONNELL LITERARY SERVICES, INC., HC#1, Box 115A, Leeds NY 12451. President/Editor: Kelly O'Donnell. Imprint is Pickles & Peanuts. **Publishes hardcover, trade and mass market paperback originals** and mass market paperback reprints. Publishes 70 titles/year. Receives 675-1,000 queries and 1,000 mss/year. 45% of books from first-time authors; 55% from unagented writers. Subsidy publishes 30% of books. Pays 10-30% royalty on wholesale price. Offers $2,000-10,000 advance. Publishes book 3 months after acceptance of ms. Simultaneous submissions OK. Reports in 1 month on queries and proposals, 2 months on mss. Book catalog and ms guidelines for #10 SASE.

Nonfiction: Biography, coffeetable book, cookbook, how-to, humor, illustrated book, children's/juvenile, reference, self-help, technical, textbook and business. Subjects include agriculture/horticulture, Americana, animals, business and economics, child guidance/parenting, computers and electronics, cooking, foods & nutrition, education, ethnic, gardening, gay/lesbian, government/politics, health/medicine, history, hobbies, language/literature, military/war, money/finance, music/dance, nature/environment, philosophy, photography, psychology, recreation, regional, religion, science, sociology, software, sports, travel, women's issues/studies. "Looking specifically for women's health titles, treatment, family—self-help. Also looking for unique adventure and first person accounts, plus biographies. Query with outline and 3 sample chapters. Reviews artwork/photos as part of freelance ms package. Writers should send photocopies and transparencies.

Recent Nonfiction Title: *The Survivors* , by Martha Ivery (breast cancer victims); *Voices*, by Sara Montanye (psychology); *Breaking Silence*, by Mary Santulli (abused children).

Fiction: Adventure, confession, erotica, ethnic, experimental, fantasy, feminist, gay/lesbian, gothic, historical, horror, humor, juvenile, literary, mainstream/contemporary, mystery, occult, picture book, plays, religious, romance (gothic, suspense western), science fiction, short story collections, suspense, western, young adult. Query with synopsis and 3 sample chapters.

Recent Fiction Title: *Pickles & Peanuts*, by Martha Ivery (juvenile); *Sands of Time*, by Teri Valentine (romance); *Dreamcatcher*, by Princess Falling Star, (romance/adventure).

Poetry: "No 'Hallmark card' poems or light verse. Looking for avant-garde, free verse and traditional." "Pays $20/page if accepted." Query with 10 sample poems.

Recent Poetry Title: *From Time to Time*, by Donna Keller (free verse); *Footprints*, by Anonymous (free verse); *Missing*, by Laura Comito (traditional).

Tips: "We need writers who can appeal to a broad, and a variety of audiences. Each writer has their own personality that suits their specific topic. Do your best, submit it, and look forward in receiving an acceptance."

ORION RESEARCH, #330, 14555 N. Scottsdale Rd., Scottsdale AZ 85254-3457. (602)-951-1114. Publisher: Roger Rohrs. Imprint is Orion Blue Books. Publishes hardcover originals. Publishes 14 titles/year. Receives 10 queries and 10 mss/year. 50% of books from first-time authors; 50% from unagented writers. Subsidy publishes 5% of books. Pays royalty on wholesale price. Simultaneous submissions OK. Query for electronic

submissions. Reports in 2 months on proposals. Book catalog and ms guidelines for #10 SASE.
Nonfiction: How-to, reference, textbook. Subjects include computers and electronics, education, photography. Query.

‡PARADIGM PUBLISHING COMPANY, P.O. Box 3877, San Diego CA 92163. (619)234-7115. Publisher: Deanna Leach. Publishes trade paperback originals. Averages 4-5 titles/year. Receives 100 queries and 50 mss/year. 95% of books from first-time authors; 100% from unagented writers. Subsidy publishes 1% of books. Pays 15% royalty on retail price after recovery of publishing cost. Publishes book 2 years after acceptance. No simultaneous submissions. Reports in 1 month on queries and proposals; 6 months on mss. Book catalog and ms guidelines free on request.
Nonfiction: How-to, humor, personal. Subjects include ethnic, gay/lesbian, health/medicine, women's issues/ studies. Query with outline. Reviews artwork/photos as part of ms package. Writers should send photocopies.
Recent Nonfiction Title: *Hey Mom, Guess What!*, by Shelly Roberts (humor gay/lesbian).
Fiction: Adventure, erotica, ethnic, feminist, gay/lesbian, humor, mystery, romance, science fiction, suspense. Submit entire ms, author bio, synopsis.
Recent Fiction Title: *Storm Shelter*, by Linda Kay Silva (mystery, lesbian).

‡PARAGON HOUSE PUBLISHERS, 370 Lexington Ave., New York NY 10017. (212)620-2820. Publisher: Michael Giampaoli. Estab. 1983. Publishes hardcover originals, trade paperback originals and reprints. Averages 25 titles/year. Receives 250 queries and 75 mss/year. 80% of books from first-time authors; 90% from unagented writers. Pays 5% royalty on wholesale price. Offers $500 advance. Publishes book 9 months after acceptance of ms. Simultaneous submissions OK. Query for electronic submissions. Reports in 1 month on queries. *Writer's Market* recommends allowing 2 months for reply. Book catalog free on request.
Nonfiction: Biography, reference, college textbook, scholarly monographs. Subjects include history, philosophy, religion. Query.
Poetry: No new or unestablished writers.

‡PARALLAX PRESS, P.O. Box 7355, Berkeley CA 94707. (510)525-0101. Editor-in-Chief: Arnold Kotler. Publishes hardcover and trade paperback originals. Publishes 10 titles/year. Receives 2,000 queries and 200 mss/year. 10% of books from first-time authors; 90% from unagented writers. Subsidy publishes 10% of books "if work is outside our target audience." Pays 5-7% royalty on wholesale price. Offers $500 advance. Publishes book 2 years after acceptance of ms. Accepts simultaneous submissions. Query for electronic submissions. Reports in 2 months on queries. Book catalog and ms guidelines free on request.
Nonfiction: Military/war (peace/war activities), religion (socially engaged Buddhism only), women's issues/ studies (eco-feminism). "We publish only socially engaged Buddhist books or nonsectarian, socially responsible religious books." Query. Reviews artwork/photos as part of ms package. Writers should send photocopies.
Tips: Audience is "adults interested in mindfulness in everyday life, spirituality, Buddhism, social activism."

PMN PUBLISHING, GFA Management, Inc., Box 47024, Indianapolis IN 46247. Fax: (317)351-1772. Publisher: George Allen. Estab. 1988. Publishes trade and mass market paperback originals and trade paperback reprints. Publishes 5-6 titles/year. Receives 24 queries and 24 mss/year. 50% of books from first-time authors; 75% from unagented writers. Subsidy publishes 25% of books. Subsidy determined by size of the market to which the work is targeted. Pays 5-10% royalty on retail price. Publishes book 18 months after acceptance of ms. Simultaneous submissions OK. Reports in 2 months on queries and proposals. Book catalog free on request.
   • PMN is now publishing *The Allen Letter*, a monthly real estate management-oriented newsletter open to freelance submissions (300-500 words).
Nonfiction: How-to, reference, self-help, technical, textbook. Subjects include business and economics, military/war, money/finance, religion, real estate. "Strongest interest is in real estate management, mobile home park management." Query or submit outline.

PRINCETON ARCHITECTURAL PRESS, 37 E. Seventh St., New York NY 10003. (212)995-9620. Fax: (212)995-9454. Editor: Clare Jacobson. Estab. 1981. Publishes hardcover and trade paperback originals and hardcover reprints. Averages 30 titles/year. Receives 200 submissions annually. 50% of books from first-time authors; 100% from unagented writers. Pays 6-10% royalty on wholesale price. Simultaneous submissions OK. Query for electronic submissions. Reports in 2-3 months. Book catalog and guidelines for 9×12 SAE with 3 first-class stamps. "Manuscripts will not be returned unless SASE is enclosed."
Nonfiction: Illustrated book, textbook. Subjects include architecture, landscape architecture, graphic design, urban planning and design. Needs texts on architecture, landscape architecture, architectural monographs, and texts to accompany a possible reprint, architectural history and urban design. Submit outline/synopsis and sample chapters or complete ms. Reviews artwork/photos as part of ms package.
Tips: "Our audience consists of architects, designers, urban planners, architectural theorists, and architectural-urban design historians, and many academicians and practitioners. We are still focusing on architecture and architectural history but would like to increase our list of books on design."

PROSTAR PUBLICATIONS, LTD., P.O. Box 67571, Los Angeles CA 90067. (310)287-2833. Editor: Peter L. Griffes. Publishes trade paperback originals and reprints. Publishes 7-8 titles/year. Receives 10 queries and 30 mss/year. 20% of books from first-time authors; 80% from unagented writers. Subsidy publishes 5% of books; depends on title subject and time of publication. Pays 15% royalty on wholesale price. Publishes book 6 months after acceptance of ms. Simultaneous submissions OK. Query for electronic submissions. Reports in 2 months. Book catalog free on request. Manuscript guidelines for #10 SASE.
Nonfiction: How-to, technical, textbook (marine titles). Subjects include recreation (marine titles) and sports (sailing). Submit proposal package. Sometimes reviews artwork/photos as part of freelance ms package. Writers should send photocopies.
Recent Nonfiction Title: *Airfare Secrets Uncovered.*

QED PRESS, Subsidiary of Comp-type, Inc., 155 Cypress St., Fort Bragg CA 95437. (707)964-9520. Fax: (707)964-7531. Senior Editor: John Fremont. Estab. 1985. Publishes hardcover originals and trade paperback originals and reprints. Publishes 5 titles. Receives 2,000 submissions/year. 75% of books from first-time authors; 75% from unagented writers. Subsidy publishes 10% of books. Decision made upon evaluation of ms. Pays 6-12% royalty on retail price. Publishes ms an average of 1 year after acceptance. Simultaneous submissions OK. Query for electronic submissions. Reports in 2 months. Book catalog for 9×12 SAE with 2 first-class stamps.
Nonfiction: Biography, cookbook, how-to, humor, self-help. "We seek books on the aging process, coping with aging, careers for older people, investments, etc." No juvenile, illustrated, photography, travel. Submit outline and sample chapters.
Fiction: Adventure, ethnic, experimental, fantasy, feminist, historical, literary, mainstream/contemporary, mystery, science fiction, short story collections, suspense. "Our thrust will be the acquisition of translated fiction by contemporary European, African and South American authors." Submit outline/synopsis and sample chapters.
Poetry: Minimal needs for poetry. No traditional, religious, rhymed or derivative poetry. Submit 3 samples.
Tips: "Our audience is older, literary, literate, involved and politically aware."

‡SCHENKMAN BOOKS, INC., 118 Main St., Rochester VT 05767. (802)767-3702. Fax: (802)767-9528. Editor-in-Chief: Joe Schenkman. Publishes hardcover and trade paperback originals and trade paperback reprints. Publishes 8-10 titles/year. Receives 100 queries and 60 mss/year. 95% of books from unagented writers. Subsidy publishes 15% of books. Pays 5-15% royalty on wholesale price. Publishes book 10 months after acceptance of ms. Simultaneous submissions OK. Query for electronic submissions. Reports in 1 month on proposals. Book catalog and ms guidelines free on request.
Nonfiction: Reference, self-help, textbook. Subjects include anthropology/archaeology, business and economics, education, language/literature, nature/environment, psychology, science, sociology, women's issues/studies, "Third World" issues. Query with cover letter, résumé, table of contents, 1 sample chapter. Reviews artwork/photos as part of freelance ms package. Writers should send photocopies.
Recent Nonfiction Title: *The Sociology of Law: A Bibliography of Theoretical Literature*, by A. Javier Treyiño (bibliography); *Police Communication in Traffic Stops*, by Angela Woodhull (training manual, handbook); *Haitian-Kreol in Ten Steps*, by Roger E. Savain (handbook).

SEVGO PRESS, 1955 22nd St., Northport AL 35476-4250. Publisher: John Seymour. Publishes hardcover and trade paperback originals. Publishes 6 titles/year. Receives 30 queries and 20 mss/year. 90% of books from first-time authors; 90% from unagented writers. Subsidy publishing determined by marketability. Pays 10% royalty on wholesale price. Publishes book 6 months after acceptance of ms. Reports in 3 months on queries. Book catalog for #10 SASE with 2 first-class stamps. Manuscript guidelines for #10 SASE.
• Sevgo Press does some subsidy publishing in form of author agreeing to purchase books at wholesale when released.
Nonfiction: Biography, cookbook, how-to, textbook. Subjects include cooking, foods and nutrition, education, history (local), military/war, regional. Query.
Fiction: Humor, drama. Query.

SKIDMORE-ROTH PUBLISHING, INC., 7730 Trade Center Dr., El Paso TX 79912. (915)877-4455. President: Linda Roth. Contact: Brenda Goodner. Estab. 1987. Publishes 40 titles/year. Receives 250 submissions/year. 50% of books first-time authors; 100% from unagented writers. Pays 5-12½% royalty on wholesale price. Publishes book an average of 9 months after acceptance. Simultaneous submissions OK. Reports in 2 months.
• Skidmore-Roth also works with authors on a subsidy arrangement.
Nonfiction: Technical, textbook. Subjects include nursing, allied health and health/medicine. Currently searching for mss in nursing and allied health. Nothing on religion, history, music/dance, travel, sports, agriculture, computers, military, politics, gay/lesbian or literature. Query. Reviews artwork/photos as part of freelance ms package.
Tips: "Anything on nursing is more likely to be published. Our audience is largely professionals in the field of medicine, nursing, allied health. If I were a writer trying to market a book today, I would look for an area that has been completely overlooked by other writers and write on that subject."

STARBOOKS PRESS, Imprint of Woldt Corp., P.O. Box 2737, Sarasota FL 34230-2737. (813)957-1281. Editor: Patrick J. Powers. Estab. 1980. Publishes trade paperback originals. Imprint averages 10-12 titles/year. Receives 30-50 submissions/year. 10% of books from first-time authors; 100% from unagented writers. Subsidy publishes 10% of books. "Subsidy deals are based on marketability and quality of work. Poetry is in this category." Pays 15% royalty based on wholesale price or buys outright for up to $150. Offers 50% average advance. Publishes book an average of 2 months after acceptance. Simultaneous submissions OK. Query for electronic submissions. Reports in up to 2 months. Book catalog free. Manuscript guidelines for 6 × 9 SAE with 2 first-class stamps.

Nonfiction: Subjects include gay and lesbian. Query or submit outline and sample chapters. Reviews artwork/photos as part of ms package.

Fiction: Erotica, gay/lesbian. "We need to produce at least ten new titles per year. Only gay and lesbian genre will be considered." Submit outline/synopsis and sample chapters (first and last pages vital).

Poetry: All poetry contracts are offered on a subsidy basis. Submit complete ms.

Tips: "Submission for one of our anthologies is in an ideal beginning. Our audience consists of gay males. We published our first lesbian anthology in 1993. If I were a writer trying to market a book today, I would keep trying to improve my work and recognize this is a business for the publisher; time is limited and suggestions should be accepted and acted upon. So often we get manuscripts which the author says cannot be edited in any way."

SUNFLOWER UNIVERSITY PRESS, Subsidiary of Journal of the West, Inc., 1531 Yuma, Box 1009, Manhattan KS 66502-4228. (913)539-1888. Publisher: Carol A. Williams. Publishes trade paperback originals and reprints. Averages 12 titles/year. Receives 250 submissions/year. 75% of books from first-time authors; 90% of books from unagented writers. Pays 10% royalty after first printing. Publishes book an average of 8 months after acceptance and contract. Reports in 2 months. Book catalog free.

Nonfiction: Biography, illustrated books, reference. Subjects include agriculture/horticulture, Americana, anthropology/archaeology, business and economics, ethnic, government/politics, health/medicine, history, language/literature, military/war, money/finance, music/dance, nature/environment, photography, recreation, regional, religion, science, sociology, sports, women's issues/studies. Our field of specialization lies in memoirs and histories of the West, and of the military, naval, and air fields; perhaps some specialized collectors' books. Query or submit 2-3 sample chapters. Reviews artwork/photos as part of the ms package (photocopies acceptable).

Fiction: Historical, western, military. "We publish a limited amount of fiction. We need narratives that are historically accurate, without a great deal of fabricated dialogue and shed light on historical incidents or events." No romance, X-rated, juvenile, stream of consciousness. Query or submit 2-3 sample chapters.

Tips: "Our audience is the informed aviation, military, or Western American history enthusiast."

UAHC PRESS, Union of American Hebrew Congregations, 838 Fifth Ave., New York NY 10021. (212)249-0100. Managing Director: Stuart L. Benick. Trade Acquisitions Editor: Aron Hirt-Manheimer. Text Acquisitions Editor: David Kasakove. Estab. 1873. Publishes hardcover and trade paperback originals. Averages 15 titles/year. 60% of books from first-time authors; 90% from unagented writers. Subsidy publishes 40% of books. Pays 5-15% royalty on wholesale price. Publishes book an average of 9 months after acceptance. Simultaneous submissions OK. Book catalog and ms guidelines for SASE.

Nonfiction: Illustrated, juvenile and Jewish textbooks. "Looking for authors that can share an enthusiasm about Judaism with young readers. We welcome first-time authors." Reviews artwork/photos as part of freelance ms package.

Tips: "We publish books that teach values."

‡VICTORY HOUSE, INC., Imprint of Victory House Publishers, P.O. Box 700238, Tulsa OK 74170. (918)747-5009. Managing Editor: Lloyd B. Hildebrand. Publishes hardcover and trade paperback originals, trade paperback reprints. Publishes 5 titles/year. Receives 500 queries and 350 mss/year. 5% of books from first-time authors; 100% from unagented writers. Subsidy publishes 10% of books. Pays negotiable royalty. Publishes book 1 year after acceptance of ms. Simultaneous submissions OK. Query for electronic submissions. Reports in 3 months on queries and proposals, 6 months on mss. Book catalog and ms guidelines for #10 SASE.

Nonfiction: Biography, coffee table book, cookbook, how-to, children's/juvenile, self-help. Subjects include psychology, regional, religion, women's issues/studies. Reviews artwork/photos as part of freelance ms package. Writers should send photocopies.

Fiction: Historical, mystery, religious.

VISTA PUBLISHING INC., 473 Broadway, Long Branch NJ 07740-5901. (908)229-6500. President: Carolyn Zagury. Publishes trade paperback originals. Estab. 1991. Publishes 6 titles/year. Receives 100 queries and 60 mss/year. 90% of books from first-time authors; 100% from unagented writers. Subsidy publishes 5% of books. "Decision to subsidy publish based on overall estimated market and shared risk factors." Pays 30-50% royalty on percentage of total net sales. Publishes book 1 year after acceptance. Simultaneous submissions OK. Query for electronic submissions. Prefers hard copy. Reports in 2 months on mss. Book catalog and ms guidelines free on request.

Nonfiction: Biography, how-to, humor, reference, self-help, textbook. Subjects include business and economics, health/medicine, psychology, women's issues/studies. Query. Submit proposal package, including complete ms. Writers should send photocopies.

Recent Nonfiction Title: *The Enemy Within*, by Anita Bush, Ph.D, RN.

Fiction: Adventure, feminist, humor, mainstream/contemporary, mystery, short story collections, suspense. Query with complete ms.

Recent Fiction Title: *When Tulips Bloom*, by Susan Miller.

Poetry: "We prefer a mix of humor and serious poetry." Submit complete ms.

Tips: Audience is nursing professionals, health care providers, women. "Be willing to take a chance and submit a manuscript for consideration. Our small press was developed to assist writers in successfully publishing. We seek the talent of nurses, healthcare providers and women authors."

‡WEATHERHILL, INC., 15th Floor, 420 Madison Ave., New York NY 10017. (212)223-3008. President: Jeff Hunter. Imprints are Weatherhill Books, Tengu Books. Editorial Director: Ray Furse. Publishes hardcover originals and trade paperback originals and reprints. Publishes 24 titles/year (20 Weatherhill, 4 Tengu). 50% of books from first-time authors; 70% from unagented writers. Subsidy publishes 5% of books. Pays 8-18% royalty on wholesale price. Offers $2,000-10,000 advance. Publishes book 1 year after acceptance of ms. No simultaneous submissions. Query for electronic submissions. Returns, postpaid, unsolicited mss if requested. Reports in 2 month. Book catalog and ms guidelines free on request.

Nonfiction: Biography, coffee table book, cookbook, how-to, humor, illustrated book, reference. Subjects include anthropology/archaeology, art/architecture, business and economics, cooking, foods and nutrition, gardening, government/politics, history, language/literature, nature/environment, philosophy, photography, sports, travel (all with Japan or East Asian orientation). "Tengu Books, a new imprint, is designed to afford a lighter, more irreverent look at Japan and the Far East. Our Weatherhill books are for the more discriminating general reader with an interest in Japan and the Far East (although we are *not* an academic publisher)." Submit outline and 2 sample chapters or proposal package, including author bio/intended market. Reviews artwork/photos as part of freelance ms package. Writers should send transparencies – duplicates and description of complete illustration possibilities.

Recent Nonfiction Title: *The Kobe Hotel*, by Saikoh Sanki.

‡WEBB RESEARCH GROUP, P.O. Box 314, Medford OR 97501. (503)664-5205. Editor-in-Chief: Bert Webber. Estab. 1973. Publishes hardcover and trade paperback originals. Publishes 11 titles/year. Receives 25 submissions/year. 25% of books are from first-time authors. "We decline to deal with agents." Subsidy publishes 10% of books through Reflected Images, (imprint for special projects and subsidy work). "Subsidy based on subject and authorship." Pays 5-10% royalty on wholesale price or makes outright purchase. Publishes book an average of 1 year after acceptance. Reports in 2 weeks on queries. *Writer's Market* recommends allowing 2 months for reply. Book catalog for #10 SAE with 2 first-class stamps.

Nonfiction: Biography, reference. Subjects include Americana (limited to Pacific Northwest and Oregon Trail), history (Pacific Northwest), military/war (WWII Japanese attack against mainland of USA only), recreation, religion, travel, Japanese-American relocation in WWII. "We are always on the lookout for photographically illustrated manuscripts on aspects of the history of the Pacific Northwest and along the Oregon Trail. We have enough books on Indians for now. We never do restaurant or camping guides but we may accept cookbooks on subsidy." Query with SASE; all unsolicited mss are returned unopened C.O.D. mail. Reviews artwork/photos as part of ms package. "Submit copies of photos with query."

Recent Nonfiction Title: *Silent Siege III: Japanese Attacks on North America in World War II*, by Bert Webber.

Tips: "Writers with first-hand knowledge of history of the Pacific Northwest or pioneer period Oregon Trail (1843-1869) have the best chance of interesting us. We do limited postal history for specialist philatelists. Our books are aimed at reference librarians who want accurate answers recorded in popular language. All books have biblio and index and we seek 9th grade readability to suit the all-American public. If I were a writer trying to market a book today, I would know what I'm writing about, not fake it, and support with a suitable bibliography. I would also have suitable quality photographs, preferably in black and white."

WESTERN BOOK/JOURNAL PRESS, Subsidiary of Journal Lithograph Co., 1470 Woodberry, San Mateo CA 94403. (415)573-8877. Executive Editor: Marie T. Mollath. Estab. 1960. Publishes hardcover and trade paperback originals and reprints. Publishes 16 titles/year. Receives 10 queries and 30 mss/year. 70% of books from first-time authors. Subsidy publishes 15% of books. Pays 10-22% royalty. Publishes book 14 months after acceptance of ms. Query for electronic submissions. Reports in 1 month on queries. *Writer's Market* recommends allowing 2 months for reply. Book catalog and ms guidelines free on request.

Nonfiction: Biography, self-help, technical. Subjects include architecture, government/politics, regional, science, historical biographies. Submit proposal package, including entire ms. *Writer's Market* recommends query with SASE first. Reviews artwork/photos as part of freelance ms package. Writers should send photocopies.

Recent Nonfiction Title: *Beginner's Guide to Hispanic Genealogy*, by Flores and Ludwig.

YE GALLEON PRESS, P.O. Box 287, Fairfield WA 99012-0287. (509)283-2422. Owner: Glen C. Adams. Estab. 1937. Publishes 25 titles/year. Subsidy publishes 25% of books. "Subsidy based on sales probabilities." Pays 5-10% royalties based on moneys actually received. No advance. Publishes book an average of 9 months after acceptance. Reports in 2 weeks on queries. *Writer's Market* recommends allowing 2 months for reply. Book catalog free.

Nonfiction: Biography (if sponsored). Subjects include Americana, history. Query. Reviews artwork/photos as part of freelance ms package.

Fiction: Historical. "I print historical fiction only if paid to do so and even then it needs to be pretty good." Query.

Tips: "We are looking for books on native Americans written from an Indian point of view. Our audience is general. A probable reader is male, college-educated, middle-aged or past, wearing glasses or collector of rare western US history. We are not likely to take any more manuscripts on a royalty basis this year as we are offered more work than we can handle."

YES INTERNATIONAL PUBLISHERS, 1317 Summit Ave., St. Paul MN 55105-2602. (612)645-6808. President: Theresa King. Publishes trade paperback originals. Publishes 3 titles/year. Receives 10 queries and 3 mss/ year. 10% of books from first-time authors; 100% from unagented writers. Pays 8-12% royalty on retail price. Offers $100-1,000 advance. Publishes book 1 year after acceptance. Reports in 1 month on queries and proposals, 1-2 months on mss. Book catalog free on request. Manuscript guidelines for #10 SASE.

Nonfiction: Self-help. Subjects include health/medicine (holistic), philosophy (transformational), psychology (transpersonal), regional (spirituality), women's issues/studies (spirituality). "We have a small budget and accept only very well written manuscripts of about 35,000-50,000 words. Writers often do not check the type of work we publish and try to convince us to publish theirs whether it fits our line or not." Query with outline and 2 sample chapters. Reviews artwork/photos as part of freelance manuscript package. Writers should send photocopies.

Tips: "Our audience is college-educated adults."

Subsidy Publishers

The following companies publish more than 50% of their books on an author-subsidy basis.

‡Aardvark Enterprises
204 Millbank Drive S.W.
Calgary, Alberta T26 2H9 Canada

Aegina Press, Inc.
59 Oak Lane
Spring Valley, Huntington WV 25704

American Literary Press
Suite 10, 11419 Cronridge Dr.
Owings Mills MD 21117

American Society for Nondestructive Testing
P.O. Box 28518
Columbus OH 43228

Authors' Unlimited
3324 Barham Blvd.
Los Angeles CA 90068

Automobile Quarterly
15040 Kutztown Rd., Box 348
Kutztown PA 19530

Barney Press
#60, 8300 Kern Canyon Rd.
Bakersfield CA 93306

Brunswick Publishing Company
P.O. Box 555
Lawrenceville VA 23868

‡Burch Street Press
63 W. Burch St., P.O. Box 152
Shippensburg PA 17257

Carlton Press, Inc.
11 W. 32nd St.
New York NY 10001

‡Common Courage Press
P.O. Box 702
Monroe ME 04951

Dorrance Publishing Co., Inc.
643 Smithfield St.
Pittsburgh PA 15222

Evanston Publishing, Inc.
1216 Hinman Ave.
Evanston IL 60202

Fairway Press
628 S. Main St.
Lima OH 45804

Fithian Press
P.O. Box 1525
Santa Barbara CA 93102

Give Books Away
2525 McKinnon Dr.
Decatur GA 30030

‡Golden Quill Press/Marshall Jones Co.
P.O. Box 2327, Barnumville Rd.
Manchester Center VT 05255-2327

The Golden Quill Press
Avery Rd.
Francestown NH 03043

Harbor House (West) Publishers, Inc.
40781 Smoke Tree Lane
Rancho Mirage CA 92270

Lucky Books
P.O. Box 1415
Winchester VA 22604

‡Pallas Press
P.O. Box 64921
Tucson AZ 85728

‡Perivale Press
13830 Erwin St.
Van Nuys CA 91401-2914

‡Only You Publications
1416 Eddingham
Lawrence KS 66046

Poetry On Wings, Inc.
P.O. Box 1000
Pear Blossom CA 93553

Prescott Press
Suite A3, 104 Row 2
Lafayette LA 70508

Proclaim Publishing
#2610, 1117 Marquette Ave.
Minneapolis MN 55403

Peter Randall Publisher
P.O. Box 4726
Portsmouth NH 03802

Red Apple Publishing
P.O. Box 101
Gig Harbor WA 98335

Rivercross Publishing, Inc.
127 E. 59th St.
New York NY 10022

‡Todd Publishing
8383 E. Evans Rd.
Scottsdale AZ 85260

Treehaus Communications, Inc.
906 W. Loveland Ave.
Loveland OH 45140

Vantage Press
516 W. 34th St.
New York NY 10001

Whitman Publishing Inc.
383 Van Gordon St.
Lakewood CO 80228

Wildstar Publishing
1550 California St.
San Francisco CA 94109

Small Presses

"Small press" is a relative term. Compared to the dozen or so conglomerates, the rest of the book publishing world may seem to be comprised of small presses. Several of the publishers listed in the Book Publishers section consider themselves small presses and cultivate the image. For our purpose of classification, the publishers listed in this section are called small presses because they publish three or fewer books per year.

The publishing opportunities are slightly more limited with the companies listed here when compared to those in the larger Book Publishers section. Small presses are usually not able to market their books as effectively as larger publishers. Their print runs and royalty arrangements are usually smaller. It boils down to money, what a publisher can afford, and in that area, small presses simply can't compete with conglomerates.

However, realistic small press publishers don't try to compete with Bantam or Random House. They realize everything about their efforts operates on a smaller scale. Most small press publishers get into book publishing for the love of it, not solely for the profit. Of course, every publisher, small or large, wants successful books. But small press publishers often measure success in different ways.

Many writers actually prefer to work with small presses. Since small publishing houses are usually begun based on the publisher's commitment to their subject matter, and since they necessarily work with far fewer authors than the conglomerates, small press authors and their books usually receive more personal attention than the larger publishers can afford to give them. Promotional dollars at the big houses tend to be siphoned toward a few books each season that they have decided are likely to succeed, leaving hundreds of "midlist" books underpromoted, and, more likely than not, destined for failure. Since small presses only commit to a very small number of books every year, they are vitally interested in the promotion and distribution of each title they publish.

Just because they publish three or fewer titles per year does not mean small press editors have the time to look at complete manuscripts. In fact, because most small presses are understaffed, the editors have even less time for submissions. The procedure for contacting a small press with your book idea is exactly the same as it is for a larger publisher. Send a one-page query with SASE first. If the press is interested in your proposal, be ready to send an outline or synopsis, and/or a sample chapter or two. Be patient with their reporting times; small presses are usually slower to respond than larger companies. You might consider simultaneous queries, as long as you note them, to compensate for the waiting game.

For more information on small presses, see *Novel & Short Story Writer's Market* and *Poet's Market* (Writer's Digest Books), and *Small Press Review* and *The International Directory of Little Magazines and Small Presses* (Dustbooks).

For a list of publishers according to their subjects of interest, see the nonfiction and fiction sections of the Book Publishers Subject Index. Information on some book publishers and producers not included in this edition of *Writer's Market* can be found in Book Publishers and Producers/Changes '94-'95.

INSIDER REPORT

Writers receive personal attention from small niche publisher

It's difficult for Barbara Brown to talk about her company, Naturegraph Press, without mentioning her late husband, Vinson Brown, a well-known naturalist and author who founded the press in 1946. He started the firm to publish materials primarily for schools to teach children about nature.

Vinson was publishing classroom materials and lecturing on nature topics at schools throughout the West when he met and married Barbara, an elementary school teacher. "Thereafter, I worked in the company and never went back to teaching," she says.

At the time, Vinson was establishing himself as both a scholarly and popular nature writer and it was his difficulties with a university press that led to his publishing one of his own books as Nature-

Barbara Brown

graph's first book. The university press was going through a period of high editorial turnover, and after three editors and three complete rewrites, Vinson decided he would do better to publish his book himself. This marked the change in Naturegraph from a publisher of auxiliary school materials to a book publisher.

Since that first book, says Brown, Naturegraph has published hundreds of nature titles and currently keeps about 100 books in print. "Originally the main focus for the press was nature books, such as *Handbook of California Birds* and *Rocks and Minerals of California*. We did a little book called *Common Edible and Useful Plants of the West* that has sold more than 132,000 copies. Then we began publishing books on Native Americans with about an equal emphasis as nature books. We also publish a few books on gardening, health and 'wit and wisdom,' but these are sidelines to our main focus."

Naturegraph publishes between two and four new books every year. The publisher receives about 400 queries or submissions a year, so the competition is very keen, says Brown. "Many such submissions are very easy to reject because they are not on a subject we handle. The biggest mistake a writer can make is not to find out first what a publisher is looking for.

"I prefer getting nice short queries, accurately to the point, describing the work. In particular I like it if writers list other works of a similar nature that have already been published and the advantages they see in theirs. It shows they've done research and have an interest in their field," she says. Brown prefers to see a query letter with an outline or sample chapters instead of a complete manuscript.

Brown looks for works that are "written simply, that can be clearly understood. I've read or tried to read scientific books where every third word is a scientific term. I guess that's needed for upper class university students or very advanced people in a particular area, but we leave that type of publishing to the university presses."

In other words, Brown looks for material that can be easily understood by the layman. "We truly do love the wilds, so we feel the more plants and animals people can identify and the more familiar they are with nature, the more likely they will be to protect their newfound friends and less likely to destroy or kill."

As a small publisher Brown appreciates authors who are willing to get involved with the promotion of their book. Many provide her with lists of contacts and lists of potential reviewers. A handful even buy books from the company at a distributor's discount and sell books themselves.

There are certain advantages to working with a small press, says Brown. "Writers get a lot of personal attention and many of our writers have become lifelong friends. There's correspondence back and forth with the editor and myself and almost all the writers I've worked with say they've seen a big improvement in their work. The deadwood gets chopped out which seems to clarify their writing, something a lot of authors cannot do for themselves."

Another important advantage is niche publishing. Naturegraph has a close relationship with its distributors and has become known by them for publishing books in specific fields. Larger companies, says Brown, may not know how to handle a particular book and are at a disadvantage because buyers do not connect their name with that type of book. In a few cases, Naturegraph was very successful with books it took over after a larger company had let them go out of print because of poor sales.

Brown says she's learned a lot about the writer's side of publishing through her husband, who published about 40 titles with a variety of publishers over the years, including Little Brown, Prentice Hall, Stanford University Press and Stackpole Books. "He never gave up. He knew that even if you are fairly established you still get rejects and many rejects come for every acceptance. There's a lot of competition even in the small press. But if you study your publishers and send the right thing to the right publisher . . . if you've done your homework and have something well written, you just have to be persistent."

—*Robin Gee*

‡ABELEXPRESS, 230 E. Main St., Carnegie PA 15106. (412)279-0672. Owner: Ken Abel. Publishes trade paperback originals for unique markets in science and health.

ACME PRESS, P.O. Box 1702, Westminster MD 21158-1702. (410)848-7577. Managing Editor: Ms. E.G. Johnston. Estab. 1991. Publishes humor. "We accept submissions on any subject as long as the material is humorous; prefer full-length novels. No cartoons or art (text only). No pornography. SASE mandatory."

ACORN PUBLISHING, 1063 S. Talmadge, Waverly NY 14892-9514. (607)565-2536. Fax: (607)565-2560. Editor: Mary O. Robb. Estab. 1985. Publishes trade paperback originals on health, recreation and general fitness. Especially interested in regional mountain biking guides for eastern US.

‡ADASTRA PRESS, 101 Strong St., Easthampton MA 01027. Contact: Gary Metras. Publishes 2-4 titles/year. Publishes poetry chapbooks (12-18 pages). Query with 5 samples in the fall; submit complete ms in February only.

AEGIS PUBLISHING GROUP, 796 Aquidneck Ave., Newport RI 02842-7202. (401)849-4200. Publisher: Robert Mastin. Estab. 1992. Reports in 2 months. "Our specialty is home or small business how-to books that will help a start-up entrepreneur succeed. Author must be an experienced authority in the subject, and the material must be very specific with helpful step-by-step advice. No fiction."

‡**AGRITECH PUBLISHING GROUP, INC.**, Division of R.G.I. Holdings Ltd., P.O. Box 950553, Mission Hills CA 91395-0553. (818)361-8889 or (818)365-1312. President/Publisher: Robert P. Griset. Imprints are Agritech Books, Equine Book Company, The Intelligent Cowboy. Publishes hardcover and trade paperback originals and reprints. Publishes 0-3 titles/year. Subjects include: agriculture/horticulture, Americana, animals, gardening, natural environment, software.

AHSAHTA PRESS, Boise State University, Dept. of English, 1910 University Dr., Boise ID 83725-1525. (208)385-1999. Fax: (208)385-4373. Co-Editor: Tom Trusky. Estab. 1974. Publishes Western American poetry in trade paperback. Reads SASE samplers annually, January-March.

‡**ALASKAN VIEWPOINT**, HCR 64 Box 453, Seward AK 99664. Editor-in-Chief: L.B. Leary. "We publish work by and about Alaskan women; miscellaneous Alaskana; fiction; nonfiction."

‡**ALTA MIRA PRESS, INC.**, P.O. Box 165, Keyport NJ 07735. Editor: Richard A. Herman. Estab. 1992. Publishes trade paperback originals. Publishes 3-4 titles/year. 100% of books from first-time authors; 100% from unagented writers. Publishes book 12-18 months after acceptance of ms. Query for electronic submissions. "We are looking for manuscripts aimed at the 45-years and older market: self-help, referral, directories."

AMERICAN CATHOLIC PRESS, 16160 S. Seton Dr., South Holland IL 60473-1863. (312)331-5845. Editorial Director: Fr. Michael Gilligan, Ph.D. Estab. 1967. Publishes hardcover originals and hardcover and paperback reprints. "Most of our sales are by direct mail, although we do work through retail outlets." Averages 4 titles/year. Pays by outright purchase of $25-100. No advance. "We publish books on the Roman Catholic liturgy—for the most part, books on religious music and educational books and pamphlets. We also publish religious songs for church use, including Psalms, as well as choral and instrumental arrangements. We are interested in new music, meant for use in church services. Books, or even pamphlets, on the Roman Catholic Mass are especially welcome. We have no interest in secular topics and are not interested in religious poetry of any kind."

AMERICAN VETERINARY PUBLICATIONS, INC., 5782 Thornwood Dr., Goleta CA 93117-3896. Publisher: Dr. Paul W. Pratt. Estab. 1920. Publishes hardcover and trade paperback originals. Publishes 2-4 titles/year. Pays royalty on net price. Publishes book 1-4 years after acceptance. No simultaneous submissions. Book catalog and ms guidelines free on request. Reference, technical, textbook, health/medicine, science. "We publish highly technical books on veterinary medicine *only*. No pet books."

‡**AMIGADGET PUBLISHING COMPANY**, P.O. Box 1696, Lexington SC 29072. Editor-in-Chief: Jay Gross. Publishes trade paperback originals. Averages 2 titles/year. "Do not send manuscript. Queries only. No books on Windows." Recent title: *Starting from Video Scratch*, by J. Gross (how-to).

ANIMA PUBLICATIONS, Imprint of Anima Books, 1053 Wilson Ave., Chambersburg PA 17201-1247. (717)267-0087. Managing Editor: Barbara D. Rotz. Estab. 1974. "Our books are read at the undergraduate level as texts in religious studies programs and by the general reading audience with an interest in Asian religions."

ANOTHER CHICAGO PRESS, P.O. Box 11223, Chicago IL 60611. Publisher: Lee Webster. Estab. 1985. Publishes fiction: ethnic, literary and short story collections.

ARCUS PUBLISHING COMPANY, P.O. Box 228, Sonoma CA 95476. (707)996-9529. Fax: (707)996-1738. Estab. 1983. Publishes personal growth and self-help books that are life-enchancing, useful, innovative and enduring. Send for quidelines. Query first.

ARIADNE PRESS, 4817 Tallahassee Ave., Rockville MD 20853-3144. (301)949-2514. President: Carol Hoover. Estab. 1976. Adventure, feminist, historical, humor, literary mainstream/contemporary fiction.

‡**ASTARTE SHELL PRESS**, P.O. Box 10453, Portland ME 04104. (207)828-1992. Contact: Sapphire. Publishes trade paperback originals. "We focus on feminist spirituality and politics, including peace and social justice issues."

AUTO BOOK PRESS, P.O. Bin 711, San Marcos CA 92079-0711. (619)744-3582. Editorial Director: William Carroll. Estab. 1955. Publishes hardcover and paperback originals. Automotive material only: technical or definitive how-to.

‡**AVIATION BOOK COMPANY,** 25133 Anza Dr., Santa Clarita CA 91355. Editor: Walter P. Winner. Publishes hardcover and trade paperback originals and reprints. Publishes 2 titles/year. Specializes in aviation books *only*.

B&B PUBLISHING, INC., P.O. Box 393, Fontana WI 53125-0393. President: William Turner. Managing Director: Lisa Turner. "Looking for supplementary educational materials for schools and libraries especially for grades K-12. Also looking for journalists interested in writing/researching state trivia books."
● This small press is also a book producer.

‡**BAY PRESS, INC.,** 115 W. Denny Way, Seattle WA 98119. Editor-in-Chief: Kimberly Barnett. Publishes trade paperback nonfiction originals on contemporary issues. Publishes 4 titles/year.

BIDDLE PUBLISHING CO., #103, P.O. Box 1305, Brunswick ME 04011. President: Julie Zimmerman. Estab. 1990. Publishes general nonfiction, including peace and social concerns, autobiography, history. Replies with SASE only.

‡**BLACK BEAR PUBLICATIONS,** 1916 Lincoln St., Croydon PA 19021-8026. (215)788-3543. Editor: A. Jeanne. Estab. 1983. Publishes poetry collections reflective of the world and our environment.

‡**BLACK HERON PRESS,** P.O. Box 95676, Seattle WA 98145. (206)363-5210. Publisher: Jerry Gold. Publishes hardcover and trade paperback originals. "Only high quality fiction. Our books have won several literary prizes. We intend to win more."

BLACK TIE PRESS, P.O. Box 440004, Houston TX 77244-0004. (713)789-5119. Publisher/Editor: Peter Gravis. Estab. 1986. Imprints are Deluxe, Matineé and Plain Editions. Publishes fiction and poetry. "We publish books not individual poems, articles, or stories. We do not encourage unsolicited fiction manuscripts."

‡**BLACK TOOTH PRESS,** 768 N. 26th St., Philadelphia PA 19130. (215)232-6611. Contact: Jim or Lisa Anderson. Publishes trade paperback originals. Averages 2 titles/year. Humor and popular culture. Submit outline. Recent title: *So Sue Me!*, by Joe Kohut. "We're looking for work which conforms to our slogan: 'Quick reading for the short-attention-span 90s!' "

‡**BLUE BUDDHA PRESS,** #365, 532 LaGuardia Place, New York NY 10012. Editor: Doctor Robert. Publishes trade paperback originals. "We're looking for fiction material in the vein of *War Assets* — multimedia projects that include photographs, illustrations, paintings and music. Read our first title, *War Assets Display Room*, by William Nowik, to see what we are looking for."

BORDER BOOKS, INC., P.O. Box 80780, Albuquerque NM 87198-0780. (505)266-8322. Publisher: Dave DeWitt. Editor: Melissa T. Stock. Estab. 1992. Publishes books on cooking, travel, gardening and the Southwest. Written query first, please.

BRETT BOOKS, INC., P.O. Box 290-627, Brooklyn NY 11229-0011. Publisher: Barbara J. Brett. Estab. 1993. Publishes general interest nonfiction books on timely subjects. Submit query letter only. Include SASE.

‡**BRIGHT MOUNTAIN BOOKS, INC.,** 138 Springside Rd., Asheville NC 28803. (704)684-8840. Editor: Cynthia F. Bright. Imprint is Historical Images. Publishes hardcover and trade paperback originals and reprints. "Our current emphasis is on regional titles, which can include nonfiction by local writers."

‡**BRIGHT RING PUBLISHING,** P.O. Box 5768, Bellingham WA 98226. (206)734-1601. Owner: Mary Ann Kohl. Publishes trade paperback originals on creative ideas for children. No crafts. Publishes 1 title/year.

‡**C.F.W. ENTERPRISES INC.,** Unique Publications, 4201 Vanowen Place, Burbank CA 91505. (818)845-2656. Manager: Bea Wong. Publishes trade paperback originals and reprints on martial arts-related topics.

‡**CADMUS EDITIONS,** P.O. Box 126, Tiburon CA 94920. Director: Jeffrey Miller. Publishes hardcover and trade paperback originals of literary fiction and poetry.

CALYX BOOKS, P.O. Box B, Corvallis OR 97339-0539. (503)753-9384. Also publishes *Calyx, A Journal of Art & Literature by Women*. Managing Editor: Margarita Donnelly. Estab. 1986 for Calyx Books; 1976 for Calyx, Inc. Publishes fine literature by women, fiction, nonfiction and poetry. Please query with SASE for submission deadlines and guidelines.

CAROUSEL PRESS, P.O. Box 6061, Albany CA 94706-0061. (510)527-5849. Editor and Publisher: Carole T. Meyers. Estab. 1976. Publishes nonfiction, family-oriented travel books.

‡**CEDI PUBLICATIONS**, Imprint of Consortium on Employment and Disability Issues, P.O. Box 10096, Arlington VA 22210. (703)795-6813. President: Bill Washburn. "We are looking for concise, documented reports which take a position on labor, insurance, and disability issues."

‡**CENTER FOR AFRO-AMERICAN STUDIES PUBLICATIONS**, University of California at Los Angeles, 160 Haines Hall, 405 Hilgard Ave., Los Angeles CA 90024-1545. (310)825-3528. Managing Editor: Toyomi Igus. Publishes hardcover and trade paperback originals. "All manuscripts should be scholarly works about the African-American experience. Authors should be able to demonstrate a thorough knowledge of the subject matter. Not interested in autobiographies, unless of an African-American personal note." Recent title: *Language & the Social Construction of Identity in Creole Situations*, edited by Marcyliena H. Morgan.

‡**CHAPEL STREET PUBLISHING**, 43 Chapel St., Seneca Falls NY 13148. (315)568-2508. Publisher: Stephen Beals. Publishes trade paperback originals. Nonfiction and fiction material "must have strong New York State connection. Prefer Central New York/Finger Lakes."

‡**CHRISTIAN MEDIA**, Box 448, Jacksonville OR 97530. (503)899-8888. Sole Proprietor: James Lloyd. Publishes trade paperback originals.

CLARITY PRESS INC., #469, 3277 Roswell Rd. NE, Atlanta GA 30305. (404)231-0649. Fax: (404)231-3899. Editorial Committee Contact: Annette Gordon. Estab. 1984. Publishes mss on minorities, human rights in US, Middle East and Africa. No fiction. Responds *only* if interested so do *not* enclose SASE.

‡**CORKSCREW PRESS, INC.**, Suite 234, 4470-107 Sunset Blvd., Los Angeles CA 90027. Editorial Director: J. Croker Norge. Estab. 1988. Publishes trade humor and humorous how-to books. Reports in 6 months.

DELANCEY PRESS, P.O. Box 40285, Philadelphia PA 19106. (215)238-9103. Editorial Director: Wesley Morrison. Estab. 1990. "We are open to reviewing all types of nonfiction. Queries by *letter* only; no initial contact by phone."

DIAMOND PRESS, Box 2458, Doylestown PA 18901. (215)345-6094. Fax: (215)345-6692. Marketing Director: Paul Johnson. Estab. 1985. Publishes trade paperback originals on softball and antiques. "We are now more interested in baseball, fast pitch softball and slow pitch softball books."

DICKENS PUBLICATIONS, 1703 Taylor St. N.W., Washington DC 20011-5312. President: Nathaniel A. Dickens. Estab. 1982. "Publishes nonfiction related to education, history, finance and various forms of fiction."

*__DIMI PRESS__, 3820 Oak Hollow Lane SE, Salem OR 97302-4774. (503)364-7698. Fax: (503)364-9727. President: Dick Lutz. Estab. 1981. Trade paperback originals of health and psychology, also certain other nonfiction titles. Subsidy publishing.

DISKOTECH, INC., Suite 210, 7930 State Line, Prairie Village KS 66208. (913)432-8606. Fax: (913)362-48659. CompuServe CIS: 72754,2773. Publisher/Editor: John Slegman. Estab. 1989. Publishes multimedia nonfiction and fiction for PC's on CD-ROM. Query first with SASE. Consider most nonfiction subjects. Considers all adult fiction genres. Recent nonfiction title: *How To Be Happily Employed in the 1990s*, by Janice Benjamin and Barbara Block. Recent fiction title: *Negative Space CVN*, (computerized video novel) by Holly Franking.
  • Diskotech, Inc. is publishing a new form of the novel, a CVN (computerized video novel), that combines print, software and video.

‡**DOWN THE SHORE PUBLISHING**, Imprint of Cormorant Books & Calendars, 534 Cedar Run Dock Rd., Cedar Run NJ 08092. Publisher: Raymond G. Fisk. Publishes hardcover originals and trade paperback originals and reprints. "As a small regional publisher, we must limit our efforts and resources to our established market: New Jersey shore and mid-Atlantic. We specialize in regional histories and pictorial, coffee table books." Query with synopsis. "We do not currently publish fiction, but will consider submissions that consider our regional market." Submit synopsis.

DUSTY DOG REVIEWS, 1904-A Gladden, Gallup NM 87301. (505)863-2398. Editor: John Pierce. Estab. 1991. Features over 75 honest and evaluative poetry book/chapbook reviews as well as literary magazine reviews from small and midrange presses in each issue. Subscription price: $4.50/yr/3 issues. Single copy price: $2. Each press editor and/or magazine editor will receive 1 free copy of the issue in which the review appears.

E.M. PRESS, INC., Box 4057, Manassas VA 22110. (703)754-0229. Editor/Publisher: Beth Miller. Estab. 1991. "We are looking for quality mainstream literature (biographies, historical events, life-experience, literary fiction) from first-time writers and veterans alike. We will consider how-to, hobby and sports material. No textbooks."

‡EARTH-LOVE PUBLISHING HOUSE, Suite 353, 3440 Youngfield St., Wheat Ridge CO 80033. (303)233-9660. Director: Laodeciae Augustine. Publishes 1-2 trade paperback originals/year on metaphysics and minerals.

EASTERN CARIBBEAN INSTITUTE, Box 1338, Frederiksted, Virgin Islands 00841-1338. (809)772-1011. Fax: (809)772-3463. President/Publisher: S.B. Jones-Hendrickson. Estab. 1982. Publishes nonfiction: biography, technical, textbook. Subjects include education, ethnic, government/politics, philosophy, economics. Fiction: ethnic, literary, plays and young adult as they pertain to the Caribbean and/or the Third World.

EASTERN PRESS, P.O. Box 881, Bloomington IN 47402-0881. Publisher: Don Lee. Estab. 1981. Publishes academic books on Asian subjects and pedagogy on languages.

‡EES PUBLICATIONS, P.O. Box 12253, Lake Park FL 33403-0235. (407)844-2102. Director: Roger Harrington. "Publishes nonfiction books on EMS education and law enforcement topics. Authors *must* have proper credentials."

‡ELDER BOOKS, 120 Montezuma Ave., P.O. Box 490, Forest Knolls CA 94933. (415)488-9002. Senior Editor: Susan Sullivan. Publishes trade paperback originals for caregivers of older adults, seniors, people dealing with Alzheimer's disease and other conditions associated with aging.

EXCALIBUR PUBLISHING, #790, 434 Avenue of Americas, New York NY 10011. (212)777-1790. Publisher: Sharon Good. "We are interested in performing arts titles."
• This company is now offering the Excalibur Book Award, with first prize a publishing contract. Write for guidelines.

‡FALL CREEK PRESS, P.O. Box 1127, Fall Creek OR 97438. (503)744-0938. Editor-in-Chief: Helen Wirth. Publishes trade paperback anthologies of original short stories. Publishes 2 titles/year (approximately 20 stores). "We solicit mss only after approving a synopsis." 30% of books from first-time authors. 98% of books from unagented writers. Pays royalty (pro-rated per anthology). "Within the context of a compelling storyline a VeriTale offers to the protagonist, and thus to the reader, an opportunity to grow spiritually. Critical to the story are the personal choices made by the protagonist which open the door to his or her personal growth."

‡FALLEN LEAF PRESS, P.O. Box 10034, Berkeley CA 94709-5034. (510)848-7805. Owner: Ann Basart. Estab. 1984. Publishes reference books on music and scores of contemporary American chamber music.

‡FATHOM PUBLISHING COMPANY, P.O. Box 200448, Anchorage AK 99520-0448. (907)272-3305. Publisher: Constance Taylor. Publishes 1-2 trade paperback originals/year on history, legal issues and reference. Manuscript guidelines for #10 SASE.

FORD-BROWN & CO., PUBLISHERS, P.O. Box 2764, Boston MA 02208-2764. Publisher: Steven Ford Brown. Estab. 1975. Publishes poetry and poetry criticism. Reports in 2 months.

FRANCISCAN PRESS, Quincy University, 1800 College Ave., Quincy IL 62301-2670. (217)228-5670. Fax: (217)228-5672. Director: Dr. Terrence J. Riddell. Estab. 1991. Publishes nonfiction books on religion.

FREE SPIRIT PUBLISHING INC., Suite 616, 400 First Ave. N., Minneapolis MN 55401-1730. (612)338-2068. President: Judy Galbraith. Editorial Assistant: M. Elizabeth Salzmann. Estab. 1983. Publishes psychology and self-help materials for children and teens, educational/parenting books for adults. "Please request a catlog and submision guidelines before submitting your work."

JOEL FRIEDLANDER, PUBLISHER, P.O. Box 3330, San Rafael CA 94912. (415)459-1311. Publisher: Joel Friedlander. Estab. 1985. Publishes hardcover and trade paperback originals on self-help and esoteric psychology. Subjects include history, philosophy and psychology. "We want popular manuscripts on East/West psychology. No economics, politics or how-to books."

FRONT ROW EXPERIENCE, 540 Discovery Bay Blvd., Byron CA 94514-9454. (510)634-5710. Fax: (510)634-5710. Editor: Frank Alexander. Estab. 1974. Imprint is Kokono. Publishes teacher/educator edition paperback originals. Only wants submissions for "Movement Education," special education and related areas.

‡GAFF PRESS, P.O. Box 1024, Astoria OR 97103-3051. (503)325-8288. Publisher: Paul Barrett. Publishes hardcover and trade paperback originals, poetry chapbooks. "Particularly interested in extraordinary ocean tales for next (third) book of sea stories." Recent title: *How to Make a Good Book.*

‡**GAMBLING TIMES INCORPORATED**, Suite 213, 16760 Stagg St., Van Nuys CA 91406. (818)781-9355. Publisher: Stanley R. Suudikoff. Publishes hardcover and trade paperback original how-to and reference books on gambling.

GEMINI PUBLISHING COMPANY, Suite 120, 14010 El Camino Real, Houston TX 77062-8024. (713)488-6866. President: Don Diebel. "We are seeking books, cassettes and videos on meeting, attracting and becoming intimate with women." Catalog for $1.

‡**GILES ROAD PRESS**, P.O. Box 212, Harrington Park NJ 07640. Publisher: Maria Langer. Publishes trade paperback originals. "Open to all topics. We are a small press publisher interested in doing limited interest books. Authors must have a clear understanding of the subject matter of their books and must provide marketing suggestions in their books and proposals." Book catalog for #10 SASE.

GMS PUBLICATIONS, 11659 Doverwood Dr., Riverside CA 92505-3216. Publisher: G. Michael Short. Estab. 1988. Publishes computer and business books in electronic format only. "No writer guidelines available."

‡**GOOD BOOK PUBLISHING COMPANY**, Box 276, Corte Madera CA 94976-0276. (415)924-8902. Publisher: Richard G. Burns. Publishes trade paperback originals and reprints on the spiritual roots of Alcoholics Anonymous.

‡**GRAPHIC ARTS PUB. INC.**, 3100 Bronson Hill Rd., Livonia NY 14487. (716)346-2776. Vice President: Donna Southworth. Publishes trade paperback originals on TQM and quality and color reproduction. Recent title: *Color Separation on the Desktop*, by Southworth and Southworth.

‡**GREAT LAKES PRESS**, P.O. Box 483, Okemos MI 48805. Managing Editor: Jeff Potter. Publishes hardcover and trade paperback originals. Publishes 4 titles/year. Pays 1-5% royalty or makes outright purchase of $500-5,000. Produces books on engineering test preparation.

GRYPHON HOUSE, INC., 3706 Otis St., Box 275, Mt. Rainier MD 20712. (301)779-6200. Editor-in-Chief: Kathy Charner. Publishes trade paperback originals of how-to and creative educational activities for teachers to do with preschool children ages 1-5.

‡**HARTWICK ELECTRONIC PRESS**, #10, 820 W. Bigelow Ave., Findlay OH 45840. Publisher: Fred Moore. Publishes multi-media books on CD-ROM. Pays 50% of net book revenue. "Our software, MultiMedia Bookstore, contains graphics and sound effects, so writers are encouraged to make creative use of these features. Demo disk available for $5. Authors should submit complete ms on disk in Word Perfect format, if possible."

‡**HEAVEN BONE PRESS**, P.O. Box 486, Chester NY 10918. Editor: Steve Hirsch. Publishes mass market paperback originals of literary fiction and poetry. Reports in 10 months.

HELIX PRESS, 4410 Hickey, Corpus Christi TX 78413. (512)852-8834. Editor: Aubrey R. McKinney. Estab. 1984. Publishes hardcover originals on science for adults.

‡**HELLS CANYON PUBLISHING**, P.O. Box 646, Halfway OR 97834. Book Division Manager: David Light. Publishes hardcover and trade paperback originals. Reports in 1 months on proposals. "We look for cutting edge issues."

HEMINGWAY WESTERN STUDIES SERIES, Boise State University, 1910 University Dr., Boise ID 83725. (208)385-1999. Editor: Tom Trusky. Publishes multiple edition artist's books which deal with Rocky Mountain political, social and environmental issues. Write for author's guidelines and catalog.

‡**HERBAL STUDIES LIBRARY**, 219 Carl St., San Francisco CA 94117. (415)564-6785. Owner: J. Rose. Publishes trade paperback originals and reprints. Averages 3 titles/year. How-to, reference and self-help. Subjects include gardening, health/medicine, herbs and aromatherapy. Query. Recent title: *Herbs for Reproductive System*, by Jeanne Rose (herbs/health).

‡**W.D. HOARD & SONS CO.**, Imprint of Hoard's Dairyman, 28 Milwaukee Ave. W., Fort Atkinson WI 53538-0801. Editor: Elvira Kan. Estab. 1870. "We primarily are a dairy publishing company, but we have had success with a veterinarian who authored two James Herriott-type humor books for us, and we would consider regional (Wisconsin) titles as well. We also have published and would like to see submissions for agricultural science texts."

‡**HORSESHOE PRESS**, 5326 Richlands Hwy., Jacksonville NC 28540. (910)324-1280. Editor: Timothy Taylor. Publishes hardcover originals. "We publish serious, well-researched historical fiction, set *before* 1900." Query.

Recent titles: *Elaine the Fair*, by Timothy Taylor; *Theodora and Her Sisters*, by Ian Dennis.

IN PRINT PUBLISHING, Suite F-2, 65 Verde Valley School Rd., Sedona AZ 86351-9033. (602)284-1370. Fax: (602)284-0534. Publisher/Editor: Tomi Keitlen. Estab. 1991. "We are interested in books that will give people hope: biographies of those that have overcome physical and mental disadvantages. No violence or sex or poetry. Particularly interested in metaphysical how-to books."

INDIANA HISTORICAL SOCIETY, 315 W. Ohio St., Indianapolis IN 46202-3299. (317)232-1882. Director of Publications: Thomas A. Mason. Estab. 1830. "We seek book-length manuscripts that are solidly researched and engagingly written on topics related to the history of Indiana." Reports in 6 months.

INTERTEXT, 2633 East 17th Ave., Anchorage AK 99508-3207. Editor: Sharon Ann Jaeger. Estab. 1982. Publishes poetry. Not currently accepting unsolicited ms.

INVERTED-A, INC., 401 Forrest Hill, Grand Prairie TX 75052. (214)264-0066. Editors: Amnon Katz. Estab. 1977. Publishes nonfiction books on a range of subjects, novellas, short story collections and poetry.

‡**IVY LEAGUE PRESS, INC.**, P.O. Box 3326, San Ramon CA 94583-8326. (510)736-0601. Fax: (510)736-0602. Editor: Maria Thomas. Publishes hardcover, trade paperback and mass market paperback originals. Subjects include health/medicine, Judaica and self-help nonfiction and medical suspense fiction. Recent nonfiction title: *Jewish Divorce Ethics*, by Bulka. Recent Fiction Title: *Allergy Shots*, by Litman.

‡**JACKSON, HART & LESLIE, INC.**, Subsidiary of Mid-List Press, 4324 12th Ave. S., Minneapolis MN 55407. (612)822-3733. Senior Editor: Lane Stiles. Publishes hardcover originals and reprints and trade paperback originals. "We only consider novels by unpublished novelists through our First Novel Series Award contest."

ALICE JAMES BOOKS, Imprint of Alice James Poetry Cooperative, 33 Richdale Ave., Cambridge MA 02140. (617)354-1408. Program Administrator: Jean Amaral. Estab. 1973. Books of poetry.

‡**THOMAS JEFFERSON UNIVERSITY PRESS**, NMSU MC111L, Kirksville MO 63501. (816)785-4665. Director: Robert V. Schnucker. Publishes 4-6 hardcover originals/year. Biography, illustrated book, textbook and monographs on Americana, anthropology/archaeology, art/architecture, government/politics, history, language/literature, military/war, philosophy, religion, sociology and translation. Recent title: *History Xn Charity*, by Hanawalt and Lindberg (Xn history).

‡**JELMAR PUBLISHING CO., INC.**, P.O. Box 488, Plainview NY 11803. (516)822-6861. President: Joel J. Shulman. Publishes hardcover originals on how-to and technical subjects. "The writer must be a specialist and recognized expert in the field."

‡**JUDAICA PRESS**, 123 Ditmas Ave., Brooklyn NY 11218. Senior Editor: Bonnie Goldman. Publishes hardcover and trade paperback originals. "We're looking for very traditional Judaica—especially children's books." Recent title: *The Torah for Children*.

LAHONTAN IMAGES, P.O. Box 1093, Susanville CA 96130-1093. (916)257-6747. Owner: Tim I. Purdy. Estab. 1986. Publishes nonfiction books pertaining to northeastern California and western Nevada.

LAWCO LTD., P.O. Box 2009, Manteca CA 95336-1209. (209)239-6006. Imprints are Money Tree and Que House. Senior Editor: Bill Thompson. Publishes nonfiction books on billiards industry. "We are also looking for books suitable for the gift market and books targeted to small businesses."

LEE & LOW BOOKS, 14th Floor, 228 E. 45th St., New York NY 10017. (212)867-6155. Publisher: Philip Lee. Editor-in-Chief: Elizabeth Szabla. Estab. 1991. "We focus on multicultural children's books. Of special interest picture book are stories set in contemporary America. We are interested in fiction as well as nonfiction." Titles recently released in 1993 include *Abuela's Weave* by Omar S. Castaneda; *Baseball Saved Us* by Ken Mochizuki; *Joshua's Masai Mask* by Dakari Hru.

‡**LIFE SURVIVAL DIGEST, INC.**, Imprint of American Surveys, Publishers, Plaza 71 W., Box 90459, Austin TX 78709. Fax: (512)288-4646. Vice President/Publishing: Stuart Ameson. Publishes 2 trade paperback originals/year on natural health.

LINCOLN SPRINGS PRESS, P.O. Box 269, Franklin Lakes NJ 07417. Contact: M. Gabrielle. Estab. 1987. Nonfiction subjects include Americana, ethnic, government/politics, history, language/literature, military/war, sociology, women's issues/studies. Fiction: ethnic, feminist, gothic, historical, literary, mainstream/contemporary, mystery, romance, short story collections.

LINTEL, P.O. Box 8609, Roanoke VA 24014-8609. (703)983-2265.. Editorial Director: Walter James Miller. Estab. 1978. Publishes experimental fiction, art poetry and selected nonfiction.

LORIEN HOUSE, P.O. Box 1112, Black Mountain NC 28711-1112. (704)669-6211. Owner/Editor: David A. Wilson. Estab. 1969. Publishes nonfiction: how-to and technical. Subjects include Americana, history, nature/environment, philosophy, science. "I need only a few manuscripts at any time and therefore am very selective." Will begin looking at mss again in 1996.

MADWOMAN PRESS, P.O. Box 690, Northboro MA 01532-0690. (508)393-3447. Editor and Publisher: Diane Benison. Estab. 1991. Publishes lesbian fiction and nonfiction. Query for further information.

MARABOU PUBLISHING, P.O. Box 1682, New York NY 10013-1682. Also 31-69 35st Astoria, NY, 11106. (718)274-6315. Sports nonfiction. "We are looking for nonfiction sports books which are geared for the historically aware. Those stories that deal with little-written about subjects will receive the most attention. Query only."

‡MARKGRAF PUBLICATIONS GROUP, The Robots Inc., P.O. Box 936, Menlo Park CA 94025. Fax: (415)940-1299. Publisher: James Hall. Estab. 1987. Publishes nonfiction books on history, government and international affairs and seriously-researched historical fiction.

‡MASEFIELD BOOKS, Suite B-54, 7210 Jordan Ave., Canoga Park CA 91303. Fax: (818)703-6087. Publisher: M. Bloomfield. Estab. 1991. Publishes nonfiction: education, government/politics, history, psychology and sociology. A modest subsidy program is available for those books with extremely limited markets.

MAUPIN HOUSE PUBLISHING, P.O. Box 90148, Gainesville FL 32607-0148. (904)373-5588. Co-Publisher: Julia Graddy. Fax: 1-800-524-0634. Publishes nonfiction books on horticulture, education, regional (Florida). "We are focusing on teacher resource books. Only classroom teachers are considered as authors."

MERRY MEN PRESS, 274 Roanoke Rd., El Cajon CA 92020-4023. Contact: Robin Hood. Estab. 1984. Publishes science fiction/fantasy, erotica in a book anthology. Reads year round. **Pays upon acceptance.** No novels looked at. Please send for guidelines.

MEYERBOOKS, PUBLISHER, P.O. Box 427, Glenwood IL 60425-0427. (708)757-4950. Publisher: David Meyer. Estab. 1976. Imprint is David Meyer Magic Books. History, reference and self-help works published on subjects of Americana, cooking and foods, health and nature. Reports in 3 months.

‡MIDDLE PASSAGE PRESS, 5517 Secrest Dr., Los Angeles CA 90043. (213)298-0266. Publisher: Barbara Bramwell. Estab. 1992. Publishes trade paperback originals."The emphasis is on contemporary issues that deal directly with the African-American Experience. No fiction."

MID-LIST PRESS, Subsidiary of Jackson, Hart & Leslie, 4324 12th Ave S., Minneapolis MN 55407-3218. Acquisitions Editor: Maria Ahrens. Estab. 1989. Mid-List Press is an independent press. In addition to publishing the annual winners of the First Novel and First Book of Poetry Series Awards, Mid-List Press publishes general interest fiction and nonfiction by first-time and established writers. Send SASE for First Series guidelines and/or general submission guidelines.

‡MORTAL PRESS, 2315 N. Alpine Rd., Rockford IL 61107-1422. (815)399-8432. Editor/Publisher: Terry James Mohaupt. Publishes hardcover originals. Publishes 1 title/year. "We will consider only works related to the fine arts, specifically literary and graphic arts, poetry or words and pictures."

MOSAIC PRESS MINIATURE BOOKS, 358 Oliver Rd., Cincinnati OH 45215-2615. (513)761-5977. Publisher: Miriam Irwin. Estab. 1977. "Publishes one nonfiction book per year. Subjects range widely. Please query."

‡MOUNT IDA PRESS, 4 Central Ave., Albany NY 12210. (518)426-5935. Publisher: Diana S. Waite. Publishes trade paperback original illustrated books on architecture.

MOUNTAIN AUTOMATION CORPORATION, P.O. Box 6020, Woodland Park CO 80866-6020. (719)687-6647. President: Claude Wiatrowski. Estab. 1976. Publishes illustrated souvenir books and videos for specific tourist attractions. "We are emphasizing videos more and books less."

MYSTIC SEAPORT MUSEUM, 75 Greenmanville Ave., Mystic CT 06355-0990. (203)572-0711. Fax: (203)572-5328. Imprint is American Maritime Library. Publications Director: Joseph Gribbins. Estab. 1970. "We need serious, well-documented biographies, studies of economic, social, artistic, or musical elements of American maritime (not naval) history; books on traditional boat and ship types and construction (how-to). We are now interested in all North American maritime history—not, as in the past, principally New England."

NATIONAL PUBLISHING COMPANY, P.O. Box 8386, Philadelphia PA 19101-8386. (215)732-1863. Fax: (215)735-5399. Editor: Peter F. Hewitt. Estab. 1863. Publishes Bibles, New Testament and foreign language New Testaments.

NATUREGRAPH PUBLISHERS, INC., P.O. Box 1075, Happy Camp CA 96039. (916)493-5353. Fax: (916)493-5240. Editor: Barbara Brown. Estab. 1946. Primarily publishes nonfiction for the layman in 6 general areas: natural history (biology, geology, ecology, astronomy); American Indian (historical and contemporary); outdoor living (backpacking, wild edibles, etc.); land and gardening (modern homesteading); crafts and how-to; holistic health (natural foods and healing arts).

NEWSAGE PRESS, Suite 150, 825 NE 20th Ave., Portland OR 97232-2275. (503)232-6794. Fax: (503)232-6891. Editorial Assistant: Betty Brickson. Estab. 1985. Publishes hardcover and trade paperback originals.

NIGHTSHADE PRESS, P.O. Box 76, Troy ME 04987-0076. (207)948-3427. Co-Editors: Carolyn Page. Estab. 1988. Publishes *Potato Eyes*, a semiannual literary magazine and 10 poetry collections/year. "We also publish one novel per year and some years we publish a short story collection." Query first for info. Reports in 2 months.
   • Poetry manuscript selection is based on the Nightshade Annual Chapbook Award Competition.

‡**NUCLEUS PUBLICATIONS**, Rt. 2, Box 49, Willow Springs MO 65793. Editor: V. McClure. Publishes trade paperback originals. "We are looking for good vegetarian cookbooks which focus on a certain topic or cuisine."

OHIO BIOLOGICAL SURVEY, Subsidiary of The Ohio State University College of Biosciences, Museum of Biological Diversity, 1315 Kinnear Rd., Columbus OH 43212-1192. (614)292-9645. Fax: (614)292-7774. Editor: Veda M. Cafazzo. Estab. 1912. "Topics limited to information about Ohio's biota."

C. OLSON & CO., P.O. Box 5100, Santa Cruz CA 95063-5100. (408)458-3365. Owner: C. Olson. Estab. 1981. "We are looking for nonfiction manuscripts or books that can be sold at natural food stores and small independent bookstores on health and on how to live a life which improves the earth's environment." Query first only, and please enclose SASE.

OMEGA PUBLICATIONS, RD 1 Box 1030E, New Lebanon NY 12125-9801.(518)794-8181. Fax: (518)794-8187. Contact: Abi'l-Khayr. Estab. 1977. "We are interested in any material related to sufism, and only that."

OPTIMUS PUBLISHING, Suite 318, 13931 N. Central Expwy., Dallas TX 75243. (214)294-2101. Managing Editor: Bill McMurray. Estab. 1990. "We are soliciting for our 'exclusive report' product line which features leisure time activities, self-help and fitness topics. All reports are of a 'how-to' nature and are 10,000-12,000 words in length. Please query first." Send #10 SASE for contributor's guidelines or $3 for guidelines and sample report.

OUR CHILD PRESS, 800 Maple Glen Lane, Wayne PA 19087-4797. (610)964-0606. Editor: Carol Hallenbeck. Estab. 1984. "We publish only adoption-related materials. Query first." Recent titles: *Don't Call Me Marda* and *Supporting An Adoption*.

‡**PACE UNIVERSITY PRESS**, One Pace Plaza, New York NY 10038. (212)346-1405. Contact: Mark Hussey. Publishes hardcover originals. "We publish scholarly work in the humanities, business, and social science fields." Recent title: *Virginia Woolf: Emerging Perspectives*, edited by Mark Hussey and Vara Neverow (conference proceeding).

‡**PACIFIC LEARNING COUNCIL**, Suite 300, 251 Post St., San Francisco CA 94108. (415)391-4135. Contact: Richard Nodine. Publishes mass market paperback originals. Publishes how-to, self-help, technical books "designed to provide important lifeskills."

‡**PANTEX INTERNATIONAL LTD.**, P.O. Box 17322, Irvine CA 92713. (714)832-3312. Fax: (714)832-5010. Manager: Jess E. Dines. Estab. 1990. Publishes nonfiction books on handwriting analysis.

PAPIER-MACHE PRESS, #14, 135 Aviation Way, Watsonville CA 95076. (408)763-1420. Fax: (408)763-1422. Submissions Editor: Shirley Coe. Estab. 1984. Publishes mostly fiction and poetry about women's issues. Query first.

‡**PARADISE PUBLICATIONS**, 8110 SW Wareham, Portland OR 97223. (503)246-1555. President: Christie Stilson. Publishes specific location travel guides.

PARTNERS IN PUBLISHING, P.O. Box 50374, Tulsa OK 74150-0374. (918)584-5906. Fax: (918)835-8258. Editor: P.M. Fielding. Estab. 1976. Publishes biography, how-to, reference, self-help, technical and textbooks on learning disabilities, special education for youth and young adults.

PAX PUBLISHING, P.O. Box 22564, San Francisco CA 94122-2564. (415)759-5658. Senior Editor: Robert Black. Publishes nonfiction books; areas include how-to, humor, self-help, business, computers, cooking, education, health/medicine, money/finance, philosophy and psychology. Submit table of contents and sample chapter. No complete mss without prior authorization.

‡**PEEL PRODUCTIONS**, P.O. Box 185-M, Molalla OR 97038-0185. (503)829-6849. Managing Editor: S. Du-Bosque. Estab. 1985. Publishes how-to, picture books, juvenile books and children's plays. Looking for how-to-draw books for ages 3-8. Query first with outline/synopsis, sample chapters and SASE.

‡**PERFECTION LEARNING CORP.**, 10520 New York Ave., Des Moines IA 50322-3775. (515)278-0133. Senior Editor: Marsha James. Estab. 1926. Imprint is Magic Key. Publishes supplemental educational material grades K-12.

‡**PERMEABLE PRESS**, #4, 47 Noe St., San Francisco CA 94114-1017. (415)255-9765. Publisher: Brian Clark. Publishes trade paperback originals. "Permeable publishes 'high risk' fiction that other publishers cannot stomach, but which is too good to go unpublished."

‡**POLLARD PRESS**, P.O. Box 19864, Jacksonville FL 32216. Owner: M.L. Lum. Publishes trade paperback and mass market paperback originals on cooking, foods and nutrition, education, hobbies, recreation and humor.

POPULAR MEDICINE PRESS, P.O. Box 1212, San Carlos CA 94070-1212. (415)594-1855. Fax: (415)594-1855. Vice President: John Bliss. Estab. 1986. Publishes books on nutrition, health and medicine. "We're less active this year and expect minimal activity in 1994-1995."

POTENTIAL DEVELOPMENT, (formerly Potentials Development for Health & Aging Services), Suite 101, 40 Hazelwood Dr., Amherst NY 14228-2223. (716)691-6601. Fax: (716)691-6620. President: C.B. Seide. Estab. 1978. Publishes paperback originals. Averages 1 title/year. Average print order for a first book is 500. Pays at least 5% royalty on sales of first 3,000 copies; 8% thereafter. "Royalty schedule presently being reviewed." Book catalog and ms guidelines for 9×12 SASE.
   ● This company has changed ownership and is looking to broaden their market and increase their royalty percentage.

‡**PRAIRIE OAK PRESS**, 2577 University Ave., Madison WI 53705. (608)238-1685. Fax: (608)238-0500. Vice President: Kristen Visser. Estab. 1991. Imprint is Prairie Classics. Publishes nonfiction biography, history and travel books about the Upper Great Lakes region, especially Wisconsin, Michigan, Illinois, Minnesota.

PROBE BOOKS, Subsidiary of Probe Ministries International, #100, 1900 Firman Dr., Richardson TX 75081-6796. (214)480-0240. Fax: (214)644-9664. Director of Publications: Rick Rood. Estab. 1973. Publishes academic, political, world view, and cultural issues from a Christian perspective. No novels, poetry, devotional prophecy, books. No unsolicited materials please. Please query by letter or phone. Reports in 6 months if return postage is supplied.

PUBLISHERS SYNDICATION INTERNATIONAL, Suite 856, 1377 K Street NW, Washington DC 20005-3033. President/Editor: A.P. Samuels. Estab. 1971. Publishes books on military history.

PUCKERBRUSH PRESS, 76 Main St., Orono ME 04473-1430. (207)581-3832 or 866-4808. Publisher/Editor: Constance Hunting. Estab. 1971. Publishes trade paperback originals of literary fiction and poetry.

‡**PURPLE FINCH PRESS**, P.O. Box 758, Dewitt NY 13214. (315)445-8087. Publisher: Nancy Benson. Publishes hardcover and trade paperback originals. "I am interested in nonfiction that deals with speech and language development, parenting, and literary criticism. I am also interested in low fat, low cholesterol cookbooks and farm type recipes for cookbooks."

‡**QUAIL RIDGE PRESS**, P.O. Box 123, Brandon MS 39043. (601)825-2063. Contact: Barney McKee. Publishes hardcover and trade paperback originals on cooking and regional guides and cookbooks. Averages 3 titles/year. Submit proposal package including 1 chapter, plans for the book. Recent title: *Only in Mississippi: A guide for the adventurous traveler*, by Lorraine Redd (guide to little-known, off-beat places around the state).

REDBRICK PRESS, P.O. Box 1895, Sonoma CA 95476-1895. Phone: 707-996-2774. Publisher: Jack Erickson. Estab. 1987. "RedBrick Press currently is publishing only books on microbreweries and specialty beers. We will expand in 1995 to include food and travel related titles."

REFERENCE PUBLICATIONS, INC., P.O. Box 344, Algonac MI 48001. (810)794-5722. Fax: (810)794-7463. Estab. 1975. Publishes Africana, Americana, and botany reference books.

RHOMBUS PUBLISHING CO., P.O. Box 806, Corrales NM 87048-0806. (505)897-3700. Submissions Editor: Benjamin Radford. Estab. 1984. Publishes nonfiction books on anthropology/archaeology, government/politics, nature/environment and Southwestern topics.

ROCKBRIDGE PUBLISHING CO., P.O. Box 351, Berryville VA 22611-0351. (703)955-3980. Fax: (703)955-4126. Publisher: Katherine Tennery. Estab. 1989. "We are developing a series of travel guides to the country roads in various Virginia counties. The self-guided tours include local history, identify geographic features, etc. We are also looking for material about the Civil War, especially biographies."

‡ROSS BOOKS, P.O. Box 4340, Berkeley CA 94704. (510)841-2474. President: Franz Ross. Publishes hardcover and trade paperback originals. "Popular science and computers are best subjects."

SAND RIVER PRESS, 1319 14th St., Los Osos CA 93402. (805)528-7347. Publisher: Bruce Miller. Estab. 1987. Publishes mostly nonfiction titles on cooking, history, literature, Native Americans, regional (California) and some literary fiction.

SANDPIPER PRESS, P.O. Box 286, Brookings OR 97415-0028. (503)469-5588. Editor: Marilyn Riddle. Estab. 1979. Query.

THE SAVANT GARDE WORKSHOP, Subsidiary of The Savant Garde Institute Ltd., 6 Union St., P.O. Box 1650, Sag Harbor NY 11963-0060. (516)725-1414. Artistic Director: Artemis Smith. "We publish books of philosophy, philosophy as literature, and avant garde thought. We are only interested in Nobel-prize-level material of extreme competence and originality. We are not a commercial publisher and are affiliated to a nonprofit educational foundation."
 • This publisher is now concentrating on 6×9 short-run on-demand monographs in author-signed perfectbound multicolor laminated covers, wholesaling at $75, as rare-edition collectibles.

SCOTS PLAID PRESS, 22-B Pine Lake Dr., Whispering Pines NC 28327-9388. Editor/Publisher: MaryBelle Campbell. Perfectbound, aesthetic paperback books, archival limited editions. Publishes biography, academic and textbooks. Subjects include anthropology/archaeology, philosophy, psychology. Accepts no unsolicited mss. Query with bio, vita and cover letter with concept and purposed use for book. Send opening page and contents page only. Enclose SASE.

SEACOAST PUBLICATIONS OF NEW ENGLAND, Suite 165, 2800A Lafayette Rd., Portsmouth NH 03801. Founder: Paul Jesep. Estab. 1992. Publishes trade paperback originals. "Books for children or adult nonfiction material all with a unique New England theme. Must be based on New England history of folklore." No fiction. Query. No phone calls. Reviews artwork/photos as part of freelance ms package.
 • More emphasis is given to topics about New Hampshire—but material on the other New England states still welcome.

‡SEA-LARK PRINT PRODUCTIONS, Subsidiary of Southwest Spirit Supply, 101 King's Lane, Commerce TX 75428-3710. (903)886-2729. Editor: Lisa Allen. Publishes hardcover and trade paperback originals. Publishes 2-3 titles/year. "We will be focusing on self-esteem, self-help books for youth and adult exceptional learners."

‡SIGNPOST BOOKS, 8912 192nd SW, Edmonds WA 98026. (206)776-0370. Publisher: Cliff Cameron. Publishes trade paperback originals. "We focus on self-propelled outdoor recreation in the Pacific Northwest (excluding hunting and fishing)."

Market conditions are constantly changing! If this is 1996 or later, buy the newest edition of Writer's Market *at your favorite bookstore or order directly from* Writer's Digest Books.

‡**SILVER MOUNTAIN PRESS**, P.O. Box 12994, Tucson AZ 85732. Editor: Jon Owens. Publishes trade paperback originals: literary and mainstream/contemporary fiction. "Our production schedule is already set for this year and next."

SILVERCAT PUBLICATIONS, Suite C, 4070 Goldfinch St., San Diego CA 92103-1865. (619)299-6774. Editor: Robert Outlaw. Estab. 1988. Publishes consumer-oriented nonfiction on topics of current interest. Responds in 2 months.
  • They have expanded their interests to include books relating to quality-of-life issues.

‡**16TH CENTURY JOURNAL PUBLISHERS**, NMSU MC111L, Kirksville MO 63501. (816)785-4665. President: Robert V. Schnucker. Publishes hardcover and trade paperback originals. Scholarly monographs on art, history, language, religion.

‡**SPECTACLE LANE PRESS INC.**, P.O. Box 34, Georgetown CT 06829. (203)762-3786. Editor: James A. Skardon. Publishes trade paperback originals and reprints. Subsidy publishes 1-2%. Reports on queries in 2 weeks. "Books should have core element of redeeming personal value and interest and appeal to identifiable customer and market."

SPHERIC HOUSE, Subsidiary of Southwest H.E.R.M. Inc., P.O. Box 40877, Tucson AZ 85717-0877. (602)623-5577. Editors: Seth Linthicum, John Linthicum. Estab. 1985. Publishes a variety of nonfiction, children's fiction and poetry. Reports in 3 months.

‡*****SPIRIT TALK**, P.O. Box 430, Browning MT 59417. (406)338-2882. Fax: (406)338-5120. Publisher/Editor: Long Standing Bear Chief. Subsidy publishes 50% of books. Reports in 1 month on queries. "We specialize in book, audio and video material that is by or about American Indians. Ours is a quarterly publication, approaching 50,000 copies. *Spirit Talk* is published in celebration of American Indian culture for a national and international audience. Write, call or fax for writer's guidelines."

STONE BRIDGE PRESS, P.O. Box 8208, Berkeley CA 94707-8208. (510)524-8732. Fax: (510)524-8711. Publisher: Peter Goodman. Estab. 1989. Publishes books on working and communicating with the Japanese, Japanese garden and design related books, Japan related literary fiction, language learning, travel and translations.

‡**STUDIO 4 PRODUCTIONS**, P.O. Box 280400, Northridge CA 91328. (818)700-2522. Editor-in-Chief: Charlie Matthews. Publishes trade paperback originals. Reports on queries in 3 months. Subjects include child guidance/parenting, humor, music/dance, self-help.

THE SUGAR HILL PRESS, 129 Sugar Hill Est. Rd., Weare NH 03281-4315. Publisher: L. Bickford. Estab. 1990. "We publish technical manuals for users of school administrative software *only*. (These are supplemental materials, not the manuals which come in the box.) A successful writer will combine technical expertise with crystal-clear prose."

THE SYSTEMSWARE CORPORATION, 973C Russell Ave., Gaithersburg MD 20879. (301)948-4890. Fax: (301)926-4243. Editor: Pat White. Estab. 1987. "We specialize in innovative books and periodicals on Knowledge Engineering or Applied Artificial Intelligence and Knowledge Based Systems. We also develop software packages."

‡**TAMARACK BOOKS, INC.**, P.O. Box 190313, Boise ID 83719-0313. (208)387-2656. Fax (208)387-2650. President/Owner: Kathy Gaudry. Publishes trade paperback originals and reprints. Cookbooks, illustrated books and nonfiction on the West for people living in the American West or interested in the West.

TAMBRA PUBLISHING, Suite D-122, 4375 W. Desert Inn, Las Vegas NV 89102-7678. Fax: (702)876-5252. Editor: Tambra Campbell. Estab. 1985. Publishes how-to books on handwriting analysis and screenwriting/screenplays.

TECHNICAL ANALYSIS OF STOCKS & COMMODITIES, Technical Analysis, Inc., 4757 California Ave. SW, Seattle WA 98116-4499. (206)938-0570. Editor: Thom Hartle. Technical Editor: John Sweeney. Estab. 1982. Publishes business and economics books and software about using charts and computers to trade stocks, options, mutual funds or commodity futures. Reports in 3 months.

‡**THIRD SIDE PRESS, INC.**, 2250 W. Farragut, Chicago IL 60625-1802. Publisher: Midge Stocker. Publishes trade paperback originals. Publishes 3-6 titles/year. "We publish books by women for women; half fiction, half nonfiction. Our nonfiction is almost exclusively health and our fiction is primarily lesbian." Recent titles include: *Cancer as a Women's Issue*, edited by Midge Stocker (anthology); *On Lill Street*, by Lynn Kanter (first novel).

TICKET TO ADVENTURE®, INC., P.O. Box 41005, St. Petersburg FL 33743-1005. Administrative Vice President: Anne Wright. Estab. 1986. Target audience is females age 17-35, college students and career changers. Publishes specific, detailed 'how to gain employment' books such as *How to Get a Job with a Cruise Line*. Writers submitting nonfiction should avoid sketchy proposal (unclear objective) and lack of demonstration of market/buyer/audience.

TIMES CHANGE PRESS, P.O. Box 1380, Ojai CA 93024-1380. (805)646-8595. Publisher: Lamar Hoover. Estab. 1970. "Our books are small format (5½×7), and nondogmatic in their approach to such topics as ecology and earth-consciousness, personal liberation, feminism, etc. We are not publishing poetry or fiction at this time."

TRAFALGAR SQUARE PUBLISHING, P.O. Box 257, N. Pomfret VT 05053-0257. (802)457-1911. Editor: Caroline Robbins. Contact: Martha Cook. Publishes nonfiction books about horses.

TURTLE PRESS, subsidiary of S.K. Productions Inc., P.O. Box 290206, Wethersfield CT 06129-0206. (203)529-7770. Editor: Cynthia Kim. Publishes trade paperback originals and reprints. Subjects include: how-to, martial arts, philosophy, self-help, sports, women's issues/studies.

‡T'WANDA BOOKS, P.O. Box 1227, Peralta NM 87042-1227. Editor: Thelma Louise. Estab. 1992. Publishes 1 title/year. Payment arrived at by mutual agreement. Fantasy, feminist, science fiction. "Looking for experiences of women in non traditional jobs that illuminate and educate." Query. SASE. Recent title: *Wild Justice*, by Ruth M. Sprague. "Our audience is all womankind and supporters who refuse to accept the definitions and limitations imposed by ancient conquerors."

UCLA-AMERICAN INDIAN STUDIES CENTER, 3220 Campbell Hall, 405 Hilgard Ave., Los Angeles CA 90024-1548. (310)825-7315. Fax: (310)206-7060. Editor: Duane Champagne. Estab. 1969. Publishes nonfiction how-to and reference books on anthropology, education, ethnic, government/politics, history, language/literature and sociology themes. Publishes poetry on Native American themes and an academic journal.

UNIVERSITY OF CALIFORNIA LOS ANGELES CENTER FOR AFRO-AMERICAN STUDIES PUBLICATIONS, 160 Haines Hall, 405 Hilgard Ave., Los Angeles CA 90024-1545. (310)825-3528. Fax: (310)206-3421. Managing Editor: Toyomi Igus. Estab. 1979. "Seeking nonfiction book-length manuscripts that have mainstream as well as scholarly or academic appeal and that focus on the African-American experience."

VALIANT PRESS, INC., P.O. Box 330568, Miami FL 33133. (305)665-1889. President: Charity Johnson. Estab. 1991. "We are interested in nonfiction books on Florida subjects."

‡VAN PATTEN PUBLISHING, 4204 SE Ogden St., Portland OR 97206. (503)775-3815. Owner: George F. Van Patten. Publishes hardcover and trade paperback originals and reprints on gardening.

VIRGINIA STATE LIBRARY AND ARCHIVES, Division of Publications and Cultural Affairs, 11th St. at Capitol Square, Richmond VA 23219-3491. (804)786-2311. Fax: (804)391-6909. Division Director: Sandra Gioia Treadway. Estab. 1823. "The Virginia State Library and Archives seeks material on the history and culture of Virginia, from the age of exploration to 1945. Submit outline and one sample chapter. Manuscripts should be restricted to a Virginia topic, and include notes and bibliography."

VISTA PUBLICATIONS, P.O. Box 661447, Miami Springs FL 33166-1447. Fax: (502)269-1003. Owner: Helen Brose. Estab. 1988. Publishes trade and mass market paperback originals. Publishes 2 titles/year. Subjects include anthropology/archaeology, government/politics, history, language/literature, regional, travel. "We specialize in books about Guatemala and Central America in English or Spanish. We are also open to works of fiction, as long as it relates to Guatemala." Submit synopsis.

VOLCANO PRESS, INC., P.O. Box 270, Volcano CA 95689-0270. (209)296-3445. Fax: (209)296-4515. Publisher: Ruth Gottstein. "We publish women's health and social issues books, and multicultural books for children that are non-racist and non-sexist."

‡VORTEX COMMUNICATIONS, Box 1008, Topanga CA 90290. (310)455-7221. President: Cynthia Riddle. Articles on health care, exercise, fitness, nutrition, spiritual well being from a holistic perspective, child care, parenting, pregnancy; 1,000 to 2,500 words.

WASATCH PUBLISHERS, 4460 Ashford Dr., Salt Lake City UT 84124-2506. (801)278-5826. Publisher: John Veranth. Estab. 1974. Publishes books on outdoor recreation in the intermountain west.
  ● Publisher has informed us they are "not taking on so many new books." Focus is on regional topics only.

WESTERN TANAGER PRESS, 1111 Pacific Ave., Santa Cruz CA 95060. (408)425-1111. Fax: (408)425-0171. Publisher: Hal Morris. Estab. 1979. Publishes historical biography, hiking and biking guides and regional history hardcover and trade paperback originals and reprints.

‡WHITEHORSE PRESS, 154 W. Brookline St., Boston MA 02118-1901. (617)241-5241. Fax: (617)241-5247. Publisher: Dan Kennedy. Estab. 1988. "We are actively seeking nonfiction books to aid motorcyclists in topics such as motorcycle safety, restoration, repair and touring. We are broadening our editorial interests to include other aspects of motorcycling. Previous focus was only motorcycle travel."

WHOLE NOTES PRESS, Imprint of *Whole Notes Magazine*, P.O. Box 1374, Las Cruces NM 88004-1374. (505)382-7446. Editor: Nancy Peters Hastings. Estab. 1988. Publishes poetry chapbooks. Submit a sampler of 3-8 poems, along with SASE.

WINGBOW PRESS, Subsidiary of Bookpeople, 7900 Edgewater Dr., Oakland CA 94621-2004. (510)632-4700. Editor: Randy Fingland. Estab. 1971. Publishes trade paperback originals. Averages 2 titles/year. Pays 7-10% royalty on retail price. Offers average $250 advance. Reference, self-help. Subjects include psychology, health, women's issues. "We are currently looking most seriously at women's studies, health, psychology, personal development. No business/finance how-to." Query or submit outline and sample chapters.

‡WOMAN IN THE MOON, P.O. Box 2087, Cupertino CA 95015. (408)738-4623. Contact: Dr. SDiane A. Bogus. Publishes hardcover and trade paperback originals and trade paperback reprints. Reports on queries in 1 month. "We are very interested in New Age topics: angels, healing, ghosts, psychic phenomena, goddess worship, spiritual biography, etc."

WORLD LEISURE, 177 Paris St., Boston MA 02128-3058. (617)569-1966. Fax: (617)561-7654. President: Charles Leocha. Reports in 2 months. "We will be publishing annual updates to *Ski Europe* and *Skiing America*. Writers planning any ski stories should contact us for possible add-on assignments at areas not covered by our staff. We also will publish general travel titles such as Travelers' Rights, Children's travel guides, guidebooks about myths and legends and self/help books such as *Getting To Know You*, and *ABCs of Life from Women Who Learned the Hard Way*.

XENOS BOOKS, Box 52152, Riverside CA 92517. (909)370-2229. Editor: Karl Kvitko. Interested chiefly in translations of 20th century literature, original experimental fiction and unusual memoirs. No children's literature, SF, PC, religious works or popular genres—detective, horror, romance, fantasy, political/espionage. "We want highly refined, strikingly original poetry and prose."

YMAA PUBLICATION CENTER, 38 Hyde Park Ave., Jamaica Plain MA 02130. (617)524-9673. Fax: (617)524-4184. Contact: David Ripianzi. Estab. 1982. "We publish exclusively Chinese philosophy, health, meditation, massage, recovery, martial arts."

Book Producers

Book producers provide services for book publishers, ranging from hiring writers to editing and delivering finished books. Most book producers possess expertise in certain areas and will specialize in producing books related to those subjects. They provide books to publishers who don't have the time or expertise to produce the books themselves (many produced books are highly illustrated and require intensive design and color-separation work). Some work with on-staff writers, but most contract writers on a per-project basis.

Most often a book producer starts with a proposal, contacts writers, editors and illustrators, assembles the book, and sends it back to the publisher. The level of involvement and the amount of work to be done on a book by the producer is negotiated in individual cases. A book publisher may simply require the specialized skill of a particular writer or editor, or a producer could put together the entire book, depending on the terms of the agreement.

Writers have a similar working relationship with book producers. Their involvement depends on how much writing the producer has been asked to provide. Writers are typically paid by the hour, by the word, or in some manner other than on a royalty basis. Writers working for book producers usually earn flat fees. Writers may not receive credit (a byline in the book, for example) for their work, either. Most of the contracts require work for hire, and writers must realize they do not own the rights to writing published under this arrangement.

The opportunities are good, though, especially for writing-related work, such as fact checking, research and editing. Writers don't have to worry about good sales. Their pay is secured under contract. Finally, writing for a book producer is a good way to broaden experience in publishing. Every book to be produced is different, and the chance to work on a range of books in a number of capacities may be the most interesting aspect of all.

Book producers most often want to see a query detailing writing experience. They keep this information on file and occasionally even share it with other producers. When they are contracted to develop a book that requires a particular writer's experience, they contact the writer. There are well over 100 book producers, but most prefer to seek writers on their own. The book producers listed in this section have expressed interest in being contacted by writers. For a list of more producers, contact the American Book Producers Association, Suite 604, 160 Fifth Ave., New York NY 10010, or look in *Literary Market Place* (R.R. Bowker).

For a list of publishers according to their subjects of interest, see the nonfiction and fiction sections of the Book Publishers Subject Index. Information on some book publishers and producers not included in this edition of *Writer's Market* can be found in Book Publishers and Producers/Changes '94-'95.

B&B PUBLISHING, INC., P.O. Box 393, Fontana WI 53125-0393. (414)275-9474. Fax: (414)275-9530. President: William Turner. Managing Editor: Lisa Turner. Publishes supplementary educational materials for grades K-12. Publishes 5-10 titles/year. 10% of books from first-time authors, 100% from unagented writers. Pays 5-10% royalty on net receipts, or makes outright purchase of $1,000. Offers $1,000 advance. Query for electronic submissions. Reports in 1 month. Promo sheets (listing titles) available for #10 SASE. Manuscript guidelines free on request.

● This company is also listed in Small Presses.

Nonfiction: Query. Reviews artwork/photos as part of freelance mss package.

Recent Nonfiction Title: *The Awesome Almanac of Wisconsin* (trade paperback).

THE BENJAMIN COMPANY, INC., 21 Dupont Ave., White Plains NY 10605-3537. (914)997-0111. Fax: (914)997-7214. President: Ted Benjamin. Estab. 1953. Produces custom-published hardcover and paperback originals. Averages 5-10 titles/year. 90-100% of books from unagented writers. "Usually commissions author to write specific book; seldom accepts proffered manuscripts." Publishes book an average of 9-12 months after acceptance. Buys mss by outright purchase. Offers advance. Simultaneous submissions OK. Query for electronic submissions. Reports in 1 month.

Nonfiction: Business/economics, cookbooks, cooking and foods, health, hobbies, how-to, self-help, sports, consumerism. "Ours is a very specialized kind of publishing—for clients (industrial and association) to use in promotional, PR, or educational programs. If an author has an idea for a book and close connections with a company that might be interested in using that book, we will be very interested in working together with the author to 'sell' the program and the idea of a special book for that company. Once published, our books often get trade distribution through a distributing publisher, so the author generally sees the book in regular book outlets as well as in the special programs undertaken by the sponsoring company. We do not encourage submission of manuscripts. We usually commission an author to write for us. The most helpful thing an author can do is to let us know what he or she has written, or what subjects he or she feels competent to write about. We will contact the author when our needs indicate that the author might be the right person to produce a needed manuscript." Query.

Recent Nonfiction Title: *Healthy Cooking with Amway Queen Cookware.*

BOOK CREATIONS INC., Schillings Crossing Rd., Canaan NY 12029. (518)781-4171. Fax: (518)781-4170. Editorial Director: Pamela Lappies. Estab. 1973. Produces trade paperback and mass market paperback originals, primarily historical fiction. Averages 15-25 titles/year. 10% of books from first-time authors; 75% from unagented writers. Pays royalty on net receipts or makes outright purchase. Advance varies with project. Reports in up to 5 months.

Nonfiction: Self-help. Subjects include cooking, foods and nutrition, health and recreation, sports. Submit résumé, publishing history and clips.

Fiction: Historicals, frontier, contemporary action/adventure, mystery, romance. Submit proposal and 50 pages of the work in progress.

● Book Creations hopes to sell more romance in the future and is therefore more interested in seeing manuscripts from that category.

Recent Fiction Title: *Darkening of the Light,* by Paul Block.

BOOKWORKS, INC., 119 S. Miami St., West Milton OH 45383. (513)698-3619. Fax: (513)698-3651. President: Nick Engler. Estab. 1984. Averages 6 titles/year. Receives 1-10 submissions/year. Less than 10% of books from first-time authors; 100% from unagented writers. Pays 2½-5% royalty on retail price. Buys mss outright for $3,000-10,000. Advance negotiable, varies. Publishes book an average of 8-18 months after acceptance. Simultaneous submissions OK. Reports in 6 weeks on queries, 2 months on mss.

Nonfiction: How-to. Subjects include woodworking, home improvement. Nothing other than woodworking/home improvement. Query or submit outline/synopsis and sample chapters. Reviews artwork/photos as part of ms package.

Tips: "We will not consider manuscripts unless written by experienced, competent craftsmen with firsthand knowledge of the subject. We publish how-to books for do-it-yourselfers, hobbyists and craftsmen."

CRACOM CORPORATION, Suite 109, 12131 Dorsett Rd., Maryland Heights MO 63043. (314)291-3988. Publisher and Editorial Director: Barbara Norwitz. Estab. 1984. Produces hardcover and trade paperback originals. Averages 6-10 titles/year. 80% of books from first-time authors; 100% from unagented writers. Pays 10-15% royalty on wholesale price. Offers variable advance. Publishes book 5-24 months after acceptance of ms. Simultaneous submissions OK. Query for electronic submissions. Reports in 3 months. Manuscript guidelines free on request.

Nonfiction: Cookbook, children's/juvenile, self-help and medical, nursing, health science textbooks and clinical references in aging and long-term care. Subjects include cooking/foods/nutrition, education, health/medicine, child abuse/incest. Submit proposal package, including description of publication, intended market, outline and 2 sample chapters. Reviews artwork/photos as part of freelance ms package. Writers should send photocopies, transparencies or prints.

A bullet introduces comments by the editor of Writer's Market indicating special information about the listing.

Recent Nonfiction Title: *Guidelines for Pediatric Emergency Drugs and Equipment*, by Wellington, Colson, Klein, Chamberlain, Wayner, Huey (emergency medicine and clinical references).

‡**THE CREATIVE SPARK**, 129 Avenida Victoria, San Clemente CA 92672. (714)366-8774. Fax: (714)366-2421. President: Mary Francis-Demarois. Produces hardcover originals. Averages 20-30 titles/year. Makes outright purchase. Offers advance. Query for electronic submissions. Reports in 3 months.
Nonfiction: Biography, humor, illustrated book, juvenile, reference, self-help. Subjects include animals, child guidance/parenting, education, ethnic, government/politics, history, sociology, sports, women's studies. Submit résumé, publishing history and clips.
Recent Nonfiction Title: *Endangered Wildlife of the World*, by Marshall Cavendish (encyclopedia).
Fiction: Any subject. Submit résumé, publishing history and clips.

‡**DESKTOP GRAFX**, 333 Brandywine Ave., Schenectady NY 12307-1121. (518)374-5841. President: Hilary Levy. Produces hardcover, trade paperback and mass market paperback originals. Averages 1-2 titles/year. 90% of books from first-time authors; 10% from unagented writers. Pays 5-20% royalty. Query for electronic submissions. Reports in 6 weeks. Book catalog and ms guidelines for SASE.
Nonfiction: How-to, self-help, software, technical, textbook. Subjects include business and economics, computer/electronics, regional, translation. Submit proposal. Reviews artwork/photos as part of ms package.
Fiction: "I would like to expand to do some fiction." Query or submit complete ms.
Tips: "I will edit, proofread and design the book—including the cover design. Please submit your manuscript on disk. Call ahead for computer requirements, etc."

DIMENSIONS & DIRECTIONS, LTD., (formerly Helena Frost Associates), Maple Rd. RR #9, Brewster NY 10509 or 301 E. 21st St., New York NY 10010. (914)279-7413. Fax: (212)353-2984. President: Helena Frost. Estab. 1970. Packages approximately 20 titles/year. Receives approximately 100 queries/year. Authors paid by flat or hourly fees or on freelance assignments. Query for electronic submissions. Reports in 3 weeks. Manuscript guidelines available per project.
Nonfiction: Textbook ancillaries, some general trade titles. Subjects include business and economics, education, government/politics, health/medicine, history, language/literature, psychology. Query.
Tips: "Although we are not interested in over-the-transom manuscripts, we do request writers' and editors' résumés with publication history and will review school-related proposals and outlines for submission to major publishers."

‡**J.K. ECKERT & CO.**, Suite 108-109, 3614 Webber St., Sarasota FL 34232-4413. (813)925-0468. Fax: (813)925-0272. Acquisitions Editor: Max Eckert. Produces hardcover originals. Averages 12-18 titles/year. 50% of books from first-time authors; 90% from unagented writers. Pays 10-50% royalty on net receipts. Query for electronic submissions. Reports usually in 2 weeks. Manuscript guidelines and list of titles in print free on request.
Nonfiction: Reference, software, technical, textbook. Subjects include business and economics, computer/electronics, health, history. Submit proposal. Reviews artwork/photos as part of ms package.
Recent Nonfiction Title: *Digital Signal Processing in Communication Systems*, VNR (professional).
Tips: "Our books are for professionals in electronics, health care and aviation/avionics, with most in design engineering disciplines. Within those constraints, we will look at anything with a definable market. Manuscripts are given a rigorous engineering-level review, so the author must be knowledgeable and coherent. The thrust should be 'how to' rather than purely academic."

‡**MICHAEL FRIEDMAN PUBLISHING GROUP**, 15 W. 26th St., New York NY 10010-1094. (212)685-6610. Fax: (212)685-1307. Editorial Director: Sharyn Rosart. Editorial Assistant: Hallie Enghorn. Estab. 1975. Packages hardcover originals working with all major publishers; publishes illustrated trade paperbacks and book/CD compilations. Produces 100 titles/year. Buys mss outright. Produces book an average of 1 year after acceptance; Friedman group responsible for all illustrative material included in book. Reports in 6 months.
Nonfiction: Illustrated coffee table books, cookbooks, how-to craft books. Subjects include Americana, animals, anthropology/archaeology, art/architecture, cooking, foods and nutrition, gardening, health and fitness, hobbies, music and entertainment, nature/environment, recreation, sports. Query.
Recent Nonfiction Title: *Herbs for Health and Healing*, by Kathi Keville.

THE K S GINIGER COMPANY INC., Suite 519, 250 W. 57th St., New York NY 10107-0599. (212)570-7499. President: Kenneth S. Giniger. Estab. 1964. Publishes hardcover, trade paperback and mass paperback originals. Averages 8 titles/year. Receives 250 submissions annually. 25% of books from first-time authors; 75% from unagented writers. Pays 5-15% royalty on retail price. Offers $3,500 average advance. Publishes book an average of 18 months after acceptance. Reports in 6 weeks on queries.
Nonfiction: Biography, coffee table book, illustrated book, reference, self-help. Subjects include business and economics, health, history, travel. "No religious books, cookbooks, personal histories or personal adventure." Query with SASE. All unsolicited mss returned unread (if postage is enclosed).

Recent Nonfiction Title: *My Favorite Prayers*, by Norman Vincent Peale.
Tips: "We look for a book whose subject interests us and which we think can achieve success in the market-place. Most of our books are based on ideas originating with us by authors we commission, but we have commissioned books from queries submitted to us."

‡**GLEASON GROUP, INC.,** 12 Main St., Norwalk CT 06851. (203)854-5895. Fax: (203)838-5452. President: Gerald Gleason. Publishes textbooks. Work-for-hire.
Nonfiction: Textbook. Subjects include computer/software.
Recent Nonfiction Titles: *WordPerfect 6.0 for DOS: A Professional Approach*; *Microsoft Word 2.0 For Windows: A Professional Approach*; *Computing Fundamentals* (all McGraw-Hill [Glencoe]).
Tips: "We are textbook packagers who occasionally use freelance tech writers to write portions of our texts."

‡**GRABER PRODUCTIONS INC.,** 60 W. 15th St., New York MI 10011. (212)929-0154. Fax: (212-929-9630. President: Eden Graber. Produces hardcover and trade paperback originals. Averages 2 books/year. 50% from agented writers. Pays outright purchase or varies by project. Query for electronic submissions.
Nonfiction: Juvenile, reference, self-help. Subjects include child guidance/parenting, gardening, health, science, sports, travel. Query.
Recent Nonfiction Titles: *Staying Healthy In A Risky Environment: The NYU Medical Center Family Guide*, *Fieldings Travellers' Medical Companion*.

GREEY DE PENCIER BOOKS, Suite 500, 175 John St., Toronto, Ontario M5T 1A7 Canada. Editor-in-Chief: Sheba Meland. Estab. 1976. Produces hardcover and trade paperback originals. Averages 12 titles/year. Receives 100 queries and 500 mss/year. 15% of books from first-time authors; 80% from unagented writers. Pays royalty on retail price. Publishes book 18 months after acceptance of ms. Simultaneous submissions OK. Query for electronic submissions. Reports in 3 months. Catalog and ms guidelines for #10 SAE.
Nonfiction: Children's/juvenile. Subjects include animals, hobbies, nature/environment, science. "We are closely affiliated with the discovery-oriented children's magazines *Owl* and *Chickadee*, and concentrate on fresh, innovative nonfiction and picture books with nature/science themes, and quality children's craft/how-to titles." Submit outline and 3 sample chapters, or proposal package, including outline, vita. Reviews art-work/photos as part of freelance ms package. Writers should send photocopies or transparencies (not originals).
Fiction: Picture books. Submit complete ms.
Tips: "To get a feeling for our style of children's publishing, take a look at some of our recent books and at *Owl* and *Chickadee* magazines. We publish Canadian authors in the main, but will occasionally publish a work from outside Canada if it strikingly fits our list."

‡**JOKES, INC.,** JSA Publications, Inc., P.O. Box 37175, Oak Park MI 48237. (810)932-0090. Editorial Director: Gwen Foss. Produces trade paperback and mass market paperback originals. Averages 15-18 titles/year. 90% of books from first-time authors; 100% from unagented writers. Makes outright purchase of $250-1,500. Offers $50-150 advance. Reports in 2 months. Book catalog and ms guidelines for #10 SASE.
Nonfiction: Humor, joke books. "We package joke books, and are looking for clean or crude jokes in these forms: one-liners, riddle-type jokes and story jokes." Jokes: submit proposal package including how many jokes, form of jokes, whether clean or crude, and several representative samples. Anecdotes and unusual facts: submit ms. Original off-color single-panel comics: submit photocopies.
Recent Nonfiction Title: *Grosser than Gross IV*, by Julius Alvin (crude jokes).

‡**JSA PUBLICATIONS, INC.,** 29205 Greening Blvd., Farmington Hills MI 48334-2945. (810)932-0090. Direc-tor: Joseph S. Ajlouny. Editor: Gwen Foss. Imprints are Push/Pull/Press, packagers of original illustrated humor books; Compositional Arts, packagers of creative nonfiction; Scrivener Press, packagers of history and travel. Packages trade paperback and mass market paperback originals. Averages 15-18 titles/year. Re-ceives 400 queries and 100 mss/year. 95% of books from first-time authors; 100% from unagented writers. Negotiates fee and advance. Simultaneous submissions OK. Reports in 1 month. Manuscript guidelines for #10 SASE.
 • Formerly publishers, this group has shifted its focus to book packaging.
Nonfiction: Popular culture, popular reference, humor, how-to, music, Americana, history, hobbies, sports. Submit proposal package including illustration samples (photcopies) and SASE.
Recent Nonfiction Titles: *The I Hate Madonna Joke Book*, by Joey West (Pinnacle).
Tips: "Your submissions must be clever!"

‡**LOUISE B. KETZ AGENCY,** 1485 First Ave., New York NY 10021. (212)535-9259. President: Louise B. Ketz. Produces hardcover originals. Averages 1-3 titles/year. 90% of books from unagented writers. Pays flat fees and honoraria. Reports in 2 months.
Nonfiction: Biography, reference. Subjects include Americana, business and economics, history, military/war, science, sports. Submit proposal.

Recent Nonfiction Title: *Encyclopedia of the American Military*, (Scribners), 3-volume reference work.
Tips: "It is important for authors to list their credentials relevant to the book they are proposing (i.e., why they are qualified to write that nonfiction work). Also helps if author defines the market (who will buy the book) and why."

LAING COMMUNICATIONS INC., 16250 NE 80th St., Redmond WA 98052-3821. (206)869-6313. Fax: (206)869-6318. Vice President/Editorial Director: Christine Laing. Estab. 1985. Imprint is Laing Research Services (industry monographs). Produces hardcover and trade paperback originals. Averages 6-10 titles/ year. 20% of books from first-time authors; 100% from unagented writers. Payment "varies dramatically since all work is sold to publishers as royalty-inclusive package." Reports in 1 month. *Writer's Market* recommends allowing 2 months for reply.
Nonfiction: History, biography, coffee table book, cookbook, how-to, illustrated book, juvenile, reference, software, technical, textbook. Subjects include Americana, corporate histories, business and economics, computers/electronics, history, science. Query. Reviews artwork/photos as part of freelance ms package. The company also manages book divisions for three firms, producing 8-12 titles annually in regional, technical and health care fields.
Recent Nonfiction Titles: *Till Victory is Won: Black Soldiers in the Civil War* (Lodestar Books).

LAMPPOST PRESS INC., P.O. Box 7042, New York NY 10128-1213. (212)876-9511. President: Roseann Hirsch. Estab. 1987. Produces hardcover, trade paperback and mass market paperback originals. Averages 25 titles/year. 50% of books from first-time authors; 85% from unagented writers. Pays 50% royalty or makes outright purchase.
Nonfiction: Biography, cookbook, how-to, humor, illustrated book, juvenile, self-help. Subjects include child guidance/parenting, cooking, foods and nutrition, gardening, health, money/finance, women's issues. Query or submit proposal. Reviews artwork/photos as part of freelance ms package.

‡LAYLA PRODUCTIONS, INC., 310 E. 44th St., New York NY 10017. (212)697-6285. Fax: (212)949-6267. President: Lori Stein. Produces hardcover and trade paperback originals. Averages 6 titles/year. 50% of books from first-time authors; 50% from unagented writers. Pays 1-5% royalty or makes outright purchase, depending on contract with publisher. Offers $2,000-10,000 advance. Query for electronic submissions. Does not return submissions, even those accompanied by SASE. Reports in 6 months.
Nonfiction: Coffee table book, cookbook, how-to, humor, illustrated book, juvenile. Subjects include Americana, cooking, foods and nutrition, gardening, history, photography, recreation. Query. Reviews artwork/ photos as part of ms package.
Recent Nonfiction Title: *American Garden Guides*, for Pantheon/Knopf (gardening how-to, illustrated).

LUCAS-EVANS BOOKS INC., 1123 Broadway, New York NY 10010. (212)929-2583. Fax: (212)929-7786. Contact: Barbara Lucas. Estab. 1984. Packages hardcover, trade paperback and mass market paperback originals for major publishers. Averages 12-15 titles/year. 20% of books from first-time authors. Pays 1-10% royalty, "depending on our contract agreement with publisher." Makes work-for-hire assignments. Offers $3,000 and up average advance. Reports in 2 months.
Nonfiction: "We are looking for series proposals and selected single juvenile books: preschool through high school." Submit query letter with credentials, discussing proposed subject. Submit entire picture book ms.
Fiction: Preschool through high school. Prefers picture books and middle grade fiction.

‡McCLANAHAN BOOK COMPANY INC., 23 W. 26th St., New York NY 10010. (212)725-1515. Fax: (212)725-5911. Executive Editor: Lauren Arieu. Produces 50-60 titles/year. 5% of books from first-time authors; 100% from unagented writers. Makes outright purchase. Query for electronic submissions. Reports within 3 months. Book catalog for 9×11 SASE.
Nonfiction: Juvenile. Submit proposal. Reviews artwork/photos as part of ms package.
Fiction: Juvenile, picture books. Submit complete ms, proposal, résumé, publishing history and clips.

‡MARKOWSKI INTERNATIONAL PUBLISHERS, One Oakglade Circle, Hummelstown PA 17036. (717)566-0468. Fax: (717)566-6423. Editor-in-Chief: Marjie Markowski. Produces hardcover and trade paperback originals. Averages 6 titles/year. 50% of books from first-time authors; 100% from unagented writers. Pays 10-15% royalty on wholesale price. Offers $1,500 advance. Does not return material. Reports in 2 months. Book catalog and ms guidelines for #10 SASE.
Nonfiction: How-to, self-help. Subjects include business and economics, health, hobbies, money/finance, psychology, sociology. Submit proposal with résumé, publishing history and clips.
Recent Nonfiction Title: *Rubber Powered Model Airplanes*.
Fiction: Juvenile, picture books. Submit proposal or entire ms with résumé, publishing history and clips.

MEGA-BOOKS OF NEW YORK, INC., 116 E. 19th St., New York NY 10003. (212)598-0909. Fax: (212)979-5074. President: Pat Fortunato. Produces trade paperback and mass market paperback originals and fiction and nonfiction for the educational market. Averages 95 titles/year. Works with first-time authors, established authors and unagented writers. Makes outright purchase for $3,000 and up. Offers 50% average advance. Free ms guidelines.

Fiction: Juvenile, mystery, young adult. Submit résumé, publishing history and clips.

Recent Fiction Titles: Nancy Drew and Hardy Boys series.

Tips: "Please be sure to obtain a current copy of our writers guidelines before writing. Please do not submit an unsolicited completed manuscript."

MENASHA RIDGE PRESS, INC., P.O. Box 43059, Birmingham AL 35243. (205)967-0566. Fax: (205)967-0580. Publisher: R.W. Sehlinger. Senior Acquisitions Editor: Leslie Cummins. Estab. 1982. Publishes hardcover and trade paperback originals. Averages 26 titles/year. Receives 600-800 submissions annually. 40% of books from first-time authors; 85% of books from unagented writers. Average print order for a first book is 4,000. Royalty and advances vary. Publishes book an average of 1 year after acceptance. Simultaneous submissions OK. Query for electronic submissions. Reports in 2 months. Book catalog for 9×12 SAE with 4 first-class stamps.

Nonfiction: How-to, humor, outdoor recreation, travel guides, small business. Subjects include business and economics, regional, recreation, adventure sports, travel. No fiction, biography or religious copies. Submit proposal, resume and clips. Reviews artwork/photos.

Recent Nonfiction Title: *Unofficial Guides* (10 travel guides) (Simon & Schuster).

Tips: "Audience: age 25-60, 14-18 years' education, white collar and professional, $30,000 median income, 75% male, 75% east of Mississippi River."

NEW ENGLAND PUBLISHING ASSOCIATES, INC., P.O. Box 5, Chester CT 06412. (203)345-READ. Fax: (203)345-3660. President: Elizabeth Frost Knappman. Vice President/Treasurer: Edward W. Knappman. Managing Editor: Larry Hand. Estab. 1982. Produces hardcover and trade paperback originals. 25% of books from first-time authors. Reports 2 months.

• New England Publishing is commissioning articles for anthologies and producing for publishers in the areas of language, literature and reference. They are also looking for authors for short books aimed at the community college level.

Recent Nonfiction Title: *Beyond Murder: The Inside Story of The Gainesville Student Murders* (NAL).

Tips: "We prefer a phone call first, followed by writing samples or résumés. If you specialize in any area, let us know. We'll try to help you with the right agency if we can't handle your work."

‡**OMNI BOOKS,** 324 W. Wendover Ave., Greensboro NC 27408. (910)275-9809. Fax: (910)275-9837. Editor-in-Chief: Stephen Levy. Produces trade paperback originals. Averages 6 titles/year. 20% of books from first-time authors; 100% from unagented writers. Pays royalty on net receipts. Reports in 3 months.

Nonfiction: Subjects include science. Query.

Recent Nonfiction Title: *Mathopedia: Omni Guide*.

‡**OTTENHEIMER PUBLISHERS, INC.,** 10 Church Lane, Baltimore MD 21208. (301)484-2100. Fax: (410)484-7591. Chairman of the Board: Allan T. Hirsh Jr. President: Allan T. Hirsh III. Contact: Tori Banks. Estab. 1890. Publishes hardcover and paperback originals and reprints. Publishes 250 titles/year. Receives 500 submissions annually. 20% of books from first-time authors; 85% of books from unagented writers. Average print order for a first book is 15,000. Negotiates royalty and advance, sometimes makes outright purchase. Publishes book an average of 9 months after acceptance. Reports in 2 months.

Fiction & Nonfiction: Cookbooks, reference, gardening, children's fiction and nonfiction, health, self-help for the layperson. Submit outline/synopsis and sample chapters or complete ms. Reviews artwork/photos as part of ms package.

Recent Nonfiction Title: *Birds of North America*.

Tips: "We're looking for nonfiction adult books and teen fiction for mass market—we're a packager."

‡**PUBLICOM, INC.,** 409 Massachusetts Ave., Acton MA 01720. (508)263-5773. Fax: (508)263-7553. Vice President, Educational Materials: Patricia Moore. Produces hardcover and trade paperback originals. Averages 1-3 titles/year. 50% of books from first-time authors; 50% from unagented writers. Pays 3-8% royalty on net receipts or makes variable outright purchase. Offers $3,000 advance. Query for electronic submissions. Reports in 6 months.

Nonfiction: Biography, how-to, illustrated book, juvenile, self-help, textbook. Subjects include business, child guidance/parenting, education, women's studies. Submit proposal, résumé, publishing history and clips.

Recent Nonfiction Title: *Say the Word!*, for New Readers Press (adult literacy manual).

‡**ANDREW ROCK & CO.,** P.O. Box 625, Newport RI 02840. (401)849-4442. Fax: (401)849-4442. President: Andrew Rock. Produces hardcover and trade paperback originals. Averages 5-10 titles/year. 50% of books from first-time authors. Pays 20-35% royalty on net receipts. Query for electronic submissions. Reports in 2 weeks. Manuscript guidelines free on request.

Nonfiction: General nonfiction. Subjects include business, economics, child guidance/parenting, health, history, Middle East. Query or submit proposal. Reviews artwork/photos as part of ms package.

Fiction: Literary, mainstream, mystery. Query.

SACHEM PUBLISHING ASSOCIATES, INC., P.O. Box 412, Guilford CT 06437-0412. (203)453-4328. Fax: (203)453-4320. President: Stephen P. Elliott. Estab. 1974. Produces hardcover originals. Averages 3 titles/year. 25% of books from first-time authors; 100% from unagented writers. Pays royalty or makes outright purchase. Query for electronic submissions. Reports in 1 month.
Nonfiction: Reference. Subjects include Americana, government/politics, history, military/war. Submit résumé and publishing history.

‡**THE STONESONG PRESS, INC.**, 211 East 51st St., New York NY 10022. (212)750-1090. President: Paul Fargis. Produces hardcover, trade and mass market paperback originals. Averages 15 titles/year. 1% of books from first-time authors; 30% from unagented writers. Pay varies from flat fee piece work to full royalty participation. Reports in 1 week.
Nonfiction: How-to, general nonfiction, illustrated book, reference. Subjects include business and economics, child guidance/parenting, cooking, foods and nutrition, gardening, health, history, money/finance, science. Submit résumé, publishing history and clips.
Recent Nonfiction Titles: *The New York Public Library Desk Reference* (Simon and Schuster); *The Family Circle Good Cooks' Book* (Simon and Schuster); *Life's Little Destruction Book* (St. Martins).
Tips: "Queries to our firm should be simple letters outlining the writer's credentials and areas of interest. *Do not send ideas or manuscripts*. A good producer will always provide and help develop the idea."

TENTH AVENUE EDITIONS, Suite 903, 625 Broadway, New York NY 10012. (212)529-8900. Fax: (212)529-7399. Managing Editor: Clive Giboire. Submissions Editor: Matthew Moore. Estab. 1984. Produces hardcover, trade paperback and mass market paperback originals. Averages 6 titles/year. Pays advance paid by publisher less our commission. Query for electronic submissions. Reports in 2 months.
Nonfiction: Biography, how-to, crafts, illustrated book, juvenile, catalogs. Subjects include music/dance, photography, women's issues/studies, art, children's. *Queries only*. Reviews artwork/photos as part of freelance ms package.
Recent Nonfiction Titles: *Earth-Friendly Crafts Series* (John Wiley & Sons).
Tips: "Send query with publishing background. Return postage a must."

‡**2M COMMUNICATIONS LTD.**, 121 W. 27th St., New York NY 10001. (212)741-1509. Fax: (212)691-4460. Editorial Director: Madeleine Morel. Produces hardcover, trade paperback and mass market paperback originals. Averages 15 titles/year. 50% of books from first-time authors; 10% from unagented writers. Pays 7-15% royalty on wholesale price. Offers $15,000 advance. Reports in 2 weeks.
Nonfiction: Biography, coffee table book, cookbook, how-to, humor, illustrated book. Subjects include child guidance/parenting, cooking, foods and nutrition, ethnic, gay/lesbian, health, psychology, women's studies. Query or submit proposal with résumé and publishing history.
Recent Nonfiction Title: *Jumping the Broom* (Holt).

DANIEL WEISS ASSOCIATES, INC., 33 W. 17th St., New York NY 10011. Fax: (212)633-1236. Editorial Assistant: Liz Craft. Estab. 1987. Produces hardcover and mass market paperback originals. Averages 120 titles/year. 20% of books from first-time authors; 20% from unagented writers. Pays 1-4% royalty on retail price; or makes outright purchase of $2,500 minimum "depending on author's experience." Offers $4,000 average advance. Reports in 2 months. Guidelines for #10 SASE.
Nonfiction: Juvenile. Submit proposal. Reviews artwork/photos as part of freelance ms package.
Fiction: Juvenile, young adult. Query.

THE WHEETLEY COMPANY, INC., Suite 300, 3201 Old Glenview Rd., Wilmette IL 60091-2942. (708)251-4422. Fax: (708)251-4668. Human Resources Manager: Linda Rogers. Estab. 1986. Produces hardcover originals for publishers of school, college and professional titles. Pays by the project. Query for electronic submissions. Does *not* return submissions, even those accompanied with SASE. Reports in 1 month.
Nonfiction: Technical, textbook. Subjects include animals, anthropology, art/architecture, business and economics, child guidance/parenting, computers/electronics, cooking, foods and nutrition, education, government/politics, health, history, language/literature, money/finance, music/dance, nature/environment, philosophy, psychology, recreation, regional, religion, science, sociology, sports, translation. Submit résumé and publishing history. Reviews artwork/photos as part of freelance ms package.

WIESER & WIESER, INC., 118 E. 25th St. New York NY 10010. (212)260-0860. Fax: (212)505-7186. Producer: George J. Wieser. Estab. 1976. Produces hardcover, trade paperback and mass market paperback originals.

For information on setting your freelance fees, see How Much Should I Charge?

Averages 25 titles/year. 10% of books from first-time authors; 90% from unagented writers. Makes outright purchase for $5,000 or other arrangement. Offers $5,000 average advance. Reports in 2 weeks. *Writer's Market* recommends allowing 2 months for reply.

Nonfiction: Coffee table book. Subjects include Americana, cooking, foods and nutrition, gardening, health, history, hobbies, military/war, nature/environment, photography, recreation, sports, travel. Query. Reviews artwork/photos only as part of freelance book package.

Tips: "Have an original idea and develop it completely before contacting us."

Book Publishers and Producers/Changes '94-'95

The following book publishers and producers were listed in the 1994 edition but do not have listings in this edition of *Writer's Market*. The majority did not respond to our request to update their listings or return a questionnaire for a new listing. If a reason was given for their exclusion, we have included it in parentheses after the listing name.

Actaeon Publishing Co.
Aglow Publications
American Nurses Publishing
APU Press (out of business)
Aquarian Press
ARCsoft Publishers
ASM International
Atheneum Publishers (merged with Scribners)
B. Klein Publications
Ballantine Books of Canada
Bantam Books Canada, Inc.
Barn Owl Books
Black Moss Press
Blackbirch Graphics, Inc.
Blockbuster Books (no longer publishes books)
Bottom Dog Press, Inc.
Broadman & Holman Press
Browndeer Press (removed by request)
Buddha Rose Publications
Calgre Press
California State University Press
Career Advancement Center (overstocked for 1995)
Carolina Wren Press
Carpenter Publishing House (no freelance proposals)
Carroll & Graf (no unsolicited mss)
Challenger Press
Chanticleer Press, Inc.
Charles Scribner's Sons
Chatham Press
Chicory Blue Press
Children's Press
Church Growth Institute
Clothespin Feber Press
Collector Books
CompCare Publishers (sold to Hazelden)
Concordia Publishing House
Creative With Words
Crisp Publications
Crown Publishing Group
Death Valley Natural History Association
Denlingers Publishers, Ltd.
Devin-Adir Publishers
Doral Publishing, Inc.
Dorling Kindersley, Inc.
Doubleday Canada Ltd.

Dragon's Den Publishing
Duke Press
Dunamis House
Durst Publications
Dutton Children's Books
E.J.M. Publishing
Eastern National Park & Monument Association
Education Associates
Fiesta City Publishers
Gallerie Publications
General Pubilshing Co., Ltd.
Global Press Works
Graphic Arts Technical Foundation
Graywolf Press
Greene Communications (out of business)
Gulf Publishing Co. (no freelance proposals)
Harcourt Brace Canada
Harian Creative Books
Harlequin Enterprises Ltd.
HarperCollins Publishers Ltd.
Health Administration Press
Health Communications, Inc.
Hillbrook House
Holiday House
Hollow Earth Publishing
Homestead Publishing (removed by request)
Houghton Mifflin Canada Ltd.
Human Kinetics Publishers, Inc.
Humanics Publishing Group
Humanities Press International, Inc.
Illuminations Press
Independence Publisher, Inc. (out of business)
Info Net Publishing
Initiatives Publishing Co.
Intercultural Press, Inc.
Intervarsity Press
Ithaca Press
Jamenair Ltd.
Jesperson Press Ltd.
Larson Publications/PBPF
Laughing Bear Press (no books)
Leadership Publishers, Inc.
Lexikos
Liberty Bell Press
Lion Publishing

Lollipop Power Books
Longmeadow Press (removed by request)
M & H Publishing Co., Inc.
Madison House Publishers, Inc, (removed by request)
Masefield Books
McGraw-Hill Ryerson Ltd.
Metal Powder Industries Foundation
Microtrend Books
N.A.L. Dutton (name change to Dutton)
NAR Publications
Nature's Design
NavPress (currently not accepting unsolicited mss)
Nelson-Hall Publishers
New Directions Publishing Corporation
New Horizons Press (out of business)
New York Niche Press
Newcastle Publishing Co. Inc.
Nightwood Editions
NordicPress (out of business)
Oddo Publishing (asked to be removed 1 year)
Oise Press
Oolichan Books
Osborne/McGraw-Hill
Pantheon Books
Parachute Press, Inc.
Parkside Publishing Corp.
Pax Publishing
Pendragon Press
Perivale Press
Phanes Press (does not accept unsolicited queries)
Pickwick Publications
Poseidon Press
Praeger Publishers
Prentice-Hall Canada, Inc., College Div.
Prentice-Hall Canada, Inc., School Div.
Press Gang Publishers
Primer Publishers
Proclaim Publishing (full subsidy)
Push/Pull/Press
Q.E.D. Publishing Group
Quarry Press
Quebec-Amerique (no English

language mss)
Quill
R&E Publishers
Red Apple Publishing (full subsidy)
Religious Education Press
Resolution Business Press
Resource Publications, Inc.
Retail Reporting Corp.
Review and Herald Publishing Association
Routledge, Inc.
Rubicon Publishing Inc.
Russell Sage Foundation (removed by request)
S.P.I. Books
Seymour Lawrence (folded)
Shorewood Books, Inc. (out of business)
Skippingstone Press, Inc.
Slawson Communications, Inc.
Sound View Press
South Wind Publishing
Space and Time (temporarily suspended)

ST Publications (removed by request)
St. Clair Press
St. John's Publishing, Inc.
Stemmer House Publishers, Inc.
Stone Wall Press, Inc. (overstocked)
Stormline Press
Student College and Publishing Division
Systems Co. (charges for review and marketing advice)
T.F.H. Books
T.F.H. Publications, Inc.
The Borgo Press
The Center for Learning
The Cottage Press (overwhelmed by submissions)
The Free Press
The Prairie Publishing Co.
The Press at California State Univ., Fresno'
The Riverdale Co., Publishers (no new titles)

The University of Calgary Press
University of Maine Press
Theatre Arts Books
Theytus Books Ltd.
Thomas Organization (full subsidy)
Thorsons
Ticknor & Fields (folded)
Transaction Books
Ulysses Travel Publications
University of Michigan Press (no outside proposals)
University of Toronto Press
University Press of America, Inc.
Viking Penguin
Waterfront Books
Western Publishing
Westernlore Press
White Cliffs Media Co.
Woodland Health Books
Woodsong Graphics (no freelance proposals)
Worldwide Library
Yankee Books (no trade books)

Consumer Magazines 280

Consumer Magazines

In the past year, a record number of consumer magazines were launched. Magazines folded, too, of course, but overall the consumer magazine industry continues to be a healthy market for the freelance writer. The start-up of hundreds of new magazines can be little else but good news for writers. But with those new magazines come ever-higher expectations from the editors responsible for filling their pages. Today's consumer magazines are tightly focused marketing vehicles aimed at very specific segments of the reading public.

When periodicals succeed in finding readers, they attract advertisers hoping to reach those same readers—those *consumers*. As long as enough advertisers find a particular magazine useful in reaching their customers, that magazine will thrive. If the magazine fails in its editorial mission—if its content does not match the interests of its intended audience—it will lose readers and advertisers and it will fold.

Consumer magazines and the freelance writer

The most important recommendation we can make to writers trying to crack the consumer magazine market, besides, of course, perfecting the craft of writing, is to work hard at understanding your target magazine's audience and angle. One of the complaints we hear most frequently from editors is that freelance writers very often send inappropriate material, i.e., material that—while it may be entertaining, well-written and timely—is simply not of interest to that magazine's readers.

You can gather clues about a magazine's readership in a number of ways:
- Start with a careful reading of the magazine's listing in this section of *Writer's Market*. Most listings offer very straightforward information about their magazine's slant and audience.
- Send for a magazine's writer's guidelines, if available. These are written by each particular magazine's editors and are usually quite specific about their needs and their readership.
- If possible, talk to an editor by phone. Many will not take phone queries, particularly those working at the higher-profile magazines. But many editors of smaller publications will spend the time to help a writer over the phone.
- Perhaps most important, read several current issues of the target magazine. Only in this way will you see firsthand the kind of stories the magazine actually buys.

Writers who can correctly and consistently discern a publication's audience and deliver stories that speak to that target readership will win out every time over writers who simply write what they write and send it where they will.

What editors want

In nonfiction, editors continue to look for short feature articles covering specialized topics. They want crisp writing and expertise. If you are not an expert in the area about which you are writing, make yourself one through research.

Always query by mail before sending your manuscript package, but keep in mind that once a piece has been accepted, many publishers now prefer to receive your submission via disk or modem so they can avoid re-keying the manuscript.

Fiction editors prefer to receive complete short story manuscripts. Writers must

INSIDER REPORT

USA Weekend seeks freshness, timeliness in stories of national interest

"The magazine is aimed at helping people deal with the changing society around them and the issues that they have to face — and it's to help them make decisions in their lives," says *USA Weekend* Managing Editor, Amy Eisman. That editorial focus means the articles that appear in this Sunday magazine running in over 400 newspapers across the country must be up-to-date, of interest to the magazine's diverse readership, and pitched with a unique, fresh angle.

Amy Eisman

"The best pieces are those that are pegged to current events of national interest," says Eisman. "The stories must look ahead and not behind, so the letters of submission should do the same. If somebody writes us a letter about a story that could have been written two years ago, we're not likely to accept that idea. Writers should be aware of the magazine's timeliness and freshness, and their letters should reflect that." Besides offering a unique look at a timely topic, what else distinguishes an effective pitch letter? "The most successful ones are those that reflect the magazine. They are clear; they get to the point right away."

For writers hoping to target specific subjects for *USA Weekend*, Eisman offers this advice: "Health stories generally cover fitness, nutrition, psychology, behavior, and health trends — not diseases. Entertainment stories are profiles and trend pieces and are often Q&As. Travel stories are service pieces and must be of national interest. Sports stories are profiles of pro athletes and trend stories and include recreational sports." The magazine will occasionally use first-person, family-related material (under its "Family" header, for instance — usually on topics of importance to baby boomers and baby busters who are coping with some kind of nineties dilemma).

To give the editor some idea of the kind of work they do, writers should include two or three clips along with their finely-tuned pitch letter.

keep in mind that marketing fiction is competitive and editors receive far more material than they can publish. For this reason, they often do not respond to submissions unless they are interested in using the story. Before submitting material, check the market's listing for fiction requirements to ensure your story is appropriate for that market. More comprehensive information on fiction markets can be found in *Novel & Short Story Writer's Market* (Writer's Digest Books).

Regardless of the type of writing you do, keep current on trends and changes in the industry. Trade magazines such as *Folio* and *Writer's Digest* will keep you abreast of start-ups and shut downs and other writing business trends.

Payment

Writers make their living by developing a good eye for detail. When it comes to marketing material, the one detail of interest to almost every writer is the question of payment. Most magazines listed here have indicated pay rates; some give very specific payment-per-word rates while others state a range. Any agreement you come to with a magazine, whether verbal or written, should specify the payment you are to receive and when you are to receive it. Some magazines pay writers only after the piece in question has been published. Others pay as soon as they have accepted a piece and are sure they are going to use it.

In *Writer's Market*, those magazines that pay on acceptance have been highlighted with the phrase — **"pays on acceptance"** — set in bold type. Payment from these markets should reach you faster than from those who pay "on publication." There is, however, some variance in the industry as to what constitutes payment "on acceptance" — some writers have told us of two- and three-month waits for checks from markets that supposedly pay "on acceptance." It is never out of line to ask an editor when you might expect to receive payment for an accepted article.

So what is a good pay rate? There are no standards; the principle of supply and demand operates at full throttle in the business of writing and publishing. As long as there are more writers than there are opportunities for publication, wages for freelancers will never skyrocket. Rates vary widely from one market to the next, however, and the news is not entirely bleak. One magazine industry source puts the average pay rate for consumer magazine feature writing at $1.25 a word, with "stories that require extensive reporting . . . more likely to be priced at $2.50 a word." In our opinion, those estimates are on the high side of current pay standards. Smaller circulation magazines and some departments of the larger magazines will pay a lower rate. As your reputation grows (along with your clip file), you may be able to command higher rates.

For more information on magazine industry trends, see Current Trends in Publishing, on page 22.

Information on some publications not included in *Writer's Market* may be found in Consumer Magazines/Changes '94-'95, located at the end of this section.

Animal

The publications in this section deal with pets, racing and show horses, and other pleasure animals and wildlife. Magazines about animals bred and raised for the market are classified in the Farm category of Trade, Technical and Professional Journals. Publications about horse racing can be found in the Sports section.

‡ADC, Animal Damage Control, Beaver Pond Publishing, P.O. Box 224, Greenville PA 16125. (412)588-3492. Editor: Rich Faler. 80% freelance written. Bimonthly magazine covering resolution of human/animal conflicts. "We want human, cost-effective how-to information written for the full- or part-time professional."

Estab. 1993. Circ. 2,000. Pays on publication. Publishes ms an average of 6 months after acceptance. Byline given. Buys first rights, one-time rights or second serial (reprint) rights. Editorial lead time 4 months. Submit seasonal material 4 months in advance. Accepts simultaneous and previously published submissions. Reports in 6 weeks on queries; 2 months on mss. Sample copy for $3. Writer's guidelines free on request.

Nonfiction How-to, interview/profile, new product, personal experience, photo feature, technical. Buys 40 mss/year. Query. Length: 500-2,500 words. Pays $30 minimum.

Photos: Send photos with submission. Reviews contact sheets, negatives, transparencies and prints. Offers no additional payment for photos accepted with ms. Captions required. Buys one-time rights.

Fillers: Anecdotes, facts, newsbreaks, short humor. Buys 20/year. Length 50-500 words. Pays $5-30.

Tips: "Select as narrow a topic as possible in the ADC field, then give a lot of meat on that one specific."

AMERICAN FARRIERS JOURNAL, P.O. Box 624, Brookfield WI 53008-0624. (414)782-4480. Fax: (414)782-1252. Editor: Frank Lessiter. Magazine published 7 times/year covering horseshoeing and horse health, related to legs and feet of horses for a professional audience of full-time and part-time horseshoers, veterinarians and horseowners. Estab. 1975. Circ. 6,000. Pays on publication. Byline given. Buys all rights. Submit material 3 months in advance. Writer's guidelines for #10 SASE.

Nonfiction: Book excerpts, general interest, historical/nostalgic, how-to, interview/profile, new product, personal experience, photo feature, technical. Buys 50 mss/year. Send complete ms. Length: 800-3,000 words. Pays 50¢/published line.

Photos: Send photos with ms. Reviews b&w contact sheets, b&w negatives, 35mm color transparencies and 8×10 b&w or color prints. Pays $15/published photo. Captions and identification of subjects required. Buys one-time rights.

ANIMALS, Massachusetts Society for the Prevention of Cruelty to Animals, 350 S. Huntington Ave., Boston MA 02130. (617)522-7400. Fax: (617)522-4885. Editor: Joni Praded. Managing Editor: Paula Abend. 90% freelance written. Bimonthly magazine publishing "articles on wildlife (American and international), domestic animals, balanced treatments of controversies involving animals, conservation, animal welfare issues, pet health and pet care." Estab. 1868. Circ. 100,000. **Pays on acceptance.** Publishes ms an average of 5 months after acceptance. Byline given. Offers negotiable kill fee. Buys one-time rights or makes work-for-hire assignments. Submit seasonal/holiday material 6 months in advance. Reports in 6 weeks. Sample copy for $2.95 and 9×12 SAE with 4 first-class stamps. Writer's guidelines for #10 SASE.

Nonfiction: Exposé, general interest, how-to, opinion and photo feature on animal and environmental issues and controversies, plus practical pet-care topics. "*Animals* does not publish breed-specific domestic pet articles or 'favorite pet' stories. Poetry and fiction are also not used." Buys 50 mss/year. Query with published clips. Length: 2,200 words maximum. "Payment for features usually starts at $350." Sometimes pays the expenses of writers on assignment.

Photos: State availability of photos with submission, if applicable. Reviews contact sheets, 35mm transparencies and 5×7 or 8×10 prints. Payment depends on usage size and quality. Captions, model releases and identification of subjects required. Buys one-time rights.

Columns/Departments: Books (book reviews of books on animals and animal-related subjects), 300 words. Buys 18 mss/year. Query with published clips. Length: 300 words maximum. "Payment usually starts at $75.

Tips: "Present a well-researched proposal. Be sure to include clips that demonstrate the quality of your writing. Stick to categories mentioned in *Animals'* editorial description. Combine well-researched facts with a lively, informative writing style. Feature stories are written almost exclusively by freelancers. We continue to seek proposals and articles that take a humane approach. Articles should concentrate on how issues affect animals, rather than humans."

‡THE ANIMALS' AGENDA, Helping People Help Animals, P.O. Box 25881, Baltimore MD 21224. (410)675-4566. Editor: K.W. Stallwood. 80% freelance written. Bimonthly magazine covering animals, cruelty-free living, vegetarianism. "Dedicated to informing people about animal rights and cruelty-free living for the purpose of inspiring action for animals. We serve a combined audience of animal advocates, interested individuals and the entire animal rights movement." Estab. 1979. Circ. 20,000. Pays on publication. Publishes ms an average of 4-6 months after acceptance. Byline given. Offers 10% kill fee. Buys first North American serial rights. Editorial lead time 2-3 months. Submit seasonal material 6-8 months in advance. Accepts simultaneous and previously published submissions. Reports in 1-2 months. Sample copy for $3. Writer's guidelines for #10 SASE.

Nonfiction: Book excerpts, exposé, general interest, interview/profile, opinion. Buys 1-10 mss/year. Query. Length: 1,000-3,000 words. Pays $100. Sometimes pays the expenses of writers on assignment.

The double dagger before a listing indicates that the listing is new in this edition. New markets are often more receptive to freelance submissions.

Photos: State availability of photos with submissions. Reviews contact sheets. Offers no additional payment for photos accepted with ms; negotiates payment individually. Captions required. Buys one-time rights.

Columns/Departments: News (investigative news on animal abuse), 1,000-1,500 words; articles (in-depth writing/treatment), 1,000-3,000 words; News & Notes (news shorts, reports, updates) 500-750 words. Buys 1-10 mss/year. Query. Pays 10¢/word.

Tips: "Please read the magazine and understand how it is structured and organized and its focus. No phone calls. Every article must be accompanied by practical action you can take. Please remember we are a not-for-profit publication."

‡APPALOOSA JOURNAL, Appaloosa Horse Club, 5070 Hwy. 8 West, P.O. Box 8403, Moscow ID 83843-0903. (208)882-5578. Fax: (208)882-8150. Editor: Debbie Pitner Moors. 10-20% freelance written. Monthly magazine covering Appaloosa horses. Estab. 1946. Circ. 14,000. Pays on publication. Publishes ms an average of 3 months after acceptance. Byline given. Buys first North American serial rights. Query for electronic submissions. Reports in 1 month on queries; 2 months on mss. Free sample copy and writer's guidelines.

Nonfiction: Essays, historical/nostalgic, how-to, humor, interview/profile, horse health, personal experience, photo feature. Buys 6-7 mss/year. Query with or without published clips, or send complete ms. Length: 400-3,000 words. Pays $100-400. Sometimes pays expenses of writers on assignment.

Photos: Send photos with submission. Payment varies. Captions and identification of subjects required.

Columns: Horse racing, endurance riding, training.

Tips: "Articles by writers with horse knowledge, news sense and photography skills are in great demand. If it's a solid article about an Appaloosa, the writer has a pretty good chance of publication. Historical breed features and "how-to" training articles are needed. A good understanding of the breed and the industry is helpful. Avoid purely sentimental, nostalgic horse owner stories. Make sure there's some substance and a unique twist."

CALIFORNIA HORSE REVIEW, P.O. Box 1238, Rancho Cordova CA 95741-1238. (916)638-1519. Fax: (916)638-1784. Editor: Jennifer Meyer. Managing Editor: Lisa Wolters. Monthly magazine covering equestrian interests. "*CHR* covers a wide spectrum—intensive veterinary investigation, trainer 'how-to' tips, breeding research updates and nutritional guidance. Editorial also devotes effort to reporting news and large state and national show results." Estab. 1963. Circ. 10,000. **Pays on acceptance.** Byline given. Buys first North American serial rights. Accepts previously published submissions. Reports in 2 months. Sample copy and writer's guidelines with SASE.

Nonfiction: General interest (West Coast equine emphasis), how-to (training, breeding, horse care, riding) and technical (riding, training). "No fiction or anything *without* a strong focal point of interest for *West Coast equestrians* in the major performance/show English and Western disciplines." Buys 25-40 mss/year. Query with published clips. Length: 500-2,500 words. Pays $50-175 for assigned articles; $25-150 for unsolicited articles. Sometimes pays telephone expenses of writers on assignment.

Photos: Send photos with submission. Reviews 3×5 or larger prints. Offers no additional payment for photos accepted with ms. Captions required. Buys one-time rights.

Tips: "Be accurate, precise and knowledgeable about horses. Our readers are not beginners but sophisticated equestrians. Elementary, overly-basic how-to's are not appropriate for us."

CAT FANCY, Fancy Publications, Inc., Box 6050, Mission Viejo CA 92690. (714)855-8822. Editor: Debbie Phillips-Donaldson. 80-90% freelance written. Monthly magazine for men and women of all ages interested in all phases of cat ownership. Estab. 1965. Circ. 303,000. Pays on publication. Publishes ms an average of 6 months after acceptance. Buys first North American serial rights. Byline given. Absolutely no simultaneous submissions. Submit seasonal/holiday material 4 months in advance. Reports in 2-3 months. Sample copy for $5.50. Writer's guidelines for SASE.

Nonfiction: Historical, medical, how-to, humor, informational, personal experience, photo feature, technical; must be cat-oriented. Buys 5-7 mss/issue. *Query first.* Length: 500-3,000 words. Pays $35-400; special rates for photo/story packages.

Photos: Photos purchased with or without accompanying ms. Pays $35 minimum for 8×10 b&w glossy and $50 minimum for color prints; $50-200 for 35mm or 2¼×2¼ color transparencies; occasionally pays more for particularly outstanding or unusual work. Send SASE for photo guidelines. Then send prints and transparencies. Model release required.

Fiction: Adventure, fantasy, historical, humorous. Nothing written with cats speaking or from cat's point of view. Buys 3-5 ms/year. *Query first.* Length: 500-3,000 words. Pays $50-400.

Fillers: Newsworthy or unusual; items with photos. Buys 5/year. Length: 500-1,000 words. Pays $35-100.

Tips: "Most of the articles we receive are profiles of the writers' own cats or profiles of cats that have recently died. We reject almost all of these stories. What we need are well-researched articles that will give our readers the information they need to better care for their cats. Please review past issues and notice the informative nature of articles before querying us with an idea. *Please query first.*"

CATS MAGAZINE, Cats Magazine Inc., P.O. Box 290037, Port Orange FL 32129-0037. (904)788-2770. Fax: (904)788-2710. Editor: Tracey Copeland. 85% freelance written. Monthly magazine for owners and lovers of cats. Estab. 1945. Circ. 149,000. Pays on publication. Byline given. Buys one-time rights. Submit seasonal/holiday material at least 6 months in advance. Reports in 3 months. Sample copy and writer's guidelines for $2 and 9×12 SAE.

Nonfiction: General interest (concerning cats); how-to (care, etc. for cats); health-related; humor; interview/profile (on cat-owning personalities); personal experience; stories about cats that live in remarkable circumstances, or have had a remarkable experience (can be historical). No talking cats, please. Send complete ms with SASE. Length 400-2,000 words. Pays $25-450.

Photos: "Professional quality photographs that effectively illustrate the chosen topic are accepted with all submissions. However, it is the perogative of the art director to choose whether or not to use the photographs along with the printed piece." Photos that accompany an article should be in the form of color slides, 2¼ transparencies or glossy prints no smaller than 5×7. Pays $50-150 total depending on size used. To be considered for a cover shot, photos should be in the form of a transparency no smaller than 2¼. Pays $150-250. Clear, color prints are accepted for the picture of the month contest. Pays $25. Identification of subjects required. Buys one-time rights.

Fiction: Fantasy, historical, mystery, science fiction, slice-of-life vignettes and suspense are only used occasionally. All fiction must involve a cat or the relationship of a cat and humans, etc. No talking cats, please. Fiction should be believable. Send complete ms. Length: 800-1,500 words. Pays $30-50.

Poetry: Free verse, light verse, traditional. Length: 4-64 lines. Pays $5-30.

Tips: "Writer must show an affinity for cats. Extremely well-written, thoroughly researched, carefully thought out articles have the best chance of being accepted. Innovative topics or a new twist on an old subject are always welcomed."

THE CHRONICLE OF THE HORSE, P.O. Box 46, Middleburg VA 22117-0046. (703)687-6341. Fax: (703)687-3937. Editor: John Strassburger. Managing Editor: Nancy Comer. 80% freelance written. Weekly magazine about horses. "We cover English riding sports, including horse showing, grand prix jumping competitions, steeplechase racing, foxhunting, dressage, endurance riding, handicapped riding and combined training. We are the official publication for the national governing bodies of many of the above sports. We feature news, how-to articles on equitation and horse care and interviews with leaders in the various fields." Estab. 1937. Circ. 23,000. **Pays for features on acceptance**; news and other items on publication. Publishes ms an average of 4 months after acceptance. Byline given. Buys first North American rights and makes work-for-hire assignments. Submit seasonal/holiday material 3 months in advance. Reports in 1 month. Sample copy for $2 and 9×12 SAE. Writer's guidelines for #10 SASE.

Nonfiction: General interest; historical/nostalgic (history of breeds, use of horses in other countries and times, art, etc.); how-to (trailer, train, design a course, save money, etc.); humor (centered on living with horses or horse people); interview/profile (of nationally known horsemen or the very unusual); technical (horse care, articles on feeding, injuries, care of foals, shoeing, etc.); news (of major competitions, clear assignment with us first). Special issues: Steeplechasing, Grand Prix Jumping, Combined Training, Dressage, Hunt Roster, Junior and Pony, Christmas. No Q&A interviews, clinic reports, Western riding articles, personal experience or wild horses. Buys 300 mss/year. Query or send complete ms. Length: 300-1,225 words. Pays $25-200.

Photos: State availability of photos. Accepts prints or color slides. Accepts color for b&w reproduction. Pays $15-30. Identification of subjects required. Buys one-time rights.

Columns/Departments: Dressage, Combined Training, Horse Show, Horse Care, Racing over Fences, Young Entry (about young riders, geared for youth), Horses and Humanities, Hunting. Query or send complete ms. Length: 300-1,225 words. Pays $25-200.

Poetry: Light verse, traditional. No free verse. Buys 30/year. Length: 5-25 lines. Pays $15.

Fillers: Anecdotes, short humor, newsbreaks, cartoons. Buys 300/year. Length: 50-175 lines. Pays $10-25.

Tips: "Get our guidelines. Our readers are sophisticated, competitive horsemen. Articles need to go beyond common knowledge. Freelancers often attempt too broad or too basic a subject. We welcome well-written news stories on major events, but clear the assignment with us."

‡DOG FANCY, Fancy Publications, Inc., P.O. Box 6050, Mission Viejo CA 92690-6050. (714)855-8822. Editor: Kim Thornton. 75% freelance written. Eager to work with unpublished writers. "We'd like to see a balance of both new and established writers." Monthly magazine for men and women of all ages interested in all phases of dog ownership. Estab. 1970. Circ. 200,000. Pays on publication. Publishes ms an average of 6-12 months after acceptance. Buys one-time rights. Byline given. Submit seasonal/holiday material 6 months in advance. Accepts previously published articles. Send tearsheet of article and information about when and where the article previously appeared. For reprints pays $75. Reports in 6-8 weeks. Sample copy for $5.50. Writer's guidelines for #10 SASE.

Nonfiction: Historical, medical, how-to, humor, informational, interview, personal experience, photo feature, profile, technical. "We'll be looking for (and paying more for) high quality writing/photo packages. Interested writers should query with topics." Buys 5 mss/issue. Query or send complete ms. Length: 750-3,000 words. Payment depends on ms quality, whether photos or other art are included, and the quality of the photos/art.

Photos: For photos purchased *without* accompanying ms, pays $15 minimum for 8×10 b&w glossy prints; $50-200 for 35mm or 2¼×2¼ color transparencies. Send prints or transparencies. Model release required.
Tips: "We're looking for the unique experience that communicates something about the dog/owner relationship—with the dog as the focus of the story, not the owner. Medical articles are assigned to veterinarians. Note that we write for a lay audience (non-technical), but we do assume a certain level of intelligence: no talking down to people. If you've never seen the type of article you're writing in *Dog Fancy*, don't expect to. No 'talking dog' articles."

THE EQUINE MARKET, Midwest Outdoors, 111 Shore Dr., Hinsdale IL 60521. (708)887-7722. Editor: Midge Koontz. 90% freelance written. Monthly tabloid covering equestrian interests. Estab. 1970. Circ. 5,000. Pays on publication. Byline given. Buys all rights or makes work-for-hire assignments. Submit seasonal/holiday material 2 months in advance. Accepts previously published material. Send photocopy of article, typed ms with rights for sale noted and information about where and when the article previously appeared. Reports in 2 months. Free sample copy and writer's guidelines.
Nonfiction: Essays, general/interest, historical/nostalgic, how-to (horse care), inspirational, interview/profile, new product, opinion, personal experience, photo feature, show reporting technical, travel. Special issues: Holiday (November-December); Farm (June); Tack Shop (September). Buys 70 mss/year. Send complete ms. Length: 500-3,000 words. Pays $25-35 for assigned articles; $25 for unsolicited articles; or may trade articles for advertising.
Photos: Send photos with submission. Reviews negatives and 3×5 prints. Offers no additional payment for photos accepted with ms. Captions and identification of subjects required.

THE GREYHOUND REVIEW, P.O. Box 543, Abilene KS 67410. (913)263-4660. Fax: (913)263-4689. Editor: Gary Guccione. Managing Editor: Tim Horan. 20% freelance written. Monthly magazine covering greyhound breeding, training and racing. Estab. 1911. Circ. 7,000. **Pays on acceptance.** Byline given. Buys first rights. Submit seasonal/holiday material 2 months in advance. Query for electronic submissions. Reports in 2 weeks on queries; 1 month on mss. *Writer's Market* recommends allowing 2 months for reply. Sample copy for $2.50. Free writer's guidelines.
Nonfiction: How-to, interview/profile, personal experience. "Articles must be targeted at the greyhound industry: from hard news, special events at racetracks to the latest medical discoveries." Do not submit gambling systems. Buys 24 mss/year. Query. Length: 1,000-10,000 words. Pays $85-150. Sometimes pays the expenses of writers on assignment.
Photos: State availability of photos with submission. Reviews 35mm transparencies and 8×10 prints. Offers $10-50/photo. Identification of subjects required. Buys one-time rights.

‡HOOF PRINT The Northeast's Equestrian Newspaper, Glens Falls Newspapers, Inc., P.O. Box 2157, Glens Falls NY 12801. (518)792-3131 ext. 257. Managing Editor: Jennifer O. Bryant. 60% freelance written. Monthly tabloid covering equestrian (horse) news and features in the Northeast. "*Hoof Print* is an all-breed, all-discipline paper for Northeastern horse owners and horse lovers. We try to offer something for everyone at every experience level and produce an information-filled, colorful, easy-to-read paper." Estab. 1992. Circ. 15,000. Pays on publication. Publishes ms an average of 4 months after acceptance. Offers approximately 50% kill fee. Buys first North American serial or second serial (reprint) rights. Editorial lead time 2 months. Submit seasonal material 3 months in advance. Accepts simultaneous and previously published submissions. Query for electronic submissions. Reports in 2-4 weeks on queries; 1-2 months on mss. Sample copy for $3. Writer's guidelines free for SASE.
Nonfiction: How-to, humor, new product, personal experience (all must relate to horses). "No articles not pertinent to Northeast horse people." Buys 60 mss/year. Query or send complete ms. Length: 500-1,500 words. Pays $25 minimum. Sometimes pays expenses of writers on assignment.
Photos: Send photos with submission. Reviews negatives, transparencies and prints. Offers $15/photo. Captions and identification of subjects required. Buys one-time rights.
Columns/Departments: The Tail End (first-person experiences with horses) 800 words; Product reviews (products of interest to horse people) 500 words. Buys 12-24 mss/year. Query or send complete ms. Pays $25-40.
Poetry: Light verse. Buys 5 poems/year. Length: 5-20 lines. Pays $15-25.
Fillers: Facts, tips, short humor. Pays $5.
Tips: "Articles about events, people, horses, farms, etc., *in our area* and of interest to our readers are always needed. Knowledge of horses usually is necessary. We offer practical advice, how-to articles, plus news, information, and a variety of features in each issue. Send for writers' guidelines and study each month's theme. Query with ideas for theme-related articles. Cover photos that reflect monthly themes are needed as well."

‡HORSE ILLUSTRATED, The Magazine for Responsible Horse Owners, Fancy Publications, Inc., P.O. Box 6050, Mission Viejo CA 92690-6050. (714)855-8822. Fax: (714)855-3045. Editor: Audrey Pavia. 90% freelance written. Prefers to work with published/established writers but will work with new/unpublished writers. Monthly magazine covering all aspects of horse ownership. "Our readers are adults, mostly women, between the ages of 18 and 40; stories should be geared to that age group and reflect responsible horse care." Estab. 1976. Circ. 180,000. Pays on publication. Publishes ms an average of 8 months after acceptance. Byline given. Buys one-time rights. Submit seasonal/holiday material 6 months in advance. Reports in 3 months. Sample copy for $3.50. Writer's guidelines for #10 SASE.

Nonfiction: How-to (horse care, training, veterinary care), humor, personal experience, photo feature. No "little girl" horse stories, "cowboy and Indian" stories or anything not *directly* relating to horses. "We are looking for longer, more authoritative, in-depth features on trends and issues in the horse industry. Such articles must be queried first with a detailed outline of the article and clips. We rarely have a need for fiction." Buys 100 mss/year. Query or send complete ms. Length: 1,000-2,500 words. Pays $100-300 for assigned articles; $50-300 for unsolicited articles.

Photos: Send photos with submission. Reviews contact sheets, 35mm transparencies and 5×7 prints. Occasionally offers additional payment for photos accepted with ms.

Tips: "Freelancers can break in at this publication with feature articles on Western and English training methods and trainer profiles (including training tips); veterinary and general care how-to articles; and horse sports articles. While we use personal experience articles (six to eight a year), they must be extremely well-written and have wide appeal; humor in such stories is a bonus. Submit photos with training and how-to articles whenever possible. We have a very good record of developing new freelancers into regular contributors/columnists. We are always looking for fresh talent, but certainly enjoy working with established writers who 'know the ropes' as well."

HORSEPLAY, Box 130, Gaithersburg MD 20884. (301)840-1866. Fax: (301)840-5722. Editor Emeritus: Cordelia Doucet. Managing Editor: Lisa Kiser. 50% freelance written. Works with published/established writers and a small number of new/unpublished writers each year. Monthly magazine covering horses and English horse sports for a readership interested in horses, show jumping, dressage, combined training, hunting and driving. 60-80 pages. Circ. 55,000. Pays at end of publication month. Buys all, first North American serial and second serial (reprint) rights. Offers kill fee. Byline given. Deadline 2 months prior to issue date. Nothing returned without SASE. Accepts previously published submissions. Send tearsheet of article and information about when and where the article previously appeared. Reports in 1 month. Sample copy for 10×13 SASE. Writer's and photographer's guidelines for #10 SASE.

Nonfiction: Instruction (various aspects of horsemanship, course designing, stable management, putting on horse shows, etc.), competitions, interview, photo feature, profile, technical. Query first. Preferred length: 1,500 words or less. Pays 10¢/word, all rights; 9¢/word, first North American serial rights; 7¢/word, second rights.

Photos: Purchased on assignment. Write captions on separate paper attached to photo. Query or send contact sheet, prints or transparencies.

Tips: Don't send fiction, Western riding, or racing articles.

I LOVE CATS, I Love Cats Publishing, 16th Floor, 950 Third Ave., New York NY 10022-2705. (212)888-1855. Editor: Lisa Sheets. 75% freelance written. Bimonthly magazine covering cats. "*I Love Cats* is a general interest cat magazine for the entire family. It caters to cat lovers of all ages. The stories in the magazine include fiction, nonfiction, how-to, humorous and columns for the cat lover." Estab. 1989. Circ. 200,000. Pays on publication. Publishes ms an average of 1 year after acceptance. Byline given. No kill fee. Buys all rights. Must sign copyright consent form. Submit seasonal material 8 months in advance. Query for electronic submissions; IBM compatible. Reports in 2 months. Sample copy for $3. Writer's guidelines for #10 SASE.

Nonfiction: Essays, how-to, humor, inspirational, interview/profile, opinion, personal experience, photo feature. No poetry. Buys 100 mss/year. Send complete ms. Length: 100-1,300 words. Pays $40-250, contributor copies or other premiums "if requested." Sometimes pays expenses of writers on assignment. Send photos with submission. Offers no additional payment for photos accepted with ms. Identification of subjects required. Buys all rights.

Fiction: Adventure, fantasy, historical, humorous, mainstream, mystery, novel excerpts, slice-of-life vignettes, suspense. "This is a family magazine. No graphic violence, pornography or other inappropriate material. *I Love Cats* is strictly 'G-rated.'" Buys 50 mss/year. Send complete ms. Length: 500-1,500 words. Pays $40-250.

Fillers: Gags to be illustrated by cartoonist and short humor. Buys 10/year. Pays $10-35.

Tips: "Please keep stories short and concise. Send complete ms with photos, if possible. I buy lots of first-time authors. Nonfiction pieces w/color photos are always in short supply. With the exception of the standing

Market conditions are constantly changing! If this is 1996 or later, buy the newest edition of Writer's Market *at your favorite bookstore or order directly from* Writer's Digest Books.

columns, the rest of the magazine is open to freelancers. Be witty, humorous or take a different approach to writing."

LONE STAR HORSE REPORT, P.O. Box 14767, Fort Worth TX 76117-0767. (817)838-8642. Fax: (817)838-6410. Editor: Henry L. King. 15-20% freelance written. Monthly magazine on horses and horse people in and around Dallas/Ft. Worth metroplex. Estab. 1983. Circ. 8,500. Pays on publication. Publishes ms an average of 2 months after acceptance. Byline given. Buys first rights and second serial (reprint) rights. Submit seasonal/holiday material 2 months in advance. Accepts reprints of previously published articles. Send tearsheet or photocopy of article or typed ms with rights for sale noted and information about when and where the article previously appeared. For reprints pays 60% of amount paid for an original article. Reports in 2 months. Sample copy for $1. Writer's guidelines for #10 SASE.
Nonfiction: Interview/profile (horsemen living in trade area); photo feature (horses, farms, arenas, facilities, people in trade area). Buys 30-40 mss/year. Query with published clips or send complete ms. Length: 200-2,000 words. Pays $15-60. Sometimes pays the expenses of writers on assignment.
Photos: State availability of photos. Pays $5 for 5×7 b&w or color prints. Buys one-time rights.
Tips: "We need reports of specific horse-related events in north Texas area such as trail rides, rodeos, play days, shows, etc., and also feature articles on horse farms, outstanding horses and/or horsemen. Since Texas now has pari-mutuel horse racing, more emphasis will be placed on coverage of racing and racehorse breeding. We report on the actions of the racing commission, locations of tracks, construction and ownership of those tracks, and the economic impact of the racing industry as new breeding farms and training facilities are established."

MUSHING, Stellar Communications, Inc., P.O. Box 149, Ester AK 99725-0149. (907)479-0454. Fax: (907)479-0454. Publisher: Todd Hoener. Managing Editor: Diane Herrmann. Bimonthly magazine on "all aspects of dog driving activities. We include information (how-to), nonfiction (entertaining), health, ethics, news and history stories." Estab. 1987. Circ. 6,000. Pays on publication. Publishes ms an average of 4 months after acceptance. Byline given. Buys first North American serial and second serial (reprint) rights. Submit seasonal/holiday material 4 months in advance. Query for electronic submissions. Reports in 1-6 months. Sample copy for $3.50. Free writer's guidelines. Call for information.
Nonfiction: Historical, how-to, humor, interview/profile, new product, personal experience, photo feature, technical, innovations, travel. Themes: Christmas, races and places, skiing, winter trips (November/December); travel, main dog sled race, recreation and work season (January/February); breeding, puppies, breakup (March/April); health and nutrition (May/June); dog packing, carting, musher interviews (July/August); equipment, events calendar, getting geared up for winter (September/October). Query with or without published clips, or send complete ms. Length: 500-3,000 words. Pays $50-250 for articles. Payment depends on quality, deadlines, experience. Sometimes pays expenses of writers on assignment.
Photos: Send photos with submission. Reviews contact sheets, transparencies, prints. Offers $20-150/photo. Captions, model releases, identification of subjects required. Buys one-time and second reprint rights. We look for good b&w and quality color for covers and specials.
Fillers: Anecdotes, facts, cartoons, newsbreaks, short humor. Length: 100-250 words. Pays $20-35.
Tips: "Read our magazine. Know something about dog-driven, dog-powered sports."

PAINT HORSE JOURNAL, American Paint Horse Association, P.O. Box 961023, Fort Worth TX 76161-0023. (817)439-3400, ext. 210. Fax: (817)439-3484. Associate Editor: Dan Streeter. 10% freelance written. Works with a small number of new/unpublished writers each year. Monthly magazine for people who raise, breed and show Paint horses. Estab. 1966. Circ. 15,000. **Pays on acceptance.** Publishes ms an average of 3 months after acceptance. Buys first North American serial rights plus reprint rights occasionally. Pays negotiable kill fee. Byline given. Phone queries OK, but prefers written query. Submit seasonal/holiday material 3 months in advance. Accepts previously published articles. Send typed ms with rights for sale noted and information about when and where the article previously appeared. For reprints, pays 20-30% of the amount paid for an original article. Reports in 1 month. Sample copy for 9×12 SAE with 5 first-class stamps. Writer's guidelines for #10 SASE.
Nonfiction: General interest (personality pieces on well-known owners of Paints); historical (Paint horses in the past — particular horses and the breed in general); how-to (train and show horses); photo feature (Paint horses). Now seeking informative well-written articles on recreational riding. Buys 4-5 mss/issue. Send complete ms. Pays $25-250.
Photos: Send photos with ms. Offers no additional payment for photos accepted with accompanying ms. Uses 3×5 or larger b&w or color glossy prints; 35mm or larger color transparencies. Captions required. Photos must illustrate article and must include Paint Horses.
Tips: "PHJ needs breeder-trainer articles, Paint horse marketing and timely articles from areas throughout the US and Canada. We are looking for more recreational and how-to articles. We are beginning to cover equine activity such as trail riding, orienteering and other outdoor events. Photos with copy are almost always essential. Well-written first person articles are welcomed. Submit items that show a definite understanding of the horse business. Be sure you understand precisely what a Paint horse is as defined by the American

Paint Horse Association. Use proper equine terminology and proper grounding in ability to communicate thoughts."

‡**PET FOCUS, America's Most Informative Pet Magazine,** Focus Publications Inc., 20 Church St., Montclair NJ 07042. (201)783-7303. Editor: Martin Fitzpatrick. Managing Editor: Thomas Happle. Copy Editor: Karin Fleming. 50% freelance written. Bimonthly consumer magazine covering pets. "We are the only multi-species pet magazine in the USA. Articles must be entertaining and informative. We try to exploit the celebrity angle of pets; top ten lists, best and worst etc.; good history/hype. The writing must be crisp and jaunty, NOT the cute, saccharin gushy poses usually associted with animals." Estab. 1991. Circ. 100,000. Pays on publication. Byline given. Buys all rights. Editorial lead time 2 months. Submit seasonal material 4 months in advance. Reports in 3-6 weeks. Sample copy free and writer's guidelines free on request.

Nonfiction: Book excerpts, essays, exposé, general interest, historical/nostalgic, humor, interview/profile, new product, photo feature, travel. "No heartworm or flea stories. No kitten up the tree stories." Buys 50-60 mss/year. Query. Length: 500-3,000 words. Pays $200 minimum for assigned articles; $50 minimum for unsolicited articles. Contributor copies for fillers, jokes, cartoons.

Photos: State availability of or send photos with submission. Reviews contact sheets, negatives, transparencies. Offers no additional payment for photos accepted with ms. Negotiages payment individually. Model releases, identification of subjects required. Buys all rights.

Columns/Departments: By individual species. Latest news, Vet breakthroughs. 1,200 words. Buys 4-5 mss/year mostly staff written. Query. Pays $200-600.

Fiction: Derek Mallone, Associate Editor. Humorous, mainstream. Buys 4 mss/year. Send complete ms. Length: 500-1,000 words. Pays $50-150.

Fillers: Fact, short humor. Length: 50 words. Pays $25.

Tips: "Our department articles on individual species must be dynamic, informative and witty. Since we appeal to all pet owners but must concentrate only four to six pages per species, the editorial has to be intriguing. Features are much more entertaining and diverse. Art, movies, theater, science, adventure can be used to pinpoint some unique aspect of pets and pet ownership. The MULTI-SPECIES concept is most important. Feature ideas have the best chance to succeed. Any article with good photo representation is a plus. *Query first.* Departments are species specific. Remember that the dog and cat person is not the same as the fish and reptile hobbyist. Try to match the species with person. Problems and solutions of keeping different species as pets are wanted most."

PETS MAGAZINE, Moorshead Publications, 10th Floor, 797 Don Mills Rd., Don Mills, Ontario M3C 3S5 Canada. (416)696-5488. Fax: (416)696-7395. Editor: Edward Zapletal. Editorial Director/Veterinarian: Dr. Tom Frisby. 50% freelance written. Bimonthly magazine on pets. Circ. 56,000 distributed by vet clinics; 7,000 personal subscriptions. Pays on publication. Publishes ms an average of 4 months after acceptance. Buys all rights. Submit seasonal/holiday material 4 months in advance. Accepts previously published submissions (sometimes). Query for electronic submissions. Sample copy for #10 SAE with 95¢ IRC or Canadian stamps. Free writer's guidelines.

Nonfiction: General interest, historical, how-to (train, bathe/groom, build dog houses, make cat toys and photograph pets), breed profile, photo feature. "No I remember Fluffy. No poetry, no fiction." Buys 40 mss/year. Query with outline. Length: 300-2,000 words. Pays 10-18¢/word (Canadian).

Photos: State availability of photos with submission. Reviews prints 3×5 and larger, b&w preferred. Offers $25/photo maximum. Identification of subjects required. Buys all rights.

Fillers: Facts. Query with samples. Buys 1-2/year. Length: 100-400 words. Pays 10-15¢/word (Canadian). "Always call or send topic outline first; we always have a backlog of freelance articles waiting to be run. Prefers factual, information pieces, not anecdotal or merely humorous, but can be written with humor; we do not cover controversial areas such as product testing, vivisection, puppy mills, pound seizure."

PURE-BRED DOGS/AMERICAN KENNEL GAZETTE, American Kennel Club, 51 Madison Ave., New York NY 10010-1603. (212)696-8241. Executive Editor: Beth Adelman. 50% freelance written. Monthly association publication on pure-bred dogs. "Material is slanted to interests of fanciers of pure-bred dogs as opposed to commercial interests or pet owners." Estab. 1889. Circ. 58,000. **Pays on acceptance of final ms.** Publishes ms an average of 6 months after acceptance. Byline given. Offers 30% kill fee. Buys first North American serial rights. Submit seasonal/holiday material 6 months in advance. Reports in up to 2 months. Sample copy and writer's guidelines for 9×12 SAE with 11 first-class stamps.

Nonfiction: General interest, historical, how-to, humor, photo feature, travel. No profiles, poetry, tributes to individual dogs, or fiction. Buys about 75 mss/year. Query with or without published clips, or send complete ms. Length: 1,000-2,500 words. Pays $100-350.

Photos: Send photos with submission. Reviews tranparencies and prints. Offers $25-100/photo. Captions required. Buys one-time rights. Photo contest guidelines for #10 SASE.

Fiction: Annual short fiction contest only. Guidelines for #10 SASE.

Tips: "Contributors should be involved in dog fancy or be expert in the area they write about (veterinary, showing, field trialing, obedience, training, dogs in legislation, dog art or history or literature). All submissions are welcome but the author must be a credible expert. Veterinary articles must be written by or with veterinarians. Humorous features are personal experiences relative to pure-bred dogs. For features generally, know the subject thoroughly and be conversant with jargon peculiar to dog sport."

THE QUARTER HORSE JOURNAL, P.O. Box 32470, Amarillo TX 79120. (806)376-4811. Fax: (806)376-8364. Editor-in-Chief: Audie Rackley. Editor: Jim Jennings. 20% freelance written. Prefers to work with published/established writers. Monthly official publication of the American Quarter Horse Association. Estab. 1948. Circ. 75,000. **Pays on acceptance.** Publishes ms an average of 3 months after acceptance. Buys first North American serial rights. Submit seasonal/holiday material 2 months in advance. Reports in 2 months. Free sample copy and writer's guidelines.
Nonfiction: Historical ("those that retain our western heritage"); how-to (fitting, grooming, showing, or anything that relates to owning, showing, or breeding); informational (educational clinics, current news); interview (feature-type stories—must be about established horses or people who have made a contribution to the business); personal opinion; and technical (equine updates, new surgery procedures, etc.). Buys 20 mss/year. Length: 800-2,500 words. Pays $150-300.
Photos: Purchased with accompanying ms. Captions required. Send prints or transparencies. Uses 5×7 or 8×10 b&w glossy prints, 2¼×2¼, 4×5 or 35 mm color transparencies. Offers no additional payment for photos accepted with accompanying ms.
Tips: "Writers must have a knowledge of the horse business."

‡THE RANCH DOG TRAINER, Stonehedge Publishing Co. Inc., 7686 State Route 17, West Plains MO 65775. (417)257-7376. Editor: Larry Conner. Managing Editor: Kathy Conner. 50% freelance written. Bimonthly magazine covering training and use of stock dogs. "Readers are farmers and ranchers who use dogs to handle livestock. Some readers are involved in competing in competitive events, working livestock with their dogs. Emphasis is made on practical use, covering all breeds of herding dogs." Estab. 1986. Circ. 2,700. Pays on publication. Byline given. Offers 25% kill fee. Buys first North American serial, all rights or makes work-for-hire assignments. Editorial lead time 4 months. Submit seasonal material 6 months in advance. Query for electronic submissions. Reports in 2 weeks on queries; 2 months on mss. Sample copy for $4. Writer's guidelines free on request.
Nonfiction: How-to train and use stockdogs, interview/profile, opinion, personal experience. "No articles about pets or show dogs." Buys 25-30 mss/year. Query with published clips. Length: 900-3,600 words. Pays minimum of $36 (4¢/word). Sometimes pays expenses of writers on assignment.
Photos: Send photos with submission. Reviews 3×5 or larger prints. Offers $5-50/photo. Identification of subjects required. Buys one-time rights.
Columns/Departments: Reviews (books or videos pertaining to stock-dog owners. Are they useful?) 900-1,800 words; Canine Health (information useful to layman) 1,800 words; Livestock Guardian Dogs (breed bio/use and training of guardian dogs—great Pyrenees, for example) 1,800 words. Buys 12 mss/year. Send complete ms. Pays $36-75 (4¢/word).
Tips: "Will work with authors who are willing to learn about stock dogs. Interviews with livestock producers who are using dogs—why a particular breed, how got started, detailed training info, etc.—are especially useful for us. Technical articles should be written by qualified professionals (i.e., canine health by veterinarians). All areas except reader-submitted sections (trial results, "Liar's Tale," letters to the editor) are open to freelancers. Generally, the more descriptive and detailed an article is, the better."

REPTILE & AMPHIBIAN MAGAZINE, RD3, Box 3709A, Pottsville PA 17901-9219. (717)622-6050. Fax: (717)622-5858. Editor: Norman Frank, D.V.M. 80% freelance written. Full-color digest-size bimonthly magazine covering reptiles and amphibians. Devoted to the amateur herpetologist who is generally college-educated and familiar with the basics of herpetology. Estab. 1989. Circ. 15,000. **Pays on acceptance.** Publishes ms an average of 4-6 months after acceptance. Byline given. Buys first North American serial, one-time and (occasionally) second serial (reprint) rights. Accepts previously published material. Send photocopy of article and information about when and where the article previously appeared. For reprints pays 100% of the amount paid for an original article. Reports in 2 months. Sample copy for $4. Writer's guidelines for #10 SASE.
Nonfiction: General interest, photo feature, technical. Publishes articles on life cycles of various reptiles and amphibians, natural history, captive care and breeding. No first-person narrative, "me-and-Joe" stories or articles by writers unfamiliar with the subject matter. "Readers are already familiar with the basics of herpetology and are usually advanced amateur hobbyists." Buys 30 mss/year. Query or send complete ms. Length: 1,500-2,000 words. Pays $75-100. Sometimes pays expenses of familiar or regular writer on assignment.
Photos: Send photos with submission whenever possible. Reviews 35mm slide transparencies, 4×6, 5×7 and 8×10 glossy prints. Offers $10 for b&w, $25 for color photos. Captions, model releases and identification of subjects required. Animals should be identified by common and/or scientific name. Buys one-time rights.
Columns/Departments: Photo Dept./Herp●Art Dept., 500-750 words; Book Review, 500-750 words. Buys 12 mss/year. Send complete ms. Pays $50-75.
Tips: "Note your personal qualifications, such as experience in the field or advanced education. Writers have the best chance selling us feature articles—know your subject and supply high quality color photos."

TROPICAL FISH HOBBYIST, "The World's Most Widely Read Aquarium Monthly," TFH Publications, Inc., 211 W. Sylvania Ave., Neptune City NJ 07753. (908)988-8400. Fax: (908)988-9635. Editor: Ray Hunziker. Managing Editor: Neal Pronek. Assistant Editor: Mary Sweeney. 75% freelance written. Monthly magazine covering the tropical fish hobby. "We favor articles well illustrated with good color slides and aimed at both the neophyte and veteran tropical fish hobbyist." Estab. 1952. Circ. 60,000. **Pays on acceptance.** Publishes ms an average of 4 months after acceptance. Byline given. Buys all rights. Submit seasonal/holiday material 4 months in advance. Accepts previously published articles. Send tearsheet of article and information about when and where the article previously appeared. For reprints pays 100% of the amount paid for an original article. Reports in 1 month. Sample copy for $3 and 9×12 SAE with 6 first-class stamps. Writer's guidelines for #10 SASE.

Nonfiction: General interest, how-to, photo feature, technical, and articles dealing with beginning and advanced aspects of the aquarium hobby. No "how I got started in the hobby" articles that impart little solid information. Buys 40-50 mss/year. Length: 500-2,500 words. Pays $25-100.

Photos: State availability of photos or send photos with ms. Pays $10 for 35mm transparencies. Identification of subjects required. "Originals returned to owner, who may market them elsewhere."

Fiction: "On occasion, we will review a fiction piece relevant to the aquarium hobby."

Tips: "We cater to a specialized readership—people knowledgeable in fish culture. Prospective authors should be familiar with subject; photography skills are a plus. It's a help if an author we've never dealt with queries first or submits a short item."

THE WESTERN HORSEMAN, World's Leading Horse Magazine Since 1936, Western Horseman, Inc., P.O. Box 7980, Colorado Springs CO 80933-7980. (719)633-5524. Editor: Pat Close. 50% freelance written. Works with a small number of new/unpublished writers each year. Monthly magazine. Estab. 1936. Circ. 224,000. **Pays on acceptance.** Publishes ms an average of 5 months after acceptance. Buys one-time and North American serial rights. Byline given. Submit seasonal/holiday material 6 months in advance. Reports in 3 weeks. Sample copy for $5. Writer's guidelines for #10 SASE. No fax material accepted.

Nonfiction: How-to (horse training, care of horses, tips, ranch/farm management, etc.) and informational (on rodeos, ranch life, historical articles of the West emphasizing horses). Buys 250 mss/year. Length: 500-2,500 words. Pays $35-400, "sometimes higher by special arrangement."

Photos: Send photos with ms. Offers no additional payment for photos. Uses 5×7 or 8×10 b&w glossy prints and 35mm transparencies. Captions required.

Tips: "Submit clean copy with professional quality photos. All copy, including computer copy, should be double-spaced. Stay away from generalities. Writing style should show a deep interest in horses coupled with a wide knowledge of the subject."

Art and Architecture

Listed here are publications about art, art history, specific art forms and architecture written for art patrons, architects, artists and art enthusiasts. Publications addressing the business and management side of the art industry are listed in the Art, Design and Collectibles category of the Trade section. Trade publications for architecture can be found in Building Interiors and Construction and Contracting sections.

THE AMERICAN ART JOURNAL, Kennedy Galleries, Inc. 5th Floor, 40 W. 57th St., New York NY 10019. (212)541-9600. Fax: (212)333-7451. Editor-in-Chief: Jayne A. Kuchna. Prefers to work with published/established writers; works with a small number of new/unpublished writers each year. Semiannual scholarly magazine of American art history of the 17th, 18th, 19th and 20th centuries, including painting, sculpture, architecture, photography, cultural history, etc., for people with a serious interest in American art, and who are already knowledgable about the subject. Readers are scholars, curators, collectors, students of American art, or persons with a strong interest in Americana. Circ. 2,000. **Pays on acceptance.** Publishes ms an average of 6 months after acceptance. Buys all rights, but will reassign rights to writer. Byline given. Reports in 2 months. Sample copy for $18.

Nonfiction: "All articles are about some phase or aspect of American art history." No how-to articles or reviews of exhibitions. No book reviews or opinion pieces. No human interest approaches to artists' lives. No articles written in a casual or "folksy" style. *Writing style must be formal and serious.* Buys 10-15 mss/year. Submit complete ms "with good cover letter." No queries. Length: 2,500-8,000 words. Pays $400-600.

Photos: Purchased with accompanying ms. Captions required. Uses b&w only. Offers no additional payment for photos accepted with accompanying ms.

Tips: "Articles *must be* scholarly, thoroughly documented, well-researched, well-written and illustrated. Whenever possible, all manuscripts must be accompanied by b&w photographs, which have been integrated into the text by the use of numbers."

AMERICAN INDIAN ART MAGAZINE, American Indian Art, Inc., 7314 E. Osborn Dr., Scottsdale AZ 85251-6417. (602)994-5445. Editor: Roanne P. Goldfein. 97% freelance written. Works with a small number of new/unpublished writers each year. Quarterly magazine covering Native American art, historic and contemporary, including new research on any aspect of Native American art north of the US/Mexico border. Estab. 1975. Circ. 20,000. Pays on publication. Publishes ms an average of 3 months after acceptance. Byline given. Buys one-time and first rights. Simultaneous queries OK. Reports in 3 weeks on queries; 3 months on mss. Writer's guidelines for #10 SASE.

Nonfiction: New research on any aspect of Native American art. No previously published work or personal interviews with artists. Buys 12-18 mss/year. Query. Length: 1,000-2,500 words. Pays $75-300.

Tips: "The magazine is devoted to all aspects of Native American art. Some of our readers are knowledgeable about the field and some know very little. We seek articles that offer something to both groups. Articles reflecting original research are preferred to those summarizing previously published information."

‡AMERICAN STYLE, Contemporary Crafts For Living and Giving, The Rosen Group, Suite 300, 3000 Chestnut Ave., Baltimore MD 21211. (410)889-2933. Editor: Laura Rosen. 50% freelance written. Semiannual magazine covering handmade American Crafts, "designed to promote and educate consumers about handmade American craft." Estab. 1994. Circ. 50,000. Pays on publication. Publishes ms an average of 6 months after acceptance. Byline given. Buys second serial (reprint) rights or all rights. Editorial lead time 4 months. Submit seasonal material 6 months in advance. Query for electronic submissions. Reports in 3 months. Sample copy for $3. Writer's guidelines for #10 SASE.

Nonfiction: General interest, interview/profile, personal experience, photo feature. Buys 4 mss/year. Query with published clips. Length: 300-2,500 words. Pays 20¢/word. Sometimes pays expenses of writers on assignment.

Photos: Send photos with submission. Reviews oversized transparencies and 35mm slides. Negotiates payment individually. Captions required.

Columns/Departments: Contact: Sharon Perfetti. Home Decorating (collecting and decorating with American crafts), 700-1,000 words. Buys 4 mss/year. Query with published clips. Pays 20¢/word.

Tips: "Contact editor about upcoming issues, article ideas. Let us know what you are sending, follow-up. All departments will be open. Concentrate on contemporary American craft art, such as ceramics, wood, fiber, glass, etc., No popsicle sticks or macramé or other hobby crafts."

ART TIMES, A Literary Journal and Resource for All the Arts, P.O. Box 730, Mount Marion NY 12456-0730. (914)246-6944. Fax: (914)246-6944. Editor: Raymond J. Steiner. 10% freelance written. Prefers to work with published/established writers; works with a small number of new/unpublished writers each year. Monthly tabloid covering the arts (visual, theatre, dance, etc.). "*Art Times* covers the art fields and is distributed in locations most frequented by those enjoying the arts. Our copies are sold at newsstands and are distributed throughout upstate New York counties as well as in most of the galleries in Soho, 57th Street and Madison Avenue in the metropolitan area; locations include theaters, galleries, museums, cultural centers and the like. Our readers are mostly over 40, affluent, art-conscious and sophisticated. Subscribers are located across US and abroad (Italy, France, Germany, Greece, Russia, etc.)." Estab. 1984. Circ. 15,000. Pays on publication. Publishes ms an average of 1 year after acceptance. Byline given. Buys first serial rights. Submit seasonal/holiday material 8 months in advance. Accepts simultaneous submissions. Reports in 3 months on queries; 6 months on mss. Sample copy for 9 × 12 SAE with 6 first-class stamps. Writer's guidelines for #10 SASE.

Fiction: "We're looking for short fiction that aspires to be *literary*. No excessive violence, sexist, off-beat, erotic, sports, or juvenile fiction." Buys 8-10 mss/year. Send complete ms. Length: 1,500 words maximum. Pays $25 maximum (honorarium) and 1 year's free subscription.

Poetry: Poet's Niche. Avant-garde, free verse, haiku, light verse, traditional. "We prefer well-crafted 'literary' poems. No excessively sentimental poetry." Buys 30-35 poems/year. Submit maximum 6 poems. Length: 20 lines maximum. Offers contributor copies and 1 year's free subscription.

Tips: "Be advised that we are presently on an approximate two year lead. We are now receiving 300-400 poems and 40-50 short stories per month. We only publish two to three poems and one story each issue. Be familiar with *Art Times* and its special audience. *Art Times* has literary leanings with articles written by a staff of scholars knowledgeable in their respective fields. Although an 'arts' publication, we observe no restrictions (other than noted) in accepting fiction/poetry other than a concern for quality writing—subjects can cover anything and not specifically arts."

THE ARTIST'S MAGAZINE, F&W Publications, Inc., 1507 Dana Ave., Cincinnati OH 45207-1005. Editor: Mary Magnus. 80% freelance written. Works with a small number of new/unpublished writers each year. Monthly magazine covering primarily two-dimensional art instruction for working artists. "Ours is a highly visual approach to teaching the serious amateur artist techniques that will help him improve his skills and market his work. The style should be crisp and immediately engaging." Circ. 250,000. **Pays on acceptance.** Publishes ms an average of 4 months after acceptance. Bionote given for feature material. Offers 20% kill fee. Buys first North American serial and second serial (reprint) rights. Accepts previously published articles "as long as noted as such." Reports in 2 months. Sample copy for $3 and 9 × 12 SAE with 3 first-class stamps. Writer's guidelines for #10 SASE.

• Writers must have working knowledge of art techniques. This magazine's most consistent need is for instructional articles written in the artist's voice. They often ask writers to forsake a byline.

Nonfiction: Instructional only—how an artist uses a particular technique, how he handles a particular subject or medium, or how he markets his work. "The emphasis must be on how the reader can learn some method of improving his artwork, or the marketing of it." No unillustrated articles; no seasonal/holiday material; no travel articles; no profiles of artists (except for "The Artist's Life," below). Buys 60 mss/year. Query first; all queries must be accompanied by slides, transparencies, prints or tearsheets of the artist's work as well as the artist's bio, and the writer's bio and clips. Length: 1,000-2,500 words. Pays $100-350 and up. Sometimes pays the expenses of writers on assignment.

Photos: "Transparencies are required with every accepted article since these are essential for our instructional format. Full captions must accompany these." Buys one-time rights.

Departments: Three departments are open to freelance writers. Strictly Business (articles dealing with the business and legal end of selling art; taxes, recordkeeping, copyright, contracts, etc.). Query first. Length: 1,800 word limit. Pays $150 and up. The Artist's Life and P.S. The Artist's Life (profiles and brief items about artists and their work; also, art-related games, puzzles and poetry). Query first with samples of artist's work for profiles; send complete ms for other items. Length: 600 words maximum. Pays $50 and up for profiles; up to $25 for brief items and poetry. P.S. (a humorous look at art from the artist's point of view, or at least sympathetic to the artist). Send complete ms. Pays $50 and up.

Tips: "Look at several current issues and read the author's guidelines carefully. Remember that our readers are fine and graphic artists."

EQUINE IMAGES, The National Magazine of Equine Art, Equine Images Ltd., P.O. Box 916, Fort Dodge IA 50501-3931. (800)247-2000, ext. 213. Fax: (800)247-2000, ext. 217. Editor: Susan J. Stocks. Publisher: Susan Badger. 80% freelance written. Bimonthly magazine of equine art. "*Equine Images* serves collectors and equine art enthusiasts. We write for a sophisticated, culturally-oriented audience." Estab. 1986. Circ. 35,000. Pays on publication. Byline given. Buys first rights and makes work-for-hire assignments. Accepts previously published articles. Send photocopy of article and information about when and where the article previously appeared. For reprints pays 50% of amount paid for an original article. Reports in 2 months. Sample copy for $6.95 and 9 × 12 SAE. Writer's guidelines for #10 SASE.

Nonfiction: Historical/nostalgic (history of the horse in art), how-to (art collections), interview/profile (equine artists, galleries, collectors), personal experience (of equine artists and collectors), photo feature (artworks or collections). "No articles about horses in general—just horse art." Buys 8-10 mss/year. Query with published clips. Length: 500-3,000 words. Pays $150-300 for assigned articles; $100-300 for unsolicited articles.

Photos: State availability of photos with submission. Writer responsible for sending visuals with finished ms. Reviews contact sheets, transparencies, prints. Offers no additional payment for photos accepted with ms. Identification of subjects required. Buys one-time rights.

Tips: "We are interested only in art-related subjects. We are looking for stories that help art collectors better understand, expand or protect their collections. The most promising categories for writers are profiles of prominent artists and equine galleries or museums. Send a good query letter with accompanying visuals, along with published clips or writing samples."

‡METROPOLIS, The Urban Magazine of Architecture and Design, Bellerophon Publications, 177 E. 87th St., New York NY 10128. (212)722-5050. Fax: (212)427-1938. Editor: Susan S. Szenasy. 75% freelance written. Monthly (except bimonthly January/February and July/August) magazine for consumers interested in architecture and design. Estab. 1981. Circ. 30,000-40,000. **Pays on acceptance.** Publishes ms an average of 6 months after acceptance. Byline given. Buys first rights or makes work-for-hire assignments. Submit calendar material 6 weeks in advance. Reports in 3-8 months. Sample copy for $4.50 including postage.

Nonfiction: Book excerpts, essays (ideas, design, residential interiors), profiles (on multi-disciplinary designers/architects). No profiles on individual architectural practices, information from public relations firms, or fine arts. Buys approximately 30 mss/year. Query with published clips. Length: 500-2,000 words. Pays $100-1,000.

Photos: State availability of or send photos with submission. Reviews contact sheets, 35mm or 4 × 5 transparencies, or 8 × 10 b&w prints. Payment offered for certain photos. Captions required. Buys one-time rights.

Columns/Departments: Insites (short takes on design and architecture), 100-600 words; pays $50-150; In Print (book review essays), 1,000-2,000 words; The Metropolis Observed (architecture and city planning news features and opinion), 750-1,500 words; pays $200-500; Visible City (historical aspects of cities), 1,500-2,500 words; pays $600-800; By Design (product design), 1,000-2,000 words; pays $600-800. Buys approximately 40 mss/year. Query with published clips.

Tips: "We're looking for ideas, what's new, the obscure or the wonderful. Keep in mind that we are interested *only* in the consumer end of architecture and design. Send query with examples of photos explaining how you see illustrations working with article. Also, be patient and don't expect an immediate answer after submission of query."

THE ORIGINAL ART REPORT, P.O. Box 1641, Chicago IL 60690-1641. Editor/Publisher: Frank Salantrie. Newsletter emphasizing "visual art conditions from the visual artists' and general public's perspectives." Estab. 1967. Pays on publication. Reports in 2 weeks. Sample copy for $1.50 and #10 SASE.

Nonfiction: Exposé (art galleries, government agencies ripping off artists, or ignoring them); historical (perspective pieces relating to now); humor (whenever possible); informational (material that is unavailable in other art publications); inspirational (acts and ideas of courage); interview (with artists, other experts; serious material on visual art conditions; no profiles); personal opinion; technical (brief items to recall traditional methods of producing art); travel (places in the world where artists are welcomed and honored); philosophical, economic, aesthetic, and artistic. "We would like to receive investigative articles on government and private arts agencies, and nonprofits, too, perhaps hiding behind status to carry on for business entities. Exclusive interest in visual fine art condition as it affects individuals, society and artists and as they affect it. Must take advocacy position. Prefer controversial subject matter and originality of treatment. Honesty and dedication to truth are absolute requirements. Also artist's position on non-art topics. No vanity profiles of artists, arts organizations and arts promoters' operations." Buys 4-5 mss/year. Query or submit complete ms. Length: 1,000 words maximum. Pays 1¢/word.

Columns/Departments: In Back of the Individual Artist. Artists express their views about non-art topics. After all, artists are in this world, too. WOW (Worth One Wow), Worth Repeating, and Worth Repeating Again. Basically, these are reprint items with introduction to give context and source, including complete name and address of publication. Looking for insightful, succinct commentary. Submit complete ms. Length: 500 words maximum and copy of item. Pays ½¢/word; In Back of Individual Artist pays 1¢/word.

Tips: "We have a stronger than ever emphasis on editorial opinion or commentary, based on fact, of the visual art condition: economics, finances, politics and manufacture of art, and the social and individual implications of and to fine art."

SOUTHWEST ART, CBH Publishing, P.O. Box 460535, Houston TX 77256-8535. (713)850-0990. Fax: (713)850-1314. Editor-in-Chief: Susan H. McGarry. Managing Editor: Jacqueline M. Pontello. 60% freelance written. Monthly fine arts magazine "directed to art collectors interested in artists, market trends and art history of the American West." Estab. 1971. Circ. 70,000. **Pays on acceptance.** Publishes ms an average of 1 year after acceptance. Byline given. Offers $125 kill fee. Submit seasonal/holiday material 8 months in advance. Accepts previously published material. Send tearsheet with information about when and where the article previously appeared. Reports in 3-6 months. Free sample copy and writer's guidelines.

Nonfiction: Book excerpts, interview/profile, opinion. No fiction or poetry. Buys 70 mss/year. Query with published clips. Length 1,400-1,600 words. Pays $400 for assigned articles. Send photos with submission.

Photos: Reviews 35mm, 2¼, 4×5 transparencies and 8×10 prints. Captions and identification of subjects required. Negotiates rights.

THEDAMU, The Black Arts Magazine, Detroit Black Arts Alliance, 13217 Livernois, Detroit MI 48238-3162. (313)931-3427. Editor: David Rambeau. Managing Editor: Titilaya Akanke. Art Director: Charles Allen. 20% freelance written. Monthly literary magazine on the arts. "We publish Afro-American feature articles on local artists." Estab. 1965. Circ. 4,000. Pays on publication. Publishes 4 months after acceptance. Byline given. Buys one-time rights. Submit seasonal/holiday material 4 months in advance. Query for electronic submissions. Accepts simultaneous and previously published submissions. Send photocopy of article and information about when and where the article previously appeared. Pays 50% of their fee for an original article. Reports in 1 month on queries; 3 months on mss. Sample copy for $2 and 6×9 SAE with 4 first-class stamps. Writer's guidelines for #10 SASE.

Nonfiction: Essays, interview/profile. Buys 20 mss/year. Send complete ms. Length: 500-1,500 words. Pays $10-25 for unsolicited articles. Pays with contributor copies or other premiums if writer agrees.

Photos: State availability of photos with submission. Reviews 5×7 prints. Offers no additional payment for photos accepted with ms. Captions, model releases and identification of subjects required. Buys one-time rights.

Tips: "Send a résumé and sample manuscript. Query for fiction, poetry, plays and film/video scenarios. Especially interested in Afro-centric cartoonists for special editions and exhibitions."

‡U.S. ART: All the News That Fits Prints, MSP Communications, Suite 500, 220 S. Sixth St., Minneapolis MN 55402. (612)339-7571. Editor/Publisher: Frank Sisser. Managing Editor: Cathy Clauson. 75% freelance written. Magazine published 10 times/year, plus annual Wildlife Art Guide and Print Guide supplements. One artist profile per issue; service articles to inform limited-edition print collectors of trends and options in the market; round-up features spotlighting a particular genre (wildlife, western, fantasy art, etc.) All artists featured must be active in the market for limited-edition prints. National circulation 55,000. Distributed primarily through galleries as a free service to their customers. Writer byline given. Pays $350-450 payment for features. Offers 25% kill fee. Departments/columns are staff-written.

• *U.S. Art* is adding a special section on original graphics, especially serigraphs.

WESTART, P.O. Box 6868, Auburn CA 95604. (916)885-0969. Editor-in-Chief: Martha Garcia. Semimonthly 20-page tabloid emphasizing art for practicing artists and artists/craftsmen; students of art and art patrons.

Estab. 1961. Circ. 5,000. Pays on publication. Buys all rights. Byline given. Phone queries OK. Free sample copy and writer's guidelines.

Nonfiction: Informational, photo feature, profile. No hobbies. Buys 6-8 mss/year. Query or submit complete ms. Include SASE for reply or return. Length: 700-800 words. Pays 50¢/column inch.

Photos: Purchased with or without accompanying ms. Send b&w prints. Pays 50¢/column inch.

Tips: "We publish information which is current — that is, we will use a review of an exhibition only if exhibition is still open on the date of publication. Therefore, reviewer must be familiar with our printing and news deadlines."

WILDLIFE ART NEWS, The International Magazine of Wildlife Art, Pothole Publications, Inc. 4725 Hwy. 7, P.O. Box 16246, St. Louis Park MN 55416-0246. (612)927-9056. Fax: (612)927-9353. Editor: Robert Koenke. Senior Editor: Rebecca Hakala Rowland. 80% freelance written. Bimonthly magazine of wildlife art and conservation. "*Wildlife Art News* is the world's largest wildlife art magazine. Features cover interviews on living artists as well as wildlife art masters, illustrators and conservation organizations. Audience is publishers, collectors, galleries, museums, show promoters worldwide." Estab. 1982. Circ. 55,000. **Pays on acceptance.** Publishes ms an average of 6 months after acceptance. Byline given. Negotiable kill fee. Buys second serial (reprint) rights. Reports in 4-6 months. Sample copy for 9 × 12 SAE with 10 first-class stamps. Writer's guidelines for #10 SASE.

Nonfiction: Buys 40 mss/year. Query with published clips. Length: 800-5,000 words. Pays $150-1,000 for assigned articles.

Columns/Departments: Buys up to 6 mss/year. Pays $100-300.

WOMEN ARTISTS NEWS, Midmarch Arts Press, 300 Riverside, New York NY 10025-5239. Editor: Judy Seigel. 70-90% freelance written. Eager to work with new/unpublished writers. Annual magazine for "artists and art historians, museum and gallery personnel, students, teachers, crafts personnel, art critics and writers." Estab. 1975. Circ. 5,000. "Token payment as funding permits." Publishes ms an average of 2 months after acceptance. Byline given. Submit seasonal material 2 months in advance. Reports in 1 month. Sample copy for $3.

Nonfiction: Features, historical, interview, book reviews, photo feature. Query or submit complete ms. Length: 500-2,500 words.

Photos: Used with or without accompanying ms. Query or submit contact sheet or prints. Pays $5 for 5 × 7 b&w prints when money is available. Captions required.

Associations

Association publications allow writers to write for national audiences while covering local stories. If your town has a Kiwanis, Lions or Rotary Club chapter, one of its projects might merit a story in the club's magazine. If you are a member of the organization, find out before you write an article if the publication pays members for stories; some associations do not. In addition, some association publications gather their own club information and rely on freelancers solely for outside features. Be sure to find out what these policies are before you submit a manuscript. Club-financed magazines that carry material not directly related to the group's activities are classified by their subject matter in the Consumer and Trade sections.

COMEDY WRITERS ASSOCIATION NEWSLETTER, P.O. Box 023304, Brooklyn NY 11202-0066. (718)855-5057. Editor: Robert Makinson. 10% freelance written. Semiannual newsletter on comedy writing for association members. Estab. 1989. **Pays on acceptance.** Publishes ms an average of 3 months after acceptance. Byline given. Buys all rights. Reports in 2 weeks on queries; 1 month on mss. Sample copy for $4. Writer's guidelines for #10 SASE.

Nonfiction: How-to, humor, opinion, personal experience. "No exaggerations about the sales that you make and what you are paid. Be accurate." Query. Length: 250-500 words. "You may submit articles and fillers and byline will be given if used. But at present payment is only made for jokes."

Photos: State availability of photos with submission. Offers no additional payment for photos accepted with ms.

Fillers: Facts. Length: 100 words maximum.

Tips: "The easiest way to be mentioned in the publication is to submit short jokes. (Payment is $1-3 per joke.)"

DISCOVERY YMCA, YMCA of the USA, 101 N. Wacker Dr., Chicago IL 60606-7386. (312)269-0523. Editor: Mary Pyke. 40% freelance written. Quarterly magazine covering the YMCA movement in 50 states. "We concentrate on how YMCAs overcome obstacles and help solve pressing social problems." Estab. 1982. Circ. 105,000. **Pays on acceptance.** Publishes ms an average of 1-2 months after acceptance. Byline given. No kill fee. Makes work-for-hire assignments. Rarely accepts unsolicited submissions.

Nonfiction: Almost exclusively features/photo essays focusing on how local YMCAs meet community service needs. "No testimonies on how wonderful the YMCA is." Buys 9-10 mss/year. Query. Length: 2,500-15,000 words. Pays $550 for assigned articles; $300 for unsolicited articles. Pays expenses of writers on assignment.

Tips: "Send three or four pieces that you are really proud of having written. I don't need to see breadth of coverage but style and complete grasp of the subject. We are trying to diversify our pool of freelancers. We very much encourage writers of color to contact us. The YMCA is an incredibly diverse organization to match."

FEDCO REPORTER, A Publication Exclusively for FEDCO Members, Box 2605, Terminal Annex, Los Angeles CA 90051. (310)946-2511, ext. 3321. Editor: John Bregoli. 90% freelance written. Works with a small number of new/unpublished writers each year. Monthly catalog/magazine for FEDCO department store members. Estab. 1940. Circ. 2 million. **Pays on acceptance.** Publishes ms an average of 4 months after acceptance. Byline given. Offers $50 kill fee. Buys all rights. Query for electronic submissions. Reports in 6 weeks. Sample copy for 9 × 12 SAE with 4 first-class stamps. Writer's guidelines for SASE.

Nonfiction: The magazine publishes material on events, personalities, anecdotes, little-known happenings of historical significance relating to Southern California. No first person narrative. Buys 85 mss/year. Query with or without published clips or send complete ms. Length: 450 words. Pays $125.

Photos: State availability of photos. Reviews b&w and color slides. Pays $25.

Tips: "We publish tightly written, well-researched stories relating to the history of Southern California, regardless of prior writing experience."

KIWANIS, 3636 Woodview Trace, Indianapolis IN 46268-3196. Fax: (317)879-0204. Managing Editor: Chuck Jonak. 85% of feature articles freelance written. Buys about 40 mss/year. Magazine published 10 times/year for business and professional persons and their families. Estab. 1915. Circ. 285,000. **Pays on acceptance.** Buys first serial rights. Offers 40% kill fee. Publishes ms an average of 6 months after acceptance. Byline given. Reports within 2 months. Sample copy and writer's guidelines for 9 × 12 SAE with 5 first-class stamps.

• Ranked as one of the best markets for freelance writers in *Writer's Digest* magazine's annual "Top 100 Markets," January 1994.

Nonfiction: Articles about social and civic betterment, small-business concerns, science, education, religion, family, youth, health, recreation, etc. Emphasis on objectivity, intelligent analysis and thorough research of contemporary issues. Positive tone preferred. Concise, lively writing, absence of clichés, and impartial presentation of controversy required. When applicable, include information and quotations from international sources. Avoid writing strictly to a US audience. "We have a continuing need for articles of international interest. In addition, we are very interested in proposals that concern helping youth, particularly prenatal through age five: day care, developmentally appropriate education, early intervention for at-risk children, parent education, safety and health." Length: 2,500-3,000 words. Pays $600-1,000. "No fiction, personal essays, profiles, travel pieces, fillers or verse of any kind. A light or humorous approach is welcomed where the subject is appropriate and all other requirements are observed." Usually pays the expenses of writers on assignment. Query first. Must include SASE for response.

Photos: "We accept photos submitted with manuscripts. Our rate for a manuscript with good photos is higher than for one without." Model release and identification of subjects required. Buys one-time rights.

Tips: "We will work with any writer who presents a strong feature article idea applicable to our magazine's audience and who will prove he or she knows the craft of writing. First, obtain writer's guidelines and a sample copy. Study for general style and content. When querying, present detailed outline of proposed manuscript's focus, direction, and editorial intent. Indicate expert sources to be used for attribution, as well as article's tone and length. Present a well-researched, smoothly written manuscript that contains a 'human quality' with the use of anecdotes, practical examples, quotations, etc."

THE LION, 300 22nd St., Oak Brook IL 60521-8842. (708)571-5466. Fax: (703)571-8890. Senior Editor: Robert Kleinfelder. 35% freelance written. Works with a small number of new/unpublished writers each year. Monthly magazine covering service club organization for Lions Club members and their families. Estab. 1917. Circ. 600,000. **Pays on acceptance.** Publishes ms an average of 5 months after acceptance. Buys all rights. Byline given. Phone queries OK. Reports in 6 weeks. Free sample copy and writer's guidelines.

Nonfiction: Informational (issues of interest to civic-minded individuals) and photo feature (must be of a Lions Club service project). No travel, biography or personal experiences. Welcomes humor, if sophisticated but clean; no sensationalism. Prefers anecdotes in articles. Buys 4 mss/issue. Query. Length: 500-2,200. Pays $50-750. Sometimes pays the expenses of writers on assignment.

Photos: Purchased with or without accompanying ms or on assignment. Captions required. Query for photos. Black and white and color glossies at least 5 × 7 or 35mm color slides. Total purchase price for ms includes payment for photos accepted with ms. "Be sure photos are clear and as candid as possible."

Tips: "Incomplete details on how the Lions involved actually carried out a project and poor quality photos are the most frequent mistakes made by writers in completing an article assignment for us. We are geared increasingly to an international audience. Writers who travel internationally could query for possible assignments, although only locally-related expenses could be paid."

THE NEIGHBORHOOD WORKS, Building Alternative Visions for the City, Center for Neighborhood Technology, 2125 W. North Ave., Chicago IL 60647. (312)278-4800, ext. 113. Fax: (312)278-3840. Editor: Patti Wolter. 75% freelance written. Bimonthly magazine focusing on community organizing around issues of housing, energy, environment, transportation and economic development. "Writers must understand the importance of empowering people in low- and moderate-income city neighborhoods to solve local problems in housing, environment and local economy." Estab. 1978. Circ. 2,500. Pays on publication. Publishes ms an average of 2-4 months after acceptance. Byline given. Buys all rights. Submit seasonal/holiday material 4 months in advance. Accepts previously published articles. Send photocopy of article. Reports in 2 months. Sample copy and writer's guidelines for 9 × 12 SAE with 3 first-class stamps.
Nonfiction: Exposés; how-to (each issue has "reproducible feature" on such topics as organizing a neighborhood recycling program); interview/profile ("of someone active on one of our issues"); personal experience ("in our issue areas, e.g, community organizing"), technical (on energy conservation and alternative energy, environmental issues). Buys about 12 mss/year. Query with résumé and published clips or send complete ms. Length: 750-2,000 words. Pays $100-500. "We pay professional writers (people who make a living at it). We don't pay nonprofessionals and students but offer them a free subscription." Pays expenses of writers on assignment by previous agreement. Please include contact names, addresses and phone numbers of people interviewed in stories.
Photos: State availability of photos with submission. Reviews contact sheets and prints. Offers $10-35/photo. Captions and identification of subjects required. Buys one-time rights.
Columns/Departments: Reproducible features (how-to articles on issues of interest to neighborhood organizations), 1,000-2,000 words. Query with published clips. Pays $100-250. Around the Nation (300-word briefs on organizing efforts), pays $35.
Tips: "We are increasingly interested in stories from cities other than Chicago (our home base)."

THE OPTIMIST MAGAZINE, Optimist International, 4494 Lindell Blvd., St. Louis MO 63108. (314)371-6000. Fax: (314)371-6006. Editor: Gary S. Bradley. 10% freelance written. Magazine published 9 times/year about the work of Optimist clubs and members for members of the Optimist clubs in the United States and Canada. Circ. 165,000. **Pays on acceptance.** Publishes ms an average of 4 months after acceptance. Buys first North American serial rights. Submit seasonal material 3 months in advance. Reports in 1 week. Sample copy and writer's guidelines for 9 × 12 SAE with 4 first-class stamps.
Nonfiction: "We want articles about the activities of local Optimist clubs. These volunteer community-service clubs are constantly involved in projects, aimed primarily at helping young people. With over 4,000 Optimist clubs in the US and Canada, writers should have ample resources. Some large metropolitan areas boast several dozen clubs. We are also interested in feature articles on individual club members who have in some way distinguished themselves, either in their club work or their personal lives. Good photos for all articles are a plus and can mean a bigger check." Buys 1-2 mss/issue. Query. "Submit a letter that conveys your ability to turn out a well-written article and tells exactly what the scope of the article will be." Length: 1,000-1,500 words. Pays $200 and up.
Photos: State availability of photos. Payment negotiated. Captions preferred. Buys all rights. "No mug shots or people lined up against the wall shaking hands."
Tips: "Find out what the Optimist clubs in your area are doing, then find out if we'd be interested in an article on a specific club project. All of our clubs are eager to talk about what they're doing. Just ask them and you'll probably have an article idea."

PERSPECTIVE, Pioneer Clubs, P.O. Box 788, Wheaton IL 60189-0788. (708)293-1600. Fax: 708-293-3053. Editor: Rebecca Powell Parat. 15% freelance written. Works with a number of new/unpublished writers each year. Triannual magazine for "volunteer leaders of clubs for girls and boys ages 2 through grade 12. Clubs are sponsored by local churches throughout North America." Estab. 1967. Circ. 24,000. **Pays on acceptance.** Publishes ms an average of 6 months after acceptance. Buys full rights for assigned articles, first North American serial rights for unsolicited mss, and second serial (reprint) rights to material originally published elsewhere. Submit seasonal/holiday material 9 months in advance. Accepts previously published material. Send photocopy of article or typed ms with rights for sale noted. Reports in 6 weeks. Writer's guidelines and sample for $1.75 and 9 × 12 SAE with 6 first-class stamps.
Nonfiction: Informational (relationship skills, leadership skills); inspirational (stories of leaders and children in Pioneer Clubs); interview (Christian education leaders, club leaders); and personal experience (of club leaders). Buys 8-12 mss/year. Byline given. Length: 500-1,500 words. Pays $25-90.
Columns/Departments: Storehouse (game, activity, outdoor activity, service project suggestions—all related to club projects for ages 2 through grade 12. Buys 4-6 mss/year. Submit complete ms. Length: 150-250 words. Pays $8-15.
Tips: "We only assign major features to writers who have previously proven that they know us and our constituency. Submit articles directly related to club work, practical in nature, i.e., ideas for leader training in communication, discipline, teaching skills. Writers who have contact with a Pioneer Club program in their

area and who are interested in working on assignment are welcome to contact us."

RECREATION NEWS, Official Publication of the League of Federal Recreation Associations, Inc., Icarus Publishers, Inc., P.O. Box 32335, Calvert Station, Washington DC 20007-0635. (202)965-6960. Editor: Sam Polson. 85% freelance written. Monthly guide to leisure-time activities for federal workers covering outdoor recreation, travel, fitness and indoor pastimes. Estab. 1979. Circ. 100,000. Pays on publication. Publishes ms an average of 8 months after acceptance. Byline given. Buys first rights and second serial (reprint) rights. Submit seasonal/holiday material 8 months in advance. Accepts simultaneous and previously published submissions. Send photocopy of article with information about where and when it previously appeared. For reprints pays $50. Reports in 1-2 months. Sample copy and writer's guidelines for 9 × 12 SAE with $1.05 postage.
Nonfiction: Articles Editor. Leisure travel (no international travel); sports; hobbies; historical/nostalgic (Washington-related); personal experience (with recreation, life in Washington). Special issues: skiing (December); education (August). Query with clips of published work. Length: 800-2,000 words. Pays from $50-300.
Photos: Photo editor. State availability of photos with query letter or ms. Uses b&w prints. Pays $25. Uses color transparency on cover only. Pays $50-125 for transparency. Captions and identification of subjects required.
Tips: "Our writers generally have a few years of professional writing experience and their work runs to the lively and conversational. We like more manuscripts in a wide range of recreational topics, including the off-beat. The areas of our publication most open to freelancers are general articles on travel and sports, both participational and spectator, also historic in the DC area."

REVIEW, A Publication of North American Benefit Association, 1338 Military St., P.O. Box 5020, Port Huron MI 48061-5020. (313)985-5191, ext. 29. Editor: Janice U. Whipple. Associate Editor: Patricia J. Samar. 30% freelance written. Works only with published/established writers. Quarterly magazine published for NABA's primarily women-membership to help them care for themselves and their families. Estab. 1892. Circ. 40,000. **Pays on acceptance.** Publishes ms an average of 1 year after acceptance. Byline given. Not copyrighted. Buys one-time, simultaneous and second serial (reprint) rights. Submit seasonal/holiday material 6 months in advance. Accepts simultaneous and previously published submissions. Send tearsheet or photocopy of article or send ms with rights for sale noted and information about when and where ms previously appeared. Reports in 2 months. Sample copy for 9 × 12 SAE with 4 first-class stamps. Writer's guidelines for #10 SASE.
Nonfiction: Looking for general interest or how-to stories of interest to women aged 25-44, such as career/employment and/or juggling work and family responsibilities in the 90s; health and fitness (mental and physical); parenting children of all ages as a parent of any age; parenting your parents; and other relevant issues. Also interested in objective news/feature stories about current events and issues pertaining to women and issues of concern to them. Profiles of outstanding prominent women—particularly those whose prominence is related to volunteerism—are also sought. Buys 4-10 mss/year. Send complete ms. Length: 1,000 to 2,000 words. Pays $150 to $500 per ms.
Photos: Not interested in photos at this time, unless accompanied by a ms. Model release and identification of subjects required.

THE ROTARIAN, Rotary International, 1560 Sherman Ave., Evanston IL 60201-1461. (708)866-3000. Fax: (708)328-8554 or (708)866-9732. Editor: Willmon L. White. Managing Editor: Charles W. Pratt. 40% freelance written. Monthly magazine for Rotarian business and professional men and women and their families, schools, libraries, hospitals, etc. "Articles should appeal to an international audience and in some way help Rotarians help other people. The organization's rationale is one of hope, encouragement and belief in the power of individuals talking and working together." Estab. 1911. Circ. 524,475. **Pays on acceptance.** Byline sometimes given. Kill fee negotiable. Buys one-time or all rights. Accepts previously published submissions. Send tearsheet or photocopy of article or typed ms with rights for sale noted and information about when and where the article previously appeared. Reports in 3 weeks. Sample copy for 9 × 12 SAE with 6 first-class stamps. Writer's guidelines for #10 SASE.
Nonfiction: Essays, general interest, humor, inspirational, photo feature, travel, business, environment. No fiction, religious or political articles. Query with published clips. Negotiates payment.
Photos: State availability of photos with submission. Reviews contact sheets and transparencies. Usually buys one-time rights.
Columns/Departments: Manager's Memo (business), Executive Health, Executive Lifestyle, Earth Diary and Trends. Length: 800 words. Query.
Tips: "Study issues, then query with SASE."

THE SAMPLE CASE, The Order of United Commercial Travelers of America, 632 N. Park St., Box 159019, Columbus OH 43215-8619. (614)228-3276. Editor: Megan Woitovich. Bimonthly magazine covering news for members of the United Commercial Travelers emphasizing fraternalism for its officers and active membership. Estab. 1888. Circ. 140,000. Pays on publication. Buys one-time rights. Reports in 3 months. Submit seasonal/holiday material 6 months in advance. Simultaneous queries and submissions OK. Accepts previously published material. Send tearsheet or photocopy of article or ms with rights for sale noted and information about where and when the article previously appeared. Pays same for reprints as for original articles.

Nonfiction: Articles on health/fitness/safety; family; hobbies/entertainment; fraternal/civic activities; business finance/insurance; travel in the US and Canada; food/cuisine.

Photos: David Knapp, Art Director. State availability of photos with ms. Prefers color prints. Pay negotiable. Captions required.

SCOUTING, Boy Scouts of America, 1325 W. Walnut Hill Lane, P.O. Box 75015, Irving TX 75015-2079. (214)580-2355. Fax: (214)580-2079. Editor: Ernest Doclar. Executive Editor: Jon Halter. 90% freelance written. Bimonthly magazine on Scouting activities for adult leaders of the Boy Scouts. Estab. 1913. Circ. 1 million. **Pays on acceptance.** Publishes ms an average of 4 months after acceptance. Byline given. Buys first North American serial rights. Submit seasonal/holiday material 4 months in advance. Reports in 2 weeks. Sample copy for $1 and #10 SAE with 4 first-class stamps. Writer's guidelines for #10 SASE.

Nonfiction: Buys 60 mss/year. Query with published clips. Length: 1,500-2,000 words. Pays $400-600 for assigned articles; $200-500 for unsolicited articles. Pays expenses of writers on assignment.

Photos: State availability of photos with submission. Reviews contact sheets and transparencies. Identification of subjects required. Buys one-time rights.

Columns/Departments: Family Quiz (quiz on topics of family interest), 1,000 words; Way it Was (Scouting history), 1,200 words. Family Talk (family—raising kids, etc.), 1,200 words. Buys 6 mss/year. Query. Pays $200-400.

SONS OF NORWAY VIKING, Sons of Norway, 1455 W. Lake St., Minneapolis MN 55408. Fax: (612)827-0658. Editor: Karin B. Miller. 50% freelance written. Prefers to work with published/established writers. Monthly membership magazine for Sons of Norway, a fraternal and cultural organization, covering Norwegian culture, heritage, history, Norwegian-American topics, modern Norwegian society, genealogy and travel. "Our audience is Norwegian-Americans (middle-aged or older) with strong interest in their heritage and anything Norwegian. Many have traveled to Norway." Estab. 1903. Circ. 70,000. **Pays on acceptance.** Publishes ms an average of 8 months after acceptance. Byline given. Offers 25% kill fee. Buys first North American serial and second serial (reprint) rights. Submit seasonal/holiday material 6 months in advance. Accepts previously published material. Send tearsheet of article. Pays 25% of amount paid for original article. Reports in 4 months. Free sample copy and writer's guidelines on request.

Nonfiction: General interest, historical/nostalgic, interview/profile, youth-related and travel—all having a Norwegian angle. "Articles should not be personal impressions nor strictly factual but well-researched and conveyed in a warm and audience-involving manner. Does it entertain *and* inform?" Buys 30 mss/year. Query. Length: 1,500 words. Generally pays $100-350.

Photos: Reviews transparencies and prints. Generally pays $50/photo; $100 for cover color photo. Identification of subjects required. Buys one-time rights.

Tips: "Show familiarity with Norwegian culture and subject matter. Our readers are knowledgeable about Norway and quick to note misstatements. Articles about modern Norway and youth are most open to freelancers."

VFW MAGAZINE, Veterans of Foreign Wars of the United States, 406 W. 34th St., Kansas City MO 64111. (816)756-3390. Fax: (816)968-1169. Editor: Rich Kolb. 40% freelance written. Monthly magazine on veterans' affairs, military history, patriotism, defense and current events. "*VFW Magazine* goes to its members worldwide, all having served honorably in the armed forces overseas from World War II through Somalia." Circ. 2.1 million. **Pays on acceptance.** Offers 50% kill fee on commissioned articles. Buys first rights. Submit seasonal/holiday material 6 months in advance. Submit detailed query letter, résumé and sample clips. Reports in 2 months. Sample copy for 9×12 SAE with 5 first-class stamps.

• *VFW Magazine* is becoming more current-events oriented.

Nonfiction: Interview/profile and veterans' affairs. Buys 25-30 mss/year. Query. Length: 1,500 words. Pays $500 maximum unless otherwise negotiated.

Photos: Send photos with submission. Reviews contact sheets, negatives, transparencies and prints. Captions, model releases and identification of subjects required. Buys first North American rights.

WOODMEN, 1700 Farnam St., Omaha NE 68102. (402)271-7211. Fax: (402)271-7269. Editor: Scott Darling. Assistant Editor: Billie Jo Foust. 10% freelance written. Works with a small number of new/unpublished writers each year. Bimonthly magazine published by Woodmen of the World Life Insurance Society for "people of all ages in all walks of life. We have both adult and child readers from all types of American families." Circ. 500,000. Not copyrighted. Buys 2-3 mss/year. **Pays on acceptance.** Byline given. Buys one-time rights. Publishes ms an average of 2 months after acceptance. Submit seasonal material 3 months in advance. Will consider simultaneous submissions. Accepts previously published articles. Send typed ms with rights for sale noted and information about when and where the article previously appeared. For reprints pays

100% of the amount paid for an original article. Reports in 5 weeks. Free sample copy. Writer's guidelines for #10 SASE.

Nonfiction: "General interest articles which appeal to the American family—travel, history, art, new products, how-to, sports, hobbies, food, home decorating, family expenses, etc. We want more 'consumer type' articles, humor, historical articles, think pieces, nostalgia, photo articles." Submit complete ms. Length: 1,500 words or less. Pays $10 minimum, 10¢/word.

Photos: Purchased with or without ms; captions optional "but suggested." Uses 8×10 glossy prints, 4×5 transparencies ("and possibly down to 35mm"). Payment "depends on use." Color and b&w prices vary according to use and quality.

Astrology, Metaphysical and New Age

Magazines in this section carry articles ranging from shamanism to extraterrestrial phenomena. The following publications regard astrology, psychic phenomena, metaphysical experiences and related subjects as sciences or as objects of serious study. Each has an individual personality and approach to these phenomena. If you want to write for these publications, be sure to read them carefully before submitting.

FATE, Llewellyn Worlwide, Ltd., P.O. Box 64383, St. Paul MN 55164-0383. Fax: (612)291-1908. 70% freelance written. Estab. 1901. Buys all rights. Byline given. Pays on publication. Sample copy and writer's guidelines for $3 and 9×12 SAE with 5 first-class stamps. Query. Reports in 3 months.

Nonfiction and Fillers: Personal psychic and mystical experiences, 400-600 words. Pays $25. Articles on parapsychology, Fortean phenomena, cryptozoology, parapsychology, spiritual healing, flying saucers, new frontiers of science, and mystical aspects of ancient civilizations, 2,000-5,000 words. Must include complete authenticating details. Prefers interesting accounts of single events rather than roundups. "We very frequently accept manuscripts from new writers; the majority are individual's first-person accounts of their own psychic/mystical/spiritual experiences. We do need to have all details, where, when, why, who and what, included for complete documentation. We ask for a notarized statement attesting to truth of the article." Pays 10¢/word. Fillers must be be fully authenticated also, and on similar topics. Length: 100-300 words.

Photos: Buys slides or prints with mss. Pays $10.

HEART DANCE, 473 Miller Ave., Mill Valley CA 94941. (415)383-2525. Editor: Ms. Randy Peyser. The largest monthly New Age calendar of events for Northern California. Monthly magazine focusing on New Age spirituality and contemporary human awareness. Estab. 1990. Circ. 50,000. Pays on publication, $25 full page articles, $5-10 quotes or excerpts, plus many copies to impress your friends with. Publishes ms an average of 1-12 months after acceptance. Byline given. You keep the copyright. Buys one-time rights. Accepts simultaneous submissions, but don't overwhelm them. Accepts previously published articles. Send photocopy of article and information about when and where the article previously appeared. For reprints pays $25. Reports back within 1 month on all submissions. Sample copy and writer's guidelines for 9×12 SASE with 98¢ postage.

Nonfiction: The focus—personal experience stories, near-death experiences, or experiences of having been touched by something greater than what we normally perceive. Humor is also welcomed. Not interested in how-to articles, or articles that refer to a specific self-help technique, specific type of spirituality or a specific religion. Not interested in poetry, UFO's, or any form of divination—astrology, numerology, etc. Articles *must be* a real heart-sharing.

Tips: "We publish the kind of articles that people cut out and put on their refrigerators, or make copies and send to their friends; articles that inspire, that really touch people's hearts and make a difference in the quality of their lives. Put your name/address/phone number on every page you submit. Extra points for typed submissions. Please send us a copy, not your original. Contact us and share your greatest gifts!"

‡NEW AGE JOURNAL, Rising Star Associates, 42 Pleasant St., Watertown MA 02172. Editor: Peggy Taylor. Editorial Manager: Lisa Horvitz. 35% freelance written. Works with a small number of new/unpublished writers each year. Bimonthly magazine emphasizing "personal fulfillment and social change. The audience we reach is college-educated, social-service/hi-tech oriented, 25-45 years of age, concerned about social values, humanitarianism and balance in personal life." Payment negotiated. Publishes ms an average of 5 months after acceptance. Byline given. Offers 25% kill fee. Buys first North American serial and reprint rights. Submit seasonal/holiday material 6 months in advance. Accepts simultaneous and previously published submissions. Send photocopy of article and information about when and where the article previously appeared. Reports in 2 months on queries. Sample copy for $5 and 9×12 SAE. Writer's guidelines for #10 SASE.

Nonfiction: Book excerpts, exposé, general interest, how-to (travel on business, select a computer, reclaim land, plant a garden, behavior, trend pieces, humor, inspirational, interview/profile, new product, food, sci-tech, nutrition, holistic health, education, personal experience. Buys 60-80 mss/year. Query with published clips. "Written queries only—no phone calls. The process of decision making takes time and involves more than one editor. An answer cannot be given over the phone." Length: 500-4,000 words. Pays $50-2,500. Pays the expenses of writers on assignment.

Photos: State availability of photos with submission. Model releases and identification of subjects required. Buys one-time rights.

Columns/Departments: Body/Mind; Reflections; First Person. Buys 60-80 mss/year. Query with published clips. Length: 750-1,500 words. Pays $100-400.

Tips: "Submit short, specific news items to the Upfront department. Query first with clips. A query is one to two paragraphs—if you need more space than that to *present* the idea, then you don't have a clear grip on it. The next open area is columns: First Person and Reflections often take first-time contributors. Read the magazine and get a sense of type of writing run in these two columns. In particular we are interested in seeing inspirational, first-person pieces that highlight an engaging idea, experience or issue. We are also looking for new cutting edge thinking."

NEW FRONTIER, Magazine of Transformation, New Frontier Education Society, 101 Cuthbert St., Philadelphia PA 19106. Editor: Sw. Virato. 80% freelance written. Monthly New Age magazine. "*New Frontier* magazine writers should embody a sense of oneness with the universe. They should come from a basic spiritual model, and essentially be a New Age person. They should see the universe and all life from a holistic view." Estab. 1980. Circ. 60,000. Pays on publication. Publishes ms an average of 6 months after acceptance. Byline given. Offers 20% kill fee or $25. Buys first North American serial, first, one-time or second serial (reprint) rights or makes work-for-hire assignments. Editorial lead time 3 months. Submit seasonal material 4 months in advance. Accepts previously published articles. Send tearsheet or photocopy of article, typed ms with rights noted and information about when and where the article previously appeared. For reprints pays 20% of the amount paid for an original article. Query for electronic submissions. MS/DOS format, MicroSoft Word, or any popular word processor program, 5¼ or 3½" floppy. Reports in 6 weeks on queries. Sample copy for $2. Writer's guidelines for #10 SASE.

Nonfiction: Book excerpts, essays, expose, general interest, historical/nostalgic, how-to, humor, inspirational, interview/profile, new product, opinion, personal experience, photo feature and "anything with awareness. Nothing dealing with hate, violence, attack, war, crime, drugs, superficial sex, pornography, meat products or unconsciousness in general." Buys 15 mss/year. Query with published clips. Length: 1,500-4,000 words. Pays $100 minimum for assigned articles, $50 for unsolicited articles or 5¢/word. Sometimes pays expenses of writers on assignment (limit agreed upon in advance).

Photos: State availability of photos with submission. Reviews contact sheets and 5×7 prints. Negotiates payment individually. Buys one-time rights.

Fillers: Newsbreaks. Buys 20/year. Length: 100-300 words. Pays $10-25.

Tips: "Our writers must have an awareness of the subject, and the subject must deal with a transformation of human consciousness in any of the following areas: astrology, ecology, spirituality, self-help, holistic health, metaphysics, health food, Eastern philosophy, yoga, cosmic consciousness, social responsibility, altered states, etc."

PARABOLA, The Magazine of Myth and Tradition, The Society for the Study of Myth and Tradition, 656 Broadway, New York NY 10012-2317. (212)505-6200. Editors: Ellen Draper/Virginia Baron. Quarterly magazine on mythology, tradition and comparative religion. "*Parabola* is devoted to the exploration of the quest for meaning as expressed in the myths, symbols, and tales of the religious traditions. Particular emphasis is on the relationship between this wisdom and contemporary life." Estab. 1976. Circ. 40,000. Pays on publication. Publishes ms 3 months after acceptance. Byline given. Offers kill fee for assigned articles only (usually $100). Buys first North American serial, first, one-time or second serial (reprint) rights. Editorial lead time 4 months. Accepts previously published and simultaneous submissions. Send photocopy of article or short story (must include copy of copyright page), information about when and where the article previously appeared. Publishes novel excerpts. Query for electronic submissions. IBM-compatible or Macintosh disks. Requires hard copy accompanying disk. Reports in 2-3 weeks on queries; on mss "variable—for articles directed to a particular theme, we usually respond the month before or the month of the deadline (so for an April 15 deadline, we are likely to respond in March or April). Articles not directed to themes may wait four months or more!" Sample copy for $6 current issue; $8 back issue. Writers guidelines and list of themes free on request.

Nonfiction: Book excerpts, essays, inspirational, personal experience, photo feature and religious. 1995— "The Stranger," deadline Jan. 15 1995; "Language," deadline Apr. 15 1995; "Eros," deadline July 15 1995; "The Soul," deadline Oct. 15. No articles not related to specific themes. Buys 4-8 mss/year. Query. Length:

The double dagger before a listing indicates that the listing is new in this edition. New markets are often more receptive to freelance submissions.

2,000-4,000 words. Pays $200 minimum. Sometimes pays expenses of writers on assignment.

Photos: State availability of photos with submission. Reviews contact sheets, any transparencies and prints. Identification of subjects required. Buys one-time rights.

Columns/Departments: Contact: David Appelbaum (book reviews); Ellen Draper/Virginia Baron (Tangents); Natalie Baan (Epicycles). Tangents (reviews of film, exhibits, dance, theater, video, music relating to theme of issue), 2,000-4,000 words; Book Reviews (reviews of current books in religion, spirituality, mythology and tradition), 500 words; Epicycles (retellings of myths and folk tales of all cultures—no fiction or made-up mythology!), under 2,000 words. Buys 2-6 unsolicited mss/year. Query. Pays $75-300.

Fiction: "We *very* rarely publish fiction; must relate to upcoming theme. Query recommended." Query.

Poetry: Free verse, traditional (must relate to theme). Buys 2-4 poems/year. Pays $50-75.

SHAMAN'S DRUM, A Journal of Experiential Shamanism, Cross-Cultural Shamanism Network, P.O. Box 430, Willits CA 95490-0430. (707)459-0486. Editor: Timothy White. Associate Editor: Carolyn Drewes. 75% freelance written. Quarterly educational magazine of cross-cultural shamanism. "*Shaman's Drum* seeks contributions directed toward a general but well-informed audience. Our intent is to expand, challenge, and refine our readers' and our understanding of shamanism in practice. Topics include indigenous medicineway practices, contemporary shamanic healers and healing practices, ecstatic spiritual practices, and contemporary shamanic psychotherapies. Our overall focus is cross-cultural, but our editorial approach is culture-specific—we prefer that authors focus on specific ethnic traditions or personal practices about which they have significant firsthand experience. We are looking for examples of not only how shamanism has transformed individual lives but also practical ways it can help ensure survival of life on the planet. We want material that captures the heart and feeling of shamanism and that can inspire people to direct action and participation, and to explore shamanism in greater depth." Estab. 1985. Circ. 18,500. Publishes ms 6 months after acceptance. Buys first North American serial and first rights. Editorial lead time 1 year. Reports in 3 months. Sample copy for $5. Writer's guidelines for #10 SASE.

Nonfiction: Book excerpts, essays, interview/profile (please query), opinion, personal experience, photo feature. *No fiction, poetry or fillers.* Buys 16 mss/year. Send complete ms. Length: 5,000-8,000. "We pay 5-10¢/word, depending on how much we have to edit. We also send two copies and tearsheets in addition to cash payment."

Photos: Send photos with submission. Reviews contact sheets, transparencies and all sizes prints. Offers $40-50/photo. Identification of subjects required. Buys one-time rights.

Columns/Departments: Contact: Judy Wells, Earth Circles Editor. Earth Circles (news format, concerned with issues, events, organizations related to shamanism, indigenous peoples and caretaking Earth. Relevant clippings also sought. Clippings paid with copies and credit line), 500-1,500 words. Buys 8 mss/year. Send complete ms. Pays 5-10¢/word. Reviews: contact Carolyn Drewes, Associate Editor (in-depth reviews of books, records/tapes/CD's about shamanism or closely related subjects such as indigenous lifestyles, ethnobotany, transpersonal healing and ecstatic spirituality), 500-1,500 words. "Please query us first and we will send *Reviewer's Guidelines*." Pays 5-10¢/word.

Tips: "All articles must have a clear relationship to shamanism, but may be on topics which have not traditionally been defined as shamanic. We prefer original material that is based on, or illustrated with, first-hand knowledge and personal experience. Articles should be well documented with descriptive examples and pertinent background information. Photographs and illustrations of high quality are always welcome and can help sell articles."

UFO MAGAZINE, A Forum on Extraordinary Theories and Phenomena, UFO Media Group, P.O. Box 1053, Sunland CA 91041. (818)951-1250. 65% freelance written. Bimonthly magazine covering UFO phenomena, events and theories. "*UFO Magazine* is the only newsstand-quality publication applying journalistic standards to the UFO subject. It is the most legitimate vehicle for UFO news and information now available to the general public." Pays on publication. Publishes ms 2-6 months after acceptance. Byline given. No kill fee. Buys one-time rights. Submit seasonal/holiday material 6 months in advance. Accepts previously published submissions. Prefer electronic submissions, IBM-compatible, ASCII. Reports in 3 months on queries. Does not return unsolicited mss. Sample copy for $5.45. Free writer's guidelines.

Nonfiction: Vicki Cooper, Editor. Book excerpts, essays, exposé, general interest, historical/nostalgic, interview/profile, opinion, personal experience, photo feature, technical. "Please, no fiction or fanatical material!" Buys 15-20 mss/year. Query. Length: 500-3,500 words. Pays $25-100 for assigned articles, or "more in some cases;" $25 maximum for unsolicited articles. "Previously unpublished UFO researchers are paid with copies unless other arrangements are made." Sometimes pays expenses of writers on assignment.

Photos: Send photos with submission. Reviews contact sheets, transparencies and 5×7 prints. Offers no additional payment for photos accepted with ms from writers. Offers $5-25/photo from professional photographers only. "Reprints can be given with credit to *UFO Magazine*."

Columns/Departments: Forum (opinion pieces usually based on factual UFO cases), 500-2,000 words; News Section (news briefs and special aspects of UFO phenomena), 500-1,500 words; International Reports (UFO news from around the world) 500-2,000 words; Book and video reviews, 250-1,000 words. Buys 15-20 mss/year. Send complete ms.

Fillers: Facts, newsbreaks. Buys 3-4/year. Pays $5-10.

Tips: "Our best submissions come from writers who have a working familiarity with the UFO subject and the research that has ensued in the modern UFO era (since 1947). But many potential contributors could also be those who have an abiding *private* fascination with UFOs along with exceptional writing skills! *UFO Magazine* is in constant need of comprehensive news-features on vital cases and/or issues concerning UFOs and related topics. The UFO subject is inextricably linked to the policies and practices of the US military and intelligence agencies, so our magazine will venture into those sensitive avenues at times."

‡**WHOLE LIFE TIMES**, Suite B, 21225 Pacific Coast Highway, Malibu CA 90265. (310)317-4200. Contact: Editor. Monthly consumer tabloid covering holistic thinking. Estab. 1979. Circ. 50,000. Pays on publication. Buys first North American serial rights. Occasionally buys reprints. Query for electronic submissions. Sample copy for $3. Writer's guidelines for #10 SASE.

Nonfiction: Book excerpts, exposé, general interest, how-to, humor, inspirational, interview/profile, spiritual, technical, travel. Buys 25 mss/year. Query with published clips or send complete ms. Length: 1,200-2,000 words. Pays 5¢/word.

Tips: "Queries should show an awareness of current topics of interest in our subject area. We are happy to see queries that address topics in a political context."

Automotive and Motorcycle

Publications in this section detail the maintenance, operation, performance, racing and judging of automobiles and recreational vehicles. Publications that treat vehicles as means of shelter instead of as a hobby or sport are classified in the Travel, Camping and Trailer category. Journals for service station operators and auto and motorcycle dealers are located in the Trade Auto and Truck section.

AMERICAN IRON MAGAZINE, TAM Communications Inc., 6 Prowitt St., Norwalk CT 06855. (203)855-0008. Fax: (203)852-9980. Managing Editor: Jonathan Gourlay. 60% freelance written. Monthly magazine covering Harley-Davidson and Indian motorcycles, with a definite emphasis on Harleys. Circ. 80,000. Pays on publication. Publishes ms an average of 6 months after acceptance. Byline given. Query for electronic submissions. Reports in 6 weeks on queries with SASE. Sample copy for $3.

Nonfiction: "Clean and non-offensive. Stories include bike features, touring stories, how-to tech stories with step-by-step photos, historical pieces, profiles, events, opinion and various topics of interest to the people who ride Harley-Davidsons." No fiction. Buys 60 mss/year. Pays $250 for touring articles with photos to first-time writers. Payment for other articles varies.

Photos: Submit color slides or large transparencies. No prints. Send SASE for return of photos.

Tips: "We're not looking for stories about the top ten biker biker bars or do-it-yourself tattoos. We're looking for articles about motorcycling, the people and the lifestyle. If you understand the Harley mystique and can write well, you've got a good chance of being published."

AMERICAN MOTORCYCLIST, American Motorcyclist Association, P.O. Box 6114, Westerville OH 43081-6114. (614)891-2425. Executive Editor: Greg Harrison. Monthly magazine for "enthusiastic motorcyclists, investing considerable time and money in the sport. We emphasize the motorcyclist, not the vehicle." Estab. 1942. Circ. 175,000. Pays on publication. Rights purchased vary with author and material. Pays 25-50% kill fee. Byline given. Query with SASE. Submit seasonal/holiday material 4 months in advance. Reports in 1 month. Free sample copy and writer's guidelines.

Nonfiction: How-to (different and/or unusual ways to use a motorcycle or have fun on one); historical (the heritage of motorcycling, particularly as it relates to the AMA); interviews (with interesting personalities in the world of motorcycling); photo feature (quality work on any aspect of motorcycling); technical articles. No product evaluations or stories on motorcycling events not sanctioned by the AMA. Buys 20-25 mss/year. Query. Length: 500 words minimum. Pays minimum $6.50/published column inch.

Photos: Purchased with or without accompanying ms or on assignment. Captions required. Query. Pays $40/photo minimum.

Tips: "Accuracy and reliability are prime factors in our work with freelancers. We emphasize the rider, not the motorcycle itself. It's always best to query us first and the further in advance the better to allow for scheduling."

AMERICAN WOMAN MOTORSCENE, (formerly *American Woman Motorsports*), American Woman Motorscene, 2830 Santa Monica Blvd., Santa Monica CA 90404. (310)829-0012. Fax: (310)453-8850. Publisher: Courtney Caldwell. Editor-at-Large: Sue Elliott. 40% freelance written. Bimonthly magazine on women in automotive. "We are geared towards working women who are purchasing the 79 million vehicles today. Estab. 1988. Circ. 50,000. Pays on publication an average of 2 months after acceptance. Byline sometimes given. Buys first rights and second serial (reprint) rights or makes work-for-hire assignments. Submit seasonal/

holiday material 4 months in advance. Accepts previously published submissions. Send tearsheet or photocopy of article and information about when and where the article previously appeared. For reprints, pays 50% of the amount paid for an original article. Query for electronic submissions. Reports in 2 months. Free sample copy.

Nonfiction: Humor, inspirational, interview/profile, new product, photo feature, travel, lifestyle. No articles depicting women in motorsports or professions that are degrading, negative or not upscale. Buys 30 mss/year. Send complete ms. Length 250-1,000 words. Pays 10¢/word for assigned articles; 7¢ for unsolicited articles. Sometimes pays expenses of writers on assignment.

Photos: Send photos with submission. Reviews contact sheets. Black and white or Kodachrome 64 preferred. Offers $10-50/photo. Captions, model releases and identification of subjects required. Buys all rights.

Columns/Departments: Lipservice (from readers); Tech Talk: (The Mall) new products; Tale End (News); 100-150 words.

Fillers: Anecdotes, facts, gags to be illustrated by cartoonist, newsbreaks, short humor. Buys 12/year. Length: 25-100 words. Negotiable.

Tips: "It helps if the writer is into motorcycles, trucks and cars. It is a special sport. If he/she is not involved in motorsports, he/she should have a positive point of view of motorsports and be willing to learn more about the subject. We are a lifestyle type of publication more than a technical magazine. Positive attitudes wanted."

AUTOMOBILE QUARTERLY, The Connoisseur's Magazine of Motoring Today, Yesterday, and Tomorrow, Kutztown Publishing Co., 15040 Kutztown Rd., Kutztown PA 19530-0348. (215)683-3169. Fax: (215)683-3287. *Note: In January 1995 the area code will change to (610).* Publishing Director: Jonathan Stein. Managing Editor: Karla Rosenbusch. Contact: John Heilig, associate editor. 85% freelance written. Quarterly magazine covering "automotive history, hardcover, excellent photography." Estab. 1962. Circ. 17,000. **Pays on acceptance.** Publishes ms an average of 1 year after acceptance. Byline given. Buys first North American serial rights. Editorial lead time 9 months. Reports in 2 weeks on queries; 2 months on mss. Sample copy for $19.95.

Nonfiction: Essays, historical/nostalgic, photo feature, technical. Buys 25 mss/year. Query. Length: 5,000-8,000 words. Pays approximately 30¢/word. Sometimes pays expenses of writers on assignment.

Photos: State availability of photos with submission. Reviews 4×5, 35mm and 120 transparencies. Buys one-time rights.

Tips: "Study the publication."

BRACKET RACING USA, 299 Market St., Saddle Brook NJ 07663. (201)712-9300. Editor: Dale Wilson. Managing Editor: Diane Boccadoro. Magazine published 8 times/year covering bracket cars and bracket racing. Estab. 1989. Circ. 45,000. Pays on publication. Publishes ms 6 months after acceptance. Byline given. Buys first North American serial rights. Query for electronic submissions. Sample copy for $3 and 9×12 SAE with 5 first-class stamps.

Nonfiction: Automotive how-to and technical. Buys 35 mss/year. Query. Length: 500-1,500 words. Pays $150/page for all articles. Sometimes pays expenses of writers on assignment.

Photos: Send photos with submission.

BRITISH CAR, P.O. Box 9099, Canoga Park CA 91309. (818)710-1234. Fax: (818)710-1877. Editor: Dave Destler. 50% freelance written. Bimonthly magazine covering British cars. "We focus upon the cars built in Britain, the people who buy them, drive them, collect them, love them. Writers must be among the aforementioned. Written by enthusiasts for enthusiasts." Estab. 1985. Circ. 30,000. Pays on publication. Publishes ms an average of 3 months after acceptance. Byline given. Buys all rights, unless other arrangements made. Submit seasonal/holiday material 4 months in advance. Query for electronic submissions. Reports in 1 month. Sample copy for $4. Writer's guidelines for #10 SASE.

• The editor is looking for more technical and restoration articles by knowledgeable enthusiasts and professionals.

Nonfiction: Historical/nostalgic; how-to (repair or restoration of a specific model or range of models, new technique or process); humor (based upon a realistic nonfiction situation); interview/profile (famous racer, designer, engineer, etc.); photo feature; technical. Buys 30 mss/year. Send complete ms. "Include SASE if submission is to be returned." Length: 750-4,500 words. Pays $2-5/column inch for assigned articles; $2-3/column inch for unsolicited articles.

Photos: Send photos with submission. Reviews transparencies and prints. Offers $15-75/photo. Captions and identification of subjects required. Buys all rights, unless otherwise arranged.

Columns/Departments: Update (newsworthy briefs of interest, not too timely for bimonthly publication), approximately 50-175 words. Buys 20 mss/year. Send complete ms.

Tips: "Thorough familiarity of subject is essential. *British Car* is read by experts and enthusiasts who can see right through superficial research. Facts are important, and must be accurate. Writers should ask themselves 'I know I'm interested in this story, but will most of *British Car's* readers appreciate it?' "

CAR AND DRIVER, 2002 Hogback Rd., Ann Arbor MI 48105-9736. (313)971-3600. Fax: (313)971-9188. Editor-in-Chief: Csaba Csere. Monthly magazine for auto enthusiasts; college-educated, professional, median

24-35 years of age. Estab. 1961. Circ. 1,100,000. **Pays on acceptance.** Rights purchased vary with author and material. Buys all rights or first North American serial rights. Reports in 2 months.

- Ranked as one of the best markets for freelance writers in *Writer's Digest* magazine's annual "Top 100 Markets," January 1994.

Nonfiction: Non-anecdotal articles about automobiles, new and old. Automotive road tests, informational articles on cars and equipment, some satire and humor and personalities, past and present, in the automotive industry and automotive sports. "Treat readers as intellectual equals. Emphasis on people as well as hardware." Informational, humor, historical, think articles and nostalgia. All road tests are staff-written. "Unsolicited manuscripts are not accepted. Query letters must be addressed to the Managing Editor. Rates are generous, but few manuscripts are purchased from outside."

Photos: Color slides and b&w photos sometimes purchased with accompanying mss.

Tips: "It is best to start off with an interesting query and to stay away from nuts-and-bolts ideas because that will be handled in-house or by an acknowledged expert. Our goal is to be absolutely without flaw in our presentation of automotive facts, but we strive to be every bit as entertaining as we are informative."

CAR AUDIO AND ELECTRONICS, Avcom Publishing, Suite 1600, 21700 Oxnard St., Woodland Hills CA 91367. (818)593-3900. Fax: (818)593-2274. Editor: William Neill. Managing Editor: Doug Newcomb. 80-90% freelance written. Monthly magazine on electronic products designed for cars. "We help people buy the best electronic products for their cars. The magazine is about electronics, how to buy, use and so on: *CA&E* explains complicated things in simple ways. Articles are accurate, easy, and fun." Estab. 1988. Circ. 122,000. **Pays on acceptance.** Publishes ms an average of 3-5 months after acceptance. Byline given. Buys all rights. Submit seasonal/holiday material 3-4 months in advance. Simultaneous submissions OK. Query for electronic submissions. Reports in 1 month. Sample copy for $3.95 and 9 × 12 SAE with 4 first-class stamps. Writer's guidelines for #10 SASE.

Nonfiction: How-to (buy electronics for your car), interview/profile, new product, opinion, photo feature, technical. Buys 60-70 mss/year. Query with or without published clips, or send complete ms. Length: 500-1,700 words. Pays $300-1,000.

Photos: Send photos with submission. Review transparencies, any size.

Tips: "Write clearly and knowledgeably about car electronics."

CAR CRAFT, Petersen Publishing Co., 6420 Wilshire Blvd., Los Angeles CA 90048. (213)782-2320. Fax: (213)782-2263. Editor: Chuck Schifsky. Monthly magazine for men and women, 18-34, "enthusiastic owners of 1949 and newer muscle cars and street machines." Circ. 400,000. Study past issues before making submissions or story suggestions. Pays generally on publication, on acceptance under special circumstances. Buys all rights. Buys 2-10 mss/year. Query.

Nonfiction: How-to articles ranging from the basics to fairly sophisticated automotive modifications. Drag racing feature stories and some general car features on modified late model automobiles. Especially interested in do-it-yourself automotive tips, suspension modifications, mileage improvers and even shop tips and homemade tools. Length: open. Pays $100-200/page.

Photos: Photos purchased with or without accompanying text. Captions suggested, but optional. Reviews 8 × 10 b&w glossy prints; 35mm or 2¼ × 2¼ color. Pays $30 for b&w, color negotiable. "Pay rate higher for complete story, i.e., photos, captions, headline, subtitle: the works, ready to go."

CHEVY HIGH PERFORMANCE, Petersen Publishing Co., 6420 Wilshire Blvd., Los Angeles CA 90048. (213)782-2000. Editor: Mike Magda. Managing Editor: Amy Diamond. 50% freelance written. Monthly magazine covering "all aspects of street, racing, restored high-performance Chevrolet vehicles with heavy emphasis on technical modifications and quality photography." Estab. 1985. Circ. 125,000. Pays on acceptance. Byline given. Offers no kill fee. Buys all rights. Submit seasonal/holiday material 6 months in advance. Query for electronic submissions. Reports in 1 month. Sample copy for 9 × 12 SAE with 5 first-class stamps.

Nonfiction: How-to, new product, photo feature, technical. "We need well-researched and photographed technical articles. Tell us how to make horse-power on a budget." Buys 60 mss/year. Query. Length: 500-2,000 words. Pays $150-1,000. Sometimes pays expenses of writers on assignment.

Photos: Send photos with submission. Reviews contact sheets, any transparencies and any prints. Offers no additional payment for photos accepted with ms. Model releases required. Buys all rights.

Columns/Departments: Buys 24 mss/year. Query. Length: 100-1,500. Pays $150-500.

Tips: "Writers must be aware of the 'street scene.' Please read the magazine closely before query. We need well-photographed step-by-step how-to technical articles. No personality profiles, fluffy features and especially personal experiences. If you don't know the difference between Z/28 and Z28 Camaros, camel-hump and 18-degree heads or what COPO and RPO stand for, there's a good chance your background isn't what we're looking for."

CLASSIC AUTO RESTORER, Fancy Publishing, Inc., P.O. Box 6050, Mission Viejo CA 92690-6050. (714)855-8822. Fax: (714)855-3045. Editor: Brian Mertz. 85% freelance written. Monthly magazine on auto restoration. "Our readers own old cars and they work on them. We help our readers by providing as much practical, how-to information as we can about restoration and old cars." Estab. 1988. Pays on publication. Publishes an average of 3 months after acceptance. Offers $50 kill fee. Buys first North American serial or one-time rights. Submit seasonal/holiday material 4 months in advance. Query for electronic submissions. Reports in 2 months. Sample copy for $5.50. Free writer's guidelines.

Nonfiction: How-to (auto restoration), new product, photo feature, technical, travel. Buys 120 mss/year. Query with or without published clips or send complete ms. Length: 200-5,000 words. Pays $100-500 for assigned articles; $75-500 for unsolicited articles.

Photos: Send photos with submission. Reviews contact sheets, transparencies and 5×7 prints. Offers no additional payment for photos accepted with ms.

Columns/Departments: Buys 12 mss/year. Send complete ms. Length: 400-1,000 words. Pays $75-200.

Tips: "Send a story. Include photos. Make it something that the magazine regularly uses. Do automotive how-tos. We need lots of them. We'll help you with them."

CLASSIC CAR DIGEST, Bemis Communication Group, Inc., 118 Pleasant St., Marblehead MA 01945. (617)639-3000. Editor: Nathan C. Ferrarelli. 50% freelance written. Quarterly magazine on classic car restoration for automobile restorers and collectors—semi-technical. Circ. 5,000. Pays on publication. Publishes ms an average of 3-6 months after acceptance. Byline given. Buys first rights. Reports in 3 months. Free sample copy and writer's guidelines.

Nonfiction: General interest, how-to (technical, about restoration), interview/profile and technical. "No fiction." Buys 10 mss/year. Query with published clips. Length: 1,500-4,000 words. Pays $150-500 for assigned articles; $100-200 for unsolicited articles. If writer has associated business, will offer free ad. Sometimes pays expenses of writers on assignment.

Photos: Send photos with submission. Reviews contact sheets and 5×7 prints. Offers $50 maximum/photo. Identification of subjects required. Buys one-time rights.

Columns/Departments: In Restoration (technical explanation) and Metalcrafting (side of each craft). Buys 8 mss/year. Send complete ms. Length: 500-1,000 words. Pays $150 maximum.

Tips: "Writer should be an avid enthusiast of classic cars and have an appreciation of craftsman's skills." Interviews with professional restorers and features about restoration facilities are areas most open to freelance writers.

‡EUROPEAN CAR, ARGUS Publishing Corp., #250, 12100 Wilshire, Los Angeles CA 90025. (310)820-3601. Fax: (310)207-9388. Editor: Greg Brown. Managing Editor: Stephanie Wolfe. 50% freelance written. Monthly magazine covering European cars. Estab. 1969. Circ. 90,000. Pays on publication. Publishes ms an average of 3-6 months after acceptance. Byline given. Buys one-time and second serial (reprint) rights. Submit seasonal/holiday material 4-5 months in advance. Simultaneous submissions OK. Query for electronic submissions. Reports in 6 months. Sample copy for $3.75. Writer's guidelines for #10 SASE.

Nonfiction: Historical/nostalgic, how-to, interview/profile, new product, photo feature, technical, travel. Query. Length: 500 words average. Pays $50-75/ms page.

Photos: Send photos with submission. Reviews contact sheets, negatives, 35mm, 2¼×2¼ transparencies, 5×7 prints. Payment depends on quality. Captions, model releases and identification of subjects required.

FOUR WHEELER MAGAZINE, 6728 Eton Ave., Canoga Park CA 91303. (818)992-4777. Fax: (818)992-4979. Editor: John Stewart. 20% freelance written. Works with a small number of new/unpublished writers each year. Monthly magazine covering four-wheel-drive vehicles, competition and travel/adventure. Estab. 1963. Circ. 355,466. Pays on publication. Publishes ms an average of 4 months after acceptance. Buys all rights. Submit seasonal/holiday material at least 4 months in advance. Query for electronic submissions. Writer's guidelines for #10 SASE.

Nonfiction: 4WD competition and travel/adventure articles, technical, how-tos, and vehicle features about unique four-wheel drives. "We like the adventure stories that bring four wheeling to life in word and photo: mud-running deserted logging roads, exploring remote, isolated trails, or hunting/fishing where the 4×4 is a necessity for success." See features by Gary Wescott and Matt Conrad for examples. Query with photos before sending complete ms. Length: 1,200-2,000 words; average 4-5 pages when published. Pays $100/page minimum for complete package.

Photos: Requires professional quality color slides and b&w prints for every article. Captions required. Prefers Kodachrome 64 or Fujichrome 50 in 35mm or 2¼ formats. "Action shots a must for all vehicle features and travel articles."

Tips: "Show us you know how to use a camera as well as the written word. The easiest way for a new writer/photographer to break in to our magazine is to read several issues of the magazine, then query with a short vehicle feature that will show his or her potential as a creative writer/photographer."

4-WHEEL & OFF-ROAD, Petersen Publishing Co., 6420 Wilshire Blvd., Los Angeles CA 90048. (213)782-2360. Editor: David Freiburger. Monthly magazine covering four-wheel-drive vehicles, "devoted to new-truck tests, buildups of custom 4×4s, coverage of 4WD racing, trail rides and other competitions." Circ. 330,000. **Pays on acceptance.** Publishes ms an average of 4 months after acceptance. Byline given. Pays 20% kill fee. Buys first North American serial rights or all rights. Submit seasonal/holiday material 4 months in advance. Reports in 3 weeks. Writer's guidelines for #10 SASE.

Nonfiction: How-to (on four-wheel-drive vehicles—engines, suspension, drive systems, etc.), new product, photo feature, technical, travel. Buys 12-16 mss/year. Send complete ms. Length: 1,000-2,500 words. Pays $200-600.

Photos: Send photos with submission. Reviews transparencies and b&w prints. Offers no additional payment for photos accepted with ms. Captions, model releases and identification of subjects required. Buys all rights.

Fillers: Anecdotes, facts, gags, newsbreaks, short humor. Buys 12-16/year. Length: 50-150 words. Pays $15-50.

Tips: "Attend 4×4 events, get to know the audience. Present material only after full research. Manuscripts should contain *all* of the facts pertinent to the story. Technical/how-to articles are most open to freelancers."

HIGH PERFORMANCE PONTIAC, CSK Publishing Co., 299 Market St., Saddle Brook NJ 07663. (201)712-9300. Editor: Richard A. Lentinello. Managing Editor: Peter Easton. Bimonthly magazine covering Pontiac cars, events and technology. "Our writers must have a knowledge of automobiles in general, and of Pontiacs in particular." Estab. 1979. Circ. 45,000 nationwide. Pays on publication. Publishes ms an average of 3 months after acceptance. Byline given. Offers negotiable kill fee. Buys first North American serial rights. Query for electronic submissions. Accepts previously published articles. Send photocopy of article and information about when and where the article previously appeared. Length: 250-2,000 words. Pays $150/page for articles. Sometimes pays expenses of writers on assignment.Reports in 3 months. Sample copy for $4.50.

Nonfiction: Historical/nostalgic, how-to (hands-on Pontiac technical articles, e.g., how to recover your GTO seats), interview/profile, new product, photo feature, technical. "We are not interested in articles about pre-'81 Pontiacs that have had Chevy engines installed (excluding Canadian Pontiacs, of course)." Buys 50 mss/year. Query with or without published clips or send complete ms.

Photos: Send photos with submission. Reviews contact sheets, negatives, transparencies and prints. Captions required. Buys one-time rights.

MOPAR MUSCLE, Dobbs Publishing Group, 3816 Industry Blvd., Lakeland FL 33811. (813)644-0449. Fax: (813)648-1187. Editor: Greg Rager. Managing Editor: Stephen Siegel. 25% freelance written. Bimonthly magazine covering Chrysler Corp. performance vehicles. "Our audience has a knowledge of and interest in Chrysler vehicles." Estab. 1987. Circ. 75,000. Pays within 30 days of publication. Byline given. Buys first rights. Submit seasonal/holiday material 6 months in advance. Query for electronic submissions. Reports in 2 weeks. Free sample copy and writer's guidelines.

Nonfiction: Historical/nostalgic, how-to/technical, humor, interview/profile, new product, personal experience, photo feature, technical. Buys 20-25 mss/year. Query with published clips. Sometimes pays expenses of writers on assignment.

Photos: Send photos with submission. Reviews contact sheets and transparencies. Model release required. Buys one-time rights.

Columns/Departments: Parts Department (new products), 50 words; Mopar Scene (news for Chrysler devotees), length varies. Buys 20-25 mss/year. Query.

Fiction: Historical, humorous. Query.

MOTOR TREND, Petersen Publishing Co., 6420 Wilshire Blvd., Los Angeles CA 90048. (213)782-2220. Editor: Leonard Emanuelson. 5-10% freelance written. Prefers to work with published/established writers. Monthly magazine for automotive enthusiasts and general interest consumers. Circ. 900,000. Publishes ms an average of 3 months after acceptance. Buys all rights. "Fact-filled query suggested for all freelancers." Reports in 1 month.

Nonfiction: Automotive and related subjects that have national appeal. Emphasis on domestic and imported cars, road tests, driving impressions, auto classics, auto, travel, racing, and high-performance features for the enthusiast. Packed with facts. Freelancers should confine queries to photo-illustrated exotic drives and other feature material; road tests and related activity are handled inhouse.

Photos: Buys photos, particularly of prototype cars and assorted automotive matter. Pays $25-500 for transparencies.

MUSCLE CARS, CSK Publishing Co., 299 Market St., Saddlebrook NJ 07663. (201)712-9300. Editor: Richard Lentinello. Managing Editor: Peter Easton. Bimonthly magazine that covers stock and modified muscle cars. Pays on publication. Byline given. Buys first North American serial rights.

Nonfiction: How-to (automotive), technical. Buys 20 mss/year. Query. Length: 1,000-10,000 words. Pays $150/page for assigned articles.

MUSCLE MUSTANGS & FAST FORDS, CSK Publishing Co., 299 Market St., Saddlebrook NJ 07663. (201)712-9300. Editor: Jim Campisano. Managing Editor: Diane Boccadoro. 40% freelance written. Magazine published 10 times/year covering late model 5-liter Mustangs and other high-performance Fords. Estab. 1988. Circ. 50,000. Pays on publication. Publishes ms an average of 6 months after acceptance. Byline given. Buys first North American serial rights. Query for electronic submissions. Reports in 3 weeks on queries; 6 weeks on mss. Sample copy for $3.50 and 9×12 SAE with 5 first-class stamps. Free writer's guidelines.

Nonfiction: How-to (automotive) and technical (automotive). Buys 50 mss/year. Query. Length: 500-1,500 words. Pays $150/magazine page for all articles. Sometimes pays expenses of writers on assignment.
Photos: Send photos with submission.

MUSTANG MONTHLY, Dobbs Publications, Inc., P.O. Box 7157, Lakeland FL 33807. (813)646-5743. Editor: Jerry Pitt. Managing Editor: Rob Reaser. 30% freelance written. Monthly magazine covering concours 1964½ through 1973 Ford Mustang, and modified 80s and 90s Mustangs. "Our average reader makes over $35,000 annually, and is 35 years of age." Estab. 1977. Circ. 85,000. Pays on publication. Publishes ms an average of 4 months after acceptance. Byline given. Buys first North American rights. No simultaneous submissions. Reports in 3 months on mss. Writers guidelines available.
Nonfiction: How-to, technical. Color car features. No seasonal, holiday, humor, fiction or material. Buys 25 mss/year. Query with or without published clips, or send complete ms. Write for guidelines first. Length: 2,500 words maximum. Pays $100-200/page. Generally uses ms within 6 months of acceptance.
Photos: Send photos with submission; photography will make or break articles. Reviews contact sheets, negatives and transparencies. No color prints. Offers $100-200/page color, $25 minimum; $10/photo b&w, $25 minimum. Captions and model releases (on our forms) "required."
Tips: "*Mustang Monthly* is looking for color features on trophy-winning original Mustangs and well-researched b&w how-to and technical articles. Our format rarely varies. A strong knowledge of early Mustangs is essential."

NATIONAL DRAGSTER, Drag Racing's Leading News Weekly, National Hot Rod Association, 2035 Financial Way, Glendora CA 91740. (818)963-8475. Fax: (818)335-4307. Editor: Phil Burgess. Managing Editor: Vicky Walker. 20% freelance written. Weekly tabloid of NHRA drag racing. "Covers NHRA drag racing—race reports, news, performance industry news, hot racing rumors—for NHRA members. Membership included with subscription." Estab. 1960. Circ. 80,000. Pays on publication. Publishes ms 1 month after acceptance. Byline given. Buys all rights. Submit seasonal/holiday material 2 months in advance. Accepts simultaneous submissions. Query for electronic submissions. Reports in 1 month. Free sample copy.
Nonfiction: General interest, historical/nostalgic, how-to, humor, interview/profile, new product, personal experience, photo feature, technical. Buys 20 mss/year. Query. Pay is negotiable. Sometimes pays expenses of writers on assignment.
Photos: State availability of photos with submission. Reviews 5×7 prints. Captions and identification of subjects required. Buys all rights.
Columns/Departments: On the Run (first-person written, ghost written by drag racers), 900-1,000 words. Buys 48 mss/year. Query. Pay is negotiable.
Tips: "Feature articles on interesting drag racing personalities or race cars are most open to freelancers."

ON TRACK, The Auto Racing Magazine of Record, OT Publishing, Inc., P.O. Box 8509, Fountain Valley CA 92728-8509. (714)966-1131. Fax: (714)556-9776. Editor: Tim Tuttle, Andrew Crask. 90% freelance written. Biweekly magazine on auto racing (no drag racing, sprint cars, etc.). Estab. 1981. Circ. 40,000. Pays on publication. Publishes ms an average of 2 months after acceptance. Byline given. Buys first North American serial rights. Query for electronic submissions. Reports on queries in 2 months. Sample copy for $2.50. Free writer's guidelines.
Nonfiction: Interview/profile, technical. Stories about race drivers with quotes from driver. Buys 3-4 mss/year. Query with published clips, or send complete ms. Length: 800-2,000 words. Pays $5.25/column inch. Sometimes pays expenses of writers on assignment.
Photos: State availability of photos with submission. Reviews 5×7 prints. Offers $12.50/photo. Captions and identification of subjects required. Buys one-time rights.

OPEN WHEEL MAGAZINE, General Media, 47 S. Main St., Ipswich MA 01938. (508)356-7030. Fax: (508)356-2492. Editor: Dick Berggren. 80% freelance written. Monthly magazine "covering sprint cars, midgets, super-modifieds and Indy cars. *OW* is an enthusiast's publication that speaks to those deeply involved in oval track automobile racing in the United States and Canada. *OW*'s primary audience is a group of men and women actively engaged in competition at the present time, those who have recently been in competition and those who plan competition soon. That audience includes drivers, car owners, sponsors and crew members who represent perhaps 50-70% of our readership. The rest who read the magazine are those in the racing trade (parts manufacturers, track operators and officials) and serious fans who see 30 or more races per year." Circ. 150,000. Pays on publication. Publishes ms an average of 6 months after acceptance. Byline given. Buys all rights. Submit seasonal material 2 months in advance. Reports in 3 weeks on queries. Sample copy for 9×12 SAE with 7 first-class stamps. Writer's guidelines for #10 SASE.
Nonfiction: General interest, historical/nostalgic, how-to, humor, interview/profile, new product, photo feature, technical. "We don't care for features that are a blow-by-blow chronology of events. The key word is interest. We want features which allow the reader to get to know the main figure very well. Our view of racing is positive. We don't think all is lost, that the sport is about to shut down and don't want stories that claim such to be the case, but we shoot straight and avoid whitewash." Buys 125 mss/year. Query with complete ms.

Photos: State availability of photos with submission. Reviews contact sheets, negatives, transparencies, prints. Buys one-time rights.

Fillers: Anecdotes, facts, short humor. Buys 100/year. Length: 1-3 pages, double-spaced. Pays $35.

Tips: "Virtually all our features are submitted without assignment. An author knows much better what's going on in his backyard than we do. We ask that you write to us before beginning a story theme. Judging of material is always a combination of a review of the story and its support illustrations. Therefore, we ask for photography to accompany the manuscript on first submission. We're especially in the market for tech."

RIDER, TL Enterprises, Inc., 3601 Calle Tecate, Camarillo CA 93012-5040. (805)389-0300. Fax: (805)389-0378. Editor: Mark Tuttle Jr.. Managing Editor: Donya Carlson. Contact: Mark Tuttle, Jr., Editor. 50% freelance written. Monthly magazine on motorcycling. "*Rider* serves owners and enthusiasts of road and street motorcycling, focusing on touring, commuting, camping and general sport street riding." Estab. 1974. Circ. 140,000. Pays on publication. Publishes ms an average of 6-12 months after acceptance. Byline given. Offers 25% kill fee. Buys first North American serial rights. Editorial lead time 4 months. Submit seasonal material 6 months in advance. Query for electronic submissions. Reports in 2 months. Sample copy for $2.95. Writer's guidelines for #10 SASE.

Nonfiction: General interest, historical/nostalgic, how-to (re: motorcycling), humor, interview/profile, personal experience. Does not want to see "fiction or articles on 'How I Began Motorcycling.' " Buys 30 mss/year. Query. Length: 500-1,500 words. Pays $100 minimum for unsolicited articles. Sometimes pays expenses of writers on assignment.

Photos: Send photos with submission. Reviews contact sheets, transparencies and 5×7 prints (b&w only). Offers no additional payment for photos accepted with ms. Captions required. Buys one-time rights.

Columns/Departments: Rides, Rallies & Clubs (favorite ride or rally), 800-1,000 words. Buys 15 mss/year. Query. Pays $100.

Tips: "We rarely accept manuscripts without photos (slides or b&w prints). Query first. Follow guidelines. We are most open to feature stories (must include excellent photography) and material for 'Rides, Rallies and Clubs.' Include information on routes, local attractions, restaurants and scenery in favorite ride submissions."

STOCK CAR RACING MAGAZINE, General Media, Box 715, Ipswich MA 01938. Editor: Dick Berggren. 80% freelance written. Eager to work with new/unpublished writers. Monthly magazine for stock car racing fans and competitors. Circ. 400,000. Pays on publication. Publishes ms an average of 3 months after acceptance. Buys all rights. Byline given. Query for electronic submissions. Reports in 6 weeks. Free writer's guidelines.

Nonfiction: General interest, historical/nostalgic, how-to, humor, interviews, new product, photo features, technical. "Uses nonfiction on stock car drivers, cars and races. We are interested in the story behind the story in stock car racing. We want interesting profiles and colorful, nationally interesting features. We are looking for more technical articles, particularly in the area of street stocks and limited sportsman." Query with or without published clips or submit complete ms. Buys 50-200 mss/year. Length: 100-6,000 words. Pays up to $450.

Photos: State availability of photos. Pays $20 for 8×10 b&w photos; up to $250 for 35mm or larger transparencies. Captions required.

Fillers: Anecdotes, short humor. Buys 100 each year. Pays $35.

Tips: "We get more queries than stories. We just don't get as much material as we want to buy. We have more room for stories than ever before. We are an excellent market with 12 issues per year. Virtually all our features are submitted without assignment. An author knows much better what's going on in his backyard than we do. We ask that you write to us before beginning a story theme. If nobody is working on the theme you wish to pursue, we'd be glad to assign it to you if it fits our needs and you are the best person for the job. Judging of material is always a combination of a review of the story and its support illustration. Therefore, we ask for photography to accompany the manuscript on first submission."

SUPER CYCLE, LFP Inc., # 300, 9171 Wilshire Blvd., Beverly Hills CA 90210. (310)274-7684. Fax: (310)274-7985. Editor: Elliot Borin. 95% freelance written. Monthly magazine covering motorcycles—Harley-Davidson. "Motorcycle events, parties, fiction stories about bikers and motorcycle legislation no foreign bike or 'bad-biker' stuff." Circ. 100,000. Pays on publication. Publishes ms an average of 6 months or longer after acceptance. Byline given. Offers no kill fee. Buys first rights. Submit seasonal/holiday material 6 months in advance. Query for electronic submissions. Reports in 2 months. Sample copy for $4 and 9×12 SAE.

Nonfiction: Interview/profile (bike builder races, etc.), personal experience (bike rally), photo feature (super customized bike with model), travel (motorcycling). "No foreign bikes, no poetry." Buys 25 mss/year. Query with or without published clips or send complete ms. Length: 200-1,500 words. Pays $200-400 for assigned articles; $200-300 for unsolicited articles. Pays in contributor copies or other premiums in trade for motorcycle painting, accessories, parts or work.

Photos: Send photos with submission. Reviews 2×2 transparencies, slides and 3×5 or 4×6 prints. Offers no additional payment for photos accepted with ms. Offers $35-50/photo with no ms. Model release required. Buys all rights.

Columns/Departments: Elliot Borin. Gearheads or Tech Tips (technical advice on motorcycles); Tattoo Time; Parties, 100-1,000 words. Buys 25 mss/year. Send complete ms. Pays $200-400.
Fiction: Adventure, humorous, mystery, romance, science fiction, Vietnam, tattoo (must all pertain to bikers). "No stories about 'bad guy' bikers." Buys 12 mss/year. Send complete ms. Length: 1,000 words maximum. Pays $200-400.
Tips: "Writers must be literate, understand bikers, type, photograph, be better than the rest!"

VETTE MAGAZINE, CSK Publishing, Inc., 299 Market St., Saddle Brook NJ 07663. (201)712-9300. Fax: (201)712-9899. Editor: D. Randy Riggs. Managing Editor: Peter Easton. 75% freelance written. Monthly magazine covering all subjects related to the Corvette automobile. "Our readership is extremely knowledgeable about the subject of Corvettes. Therefore, writers must know the subject thoroughly and be good at fact checking." Estab. 1976. Circ. 65,000. Offers 50% kill fee. Buys first North American serial rights. Submit seasonal/holiday material 4 months in advance. Query for electronic submissions. Reports in 6 weeks. Sample copy for 9 × 12 SAE with 6 first-class stamps. Writer's guidelines for #10 SASE.
Nonfiction: General interest, historical/nostalgic, how-to, interview/profile, new product, personal experience, photo feature, technical, travel. Buys 120 mss/year. Query with published clips. Length: 400-2,700 words. Pays $150-750 for assigned articles; $100-350 for unsolicited articles. Sometimes pays expenses of writers on assignment.
Photos: State availability of photos with submission. Reviews contact sheets. Offers no additional payment for photos accepted with ms. Captions and model releases required. Buys one-time rights.
Columns/Departments: Reviews (books/videos), 400-500 words. Buys 12 mss/year. Query. Pays $50-150.
Fiction: Adventure, fantasy, slice-of-life vignettes. Buys 2 mss/year. Query with published clips. Length: 400-2,500 words. Pays $100-500.

‡WOMEN WITH WHEELS, Newsletter For Women on Automobiles, Women With Wheels, Suite A, 1718 Northfield Square, Northfield IL 60093. (708)501-3519. Editor: Susan Frissell, Ph.D. Quarterly consumer newsletter covering automobiles. "*WWW* is written for women. It caters to women who not only purchase their own automobiles, but are also responsible for maintaining them. *WWW* is written to educate and inform women in a jargon-free style. Audience is from 18-75 years old, with average income of over $31,000, for the most part college educated." Estab. 1989. Circ. 200. Pays on publication. Publishes ms an average of 2-3 months after acceptance. Byline given. Buys first North American serial or one-time rights. Editorial lead time 2 months. Submit seasonal material 2-3 months in advance. Accepts simultaneous and previously published submissions. Reports in 1 month on queries; 2 months on mss. Sample copy for 8½ × 11 SAE with 4 first-class stamps. Writer's guidelines for #10 SASE.
Nonfiction: Book excerpts, historical/nostalgic, how-to, humor, interview/profile, new product, opinion, personal experience, technical. Special issues: auto show/new model coverage (February); national car care month (October). "Nothing loaded with automotive jargon." Buys 5 mss/year. Send complete ms. Length: 100-200 words. Pays $5 for assigned articles; $3.50 for unsolicited articles.
Photos: State availability of photos with submission. Reviews 3½ × 5 prints. Offers no additional payment for photos accepted with ms. Captions and identification of subjects required. Buys one-time rights.
Columns/Departments: New Products (auto-related) 50-200 words; Autosmarts (up and coming Automotive trends), 100-300 words; Features (personal stories about women in auto-related fields), 500-1,500 words. Buys 5 mss/year. Pays $3.50-10.
Fillers: Anecdotes, facts, newsbreaks, short humor. Buys 50/year. Length: 25-100 words. Pays $1-5.
Tips: "Request a copy of author's guidelines. All departments are open to freelancers. Looking to increase our freelance percentage with new and/or established writers. Also interested in students writing on auto-related topics looking to build a portfolio. Will also consider 'personal' stories about car buying, maintenance experiences, etc. – good and bad. Looking for 'how-to' and personal stories about women in auto-related fields and endeavors, mostly. Always up for something new and innovative. Real open to experimenting! Send it, we'll look at it!"

Aviation

Professional and private pilots and aviation enthusiasts read the publications in this section. Editors want material for audiences knowledgeable about commercial aviation. Magazines for passengers of commercial airlines are grouped in the Inflight category. Technical aviation and space journals and publications for airport operators, aircraft dealers and others in aviation businesses are listed under Aviation and Space in the Trade section.

AIR & SPACE/SMITHSONIAN MAGAZINE, 10th Floor, 370 L'Enfant Promenade SW, Washington DC 20024-2518. (202)287-3733. Fax: (202)287-3163. Editor: George Larson. Managing Editor: Tom Huntington. 80%

freelance written. Prefers to work with published/established writers. Bimonthly magazine covering aviation and aerospace for a non-technical audience. "Features are slanted to a technically curious, but not necessarily technically knowledgeable audience. We are looking for unique angles to aviation/aerospace stories, history, events, personalities, current and future technologies, that emphasize the human-interest aspect." Estab. 1985. Circ. 310,000. **Pays on acceptance.** Byline given. Offers kill fee. Buys first North American serial rights. Adapts from previously published or soon to be published books and other works. Send photocopy of article, including information about when and where the article previously appeared. Reports in 2-3 months. Sample copy for $3.50 and 9½ × 13 SASE. Free writer's guidelines.

   • The editors are actively seeking stories covering space and the history of the involvement of minorities in aviation and space.

Nonfiction: Book excerpts, essays, general interest (on aviation/aerospace), historical/nostalgic, how-to, humor, interview/profile, photo feature, technical. Buys 50 mss/year. Query with published clips. Length: 1,500-3,000 words. Pays $2,000 average. Pays the expenses of writers on assignment.

Photos: State availability of illustrations with submission. Reviews 35mm transparencies. Refuses unsolicited material.

Columns/Departments: Above and Beyond (first person), 1,500-2,000 words; Flights and Fancy (whimsy), approximately 1,200 words; Oldies & Oddities (weird, wonderful or old), 1,200 words; Collections (profiles of unique museums), 1,200 words. Buys 25 mss/year. Query with published clips. Pays $1,000 maximum. Soundings (brief items, timely but not breaking news), 500-700 words. Pays $300.

Tips: "Soundings is the section most open to freelancers."

AIR LINE PILOT, Air Line Pilots Association, 535 Herndon Parkway, P.O. Box 1169, Herndon VA 22070. (703)689-4176. Editor: Esperison Martinez, Jr. 10% freelance written. Prefers to work with published/established writers; works with a small number of new/unpublished writers each year. Monthly magazine for airline pilots covering "commercial aviation industry information — economics, avionics, equipment, systems, safety — that affects a pilot's life in professional sense." Also includes information about management/labor relations trends, contract negotiations, etc. Estab. 1931. Circ. 62,000. **Pays on acceptance.** Publishes ms an average of 6 months after acceptance. Offers 50% kill fee. Buys all rights. Submit seasonal/holiday material 6 months in advance. Query for electronic submissions. Reports in 2 months. Sample copy for $2. Writer's guidelines for #10 SASE.

Nonfiction: Humor, inspirational, photo feature, technical. "We are backlogged with historical submissions and prefer not to receive unsolicited submissions at this time." Buys 20 mss/year. Query with or without published clips, or send complete ms. Length: 700-3,000 words. Pays $200-600 for assigned articles; pays $50-600 for unsolicited articles.

Photos: Send photos with submission. Reviews contact sheets, 35mm transparencies and 8 × 10 prints. Offers $10-35/photo. Identification of subjects required. Buys one-time rights.

Tips: "For our feature section, we seek aviation industry information that affects the life of a professional airline pilot from a career standpoint. We also seek material that affects a pilot's life from a job security and work environment standpoint. Any airline pilot featured in an article must be an Air Line Pilot Association member in good standing."

BALLOON LIFE, Balloon Life Magazine, Inc., 2145 Dale Ave., Sacramento CA 95815-3632. (916)922-9648. Fax: (916)922-4730. Editor: Tom Hamilton. 75% freelance written. Monthly magazine for sport of hot air ballooning. Estab. 1986. Circ. 4,000. Pays on publication. Byline given. Offers 50-100% kill fee. Buys first North American serial or second serial (reprint) rights. Submit seasonal/holiday material 3-4 months in advance. Accepts previously published material. Send photocopy or article of short story. For reprints pays 100% of amount paid for original article. Query for electronic submissions. Reports in 3 weeks on queries; 1 month on mss. *Writer's Market* recommends allowing 2 months for reply. Sample copy for 9 × 12 SAE with $2 postage. Writer's guidelines for #10 SASE.

Nonfiction: Book excerpts, general interest, how-to (flying hot air balloons, equipment techniques), interview/profile, new product, letters to the editor, technical. Buys 150 mss/year. Query with or without published clips, or send complete ms. Length: 800-5,000 words. Pays $50-75 for assigned articles; $25-50 for unsolicited articles. Sometimes pays expenses of writers on assignment.

Photos: Send photos with submission. Reviews transparencies, prints. Offers $15-50/photo. Identification of subjects required. Buys one-time rights.

Columns/Departments: Hangar Flying (real life flying experience that others can learn from), 800-1,500 words; Preflight (a news and information column), 100-500 words; Logbook (recent balloon events — events that have taken place in last 3-4 months), 300-500 words. Buys 60 mss/year. Send complete ms. Pays $15-50.

Fiction: Humorous. Buys 3-5 mss/year. Send complete ms. Length: 800-1,500 words. Pays $50.

Tips: "This magazine slants toward the technical side of ballooning. We are interested in articles that help to educate and provide safety information. Also stories with manufacturers, important individuals and/or of historic events and technological advances important to ballooning. The magazine attempts to present articles that show 'how-to' (fly, business opportunities, weather, equipment). Both our Feature Stories section and Logbook section are where most manuscripts are purchased."

CAREER PILOT, FAPA, 4959 Massachusetts Blvd., Atlanta GA 30337-6607. (404)997-8097. Assistant Editor: David Jones. 80% freelance written. Monthly magazine covering aviation. "A career advisory magazine as a service to FAPA members. Readers largely are career pilots who are working toward their professional goals. Articles cover topics such as recent developments in aviation law and medicine, changes in the industry, job interview techniques and how to get pilot jobs." Estab. 1983. Circ. 13,500. Pays prior to publication. Publishes ms an average of 3-4 months after acceptance. Byline given. Offers 50% kill fee. Buys all rights. Simultaneous and previously published submissions OK. Send tearsheet or photocopy of article, typed ms with rights for sale noted and information about when and where the article previously appeared. For reprints pays 50% of the amount paid for an original article. Query for electronic submissions. Reports in 3 months.
Nonfiction: How-to (get hired by an airline), interview/profile (aviation related), personal experience (aviation related). Special issue: Corporate Aviation (September). "No humor, cartoons or fiction." Buys 60 mss/year. Query with clips or send complete ms. Length: 2,500 words. "Pays 18¢/word with $50 bonus for meeting deadlines." Sometimes pays expenses of writers on assignment.
Photos: State availability of photos with submission. Reviews prints. Offers no additional payment for photos accepted with ms. Captions and identification of subjects required.
Tips: "Send articles and clips that are aviation/business related. Express your interest in writing for our publication on a semi-regular basis."

CESSNA OWNER MAGAZINE, Jones Publishing, Inc., N7450 Aanstad Rd., P.O. Box 5000, Iola WI 54945. (715)445-5000. Editor: Gregory Bayer. 90% freelance written. Monthly magazine covering Cessna single and twin engine aircraft. "*Cessna Owner Magazine* is the official publication of the Cessna Owner Organization (C.O.O.). Therefore, our readers are Cessna aircraft owners, renters, pilots, and enthusiasts. Articles should deal with buying/selling, flying, maintaining, or modifying Cessnas. The purpose of our magazine is to promote safe, fun, and affordable flying." Estab. 1975. Circ. 5,555. Pays on publication. Publishes ms an average of 3 months after acceptance. Byline given. Buys first, one-time or second serial (reprint) rights or makes work-for-hire assignment on occasion. Editorial lead time 1 month. Submit seasonal material 3 months in advance. Accepts previously published submissions. Reports in 2 weeks on queries; 1 month on mss. Sample copy and writer's guidelines free on request.
Nonfiction: Historical/nostalgic (of specific Cessna models), how-to (aircraft repairs and maintenance), humor, interview/profile, new product, personal experience, photo feature, technical (aircraft engines and airframes), travel. "We are always looking for articles about Cessna aircraft modifications. We also greatly need articles on Cessna twin-engine aircraft. April, July, and November are always big issues for us, because we attend various airshows during these months and distribute free magazines. Feature articles on unusual, highly-modified, or vintage Cessnas are especially welcome during these months. Good photos are also a must for these special issues." Buys 24 mss/year. Query. Length: 1,500-3,500 words. Pays 8¢/word minimum for assigned articles; 5¢/word minimum for unsolicited articles.
Photos: Send photos with submission. Reviews 3×5 and larger prints. Offers no additional payment for photos accepted with ms or negotiates payment individually (on occasion). Captions and identification of subjects required.
Columns/Departments: Member's Corner (a feature article about a Cessna Owner Organization member and his/her plane), 1,000-1,500 words; Tailfeathers (humor/aviations "lighter" side), 1,500-3,000 words; Book Reviews, 1,000 words. Buys 6 mss/year. Query. Pays 5-12¢/word maximum.
Tips: "Always submit a hard copy and ASCII formatted computer disk (when possible). Color photos mean a lot to us, and manuscripts stand a much better chance of being published when accompanied by photos. Visit our booth at the major airshows (Osh Kosh, Sun 'n Fun, AOPA) and get to know our staff. Shows are also great places to find story leads. Freelancers can best get published by submitting articles on aircraft modifications, vintage planes, restorations, flight reports, twin-engine Cessnas, etc. We need articles on *women* who fly Cessna aircraft!"

FLYING, Hachette Filipacchi Magazine, Inc., 2nd Floor, 500 W. Putnam Ave., Greenwich CT 06830. (203)622-2700. Editor: J. "Mac" MacClellan. 2-3% freelance written. Monthly magazine. Circ. 322,096. **Pays on acceptance.** Publishes ms an average of 3 months after acceptance. Buys first North American serial rights, but with exclusivity for 2 years. Reports in 3 weeks on queries; 5 weeks on mss. "Writers should be pilots and know first-hand what they are writing about." Query with or without published clips or send complete ms. Length: 4 pages typeset maximum. Pay varies, $1,200 maximum.

GENERAL AVIATION NEWS & FLYER, N.W. Flyer, Inc., P.O. Box 39099, Tacoma WA 98439-0099. (206)471-9888. Fax: (206)471-9911. Editor: Dave Sclair. 30% freelance written. Prefers to work with published/established writers. Biweekly tabloid covering general aviation. Provides "coverage of aviation news, activities, regulations and politics of general and sport aviation with emphasis on timely features of interest to pilots and aircraft owners." Estab. 1949. Circ. 35,000. Pays 1 month after publication. Publishes ms an average of 3 months after acceptance. Byline given. Buys one-time and first North American serial rights; on occasion second serial (reprint) rights. Submit seasonal/holiday material 2 months in advance. Accepts previously published submissions from noncompetitive publications if so noted. Query for electronic submissions. Reports in 1-2 months. Sample copy for $3.50. Writer's and style guidelines for #10 SASE.

Nonfiction: Features of current interest about aviation businesses, developments at airports, new products and services, safety, flying technique and maintenance. "Good medium-length reports on current events—controversies at airports, problems with air traffic control, FAA, etc. We want solid news coverage of breaking stories." Query first on historical, nostalgic features and profiles/interviews. Many special sections throughout the year; send SASE for list. Buys 100 mss/year. Query or send complete ms. Length: 500-2,000 words. Pays up to $3/printed column inch maximum. Rarely pays the expenses of writers on assignment.

Photos: "Good pics a must." Send photos (b&w or color prints preferred, no slides) with ms. Captions and photographer's ID required. Pays $10/b&w photo used.

Tips: "We always are looking for features on places to fly and interviews or features about people and businesses using airplanes in unusual ways. Travel features must include information on what to do once you've arrived, with addresses from which readers can get more information. Get direct quotations from the principals involved in the story. We want current, first-hand information."

PIPERS MAGAZINE, Jones Publishing, Inc., N7450 Aanstad Rd., P.O. Box 5000, Iola WI 54945. (715)445-5000. Editor: Gregory Bayer. 90% freelance written. Monthly magazine covering Piper single and twin engine aircraft. "Pipers Magazine is the official publication of the Piper Owner Society (P.O.S). Therefore, our readers are Piper aircraft owners, renters, pilots, mechanics and enthusiasts. Articles should deal with buying/selling, flying, maintaining, insuring, or modifying Pipers. The purpose of our magazine is to promote safe, fun and affordable flying." Estab. 1988. Circ. 3,158. Pays on publication. Publishes ms an average of 3 months after acceptance. Buys first, one-time or second serial (reprint) rights or makes work-for-hire assignment on occasion. Editorial lead time 1 month. Submit seasonal material 3 months in advance. Accepts previously published submissions. Query for electronic submissions. Reports in 2 weeks on queries;1 month on mss. Sample copy and writer's guidelines free on request.

Nonfiction: Historical/nostalgic (of specific models of Pipers), how-to (aircraft repairs & maintenance), humor, interview/profile (industry leaders), new product, personal experience, photo feature, technical (aircraft engines and airframes), travel. We are always looking for articles about Piper aircraft modifications. We also are in great need of articles on Piper twin engine aircraft, and late-model Pipers. April, July, and November are always big issues for us, because we attend airshows during these months and distribute free magazines. Feature articles on unusual, highly-modified, vintage, late-model, or ski/float equipped Pipers are especially welcome. Good photos are a must for these special "show issues." Buys 24 mss/year. Query. Length: 1,500-3,500 words. Pays 8¢/word for assigned articles, 5¢/word for unsolicited articles.

Photos: Send photos with submissions. Reviews transparencies, 3×5 and larger prints. Offers no additional payment for photos accepted with; or negotiates payment individually. Captions, identification of subjects required.

Columns/Departments: Member's Corner (feature article about a Piper Owner Society member and his/her plane), 1,000-1,500 words; Tailfeathers (humor/aviation's "lighter" side), 1,500-3,000 words; Book Reviews, 1,000 words. Buys 6 mss/year. Query. Pays 5¢-12¢ word.

Tips: "Always submit a hard copy and an ASCII formatted computer disk when possible. Color photos mean a lot to us, and manuscripts stand a much greater chance of being published when accompanied by photos. Visit our booth at the major airshows (OshKosh, Sun 'n Fun, AOPA) and get to know our staff. Shows are also great places to find story leads. Freelancers can best get published by submitting articles on aircraft modifications, vintage planes, late-model planes, restorations, twin-engine Pipers, etc. We need articles on *women* who fly Piper aircraft!"

PLANE AND PILOT, Werner Publishing Corp., Suite 1220, 12121 Wilshire Blvd., Los Angeles CA 90025. (310)820-1500. Fax: (310)826-5008. Editor: Steve Werner. Managing Editor: James Lawrence. 100% freelance written. Monthly magazine that covers general aviation. "We think a spirited, conversational writing style is most entertaining for our readers. We are read by private and corporate pilots, instructors, students, mechanics and technicians—everyone involved or interested in general aviation." Estab. 1964. Circ. 130,000. Pays on publication. Publishes ms an average of 3 months after acceptance. Byline given. Kill fee negotiable. Buys all rights. Submit seasonal material 4 months in advance. Accepts previously published material. Send photocopy of article or typed ms with rights for sale noted and include information about when and where the article previously appeared. For reprints pays 50% of the amount paid for an original article. Query for electronic submissions. Reports in 2 months. Sample copy for $2.95. Free writer's guidelines.

Nonfiction: Book excerpts, essays, general interest, how-to, humor, inspirational, new product, personal experience, technical, travel, pilot proficiency and pilot reports on aircraft. Buys 150 mss/year. Send complete ms. Length: 1,000-2,500 words. Pays $200-500. Pays expenses of writers on assignment.

Photos: Send photos with submission. Reviews transparencies and prints. Offers $50-300/photo. Captions and identification of subjects required. Buys all rights.

Columns/Departments: Associate Editor: Kristi Johnson. Readback (any newsworthy items on aircraft and/or people in aviation), 100-300 words; Flight I'll Never Forget (a particularly difficult or wonderful flight), 1,000-1,500 words; Jobs & Schools (a feature or an interesting school or program in aviation), 1,000-1,500 words; and Travel (any traveling done in piston-engine aircraft), 1,000-2,500 words. Buys 30 mss/year. Send complete ms. Length: 1,000-2,500 words. Pays $200-500.

PRIVATE PILOT, Fancy Publications Corp., P.O. Box 6050, Mission Viejo CA 92690-6050. (714)855-8822. Fax: (714)855-3045. Editor: Mary F. Silitch. 75% freelance written. Works with a small number of new/unpublished writers each year. For owner/pilots of private aircraft, for student pilots and others aspiring to attain additional ratings and experience. "We take a unique, but limited view within our field." Estab. 1964. Circ. 105,000. Buys first North American serial rights. Pays on publication. Publishes ms average of 6 months after acceptance. No simultaneous submissions. Query for electronic submissions. Reports in 2 months. Sample copy for $4. Writer's guidelines for SASE.

Nonfiction: Material on techniques of flying, developments in aviation, product and specific airplane test reports, travel by aircraft, and development and use of airports. All must be related to general aviation field. Buys about 60-90 mss/year. Query. Length: 1,000-4,000 words. Pays $75-300.

Photos: Pays $50 for four-color prints or transparencies purchased with ms or on assignment. Pays $300 for color transparencies used on cover.

• There is a greater emphasis on quality photography at this magazine.

Tips: "Freelancer must know the subject about which he is writing and use good grammar; remember that we try to relate to the middle segment of the business/pleasure flying public. We see too many 'first flight' type of articles. Most writers do not do enough research on their subject. We would like to see more material on business-related flying, more on people involved in flying."

PROFESSIONAL PILOT, Queensmith Communications, 3014 Colvin St., Alexandria VA 22314. (703)370-0606. Fax: (703)370-7082. Editor: Clifton Stroud. 75% freelance written. Monthly magazine on major and regional airline, corporate, military and various other types of professional aviation. "Our readers are commercial pilots with highest ratings and the editorial content reflects their knowledge and experience." Estab. 1967. Circ. 35,000. **Pays on acceptance.** Publishes ms an average of 3 months after acceptance. Byline given. Kill fee negotiable. Buys all rights. Free sample copy.

Nonfiction: How-to (avionics and aircraft flight checks), humor, interview/profile, personal experience (if a lesson for professional pilots), photo feature, technical (avionics, weather, engines, aircraft). All issues have a theme such as regional airline operations, maintenance, jet aircraft, helicopters, etc. Buys 40 mss/year. Query. Length: 750-2,500. Pays $200-1,000. Sometimes pays expenses of writers on assignment.

Photos: Send photos with submission. Prefers transparencies. Offers no additional payment for photos accepted with ms. Captions and identification of subjects required. Buys all rights.

Columns/Departments: Pireps (aviation news), 300-500 words. Buys 12 mss/year. Query. Pays $100-250.

Tips: Query first. "Freelancer should have background in aviation that will make his articles believable to highly qualified pilots of commercial aircraft. We are placing a greater emphasis on airline operations, management and pilot concerns."

Business and Finance

Business publications give executives and consumers a range of information from local business news and trends to national overviews and laws that affect them. National and regional publications are listed below in separate categories. Magazines that have a technical slant are in the Trade section under Business Management, Finance or Management and Supervision categories.

National

‡BUSINESS 95, Success Strategies For Small Business, Group IV Communications, Inc., #100, 125 Auburn Ct., Thousand Oaks CA 91362-3617. (805)496-6156. Editor: Daniel Kehrer. Editorial Director: Don Phillipson. Articles Editor: Frances Huffman. 75% freelance written. Bimonthly magazine for small and independent business. "We publish only practical articles of interest to small business owners all across America; also some small business owner profiles." Estab. 1989. Circ. 630,000. **Pays on acceptance.** Publishes ms an average of 4 months after acceptance. Byline given. Offers 25% kill fee. First and non-exclusive reprint rights. Simultaneous queries OK. Reports in 3 months. Sample copy for $4. Writer's guidelines for #10 SASE. All submissions will also be considered for *I.B.*, also published by Group IV.

Nonfiction: How-to articles for operating a small business. No "generic" business articles, articles on big business, articles on how to start a business or general articles on economic theory. Buys 80-100 mss/year. Query with résumé and published clips; do not send ms. Length: 1,000-2,000 words. Pays $500-1,500 for assigned articles. Pays expenses of writers on assignment.

Columns/Departments: Tax Tactics, Small Business Computing, Marketing Moves, Ad-visor, Banking & Finance, Business Cost-Savers, all 1,000-2,000 words. Buys 40-50 mss/year. Query with résumé and published clips. Pays $500-1,500.

Tips: "Talk to small business owners anywhere in America about what they want to read, what concerns or interests them in running a business. All areas open, but we use primarily professional business writers with top credentials in the field."

BUSINESS START-UPS, Entrepreneur Group, Inc., 2392 Morse Ave., Irvine CA 92714. (714)261-2083. Editor: Rieva Lesonsky. 20-25% freelance written. Monthly magazine on small business. "Provides how-to information for starting a small business, running a small business during the 'early' years and profiles of entrepreneurs who have started successful small businesses." Estab. 1989. Circ. 210,000. **Pays on acceptance.** Byline given. Offers 20% kill fee. Buys first time international rights. Submit seasonal/holiday material 6 months in advance. Reports in 2 months on queries. Sample copy for $3. Writer's guidelines for SASE. Please write: "Attn: Writer's Guidelines" on envelope.
Nonfiction: "We are especially seeking how-to articles for starting a small business. Please read the magazine and writer's guidelines first before querying." Interview/profiles on entrepreneurs. Query. Length: 1,800. Pays $300.
Photos: State availability of photos with submission. Identification of subjects required.

BUSINESS TODAY, Meridian International, Inc., P.O. Box 10010, Ogden UT 84409. (801)394-9446. 40% freelance written. Monthly magazine covering all aspects of business. Particularly interested in tips to small/medium business managers. **Pays on acceptance.** Publishes ms an average of 3 months after acceptance. Byline given. Buys first rights, second serial (reprint) rights and nonexclusive reprint rights. Reports in 2 months with SASE. Sample copy for $1 and 9×12 SAE. Writer's guidelines for #10 SASE. All requests for samples and guidelines, and queries should be addressed Attn: Editorial Staff.
Nonfiction: General interest articles about employee relations, management principles, trends in finance, technology, ergonomics, and "how to do it better" stories. Articles covering up-to-date practical business information are welcome. Cover stories are often profiles of people who have expertise and success in a specific aspect of business. Buys 40 mss/year. Query. Length: 1,000 words. Pays 15¢/word for first rights plus non-exclusive reprint rights. Payment for second rights is 10¢/word.
Photos: Send photos with ms. Reviews 35mm or larger transparencies and 5×7 or 8×10 color prints. Pays $35 for inside photo; pays $50 for cover photo. Captions, model releases and identification of subjects required.
Tips: "We're looking for meaty, hard-core business articles with practical applications. Profiles should be prominent business-people, preferably Fortune-500 league. The key is a well-written query letter that: 1) demonstrates that the subject of the article is tried-and-true and has national appeal, 2) shows that the article will have a clear, focused theme, 3) gives evidence that the writer/photographer is a professional, even if a beginner."

BUSINESS WEEK, McGraw Hill, 1221 Avenue of the Americas, New York NY 10020. Weekly publication covering news and trends in the world of business. This magazine did not respond to our request for information. Query before submitting.

THE ECONOMIC MONITOR, The Charles B McFadden Co., Inc., P.O. Box 2268, Winter Park FL 32790. (407)629-4548. Fax: (407)629-0762. 50% freelance written. Quarterly magazine on economics and national economic policy. "*The Economic Monitor* publishes articles that explain economic issues in lay terms. It observes and comments on national economic and social policy from a conservative free-market viewpoint." Estab. 1990. Circ. 500. Pays on publication. Publishes ms an average of 3 months after acceptance. Buys one-time rights. Editorial lead time 3 months. Accepts simultaneous and previously published submissions. Reports in 3 weeks on queries; 1 month on mss (prefer query first). Sample copy for 9×12 SAE with 2 first-class stamps. Writer's guidelines for #10 SASE.
Nonfiction: Book excerpts, essays, exposé, humor, interview/profile and opinion. "No opinion pieces that are not backed by research." Buys 16 mss/year. Query with published clips. Length: 500-2,500 words. Pays $50 minimum for assigned articles; $25 for unsolicited articles. Pays contributor copies "in addition to any cash stipend. Sometimes will pay in copies for unpublished or published book excerpts that the author can use for publicity/exposure."
Columns/Departments: The Press (media bias), 700-1,000 words. Buys 2 mss/year. Query with published clips. Pays $25-50.
Tips: "The Monitor is a not-for-profit project. We eagerly seek new conservative writers. Although we only offer small stipends at present, we are looking for material that is suitable for expansion into books and/or syndication. Anything we use must be well researched and backed by facts. We look for tight, well-written copy. We are particularly interested in these subjects: (1) liberal media bias; (2) effect of tax policy on gross domestic product; and (3) how government transfers the cost of its social programs to business."

ENTREPRENEUR MAGAZINE, 2392 Morse Ave., Irvine CA 92714. Fax: (714)755-4211. Editor: Rieva Lesonsky. 40% freelance written. "Readers are small business owners seeking information on running a better business." Circ. 380,000. **Pays on acceptance.** Publishes ms an average of 3-5 months after acceptance. Buys first international rights. Byline given. Submit seasonal/holiday material 6 months in advance of issue date.

Reports in 2 months. Sample copy for $3. Writer's guidelines for #10 SASE. Please write "Attn: Writer's Guidelines" on envelope.

Nonfiction: How-to (information on running a business, profiles of unique entrepreneurs). Buys 60-70 mss/year. Query with clips of published work and SASE. Length: 2,000 words. Payment varies.

Photos: "We use color transparencies to illustrate articles. Please state availability with query." Uses standard color transparencies. Buys various rights. Model release required.

Tips: "Read several issues of the magazine! Study the feature articles. (Columns are not open to freelancers.) It's so exciting when a writer goes beyond the typical, flat "business magazine query" — how to write a press release, how to negotiate with vendors, etc. — and instead investigates a current trend and then develops a story on how that trend affects small business."

EXECUTIVE FEMALE, NAFE, 4th Floor, 30 Irving Place, New York NY 10003. (212)645-0770. Fax: (212)477-2200. Editor-in-Chief: Basia Hellwig. Executive Editor: Patti Watts. Assistant Managing Editor: Dorian Burden. Assistant Editor: Melissa Wahl. 60% freelance written. Bimonthly magazine emphasizing "useful career, business and financial information for the upwardly mobile female." Prefers to work with published/established writers. Estab. 1975. Circ. 200,000. Byline given. **Pays on acceptance.** Publishes ms an average of 2 months after acceptance. Submit seasonal/holiday material 6 months in advance. Buys first rights, second serial (reprint) rights to material originally published elsewhere. Accepts previously published material. Send photocopy of article or typed ms with rights for sale noted and information about when and where the article previously appeared. Pays 25% of amount paid for an original article. Reports in 2 months. Sample copy for $2.50. Writer's guidelines for #10 SASE.

Nonfiction: "Articles on any aspect of career advancement and financial planning are welcomed." Needs how-tos for managers and articles about coping on the job, trends in the workplace, financial planning, trouble shooting, business communication, time and stress management, career goal-setting and get-ahead strategies. Written queries only. Submit photos with ms (b&w prints or transparencies) or include suggestions for artwork. Length: 800-2,000 words. Pays 50¢/word. Pays for local travel and telephone calls.

Columns/Departments: Your Money (savings, financial advice, economic trends, interesting tips); Managing Smart (tips on managing people, getting ahead); and Your Business (entrepreneurial stories). Buys 20 mss/year. Query with published clips or send complete ms. Length: 250-1,000 words. Pays 50¢/word.

‡HOMEWORKING MOTHERS, Mothers' Home Business Network, Box 423, East Meadow NY 11554-0423. Attn: Editorial Submission. (516)997-7394. Fax: (516)997-0839. Editor: Georganne Fiumara. 25% freelance written. Will work with new/unpublished writers. Quarterly newsletter "written for mothers who have home businesses or would like to. These mothers want to work at home so that they can spend more time with their children." Circ. 10,000. Pays on publication. Publishes ms an average of 3-6 months after acceptance. Byline given. Buys one-time rights. Submit seasonal/holiday material 8 months in advance. Accepts simultaneous and previously published submissions. Send photocopy of article and information about when and where the article previously appeared. For reprints pays 100% of the amount paid for an original article. Reports in 1 month on queries; 6 weeks on mss. Sample copy for $5 and #10 SAE with 75¢ postage.

Nonfiction: Book excerpts, essays, how-to, humor, inspirational, personal experience, technical — *home business information* "all relating to working at home or home-based businesses." No articles about questionable home business opportunities. Buys 5-10 mss/year. Query with published clips, or send complete ms. Length: 300-1,000 words. Payment varies. Sometimes pays writers with contributor copies or in advertising or promoting a writer's business if applicable. "We would like to receive in-depth descriptions of one home business possibility, i.e., bookkeeping, commercial art, etc. — at least 3,000 words to be published in booklet form. (Pays $150 and buys all rights)."

Columns/Departments: It's My Business (mothers describe their businesses, how they got started, and how they handle work and children at the same time); Advice for Homeworking Mothers (business, marketing and tax basics written by professionals); Considering the Possibilities (ideas and descriptions of legitimate home business opportunities); A Look at a Book (excerpts from books describing some aspect of working at home or popular work-at-home professions); Time Out for Kids (inspirational material to help mothers cope with working at home). Length varies, but average 500 words. Buys 4 mss/year. Send complete ms.

Poetry: Free verse, light verse, traditional. "About being a mother working at home or home business." Submit maximum 5 poems. Pays $5.

Fillers: Facts and newsbreaks "about working at home for 'Marketing, Managing and More' page." Length: 150 words maximum. Pays $10.

Tips: "We prefer that the writer have personal experience with this lifestyle or be an expert in the field when giving general home business information. It's My Business and Time Out for Kids are most open to freelancers. Writers should read *HM* before trying to write for us."

I.B. (Independent Business, America's Small Business Magazine, Group IV Communications, Inc., #100, 125 Auburn Ct., Thousand Oaks CA 91362-3617. (805)496-6156. Editor: Daniel Kehrer. Editorial Director: Don Phillipson. Articles Editor: Frances Huffman. 75% freelance written. Bimonthly magazine for small and independent business. "We publish only practical articles of interest to small business owners all across America; also some small business owner profiles." Estab. 1989. Circ. 630,000. **Pays on acceptance.**

Publishes ms an average of 4 months after acceptance. Byline given. Offers 25% kill fee. First and non-exclusive reprint rights. Simultaneous queries OK. Reports in 3 months. Sample copy for $4. Writer's guidelines for #10 SASE. All submissions will also be considered for I.B., also published by Group IV.

Nonfiction: How-to articles for operating a small business. No "generic" business articles, articles on big business, articles on how to start a business or general articles on economic theory. Buys 80-100 mss/year. Query with résumé and published clips; do not send mss. Length: 1,000-2,000 words. Pays $500-1,500 for assigned articles. Pays expenses of writers on assignment.

Columns/Departments: Tax Tactics, Small Business Computing, Marketing Moves, Ad-visor, Banking & Finance, Business Cost-Savers, all 1,000-2,000 words. Buys 40-50 mss/year. Query with résumé and published clips. Pays $500-1,500.

Tips: "Talk to small business owners anywhere in America about what they want to read, what concerns or interests them in running a business. All areas open, but we use primarily professional business writers with top credentials in the field."

INCOME OPPORTUNITIES, IO Publications, 1500 Broadway, New York NY 10036-4015. (212)642-0600. Fax: (212)302-8269. Editor: Stephen Wagner. Managing Editor: Arthur Blougouras. 90% freelance written. Monthly magazine covering small business. Estab. 1956. Circ. 425,000. **Pays on acceptance.** Publishes ms an average of 5 months after acceptance. Byline given. Buys second serial (reprint) or all rights and makes work-for-hire assignments. Submit seasonal/holiday material 6 months in advance. Query for electronic submissions. Reports in 3 weeks on queries, 1 month on mss. *Writer's Market* recommends allowing 2 months for reply. Free sample copy. Writer's guidelines for #10 SASE.

Nonfiction: How-to (start a small or home business), new product (for mail order, flea market sales). Need freelance material for 2 home business issues. No purely inspirational articles. Buys 100 mss/year. Query. Length: 600-2,500 words. Pays $100-350. Sometimes pays expenses of writers on assignment.

Photos: Send photos with submission. Offers no additional payment for photos accepted with ms. Identification of subjects required. Buys all rights.

Tips: Areas most open to freelancers are "profiles of successful small-business operators. Details of how they started, start-up costs, how they operate, advertising methods, tools, materials, equipment needed, projected or actual earnings, advice to readers for success."

MONEY, Time & Life Bldg., Rockefeller Center, New York NY 10020. Monthly publication covering investment and other money-related topics. This magazine did not respond to our request for information. Query before submitting.

NATION'S BUSINESS, US Chamber of Commerce, 1615 H St. NW, Washington DC 20062-2000. (202)463-5650. Fax: (202)887-3437. Editor: Robert T. Gray. Managing Editor: Mary McElveen. 50% freelance written. Monthly magazine covering management of small businesses. Estab. 1912. Circ. 865,000. **Pays on acceptance.** Publishes ms an average of 6 months after acceptance. Byline given. Kill fee negotiable. Buys all rights. Query for electronic submissions. Accepts previously published articles. Send tearsheet or photocopy of article or typed ms with rights for sale noted and information about when and where the article previously appeared. Reports in 1 month. Sample copy for $2.50. Free writer's guidelines.

• Ranked as one of the best markets for freelance writers in *Writer's Digest* magazine's annual "Top 100 Markets," January 1994.

Nonfiction: Book excerpts, how-to, new product, personal experience. No opinion or corporate personnel. Buys 100 mss/year. Query. Length: 250-3,000 words. Pays $100-2,000. Sometimes pays expenses of writers on assignment.

OWNER-MANAGER, P.O. Box 1521, Wall St. Station, New York NY 10268-1521. (212)323-8056. Editor: Charles Riley II. Managing Editor: Jeff Deasy. Publisher: V. Ricasio. 20% freelance written. Bimonthly magazine for business and enterprise. "Our readers are owners who manage their own companies. The editorial mission is to provide them with information to manage their businesses, but not merely to become better businessmen but fulfilled individuals as well." Estab. 1992. Circ. 10,000. Pays on publication. Publishes ms an average of 4 months after acceptance. Byline given. Offers 30% kill fee. Buys first rights or second serial rights. Editorial lead time 2 months. Submit seasonal material 3 months in advance. Accepts previously published submissions. Query for electronic submissions. Sample copy for 8½×11 SAE with 1 first-class stamp. Writer's guideliines for #10 SASE.

Nonfiction: Book excerpts, essays, general interest, how-to (not detailed guide but why such actions are needed), interview/profile, opinion, technical. Buys 8 mss/year. Send complete ms. Length: 2,500-5,000 words. Pays $1,000 minimum for assigned articles, $350 minimum for unsolicited articles.

Photos: State availability of photos with submission. Reviews prints. Negotiates payment individually. Captions required. Buys one-time rights.

Columns/Departments: Buys 4 mss/year. Query. Pays $250-500.

Tips: "Cover stories are most open to freelancers."

PROFIT, The Magazine for Canadian Entrepreneurs, CB Media Limited, 5th Floor, 777 Bay St., Toronto, Ontario Canada M5W 1A7. (416)596-5999. Editor: Rick Spence. 80% freelance written. Quarterly magazine covering small and medium business. "We specialize in specific, useful information that helps our readers manage their businesses better. We want Canadian stories only." Estab. 1982. Circ. 110,000. **Pays on acceptance.** Publishes ms an average of 1-2 months after acceptance. Byline given. Kill fee varies. Buys first North American serial rights and database rights. Submit seasonal/holiday material 6 months in advance. Query for electronic submissions. Reports in 1 month on queries; 2-6 weeks on mss. Sample copy for 9×12 SAE with 84¢ postage (Canadian). Free writer's guidelines.
Nonfiction: How-to (business management tips), strategies and Canadian business profiles. Buys 50 mss/year. Query with published clips. Length: 800-2,000 words. Pays $500-2,000 (Canadian). Pays expenses of writers on assignment. State availability of photos with submission.
Columns/Departments: Innovators (interesting new Canadian products, inventions or services), 200 words; Finance (info on raising capital in Canada), 700 words; Marketing (marketing strategies for independent business), 700 words. Buys 80 mss/year. Query with published clips. Length: 200-800 words. Pays $150-600 (Canadian).
Tips: "We're wide open to freelancers with good ideas and some knowledge of business. Read the magazine and understand it before submitting your ideas."

‡REPORT ON BUSINESS MAGAZINE, Globe and Mail, 444 Front St. W., Toronto Ontario M5V 2S9 Canada. (416)585-5499. Editor: David Olive. 50% freelance written. Monthly "business magazine like *Forbes* or *Manhattan, Inc.* which tries to capture major trends and personalities." Circ. 300,000. **Pays on acceptance.** Publishes ms an average of 4 months after acceptance. Byline given. Offers 50% kill fee. Buys first North American serial rights. Query for electronic submissions. Reports in 3 weeks. Free sample copy.
Nonfiction: Book excerpts, exposé, interview/profile, new product, photo feature. Buys 30 mss/year. Query with published clips. Length: 2,000-4,000 words. Pays $200-3,000. Pays expenses of writers on assignment.
Tips: "For features send a one-page story proposal. We prefer to write about personalities involved in corporate events."

TECHNICAL ANALYSIS OF STOCKS & COMMODITIES, The Trader's Magazine, Technical Analysis, Inc., 4757 California Ave. SW, Seattle WA 98116-4499. (206)938-0570. Publisher: Jack K. Hutson. 75% freelance written. Eager to work with new/unpublished writers. Magazine covers methods of investing and trading stocks, bonds and commodities (futures), options, mutual funds and precious metals. Estab. 1982. Circ. 42,000. Pays on publication. Publishes ms an average of 3 months after acceptance. Byline given. Offers 50% kill fee. Buys all rights; however, second serial (reprint) rights revert to the author, provided copyright credit is given. Accepts previously published submissions. Send tearsheet or photocopy of article or typed ms with rights for sale noted and information about when and where the article appeared. Query for electronic submissions. Reports in 3 weeks on queries; 1 month on mss. Sample copy for $5. Writer's guidelines for #10 SASE.
Nonfiction: Thomas R. Hartle, editor. Reviews (new software or hardware that can make a trader's life easier, comparative reviews of software books, services, etc.); how-to (trade); technical (trading and software aids to trading); utilities (charting or computer programs, surveys, statistics or information to help the trader study or interpret market movements); humor (unusual incidents of market occurrences, cartoons). "No newsletter-type, buy-sell recommendations. The article subject must relate to trading psychology, technical analysis, charting or a numerical technique used to trade securities or futures. Virtually requires graphics with every article." Buys 150 mss/year. Query with published clips if available or send complete ms. Length: 1,000-4,000 words. Pays $100-500. (Applies per inch base rate and premium rate—write for information). Sometimes pays expenses of writers on assignment.
Photos: Christine M. Morrison, photo editor. State availability of photos. Pays $20-150 for b&w or color negatives with prints or positive slides. Captions, model releases and identification of subjects required. Buys one-time and reprint rights.
Columns/Departments: Buys 100 mss/year. Query. Length: 800-1,600 words. Pays $50-300.
Fillers: Karen Webb, fillers editor. Jokes and cartoons on investment humor. Must relate to trading stocks, bonds, options, mutual funds or commodities. Buys 20/year. Length: 500 words. Pays $20-50.
Tips: "Describe how to use technical analysis, charting or computer work in day-to-day trading of stocks, bonds, mutual funds, options or commodities. A blow-by-blow account of how a trade was made, including the trader's thought processes, is, to our subscribers, the very best received story. One of our prime considerations is to instruct in a manner that the lay person can comprehend. We are not hyper-critical of writing style. The completeness and accuracy of submitted material are of the utmost consideration. Write for detailed writer's guidelines."

‡WORKING AT HOME, P.O.Box 200504, Cartersville GA 30120. Editor: Mrs. H.C. McGarity. 20% freelance written. Triannual newsletter covering ideas for small home-based business. "Offers wide variety of suggestions for and descriptions of, businesses for home-bound people to start in their homes. Many may be started with little money, sometimes no money." Estab. 1985. Circ. under 400. **Pays on acceptance.** Publishes ms an average of 3 months after acceptance. Byline given. Buys first North American serial rights. Editorial lead time 3 months. Submit seasonal material 4 months in advance. Accepts simultaneous and previously published submissions. Reports in 2 weeks on queries, 1 month on mss. Sample copy for $2.75 (in US); $3.75 elsewhere. Writer's guidelines for #10 SASE.

Nonfiction: How-to (start a small home business on small or no investment), new products, personal experience. "Nothing on franchise ideas or high-investment schemes." Buys 2-3 mss/year. Query. Length: 300-400 words. Pay 4¢/word.

Photos: State availability of photos with submission. Reviews contact sheets. Negotiates payment individually. Captions, model releases, identification of subjects required. Buys one-time rights.

Tips: "Keep submissions short and succinct."

YOUR MONEY, Consumers Digest Inc., 5705 N. Lincoln Ave., Chicago IL 60659. (312)275-3590. Editor: Dennis Fertig. 75% freelance written. Bimonthly magazine on personal finance. "We cover the broad range of topics associated with personal finance—spending, saving, investing earning, etc." Estab. 1979. Circ. 385,000. **Pays on acceptance.** Publishes ms an average of 2 months after acceptance. Byline given. Offers 50% kill fee. Buys first rights and second serial (reprint) rights. Reports in 3 months on queries. Do not send computer disks. Sample copy and writer's guidelines for 9 × 12 SAE with $1 postage. Writer's guidelines for #10 SASE.

Nonfiction: How-to. "No first-person success stories or profiles of one company." Buys 25 mss/year. Send complete ms or query and clips. Include stamped, self-addressed postcard for more prompt response. Length: 1,500-2,500 words. Pays 35¢/word for assigned articles. Pays expenses of writers on assignment.

Tips: "Know the subject matter. Develop real sources in the investment community. Demonstrate a reader-friendly style that will help make the sometimes complicated subject of investing more accessible to the average person. Fill manuscripts with real-life examples of people who actually have done the kinds of things discussed—people we can later photograph."

Regional

ADCOM MAGAZINE New England's Own Advertising and Marketing Magazine, 18 Imperial Place, Providence RI 02903. (401)751-6550. Fax: (401)751-6703. Editor: Karen Sullivan. 10% freelance written. Monthly magazine covering advertising, marketing, media and PR. "*Adcom Magazine* provides information and features on advertising, marketing, media, PR and related fields within New England. Primary freelance need: case studies and strategies. Readership: ad agencies, corporate advertising staff." Estab. 1976. Circ. 9,000. Pays 30 days after publication. Publishes ms an average of 2 months after acceptance. Byline given. No kill fee. Buys first rights or second serial (reprint) rights. Submit seasonal/holiday material 3 months in advance. Accepts simultaneous and previously published submissions. Send photocopy of article and information about when and where the article previously appeared. Query for electronic submissions. Reports in 1 month. Sample copy for 9 × 12 SAE with 6 first-class stamps.

Nonfiction: How-to, opinion, strategies, case studies, industry overviews. Buys 10 mss/year. Query with published clips. Length: 500-3,000 words. Pays $75-350 for assigned articles; $25-50 for unsolicited articles.

Photos: State availability of photos with submission. Reviews contact sheets, transparencies and 5 × 7 prints. Offers $10-20/photo. Captions, model releases and identification of subjects required. Buys one-time rights.

Columns/Departments: Case Study (case study of a company's advertising/marketing program; must be a New England company), 1,200-3,000 words; Strategies ("how-to" or explanatory articles that relate to advertising, PR, marketing, direct marketing or media), 400-700 words; Industry Overview (an overview of marketing/advertising within specific industries in New England), 700-2,500 words. Buys 10 mss/year. Query with published clips. Length: 400-3,000 words. Pays $50-350.

Tips: "Call the editor. When she's not on deadline she's happy to brainstorm with prospective contributors. Best to send her a letter with clips first, though. Remember—submissions must have New England focus. Good luck!"

BOSTON BUSINESS JOURNAL, P&L Publications, 200 High St., Boston MA 02110-3036. (617)330-1000. Fax: (617)330-1016. Editor: Charles Heschmeyer. 20% freelance written. Weekly newspaper covering business in Greater Boston. "Our audience is top managers at small, medium and Fortune 500 companies." Circ. 22,000. Pays on publication. Publishes ms an average of 2 weeks after acceptance. Byline given. Offers 50% kill fee. Buys all rights. Query for electronic submissions. Reports in 1 week on queries. Does not accept unsolicited mss.

Nonfiction: Freelancers used for special focus sections on hotels, health care, real estate, construction, computers and the office. Buys 50 mss/year. Query with published clips. Length: 800-1,000 words. Pays $155 for assigned articles.

Photos: State availability of photos with submission. Reviews 8 × 10 prints. Pays $40-55/photo. Identification of subjects required. Buys one-time and reprint rights.

Tips: "Look for hard news angle versus feature angle. Use 'numbers' liberally in the story. We prefer submissions on computer disk (call for specifics). We are only interested in local builders stories written by local writers."

BOULDER COUNTY BUSINESS REPORT, Suite D, 4885 Riverbend Rd., Boulder CO 80301-2617. (303)440-4950. Fax: (303)440-8954. Editor: Jerry W. Lewis. 75% freelance written. Prefers to work with published/established writers; works with a small number of new/unpublished writers each year. Monthly newspaper covering Boulder County business issues. Offers "news tailored to a monthly theme and read primarily by Colorado businesspeople and by some investors nationwide. Philosophy: Descriptive, well-written articles that reach behind the scene to examine area's business activity." Estab. 1982. Circ. 18,000. Pays on publication. Publishes ms an average of 1 month after acceptance. Byline given. Buys one-time rights and second serial (reprint) rights. Query for electronic submissions. Reports in 1 month on queries; 2 weeks on mss. *Writer's Market* recommends allowing 2 months for reply. Sample copy for $1.44.
Nonfiction: Interview/profile, new product, examination of competition in a particular line of business. "All our issues are written around one or two monthly themes. No articles are accepted in which the subject has not been pursued in depth and both sides of an issue presented in a writing style with flair." Buys 120 mss/year. Query with published clips. Length: 250-2,000 words. Pays $50-300.
Photos: State availability of photos with query letter. Reviews b&w contact sheets. Pays $10 maximum for b&w contact sheet. Identification of subjects required. Buys one-time rights and reprint rights.
Tips: "Must be able to localize a subject. In-depth articles are written by assignment. The freelancer located in the Colorado area has an excellent chance here."

BUSINESS, Omni Media, 2065 Cantu Court, Sarasota FL 34232. (813)378-9048. Editor: Deborah Robbins Millman. 60% freelance written. Bimonthly magazine for business. "We are a regional business magazine covering Sarasota and Manatee counties in Florida." Circ. 10,000. Pays on publication. Publishes ms an average of 2 months after acceptance. Byline given. Makes work-for-hire assignments. Editorial lead time 2 months. Submit seasonal material 2-3 months in advance. Prefers WordPerfect 4.0 5¼" disks.
Nonfiction: Book excerpts, essays, how-to, interview/profile, travel and business advice. No fiction. Buys 30-40 mss/year. Query with published clips. Length: 1,000-3,500 words. Pays $0-150. Pays with contributor's copies "if unsolicited article of interest for which we have not budgeted funds."
Photos: Send photos with submission. Offers no additional payment for photos accepted with ms in most cases but negotiates payment individually in some cases. Captions and identification of subjects required. Buys one-time rights.
Tips: "Send a résumé and writing sample, plus any story ideas."

BUSINESS NEW HAMPSHIRE MAGAZINE, Suite 201, 404 Chestnut St., Manchester NH 03101-1831. Editor: Robin Baskerville. 50% freelance written. Monthly magazine with focus on business, politics and people of New Hampshire. "Our audience consists of the owners and top managers of New Hampshire businesses." Estab. 1983. Circ. 13,000. Pays on publication. Publishes ms an average of 2 months after acceptance. Byline given. Writer's guidelines available to likely contributors.
Nonfiction: Features—how-to, interview/profile. Buys 24 mss/year. Query with published clips and résumé. "No unsolicited manuscript; interested in local writers only." Length: 750-2,500 words. $75-250 for assigned articles.
Photos: Both b&w and color photos used. Pays $40-80. Buys one-time rights.
Tips: "I *always* want clips and résumé with queries. Freelance stories are almost always assigned. Stories *must* be local to New Hampshire."

‡COLORADO BUSINESS, Wiesner Inc., 7009 S. Potomac St., Englewood CO 80112. (303)397-7600. Editor: Julie Hutchinson. 75% freelance written. Monthly magazine covering Colorado-based businesses. Estab. 1973. Circ. 20,000. **Pays on acceptance.** Publishes ms an average of 3 months after acceptance. Byline given. Offers 50% kill fee. Buys first rights. Editorial lead time 3 months. Submit seasonal material 6 months in advance. Query for electronic submissions. Reports in 1 month on queries.
Nonfiction: Business, general interest, historical/nostalgic, how-to, interview/profile, new product, opinion, personal experience, photo feature, technical. Buys 40 mss/year. Query with published clips. Length: 700-4,000 words. Pays $200 for assigned articles; $50 for unsolicited articles. Sometimes pays expenses of writers on assignment.
Photos: State availability of photos with submission. Reviews contact sheets, transparencies. Negotiates payment individually. Captions, identification of subjects required. Buys one-time rights.
Columns/Departments: Buys 24 mss/year. Query with published clips. Pays $50-200.
Tips: "Know the magazine before you pitch me. Solid story ideas specifically geared to Colorado audience. No boring stories. No corporatese."

CORPORATE CLEVELAND, Business Journal Publishing Co., 3rd Floor, 1720 Euclid Ave., Cleveland OH 44115. (216)621-1644. Fax: (216)621-5918. Publisher/Editor: Richard J. Osborne. Executive Editor: Edward J. Walsh. 25% freelance written. Prefers to work with published/established writers based in Northeast Ohio. Monthly magazine covering general business topics. "*Corporate Cleveland* serves Northeast Ohio. Readers are business executives in the area engaged in manufacturing, agriculture, mining, construction, transportation, communications, utilities, retail and wholesale trade, services and government." Estab. 1991. Circ. 31,000. Pays for features on publication. Query first.

Nonfiction: General interest, how-to, interview/profile, opinion, personal experience. "In all cases, write with the Northeast Ohio executive in mind. Stories should give readers useful information on business within the state, trends in management, ways to manage better or other developments that would affect them in their professional careers." Buys 14-20 mss/year. Query with published clips. Length: 800-2,500 words. Pays $75 minimum. Sometimes pays expenses of writers on assignment. All specifics must be negotiated in advance.
Photos: State availability of photos. Reviews b&w and color transparencies and prints. Captions and identification of subjects required. Buys variable rights.
Columns/Departments: News and People (profiles of business execs). Query with published clips. Length: 100-600 words. Pay varies.
Tips: "Features are most open to freelancers. Come up with new ideas or information for our readers: executives in manufacturing and service industries. Writers should be aware of the trend toward specialization in magazine publishing with strong emphasis on people in coverage."

‡**FLORIDA TREND, Magazine of Florida Business and Finance,** Box 611, St. Petersburg FL 33731. (813)821-5800. Publisher: Lynda Keever. Monthly magazine covering business economics and public policy for Florida business people and investors. Circ. 50,000. Pays on final acceptance. Byline given. Buys first North American serial rights. Reports in 2 months. Sample copy for $3.50 plus tax and postage.
Nonfiction: Business and finance. Buys 10-12 mss/year. Query with or without published clips. Length: 1,200-2,500 words. Manuscripts not returned.

MONEY SAVING IDEAS, The National Research Bureau Inc., P.O. Box 1, Burlington IA 52601-0001. (319)752-5415. Fax: (319)752-3421. Editor: Nancy Heinzel. 75% freelance written. Quarterly magazine that features money saving strategies. "We are interested in money saving tips on various subjects (insurance, travel, heating/cooling, buying a house, ways to cut costs and balance checkbooks). Our audience is mainly industrial and office workers." Estab. 1948. Pays on publication. Publishes ms an average of 1 year after acceptance. Byline given. Buys all rights. Sample copy and writers guidelines for #10 SAE with 2 first-class stamps. Writer's guidelines for #10 SASE.
Nonfiction: How-to (save on grocery bills, heating/cooling bills, car expenses, insurance, travel). Query with or without published clips, or send complete ms. Length: 500-700 words. Pays 4¢/word.
Tips: "Follow our guidelines. Keep articles to stated length, double-spaced, neatly typed. If writer wishes rejected manuscript returned include SASE. Name, address and word length should appear on first page."

OREGON BUSINESS, Oregon Business Media, Suite 407, 921 SW Morrison, Portland OR 97205. (503)223-0304. Fax: (503)221-6544. Editor: Kathy Dimond. 20% freelance written. Monthly magazine covering business in Oregon. Estab. 1981. Circ. 20,000. Pays on publication. Publishes ms an average of 3 months after acceptance. Byline given. Buys first rights. No simultaneous submissions or previously published submissions. Reports in 2 months. Sample copy for 9 × 12 SAE with 5 first-class stamps.
Nonfiction: Statewide business magazine. Focus is on world trade, finance, family businesses, government regulations, and management issues. Geared to needs and interests of *Oregon* businesses and "helping Oregon companies grow." Virtually all freelance is assigned—query first. Buys 25 mss/year. Length: 600-2,000 words. Pays $100-400 depending on length of assignment.
Photos: D.C. Jesse Burkhardt, photo editor. "Always looking for new talent, and creativity—especially outside of Portland." Pays $75/assignment, and expenses.

‡**REGARDIES: THE MAGAZINE OF WASHINGTON BUSINESS,** 1010 Wisconsin Ave. NW, Washington DC 20007. (202)342-0410. Editor: Richard Blow. 80% freelance written. Works with a small number of new/unpublished writers each year. Monthly magazine covering business and general features in the Washington DC metropolitan area for Washington business executives. Circ. 60,000. Pays within 30 days after publication. Publishes ms an average of 2 months after acceptance. Byline given. Offers variable kill fee. Buys first serial and second serial (reprint) rights. Submit seasonal/holiday material 3 months in advance. Reports in 3 weeks. Sample copy for $8 and 9 × 12 SAE.
Nonfiction: Profiles (of business leaders), investigative reporting, real estate, advertising, politics, lifestyle, media, retailing, communications, labor and financial issues—all on the Washington business scene. "If it is not the kind of story that could just as easily run in a good city magazine or a national magazine like *Harper's, Atlantic, Esquire,* etc., I don't want to see it." Also buys book mss for excerpt. No how-to. Narrative nonfiction only. Buys 90 mss/year. Length: 4,000 words average. Buys 5-6/issue. Pays negotiable rate. Pays the expenses of writers on assignment.
Columns/Departments: Length: 1,500 words average. Buys 8-12/issue. Pays negotiable rates.
Tips: "The most frequent mistake writers make is not including enough information and data about business which, with public companies, is easy enough to find. This results in flawed analysis and a willingness to accept the 'official line.' "

ROCHESTER BUSINESS MAGAZINE, Rochester Business, Inc., 1600 Lyell Ave., Rochester NY 14606-2395. (716)458-8280. Fax: (716)458-9831. Editor: Kristina Hutch. 25% freelance written. Monthly magazine. "*RBM* is a colorful tutorial business publication targeted specifically toward business owners and upper-level manag-

ers in the Rochester metropolitan area. Our audience is comprised of upscale decision-makers with keen interest in the 'how-to' of business. Some features deal with lifestyle, golf, cultural focus, etc." Estab. 1984. Circ. 11,000. Pays on publication. Publishes ms an average of 6 months after acceptance. Byline given. Buys all rights. Accepts previously published material. Send typed ms with rights for sale noted and information about when and where the article previously appeared. For reprints pays 100% of the amount paid for an original article. Reports in 1 month. Sample copy and writer's guidelines for SAE with 6 first-class stamps.
Nonfiction: Essays, historical/nostalgic, how-to, humor, interview/profile, personal experience, all with business slant. Buys 12-24 mss/year. Query with published clips. Length: 1,500 words maximum. Pays $50-100.
Photos: State availability of photos with submission. Offers no additional payment for photos accepted with ms. Captions required.

Career, College and Alumni

Three types of magazines are listed in this section: university publications written for students, alumni and friends of a specific institution; publications about college life for students; and publications on career and job opportunities. Literary magazines published by colleges and universities are listed in the Literary and "Little" section.

‡**AMERICAN CAREERS**, Career Communications, Inc., 6701 W. 64th St., Overland Park KS 66202. Editorial Consultant: Mary Pitchford. 10% freelance written. Middle school and high school student publication published 3 times during school year covering careers, career statistics, skills needed to get jobs. "*American Careers* is a paid-circulation magazine purchased for high school students to promote career exploration and career education. Most stories are provided at no charge by authorization in business, education and government. We assign some stories to freelancers and purchase some first-time, one-time rights." Estab. 1990. Circ. 500,000. Payment depends on whether assignment or submission. Byline sometimes given. Buys first, one-time or second serial (reprint) rights and makes work-for-hire assignments. Accepts previously published submissions. Query for electronic submissions. Reports in 1 month. Sample copy and writer's guidelines free on request.
Nonfiction: Career and education features. Special issue: health careers. Buys 6 mss/year. Query with published clips. Length: 350-750 words. Negotiates payment. Pays expenses of writers on assignment.
Photos: State availability of photos with submission. Reviews contact sheets. Negotiates payment individually. Captions, model releases and identification of subjects required. Buys one-time rights.
Columns/Departments: Reality Check (brief facts, statistics, how-to ideas on careers, job hunting and other career-related information.) Length: 25-100 words. Some reviewing of current related books, video software. Buys 6 mss/year. Negotiates payment.
Tips: "Letters of introduction or query letters with samples are ways we get to know writers. Samples should include how-to articles or career articles. Articles written for publication for teenagers also would make good samples. Short feature articles on careers, career-related how-to articles and self-assessment tools (10-20 point quizzes with scoring information) are primarily what we publish."

THE BLACK COLLEGIAN, The Career & Self Development Magazine for African American Students, Black Collegiate Services, Inc., 1240 S. Broad St., New Orleans LA 70125. (504)821-5694. Fax: (504)821-5713. Editor: Kuumba F. Kazi. 25% freelance written. Magazine published bimonthly during school year for African-American college students and recent graduates with an interest in career and job information, African-American cultural awareness, personalities, history, trends and current events. Estab. 1970. Circ. 121,000. Buys one-time rights. Byline given. Pays on publication. Submit seasonal and special interest material 2 months in advance of issue date. Special Issues: Careers (September); Computers/Grad School and Travel/Summer programs (November); Engineering and Black History (January); Jobs (March). Reports in 3-6 months. Sample copy $for 4 and 9 × 12 SAE. Writer's guidelines for #10 SASE.
Nonfiction: Material on careers, sports, black history, news analysis. Articles on problems and opportunities confronting African-American college students and recent graduates. Book excerpts, exposé, general interest, historical/nostalgic, how-to (develop employability), opinion, personal experience, profile, inspirational. Buys 40 mss/year (6 unsolicited). Query with published clips or send complete ms. Length: 500-1,500 words. Pays $100-500.
Photos: State availability of or send photos with query or ms. Black and white photos or color transparencies purchased with or without ms. 8 × 10 prints preferred. Captions, model releases and identification of subjects required. Pays $35/b&w; $50/color.

CAREER FOCUS, For Today's Professional, Communications Publishing Group, Inc., 250 Mark Twain Tower, 106 W. 11th St., Kansas City MO 64105-1806. (816)221-4404. Fax: (516)273-8936. Editor: Georgia Clark. 40% freelance written. Monthly magazine "devoted to providing positive insight, information, guidance and motivation to assist Blacks and Hispanics (ages 21-40) in their career development and attainment of goals." Estab. 1988. Circ. 250,000. Pays on publication. Byline often given. Buys second serial (reprint) rights and makes work-for-hire assignments. Submit seasonal/holiday material 6 months in advance. Accepts simultaneous and previously published submissions. Send tearsheet of article and information about when and where the article previously appeared. For reprints pays 50% of the amount paid for an original article. Reports in 2 months. Sample copy for 9 × 12 SAE with 4 first-class stamps. Writer's guidelines for #10 SASE.

Nonfiction: Book excerpts, general interest, historical, how-to, humor, inspirational, interview/profile, personal experience, photo feature, technical, travel. Length: 750-2,000 words. Pays $150-400 for assigned articles; 10¢/word for unsolicited articles. Sometimes pays expenses of writers on assignment.

Photos: State availability of photos with submission. Reviews transparencies. Pays $20-25/photo. Captions, model releases and identification of subjects required. Buys all rights.

Columns/Departments: Profiles (striving and successful Black and Hispanic young adult, ages 21-40). Buys 15 mss/year. Send complete ms. Length: 500-1,000 words. Pays $50-250.

Fiction: Adventure, ethnic, historical, humorous, mainstream, slice-of-life vignettes. Buys 3 mss/year. Send complete ms. Length: 1,500-5,000 words. Pays $100-400.

Poetry: Free verse. Buys 4/year. Length: 10-25 lines. Pays $10-50.

Fillers: Anecdotes, facts, gags to be illustrated by cartoonist, newsbreaks, short humor. Buys 10/year. Length: 25-250 words. Pays $25-100.

Tips: For new writers: Submit full ms that is double-spaced; clean copy only. If available, send clips of previously published works and résumé. Should state when available to write. Most open to freelancers are profiles of successful and striving persons including photos. Profile must be of a Black or Hispanic adult living in the US. Include on first page of ms name, address phone, Social Security number and number of words in article.

CAREER WOMAN, For Entry-Level and Professional Women, Equal Opportunity Publications, Inc., Suite 420, 150 Motor Pkwy., Hauppauge NY 11788-5145. (516)273-8743. Fax: (516)273-8936. Editor: Eileen Nester. Estab. 1973. 80% freelance written. Works with new/unpublished writers each year. Triannual magazine covering career-guidance for college women. Strives to "bridge the gap between college life and the working world—with advice ranging from conducting an effective job search to surviving the first several years on the job to finding a balance between personal and professional lives." Audience is 60% college juniors and seniors, 40% working graduates. Circ. 10,500. Controlled circulation, distributed through college guidance and placement offices. Pays on publication. Publishes ms an average of 3-12 months after acceptance. Byline given. Buys first North American rights. Simultaneous queries and submissions OK. Reports in 2 months. Sample copy and writer's guidelines for 9 × 12 SAE with 5 first-class stamps.

Nonfiction: "We want career-related articles describing for a college-educated woman the how-tos of obtaining a professional position and advancing her career." Looks for practical features detailing self-evaluation techniques, the job-search process and advice for succeeding on the job. Emphasizes role-model profiles of successful career women. Needs mss presenting information on professions offering opportunities to young women—especially the growth professions of the future. Special issues emphasize career opportunities for women in fields such as health care, communications, sales, marketing, banking, insurance, finance, science, engineering and computers. Query first.

Photos: Send with ms. Prefers 35mm color slides, but will accept b&w prints. Captions and identification of subjects required. Buys all rights.

Tips: "The best way to get published is to find a unique approach to common topics. Remember that you are addressing a group of women new to the workforce. They need advice on virtually every career-guidance topic."

CAREERS & COLLEGES MAGAZINE, E.M. Guild, Inc., 6th Floor, 989 Avenue of Americas, New York NY 10018. (212)563-4688. Editor-in-Chief/Publisher: June Rogoznica. Senior Editor: Don Rauf. Contact: June Rogoznica. 85-95% freelance written. Quarterly magazine for education, careers and life choices for high school students. "*Careers & Colleges* is a magazine that believes in young people. It believes that they have the power—and responsibility—to shape their own futures. That is why each issue provides high school juniors and seniors with useful, thought-provoking reading on career choices, life values, higher education and other topics that will help them enjoy profitable and self-respecting work." Estab. 1980. Circ. 500,000. **Pays on acceptance.** Byline given. Offers 20% kill fee. Buys first North American serial rights. Editorial lead time 6 months. Submit seasonal material 6 months in advance. Accepts previously published articles. Send photocopy of article. Reports in 1 month on queries. Sample copy for $2.50 and 9 × 12 SAE with 5 first-class stamps. Writer's guidelines for #10 SASE.

Nonfiction: Book excerpts, how-to (job or college related), interview/profile (teen role models). May publish a Spring issue on summer jobs and other employment opportunities for young adults. "No personal essays, life experiences or fiction." Buys 36-52 mss/year. Query with published clips. Length: 600-1,500 words. Pays $150 minimum. Sometimes pays expenses of writers on assignment (limit agreed upon in advance).

Photos: State availability of photos with submission. Negotiates payment individually. Buys one-time rights.

Columns/Departments: MoneyWise (strategies and resources for financing education beyond high school), 600-800 words; Career Watch (profiles of growth careers/interview plus statistics), 800 words. Buys 18-24 mss/year. Query with or without published clips. Pays $150-350.

Tips: "Be sure to request writer's guidelines. Follow guidelines specifically. No unsolicited manuscripts are accepted. Send a one-page query and clips. Examine other teen magazines for current topic ideas. Many opportunities exist in our career profile section—pay is low, but it is a good testing ground for us to gauge a writer's ability—strong performance here can lead to bigger articles. Query about growth careers that we have not covered in the past (consult magazine's Career Watch Index)."

CAREERS & MAJORS (for College Students), Oxendine Publishing, Inc., P.O. Box 14081, Gainesville FL 32604-2081. (904)373-6907. Editor: W.H. "Butch" Oxendine Jr.. Managing Editor: Kay Quinn. 35% freelance written. Quarterly magazine for college careers and job opportunities. Estab. 1983. Circ. 17,000. Pays on publication. Publishes ms an average of 2-3 months after acceptance. Byline given. Buys all rights. Submit seasonal/holiday material 4 months in advance. Accepts simultaneous and previously published submissions. Send photocopy of article. Query for electronic submissions; prefers IBM. Reports in 1 month on queries. Sample copy for 8 × 11 SAE with 3 first-class stamps. For query/response and/or writer's guidelines send SASE.
Nonfiction: How-to, humor, new product, opinion. "No lengthy individual profiles or articles without primary and secondary sources of attribution." Buys 10 mss/year. Query with published clips. Length: 250-1,000 words. Pays $35 maximum. Pays contributor copies to students or first-time writers. State availability of photos with submission. Reviews contact sheets, negatives and transparencies; size "doesn't matter." Offers $50/photo maximum. Captions, model releases and identification of subjects required. Buys all rights.
Columns/Departments: College Living (various aspects of college life, general short humor oriented to high school or college students), 250-1,000 words; Buys 10 mss/year. Query. Length: 250-1,000 words. Pays $35 maximum.
Fillers: Facts, newsbreaks, short humor. Buys 10/year. Length: 100-500 words. Pays $35 maximum.
Tips: "Read other high school and college publications for current issues, interests. Send manuscripts or outlines for review. All sections open to freelance work. Always looking for lighter, humorous articles, as well as features on Florida colleges and universities, careers, jobs. Multi-sourced (5-10) articles best."

CARNEGIE MELLON MAGAZINE, Carnegie Mellon University, 5017 Forbes Ave., Pittsburgh PA 15213-3890. (412)268-2132. Fax: (412)268-6929. Editor: Ann Curran. Estab. 1900. Quarterly alumni publication covering university activities, alumni profiles, etc. Circ, 56,000. **Pays on acceptance.** Byline given. Not copyrighted. Reports in 1 month.
Nonfiction: Book reviews (faculty alumni), general interest, humor, interview/profile, photo feature. "We use general interest stories linked to Carnegie Mellon activities and research." No unsolicited mss. Buys 5 features and 5-10 alumni profiles/year. Query with published clips. Length: 800-2,000 words. Pays $100-400 or negotiable rate. Sample copy for $2 and 9 × 12 SAE.
Poetry: Avant-garde or traditional. No previously published poetry. No payment.

CIRCLE K MAGAZINE, 3636 Woodview Trace, Indianapolis IN 46268-3196. Fax: (317)879-0204. Executive Editor: Nicholas K. Drake. 60% freelance written. "Our readership consists almost entirely of above-average college students interested in voluntary community service and leadership development. They are politically and socially aware and have a wide range of interests." Published 5 times/year. Circ. 15,000. **Pays on acceptance.** Normally buys first North American serial rights. Byline given. Submit seasonal/holiday material 6 months in advance. Reports in 2 months. Sample copy and writer's guidelines for large SAE with 3 first-class stamps.
Nonfiction: Articles published in *Circle K* are of 2 types—serious and light nonfiction. "We are interested in general interest articles on topics concerning college students and their lifestyles, as well as articles dealing with careers, community concerns and leadership development. No first person confessions, family histories or travel pieces." Query. Length: 800-1,900 words. Pays $150-400.
Photos: Purchased with accompanying ms. Captions required. Total purchase price for ms includes payment for photos.
Tips: "Query should indicate author's familiarity with the field and sources. Subject treatment must be objective and in-depth, and articles should include illustrative examples and quotes from persons involved in the subject or qualified to speak on it. We are open to working with new writers who present a good article idea and demonstrate that they've done their homework concerning the article subject itself, as well as concerning our magazine's style. We're interested in college-oriented trends, for example, entrepreneur schooling is now a major shift; rising censorship on campus; high-tech classrooms; virtual reality; music; leisure; and health issues."

COLLEGE MONTHLY, 381 Main St., Worcester MA 01608. (508)753-2550. Editor: Maureen Castillo. Managing Editor: Randy Cohen. 25% freelance written. Magazine published 8 times/year covering college lifestyle and entertainment. Estab. 1986. Circ. 73,000. Pays on publication. Byline given. Offers $5 kill fee. Buys one-time rights. Query for electronic submissions. Free sample copy and writer's guidelines with 9 × 12 SAE and 6 first-class stamps.

Nonfiction: Humor, interview/profile, opinion, personal experience, travel. Query with published clips. Length: 500-2,000 words. Pays $25-100 for assigned articles; $5-25 for unsolicited articles. Sometimes pays the expenses of writers on assignment.

Photos: State availability of photos with submission. Offers no additional payment for photos accepted with ms. Caption required. Buys one-time rights.

Columns/Departments: Fashion (trends in the college market for clothes); Lifestyle (off-the-wall things students do); Sports (national sports and college); Politics (national level/hot social issues), all 500-750 words.

Fillers: Newsbreaks, short humor. Length: 100 words. Pays $5-25.

Tips: "We are looking for more fashion, education and sports articles."

COLLEGE PREVIEW, A Guide for College-Bound Students, Communications Publishing Group, 250 Mark Twain Tower, 106 W. 11th St., Kansas City MO 64105-1806. (816)221-4404. Fax: (816)221-1112. Editor: Georgia Clark. 40% freelance written. Quarterly educational and career source guide. "Contemporary guide designed to inform and motivate Black and Hispanic young adults, ages 16-21 years old about college preparation, career planning and life survival skills." Estab. 1985. Circ. 600,000. Pays on publication. Byline often given. Buys first serial and second serial (reprint) rights or makes work-for-hire assignments. Submit seasonal/holiday material 6 months in advance. Accepts simultaneous and previously published submissions. Send tearsheet or photocopy of article or short story or typed ms with rights for sale noted and information about when and where the article previously appeared. For reprints, pays 50% of the amount paid for an original article. Reports in 2 months. Sample copy for 9 × 12 SAE with 4 first-class stamps. Writer's guidelines for #10 SASE.

Nonfiction: Book excerpts or reviews, general interest, how-to (dealing with careers or education), humor, inspirational, interview/profile (celebrity or "up and coming" young adult), new product (as it relates to young adult market), personal experience, photo feature, technical, travel. Send complete ms. Length: 750-2,000 words. Pays $150-400 for assigned articles; 10¢/word for unsolicited articles. Sometimes pays expenses of writers on assignment.

Photos: State availability of photos with submission. Reviews transparencies. Offers $20-$25/photo. Captions, model releases and identification of subjects required. Will return photos—send SASE.

Columns/Departments: Profiles of Achievement (striving and successful minority young adults ages 16-35 in various careers). Buys 30 mss/year. Send complete ms. Length: 500-1,500. Pays 10¢/word.

Fiction: Adventure, ethnic, historical, humorous, mainstream, slice-of-life vignettes. Buys 3 mss/year. Send complete ms. Length: 1,000-5,000 words. Pays $100-400.

Poetry: Free verse. Buys 5 poems/year. Submit maximum 5 poems. Length: 10-25 lines. Pays $10-50.

Fillers: Anecdotes, facts, gags to be illustrated by cartoonist, newsbreaks, short humor. Buys 10/year. Length: 25-250 words. Pays $25-100.

Tips: For new writers—send complete ms that is double spaced; clean copy only. If available, send clips of previously published works and résumé. Should state when available to write. Include on first page of ms name, address, phone, Social Security number, word count and SASE.

DIRECT AIM, A Resource Guide for Vocational/Technical Graduates, Communications Publishing Group, #250, 106 W. 11th St., Kansas City MO 64105-1806. (816)221-4404. Fax: (816)221-1112. Publisher: Georgia Clark. 40% freelance written. Quarterly educational and career source guide for Black and Hispanic college students at traditional, non-traditional, vocational and technical institutions. "This magazine informs students about college survival skills and planning for a future in the professional world." Buys second serial (reprint) rights or makes work-for-hire assignments. Submit seasonal/holiday material 6 months in advance. Accepts simultaneous and previously published submissions. Send tearsheet of article or short story or typed ms with rights for sale noted and information about when and where the article previously appeared. For reprints pays 50% of the amount paid for an original article. Reports in 2 months. Sample copy for 9 × 12 SAE with 4 first-class stamps. Writer's guidelines for #10 SASE.

Nonfiction: Book excerpts or reviews, general interest, how-to (dealing with careers or education), humor, inspirational, interview/profile (celebrity or "up and coming" young adult), new product (as it relates to young adult market), personal experience, photo feature, technical, travel. Query or send complete ms. Length: 750-2,000 words. Pays $150-400 for assigned articles; 10¢/word for unsolicited articles. Sometimes pays expenses of writers on assignment.

Photos: State availability of photos with submission. Reviews transparencies. Offers $20-25/photo. Captions, model releases and identification of subjects required. Will return photos.

Columns/Departments: Profiles of Achievement (striving and successful minority young adult age 18-35 in various technical careers). Buys 25 mss/year. Send complete ms. Length: 500-1,500. Pays $50-250.

Fiction: Publishes novel excerpts. Adventure, ethnic, historical, humorous, mainstream, slice-of-life vignettes. Buys 3 mss/year. Send complete ms. Length: 1,000-5,000 words. Pays $100-400.

Poetry: Free verse. Buys 5 poems/year. Submit maximum 5 poems. Length: 10-25 lines. Pays $10-50.

Fillers: Anecdotes, facts, gags to be illustrated by cartoonist, newsbreaks, short humor. Buys 30/year. Length: 25-250 words. Pays $25-100.

Tips: For new writers—send complete ms that is double spaced; clean copy only. If available, send clips of previously published works and résumé. Should state when available to write. Include on first page of ms name, address, phone, Social Security number and word count. Photo availability is important.

EQUAL OPPORTUNITY, The Nation's Only Multi-Ethnic Recruitment Magazine for Black, Hispanic, Native American & Asian American College Grads, Equal Opportunity Publications, Inc., Suite 420, 150 Motor Pkwy., Hauppauge NY 11788-5145. (516)273-0066. Fax: (516)273-8936. Editor: James Schneider. 50% freelance written. Prefers to work with published/established writers. Triannual magazine covering career guidance for minorities. "Our audience is 90% college juniors and seniors; 10% working graduates. An understanding of educational and career problems of minorities is essential." Estab. 1967. Circ. 15,000. Controlled circulation, distributed through college guidance and placement offices. Pays on publication. Publishes ms an average of 6 months after acceptance. Byline given. Buys first rights. Deadline dates: Fall (June 10); Winter (September 15); Spring (January 1). Accepts simultaneous queries and previously published submissions. Sample copy and writer's guidelines for 9 × 12 SAE with 5 first-class stamps.

Nonfiction: Book excerpts and articles (job search techniques, role models); general interest (specific minority concerns); how-to (job-hunting skills, personal finance, better living, coping with discrimination); humor (student or career related); interview/profile (minority role models); opinion (problems of minorities); personal experience (professional and student study and career experiences); technical (on career fields offering opportunities for minorities); travel (on overseas job opportunities); and coverage of Black, Hispanic, Native American and Asian American interests. Special issues include career opportunities for minorities in industry and government in fields such as banking, insurance, finance, communications, sales, marketing, engineering, computers, military and defense. Query or send complete ms. Length: 1,000-1,500 words. Sometimes pays expenses of writers on assignment. Pays 10¢/word.

Photos: Prefers 35mm color slides and b&w. Captions and identification of subjects required. Buys all rights. Pays $15/photo use.

Tips: "Articles must be geared toward questions and answers faced by minority and women students."

FIRST OPPORTUNITY, A Guide for Vocational/Technical Students, Communications Publishing Group, 250 Mark Twain Tower, 106 W. 11th St., Kansas City MO 64105-1806. (816)221-4404. Editor: Georgia Clark. 40% freelance written. Biannual resource publication focusing on advanced vocational/technical educational opportunities and career preparation for Black and Hispanic young adults, ages 16-21. Circ. 500,000. Pays on publication. Byline sometimes given. Buys second serial (reprint) rights or makes work-for-hire assignments. Submit seasonal/holiday material 6 months in advance. Accepts simultaneous and previously published submissions. Send tearsheet of article or typed ms with rights for sale noted and information about when and where the article previously appeared. For reprints, pays 50% of the amount paid for an original article. Reports in 2 months. Sample copy for 9 × 12 SAE with 4 first-class stamps. Writer's guidelines for #10 SASE.

Nonfiction: Book excerpts or reviews, general interest, how-to (dealing with careers or education), humor, inspirational, interview/profile (celebrity or "up and coming" young adult), new product (as it relates to young adult market), personal experience, photo feature, technical, travel. Length: 750-2,000 words. Pays $150-400 for assigned articles; 10¢/word for unsolicited articles. Sometimes pays expenses of writers on assignment.

Photos: State availability of photos with submission. Prefers transparencies. Offers $20-25/photo. Captions, model releases, identification of subjects required. Buys all rights.

Columns/Departments: Profiles of Achievement (striving and successful minority young adult, age 16-35 in various vocational or technical careers). Buys 15 mss/year. Send complete ms. Length: 500-1,500. Pays $50-250.

Fiction: Adventure, ethnic, historical, humorous, mainstream, slice-of-life vignettes. Buys 3 mss/year. Send complete ms. Length: 1,000-5,000 words. Pays $100-400.

Poetry: Free verse. Buys 5 poems/year. Submit maximum 5 poems. Length: 10-25 lines. Pays $10-50.

Fillers: Anecdotes, facts, gags to be illustrated by cartoonist, newsbreaks, short humor. Buys 10/year. Length: 25-250 words. Pays $25-100.

Tips: For new writers—send complete ms that is double spaced; clean copy only. If available, send clips of previously published works and résumé. Should state when available to write. Include on first page of ms name, address, phone, Social Security number and word count. Photo availability is important.

FLORIDA LEADER (for college students), P.O. Box 14081, Gainesville FL 32604. (904)373-6907. Fax: (904)373-8120. Publisher: W.H. "Butch" Oxendine, Jr. Editor: Kay Quinn. 25% freelance written. Quarterly "college magazine, feature-oriented, especially activities, events, interests and issues pertaining to college students." Estab. 1981. Circ. 27,000. Publishes ms an average of 2 months after acceptance. Byline given. Submit seasonal/holiday material 6 months in advance. Query for electronic submissions. Reports in 2 months on queries. Sample copy and writer's guidelines for 9 × 12 SAE with 5 first-class stamps.

Nonfiction: How-to, humor, interview/profile, feature—all multi-sourced and Florida college related. Special issues: Careers and Majors (January, June); Florida Leader high school edition (August, January, May); Transfer (for community college transfers, November, July); Returning Student (for nontraditional-age students, July); Student Leader (October, March—pays double). Query with SASE. Length: 500 words or less. Payment varies. Sometimes pays expenses of writers on assignment.

Photos: State availability of photos with submission. Reviews negatives and transparencies. Captions, model releases, identification of subjects requested.

FORDHAM MAGAZINE, Fordham University, Suite 313, 113 W. 60th St., New York NY 10023-7404. (212)636-6530. Fax: (212)765-2976. Editor: Michael Gates. 50% freelance written. Quarterly magazine on Fordham University and its alumni. "We use profiles of our alumni—e.g. actor Denzel Washington, author Mary Higgins Clark—and discuss how education influenced their careers." **Pays on acceptance.** Estab. 1966. Publishes ms an average of 6 months after acceptance. Byline given. Offers 25% kill fee. Submit seasonal/holiday material 6 months in advance. Accepts previously published material. Send photocopy of article and information about when and where the article appeared. Reports in 3 months on queries; 3-4 months on mss. Sample copy for 9×12 SAE with 6 first-class stamps. Writer's guidelines for SASE.

Nonfiction: Book excerpts, essays, historical/nostalgic, interview/profile (alumni, faculty, students), photo feature. All must be specific to Fordham University or its alumni. Buys 12 mss/year. Query with published clips. Length: 1,000-2,500. Pays $250-500 for assigned articles; $50-250 for unsolicited articles. Sometimes pays expenses of writers on assignment.

Fiction: "We haven't published novel excerpts yet, but I think we would if it was of excellent quality and/or Fordham-related in some way."

Photos: State availability of photos with submission. Reviews contact sheets, transparencies, prints. Offers additional payment for photos accepted with ms. Identification of subjects required.

Tips: "Research our alumni and see if there is a noted or interesting personality you might interview—someone who might live in your area."

‡INSIDER MAGAZINE, Inmate Graphics, 4124 Oakton St., Skokie IL 60076. (708)328-9925. Managing Editor: Sarah Fister. 80% freelance written. Monthly magazine covering general interest for college students. "All of our stories are directed to college students, specifically Campus Life, Music, Careers and other features of interest." Estab. 1984. Circ. 1 million. Pays on publication. Publishes ms an average of 3 months after acceptance. Byline given. Buys all rights. Editorial lead time 2½ months. Submit seasonal material 4 months in advance. Accepts simultaneous and previously published submissions (sometimes with rewrites). Query for electronic submissions. Reports in 1-2 months. Sample copy and writer's guidelines free.

Nonfiction: Essays (occasionally), exposé, general interest, how-to, humor, interview/profile, new product, opinion (occasionally), personal experience (occasionally), photo feature, travel. "Every month has a loose theme. It's listed at end of guidelines." Query with published clips or send complete ms. Length: 300-1,200 words. Pays 1¢/word. Sometimes pays expenses of writers on assignment.

Photos: Send photos with submission. Review prints. Offers no additional payment for photos accepted with ms. Captions, model releases, identification of subjects required.

Fillers: Anecdotes, facts, gags to be illustrated by cartoonist, newsbreaks, short humor. Pays 1-5¢/word.

Tips: "All our sections are open to freelancers especially students. This publication is designed to give young writers experience in freelancing."

JOURNEY, A Success Guide for College and Career Bound Students, Communications Publishing Group, 250 Mark Twain Tower, 106 W. 11th St., Kansas City MO 64105-1806. (816)221-4404. Fax: (816)221-1112. Editor: Georgia Clark. 40% freelance written. Biannual educational and career source guide for Asian-American high school and college students (ages 16-25) who have indicated a desire to pursue higher education through college, vocational and technical or proprietary schools. Estab. 1982. Circ. 200,000. Pays on publication. Byline sometimes given. Buys second serial (reprint) rights or makes work-for-hire assignments. Submit seasonal/holiday material 6 months in advance. Accepts simultaneous and previously published submissions. Send typed ms with rights for sale noted and information about when and where the article previously appeared. For reprints pays 50% of the amount paid for an original article. Reports in 3 months. Sample copy for 9×12 SAE with 4 first-class stamps. Writer's guidelines for #10 SASE.

Nonfiction: Book excerpts or reviews, general interest, how-to (dealing with careers or education), humor, inspirational, interview/profile (celebrity or "up and coming" young adult), new product (as it relates to young adult market), personal experience, photo feature, sports, technical, travel. First time writers with *Journey* must submit complete ms for consideration. Length: 750-2,000 words. Pays $150-400 for assigned articles; 10¢/word for unsolicited articles. Sometimes pays expenses of writers on assignment.

Photos: State availability of photos with submission. Prefers transparencies. Offers $20-25/photo. Captions, model releases and identification of subjects required. Buys all or one-time rights.

Columns/Departments: Profiles of Achievement (striving and successful minority young adult, age 16-35 in various careers). Buys 15 mss/year. Send complete ms. Length: 500-1,500. Pays $50-200.

Fiction: Publishes novel exerpts. Adventure, ethnic, historical, humorous, mainstream, slice-of-life vignettes. Buys 3 mss/year. Send complete ms. Length: 1,000-3,000 words. Pays $100-400.

Poetry: Free verse. Buys 5/year. Submit up to 5 poems at one time. Length: 10-25 lines. Pays $10-50.

Fillers: Anecdotes, facts, gags to be illustrated by cartoonist, newsbreaks, short humor. Buys 10/year. Length: 25-250 words. Pays $25-100.

Tips: For new writers—must submit complete ms that is double spaced; clean copy only. If available, send clippings of previously published works and résumé. Should state when available to write. Include on first page your name, address, phone, Social Security number and word count. Availability of photos enhances your chances. "We desperately need more material dealing with concerns of Asian-American students."

MISSISSIPPI STATE ALUMNUS, Mississippi State University, Alumni Association, Editorial Office, P.O. Box 5328, Mississippi State MS 39762-5328. (601)325-3442. Fax: (601)325-7455. Editor: Allen Snow. Up to 10% freelance written. Works with small number of new/unpublished writers each year. Triannual magazine for well-educated audience emphasizing articles about Mississippi State graduates and former students. Estab. 1927. Circ. 57,000. Pays on publication. Publishes ms 6 months after acceptance. Buys one-time rights. Byline given. Accepts simultaneous and previously published submissions OK. Reports in 2 months. Sample copy for 9 × 12 SAE with 5 first-class stamps.

Nonfiction: Historical, informational, interview (with MSU grads), nostalgia (early days at MSU), personal experience, profile (by MSU grads, but must be of wide interest to other grads). Buys 1-3 mss/year. Send complete ms. Length: 500-2,000 words. Pays $50-100 (including photos, if used).

Photos: Offers no additional payment for photos purchased with accompanying ms. Captions required. Uses 5 × 7 and 8 × 10 b&w photos and color transparencies of any size.

Columns/Departments: Statements, "a section of the *Mississippi State Alumnus* that features briefs about alumni achievements and professional or business advancement. There is no payment for Statements briefs."

Tips: "All stories *must* be about Mississippi State University or its alumni. We're putting more emphasis on people and events on the campus — teaching, research and public service projects. But we're still eager to receive good stories about alumni in all parts of the world. We welcome articles about MSU grads in interesting occupations and have used stories on off-shore drillers, miners, horse trainers, etc. We also want profiles on prominent MSU alumni. We're using more short features (500-700 words) to vary the length of our articles in each issue. We pay $25-50 for these, including one b&w photo."

NOTRE DAME MAGAZINE, University of Notre Dame, Room 415, Administration Bldg., Notre Dame IN 46556-0775. (219)631-5335. Fax: (219)631-6947. Editor: Walton R. Collins. Managing Editor: Kerry Temple. 75% freelance written. Quarterly magazine covering news of Notre Dame and education and issues affecting the Roman Catholic Church. "We are interested in the moral, ethical and spiritual issues of the day and how Christians live in today's world. We are universal in scope, Catholic in viewpoint and serve Notre Dame alumni, friends and other constituencies." Estab. 1972. Circ. 120,000. **Pays on acceptance.** Publishes ms an average of 1 year after acceptance. Byline given. Kill fee negotiable. Buys first rights. Simultaneous queries OK. Query for electronic submissions. Reports in 1 month. Free sample copy.

Nonfiction: Opinion, personal experience, religion. Buys 35 mss/year. Query with clips of published work. Length: 600-3,000 words. Pays $250-1,500. Sometimes pays the expenses of writers on assignment.

Photos: State availability of photos. Reviews b&w contact sheets, transparencies and 8 × 10 prints. Model releases and identification of subjects required. Buys one-time rights.

OREGON QUARTERLY, The Magazine of the University of Oregon, University of Oregon, 130 Chapman Hall, Eugene OR 97403-5228. (503)346-5047. Fax: (503)346-2220. Editor: Tom Hager. Managing Editor: Mike Lee. 50% freelance written. Quarterly university magazine of people and ideas at the University of Oregon. Estab. 1919. Circ. 95,000. Pays on publication. Publishes ms an average of 3 months after acceptance. Byline given. Offers 20% kill fee. Buys first North American serial rights. Accepts previously published material. Send photocopy of article and information about when and where the article previously appeared. Query for electronic submissions. Reports in 2 months. Sample copy for 9 × 12 SAE with 4 first-class stamps.

Nonfiction: Northwest issues and culture from the perspective of UO alumni and faculty. Buys 30 mss/year. Query with published clips. Length: 250-2,500 words. Pays $50-500. Sometimes pays expenses of writers on assignment.

Photos: State availability of photos with submission. Reviews 8 × 10 prints. Offers $10-25/photo. Identification of subjects required. Buys one-time rights.

Tips: "Query with strong, colorful lead; clips."

‡THE OREGON STATER, Oregon State University Alumni Association, ADS 416, OSU, Corvallis OR 97331. (503)737-0780. Editor: George Edmonston Jr. 20% freelance written. Tabloid covering news of Oregon State University and its alumni. Estab. 1915. Circ. 16,000. **Pays on acceptance.** Byline given. Buys one-time rights. Editorial lead time 4 months. Submit seasonal material 3 months in advance. Reports in 2 weeks on queries; 3 months on mss. Sample copy and writer's guidelines free on request.

Nonfiction: General interest, historical/nostalgic, humor, inspirational, interview/profile, personal experience, photo feature. Buys 40 mss/year. Query with or without published clips. Length: 2,000 words maximum. Pays $50-1,000. Pays expenses of writers on assignment.

Photos: Send photos with submission. Offers no additional payment for photos accepted with ms. Captions, model releases and identification of subjects required. Buys one-time rights.

‡THE PENN STATER, Penn State Alumni Association, 105 Old Main, University Park PA 16802. (814)865-2709. Editor: Debbie Williams Ream. 75% freelance written. Bimonthly magazine covering Penn State and Penn Staters. "All of our readers are members of the Penn State Alumni Association. They are highly educated, but view our publication as 'easy reading' and a link back to their alma mater. There is a lot of pride in knowing that one out of every 750 Americans went to Penn State." Estab. 1910. Circ. 120,000. **Pays on acceptance.** Publishes ms an average of 4 months after acceptance. Byline given. Offers 50% kill fee. Buys first North American serial rights or second serial (reprint) rights. Editorial lead time 3 months. Submit seasonal material 4-5 months in advance. Accepts simultaneous and previously published submissions. Query for electronic submissions. Reports in 1 month on queries; 2 months on mss. Sample copy and writer's guidelines free on request.

Nonfiction: Book excerpts (by Penn Staters), general interest, historical/nostalgic, humor, interview/profile, personal experience (sometimes), photo feature, science/research. Buys 20 mss/year. Query with published clips. Length: 750-4,000 words. Pays $150. Sometimes pays expenses of writers on assignment.

Photos: Send photos with submission. Reviews transparencies and prints. Negotiates payment individually. Captions required. Buys one-time rights.

Tips: "We're always looking for stories from out of state. Stories that have some national slant, that consider a national view of an issue, and somehow involve a Penn Stater are desirable. Profiles of unusual or successful alumni are an 'easy in.' We accept freelance articles almost exclusively for our features section. Generally we run three to four features per issue, plus a photo feature and nostalgia/history piece."

‡PORTLAND MAGAZINE, The University of Portland Quarterly, 5000 N. Willamette Blvd., Portland OR 97203. Editor: Brian Doyle. 70% freelance written. Quarterly magazine covering University of Portland news, issues, concerns. Generally features are about spirituality (esp. Catholicism), the Northwest, higher education, or the University itself. Estab. 1985. Circ. 25,000. Pays on publication. Publishes ms an average of 3 months after acceptance. Byline given. Buys first North American serial rights. Editorial lead time 6-8 months. Submit seasonal material 8 months in advance. Reports in 1 month on queries. Sample copy and writer's guidelines free on request.

Nonfiction: Book excerpts, essays, general interest, interview/profile, opinion, personal experience, religious. Buys 6 mss/year. Query with published clips or send complete ms. Length: 1,000-3,000 words. Pays $100-500. Sometimes pays expenses of writers on assignment.

THE PURDUE ALUMNUS, Purdue Alumni Association, Purdue Memorial Union 160, 101 N. Grant St., West Lafayette IN 47906-6212. (317)494-5184. Fax: (317)494-9179. Editor: Tim Newton. 75% freelance written. Prefers to work with published/established writers; works with small number of new/unpublished writers each year. Magazine published 9 times/year covering subjects of interest to Purdue University alumni. Estab. 1912. Circ. 65,000. Pays on publication. Publishes ms an average of 2 months after acceptance. Byline given. Buys first rights and makes work-for-hire assignments. Submit seasonal/holiday material 6 months in advance. Accepts simultaneous and previously published submissions. Reports in 2 weeks on queries; 1 month on mss. Sample copy for 9 × 12 SAE with 2 first-class stamps.

Nonfiction: Book excerpts, general interest, historical/nostalgic, humor, interview/profile, personal experience. Focus is on alumni, campus news, issues and opinions of interest to 65,000 members of the Alumni Association. Feature style, primarily university-oriented. Issues relevant to education. Buys 12-20 mss/year. Length: 1,500-2,500 words. Pays $250-500. Pays expenses of writers on assignment.

Photos: State availability of photos. Reviews b&w contact sheet or 5 × 7 prints.

Tips: "We have 280,000 living, breathing Purdue alumni. If you can find a good story about one of them, we're interested. We use local freelancers to do campus pieces."

RIPON COLLEGE MAGAZINE, P.O. Box 248, Ripon WI 54971-0248. (414)748-8364. Fax: (414)748-9262. Editor: Loren J. Boone. 15% freelance written. Quarterly magazine that "contains information relating to Ripon College and is mailed to alumni and friends of the college." Estab. 1851. Circ. 14,000. Pays on publication. Publishes ms an average of 3 months after acceptance. Byline given. Not copyrighted. Makes work-for-hire assignments. Query for electronic submissions. Reports in 2 weeks.

Nonfiction: Historical/nostalgic, interview/profile. Buys 4 mss/year. Query with or without published clips, or send complete ms. Length: 250-1,000 words. Pays $25-350.

Photos: State availability of photos with submission. Reviews contact sheets. Offers additional payment for photos accepted with ms. Captions and model releases are required. Buys one-time rights.

Tips: "Story ideas must have a direct connection to Ripon College."

SCORECARD, Falsoft, Inc., 9509 US Highway 42, P.O. Box 385, Prospect KY 40059. (502)228-4492. Fax: (502)228-5121. Editor: John Crawley. 50% freelance written. Prefers to work with published/established writers. Weekly sports fan tabloid covering University of Louisville sports only. Estab. 1982. Circ. 7,500. Pays on publication. Publishes ms an average of 1 month after acceptance. Byline given. Buys first rights. Submit seasonal/holiday material 1 month in advance. Accepts previously published submissions "rarely". Reports in 2 weeks. Free sample copy and writer's guidelines.

Nonfiction: Assigned to contributing editors. Buys 100 mss/year. Query with published clips. Length: 750-1,500 words. Pays $20-50. Sometimes pays expenses of writers on assignment.

Photos: State availability of photos.

Columns/Departments: Notes Page (tidbits relevant to University of Louisville sports program or former players or teams). Buys 25 mss/year. Length: Approximately 100 words. Pay undetermined.

Tips: "Be very familiar with history and tradition of University of Louisville sports program. Contact us with story ideas. Know the subject."

SHIPMATE, U.S. Naval Academy Alumni Association Magazine, 247 King George St., Annapolis MD 21402-1306. (410)263-4469. Editor: Cdr. D.E. Church USN (retired). 100% freelance written. Magazine published 10 times/year by and for alumni of the US Naval Academy. Estab. 1938. Circ. 35,500. Pays on publication. Byline given. Buys first North American serial rights. Submit seasonal/holiday material 10 months in advance. Reports in 1 week. Sample copy for 9 × 12 SAE with 6 first-class stamps.

Nonfiction: Buys 50 mss/year. Send complete ms. Length: 2,000-7,500 words. Pays $100 for unsolicited articles.

Photos: Send photos with submission. Offers no additional payment for photos accepted with ms. Identification of subjects required. Buys one-time rights.

Tips: "The writer should be a Naval Academy alumnus (not necessarily a graduate) with first-hand experience of events in the Naval Service."

THE STUDENT, 127 Ninth Ave. N., Nashville TN 37234. Acting Editor: Gina Howard. 10% freelance written. Works with a small number of new/unpublished writers each year. Publication of National Student Ministry Department of The Sunday School Board of the Southern Baptist Convention. Monthly magazine for college students, focusing on freshman and sophomore levels. Estab. 1922. Circ. 40,000. Buys all rights. **Pays on acceptance.** Publishes ms an average of 10 months after acceptance. Manuscripts should be double-spaced on white paper with 50-space line, 25 lines/page. Sources for quotes and statistics should be given for verification. Reports usually within 2 months. Sample copy and guidelines for 9 × 12 SAE with 3 first-class stamps.

Nonfiction: Contemporary questions, problems, and issues facing college students viewed from a Christian perspective to develop high moral and ethical values. Cultivating interpersonal relationships, developing self-esteem, dealing with the academic struggle, coping with rejection, learning how to love and developing a personal relationship with Jesus Christ. Prefers complete ms rather than query. Length: 1,000 words maximum. Pays 5½¢/word after editing with reserved right to edit accepted material.

Fiction: Satire and parody on college life, humorous episodes; emphasize clean fun and the ability to grow and be uplifted through humor. Contemporary fiction involving student life, on campus as well as off. Length: 1,000 words. Pays 5½¢/word.

TEXAS ALCALDE, P.O. Box 7278, Austin TX 78713-7278. (512)471-3799. Fax: (512)471-8088. Acting Editor: Mr. Aurel Seale. 20% freelance written. Works with a small number of new/unpublished writers each year. Bimonthly magazine of the University of Texas. Estab. 1913. Circ. 55,000. Pays on publication. Publishes ms an average of 6 months after acceptance. Buys all rights. Submit seasonal/holiday material 5 months in advance. Query for electronic submissions. Reports in 1 month. Sample copy for $1.50 and 8½ × 11 SAE with $1.30 postage. Writer's guidelines for #10 SASE.

• *Texas Alcade* is now more willing to work with beginners.

Nonfiction: General interest; historical (University of Texas, research and faculty profile); humor (humorous Texas subjects); nostalgia (University of Texas traditions); profile (students, faculty, alumni); technical (University of Texas research on a subject or product). No subjects lacking taste or quality, or not connected with the University of Texas. Buys 12 mss/year. Query. Length: 1,000-2,400 words. Pays according to importance of article.

TRANSFER (for community college students), Oxendine Publishing, Inc., P.O. Box 14081, Gainesville FL 32604-2081. (904)373-6907. Editor: W.H. "Butch" Oxendine Jr.. Managing Editor: Kay Quinn. 50% freelance written. Semiannual magazine "easing the transition from 2-year to 4-year schools." Estab. 1992. Circ. 20,000. Pays on publication. Publishes ms an average of 2-3 months after acceptance. Byline given. Buys all rights. Submit seasonal/holiday material 4 months in advance. Accepts previously published material. Query for electronic submissions; prefers IBM. Reports in 1-2 months. Sample copy for 8 × 11 SAE with 3 first-class stamps. For query response and/or writer's guidelines send #10 SASE.

Nonfiction: How-to, humor, new product, opinion. "No lengthy individual's profiles, or articles without primary and secondary sources attribution." Buys 10 mss/year. Query. Length: 250-1,000 words. Pays $35 maximum. Pays with contributors copies to students or first-time writers.

 A bullet introduces comments by the editor of Writer's Market *indicating special information about the listing.*

Photos: State availability of photos with submission. Send photos with submission. Reviews contact sheets, negatives, transparencies. Offers $50/photo maximum. Captions, model releases, identification of subjects required. Buys all rights.

Columns/Departments: Transfer Student Trials, 250-1,000 words; Finding Financial Aid, 250-1,000 words. Query. Pays $35 maximum.

Fillers: Facts, newsbreaks, short humor. Buys 10/year. Length: 100-500 words. Pays $35 maximum.

Tips: "Read other high school and college publications for current issues, interests. Send manuscripts or outlines for review. All sections open to freelance work. Always looking for lighter, humorous articles, as well as features on Florida colleges and universities, careers, jobs. Multi-sourced (5-10) articles are best."

VISIONS, A Success Guide for Native American Students, Communications Publishing Group, 250 Mark Twain Tower, 106 W. 11th St., Kansas City MO 64105-1806. (816)221-4404. Fax: (816)221-1112. Editor: Georgia Clark. 40% freelance written. Biannual education and career source guide designed for Native American students who want to pursue a higher education through colleges, vocational and technical schools or proprietary schools, to focus on insight, motivational and career planning informations. For young adults, ages 16-25. Circ. 100,000. Pays on publication. Byline sometimes given. Buys second serial (reprint) rights or makes work-for-hire assignments. Submit seasonal/holiday material 6 months in advance. Accepts simultaneous and previously published submissions. Send typed ms with rights for sale noted and information about when and where the article previously appeared. For reprints, pays 50% of the amount paid for an original article. Reports in 2 months. Sample copy for 9×12 SAE with 4 first-class stamps. Writer's guidelines for #10 SASE.

Nonfiction: Book excerpts or reviews, general interest, how-to, humor, inspirational, interview/profile, new product, personal experience, photo feature, technical, travel, sports. Query or send complete ms. Length: 750-2,000 words. Pays $150-400 for assigned articles; 10¢/word for unsolicited articles. Sometimes pays expenses of writers on assignment.

Photos: State availability of photos with submission. Reviews transparencies. Offers $20-25/photo. Captions, model releases, and identification of subjects required. Buys all rights.

Columns/Departments: Profiles of Achievement (striving and successful Native American young adults, age 16-35, in various careers). Length: 500-1,500 words. Buys 15 mss/year. Send complete ms. Pays $50-250.

Fiction: Adventure, ethnic, historical, humorous, mainstream, slice-of-life vignettes. Buys 3 mss/year. Send complete ms. Length: 1,000-5,000 words. Pays $100-400.

Poetry: Free verse. Buys 5 poems/year. Submit up to 5 poems at one time. Length: 10-25 lines. Pays $10-50.

Fillers: Anecdotes, facts, gags to be illustrated by cartoonist, newsbreaks, short humor. Buys 10 fillers/year. Length: 25-250 words. Pays $25-100.

Tips: For new writers—submit complete manuscript that is double spaced; clean copy only. If available, send clippings of previously published works and résumé. Should state when available to write. Include on first page of manuscript your name, address, phone, Social Security number and word count. Availability of photos will enhance your chances.

WHAT MAKES PEOPLE SUCCESSFUL, The National Research Bureau, Inc., P.O. Box 1, Burlington IA 52601-0001. (319)752-5415. Fax: (319)752-3421. Editor: Nancy Heinzel. 75% freelance written. Eager to work with new/unpublished writers and works with a small number each year. Quarterly magazine. Estab. 1948. Pays on publication. Publishes ms an average of 1 year after acceptance. Buys all rights. Submit seasonal/holiday material 8 months in advance of issue date. Sample copy and writer's guidelines for #10 SAE with 2 first-class stamps.

Nonfiction: How-to (be successful); general interest (personality, employee morale, guides to successful living, biographies of successful persons, etc.); experience; opinion. No material on health. Buys 3-4 mss/issue. Query with outline. Length: 500-700 words. Pays 4¢/word.

Tips: Short articles (rather than major features) have a better chance of acceptance because all articles are short.

WPI JOURNAL, Worcester Polytechnic Institute, 100 Institute Rd., Worcester MA 01609-2280. Fax: (508)831-5604. Editor: Michael Dorsey. 20% freelance written. Quarterly alumni magazine covering science and engineering/education/business personalities for 20,000 alumni, primarily engineers, scientists, managers, national media. Estab. 1897. Circ. 24,500. Pays on publication. Publishes ms an average of 6 months after acceptance. Byline given. Buys one-time rights. Submit seasonal/holiday material 6 months in advance. Accepts simultaneous and previously published submissions. Query for electronic submissions. Requires hard copy also. Reports in 1 month on queries.

Nonfiction: Interview/profile (people in engineering, science); photo feature; features on science, engineering and management. Query with published clips. Length: 1,000-4,000 words. Pays negotiable rate. Sometimes pays the expenses of writers on assignment.

Photos: State availability of photos with query or ms. Reviews b&w contact sheets. Pays negotiable rate. Captions required.

Tips: "Submit outline of story and/or ms of story idea or published work. Features are most open to freelancers. Keep in mind that this is an alumni magazine, so most articles focus on the college and its community."

Child Care and Parental Guidance

Some publications in this section are general interest parenting magazines while others for child care providers combine care information with business tips. Other markets that buy articles about child care and the family are included in the Religious and Women's sections and in the Trade Education section. Publications for children can be found in the Juvenile section.

ATLANTA PARENT/ATLANTA BABY, Suite 506, 4330 Georgetown Square II, Atlanta GA 30338-6217. (404)454-7599. Editor: Liz White. Managing Editor: Peggy Middendorf. 100% freelance written. Monthly tabloid covering parenting of children from birth-14 years old. Offers "down-to-earth help for parents." Estab. 1983. Circ. 55,000. Pays on publication. Publishes ms 3 months after acceptance. Byline given. Buys one-time rights. Submit seasonal material 6 months in advance. Accepts previously published articles. Send photocopy of article or typed ms with rights for sale noted and information about when and where the article previously appeared. For reprints pays 50-70% of the amount paid for an original article. Query for electronic submissions. Reports in 3 months. Sample copy for $2.
Nonfiction: General interest, how-to, humor, interview/profile, travel. Special issues: Private school (January); Birthday parties (February); Camp (March/April); Maternity and Mothering (May); Child care (July); Back-to-school (August); Drugs (October); Holidays (November/December). Does not want first person accounts or philosophical discussions. Buys 60 mss/year. Query with or without published clips, or send complete ms. Length: 700-2,100 words. Pays $15-30. Sometimes pays expenses of writers on assignment.
Photos: State availability of photos with submission and send photocopies. Reviews 3×5 photos "b&w preferably." Offers $5/photo. Buys one-time rights.
Columns/Departments: Pack up and go (travel), 700-1,500. Buys 8-10 mss/year. Send complete ms. Length: 700-1,500 words. Pays $15-30.
Tips: "Articles should be geared to problems or situations of families and parents. Should include down-to-earth tips and clearly written. No philosophical discussions or first person narratives."

BABY CONNECTION NEWS JOURNAL, a newspaper for new and expectant famillies, Parent Education for Infant Development, Post Office Drawer 13320, San Antonio TX 78213. Editor: Gina Morris. Managing Editor: Ed Boyd. Editorial contact: Gina Morris. 100% freelance written. Quarterly newspaper/tabloid covering infant sensory development. Newspaper "explores issues of pregnancy, childbirth and specifically the infant's first year of development." Estab. 1986. Circ. 45,000. Pays on publication. Publishes ms an average of 6 months after acceptance. Byline given. Buys one-time rights. Editorial lead time 6-9 months. Submit seasonal material "anytime." Accepts simultaneous and previously published submissions. Send tearsheet or photocopy of article or typed ms with rights for sale noted and information about when and where the article previously appeared. For reprints pays 100% of the amount paid for an original article. Reports in 2 months. Sample copy for $3.75 and 10×13 SAE with 5 first-class stamps.
Nonfiction: Essays, humor, inspirational, new product, personal experience. "No poetry. No weird, mystic, rambling articles. No harsh or judgemental articles." Buys 36-48 mss/year. Send complete ms. Length: 600-1,500 words. Pays $10. Sometimes pays contributor's copies "as an addition to payment."
Photos: State availability of photos with submission. Reviews contact sheets, negatives, 4×6 prints. Offers $5-10/photo. Negotiates payment individually. Identification of subjects required. Buys one-time rights.
Columns/Departments: Baby Universe (news around the globe—infant related), 75-150 words; News News News (products new on the market for babies), 250-300 words. Buys 12 mss/year. Send complete ms. Pays $5-10.
Fiction: Adventure, humorous, romance, slice-of-life vignettes. "All articles with any slant must pertain to infancy issues." Buys 8-10 mss/year. Send complete ms. Length 600-1,000 words. Pays $10.
Fillers: Anecdotes, facts, newsbreaks, short humor. Buys 36/year. Length: 40-180 words. Pays $5.
Tips: "State that your submission is via *Writer's Market* for special attention, be patient in allowing time for response. Always include brief bio with your submission—something that will endear you to our readers, male perspective encouraged. We prefer articles on infant development such as growth, stages, mental, social, physical, etc. Write as though you are in your kitchen talking to your best friend. Make a difference in our readers' lives, give emotional support, humor a big plus. Be personal and detailed. Read our focus twice to be sure you submit what we need. If you are zeroed in on what we can use—you have an excellent chance of being published."

BAY AREA PARENT MAGAZINE, Bay Area Publishing Group Inc., 401 "A" Alberto Way, Los Gatos CA 95032-5404. Fax: (408)356-4903. Editor: Lynn Berardo. 80% freelance written. Works with locally-based published/established writers and some non-local writers. Monthly tabloid of resource information for parents and teachers. Circ 70,000. Pays on publication. Publishes ms an average of 3 months after acceptance. Byline given. Buys one-time rights. Submit seasonal/holiday material 3 months in advance. Accepts simultaneous and previously published submissions. Send typed ms with rights for sale noted and information about when and where the article previously appeared. Query for electronic submissions. Sample copy for 9 × 12 SAE with 6 first-class stamps. Writer's guidelines for #10 SASE.

Nonfiction: Book excerpts (related to our interest group); exposé (health, psychology); historical/nostalgic ("History of Diapers"); how-to (related to kids/parenting); humor; interview/profile; photo feature; travel (with kids, family). Special issues: Music (March); Art and Kid's Birthdays (April); Summer Camps and Vacations (May); Family Fun and Health and Medicine (June); Working Parents (July); Fashion and Sports (August); Back-to-School (September). No opinion or religious articles. Buys 45-60 mss/year. Query or send complete ms. Length: 150-1,500 words. Pays 6¢/word. Sometimes pays expenses of writers on assignment.

Photos: State availability of photos. Prefers b&w contact sheets and/or 3 × 5 b&w prints. Pays $5-25. Model release required. Buys one-time rights.

Columns/Departments: Child Care, Family Travel, Birthday Party Ideas, Baby Page, Toddler Page, Adolescent Kids. Buys 36 mss/year. Send complete ms. Length: 400-1,200 words. Pays $20-75.

Tips: "Submit new, fresh information concisely written and accurately researched. We also produce *Bay Area Baby Magazine*, a semiannual publication and *Valley Parent* Magazine, which focuses on central Contra Costa County and southern Alameda County."

‡**BIRACIAL CHILD**, Interrace Publications, P.O. Box 12048, Atlanta GA 30355. (404)364-9690. Editor: Candy Miller. 60% freelance written. Quarterly magazine covering biracial/mixed-race and transracial adoption parenting. "Parenting issues specific to interracial families with biracial (mixed-race) children/teens. Also, transracial adoption and interracial step-families." Estab. 1994. Circ. 3,000. Pays on publication. Byline given. Buys first rights, second serial rights or makes work-for-hire assignments. Submit seasonal material 3 months in advance. Accepts simultaneous and previously published submissions. Query for electronic submissions. Reports in 1-2 months. Sample copy for $2 and 9 × 12 SAE with $1 postage. Writer's guidelines for #10 SASE.

Nonfiction: Essays, general interest, historical/nostalgic, how-to, humor, inspirational, interview/profile, new product, opinion, personal experience, photo feature. Buys 12-20 mss/year. Query. Length: 200-3,200 words. Pays $20-50 for assigned articles; $50-75 for cover stories. Sometimes pays expenses of writers on assignment.

Photos: State availability of photos with submission. Negotiates payment individually. Identification of subjects required. Buys one-time rights.

Columns/Departments: Buys 4 mss/year. Query. Pays $15.

Fiction: Ethnic, historical, humorous, slice-of-life vignettes. Buys 4 mss/year. Query. Length: 800-1,600 words. Pays $10-25.

CHILD, NY Times Co. Women's Magazine, 110 Fifth Ave., New York NY 10011. (212)463-1000. Editor: Freddi Greenberg. Executive Editor: Mary Beth Jordan. 95% freelance written. Monthly magazine for parenting. Estab. 1986. Circ. 650,000. **Pays on acceptance.** Byline given. Offers 25% kill fee. Buys first North American serial, first, one-time and second serial (reprint) rights. Editorial lead time 3 months. Submit seasonal material 6 months in advance. Accepts simultaneous submissions. Reports in 2 months. Sample copy for $3.95. Writer's guidelines free on request.

  • Ranked as one of the best markets for freelance writers in *Writer's Digest* magazine's annual "Top 100 Markets," January 1994.

Nonfiction: Book excerpts, general interest, interview/profile, new product, photo feature. No poetry. Query with published clips. Length: 250 words minimum. Payment negotiable. Pays expenses of writers on assignment.

Photos: State availability of photos with submission. Reviews transparencies. Negotiates payment individually. Buys one-time rights.

Columns/Departments: Articles editor: Miriam Arond. Love, Dad (fathers' perspective); Child of Mine (mothers' or fathers' perspective). Query with published clips.

CHRISTIAN PARENTING TODAY, Good Family Magazines, P.O. Box 850, 548 Sisters Pkwy., Sisters OR 97759-0850. (503)549-8261. Editor: David Kopp. Managing Editor: Brad Lewis. 50% freelance written. Bimonthly magazine covering parenting today's children. "*Christian Parenting Today* is a positive, practical magazine that targets real needs of the contemporary family with authoritative articles based on fresh research and the timeless truths of the Bible. *CPT*'s readers represent the broad spectrum of Christians who seek intelligent answers to the new demands of parenting in the 90s." Estab. 1988. Circ. 250,000. Pays on acceptance or publication. Byline given. Buys first North American serial or second serial (reprint) rights. Submit seasonal/holiday material 6 months in advance. Query for electronic submissions. Simultaneous submissions discouraged. Accepts previously published material. Send tearsheet or photocopy of article, or typed ms with rights for sale noted and information about when and where the article previously appeared. For reprints pays 25% of the amount paid for an original article. Reports in 2 months. Sample copy for 9 × 12 SASE with 7 first-class stamps. Writer's guidelines for #10 SASE.

Nonfiction: Book excerpts, how-to, humor, inspirational, religious. Buys 50 mss/year. Query. Length: 750-2,000 words. Pays 15-25¢/word. Sometimes pays expenses of writers on assignment.

Photos: State availability of photos with submission. Do not submit photos without permission. Reviews transparencies. Model release required. Buys one-time rights.

Columns/Departments: Parent Exchange (family-tested parenting ideas from our readers), 25-100 words; Life In Our House (entertaining, true, humorous stories about your family), 25-100 words. Buys 120 mss/year. Send complete ms. Pays $25-40. No SASE required. Submissions become property of CPT.

Tips: "Our readers are active evangelical Christians from the broad spectrum of Protestant and Roman Catholic traditions. We are *not* interested in advocating any denominational bias. Our readers want authority, conciseness, problem-solving, entertainment, encouragement and surprise. They also require a clear biblical basis for advice. We are unable to acknowledge unsolicited manuscripts without SASE."

‡**DIVORCED PARENTS X-CHANGE**, P.O. Box 1127, Athens OH 45701-1127. Editor: Terri Andrews. 25-50% freelance written. Monthly newsletter for members of the Divorced Parents X-Change covering divorce, step parenting, legal news and updates, child custody, child support etc. "Our readership is composed of divorced and divorcing parents, stepparents, counselors, attorneys, judges, and teachers. We cover all areas of divorce, such as legal issues, child care, relationships, and single parenting. Our publication is positive, supportive, upbeat, and helpful. We focus on equality for parents and cooperation. We also focus on the adversarial court system and its faults—and then offer alternatives to these problems that do not include litigation." Estab. 1993. Pays on publication. Publishes ms an average of 3 months after acceptance. Byline given. Buys all rights and makes work-for-hire assignments. Editorial lead time 3 months. Submit seasonal material 3 months in advance. Accepts simultaneous and previously published submissions. Reports in 4-6 weeks on queries; 2-4 months on mss. Sample copy free on request. Writer's guidelines for #10 SASE.

Nonfiction: Book excerpts (of divorce and related books), essays, exposé, general interest, historical/nostalgic (of divorce), how-to (find an attorney), humor (for "strange stories from divorce court" column), interview/profile (of prominent person who deals with divorce: judges, mediators, etc.). "We do not want any articles about pitiful stories of parents who are going through a bad time and want sympathy. The DPX tries to focus on positive aspects of life after divorce—not the negatives." Query or send complete ms. Length: 2,500 words maximum. Pays 1¢/word minimum.

Columns/Departments: Contact: Columns Submissions. My Child And I (positive activities, advice and information for parents); Strange Stories from Divorce Court (unusual stories about divorced and divorcing couples); The Law and You (focusing on a legal issue (federal law) that is relevant to all divorced parents (must be accompanied by sources). Buys 12/year for each subject. Query or send complete ms. Pays 1¢/word.

Fillers: Anecdotes, facts, newsbreaks, short humor. Length: 200-500 words. Pays 1¢/word maximum.

Tips: "Articles must deal with an issue of interest to parents. Be familiar with our newsletter and its readership before trying to write for us. We publish constructive, optimistic, and helpful pieces that present alternative solutions and new ideas for coping with and solving the problems that confront divorced, step, and single parents. Include a SASE or we cannot write you back. We'd be more than happy to look at anything that would be of interest to divorced and stepparents as well articles about grandparents rights. The best articles are the shortest, yet in-depth, pieces. The shorter, the better."

‡**FAMILY LIFE**, 1290 Avenue of the Americas, New York NY 10104. Editor: Nancy Evans. Contact: Linette Andréa. 90% freelance written. Bimonthly magazine for parents of children ages 3-12. Estab. 1993. Circ. 160,000. Pays on publication. Publishes ms an average of 4 months. Byline given. Offers 25% kill fee. Buys first North American rights. Editorial lead time 5 months. Submit seasonal material 8 months in advance. Accepts simultaneous submissions. Reports in 6 weeks on queries. Sample copy for $3. Writer's guidelines for #10 SASE.

Nonfiction: Book excerpts, essays, general interest, new product, personal experience, photo feature, travel. Does not want to see articles about children under 3 or childbirth. Query with published clips. Pays $1/word. Pays expenses of writers on assignment.

Photos: State availability of photos with submission. Reviews transparencies. Negotiates payment individually. Buys one-time rights.

Columns/Departments: Elizabeth Kraft. Query with published clips. Pays $1/word minimum.

FAMILY TIMES, Family Times, Inc., 1900 Super Five Lane, Wilmington DE 19802. (302)575-0935. Editor: Alison Garber. Assistant Editor: Ainee Pamintuan. 25% freelance written. Monthly tabloid for parenting. "Our targeted distribution is to parents via a controlled network of area schools, daycares, pediatricians and places where families congregate. We only want articles related to parenting, children's issues and enhancing family life." Estab. 1991. Circ. 50,000. Pays on publication. Publishes ms an average of 2 months after acceptance. Byline given. Buys one-time or second serial (reprint) rights. Editorial lead time 2 months. Submit seasonal material 2 months in advance. Accepts simultaneous and previously published submissions. Query for electronic submissions. Prefers Mac diskette. Reports in 1 month on mss. Sample copy for 3 first-class stamps.

Nonfiction: Book excerpts, how-to parenting, inspirational, interview/profile, new product, opinion, personal experience, photo feature, travel, children, parenting. Special issues: Schools (October); Camps (February);

Maternity (July); Holiday (December); Fitness (March); Birthday (May); Back to School (August). Buys 48 mss/year. Send complete ms. Length: 350-1,200 words. Pays $30 minimum for assigned articles; $25 for unsolicited articles. Sometimes pays expenses of writers on assignment.

Photos: State availability of photos with submission. Negotiates payment individually. Identification of subjects required. Buys one-time rights.

Columns/Departments: Pays $25-50.

Tips: "Work with other members of PPA (Parenting Publications of America). Since we all share our writers and watch others' work. We pay little but you can sell the same story to 30+ other publications in different markets. We are most open to general features."

‡**GRAND RAPIDS PARENT MAGAZINE,** Gemini Publications, 549 Ottawa NW, Grand Rapids MI 49503. (616)459-4545. Editor: Carole Valade Smith. 90% freelance written. Monthly magazine. "Written for parents in the West Michigan area." Estab. 1989. Circ. 12,000. Pays on publication. Byline given. Offers $25 kill fee. Buys first North American serial rights, simultaneous rights, all rights or makes work-for-hire assignments. Editorial lead time 2-3 months. Submit seasonal material 4 months in advance. Accepts simultaneous submissions. Query for electronic submissions. Reports in 2 months on queries; 6 months on mss. Writer's guidelines for #10 SASE.

Nonfiction: General interest, historical/nostalgic, how-to, inspirational, interview/profile, new product, opinion, personal experience, photo feature, religious, travel. Buys 20-30 mss/year. Query. Length: 500-1,500 words. Pays $25. Sometimes pays expenses of writers on assignment.

Photos: State availabililty of photos with submission. Reviews contact sheets. Offers $25/photo. Captions, model releases and identification of subjects required. Buys one-time or all rights.

Columns/Departments: All local: law, finance, humor, opinion, mental health. Pays $25.

GROWING PARENT, Dunn & Hargitt, Inc., P.O. Box 620, Lafayette IN 47902-0620. (317)423-2624. Fax: (317)423-4495. Editor: Nancy Kleckner. 40-50% freelance written. Works with a small number of new/unpublished writers each year. "We do receive a lot of unsolicited submissions but have had excellent results in working with some unpublished writers. So, we're always happy to look at material and hope to find one or two jewels each year." Monthly newsletter which focuses on parents—the issues, problems, and choices they face as their children grow. "We want to look at the parent as an adult and help encourage his or her growth not only as a parent but as an individual." Estab. 1967. **Pays on acceptance.** Publishes ms an average of 6 months after acceptance. Byline given. Buys first North American serial rights; maintains exclusive rights for three months. Submit seasonal/holiday material 6 months in advance. Accepts previously published material. Send photocopy of article and information about when and where it previously appeared. Reports in 2 weeks. Sample copy and writer's guidelines for 5×8 SAE with 2 first-class stamps.

Nonfiction: "We are looking for informational articles written in an easy-to-read, concise style. We would like to see articles that help parents deal with the stresses they face in everyday life—positive, upbeat, how-to-cope suggestions. We rarely use humorous pieces, fiction or personal experience articles. Writers should keep in mind that most of our readers have children under three years of age." Buys 15-20 mss/year. Query. Length: 1,000-1,500 words; will look at shorter pieces. Pays 10-15¢/word (depends on article).

Tips: "Submit a very specific query letter with samples."

HEALTHY KIDS, Cahners Publishing, 249 W. 17th St., New York NY 10011. Managing Editor: Ellen Wlody. 90% freelance written. Bimonthly magazine covering children's health. Estab. 1989. Circ. 1.5 million. **Pays on acceptance.** Byline given. Buys first rights. Submit seasonal/holiday material at least 6 months in advance. Reports in 1 month on queries. Free sample copy and writer's guidelines for SASE.

Nonfiction: How-to help your child develop as a person, keep safe, keep healthy. No poetry, fiction, travel or product endorsement. Buys 30 mss/year. Query. Length: 1,500-2,000 words. Pays $500-1,000. Pays expenses of writers on assignment. Does not accept unsolicited mss.

Columns/Departments: Buys 30 mss/year. Query. Length: 1,500-2,000 words. Pays $500-750.

HOME EDUCATION MAGAZINE, P.O. Box 1083, Tonasket WA 98855-1083. Editors: Mark J. Hegener and Helen E. Hegener. 80% freelance written. Eager to work with new/unpublished writers each year. Bimonthly magazine covering home-based education. "We feature articles which address the concerns of parents who want to take a direct involvement in the education of their children—concerns such as socialization, how to find curriculums and materials, testing and evaluation, how to tell when your child is ready to begin reading, what to do when homeschooling is difficult, teaching advanced subjects, etc." Estab. 1983. Circ. 7,200. Pays on publication. Publishes ms an average of 2 months after acceptance. Byline given. ("Please include a 30-50 word credit with your article.") Buys first North American serial, first, one-time, second serial (reprint) and simultaneous rights and makes work-for-hire assignments. Submit seasonal/holiday material 6 months in advance. Accepts simultaneous and previously published submissions. Query for electronic submission requirements. Reports in 2 months. Sample copy for $4.50. Writer's guidelines for #10 SASE.

Nonfiction: Book excerpts, essays, how-to (related to home schooling), humor, inspirational, interview/profile, personal experience, photo features, technical. Buys 40-50 mss/year. Query with or without published clips, or send complete ms. Length: 750-3,500 words. Pays 45¢/column inch. Sometimes pays expenses of writers on assignment.

Photos: Send photos with submission. Reviews 5×7, 35mm prints and b&w snapshots; color transparencies for covers $25 each. Write for photo rates. Identification of subjects required. Buys one-time rights.

Tips: SASE. "We would like to see how-to articles (that don't preach, just present options); articles on testing, accountability, working with the public schools, socialization, learning disabilities, resources, support groups, legislation and humor. We need answers to the questions that homeschoolers ask."

HOME LIFE, Sunday School Board, 127 9th Ave. N., Nashville TN 37234. (615)251-2271. Editor-in-Chief: Charlie Warren. 50% freelance written. Prefers to work with published/established writers, but will work with new/unpublished writers. Monthly magazine emphasizing Christian marriage and family life for married adults of all ages, but especially newlyweds and middle-aged marrieds. Estab. 1947. Circ. 615,000. **Pays on acceptance.** Publishes ms an average of 15 months after acceptance. Buys first, first North American serial and all rights. Byline given. Query. Submit seasonal/holiday material 1 year in advance. Reports in 2 weeks on queries; 3 months on mss. Sample copy for $1. Writer's guidelines for #10 SASE.

Nonfiction: How-to (good articles on marriage and family life); informational (about some current family-related issue of national significance such as "Television and the Christian Family" or "Whatever Happened to Family Worship?"); personal experience (informed articles by people who have solved marriage and family problems in healthy, constructive ways). "No column material. We are not interested in material that will not in some way enrich Christian marriage or family life. We are interested in articles on fun family activities for a new department called Family Time." Buys 100-150 mss/year. Query or submit complete ms. Length: 600-1,800 words. Pays $75-275.

Fiction: "Fiction should be family-related and should show a strong moral about how families face and solve problems constructively." Buys 12-20 mss/year. Submit complete ms. Length: 1,500-1,800 words. Pays from $150.

Tips: "Study the magazine to see our unique slant on Christian family life. We prefer a life-centered case study approach, rather than theoretical essays on family life. Our top priority is marriage enrichment material."

L.A. PARENT, The Magazine for Parents in Southern California, P.O. Box 3204, Burbank CA 91504. (818)846-0400. Fax: (818)841-4380. Editor: Jack Bierman. Managing Editor: David Jamieson. 80% freelance written. Prefers to work with published/established writers, but works with a small number of new/unpublished writers each year. Monthly tabloid covering parenting. Estab. 1980. Circ. 200,000. **Pays on acceptance.** Publishes ms an average of 4 months after acceptance. Byline given. Buys first and reprint rights. Submit seasonal/holiday material 3 months in advance. Accepts simultaneous queries and previously published submissions. Send tearsheet of article and information about when and where the article previously appeared. For reprints pays 33% of the amount paid for an original article. Query for electronic submissions. Reports in 2 months. Sample copy and writer's guidelines for $2 and 11×14 SAE with 5 first-class stamps.

Nonfiction: David Jamieson, articles editor. General interest, how-to. "We focus on generic parenting for ages 0-10 and southern California activities for families, and do round-up pieces, i.e., a guide to private schools, art opportunities." Buys 60-75 mss/year. Query with clips of published work. Length: 700-1,200 words. Pays $200-300 plus expenses.

Tips: "We will be using more contemporary articles on parenting's challenges. If you can write for a 'city magazine' in tone and accuracy, you may write for us. The 'Baby Boom' has created a need for more generic parenting material. We look for a sophisticated tone in covering the joys and demands of being a mom or dad in the 90s."

LADIES' HOME JOURNAL PARENT'S DIGEST, Meredith Corporation, 100 Park Ave., New York NY 10017. (212)351-3500. Editor: Mary Mohler. Managing Editor: Carolyn B. Noyes. 75% freelance written. Quarterly magazine for childrearing and parenting. "This is a digest of materials that have previously appeared in books, newspapers or on the air." Estab. 1991. Circ. 400,000. **Pays on acceptance.** Byline given. Buys first North American serial, second serial (reprint) or all rights. Submit seasonal material 6 months in advance. Accepts previously published submissions. Reports in 6 weeks on queries.

Nonfiction: Book excerpts, essays, humor, new product, travel. Buys 50 mss/year. Query with published clips. Length: 250-2,500 words. Payment negotiable for previously published material. Sometimes pays expenses of writers on assignment (limit agreed upon in advance).

Photos: State availability of photos with submission. Negotiates payment individually. Model release and identification of subjects required.

LONG ISLAND PARENTING NEWS, RDM Publishing, P.O. Box 214, Island Park NY 11558. (516)889-5510. Fax: (516)889-5513. Editor: Pat Simms-Elias. Managing Editor: Andrew Elias. 70% freelance written. Free

For explanation of symbols, see the Key to Symbols and Abbreviations. For unfamiliar words, see the Glossary.

community newspaper published monthly covering parenting, children and family issues. "A publication for concerned parents with active families and young children. Our slogan is: 'For parents who care to know.' " Estab. 1989. Circ. 50,000. Pays on publication. Publishes ms an average of 3 months after acceptance. Byline given (also 1-3 line bio, if appropriate). Buys one-time rights. Accepts simultaneous and previously published submissions. Send photocopy of article and information about when and where the article previously appeared. Pays 75-100% of their fee for an original article. Reports in 3 months. Sample copy for $3 and 9×12 SAE with 5 first-class stamps. Free writer's guidelines.

Nonfiction: Essays, general interest, humor, interview/profile, travel. Will need articles covering childcare, childbirth/maternity, schools, camps and back-to-school. Buys 20-30 mss/year. Query with or without published clips, or send complete ms. Length: 350-2,000 words. Pays $25-150. "Sometimes trade article for advertising space." Sometimes pays expenses of writers on assignment.

Photos: Send photos with submission. Reviews 4×5 prints. Offers $5-50/photo. Captions required. Buys one-time rights.

Columns/Departments: Off The Shelf (book reviews); Fun & Games (toy and game reviews); KidVid (reviews of kids' video); The Beat (reviews of kids' music); Monitor (reviews of computer hardware and software for kids); Big Screen (reviews of kids' films); Soon Come (for expectant parents); Educaring (parenting info and advice); Something Special (for parents of kids with special needs); Growing Up (family health issues); On the Ball (sports for kids); Perspectives (essays on family life); Words Worth (storytelling); Getaway (family travel). Buys 20-30 mss/year. Send complete ms. Length: 500-1,000 words. Pays 25-150.

Fillers: Facts and newsbreaks. Buys 1-10/year. Length: 200-500. Pays $10-25.

METROKIDS MAGAZINE, The Resource for Parents and Children in the Delaware Valley, Kidstuff Publications, Inc., Riverview Plaza, 1400 S. Columbus Blvd., Philadelphia PA 19147. (215)551-3200. Editor: Frank Lewis. 80% freelance written. Monthly tabloid that provides information for parents and kids in Philadelphia and surrounding counties. Estab. 1990. Circ. 70,000. Pays on publication. Byline given. Buys one-time rights. Submit seasonal/holiday material 4 months in advance. Accepts previously published submissions. Send tearsheet or photocopy of article and information about when and where the article previously appeared. For reprints pays 75-80% of the amount paid for an original article. Query for electronic submissions. Reports in up to 8 months on queries. Sample copy for 9×12 SAE with 4 first-class stamps. Writer's guidelines for #10 SASE.

Nonfiction: General interest, how-to, humor, new product, travel. "Each issue has a focus (for example: finance, extra-curricular lessons for kids, health and nutrition, new babies, birthdays, child care, etc.)." Buys 20 mss/year. Query with or without published clips. Length: 750 words maximum. Pays $1-50. Sometimes pays expenses of writers on assignment.

Photos: State availability of photos with submission. Captions required. Buys one-time rights.

Columns/Departments: Away We Go (travel), 500 words; On Call (medical), 500 words; Book Beat (book reviews), 500 words; SOS (In search of software), 500 words. Buys 25 mss/year. Query. Pays $1-50.

Tips: "Send a query letter several months before a scheduled topical issue; then follow-up with a telephone call. We are interested in receiving feature articles (on specified topics) or material for our regular columns (which should have a regional/seasonal base). 1995 editorial calendar available on request."

PARENT LIFE, (formerly *Living with Preschoolers* and *Living with Children*), Baptist Sunday School Board, 127 Ninth Ave. N., Nashville TN 37234. (615)251-2229. Fax: (615)251-5058. Contact Editor. 30% freelance written. Works with a small number of new/unpublished writers each year. Monthly magazine covering parenting issues for parents of children (infants through 12-year-olds), "written and designed from a Christian perspective." Estab. 1994. Circ. 152,000. **Pays on acceptance.** Byline given. "We generally buy all rights to manuscripts. First and reprint rights may be negotiated at a lower rate of pay." Submit seasonal/holiday material 1 year in advance. Accepts previously published submissions (on limited basis). Résumés and queries only. Reports in 1 month on queries; 2 months on mss. Sample copy for 9×12 SASE. Free writer's guidelines.

PARENTING MAGAZINE, 17th Floor, 301 Howard, San Francisco CA 94105. (415)546-7575. Fax: (415)546-0578. Executive Editor: Anne Krueger. Managing Editor: Bruce Raskin. Editor: Steve Reddicliffe. Magazine published 10 times/year "for parents of children from birth to ten years old, with the most emphasis put on the under-sixes." Estab. 1987. **Pays on acceptance.** Byline given. Offers 25% kill fee. Buys first rights. Query for electronic submissions. Reports in 1 month. Sample copy for $1.95 and 9×12 SAE with 5 first-class stamps. Writer's guidelines for #10 SASE.

• Ranked as one of the best markets for freelance writers in *Writer's Digest* magazine's annual "Top 100 Markets," January 1994.

Nonfiction: Articles editor. Book excerpts, humor, investigative reports, personal experience, photo feature. Buys 20-30 features/year. Query with or without published clips, or send complete ms. Length: 1,000-3,500 words. Pays $500-2,000. Sometimes pays expenses of writers on assignment.

Columns/Departments: News and Reviews (news items relating to children/family), 100-400 words; Ages and Stages (health, nutrition, new products and service stories), 100-500 words; Passages (parental rites of passage), 850 words; Up in Arms (opinion, 850 words). Buys 50-60 mss/year. Pays $50-500.

PARENTS MAGAZINE, 685 Third Ave., New York NY 10017. Fax: (212)867-4583. Editor-in-Chief: Ann Pleshette Murphy. 25% freelance written. Monthly. Estab. 1926. Circ. 1,740,000. **Pays on acceptance.** Publishes ms an average of 8 months after acceptance. Usually buys first serial or first North American serial rights; sometimes buys all rights. Pays 25% kill fee. Reports in approximately 2 months. Sample copy for $2. Writer's guidelines for #10 SASE.

Nonfiction: "We are interested in well-documented articles on the development and behavior of preschool, school-age and adolescent children and their parents; good, practical guides to the routines of baby care; articles that offer professional insights into family and marriage relationships; reports of new trends and significant research findings in education and in mental and physical health; and articles encouraging informed citizen action on matters of social concern. Especially need articles on women's issues, pregnancy, birth, baby care and early childhood. We prefer a warm, colloquial style of writing, one which avoids the extremes of either slang or technical jargon. Anecdotes and examples should be used to illustrate points which can then be summed up by straight exposition." Query. Length: 2,500 words maximum. Payment varies. Sometimes pays the expenses of writers on assignment.

PARENTS' PRESS, The Monthly Newspaper for Bay Area Parents, 1454 Sixth St., Berkeley CA 94710. (510)524-1602. Editor: Dixie M. Jordan. Managing Editor: Lynn Verbeek. 50% freelance written. Monthly tabloid for parents. Estab. 1980. Circ. 75,000. Pays within 60 days of publication. Publishes ms an average of 6 months after acceptance. Kill fee varies (individually negotiated). Buys first rights, second serial (reprint) and almost always Northern California Exclusive rights. Accepts previously published material. Send photocopy of article or typed ms with rights for sale noted and information about when and where the article previously appeared. For reprints pays 10-25% of amount paid for an original article. Submit seasonal material 6 months in advance. Reports in 2 months. Sample copy for $3. Writer's guidelines for #10 SASE.

Nonfiction: Book excerpts (family, children), how-to (parent, raise children, nutrition, health, etc.), humor (family life, children), interview/profile (of Bay Area residents, focus on their roles as parents), travel (family), family resources and activities. "Annual issues include Pregnancy and Birth, Travel, Back-to-School, Children's Health. Write for planned topic or suggest one. We require a strong Bay Area focus where appropriate. Please don't send 'generic' stories. While we publish researched articles which spring from personal experience, we do not publish strictly personal essays. Please, no birth stories." Buys 30-50 mss/year. Query with or without published clips, or send complete ms. Length: 300-3,000 words; 1,500-2,000 average. Pays $50-150 for assigned articles; $25-125 for unsolicited articles. Will negotiate fees for special projects written by Bay Area journalists.

Photos: State availability of photos with submission. Reviews prints, any size, b&w only. Offers $10-15/photo. Model release and identification of subject required. Buys one-time rights.

Columns/Departments: Books (reviews of parenting and children's books, preferably by San Francisco Bay Area authors, publishers). Buys 12-24 mss/year. Send complete ms. Length: 100-750 words. Pays $15-25.

Tips: "All sections of Parents' Press are open to freelancers, but we are protective of our regular columnists' turf (children's health, women's health, infant and child behavior), so we ask writers to query whether a topic has been addressed in the last three years. Best bets to break in are family activities, education, nutrition, family dynamics and issues. While we prefer articles written by experts, we welcome well-researched journalism."

PEDIATRICS FOR PARENTS, The Newsletter for Caring Parents, Pediatrics for Parents, Inc., P.O. Box 1069, Bangor ME 04402-1069. (207)942-6212. Fax: (207)947-3134. Editor: Richard J. Sagall, M.D. 20% freelance written. Eager to work with new/unpublished writers. Monthly newsletter covering medical aspects of rearing children and educating parents about children's health. Estab. 1981. Circ. 2,000. Pays on publication. Publishes ms an average of 3-4 months after acceptance. Byline given. Buys first North American serial rights, first and second rights to the same material, and second (reprint) rights to material originally published elsewhere. Rights always include right to publish article in books on "Best of . . ." series. Submit seasonal/holiday material 6 months in advance. Accepts simultaneous queries and previously published submissions. Query for electronic submissions. Reports in 1 month on queries; 6 weeks on mss. Sample copy for $2. Writer's guidelines for #10 SAE with 2 first-class stamps.

Nonfiction: Book reviews, how-to (feed healthy kids, exercise, practice wellness, etc.), new product, technical (explaining medical concepts in shirtsleeve language). No general parenting articles. Query with published clips or submit complete ms. Length: 25-1,000 words. Pays 2-5¢/edited word.

Columns/Departments: Book reviews; Please Send Me (material available to parents for free or at nominal cost); Pedia-Tricks (medically-oriented parenting tips that work). Send complete ms. Pays $15-250. Pays 2¢/edited word.

Tips: "We are dedicated to taking the mystery out of medicine for young parents. Therefore, we write in clear and understandable language (but not simplistic language) to help people understand and deal intelligently with complex disease processes, treatments, prevention, wellness, etc. Our articles must be well researched and documented. Detailed references must always be attached to any article for documentation, but not for publication. We strongly urge freelancers to read one or two issues before writing."

SAN DIEGO FAMILY PRESS, San Diego County's Leading Resource for Parents & Educators Who Care!, P.O. Box 23960, San Diego CA 92193-0960. Editor: Sharon Bay. Contact: Dina Madruga, Assistant Editor. 75% freelance written. Monthly magazine for parenting and family issues. "*SDFP* strives to provide informative, educational articles emphasizing positive parenting for our typical readership of educated mothers, ages 25-45, with an upper-level income. Most articles are factual and practical, some are humor and personal experience. Editorial emphasis is uplifting and positive." Estab. 1983. Circ. 65,000. Pays on publication. Publishes ms an average of 5 months after acceptance. Byline given. Buys first, one-time or second serial (reprint) rights. Editorial lead time 1 month. Submit seasonal material 3 months in advance. Reports in 6-8 weeks on queries; 2-3 months on mss. Sample copy for $3.50. Writer's guidelines for #10 SASE.

Nonfiction: How-to, parenting, new baby help, enhancing education, family activities, interview/profile (influential or noted persons or experts included in parenting or the welfare of children) and articles of specific interest to or regarding. San Diego (for California) families/children/parents/educators. "No rambling, personal experience pieces." Buys 75 mss/year. Send complete ms. Length: 1,200 maximum words. Pays $1.25/column inch. "Byline and contributor copies if writer prefers."

Photos: State availability of photos with submission. Reviews contact sheets and 3½×5 or 5×7 prints. Negotiates payment individually. Identification of subjects preferred. Buys one-time rights.

Columns/Departments: Kids' Books (topical book reviews), 800 words. Buys 12 mss/year. Query with published clips. Pays $1.25/column inch minimum.

Fillers: Facts and newsbreaks (specific to the family market). Buys 10/year. Length: 50-200 words. Pays $1.25/column inch minimum, $25 maximum.

SESAME STREET PARENTS, Children's Television Workshop, 1 Lincoln Plaza, New York NY 10023. (212)595-3456. Fax: (212)875-6105. Editor-in-Chief: Ira Wolfman. 80% freelance written. Magazine published 10 times/year for parents of preschoolers that accompanies every issue of Sesame Street Magazine. Circ. 1.2 million. **Pays on acceptance.** Byline given. Offers 33% kill fee. Buys varying rights. Submit seasonal/holiday material 7 months in advance. Accepts previously published articles. Send typed ms with rights for sale noted and information about when and where the article previously appeared. For reprints pays 75% of the amount paid for an original article. Reports in 1 month on queries. Sample copy for 9×12 SAE with 6 first-class stamps. Writer's guidelines for #10 SASE.

• Ranked as one of the best markets for freelance writers in *Writer's Digest* magazine's annual "Top 100 Markets," January 1994.

Nonfiction: Child development/parenting, how-to (practical tips for parents of preschoolers), interview/profile, personal experience, book excerpts, essays, photo feature, travel (with children). Buys 100 mss/year. Query with published clips, or send complete ms. Length: 500-2,000 words. Pays $300-2,000 for articles.

Photos: State availability of photos with submission. Model releases, identification of subjects required. Buys one-time or all rights.

‡SMARTKIDS, The Newsletter for Raising Intelligent Children, SmartKids Enterprise, P.O. Box 114, LaVerne CA 91750. Editor: Michelle Dowd. Managing Editor: Scott Lukesh. 50% freelance written. Bimonthly newsletter covering educational objectives. "The *SmartKids* newsletter is for intelligent, educated parents who want to give their children every advantage. All material should be up-to-date and informed." Estab. 1993. Circ. 1,000. Pays on publication. Publishes ms an average of 3 months after acceptance. Byline given. Buys first rights. Submit seasonal material 6 months in advance. Accepts simultaneous submissions. Reports in 3 weeks. Sample copy and writer's guidelines for $2.

Nonfiction: Essays, how-to (tips on parenting), opinion, personal experience. Special holiday issue in November. Submit mss by June. No book reviews. Buys 18 mss/year. Send complete ms. Length: 500-1,000 words. Pays 5¢/word minimum.

Columns/Departments: Science (activities to be done together), 750 words; Activities (things to do for parents and children to share), 750 words. Buys 6 mss/year. Pays $10-100.

Tips: "Submit new, fresh information intelligently and concisely written and accurately researched. We have an educated readership and it is crucial not to talk down to them. We are eager to work with new and unpublished writers who have original and interesting information for our readers. We are currently looking for articles about major political issues or current events that affect families. We are also open to analyses of recent psychological, philosophical, or sociological studies about child-rearing (particularly for elementary age children)."

‡SOUTH FLORIDA PARENTING, Suite R, 4200 Aurora St., Coral Gables FL 33146. (305)448-6003. Editor: Ken Roberts. Contact: Deborah Z. Roffino. 90% freelance written. Monthly magazine covering parenting, family. Estab. 1989. Circ. 100,000. Pays on publication. Publishes ms an average of 3 months after acceptance. Byline given. Buys one-time rights or second serial (reprint) rights. Editorial lead time 3 months. Submit seasonal material 3 months in advance. Accepts simultaneous and previously published submissions if not published in our circulation area. Query for electronic submissions. Reports in 2 weeks on queries; 1 month on mss. Sample copy and writer's guidelines free on request.

Nonfiction: General interest, how-to, humor, interview/profile, new product, personal experience. Special issues: Maternity, Special Needs Children, Travel. Buys 24 mss/year. Send complete ms. Length: 600-1,800 words. Pays $100 for articles; $25 for reprints. Sometimes pays expenses of writers on assignment.

Photos: State availability of photos with submission. Offers no additional payment for photos accepted with ms.

Tips: "A unique approach to a universal parenting concern will be considered for publication. Profiles or interviews of courageous parents, unparalleled parents are sought. Opinion pieces on child rearing should be supported by experts and research should be listed."

TODAY'S FAMILY, Suite 328, 3585 N. Lexington Ave., Arden Hills MN 55126. (612)486-7820. Managing Editor: Valerie Hockert. 65% freelance written. Bimonthly magazine covering family social issues. Estab. 1991. Circ. 50,000. Pays on publication. Publishes ms 4 months after acceptance. Byline given. No kill fee. Buys first North American serial rights. Submit seasonal material 6 months in advance. Reports in 3 weeks on queries; 6 weeks on mss. Sample copy for $4. Writer's guidelines for #10 SASE.

Nonfiction: General interest, how-to, interview/profile, educational. "No fiction or personal essays." Buys 50 mss/year. Query. Length: 750-1,200 words. "Payment for assigned articles is negotiable." Pays $10-50 for unsolicited articles. Sometimes pays expenses of writers on assignment.

Photos: State availability of photos with submission. Reviews contact sheets and transparencies. Offers $5/photo minimum. Captions, model releases and identification of subjects required. Buys one-time rights.

Tips: "We like to see new ideas and new approaches to subjects of great concern to the family of today."

TWINS, The Magazine for Parents of Multiples, P.O. Box 12045, Overland Park KS 66282-2045. (913)722-1090. Fax: (913)722-1767. Editor-in-Chief: Barbara C. Unell. 100% freelance written. Eager to work with new/unpublished writers. Bimonthly international magazine designed to give professional guidance to help multiples, their parents and those professionals who care for them learn about twin facts and research. Estab. 1984. Circ. 56,000. Pays on publication. Publishes ms an average of 6 months after acceptance. Byline given. Buys all rights. Accepts previously published articles. Send photocopy of article or typed ms with rights for sale noted and information about when and where the article previously appeared. Submit seasonal/holiday material 10 months in advance. Reports in 6 weeks on queries; 2 months on mss. Sample copy for $5. Writer's guidelines for #10 SASE.

Nonfiction: Book excerpts, general interest, how-to, humor, interview/profile, personal experience, photo feature. "No articles that substitute the word 'twin' for 'child' — those that simply apply the same research to twins that applies to singletons without any facts backing up the reason to do so." Buys 150 mss/year. Query with or without published clips, or send complete ms. Length: 1,250-3,000 words. Payment varies; sometimes pays in contributor copies or premiums instead of cash. Sometimes pays the expenses of writers on assignment.

Photos: Send photos with submission. Reviews contact sheets, 4×5 transparencies, all size prints. Captions, model releases, identification of subjects required. Buys all rights.

Columns/Departments: Resources, Supertwins, Prematurity, Family Health, Twice as Funny, Double Focus (series from pregnancy through adolescence), Personal Perspective (first-person accounts of beliefs about a certain aspect of parenting multiples), Over the Back Fence (specific tips that have worked for the writer in raising multiples), Research, On Being Twins (first-person accounts of growing up as a twin), On Being Parents of Twins (first-person accounts of the experience of parenting twins), Double Takes (fun photographs of twins), Education Matters. Buys 70 mss/year. Query with published clips. Length: 1,250-2,000 words. Payment varies.

Fillers: Anecdotes, short humor. Length: 75-750 words. Payment varies.

Tips: "Features and columns are both open to freelancers. Columnists write for *Twins* on a continuous basis, so the column becomes their column. We are looking for a wide variety of the latest, well-researched practical information. There is no other magazine of this type directed to this market. We are interested in personal interviews with celebrity twins or celebrity parents of twins, tips on rearing twins from experienced parents and/or twins themselves and reports on national and international research studies involving twins."

WORKING MOTHER MAGAZINE, Lang Communications, 230 Park Ave., New York NY 10169. (212)551-9500. Editor: Judsen Culbreth. Executive Editor: Mary McLaughlin. 90% freelance written. Prefers to work with published/established writers; works with a small number of new/unpublished writers each year. Monthly magazine for women who balance a career with the concerns of parenting. Circ. 850,000. **Pays on acceptance.** Publishes ms an average of 4 months after acceptance. Byline given. Buys first North American Serial and all rights. Pays 20% kill fee. Submit seasonal/holiday material 6 months in advance. Reports in 6 weeks. Sample copy for $1.95. Writer's guidelines for SASE.

Nonfiction: Service, humor, child development, material pertinent to the working mother's predicament. Send query to attention of *Working Mother Magazine.* Buys 9-10 mss/issue. Length: 750-2,000 words. Pays $300-1,800. "We pay more to people who write for us regularly." Pays the expenses of writers on assignment.

Tips: "We are looking for pieces that help the reader. In other words, we don't simply report on a trend without discussing how it specifically affects our readers' lives and how they can handle the effects. Where can they look for help if necessary?"

Comic Books

Comic books aren't just for kids. Today, this medium also attracts a reader who is older and wants stories presented visually on a wide variety of topics. In addition, some instruction manuals, classics and other stories are being produced in a comic book format.

This doesn't mean you have to be an artist to write for comic books. Most of these publishers want to see a synopsis of one to two double-spaced pages. Be concise. Comics use few words and rely on graphics as well as words to forward the plot.

Once your synopsis is accepted, either an artist will draw the story from your plot, returning these pages to you for dialogue and captions, or you will be expected to write a script. Scripts run approximately 23 typewritten pages and include suggestions for artwork as well as dialogue. Try to imagine your story on actual comic book pages and divide your script accordingly. The average comic has six panels per page, with a maximum of 35 words per panel.

If you're submitting a proposal to Marvel, your story should center on an already established character. If you're dealing with an independent publisher, characters are often the property of their creators. Your proposal should be for a new series. Include a background sheet for main characters who will appear regularly, listing origins, weaknesses, powers or other information that will make your character unique. Indicate an overall theme or direction for your series. Submit story ideas for the first three issues. If you're really ambitious, you may also include a script for your first issue. As with all markets, read a sample copy before making a submission. The best markets may be those you currently read, so consider submitting to them even if they aren't listed in this section.

CARTOON WORLD, P.O. Box 30367, Dept. WM, Lincoln NE 68503. Editor: George Hartman. 100% freelance written. Works with published/established writers and a small number of new/unpublished writers each year. "Monthly newsletter for professional and amateur cartoonists who are serious and want to utilize new cartoon markets in each issue." Buys only from paid subscribers. Circ. 150-300. **Pays on acceptance.** Publishes ms an average of 2 months after acceptance. Byline given. Buys second (reprint) rights to material originally published elsewhere. Accepts previously published articles. Send tearsheet or photocopy of article or typed ms with rights for sale noted and information about when and where the article previously appeared. For reprints pays 25% of the amount paid for an original article. Not copyrighted. Submit seasonal/holiday material 3 months in advance. Simultaneous submissions OK. Reports in 1 month. Sample copy for $5.
Nonfiction: "We want only positive articles about the business of cartooning and gag writing." Buys 10 mss/year. Query. Length: 1,000 words. Pays $5/page.

COMICS SCENE, Starlog Group, 8th Floor, 475 Park Ave. S., New York NY 10016. (212)689-2830. Fax: (212)889-7933. Editor: David McDonnell. Magazine published 9 times/year on comic books, strips, cartoons, those who create them and TV/movie adaptations of both. Estab. 1981. Pays on publication. Byline given. Offers 25% kill fee. Buys all rights or second serial (reprint) rights. Submit seasonal/holiday material 6 months in advance. Absolutely *no* simultaneous submissions. Reports in 6 weeks on queries; 2 months on mss. Sample copy for $5. Writer's guidelines for #10 SASE. *No* queries by phone for *any* reason whatsoever.

ALWAYS submit unsolicited manuscripts or queries with a self-addressed, stamped envelope (SASE) within your country or a self-addressed envelope with International Reply Coupons (IRC) purchased from the post office for other countries.

Nonfiction: Book excerpts, historical/nostalgic, interview/profile, new product, personal experience. Buys 90 mss/year. Query with published clips. Length: 750-3,500 words. Pays $150-250. Sidebars $50-75. Does *not* publish fiction or comics stories and strips. Rarely buys reprints.

Photos: State availability of photos and comic strip/book/animation artwork with submission. Reviews contact sheets, transparencies and 8×10 prints. Offers $10-25 for original photos. Captions, model releases, identification of subjects required. Buys all rights.

Columns/Departments: The Comics Reporter ("newsy" mini-interview with writer, director, producer of TV series/movie adaptations of comic books and strips). Buys 10-12 mss/year. Query with published clips. Length: 100-750 words. Pays $15-50.

Tips: "We *really* need coverage of independent comics companies' products and creators. We need interviews with specific comic strip creators. Most any writer can break in with interviews with hot comic book writers and artists (we really *need* more of the hot ones) – and with comic book creators who don't work for the big two companies. We do *not* want nostalgic items or interviews. Do not burden us with your own personal comic book stories or artwork. We don't have time to evaluate them and can't provide critiques or advice. Get interviews we can't get or haven't thought to pursue. Out-thinking overworked editors is an almost certain way to sell a story."

MARVEL COMICS, 387 Park Ave. S., New York NY 10016. (212)696-0808. Editor-in-Chief: Tom DeFalco. 99% freelance written. Publishes 60 comics and magazines/month, 6-12 graphic novels/year, and specials, storybooks, industrials, and paperbacks for all ages. Over 9 million copies sold/month. Pays a flat fee for most projects, plus a royalty type incentive based upon sales. Also works on advance/royalty basis on many projects. **Pays on acceptance.** Publishes ms an average of 6 months after acceptance. Byline given. Offers variable kill fee. Rights purchased depend upon format and material. Submit seasonal/holiday material 1 year in advance. Accepts simultaneous submissions. Reports in 6 months. Writer's guidelines for #10 SASE. Additional guidelines on request.
  • Marvel Comics no longer accepts unsolicited mss.

Fiction: Super hero, action-adventure, science fiction, fantasy and other material. Only comics. Buys 600-800 mss/year. Query with brief plot synopses only. Do not send scripts, short stories or long outlines. A plot synopsis should be less than two typed pages; send two synopses at most. Pays expenses of writers on assignment.

Consumer Service and Business Opportunity

Some of these magazines are geared to investing earnings or starting a new business; others show how to make economical purchases. Publications for business executives and consumers interested in business topics are listed under Business and Finance. Those on how to run specific businesses are classified by category in the Trade section.

JERRY BUCHANAN'S INFO MARKETING REPORT, TOWERS Club Press, Inc., P.O. Box 2038, Vancouver WA 98668-2038. (206)574-3084. Fax: (206)576-8969. Editor: Jerry Buchanan. 5-10% freelance written. Works with a small number of unpublished writers each year. Monthly of 10 or more pages on entrepreneurial enterprises, reporting especially on self-publishing of how-to reports, books, audio and video tapes, seminars, etc. "By-passing big trade publishers and marketing your own work directly to consumer (mail order predominantly)." Estab. 1974. Circ. 10,000. Pays on publication. Publishes ms an average of 2 months after acceptance. Byline given. Buys one-time rights. Fax submissions accepted of no more than 3 pages. Accepts previously published articles. Send photocopy of article and information about when and where the article previously appeared. For reprints pays 50% of the amount paid for an original article. Reports in 2 weeks. Sample copy for $15 and 6×9 SASE.

Nonfiction: Exposé (of mail order fraud); how-to (personal experience in self-publishing and marketing); book reviews of new self-published nonfiction how-to-do-it books (must include name and address of author). "Welcomes well-written articles of successful self-publishing/marketing ventures. Must be current, and preferably written by the person who actually did the work and reaped the rewards. There's very little we will not consider, *if* it pertains to unique money-making enterprises that can be operated from the home." Buys 10 mss/year. Send complete ms. Length: 500-1,500 words. Pays $150-250. Pays extra for b&w photo and bonus for excellence in longer ms.

Tips: "The most frequent mistake made by writers in completing an article for us is that they think they can simply rewrite a newspaper article and be accepted. That is only the start. We want them to find the article about a successful self-publishing enterprise, and then go out and interview the principal for a more detailed how-to article, including names and addresses. We prefer that writer actually interview a successful self-publisher. Articles should include how idea first came to subject; how they implemented and financed and promoted the project; how long it took to show a profit and some of the stumbling blocks they overcame; how many persons participated in the production and promotion; and how much money was invested (approximately) and other pertinent how-to elements of the story. Glossy photos (b&w) of principals at work in their offices will help sell article."

CONSUMERS DIGEST MAGAZINE, for People who Demand Value, Consumers Digest, Inc., 5705 N. Lincoln Ave., Chicago IL 60659. (312)275-3590. Editor: John K. Manos. 70% freelance written. Bimonthly magazine offering "practical advice on subjects of interest to consumers: products and services, automobiles, health, fitness, consumer legal affairs, personal money management, etc." Estab. 1959. Circ. 1.3 million. **Pays on acceptance.** Publishes ms an average of 3 months after acceptance. Byline given. Offers 50% kill fee. Buys all rights. Submit seasonal material 6 months in advance. Accepts simultaneous submissions. Query for electronic submissions. Reports in 6 weeks on queries; 3 months on mss. Sample copy for 9 × 12 SAE with 6 first-class stamps. Free writer's guidelines.

Nonfiction: Elliott H. McCleary, articles editor. Exposé, general interest, how-to (financial, purchasing), new product, travel, health, fitness. Buys 50 mss/year. Query with published clips. Length: 1,000-3,500 words. Pays $400-3,500 for assigned articles; $400-1,700 for unsolicited articles. Sometimes pays expenses of writers on assignment.

Photos: State availability of photos with submission. Reviews transparencies. Pays $100-500/photo. Captions, model releases and identification of subjects required. Buys all rights.

Columns/Departments: Mary S. Butler, column editor. Consumerscope (brief items of general interest to consumers—auto news, travel tips, the environment, smart shopping, news you can use). Buys 10 mss/year. Query. Length: 100-500 words. Pays $75-200.

Tips: "Keep the queries brief and tightly focused. Read our writer's guidelines first and request an index of past articles for trends and to avoid repeating subjects. Focus on subjects of broad national appeal. Stress personal expertise in proposed subject area."

‡CRIME PREVENTION, The consumer guide to home, vehicle and personal security, National Publishing Co., 1533 Burgundy Pkwy., Streamwood IL 60107. (708)837-2044. Managing Editor: Tom Scroogy. 80% freelance written. Quarterly tabloid covering crime prevention and security. "*CP* is written in an informative and entertaining style designed to educate ordinary people how to make themselves safer from crime." Estab. 1994. Circ. 250,000. Pays on publication. Publishes ms an average of 3 months after acceptance. Byline given. Buys first North American serial rights. Editorial lead time 3 months. Submit seasonal material 6 months in advance. Accepts simultaneous and previously published submissions. Reports in 1 month. Sample copy for 10 × 12 SASE. Writer's guidelines free on request.

Nonfiction: Book excerpts, how-to (secure homes, vehicles, property), interview/profile, new product, personal experience, photo feature. Buys 60 mss/year. Send complete ms. Length: 500-1,500 words. Pays $100. Sometimes pays expenses of writers on assignment.

Photos: Reviews 5 × 7 prints. Offers no additional payment for photos accepted with ms. Captions, model releases required.

Tips: "Have a particular angle on crime prevention in mind and call the Managing Editor."

ECONOMIC FACTS, The National Research Bureau, Inc., P.O. Box 1, Burlington IA 52601-0001. (319)752-5415. Fax: (319)752-3421. Editor: Nancy Heinzel. 75% freelance written. Eager to work with new/unpublished writers; works with a small number of new/unpublished writers each year. Published 4 times/year. Estab. 1948. Pays on publication. Publishes ms an average of 1 year after acceptance. Buys all rights. Byline given. Sample copy and writer's guidelines for #10 SAE with 2 first-class stamps.

Nonfiction: General interest (private enterprise, government data, graphs, taxes and health care). Buys 10 mss/year. Query with outline of article. Length: 500-700 words. Pays 4¢/word.

‡HOME OFFICE OPPORTUNITIES, Deneb Publishing, P.O.Box 780, Lyman WY 82937. (307)786-4513. Editor: Diane Wolverton. 90% freelance written. Bimonthly magazine covering topics of interest to home business owners and telecommuters. "*Home Office Opportunities* offers how-to information, ideas, profiles, resources and motivation to individuals who work at home." Estab. 1990. Circ. 500. **Pays on acceptance.** Publishes ms 4-6 months after acceptance. Byline given. Buys first North American serial rights or second serial (reprint) rights. Editorial lead time 4 months. Submit seasonal material 6 months in advance Accepts simultaneous and previously published submissions. Reports in 1 month on queries; 2-3 months on mss. Sample copy for $2. Writer's guidelines for #10 SASE.

Nonfiction: How-to (effectively run home office), humor (related to working at home), interview/profile, personal experience, and technical (home business topics and telecommuting). "We like lots of specifics—ideas readers can actually put to work in their businesses." Buys 50 mss/year. Query; send complete ms for humor. Length: 400-2,000 words. Pays 1¢/word.

Photos: State availability of photos with submission. Reviews 5 × 7 b&w prints. Offers $3-5/photo. Captions required. Buys one-time rights.

Fiction: Business fiction. Buys 6 mss/year. Send complete ms. Length: 2,000 words maximum. Pays 1¢/word. "Short stories should have a business orientation, a business-savvy central character, and a conclusion that makes the reader feel good about being in business. Entertain while demonstrating solid business principles. Surprise us! Delight us."

Fillers: Facts. Buys 6-12/year.Length: 50-250 words. Pays $1-3.
Tips: Looking for "profiles of people operating successful and interesting home businesses or working at home for a large corporation. Make the profile come alive—not just dry facts or feature information that would run in a community newspaper."

‡INCOME PLUS MAGAZINE, Opportunity Associates, Suite 303, 73 Spring St., New York NY 10012. (212)925-3180. Fax: (212)925-3108. Editor: Donna Ruffini. 33-50% freelance written. Monthly magazine on small business and money-making ideas. Provides "hands-on service to help small business owners, home office owners and entrepreneurs successfully start up and run their enterprises. Focus on francising, mail order." Estab. 1989. Circ. 200,000. Pays on publication. Byline given. Offers 20% kill fee. Buys first North American serial rights. Query for electronic submissions. Reports in 6 weeks. Sample copy for $2 and 1 first-class stamp. Writer's guidelines for 1 first-class stamp.
Nonfiction: How-to (business, finance, home office, technical start-up). Buys 48 mss/year. Query with published clips. Length: 1,500-2,500 words. Pays $50-750. Sometimes pays expenses of writers on assignment.
Photos: State availability of photos with submission. Offers no additional payment for photos accepted with ms.
Columns/Departments: Legal and You The Boss (original reporting with real example of business owners to back up point of story); Home Business Marketing (service with easily and immediately applicable advice. Frequent use of bullets); 1,200 words. Buys 24 mss/year. Query with published clips. Pays $50-350.

KIPLINGER'S PERSONAL FINANCE, (formerly *Changing Times*), 1729 H St. NW, Washington DC 20006. Editor: Ted Miller. Less than 10% freelance written. Prefers to work with published/established writers. Monthly magazine for general, adult audience interested in personal finance and consumer information. Estab. 1947. Circ. 1 million. **Pays on acceptance.** Publishes ms an average of 2 months after acceptance. Buys all rights. Reports in 1 month. Query for electronic submissions. Thorough documentation required for fact-checking.
Nonfiction: "Most material is staff-written, but we accept some freelance." Query with clips of published work. Pays expenses of writers on assignment.
Tips: "We are looking for a heavy emphasis on personal finance topics."

‡LIVING SAFETY, A Canada Safety Council publication for safety in the home, traffic and recreational environments, #6-2750 Stevenage Dr., Ottawa, Ontario K1G 3N2 Canada. (613)739-1535. Editor: Heather Totten. 65% freelance written. Quarterly magazine covering off-the-job safety. "Off-the job health and safety magazine covering topics in the home, traffic and recreational environments. Audience is the Canadian employee and his/her family." Estab. 1983. Circ. 105,000. **Pays on acceptance.** Publishes ms an average of 2 months after acceptance. Byline given. Buys all rights. Editorial lead time 4 months. Submit seasonal material 6 months in advance. Accepts simultaneous and previously published submissions. Reports in 3-4 weeks on queries. Sample copy and writer's guidelines free on request.
Nonfiction: General interest, how-to (safety tips, health tips), personal experience. Buys 24 mss/year. Query with published clips. Length: 1,000-2,500 words. Pays $500 maximum. Sometimes pays expenses of writers on assignment.
Photos: State availability of photos with submission. Reviews contact sheet, negatives, transparencies, prints. Offers no additional payment for photos accepted with ms. Identification of subjects required.
Tips: "Send intro letter, query, résumé and published clips (magazine preferable). Wait for a phone call from editor."

Contemporary Culture

These magazines combine politics, gossip, fashion and entertainment in a single package. Their approach to institutions is typically irreverent and the target is primarily a young adult audience. Although most of the magazines are centered in large metropolitan areas, some have a following throughout the country.

BOMB MAGAZINE, Artists Writers Actors Directors, New Art Publications, Suite 1002A, 594 Broadway, New York NY 10012. (212)431-3943. Editor-in-Chief: Betsy Sussler. 2% freelance accepted. Quarterly magazine covers literature, art, theater, film and music. "We are interested in interviews *between* professionals." Estab. 1981. Circ. 12,000. Pays on publication. Publishes ms an average of 6 months after acceptance. Byline given. Buys one-time rights. Reports in 4 months. Sample copy for $5 with $2.90 postage.
Nonfiction: Book excerpts. "Literature *only*." Length: 250-5,000 words. Pays $100 minimum.
Photos: Offers $100/photo minimum. Captions required. Buys one-time rights.
Fiction: Experimental and novel excerpts. "No commercial fiction." Buys 28 mss/year. Send complete ms. Length: 250-5,000. Pays $100 minimum. Publishes novel excerpts.
Poetry: Avant-garde. Buys 10 poems/year. Submit maximum 6 poems. Pays $50 minimum.

‡BRUTARIAN, The Magazine That Dares To Be Lame, Box 25222, Arlington VA 22202. Editor: Dominick Salemi. 100% freelance written. Quarterly magazine covering popular and unpopular culture. "A healthy knowledge of the great works of antiquity and an equally healthy contempt for most of what passes today as culture." Estab. 1991. Circ. 2,000. Pays on publication. Publishes ms an average of 3 months after acceptance. Byline given. Buys first or one-time rights. Editorial lead time 2 months. Submit seasonal material 6 months in advance. Accepts previously published submissions. Reports in 1 week on queries; 2 months on mss. Sample copy for $4. Writer's guidelines free on request.

Nonfiction: Book excerpts, essays, exposé, general interest, historical/nostalgic, humor, interview/profile, reviews of books, film and music. Buys 10-20 feature articles/year. Send complete ms. Length: 1,000-10,000 words. Pays $100. Sometimes pays expenses of writers on assignment.

Photos: State availability of photos with submission. Reviews contact sheets. Offers no additional payment for photos accepted with ms. Caption, model releases, identification of subjects required. Buys one-time rights.

Columns/Departments: Celluloid Void (critiques of cult and obscure films), 500 words; Brut Library (critiques of books), 500 words; Audio Depravation (short critiques of odd and R&R music), 50-100 words. Buys "hundreds" of mss/year. Send complete ms. Pays $5-25.

Fiction: Adventure, confession, erotica, experimental, fantasy, horror, humorous, mystery, novel excerpts, science fiction, slice-of-life vignettes, suspense. Buys 4-10 mss/year. Send complete ms. Length: 1,000-10,000 words. Pays $100-500.

Poetry: Avant-garde, free verse, light verse, traditional. Buys 10-15 poems/year. Submit maximum 10 poems. Length: 25-1,000. Pays $20-200.

Tips: "Send résumé with completed manuscript. Avoid dry tone and excessive scholasticism. Do not cover topics or issues which have been done to death unless you have a fresh approach or new insights on the subject."

CANADIAN DIMENSION, Dimension Publications Inc., #707-228 Notre Dame Ave., Winnipeg, Manitoba, R3B 1N7 Canada. Fax: (204)943-4617. 80% freelance written. Bimonthly magazine "that makes sense of the world. We bring a socialist perspective to bear on events across Canada and around the world. Our contributors provide in-depth coverage on popular movements, peace, labour, women, aboriginal justice, environment, third world and eastern Europe." Estab. 1963. Circ. 4,000. Pays on publication. Publishes ms an average of 6 months after acceptance. Copyrighted by CD after publication. Simultaneous submissions OK. Reports in 6 weeks on queries. Sample copy for $2. Writer's guidelines for #10 SAE with IRC.

Nonfiction: Interview/profile, opinion, reviews, political commentary and analysis, journalistic style. Buys 8 mss/year. Length: 500-2,000 words. Pays $25-100.

FRANCE TODAY, FrancePress Inc., 1051 Divisadero St., San Francisco CA 94115. (415)921-5100. Editor: Anne Prah-Perochon. Associate Publisher: Allyn Kaufmann. 90% freelance written. Tabloid published 10 times/year covering contemporary France. "*France Today* is a feature publication on contemporary France including sociocultural analysis, business, trends, current events and travel." Estab. 1989. Circ. 7,500. Pays on publication. Publishes ms an average of 3-5 months after acceptance. Byline given. Buys first, first North American serial and second serial (reprint) rights. Submit seasonal/holiday material 4 months in advance. Accepts previously published and simultaneous submissions. Send tearsheet or photocopy of article or typed ms with rights for sale noted and information about when and where the article previously appeared. Reports in 3 months. Sample copy and writer's guidelines for 10×13 SAE with 3 first-class stamps.

Nonfiction: Essays, exposé, general interest, historical, humor, interview/profile, personal experience, travel. "No travel pieces about well-known tourist attractions." Buys 50% mss/year. Query with or without published clips, or send complete ms. Length: 500-1,500 words. Pays $150-250. Pays expenses of writers on assignment "if actually assigned. Not for unsolicited pieces."

Photos: Offers $25/photo. Identification of subjects required. Buys one-time rights.

Columns/Departments: Letter from Paris (current issues, trends, tones of Paris), 1100 words; and En Route (itinerary of approx. 1,500 words including sidebar). Query with published clips and send complete ms. Length: 500-1,100 words. Pays $150-225.

GRAY AREAS, Examining The Gray Areas of Life, Gray Areas, Inc., P.O. Box 808, Broomall PA 19008-0808. (215)353-8238. Editor: Netta Gilboa. 50% freelance written. Quarterly magazine covering music, popular culture, technology and law. "We are interested in exploring all points of view about subjects which are illegal, potentially illegal, immoral and/or controversial." Estab. 1991. Circ. 10,000. Pays on publication. Publishes ms 6-9 months after acceptance. Buys first North American serial, one-time and second serial (reprint) rights. Accepts previously published material. Send photocopy of article and information about when and where the article previously appeared. For reprints pays 10% of the amount paid for an original article. Editorial lead time 3-6 months. Accepts electronic submissions. Reports in 1 month on queries. Sample copy for $5.

● The editor notes that *Writer's Market* has been the single best source for finding articles.

Nonfiction: Essays, exposé, general interviews/profile, opinion, personal experience. "No poetry, short stories or fiction." Query. Payment negotiable. "If we want it, we'll pay requested fees." Pays with contributor copies if writer is a newcomer interested in building a portfolio.

Photos: State availability of photos with submission. Reviews prints only, any size. Negotiates payment individually. "We pay for one-time use of all photos published." Model releases and identification of subjects required. Buys one-time rights.

Columns/Departments: CD reviews (rock, pop, folk, world, etc., no classical), no word limit; concert reviews (no classical, country or opera), no word limit; "Would like to add regular columns on law, crime and AIDS." Query. Payment negotiable.

Tips: "1. We are actively looking for freelancers as we are new and writing most of *Gray Areas* ourselves. 2. We prefer letters to phone calls and will answer all letters which include an SASE. 3. We use freelancers based on an ability to adhere to deadlines (which are loose as we are a quarterly) and based on their knowledge of our specialized subject matter. 4. We do not discriminate against freelancers for lack of prior publications, not having a computer or typewriter, etc. We need people with legal expertise, experience with criminals and/or law enforcement and with access to celebrities. We also need people whose tastes and political viewpoints differ from our own. Our readers have only one thing in common—an open mind. They want to read a broad spectrum of articles that disagree with each other. 5. Please read the magazine! We don't print fluff and have no word limits. In-depth articles are of more interest than traditional 750-2,000 word pieces."

HIGH TIMES, Trans High Corp., 5th Floor, 235 Park Ave. S., New York NY 10003-1405. (212)972-8484. Fax: (212)475-7604. Editor: Steve Hager. News Editor: Bill Weinberg. 75% freelance written. Monthly magazine covering marijuana and the counterculture. Estab. 1974. Circ. 250,000. Pays on publication. Byline given. Offers 20% kill fee. Buys one-time or all rights or makes work-for-hire assignments. Submit seasonal/holiday material 6 months in advance. Accepts previously published and simultaneous submissions. Send tearsheet of article or typed ms with rights for sale noted. For reprints pays in ad trade. Reports in 1 month on queries; 4 months on mss. Sample copy for $5 and #10 SASE. Writer's guidelines for SASE.

• No longer accepts fiction.

Nonfiction: Book excerpts, exposé, humor, interview/profile, new product, personal experience, photo feature, travel. Buys 30 mss/year. Send complete ms. Length: 1,000-10,000 words. Pays $150-400. Sometimes pays in trade for advertisements. Sometimes pays expenses of writers on assignment.

Photos: Malcolm Mackinnon, photo editor. Send photos with submission. Pays $50-300. Captions, model release, identification of subjects required. Buys all rights or one-time use.

Columns/Departments: Steve Bloom, music editor. Nate Eaton, cultivation editor. Peter Gorman, views editor. Drug related books; drug related news. Buys 10 mss/year. Query with published clips. Length: 100-2,000 words. Pays $25-300.

Fillers: Gags to be illustrated by cartoonist, newsbreaks, short humor. Buys 10 mss/year. Length: 100-500 words. Pays $10-50. Cartoon Editor: John Holmstrom.

Tips: "All sections are open to good, professional writers."

‡IN CONTEXT, A Quarterly of Humane Sustainable Culture, Context Institute, P.O. Box 11470, Bainbridge Island WA 98110. (206)842-0216. Editor: Robert Gilman. 10% freelance written. Quarterly magazine covering humane, sustainable culture. "We are looking for solution-oriented material. Our publication's purpose is to provide the tools and vision that could make possible a humane, sustainable world. We are particularly interested in examples of things that are now working in that direction—especially at the community or business scale." Estab. 1983. Circ. 12,000. Pays on publication. Publishes ms an average of 3 months after acceptance. Byline given. Buys variable rights. Editorial lead time 5 months. Accepts simultaneous and previously published submissions. Query for electronic submissions. Variable reporting time. Sample copy for $6. Writer's guidelines for #10 SASE.

Nonfiction: Book excerpts, essays, how-to (be more sustainable), humor, interview/profile, opinion, personal experience, photo feature, religious, technical, innovations (technical or social). "Each issue focuses on a special theme. Writers should send SASE for concept memo." Buys 8 mss/year. Query with published clips. Length: 400-3,600 words. Pays $20-80. Sometimes pays expenses of writers on assignment.

Photos: State availability of photos with submission. Reviews contact sheets, negatives, transparencies, prints. Offers $10-125/photo. Buys one-time rights.

Columns/Departments: Planetary Pulse (the progress of sustainability—usually at a community or business scale), 600-700 words; Facts Out of Context (one sentence facts). Buys 5-6 mss/year. Query with published clips. Pays $20.

Poetry: Avant-garde, free verse, haiku, light verse, traditional. Buys 2-3 poems/year, generally related to issue theme.

Tips: "Send SASE for concept memos of upcoming issue themes. Most of our material is related to a specific theme, so even excellent material outside of the themes may not be accepted."

‡NEW HAVEN ADVOCATE, New Haven's News & Arts Weekly, New Mass Media Inc., 1 Long.Wharf Dr., New Haven CT 06571. (203)789-0010. Editor: Joshua Mamis. 10% freelance written. Alternative weekly tabloid. "Alternative, investigative, cultural reporting with a strong voice. We like to shake things up." Estab. 1975. Circ. 55,000. Pays on publication. Byline given. Offers 50% kill fee. Buys one-time rights. Editorial lead time 1 month. Submit seasonal material 2 months in advance. Accepts simultaneous submissions. Query for electronic submissions. Reports in 1 month on queries. Sample copy free on request.

Nonfiction: Book excerpts, essays, exposé, general interest, humor, interview/profile. Buys 15-20 mss/year. Query with published clips. Length: 750-2,000 words. Pays $50-150. Sometimes pays expenses of writers on assignment.

Photos: Freelancers should state availability of photos with submission. Captions, model releases, identification of subjects required. Buys one-time rights.

Tips: "Strong Connecticut angle; strong literary voice, controversial, easy-reading, contemporary, etc."

‡**OUT**, Suite 600, 110 Greene St., New York NY 10012. Editors: Michael Goff, Sarah Pettit. 80% freelance written. Monthly "national gay and lesbian general-interest magazine. Our subjects range from current affairs to culture, from fitness to finance. Stories may be anywhere from 50-word items to 8,000-word investigative features." Estab. 1992. Circ. 85,000. Pays on publication. Publishes ms an average of 3 months after acceptance. Byline given. Offers 25% kill fee. Buys first North American serial rights, second serial (reprint) rights for anthologies (additional fee paid) and 30-day reprint rights (additional fee paid if applicable). Editorial lead time 3 months. Submit seasonal material 4-5 months in advance. Accepts simultaneous submissions and previously published submissions (infrequently). Reports in 6 weeks on queries; 2 months on mss. Sample copy for $6. Writer's guidelines. for #10 SASE.

Nonfiction: Book excerpts, essays, exposé, general interest, historical/nostalgic, humor, interview/profile, new product, opinion, personal experience, photo feature, travel, fashion/lifestyle. Buys 200 mss/year. Query with published clips. Length: 50-10,000 words. Pays 50¢/word. Sometimes pays expenses of writers on assignment.

Photos: State availability of photos with submission. Reviews contact sheets, transparencies, prints. Negotiates payment individually. Captions, model releases, identification of subjects required. Buys one-time rights.

Poetry: Anecdotes, facts, newsbreaks. Buys 20/year. Length: 25-100 words. Pays $50-100.

Tips: "OUT's contributors include editors and writers from the country's top consumer titles: skilled reporters, columnists, and writers with distinctive voices and specific expertise in the fields they cover. But while published clips and relevant experience are a must, the magazine also seeks out fresh, young voices. The best guide to the kind of stories we publish is to review our recent issues — is there a place for the story you have in mind? Be aware of our long lead time."

‡**PROSCENIUM, Canada's Arts & Culture News Magazine,** Canadian Conference of the Arts. 189 Laurier Ave. E., Ottawa, Ontario K1N 6P1 Canada. (613)238-3561. Editor: Jocelyne Dubois. 40% freelance written. Quarterly magazine covering arts and culture. "We write for artists, arts administrators and culture workers interested in federal/provincial arts/culture policy and its development." Estab. 1991. Circ. 2,500. Pays on publication. Publishes ms an average of 3 months after acceptance. Byline given. Buys one-time rights. Editorial lead time 3 months. Accepts previously published submissions. Query for electronic submissions. Sample copy for $3.95 (Canadian).

Nonfiction: Essays, interview/profile, opinion. "No fiction, poetry, book reviews, film/music reviews." Buys 4-5 mss/year. Query. Length 800-1,200 words. Pays $250 minimum for assigned articles; $200 minimum for unsolicited articles. Sometimes pays expenses of writers on assignment.

Photos: Send photos with submission. Identification of subjects required. Buys one-time rights.

Fillers: Gags to be illustrated by cartoonist. Buys 3/year. Pays $100-150.

Tips: "Call or write with ideas and story outline. We don't have a lot of room for freelance — maybe two articles per issue. Call to find out what upcoming themes are and see if you have ideas that can work in that theme."

‡**PUBLIC**, Public Access, #307, 192 Spadina Ave., Toronto, Ontario M5T 2C2 Canada. (416)868-1161. Editors: Marc De Guerre, Tom Taylor. 100% freelance written. Semiannual journal covering contemporary art and culture issues. "*Public* is an interdisciplinary journal combining scholarly and critical writing in cultural studies with artistic practices from the visual arts, performance and literature." Estab. 1987. Circ. 2,000. Pays on publication. Publishes ms an average of 3-6 months after acceptance. Byline given. Buys all rights. Editorial lead time 3-6 months. Submit seasonal material 3-6 months in advance. Accepts previously published submissions. Query for electronic submissions. Reports in 3 months on queries. Writer's guidelines free on request.

Nonfiction: Essays, photo feature, academic articles on arts and cultural issues. Buys 10 mss/year. Query or send complete ms. Length: 5,000-10,000 words. Pays $300.

Photos: Send photos with submission. Reviews transparencies, prints. Offers no additional payment for photos accepted with ms. Captions, identification of subjects required. Buys all rights.

Detective and Crime

Fans of detective stories want to read accounts of actual criminal cases, detective work and espionage. The following magazines specialize in nonfiction, but a few buy some fiction. Markets specializing in crime fiction are listed under Mystery publications.

BACK CHANNELS, Kross Research & Publications, P.O. Box 9, Franklin Park NJ 08823-0009. (908)297-7923. Editor: Peter Kross. 90% freelance written. Quarterly magazine that covers espionage, conspiracies and history. "We publish nonfiction articles on: espionage, assassinations, conspiracies, historical pieces and book reviews." Estab. 1991. Pays on publication. Byline given. Offers $15 kill fee. Buys first North American serial rights. Submit seasonal material 6 months in advance. Accepts simultaneous submissions. Reports in 1 month. Sample copy for $5 and 9 × 12 SAE with 4 first-class stamps. Free writer's guidelines.
Nonfiction: Exposé, historical/nostalgic, interview/profile. No fiction. No photos. Buys 20 mss/year. Query with or without published clips, or send complete ms. Length: 1,000-1,200 words or 10 pages double spaced. Pays $25 for articles.
Fillers: Facts, newsbreaks. Buys 10/year. Length: 40-50 words. Pays $5.
Tips: "Read daily papers and books dealing with current events, historical and modern spying and conspiracies. We are looking for stories on Kennedy and King assassinations or current espionage cases. Will also accept book reviews."

DETECTIVE CASES, Detective Files Group, 1350 Sherbrooke St. W., Montreal, Quebec H3G 2T4 Canada. Editor-in-Chief: Dominick A. Merle. Bimonthly magazine. See *Detective Files*.

DETECTIVE DRAGNET, Detective Files Group, 1350 Sherbrooke St. W., Montreal, Quebec H3G 2T4 Canada. Editor-in-Chief: Dominick A. Merle. Bimonthly 72-page magazine. See *Detective Files*.

DETECTIVE FILES, Detective Files Group, 1350 Sherbrooke St. W., Montreal, Quebec H3G 2T4 Canada. Editor-in-Chief: Dominick A. Merle. Estab. 1930. 100% freelance written. Bimonthly magazine; 72 pages. **Pays on acceptance.** Publishes ms an average of 3-6 months after acceptance. Buys all rights. Reports in 1 month. Sample copy and writer's guidelines for SAE with IRCs.
Nonfiction: True crime stories. "Do a thorough job; don't double-sell (sell the same article to more than one market); deliver, and you can have a steady market. Neatness, clarity and pace will help you make the sale." Query. Length: 3,500-6,000 words. Pays $250-350.
Photos: Purchased with accompanying ms; no additional payment.

HEADQUARTERS DETECTIVE, Detective Files Group, 1350 Sherbrooke St. W., Montreal, Quebec H3G 2T4 Canada. Editor-in-Chief: Dominick A. Merle. Bimonthly magazine; 72 pages. See *Detective Files*.

INSIDE DETECTIVE, Official Detective Group, R.G.H. Publishing Corp., 460 W. 34th St., New York NY 10001. (212)947-6500. Editor-in-Chief: Rose Mandelsberg. Managing Editor: Christofer Pierson. Magazine published 7 times/year. Circ. 90,000. **Pays on acceptance.** Publishes ms an average of 3 months after acceptance. Byline given. Buys first rights and one-time world rights. Query for electronic submissions. Reports in 2 weeks. Free writer's guidelines.
Nonfiction: Buys 120 mss/year. Query. Pays $250. Length: 5,000-6,000 words (approximately 20 typed pages).

P. I. MAGAZINE, America's Private Investigation Journal, 755 Bronx, Toledo OH 43609. (419)382-0967. Editor: Bob Mackowiak. 75% freelance written. "Not a trade journal. Audience includes professional investigators and mystery/private eye fans. Estab. 1988. Circ. 3,000. Pays on publication. Publishes ms an average of 3 months after acceptance. Buys one-time rights. Submit seasonal/holiday material 3 months in advance. Simultaneous submissions OK. Reports in 3 months on queries; 4 months on mss. Sample copy for $5.75.
Nonfiction: Interview/profile, personal experience and accounts of real cases. Buys 4-10 mss/year. Send complete ms. Length: 1,500 words. Pays $50 for unsolicited articles.
Photos: Send photos with submission. May offer additional payment for photos accepted with ms. Model releases and identification of subjects required. Buys one-time rights.
Tips: "The best way to get published in *P.I.* is to write a detailed story about a professional private detective's true-life case."

STARTLING DETECTIVE, Detective Files Group, 1350 Sherbrooke St. W., Montreal, Quebec H3G 2T4 Canada. Editor-in-Chief: Dominick A. Merle. Bimonthly 72-page magazine. See *Detective Files*.

TRUE POLICE CASES, Detective Files Group, 1350 Sherbrooke St. W., Montreal, Quebec H3G 2T4 Canada. Editor-in-Chief: Dominick A. Merle. Bimonthly 72-page magazine. Buys all rights. See *Detective Files*.

Disabilities

These magazines are geared toward disabled persons and those who care for or teach them. A knowledge of disabilities and lifestyles is important for writers trying to break in to this field; editors regularly discard material that does not have a realistic focus.

Some of these magazines will accept manuscripts only from disabled persons or those with a background in caring for disabled persons.

ACCENT ON LIVING, P.O. Box 700, Bloomington IL 61702-0700. (309)378-2961. Fax: (309)378-4420. Editor: Betty Garee. 75% freelance written. Eager to work with new/unpublished writers. Quarterly magazine for physically disabled persons and rehabilitation professionals. Estab. 1956. Circ. 20,000. Buys first and second (reprint) rights. Byline usually given. Buys 50-60 unsolicited mss/year. Pays on publication. Publishes ms an average of 6 months after acceptance. Reports in 1 month. Sample copy and writer's guidelines $3 for #10 SAE with 7 first-class stamps. Writer's guidelines for #10 SASE.

Nonfiction: Articles about new devices that would make a disabled person with limited physical mobility more independent; should include description, availability and photos. Medical breakthroughs for disabled people. Intelligent discussion articles on acceptance of physically disabled persons in normal living situations; topics may be architectural barriers, housing, transportation, educational or job opportunities, organizations, or other areas. How-to articles concerning everyday living, giving specific, helpful information so the reader can carry out the idea himself/herself. News articles about active disabled persons or groups. Good strong interviews. Vacations, accessible places to go, sports, organizations, humorous incidents, self improvement and sexual or personal adjustment — all related to physically handicapped persons. No religious-type articles. "We are looking for upbeat material." Query. Length: 250-1,000 words. Pays 10¢/word for article as it appears in magazine (after editing and/or condensing by staff).

Photos: Pays $10 minimum for b&w photos purchased with accompanying captions. Amount will depend on quality of photos and subject matter. Pays $50 and up for four-color slides used on cover. "We need good-quality transparencies or slides with submissions — or b&w photos."

Tips: "Ask a friend who is disabled to read your article before sending it to *Accent*. Make sure that he/she understands your major points and the sequence or procedure."

ARTHRITIS TODAY, Arthritis Foundation. 1314 Spring St. NW, Atlanta GA 30309. (404)872-7100. Fax: (404)872-9559. Editor: Cindy T. McDaniel. Managing Editor: Tracy Ballew. 70% freelance written. Bi-monthly magazine about living with arthritis; latest in research/treatment. "*Arthritis Today* is written for the 37 million Americans who have arthritis and for the millions of others whose lives are touched by an arthritis-related disease. The editorial content is designed to help the person with arthritis live a more productive, independent and painfree life. The articles are upbeat and provide practical advice, information and inspiration." Estab. 1987. Circ. 500,000. Buys first North American serial rights but requires unlimited reprint rights in Arthritis Foundation publications. Submit seasonal/holiday material 6 months in advance. Accepts simultaneous and previously published submissions. Send photocopy of article with rights for sale noted and information about when and where the article previously appeared. For reprints pays 25-50% of the amount paid for an original article. Reports in 1 month on queries; 2 months on mss. Sample copy for 9 × 11 SAE with 4 first-class stamps. Writer's guidelines for #10 SASE.

• *Arthritis Today* is looking for more general health and lifestyle topics.

Nonfiction: General interest, how-to (tips on any aspect of living with arthritis), inspirational, interview/profile, opinion, personal experience, photo feature, technical, nutrition, general health and lifestyle. Buys 45 mss/year. Query with published clips. Length: 1,000-2,500. Pays $450-1,000. Sometimes pays expenses of writers on assignment.

Photos: Submit slides, tearsheets or prints for consideration. Assignments range between $100-300/photo, reprints $50. Captions, model releases, identification of subjects required. Buy one-time North American serial rights.

Columns/Departments: Quick Takes (general news and information); Scientific Frontier (research news about arthritis), 200-600 words. Buys 16-20 mss/year. Query with published clips. Pays $75-250.

Tips: "In addition to articles specifically about living with arthritis, we look for articles to appeal to an older audience on subjects such as hobbies, general health, lifestyle, etc."

CAREERS & the disABLED, Equal Opportunity Publications, Suite 420, 150 Motor Pkwy., Hauppauge, NY 11788-5145. (516)273-0066. Fax: (516)273-8936. Editor: James Schneider. 60% freelance written. Triannual career guidance magazine that is distributed through college campuses for disabled college students and professionals. Deadline dates: April 1 (Fall); October 1 (Winter); January 1 (Spring). "The magazine offers role-model profiles and career guidance articles geared toward disabled college students and professionals." Pays on publication. Publishes ms an average of 6 months after acceptance. Estab. 1967. Circ. 15,000. Byline given. Buys first rights. Accepts simultaneous and previously published submissions. Reports in 2 weeks. Sample copy and writer's guidelines for 9 × 12 SAE with 5 first-class stamps.

Nonfiction: General interest, interview/profile, opinion, personal experience. Buys 15 mss/year. Query. Length: 1,000-1,500 words. Pays 10¢/word. Sometimes pays the expenses of writers on assignment.

Photos: State availability of photos with submission. Reviews prints. Offers $15/photo and/or color slides. Captions. Buys one-time rights.

Tips: "Be as targeted as possible. Role model profiles which offer advice to disabled college students are most needed."

DIABETES SELF-MANAGEMENT, R.A. Rapaport Publishing, Inc., Suite 800, 150 W. 22nd St., New York NY 10011-2421. (212)989-0200. Fax: (212)989-4786. Editor: James Hazlett. 20% freelance written. Bimonthly magazine about diabetes. "We publish how-to health care articles for motivated, intelligent readers who have diabetes and who are actively involved in their own health care management. All articles must have immediate application to their daily living." Estab. 1983. Circ. 285,000. Pays on publication. Publishes ms an average of 3 months after acceptance. Byline given. Offers 20% kill fee. Buys all rights. Submit seasonal/holiday material 6 months in advance. Query for electronic submissions. Reports in 1 month. Sample copy for $3.50 and 9×12 SAE with 6 first-class stamps. Writer's guidelines for #10 SASE.
Nonfiction: How-to (exercise, nutrition, diabetes self-care, product surveys), technical (reviews of products available, foods sold by brand name), travel (considerations and prep for people with diabetes). Buys 10-12 mss/year. Query with published clips. Length: 2,000-4,000 words. Pays $400-600 for assigned articles; $200-600 for unsolicited articles.
Tips: "The rule of thumb for any article we publish is that it must be clear, concise, useful and instructive, and it must have immediate application to the lives of our readers."

INDEPENDENT LIVING, Connecting Dealers and People with Special Needs, Equal Opportunity Publications, Inc. Suite 420, 150 Motor Pkwy., Hauppauge NY 11788-5145. (516)-273-8743. Fax: (516)273-8936. Editor: Anne Kelly. 75% freelance written. Bimonthly magazine on home health care, rehabilitation and disability issues. "*Independent Living* magazine is written for persons with disabilities and the home care dealers, manufacturers, and health care professionals who serve their special needs." Estab. 1968. Circ. 35,000. Pays on publication. Byline given. Buys First North American serial rights. Reports in 3 months. Free sample copy and writer's guidelines.
Nonfiction: Essays, how-to, humor, inspirational, interview/profile, new product, opinion, personal experience, cartoons, travel. Buys 40 mss/year. Query. Length: 500-1,500 words. Pays 10¢/word.
Photos: Send photos with submission. Reviews prints. Offers $15/photo. Prefers 35mm color slides. Captions and identification of subjects required. Buys all rights.
Tips: "The best way to have a manuscript published is to first send a detailed query on a subject related to the home health care and independent lifestyles of persons who have disabilities. We also need articles on innovative ways that home health care dealers are meeting their clients needs, as well as profiles of people with disabilities who are successful."

KALEIDOSCOPE: International Magazine of Literature, Fine Arts, and Disability, Kaleidoscope Press, 326 Locust St., Akron OH 44302-1876. (216)762-9755. Fax: (216)762-0912. Editor-in-Chief: Dr. Darshan Perusek. Subscribers include individuals, agencies and organizations that assist people with disabilities and many university and public libraries. Estab. 1979. Circ. 1,500. 75% freelance written. Eager to work with new/unpublished writers. Byline given. Accepts previously published material. Send typed ms with rights for sale noted and information about when and where the article previously appeared. Publishes novel excerpts. Rights return to author upon publication. Appreciate work by established writers as well. Especially interested in work by writers with a disability. Features writers both with and without disabilities. Writers without a disability must limit themselves to our focus, while those with a disability may explore any topic (although we prefer original perspectives about experiences with disability). Submit photocopies with SASE for return of work. Please type submissions. All submissions should be accompanied by an autobiographical sketch. May include art or photos that enhance works, prefer b&w with high contrast. Reports in 3 weeks, acceptance or rejection may take 6 months. Pays $10-125 plus 2 copies. Sample copy for $4 prepaid. Guidelines free for SASE.
Nonfiction or Fiction: Publishes 8-14 mss/year. Maximum 5,000 words. Personal experience essays, book reviews and articles related to disability. Short stories, excerpts. Traditional and experimental styles. Works should explore experiences with disability. Use people-first language.
Poetry: Limit 5 poems/submission. Publishes 12-20 poems/year. Do not get caught up in rhyme scheme. High quality with strong imagery and evocative language. Will review any style.
Tips: Inquire about future themes of upcoming issues. Sample copy very helpful. Works should not use stereotyping, patronizing or offending language about disability. We seek fresh imagery and thought-provoking language.

MAINSTREAM, Magazine of the Able-Disabled, Exploding Myths, Inc., 2973 Beech St., San Diego CA 92102. (619)234-3138. Editor: Cyndi Jones. Managing Editor: William Strothers. 100% freelance written.

Always check the most recent copy of a magazine for the address and editor's name before you send in a query or manuscript.

Eager to develop writers who have a disability. Magazine published 10 times/year (monthly except January and June) covering disability-related topics, written for active and upscale disabled consumers. Estab. 1975. Circ. 18,200. Pays on publication. Publishes ms an average of 3 months after acceptance. Byline given. Buys all rights. Submit seasonal/holiday material 4 months in advance. Accepts previously published material. Send photocopy or tearsheet of article or short story or typed ms with rights for sale noted and information about when and where the article previously appeared. Payment varies. Reports in 4 months. Sample copy for $4.50 or 9 × 12 SAE and $3 with 6 first-class stamps. Writer's guidelines for #10 SASE.

Nonfiction: Book excerpts, exposé, how-to (daily independent living tips), humor, interview/profile, personal experience (dealing with problems/solutions), photo feature, technology, computers, travel, politics and legislation. "All must be disability-related, directed to disabled consumers." *NO* articles on " 'my favorite disabled character', 'my most inspirational disabled person', 'poster child stories.' " Buys 65 mss/year. Query with or without published clips and send complete ms. Length: 8-12 pages. Pays $100-150. May pay subscription if writer requests.

Photos: State availability of photos with submission. Reviews contact sheets, 1½ × ¾ transparencies and 5 × 7 or larger prints. Offers $20-25/b&w photo. Captions, identification of subjects required. Buys all rights.

Columns/Departments: Creative Solutions (unusual solutions to common aggravating problems); Personal Page (deals with personal relations: dating, meeting people). Buys 10 mss/year. Send complete ms. Length: 500-800 words. Pays $75. "We also are looking for disability rights cartoons."

Fiction: Humorous. Must be disability-related. Buys 4 mss/year. Send complete ms. Length: 800-1,200 words. Pays $75.

Tips: "It seems that politics and disability are becoming more important. Please include your phone number on cover page. We accept 5.25 or 3.5″ floppy discs — ASCII, Wordperfect, Wordstar-IBM."

NEW MOBILITY, 6133 Bristol Park Way, Culver City CA 90231. (310)337-9717. Contact: Jean Dobbs, Associate Editor. 40% freelance written. Bimonthly magazine for people who use wheelchairs. "*New Mobility* covers the lifestyles of *active* wheelchair users with articles on health and medicine; sports, recreation and travel; equipment and technology; relationships, family and sexual issues; personalities; civil rights and legal issues. Writers should address issues with solid reporting and strong voice." Estab. 1989. Circ. 20,000. Pays 30 days after publication (10¢/word). Publishes ms an average of 6 months after acceptance. Byline given. Offers 50% kill fee. Buys first North American serial rights. Editorial lead time 6 months. Accepts simultaneous and previously published submissions only if material does not appear in other disability publications and is rewritten. Send photocopy of article or typed ms with rights for sale noted, information about when and where the article previously appeared. For reprints pays 100% of the amount paid for an original article "because we require additional work." Query for electronic submissions. Reports in 3 months. Sample copy $5. Writer's guidelines for #10 SASE.

• *New Mobility* has added more stories on multiple sclerosis.

Nonfiction: Essays, exposé, humor, interview/profile, new product, opinion, photo feature, travel and medical feature. "No inspirational tear-jerkers." Buys 30 mss/year. Query with 1-2 published clips. Length: 700-2,000 words. Pays 10¢/word. Sometimes pays expenses of writers on assignment.

Photos: State availability of photos with submission. Reviews contact sheets, transparencies and prints. Negotiates payment individually. Identification of subjects required. Buys one-time rights.

Columns/Departments: My Spin (opinion piece on disability-related topic), 700 words; Media (reviews of books, videos on disability), 300-400 words; People (personality profiles of people w/disabilities), 300-700 words. Buys 20 mss/year. Query with published clips. Send complete ms. Pays $30-70.

Tips: "Avoid 'courageous' or 'inspiring' tales of people who 'overcome' their disability. Writers don't have to be disabled to write for this magazine, but they should be familiar with the issues people with disabilities face. Most of our readers have disabilities, so write for this audience. We are most open to personality profiles, either for our short People department or as feature articles. In all of our departments, we like to see adventurous people, irreverent opinions and lively writing. Don't be afraid to let your *voice* come through."

PEOPLENET, "Where People Meet People," P.O. Box 897, Levittown NY 11756-0911. (516)579-4043. Editor: Robert Mauro. 10% freelance written. Triannual networking newsletter for *disabled* singles. "Covers relationships, mainly of disabled singles. I am looking for articles, poems and short shorts about disabled singles — people who want to meet people for friendship and romance." Estab. 1987. Circ. 200. **Pays on acceptance.** Publishes ms an average of 1 year after acceptance. Byline given. No kill fee. Buys first rights. Submit seasonal/holiday material 1 year in advance. Query for electronic submissions. Reports immediately. Sample copy for $3 and #10 SAE with 52¢ postage. Writer's guidelines for #10 SASE.

Nonfiction: How-to (deal with rejection, low self-esteem), humor, other (disabled singles and relationships). Does not want to see articles on "super-crips." Buys 1-3 mss/year. Send complete ms. Length: 500-750 words. Pays $5-7.50 plus 1 copy for unsolicited articles.

Columns/Departments: Real Crip Sex (discussion in explicit detail of ways to make love despite disability), 750 words; Dating Scene (ways and means and problems of dating), 500-750 words; Coping Scene (coping with rejection, low self-esteem, low energy), 500-750 words. Buys 1-3 mss/year. Send complete ms. Length: 500-750 words. Pays $5-7.50.

Fiction: Experimental, fantasy, humorous, romance, slice-of-life vignettes. Does not want to see "anything that does not have a disabled character in it." Buys 1-2 mss/year. Send complete ms. Length: 500-1,000 words. Pays $5-10.

Poetry: Avant-garde, free verse, haiku, light verse, traditional. "Anything that is romantic. No 'song lyrics' or 'greeting card' poetry!" Buys 3-6 poems/year. Submit maximum 4 poems. Length: 4-10 lines. Pays $1-5.

Fillers: Gags, short humor. Buys 3-6 mss/year. Length: 100-500 words.

Tips: "We want *professionally* submitted pieces. I'd love to see some good cartoons on *the dilemmas of dating for the disabled*. All areas are open. But we want good material that will instruct, entertain and make a reader *think*."

‡**A POSITIVE APPROACH, A Christian Magazine For People With Disabilities**, P.O. Box 910, Millville NJ 08332. (609)451-4777. Managing Editor: Pat Swart. 90% freelance written. Quarterly magazine covering physical disability. "Profiles needed no product endorsement articles. Writing to and about those with disabilities is important, not talking down to them. Please do not use 'wheelchair-bound', or 'cripple'. Wheelchairs are for mobility. Use term "people" first, disability last." Estab. 1986. Circ. 36,700. Pays on publication. Byline given. Buys one-time or simultaneous rights or makes work-for-hire assignments. Editorial lead time 4 months. Submit seasonal material 3-4 months in advance. Accepts simultaneous and previously published submissions. Reports in 2 weeks on queries; 1 month on mss. Sample copy for $2. Writer's guidelines for #10 SASE.

Nonfiction: General interest, humor, inspirational, interview/profile, personal experience, photo feature, travel (all must be related to disability). Query with published clips or send complete ms. Length: 500-800 words. Pays $50.

Photos: Send photos with submission. Reviews any b&w prints. Offers no additional payment for photos accepted with ms. Identification of subjects required.

Entertainment

This category's publications cover live, filmed or videotaped entertainment, including home video, TV, dance, theater and adult entertainment. In addition to celebrity interviews, most publications want solid reporting on trends and upcoming productions. Magazines in the Contemporary Culture section also use articles on entertainment. For those publications with an emphasis on music and musicians, see the Music section.

‡**AUDIENCE, Program Guide for the Performing Arts**, Fearless Designs, Inc., Suite 206, 622 E. Main, Louisville KY 40202. (502)581-9713. Contact: Aggie Hollkamp. 80% freelance written. Monthly program guide covering performing arts. "We publish articles relating to dance, theater, music and other items relating to the arts." Estab. 1993. Circ. 500,000. Pays on publication. Publishes ms an average of 1 month after acceptance. Byline given. Offers 50% kill fee. Buys one-time rights. Editorial lead time 1 month. Submit seasonal material 2-3 months in advance. Accepts simultaneous and previously published submissions. Query for electronic submissions. Reports in 1 month on queries. Writer's guidelines for #10 SASE.

Nonfiction: Contact: Kay Tull. General interest, historical/nostalgic, inspirational, interview/profile, opinion, personal experience, photo feature. Buys 12 mss/year. Query with published clips. Length: 2,500 words maximum. Pays $250 for assigned articles; $200 for unsolicited articles. Sometimes pays expenses of writers on assignment.

Photos: State availability of photos with submission. Reviews contact sheets, transparencies. Captions, model releases, identification of subjects requried. Buys one-time rights.

Fillers: Anecdotes, facts, gags to be illustrated by cartoonist, newsbreaks, short humor. Buys 5-10/year. Pays $50-100.

Tips: "Broad interest, scoops, profiles, arts business related articles will be more likely to be accepted. Local and regional interest would get special attention but national is also requested."

‡**THE CD-ROM REPORTER**, The Centos Company, Suite 161, 5024 Katella Ave., Los Alamitos CA 90720. Editor: Rob Kerbs. 60% freelance written. Bimonthly review guide covering consumer-oriented CD-ROMs. Circ. 7,000. Pays on publication. Publishes ms an average of 2 months after acceptance. Byline given. Buys all rights. Reports in 3 weeks on queries; 1 month on mss. Sample copy for $5. Writer's guidelines for #10 SASE.

Nonfiction: Interview/profile (personalities included in CD-ROM), new product (new CD-ROM products), opinion (CD-ROM reviews, CD audiovisuals, critical essays). Length: 500-2,000 words. Pays 3¢/word plus copies.

Photos: State availability of photos with submission. Offers no additional payment for photos accepted with ms. Identification of subjects required.

Columns/Departments: Technically close-up conceptual pieces—minimal computer talk.

Tips: "The CD-ROM Reporter is a consumer-oriented publication committed to the CD-ROM industry. The goal is to provide clear, concise and useful information to the CD-ROM viewing public. Please view past issues of our periodical to get an idea of what we are looking for. We are NOT looking for articles written in technical contexts or forms. 'Consumer oriented' are the two key words to keep in mind when writing for us."

‡CHILD STARS MAGAZINE, P.O. Box 55328, Stockton CA 95205. (209)942-2131. Editor: Joe Kraus. 50% freelance written. Quarterly magazine covering child stars (movie/TV), "but we are open to other fields." "Our publication is for fans of child stars past and present. It is written for adults, not kids, although many kids do subscribe. Child stars don't have to be superstars. They can be new to the business and up-and-coming. More often than not our readers are movie/TV buffs and movie memorabilia collectors." Estb. 1993. Circ. 5,000. Pays on publication. Byline given. Offers 75% kill fee. Buys one-time rights. Editorial lead time 3 months. Submit seasonal material 4 months in advance. Accepts simultaneous and previously published submissions. Reports in 2 weeks on queries; 1 month on mss. Sample copy for $4. Writer's guidelines free on request.

Nonfiction: Book excerpts, general interest, historical/nostalgic, humor, inspirational, interview/profile, opinion, personal experience. "Keep it positive and upbeat." Buys 30 mss/year. Query but will accept complete ms. Length: 400-2,000 words. Pays $25-100. Sometimes pays expenses of writers on assignment.

Photos: Send photos with submission. Reviews contact sheets, transparencies, prints. Offers $10/photo if original, we pay $5/photo if supplied by the child star. Captions required. Buys one-time rights.

Tips: "In most publications you need that great idea—not here. All you need is to come up with a name of a child star (past or present) which we haven't covered before. On child stars who have died, all you need do is some research. On living past or present child stars an interview is most often required, but this can be done on the telephone. Most of our readers are adults, but we have many teen and pre-teen readers as well. Our focus is on the positive. We do not publish tabloid or teen magazine style articles."

CINEASTE, America's Leading Magazine on the Art and Politics of the Cinema, Cineaste Publishers, Inc., #1601, 200 Park Ave. S., New York NY 10003-1503. (212)982-1241. Editor-in-Chief: Gary Crowdus. 50% freelance written. Quarterly magazine on motion pictures, offering "social and political perspective on the cinema." Estab. 1967. Circ. 8,000. Pays on publication. Publishes ms an average of 3 months after acceptance. Byline given. Offers 50% kill fee. Buys first North American serial rights. Reports in 3 weeks on queries; 2 months on mss. Sample copy for $5. Writer's guidelines for #10 SASE.

Nonfiction: Essays, interview/profile, criticism. Buys 40-50 mss/year. Query with or without published clips, or send complete ms. Length: 3,000-6,000 words. Pays $20.

Photos: State availability of photos with submissions. Reviews prints. Offers no additional payment for photos accepted with ms. Identification of subjects required.

CINEFANTASTIQUE MAGAZINE, The review of horror, fantasy and science fiction films, P.O. Box 270, Oak Park IL 60303. (708)366-5566. Editor: Frederick S. Clarke. 100% freelance written. Willing to work with new/unpublished writers. Bimonthly magazine covering horror, fantasy and science fiction films. Estab. 1970. Circ. 60,000. Pays on publication. Publishes ms an average of 6 months after acceptance. Byline given. Buys all rights. Simultaneous queries OK. Reports in 2 months or longer. Sample copy for $7 and 9 × 12 SAE. "Enclose SASE if you want your manuscript back."

Nonfiction: Historical/nostalgic (retrospects of film classics); interview/profile (film personalities); new product (new film projects); opinion (film reviews, critical essays); technical (how films are made). Buys 100-125 mss/year. Query with published clips. Length: 1,000-10,000 words. Sometimes pays the expenses of writers on assignment.

Photos: State availability of photos with query letter or ms.

Tips: "Study the magazine to see the kinds of stories we publish. Develop original story suggestions; develop access to film industry personnel; submit reviews that show a perceptive point of view."

COUNTRY AMERICA, Meredith Publishing Corporation, 1716 Locust, Des Moines IA 50309-3023. (515)284-2910. Fax: (515)284-3035. Editor: Danita Allen. Managing Editor: Bill Eftink. Magazine published 10 times/year covering country entertainment/lifestyle. Estab. 1989. Circ. 1,000,000. **Pays on acceptance.** Byline given. Buys all rights (lifetime). Submit seasonal/holiday material 8 months in advance. Accepts previously published submissions "if notified." Reports in 3 months. Free writer's guidelines.

• Ranked as one of the best markets for freelance writers in *Writer's Digest* magazine's annual "Top 100 Markets," January 1994.

Nonfiction: Garden/food, general interest, historical/nostalgic, how-to (home improvement), interview/profile (country music entertainers), photo feature, travel. Special issues: Christmas, travel, wildlife/conservation, country music. Buys 130 mss/year. Query. Pays $100-1,000 for assigned articles. Sometimes pays expenses of writers on assignment.

Photos: State availability of photos with submission. Reviews contact sheets, negatives, 35mm transparencies. Offers $50-500/photo. Captions and identification of subjects required. Buys all rights.

Fillers: Short humor. Country curiosities that deal with animals, people, crafts, etc.
Tips: "Think visually. Our publication will be light on text and heavy on photos. Be general; this is a general interest publication meant to be read by every member of the family. We are a service-oriented publication; please stress how-to sidebars and include addresses and phone numbers to help readers find out more."

DANCE CONNECTION, 603, 815 First St. SW, Calgary, Alberta T2P 1N3 Canada. (403)237-7327. Fax: (403)237-7327. Editor: Heather Elton. 75% freelance written. Magazine published 5 times/year devoted to dance with a broad editorial scope reflecting a deep commitment to a view of dance that embraces its diversity of style and function. Articles have ranged in subject matter from the role of dance in Plains Indian culture, to an inquest into the death of Giselle, to postmodern dance. Estab. 1983. Circ. 5,000. Pays on publication. Byline given. Buys first rights or second serial (reprint) rights. Submit seasonal material 3 months in advance. Accepts simultaneous and previously published submissions. Send tearsheet or photocopy of article and information about when and where the article previously appeared. For reprints pays 50% of the amount paid for an original article. Query for electronic submissions. Reports in 3 months. Sample copy for 9 × 12 SAE with 3 IRCs.
Nonfiction: A variety of writing styles including criticism, essay, exposé, general interest, historical/nostalgic, humor, opinion, interview, performance review, forum debate, literature and photo feature. Query with published clips, or send complete ms. Length 800-2,500 words. Pays $5-250.
Fiction: Literature and poetry relating to dance. No poems about ballet. Publishes novel excerpts.
Columns/Departments: Performance Reviews, Book Reviews, Dance News, Calendar.

DANCE MAGAZINE, 33 W. 60th St., New York NY 10023. (212)245-9050. Fax: (212)956-6487. Editor-in-Chief: Richard Philp. 25% freelance written. Monthly magazine covering dance. Estab. 1927. Circ. 51,000. Pays on publication. Byline given. Offers up to $150 kill fee (varies). Makes work-for-hire assignments. Submit seasonal/holiday material 4 months in advance. Reports in "weeks." Sample copy and writer's guidelines for 9 × 12 SASE.
Nonfiction: Interview/profile. Buys 50 mss/year. Query with published clips or send complete ms. Length: 300-2,000 words. Pays $15-350. Sometimes pays expenses of writers on assignment.
Photos: State availability of photos with submission. Reviews transparencies and prints. Offers $25-285/photo. Captions and identification of subjects required. Buys one-time rights.
Columns/Departments: Presstime News (topical, short articles on current dance world events), 75-400 words. Buys 40 mss/year. Query with published clips. Pays $20-75.
Tips: Writers must have "thorough knowledge of dance and take a sophisticated approach."

DRAMATICS MAGAZINE, Educational Theatre Association, 3368 Central Pkwy., Cincinnati OH 45225-2392. (513)559-1996. Editor-in-Chief: Donald Corathers. 70% freelance written. Works with small number of new/unpublished writers. For theater arts students, teachers and others interested in theater arts education. Magazine published monthly, September-May. Estab. 1929. Circ. 35,000. **Pays on acceptance.** Publishes ms an average of 3 months after acceptance. Buys first North American serial rights. Byline given. Submit seasonal/holiday material 3 months in advance. Accepts simultaneous and previously published submissions. Send tearsheet or photocopy of article or play, or typed ms with rights for sale noted and information about when and where the article previously appeared. Pays 50% of their fee for an original article. Query for electronic submissions. Reports in 3 months; may be longer on unsolicited mss. Sample copy for 9 × 12 SAE with 5 first-class stamps. Free writer's guidelines.
Nonfiction: How-to (technical theater, directing, acting, etc.), informational, interview, photo feature, humorous, profile, technical. Buys 30 mss/year. Submit complete ms. Length: 750-3,000 words. Pays $50-300. Rarely pays expenses of writers on assignment.
Photos: Purchased with accompanying ms. Uses b&w photos and transparencies. Query. Total purchase price for ms usually includes payment for photos.
Fiction: Drama (one-act and full-length plays). "No plays for children, Christmas plays or plays written with no attention paid to the conventions of theater." Prefers unpublished scripts that have been produced at least once. Buys 5-9 mss/year. Send complete ms. Pays $100-400.
Tips: "The best way to break in is to know our audience—drama students, teachers and others interested in theater—and to write for them. Writers who have some practical experience in theater, especially in technical areas, have a leg-up here, but we'll work with anybody who has a good idea. Some freelancers have become regular contributors. Others ignore style suggestions included in our writer's guidelines."

EAST END LIGHTS, The Quarterly Magazine for Elton John Fans, Voice Communications Corp., P.O. Box 760, New Baltimore MI 48047. (313)949-7900. Fax: (313)949-2217. Editor: Tom Stanton. 90% freelance written. Quarterly magazine covering British rock star Elton John. "In one way or another, a story must relate to Elton John, his activities or associates (past and present). We appeal to discriminating Elton fans. No gushing fanzine material. No current concert reviews." Estab. 1990. Circ. 1,000. Pays 3 weeks after publication. Publishes ms an average of 2-3 months after acceptance. Byline given. Offers 100% kill fee. Buys first rights and second serial (reprint) rights. Submit seasonal material 2-3 months in advance. Reports in 2 months. Sample copy for $2. Free writer's guidelines.

Nonfiction: Book excerpts, essays, exposé, general interest, historical/nostalgic, humor and interview/profile. Buys 20 mss/year. Query with or without published clips or send complete ms. Length: 400-1,000 words. Pays $50-200 for assigned articles; $40-150 for unsolicited articles. Pays with contributor copies only if the writer requests. Sometimes pays the expenses of writers on assignment.

Photos: State availability of photos with submission. Reviews negatives and 5×7 prints. Offers $40-75/photo. Identification of subjects required. Buys one-time rights and all rights.

Columns/Departments: Clippings (non-wire references to Elton John in other publications), maximum 200 words. Buys 12 mss/year. Send complete ms. Length: 50-200 words. Pays $10-20.

Tips: "Approach with a well-thought-out story idea. We'll provide direction. All areas equally open. We prefer interviews with Elton-related personalities—past or present. We are particularly interested in music/memorabilia collecting of Elton material."

EMMY MAGAZINE, Academy of Television Arts & Sciences, 5220 Lankershim Blvd., North Hollywood CA 91601-3109. (818)754-2800. Fax: (818)761-2827. Editor/Publisher: Hank Rieger. Managing Editor: Gail Polevoi. 100% freelance written. Prefers to work with published established writers. Bimonthly magazine on television for TV professionals and enthusiasts. Circ. 12,000. Pays on publication or within 6 months. Publishes ms an average of 4 months after acceptance. Byline given. Offers 25% kill fee. Buys first North American serial rights. Reports in 1 month. Sample copy for 9×12 SAE with 6 first-class stamps.

Nonfiction: Articles on issues, trends, and VIPs (especially those behind the scenes) in broadcast and cable TV; programming; new technology; and important international developments. "We require TV industry expertise and clear, lively writing." Length: 2,000 words. Pay $750-950. Pays some expenses of writers on assignment.

Columns/Departments: Most written by regulars, but newcomers can break into CloseUps, Viewpoint or Innerviews. Length: 500-1,500 words, depending on department. Pays $250-600.

Tips: Study publication; query in writing with published clips. No fanzine or academic approaches, please.

FANGORIA: Horror in Entertainment, Starlog Communications, Inc., 475 Park Ave. S., 8th Floor, New York NY 10016. (212)689-2830. Fax: (212)889-7933. Editor: Anthony Timpone. 95% freelance written. Works with a small number of new/unpublished writers each year. Magazine published 10 times/year covering horror films, TV projects, comics, videos and literature and those who create them. Estab. 1979. Pays on publication. Publishes ms an average of 3 months after acceptance. Byline given. Buys all rights. Submit seasonal/holiday material 6 months in advance. Query for electronic submissions. Reports in 6 weeks. "We provide an assignment sheet (deadlines, info) to writers, thus authorizing queried stories that we're buying." Sample copy for $4.95 and 10×13 SAE with 4 first-class stamps. Writers' guidelines for #10 SASE.

Nonfiction: Book excerpts, interview/profile of movie directors, makeup FX artists, screenwriters, producers, actors, noted horror novelists and others—with genre credits. No "think" pieces, opinion pieces, reviews (excluding books), or sub-theme overviews (i.e., vampire in the cinema). Buys 100 mss/year. Query with published clips. Length: 1,000-3,000 words. Pays $100-225. Rarely pays the expenses of writers on assignment. Avoids articles on science fiction films—see listing for sister magazine *Starlog* in *Writer's Market* science fiction magazine section.

Photos: State availability of photos. Reviews b&w and color prints and transparencies. "No separate payment for photos provided by film studios." Captions and identification of subjects required. Photo credit given. Buys all rights.

Columns/Departments: Monster Invasion (news about new film productions; must be exclusive, early information; also mini-interviews with filmmakers and novelists). Query with published clips. Length: 300-500 words. Pays $45-75.

Fiction: "We do *not* publish any fiction or poetry. *Don't* send any."

Tips: "Other than recommending that you study one or several copies of *Fangoria*, we can only describe it as a horror film magazine consisting primarily of interviews with technicians and filmmakers in the field. Be sure to stress the interview subjects' words—not your own opinions as much. We're very interested in small, independent filmmakers working outside of Hollywood. These people are usually more accessible to writers, and more cooperative. *Fangoria* is also sort of a *de facto* bible for youngsters interested in movie makeup careers and for young filmmakers. We are devoted only to *reel* horrors—the fakery of films, the imagery of the horror fiction of a Stephen King or a Clive Barker—*we do not* want nor would we *ever* publish articles on real-life horrors, murders, etc. A writer must *like* and *enjoy* horror films and horror fiction to work for us. If the photos in *Fangoria* disgust you, if the sight of (*stage*) blood repels you, if you feel 'superior' to horror (and its fans), you aren't a writer for us and we certainly aren't the market for you."

‡FILM COMMENT, Film Society of Lincoln Center, 70 Lincoln Center Plaza, New York NY 10023. (212)875-5610. Editor: Richard T. Jameson. 100% freelance written. Bimonthly magazine covering film criticism and film history. "*FC* publishes authoritative, personal writing (not journalism) reflecting experience of and involvement with film as an art form." Estab. 1962. Circ. 30,000. Pays on publication. Publishes ms an average of 2 months after acceptance. Byline given. Offers 50% kill fee (assigned articles only). Editorial lead time 1½ months. Accepts simultaneous submissions. Query for electronic submissions. Reports in 1-2 weeks on queries. Writer's guidelines free on request.

Nonfiction: Essays, historical/nostalgic, interview/profile, opinion, personal experience. Buys 100 mss/year. Send complete ms. "We respond to queries, but rarely *assign* a writer we don't know." Length: 800-8,000 words. Pays $200 for assigned articles; $100 for unsolicited articles.

Photos: State availability of photos with submission. Offers no additional payment for photos accepted with ms. Buys one-time rights.

Columns/Departments: Life With Video (impact of video on availability and experience of films; video as new imaginative dimension), 1,000-2,000 words. Pays $250 and up.

Tips: "Demonstrate ability and inclination to write FC-worthy articles. We read and consider everything we get, and we do print unknowns and first-timers. Probably the writer with a shorter submission (1,000-2,000 words) has a better chance than with an epic article that would fill half the issue."

FILM QUARTERLY, University of California Press, Berkeley CA 94720. (510)601-9070. Fax: (510)601-9036. Editor: Ann Martin. 100% freelance written. Eager to work with new/unpublished writers. Quarterly. Estab. 1958. Byline given. Pays on publication. Buys all rights. Publishes ms an average of 6-12 months after acceptance. Query. Reports in 5 months. Sample copy and writer's guidelines for SASE.

Nonfiction: Articles on style and structure in films, articles analyzing the work of important directors, historical articles on development of the film as art, reviews of current films and detailed analyses of classics and book reviews of film books. Must be familiar with the past and present of the art; must be competently, although not necessarily breezily, written; must deal with important problems of the art. "We write for people who like to think and talk seriously about films, as well as simply view them and enjoy them. We use no personality pieces or reportage pieces. Interviews usually work for us only when conducted by someone familiar with most of a filmmaker's work. (We don't use performer interviews.)" Length: 6,000 words maximum. Pay is about 2¢/word.

Tips: "*Film Quarterly* is a specialized academic journal of film criticism, though it is also a magazine (with pictures) sold in bookstores. It is read by film teachers, students, and die-hard movie buffs, so unless you fall into one of those categories, it is very hard to write for us. Currently, we are especially looking for material on independent, documentary, etc., films not written about in the national film reviewing columns."

KPBS On Air, San Diego's Guide to Public Broadcasting, KPBS-TV/FM, Suite 16, 5164 College Ave., San Diego CA 92115. Mailing address: KPBS Radio/TV, San Diego CA 92182-0527. (619)594-3766. Fax: (619)265-6417. Editor: Michael Good. 15% freelance written. Monthly magazine on public broadcasting programming and San Diego arts. "Our readers are very intelligent, sophisticated and rather mature. Your writing should be, too." Estab. 1970. Circ. 62,000. Pays on publication. Publishes ms an average of 1 month after acceptance. Byline given. Pays 50% kill fee. Not copyrighted. Buys first North American serial rights. Submit seasonal/holiday material 3 months in advance. Accepts previously published materials. Send tearsheet or photocopy of article or typed ms with rights for sale noted and information about when and where the article previously appeared. For reprints pays 50-100% of the amount paid for an original article. Query for electronic submissions. Reports in 3 months. Sample copy for 9 × 12 SAE with 4 first-class stamps.

Nonfiction: Interview/profile of PBS personalities and/or artists performing in San Diego, opinion, profiles of public TV and radio personalities, backgrounds on upcoming programs. Nothing over 1,500 words. Buys 60 mss/year. Query with published clips. Length: 300-1,500 words. Pays 20¢/word; 25¢/word if the article is received via modem or computer disk. Sometimes pays expenses of writers on assignment.

Photos: State availability of photos with submission. Reviews transparencies and 5 × 7 prints. Offers $30-300/photo. Identification of subjects required. Buys one-time rights.

Columns/Departments: On the Town (upcoming arts events in San Diego), 800 words; Short Takes (backgrounds on public TV shows), 500 words; Radio Notes (backgrounders on public radio shows), 500 words. Buys 35 mss/year. Query or query with published clips. Length: 300-800 words. Pays 20¢/word; 25¢/word if the article is received via modem or computer disk.

Tips: "Feature stories for national writers are most open to freelancers. Arts stories for San Diego writers are most open. Read the magazine, then talk to me."

MOVIE MARKETPLACE, World Publishing, 990 Grove St., Evanston IL 60201. (708)491-6440. Editor: Robert Meyers. 90% freelance written. Bimonthly magazine featuring video and movie subjects. Estab. 1987. Circ. 100,000. **Pays on acceptance.** Byline given. Offers $100 kill fee. Buys first North American serial rights. Submit seasonal/holiday material 6 months in advance. Accepts simultaneous and previously published submissions. Reports in 3 weeks. Sample copy for $2.50 and 9 × 11 SASE.

Nonfiction: Interview/profile, movie-video topics. Query with published clips. Length: 350 words, short; 750-900 words, long. Pays $100-200 for assigned articles.

Photos: State availability of or send photos (b&w only) with submission. Reviews contact sheets. Offers no additional payment for photos accepted with ms. Identification of subjects required. Buys first North American serial rights only.

NEW YORK/LONG ISLAND UPDATE, 151 Alkier St., Brentwood NY 11717. (516)435-8890. Fax: (516)435-8925. Editor: Cheryl Ann Meglio. Managing Editor: Allison A. Whitney. 60% freelance written. Monthly magazine covering "regional entertainment interests as well as national interests." Estab. 1980. Circ. 60,000.

Pays on publication. Publishes ms an average of 4 months after acceptance. Byline given. Buys all rights. Submit seasonal/holiday material 4 months in advance. Query for electronic submissions. Reports in 10 weeks on queries. Free sample copy and writer's guidelines.

Nonfiction: General interest, humor, interview/profile, new product, travel. Buys 60 mss/year. Query with published clips. Length: 250-1,500 words. Pays $25-125.

Columns/Departments: Nightcap (humor piece), 700 words. Query with published clips. Pays $50.

Fiction: Humorous. Buys 8 mss/year. Length: 700 maximum words. Pays $50 maximum.

PALMER VIDEO MAGAZINE, 1767 Morris Ave., Union NJ 07083. (908)686-3030. Fax: (908)686-2151. Editor: Susan Baar. 15% freelance written. Monthly magazine covering video and film related topics. *"The Palmer Video Magazine* is a 32-page magazine designed exclusively for Palmer Video members. It is both entertaining and informative as it pertains to film and video." Estab. 1983. Circ. 200,000. Pays 30 days after receipt of article. Publishes ms 1 month after acceptance. Makes work-for-hire assignments. Submit seasonal/holiday material 2 months in advance. Accepts simultaneous and previously published submissions. Send typed ms with rights for sale noted and information about when and where the article previously appeared. Reports in 2 months. Free sample copy and writer's guidelines.

Nonfiction: How-to (video related), interview/profile (film related), technical (video related). Buys 40 mss/year. Query with published clips. Length: 500-2,000 words. Pays $50-200 for assigned articles.

Photos: State availability of photos with submission. Offers no additional payment for photos accepted with ms.

Columns/Departments: Profile (interviews of profiles on actors/directors, etc.), 1,000 words; Cinemascope (article pertaining to film genre), 1,000-2,000 words. Buys 40 mss/year. Query with published clips. Pays $50-200.

PEOPLE MAGAZINE, Time-Warner, Inc., Time & Life Bldg., Rockefeller Center, New York NY 10020. Weekly publication covering popular culture for a general audience. This magazine did not respond to our request for information. Query before submitting.

PERFORMING ARTS MAGAZINE, 3539 Motor Ave., Los Angeles CA 90034. (310)839-8000. Editor: Dana Kitaj. 100% freelance written. Monthly magazine covering theater, music, dance, visual art. "We publish general pieces on the arts of a historical or 'current-events' nature." Estab. 1965. Circ. 700,000. Pays on publication. Publishes ms an average of 2 months after acceptance. Offers $150 kill fee. Buys one-time rights. Submit seasonal/holiday material 3 months in advance. Accepts previously published submissions. Sample copy for 9 × 12 SASE.

Nonfiction: Book excerpts (on the Arts), general interest (theater, dance, opera), historical/nostalgic, interview/profile (performers, artists), travel. No critical texts, religious, political essays or reviews. Buys 60 mss/year. Query with published clips. Length: 1,500-3,000 words. Pays $500-1,000. Sometimes pays expenses of writers on assignment.

Photos: State availability of photos with submission. Reviews transparencies. Offers no additional payment for photos accepted with ms. Buys one-time rights.

Tips: "Theater, dance and music on the West Coast are our main interests. Write broad information pieces or interviews."

THE PLAY MACHINE, P.O. Box 330507, Houston TX 77233-0507. Editor: Norman Clark Stewart Jr. 90% freelance written. Quarterly tabloid of recreation/adult play. Estab. 1990. Circ. 1,000. Pays on publication. Byline given. Buys first North American, one-time or second serial (reprint) rights. Submit seasonal/holiday material 8 months in advance. Accepts simultaneous and previously published submissions. Reports in 8 months on mss. Sample copy for 9 × 12 SAE with 4 first-class stamps. Writer's guidelines for #10 SAE with 2 first-class stamps.

Nonfiction: How-to (play or have fun), humor (not satire—playful), interview/profile (with pranksters/jokers or genius in relation to fun), new product (recreational/hobby, etc.). Nothing that is not fun, playful or related to recreation—nothing serious. Buys 20-100 mss/year. Send complete ms. Length: 3,500 words maximum. Pays $50 maximum for unsolicited articles.

Photos: Send photos with submission. Offers no additional payment for photos accepted with ms. Model releases and identification of subjects required. Buys one-time rights.

Fillers: Anecdotes, facts, gags to be illustrated by cartoonist, short humor. Buys 200/year. Pays $5 maximum.

Tips: "Have fun writing the submissions."

‡PLAY MAGAZINE, Milor Entertainment Group, 3620 NW 43rd St., Gainesville FL 32606. (904)375-3705. Editor: Bill Stevenson. Managing Editor: Roy Parkhurst. 100% freelance written. Quarterly consumer magazine covering educational entertainment products. "Interactive entertainment-oriented products. Geared towards parents. Cover music, video, software, travel, medical, toys." Estab. 1992. Circ. 120,000. Pays on publication. Byline given. Offers 50% kill fee. Buys first North American serial rights. Editorial lead time 6 months. Submit seasonal material 3 months in advance. Accepts simultaneous submissions. Query for electronic submissions. Reports in 2 months. Sample copy for 11×14 SAE with 10 first-class stamps. Writer's guidelines free on request.

Nonfiction: General interest, how-to (creative learning projects), interview/profile, new product (big one), technical, travel, medical (M.D.'s). "Virtually all freelance" material. Query with published clips. Length: 300-3,000 words. Pays 20¢/word. Sometimes pays expenses of writers on assignment.

Photos: Send photos with submission. Negotiates payment individually.

Columns/Departments: Play ground (review of new products), 100-300 words; Toys (seasonal), 1,000-2,000 words; Computers, music, video, 1,000-2,000 words. Buys 50 mss/year. Query with published clips. Pays 20-30¢/word.

Tips: "Query with clips. Edutainment is a relatively new concept. Find an interesting angle."

SATELLITE ORBIT, Commtek Communications Corp., Suite 600, 8330 Boone Blvd., Vienna VA 22182. (703)827-0511. Fax: (703)356-6179. Publisher: John Misrasi. Editor: Phillip Swann. 25% freelance written. Monthly magazine. Estab. 1979. **Pays on acceptance.** Publishes an average of 3 months after acceptance. Kill fee varies. Reports in 1 month. Accepts previously published material.

Nonfiction: "Wants to see articles on satellite programming, equipment, television trends, sports and celebrity interviews." Query with published clips. Length: 700 words. Pay varies.

SOAP OPERA DIGEST, K-III Magazines, 45 W. 25 St., New York NY 10010. Editors: Lynn Leahey. Managing Editors: Jason Bonderoff, Roberta Caploe. 20% freelance written. Bimonthly magazine covering soap operas. "Extensive knowledge of daytime and prime time soap operas is required." Estab. 1975. Circ. 1,000,000. **Pays on acceptance.** Publishes ms an average of 3 months after acceptance. Byline given. Offers 30% kill fee. Buys first North American serial and second serial (reprint) rights. Submit seasonal/holiday material 4 months in advance. Reports in 1 month. Writer's guidelines for #10 SASE.

Nonfiction: Interview/profile. No essays. Buys 30 mss/year. Query with published clips. Length: 1,000-2,000 words. Pays $250-500 for assigned articles; $150-250 for unsolicited articles. Sometimes pays expenses of writers on assignment.

Photos: Offers no additional payment for photos accepted with ms. Buys all rights.

SOAP OPERA UPDATE, The Magazine of Stars and Stories, 270 Sylvan Ave., Englewood Cliffs NJ 07632. (201)569-6699. Fax: (201)569-2510. Editors: Dawn Mazzurco, Richard Spencer. 25% freelance written. Bi-weekly magazine on daytime serials. "We cover the world of soap operas with preview information, in-depth interviews and exclusive photos. Feature interviews, history, character sketches, events where soap stars are seen and participate." Estab. 1988. Pays on publication. Byline given. Buys first North American serial rights. Submit seasonal/holiday material 3 months in advance. Accepts simultaneous submissions. Reports in 1 month.

Nonfiction: Humor, interview/profile. "Only articles directly about actors, shows or history of a soap opera." Buys 100 mss/year. Query with published clips. Length: 750-2,200 words. Pays $200. Sometimes pays expenses of writers on assignment.

Photos: State availability of photos with submission. Reviews transparencies. Offers $25. Captions and identification of subjects required. Buys all rights.

Tips: "Come up with fresh, new approaches to stories about soap operas and their people. Submit ideas and clips. Take a serious approach; don't talk down to the reader. All articles must be well written and the writer knowledgeable about his subject matter."

‡SOUND & IMAGE, Hachette Filipacchi Magazines, Inc., 45th Floor, 1633 Broadway, New York NY 10019. (212)767-6020. Editor: Bill Wolfe. 80% freelance written. Quarterly magazine covering home entertainment and electronics. "*Sound & Image* reports on how average Americans can get the most entertainment value from home electronics systems, as well as emerging technologies, software, and lifestyle/cultural issues related to technology and media, audio, video, computers, etc." Estab. 1990. Circ. 50,000. **Pays on acceptance.** Publishes ms an average of 2 months after acceptance. Byline given. Offers 50% kill fee. Buys first North American serial rights. Editorial lead time 3 months. Submit seasonal material 3 months in advance. Accepts simultaneous submissions. Query for electronic submissions.

Nonfiction: Exposé (bad business deals, misuse of technology, etc.); how-to (buy and use electronic home-entertainment systems); humor (brief satires of TV, movies, etc.); interview/profiles (media/technology movers); new product (audio, video, computer, gadgets); opinion (technology and media's effect on society); technical (reviews of equipment, new technology). Buys 80 mss/year. Query with published clips. Length: 1,200-4,000 words. Pays $500-2,000. Sometimes pays expenses of writers on assignment.

Photos: State availability of photos at time of query. Reviews 4×5 transparencies. Negotiates payment individually. Model releases, identification of subjects required. Buys one-time rights.

Columns/Departments: Technology (new trends in home entertainment (5 per issue), 500-1,500 words; Preview (advance info on groundbreaking development), 200-300 words; Last Call (personal slant on elec. home ent, media, technology), 750 words. Buys 40 mss/year. Query with published clips. Pays $300-1,000.

Fiction: Fantasy (futurist science fiction); science fiction (how our lives/world will change as technology matures); slice-of-life vignettes (relating to electronic home entertainment). Will consider queries. Query with published clips. Length: 750-3,000 words. Pays $300-3,000.

Fillers: Facts, newsbreaks, celebrity blurbs. Buys 50/year. Length: 50-200 words. Pays $25-200.

Tips: "Discuss your subject from a position of expertise and write with a hip, pointed style. Queries should include a linear outline that demonstrates that the story will have a beginning, middle, and end. An ability to get quotes from appropriate luminaries is a big plus."

‡**TDR; The Drama Review: The Journal of Performance Studies,** New York University, 6th Floor, 721 Broadway, New York NY 10003. (212)998-1626. Managing Editor: Annemarie Bean. Editor: Richard Schechner. 95% freelance written. Works with a small number of new/unpublished writers each year. Quarterly magazine with "emphasis not only on theater but also dance, ritual, musical performance, mime, and other facets of performative behavior. For avant-garde community, students and professors of anthropology, performance studies and related fields. Political material is welcome." Estab. 1954. Circ. 7,000. Pays on publication. Submit material 6 months in advance. Accepts previously published submissions (if published in another language). Reports in 3 months. Publishes ms an average of 6 months after acceptance. Sample copy for $10 (from MIT Press). Free writer's guidelines.

Nonfiction: Annemarie Bean, managing editor. Buys 10 mss/issue. Query by letter only. Pay determined by page count. Submit both hard copy and disk (Word or WordPerfect).

Photos: State availability of photos and artwork with submission. Prefers 5 × 7 b&w photos. Captions required.

Tips: "*TDR* is a place where contrasting ideas and opinions meet. A forum for writing about performances and the social, economic and political contexts in which performances happen. The editors want interdisciplinary, intercultural, multivocal, eclectic submissions."

‡**THEATREFORUM, International Theatre Journal,** UCSD Department of Theatre, 9500 Gilman Dr., La Jolla CA 92093. (619)534-6598. Editor: Jim Carmody. 75% freelance written. Semiannual magazine covering performance, theatrical and otherwise. "*TheatreForum* is an international journal of theater and performance art and dance theater and music theater and forms yet to be devised. We publish performance texts, interviews with artists on their creative process, and articles about innovative productions and groups. Written by and for members of both the academic and artistic community, we represent a wide variety of aesthetic and cultural interests." Estab. 1992. Circ. 2,000. Pays on publication. Byline given. Buys one-time rights or anthology rights for scripts. Editorial lead time 4 months. Query for electronic submissions. Reports in 1 month on queries; 2 months on mss. Sample copy for $5. Writer's guidelines for #10 SASE.

Nonfiction: Essays, interview/profile, photo feature, performance criticism. Buys 10-12 mss/year. Query with published clips. Length: 1,000-5,000 words. Pays 5¢/word.

Photos: State availability of photos with submission. Negotiates payment individually. Identification of subjects required. Buys one-time rights.

Fiction: Previously published plays are not considered. Buys 4-6 mss/year. Query with published clips. Pays $200 for fiction.

Tips: "We are interested in documenting, discussing, and disseminating innovative and provocative theaterworks. Non-traditional and inventive texts (plays) are welcome. We also publish in-depth analyses of innovative theatrical productions. We are interested in finding artists who want to write about other artists."

TV GUIDE, 1211 Avenue of the Americas, New York NY 10036. Editor (National Section): Barry Golson. Managing Editor: Jack Curry. 50% freelance written. Prefers to work with published/established writers but works with a small number of new/unpublished writers each year. Weekly. Circ. 14 million. Publishes ms an average of 1 month after acceptance.

Nonfiction: Wants offbeat articles about TV people and shows. This magazine is not interested in fan material. Also wants stories on the newest trends of television, but they must be written in clear, lively English. Study publication. Length: 1,000-2,000 words.

Photos: Uses professional high-quality photos, normally shot on assignment by photographers chosen by *TV Guide.* Prefers color. Pays $350 day rate against page rates — $450 for 2 pages or less.

VIDEO, 460 W. 34th St., New York NY 10001. (212)947-6500. Fax: (212)947-6727. Editor: James M. Barry. Managing Editor: Stan Pinkwas. 50% freelance written. Prefers to work with published/established writers; works with a small number of new/unpublished writers each year. Monthly magazine covering home video equipment, technology and prerecorded tapes. Circ. 350,000. **Pays on acceptance.** Publishes ms an average of 3 months after acceptance. Byline given. Buys first North American serial rights. Query for electronic submissions. Reports in 3 weeks on queries; 1 month on mss.

Nonfiction: Buys 50 mss/year. Query with published clips. Pays $300-1,000. Sometimes pays the expenses of writers on assignment.

Tips: The entire feature area is open to freelancers. Write a brilliant query and send samples of published articles.

VIDEOMANIA, "The Video Collector's Newspaper," Legs Of Stone Publishing Co., P.O. Box 47, Princeton WI 54968-0047. Editor: Bob Katerzynske. 75% freelance written. Eager to work with new/unpublished writers. Monthly tabloid for the home video hobbyist. "Our readers are very much 'into' home video: they like reading about it — including both video hardware and software — 98% also collect video (movies, vintage TV, etc.)." Estab. 1981. Circ. 5,000. Pays on publication. Publishes ms an average of 3-6 months after acceptance. Byline given. Buys all rights; may reassign. Submit seasonal/holiday material 6 months in advance. Reports in 1-3 months on mss. Accepts previously published material. Send tearsheet of article or short story, or typed ms with rights for sale noted and information about when and where the article previously appeared, signed permission to reprint. Pays 100% of their fee for an original article. Sample copy for 9 × 12 SAE with 9 first-class stamps. Writer's guidelines for #10 SASE.

● This magazine reports they are receiving a large amount of poetry. They do not want any poetry.

Nonfiction: Book excerpts, videotape and book reviews, exposé, general interest, historical/nostalgic, how-to, humor, interview/profile, new product, opinion, personal experience, photo feature, technical, travel. "All articles should deal with video and/or film. We always have special holiday issues in November and December." No "*complicated* technical pieces." Buys 24 mss/year. Send complete ms. Length: 200-400 words. Video reviews under 100 words. Pays $2.50 maximum. "Contributor copies also used for payment."

Photos: Send photos with submissions. Reviews contact sheets and 3 × 5 prints. Offers no additional payment for photos accepted with ms. Model releases and identification of subjects required. Buys all rights; may reassign.

Fiction: Adventure, horror, humorous. "We want short, video-related fiction only on an occasional basis. Since we aim for a general readership, we do not want any pornographic material." Buys 5 mss/year. Send complete ms. Length: 200-400 words. Pays $2.50 maximum plus copies.

Tips: "We want to offer more reviews and articles on offbeat, obscure and rare movies, videos and stars. Write in a plain, easy-to-understand style. We're not looking for a highhanded, knock-'em-dead writing style . . . just something good! We want more short video, film and book reviews by freelancers."

Ethnic/Minority

Ideas and concerns of interest to specific nationalities and religions are covered by publications in this category. General interest lifestyle magazines for these groups are also included. Many ethnic publications are locally-oriented or highly specialized and do not wish to be listed in a national publication such as *Writer's Market*. Query the editor of an ethnic publication with which you're familiar before submitting a manuscript, but do not consider these markets closed because they are not listed in this section. Additional markets for writing with an ethnic orientation are located in the following sections: Career, College and Alumni; Juvenile; Men's; Women's; and Teen and Young Adult.

‡**AFRICAN CONTINENT NEWS,** #201-202, 318 Cleveland Ave. NW, Canton OH 44702. (216)453-5550. Editor/Publisher: Isaiah Jackson. Managing Editor: John Misha. 95% freelance written. Monthly newspaper covering news that affects Africa, Africans and the entire Black race. Estab. 1989. Circ. 11,000. Pays on publication. Publishes ms an average of 3 months after acceptance. Byline given. Not copyrighted. Buys first North American serial rights, one-time rights or simultaneous rights. Submit seasonal/holiday material 4 months in advance. Reports in 3 months. Writer's guidelines for SASE.

Nonfiction: Exposé, general interest, historical/nostalgic, humor, inspirational, interview/profile, opinion, personal experience, photo feature, travel, food, political and economy. Buys 36 mss/year. Send complete ms. Length: 1,000-3,000 words. Pays $20-200. Sometimes pays expenses of writers on assignment.

Photos: Send photos or state availability of photos with submission. Reviews b&w or color prints. Offers $5/photo. Captions, model releases, identification of subjects required. Buys all rights.

Columns/Departments: Food (cooking and review African food and restaurants); Marriage, Political and Economy; all 250-400 words. Send complete ms. Length: 250-400 words. Pays $15.

Poetry: Traditional. Offers no payment.

Fillers: Facts, short humor. Offers no payment.

Tips: "Submit with a note about interest in African affairs. We are interested in articles that offer an African-American perspective on African affairs. Human interest stories are the most open to freelancers. We like articles dealing with current issues involving Africa and the Africans."

AFRICAN-AMERICAN HERITAGE, Dellco Publishing Company, Suite 103, 8443 S. Crenshaw Blvd., Inglewood CA 90305. (213)752-3706. Editor: Dennis W. DeLoach. 30% freelance written. Quarterly magazine looking for "positive, informative, educational articles that build self-esteem, pride and an appreciation for the richness of culture and history." Estab. 1978. Circ. 25,000. Pays on publication. Publishes ms an average of 3-6 months after acceptance. Byline given. Offers 25% kill fee. Buys First North American serial, one-time or simultaneous rights. Submit seasonal/holiday material 6 months in advance. Accepts simultaneous and previously published submissions. Reports in 1 month on queries; 2 months on mss. Sample copy for 9×12 SASE. Writer's guidelines for SAE with 4 first-class stamps.

Nonfiction: Book excerpts, essays, general interest, historical/nostalgic, how-to, humor, inspirational, interview/profile, new product, opinion, personal experience, photo feature, religious, travel. Special issue: Black History Month (February). Buys 6 mss/year. Query. Length: 200-2,000 words. Pays $25-300 for assigned articles. Sometimes pays expenses of writers on assignment.

Photos: State availability of photos with submission. Reviews 5×7 prints. Offers no additional payment for photos accepted with ms. Identification of subject required. Buys one-time rights.

Columns/Departments: History (historical profiles); Commentary (letters to the editor); Interviews (personalities, unusual careers, positive experiences); Short Stories (well written, entertaining). Length: 2,000 words maximum. Buys 12 mss/year. Query. Pays $25-300.

Fiction: Adventure, ethnic, historical, humorous, mystery, religious, romance and slice-of-life vignettes. "No erotica, horror or fantasy." Buys 6 mss/year. Query. Length: 200-2,000 words. Pays $25-300.

Poetry: Avant-garde, free verse, Haiku, light verse and traditional. Buys 60 poems/year. Submit maximum 5 poems. Length: 4-36 lines. Pays $10-25.

Fillers: Anecdotes and facts. Buys 12/year. Length: 10-200 words. Pays $25-100.

AIM MAGAZINE, AIM Publishing Company, 7308 S. Eberhart Ave., Chicago IL 60620-0554. (312)874-6184. Editor: Ruth Apilado. Managing Editor: Dr. Myron Apilado. Estab. 1975. 75% freelance written. Works with a small number of new/unpublished writers each year. Quarterly magazine on social betterment that promotes racial harmony and peace for high school, college and general audience. Circ. 10,000. Pays on publication. Publishes ms an average of 3 months after acceptance. Offers 60% kill fee. Not copyrighted. Buys one-time rights. Submit seasonal/holiday material 6 months in advance. Simultaneous queries and submissions OK. Reports in 2 months on queries. Sample copy and writer's guidelines for $4 and 9×12 SAE with $1.31 postage.

Nonfiction: Exposé (education); general interest (social significance); historical/nostalgic (Black or Indian); how-to (create a more equitable society); profile (one who is making social contributions to community); book reviews and reviews of plays "that reflect our ethnic/minority orientation." No religious material. Buys 16 mss/year. Send complete ms. Length: 500-800 words. Pays $25-35.

Photos: Reviews b&w prints. Captions, identification of subjects required.

Fiction: Ethnic, historical, mainstream, suspense. "Fiction that teaches the brotherhood of man." Buys 20 mss/year. Send complete ms. Length: 1,000-1,500 words. Pays $25-35.

Poetry: Avant-garde, free verse, light verse. No "preachy" poetry. Buys 20 poems/year. Submit maximum 5 poems. Length: 15-30 lines. Pays $3-5.

Fillers: Jokes, anecdotes, newsbreaks. Buys 30/year. Length: 50-100 words. Pays $5.

Tips: "Interview anyone of any age who unselfishly is making an unusual contribution to the lives of less fortunate individuals. Include photo and background of person. We look at the nations of the world as part of one family. Short stories and historical pieces about Blacks and Indians are the areas most open to freelancers. Subject matter of submission is of paramount concern for us rather than writing style. Articles and stories showing the similarity in the lives of people with different racial backgrounds are desired."

THE AMERICAN CITIZEN ITALIAN PRESS, 13681 V St., Omaha NE 68137. (402)896-0403. Fax: (402)895-7820. Publisher/Editor: Diana C. Failla. 80% freelance written. Quarterly newspaper of Italian-American news/stories. Estab. 1923. Circ. 8,490. Pays on publication. Publishes ms an average of 3 months after acceptance. Byline given. Not copyrighted. Buys first North American serial rights. Submit seasonal/holiday material 2 months in advance. Accepts previously published submissions. Send photocopy of article or typed ms with rights for sale noted and information about when and where the article previously appeared. For reprints pays 80% of amount paid for an original article. Reports in 4 months. Sample copy for 10×13 SAE with $1.50 postage. Writer's guidelines for #10 SAE with 2 first-class stamps.

Nonfiction: Book excerpts, general interest, historical/nostalgic, opinion, photo feature, celebrity pieces, travel, fashions, profiles, sports (Italian players). Query with published clips. Length: 400-600 words. Pays $15-25. Pays more for in-depth pieces.

Photos: State availability of photos. Reviews b&w prints. Pays $5. Captions and identification of subjects required. Buys all rights.

For explanation of symbols, see the Key to Symbols and Abbreviations. For unfamiliar words, see the Glossary.

Columns/Departments: Query.
Fiction: Query. Pays $15-20. Sometimes publishes novel excerpts.
Poetry: Submit maximum 5 poems. Pays $5-10.
Tips: "Human interest stories are the most open to freelancers. We like work dealing with current issues involving those of Italian/American descent."

AMERICAN VISIONS, The Magazine of Afro-American Culture, 2101 S Street, Washington DC 20008. (202)462-1779. Managing Editor: Joanne Harris. 75% freelance written. Bimonthly magazine on African-American art, culture and history. "Editorial is reportorial, current, objective, 'pop-scholarly'. Audience is ages 25-54, mostly black, college educated." Estab. 1986. Circ. 125,000. Pays 30 days after publication. Publishes ms an average of 2 months after acceptance. Byline given. Offers 25% kill fee. Buys first North American, one-time and second serial (reprint) rights. Submit seasonal/holiday material 5 months in advance. Accepts simultaneous and previously published submissions. Query for electronic submissions. Reports in 2-3 months. Free sample copy and writer's guidelines with SASE.
Nonfiction: Book excerpts, general interest, historical/nostalgic, interview/profile literature, photo feature, travel. Publishes travel supplements – domestic, Africa, Europe, Canada, Mexico. No fiction, poetry, personal experience or opinion. Buys about 60-70 mss/year. Query with or without published clips or send complete ms. Length: 500-2,500 words. Pays $100-600 for assigned articles; $100-400 for unsolicited articles. Sometimes pays expenses of writers on assignment.
Photos: State availability of photos with submission. Reviews contact sheets, 3×5 transparencies, and 3×5 or 8×10 prints. Offers $15 minimum. Identification of subjects required. Buys one-time rights.
Columns/Departments: Books, Cuisine, Film, Music, Profile, Travel, 750-1,750 words. Buys about 40 mss/ year. Query or send complete ms. Pays $100-400.
Tips: "Little-known but terribly interesting information about black history and culture is desired. Aim at an upscale audience. Send ms with credentials." Looking for writers who are enthusiastic about their topics.

‡ARARAT, 585 Saddle River Rd., Saddle Brook NJ 07662. Editor-in-Chief: Leo Hamalian. 80% freelance written. Quarterly magazine emphasizing Armenian life and culture for Americans of Armenian descent and Armenian immigrants. "Most are well-educated; some are Old World." Circ. 2,200. Pays on publication. Publishes ms an average of 1 year after acceptance. Buys first North American serial rights and second (reprint) rights to material originally published elsewhere. Submit seasonal/holiday material at least 3 months in advance. Accepts previously published material. Reports in 6 weeks. Sample copy for $7 and 4 first-class stamps.
Nonfiction: Historical (history of Armenian people, of leaders, etc.); interviews (with prominent or interesting Armenians in any field, but articles are preferred); profile (on subjects relating to Armenian life and culture); personal experience (revealing aspects of typical Armenian life); and travel (in Armenia and Armenian communities throughout the world and the US). Buys 3 mss/issue. Query. Length: 1,000-6,000 words. Pays $25-100.
Columns/Departments: Reviews of books by Armenians or relating to Armenians. Buys 6/issue. Query. Pays $25. Open to suggestions for new columns/departments.
Fiction: Any stories dealing with Armenian life in America or in the old country. Buys 4 mss/year. Query. Length: 2,000-5,000 words. Pays $50-100.
Poetry: Any verse that is Armenian in theme. Buys 6/issue. Pays $10.
Tips: "Read the magazine, and write about the kind of subjects we are obviously interested in, e.g., Kirlian photography, Aram Avakian's films, etc. Remember that we have become almost totally ethnic in subject matter, but we want articles that present (to the rest of the world) the Armenian in an interesting way. The most frequent mistake made by writers in completing an article for us is that they are not sufficiently versed in Armenian history/culture. The articles are too superficial for our audience. We also accept articles or stories dealing with Armenia's neighboring nations and adopted homelands."

THE B'NAI B'RITH INTERNATIONAL, JEWISH MONTHLY, 1640 Rhode Island Ave. NW, Washington DC 20036. (202)857-6645. Editor: Jeff Rubin. 50% freelance written. Magazine published 80 times/year covering Jewish affairs. Estab. 1886. Circ. 185,000. **Pays on acceptance.** Publishes ms an average of 3 months after acceptance. Byline given. Kill fee depends on rate of payment. Buys first North American serial rights. Submit seasonal/holiday material 6 months in advance. Query for electronic submissions. Reports in 2 weeks. Sample copy for $2 and 9×13 SAE with 2 first-class stamps. Free writer's guidelines.
Nonfiction: Book excerpts, essay, exposé, general interest, historical, inspirational, interview/profile, photo feature, travel. Buys 40-50 mss/year. Query with published clips. Length: 750-3,000 words. Pays $50-750 for assigned articles; $50-500 for unsolicited articles. Sometimes pays expenses of writers on assignment.
Photos: State availability of photos with submission. Reviews contact sheets, 2×3 transparencies and prints. Payment depends on quality and type of photograph. Identification of subjects required. Buys one-time rights.
  • No longer publishes fiction.

Tips: "Writers should submit clips with their queries. The best way to break in to the *Jewish Monthly* is to submit a range of good story ideas accompanied by clips. We aim to establish relationships with writers and we tend to be loyal. All sections are equally open."

CLASS, R.E. John-Sandy Ltd., 900 Broadway, New York NY 10003. (212)677-3055. Executive Editor: Denolyn Carroll. 25% freelance written. Monthly "general interest publication geared toward Caribbean, Latin and African Americans between ages 18-49." Estab. 1979. Circ. 250,000. Pays 45 days after publication. Byline given. Buys first North American serial and second serial (reprint) rights. Submit seasonal/holiday material 3 months in advance. Reports in 6 weeks. Sample copy for 9 × 12 SAE with 4 first-class stamps. Writer's guidelines for #10 SASE.
Nonfiction: Exposé, general interest, historical/nostalgic, interview/profile, religious, travel. Query with published clips. Length: 500-1,300 words. Pays 10¢/word maximum. Sometimes pays expenses of writers on assignment.
Photos: Send photos with submission. Offers no additional payment for photos accepted with ms. Captions, model releases and identification of subjects required. Buys all rights.
Columns/Departments: Length: 500-1,300 words. Pays 10¢/word maximum.
Poetry: Buys 10-20 poems/year. Submit maximum 5 poems. Pays $10 maximum.

CONGRESS MONTHLY, American Jewish Congress, 15 E. 84th St., New York NY 10028. (212)879-4500. Editor: Maier Deshell. 90% freelance written. Magazine published 7 times/year covering topics of concern to the American Jewish community representing a wide range of views. Distributed mainly to the members of the American Jewish Congress. "Readers are intellectual, Jewish, involved." Estab. 1933. Circ. 35,000. Pays on publication. Publishes ms an average of 3 months after acceptance. Byline given. Buys one-time rights. Submit seasonal/holiday material 2 months in advance. No previously published submissions. Reports in 2 months.
Nonfiction: General interest ("current topical issues geared toward our audience"). No technical material. Send complete ms. Length: 2,000 words maximum. Pays $100-150/article.
Photos: State availability of photos. Reviews b&w prints. "Photos are paid for with payment for ms."
Columns/Departments: Book, film, art and music reviews. Send complete ms. Length: 1,000 words maximum. Pays $100-150/article.

EBONY MAGAZINE, 820 S. Michigan Ave., Chicago IL 60605. (312)322-9200. Publisher: John H. Johnson. Executive Editor: Lerone Bennett, Jr. 10% freelance written. For Black readers of the US, Africa and the Caribbean. Monthly. Circ. 1.8 million. Buys first North American serial and all rights. Buys about 10 mss/year. Pays on publication. Publishes ms an average of 3 months after acceptance. Submit seasonal material 2 months in advance. Query the Ebony Editorial Committee. Reports in 1 month.
Nonfiction: Achievement and human interest stories about, or of concern to, Black readers. Interviews, profiles, humor pieces. Length: 1,500 words maximum. "Study magazine and needs carefully. Perhaps one out of 50 submissions interests us. Most are totally irrelevant to our needs and are simply returned." Pays $200 minimum. Sometimes pays the expenses of writers on assignment.
Photos: Purchased with mss, and with captions only. Buys 8 × 10 glossy prints, color transparencies, 35mm color. Submit negatives and contact sheets when possible. Offers no additional payment for photos accepted with mss.

EMERGE, Black America's Newsmagazine, Emerge Communications, Inc., Suite 2200, 1700 N. Moore St., Arlington VA 22009. (703)875-0430. Fax: (703)516-6406. Editor: Geore E. Curry. Managing Editor: Florestine Purnell. 80% freelance written. African-American news monthly. "*Emerge* is a general interest publication reporting on a wide variety of issues from health to sports to politics, almost anything that affects Black Americans. Our audience is comprised primarily of African-Americans 25-49, individual income of $35,000, professional and college educated." Estab. 1989. Circ. 200,000. **Pays on acceptance.** Publishes ms an average of 3 months after acceptance. Byline given. Offers 25% kill fee. Buys first North American serial rights. Submit seasonal material 6 months in advance. Query for electronic submissions. Reports in 5 weeks. Sample copy for $3 and 9 × 12 SAE. Writer's guidelines for #10 SAE with 2 first-class stamps.
  • Ranked as one of the best markets for freelance writers in *Writer's Digest* magazine's annual "Top 100 Markets," January 1994.
Nonfiction: Essays, exposé, general interest, historical/nostalgic, humor, interview/profile, technical, travel. "We are not interested in standard celebrity pieces that lack indepth reporting as well as analysis, or pieces dealing with interpersonal relationships." Query with published clips. Length: 600-2,000 words. Pays 60-75¢/word.
Photos: State availability of photos with submission. Reviews contact sheets. Negotiated payment. Captions, model releases, and indentification of subjects required. Buys one-time rights.
Columns/Departments: Query.
Tips: "If a writer doesn't have a completed manuscript, then he should mail a query letter with clips. No phone calls. First-time authors should be extremely sensitive to the *Emerge* style and fit within these guidelines as closely as possible. We do not like to re-write or re-edit pieces. We are a news monthly so articles must

be written with a 3 month lead time in mind. If an assignment is given and another one is desired, writers must assist our research department during fact checking process and closing. Read at least six issues of the publication before submitting ideas."

EXITO, News and Sun Sentinel Company, #212, 8323 NW 12th St., Miami FL 33126. (305)597-5000. Editor: Humberto Cruz. 30% freelance written. Weekly tabloid that covers topics of general interest. "We reach bilingual, bicultural Hispanics, ages 25-54." Estab. 1991. Circ. 80,000. Pays on publication. Byline given. Buys one-time and second serial (reprint) rights. Submit seasonal/holiday material 6 months in advance. Accepts simultaneous submissions. Query for electronic submissions. Reports in 1 month. *Writer's Market* recommends allowing 2 months for reply. Sample copy for 9×12 SAE with 6 first-class stamps.
Nonfiction: Christina Arencibia (travel articles), Humberto Cruz (general interest), Magaly Rubiera (lifestyle, health). General interest, how-to, interview/profile, new product, religious, travel. Buys 200 mss/year. Query with or without published clips or send complete ms. Length: 1,700 words. Pays $75 for articles.
Photos: State availability of photos with submission. Reviews transparencies. Captions and identification of subjects required. Buys one-time rights.
Tips: *Exito* only accepts mss written in Spanish. "We are particularly interested in articles on travel."

HADASSAH MAGAZINE, 50 W. 58th St., New York NY 10019. Executive Editor: Alan M. Tigay. 90% freelance written. Works with small number of new/unpublished writers each year. Monthly, (except combined issues June/July and August/September). Circ. 334,000. Buys first rights (with travel and family articles, buys all rights). Free sample copy and writer's guidelines with SASE.
Nonfiction: Primarily concerned with Israel, Jewish communities around the world and American civic affairs as relates to the Jewish community. "We are also open to art stories that explore trends in Jewish art, literature, theater, etc. Will not assign/commission a story to a first-time writer for Hadassah." Buys 10 unsolicited mss/year. No phone queries. Send query and writing samples. Length: 1,500-2,000 words. Pays $200-400, less for reviews. Sometimes pays the expenses of writers on assignment.
Photos: "We buy photos only to illustrate articles, with the exception of outstanding color from Israel which we use on our covers. We pay $175 and up for a suitable cover photo." Offers $50 for first photo; $35 for each additional. "Always interested in striking cover (color) photos, especially of Israel and Jerusalem."
Columns/Departments: "We have a Family column and a Travel column, but a query for topic or destination should be submitted first to make sure the area is of interest and the story follows our format."
Fiction: Contact Joan Michel. Short stories with strong plots and positive Jewish values. No personal memoirs, "schmaltzy" or women's magazine fiction. "We continue to buy very little fiction because of a backlog." Length: 3,000 words maximum. Pays $300 minimum. "Require proper size SASE."
Tips: "We are interested in reading articles that offer an American perspective on Jewish affairs (1,500 words). For example, a look at the presidential candidates from a Jewish perspective. Send query of topic first."

HERITAGE FLORIDA JEWISH NEWS, P.O. Box 300742, Fern Park FL 32730-0742. (407)834-8787. Fax: (407)831-0507. Associate Editor: Vivian Gallimore. Publisher/Editor: Jeffrey Gaeser. 20% freelance written. Weekly tabloid on Jewish subjects of local, national and international scope, except for special issues. "Covers news of local, national and international scope of interest to Jewish readers and not likely to be found in other publications." Estab. 1976. Circ. 3,500. Pays on publication. Publishes ms an average of 2 months after acceptance. Byline given. Buys first North American serial, first, one-time, second serial (reprint) or simultaneous rights. Submit seasonal/holiday material 3 months in advance. Publishes reprints of previously published material. Send typed ms with rights for sale noted. Reports in 1 month. Sample copy for $1 and 9×12 SASE.
Nonfiction: General interest, interview/profile, opinion, photo feature, religious, travel. "Especially needs articles for these annual issues: Rosh Hashanah, Financial, Chanukah, Celebration (wedding and bar mitzvah), Passover, Health and Fitness, Education, Travel. No fiction, poems, first-person experiences." Buys 50 mss/year. Send complete ms. Length: 500-1,000 words. Pays 50¢/column inch.
Photos: State availability of photos with submission. Reviews b&w prints up to 8×10. Offers $5/photo. Captions and identification of subjects required. Buys one-time rights.

THE HIGHLANDER, Angus J. Ray Associates, Inc., P.O. Box 397, Barrington IL 60011-0397. (708)382-1035. Editor: Angus J. Ray. 50% freelance written. Works with a small number of new/unpublished writers each year. Bimonthly magazine covering Scottish history, clans, genealogy, travel/history, and Scottish/American activities. Estab. 1961. Circ. 40,000. **Pays on acceptance.** Publishes ms an average of 6 months after acceptance. Byline given. Buys first North American serial and second serial (reprint) rights. Submit seasonal/holiday material 6 months in advance. Accepts previously published submissions. Send tearsheet or photocopy of article. For reprints pays 50% of amount paid for an original article. Reports in 1 month. Sample copy for $2. Free writer's guidelines.
Nonfiction: Historical/nostalgic. "No fiction; no articles unrelated to Scotland." Buys 50 mss/year. Query. Length: 750-2,000 words. Pays $75-150.

Photos: State availability of photos. Pays $5-10 for 8 × 10 b&w prints or transparencies. Reviews b&w contact sheets. Identification of subjects required. Buys one-time rights.
Tips: "Submit something that has appeared elsewhere."

HISPANIC, Suite 410, 111 Massachusetts Ave., NW, Washington DC 20001. (202)682-3000. Fax: (202)682-4091. Editor: Alfredo J. Estrada. Contact: Managing Editor. 90% freelance written. Monthly magazine for the Hispanic community. "HISPANIC is a general interest, lifestyle, entertainment, upbeat, role model publication." Estab. 1987. Circ. 250,000. Pays on publication. Publishes ms an average of 4 months after acceptance. Byline given. Offers 25% kill fee. Buys all rights. Submit seasonal/holiday material 4 months in advance. Free sample copy and writer's guidelines.
 • This magazine will be moving to Austin, Texas.
Nonfiction: General interest, historical/nostalgic, humor, interview/profile, opinion, personal experience, photo feature and travel. Buys 200 mss/year. Query. Length: 50-3,000 words. Pays $50-600. Pays writers phone expenses, "but these must be cleared with editors first."
Photos: State availability of photos with submission. Reviews transparencies. Offers $25-600/photo. Captions, model releases and identification of subjects required. Buys one-time rights.
Columns/Departments: Forum (political opinion and analysis), cars, money, career, business and reviews. All columns are approximately 500 words but vary in fee.

HISPANIC BUSINESS, Hispanic Business, Inc., 360 S. Hope Ave., Santa Barbara CA 93105. (805)682-5843. Publisher: Jesus Chavarria. Managing Editor: Hector Cantu. 20% freelance written. Monthly trade magazine "written for and about Hispanic CEO's, managers and professionals." Estab. 1979. Circ. 165,000. Pays on publication. Byline given. Kill fee varies. Buys all rights. Submit seasonal/holiday material 3 months in advance. Query for electronic submissions. Reports in 2 weeks. Sample copy for $5. Writer's guidelines for $1.75 and #10 SASE.
Nonfiction: Interview/profile. Buys 36 mss/year. Query with published clips. Length: 750-3,000 words. Pays $225-900 for assigned articles; $195-780 for unsolicited articles. Sometimes pays the expenses of writers on assignment.
Photos: State availability of photos with submission. Reviews transparencies. Offers no additional payment for photos accepted with ms. Identification of subjects required. Buys all rights.
Tips: "We are looking for business writers with close ties to their local Hispanic community."

INSIDE, The Jewish Exponent Magazine, Jewish Federation of Greater Philadelphia, 226 S. 16th St., Philadelphia PA 19102. (215)893-5700. Fax: (215)546-3957. Editor: Jane Biberman. Managing Editor: Martha Ledger. 95% freelance written (by assignment). Works with published/established writers and a small number of new/unpublished writers each year. Quarterly Jewish community magazine for a general interest Jewish readership 25 years of age and older. Estab. 1979. Circ. 75,000. **Pays on acceptance.** Offers 20% kill fee. Publishes ms an average of 2 months after acceptance. Byline given. Buys first rights. Reprint possibilities with our licensees. Submit seasonal/holiday material 3 months in advance. Reports in 2 weeks on queries; 1 month on mss. Sample copy for $5 and 9 × 12 SAE. Writer's guidelines for #10 SASE.
Nonfiction: Book excerpts, general interest, historical/nostalgic, humor, interview/profile, personal experience, religious. Philadelphia angle desirable. Buys 12 unsolicited mss/year. Query. Length: 1,000-3,500 words. Pays $100-1,000.
Photos: State availability of photos with submission. Identification of subjects required. Buys first rights.
Fiction: Short stories. Query.
Tips: "Personalities — very well known — and serious issues of concern to Jewish community needed."

‡INTERNATIONAL EXAMINER, 622 S. Washington, Seattle WA 98104. (206)624-3925. Editor: Jeff J. Lin. 25% freelance written. Biweekly newspaper covering Asian-American issues and stories. "We write about Asian-American issues and things of interest to *Asian-Americans*. We do not want stuff about *Asian* things (stories on your trip to China, Japanese Tea Ceremony, etc. will be rejected). Yes, we are in English." Estab. 1974. Circ. 12,000. Pays on publication. Publishes ms an average of 1 months after acceptance. Buys one-time rights. Editorial lead time 1 month. Submit seasonal material 1 month in advance. Accepts simultaneous and previously published submissions (as long as not published in same area). Sample copy for #10 SASE.
Nonfiction: Essays, exposé, general interest, historical/nostalgic, humor, interview/profile, opinion, personal experience, photo feature. Buys 50 mss/year. Query with published clips. Length: depends on subject, 750-5,000 words. Pays $25. Sometimes pays expenses of writers on assignment.
Photos: State availability of photos with submission. Reviews contact sheets. Negotiates payment individually. Captions, identification of subjects required, Buys one-time rights.
Fiction: Asian-American authored fiction. Buys 1-2 mss/year. Query.
Tips: "Write decent, suitable material on a subject of interest to Asian-American community. All submissions are reviewed; all good ones are contacted. Also helps to call and run idea by editor before or after sending submissions."

‡**INTERRACE MAGAZINE**, Interrace Publications, P.O. Box 12048, Atlanta GA 30355. (404)364-9690. Editor: Candy Mills. Contact: Gabe Grosz. 70% freelance written. Bimonthly magazine covering interracial/multiracial topics. "We cover all aspects dealing with interracial couples and families; people who are mixed-race." Estab. 1989. Circ. 25,000. Pays on publication. Publishes ms an average of 1-3 months after acceptance. Byline given. Buys first rights or makes work-for-hire assignments. Submit seasonal material 3 months in advance. Accepts simultaneous and previously published submissions. Query for electronic submissions. Reports in 1-2 months on queries; 2-3 months on mss. Sample copy for $2 and 9 × 12 SAE with $1 postage. Writer's guidelines for #10 SASE.

Nonfiction: Essays, exposé, general interest, historical/nostalgic, humor, inspirational, interview/profile, new product, opinion, personal experience, photo feature, travel. Buys 30-40 mss/year. Query. Length: 200-4,800 words. Pays $20-50 for assigned articles; $50-75 for cover stories. Sometimes pays expenses of writers on assignment. Freelancers should state availability of photos with submission. Negotiates payment individually. Identification of subjects required. Buys one-time rights.

Columns/Departments: Buys 3-5 mss/year. Query. Pays $20.

Fiction: Ethnic, historical, humorous, romance, slice-of-life vignettes. Buys 8 mss/year. Query. Length: 800-2,400 words. Pays $20-40.

JEWISH ACTION, Union of Orthodox Jewish Congregations of America, 18th Floor, 333 Seventh Ave., New York NY 10001-5072. (212)563-4000, ext. 146, 147. Fax: (212)564-9058. Editor: Charlotte Friedland. Assistant Editor: Elissa Feldman. 80% freelance written. "Quarterly magazine offering a vibrant approach to Jewish issues, Orthodox lifestyle and values." Circ. 45,000. Pays 4-6 weeks after publication. Byline given. Submit seasonal/holiday material 4 months in advance. Reports in 5 months. Sample copy and guidelines for 9 × 12 SAE with 5 first-class stamps.

Nonfiction: Current Jewish issues, history, biography, art, inspirational, humor, book reviews. Query with published clips. Length: 1,500-2,500 words. Pays $100-300 for assigned articles; $75-150 for unsolicited articles. Buys 30-40 mss/year.

Fiction: Must have relevance to Orthodox reader. Length: 1,000-2,000 words.

Poetry: Limited number accepted. Pays $25-75.

Columns/Departments: Student Voice (about Jewish life on campus), 1,000 words. Buys 4 mss/year. Just Between Us (personal opinion on current Jewish life and issues), 1,000 words. Buys 4 mss/year. Jewish Living (section pertaining to holidays, contemporary Jewish practices), 1,000-1,500 words. Buys 10 mss/year.

Photos: Send photos with submission. Identification of subjects required.

Tips: "Remember that your reader is well-educated and has a strong commitment to Orthodox Judaism. Articles on the Holocaust, holidays, Israel and other common topics should offer a fresh insight."

JEWISH NEWS OF GREATER PHOENIX, Phoenix Jewish News, Inc., P.O. Box 26590, Phoenix AZ 85068-6590. (602)870-9470. Fax: (602)870-0426. Executive Editor: Flo Eckstein. Managing Editor: Leni Reiss. 5% freelance written. Prefers to work with published/established writers. Weekly tabloid covering subjects of interest to Jewish readers. Estab. 1948. Circ. 7,000. Publishes ms an average of 3 months after acceptance. Byline given. Submit seasonal/holiday material 3 months in advance. Accepts simultaneous and previously published submissions. Send typed ms with rights for sale noted and information about when and where the article previously appeared. Sample copy for $1.

Nonfiction: General interest, issue analysis, interview/profile, opinion, personal experience, photo feature, travel. Special sections include Fashion and Health, House and Home, Back to School, Summer Camps, Party Planning, Bridal, Adult Lifestyles, Travel, Business and Finance, and Jewish Holidays. Send complete ms. Length: 1,000-2,500 words. Pays $15-50 for simultaneous rights; $1.50/column inch for first serial rights.

Photos: Send photos with query or ms. Pays $10 for 8 × 10 b&w prints. Captions required.

Tips: "We are looking for lifestyle and issue-oriented pieces of particular interest to Jewish readers. Our newspaper reaches across the religious, political, social and economic spectrum of Jewish residents in this burgeoning Southwestern metropolitan area. We stay away from cute stories as well as ponderous submissions."

MIDSTREAM, A Monthly Jewish Review, 110 E. 59 St., New York NY 10022-1373. Editor: Joel Carmichael. 90% freelance written. Works with a small number of new/unpublished writers each year. Monthly magazine. "*Midstream* magazine is the Zionist periodical of record; in fact, there is no other journal of its kind which publishes Zionist historiography on a monthly basis in the world." Estab. 1954. Circ. 10,000. Buys first North American serial rights. Byline given. Pays after publication. Publishes ms an average of 6 months after acceptance. Reports in 3 months. Fiction guidelines for #10 SASE.

Nonfiction: "Articles offering a critical interpretation of the past, searching examination of the present, and affording a medium for independent opinion and creative cultural expression. Articles on the political and social scene in Israel, on Jews in Russia, the US and elsewhere. Pays 5¢/word.

Fiction: Primarily of Jewish and related content. Pays 5¢/word.

Tips: "A book review is a good way to start. Send us a sample review or a clip, let us know your area of interest, suggest books you would like to review. For longer articles, give a brief account of your background or credentials in this field. Send query describing article or ms with cover letter. Since we are a monthly, we look for critical analysis rather than a 'journalistic' approach."

NA'AMAT WOMAN, Magazine of NA'AMAT USA, the Women's Labor Zionist Organization of America, NA'AMAT USA, 200 Madison Ave., New York NY 10016. (212)725-8010. Editor: Judith A. Sokoloff. 80% freelance written. Magazine published 5 times/year covering Jewish themes and issues; Israel; women's issues; Labor Zionism; and social, political and economic issues. Estab. 1926. Circ. 30,000. Pays on publication. Byline given. Not copyrighted. Buys first North American serial, one-time, first serial and second serial (reprint) rights to book excerpts and makes work-for-hire assignments. Reports in 3 months. Writer's guidelines for SASE.
Nonfiction: Exposé, general interest (Jewish), historical/nostalgic, interview/profile, opinion, personal experience, photo feature, travel (Israel), art and music. "All articles must be of particular interest to the Jewish community." Buys 35 mss/year. Query with clips of published work or send complete ms. Pays 10¢/word.
Photos: State availability of photos. Pays $10-30 for 4×5 or 5×7 prints. Captions, identification of subjects required. Buys one-time rights.
Columns/Departments: Film and book reviews with Jewish themes. Buys 20-25 mss/year. Query with clips of published work or send complete ms. Pays 10¢/word.
Fiction: Historical/nostalgic, humorous, women-oriented and novel excerpts. "Good intelligent fiction with Jewish slant. No maudlin nostalgia or trite humor." Buys 3 mss/year. Send complete ms. Length: 1,200-3,000 words. Pays 10¢/word.

NATIVE PEOPLES MAGAZINE, The Arts and Lifeways, Suite C-224, 5333 N. Seventh St., Phoenix AZ 85014-2804. (602)252-2236. Fax: (602)265-3113. Editorial Coordinator: Rebeca Withers. Editor: Gary Avey. Quarterly magazine on Native Americans. "The primary purpose of this magazine is to offer a sensitive portrayal of the arts and lifeways of native peoples of the Americas." Estab. 1987. Circ. 108,000. Pays on publication. Byline given. Buys one-time rights. Query for electronic submissions. Reports in 1 month on queries; 2 months on mss. Sample copy for 9×12 SAE with 5 first-class stamps. Free writer's guidelines. "Extremely high quality reproduction with full-color throughout."
Nonfiction: Book excerpts, historical/nostalgic, interview/profile, personal experience, photo feature. Buys 35 mss/year. Query with published clips. Length: 1,800-2,200 words. Pays 25¢/word. Publishes nonfiction book excerpts.
Photos: State availability of photos with submission. Reviews transparencies (all formats). Offers $45-150 per page rates. Identification of subjects required. Buys one-time rights.

POLISH AMERICAN JOURNAL, Polonia's Voice, Panagraphics, Inc., 1275 Harlem Rd., Buffalo NY 14206-1980. (716)893-5771. Fax: (716)893-5783. Editor: Mark A. Kohan. Managing Editor: Paulette T. Kulbacki. 20% freelance written. Monthly tabloid for Polonia (Polish and Polish-American events, people, etc.). "Stories should be about Polish-Americans active in their community on either a local or national level. Prefer biographies/histories of these people or essays on their accomplishments." Estab. 1911. Circ. 20,000. Pays at end of publication quarter (March, June, September, December). Publishes ms 3-4 months after acceptance. Byline given. Reports in 2 months. Offers $2 kill fee. Not copyrighted. Buys one-time rights. Submit seasonal/holiday material 3 months in advance. Accepts previously published submissions. Query for electronic submissions. Sample copy for 9×12 SAE with 3 first-class stamps.
Nonfiction: Exposé (story on Polish-Americans), general interest (community news), historical/nostalgic (retrospectives on events), how-to (organize groups, etc.), interview/profile (background on local Pol-Ams), opinion (historical observations, anti-defamation, etc.), personal experience (growing up Polish-American). Special issues on Easter and Christmas celebrations—how practiced in other areas; travel to Poland, airfare and comparisons, etc.; salute to prominent Polish-American business leaders, clergy, media personalities, etc. Buys 6-8 mss/year. Query. Length: 200-1,000 words. Pays $10-25. Sometimes pays expenses of writers on assignment.
Photos: State availability of photos with submission. Reviews 8½×11 prints. Offers $2-7.50 per solicited photo. Identification of subjects required. Buys one-time rights.
Columns/Departments: Forum/Viewpoints (observations on recent decisions/events), 750 words maximum; culture (music/art developments), 750 words maximum; scholarships/studies (grants and programs available), 750 words maximum. Buys 6 mss/year. Query. Pays $10-25.
Fillers: Anecdotes, facts, gags to be illustrated by cartoonist, newsbreaks, short humor. Buys 10/year. Length: 50-250 words. Pays $2-10.
Tips: "We want articles which encourage people to participate and get involved with Polonia—from investments in Poland to 'how-to' pieces on egg dying. Travel stories will be returned unread. Freelancers who can provide light or humorous copy are most welcome."

SCANDINAVIAN REVIEW, The American-Scandinavian Foundation, 725 Park Ave., New York NY 10021. (212)879-9779. Fax: (212)249-3444. Editor: Adrienne Gynongy. 75% freelance written. Triannual magazine for contemporary Scandinavia. Audience: members, embassies, consulates, libraries. Slant: popular coverage of contemporary affairs in Scandinavia. Estab. 1913. Circ. 3,500. Pays on publication. Publishes ms 2 months after acceptance. Byline given. Buys first North American serial and second serial (reprint) rights. Editorial lead time 3 months. Submit seasonal material 3 months in advance. Accepts previously published submissions. Query for electronic submissions. Reports in 6 weeks on queries. Sample copy and writer's guidelines free on request.

Nonfiction: General interest, interview/profile, photo feature, travel (must have Scandinavia as topic focus). Special issue on Scandinavian travel. *No pornography.* Buys 30 mss/year. Query with published clips. Length: 1,500-2,000 words. Pays $300 max. Pays contributor's copies (at writer's request).

Photos: State availability of photos with submission or send photos with submission. Reviews 3×5 transparencies or 3×5 prints. Pays $25-50/photo; negotiates payment individually. Captions required. Buys one-time rights.

THE UKRAINIAN WEEKLY, Ukrainian National Association, 30 Montgomery St., Jersey City NJ 07302-3821. (201)434-0237. Editor-in-Chief: Roma Hadzewycz. 30% freelance written (mostly by a corps of regular contributors). Weekly tabloid covering news and issues of concern to Ukrainian community, primarily in North America but also around the world, and events in Ukraine. "We have a news bureau in Kyyiv, capital of Ukraine." Estab. 1933. Circ. 11,000. Pays on publication. Publishes ms an average of 1-2 months after acceptance. Byline given. Buys first North American serial and second serial (reprint) rights or makes work-for-hire assignments. Submit seasonal/holiday material 1 month in advance. Accepts previously published material. Send typed ms with rights for sale noted and information about when and where the article previously appeared. Pays 25-50% of amount paid for an original article. Reports in 1 month. Free sample copy for 9×12 SAE with 3 first-class stamps.

Nonfiction: Book excerpts, essays, exposé, general interest, historical/nostalgic, interview/profile, opinion, personal experience, photo feature, news events. Special issues: Easter, Christmas, anniversary of Ukraine's independence (August 24, 1991) (proclamation) and December 1, 1991 (referendum), student scholarships, anniversary of Chornobyl nuclear accident and year-end review of news. Buys 80 mss/year. Query with published clips. Length: 500-2,000 words. Pays $45-100 for assigned articles. Pays $25-100 for unsolicited articles. Sometimes pays the expenses of writers on assignment.

Photos: Send photos with submission. Reviews contact sheets, negatives and 3×5, 5×7 or 8×10 prints. Offers no additional payment for photos accepted with ms.

Columns/Departments: News & Views (commentary on news events), 500-1,000 words. Buys 10 mss/year. Query. Pays $25-50.

Tips: "Become acquainted with the Ukrainian community in the US and Canada. The area of our publication most open to freelancers is community news—coverage of local events. We'll put more emphasis on events in Ukraine now that it has re-established its independence."

VISTA, The Hispanic Magazine (Florida), Suite 600, 999 Ponce de Leon Blvd., Coral Gables FL 33134. (305)442-2462. Fax: (305)443-7650. Regional Editor: Carmen Teresa Roiz. 95% freelance written. Prefers to work with published/established writers. An English-language monthly directed at Hispanic Americans. Appears as a supplement to 38 newspapers across the country with a combined circulation of 1.1 million in cities with large Latin populations. Estab. 1985. Pays on publication. Publishes ms an average of 4 months after acceptance. Byline given. Offers 25% kill fee. Buys first rights. Submit seasonal/holiday material 6 months in advance. Reports in 2 weeks on queries; 1 month on mss. Sample copy and writer's guidelines for 3 first-class stamps.

Nonfiction: General interest, historical, inspirational, interview/profile, opinion, travel. No articles without a Hispanic-American angle. Buys 90 mss/year. Query with published clips. Length: 100-1,500 words. Pays $50-500. Sometimes pays the expenses of writers on assignment.

Photos: State availability of photos with submission. Reviews contact sheets, negatives, transparencies and prints. Negotiates payment. Identification of subjects required. Buys one-time rights.

Columns/Departments: Vistascopes and Newsnotes (Hispanic people in the news), 250 words; Voices (personal views on matters affecting Hispanic Americans), 500 words. Buys 48 mss/year. Query with published clips. Length: 100-750 words. Pays $50-200.

Tips: "Be aware of topics and personalities of interest to Hispanic readers. We need profiles of Hispanic Americans in unusual or atypical roles and jobs. Anticipate events; profiles should tell the reader what the subject will be doing at the time of publication. Keep topics upbeat and positive: no stories on drugs, crimes. A light, breezy touch is needed for the profiles. Express your opinion in the Voices pages but be scrupulously impartial and accurate when writing articles of general interest."

Food and Drink

Magazines appealing to gourmets, health-conscious consumers and vegetarians are classified here. Journals aimed at food processing, manufacturing and retailing are in the Trade section. Many magazines in General Interest and Women's categories also buy articles on food topics.

BEST RECIPES MAGAZINE, Stauffer Magazine Group, 1503 SW 42nd St., Topeka KS 66609-1265. (913)274-4300. Editor-in-Chief: Roberta J. Peterson. 20% freelance written. Bimonthly magazine with emphasis on recipes from a middle America perspective — *not* a high-income lifestyle or exotic cooking publication. Estab. 1987. Circ. 250,000. Pays on publication. Publishes average of 6 months after acceptance. Byline given. Buys first rights or makes work-for-hire assignments. Occasionally buys reprint rights if first publication was to extremely local or regional audience. Send tearsheet of article or typed ms with rights for sale noted and information about when and where the article previously appeared. For reprints pays 60% of the amount paid for an original article. Submit seasonal material one year in advance. Reports in 4 months on queries. Sample copy and writer's guidelines for $2.75 and 11 × 14 SAE with 5 first-class stamps.

Nonfiction: *Best Recipes* seeks articles about creative, interesting or famous people who cook or practical cooking advice, such as healthful ways to update grandma's recipes or adapting home cooking to the microwave. Top quality, professional color photography enhances acceptability of articles. Black and white line drawings also desirable for some stories, such as how-tos. Buys 8-10 mss a year. Length 800 words maximum. Pays $75 to $200 for unsolicited articles.

Tips: Do not send anything not related to foods, recipes, cooking tips. ALL stories (even tips, how-tos) should include practical, tested recipes.

BON APPETIT, America's Food and Entertaining Magazine, Condé Nast Publications, Inc., 6300 Wilshire Blvd., Los Angeles CA 90048. (213)965-3600. Fax: (213)937-1206. Executive Editor: Barbara Fairchild. Editor-in-Chief: William J. Garry. 10% freelance written. Monthly magazine that covers fine food, restaurants and home entertaining. "*Bon Appetit* readers are upscale food enthusiasts and sophisticated travelers. They eat out often and entertain four to six times a month." Estab. 1975. Circ. 1,331,853. **Pays on acceptance**. Byline given. Negotiates rights. Submit seasonal/holiday material 1 year in advance. No simultaneous or previously published submissions. Reports in 6 weeks on queries. Writer's guidelines for #10 SASE.

Nonfiction: Travel (restaurant or food-related), food feature, dessert feature. "No cartoons, quizzes, poetry, historic food features or obscure food subjects." Buys 45 mss/year. Query with published clips. Length: 750-2,000 words. Pays $500-1,800. Sometimes pays expenses of writers on assignment.

Photos: Never send photos.

Tips: "We are most interested in receiving travel or restaurant stories from freelancers. They must have a good knowledge of food (as shown in accompanying clips) and a light, lively style with humor. Nothing long and pedantic please."

CHILE PEPPER, The Magazine of Spicy Foods, Out West Publishing Company, 5106 Grand NE, P.O. Box 80780, Albuquerque NM 87198-0780. (505)266-8322. Fax: (505)266-2127. Associate Editor: Melissa Stock. 25-30% freelance written. Bimonthly magazine on spicy foods. "The magazine is devoted to spicy foods, and most articles include recipes. We have a very devoted readership who love their food hot!" Estab. 1986. Circ. 80,000. Pays on publication. Offers 50% kill fee. Buys first and second rights. Submit seasonal/holiday material 6 months in advance. Accepts previously published submissions. Send tearsheet or photocopy of article and information about when and where the article previously appeared. For reprints pays 25% of the amount paid for an original article. Query for electronic submissions. Reports in 2 months. Sample copy for 9 × 12 SAE with 5 first-class stamps. Writer's guidelines for #10 SASE.

Nonfiction: Book excerpts (cookbooks), how-to (cooking and gardening with spicy foods), humor (having to do with spicy foods), new product (hot products), travel (having to do with spicy foods). Buys 20 mss/year. Query. Length: 1,000-3,000 words. Pays $150 minimum for assigned articles; $100 for unsolicited articles. Sometimes pays expenses of writers on assignment.

Photos: State availability of photos with submission. Reviews contact sheets, negatives, transparencies and prints. Offers $25 minimum/photo. Captions and identification of subjects required. Buys one-time rights.

Tips: "We're always interested in queries from *food* writers. Articles about spicy foods with six to eight recipes are just right. No fillers. Need exotic location travel/food pieces."

COOKING LIGHT, The Magazine of Food and Fitness, Southern Living, Inc. P.O. Box 1748, Birmingham AL 35201-1681. (205)877-6000. Executive Editor: Deborah Lowery. Editor: Douglas Crichton. Managing Editor: Nathalie Dearing. 75% freelance written. Bimonthly magazine on healthy recipes and fitness information. "*Cooking Light* is a positive approach to a healthier lifestyle. It's written for healthy people on regular diets who are counting calories or trying to make calories count toward better nutrition. Moderation, balance and variety are emphasized. The writing style is fresh, upbeat and encouraging, emphasizing that eating a balanced, varied, lower-calorie diet and exercising regularly do not have to be boring." Estab. 1987. Circ. 1.1 million. **Pays on acceptance**. Publishes ms an average of 1 year after acceptance. Byline sometimes given. Offers 25% of original contract fee as kill fee. Submit seasonal/holiday material 1 year in advance. Reports in 1 year.

For information on setting your freelance fees, see How Much Should I Charge?

• Ranked as one of the best markets for freelance writers in *Writer's Digest* magazine's annual "Top 100 Markets," January 1994.

Nonfiction: Personal experience on nutrition, healthy recipes, fitness/exercise. Back up material a must. Buys 150 mss/year. Query with published clips. Length: 400-2,000 words. Pays $250-2,000 for assigned articles. Pays expenses of writers on assignment.

Columns/Departments: Try On a Sport (introducing readers to new sports as well as new ways to view old sports), 1,000 words; Indulgences (focuses on vanity, body care and healthy indulgences, such as masks, bath oils, skin and nail care tips), 1,000 words; Attitudes (on the human mind at work; psychology, changing attitudes, trends and other issues involving the mind), 1,000 words; Health Matters (focuses on wide range of health issues), 1,000 words; I Did It (about how a reader overcame an obstacle and rewarded herself), 1,000 words; Walk Talk (ways to make the most of our readers' number one exercise), 1,000 words; Profile (of persons who exhibit an exemplary healthy lifestyle. These can be celebrities or unknown people with a message.) 1,000 words; Food for Thought (collection of food-related articles on the following topics—mini profile on a chef, restaurant and eating-out trends, food products and equipment, cooking tips and diet concerns) 250-350 words, short, 400-500 words, long. Buys 30 mss/year. Query. Pays $50-2,000.

Tips: "Emphasis should be on achieving a healthier lifestyle through food, nutrition, fitness, exercise information. In submitting queries, include information on professional background. Food writers should include examples of healthy recipes which meet the guidelines of *Cooking Light*."

EATING WELL, The Magazine of Food and Health, Telemedia Communications (US) Inc., P.O. Box 1001, Charlotte VT 05445-1001. (802)425-3961. Fax: (802)425-3307. Editor: Scott Mowbray. Food Editor: Susan Stuck. 90% freelance written. Bimonthly magazine covering food, health. Estab. 1989. Circ. 525,000. Pays 45 days after acceptance. Publishes ms an average of 6 months after acceptance. Byline given. Offers 25% kill fee. Buys first North American serial and second serial (reprint) rights. Submit seasonal/holiday material 1 year in advance. Reports in 2 months.

Nonfiction: Scott Mowbray. Book excerpts, nutrition, cooking, interview/profile, food, travel. Query with published clips. Length: 2,000-4,000 words. Pays $1,500-3,500. Pays expenses of writers on assignment.

Photos: State availability of photos with submission. Reviews transparencies. Offers $50-250/photo. Captions and identification of subjects required. Buys one-time rights.

Columns/Departments: Mary Hegarty. Nutrition Report (timely nutrition research news), 150-400 words; and Observer (current news in the food world), 150-400 words. Buys 60 mss/year. Query. Pays $200-300.

Tips: "We invite experienced, published science writers to do a broad range of in-depth, innovative food-health-nutrition features. Read the magazine first."

‡FINE COOKING, The Taunton Press, P.O. Box 5506, 63 S. Main St., Newtown CT 06470. (203)426-8171. Editor: Jan Wahlin. Contact: Martha Holmberg. Bimonthly magazine focusing exclusively on cooking. "*Fine Cooking* is a magazine for people who are passionate about the craft of cooking. Most readers are avid home cooks, though many are professionals. Our writers are not necessarily professional writers. It is more important to us that they are experienced cooks with first-hand knowledge and information to share." Estab. 1993. Circ. 85,000. Pays on publication. Byline given. Offers $150 kill fee or page rate. Buys one-time rights. Editorial lead time 6-9 months. Submit seasonal material 9 months in advance. Query for electronic submissions. Reports in 6 weeks on queries. Sample copy for $4.95. Writer's guidelines free on request.

Nonfiction: How-to, humor, personal experience. Buys approximately 40 mss/year. Query. Pay varies. Sometimes pays expenses of writers on assignment.

Columns/Departments: Suzanne Roman. Tidbits (humor), 600-700 words; Tips (shortcuts), 100 words; Basics (techniques), 400-600 words. Query. Pays $25-50.

Tips: "Our entire magazine is written by experienced cooks—articles, Q&A, Tips, Flavorings, Basics, Tidbits and Food Science. We welcome submissions in all these areas. Unless you have first-hand experience, we're not the right magazine for you."

FOOD & WINE, American Express Publishing Corp., 1120 Avenue of the Americas, New York NY 10036. (212)382-5618. Editor: Mary Simons. Managing Editor: Mary Ellen Ward. Monthly magazine for "active people for whom eating, drinking, entertaining, dining out, travel and all the related equipment and trappings are central to their lifestyle." Estab. 1978. Circ. 725,000. **Pays on acceptance.** Byline given. Offers 25% kill fee. Buys first world rights. Submit seasonal/holiday material 9 months in advance. Query for electronic submissions. Reports in 3 weeks on queries; 2 weeks on mss. Sample copy for $5. Writer's guidelines for #10 SASE.

• Ranked as one of the best markets for freelance writers in *Writer's Digest* magazine's annual "Top 100 Markets," January 1994.

Nonfiction: Essays, how-to, humor, kitchen and dining room design, travel. Query with published clips. Buys 125 mss/year. Length: 1,000-3,000 words. Pays $800-2,000. Pays expenses of writers on assignment.

Photos: State availability of photos with submission. No unsolicited photos or art. Offers $100-450 page rate per photo. Model releases and identification of subjects required. Buys one-time rights.

Columns/Departments: What's Up, Dining Out, The Hungry Traveler, Cooking Wisdom, Setting the Scene, Low-fat Cooking, Dinner for a Busy Weeknight, Wines & Spirits, Food & Health. Buys 120 mss/year. Query with published clips. Length: 800-3,000 words. Pays $800-2,000.
Tips: "Good service, good writing, up-to-date information, interesting article approach and appropriate point of view for *F&W*'s audience are important elements to keep in mind. Look over several recent issues before writing query."

GOURMET, 560 Lexington Ave., New York NY 10022. Monthly publication covering cooking, entertaining, travel and culture. This magazine did not respond to our request for information. Query before submitting.

KASHRUS MAGAZINE, The Bimonthly for the Kosher Consumer and the Trade, Yeshiva Birkas Reuven, P.O. Box 204, Parkville Station, Brooklyn NY 11204. (718)336-8544. Editor: Rabbi Yosef Wikler. 25% freelance written. Prefers to work with published/established writers, but will work with new/unpublished writers. Bimonthly magazine covering kosher food industry and food production. Estab. 1980. Circ. 10,000. Pays on publication. Publishes ms an average of 2 months after acceptance. Byline given. Offers 50% kill fee. Buys first or second serial (reprint) rights. Submit seasonal/holiday material 2 months in advance. Simultaneous and previously published submissions OK. Prefers submissions in major word processing programs on disk with accompanying hard copy. Reports in 1 week on queries; 2 weeks on mss. *Writer's Market* recommends allowing 2 months for reply. Sample copy for $2. Professional discount on subscription: $15/10 issues (regularly $27).
Nonfiction: General interest, interview/profile, new product, personal experience, photo feature, religious, technical and travel. Special issues feature; International Kosher Travel (October) and Passover (March). Buys 8-12 mss/year. Query with published clips. Length: 1,000-1,500 words. Pays $100-250 for assigned articles; pays up to $100 for unsolicited articles. Sometimes pays the expenses of writers on assignment. Reprints OK; send tearsheet or photocopy of article. Pays 25% of their fee for an original article.
Photos: State availability of photos with submission. Offers no additional payment for photos accepted with ms. Buys one-time rights.
Columns/Departments: Book Review (cook books, food technology, kosher food), 250-500 words; People in the News (interviews with kosher personalities), 1,000-1,500 words; Regional Kosher Supervision (report on kosher supervision in a city or community), 1,000-1,500 words; Food Technology (new technology or current technology with accompanying pictures), 1,000-1,500 words; Travel (international, national), must include Kosher information and Jewish communities, 1,000-1,500 words; and Regional Kosher Cooking, 1,000-1,500 words.Buys 8-12 mss/year. Query with published clips. Pays $50-250.
Tips: "*Kashrus Magazine* will do more writing on general food technology, production, and merchandising as well as human interest travelogs and regional writing in 1995 than we have done in the past. Areas most open to freelancers are interviews, food technology, regional reporting and travel. We welcome stories on the availability and quality of Kosher foods and services in communities across the US and throughout the world. Some of our best stories have been by non-Jewish writers about kosher observance in their region."

‡QUICK 'N EASY COUNTRY COOKIN', Parkside Publications Inc., P.O. Box 66, Davis SD 57021. (605)238-5704. Editor: Pam Schrag. 75% freelance written. Bimonthly magazine covering cooking and daily life. Estab. 1986. Circ. 43,000. Pays on publication. Byline given. Buys one-time rights. Editorial lead time 4 months. Submit seasonal material 4-5 months in advance. Accepts simultaneous submissions. Sample copy and writer's guidelines free on request.
Nonfiction: General interest, humor, inspirational, interview/profile, personal experience, photo feature, religious. Buys 80 mss/year. Send complete ms. Length: 300-500 words. Pays $10.
Photos: Send photos with submission. Reviews negatives and 4×5 prints. Offers no additional payment for photos accepted with ms. Buys one-time rights.
Columns/Departments: Cooks of the month (background on person and recipes), 200 words with photo; Food for Thought (a nondenominational spiritual message), 200-300 words. Buys 40 mss/year. Send complete ms. Pays $5-10.
Fiction: Humorous, religious. Buys 20 mss/year. Send complete ms. Length: 100-400 words. Pays $10.
Poetry: All types. Buys 10 poems/year. Length: 5-30 lines. Pays $5.
Fillers: Anecdotes, facts, short humor. Buys 10/year. Length: 50-150 words. Pays $5-10.
Tips: "We enjoy articles of all varieties from a humorous event with a vacuum cleaner or a garden on the balcony. Other articles on people that collect unique items or restoring items. Mainly we enjoy articles with real down-to-earth humor or information. Our publication is very seasonal and we will hold article for a year for consideration before we return or contact writer on a scheduled time slot."

VEGETARIAN GOURMET, Chitra Publications, 2 Public Ave., Montrose PA 18801. (717)278-1984. Editor: Jessica Dubey. 75% freelance written. Quarterly magazine on seasonal vegetarian cooking with additional low-fat issue. "An entertaining and practical how-to guide to cooking food that is delicious and healthful." Estab. 1991. Circ. 75,000. Pays on publication. Publishes ms an average of 1-3 months after acceptance. Byline given. Kill fee offered "depends on price ordinarily paid for accepted ms." Buys one-time rights and second serial (reprint) rights. Submit seasonal material 5-6 months in advance. Query for electronic submissions. Reports in 3 weeks on queries; 6 weeks on mss. Sample copy free on request. Writer's guidelines for #10 SASE.

Nonfiction: How-to (cooking), book and restaurant reviews. "No previously published or non-vegetarian material; no articles not directly related to food or cooking." Buys approximately 40 mss/year. Send complete ms. Length: 400-1,000 words. Pays $175-250. Sometimes pays expenses of writers on assignment.

Photos: Send photos with submission. Reviews 2 1/4 transparencies. Offers $25-50/photo. Captions required. Buys one-time rights.

Columns/Departments: International fare (vegetarian cuisine of a foreign country), 800 words; desserts (vegetarian dessert made with natural sweeteners), 800 words; extraordinary vegetables (introduce one or more less familiar vegetables), 800 words; entertainment (unique ways of entertaining with vegetarian food), 800 words; VG visits (profile of a vegetarian restaurant), 500-700 words; cook for kids (fun ideas for vegetarian meals for kids), 400-600 words; fast foods (dishes that can be made quickly with a particular food), 400-500 words. Buys 40 mss/year. Send complete ms. Pays $75-250.

Tips: "Submit a completed ms along with recipe blurbs, photos (if available) and information on less familiar ingredients (what they are and how to obtain them). Include useful cooking tips and nutritional value of food(s) you are writing about. All departments open to freelance."

WINE SPECTATOR, M. Shanken Communications, Inc., 387 Park Ave. S., New York NY 10016. (212)684-4224. Fax: (212)684-5424. Managing Editor: Jim Gordon. 20% freelance written. Prefers to work with published/established writers. Biweekly consumer news magazine covering wine. Estab. 1976. Circ. 120,000. Pays within 30 days of publication. Publishes ms an average of 2 months after acceptance. Byline given. Buys all rights and makes work-for-hire assignments. Submit seasonal/holiday material 4 months in advance. Query for electronic submissions. Reports in 3 months. Sample copy for $2.50. Free writer's guidelines.

Nonfiction: General interest (news about wine or wine events); interview/profile (of wine, vintners, wineries); opinion; travel, dining and other lifestyle pieces; photo feature. No "winery promotional pieces or articles by writers who lack sufficient knowledge to write below just surface data." Query. Length: 100-2,000 words average. Pays $50-500.

Photos: Send photos with ms. Pays $75 minimum for color transparencies. Captions, model releases and identification of subjects required. Buys all rights.

Tips: "A solid knowledge of wine is a must. Query letters essential, detailing the story idea. New, refreshing ideas which have not been covered before stand a good chance of acceptance. *Wine Spectator* is a consumer-oriented *news magazine*, but we are interested in some trade stories; brevity is essential."

Games and Puzzles

These publications are written by and for game enthusiasts interested in both traditional games and word puzzles and newer role-playing adventure, computer and video games. Additional home video game publications are listed in the Entertainment section. Other puzzle markets may be found in the Juvenile section.

bePUZZLED, Mystery Jigsaw Puzzles, 22 E. Newberry Rd., Bloomfield CT 06002. (203)769-5700. President: Mary Ann Lombard. Creative Director: Richard DeZinno. 100% freelance written. Mystery jigsaw puzzle using short mystery stories published 2-4 times/year. Covers mystery, suspense, adventure for children and adults. Estab. 1987. Pays on completion. Publishes ms an average of 9 months after acceptance. Byline given (sometimes pen name required). Buys all rights. Submit seasonal/holiday material 9 months in advance. Accepts simultaneous submissions. Reports in 2 weeks on queries; 3 months on mss. Free writer's guidelines with SASE.

Fiction: Adventure, humorous, mainstream, mystery, suspense (*exact* subject within genre above is released to writers as available.) Buys 10 mss/year. Query. Length: 3,500-5,500 words. Pays $250-2,000.

Fillers: "Writers must follow submission format as outlined in writer's guidelines. We incorporate short mystery stories and jigsaw puzzles into a game where the clues to solve the mystery are cleverly hidden in both the short story and the puzzle picture. Writer must be able to integrate the clues in the written piece to these to appear in puzzle picture. Playing one of our games helps to clarify how we like to 'marry' the story clues and the visual clues in the puzzle."

CHESS LIFE, United States Chess Federation, 186 Route 9W, New Windsor NY 12553-7698. (914)562-8350. Fax: (914)561-2437. Editor: Glenn Petersen. 15% freelance written. Works with a small number of new/unpublished writers each year. Monthly magazine covering the chess world. Estab. 1939. Circ. 70,000. Pays variable fee. Publishes ms an average of 5 months after acceptance. Byline given. Offers kill fee. Buys first or negotiable rights. Submit seasonal/holiday material 8 months in advance. Accepts simultaneous and previously published submissions. Send typed ms with rights for sale noted and information about when and where the article previously appeared.

Reports in 3 months. Sample copy and writer's guidelines for 9×11 SAE with 5 first-class stamps.

Nonfiction: General interest, historical, interview/profile, technical—all must have some relation to chess. No "stories about personal experiences with chess." Buys 30-40 mss/year. Query with samples "if new to publication." Length: 3,000 words maximum. Sometimes pays the expenses of writers on assignment.
Photos: Reviews b&w contact sheets and prints, and color prints and slides. Captions, model releases and identification of subjects required. Buys all or negotiable rights.
Fiction: "Chess-related, high quality." Buys 2-3 mss/year. Pays variable fee.
Tips: "Articles must be written from an informed point of view—not from view of the curious amateur. Most of our writers are specialized in that they have sound credentials as chessplayers. Freelancers in major population areas (except New York and Los Angeles, which we already have covered) who are interested in short personality profiles and perhaps news reporting have the best opportunities. We're looking for more personality pieces on chessplayers around the country; not just the stars, but local masters, talented youths, and dedicated volunteers. Freelancers interested in such pieces might let us know of their interest and their range. Could be we know of an interesting story in their territory that needs covering."

COMPUTER GAMING WORLD, The Premier Computer Game Magazine, Golden Empire Publications, Inc., #260, 130 Chaparral Court, Anaheim CA 92808-2238. (714)283-3000. Fax: (714)283-3444. Editor: Chris Lombardi. 75% freelance written. Works with a small number of new/unpublished writers each year. Monthly magazine covering computer games. "*CGW* is read by an adult audience looking for detailed reviews and information on strategy, adventure and action games." Estab. 1981. Circ. 105,000. Pays on publication. Publishes ms an average of 3 months after acceptance. Byline given. Buys first rights. Submit seasonal/holiday material 4 months in advance. Electronic submissions preferred, but not required. Query first. Reports in 4 months. Sample copy for $3.50. Free writer's guidelines.
Nonfiction: Reviews, strategy tips, industry insights. Buys 60 mss/year. Query. Length: 750-2,000 words. Pays $.10 per word. Sometimes pays the expenses of writers on assignment.

DRAGON MAGAZINE, TSR, Inc., P.O. Box 111, 201 Sheridan Springs Rd., Lake Geneva WI 53147-0111. (414)248-3625. Fax: (414)248-0389. Editor: Dale Donovan. Monthly magazine of fantasy and science-fiction role-playing games. 90% freelance written. Eager to work with published/established writers as well as new/unpublished writers. "Most of our readers are intelligent, imaginative teenage males." Estab. 1976. Circ. about 100,000, primarily across the US, Canada and Great Britain. Byline given. Offers kill fee. Submit seasonal/holiday material 8 months in advance. Pays on publication for articles to which all rights are purchased; pays on acceptance for articles to which first/worldwide rights in English are purchased. Publishing dates vary from 1-24 months after acceptance. Reports in 3 months. Sample copy $4.50. Writer's guidelines for #10 SAE with 1 first-class stamp.
Nonfiction: Articles on the hobby of science fiction and fantasy role-playing. No general articles on gaming hobby. "Our article needs are *very* specialized. Writers should be experienced in gaming hobby and role-playing. No strong sexual overtones or graphic depictions of violence." Buys 120 mss/year. Query. Length: 1,000-8,000 words. Pays $50-500 for assigned articles; $5-400 for unsolicited articles.
Fiction: Barbara G. Young, fiction editor. Fantasy only."No strong sexual overtones or graphic depictions of violence." Buys 12 mss/year. Send complete ms. Length: 2,000-8,000 words. Pays 6-8¢/word.
Tips: "*Dragon Magazine* is *not* a periodical that the 'average reader' appreciates or understands. A writer must *be* a reader and must share the serious interest in gaming our readers possess."

GAME INFORMER MAGAZINE, for Video Game Enthusiasts, Sunrise Publications, 10120 West 76th St., Eden Prairie MN 55344. (612)946-7245. Editor: Andy McNamara. 10% freelance written. Bimonthly magazine for video game industry. Estab. 1991. Circ. 200,000. Pays on publication. Publishes ms an average of 3 months after acceptance. Byline given. Offers 50% kill fee. Buys first and one-time rights. Editorial lead time 3 months. Submit seasonal material 3-4 months in advance. Accepts simultaneous submissions. Query for electronic submissions. Sample copy and writer's guidelines free on request.
Nonfiction: Essays, general interest, historical/nostalgic, how-to, interview/profile, new product, opinion, technical, game strategies. Publishes year-end tip and strategy guide (deadline mid-October). No game reviews. Buys 4 mss/year. Query with published clips. Length: 500-2,000 words. Pays $50 for assigned articles.
Photos: State availability of photos with submission. Reviews 2×2 transparencies and 3×5 prints. Negotiates payment individually. Identification of subjects required. Buys one-time rights.
Columns/Departments: Query. Pays $25-150.
Fillers: Facts, gags to be illustrated by cartoonist, newsbreaks. Buys 6/year. Length negotiable. Pay negotiable.
Tips: "We appreciate queries prior to manuscript submissions, as we prefer to assign articles or discuss them first. It is best to call with one or two story ideas in mind. We are a very topic-specific publication and look for writers with expertise in a given area. However, the writing style must be open and appeal to a broad age range. We often look for special interest or focus articles on a given aspect of the very dynamic industry that we cover. Technical hardware features or company profiles are also welcome."

GIANT CROSSWORDS, Scrambl-Gram, Inc., Puzzle Buffs International, 1772 State Rd., Cuyahoga Falls OH 44223-1200. (216)923-2397. Editor: C.R. Elum. Submissions Editor: W. Bowers. 40% freelance written. Eager to work with new/unpublished writers. Quarterly crossword puzzle and word game magazine. Estab. 1970.

Pays on acceptance. Publishes ms an average of 1 month after acceptance. No byline given. Buys all rights. Simultaneous queries OK. Accepts previously published materials. Send information about when and where the article previously appeared. Reports in 1 month. "We offer constructors' kits, master grids, clue sheets and a 'how-to-make-crosswords' book for $37.50 postpaid." Send #10 SASE for details.

Nonfiction: Crosswords and word games only. Query. Pays according to size of puzzle and/or clues.

Tips: "We are expanding our syndication of original crosswords and our publishing schedule to include new titles and extra issues of current puzzle books."

SCHOOL MATES, United States Chess Federation, 186 Rte. 9W, New Windsor NY 12553-5794. (914)562-8350 ext. 152. Fax: (914)561-CHES (2437). Editor: Carl Simmons. Contact: Cheryl Lemire, Assistant Editor. 10% freelance written. Bimonthly magazine of chess for the beginning (some intermediate) player. Includes instruction, player profiles, chess tournament coverage, listings. Estab. 1987. Circ. 21,009. Pays on publication. Publishes ms an average of 6 months after acceptance. Byline given. Publication copyrighted "but not filed with Library of Congress." Buys first rights. Editorial lead time 2 months. Submit seasonal material 2-3 months in advance. Accepts simultaneous and previously published submissions. Send tearsheet or photocopy of article or typed ms with rights for sale noted and information about when and where the article previously appeared. For reprints pays 100% of the amount paid for an original article. Query for electronic submissions. Reports in "anywhere from 1 week to 6 months." Sample copy and writer's guidelines free on request.

Nonfiction: How-to, humor, personal experience (chess, but not "my first tournament"), photo feature, technical, travel and any other chess related item. "No poetry; no fiction; no sex, drugs, rock 'n roll." Buys 1-2 mss/year. Query. Length: 250-1,000 words. Pays $40/1,000 words. "We are not-for-profit; we try to make up for low $ rate with complimentary copies." Sometimes pays expenses of writers on assignment.

Photos: Send photos with submission. Reviews prints. Offers $25/photo for first time rights. Captions and identification of subjects required. Buys one-time rights, pays $15 for subsequent use.

Columns/Departments: Test Your Tactics/Winning Chess Tactics (explanation, with diagrams, of chess tactics; 8 diagrammed chess problems, e.g. "white to play and win in 2 moves"), 270 words; Basic Chess (chess instruction for beginners). Query with published clips. Pays $40/1,000 words.

Tips: "Know your subject; chess is a technical subject, and you can't fake it. Human interest stories on famous chess players or young chess players can be 'softer,' but always remember you are writing for children, and make it lively. We use the Frye readability scale (3rd-6th grade reading level), and items written on the appropriate reading level do stand out immediately! We are most open to human interest stories, puzzles, cartoons, photos. We are always looking for an unusual angle, e.g. (wild example) a kid who plays chess while surfing, or (more likely) a blind kid and how she plays chess with her specially-made chess pieces and board, etc."

General Interest

General interest magazines need writers who can appeal to a broad audience—teens and senior citizens, wealthy readers and the unemployed. Each magazine still has a personality that suits its audience—one that a writer should study before sending material to an editor. Other markets for general interest material are in these Consumer categories: Ethnic/Minority, Inflight, Men's, Regional and Women's. General interest magazines that are geared toward a specific group (such as doctors) are listed in Trade in their respective sections.

THE AMERICAN LEGION MAGAZINE, P.O. Box 1055, Indianapolis IN 46206-1055. (317)635-8411. Editor: John Greenwald. Monthly. 95% freelance written. Prefers to work with published/established writers, but works with a small number of new/unpublished writers each year. Estab. 1919. Circ. 2.9 million. Buys first North American serial rights. Reports on submissions "promptly." **Pays on acceptance.** Publishes ms an average of 6 months after acceptance. Byline given. Reports in 2 months. Sample copy for 9×12 SAE with 6 first-class stamps. Writer's guidelines for #10 SASE.

• Ranked as one of the best markets for freelance writers in *Writer's Digest* magazine's annual "Top 100 Markets," January 1994.

Nonfiction: Query first, considers some unsolicited ms. Query should explain the subject or issue, article's angle and organization, writer's qualifications and experts to be interviewed. Well-reported articles or expert commentaries cover issues/trends in world/national affairs, contemporary problems, general interest, sharply-focused feature subjects. Monthly Q&A with national figures/experts. Few personality profiles. No regional topics. Buys 75 mss/year. Length: 1,000-2,000 words. Pays $600-2,000. Pays phone expenses of writers on assignment.

Photos: On assignment.

Tips: "Queries by new writers should include clips/background/expertise; no longer than 1½ pages. Submit suitable material showing you have read several issues. *The American Legion Magazine* considers itself '*the* magazine for a strong America.' Reflect this theme (which includes economy, educational system, moral fiber, social issues, infrastructure, technology and national defense/security). We are a general interest, national magazine, not a strictly military magazine. No unsolicited jokes."

THE AMERICAN SCHOLAR, The Phi Beta Kappa Society, 1811 Q Street NW, Washington DC 20009-9974. (202)265-3808. Editor: Joseph Epstein. Managing Editor: Jean Stipicevic. 100% freelance written. Intellectual quarterly. "Our writers are specialists writing for the college-educated public." Estab. 1932. Circ. 26,000. Pays after author has seen edited piece in galleys. Byline given. Offers 50% kill fee. Buys first rights. Submit seasonal/holiday material 6 months in advance. Reports in 2 weeks on queries; 2 months on ms. Sample copy for $6.50. Writer's guidelines for #10 SASE.
Nonfiction: Book excerpts (prior to publication only), essays, historical/nostalgic, humor. Buys 40 mss/year. Query. Length: 3,000-5,000 words. Pays $500.
Columns/Departments: Buys 16 mss/year. Query. Length: 3,000-5,000 words. Pays $500.
Poetry: Sandra Costich, poetry editor. Buys 20/year. Submit maximum 3 poems. Length: 34-75 lines. Pays $50. "Write for guidelines."
Tips: "The section most open to freelancers is the book review section. Query and send samples of reviews written."

‡AMERICAN TIMES/PRIME TIMES, For The Ways We Live, Grote Publishing, Suite 207, 634 W. Main St., Madison WI 53703-2697. Editor: Barbara Walsh. 30% freelance written. Quarterly association-sponsored publication for financial institutions. "*American Times* is a topical magazine of broad appeal, available to the general public but mainly distributed to older adult club members of financial institutions. It offers investigative reporting, interviews, and timely articles on health, finance, travel, outdoor sports, consumer issues, lifestyle, home arts, science, and technology, specializing in articles that are quintessentially 'American' in flavor." Estab. 1979 (*Prime Times*), 1993 (*American Times*). Circ. 120,000. Pays on publication. Publishes an average of 3-7 months after acceptance. Byline given. Buys first North American serial rights, one-time rights (photos) and second serial (reprint) rights. Editorial lead time 7 months. Submit seasonal material 7 months in advance. Query for electronic submissions. Reports in 6 weeks on queries; 2 months on mss. Sample copy for $4, and 9×12 SAE with 5 first-class stamps. Writer's guidelines for #10 SASE.
Nonfiction: Book excerpts, general interest, historical, humor, interview/profile, new product, photo feature, travel. "No nostalgia pieces, medical or financial pieces based solely on personal anecdotes, or personal opinion essays." Buys 4-10 mss/year. Prefers to see complete ms. Length: 1,200-2,000 words. Pays $250 minimum for full-length assigned articles; $100 minimum for unsolicited articles.
Photos: State availability of or send photos with submission. Reviews contact sheets, transparencies and prints. Negotiates payment individually. Model releases and identification of subjects required. Buys one-time rights.
Tips: "Articles that contain useful, well-documented, up-to-date information have the best chance of publication. Don't send personal essays, or articles that repeat information readily available in mainstream media. Articles on health and medical issues *must* be founded in sound scientific method and include current data. You must be able to document your research. Make it easy for us to make a decision on your submission. If the article is written, submit the entire thing—manuscript with professional-quality photos. If you query, be specific. Write part of it in the style in which you would write the article. Be sure to enclose clips. With every article we publish, something about the story must lend itself to strong graphic representation."

THE ATLANTIC, 745 Boylston St., Boston MA 02116. (617)536-9500. Editor: William Whitworth. Managing Editor: Cullen Murphy. Monthly magazine of arts and public affairs. Circ. 500,000. Pays on acceptance. Byline given. Buys first North American serial rights. Simultaneous submissions discouraged. Reporting time varies. All unsolicited mss must be accompanied by SASE.
• Writers should be aware that this is not a market for beginner's work (nonfiction and fiction), nor is it truly for intermediate work. Study this magazine before sending only your best, most professional work. Ranked as one of the best markets for fiction writers in *Writer's Digest* magazine's biannual "Fiction 50," June 1994.
Nonfiction: Book excerpts, essays, general interest, humor, personal experience, religious, travel. Query with or without published clips or send complete ms. Length: 1,000-6,000 words. Payment varies. Sometimes pays expenses of writers on assignment.
Fiction: C. Michael Curtis, fiction editor. Buys 12-15 mss/year. Send complete ms. Length: 2,000-6,000 words preferred. Payment $2,500.
Poetry: Peter Davison, poetry editor. Buys 40-60 poems/year.

A BETTER LIFE FOR YOU, The National Research Bureau, Inc., P.O. Box 1, Burlington IA 52601-0001. (319)752-5415. Fax: (319)752-3421. Editor: Nancy Heinzel. 75% freelance written. Works with a small number of new/unpublished writers each year. Quarterly magazine. Estab. 1948. Pays on publication. Publishes ms an average of 1 year after acceptance. Buys all rights. Submit seasonal/holiday material 7 months in advance of issue date. Sample copy and writer's guidelines for #10 SAE with 2 first-class stamps.

Nonfiction: General interest (steps to better health, on-the-job attitudes); how-to (perform better on the job, do home repair jobs, and keep up maintenance on a car). Buys 10-12 mss/year. Query or send outline. Length: 500-700 words. Pays 4¢/word.

Tips: "Writers have a better chance of breaking in at our publication with short articles."

CAPPER'S, Stauffer Communications, Inc., 1503 SW 42nd St., Topeka KS 66609-1265. (913)274-4346. Editor: Nancy Peavler. Associate Editor: Cheryl Ptacek. 25% freelance written. Works with a small number of new/ unpublished writers each year. Biweekly tabloid emphasizing home and family for readers who live in small towns and on farms. Estab. 1879. Circ. 375,000. **Pays for poetry on acceptance;** articles on publication. Publishes ms an average of 6 months after acceptance. Buys first serial rights only. Submit seasonal/holiday material at least 2 months in advance. Accepts previously published material. Send typed ms with rights for sale noted and information about when and where the article previously appeared. For reprints pays 100% of the amount paid for an original article. Reports in 3-4 months; 8-10 months for serialized novels. Sample copy for $1. Writer's guidelines for #10 SASE.

Nonfiction: Historical (local museums, etc.), inspirational, nostalgia, travel (local slants), people stories (accomplishments, collections, etc.). Buys 50 mss/year. Submit complete ms. Length: 700 words maximum. Pays $1.50/inch.

Photos: Purchased with accompanying ms. Submit prints. Pays $10-15 for 8×10 or 5×7 b&w glossy prints. Total purchase price for ms includes payment for photos. Limited market for color photos (35mm color slides); pays $35-40 each.

Columns/Departments: Heart of the Home (homemakers' letters, recipes, hints); Hometown Heartbeat (descriptive). Submit complete ms. Length: 300 words maximum. Pays $1-7.

Fiction: "We buy very few fiction pieces—longer than short stories, shorter than novels." Adventure and romance mss. No explicit sex, violence or profanity. Buys 4-5 mss/year. Query. Pays $75-400 for 7,500-60,000 words.

Poetry: Free verse, haiku, light verse, traditional, nature, inspiration. "The poems that appear in *Capper's* are not too difficult to read. They're easy to grasp. We're looking for everyday events and down-to-earth themes." Buys 4-5/issue. Limit submissions to batches of 5-6. Length: 4-16 lines. Pays $5-10.

Tips: "Study a few issues of our publication. Most rejections are for material that is too long, unsuitable or out of character for our paper (too sexy, too much profanity, etc.). On occasion, we must cut material to fit column space."

THE CHRISTIAN SCIENCE MONITOR, 1 Norway St., Boston MA 02115. (617)450-2000. Contact: Submissions. International newspaper issued daily except Saturdays, Sundays and holidays in North America; weekly international edition. Estab. 1908. Circ. 110,000. Buys all newspaper rights worldwide for 3 months following publication. Buys limited number of mss, "top quality only." Publishes original (exclusive) material only. Pays on publication. Reports in 1 month. Submit complete original ms or letter of inquiry. Writer's guidelines for #10 SASE.

Nonfiction: Lawrence J. Goodrich, feature editor. In-depth features and essays. Please query by mail before sending mss. "Style should be bright but not cute, concise but thoroughly researched. Try to humanize news or feature writing so reader identifies with it. Avoid sensationalism, crime and disaster. Accent constructive, solution-oriented treatment of subjects." Home Forum page buys essays of 400-900 words. Pays $150 average. Education, arts, environment, food, science and technology pages will consider articles not usually more than 800 words appropriate to respective subjects. No medical stories." Pays $150-200.

Poetry: Traditional, blank and free verse. Seeks non-religious poetry of high quality and of all lengths up to 75 lines. Pays $35-75 average.

Tips: "We prefer neatly typed originals. No handwritten copy. Enclosing an SAE and postage with ms is a must."

DESTINATION DISCOVERY The Magazine of the Discovery Channel, Discovery Publishing, Inc., 7700 Wisconsin Ave., Bethesda MD 20814. Editor: Rebecca Farwell. Managing Editor: Kathy H. Ely. Contact: Jody Bettencourt. 95% freelance written. Monthly magazine of general interest, inspired by television network. Estab. 1985. Circ. 200,000. **Pays on acceptance.** Byline given. Offers 20% kill fee. Buys first North American serial rights. Editorial lead time 6 months. Accepts simultaneous submissions. Query for electronic submissions. Prefers Microsoft Word or IBM Wordperfect. Reports in 2 months. Sample copy for $2.50. Writer's guidelines free on request.

• Ranked as one of the best markets for freelance writers in *Writer's Digest* magazine's annual "Top 100 Markets," January 1994.

Nonfiction: Literary: essays, general interest, historical/nostalgic, interview/profile, personal experience, photo feature, travel. No poetry, fiction, humor, how-to articles or travelogues. Buys 100+ mss/year. Query with published clips. Length: 400-4,000 words. Pays 25¢/word minimum. "Variable with experience and reporting." Sometimes pays expenses of writers on assignment (limit agreed upon in advance).

Photos: State availability of photos with submission. Reviews contact sheets, negatives, transparencies and prints. Negotiates payment individually. Identification of subjects required. Buys one-time rights.

Columns/Departments: Green Alert (environmental), 900 words; and Eureka! (science discoveries), 900 words. Buys 30+ mss/year. Query with published clips. Pays $500.

Tips: "All areas are open to freelancers, though newcomers usually start in our 'There & Back section, or on one of our columns."

EQUINOX: THE MAGAZINE OF CANADIAN DISCOVERY, Telemedia Communications, Inc., 7 Queen Victoria Rd., Camden East, Ontario K0K 1J0 Canada. (613)378-6661. Editor: Jim Cormier. Associate Editor: Eileen Whitney. Bimonthly magazine "publishing in-depth profiles of people, places and wildlife to show readers the real stories behind subjects of general interest in the fields of science and geography." Estab. 1982. Circ. 175,000. **Pays on acceptance.** Byline given. Offers 50% kill fee. Buys first North American serial rights only. Submit seasonal queries 1 year in advance. Reports in 2 months. Sample copy for $5 and #10 SAE with 48¢ Canadian postage. Writer's guidelines for #10 SASE.

Nonfiction: Book excerpts (occasionally), geography, science, art, natural history and environment, no travel articles. Buys 40 mss/year. Query. Length: 1,500-5,000 words. Pays $1,750-3,000 negotiated.

Photos: Send photos with ms. Reviews color transparencies—must be of professional quality; no prints or negatives. Captions and identification of subjects required.

Columns/Departments: Nexus (current science that isn't covered by daily media); Habitat (Canadian environmental stories not covered by daily media). Buys 80 mss/year. Query with clips of published work. Length: 200-800 words. Pays $250-500.

Tips: "Submit ideas for short photo essays as well as longer features."

FRIENDLY EXCHANGE, The Aegis Group: Publishers, Friendly Exchange Business Office, P.O. Box 2120, Warren MI 48090-2120. Publication Office: (810)558-7226. Editor: (702)786-7419. Editor: Adele Malott. 80% freelance written. Works with a small number of new/unpublished writers each year. Quarterly magazine for policyholders of Farmers Insurance Group of Companies exploring travel and leisure topics of interest to active families. "These are traditional families (median adult age 39) who live primarily in the area bounded by Ohio on the east and the Pacific Ocean on the west. New states added recently include Tennessee, Alabama, and Virginia." Estab. 1981. Circ. 5.7 million. **Pays on acceptance.** Publishes ms an average of 5 months after acceptance. Offers 25% kill fee. Buys all rights. Submit seasonal/holiday material 1 year in advance. Simultaneous queries OK. Query for electronic submissions. Reports in 2 months. Sample copy for 9×12 SAE with 5 first-class stamps. Writer's guidelines for #10 SASE.

Nonfiction: "Domestic travel and leisure topics of interest to the family can be addressed from many different perspectives, including health and safety, consumerism, heritage and education. Articles offer a service to readers and encourage them to take some positive action such as taking a trip. Style is colorful, warm and inviting, making liberal use of anecdotes and quotes. The only first-person articles used are those assigned; all others in third person. Only domestic travel locations are considered. Buys 8 mss/issue. Query. Length: 600-1,500 words. Pays $500-1,000/article, plus agreed-upon expenses.

Photos: Art director. Pays $150-250 for 35mm color transparencies; $50 for b&w prints. Cover photo payment negotiable. Pays on publication.

Columns/Departments: All columns and departments rely on reader-generated materials; none used from professional writers.

Tips: "We concentrate exclusively on the travel and leisure hours of our readers. Do not use destination approach in travel pieces—instead, for example, tell us about the people, activities, or events that make the location special. We prefer to go for a small slice rather than the whole pie, and we are just as interested in the cook who made it or the person who will be eating it as we are in the pie itself. Concentrate on what families can do together."

FUTURIFIC MAGAZINE, Terrace 3, 150 Haven Ave., New York NY 10032. (212)297-0502. Editor-in-Chief: Balint Szent-Miklosy. 50-75% freelance written. Monthly. "Futurific, Inc. 'Foundation for Optimism,' is an independent, nonprofit organization set up in 1976 to study the future, and *Futurific Magazine* is its monthly report on findings. We report on what is coming in all areas of life from international affairs to the arts and sciences. Readership cuts across all income levels and includes leadership, in all areas of society." Estab. 1976. Circ. 10,000. Pays on publication. Publishes ms an average of 1 month after acceptance. Byline given in most cases. Buys one-time rights and will negotiate reprints. Reports within 1 month. Sample copy for $5 and 9×12 SAE with 4 first-class stamps. Writer's guidelines alone for #10 SASE.

Nonfiction: "All subjects must deal with the future: book, movie, theater, hardware and software reviews, general interest, how to forecast the future—seriously, humor, interview/profile, new product, photo feature, technical. *No historical, how-to, opinion or gloom and doom.*" Send complete ms. Length: 5,000 words maximum. Payment negotiable.

Photos: Send photos with ms. Reviews b&w prints. Pay negotiable. Identification of subjects required.

Columns/Departments: Medical breakthroughs, new products, inventions, book, movie, theater and software reviews, etc. "Anything that is new or about to be new." Send complete ms.

Poetry: Avant-garde, free verse, haiku, light verse, traditional. "Must deal with the future. No gloom and doom or sad poetry." Buys 6/year. Submit unlimited number of poems. Length: open. Pays in copies.

Fillers: Clippings, jokes, gags, anecdotes, short humor, newsbreaks. "Must deal with the future." Length: open. Pays in copies.
Tips: "It's not who you are, it's what you have to say that counts with us. We seek to maintain a light-hearted, professional look at forecasting. Be upbeat and *show a loving expectation for the marvels of human achievement.* Take any subject or concern you find in regular news magazines and extrapolate as to what the future will be. Use imagination. Get involved in the excitement of the international developments, social interaction. *Write the solution* — not the problem."

GRIT, America's Family Magazine, Stauffer Magazine Group, 1503 SW 42nd St., Topeka KS 66609-1265. (913)274-4300. Editor-in-Chief: Roberta J. Peterson. 60% freelance written. Open to new writers. *"Grit* is Good News. As a wholesome, family-oriented magazine published for more than a century and distributed nationally, *Grit* is characterized by old-fashioned friendliness. *Grit's* goal is to offer helpful and uplifting information in an appealing, interesting and readable manner. Our readers cherish family values and appreciate practical and innovative ideas. Many of them live in small towns and rural areas across the country; others live in cities but share many of the values typical of small-town America." Estab. 1882. Circ. 400,000. Pays on publication. Publishes ms an average of 2 months after acceptance. Byline given. Buys first rights. Occasionally buys reprint rights if first publication was to extremely local or regional audience. Submit seasonal material 8 months in advance. Reports in 2 months on queries. Sample copy and writer's guidelines for $2 and 11 × 14 SAE with 4 first-class stamps.
Nonfiction: Most in need of cover stories (timely, newsworthy, but with a *Grit* angle); *Grit* People, Americana and human interest features, Home, Consumer, Health, Friends and Family, and travel stories. Also need touching, humorous or off-beat shorts with art (color or b&w). Each of these represents a specific department in the magazine; writers will best be able to successfully sell their work by becoming familiar with the publication. Pays minimum of 22¢/word for assigned articles (average $150-300 for a feature, more with photos), less for unsolicited mss or reprints. Main features run 1,000 to 1,500 words, sidebars often additional; department features average 500-900 words.
Fiction: Short stories, 2,500 words; may also purchase accompanying art if of high quality and appropriate occasionally publishes shorter or longer work also. Send complete ms with SASE. Note Fiction Dept. on envelope!
Photos: Professional quality photos (b&w prints or color slides) increase acceptability of articles. Black and white prints *required* with *Grit* People submissions. Photos: $35-200 each, dependent on quality, placement and color/b&w.
Tips: "With the exception of *Grit* People submissions, articles should be nationalized with several sources identified fully. Third-person accounts are preferred. Information in sidebar or graphic form is appropriate for many stories. *Grit* readers enjoy lists of tips, resources, or questions that help them understand the topic, for example, 5 ways to . . . *Grit* stories should be helpful and conversational with an upbeat approach. Preferred to queries: Submit a list of several brief but developed story ideas by department/feature along with a brief bio and examples of your published work."

HARPER'S MAGAZINE, 11th Floor, 666 Broadway, New York NY 10012. (212)614-6500. Fax: (212)228-5889. Editor: Lewis H. Lapham. 40% freelance written. Monthly magazine for well-educated, socially concerned, widely read men and women who value ideas and good writing. Estab. 1850. Circ. 205,000. Rights purchased vary with author and material. Accepts previously published articles. Send tearsheet or photocopy of article, or typed ms with rights for sale noted and information about when and where the article previously appeared. Pays negotiable kill fee. **Pays on acceptance.** Reports in 2 weeks. Publishes ms an average of 3 months after acceptance. Sample copy for $2.95.
   • Ranked as one of the best markets for freelance writers in *Writer's Digest* magazine's annual "Top 100 Markets," January 1994.
Nonfiction: "For writers working with agents or who will query first only, our requirements are: public affairs, literary, international and local reporting and humor." No interviews; no profiles. Complete ms and query must include SASE. No unsolicited poems will be accepted. Publishes one major report per issue. Length: 4,000-6,000 words. Publishes one major essay/issue. Length: 4,000-6,000 words. "These should be construed as topical essays on all manner of subjects (politics, the arts, crime, business, etc.) to which the author can bring the force of passionately informed statement."
Fiction: Publishes one short story/month. Generally pays 50¢-$1/word.
Photos: Deborah Rust, Art Director. Occasionally purchased with mss; others by assignment. Pays $50-500.

IDEALS MAGAZINE, Ideals Publications Inc., P.O. Box 48000, Nashville TN 37214. (615)231-6740. Publisher: Patricia Pingry. Editor: Lisa Thompson. 95% freelance written. Published 8 times a year. "Our readers are generally conservative, educated women over 50. The magazine is mainly light poetry and short articles with a nostalgic theme. Issues are seasonally oriented and thematic." Pays on publication. Publishes ms an average of 1 year after acceptance. Byline given. Buys one-time, worldwide serial and subsidiary rights. Submit seasonal/holiday material 8 months in advance. Accepts simultaneous and previously published submissions. Send tearsheet or photocopy of article or short story and information about when and where the article previously appeared. Pays 100% of amount paid for an original article. Reports in 3 months. Sample copy for $4. Writer's guidelines for #10 SASE.

Nonfiction: Essays, historical/nostalgic, humor, inspirational, personal experience. "No down-beat articles." Buys 20 mss/year. Query with or without published clips, or send complete ms. Length: 800-1,000 words.

Photos: Send SASE for guidelines. Reviews tearsheets only. Offers no additional payment for photos accepted with ms. Captions, model releases and identification of subjects required. Buys one-time rights. Payment varies.

Fiction: Slice-of-life vignettes. Buys 10 mss/year. Length: 800-1,000 words.

Poetry: Light verse, traditional. "No erotica or depressing poetry." Buys 250/year. Submit maximum 15 poems, 20-30 lines.

Tips: "Poetry is the area of our publication most open to freelancers. It must be oriented around a season or theme. Nostalgia is an underlying theme of every issue. Poetry must be optimistic."

KNOWLEDGE, Official Publication of the World Olympiads of Knowledge, Knowledge, Inc., 3863 Southwest Loop 820, S 100, Ft. Worth TX 76133-2063. (817)292-4272. Fax: (817)294-2893. Editor: Dr. O.A. Battista. Managing Editor: Elizabeth Ann Battista. 90% freelance written. Quarterly magazine for lay and professional audiences of all occupations. Estab. 1985. Circ. 3,000. Pays on publication. Publishes ms an average of 6 months after acceptance. Buys all rights. "We will reassign rights to a writer after a given period." Accepts previously published articles. Send photocopy of article. Byline given. Submit seasonal/holiday material 6 months in advance. Reports in 1 month. Sample copy for $6. Writer's guidelines for #10 SASE.

Nonfiction: Informational—original new knowledge that will prove mentally or physically beneficial to all readers. Buys 30 unsolicited mss/year. Query. Length: 1,500-2,000 words maximum. Pays $100 minimum. Sometimes pays the expenses of writers on assignment.

Columns/Departments: Journal section uses maverick and speculative ideas that other magazines will not publish and reference. Payment is made, on publication, at the following minimum rates: Feature Articles $100. Why Don't They, $50; Salutes, $25; New Vignettes, $25; Quotes To Ponder, $10; and Facts, $5.

Tips: "The editors of *Knowledge* welcome submissions from contributors. Manuscripts and art material will be carefully considered but received *only* with the unequivocal understanding that the magazine will not be responsible for loss or injury. Material from a published source should have the publication's name, date and page number. Submissions cannot be acknowledged and will be returned only when accompanied by a SASE having adequate postage."

LEFTHANDER MAGAZINE, Lefthander International, P.O. Box 8249, Topeka KS 66608-0249. (913)234-2177. Managing Editor: Kim Kipers. 80% freelance written. Eager to work with new/unpublished writers. Bimonthly magazine for "lefthanded people of all ages and interests in 50 US states and 12 foreign countries. The one thing they have in common is an interest in lefthandedness." Estab. 1975. Circ. 26,000. Pays on publication. Publishes ms an average of 4 months after acceptance. Byline usually given. Offers 25% kill fee. Rights negotiable. Simultaneous queries OK. Reports on queries in 2 months. Sample copy for $2 and 9 × 12 SAE. Writer's guidelines for #10 SASE.

Nonfiction: Interviews with famous lefthanders; features about lefthanders with interesting talents and occupations; how-to features (sports, crafts, hobbies for lefties); research on handedness and brain dominance; exposé on discrimination against lefthanders in the work world; features on occupations and careers attracting lefties; education features relating to ambidextrous right brain teaching methods. Buys 50-60 mss/year. Length: 1,500-2,000 words for features. Pays $85-100. Buys 6 personal experience shorts/year. Pays $25. Pays expenses of writer on assignment. Query with SASE.

Photos: State availability of photos for features. Pays $10-15 for good contrast b&w glossies. Rights negotiable.

Tips: "All material must have a lefthanded hook. We prefer practical, self-help and self-awareness types of editorial content of general interest."

LEISURE WORLD, Ontario Motorist Publishing Company, 1253 Ouellette Ave., Box 580, Windsor, Ontario N8X 1J3 Canada. (519)971-3208. Fax: (519)977-1197. Editor: Douglas O'Neil. 30% freelance written. Bimonthly magazine distributed to members of the Canadian Automobile Association in southwestern and midwestern Ontario, the Niagara Peninsula and the maritime provinces. Editorial content is focused on travel, entertainment and leisure time pursuits of interest to CAA members." Estab. 1988. Circ. 321,000. Pays on publication. Publishes ms an average of 2 months after acceptance. Buys first rights and second serial (reprint) rights. Submit seasonal/holiday material 4 months in advance. Accepts previously published material. Send information about when and where the article previously appeared. Pays 100% of amount paid for original article. Reports in 2 months. Sample copy for $2. Free writer's guidelines.

Nonfiction: Lifestyle, humor, travel. Buys 20 mss/year. Send complete ms. Length: 800-1,500 words. Pays $50-200.

Photos: Reviews negatives. Offers $40/photo. Captions, model releases required. Buys one-time rights.
Columns/Departments: Query with published clips. Length: 800 words. Pays $50-100.
Tips: "We are most interested in travel destination articles that offer a personal, subjective and positive point of view on international (including US) destinations. Good quality color slides are a must."

LIFE, Time & Life Bldg., Rockefeller Center, New York NY 10020. (212)522-1212. Managing Editor: Daniel Okrent. Articles: Assistant Managing Editor: Jay D. Lovinger. 10% freelance written. Prefers to work with published/established writers; works with a very small number of new/unpublished writers each year. Monthly general interest picture magazine for people of all ages, backgrounds and interests. Estab. 1936. Circ. 1.5 million. **Pays on acceptance.** Publishes an average of 3 months after acceptance. Byline given. Buys first North American serial rights. Submit seasonal material 4 months in advance. Simultaneous submissions OK. Reports in 2 months.
  ● Although this magazine is better known for its photos than its articles, the writing nonetheless is
    of exceptional quality.
Nonfiction: "We've done articles on anything in the world of interest to the general reader and on people of importance. It's extremely difficult to break in since we buy so few articles. Most of the magazine is pictures. We're looking for very high quality writing. We select writers whom we think match the subject they are writing about." Query with clips of previously published work. Length: 1,000-4,000 words.

MACLEAN'S, Canada's Weekly News Magazine, Maclean Hunter Ltd., 777 Bay St., Toronto, Ontario M5W 1A7, Canada. Weekly publication covering Canadian and international news. This magazine did not respond to our request for information. Query before submitting.

MERIDIAN'S LIFESTYLES, Meridian International, Inc., Box 10010, Ogden UT 84409. (801)394-9446. 40% freelance written. Monthly inhouse magazine featuring personality profiles. **Pays on acceptance.** Publishes ms an average of 8 months after acceptance. Byline given. Buys first rights, second serial (reprint) rights and non-exclusive reprint rights. Accepts simultaneous and previously published submissions (written query first). Query first. Reports in 2 months with SASE. Sample copy for $1 and 9 × 12 SAE. Writer's guidelines for #10 SASE. All requests for sample copies, guidelines and queries should be addressed Attn: Editorial Staff.
Nonfiction: Personality profiles of nationally recognized celebrities in sports, entertainment and fine arts. "Celebrities must have positive values and make a contribution, beyond their good looks, to society. These are cover features – photogenic appeal needed." Buys 40 mss/year. Query. Length: 1,000 words. Pays 15¢/word for first rights plus non-exclusive reprint rights. Payment for second rights is 10¢/word.
Photos: Send photos with ms. Pays $35/inside photo, $50/cover photo. Reviews 35mm or larger transparencies and 5 × 7 or 8 × 10 sharp color prints. Prefers transparencies. Captions, model releases and identification of subjects required.
Tips: "The key is a well-written query letter that: 1) demonstrates that the subject of the article has national appeal; 2) shows that a profile of the person interviewed will have a clear, focused theme; 3) gives evidence that the writer/photographer is a professional, even if a beginner."

MONDO 2000, Fun City MegaMedia, P.O. Box 10171, Berkeley CA 94709. (510)845-9018. Editor: Wes Thomas. Managing Editor: Paul McEnry. Contact: Jas Morgan. 75% freelance written. Quarterly magazine for cutting edge technology, music, arts, fashion. Estab. 1989. Circ. 100,000. Pays on publication. Byline given; name in lights. Buys first and second rights. Editorial lead time 3 months. Submit seasonal material 2 months in advance. Electronic submissions to: Mondo@well.sf.ca. Reports in 2 weeks on queries; 1 month on mss. Sample copy for $7. Writer's guidelines free on request.
Nonfiction: Book excerpts, essays, exposé, how-to, interview/profile, new product, technical. "No fiction, poetry, lame humor." Query with published clips. Length: 650-3,900 words. Pays 20¢/word.
Photos: Bart Nagel, art director. Send photos with submission. Reviews transparencies, 35mm, color photocopies. Negotiates payment individually. Identification of subjects required. Buys first and second rights.
Columns/Departments: Contact: St. Jude Milhon, Senior Editor (510)540-8775. Street Tech (garage level, do it yourself high tech), 1,300 words and Reviews (books, software, film, computer games), 650-1,300 words. Buys 12 mss/year. Query with published clips. Pays $32.50 minimum, $130 maximum.
Tips: "Interviews, street tech, tech items, reviews are most open to freelancers. Must be *hot* – cutting edge, near future, non-mainstream, bizarre, intellectually stimulating, funny."

NATIONAL GEOGRAPHIC MAGAZINE, 1145 17th St. NW, Washington DC 20036. (202)857-7000. Editor: William Graves. Approximately 50% freelance written. Prefers to work with published/established writers. Monthly magazine for members of the National Geographic Society. Estab. 1888. Circ. 9.5 million.
  ● Ranked as one of the best markets for freelance writers in *Writer's Digest* magazine's annual "Top
    100 Markets," January 1994.
Nonfiction: *National Geographic* publishes general interest, illustrated articles on science, natural history, exploration, politics and geographical regions. Almost half of the articles are staff-written. Of the freelance writers assigned, some are experts in their fields; the remainder are established professionals. Fewer than 1% of unsolicited queries result in assignments. Query (500 words) by letter, not by phone, to Associate

Editor Robert Poole. Do not send mss. Before querying, study recent issues and check a *Geographic Index* at a library since the magazine seldom returns to regions or subjects covered within the past 10 years. Pays expenses of writers on assignment.

Photos: Photographers should query in care of the Photographic Division.

THE NEW YORKER, 20 W. 43rd St., New York NY 10036-7441. Editor: Tina Brown. Weekly. Estab. 1925. Circ. 600,000.

- *The New Yorker* is one of today's premier markets for top-notch nonfiction, fiction and poetry. The magazine did not respond to our request for information. Query before submitting. The editors deal with a tremendous number of submissions every week; writers hoping to crack this market shoud be prepared to wait at least two or three months for a reply.

‡NIGHT OWL'S NEWSLETTER, Night Owl Network, P.O. Box 488, LaPorte TX 77572-0488. Editor: Robin Parker. Managing Editor: Debbie Jordan. 100% freelance written. Quarterly newsletter for night owls. "Night Owl's Newsletter offers information and support for and about night people. We present the "big picture" of the night community while working for dignity for night owls." Estab. 1990. Circ. 250. Pays on publication. Publishes ms an average of 1 year after acceptance. Byline given. Buys one-time rights. Submit seasonal material 6 months in advance. Accepts simultaneous and previously published submissions. Reports in 2-3 months on mss. Sample copy for $3.50. Writer's guidelines for #10 SASE.

Nonfiction: Book excerpts, essays, humor, interview/profile, opinion, personal experience, anything about night people, owls and other night subjects. Special articles or issues will be "Am I a Night Owl or Do I Just Have Insomnia?"; "Drugs and Sleep", "When Owls and Larks Marry." "We have enough of the personal-experience pieces about being up when everyone is asleep; we're looking for those with a new slant—a twist! Buys 4 mss/year. Send complete ms. Length: 250-1,000 words. Pays $1 minimum for unsolicited articles plus contributor copy.

Fiction: Anything. Any form, but must have some connection to night and night people. Buys 4 mss/year. Send complete ms. Length: 250-1,000 words. Pays $1 plus 1 contributor copy.

Fillers: Anecdotes, facts, newsbreaks, short humor (must be related to night and night people). Length: 250 words. Pays $1 minimum.

Tips: "We consider all submissions equally. We especially need factual articles on various aspects of what it is like to be a night person. To date—all such articles have been written by publisher—but we want some by others that are well-researched and well-written. Read back issues to understand our message. Open in all areas, especially well-researched and well-written articles on all aspects of the night owl experience and the "big picture" for night people."

NOSTALGIA, A Sentimental State of Mind, Nostalgia Publications, P.O. Box 2224, Orangeburg SC 29116-2224. Editor: Connie L. Martin. 100% freelance written. Semiannual magazine for poetry and true short stories. "True, personal experiences that relate faith, struggle, hope, success, failure and rising above problems common to all." Estab. 1986. Circ. 1,000. Pays on publication. Publishes ms an average 6-12 months after acceptance. Byline given. Buys one-time rights. Submit seasonal material 6 months in advance. Accepts previously published material. Send tearsheet or photocopy of article or short story, typed ms with rights for sale noted and information about when and where the article previously appeared. Reports in 4-6 weeks on queries. Sample copy for $3. Writer's guidelines for #10 SASE.

Nonfiction: General interest, historical/nostalgic, humor, inspirational, opinion, personal experience, photo feature, religious, travel. Does not want to see "anything with profanity or sexual references." Buys 7-8 mss/year. Send complete ms. Length: 1,000 words. Pays $25 minimum. Pays contributor copies "if copies are preferred."

Photos: State availability of photos with submission. Offers no additional payment for photos with ms.

Poetry: Free verse, haiku, light verse, traditional, modern prose. "No ballads—no profanity—no sexual references." Submit 3 poems maximum. Pays $200 annually. Nostalgia Poetry Award. Entry fee $3 reserves future copy, covers 3 poems. Honorable Mentions published. Deadlines: June 30 and December 31.

OUT WEST, America's On the Road Newspaper, Suite 11, 408 Broad St., Nevada City CA 95959. (916)478-9080. Fax: (916)478-9082. Editor: Chuck Woodbury. 30% freelance written. Quarterly tabloid for general audience. Estab. 1988. Circ. 12,000. Pays on acceptance or publication (negotiated). Byline given. Buys one-time or reprint rights. Submit seasonal/holiday material 4 months in advance. Accepts simultaneous and previously published submissions. Send tearsheet or photocopy of article, or typed ms with rights for sale noted and information about when and where the article previously appeared. For reprints, pays 50-75% of the amount paid for an original article. Reports in 2 months. Sample copy for $2.50. Writer's guidelines for #10 SASE.

Nonfiction: Essays, historical, humor, photo feature, profiles, travel, but always relating to the rural West. Readers are travelers and armchair travelers interested in what's along the back roads and old 2-lane highways of the non-urban West. Articles about old cafes, motels, hotels, roadside trading posts, drive-in theaters, highways of yesteryear like Route 66 and good roadtrips are especially welcome. No foreign travel. Query or send complete ms. Length: 300-1,000 words. Pays $25-100.

Photos: Black and white only; prefers 5×7 or 8×10 prints. Buys stand-alone photos of funny things and signs along the road. Pays $5-30.

Columns/Departments: Western wildlife, roadfood, roadtrips, rural museums and attractions, tourist railroads, Alaska, Death Valley, ghost towns, western history, western tours and off-beat attractions. Length: 400-600 words. Pays $25-35.

Fillers: Anecdotes, short humor, unusual Western historical facts, funny small business slogans, cartoons, travel tips, book, video reviews. Length 25-150 words. Pays $2-20.

Tips: "It's very important to read the publication before submitting work. No how-to articles. *Out West* is not an RV or senior publication."

PARADE, Parade Publications, Inc., 711 Third Ave., New York NY 10017. (212)573-7000. Editor: Walter Anderson. Weekly magazine for a general interest audience. 90% freelance written. Circ. 37 million. **Pays on acceptance.** Publishes ms an average of 3 months after acceptance. Kill fee varies in amount. Buys first North American serial rights. Reports in 5 weeks on queries. Writer's guidelines for #10 SAE.

Nonfiction: General interest (on health, trends, social issues, business or anything of interest to a broad general audience); interview/profile (of news figures, celebrities and people of national significance); and "provocative topical pieces of news value." Spot news events are not accepted, as *Parade* has a 6-week lead time. No fiction, fashion, travel, poetry, quizzes or fillers. Address single-page queries to Articles Correspondent. Length: 800-1,500 words. Pays $2,500 minimum. Pays expenses of writers on assignment.

Tips: "Send a well-researched, well-written three-paragraph query targeted to our market. Please, no phone queries. We're interested in well-written exclusive mss on topics of news interest. The most frequent mistake made by writers in completing an article for us is not adhering to the suggestions made by the editor when the article was assigned."

POOR KATY'S ALMANAC: HOME OF PULP FICTION . . . AND MORE!, (formerly *Katy's Cab*), Katy's Cab Publications, P.O. Box 3031, Anaheim CA 92801-3031. Editor: Katy Oviatt. Editorial contact: Noel Clancy, associate editor. 90% freelance written. Bimonthly magazine for taxicab drivers and passengers. Estab. 1992. Circ. 500. **Pays on acceptance.** Publishes ms an average of 4 months after acceptance. Byline given. Rights negotiated. Editorial lead time 2-4 months. Submit seasonal material 6 months in advance. Accepts simultaneous and previously published submissions. Reports in 3 months. Sample copy for $2 (bulk quantities at reduced prices to taxicab companies). Writer's guidelines for #10 SASE.

Nonfiction: Katy Oviatt, managing editor. General interest, historical/nostalgic, how-to (self-protection, customer service, public service, handle difficult passengers, prevent drunk drivers), humor, inspirational, interview/profile, new product (taxi related), opinion, personal experience, travel, consumer advice, "Cab Driver of the Month" biographies. "April is 'dispatcher appreciation'; May is 'peace officer appreciation'; and the usual seasonal events." No lengthy pieces. Buys 24-36 mss/year. Send complete ms. Length: 200-1,000 words. Pays in copies, unless otherwise negotiated.

Photos: Send photos with submission. "Prefers 5×7 or smaller; b&w works best. Also need color photos of taxicabs for 2¼" campaign buttons and postcards. Negotiates payment individually. Captions, model releases, identification of subjects required. Buys all rights unless otherwise negotiated.

Columns/Departments: From My Taxi (op-ed by active or retired cab drivers), 200-1,000 words; Tips on Tips (tells cab drivers how to earn bigger, better tips—practical advice), 100-500 words. Buys 12-24 mss/year. Send complete ms. Pays in copies, unless otherwise negotiated.

Fiction: Juanita Wilcox, fiction editor. Adventure, experimental, fantasy, historical, humorous, mainstream, mystery, science fiction, serials, slice-of-life vignettes, suspense, western. "No gratuitous violence; no minority or gender bashing (unless used in quotes by an ignorant character who suffers from his/her attitude in some way); no explicit sex; watch the foul language unless it's really necessary." Buys 12-24 mss/year. Send complete ms. Length: 200-2,000 words. Pays in copies, unless otherwise negotiated.

Poetry: Noel Clancy, associate editor. Light verse, traditional, "limerick of the month." Buys 24 poems/year. Submit maximum 4 poems. Length: 2-10 lines. Pays in copies, unless otherwise negotiated.

Fillers: Katy Oviatt, managing editor. Anecdotes, facts, gags to be illustrated by cartoonist, ideas for 2¼" round campaign-type buttons, newsbreaks, short humor, trivia (short question and answer), puzzles, illustrated cartoons. Buys 35/year. Length varies. Pays $1.

Tips: "Keep material clean. *Katy's Kab* is decent enough for cab drivers to hand to their passengers as a public-relations gift. (We do use material with mature themes, but not in the magazine. Send to our "anthology" department). No reply without SASE. We are most open to fiction! All genres are welcome, because we want to emulate the old pulp magazines from the fifties. This year we have a new need for gags and ideas for our line of 2½" campaign-type buttons and postcards. They are general purpose; taxicab-related; and custom-ordered; and will be illustrated by freelance artists. If interested, send gag or idea to our 'Button Department.' Gag payment is usually $1 (one dollar) per contracted idea."

READER'S DIGEST, Pleasantville NY 10570. Monthly. Circ. 15 million. Publishes general interest articles "as varied as all human experience." The *Digest* does not read or return unsolicited mss. Address proposals and tearsheets of published articles to the editors. Considers only previously published articles; pays $1,200/ *Digest* page for World Digest rights. (Usually split 50/50 between original publisher and writer.) Tearsheets of submitted article must include name of original publisher and date of publication.

Columns/Departments: "Original contributions become the property of *Reader's Digest* upon acceptance and payment. Life-in-these-United States contributions must be true, unpublished stories from one's own experience, revealing adult human nature, and providing appealing or humorous sidelights on the American scene." Length: 300 words maximum. Pays $400 on publication. True and unpublished stories are also solicited for Humor in Uniform, Campus Comedy and All in a Day's Work. Length: 300 words maximum. Pays $400 on publication. Towards More Picturesque Speech—the first contributor of each item used in this department is paid $50 for original material, $35 for reprints. Contributions should be dated, and the source must be given. For items used in Laughter, the Best Medicine, Personal Glimpses, Quotable Quotes, and elsewhere in the magazine payment is as follows; to the *first* contributor of each from a published source, $35. For original material, $30/*Digest* two-column line, with a minimum payment of $50. Send complete anecdotes to excerpt editor."

  • Ranked as one of the best markets for freelance writers in *Writer's Digest* magazine's annual "Top 100 Markets," January 1994.

‡**READER'S DIGEST (CANADA)**, 215 Redfern, Westmount, Quebec H3Z 2V9 Canada. (514)934-0751. Editor-in-Chief: Alexander Farrell. Managing Editor: Robert Cameron. 10-25% freelance written. Monthly magazine of general interest articles and subjects. Estab. 1948. Circ. 1.3 million. **Pays on acceptance** for original works. Pays on publication for "pickups." Byline given. Offers $500 (Canadian) kill fee. Buys one-time rights (for reprints), all rights (for original articles). Submit seasonal/holiday material 4-5 months in advance. Accepts previously published submissions. Query for electronic submissions. Reports in 5 weeks on queries. Writer's guidelines for #10 SASE with Canadian postage or #10 SAE with 1 IRC.
Nonfiction: General interest, how-to (general interest), inspirational, personal experience. "No fiction, poetry or articles too specialized, technical or esoteric—read *Reader's Digest* to see what kind of articles we want." Query with published clips to Managing Editor. Length: 3,000-5,000 words. Pays a minimum of $2,700 for assigned articles. Pays expenses of writers on assignment.
Photos: State availability of photos with submission.
Tips: "*Reader's Digest* usually finds its freelance writers through other well-known publications in which they have previously been published. There are guidelines available and writers should read *Reader's Digest* to see what kind of stories we look for and how they are written. WE DO NOT ACCEPT UNSOLICITED MANUSCRIPTS."

‡**READERS REVIEW**, The National Research Bureau, Inc., P.O. Box 1, Burlington IA 52601-0001. (319)752-5415. Fax: (319)752-3421. Editor: Nancy Heinzel. 75% freelance written. Works with a small number of new/unpublished writers each year, and is eager to work with new/unpublished writers. Quarterly magazine. Estab. 1948. Pays on publication. Publishes ms an average of 1 year after acceptance. Buys all rights. Submit seasonal/holiday material 7 months in advance of issue date. Sample copy and writers guidelines for #10 SAE with 2 first-class stamps.
Nonfiction: General interest (steps to better health, attitudes on the job); how-to (perform better on the job, do home repairs, car maintenance); travel. Buys 10-12 mss/year. Query with outline or submit complete ms. Length: 500-700 words. Pays 4¢/word.
Tips: "Writers have a better chance of breaking in at our publication with short articles."

REAL PEOPLE, The Magazine of Celebrities and Interesting People, Main Street Publishing Co., Inc., 16th Floor, 950 Third Ave. New York NY 10022-2705. (212)371-4932. Fax: (212)838-8420. Editor: Alex Polner. 75% freelance written. Bimonthly magazine for ages 35 and up focusing on celebs and show business, but also interesting people who might appeal to a national audience. Estab. 1988. Circ. 125,000. Pays on publication. Byline given. Pays 33% kill fee. Buys all rights. Submit seasonal/holiday material 6 months in advance. Reports within 1 month. Sample copy for $3.50 and 8×11 SAE with 3 first-class stamps. Writer's guidelines for #10 SASE.
Nonfiction: Interview/profile. Buys 80 mss/year. Query with published clips (and SAE). Length: 500-2,000 words. Pays $150-500 for assigned articles; $100-250 for unsolicited articles.
Columns/Departments: Newsworthy shorts—up to 200 words. "We are doing more shorter (75-250 word) pieces for our 'Real Shorts' column." Pays $25-50.
Photos: State availability of photos with submissions. Reviews 5×7 prints and/or slides. Offers no additional payment for photos accepted with ms. Captions, model releases and identification of subjects required. Buys one-time rights.

‡**REUNIONS MAGAZINE**, P.O. Box 11727, Milwaukee WI 53211-0727. (414)263-4567. Editor: Carol Burns. 75% freelance written. Quarterly magazine covering reunions—all aspects, all types. "*Reunions Magazine* is primarily for those actively involved with class, family and military reunions or ongoing adoptive or genealogical searchers. We want easy, practical ideas about organizing, planning, researching/searching, attending or promoting reunions." Estab. 1990. Circ. 5,000. Pays on publication. Publishes ms an average of 9 months after acceptance. Byline given. Buys one-time rights. Editorial lead time 6 months. Submit seasonal material 9 months in advance. Accepts previously published submissions. Query for electronic submissions. Reports

in 3 months on queries. Sample copy free. Writer's guidelines for #10 SASE.
Nonfiction: Historical/nostalgic, how-to, humor, interview/profile, new product, personal experience, photo feature, travel, reunion recipes with reunion anecdote—all must be reunion-related. Special issues: African-American family reunions; reunions in various sections of the US; ethnic reunions. Buys 12 mss/year. Query with published clips. Length: 500-2,000 words. Pays $25 minimum. Pays expenses of writers on assignment.
Photos: State availability of photos with submission. Reviews contact sheets, negatives, 35mm transparencies and prints. Offers no additional payment for photos accepted with ms. Captions, model releases and identification of subjects required. Buys one-time rights.
Fillers: Anecdotes, facts, newsbreaks, short humor—all reunion related. Buys 8/year. Length: 50-250 words. Pays $5.
Tips: "Write a lively account of an interesting or unusual reunion, either upcoming or as soon afterward as possible. Tell readers why this reunion is special, what went into planning it and how attendees reacted. Our *Masterplan* section is a great place for a freelancer to start. Send us how-tos or tips on any aspect of reunions. Open your minds to different types of reunions—they're all around!"

‡ROBB REPORT, The Magazine for the Affluent Lifestyle, 1 Acton Place, Acton MA 01720. (508)263-7749. Fax: (508)263-0722. Editor: Robert Feeman. Managing Editor: Janice Stillman. 60% freelance written. Monthly magazine. "We are a lifestyle magazine geared toward active, affluent readers. Addresses upscale autos, luxury travel, boating, technology, lifestyles, personal style, sports, investments, collectibles." Estab. 1975. Circ. 80,000. Pays on publication. Byline given. Offers 50% kill fee. Buys all rights or first North American serial rights. Submit seasonal/holiday material 5 months in advance. Query for electronic submissions. Reports in 2 months on queries; 1 month on mss. Sample copy for $6. Writer's guidelines for #10 SASE.
Nonfiction: General interest (autos, lifestyle, etc.), interview/profile (business), new product (autos, boats, consumer electronics), travel (international and domestic). No essays, personal travel experiences, bargain travel. Buys 60 mss/year. Query with published clips if available. Length: 1,500-3,500 words. Pays $500-850. Sometimes pays expenses of writers on assignment.
Photos: State availability of photos with submission. Payment depends on article. Buys one-time rights.
Tips: "Study the magazine. We are geared exclusively to affluent readers. All article submissions should be targeted at that audience. We are now interested in business and sports profiles."

THE SATURDAY EVENING POST, The Saturday Evening Post Society, 1100 Waterway Blvd., Indianapolis IN 46202. (317)636-8881. Editor: Cory SerVaas, M.D. Managing Editor: Ted Kreiter. 30% freelance written. Bimonthly general interest, "family-oriented magazine focusing on physical fitness, preventive medicine." Estab. 1728. Circ. 570,000. Pays on publication. Publishes ms an average of 3 months after acceptance. Byline given. Buys second serial (reprint) and all rights. Submit seasonal/holiday material 4 months in advance. Accepts simultaneous and previously published submissions. Query for electronic submissions. Reports in 1 month on queries; 6 weeks on mss. Writer's guidelines for #10 SASE.
Nonfiction: Book excerpts, general interest, how-to (gardening, home improvement), humor, interview/profile, travel. "No political articles or articles containing sexual innuendo or hypersophistication." Buys 50 mss/year. Query with or without published clips, or send complete ms. Length: 750-2,500 words. Pays $200 minimum, negotiable maximum for assigned articles. Sometimes pays expenses of writers on assignment.
Photos: State availability of photos with submission. Reviews negatives and transparencies. Offers $50 minimum, negotiable maxmium per photo. Model release, identification required. Buys one-time or all rights.
Columns/Departments: Travel (destinations), 750-1,500. Buys 16 mss/year. Query with published clips or send complete ms. Length: 750-1,500 words. Pays $200 minimum, negotiable maximum.
Fiction: Jack Gramling, fiction editor. Historical, humorous, mainstream, mystery, science fiction, western. "No sexual innuendo or profane expletives." Send complete ms. Length: 1,000-2,500 words. Pays $150 minimum, negotiable maximum.
Poetry: Light verse.
Fillers: PostScripts Editor: Steve Pettinga. Anecdotes, short humor. Buys 200/year. Length 300 words. Pays $15.
Tips: "Areas most open to freelancers are Health, PostScripts and Travel. For travel we like text-photo packages, pragmatic tips, side bars and safe rather than exotic destinations. Query by mail, not phone. Send clips."

SELECTED READING, The National Research Bureau, Inc., P.O. Box 1, Burlington IA 52601-0001. (319)752-5415. Fax: (319)752-3421. Editor: Nancy Heinzel. 75% freelance written. Works with a small number of new/unpublished writers each year. Quarterly magazine. Estab. 1948. Pays on publication. Publishes ms an average of 1 year after acceptance. Buys all rights. Submit seasonal/holiday material 7 months in advance of issue date. Sample copy and writer's guidelines for #10 SAE with 2 first-class stamps.
Nonfiction: General interest (economics, health, safety, working relationships), how-to, travel (out-of-the way places). No material on car repair. Buys 10-12 mss/year. Query. Short outline or synopsis is best; lists of titles are no help. Length: 500-700 words. Pays 4¢/word.
Tips: "Writers have a better chance of breaking in at our publication with short articles."

‡**SILVER CIRCLE**, Home Savings of America, 4900 Rivergrade, Irwindale CA 91706. Editor: Jay A. Binkly. 80% freelance written. Consumer magazine published 3 times/year. "Despite the magazine's title, editorial is *not* the stereotypical senior fare. Articles that are aimed solely at *seniors* are rejected 99% of the time. Articles should have broad demographic appeal. Along with gardening and financial planning, subjects that have appeared in the magazine include computer software, heli-hiking tours, home fitness centers, high-tech new-car options, video cameras, investment scams, party planning, etc. Our editorial mission is to provide our readers with practical, relevant, upbeat consumer service information." Estab. 1974. Circ. 575,000. **Pays on acceptance.** Byline given. Offers 20% kill fee. Buys first North American serial rights. Editorial lead time 5 months. Submit seasonal material 5 months in advance. Accepts simultaneous and previously published submissions. Query for electronic submissions. Reports in 3 weeks on queries; 1 month on mss. Sample copy for 8½×11 SASE. Writer's guidelines for #10 SASE.

Nonfiction: How-to, new product, travel. Buys 15 mss/year. Query with published clips. Length: 800-3,000 words. Pays $150 minimum for assigned articles; $1,500 minimum for unsolicited articles. Sometimes pays expenses of writers on assignment.

Photos: Send photos with submissions. Offers $35-500/photo. Captions required. Buys one-time rights.

Columns/Departments: To Your Health (practical health items), 500 words; Minding Your Money (practical money items), 500 words; Travel Notes (practical travel items), 500 words. Buys 100 mss/year. Pays $35-100.

SMITHSONIAN MAGAZINE, 900 Jefferson Dr., Washington DC 20560. Articles Editor: Marlane A. Liddell. 90% freelance written. Prefers to work with published/established writers. Monthly magazine for "associate members of the Smithsonian Institution; 85% with college education." Circ. 3 million. Buys first North American serial rights. "Payment for each article to be negotiated depending on our needs and the article's length and excellence." **Pays on acceptance.** Publishes ms an average of 6 months after acceptance. Submit seasonal material 3 months in advance. Reports in 2 months. Sample copy for $3 % Judy Smith. Writer's guidelines for #10 SASE.

• Ranked as one of the best markets for freelance writers in *Writer's Digest* magazine's annual "Top 100 Markets," January 1994.

Nonfiction: "Our mandate from the Smithsonian Institution says we are to be interested in the same things which now interest or should interest the Institution: cultural and fine arts, history, natural sciences, hard sciences, etc." Query. Back Page humor: 750 words; full length article 3,500-4,500 words. Payment negotiable. Pays expenses of writers on assignment.

Photos: Purchased with or without ms and on assignment. Captions required. Pays $400/full color page.

THE STAR, 660 White Plains Rd., Tarrytown NY 10591. (914)332-5000. Fax: (914)332-5043. Editor: Richard Kaplan. Executive Editor: Steve LeGrice. 40% freelance written. Prefers to work with published/established writers. Weekly magazine "for every family; all the family—kids, teenagers, young parents and grandparents." Estab. 1974. Circ. 2.8 million. Publishes ms an average of 1 month after acceptance. Buys first North American serial, occasionally second serial book rights. Query for electronic submissions. Reports in 2 months. Pays expenses of writers on assignment.

Nonfiction: Exposé (government waste, consumer, education, anything affecting family); general interest (human interest, consumerism, informational, family and women's interest); how-to (psychological, practical on all subjects affecting readers); interview (celebrity or human interest); new product; photo feature; profile (celebrity or national figure); health; medical; diet. No first-person articles. Query or submit complete ms. Length: 500-1,000 words. Pays $50-1,500.

Photos: Alistair Duncan, photo editor. State availability of photos with query or ms. Pays $25-100 for 8×10 b&w glossy prints, contact sheets or negatives; $150-1,000 for 35mm color transparencies. Captions required. Buys one-time or all rights.

THE SUN, A Magazine of Ideas, The Sun Publishing Company, 107 N. Roberson St., Chapel Hill NC 27516. (919)942-5282. Editor: Sy Safransky. 90% freelance written. Monthly general interest magazine. "We are open to all kinds of writing, though we favor work of a personal nature." Estab. 1974. Circ. 20,000. Pays on publication. Publishes ms an average of 6 months after acceptance. Byline given. Buys first or one-time rights. Accepts previously published submissions. Reports in 1 month on queries; 3-5 months on mss. Sample copy for $3 and SASE. Free writer's guidelines.

Nonfiction: Book excerpts, essays, expose, general interest, interview, opinion, personal experience, spiritual. Buys 24 mss/year. Send complete ms. Length: 10,000 words maximum. Pays $100-200. "Complimentary subscription is given in addition to payment."

Photos: Send b&w photos with submission. Offers $25-50/photo. Model releases preferred. Buys one-time rights.

Fiction: Experimental, humorous, literary, mainstream, novel excerpts. "We avoid stereotypical genre pieces like sci-fi, romance, western and horror. Read an issue before submitting." Buys 30 mss/year. Send complete ms. Length: 10,000 words maximum. Pays $100 for original fiction.

Poetry: Free verse, prose poems, short and long poems. Buys 24 poems/year. Submit 6 poems maximum. Pays $25.

TIME, Time & Life Bldg., Rockefeller Center, New York NY 10020-1393. Weekly publication covering news and popular culture. This magazine did not respond to our request for information. Query before submitting.

‡TOWN AND COUNTRY, 1700 Broadway, New York NY 10019. (212)903-5000. Managing Editor: Jon Rizzi. For upper-income Americans. Monthly. Circ. 530,000. **Pays on acceptance.** Not a large market for freelancers. Always query first.
Nonfiction: Ron Javers, editor-in-chief. "We're always trying to find ideas that can be developed into good articles that will make appealing cover lines." Wants provocative and controversial pieces. Length: 1,500-2,000 words. Pay varies. Also buys shorter pieces for which pay varies.

‡USA WEEKEND, Gannett Co., Inc., 1000 Wilson Blvd., Arlington VA 22229. Editor: Marcia Bullard. 70% freelance written. Weekly Friday-Sunday newspaper magazine. Estab. 1985. Circ. 15 million. **Pays on acceptance.** Publishes ms an average of 3 months after acceptance. Byline given. Offers 25% kill fee. Buys first worldwide serial rights. Submit seasonal material 5 months in advance. Query for electronic submissions. Reports in 5 weeks.
Nonfiction: Food and Family Issues (contact: Connie Kurz); Trends and Entertainment (contact: Gayle Carter); Recreation (contact: John Butterfield); Cover Stories (contact: Dan Olmsted). Also looking for book excerpts, general interest articles, how-to, interview/profile, travel, food, recreation. No first-person essays, historic pieces or retrospective pieces. Buys 200 mss/year. Query with published clips. No unsolicited mss accepted. Length: 50-2,000 words. Pays $75-2,000. Sometimes pays expenses of writers on assignment.
Photos: State availability of photos with submission.
Columns/Departments: Food, Travel, Entertainment, Books, Recreation. "All stories must be pegged to an upcoming event, must report new and refreshing trends in the field and must include high profile people." Length: 50-1,000 words. Query with published clips. Pays $250-500.
Tips: "We are looking for authoritative, lively articles that blend the author's expertise with our style. All articles must have a broad, timely appeal. One-page query should include peg or timeliness of the subject matter. We generally look for sidebar material to accompany each article."

‡THE WORLD & I, A Chronicle of Our Changing Era, News World Communications, Inc., 2800 New York Ave. NE, Washington DC 20002. (202)635-4000. Fax: (202)269-9353. Editor: Morton A. Kaplan. Executive Editor: Michael Marshall. Contact: Gary Rowe. 90% freelance written. Publishing more than 100 articles each month, this is a broad interest magazine for the thinking person. Estab. 1986. Circ. 30,000. Pays on publication. Publishes ms an average of 6 months after acceptance. Byline given. Offers 20% kill fee. Buys all rights. Submit seasonal material 5 months in advance. Accepts previously published material. Send tearsheet or photocopy of article, typed ms with rights for sale noted and information about when and where the article previously appeared. Query for electronic submissions. Reports in 6 weeks on queries; 10 weeks on mss. Sample copy for $5 and 9×12 SASE. Writer's guidelines for #10 SASE.
Nonfiction: "Description of Sections: Current Issues: Politics, economics and strategic trends covered in a variety of approaches, including special report, analysis, commentary and photo essay. The Arts: International coverage of music, dance, theater, film, television, design, architecture, photography, poetry, painting and sculpture—through reviews, features, essays and a 10-page Gallery of full-color reproductions. Life: Articles on well-known and respected people, cultural trends, adventure, travel, family and youth issues, education, consumer issues, gardens, home, health and food. Natural Science: Covers the latest in science and technology, relating it to the social and historical context, under these headings: At the Edge, Impacts, Nature Walk, Science and Spirit, Science and Values, Scientists: Past and Present, Crucibles of Science and Science Essay. Book World: Excerpts from important, timely books (followed by commentaries) and 10-12 scholarly reviews of significant new books each month, including untranslated works from abroad. Covers current affairs, intellectual issues, contemporary fiction, history, moral/religious issues and the social sciences. Currents in Modern Thought: Examines scholarly research and theoretical debate across the wide range of disciplines in the humanities and social sciences. Featured themes are explored by several contributors. Investigates theoretical issues raised by certain current events, and offers contemporary reflection on issues drawn from the whole history of human thought. Culture: Surveys the world's people in these subsections: Peoples (their unique characteristics and cultural symbols), Crossroads (changes brought by the meeting of cultures), Patterns (photo essay depicting the daily life of a distinct culture), Folk Wisdom (folklore and practical wisdom and their present forms), and Heritage (multicultural backgrounds of the American people and how they are bound to the world. Photo Essay: The 10-page Life and Ideals dramatizes a human story of obstacles overcome in the pursuit of an ideal. Three other photo essays appear each month: Focus (Current Issues), Gallery (The Arts), and Patterns (Culture). 'No *National Enquirer*-type articles.' " Buys 1,200 mss/year. Query with published clips. Length: 1,000-5,000 words. Pays 10-20¢/word. Sometimes pays expenses of writers on assignment. First-person work is discouraged.
Poetry: Query arts editor. Avant-garde, free verse, haiku, light verse, traditional. Buys 6-12 poems/year. Submit maximum 5 poems. Pays $25-50.
Photos: State availability of photos with submission. Reivews contact sheets, transparencies and prints. Payment negotiable. Model releases and identification of subjects required. Buys one-time rights.

Tips: "Send a short query letter with a viable story idea (no unsolicited mss, please!) for a specific section and/or subsection."

Health and Fitness

The magazines listed here specialize in covering health and fitness topics for a general audience. Many focus not as much on exercise as on general "healthy lifestyle" topics. Magazines covering health topics from a medical perspective are listed in the Medical category of Trade. Also see the Sports/Miscellaneous section where publications dealing with health and particular sports may be listed. For magazines that cover healthy eating, refer to the Food and Drink section. Many general interest publications are also potential markets for health or fitness articles.

AMERICAN HEALTH MAGAZINE, Fitness of Body and Mind, Reader's Digest Corp., 28 W. 23rd St., New York NY 10010. (212)366-8900. Editor: Carey Winfrey. Executive Editor: Judith Groch. 70% freelance written. General interest health magazine published 10 times/year covering both scientific and "lifestyle" aspects of health, including medicine, fitness, nutrition and psychology. Estab. 1982. Circ. 800,000. **Pays on acceptance.** Publishes ms an average of 4-6 months after acceptance. Byline or tagline given. Offers 25% kill fee. Buys first North American serial rights. Reports in 6 weeks. Sample copy for $3. Writer's guidelines for #10 SASE.
  • Ranked as one of the best markets for freelance writers in *Writer's Digest* magazine's annual "Top 100 Markets," January 1994.
Nonfiction: Mail to Editorial/Features. News-based articles usually with a service angle; well-written pieces with an investigative or unusual slant; humor; profiles (health or fitness related). No mechanical research reports, quick weight-loss plans or unproven treatments. "Stories should be written clearly, without jargon. Information should be new, authoritative and helpful to readers." Buys 60-70 mss/year (plus many more news items). Query with 2 clips of published work. Length: 1,000-3,000 words. Payment varies. Pays the expenses of writers on assignment.
Photos: Pays $100-600 for 35mm transparencies and 8 × 10 prints "depending on use." Captions and identification of subjects required. Buys one-time rights.
Columns/Departments: Mail to Editorial/News, Medicine, Fitness, Nutrition, The Mind, Environment, Family, Dental, Looking Good. Other news sections included from time to time. Buys about 300 mss/year. Query with clips of published work. Pays $150-250 upon acceptance.
Tips: "*American Health* has no full-time staff writers; we rely on outside contributors for most of our articles. The magazine needs good ideas and good articles from experienced journalists and writers. Feature queries should be short (no longer than a page) and to the point. Give us a good angle and a paragraph of background. Queries only. We are not responsibe for material not accompanied by a SASE."

BETTER HEALTH, Better Health Press, 1450 Chapel St., New Haven CT 06511-4440. (203)789-3972. Publishing Director: James F. Malerba. 100% freelance written. Prefers to work with published/established writers; will consider new/unpublished writers. Bimonthly magazine devoted to health and wellness issues, as opposed to medical issues. Estab. 1979. Circ. 450,000. Pays on publication. Byline given. Offers $75 kill fee. Buys first rights. Query first; do not send article. Sample copy for $2.50. Writer's guidelines for #10 SASE.
Nonfiction: Wellness/prevention issues are of prime interest. New medical techniques or nonmainstream practices are not considered. No fillers, poems, quizzes, seasonal, heavy humor, inspirational or personal experience. Length: 2,500-3,000 words. Pays $300-500. Does not offer additional payment for photos, research costs, etc. No dot matrix.
Tips: "We look for upbeat health and wellness features of interest to a general audience, such as women's health issues, infertility, senior concerns and so forth. Absolutely no articles that are not well-researched through medical doctors at the Hospital of Saint Raphael (our parent organization), or similar local health and wellness authorities. Queries not accompanied with an SASE will be consigned to the wastebasket, unread."

BODYWISE, Magazine of Fitness, Diet, and Preventative Medicine, Prestige Publications, Inc., 4151 Knob Dr., Eagan MN 55122. (612)452-0571. Fax: (612)454-5791. Editor: Carla Waldemar. Managing Editor: Tony Gunderson. 60% freelance written. Bimonthly magazine. "Articles should include what is *now* in fitness, diet, or medicine. Our audience is active adults ages 20-35 who want to take an active role in fitness and health." Estab. 1990. Circ. 200,000. Pays on publication. Byline given. Buys all rights. Accepts previously published articles. Send photocopy of article or typed ms with rights for sale noted and information about when and where the article previously appeared. Submit seasonal material 3 months in advance. Query for electronic submissions. Reports in 2 months. Writer's guidelines for #10 SAE with 4 first-class stamps.

• *Bodywise* would like to see personal accounts from men and women who have succeeded in a significant fitness or weight loss goal. Article should include photos.

Nonfiction: Book excerpts, general interest, how-to, inspirational, new product, exercise, nutrition, health discoveries; sidebars welcome. Length: 900-3,000 words. Pays $250-350/article. "*Bodywise* specials and *Today's Lifestyles* are short single subjects that offer authors the opportunity to submit or write on a work-for-hire single subject: fitness, health, diet and cookbooks. Books pay from $1,500-2,500. November focus of *Today's Lifestyles* will be '30 Day Shape Up!' " Query.

Photos: Send photos with submission. Reviews transparencies. Offers $100-350/photo. Buys one-time rights.

‡COMMON GROUND MAGAZINE, Ontario's Quarterly Guide to Natural Foods & Lifestyles, New Age Times Ink, 356 DuPont St., Toronto, Ontario M5R 1V9 Canada. Editor: Julia Wood Ford. 50% freelance written. Quarterly magazine covering holistic health, nutritional medicine. "We give top priority to well-researched articles on nutritional medicine, healing properties of foods and herbs, environmental health issues, natural lifestyles, alternative healing for cancer, arthritis, heart disease, etc. Organic foods and issues. Estab. 1985. Circ. 44,000. Pays on publication. Publishes ms 2-3 months after acceptance. Byline given. Buys first rights, one-time rights or second serial (reprint) rights. Editorial lead time 2-3 months. Submit seasonal material 2-3 months in advance. Accepts simultaneous and previously published submissions. Reports "when we have time." Sample copy for $2. Writer's guidelines free on request by phone.

Nonfiction: Book excerpts, exposé, how-to (on self-health care), inspirational, personal experience. "Nothing endorsing drugs, surgery, pharmaceuticals. No submissions from public relations firms." Buys 8-12 mss/year. Query with or without published clips. Length 1,000-1,800 words. Pays 10¢/word. Sometimes pays expenses of writers on assignment.

Photos: Send photos with submission. Offers $25-30/photo. Identification of subjects required. Buys one-time rights.

Fillers: Facts, newsbreaks.

Tips: "Must have a good working knowledge of subject area and be patient if not responded to immediately. Features are most open to freelancers. Write well, give me the facts, but do it in layman's terms. A sense of humor doesn't hurt. All material must be relevant to our *Canadian* readership audience."

COUNTDOWN, Juvenile Diabetes Foundation, 432 Park Ave. S., New York NY 10016-8013. (212)889-7575. Fax: (212)532-8791. Editor: Sandy Dylak. 75% freelance written. Quarterly magazine focusing on medical research. "*Countdown* is published for people interested in diabetes research. Written for a lay audience. Often, stories are interpretation of highly technical biomedical research." Estab. 1970. Circ. 150,000. **Pays on acceptance.** Byline given. Buys first rights. Editorial lead time 3 months. Submit seasonal material 3 months in advance. Accepts simultaneous and previously published submissions. Send photocopy of article. For reprints pays 50% of the amount paid for an original article. Query for electronic submissions. Prefers disc—any format. Reports in 1 month. Sample copy free on request.

Nonfiction: Essays, general interest, how-to, interview/profile, new product and personal experience. "All articles must relate to diabetes. 95% published freelance stories are assigned." Buys 15 mss/year. Query with published clips. Length: 500-2,500 words. Pays $500 minimum for assigned articles. Pays expenses of writers on assignment.

Photos: Send photos with submission. Reviews transparencies and prints. Negotiates payment individually. Captions, model releases and identification of subjects required. Buys one-time rights.

Tips: "Knowledge of biomedical research, specifically immunology and genetics, is necessary. We are most open to feature stories and profiles."

FDA CONSUMER, 5600 Fishers Lane, Rockville MD 20857. (301)443-3220. Editor: Judith Levine Willis. 30% freelance written. Prefers to work with experienced health and medical writers. Monthly magazine (January/February and July/August issues combined) for general public interested in health issues. A federal government publication (Food and Drug Administration). Circ. 28,000. Pays after acceptance. Publishes ms an average of 3 months after acceptance. Byline given. Not copyrighted. Pays 50% kill fee. "All rights must be assigned to the USA so that the articles may be reprinted without permission." Query with résumé and clips only. Buys 15-20 freelance mss/year. "We cannot be responsible for any work by writer not agreed upon by prior contract." Free sample copy.

Nonfiction: "Upbeat feature articles of an educational nature about FDA regulated products and specific FDA programs and actions to protect the consumer's health and pocketbook. Articles based on health topics connected to food, drugs, medical devices, and other products regulated by FDA. All articles subject to clearance by the appropriate FDA experts as well as acceptance by the editor. All articles based on prior arrangement by contract." Length: 2,000-2,500 words. Pays $800-950 for "first-timers," $1,200 for those who have previously published in *FDA Consumer*. Pays phone and mailing expenses.

Photos: Black and white photos are purchased on assignment only.

Tips: "Besides reading the feature articles in *FDA Consumer*, a writer can best determine whether his/her style and expertise suit our needs by submitting a résumé and clips; story suggestions are unnecessary as most are internally generated."

HEALTH, Time Publishing Ventures, 18th Floor, 301 Howard St., San Francisco CA 94105. (415)512-9100. Editor: Eric Schrier. Send submissions to: Katherine Lee, editorial assistant. Magazine published 7 times/ year on health, fitness, and nutrition. "Our readers are predominantly college-educated women in their 30s and 40s. Edited to focus not on illness, but on events, ideas and people." Estab. 1987. Circ. 900,000. **Pays on acceptance.** Byline given for features. Offers 25% kill fee. Buys first North American serial rights. Submit seasonal material 5 months in advance. Accepts simultaneous submissions. Reports in 2 months on queries. Sample copy for $5. Writer's guidelines for #10 SASE. "No phone calls, please."
   • *Health* stresses that writers must send for guidelines before sending a query, and that only queries that closely follow the guidelines get passed on to editors.
Nonfiction: "Articles should not be too narrow. They should offer practical advice and give clear explanations." Buys 50-60 mss/year. "No unsolicited manuscripts, please." Query with published clips. Length: 1,200 words. Pays $1,800 for assigned articles. Pays the expenses of writers on assignment.
Departments: Food, Mind, Vanities, Fitness, Family. Length: 1,200-1,500 words. Buys 25 mss/year. Query with published clips. Pays $1,800.
Tips: "Keep the focus narrow and the appeal broad. A query that starts with an unusual local event and hooks it legitimately to some national trend or concern is bound to get our attention. Show, don't tell. Use quotes, examples and statistics to show why the topic is important and why the approach is workable. We always look for clear evidence of credible research findings pointing to meaningful options for our readers. Freelancers have the best chance of getting published in departments."

LET'S LIVE MAGAZINE, Hilltopper Publications, Inc., 320 N. Larchmont Blvd., P.O. Box 74908, Los Angeles CA 90004-3030. (213)469-3901. Fax: (213)469-9597. Editor: Patty Padilla-Gallagher. Monthly magazine emphasizing nutrition. 15% freelance written. Works with a small number of new/unpublished writers each year. Estab. 1933. Circ. 850,000. Pays 1 month after publication. Publishes ms an average of 4 months after acceptance. Buys first world serial rights. Byline given. Submit seasonal/holiday material 6 months in advance. Reports in 2 months on queries; 3 months on mss. Sample copy for $2.50 for 10 × 13 SAE with 6 first-class stamps. Writer's guidelines for #10 SASE.
Nonfiction: General interest (effects of vitamins, minerals and nutrients in improvement of health or afflictions); historical (documentation of experiments or treatment establishing value of nutrients as boon to health); how-to (acquire strength and vitality, improve health of adults and/or children and prepare tasty health-food meals); interview (benefits of research in establishing prevention as key to good health); personal opinion (views of orthomolecular doctors or their patients on value of health foods toward maintaining good health); profile (background and/or medical history of preventive medicine, M.D.s or Ph.D.s, in advancement of nutrition). Manuscripts must be well-researched, reliably documented and written in a clear, readable style. Buys 2-4 mss/issue. Query with published clips. Length: 1,000-1,200 words. Pays $150. Sometimes pays expenses of writers on assignment.
Photos: Send photos with ms. Pays $17.50 for 8 × 10 b&w glossy prints; $35 for 8 × 10 color prints and 35mm transparencies. Captions and model releases required.
Tips: "We want writers with experience in researching nonsurgical medical subjects and interviewing experts with the ability to simplify technical and clinical information for the layman. A captivating lead and structural flow are essential. The most frequent mistakes made by writers are in writing articles that are too technical; in poor style; written for the wrong audience (publication not thoroughly studied), or have unreliable documentation or overzealous faith in the topic reflected by flimsy research and inappropriate tone."

LONGEVITY, General Media International, Inc., 1965 Broadway, New York NY 10023-5965. (212)496-6100. Fax: (212)580-3693. Editor-in-Chief: Susan Millar Perry. Monthly magazine on medicine, health, fitness and life extension research. "*Longevity* is written for a baby-boomer audience who want to prolong their ability to lead a productive, vibrant, healthy life and to look as good as they feel at their best." Estab. 1989. Circ. 375,000. **Pays on acceptance.** Publishes ms an average of 2 months after acceptance. Byline given. Offers 25% kill fee. Makes work-for-hire assignments. Query for electronic submissions. Reports in 3 months. Sample copy for #10 SAE with 4 first-class stamps.
   • Ranked as one of the best markets for freelance writers in *Writer's Digest* magazine's annual "Top 100 Markets," January 1994.
Nonfiction: Consumer trends in anti-aging, new products, health. Query. Length: 150-2,000 words. Pays $100-2,500. Pays expenses of writers on assignment.
Columns/Departments: Antiaging News; Outer Limits; Looks Savers; Childwise; Air, Earth & Water; Marketing Youth; Medicine; The Intelligent Eater; Mind Body Spirit; Love & Longevity; In Shape; Long Life Ideas and Health Style Setters.

MASSAGE MAGAZINE, Keeping Those Who Touch—In Touch, Noah Publishing Co., P.O. Box 1500, Davis CA 95617-1500. (916)757-6033. Fax: (916)757-6041. Publisher: Robert Calvert. Managing Editor: Karen Menehan. Senior Editor: Melissa B. Mower. 80% freelance written. Prefers to work with published/ established writers, but works with a number of new/unpublished writers each year. Bimonthly magazine on massage-bodywork and related healing arts. Estab. 1985. Circ. 50,000. Pays 30 days after publication. Publishes ms an average of 6 months after acceptance. Byline given. Buys first North American rights. Accepts previously published submissions. Send tearsheet or photocopy of article, or typed ms with rights for sale noted. For reprints pays variable amount. Reports in 1 month on queries; 2 months on mss. Sample copy for $5. Free writer's guidelines.

Nonfiction: General interest, historical/nostalgic, how-to, humor, experiential, inspirational, interview/profile, new product, photo feature, technical, travel. Length: 600-2,000 words. Pays $50-100 for assigned articles; $25-50 for unassigned. Sometimes pays the expenses of writers on assignment.

Photos: Send photos with submission. Offers $10-25/photo. Identification of subjects required. Buys one-time rights.

Columns/Departments: Touching Tales (experiential); Insurance; Table Talk (news briefs); Kneading Advice; Practice Building (business); In Touch with Associations (convention highlights); In Review/On Video (product, book, and video reviews); Technique; Body/mind; Convention Calendar (association convention listings). Length: 800-1,200 words. Pays $35-75 for most of these columns.

Fillers: Anecdotes, facts, news briefs, short humor. Length: 100 words. Pays $25 maximum.

MEN'S FITNESS, Men's Fitness, Inc., 21100 Erwin St., Woodland Hills CA 91367-3712. (818)884-6800. Fax: (818)704-5734. Editor-in-Chief: Peter Sikowitz. Editorial Assistant: Ann Lion. 95% freelance written. Works with small number of new/unpublished writers each year. Monthly magazine for health-conscious men ages 18-45. Provides reliable, entertaining guidance for the active male in all areas of lifestyle. Pays 1 month after acceptance. Publishes ms an average of 4 months after acceptance. Offers 33% kill fee. Buys all rights. Submit seasonal material 4 months in advance. Reports in 2 months. Writer's guidelines for 9 × 12 SAE. Query before sending ms.

  • Ranked as one of the best markets for freelance writers in *Writer's Digest* magazine's annual "Top 100 Markets," January 1994.

Nonfiction: Service, informative, inspirational and scientific studies written for men. Few interviews or regional news unless extraordinary. Query with published clips. Length: 1,200-1,800 words. Pays $500-1,000.

Columns/Departments: Nutrition, Mind, Appearance, Sexuality, Health. Length: 1,200-1,500 words. Pays $400-500.

Tips: "Be sure to know the magazine before sending in queries."

MUSCLE MAG INTERNATIONAL, 6465 Airport Rd., Mississauga, Ontario L4V 1E4 Canada. Editor: Johnny Fitness. 80% freelance written. "We do not care if a writer is known or unknown; published or unpublished. We simply want good instructional articles on bodybuilding." Monthly magazine for 16- to 60-year-old men and women interested in physical fitness and overall body improvement. Estab. 1972. Circ. 300,000. Buys all rights. **Pays on acceptance.** Publishes ms an average of 4 months after acceptance. Byline given. Buys 200 mss/year. Sample copy for $5 and 9 × 12 SAE. Reports in 2 months. Submit complete ms with IRCs.

Nonfiction: Articles on ideal physical proportions and importance of supplements in the diet, training for muscle size. Should be helpful and instructional and appeal to young men and women who want to live life in a vigorous and healthy style. "We would like to see articles for the physical culturist on new muscle building techniques or an article on fitness testing." Informational, how-to, personal experience, interview, profile, inspirational, humor, historical, expose, nostalgia, personal opinion, photo, spot news, new product, merchandising technique. "Also now actively looking for good instructional articles on Hardcore Fitness." Length: 1,200-1,600 words. Pays 20¢/word. Sometimes pays the expenses of writers on assignment.

Columns/Departments: Nutrition Talk (eating for top results) Shaping Up (improving fitness and stamina). Length: 1,300 words. Pays 20¢/word.

Photos: Color and b&w photos are purchased with or without ms. Pays $25 for 8 × 10 glossy exercise photos; $20 for 8 × 10 b&w posing shots. Pays $200-500 for color cover and $30 for color used inside magazine (transparencies). More for "special" or "outstanding" work.

Fillers: Newsbreaks, puzzles, quotes of the champs. Length: open. Pays $5 minimum.

Tips: "The best way to break in is to seek out the muscle-building 'stars' and do in-depth interviews with biography in mind. Color training picture support essential. Writers have to make their articles informative in that readers can apply them to help gain bodybuilding success. Specific fitness articles should quote experts and/or use scientific studies to strengthen their theories."

NAUTILUS "America's Fitness Magazine," Nautilus International, Suite 150, 9800 W. Kincey Ave., Huntersville NC 28078. (704)875-7208. Fax: (704)875-7215. Editor: Amy Stoneman. 95% freelance written. Quarterly magazine for fitness/wellness. "Editorial mission is guided toward educational, informative articles related to general wellness and the benefits of exercise. Special emphasis in many articles is geared toward strength training. Content includes medical columns, 'how-to' exercise articles, adventure/travel pieces, recipe columns and general, fitness-related subjects." Estab. 1992. Circ. 100,000. **Pays on acceptance.** Publishes ms an average of 4-5 months after acceptance. Buys first North American serial rights. Editorial lead time 6 months. Submit seasonal material 4-5 months in advance. Sample copy and writer's guidelines free on request.

Nonfiction: General interest, how-to, inspirational, interview/profile, opinion, personal experience. "No fiction." Buys 60 mss/year. Query with published clips. Length: 800-2,500 words. Pays $200 minimum. Sometimes pays expenses of writers on assignment.

Photos: Send photos with submission. Negotiates payment individually. Model releases, identification of subjects required.

Columns/Departments: Medical Q&A (exercise-related issues, medical problems), 800-1,500 words; Strength Training ("how-to" routines), 800-1,500 words. Buys 8-10 mss/year. Query with published clips. Pays $200-500.

Tips: "We appreciate any articles ideas, especially timely, innovative subjects related to fitness. Because virtually entire book is freelanced, opportunities are wide for authors. Articles generally are geared toward educational, informative nature."

NEW LIVING, Sports, Health & Fitness News That's Good For You, P.O. Box 1519, Stony Brook NY 11790-0909. (516)981-7232. Fax: (516)585-4606. Editor: Christine Lynn Harvey. 20% freelance written. Monthly tabloid covering health, fitness and leisure sports. *"New Living* readers are mainstream, health conscious consumers who are also multi-sport fitness enthusiasts, not necessarily competitive athletes." Estab. 1991. Circ. 50,000. Byline and bio notes given. Buys all rights or makes work-for-hire assignments. Submit seasonal material 2 months in advance. Accepts previously published material. Send photocoy of article. For reprints pays 10% of the amount paid for an original article. "We do not necessarily report back." Sample copy for $1.25 and 9×12 SAE. Editorial calendar for #10 SASE.

Nonfiction: General interest, how-to (health, fitness related), interview/profile (with sports and fitness personalities), photo feature. "No articles referring to other books or articles." Buys 20 mss/year. Query with published clips. Length: 500-1,500 words. Sometimes pays in contributor copies.

Photos: Send photos with submission. Offers $25/photo. Identification of subjects required. Buys all rights.

Columns/Departments: Golf, Tennis, Cycling, Running, Sports Medicine, Nutrition, Health, Recipes, Exercise Tips, Beauty. Length: 100-500 words. Buys 150 mss/year. Query. Pays $25-100.

Fillers: Facts, gags to be illustrated by cartoonist. Buys 100/year. Length: 25-100 words. Pays $5-25.

Tips: "Query with samples of previously published clips first and tell us why the proposed article is worth publishing."

‡PERSONAL FITNESS & WEIGHT LOSS MAGAZINE, Fitness and Health for Adults over 30, Publication Partners, Inc., 4151 Knob Dr., Eagan MN 55122. Editor: Carla Waldemar. Publisher: Russ Moore. 35% freelance written. Quarterly. "Articles should include what is new in health, fitness, and diet. Our audience is adults over 30 who want to stay young and fit, adults who want to take an active part in health and fitness." Estab. 1988. Circ. 150,000. Pays on publication. Byline given. Buys all rights. Submit seasonal material 3 months in advance. Accepts previously published submissions. Send photocopy of article or typed ms and information about when and where the article previously appeared. Writer's guidelines for #10 SAE with 4 first-class stamps.

Nonfiction: Book excerpts, general interest, how-to, exercise, health. Pays $200-300. Personal fitness, diet, lowfat cookbooks, and exercise are short single subjects that offer authors the opportunity to submit or write on a work-for-hire basis. Pays $650-2,000 for books.

Photos: State availability of photos with submission. Reviews transparencies. Offers $50-200/photo. Buys one-time rights.

THE PHOENIX, Recovery, Renewal and Growth, 3307 14th Ave. S., Minneapolis MN 55407-2206. (612)722-1149. Editor: Rosanne Bane. Publisher: Fran Jackson. 100% freelance written. Monthly tabloid covering recovery and personal growth. Estab. 1981. Circ. 100,000. Pays on publication. Byline given. Offers 25% kill fee. Buys one-time or simultaneous rights. Query seasonal/holiday material 4 months in advance. Accepts simultaneous and previously published submissions. Send photocopy or typed ms with rights for sale noted and information about when and where article previously appeared. For reprints pays 50-100% of the amount paid for an original article. Pays 50-100% of their fee for an original article. Query for electronic submissions. Reports on rejections within 1 month; possible acceptance or assignments can take up to a year. Sample copy, writer's guidelines and editorial calendar for 9×12 SAE with 4 first-class stamps.

Nonfiction: Essays, how-to, humor, inspirational, interview/profile and opinion. Buys 60 mss/year. Query. Length: 800-2,000 words. Pays $35-150. Sometimes pays expenses of writers on assignment. Send photos with submission. Payment for photos accepted with ms. Identification of subjects required.

Tips: "We do work with new writers and have been delighted to help our writers grow into larger, better paying markets over the years. But please know who we are and who our readers are. Please, don't send an article about your cousin's 'recovery' from having her appendix removed. That isn't what we mean by 'recovery.' Our readers are committed to personal and spiritual growth; many of them are members of 12 Step groups or other self-help programs. Their interests are usually beyond Stage I Recovery. (If you don't know what that means, you need to find out.) If you want to reach our audience, STUDY a sample copy, guidelines and editorial calendar first, then QUERY. Every other month the issue has a theme, for example, Healthy Sexuality, Parenting in Recovery or Recovery from Gambling Addition. Queries that address a theme have the best chance of being published. We emphasize articles/interviews that contain useful, practical information. Shorter pieces (800-1,000 words) are much easier to place. We are open to short, first-person stories of recovery and growth, but again, please take a look at the kinds of stories we've published in the past to get a feel for what we're looking for."

SHAPE MAGAZINE, Weider Health & Fitness, 21100 Erwin St., Woodland Hills CA 91367. (818)595-0593. Fax: (818)704-5734. Editor: Barbara Harris. 10% freelance written. Prefers to work with published/established writers, but will consider new/unpublished writers. Monthly magazine covering women's health and fitness. Estab. 1981. Circ. 800,000. Pays on publication. Publishes ms an average of 6 months after acceptance. Offers 33% kill fee. Buys all rights and reprint rights. Submit seasonal/holiday material 8 months in advance. Accepts previously published material. Send photocopy of article and information about when and where the article previously appeared. Reports in 2 months. Sample copy for 9 × 12 SAE and 4 first-class stamps.
Nonfiction: Book excerpts; exposé (health, fitness related); how-to (get fit); interview/profile (of fit women); health/fitness; humor. "We use some health and fitness articles written by professionals in their specific fields. No articles that haven't been queried first." Query with clips of published work. Length: 500-2,000 words. Pays negotiable fee. Pays expenses of writers on assignment.

SOBER TIMES, The Recovery Magazine, Sober Times Inc., 6306 E. Green Lake Way N., Seattle WA 98103. (206)523-8005. Fax: (206)523-8085. Publisher: Gerauld D. Miller. 70% freelance written. Monthly tabloid on recovery from addictions. "*Sober Times* provides information about recovery from drug, alcohol and other addictive behavior, and it champions sober, sane and healthy lifestyles." Estab. 1987. Circ. 42,000. Pays on publication. Publishes ms an average of 2 months after acceptance. Byline given. Buys all rights and makes work-for-hire assignments. Submit seasonal/holiday material 3 months in advance. Reports in 2 months. Send SASE for writer's guidelines. Sample copy for $3 and 9 × 12 SAE with 4 first-class stamps.
Nonfiction: Essays, general interest, humor, interview/profile, opinion, personal experience, photo feature. "No fiction or poetry will be considered. No medical or psychological jargon." Buys 90 mss/year. Send complete ms. Length: 900-2,000 words. Pays $50+.
Photos: Send photos with submission. Reviews prints only. Offers no additional payment for photos accepted with ms. Identification of subjects required. Buys one-time rights.
Tips: "Send in finished ms with any prints. They will only be returned if accompanied by SASE. Most accepted articles are under 1,000 words. Celebrity interviews should focus on recovery from addiction."

TOTAL HEALTH, Body, Mind and Spirit, Trio Publications, Suite 300, 6001 Topanga Canyon Blvd., Woodland Hills CA 91367. (818)887-6484. Fax: (818)887-7960. Editor: Robert L. Smith. Managing Editor: Rosemary Hofer. Prefers to work with published/established writers. 80% freelance written. Bimonthly magazine covering fitness, diet (weight loss), nutrition and mental health—"a family magazine about wholeness." Estab. 1978. Circ. 90,000. Pays on publication. Publishes ms an average of 2 months after acceptance. Byline given. Buys all rights. Submit seasonal/holiday material 4 months in advance. Reports in 2 months. Sample copy for $1 and 9 × 12 SAE with 5 first-class stamps. Writer's guidelines for #10 SASE.
Nonfiction: Exposé, how-to (pertaining to health and fitness), religious (Judeo-Christian). Especially needs articles on skin and body care and power of positive thinking articles. No personal experience articles. Buys 48 mss/year. Send complete ms. Length: 1,500-2,000 words. Pays $50-75. Sometimes pays the expenses of writers on assignment.
Photos: Send photos with submission. Offers no additional payment for photos accepted with ms. Captions, model releases and identification of subjects required.
Tips: "Feature-length articles are most open to freelancers. We are looking for more self help, prevention articles."

‡TRAVELFIT, Magazine of Travel and Fitness, Prestige Publications, Inc., 4151 Knob Dr., Eagan MN 55122. (612)452-0571. Editor: Carla Waldemar. 50% freelance written. Quarterly magazine covering what is new in fitness and diet as it relates to travel. "Our audience is active adults of all ages who enjoy travel and desire active vacations that allow them to maintain their exercise and diet routines. Adventure and active vacation articles are requested. How-to travel and exercise should include photos." Estab. 1990. Circ. 150,000. Pays on publication. Byline given. Buys all rights. Submit seasonal material 6 months in advance. Accepts previously published submissions. Send photocopy of article, or typed ms with rights for sale noted and information about when and where the article previously appeared. Writer's guidelines for #10 SAE with 4 first-class stamps.
Nonfiction: Book excerpts, general interest, how-to, nutrition, health discussions. Length: 1,000-3,000 words. Pays $50-300.
Photos: State availability of photos with submission. Reviews transparencies. Offers $50-100/photo. Buys one-time rights.

VEGETARIAN JOURNAL, P.O. Box 1463, Baltimore MD 21203-1946. (410)366-VEGE. Editors: Charles Stahler and Debra Wasserman. Bimonthly journal on vegetarianism. "*Vegetarian* issues include health, nutrition, ethics and world hunger. Articles related to nutrition should be documented by established (mainstream) nutrition studies." Estab. 1982. Circ. 20,000. **Pays on acceptance.** Publishes ms an average of 5 months after acceptance. Byline given. Makes work-for-hire assignments. Submit seasonal/holiday material 6 months in advance. Reports in 1 month. Sample copy for $3. Writer's guidelines for SASE.
Nonfiction: Book excerpts, exposé, how-to, interview/profile, new products, travel. "At present we are only looking for in-depth articles on selected nutrition subjects from registered dietitians or M.D.'s and in-depth

food-related environmental articles from environmental scientists with advanced degrees. Please query with your background. Possibly some in-depth practical and researched articles from others. No miracle cures or use of supplements." Buys 1-5 mss/year. Query with or without published clips or send complete ms. Length: 2,500-8,250 words. Pays $100-300. Sometimes pays writers with contributor copies or other premiums "if not a specific agreed upon in-depth article." Sometimes pays the expenses of writers on assignment.

Photos: Send photos with submission. Reviews prints. Identification of subjects required. Buys one-time rights.

Poetry: Avant-garde, free verse, haiku, light verse, traditional. "Poetry should be related to vegetarianism, world hunger or animal rights. No graphic animal abuse. We do not want to see the word blood in any form." Pays in copies.

Tips: "We are most open to vegan-oriented medical professionals or vegetarian/animal rights activists who are new to freelancing."

VEGETARIAN TIMES, 4 High Ridge Park, Stamford CT 06905. (203)321-1776. Fax: (203)322-1966. Managing Editor: Joanne McAllister Smart. 50% freelance written. Prefers to work with published/established writers; works with small number of new/unpublished writers each year. Monthly magazine. Circ. 300,000. Buys first serial or all rights. Byline given unless extensive revisions are required or material is incorporated into a larger article. **Pays on acceptance.** Publishes ms an average of 4 months after acceptance. Submit seasonal material 6 months in advance. Reports in 3 months. Query. Sample copy for $3. Writer's guidelines for #10 SASE.

Nonfiction: Features articles that inform readers about how vegetarianism relates to diet, cooking, lifestyle, health, consumer choices, natural foods, environmental concerns and animal welfare. "All material should be well-documented and researched, and written in a sophisticated and lively style." Informational, how-to, personal experience, interview, profile, investigative. Length: average 2,000 words. Pays flat rate of $100-1,000, sometimes higher, depending on length and difficulty of piece. Will also use 200-500-word items for news department. Sometimes pays expenses of writers on assignment.

Photos: Payment negotiated/photo.

Tips: "You don't have to be a vegetarian to write for *Vegetarian Times*, but it is vital that your article have a vegetarian perspective. The best way to pick up that slant is to read several issues of the magazine (no doubt a tip you've heard over and over). We are looking for stories that go beyond the obvious 'Why I Became a Vegetarian.' A well-written provocative query plus samples of your best writing will increase your chances of publication."

VIBRANT LIFE, A Magazine for Healthful Living, Review and Herald Publishing Assn., 55 W. Oak Ridge Dr., Hagerstown MD 21740-7390. (301)791-7000. Fax: (301)791-7012. Editor: Barbara Jackson-Hall. 20% freelance written. Enjoys working with published/established writers; works with a small number of new/unpublished writers each year. Bimonthly magazine covering health articles (especially from a prevention angle and with a Christian slant). Estab. 1845. Circ. 50,000. **Pays on acceptance.** "The average length of time between acceptance of a freelance-written manuscript and publication of the material depends upon the topics; some immediately used; others up to 2 years." Byline always given. Buys first serial, first World serial, or sometimes second serial (reprint) rights. Accepts previously published material. Send tearsheet of article and information about when and where the article previously appeared. For reprints pays 50% of the amount paid for an original article. Submit seasonal/holiday material 6 months in advance. Reports in 2 months. Sample copy for $1. Writer's guidelines for #10 SASE.

Nonfiction: Interview/profile (with personalities on health). "We seek practical articles promoting better health and a more fulfilled life. We especially like features on breakthroughs in medicine, and most aspects of health." Buys 20-25 mss/year. Send complete ms. Length: 750-1,800 words. Pays $125-250.

Photos: Send photos with ms. Needs 35mm transparencies. Not interested in b&w photos.

Tips: "*Vibrant Life* is published for baby boomers, particularly women and young professionals, age 30-45. Articles must be written in an interesting, easy-to-read style. Information must be reliable; no faddism. We are more conservative than other magazines in our field. Request a sample copy, and study the magazine and writer's guidelines."

VIM & VIGOR, America's Family Health Magazine, Suite 11, 8805 N. 23rd Ave., Phoenix AZ 85021. (602)395-5850. Fax: (602)395-5853. Editor: Fred Petrovsky. 75% freelance written. Quarterly magazine covering health and healthcare. Estab. 1985. Circ. 900,000. **Pays on acceptance.** Publishes ms an average of 3 months after acceptance. Byline given. Buys all rights. Accepts previously published material. Send photocopy of article and information about when and where the article previously appeared. Pays 50% of their fee for an original article. Query for electronic submissions. Reports in 2 weeks on queries. Sample copy for 9×12 SAE with 8 first-class stamps. Writer's guidelines for #10 SASE.

Nonfiction: Health, diseases and healthcare. "Don't send complete manuscripts. All articles are assigned to freelance writers. Send samples of your style." Buys 4 mss/year. Query with published clips. Length: 2,000 words. Pays $450. Pays expenses of writers on assignment.

Photos: Send photos with submission. Reviews contact sheets and any size transparencies. Offers no additional payment for photos accepted with ms. Captions, model releases, identification of subjects required. Buys one-time rights.
Tips: "We rarely accept suggested story ideas."

WEIGHT WATCHERS MAGAZINE, 11th Floor, 360 Lexington Ave., New York NY 10017. Fax: (212)687-4398. Editor-in-Chief: Lee Haiken. Health Editor: Deborah Kogz. Contact Managing Editor: Nancy Gagliardi, Food Editor: Joyce Handley. Associate Features Editor: Catherine Censor. Beauty & Fitness Editor: Betty Solo. 80% freelance written. Works with a small number of new/unpublished writers each year. Monthly magazine for those interested in "weight loss and weight-related issues. Interested in any article normally found in women's magazines as long as they have a 'weight angle'." Estab. 1968. Circ. 1 million. Buys first North American serial rights only. **Pays on acceptance.** Publishes ms an average of 6 months after acceptance. Reports in 6 months. Sample copy and writer's guidelines $1.95 for 9×12 SAE.
Nonfiction: "We are interested in general health and medical articles; nutrition pieces based on documented research results; fitness stories that feature a wide variety of topics appealing to everyone from beginning to seasoned exercisers; and weight loss stories that focus on interesting people and situations. While our articles are authoritative, they are written in a friendly service style. A humorous tone is acceptable as long as it is in good taste. To expedite the fact-checking process, we require a second copy of your manuscript that is annotated in the margins with the telephone numbers of all interview subjects, with citations from such written sources as books, journal articles, magazines, newsletters, newspapers, or press releases. You must attach photocopies of these sources to the annotated manuscript with relevant passages highlighted and referenced to your margin notes. We will be happy to reimburse you for copying costs." Send detailed queries with published clips and SASE. No full-length mss; send feature ideas, as well as before-and-after weight loss story ideas dealing with "real people." Length: 750-1,500 words. Pays $350-800.
Tips: "Though we prefer working with established writers, *Weight Watchers Magazine* welcomes new writers as well. As long as your query is tightly written, shows style and attention to detail, and gives evidence that you are knowledgeable about the topic. When developing a story for us, keep in mind that we prefer interview subjects to be medical professionals with university appointments who have published in their field of expertise."

YOUR HEALTH, Globe Communications Corp., 5401 NW Broken Sound Blvd., Boca Raton FL 33487. (407)997-7733. Editor: Susan Gregg. Associate Editor: Lisa Rappa. 70% freelance written. Semimonthly magazine on health and fitness. "*Your Health* is a lay-person magazine covering the entire gamut of health, fitness and medicine." Estab. 1962. Circ. 50,000. Pays on publication. Byline given. Buys first North American serial and second serial (reprint) rights. Submit seasonal/holiday material 3 months in advance. Accepts previously published submissions. Send photocopy of article and information about when and where the article previously appeared. Reports in 1 month on queries; 6 weeks on mss. Free sample copy and writer's guidelines.
Nonfiction: Book excerpts, general interest, how-to (on general health and fitness topics), inspirational, interview/profile, medical breakthroughs, natural healing and alternative medicine, new products. "Give us something new and different." Buys 75-100 mss/year. Query with published clips or send complete ms. Length: 300-2,000 words. Pays $25-150.
Photos: Send photos with submission. Reviews contact sheets, negatives, transparencies, prints. Offers $50-100/photo. Captions, model releases, identification of subjects required. Buys one-time rights.
Tips: "Freelancers can best break in by offering us stories of national interest that we won't find through other channels, such as wire services. Well-written self-help articles, especially ones that focus on natural prevention and cures are always welcome."

YOUR HEALTH, Meridian International, Inc., Box 10010, Ogden UT 84409. (801)394-9446. 65% freelance written. Monthly inhouse magazine covering personal health, customized with special imprint titles for various businesses, organizations and associations. "Articles should be timeless, noncontroversial, upscale and positive, and the subject matter should have national appeal." Circ. 40,000. **Pays on acceptance.** Publishes ms an average of 3 months after acceptance. Byline given. Buys first rights, second serial (reprint) and non-exclusive reprint rights. Accepts simultaneous and previously published submissions. Reports in 2 months with SASE. Sample copy for $1 and 9×12 SAE. Writer's guidelines with #10 SASE. (All requests for sample copies and guidelines and queries should be addressed Attention: Editorial Staff.)
Nonfiction: "Health care needs, particularly for mature reader. Medical technology; common maladies and survey of preventive or non-drug treatments; low-impact fitness activities; nutrition with recipes; positive aspects of hospital, nursing home, and home care by visiting nurse. Profiles on exceptional health care professionals or people coping with disability or illness. Photo support with healthy looking people is imperative. No chiropractic, acupuncture, podiatry or herbal treatments. Material must be endorsed by AMA or ADA. All articles are reviewed by a medical board for accuracy. Medical conclusions should be footnoted for fact-checking." Buys 40 mss/year. Query by mail. Length: 1,000 words. Pays 15¢/word for first rights plus non-exclusive reprint rights. Payment for second rights 10¢/word. Authors retain the right to resell material after it is printed by *Your Health*.

Photos: Send photos with ms. Reviews 35mm and 2¼ × 2¼ transparencies and 5 × 7 or 8 × 10 color prints. Offers $35/inside photo and $50/cover photo. Captions, model releases, identification of subjects required.

Tips: "The key for the freelancer is a well-written query letter that demonstrates that the subject of the article has national appeal; establishes that any medical claims are based on interviews with experts and/or reliable documented sources; shows that the article will have a clear, focused theme; top-quality color photos; and gives evidence that the writer/photographer is a professional, even if a beginner. The best way to get started as a contributor to *Your Health* is to prove that you can submit a well-focused article, based on facts, along with a variety of beautiful color transparencies to illustrate the story. Material is reviewed by a medical board and must be approved by them."

YOUR HEALTH & FITNESS, General Learning Corp., 60 Revere Dr., Northbrook IL 60062-1563. (708)205-3000. Senior Editor: Carol Lezak. 90-95% freelance written. Prefers to work with published/established writers. Quarterly magazine covering health and fitness. Needs "general, educational material on health, fitness and safety that can be read and understood easily by the layman." Estab. 1969. Circ. 1 million. Pays after publication. Publishes ms an average of 6 months after acceptance. No byline given (contributing editor status given in masthead). Offers 50% kill fee. Buys all rights. Reports in 1 year.

Nonfiction: General interest. "All article topics assigned. No queries; if you're interested in writing for the magazine, send a cover letter, résumé, curriculum vitae and writing samples. All topics are determined a year in advance of publication by editors; no unsolicited manuscripts." Buys approximately 65 mss/year. Length: 350-850 words. Pays $100-400 for assigned articles.

Photos: Offers no additional payment for photos accepted with ms.

Tips: "Write to a general audience that has only a surface knowledge of health and fitness topics. Possible subjects include exercise and fitness, psychology, nutrition, safety, disease, drug data, and health concerns."

History

Listed here are magazines and other periodicals written for historical collectors, genealogy enthusiasts, historic preservationists and researchers. Editors of history magazines look for fresh accounts of past events in a readable style. Some publications cover an era, such as the Civil War, or a region, while others specialize in historic preservation.

AMERICAN HERITAGE, 60 Fifth Ave., New York NY 10011. (212)206-5500. Fax: (212)620-2332. Editor: Richard Snow. 70% freelance written. Magazine published 8 times/year. Circ. 300,000. Usually buys first North American rights or all rights. Byline given. **Pays on acceptance.** Publishes ms an average of 6-12 months after acceptance. Before submitting material, "check our index to see whether we have already treated the subject." Submit seasonal material 1 year in advance. Reports in 1 month. Writer's guidelines for #10 SASE.

• Ranked as one of the best markets for freelance writers in *Writer's Digest* magazine's annual "Top 100 Markets," January 1994.

Nonfiction: Wants "historical articles by scholars or journalists intended for intelligent lay readers rather than for professional historians." Emphasis is on authenticity, accuracy and verve. "Interesting documents, photographs and drawings are always welcome. Query. Style should stress readability and accuracy." Buys 30 unsolicited mss/year. Length: 1,500-5,000 words. Sometimes pays the expenses of writers on assignment.

Tips: "We have over the years published quite a few 'firsts' from young writers whose historical knowledge, research methods and writing skills met our standards. The scope and ambition of a new writer tell us a lot about his or her future usefulness to us. A major article gives us a better idea of the writer's value. Everything depends on the quality of the material. We don't really care whether the author is 20 and unknown, or 80 and famous, or vice versa."

AMERICAN HISTORY, P.O. Box 8200, Harrisburg PA 17105-8200. (717)657-9555. Fax: (717)657-9526. Editor: Ed Holm. 60% freelance written. Bimonthly magazine of cultural, social, military and political history published for a general audience. Estab. 1966. Circ. 160,000. **Pays on acceptance.** Byline given. Buys all rights. Query for electronic submissions. Reports in 10 weeks on queries. Writer's guidelines for #10 SASE. Sample copy and guidelines for $4 (includes 3rd class postage) or $3.50 and 9 × 12 SAE with 4 first-class stamps.

Nonfiction: Regular features include American Profiles (biographies of noteworthy historical figures); Artifacts (stories behind historical objects); Portfolio (pictorial features on artists, photographers and graphic subjects); Digging Up History (coverage of recent major archaeological and historical discoveries); Testaments to the Past (living history articles on major restored historical sites). "Material is presented on a popular rather than a scholarly level." Writers are required to query before submitting ms. "Query letters should be limited to a concise 1-2 page proposal defining your article with an emphasis on its unique qualities." Buys 10-15 mss/year. Length: 1,000-5,000 words depending on type of article. Pays $200-1,000. Sometimes pays the expenses of writers on assignment.

Photos: Welcomes suggestions for illustrations. Pays for the reproduced color illustrations that the author provides.

Tips: "Key prerequisites for publication are thorough research and accurate presentation, precise English usage and sound organization, a lively style, and a high level of human interest. Submissions received without return postage will not be considered or returned. Inappropriate materials include: fiction, book reviews, travelogues, personal/family narratives not of national significance, articles about collectibles/antiques, living artists, local/individual historic buildings/landmarks and articles of a current editorial nature."

AMERICA'S CIVIL WAR, Cowles History Group, Suite 300, 602 S. King St., Leesburg VA 22075. (703)771-9400. Editor: Roy Morris, Jr. 95% freelance written. Bimonthly magazine of "popular history and straight historical narrative for both the general reader and the Civil War buff." Estab. 1988. Circ. 125,000. Pays on publication. Publishes ms up to 2 years after acceptance. Byline given. Buys first North American serial rights. Query for electronic submissions. Reports in 3 months on queries; 6 months on mss. Sample copy for $3.95. Writer's guidelines for #10 SASE.

Nonfiction: Book excerpts, historical, travel. No fiction or poetry. Buys 48 mss/year. Query. Length: 4,000 words maximum. Pays $300 maximum.

Photos: Send photos with submission. Payment for photos negotiable. Captions and identification of subjects required. Buys one-time rights.

Columns/Departments: Personality (probes); Ordnance (about weapons used); Commands (about units); Travel (about appropriate historical sites). Buys 24 mss/year. Query. Length: 2,000 words. Pays up to $150.

ANCESTRY MAGAZINE, (formerly *Ancestry Newsletter*), Ancestry, Inc., P.O. Box 476, Salt Lake City UT 84110-0476. (801)531-1790. Fax: (801)531-1798. Editor: Loretto Szvcs. 95% freelance written. Eager to work with new/unpublished writers. Bimonthly magazine covering genealogy and family history. "We publish practical, instructional and informative pieces specifically applicable to the field of genealogy. Our audience comprises active genealogists, both hobbyists and professionals." Estab. 1984. Circ. 8,200. Pays on publication. Publishes ms an average of 9 months after acceptance. Byline given. Buys first North American serial or all rights. Submit seasonal/holiday material 4 months in advance. Accepts simultaneous submissions. Reports in 2 weeks. Sample copy and writer's guidelines for 9 × 12 SAE with 3 first-class stamps.

Nonfiction: General interest (genealogical); historical; how-to (genealogical research techniques); instructional; photo feature (genealogically related). No unpublished or published family histories, genealogies, the "story of my great-grandmother" or personal experiences. Buys 25-30 mss/year. Send complete ms. Length: 1,500-4,000 words. Pays $25-75.

Photos: Send high-quality photos (preferably color) with submission. Reviews both b&w and color transparencies or prints, 35mm to 8 × 10. Offers no additional payment for photos accepted with ms. Identification of subjects required. Buys one-time rights.

Tips: "You don't have to be famous, but you must know something about genealogy. Our readers crave any information which might assist them in their ancestral quest."

THE ARTILLERYMAN, Cutter & Locke, Inc., Publishers, RR 1 Box 36, Tunbridge VT 05077. (802)889-3500. Editor: C. Peter Jorgensen. 60% freelance written. Quarterly magazine covering antique artillery, fortifications and crew-served weapons 1750 to 1900 for competition shooters, collectors and living history reenactors using artillery. "Emphasis on Revolutionary War and Civil War but includes everyone interested in pre-1900 artillery and fortifications, preservation, construction of replicas, etc." Estab. 1979. Circ. 2,200. Pays on publication. Publishes ms an average of 6 months after acceptance. Byline given. Not copyrighted. Buys one-time rights. Accepts simultaneous and previously published submissions. Reports in 3 weeks. Sample copy and writer's guidelines for 9 × 12 SAE with 4 first-class stamps.

Nonfiction: Historical; how-to (reproduce ordnance equipment/sights/implements/tools/accessories, etc.); interview/profile; new product; opinion (must be accompanied by detailed background of writer and include references); personal experience; photo feature; technical (must have footnotes); travel (where to find interesting antique cannon). Interested in "artillery *only*, for sophisticated readers. Not interested in other weapons, battles in general." Buys 24-30 mss/year. Send complete ms. Length: 300 words minimum. Pays $20-60. Sometimes pays the expenses of writers on assignment.

Photos: Send photos with ms. Pays $5 for 5 × 7 and larger b&w prints. Captions, identification of subjects required.

Tips: "We regularly use freelance contributions for Places-to-Visit, Cannon Safety, The Workshop and Unit Profiles departments. Also need pieces on unusual cannon or cannon with a known and unique history. To judge whether writing style and/or expertise will suit our needs, writers should ask themselves if they could knowledgably talk *artillery* with an expert. Subject matter is of more concern than writer's background."

For information on setting your freelance fees, see How Much Should I Charge?

‡**CANADIAN WEST**, P.O. Box 3399, Langley, British Columbia V3A 4R7 Canada. (604)534-9378. Editor-in-Chief: Garnet Basque. 80-100% freelance written. Works with a small number of new/unpublished writers each year. Quarterly magazine emphasizing pioneer history, primarily of British Columbia, Alberta and the Yukon. Estab. 1981. Circ. 8,000. Pays on publication. Publishes ms an average of 6 months after acceptance. Buys first North American serial rights. Phone queries OK. Accepts previously published material. Send typed ms with rights for sale noted and information about when and where the article previously appeared. For reprints pays 50% of the amount paid for an original article. Query for electronic submissions. Reports in 2 months. Sample copy and writer's guidelines for $1.50 and 9×12 SAE.

Nonfiction: How-to (related to gold panning and dredging); historical (pioneers, shipwrecks, massacres, battles, exploration, logging, Indians, ghost towns, mining camps, gold rushes and railroads). Interested in an occasional US based article from states bordering British Columbia when the story also involves some aspect of Canadian history. No American locale articles. Buys 28 mss/year. Submit complete ms. Length: 2,000-3,500 words. Pays $100-300.

Photos: All mss must include photos or other artwork. Submit photos with ms. Pays $10/b&w photo and $20/color photo. Captions preferred. "Photographs are kept for future reference with the right to re-use. However, we do not forbid other uses, generally, as these are historical prints from archives."

Columns/Departments: Open to suggestions for new columns/departments.

CHICAGO HISTORY, The Magazine of the Chicago Historical Society, Chicago Historical Society, Clark St. at North Ave., Chicago IL 60614-6099. (312)642-4600. Fax: (312)266-2077. Acting Editor: Claudia Lamm Wood. Assistant Editor: Rosemary Adams. 100% freelance written. Works with a small number of new/unpublished writers each year. Triannual magazine covering Chicago history: cultural, political, economic, social and architectural. Estab. 1945. Circ. 9,500. Pays on publication. Publishes ms an average of 1 year after acceptance. Byline given. Buys all rights. Submit seasonal/holiday material 9 months in advance. Query for electronic submissions. Reports in 4 months. Sample copy for $3.50 and 9×12 SAE with 3 first-class stamps. Free writer's guidelines.

Nonfiction: Book excerpts, essays, historical, photo feature. Articles should be "analytical, informative, and directed at a popular audience with a special interest in history." No "cute" articles. Buys 8-12 mss/year. Query or send complete ms. Length: approximately 4,500 words. Pays $150-250.

Photos: Send photos with submission and submit photocopies. Would prefer no originals. Offers no additional payment for photos accepted with ms. Identification of subjects required.

Tips: "A freelancer can best break in by 1) calling to discuss an article idea with editor; and 2) submitting a detailed outline of proposed article. All sections of *Chicago History* are open to freelancers, but we suggest that authors do not undertake to write articles for the magazine unless they have considerable knowledge of the subject and are willing to research it in some detail. We require a footnoted manuscript, although we do not publish the notes."

CIVIL WAR TIMES ILLUSTRATED, P.O. Box 8200, Harrisburg PA 17105-8200. (717)657-9555. Fax: (717)657-9526. Editor: John E. Stanchak. 90% freelance written. Works with a small number of new/unpublished writers each year. Bimonthly magazine. Estab. 1961. Circ. 176,000. **Pays on acceptance.** Publishes ms an average of 12-18 months after acceptance. Buys all, first or one-time rights, or makes work-for-hire assignments. Submit seasonal/holiday material 1 year in advance. Query for electronic submissions. Reports in 2 weeks on queries; 4 months on mss. Sample copy for $3.50. Free writer's guidelines.

Nonfiction: Profile, photo feature, Civil War historical material. "Positively no fiction or poetry." Buys 20 freelance mss/year. Length: 2,500-5,000 words. Query. Pays $75-600. Sometimes pays the expenses of writers on assignment.

Photos: W. Douglas Shirk, art director. Send photos. Pays $5-50 for 8×10 b&w glossy prints and copies of Civil War photos; $1,000-1,500 for 4-color cover photos; $100-250 for color photos for interior use.

Tips: "We're very open to new submissions. Query us after reading several back issues, then submit illustration and art possibilities along with the query letter for the best 'in.' Never base the narrative solely on family stories or accounts. Submissions must be written in a popular style but based on solid academic research. Manuscripts are required to have marginal source annotations."

‡**LOUIS L'AMOUR WESTERN MAGAZINE**, Dell Magazines, 1540 Broadway, New York NY 10036. (212)782-8532. Editor: Elana Lore. 100% freelance written. Bimonthly magazine covering western fiction. "*LLWM* publishes the best of new, never before published western fiction being written today. We focus on the traditional western, but consider modern, mystery-oriented, Native American, and other types of western fiction. Our audience is 70% male, 35-64, living mostly in nonurban areas across the US and in Canada." Estab. 1993. **Pays on acceptance.** Publishes ms an average of 6 months after acceptance. Byline given. Buys first serial and anthology rights. Editorial lead time 6-8 months. Submit seasonal material 6-8 months in advance. Accepts simultaneous submissions. Reports in 1 month on queries; 2-3 months on mss. Sample copy for $3.95. Writer's guidelines for #10 SASE.

Nonfiction: Historical/nostalgic (profiles of western historical figures), interview/profile, travel (in the West). Buys 18 mss/year. Query with published clips. Length: 2,500-3,000 words. Pays 8¢/word. Sometimes pays expanses of writers on assignment.

Photos: State availability of photos with submission. Negotiates payment individually.

Columns/Departments: Interview (current western figures), 2,500-3,000 words; Frontier Profile (historical western figures), 2,500-3,000 words; Western Travel (combination of modern/historical info on locations, done by experts in the area), 2,500-3,000 words. Buys 18 mss/year. Query with published clips. Pays 8¢/word.

Fiction: Western. Buys 50 mss/year. Send complete ms. **Length:** 12,000 words maximum. Pays 8¢/word.

Tips: "For fiction, do your historical research to make sure your story is accurate. Avoid writing about well-known historical figures in your work. For nonfiction, also, avoid querying us about well-known historical figures. We want people and places that aren't already well-known to our readership."

‡**THE LINCHPIN, For Memoirists, Genealogists, And Family Historians,** EJP Publishing Co., P.O. Box 44268, Tucson AZ 85733. Editor: Ethel Jackson Price. 60% freelance written. Quarterly newsletter "for memoirists, genealogists, and family historians. Other than that, we vary. Some articles are more technical than others but all must be 'reader friendly'." Estab. 1991. Circ. 1,281. Pays some on acceptance, some on publication. Publishes ms an average of 6 months after acceptance. Byline given. Buys second serial (reprint) rights, all rights or makes work-for-hire assignments. Submit seasonal material 4 months in advance. Accepts previously published submissions. Reports in 3 weeks on queries; 2 months on mss. Sample copy for #10 SAE and 2 first-class stamps. Writer's guidelines free on request.

Nonfiction: Book excerpts, essays, general interest, historical/nostalgic, how-to, humor, interview/profile, new product, personal experience, book reviews (but write first). Special issues: State-by-State collection of articles re: colorful characters and events. Query always. Length: 800 words maximum. Pays $30.

Columns/Departments: Books, etc. (reviews) up to 800 words. Buys at least 4 mss/year. Query always. Pays $10-30.

Fillers: Facts, newsbreaks. Length: 100 words maximum. Pays $10.

Tips: "We strongly encourage the novice writer who may or may not be previously published. We just as strongly suggest that anyone wanting to write for us requests our list of suggested ideas. Otherwise, we're quite flexible."

MAIL CALL, The Most Stirring Newsletter for Civil War Enthusiasts, P.O. Box 5031, South Hackensack NJ 07606-5031. (201)296-0419. Managing Editor: Anna Pansini. Publisher: Chris Jackson. 25% freelance written. Bimonthly hobbyist newsletter covering Civil War in America "for Civil War enthusiasts interested in reading and writing first account impressions of soldiers, Union and Confederate, as well as today's reenactors and historians." Estab. 1990. Circ. 500. Pays on publication. Publishes ms 6-12 months after acceptance. Byline given "plus short bio or background." Offers 50% kill fee. Buys one-time rights. Editorial lead time 6 months. Submit seasonal material 6 months in advance. Accepts simultaneous and previously published submissions. Send photocopy of article or typed ms with rights for sale noted and information about when and where the article previously appeared. For reprints, pays 25% of the amount paid for an original article. Reports in 4 months. Sample copy and writer's guidelines for $5.

Nonfiction: Book excerpts, essays, exposé, general interest, historical/nostalgic, how-to, humor, inspirational, interview/profile, opinion, personal experience, religious, travel, poetry, song lyrics, quotes. "No stories which only touch or mention Civil War themes. We prefer articles where Civil War theme is central." Buys 10 mss/year. Query. Length: 500-5,000 words. Pays $25 minimum for assigned articles; $5 minimum for unsolicited articles. "Pays contributor copies for anything other than personal experience." Sometimes pays expenses of writers on assignment.

Columns/Departments: Open Letters (personal experience). Buys 4 mss/year. Query. Pays $5-100.

Fiction: Adventure, condensed novels, ethnic, historical, horror, humorous, mainstream, novel excerpts, religious, romance, science fiction, slice-of-life vignettes, suspense, western, Civil War. Articles where Civil War theme is central. Buys 2 mss/year. Query. Length: 500-2,500 words. Pays copies to $50 maximum.

Poetry: Free verse, traditional. Buys 4 poems/year. Submit unlimited number of poems. Length: 2-100 lines. Pays $5-50.

Fillers: Anecdotes, facts, gags, illustrations, newsbreaks, short humor. Buys 5/year. Length: 10-500 words. Pays $5-25.

Tips: "Writers should be familiar with Civil War history, books or movies, music, sites, battlefields or reenacting."

MEDIA HISTORY DIGEST, % *Editor and Publisher,* 11 W. 19th St., New York NY 10011-4234. Editor: Hiley H. Ward. 100% freelance written. Semiannual (will probably return to being quarterly) magazine. Estab. 1980. Circ. 2,000. Pays on publication. Publishes ms an average of 4 months after acceptance. Byline given. Buys first or second serial (reprint) rights. Submit seasonal/holiday material 8 months in advance. Accepts previously published submissions. Reports in 3 months. Sample copy for $3.75.

Nonfiction: Historical/nostalgic (media); humor (media history); puzzles (media history). Buys 15 mss/year. Query. Length: 1,500-3,000 words. Pays $125 for assigned articles; $100 for unsolicited articles. Pays in contributor copies for articles prepared by university graduate students. Sometimes pays the expenses of writers on assignment.

Photos: Send photos with submission. Buys first or reprint rights.

Columns/Departments: Quiz Page (media history) and "Media Hysteria" (media history humor). Query. Pays $50-125 for humor; $25 for puzzles.

Fillers: Anecdotes and short humor on topics of media history.

Tips: "Send in-depth enterprising material targeted for our specialty—media history, pre-1970."

MILITARY HISTORY, Cowles History Group, #300, 602 S. King St. Leesburg VA 22075. (703)771-9400. Editor: C. Brian Kelly. 95% freelance written. Circ. 200,000. "We'll work with anyone, established or not, who can provide the goods and convince us as to its accuracy." Bimonthly magazine covering all military history of the world. "We strive to give the general reader accurate, highly readable, often narrative popular history, richly accompanied by period art." Pays on publication. Publishes ms 1-2 years after acceptance. Byline given. Buys all rights. Submit anniversary material 1 year in advance. Reports in 3 months on queries; 6 months on mss. Sample copy for $3.95. Writer's guidelines for #10 SASE.

Nonfiction: Historical; interview (military figures of commanding interest); personal experience (only occasionally). Buys 18 mss, plus 6 interviews/year. Query with published clips. "To propose an article, submit a short, self-explanatory query summarizing the story proposed, its highlights and/or significance. State also your own expertise, access to sources or proposed means of developing the pertinent information." Length: 4,000 words. Pays $400.

Columns/Departments: Espionage, weaponry, perspectives, personality, travel (with military history of the place) and books—all relating to military history. Buys 24 mss/year. Query with published clips. Length: 2,000 words. Pays $200.

Tips: "We would like journalistically 'pure' submissions that adhere to basics, such as full name at first reference, same with rank, and definition of prior or related events, issues cited as context or obscure military 'hardware.' Read the magazine, discover our style, and avoid subjects already covered. Pick stories with strong art possibilities (*real* art and photos), send photocopies, tell us where to order the art. Avoid historical overview, focus upon an event with appropriate and accurate context. Provide bibliography. Tell the story in popular but elegant style."

OLD MILL NEWS, Society for the Preservation of Old Mills, 604 Ensley Dr., Rt. 29, Knoxville TN 37920. (615)577-7757. Editor: Michael LaForest. 40% freelance written. Quarterly magazine covering "water, wind, animal and steam power mills (usually grist mills)." Estab. 1972. Circ. 2,500. **Pays on acceptance.** Byline given. Buys first North American serial or first rights. Accepts simultaneous submissions. Reports in 1 month. Sample copy for $3.

Nonfiction: Historical, technical. "No poetry, recipes, mills converted to houses, commercial or alternative uses, nostalgia." Buys 8 mss/year. Query with or without published clips, or send complete ms. Length: 400-1,000 words. Pays $15-50.

Photos: Send photos with submission. "At least one recent photograph of subject is highly recommended." Uses b&w or color prints only; no transparencies. Offers $5-10/photo. Identification of subjects required. Buys one-time rights.

Fillers: Short humor. Buys 3-4/year. Length: 50-200 words. Pays $10 maximum.

Tips: "An interview with the mill owner/operator is usually necessary. Accurate presentation of the facts and good English are required."

‡OLD WEST, Western Publications, P.O. Box 2107, Stillwater OK 74076. (405)743-3370. Editor: John Joerschke. 100% freelance written. Quarterly magazine covering Western American history. Estab. 1964. Circ. 30,000. **Pays on acceptance.** Publishes ms an average of 6 months after acceptance. Byline given. Buys first North American serial rights. Editorial lead time 5 months. Submit seasonal material 6 months in advance. Reports in 6 weeks on queries. Sample copy for $2. Writer's guidelines for #10 SASE.

Nonfiction: Historical/nostalgic, travel. Buys 120 mss/year. Query. Length: 750-4,000 words. Pays 3¢/word minimum.

Photos: Send photos with submission. Reviews contact sheets, 35mm or larger transparencies, 4×5 or larger prints. Offers $10/photo. Captions required. Buys one-time rights.

Columns/Departments: Going Western (places or events in the West, travel related), 750-1,000 words. Buys 8-10 mss/year. Query. Pays 3¢/word minimum.

Tip: "While we publish stories about old West legends such as Wyatt Earp, Jesse James, and Billy the Kid, we need stories about unusual incidents and characters. Make sure research is original and thorough. Please query before submission."

PERSIMMON HILL, 1700 NE 63rd St., Oklahoma City OK 73111. Fax: (405)478-4714. Editor: M.J. Van Deventer. 70% freelance written. Prefers to work with published/established writers; works with a small number of new/unpublished writers each year. Quarterly magazine for an audience interested in Western art, Western history, ranching and rodeo, including historians, artists, ranchers, art galleries, schools, and libraries. Publication of the National Cowboy Hall of Fame and Western Heritage Center. Estab. 1970. Circ. 15,000. Buys first rights. Byline given. Buys 35-50 mss/year. Pays on publication. Publishes ms an average of

6 months-2 years after acceptance. Reports in 3 months. Sample copy for $7 and 8 first-class stamps. Writer's guidelines for #10 SASE.

• *Persimmon Hill* needs reviewers for book review column.

Nonfiction: Historical and contemporary articles on famous Western figures connected with pioneering the American West, Western art, rodeo, cowboys, etc. (or biographies of such people), stories of Western flora and animal life and environmental subjects. "We want thoroughly researched and historically authentic material written in a popular style. May have a humorous approach to subject. No broad, sweeping, superficial pieces; i.e., the California Gold Rush or rehashed pieces on Billy the Kid, etc." Length: 1,500 words. Query with clips. Pays $100-250; special work negotiated.

Photos: Black and white glossy prints or color transparencies purchased with ms, or on assignment. Pays according to quality and importance for b&w and color photos. Suggested captions required.

Tips: "Excellent illustrations for articles are essential! No telephone queries."

PRESERVATION NEWS, National Trust for Historic Preservation, 1785 Massachusetts Ave. NW, Washington DC 20036. (202)673-4075. Executive Editor: Arnold M. Berke. 30% freelance written. Prefers to work with published/established writers. Bimonthly tabloid covering preservation of historic buildings in the US. "We cover proposed or completed preservation projects and controversies involving historic buildings and districts. Most entries are news stories, features or opinion pieces." Circ. 200,000. Pays on publication. Publishes ms an average of 1 month after acceptance. Byline given. Offers variable kill fee. Buys one-time rights. Simultaneous queries OK. Reports in 2 months on queries. Sample copy for $1 for 11 × 13 SAE and 56¢ postage.

• *Preservation News* will be merging with *Historic Preservation* magazine.

Nonfiction: News, interview/profile, opinion, humor, personal experience, photo feature, travel. Buys 16 mss/year. Query with published clips. Length: 500-1,400 words. Pays $150-450. Sometimes pays the expenses of writers on assignment, but not long-distance travel.

Photos: Send photos with query or ms. Reviews b&w contact sheets, b&w or color prints and slides. Pays $25-100. Identification of subjects required. Credits given.

Columns/Departments: "We seek reporters who can give a historic preservation slant on development conflict throughout the United States. We also are looking for foreign coverage." Buys 8 mss/year. Query with published clips. Length: 800-1,400 words. Pays $150-450.

Tips: "Do not send or propose histories of buildings, descriptive accounts of cities or towns or long-winded treatises on any subjects. This is a *newspaper*. Proposals for coverage of fast-breaking events are especially welcome."

TIMELINE, Ohio Historical Society, 1982 Velma Ave., Columbus OH 43211-2497. (614)297-2360. Fax: (614)297-2411. Editor: Christopher S. Duckworth. 90% freelance written. Works with a small number of new/unpublished writers each year. Bimonthly magazine covering history, natural history, archaeology and fine and decorative arts. Estab. 1885. Circ. 17,500. **Pays on acceptance.** Publishes ms an average of 1 year after acceptance. Byline given. Offers $75 minimum kill fee. Buys first North American serial or all rights. Submit seasonal/holiday material 6 months in advance. Query for electronic submissions. Reports in 3 weeks on queries; 6 weeks on mss. Sample copy for $5 and 9 × 12 SAE. Writer's guidelines for #10 SASE.

Nonfiction: Book excerpts, essays, historical, profile (of individuals), photo feature. Buys 22 mss/year. Query. Length: 500-6,000 words. Pays $100-900.

Photos: Send photos with submission. Will not consider submissions without ideas for illustration. Reviews contact sheets, transparencies, 8 × 10 prints. Captions, model releases, and identification of subjects required. Buys one-time rights.

Tips: "We want crisply written, authoritative narratives for the intelligent lay reader. An Ohio slant may strengthen a submission, but it is not indispensable. Contributors must know enough about their subject to explain it clearly and in an interesting fashion. We use high-quality illustration with all features. If appropriate illustration is unavailable, we can't use the feature. The writer who sends illustration ideas with a manuscript has an advantage, but an often-published illustration won't attract us."

TRACES OF INDIANA AND MIDWESTERN HISTORY, Indiana Historical Society, 315 W Ohio St., Indianapolis IN 46202-3299. (317)232-1884. Fax: (317)233-3109. Executive Editor: Thomas Mason. Managing Editor: Kent Calder. 80% freelance written. Quarterly magazine on Indiana and Midwestern history. Estab. 1989. Circ. 11,000. **Pays on acceptance.** Publishes ms an average of 6 months after acceptance. Byline given. Buys one-time rights. Submit seasonal/holiday material 1 year in advance. Accepts previously published submissions. Reports in 3 months on mss. Sample copy for $5 and 9 × 12 SAE with 6 first-class stamps. Writer's guidelines for #10 SASE.

Nonfiction: Book excerpts, historical essays, photo features. Buys 20 mss/year. Send complete ms. Length: 2,000-3,000 words. Pays $100-500.

Photos: Send photos with submission. Reviews contact sheets, transparencies and prints. Pays "reasonable photographic expenses." Captions, model releases and identification of subjects required. Buys one-time rights.

Tips: "Freelancers should be aware of prerequisites for writing history in general and popular history in particular. Should have some awareness of other magazines of this type published by midwestern and western historical societies. Preference is given to subjects with an Indiana connection. Quality of potential illustration is also important."

TRUE WEST, Western Periodicals, Inc., P.O. Box 2107, Stillwater OK 74076-2107. (405)743-3370. Editor: John Joerschke. 100% freelance written. Works with a small number of new/unpublished writers each year. Magazine on Western American history before 1940. "We want reliable research on significant historical topics written in lively prose for an informed general audience." Estab. 1953. Circ. 30,000. **Pays on acceptance.** Publishes ms an average of 4 months after acceptance. Byline given. Buys first North American serial rights. Submit seasonal/holiday material 6 months in advance. Simultaneous queries OK. Reports in 1 month on queries; 2 months on mss. Sample copy for $2 and 9×12 SAE. Writer's guidelines for #10 SASE.
Nonfiction: Historical/nostalgic, how-to, photo feature, travel. "We do not want rehashes of worn-out stories, historical fiction or history written in a fictional style." Buys 150 mss/year. Query. Length: 500-4,500 words. Pays 3-6¢/word.
Photos: Send photos with accompanying query or ms. Pays $10 for b&w prints. Identification of subjects required. Buys one-time rights.
Columns/Departments: Western Roundup—200-300-word short articles on historically oriented places to go and things to do in the West. Should include one b&w print. Buys 12-16 mss/year. Send complete ms. Pays $35.
Tips: "Do original research on fresh topics. Stay away from controversial subjects unless you are truly knowledgable in the field. Read our magazines and follow our guidelines. A freelancer is most likely to break in with us by submitting thoroughly researched, lively prose on relatively obscure topics. First person accounts rarely fill our needs."

VIKINGSHIP, Suite 103, 128 Asbury Ave., Evanston IL 60202-3886. (708)733-0332. Editor: W.R. Anderson. 25% freelance written. Quarterly historical newsletter "focusing on Medieval evidence of Norse Vikings in America." Estab. 1962. Circ. 1,240. **Pays on acceptance.** Byline sometimes given. Buys one-time rights. Accepts previously published submissions. Send tearsheet of article and information about when and where the article previously appeared. Reports in 2 weeks on queries. Sample copy for $1 and #10 SAE with 2 first-class stamps.
Nonfiction: Exposé, general interest. "No rehash of textbook/encyclopedia data, which is generally known and largely false." Buys 3 mss/year. Query. Length: 100-2,000 words. Pays $10-200. Sometimes offers membership dues in lieu of small payment.
Photos: Send photos with submission. Reviews contact sheets and 5×7 prints. Offers $10/photo. Captions, model releases and identification of subjects required. Buys one-time rights.

VIRGINIA CAVALCADE, Virginia State Library and Archives, Richmond VA 23219-3491. (804)786-2312. Editor: Edward D.C. Campbell, Jr.. Quarterly magazine primarily for readers with an interest in Virginia history. 90% freelance written. "Both established and new writers are invited to submit articles." Estab. 1951. Circ. 9,000. Buys all rights. Byline given. **Pays on acceptance.** Publishes ms an average of 1 year after acceptance. Submit seasonal material 18 months in advance. Reports in 6 weeks. Sample copy for $3. Free writer's guidelines.
Nonfiction: "We welcome readable and factually accurate articles that are relevant to some phase of Virginia history. Art, architecture, literature, education, business, technology and transportation are all acceptable subjects, as well as political and military affairs. Articles must be based on thorough, scholarly research. We require foot- or end notes but do not publish them. Any period from the age of exploration to the mid-20th century, and any geographical section or area of the state may be represented. Must deal with subjects that will appeal to a broad readership. Articles must be suitable for illustration, although it is not necessary that the author provide the pictures. If the author does have pertinent illustrations or knows their location, the editor appreciates information concerning them." Buys 12-15 mss/year. Query. Length: 3,500-4,500 words. Pays $100.
Photos: Uses 8×10 b&w glossy prints; transparencies should be at least 4×5.
Tips: "*Cavalcade* employs a narrative, anecdotal style. Too many submissions are written for an academic audience or are simply not sufficiently gripping."

WESTERN TALES, P.O. Box 33842, Granada Hills CA 91394. Editor: Dorman Nelson. Managing Editor: Mariann Kumke. Editor/Publisher: Dorman Nelson. 100% freelance written. Quarterly historical/western fiction literary magazine. Estab. 1993. Circ. 5,000 (1st printing). **Pays on acceptance.** Byline given. Buys first North American serial and/or second serial (reprint) rights. Publishes novel excerpts. Editorial lead time 6 months. Accepts previously published submissions. Send photocopy of article or short story and information about when and where the article previously appeared. For reprints pays same amount paid for an original article. Reports in 2 weeks on queries; 3 months on mss. Sample copy for $6. Writer's guidelines for #10 SASE.
Nonfiction: Book excerpts, general interest (western), historical/nostalgic, shorts, humor. Special issues: Edgar Rice Burroughs; Women Western Writers; individual Western Writers; Native American Writers. Buys up to 50 mss/year. Query with or without published clips. Pays $25.

Photos: Send photos with submission. Reviews contact sheets or 5 × 7 prints (no larger). Negotiates payment individually. Buys one-time rights. "Note: western oriented photos only."

Columns/Departments: Music (country/western/bluegrass reviews); Events (events around country – rodeos, pow-wows, round-ups etc.Review (review of western poetry – books, notes and writer's bios). Buys 12 each mss/year. Query. Negotiates payment.

Fiction: Adventure (western), historical, humorous (western), romance (western), slice-of-life vignettes, western. Buys 65 mss/year. Query with or without published clips, or send complete ms. Pays $100-negotiable maximum.

Poetry: Western-flavor. Buys to 50 poems/year. Submit maximum 3 poems. Length to 20 lines. Pays $25-negotiable maximum.

Tips: "Write a good tale and send'er in! Note: The mainline is short western stories of fiction!"

WILD WEST, Cowles History Group, #300, 602 S. King St., Leesburg VA 22075. (703)771-9400. Editor: William M. Vogt. 95% freelance written. Bimonthly magazine on history of the American West. *"Wild West* covers the popular (narrative) history of the American West – events, trends, personalities, anything of general interest." Estab. 1988. Circ. 125,000. Pays on publication. Byline given. Buys all rights. Submit seasonal/holiday material 1 year in advance. Query for electronic submissions. Sample copy for $3.95. Writer's guidelines for #10 SASE.

Nonfiction: Historical/nostalgic, humor, travel. No fiction or poetry – nothing current. Buys 24 mss/year. Query. Length: 4,000 words. Pays $300.

Photos: Send photos with submission. Captions, identification of subjects required. Buys one-time rights or all rights.

Columns/Departments: Travel; Gun Fighters & Lawmen; Personalities; Warriors & Chiefs; Artist West; Books Reviews. Buys 16 mss/year. Length: 2,000. Pays $150 for departments, by the word for book reviews.

YESTERDAY'S MAGAZETTE, The Magazine of Memories, Independent Publishing Co., P.O. Box 15126, Sarasota FL 34277-1526. Editor: Ned Burke. 95% freelance written. Bimonthly magazine of nostalgia. Estab. 1973. Circ. 2,500. Pays on publication. Publishes ms an average of 6 months after acceptance. Byline given. Buys first rights. Submit seasonal/holiday material 4 months in advance. Reports in 2 months. Sample copy for $3 and 9 × 12 SAE with 4 first-class stamps. Free writer's guidelines.

• *Yesterday's Magazette* needs shorter articles, 500-1,000 words with photos or artwork.

Nonfiction: General interest, historical/nostalgic, humor, inspirational, interview/profile ('yesterday' celebrities), opinion, personal experience, photo feature. Special issues: "Christmas" (deadline November 15, featuring "My Favorite Christmas Memory"); traditional poetry issue (May, deadline April 15). Buys 100 mss/year. Send complete ms. Length: 100-1,500 words. Pays $5-25 for unsolicited articles. Pays for most short articles, poems, etc.

Photos: Send photos with submission. Reviews 5 × 7 prints. Offers no additional payment for photos accepted with ms. Identification of subjects required. Buys one-time rights. "Write for details on our new 'Miss Yesterday' contest." SASE required.

Columns/Departments: The Way We Were (a look at certain period of time – 40s, 50s, etc.); When I Was a Kid (childhood memories); In A Word (objects from the past – 'ice box', etc.); Yesterday Trivia (quiz on old movie stars, TV shows, etc.); all 300-750 words. Buys 12 mss/year. Send complete ms. Length: 500-750 words. Pays $5-10.

Fiction: Historical, humorous, slice-of-life vignettes. "No modern settings." Buys 4 mss/year. Send complete ms. Length: 750-2,500 words. Pays $5-25.

Poetry: Traditional. Nothing other than traditional. Buys 50 poems/year. Submit maximum 5 poems. Length: 4-32 lines. Pays $5 and/or contributor copies.

Fillers: Anecdotes, short humor. Buys 5/year. Length: 50-250 words. Pays $5 and/or contributor copies.

Tips: "We would like to see more 40s, 50s and 60s pieces, especially with photos. It's hard to reject any story with a good photo. All areas are open, especially 'Plain Folks Page' which uses letters, comments and opinions of readers."

Hobby and Craft

Magazines in this category range from home video to cross stitch. Craftspeople and hobbyists who read these magazines want new ideas while collectors need to know what is most valuable and why. Collectors, do-it-yourselfers and craftspeople look to these magazines for inspiration and information. Publications covering antiques and miniatures are also listed here. Publications covering the business side of antiques and collectibles are listed in the Trade Art, Design and Collectibles section.

THE AMERICAN COLLECTORS JOURNAL, P.O. Box 407, Kewanee IL 61443-0407. (308)852-2602. Editor: Carol Savidge. 55% freelance written. Eager to work with new/unpublished writers. Bimonthly tabloid covering antiques and collectibles. Estab. 1980. Circ. 51,841. Pays on publication. Publishes ms an average of 8 months after acceptance. Byline given. Not copyrighted. Buys first North American serial rights. Submit seasonal/holiday material 6 months in advance. Reports in 1 month. Sample copy for 6×9 SAE with 4 first-class stamps.
Nonfiction: Carol Savidge, articles editor. General interest, interview/profile, photo feature, technical. Buys 12-20 mss/year. Query or send complete ms. Pays $10-35 for unsolicited articles.
Photos: Send photos with submission. Reviews 5×7 prints. Offers no additional payment for photos accepted with ms. Captions required. Buys one-time rights.
Tips: "We are looking for submissions with photos in all areas of collecting and antiquing, unusual collections, details on a particular kind of collecting or information on antiques."

‡AMERICAN SQUARE DANCE MAGAZINE, Sanborn Enterprises, 661 Middlefield Rd., Salinas CA 93906. Editor: Jon Sanborn. 50% freelance written. Monthly magazine covering square, round, country-western, clogging, contra dance. Estab. 1945. Circ. 16,000. Pays on publication. Publishes ms an average of 4 months after acceptance. Byline given. Buys one-time rights. Editorial lead time 3 months. Submit seasonal material 6-8 months in advance. Accepts simultaneous and previously published submissions. Reports in 6 weeks on queries. Sample copy for $2. Writer's guidelines for #10 SASE.
Nonfiction: Book excerpts, exposé, personal experience, photo feature, travel. Buys 5 mss/year. Query with published clips. Length: 600-1,000 words. Pays $70 minimum for assigned articles; $25 minimum for unsolicited articles.
Columns/Departments: Pays $25-60.

AMERICAN WOODWORKER, Rodale Press, Inc., 33 E. Minor St., Emmaus PA 18098-0099. (215)967-5171. Fax: (215)967-8956. Editor/Publisher: David Sloan. Managing Editor: Kevin Ireland. 70% freelance written. Bimonthly magazine. "*American Woodworker* is a how-to magazine edited for the woodworking enthusiast who wants to improve his/her skills. We strive to motivate, challenge and entertain." Estab. 1985. Circ. 300,000. Pays on publication. Publishes ms an average of 6 months after acceptance. Byline given. Offers $100 kill fee. Buys one-time and second serial (reprint) rights. Accepts previously published material. Send photocopy of article or typed ms with rights for sale noted. Submit seasonal material 8 months in advance. Query for electronic submissions. Reports in 1 month. Free sample copy and writer's guidelines.
Nonfiction: Essays, historical/nostalgic, how-to (woodworking projects and techniques), humor, inspirational, interview/profile, new product, personal experience, photo feature, technical. ("All articles must have woodworking theme.") Buys 30 mss/year. Query. Length: up to 2,500 words. Pays new authors base rate of $150/published page. Sometimes pays expenses of writers on assignment.
Photos: Send photos with submission. Reviews 35mm or larger transparencies. Offers no additional payment for photos accepted with ms. Model releases required. Buys one-time rights.
Columns/Departments: Final Pass (woodworking news and nonsense, 1,000 word max). Buys 10 mss/year. Send complete ms. Pays $100-300.
Poetry: Avant-garde, free verse, Haiku, light verse, traditional. "All poetry must have workworking or craftsmanship theme." Buys 1 poem/year. Submit maximum 5 poems. Pays $50-100.
Tips: "Reading the publication is the only real way to get a feel for the niche market *American Woodworker* represents and the needs and interests of our readers. Magazine editorial targets the serious woodworking enthusiast who wishes to improve his/her skills. Feature stories and articles most accessible for freelancers. Articles should be technically accurate, well organized and reflect the needs and interests of the amateur woodworking enthusiast."

ANTIQUE REVIEW, P.O. Box 538, Worthington OH 43085-0538. Editor: Charles Muller. (614)885-9757. Fax: (614)885-9762. 60% freelance written. Eager to work with new/unpublished writers. Monthly tabloid for an antique-oriented readership, "generally well-educated, interested in Early American furniture and decorative arts, as well as folk art." Estab. 1975. Circ. 11,000. Pays on publication date assigned at time of purchase. Publishes ms an average of 3 months after acceptance. Buys first North American serial and second (reprint) rights to material originally published in dissimilar publications. Accepts previously published material if not first printed in competitive publications. Send tearsheet or photocopy of article. For reprints pays 100% of the amount paid for an original article. Byline given. Phone queries OK. Reports in 3 months. Free sample copy and writer's guidelines for #10 SASE.
Nonfiction: "The articles we desire concern history and production of furniture, pottery, china, and other quality Americana. In some cases, contemporary folk art items are acceptable. We are also interested in reporting on antiques shows and auctions with statements on conditions and prices. We do not want articles on contemporary collectibles." Buys 5-8 mss/issue. Query with clips of published work. Query should show "author's familiarity with antiques, an interest in the historical development of artifacts relating to early America and an awareness of antiques market." Length: 200-2,000 words. Pays $100-200. Sometimes pays the expenses of writers on assignment.

Photos: Send photos with query. Payment included in ms price. Uses 3 × 5 or larger glossy b&w prints. Color acceptable. Captions required. Articles with photographs receive preference.

Tips: "Give us a call and let us know of specific interests. We are more concerned with the background in antiques than in writing abilities. The writing can be edited, but the knowledge imparted is of primary interest. A frequent mistake is being too general, not becoming deeply involved in the topic and its research. We are interested in primary research into America's historic material culture."

ANTIQUES & AUCTION NEWS, Route 230 West, P.O. Box 500, Mount Joy PA 17552. (717)653-1833, ext. 254. Editor: Doris Ann Johnson. Works with a very small number of new/unpublished writers each year. Weekly tabloid for dealers and buyers of antiques, nostalgics and collectibles, and those who follow antique shows, shops and auctions. Estab. 1969. Circ. 35,000. Pays on publication. Submit seasonal/holiday material 3 months in advance. Free sample copy available if you mention *Writer's Market*. Writer's guidelines for #10 SASE.

Nonfiction: "Our readers are interested in collectibles and antiques dating approximately from the Civil War to the present, originating in the US or western Europe. We will consider a few stories per year if they are well-written, slanted toward helping collectors, buyers, dealers and readers learn more about the field. This could be an historical perspective, a specific area of collecting, an especially interesting antique or unusual collection. Issues have included material on old Christmas ornaments, antique love tokens, collections of fans, pencils and pottery, and 'The Man from U.N.C.L.E.' books and magazines. Articles may be how-to, informational research, news and reporting and even an occasional photo feature." Call or write before submitting any ms. Length: 1,000 words or less preferred, but will consider up to 2,000 words. Pays $15 for articles with usable photos; $20 for front page.

Photos: Purchased as part of ms package. "We prefer b&w photos, usually of a single item against a simple background. Color photos can be used if there is good contrast between darks and lights." Captions required. Photos are returned.

‡**BANK NOTE REPORTER**, Krause Publications, 700 E. State St., Iola WI 54990-0001. (715)445-2214. Fax: (715)445-4087. Editor: David Harper. 30% freelance written. Works with a small number of new/unpublished writers each year. Monthly tabloid for advanced collectors of US and world paper money. Estab. 1952. Circ. 5,600. Pays on publication. Publishes ms an average of 3 months after acceptance. Byline given. Buys first North American serial and reprint rights. Query for electronic submissions. Reports in 2 months. Sample copy for 9 × 12 SAE and postage.

Nonfiction: "We review articles covering any phase of paper money collecting including investing, display, storage, history, art, story behind a particular piece of paper money and the business of paper money." News items not solicited. "Our staff covers the hard news." Buys 6 mss/issue. Send complete ms. Length: 500-3,000 words. Pays 3¢/word to first-time contributors; negotiates fee for later articles.

Photos: Pays $5 for 5 × 7 b&w glossy prints. Captions and model releases required.

Tips: "The writer has a better chance of breaking in at our publication with short articles due to the technical nature of the subject matter and sophistication of our readers. Material about bank notes used in a writer's locale would be interesting, useful, encouraged. We like new names."

BECKETT BASEBALL CARD MONTHLY, Statabase, Inc., 15850 Dallas Pkwy., Dallas TX 75248. (214)991-6657. Fax: (214)991-8930. Editor: Dr. James Beckett. Managing Editor: Jay Johnson. 85% freelance written. Monthly magazine on baseball card and sports memorabilia collecting. "Our readers expect our publication to be entertaining and informative. Our slant is that hobbies are fun and rewarding. Especially wanted are how-to-collect articles." Estab. 1984. Circ. 750,000. **Pays on acceptance.** Publishes ms an average of 4 months after acceptance. Byline given. Pays $50 kill fee. Buys first North American serial rights. Submit seasonal/holiday material 6 months in advance. "No simultaneous submissions, please!" Reports in 1 month. Sample copy for $2.95. Free writer's guidelines.

Nonfiction: Book excerpts, historical/nostalgic, how-to, humor, interview/profile, new product, opinion, personal experience, photo feature, technical. Special issues: Spring training (February); season preview (April); All-Star game (July); stay in school (August); World Series (October). No articles that emphasize speculative prices and investments. Buys 145 mss/year. Send complete ms. Length: 300-1,500 words. Pays $100-400 for assigned articles; $50-200 for unsolicited articles. Sometimes pays expenses of writers on assignment.

Photos: Send photos with submission. Reviews 35mm transparencies, 5 × 7 or larger prints. Offers $10-300/photo. Captions, model releases and identification of subjects required. Buys one-time rights.

Fiction: Humorous only.

Tips: "A writer for *Beckett Baseball Card Monthly* should be an avid sports fan and/or a collector with an enthusiasm for sharing his/her interests with others. Articles must be factual, but not overly statistic-laden. First person (not research) articles presenting the writer's personal experiences told with wit and humor, and emphasizing the stars of the game, are *always* wanted. Acceptable articles must be of interest to our two basic reader segments: teenaged boys and their middle-aged fathers who are re-experiencing a nostalgic renaissance of their own childhoods. Prospective writers should write down to neither group!"

BECKETT BASKETBALL MONTHLY, Statabase, Inc., 15850 Dallas Pkwy., Dallas TX 75248. (214)991-6657. Fax: (214)991-8930. Editor: Dr. James Beckett. Managing Editor: Jay Johnson. 85% freelance written. Monthly magazine on basketball card and sports memorabilia collecting. "Our readers expect our publication to be entertaining and informative. Our slant is that hobbies are fun and rewarding. Especially wanted are articles dealing directly with the hobby of basketball card collecting." Estab. 1990. Circ. 450,000. **Pays on acceptance.** Publishes ms an average of 4 months after acceptance. Byline given. Pays $50 kill fee. Buys first North American serial rights. Submit seasonal/holiday material 6 months in advance. "No simultaneous submissions, please!" Reports in 1 month. Sample copy for $2.95. Free writer's guidelines.

Nonfiction: Book excerpts, historical/nostalgic, how-to, humor, interview/profile, new product, opinion, personal experience, photo feature, technical. Special issues: All Star game, stay in school (February); playoffs (June); new card sets (September). No articles that emphasize speculative prices and investments. Buys 145 mss/year. Send complete ms. Length: 300-1,500 words. Pays $100-400 for assigned articles; $100-200 for unsolicited articles. Sometimes pays expenses of writers on assignment.

Photos: Send photos with submission. Reviews 35mm transparencies, 5×7 or larger prints. Offers $10-300/photo. Captions, model releases and identification of subjects required. Buys one-time rights.

Fiction: Humorous only.

Tips: "A writer for *Beckett Basketball Monthly* should be an avid sports fan and/or a collector with an enthusiasm for sharing his/her interests with others. Articles must be factual, but not overly statistic-laden. First person (not research) articles presenting the writer's personal experiences told with wit and humor, and emphasizing the stars of the game, are *always* wanted. Acceptable articles must be of interest to our two basic reader segments: late teenaged boys and their fathers who are re-experiencing a nostalgic renaissance of their own childhoods. Prospective writers should write down to neither group!"

BECKETT FOCUS ON FUTURE STARS, Statabase, Inc., 15850 Dallas Pkwy., Dallas TX 75248. (214)991-6657. Fax: (214)991-8930. Editor: Dr. James Beckett. Managing Editor: Jay Johnson. 85% freelance written. Monthly magazine offering superstar coverage of young, outstanding players in baseball (major-league rookies, minor league stars and college), basketball (college), football (college) and hockey (juniors and college), with an emphasis on collecting sports cards and memorabilia. "Our readers expect our publication to be entertaining and informative. Our slant is that hobbies are fun and rewarding. Especially wanted are how-to collect articles." Estab. 1991. Circ. 100,000. **Pays on acceptance.** Publishes ms an average of 4 months after acceptance. Byline given. Pays $50 kill fee. Buys first North American serial rights. Submit seasonal/holiday material 8 months in advance. "No simultaneous submissions, please!" Reports in 1 month. Sample copy for $2.95. Free writer's guidelines.

Nonfiction: Book excerpts, historical/nostalgic, how-to, humor, interview/profile, new product, opinion, personal experience, photo feature, technical. Special issues: card sets in review (January); stay in school (February); draft special (June). No articles that emphasize speculative prices and investments on cards. Buys 145 mss/year. Send complete ms. Length: 300-1,500 words. Pays $100-400 for assigned articles; $50-200 for unsolicited articles. Sometimes pays expenses of writers on assignment.

Photos: Send photos with submission. Reviews 35mm transparencies, 5×7 or larger prints. Offers $25-300/photo. Captions, model releases and identification of subjects required. Buys one-time rights.

Fiction: Humorous only

Tips: "A writer for *Beckett Focus on Future Stars* should be an avid sports fan and/or a collector with an enthusiasm for sharing his/her interests with others. Articles must be factual, but not overly statistic-laden. First person (not research) articles presenting the writer's personal experiences told with wit and humor, and emphasizing the stars of the game, are *always* wanted. Acceptable articles must be of interest to our two basic reader segments: teenaged boys and their middle-aged fathers who are re-experiencing a nostalgic renaissance of their own childhoods. Prospective writers should write down to neither group!"

BECKETT FOOTBALL CARD MONTHLY, Statabase, Inc., 15850 Dallas Pkwy., Dallas TX 75248. (214)991-6657. Fax: (214)991-8930. Editor: Dr. James Beckett. Managing Editor: Jay Johnson. 85% freelance written. Monthly magazine on football card and sports memorabilia collecting. "Our readers expect our publication to be entertaining and informative. Our slant is that hobbies are fun and rewarding. Especially wanted are how-to collect articles." Estab. 1989. Circ. 250,000. **Pays on acceptance.** Publishes ms an average of 4 months after acceptance. Byline given. Pays $50 kill fee. Buys first North American serial rights. Submit seasonal/holiday material 6 months in advance. "No simultaneous submissions, please!" Reports in 1 month. Sample copy for $2.95. Free writer's guidelines.

Nonfiction: Book excerpts, historical/nostalgic, how-to, humor, interview/profile, new product, opinion, personal experience, photo feature, technical. Special issues: Super Bowl (January); Pro Bowl (February); NFL draft (April); stay in school (August) preview (September). No articles that emphasize speculative prices and investments. Buys 145 mss/year. Send complete ms. Length: 300-1,500 words. Pays $100-400 for assigned articles; $50-200 for unsolicited articles. Sometimes pays expenses of writers on assignment.

Photos: Send photos with submission. Reviews 35mm transparencies, 5×7 or larger prints. Offers $10-300/photo. Captions, model releases and identification of subjects required. Buys one-time rights.

Fiction: Humorous only.

Tips: "A writer for *Beckett Football Card Monthly* should be an avid sports fan and/or a collector with an enthusiasm for sharing his/her interests with others. Articles must be factual, but not overly statistic-laden. Acceptable articles must be of interest to our two basic reader segments: teenaged boys and their middle-aged fathers who are re-experiencing a nostalgic renaissance of their own childhoods. Prospective writers should write down to neither group!"

BECKETT HOCKEY MONTHLY, Statabase, Inc., 15850 Dallas Pkwy., Dallas TX 75248. (214)991-6657. Fax: (214)991-8930. Editor: Dr. James Beckett. Managing Editor: Jay Johnson. 85% freelance written. Monthly magazine on hockey, hockey card and memorabilia collecting. "Our readers expect our publication to be entertaining and informative. Our slant is that hobbies are for fun and rewarding. Especially wanted are how-to collect articles." Estab. 1990. Circ. 200,000. **Pays on acceptance.** Publishes ms an average of 3 months after acceptance. Byline given. Pays $50 kill fee. Buys first North American serial rights. Submit seasonal/holiday material 6 months in advance. "No simultaneous submissions, please!" Reports in 1 month. Sample copy for $2.95. Free writer's guidelines.

Nonfiction: Book excerpts, historical/nostalgic, how-to, humor, interview/profile, new product, opinion, personal experience, photo feature, technical. Special issues: All-Star game (February); Stanley Cup preview (April); draft (June); season preview (October). No articles that emphasize speculative prices and investments. Buys 145 mss/year. Send complete ms. Length: 300-1,500 words. Pays $100-400 for assigned articles; $50-200 for unsolicited articles. Sometimes pays expenses of writers on assignment.

Photos: Send photos with submission. Reviews 35mm transparencies, 5 × 7 or larger prints. Offers $10-300/photo. Captions, model releases and identification of subjects required. Buys one-time rights.

Fiction: Humorous only.

Tips: "A writer for *Beckett Hockey Monthly* should be an avid sports fan and/or a collector with an enthusiasm for sharing his/her interests with others. Articles must be factual, but not overly statistic-laden. Acceptable articles must be of interest to our two basic reader segments: teenaged boys and their middle-aged fathers who are re-experiencing a nostalgic renaissance of their own childhoods. Prospective writers should write down to neither group!"

THE BLADE MAGAZINE, Blade Publications, P.O. Box 22007, Chattanooga TN 37422. Fax: (615)892-7254. Publisher: Bruce Voyles. Editor: Steve Shackleford. 90% freelance written. Magazine published 8 times/year for knife enthusiasts who want to know as much as possible about quality knives and edged weapons. Estab. 1973. Pays on publication. Publishes ms an average of 6 months after acceptance. Buys all rights. Submit seasonal/holiday material 6 months in advance. Accepts previously published submissions if not run in other knife publications. Send tearsheet of article or typed ms with rights for sale noted and information about when and where the article previously appeared. For reprints pays 90% of the amount paid for an original article. Reports in 2 months. Sample copy for $3.25. Writer's guidelines for #10 SASE.

● *Blade Magazine* is putting more emphasis on new products, knife accessories, knife steels, knife handles, knives and celebrities, knives in the movies.

Nonfiction: How-to; historical (on knives and weapons); adventure on a knife theme; celebrities who own knives; knives featured in movies with shots from the movie, etc.; new product; nostalgia; personal experience; photo feature; profile; technical. "We would also like to receive articles on knives in adventuresome life-saving situations." No poetry. Buys 75 unsolicited mss/year. "We evaluate complete manuscripts and make our decision on that basis." Length: 500-1,000 words, longer if content warrants it. Pays $200/story minimum; more for "better" writers. "We will pay top dollar in the knife market." Sometimes pays the expenses of writers on assignment.

Photos: Send photos with ms. Pays $5 for 8 × 10 b&w glossy prints, $25-75 for 35mm color transparencies. Captions required. "Photos are critical for story acceptance."

Tips: "We are always willing to read submissions from anyone who has read a few copies and studied the market. The ideal article for us is a piece bringing out the romance, legend, and love of man's oldest tool — the knife. We like articles that place knives in peoples' hands — in life saving situations, adventure modes, etc. (Nothing gory or with the knife as the villain.) People and knives are good copy. We are getting more and better written articles from writers who are reading the publication beforehand. That makes for a harder sell for the quickie writer not willing to do his homework."

COINS, Krause Publications, 700 E. State St., Iola WI 54990-0001. (715)445-2214. Fax: (715)445-4087. Editor: Alan Herbert. 50% freelance written. Eager to work with new/unpublished writers. Monthly magazine about US and foreign coins for all levels of collectors, investors and dealers. Estab. 1952. Circ. 71,000. Reports in 2 months. Free sample copy and writer's guidelines.

Nonfiction: "We're looking for stories that will help coin collectors pursue their hobby in today's market. Stories should include what's available in the series being discussed, its value in today's market, and tips for buying that material." Buys 4 mss/issue. Query first. Length: 500-2,500 words. Pays 3¢/word to first-time contributors; fee negotiated for later articles.

Photos: Pays $5 minimum for b&w prints; $25 minimum for 35mm transparencies. Captions and model releases required. Buys first rights.

COLLECTOR EDITIONS, Collector Communications Corp., 170 Fifth Ave., New York NY 10010-5911. (212)989-8700. Fax: (212)645-8976. Editor: Joan Muyskens Pursley. 40% freelance written. Works with a small number of new/unpublished writers each year. Bimonthly magazine on porcelain and glass collectibles and limited-edition prints. "We specialize in contemporary (post-war ceramic and glass) collectibles, including reproductions, but also publish articles about antiques, if they are being reproduced today and are generally available." Estab. 1973. Circ. 75,000. Buys first North American serial rights. "First assignments are always done on a speculative basis." Pays within 30 days of acceptance. Publishes ms an average of 6 months after acceptance. Reports in 2 months. Sample copy for $2. Writer's guidelines for #10 SASE.

Nonfiction: "Short features about collecting, written in tight, newsy style. We specialize in contemporary (postwar) collectibles. Values for pieces being written about should be included." Informational, interview, profile, exposé, nostalgia. Buys 15-20 mss/year. Query with sample photos. Length: 500-1,500 words. Pays $100-300. Sometimes pays expenses of writers on assignment.

Columns/Departments: Staff written; not interested in freelance columns.

Photos: B&w and color photos purchased with accompanying ms with no additional payment. Captions are required. "We want clear, distinct, full-frame images that say something."

Tips: "Unfamiliarity with the field is the most frequent mistake made by writers in completing an article for us."

COLLECTORS NEWS & THE ANTIQUE REPORTER, P.O. Box 156, Grundy Center IA 50638-0156. (319)824-6981. Fax: (319)824-3414. Editor: Linda Kruger. 20% freelance written. Estab. 1959. Works with a small number of new/unpublished writers each year. Monthly magazine-size publication on newsprint covering antiques, collectibles and nostalgic memorabilia. Circ. 13,000. Byline given. Pays on publication. Publishes ms an average of 1 year after acceptance. Buys first rights and makes work-for-hire assignments. Submit seasonal/holiday material 3 months in advance. Reports in 2 weeks on queries; 6 weeks on mss. Sample copy for $3 for 9×12 SAE. Free writer's guidelines.

Nonfiction: General interest (any subject re: collectibles, antique to modern); historical/nostalgic (relating to collections or collectors); how-to (display your collection, care for, restore, appraise, locate, add to, etc.); interview/profile (covering individual collectors and their hobbies, unique or extensive; celebrity collectors, and limited edition artists); technical (in-depth analysis of a particular antique, collectible or collecting field); and travel (coverage of special interest or regional shows, seminars, conventions – or major antique shows, flea markets; places collectors can visit, tours they can take, museums, etc.). Special issues: show/flea market (January, June) and usual seasonal emphasis. Buys 100 mss/year. Query with sample of writing. Length: 800-1,000 words. Pays $1/column inch.

Photos: Reviews color or b&w prints. Payment for photos included in payment for ms. Captions required. Buys first rights.

Tips: Articles most open to freelancers are on farm/country/rural collectibles; celebrity collectors; collectors with unique and/or extensive collections; music collectibles; transportation collectibles; advertising collectibles; bottles; glass, china and silver; primitives; furniture; toys; black memorabilia; political collectibles; and movie memorabilia.

‡COLLECTOR'S SPORTSLOOK, Wizard Press, 151 Wells Ave., Congers NY 10920-2064. (914)268-2000. Editor-in-Chief: Tucker Smith. Associate Editor: Scott Gramling. 40% freelance written. Monthly magazine covering sports trading cards and collectibles. "Anything that has to do with collecting sports and non-sports memorabilia is fair game in *Collector's Sportslook*. Commentary, exposé, informative and how-to articles are all accepted for consideration. In addition, we are always interested in stories about the history of sports and non-sports topics, if there is a genuine collecting angle. Original art, cartoons and short stories that pertain to collecting are also accepted for consideration." Estab. 1993. Circ. 150,000. Pays on publication. Byline given. Offers 50% kill fee. Editorial lead time 4 months. Submit seasonal material 4 months in advance. Accepts simultaneous submissions. Query for electronic submissions. Reports in 6 weeks on queries; 3 months on mss. Sample copy and writer's guidelines free on request.

Nonfiction: Payment ranges from $50-1,500, according to writer's guidelines.

Columns/Departments: Scott Gramling, Associate Editor. Market Watch (vignettes of interesting sports stars, sports places, and other sports-related topics), 300 words. Buys 20 mss/year. Send complete ms. Pays $50-150.

Fillers: Scott Gramling, Associate Editor. Anecdotes, facts, gags, newsbreaks, short humor. Buys 20/year. Length: 25-300 words. Pays $25-150.

Tips: "Areas most open to freelancers include vignettes, short anecdotes and off-beat stories about sports, athletes and/or collectibles. When writing, keep in mind that *Sportslook*'s goal is to 'put the fun back into collecting.' "

‡CRAFTING TODAY, M.S.C. Publishing, Inc., 243 Newton-Sparta Rd., Newton NJ 07860. (201)383-8080. Editor: Deborah McGowan. Contact: Linda Dunlap. Bimonthly magazine covering beginner to intermediate level crafts. Estab. 1989. Circ. 80,000. Pays on publication. Publishes ms an average of 3-6 months after acceptance. Byline given. Buys first rights and second serial (reprint) rights. Editorial lead time 6 months. Submit seasonal material 6 months in advance. No simultaneous submissions. Accepts previously published submissions occasionally. Sample copy for 9 × 12 SAE with 6 first-class stamps. Writer's guidelines for #10 SASE.

Nonfiction: How-to (crafts). Special issues: Americana Designs cross stitch collectibles, Homestead Classics Christmas crafts. Buys 3 mss/year. Query. Length: 700-1,500 words. Pays 10¢/word.

CRAFTS MAGAZINE, PJS Publications Inc., News Plaza, Box 1790, Peoria IL 61656. (309)682-6626. Fax: (309)682-7394. Editor: Judith Brossart. Monthly magazine. Circ. 400,000. **Pays on acceptance.** Publishes ms an average of 3 months after acceptance. Buys all rights. Reports in 2 months. "We do how-to only; we don't have special features in our magazine." Send query with photo or sketch first. Pays $75-400.

CRAFTS 'N' THINGS, Clapper Communications Companies, Suite 1000, 701 Lee St., Des Plaines IL 60016-4570. (708)297-7400. Fax: (708)297-8528. Editor: Julie Stephani. 80% freelance written. How-to and craft project magazine published 10 times/year. "We publish instruction for craft projects for beginners to intermediate level hobbyists." Estab. 1975. Circ. 300,000. Pays on publication. Publishes ms an average of 4 months after acceptance. Byline given. Offers $50 kill fee. Buys first, second serial (reprint) or all rights. Accepts previously published material. Send photocopy of article and information about when and where the article previously appeared. Submit seasonal material 6 months in advance. Simultaneous submissions not encouraged, please notify. Free sample copy and writer's guidelines.

Nonfiction: How-to (craft projects), new product (for product review column). Send SASE for list of issue themes. Buys 240 mss/year. Send complete ms with photos and instructions. Pays $50-250. Offers listing exchange as a product source instead of payment in some cases.

Columns/Departments: Bright Ideas (original ideas for working better with crafts—hints and tips). Buys 30 mss/year. Send complete ms. Length: 25-50 words. Pays $20.

Tips: "Query for guidelines and listing of themes and deadlines. How-to articles are the best bet for freelancers."

‡**CRAFTWORKS, For The Home,** All American Crafts Publishing, 243 Newton-Sparta Rd., Newton NJ 07860. (201)383-8080. Editor: Matthew Jones. 90% freelance written. Monthly magazine covering craft how-to's. "*Craftworks* accepts articles relating to projects, ideas, tips, and techniques for general crafting, including painting, cross stitch, needlework, basketry, woodworking, stained glass, crochet, paper art, etc." Estab. 1985. Circ. 300,000. Pays on publication. Publishes ms an average of 3-6 months after acceptance. Byline given. Buys first rights and second serial (reprint) rights. Editorial lead time 3-6 months. Submit seasonal material 3 months in advance. No simultaneous submissions. Accepts previously published submissions occasionally. Query for electronic submissions. Reports in 2-4 weeks on queries. Sample copy for 9 × 12 SAE with 6 first-class stamps. Writer's guidelines for #10 SASE.

Nonfiction: How-to. Buys 125 mss/year. Length: 1,500 words maximum. Pays $50-150.

Photos: Send photos with submission.

‡**CREATIVE WOODWORKS & CRAFTS,** MSC Publishing, Inc., 243 Newton-Sparta Rd., Newton NJ 07860. (201)383-8080. Editor: Robert A. Becker. Bimonthly magazine covering woodworking. "This is a how-to publication; instructions must be clear, concise, and easy-to-follow. Only original designs accepted. They range from beginner to expert. Clean, accurate; complete patterns with all sizes must accompany instructions. Prefer full size (or 1″ grid overlay to reduce)." Estab. 1988. Circ. 95,000. Pays on publication. Publishes ms an average of 3-6 months after acceptance. Byline given. Buys first rights and reprint rights. Editorial lead time 6 months. Submit seasonal material 8 months in advance. No simultaneous submissions. Accepts previously published submissions occasionally. Reports in 3 weeks on queries. Sample copy for 9 × 12 SAE with 6 first-class stamps. Writer's guidelines for #10 SASE.

Nonfiction: How-to. Buys 8-10 mss/year. Query. Length: 1,000-3,000 words. Pays $125 for assigned articles; $50 and up for unsolicited articles.

Photos: Send photos or transparencies for review with submission. Actual sample will be requested after review. Negotiates payment individually. Captions, model releases, identification of subjects required.

Columns/Departments: Basic Woodworking (how-to articles on how to use wood working machinery, tools, and wood techniques), 1,500-2,000. Buys 6 mss/year. Query. Pays $75-200.

Tips: "Keep all copy, instructions, drawings, etc. as clean as possible—no errors or inferior or illegible writing. All instructions should be clear, concise, and, if they are already in the magazine's format, it is a big plus."

‡**CROCHET FANTASY,** All American Crafts, Inc., 243 Newton-Sparta Rd., Newton NJ 07860-2748. (201)383-8080. Fax: (201)383-8133. Editorial Director: Camille Pomaco. Editor: Janice Edsall. Crochet magazine published 8 times/year. Estab. 1982. "Each issue includes a variety of sweaters, doilies, afghans and other items." Pays on publication. Publishes ms an average of 6 months after acceptance. Byline given. Buys first rights, second serial (reprint) rights or all rights. Submit seasonal/holiday material 8 months in advance. Query for electronic submissions. Reports in 2 months on queries. Sample copy for 9 × 12 SAE. Writer's guidelines for #10 SASE.

Nonfiction: How-to, humor, personal experience, technical. Buys 2 mss/year. Query. Length: 500-3,000 words. Pays 7-10¢/word for assigned articles.

Photos: Send photos with submission. Reviews all sizes transparencies and prints. Offers no additional payment for photos accepted with ms. Model releases required. Buys all rights.

Columns/Departments: Stitch Wit (crochet hints, crochet anecdotes, etc.), 50-500 words. Pays $5 per published hint.

‡**CROCHET WORLD,** House of White Birches, P.O. Box 776, Henniker NH 03242. Editor: Susan Hankins. 100% freelance written. Bimonthly magazine covering crochet patterns. "Crochet World is a pattern magazine devoted to the art of crochet. We also feature a Q&A column, letters (swap shop) column and occasionally non-pattern manuscripts, but it must be devoted to crochet." Estab. 1978. Circ. 75,000. Pays on publication. Byline given. Buys all rights. Editorial lead time 4 months. Submit seasonal material 6 months in advance. Query for electronic submissions. Reports in 1 month. Sample copy for $2. Writer's guidelines free on request.

Nonfiction: How-to (crochet). Special issue: Christmas Annual (June—material by April 15). Buys 0-2 mss/year. Send complete ms. Length: 500-1,500 words. Pays $50.

Columns/Departments: Touch of Style (crocheted clothing); It's a Snap! (quick one-night simple patterns); Pattern of the Month, first and second prize each issue. Buys dozens of mss/year. Send complete pattern. Pays $40-300.

Poetry: Strictly crochet-related. Buys 0-10 poems/year. Submit maximum 2 poems. Length: 6-20 lines. Pays $10-20.

Fillers: Anecdotes, facts, gags to be illustrated by cartoonist, short humor. Buys 0-10/year. Length: 25-200 words. Pays $10-20.

Tips: "Be aware that this is a pattern generated magazine for crochet designs. I prefer the actual item sent along with the complete directions/graphs etc. over queries. In some cases a photo submission or good sketch will do. Crocheted designs must be well made and directions must be complete. Write for my Designer's Guidelines which details how to submit designs. Non-crochet items, such as fillers, poetry *must* be crochet related, not knit, not sewing etc."

CROSS STITCH SAMPLER, Sampler Publications, P.O. Box 413, Chester Heights PA 19017-0413. (215)358-9242. Fax: (215)558-9340. Editor: Deborah N. DeSimone. Quarterly magazine on needlework and counted thread. Estab. 1983. Circ. 156,000. Pays on publication. Publishes ms an average of 3 months after acceptance. Byline given. Buys all rights (negotiable). Rarely publishes reprints of previously published articles. Send photocopy of article and information about when and where the article previously appeared. For reprints pays 50% of the amount paid for an original article. Reports in 3 months. Sample copy for 9×12 SAE with $1.67 postage.

Nonfiction: General interest, historical/nostalgic, inspirational, interview/profile, personal experience, photo feature. Buys 6-10 mss/year. Send complete ms. Pays $75-300+.

Photos: Send photos with submission. Reviews contact sheets, 4×5 transparencies and 3×5 prints. May offer additional payment for photos accepted with ms. Captions and identification of subjects required. Buys one-time rights.

DECORATIVE ARTIST'S WORKBOOK, F&W Publications, Inc., 1507 Dana Ave., Cincinnati OH 45207-1005. Editor: Sandra Carpenter Forbes. Estab. 1987. 50% freelance written. Bimonthly magazine covering decorative painting projects and products of all sorts. Offers "straightforward, personal instruction in the techniques of decorative painting." Circ. 88,000. **Pays on acceptance.** Byline given. Offers 20% kill fee. Buys first North American serial rights. Submit seasonal/holiday material 8 months in advance. Reports in 1 month. Sample copy for $3.65 and 9×12 SAE with 5 first-class stamps.

Nonfiction: How-to (related to decorative painting projects), new products, techniques, artist profiles. Buys 30 mss/year. Query with slides or photos. Length: 1,200-1,800 words. Pays 10-12¢/word.

Photos: State availability of or send photos with submission. Reviews 35mm, 4×5 transparencies and quality photos. Offers no additional payment for photos accepted with ms. Captions required. Buys one-time rights.

Fillers: Anecdotes, facts, short humor. Buys 15/year. Length: 50-200 words. Pays $10-25.

Tips: "The more you know—and can prove you know—about decorative painting, crafting and home decor, the better your chances. I'm looking for experts in the field who, through their own experience, can artfully describe the techniques involved. How-to articles are most open to freelancers. Be sure to query with slides or transparencies, and show that you understand the extensive graphic requirements for these pieces and are able to provide progressives—slides or illustrations that show works in progress."

‡**DOLL COLLECTOR'S PRICE GUIDE,** House of White Birches, 306 E. Parr Rd., Berne IN 46711. (219)589-8741. Editor: Cary Raesher. Quarterly magazine covering doll collecting. Audience is interested in informative articles about collecting and investing in dolls, museum exhibits, doll history, etc. Estab. 1991. Circ. 43,985. Pays pre-publication. Byline given. Buys first, one-time or all rights. Editorial lead time 6 months. Accepts previously published submissions. Reports in 2 months. Sample copy for $2. Writer's guidelines for #10 SASE.

Nonfiction: Historical/nostalgic. Buys 20 mss/year. Send complete ms. Pays $50.

Photos: Send photos with submission. Captions and identification of subjects required.

DOLL WORLD The Magazine for Doll Lovers, House of White Birches, 306 E. Parr Rd., Berne IN 46711. (219)589-8741. Fax: (219)589-8093. Editor: Cary Raesner. 90% freelance written. Bimonthly magazine covering doll collecting, restoration. "Interested in informative articles about doll history and costumes, interviews with doll artists and collectors, and how-to articles." Estab. 1978. Circ. 54,000. Pays pre-publication. Byline given. Buys first or one-time rights. Submit seasonal/holiday material 6 months in advance. Accepts previously published submissions. Reports in 6-8 weeks on queries; 2 months on mss. Sample copy for $2.95. Writer's guidelines for SASE.
Nonfiction: How-to, interview/profile. Buys 100 mss/year. Send complete ms. Pays $50.
Photos: Send photos with submission. Captions and identification of subjects required. Buys one-time or all rights.
Tips: "Choose a specific manufacturer and talk about his dolls or a specific doll—modern or antique—and explore its history and styles made."

DOLLS, The Collector's Magazine, Collector Communications Corp., 170 Fifth Ave., New York NY 10010-5911. (212)989-8700. Fax: (212)645-8976. Managing Editor: Karen Bischoff. 75% freelance written. Works with a small number of new/unpublished writers each year. Magazine published 10 times/year covering doll collecting "for collectors of antique, contemporary manufacturer and artist dolls. We publish well-researched, professionally written articles illustrated with photographs of high quality, color or b&w." Estab. 1982. Circ. 120,000. Pays within 1 month of acceptance. Publishes ms an average of 9 months after acceptance. Byline given. "Almost all first manuscripts are on speculation. We rarely kill assigned stories, but kill fee would be about 33% of article fee." Buys first North American serial or second serial rights if piece has appeared in a non-competing publication. Submit seasonal/holiday material 6 months in advance. Accepts previously published material. Send typed ms with rights for sale noted and information about when and where the article previously appeared. For reprints pays 50% of the amount paid for an original article. Reports in 2 months. Sample copy for $2. Writer's guidelines for #10 SASE.
Nonfiction: Book excerpts; historical (with collecting angle); interview/profile (on doll artists); new product (just photos and captions; "we do not pay for these, but regard them as publicity"); technical (doll restoration advice by experts only); travel (museums and collections around the world). "No sentimental, uninformed 'my doll collection' or trade magazine-type stories on shops, etc. Our readers are knowledgeable collectors." Query with clips. Length: 500-2,500 words. Pays $100-350. Sometimes pays expenses of writers on assignment.
Photos: Send photos with accompanying query or ms. Reviews 4×5 transparencies; 4×5 or 8×10 b&w prints and 35mm slides. "We do not buy photographs submitted without manuscripts unless we have assigned them; we pay for the manuscript/photos package in one fee." Captions required. Buys one-time rights.
Columns/Departments: Doll Views—a miscellany of news and views of the doll world includes reports on upcoming or recently held events. "*Not* the place for new dolls, auction prices or dates; we have regular contributors or staff assigned to those columns." Query with clips if available or send complete ms. Length: 200-500 words. Pays $25-75. Doll Views items are given an endsig.
Fillers: "We don't use fillers but would consider them if we got something good. Hints on restoring, for example, or a nice illustration." Length: 500 words maximum. Pays $25-75.
Tips: "We need experts in the field who are also good writers. Freelancers who are not experts should know their particular story thoroughly and do background research to get the facts correct. Well-written queries from writers outside the NYC area are especially welcomed. Non-experts should stay away from technical or specific subjects (restoration, price trends). Short profiles of artists or a story of a local museum collection, with good photos, might catch our interest. Editors want to know they are getting something from a writer they cannot get from anyone else. Good writing should be a given, a starting point. After that, it's what you know."

EARLY AMERICAN LIFE, Cowles Magazines, Inc., P.O. Box 8200, Harrisburg PA 17105-8200. Fax: (717)657-9552. Editor: Mimi Handler. 20% freelance written. Bimonthly magazine for "people who are interested in capturing the warmth and beauty of the 1600 to 1840 period and using it in their homes and lives today. They are interested in arts, crafts, travel, restoration and collecting." Estab. 1970. Circ. 150,000. Buys first North American serial rights. Buys 40 mss/year. **Pays on acceptance.** Publishes ms an average of 1 year after acceptance. Accepts previously published articles. Send typed ms with rights for sale noted and information about when and where the article previously appeared. Reports in 3 months. Sample copy and writer's guidelines for 9×12 SAE with 4 first-class stamps. Query or submit complete ms with SASE.
Nonfiction: "Social history (the story of the people, not epic heroes and battles), travel to historic sites, country inns, antiques and reproductions, refinishing and restoration, architecture and decorating. We try to entertain as we inform. While we're always on the lookout for good pieces on any of our subjects, the 'travel to historic sites' theme is most frequently submitted. Would like to see more on how real people did something great to their homes." Buys 40 mss/year. Query or submit complete ms. Length: 750-3,000 words. Pays $100-600. Pays expenses of writers on assignment.
Photos: Pays $10 for 5×7 (and up) b&w photos used with mss, minimum of $25 for color. Prefers 2¼×2¼ and up, but can work from 35mm.
Tips: "Our readers are eager for ideas on how to bring early America into their lives. Conceive a new approach to satisfy their related interests in arts, crafts, travel to historic sites, and especially in houses

decorated in the early American style. Write to entertain and inform at the same time, and be prepared to help us with illustrations, or sources for them."

EDGES, The Official Publication of the International Blade Collectors Association, Blade Publications, P.O. Box 22207, Chattanooga TN 37421. Fax: (615)892-7254. Editor: J. Bruce Voyles. Quarterly newsletter covering the knife business and knife collecting. Circ. 20,000. Pays on publication. Byline given. Buys all rights. Submit seasonal/holiday material 6 months in advance. Accepts previously published submissions "as long as they are exclusive to our market." Send photocopy of article and information about when and where the article previously appeared. For reprints, pays 100% of the amount paid for an original article. Reports in 5 months. Acknowledges receipt of queries and ms in 2 months. Sample copy for $1.

Nonfiction: "Emphasis on knife values with each story containing an extensive collector value chart with values on each knife." Book excerpts, exposé, general interest, historical (well-researched), how-to, humor, new product, opinion, personal experience, photo feature, technical. "We look for articles on all aspects of the knife business, including technological advances, profiles, knife shows, and well-researched history. Ours is not a hard market to break into if the writer is willing to do a little research. To have a copy is almost a requirement." Buys 150 mss/year. Send complete ms. Length: 50-3,000 words "or more if material warrants additional length." Pays $150/story, minimum.

Photos: Story payment includes pictures. Captions and model release required (if persons are identifiable).

Fillers: Clippings, anecdotes and newsbreaks.

Tips: "If writers haven't studied the publication they shouldn't bother to submit an article. If they have studied it, we're an easy market to sell to." Buys 80% of the articles geared to "the knife business."

ELECTRONICS NOW, Gernsback Publications, Inc., 500 B Bi-County Blvd., Farmingdale NY 11735. (516)293-3000. Editor: Brian C. Fenton. 75% freelance written. Monthly magazine on electronics technology and electronics construction. Estab. 1929. Circ. 175,000. **Pays on acceptance.** Publishes ms an average of 6 months after acceptance. Byline given. Buys all rights. Submit seasonal/holiday material 5-6 months in advance. Query for electronic submissions. Reports in 2 months on queries; 4 months on mss. Free sample copy and writer's guidelines.

Nonfiction: How-to (electronic project construction), humor (cartoons), new product. Buys 150-200 mss/year. Send complete ms. Length: 1,000-10,000 words. Pays $200-800 for assigned articles; $100-800 for unsolicited articles.

Photos: Send photos with submission. Offers no additional payment for photos accepted with ms. Captions, model releases and identification of subjects required. Buys all rights.

FIBERARTS, The Magazine of Textiles, Altamont Press, 50 College St., Asheville NC 28801. (704)253-0467. Fax: (704)253-7952. Editor: Ann Batchelder. 100% freelance written. Eager to work with new/unpublished writers. Magazine published 5 times/year covering textiles as art and craft (weaving, quilting, surface design, stitchery, knitting, fashion, crochet, etc.) for textile artists, craftspeople, hobbyists, teachers, museum and gallery staffs, collectors and enthusiasts. Estab. 1975. Circ. 23,000. Pays 60 days after publication. Publishes ms an average of 4 months after acceptance. Byline given. Buys first rights. Editorial guidelines and style sheet available. Sample copy for $4.50 and 10×12 SAE with 2 first-class stamps. Writer's guidelines for #10 SAE with 2 first-class stamps.

Nonfiction: Historical, artist interview/profile, opinion, photo feature, technical, education, trends, exhibition reviews, textile news. Query. "Please be very specific about your proposal. Also an important consideration in accepting an article is the kind of photos—35mm slides and/or b&w glossies—that you can provide as illustration. We like to see photos in advance." Length: 250-2,000 words. Pays $40-300, depending on article. Rarely pays the expenses of writers on assignment or for photos.

Tips: "Our writers are very familiar with the textile field, and this is what we look for in a new writer. Familiarity with textile techniques, history or events determines clarity of an article more than a particular style of writing. The writer should also be familiar with *Fiberarts*, the magazine."

‡THE FIBERFEST MAGAZINE, Stony Lonesome Press, P.O. Box 112, Hastings MI 49325. (616)765-3047. Editor: Sue Drummond. Contact: Kathy Maurer. 10% freelance written. Quarterly magazine covering natural fibers-wool, mohair, angora, alpaca. "Devoted to fiber animal husbandry, processing and producing natural fiber products and marketing natural fibers." Estab. 1993. Circ. 2,000. Pays on publication. Publishes ms an average of 3 months after acceptance. Offers $10 kill fee. Buys first rights. Editorial lead time 3 months. Submit seasonal material 3 months in advance. Reports in 2 weeks on queries. Sample copy for $5 and $2 postage. Writer's guidelines free on request.

Nonfiction: Essays, general interest, historical/nostalgic, how-to, humor, interview/profile, new product, opinion, personal experience, photo feature. Buys 20 mss/year. Query. Length: 1,000-1,500 words. Pays $50. Sometimes pays expenses of writers on assignment.

Photos: Send photos with submission. Reviews contact sheets. Offers $5-10/photo. Captions required. Buys one-time rights.

Poetry: Free verse, light verse, traditional. Must be natural fiber related. Buys 2 poems/year. Submit maximum 5 poems. Length: 5-25 lines. Pays $10-50.

Fillers: Anecdotes, facts, short humor, cartoons, drawings. Buys 10/year. Length: 500 words. Pays $10-50.

FINE WOODWORKING, The Taunton Press, P.O. Box 5506, Newtown CT 06470-5506. (203)426-8171. Fax: (203)426-3434. Editor: William Sampson. Bimonthly magazine on woodworking in the small shop. "All writers are also skilled woodworkers. It's more important that a contributor be a woodworker than a writer. Our editors (also woodworkers) will fix the words." Estab. 1975. Circ. 292,000. Pays on publication. Byline given. Kill fee varies; "editorial discretion." Buys first rights and rights to republish in anthologies and use in promo pieces. Submit seasonal/holiday material 6 months in advance. Accepts simultaneous submissions. Query for electronic submissions. Reports in 2 months. Sample copy for $5.50 and 10 first-class stamps. Free writer's guidelines.
Nonfiction: How-to (woodworking). Buys 120 mss/year. "No specs—our editors would rather see more than less." Pays $150/magazine page. Sometimes pays expenses of writers on assignment.
Photos: Send photos with submission. Reviews contact sheets, negatives, transparencies and prints. Captions, model releases and identification of subjects required. Buys one-time rights.
Columns/Departments: Notes & Comment (topics of interest to woodworkers); Question & Answer (woodworking Q & A); Follow-Up (information on past articles/readers' comments); Methods of Work (shop tips); Tool Forum (short reviews of new tools). Buys 400 items/year. Length varies. Pays $10-150/published page.
Tips: "Send for authors guidelines and follow them. Stories about woodworking reported by non-woodworkers *not* used. Our magazine is essentially reader-written by woodworkers."

FINESCALE MODELER, Kalmbach Publishing Co., 21027 Crossroads Circle, P.O. Box 1612, Waukesha WI 53187. (414)796-8776. Fax: (414)796-1383. Editor: Bob Hayden. 80% freelance written. Eager to work with new/unpublished writers. Magazine published 8 times/year "devoted to how-to-do-it modeling information for scale model builders who build non-operating aircraft, tanks, boats, automobiles, figures, dioramas, and science fiction and fantasy models." Circ. 85,000. **Pays on acceptance.** Publishes ms an average of 14 months after acceptance. Byline given. Buys all rights. Reports in 6 weeks on queries; 3 months on mss. Sample copy for 9×12 SAE with 3 first-class stamps. Free writer's guidelines.
Nonfiction: How-to (build scale models); technical (research information for building models). Query or send complete ms. Length: 750-3,000 words. Pays $40/published page minimum.
  ● This magazine is especially looking for how-to articles for car modelers.
Photos: Send photos with ms. Pays $7.50 minimum for transparencies and $5 minimum for 5×7 b&w prints. Captions and identification of subjects required. Buys one-time rights.
Columns/Departments: *FSM* Showcase (photos plus description of model); *FSM* Tips and Techniques (model building hints and tips). Buys 25-50 Tips and Techniques/year. Query or send complete ms. Length: 100-1,000 words. Pays $10-20.
Tips: "A freelancer can best break in first through hints and tips, then through feature articles. Most people who write for *FSM* are modelers first, writers second. This is a specialty magazine for a special, quite expert audience. Essentially, 99% of our writers will come from that audience."

‡GEM SHOW NEWS, Shows of Integrity, 19 River St., Cooperstown KY 13326. (607)547-2604. Publisher: Edward J. Tripp. Editor: Judi Tripp. Managing Editor: Stacy Hobbs. 50% freelance written. Annual newspaper on precious stones, mineral collecting and jewelry. "Slant should be gem/collectible investments including gold, gold coins, silver, silver jewelry and original silver designs." Estab. 1979. Circ. 30,000. **Pays on acceptance.** Publishes ms an average of 2 months after acceptance. Byline given. Publication not copyrighted. Buys first rights and makes work-for-hire assignments. Submit seasonal/holiday material 4 months in advance. Accepts simultaneous and previously published submissions. Send typed ms with rights for sale noted. For reprints pays 50% of the amount paid for an original article. Reports in 4 months. Sample copy for 9×12 SAE with 5 first-class stamps. Writer's guidelines for #10 SASE.
Nonfiction: How-to (gem collecting; gem cutting/collecting), humor, interview/profile, new product, personal experience, photo feature, technical, travel. Buys 30 mss/year. Send complete ms; include word count for faster payment. Length: 1,000-3,000 words. Pays $50-150.
Photos: Send photos with submission. Reviews prints (3×5). Offers $5-10/photo. Captions, model releases and identification of subjects required. Buys one-time rights.
Fillers: Anecdotes, facts, gags to be illustrated by cartoonist, newsbreaks, short humor. Buys 30 mss/year. Length: 500 words maximum. Pays $10-25.
Tips: "Attend gem and jewelry shows to see the interest in this field. The gem and mineral collecting field is the second most popular hobby (second only to coin and stamp collecting) in the US. All areas are open, including current fads and trends such as articles on the current quartz crystals and crystal healing craze and related subjects. Since this is an annual issue publication (December/January), please submit articles in September or October only."

GOLD AND TREASURE HUNTER, (formerly *Modern Gold Miner and Treasure Hunter*), 27 Davis Rd., P.O. Box 47, Happy Camp CA 96039-0047. (916)493-2062. Fax: (916)493-2095. Editor: Dave McCracken. Managing Editor: Janice Trombetta. Bimonthly magazine on small-scale gold mining and treasure hunting. "We want interesting fact and fiction stories and articles about small-scale mining, treasure hunting, camping and the great outdoors." Estab. 1987. Circ. 50,000. Pays on publication. Buys all rights. Submit seasonal/holiday material 4 months in advance. Accepts previously published articles. Send tearsheet or photocopy of article or typed ms with rights for sale noted and information about when and where the article previously appeared. For reprints pays 50% of the amount paid for an original article. Query for electronic submissions. Reports in 1 month. Sample copy for 9×12 SAE with $1.45 postage. Free writer's guidelines.

Nonfiction: How-to, humor, inspirational, interview/profile, new product, personal experience, photo feature, travel. "No promotional articles concerning industry products." Buys 125 mss/year. Send complete ms. Length: 1,500-2,500 words. Pays $25-150.

Photos: Send photos with submission. Reviews any size transparencies and prints. Pays $10-50/photo. Captions are required. Buys all rights.

Fiction: Adventure, experimental, fantasy, historical, horror, humorous, mystery, suspense, western.

Tips: "Our general readership is comprised mostly of individuals who are actively involved in gold mining and treasure hunting, or people who are interested in reading about others who are active and successful in the field. True stories of actual discoveries, along with good color photos — particularly of gold — are preferred. Also, valuable how-to information on new and workable field techniques, preferably accompanied by supporting illustrations and/or photos."

HOME MECHANIX, 2 Park Ave., New York NY 10016. (212)779-5000. Editor: Michael Chotiner. Contact: Natalie Posner. 50% freelance written. Prefers to work with published/established writers. "If it's good, and it fits the type of material we're currently publishing, we're interested, whether writer is new or experienced." Magazine published 10 times/year for the active home and car owner. "Articles emphasize an active, home-oriented lifestyle. Includes information useful for maintenance, repair and renovation to the home and family car. Information on how to buy, how to select products useful to homeowners/car owners. Emphasis in home-oriented articles is on good design, inventive solutions to styling and space problems, useful home-workshop projects." Estab. 1928. Circ. 1 million. **Pays on acceptance.** Publishes ms an average of 6 months after acceptance. Byline given. Buys first North American serial rights. Reports in 3 months. Query.

• Ranked as one of the best markets for freelance writers in *Writer's Digest* magazine's annual "Top 100 Markets," January 1994.

Nonfiction: Feature articles relating to homeowner/car owner, 1,500-2,500 words. "This may include personal home-renovation projects, professional advice on interior design, reports on different or unusual construction methods, energy-related subjects, outdoor/backyard projects, etc. No high-tech subjects such as aerospace, electronics, photography or military hardware. Most of our automotive features are written by experts in the field, but fillers, tips, how-to repair, or modification articles on the family car are welcome. Articles on construction, tool use, refinishing techniques, etc., are also sought. Pays $300 minimum for features; fees based on number of printed pages, photos accompanying mss., etc." Pays expenses of writers on assignment.

Photos: Photos should accompany mss. Pays $600 and up for transparencies for cover. Inside color: $300/1 page, $500/2, $700/3, etc. Captions and model releases required.

Tips: "The most frequent mistake made by writers in completing an article assignment for *Home Mechanix* is not taking the time to understand its editorial focus and special needs."

THE HOME SHOP MACHINIST, 2779 Aero Park Dr., P.O. Box 1810, Traverse City MI 49685. (616)946-3712. Fax: (616)946-3289. Editor: Joe D. Rice. 95% freelance written. Bimonthly magazine covering machining and metalworking for the hobbyist. Circ. 24,500. Pays on publication. Publishes ms an average of 18 months after acceptance. Byline given. Buys first North American serial rights only. Accepts simultaneous submissions. Reports in 2 months. Free sample copy and writer's guidelines for 9×12 SASE.

Nonfiction: How-to (projects designed to upgrade present shop equipment or hobby model projects that require machining), technical (should pertain to metalworking, machining, drafting, layout, welding or foundry work for the hobbyist). No fiction. Buys 50 mss/year. Query or send complete ms. Length: open — "whatever it takes to do a thorough job." Pays $40/published page, plus $9/published photo.

Photos: Send photos with ms. Pays $9-40 for 5×7 b&w prints; $70/page for camera-ready art; $40 for b&w cover photo. Captions and identification of subjects required.

Columns/Departments: Book Reviews; New Product Reviews; Micro-Machining; Foundry. "Writer should become familiar with our magazine before submitting. Query first." Buys 25-30 mss/year. Length: 600-1,500 words. Pays $40-70/page.

Fillers: Machining tips/shortcuts. No news clippings. Buys 12-15/year. Length: 100-300 words. Pays $30-48.

Tips: "The writer should be experienced in the area of metalworking and machining; should be extremely thorough in explanations of methods, processes — always with an eye to safety; and should provide good quality b&w photos and/or clear drawings to aid in description. Visuals are of increasing importance to our readers. Carefully planned photos, drawings and charts will carry a submission to our magazine much farther along the path to publication."

JUGGLER'S WORLD, International Jugglers Association, Box 443, Davidson NC 28036-0443. (704)892-1296. Fax: (704)892-2499. Editor: Bill Giduz. 25% freelance written. Quarterly magazine on juggling. "*Juggler's World* publishes news, feature articles, fiction and poetry that relates to juggling. We also encourage 'how-to' articles describing how to learn various juggling tricks." Circ. 3,500. **Pays on acceptance.** Publishes ms an average of 6 months after acceptance. Byline given. Buys all rights. Submit seasonal/holiday material 6 months in advance. Accepts simultaneous and previously published submissions. Send photocopy of article. For reprints, pays 50% of the amound paid for an original article. Query for electronic submissions. Reports in 6 weeks. Sample copy for 9×12 SAE with 5 first-class stamps. Writer's guidelines for #10 SASE.

Nonfiction: Essays, general interest, historical/nostalgic, how-to, humor, interview/profile, opinion, personal experience, photo feature, travel. Buys 3 mss/year. Query. Length: 500-2,000 words. Pays $50-100 for assigned articles. Pays expenses of writers on assignment.

Photos: Send photos with submission. Reviews contact sheets, negatives and prints. Offers no additional payment for photos accepted with ms. Captions required. Buys one-time rights.

Fiction: Ken Letko, fiction editor. Adventure, fantasy, historical, humorous, science fiction, slice-of-life vignettes. Buys 2 mss/year. Query. Length: 250-1,000 words. Pays $25-50.

Tips: "The best approach is a feature article or an interview with a leading juggler. Article should include both human interest material (describe the performer as an individual) and technical juggling information to make clear to a knowledgeable audience the exact tricks and skits performed."

KITPLANES, For designers, builders and pilots of experimental aircraft, Fancy Publications, P.O. Box 6050, Mission Viejo CA 92690. (714)855-8822. Fax: (714)855-3045. Editor: Dave Martin. Managing Editor: Keith Beveridge. 70% freelance written. Eager to work with new/unpublished writers. Monthly magazine covering self-construction of private aircraft for pilots and builders. Estab. 1972. Circ. 85,000. Pays on publication. Publishes ms an average of 3 months after acceptance. Byline given. Offers negotiable kill fee. Buys first North American serial rights. Submit seasonal/holiday material 6 months in advance. Query for electronic submissions. Reports in 2 weeks on queries; 6 weeks on mss. Sample copy for $3. Free writer's guidelines.

Nonfiction: How-to, interview/profile, new product, personal experience, photo feature, technical, general interest. "We are looking for articles on specific construction techniques, the use of tools, both hand and power, in aircraft building, the relative merits of various materials, conversions of engines from automobiles for aviation use, installation of instruments and electronics." No general-interest aviation articles, or "My First Solo" type of articles. Buys 80 mss/year. Query. Length: 500-5,000 words. Pays $100-400, including story photos.

Photos: State availability of or send photos with query or ms. Pays $250 for cover photos. Captions and identification of subjects required. Buys one-time rights.

Tips: "*Kitplanes* contains very specific information—a writer must be extremely knowledgeable in the field. Major features are entrusted only to known writers. I cannot emphasize enough that articles must be directed at the individual aircraft builder. We need more 'how-to' photo features in all areas of homebuilt aircraft."

THE LEATHER CRAFTERS & SADDLERS JOURNAL, 4307 Oak Dr., Rhinelander WI 54501-9717. (715)362-5393. Fax: (715)362-5393. Editor: William R. Reis. Managing Editor: Dorothea Reis. 100% freelance written. Bimonthly craft magazine. "Aid to craftsmen using leather as the base medium. All age groups and skill levels from beginners to master carvers and artisans." Estab. 1990. Circ. 6,000. Pays on publication. Publishes ms an average of 2 months after acceptance. Byline given. "All assigned articles subject to review for acceptance by editor." Buys first North American serial and second serial (reprint) rights. Submit seasonal/holiday material 6 months in advance. Accepts simultaneous and previously published submissions. Send tearsheet or photocopy of article. Pays 50% of original article fee. Reports in 1 month. Sample copy for $4.50. Writer's guidelines for #10 SASE.

Nonfiction: How-to (crafts and arts and any other projects using leather). "I want only articles that include hands-on, step-by-step, how-to information." Buys 75 mss/year. Send complete ms. Length: 500-2,500 words. Pays $20-200 for assigned articles; $20-150 for unsolicited articles. Send good contrast color print photos and full size patterns and/or full-size photo-carve patterns with submission. Lack of these reduces payment amount. Captions required.

Columns/Departments: Beginners, Intermediate, Artists, Western Design, Saddlemakers, International Design and Letters (the open exchange of information between all peoples). Length: 500-2,500 on all. Buys 75 mss/year. Send complete ms. Pays 5¢/word.

Fillers: Anecdotes, facts, gags illustrated by cartoonist, newsbreaks. Length: 25-200 words. Pays $3-10.

Tips: "We want to work with people who understand and know leathercraft and are interested in passing on their knowledge to others. We would prefer to interview people who have achieved a high level in leathercraft skill."

LINN'S STAMP NEWS, Amos Press, 911 Vandemark Rd., P.O. Box 29, Sidney OH 45365. (513)498-0801. Fax: (513)498-0814. Editor: Michael Laurence. Managing Editor: Elaine Boughner. 50% freelance written. Weekly tabloid on the stamp collecting hobby. "All articles must be about philatelic collectibles." Estab. 1928. Circ. 75,000. Pays on publication. Publishes ms an average of 1 month after acceptance. Byline given. Buys first North American serial rights. Submit seasonal/holiday material 2 months in advance. Reports in 2 weeks on mss. Free sample copy. Writer's guidelines for #10 SAE with 2 first-class stamps.

Nonfiction: General interest, historical/nostalgic, how-to, interview/profile, technical. "No articles merely giving information on background of stamp subject. Must have philatelic information included." Buys 300 mss/year. Send complete ms. Length: 500 words maximum. Pays $10-50. Rarely pays expenses of writers on assignment.

Photos: Send photos with submission. Prefers glossy b&w prints. Offers no additional payment for photos accepted with ms. Captions required. Buys all rights.

LIVE STEAM, Live Steam, Inc., 2779 Aero Park Dr., Box 629, Traverse City MI 49685. (616)946-3712. Fax: (616)946-3289. Editor: Joe D. Rice. 90% freelance written. Eager to work with new/unpublished writers. Bimonthly magazine covering steam-powered models and full-size engines (i.e., locomotives, traction, cars, boats, stationary, etc.) "Our readers are hobbyists, many of whom are building their engines from scratch. We are interested in anything that has to do with the world of live steam-powered machinery." Circ. 12,800. Pays on publication. Publishes ms an average of 18 months after acceptance. Byline given. Buys first North American serial rights only. Reports in 3 weeks. Free sample copy and writer's guidelines.

Nonfiction: Historical/nostalgic, how-to (build projects powered by steam), new product, personal experience, photo feature, technical (must be within the context of steam-powered machinery or on machining techniques). No fiction. Buys 50 mss/year. Query or send complete ms. Length: 500-3,000 words. Pays $30-500/published page. Sometimes pays the expenses of writers on assignment.

Photos: Send photos with ms. Pays $50/page of finished art. Pays $8 for 5×7 b&w prints; $40 for color cover. Captions and identification of subjects required.

Columns/Departments: Steam traction engines, steamboats, stationary steam, steam autos. Buys 6-8 mss/year. Query. Length: 1,000-3,000 words. Pays $20-50.

Tips: "At least half of all our material is from the freelancer. Requesting a sample copy and author's guide will be a good place to start. The writer must be well-versed in the nature of live steam equipment and the hobby of scale modeling such equipment. Technical and historical accuracy is an absolute must. Often, good articles are weakened or spoiled by mediocre or poor quality photos. Freelancers must learn to take a *good* photograph."

LOOSE CHANGE, Mead Publishing Co., 1515 S. Commerce St., Las Vegas NV 89102-2703. (702)387-8750. Publisher: Daniel R. Mead. 5-10% freelance written. Eager to work with new/unpublished writers. Magazine published 10 times/year covering gaming and coin-operated machines: slot machines; trade stimulators; jukeboxes; gumball and peanut vendors; pinballs; scales, etc. "Our audience is predominantly male. Readers are all collectors or enthusiasts of coin-operated machines, particularly slot machines and jukeboxes. Subscribers are, in general, not heavy readers." Circ. 3,000. **Pays on acceptance.** Publishes ms an average of 2-3 months after acceptance. Byline given. Prefers to buy all rights, but also buys first and reprint rights. "We may allow author to reprint upon request in noncompetitive publications." Accepts previously published submissions; must be accompanied by complete list of previous sales, including sale dates. Query for electronic submissions. Reports in 1 month on queries; 6 weeks on mss. Sample copy for $1.50. Writer's guidelines for #10 SASE.

Nonfiction: Historical/nostalgic, how-to, interview/profile, opinion, personal experience, photo feature, technical. "Articles illustrated with clear, black and white photos are always considered much more favorably than articles without photos (we have a picture-oriented audience). The writer must be knowledgeable about subject matter because our readers are knowledgeable and will spot inaccuracies." Buys up to 10 mss/year. Length: 900-6,000 words; 3,500-12,000 for cover stories. Pays $100 maximum, inside stories; $200 maximum, cover (feature) stories.

Photos: "Captions should tell a complete story without reference to the body text." Send photos with ms. Reviews 8×10 and 5×7 b&w glossy prints. Captions required. "Purchase price for articles includes payment for photos."

Fiction: "All fiction must have a gambling/coin-operated-machine angle. Very low emphasis is placed on fiction. Fiction must be exceptional to be acceptable to our readers." Buys maximum 4 mss/year. Send complete ms. Length: 800-2,500 words. Pays $60 maximum.

LOST TREASURE, INC., P.O. Box 1589, Grove OK 74344. Managing Editor: Grace Michael. 75% freelance written. Monthly, bimonthly and annual magazines covering lost treasure. Estab. 1966. Circ. 55,000. Buys all rights. Byline given. Buys 225+ mss/year. Queries welcome. Length: 1,200-1,800 words. Pays on publication (4¢/word). No simultaneous submissions. Reports in 2 months. Queries welcome. Writers guidelines for #10 SASE. Sample copies (all 3 magazines) and guidelines for 10×13 SAE with $2.90 postage.

Nonfiction: 1) *Lost Treasure*, a monthly publication, is composed of lost treasure stories, legends, folklore, and how-to articles. 2) *Treasure Facts*, a bimonthly publication, consists of how-to information for treasure hunters, treasure hunting club news, who's who in treasure hunting, tips, etc. 3) *Treasure Cache*, an annual publication, contains stories about documented treasure caches with a sidebar from the author telling the reader how-to search for the cache highlighted in the story.

Photos: Black and white glossy prints with mss help sell your story. Pays $5/published photo. Cover photos pay $100/published photo; must be 35mm color slides, vertical. Captions required.

Tips: We are only interested in treasures that can be found with metal detectors. Queries welcome but not required. If you write about famous treasures and lost mines, be sure we haven't used your selected topic recently and story must have a new slant or new information. Source documentation required. How-To's should cover some aspect of treasure hunting and how-to steps should be clearly defined. If you have a

Treasure Cache story we will, if necessary, help the author with the sidebar telling how to search for the cache in the story.

MANUSCRIPTS, The Manuscript Society, Department of History, University of South Carolina, Columbia SC 29208. (803)777-6525. Editor: David R. Chesnutt. 10% freelance written. Quarterly magazine for collectors of autographs and mss. Estab. 1948. Circ. 1,500. **Pays on acceptance.** Publishes ms an average of 6-18 months after acceptance. Byline given. Buys first publication rights. Query for electronic submissions. Reports in 1 month. Sample copy for 6½×9½ SAE with 5 first-class stamps.
Nonfiction: Historical, personal experience, photo feature. Buys 4-6 mss/year. Query. Length: 1,500-3,000 words. Pays $50-250 for unsolicited articles.
Photos: Send photos with submission. Reviews contact sheets and prints. Offers $15-30/photo. Captions and identification of subjects required. Buys one-time rights.
Tips: "The Society is a mix of autograph collectors, dealers and scholars who are interested in manuscripts. Good illustrations of manuscript material are essential. Unusual documents are most often the basis of articles. Scholarly apparatus may be used but is not required. Articles about significant collections of documents (or unusual collections) would be welcomed. Please query first."

MINIATURE QUILTS, Chitra Publications, 2 Public Ave., Montrose PA 18801. (717)278-1984. Fax: (717)278-2223. Editor: Patti Bachelder. 40% freelance written. Quarterly magazine on miniature quilts. "We seek patterns and articles of an instructional nature (all techniques), profiles of talented quiltmakers and informational articles on all aspects of miniature quilts. Miniature is defined as quilts made up of blocks smaller than five inches." Estab. 1990. Circ. 50,000. Pays on publication. Publishes ms an average of 6 months after acceptance. Byline given. Buys second serial (reprint) rights. Submit seasonal/holiday material 6-8 months in advance. Query for electronic submissions. Reports in 2 months on queries and mss. Free sample copy and writer's guidelines.
Columns/Departments: Book and product reviews (focused on miniature quilts, currently written by one writer). Length: 800-1,600 words.
Photos: Send photos with submission. Reviews transparencies. Offers $20/photo. Captions, model releases and identification of subjects required. Buys all rights.
Tips: "Publication hinges on good photo quality. Query with ideas; send samples of prior work."

MODEL RAILROADER, P.O. Box 1612, Waukesha WI 53187. Editor: Andy Sperandeo. Monthly for hobbyists interested in scale model railroading. Buys exclusive rights. "Study publication before submitting material." Reports on submissions within 1 month.
Nonfiction: Wants construction articles on specific model railroad projects (structures, cars, locomotives, scenery, benchwork, etc.). Also photo stories showing model railroads. Query. First-hand knowledge of subject almost always necessary for acceptable slant. Pays base rate of $90/page.
Photos: Buys photos with detailed descriptive captions only. Pays $10 and up, depending on size and use. Pays double b&w rate for color; full color cover earns $200.

MONITORING TIMES, Grove Enterprises Inc., P.O. Box 98, Brasstown NC 28902-0098. (704)837-9200. Fax: (704)837-2216. Managing Editor: Rachel Baughn. Publisher: Robert Grove. 80% freelance written. Monthly magazine for radio hobbyists. Estab. 1982. Circ. 30,000. Pays 30-60 days before date of publication. Publishes ms an average of 4 months after acceptance. Byline given. Buys first North American serial rights and limited reprint rights. Submit seasonal/holiday material 4 months in advance. Accepts previously published submissions. Send photocopy of article and information about when and where the article previously appeared. Pays 25% of amount paid for an original article. Reports in 1 month. Sample copy and writer's guidelines for 9×12 SAE and 9 first-class stamps.
Nonfiction: General interest, how-to, humor, interview/profile, personal experience, photo feature, technical. Buys 275 mss/year. Query. Length: 1,000-2,500 words. Pays $150-200.
Photos: Send photos with submission. Offers $10-25/photo. Captions required. Buys one-time rights.
Columns/Departments: "Query managing editor."

MOUNTAIN STATES COLLECTOR, Spree Publishing, P.O. Box 2525, Evergreen CO 80439. Fax: (303)674-1253. Editor: Carol Mac Dougall. Managing Editor: Peg DeStefano. 85% freelance written. Monthly tabloid covering antiques and collectibles. Estab. 1970. Circ. 10,000. Pays on publication. Publishes ms an average of 6 months after acceptance. Byline given. Not copyrighted. Buys first, one-time or second serial (reprint) rights. Submit seasonal/holiday material at least 3 months in advance. Accepts simultaneous and previously published submissions. Send typed ms with rights for sale noted. Pays 100% of their fee for an original article. Reports in 4 months. Sample copy for 9×12 SAE with 4 first-class stamps. Writer's guidelines for #10 SASE.
Nonfiction: About antiques and/or collectibles—book excerpts, historical/nostalgic, how-to (collect), interview/profile (of collectors) and photo feature. Buys 75 mss/year. Query with or without published clips, or send complete ms. Length: 500-1,500 words. Pays $15. Sometimes pays the expenses of writers on assignment (mileage, phone—not long distance travel).

Photos: Send photos with submission. Reviews contact sheets, and 5×7 b&w prints. Offers $5/photo used. Captions preferred. Buys one-time rights.

Tips: "Writers should know their topics well or be prepared to do in-depth interviews with collectors. We prefer a down-home approach. We need articles on antiques, collectors and collections; how-to articles on collecting; how a collector can get started; or clubs for collectors. We would like to see more articles in 1994 with high-quality b&w photos."

THE NUMISMATIST, American Numismatic Association, 818 N. Cascade Ave., Colorado Springs CO 80903-3279. (719)632-2646. Fax: (719)634-4085. Editor/Publisher: Barbara Gregory. Monthly magazine "for collectors of coins, medals, tokens and paper money." Estab. 1888. Circ. 28,000. Pays on publication. Publishes ms an average of 1 year after acceptance. Byline given. Buys first North American serial or second serial (reprint) rights. Accepts previously published submissions. Send photocopy of article and information about when and where the article previously appeared. Pays 100% of amount paid for an original article. Submit seasonal/holiday material 1 year in advance. Reports in 2 months. Sample copy and writer's guidelines for 9×12 SAE with 5 first-class stamps.

Nonfiction: Essays, exposé, general interest, historical/nostalgic, humor, interview/profile, new product, opinion, personal experience, photo feature, technical. No articles that are lengthy or non-numismatic. Buys 48-60 mss/year. Send complete ms. Length: 1,000-3,500 words. Pays "on rate-per-published-page basis." Sometimes pays the expenses of writers on assignment.

Photos: Send b&w photos with ms. Reviews contact sheets, 4×5 or 5×7 prints. Offers $2.50-5/photo. Captions and identification of subjects required. Buys one-time rights.

Columns/Departments: Buys 72 mss/year. Length: 775-2,000 words. "Pays negotiable flat fee per column."

NUTSHELL NEWS, For creators and collectors of scale miniatures, Kalmbach Publishing Co., 21027 Crossroads Circle, Waukesha WI 53187-9951. (414)796-8776. Fax: (414)796-1383. Editor: Sybil Harp. 50% freelance written. Monthly magazine covering dollhouse scale miniatures. "*Nutshell News* is aimed at serious, adult hobbyists. Our readers take their miniatures seriously and do not regard them as toys. We avoid 'cutesiness' and treat our subject as a serious art form and/or an engaging leisure interest." Estab. 1971. Circ. 40,000. Pays advance fee on acceptance and balance on publication. Byline given. Offers $25 kill fee. Buys all rights but will revert rights by agreement. Submit seasonal/holiday material 1 year in advance. Reports in 3 weeks on queries; 2 months on mss. Sample copy for $3.50. Writer's guidelines for #10 SASE.

Nonfiction: How-to miniature projects in 1", ½", ¼" scales, interview/profile (artisans or collectors), photo feature (dollhouses, collections, museums). Special issues: smaller scales annual ½", ¼" or smaller scales (May); kitcrafting—customizing kits or commercial miniatures, a how-to issue (August). No articles on miniature shops or essays. Buys 120 mss/year. Query. Length: 1,000-1,500 words for features, how-to's may be longer. "Payment varies, but averages $150 for features, more for long how-to's." Sometimes pays expenses of writers on assignment.

Photos: Send photos with submission. Requires 35mm slides and larger, 3×5 prints. "Photos are paid for with manuscript. Seldom buy individual photos." Captions preferred; identification of subjects required. Buys all rights.

Tips: "It is essential that writers for *Nutshell News* be active miniaturists, or at least very knowledgeable about the hobby. Our readership is intensely interested in miniatures and will discern lack of knowledge or enthusiasm on the part of an author. A writer can best break in to *Nutshell News* by convincing me that he/ she knows and is interested in miniatures, and by sending photos and/or clippings to substantiate that. Photographs are extremely important. They must be sharp and properly exposed to reveal details. For articles about subjects in the Chicago/Milwaukee area, we can usually send our staff photographer."

‡PAINTWORKS, Discovery Magazine For Decorative Painters, All American Crafts Publishing, 243 Newton-Sparta Rd., Newton NJ 07860. (201)383-8080. Editor: Matthew T. Jones. 90% freelance written. Bimonthly magazine covering decorative painting. "*Paintworks* accepts articles related to decorative painting projects, ideas, tips, and techniques, including folk art, stenciling, rosemaling, faux finishing, silk painting, and tinware in oils and acrylics." Estab. 1991. Circ. 100,000. Pays on publication. Publishes ms an average of 3-6 months after acceptance. Byline given. Buys first rights and second serial (reprint) rights. Editorial lead time 3-6 months. Submit seasonal material 3 months in advance. No simultaneous submissions. Accepts previously published submissions occasionally. Reports in 2-4 weeks on queries. Sample copy for 9×12 SAE with 6 first-class stamps. Writer's guidelines for #10 SASE.

Nonfiction: How-to. Buys 75-100 mss/year. Query. Length: 1,500 words maximum. Pays 10¢/word.

Tips: "Send photos of finished projects for sale as how-to articles."

PAPER COLLECTORS MARKETPLACE, Watson Graphic Designs, Inc., P.O. Box 128, Scandinavia WI 54977-0128. (715)467-2379. Fax: (715)467-2243. Publisher: Doug Watson. 100% freelance written. Monthly magazine on paper collectibles. "All articles must relate to the hobby in some form. Whenever possible values should be given for the collectibles mentioned in the article." Estab. 1987. Circ. 4,000. Pays on publication. Byline given. Offers 25% kill fee on commissioned articles. Buys first North American serial rights. Submit

seasonal/holiday material 2 months in advance. Reports in 2 weeks. Free sample copy. Writer's guidelines for #10 SASE.
Nonfiction: Historical/nostalgic, how-to, photo feature, technical. Buys 60 mss/year. Query with published clips. Length: 1,000-2,000 words. Pays 3-5¢/word.
Photos: Send photos with submissions. Offers no additional payment for photos accepted with ms. Captions, model releases and identification of subjects required. Buys one-time rights.

THE PEN AND QUILL, Universal Autograph Collectors Club (UACC), P.O. Box 6181, Washington DC 20044-6181. (202)332-7388. Editor: Bob Erickson. 20% freelance written. Bimonthly magazine of autograph collecting. All articles must advance the hobby of autograph collecting in some manner. Estab. 1966. Circ. 1,900. Pays on publication. Publishes ms an average of 6 months after acceptance. Byline given. Buys first North American serial rights. Submit seasonal/holiday material 4 months in advance. Sample copy for $5.
Nonfiction: General interest, historical/nostalgic, interview/profile. Buys 4 mss/year. Send complete ms. Length: 500-2,500 words. Pays $20-100.
Photos: Send photos with submission. Offers no additional payment for photos accepted with ms. Captions and identification of subjects required. Buys one-time rights.

POPULAR ELECTRONICS, Gernsback Publications, Inc., 500B Bi-County Blvd., Farmingdale NY 11735-3918. (516)293-3000. Fax: (516)293-3115. Editor: Carl Laron. 80% freelance written. Monthly magazine covering hobby electronics—"features, projects, ideas related to audio, radio, experimenting, test equipment, antique radio, communications, consumer electronics, state-of-the-art, etc." Circ. 87,877. **Pays on acceptance.** Byline given. Buys all rights. Submit seasonal/holiday material 6 months in advance. Query for electronic submissions. Reports in 1 month. Free sample copy, "include mailing label." Writer's guidelines for #10 SASE.
Nonfiction: General interest, how-to, photo feature, technical. Buys 200 mss/year. Query or send complete ms. Length: 1,000-3,500 words. Pays $100-500.
Photos: Send photos with submission. "Wants b&w glossy photos." Offers no additional payment for photos accepted with ms. Captions required. Buys all rights.
Tips: "All areas are open to freelancers. Project-type articles and other 'how-to' articles have best success."

POPULAR ELECTRONICS HOBBYISTS HANDBOOK, Gernsback Publications, Inc., 500 B Bi-County Blvd., Farmingdale NY 11735-3918. (516)293-3000. Fax: (516)293-3115. Editor: Julian S. Martin. 95% freelance written. Semiannual magazine on hobby electronics. Estab. 1989. Circ. 125,000. **Pays on acceptance.** Byline given. Buys all rights. Submit seasonal/holiday material 6 months in advance. Query for electronic submissions. Reports in 2 weeks.
Nonfiction: General interest, historical/nostalgic, how-to (build projects, fix consumer products, etc., all of which must be electronics oriented), photo feature, technical. "No product reviews!" Buys 20-30 mss/year. Send complete ms. Length: 1,000-5,000 words. Pays $100-500 for assigned articles; $100-500 for unsolicited articles.
Photos: Send photos with submission. "We want b&w glossy photos." Reviews 5×7 or 8×10 b&w prints. Offers no additional payment for photos accepted with ms. Captions and model releases are required. Buys all rights.
Tips: "Read the magazine. Know and understand the subject matter. Write it. Submit it."

POPULAR MECHANICS, Hearst Corp., 3rd Floor, 224 W. 57th St., New York NY 10019. (212)649-2000. Editor: Joe Oldham. Managing Editor: Deborah Frank. 50% freelance written. Monthly magazine on automotive, home improvement, science, boating, outdoors, electronics. "We are a men's service magazine that tries to address the diverse interests of today's male, providing him with information to improve the way he lives. We cover stories from do-it-yourself projects to technological advances in aerospace, military, automotive and so on." Estab. 1902. Circ. 1.6 million. **Pays on acceptance.** Publishes ms an average of 6 months after acceptance. Byline given. Offers 25% kill fee. Buys all rights. Submit seasonal/holiday material 6 months in advance. Query. Reports in 2 weeks on queries; 1 month on mss. Sample copy and writer's guidelines for 9×12 SASE.
Nonfiction: General interest, how-to (shop projects, car fix-its), new product, technical. Special issues: Design and Engineering Awards (January); Boating Guide (February); Home Improvement Guide (April); Car Care Guide (May); Automotive Parts & Accessories Guide (October); Woodworking Guide (November). No historical, editorial or critique pieces. Buys 24 mss/year. Query with or without published clips or send complete ms. Length: 500-3,000 words. Pays $500-1,500 for assigned articles; $15-1,000 for unsolicited articles. Sometimes pays expenses of writers on assignment.
Photos: Send photos with submission. Reviews 5×7 transparencies and prints. Offers no additional payment for photos accepted with ms. Captions, model releases and identification of subjects required. Buys first and exclusive publication rights in the US during on-sale period of issue in which photos appear plus 90 days after.
Columns/Departments: New Cars (latest and hottest cars out of Detroit and Europe), Car Care (Maintenance basics, How It Works, Fix-Its and New products: send to Mike Allen. Electronics, Audio, Home Video, Computers, Photography: send to Frank Vizard. Boating (new equipment, how-tos, fishing tips), Outdoors

(gear, vehicles, outdoor adventures): send to Joe Skorupa. Home & Shop Journal: send to Steve Willson. Science (latest developments), Tech Update (breakthroughs) and Aviation (sport aviation, homebuilt aircraft, new commercial aircraft, civil aeronautics): send to Abe Dane. All columns are about 1,000 words.

POPULAR WOODWORKING, EGW Publishing Co., 1041 Shary Circle, Concord CA 94518-2407. (510)671-9852. Fax: (510)671-0692. Editor: Robert C. Cook. 40% freelance written. Eager to work with new/unpublished writers. Bimonthly magazine covering woodworking. "Our readers are the woodworking hobbyist and small woodshop owner. Writers should have a knowledge of woodworking, or be able to communicate information gained from woodworkers." Estab. 1981. Circ. 284,000. Pays half on acceptance, and the balance plus 3 copies on publication. Publishes ms an average of 10-12 months after acceptance. Byline given. Buys all and first serial and sometimes second-time rights. Submit seasonal/holiday material 6 months in advance. Reports in 2 months. Sample copy and writer's guidelines for $4.50 and 9 × 12 SAE with 6 first-class stamps.
Nonfiction: How-to (on woodworking projects, with plans); humor (woodworking anecdotes); technical (woodworking techniques). "No home-maintenance articles or shop horror stories." Buys 100 mss/year. Query with or without published clips or send complete ms. Pays $500-1,000 for large, complex projects, and $100-500 for simpler projects and other features.
Photos: Send photos with submission. Reviews color only, 4 × 5 transparencies, 5 × 7 glossy prints and 35mm slides. Offers no additional payment for photos accepted with ms; extra for quality cover photos. Need sharp close-up color photos of woodworkers demonstrating a technique. Captions and identification of subjects required.
Columns/Departments: Jig Journal (how to make special fixtures to help a tool do a task), 500-1,500 words. Buys 6 mss/year. Query.
Fillers: Anecdotes, facts, short humor, shop tips. Buys 15/year. Length: 50-500 words.
Tips: "Show a technical knowledge of woodworking. We really need project with plans articles. Describe the steps in making a piece of furniture (or other project). Provide a cutting list and a rough diagram (we can redraw). If the writer is not a woodworker, he should have help from a woodworker to make sure the technical information is correct."

‡POSTCARD COLLECTOR, Jones Publishing, Inc., P.O. Box 337, Iola WI 54945-0337. (715)445-5000. Fax: (715)445-4053. Editor: Deborah Lengkeek. 70% freelance written. Monthly magazine. "Publication is for postcard collectors; all editorial content relates to postcards in some way." Estab. 1986. Circ. 6,000. Pays on publication. Publishes ms an average of 6 months after acceptance. Byline given. Buys one-time, first or second serial rights. Submit seasonal/holiday material 3 months in advance. Accepts previously published submissions. Reports in 2 weeks on queries; 1 month on mss. Sample copy and writer's guidelines for 9 × 12 SAE with 4 first-class stamps.
Nonfiction: General interest, historical/nostalgic, how-to (e.g. preservatives), new product, opinion, personal experience, photo feature, travel. Buys 60 mss/year. Send complete ms. Length: 200-1,800 words. Pays 5¢/word for assigned articles; 3-5¢/word for unsolicited articles.
Photos: State availability of postcards with submission. Offers $1-3/photo. Captions and identification of subjects required. Buys perpetual, but nonexclusive rights.
Columns/Departments: 50-150 words. Buys 60 mss/year. Query. Pay is negotiable.
Tips: "We publish information about postcards written by expert topical specialists. The writer must be knowledgable about postcards and have acquired 'expert' information. We plan more complete listings of postcard sets and series—old and new." Areas most open to freelancers are feature-length articles on specialized areas (600-1,800 words) with 1-10 illustrations.

QST, American Radio Relay League, Inc., 225 Main St., Newington CT 06111-1494. (203)666-1541. Fax: (203)665-7531. Editor: Mark Wilson. Contact Assistant Managing Editor: Kirk Kleinschmidt. 60% freelance written. Monthly magazine covering amateur radio interests and technology. "Ours are topics of interest to radio amateurs and persons in the electronics and communications fields." Estab. 1914. Circ. 165,000. Pays on publication. Publishes ms an average of 4 months after acceptance. Byline given. Usually buys all rights. Submit seasonal/holiday material 5 months in advance. Query for electronic submissions. Reports in 3 weeks on queries. Free sample copy and writer's guidelines for 10 × 13 SAE with 5 first-class stamps.
Nonfiction: General interest, how-to, humor, new products, personal experience, photo feature, technical (anything to do with amateur radio). Buys 50 mss/year. Query with or without published clips, or send complete ms. Length: no minimum or maximum. Pays $65/published page. Sometimes pays expenses of writers on assignment.
Photos: Send photos with submission. Sometimes offers additional payment for photos accepted with ms or for cover. Captions, model releases and identification of subjects required. Usually buys all rights.
Columns/Departments: Hints and Kinks (hints/time saving procedures/circuits/associated with amateur radio), 50-200 words. Buys 100 mss/year. Send complete ms. Pays $20.
Tips: "Write with an idea, ask for sample copy and writer's guide. Technical and general interest to amateur operators, communications and electronics are most open."

QUICK & EASY CRAFTS, For Today's Crafty Women, House of White Birches, 306 E. Parr Rd., Berne IN 46711. (219)589-8741. Fax: (219)589-8093. Editor: Beth Schwartz Wheeler. 90% freelance written. Bimonthly magazine covering crafts that are upscale but easily and quickly done. "Our audience does not mind spending money on craft items to use in their projects but they don't have lots of time to spend." Estab. 1979. Circ. 380,000. Pays mid-production. Byline given. Buys all rights. Submit seasonal/holiday material 1 year in advance. Reports in 2 weeks on queries. Sample copy for $2. Free writer's guidelines.
Nonfiction: How-to. No profiles of other crafters. Buys 150 mss/year. Send complete ms. Pays $25-250.
Tips: "Manuscript should include complete instructions for project. Send good, clear photo."

QUILT WORLD, House of White Birches, 306 E. Parr Rd., Berne IN 46711. (219)589-8741. Fax: (207)794-3290. Editor: Sandra L. Hatch. 100% freelance written. Works with a small number of new/unpublished writers each year. Bimonthly magazine covering quilting. "We publish articles on quilting techniques, profiles of quilters and coverage of quilt shows. Reader is 30-70 years old, midwestern." Circ. 130,000. Pays on publication. Publishes ms an average of 6 months after acceptance. Byline given. Buys all, first, one-time and second serial (reprint) rights. Submit seasonal/holiday material 9 months in advance. Accepts previously published material. Send photocopy of article and information about when and where it previously appeared. Query for electronic submissions. Reports in 1 month. Sample copy for $3. Writer's guidelines for #10 SASE.
Nonfiction: How-to, interview/profile (quilters), technical, new product (quilt products), photo feature. Buys 18-24 mss/year. Query. Length: open. Pays $35-100.
Photos: Send photos with submission. Reviews transparencies and prints. Offers $15/photo (except covers). Identification of subjects required. Buys all or one-time rights.
Tips: "Send list of previous articles published with résumé and a SASE. List ideas which you plan to base your articles around."

QUILTER'S NEWSLETTER MAGAZINE, P.O. Box 394, Wheatridge CO 80034-0394. Fax: (303)420-7358. Editor: Bonnie Leman. Magazine published 10 times/year. Estab. 1969. Circ. 200,000. Buys first North American serial rights or second rights. Buys about 15 mss/year. Pays on publication, sometimes on acceptance. Reports in 2 months. Free sample copy.
Nonfiction: "We are interested in articles on the subject of quilts and quiltmakers *only*. We are not interested in anything relating to 'Grandma's Scrap Quilts' but could use fresh material." Submit complete ms. Pays 10¢/word minimum, usually more.
Photos: Additional payment for photos depends on quality.
Fillers: Related to quilts and quiltmakers only.
Tips: "Be specific, brief, and professional in tone. Study our magazine to learn the kind of thing we like. Send us material which fits into our format but which is different enough to be interesting. Realize that we think we're the best quilt magazine on the market and that we're aspiring to be even better, then send us the cream off the top of your quilt material."

QUILTING INTERNATIONAL, A Showcase of Collectible Quilts & Contemporary Fiber Art, All American Crafts, Inc., 243 Newton-Sparta Rd., Newton NJ 07860. (201)383-8080. Fax: (201)383-8133. Editorial Director: Camille Pomaco. Editor: Marion Buccieri. 50% freelance written. Bimonthly quilts and quilting magazine. "We feature articles that inform and inspire quilters and fabric artists, showcasing both pieced and appliqued items, antique and contemporary. Articles that emphasize international trends and exhibits in the expanding world of quilting as a fiber art are welcome." Estab. 1987. Pays on publication. Publishes ms an average of 6 months after acceptance. Byline given. Buys first North American serial rights. Editorial lad time 4 months. Submit seasonal/holiday material 6 months in advance. Reports in 6-8 weeks on queries. Sample copy for 9 × 12 SAE with 4 first-class stamps. Free writer's guidelines for #10 SASE.
Nonfiction: Quilts and patterns; quilt exhibits, international and local quilt events, general interest, historical, how-to, inspirational, interview/profile, personal experience, photo feature (all as related to quilts and quilting). No poetry or fiction. Query. Length: 1,000-1500 words. Pays 10-15¢/word. Sometimes pays expenses of writers on assignment.
Photos: Send photos with submission. Reviews 4 × 5 transparencies or 3 × 5 prints. Pays $15-30. Captions required. Buys one-time rights.
Fillers: Anecdotes, gags to be illustrated by cartoonist, short humor. Buys 6-12/year. Length: 100-300 words. Pays 10¢/word.
Tips: "Good quality slides or chromes of beautiful quilts are highly desirable. We want articles about specific quilts and the quilters involved."

QUILTING TODAY MAGAZINE, The International Quilt Magazine, Chitra Publications, 2 Public Ave., Montrose PA 18801. (717)278-1984. Fax: (717)278-2223. Editor: Patti Bachelder. 80% freelance written. Bimonthly magazine on quilting, traditional and contemporary. "We seek articles that will cover one or two full pages (800 words each); informative to the general quilting public, present new ideas, interviews, instructional, etc." Estab. 1986. Circ. 90,000. Pays on publication. Publishes ms an average of 6 months after acceptance. Byline given. Buys second serial (reprint) rights and makes work-for-hire assignments. Submit seasonal/holiday material 6-8 months in advance. Query for electronic submissions. Reports in 1 month on

queries; 2 months on mss. Free sample copy and writer's guidelines for 9 × 12 SAE with 6 first-class stamps.
Nonfiction: Books excerpts, essays, how-to (for various quilting techniques), humor, interview/profile, new product, opinion, personal experience, photo feature. "No articles about family history related to a quilt or quilts unless the quilt is a masterpiece of color and design, impeccable workmanship." Buys 20-30 mss/year. Query with or without published clips or send complete mss. Length: 800-1,600 words. Pays $50-75/page. Sometimes pays expenses of writers on assignment.
Photos: Send photos with submission. Reviews 35mm slides and larger transparencies. Offers $20/photo. Captions, identification of subjects required. Buys all rights unless rented from a museum.
Columns/Departments: Book and product reviews, 300 words maximum; Quilters Lesson Book (instructional), 800-1,600 words. Buys 10-12 ms/year. Send complete ms. Pays up to $75/column.
Fiction: Fantasy, historical, humorous. Buys 1 mss/year. Send complete ms. Length: 300-1,600 words. Pays $50-75/page.
Tips: "Query with ideas; send samples of prior work so that we can assess and suggest assignment. Our publications appeal to traditional quilters (generally middle-aged) who use the patterns in each issue. Must have excellent photos."

RAILROAD MODEL CRAFTSMAN, Box 700, Newton NJ 07860. (201)383-3355. Fax: (201)383-4064. Editor: William C. Schaumburg. 75% freelance written. Works with a small number of new/unpublished writers each year. Monthly magazine for model railroad hobbyists, in all scales and gauges. Circ. 97,000. Buys all rights. Buys 50-100 mss/year. Pays on publication. Publishes ms an average of 9 months after acceptance. Submit seasonal material 6 months in advance. Sample copy for $2. Writer's and photographer's guidelines for SASE.
Nonfiction: "How-to and descriptive model railroad features written by persons who did the work are preferred. Almost all our features and articles are written by active model railroaders. It is difficult for non-modelers to know how to approach writing for this field." Pays minimum of $1.75/column inch of copy ($50/page).
Photos: Purchased with or without mss. Buys sharp 8 × 10 glossy prints and 35mm or larger transparencies. Pays minimum of $10 for photos or $5/diagonal inch. $200 for covers, which must tie in with article in that issue. Caption information required.
Tips: "We would like to emphasize modeling based on actual prototypes of equipment and industries as well as prototype studies of them."

SCOTT STAMP MONTHLY, Amos Press, Inc., P.O. Box 828, 2280 Industrial Blvd., Sidney OH 45365-0828. Fax: (513)498-0808. Editor: Wayne L. Youngblood. 70% freelance written. Works with a small number of new/unpublished writers each year. Monthly magazine for stamp collectors, from the beginner to the sophisticated philatelist. "The *Scott Stamp Monthly* provides collectors with new Scott catalog numbers, entertaining and educational reading. All stories must primarily be about the stamps saved by collectors, and secondarily historical or topical." Estab. 1920. Circ. 22,000. Pays on publication. Publishes ms an average of 2-3 months after acceptance. Byline given. Buys first North American serial rights. Editorial lead time 2-3 months. Submit seasonal or holiday material at least 5 months in advance. Query for electronic submissions. Prefers ASCII-based, preferably Xy-write. Reports in 1-2 months. Sample copy for 9 × 12 SAE with 5 first-class stamps. Writer's guidelines for #10 SASE.
Nonfiction: General interest, historical/nostalgic, how-to, opinion, personal experience, photo feature, technical (all must be stamp-related). "I do not want to see general articles that are only loosely tied to stamp collecting. This includes historical pieces tied to stamps only by illustration." Buys 65+ mss/year. Query with published clips. Length: 800-2,500 words. Pays $75 minimum.
Photos: Send photos with submission. Reviews contact sheets and 5 × 7 or larger prints. Offers no additional payment for photos accepted with ms. Buys one-time rights.
Columns: To Err is Divine (design errors on stamps), 30-40 words; The Odd Lot (unusual or ironic stamp articles) 700-1,000 words. Buys 60 mss/year. Pays $25 for design errors, $75 maximum.
Fiction: Adventure, fantasy, historical, suspense. "No pat formulas. We rarely buy fiction and are very choosy about what we accept." Buys 2-3 mss/year. Query with published clips. Length: 800-2,500 words. Pays $75-125.
Fillers: Anecdotes, facts. Length: 50-600 words. Payment negotiable.
Tips: "I seriously doubt that anyone who is not a stamp collector will get material published. Articles must display an understanding of the hobby and a sensitivity to collectors' needs. I can't stress enough that articles should be primarily about the stamps themselves. We are more in need of features than anything else. Although not required, it would be most helpful for freelancers to frequently consult the Associated Press style book. This will result in fewer editorial changes, and a greater chance of acceptance."

SEW NEWS, The Fashion Magazine for People Who Sew, PJS Publications, Inc., News Plaza, P.O. Box 1790, Peoria IL 61656. (309)682-6626. Fax: (309)682-7394. Editor: Linda Turner Griepentrog. 90% freelance written. Works with a small number of new/unpublished writers each year. Monthly magazine covering fashion-sewing. "Our magazine is for the beginning home sewer to the professional dressmaker. It expresses the fun, creativity and excitement of sewing." Estab. 1980. Circ. 261,000. **Pays on acceptance.** Publishes ms an average of 6 months after acceptance. Byline given. Buys all rights. Submit seasonal/holiday material 6 months in advance. Reports in 2 months. Sample copy for $3.95. Writer's guidelines for #10 SAE with 2 first-class stamps.

Nonfiction: How-to (sewing techniques), interview/profile (interesting personalities in home-sewing field). Buys 200-240 ms/year. Query with published clips if available. Length: 500-2,000 words. Pays $25-500. Rarely pays expenses of writers on assignment.

Photos: Send photos. Prefers b&w, color photographs or slides. Payment included in ms price. Identification of subjects required. Buys all rights.

Tips: "Query first with writing sample and outline of proposed story. Areas most open to freelancers are how-to and sewing techniques; give explicit, step-by-step instructions plus rough art."

‡**SHUTTLE SPINDLE & DYEPOT**, Handweavers Guild of America, Suite 702, 2402 University Ave., St. Paul MN 55114. (612)646-0802. Fax: (612)646-0806. E-mail: 73744.202 CompuServe.com. Editor: Sandra Bowles. 60% freelance written. Quarterly magazine covering handweaving, spinning and dyeing and related fiber art. "We take the practical and aesthetic approach to handweaving, handspinning, and related textile arts." Estab. 1969. Pays on publication. Publishes ms 15 months after acceptance. Byline given. Buys first North American serial rights. Submit seasonal material 1 year in advance. Rarely accepts previously published submissions. Reports in 2 months. Sample copy for $6.50. Free writer's guidelines.

Nonfiction: How-to, interview/profile, personal experience, photo feature, technical. "We want interesting, practical, technical information in our field." Buys 30 mss/year. Query with or without published clips, or send complete ms. Length: 500-1,200 words. Pays $25-125.

Photos: State availability of slides or transparencies or b&w photos with submission. Reviews contact sheets and transparencies.

Tips: "We read all submissions."

SPIN-OFF, Interweave Press, 201 E. 4th St., Loveland CO 80537. (303)669-7672. Fax: (303)667-8317. Editor: Deborah Robson. 10-20% freelance written. Quarterly magazine covering handspinning, dyeing, techniques and projects for using handspun fibers. Audience includes "practicing textile/fiber craftsworkers. Article should show considerable depth of knowledge of subject, although the tone should be informal and accessible." Estab. 1975. Circ. 15,000. Pays on publication. Publishes ms an average of 1 year after acceptance. Byline given. Buys first North American serial rights. Sample copy for $4.50 and 9 × 12 SAE. Writer's guidelines for #10 SAE and 2 first-class stamps.

Nonfiction: Historical, how-to (spinning; and knitted, crocheted and woven projects from handspun fibers with instructions); interview/profile (of successful and/or interesting handspinners); technical (on spinning, dyeing or fiber technology, use, properties). "All articles must contain a high level of in-depth information. Our readers are very knowledgeable about these subjects." Query. Length: 2,000 words. Pays $15-100.

Photos: Send photos. Identification of subjects and releases required.

Tips: "You should display knowledge of your subject, but you can tailor your article to reach beginning, intermediate or advanced spinners. Try for thoughtful organization, a personal informal style, and an article or series segment that is self-contained. New approaches to familiar topics are welcomed."

SPORTS COLLECTORS DIGEST, Krause Publications, 700 E. State St., Iola WI 54990. (715)445-2214. Fax: (715)445-4087. Editor: Tom Mortenson. Estab. 1952. 50% freelance written. Works with a small number of new/unpublished writers each year. Weekly sports memorabilia magazine. "We serve collectors of sports memorabilia—baseball cards, yearbooks, programs, autographs, jerseys, bats, balls, books, magazines, ticket stubs, etc." Estab. 1952. Circ. 52,000. Pays after publication. Publishes ms an average of 3 months after acceptance. Byline given. Buys first North American serial rights only. Submit seasonal/holiday material 3 months in advance. Accepts previously published material; send tearsheet of article. Pays 100% of their fee for an original article. Reports in 5 weeks on queries; 2 months on mss. Free sample copy. Writer's guidelines for #10 SASE.

Nonfiction: General interest (new card issues, research on older sets); historical/nostalgic (old stadiums, old collectibles, etc.); how-to (buy cards, sell cards and other collectibles, display collectibles, ways to get autographs, jerseys and other memorabilia); interview/profile (well-known collectors, ball players—but must focus on collectibles); new product (new card sets); personal experience ("what I collect and why"-type stories). No sports stories. "We are not competing with *The Sporting News, Sports Illustrated* or your daily paper. Sports collectibles only." Buys 100-200 mss/year. Query. Length: 300-3,000 words; prefers 1,000 words. Pays $50-125.

Photos: Unusual collectibles. Send photos. Pays $5-15 for b&w prints. Identification of subjects required. Buys all rights.

Columns/Departments: "We have all the columnists we need but welcome ideas for new columns." Buys 100-150 mss/year. Query. Length: 600-3,000 words. Pays $70-90.

Tips: "If you are a collector, you know what collectors are interested in. Write about it. No shallow, puff pieces; our readers are too smart for that. Only well-researched articles about sports memorabilia and collecting. Some sports nostalgia pieces are OK. Write only about the areas you know about."

STAMP COLLECTOR, For People Who Love Philately, Division of Van Dahl Publications, Capital Cities/ABC, Inc., P.O. Box 10, Albany OR 97321-0006. (503)928-3569. Fax: (503)967-7262. Editor: Ken Palke. 70% freelance written. Weekly tabloid covering philately. "Stamp Collector is dedicated to promoting the growth and enjoyment of philately through the exchange of information and ideas. All shades of opinion are published to provide the widest possible view of the hobby." Estab. 1931. Circ. 18,500. Pays on publication. Byline given. Buys all rights. Submit seasonal/holiday material 1½ months in advance. Query for electronic submissions. Call for details. Reports in 2 months. Sample copy and writer's guidelines upon request for 9 × 12 SAE with 4 first-class stamps.

Nonfiction: "No general articles on world history, world geography, lengthy articles about one particular stamp, puzzles, games, quizzes, etc." Buys 500 mss/year. Query. Pays $30-50. Sometimes pays the expenses of writers on assignment. Send photos, stamps or clear photocopies with submission. Buys all rights. Send SASE with unsolicited mss.

Columns/Departments: Guest Editorials, 1,000 words. Buys 15 mss/year. Send complete ms. Pays $30.

Tips: "Be a stamp collector or stamp dealer with some specific area of interest and/or expertise. Find a subject (stamps of a particular country, time period, designer, subject matter portrayed, printing method, etc.) that you are interested in and knowledgeable about, and in which our average reader would be interested. Our average reader is well-educated, intelligent, professional with diverse interests in postal services, printing methods, politics, geography, history, anthropology, economics, arts, etc."

SUNSHINE ARTISTS, America's Art & Craft Show Magazine, Sunshine Artists USA Inc., 1736 N. Highway 427, Longwood FL 32750-3410. (407)332-4944. Fax: (407)332-9672. Editor: Jeffrey D. Prutsman. Executive Editor: Kristine Petterson. Managing Editor: Merry Holden Mott. Monthly magazine covering art shows in the United States. "We are the premier marketing/reference magazine for those professional artists and crafts professionals who earn their living through art shows nationwide. We list more than 4,000 shows annually, critique many of them and publish articles on marketing, selling and other issues of concern to professional show circuit artists." Estab. 1972. Circ. 14,000. Pays on publication. Publishes ms an average of 3 months after acceptance. Byline given. Buys first North American serial rights. Reports within 2 months. Sample copy for $5.

Nonfiction: "We publish articles of interest to artists and crafts professionals who travel the art show circuit. Current topics include marketing, computers and RV living." No how-to. Buys 5-10 freelance mss/year. Query or ms. Length: 1,000-2,000 words. Pays $50-150 for accepted articles.

Photos: Send photos with submission. Black and white photos only. Offers no additional payment for photos accepted with ms. Captions, model releases and identification of subjects required.

TEDDY BEAR REVIEW, Collector Communications Corp., 170 Fifth Ave., New York NY 10010. (212)989-8700. Editor: Stephen L. Cronk. 75% freelance written. Works with a small number of new/unpublished writers each year. Bimonthly magazine on teddy bears. Estab. 1985. Pays 30 days after acceptance. Byline given. Buys first North American serial rights. Submit seasonal/holiday material 6 months in advance. Accepts previously published material. Send photocopy of article and information about when and where the article previously appeared. Sample copy and writer's guidelines for $2 and 9 × 12 SAE.

Nonfiction: Book excerpts, historical, how-to, interview/profile. No nostalgia on childhood teddy bears. Buys 30-40 mss/year. Query with published clips. Length: 500-1,500 words. Pays $75-200. Sometimes pays the expenses of writers on assignment "if approved ahead of time."

Photos: Send photos with submission. Reviews transparencies and b&w prints. Offers no additional payment for photos accepted with ms. Captions required. Buys one-time rights.

Tips: "We are interested in good, professional writers around the country with a strong knowledge of teddy bears. Historical profile of bear companies, profiles of contemporary artists and knowledgeable reports on museum collections are of interest."

‡THREADS, Taunton Press, 63 S. Main St., P.O. Box 5506, Newtown CT 06470. (203)426-8171. Editor: Amy Yanagi. Bimonthly magazine covering garment construction (sewing, knitting) and related fabric crafts (quilting and embroidery). "We're seeking proposals from hands-on authors who first and foremost have a skill. Being an experienced writer is of secondary consideration." Estab. 1985. Circ. 150,000. Pays $150/page. Byline given. Offers $150 kill fee. Buys one-time rights or reprint rights in article collections. Editorial lead time 4 months minimum. Query for electronic submissions. Reports in 1-2 months. Writer's guidelines free on request.

Nonfiction: "We prefer first-person experience."

Columns/Departments: Notes (current events, new products, opinions); Book reviews; Tips; Yarns (stories of a humorous nature). Query. Pays $150/page.

Tips: "Send us a proposal (outline) with photos of your own work (garments, samplers, etc. . .)"

TRADITIONAL QUILTWORKS, The Pattern Magazine for Creative Quilters, Chitra Publications, 2 Public Ave., Montrose PA 18801. (717)278-1984. Fax: (717)278-2223. Editor: Patti Bachelder. 60% freelance written. Bimonthly magazine on quilting. "We seek articles of an instructional nature, profiles of talented teachers, articles on the history of specific areas of quiltmaking (patterns, fiber, regional, etc.)." Estab. 1988. Circ.

90,000. Pays on publication. Publishes ms an average of 6 months after acceptance. Byline given. Buys second serial (reprint) rights. Submit seasonal/holiday material 6-8 months in advance. Query for electronic submissions. Reports in 2 months. Sample copy and writer's guidelines for 9×12 SASE and 6 first-class stamps.

Nonfiction: Historical, instructional, quilting education. "No light-hearted entertainment." Buys 12-18 mss/year. Query with or without published clips, or send complete ms. Length: 1,600 words maximum. Pays $75/page.

Photos: Send photos with submission. Reviews transparencies (color). Offers $20 per photo. Captions, model releases and identification of subjects required. Buys all rights.

Tips: "Query with ideas; send samples of prior work so that we can assess and suggest assignment. Our publications appeal to traditional quilters, generally middle-aged and mostly who use the patterns in the magazine. Publication hinges on good photo quality."

‡**TREASURE**, Double Eagle Publishing Co., P.O. Box 489, Yucaipa CA 92399. Fax: (909)795-9458. Editor: Lee Chandler. Monthly magazine covering treasure hunting and metal detecting. 90% freelance written. Eager to work with new/unpublished writers. Circ. 40,000. Pays 2-3 months after publication. Publishes ms an average of 6 months after acceptance. Buys all rights. Byline given. Phone queries OK. Submit seasonal/holiday material 4 months in advance. Accepts previously published articles. Send photocopy of article or typed ms with rights for sale noted. Query for electronic submissions. Reports in 2 months. Sample copy for 9×12 SAE and $1.05 postage. Writer's guidelines for SAE and $1.

Nonfiction: How-to (coinshooting and treasure hunting tips); informational and historical (location of lost treasures with emphasis on the lesser-known); interviews (with treasure hunters); profiles (successful treasure hunters and metal detector hobbyists); personal experience (treasure hunting); technical (advice on use of metal detectors and metal detector designs). "We would like more coverage of archaeological finds, both professional and amateur, and more reports on recently found caches, whether located purposefully or accidentally—both types should be accompanied by photos of the finds." Buys 6-8 mss/issue. Send complete ms. Length: 300-3,000 words. Pays $30-200. "Our rate of payment varies considerably depending upon the proficiency of the author, the quality of the photographs, the importance of the subject matter, and the amount of useful information given."

Photos: Offers no additional payment for 5×7 or 8×10 b&w glossy prints used with mss. Pays $75 minimum for color transparencies (35mm or 2¼×2¼). Color for cover only. "Clear photos and other illustrations are a must." Model release required.

Tips: "We hope to increase our news coverage of archaeological digs and cache finds, opening the doors to writers who would like simply to use their journalistic skills to report a specific event. No great knowledge of treasure hunting will be necessary. The most frequent mistakes made by writers in completing an article for *Treasure* are failure to list sources of information and to supply illustrations or photos with a story."

TREASURE CHEST, The Information Source & Marketplace for Collectors and Dealers of Antiques and Collectibles, Venture Publishing Co., Suite 414, 2112 Broadway, New York NY 10023. (212)496-2234. Editor: Howard E. Fischer. 100% freelance written. Monthly newspaper on antiques and collectibles. Estab. 1988. Circ. 50,000. Pays on publication. Publishes ms an average of 3 months after acceptance. Byline given. Buys first rights and second serial (reprint) rights. Accepts previously published material. Send tearsheet or photocopy of article and information about when and where the article previously appeared. For reprints pays 60% of the amount paid for original article. Reports in 2 months on mss. Sample copy for 9×12 SAE with $2. Writer's guidelines for #10 SASE.

Nonfiction: How-to (detect reproductions, find new sources of items, etc.), humor, personal experience, photo feature. Primarily interested in feature articles on a specific field of antiques or collectibles which includes a general overview of that field. Buys 35 mss/year. Send complete ms. Length: 1,000 words. Pays $30. Payment in contributor copies or other premiums negotiable.

Fillers: Anecdotes, facts, gags to be illustrated by cartoonist, short humor. Buys 12/year. Length: 100-350 words. Pays $10.

Tips: "Learn about your subject by interviewing experts—appraisers, curators, dealers."

THE TRUMPETER, Croatian Philatelic Society, 1512 Lancelot, Borger TX 79007-6341. (806)273-7225. Editor: Eck Spahich. 80% freelance written. Eager to work with new/unpublished writers. Quarterly magazine covering stamps, coins, currency, military decorations and collectibles of the Balkans and central Europe. Estab. 1972. Circ. 800. Pays on publication. Publishes ms an average of 9 months after acceptance. Byline given. Buys first and one-time rights. Submit seasonal/holiday material 6 months in advance. Accepts simultaneous and previously published submissions. For reprints pays 50% of amount paid for an original article. Reports in 2 months. Sample copy for $4. Writer's guidelines for #10 SASE.

Nonfiction: Book excerpts, general interest, historical/nostalgic, how-to (on detecting forged stamps, currency etc.) interview/profile, photo feature, travel. Buys 15-20 mss/year. Send complete ms. Length: 500-1,500 words. Pays $25-50 for assigned articles; $5-25 for unsolicited articles. Sometimes pays the expenses of writers on assignment.

Photos: Send photos with submission. Reviews 3×5 prints. Offers $5-10/photo. Captions and identification of subjects required. Buys one-time rights.

Columns/Departments: Book Reviews (stamps, coins, currency of Balkans), 200-400 words; Forgeries (emphasis on pre-1945 period), 500-1,000 words. Buys 10 mss/year. Send complete ms. Length: 100-300 words. Pays $5-25.

Fillers: Facts. Buys 15-20/year. Length: 20-50 words. Pays $1-5.

Tips: "We desperately need features on Zara, Montenegro, Serbia, Bulgaria, Bosnia, Croatia, Romania and Laibach."

VIDEOMAKER, Camcorders, Editing, Desktop Video, Audio and Video Production, Videomaker Inc., P.O. Box 4591, Chico CA 95927. (916)891-8410. Fax: (916)891-8443. Editor: Stephen Muratore. Managing Editor: Paula Munier Lee. 75% freelance written. Monthly magazine on video production. "Our audience encompasses video camera users ranging from broadcast and cable TV producers to special-event videographers to video hobbyists . . . labeled professional, industrial, 'prosumer' and consumer. Editorial emphasis is on video*making* (production and exposure), *not* reviews of commercial videos. Personal video phenomenon is a young 'movement'; readership is encouraged to participate — get in on the act, join the fun." Estab. 1986. Circ. 75,000. Pays on publication. Publishes ms an average of 4-6 months after acceptance. Byline given. Buys all rights. Submit seasonal/holiday material 6 months in advance. Accepts simultaneous and previously published submissions. Query for electronic submissions. Reports in 3 months. Sample copy for 9×12 SAE with 9 first-class stamps. Free writer's guidelines.

Nonfiction: How-to (tools, tips, techniques for better videomaking); interview/profile (notable videomakers); product probe (review of latest and greatest or innovative); personal experience (lessons to benefit other videomakers); technical (state-of-the-art audio/video). Articles with comprehensive coverage of product line or aspect of videomaking preferred. Buys 70 mss/year. Query with or without published clips, or send complete ms. Length: open. Pays $150-300, negotiable.

Photos: Send photos and/or other artwork with submissions. Reviews contact sheets, transparencies and prints. Captions required. Payment for photos accepted with ms included as package compensation. Buys one-time rights.

Columns/Departments: Desktop Video (state-of-the-art products, applications, potentials for computer-video interface); Profile (highlights videomakers using medium in unique/worthwhile ways); Book/Tape Mode (brief reviews of current works pertaining to video production); Camera Work (tools and tips for beginning videomakers); Video for Hire (money-making opportunities); Edit Points (tools and techniques for successful video editing). Buys 40 mss/year. Pays $35-200.

Fillers: Anecdotes, facts, cartoons, newsbreaks, short humor. Negotiable pay.

Tips: "Comprehensiveness a must. Article on shooting tips covers *all* angles. Buyer's guide to special-effect generators cites *all* models available. Magazine strives for an 'all-or-none' approach. Most topics covered once (twice tops) per year, so we must be thorough. Manuscript/photo package submissions helpful. *Videomaker* wants videomaking to be fulfilling and fun."

VOGUE KNITTING, Butterick Company, 161 Sixth Ave., New York NY 10013-1205. Fax: (212)620-2736. Editor: Nancy J. Thomas. Associate Managing Editor: Ruth Tobacco. 25% freelance written. Quarterly magazine that covers knitting. "High fashion magazine with projects for knitters of all levels. In-depth features on techniques, knitting around the world, interviews, bios and other articles of interest to well-informed readers." Estab. 1982. Circ. 200,000. **Pays on acceptance.** Publishes ms an average of 4 months after acceptance. Buys all rights. Editorial lead time 6 months. Submit seasonal material 6 months in advance. Accepts simultaneous submissions. Query for electronic submissions. Prefers IBM WordPerfect. Requires hard copy with electronic submission. Writer's guidelines free on request.

Nonfiction: Essays, general interest, historical/nostalgic, how-to, interview/profile, personal experience, photo feature, technical, travel. Buys 25 mss/year. Query. Length: 600-1,200 words. Pays $250 minimum.

Photos: Send photos with submission. Reviews 3×5 transparencies. Negotiates payment individually. Captions, model releases and identification of subjects required. Buys all rights.

WEEKEND WOODCRAFTS, Easy Projects to Build & Finish, EGW International, 1041 Shary Circle, Concord CA 94518. (510)671-9852. Fax: (510)671-0692. Editor: Ben Green. Bimonthly magazine of woodworking and finishing. "*Weekend Woodcrafts* is the hobbyist's source for easy projects to build and finish." Estab. 1992. Circ. 140,000. **Pays on acceptance.** Publishes ms an average of 9 months after acceptance. No byline. Buys first North American serial rights. Editorial lead time 6 months. Submit seasonal material 6 months in advance. Reports in up to 2 months. Buys project designs and step-by-step construction photos.

Tips: "Go through the magazine to get an idea of the type of project we're looking for."

WESTERN & EASTERN TREASURES, People's Publishing Co., Inc., P.O. Box 1095, Arcata CA 95521-1095. Fax: (707)822-0973. Editor: Rosemary Anderson. Monthly magazine covering treasure hunting and metal detecting for all ages, entire range of education, coast-to-coast readership. 90% freelance written. Estab. 1966. Circ. 70,000. Pays on publication. Publishes ms an average of 1 year after acceptance. Buys all rights. Reports in 3 months. Sample copy and writer's guidelines for $2 and 9×12 SAE with 8 first-class stamps.

Nonfiction: How-to "hands on" use of metal detecting equipment, how to locate coins, jewelry and relics, prospect for gold, where to look for treasures, rocks and gems, etc., "first-person" experiences. "No purely historical manuscripts or manuscripts that require two-part segments or more." Buys 200 unsolicited mss/year. Submit complete ms. Length: maximum 1,500 words. Pays 2¢/word—negotiable.

Photos: Purchased with accompanying ms. Captions required. Submit b&w prints (preferred), color prints or 35mm Kodachrome transparencies. Pays $5 maximum for 3×5 and up b&w glossy prints; $50 and up for 35mm Kodachrome cover slides. Model releases required.

Tips: "The writer has a better chance of breaking in at our publication with short articles and fillers as these give the readers a chance to respond to the writer. The publisher relies heavily on reader reaction. Not adhering to word limit is the main mistake made by writers in completing an article for us. Writers must clearly cover the subjects described above in 1,500 words or less."

‡WOMEN'S HOUSEHOLD CROCHET, House of White Birches, Inc., 306 E. Parr Rd., Berne IN 46711-0776. Editor: Susan Hankins. 99% freelance written. Quarterly magazine for "crochet lovers—young and old, city and country, thread and yarn lovers alike. Our readers crochet for necessity as well as pleasure. Articles are 99% pattern-oriented. We need patterns for all expertise levels—beginner to expert. No knit patterns please." Estab. 1962. Circ. 75,000. Pays on publication. Publishes ms an average of 3-12 months after acceptance. Byline given. Buys all rights. Submit seasonal/holiday material 6 months in advance. Reports in 1 month on queries; 6 weeks on mss. Sample copy for $2 with 9 × 12 SAE and 3 first-class stamps. Free writer's guidelines.

Photos: Buys no photos. Must send crocheted item for staff photography.

Columns/Departments: Editor's Choice Contest (1st and 2nd prizes chosen each issue for crochet design). Buys 8 mss/year. Send complete ms. Length: 500-2,000 words. Pays competitive designer rates.

Poetry: Light verse, traditional (all related to crochet!). "No long poems over 20 lines. Nothing of a sexual nature." Buys 6 poems/year. Submit maximum 2 poems. Length: 5-20 lines. Pays $5-20.

Fillers: Anecdotes, crochet cartoons, facts, short humor. Buys 4-6/year. Length: 35-70 words. Pays $5-20.

Tips: "We only buy crochet patterns. No longer interested in non-pattern mss."

WOODSHOP NEWS, Soundings Publications Inc., 35 Pratt St., Essex CT 06426-1185. (203)767-8227. Fax: (203)767-1048. Editor: Ian C. Bowen. Senior Editor: Thomas Clark. 20% freelance written. Monthly tabloid "covering woodworking for professionals and hobbyists. Solid business news and features about woodworking companies. Feature stories about interesting amateur woodworkers. Some how-to articles." Estab. 1986. Circ. 100,000. Pays on publication. Publishes ms an average of 2-3 months after acceptance. Byline given. Offers 25% kill fee. Buys first North American serial rights. Submit seasonal/holiday material 4 months in advance. Accepts simultaneous submissions. Query for electronic submissions. Reports in 3 weeks on queries; 1 month on mss. Free sample copy and writer's guidelines.

• *Woodshop News* needs writers in major cities in all regions except the Northeast. Also looking for more editorial opinion pieces.

Nonfiction: How-to (query first), interview/profile, new product, opinion, personal experience, photo feature. No general interest profiles of "folksy" woodworkers. Buys 50-75 mss/year. Query with published clips. Length: 100-1,800 words. Pays $30-400 for assigned articles; $30-200 for unsolicited articles. Pays expenses of writers on assignment.

Photos: Send photos with submission. Reviews contact sheets and prints. Offers $20-35/photo. Captions and identification of subjects required. Buys one-time rights.

Columns/Departments: Pro Shop (business advice, marketing, employee relations, taxes etc. for the professional written by an established professional in the field). Length: 1,200-1,500 words. Buys 12 mss/year. Query. Pays $200-350.

Tips: "The best way to start is a profile of a business or hobbyist woodworker in your area. Find a unique angle about the person or business and stress this as the theme of your article. Avoid a broad, general-interest theme that would be more appropriate to a daily newspaper. Our readers are woodworkers who want more depth and more specifics than would a general readership. If you are profiling a business, we need standard business information such as gross annual earnings/sales, customer base, product line and prices, marketing strategy, etc. Black and white 35 mm photos are a must. We need more freelance writers from the Mid-Atlantic, Midwest and West Coast."

WOODWORK, A magazine for all woodworkers, Ross Periodicals, P.O. Box 1529, Ross CA 94957-1529. (415)382-0580. Fax: (415)382-0587. Editor: John McDonald. Publisher: Tom Toldrian. 90% freelance written. Bimonthly magazine covering woodworking. "We are aiming at a broad audience of woodworkers, from the home enthusiast/hobbyist to more advanced." Estab. 1986. Circ. 100,000. Pays on publication. Byline given. Buys first North American serial and second serial (reprint) rights. Accepts previously published material. Send tearsheet or photocopy of article or typed ms with rights for sale noted and information about when and where the article previously appeared. Pays 25% of amount paid for an original article. Reports in 2 months. Sample copy for $3 and 9 × 12 SAE with 6 first-class stamps. Writer's guidelines for #10 SASE.

Nonfiction: How-to (simple or complex, making attractive furniture), interview/profile (of established woodworkers that make attractive furniture), photo feature (of interest to woodworkers), technical (tools, techniques). "Do not send a how-to unless you are a woodworker." Buys 40 mss/year. Query first. Length: 1,500-3,000 words. Pays $150/published page.

Photos: Send photos with submission. Reviews 35mm slides. Offers no additional payment for photos accepted with ms. Captions and identification of subjects required. Buys one-time rights.

Columns/Departments: Feature articles 1,500-3,000 words. From non-woodworking freelancers, we use interview/profiles of established woodworkers. Bring out woodworker's philosophy about the craft, opinions about what is happening currently. Good photos of attractive furniture a must. Section on how-to desirable. Query with published clips. Pays $600-1,500 at $150/published page.

Fillers: Anecdotes, facts, newsbreaks, short humor. Length: 1,000 words. Pays $150 maximum.

Tips: "If you are not a woodworker, the interview/profile is your best, really only chance. Good writing is essential as are good photos. The interview must be entertaining, but informative and pertinent to woodworkers' interests."

‡WORKBASKET, The World's Largest Needlework and Crafts Magazine, KC Publishing, Suite 310, 700 W. 47th St., Kansas City MO 64112. (816)531-5730. Executive Editor: Kay M. Olson. 75% freelance written. Bimonthly magazine covering needlework and crafts. "A variety of needlework patterns and craft projects for all levels, beginners to experienced." Estab. 1935. Circ. 750,000. **Pays on acceptance.** Byline given. Buys first rights. Editorial lead time 6-12 months. Submit seasonal material 18-24 months in advance. Accepts previously published submissions occasionally. Reports in 4 months. Sample copy for $2.95. Writer's guidelines free on request.

Nonfiction: How-to. Buys 50 mss/year. Query. Payment varies depending on complexity of the project.

Tips: "Bazaar-type items are accepted for $25 payment of project idea."

WORKBENCH, Suite 310, 700 W. 47th St., Kansas City MO 64112. (816)531-5730. Fax: (816)531-3873. Executive Editor: Robert N. Hoffman. 75% freelance written. Prefers to work with published/established writers; but works with a small number of new/unpublished writers each year. For woodworkers and home improvement do-it-yourselfers. Estab. 1957. Circ. 750,000. **Pays on acceptance.** Publishes ms an average of 1 year after acceptance. Byline given. Buys all rights. Reports in 3 months. Sample copy for 9 × 12 SAE with 6 first-class stamps. Free writer's guidelines.

Nonfiction: "We have continued emphasis on do-it-yourself woodworking, home improvement and home maintenance projects. We provide in-progress photos, technical drawings and how-to text for all projects. We are very strong in woodworking, cabinetmaking and classic furniture construction. Projects range from simple toys to reproductions of furniture now in museums. We would like to receive woodworking projects that can be duplicated by both beginning do-it-yourselfers and advanced woodworkers." Query. Pays $175/published page or more depending on quality of submission. Additional payment for good color photos. "If you can consistently provide good material, including photos, your rates will go up and you will get assignments."

Columns/Departments: Shop Tips bring $25 with a line drawing and/or b&w photo.

Tips: "Our magazine focuses on woodworking, covering all levels of ability, and home improvement projects from the do-it-yourselfer's viewpoint, emphasizing the most up-to-date materials and procedures. We would like to receive articles on home improvements and remodeling, and/or simple contemporary furniture. We place a heavy emphasis on projects that are both functional and classic in design. We can photograph projects worthy for publication, so feel free to send snapshots."

‡WORLD COIN NEWS, Krause Publications, 700 E. State, Iola WI 54990-0001. (715)445-2214. Fax: (715)445-4087. Editor: David C. Harper. 30% freelance written. Works with a small number of new/unpublished writers each year. Weekly newsmagazine about non-US coin collecting for novices and advanced collectors of foreign coins, medals, and other numismatic items. Estab. 1952. Circ. 10,000. Pays on publication. Publishes ms an average of 1 month after acceptance. Byline given. Buys first North American serial rights and reprint rights. Submit seasonal material 2 months in advance. Accepts simultaneous submissions. Reports in 1 month. Free sample copy.

Nonfiction: "Send us timely news stories related to collecting foreign coins and current information on coin values and markets." Send complete ms. Buys 30 mss/year. Length: 500-2,000 words. Pays 3¢/word to first-time contributors; fees negotiated for later articles.

Photos: Send photos with ms. Pays $5 minimum for b&w prints. Captions and model release required. Buys first rights and reprint rights.

YESTERYEAR, Yesteryear Publications, P.O. Box 2, Princeton WI 54968. (414)787-4808. Editor: Michael Jacobi. Prefers to work with published/established writers. For antique dealers and collectors, people interested in collecting just about anything. Monthly tabloid. Estab. 1976. Circ. 8,000. Pays on publication. Publishes ms an average of 3 months after acceptance. Buys one-time rights. Byline given. Submit seasonal/holiday material 3 months in advance. Accepts simultaneous and previously published submissions. Send photocopy of article and information about when and where the article previously appeared. Pays 100% of amount paid for an original article. Reports in 1 month. Sample copy for $2.

Nonfiction: General interest (basically, anything pertaining to antiques and collectible items); how-to (refinishing antiques, how to collect). The more specific and detailed, the better. "We do not want personal experience or opinion articles." Buys 3 mss/year. Send complete ms. Pays $10-25.

Photos: Send photos with ms. Pays $5 for 5×7 b&w glossy or matte color prints. Captions preferred.

Home and Garden

Some magazines here concentrate on gardens; others on the how-to of interior design. Still others focus on homes and gardens in specific regions of the country. Be sure to read the publication to determine its focus before submitting a manuscript or query.

AMERICAN HORTICULTURIST, Publication of the American Horticultural Society, 7931 E. Blvd. Dr., Alexandria VA 22308-1300. (703)768-5700. Fax: (703)768-7533. Editor: Kathleen Fisher. 90% freelance written. Bimonthly magazine covering gardening. Estab. 1922. Circ. 25,000. Pays on publication. Publishes ms an average of 6 months after acceptance. Byline given. Buys first North American serial rights. Submit seasonal/holiday material 6 months in advance. Reports in 3 months on queries, if SASE included. Sample copy for $3. Free writer's guidelines.
  • *American Horticulturist* is putting greater stress on environmentally-responsible gardening. They are using fewer photos, trying to do more writing inhouse.

Nonfiction: Book excerpts, historical, children and nature, plants and health, city gardening, humor, interview/profile, personal experience, technical (explain science of horticulture to lay audience). Buys 30-40 mss/year. Query with published clips. Length: 1,000-2,500 words. Pays $100-400. Pays with contributor copies or other premiums when other horticultural organizations contribute articles.

Photos: Send photos with query. Pays $50-75/photo. Captions required. Buys one-time rights.

Tips: "We are read by sophisticated gardeners, but also want to interest beginning gardeners. Subjects should be unusual plants, recent breakthroughs in breeding, experts in the field, translated for lay readers."

ATLANTA HOMES AND LIFESTYLES, Suite 580, 5775-B Glenridge Dr., Atlanta GA 30328. (404)252-6670. Fax: (404)252-6673. Editor: Barbara S. Tapp. 65% freelance written. Bimonthly magazine on shelter design, lifestyle in the home. "*Atlanta Homes and Lifestyles* is designed for the action-oriented, well-educated reader who enjoys his/her shelter, its design and construction, its environment, and living and entertaining in it." Estab. 1983. Pays on publication. Byline given. Publishes ms an average of 6 months after acceptance. Pays 25% kill fee. Buys all rights. Accepts previously published material. Send tearsheet or photocopy of article and information about where and when it previously appeared. For reprints pays 50% of amount paid for original article. Reports in 3 months. Sample copy for $3.50.

Nonfiction: Historical, interview/profile, new products, well-designed homes, antiques (then and now), photo features, gardens, local art, remodeling, food, preservation, entertaining. "We do not want articles outside respective market area, not written for magazine format, or that are excessively controversial, investigative or that cannot be appropriately illustrated with attractive photography." Buys 35 mss/year. Query with published clips. Length: 750-1,000 words. Pays $350 for features. Sometimes pays expenses of writers on assignment "if agreed upon in advance of assignment."

Photos: Send photos with submission; most photography is assigned. Reviews transparencies. Offers $40-50/photo. Captions, model releases, and identification of subjects required. Buys one-time rights.

Columns/Departments: Antiques, Quick Fix (simple remodeling ideas), Cheap Chic (stylish decorating that is easy on the wallet), Digging In (outdoor solutions from Atlanta's gardeners), Big Fix (more extensive remodeling projects), Short Takes (news and finds about the people and products in home-related businesses in and around Atlanta), Home Eco, Home Tech, Real Estate News, Interior Elements (hot new furnishings on the market), Weekender (long or short weekend getaway subjects). Query with published clips. Buys 25-30 mss/year. Length: 350-500 words. Pays $50-200.

‡BACKHOME: Hands On & Down to Earth, Wordsworth Communications, Inc., P.O. Box 70, Hendersonville NC 28792. (704)696-3838. Editor: Lorna K. Loveless. 80% freelance written. Quarterly magazine covering self-sufficiency in home, garden, shop and community. "*BackHome* encourages readers to take more control over their lives by doing more for themselves: productive organic gardening; building and repairing their homes; utilizing alternative energy systems; raising crops and livestock; building furniture; toys and games and other projects; creative cooking. *BackHome* promotes respect for family activities, community programs and the environment." Estab. 1990. Circ. 18,000. Pays on publication. Publishes ms 3-12 months after acceptance. Byline given. Offers $25 kill fee at publisher's discretion. Buys first North American serial rights. Editorial lead time 3 months. Submit seasonal material 3-6 months in advance. Accepts previously published submissions. Query for electronic submissions. Prefers ASCII WP Wordstar, MS Word, MacWrite. Reports in 4-6 weeks on queries; 1-2 months on mss. Sample copy for $4.50. Writer's guidelines free on request.

Nonfiction: How-to (gardening, construction, energy, home business), interview/profile, personal experience, technical, self-sufficiency. Buys 80 mss/year. Query. Length: 350-5,000 words. Pays $100 minimum for assigned articles; $35 minimum for unsolicited articles.

Photos: Send photos with submission. Reviews 5×7 prints. Offers no additional payment for photos accepted with ms. Identification of subjects required. Buys one-time rights.

Columns/Departments: FeedBack (new products; book, tape and video reviews), 250 words. Buys 4 mss/year. Query. Pays $25-50.

Tips: "Be very specific in relating personal experiences in the areas of gardening, energy, and homebuilding how-to. Third-person approaches to others' experiences are also acceptable but somewhat less desireable. Clear b&w or color photo prints help immensely when deciding upon what is accepted, especially those in which people are prominent."

BACKWOODS HOME MAGAZINE, INC., #213, 1257 Siskiyou Blvd., Ashland OR 97520. Editor: Dave Duffy. 80% freelance written. Bimonthly magazine covering house building, alternate energy, gardening, health and self-sufficiency. "We write for the person who values independence above all else. Our readers want to build their own homes, generate their own electricity, grow their own food and in general stand on their own two feet." Estab. 1989. Circ. 85,000. **Pays on acceptance.** Publishes ms an average of 2 months after acceptance. Byline given. Offers 15% kill fee. Buys first rights and second serial (reprint) rights or makes work-for-hire assignments. Submit seasonal/holiday material 6 months in advance. Accepts previously published submissions. Query for electronic submissions. Reports in 2 weeks. Sample copy for $2 and 9×12 SAE with 6 first-class stamps. Writer's guidelines for #10 SASE.

Nonfiction: Historical/nostalgic, how-to (about country things, alternate energy), humor, interview/profile (of independent people), new product (alternate energy), personal experience, photo feature (about country things), technical (about alternate energy production, building a house). "No opinion, exposé or religious articles." Buys 50 mss/year. Query with or without published clips or send complete ms. Length: 300-3,000 words. Pays $15-300.

Photos: Send photos with submission. Reviews 3×5 or larger prints. Identification of subjects required. Buys one-time rights.

Columns/Departments: Book Review (alternate energy/house building/gardening), 300-400 words; Recipes (country cooking), 150 words; Alternate Energy (solar cells, hydro, generator), 600-3,000 words; Gardening (organic), 600-1,800 words; Home Building (do-it-yourself), 600-2,800 words. Buys 30-40 mss/year. Send complete ms. Pays up to $300.

Poetry: Free verse, haiku, light verse, traditional. Buys 15 poems/year. Length: 3-25 lines. Pays $5.

Tips: "We insist on accuracy in nonfiction articles. Writers must know the subject. We are basically a country magazine that tries to show people how to do things that make country life more pleasant."

BETTER HOMES AND GARDENS, 1716 Locust St., Des Moines IA 50309-3023. (515)284-3000. Editor-in-Chief: Jean Lem Mon. Editor (Building): Anne McCloskey. Editor (Furnishings): Denise Caringer. Editor-in-Chief: Jean Lem MonEditor (Foods): Nancy Byal. Editor (Travel): Lois Naylor. Editor (Garden Outdoor Living): Doug Jimerson. Editor (Health & Education): Paul Krantz. Editor (Money Management, Automotive, Features): Margaret Daly. 10-15% freelance written. **Pays on acceptance.** Buys all rights. "We read all freelance articles, but much prefer to see a letter of query rather than a finished manuscript."

Nonfiction: Travel, education, health, cars, money management, home entertainment. "We do not deal with political subjects or with areas not connected with the home, community, and family." Pays rates "based on estimate of length, quality and importance." No poetry.

• Most stories published by this magazine go through a lengthy process of development involving both editor and writer. Some editors will consider *only* query letters, not unsolicited manuscripts.

Tips: Direct queries to the department that best suits your story line.

COLORADO HOMES & LIFESTYLES, 7009 S. Potomac St., Englewood CO 80112-4029. (303)397-7600. Fax: (303)397-7619. Editor: Laurel Lund. Assistant Editor: Lisha Bridges. Publisher: Pat Cooley. 50% freelance written. Bimonthly magazine covering Colorado homes and lifestyles for upper-middle-class and high income households as well as designers, decorators and architects. Circ. 30,000. **Pays on acceptance.** Publishes ms an average of 4 months after acceptance. Byline given. Buys all rights. Submit seasonal/holiday material 6 months in advance. Simultaneous queries OK. Query for electronic submissions. Reports in 3 months.

Nonfiction: Fine homes and furnishings, regional interior design trends, interesting personalities and lifestyles, gardening and plants—all with a Colorado slant. Buys 30 mss/year. Send complete ms. Length: 1,000-1,500 words. "For unique, well-researched feature stories, pay is $150-200. For regular departments, $125-140." Sometimes pays the expenses of writers on assignment.

Photos: Send photos with ms. Reviews 35mm, 4×5 and 2¼ color transparencies and b&w glossy prints. Identification of subjects required. Please include photographic credits.

Tips: "The more interesting and unique the subject the better. A frequent mistake made by writers is failure to provide material with a style and slant appropriate for the magazine, due to poor understanding of the focus of the magazine."

COTTAGE LIFE, Quarto Communications, Suite 408, 111 Queen St. E., Toronto, Ontario M5C 1S2 Canada. (416)360-6880. Fax: (416)360-6814. Editor: Ann Vanderhoof. Managing Editor: David Zimmer. 80% freelance written. Bimonthly magazine covering waterfront cottaging. "*Cottage Life* is written and designed for the people who own and spend time at cottages throughout Canada and bordering US states." Estab. 1988. Circ. 70,000. **Pays on acceptance.** Publishes ms an average of 2 months after acceptance. Byline given. Buys first North American serial rights. Query for electronic submissions.
Nonfiction: Book excerpts, exposé, historical/nostalgic, how-to, humor, interview/profile, personal experience, photo feature, technical. Buys 90 mss/year. Query with published clips. Length: 150-3,500 words. Pays $100-2,200 for assigned articles. Pays $50-1,000 for unsolicited articles. Sometimes pays expenses of writers on assignment. Query first.
Columns/Departments: Cooking, Real Estate, Fishing, Nature, Watersports, Personal Experience and Issues. Length: 150-1200 words. Query with published clips. Pays $100-750.

COUNTRY HOME, Meredith Corp., Locust at 17th, Des Moines IA 50336. Bimonthly publication covering country living. This magazine did not respond to our request for information. Query before submitting.

‡COUNTRY HOME AND GARDENS, Magazine for Beautiful Homes and Bountiful Gardens, Prestige Publications, Inc., 4151 Knob Dr., Eagan MN 55122. (612)452-0571. Editor: Carla Waldemar. Publisher: Russ Moore. 40% freelance written. Bimonthly magazine. "Articles should include what's new in decorating, collectibles, country inn travel, do-it-yourself home projects, crafts, gardening tips and new products. Our audience is men and women 25-60 who are interested in making the most of their home experience." Estab. 1993. Circ. 200,000. Pays on publication. Byline given. Buys all rights. Submit seasonal material 3 months in advance. Accepts previously published submissions. Send photocopy of article or typed ms with rights for sale noted and information about when and where the article previously appeared. For reprints pays $50-100.
Photos: State availability of photos with submission. Reviews transparencies. Offers $50-200/photo. Buys one-time rights.

COUNTRY LIVING, Hearst Corp., 224 W. 57th St., New York NY 10019. Monthly publication covering country lifestyles. This magazine did not respond to our request for information. Query before submitting.

‡DESIGN TIMES, Beautiful Interiors of the Northeast, Regis Publishing Co., Inc., Suite 828, 1 Design Center Place, Boston MA 02210. (617)859-9690. Editor: Emily Crawford. 60% freelance written. Bimonthly magazine covering residential interior design in Northeast. "Show, don't tell. Readers want to look over the shoulders of professional interior designers. Avoid clichés. Love design." Estab. 1988. Circ. 15,000. Pays on publication. Publishes ms an average of 4 months after acceptance. Byline given. Offers 10% kill fee. Buys all rights. Editorial lead time 3 months. Submit seasonal material 6 months in advance. Accepts simultaneous submissions. Query for electronic submissions. Reports in 1 month. Sample copy for 10×13 SAE with 10 first-class stamps.
Nonfiction: Residential interiors (Northeast only). Buys 25 mss/year. Query with published clips. Length: 1,200-3,000 words. Pays $100. Sometimes pays the expenses of writers on assignment.
Photos: State availability of photos with submission. Reviews 4×5 transparencies, 9×10 prints. Negotiates payment individually. Caption, model releases, identification of subject required. Buys one-time rights.
Columns/Departments: Pays $100-150.
Tips: "A Northeast home owned by a well-known personality or designer would be a good feature query."

FAMILY LIVING, The Trade Magazine for Homeowners, P.O. Box 18507, Anaheim Hills CA 92817-8507. (714)632-9810. Editor: Eva Sandstrom. 5% freelance written. Bimonthly magazine for the homeowner market. Estab. 1980. Circ. 1,000,000. Pays on publication. Byline given. Makes work-for-hire assignments. Submit seasonal/holiday material 4 months in advance. Accepts simultaneous and previously published submissions. Send tearsheet of article. Sample copy for $1.
Nonfiction: General interest, how-to, new product, travel. "No political or fiction material." Buys 1-2 mss/year. Query. Length: 100-600 words. Pays $50-150 for assigned articles. Sometimes pays the expenses of writers on assignments.
Photos: Send photos with submission. Offers no additional payment for photos accepted with ms. Identification of subjects required. Buys one-time rights.

FINE GARDENING, Taunton Press, 63 S. Main St., P.O. Box 5506, Newtown CT 06470-5506. 1-800-243-7252. Fax: (203)426-3434. Editor: Nancy Beaubaire. Bimonthly magazine on gardening. "Focus is broad subject of landscape and ornamental gardening, with secondary interest in food gardening. Articles written by avid gardeners—first person, hands-on-gardening experiences." Estab. 1988. Circ. 175,000. Pays on publication. Byline given. Buys first North American serial rights. Receipt of work notice sent immediately. Decision made within a few months. Free writer's guidelines.
Nonfiction: Book review, essays, how-to, opinion, personal experience, photo feature. Buys 50-60 mss/year. Query. Length: 1,000-3,000 words. Pays $150/page.

on garden products. We also need more in-depth reports on major architecture, environmental, and social aspects of life in San Diego and the border area."

‡SPROUTLETTER, Sprouting Publications, P.O. Box 62, Ashland OR 97520. (503)488-2326. Editor: Michael Linden. 50% freelance written. Quarterly newsletter covering sprouting, live foods, indoor food gardening. "We emphasize growing foods (especially sprouts) indoors for health, economy, nutrition and food self-sufficiency. We also cover topics related to sprouting, live foods and holistic health." Estab. 1980. Circ. 2,500. Pays on publication. Publishes ms an average of 3 months after acceptance. Byline given. Buys North American serial and second (reprint) rights. Submit seasonal/holiday material 4 months in advance. Accepts previously published submissions. Reports in 2 weeks on queries; 3 weeks on mss. Sample copy for $3.
• *Sproutletter* has substantially increased its payment (from $15-50 to $50-75 for nonfiction article) and the number of fillers it buys each year (5-6 to over 100).
Nonfiction: General interest (raw foods, algae, sprouting, holistic health, algae); how-to (grow sprouts, all kinds of foods indoors; build devices for sprouting or indoor gardening); personal experience (in sprouting or related areas); technical (experiments with growing sprouts). No common health food/vitamin articles or growing ornamental plants indoors (as opposed to food producing plants). Buys 4-6 mss/year. Query. Length: 500-2,400 words. Pays $50-75. Trades for merchandise are also considered.
Columns/Departments: "Will consider innovative regular columnists." Book Reviews (books oriented toward sprouts, nutrition or holistic health). Reviews are short and informative. News Items (interesting news items relating to sprouts or live foods); Recipes (mostly raw foods). Buys 5-10 mss/year. Query. Length: 100-450 words. Pays $15-30.
Fillers: In all areas already mentioned. Buys 100. Length: 50-150 words. Pays $10 and free subscription.
Tips: "Writers should have a sincere interest in holistic health and in natural whole foods. We like tight writing which is optimistic, interesting and informative. Consumers are demanding more thorough and accurate information. Articles should cover any given subject in depth in an enjoyable and inspiring manner. A frequent mistake is that the subject matter is not appropriate. Also buys cartoon strips and singles. Will consider series."

TEXAS GARDENER, The Magazine for Texas Gardeners, by Texas Gardeners, Suntex Communications, Inc., P.O. Box 9005, Waco TX 76714-9005. (817)772-1270. Editor: Chris S. Corby. Managing Editors: Gloria Gonzales. 80% freelance written. Works with a small number of new/unpublished writers each year. Bi-monthly magazine covering vegetable and fruit production, ornamentals and home landscape information for home gardeners in Texas. Estab. 1981. Circ. 37,000. Pays on publication. Publishes ms an average of 4 months after acceptance. Byline given. Buys first North American serial and all rights. Submit seasonal/holiday material 6 months in advance. Query for electronic submissions. Reports in 2 months. Sample copy for $2.75 and SAE with 5 first-class stamps. Writer's guidelines for #10 SASE.
Nonfiction: How-to, humor, interview/profile, photo feature. "We use feature articles that relate to Texas gardeners. We also like personality profiles on hobby gardeners and professional horticulturists who are doing something unique." Buys 50-100 mss/year. Query with clips of published work. Length: 800-2,400 words. Pays $50-200.
Photos: "We prefer superb color and b&w photos; 90% of photos used are color." Send photos. Pays negotiable rates for 2¼ or 35mm color transparencies and 8×10 b&w prints and contact sheets. Model release and identification of subjects required.
Tips: "First, be a Texan. Then come up with a good idea of interest to home gardeners in this state. Be specific. Stick to feature topics like 'How Alley Gardening Became a Texas Tradition.' Leave topics like 'How to Control Fire Blight' to the experts. High quality photos could make the difference. We would like to add several writers to our group of regular contributors and would make assignments on a regular basis. Fillers are easy to come up with in-house. We want good writers who can produce accurate and interesting copy. Frequent mistakes made by writers in completing an article assignment for us are that articles are not slanted toward Texas gardening, show inaccurate or too little gardening information or lack good writing style. We will be doing more 'people' features and articles on ornamentals."

YOUR HOME, Meridian International, Inc., Box 10010, Ogden UT 84409. (801)394-9446. 65% freelance written. Monthly inhouse magazine covering home/garden subjects. **Pays on acceptance.** Publishes ms an average of 3 months after acceptance. Byline given. Buys first rights, second serial (reprint) rights and nonexclusive reprint rights. Editorial lead time 8 months. Submit seasonal material 10 months in advance. Accepts simultaneous and previously published submissions. Reports in 2 months with SASE. Sample copy for $1 and 9×12 SAE. Writer's guidelines with #10 SASE. All requests for samples and guidelines and queries should be addressed Attn: Editorial Staff.
Nonfiction: General interest articles about fresh ideas in home decor, ranging from floor and wall coverings to home furnishings. Subject matter includes the latest in home construction (exteriors, interiors, building materials, design), the outdoors at home (landscaping, pools, patios, gardening), remodeling projects, home management, home buying and selling. "No do-it-yourself pieces." Written query. Buys 40 mss/year. Length: 1,000 words. Pays 15¢/word for first rights plus nonexclusive reprint rights. Payment for second serial rights 10¢/word.

Photos: Send photos with submission. Reviews 35mm transparencies. Buys serial rights.
Columns/Department: Book reviews (on gardening); Gleanings (essays, stories, opinions, research); Last Word (essays/serious, humorous, fact or fiction). Query. Length: 250-1,000 words. Pays $25-150.
Tips: "It's most important to have solid first-hand experience as a gardener. Tell us what you've done with your own landscape and plants."

FLOWER AND GARDEN MAGAZINE, Suite 310, 700 W. 47th St., Kansas City MO 64112. Fax: (816)531-3873. Editor: Kay Melchisedech Olson. 50% freelance written. Works with a small number of new/unpublished writers each year. Bimonthly picture magazine for home gardeners. Estab. 1957. Circ. 600,000. Buys first time nonexclusive reprint rights. Sometimes accepts previously published articles. Send typed ms with rights for sale noted, including information about when and where the article previously appeared. Byline given. **Pays on acceptance.** Publishes ms an average of 1 year after acceptance. Reports in 2 months. Sample copy for $2.95 and 10×13 SAE. Writer's guidelines for #10 SASE.
Nonfiction: Interested in illustrated articles on how to do certain types of gardening and descriptive articles about individual plants. Flower arranging, landscape design, house plants and patio gardening are other aspects covered. "The approach we stress is practical (how-to-do-it, what-to-do-it-with). We emphasize plain talk, clarity and economy of words. An article should be tailored for a national audience." Buys 20-30 mss/year. Query. Length: 500-1,500 words. Rates vary depending on quality and kind of material.
Photos: Buys transparencies, 35mm and larger. Photos are paid for on publication.
Tips: "The prospective author needs good grounding in gardening practice and literature. Offer well-researched and well-written material appropriate to the experience level of our audience. Use botanical names as well as common. Photographs help sell the story. Describe special qualifications for writing the particular proposed subject."

THE HERB COMPANION, Interweave Press, 201 E. Fourth St., Loveland CO 80537-5655. (303)669-7672. Fax: (303)667-8317. Editor: Linda Ligon. Managing Editor: David Merrill. 80% freelance written. Bimonthly magazine about herbs: culture, history, culinary use, crafts and some medicinal. Audience includes a wide range of herb enthusiasts. Circ. 110,000. Pays on publication. Byline given. Buys first North American serial rights. Reports in 2 months. Query in writing. Length: 6-12 pages. Typical payment is $100/published page. Sample copy for $4. Writer's guidelines for #10 SASE.
Photos: Send photos.
Tips: "Articles must show depth and working knowledge of the subject, though tone should be informal and accessible."

HERB QUARTERLY, P.O. Box 689, San Anselmo CA 94960-0689. Fax: (415)455-9541. Publisher: James Keough. 80% freelance written. Quarterly magazine for herb enthusiasts. Estab. 1979. Circ. 35,000. Pays on publication. Publishes ms an average of 6 months after acceptance. Buys first North American serial and second (reprint) rights. Query for electronic submissions. Query letters recommended. Reports in 2 months. Sample copy for $5 and 9×12 SASE. Writer's guidelines for #10 SASE.
Nonfiction: Gardening (landscaping, herb garden design, propagation, harvesting); medicinal and cosmetic use of herbs; crafts; cooking; historical (folklore, focused piece on particular period—*not* general survey); interview of a famous person involved with herbs or folksy herbalist; personal experience; photo essay ("cover quality" 8×10 b&w or color prints). "We are particularly interested in herb garden design, contemporary or historical." No fiction. Send double-spaced ms. Length: 1,000-3,500 words. Pays $75-250.
Tips: "Our best submissions are narrowly focused on herbs with much practical information on cultivation and use for the experienced gardener."

HOME MAGAZINE, The Magazine of Remodeling and Decorating, 44th Floor, 1633 Broadway, New York NY 10019. Editor/Director: Gale C. Steves. Articles Editor: Linda Lentz. 80% freelance written. Monthly magazine covering remodeling, decorating, architecture, entertaining, building and gardens. Estab. 1981. Circ. 1 million. **Pays on acceptance.** Publishes ms an average of 3-6 months after acceptance. Offers negotiable kill fee. Buys all rights. Submit seasonal/holiday material 6-13 months in advance. Reports immediately. Free sample copy and writer's guidelines.
Nonfiction: Linda Lentz, articles editor. Essays, how-to, interview/profile, personal experience, photo feature, technical. Buys 100-120 mss/year. Query with published clips. Length: 500-1,500 words. Negotiates payment.

HOMES MAGAZINE, Homes Publishing Group, 178 Main St., Unionville, Ontario L3R 2G9 Canada. (905)479-4663. Editor: Risë Levy. 40% freelance written. Magazine published 8 times/year for new home buyers. "*Homes Magazine* is a new-home guide for the Greater Toronto/Ontario area." Estab. 1985. Circ. 100,000. Pays 30 days after publication. Publishes ms an average of 3 months after acceptance. Byline given. Offers 50% kill fee. Buys all rights (unless otherwise arranged). Accepts previously published articles or short stories. Send photocopy of article. For reprints, pays 10% of the amount paid for an original article. Submit seasonal/holiday material 4 months in advance. Query for electronic submissions. Free sample copy.

Nonfiction: Book excerpts, general interest, interview/profile, new product, photo feature. No fiction. Payment varies; please inquire.

Photos: State availability of or send photos with submission. Reviews transparencies and prints. Offers no additional payment for photos accepted with ms. Model releases and identification of subjects required. Buys one-time rights.

Tips: "Department columns are written by staff writers. Features are most often written by freelancers."

LOG HOME LIVING, Home Buyer Publications Inc., P.O. Box 220039, Chantilly VA 22022. (703)222-9411. Editor: Roland Sweet. Less than 20% freelance written. Bimonthly magazine "for people who own or are planning to build contemporary manufactured and handcrafted kit log homes. Our audience is married couples 35-50 years old." Estab. 1989. **Pays on acceptance.** Publishes ms an average of 1 year after acceptance. Byline given. Buys one-time rights. Submit seasonal/holiday material 9-12 months in advance. Accepts previously published submissions. Send photocopy of article. Pays 50% of amount paid for an original article. Reports in 6 months. Sample copy for $3.50. Writer's guidelines for #10 SASE.

Nonfiction: How-to (buy or build log home), interview/profile (log home owners), photo feature (log homes), technical (design/decor topics). "We do not want historical/nostalgic material." Buys 4-6 mss/year. Query with published clips. Length: 750-1,500 words. Pays $100-500. Sometimes pays expenses of writers on assignment.

Photos: Send photos with submission. Reviews contact sheets, 2½ × 2½ transparencies and 4 × 5 transparencies. Offers $50-100/photo. Captions, model releases and identification of subjects required. Buys one-time rights.

Tips: "Owner profiles are most open to freelancers. Reveal how they planned for, designed and bought/built their dream home; how they decorated it; how they like it; advice for others thinking of buying."

MIDWEST LIVING, Meredith Corp., 1912 Grand Ave., Des Moines IA 50309. Bimonthly publication covering lifestyle and home subjects of interest to Midwestern readers. This magazine did not respond to our request for information. Query before submitting.

MUIR'S ORIGINAL LOG HOME GUIDE FOR BUILDERS & BUYERS, Muir Publishing Company Inc., 164 Middle Creek Rd., Cosby TN 37722. (615)487-2256. Fax: (615)487-3249. Editor: Doris Muir. 65% freelance written. Quarterly magazine covering the buying and building of log homes. "We publish for persons who want to buy or build their own log home. Unlike conventional housing, it is possible for the average person to build his/her own log home. Articles should aim at providing help in this or describe the experiences of someone who has built a log home." Estab. 1917. Circ. 170,000. Pays on publication. Publishes ms an average of 6 months after acceptance. Byline given. Buys first North American rights. Submit seasonal/holiday material 4 months in advance. Accepts simultaneous and previously published submissions, if noted. Send photocopy of article or typed ms with rights for sale noted and information about when and where the article previously appeared. For reprints, pays 50% of the amount paid for an original article. Query for electronic submissions. Reports in 2 weeks. Sample copy for $3 (postage included). Writer's guidelines for SASE.

Nonfiction: General interest; historical/nostalgic (log home historic sites, restoration of old log structures); how-to (anything to do with building log homes); inspirational (sweat equity—encouraging people that they can build their own home for less cost); interview/profile (with persons who have built their own log homes); new product (or new company manufacturing log homes—check with us first); personal experience (author's own experience with building his own log home, with photos is ideal); photo feature (on log home decor, author or anyone else building his own log home); technical (for "Techno-log" section: specific construction details, i.e., new log buiding details, joining systems). Also, "would like photo/interview/profile stories on famous persons and their log homes—how they did it, where they got their logs, etc." Interested in log commercial structures. "Please no exaggeration—this is a truthful, back-to-basics type of magazine trying to help the person interested in log homes." Buys 25 mss/year. Query with clips of published work or send complete ms. "Prefer queries first with photo of subject house." Length: open. Pays 10-25¢/word, depending on quality.

Photos: Slides, transparencies or color prints, $5-50, depending on quality. "All payments are arranged with individual author/submitter." Captions and identification of subjects required. Buys first North American rights unless otherwise arranged.

Columns/Departments: Pro-Log (short news pieces of interest to the log-building world); Techno-Log (technical articles, i.e., solar energy systems; any illustrations welcome); Book-Log (book reviews only, on books related to log building and alternate energy; "check with us first"); Chrono-Log (features on historic log buildings); Decor (practical information on how to finish and furnish a log house). Buys possible 50-75 mss/year. Query with clips of published work or send complete ms. Length: 100-1,000 words or more. "All payments are arranged with individual author/submitter." Enclose SASE.

Tips: "The writer may have a better chance of breaking in at our publication with short articles and fillers since writing well on log homes requires some prior knowledge of subject. The most frequent mistakes made by writers in completing an article assignment for us are not doing enough research or not having understanding of the subject; not people-oriented enough; angled toward wrong audience. They don't study the publication before they submit manuscripts."

NATIONAL GARDENING, National Gardening Association, 180 Flynn Ave., Burlington VT 05401. (802)863-1308. Fax: (802)863-5962. Editor: Michael MacCaskey. Managing Editor: Vicky Congdon. 80% freelance written. Willing to work with new/unpublished writers. Bimonthly magazine covering all aspects of food gardening and ornamentals. "We publish not only how-to garden techniques, but also news that affects home gardeners, like breeding advancements and new variety releases. Detailed, experienced-based articles with carefully worked-out techniques for planting, growing, harvesting and using garden fruits and vegetables sought as well as profiles of expert gardeners in this country's many growing regions. Our material is for both experienced and beginning gardeners." Estab. 1979. Circ. 250,000. **Pays on acceptance.** Publishes ms an average of 9 months after acceptance. Byline given. Buys first serial and occasionally second (reprint) rights to material originally published elsewhere. Reports in 2 months. Sample copy for $3. Writer's guidelines for #10 SASE.

Nonfiction: How-to, humor, interview/profile, pest profiles, opinion, personal experience, recipes. Buys 50-60 mss/year. Query first. Length: 500-2,500 words. Pays 25¢/word. Sometimes pays the expenses of writers on assignment; must have prior approval.

Photos: Vicky Congdon, managing editor. Send photos with ms. Pays $20-40 for b&w photos; $50 for color slides. Captions, model releases and identification of subjects required.

Tips: "Take the time to study the style of the magazine—the focus of the features and the various departments. Keep in mind that you'll be addressing a national audience."

ORGANIC GARDENING, Rodale Press, 33 E. Minor, Emmaus PA 18098. (610)967-5171. Managing Editor: Matt Damsker. 30% freelance written. Published 9 times/year. Pays between acceptance and publication. Buys all rights. Reports in 2 months on queries; 1 month on mss.

Nonfiction: "Our title says it all. We seem to put more emphasis on the gardening aspect." Query with published clips and outline. Pays 50¢/word.

‡PLANT & GARDEN, Canada's Practical Gardening Magazine, (formerly *TLC... for Plants*), Gardenvale Publishing Co. Ltd., 1 Pacifique, Ste. Anne de Bellevue, Quebec H9X 1C5 Canada. (514)457-2744. Editor: Kathryn Spracklin. 95% freelance written. Quarterly magazine covering gardening in Canada. "We are a *practical* gardening magazine focusing on how-to, step-by-step type articles on all aspects of garden and houseplant care. Readers are both novice and experienced Canadian gardeners." Estab. 1988. Circ. 36,000. Pays on publication. Publishes ms 4 months after acceptance. Byline given. Offers 50% kill fee. Buys first North American serial rights. Editorial lead time 4 months. Submit seasonal material 4 months in advance. Accepts simultaneous submissions. Query for electronic submissions. Reports in 2 months. Sample copy free on request. Writer's guidelines for SAE and IRC or, preferably, SAE with 43¢ first-class Canadian stamp.

Nonfiction: Historical/nostalgic, how-to, humor, interview/profile, new product, personal experience—garden-related topics only. No religious/travel outside Canada. Buys 60 mss/year. Query with published clips. Length: 600-1,800 words. Pays $75 minimum (600 words). Sometimes pays expenses of writers on assignment.

Photos: Send photos with submission. Reviews negatives and 4 × 5 transparencies. Offers no additional payment for photos accepted with ms. Captions required. Buys one-time rights.

Columns/Departments: Profile (profiles of gardens and/or gardeners); Hydroponics (how-to for home gardener); Junior Gardener (how-to/ideas for kids and gardening); Down to Earth (humor/essay on gardening); Herb Garden (herb profiles). Length: 600-800 words. Buys 16 mss/year. Query with published clips. Pays $75-150.

Tips: "Please be knowledgeable about gardening—not just a freelance writer. Be accurate and focus on plants/techniques that are appropriate to Canada and be as down to earth as possible. We want good quality writing and interesting subject matter. Areas most open to freelancers are Down to Earth and Profile. We are especially looking for garden profiles from outside Ontario and Quebec (West Coast and Maritimes)."

SAN DIEGO HOME/GARDEN LIFESTYLES, Mckinnon Enterprises, Box 719001, San Diego CA 92171-9001. (714)233-4567. Fax: (619)233-1004. Editor: Dirk Sutro. Senior Editor: Phyllis Van Doren. 50% freelance written. Works with a small number of new/unpublished writers each year. Monthly magazine covering homes, gardens, food, intriguing people, business and real estate, art, culture, and local travel for residents of San Diego city and county. Estab. 1979. Circ. 45,000. **Pays on acceptance.** Publishes ms an average of 3 months after acceptance. Byline given. Buys first North American serial rights only. Submit seasonal material 3 months in advance. Reports in 3 months. Sample copy for $4.

● With addition of *Lifestyles* to its name this publication now covers people, controversies and places it didn't before.

Nonfiction: Residential architecture and interior design (San Diego-area homes only); remodeling (must be well-designed—little do-it-yourself); residential landscape design; furniture; other features oriented towards upscale readers interested in living the cultured good life in San Diego. Articles must have local angle. Buys up to 5 unsolicited mss/year. Query with published clips. Length: 700-2,000 words. Pays $50-350.

Tips: "No out-of-town, out-of-state subject material. Most freelance work is accepted from local writers. Gear stories to the unique quality of San Diego. We try to offer only information unique to San Diego—people, places, shops, resources, etc. We plan more food and entertaining-at-home articles and more articles

Photos: Send photos with ms. Reviews 35mm or larger transparencies and 5×7 or 8×10 "sharp, professional-looking" color prints. Pays $35 for inside photo; pays $50 for cover photo. Captions, model releases and identification of subjects required.
Tips: "Always looking for upscale, universal pieces. No do-it-yourself articles. The key is a well-written query letter that: (1) demonstrates that the subject of the article is practical and useful and has national appeal; (2) shows that the article will have a clear, focused theme and will be based on interviews with experts; (3) outlines the availability (from the writer, a photographer or a PR source) of top-quality color photos. If you are a professional writer, send clips; we do also publish first-time writers."

Humor

Publications listed here specialize in gaglines or prose humor, some for readers and others for performers or speakers. Other publications that use humor can be found in nearly every category in this book. Some have special needs for major humor pieces; some use humor as fillers; many others are interested in material that meets their ordinary fiction or nonfiction requirements but also has a humorous slant. The majority of humor articles must be submitted as complete manuscripts on speculation because editors usually can't know from a query whether or not the piece will be right for them.

‡**THE COMEDY MAGAZINE**, Quality Services, 5290 Overpass Rd., Santa Barbara CA 93111. (805)964-7841. Contact: Paula Brown. 30-40% freelance written. Bimonthly magazine featuring comedy, funny one liners, captions. "We are looking for good clean comedy. Funny looks at everyday life situations and any topical subject are best. Our magazine is an accumulation of jokes, cartoons and articles on comedians working today. Our audience or target group is men 21-49 and women 21-35." Estab. 1993. Circ. 35,000. Pays on publication. Publishes ms an average of months after acceptance. Byline sometimes given. Buys one-time rights. Submit seasonal material 2-3 months in advance. Accepts simultaneous and previously published submissions. Call for writer's guidelines.
Nonfiction: Book excerpts, essays, exposé, general interest, historical/nostalgic, how-to, humor, inspirational, interview/profile, new product, opinion, personal experience, photo feature, religious, technical, travel (all must have humor emphasis). Query with published clips. Length: 1-2 typed pages maximum. Pay varies.
Photos: State availability of photos with submission. Reviews transparencies or prints no larger than 8×10. Offers no additional payment for photos accepted with ms. Model releases, identification of subjects required. Buys one-time rights.
Columns/Departments: Reader Photo, Joke Page, Political Humor, Advice column. Query with published clips. Pay varies.
Fiction: Humorous.
Poetry: Humorous. Length: 1 page.
Fillers: Anecdotes, gags to be illustrated by cartoonist, short humor. Buys 30-40/year. Length: half page. Pay varies, about $25/cartoon.
Tips: "The best approach is to be professional and save your humor for your submission."

FUNNY TIMES, A Monthly Humor Review, Funny Times, Inc., P.O. Box 18530, Cleveland Heights OH 44118. (216)371-8600. Editors: Raymond Lesser, Susan Wolpert. 10% freelance written. Monthly tabloid for humor. *"Funny Times* is a monthly review of America's funniest cartoonists and writers. We are the *Reader's Digest* of modern American humor with a progressive/peace oriented/environmental/politically activist slant." Estab. 1985. Circ. 43,000. Pays on publication. Publishes ms an average of 3 months after acceptance. Byline given. Buys one-time or second serial (reprint) rights. Editorial lead time 2 months. Accepts simultaneous and previously published submissions. Reports in 2 months on mss. Sample copy for $2.50 or 9×12 SAE with 4 first-class stamps. Writer's guidelines for #10 SASE.
Nonfiction: Essays (funny), humor, interview/profile, opinion (humorous), personal experience (absolutely funny). "We only publish humor or interviews with funny people (comedians, comic actors, cartoonists, etc.). Everything we publish is very funny. If your piece isn't extremely funny then don't bother to send it. Don't send us anything that's not outrageously funny. Don't send anything that other people haven't already read and told you they laughed so hard they peed their pants." Buys 36 mss/year. Send complete ms. Length: 1,000 words. Pays $20 minimum for unsolicited articles.
Fiction: Humorous. Buys 6 mss/year. Query with published clips. Length: 5,000 words. Pays $20-150.
Fillers: Short humor. Buys 6/year. Pays $20.
Tips: "Send us a small packet (1-3 items) of only your very funniest stuff. If this makes us laugh we'll be glad to ask for more. We particularly welcome previously published material that has been well-received elsewhere."

THE JOE BOB REPORT, (formerly *We Are The Weird*), Briggs Museum of American Culture, P.O. Box 2002, Dallas TX 75221. Fax: (214)368-2310. Editor: Joe Bob Briggs. Assistant Editor: Tanja Lindstrom. 5% freelance written. Biweekly newsletter/fanzine covering Joe Bob Briggs, popular culture and film. "Radical humor in the spirit of syndicated columnist and TV personality Joe Bob Briggs." Estab. 1985. Circ. 3,500. Pays on publication. Publishes ms an average of 1 month after acceptance. Byline given. Buys first North American serial and second serial (reprint) rights. Submit seasonal/holiday material 2-3 months in advance. Accepts simultaneous and previously published submissions. Query for electronic submissions. Sample copy for #10 SAE with 2 first-class stamps.

Nonfiction: Essays, humor, opinion, personal experience. Buys 10 mss/year. Send complete ms. Length: 2,000 words maximum. Pays $25 maximum. Pays in contributor copies or other premiums when the writer requests it.

Photos: Send photos with submission. Offers $5-25/photo. Model releases and identification of subjects required. Buys all rights.

Fiction: Fantasy, horror, humorous, slice-of-life vignettes. Buys 5 mss/year. Send complete ms. Length: 2,000 maximum words. Pays $25 maximum.

Poetry: Avant-garde, free verse, Haiku, light verse, traditional. Buys 5 poems/year. Pays $25 maximum.

Fillers: Anecdotes, facts, short humor. Buys 5/year. Length: 25 words maximum.

Tips: "Anything that makes us laugh will get our attention. We are most open to poems or short essays (500 words or less). They should be humorous or deal with popular culture, especially the fields of movies, music and stand-up comedy."

LAF!, Scher Maihem Publishing, Ltd., P.O. Box 313, Avilla IN 46710-0313. Submissions Editor: Fran Glass. 100% freelance written. Monthly tabloid that features modern life humor for baby boomers. Estab. 1991. Circ. 500. Pays within 30 days of publication. Buys first or second serial (reprint) rights. Submit seasonal/holiday material 6 months in advance. No simultaneous submissions. Reports in 3 months. Sample copy for 9×12 SASE with 2 first-class stamps. Writer's guidelines for #10 SASE.

• *Laf!* also sponsors the Loudest Laf! Laurel contest.

Fillers: Humor, cartoons. "No religious, political, sexually or racially offensive humor. No poems." Buys 60 mss/year. Send complete ms. Length: 200-500 words. Pays $5-15. No series.

Tips: "If your humor writing appeals to people ages 45 and younger who live in small towns and the suburbs, send it. Our audience is broad, so the writing and subject must have wide appeal. We highly suggest writers take a look at the magazine and guidelines first."

LATEST JOKES, P.O. Box 3304, Brooklyn NY 11202-0066. (718)855-5057. Editor: Robert Makinson. Estab. 1974. 20% freelance written. Bimonthly newsletter of humor for TV and radio personalities, comedians and professional speakers. **Pays on acceptance.** Byline given. Buys all rights. Submit seasonal/holiday material 3 months in advance. Reports in 2 months. Sample copy for $3 and SASE.

Nonfiction: Humor (short jokes). No "stupid, obvious, non-funny vulgar humor. Jokes about human tragedy also unwelcome." Send complete ms. Pays $1-3/joke.

Fiction: Humorous jokes. Pays $1-3.

Poetry: Light verse (humorous). Submit maximum 3 poems at one time. Line length: 2-8 lines. Pays 25¢/line.

Tips: "No famous personality jokes. Clever statements are not enough. Be original and surprising."

MAD MAGAZINE, 485 MADison Ave., New York NY 10022-5852. (212)752-7685. Editors: Nick Meglin, John Ficarra. 100% freelance written. Magazine published 8 times/year. Estab. 1952. Circ. 1 million. **Pays on acceptance.** Publishes ms an average of 6 months after acceptance. Byline given. Buys all rights. Submit seasonal/holiday material 6 months in advance. Reports in 6-10 weeks. Writer's guidelines for #10 SASE.

Nonfiction: Satire, parody. "We're always on the lookout for new ways to spoof and to poke fun at hot trends. We're *not* interested in formats we're already doing or have done to death like 'what they say and what they really mean.'" Buys 400 mss/year. "Submit a premise with three or four examples of how you intend to carry it through, describing the action and visual content. Rough sketches not necessary. One-page gags: two to eight panel cartoon continuities at minimum very funny, maximum hilarious!" Pays minimum of $400/*MAD* page. "*Don't* send riddles, advice columns, TV or movie satires, book manuscripts, top ten lists, articles about Alfred E. Neuman, poetry, essays, short stories or other text pieces."

Tips: "Have fun! Remember to think visually! Surprise us! Freelancers can best break in with nontopical material. Include SASE with each submission. Originality is prized. We like outrageous, silly and/or satirical humor."

‡THE RAGAMUFFIN, Doing for journalism what elevator shoes did for rock & roll, P.O. Box 21707, Cleveland OH 44121-0707. (216)932-7923. Editor: Mark Hentemann. Managing Editor: Ken Dodd. Contact: Margaret O'Shae-Vyorass, managing stapler. 80% freelance written. Quarterly tabloid covering college humor. Estab. 1989. Circ. 51,000. Pays on publication. Publishes ms an average of 4 months after acceptance. Byline sometimes given. Buys one-time rights and second serial (reprint) rights. Editorial lead time 4 months. Accepts simultaneous and previously published submissions. For electronic submissions, query to: ximinez@-

aol.com. Reports in 3 months on mss. Sample copy for 9 × 12 SAE and 2 first-class stamps. Writer's guidelines free on request.

Nonfiction: Humor. Query. Pays 20¢/word for feature or articles; $12/classified, letter to the editor, or horoscope published; $30/cartoon published.

Photos: State availability of photos with submission. Negotiates payment individually. Buys one-time rights.

Columns/Departments: Letters to Editor (parody), 3-50 words; Horoscopes (parody), 45 words; Classifieds (parody), 25 words. Buys 150 mss/year. Send complete ms. Pays $12.

Fiction: Humorous. "Nothing serious." Buys 12 mss/year. Query. Length: 10-1,500 words. Pays $25-225.

Poetry: Parody. "No serious poetry." Buys 6 poems/year. Submit maximum 5 poems. Pays 15¢/word.

Fillers: Buys 20/year. Length: 5-300 words. Pays $12-45.

Tips: "Unconventional humor is more prone to be chosen than conventional. Originality carries a lot of weight. The most popular pieces are either the sublimely stupid, or mind-bendingly contradictory. Or better yet, something that cleverly flames on the real-life situation of college life. What is suggested to new writers is that they begin with the fillers, letters to the editor, classifieds, or horoscopes. Once they publish ten of these, they become a contributing editor, and we work with them on assignments."

SPEAKERS IDEA FILE, 165 W. 47th St., New York NY 10036. Humor Editor: Gary Apple. For "business communicators of all types—politicians, CEO's, salespeople, teachers, toastmasters, etc." Estab. 1972. Pays on publication. Buys all rights. Reports in 1 month. Writer's guidelines for SASE.

Fillers: "In our humor section, we publish funny one-liners and short jokes that public speakers can use in their presentations. These include jokes about news events, celebrities, trends, families, business, and finance. We also run jokes specifically geared toward the public speaking environment: jokes for beginning and ending a speech, introductions, hecklers, roasts, retirement, and so on." Pays $12/joke.

Tips: "The material that you send *must be original*. Do not send jokes you've heard somewhere, only truly funny jokes you've written yourself. Please submit no more than fifteen jokes at one time. Enclose a SASE for the return of your material. We're always looking for new, funny writers."

Inflight

Most major inflight magazines cater to business travelers and vacationers who will be reading, during the flight, about the airline's destinations and other items of general interest.

ABOARD MAGAZINE, Suite 220, 100 Almeria, Coral Gables FL 33134. Fax: (305)441-9739. Editor: Robert Cusin. 20% freelance written. Bimonthly bilingual inflight magazine designed to reach travelers to and from Latin America, carried on 11 major Latin-American airlines. Estab. 1976. Circ. 89,000. Pays on publication. Byline given. Buys one-time or simultaneous rights or makes work-for-hire assignments. Accepts simultaneous and previously published submissions. Send photocopy of article. For reprints pays same amount paid for original. Reports in 1 month. "SASE please."

Nonfiction: General interest, new product, business, science, art, fashion, photo feature, technical, travel. "No controversial or political material." Buys 50 mss/year. Length: 1,200-1,500 words. Pays $100-150. Sometimes pays expenses of writers on assignment.

Photos: Send photos with submission, 35mm slides or transparencies only. Reviews transparencies. Offers no additional payment for photos accepted with ms. Offers $20/photo minimum. Identification of subjects required. Buys one-time rights.

Fillers: Facts. Buys 6/year. Length: 800-1,200 words. Pays $100.

Tips: "Send article with photos. We need lots of travel material on Ecuador, Bolivia, El Salvador, Honduras, Peru, Guatemala and the Dominican Republic, Uruguay, Nicaragua, Paraguay."

‡AL BURAQ, The Inflight Magazine for Kuwait Airways, Fortune Promoseven, P.O. Box 5989, Manama, Bahrain. (973)250148 x635. Editor: Gregory O. Jones. 60% freelance written. Monthly magazine covering travel, general interest. "*Al Buraq* exists to promote Kuwait Airways and travel to destinations served by Kuwait Airways. Remember to keep stories brief and interesting; remember that one half the magazine is in Arabic for a Middle Eastern audience." Estab. 1989. Circ. 50,000. Pays on publication. Publishes ms an average of 3 months after acceptance. Byline given. Offers 50% kill fee. Buys first, one-time, second serial (reprint) or Arabic language rights. Editorial lead time 4 months. Submit seasonal material 4 months in advance. Accepts previously published submissions. Query for electronic submissions. Reports in 1 month. Sample copy for 8½ × 12 SAE with 2 IRCs. Writer's guidelines free on request.

Nonfiction: General interest, interview/profile, photo feature, travel. "No humor, politics, sex or religious overtones. Humor translates poorly, the rest are not usable." Buys 40 mss/year. Query with published clips. Length: 400-1,200 words. Pays $120. Sometimes pays expenses of writers on assignment.

Photos: Ideally, send photos with submission. Reviews contact sheets, transparencies and prints (5 × 7 minimum). Offers $50-200/photo. Captions required. Buys one-time rights.

Tips: "Send for contributor notes and sample copy. Remember where we are published. The article may be published in Arabic, and will definitely be read by non-Americans; therefore, all American slang or 'in-terms' should either be avoided or explained. Write internationally, appeal personally. Stories complete with pictures and on diskettes go to the head of the queue. Always welcome well-written, competently-illustrated, succinct feature articles pertinent to our readers. *Al Buraq* is a good market for the fledgling writer."

AMERICA WEST AIRLINES MAGAZINE, Skyword Marketing, Inc., Suite 240, 7500 N. Dreamy Draw Dr., Phoenix AZ 85020-4660. (602)997-7200. Editor: Michael Derr. 90% freelance written. Works with small number of new/unpublished writers each year. Monthly "general interest magazine, with substantial business editorial, emphasizing the western and southwestern US. Some Midwestern, Northwestern and Eastern subjects also appropriate. We look for innovative, newsworthy and unconventional subject matter." Estab. 1986. Query with published clips and SASE. No unsolicited mss. Pays on publication. Publishes ms an average of 4 months after acceptance. Byline given. Offers 15% kill fee. Buys first North American rights. Submit seasonal/holiday material 6-8 months in advance. Accepts simultaneous submissions, if indicated. Reports in 1 month on queries; 5 weeks on mss. Sample copy for $3. Writer's guidelines for 9 × 12 SAE with 3 first-class stamps.
  • Ranked as one of the best markets for freelance writers in *Writer's Digest* magazine's annual "Top 100 Markets," January 1994.
Nonfiction: General interest, creative leisure, profile, photo feature, science, sports, business issues, entre-preneurs, nature, arts, travel, trends. Also considers essays and humor. No puzzles, reviews or highly contro-versial features. Buys 130-140 mss/year. Length: 300-2,200. Pays $150-900. Pays some expenses.
Photos: State availability of original photography. Offers $50-250/photo. Captions, model releases and identi-fication of subjects required. Buys one-time rights.

AMERICAN WAY, P.O. Box 619640, Dallas/Fort Worth Airport TX 75261-9640. (817)967-1804. Fax: (817)967-1571. Editor: John H. Ostdick. Assistant Editor: Tim Rogers. 98% freelance written. Prefers to work with published/established writers. Biweekly inflight magazine for passengers flying with American Airlines. Estab. 1966. **Pays on acceptance.** Publishes ms an average of 4 months after acceptance. Buys first serial rights. Reports in 5 months.
  • Ranked as one of the best markets for freelance writers in *Writer's Digest* magazine's annual "Top 100 Markets," January 1994.
Nonfiction: Trends in business, the arts and entertainment industries, sports, technology, food, science, medicine, travel, Q&As with interesting people. "We are amenable to almost any subject that would be interesting, entertaining or useful to a passenger of American Airlines." Also humor, trivia, trends, and will consider a variety of ideas. Buys 450 mss/year. Query with published clips. Length: 1,000-3,500 words. Pays $850 and up. Usually pays some expenses for writers on assignment.
Fiction: Jeff Posey, editor. Length: 2,500 words maximum. Payment varies.

‡THE AUSTRALIAN WAY, Qantas Inflight Magazine, David Syme & Co. Ltd., 250 Spencer St., Melbourne Victoria 3000 Australia. Editor: Brian Courtis. 80% freelance written. Monthly magazine. "*The Australian Way* caters to Qantas Airways passengers travelling on both internal Australian routes and overseas. It provides articles on international events, travel, the arts, science and technology, sport, natural history and humor. The focus is on elegant writing and high-quality photography." Estab. 1993. Circ. 900,000. Pays on publication. Publishes ms an average of 3 months after acceptance. Byline given. Buys first rights. Editorial lead time 3 months. Submit seasonal material 4 months in advance. Query for electronic submissions.
Nonfiction: General interest, historical/nostalgic, interview/profile, photo feature, travel. Query with pub-lished clips. Buys 200 mss/year. Length: 800-2,000 words. Pays $500 (Australian) for assigned articles; $400 (Australian) for unsolicited articles.
Photos: State availability of photos with submission. Reviews transparencies and prints. Negotiates payment individually. Captions and identification of subjects required. Buys all rights if commissioned; one-time rights if unsolicited.
Columns/Departments: Contact: Michelle Fincke. Carousel (unusual news, facts, happenings that interest travellers—trends or personalities etc.) 150 words. Query. Pays $100-250 Australian.
Tips: "Writers should entertain as well as inform both an Australian and international readership. Features can be of general interest, about personalities, or on cultural, business or sporting interests. The magazine tends to avoid travel 'destination' pieces *per se*, though it carries appropriate stories that use these locations as backdrops."

Always check the most recent copy of a magazine for the address and editor's name before you send in a query or manuscript.

‡GOLDEN FALCON, Fortune Promoseven, P.O. Box 5989, Manama, Bahrain. (973)250148 x635. Fax: (973)271451. Editor: Gregory O. Jones. 60% freelance written. Monthly magazine covering travel, general interest for Gulf Air. Estab. 1988 (relaunched July 1993). Circ. 50,000. Pays on publication. Publishes ms an average of 4 months after acceptance. Byline given. Offers 50% kill fee. Buys first, one-time, second serial (reprint) or Arabic language rights. Editorial lead time 4 months. Submit seasonal material 5 months in advance. Accepts previously published submissions. Query for electronic submissions. Reports in 1 month. Sample copy for 8½ × 12 SAE with 2 IRCs. Writer's guidelines free on request.

Nonfiction: General interest, historical/nostalgic, interview/profile, photo feature, travel. "No humor, politics, sex or religion. Humor translates poorly, the other three are unusable." Buys 50 mss/year. Query with published clips. Length: 400-1,500 words. Pays $120. Sometimes pays the expenses of writers on assignment.

Photos: State availability of photos with submission. Reviews contact sheets, transparencies and prints (5 × 7 minimum). Offers $50-200/photo. Captions required. Buys one-time rights.

Columns/Departments: Technology (popular science, new gadgets), 300-500 words and photos; Business (no bad news—upbeat and optimistic), 300-500 words and photos; The Arts/Music/Show Biz (personalities, history, mini-articles), 300-500 words and photos. Buys 48 mss/year. Query with published clips. Pays $110-140.

Tips: "Read contributor notes carefully. Remember where we are published. National and religious sensibilities must be observed. The articles will be read by non-Americans, so avoid American-isms and slang. Write internationally, appeal individually. Stories which are complete with captioned photos and computer disk go to the head of the queue. Send for destination list and produce stories from places where travel companies do *not* send writers for 'familiarization trips.' Short columns, easily researched, complete with one picture, can be produced quickly. We have a prodigious appetite for them and they can be assembled from assorted manufacturers' and companies' press releases. Motoring column must refrain from mention of a single company. Prefer three or more."

‡HEMISPHERES, Pace Communications for United Airlines, 1301 Carolina St., Greensboro NC 27401. (910)378-6065. Editor: Kate Coreer. Managing Editor: Sheryl Miller. 95% freelance written. Monthly magazine for inflight passengers covering travel and business—a global perspective with information for the professional who travels frequently. Estab. 1992. Circ. 500,000. **Pays on acceptance.** Publishes ms 4-12 months after acceptance. Byline given. Offers 20% kill fee. Buys first, worldwide rights. Editorial lead time 4-8 months. Submit seasonal material 6-8 months in advance. Reports in 6-10 weeks on queries; 2-4 months on mss. Sample copy for $5. Writer's guidelines for #10 SASE.

Nonfiction: Book excerpts, general interest, humor, personal experience. No "What I did (or am going to do) on a trip to. . . . " Query with published clips. Length: 500-3,000 words. Negotiates payment individually.

Photos: State availability of photos with submission. Reviews transparencies "only when we request them." Negotiates payment individually. Captions, model releases and identification of subjects required. Buys one-time rights.

Columns/Departments: Making a Difference (Q&A interview with world leaders, movers and shakers); On Location (1-sentence "25 Fun Facts" about a city, state, country or destination); Executive Secrets (things that top executives know—e.g., business strategies); Case Study (business strategies of international companies or organizations); Weekend Breakaway (physically active getaway—hiking, windsurfing, etc.— just outside a major city); Roving Gourmet (insider's guide to interesting eating in major city, resort area, or region; Collecting (photo with lengthy caption or occasional 800-word story on collections and collecting with emphasis on travel); Eye on Sports (global look at anything of interest in sports); Vintage Traveler (options for mature, experienced travelers); Savvy Shopper (insider's tour of best places in the world to shop); Science and Technology alternates with Computers (substantive, insightful story); Aviation Journal (for those fascinated with aviation); Of Grape And Grain (wine and spirits with emphasis on education); Show Business (films, music and entertainment); Musings (humor or just curious musings); Quick Quiz (tests to amuse and educate); Travel News (brief, practical, invaluable, trend-oriented tips). Length: 800-1,400 words. Query with published clips.

Fiction: Adventure, humorous, mainstream, slice-of-life vignettes. Buys 4 mss/year. Query. Length: 500-2,000 words. Negotiates payment individually.

‡MIDWEST EXPRESS MAGAZINE, Paradigm Communications Group, Suite 250, 2701 First Ave., Seattle WA 98121. Editor: Eric Lucas. 90% freelance written. Bimonthly magazine for Midwest Express Airlines. "Postive depiction of the changing economy and culture of the US, plus travel and leisure features." Estab. 1993. Circ: 32,000. Pays on publication. Byline given. Offers 33% kill fee. Buys first North American serial rights. Editorial lead time 3-9 months. Submit seasonal material 1 year in advance. Accepts simultaneous submissions. Query for electronic submissions. Reports in 4-6 weeks on queries. Sample copy for #10 SASE. Writer's guidelines free on request.

Nonfiction: Travel (business, some sports and leisure). "Need good ideas for golf articles in Spring." Buys 20-25 mss/year. Query with published clips and resume. Length: 250-3,000 words. Pays $100 minimum. Sometimes pays expenses of writers on assignment.

Columns/Departments: Todd Powell, associate editor. Preview (arts and events), 200-400 words; Portfolio (business-queries to Eric Lucas), 200-500 words. Buys 12-15 mss/year. Query with published clips. Pays $100-150.

Tips: "Article ideas *must* encompass areas within the airline's route system. We buy quality writing from reliable writers. Editorial philosophy emphasizes innovation and positive outlook. Do not send manuscripts unless you have no clips."

‡NORTHWEST AIRLINES WORLD TRAVELER, Skies America Publishing Co., 7730 SW Mohawk, Tualatin OR 97062. (503)691-1955. Editor: Terri Wallo. 90% freelance written. Monthly business and travel editorial magazine. Estab. 1969. Circ. 350,000. Pays on publication. Publishes ms an average of 3 months after acceptance. Byline given. Offers 100% kill fee. Buys first North American serial rights. Editorial lead time 3 months. Submit seasonal material 6 months in advance. Accepts simultaneous submissions. Query for electronic submissions. Reports in 6 weeks on queries; 2 months on mss. Sample copy for $3. Writer's guidelines for #10 SASE.

Nonfiction: Book excerpts, humor, interview/profile, personal experience. Buys 3 mss/year. Query. Length: 1,000-2,000 words. Pays $850 for assigned articles; $500 for unsolicited articles.

Photos: State availability of photos with submission. Reviews transparencies. Negotiates payment individually. Identification of subjects required. Buys one-time rights.

Fillers: Facts, newsbreaks. Buys 10/year. Length: 200 minimum. Pays $100.

SKY, Inflight Magazine of Delta Air Lines, Halsey Publishing Co., 600 Corporate Dr., Ft. Lauderdale FL 33334. (305)776-0066. Editor: Lidia De Leon. Managing Editor: Barbara Whelehan. 90% freelance written. Monthly magazine. "Delta *SKY* is a general interest, nationally/internationally-oriented magazine with the main purpose to entertain and inform business and leisure travelers aboard Delta Air Lines." Estab. 1971. Circ. 500,000. **Pays on acceptance.** Publishes ms an average of 2 months after acceptance. Byline given. Offers 100% kill fee when cancellation is through no fault of the writer. Buys one-time rights. Submit seasonal/holiday material 9 months in advance. Accepts simultaneous submissions. Query for electronic submissions. Reports in 1 month. Sample copy for 9 × 12 SAE. Writer's guidelines for #10 SASE.

• Ranked as one of the best markets for freelance writers in *Writer's Digest* magazine's annual "Top 100 Markets," January 1994.

Nonfiction: General interest, photo feature. "No opinion, religious, reviews, poetry, fiction or fillers." Buys 200-250 mss/year. Query with published clips. Length: 1700-2500 words. Pays $500-700 for assigned articles; $400-500 for unsolicited articles. Pays expenses of writers on assignment.

Photos: State availability of photos with submission. Reviews 4 × 5 transparencies and 5 × 7 prints. Offers varying rates on photos. Captions, model releases and identification of subject required. Buys one-time rights.

Columns/Departments: Management (managerial techniques, methods of topical nature); Living (subjects of topical, contemporary interest); Finance (personal finance, tips). Buys 50-60 mss/year. Query. Length: 1500-1700 words. Pays $400-500.

Tips: "Send a well detailed query tied in to one of the feature or column categories of the magazine. Since our lead times call for planning of editorial content 6-9 months in advance, that should also be kept in mind when proposing story ideas. All feature story and column/department categories are open to freelancers, with the exceptions of Travel (areas are predetermined by the airline) and the executive Profile Series (which is also predetermined)."

WASHINGTON FLYER MAGAZINE, #111, 11 Canal Center Plaza, Alexandria VA 22314. (703)739-9292. Editor: Brian T. Cook. Associate Editors: Laurie McLaughlin, Stephen Soltis. 40% freelance written. Bimonthly in-airport magazine for business and pleasure travelers at Washington National and Washington Dulles International airports. "Primarily affluent, well-educated audience that flies frequently in and out of Washington, DC." Estab. 1989. Circ. 160,620. **Pays on acceptance.** Byline given. Buys first North American rights. Submit seasonal/holiday material 4 months in advance. Query for electronic submissions. Reports in approximately 2½ months. Sample copy and writer's guidelines for 9 × 12 SAE with 9 first-class stamps.

• *Washington Flyer* has brought more work inhouse, reducing its need for new freelancers, e.g., last edition they were 80% freelance written, this edition, 40%.

Nonfiction: General interest, interview/profile, travel, business. Buys 20-30 mss/year. Query with published clips. Length: 300-1,200 words. Pays $100-600. Sometimes pays expenses of writers on assignment.

Photos: State availability of photos with submission. Reviews negatives and transparencies (almost always color). Will consider additional payment for top-quality photos accepted with ms. Identification of subjects required. Buys one-time rights.

Tips: "Know the Washington market and issues relating to frequent business/pleasure travelers as we move toward a global economy."

Juvenile

Just as children change and grow, so do juvenile magazines. Children's magazine editors stress that writers must read recent issues. This section lists publications for children ages 2-12. Magazines for young people 13-19 appear in the Teen and Young

Adult category. Many of the following publications are produced by religious groups and, where possible, the specific denomination is given. A directory for juvenile markets, *Children's Writer's and Illustrator's Market*, is available from Writer's Digest Books.

BOYS' LIFE, Boy Scouts of America, P.O. Box 152079, Irving TX 75015-2079. Editor: Tom Stuckey. 75% freelance written. Prefers to work with published/established writers; works with small number of new/unpublished writers each year. Monthly magazine covering activities of interest to all boys ages 8-18. Most readers are Scouts or Cub Scouts. Estab. 1911. Circ 1.3 million. **Pays on acceptance.** Publishes ms an average of 6-12 months after acceptance. Buys one-time rights. Reports in 4-6 weeks. Sample copy for $2.50 and 9 × 12 SAE. Writer's guidelines for #10 SASE.
  • Ranked as one of the best markets for freelance writers in *Writer's Digest* magazine's annual "Top 100 Markets," January 1994, and for fiction writers in its biannual "Fiction 50," June 1994.
Nonfiction: Major articles run 750-1,500 words; preferred length is about 1,000 words including sidebars and boxes. Pays minimum $500 for major article text. Uses strong photo features with about 500 words of text. Separate payment or assignment for photos. "Much better rates if you really know how to write for our market." Buys 60 major articles/year. Also needs how-to features and hobby and crafts ideas. Query all nonfiction ideas in writing with SASE. Pays expenses of writers on assignment. Also buys freelance comics pages and scripts. Query first in writing, not by phone.
Columns: "Food, Health, Pets, Bicycling, Sports, Electronics, Space and Aviation, Science, Entertainment, Music, History, Cars and Magic are some of the columns for which we use 400-600 words of text. This is a good place to show us what you can do. Query first in writing." Pays $150-350. Buys 75-80 columns/year.
Fiction: Short stories 1,000-1,500 words; rarely longer. Send complete ms with SASE. Pays $500 minimum. Buys 15 short stories/year.
Tips: "We strongly recommend reading at least 12 issues of the magazine and learning something about the programs of the Boy Scouts of America before you submit queries. We are a good market for any writer willing to do the necessary homework."

CALLIOPE: The World History Magazine for Young People, Cobblestone Publishing, Inc., 7 School St., Peterborough NH 03458-1454. (603)924-7209. Fax: (603)924-7380. Editor-in-Chief: Carolyn P. Yoder. Editors: Rosalie and Charles Baker. 50% freelance written. Prefers to work with published/established writers. Magazine published 5 times/year covering world history through 1800 AD for 8- to 14-year-olds. Articles must relate to the issue's theme. Pays on publication. Byline given. Buys all rights. Accepts simultaneous submissions. Previously published submissions rarely accepted. Sample copy for $3.95 and 7½ × 10½ SAE with 5 first-class stamps. Writer's guidelines for SASE.
Nonfiction: Essays, general interest, historical/nostalgic, how-to (activities), recipes, humor, interview/profile, personal experience, photo feature, technical, travel. Articles must relate to the theme. No religious, pornographic, biased or sophisticated submissions. Buys approximately 30-40 mss/year. Query with published clips. Feature articles 700-800 words. Pays 14-17¢/printed word. Supplemental nonfiction 300-600 words. Pays 10-13¢/printed word.
Photos: State availability of photos with submission. Reviews contact sheets, color slides and b&w prints. Buys one-time rights. Pays $15-50 for b&w (color cover negotiated).
Fiction: All fiction must be theme-related. Buys 10 mss/year. Query with published clips. Length: up to 800 words. Pays 10-17¢/word.
Poetry: Light verse, traditional. No religious or pornographic poetry or poetry not related to the theme. Submit maximum 1 poem. Pays on individual basis. Poetry, up to 100 lines.
Columns/Departments: Puzzles and Games (no word finds); crossword and other word puzzles using the vocabulary of the issue's themes; mazes and picture puzzles that relate to the theme. Pays on an individual basis.
Tips: "Writers must have an appreciation and understanding of world history. Writers must not condescend to our readers."

CHICKADEE MAGAZINE, For Young Children from *OWL*, Owl Communications, Suite 500, 179 John St., Toronto, Ontario M5T 3G5 Canada. (416)971-5275. Editor: Lizann Flatt. 25% freelance written. Magazine published 10 times/year (except July and August) for 3-9-year-olds. "We aim to interest young children in the world around them in an entertaining and lively way." Estab. 1979. Circ. 110,000 Canada and US. **Pays on acceptance.** Byline given. Buys all rights. Submit seasonal/holiday material up to 1 year in advance. Reports in 2 months. Sample copy for $3.50 and SAE ($1 money order or IRC's). Writer's guidelines for SAE.
Nonfiction: How-to (easy and unusual arts and crafts); personal experience (real children in real situations); photo feature (wildlife features). No articles for older children; no religious or moralistic features.
Photos: Send photos with ms. Reviews 35mm transparencies. Identification of subjects required.
Fiction: Adventure (relating to the 3-9-year-old), humor. No talking animal stories or religious articles. Send complete ms with $1 money order for handling and return postage. Pays $210 (US).

Tips: "A frequent mistake made by writers is trying to teach too much—not enough entertainment and fun."

CHILD LIFE, Children's Better Health Institute, P.O. Box 567, Indianapolis IN 46206-0567. (317)636-8881. Fax: (317)684-8094. Editor: Lise Hoffman. 90% freelance written. Bimonthly magazine (except monthly March, June, September, December) covering "general topics of interest to children—emphasis on health preferred but not necessary." Pays on publication. Publishes ms an average of 6 months after acceptance. Byline given. Buys all rights. Submit seasonal/holiday material 8 months in advance. Reports in 2 months. Sample copy for $1.25. Writer's guidelines for #10 SASE.
Nonfiction: How-to (simple crafts), anything children might like—health topics preferred. Buys 20 mss/year. Send complete ms. Length: 400-1,000. Pays 12¢/word (approximately).
Photos: Send photos only with accompanying editorial material. Reviews transparencies. Offers $30 for inside color photo, $50 for front cover. Captions, model releases and identification of subjects required. Buys one-time rights.
Columns/Departments: Regular columns especially hospitable to freelancers include "One World, Fun World: Games from the Global Village," "Odd Jobs, "Odd Hobbies" and "ChowTime," (a recipe column). Query for descriptions with #10 SASE.
Fiction: Adventure, fantasy, historical, humorous, multicultural, mystery, science fiction, suspense. All must be geared to children (9-11 years old). Buys 20-25 mss/year. Send complete ms. Length: 400-900 words. Pays 12¢/word (approximately).
Poetry: Free verse, haiku, light verse, traditional. No long "deep" poetry not suited for children. Buys 8 poems/year. Submit maximum 5 poems. Pays approximately $2/line.
Fillers: "Constant, ongoing demand for puzzles, games, mazes, etc." Variable pay.
Tips: "Present health-related items in an interesting, non-textbook manner. The approach to health fiction can be subtle—tell a good story first. We also consider non-health items—make them fresh and enjoyable for children."

CHILDREN'S DIGEST, Children's Better Health Institute, P.O. Box 567, Indianapolis IN 46206-0567. (317)636-8881. Editor: Sandy Grieshop. 85% freelance written. Works with a small number of new/unpublished writers each year. Magazine published 8 times/year covering children's health for preteen children. Estab. 1950. Pays on publication. Publishes ms an average of 1 year after acceptance. Byline given. Buys all rights. Submit seasonal/holiday material 8 months in advance. Submit *only* complete mss. "No queries, please." Reports in 2 months. Sample copy for $1.25. Writer's guidelines for #10 SASE.
Nonfiction: Historical, interview/profile (biographical), craft ideas, health, nutrition, fitness and sports. "We're especially interested in factual features that teach readers about fitness and sports or encourage them to develop better health habits. We are *not* interested in material that is simply rewritten from encyclopedias. We try to present our health material in a way that instructs *and* entertains the reader." Buys 15-20 mss/year. Send complete ms. Length: 500-1,200 words. Pays up to 12¢/word. Sometimes pays the expenses of writers on assignment.
Photos: State availability of full color or b&w photos. Payment varies. Model releases and identification of subjects required. Buys one-time rights.
Fiction: Adventure, humorous, mainstream, mystery. Stories should appeal to both boys and girls. "We need some stories that incorporate a health theme. However, we don't want stories that preach, preferring instead stories with implied morals. We like a light or humorous approach." Buys 15-20 mss/year. Length: 500-1,500 words. Pays up to 12¢/word.
Poetry: Pays $15 minimum.
Tips: "Many of our readers have working mothers and/or come from single-parent homes. We need more stories that reflect these changing times while communicating good values."

CHILDREN'S PLAYMATE, Children's Better Health Institute, P.O. Box 567, Indianapolis IN 46206-0567. (317)636-8881. Editor: Lisa Hoffman. 75% freelance written. Eager to work with new/unpublished writers. Magazine published 8 times/year. "We are looking for articles, stories, and activities with a health, sports, fitness or nutritionally oriented theme. We also publish general interest fiction and nonfiction. We try to present our material in a positive light, and we try to incorporate humor and a light approach wherever possible without minimizing the seriousness of what we are saying." For children ages 6-8. Estab. 1928. Buys all rights. Byline given. Pays on publication. Publishes ms an average of 1 year after acceptance. Submit seasonal material 8 months in advance. Reports in 8-10 weeks. Sometimes may hold mss for up to 1 year, with author's permission. "Material will not be returned unless accompanied by a SASE." Sample copy for $1.25. Writer's guidelines for #10 SASE.
Nonfiction: 500 words maximum. "A feature may be an interesting presentation on animals, people, events, objects or places, especially about good health, exercise, proper nutrition and safety. Include word count. Buys 40 mss/year. "We would very much like to see more nonfiction features on people (kids primarily) and places and events. We do not consider outlines. Reading the whole manuscript is the only way to give fair consideration. The editors cannot criticize, offer suggestions, or review unsolicited material that is not accepted." No queries. Pays up to 17¢/word.

Fiction: Short stories for beginning readers, not over 700 words. Seasonal stories with holiday themes. Humorous stories, unusual plots. "We are interested in stories about children in different cultures and stories about lesser-known holidays (not just Christmas, Thanksgiving, Halloween, Hanukkah)." Vocabulary suitable for ages 6-8. Submit complete ms. Pays up to 17¢/word. Include word count with stories.

Fillers: Recipes, puzzles, dot-to-dots, color-ins, hidden pictures, mazes. Buys 30 fillers/year. Payment varies. Prefers camera-ready activities. Activity guidelines for #10 SASE.

Tips: Especially interested in features, stories, poems and articles about special holidays, particularly noteworthy or interesting kids, customs and events.

CLUBHOUSE, Your Story Hour, P.O. Box 15, Berrien Springs MI 49103. (616)471-3701. Editor: Elaine Trumbo. 75% freelance written. Works with a small number of new/unpublished writers each year. Monthly magazine covering many subjects with Christian approach, though not associated with a church. "Stories and features for fun for 9-14 year-olds. Main objective: To provide a psychologically 'up' magazine that lets kids know that they are acceptable, 'neat' people." Estab. 1951. Circ. 4,000. Pays on acceptance within about 6 months. Publishes ms an average of 1 year after acceptance. Byline given. Buys first serial rights or first North American serial rights, one-time rights, simultaneous rights, and second serial (reprint) rights. Accepts simultaneous and previously published submissions. Send tearsheet, photocopy or typed ms of article. For reprints, pays 100% of amount paid for original article. Reports in 4-8 weeks. Sample copy for 6×9 SAE and 3 first-class stamps. Writer's guidelines for #10 SASE.

• *Clubhouse* has reduced its number of pages but is being published monthly instead of bimonthly.

Nonfiction: How-to (crafts), personal experience, recipes (without sugar or artificial flavors and colors). "No stories in which kids start out 'bad' and by peer or adult pressure or circumstances are changed into 'good' people." Send complete ms. Length: 750-800 words ($25); 1,000-1,200 words ($30); feature story, 1,200 words ($35).

Photos: Send photos with ms. Pays on publication according to published size. Buys one-time rights.

Columns/Departments: Body Shop (short stories or "ad" type material that is anti-smoking, drugs and alcohol and pro-good nutrition, etc.), 1,000 words maximum; Jr. Detective (secret codes, word search, deduction problems, hidden pictures, etc.), 400 words maximum. Buys 12 mss/year. Send complete ms. Pays $10-30.

Fiction: Adventure, historical, humorous, mainstream. "Stories should depict bravery, kindness, etc., without a preachy attitude." No science fiction, romance, confession or mystery. Cannot use Santa-elves, Halloween or Easter Bunny material. Buys 30 mss/year. Send query or complete ms (prefers ms). Length: 750-800 words ($20); 1,000-1,200 words ($30); lead story ($35).

Poetry: Free verse, light verse, traditional. Buys 6-10/year. Submit maximum 5 poems. Length: 4-24 lines. Pays $5-20.

Fillers: Cartoons. Buys 18/year. Pay $12 maximum.

Tips: "Send all material during March or April. By the end of June acceptance or rejection notices will be sent. Material chosen will probably appear the following year. Basically, kids are more and more informed and aware of the world around them. This means that characters in stories for *Clubhouse* should not seem too simple, yet maintain the wonder and joy of youth."

COBBLESTONE: The History Magazine for Young People, Cobblestone Publishing, Inc., 7 School St., Peterborough NH 03458-1457. (603)924-7209. Fax: (603)924-7380. Editor-in-Chief: Carolyn P. Yoder. Editor: Samuel A. Mead. 100% (except letters and departments) freelance written (approximately 2 issues/year are by assignment only). Prefers to work with published/established writers. Monthly magazine (except July and August) covering American history for children ages 8-14. "Each issue presents a particular theme, from different angles, making it exciting as well as informative. Half of all subscriptions are for schools." Circ. 38,000. Pays on publication. Publishes ms an average of 4 months after acceptance. Byline given. Buys all rights or makes work-for-hire assignments. All material must relate to monthly theme. Accepts simultaneous and previously published submissions. Sample copy for $3.95 and 7½×10½ SAE with 5 first-class stamps. Writer's guidelines for SASE.

Nonfiction: Historical/nostalgic, how-to, interview, plays, biography, recipes, activities, personal experience. "Request a copy of the writer's guidelines to find out specific issue themes in upcoming months." No material that editorializes rather than reports. Buys 5-8 mss/issue. Length: Feature articles 700-800 words. Pays 14-17¢/printed word. Supplemental nonfiction 300-600 words. Pays up to 10-13¢/printed word. Query with published clips, outline and bibliography.

Fiction: Adventure, historical, humorous, biographical fiction. "Has to be very strong and accurate." Buys 1-2 mss/issue. Length: up to 800 words. Request free editorial guidelines that explain upcoming issue themes and give query deadlines. "Message" must be smoothly integrated with the story. Query with written samples. Pays 10-17¢/printed word.

Poetry: Free verse, light verse, traditional. Submit maximum 2 poems. Length: up to 100 lines. Pays on an individual basis. Must relate to theme.

Columns/Departments: Puzzles and Games (no word finds); crossword and other word puzzles using the vocabulary of the issue's theme; mazes and picture puzzles that relate to the theme. Pays on an individual basis.

Tips: "All material is considered on the basis of merit and appropriateness to theme. Query should state idea for material simply, with rationale for why material is applicable to theme. Request writer's guidelines (includes themes and query deadlines) before submitting a query. Include SASE."

CRICKET, Carus Publishing Co., P.O. Box 300, Peru IL 61354-0300. (815)224-6643. Editor-in-Chief: Marianne Carus. Monthly magazine. Estab. 1973. Circ. 100,000. Pays on publication. Byline given. Buys first publication rights in the English language. Submit seasonal/holiday material 1 year in advance. Accepts previously published submissions. Send typed ms with rights for sale noted and information about when and where the article previously appeared. For reprints pays 50% of the amount paid for original article. Reports in 3 months. Sample copy and writer's guidelines for $4 and 9 × 12 SAE. Writer's guidelines only for #10 SASE.
  • Ranked as one of the best markets for fiction writers in *Writer's Digest* magazine's biannual "Fiction 50," June 1994. *Cricket* is looking for more fiction and nonfiction for the older end of its age range.
Nonfiction: Adventure, biography, foreign culture, geography, history, science, social science, sports, technology, travel. (A short bibliography is required for *all* nonfiction articles.) Send complete ms. Length: 200-1,200 words. Pays up to 25¢/word.
Fiction: Adventure, ethnic, fairy tales, fantasy, historical, humorous, mystery, novel excerpts, science fiction, suspense, western. No didactic, sex, religious or horror stories. Buys 24-36 mss/year. Send complete ms. Length: 200-1,500 words. Pays up to 25¢/word.
Poetry: Buys 8-10 poems/year. Length: 25 lines maximum. Pays up to $3/line on publication.

CRUSADER MAGAZINE, P.O. Box 7259, Grand Rapids MI 49510-7259. Fax: (616)241-5558. Editor: G. Richard Broene. 40% freelance written. Works with a small number of new/unpublished writers each year. Magazine published 7 times/year. "*Crusader Magazine* shows boys (9-14) how God is at work in their lives and in the world around them." Estab. 1958. Circ. 14,000. Buys 20-25 mss/year. **Pays on acceptance.** Byline given. Publishes ms an average of 8 months after acceptance. Rights purchased vary with author and material; buys first serial, one-time, second serial (reprint) and simultaneous rights. Submit seasonal material (Christmas, Easter) at least 5 months in advance. Accepts simultaneous submissions. Reports in 2 months. Sample copy and writer's guidelines for 9 × 12 SAE with 3 first-class stamps.
Nonfiction: Articles about young boys' interests: sports, outdoor activities, bike riding, science, crafts, etc., and problems. Emphasis is on a Christian multi-racial perspective, but no simplistic moralisms. Informational, how-to, personal experience, interview, profile, inspirational, humor. Submit complete ms. Length: 500-1,500 words. Pays 2-5¢/word.
Photos: Pays $4-25 for b&w photos purchased with mss.
Fiction: "Considerable fiction is used. Fast-moving stories that appeal to a boy's sense of adventure or sense of humor are welcome. Avoid preachiness. Avoid simplistic answers to complicated problems. Avoid long dialogue and little action." Length: 900-1,500 words. Pays 2¢/word minimum.
Fillers: Uses short humor and any type of puzzles as fillers.

‡CURRENT HEALTH 1, The Beginning Guide to Health Education, General Learning Corporation, 60 Revere Dr., Northbrook IL 60062-1563. (708)205-3000. Executive Editor: Laura Ruekberg. 95% freelance written. An educational health periodical published monthly, September-May. "Our audience is 4th-7th grade health education students. Articles should be written at a 5th grade reading level. As a curriculum supplementary publication, info should be accurate, timely, accessible and highly readable." Estab. 1976. Circ. 100,000. Pays on publication. Publishes ms an average of 9 months after acceptance. Buys all rights.
Nonfiction: Health curriculum. Buys 100 mss/year. "We accept no queries or unsolicited mss. *Articles are on assignment only.* Send introductory letter, résumé and clips." Length: 800-2,000 words. Pays $100-400 for assigned articles.
Tips: "We are looking for good writers with an education and health background preferably, who can write for the age group in a firm, accessible, and medically/scientifically accurate way. Ideally, the writer should be an expert in the area in which he or she is writing. Topics open to freelancers are disease, drugs, fitness and exercise, psychology, safety, nutrition and personal health."

DISCOVERIES, 6401 The Paseo, Kansas City MO 64131. Fax: (816)333-4439. Editor: Latta Jo Knapp. Mostly freelance written. For boys and girls ages 8-9. Weekly. Estab. 1974. Publishes ms an average of 1 year after acceptance. Buys all rights. "Minimal comments on pre-printed form are made on rejected material." Reports in 3 months. Sample copy and guidelines for #10 SASE.
Fiction: Stories with Christian emphasis on high ideals, wholesome social relationships and activities, right choices, Sabbath observance, church loyalty and missions. *Discoveries* extends the Sunday School lesson with life-related stories of 3rd and 4th grade children. Informal style. Submit complete ms. Length: 500-700 words. Pays 5¢/word.

DOLPHIN LOG, The Cousteau Society, Suite 402, 870 Greenbrier Circle, Chesapeake VA 23320-2641. (804)523-9335. Editor: Elizabeth Foley. 30-40% freelance written. Prefers to work with published/established writers; works with a small number of new/unpublished writers each year. Bimonthly nonfiction magazine covering marine biology, ecology, natural history and the environment. "*Dolphin Log* is an educational publication for children ages 7-13 offered by The Cousteau Society. Subject matter encompasses all areas that can be related to our global water system. The philosophy of the magazine is to delight, instruct and instill an environmental ethic and understanding of the interconnectedness of living organisms, including people." Estab. 1981. Circ. 80,000. Pays on publication. Publishes ms an average of 1 year after acceptance. Byline given. Buys one-time, reprint and translation rights. Reports in 2 months. Sample copy for $2 and 9×12 SAE with 3 first-class stamps. Writer's guidelines for SASE. (Make checks payable to The Cousteau Society.)

Nonfiction: General interest (per guidelines); how-to (water-related crafts or science); photo feature (marine subject). "Of special interest are articles on specific marine creatures, and games involving an ocean/water-related theme which develop math, reading and comprehension skills. Experiments that can be conducted at home and demonstrate a phenomenon or principle of science are wanted as are clever crafts or art projects which also can be tied to an ocean theme. No 'talking' animals. First-person accounts are discouraged, as are fictional narratives and articles that address the reader." Buys 8-12 mss/year. Query or send complete ms. Length: 400-600 words. Pays $50-150.

Photos: Send photos with query or ms (duplicates only). Prefers underwater animals, water photos with children, photos that explain text. Pays $25-200/photo. Identification of subjects required. Buys one-time and translation rights.

Columns/Departments: Discovery (science experiments or crafts a young person can easily do at home), 50-250 words; Creature Feature (lively article on one specific marine animal), 200-300 words. Buys 1 mss/year. Send complete ms. Pays $25-100.

Poetry: No "talking" animals or dark or religious themes. Buys 1-2 poems/year. Pays $10-100.

Tips: "Find a lively way to relate scientific facts to children without anthropomorphizing. We need to know material is accurate and current. Articles should feature an interesting marine creature and contain factual material that's fun to read. We are always interested in material that draws information from current scientific research."

THE FRIEND, 50 E. North Temple, Salt Lake City UT 84150. Managing Editor: Vivian Paulsen. 50% freelance written. Eager to work with new/unpublished writers as well as established writers. Appeals to children ages 3-11. Monthly publication of The Church of Jesus Christ of Latter-Day Saints. Circ. 280,000. **Pays on acceptance.** Buys all rights. Submit seasonal material 8 months in advance. Sample copy and writer's guidelines for 75¢ and 9×12 SAE with 4 first-class stamps.

Nonfiction: Subjects of current interest, science, nature, pets, sports, foreign countries, things to make and do. Special issues: Christmas, Easter. "Submit only complete manuscript—no queries, please." No simultaneous submissions. Length: 1,000 words maximum. Pays 9¢/word minimum.

Fiction: Seasonal and holiday stories, stories about other countries and their children. Wholesome and optimistic; high motive, plot and action. Character-building stories preferred. Length: 1,200 words maximum. Stories for younger children should not exceed 250 words. Pays 9¢/word minimum.

Poetry: Serious, humorous, holiday. Any form with child appeal. Pays $25.

Tips: "Do you remember how it feels to be a child? Can you write stories that appeal to children ages 3-11 in today's world? We're interested in stories with an international flavor and those that focus on present-day problems. Send material of high literary quality slanted to our editorial requirements. Let the child solve the problem—not some helpful, all-wise adult. No overt moralizing. Nonfiction should be creatively presented—not an array of facts strung together. Beware of being cutesy."

HIGHLIGHTS FOR CHILDREN, 803 Church St., Honesdale PA 18431-1824. Fax: (717)253-0179. Editor: Kent L. Brown Jr. Manuscript Coordinator: Beth Troop. 80% freelance written. Monthly magazine for children ages 2-12. Estab. 1946. Circ. 2.8 million. **Pays on acceptance.** Buys all rights. Reports in about 2 months. Free sample copy. Writer's guidelines for #10 SASE.

● Ranked as one of the best markets for freelance writers in *Writer's Digest* magazine's annual "Top 100 Markets," January 1994 and as one of the best for fiction writers in its biannual "Fiction 50," June 1994.

Nonfiction: "We need articles on science, technology and nature written by persons with strong backgrounds in those fields. Contributions always welcomed from new writers, especially engineers, scientists, historians, teachers, etc., who can make useful, interesting facts accessible to children. Also writers who have lived abroad and can interpret the ways of life, especially of children, in other countries in ways that will foster world brotherhood. Sports material, biographies and articles of general interest to children. Direct, original approach, simple style, interesting content, not rewritten from encyclopedias. State background and qualifications for writing factual articles submitted. Include references or sources of information. Length: 900 words maximum. Pays $125 minimum. Also buys original party plans for children ages 7-12, clearly described in 300-600 words, including drawings or samples of items to be illustrated. Also, novel but tested ideas in crafts, with clear directions and made-up models. Projects must require only free or inexpensive, easy-to-obtain materials. Especially desirable if easy enough for early primary grades. Also, fingerplays with lots of action, easy for very young children to grasp and to dramatize. Avoid wordiness. We need creative-thinking puzzles that can be illustrated, optical illusions, brain teasers, games of physical agility and other 'fun' activities." Pays minimum $35 for party plans; $20 for crafts ideas; $25 for fingerplays.

Fiction: Unusual, meaningful stories appealing to both girls and boys, ages 2-12. "Vivid, full of action. Engaging plot, strong characterization, lively language." Prefers stories in which a child protagonist solves a dilemma through his or her own resources. Seeks stories that the child ages 8-12 will eagerly read, and the child ages 2-7 will begin to read and/or will like to hear when read aloud (400-900 words). "We publish stories in the suspense/adventure/mystery, fantasy and humor category, all requiring interesting plot and a number of illustration possiblities. Also need rebuses (picture stories 125 words or under), stories with urban settings, stories for beginning readers (100-400 words), sports and horse stories and retold folk tales. We also would like to see more material of 1-page length (300-500 words), both fiction and factual. War, crime and violence are taboo." Pays $120 minimum.

Tips: "We are pleased that many authors of children's literature report that their first published work was in the pages of *Highlights*. It is not our policy to consider fiction on the strength of the reputation of the author. We judge each submission on its own merits. With factual material, however, we do prefer that writers be authorities in their field or people with first-hand experience. In this manner we can avoid the encyclopedic article that merely restates information readily available elsewhere. We don't make assignments. Query with simple letter to establish whether the nonfiction *subject* is likely to be of interest. A beginning writer should first become familiar with the type of material that *Highlights* publishes. Include special qualifications, if any, of author. Write for the child, not the editor."

HOPSCOTCH, The Magazine for Girls, Bluffton News Publishing & Printing Co., P.O. Box 164, Bluffton OH 45817-0164. (419)358-4610. Fax: (419)358-5027. Editor: Marilyn B. Edwards. Editor's Assistant: Jeannie Badertscher. 90% freelance written. Bimonthly magazine on basic subjects of interest to young girls. "*HOPSCOTCH* is a digest-size magazine with a four-color cover and two-color format inside. It is designed for girls ages 6-12 and features pets, crafts, hobbies, games, science, fiction, history, puzzles, careers, etc." Estab. 1989. Pays on publication. Byline given. Buys first and second rights. Submit seasonal/holiday material 6-8 months in advance. Accepts simultaneous and previously published submissions. Send tearsheet or photocopy of article. For reprints pays 100% of the amount paid for original article. Reports in 3 weeks on queries; 2 months on mss. Sample copy for $3. Writer's guidelines, current theme list and needs for #10 SASE.

• Ranked as one of the best markets for fiction writers in *Writer's Digest* magazine's biannual "Fiction 50," June 1994.

Nonfiction: Book excerpts, general interest, historical/nostalgic, how-to (crafts), humor, inspirational, interview/profile, personal experience, pets, games, fiction, careers, sports, cooking. "No fashion, hairstyles, sex or dating articles." Buys 60 mss/year. Send complete ms. Length: 400-1,100 words. Pays $30-100.

Photos: Send photos with submission. Prefers b&w photos, but color photos accepted. Offers $7.50-10/photo. Captions, model releases and identification of subjects required. Buys one-time rights.

Columns/Departments: Science—nature, crafts, pets, cooking (basic), 400-1,000 words. Send complete ms. Pays $25-60.

Fiction: Adventure, fantasy, historical, humorous, mainstream, mystery, novel excerpts, suspense. Buys 15 mss/year. Send complete ms. Length: 600-1,000 words. Pays $30-70.

Poetry: Free verse, light verse, traditional. "No experimental or obscure poetry." Submit maximum 6 poems. Pays $10-30.

Tips: "Almost all sections are open to freelancers. Freelancers should remember that *HOPSCOTCH* is a bit old-fashioned, appealing to *young* girls (6-12). We cherish nonfiction pieces that have a young girl or young girls directly involved in unusual and/or worthwhile activities. Any piece accompanied by decent photos stands an even better chance of being accepted."

HUMPTY DUMPTY'S MAGAZINE, Children's Better Health Institute, P.O. Box 567, Indianapolis IN 46206-0567. Editor: Janet Hoover. 90% freelance written. "We try not to be overly influenced by an author's credits, preferring instead to judge each submission on its own merit." Bimonthly magazine (monthly March, June, September, December) covering health, nutrition, hygiene, exercise and safety for children ages 4-6. Pays on publication. Publishes ms at least 8 months after acceptance. Buys all rights (but will return one-time book rights if author has name of interested publisher and tentative date of publication). Submit seasonal material 8 months in advance. Reports in 3 months. Sample copy for $1.25. Writer's guidelines for #10 SASE.

Nonfiction: "We are open to nonfiction on almost any age-appropriate subject, but we especially need material with a health theme—nutrition, safety, exercise, hygiene. We're looking for articles that encourage readers to develop better health habits without preaching. Very simple factual articles that creatively teach readers about their bodies. We use simple crafts, some with holiday themes. We also use several puzzles and activities in each issue—dot-to-dot, hidden pictures and other activities that promote following instructions, developing finger dexterity and working with numbers and letters. Submit complete ms with word count and Social Security number. Length: 600 words maximum. Pays 10-20¢/word.

Fiction: "We use some stories in rhyme and a few easy-to-read stories for the beginning reader. All stories should work well as read alouds. Currently we need sports/fitness stories and seasonal stories with holiday themes. We use contemporary stories and fantasy, some employing a health theme. We try to present our health material in a positive light, incorporating humor and a light approach wherever possible. Avoid stereotyping. Characters in contemporary stories should be realistic and up-to-date. Remember, many of our readers have working mothers and/or come from single-parent homes. We need more stories that reflect these changing times but at the same time communicate good, wholesome values." Submit complete ms with word count and Social Security number. Length: 600 words maximum. Pays 10-20¢/word.

Poetry: Short, simple poems. Pays $15 minimum.

Tips: "Writing for *Humpty Dumpty* is similar to writing picture book manuscripts. There must be a great economy of words. We strive for at least 50% art per page (in stories and articles), so space for text is limited. Because the illustrations are so important, stories should lend themselves well to visual imagery."

JACK AND JILL, Children's Better Health Institute, P.O. Box 567, Indianapolis IN 46206-0567. (317)636-8881. Editor: Steve Charles. 70% freelance written. Magazine published 8 times/year for children ages 7-10. Pays on publication. Publishes ms an average of 8 months after acceptance. Buys all rights. Byline given. Submit seasonal material 8 months in advance. Reports in 10 weeks. May hold material being seriously considered for up to 1 year. "Material will not be returned unless accompanied by SASE with sufficient postage." Sample copy for $1.25. Writer's guidelines for #10 SASE.

Nonfiction: "Because we want to encourage youngsters to read for pleasure and for information, we are interested in material that will challenge a young child's intelligence *and* be enjoyable reading. Our emphasis is on good health, and we are in particular need of articles, stories, and activities with health, safety, exercise and nutrition themes. We try to present our health material in a positive light—incorporating humor and a light approach wherever possible without minimizing the seriousness of what we are saying." Straight factual articles are OK if they are short and interestingly written. "We would rather see, however, more creative alternatives to the straight factual article. For instance, we'd be interested in seeing a health message or facts presented in articles featuring positive role models for readers. Many of the personalities children admire—athletes, musicians, and film or TV stars—are fitness or nutrition buffs. Many have kicked drugs, alcohol or smoking habits and are outspoken about the dangers of these vices. Color slides, transparencies or b&w photos accompanying this type of article would greatly enhance salability." Buys 10-15 nonfiction mss/year. Length: 500-800 words. Pays a minimum of 10¢/word.

Photos: When appropriate, photos should accompany ms. Reviews sharp, contrasting b&w glossy prints. Sometimes uses color slides, transparencies or good color prints. Pays $20 for b&w, $35 for color, minimum of $50 for cover. Buys one-time rights.

Fiction: May include, but is not limited to, realistic stories, fantasy adventure—set in past, present or future. "All stories need a well-developed plot, action and incident. Humor is highly desirable. Stories that deal with a health theme need not have health as the primary subject." Length: 500-800 words (short stories). Pays 10¢/word minimum. Buys 20-25 mss/year.

Fillers: Puzzles (including various kinds of word and crossword puzzles), poems, games, science projects, and creative craft projects. Instructions for activities should be clearly and simply written and accompanied by models or diagram sketches. "We also have a need for recipes. Ingredients should be healthful; avoid sugar, salt, chocolate, red meat and fats as much as possible. In all material, avoid references to eating sugary foods, such as candy, cakes, cookies and soft drinks."

Tips: "We are constantly looking for new writers who can tell good stories with interesting slants—stories that are not full of out-dated and time-worn expressions. Our best authors are writers who know what today's children are like. Keep in mind that our readers are becoming 'computer literate', living in an age of rapidly developing technology. They are exploring career possibilities that may be new and unfamiliar to our generation. They are faced with tough decisions about drug and alcohol use. Many of them are latch-key children because both parents work or they come from single-parent homes. We need more stories and articles that reflect these changing times but that also communicate good, wholesome values. Obtain *current* issues of the magazines and *study* them to determine our present needs and editorial style."

‡JUNIOR TRAILS, Gospel Publishing House, 1445 Boonville Ave., Springfield MO 65802-1894. (417)862-2781. Editor: Sinda S. Zinn. 100% freelance written. Eager to work with new/unpublished writers. Weekly tabloid covering religious fiction; and biographical, historical and scientific articles with a spiritual emphasis for boys and girls ages 10-11. Circ. 65,000. **Pays on acceptance.** Publishes ms an average of 9-12 months after acceptance. Byline given. Not copyrighted. Buys simultaneous rights, first rights, or second (reprint) rights. Submit seasonal/holiday material 15 months in advance. Provide word count. Accepts simultaneous and previously published submissions. Send typed ms with rights for sale noted and information about where and when the piece previously appeared. For reprints pays 66% of amount paid for original article. Reports in 1 month on mss. Sample copy and writer's guidelines for 9×12 SAE with 2 first-class stamps.

Nonfiction: Biographical, historical, scientific (with spiritual lesson or emphasis). "Junior-age children need to be alerted to the dangers of drugs, alcohol, smoking, etc. They need positive guidelines and believable examples relating to living a Christian life in an ever-changing world." Buys 20-30 mss/year. Send complete ms. Length: 500-800 words. Pays 2-3¢/word.

Fiction: Adventure (with spiritual lesson or application); religious. "We're looking for fiction that presents believable characters working out their problems according to Biblical principles. No fictionalized accounts of Bible stories or events." Buys 60-80 mss/year. Send complete ms. Length: 1,000-1,500 words. Pays 2-3¢/word.

Poetry: Free verse, light verse. Buys 30-40 mss/year. Pays 20¢/line.

Fillers: Anecdotes (with spiritual emphasis). Buys 15-20/year. Length: 200 words maximum. Pays 2-3¢/word.

Tips: "We like to receive stories showing contemporary children positively facing today's world. These stories show children who are aware of their world and who find a moral solution to their problems through the guidance of God's Word. They are not 'super children' in themselves. They are average children learning how to face life through God's help. We tend to get settings in stories that are out of step with today's society. We will tend to turn more and more to purely contemporary settings unless we are using a historical or biographical story. We will have the setting, characters and plot agree with each other in order to make it more believable to our audience."

LADYBUG, the Magazine for Young Children, Carus Publishing Co., P.O. Box 300, Peru IL 61354-0300. (815)224-6643. Editor-in-Chief: Marianne Carus. Associate Editor: Paula Morrow. Monthly general interest magazine for children (ages 2-6). "We look for quality writing—quality literature, no matter the subject." Estab. 1973. Circ. 130,000. Pays on publication. Byline given. All accepted mss are published. Buys first publication rights in the English language. Submit seasonal/holiday material 1 year in advance. Accepts simultaneous submissions. Do not query; send completed ms. Reports in 3 months. Sample copy and guidelines for $4 and 9×12 SAE. Guidelines only for #10 SASE.

   • *Ladybug* is now publishing a parents' insert in the magazine and is accepting material for that section. Study issues since October 1993 before submitting. Do not query; send complete ms.

Columns/Departments: Can You Do This?, 2-3 pages; The World Around You, 2-3 pages. Buys 35 mss/year. Send complete ms. "Most *Ladybug* nonfiction is in the form of illustration. We'd like more simple science, how-things-work and behind-the-scenes on a preschool level. Maximum length 250-300 words."

Fiction: Adventure, ethnic, fantasy, folkore, humorous, mainstream, mystery. Buys 30 mss/year. Send complete ms. Length: 850 maximum words. Pays up to 25¢/word.

Poetry: Light verse, traditional, humorous. Buys 20 poems/year. Submit *maximum* 5 poems. Length: 20 lines maximum. Pays up to $3/line.

Fillers: Anecdotes, facts, short humor. Buys 10/year. Length: 250 (approximately) maximum words. Pays up to 25¢/word. We welcome interactive activities: rebuses, up to 100 words; *original* fingerplays and action rhymes (up to 8 lines).

Tips: "Reread a manuscript *before* sending it in. Be sure to keep within specified word limits. Study back issues before submitting to learn about the types of material we're looking for. Writing style is paramount. We look for rich, evocative language and a sense of joy or wonder. Remember that you're writing for pre-schoolers—be age-appropriate but not condescending. A story must hold enjoyment for both parent and child through repeated read-aloud sessions. Remember that we live in a multicultural world. People come in all colors, sizes, physical conditions and have special needs. Be inclusive!"

NOAH'S ARK, A Newspaper for Jewish Children, 8323 Southwest Freeway #250, Houston TX 77074. (713)771-7144. Editors: Debbie Israel Dubin, Linda Freedman Block. Monthly tabloid that "captures readers' interest and reinforces learning about Jewish history, holidays, laws and culture through articles, stories, recipes, games, crafts, projects, Hebrew column and more." For Jewish children, ages 6-12. Circ. 450,000. **Pays on acceptance.** Byline given. Buys first North American serial rights. Submit seasonal/holiday material 4 months in advance. Accepts simultaneous submissions. Reports in 6 weeks on queries; 2 months on mss. Sample copy and writer's guidelines for #10 SASE.

Nonfiction: Historical/nostalgic, craft projects, recipes, humor, interview/profile. Send complete ms. Length: 350 words maximum. Usually pays 5¢/word.

Photos: State availability of or send photos with submission. Offers no additional payment for photos accepted with ms. Identification of subjects required. Buys one-time rights.

Fiction: All must be of Jewish interest: historical, humorous, religious (Jewish), slice-of-life vignettes. Any and all suitable for Jewish children. Buys 2-3 mss/year. Send complete ms. Length: 600 words maximum. Pays 5¢/word.

Poetry: Light verse, traditional. Buys 1 poem/year. Submit maximum 1 poem. Payment varies.

Fillers: All must be of Jewish interest: anecdotes, facts, gags, short humor, games. Buys 3-5/year. Payment varies.

Tips: "We're just looking for high quality material suitable for entertainment as well as supplemental religious school use." Encourages freelancers to take an "unusual approach to writing about holidays. All submissions must have Jewish content and positive Jewish values. Content should not be exclusively for an American audience."

ON THE LINE, Mennonite Publishing House, 616 Walnut Ave., Scottdale PA 15683-1999. (412)887-8500. Fax: (412)887-3111. Editor: Mary Clemens Meyer. 90% freelance written. Works with a small number of new/unpublished writers each year. Weekly magazine for children ages 10-14. Estab. 1908. Circ. 8,500. **Pays on acceptance.** Publishes ms an average of 1 year after acceptance. Byline given. Buys one-time rights. Submit seasonal/holiday material 6 months in advance. Accepts simultaneous and previously published submissions. Reports in 1 month. Sample copy for 9×12 SAE with 2 first-class stamps.

Nonfiction: How-to (things to make with easy-to-get materials); informational (350-500 word articles on wonders of nature, people who have made outstanding contributions). Buys 95 unsolicited mss/year. Send complete ms. Length: 500-900 words. Pays $10-30.

Photos: Photos purchased with or without ms. Pays $10-40 for 8 × 10 b&w photos. Total purchase price for ms includes payment for photos.

Fiction: Adventure, humorous, religious. Buys 52 mss/year. Send complete ms. Length: 1,000-1,500 words. Pays 2-4¢/word.

Poetry: Light verse, religious. Length: 3-12 lines. Pays $5-15.

Tips: "Study the publication first. We need short well-written how-to and craft articles. Don't send query; we prefer to see the complete manuscript."

OWL MAGAZINE, The Discovery Magazine for Children, Owl Communications, Suite 500, 179 John St., Toronto, Ontario M5T 3G5 Canada. (416)971-5275. Editor: Debora Pearson. 25% freelance written. Works with small number of new writers each year. Magazine published 10 times/year (no July or August issues) covering science and nature. Aims to interest children in their environment through accurate, factual information about the world presented in an easy, lively style. Estab. 1976. Circ. 160,000. **Pays on acceptance.** Publishes ms an average of 3 months after acceptance. Byline given. Buys all rights. Submit seasonal/holiday material 1 year in advance. Reports in 10 weeks. Sample copy for $4.28. Writer's guidelines for SAE (large envelope if requesting sample copy) and money order for $1 postage (no stamps please).

Nonfiction: Personal experience (real life children in real situations); photo feature (natural science, international wildlife, and outdoor features); science and environmental features. No problem stories with drugs, sex or moralistic views, or talking animal stories. Query with clips of published work.

Photos: State availability of photos. Reviews 35mm transparencies. Identification of subjects required. Send for photo package before submitting material.

Tips: "Write for editorial guidelines first. Review back issues of the magazine for content and style. Know your topic and approach it from an unusual perspective. Our magazine never talks down to children."

POCKETS, The Upper Room, P.O. Box 189, Nashville TN 37202-0189. (615)340-7333. Fax: (615)340-7006. Editor: Janet R. McNish. Associate Editor: Lynn Gilliam. 50% freelance written. Eager to work with new/unpublished writers. Monthly magazine (except January/February issues) covering children's and families spiritual formation. "We are a Christian, non-denominational publication for children 6 to 12 years of age." Estab. 1981. Circ. 70,000. **Pays on acceptance.** Byline given. Offers 4¢/word kill fee. Buys first North American serial rights. Submit seasonal/holiday material 1 year in advance. Accepts previously published material. Send typed ms with rights for sale noted. For reprints pays 100% of amount paid for original article. Reports in 10 weeks on mss. Sample copy for 7½ × 10½ SAE with 4 first-class stamps. Writer's guidelines and themes for #10 SASE.

Nonfiction: Interview/profile, religious (retold scripture stories), personal experience. List of themes for special issues available with SASE. No violence or romance. Buys 5 mss/year. Send complete ms. Length: 600-1,500 words. Pays 12¢/word.

Photos: Send photos with submission. Prefer no photos unless they accompany an article. Reviews contact sheets, transparencies and prints. Offers $25-50/photo. Buys one-time rights.

Columns Departments: Refrigerator Door (poetry and prayer related to themes), 25 lines; Pocketsful of Love (family communications activities), 300 words; Activities/Games ($25 and up); Peacemakers at Work (profiles of people, particularly children, working for peace, justice and ecological concerns), 300-800 words. Buys 20 mss/year. Send complete ms. Pays 12¢/word; recipes $25.

Fiction: Adventure, ethnic, slice-of-life. "Stories should reflect the child's everyday experiences through a Christian approach. This is often more acceptable when stories are not preachy or overtly Christian." Buys 22 mss/year. Send complete ms. Length: 750-1,600 words. Pays 12¢/word and up.

Poetry: Buys 8 poems/year. Length: 4-25 lines. Pays $25-50.

Tips: "Theme stories, role models and retold scripture stories are most open to freelancers. We are also looking for nonfiction stories about children involved in peace/justic/ecology efforts. Poetry is also open, but we rarely receive an acceptable poem. It's very helpful if writers send for our themes. These are *not* the same as writer's guidelines."

POWER AND LIGHT, 6401 The Paseo, Kansas City MO 64131. Fax: (816)333-4439. Editor: Beula Postlewait. Mostly freelance written. Weekly magazine for boys and girls ages 11-12 using WordAction Sunday School curriculum. Estab. 1992. Publishes ms an average of 1 year after acceptance. Buys multiple use rights. "Minimal comments on pre-printed form are made on rejected material." Accepts previously published material. Send typed ms with rights for sale noted and information about when and where article previously appeared. For reprints pays 3½¢/word. Reports in 3 months. Sample copy and guidelines for SASE.

Fiction: Stories with Christian emphasis on high ideals, wholesome social relationships and activities, right choices, Sabbath observance and church loyalty. Informal style. Submit complete ms. Length: 500-700 words. Pays 5¢/word.

Tips: "All themes and outcomes should conform to the theology and practices of the Church of the Nazarene."

R-A-D-A-R, 8121 Hamilton Ave., Cincinnati OH 45231. (513)931-4050. Editor: Margaret Williams. 75% freelance written. Prefers to work with published/established writers; works with a small number of new/ unpublished writers each year. Weekly for children in grades 3-6 in Christian Sunday schools. Estab. 1866 (publishing house). Rights purchased varies with author and material; prefers buying first serial rights, but will buy second (reprint) rights. Occasionally overstocked. **Pays on acceptance.** Publishes ms an average of 6-12 months after acceptance. Submit seasonal material 1 year in advance. Reports in 2 months. Free sample copy. Writer's guidelines for #10 SASE.
Nonfiction: Articles on hobbies and handicrafts, nature, famous people, seasonal subjects, etc., written from a Christian viewpoint. No articles about historical figures with an absence of religious implication. Length: 500-1,000 words. Pays 3-7¢/word maximum.
Fiction: Short stories of heroism, adventure, travel, mystery, animals, biography. "True or possible plots stressing clean, wholesome, Christian character-building ideas, but not preachy. Make prayer, church attendance and Christian living a natural part of the story. We correlate our fiction and other features with a definite Bible lesson. Writers who want to meet our needs should send for a theme list." No talking animal stories, science fiction, Halloween stories or first-person stories from an adult's viewpoint. Length: up to 1,000 words. Pays 3-7¢/word maximum.

RANGER RICK, National Wildlife Federation, 1400 16th St. NW, Washington DC 20036. (703)790-4274. Editor: Gerald Bishop. 40% freelance written. Works with a small number of new/unpublished writers each year. Monthly magazine for children from ages 6-12, with the greatest concentration in the 7-10 age bracket. Buys all world rights unless other arrangements made. Byline given "but occasionally, for very brief pieces, we will identify author by name at the end. Contributions to regular columns usually are not bylined." Estab. 1967. **Pays on acceptance.** Publishes ms an average of 18 months after acceptance. Reports in 6 weeks. "Anything written with a specific month in mind should be in our hands at least 10 months before that issue date." Writer's guidelines for #10 SASE.
Nonfiction: "Articles may be written on anything related to nature, conservation, the outdoors, environmental problems or natural science. Please avoid articles about animal rehabilitation, unless the species are endangered." Buys 25-35 unsolicited mss/year. Query. Pays from $50-575, depending on length, quality and content (maximum length, 900 words). Unless you are an expert in the field or are writing from direct personal experience, all factual information must be footnoted and backed up with current, reliable references.
Fiction: "Same categories as nonfiction plus fantasy and science fiction. The attributing of human qualities to animals is limited to our regular feature, 'The Adventures of Ranger Rick,' so please do not humanize wildlife. We discourage keeping wildlife as pets."
Photos: "Photographs, when used, are paid for separately. It is not necessary that illustrations accompany material."
Tips: "In your query letter, include details of what manuscript will cover; sample lead; evidence that you can write playfully and with great enthusiasm, conviction and excitement (formal, serious, dull queries indicate otherwise). Think of an exciting subject we haven't done recently, sell it effectively with query, and produce a manuscript of highest quality. Read past issues to learn successful styles and unique approaches to subjects.

SHOFAR MAGAZINE, 43 Northcote Dr., Melville NY 11747-3924. (516)643-4598. Fax: (516)643-4598. Managing Editor: Gerald H. Grayson. 80-90% freelance written. Monthly children's magazine on Jewish subjects. Estab. 1984. Circ. 17,000. Pays on publication. Byline given. Buys one-time rights. Submit seasonal/holiday material 6 months in advance. Accepts simultaneous submissions. Reports in 2 months. Sample copy and writer's guidelines for 9×12 SAE with 4 first-class stamps.
Nonfiction: Dr. Gerald H. Grayson, publisher. Historical/nostalgic, humor, inspirational, interview/profile, personal experience, photo feature, religious, travel. Buys 15 mss/year. Send complete ms. Length: 750-1,000 words. Pays 7-10¢/word. Sometimes pays the expenses of writers on assignment.
Photos: State availability of or send photos with submission. Offers $10-50/photo. Identification of subjects required. Buys one-time rights.
Fiction: Adventure, historical, humorous, religious. Buys 15 mss/year. Send complete ms. Length: 750-1,000 words. Pays 7-10¢/word.
Poetry: Free verse, light verse, traditional. Buys 4-5 poems/year. Length: 8-50 words. Pays 7-10¢/word.
Tips: "Submissions must be on a Jewish theme and should be geared to readers who are 8 to 12 years old."

SPORTS ILLUSTRATED FOR KIDS, Time-Warner, Time & Life Building, New York NY 10020. (212)522-5437. Fax: (212)522-0120. Managing Editor: Craig Neff. 50% freelance written. Monthly magazine on sports for children 8 years old and up. Content is divided 50/50 between sports as played by kids, and sports as played by professionals. Estab. 1989. **Pays on acceptance.** Publishes ms an average of 3 months after acceptance. Byline given. Offers 25% kill fee. Buys all rights. Sample copy for $1.95. Writer's guidelines for SAE.
  ● Ranked as one of the best markets for freelance writers in *Writer's Digest* magazine's annual "Top 100 Markets," January 1994.
Nonfiction: Patricia Berry, articles editor. Games, general interest, how-to, humor, inspirational, interview/profile, photo feature, puzzles. Buys 15 mss/year. Query with published clips. Length: 100-1,500 words. Pays

$75-1,000 for assigned articles; $75-800 for unsolicited articles. Pays expenses of writers on assignment.
Photos: State availability of photos with submission. Buys one-time rights.
Columns/Departments: The Worst Day I Ever Had (tells about day in pro athlete's life when all seemed hopeless), 500-600 words; Hotshots (young [8-13] athlete getting good things out of sports), 100-250 words; Quick Kicks (short, fresh news about kids doing awaiting things, on and off the field), 100-250 words. Buys 10-15 mss/year. Query with published clips. Pays $75-600.

STONE SOUP, The Magazine by Children, Children's Art Foundation, P.O. Box 83, Santa Cruz CA 95063-0083. (408)426-5557. Fax: (408)426-1161. Editor: Ms. Gerry Mandel. 100% freelance written. Bimonthly magazine of writing and art by children, including fiction, poetry, book reviews, and art by children through age 13. Estab. 1973. Audience is children, teachers, parents, writers, artists. "We have a preference for writing and art based on real-life experiences; no formula stories or poems." Pays on publication. Publishes ms an average of 3 months after acceptance. Buys all rights. Submit seasonal/holiday material 6 months in advance. Reports in 1 month. Sample copy for $4. Writer's guidelines with SASE.
Nonfiction: Book reviews. Buys 10 mss/year. Query. Pays $15 for assigned articles.
Fiction: Adventure, ethnic, experimental, fantasy, historical, humorous, mystery, science fiction, slice-of-life vignettes, suspense. "We do not like assignments or formula stories of any kind." Accepts 55 mss/year. Send complete ms. Pays $10 for stories. Authors also receive 2 copies and discounts on additional copies and on subscriptions.
Poetry: Avant-garde, free verse. Accepts 20 poems/year. Pays $10/poem. (Same discounts apply.)
Tips: "We can't emphasize enough how important it is to read a couple of issues of the magazine. We have a strong preference for writing on subjects that mean a lot to the author. If you feel strongly about something that happened to you or something you observed, use that feeling as the basis for your story or poem. Stories should have good descriptions, realistic dialogue and a point to make. In a poem, each word must be chosen carefully. Your poem should present a view of your subject and a way of using words that are special and all your own."

STORY FRIENDS, Mennonite Publishing House, 616 Walnut Ave., Scottdale PA 15683-1999. (412)887-8500. Fax: (412)887-3111. Editor: Marjorie Waybill. 80% freelance written. Monthly story paper in weekly parts for children ages 4-9. "*Story Friends* is planned to provide wholesome Christian reading for the 4- to 9-year-old. Practical life stories are included to teach moral values and remind the children that God is at work today. Activities introduce children to the Bible and its message for them." Estab. 1905. Circ. 9,000. **Pays on acceptance.** Publishes ms an average of 1 year after acceptance. Byline given. Publication not copyrighted. Buys one-time and second serial (reprint) rights. Submit seasonal/holiday material 6 months in advance. Accepts simultaneous and previously published submissions. Send typed ms with rights for sale noted. Reports in 1 month. Sample copy for 9×12 SAE with 2 first-class stamps. Writer's guidelines for #10 SASE.
Nonfiction: How-to (craft ideas for young children), photo feature. Buys 20 mss/year. Send complete ms. Length: 300-500 words. Pays 3-5¢/word.
Photos: Send photos with submission. Reviews 8½×11 b&w prints. Offers $20-25/photo. Model releases required. Buys one-time rights.
Fiction: See writer's guidelines for *Story Friends.* Buys 50 mss/year. Send complete ms. Length: 300-800 words. Pays 3-5¢/word.
Poetry: Traditional. Buys 20 poems/year. Length: 4-16 lines. Pays $5-10/poem.
Tips: "Send stories that children from a variety of ethnic backgrounds can relate to; stories that deal with experiences similar to all children. For example, all children have fears but their fears may vary depending on where they live."

3-2-1 CONTACT, Children's Television Workshop, 1 Lincoln Plaza, New York NY 10023. (212)595-3456. Fax: (212)875-6105. Editor-in-Chief: Jonathan Rosenbloom. Editor: Curtis Slepian. 40% freelance written. Magazine published 10 times/year covering science and technology for children ages 8-14. Estab. 1979. Circ. 400,000. **Pays on acceptance.** Publishes ms an average of 6 months after acceptance. Buys all rights "with some exceptions." Submit seasonal material 8 months in advance. Accepts simultaneous and previously published submissions if so indicated. Reports in 1 month. Sample copy for $1.75 and 9×12 SAE with 2 first-class stamps. Writer's guidelines for #10 SASE.
Nonfiction: General interest (space exploration, the human body, animals, computers and the new technology, current science issues); profile (of interesting scientists or children involved in science or with computers); photo feature (centered around a science theme); role models of women and minority scientists. No articles on travel not related to science. Buys 5 unsolicited mss/year. Query with published clips. Length: 700-1,000 words. Pays $150-500. Sometimes pays expenses of writers on assignment.
Photos: Do *not* send photos on spec.
Tips: "I prefer a short query, without ms, that makes it clear that an article is interesting. When sending an article, include your telephone number. Don't call us, we'll call you. Many submissions we receive are more like college research papers than feature stories. We like articles in which writers have interviewed kids or scientists, or discovered exciting events with a scientific angle. Library research is necessary; but if that's all

you're doing, you aren't giving us anything we can't get ourselves. If your story needs a bibliography, chances are, it's not right for us."

TOUCH, P.O. Box 7259, Grand Rapids MI 49510. Editor: Joanne Ilbrink. 80% freelance written. Prefers to work with published/established writers. Monthly magazine "to show girls ages 7-14 how God is at work in their lives and in the world around them. The May/June issue annually features material written by our readers." Estab. 1972. Circ. 15,500. **Pays on acceptance.** Publishes ms an average of 1 year after acceptance. Byline given. Buys second serial (reprint) and first North American serial rights. Submit seasonal/holiday material 9 months in advance. Accepts simultaneous and previously published submissions. Reports in 2 months. Sample copy and writer's guidelines for 9 × 12 SAE with 3 first-class stamps.

Nonfiction: How-to (crafts girls can make easily and inexpensively); informational (write for issue themes); humor (need much more); inspirational (seasonal and holiday); interview; multicultural materials; travel; personal experience (avoid the testimony approach); photo feature (query first). "Because our magazine is published around a monthly theme, requesting the letter we send out twice a year to our established freelancers would be most helpful. We do not want easy solutions or quick character changes from bad to good. No pietistic characters. Constant mention of God is not necessary if the moral tone of the story is positive. We do not want stories that always have a good ending." Buys 36-45 unsolicited mss/year. Submit complete ms. Length: 100-1,000 words. Pays 2½-5¢/word, depending on the amount of editing.

Photos: Purchased with or without ms. Reviews 5 × 7 or 8 × 10 clear b&w glossy prints. Appreciate multicultural subjects. Pays $20-50 on publication.

Fiction: Adventure (that girls could experience in their hometowns or places they might realistically visit); humorous; mystery (believable only); romance (stories that deal with awakening awareness of boys are appreciated); suspense (can be serialized); religious (nothing preachy). Buys 30 mss/year. Submit complete ms. Length: 300-1,000 words. Pays 2½-5¢/word.

Poetry: Free verse, haiku, light verse, traditional. Buys 10/year. Length: 30 lines maximum. Pays $5-15 minimum.

Fillers: Puzzles, short humor, cartoons. Buys 3/issue. Pays $7-15.

Tips: "Prefers not to see anything on the adult level, secular material or violence. Writers frequently oversimplify the articles and often write with a Pollyanna attitude. An author should be able to see his/her writing style as exciting and appealing to girls ages 7-14. The style can be fun, but also teach a truth. The subject should be current and important to *Touch* readers. We would like to receive material that features a multicultural slant."

TURTLE MAGAZINE FOR PRESCHOOL KIDS, Children's Better Health Institute, P.O. Box 567, Indianapolis IN 46206-0567. (317)636-8881. Editor: Elizabeth A. Rinck. 90% freelance written. Bimonthly magazine (monthly March, June, September, December). General interest, interactive magazine with the purpose of helping preschoolers develop healthy minds and healthy bodies. Pays on publication. May hold mss for up to 1 year before acceptance/publication. Byline given. Buys all rights. Submit seasonal/holiday material 8 months in advance. Reports in 10 weeks. Sample copy for $1.25. Writer's guidelines for #10 SASE.

Nonfiction: "Uses very simple science experiments. Would like to see some short, simple nature articles — especially interested in subjects of gardening and environmental awareness."

Fiction: Fantasy, humorous, realistic stories. All should have single-focus story lines and work well as read-alouds. "Most of the stories we use will have a character-building bent, but they should not be preachy or overly moralistic. We are in constant need of stories that will help a preschooler grow to a greater appreciation of his/her body and what it can do; stories that encourage active, vigorous play; stories that teach fundamental lessons about good health without being too heavy-handed. We're no longer buying many stories about 'generic' turtles, as we now have PokeyToes, our own turtle character. All stories should 'move along' and lend themselves well to illustration. Writing should be energetic, enthusiastic and creative — like preschoolers themselves."

Poetry: We're especially looking for action rhymes to foster creative movement in preschoolers. We also use original finger plays, stories in rhyme and short verse.

Tips: "We are trying to include more material for our youngest readers. We'd like to see some well-executed ideas for teaching basic concepts to 2- and 3-year-olds. We're open to counting and alphabet stories, but they must be handled in a new, fresh way. All material must first be entertaining; otherwise all efforts to teach will be wasted."

Market conditions are constantly changing! If this is 1996 or later, buy the newest edition of Writer's Market *at your favorite bookstore or order directly from* Writer's Digest Books.

VENTURE, Christian Service Brigade, P.O. Box 150, Wheaton IL 60189-0150. (708)665-0630. Fax: (708)665-0372. Editor: Deborah Christensen. 30% freelance written. Works with a small number of new/unpublished writers each year. Bimonthly company publication "published to support and compliment CSB's Stockade and Battalion programs. We aim to provide wholesome, entertaining reading for boys ages 10-15." Estab. 1959. Circ. 19,000. Pays on publication. Publishes ms an average of 6 months after acceptance, sometimes longer. Byline given. Offers $35 kill fee. Buys first North American serial, one-time and second serial (reprint) rights. Submit seasonal/holiday material 6 months in advance. Accepts previously published submissions. Send typed ms with rights for sale noted. For reprints pays 75% of amount paid for original article. Reports in 1 week. Sample copy for $1.85 and 9 × 12 SAE with 4 first-class stamps. Writer's guidelines for #10 SASE.
  • *Venture* is using more reprints.
Nonfiction: General interest, humor, inspirational, interview/profile, personal experience, photo feature, religious. Buys 18-20 mss/year. Send complete ms. Length: 500-1,000 words. Pays $75-150 for assigned articles; $40-100 for unsolicited articles. Sometimes pays expenses of writers on assignment.
Photos: Send photos with submission. Reviews contact sheets and 5 × 7 prints. Offers $35-125/photo. Buys one-time rights.
Fiction: Adventure, humorous, mystery, religious. Buys 10-12 mss/year. Send complete ms. Length: 1,000 words. Pays $40-100.
Tips: "Talk to young boys. Find out the things that interest them and write about those things. We are looking for material relating to our theme: Building Men to Serve Christ. We prefer shorter (1,000 words) pieces. Writers *must* weave Christianity throughout the story in a natural way, without preaching or token prayers. How does a boy's faith in Christ influence the way he responds to a situation."

WONDER TIME, 6401 The Paseo, Kansas City MO 64131. (816)333-7000. Fax: (816)333-4439. Editor: Lois Perrigo. Editorial Assistant: Teresa Gillihan. 75% freelance written. "Willing to read and consider appropriate freelance submissions." Published weekly by WordAction for children ages 6-8. Estab. early 1900s. Pays on publication. Publishes ms an average of 1 year after acceptance. Byline given. Buys rights to reuse and all rights for curriculum assignments. Reports in 1 month. Sample copy and writer's guidelines for 9 × 12 SAE with 2 first-class stamps.
Fiction: Buys stories portraying Christian attitudes without being preachy. Uses stories for special days— stories teaching honesty, truthfulness, kindness, helpfulness or other important spiritual truths, and avoiding symbolism. Also, stories about real life problems children face today. "God should be spoken of as our Father who loves and cares for us; Jesus, as our Lord and Savior." Buys 52/mss year. Length: 250-350 words. Pays $25 on publication.
Poetry: Uses verse which has seasonal or Christian emphasis. Length: 4-8 lines. Pays 25¢/line, minimum $3.
Tips: "Any stories that allude to church doctrine must be in keeping with Wesleyan beliefs. Any type of fantasy must be in good taste and easily recognizable."

Men's

Many, though not all, magazines in this section typically focus on pictorial layouts accompanied by stories and articles of a sexual nature. Most also offer non-sexual features on topics of interest to men. Magazines that also use material slanted toward men can be found in Business and Finance, Child Care and Parental Guidance, General Interest, Relationships, Military and Sports sections.

CHIC MAGAZINE, HG Publications, Suite 300, 9171 Wilshire Blvd., Beverly Hills CA 90210-5530. Executive Editor: Doug Oliver. 40% freelance written. Monthly magazine for men, ages 20-35 years, college-educated and interested in current affairs, entertainment and sex. Estab. 1976. Circ. 50,000. Pays 1 month after acceptance. Publishes ms an average of 3 months after acceptance. Buys all rights. Offers 20% kill fee. Byline given unless writer requests otherwise. Reports in 2 months. Writer's guidelines for #10 SASE.
Nonfiction: Sex-related topics of current national interest, interview (off-beat personalities in news and entertainment), celebrity profiles. Buys 12-18 mss/year. Query. Length: 3,000 words. Pays $750. Sometimes pays the expenses of writers on assignment.
Columns/Departments: Third Degree (short Q&As with unusual people), 2,000 words. Pays $350. My Confession (first-person sexual experiences), 1,000 words. Pays $25.
Fiction: Length: 3,000 words. Pays $500. "We buy stories with emphasis on erotic themes. These may be adventure, action, mystery, horror or humorous stories, but the tone and theme must involve sex and eroticism. The erotic nature of the story should not be subordinate to the characterizations and plot; the main graphically depicted sex slant should be 1½ pages in length, and must grow logically from the people and the plot, not be contrived or forced."
Tips: "We do not buy poetry or non-erotic science fiction. Refrain from stories with drug themes, sex with minors, male sexuality, incest and bestiality."

ESQUIRE, 250 W. 55th St., New York NY 10019. (212)649-4020. Editor-in-Chief: Edward Kosner. 99% freelance written. Monthly. Estab. 1933. **Pays on acceptance.** Publishes ms an average of 6 months after acceptance. Usually buys first serial rights. Reports in up to 2 months. "We depend chiefly on solicited contributions and material from literary agencies. We are unable to accept responsibility for unsolicited material." Query.

Nonfiction: Articles vary in length, but features usually average 2,000-5,000 words. Articles should be slanted for sophisticated, intelligent readers; however, not highbrow in the restrictive sense. Wide range of subject matter. Rates vary depending on length, quality, etc. Query. Sometimes pays expenses of writers on assignment.

Photos: Marianne Butler, photo editor. Payment depends on how photo is used. Guarantee on acceptance. Buys first periodical publication rights.

Fiction: L. Rust Hills, fiction editor. "Literary excellence is our only criterion." Discourages genre fiction (horror, science fiction, murder mystery, etc.), and does not use poetry. Length: about 1,000-6,000 words.

Tips: "The writer sometimes has a better chance of breaking in at *Esquire* with short, lesser-paying articles (rather than with major features) because we need more short pieces."

FLING INTERNATIONAL, Relim Publishing Co., Inc., 550 Miller Ave., Mill Valley CA 94941. (415)383-5464. Editor: Arv Miller. Managing Editor: Ted Albert. 30% freelance written. Prefers to work with published/ established writers. Quarterly men's sophisticate magazine. Young male audience of adults ages 18-34. Estab. 1957. Circ. 100,000. Pays before publication. Publishes ms an average of 6 months after acceptance. Buys first North American serial and second serial (reprint) rights or makes work-for-hire assignments. Submit seasonal material 8 months in advance. Does not consider multiple submissions. Reports in 3 weeks on queries; 1 month on mss. Sample copy for $5. Writer's guidelines for SASE.

Nonfiction: Exposé, how-to (better relationships with women, better lovers), interview/profile, sports, finance, taboo sex articles. Buys 15 mss/year. Query. Length: 1,500-3,000 words. Pays $150-350. Sometimes pays expenses of writers on assignment.

Photos: Send photos with query. Reviews 35mm color transparencies. Pays $10-25 for b&w; $20-35 for color. Model releases required. Buys one-time rights.

Columns/Departments: Buys 12 mss/year. Query or send complete ms. Length: 100-200 words. Pays $35-150.

Fiction: Sexually oriented, strong male-female relationship. Lots of written detail about female's abundant chest-size a must. No science fiction, western, plotless, private-eye, "dated" or adventure. Buys 6 mss/year. Send complete ms. Length: 2,000-3,000 words. Pays $135-200.

• No longer accepting fillers.

Tips: "Nonfiction and fiction are wide open areas to freelancers. Always query with one-page letter to the editor before proceeding with any writing. Also send a sample photocopy of published material, similar to suggestion."

GALLERY MAGAZINE, Montcalm Publishing Corp., 401 Park Ave. S., New York NY 10016-8802. (212)779-8900. Fax: (212)725-7215. Editorial Director: Barry Janoff. Managing Editor: Rich Friedman. 50% freelance written. Prefers to work with published/established writers. Monthly magazine "focusing on features of interest to the young American man." Estab. 1972. Circ. 500,000. Pays 50% on acceptance, 50% on publication. Byline given. Pays 25% kill fee. Buys first North American serial rights or makes work-for-hire assignments. Submit seasonal/holiday material 6 months in advance. Reports in 1 month on queries; 2 months on mss. Sample copy for $6.95 (add $2 for Canadian and foreign orders). Writer's guidelines for SASE.

Nonfiction: Investigative pieces, general interest, how-to, humor, interview, new products, profile. "We *do not* want to see pornographic articles." Buys 4-5 mss/issue. Query or send complete mss. Length: 1,000-3,000 words. Pays $300-2,000. "Special prices negotiated." Sometimes pays expenses of writers on assignment.

Photos: Send photos with accompanying mss. Pay varies for b&w or color contact sheets and negatives. Buys one-time rights. Captions preferred; model release required.

Fiction: Adventure, erotica (special guidelines available), experimental, humorous, mainstream, mystery, suspense. Buys 1 ms/issue. Send complete ms. Length: 1,000-3,000 words. Pays $350-500.

• Publisher reports staff writers are producing more of this magazine's regular features.

GENESIS, Jakel Corp., 20th Floor, 1776 Broadway, New York NY 10019. (212)265-3500. Publisher/Editor: Michael Banka. 85% freelance written. Men's magazine published 14 times/year. "We are interested in headline and behind-the-headlines articles on sexual or controversial subjects of interest to men." Estab. 1973. Circ. 425,000. Pays 60 days after acceptance. Publishes ms an average of 3 months after acceptance. Byline given. Offers 25% kill fee. Buys second serial (reprint) and English worldwide rights (may revert to writer upon request). Submit seasonal material 6 months in advance. Accepts simultaneous submissions. Reports in 3 months. Writer's guidelines for #10 SASE.

Nonfiction: Exposé; humor; interview/profile; photo feature; erotica; film, music and book reviews; comment on contemporary relationships; automotive. "With the exception of the entertainment reviews, one exposé-style piece and one automotive piece/issue, all editorial in *Genesis* has a sexual orientation." Buys 60 mss/

year. Query with published clips. First-time writers must submit ms on spec. Length: 1,500-2,000 words. Pays $300-700 for assigned articles; $100-500 for unsolicited articles.

Photos: Send photos with submission. Reviews transparencies (no fixed size requirements) and prints. Offers $50-100/photo. Model releases and identification of subjects required. Buys English worldwide and second serial (reprint) rights.

Columns/Departments: Film, music and book reviews, 500-750 words; 'On the Couch' (sexual confessions from woman's point of view), 750-1,000 words. Buys 65 mss/year. Query with published clips. First-time writers must submit ms on spec. Pays $75-350.

Tips: "Because we accept only a small number of nonsex-related articles, freelancers' best chance to break in is to write sex features or contribute to the entertainment pages; we have a partciular need for 300-500 word articles on film and TV. When writing about sexual issues or lifestyles, writers should offer their own opinions on the subject rather than provide drably objective overviews. First-person point-of-view is strongly recommended. Writing must be sexually explicit with a minimum amount of 'lead in.' "

GENT, "Home of the D-Cups," Dugent Publishing Corp., Suite 600, 2600 Douglas Rd., Coral Gables FL 33134. Managing Editor: Steve Dorfman. Contact: Steve Dorfman. 80% freelance written. Monthly men's sophisticate magazine with emphasis on big breasts. Estab. 1960. Circ. 150,000. Pays on publication. Byline given. Buys first North American serial or second serial (reprint) rights. Editorial lead time 4 months. Submit seasonal material 6 months in advance. Accepts previously published submissions. Reports in 2 weeks on queries; 3 months on mss. Sample copy for $5. Writer's guidelines for #10 SASE.

Nonfiction: How-to ("anything sexually related"), personal experience ("any and all sexually related matters"). Buys 13 mss/year. Query. Length: 2,000-3,500 words. Pays $250.

Photos: Send photos with submission. Reviews 35mm transparencies. Negotiates payment individually. Model releases and identification of subjects required. Buys first North American with reprint rights.

Fiction: Erotica, fantasy. Buys 26 mss/year. Send complete ms. Length: 2,000-3,500 words. Pays $200-250.

GENTLEMEN'S QUARTERLY, Condé Nast, 350 Madison Ave., New York NY 10017. (212)880-8800. Editor-in-Chief: Arthur Cooper. Managing Editor: Martin Beiser. 60% freelance written. Circ. 700,000. Monthly magazine emphasizing fashion, general interest and service features for men ages 25-45 with a large discretionary income. **Pays on acceptance.** Byline given. Pays 25% kill fee. Submit seasonal/holiday material 6 months in advance. Reports in 1 month.

Nonfiction: Politics, personality profiles, lifestyles, trends, grooming, nutrition, health and fitness, sports, travel, money, investment and business matters. Buys 4-6 mss/issue. Query with published clips. Length: 1,500-4,000 words. Pay varies.

Columns/Departments: Martin Beiser, managing editor. Private Lives, Health and Games (sports). Query with published clips. Length: 1,000-2,500 words. Pay varies.

Tips: "Major features are usually assigned to well-established, known writers. Pieces are almost always solicited. The best way to break in is through the columns, especially Games, Health or Humor."

HEARTLAND USA, % PeakMedia, P.O. Box 925, Hailey ID 83333-0925. (208)788-4500. Fax: (208)788-5098. Editor: Brad Pearson. Managing Editor: Clarence Stilwill. 50% freelance written. Quarterly magazine for working men. "*Heartland USA* is a general interest, lifestyle magazine for working men 18 to 53. It covers spectator sports (primarily motor sports, football, baseball and basketball, hunting, fishing, how-to, travel, music, gardening, the environment, human interest, etc.), emphasizing the upbeat or humorous." Estab. 1991. Circ. 1,000,000. **Pays on acceptance.** Byline given. Offers 20% kill fee. Buys first North American serial and second serial (reprint) rights. Submit seasonal material 6 months in advance. Accepts simultaneous and previously published submissions. Send tearsheet or photocopy of article, typed ms with rights for sale noted and information about when and where the article previously appeared. Query for electronic submissions. Reports in 1 month on queries. Sample copy for 9 × 12 SAE with 10 first-class stamps. Free writer's guidelines.

Nonfiction: Book excerpts, general interest, historical/nostalgic, how-to, humor, inspirational, interview/profile, new product, personal experience, photo feature, technical, travel. "No fiction or dry expository pieces." Buys 30 mss/year. Query with or without published clips or send complete ms. Length: 350-1,200 words. Pays 80¢ to $1/word for assigned articles; 25-80¢/word for unsolicited articles. Sometimes pays expenses of writers on assignment.

Photos: Send photos with submission. Reviews transparencies. Identification of subjects required. Buys one-time rights.

Tips: "Features with the possibility of strong photographic support are open to freelancers, as are our shorter departments. We look for a relaxed, jocular, easy-to-read style, and look favorably on the liberal use of anecdote or interesting quotations."

HIGH SOCIETY MAGAZINE, Drake Publishers, 801 Second Ave., New York NY 10017. (212)661-7878/ Editor: Vincent Stevens. Managing Editor: Robert See. 50% freelance written. Men's sophisticate magazine emphasizing men's entertainment. "Everything of interest to the American male." Estab. 1976. Circ. 400,000. **Pays on acceptance.** Byline given. Offers $200 kill fee. Buys first North American serial rights. Submit seasonal material 6 months in advance. Accepts simultaneous submissions. Reports in 2 weeks on queries. Sample copy for $2 and 9 × 12 SAE.

Nonfiction: Book excerpts, exposé, general interest, interview/profile, photo feature. Buys 60 mss/year. Query with or without published clips, or send complete ms. Length: 1,500-3,000 words. Pays $300-800 for assigned articles; $200-500 for unsolicited articles. Sometimes pays expenses of writers on assignment.

Photos: Send photos with submission. Reviews 2¼ × 2¼ transparencies and 8 × 10 prints. Offers $200/photo. Captions, model releases and identification of subjects required. Buys one-time rights.

Columns/Departments: Private Passions (first person sexual accounts), 600 words; Bad Guys (crime related exposes), 1,800 words; Sex & Music (biographies of female celebs in music business), 1,000 words. Buys 60 mss/year. Query with published clips. Pays $150-800.

‡**HUSTLER,** HG Inc., Suite 300, 9171 Wilshire Blvd., Beverly Hills CA 90210. Editor: Allan MacDonell. 60% freelance written. Magazine published 13 times/year. "*Hustler* is the no-nonsense men's magazine. Our audience does not need to be told whether to wear their trousers cuffed or plain. The *Hustler* reader expects honest, unflinching looks at hard topics—sexual, social, political, personality profile, true crime." Estab. 1974. Circ. 750,000. Pays as boards ship to printer. Publishes ms an average of 3 months after acceptance. Byline given. Offers 20% kill fee. Buys all rights. Editorial lead time 4 months. Submit seasonal material 6 months in advance. Reports in 2 weeks on queries; 1 month on mss. Writer's guidelines for #10 SASE.

Nonfiction: Book excerpts, exposé, general interest, how-to, interview/profile, personal experience, trends. Buys 30 mss/yer. Query. Length: 3,500-4,000 words. Pays $1,500 for assigned articles; $1,000 for unsolicited articles. Sometimes pays expenses of writers on assignment.

Columns/Departments: Tim Power. Sex Play (some aspect of sex that can be encapsulated in a limited space), 2,500 words. Buys 13 mss/year. Send complete ms. Pays $500.

Fiction: Tim Power. "Difficult fiction market. Must have two sex scenes; yet not be rote or boring." Buys 2 mss/year. Send complete ms. Length: 3,000-3,500. Pays $700-1,000.

Fillers: Pays $50-100. Jokes and "Graffilthy," bathroom-wall humor.

Tips: "Don't try and mimic the *Hustler* style. If a writer needs to be molded into our voice, we'll do a better job of it than he or she will."

HUSTLER BUSTY BEAUTIES, America's Breast Magazine, HG Publications, Inc., Suite 300, 9171 Wilshire Blvd., Beverly Hills CA 90210. (213)858-7100. Fax: (213)275-3857. Editor: N. Morgen Hagen. 40% freelance written. Men's monthly sophisticate magazine. "*Hustler Busty Beauties* is an adult title that showcases attractive large-breasted women with accompanying erotic fiction, reader letters, humor." Estab. 1974. Circ. 180,000. Pays on publication. Publishes ms an average of 6 months after acceptance. Byline given. Buys all rights. Reports in 1 month. Sample copy for $6 and 9 × 12 SAE. Free writer's guidelines.

Columns/Departments: LewDDD Letters (erotic experiences involving large-breasted women from first-person point-of-view), 500-1,000 words. Buys 24-36 mss year. Send complete ms. Pays $50-75.

Fiction: Adventure, erotica, fantasy, humorous, mystery, science fiction, suspense. "No violent stories or stories without a bosomy female character." Buys 12 mss year. Send complete ms. Length: 750-2,500 words. Pays $250-500.

Jokes: Appropriate for audience. Pays $10-25.

NUGGET, Dugent Publishing Corp., Suite 600, 2600 Douglas Rd., Coral Gables FL 33134. Managing Editor: Nye Willden. Contact: Christopher James, editor-in-chief. 100% freelance written. Men's/adult magazine published 8 times a year covering fetish and kink. "*Nugget* is a one-of-a-kind publication which appeals to daring, open-minded adults who enjoy all forms of both kinky, alternative sex (catfighting, transvestism, fetishism, bi-sexuality, etc.) and conventional sex." Estab. 1960. Circ. 28,097. Pays on publication. Publishes ms an average of 1 year after acceptance. Byline given. Buys first North American serial rights. Editorial lead time 5 months. Submit seasonal material 1 year in advance. Accepts simultaneous submissions. Reports in 2 weeks on queries; 2 months on mss. Sample copy for $3. Writer's guidelines free on request.

Nonfiction: Interview/profile, sexual matters/trends (fetish and kink angle). Buys 4 mss/year. Query. Length: 2,000-3,000 words. Pays $200 minimum.

Photos: Send photos with submission. Reviews transparencies. Offers no additional payment for photos accepted with ms. Model releases required. Buys one-time second rights.

Fiction: Erotica, fantasy. Buys 20 mss/year. Send complete ms. Length: 2,000-3,000 words. Pays $200-250.

Tips: Most open to fiction submissions. (Follow readers guidelines for suitable topics.)

OPTIONS, AJA Publishing, P.O. Box 470, Port Chester NY 10573. (914)939-2111. Editor: Don Stone. Associate Editor: Diana Sheridan. Mostly freelance written. Sexually explicit magazine for and about bisexuals and homosexuals, published 10 times/year. "Articles, stories and letters about bisexuality. Positive approach.

For explanation of symbols, see the Key to Symbols and Abbreviations. For unfamiliar words, see the Glossary.

Safe-sex encounters unless the story clearly pre-dates the AIDS situation." Estab. 1977. Circ. 100,000. Pays on publication. Publishes mss an average of 10 months after acceptance. Byline given, usually pseudonymous. Buys all rights. Submit seasonal material 8 months in advance; buys very little seasonal material. Reports in 3 weeks. Sample copy for $2.95 and 6×9 SAE with 5 first-class stamps. Writer's guidelines for SASE.

Nonfiction: Essays (occasional), how-to, humor, interview/profile, opinion, personal experience (especially). All must be bisexually or gay related. Does not want "anything not bisexually/gay related, anything negative, anything opposed to safe sex, anything dry/boring/ponderous/pedantic. Write even serious topics informally if not lightly." Buys 10 nonfiction mss/year. Send complete ms. Length: 2,000-3,000. Pays $100.

Photos: Reviews transparencies and prints. Pays $20 for b&w photos; $200 for full color. Black and white or color sets $150. Previously published photos acceptable.

Fiction: "We don't usually get enough true first-person stories and need to buy some from writers. They must be bisexual, usually man/man, hot and believable. They must not read like fiction." Buys 70 fiction mss/year. Send complete ms. Length: 2,000-3,000. Pays $100.

Tips: "We use many more male/male pieces than female/female. Use only one serious article per issue. A serious/humorous approach is good here, but only if it's natural to you; don't make an effort for it. No longer buying 'letters'. We get enough real ones."

PENTHOUSE, General Media, 1965 Broadway, New York NY 10023. Monthly publication covering style, culture and fashion for men. This magazine did not respond to our request for information. Query before submitting.

PLAYBOY, 680 N. Lakeshore Dr., Chicago IL 60611. Monthly publication covering fashion, style and popular culture for men. This magazine did not respond to our request for information. Query before submitting.

‡PLUMPERS & BIG WOMEN, Dugent Publishing Corp., 2600 Douglas Rd., Coral Gables FL 33134. Managing Editor: Nye Willden. Contact: E. L. Mullins, editor. 100% freelance written. Bimonthly magazine covering large women and the men who admire them. "*Plumpers* is an adult men's magazine devoted to obese women — nude female models, articles and fiction about plump women and topics directed to the thousands of 'plumper' lovers." Estab. 1993. Circ. 100,000. Pays on publication. Publishes ms an average of 3 months after acceptance. Byline given. Offers 50% or $125 kill fee. Buys first North American or second serial (reprint) rights. Editorial lead time 3 months. Submit seasonal material 4 months in advance. Accepts previously published submissions. Query for electronic submissions. Reports in 3 weeks on queries; 1 month on mss. Sample copy for $3. Writer's guidelines free on request.

Nonfiction: Book excerpts, general interest, how-to, interview/profile, opinion, personal experience, photo feature. "We don't publish anything not related to fat women." Buys 6-8 mss/year. Query. Length: 1,500 words. Pays $250. Sometimes pays expenses of writers on assignment.

Photos: State availability of photos with submission. Reviews 35mm transparencies and prints. Negotiates payment individually. Model releases and identification of subjects required. Buys one-time rights.

Fiction: Erotica, romance. Buys 6-8 mss/year. Send complete ms. Length: 1,200-1,500 words. Pays $250.

Tips: "Must have a very positive approach to large women and be able to convey that in stories and articles (*and* photos)."

SCREW, P.O. Box 432, Old Chelsea Station, New York NY 10113. Managing Editor: Manny Neuhaus. 95% freelance written. Eager to work with new/unpublished writers. Weekly tabloid newspaper for a predominantly male, college-educated audience, 21-mid-40s. Estab. 1968. Circ. 125,000. Pays on publication. Publishes ms an average of 3 months after acceptance. Byline given. Buys all rights. Reports in 3 months. Free sample copy and writer's guidelines.

Nonfiction: "Sexually-related news, humor, how-to articles, first-person and true confessions. Frank and explicit treatment of all areas of sex; outrageous and irreverent attitudes combined with hard information, news and consumer reports. Our style is unique. Writers should check several recent issues." Buys 150-200 mss/year. Will also consider material for Letter From . . ., a consumer-oriented wrap-up of commercial sex scene in cities around the country; submit complete ms or query. Length: 1,000-3,000 words. Pays $100-250. Also, My Scene, a sexual true confession. Length: 1,000-2,500 words. Pays $40.

Photos: Reviews b&w glossy prints (8×10 or 11×14) purchased with or without mss or on assignment. Pays $10-50.

Tips: "All manuscripts get careful attention. Those written in *Screw* style on sexual topics have the best chance. I anticipate a need for more aggressive, insightful political humor."

‡SUGAH, Dugent Publishing Corp., 2600 Douglas Rd., Coral Gables FL 33134. Editor: Al Noland. Contact: Nye Willden, managing editor. 100% freelance written. Bimonthly magazine covering black interest articles/fiction. "*Sugah* is a black-oriented men's magazine with models, articles and stories for those interested in Afro-American culture and topics." Estab. 1993. Circ. 50,000. Pays on publication. Byline given. Offers 50% or $150 kill fee. Buys first North American and second serial (reprint) rights. Editorial lead time 3 months. Submit seasonal material 4 months in advance. Accepts previously published submissions. Query for electronic submissions. Reports in 3 weeks on queries; 1 month on mss. Sample copy for $3. Writer's guidelines free on request.

Nonfiction: General interest, historical/nostalgic, humor, interview/profile, personal experience, travel. Buys 6 mss/year. Query. Length: 1,200-1,500 words. Pays $250-300. Sometimes pays expenses of writers on assignment.

Photos: State availability of photos with submission. Reviews 35mm or 2×2 transparencies and 3×5 prints. Offers no additional payment for photos accepted with ms. Identification of subjects required. Buys one-time rights.

Fiction: Erotica, ethnic, romance. "Nothing without black characters." Buys 6 mss/year. Send complete ms. Length: 1,200-1,500 words. Pays $250.

Tips: "Articles and stories must be of interest to the educated 20-30-year-old black male (or female) and those who are interested in black women, erotica and culture."

‡**SWANK,** Swank Publications, 210 Route 4 East, Paramus NJ 07652. (201)843-4004. Fax: (201)843-8636. Editor: Paul Gambino. 75% freelance written. Works with new/unpublished writers. Monthly magazine on "sex and sensationalism, lurid. High quality adult erotic entertainment." Audience of men ages 18-38, high school and some college education, medium income, skilled blue-collar professionals, union men, some white-collar. Estab. 1954. Circ. 400,000. Pays on publication. Publishes ms an average of 4 months after acceptance. Byline given, pseudonym if wanted. Buys first North American serial rights. Submit seasonal material 6 months in advance. Reports in 3 weeks on queries; 1 month on mss. Sample copy for $5.95. Writer's guidelines for SASE.

Nonfiction: Exposé (researched), adventure must be accompanied by color photographs. "We buy articles on sex-related topics, which don't need to be accompanied by photos." Interested in lifestyle (unusual) pieces. Buys photo pieces on autos, action, adventure. Buys 34 mss/year. Query with or without published clips. Pays $350-500. Sometimes pays the expenses of writers on assignment. "It is strongly recommended that a sample copy is reviewed before submitting material."

Photos: Bruce Perez, photo editor. Send photos. "If you have good photographs of an interesting adventure/lifestyle subject, the writing that accompanies is bought almost automatically." Model releases required.

THE JAMES WHITE REVIEW, A Gay Men's Literary Quarterly, P.O. Box 3356, Butler Quarter, Minneapolis MN 55403. (612)339-8317. Editor: Phil Willkie. Managing Editor: Bayne Holley. 100% freelance written. Quarterly tabloid covering gay men. Estab. 1983. Circ. 4,000. Byilne given. Buys first North American serial rights. Editorial lead time 3 months. Submit seasonal material 3 months in advance. Query for electronic submissions. Reports in 3 months on queries. Sample copy for $3. Writer's guidelines for #10 SASE.

Nonfiction: Book excerpts and essays. Buys 4 mss/year. Send complete ms. Length: 2,000 words maximum. Pays $50 minimum.

Photos: Send photos with submission. Reviews prints. Negotiates payment individually. Buys one-time rights.

Fiction: Confession, erotica, experimental, fantasy, historical, novel excerpts and serialized novels. Buys 20 mss/year. Send complete ms. Length: 2,000 words maximum. Pays $50 maximum.

Poetry: Cliff Mayhood, poetry editor. Avant-garde, free verse, light verse and traditional. Buys 80 poems/year. Submit maximum 10 poems. Pays $20.

Military

These publications emphasize military or paramilitary subjects or other aspects of military life. Technical and semitechnical publications for military commanders, personnel and planners, as well as those for military families and civilians interested in Armed Forces activities are listed here. Publications covering military history can be found in the History section.

AMERICAN SURVIVAL GUIDE, McMullen & Yee Publishing, Inc., 774 S. Placentia Ave., Placentia CA 92670-6832. Editor: Jim Benson. 50% freelance written. Monthly magazine covering "self-reliance, defense, meeting day-to-day and possible future threats—survivalism for survivalists." Circ. 72,000. Pays on publication. Publishes ms up to 1 year after acceptance. Byline given. Submit seasonal material 5 months in advance. Sample copy for $3.50. Writer's guidelines for SASE. Articles should be submitted on computer floppy disk, either 3½ or 5¼ inch floppy with hard copy included. Microsoft Word files are preferred but other software text files will work such as Word Pefect.

Nonfiction: Exposé (political); how-to; interview/profile; personal experience (how I survived); photo feature (equipment and techniques related to survival in all possible situations); emergency medical; health and fitness; communications; transportation; food preservation; water purification; self-defense; terrorism; nuclear dangers; nutrition; tools; shelter; etc. "No general articles about how to survive. We want specifics and single subjects." Buys 60-100 mss/year. Query or send complete ms. Length: 1,500-2,000 words. Pays $140-350. Sometimes pays some expenses of writers on assignment.

Photos: Send photos with ms. "One of the most frequent mistakes made by writers in completing an article assignment for us is sending photo submissions that are inadequate." Captions, model releases and identification of subjects mandatory. Buys all rights.
Tips: "Prepare material of value to individuals who wish to sustain human life no matter what the circumstance. This magazine is a text and reference."

ARMY MAGAZINE, 2425 Wilson Blvd., Arlington VA 22201-3385. (703)841-4300. Fax: (703)525-9039. Managing Editor: Mary Blake French. 70% freelance written. Prefers to work with published/established writers. Monthly magazine emphasizing military interests. Estab. 1904. Circ. 130,000. Pays on publication. Publishes ms an average of 5 months after acceptance. Buys all rights. Byline given except for back-up research. Submit seasonal/holiday material 3 months in advance. Sample copy and writer's guidelines for 9×12 SAE with $1 postage.
Nonfiction: Historical (military and original); humor (military feature-length articles and anecdotes); interview; new product; nostalgia; personal experience dealing especially with the most recent conflicts in which the US Army has been involved (Desert Storm, Panama, Grenada); photo feature; profile; technical. No rehashed history. "We would like to see more pieces about little-known episodes involving interesting military personalities. We especially want material lending itself to heavy, contributor-supplied photographic treatment. The first thing a contributor should recognize is that our readership is very savvy militarily. 'Gee-whiz' personal reminiscences get short shrift, unless they hold their own in a company in which long military service, heroism and unusual experiences are commonplace. At the same time, Army readers like a well-written story with a fresh slant, whether it is about an experience in a foxhole or the fortunes of a corps in battle." Buys 12 mss/issue. Submit complete ms. Length: 3,500 words, but shorter items, especially in 1,500 to 2,500 range, often have better chance of getting published. Pays 12-18¢/word.
Photos: Submit photo material with accompanying ms. Pays $25-50 for 8×10 b&w glossy prints; $50-350 for 8×10 color glossy prints or 2¼×2¼ transparencies; will also accept 35mm. Captions preferred. Buys all rights. Pays $35-50 for cartoon with strong military slant.
Columns/Departments: Military news, books, comment (*New Yorker*-type "Talk of the Town" items). Buys 8/issue. Submit complete ms. Length: 1,000 words. Pays $40-150.

ASIA-PACIFIC DEFENSE FORUM, Commander-in-Chief, U.S. Pacific Command, Box 64013, Camp H.M. Smith HI 96861-4013. (808)477-0760/1454. Fax: (808)477-6247. Editor-in-Chief: Lt. Col. (Ret.) Paul R. Stankiewicz. Editor: Major Ricardo Finney. 12% (maximum) freelance written. Quarterly magazine for foreign military officers in 51 Asian-Pacific, Indian Ocean and other countries; all services—Army, Navy, Air Force and Marines. Secondary audience—government officials, media and academicians concerned with defense issues. "We seek to keep readers abreast of current status of US forces and of US national security policies in the Asia-Pacific area, and to enhance regional dialogue on military subjects." Estab. 1976. Circ. 34,000. **Pays on acceptance.** Publishes ms an average of 4 months after acceptance. Byline given. Buys simultaneous, second serial (reprint) or one-time rights. Accepts simultaneous and previously published submissions. Send tearsheet or photocopy of article and information about when and where the article previously appeared. Reports in 3 weeks on queries; 10 weeks on mss. Free sample copy and writer's guidelines (send self-addressed label).
Nonfiction: General interest (current type forces and weapons systems, strategic balance and regional security issues and Asian-Pacific armed forces); historical (rarely used); how-to (training, leadership, force employment procedures, organization); interview; personal experience (rarely used). "We do not want overly technical weapons/equipment descriptions, overly scholarly articles, controversial policy, or budget matters; nor do we seek discussion of in-house problem areas. We do not deal with military social life, base activities or PR-type personalities/job descriptions." Buys 2-4 mss/year. Query or send complete ms. Length: 1,000-3,000 words. Pays $100-300.
Photos: Send photos with query or ms. "We provide nearly all photos; however, we will consider good quality photos with manuscripts." Reviews color, b&w glossy prints or 35mm color transparencies. Offers no additional payment for photos accompanying mss. Photo credits given. Captions required. Buys one-time rights.
Tips: "Don't write in a flashy, Sunday supplement style. Our audience is relatively staid, and fact-oriented articles requiring a newspaper/journalistic approach are used more than a normal magazine style. Provide material that is truly foreign audience-oriented and easily illustrated with photos."

‡FAMILY MAGAZINE, The Magazine for Military Wives, PABCO, 169 Lexington Ave., New York NY 10016. (212)545-9740. Executive Editor: Liz DeFranco. 85% freelance written. Monthly magazine covering military family life. "All subjects covered must be germane to the military family or the military wife. All services mentioned must be accessible to military families. Any products or services should tie in with the PX/BX or commissary." Estab. 1958. Circ. 600,000. Pays on publication. Publishes ms an average of 4 months after acceptance. Byline given. Buys first North American serial rights and makes work-for-hire assignments. Editorial lead time 3 months. Submit seasonal material 6 months in advance. Accepts simultaneous submissions. Query for electronic submissions. Reports in 6 weeks on queries; 2 months on mss. Sample copy for $1.25 and 9×12 SASE. Writer's guidelines for #10 SASE.

Nonfiction: General interest, humor, interview/profile, new product, personal experience, photo feature, travel, military/family. Special issues: military retirees, active duty military women. Buys 35 mss/year. Send complete ms. Length: 1,000-3,000 words. Pays $50.

Photos: State availability of photos with submission. Reviews transparencies and prints. Negotiates payment individually. Buys one-time rights.

Columns/Departments: Comstore Cookery (recipes), 10-15 recipes plus text; Travel (things to do with children), 2,000-3,000 words; FAMILY Kid (children's puzzles, games, etc.), graphics (1 page). Buys 30 mss/year. Send complete ms. Pays $50-150.

Fillers: Short humor, travel tips, cooking tips. Buys 2/year. Length: 50-250 words. Pays $25.

Tips: "Request a copy of the magazine before submitting. Don't send manuscripts that have made the rounds and are over-photocopied and messy. Have someone else read it for feedback before sending it out. Know the military market or the subject well."

MARINE CORPS GAZETTE, Professional Magazine for United States Marines, Marine Corps Association, P.O. Box 1775, Quantico VA 22134. (703)640-6161, (800)336-0291. Fax: (703)640-0823. Editor: Col. John E. Greenwood, USMC (Ret.). Managing Editor: Lt. Col. Steven M. Crittenden, USMC (Ret.). Less than 5% freelance written. "Will continue to welcome and respond to queries, but will be selective due to large backlog from Marine authors." Monthly magazine. "*Gazette* serves as a forum in which serving Marine officers exchange ideas and viewpoints on professional military matters." Estab. 1916. Circ. 36,600. No payment for articles unless author is commissioned by Editor. Publishes ms an average of 6 months after acceptance. Byline given. Buys all rights. Accepts previously published submissions. Send tearsheet of article or typed ms with rights for sale noted and information about when and where the article previously appeared. For reprints pays 100% of their fee for an original article. Reports in 3 weeks on queries; 2 months on mss. Free sample copy and writer's guidelines.

Nonfiction: Historical/nostalgic (Marine Corps operations only); technical (Marine Corps related equipment). "The magazine is a professional journal oriented toward hard skills, factual treatment, technical detail—no market for lightweight puff pieces—analysis of doctrine, lessons learned goes well. A very strong Marine Corps background and influence are normally prerequisites for publication." Query or send complete ms. Length: 2,500-5,000 words.

Photos: "We welcome photos and charts. Photos need not be original, nor have been taken by the author, but they must support the article."

Columns/Departments: Book Reviews (of interest and importance to Marines); Ideas and Issues (an assortment of topical articles, e.g., opinion or argument, ideas of better ways to accomplish tasks, reports on weapons and equipment, strategies and tactics, etc., also short vignettes on history of Corps). Publishes 60-plus book reviews/year; author receives book for 750-word book review. Publishes over 150 Ideas and Issues mss/year.

Tips: "Book reviews or short articles (500-1,500 words) on Marine Corps related hardware or technological development are the best way to break in. Sections/departments most open to freelancers are Book Reviews and Ideas & Issues sections—query first. We are not much of a market for those outside US Marine Corps or who are not closely associated with current Marine activities. All manuscripts should be double-spaced and accompanied by a floppy disk if possible."

MILITARY LIFESTYLE, Downey Communications, Inc., Suite 710, 4800 Montgomery Lane, Bethesda MD 20814-5341. (301)718-7600. Fax: (301)718-7652. Editor: Hope M. Daniels. 80% freelance written. Works with equal balance of published and unpublished writers. Monthly magazine for military families in the US and overseas. Estab. 1969. Circ. 100,000. Pays on publication. Publishes ms an average of 4 months after acceptance. Buys first North American serial rights. Submit seasonal material at least 8 months in advance. Reports in approximately 3 months. Sample copy for $1.50 and 9×12 SASE with adequate postage for a magazine. Writer's guidelines for #10 SASE.

• This publication has become a monthly and nearly tripled the size of each issue. They report an increased need for freelance submissions. Ranked as one of the best markets for freelance writers in *Writer's Digest* magazine's annual "Top 100 Markets," January 1994.

Nonfiction: "All articles must have special interest for military families. General interest articles are OK if they reflect situations our readers can relate to." Food, entertaining, profiles, childraising, health, home decor, travel, finances, second careers, housing and real estate. "Query letter should name sources, describe focus of article, use a few sample quotes from sources, indicate length, and should describe writer's own qualifications for doing the piece." Length: approximately 1,500 words. Pay varies. Negotiates expenses on a case-by-case basis.

Photos: Judi Connelly, art director. Purchased with accompanying ms and on assignment. Uses 35mm or larger transparencies. Captions and model releases are required.

Columns/Departments: Your Point of View—personal experience pieces by military family members. Also, Your Pet, Your Money and Your Family. Query. Length: 800-1,200 words. Rates vary.

Fiction: Slice-of-life, family situation, contemporary tableaux. "Military family life or relationship themes only." Buys 6-8 mss/year. Query. Length: 1,200-1,500 words. Pay varies.

Tips: "We are a magazine for active duty and retired military families. Our editorial attempts enthusiastically to reflect that. Our ideal contributor is a military family member who can write. However, I'm always impressed by a writer who has analyzed the market and can suggest some possible new angles for us. Sensitivity to military issues is a must for our contributors, as is the ability to write good personality profiles and/or do thorough research about military family life. We don't purchase household hints, historical articles, poetry, WW II-era material or parenting advice that is too personal and limited only to the writer's own experience."

‡**NAVY TIMES,** Times Journal, 6883 Commercial Dr., Springfield VA 22159. (703)750-8636. Fax: (703)750-8622. Editor: Tobias Naegele. Managing Editor: Jean Reid Norman. Weekly newspaper covering sea services. News and features of men and women in the Navy, Coast Guard and Marine Corps. Estab. 1950. Circ. 90,000. **Pays on acceptance.** Byline given. Buys first North American serial or second serial (reprint) rights. Submit seasonal material 2 months in advance. Reports in 2 months. Free writer's guidelines.
Nonfiction: Historical/nostalgic, opinion. No poetry. Buys 100 mss/year. Query. Length: 500-1,000 words. Pays $50-500. Sometimes pays expenses of writers on assignment.
Photos: Send photos with submission. Offers $20-100/photo. Captions and identification of subjects required. Buys one-time rights.

OFF DUTY MAGAZINE, Suite C-2, 3303 Harbor Blvd., Costa Mesa CA 92626-1500. (714)549-7172. Fax: (714)549-4222. Editorial Director: Jim Shaw. Managing Editor: Gary Burch. 30% freelance written. Monthly magazine covering the leisure-time activities and interests of the military community. "Our audience is solely military members and their families; many of our articles could appear in other consumer magazines, but we always slant them toward the military; i.e. where to get a military discount when traveling." Estab. 1970. Circ. 582,000. **Pays on acceptance.** Publishes ms an average of 3 months after acceptance. Byline given. Buys one-time rights. Submit seasonal material at least 4 months in advance. Accepts simultaneous and previously published submissions. Send tearsheet or photocopy of article and information about when and where the article previously appeared. Reports in 2 months on queries. Sample copy for 9 × 12 SAE with 6 first class stamps. Writer's guidelines for SASE.
Nonfiction: Humor (military), interview/profile (music and entertainment), travel, finance, lifestyle (with a military angle). "Must be familiar with *Off Duty* and its needs." Buys 30-40 mss/year. Query. Length: 800-2,100 words. Pays $160-420 for assigned articles.
  • Publisher is not interested in seeing World War II reminiscences.
Photos: Send photos with submission. Reviews contact sheets and 35mm transparencies. Offers $50-300 (cover)/photo. Captions and identifiction of subjects required. Buys one-time rights.
Tips: "Get to know the military community and its interests beyond the stereotypes. Travel—query with the idea of getting on our next year's editorial calendar. We choose our primary topics at least 6 months prior to its start."

OVERSEAS!, Military Consumer Today, Inc., Kolpingstr 1, 69172 Leimen, West Germany 011-49-6224-7060. Fax: 011-49-6224-70616. Editor: Greg Ballinger. Eager to work with new/unpublished writers. Monthly magazine. "*Overseas!* is aimed at the US military in Europe. It is the leading military lifestyle magazine slanted toward living in Europe." Estab. 1973. Circ. 52,000. Pays on publication. Publishes ms an average of 3 months after acceptance. Byline given. Publishes photos, bio of new writers in editor's column. Offers kill fee depending on circumstances and writer. Buys one-time rights. Submit seasonal/holiday material at least 4 months in advance. Accepts simultaneous and previously published submissions. Reports in 2 months. Sample copy for 9 × 12 SAE with 5 IRCs. Writer's guidelines for SAE and 1 IRC.
Nonfiction: General interest (lifestyle for men and other topics); interview/profile (music, personality interviews; current music stars); travel (European, first person adventure; write toward male audience). No articles that are drug- or sex-related. No cathedrals or museums of Europe stories. Query with or without published clips, or send complete ms. Length: 750-2,000 words. Pays 10¢/word.
Tips: "We would like more submissions on travel in Europe. Writing should be lively, interesting, with lots of good information. We anticipate a change in the length of articles. Articles will be shorter and livelier with more sidebars because readers don't have time to read longer articles."

PARAMETERS: U.S. Army War College Quarterly, U.S. Army War College, Carlisle Barracks PA 17013-5050. (717)245-4943. Editor: Col. John J. Madigan, U.S. Army Retired. 100% freelance written. Prefers to work with published/established writers or experts in the field. Readership consists of senior leadership of US defense establishment, both uniformed and civilian, plus members of the media, government, industry and academia interested in national and international security affairs, military strategy, military leadership and management, art and science of warfare, and military history (provided it has contemporary relevance). Most readers possess a graduate degree. Estab. 1971. Circ. 12,000. Not copyrighted; unless copyrighted by author, articles may be reprinted with appropriate credits. Buys first serial rights. Byline given. Pays on publication. Publishes ms an average of 6 months after acceptance. Reports in 6 weeks. Free sample copy and writer's guidelines.
Nonfiction: Articles are preferred that deal with current security issues, employ critical analysis and provide solutions or recommendations. Liveliness and verve, consistent with scholarly integrity, appreciated. Theses,

studies and academic course papers should be adapted to article form prior to submission. Documentation in complete endnotes. Submit complete ms. Length: 4,500 words average, preferably less. Pays $150 average (including visuals).

Tips: "Make it short; keep it interesting; get criticism and revise accordingly. Tackle a subject only if you are an authority."

‡**PERIODICAL,** Journal of America's Military Past, 10206 Lariston Lane, Silver Spring MD 20903-1311. Editor-in-Chief: Logan C. Osterndorf. 90% freelance written. Works with a small number of new/unpublished writers each year. Quarterly magazine emphasizing old and abandoned forts, posts and military installations; military subjects for a professional, knowledgeable readership interested in one-time defense sites or other military installations. Circ. 1,500. Pays on publication. Publishes ms an average of 6 months after acceptance. Buys one-time rights. Accepts simultaneous and previously published submissions (if published a long time ago). Reports in 3 weeks. Writer's guidelines for #10 SASE.

Nonfiction: Historical, personal experience, photo feature, technical (relating to posts, their construction/ operation and military matters). Buys 4-6 mss/issue. Query or send complete ms. Length: 300-4,000 words. Pays $2/published page minimum.

Photos: Purchased with or without ms. Query. Reviews glossy, single-weight b&w prints. Offers no additional payment for photos accepted with accompanying ms. Captions required.

Tips: "We plan more emphasis on appeal to professional military audience and military historians."

THE RETIRED OFFICER MAGAZINE, 201 N. Washington St., Alexandria VA 22314-2539. (800)245-8762. Fax: (703)838-8179. Editor: Col. Charles D. Cooper, USAF-Ret. Managing Editor: Julia Leigh. 60% freelance written. Prefers to work with published/established writers. Monthly magazine for officers of the 7 uniformed services and their families. Estab. 1945. Circ. 395,000. **Pays on acceptance.** Publishes ms an average of 9-12 months after acceptance. Byline given. Buys first serial rights. Submit seasonal material (holiday stories with a military theme) at least 9-12 months in advance. Reports on material accepted for publication within 3 months. Sample copy and writer's guidelines for 9 × 12 SAE with 6 first class stamps.

Nonfiction: Current military/political affairs, health and wellness, recent military history, travel, second-career job opportunities, military family lifestyle. Also, upbeat articles on aging, issues pertinent to a retired military officer's milieu. "We rarely accept unsolicited manuscripts. We look for detailed query letters with résumé and sample clips attached. We do not publish poetry or fillers." Buys 48 mss/year. Length: 800-2,000 words. Pays up to $1,000.

Photos: Query with list of stock photo subjects. Reviews 8 × 10 b&w photos (normal halftone). Original slides or transparencies must be suitable for color separation. Pays up to $125 for inside color; up to $200 for cover.

Tips: "Our readers are 55-65. We never write about them as senior citizens, yet we look for upbeat stories that take into consideration the demographic characteristics of their age group. An author who can submit a complete package of story and photos is valuable to us."

SOLDIER OF FORTUNE, The Journal of Professional Adventurers, Omega Group, Ltd., P.O. Box 693, Boulder CO 80306-0693. (303)449-3750. Fax: (303)444-5617. Managing Editor: Tom Slizewski. Assistant Editor: Lynne Robertson. 50% freelance written. Monthly magazine covering military, paramilitary, police, combat subjects and action/adventure. "We are an action-oriented magazine; we cover combat hot spots around the world such as Afghanistan, El Salvador, Angola, etc. We also provide timely features on state-of-the-art weapons and equipment; elite military and police units; and historical military operations. Reader-ship is primarily active-duty military, veterans and law enforcement." Estab. 1975. Circ. 175,000. Byline given. Offers 25% kill fee. Buys all rights; will negotiate. Accepts previously published submissions. Send tearsheet of article and information about when and where it previously appeared. For reprints, pays 100% of their fee for an original article. Submit seasonal material 5 months in advance. Reports in 3 weeks on queries; 1 month on mss. Sample copy for $5. Writer's guidelines for #10 SASE. Send mss to articles editor; queries to managing editor.

Nonfiction: Exposé; general interest; historical/nostalgic; how-to (on weapons and their skilled use); humor; profile; new product; personal experience; novel excerpts; photo feature ("number one on our list"); techni-cal; travel; combat reports; military unit reports and solid Vietnam and Operation Desert Storm articles. "No 'How I won the war' pieces; no op-ed pieces *unless* they are fully and factually backgrounded; no knife articles (staff assignments only). *All* submitted articles should have good art; art will sell us on an article." Buys 75 mss/year. Query with or without published clips or send complete ms. Length: 2,000-3,000 words. Pays $150-250/page. Sometimes pays the expenses of writers on assignment.

Photos: Send photos with submission (copies only, no originals). Reviews contact sheets and transparencies. Offers no additional payment for photos accepted with ms. Pays $500 for cover photo. Captions and identifica-tion of subjects required. Buys one-time rights.

Columns/Departments: Lynn Robertson, articles editor. Combat craft (how-to military and police survival skills) and I Was There (first-person accounts of the arcane or unusual based in a combat or law enforcement environment), both 600-800 words. Buys 16 mss/year. Send complete ms. Length: 600-800 words. Combat craft pays $200; I was There $100.

Fillers: Bulletin Board editor. Newsbreaks; military/paramilitary related, *"has* to be documented." Length: 100-250 words. Pays $25.

Tips: "Submit a professionally prepared, complete package. All artwork with cutlines, double-spaced typed manuscript with 5.25 or 3.5 IBM-compatible disc, if available, cover letter including synopsis of article, supporting documentation where applicable, etc. Manuscript must be factual; writers have to do their homework and get all their facts straight. One error means rejection. We will work with authors over the phone or by letter, tell them if their ideas have merit for an acceptable article, and help them fine-tune their work. I Was There is a good place for freelancers to start. Vietnam features, if carefully researched and art heavy, will always get a careful look. Combat reports, again, with good art, are number one in our book and stand the best chance of being accepted. Military unit reports from around the world are well received as are law enforcement articles (units, police in action). If you write for us, be complete and factual; pros read *Soldier of Fortune*, and are *very* quick to let us know if we (and the author) err. We will be Operation Desert Storm-oriented for years to come, in terms of first-person accounts and incisive combat reports. Read a current issue to see where we're taking the magazine in the 1990s."

TIMES NEWS SERVICE, (formerly *Army Times*), Army Times Publishing Co., Springfield VA 22159-0200. (703)750-8725. Fax: (703)750-8612. Deputy Editor: Margaret Roth. Managing Editor: Roger Hyneman. 15% freelance written. Willing to work with new/unpublished writers. Manages weekly lifestyle section of Army, Navy and Air Force Times covering current lifestyles and problems of career military families around the world. Circ. 305,000. **Pays on acceptance.** Publishes ms an average of 2 months after acceptance. Byline given. Buys first worldwide rights. Submit seasonal material 3 months in advance. Query for electronic submissions. Reports in about 1 month. Writer's guidelines for #10 SASE.

Nonfiction: Exposé (current military); interview/profile (military); personal experience (military only); travel (of military interest). Buys about 200 mss/year. Query with published clips. Length: 500-2,000 words. Pays $100-275. Sometimes pays the expenses of writers on assignment.

Photos: Send photos or send photos with ms. Reviews 35mm color contact sheets and prints. Captions, model releases and identification of subjects required.

Tips: "In your query write a detailed description of story and how it will be told. A tentative lead is nice. A military angle is crucial. Just one good story 'breaks in' a freelancer. Follow the outline you propose in your query letter and humanize articles with quotes and examples."

VIETNAM, Cowles History Group, #300, 602 S. King St., Leesburg VA 22075. (703)771-9400. Editor: Colonel Harry G. Summers, Jr. Managing Editor: Kenneth Phillips. 80-90% freelance written. Quarterly magazine on military aspects of the Vietnam War. "Without debating the wisdom of US involvement, pro or con, our objective is to tell the story of the military events, weaponry and personalities of the war, as it happened." Estab. 1988. Circ. 140,000. Pays on publication. Publishes ms up to 2 years after acceptance. Byline given. Buys all rights. Query for electronic submissions. Reports in 3 months on queries; 6 months on mss. Sample copy for $3.95. Writer's guidelines for #10 SASE.

Nonfiction: Book excerpts (if original), historical, interview, personal/experience, military history. "Absolutely no fiction or poetry; we want straight history, as much personal narrative as possible, but not the gung-ho, shoot-em-up variety, either." Buys 50 mss/year. Query. Length: 4,000 words maximum. Pays $300 for features.

Photos: Send photos with submission. Pays up to $100/photo, depending on use. Identification of subjects required. Buys one-time rights.

Columns/Departments: Arsenal (about weapons used, all sides); Personality (profiles of the players, all sides); Fighting Forces (about various units or types of unites: air, sea, rescue); Perspectives. Query. Length: 2,000 words. Pays $150.

WORLD WAR II, Cowles History Group, #300, 602 S. King St., Leesburg VA 22075. (703)771-9400. Editor: Michael Haskew. Managing Editor: Roger L. Vance. 95% freelance written. Prefers to work with published/established writers. Bimonthly magazine covering "military operations in World War II—events, personalities, strategy, national policy, etc." Estab. 1983. Circ. 220,000. Pays on publication. Publishes ms an average of 1-2 years after acceptance. Byline given. Buys all rights. Submit anniversary-related material 1 year in advance. Reports in 3 months on queries; 6 months or more on mss. Sample copy for $4. Writer's guidelines for #10 SASE.

Nonfiction: World War II military history. No fiction. Buys 24 mss/year. Query. Length: 4,000 words. Pays $200.

Photos: State availability of art and photos with submission. (For photos and other art, send photocopies and cite sources. "We'll order.") Sometimes offers additional payment for photos accepted with ms. Captions and identification of subjects required. Buys one-time rights.

Columns/Department: Undercover (espionage, resistance, sabotage, intelligence gathering, behind the lines, etc.); Personalities (WW II personalities of interest); Armaments (weapons, their use and development), all 2,000 words. Book reviews, 300-750 words. Buys 18 mss/year (plus book reviews). Query. Pays $100.

Tips: "List your sources and suggest further readings in standard format at the end of your piece—as a bibliography for our files in case of factual challenge or dispute. All submissions are on speculation. When the story's right, but the writing isn't, we'll pay a small research fee for use of the information in our own style and language."

Music

Music fans follow the latest industry news in these publications. Types of music and musicians or specific instruments are the sole focus of some magazines. Publications geared to the music industry and professionals can be found in the Trade Music section. Additional music and dance markets are found in the Entertainment section.

THE ABSOLUTE SOUND, The Journal of The High End, P.O. Box 360, Sea Cliff NY 11579. (516)676-2830. Fax: (516)676-5469. Editor-in-Chief: Harry Pearson, Jr. Managing Editor: Frank Doris. 10% freelance written. Works with a small number of new/unpublished writers each year. Magazine published 8 times/year covering the music reproduction business, audio equipment and records for "up-scale, high tech men and women, ages 20-100, serious music lovers." Estab. 1973. Pays on publication. Byline given. Buys all rights. Accepts previously published submissions. Send tearsheet or photocopy of article and information about when and where the article previously appeared. Pays 25-50% of their fee for an original article. Reports in 4 months. Query for electronic submissions. Sample copy for $7.50.
• *The Absolute Sound* would like more industry reporting, as well as interviews with industry people.
   This magazine has increased its frequency from 6-8 issues/year. They report they need more queries.
Nonfiction: Exposé (of bad commercial audio practices); interview/profile (famous recording engineers, famous conductors); new product (audio); opinion (audio and record reviews); technical (how to improve your stereo system). Special Recordings issue. No puff pieces about industry. No newspaper clippings. Query with published clips. Length: 250-5,000 words. Pays $125-1,000. Sometimes pays the expenses of writers on assignment.
Columns/Departments: Audio Musings (satires), Reports from Overseas (audio shows, celebrities, record companies). Buys 8 mss/year. Length: 250-750 words. Pays $125-200.
Tips: "Writers should know about audio, recordings and the engineering of same, as well as live music. The approach is *literate*, witty, investigative, good journalism."

AMERICAN SONGWRITER, 121 17th Ave. S., Nashville TN 37203-2707. (615)244-6065. Fax: (615)742-1123. Editor: Vernell Hackett. Managing Editor: Deborah Price. 30% freelance written. Bimonthly magazine educating amateur songwriters while informing professionals. Estab. 1984. Circ. 5,000. Pays on publication. Publishes ms an average of 2 months after acceptance. Offers $10 kill fee. Buys first North American serial rights. Accepts simultaneous and previously published submissions. Send photocopy of article or typed ms with rights for sale noted. Pays 50% of amount paid for an original article. Query for electronic submissions. Reports in 2 months. Sample copy for $3. Writer's guidelines for SAE.
Nonfiction: General interest, interview/profile, new product, technical. "No fiction." Buys 20 mss/year. Query with published clips. Length: 300-1,200 words. Pays $25-50 for assigned articles.
Photos: Send photos with submission. Reviews 3 × 5 prints. Offers no additional payment for photos accepted with ms. Identification of subjects required. Buys one-time rights.

BAM, Rock and Video/the California Music Magazine, BAM Publications, 3470 Burkirk Ave., Pleasant Hill CA 94523. (510)934-3700. Editors: Steve Stolder, Bill Holdship. 60% freelance written. Biweekly tabloid. Circ. 110,000. Pays on publication. Publishes ms an average of 1 month after acceptance. Byline given. Offers negotiable kill fee. Buys first North American serial rights. Accepts previously pubished articles. Send typed ms with rights for sale noted and information about when and where the article previously appeared. For reprints, pays 100% of the amount paid for original article. Submit seasonal material 3 months in advance. Reports in 3 weeks. Sample copy for $2.
Nonfiction: Book excerpts, interview/profiles, record reviews, new product reviews. Buys 100 mss/year. Query with published clips. Length: 1,500-5,000 words. Pays $40-300. Sometimes pays expenses of writers on assignment.
Tips: "*BAM*'s focus is on both the personality and the craft of musicians. Writers should concentrate on bringing out their subject's special traits and avoid bland, clichéd descriptions and quotes. Clear, crisp writing is essential. Many potential *BAM* writers try to be too clever and end up sounding stupid. Also, it helps to have a clear focus. Many writers tend to ramble and simply string quotes together."

BANJO NEWSLETTER, P.O. Box 3418, Annapolis MD 21403-0418. (410)482-6278. Editor: Don Nitchie. 10% freelance written. Monthly magazine covering the "instructional and historical treatment of the 5-string banjo. Covers all aspects of the instrument. Tablature is used for musical examples." Estab. 1973. Circ. 7,000. Pays on publication. Byline given. Buys one-time rights. Accepts previously published submissions. Send typed ms with rights for sale noted and information about when and where the article previously appeared. Pays 100% of amount paid for an original article. Query for electronic submissions. Reports in 1 month on queries. Sample copy for $1.

Nonfiction: Interviews with 5-string banjo players, banjo builders, shop owners, etc. No humorous fiction from anyone unfamiliar with the popular music field. Buys 6 mss/year. Query. Length: 500-4,000 words. Pays $20-100. Sometimes pays writers with contributor copies or other premiums "if that is what writer wants." Very seldom pays expenses of writers on assignment. "We can arrange for press tickets to musical events."

Photos: Send photos with submission. Reviews b&w prints. Offers $10-40/photo. Captions and identification of subjects required whenever possible. Buys one-time rights.

Columns/Departments: Buys 60 mss/year. Query. Length: 500-750 words. Payment varies.

Poetry: Don Nitchie, poetry editor: Rt. 1, Box 289, Chilwark MA 02535. Buys 2 poems/year. Submit maximum 1 poem at one time.

Tips: "The writer should be motivated by being a student of the 5-string banjo or interested in the folk or bluegrass music fields where 5-string banjo is featured. Writers should be able to read and write banjo tablature and know various musicians or others in the field."

BLUEGRASS UNLIMITED, Bluegrass Unlimited, Inc., P.O. Box 111, Broad Run VA 22014-0111. (703)349-8181. Fax: (703)341-0011. Editor: Peter V. Kuykendall. Managing Editor: Sharon Watts. 80% freelance written. Prefers to work with published/established writers. Monthly magazine on bluegrass and old-time country music. Estab. 1966. Circ. 23,500. Pays on publication. Publishes ms an average of 4 months after acceptance. Byline given. Kill fee negotiated. Buys first North American serial, one-time, all rights and second serial (reprint) rights. Accepts previously published submissions. Send photocopy or typed ms with rights for sale noted and information about when and where the article previously appeared. Pays 70-80% of amount paid for an original article. Submit seasonal material 4 months in advance. Reports in 2 weeks on queries; 2 months on mss. Free sample copy and writer's guidelines for #10 SASE.

Nonfiction: General interest, historical/nostalgic, how-to, interview/profile, personal experience, photo feature, travel. No "fan" style articles. Buys 75-80 mss/year. Query with or without published clips. No set word length. Pays 6-8¢/word.

Photos: State availability of or send photos with query. Reviews 35mm transparencies and 3×5, 5×7 and 8×10 b&w and color prints. Pays $50-150 for transparencies; $25-50 for b&w prints; $50-150 for color prints. Identification of subjects required. Buys one-time and all rights.

Fiction: Ethnic, humorous. Buys 3-5 mss/year. Query. No set word length. Pays 6-8¢/word.

Tips: "We would prefer that articles be informational, based on personal experience or an interview with lots of quotes from subject, profile, humor, etc."

B-SIDE MAGAZINE, P.O. Box 1860, Burlington NJ 08016. Editor: Carol L. Schutzbank. Managing Editor: Sandra Garcia. Contact: Carol Schutzbank. 60% freelance written. Bimonthly magazine covering music and related subjects of interest. "*B-Side* bridges the gap between "home-grown" fanzines and the more slick, commercial music magazines." Estab. 1986. Circ. 30,000. Pays varies according to assignment. Byline given. Buys first rights. Query for electronic submissions. Reports in 1-2 months on queries; 1-4 months on mss. Sample copy for $5. Writer's guidelines for #10 SASE.

Nonfiction: Exposé, general interest, new product, interviews, reviews. Pay varies.

Photos: State availability of photos with submission. Reviews contact sheets. Negotiates payment indiviaully. Identification of subjects required. Buys one-time rights.

Tips: "Read our magazine and learn who we are. Too many writers 'scan' us without paying attention to what sets us apart from our competitirs. Read the magazine thoroughly. Good for breaking in are small profile pieces on emerging acts, topics, issues."

CLASSICAL MUSIC MAGAZINE, Suite 207, 121 Lakeshore Rd. E., Mississauga, Ontario L5G 1E5 Canada. Publisher: Anthony D. Copperthwaite. Associate Editor: C. Cooperthwaite. 90% freelance written. Prefers to work with published/established writers but works with a small number of new/unpublished writers each year. Magazine published 5 times/year. Estab. 1978. Circ. 10,000. Pays on publication. Publishes ms an average of 4 months after acceptance. Byline given. Buys first North American serial, one-time and second serial (reprint) rights. Submit seasonal material 4 months in advance. Accepts previously published submissions. Query for electronic submissions. Reports in 6 months. Sample copy and writer's guidelines for $5 and 9×12 SAE.

Nonfiction: Interviews, personality profiles, book reviews, historical articles, some human interest stories. "All articles should pertain to the world of classical music. No academic analysis or short pieces of family experiences." Query with published clips; phone queries OK. Unsolicited articles will not be returned. Length: 500 words or less pays $35-75; 1,500-3,500 words pays $100-500 (Canadian funds). Sometimes pays expenses of writers on assignment.

Photos: Quality photos or illustrations purchased with article. No posed promotion photos. Captions required. Buys one-time rights with article.

Tips: "Send a sample of your writing with suggested subjects. A solidly researched historical article with source references, or an interview with photographs with a famous classical music personality are your best bets."

COUNTRY SONG ROUNDUP, Country Song Roundup, Inc., Suite 401, 210 Route 4 East, Paramus NJ 07652-5116. (201)843-4004. Fax: (201)843-8636. Editor: Celeste R. Gomes. Assistant Editor: Jennifer Fusco-Giacobbe. Contact: Celeste R. Gomes. 10% freelance written. Monthly magazine covering country music. "Our magazine is for the country music fan and songwriter. The slant of our articles is on the music, the songs; the artistic side. At times, we cover the private side of an artist." Estab: 1949. Circ. 200,000. Pays on publication. Publishes ms an average of 6 months after acceptance. Byline given. Offer 50% kill fee or $50. Buys first rights and second serial (reprint) rights. Editorial lead time 3 months. Submit seasonal material 6 months in advance. Query for assignments. "No phone calls please." Reports in 2 weeks on queries; 2 months on mss. Sample copy for $2.95. Writer's guidelines for #10 SASE.
Nonfiction: Interview/profile of country artists. "No profiles on new artists—they're done inhouse. No personal experience articles, reviews of any kind or Question and Answer articles." Buys 25-30 mss/year. Query with published clips. Length: 1,000-1,200 words. Pays $100 minimum. "Besides regular fee ($100) a copy of the issue in which article appears is sent to the writer."

‡GUITAR PLAYER MAGAZINE, GPI Publications, Suite 100, 411 Borel Ave., San Mateo CA 95112. (415)358-9216. Editor: Joe Gore. 70% freelance written. Monthly magazine for persons "interested in guitars, guitarists, manufacturers, guitar builders, bass players, equipment, careers, etc." Circ. 150,000. Buys first serial and limited reprint rights. **Pays on acceptance.** Publishes ms an average of 3 months after acceptance. Byline given. Reports in 6 weeks. Writer's guidelines for #10 SASE.
Nonfiction: Publishes "wide variety of articles pertaining to guitars and guitarists: interviews, guitar craftsmen profiles, how-to features—anything amateur and professional guitarists would find fascinating and/or helpful. On interviews with 'name' performers, be as technical as possible regarding strings, guitars, techniques, etc. We're not a pop culture magazine, but a magazine for musicians." Also buys features on such subjects as a guitar museum, role of the guitar in elementary education, personal reminiscences of past greats, technical gadgets and how to work them, analysis of flamenco, etc. Buys 30-40 mss/year. Query. Length: open. Payment varies. Sometimes pays expenses of writers on assignment.
Photos: Reviews b&w glossy prints. Buys 35mm color transparencies. Payment varies. Buys one time rights.

HIT PARADER, #220, 63 Grand Ave., River Edge NJ 07661. (210)487-6124. Editor: Andy Secher. Managing Editor: Anne Leighton. 5% freelance written. Monthly magazine covering heavy metal music. "We look for writers who have access to the biggest names in heavy metal music." Estab. 1943. Circ. 200,000. Pays on publication. Publishes ms an average of 4 months after acceptance. Byline given. Buys all rights. Submit seasonal material 4 months in advance. Reports in 2 months on queries. Sample copy for 9×12 SAE with 5 first-class stamps.
Nonfiction: General interest, interview/profile. Buys 3-5 mss/year. Query with published clips. Length: 600-800 words. Pays $75-140. Lifestyle-oriented and hardball pieces. "Study and really know the bands to get new angles on story ideas."
Photos: Reviews transparencies, 5×7 and 8×10 b&w prints and Kodachrome 64 slides. Offers $25-200/photo. Buys one-time rights. "We don't work with new photographers."
Tips: "Interview big names in metal, get published in other publications. We don't take chances on new writers."

HOME & STUDIO RECORDING, The Magazine for the Recording Musician, Music Maker Publications, #200, 7318 Topanga Canyon Blvd., Canoga Park CA 91303-1242. (818)346-3404. Fax: (818)346-3597. Editor: Nick Batzdorf. 33% freelance written. Monthly magazine of technical and practical info to help musicians make better recordings. Estab. 1987. Circ. 40,000. Pays on publication. Publishes ms an average of 4 months after acceptance. Byline given. Buys first rights. Query for electronic submissions. Reports in 3 weeks on queries. Sample copy for $2.95 and 9×12 SAE with 5 first-class stamps. Writer's guidelines for #10 SASE.
Nonfiction: How-to, personal experience, technical. Buys 36 mss/year. Query. Length: up to 4,000 words. Pays $71.50-440.
Photos: Send photos with submission. Reviews contact sheets, negatives and transparencies. Offers no additional payment for photos accepted with ms. Buys one-time rights.
Tips: "Freelancer needs to have good knowledge of subject matter. Particularly interested in technical applications of equipment and recording techniques. We are also publishing new Spanish language version. We're interested in technical interviews with Latin American artists, recording engineers, etc. involved in recording—who are recognizable names."

ILLINOIS ENTERTAINER, Suite 150, 2250 E. Devon, Des Plaines IL 60018. (708)298-9333. Fax: (708)298-7973. Editor: Michael C. Harris. 95% freelance written. Prefers to work with published/established writers but open to new writers with "style." Monthly tabloid covering music and entertainment for consumers within 100-mile radius of Chicago. Estab. 1974. Circ. 80,000. Pays on publication. Publishes ms an average of 2 months after acceptance. Byline given. Offers 10% kill fee. Buys one-time rights. Accepts previously published articles. Send tearsheet or photocopy of article and information about when and where the article previously appeared. For reprints, pays 100% of the amount paid for an original article. Reports in 1-2 months. Sample copy for $5.

Nonfiction: Interview/profile (of entertainment figures). Buys 75 mss/year. Query with published clips. Length: 500-2,000 words. Pays $15-100. Sometimes pays expenses of writers on assignment.

Photos: Send photos. Pays $20-30 for 5 × 7 or 8 × 10 b&w prints; $125 for color cover photo, both on publication only. Captions and identification of subjects required.

Columns/Departments: Spins (record reviews stress record over band or genre). Buys 200 mss/year. Query with published clips. Length: 150-250 words. Pays $8-40.

Tips: "Send clips (published or unpublished) with phone number, and be patient. Full staff has seniority, but if you know the ins and outs of the entertainment biz, and can balance that knowledge with a broad sense of humor, then you'll have a chance. Also, *IE* is more interested in alternative music than the pop-pap you can hear/read about everywhere else."

INTERNATIONAL MUSICIAN, American Federation of Musicians, Suite 600, Paramount Building, 1501 Broadway, New York NY 10036. (212)869-1330. Fax: (212)302-4374. Editor: Stephen R. Sprague. Managing Editor: Jessica Roe. 10% freelance written. Prefers to work with published/established writers. Monthly magazine for professional musicians. Estab. 1900. **Pays on acceptance.** Publishes ms an average of 3 months after acceptance. Byline given. Accepts previously published material. Send typed ms with rights for sale noted. Pays 60% of amount paid for an original article. Reports in 3 months.

Nonfiction: Articles on prominent instrumentalists (classical, jazz, rock or country) who are members of the American Federation of Musicians. Send complete ms. Length: 1,500 words maximum.

JAZZ TIMES, Jazz Times, Inc., #303, 7961 Eastern Ave., Silver Spring MD 20910. (301)588-4114. Editor: Mike Joyce. Associate Publisher: Lee Mergner. 20% freelance written. Magazine published 10 times/year covering jazz (& blues) music. Estab. 1970. Circ. 74,000. Pays on publication. Byline given. Buys first North American serial rights. Sample copy for $4.

Nonfiction: Jazz, guitar, bass, piano, sax, festival, blues. Buys 60 mss/year. Query. Length: 1,000-2,500 words. Pays 10¢/word. Sometimes pays expenses of writers on assignment.

Photos: Send photos with submission. Buys one-time rights.

‡JAZZIZ MAGAZINE, Jazziz Magazine Inc., 3620 NW 43rd St., Gainesville FL 32606. (904)375-3705. Editor: Bill Stevenson. Managing Editor: Roy Parkhurst. 100% freelance written. Bimonthly magazine. Adult oriented music—jazz, world beat, New Age, blues, what's new and innovative. Estab. 1984. Circ. 100,000. Pays on publication. Publishes ms an average of 2 months after acceptance. Byline given. Offers 50% kill fee. Buys first North American serial rights. Editorial lead time 6 months. Submit seasonal material 3 months in advance. Accepts simultaneous submissions. Query for electronic submissions. Reports in 2 weeks on queries; 2 months on mss. Sample copy for $2.90 and 11 × 14 SAE. Writers guidelines free on request.

Nonfiction: General interest (music), historical/nostalgic, interview/profile, new product, opinion, technical. Buys 100 mss/year. Query with published clips. Length: 300-4,000 words. Pays 12¢/word. Sometimes pays expenses of writers on assignment.

Photos: Send photos with submission. Negotiates payment individually.

Columns/Departments: Prelude (new artist release), 300 words; Coda (short artist profiles), 800 words; various topical review columns, 300-1,200 words. Buys 300 mss/year. Query with published clips. Pays 12¢/word.

Tips: "Query us. Get our writer's guidelines. Call or write us *after* you've become familiar with our publication and have definate ideas to discuss." All areas open to freelancers. "Know what you're talking (writing) about."

THE MISSISSIPPI RAG, "The Voice of Traditional Jazz and Ragtime," 6500 Nicollet Ave. S., Minneapolis MN 55423-1673. (612)861-2446 or (612)920-0312. Fax: (612)861-4621. Editor: Leslie Johnson. 70% freelance written. Works with small number of new/unpublished writers each year, "but most of our writers have been with us for years." Monthly tabloid covering traditional jazz and ragtime. Estab. 1973. Circ. 12,000. Pays on publication. Publishes ms an average of 4 months after acceptance. Byline given. Buys all rights, "but writer may negotiate if he wishes to use material later." Submit seasonal material 3 months in advance. Reports in 3-6 months. Sample copy and writer's guidelines for 9 × 12 SAE with 5 first-class stamps.

Nonfiction: Historical, interview/profile, personal experience, photo features, current jazz and ragtime news, festival coverage, book, video and record reviews, gigs and festival listings. Reviews are always assigned. No "long-winded essays on jazz or superficial pieces on local ice cream social Dixieland bands." Buy 24-30 mss/year. Query with or without published clips, or send complete ms. Length: 1,000-6,500 words. Pays 2¢/word.

Photos: Send photos with submission. Prefers b&w 5 × 7 or 8 × 10 prints. Offers $5 photo/minimum. Identification of subjects required. Buys one-time rights.

Columns/Departments: Book and Record reviews. Buys 60 assigned mss/year. Query with published clips. Pays 2¢/word.

Tips: "Become familiar with the jazz world. The *Rag* is read by musicians, jazz/ragtime writers, historians and jazz/ragtime buffs. We want articles that have depth—solid facts and a good basic grasp of jazz and/or ragtime history. Not for the novice jazz writer. Interviews with jazz and ragtime performers are most open to freelancers. It's wise to query first because we have already covered so many performers."

MODERN DRUMMER, 870 Pompton Ave., Cedar Grove NJ 07009. (201)239-4140. Fax: (201)239-7139. Editor-in-Chief: Ronald Spagnardi. Features Editor: William F. Miller. Managing Editor: Rick Van Horn. Monthly magazine for "student, semi-pro and professional drummers at all ages and levels of playing ability, with varied specialized interests within the field." 60% freelance written. Circ. 95,000. Pays on publication. Publishes ms an average of 3 months after acceptance. Buys all rights. Accepts previously published submissions. Reports in 2 weeks. Sample copy for $3.95. Free writer's guidelines.
Nonfiction: How-to, informational, interview, new product, personal experience, technical. "All submissions must appeal to the specialized interests of drummers." Buys 20-30 mss/year. Query or submit complete ms. Length: 5,000-8,000 words. Pays $200-500.
Photos: Purchased with accompanying ms. Reviews 8×10 b&w prints and color transparencies.
Columns/Departments: Jazz Drummers Workshop, Rock Perspectives, In The Studio, Show Drummers Seminar, Teachers Forum, Drum Soloist, The Jobbing Drummer, Strictly Technique, Book Reviews, Record Reviews, Video Reviews, Shop Talk. "Technical knowledge of area required for most columns." Buys 40-50 mss/year. Query or submit complete ms. Length: 500-2,500 words. Pays $25-150.

MUSICIAN, Billboard Publications, 11th Floor, 1515 Broadway, New York NY 10036. (212)536-5208. Editor: Bill Flanagan. Senior Editors: Keith Powers, Ted Greenwald, Mark Rowland. 85% freelance written. Monthly magazine covering contemporary music, especially rock, pop and jazz. Estab. 1976. Circ. 170,000. Pays on publication. Byline given. Offers 25-33% kill fee. Buys first world serial rights. Submit seasonal material 3 months in advance.
Nonfiction: All music-related: book excerpts, exposé, historical, how-to (recording and performing), humor, interview/profile, new product, technical. Buys 150 mss/year. Query with published clips. Length: 300-10,000 words. Payment negotiable. Pays expenses of writers on assignment.
Photos: Assigns photo shoots. Uses some stock. Offers $50-300/photo.
Columns/Departments: Jazz (jazz artists or works), 1,000-5,000 words; Reviews (record reviews), 300-500 words; Rough Mix (short, newsy stories), 300 words; Working Musician (technical "trade" angles on musicians), 1,000-3,000 words. Query with published clips. Length 300-1,500 words.
Tips: "Be aware of special music writers' style; don't gush, be somewhat skeptical; get the best quotes you can and save the arcane criticism for reviews; know and apply Strunk and White; be interesting. Please send *published* clips; we don't want to be anyone's first publication. Our writing is considered excellent (in all modesty), even though we don't pay as much as we'd like. We recognize National Writers Union."

ONE SHOT, The Magazine of One-Hit Wonders, One Shot Enterprises, Contract Station 6, Box 145, Denver CO 80203. Editor: Steve Rosen. 80% freelance written. Eager to work with new/unpublished writers. "*One Shot* is dedicated to remembering now-obscure or under-appreciated performers of rock and related musics; expecially the one-hit wonders. Uses interviews, essays and journalism." Estab. 1986. Circ. 200. **Pays on acceptance.** Publishes ms up to 1 year after acceptance. Byline given. Buys one-time, second serial (reprint) or simultaneous rights, and makes work-for-hire assignments. Accepts simultaneous and previously published submissions. Send typed ms with rights for sale noted. For reprints pays 75% of their fee for an original article. Reports in 1 month. Sample copy for $4. Writer's guidelines for #10 SASE.
Nonfiction: Book excerpts, essays, exposé, general interest, historical/nostalgic, interview/profile, opinion, personal experience, travel. No religious/inspirational articles. Buys 16 mss/year. Query. Length: 2,500 maximum words. Pays up to $100 for most articles, will pay more for longer features. Sometimes pays expenses of writers on assignment.
  ● This magazine only publishes journalism/essays related to rock 'n' roll one-hit wonders. It previously took journalism/fiction/essays/poetry related to all types of "neglected" rock 'n' roll.
Photos: Send photos with submission. Reviews contact sheets and 8½×11 prints. Offers additional payment for photos accepted with ms. Buys one-time rights.
Columns/Departments: Speak, Memory! (personal experiences with now-obscure rock, etc., performers); Buys 10 mss/year. Query with or without published clips, or send complete ms. Length: 1,000 maximum words. Pays up to $100.
Tips: "*One Shot* needs 'Where are They Now' articles on one- or two-hit performers who were once popular. Those pieces should include interviews with the performer and others; and provide a sense of 'being there'. *One Shot* will pay for such stories. Just send me a note explaining your interests, and I'll respond with detailed suggestions. I won't disqualify anyone for not following procedures; I want to encourage a body of work on this topic."

PULSE!, Tower Records, 2500 Del Monte W., Sacramento CA 95691. (916)373-2450. Editor: Mike Farrace. Contact: Suzanne Mikesell. 80% freelance written. Works with a SMALL number of new/unpublished writers each year. Monthly magazine covering recorded music, film, video, video games and interactive multimedia.

Estab. 1983. Circ. 290,000. Pays on publication. Publishes ms an average of 8 months after acceptance. Byline given. Buys first serial rights. Reports in 2 months. Sample copy for 12×15 SAE with 8 first-class stamps. Also publishes a bimonthly classical music magazine titled *Classical Pulse!*

Nonfiction: Feature stories, interview/profile (angled toward subject's taste in music, such as 10 favorite albums, first record ever bought, anecdotes about early record-buying experiences). Always looking for concise news items and commentary about nonpopular musical genres. Buys 200-250 mss/year. Query or send complete ms. Length: 200-2,500 words. Pays $20-1,000.

Photos: Send photos. Captions and identification of subjects required. Buys one-time rights.

Fillers: Newsbreaks.

Tips: "Break in with 200- to 400-word news-oriented stories on recording artists or on fast breaking, record-related news, personnel changes, unusual match-ups, reissues of great material. Any kind of music. The more obscure genres on independent labels are the hardest for us to cover, so they stand a good chance of being used."

RELIX MAGAZINE, Music for the Mind, P.O. Box 94, Brooklyn NY 11229. Editor: Toni A. Brown. Fax: (718)692-4345. 60% freelance written. Eager to work with new/unpublished writers. Bimonthly magazine covering rock 'n' roll music and specializing in Grateful Dead and other San Francisco and 60s related groups for readers ages 15-65. Estab. 1974. Circ. 60,000. Pays on publication. Publishes ms an average of 6 months after acceptance. Byline given. Buys all rights. Reports in 1 year. Accepts previously published material. Send typed ms with rights for sale noted and information about when and where the article previously appeared. Sample copy for $3.

Nonfiction: Historical/nostalgic, interview/profile, new product, personal experience, photo feature, technical. Special issues: year-end special. Query with published clips if available or send complete ms. Length open. Pays $1.75/column inch.

Fiction: Publishes novel excerpts.

Columns/Departments: Query with published clips, if available, or send complete ms. Pays variable rates.

Tips: "The most rewarding aspects of working with freelance writers are fresh writing and new outlooks."

THE $ENSIBLE SOUND, 403 Darwin Dr., Snyder NY 14226. (716)839-2199. Fax: (716)839-2264. Publisher: John A. Horan. 80% freelance written. Eager to work with new/unpublished writers. Quarterly magazine for "high fidelity enthusiasts, many having a high fidelity industry-related jobs." Circ. 12,800. **Pays on acceptance.** Publishes ms an average of 6 months after acceptance. Byline given. Buys all rights. Accepts simultaneous and previously published submissions. Send typed ms with rights for sale noted. Reports in 2 weeks. Sample copy for $2, or free with writing sample, outline and ideas.

Nonfiction: Exposé; how-to; general interest; humor; historical; interview (people in hi-fi business, manufacturers or retail); new product (all types of new audio equipment); nostalgia (articles and opinion on older equipment); personal experience (with various types of audio equipment); photo feature (on installation, or how-to tips); profile (of hi-fi equipment); technical (pertaining to audio). "Subjective evaluations of hi-fi equipment make up 70% of our publication. We will accept 10/issue." Buys 8 mss/year. Submit outline. Pays $25 maximum. Pays expenses of writers on assignment.

Columns/Departments: Bits & Pieces (short items of interest to hi-fi hobbyists); Ramblings (do-it-yourself tips on bettering existing systems); Record Reviews (of records which would be of interest to audiophiles and recordings of an unusual nature). Query. Length: 25-400 words. Pays $10/page.

SOUNDTRACK, The Journal of the Independent Music Association, SoundTrack Publishing, P.O. Box 609, Ringwood NJ 07456. (201)831-1317. Fax: (201)831-8672. Editor: Don Kulak. 60% freelance written. Bimonthly music and business magazine. Estab. 1988. Circ. 10,000. Pays on publication. Publishes ms an average of 2-3 months after acceptance. Byline sometimes given. Buys first rights and second serial (reprint) rights. Submit seasonal/holiday material 4 months in advance. Accepts simultaneous and previously published submissions. Reports in 1 week on queries; 3 weeks on mss. Free sample copy and writer's guidelines for 9×12 SAE with $2 postage.

Nonfiction: Book excerpts, exposé, how-to, interview/profile, opinion, technical. Buys 36 mss/year. Query with published clips. Length: 1,000-2,000 words.. Pays $50-200 for assigned articles. No unsolicited mss. Sometimes pays writers with contributor copies or other premiums rather than cash by "mutually beneficial agreement." Sometimes pays expenses of writers on assignment.

Photos: Send photos with submissions. Offers $10-20/photo. Buys all rights.

Columns/Departments: The Business of Music (promotion, distribution, forming a record label; alternative markets—film scores, jingles, etc.; how-to's on generating more income from own music); and Sound Input (in-depth and objective reporting on audio equipment and technology, emphasizing acoustical ramifications, also, cassette, record and CD manufacturing). Buys 24 mss/year. Query with published clips. Length: 1,000-2,000 words.

Tips: "Write a letter explaining background, interests, and areas of special study and what you hope to get out of writing for our publication. All sections are open to freelancers. Writing should be fluid and direct. We would like more how-to information on record marketing and distribution."

STEREO REVIEW, Hachette Filipacchi Magazines, Inc., 1633 Broadway, New York NY 10019. (212)767-6000. Editor-in-Chief: Louise Boundas. Executive Editor: Michael Riggs. Classical Music Editor: Robert Ripps. Popular Music Editor: Steve Simels. 65% freelance written, almost entirely by established contributing editors, and on assignment. Monthly magazine. Estab. 1958. Circ. 500,000. **Pays on acceptance.** Publishes ms an average of 5 months after acceptance. Byline given. Buys first North American serial or all rights. Reports in 5 months. Sample copy for 9×12 SAE with 11 first-class stamps.
Nonfiction: Equipment and music reviews, how-to-buy, how-to-use, stereo, interview/profile. Buys approximately 25 mss/year. Query with published clips. Length: 1,500-3,000 words. Pays $500-1,000 for assigned articles.
Tips: "Send proposals or outlines, rather than completed articles, along with published clips to establish writing ability. Publisher assumes no responsibility for return or safety of unsolicited art, photos or manuscripts."

TRADITION, Prairie Press, Box 438, Walnut IA 51577. (712)366-1136. Editor: Robert Everhart. 20% freelance written. Bimonthly magazine emphasizing traditional country music and other aspects of pioneer living. Circ. 2,500. Pays on publication. Not copyrighted. Byline given. Buys one-time rights. Submit seasonal/holiday material 6 months in advance. Accepts simultaneous and previously published submissions. Reports in 1 month. Sample copy for $1.
Nonfiction: Historical (relating to country music); how-to (play, write, or perform country music); inspirational (on country gospel); interview (with traditional country performers); nostalgia (pioneer living); personal experience (country music); travel (in connection with country music contests or festivals). Query. Length: 800-1,200 words. Pays $10-15.
Photos: Send photos with query. Payment included in ms price. Reviews 5×7 b&w prints. Captions and model releases required. Buys one-time rights.
Poetry: Free verse and traditional. Buys 4 poems/year. Length: 5-20 lines. Submit maximum 2 poems with SASE. Pays $2-5.
Fillers: Clippings, jokes and anecdotes. Buys 5/year. Length: 15-50 words. Pays $5-10.
Tips: "Material must be concerned with what we term 'real' country music as opposed to today's 'pop' country music. Freelancer must be knowledgable of the subject; many writers don't even know who the father of country music is, let alone write about him."

Mystery

These magazines buy fictional accounts of crime, detective work and mystery. Skim through other sections to identify markets for fiction; some will consider mysteries. For nonfiction crime markets, refer to the Detective section.

ALFRED HITCHCOCK MYSTERY MAGAZINE, Bantam Doubleday Dell, 1540 Broadway, New York NY 10036. Editor: Cathleen Jordan. Magazine published 13 times/year featuring mystery fiction. Circ. 230,000. **Pays on acceptance.** Byline given. Buys first, first anthology and foreign rights. Submit seasonal/holiday material 7 months in advance. Reports in 2 months. Writer's guidelines for SASE.
  ● Ranked as one of the best markets for fiction writers in *Writer's Digest* magazine's biannual "Fiction 50," June 1994.
Fiction: Original and well-written mystery and crime fiction. Length: up to 14,000 words.

ELLERY QUEEN'S MYSTERY MAGAZINE, Bantam Doubleday Dell, 1540 Broadway, New York NY 10036. Editor: Janet Hutchings. 100% freelance written. Magazine published 13 times/year featuring mystery fiction. Estab. 1941. Circ. 279,000. **Pays on acceptance.** Publishes ms an average of 6 months after acceptance. Byline given. Buys first serial or second serial (reprint) rights. Accepts simultaneous submissions. Reports in 3 months. Writer's guidelines for #10 SASE.
  ● Ranked as one of the best markets for fiction writers in *Writer's Digest* magazine's biannual "Fiction 50," June 1994.
Fiction: Special consideration will be given to "anything timely and original. We publish every type of mystery: the suspense story, the psychological study, the private-eye story, the deductive puzzle—the gamut of crime and detection from the realistic (including stories of police procedure) to the more imaginative (including 'locked rooms' and impossible crimes). We always need detective stories, and do not want sex, sadism or sensationalism-for-the-sake-of-sensationalism." No gore or horror; seldom publishes parodies or pastiches. Buys up to 13 mss/issue. Length: 6,000 words maximum; occasionally higher but not often. Also buys 2-3 short novels/year of up to 17,000 words, by established authors and minute mysteries of 250 words. Pays 3-8¢/word.
Poetry: Short mystery verses, limericks. Length: 1 page, double-spaced maximum.
Tips: "We have a Department of First Stories to encourage writers whose fiction has never before been in print. We publish an average of 13 first stories every year."

‡**NEW MYSTERY, The World's Best Mystery,** Crime and Suspense Stories, #2001, 175 Fifth Ave., New York NY 10010. Editor: Linda Wong. 100% freelance written. Quarterly magazine featuring mystery short stories and book reviews. Estab. 1989. Circ. 80,000. **Pays on acceptance.** Publishes ms an average of 6 months after acceptance. Byline given. Buys first North American serial or all rights. Editorial lead time 6 months. Submit seasonal material 1 year in advance. Accepts simultaneous submissions. Query for electronic submissions. Reports in 2 months on mss. Sample copy for $5 and 9 × 12 SAE with $1.05 postage.
Nonfiction: New product, short book reviews. Buys 40 mss/year. Send complete ms. Length: 250-2,000 words. Pays $20-50.
Fiction: Humorous, mystery, suspense. Buys 50 mss/year. Send complete ms. Length: 2,000-6,000 words. Pays $50-500.
Fillers: Acrostic or crossword puzzles. Pays $25-50.

Nature, Conservation and Ecology

These publications promote reader awareness of the natural environment, wildlife, nature preserves and ecosystems. Many of these "green magazines" also concentrate on recycling and related issues. They do not publish recreation or travel articles except as they relate to conservation or nature. Other markets for this kind of material can be found in the Regional; Sports; and Travel, Camping and Trailer categories, although magazines listed there require that nature or conservation articles be slanted to their specialized subject matter and audience. Some juvenile and teen publications also buy nature-related material for young audiences. For more information on recycling publications, turn to the Resources and Waste Reduction section in Trade.

ALTERNATIVES, P.O. Box 566822, Atlanta GA 30356. (404)973-1994. Editor: Rochel Haigh Blehr. 100% freelance written. Monthly newspaper of environmental/alternative health issues. Estab. 1989. Circ. 45,000. Pays on publication. Byline given. Buys first North American serial rights. Editorial lead time 1 month. Submit seasonal material 2 months in advance. Accepts simultaneous submissions. Sample copy free on request. Writer's guidelines for #10 SASE.
Nonfiction: Environment. Buys 420 mss/year. Send complete ms. Length: 1,000-1,500 words. Pays $50 minimum for unsolicited articles.
Photos: State availability of or send photos with submission. Reviews 5 × 7 prints. Identification of subjects required.
Tips: "All submissions are read. They should be hard news AP style, with pros and cons. Topics must cover environment and alternative health. No personal opinion or personal agendas will be considered."

‡**AMC OUTDOORS, The Magazine of the Appalachian Mountain Club,** Appalachian Mountain Club, 5 Joy St., Boston MA 02108. (617)523-0655 ext. 312. Editor/Publisher: Catherine K. Buni. 90% freelance written. Monthly magazine covering outdoor recreation and conservation issues. Estab. 1907. Circ. 60,000. Pays on publication. Publishes ms an average of 3 months after acceptance. Byline given. Offers 25% kill fee. Buys all rights. Editorial lead time 3 months. Submit seasonal material 4 months in advance. Query for electronic submissions. Reports in 1 month on queries; 2 months on mss. Sample copy for #10 SASE. Writer's guidelines free on request.
Nonfiction: Book excerpts, essays, exposé, general interest, historical/nostalgic, how-to, interview/profile, opinion, personal experience, photo feature, technical, travel. Special issues: Northern Forest Report (April) featuring the northern areas of New York, New Hampshire, Vermont, and Maine, and protection efforts for these areas. Buys 10 mss/year. Query with or without published clips. Length: 500-3,000 words. Pays $50. Sometimes pays expenses of writers on assignment.
Photos: State availability of photos with submission. Reviews contact sheets, transparencies and prints. Model releases and identification of subjects required.
Columns/Departments: Contact: Kimberly Ridley. News (environmental/outdoor recreation coverage of northeast), 1,300 words. Buys 20 mss/year. Query. Pays $50-500.

AMERICAN FORESTS, American Forests, 1516 P St. NW, Washington DC 20005. (202)667-3300. Fax: (202)667-7751. Editor: Bill Rooney. 70% freelance written. Bimonthly magazine "of trees and forests, published by a nonprofit citizens' organization for the advancement of intelligent management and use of our forests, soil, water, wildlife and all other natural resources necessary for an environment of high quality." Estab. 1895. Circ. 30,000. **Pays on acceptance.** Publishes ms an average of 4-8 months after acceptance. Byline given. Buys one-time rights. Accepts previously published articles. Send tearsheet of article or typed ms with rights for sale noted and information about when and where the article previously appeared. For reprints, pays 50% of the amount paid for an original article. Written queries preferred. Submit seasonal

material 5 months in advance. Reports in 2 months. Sample copy for $1.20. Writer's guidelines for SASE.
Nonfiction: General interest, historical, how-to, humor, inspirational. All articles should emphasize trees, forests, forestry and related issues. Buys 7-10 mss/issue. Query. Length: 2,000 words. Pays $300-700.
Photos: Send photos. Offers no additional payment for photos accompanying ms. Uses 8×10 b&w glossy prints; 35mm or larger transparencies, originals only. Captions required. Buys one-time rights.
Tips: "Query should have honesty and information on photo support."

‡THE AMICUS JOURNAL, Natural Resources Defense Council, 40 W. 20th St., New York NY 10011. (212)727-2700. Editor: Kathrin Day Lassila. 80% freelance written. Quarterly magazine covering national and international environmental policy. *"The Amicus Journal* is intended to provide the general public with a journal of thought and opinion on environmental affairs, particularly those relating to policies of national and international significance. Estab. 1979. Estab. 170,000. Pays on acceptance. Publishes ms an average of 6 months after acceptance. Offers 30% kill fee. Buys first North American serial rights. Submit seasonal material 6 months in advance. Query for electronic submissions. Prefer modem at 1200 baud. Reports in 6 weeks on queries. Sample copy for 9×12 SAE with $1.44 postage. Writer's guidelines free on request.
Nonfiction: Exposé, interview/profile, book reviews. Query with published clips. Length: 200-1,500 words. Pay negotiable. Sometimes pays expenses of writers on assignment.
Photos: State availability of photos with submission. Reviews contact sheets, color transparencies, 8×10 b&w prints. Negotiates payment individually. Captions, model releases, identification of subjects required. Buys one-time rights.
Columns/Departments: News & Comment (summary reporting of environmental issues, usually tied to topical items), 200-500 words; Book Reviews (in-depth reporting on issues and personalities, well-informed essays on books of general interest to environmentalists interested in policy and history), 500-1,000 words. Buys 25 mss/year. Query with published clips. Pay negotiable.
Poetry: Brian Swann. Avant-garde, free verse, haiku. All poetry should be rooted in nature. Must submit with SASE. Buys 16 poems/year. Pays $25.
Tips: "Please stay up to date on environmental issues, and review *The Amicus Journal* before submitting queries. Except for editorials all departments are open to freelance writers. Queries should precede manuscripts, and manuscripts should conform to the Chicago Manual of Style. Writers are asked to be sensitive to tone. As a policy magazine, we do not publish articles of a personal or satirical nature."

APPALACHIAN TRAILWAY NEWS, Appalachian Trail Conference, P.O. Box 807, Harpers Ferry WV 25425-0807. (304)535-6331. Fax: (304)535-2667. Editor: Judith Jenner. 50% freelance written. Bimonthly magazine. Estab. 1925. Circ. 26,000. **Pays on acceptance.** Byline given. Buys first North American serial or second serial (reprint) rights. Accepts previously published submissions. Send photocopy of article or typed ms with rights for sale noted and information about when and where the article previously appeared. Reports in 2 months. Sample copy for $2.50 includes guidelines. Writer's guidelines only for SASE.
● Articles must relate to Appalachian Trail.
Nonfiction: Essays, general interest, historical/nostalgic, how-to, humor, inspirational, interview/profile, photo feature, technical, travel. No poetry or religious materials. Buys 15-20 mss/year. Query with or without published clips, or send complete ms. Length: 250-3,000 words. Pays $25-300. Pays expenses of writers on assignment. Publishes, but does not pay for "hiking reflections."
Photos: State availability of b&w photos with submission. Reviews contact sheets, negatives and 5×7 prints. Offers $25-125/photo. Identification of subjects required. Negotiates future use by Appalachian Trail Conference.
Tips: "Contributors should display an obvious knowledge of or interest in the Appalachian Trail. Those who live in the vicinity of the Trail may opt for an assigned story and should present credentials and subject of interest to the editor."

ARCHIPELAGO, The Society for Ocean Studies, P.O. Box 510266, Key Colony Beach FL 33051-0266. (305)743-6155. Editor: Robert O. Stafford. Publisher: Phil Edwards. Quarterly newsletter covering the oceans. "Our readers are educated, upscale laymen with an interest in marine matters. We run informative stories on just about any subject related to the sea." Estab. 1986. Circ. 200. Pays on publication. Publishes ms an average of 3 months after acceptance. Byline given. Buys first North American serial rights. Accepts simultaneous submissions. Reports in 2 weeks. Sample copy and writer's guidelines for #10 SASE.
Nonfiction: "No high tech material with specialized jargon, highly localized interest or very broad subject matter." Buys 4-5 mss/year. Query. Length: 1,000-1,500 words. Pays $50.
Photos: Discourages photos; prefers line drawings for illustration. State availabity of photos with submission. Offers no additional payment for photos accepted with ms. Buys one-time rights.

A bullet introduces comments by the editor of Writer's Market *indicating special information about the listing.*

Tips: "We are looking for general interest articles related to marine matters: oceanography, biology, chemistry, archaeology, history, meteorology, etc."

AUDUBON, The Magazine of the National Audubon Society, National Audubon Society, 700 Broadway, New York NY 10003-9501. Fax: (212)755-3752. Editor: Michael W. Robbins. 85% freelance written. Bimonthly magazine. Estab. 1887. Circ. 430,000. **Pays on acceptance.** Byline given. Buys first North American serial rights, second serial (reprint) rights on occasion. Query before submission. Reports in 3 months. Sample copy for $4 and 9 × 12 SAE with 10 first-class stamps or $5 for magazine and postage. Writer's guidelines for #10 SASE.
 • Ranked as one of the best markets for freelance writers in *Writer's Digest* magazine's annual "Top 100 Markets," January 1994.

Nonfiction: Essays, investigative, historical, humor, interview/profile, opinion, photo feature, book excerpts (well in advance of publication). Length: 250-4,000 words. Pays $250-4,000. Pays expenses of writers on assignment.

Photos: Query with photographic idea before submitting slides. Reviews 35mm transparencies. Offers page rates per photo on publication. Captions and identification of subjects required. Write for photo guidelines.

BIRD WATCHER'S DIGEST, Pardson Corp., P.O. Box 110, Marietta OH 45750. Editor: Mary Beacom Bowers. 60% freelance written. Works with a small number of new/unpublished writers each year. Bimonthly magazine covering natural history—birds and bird watching. "*BWD* is a nontechnical magazine interpreting ornithological material for amateur observers, including the knowledgeable birder, the serious novice and the backyard bird watcher; we strive to provide good reading and good ornithology." Estab. 1978. Circ. 85,000. Pays on publication. Publishes ms an average of 1 year after acceptance. Byline given. Buys one-time, first serial and second serial (reprint) rights. Submit seasonal material 6 months in advance. Accepts previously published submissions. Reports in 2 months. Sample copy for $3. Writer's guidelines for #10 SASE.

Nonfiction: Book excerpts, how-to (relating to birds, feeding and attracting, etc.), humor, personal experience, travel (limited—we get many). "We are especially interested in fresh, lively accounts of closely observed bird behavior and displays and of bird watching experiences and expeditions. We often need material on less common species or on unusual or previously unreported behavior of common species." No articles on pet or caged birds; none on raising a baby bird. Buys 75-90 mss/year. Send complete ms. All submissions must be accompanied by SASE. Length: 600-3,500 words. Pays from $50.

Photos: Send photos with ms. Pays $10 minimum for b&w prints; $50 minimum for transparencies. Buys one-time rights.

Poetry: Avant-garde, free verse, light verse, traditional. No haiku. Buys 12-18 poems/year. Submit maximum 3 poems. Length 8-20 lines. Pays $10.

Tips: "We are aimed at an audience ranging from the backyard bird watcher to the very knowledgeable birder; we include in each issue material that will appeal at various levels. We always strive for a good geographical spread, with material from every section of the country. We leave very technical matters to others, but we want facts and accuracy, depth and quality, directed at the veteran bird watcher and at the enthusiastic novice. We stress the joys and pleasures of bird watching, its environmental contribution, and its value for the individual and society."

‡BOREALIS: The Magazine of the Canadian Parks and Wilderness Society, Box 1359, Edmonton, Alberta T5J 2N2 Canada. Editor: David Dodge. 50% freelance written. Quarterly magazine covering wilderness and ecological issues. "*Borealis* provides coverage of wilderness and ecological issues in a popular, visually-oriented format." Estab. 1965. Circ. 15,000. Pays on publication. Byline given. Buys first North American serial rights. Editorial lead time 6 months. Submit seasonal material 9-12 months in advance. Accepts simultaneous submissions. Reports in 2 months on queries. Sample copy for $5 (includes postage). Writer's guidelines for #10 SASE.

Nonfiction: Essays, exposé, general interest, historical/nostalgic, humor, inspirational, interview/profile, opinion, personal experience, photo feature. Buys 10-20 mss/year. Query with published clips. Length: 100-4,000 words. Pays 15¢/word. Sometimes pays expenses of writers on assignment.

Photos: State availability of photos with submission. Negotiates payment individually. Captions and identification of subjects required. Buys one-time rights.

Columns/Departments: Canada File (news shorts about wilderness, ecological issues); Book reviews (books about wilderness, ecological issues and nature); 100-500 words. No pay.

E THE ENVIRONMENTAL MAGAZINE, Earth Action Network, P.O. Box 5098, Westport CT 06881-5098. (203)854-5559. Fax: (203)866-0602. Editor: Doug Moss. Contact: Elissa Wolfson, managing editor. 80% freelance written. Bimonthly magazine on environmentalism. "*E Magazine* was formed for the purpose of acting as a clearinghouse of information, news and commentary on environmental issues." Estab. 1990. Circ. 50,000. Pays on publication. Byline given. Offers 50% kill fee. Buys first North American serial rights. Editorial lead time 3 months. Submit seasonal material 3-6 months in advance. Accepts simultaneous submissions and occasionally previously published articles. Send tearsheet or photocopy of article or typed ms with rights for sale noted and information about when and where the article previously appeared. Query for all submissions. Sample copy for $4. Writer's guidelines for #10 SASE.

Nonfiction: Exposé (environmental), how-to (the "Environmentalist" section), interview/profile, new product, opinion. No fiction or poetry. Buys 100 mss/year. Query with published clips. Length: 100-5,000 words. Pays 20¢/word, negotiable. On spec or free contributions welcome. Sometimes pays telephone expenses of writers on assignment.

Photos: Send photos with submission, or send photos with submission (if available). Reviews printed samples, e.g., magazine tearsheet, postcards, etc. to be kept on file. Negotiates payment individually. Identification of subjects required. Buys one-time rights.

Columns/Departments: In Brief/Currents (environmental news stories/trends), 400-1,000 words; Consumer News (environmentally sound products/trends), 1,200 words; Food and Health (ecological and health impacts of dietary choices), 1,200 words; the Environmentalist (how-to eco lifestyle tips), 1,000 words; Book Reviews (environmental books), 1,200 words; Interviews (environmental leaders), 2,000 words. Buys 100 mss/year. Query with published clips. Pays 20¢/word, negotiable. On spec or free contributions welcome.

Tips: "Contact us to obtain writer's guidelines and back issues of our magazine. Tailor your query according to the department/section you feel it would be best suited for. Articles must be lively, well-researched, and relevant to a mainstream, national readership."

‡**EARTHKEEPER, Canada's Environmental Magazine,** P.O. Box 1649, Guelph, Ontario N1H 6R7 Canada. Editor: Scott Black. 90% freelance written. Bimonthly magazine covering the environment. "*Earthkeeper* is a national environmental magazine which covers issues of interest to the average consumer. Articles are well-researched, and the editorial approach is positive and constructive." Estab. 1990. Circ. 11,000. Pays on publication. Publishes ms an average of 4 months after acceptance. Byline given. Offers 50% kill fee. Buys first North American serial or one-time rights. Editorial lead time 6 months. Submit seasonal material 8 months in advance. Accepts simultaneous submissions. Reports in 1 month. Sample copy for $3.95. Writer's guidelines for #10 SASE.

Nonfiction: General interest, historical/nostalgic, humor, inspirational, interview/profile, new product, opinion, personal experience, photo feature. religious, technical, travel. Buys 48 mss/year. Query with published clips. Length: 300-2,500 words. Sometimes pays expenses of writers on assignment.

Photos: State availability of photos with submission. Reviews 3½ × 5 prints. Offers $25-100/photo. Captions, model releases and identification of subjects required. Buys one-time rights.

Fillers: Facts. Buys 10/year. Length: 300-750 words. Pays $25-50.

ENVIRONMENT, Heldref Publications, 1319 18th St. NW, Washington DC 20036-1802. Managing Editor: Barbara T. Richman. 2% freelance written. Magazine published 10 times/year for high school and college students and teachers, scientists, business and government executives, teachers, citizens, interested in environment or effects of technology and science in public affairs. Estab. 1958. Circ. 12,500. Buys all rights. Byline given. Pays on publication to professional writers. Publishes ms an average of 4 months after acceptance. Reports in 3 months. Query or submit 3 double-spaced copies of complete ms. Sample copy for $6.75.

Nonfiction: Scientific and environmental material, effects of technology on society. Preferred length: 4,000-5,000 words for full-length article. Pays $100-300, depending on material. Also accepts shorter articles (1,000-1,700 words) for "Overview" section. Pays $100. "All full-length articles must offer readers authoritative analyses of key environmental problems. Articles must be annotated (referenced), and all conclusions must follow logically from the facts and arguments presented." Prefers articles centering around policy-oriented, public decision-making, scientific and technological issues.

HIGH COUNTRY NEWS, High Country Foundation, P.O. Box 1090, Paonia CO 81428-1090. (303)527-4898. Editor: Betsy Marston. 80% freelance written. Works with a small number of new/unpublished writers each year. Biweekly tabloid covering environment and natural resource issues in the Rocky Mountain states for environmentalists, politicians, companies, college classes, government agencies, etc. Estab. 1970. Circ. 14,500. Pays on publication. Publishes ms an average of 2 months after acceptance. Byline given. Buys one-time rights. Reports in 1 month. Free sample copy and writer's guidelines.

Nonfiction: Reporting (local issues with regional importance); exposé (government, corporate); interview/profile; opinion; personal experience; centerspread photo feature. Special issues include those on states in the region. Buys 100 mss/year. Query. Length: 3,000 words maximum. Pays 15-20¢/word. Sometimes pays expenses of writers on assignment.

• This magazine has increased its pay rates since last being listed.

Photos: Send photos with ms. Prefers b&w prints. Captions and identification of subjects required.

Poetry: Chip Rawlins, poetry editor, P.O. Box 1262, Pinedale WY 82941. Avant-garde, free verse, haiku, light verse, traditional. Pays in contributor copies.

For information on setting your freelance fees, see How Much Should I Charge?

Tips: "We use a lot of freelance material, though very little from outside the Rockies. Start by writing a query letter."

‡**THE INLAND SEA**, The Inland Sea Society, 12833E 5th 13, Maple WI 54854. (715)364-8533. Editor: Tom Hastings. 75% freelance written. Quarterly covering recreation on and protection of Lake Superior. "We are most receptive to journal entries of the writer who has kayaked or sailed around all or part of Lake Superior." Estab. 1990. Circ. 2,500. Pays on publication. Byline given. Offers 50% kill fee. Buys first North American serial rights. Editorial lead time 2 months. Submit seasonal material 1-6 months in advance. Query for electronic submissions. Reports in 3 weeks on queries. Sample copy for $2 and #10 SASE. Writer's guidelines free on request.

Nonfiction: Book excerpts, essays, exposé, how-to ("sail tips" "paddle tips"), personal experience, travel. "No diatribes, nothing not about the Lake Superior watershed." Buys 12 mss/year. Send complete ms. Length: 300-900 words. Pays $10-30.

Photos: Send photos with submission. Reviews 5×7, 4×6, 8×10 prints. Offers $10 minimum. Captions required. Buys one-time rights.

Columns/Departments: Lake Journal (journal entry of kayaker or sailor), 300-900 words; Paddle Tips (safety, boat repair, paddling instruction), 300-900 words. Buys 12 mss/year. Send complete ms. Pays $20-30.

Tips: "The Inland Sea Society stresses ecotourism, sustainable development, kayaking, water quality of Lake Superior, sailing, and the beauty and power of this body of water that contains a full 10% of the freshwater in the world. Paddle/sail tips and journal entries sections are most open to freelancers."

INTERNATIONAL WILDLIFE, National Wildlife Federation, 8925 Leesburg Pike, Vienna VA 22184-0001. Editor: Jonathan Fisher. 85% freelance written. Prefers to work with published/established writers. Bimonthly for persons interested in natural history and the environment in countries outside the US. Estab. 1971. Circ. 380,000. **Pays on acceptance.** Publishes ms an average of 4 months after acceptance. Usually buys all rights to text. "We are now assigning most articles but will consider detailed proposals for quality feature material of interest to a broad audience." Reports in 6 weeks. Writer's guidelines for #10 SASE.

Nonfiction: Focuses on world wildlife, environmental problems and peoples' relationship to the natural world as reflected in such issues as population control, pollution, resource utilization, food production, etc. Stories deal with non-US subjects. Especially interested in articles on animal behavior and other natural history, first-person experiences by scientists in the field, well-reported coverage of wildlife-status case studies which also raise broader themes about international conservation and timely issues. Query. Length: 2,000-2,500 words. Also in the market for short, 750-word "one pagers." Examine past issue for style and subject matter. Pays $1,500 minimum for long features. Sometimes pays expenses of writers on assignment.

Photos: Purchases top-quality color photos; prefers packages of related photos and text, but single shots of exceptional interest and sequences also considered. Prefers Kodachrome or Fujichrome transparencies. Buys one-time rights.

MICHIGAN NATURAL RESOURCES MAGAZINE, Kolka & Robb, Inc, Suite 1386, 30600 Telegraph Rd., Bingham Farms MI 48025. (810)642-9580. Editor: Richard Morscheck. 50% freelance written. Works with a small number of new/unpublished writers each year. Bimonthly magazine covering natural resources in the Great Lakes area. Estab. 1931. Circ. 100,000. **Pays on acceptance.** Publishes ms an average of 9 months after acceptance. Byline given. Buys first rights. Submit seasonal/holiday material 1 year in advance. Reports in 2 months. Sample copy for $4 and 9×12 SAE. Writer's guidelines for #10 SASE.

Nonfiction: "All material must pertain to this region's natural resources: lakes, rivers, wildlife, flora and special features. No personal experience." Buys 15 mss/year. Query with clips of published work. Length: 1,000-3,000 words. Pays $150-500. Sometimes pays the expenses of writers on assignment.

Photos: Photos submitted with an article can help sell it, but they must be of professional quality and razor sharp in focus. Send photos with ms. Pays $50-250 for 35mm transparencies; Fuji or Kodachrome preferred. Identification of subjects required. Buys one-time rights.

Tips: "We hope to exemplify why Michigan's natural resources are valuable to people and vice versa. We also strongly suggest that prospective writers familiarize themselves with past issues of the magazine before sending us material to review."

NATIONAL PARKS, 1776 Massachusetts Ave. NW, Washington DC 20036. (202)223-6722. Fax: (202)659-0650. Editor: Sue Dodge. 85% freelance written. Prefers to work with published/established writers. Bimonthly magazine for a highly educated audience interested in preservation of National Park System units, natural areas, and protection of wildlife habitat. Estab. 1919. Circ. 350,000. **Pays on acceptance.** Publishes ms an average of 5 months after acceptance. Buys first North American serial and second serial (reprint) rights. Reports in 3 months. Sample copy for $3 and 9×12 SAE. Writer's guidelines for #10 SASE.

• Ranked as one of the best markets for freelance writers in *Writer's Digest* magazine's annual "Top 100 Markets," January 1994.

Nonfiction: Exposé (on threats, wildlife problems in national parks); descriptive articles about new or proposed national parks and wilderness parks; natural history pieces describing park geology wildlife, or plants. All material must relate to national parks. No poetry, philosophical essays or first person narratives. "Queries are welcome, but unsolicited manuscripts are not accepted." Length: 2,000-3,000 words. Pays $800 for full-length features; $350 for serial articles.

Photos: $100-250 for transparencies. Captions required. Buys first North American serial rights.

NATIONAL WILDLIFE, National Wildlife Federation, 8925 Leesburg Pike, Vienna VA 22184-0001. (703)790-4524. Editor-in-Chief: Bob Strohm. Editor: Mark Wexler. 75% freelance written, "but assigns almost all material based on staff ideas. Assigns few unsolicited queries." Bimonthly magazine on wildlife, natural history and environment. "Our purpose is to promote wise use of the nation's natural resources and to conserve and protect wildlife and its habitat. We reach a broad audience that is largely interested in wildlife conservation and nature photography. We avoid too much scientific detail and prefer anecdotal, natural history material." Estab. 1963. Circ. 660,000. **Pays on acceptance.** Publishes ms an average of 1 year after acceptance. Offers 25% kill fee. Buys all rights. Submit seasonal material 8 months in advance. Reports in 6 weeks. Writer's guidelines for #10 SASE.

Nonfiction: General interest (2,500-word features on wildlife, new discoveries, behavior, or the environment); how-to (an outdoor or nature related activity); personal experience (outdoor adventure); photo feature (wildlife); short 700-word features on an unusual individual or new scientific discovery relating to nature. Buys 50 mss/year. Query with or without published clips. Length: 750-2,500 words. Pays $500-2,000. Sometimes pays expenses of writers on assignment.

Photos: John Nuhn, photo editor. Send photos or send photos with query. Prefers Kodachrome or Fujichrome transparencies. Buys one-time rights.

Tips: "Writers can break in with us more readily by proposing subjects (initially) that will take only one or two pages in the magazine (short features)."

NATURAL HISTORY, Natural History Magazine, Central Park W. at 79th St., New York NY 10024. Editor: Alan P. Ternes. 15% freelance written. Monthly magazine for well-educated, ecologically aware audience: professional people, scientists and scholars. Circ. 500,000. Pays on publication. Publishes ms an average of 3 months after acceptance. Byline given. Buys first serial rights and becomes agent for second serial (reprint) rights. Submit seasonal material at least 6 months in advance.

Nonfiction: Uses all types of scientific articles except chemistry and physics—emphasis is on the biological sciences and anthropology. Prefers professional scientists as authors. "We always want to see new research findings in almost all the branches of the natural sciences—anthropology, archeology, zoology and ornithology. We find that it is particularly difficult to get something new in herpetology (amphibians and reptiles) or entomology (insects), and we would like to see material in those fields. We lean heavily toward writers who are scientists. We expect high standards of writing and research. We favor an ecological slant in most of our pieces, but do not generally lobby for causes, environmental or other. The writer should have a deep knowledge of his subject, then submit original ideas either in query or by manuscript. Acceptance is more likely if article is accompanied by high-quality photographs." Buys 60 mss/year. Query or submit complete ms. Length: 1,500-3,000 words. Pays $750-1,000, plus additional payment for photos used.

Photos: Rarely uses 8×10 b&w glossy prints; pays $125/page maximum. Much color is used; pays $300 for inside and up to $500 for cover. Buys one-time rights.

Tips: "Learn about something in depth before you bother writing about it."

‡NATURE CANADA, Canadian Nature Federation, Suite 520, 1 Nicholas St., Ottawa, Ontario KIN 7B7 Canada. Editor: Barbara Stevenson. Quarterly membership magazine covering conservation, natural history and environmental/naturalist community. "*Nature Canada* is written for an audience interested in nature. Its content supports the Canadian Nature Federation's philosophy that all species have a right to exist regardless of their usefulness to humans. We promote the awareness, understanding and enjoyment of nature." Estab. 1971. Circ. 20,000. Pays on publication. Publishes ms an average of 3 months after acceptance. Byline given. Offers $100 kill fee. Buys one-time rights. Editorial lead time 3 months. Submit seasonal material 6 months in advance. Reports in 1-3 months on mss. Sample copy for $5. Writer's guidelines free on request.

Nonfiction: Canadian environmental issues and natural history. Special issues: backyard habitat—how to attract wildlife species and naturalize your backyard (Canadian focus). Buys 20 mss/year. Query with published clips. Length: 2,000-4,000 words. Pays 25¢/word (Canadian).

Photos: State availability of photos with submission. Offers $40-100/photo (Canadian). Identification of subjects required. Buys one-time rights.

Columns/Departments: The Green Gardener (naturalizing your backyard), 1,200 words; Discovery (newly discovered or little-known facts about wild species), 800-1,500 words; Connections (Canadians making a difference for the environment), 1,000-1,500 words. Buys 16 mss/year. Query with published clips. Pays 25¢/ (Canadian)/word.

Tips: "Our readers are knowledgeable about nature and the environment so contributors should have a good understanding of the subject. We also deal exclusively with Canadian issues and species."

OUTDOOR AMERICA, Level B, 1401 Wilson Blvd., Arlington VA 22209-2318. (703)528-1818. Fax: (703)528-1836. Editor: Michael E. Diegel. 20% freelance written. Prefers to work with published/established writers but is open to new writers who send complete mss. Quarterly magazine about natural resource conservation and outdoor recreation for sports enthusiasts and local conservationists who are members of the Izaak Walton League. Estab. 1922. Circ. 50,000. Pays on publication. Publishes ms an average of 4 months after acceptance. Byline and brief bio given. Buys one-time North American rights, depending on arrangements with author. Query first. Submit seasonal material 6 months in advance. Reports in 1 month, often sooner. Sample copy for $1.50 and 9 × 12 SAE. Writer's guidelines for SASE.
Nonfiction: "We are interested in thoroughly researched, well-written pieces on current natural resource and recreation issues of *national importance* (threats to water, fisheries, wildlife habitat, air, public lands, soil, etc.); articles on wildlife management controversies; natural history articles; humor pieces on outdoor recreation themes (fishing, hunting, camping, ethical outdoor behavior, etc.)." Length: 900-2,000 words. Payment: 20¢/word.
  • The editor of this magazine would like to see more environmental investigative, natural history and outdoor recreation queries.
Photos: Reviews 5 × 7 b&w glossy prints and 35mm and larger transparencies. Additional payment for photos with ms negotiated. Pays $225 for cover. Captions and model releases (for models under age 18) required. Buys one-time rights.
Tips: "Writers should obtain guidelines and sample issue *before* querying us. They will understand our needs and editorial focus much better if they've done this. Most ideas I receive aren't worth a 2,000-word feature. I'm looking for writers who have a real voice and can write with a national audience of informed conservationists in mind."

PACIFIC DISCOVERY, California Academy of Sciences, Golden Gate Park, San Francisco CA 94118-4599. (415)750-7116. Fax: (415)750-7106. Editor: Keith Howell. 100% freelance written. Prefers to work with published/established writers. "Quarterly journal of nature and culture in California, the West, the Pacific and Pacific Rim countries read by scientists, naturalists, teachers, students, and others having a keen interest in knowing the natural world more thoroughly." Estab. 1948. Circ. 30,000. Buys first North American serial rights. Pays on publication. Query for electronic submissions. Reports within 2 months. Sample copy for 9 × 12 SAE with 5 first-class stamps. Writer's guidelines for #10 SASE.
Nonfiction: "Subjects of articles include behavior and natural history of animals and plants, ecology, evolution, anthropology, indigenous cultures, geology, paleontology, biogeography, taxonomy and related topics in the natural sciences. Occasional articles are published on the history of natural science, exploration, astronomy and archaeology. Emphasis is on current research findings. Authors need not be scientists; however, all articles must be based, at least in part, on firsthand fieldwork. Accuracy is crucial." Query with 100-word summary of projected article for review before preparing finished ms. Length: 800-4,000 words. Pays 25¢/word.
Photos: Send photos with submission "even if an author judges that his own photos should not be reproduced. Referrals to professional photographers with coverage of the subject will be greatly appreciated." Reviews 35mm, 4 × 5 or other transparencies or 8 × 10 b&w glossy prints. Offers $75-175 and $200 for the cover. Buys one-time rights.

SIERRA, 730 Polk St., San Francisco CA 94109-7813. (415)923-5656. Fax: (415)776-4868. Editor-in-Chief: Jonathan F. King. Deputy Editor: Annie Stine. Senior Editors: Joan Hamilton, Reed McManus. Associate Editors: Mark Mardon, Paul Rauber. Managing Editor: Marc Lecard. Works with a small number of new/unpublished writers each year. Bimonthly magazine emphasizing conservation and environmental politics for people who are well educated, activist, outdoor-oriented and politically well informed with a dedication to conservation. Estab. 1893. Circ. 500,000. **Pays on acceptance.** Publishes ms an average of 4 months after acceptance. Byline given. Buys first North American serial rights. Query for electronic submissions. Reports in 2 months.
  • Ranked as one of the best markets for freelance writers in *Writer's Digest* magazine's annual "Top 100 Markets," January 1994. Editor reports no interest in seeing outdoor how-to or equipment articles.
Nonfiction: Exposé (well-documented on environmental issues of national importance such as energy, wilderness, forests, etc.); general interest (well-researched nontechnical pieces on areas of particular environmental concern); photo feature (photo essays on threatened or scenic areas); journalistic treatments of semi-technical topics (energy sources, wildlife management, land use, waste management, etc.). No "My trip to . . ." or "why we must save wildlife/nature" articles; no poetry or general superficial essays on environmentalism; no reporting on purely local environmental issues. Buys 5-6 mss/issue. Query with published clips. Length: 800-3,000 words. Pays $450-2,000. Pays limited expenses of writers on assignment.
Photos: Lacey Tuttle Brown, art and production manager. Send photos. Pays $300 maximum for transparencies; more for cover photos. Buys one-time rights.
Tips: "Queries should include an outline of how the topic would be covered and a mention of the political appropriateness and timeliness of the article. Statements of the writer's qualifications should be included."

SNOWY EGRET, The Fair Press, P.O. Box 9, Bowling Green IN 47833. (812)829-1910. Editors: Philip Repp, Michael Aycock. 95% freelance written. Semiannual magazine of natural history from literary, artistic, philosophical and historical perspectives. "We are interested in works that celebrate the abundance and beauty of nature, encourage a love and respect for the natural world, and examine the variety of ways through which human beings connect psychologically and spiritually with living things and landscape. Circ. 500. Pays on publication. Publishes ms an average of 1 year after acceptance. Buys first North American serial and one-time rights. Submit seasonal material 6 months in advance. Accepts simultaneous submissions. Reports in 3 months. Sample copy for $8 and 9 × 12 SAE. Writer's guidelines for 6 × 9 SASE.

Nonfiction: Essays, general interest, historical, interview/profile, opinion, personal experience, travel. "No topical, dated articles, highly scientific or technical pieces." Buys 20 mss/year. Send complete ms. Length: 500-10,000. Pays $2/page.

Fiction: Literary with natural history orientation. "No popular and genre fiction." Buys up to 10 mss/year. Send complete ms. Length: 500-10,000. Pays $2/page.

Poetry: Nature-oriented: avant-garde, free verse, haiku, traditional. Buys 20 poems/year. Pays $4/poem to $4/page.

Tips: "Make sure that all assertions, ideas, messages, etc. are thoroughly rooted in detailed observations and shared with the reader through description, dialogue, and narrative. The reader needs to see what you've seen, live what you've lived. Whenever possible the subject shown should be allowed to carry its own message, to speak for itself. We look for book reviews, essays, poetry, fiction, conservation and environmental studies based on first-hand observations of plants and animals that show an awareness of detail and a thorough-going familiarity with the organisms or habitats in question."

SUMMIT, 1221 May St., Hood River OR 97031. (503)387-2200. Editor: John Harlin. 100% freelance written. Bimonthly magazine covering mountain culture, environment and sport. "Sophisticated, inspired, introspective and passionate writing for an educated audience with high literary standards. The writing must relate to the mountain world, but this can be treated broadly." Estab. 1990. Pays 3 months prior to publication or on acceptance. Publishes ms an average of 3-9 months after acceptance. Byline given. Offers 25% kill fee. Buys first North American serial, first, second serial (reprint) or simultaneous rights. Submit seasonal material 3-12 months in advance. Accepts simultaneous and previously published submissions. Send tearsheet or photocopy of article or short story or typed ms with rights for sale noted and information about when and where the article previously appeared. Reports in 2 months. Sample copy for $6 and 9 × 12 SAE with 10 first-class stamps "or send $8 w/SAE and we'll stamp." Writer's guidelines for #10 SASE.

Nonfiction: Book excerpts, essays, exposé, general interest, historical/nostalgic, humor, inspirational, interview/profile, opinion, personal experience, photo feature, travel. "No what-I-did stories that don't have strong literary content." Buys 30 mss/year. Query with or without published clips or send complete ms. Length: 100-4,000 words. Pays $50-800.

Photos: Send photos with query or ms. Send photos with submission. Reviews contact sheets, transparencies and prints. Offers $50-175/photo, $300 for cover. Identification of subjects required. Buys one-time rights.

Columns/Departments: Mountain Times and Scree (news and essays on mountain world), 50-1,500 words. Buys 25 mss/year. Query with published clips or send complete ms. Pays $50-300. The Summit Guide (mountain travel guide to destinations and techniques). Query stating fields of expertise. 50-1,500 words. Pays $50-700.

Poetry: Pays $50-200. Buys only occasionally. Must be mountain-related.

Fillers: Facts and short humor. Pays $50 minimum.

Tips: "If we don't know the writer, submitting complete manuscripts or partial manuscripts helps. Published clips help, but we distrust them because they've already been edited. Know the magazine, *know your subject* and *know your writing*. Mountain Times news pieces and essays can be about any place and anything in the mountain world but must be entertaining or provocative. Previously published material from non-competing magazines is welcome. Send published piece with date and source."

WILDLIFE CONSERVATION MAGAZINE, Wildlife Conservation Society, 185th St. and Southern Blvd., Bronx NY 10460-1068. (212)220-5121. Editor: Joan Downs. 90% freelance written. Bimonthly magazine covering wildlife. Estab. 1895. Circ. 141,858. **Pays on acceptance.** Publishes ms an average of 1 year or more after acceptance. Byline given. Buys first North American serial rights. Submit seasonal material 1 year in advance. Accepts simultaneous submissions. Reports in 2 months on queries; 3 months on mss. Sample copy for $2.95 and 9 × 12 SAE with 6 first-class stamps. Writer's guidelines for SASE.

● Ranked as one of the best markets for freelance writers in *Writer's Digest* magazine's annual "Top 100 Markets," January 1994.

Nonfiction: Nancy Simmons, senior editor. Essays, personal experience, wildlife articles. No pet or any domestic animal stories. Buys 12 mss/year. Query. Length 1,500-2,500 words. Pays $750-3,000 for assigned articles; $500-1,000 for unsolicited articles.

Photos: Send photos with submission. Reviews transparencies. Buys one-time rights.

ZOO LIFE, Zoos, Aquariums, and Wildlife Parks, Ingle Publishing Co., 11661 San Vicente Blvd., Los Angeles CA 90049. (310)820-8841. Editor: Mary Batten. Managing Editor: Jody Ingle. 75% freelance written.

"Quarterly magazine devoted to those readers interested in the conservation, education, research and captive-breeding efforts of zoos, aquariums and wildlife parks. Our articles appeal to educated adults as well as children; in short, to anyone who enjoys zoos and the animals in them." Estab. 1989. Circ. 80,000. Pays on publication. Publishes ms an average of 6 months after acceptance. Byline given. Buys one-time or second serial (reprint) rights. Submit seasonal material 1 year in advance. Accepts simultaneous and previously published submissions. Reports in 1 month on queries; 2 months on mss. Sample copy for $3.95 and 9×12 SAE with 10 first-class stamps. Free writer's guidelines.

Nonfiction: Book excerpts, essays, general interest, historical/nostalgic, how-to (photography), interview/profile, opinion, photo feature, travel. "Please, no general trips through a zoo exhibit; we prefer in-depth focus on a zoo animal, new research on animal behavior, exhibit, program, or personality." Buys 45 mss/year. Query with published clips. Length: 500-2,000 words. Pays $600 maximum for assigned articles.

Photos: Send photos with submission. Reviews 35mm or 4×5 transparencies. Payment negotiable. Identification of subjects required. Buys one-time rights.

Columns/Departments: Arkwatch (column devoted to zoos' captive-breeding programs), 1,200 words; Reviews (book, video reviews of relevant titles), 500-700 words; Zoo Views (opinion, usually on conservation or zoo issues, usually written by professionals), 1,200 words. Buys 8 mss/year. Query with published clips. Length: 500-1,200 words. Pays $150-360.

Tips: "Querying with samples is the writer's best bet. Also, familiarity with the magazine and the articles it has *already* published is advised. We are looking for well-researched pieces featuring interviews with zoo experts or other authorities on animal conservation."

Personal Computers

Personal computer magazines continue to evolve. The most successful have a strong focus on a particular family of computers or widely-used applications and carefully target a specific type of computer use. Magazines serving MS-DOS and Macintosh families of computers are expected to grow, while new technology will also offer opportunities for new titles. Some of the magazines offer an online service for readers in which they can get the magazine alone or with a supplement on computer disk. Be sure you see the most recent issue of a magazine before submitting material.

AMAZING COMPUTING, PiM Publications, Inc., P.O. Box 2140, Fall River MA 02722-2140. (508)678-4200. Fax: (508)675-6002. Managing Editor: Donald D. Hicks. 90% freelance written. Monthly magazine for the Commodore Amiga computer system user. Circ. 35,000. Pays on publication. Publishes ms an average of 2-4 months after acceptance. Byline given. Buys all rights. Query for electronic submissions. Reports in 2 months. Sample copy for $5. Free writer's guidelines.

Nonfiction: How-to, new product, technical, reviews, tutorials. Buys 200 mss/year. Query. Length: 1,000 words minimum. Pays $65 minimum/page.

Photos: Send photos with submission. Reviews 4×6 prints. Offers $25/photo. Captions required. Buys all rights.

Columns/Departments: Reviews and Programs. Buys 100 mss/year. Query. Length: 1,000-3,000 words.

BYTE MAGAZINE, 1 Phoenix Mill Lane, Peterborough NH 03458-0809. (603)924-9281. Fax: (603)924-2550. Editor: Dennis Allen. Monthly magazine covering personal computers for professional users of computers. 50% freelance written. Estab. 1975. Circ. 515,000. **Pays on acceptance.** Byline given. Buys all rights. Reports on rejections in 6 weeks; 3 months if accepted. Electronic submissions accepted, IBM or Macintosh compatible. Sample copy for $3.50. Writer's guidelines for #10 SASE.

Nonfiction: News, reviews, in-depth discussions of topics related to microcomputers or technology. Buys 160 mss/year. Query. Length: 1,500-5,000 words. Pay is $350-1,000 for assigned articles; $500-750 for unassigned.

Tips: "Always interested in hearing from freelancers who are technically astute users of personal computers. Especially interested in stories on new computing technologies, from anywhere in the world. Read several issues of BYTE to see what we cover, and how we cover it. Read technical journals to stay on the cutting edge of new technology and trends. Send us a proposal with a short outline of an article explaining some new technology, software trend, and the relevance to advanced business users of personal computers. Our readers want accurate, useful, technical information; not fluff and not meaningless data presented without insight or analysis."

‡COMPUSERVE MAGAZINE, 5000 Arlington Centre Blvd., Columbus OH 43220. (614)457-8600. Editor: Kassie Rose. 75% freelance written. Monthly membership magazine covering how to get the most from the CompuServe Information Service. "The editorial content shows members how to use the CompuServe Information Service. Departments address how the online connection can benefit them in using hardware and software, managing business (whether corporate or home-based), and pursuing hobbies, travel or other interests. The audience is 90% male (74% of whom are married) with an average annual income of $86,200. Ninety percent are professionals, managers, executives or proprietors." Estab. 1981. Circ. 1 million. Pays on publication. Publishes ms an average of 4 months after acceptance. Byline given. Offers 50% kill fee. Buys first North American serial rights. Editorial lead time 4 months. Query for electronic submissions. Reports in 1 month on queries. Sample copy free on request.

Nonfiction: Technical, travel. "Each article relates to how members can use CIS to accomplish something, whether planning a trip or getting advice on buying hardware." Buys 120 mss/year. Query with published clips. Length: 1,200-4,000 words. Pays $500.

Photos: Send photos with submission. Reviews transparencies and prints up to 5 × 7. Model releases, identification of subjects required. Buys all rights.

Columns/Departments: Contact: Cathryn Conroy. Book Reviews (computer industry books), 300 words. Buys 100 mss/year. Query with published clips. Pays $75.

Tips: "Freelancers should familiarize themselves with the magazine's focus and style and, if possible, with the information service itself. They should then send a cover letter, résumé and appropriate clips to the editor, outlining areas of technical or other expertise. The magazine's departments (Computing Services, Personal Enterprise and Random Access) are the most open to new freelancers. In all cases, the stories are heavily driven by member examples, with supporting advice from experts who belong to the information service."

‡COMPUTOREDGE, San Diego's Computer Magazine, The Byte Buyer, Inc., P.O. Box 83086, San Diego CA 92138. (619)573-0315. Fax: (619)573-0205. Managing Editor: Leah Steward. 90% freelance written. Weekly magazine on computers. "We cater to the novice/beginner/first-time computer buyer. Humor is welcome." Estab. 1983. Circ. 90,000. Pays on publication. Net 30 day payment after publication. Byline given. Offers $15 kill fee. Buys first North American serial rights. Submit seasonal material 2 months in advance. Query for electronic submissions. Reports in 2 months. Writer's guidelines and an editorial calendar for #10 SASE "or call (619)573-1675 with your modem and download writer's guidelines. Read sample issue online." Sample issue for $1.75 postage.

Nonfiction: General interest (computer), how-to, humor, personal experience. Buys 80 mss/year. Send complete ms. Length: 900-1,200 words. Pays 8-10¢/word for assigned articles. Pays 5-10¢/word for unsolicited articles.

Photos: Send photos with submission. Captions and identification of subjects required. Buys one-time rights.

Columns/Departments: Beyond Personal Computing (a reader's personal experience). Buys 80 mss/year. Send complete ms. Length: 500-1,000 words. Pays $50.

Fiction: Confession, fantasy, slice-of-life vignettes. No poetry. Buys 20 mss/year. Send complete ms. Length: 900-1,200 words. Pays 8-10¢/word.

Tips: "Be relentless. Convey technical information in an understandable, interesting way. We like light material, but not fluff. Write as if you're speaking with a friend. Avoid the typical 'Love at First Byte' article. Avoid the 'How My Grandmother Loves Her New Computer' article. We do not accept poetry. Avoid sexual mnuendoes/metaphors. Reading a sample issue is advised."

‡ELECTRONIC ENTERTAINMENT, the Interactive Resource for the Electronic Age, IDG Communications, #700, 951 Mariners Island Blvd., San Mateo CA 94404. (415)349-4300. Contact: Fredric Paul. 60% freelance written. Monthly magazine covering multimedia entertainment, family computing. Estab. 1993. Circ. 150,000. **Pays on acceptance.** Publishes ms an average of 3 months after acceptance. Byline given. Buys all rights. Editorial lead time 3 months. Submit seasonal material 6 months in advance. Query for electronic submissions.

Nonfiction: Book excerpts, exposé, general interest, historical/nostalgic, how-to, humor, interview/profile, new product, opinion, personal experience, photo feature, technical. Query with published clips. Length: 100-4,000 words. Pays $50-1,000.

Photos: Send photos with submission. Reviews negatives, transparencies or computer files. Offers no additional payment for photos accepted with ms. Captions required. Buys all rights.

Columns/Departments: State of the Game (game reviews), 400-600 words. Buys 12 mss/year. Query with published clips. Pays $50-150.

Fiction: Science fiction, techno-humor. Query with published clips or send complete ms.

Fillers: Contact: Donna Meyerson. Anecdotes, facts, short humor. Length: 25-100 words. Pays $25.

Tips: "Read the magazine, know something about the field, have proven writing skills, and propose ideas with fresh angles."

GENEALOGICAL COMPUTING, Ancestry Inc., P.O. Box 476, Salt Lake City UT 84110. (801)531-1790. Fax: (801)531-1798. Editor: Dennis M. Sampson. 50% freelance written. Quarterly magazine on genealogy, using computers. Designed for genealogists who use computers for records management. "We publish articles on all types of computers: PC, Macintosh, Apple II, etc." Estab. 1981. Circ. 4,500. Pays on publication. Publishes ms an average of 4 months after acceptance. Byline given. Buys all rights. Query for electronic submissions. Reports in 2 months.

Nonfiction: New product, personal experience (with software), technical (telecommunications, data exchange, data base development) how-to, reviews, opinion, programming. "Articles on pure genealogy cannot be accepted; this also applies to straight computer technology." Query with outline/summary. Length: 1,000-4,000 words. Pays $100.

Tips: "We need how-to articles describing methods of managing genealogical information with your computer. We accept a *limited* number of pertinent BASIC programs or programming ideas for publication."

‡LINK-UP, The Newsmagazine for Users of Online Services and CD-ROM, Learned Information, Inc., 2222 River Dr., King George VA 22485. CompuServe: #72105,1753. Editor: Loraine Page. 70% freelance written. Bimonthly tabloid covering online communications and electronic information. "Our readers have modems or CD-ROM drives. We need articles on what they can do with them. Our primary audience is business users. What databases can they log onto to gain a business edge? What new CD-ROM titles are worthy of investing in? We also cover personal and educational use." Estab. 1980. Circ. 10,000. Pays on publication. Publishes ms an average of 2 months after acceptance. Byline given. Offers 50% kill fee. Buys first rights. Editorial lead time 2 months. Submit seasonal material 3 months in advance. Accepts simultaneous submissions. Query for electronic submissions. Reports in 3 months. Sample copy for $2. Writer's guidelines free on request.

Nonfiction: Essays, how-to, humor, personal experience. Buys 40 mss/year. Query with published clips. Length: 500-1,500 words. Pays $90-220. Sometimes pays half the phone expenses of writers on assignment, but only by special arrangment.

Tips: "Be on target. Reading several issues of the magazine is crucial."

‡MACLINE, Delaware Valley's Adventure Mac Magazine, Simmons Business Systems, P.O. Box 845, Lansdowne PA 19050. Contact: Brian Pomeroy. 75% freelance written. Bimonthly magazine covering Apple Macintosh computers. Estab. 1991. Circ. 11,000. **Pays on acceptance.** Byline given. Buys one-time rights. Editorial lead time 4 months. Submit seasonal material 4 months in advance. Accepts simultaneous and previously published submissions. Query for electronic submissions. Reports in 1 month. Sample copy for 9 × 12 SAE with 3 first-class stamps. Writer's guidelines for #10 SASE.

Nonfiction: Book excerpts, exposé, how-to, interview/profile, new product, photo feature, technical. Special issue: Macworld Expo (August). Buys 10 mss/year. Query. Length: 250-1,500 words. Pays $50 for assigned articles; $25 for unsolicited articles. Sometimes pays expenses of writers on assignment.

Photos: State availability of photos with submission. Reviews contact sheets. Negotiates payment individually. Captions and model releases required. Buys one-time rights.

Columns/Departments: Technology update (new products and techniques), 500 words; Questions & Answers (answers to Mac problems), 500 words. Buys 6 mss/year. Query. Pays $25-50.

Tips: "We are always looking for stories on how users can better utilize their Mac equipment. Stories on tips and techniques for better productivity are always welcome, as are profiles of Mac users who use their Macs in unusual or unique ways."

‡MACPOWER MAGAZINE, The Magazine for the Macintosh PowerBook and Newton, Hollow Earth Publishing, P.O. Box 1355, Boston MA 02205-1355. Editor: Heilan Yvette Grimes. 95% freelance written. Monthly magazine covering PowerBooks and Newton. "We offer helpful information about the PowerBook and Newton." Estab. 1994. Circ. 35,000. **Pays on acceptance.** Byline given. Buys all rights and makes work-for-hire assignments. Editorial lead time 2 months. Submit seasonal material 5 months in advance. Query for electronic submissions. Reports in 2 weeks on queries; 1 month on mss. Sample copy for 9 × 12 SAE with 3 first-class stamps. Writer's guidelines for #10 SASE.

Nonfiction: Book excerpts, general interest, historical/nostalgic, how-to, humor, interview/profile, new product, personal experience, technical. Query. Length: 300+ words. Pays per page, negotiated. Sometimes pays expenses of writers on assignment.

Photos: Send photos with submission. Reviews transparencies. (Prefer electronic PICT or TIFF files.) Negotiates payment individually. Captions, model releases and identification of subjects required. Buys all rights.

Columns/Departments: "We are interested in Help columns on individual topics. Check the magazine for an idea of what we publish." Buys 60 mss/year. Query with published clips.

Fillers: Anecdotes, facts, gags to be illustrated by cartoonist, newsbreaks, short humor. Length: 20-50 words.

Tips: "Contact us in writing first. Know your subject and have something interesting to say. Reviews and new ideas are most open to freelancers."

MICRO COMPUTER JOURNAL, The Practical Magazine for Personal Computers & Microcontrollers, CQ Communications, 76 N. Broadway, Hicksville NY 11801. (516)681-2922. Fax: (516)681-2926. 90% freelance written. Editor: Art Salzberg. Managing Editor: Alex Burawa. Bimonthly magazine covering single-board computers, microcontrolled electronic devices, software, personal computers, electronic circuitry, construction projects and technology for readers with a technical affinity. Estab. 1984. Circ. 50,000. Pays on publication. Publishes ms an average of 3 months after acceptance. Byline given. Offers 25% kill fee. Buys first North American serial rights. Reports in 2 weeks on queries; 3 weeks on mss. *Writer's Market* recommends allowing 2 months for reply. Sample copy for $1 and 9 × 12 SAE. Writer's guidelines for #10 SASE.

Nonfiction: How-to (construction projects, applications, computer enhancements, upgrading and trouble-shooting); new product (reviews); opinion (experiences with computer products); technical (features and tutorials: circuits, applications). "Articles must be technically accurate. Writing should be 'loose,' not text-bookish." No long computer programs. Buys 125 mss/year. Query. Length: 500-4,000 words. Pays $90-150/published page. Sometimes pays expenses of writers on assignment.

Photos: Send photos with query or ms. Reviews transparencies and 5×7 b&w prints. Captions, model releases, and identification of subjects required. Buys first North American rights.

Tips: "The writer must have technical or applications acumen and well-researched material. Articles should reflect the latest products and technology. Sharp, interesting photos are helpful, as are rough, clean illustrations for re-drawing. Cover useful improvements to existing personal computers. Areas most open to freelancers include feature articles, technical tutorials, and projects to build. Some writers exhibit problems with longer pieces due to limited technical knowledge and/or poor organization. We can accept more short pieces. For electronic submissions, use Electronic mailbox, Micro Computer Journal on MCI Mail."

MICROpendium, Covering the TI99/4A, Myarc 9640 compatibles, Burns-Koloen Communications Inc., P.O. Box 1343, Round Rock TX 78680-1343. (512)255-1512. Editor: Laura Burns. 40% freelance written. Eager to work with new/unpublished writers. Monthly magazine for users of the "orphaned" TI99/4A. "We are interested in helping users get the most out of their home computers." Estab. 1984. Circ. 4,000. Pays on publication. Publishes ms an average of 2-3 months after acceptance. Byline given. Buys second serial rights. Accepts previously published articles. Send tearsheet or photocopy of article. Include information about when and where the article previously appeared. For reprints, payment varies. Query for electronic submission. Reports in 2 weeks on queries; 2 months on manuscripts. Sample copy and writer's guidelines for 9×12 SAE with 3 first-class stamps.

Nonfiction: Book excerpts, how-to (computer applications), interview/profile (of computer "personalities," e.g. a software developer concentrating more on "how-to" than personality), opinion (product reviews, hardware and software). Buys 30-50 mss/year. Query with or without published clips, or send complete ms. "We can do some articles as a series if they are lengthy, yet worthwhile." Pays $10-150, depending on length. No pay for product announcements. Sometimes pays the expenses of writers on assignment.

Photos: Send photos with submission. Reviews contact sheets, negatives, transparencies, and prints (b&w preferred). Buys negotiable rights.

Columns/Departments: User Notes (tips and brief routines for the computer), 100 words and up. Buys 35-40 mss/year. Send complete ms. Pays $10.

Tips: "The area most open to freelancers is product reviews on hardware and software. The writer should be a sophisticated TI99/4A computer user. We are more interested in advising our readers of the availability of good products than in 'panning' poor ones. We are interested in coverage of the Geneve 9640 by Myarc. We are not at all interested in general computer or technology-related articles unrelated to TI or Myarc computers."

ONLINE ACCESS, The Magazine that Makes Modems Work, Chicago Fine Print, Inc., Suite 203, 920 N. Franklin, Chicago IL 60610. Fax: (312)573-0520. Editor: Carol Freer. Associate Publisher: Kathy McCabe. 90% freelance written. Magazine, guide and directory that covers the online computer industry for computer owners who use modems. Ten publications/year including four issues devoted to bulletin board systems. "Online Access is the largest circulation international magazine for people interested in learning about online services and commercial databases for both personal and business applications." Pays on publication. Publishes ms an average of 2 months after acceptance. Byline given. Offers $50 kill fee. Buys first rights or second serial (reprint) rights. Submit seasonal/holiday material 6 months in advance. "Query for electronic submissions." Reports in 1 month on queries; 3 weeks on mss. *Writer's Market* recommends allowing 2 months for reply. Sample copy for $4.95.

Nonfiction: General interest (online industry); how-to (use a particular online service); humor; interview/profile (of major industry figures); new product (but *not* hardware!); opinion (about current online industry issues); personal experience (if relevant); photo feature. "No overly technical pieces; no step-by-step guides to searching databases. Please don't write about your terrific new modem!" Query with published clips. Length: 1,500-2,500 words. Pays $100-500. Pays in contributor copies by mutual agreement before assignment is given. Sometimes pays expenses of writers on assignment.

Photos: Send photos with submission. Reviews 5×7 transparencies and prints. Offers no additional payment for photos accepted with ms. Captions, model releases and identification of subjects required. Buys one-time rights.

Tips: "We are seeking more articles about bulletin board systems."

PC/COMPUTING, Ziff-Davis Publishing Co., 19th Floor, 950 Tower Lane, Foster City CA 94404-2121. (415)578-7000. Fax: (415)578-7029. Editor: Bill Roberts. Monthly magazine for business users of desktop computers. Estab. 1988. Circ. 850,000. **Pays on acceptance.** Byline given. Offers negotiable kill fee. Makes work-for-hire assignments. Query for electronic submissions. Reports in 1 month. Sample copy for $2.95. Writer's guidelines for #10 SASE.

• Ziff-Davis Publishing Company has created an electronic information service called the Interchange

Online Network that draws on the contents of its various computer magazines, including *PC Magazine*, *PC Computing*, *PC Week*, *Mac User*, *Mac Week*, *Computer Shopper* and *Computer Gaming World*.
Nonfiction: Book excerpts, how-to, new product and technical. Query with published clips. Payment negotiable. Sometimes pays expenses of writers on assignment.
Tips: "We're looking for helpful, specific information that appeals to advanced users of PCs. No novice material. Writers must be knowledgeable about personal computers." Queries to Howard Baldwin, Senior Editor, at MCImail 644-2491 (e-mail), with clips following by US mail. No phone queries.

‡**PC GRAPHICS & VIDEO,** Advanstar Communications, 859 Willamette St., Eugene OR 97401. (503)343-1200. Editor: David B. Brooks. 30-40% freelance written. Monthly magazine covering personal computer graphics and video. "*PC Graphics & Video* addresses hardware, software, techniques, resources, isssues in personal computer industry and use of IBM compatibles for pre-press, multimedia, digital video." Estab. 1992 (formerly *High Color*). Circ. 75,000. Pays on publication. Publishes ms an average of 2-3 months after acceptance. Negotiable kill fee. Buys first and collateral rights. Editorial lead time 2 months. Query for electronic submissions. Sample copy and writer's guidelines free on request.
Nonfiction: How-to, interview/profile, new product, technical. Query with published clips. Length: 750-3,000 words. Pays $250 per published page including photos.
Photos: Send photos with submission. Reviews digital prints. Captions, model releases and identification of subjects required. Buys one-time and collateral rights.

PC WORLD, PCW Communications, Inc., 501 2nd St., San Francisco CA 94107. (415)243-0500. Editor-in-Chief: Phil Lemmons. 60% freelance written. Monthly magazine covering IBM Personal Computers and compatibles. Circ. 915,000. **Pays on acceptance.** Byline given. Offers negotiable kill fee. Buys all rights. Query for electronic submissions. Free writer's guidelines.
Nonfiction: *PC World* is composed of 4 departments: News, How-tos, Review and Features. Reviews critically and objectively analyzes new hardware and software. How-tos gives readers instructions for improving their PC productivity. Features help readers understand the impact of PC technology on their business lives. News keeps readers apprised of new products, trends and industry events." Articles must focus on the IBM PC or compatibles. Query with or without published clips or send complete ms. Buys 50 mss/year. Length: 1,500-2,500 words. Pays $50-2,000. Does not accept unsolicited mss.
Tips: "Familiarity with the IBM PC or technical knowledge about its operations—coupled with a solid understanding of business needs—often determines whether we accept a query. Send all queries to the attention of Proposals—Editorial Department."

PCM, The Personal Computing Magazine for Tandy Computer Users, Falsoft, Inc., Falsoft Bldg., 9509 US Highway 42, Box 385, Prospect KY 40059-0385. (502)228-4492. Fax: (502)228-5121. Editor: Lawrence C. Falk. Managing Editor: Sue Fomby. 50% freelance written. Monthly magazine for owners of the Tandy Model 100, 200 and 600 portable computer and the Tandy 1000, 1200, 2000, 3000, 4000 and 5000. Estab. 1983. Circ. 80,000. Pays on publication. Publishes ms an average of 3 months after acceptance. Byline given. Buys all rights and rights for disk service reprint. Submit seasonal material 4 months in advance. Query for electronic submissions. Reports in 2 months. Free writer's guidelines.
Nonfiction: Julie Hutchinson, submissions editor. "We prefer how-to articles with programs." No general interest material. Buys 80 mss/year. Send complete ms. "Do not query." Length: 300 words minimum.
Photos: Send photos. Can use .PCXs.
Tips: "At this time we are only interested in submissions for the Tandy MS-DOS and portable computers. Strong preference is given to submissions accompanied by brief program listings. All listings must be submitted on disk as well as in hard copy form."

PUBLISH, The Art and Technology of Electronic Publishing, MultiMedia Communications, Inc., 501 Second St., San Francisco CA 94107. (415)243-0600. Editor-in-Chief: Jake Widman. 50% freelance written. Monthly magazine on desktop publishing and presentations. Estab. 1986. Circ. 107,000. Pays on publication. Publishes ms an average of 4-5 months after acceptance. Byline given. Buys first international rights. Query for electronic submissions. Reports in 3 weeks. Writer's guidelines for #10 SASE.
Nonfiction: Book excerpts, product reviews, how-to (publishing topics), news, new products, technical tips. Buys 120 mss/year. Query with published clips. Length: 300-2,500 words. No unsolicited mss.
Photos: Send photos with submission. Reviews contact sheets. Captions and identification of subjects required.

‡**WIRED MAGAZINE,** 544 Second St., San Francisco CA 94107. (415)904-0660. Editor & Publisher: Louis Rossetto. Contact: John Battelle, Managing Editor. 95% freelance written. Monthly magazine covering technology and digital culture. "We cover the digital revolution and related advances in computers, communications and lifestyles." Estab. 1993. Circ. 180,000. Pays on publication. Publishes ms an average of 2 months after acceptance. Byline given. Offers 25% kill fee. Buys first North American serial rights, global rights with 25% payment. Editorial lead time 2 months. Query for electronic submissions. Reports in 3 weeks on queries. Sample copy for $4.95. Writer's guidelines for #10 SASE.

Nonfiction: Essays, interview/profile, opinion. "No poetry or trade articles." Buys 85 features, 130 short pieces, 200 reviews, 36 essays and 50 other mss/year. Query. Pays expenses of writers on assignment.

‡WORDPERFECT FOR WINDOWS MAGAZINE, WordPerfect Publishing Corp., 270 W. Center St., Orem UT 84057-4683. (801)226-5555. Fax: (801)226-8804. Editorial Director: Clair F. Rees. Editor-in-Chief: Jeff Hadfield. 60% freelance written. Monthly magazine of "how-to" articles for users of WordPerfect for Windows and compatible software. Estab. 1991. Circ. 100,000. Publishes ms an average of 6-8 months after acceptance. Byline given. Pays negotiable kill fee. Buys first and secondary world rights. Submit seasonal material 8 months in advance. Query. Reports in 2 months. Sample copy for 9 × 12 SAE with 7 first-class stamps. Free writers guidelines.
Nonfiction: How-to, step-by-step applications (with keystrokes and screenshots in PCX format), humor, interview/company profile, new product, technical. "Easy-to-understand articles written with *minimum* jargon. Articles should provide readers good, useful information about word processing and other computer functions." Buys 120-160 mss/year. Query with or without published clips. Length: 800-1,800 words.
Columns/Departments: Desktop Publishing, Printing, 1,000-1,400 words; Basics (tips for beginners), 1,000-1,400 words; Out the Window (humor), Buys 90-120 mss/year. Query with published clips. Pays $400-700 on acceptance.
Tips: "Studying publication provides best information. We're looking for writers who can both inform *and* entertain our specialized group of readers."

WORDPERFECT, THE MAGAZINE, WordPerfect Publishing Corp., 270 W. Center St., Orem UT 84057-4683. (801)226-5555. Fax: (801)226-8804. Editorial Director: Clair F. Rees. Editor-in-Chief: Lisa Bearnson. 70% freelance written. Monthly magazine of "how-to" articles for users of various WordPerfect computer software. Estab. 1988. Circ. 275,000. Publishes ms an average of 6-8 months after acceptance. Byline given. Negotiable kill fee. Buys first and secondary world rights. Submit seasonal/holiday material 8 months in advance. Query for electronic submissions only. Reports in 2 months. Sample copy for 9 × 12 SAE with 7 first-class stamps. Free writer's guidelines.
Nonfiction: How-to, step-by-step applications (with keystrokes), humor, interview/company profile, new product, technical. "Easy-to-understand articles written with *minimum* jargon. Articles should provide readers good, useful information about word processing and other computer functions." Buys 120-160 mss/year. Query with or without published clips. Length: 800-1,800 words.
Photos: Send photos with submission. Reviews transparencies (35mm or larger). Offers no additional payment for photos accepted with ms. Captions and identification of subjects required. Buys one-time rights.
Columns/Departments: Macro Magic (WordPerfect macros), 1,000-1,400 words; Back to Basics (tips for beginners), 1,000-1,400 words; Final Keystrokes (humor), 800 words. Buys 90-120 mss/year. Query with published clips. Pays $400-700, on acceptance.
Tips: "Studying publication provides best information. We're looking for writers who can both inform *and* entertain our specialized group of readers."

Photography

Readers of these magazines use their cameras as a hobby and for weekend assignments. To write for these publications, you should have expertise in photography. Magazines geared to the professional photographer can be found in the Photography Trade section.

AMERICAN PHOTO, Hachette Filipacchi Magazines, Inc., Dept. WM, 1633 Broadway, New York NY 10019. (212)767-6273. Editor: David Schonauer. Executive Editor: Sudie Redmond. Bimonthly magazine for advanced amateur, sophisticated general interest and professional photographers. **Pays on acceptance.** Byline given. Buys first North American serial rights. Sample copy for $5.70 (includes postage). Writer's guidelines for #10 SASE.
Nonfiction: Length: 500-2,500 words. Query first. Sometimes pays writers expenses on assignment (reasonable). No how-to stories on equipment.
Columns/Departments: Buys 10-30 mss/year. Length: 700 words maximum.

‡BLACKFLASH, P.G. Press, 2nd Floor, 12 23rd St. E., Saskatoon, Saskatchewan S7K 0H5 Canada. (306)244-8018. Editor: Wallace Polsom. Managing Editor: Monte Greenshields. Quarterly magazine covering issues in contemporary photography. Estab. 1982. Circ. 1,700. **Pays on acceptance.** Byline given. Offers 50% kill fee. Editorial lead time 6 months. Submit seasonal material 6 months in advance. Query for electronic submissions. Prefers WordPerfect 5.1. Reports in 1 month on queries; 2 months on mss. Sample copy for $3.75. Writer's guidelines for #10 SASE.
Nonfiction: Jeff Gee, publications coordinator. Essays, opinion. Send complete ms. Length: 2,500-3,000 words. Pays $350 minimum for assigned articles; $150 for unsolicited articles.

Photos: Send photos with submission. Offers no additional payment for photos accepted with ms.
Columns/Departments: Jeff Gee, publications coordinator. Articles on photographic artists, book reviews, exhibition reviews, all 2,500-3,000 words. Articles are assigned. Query with published clips or send complete ms.
Tips: "All articles written to date have been assigned. We are interested in articles about contemporary photography to use if a deadline has been blown. Writers should submit an article (sample) and a cv for review. We are in the process of building a writers' file for assignments."

DARKROOM & CREATIVE CAMERA TECHNIQUES, Preston Publications, Inc., P.O. Box 48312, 7800 Merrimac Ave., Niles IL 60714. (708)965-0566. Fax: (708)965-7639. Publisher: Seaton Preston. Editor: David Alan Jay. 85% freelance written. Bimonthly publication covering the most technical aspects of photography: photochemistry, lighting, optics, processing and printing, Zone System, special effects, sensitometry, etc. Aimed at advanced workers. Prefers to work with experienced photographer-writers; happy to work with excellent photographers whose writing skills are lacking. "Article conclusions often require experimental support." Estab. 1979. Circ. 45,000. Pays within about 2 weeks of publication. Publishes ms an average of 6 months after acceptance. Byline given. Buys one-time rights. Query for electronic submissions. Sample copy for $4.50. Writer's guidelines with #10 SASE.
Nonfiction: Special interest articles within above listed topics; how-to, technical product reviews, photo features. Query or send complete ms. Length open, but most features run approximately 2,500 words or 3-4 magazine pages. Pays $100/published page for well-researched technical articles.
Photos: "Don't send photos with ms. Will request them at a later date." Manuscript payment includes payment for photos. Prefers transparencies and 8×10 b&w prints. Captions, model releases (where appropriate) and technical information required. Buys one-time rights.
Tips: "We like serious photographic articles with a creative or technical bent. Successful writers for our magazine are doing what they write about. Also, any ms that addresses a serious problem facing many photographers will get our immediate attention."

NATURE PHOTOGRAPHER, Nature Photographer Publishing Co., Inc., P.O. Box 2037, West Palm Beach FL 33402-2037. (407)586-7332. Fax: (407)586-9521. Editor: Evamarie Mathaey. 45% freelance written. Bimonthly magazine "emphasizing nature photography that uses low-impact techniques and ethics. Articles include how-to, travel to world-wide wilderness locations and how nature photography can be used to benefit the environment and environmental education of the public." Estab. 1990. Circ. 15,000. Pays on publication. Buys one-time rights. Submit seasonal material 8 months in advance. Accepts simultaneous and previously published submissions. Send photocopy of article and information about when and where the article previously appeared. For reprints, pays 75% of the amount paid for an original article. Reports in 2 months. Sample copy for 9×12 SAE with 6 first-class stamps. Writer's guidelines for #10 SASE.
Nonfiction: How-to (underwater, exposure, creative techniques, techniques to make photography easier, low-impact techniques, macro photography, large-format, wildlife), photo feature, technical, travel. No articles about photographing in zoos or on game farms. Buys 12-18 mss/year. Query with published clips or writing samples. Length: 750-2,500 words. Pays $75-150.
Photos: Send photos with submission. Reviews 35mm, 2¼ and 4×5 transparencies. Offers no additional payment for photos accepted with ms. Identification of subjects required. Buys one-time rights.
Tips: "Query with original, well-thought out ideas and good writing samples. Make sure you send SASE. Areas most open to freelancers are travel, how-to and conservation. Must have good, solid research and knowledge of subject."

SHUTTERBUG MAGAZINE, Patch Communications, 5211 S. Washington Ave., Titusville FL 32780. (407)268-5010. Editor: Bob Shell. Managing Editor: Bonnie Paulk. Contact: Bob Shell. 100% freelance written. Monthly magazine covering photography. "Provides how-to articles for advanced amateur to professional photographers." Estab. 1970. Circ. 100,000. Byline given. Buys first rights and second serial (reprint) rights. Editorial lead time 6 months. Submit seasonal material at least 6 months in advance. Accepts previously published submissions. Reports in 6-8 weeks on queries. Sample copy free on request. Writer's guidelines for #10 SASE.
Nonfiction: Historical/nostalgic (photography), how-to (photography), humor, interview/profile, new product, photo feature, technical. "All photo related." *No unsolicited articles.* Buys 60+ mss/year. Query. Pays $300 minimum for assigned articles; $200 minimum for unsolicited articles. Pays expenses of writers on assignment.
Photos: Send photos with submission. Reviews any transparencies, 8×10 prints. Offers no additional payment for photos accepted with ms. Captions and model releases required. Buys one-time rights.
Tips: "Submit only material similar in style to that in our magazine. All sections open to freelancers."

WILDLIFE PHOTOGRAPHY, P.O. Box 224, Greenville PA 16125. (412)588-3492. Editor: Rich Faler. 90% freelance written. Eager to work with new/unpublished writers. Bimonthly magazine "dedicated to the pursuit and capture of wildlife on film. Emphasis on how-to." Estab. 1985. Circ. 3,000. Pays on publication. Publishes ms an average of 1 year after acceptance. Byline given. Buys first, one-time or second serial (reprint) rights.

Submit seasonal/holiday material 4 months in advance. Accepts simultaneous and previously published submissions. Send tearsheet or photocopy of article, and information about when and where the article previously appeared. Reports in 2 weeks on queries; 6 weeks on mss. Sample copy for $2 and 9×12 SAE. Free writer's guidelines.

Nonfiction: Book excerpts, how-to (work with animals to take a good photo), interview/profile (of professionals), new product (of particular interest to wildlife photography), personal experience (with cameras in the field), travel (where to find superb photo opportunities of plants and animals). No fiction or photography of pets, sports and scenery. Buys 30 mss/year. Query or send complete ms. Length: 500-3,000 words. Pays $30-100.

Photos: Send sharp photos with submission. Reviews contact sheets, negatives, transparencies, 5×7 prints as part of ms package. Photos accepted only with ms. Offers no additional payment for photos. Captions and identification of subjects required. Buys one-time rights.

Fillers: Anecdotes, facts. Buys 12/year. Length: 50-200 words. Pays $5-15.

Tips: "Give solid how-to info on how to photograph a specific species of wild animal. Send photos, not only of the subject, but of the photographer and his gear in action. The area of our publication most open to freelancers is feature articles."

Politics and World Affairs

These publications cover politics for the reader interested in current events. Other publications that will consider articles about politics and world affairs are listed under Business and Finance, Contemporary Culture, Regional and General Interest. For listings of publications geared toward the professional, see Government and Public Service in the Trade section.

‡**AFRICA REPORT**, 833 United Nations Plaza, New York NY 10017. (212)949-5666. Fax: (212)682-6174. Editor: Margaret A. Novicki. 60% freelance written. Prefers to work with published/established writers. A bimonthly magazine for U.S. citizens and residents with a special interest in African affairs for professional, business, academic or personal reasons. Not tourist-related. Circ. 10,500. Pays on publication. Publishes ms an average of 2 months after acceptance. Rights purchased vary with author and material; usually buys all rights, very occasionally first serial rights. Byline given unless otherwise requested. Sample copy for $5.50; free writer's guidelines.

Nonfiction: Interested in "African political, economic and cultural affairs, especially in relation to U.S. foreign policy and business objectives. Style should be journalistic but not academic or light. Articles should not be polemical or long on rhetoric but may be committed to a strong viewpoint. I do not want tourism articles." Would like to see in-depth topical analyses of lesser known African countries, based on residence or several months' stay in the country. Buys 5 unsolicited mss/year. Pays $150-250.

Photos: Photos purchased with or without accompanying mss with extra payment. Reviews b&w only. Pays $25. Submit 12×8 "half-plate."

Tips: "Read *Africa Report* and other international journals regularly. Become an expert on an African or Africa-related topic. Make sure your submissions fit the style, length and level of *Africa Report*."

CALIFORNIA JOURNAL, 2101 K St., Sacramento CA 95816. (916)444-2840. Editor: Richard Zeiger. Managing Editor: A.G. Block. 20% freelance written. Prefers to work with published/established writers. Monthly magazine that emphasizes analysis of California politics and government. Estab. 1970. Circ. 20,000. Pays on publication. Publishes ms an average of 2 months after acceptance. Byline given. Buys all rights. Query for electronic submissions. Writer's guidelines for #10 SASE.

Nonfiction: Profiles of state and local government and political analysis. No outright advocacy pieces. Buys 25 unsolicited mss/year. Query. Length: 900-3,000 words. Pays $150-1,000. Sometimes pays the expenses of writers on assignment.

CHURCH & STATE, Americans United for Separation of Church and State, 8120 Fenton St., Silver Spring MD 20910-4781. (301)589-3707. Fax: (301)495-9173. Managing Editor: Joseph Conn. 10% freelance written. Prefers to work with published/established writers. Monthly magazine emphasizing religious liberty and church/state relations matters. Strongly advocates separation of church and state. Readership "includes the whole spectrum, but is predominantly Protestant and well-educated." Estab. 1947. Circ. 33,000. **Pays on acceptance.** Publishes ms an average of 2 months after acceptance. Buys all rights. Accepts simultaneous and previously published submissions. Send tearsheet or photocopy or typed ms with rights for sale noted and information about when and where the article previously appeared. Reports in 2 months. Sample copy and writer's guidelines for 9×12 SAE with 3 first-class stamps.

Nonfiction: Exposé, general interest, historical, interview. Buys 11 mss/year. Query. Length: 3,000 words maximum. Pays negotiable fee.

Photos: Send photos with query. Pays negotiable fee for b&w prints. Captions preferred. Buys one-time rights.
Tips: "We're looking for feature articles on underreported local church-state controversies. We also consider 'viewpoint' essays that offer a unique or personal take on church-state issues."

COMMONWEAL, A Review of Public Affairs, Religion, Literature and the Arts, Commonweal Foundation, 15 Dutch St., New York NY 10038. (212)732-0800. Editor: Margaret O'Brien Steinfels. Contact: Patrick Jordan, managing editor. Biweekly magazine. Estab. 1924. Circ. 18,000. **Pays on acceptance.** Byline given. Buys all rights. Submit seasonal material 2 months in advance. Reports in 2 months. Free sample copy.
Nonfiction: Essays, general interest, interview/profile, personal experience, religious. Buys 20 mss/year. Query with published clips. Length: 1,200-3,000 words. Pays $75-100.
Poetry: Rosemary Deen, poetry editor. Free verse, traditional. Buys 25-30 poems/year. Pays 75¢/line.

CURRENT WORLD LEADERS, International Issues, International Academy at Santa Barbara, Suite D, 800 Garden St., Santa Barbara CA 93101-1552. (805)965-5010. Fax: (805)965-6071. Editorial Director: Thomas S. Garrison. 25% freelance written. Bimonthly magazine covering international and comparative politics. "We cover several perspectives for each issue topic. We welcome papers that present a particular point of view on current international political issues. Our main audience is college-level teachers and students." Estab. 1957. Pays on publication. Publishes ms an average of 4 months after acceptance. Byline given. No kill fee. Buys first rights. Accepts simultaneous and previously published submissions. Query for electronic submissions. Reports in 3 weeks on queries. Free sample copy and writer's guidelines for 6×9 SAE with 5 first-class stamps.
Nonfiction: Essays (political), opinion (political). "Articles must have a political theme." Buys 3-5 mss/year. Length: 4,500-10,000 words. Pays $25-100.
  • No longer seeking photos or photo features.
Tips: "Write and ask for our writers guidelines and our annual Call for Papers. Know your topic."

EMPIRE STATE REPORT, The magazine of politics and public policy in New York State, 3rd Floor, 4 Central Ave., Albany NY 12210. (518)465-5502. Fax: (518)465-9822. Editor: Jeff Plungis. 50% freelance written. Monthly magazine providing "timely political and public policy features for local and statewide public officials in New York State. Anything that would be of interest to them is of interest to us." Estab. 1983. Circ. 12,000. Pays 2 months after publication. Byline given. Buys first North American serial rights. Query for electronic submissions. Reports in 1 month on queries; 2 months on mss. Sample copy for $3.50 with #10 SASE.
Nonfiction: Essays, exposé, interview/profile and opinion. "Writers should send for our editorial calendar." Buys 48 mss/year. Query with published clips. Length: 750-3,000 words. Pays $35-400 for assigned articles. Sometimes pays expenses of writers on assignment.
Photos: Send photos with submission. Reviews any size prints. Offers $50-100/photo. Identification of subjects required. Buys one-time rights.
Columns/Departments: New York Digest (short news stories about state politics), 300-900 words; Perspective (opinion pieces), 750-800 words. Buys 24 mss/year. Query. Length: 750-1,000 words. Pays $50-100.
Tips: "Send us a query. If we are not already working on the idea, and if the query is well written, we might work something out with the writer. Writers have the best chance selling something for New York Digest."

EUROPE, 2100 M St. NW, 7th Floor, Washington DC 20037. (202)862-9555. Fax: (202)429-1766. Editor: Robert Guttman. Managing Editor: Peter Gwin. 75% freelance written. Magazine published 10 times/year for anyone with a professional or personal interest in Europe and European/US relations. Estab. 1963. Circ. 25,000. Pays on publication. Publishes ms an average of 2 to 3 months after acceptance. Buys first serial and all rights. Submit seasonal material 3 months in advance. Reports in 6 months.
Nonfiction: Interested in current affairs (with emphasis on economics, business and politics), the Single Market and Europe's relations with the rest of the world. Publishes monthly cultural travel pieces, with European angle. "High quality writing a must. We publish articles that might be useful to people with a professional interest in Europe." Query or submit complete ms or article outline. Include résumé of author's background and qualifications. Length: 500-2,000 words. Pays $150-500.
  • This magazine is accepting more freelance articles and has increased its pay rates for them. The editor is encouraging more queries.
Photos: Photos purchased with or without accompanying mss. Buys b&w and color. Pays $25-35 for b&w print, any size; $100 for inside use of transparencies; $450 for color used on cover; per job negotiable.

FREEDOM MAGAZINE, Church of Scientology, Suite 1200, 6331 Hollywood Blvd., Los Angeles CA 90028. (213)960-3500. Editor: Thomas G. Whittle. 20% freelance written. Monthly magazine "dedicated to investigative reporting in the public interest," with emphasis on hard news, current events and investigative reporting. Circ. 110,000. Pays on publication. Publishes ms an average of 3 months after acceptance. Rights purchased vary with author and material. Submit seasonal material 4 months in advance. Responds in 2-3 weeks. Sample copy on request.

Nonfiction: National and international news, investigative reporting, business news. Highlights individuals who are championing the cause of human rights in a special "Leaders in the Field of Human Rights" feature. Articles have exposéd misconduct and abuses by officials in CIA and other agencies. Harmful effects of psychiatric drugs such as Prozac have been examined in depth. Query with detailed outline, including statement of whether the information has appeared elsewhere. Enclosing clips of other stories you have published may help your chances of acceptance. Length: 800-3,000 words. Pays $100-250, occasionally more.

Photos: Send photos with submission. Color: 35mm slides but prefers 2¼×5 inch transparencies; b&w: 8×10 or 5×7 prints. Offers $20-100/photo. Captions required. Buys one-time rights.

‡**NACLA REPORT ON THE AMERICAS,** North American Congress on Latin America, 475 Riverside Dr., Room 454, New York NY 10115. (212)870-3146. Editor: Fred Rosen. Associate Editor: Deidre McFadyen. 75% freelance written. Bimonthly magazine on Latin America, the Caribbean and US foreign policy. Estab. 1966. Circ. 11,000. Pays on publication. Byline given. Offers 25% kill fee. Buys one-time rights. Accepts simultaneous submissions. Query for electronic submissions. Reports in 2 months. Sample copy for $5.75.

Nonfiction: Exposé and features emphasizing analysis. Buys 25 mss/year. Query with published clips or send complete ms. Length: 2,000-3,000 words. Pays 12¢/published word. Reprints OK; send photocopy of article and information about when and where the article previously appeared. Pays negotiable rate for reprints.

Photos: Send photos with submission. Reviews contact sheets and prints (5×7). Pays $25 minimum. Identification of subjects required. Buys one-time rights.

THE NATION, 72 Fifth Ave., New York NY 10011-8046. Fax: (212)463-9712. Editor: Katrina Vanden Heuvel. 75% freelance written. Estab. 1865. Works with a small number of new/unpublished writers each year. Weekly. Buys first serial rights. Query for electronic submissions. Free sample copy and writer's guidelines for 6×9 SASE.

Nonfiction: "We welcome all articles dealing with the social scene, from an independent perspective." Queries encouraged. Buys 100 mss/year. Length: 2,500 words maximum. Modest rates. Sometimes pays expenses of writers on assignment.

Tips: "We are firmly committed to reporting on the issues of labor, national politics, business, consumer affairs, environmental politics, civil liberties and foreign affairs."

NATIONAL REVIEW, National Review Inc., Dept. WM, 150 E. 35th St., New York NY 10016. (212)679-7330. Editor: John O'Sullivan. Managing Editor: Linda Bridges. 60% freelance written. Biweekly political and cultural journal of conservative opinion. "While we sometimes publish symposia including liberal or even leftist opinion, most of what we publish has a conservative or libertarian angle." Estab. 1955. Circ. 270,000. Pays on publication. Byline given. Offers 50% kill fee "on pieces definitely accepted." Buys first, one-time, second serial or simultaneous rights. Submit seasonal/holiday material 2 months in advance. Reports in 2 weeks on queries; 3 months on mss. Free sample copy.

Nonfiction: Rich Lowry, articles editor. Essays, exposés (of government boondoggles), interview/profile, religious. No editorial-type pure opinion. Buys 130 mss/year. Query. Length: 500-3,000 words. Pays $100-1,000 for assigned articles; $100-600 for unsolicited articles. Sometimes pays expenses of writers on assignment.

Columns/Departments: David Klinghoffer, literary editor. Book reviews (conservative political where applicable) and arts pieces. Buys 130 mss/year. Query. Length: 800-1,200 words. Pays $225-300.

Tips: "Always query. We accept phone queries. Double-space manuscripts. We expect a fairly conservative point of view, but don't want a lot of editorializing. And we prefer pieces that are a bit more essayistic than a standard newspaper report."

NEW JERSEY REPORTER, A Journal of Public Issues, The Center for Analysis of Public Issues, 16 Vandeventer Ave., Princeton NJ 08542. (609)924-9750. Fax: (609)924-0363. Managing Editor: Lee Seglem. 60% freelance written. Prefers to work with published/established writers but will consider submissions from others. Bimonthly magazine covering New Jersey politics, public affairs and public issues. *"New Jersey Reporter* is a hard-hitting and highly respected magazine published for people who take an active interest in New Jersey politics and public affairs, and who want to know more about what's going on than what newspapers and television newscasts are able to tell them. We publish a great variety of stories ranging from analysis to exposé." Estab. 1970. Circ. 2,200. Pays on publication. Byline given. Buys all rights. Reports in 1 month. Sample copy available on request.

• This magazine is using more freelance writing now than ever before.

Nonfiction: Book excerpts, exposé, interview/profile, opinion. "We like articles from specialists (in planning, politics, economics, corruption, etc.) – particularly if written by professional journalists – but we reject stories that do not read well because of jargon or too little attention to the actual writing of the piece. Our magazine is interesting as well as informative." Buys 18-25 mss/year. Query with published clips. Length: 1,800-4,500 words. Pays $100-500.

Tips: "Queries should be specific about how the prospective story is an issue that affects or will affect the people of New Jersey and its government. The writer's résumé should be included. Stories – unless they are specifically meant to be opinion – should come to a conclusion but avoid a 'holier than thou' or preachy tone. Allegations should be scrupulously substantiated. Our magazine represents a good opportunity for freelancers to acquire great clips. Our publication specializes in longer, more detailed, analytical features. The most frequent mistake made by writers in completing an article for us is too much personal opinion versus reasoned advocacy. We are less interested in opinion than in analysis based on sound reasoning and fact. *New Jersey Reporter* is a well-respected publication, and many of our writers go on to nationally respected newspapers and magazines."

‡**NORTH-SOUTH, The Magazine of the Americas,** North-South Center, University Of Miami, P.O. Box 248014, Coral Gables FL 33124-3211. (305)284-8909. Editor: Jaime Suchlicki. Managing Editor: Susan Latuszynski. 100% freelance written. Bimonthly magazine on hemispheric issues — trade, debt, environment, politics. *Editor's note: Published in English and Spanish editions.* Estab. 1991. Circ. 10,000. Pays on publication. Byline given. Makes work-for-hire assignments. Reports in 1 month.
Nonfiction: "Freelancers must have heavy professional experience in Latin America — so nothing from 'amateurs.' " Buys 6 mss/year. Query. Length: 1,200-1,800. Pays $150-300.
Photos: Send photos with submission. Payment negotiable. Captions required. Buys one-time rights.

‡**POLICY REVIEW,** The Heritage Foundation, 214 Massachusetts Ave. NE, Washington DC 20002. (202)546-4400. Editor: Adam Meyerson. Managing Editor: Margaret D. Bonilla. Quarterly magazine for conservative ideas about politics and policy. "We have been described as 'the most thoughtful, the most influential and the most provocative publication of the intellectual right.' " Estab. 1977. Circ. 23,000. Pays on publication. Byline given.
Nonfiction: "We are especially interested in freelance articles on how public policies affect families and communities." Buys 4 mss/year. Send complete ms. Length: 2,000-6,000 words. Average payment of $500 per article.

THE PRAGMATIST, A Utilitarian Approach, P.O. Box 392, Forest Grove PA 18922-0392. Fax: (215)348-8006. Editor: Jorge Amador. Publisher: Hans G. Schroeder. 67% freelance written. Bimonthly magazine on politics and current affairs. "*The Pragmatist* is a free-market magazine with a social conscience. We explore the practical benefits of tolerance, civil liberties and the market order, with emphasis on helping the poor and the underprivileged." Estab. 1983. Circ. 1,250. Pays on publication. Publishes ms an average of 4 months after acceptance. Byline given. Publication not copyrighted "but will run copyright notice for individual author on request." Buys first rights and/or second serial (reprint) rights. Submit seasonal material 6 months in advance. Accepts previously published submissions. Send tearsheet or photocopy of article or typed ms with rights for sale noted and information about when and where the article previously appeared. Pays 100% of their fee for an original article. Query for electronic submissions. Reports in 2 months. Sample copy for $3 and 9 × 12 SAE with 3 first-class stamps. Writer's guidelines for #10 SASE.
Nonfiction: Essays, humor, opinion. "*The Pragmatist* is solution-oriented. We seek facts and figures, not moralizing or abstract philosophy, and focus on the issues, not personalities. Recent articles have explored alternatives to socialized military defense and examined the hazards of drug prohibition." Buys 24 mss/year. Query with published clips or send complete ms. Length: 500-2,500 words. Pays 1¢/published word plus copies.
Columns/Departments: Book Review (history/current affairs, dealing with the dangers of power or the benefits of civil liberties and market relations). Buys 10-15 mss/year. Query with published clips or send complete ms. Length: 1,000-1,500 words. Pays 1¢/published word copies.
Fiction: "We use very little fiction, and then only if it makes a political point."
Tips: "We welcome new writers. Most of our authors are established, but the most important article criteria are clear writing and sound reasoning backed up by facts. Write for an educated lay audience, not first-graders or academics. Polite correspondence gets answered first. No phone calls, please. Don't get discouraged by initial rejections; keep working on your writing and your targeting."

THE PROGRESSIVE, 409 E. Main St., Madison WI 53703-2899. (608)257-4626. Fax: (608)257-3373. Editor: Erwin Knoll. 75% freelance written. Monthly. Estab. 1909. Pays on publication. Publishes ms an average of 6 weeks after acceptance. Byline given. Buys all rights. Reports in 1 month. Sample copy for 9 × 12 SAE with 4 first-class stamps. Writer's guidelines for #10 SASE.
Nonfiction: Primarily interested in articles which interpret, from a progressive point of view, domestic and world affairs. Occasional lighter features. "*The Progressive* is a *political* publication. General-interest material is inappropriate." Query. Length: 3,000 words maximum. Pays $100-300.

 The double dagger before a listing indicates that the listing is new in this edition. New markets are often more receptive to freelance submissions.

Tips: "Display some familiarity with our magazine, its interests and concerns, its format and style. We want query letters that fully describe the proposed article without attempting to sell it—and that give an indication of the writer's competence to deal with the subject."

SOUTHERN EXPOSURE, P.O. Box 531, Durham NC 27702. (919)419-8311. Contact: Editor. Quarterly journal for well educated Southerners of all ages interested in "left-liberal" political perspective and the South. Estab. 1970. Circ. 7,500. Pays on publication. Buys all rights. Offers kill fee. Byline given. Will consider simultaneous submissions. Submit seasonal material 6 months in advance. Reports in 3 months. "Query is appreciated, but not required." Sample copy for $4. Writer's guidelines for #10 SASE.
Nonfiction: "Ours is one of the few publications about the South *not* aimed at business or upper-class people; it appeals to all segments of the population. *And*, it is used as a resource—sold as a magazine and then as a book—so it rarely becomes dated." Needs investigative articles about the following subjects as related to the South: politics, energy, institutional power from prisons to universities, women, labor, Afro-Americans and the economy. Informational interview, profile, historical, think articles, exposé, opinion, book reviews. Length: 4,500 words maximum. Pays $50-200. Smaller fee for short items.
Photos: "Very rarely purchase photos, as we have a large number of photographers working for us." 8×10 b&w preferred; no color. Payment negotiable.
Tips: "Because we are publishing shorter issues on a quarterly basis, we are looking for clear and thoughtful writing, articles that relate specific experiences of individual Southerners or grass roots groups to larger issues."

TOWARD FREEDOM, A progressive perspective on world events, Toward Freedom Inc., 209 College St., Burlington VT 05401. (802)658-2523. Fax: (802)658-3738. Editor: Greg Guma. 75% freelance written. Political journal published 8 times/year covering political/cultural analysis, focus on Third world and Europe. "*Toward Freedom* is an internationalist newsletter with a progressive perspective on political, cultural and environmental issues in the Third World and Europe. Also covers the United Nations, the Non-aligned Movement and US foreign policy." Estab. 1952. Byline given. Circ. 2,000. Pays on publication. Kill fee "rare–negotiable." Buys first North American serial and one-time rights. Editorial lead time 1 month. Query for electronic submissions. Reports in 2 weeks on queries; 1 month on mss. *Writer's Market* recommends allowing 2 months for reply. Sample copy for $3. Writer's guidelines free on request.
Nonfiction: Book reviews, interview/profile, opinion, personal experience, travel, foreign, political analysis—women's issues. Special issue: Women's Issue (March). No religious, how-to, fiction. Buys 80-100 mss/year. Query. Length: 700-2,000 words. Pays 10¢/word for all used.
Photos: Send photos with submission, if available. Reviews any prints. Offers $25 maximum/photo. Identification of subjects required. Buys one-time rights.
Columns/Departments: Book Review (Third World/European writers; political), 800-1,000 words. Buys 8-10 mss/year. Query. Pays 10¢/word. Commentary column, 900-1,000 words. Buys 8/year. Pays 10¢/word.
Tips: "Except for book or other reviews, writers must be knowledgeable about country, political situation, foreign policy, etc., on which they are writing. Occasional cultural 'travelogues' accepted, especially those that would enlighten our readers about a foreign way of life. Writing must be professional."

WASHINGTON MONTHLY, The Washington Monthly Company, 1611 Connecticut Ave. NW, Washington DC 20009. (202)462-0128. Editor: Charles Peters. Managing Editor: David Segal. Contact: David Segal. 80% freelance written. Monthly magazine covering political commentary, Washington news. Estab. 1969. Circ. 30,000. Pays on publication. Publishess ms an average of 3-5 months after acceptance. Byline given. Buys all rights. Editorial lead time 1½ months. Submit seasonal material 2 months in advance. Query for electronic submissions. Reports in 1 week on queries; 1 month on mss. *Writer's Market* recommends allowing 2 months for reply. Sample copy for $3.95 and SASE. Writer's guidelines free on request.
Nonfiction: Book excerpts, essays, exposé, historical/nostalgic, interview/profile, opinion, personal experience, "anything exposing frauds of government—interesting memos—government foibles." Buys 30 mss/year. Query. Length: 1,500-5,000 words. Pays 10¢/word.
Photos: Send photos with submission. Negotiates payment individually. Captions, model releases and identification of subjects required.
Fillers: R. Carey Jones. Anecdotes, facts, gags to be illustrated by cartoonist, newsbreaks, short humor. Accepted de gratis. Length: 15-100 words.
Tips: "Freelancers should read previous issues and articles of *The Washington Monthly* to gain an understanding of its journalistic purpose and intent."

WILSON QUARTERLY, Woodrow Wilson International Center for Scholars, Suite 704, 901 D Street SW, Washington DC 20024-2169. (202)287-3000. Editor: Jay Tolson. Managing Editor: James Carman. 25% freelance written. Scholarly magazine that "tries to present the world of scholarly thought and research to a non-academic, but educated audience." Recent articles have ranged from 'American Finance' to a profile of G.K. Chesterton." Estab. 1976. Circ. 70,000. Pays on publication. Byline given. Pays negotiable kill fee. Buys first rights. Accepts previously published submissions. Send photocopy of article. For reprints, payment varies. Query for electronic submissions. Reports in 6 weeks. Sample copy for $7.

Nonfiction: Scholarly research. No fiction, poetry, or academic theses. Buys 10 mss/year. Query. Length: 3,000 words. Pays $500-1,200 for assigned articles; $300-1,000 for unsolicited articles.

Photos: Send photos with submission. Offers no additional payment for photos accepted with ms. Captions, model releases and identification of subjects required. Buys one-time rights.

Columns/Departments: Current Books (freelance reviews; must query for assignment). Buys 20 mss/year. Query with published clips. Length: 300-500 words. Pays $20-100.

Tips "Independent essays are the best for freelancers. Writers should definitely read the magazine before submitting any article, and should query if at all possible. Often we reject manuscripts because they do not fit in with our editorial content or overlap with other articles already assigned. We are particularly interested in articles that contain new, independent scholarly research, but are written with a journalistic flavor."

‡**WORLD POLICY JOURNAL,** World Policy Institute, Suite 413, 65 Fifth Ave., New York NY 10003. (212)229-5808. Fax: (212)229-5579. Editor: James Chace. Estab. 1983. 10% freelance written. "We are eager to work with new or unpublished writers as well as more established writers." A quarterly journal covering international politics, economics, and security issues, as well as historical and cultural essays, book reviews, profiles, and first-person reporting from regions not covered in the general media. "We hope to bring a new sense of imagination, principle and proportion, as well as a restored sense of reality and direction to America's discussion of its role in the world." Circ. 8,000. Pays on publication. Publishes ms an average of 3 months after acceptance. Byline given. Offers variable kill fee. Buys all rights. Reports in 2 months. Sample copy for $7.50 and 9×12 SAE with 10 first-class stamps.

Nonfiction: Articles that "define policies that reflect the shared needs and interests of all nations of the world." Query. Length: 20-30 pages (8,000 words maximum). Pays variable commission rate.

Tips: "By providing a forum for many younger or previously unheard voices, including those from Europe, Asia, Africa and Latin America, we hope to replace lingering illusions and fears with new priorities and aspirations. Articles submitted on speculation very rarely suit our particular needs."

Psychology and Self-Improvement

These publications focus on psychological topics, how and why readers can improve their own outlooks, and how to understand people in general. Many General Interest, Men's and Women's publications also publish articles in these areas.

CHANGES MAGAZINE, the US Journal, Inc., 3201 SW 15th St., Deerfield Beach FL 33442-8190. (800)851-9100. Fax: (305)360-0034. Managing Editor: Jeffrey Laign. 10% freelance written. Bimonthly magazine covering self-help and recovery. "We want to help people to improve their lives." Estab. 1986. Circ. 100,000. Pays on publication. Publishes ms an average of 4 months after acceptance. Byline given. Pays $25 kill fee. Buys first North American serial rights. Submit seasonal material 6 months in advance. Accepts simultaneous and previously published submissions discouraged. Query for electronic submissions. Reports in 2-4 months. Sample copy for $3.95. Writer's guidelines for #10 SASE.

Nonfiction: Personal experience, recovery/therapy and investigative pieces. We must approve interviews. No religious material, self-advertisements or reviews of books. Buys 15-20 mss/year. Query. Length: 500-2,000 words. Pays 15¢/word. Pays poetry and personal experience pieces with contributor's copies.

Photos: Send photos with submission. Reviews 5×7 prints. Payment negotiable. Model releases required. Buys one-time rights.

Fiction: "Stories of triumph: We look for insightful fiction which casts the magazine's serious subjects in unique ways." Pays $100. Length: 2,000 words maximum.

Poetry: Avant-garde, free verse, light verse. Pays in contributor's copies.

Tips: "Query by mail. Show a willingness and skill for talking to a variety of sources, tying in a current event, if applicable. Use a friendly, conversational style, but don't assume your readers are disinterested in the deeper aspects of your story."

THE HEALING WOMAN, The monthly newsletter for women survivors of childhood sexual abuse, P.O. Box 3038, Moss Beach CA 94038. (415)728-0339. Fax: (415)728-1324. Editor: Margot Silk Forrest. 70% freelance written. Monthly newsletter covering recovery from childhood sexual abuse. "Submissions accepted only from writers with personal or professional experience with childhood sexual abuse. We are looking for intelligent, honest and compassionate articles on topics of interest to survivors. We also publish first-person stories, poetry, interviews and book reviews." Estab. 1992. Circ. 5,000. **Pays on acceptance.** Publishes ms an average of 3-8 months after acceptance. Byline given. Offers 50% kill fee. Buys first North American serial rights. Editorial lead time 4 months. Submit seasonal material 4 months in advance. Accepts previously published submissions. Send photocopy of article and information about when and where the article previously appeared. For reprints pays 100% of the amount paid for an original article. Query for electronic submissions. Reports in 3-4 weeks on queries. Writer's guidelines for #10 SASE.

Nonfiction: Book excerpts, essays, general interest, interview/profile, opinion, personal experience. "No articles on topics with which the writer has not had first-hand experience. If you've been there, you can write about it for us. If not, don't write about it." Buys 30 mss/year. Query with published clips. Length: 300-1,500 words. Pays $25-50. "Pays in copies for poems, short first-person pieces."

Photos: Send photos with submission. Negotiates payment for photos individually. Identification of subjects required. Buys one-time rights.

Columns/Departments: Book Reviews (books or accounts of incest survivors, therapy for incest survivors), 500-600 words; and Survivors Speak Out (first-person stories of recovery), 300-500 words.

Poetry: No *long* poems preoccupied with painful aspects of sexual abuse. Buys 25 poems/year, but pays only in copies.

Tips: "Although our subject matter is painful, *The Healing Woman* is not about suffering—it's about healing. Our department called 'Survivors Speak Out' features short, honest, insightful first-person essays with a conversational tone. We are happy to work with unpublished writers in this department."

LOTUS, JOURNAL FOR PERSONAL TRANSFORMATION, Lotus, Inc., Suite 157, 4421 West Okmulgee, Muskogee OK 74401. (918)683-4560. Editor: Mary Nurrie Stearns. 20% freelance written. Magazine of personal and spiritual transformation published 5 times/year. Estab. 1991. Circ. 29,000. Pays on publication. Publishes ms an average of 4 months after acceptance. Byline given. Offers 25% kill fee. Buys first North American serial, first rights, one-time or second serial (reprint) rights. Submit seasonal material 4 months in advance. Accepts simultaneous and previously published submissions. Query for electronic submissions. Reports in 6 weeks. Sample copy for $5.95. Writer's guidelines for SASE.

Nonfiction: Essays, inspirational, interview/profile, religious. Buys 8 mss/year. Send complete ms. Length: 500-5,000 words. Pays $50-500. Pays in contributor's copies if requested.

Photos: Send photos with submission. Reviews contact sheets and 8×10 prints. Pays $15-85/photo. Buys one-time rights.

Columns/Departments: Reviews. "We review films and books that deal with personal and spiritual transformation." Length: 500-1250 words. Buys 16 mss/year. Send complete ms. Pays $25-100.

Tips: "We look for writings that are not dogmatic in content and that will appeal to individuals from most any religious background."

ROSICRUCIAN DIGEST, Rosicrucian Order, AMORC, Rosicrucian Park, San Jose CA 95191-0001. (408)947-3600. Editor-in-Chief: Robin M. Thompson. 50% freelance written. Works with a small number of new/unpublished writers each year. Quarterly magazine emphasizing mysticism, science and the arts for "men and women of all ages, seeking answers to life's questions." **Pays on acceptance.** Publishes ms an average of 5-6 months after acceptance. Buys first serial and second serial (reprint) rights. Byline given. Submit seasonal material 5 months in advance. Accepts previously published submissions. Reports in 2 months. Free sample copy. Writer's guidelines for #10 SASE.

Nonfiction: How to deal with life—and all it brings us—in a positive and constructive way. Informational articles—new ideas and developments in science, the arts, philosophy and thought. Historical sketches, biographies, human interest, psychology, philosophical and inspirational articles. No religious, astrological or political material or articles promoting a particular group or system of thought. Buys variable amount of mss/year. Query. Length: 1,000-1,500 words. Pays 6¢/word.

Photos: Purchased with accompanying ms. Send prints. Pays $10/8×10 b&w glossy print.

Fillers: Short inspirational or uplifting (not religious) anecdotes or experiences. Buys 6/year. Query. Length: 22-250 words. Pays 2¢/word.

Tips: "We are looking for well-written articles with a positive, constructive approach to life in these trying times. This seems to be a time of indecision and apathy in many areas, and we are encouraged when we read an article that lets the reader know that he/she can get involved, take positive action, make a change in his/her life. We are also looking for articles about how other cultures outside our own deal with the big questions, problems, and changes in life, i.e., the questions of 'Who am I?' 'Where do I fit in?', the role of elders in passing on culture to new generations, philosophical aspects of other cultures that can help us grow today."

SCIENCE OF MIND MAGAZINE, 3251 W. Sixth St., P.O. Box 75127, Los Angeles CA 90075. (213)388-2181. Editor: Sandra Sarr. 30% freelance written. Monthly magazine that features articles on spirituality, self-help and inspiration. "Our publication centers on oneness of all life and spiritual empowerment through the application of Science of Mind principles." Pays on publication. Publishes ms an average of 5 months after acceptance. Byline given. Buys first North American serial rights. Submit seasonal material 6 months in advance. Reports in 6 weeks on queries; 2-3 months on mss. Free writer's guidelines.

• *Science of Mind* often fits manuscript topic into monthly themes.

Nonfiction: Book excerpts, inspirational, personal experience of Science of Mind, spiritual. Buys 35-45 mss/year. Query or send complete ms. Length: 750-2,000 words. Pays $25/printed page. Pays in contributors copies for some special features written by readers.

Photos: Reviews 35mm transparencies and 5×7 or 8×10 b&w prints. Buys one-time rights.

Poetry: Inspirational and Science of Mind oriented. "We are not interested in poetry not related to Science of Mind principles." Buys 10-15 poems/year. Length: 7-25 lines. Pays $25.

Tips: "We are interested in first person experiences of a spiritual nature having to do with the Science of Mind."

Regional

Many regional publications rely on staff-written material, but others accept work from freelance writers who live in or know the region. Some of these magazines are among the bestselling magazines in a particular area and are read carefully, so writers must be able to supply accurate, up-to-date material. The best regional publication to target with your submissions is usually the one in your hometown, whether it's a city or state magazine or a Sunday supplement in a newspaper. Since you are familiar with the region, it is easier to propose suitable story ideas.

Listed first are general interest magazines slanted toward residents of and visitors to a particular region. Next, regional publications are categorized alphabetically by state, followed by Canada. Publications that report on the business climate of a region are grouped in the regional division of the Business and Finance category. Recreation and travel publications specific to a geographical area are listed in the Travel, Camping and Trailer section. Keep in mind also that many regional publications specialize in specific areas, and are listed according to those sections. Regional publications are not listed if they only accept material from a select group of freelancers in their area or if they did not want to receive the number of queries and manuscripts a national listing would attract. If you know of a regional magazine that is not listed, approach it by asking for writer's guidelines before you send unsolicited material.

General

‡**AAA WORLD,** (formerly *Maine Motorist*), AAA Maine, P.O. Box 3544, Portland ME 04104-3544. (207)780-6831. Fax: (207)780-6914. Editor: Ellen Kornetsky. 1% freelance written. Bimonthly magazine on travel, car care, AAA news. *Editor's note: This magazine is now partially syndicated.* "Our readers enjoy learning about travel opportunities in the New England region and elsewhere. In addition, they enjoy topics of interest to automobile owners." Estab. 1910. Circ. 150,000. Pays on publication. Publishes ms an average of 4 months after acceptance. Byline given. Not copyrighted. Buys simultaneous rights; makes work-for-hire assignments. Submit seasonal material 6 months in advance. Accepts simultaneous submissions. Reports in 4 months. Sample copy for 9 × 12 SAE and 5 first-class stamps.
  • Ranked as one of the best markets for freelance writers in *Writer's Digest* magazine's annual "Top 100 Markets," January 1994.
Nonfiction: Historical/nostalgic (travel), how-to (car care, travel), travel (New England, US and foreign). No exotic travel destinations that cost a great deal. Send complete ms. Length: 500-800 words. Pays $100.
Photos: Send photos. Reviews 5 × 7 transparencies. Pays $15 for b&w; $35 for color. Captions required. Buys one-time rights.
Tips: "Travel (particularly New England regional) material is most needed. Interesting travel options are appreciated."

THE APPALACHIAN LOG, Appalachian Log Publishing Company, P.O. Box 20297, Charleston WV 25362-1297. (304)342-5789. Editor: Ron Gregory. 50% freelance written. Works with new/unpublished writers. Monthly magazine covering southern Appalachia. "*The Appalachian Log* is dedicated to promoting the people and places of Southern Appalachia. We publish only 'positive' articles concerning our region. We are *not* interested in religious or political material." Estab. 1992. Circ. 5,000. Pays on publication. Publishes ms an average of 3 months after acceptance. Byline given. Offers 10% kill fee or $10. Not copyrighted. Buys first, one-time, second serial (reprint) or simultaneous rights. Editorial lead time 2 months. Submit seasonal material 2 months in advance. Accepts simultaneous and previously published submissions. Query for electronic submissions. Reports in 3 weeks on queries; 3 months on mss. Sample copy for $1.50. Writer's guidelines for #10 SASE.
Nonfiction: Book excerpts, essays, historical/nostalgic, humor, inspirational, interview/profile, personal experience, photo feature, travel, genealogy. Special issues include snow skiing in the Southern Appalachians, festivals in Southern Appalachia, whitewater Rafting in Southern Appalachians. "No religious, exposé or opinion pieces. (We are no longer interested in political/opinion articles.)" Buys 30 mss/year. Send complete ms. Length: 300 words minimum. Pays $50 minimum for assigned articles; $10 minimum for unsolicited articles. Sometimes pays expenses of writers on assignment.

Photos: Send photos with submission. Reviews contact sheets. Captions required. Buys one-time rights.

Columns/Departments: Betty Gregory, publisher. Family History (genealogy), 1,000-2,000 words. Buys 4 mss/year. Query. Pays $20-50.

Fiction: Condensed novels, historical, humorous, mainstream, slice-of-life vignettes. No religious or erotic material. Buys 10 mss/year. Send complete ms. Length: 500-5,000 words. Pays $25-200.

Poetry: Betty Gregory, publisher. Avant-garde, free verse, light verse, traditional. Buys 40 poems/year. Length: 10-80 lines. Pays $7.50-30.

Fillers: Anecdotes, facts, short humor. Buys 15/year. Length: 25-250 words. Pays $5-50.

Tips: "Cover letters that give some indication of the author's knowledge of our region are helpful. All articles and submissions should, likewise, display the author's familiarity with Southern Appalachia. Details — particularly nostalgic ones — must be authentic and correct. Fiction and nonfiction short stories or longer works that can be serialized appeal to us. Writers in this area should be clear in their storyline (no 'hidden' meanings) and should keep in mind that our magazine loves Southern Appalachia and its people."

BLUE RIDGE COUNTRY, Leisure Publishing, P.O. Box 21535, Roanoke VA 24018-9900. (703)989-6138. Fax: (703)989-7603. Editor: Kurt Rheinheimer. 75% freelance written. Bimonthly magazine on the Blue Ridge region from Maryland to Georgia. "The magazine is designed to celebrate the history, heritage and beauty of the Blue Ridge region. It is aimed at the adult, upscale readers who enjoy living or traveling in the mountain regions of Virginia, North Carolina, West Virginia, Maryland, Kentucky, Tennessee, South Carolina and Georgia." Estab. 1972. Circ. 75,000. Pays on publication. Publishes ms an average of 6-8 months after acceptance. Byline given. Offers $50 kill fee for commissioned pieces only. Buys first and second serial (reprint) rights. Submit seasonal material 6 months in advance. Query for electronic submissions. Reports in 2 months. Sample copy for 9×12 SAE with 6 first-class stamps. Writer's guidelines for #10 SASE.

Nonfiction: General interest, historical/nostalgic, interview/profile, personal experience, photo feature, travel, history. Buys 25-30 mss/year. Query with or without published clips or send complete ms. Length: 500-1,800 words. Pays $50-250 for assigned articles; $25-250 for unsolicited articles.

● This magazine is looking for more photo-essays and shorter pieces.

Photos: Send photos with submission. Prefers transparencies. Offers $10-25/photo and $100 for cover photo. Identification of subjects required. Buys all rights.

Columns/Departments: Country Roads (stories on people, events, ecology, history, antiques, books), Mountain Living (profiles of cooks and their recipes, garden tips, weather info), GreenWatch (ecology news and tips); 50-200 words. Buys 12-24 mss/year. Query. Pays $10-40.

Tips: "Freelancers needed for departmental shorts and 'macro' issues affecting whole region. Need field reporters from all areas of Blue Ridge region. Also, we need updates on the Blue Ridge Parkway, Appalachian Trail, national forests, ecological issues, preservation movements."

‡MID-ATLANTIC COUNTRY, ESS Ventures, Inc., Suite 120, 6401 Golden Triangle Dr., Greenbelt MD 20770-3225. (301)220-2300. Editor: Tim Sayles. Managing Editor: Carolyn Anderson. Senior Editor: Sara Lowen. 80% freelance written. Monthly consumer publication covering travel, leisure and lifestyle (Mid-Atlantic). Estab. 1980. Coverage includes New Jersey, Pennsylvania, Delaware, Maryland, the District of Columbia, Virginia, West Virginia and North Carolina. Edited for affluent, suburban residents of the region's major markets. Explores opportunities for quality leisure at home and away. Features and columns are devoted to four main editorial categories: travel; leisure and the outdoors; regional people and profiles; and home and garden, including properties and interiors, food, restaurants and entertaining. Circ. 122,022. **Pays on acceptance.** Byline given. Buys first North American serial rights, one-time rights, or second serial (reprint) rights. Offers 33% kill fee. Submit seasonal material 12 months in advance. Query for electronic submissions. Accepts previously published submissions. Send typed ms with rights for sale noted and information about when and where the article previously appeared. Pays 50% of the amount paid for an original article. Reports in 3 months. Sample copy for 10×12 SASE.

Nonfiction: Contact: Editorial Queries. Book excerpts, essays, historical/nostalgic, profile (regional), photo feature (landscapes, small towns), travel. Not interested in subjects outside Mid-Atlantic states. Rarely consider pieces over 4,000 words. Query with published clips. Length: 1,000-3,000 words. Pays $50-200 for assigned articles. Pays expenses of writers on assignment.

Photos: Send photos with submission. Offers $200/photo maximum, $300 day rate. Captions, model releases, identification of subjects required. Buys one-time rights.

Columns/Departments: Tastings (restaurant reviews), Country Inns (Country Inn reviews), Sporting Life (sports, recreation, adventures). Buys 30 mss/year. Query with published clips. Length: 1,000-1,750 words. Pays $150-350.

Tips: "We like voice, an instinct for narrative and stylish writing. We respond to fresh ideas, surprising angles on what might otherwise be the same old stuff. EXTRAS — The 50-350 word short items upfront are always fertile territory for freelancers, but the pay is typically low."

NORTHWEST PARKS & WILDLIFE, Educational Publications Foundation, P.O. Box 18000, Florence OR 97439-0130. (800)348-8401. Fax: (503)997-1124. Editor: Dave Peden. Managing Editor: Judy Fleagle. 75% freelance written. Bimonthly regional magazine for Washington, Oregon, British Columbia, Idaho and occasionally Alaska, W. Montana and N. California. Estab. 1991. Circ. 25,000. Pays on publication. Publishes ms an average of 6-12 months after acceptance. Byline given. Offers 33% kill fee. Buys first North American serial rights. Submit seasonal material 6 months in advance. Query for electronic submissions. Reports on queries in 1 month and ms in 3 months. Sample copy for $4.50. Writer's guidelines for #10 SASE.

Nonfiction: General interest, interview/profile, personal experience, photo feature, wildlife and wilderness areas, profiles of parks. "Any article not related to Pacific Northwest will be returned." Buys 100 mss/year. Query with published clips. Length: 500-2,000 words. Pays $50-350 plus 2-5 contributor's copies.

Photos: Send photos with submission. Reviews 35mm or larger transparencies. Prefers to buy photo-text packages. Captions, model releases, photo credits and identification of subjects required. Buys one-time rights.

Fillers: Newsbreaks. Uses 45/year. Length: 300-500 words. No payment for fillers.

Tips: "Slant articles for readers not living in Pacific Northwest. Keep articles informative rather than travel oriented. Do give directions and contact information for 'GettingThere' section at end of article. An articulate query of one page is appreciated rather than a ms. Articles of 800-1,000 words with photos are easiest to fit in. Articles of 400 words with good horizontal photo are needed for back page section. Accurate captions and photo credits on separate sheet from photos are appreciated."

‡**NORTHWEST TRAVEL,** Northwest Regional Magazines, P.O. Box 18000, Florence OR 97439. (503)997-8401. Editor: Dave Peden. Managing Editor: Judy Fleagle. 50% freelance written. Bimonthly consumer magazine covering the Pacific Northwest. "We like energetic writing about popular activities and destinations in the Northwest. Northwest Travel aims to give readers practical ideas on where to go in the region. Magazine covers Oregon, Washington, Idaho, B.C.; occasionally Alaska and western Montana." Estab. 1991. Circ. 50,000. Pays on publication. Publishes ms an average of 6-8 months after acceptance. Offers 33% kill fee. Buys first North American serial rights or second serial (reprint) rights. Submit seasonal material 6 months in advance. Accepts simultaneous and previously published submissions. Query for electronic submissions. Reports in 1½ months on mss (but prefer queries); 1½ months on queries. Sample copy for $4.50. Writer's guidelines for #10 SASE.

Nonfiction: Book excerpts, general interest, historical/nostalgic, interview/profile (rarely), photo feature, travel (only in Northwest region). "No cliche-ridden pieces on places that everyone covers." Buys 40-50 mss/year. Query with or without published clips. Length: 300-2,500 words. Pays $125 minimum for assigned articles; $50 minimum for unsolicited articles.

Photos: State availability of photos with submission. Reviews transparencies (prefer dupes). Negotiates payment individually. Captions, model releases, credits and identification of subjects required. Buys one-time rights.

Columns/Departments: Restaurant Reviews 1,000 words. Pays $125. Worth A Stop (brief items describing places "worth a stop," 300-500 words. Buys 25-30 mss/year. Send complete ms. Pays $50-125.

Fillers: Anecdotes, facts. Length: 50-200 words. Pays $25-50.

Tips: "Write fresh, lively copy (avoid cliches) and cover exciting travel topics in the region that haven't been covered in other magazines. A story with stunning photos will get serious consideration. Areas most open to freelancers are Worth A Stop and Restaurant Reviews. Take us to fascinating, interesting, fun places we might not otherwise discover."

NOW AND THEN, Center for Appalachian Studies and Services, East Tennessee State University, P.O. Box 70556, Johnson City TN 37614-0556. (615)929-5348. Fax: (615)929-5348. Editor: Pat Arnow. 80% freelance written. Triannual regional magazine. Estab. 1984. Circ. 1,500. Pays on publication. Publishes ms an average of 6 months after acceptance. Byline given. Buys one-time rights. Accepts simultaneous submissions. Send typed ms with rights for sale noted. Reports in 1 month on queries; 4 months on mss. Sample copy for $3.50. Writer's guidelines for #10 SASE.

Nonfiction: Book excerpts, essays, historical, humor, interview/profile, personal experience, photo feature. "We do have a special focus in each issue—we've featured Appalachian Blacks, Cherokees, women, music and veterans. Write for future themes. Stereotypes, generalizations, sentimental writing are rejected. It must have to do with Appalachia." Buys 8 mss/year. Query with or without published clips or send complete ms. Length: 2,500 words. Pays $15-60 for assigned articles; $10-60 for unsolicited articles. Sometimes pays expenses of writers on assignment.

Photos: Send photos with submission. Reviews contact sheets and prints. Sometimes can offer additional payment for photos accepted with ms. Captions, model releases and identification of subjects required. Buys one-time rights.

Fiction: Ethnic, experimental, historical, humorous, novel excerpts, slice-of-life vignettes. Buys 3 mss/year. Send complete ms. Length: 2,500 words maximum. Pays $10-50. Must have some relation to theme issues.

Poetry: Avant-garde, free verse. Buys 30-35 poems/year. Pays 2 contributor's copies and a year subscription. Send no more than 5 poems at a time.

Tips: "Everything we publish has something to do with life in Appalachia present and past. Profiles of people living and working in the region, short stories that convey the reality of life in Appalachia (which can include malls, children who wear shoes and watch MTV) are the kinds of things we're looking for."

YANKEE, Yankee Publishing Inc., P.O. Box 520, Dublin NH 03444-0520. (603)563-8111. Editor: Judson D. Hale, Sr.. Managing Editor: Tim Clark. 50% freelance written. Monthly magazine that features articles on New England. "Our mission is to express and perhaps, indirectly, preserve the New England culture—and to do so in an entertaining way. Our audience is national, and has one thing in common—they love New England." Estab. 1935. Circ. 700,000. Pays within 30 days of acceptance. Byline given. Offers 33% kill fee. Buys first rights. Submit seasonal material 5 months in advance. Accepts simultaneous submissions. Send tearsheet, photocopy of article or short story, typed ms with rights for sale noted and information about when and where the material previously appeared. For reprints pays 100% of the amount paid for an original article. Query for electronic submissions." Reports in 2 months on queries. Writer's guidelines for #10 SASE.
• Ranked as one of the best markets for freelance writers in *Writer's Digest* magazine's annual "Top 100 Markets," January 1994.
Nonfiction: Lauri Grotstein, assistant editor. Essays, general interest, historical/nostalgic, humor, interview/profile, personal experience. "No 'good old days' pieces, no dialect humor and nothing outside New England!" Buys 30 mss/year. Query with published clips. Length: 250-2,500 words. Pays $50-2,000 for assigned articles; $50-500 for unsolicited articles. Sometimes pays expenses of writers on assignment.
Photos: Send photos with submission. Reviews contact sheets and transparencies. Offers $50-150/photo. Identification of subjects required. Buys one-time rights.
Columns/Departments: New England Sampler (short bits on interesting people, anecdotes, lost and found), 100-400 words; Yankee's Home Companion (short pieces about home-related items), 100-400 words; I Remember (nostalgia focused on specific incidents), 400-500 words. Buys 80 mss/year. Query with published clips. Pays $50-400.
Fiction: Edie Clark, fiction editor. "We publish high-quality literary fiction that explores human issues and concerns in a specific place—New England." Publishes novel excerpts. Buys 6 mss/year. Send complete ms. Length: 500-2,500 words. Pays $1,000.
Poetry: Jean Burden, poetry editor. "We don't choose poetry by type. We look for the best. No inspirational, holiday-oriented, epic, limericks, etc." Buys 40 poems/year. Submit maximum 3 poems. Length: 2-20 lines. Pays $50.
Tips: "Submit lots of ideas. Don't censor yourself—let *us* decide whether an idea is good or bad. We might surprise you. Remember we've been publishing for 57 years, so chances are we've already done every 'classic' New England subject. Try to surprise us—it isn't easy. These departments are most open to freelancers: New England Sampler; Home Companion; I Remember. Study the ones we publish—the format should be apparent. Surprise us!"

Alabama

ALABAMA HERITAGE, University of Alabama, Box 870342, Tuscaloosa AL 35487-0342. (205)348-7467. Fax: (205)348-7434. Editor: Suzanne Wolfe. 50% freelance written. Quarterly magazine on Alabama history and culture. "*Alabama Heritage* is a nonprofit historical quarterly published by the University of Alabama for the intelligent lay reader. We are interested in lively, well written and thoroughly researched articles on Alabama/Southern history and culture. Readability and accuracy are essential." Estab. 1986. Pays on publication. Byline given. Buys first rights and second serial (reprint) rights. Query for electronic submissions. Reports in 1 month. *Writer's Market* recommends allowing 2 months for reply. Sample copy for $5. Writer's guidelines for #10 SASE.
Nonfiction: Historical. "We do not want fiction, poetry, book reviews, articles on current events or living artists and personal/family reminiscences." Buys 10 mss/year. Query. Length: 1,500-5,000 words. Pays $100 minimum. Also sends 10 copies to each author plus 1-year subscription.
Photos: Reviews contact sheets. Identification of subjects required. Buys one-time rights.
Tips: "Authors need to remember that we regard history as a fascinating subject, not as a dry recounting of dates and facts. Articles that are lively and engaging, in addition to being well researched, will find interested readers among our editors. No term papers, please. All areas of our magazine are open to freelance writers. Best approach is a written query."

ALABAMA LIVING, Alabama Rural Electric Assn., P.O. Box 244014, Montgomery AL 36124. (205)215-2732. Editor: Darryl Gates. 10% freelance written. Monthly magazine covering rural electric consumers. "Our magazine is an editorially balanced, informational and educational service to members of rural electric cooperatives. Our mix regularly includes Alabama history, nostalgia, gardening, outdoor and consumer pieces." Estab. 1948. Pays on publication. Publishes ms an average of 3 months after acceptance. Byline given. Publication is not copyrighted. Buys second serial (reprint) rights. Editorial lead time 3 months. Submit seasonal material 4 months in advance. Accepts simultaneous and previously published submissions. Send information about when and where the article previously appeared. Pays 100% of the amount paid for an original article. Reports in 1 month on queries. Sample copy free on request.
Nonfiction: Historical/nostalgic, rural-oriented. Buys 6 mss/year. Send complete ms (copy). Length: 300-750 words. Pays $100 minimum for assigned articles; $40 minimum for unsolicited articles.

Tips: "The best way to break into *Alabama Living* is to give us a bit of history or nostalgia about Alabama or the Southeast."

Alaska

ALASKA, The Magazine of Life on the Last Frontier, Suite 200, 808 E St., Anchorage AK 99501-9963. (907)272-6070. Fax: (907)272-6070. Editor: Tobin Morrison. Managing Editor: Nolan Hester. 80% freelance written. Eager to work with new/unpublished writers. Monthly magazine covering topics "uniquely Alaskan." Estab. 1935. Circ. 235,000. **Pays on acceptance.** Publishes ms an average of 6 months after acceptance. Byline given. Buys first or one-time rights. Submit seasonal material 1 year in advance. Query for electronic submissions. Reports in 2 months. Sample copy for $3 and 9×12 SAE with 7 first-class stamps. Writer's guidelines for #10 SASE.
   • Ranked as one of the best markets for freelance writers in *Writer's Digest* magazine's annual "Top 100 Markets," January 1994.
Nonfiction: Historical/nostalgic, adventure, how-to (on anything Alaskan), humor, interview/profile, personal experience, photo feature. Also travel articles and Alaska destination stories. Does not accept fiction or poetry. Buys 60 mss/year. Query. Length: 100-2,500 words. Pays $100-1,250 depending upon length. Pays expenses of writers on assignment.
Photos: Send photos with submission. Reviews 35mm or larger transparencies. Captions and identification of subjects required.
Tips: "We are placing even more emphasis on natural history, adventure and profiles."

Arizona

ARIZONA HIGHWAYS, 2039 W. Lewis Ave., Phoenix AZ 85009-9988. (602)258-6641. Fax: (602)254-4505. Managing Editor: Richard G. Stahl. 90% freelance written. Prefers to work with published/established writers. State-owned magazine designed to help attract tourists into and through the state. Estab. 1925. **Pays on acceptance.** Reports in up to 3 months. Writer's guidelines for SASE.
   • Ranked as one of the best markets for freelance writers in *Writer's Digest* magazine's annual "Top 100 Markets," January 1994.
Nonfiction: Feature subjects include narratives and exposition dealing with history, anthropology, nature, wildlife, armchair travel, out of the way places, small towns, old west history, Indian arts and crafts, travel, etc. Travel articles are experience-based. All must be oriented toward Arizona and the Southwest. Buys 6 mss/issue. Buys first serial rights. Query with "a lead paragraph and brief outline of story. We deal with professionals only, so include list of current credits." Length: 600-2,000 words. Pays 35-55¢/word. Sometimes pays expenses of writers on assignment.
Photos: "We will use transparencies of 2¼, 4×5 or larger, and 35mm when they display exceptional quality or content. We prefer 35mm Kodachrome. Each transparency *must* be accompanied by information attached to each photograph: where, when, what. No photography will be reviewed by the editors unless the photographer's name appears on *each* and *every* transparency." Pays $80-350 for "selected" transparencies. Buys one-time rights.
Columns/Departments: New departments in the magazine include Focus on Nature, Along the Way, Back-Road Adventure, Legends of the Lost, Hike of the Month and Arizona Humor. "Back Road and Hikes also must be experience-based."
Tips: "Writing must be of professional quality, warm, sincere, in-depth, well-peopled and accurate. Avoid themes that describe first trips to Arizona, the Grand Canyon, the desert, Colorado River running, etc. Emphasis is to be on Arizona adventure and romance as well as flora and fauna, when appropriate, and themes that can be photographed. Double check your manuscript for accuracy."

PHOENIX, Media America Corporation, #B-200, 5555 N. 7th Ave., Phoenix AZ 85013-1755. (602)207-3750. Fax: (602)207-3777. Editor/Publisher: Richard S. Vonier. Managing Editor: Beth Deveny. 70% freelance written. Monthly magazine covering southwest, state of Arizona, metro Phoenix. Estab. 1966. Circ. 50,000. Pays on acceptance or publication. Publishes ms an average of 5 months after acceptance. Byline given. Negotiable kill fee. Buys first North American serial rights and one-time rights. Submit seasonal material 4 months in advance. Accepts simultaneous and previously published submissions. Send tearsheet or photocopy of article and/or typed ms with rights for sale noted and information about when and where the article previously appeared. Pays 50% of their fee for an original article. Query for electronic submissions. Reports in 2 months. Sample copy for $1.95 and 9×12 SAE with 5 first-class stamps.
Nonfiction: Book excerpts, essays, investigative, general interest, historical/nostalgic, how-to, humor, inspirational, interview/profile, opinion, personal experience, photo feature, religious, technical, travel, other. "No material dealing with travel outside the region or other subjects that don't have an effect on the area." Buys 35-65 mss/year. Query with published clips. Pays $50-1,500 for assigned articles; $50-500 for unsolicited articles. Sometimes pays expenses of writers on assignment.
Photos: Send photos with submissions. Reviews contact sheets, negatives, transparencies, prints. Offers $25-100/photo. Captions, model releases and identification of subjects required. Buys one-time rights.

Tips: "We have no published guidelines. Articles should be of local or regional interest with vivid descriptions that put the reader in the story and present new information or a new way of looking at things. We are not afraid of opinion."

TUCSON LIFESTYLE, Citizen Publishing Company of Wisconsin, Inc., dba Old Pueblo Press, Suite 12, 7000 E. Tanque Verde Rd., Tucson AZ 85715-5318. (602)721-2929. Fax: (602)721-8665. Editor-in-Chief: Sue Giles. 90% freelance written. Prefers to work with published/established writers. Monthly magazine covering city-related events and topics. Estab. 1982. Circ. 27,000. **Pays on acceptance.** Publishes ms an average of 6 months after acceptance. Byline given. Buys first rights and second serial (reprint) rights. Submit seasonal material 1 year in advance. Reports in 6 months. Accepts previously published submissions. Send typed ms with rights for sale noted and information about when and where the article previously appeared. Pays 25-50% of the amount paid for an original article. Sample copy for $3.20. Free writer's guidelines.
Nonfiction: All stories need a Tucson angle. Historical/nostalgic, humor, interview/profile, personal experience, travel, local stories. Special issue: Christmas (December). "We do not accept *anything* that does not pertain to Tucson or Arizona." Buys 100 mss/year. Query. Pays $50-300. Sometimes pays expenses of writers on assignment.
Photos: Reviews contact sheets, 2¼×2¼ transparencies and 5×7 prints. Offers $25-100/photo. Identification of subjects required. Buys one-time rights.
Columns/Departments: In Business—articles on Tucson businesses and business people; Southwest Homes (environmental living in Tucson: homes, offices). Buys 36 mss/year. Query. Pays $100-200.
Tips: Features are most open to freelancers. " 'Style' is not of paramount importance; good, clean copy with interesting lead is a 'must.' "

California

BUZZ, The Talk of Los Angeles, Suite 450, 11835 W. Olympic Blvd., Los Angeles CA 90064-5000. (310)473-2721. Editor-in-Chief: Allan Mayer. 80% freelance written. Monthly magazine for Los Angeles. "We are looking for lively, provocative, insightful journalism, essays and fiction of and for Los Angeles." Estab. 1990. Circ. 75,000. Pays within 30 days of acceptance. Byline given. Offers 25% kill fee. Buys first North American serial rights. Submit seasonal material 4 months in advance. Query for electronic submissions. Reports in 3 months. Sample copy for $2.50 and 10×13 SAE with 10 first-class stamps.
 • Ranked as one of the best markets for freelance writers in *Writer's Digest* magazine's annual "Top 100 Markets," January 1994 and as one of the best markets for fiction writers in its biannual "Fiction 50," June 1994.
Nonfiction: Greg Critser, deputy editor. Book excerpts, essays, general interest, interview/profile. "No satirical essays, book/movie/theater reviews or personal memoirs." Buys 30 mss/year. Query with published clips. Length: 2,500-4,000 words. Pays $2,000-5,000. Sometimes pays expenses of writers on assignment.
Photos: Send photos with submission. Photos are assigned separately. Model releases and identification of subjects required. Buys one-time rights.
Columns/Departments: Susan Gordon, senior editor. "What's the Buzz" (witty, "Talk of the Town"-like pieces on personalities, trends and events in L.A.), 300-1,000 words. Buys 60 mss/year. Query with published clips. Pays $200-1,000.
Fiction: Renee Vogel, fiction editor. "We are interested in any type fiction by L.A. writers, and in fiction relevant to L.A. by non-L.A.-based writers. No fiction that has no connection with L.A." Publishes novel excerpts. Buys 10 mss/year. Send complete ms. Length: 1,500-4,000 words. Pays $1,000-2,500.
Tips: "The 'What's the Buzz' section is the best place to break into *Buzz*. Freelancers should keep in mind that we're looking for national-quality works."

‡THE EAST BAY MONTHLY, The Berkeley Monthly, Inc., 1301 59th St., Emeryville CA 94608. (510)658-9811. Editor: Tim Devaney. 95% freelance written. Monthly tabloid. "We like stories about local people and issues, but we also accept ideas for articles about topics that range beyond the East Bay's borders or have little or nothing to do with the region." Estab. 1970. Circ. 75,000. Pays on publication. Byline given. Offers 25% kill fee. Buys first rights or second serial (reprint) rights. Editorial lead time 2 months. Submit seasonal material 2 months in advance. Accepts simultaneous and previously published submissions. Reports in 1 month. Sample copy for $1. Writer's guidelines for #10 SASE.
Nonfiction: Essays, exposé, general interest, historical/nostalgic, humor, interview/profile, opinion, personal experience, photo feature, travel. Buys 55 mss/year. Query with published clips. Length: 1,500-3,000 words. Pays 10¢/word.
Photos: State availability of photos with submission. Reviews contact sheets, 4×5 transparencies, 8×10 prints. Negotiates payment individually. Identification of subjects required. Buys one-time rights.
Columns/Departments: Shopping Around (local retail news), 2,000 words; Food for Thought (local food news), 2,000 words; First Person, 2,000 words. Buys 15 mss/year. Query with published clips. Pays 10¢/word.

LOS ANGELES MAGAZINE, ABC/Capital Cities, 1888 Century Park East, Los Angeles CA 90067. (310)557-7569. Fax: (310)557-7517. Executive Editor: Rodger Claire. Editor: Lew Harris. 98% freelance written.

Monthly magazine about southern California. "The primary editorial role of the magazine is to aid a literate, upscale audience in getting the most out of life in the Los Angeles area." Estab. 1963. Circ. 174,000. Pays on publication. Publishes ms an average of 4 months after acceptance. Byline given. Offers 30% kill fee. Buys first North American serial rights. Submit seasonal material 6 months in advance. Reports in 3 months. Sample copy for $5. Writer's guidelines for #10 SASE.

  • Ranked as one of the best markets for freelance writers in *Writer's Digest* magazine's annual "Top 100 Markets," January 1994.

Nonfiction: Book excerpts (about L.A. or by famous L.A. author); exposé (any local issue); general interest; historical/nostalgic (about L.A. or Hollywood); interview/profile (about L.A. person). Buys up to 100 mss/year. Query with published clips. Length: 250-3,500 words. Pays $50-2,000. Sometimes pays expenses of writers on assignment.

Photos: Nancie Clare, photo editor. Send photos.

Columns/Departments: Buys 170 mss/year. Query with published clips. Length: 250-1,200 words. Pays $50-600.

LOS ANGELES READER, Suite 301, 5550 Wilshire Blvd., Los Angeles CA 90036-3389. (213)965-7430. Fax: (213)933-0281. Editor: James Vowell. Managing Editor: Erik Himmelsbach. 85% freelance written. Weekly tabloid of features and reviews for "intelligent young Los Angelenos interested in politics, the arts and popular culture." Estab. 1978. Circ. 90,000. Pays on publication. Publishes ms an average of 60 days after publication. Byline given. Buys one-time rights. Accepts previously published submissions. Send photocopy of article, typed ms with rights for sale noted and information about when and where the article previously appeared. Pays 50% of their fee for an original article. Query for electronic submissions. Reports in 2 months. Sample copy for $1 for 9×12 SAE with 2 first-class stamps.

Nonfiction: General interest, journalism, interview/profile, personal experience, photo features—all with strong local slant. Buys "scores" of mss/year. Send complete ms or query. Length: 200-3,500 words. Pays $25-300.

Tips: "Break in with submissions for our Cityside page which uses short (400-800 word) news items on Los Angeles happenings, personalities and trends. Try to have some conflict in submissions: 'x exists' is not as good a story as 'x is struggling with y over z.' Stories must have Los Angeles angle. We much prefer submissions in electronic form."

LOS ANGELES TIMES MAGAZINE, *Los Angeles Times*, Times Mirror Sq., Los Angeles CA 90053. (213)237-7000. Fax: (213)237-7386. Editor: Bret Israel. 50% freelance written. Weekly magazine of regional general interest. Circ. 1,164,388. Payment schedule varies. Publishes ms an average of 2 months after acceptance. Byline given. Buys first North American serial rights. Submit seasonal material 3 months in advance. Accepts simultaneous queries and submissions. Reports in 1-2 months. Sample copy and writer's guidelines are free.

Nonfiction: General interest, investigative and narrative journalism, interview/profiles, reported essays. Covers California, the West, the nation and the world. Written queries only. Queries must include clips. Length: 2,500-4,500 words. Pays agreed upon expenses.

Photos: Query first. Reviews color transparencies and b&w prints. Payment varies. Captions, model releases and identification of subjects required. Buys one-time rights.

Tips: "Prospective contributors should know their subject well and be able to explain why a story merits publication. Previous national magazine writing experience preferred."

METRO, Metro Publishing Inc., 550 S. 1st St., San Jose CA 95113-2806. (408)298-8000. Editor: Dan Pulcrano. Managing Editor: Sharan Street. 35-50% freelance written. Weekly alternative newspaper. "*Metro* is for a sophisticated urban audience—stories must be more in-depth with an unusual slant not covered in daily newspapers." Estab. 1985. Circ. 85,000. Pays on publication from one week to two months. Publishes ms after acceptance. Byline given. Offers kill fee with assignment memorandum signed by editor. Buys first North American serial and second serial (reprint) rights—non-exclusive. Submit seasonal material 3 months in advance. Accepts previously published material. Send photocopy of article including information about when and where the article previously appeared. Pays $25-200 for reprints. Query for electronic submissions. Reports in 2 months on queries; 4 months on mss. Sample copy for $3. Writer's guidelines for #10 SASE.

Nonfiction: Book excerpt, exposé, interview/profile (particularly entertainment oriented). Some sort of local angle preferred. Special issues: Wedding Feature, Health and Fitness, Spring and Fall Fashion. Buys 75 mss/year. Query with published clips. Length: 500-4,000 words. Pays $50-500 for articles. Sometimes pays expenses of writers on assignment.

Photos: Send photos with submission. Reviews contact sheets, negatives, any size transparencies and prints. Offers $25-50/photo, more if used on cover. Captions, model releases and identification of subjects required. Buys one-time rights.

Columns/Departments: MetroMenu (copy related to food, dining out), 500-1,000 words; MetroGuide (entertainment features, interviews), 500-1,500 words. Buys 100 mss/year. Query with published clips. Pays $25-75.

Tips: "Seasonal features are most likely to be published, but we take only the best stuff. Stories on local news events or national news events with a local angle will also be considered. Preferred submission format is Macintosh disk with accompanying printout."

ORANGE COAST MAGAZINE, The Magazine of Orange County, Orange Coast Kommunications Inc., Suite 8, 245-D Fischer Ave., Costa Mesa CA 92626-4514. (714)545-1900. Fax: (714)545-1932. Editor: Robin Manougian. Managing Editor: Allison Joyce. 95% freelance written. Monthly magazine "designed to inform and enlighten the educated, upscale residents of Orange County, California; highly graphic and well-researched." Estab. 1974. Circ. 40,000. **Pays on acceptance.** Publishes ms an average of 4 months after acceptance. Byline given. Buys first serial rights. Submit seasonal material at least 6 months in advance. Accepts simultaneous submissions. Reports in 2 months. Sample copy for $2.95 and 10 × 12 SAE with 8 first-class stamps. Writer's guidelines for SASE.
Nonfiction: Exposé (Orange County government, politics, business, crime), general interest (with Orange County focus),; historical/nostalgic, guides to activities and services, interview/profile (prominent Orange County citizens), local sports, travel. Special issues: Dining and Entertainment (March); Health and Fitness (January); Resort Guide (November); Home and Garden (June); Holiday (December). Buys 100 mss/year. Query or send complete ms. Absolutely no phone queries. Length: 1,000-3,000 words. Pays $250 maximum.
Columns/Departments: Business statistics. Most departments are not open to freelancers. Buys 200 mss/ year. Query or send complete ms. *Absolutely no phone queries*. Length: 1,000-2,000 words. Pays $150 maximum.
Fiction: Buys only under rare circumstances. Send complete ms. Length: 1,000-5,000 words. Pays $250.
Tips: "Most features are assigned to writers we've worked with before. Don't try to sell us 'generic' journalism. *Orange Coast* prefers articles with specific and unusual angles that in some way include Orange County. A lot of freelance writers ignore our Orange County focus. We get far too many generalized manuscripts."

PALM SPRINGS LIFE, Desert Publications, Inc., P.O. Box 2724, Palm Springs CA 92263-2724. (619)325-2333. Fax: (619)325-7008. Editor: Jamie Pricer. Estab. 1958. 30% freelance written. Monthly magazine covering "affluent resort/southern California/Palm Springs desert resorts. *Palm Springs Life* is a luxurious magazine aimed at the 'affluence' market. Surveys show that our readership has a median age of 50.1, a median household income of $190,000, a primary home worth $275,150 and a second home worth $190,500." Circ. 24,000. Pays on publication. Publishes ms an average of 3 months after acceptance. Byline given. Buys all rights (negotiable). Submit seasonal material 4 months in advance. Accepts simultaneous and previously published submissions. Query for electronic submissions. Reports in 3 months. Sample copy for $6.
Nonfiction: General interest, historical/nostalgic, humor, interview/profile, new product, photo feature, travel. Special issues: Real Estate (May); Home and Garden (May); Health (July); Desert Living Annual/ Coachella Valley focus (September); Desert Progress (October); Arts & Culture (November); Holiday Shopping (December). Query with published clips. Length: 700-1,200 words. Pays 20¢/word. Sometimes pays the expenses of writers on assignment.
  • Increased focus on desert region and business writing opportunities.
Photos: Reviews 2¼ × 2¼, 4 × 5, 35mm transparencies. Offers $50-500 (for cover). Captions, model releases and identification of subjects required.
Tips: "*Palm Springs Life* publishes articles about dining, fashion, food, wine, beauty, health, business, sports (especially tennis and golf) and the lifestyle of the powerful, rich and famous. We are always interested in new ways to enjoy wealth, display luxury and consume it. We want to hear what's 'in' and what's 'out,' what's new in Palm Springs and the Coachella Valley, and how to solve problems experienced by our readers."

PALO ALTO WEEKLY, Embarcadero Publishing Co., 703 High St., P.O. Box 1610, Palo Alto CA 94302. (415)326-8210. Fax: (415)326-3928. Editor: Paul Gullixson. 5% freelance written. Semiweekly tabloid focusing on local issues and local sources. Estab. 1979. Circ. 48,000. Pays on publication. Publishes ms an average of 1 month after acceptance. Byline given. Offers 50% kill fee. Buys first rights. Submit seasonal/holiday material 2 months in advance. Reports in 2 weeks. Sample copy for 9 × 12 SAE with 2 first-class stamps.
Nonfiction: General interest, historical/nostalgic, interview/profile, photo feature. Special issues: Together (weddings – mid February); Interiors (May, October). Nothing that is not local; no travel. Buys 25 mss/year. Query with published clips. Length: 700-1,000 words. Pays $25-40.
Photos: Send photos with submission. Reviews contact sheets and 5 × 7 prints. Offers $10 minimum/photo. Captions, model releases and identification of subjects required. Buys one-time rights.
Tips: "Writers have the best chance if they live within circulation area and know publication and area well. DON'T send generic, broad-based pieces. The most open sections are food, interiors and sports. Keep it LOCAL."

SACRAMENTO MAGAZINE, 4471 D St., Sacramento CA 95819. Fax: (916)452-6061. Editor: Krista Minard. Managing Editor: Sigrid Bathen. 100% freelance written. Works with a small number of new/unpublished writers each year. Monthly magazine emphasizing a strong local angle on politics, local issues, human interest and consumer items for readers in the middle to high income brackets. Estab. 1975. Pays on publication. Publishes ms an average of 3 months after acceptance. Rights vary; generally buys first North American serial rights, rarely second serial (reprint) rights. No reprints. Reports in 2 months. Sample copy for $4.50. Writer's guidelines for #10 SASE.

Nonfiction: Local issues vital to Sacramento quality of life. Buys 5 unsolicited feature mss/year. Query first in writing. Length: 1,500-3,000 words, depending on author, subject matter and treatment. Sometimes pays expenses of writers on assignment.

Photos: Send photos. Payment varies depending on photographer, subject matter and treatment. Captions (including IDs, location and date) required. Buys one-time rights.

Columns/Departments: Business, home and garden, media, parenting, first person essays, regional travel, gourmet, profile, sports, city arts (1,000-1,800 words); and City Lights (250-400 words).

SAN FRANCISCO BAY GUARDIAN, 520 Hampshire St., San Francisco CA 94110-1417. (415)255-3100. Fax: (415)255-8762. Editor/Publisher: Bruce Brugmann. 40% freelance written. Works with a small number of new/unpublished writers each year. Weekly news magazine specializing in investigative, consumer and life-style reporting for a sophisticated, urban audience. Estab. 1966. Circ. 140,000. Pays 1 month after publication. Publishes ms an average of 2 months after acceptance. Byline given. Buys 200 mss/year. Buys first rights. No simultaneous or multiple submissions. Query for electronic submissions. Reports in 2 months.

Nonfiction: Pia Hinckle, news editor; Tommy Tompkins, arts editor; Miriam Wolf, features editor. Publishes "incisive local news stories, investigative reports, features, analysis and interpretation, how-to, consumer and entertainment reviews. Most stories have a Bay Area angle." Freelance material should have a "public interest advocacy journalism approach." Sometimes pays the expenses of writers on assignment.

Photos: Mark Evans, art director. Purchased with or without mss.

Tips: "Work with our volunteer and intern projects in investigative, political and consumer reporting. We teach the techniques and send interns out to do investigative research. We like to talk to writers in our office before they begin doing a story."

THE SAN GABRIEL VALLEY MAGAZINE, Miller Books, 2908 W. Valley Blvd., Alhambra CA 91803. (213)284-7607. Fax: (818)284-7607. Editor: Joseph Miller. 75% freelance written. Bimonthly magazine for middle- to upper-income people who dine out often at better restaurants in Los Angeles County. Estab. 1962. Circ. 3,400. Pays on publication. Publishes ms an average of 45 days after acceptance. Buys simultaneous, second serial (reprint) and one-time rights. Phone queries OK. Submit seasonal material 1 month in advance. Accepts simultaneous and previously published submissions. Send tearsheet or photocopy of article or short story. Pays same as for original material. Reports in 1 month. Sample copy for $1.

Nonfiction: Exposé (political), informational (restaurants in the Valley), inspirational (success stories and positive thinking), interview (successful people and how they made it), profile (political leaders in the San Gabriel Valley), travel (places in the Valley). Interested in 500-word humor articles. Buys 18 unsolicited mss/year. Length: 500-10,000 words. Pays 5¢/word.

Columns/Departments: Restaurants, Education, Valley News, Valley Personality. Buys 2 mss/issue. Send complete ms. Length: 500-1,500 words. Pays 5¢/word.

Fiction: Historical (successful people), western (articles about Los Angeles County). Buys 2 mss/issue. Send complete ms. Length: 500-10,000 words. Pays 5¢/word.

Tips: "Send us a good personal success story about a Valley or a California personality. We are also interested in articles on positive thinking."

‡VENTURA COUNTY & COAST REPORTER, VCR Inc., Suite 213, 1583 Spinnaker Dr., Ventura CA 93001. (805)658-2244. Fax: (805)658-7803. Editor: Nancy Cloutier. 12% freelance written. Works with a small number of new/unpublished writers each year. Weekly tabloid covering local news. Circ. 35,000. Pays on publication. Publishes ms an average of 2 weeks after acceptance. Byline given. Buys first North American serial rights. Reports in 3 weeks.

Nonfiction: General interest (local slant), humor, interview/profile, travel (local—within 500 miles). Local (Ventura County) slant predominates. Length: 2-5 double-spaced typewritten pages. Pays $10-25.

Photos: Send photos with ms. Reviews b&w contact sheet.

Columns/Departments: Entertainment, Sports, Dining News, Real Estate, Boating Experience (Southern California). Send complete ms. Pays $10-25.

Tips: "As long as topics are up-beat with local slant, we'll consider them."

Colorado

ASPEN MAGAZINE, Ridge Publications, P.O. Box G-3, Aspen CO 81612. (303)920-4040. Fax: (303)920-4044. Editor: Janet C. O'Grady. Managing Editor: Rebecca Bennett. 85% freelance written. "We rarely accept submissions by new freelance writers." Bimonthly magazine covering Aspen and the Roaring Fork Valley. Estab. 1974. Circ. 16,000. Pays within 30 days of publication. Byline given. Kill fee varies. Buys first North American serial rights. Query for electronic submissions. Reports in 6 months. Sample copy for 9 × 12 SAE with 10 first-class stamps. Writer's guidelines for #10 SASE.

Nonfiction: Essay, historical, interview/profile, photo feature, enrivonmental and local issues, architecture and design, sports and outdoors, arts. "We do not publish general interest articles without a strong Aspen hook. We do not publish 'theme' (skiing in Aspen) or anniversary (40th year of Aspen Music Festival)." Buys 30-60 mss/year. Query with published clips. Length: 50-4,000 words. Pays $50-1,000.

Photos: Send photos with submission. Reviews contact sheets, negatives, transparencies, prints. Model release and identification of subjects required.

Columns/Departments: Town and mountain news, sports, business, travel, health, beauty, fitness, art news. "We rarely accept freelance travel stories. Virtually all travel is written in-house." Query with published clips. Length: 200-1,500. Pays $50-150.

‡FLATIRONS, The Boulder Magazine, Steamboat Communications Group Inc., Suite 205, 5775 Flatiron Pkwy., Boulder CO 80301-5730. (303)449-1847. Editor: Rolly Wahl. Contact: Leland Rucker, Managing Editor. 80% freelance written. Semiannual magazine covering Boulder and Boulder County region. "*Flatirons—The Boulder Magazine* showcases the people, events, lifestyles, interests and history of Boulder and Boulder County. Our readers are generally well-educated, well-traveled, active people in the area or visiting the region from all 50 states and many foreign countries. Writing should be fresh, entertaining and informative." Estab. 1993. Circ. 30,000. Pays on publication. Publishes ms an average of 3 months after acceptance. Byline given. Offers 100% kill fee. Buys one-time rights. Editorial lead time 8-12 months. Submit seasonal material 8-12 months in advance. Accepts simultaneous and previously published submissions. Query for electronic submissions. Reports in 1 month on queries; 2 months on mss. Sample copy for $5.95 and SASE. Writer's guidelines free on request.

Nonfiction: Essays, general interest, historical/nostalgic, humor, interview/profile, personal experience, photo feature. "No poetry." Buys 10-15 mss/year. Query with published clips. Length: 500-3,000 words. Pays $100 for assigned articles; $50 for unsolicited articles. Sometimes pays expenses of writers on assignment.

Photos: State availability of photos with submission. Reviews transparencies. Offers $50-250/photo. Captions, model releases and identification of subjects required. Buys one-time rights.

Tips: "(1) It is essential for writers to study current and past issues of our magazine to become familiar with type and balance of subject matter and angles. (2) It is also helpful for writers to have visited our region to capture the unique 'sense of place' aspects we try to share with readers. (3) We try to make subjects and treatments 'timeless' in nature because the magazine is a 'keeper' with a multi-year shelf life. Western lifestyles and regional history are very popular topics for our readers. So are nature (including environmental subjects), sports and recreation. Please query first with ideas to make sure subjects are fresh and appropriate."

‡STEAMBOAT MAGAZINE, Mac Media Inc., 2955 Village Dr., P.O. Box 4328, Steamboat Springs CO 80477. (303)879-5250 ext. 12. Editor: Rolly Wahl. 80% freelance written. Semiannual magazine covering Steamboat Springs and Northwest Colorado region. "Steamboat Magazine showcases the history, people, lifestyles and interests of Northwest Colorado. Our readers are generally well educated, well travelled, active people visiting our region to ski in winter and recreate in summer. They come from all 50 states and many foreign countries. Writing should be fresh, entertaining and informative." Estab. 1978. Circ. 20,000. Pays on publication. Publishes ms an average of 3 months after acceptance. Byline given. Offers 100% kill fee. Buys one-time rights. Editorial lead time 8-12 months. Submit seasonal material 6-12 months in advance. Accepts simultaneous and previously published submissions. Query for electronic submissions. Reports in 1 month on queries; 2 months on mss. Sample copy for $5.95 and SAE with 10 first-class stamps. Writer's guidelines free on request.

Nonfiction: Essays, general interest, historical/nostalgic, humor, interview/profile, personal experience, photo feature. Buys 10-15 mss/year. Query with published clips. Length: 500-3,000 words. Pays $100-500 for assigned articles; $50-300 for unsolicited articles. Sometimes pays expenses of writers on assignment.

Photos: State availability of photos with submission. Reviews transparencies. Offers $50-250/photo. Captions, model releases, identification of subjects required. Buys one-time rights.

Tips: "Western lifestyles and regional history are very popular topics for our readers. So is nature (including environmental subjects) and sports and recreation. Please query first with ideas to make sure subjects are fresh and appropriate. We try to make subjects and treatments "timeless" in nature, because our magazine is a "keeper" with a multi-year shelf life."

‡VAIL MAGAZINE, Flatirons/Vail L.L.C., P.O. Box 4328, Steamboat Springs CO 80477. (303)476-6600. Editor: Don Berger. 80% freelance written. Semiannual magazine covering Vail, Central Rocky Mountains, and mountain living. "*Vail Magazine* showcases the lifestyles and history of the Vail Valley. We are particularly interested in personality profiles, home and design features, the arts, winter and summer recreation and adventure stories, and environmental articles." Estab. 1975. Circ. 30,000. Pays on publication. Publishes ms an average of 3 months after acceptance. Byline given. Offers 100% kill fee. Buys one-time rights. Editorial lead time 8-12 months. Submit seasonal material 8-12 months in advance. Accepts simultaneous submissions. Query for electronic submissions. Reports in 1 month on queries; 2 months on mss. Sample copy for $5.95 and SAE with 10 first-class stamps. Writer's guidelines free on request.

Nonfiction: Essays, general interest, historical/nostalgic, humor, interview/profile, personal experience, photo feature. Buys 20-25 mss/year. Query with published clips. Length: 500-3,000 words. Pays $100 for assigned articles; $50 for unsolicited articles. Sometimes pays expenses of writers on assignment.

Photos: State availability of photos with submission. Reviews transparencies. Offers $50-250/photo. Captions, model releases and identification of subjects required. Buys one-time rights.

Tips: "Be familiar with the Vail Valley and its 'personality.' Approach a story that will be relevant for several years to come. We produce a magazine that is a 'keeper.' "

Connecticut

‡CENTERSTAGE, (formerly *Metropolitan Hartford*), 196 Trumbull St., Hartford CT 06103-2207. (203)560-2699. Editor: Kenneth Ross. Mostly staff written. Bimonthly magazine covering performing arts in Connecticut. Estab. 1993. Circ. 70,000. Pays on publication. Publishes ms an average of 3 months after acceptance. Byline or signature line given. Offers 15% kill fee. Buys first North American serial rights. Reports in 1-2 months. Sample copy for $2.50 and 9 × 12 SAE with 6 first-class stamps.

Nonfiction: Articles about performing arts or visual arts organizations in Connecticut or about people involved in performing or visual arts in Connecticut. Our emphasis is on classical music, opera, ballet, theater (including musicals), pop, cabaret. We occasionally publish essays on the arts. Query with published clips. Length: 300-1,800 words. Pays $100-500. Sometimes pays expenses of writers on assignment. Consideration given only to subjects relating to performing or visual arts in Connecticut.

Photos: State availability of, or send photos with submission. Reviews transparencies and prints. Model releases and identification of subjects required. Buys one-time rights.

Fiction: Seldom prints fiction, but considers stories that relate to Connecticut arts.

CONNECTICUT MAGAZINE, Communications International, 789 Reservoir Ave., Bridgeport CT 06606. (203)374-5488. Fax: (203)371-6561. Editor: Charles Monagan. Managing Editor: Dale Salm. 80% freelance written. Prefers to work with published/established writers who know the state and live/have lived here. Monthly magazine covering the state of Connecticut "for an affluent, sophisticated, suburban audience. We want only articles that pertain to living in Connecticut." Estab. 1971. Circ. 85,000. Pays on publication. Publishes ms an average of 3-4 months after acceptance. Byline given. Offers 20% kill fee. Buys first North American serial rights. Submit seasonal/holiday material 4 months in advance. Reports in 6 weeks on queries. Writer's guidelines for #10 SASE.

Nonfiction: Book excerpts, exposé, general interest, interview/profile, other topics of service to Connecticut readers. No personal essays. Buys 50 mss/year. Query with published clips. Length: 2,500-4,200 words. Pays $600-1,200. Sometimes pays the expenses of writers on assignment.

Photos: Send photos with submission. Reviews contact sheets and transparencies. Offers $50 minimum/photo. Model releases and identification of subjects required. Buys one-time rights.

Columns/Departments: Business, Health, Politics, Connecticut Guide, Arts, Gardening, Environment, Education, People, Sports, Media. Buys 50 mss/year. Query with published clips. Length: 1,500-2,500 words. Pays $300-600.

Fillers: Around and About editor—Valerie Schroth, senior editor. Short pieces about Connecticut trends, curiosities, interesting short subjects, etc. Buys 50/year. Length: 150-400 words. Pays $75.

Tips: "Make certain that your idea is not something that has been covered to death by the local press and can withstand a time lag of a few months. Freelancers can best break in with Around and About; find a Connecticut story that is offbeat and write it up in a fun, lighthearted, interesting manner. Again, we don't want something that has already received a lot of press."

NORTHEAST MAGAZINE, *The Hartford Courant*, 285 Broad St., Hartford CT 06115-2510. (203)241-3700. Editor: Lary Bloom. 50% freelance written. Eager to work with new/unpublished writers. Weekly magazine for a Connecticut audience. Estab. 1982. Circ. 300,000. **Pays on acceptance.** Publishes ms an average of 10 months after acceptance. Byline given. Buys one-time rights. Reports in 3 months.

• Ranked as one of the best markets for freelance writers in *Writer's Digest* magazine's annual "Top 100 Markets," January 1994 and as one of the best markets for fiction writers in its biannual "Fiction 50," June 1994.

Nonfiction: General interest (has to have strong Connecticut tie-in); in-depth investigation of stories behind news (has to have strong Connecticut tie-in); historical/nostalgic; interview/profile (of famous or important people with Connecticut ties); personal essays (humorous or anecdotal). No poetry. Buys 50 mss/year. Length: 750-2,500 words. Pays $200-1,500.

Photos: Most assigned; state availability of photos. "Do not send originals."

Fiction: Well-written, original short stories and (rarely) novel excerpts. Length: 750-1,500 words.

Tips: "Less space available for all types of writing means our standards for acceptance will be much higher. We can only print three to four short stories a year."

District of Columbia

THE WASHINGTON POST, 1150 15th St. NW, Washington DC 20071. (202)334-7750. Travel Editor: Linda L. Halsey. 60% freelance written. Prefers to work with published/established writers. Weekly newspaper travel section (Sunday). Pays on publication. Publishes ms an average of 3-6 months after acceptance. Byline given. "We are now emphasizing staff-written articles as well as quality writing from other sources. Stories are rarely assigned; all material comes in on speculation; there is no fixed kill fee." Buys only first North American serial rights. Travel must not be subsidized in any way. Usually reports in 1 month. *Writer's Market* recommends allowing 2 months for reply.

Nonfiction: Emphasis is on travel writing with a strong sense of place, color, anecdote and history. Query with published clips. Length: 1,500-2,500 words, plus sidebar for practical information.

Photos: State availability of photos with ms.

THE WASHINGTON POST MAGAZINE, *The Washington Post*, 1150 15th St. NW, Washington DC 20071. (202)334-7374. Managing Editor: Liza Mundy. 40% freelance written. Prefers to work with published/established writers. Weekly magazine featuring articles of interest to Washington readers. Circ. 1.2 million (Sunday). Average issue includes 2 feature articles. **Pays on acceptance.** Publishes ms an average of 2 months after acceptance. Byline given. Buys all rights or first North American serial rights, depending on fee. Submit seasonal material 4 months in advance. Reports in 6 weeks. Sample copy for 9 × 12 SAE with 2 first-class stamps.

Nonfiction: Controversial and consequential articles with a strong Washington angle. Query with published clips. Length: 1,500-6,500 words. Pays $250-up; competitive with major national magazine rates. Pays expenses of writers on assignment.

Photos: Reviews 4 × 5 or larger b&w glossy prints and 35mm or larger color transparencies. Model releases required.

Tips: "Always send SASE for return of material."

THE WASHINGTONIAN MAGAZINE, Suite 200, 1828 L St. NW, Washington DC 20036-5169. Editor: John A. Limpert. Assistant Editor: Carrie Wiklund. 20% freelance written. Prefers to work with published/established writers who live in the Washington area. Monthly magazine for active, affluent and well-educated audience. Estab. 1965. Circ. 157,055. Buys first rights only. Pays on publication. Publishes ms an average of 2 months after acceptance. Accepts simultaneous submissions. Reports in 3 months. Sample copy for $5 and 9 × 12 SAE. Writer's guidelines for #10 SASE.

● The editors have specified that they do not take much freelance work.

Nonfiction: "*The Washingtonian* is written for Washingtonians. The subject matter is anything we feel might interest people interested in the mind and manners of the city. The only thing we ask is thoughtfulness and that no subject be treated too reverently. Audience is literate. We assume considerable sophistication about the city and a sense of humor." Buys how-to, personal experience, interview/profile, humor, think pieces, exposés. Buys 40 mss/year. Length: 1,000-7,000 words; average feature 4,000 words. Pays 50¢/word. Sometimes pays the expenses of writers on assignment. Query or submit complete ms.

Photos: Photos rarely purchased with mss.

Florida

BOCA RATON MAGAZINE, JES Publishing, Suite 100, 6413 Congress Ave., Boca Raton FL 33487. (407)997-8683. Fax: (407)997-8909. Editor: Marie Speed. 70% freelance written. Bimonthly magazine covering Boca Raton lifestyles. "Ours is a lifestyle magazine devoted to the residents of South Florida, featuring fashion, interior design, food, people, places and issues that shape the affluent South Florida market." Estab. 1981. Circ. 20,000. **Pays on acceptance.** Publishes ms an average of 3 months after acceptance. Byline given. Offers $50 kill fee. Buys second serial (reprint) rights. Submit seasonal material 7 months in advance. Accepts simultaneous and previously published submissions. Send tearsheet of article. Pays 50% of amount paid for an original article. Query for electronic submission. Reports in 1 month. Sample copy for $3.95 for 10 × 13 SAE with 10 first-class stamps. Writer's guidelines for #10 SASE.

● No longer publishes fiction.

Nonfiction: General interest, historical/nostalgic, humor, interview/profile, photo feature, travel. Query with or without published clips, or send complete ms. Length: 800-2,500 words. Pays $50-500 for assigned articles; $50-300 for unsolicited articles. Sometimes pays expenses of writers on assignment.

Photos: Send photos with submission.

Columns/Departments: Body & Soul (health, fitness and beauty column, general interest), 1,000 words; Family Room (family and social interactions), 1,000 words; Humor (South Florida topics), 600-1,200 words. Buys 6 mss/year. Query with published clips or send complete ms. Length: 600-1,500 words. Pays $50-250.

FLORIDA KEYS MAGAZINE, Gibbons Publishing, Inc., P.O. Box 2921, Key Largo FL 33037-7921. (800)273-1026. Fax: (305)451-5201. Editor: Gibbons D. Cline. Contact: Diane Thompson, associate editor. Key West Office: P.O. Box 6524, Key West FL 33040-6524. (305)296-7300. 75% freelance written. Bimonthly magazine for lifestyle in the Florida Keys. "*FKM* caters to full-time residents of the Florida Keys. These are people with a unique lifestyle and a rich, colorful history." Estab. 1978. Circ. 10,000. Pays on publication. Publishes ms an average of 4-6 months after acceptance. Byline given. Buys first North American serial, first or all rights. Editorial lead time 4-6 months. Submit seasonal material at least 6 months in advance. Query for electronic submissions. Reports in 3-4 weeks on queries; 1-6 months on mss. Sample copy for $2.50. Writer's guidelines free on request.

Nonfiction: General interest, historical/nostalgic, how-to (water sports, home improvement, gardening, crafts), humor, interview/profile (keys residents *only*), travel. Special issues: Fantasy Fest-Key West (Halloween); Real Estate. "No erotica or personal experiences in the Keys ... please do not send Hemingway-related stories or stories regarding your Keys vacation!" Buys 20-30 mss/year. Query with published clips. Length: 500-2,000 words. Pays $2/column inch minimum.

Photos: Send photos with submissions. Reviews transparencies (any size), prints, slides. Offers no additional payment for photos accepted with ms. Model releases and identification of subjects required. Buys all rights.

Columns/Departments: Dining Guide (Keys recipes, restaurant reviews), 1,200 words; Eco-Watch (environmental issues in Florida Keys), 1,200 words; Entertainment (reviews books, movies, music pertaining to Keys), 1,200 words. Buys 5-10 mss/year. Query with published clips. Pays $2/column inch.

Tips: "It is difficult to write about Keys unless writer is resident of Monroe County, Florida, or frequent visitor. Must be familiar with unique atmosphere and lifestyle of Florida Keys. Request résumé to be submitted with query and/or mss. If author is unfamiliar with Keys, massive research is suggested (strongly). We are most open to new and unusual angles on fishing, boating, diving, snorkeling, sailing, shelling, sunbathing and Keys special events. Health and environmental articles are welcome. Home & Garden and Arts & Crafts are easy to write with research."

FLORIDA LIVING, North Florida Publishing Co. Inc., Suite 6, 102 NE Tenth Ave., Gainesville FL 32601-2322. (904)372-3453. Editor: John Paul Jones. Managing Editor: Holly M. Hays. Monthly lifestyle magazine covering Florida subjects for Floridians and would be Floridians. Estab. 1981. Circ. 25,000. Publishes ms an average of 3-6 months after acceptance. Byline given. No kill fee. Buys one-time rights. Submit seasonal/holiday material 3-12 months in advance. Reports in 2 months. Writer's guidelines sent on request with SASE.

Nonfiction: General Florida interest, historical/nostalgic, interview/profile, personal experience, travel, out-of-the-way Florida places. Buys 50-60 mss/year. Query. Length: 500-1,500 words. Pays $25-200 for assigned articles; $25-100 for unsolicited articles.

Photos: Send photos with submission. Reviews 3×5 color prints. Offers up to $10/photo. Captions required. Buys one-time rights.

Fiction: Historical. Buys 2-3 mss/year. Send complete ms. Length: 1,000-3,000 words. Pays $50-200.

FOLIO WEEKLY, Folio Publishing Inc., Suite 11, 9456 Phillips Highway, Jacksonville FL 32256. (904)260-9770. Fax: (904)260-9773. Editor: Tim Thornton. 50% freelance written. Weekly news and opinion tabloid. Estab 1987. Circ. 31,000. Pays on publication. Publishes ms an average of 1-2 months after acceptance. Byline given. Offers 50% kill fee. Buys first North American serial or second serial (reprint) rights or makes work-for-hire assignments. Submit seasonal material 4 months in advance. Accepts simultaneous and previously published submissions. Send photocopy of article and information about when and where the article previously appeared. Pays 50% of the amount paid for an original article. Reports in 2 months. Sample copy for 9×12 SAE.

Nonfiction: Buys 40 mss/year. Query with published clips. Length: 2,000-3,000 words. Pays $150-200 for assigned articles.

Photos: Send photos with submission. Captions, model releases, identification of subjects required.

Columns/Departments: Backpage (locally oriented editorials), 900 words.

Tips: "*Folio* serves a concerned, bright, hip readership that's interested in the environment, politics and the arts. Good, clear, gripping writing is important, but it's more important to get the facts straight. If it's not related to Northeast Florida, we're not interested. We're serious, but we have a sense of humor."

ISLAND LIFE, The Enchanting Barrier Islands of Florida's Southwest Gulf Coast, Island Life Publications, P.O. Box 929, Sanibel FL 33957. Editor: Joan Hooper. Editorial Associate: Susan Shores. 40% freelance written. Prefers to work with published/established writers, but works with a small number of new/unpublished writers each year. Quarterly magazine of the Barrier Islands Sanibel, Captiva, Marco, for upper-income residents and vacationers of Florida's Gulf Coast area. Estab. 1980. Circ. 20,000. Pays on publication. Publishes ms an average of 1 year after acceptance. Byline given. Buys first serial and second serial (reprint) rights. Accepts simultaneous submissions. Reports in 1 month on queries; 3 months on mss.

Nonfiction: General interest, historical. "Travel and interview/profile done by staff. Our past use of freelance work has been heavily on Florida wildlife (plant and animal), Florida cuisine, and Florida parks and conservancies. We are a regional magazine. No fiction or first-person experiences. No poetry. Our editorial emphasis is on the history, culture, wildlife, art, scenic, sports, social and leisure activities of the area." Buys 10-20 mss/year. Query with ms and photos. Length: 500-1,500 words. Pays 3-8¢/word.

Photos: Send photos with ms. No additional payment. Captions, model releases, identification of subjects required.

Tips: "Submissions are rejected, most often, when writer sends other than SW Florida focus."

‡JACKSONVILLE, (formerly *Jacksonville Today*), White Publishing Co., Suite 300, 1650 Prudential Dr., Jacksonville FL 32207. (904)396-8666. Editor: Larry Marscheck. 80% freelance written. Consumer magazine published 10 times/year covering life and business on Florida's First Coast. "City/regional magazine for Jacksonville and the Beaches, Orange Park, St. Augustine and Amelia Island, Florida. Targets upwardly mobile residents. Estab. 1985. Circ. 25,000. Pays on publication. Byline given. Offers 25-33% kill fee. Buys first North American serial rights or second serial (reprint) rights. Editorial lead time 3 months. Submit seasonal 4 months in advance. Accepts previously published submissions. Send photocopy of article and include information about when and where it first appeared. Query for electronic submissions. Reports in 2-4 weeks on queries; 1 month on mss. Sample copy for $5 (includes postage). Writer's guidelines free on request.

Nonfiction: Book excerpts, exposé, general interest, historical/nostalgic, how-to (service articles), humor, interview/profile, personal experience, photo feature, travel, local business successes, trends, personalities, how things work. "First Coast Guide is July/August issue—essentially a city guide for Northeast Florida region. All articles must have relevance to Jacksonville and Florida's First Coast (Duval, Clay, St. Johns, Nassau, Baker counties). Buys 50 mss/year. Query with published clips. Length: 1,200-3,000 words. Pays $50-500 for feature-length pieces. Sometimes pays expenses of writers on assignment.

Photos: State availability of photos with submission. Reviews contact sheets, transparencies. Negotiates payment individually. Captions, model releases required. Buys one-time rights.

Columns/Departments: Business (trends, success stories, personalities), 1,000-1,250 words; Health (trends, emphasis on people, hopeful outlooks), 1,000-1,200 words; Real Estate (service), 1,000-1,200 words; Yesterday (historical), 300 words. Buys 40 mss/year. Pays $200-300.

Fiction: Adventure, condensed novels, historical, humorous, mainstream, mystery, novel excerpts, science fiction, slice-of-life vignettes, all must have Jacksonville or Northeast Florida setting and/or characters. Buys 1 or more mss/year. Send complete ms. Length: 1,000 words. Pays $250-500. "It should be noted that we have bought only a few fiction pieces since publication began. We are open to buying more, if they are well-written and relevant to our area."

Tips: "We are a writer's magazine, therefore we demand writing that tells a story with flair. While the whole magazine is open to freelancers, new writers can break in via 'short takes'—50-300 word stories about trends, phenomena and people in the First Coast area."

ORLANDO MAGAZINE, Orlando Media Affiliates, P.O. Box 2207, Suite 130, 341 N. Maitland Ave., Orlando FL 32802-9999. (407)539-3939. Fax: (407)539-0533. 10% freelance written. Monthly magazine covering lifestyle, home and garden and business. Estab. 1946. Circ. 35,000. Pays on publication. Publishes ms an average of 2 months after acceptance. Byline given. Offers kill fee. Submit seasonal/holiday material 4-6 months in advance. Accepts simultaneous submissions. Reports in 2 months. Free sample copy and writer's guidelines.

Nonfiction: Exposé, how-to (business), interview. Buys 12-15 mss/year. Send complete ms. Length: 1,000-2,500 words. Pays $100-450 for articles. "Looking for stories that locally reflect national trends in lifestyles, home and garden and business. Publish at least one issue-oriented story per month."

Photos: Send photos with submission. Reviews transparencies. Offers $5/photo. Captions and identification of subjects required. Buys one-time rights.

Columns/Departments: Sports, health, fitness, arts and virtually all business topics. All submissions should have local slant. Length: 1,200-1,500. Buys 12-15 mss/year. Pays $200-350.

PALM BEACH ILLUSTRATED, Palm Beach Media Group, 1016 N. Dixie Hwy., West Palm Beach FL 33401. (407)659-0210. Editor: Judy DiEdwardo. 80% freelance written. Magazine published 10 times/year for upscale lifestyle. Estab. 1952. Circ. 25,000. Pays on publication. Byline given. Buys first North American serial and/or second serial (reprint) rights. Editorial lead time 3 months. Submit seasonal material 3 months in advance. Accepts simultaneous and previously published submissions. Query for electronic submissions. Reports in 2 months on queries. Writer's guidelines for #10 SASE.

Nonfiction: General interest, historical/nostalgic, humor, interview/profile, photo feature, travel. "No budget travel, please. Our readers travel to—and are interested in—the exotic places of the world." Buys 12-20 mss/year. Query with published clips. Length: 500-1,500 words. Pays $100 minimum.

Photos: Send photos with submission. Captions, model releases, identification of subjects required. Buys one-time (exclusive use) rights.

Tips: "Read us first before submitting. Though we focus on the Palm Beach lifestyle, our readership has interests that are of national/international concern and interest. Travel, lifestyle, profiles, interviews are the top freelance-supported areas, however, we do consider submissions for other areas."

ALWAYS submit unsolicited manuscripts or queries with a self-addressed, stamped envelope (SASE) within your country or a self-addressed envelope with International Reply Coupons (IRC) purchased from the post office for other countries.

‡PALM BEACH LIFE, Palm Beach Newspapers Inc./Cox Enterprises, 265 Royal Poinciana Way, Palm Beach FL 33480-4063. (407)820-4750. Fax: (407)655-4594. Managing Editor: Michael J. Gaeta. 100% freelance written. Monthly magazine, a regional publication for Palm Beach County and South Florida. Estab. 1906. Circ. 26,000. **Pays on acceptance.** Publishes ms an average of 3 months after acceptance. Byline given. Buys first North American serial rights. Submit seasonal/holiday material 6 months in advance. Query for electronic submission. Reports in 1 month.

Nonfiction: Essays, exposé, general interest, historical/nostalgic, humor, interview/profile, photo feature, travel. Buys 100 mss/year. Query with published clips. Length: 900-5,000 words. Pays $150-700 for assigned articles; $75-400 for unsolicited articles. Sometimes pays expenses of writers on assignment (depending on agreed-upon fee).

Photos: Send photos with submission. Reviews transparencies. Offers $35-200 per photo. Captions, model releases, identification of subjects required. Buys one-time rights.

Columns/Departments: Travel (specifically focused topical travel pieces), 1,500 words; High Profile (profiles of people of interest to readers in our region), 2,500 words. Buys 36 mss/year. Query with published clips. Pays $75-400.

PENSACOLA MAGAZINE, PEC Printing and Publishing, 2101 W. Government St., Pensacola FL 32501. (904)438-5421. Editor: Donna Peoples. 100% freelance written. Monthly magazine for news about city of Pensacola. Estab. 1983. Pays on acceptance. Publishes ms an average of 2 months after acceptance. Byline given. Offers 25% kill fee. Buys one-time or second serial (reprint) rights or makes work-for-hire assignments. Editorial lead time 2 months. Submit seasonal material 3-4 months in advance. Accepts simultaneous and previously published submissions. Query for electronic submissions. Reports in 3 weeks on queries; 1 month on mss. *Writer's Market* recommends allowing 2 months for reply. Sample copy for $3.

Nonfiction: General interest, historical/nostalgic, how-to, humor, interview/profile (of Pensacola residents), photo feature, travel. Does not want to see anything other than travel or holiday material; rarely runs stories that don't relate to Pensacola. Buys 80 mss/year. Query with published clips. Length: 800-1,500 words. Pays 7¢/word.

Photos: Send photos with submission. Reviews contact sheets, transparencies and prints. Offers $25/photo minimum. Negotiates payment individually. Captions, model releases and identification of subjects required. Buys one-time rights.

SENIOR VOICE OF FLORIDA, Florida's Leading Newspaper for Active Mature Adults, Suncoast Publishing Group, Suite E, 6281 39th St. N., Pinellas Park FL 34665-6040. Publisher: Donna Castellanos. Editor: Nancy Yost. 25% freelance written. Prefers to work with published/established writers. Monthly newspaper for mature adults 50 years of age and over. Estab. 1981. Circ. 50,000. Pays on publication. Publishes ms an average of 3 months after acceptance. Byline given. Buys one-time rights. Submit seasonal material 3 months in advance. Accepts simultaneous and previously published submissions. Reports in 2 months. Sample copy for $1 and 10×13 SAE with 6 first-class stamps.

Nonfiction: Exposé, general interest, historical/nostalgic, how-to, humor, inspirational, interview/profile, opinion, photo feature, travel, health, finance, all slanted to a senior audience. Buys 10 mss/year. Query or send complete ms. Length: 300-600 words. Pays $15.

Photos: Send photos with submission. Reviews 3×5 color and 5×7 b&w prints. Identification of subjects required.

Columns/Departments: Travel (senior slant) and V.I.P. Profiles (mature adults). Buys 10 mss/year. Send complete ms. Length: 300-600 words. Pays $15.

Fillers: Anecdotes, facts, cartoons, gags to be illustrated by cartoonist, short humor. Buys 10/year. Length: 150-250 words. Pays $10.

Tips: "Our service area is the Florida Gulf Coast, an area with a high population of resident retirees and repeat visitors who are 50 plus. We are interested primarily in serving their needs. In writing for that readership, keep their interests in mind. What they are interested in, we are interested in. We like a clean, concise writing style. Photos are important."

SUNSHINE: THE MAGAZINE OF SOUTH FLORIDA, The Sun-Sentinel Co., 200 E. Las Olas Blvd., Fort Lauderdale FL 33301-2293. (305)356-4685. Editor: John Parkyn. 60% freelance written. Prefers to work with published/established writers, but works with a small number of new/unpublished writers each year. General interest Sunday magazine "for the *Sun-Sentinel's* 800,000 readers in South Florida." Circ. 360,000. Pays within 1 month of acceptance. Publishes ms an average of 2 months after acceptance. Byline given. Offers 25% kill fee for assigned material. Buys first serial rights or one-time rights in the state of Florida. Submit seasonal/holiday material 2 months in advance. Accepts simultaneous and previously published submissions. Send tearsheet or photocopy of article or typed ms with rights for sale noted and information about when and where the article previously appeared. Reports in 1 month on queries; 2 months on mss. Free sample copy and writer's guidelines.

Nonfiction: General interest, interview/profile, travel. "Articles must be relevant to the interests of adults living in South Florida." Buys about 150 mss/year. Query with published clips. Length: 1,000-3,000 words; preferred length 2,000-2,500 words. Pays 25¢/word to $1,000 maximum.

Photos: Send photos. Pays negotiable rate for 35mm and 2¼ color slides. Captions and identification of subjects required; model releases required for sensitive material. Buys one-time rights for the state of Florida.
Tips: "Do not phone, but do include your phone number on query letter. Keep your writing tight and concise — readers don't have the time to wade through masses of 'pretty' prose. We are always in the market for first-rate profiles, human-interest stories and travel stories (which usually spotlight destinations within easy access of South Florida, e.g. Southeastern US, Caribbean, Central America). Freelancers should also consider our 1,100-word 'First Person' feature, which describes personal experiences of unusual interest."

‡**TALLAHASSEE MAGAZINE,** 1725 E. Mahan Dr., P.O. Box 1837, Tallahassee FL 32302. (904)878-0554. Editor: A. David Fiore. 90% freelance written. Bimonthly magazine. Estab. 1979. Circ. 19,000. **Pays on acceptance.** Byline given. Offers 25% kill fee. Buys first North American serial rights. Submit seasonal material 6 months in advance. Accepts simultaneous and previously published submissions. Query for electronic submissions. Reports in 3 months on queries. Sample copy for $2.95 and 9 × 12 SAE with 7 first-class stamps. Writer's guidelines for #10 SASE.
Nonfiction: General interest, historical/nostalgic, humor, interview/profile, photo feature and travel. No fiction or poetry. Buys 85 mss/year. Query with published clips. Length: 800-1,500 words. Pays $175-250.
Photos: Send photos with submission. Reviews contact sheets, 2¼ or 35mm transparencies and 3 × 5 prints. Offers $25-35 photo. Model releases and identification of subjects required. Buys one-time rights.
Columns/Departments: Sports; Your Money; People; Food; Family Matters; Down to Business. Buys 50 mss/year. Query with published clips. Length: 800-1,000 words. Pays $150-160.
Tips: "We are looking for short queries with clips to support writing style and experience."

‡**TROPIC MAGAZINE, Sunday Magazine of the Miami Herald,** Knight Ridder, 1 Herald Plaza, Miami FL 33132-1693. (305)376-3432. Editor: Bill Rose. Executive Editor: Tom Shroder. 20% freelance written. Works with small number of new/unpublished writers each year. Weekly magazine covering general interest, locally oriented topics for local readers. Circ. 500,000. Pays on publication. Publishes ms an average of 2 months after acceptance. Byline given. Buys first serial rights. Submit seasonal material 2 months in advance. Accepts previously published submissions. Send typed ms with rights for sale noted and information about when and where the article previously appeared. Pays 50% of the amount paid for an original article. Reports in 3 months. Sample copy for 11 × 14 SAE.
Nonfiction: General interest, interview/profile (first person), personal experience. No fiction or poetry. Buys 20 mss/year. Query with published clips or send complete ms with SASE. Length: 1,500-3,000 words. Pays $200-1,000/article.
Photos: Janet Santelices, art director. Send photos.

WATERFRONT NEWS, Ziegler Publishing Co., Inc., 1523 S. Andrews Ave., Ft. Lauderdale FL 33316-2507. (305)524-9450. Fax: (305)524-9464. Editor: John Ziegler. 75% freelance written. Monthly tabloid covering marine and boating topics for the Greater Ft. Lauderdale waterfront community. Estab. 1984. Circ. 42,000. Pays on publication. Publishes ms an average of 2 months after acceptance. Byline given. Buys first serial, second serial (reprint) rights or simultaneous rights in certain circumstances. Submit seasonal material 3 months in advance. Accepts previously published submissions. Send information about when and where the article previously appeared. Pays negotiable fee for reprints. Reports in 1 month on queries. *Writer's Market* recommends allowing 2 months for reply. Sample copy for 9 × 12 SAE with 4 first-class stamps. Free writer's guidelines.
Nonfiction: Historical/nostalgic (nautical or Southern Florida); new marine products; opinion (on marine topics); technical (on marine topics); marine travel. Buys 50 mss/year. Query with or without published clips or send complete ms. Length: 500-1,000 words. Pays $50-200 for assigned articles; $25-200 for unsolicited articles. Sometimes pays the expenses of writers on assignment.
Photos: Send photos or send photos with submission. Reviews contact sheets and 3 × 5 or larger prints. Offers $5/photo. Buys one-time rights.
Columns/Departments: Query with published clips. Length 500-1,000 words. Pays $25-100.
Fillers: Anecdotes, facts, nautical one-liners to be illustrated by cartoonist, newsbriefs, short humor. Buys 12/year. Length 100-500 words. Pays $10-200.
Tips: "Nonfiction marine, nautical or South Florida stories only. No fiction or poetry. Keep it under 1,000 words. Photos or illustrations help. Send for a sample copy of *Waterfront News* so you can acquaint yourself with our publication and our unique audience."

Georgia

‡**GEORGIA JOURNAL,** Grimes Publications, Inc., P.O. Box 27, Athens GA 30603-0027. Fax: (706)354-6824. Editor: Conoly Hester. 75% freelance written. Works with a small number of new/unpublished writers each year. Quarterly magazine covering the state of Georgia. Estab. 1980. Circ. 12,000. Please query first. Pays on publication. Publishes ms an average of 6-12 months after acceptance. Byline given. Buys first serial rights. Submit seasonal material 6 months in advance. Reports in 6 months. Sample copy for $3.50. Writer's guidelines for #10 SASE.

Nonfiction: We are interested in almost everything going on within Georgia, particularly history, tourist attractions, personalities, gardening, house restorations, arts, events. We prefer pieces that are current with a strong human interest slant. Nothing risque. When we tell readers about places they may wish to go, or activities they may wish to take part in, we give them directions, use maps, include other points of interest in the vicinity. Buys 30-40 mss/year. Query. Length: 800-2,000 words. Pays $50-300. Reprints OK; send tearsheet of article or computer disk if possible and information about when and where the article previously appeared. Pays 50% of their fee for an original article.

Photos: Send photos or send photos with query or ms. Sharp 8 × 10 b&w glossies and/or color slides. Captions, model releases, identification of subjects required.

Columns/Departments: Books and writers; interesting or historic houses/buildings for sale; Commentary section; Exploring Georgia—uses shorter pieces; Calendar of events; reviews of restaurants, B&Bs and historic inns.

Poetry: Janice Moore, poetry editor. Free verse, haiku, light verse, traditional. Uses poetry from or dealing with the South which is suitable for a general audience. Uses 20 poems/year. Submit maximum 4 poems. Length: 25 lines. Pays in copies.

Hawaii

ALOHA, THE MAGAZINE OF HAWAII AND THE PACIFIC, Davick Publications, 4th Floor, 720 Kapiolani Blvd., Honolulu HI 96813. (808)593-1191. Fax: (808)593-1327. Editorial Director: Cheryl Tsutsumi. 50% freelance written. Bimonthly regional magazine of international interest. "Most of our readers do not live in Hawaii, although most readers have been to the Islands at least once. The magazine is directed primarily to residents of Hawaii in the belief that presenting material to an immediate critical audience will result in a true and accurate presentation that can be appreciated by everyone. *ALOHA* is not a tourist publication and is not geared to such a readership, although travelers will find it to be of great value." Estab. 1977. Circ. 65,000. Pays on publication. Publishes ms an average of 6 months after acceptance; unsolicited ms can take a year or more. Byline given. Offers variable kill fee. Buys first rights. Submit seasonal material 1 year in advance. Reports in 2 months. Sample copy for $3.95 and SASE. Free writer's guidelines.

Nonfiction: Book excerpts, historical/nostalgic (historical articles must be researched with bibliography), interview/profile, photo features. Subjects include the arts, business, flora and fauna, people, sports, destinations, food, interiors, history of Hawaii. "We don't want stories of a tourist's experiences in Waikiki or odes to beautiful scenery. We don't want an outsider's impressions of Hawaii, written for outsiders." Buys 24 mss/year. Query with published clips. Length: 1,000-4,000 words. Pay ranges from $200-500. Sometimes pays expenses of writers on assignment.

Photos: Send photos with query. Pays $25 for b&w prints; prefers negatives and contact sheets. Pays $60 for 35mm (minimum size) color transparencies used inside; $125 for double-page bleeds; $250 for color transparencies used as cover art. "*ALOHA* features Beautiful Hawaii, a collection of photographs illustrating that theme, in every issue. A second photo essay by a sole photographer on a theme of his/her own choosing is also published occasionally. Queries are essential for the sole photographer essay." Model releases and identification of subjects are required. Buys one-time rights.

Fiction: Ethnic, historical. "Fiction depicting a tourist's adventures in Waikiki is not what we're looking for. As a general statement, we welcome material reflecting the true Hawaiian experience." Buys 2 mss/year. Send complete ms. Length: 1,000-2,500 words. Pays $300.

Poetry: Haiku, light verse, traditional. No seasonal poetry or poetry related to other areas of the world. Buys 6 poems/year. Submit maximum 6 poems. Prefers "shorter poetry"—20 lines or less. Pays $30.

Tips: "Read *ALOHA*. Be meticulous in your research and have good illustrative material available to accompany your text."

HAWAII MAGAZINE, Fancy Publications, Inc., P.O. Box 6050, Mission Viejo CA 92690. (714)855-8822. Editor: Dennis Shattuck. Managing Editor: Julie Applebaum. 60% freelance written. Bimonthly magazine covering The Islands of Hawaii. "*Hawaii Magazine* is written for people all over the world who visit and enjoy the culture, people and places of the Hawaiian Islands." Estab. 1984. Circ. 71,000. Pays on publication. Byline given. Buys first North American serial rights. Submit seasonal material 6 months in advance. Query for electronic submissions. Reports in 1 month on queries; 6 weeks on mss. Sample copy for $3.95. Free writer's guidelines.

Nonfiction: General interest, historical/nostalgic, how-to, interview/profile, personal experience, photo feature, travel. "No articles on the following: first trip to Hawaii—How I discovered the Islands, the Hula, Poi, or Luaus." Buys 66 mss/year. Query with or without published clips or send complete ms. Length: 4,000 words maximum. Pays $100-500 for assigned articles.

Photos: Send photos with submission. Reviews contact sheets and transparencies. Offers $35-250 per photo. Identification of subjects preferred. Buys one-time rights.

Columns/Departments: Backdoor Hawaii (humorous look at the islands), 800-1,200 words; Hopping the Islands (news, general interest items), 100-200 words. Buys 6-12 mss/year. Query. Length: 800-1,500 words. Pays $100-200.

Tips: "Freelancers must be knowledgeable about Island subjects, virtual authorities on them. We see far too many first-person, wonderful-experience types of gushing articles. We buy articles only from people who are thoroughly grounded in the subject on which they are writing."

HONOLULU, Honolulu Publishing Co., Ltd., 36 Merchant St., Honolulu HI 96813. (808)524-7400. Fax: (808)531-2306. Editor/Publisher: John Alves. Executive Editor: John Heckathorn. Managing Editor: Janice Otaguro. 20% freelance written. Prefers to work with published/established writers. Monthly magazine covering general interest topics relating to Hawaii. Estab. 1888. Circ. 75,000. **Pays on acceptance.** Publishes ms an average of 4 months after acceptance. Byline given. Buys first serial rights. Submit seasonal material 5 months in advance. Accepts simultaneous submissions. Reports in 2 months. Sample copy for $2 and 9 × 12 SAE with 8 first-class stamps. Free writer's guidelines.

● This magazine is now requiring samples of previously published work.

Nonfiction: Exposé, general interest, historical/nostalgic, photo feature — all Hawaii-related. "We run regular features on fashion, interior design, Neighbor Island, travel, politics, dining and arts, plus other timely, provocative articles. No personal experience articles." Buys 10 mss/year. Query with published clips if available. Length: 2,000-4,000 words. Pays $500. Sometimes pays expenses of writers on assignment.

Photos: Teresa Black, photo editor. Send photos. Pays $15 maximum for b&w contact sheet; $25 maximum for 35mm transparencies. Captions and identification of subjects required. Buys one-time rights.

Columns/Departments: Calabash (light, "newsy," timely, humorous column on any Hawaii-related subject). Buys 15 mss/year. Query with published clips or send complete ms. Length: 250-1,000 words. Pays $35.

Illinois

CHICAGO LIFE, P.O. Box 11311, Chicago IL 60611-0311. Editor: Pam Berns. Contact: Paula Lyon, managing editor. 95% freelance written. Bimonthly magazine on Chicago life. Estab. 1984. Circ. 60,000. Pays on publication. Byline given. Kill fee varies. Submit seasonal/holiday material 8 months in advance. Accepts simultaneous and previously published submissions. Send tearsheet or photocopy of article and information about when and where the article previously appeared. Pays 100% of the amount paid for an original article. Reports in 3 months. Sample copy for 9 × 12 SAE with 7 first-class stamps.

Nonfiction: Book excerpts, essays, exposé, how-to, photo feature, travel. Buys 50 mss/year. Send complete ms. Length: 400-1,200 words. Pays $30 for unsolicited articles. Sometimes pays the expenses of writers on assignment.

Photos: Send photos with submission. Reviews contact sheets, negatives, transparencies, prints. Offers $15-30/photo. Buys one-time rights.

Columns/Departments: Law, Book Reviews, Travel. Send complete ms. Length: 500 words. Pays $30.

Fillers: Facts. Pays $15-30.

Tips: "Please send finished work with visuals (photos, if possible). Topics open include travel, self improvement, how-to-do almost anything, entrepreneurs, how to get rich, beautiful, more well-informed."

CHICAGO MAGAZINE, 414 N. Orleans, Chicago IL 60610-4409. Managing Editor: Shane Tritsch. 40% freelance written. Prefers to work with published/established writers. Monthly magazine for an audience which is "95% from Chicago area; 90% college educated; upper income, overriding interests in the arts, politics, dining, good life in the city and suburbs. Most are in 25-50 age bracket, well-read and articulate." Estab. 1968. Circ. 165,000. **Pays on acceptance.** Publishes ms an average of 6 months after acceptance. Submit seasonal material 4 months in advance. Reports in 1 month. Query; indicate "specifics, knowledge of city and market, and demonstrable access to sources." For sample copy, send $3 to Circulation Dept. Writer's guidelines for #10 SASE.

● Ranked as one of the best markets for freelance writers in *Writer's Digest* magazine's annual "Top 100 Markets," January 1994.

Nonfiction: "On themes relating to the quality of life in Chicago: past, present, and future." Writers should have "a general awareness that the readers will be concerned, influential longtime Chicagoans reading what the writer has to say about their city. We generally publish material too comprehensive for daily newspapers." Personal experience and think pieces, profiles, humor, spot news, historical articles, exposés. Buys about 50 mss/year. Length: 500-6,000 words. Pays $100-$2,500. Pays expenses of writers on assignment.

Photos: Reviews b&w glossy prints, 35mm color transparencies or color prints. Usually assigned separately, not acquired from writers.

Tips: "Submit detailed queries, be business-like and avoid clichéd ideas."

THE CHICAGO TRIBUNE MAGAZINE, Chicago Tribune Co., 435 N. Michigan Ave., Chicago IL 60611. (312)222-3573. Editor: Denis Gosselin. Managing Editor: Douglas Balz. 50% freelance written. Weekly Sunday magazine. "We look for unique, compelling, all-researched, eloquently written articles on subjects of general interest." Circ. 1.3 million. Pays on publication. Publishes ms an average of 2 months after acceptance. Offers $250 kill fee. Buys one-time rights. Submit seasonal/holiday material 6 months in advance. Query for electronic submissions. Reports in 1 month on queries; 6 weeks on mss.

Nonfiction: Book excerpts, exposé, general interest, interview/profile, photo feature, technical, travel. Buys 35 mss/year. Query or send complete ms. Length: 2,500-5,000 words. Pays $750-1,000. Sometimes pays the expenses of writers on assignment.

Photos: Send photos with submission. Payment varies for photos. Captions and identification of subjects required. Buys one-time rights.

Columns/Departments: First Person (Chicago area subjects only, talking about their occupations), 1,000 words; Chicago Voices (present or former high-profile Chicago area residents with their observations on or reminiscences of the city of Chicago), 1,000 words. Buys 40 mss/year. Query. pays $250. Buys 52 mss/year. Query. Pays $250.

Fiction: Length: 1,500-2,000 words. Pays $750-1,000.

NORTH SHORE, The Magazine of Chicago's North and Northwest Suburbs, PB Communications, 874 Green Bay Rd., Winnetka IL 60093. (708)441-7892. Publisher: Asher Birnbaum. Managing Editor: Karen Titus. 75% freelance written. Monthly magazine. "Our readers are a diverse lot, from middle-class communities to some of the country's wealthiest zip codes. But they all have one thing in common—our proximity to Chicago." Pays on publication. Publishes ms an average of 3 months after acceptance. Byline given. Offers 50% kill fee. Buys first North American serial rights. Submit seasonal material 5 months in advance. Accepts previously published submissions. Reports in 3 months. Free writer's guidelines for #10 SASE.

Nonfiction: Book excerpts, exposé, general interest, how-to, interview/profile, photo feature, travel. Special issues: Weddings (January, July); Fitness (February); Homes/Gardens (March, June, September, December); Weekend Travel (May); Nursing/Retirement Homes (August); Dining and Nightlife (October). Buys 50 mss/year. Query with published clips. Length: 500-4,000 words. Pays $100-800. Sometimes pays expenses of writers on assignment.

Photos: Send photos with submission. Reviews contact sheets, negatives, transparencies, prints. Offers $25-100/photo. Identification of subjects required. Buys one-time rights.

Columns/Departments: "Prelude" (shorter items of local interest), 250 words. Buys 12 mss/year. Query with published clips. Pays $50.

Tips: "We're always looking for something of local interest that's fresh and hasn't been reported elsewhere. Look for local angle. Offer us a story that's exclusive in the crowded Chicago-area media marketplace. Well-written feature stories have the best chance of being published. We cover all of Chicago's north and northwest suburbs together with some Chicago material, not just the North Shore."

‡THIRD WORD, Chicago's Arts & Entertainment Magazine, Third Word Publishing, Inc., Suite 205, 25 E. Delaware, Chicago IL 60611. (312)642-0288. Editor: Brendan Baber. Managing Editor: Tracey Pepper. 100% freelance written. Bimonthly consumer magazine covering arts and entertainment in Chicago. "We're looking for fun, personality-driven articles.We like over-the-top work." Estab. 1993. Circ. 20,000. Pays on publication. Publishes ms an average of 2 months after acceptance. Byline given. Buys first North American serial rights. Editorial lead time 2 months. Submit seasonal material 4 months in advance. Accepts simultaneous submissions. Query for electronic submissions. Reports in 3 weeks on queries. Sample copy for $2. Writer's guidelines free on request.

Nonfiction: Exposé, humor, interview/profile, personal experience. Buys 60 mss/year. Query with published clips. Length: 1,800-2,500 words. Pays $50-100. Sometimes pays expenses of writers on assignment.

Photos: State availability of photos with submission. Reviews contact sheets. Negotiates payment individually. Identification of subjects required. Buys one-time rights.

Fiction: Ethnic, experimental, humorous. Send complete ms. Length: 500-1,200 words. Pays $50.

Poetry: Avant-garde, free verse, light verse, traditional. "We have an especial loathing for dull, windy, navel-gazing." Buys 6 poems/year. Length: 20-60 lines. Pays $50.

Tips: Amuse us. Don't bother sending a résumé. Show us your voice—we don't follow the AP style. We want to hear *you* in your writing.

‡WINDY CITY SPORTS MAGAZINE, Chicago Sports Resources, 1450 W. Randolph, Chicago IL 60607. (312)421-1551. Fax: (312)421-1454. Editor: Shelley Hill. 75% freelance written. Monthly magazine covering amateur, participatory sports. "Windy City Sports Magazine is a 70-100 page monthly magazine covering amateur, participatory, endurance sports in the Chicago metropolitan area. We cover running, cycling, in-line skating, outdoor sports; we do not cover professional football, basketball, etc." Estab. 1987. Circ. 100,000. "We pay on acceptance if assigned, on publication if submitted." Byline given. Offers 50% kill fee. Buys one-time rights. Editorial lead time 2 months. Submit seasonal material 2 months in advance. Accepts simultaneous and previously published submissions. Send photocopy of article, typed ms with rights for sale noted and information about when and where the article previously appeared. Payment varies. Query for electronic submissions. Reports in 1 month. Send $2 or SASE (manila) with $2 postage. Writer's guidelines free on request.

Nonfiction: Book excerpts, essays, general interest, historical/nostalgic, how-to, humor, inspirational, interview/profile, new product, opinion (does not mean letters to the editor), personal experience, technical, travel. "No articles on professional sports." Query with published clips. Length: 700-1,200 words. Pays $75-150. Sometimes pays expenses of writers on assignment.

Photos: Freelancers should state availability of photos with submission. Send photos with submission. Reviews b&w photos. Negotiates payment individually. Captions and identification of subject required. Buys one-time rights.

Columns/Departments: Running, women's nutrition, cycling, road trip, sports medicine, fitness centers. 800-1,000 words for all columns. Buys 70 mss/year. Query with published clips. Send complete ms. Pays $75-125.

Poetry: Anything. "Must be sports-related."

Fillers: Anecdotes, facts, cartoons, short humor. Buys 25/year. Length: 50-250 words. Pays $25-100. "I love cartoons!"

Tips: "It helps to be active in the sport the writer chooses to write about. Being a runner when writing a running article gives extra credentials. The columns/departments are most open to freelancers. I must fill these columns every month, 11 times per year. I run out of ideas quickly. Also, be aware of the season when pitching ideas."

Indiana

ARTS INDIANA, Arts Indiana, Inc. Suite 701, 47 S. Pennsylvania, Indianapolis IN 46204-3622. (317)632-7894. Fax: (317)632-7966. Editor: Hank Nuwer. 80% freelance written. Monthly (September-June) magazine on artists, writers, performers and arts organizations working in Indiana—literary, visual and performing. Estab. 1978. Circ. 10,000. **Pays on acceptance.** Publishes ms an average of 3 months after acceptance. Byline given. Offers 20% kill fee. Buys first North American serial rights. Submit seasonal material 4 months in advance. Reports in 1-3 weeks. Sample copy available for $3.
Nonfiction: Essays, historical/nostalgic, interview/profile, opinion, photo feature, interviews with reviews (Q & A format). "No straight news reportage." Query with published clips. Length: 1,000-3,000 words. Pays $50-300 for articles. Sometimes pays expenses of writer on assignment.
Photos: Send b&w photos with submission. Reviews 5×7 or larger prints. Sometimes offers additional payment for photos accepted with ms. Captions and identification of subjects required. Buys one-time rights.
Tips: "We are looking for people-oriented and issue-oriented articles. Articles about people should reveal personality as well as describe work."

INDIANAPOLIS MONTHLY, Emmis Publishing Corp., Suite 1200, 950 N. Meridian St., Indianapolis IN 46204. (317)237-9288. Fax: (317)237-9426.Editor-in-Chief: Deborah Paul. Editor: Sam Stall. 50% freelance written. Prefers to work with published/established writers. Monthly magazine of "upbeat material reflecting current trends. Heavy on lifestyle, homes and fashion. Material must be regional (Indianapolis and/or Indiana) in appeal." Estab. 1977. Circ. 40,000. Pays on publication. Publishes ms an average of 2 months after acceptance. Byline given. Offers 50% kill fee in some cases. Buys first North American serial rights and makes work-for-hire assignments. Submit seasonal material 3 months in advance. Accepts previously published submissions if published in a non-competing market. Send photocopy of article or typed ms with rights for sale noted and information about when and where the article previously appeared. Pays 100% of the amount paid for an original article. Reports in 2 months. Sample copy for $3.05 and 9×12 SAE. Writers' guideliines for #10 SASE.
Nonfiction: General interest, interview/profile, photo feature, but only with a strong Indianapolis or Indiana angle. No poetry, fiction or domestic humor; no "How Indy Has Changed Since I Left Town" or "An Outsider's View of the 500" stories. Buys 50 mss/year. Query with published clips or send complete ms. Length: 200-6,000 words. Pays $50-500.
Photos: Send photos with submission. Offers $50 minimum/photo. Identification of subjects required. Buys one-time rights.
Columns/Departments: Around the Circle; 9 to 5 (profile of person with intriguing job); Sport (star athletes and trendy activities); Health (new technology; local sources); Controversy; Hoosiers at Large; Peoplescape; Coping (overcoming adversity). "Again, a local angle is the key." Query with published clips or send complete mss. Pays $150-300.
Tips: "Tell us something we didn't know about Indianapolis. Find a trendy subject with a strong Indianapolis (or Indiana) angle and sell it with a punchy query and a few of your best clips. Don't confuse 'general interest' with 'generic interest'—all material must focus sharply on Indianapolis and/or Indiana. Topics, however, can vary from serious to wacky: Recent issues have included everything from a feature story about college basketball star Damon Bailey to a two-paragraph piece on an Indiana gardening supply house that sells insects by mail. Best breaking-in topics for freelancers are Around the Circle (short takes on trendy local topics); Hoosiers at Large (Indiana natives relate first-person experiences); Peoplescape (one-paragraph back page feature about interesting resident). Fax queries OK; no phone queries please."
• This magazine will consider nonfiction book excerpts of material relevant to their readers.

Kansas

KANSAS!, Kansas Department of Economic Development, Suite 1300, 700 SW Harrison, Topeka KS 66603-3957. (913)296-3479. Editor: Andrea Glenn. 90% freelance written. Quarterly magazine emphasizing Kansas "people and places for all ages, occupations and interests." Estab. 1945. Circ. 54,000. **Pays on acceptance.** Publishes ms an average of 1 year after acceptance. Byline given. Buys one-time rights. Submit seasonal material 8 months in advance. Reports in 2 months. Sample copy and writer's guidelines available.

Nonfiction: General interest, interview, photo feature, travel. "Material must be Kansas-oriented and have good potential for color photographs. We feature stories about Kansas people, places and events that can be enjoyed by the general public. In other words, events must be open to the public, places also. People featured must have interesting crafts, etc. Query letter should clearly outline story in mind. I'm especially interested in Kansas freelancers who can supply their own photos." Length: 750-1,250 words. Pays $150-250. Sometimes pays expenses of writers on assignment.

Photos: "We are a full-color photo/manuscript publication." Send photos with query. Pays $50-75 (generally included in ms rate) for 35mm or larger format transparencies. Captions required.

Tips: "History and nostalgia stories do not fit into our format because they can't be illustrated well with color photography."

Kentucky

BACK HOME IN KENTUCKY, Greysmith Publishing Inc., P.O. Box 681629, Franklin TN 37068-1629. (615)794-4338. Fax: (615)790-6188. Editor: Nanci P. Gregg. 50% freelance written. Bimonthly magazine covering Kentucky heritage, people, places, events. We reach Kentuckians and "displaced" Kentuckians living outside the state. Estab. 1977. Pays on publication. Publishes ms an average of 8 months after acceptance. Byline given. Buys first North American serial rights. Submit seasonal material 8 months in advance. Reprints OK; send tearsheet or photocopy of article, typed ms with rights for sale noted and information about when and where the article previously appeared. Pays 75% of their fee for an original article. Query for electronic submissions. Reports in 2 months. Sample copy for $2.50 and 9 × 12 SAE with 5 first-class stamps. Writer's guidelines for #10 SASE.

Nonfiction: Historical (Kentucky related), how-to (might be gardening or crafts), interview/profile (noted or unusual Kentuckians), photo feature (Kentucky places and events), travel (unusual/little known Kentucky places). No inspirational or religion—all must be Kentucky related. Buys 25 mss/year. Query with or without published clips or send complete ms. Length: 500-2,000 words. Pays $25-100 for assigned articles; $15-50 for unsolicited articles. "In addition to normal payment, writers receive 4 copies of issue containing their article." Sometimes pays expenses of writers on assignment.

Photos: Send photos with submission. Reviews transparencies and 5 × 7 prints. Offers no additional payment for photos accepted with ms. Model releases and identification of subjects required. Rights purchased depends on situation. Also looking for color transparencies for covers. Vertical format. Pays $50-150.

Columns/Departments: Kentucky travel, Kentucky crafts, Kentucky gardening. Buys 10-12 mss/year. Query with published clips. Length: 500-750 words. Pays $15-40.

Tips: "We work mostly with unpublished writers who have a feel for Kentucky—its people, places, events, etc. The areas most open to freelancers are little known places in Kentucky, unusual history, and profiles of interesting, unusual Kentuckians."

KENTUCKY LIVING, P.O. Box 32170, Louisville KY 40232-0170. (502)451-2430. Fax: (502)459-1611. Editor: Gary W. Luhr. Mostly freelance written. Prefers to work with published/established writers. Monthly feature magazine primarily for Kentucky residents. Estab. 1948. Circ. 380,000. **Pays on acceptance.** Publishes ms on average of 4-12 months after acceptance. Byline given. Buys first serial rights for Kentucky. Submit seasonal material at least 6 months in advance. Will consider previously published and simultaneous submissions (if previously published and/or submitted outside Kentucky). Reports in 1 month. Sample copy for 9 × 12 SAE with 4 first-class stamps. Writer's guidelines for #10 SASE.

Nonfiction: Prefers Kentucky-related profiles (people, places or events), history, biography, recreation, travel, leisure, lifestyle articles, book excerpts. Buys 18-24 mss/year. Query or send complete ms. Pays $75 to $125 for "short" features (600-800 words) used in section known as "Kentucky Fare." For major articles (800-2,000 words) pays $150 to $350. Sometimes pays the expenses of writers on assignment.

Photos: State availability of or send photos with submission or advise as to availability. Reviews color slides and b&w prints. Identification of subjects required. Payment for photos included in payment for ms. Pays extra if photo used on cover.

Tips: "The quality of writing and reporting (factual, objective, thorough) is considered in setting payment price. We prefer well-documented pieces filled with quotes and anecdotes. Avoid boosterism. Well-researched, well-written feature articles, particularly on subjects of a serious nature, are given preference over light-weight material."

Louisiana

SUNDAY ADVOCATE MAGAZINE, P.O. Box 588, Baton Rouge LA 70821-0588. (504)383-1111, ext. 350. Fax: (504)388-0351. Newsfeatures Editor: Freda Yarbrough. 5% freelance written. "We are backlogged but still welcome submissions." Byline given. Estab. 1925. Pays on publication. Publishes ms up to 3 months after acceptance. Query for electronic submissions.

Nonfiction and Photos: Well-illustrated, short articles; must have local, area or Louisiana angle, in that order of preference. Also interested in travel pieces. Photos purchased with mss. Pays $100-200.
Tips: "Styles and subject matter may vary. Local interest is most important. No more than 4-5 typed, double-spaced pages."

Maine

ISLESBORO ISLAND NEWS, Islesboro Publishing, HCR 227, Islesboro ME 04848. (207)734-6745. Fax: (207)734-6519. Publisher: Agatha Cabaniss. 20% freelance written. Monthly tabloid on Penobscot Bay islands and people. Estab. 1985. **Pays on acceptance.** Byline given. Buys one-time rights. Sample copy for $2. Writer's guidelines for #10 SAE with 3 first-class stamps.
Nonfiction: Articles about contemporary issues on the islands, historical pieces, personality profiles, arts, lifestyles and businesses on the islands. Any story must have a definite Maine island connection. No travel pieces. Query or send complete ms. Pays $20-50.
Photos: Send photos with submission.
Tips: "Writers must know the Penobscot Bay Islands. We are not interested in pieces of a generic island nature unless they relate to development problems, or the viability of the islands as year round communities. We do not want 'vacation on a romantic island,' but we are interested in island historical pieces."

Maryland

BALTIMORE MAGAZINE, Suite 1000, 16 S. Calvert St., Baltimore MD 21202. (410)752-7375. Fax: (410)625-0280. Editor: Ramsey Flynn. Managing Editor: Margaret Guroff. 30-40% freelance written. Monthly magazine covering the Baltimore area. "Pieces must address an educated, active, affluent reader and must have a very strong Baltimore angle." Estab. 1907. Circ. 50,000. Pays within 60 days of acceptance. Byline given. Offers 30% kill fee. Buys first rights. Submit seasonal/holiday material 4 months in advance. Query for electronic submissions. Reports in 2 months on queries; 2 weeks on assigned mss; 3 months on unsolicited mss. Sample copy for $2.05 and 9 × 12 SAE with $2.40 postage. Writer's guidelines for a business-sized SASE.
Nonfiction: Margaret Guroff. Book excerpt (Baltimore subject or Baltimore author), essays (Baltimore subject), exposé (Baltimore subject), humor (Baltimore focus), interview/profile (w/Baltimorean), personal experience (Baltimore focus), photo feature, travel (local and regional to Maryland *only*). "Nothing that lacks a strong Baltimore focus or angle." Query with published clips or send complete ms. Length: 200-4,500 words. Pays $25-2,500 for assigned articles; $25-500 for unsolicited articles. Sometimes pays expenses of writers on assignment.
Tips: "Writers who live in the Baltimore area can send résumé and published clips to be considered for first assignment. Must show an understanding of writing that is suitable to an educated magazine reader and show ability to write with authority, describe scenes, help reader experience the subject. Too many writers send us newspaper-style articles, instead. We are seeking: 1) *Human interest features* — strong, even dramatic profiles of Baltimoreans of interest to our readers. 2) *First person accounts* of experience in Baltimore, or experiences of a Baltimore resident. 3) *Consumer* — according to our editorial needs, and with Baltimore sources." Writers new to us have most success with small humorous stories and 1,000-word personal essays that exhibit risky, original thought.

CHESAPEAKE BAY MAGAZINE, 1819 Bay Ridge Ave., Annapolis MD 21403. (410)263-2662. Editor: Jean Waller. 40% freelance written. Works with a small number of new/unpublished writers each year. Monthly regional publication for "those who enjoy reading about the Chesapeake and its tributaries. Our readers are yachtsmen, boating families, fishermen, ecologists — anyone who is part of Chesapeake Bay life." Circ. 33,000. Pays on publication. Publishes ms an average of 10-14 months after acceptance. Buys first North American serial rights and all rights. Submit seasonal material 6-8 months in advance. Reports in 2 months. Sample copy for $2.95. Writer's guidelines for SASE.
Nonfiction: "All material must be about the Chesapeake Bay area — land or water." How-to (fishing and sports pertinent to Chesapeake Bay); general interest; humor (welcomed, but don't send any "dumb boater" stories where common safety is ignored); historical; interviews (with interesting people who have contributed in some way to Chesapeake Bay life: authors, historians, sailors, oystermen, etc.); nostalgia (accurate, informative and well-paced — no maudlin ramblings about "the good old days"); personal experience (drawn from experiences in boating situations, adventures, events in our geographical area); photo feature (with accompanying ms); profile (on natives of Chesapeake Bay); technical (relating to boating, fishing); Chesapeake Bay folklore. "We do not want material written by those unfamiliar with the Bay area, or general sea stories." Buys 25 unsolicited mss/year. Query or submit complete ms. Length: 1,000-2,500 words. Pays $100-150.
Photos: Chris Gill, art director. Submit photo material with ms. Reviews 8 × 10 b&w glossy prints and color transparencies. Pays $200 for 35mm, 2¼ × 2¼ or 4 × 5 color transparencies used for cover photos; $15-75 for color photo used inside. Captions and model releases required. Buys one-time rights with reprint permission.
Tips: "We are a regional publication entirely about the Chesapeake Bay and its tributaries. Our readers are true 'Bay' lovers, and look for stories written by others who obviously share this love. We are particularly

interested in material from the Lower Bay (Virginia) area and the Upper Bay (Maryland/Delaware) area. We are looking for personal experience Chesapeake boating articles/stories, especially from power boaters."

MARYLAND MAGAZINE, 13th Floor, 100 S. Charles St., Baltimore MD 21201. (410)539-3100. Fax: (410)539-3188. Publisher: Gerry Hartung. Editorial Director: Michelle Scoville Burke. 95% freelance written. Prefers to work with published/established writers. Bimonthly magazine covering Maryland's history, culture, personalities, travel. Estab. 1968. Circ. 35,000. Pays within 45 days of acceptance. Publishes ms 3-6 months after acceptance. Byline given. Offers 25% kill fee. Buys first North American rights. Editorial lead time 2 months. Submit seasonal/holiday material 1 year in advance. Accepts simultaneous submissions. Query for electronic submissions. Reports in 6 weeks on queries; 3 months on mss. Sample copy for $3.50. Writer's guidelines for #10 SASE.
Nonfiction: General interest, historical/nostalgic, humor, interview/profile, photo feature and travel. Articles on any facet of Maryland life. "We publish an annual golf guide and an annual calendar." No fiction, poetry or controversial material or any topic *not* dealing with the state of Maryland; no trendy topics, or one that has received much publicity elsewhere. Buys 54 mss/year. Query with published clips or send complete ms. Length: 500-2,500 words. Pays 20-40¢/word. Sometimes pays expenses of writers on assignment.
Photos: Freelancers should state availability of photos with submission. Send photos with submission. Reviews contact sheets, negatives, transparencies, prints. Negotiates payment individually. Captions required. Buys one-time rights (plus promotional rights).
Columns/Departments: Bookshelf (Maryland-related book reviews), 200-300 words; Marylanders Through & Through (profile of interesting Marylander), 500 words; At Home (review of historic or culturally significant home), 1,500 words. Buys 24 mss/year. Query with published clips. Pays 20-40¢/word.
Tips: "All sections are open to freelancers. Thoroughly research your topic and give sources (when applicable)."

WARM WELCOMES MAGAZINE, Warm Welcomes Inc., P.O. Box 1066, Hagerstown MD 21741-1066. (301)797-9276. Fax: (301)797-1065. Editor: Winnie Wagaman. 25% freelance written. Monthly magazine that covers history, culture, events and people of the areas surrounding the state of Maryland. Our audience consists of upper- and middle-income professionals in Maryland, South Central Pennsylvania, Virginia, Washington, D.C. and West Virginia. Estab. 1989. Circ. 20,000. Pays on publication. Publishes ms an average of 3 months after acceptance. Byline given. Kill fee varies. Buys exclusive rights. Submit seasonal material 6 months in advance. Accepts simultaneous and previously published submissions. Send photocopy of article or typed ms with rights for sale noted and information about when and where the article previously appeared. Pays 100% of the amount paid for an original article. Query for electronic submissions. Reports in 3 months. Sample copy for 6×9 SAE with 4 first-class stamps. Writer's guidelines for #10 SASE.
Nonfiction: General interest, historical/nostalgic, interview/profile, travel (limited). "We accept only material related to our area's history, people and locations." Buys 12 mss/year. Query with or without published clips or send complete ms. Length: 600-1,200 words. Pays $25-75 for assigned articles; $25-50 for unsolicited articles.
Photos: Send photos with submission. Reviews contact sheets and 5×7 b&w prints. Pays $10-25. Identification of subjects required. Buys one-time rights.
Tips: "Writers can best approach our publication with a well-written query or ms pertaining to the area—something that shows they know their subject and the audience they are writing for. Interview/profile pieces have the best chance of being picked up for publication."

Massachusetts

‡BERKSHIRE, New England's Best Side, Berkshire Publishing Inc., P.O. Box 97, Jay NY 12941. Editor: Marisa Giannetti. 90% freelance written. Quarterly magazine covering Berkshire region of Massachusetts/New York/Vermont/Connecticut. "Articles and photographs must be related to the Berkshire region of western Massachusetts, eastern New York, northwest Connecticut and southern Vermont." Estab. 1980. Circ. 25,000. Pays within 60 days of publication. Publishes ms 3-6 months after acceptance. Byline given. Offers 20% kill fee. Buys first North American serial rights. Editorial lead time 4 months. Submit seasonal material at least 3 months in advance. Query for electronic submissions. Reports in 3 months on queries. Sample copy free on request.
Nonfiction: Book excerpts, cultural events, general interest, historical/nostalgia, humor, interview/profile, new product, photo feature, regional issues, sports, travel. "No fiction or poetry." Buys 40 mss/year. Query with or without published clips. Length: 500-5,000 words. Pays $500 minimum for assigned articles; $50 minimum for unsolicited articles. Sometimes pays expenses of writers on assignment.
Photos: State availability of photos with submission. Reviews contact sheets, negatives and transparencies. Negotiates payment individually. Captions and identification of subjects required. Buys one-time rights.
Columns/Departments: Neighbors (local people of real interest), 1,500 words; Almanac (news items of interest to region), 100-500 words; Real Estate (properties on the market in Berkshires), 2,000 words. Buys 15 mss/year. Query with or without published clips. Pays $50-650.

Tips: "Be very familiar with the Berkshire region and only query about subjects that suit us. Ask yourself what's the Berkshire connection before even proceeding with a query—and make sure it's a *strong* connection. Don't phone in queries—you will get nowhere with me! Berkshire Almanac (short newsy items and new products, businesses, trends) and Real Estate stories are best way to try to get published."

BOSTON GLOBE MAGAZINE, *Boston Globe,* Boston MA 02107. Editor-in-Chief: Ms. Ande Zellman. Assistant Editor: Fiona Luis. 50% freelance written. Weekly magazine. Circ. 805,099. **Pays on acceptance.** Publishes ms an average of 2 months after acceptance. No reprints of any kind. Buys first serial rights. Submit seasonal material 3 months in advance. SASE must be included with ms or queries for return. Reports in 1 month. Sample copy for 9×12 SAE with 2 first-class stamps.
   • Ranked as one of the best markets for freelance writers in *Writer's Digest* magazine's annual "Top 100 Markets," January 1994.
Nonfiction: Exposé (variety of issues including political, economic, scientific, medical and the arts), interview (not Q&A), profile, book excerpts (first serial rights only). No travelogs. Buys up to 100 mss/year. Query. Length: 2,000-5,000 words. Payment negotiable.
Photos: Purchased with accompanying ms or on assignment. Reviews contact sheets. Pays standard rates according to size used. Captions required.

‡THE BOSTON PHOENIX, 126 Brookline Ave., Boston MA 02215. (617)536-5390. Fax: (617)859-8201. Editor: Peter Kadzis. Contacts: Dan Kennedy (news); Caroline Knapp (features); Ted Drozdowski (arts). 40% freelance written. Weekly alternative newspaper for 18-40 age group, educated post-counterculture. Estab. 1966. Circ. 139,000. Buys first serial rights. Pays on publication. Offers kill fee. Publishes ms an average of 1 month after acceptance. Byline given. Reports in 2 months. Sample copy for $1.50.
   • *Boston Phoenix* has a monthly supplement (*One in Ten*) on gay and lesbian issues. Supplements editor is Robert Sullivan.
Nonfiction: News (local coverage, national, some international affairs, features, think pieces and profiles), lifestyle (features, service pieces, consumer-oriented tips, medical, food, some humor if topical, etc.), arts (reviews, essays, interviews), supplements (coverage of special-interest areas, e.g., skiing, book reviews, seasonal, recreation, education). Query section editor. "Liveliness, accuracy, and great literacy are absolutely required." No fiction. Poetry OK. Query letter preferable to ms. Pays 4¢/word and up. Sometimes pays the expenses of writers on assignment.

CAPE COD LIFE, Including Martha's Vineyard and Nantucket, Cape Cod Life, Inc., P.O. Box 767, Cataumet MA 02534-0767. (508)564-4466. Fax: (508)564-4470. Editor: Brian F. Shortsleeve. 80% freelance written. Bimonthly magazine focusing on "area lifestyle, history and culture, people and places, business and industry, and issues and answers." Readers are "year-round and summer residents of Cape Cod as well as non-residents who spend their leisure time on the Cape." Circ. 35,000. Pays 30 days after publication. Byline given. Offers 20% kill fee. Buys first North American serial rights or makes work-for-hire assignments. Submit seasonal/holiday material 6 months in advance. Simultaneous queries OK. Reports in 2-6 months on queries and ms. Sample copy for $3.75. Writer's guidelines for #10 SASE.
Nonfiction: General interest, historical, gardening, interview/profile, photo feature, travel, marine, nautical, nature, arts, antiques. Buys 20 mss/year. Query with or without published clips. Length: 1,000-4,000 words. Pays $100-400.
Photos: Send photos with query. Pays $25-200 for photos. Captions and identification of subjects required. Buys first rights with right to reprint.
Tips: "Freelancers submitting *quality* spec articles with a Cape Cod angle have a good chance at publication. We do like to see a wide selection of writer's clips before giving assignments. We accept more spec work written about Cape and Islands history than any other area."

PROVINCETOWN ARTS, Provincetown Arts, Inc., 650 Commercial St., Provincetown MA 02657. (508)487-3167. Editor: Christopher Busa. Contact: Christopher Busa. 90% freelance written. Annual magazine for contemporary art and writing. "*Provincetown Arts* focuses broadly on the artists and writers who inhabit or visit the Lower Cape, and seeks to stimulate creative activity and enhance public awareness of the cultural life of the nation's oldest continuous art colony. Drawing upon a 75-year tradition rich in visual art, literature, and theater, *Provincetown Arts* offers a unique blend of interviews, fiction, visual features, reporting, and poetry." Estab. 1985. Circ. 8,000. Pays on publication. Publishes ms an average of 4 months after acceptance. Offers 50% kill fee. Buys one-time and second serial (reprint) rights. Editorial lead time 4-6 months. Submit seasonal material 6 months in advance. Query for electronic submissions. Reports in 3 weeks on queries; 2 months on mss. Sample copy for $10. Writer's guidelines for #10 SASE.
Nonfiction: Book excerpts, essays, humor, interview/profile. Buys 40 mss/year. Send complete ms. Length: 1,500-4,000 words. Pays $150 minimum for assigned articles; $125 minimum for unsolicited articles. Sometimes pays expenses of writers on assignment.
Photos: Send photos with submission. Reviews 8×10 prints. Offers $20-100/photo. Identification of subjects required. Buys one-time rights.

Fiction: Mainstream. Also publishes novel excerpts. Buys 7 mss/year. Send complete ms. Length: 500-5,000 words. Pays $75-300.
Poetry: Buys 25 poems/year. Submit maximum 3 poems. Pays $25-150.

WORCESTER MAGAZINE, 172 Shrewsbury St., Worcester MA 01604-4636. Senior Editor: Paul Della Valle. 10% freelance written. Weekly tabloid emphasizing the central Massachusetts region. Estab. 1976. Circ. 40,000. Pays on publication. Publishes ms an average of 3 weeks after acceptance. Byline given. Buys all rights. Submit seasonal material 2 months in advance. No simultaneous submissions. Does not report on unsolicited material.
Nonfiction: Exposé (area government, corporate), how-to (concerning the area, homes, vacations), interview (local), personal experience, opinion (local), photo feature. "We are interested in any piece with a local angle." Buys 75 mss/year. Length: 500-1,500 words. Pays $35-250.
Photos: Send photos with query. Pays $10 for b&w photos. Captions preferred; model release required. Buys all rights.

Michigan

ABOVE THE BRIDGE MAGAZINE, 120 McLaughlin Rd., Skandia MI 49885. Editor: Lynn DeLoughary St. Arnaud. 100% freelance written. Quarterly magazine on the Upper Peninsula of Michigan. "Most material, including fiction, has an Upper Peninsula of Michigan slant. Our readership is past and present Upper Peninsula residents." Circ. 2,000. Pays on publication. Publishes ms an average of 6 months after acceptance. Byline given. Buys one-time rights. Submit seasonal/holiday material 6 months in advance. Accepts previously published submissions. Send typed ms with rights for sale noted and information about when and where the article previously appeared. For reprints, pays 100% of the amount paid for an original article. Query for electronic submissions. Reports in 5 months. Sample copy for $3.50. Writer's guidelines for #10 SASE.
Nonfiction: Book excerpts (books on Upper Peninsula or UP writer), essays, historical/nostalgic (UP), interview/profile (UP personality or business), personal experience, photo feature (UP). Note: Travel by assignment only. "This is a family magazine; therefore, no material in poor taste." Buys 60 mss/year. Send complete ms. Length: 1,000-2,500 words. Pays 2¢/word.
Photos: Send photos with submission. Reviews prints (5×7 or larger). Offers $5 ($15-20 if used for cover). Captions, model releases, identification of subjects required. Buys one-time rights.
Fiction: Ethnic (UP heritage), humorous, mainstream, mystery. No horror or erotica. "Material set in UP has preference for publication. Accepts children's fiction." Buys 12 mss/year. Send complete ms. Length: 2,000 words (1,000 maximum for children's). Pays 2¢/word.
Poetry: Free verse, haiku, light verse, traditional. No erotica. Buys 20 poems/year. Shorter poetry preferred. Pays $5.
Fillers: Anecdotes, short humor. Buys 25/year. Length: 100-500 words. Pays 2¢/word maximum.
Tips: "Material on the shorter end of our requirements has a better chance for publication. We're very well-stocked at the moment. We can't use material by out-of-state writers with content not tied to Upper Peninsula of Michigan. Know the area and people, read the magazine. Most material received is too long. Stick to our guidelines. We love to publish well written material by previously unpublished writers."

ANN ARBOR OBSERVER, Ann Arbor Observer Company, 201 E. Catherine, Ann Arbor MI 48104. Fax: (313)769-3375. Editor: John Hilton. 50% freelance written. Works with a small number of new/unpublished writers each year. Monthly magazine featuring stories about people and events in Ann Arbor. Estab. 1976. Circ. 56,000. Pays on publication. Publishes ms an average of 2 months after acceptance. Byline given. Query for electronic submissions. Reports in 3 weeks on queries; "several months" on mss. Sample copy for 12½ × 15 SAE with $3 postage. Free writer's guidelines.
Nonfiction: Historical, investigative features, profiles, brief vignettes. Must pertain to Ann Arbor. Buys 75 mss/year. Length: 100-7,000 words. Pays up to $1,000/article. Sometimes pays expenses of writers on assignment.
Tips: "If you have an idea for a story, write a 100-200-word description telling us why the story is interesting. We are most open to intelligent, insightful features of up to 5,000 words about interesting aspects of life in Ann Arbor."

DETROIT MONTHLY, Crain Communications, 1400 Woodbridge, Detroit MI 48207. (313)446-6000. Fax: (313)446-1687. Editor: John Barron. 50% freelance written. Monthly magazine. "We are a city magazine for educated, reasonably well-to-do, intellectually curious Detroiters." Estab. 1978. Circ. 100,000. **Pays on acceptance.** Byline given. Offers negotiable kill fee. Buys first North American serial rights. Accepts previously published submissions. Send tearsheet or photocopy of article. For reprints, pays 15-25% of the amount pays for an original article. Submit seasonal material 4 months in advance. Query for electronic submissions. Reports in 2 months.
Nonfiction: Book excerpts, exposé. Buys 25 mss/year. Query with published clips. Length: 1,000-5,000 words. Pays $100-1,200. Sometimes pays the expenses of writers on assignment.
Photos: Send photos with submission.

GRAND RAPIDS MAGAZINE, 549 Ottawa Ave. NW, Grand Rapids MI 49503-1444. (616)459-4545. Fax: (616)459-4800. Publisher: John H. Zwarensteyn. Editor: Carole Valade Smith. 70% freelance written. Eager to work with new writers. Monthly general feature magazine serving Western Michigan. Estab. 1964. Circ. 12,000. Pays on 15th of month of publication. Publishes ms an average of 4 months after acceptance. Buys first serial rights. Phone queries OK. Submit seasonal material 3 months in advance. Accepts previously published submissions. Query for electronic submissions. Reports in 3 months. Sample copy for $2 and 6 first-class stamps.
  • This magazine is using fewer staff writers and more freelance writers than before.
Nonfiction: Western Michigan writers preferred. Western Michigan subjects only: government, labor, investigative, criminal justice, environment, health/medical, education, general interest, historical, interview/profile, nostalgia. Inspirational and personal experience pieces discouraged. No breezy, self-centered "human" pieces or "pieces not only light on style but light on hard information." Humor appreciated but must be specific to region. "If you live here, see the managing editor before you write. If you don't, send a query letter with published clips, or phone." Length: 500-4,000 words. Pays $35-200. Sometimes pays the expenses of writers on assignment.
Photos: Send photos. Pays $25 minimum for 5×7 glossy print and $35 minimum for 35 or 120mm transparency. Captions and model releases required.
Tips: "Television has forced city/regional magazines to be less provincial and more broad-based in their approach. People's interests seem to be evening out from region to region. The subject matters should remain largely local, but national trends must be recognized in style and content. And we must *entertain* as well as inform."

MICHIGAN COUNTRY LINES, Michigan Electric Cooperative Association, 2859 W. Jolly Rd., Okemos MI 48864. (517)351-6322. Fax: (517)351-6396. Editor: Michael Buda. Managing Editor: Gail Knudtson. 10% freelance written. Bimonthly magazine covering rural Michigan. Estab. 1980. Circ. 170,000. Pays on publication. Publishes ms an average of 4 months after acceptance. Byline given. Buys one-time and second serial (reprint) rights. Submit seasonal material 3 months in advance. Query for electronic submissions. Reports in 2 months. Free sample copy.
Nonfiction: Personalities, how-to (rural living), photo feature. No product or out-of-state. Buys 6 mss/year. Send complete ms. Length: 700-1,500 words. Pays $200 for assigned articles; $150 unsolicited articles. Pays expenses of writers on assignment.
Photos: Send photos with submission. Reviews contact sheets, 35mm transparencies and 3×5 prints. Offers $10-15/photo. Captions, model releases and identification of subjects required. Buys one-time rights.
Tips: "Features are most open to freelancers. We no longer need historical/nostalgic articles."

Minnesota

LAKE SUPERIOR MAGAZINE, Lake Superior Port Cities, Inc., P.O. Box 16417, Duluth MN 55816-0417. (218)722-5002. Fax: (218)722-4096. Editor: Paul L. Hayden. 60% freelance written. Works with a small number of new/unpublished writers each year. Bimonthly regional magazine covering contemporary and historic people, places and current events around Lake Superior. Estab. 1979. Circ. 20,000. Pays on publication. Publishes ms an average of 10 months after acceptance. Byline given. Offers $25 kill fee. Buys first North American serial and some second rights. Submit seasonal material 1 year in advance. Query for electronic submissions. Reports in 2 months. Sample copy for $3.95 and 5 first-class stamps. Writer's guidelines for #10 SASE.
Nonfiction: Book excerpts, general interest, historic/nostalgic, humor, interview/profile (local), personal experience, photo feature (local), travel (local), city profiles, regional business, some investigative. Buys 45 mss/year. Query with published clips. Length 300-2,200 words. Pays $80-400. Sometimes pays the expenses of writers on assignment.
Photos: Quality photography is our hallmark. Send photos with submission. Reviews contact sheets, 2×2 transparencies, 4×5 prints. Offers $20 for b&w and $35 for color. $75 for covers. Captions, model releases, identification of subjects required.
Columns/Departments: Current events and things to do (for Events Calendar section), short, less than 300 words; Around The Circle (media reviews and short pieces on Lake Superior or Great Lakes environmental issues and themes and letters and short pieces on events and highlights of the Lake Superior Region); I Remember (nostalgic lake-specific pieces), up to 1,100 words; Life Lines (single personality profile with b&w), up to 700 words. Other headings include Destinations, Nature, Wilderness Living, Heritage, Shipwreck, House For Sale. Buys 20 mss/year. Query with published clips. Pays $10-75.
Fiction: Ethnic, historic, humorous, mainstream, novel excerpts, slice-of-life vignettes, ghost stories. Must be regionally targeted in nature. Buys only 2-3 mss/year. Query with published clips. Length: 300-2,500 words. Pays $1-125.
Tips: "Well-researched queries are attended to. We actively seek queries from writers in Lake Superior communities. We prefer manuscripts to queries. Provide enough information on why the subject is important to the region and our readers, or why and how something is unique. We want details. The writer must have a thorough knowledge of the subject and how it relates to our region. We prefer a fresh, unused approach

to the subject which provides the reader with an emotional involvement. Almost all of our articles feature quality photography, color or black and white. It is a prerequisite of all nonfiction. All submissions should include a *short* biography of author/photographer."

‡MINNESOTA CALLS MAGAZINE, The Magazine About Life In Minnesota, Minnesota Calls, Inc., Suite 205, 101 W. Second St., Duluth MN 55802. (218)722-7761. Editor: Jo Ann Paull. Editorial contact (submissions): Tony Rogers, associate editor. 65% freelance written. Bimonthly consumer magazine covering people, places and events in Minnesota. "Stories about Minnesota's culture, history, environment, and lifestyles. We like humorous and offbeat stories or events. Things that make Minnesota such a terrific place to live." Estab. 1990. Circ. 20,000. Pays on publication. Byline given. Buys first North American serial rights. Editorial lead time 3 months. Submit seasonal material 4 months in advance. Accepts simultaneous and previously published submissions. Reports in 2 months on queries; 2 months on mss. Sample copy for $5.50. Writer's guidelines for #10 SASE.
Nonfiction: Essays, exposé, general interest, historical/nostalgic, humor, interview/profile, new product, personal experience, photo feature, travel. "Not interested in anything that focuses too heavily on the Twin Cities metro area." Buys 120 mss/year. Query. Length: 500-2,000 words. Pays $50. Sometimes pays expenses of writers on assignment.
Photos: Send photos with submission. Reviews transparencies and prints. Negotiates payment individually. Identification of subjects required. Buys one-time rights.
Columns/Departments: Country Roads, City Streets (offbeat/humorous places or news), 500 words; Great Outdoors (outdoor/nature stories), 500 words. Buys 60 mss/year. Query. Pays $50-100.
Fiction: Adventure, historical, humorous, slice-of-life vignettes. Buys 2 mss/year. Send complete ms. Length: 750-2,000 words. Pays $150-350.
Tips: "Read the magazine. We rarely accept stories from "Big City" people who have "discovered" Minnesota. Some of the more open sections are Country Road, City Streets and Great Outdoors. Look for subjects that really say 'Minnesota.' Humor is always good."

MPLS. ST. PAUL MAGAZINE, Suite 500, 220 S. Sixth St., Pillsbury Center-South Tower, Minneapolis MN 55402-4507. (612)339-7571. Fax: (612)339-5806. Editor: Brian Anderson. Executive Editor: Sylvia Paine Lindman. Managing Editor: Claude Peck. 70% freelance written. Monthly general interest magazine covering the metropolitan area of Minneapolis/St. Paul and aimed at college-educated professionals who enjoy living in the area and taking advantage of the cultural, entertainment and dining out opportunities. Reports on people and issues of importance to the community. Estab. 1978. Circ. 64,000. **Pays on acceptance.** Publishes ms an average of 3 months after acceptance. Byline given. Offers 25% kill fee. Buys first North American serial rights. Submit seasonal material 5 months in advance. Query for electronic submissions. Reports in 1 month. Sample copy for $4.18.
Nonfiction: Book excerpts, general interest, historical/nostalgic, interview/profile (local), new product, photo feature (local), travel (regional). Buys 200 mss/year. Query with published clips. Length: 1,000-4,000 words. Pays $100-1,200. Sometimes pays expenses of writers on assignment.
Photos: Jim Nelson, photo editor.
Columns/Departments: Nostalgia (Minnesota historical); Home (interior design, local). Query with published clips. Length: 750-2,000 words. Pays $100-400.

Mississippi

MISSISSIPPI, Downhome Publications, 5 Lakeland Circle, P.O. Box 16445, Jackson MS 39216. (601)982-8418. Editor: Ann Becker. 95% freelance written. Bimonthly magazine "focuses almost exclusively on positive aspects of Mississippi—people, places, events." Estab. 1982. Circ. 25,000. Pays on publication. Publishes ms an average of 6 months after acceptance. Byline given. Offers $75 kill fee. Buys one-time rights. Submit seasonal material 1 year in advance. Query for electronic submissions. Reports in 3 months. Sample copy for $3.75. Writer's guidelines for #10 SASE.
Nonfiction: Essays, general interest, historical/nostalgic, interview/profile, personal experience, photo feature, travel. No essays on Southern accents or Southerners in the North. Buys 72 mss/year. Query with published clips. Length: 500-2,000 words. Pays $50-500.
Photos: Send photos with submission. Reviews contact sheets, 2¼ × 2¼ transparencies and 4 × 5 prints. Offers $25-100/photo. Captions, model releases and identification of subjects required. Buys one-time rights.
Columns/Departments: Travel, People, Music, Heritage, Sports, Business, Art, Outdoors, Homes and Gardens (focuses on Mississippi people, places or events), 1,500 words each. Buys 35 mss/year. Query with published clips. Length: 500-1,500 words. Pays $125.
Tips: "Query by mail. Query should give some idea of how story would read. Including a lead is good. Be patient. Be aware of past articles—we only feature a subject once. All departments are good starting points. Be sure subject has *state*wide interest. Be sure subject has good reputation in field."

Missouri

MISSOURI MAGAZINE, Box 28830, St. Louis MO 63123-0030. (314)638-4050. Fax: (618)476-1616. Editor: Tony Nolan Adrignola. Quarterly magazine covering Missouri-oriented topics. "We prefer human-interest articles unique to Missouri—from historical pieces to profiles of people and places in Missouri today." Estab. 1974. Circ. 15,000. Pays on publication. Byline given. Buys first rights. Accepts simultaneous and previously published submissions. Send tearsheet or photocopy of article and SASE. For reprints pays 50% of the amount paid for an original article. Submit seasonal material 6 months in advance. Query for electronic submissions. Reports in 1 month queries; 3 months on mss. Sample copy for $4.95. Free writer's guidelines.
Nonfiction: General interest, historical/nostalgic, interview/profile, photo feature, travel, Missouri geology, natural history, wildlife. No fiction. Buys 28 mss/year. Send complete ms. Length: 1,500-3,000 words. Pays 5¢/word for articles; $75-200 for unsolicited articles. Sometimes pays in trade out with ads.
Photos: Send photos with submission. Reviews 2¼ × 2¼ transparencies. Offers $5-25/photo. Captions, model releases, identification of subjects required. Buys one-time rights.
Columns/Departments: Bed & Breakfast Review (reviews B&Bs in Missouri—unique, 'quality' establishments), 300 words; Best Foot Forward (listing of exemplary establishments or services in Missouri), 50-100 words. Buys 28 mss/year. Send complete ms. Length 50-300 words. Pays $10-25.
Fillers: Facts. Buys 40/year. Length: 50-100 words. Pays $5-25.
Tips: "Send complete manuscript—professionally written with photos of excellent quality. SASE."

PITCH WEEKLY, News and Entertainment for Metro Kansas City, (formerly *Pitch*), Pitch Publishing, Inc., 3701 Summit, Kansas City MO 64111-2826. (816)561-6061. Fax: (816)756-0502. Editor: Bruce Rodgers. 75% freelance written. Weekly alternative newspaper that covers arts, entertainment, politics and social and cultural awareness in Kansas City. Estab. 1980. Circ. 61,000. Pays 1 month from publication. Buys first or one-time rights or makes work-for-hire assignments. Editorial lead time 1 month. Submit seasonal material 2 months in advance. *Query First!* Accepts previously published submissions. Send photocopy of article or typed ms with rights for sale noted and information about when and where the article previously appeared. Pays 50% of the amount paid for an original article. Reports in 2 months on queries.
Nonfiction: Exposé, humor, interview/profile, opinion, news, photo feature. Buys 40-50 mss/year. Query with published clips. Length: 700. Pays $25 minimum. Sometimes pays expenses of writers on assignment (limit agreed upon in advance). Prefer nonfiction with local hook.
Photos: Send photos with submission. Reviews contact sheets. Offers no additional payment for photos accepted with ms. Captions and identification of subjects required. Buys one-time rights.
Fiction: Holiday-theme fiction published on Christmas, Thanksgiving, Valentine's Day. "Must be slightly off-beat and good." Length: 1,500-2,000 words. Payment $75.
Tips: "Approach us with unusual angles on current political topics of responsible social documentary. Send well-written, clear, concise query with identifiable direction of proposed piece and SASE for reply or return. Previous publication in AAN paper a plus. We're looking for features and secondary features: current events in visual and performing arts (include new trends, etc.); social issues (OK to have an opinion as long as facts are well-documented); liberal politics."

‡RIVER HILLS TRAVELER, Todd Publishing, Route 2 Box 2304, Piedmont MO 63957. (314)223-7143. Editor: Bob Todd. 60% freelance written. Monthly consumer tabloid covering fishing, hunting, camping and southern Missouri. "We are about outdoor sports and nature in the southeast quarter of Missouri. Topics like those in *Field & Stream* and *National Geographic*." Estab. 1973. Circ. 7,500. Pays on publication. Publishes ms an average of 2 months after acceptance. Byline given. Buys one-time rights. Editorial lead time 2 months. Submit seasonal material 1-12 months in advance. Accepts simultaneous and previouly published submissions. Query for electronic submissions. Reports in 1 month. Sample copy and writer's guidelines free on request.
Nonfiction: Historical/nostalgic, how-to, humor, opinion, personal experience. photo feature, technical, travel. "No stories about other geographic areas." Buys 80 mss/year. Query with writing samples. Length: 1,500 maximum words. Pays $25. Sometimes pays expenses of writers on assignment.
Photos: Send photos with submission. Reviews contact sheets and prints. Negotiates payment individually. Identification of subjects required. Buys one-time rights.
Fillers: Gags. Pays $10.
Tips: "We are a 'poor man's version' of *Field & Stream* and *National Geographic*—about the eastern Missouri Ozarks."

SPRINGFIELD! MAGAZINE, Springfield Communications Inc., P.O. Box 4749, Springfield MO 65808-4749. (417)882-4917. Editor: Robert C. Glazier. 85% freelance written. Works with a small number of new/unpublished writers each year; eager to work with new/unpublished writers. Monthly magazine. "This is an extremely local and provincial magazine. No *general* interest articles." Estab. 1979. Circ. 10,000. Pays on publication. Publishes ms an average of 6 months after acceptance. Byline given. Buys first serial rights. Submit seasonal/holiday material 6-12 months in advance. Simultaneous queries OK. Reports in 3 months on queries; 6 months on mss. Sample copy for $5 and 9½ × 12½ SAE.

Nonfiction: Book excerpts (by Springfield authors only), exposé (local topics only), historical/nostalgic (top priority but must be local history), how-to (local interest only), humor (if local angle), interview/profile (needs more on females than on males), personal experience (local angle), photo feature (local photos), travel (1 page/month). No material that could appeal to any other magazine anywhere else. Buys 150 mss/year. Query with published clips or send complete ms. Length: 500-5,000 words. Pays $25-250. Sometimes pays expenses of writers on assignment.

• They need more female profiles and *local* historical pieces.

Photos: Send photos or send photos with query or ms. Reviews b&w and color contact sheets, 4×5 color transparencies, 5×7 b&w prints. Pays $5-35 for b&w, $10-50 for color. Captions, model releases, identification of subjects required. Buys one-time rights.

Columns/Departments: Buys 250 mss/year. Query or send complete ms. Length varies widely but usually 500-2,500 words.

Tips: "We prefer that a writer read eight or ten copies of our magazine prior to submitting any material for our consideration. The magazine's greatest need is for features which comment on these times in Springfield. We are overstocked with nostalgic pieces right now. We also are much in need of profiles about young women and men of distinction."

STL: Magazine, St. Louis Regional Educational and Public Television Commission, 6996 Millbrook Blvd., St. Louis MO 63130-4944. (314)726-7685. Fax: (314)726-0677. Editor: Gayle R. McIntosh. Contact: Terri Gates, managing editor. Monthly magazine focusing on history, education, arts and culture of metropolitan area, including information on local public television station programming. Estab. 1991. Circ. 50,000. Pays on publication. Publishes ms an average of 2 months after acceptance. Byline given. Buys one-time rights. Submit seasonal material 6 months in advance. Accepts simultaneous and previously published submissions. Send photocopy of article or typed ms with rights for sale noted and information about when and where the article previously appeared. Fee negotiable. Query for electronic submissions. Reports in 6 months on queries. Free sample copy for 9×12 SAE with 4 first-class stamps.

Nonfiction: Book excerpts, historical/nostalgic, how-to (garden, home, cooking), interview/profile, personal experience, travel. Buys 12 mss/year. Query with published clips. Length: 1,000-2,500 words. Pays $75-300. Publishes novel excerpts occasionally. Use only material by local writer; or writer featured in PBS or local programming; or about topic of local interest.

• *STL* is using more local writers.

Photos: Send photos with submission. Offers no additional payment for photos accepted with ms. Identification of subjects required. Buys one-time rights.

Columns: Special interest in health and issues related to older readership. Must have local focus. Buys 12 mss/year. Query with published clips. Length: 500-750 words. Pays $50-75.

Montana

MONTANA MAGAZINE, American Geographic Publishing, P.O. Box 5630, Helena MT 59604-5630. (406)443-2842. Fax: (406)443-5480. Editor: Beverly R. Magley. 90% freelance written. Bimonthly "strictly Montana-oriented magazine that features community and personality profiles, contemporary issues, travel pieces." Estab. 1970. Circ. 69,000. Publishes ms an average of 8-12 months after acceptance. Byline given. Offers $50-100 kill fee on assigned stories only. Buys one-time rights. Submit seasonal material at least 6 months in advance. Accepts simultaneous submissions. Send information about when and where the article previously appeared. Pays 50% of their fee for an original article. Reports in 2 months. Sample copy for $3. Writer's guidelines for #10 SASE.

Nonfiction: Essays, general interest, interview/profile, photo feature, travel. Special features on summer and winter destination points. Query by January for summer material; July for winter material. No 'me and Joe' hiking and hunting tales; no blood-and-guts hunting stories; no poetry; no fiction; no sentimental essays. Buys 30 mss/year. Query. Length: 300-4,500 words. Pays 15¢/word for articles. Sometimes pays the expenses of writers on assignment.

Photos: Send photos with submission. Reviews contact sheets, 35mm or larger format transparencies, 5×7 prints. Offers additional payment for photos accepted with ms. Captions, model releases, identification of subjects required. Buys one-time rights.

Columns/Departments: Over the Weekend (destination points of interest to travelers, family weekends and exploring trips to take), 500-1,000 words plus b&w or color photo; Food and Lodging (great places to eat; interesting hotels, resorts, etc.), 700-1,000 words plus b&w or color photo; Made in MT (successful cottage industries), 700-1,000 words plus b&w or color photo. Humor 800-1,000 words. Query.

Nevada

NEVADA MAGAZINE, 1800 E. Hwy. 50, Carson City NV 89710-0005. (702)687-5416. Fax: (702)687-6159. Publisher: Rich Moreno. Editor: David Moore. Contact: Carolyn Graham, associate editor. 50% freelance written. Works with a small number of new/unpublished writers each year. Bimonthly magazine published by the state of Nevada to promote tourism in the state. Estab. 1936. Circ. 100,000. Pays on publication.

Publishes ms an average of 6 months after acceptance. Byline given. Buys first North American serial rights. Phone queries OK. Submit seasonal material at least 6 months in advance. Query for electronic submissions. Word processing and page layout on Macintosh. Reports in 1 month. Sample copy for $1. Free writer's guidelines.

Nonfiction: Nevada topics only. Historical, nostalgia, photo feature, people profile, recreational, travel, think pieces. "We welcome stories and photos on speculation." Publishes nonfiction book excerpts. Buys 40 unsolicited mss/year. Submit complete ms or queries to Associate Editor, Carolyn Graham. Length: 500-2,000 words. Pays $75-300.

Photos: Paul AlLée, art director. Send photo material with accompanying ms. Pays $10-50 for 8 × 10 glossy prints; $15-75 for color transparencies. Name, address and caption should appear on each photo or slide. Buys one-time rights.

Tips: "Keep in mind that the magazine's purpose is to promote tourism in Nevada. Keys to higher payments are quality and editing effort (more than length). Send cover letter; no photocopies. We look for a light, enthusiastic tone of voice without being too cute; articles bolstered by amazing facts and thorough research; and unique angles on Nevada subjects."

New Jersey

ATLANTIC CITY MAGAZINE, P.O. Box 2100, Pleasantville NJ 08232-1924. (609)272-7900. Fax: (609)272-7910. Editor: Ken Weatherford. 80% freelance written. Works with small number of new/unpublished writers each year. Monthly regional magazine covering issues pertinent to the Jersey Shore area. Estab. 1978. Circ. 50,000. Pays on publication. Publishes ms an average of 4 months after acceptance. Byline given. Buys one-time rights. Offers variable kill fee. Accepts previously published submissions. Send typed ms with rights for sale noted and information about when and where the article previously appeared. Pays 50% of their fee for an original article. Submit seasonal material 6 months in advance. Reports in 6 weeks. Sample copy for $3 and 9 × 12 SAE with 6 first-class stamps. Writer's guidelines for SASE.

Nonfiction: Entertainment, general interest, recreation, history, lifestyle, interview/profile, photo feature, trends. "No hard news or investigative pieces. No travel pieces or any article without a South Jersey shore area/Atlantic City slant." Query. Length: 100-3,000 words. Pays $50-700 for assigned articles; $50-500 for unsolicited articles. Sometimes pays the expenses of writers on assignment.

Photos: Send photos. Reviews contact sheets, negatives, 2¼ × 2¼ transparencies, 8 × 10 prints. Pay varies. Captions, model releases, identification of subjects required. Buys one-time rights.

Columns/Departments: Art, Business, Entertainment, Sports, Dining, History, Style, Real Estate. Query with published clips. Length: 500-2,000 words. Pays $150-400.

Tips: "Our readers are a broad base of local residents and visiting tourists. We need stories that will appeal to both audiences."

NEW JERSEY MONTHLY, P.O. Box 920, Morristown NJ 07963-0920. (201)539-8230. Editor: Jenny De Monte. 50% freelance written. Monthly magazine covering "almost anything that's New Jersey related." Estab. 1976. Circ. 87,000. Pays on completion of fact-checking. Byline given. Offers 10-30% kill fee. Buys first rights. Submit seasonal material 6 months in advance. Reports in 3 months. Sample copy for $5.95 (% Back Issue Dept.); writer's guidelines for #10 SASE.

● Ranked as one of the best markets for freelance writers in *Writer's Digest* magazine's annual "Top 100 Markets," January 1994.

Nonfiction: Book excerpts, essays, exposé, general interest, historical, humor, interview/profile, opinion, personal experience, travel. Special issues: Dining Out (February and August); Real Estate (March); Home & Garden (April); Great Weekends (May); Shore Guide (June); Fall Getaways (October); Holiday Shopping & Entertaining (November). "No experience pieces from people who used to live in New Jersey or general pieces that have no New Jersey angle." Buys 96 mss/year. Query with published magazine clips and SASE. Length: 200-3,000 words. Pays 30¢/word and up. Pays reasonable expenses of writers on assignment with prior approval.

● This magazine continues to look for strong investigative reporters with novelistic style and solid knowledge of New Jersey issues.

Photos: Send photos with submission. Payment negotiated. Identification of subjects and return postage required. "Submit dupes only. Drop off for portfolios on Wednesdays only. The magazine accepts no responsibility for unsolicited photography, artwork or cartoons." Buys exclusive first serial or one-time rights.

Columns/Departments: Business (company profile, trends, individual profiles); Health & Fitness (trends, personal experience, service); Home & Garden (homes, gardens, trends, profiles, etc.); Travel (in and out-of-state). Buys 36 mss/year. Query with published clips. Length: 750-1,500 words. Pays 30¢ and up/word.

Tips: "To break in, we suggest contributing briefs to our front-of-the-book section, 'Garden Variety' (light, off-beat items, trends, people, things; short service items, such as the 10 best NJ-made ice creams; short issue-oriented items; gossip; media notes). We pay a flat fee, from $50-150."

‡**NEW JERSEY OUTDOORS,** New Jersey Department of Environmental Protection and Energy, CN 402, Trenton NJ 08625. (609)777-4182. Editor: Beth Kuhles. 50% freelance written. Quarterly consumer magazine

covering outdoor activities, history and culture in N.J. *"New Jersey Outdoors* celebrates the natural and historic resources of New Jersey with articles and photography on wildlife, nature, historic treasures, recreation, fishing, hunting, conservation and environmental protection." Estab. 1950. Circ. 30,000. Pays on publication. Byline given. Buys one-time rights. Editorial lead time 6 months. Submit seasonal material 6 months in advance. Accepts simultaneous and previously published submissions. Query for electronic submissions. Reports in 3 months on queries. Sample copy free on request. Writer's guidelines for #10 SASE.

Nonfiction: General interest, historical/nostalgic, how-to, interview/profile, personal experience, photo feature. *"New Jersey Outdoors* is not interested in articles showing disregard for the environment or in items demonstrating unskilled persons taking extraordinary risks." Buys 30-40 mss/year. Query with published clips. Length: 600-2,000 words. Pays $100-500. Sometimes pays expenses of writers on assignment.

Photos: State availability of photos with submission. Reviews contact sheets, negatives, transparencies. Offers $20-125/photo. Captions and identification of subjects required. Buys one-time rights.

Columns/Departments: Afield (first person outdoor activities), 800 words; Cityscape (environmental activities in cities or suburbs), 800 words; Gardens (gardens or gardening tips), 800 words; Outings (trips to specific N.J. locations), 800 words; Profile (people who make a difference in environment), 800 words; Volunteers (volunteers for environment), 800 words. Buys 25 mss/year. Query with published clips. Pays $100-500.

Tips: *"New Jersey Outdoors* generally publishes season-specific articles, which are planned six months in advance. Stories should be accompanied by *great* photography. Articles *must* relate to New Jersey."

THE SANDPAPER, Newsmagazine of the Jersey Shore, The SandPaper, Inc., 1816 Long Beach Blvd., Surf City NJ 08008-5461. (609)494-2034. Fax: (609)494-1437. Editor: Curt Travers. Freelance Submissions Editor: Gail Travers. 50% freelance written. Weekly tabloid covering subjects of interest to Jersey shore residents and visitors. *"The SandPaper* publishes three editions covering many of the Jersey Shore's finest resort communities including Long Beach Island, Cape May and Ocean City, New Jersey. Each issue includes a mix of news, human interest features, opinion columns and entertainment/calendar listings." Estab. 1976. Circ. 60,000. Pays on publication. Publishes ms an average of 1 month after acceptance. Byline given. Offers 100% kill fee. Buys first or all rights. Submit seasonal material 3 months in advance. Accepts simultaneous and previously published submissions. Send photocopy of article and information about when and where it previously appeared. Pays 25-50% of their fee for an original article.. Reports in 1 month. Sample copy for 9×12 SAE with 8 first-class stamps.

Nonfiction: Essays, general interest, historical/nostalgic, humor, opinion, environmental submissions relating to the ocean, wetlands and pinelands. Must pertain to New Jersey shore locale. Also, arts, entertainment news, reviews if they have a Jersey shore angle. Buys 10 mss/year. Send complete ms. Length: 200-2,000 words. Pays $25-200. Sometimes pays the expenses of writers on assignment.

Photos: Send photos with submission. Offers $8-25/photo. Buys one-time or all rights.

Columns/Departments: SpeakEasy (opinion and slice-of-life; often humorous); Commentary (forum for social science perspectives); both 1,000-1,500 words, preferably with local or Jersey shore angle. Buys 50 mss/year. Send complete ms. Pays $30.

Tips: "Anything of interest to sun worshippers, beach walkers, nature watchers, water sports lovers is of potential interest to us. There is an increasing coverage of environmental issues. The opinion page and columns are most open to freelancers. We are steadily increasing the amount of entertainment-related material in our publication. Articles on history of the shore area are always in demand."

New Mexico

NEW MEXICO MAGAZINE, Lew Wallace Bldg., 495 Old Santa Fe Trail, Santa Fe NM 87503. Editor-in-Chief: Emily Drabanski. Editor: Jon Bowman. Associate Editors: Walter K. Lopez, Camille Flores-Turney. 80% freelance written. Monthly magazine emphasizing New Mexico for a college-educated readership, above average income, interested in the Southwest. Estab. 1922. Circ. 125,000. **Pays on acceptance.** Publishes ms an average of 6 months to a year after acceptance. Buys first North American serial rights. Submit seasonal material 1 year in advance. Reports in 2 months. Sample copy for $2.95. Free writer's guidelines.

Nonfiction: New Mexico subjects of interest to travelers. Historical, cultural, informational articles. "We are looking for more short, light and bright stories for the 'Asi Es Nuevo Mexico' section." No columns, cartoons, poetry or non-New Mexico subjects. Buys 5-7 mss/issue. Query with 3 published writing samples. No phone or fax queries. Length: 250-2,000 words. Pays $100-500.

  • This magazine rarely publishes reprints but sometimes publishes excerpts from novels and nonfiction books.

Photos: Purchased with accompanying ms or on assignment. Query or send contact sheet or transparencies. Pays $50-80 for 8×10 b&w glossy prints; $50-150 for 35mm—prefers Kodachrome. Photos should be in plastic-pocketed viewing sheets. Captions and model releases required. Mail photos to Art Director John Vaughan. Buys one-time rights.

Tips: "Send a superb short (300 words) manuscript on a little-known person, event, aspect of history or place to see in New Mexico. Faulty research will ruin a writer's chances for the future. Good style, good grammar. No generalized odes to the state or the Southwest. No sentimentalized, paternalistic views of Indians or Hispanics. No glib, gimmicky 'travel brochure' writing. No first-person vacation stories. We're always looking for well-researched pieces on unusual aspects of New Mexico history. Lively writing."

New York

ADIRONDACK LIFE, P.O. Box 97, Jay NY 12941-0097. Fax: (518)946-7461. Editor: Tom Hughes. 70% freelance written. Prefers to work with published/established writers. Emphasizes the Adirondack region and the North Country of New York State in articles concerning outdoor activities, history, and natural history directly related to the Adirondacks. Publishes 7 issues/year, including special Annual Outdoor Guide. Estab. 1970. Circ. 50,000. Pays 45 days after acceptance. Publishes ms an average of 6 months after acceptance. Buys one-time rights. Byline given. Submit seasonal material 1 year in advance. Reports in 1 month. Sample copy for 9 × 12 SAE with 8 first-class stamps. Writer's guidelines for #10 SASE.
Nonfiction: "*Adirondack Life* attempts to capture the unique flavor and ethos of the Adirondack mountains and North Country region through feature articles directly pertaining to the qualities of the area and through department articles examining specific aspects. Example: Barkeater: personal essay; Special Places: unique spots in the Adirondacks; Working: careers in the Adirondacks and Wilderness: environmental issues, personal experiences." Buys 20-25 unsolicited mss/year. Query. Length: for features, 5,000 words maximum; for departments, 1,800 words. Pays up to 25¢/word. Sometimes pays expenses of writers on assignment.
• Also considers novel excerpts in its subject matter.
Photos: All photos must have been taken in the Adirondacks. Each issue contains a photo feature. Purchased with or without ms or on assignment. All photos must be identified as to subject or locale and must bear photographer's name. Submit color slides or b&w prints. Pays $25 for b&w prints; $50 for transparencies; $300 for cover (color only, vertical in format). Credit line given.
Tips: "We are looking for clear, concise, well-organized manuscripts, that are strictly Adirondack in subject."

BUFFALO SPREE MAGAZINE, Spree Publishing Co., Inc., Dept. WM, 4511 Harlem Rd., Buffalo NY 14226-3859. (716)839-3405. Editor: Johanna V. Shotell. Contact: Alyssa Chase, associate editor. 90% freelance written. Quarterly literary, consumer-oriented, city magazine. Estab. 1967. Circ. 21,000. Pays on publication. Publishes ms an average of 6-12 months after acceptance. Byline given. Buys first North American serial rights. Submit seasonal material 9-12 months in advance. Reports in 6 months on mss. Sample copy for $2 and 9 × 12 SAE with 9 first-class stamps.
Nonfiction: Essays, interview/profile, historical/nostalgic, humor, personal experience, travel. Buys 50 mss/year. Send complete ms. Length: 600-2,000 words. Pays $100-150 for unsolicited articles.
Photos: Send photos with submission. Reviews prints (any size). Offers no additional payment for photos accepted with ms. Captions required. Buys one-time rights.
Fiction: Experimental, mainstream. "No pornographic or religious manuscripts." Buys 60 mss/year. Send complete ms. Length: 500-2,000 words. Pays $100-150.
Poetry: Janet Goldenberg, poetry editor. Buys 24 poems/year. Submit maximum 4 poems. Length: 50 lines maximum. Pays $25.

CITY LIMITS, City Limits Community Information Service, Inc., 40 Prince St., New York NY 10012. (212)925-9820. Fax: (212)996-3407. Editor: Andrew White. Senior Editor: Jill Kirschenbaum. Associate Editor: Steve Mitra. 50% freelance written. Works with a small number of new/unpublished writers each year. Monthly magazine covering housing and related urban issues. "We cover news and issues in New York City as they relate to the city's poor, moderate and middle-income residents." Estab. 1976. Circ. 5,000. Pays on publication. Publishes ms an average of 1-2 months after acceptance. Byline given. Buys first North American serial, one-time, or second serial (reprint) rights. Query for electronic submissions. Reports in 3 weeks. Sample copy for $2.
Nonfiction: Exposé, interview/profile, opinion, hard news, community profile. "No fluff, no propaganda." Length: 600-2,500 words. Pays $50-150. Sometimes pays expenses of writers on assignment.
Photos: Reviews contact sheets and 5 × 7 prints. Offers $10-40/photo, cover only. Identification of subjects required. Buys one-time rights.
Columns/Departments: Short Term Notes (brief descriptions of programs, policies, events, etc.), 250-400 words; Book Reviews (housing, urban development, planning, etc.), 250-600 words; Pipeline (covers community organizations, new programs, government policies, etc.), 600-800 words; People (who are active in organizations, community groups, etc.), 600-800 words; Organize (groups involved in housing, job programs, health care, etc.), 600-800 words. Buys 50-75 mss/year. Query with published clips or send complete ms. Pays $25-100.
Tips: "We are open to a wide range of story ideas in the community development field. If you don't have particular expertise in housing, urban planning etc., start with a community profile or pertinent book or film review. Short Term Notes is also good for anyone with reporting skills. We're looking for writing that is serious and informed but not academic or heavy handed."

HUDSON VALLEY MAGAZINE, Suburban Publishing, P.O. Box 429, Poughkeepsie NY 12601-3109. (914)485-7844. Fax: (914)485-5975. Editor-in-Chief: Susan Agrest. Monthly magazine. Estab. 1971. Circ. 27,000. Pays on publication. Byline given. Offers 25% kill fee. Buys first North American serial rights or first rights. Submit seasonal material 3 months in advance. Query for electronic submissions. Accepts previously published submissions. Send tearsheet, photocopy of article or short story and information about when and where the material previously appeared. Reports in 6 months. Sample copy for $1 and 11×14 SAE with 4 first-class stamps.

Nonfiction: Only articles related to the Hudson Valley. Book excerpts, exposé, general interest, historical/nostalgic, how-to, humor, interview/profile, new product, opinion, photo feature, travel, business. Buys 150 mss/year. Query with published clips. Length: 300-3,500 words. Pays $25-800 for assigned articles.

Photos: Send photos with submission. Captions, model releases, identification of subjects required.

Columns/Departments: Open Season (advocacy/editorial); Environs (environmental); Pleasure Grounds; Charmed Places (homes); and Slice of Life (essays). Query with published clips. Length: 1,200-1,500 words. Pays $75-200.

Fiction: Novel excerpts rarely accepted.

Fillers: Anecdotes, facts, newsbreaks. Buys 36/year. Length: 300-500 words. Pays $25-50.

Tips: "Send a letter, résumé, sample of best writing and queries. No manuscripts. Factual accuracy imperative."

NEW YORK MAGAZINE, K-III Magazine Corp., 755 Second Ave., New York NY 10017-5998. (212)880-0700. Editor: Kurt Andersen. Managing Editor: Sarah Jewler. 25% freelance written. Weekly magazine focusing on current events in the New York metropolitan area. Circ. 433,813. **Pays on acceptance.** Offers 10% kill fee. Buys first North American serial rights. Submit seasonal material 2 months in advance. Reports in 1 month. Sample copy for $3.50. Writer's guidelines for SASE.

Nonfiction: Exposé, general interest, profile, new product, personal experience, travel. Query. Pays 75¢-$1.25/word. Pays expenses of writers on assignment.

Tips: "Submit a detailed query to Sarah Jewler, *New York*'s managing editor. If there is sufficient interest in the proposed piece, the article will be assigned."

NEWSDAY, Melville NY 11747-4250. Viewpoints Editor: Noel Rubinton. Opinion section of daily newspaper. Byline given. Estab. 1940.

Nonfiction: Seeks "opinion on current events, trends, issues—whether national or local, government or lifestyle. Must be timely, pertinent, articulate and opinionated. Preference for authors within the circulation area including New York City." Length: 700-800 words. Pays $150-200.

Tips: "It helps for prospective authors to be familiar with our paper and section."

SPOTLIGHT MAGAZINE, Meadown Publications Inc., 126 Library Lane, Mamaroneck NY 10543. (914)381-4740. Fax: (914)381-4641. Editor: Marcia Hecht. 10% freelance written. Monthly magazine of general interest. Audience is "anyone who's literate in the NY-NJ-CT tristate area. We try to appeal to a broad audience throughout our publication area." Estab. 1977. Circ. 73,000. Pays on publication. Byline given. Buys first rights. Editorial lead time 3 months. Submit seasonal material 5 months in advance. Query for electronic submissions. Reports in 3 weeks on queries; 2 months on mss. Sample copy for $3. Writer's guidelines for #10 SASE.

Nonfiction: Book excerpts, essays, exposé, general interest, historical/nostalgic, how-to, humor, inspirational, interview/profile, new product, photo feature, travel, illustrations. Publishes annual special-interest guides: Wedding (February, June, September); Dining (December); Home Design (April, October); Parenting (May); Travel (June, November); Health (July, January); Education (January, August); Holiday Gifts (December). Does not want to see fiction or poetry. Buys 5-10 mss/year. Query. Pays $50 minimum. Sometimes pays expenses of writers on assignment.

Photos: State availability of or send photos with submission. Reviews transparencies and prints. Negotiates payment individually. Captions, model releases, identification of subjects required (when appropriate). Buys one-time rights.

Columns/Departments: 'Spotlight' (profiles), 600-750 words. Buys 3-5 mss/year. Query. Pays $75.

Tips: "Write a letter asking for info."

‡SYRACUSE NEW TIMES, A. Zimmer Ltd., 1415 W. Genesee St., Syracuse NY 13204. Editor: Mike Greenstein. 50% freelance written. Weekly tabloid covering news, sports, arts and entertainment. "*The New Times* is an alternative weekly that can be topical, provocative, irreverent and intensely local." Estab. 1969. Circ. 45,000. Pays on publication. Publishes ms an average of 1 month after acceptance. Byline given. Buys one-time rights. Editorial lead time 3 months. Submit seasonal material 3 months in advance. Accepts simultaneous and previously published submissions. Query for electronic submissions. Reports in 2 weeks on queries; 1 month on mss. Sample copy for 9×11 SAE with 2 first-class stamps. Writer's guidelines for #10 SASE.

Nonfiction: Essays, general interest. Buys 200 mss/year. Query with published clips. Length: 250-2,500 words. Pays $25.

Photos: State availability of photos or send photos with submission. Reviews 8×10 prints. Offers $10-25/photo or negotiates payment individually. Identification of subjects required. Buys one-time rights.

Tips: "Move to Syracuse and query with strong idea."

North Carolina

CHARLOTTE MAGAZINE, The New Charlotte Magazine, Inc., P.O. Box 11048, Charlotte NC 28220-1048. (704)366-5000. Editor: Bob Dill. 90% freelance written. Bimonthly magazine for Charlotte and regional NC lifestyles. "Though expanding, our current readership is largely female, 25-50. Our audience as a whole is urban, upscale, well-educated, and an ad mixture of native Charlotte or N. Carolinians and young, mobile professionals making a warmer life in the sunbelt." Estab. 1978. Circ. 20,000. Pays on publication. Publishes ms an average of 1-2 months after acceptance. Byline given. Buys first North American serial rights. Editorial lead time 2 months. Submit seasonal material 4 months in advance. Accepts simultaneous and previously published submissions. Query for electronic submissions. Reports in 2 weeks on queries. Sample copy for 9 × 12 SAE. Writer's guidelines for #10 SASE.
Nonfiction: Essays, exposé, general interest, historical/nostalgic, how-to, humor, interview/profile, personal experience, photo feature, travel. "No generic how-to, pieces with no Charlotte or regional connection, humor with no Charlotte connection or syndicated (self or otherwise) material." Buys 30 mss/year. Query with published clips. Length: 750-2,500 words. Pays 12¢/word. Pays in contributor's copies "At request of the writers. Not usual, though it has happened." Sometimes pays expenses of writers on assignment.
Photos: Send photos with submission. Reviews transparencies and prints. Negotiates payment individually. Model releases and identification of subjects required. Buys one-time rights.
Columns/Departments: Essays (well written, humorous short essays on topics of interest to people who live in Charlotte), 750-1,000 words. Pays 12¢/word minimum; negotiable.
Fiction: "We run fiction once a year in our summer reading issue." Buys 1-2 mss/year. Query.
Poetry: "We are considering poetry (short) by Charlotte poets only."
Tips: "For us, a strong feature idea is the best way to break in. New or interesting Charlotte or NC slants on travel, fashion, personalities, are sought constantly here."

THE STATE, Down Home in North Carolina, Suite 2200, 128 S. Tryon St., Charlotte NC 28202. Fax: (704)375-8129. Managing Editor: Scott Smith. 90% freelance written. Monthly. Circ. 23,000. Publishes ms an average of 6-12 months after acceptance. Byline given. No kill fee. Buys first serial rights. Pays on publication. Submit seasonal material 8-12 months in advance. Reports in 2 months. Sample copy for $2.50.
Nonfiction: General articles about places, people, events, history, nostalgia, general interest in North Carolina. Emphasis on travel in North Carolina. Will use humor if related to region. Length: 700-2,000 words average. Pays $125-150 for assigned articles; $75-125 for unsolicited articles.
Photos: Send photos with submission. Reviews contact sheets and transparencies. Offers no additional payment for photos. Captions and identification of subjects required. Buys one-time rights.
Columns/Departments: The State We're In (newsbriefs about current events in NC; most have travel, historic or environmental slant), 150-500 words. Buys 10 mss/year. Pays $25.

Ohio

BEACON MAGAZINE, Akron Beacon Journal, P.O. Box 640, Akron OH 44309-0640. (216)996-3586. Editor: Ann Sheldon Mezger. 25% freelance written. Works with a small number of new/unpublished writers each year. Sunday newspaper magazine of general interest articles with a focus on Northeast Ohio. Circ. 225,000. Pays on publication. Publishes ms an average of 2 months after acceptance. Byline given. Offers 50% kill fee. Buys one-time, simultaneous and second serial (reprint) rights. Submit seasonal material 3 months in advance. Accepts simultaneous and previously published submissions. Send typed ms with rights for sale noted and information about when and where the article previously appeared. Pays 50% of their fee for an original article. Reports in 1 month. Free sample copy and writer's guidelines.
Nonfiction: General interest, historical/nostalgic, short humor, and interview/profile. Buys 50 mss/year. Query with or without published clips. Include Social Security number with story submission. Length: 500-3,000 words. Pays $75-550. Sometimes pays expenses of writers on assignment.
Photos: Send photos. Pays $25-50 for 35mm color transparencies and 8 × 10 b&w prints. Captions and identification of subjects required. Buys one-time rights.

BEND OF THE RIVER MAGAZINE, P.O. Box 39, Perrysburg OH 43552-0039. (419)874-7534. Fax: (419)874-1466. Publisher: R. Lee Raizk. 90% freelance written. Eager to work with new/unpublished writers. "We buy material that we like whether by an experienced writer or not." Monthly magazine for readers interested in Ohio history, antiques, etc. Estab. 1972. Circ. 4,500. Pays on publication. Publishes ms an average of 6 months after acceptance. Byline given. Buys one-time rights. Submit seasonal material 2 months in advance; deadline for holiday issue is November 1. Reports in up to 6 months. Sample copy for $1.50.
Nonfiction: "We deal heavily in Northwestern Ohio history. We are looking for well-researched articles about local history and nostalgia. We'd like to see interviews with historical (Ohio) authorities; articles about grass roots farmers, famous people from Ohio like Doris Day, Gloria Steinem, etc. and preservation. Buys 75 unsolicited mss/year. Submit complete ms or send query. Length: 1,500 words. Pays $10-25.

Photos: Purchases b&w or color photos with accompanying mss. Pays $2 minimum. Captions required.
Tips: "Any Toledo area, well-researched history will be put on top of the heap. We like articles about historical topics treated in down-to-earth conversational tones. If you send a picture with manuscript, it gets an A+! We pay a small amount but usually use our writers often and through the years. We're loyal."

CINCINNATI MAGAZINE, 409 Broadway, Cincinnati OH 45202-3340. (513)421-4300. Editorial Director: Felix Winternitz. Homes Editor: Linda Vaccariello. Food Editor: Lilia F. Brady. Monthly magazine emphasizing Cincinnati living. Circ. 32,000. **Pays on acceptance.** Byline given. Buys first rights. Submit seasonal material 4 months in advance. Accepts simultaneous and previously published submissions. Send photocopy of article and information about when and where the article previously appeared. For reprints pays 33% of the amount paid for an original article. Reports in 2 months.
Nonfiction: Profiles of Cincinnati celebrities, local business, trend stories. Buys 1 ms/issue. Query. Length: 2,000-4,000 words. Pays $150-400.
Columns/Departments: Cincinnati dining, media, arts and entertainment, people, politics, sports. Buys 2 mss/issue. Query. Length: 750-1,500 words. Pays $75-150.
Tips: "We do special features each month. January (Homes); February (Dining out, restaurants); March (Health, Personal finance); April (Home and Fashion); May (Environment and Golf); June (Health); July (Food and Homes); August (Fashion); September (Homes); October (Best and Worst); November (Automotive Guide and Fashion); December (City guide). We also have a special issue in August where we feature a local fiction contest."

‡**NORTHERN OHIO LIVE,** LIVE Publishing Co., 11320 Juniper Rd., Cleveland OH 44106. (216)721-1800. Managing Editor: Shari M. Sweeney. Contact: Michael von Glahn, editor. 70% freelance written. Monthly magazine covering Northern Ohio's arts, entertainment, education and dining. "*Live*'s reader demographic is mid-30s to 50s, though we're working to bring in the late 20s. Our readers are well-educated, many with advanced degrees. They're interested in Northern Ohio's cultural scene and support it." Estab. 1980. Circ. 32,000. Pays 20th of publication month. Publishes ms an average of 1 month after acceptance. Byline given. Offers 50% kill fee. Buys first North American serial rights. Editorial lead time 2 months. Submit seasonal material 3-4 months in advance. Query for electronic submissions. Reports in 3 weeks on queries; 2 months on mss. Sample copy for $2.
Nonfiction: Essays, exposé, general interest, humor, interview/profile, photo feature, travel. All should have a Northern Ohio slant and preferably an arts focus. Special issues: Gourmet Guide (restaurants) (May); Gallery Tour (May, October); After 5 (nightlife) (November). "No business/corporate articles, stories outside Northern Ohio." Buys 100 mss/year. Query with published clips. Length: 1,000-3,500 words. Pays $100. Sometimes pays expenses of writers on assignment.
Photos: State availability of photos with submission. Reviews contact sheets, 4×5 transparencies and 3×5 prints. Negotiates payment individually. Identification of subjects required. Buys one-time rights.
Columns/Departments: News & Reviews (arts previews, personality profiles, general interest), 1,000-1,800 words. Buys 60-70 mss/year. Query with published clips. Pays $100-150.

OHIO MAGAZINE, Ohio Magazine, Inc., Subsidiary of Dispatch Printing Co., 62 E. Broad St., Columbus OH 43215-3522. (614)461-5083. Editor: Casandra Ring. 40% freelance written. Works with a small number of new/unpublished writers each year. Monthly magazine emphasizing news and feature material of Ohio for an educated, urban and urbane readership. Estab. 1978. Circ. 100,000. Pays on publication. Publishes ms an average of 5 months after acceptance. Buys all, second serial (reprint), one-time, first North American serial or first serial rights. Byline given except on short articles appearing in sections. Submit seasonal material minimum 6 months in advance. Accepts previously published submissions. Send tearsheet or photocopy of article and information about when and where it previously appeared. Pays 50% of their fee for an original article. Reports in 2 months. Sample copy for $3 and 9×12 SAE. Writer's guidelines for #10 SASE.
Nonfiction: Features: 2,000-8,000 words. Pays $800-1,400. Cover pieces $650-1,200. Sometimes pays expenses of writers on assignment.
Columns/Departments: Ohioans (should be offbeat with solid news interest; 1,000-2,000 words, pays $300-500); Business (covering business related news items, profiles of prominent people in business community, personal finance—all Ohio angle; 1,000 words and up, pays $300-500); Environment (issues related to Ohio and Ohioans, 1,000-2,000 words, pays $400-700). Buys minimum 40 unsolicited mss/year.
Photos: Brooke Wenstrup, art director. Rate negotiable.
Tips: "Freelancers should send a brief prospectus if complete ms is not ready for submission. All articles should have a definite Ohio application. We need more columns and short features—especially original profile ideas."

PLAIN DEALER MAGAZINE, Plain Dealer Publishing Co., 1801 Superior Ave., Cleveland OH 44114. (216)344-4546. Fax: (216)999-6354. Editor: Anne Gordon. 30% freelance written. Sunday weekly/general interest newspaper magazine focusing on Cleveland and northeastern Ohio. Circ. 550,000. Pays on publication. Publishes ms an average of 2-3 months after acceptance. Byline given. Buys first or one-time rights. Submit seasonal/holiday material 3 months in advance. Occasionally accepts previously published submissions. Send typed ms with rights for sale noted and information about when and where the article previously appeared. Reports in 1 month on queries; 2 months on mss. Sample copy for $1.

Nonfiction: Profiles, in-depth features, essays, exposé, historical/nostalgic, humor, personal experience. Must focus on northeast Ohio, people, places and issues of the area. Buys 20 mss/year. Query with published clips or send complete ms. Manuscripts must be double-spaced and should include a daytime telephone number. Length: 800-3,000 words. Pays $150-500.

Photos: Send photos with submission. Buys one-time rights.

Tips: "We're always looking for good writers and good stories."

Oklahoma

OKLAHOMA TODAY, P.O. Box 53384, Oklahoma City OK 73152-9971. Fax: (405)521-3992. Editor: Jeanne M. Devlin. 80% freelance written. Works with a small number of new/unpublished writers each year. Bimonthly magazine covering people, places and things Oklahoman. "We are interested in showing off the best Oklahoma has to offer; we're pretty serious about our travel slant but regularly run history, nature and personality profiles." Estab. 1956. Circ. 45,000. **Pays on final acceptance.** Publishes ms an average of 6 months after acceptance. Byline given. Buys first serial rights. Submit seasonal material 1 year in advance "depending on photographic requirements." Accepts previously published submissions. Send tearsheet of article or typed ms with rights for sale noted and information about when and where the article previously appeared. Reports in 3-4 months. Sample copy for $2.50 and 9×12 SASE. Writer's guidelines for #10 SASE.

Nonfiction: Book excerpts (pre-publication only, on Oklahoma topics); photo feature and travel (in Oklahoma). Buys 40-60 mss/year. Query with published clips; no phone queries. Length: 1,000-3,000 words. Pays $25-750.

• This market is seeking a variety of styles, from first person to essay.

Photos: High-quality transparencies, b&w prints. "We are especially interested in developing contacts with photographers who either live in Oklahoma or have shot here. Send samples and price range." Free photo guidelines with SASE. Pays $50-100 for b&w and $50-750 for color; reviews 2¼ and 35mm color transparencies. Model releases, identification of subjects, other information for captions required. Buys one-time rights plus right to use photos for promotional purposes.

Tips: "The best way to become a regular contributor to *Oklahoma Today* is to query us with one or more story ideas, each developed to give us an idea of your proposed slant. We're looking for *lively*, concise, well-researched and reported stories, stories that don't need to be heavily edited and are not newspaper style. We have a two-person editorial staff, and freelancers who can write and have done their homework get called again and again."

Oregon

CASCADES EAST, P.O. Box 5784, Bend OR 97708-5784. (503)382-0127. Fax: (503)382-7057. Editor: Geoff Hill. Contact: Kim Hill, associate publisher. 90% freelance written. Prefers to work with published/established writers. Quarterly magazine for "all ages as long as they are interested in outdoor recreation in central Oregon: fishing, hunting, sight-seeing, golf, tennis, hiking, bicycling, mountain climbing, backpacking, rockhounding, skiing, snowmobiling, etc." Estab. 1972. Circ. 10,000 (distributed throughout area resorts and motels and to subscribers). Pays on publication. Publishes ms an average of 6 months after acceptance. Buys all rights. Byline given. Submit seasonal material 6 months in advance. Reports in 3 months. Sample copy and writer's guidelines for $4 and 9×12 SAE.

Nonfiction: General interest (first person experiences in outdoor central Oregon—with photos, can be dramatic, humorous or factual), historical (for feature, "Little Known Tales from Oregon History," with b&w photos), personal experience (needed on outdoor subjects: dramatic, humorous or factual). "No articles that are too general, sight-seeing articles that come from a travel folder, or outdoor articles without the first-person approach." Buys 20-30 unsolicited mss/year. Query. Length: 1,000-3,000 words. Pays 5-10¢/word.

Photos: "Old photos will greatly enhance chances of selling a historical feature. First-person articles need b&w photos, also." Pays $10-25 for b&w; $15-100 for transparencies. Captions preferred. Buys one-time rights.

Tips: "Submit stories a year or so in advance of publication. We are seasonal and must plan editorials for summer '94 in the spring of '93, etc., in case seasonal photos are needed."

OREGON COAST, The Bi-Monthly Magazine of Coastal Living, 1525 12th St., Florence OR 97439-0130. (800)348-8401. Managing Editor: Judy Fleagle. Senior Editor: Dave Peden. 75% freelance written. Bimonthly magazine covering the Oregon Coast. Estab. 1982. Circ. 65,000. Pays on publication. Publishes ms an average of 6-12 months after acceptance. Byline given. Offers 33% kill fee. Buys first North American serial rights. Submit seasonal material 6 months in advance. Query for electronic submissions. Reports in 1 month on queries; 3 months on mss. Sample copy for $4.50. Writer's guidelines for #10 SASE.

Nonfiction: "A true regional with general interest, historical/nostalgic, humor, interview/profile, personal experience, photo feature, travel and nature as pertains to Oregon Coast." Buys 60 mss/year. Query with published clips. Length: 500-2,000 words. Pays $75-350 plus 2-5 contributor copies.

Photos: Send photos with submission. Reviews 35mm or larger transparencies and 3 × 5 or larger prints. Offers no additional payment for photos accepted with ms. Photo submissions with no ms for stand alone or cover photos. Captions, model releases, photo credits, identification of subjects required. Buys one-time rights.

Fillers: Newsbreaks (no-fee basis) and short articles. Buys 12/year. Length: 300-500 words. Pays $35-50.

Tips: "Slant article for readers who do not live at the Oregon Coast. At least one historical article is used in each issue. Manuscript/photo packages are preferred over mss with no photos. List photo credits and captions for each print or slide. Check all facts, proper names and numbers carefully in photo/ms packages."

‡OREGON PARKS, Educational Publications Foundation, P.O. Box 18000, Florence OR 97439. (503)997-8401. Editor: Dave Peden. Managing Editor: Judy Fleagle. Editorial contact (submissions): Dave Peden or Judy Fleagle. 50% freelance written. Consumer publication. Bimonthly trade magazine covering parklands in Oregon/other public lands. "The magazine, which was begun with the active participation of the state parks department, aims to inform Oregonians and visitors about the parks and public lands in Oregon, their facilities, services, and issues." Estab. 1993. Circ. 20,000. Pays on publication. Byline given. Offers 33% kill fee. Buys first North American serial rights (for ms and ms/photo packages). Editorial lead time 4-6 months. Submit seasonal material 6 months in advance. Query for electronic submissions. Reports in 6 weeks on queries. Sample copy for $4.50. Writer's guidelines for #10 SASE.

Nonfiction: General interest, historical/nostalgic, photo feature, travel. "No interest in non-Oregon articles, or articles on wilderness areas in Oregon. Don't need spotted owl stories." Buys 45-55 mss/year. Query with or without published clips. Length: 500-2,000 words. Pays $75 minimum for unsolicited articles.

Photos: State availability of photos with query. Reviews transparencies. Captions, model releases (if person is readily identifiable) and credits required.

Tips: "Looking for interesting activity-oriented articles placed in parks (not necessarily state parks) and forestlands in Oregon. Lively writing and great photos are the best entree to the magazine. Pick a city or county park that you think is great, but not well known outside of your local area. Query first and have photos available — transparencies if possible."

Pennsylvania

PENNSYLVANIA, Pennsylvania Magazine Co., P.O. Box 576, Camp Hill PA 17001-0576. (717)761-6620. Publisher: Albert E. Holliday. Managing Editor: Joan Holliday. 90% freelance written. Bimonthly magazine. Estab. 1981. Circ. 40,000. Pays on acceptance except for articles (by authors unknown to us) sent on speculation. Publishes ms an average of 6-12 months after acceptance. Byline given. Offers 25% kill fee for assigned articles. Buys first North American serial or one-time rights. Accepts previously published submissions. Send tearsheet or photocopy of article and information about when and where the article previously appeared. Pays 50% of their fee for an original article. Reports in 1 month. Sample copy for $2.95. Writer's guidelines for #10 SASE.

Nonfiction: General interest, historical/nostalgic, photo feature, travel — all dealing with or related to Pennsylvania. Nothing on Amish topics, hunting or skiing. Buys 50-75 mss/year. Query. Length: 250-2,500 words. Pays $50-400. Sometimes pays the expenses of writers on assignment. All articles must be illustrated; send photocopies of possible illustrations with query or mss. *Will not consider without illustrations.*

Photos: Reviews 35mm and 2¼ color transparencies (no originals) and 5 × 7 to 8 × 10 color and b&w prints. Pays $15-50 for inside photos; up to $100 for covers. Captions required. Buys one-time rights.

Columns/Departments: Panorama (short items about people, unusual events); Made in Pennsylvania (short items about family and individually owned consumer-related businesses); Almanac (short historical items). All must be illustrated.

‡PENNSYLVANIA HERITAGE, Pennsylvania Historical and Museum Commission, P.O. Box 1026, Harrisburg PA 17108-1026. (717)787-7522. Fax: (717)787-8312. Editor: Michael J. O'Malley III. 90% freelance written. Prefers to work with published/established writers. Quarterly magazine. "*Pennsylvania Heritage* introduces readers to Pennsylvania's rich culture and historic legacy, educates and sensitizes them to the value of preserving that heritage and entertains and involves them in such as way as to ensure that Pennsylvania's past has a future. The magazine is intended for intelligent lay readers." Estab. 1974. Circ. 10,000. **Pays on acceptance.** Publishes ms an average of 1 year after acceptance. Byline given. Buys all rights. Accepts simultaneous queries and submissions. Reports in 6 weeks on queries; 3-6 months on mss. Sample copy for $5 and 9 × 12 SAE; writer's guidelines for #10 SASE.

Nonfiction: Art, science, biographies, industry, business, politics, transportation, military, historic preservation, archaeology, photography, etc. No articles which in no way relate to Pennsylvania history or culture. "Our format requires feature-length articles. Manuscripts with illustrations are especially sought for publication. We are now looking for shorter (2,000 words) manuscripts that are heavily illustrated with *Publication-quality* photographs or artwork." Buys 20-24 mss/year. Query; prefers to see mss of shorter pieces. Length: 2,000-3,500 words. Pays $300-750.

Photos: State availability of, or send photos with query or ms. Pays $25-100 for transparencies; $5-10 for b&w photos. Captions and identification of subjects required. Buys one-time rights.

Tips: "We are looking for well-written, interesting material that pertains to any aspect of Pennsylvania history or culture. Potential contributors should realize that, although our articles are popularly styled, they are not light, puffy or breezy; in fact they demand strident documentation and substantiation (sans footnotes). The most frequent mistake made by writers in completing articles for us is making them either too scholarly or too nostalgic. We want material which educates, but also entertains. Authors should make history readable and entertaining."

PITTSBURGH MAGAZINE, QED Communications, Inc., 4802 5th Ave., Pittsburgh PA 15213. (412)622-1360. Fax: (412)622-7066. No phone queries. Send queries to Michelle Pilecki, Managing Editor. 60% freelance written. Prefers to work with published/established writers. The magazine is purchased on newsstands and by subscription and is given to those who contribute $40 or more a year to public TV in western Pennsylvania. Estab. 1970. Circ. 65,000. Pays on publication. Publishes ms an average of 2 months after acceptance. Buys first North American serial rights and second serial (reprint) rights. Offers kill fee. Byline given. Submit seasonal material 6 months in advance. Query for electronic submissions. Reports in 2 months. Sample copy for $2 (old back issues).
  • Editor reports a need for more hard news and more stories geared to young readers.
Nonfiction: Exposé, lifestyle, sports, informational, service, business, medical, profile. Must have regional angle. Query with outline. Length: 2,500 words or less. Pays $100-1,200.
Photos: Query for photos. Model releases required. Sometimes pays the expenses of writers on assignment.

Rhode Island

RHODE ISLAND MONTHLY, Dept. WM, 18 Imperial Place, Providence RI 02903-4641. (401)421-2552. Fax: (401)831-5624. Editor: Dan Kaplan. Managing Editor: Vicki Sanders. 90% freelance written. Monthly magazine on Rhode Island living. Estab. 1988. Circ. 26,000. Pays on publication. Publishes ms an average of 2 months after acceptance. Byline given. Kill fee varies. Buys first rights. Submit seasonal material 4 months in advance. Query for electronic submissions. Sample copy for $2.50 for 9 × 12 SAE with $1.52 postage.
Nonfiction: Profiles, human interest features, exposé, photo feature. "We do not want material unrelated to Rhode Island." Buys 48 mss/year. Query with published clips. Length: 200-6,000 words. Pays $100-1,000. Pays expenses of writers on assignment for stories over $400.
Photos: Send photos with submission. Reviews contact sheets and 5 × 7 prints. Offers $50-200. Captions, model releases and identification of subjects required. Buys one-time rights.

THE RHODE ISLANDER MAGAZINE, Providence Journal Co., 75 Fountain St., Providence RI 02902. (401)277-7349. Fax: (401)277-7346. Editor: Elliot Krieger. 50% freelance written. Weekly Sunday supplement magazine about news of Rhode Island and New England. Estab. 1946. Circ. 250,000. Pays on publication. Byline given. Buys first North American serial rights. Submit seasonal/holiday 3 months in advance. Accepts simultaneous and previously published submissions. Send tearsheet or send typed ms with rights for sale noted. For reprints pays 50% of the amount paid for an original article. Query for electronic submissions. Reports in 1 month on queries.
  • This magazine is currently seeking more short pieces, containing less than 500 words.
Nonfiction: Book excerpts, exposé, general interest, historical/nostalgic, interview/profile, photo feature. "We are strictly a regional news magazine." No fiction or poetry. Buys 100 mss/year. Query. Length: 250-5,000. Pays $50-500.
Photos: Send photos with submission. Offers $25-100/photo. Captions and identification of subjects required.

South Carolina

CHARLESTON MAGAZINE, P.O. Box 21770, Charleston SC 29413-1770. (803)722-8018. Fax: (803)722-8116. Editors: Dawn Leggett. Associate Editor: Louise Chase. 95% freelance written. Monthly magazine covering the Lowcountry South Carolina, the South as a region. "Consumer magazine with a general focus each issue that reflects an essential element of Charleston life and Lowcountry living. Estab. 1986. Circ. 20,000. Pays on publication. Publishes ms an average of 3 months after acceptance. Byline given. Buys one-time rights. Submit seasonal material 4 months in advance. Query for electronic submissions. Reports in 2 months. Sample copies for 9 × 12 SAE with 5 first-class stamps. Free writer's guidelines.
Nonfiction: Book excerpts, essays, general interest, historical/nostalgic, humor, food, architecture, sports, interview/profile, opinion, personal experience, photo feature, travel, current events, art. "Each issue has a focus—these themes are listed in our writer's guidelines. Not interested in general interest articles. Must pertain to the Charleston area or, at their broadest scope, the South as a region." Buys 120 mss/year. Query with published clips. Length: 150-1,500 words. Pays 10¢/published word. Sometimes pays expenses of writers on assignment.
Photos: Send photos with submission if available. Reviews contact sheets, transparencies, slides. Offers $35 maximum/photo. Captions and identification of subjects required. Buys one-time rights.
Columns/Departments: Channel Markers (general interest), 50-150 words; Hindsight (historical perspectives and local Lowcountry interest), 1,000-1,200 words; First Person (profile—people of local interest), 1,000-

1,200 words; Art (features a successful or innovative artist), 1,000-1,200 words; Architecture (renovations, restorations or new constructions of Lowcountry houses), 1,000 words; sporting Life (humorous, adventurous tales of life outdoors), 1,000-1,200 words; Southern View (expanded editorial page in which a person expresses his or her view on the South), 750 words; Great Tastes (thought-provoking pieces on regional food), 1,000-1,200 words.
Tips: "Follow our writer's guidelines. Areas most open to freelancers are Columns/Departments and features. Should be of local interest."

SANDLAPPER, The Magazine of South Carolina, RPW Publishing Corp, P.O. Box 1108, Lexington SC 29071-1108. (803)359-9954. Fax: (803)957-8226. Editor: Robert P. Wilkins. Managing Editor: Daniel E. Harmon. 35% freelance written. Quarterly feature magazine focusing on the positive aspects of South Carolina. Estab. 1989. Circ. 5,000. Pays during the dateline period. Publishes ms an average of 4 months after acceptance. Byline given. Buys first North American serial rights and the right to reprint. Submit seasonal material 6 months in advance. Query for electronic submissions. Free writer's guidelines.
Nonfiction: Feature articles and photo essays about South Carolina's interesting people, places, cuisine, things to do. Occasional history articles. Query. Length: 600-5,000 words. Pays $50-500. Sometimes pays the expenses of writers on assignment.
Tips: "We're not interested in articles about topical issues, politics, crime or commercial ventures. Humorous angles are encouraged. Avoid first-person nostalgia and remembrances of places that no longer exist."

South Dakota

DAKOTA OUTDOORS, South Dakota, Hipple Publishing Co., P.O. Box 669, 333 W. Dakota Ave., Pierre SD 57501-0669. (605)224-7301. Fax: (605)224-9210. Editor: Kevin Hipple. 50% freelance written. Monthly magazine on Dakota outdoor life. Estab. 1975. Circ. 6,500. Pays on publication. Publishes ms an average of 2 months after acceptance. Byline given. Submit seasonal material 3 months in advance. Accepts simultaneous and previously published submissions (if notified). Send photocopy of article or typed ms with rights for sale noted and information about when and where the article previously appeared. Pays 50% of their fee for an original article. Query for electronic submissions. Reports in 3 months. Sample copy for 9×12 SAE with 3 first-class stamps.
Nonfiction: General interest, how-to, humor, interview/profile, new product, opinion, personal experience, photo feature, technical (all on outdoor topics—prefer in Dakotas). Buys 50 mss/year. Query with or without published clips, or send complete ms. Length: 200-1,000 words. Pays $5-50 for assigned articles; $40 maximum for unsolicited articles. Sometimes pays in contributor copies or other premiums (inquire).
Photos: Send photos with submission. Reviews 5×7 prints. Offers no additional payment for photos accepted with ms. Identification of subjects preferred. Buys one-time rights.
Fillers: Anecdotes, facts, gags to be illustrated by cartoonist, newsbreaks, short humor. Buys 10/year. Also publishes line drawings of fish and game. Prefers 5×7 prints.
Tips: "Submit samples of manuscript or previous works for consideration; photos or illustrations with manuscript are helpful."

Tennessee

MEMPHIS, MM Corporation, P.O. Box 256, Memphis TN 38101-0256. (901)521-9000. Fax: (901)521-0129. Editor: Tim Sampson. 60% freelance written. Works with a small number of new/unpublished writers. Estab. 1976. Circ. 21,917. Pays on publication. Publishes ms an average of 3 months after acceptance. Byline given. Buys first North American serial rights. Offers 20% kill fee. Accepts simultaneous submissions. Reports in 2 months. Sample copy for 9×12 SAE with 9 first-class stamps. Writer's guidelines for SASE.
Nonfiction: Exposé, general interest, historical, how-to, humor, interview, profile. "Virtually all of our material has strong Memphis area connections." Buys 25 freelance mss/year. Query or submit complete ms or published clips. Length: 500-5,000 words. Pays $50-500. Sometimes pays expenses of writers on assignment.
Tips: "The kinds of manuscripts we most need have a sense of story (i.e., plot, suspense, character), an abundance of evocative images to bring that story alive, and a sensitivity to issues at work in Memphis. The most frequent mistakes made by writers in completing an article for us are lack of focus, lack of organization, factual gaps and failure to capture the magazine's style. Tough investigative pieces would be especially welcomed."

Texas

DALLAS LIFE MAGAZINE, Sunday Magazine of *The Dallas Morning News*, Communications Center, P.O. Box 655237, Dallas TX 75265. (214)977-8432. Managing Editor: Mike Maza. Weekly magazine. "We are a lively, topical, sometimes controversial city magazine devoted to informing, enlightening and entertaining our urban Sunbelt readers with material that is specifically relevant to Dallas lifestyles and interests." **Pays on acceptance.** Byline given. Buys first North American serial rights or simultaneous rights. Accepts simultaneous submissions ("if not competitive in our area"). Reports in 2 months.

Nonfiction: General interest, humor (short), interview/profile. "All material must, repeat *must*, have a Dallas metropolitan area frame of reference." Special issues: spring and fall home furnishings. Buys 5-10 unsolicited mss/year. Query with published clips or send complete ms. Length: 1,200-3,000 words. Pays $350-1,200.

HOUSTON LIFE MAGAZINE, (formerly *Houston Metropolitan Magazine*), P.O. Box 25386, Houston TX 77265-5386. (713)524-3000. Editor: David Walker. 85% freelance written. Monthly city magazine distributed in the *Houston Post*. Estab. 1974. Circ. 350,000. **Pays on acceptance.** Publishes ms an average of 3 months after acceptance. Byline given. Offers 25% kill fee. Buys first North American serial rights. Submit seasonal material 6 months in advance. Query for electronic submissions. Accepts simultaneous and previously published submissions. Send tearsheet or photocopy of article or typed ms with rights for sale noted and information about when and where the article previously appeared. Reports in 2 weeks on queries; 2 months on mss.

Nonfiction: Home design, gardening, regional travel, health and fitness, profiles, lifestyle/entertainment, food features, visual stories. "We cover Galveston and the Texas Hill Country as well as Houston." Query with published clips or send complete ms. Length: 300-2,500 words. Pays $50-1,000.

Photos: Audrey Satterwhite, art director. Send photos with submission. Buys one-time rights. "Also assigns photographers at day or job rates."

Tips: "Submit clips demonstrating strong writing and reporting skills with detailed queries, bearing in mind that this is a city magazine. Our intent is to be a lively, informative city book, addressing the issues and people who affect our lives objectively and fairly. But also with affection and, where suitable, a sense of humor. Only those familiar with the Houston metropolitan area should approach us."

‡INNER-VIEW, Texas Literary Magazine, Inner-View Publishing Co., Inc., P.O. Box 66156, Houston TX 77266-6127. (713)527-0606. Editor: Kit van Cleave. 20% freelance written. Works with small number of new/unpublished writers each year. We want to let those writers who may be new in Texas or are coming here know that we are here and will work with them." Estab. 1980. Circ. 35,000. Pays on publication. Publishes ms an average of 2 months after acceptance. Byline given. Buys first North American serial rights, first rights or one-time rights. Submit seasonal material 1 month in advance. Accepts simultaneous submissions. Reports in 2 months. Sample copy for 9 × 12 SAE with 7 first-class stamps.

Nonfiction: Interview/profile, movie reviews. Plans special holiday issues. Query. Length: 1-7 pages. Pays $20-50.

Photos: Send photos with submission. Reviews 8 × 10 or 5 × 7 prints. Offers no additional payment for photos accepted with ms. Captions required. Buys one-time rights.

Columns/Departments: Movie Reviews. Buys 50 mss/year. Query. Length: 1-2 pages.

TEXAS PARKS & WILDLIFE, Suite 120, 3000 South I.H. 35, Austin TX 78704. (512)707-1833. Fax: (512)707-1913. Editor: David Baxter. Managing Editor: Mary-Love Bigony. Contact: Jim Cox, senior editor. 80% freelance written. Monthly magazine featuring articles about Texas hunting, fishing, outdoor recreation, game and nongame wildlife, state parks, environmental issues. All articles must be about Texas. Estab. 1942. Circ. 180,000. **Pays on acceptance.** Publishes ms an average of 6 months after acceptance. Byline given. Kill fee determined by editor, usually $200-250. Buys first rights. Submit seasonal material 6 months in advance. Query for electronic submissions. Reports in 1 month on queries; 3 months on mss. Free sample copy and writer's guidelines.

Nonfiction: Jim Cox, articles editor. General interest (Texas only), historical/nostalgic, how-to (outdoor activities), interview/profile, photo feature, travel (state parks). Buys 60 mss/year. Query with published clips. Length: 250-2,500 words. Pays $600 maximum.

Photos: Send photos with submission. Reviews transparencies. Offers $65-350 maximum/photo. Captions and identification of subjects required. Buys one-time rights.

Columns/Departments: Outdoor Heritage Series (focus on an individual's commitment and contributions to the conservation of Texas's environment or wildlife), 500-1,000 words. Buys 6 mss/year. Query with published clips. Pays $100-300. Monthly departments: hunting and fishing, the environment, young naturalist, places to go. Maximum 1,000 words.

Tips: "Read outdoor pages of statewide newspapers to keep abreast of news items that can lead to story ideas. Feel free to include more than one story idea in one query letter. All areas are open to freelancers. All articles must have a Texas focus."

Always check the most recent copy of a magazine for the address and editor's name before you send in a query or manuscript.

Utah

SALT LAKE CITY, Suite A, 1270 West 2320 S., Salt Lake City UT 84119-1449. (801)975-1927. Fax: (801)975-1982. Editor: Ellen Fagg. Managing Editor: Jane Chapman Martin. 60% freelance written. Bimonthly magazine. "Ours is a lifestyle magazine, focusing on the people, issues and places that make Utah and the Intermountain West unique. Our audience is mainly educated, affluent, ages 25-55. Our pieces are generally positive, or at the very least suggestive of solutions. Again, we focus heavily on people." Estab. 1989. Circ. 15,000. Pays on publication. Publishes ms an average of 3-6 months after acceptance. Byline given. Offers $25 kill fee. Buys first North American serial or second serial (reprint) rights. Submit seasonal material 6 months in advance. Accepts simultaneous and previously published submissions. Send photocopy or typed ms with rights for sale noted and information about when and where material previously appeared. Query for electronic submissions. Reports in 1-3 months on mss. Free sample copy and writer's guidelines. AP style.

Nonfiction: Essays (health, family matters, financial), general interest, historical/nostalgic (pertaining to Utah and Intermountain West), humor, interview/profile (famous or powerful people associated with Utah business, politics, media), personal experience, photo feature (fashion available in Utah stores or cuisine of anywhere in world), travel (anywhere exotic in the world). "No movie reviews or current news subjects, please." Even essays need a tight local angle. Buys 5 mss/year. Query with published clips or send complete ms. Length: 800-2,000 words. Pays $75-400 for assigned articles; $75-250 for unsolicited articles. "A major feature is negotiable."

Photos: Send photos with submission. Reviews transparencies (size not important). Captions, model releases, identification of subjects required. Payment and rights negotiable. Don't send original negs/transparencies unless requested.

Columns/Departments: Up Close (standard personality profile), 1,200-1,500 words; Travel (exotic world travel/preferable to include excellent photography), 2,000 words; Q & A of famous person, 1,200-1,500 words; Executive Signature (profile, business slant of major Utah entrepeneur); and Food (recipes must be included), 1,000-1,500 words. Buys 5-10 mss/year. Query with published clips or send complete ms. Pays $75-250.

• No longer accepting unsolicited fiction and poetry. Also writing more articles inhouse. They are overstocked in travel pieces, and are only considering stories from well-known Utah writers.

Tips: "Well-written, neatly typed, well-researched, complete manuscripts that come across my desk are most likely to be published if they fit our format. They are a godsend. Writers have the best chance of selling us humor, eye-openers, family topics and small features on topics of general interest to Utahns and American western living. For example, we have covered mountainwest recreation, child abuse, education, earthquakes, air pollution, Native American issues. Every story is tightly angled to a local audience. Please write for a free sample copy if you have never read our magazine."

Vermont

VERMONT LIFE MAGAZINE, 6 Baldwin St., Montpelier VT 05602-2109. (802)828-3241. Editor-in-Chief: Thomas K. Slayton. 90% freelance written. Prefers to work with published/established writers. Quarterly magazine. Estab. 1946. Circ. 90,000. Publishes ms an average of 9 months after acceptance. Byline given. Offers kill fee. Buys first serial rights. Submit seasonal material 1 year in advance. Simultaneous queries OK. Reports in 1 month. *Writer's Market* recommends allowing 2 months for reply. Writer's guidelines for #10 SASE.

• Ranked as one of the best markets for freelance writers in *Writer's Digest* magazine's annual "Top 100 Markets," January 1994.

Nonfiction: Wants articles on today's Vermont, those which portray a typical or, if possible, unique aspect of the state or its people. Style should be literate, clear and concise. Subtle humor favored. No "Vermont clichés"—maple syrup, town meetings or stereotyped natives. Buys 60 mss/year. Query by letter essential. Length: 1,500 words average. Pays 20¢/word. Seldom pays expenses of writers on assignment.

Photos: Buys photographs with mss; buys seasonal photographs alone. Prefers b&w contact sheets to look at first on assigned material. Color submissions must be 4×5 or 35mm transparencies. Pays $75-150 inside color; $200 for cover. Gives assignments but only with experienced photographers. Query in writing. Captions, model releases, identification of subjects required. Buys one-time rights, but often negotiates for re-use rights.

Tips: "Writers who read our magazine are given more consideration because they understand that we want authentic articles about Vermont. If a writer has a genuine working knowledge of Vermont, his or her work usually shows it. Vermont is changing and there is much concern here about what this state will be like in years ahead. It is a beautiful, environmentally sound place now and the vast majority of residents want to keep it so. Articles reflecting such concerns in an intelligent, authoritative, non-hysterical way will be given very careful consideration. The growth of tourism makes *Vermont Life* interested in intelligent articles about specific places in Vermont, their history and attractions to the traveling public."

VERMONT MAGAZINE, P.O. Box 288, Bristol VT 05443-0288. (802)453-3200. Editor: John S. Rosenberg. Bimonthly magazine about Vermont. Estab. 1989. Buys first North American serial rights. Submit all material

5-6 months in advance; must query first. Reports in 2 weeks. Writer's guidelines for #10 SASE.

Nonfiction: Journalism and reporting, book excerpts (pre- or post-book publication), essays, exposé, general interest, how-to, humor, interview/profile, photo feature, calendar. All material must be about contemporary Vermont. Buys 30 mss/year but most are assigned by the editor. Query with published clips. Length: 900-3,500 words. Pays $200-800. Sometimes pays expenses of writers on assignment. Rarely publishes reprints.

Photos: Vermont subjects a must. Send photos and illustrations to Elaine Bradley, art director. Reviews contact sheets, 35mm transparencies, 8 × 10 b&w prints. Captions, model releases (if possible), identification of subjects required. Buys one-time rights.

Fiction: Publishes novel excerpts and stories about Vermont (1-2/year, maximum).

Tips: "Our readers *know* their state well, and they know the 'real' Vermont can't be slipped inside a glib and glossy brochure. We're interested in serious journalism on major issues, plus coverage of arts, outdoors, living, nature, architecture."

‡**VERMONT TIMES, Statewide Weekly,** P.O. Box 940, Webster Rd., Shelburne VT 05482. (802)985-2400. Fax: (802)985-2490. Editor: Dan Hickey. Arts and Features Editor: Paula Rootly. 80% freelance written. Works with a small number of new/unpublished writers each year. A locally oriented weekly paper covering Vermont politics, environment, arts, etc. Estab. 1990. Circ. 42,000. Pays on publication. Byline given. Offers 25% kill fee only after written acceptance. Buys first serial rights. Submit seasonal material 1 month in advance. Accepts simultaneous queries and previously published submissions. Query for electronic submissions. Reports in 1 month.

Nonfiction: Articles (profiles, exposés, opinion pieces) must have a Vermont angle. Buys about 10 mss/year. Query with published clips. Length: 500-2,500 words. Pays $30-250.

Photos: Pays $10-30 for b&w contact sheets and negatives. Captions, model releases, identification of subject required. Buys one-time rights.

Tips: "Short news stories are most open to freelancers. Knowledge of Vermont politics is essential."

Virginia

NOVASCOPE, Novascope, Inc., P.O. Box 1590, Middleburg VA 22117-1590. (703)687-3314. Fax: (703)687-4113. Editors: Mark Smith and Joy Smith. 75% freelance written. Monthly magazine on human interest, environmental issues, history and events pertinent to northern Virginia. Estab. 1985. Circ. 15,000. Pays on publication. Byline given. Buys first North American serial rights. Submit seasonal material 3 months in advance. Accepts simultaneous submissions. Reports in 3 months. Free sample copy and writer's guidelines.

Nonfiction: General interest, historical, interview/profile, all pertinent to northern Virginia. Buys 50 mss/year. Query with published clips. Length: 1,000 words maximum. Pays $50 maximum for unsolicited articles.

Photos: State availability of photos with submission. Reviews 35mm transparencies. Offers $10 maximum/photo. Identification of subjects required. Buys one-time rights.

THE ROANOKER, Leisure Publishing Co., 3424 Brambleton Ave., P.O. Box 21535, Roanoke VA 24018-9900. (703)989-6138. Fax: (703)989-7603. Editor: Kurt Rheinheimer. 75% freelance written. Works with a small number of new/unpublished writers each year. Magazine published 10 times/year covering people and events of Western Virginia. "*The Roanoker* is a general interest city magazine edited for the people of Roanoke, Virginia and the surrounding area. Our readers are primarily upper-income, well-educated professionals between the ages of 35 and 60. Coverage ranges from hard news and consumer information to restaurant reviews and local history." Estab. 1974. Circ. 14,000. Pays on publication. Publishes ms an average of 4 months after acceptance. Byline given. Buys all rights; makes work-for-hire assignments. Submit seasonal material 4 months in advance. Reports in 2 months. Sample copy for $2 and 9 × 12 SAE with 5 first-class stamps.

Nonfiction: Exposé, historical/nostalgic, how-to (live better in western Virginia), interview/profile (of well-known area personalities), photo feature, travel (Virginia and surrounding states). "Were looking for more photo feature stories based in western Virginia. We place special emphasis on consumer-related issues and how-to articles." Periodic special sections on fashion, real estate, media, banking, investing. Buys 60 mss/year. Query with published clips or send complete ms. Length: 1,400 words maximum. Pays $35-200.

● This magazine is looking for shorter pieces than before.

Photos: Send photos with ms. Reviews color transparencies. Pays $5-10 for 5 × 7 or 8 × 10 b&w prints; $10 maximum for 5 × 7 or 8 × 10 color prints. Captions and model releases required. Rights purchased vary.

Tips: "It helps if freelancer lives in the area. The most frequent mistake made by writers in completing an article for us is not having enough Roanoke-area focus: use of area experts, sources, slants, etc."

Washington

PACIFIC NORTHWEST, Adams Publishing of the Pacific Northwest, Suite 101, 701 Dexter Ave. N., Seattle WA 98109-4339. (206)284-1750. Fax: (206)284-2550. Editor: Ann Naumann. 80% freelance written. "*Pacific Northwest* is published 10 times/year, directed primarily at longtime residents of Oregon, Washington, Idaho, western Montana, Alaska, northern California, western Alberta and British Columbia." Estab. 1966. Circ.

86,885. Pays on publication. Publishes ms an average of 4 months after acceptance. Byline given. Offers kill fee. Buys first North American serial rights. Submit seasonal material 6 months in advance. Query for electronic submissions. Accepts previously published submissions. Send photocopy of article or short story. For reprints pays 50% of the amount paid for an original article. Reports in 6 weeks. Sample copy for $4. Free writer's guidelines.

Nonfiction: Book excerpts (Northwest), exposé, general interest, interview/profile, personal experience, photo feature, travel, business, and arts. No self-help. Buys 180 mss/year. Query with published clips. Length: 300-2,500 words. Pays $100-1,000 for assigned articles. Sometimes pays expenses of writers on assignment.

Photos: Send photos with submission. Reviews contact sheets. Offers $50-250/photo. Identification of subjects required. Buys one-time rights.

Columns/Departments: EcoHeroes (regional environmental leader profiles), 1,000 words; Gearing Up (outdoor activity how-to), 1,000 words; and Weekends (regional getaways), 500-1,200 words. Buys 90 mss/year. Query with published clips. Pays $150-300.

‡SEATTLE, Adams Publishing of the Pacific Northwest, Suite 101, 701 Dexter Ave. N, Seattle WA 98109. (206)284-1750. Editor: Giselle Smith. 90% freelance written. Bimonthly magazine serving the Greater Seattle area, from Bellevue to Vashon, from Edmonds to Kent. Articles for the magazine should be written with our readership in mind. They are interested in the arts, social issues, their homes and gardens and in maintaining the region's high quality of life. Estab. 1992. Circ. 33,570. Pays on publication. Publishes ms an average of 4 months after acceptance. Byline given. Offers 33% kill fee. Buys first rights or second serial (reprint) rights. Editorial lead time 4 months. Submit seasonal material 6 months in advance. Reports in 6 weeks on queries; 2 months on mss. Sample copy and writer's guidelines for #10 SASE.

Nonfiction: Book excerpts, general interest, interview/profile, photo feature, local interest. Buys 60-75 mss/year. Query with published clips. Length: 200-2,500 words. Pays $75 minimum for assigned articles; $50 minimum for unsolicited articles. Sometimes pays expenses of writers on assignment.

Photos: State availability of photos with submission. Negotiates payment individually. Buys one-time rights.

Columns/Departments: Home and Garden, Nightlife, Dining, Style, Neighborhood, Private Eye. Query with published clips. Pays $150-300.

SEATTLE WEEKLY, Sasquatch Publishing, Suite 300, 108 Western Ave., Seattle WA 98104. (206)623-0500. Editor: Knute Berger. 20% freelance written. Eager to work with new/unpublished writers, especially those in the region. Weekly tabloid covering arts, politics, food, business and books with local and regional emphasis. Estab. 1976. Circ. 37,000. Pays 1 week after publication. Publishes ms an average of 1 month after acceptance. Byline given. Offers variable kill fee. Buys first North American serial rights. Submit seasonal material minimum 2 months in advance. Simultaneous queries OK. Reports in 1 month. *Writer's Market* recommends allowing 2 months for reply. Sample copy for $2. Writer's guidelines for #10 SASE.

Nonfiction: Book excerpts, exposé, general interest, historical/nostalgic (Northwest), humor, interview/profile, opinion, arts-related essays. Buys 6-8 cover stories/year. Query with résumé and published clips. Length: 700-4,000 words. Pays $75-800. Sometimes pays the expenses of writers on assignment.

Tips: "The *Seattle Weekly* publishes stories on Northwest politics and art, usually written by regional and local writers, for a mostly upscale, urban audience; writing is high-quality magazine style."

West Virginia

WONDERFUL WEST VIRGINIA, State of West Virginia Dept. of Natural Resources, Bldg. 3, 1900 Kanawha Blvd. E., State Capital Complex, Charleston WV 25305-0669. (304)558-9152. Editor: Nancy Clark. 95% freelance written. Monthly magazine of "general interest, show-piece quality, portraying a positive image of West Virginia, with emphasis on outdoor/natural resources subjects." Estab. 1970. Circ. 63,000. **Pays on acceptance.** Publishes ms an average of 24 months after acceptance. Byline given. Offers 5¢/word kill fee. Buys first or second rights. Submit seasonal material 6 months in advance. Reports in 3 months. Sample copy for $3.25. Free writer's guidelines.

Nonfiction: General interest, natural resources, historical/nostalgic, photo feature, travel. "No outsider's views of West Virginia and its people; nothing negative or about poor, ignorant 'hillbilly' types of people or places. 'No Me and Joe hunting and fishing' stories." Buys 50 mss/year. Query. Length: 500-2,000 words. Pays $50-300.

• Looking especially for shorter articles (1,000 words or fewer).

Photos: Photos are taken by staff photographer, if feasible. Will consider photos with submission. Reviews 35mm or larger transparencies. Offers $75/color photo. Captions, model releases, identification of subjects required. Buys one-time rights.

Tips: "Read Guidelines for Writers. Write an article especially for readers who love West Virginia about an interesting place or event in West Virginia. Entire publication is open to freelancers. Need more stories on outdoor recreation (no hunting and fishing). We are only interested in articles from writers with a personal knowledge of West Virginia. We are presently scheduling stories into 1996 and 1997 issues. Query us as to subject first."

Wisconsin

MILWAUKEE MAGAZINE, 312 E. Buffalo St., Milwaukee WI 53202. (414)273-1101. Fax: (414)273-0016. Editor: John Fennell. 40% freelance written. Monthly magazine covering Milwaukee and surrounding region. "We publish stories about Milwaukee, of service to Milwaukee-area residents and exploring the area's changing lifestyle, business, arts, politics and dining." Circ. 40,000. Pays on publication. Publishes ms an average of 2 months after acceptance. Byline given. Offers 20% kill fee. Buys first rights. Submit seasonal material 5-6 months in advance. Query for electronic submissions. Reports in 6 weeks on queries. *Writer's Market* recommends allowing 2 months for reply. Sample copy for $4.
Nonfiction: Book excerpts, essays, exposé, general interest, historical/nostalgic, interview/profile, photo feature, travel, food and dining and other services. "No articles without a strong Milwaukee or Wisconsin angle." Buys 30-50 mss/year. Query with published clips. Length: 1,500-5,000 words. Pays $600-1,000. Sometimes pays expenses of writers on assignment.
Photos: Send photos with submission. Reviews contact sheets, negatives, any transparencies and any prints. Offers no set rate per photo. Identification of subjects required. Buys one-time rights.
Columns/Departments: Steve Filmanowicz, departments editor. Insider (inside information on Milwaukee), 200-700 words. Buys 60 mss/year. Query with published clips. Pays $30-125.
Tips: "Pitch something for the Insider, or suggest a compelling profile we haven't already done and submit clips that prove you can do the job. The department most open is Insider. Think short, lively, offbeat, fresh, people-oriented."

WISCONSIN, *The Milwaukee Journal Magazine*, P.O. Box 661, Milwaukee WI 53201-0661. (414)224-2341. Fax: (414)224-2047. Editor: Alan Borsuk. 20% freelance written. Prefers to work with published/established writers. Weekly general interest magazine appealing to readers living in Wisconsin. Estab. 1969. Circ. 500,000. Pays on publication. Publishes ms an average of 4 months after acceptance. Byline given. Buys first serial rights. Submit seasonal material 4 months in advance. Simultaneous queries OK. Reports in 2 months on queries; 6 months on mss. Sample copy and writer's guidelines for 9 × 12 SAE with 2 first-class stamps.
Nonfiction: Exposé, general interest, humor, interview/profile, opinion, personal experience, photo feature, with Wisconsin angles in most cases. Buys 50 mss/year. Query. Length: 500-2,500 words. Pays $75-600. Sometimes pays expenses of writers on assignment.
Photos: Send photos.
Columns/Departments: Opinion, Humor, Essays. Buys 50 mss/year. Length: 300-1,000 words. Pays $100-200.
Tips: "We are primarily Wisconsin-oriented and are becoming more news-oriented."

WISCONSIN OUTDOOR JOURNAL, Krause Publications, 700 E. State St., Iola WI 54990-0001. (715)445-2214. Fax: (715)445-4087. Editor: Steve Heiting. 95% freelance written. Magazine published 8 times/year. "*Wisconsin Outdoor Journal* is more than a straight hook-and-bullet magazine. Though *WOJ* carries how-to and where-to information, it also prints narratives, nature features and state history pieces to give our readers a better appreciation of Wisconsin's outdoors." Estab. 1987. Circ. 48,000. **Pays on acceptance.** Byline given. Buys first North American serial rights. Submit seasonal material 1 year in advance. Reports in 6 weeks. *Writer's Market* recommends allowing 2 months for reply. Sample copy for 9 × 12 SAE with 7 first-class stamps. Writer's guidelines for #10 SASE.
Nonfiction: Book excerpts, essays, historical/nostalgic, how-to, humor, interview/profile, personal experience, photo feature. No articles outside of the geographic boundaries of Wisconsin. Buys 80 mss/year. Query. Send complete ms. "Established writers may query, otherwise I prefer to see the complete ms." Length: 1,500-2,000 words. Pays $100-250.
Photos: Send photos with submission. Reviews 35mm transparencies. Offers no additional payment. Captions required. Buys one-time rights. Photos without mss pay from $10-150. Credit line given.
Fiction: Adventure, historical, humorous. "No eulogies of a good hunting dog." Buys 10 mss/year. Send complete ms. Length: 1,500-2,000 words. Pays $100-250.
Tips: "Writers need to know Wisconsin intimately—stories that appear as regionals in other magazines probably won't be printed within *WOJ*'s pages."

WISCONSIN TRAILS, P.O. Box 5650, Madison WI 53705-1056. (608)231-2444. Fax: (608)231-1557. Associate Editor: Lucy J. Rhodes. 40% freelance written. Prefers to work with published/established writers. Bimonthly magazine for readers interested in Wisconsin; its contemporary issues, personalities, recreation, history, natural beauty and the arts. Estab. 1959. Circ. 55,000. Buys first serial rights, one-time rights occasionally. Pays on publication. Submit seasonal material at least 1 year in advance. Publishes ms an average of 6 months after acceptance. Byline given. Reports in 2 months. Sample copy for 9 × 12 SASE with 10 first-class stamps. Writer's guidelines for #10 SASE.
Nonfiction: "Our articles focus on some aspect of Wisconsin life; an interesting town or event, a person or industry, history or the arts and especially outdoor recreation. We do not use first-person essays or biographies about people who were born in Wisconsin but made their fortunes elsewhere. No poetry. No articles that are too local for our regional audience, or articles about obvious places to visit in Wisconsin. We need

more articles about the new and little-known." Buys 3 unsolicited mss/year. Query or send outline. Length: 1,000-3,000 words. Pays $150-500 (negotiable), depending on assignment length and quality. Sometimes pays expenses of writers on assignment.

Photos: Purchased with or without mss or on assignment. Uses 35mm transparencies; larger format OK. Color photos usually illustrate an activity, event, region or striking scenery. Prefer photos with people in scenery. Black and white photos usually illustrate a given article. Pays $50 each for b&w on publication. Pays $50-75 for inside color; $100-200 for covers. Captions preferred.

Tips: "We're looking for active articles about people, places, events and outdoor adventures in Wisconsin. We want to publish one in-depth article of state-wide interest or concern per issue, and several short (600-1,500 word) articles about short trips, recreational opportunities, restaurants, inns and cultural activities. We will be looking for more articles about out-of-the-way places in Wisconsin that are exceptional in some way."

Canada

CANADIAN GEOGRAPHIC, 39 McArthur Ave., Ottawa, Ontario K1L 8L7 Canada. (613)745-4629. Fax: (613)744-0947. Editor: Ian Darragh. Managing Editor: Eric Harris. Contact: Monique Roy-Sole. 90% freelance written. Works with a small number of new/unpublished writers each year. Estab. 1930. Circ. 245,000. Bimonthly magazine. **Pays on acceptance.** Publishes ms an average of 3 months after acceptance. Buys first Canadian rights; interested only in first-time publication. Reports in 1 month. Sample copy for $3.95 (Canada.) and 9×12 SAE. Free writer's guidelines.

Nonfiction: Buys authoritative geographical articles, in the broad geographical sense, written for the average person, not for a scientific audience. Predominantly Canadian subjects by Canadian authors. Buys 30-45 mss/year. *Always query first in writing and enclose a SASE.* Cannot reply personally to all unsolicited proposals. Length: 1,500-3,000 words. Pays 50¢/word minimum. Usual payment for articles ranges between $1,000-3,000. Higher fees reserved for commissioned articles. Sometimes pays the expenses of writers on assignment.

• They need articles on earth sciences.

Photos: Pays $75-400 for color photos, depending on published size.

THE GEORGIA STRAIGHT, Vancouver Free Press Publishing Corp., 2nd Floor, 1235 W. Pender St., Vancouver, British Columbia V6E 2V6 Canada. (604)681-2000. Fax: (604)681-0272. Managing Editor: Charles Campbell. 100% freelance written. Weekly tabloid on arts, entertainment, lifestyle and civic issues. Estab. 1967. Circ. 100,000. Pays on publication. Byline given. Offers 75-100% kill fee. Buys first North American serial or second serial (reprint) rights. Accepts simultaneous and previously published submissions. Send typed ms with rights for sale noted and information about when and where the article previously appeared. Pays 50-100% of their fee for an original article. Reports in 1 month. *Writer's Market* recommends allowing 2 months for reply. Sample copy for $1 and 9×12 SAE.

Nonfiction: General interest, humor, interview/profile, travel, arts and entertainment. Buys 600 mss/year. Query with published clips. Length: 250-4,000 words. Pays $40-800. Sometimes pays expenses of writers on assignment.

Photos: Send photos with submission. Reviews, contact sheets, transparencies and 8×10 prints. Offers $35-150/photo. Captions, model releases and identification of subjects required. Buys one-time rights.

Tips: "Be aware of entertainment events in the Vancouver area and expansion of our news coverage. Most stories relate to those events. We don't return American manuscripts because Canadian postage is not generally provided."

‡MONARCHY CANADA, Monarchist League of Canada, Suite 206, 3050 Yonge St., Toronto, Ontario M4V 1K6 Canada. (416)482-4157. Editor: Arthur Bousfield. Quarterly magazine covering royalty. "All aspects of constitutional monarchy in Canada and Commonwealth—political, constitutional, social, artistic, cultural dimensions." Estab. 1970. Circ. 10,000. Pays on publication. Publishes ms 3-6 months after acceptance. Byline given. Buys first rights. Editorial lead time 3-6 months. Submit seasonal material 6 months in advance. Accepts simultaneous and previously published submissions. Reports in 1 month on queries; 2 months on mss. Sample copy and writer's guidelines free on request.

Nonfiction: Essays, general interest, historical/nostalgic, humor, interview/profile, opinion, personal experience, travel (if monarchy-related). Buys 2-4 mss/year. Query. Length: 200-10,000 words. Pays $50. Pays expenses of writers on assignment.

Photos: State availability of photos with submission. Reviews 3×5 or larger prints. Offers no additional payment for photos accepted with ms. Buys one-time rights.

Fillers: Anecdotes, facts, short humor. Buys 2-4/year. Length: 50-350 words. Pays $25-50.

Tips: Looking for "unusual aspects of monarchy *with Canadian slant.*"

OTTAWA MAGAZINE, Ottawa Magazine Inc., 192 Bank St., Ottawa, Ontario K2P 1W8 Canada. (613)234-7751. Fax: (613)234-9226. Editor: Rosa Harris Adler. 80% freelance written. Prefers to work with published/established writers. Magazine published 9 times/year, covering life in Ottawa and environs. "*Ottawa Magazine* reflects the interest and lifestyles of its readers who tend to be married, ages 35-55, upwardly mobile and

urban." Circ. 40,000. **Pays on acceptance.** Publishes ms an average of 6 months after acceptance. Byline given. "Kill fee depends on agreed-upon fee; very seldom used." Buys first North American serial and second serial (reprint) rights. Accepts previously published submissions. Reports in 2 months. Sample copy for $2.25.
Nonfiction: Book excerpts (by local authors or about regional issues); exposé (federal or regional government, education); general interest; interview/profile (on Ottawans who have established national or international reputations); photo feature (for recurring section called Freezeframe); travel (recent examples are Brazil, Trinidad & Tobago, Copenhagen). "No articles better suited to a national or special interest publication." Buys 100 mss/year. Query with published clips. Length: 1,500-2,000 words. Pays $500/1,000 (Canadian).
Tips: "A phone call to our associate editor is the best way to assure that queries receive prompt attention. Once a query interests me the writer is assigned a detailed 'treatment' of the proposed piece which is used to determine viability of story. We will be concentrating on more issue-type stories with good, solid fact-researched base, also doing more fluffy pieces—best and worst of Ottawa—that sort of stuff. Harder for out-of-town writers to furnish. The writer should strive to inject a personal style and avoid newspaper-style reportage. *Ottawa Magazine* also doesn't stoop to boosterism and points out the bad along with the good. Good prospects for US writers are interiors (house and garden type), gardening (for Northern climate), leisure/lifestyles. Reprints OK."

‡**UP HERE, Life in Canada's North,** OUTCROP The Northern Publishers, Box 1350, Yellowknife, Northwest Territories X1A 2N9 Canada. (403)920-4652. 50% freelance written. Bimonthly magazine covering general interest about Canada's North. "We publish features, columns and shorts about people, wildlife, native cultures, travel and adventure in Northern Canada, with an occasional swing into Alaska. Be informative, but entertaining." Estab. 1984. Circ. 37,500. Pays on publication. Publishes ms an average of 4 months after acceptance. Offers $100 (Canadian) kill fee. Buys first North American serial rights. Editorial lead time 4 months. Submit seasonal material 6 months in advance. Query for electronic submissions. Reports in 4 months. Sample copy for $3 (Canadian). Writer's guidelines free on request.
Nonfiction: Historical/nostalgic, interview/profile, personal experience, photo feature, travel. Buys 40 mss/year. Send complete ms. Length: 750-3,000 words. Pays $250 for assigned articles; $150 for unsolicited articles. Sometimes pays expenses of writers on assignment.
Photos: Send photos with submission. Reviews transparencies and prints. Offers $35-150/photo. Captions required. Buys one-time rights.
Columns/Departments: Photography (how-to for amateurs), 1,250 words; Natural North (wildlife—the land, environment), 1,250-1,800 words; On the Road (driving in Northern regions, RV, etc.), 750-1,800 words. Buys 12 mss/year. Send complete ms. Pays $150-350.
Tips: "You must have lived in or visited Canada's North (the Northwest Territories, Yukon, the extreme north of British Columbia, Alberta, etc.). We like well-researched, concrete adventure pieces, insights about Northern people and lifestyles, readable natural history. Features are most open to freelancers—travel, adventure and so on. Top-quality photos can sell a piece better than any other factor."

‡**WESTERN PEOPLE, Supplement to the Western Producer,** Western Producer Publications, Box 2500, Saskatoon, Saskatchewan S7K 2C4 Canada. (306)665-3500. Managing Editor: Michael Gillgannon. Weekly farm newspaper supplement covering rural Western Canada. "Our magazine reflects the life and people of rural Western Canada both in the present and historically." Estab. 1978. Circ. 100,000. **Pays on acceptance.** Publishes ms an average of 6 months after acceptance. Byline given. Buys first rights. Submit seasonal material 3 months in advance. Reports in 3 weeks. Sample copy for 9 × 12 SAE and 3 IRCs. Writer's guidelines for #10 SAE and 2 IRCs.
Nonfiction: General interest, historical/nostalgic, humor, interview/profile, personal experience, photo feature. Buys 225 mss/year. Send complete ms. Length: 500-2,500 words. Pays $100-300.
Photos: Send photos with submission. Reviews transparencies and prints. Captions and identification of subjects required. No stand-alone photos.
Fiction: Adventure, historical, humorous, mainstream, mystery, romance, suspense, western stories reflecting life in rural western Canada. Buys 25 mss/year. Send complete ms. Length: 1,000-2,000 words. Pays $150-250.
Poetry: Free verse, traditional, haiku, light verse. Buys 75 poems/year. Submit maximum 3 poems. Length: 4-50 lines. Pays $15-50.
Tips: "Western Canada is geographically very large. The approach for writing about an interesting individual is to introduce that person *neighbor-to-neighbor* to our readers."

‡**THE WESTERN PRODUCER,** Western Producer Publications, Box 2500, 2310 Millar Ave., Saskatoon, Saskatchewan S7K 2C4 Canada. (306)665-3500. Fax: (306)653-1255 or News Fax: (306)934-2401. Editor: Garry Fairbairn. Managing Editor: Elaine Shein. Contact: Barb Glen, news editor. 30% freelance written. Weekly newspaper covering agriculture and rural life. Publishes "informative material for 105,000 western Canadian farm familes." Pays on publication. Byline given. Kill fee varies. Not copyrighted. Buys one-time rights. Submit seasonal material 2 months in advance. Accepts simultaneous and previously published submissions. Query for electronic submissions. Reports in 1 week on queries; 1-2 months on mss. Sample copy for 11 × 14 SAE with IRC. Writer's guidelines for #10 SAE.

Nonfiction: General interest, historical/nostalgic, how-to (on farm machinery or construction), humor, new product, technical, production, markets info, on-farm features, rural cartoons. Special supplements throughout the year, including livestock and seed varieties. Nothing "non-Canadian, over 1,500 words." Buys 600 mss/year. Query. Length: 2,000 words. Pays $100-400 for assigned articles; pays $150 maximum for unsolicited articles. Sometimes pays the expenses of writers on assignment.
Photos: Send photos with submission. Reviews contact sheets, negatives, transparencies, prints. Offers $20-40/b&w photos, $35-100/color photos. Captions required. Buys one-time rights.
Columns/Departments: Michael Gillgannon, editor. Western People (magazine insert focusing on Western Canadian personalities, hobbies, history, fiction), 500-2,000 words. Buys 350 mss/year. Query. Length: 500-2,000 words. Pays $50-500.
Fiction: Ethnic, historical, humorous, slice-of-life vignettes, western, rural settings. No non-western Canadian subjects. Buys 40 mss/year. Query. Length: 500-2,000. Pays $50-500.
Poetry: Free verse, light verse, traditional. Buys 20 poems/year. Length: 10-100 lines. Pays $10-100.
Tips: "Use CP/AP/UPI style and a fresh ribbon." Areas most open to freelancers are "cartoons, on-farm profiles, rural Canadian personalities."

WHERE VICTORIA/ESSENTIAL VICTORIA, Key Pacific Publishers Co. Ltd., 3rd Floor, 1001 Wharf St., Victoria, British Columbia V8W 1T6 Canada. (604)388-4324. Editor: Anna Feindel. Editorial Director: Janice Strong. 40% freelance written. Monthly magazine on Victoria and Vancouver Island. Estab. 1975. Circ. 30,000. Pays on publication. Publishes ms an average of 1-2 months after acceptance. Byline given. Buys first North American serial and all rights. Query for electronic submissions. Accepts previously published submissions. Send photocopy of article and information about when and where the article previously appeared. Pays 75% of their fee for an original article. Reports in 3 months. Free sample copy.
Nonfiction: General interest, travel. Essential Victoria. Buys 30 mss/year. Query with published clips. Length: 500-2,500 words. Pays 20-40¢/word.
Photos: Send photos with submission. Reviews contact sheets, transparencies, prints. Offers $50-150/photo. Model releases and identification of subjects required. Buys one-time rights.

Relationships

These publications focus on lifestyles and relationships. They are read and often written by single people, gays and lesbians and those interested in these lifestyles or in alternative outlooks. They may offer writers a forum for unconventional views or serve as a voice for particular audiences or causes.

ATLANTA SINGLES MAGAZINE, Hudson Brooke Publishing, Inc., Suite 304N, 180 Allen Rd., Atlanta GA 30328. (404)256-9411. Fax: (404)256-9719. Editor: Cheryl Fenton. 10% freelance written. Works with a small number of new/unpublished writers each year. Bimonthly magazine for single, widowed or divorced adults, medium to high income level, many business and professionally oriented; single parents, ages 25 to 55. Estab. 1977. Circ. 15,000. Pays on publication. Publishes ms an average of 6 months after acceptance. Byline given. Buys one-time, second serial (reprint) and simultaneous rights. Submit seasonal material 6 months in advance. Accepts simultaneous and previously submissions. Send tearsheet or photocopy of article and information about when and where the article previously appeared. Pays 50% of their fee for an original article. Reports in 1 month. Sample copy for $2 and 8×10 SAE with 7 first-class stamps. Writer's guidelines for #10 SASE.
Nonfiction: General interest, humor, personal experience, photo feature, travel. No fiction or pornography. Buys 5 mss/year. Send complete ms. Length: 600-1,200 words. Pays $50-150 for unsolicited articles; sometimes trades for personal ad.
Photos: Send photos with submission. Cover photos also considered. Reviews prints. Offers no additional payment for photos accepted with ms. Model releases and identification of subjects required. Buys one-time rights.
Columns/Departments: Will consider ideas. Query. Length: 600-800 words. Pays $25-150/column or department.
Tips: "We are open to articles on *any* subject that would be of interest to singles. For example, travel, autos, movies, love stories, fashion, investments, real estate, etc. Although singles are interested in topics like self-awareness, being single again, and dating, they are also interested in many of the same subjects that married people are, such as those listed."

BAY WINDOWS, New England's Largest Gay and Lesbian Newspaper, Bay Windows, Inc., 1523 Washington St., Boston MA 02118-2034. (617)266-6670. Fax: (617)266-5973. Editor: Jeff Epperly. Arts Editor: Ruby Kikel. 30-40% freelance written. Weekly newspaper of gay news and concerns. "*Bay Windows* covers predominantly news of New England, but will print non-local news and features depending on the newsworthiness of the story. We feature hard news, opinion, news analysis, arts reviews and interviews." Estab. 1983. Publishes ms within 2 months of acceptance, pays within 2 months of publication. Byline given. Offers

50% kill fee. Rights obtained varies, usually first serial rights. Simultaneous submissions accepted if other submissions are outside of New England. Submit seasonal material 3 months in advance. Accepts previously published submissions. Send typed ms with rights for sale noted and information about when and where the article previously appeared. Pays 75% of their fee for an original article. Reports in 3 months. Sample copy for $5. Writer's guidelines for #10 SASE.

Nonfiction: Hard news, general interest with a gay slant, interview/profile, opinion, photo features. Publishes 200 mss/year. Query with published clips or send complete ms. Length: 500-1,500 words. Pay varies: $25-100 news; $10-60 arts.

Photos: $25/published photo, b&w photos only. Model releases and identification of subjects required.

Columns/Departments: Film, music, dance, books, art. Length: 500-1,500 words. Buys 200 mss/year. Pays $10-100.

• Looking for more humor.

Poetry: All varieties. Publishes 50 poems per year. Length: 10-30 lines. No payment.

Tips: "Too much gay-oriented writing is laden with the clichés and catch phrases of the movement. Writers must have intimate knowledge of gay community; however, this should not mean that standard English usage is not required. We look for writers with new—even controversial perspectives on the lives of gay men and lesbians. While we assume gay is good, we will print stories which examine problems within the community and movement. No pornography or erotica."

DRUMMER, Desmodus, Inc., P.O. Box 410390, San Francisco CA 94141-0390. (415)252-1195. Fax: (415)252-9574. Managing Editor: Marcus Wonacott. 50% freelance written. Gay male leather and related fetish erotica/news. Monthly magazine publishes "erotic aspects of leather and other masculine fetishes for gay men." Estab. 1976. Circ. 45,000. Pays 30 days past publication. Publishes ms an average of 3 months after acceptance. Byline given. Buys first North American serial rights or makes work-for-hire assignments. Submit seasonal/holiday material 9 months in advance. Accepts previously published submissions. Reports in 1 month on queries; in 3 months on mss. Sample copy for $6. Writer's guidelines for #10 SASE.

Nonfiction: Book excerpts, essays, historical/nostalgic, how-to, humor, interview/profile, new product, opinion, personal experience, photo feature, technical, travel. No feminine-slanted or heterosexual pieces. Buys 25 mss/year. Query with or without published clips or send complete ms. Prefer disk (DOS) along with ms. Length: 1,000-15,000 words. Pays $50-200 for assigned articles; $50-100 for unsolicited articles. Rarely pays expenses of writers on assignment.

Photos: Send photos with submission (photocopies OK). Reviews contact sheets and transparencies. Offers $25-50/photo. Model releases and identification of subjects required. Buys one-time rights or all rights.

Fiction: Adventure, erotica, ethnic, fantasy, historical, horror, humorous, mystery, novel excerpts, science fiction, slice-of-life vignettes, suspense, western. Must have gay "macho" erotic elements. Buys 60-75 mss/year. Send complete ms. Prefer disk (DOS) along with ms. Length: 1,000-20,000 words. Occasionally serializes stories. Pays $100.

Fillers: Anecdotes, facts, gags, cartoons, newsbreaks. Ms must be scannable. Buys 50/year. Length: 10-100 words. pay $10-50.

Tips: "All they have to do is write—but they must be knowledgable about some aspect of the scene. While the magazine is aimed at gay men, we welcome contributions from straight men and from straight, bisexual and gay women who understand leather, SM and kinky erotic fetishes. Fiction is most open to freelancers."

FIRST HAND, Experiences For Loving Men, Firsthand, Ltd., 310 Cedar Lane, Teaneck NJ 07666. (201)836-9177. Fax: (201)836-5055. Editor: Bob Harris. Publisher: Jackie Lewis. 75% freelance written. Eager to work with new/unpublished writers. Monthly magazine of homosexual erotica. Estab. 1980. Circ. 70,000. Pays 6 months after acceptance or on publication, whichever comes first. Publishes ms an average of 8 months after acceptance. Byline given. Buys all rights (exceptions made) and second serial (reprint) rights. Submit seasonal material 10 months in advance. Reports in 4 months. Sample copy for $5. Writer's guidelines for #10 SASE.

Columns/Departments: Survival Kit (short nonfiction articles, up to 1,000 words, featuring practical information on safe sex practices, health, travel, psychology, law, fashion, and other advice/consumer/lifestyle topics of interest to gay or single men). "For this section, we sometimes also buy reprint rights to appropriate articles previously published in local gay newspapers around the country." Infotainment (short reviews up to 1,000 words on books, film, TV, video, theater, performance art, museums, etc.). Reviews must have a gay angle. Query; include photocopy if previously published article. Pays $35-70, depending on length, if original; if reprint, pays half that rate.

Fiction: Erotic fiction up to 5,000 words, average 2,000-3,000 words. "We prefer fiction in the first person which is believable—stories based on the writer's actual experience have the best chance. We're not interested in stories which involve underage characters in sexual situations. Other taboos include bestiality, rape—except in prison stories, as rape is an unavoidable reality in prison—and heavy drug use. Writers with questions about what we can and cannot depict should write for our guidelines, which go into this in more detail. We print mostly self-contained stories; we will look at novel excerpts, but only if they stand on their own."

Poetry: Free verse and light verse. Buys 12/year. Submit maximum 5 poems. Length: 10-30 lines. Pays $25.

Tips: "*First Hand* is a very reader-oriented publication for gay men. Half of each issue is made up of letters from our readers describing their personal experiences, fantasies and feelings. Our readers are from all walks of life, all races and ethnic backgrounds, all classes, all religious and political affiliations, and so on. They are very diverse, and many live in far-flung rural areas or small towns; for some of them, our magazines are the primary source of contact with gay life, in some cases the only support for their gay identity. Our readers are very loyal and save every issue. We return that loyalty by trying to reflect their interests—for instance, by striving to avoid the exclusively big-city bias so common to national gay publications. So bear in mind the diversity of the audience when you write."

FORUM, The International Journal of Human Relations, General Media Inc., 1965 Broadway, New York, NY 10023. (212)496-6100. Editor: V.K. McCarty. 100% freelance written. Works with small number of new/ unpublished writers each year. Monthly magazine. "*Forum* is the only serious publication in the US to cover human sexuality in all its aspects for the layman—not only the erotic, but the medical, political, legal, etc." Circ. 300,000. **Pays on acceptance.** Publishes ms an average of 6-12 months after acceptance. Byline given. "Pseudonym mandatory for first-person sex stories." Offers 25% kill fee. Buys all rights. Submit seasonal/ holiday material 6 months in advance. Reports in 2 months on mss.
Nonfiction: Book excerpts, personal experience, essays or scientifically researched articles on all aspects of sex and sexuality. Buys 100 mss/year. Query or send complete ms. Length: 2,000-3,000 words. Pay varies.
Fiction: "Excellent erotic fiction is considered. Letters detailing sexual adventures are sent in by our readers, and we make no payment for them. We do not publish poetry."

THE GUIDE, To Gay Travel, Entertainment, Politics and Sex, Fidelity Publishing, P.O. Box 593, Boston MA 02199-0593. (617)266-8557. Fax: (617)266-1125. Editor: French Wall. 50% freelance written. Monthly magazine on the gay and lesbian community. Estab. 1981. Circ. 30,000. **Pays on acceptance.** Publishes ms an average of 2 months after acceptance. Kill fee negotiable. Buys all rights. Submit seasonal material 2 months in advance. Accepts simultaneous submissions. Reports in 3 months. Sample copy for 9 × 12 SAE with 8 first-class stamps. Writer's guidelines for #10 SASE.
Nonfiction: Book excerpts (if yet unpublished), essays, exposé, general interest, historical/nostalgic, humor, interview/profile, opinion, personal experience, photo feature, religious. Buys 24 mss/year. Query with or without published clips or send complete ms. Length: 500-5,000 words. Pays $50-180.
Photos: Send photos with submission. Reviews contact sheets. Offers no additional payment for photos accepted with ms (although sometimes negotiable). Captions, model releases, identification of subjects preferred; releases required sometimes. Buys one-time rights.
Tips: "Brevity, humor and militancy appreciated."

GUYS, First Hand Ltd., P.O. Box 1314, Teaneck NJ 07666-3441. (201)836-9177. Fax: (201)836-5055. Editor: William Spencer. 80% freelance written. Monthly magazine of erotica for gay men. "A positive, romantic approach to gay sex." Estab. 1988. Circ. 60,000. Pays on publication. Publishes ms an average of 1 year after acceptance. Byline given. Buys first North American serial or all rights. Submit seasonal material 10 months in advance. Accepts previously published submissions. Send photocopy of article or short story or typed ms with rights for sale noted. Pays 50% of their fee for an original article. Reports in 2-6 months. Sample copy for $5. Writer's guidelines for #10 SASE.
Columns/Departments: Starstruck (Hollywood with a gay angle), 1,250-1,500 words; Point of view (op/ed), 1,000-1,500 words. Buys 12 mss/year. Query. Pays $75-100.
Fiction: Erotica. Buys 72 mss/year. Length: 1,000-10,000 words. Pays $75-250.

IN TOUCH FOR MEN, In Touch International, Inc., 13122 Saticoy St., North Hollywood CA 91605-3402. (818)764-2288. Fax: (818)764-2307. Editor: D. DiFranco. 80% freelance written. Works with a small number of new/unpublished writers each year. Monthly magazine covering the gay male lifestyle, gay male humor and erotica. Estab. 1973. Circ. 70,000. Pays on publication. Byline given, pseudonym OK. Buys one-time rights. Accepts simultaneous submissions. Reports in 2 months. Sample copy for $5.95. Writer's guidelines for #10 SASE.
Nonfiction: Buys 36 mss/year. Send complete ms. Length: 3,000-3,500 words. Pays $25-75.
• Needs more lifestyle features.
Photos: Send photos with submission. Reviews contact sheets, transparencies, prints. Offers $35/photo. Captions, model releases, identification of subjects required. Buys one-time rights.
Fiction: Erotica, novel excerpts; all must be gay male erotica. Buys 36 mss/year. Send complete ms. Length: 3,000-3,500 words. Pays $75 maximum.
Fillers: Short humor. Buys 12/year. Length: 1,500-3,500 words. Pays $50-75.
Tips: "Our publication features male nude photos plus three fiction pieces, several articles, cartoons, humorous comments on items from the media, photo features. We try to present the positive aspects of the gay lifestyle, with an emphasis on humor. Humorous pieces may be erotic in nature. We are open to all submissions that fit our gay male format; the emphasis, however, is on humor and the upbeat. We receive many fiction manuscripts but not nearly enough articles and humor."

LAMBDA BOOK REPORT, A Review of Contemporary Gay and Lesbian Literature, Lambda Rising, Inc., 1625 Connecticut Ave. NW, Washington DC 20009-1013. (202)462-7924. Fax: (202)462-7257. Senior

Editor: Jim Marks. Assistant Editor: Kanani Kauka. Managing Editor: Leslie Smith. 90% freelance written. Bimonthly magazine that covers gay/lesbian literature. "*Lambda Book Report* devotes its entire contents to the discussion of gay and lesbian books and authors. Any other submissions would be inappropriate." Estab. 1987. Circ. 11,000. Pays 30 days after publication. Byline given. Buys first rights. Query for electronic submissions. Reports in 2 month. Sample copy for $3.95 and 9×12 SAE with 5 first-class stamps. Free writer's guidelines.

Nonfiction: Book excerpts, essays (on gay literature), interview/profile (of authors), book reviews. "No historical essays, fiction or poetry." Query with published clips. Length: 200-2,000 words. Pays $15-125 for assigned articles; $5-25 for unsolicited articles.

Photos: Send photos with submission. Reviews contact sheets. Offers $10-25/photo. Model releases required. Buys one-time rights.

Tips: "Assignments go to writers who query with 2-3 published book reviews and/or interviews. It is helpful if the writer is familiar with gay and lesbian literature and can write intelligently and objectively on the field. Review section is most open. Writers should demonstrate with clips their scope of knowledge, ability and interest in reviewing gay books."

LIBIDO, The Journal of Sex & Sensibility, Libido, Inc., 5318 N. Paulina St., Chicago IL 60640, Editor: Marianna Beck. Managing Editor: Jack Hafferkamp. Submissions Editor: J.L. Beck. 50% freelance written. Quarterly magazine covering literate erotica. "*Libido* is about sexuality. Orientation is not an issue, writing ability is. The aim is to enlighten as often as it is to arouse. Humor—sharp and smart—is important, so are safer sex contexts." Estab. 1988. Circ. 9,000. Pays on publication. Byline given. Kill fee "rare, but negotiable." Buys one-time or second serial (reprint) rights. Editorial lead time 3 months. Submit seasonal material 4 months in advance. Accepts previously published submissions. Send tearsheet of article or short story and information about when and where the material previously appeared. Payment negotiable. Reports in 3-6 months. Sample copy for $7. Writer's guidelines for #10 SASE.

Nonfiction: Book excerpts, essays, historical/nostalgic, humor, photo feature, travel. "No violence, sexism or misty memoirs." Buys 10-20 mss/year. Send complete ms. Length: 300-2,500 words. Pays $50 minimum for assigned articles; $15 minimum for unsolicited articles. Pays contributor copies "when money isn't an issue and copies or other considerations have equal or higher value." Sometimes pays expenses of writers on assignment.

Photos: Send photos with submission. Reviews contact sheets and 5×7 and 8×10 prints. Negotiates payment individually. Model releases required. Buys one-time rights.

Fiction: Erotica, novel excerpts. Buys 10 mss/year. Send complete ms. Length: 800-2,500 words. Pays $20-50.

Poetry: Uses humorous short erotic poetry. No limericks. Buys 10 poems/year. Submit maximum 3 poems. Pays $15.

Tips: "Send us a manuscript—make it short, sharp and with a lead that makes us want to read. If we're not hooked by paragraph three, we reject the manuscript."

METRO SINGLES LIFESTYLES, Metro Publications, Dept. WM, P.O. Box 28203, Kansas City MO 64118. (816)436-8424. Editor: Robert L. Huffstutter. 40% freelance written. Eager to work with new/unpublished writers and photographers. Bimonthly tabloid covering singles lifestyles. Estab. 1984. **Pays on acceptance.** Publishes ms an average of 2 months after acceptance. Byline given with photo optional. Buys one-time and second serial (reprint) rights. Submit seasonal material 3 months in advance. Reports in 6 weeks. Sample copy for $3 and 9×12 SAE with 5 first-class stamps.

Nonfiction: Essay, general interest, how-to (on meeting the ideal mate, recovering from divorce, etc.), inspirational, interview/profile, personal experience, photo feature. Buys 6-12 mss/year. Send complete ms. Length: 700-1,200 words. Pays $100 maximum for assigned articles; pays $20-50 for unsolicited articles. Will pay in copies or other if writer prefers.

Photos: Pays up to $100 for photo layouts (10-12 photos). Subject matter suggested includes swimwear fashion, recreational events, "day in the life of an American single," etc. Reviews 3×5 and 8×10 color or b&w prints. Model releases of close-up or fashion shots required. Buys one-time and reprint rights. **Pays on acceptance.**

Columns/Departments: Movie Reviews, Lifestyles, Singles Events, Book Reviews (about singles), all 400-1,000 words. Buys 9-12 mss/year. Send complete ms. Pays $20-50.

Fiction: Confession, humorous, romance, slice-of-life vignettes. Buys 6-12 mss/year. Send complete ms. Length: 700-1,200 words. Pays $20-50.

Poetry: Free verse and light verse. Buys 40-60 poems/year. Submit maximum 3 poems. Length: 21 lines. Pays in complimentary copies and subscriptions for poetry. Byline given.

Tips: "A freelancer can best approach and break in to our publication with positive articles, photo features about singles and positive fiction about singles. Photos and short bios of singles (blue collar, white collar, and professional) at work needed. Photos and a few lines about singles enjoying recreation (swimming, sports, chess, etc.) always welcome. Color photos, close-up, are suitable."

MOM GUESS WHAT NEWSPAPER, 1725 L St., Sacramento CA 95814. (916)441-6397. Editor: Linda Birner. 80% freelance written. Works with small number of new/unpublished writers each year. Biweekly tabloid covering gay rights and gay lifestyles. Estab. 1978. Circ. 21,000. Publishes ms an average of 3 months after acceptance. Byline given. Buys all rights. Submit seasonal material 3 months in advance. Reports in 2 months. Sample copy for $1. Writer's guidelines for 10×13 SAE with 4 first-class stamps.
Nonfiction: Interview/profile and photo feature of international, national or local scope. Buys 8 mss/year. Query. Length: 200-1,500 words. Payment depends on article. Pays expenses of writers on special assignment.
Photos: Send photos with submission. Reviews 5×7 prints. Offers no additional payment for photos accepted with ms. Captions and identification of subjects required. Buys one-time rights.
Columns/Departments: News, Restaurants, Political, Health, Film, Video, Book Reviews. Buys 12 mss/ year. Query. Payment depends on article.

‡ON THE SCENE MAGAZINE, 3507 Wyoming NE, Albuquerque NM 87111-4427. (505)299-4401. Editor: Gail Skinner. 60% freelance written. Eager to work with new/unpublished writers. Monthly tabloid covering lifestyles for all ages. Estab. 1979. Pays on publication. Publishes ms within 12 months after acceptance. Byline given. Submit seasonal material 3 months in advance. Query for electronic submissions. Accepts previously published submissions. Send photocopy of article or typed ms with rights for sale noted. Pays 80% of the amount paid for an original article. Reports in 3 months. Sample copy for $3 and 9×12 SAE with 5 first-class stamps. Writer's guidelines for #10 SASE.
Nonfiction: General interest, how-to, humor, inspirational, opinion, personal experience, relationships, consumer guide, travel, finance, real estate, parenting, astrology. No suggestive or pornographic material. Buys 60 mss/year. Send complete ms. "Ms returned only if adequate SASE is included." Also publishes some fiction. Length: 500-1,200 words. Pays $20-60.
Photos: Send photos with ms. Captions, model releases, identification of subjects required.
Tips: "We are looking for articles that deal with every aspect of living—whether on a local or national level. Our readers are of above-average intelligence, income and education. The majority of our articles are chosen from 'relationships,' 'humor' and seasonal submissions."

SINGLELIFE MAGAZINE, SingleLife Enterprises, Inc., 606 W. Wisconsin Ave., Milwaukee WI 53203-1992. (414)271-9700. Fax: (414)271-5263. Editor: Gail Levine. 40% freelance written. Prefers to work with published/established writers. Bimonthly magazine covering single lifestyles. Estab. 1982. Circ. 22,000. Pays on publication. Publishes ms an average of 4-6 months after acceptance. Byline given. Buys one-time second serial (reprint) rights. Submit seasonal material 4 months in advance. Accepts previously published submissions. Send typed ms with rights for sale noted and information about when and where the article previously appeared. Pays 75% of their fee for an original article. Reports in 2 months. Sample copy and writer's guidelines for $3.50. Writer's guidelines for #10 SASE.
Nonfiction: Upbeat and in-depth articles on significant areas of interest to single people such as male/ female relationships, travel, health, sports, food, single parenting, humor, finances, places to go and things to do. Prefers third person point of view and ms to query letter. "Our readers are between 25 and 50." Length: 1,000-1,500 words. Pays $60-100.
• No longer publishing fiction or poetry.
Tips: "The easiest way to get in is to write something humorous or insightful, or both."

TWN, South Florida's Weekly Gay Alternative, (formerly *The Weekly News*), 901 NE 79th St., Miami FL 33138. (305)757-6333. Fax: (305)756-6488. Editor: Steven R. Biller. 40% freelance written. Weekly gay tabloid. Circ. 34,000. Pays on publication. Byline given. Buys one-time rights. Submit seasonal material 2 months in advance. Accepts simultaneous and previously published submissions. Send tearsheet or typed ms with rights for sale noted and information about when and where the article previously appeared. Usually pays 100% of the amount paid for an original article. Guidelines for SASE. Sample copy for 10×13 SAE with 6 first-class stamps.
Nonfiction: Exposé, humor, interview/profile. Buys 8 mss/year. Send complete ms. Pays $25-500. Sometimes pays the expenses of writers on assignment.
Photos: Send photos with submission. Reviews 3×5 prints. Offers $5-20/photo. Buys first and future use.
Columns/Departments: Send complete ms. Length: 700 words maximum. Pays $15-30.
• Publication has been reformatted to serve readers in South Florida.

THE WASHINGTON BLADE, Washington Blade, Inc., 1408 U St., NW, Washington DC 20009-3916. (202)797-7000. Fax: (202)797-7040. Senior Editor: Lisa M. Keen. 20% freelance written. Weekly news tabloid covering the gay/lesbian community. "Articles (subjects) should be written from or directed to a gay perspective." Estab. 1969. Circ. 40,500. Pays in 1 month. Publishes ms an average of 1 month after acceptance. Byline given. Offers $15 kill fee. Buys first North American serial rights. Submit seasonal material 1 month in advance. Reports in 1-2 months. Sample copy and writer's guidelines for 9×12 SAE with 6 first-class stamps.
Nonfiction: Exposé (of government, private agency, church, etc., handling of gay-related issues); historical/ nostalgic; interview/profile (of gay community/political leaders; persons, gay or nongay, in positions to affect gay issues; outstanding achievers who happen to be gay; those who incorporate the gay lifestyle into their

professions); photo feature (on a nationally or internationally historic gay event); travel (on locales that welcome or cater to the gay traveler). *The Washington Blade* basically covers 2 areas: news and lifestyle. News coverage of D.C. metropolitan area gay community, local and federal government actions relating to gays, as well as national news of interest to gays. Section also includes features on current events. Special issues: annual gay pride (early June). No sexually explicit material. Articles of interest to the community must include and be written for both gay men and lesbians. Buys 30 mss/year, average. Query with published clips and résumé. Length: 500-1,500 words. Pays 5-10¢/word. Sometimes pays the expenses of writers on assignment.

Photos: "A photo or graphic with feature/lifestyle articles is particularly important. Photos with news stories are appreciated." Send photos. Reviews b&w contact sheets and 5×7 glossy prints. Pays $25 minimum. Captions preferred; model releases required. On assignment, photographer paid mutually agreed upon fee, with expenses reimbursed. Publication retains all rights.

Tips: "Send good examples of your writing and know the paper before you submit a manuscript for publication. We get a lot of submissions which are entirely inappropriate. We're looking for more features, but fewer AIDS-related features. Greatest opportunity for freelancers resides in current events, features, interviews and book reviews."

Religious

Religious magazines focus on a variety of subjects, styles and beliefs. Many are publishing articles relating to current topics such as AIDS, cults, or substance abuse. Fewer religious publications are considering poems and personal experience articles, but many emphasize special ministries to singles, seniors or other special interest groups. Such diversity makes reading each magazine essential for the writer hoping to break in. Educational and inspirational material of interest to church members, workers and leaders within a denomination or religion is needed by the publications in this category. Publications intended to assist professional religious workers in teaching and managing church affairs are classified in Church Administration and Ministry in the Trade section. Religious magazines for children and teenagers can be found in the Juvenile and Teen and Young Adult classifications. Other religious publications can be found in the Ethnic/Minority section as well.

AMERICA, 106 W. 56th St., New York NY 10019. (212)581-4640. Editor: Rev. George W. Hunt. Published weekly for adult, educated, largely Roman Catholic audience. Estab. 1909. **Pays on acceptance.** Byline given. Usually buys all rights. Reports in 3 weeks. Free writer's guidelines.
Nonfiction: "We publish a wide variety of material on politics, economics, ecology, and so forth. We are not a parochial publication, but almost all of our pieces make some moral or religious point. We are not interested in purely informational pieces or personal narratives which are self-contained and have no larger moral interest." Articles on literature, current political, social events. Length: 1,500-2,000 words. Pays $50-100.
Poetry: Length: 15-30 lines. Patrick Samway, S.J., poetry editor.

THE ANNALS OF SAINT ANNE DE BEAUPRÉ, Redemptorist Fathers, P.O. Box 1000, St. Anne De Beaupré, Quebec G0A 3C0 Canada. (418)827-4538. Fax: (418)827-4530. Editor: Roch Achard C.Ss.R. 80% freelance written. Works with a small number of new/unpublished writers each year. Monthly magazine on religion. "Our aim is to promote devotion to St. Anne and Catholic family values." Estab. 1878. Circ. 45,000. **Pays on acceptance.** Publishes ms an average of 1-2 years after acceptance. Byline given. Buys first North American rights only. Submit seasonal material 3 months in advance. Reports in 2-3 weeks. Free sample copy and writer's guidelines. We never accept simultaneous submissions or reprints.
Nonfiction: Exposé, general interest, inspirational, personal experience. No articles without spiritual thrust. Buys 30 mss/year. Send complete ms. Length: 500-1,500 words. Pays 3-4¢/word.
Fiction: Religious. Buys 15 mss/year. Send complete ms. Length: 500-1,500 words. Pays 3-4¢/word.
Poetry: "Our poetry 'bank' is full and we will not be accepting any new items for the next year or so."
Tips: "Write something educational, inspirational, objective and uplifting. Reporting rather than analysis is simply not remarkable. Please ensure that your ms is typed, double-spaced, legible. Include a pertinent photo, if possible."

THE ASSOCIATE REFORMED PRESBYTERIAN, Associate Reformed Presbyterian General Synod, 1 Cleveland St., Greenville SC 29601-3696. (803)232-8297. Editor: Ben Johnston. 5% freelance written. Works with a small number of new/unpublished writers each year. Christian magazine serving a conservative, evangelical and Reformed denomination, most of whose members are in the Southeast US. Estab. 1976. Circ. 6,300. **Pays on acceptance.** Publishes ms an average of 4 months after acceptance. Byline given. Not copyrighted.

Buys first, one-time, or second serial (reprint) rights. Submit seasonal material 4 months in advance. Accepts simultaneous and previously published submissions. Send tearsheet or photocopy of article or short story or typed ms with rights for sale noted and information about when and where the article previously appeared. For reprints, pays 100% of the amount paid for an original article. Reports in 1 month. Sample copy for $1.50. Writer's guidelines for #10 SASE.

Nonfiction: Book excerpts, essays, inspirational, opinion, personal experience, religious. Buys 10-15 mss/year. Query. Length: 400-2,000 words. Pays $70 maximum.

Photos: State availability of photos with submission. Reviews 5×7 reprints. Offers $25 maximum/photo. Captions and identification of subjects required. Buys one-time rights.

Fiction: Religious and children's. Pays $50 maximum.

Tips: "Feature articles are the area of our publication most open to freelancers. Focus on a contemporary problem and offer Bible-based solutions to it. Provide information that would help a Christian struggling in his daily walk. Writers should understand that we are denominational, conservative, evangelical, Reformed and Presbyterian. A writer who appreciates these nuances would stand a much better chance of being published here than one who does not."

‡BAPTIST LEADER, P.O. Box 851, Valley Forge PA 19482-0851. (610)768-2153. Editor: Linda Isham. For pastors, teachers, lay leaders and Christian education staff in churches. 5% freelance written. Works with several new/unpublished writers each year. Quarterly. Estab. 1939. Pays on publication. Publishes ms an average of 8 months after acceptance. Editorial lead time 8 months. Accepts previously published submissions. Send typed ms with rights for sale noted and information about when and where the article previously appeared. Pays 100% of their fee for an original article. Sample copy for $1.50. Writer's guidelines for #10 SASE.

Nonfiction: Educational topics. How-to articles and programs for local church teachers and leaders. Length: 1,500-2,000 words. Pays $25-75.

Tips: "Emphasis on Christian education administration and planning and articles for all church leaders."

BIBLICAL ILLUSTRATOR, The Sunday School Board, 127 Ninth Ave. N., Nashville TN 37234. Fax: (615)251-2795. Design Editor: James D. McLemore. "Articles are designed to coordinate with other Southern Baptist periodicals. Unsolicited mss are rarely applicable. Inquire first." Reports in 2 months. Sample copy for 9×12 SAE with 3 first-class stamps.

‡CAMPUS LIFE, Christianity Today, Inc., 465 Gundersen Dr., Carol Stream IL 60188. (708)260-6200. Editor: Harold Smith. Contact: Christopher Lutes, manuscripts editor. 35% freelance written. Magazine published ten times/year for the Christian life as it related to today's teen. "*Campus Life* is a magazine for high-school and college age teenagers. Our editorial slant is not overtly religious. The indirect style is intended to create a safety zone with our readers and to reflect our philosophy that God is interested in all of life. Therefore, we publish 'message stories' side by side with general interest, humor, etc." Estab. 1942. Circ. 120,000. **Pays on acceptance.** Publishes ms an average of 4-5 months after acceptance. Byline given. Offers 50% kill fee. Buys first and one-time rights. Editorial lead time 4 months. Submit seasonal material 4-5 months in advance. Accepts simultaneous and previously published submissions. Reports in 3-5 weeks on queries; 1-2 months on mss. Sample copy for $2 and 8×10 SAE with 3 first-class stamps. Writer's guidelines for #10 SASE.

Nonfiction: Humor, personal experience, photo feature. The *Christian* college experience. Buys 10-20 mss/year. Query with published clips. Length: 250-2,500 words. Pays 10-20¢ minimum.

Photos: State availability of photos with submission. Reviews contact sheets, transparencies, 5×7 prints. Negotiates payment individually. Model release required. Buys one-time rights.

Columns/Departments: Making the Grade (tips and information for today's student), 50-250 words. Query with published clips. Pays $10-125.

Fiction: Buys 1-5 mss/year. Query. Length: 1,000-3,500 words. Pays 10-20¢/word.

Poetry: Free verse. "No material that does not 'communicate' to the average teenager." Buys 1-5 poems/year. Submit maximum 2 poems. Length: 5-20 lines. Pays $25-50.

Fillers: Anecdotes, facts, short humor. Buys 3-5/year. Length: $25-250 words. Pays $10-50.

Tips: "The best way to break in to *Campus Life* is through writing first-person or as-told-to first-person stories. But query first—with theme info, telling way this story would work for our audience. We are seeking humor: high school experiences with a "Dave Barry" flair, first-person, capturing a teen's everyday 'life lesson' experience."

‡CATHOLIC HERITAGE, Our Sunday Visitor, Inc., 200 Noll Plaza, Huntington IN 46750. (219)356-8400. Managing Editor: Richard Beemer. Contact: Robert P. Lockwood, editor. 25% freelance written. Bimonthly magazine covering the Catholic faith. "Explores the history and heritage of the Catholic faith with special emphasis on its impact on culture." Estab. 1991. Circ. 25,000. **Pays on acceptance.** Publishes ms an average of 1 year after acceptance. Byline given. Offers 33% or $50-75 kill fee. Buys first North American serial rights. Editorial lead time 6 months. Submit seasonal material 6 months in advance. Accepts previously published submissions. Reports in 3 weeks on queries; 1 month on mss. Sample copy free on request.

Nonfiction: Book excerpts, general interest, humor, interview/profile, photo feature, religious, travel, Church history. "No nostalgia pieces about what it was like growing up Catholic or about life in the Church prior to Vatican II." Buys 15 mss/year. Query. Length: 1,000-2,000 words. Pays $200. Sometimes pays expenses of writers on assignment.

Photos: State availability of photos with submission. Reviews prints. Negotiates payment individually. Captions required. Buys one-time rights.

Tips: "Write solid queries that take an aspect of the Catholic heritage and apply it to developments today. Show a good knowledge of the Church and a flair for historical writing. General features are most open to freelancers."

CATHOLIC NEAR EAST MAGAZINE, Catholic Near East Welfare Association, 1011 First Ave., New York NY 10022-4195. (212)826-1480. Fax: (212)838-1344. Editor: Michael La Città. 50% freelance written. Bimonthly magazine for a Catholic audience with interest in the Near East, particularly its current religious, cultural and political aspects. Estab. 1926. Circ. 100,000. **Pays on acceptance.** Publishes ms an average of 4 months after acceptance. Byline given. Buys all rights. Reports in 2 months. Sample copy and writer's guidelines for 7½×10½ SAE with 2 first-class stamps.

Nonfiction: "Cultural, devotional, political, historical material on the Near East, with an emphasis on the Eastern Christian churches. Style should be simple, factual, concise. Articles must stem from personal acquaintance with subject matter, or thorough up-to-date research." Length: 1,200-1,800 words. Pays 20¢/word.

Photos: "Photographs to accompany manuscript are welcome; they should illustrate the people, places, ceremonies, etc. which are described in the article. We prefer color transparencies but occasionally use b&w. Pay varies depending on use – scale from $50-300."

Tips: "We are interested in current events in the regions listed above as they affect the cultural, political and religious lives of people."

CHICAGO STUDIES, Box 665, Mundelein IL 60060. (708)566-1462. Editor: Rev. George J. Dyer. 50% freelance written. Triannual magazine for Roman Catholic priests and religious educators. Estab. 1962. Circ. 5,000. **Pays on acceptance.** Buys all rights. Reports in 2 months. Sample copy for $5. Free writer's guidelines.

Nonfiction: Nontechnical discussion of theological, Biblical, ethical topics. Articles aimed at a nontechnical presentation of the contemporary scholarship in those fields. Submit complete ms. Buys 30 mss/year. Length: 3,000-4,000 words. Pays $35-100.

THE CHRISTIAN CENTURY, 407 S. Dearborn St., Chicago IL 60605-1150. (312)427-5380. Editor: James M. Wall. Senior Editors: Martin E. Marty and Dean Peerman. Managing Editor: David Heim. 70% freelance written. Eager to work with new/unpublished writers. Weekly magazine for ecumenically-minded, progressive church people, both clergy and lay. Circ. 37,000. Pays on publication. Publishes ms an average of 2 months after acceptance. Usually buys all rights. Reports in 2 months. Sample copy available for $2. All queries, mss should be accompanied by SASE.

Nonfiction: "We use articles dealing with social problems, ethical dilemmas, political issues, international affairs and the arts, as well as with theological and ecclesiastical matters. We focus on concerns that arise at the juncture between church and society, or church and culture." Query appreciated, but not essential. Length: 2,500 words maximum. Payment varies, but averages $30/page.

CHRISTIAN EDUCATION COUNSELOR, (formerly *Sunday School Counselor*), General Council of the Assemblies of God, 1445 Boonville, Springfield MO 65802-1894. (417)862-2781. Editor: Sylvia Lee. 60% freelance written. Works with small number of new/unpublished writers each year. Monthly magazine on religious education in the local church – the official Sunday school voice of the Assemblies of God channeling programs and help to local, primarily lay, leadership. Estab. 1994. Circ. 35,000. **Pays on acceptance.** Publishes ms an average of 9 months after acceptance. Byline given. Offers variable kill fee. Buys first North American serial, one-time, all, simultaneous, first serial or second serial (reprint) rights; makes work-for-hire assignments. Submit seasonal material 7 months in advance. Accepts simultaneous and previously published submissions. Send typed ms with rights for sale noted and information about when and where the article previously appeared. Pays 50% of their fee for an original article. Reports in 1 month. Free sample copy and writer's guidelines for SASE.

Nonfiction: How-to, inspirational, interview/profile, personal experience, photo feature. All related to religious education in the local church. Buys 100 mss/year. Send complete ms. Length: 300-1,800 words. Pays $25-150.

Photos: Send photos with ms. Reviews b&w and color prints. Model releases and identification of subjects required. Buys one-time rights.

• Looking for more photo-illustrated mss.

CHRISTIAN HOME & SCHOOL, Christian Schools International, 3350 East Paris Ave. SE, Grand Rapids MI 49512. (616)957-1070, ext. 234. Executive Editor: Gordon L. Bordewyk. Senior Editor: Roger Schmurr. 30% freelance written. Works with a small number of new/unpublished writers each year. Bimonthly magazine published 6 times/year covering family life and Christian education. "For parents who support Christian education. We feature material on a wide range of topics of interest to parents." Estab. 1922. Pays on publication. Publishes ms an average of 4 months after acceptance. Byline given. Buys first North American serial rights. Submit seasonal material 4 months in advance. Simultaneous queries OK. Reports in 1 month. Sample copy for 9 × 12 SAE with 4 first-class stamps. Writer's guidelines for #10 SASE.

Nonfiction: Book excerpts, interview/profile, opinion, personal experience, articles on parenting and school life. "We publish features on issues which affect the home and school and profiles on interesting individuals, providing that the profile appeals to our readers and is not a tribute or eulogy of that person." Buys 40 mss/year. Send complete ms. Length: 500-2,000 words. Pays $75-150. Sometimes pays the expenses of writers on assignment.

Photos: "If you have any color photos appropriate for your article, send them along."

Tips: "Features are the area most open to freelancers. We are publishing articles that deal with contemporary issues that affect parents. Use an informal easy-to-read style rather than a philosophical, academic tone. Try to incorporate vivid imagery and concrete, practical examples from real life."

CHRISTIAN READER, A Digest of the Best in Christian Reading, Christianity Today, 465 Gundersen Dr., Carol Stream IL 60188. (708)260-6200. Fax: (708)260-0114. Editor: Bonne Steffen. 80% freelance written. Bimonthly magazine for "evangelical Christian audience, especially women 45 and older." Estab. 1963. Circ. 245,000. **Pays first rights on acceptance;** pays reprints on publication. Byline given. Buys first North American serial, first or second serial (reprint) rights. Editorial lead time 6 months. Submit seasonal material 9 months in advance. Accepts previously published submissions. Send tearsheet or photocopy of article or typed manuscript with rights for sale noted and information about when and where the article previously appeared. Pays 50% of the amount paid for an original article. Reports in 2 weeks on mss; 1 month on queries. Sample copy for 5 × 8 SAE with 2 first-class stamps. Writer's guidelines for #10 SASE.

Nonfiction: Book excerpts, humor, inspirational, personal experience, religious. Buys 120 mss/year. Query. Length: 500-1,500 words. Pays $50-100 for original articles, depending on length; $30-50 for reprinted articles. Pays expenses of writers on assignment.

Photos: State availability of photos with submission. Reviews 35mm 4 × 6 transparencies. Negotiates payment individually. Buys one-time rights.

Columns/Departments: Bonnie Rice: editorial coordinator. Lite Fare (adult church humor), 25-150 words; and Kids of the Kingdom (kids say and do funny things), 25-150 words; Rolling Down the Aisle (humorous wedding tales), 25-250 words. Buys 150 mss/year. Send complete ms. Pays $25.

‡THE CHRISTIAN RESPONSE, Christian Writers of America, Route 2 Box 1, P.O. Box 125, Staples MN 56479. (218)894-1165. Editor: Hap Corbett. 15% freelance written. Bimonthly consumer newsletter covering religion – Christianity. "Exposes incidents of Christians or Christianity being misrepresented or unfairly treated in the media." Estab. 1993. Circ. 200. **Pays on acceptance.** Publishes ms an average of 2-6 months after acceptance. Buys first rights or simultaneous rights. Editorial lead time 2 months. Submit seasonal material 6 months in advance. Accepts simultaneous and previously published submissions. Reports in 3 weeks on queries; 1 month on mss. Sample copy for $1.

Nonfiction: Religious. Length: 200 maximum words. Pays $5-20 minimum for unsolicited articles.

Fillers: Length: 10-25 words. Pays $5-10.

Tips: "Our organization encourages Christians in all aspects of writing but our main emphasis is on short, snappy letters, preferably under 200 words – ideally under 100."

CHRISTIAN SINGLE, Family Ministry Dept., Baptist Sunday School Board, 127 9th Ave. N., Nashville TN 37234. (615)251-4124. Editor: Stephen Felts. Contact: Leigh Neely, assistant editor. 30% freelance written. Prefers to work with published/established writers. Monthly "contemporary Christian magazine that seeks to give substantive information to singles for living the abundant life. It seeks to be constructive and creative in approach." Estab. 1979. Circ. 70,000. **Pays on acceptance.** Publishes ms 6-12 months after acceptance. Byline given. Buys all rights or makes work-for-hire assignments. Submit seasonal material 6 months in advance. Reports in 2 months. Accepts previously published submissions. Send typed ms with rights for sale noted. Pays 75% of their fee for an original article. Sample copy and writer's guidelines for 9 × 12 SASE with 4 first-class stamps.

Nonfiction: Humor (good, clean humor that applies to Christian singles), how-to (specific subjects which apply to singles), inspirational (of the personal experience type), high adventure personal experience (of single adults), photo feature (on outstanding Christian singles), financial articles targeted to single adults. Buys 60-75 unsolicited mss/year. Query with published clips. Length: 600-1,200 words. Payment negotiable.

Fiction: "We are also looking for fiction suitable for our target audience."

Tips: "We are looking for people who experience single living from a positive, Christian perspective."

• They want more experienced writers and want submissions on disk, with accompanying hard copy.

‡CHRISTIAN SOCIAL ACTION, 100 Maryland Ave. NE, Washington DC 20002. (202)488-5621. Fax: (202)488-5619. Editor: Lee Ranck. 2% freelance written. Works with a small number of new/unpublished writers each year. Monthly for "United Methodist clergy and lay people interested in in-depth analysis of social issues, with emphasis on the church's role or involvement in these issues." Circ. 2,500. May buy all rights. Pays on publication. Publishes ms an average of 2 months after acceptance. Rights purchased vary with author and material. Returns rejected material in 4-5 weeks. Reports on material accepted for publication in a month. Free sample copy and writer's guidelines for #10 SASE.

Nonfiction: "This is the social action publication of The United Methodist Church published by the denomination's General Board of Church and Society. Our publication tries to relate social issues to the church— what the church can do, is doing; why the church should be involved. We only accept articles relating to social issues, e.g., war, draft, peace, race relations, welfare, police/community relations, labor, population problems, drug and alcohol problems." No devotional, 'religious,' superficial material, highly technical articles, personal experiences or poetry. Buys 25-30 mss/year. "Query to show that writer has expertise on a particular social issue, give credentials, and reflect a readable writing style." Query or submit complete ms. Length: 2,000 words maximum. Pays $75-125. Sometimes pays the expenses of writers on assignment.

Tips: "Write on social issues, but not superficially; we're more interested in finding an expert who can write (e.g., on human rights, alcohol problems, peace issues) than a writer who attempts to research a complex issue."

CHRISTIANITY TODAY, 465 Gundersen Dr., Carol Stream IL 60188-2498. Fax: (708)260-0114. Administrative Editor: Carol Thiessen. 80% freelance written. Works with a small number of new/unpublished writers each year. Semimonthly magazine emphasizing orthodox, evangelical religion. Estab. 1956. Circ. 180,000. Publishes ms an average of 6 months after acceptance. Usually buys first serial rights. Submit seasonal material at least 8 months in advance. Accepts previously published submissions. Send photocopy of article or typed manuscript with rights for sale noted and information about when and where the article previously appeared. Pays 25% of the amount paid for an original article. Reports in 3 months. Sample copy and writer's guidelines for 9×12 SAE with 3 first-class stamps.

Nonfiction: Theological, ethical, historical, informational (not merely inspirational). Buys 4 mss/issue. *Query only.* Unsolicited mss not accepted and not returned. Length: 1,000-4,000 words. Pays negotiable rates. Sometimes pays the expenses of writers on assignment. Accepts previously published submissions. Send typed ms with rights for sale noted and information about when and where the article previously appeared. Pays 25% of their fee for an original article.

Columns/Departments: Church in Action (profiles of not-so-well-known Christians involved in significant or offbeat services). Buys 7 mss/year. Query only. Length: 900-1,000 words.

Tips: "We are developing more of our own manuscripts and requiring a much more professional quality of others. Queries without SASE will not be answered and manuscripts not containing SASE will not be returned."

CHRYSALIS, Journal of Spiritual Discovery, P.O. Box 549, West Chester PA 19381-0549. Send inquiries and mss directly to the editorial office: Route 1, Box 184, Dillwyn VA 23936-9616. Editor: Carol S. Lawson. Managing Editor: Susanna van Rensselaer. 50% freelance written. Triannual literary magazine on spiritually related topics. "*It is very important to send for writer's guidelines and sample copies before submitting.* Content of fiction, articles, reviews, poetry, etc., should be directly focused on that issue's theme and directed to the educated, intellectually curious reader." Estab. 1985. Circ. 3,000. Pays at page-proof stage. Publishes ms an average of 9 months after acceptance. Byline given. Buys first rights and makes work-for-hire assignments. Reports in 1 month on queries; 3 months on mss. Sample copy for $5 and 9×12 SAE. Writer's guidelines and copy deadlines for SASE.

Nonfiction: Essays and interview/profile. Upcoming themes: Windows (Spring 1995); Play (Summer 1995); The Good Life (Autumn 1995); Symbols (Spring 1996). Buys 15 mss/year. Query. Length: 750-2,500 words. Pays $50-250 for assigned articles; $50-150 for unsolicited articles.

Photos and Illustrations: Send suggestions for illustrations with submission. Offers no additional payment for photos accepted with ms. Captions and identification of subjects required. Buys original artwork for cover and inside copy, b&w illustrations related to theme; pays $25-150. Buys one-time rights.

Columns/Departments: Fringe Benefits (book, film, art, video reviews relevant to *Chrysalis* subject matter), 350-500 words. Buys 12 mss/year. Length: 350-2,000. Pays $50-250.

Fiction: Phoebe Loughrey, fiction editor. Adventure, experimental, historical, mainstream, mystery, science fiction, related to theme of issue. Buys 6 mss/year. Query. Length: 500-2,500 words. Short fiction more likely to be published. Pays $50-150.

Poetry: Avante-garde and traditional *but not religious.* Buys 10 poems/year. Pays $25. Submit maximum 6.

THE CHURCH HERALD, 4500 60th St. SE, Grand Rapids MI 49512-9642. Editor: Jeffrey Japinga. Managing Editor: Christina Van Eyl. 5% freelance written. Prefers to work with published/established writers. Monthly magazine covering contemporary Christian life. "*The Church Herald* is the denominational publication of the Reformed Church in America, a Protestant denomination in the Presbyterian-Reformed family of churches. We will consider carefully researched and well-written articles on almost any subject, but they all must have a distinctively Christian perspective and must have a specific connection with our intended denominational audience." Circ. 108,000. **Pays on acceptance.** Publishes ms an average of 3 months after acceptance. Byline given. Offers 50% kill fee. Buys first, one-time, second serial (reprint), simultaneous and all rights. Submit seasonal material 6 months in advance. Accepts simultaneous and previously published submissions. Query for electronic submissions. Reports in 1 month on queries; 2 months on mss. Sample copy and writer's guidelines for $2 and 9 × 12 SAE.

Nonfiction: Essays, general interest, humor, inspirational, personal experience, religious. Buys 15 mss/year. Queries only; unsolicited mss returned. Length: 400-1,500 words. Pays $50-200 for assigned articles. Pays $50-150 for unsolicited articles. Pays expenses of writers on assignment.

Photos: State availability of photos with submission. Reviews color transparencies and 8 × 10 b&w prints. Offers $25-50/photo. Model releases required. Buys one-time rights.

Fiction: Religious. "We consider good fiction written from a Christian perspective. Avoid pious sentimentality and obvious plots." Buys 1 ms/year. Send complete ms. Length: 400-1,500 words. Pays $45-120.

• No longer considering poetry.

Tips: "Research articles carefully. Superficial articles are immediately recognizable; they cannot be disguised by big words or professional jargon. Writers need not have personally experienced everything they write about, but they must have done careful research. Also, what our readers want are new solutions to recognized problems; be specific. If a writer doesn't have any, he or she should try another subject. Section most open to freelancers is feature articles on issues of faith or Christian living."

COLUMBIA, 1 Columbus Plaza, New Haven CT 06507. (203)772-2130. Editor: Richard McMunn. Monthly magazine for Catholic families. Caters particularly to members of the Knights of Columbus. Estab. 1921. Circ. 1.5 million. **Pays on acceptance.** Buys first serial rights. Free sample copy and writer's guidelines.

Nonfiction and Photos: Fact articles directed to the Catholic layman and his family dealing with current events, social problems, Catholic apostolic activities, education, ecumenism, rearing a family, literature, science, arts, sports and leisure. Color glossy prints, transparencies or contact prints with negatives are required for illustration. Articles without ample illustrative material are not given consideration. Pays up to $500, including photos. Buys 30 mss/year. Query. Length: 1,000-1,500 words.

COMMENTS, From the Friends, P.O. Box 840, Stoughton MA 02072-0840. Editor: David A. Reed. 10% freelance written. Quarterly Christian newsletter written especially for "Jehovah's Witnesses, ex-Jehovah's Witnesses and persons concerned about Jehovah's Witness, relatives, friends, and neighbors." Estab. 1981. Circ. 1,500. Pays on publication. Publishes ms an average of 3 months after acceptance. Byline sometimes given. Buys second serial (reprint) and simultaneous rights. Submit seasonal/holiday material 4 months in advance. Accepts simultaneous and previously published submissions. Send photocopy of article or typed manuscript with rights for sale noted. Pays 50% of their fee for an original article. Query for electronic submissions. Reports in 1 month on mss. *Writer's Market* recommends allowing 2 months for reply. Sample copy for $1 and #10 SAE with 2 first-class stamps. Writer's guidelines for #10 SAE with 2 first-class stamps.

Nonfiction: Book excerpts, essays, exposé, how-to (witnessing tips), humor, inspirational (aimed at JW's and ex-JW's *only*), interview/profile, personal experience, religious, book reviews of books on cults only. "No general religious material not written specifically for our unique readership." Buys 4 mss/year. Send complete ms. Length: 200-1,000 words. Pays $2-20. May pay with contributor copies rather than a cash payment "when a writer contributes an article as a gift to this ministry."

Columns/Departments: Witnessing Tips (brief, powerful and effective approaches), 250-300 words; News Briefs (current events involving Jehovah's Witnesses and ex-Jehovah's Witnesses), 60-240 words. Buys 4 mss/year. Send complete ms. Length: 60-300 words. Pays $2-10.

Fillers: Facts, newsbreaks, quotes. Buys 4/year. Length: 10-50 words. Pays $1-5.

Tips: "Acquaint us with your background that qualifies you to write in this field. Write well-documented, germane articles in layman's language. We reject all material that is not specifically about Jehovah's Witnesses. We publish nothing else."

‡COMPASS: A JESUIT JOURNAL, Jesuit Fathers of Upper Canada, #300, 10 St. Mary St., Toronto, Ontario M4Y 1P9 Canada.(416)921-0653. Editor: Robert Chodos. Managing Editor: Martin Royackers, SJ. 80% freelance written. Bimonthly magazine covering religious affairs, "directed at an informed general audience, made up primarily but by no means exclusively of Canadian Catholics. It provides an ethical perspective on contemporary social and religious affairs." Estab. 1983. Circ. 3,500. Pays on publication. Byline given. Offers 50% kill fee. Buys first rights. Editorial lead time 4 months. Submit seasonal material 4 months in advance. Query for electronic submissions. Reports in 3 months. Sample copy and writer's guidelines for $2.

Nonfiction: Essays, general interest, opinion, personal experience, religious. Special issues: 1950s (March 1995), Work (May 1995). Buys 50 mss/year. Query with published clips. Length: 750-2,000 words. Pays $100.

Photos: State availability of photos with submission. Offers no additional payment for photos accepted with ms. Identification of subjects required. Buys one-time rights.

Columns/Departments: Testament (commentary on Scripture); Colloquy (relationship between theology and daily life); Disputation (comment on articles previously appearing in *Compass*). Length: 750 words. Buys 18 mss/year. Query. Pays $50-150.

Fiction: Mainstream, religious. Buys 2 mss/year. Send complete ms. Length: 1,000-2,500 words. Pays $100-350.

Poetry: Free verse, traditional. Buys 1 poem/year. Submit maximum 10 poems. Length: 50 lines maximum. Pays $50-100.

Fillers: Jack Costello, SJ, Points editor. Anecdotes, short humor. Buys 12/year. Length: 20-100 words. Pays 1 year subscription to *Compass*.

Tips: "*Compass* publishes theme issues. The best chance of being published is to get a list of upcoming themes and gear proposals to them. All sections are open to freelancers."

CONSCIENCE, A Newsjournal of Prochoice Catholic Opinion, Catholics for a Free Choice, Suite 301, 1436 U St. NW, Washington DC 20009-3997. (202)986-6093. Editor: Maggie Hume. 80% freelance written. Willing to work with new/unpublished writers. Quarterly newsjournal covering reproductive health and rights, including but not limited to abortion rights in the church, and church-state issues in US and worldwide. "A feminist, pro-choice perspective is a must, and knowledge of Christianity and specifically Catholicism is helpful." Estab. 1980. Circ. 12,000. Pays on publication. Publishes ms an average of 4 months after acceptance. Byline given. Buys first North American serial rights; makes work-for-hire assignments. Submit seasonal material 6 months in advance. Sometimes accepts previously published submission. Send tearsheet or photocopy of article or typed manuscript with rights for sale noted and information about when and where the article previously appeared. Pays 20-30% of their fee for an original article. Query for electronic submissions. Reports in 4 months. Sample copy for 9 × 12 SASE with 98¢ postage. Writer's guidelines for #10 SASE.

● This magazine is increasingly international in focus.

Nonfiction: Book excerpts, interview/profile, opinion, issue anaylsis, a small amount of personal experience. Especially needs material that recognizes the complexity of reproductive issues and decisions, and offers original, honest insight. Buys 8-12 mss/year. Query with published clips or send complete ms. Length: 1,000-3,500 words. Pays $25-150. "Writers should be aware that we are a nonprofit organization." Sometimes pays the expenses of writers on assignment.

Photos: State availability of photos with query or ms. Prefers b&w prints. Identification of subjects required.

Columns/Departments: Book reviews. Buys 6-10 mss/year. Query first preferred; send complete ms. Length: 600-1,200 words. Pays $25-50.

Fillers: Newsbreaks. Uses 6/year. Length: 100-300 words. $25-35.

Tips: "Say something new on the issue of abortion, or sexuality, or the role of religion or the Catholic church, or women's status in the church. Thoughtful, well-researched and well-argued articles needed. The most frequent mistakes made by writers in submitting an article to us are lack of originality and wordiness."

CORNERSTONE, Cornerstone Communications, Inc., 939 W. Wilson, Chicago IL 60640-5718. Editor: Dawn Herrin. Submissions Editor: Jennifer Ingerson. 10% freelance written. Eager to work with new/unpublished writers. 3-6 issues/year. Magazine covers contemporary issues in the light of Evangelical Christianity. Estab. 1972. Circ. 50,000. Pays after publication. Byline given. Buys first serial rights. Submit seasonal material 6 months in advance. Accepts simultaneous and previously published submissions. Manuscripts *not* returned. "Send copies, not originals. If work is considered for publication, we will contact." Reports in 8-12 weeks. Sample copy and writer's guidelines for 8½ × 11 envelope with 5 first-class stamps.

Nonfiction: Essays, personal experience, religious. Buys 1-2 mss/year. Query. 2,700 words maximum. Pays negotiable rate, 8-10¢/word. Sometimes pays the expenses of writers on assignment.

Photos: Send photos with accompanying ms. Reviews 8 × 10 b&w and color prints and 35mm slides. Identification of subjects required. Buys negotiable rights.

Columns/Departments: Music (interview with artists, mainly rock, focusing on artist's world view and value system as expressed in his/her music), Current Events, Personalities, Film and Book Reviews (focuses on meaning as compared and contrasted to biblical values). Buys 1-4 mss/year. Query. Length: 100-2,500 words (negotiable). Pays negotiable rate, 8-10¢/word.

Fiction: "Articles may express Christian world view but should not be unrealistic or 'syrupy.' Other than porn, the sky's the limit. We want fiction as creative as the Creator." Buys 1-4 mss/year. Send complete ms. Length: 250-2,500 words (negotiable). Pays negotiable rate, 8-10¢/word.

Poetry: Avant-garde, free verse, haiku, light verse, traditional. No limits *except* for epic poetry ("We've not the room!"). Buys 10-50 poems/year. Submit maximum 5 poems. Payment negotiated. 1-15 lines: $10. Over 15 lines: $25.

Tips: "A display of creativity which expresses a biblical world view without cliches or cheap shots at non-Christians is the ideal. We are known as one of the most avant-garde magazines in the Christian market, yet attempt to express orthodox beliefs in language of the '90s. *Any* writer who does this may well be published by *Cornerstone*. Creative fiction is begging for more Christian participation. We anticipate such contributions gladly. Interviews where well-known personalities respond to the gospel are also strong publication possibilities."

THE COVENANT COMPANION, Covenant Publications of the Evangelical Covenant Church, 5101 N. Francisco Ave., Chicago IL 60625. (312)784-3000. Fax: (312)784-4366. Editor: James R. Hawkinson. 10-15% freelance written. "As the official monthly organ of The Evangelical Covenant Church, we seek to inform, stimulate and gather the denomination we serve by putting Covenants in touch with each other and assisting them in interpreting contemporary issues. We also seek to inform them on events in the church. Our background is evangelical and our emphasis is on Christian commitment and life." Circ. 23,500. Publishes ms an average of 2 months after acceptance. Byline given. Buys first or all rights. Submit seasonal material 4 months in advance. Accepts simultaneous and previously published submissions. Query for electronic submissions. Sample copy for $2.25 and 9 × 12 SASE. Writer's guidelines for #10 SASE. Unused mss returned only if accompanied by SASE.

Nonfiction: Humor, inspirational, religious. Buys 20-25 mss/year. Send complete ms. Length: 500-2,000 words. Pays $15-50 for assigned articles; pays $15-35 for unsolicited articles.

Photos: Send photos with submissions. Reviews prints. Offers no additonal payment for photos accepted with ms. Identification of subjects required. Buys one-time rights.

Poetry: Traditional. Buys 10-15 poems/year. Submit maximum 10 poems. Pays $10-15.

Tips: "Seasonal articles related to church year and on national holidays are welcome."

‡DAILY MEDITATION, Box 2710, San Antonio TX 78299. Editor: Ruth S. Paterson. Quarterly. Byline given. Rights purchased vary. **Pays on acceptance.** Submit seasonal material 6 months in advance. Sample copy for $1.

Nonfiction: "Inspirational, self-improvement and nonsectarian religious articles, showing the path to greater spiritual growth." Length: 750-1,600 words. Pays 1½-2¢/word.

Fillers: Length: 400 words maximum.

Poetry: Inspirational. Length: 16 lines maximum. Pays 14¢/line.

Tips: "All our material is freelance except our meditations, which are staff written. We buy approximately 250 manuscripts per year. We must see finished manuscripts; no queries, please. Checking copy is sent upon publication."

THE DOOR, Box 118, N. 30th St., Waco TX 76710. (916)842-2701. Contact: Bob Darden. (817)752-1468. 50% freelance written. Works with a small number of new/unpublished writers each year. Bimonthly magazine for men and women connected with the church. Circ. 11,000. Pays on publication. Publishes an average of 1 year after acceptance. Buys first rights. Accepts previously published articles. Send typed ms with rights for sale noted and information about when and where the article previously appeared. Reports in 3 months. Sample copy for $4. Writer's guidelines for SASE.

Nonfiction: Satirical articles on church renewal, Christianity and organized religion. Few book reviews. Buys about 30 mss/year. Submit complete ms. Length: 1,500 words maximum, 750-1,000 preferred. Pays $60-200. Sometimes pays expenses of writers on assignments.

Tips: "We look for someone who is clever, on our wave length, and has some savvy about the evangelical church. We are very picky and highly selective. The writer has a better chance of breaking in with our publication with short articles and fillers since we are a bimonthly publication with numerous regular features and the magazine is only 36 pages. The most frequent mistake made by writers is that they do not understand satire. They see we are a humor magazine and consequently come off funny/cute (like *Reader's Digest*) rather than funny/satirical (like *National Lampoon*)."

EPISCOPAL LIFE, Episcopal Church in the United States, 815 Second Ave., New York NY 10017. (212)922-5398. Editor: Jerrold F. Hames. Managing Editor: Edward P. Stannard. 35% freelance written. Monthly tabloid of news, information, viewpoints of Episcopal Church and ecumenical interest to Episcopalians in the US. Estab. 1990. Circ. 180,000. Pays on publication. Publishes an average of 2 months after acceptance. Byline given. Offers 50% kill fee. Buys one-time rights and makes work-for-hire assignments. Submit seasonal material 4 months in advance. Accepts simultaneous and previously published submissions. Query for electronic submissions. Reports in 1 month. Free sample copy.

Nonfiction: Inspirational, interview/profile, religious. Needs freelance material for Christmas, Easter, education issue, book issue and environmental issue. No first-person articles. Buys 12 mss/year. Query with published clips. Length: 250-1,200 words. Pays $50-300. Pays expenses of writers on assignment.

Photos: State availability of photos with submission. Offers $50-75/photo. Identification of subjects required. Buys one-time rights.

Columns/Departments: Nan Cobbey, departments editor. Buys 36 mss/year. Query with published clips. Length: 300-600 words. Pays $35-75.

EVANGEL, Free Methodist Publishing House, P.O. Box 535002, Indianapolis IN 46253-5002. (317)244-3660. Fax: (317)244-1247. Editor: Carolyn Smith. 100% freelance written. Weekly magazine. Estab. 1897. Circ. 26,000. Pays on publication. Publishes an average of 1 year after acceptance. Buys simultaneous, second serial (reprint) or one-time rights. Submit seasonal material 9 months in advance. Reports in 1 month. Sample copy and writer's guidelines for 6 × 9 SAE with 2 first-class stamps.

Nonfiction: Interview (with ordinary person who is doing something extraordinary in his community, in service to others), profile (of missionary or one from similar service profession who is contributing significantly to society), personal experience (finding a solution to a problem common to young adults; coping with handicapped child, for instance, or with a neighborhood problem. Story of how God-given strength or insight saved a situation). Buys 100 mss/year. Submit complete ms. Length: 300-1,000 words. Pays 4¢/word.

Photos: Purchased with accompanying ms. Captions required. Send prints. Pays $10 for 8 × 10 b&w glossy prints.
Fiction: Religious themes dealing with contemporary issues dealt with from a Christian frame of reference. Story must "go somewhere." Buys 50 mss/year. Submit complete ms.
Poetry: Free verse, haiku, light verse, traditional, religious. Buys 50 poems/year. Submit maximum 6 poems. Length: 4-24 lines. Pays $10.
Tips: "Seasonal material will get a second look (won't be rejected so easily). Write an attention grabbing lead followed by an article that says something worthwhile. Relate the lead to some of the universal needs of the reader—promise in that lead to help the reader in some way. Lack of SASE brands author as a nonprofessional; I seldom even bother to read the script." Prefers non-justified righthand margin.

EVANGELIZING TODAY'S CHILD, Child Evangelism Fellowship Inc., Box 348, Warrenton MO 63383-0348. (314)456-4321. Editor: Elsie Lippy. 50% freelance written. Prefers to work with published/established writers. Bimonthly magazine. Our purpose is to equip Christians to win the world's children to Christ and disciple them. Our readership is Sunday school teachers, Christian education leaders and children's workers in every phase of Christian ministry to children up to 12 years old." Estab. 1942. Circ. 22,000. Pays within 90 days of acceptance. Publishes ms an average of 6 months after acceptance. Byline given. Pays a kill fee if assigned. Buys first serial rights. Submit seasonal material 6 months in advance. Accepts previously published submissions. Send tearsheet of article; pays 35% of original article fee. Reports in 2 months. Sample copy for 9 × 12 SAE with 5 first-class stamps. Writer's guidelines for SASE.
Nonfiction: Unsolicited articles welcomed from writers with Christian education training or current experience in working with children. Buys 35 mss/year. Query. Length: 1,200-1,500. Pays 8-12¢/word.
Photos: Submissions of photos on speculation accepted. Needs photos of children or related subjects. Pays $35 for 8 × 10 b&w glossy prints; $45 for inside color prints or transparencies, $125 for cover transparencies.

THE FAMILY—A Catholic perspective, Daughters of St. Paul, 50 St. Paul's Ave., Boston MA 02130. (617)522-8911. Editor: Sr. Mary Lea Hill. Contact: Sr. Theresa Frances, managing editor. Monthly magazine on Catholic family life. "*The Family* magazine stresses the special place of the family within society as an irreplaceable center of life, love and faith. Articles on timely, pertinent issues help families approach today's challenges with a faith perspective and a spirit of commitment to the Gospel of Jesus Christ." Estab. 1952. Pays on publication. Publishes ms an average of 12 months after acceptance. Byline given. Buys first and second serial (reprint) rights. Submit seasonal material 9 months in advance. Accepts previously published submissions. Send tearsheet or typed ms with rights for sale noted and information about when and where material previously appeared. Pays 60% of the amount paid for an original article or story. Reports in 3 months. Sample copy for $1.75 and 9 × 12 SAE with 5 first-class stamps. Writer's guidelines for #10 SASE. "No simultaneous submissions. We do not review manuscripts in the months of July or August."
Nonfiction: Humor, inspirational, interview/profile, religious. Buys 40 mss/year. Send complete ms. Length: 500-1,500 words. Pays $50-125. Also may pay in contributor's copies.
Photos: Send photos with submission. Reviews 4 × 5 transparencies. Captions, model releases, identification of subjects required. Buys one-time rights.
Fiction: Humorous, religious, slice-of-life vignettes, family. Buys 12 mss/year. Send complete ms. Length: 1,000-2,000 words. Pays $50-125.
Fillers: Anecdotes, short humor. Buys 15/year. Length: 50-200 words. Pays $10-20.

THE FAMILY DIGEST, P.O. Box 40137, Fort Wayne IN 46804. Editor: Corine B. Erlandson. 95% freelance written. Bimonthly digest-sized magazine. "*The Family Digest* is geared to the joy and fulfillment of the Catholic family, and its relationship to the Catholic parish." Estab. 1945. Circ. 150,000. **Pays on acceptance.** Publishes ms usually within 12 months after acceptance. Byline given. Buys first North American rights. Submit seasonal material 7 months in advance. Reports in 4-6 weeks. Sample copy and writer's guidelines for 6 × 9 SAE with 2 first-class stamps.
Nonfiction: Family life, parish life, how-to, seasonal, inspirational, prayer life, Catholic traditions. Send ms with SASE. No poetry or fiction. Buys 55 unsolicited mss/year. Length: 750-1,100 words. Pays 5¢/word.
Fillers: Anecdotes, short humor. Buys 5/issue. Length: 50-100 words maximum. Cartoons: Publishes 5-8 cartoons/issue, related to family and Catholic parish life. Also, tasteful religious humor. Pays $10/cartoon, on acceptance.
Tips: "Prospective freelance contributors should be familiar with the publication, and the types of articles accepted and published. We rarely use reprints; we prefer fresh material that will hold up over time and is not tied to an event in the news. We are more oriented to families with kids and the problems such families face as parents raise their children in the Catholic faith within a secular society. Articles on family and parish life, including seasonal articles, how-to pieces, inspirational and humorous stories, will be gladly reviewed for possible publication."

GROUP MAGAZINE, P.O. Box 481, Loveland CO 80538. (303)669-3836. Fax: (303)669-3269. Editor: Rick Lawrence. Managing Editor: Cindy Parolini. 60% freelance written. Magazine published 8 times/year covering youth ministry. "Writers must be actively involved in youth ministry. Articles we accept are practical, not theoretical, and focused for local church youth workers." Estab. 1974. Circ. 57,000. **Pays on acceptance.** Publishes ms an average of 6 months after acceptance. Byline given. Offers $20 kill fee. Buys all rights. Submit seasonal material 7 months in advance. Reports in 1-2 months. Sample copy for 9 × 12 SAE with 3 first-class stamps. Writer's guidelines for 9 × 12 SAE with 2 first-class stamps.

Nonfiction: How-to (youth ministry issues). No personal testimony, theological or lecture-style articles. Buys 50-60 mss/year. Query. Length: 500-1,800 words. Pays $75-200. Sometimes pays for phone calls on agreement.

• Looking for more mini-articles that are practical and tip-oriented; no more than 250 words.

Photos: State availability of photos with submission. Model releases and identification of subjects required. Buys all rights.

GUIDEPOSTS MAGAZINE, 16 E. 34th St., New York NY 10016-4397. Editor: Fulton Oursler, Jr. 30% freelance written. "Works with a small number of new/unpublished writers each year. *Guideposts* is an inspirational monthly magazine for people of all faiths, in which men and women from all walks of life tell in first-person narrative how they overcame obstacles, rose above failures, handled sorrow, learned to master themselves and became more effective people through faith in God." Estab. 1945. Publishes ms an "indefinite" number of months after acceptance. Pays 25% kill fee for assigned articles. "Most of our stories are ghosted articles, so the writer would not get a byline unless it was his/her own story." Buys all rights and second serial (reprint) rights. Reports in 1-2 months.

Nonfiction and Fillers: Articles and features should be written in simple, anecdotal style with an emphasis on human interest. Short mss of approximately 250-750 words (pays $50-200) considered for such features as Quiet People and general one-page stories. Address short items to Colleen Hughes. For full-length mss, 750-1,500 words, pays $200-400. All mss should be typed, double-spaced and accompanied by SASE. Annually awards scholarships to high school juniors and seniors in writing contest. Buys 40-60 unsolicited mss/year. Pays expenses of writers on assignment.

Tips: "Study the magazine before you try to write for it. Each story must make a single spiritual point. The freelancer would have the best chance of breaking in by aiming for a one- or two-page article. Sensitively written anecdotes are extremely useful. And it is much easier to just sit down and write them than to have to go through the process of preparing a query. They should be warm, well written, intelligent and upbeat. We like personal narratives that are true and have some universal relevance, but the religious element does not have to be driven home with a sledge hammer. A writer succeeds with us if he or she can write a true article in short-story form with scenes, drama, tension and a resolution of the problem presented."

‡HINDUISM TODAY, Himalayan Academy, 107 Kaholalele Rd., Kapaa HI 96746. (808)822-7032. Publisher: H.H. Sivaya Subramuniya-Swami. Editor: Rev. Palaniswami. Managing Editor: Rev. Arumugaswami. 25% freelance written. Monthly tabloid covering Hindu spirituality and related areas. "Our philosophy is to inform and inspire Hindus worldwide, dispel myths, illusions and disinformation about Hinduism, protect, preserve and promote Hindu religion." Estab. 1979. Circ. 220,000 in 9 editions: North America, UK/Europe, Malaysia, Mauritius, Africa, India, Singapore, Netherlands (Dutch) and India (Hindi language). Pays 30 days after publication. Publishes ms an average of 2 months after acceptance. Byline given. $25 kill fee. Buys all rights. Accepts previously published submissions. Query for electronic submissions. Reports in 3 months. Free sample copy and writer's guidelines.

Nonfiction: Book excerpts, essays, exposé, general interest, historical/nostalgic, humor, inspirational, interview/profile, personal experience, photo feature, religious. "Nothing that is all politics." Buys 60 mss/year. Query with published clips. Length: 500-2,000 words. Pays 6¢/word. Sometimes pays expenses of writers on assignment.

Photos: Send photos with submission. Reviews 4 × 6 prints. Offers $10 minimum; negotiable maximum per photo. Captions and identification of subjects required. Buys all rights.

Fillers: Anecdotes, facts, newsbreaks. Buys 80/year. Length: 30-200 words. Pays $5-20.

Tips: "We need people who can do first-hand reports on events and people of interest to Hindus and spiritual seekers drawn toward Eastern traditions. Feature articles are most open to freelancers."

HOME TIMES, A Good Little Newspaper, Neighbor News, Inc., #12, 3676 Collin Dr., West Palm Beach FL 33406. (407)439-3509. Editor: Dennis Lombard. 80% freelance written. Weekly tabloid of conservative, pro-Christian news and views. "*Home Times* is a conservative newspaper written for the general public but with a pro-Christian, family-values slant. It is not religious or preachy." Estab. 1988. Circ. 20,000. Pays on publication. Publishes ms an average of 2 months after acceptance. Byline given. No kill fee. Buys one-time rights or makes work for hire assignments. Editorial lead time 1 month. Submit seasonal material 1 month in advance. Accepts simultaneous and previously published submissions. Send tearsheet or photocopy of article or short story or typed ms with rights for sale noted and information about when and where the material previously appeared. Pays up to 100% of amount paid for an original article. Reports in 1 week. *Writer's Market* recommends allowing 2 months for reply. Sample copy for $3 and 9 × 12 SASE with 4 stamps. Writer's guidelines for #10 SASE.

• Editor reports that moving to weekly publication will more than double this publication's needs.

Nonfiction: Current events, essays, general interest, historical/nostalgic, how-to, humor, inspirational, interview/profile, opinion, personal experience, photo feature, religious, travel. "Nothing preachy, moralistic, religious or with churchy slant." Buys 50 mss/year. Send complete ms. Length: to 900 maximum words. Pays $5 minimum. Pays contributor's copies on mutual agreement. Sometimes pays expenses of writers on assignment.

Photos: Send photos with submission. Reviews 4×5 prints. Offers $5-10/photo. Captions, model releases, identification of subjects required. Buys one-time rights.

Columns/Departments: Buys 50 mss/year. Send complete ms. Pays $5-15.

Fiction: Historical, humorous, mainstream, religious, issue-oriented contemporary. "Nothing preachy, moralistic." Buys 5 mss/year. Send complete ms. Length: 500-1,200 words. Pays $5-25.

Poetry: Free verse, light verse, traditional. Buys 10 poems/year. Submit maximum 3 poems. Length: 2-24 lines. Pays $5-10.

Fillers: Anecdotes, facts, newsbreaks, short humor. Uses 25/year. Length: to 100 words.

Tips: "We encourage new writers. We are different from ordinary news or religious publications. We strongly suggest you read guidelines and sample issues. (3 issues for $3 and 9×12 SASE w/3 stamps; writer's subscription 12 issues plus 3 samples for $9.) We are most open to material for new columns; journalists covering hard news in major news centers—with a Conservative slant."

THE JEWISH WEEKLY NEWS, Or V'Shalom, Inc., P.O. Box 1569, Springfield MA 01101-1569. (413)739-4771. Editor: Kenneth G. White. 25% freelance written. Jewish news and features, secular and non-secular; World Judaism; arts (New England based). Estab. 1945. Circ. 2,500. Pays on publication. Publishes ms an average of 2 months after acceptance. Byline given. Not copyrighted. Buys first North American serial rights and second serial (reprint) rights. Submit seasonal material 2 months in advance. Accepts simultaneous and previously published submissions. Send photocopy of article or typed ms with rights for sale noted and information about when and where the article previously appeared. Pays 100% of the amount paid for an original article. Query for electronic submissions. Reports in 3 months. Sample copy for 9×12 SAE with 5 first-class stamps.

Nonfiction: Interview/profile, religious, travel. Special issues: Jewish New Year (September); Chanukah (December); Bridal (Winter/Fall); Bar/Bat Mitzvahs (May). Buys 20 mss/year. Query with published clips. Length: 300-1,000 words. Pays $15-25/article.

Photos: Send photos with submission. Reviews 5×7 prints. Offers no additional payment for photos accepted with ms. Identification of subjects required.

Columns/Departments: Jewish Kitchen (Kosher recipes), 300-500 words. Buys 10 mss/year. Query with published clips. Length: 300-5,000 words. Pays $15-25/article.

LIGHT AND LIFE MAGAZINE, Free Methodist Church of North America, P.O. Box 535002, Indianapolis IN 46253-5002. Fax: (317)244-1247. Editor: Bob Haslam. 35% freelance written. Works with a small number of new/unpublished writers each year. Monthly magazine emphasizing evangelical Christianity with Wesleyan slant for a cross section of adults. Estab. 1868. Circ. 30,000. Pays on publication. Publishes ms an average of 6 months after acceptance. Byline given. Prefers first serial rights; rarely buys second serial (reprint) rights. Submit seasonal material 6 months in advance. Reports in 6 weeks. Sample copy and guidelines for $1.50. Writer's guidelines for SASE.

Nonfiction: "We need fresh, upbeat articles showing the average layperson how to be Christ-like at home, work and play." Submit complete ms. Buys 50-60 unsolicited ms/year. Pays 4¢/word. Length: 500-600 or 1,000-1,200 words.

Photos: Purchased without accompanying ms. Send prints or slides. Pays $5-35 for color or b&w photos.

LIGUORIAN, Liguori MO 63057-9999. Fax: (314)464-8449. Editor: Rev. Allan Weinert. Managing Editor: Susan M. Schuster. 25% freelance written. Prefers to work with published/established writers. Monthly magazine for families with Catholic religious convictions. Estab. 1913. Circ. 400,000. **Pays on acceptance.** Byline given "except on short fillers and jokes." Buys all rights but will reassign rights to author *after* publication upon written request. Submit seasonal material 6 months in advance. Query for electronic submissions. Reports in up to 6 months. Sample copy and writer's guidelines for 6×9 SAE with 3 first-class stamps.

Nonfiction: "Pastoral, practical and personal approach to the problems and challenges of people today. No travelogue approach or unresearched ventures into controversial areas. Also, no material found in secular publications—fad subjects that already get enough press, pop psychology, negative or put-down articles." Buys 60 unsolicited mss/year. Buys 12 fiction mss/year. Length: 400-2,000 words. Pays 10-12¢/word. Sometimes pays expenses of writers on assignment.

Photos: Photographs on assignment only unless submitted with and specific to article.

LIVE, 1445 Boonville Ave., Springfield MO 65802-1894. (417)862-2781. Fax: (417)862-8558. Adult Editor: Paul W. Smith. 100% freelance written. Works with several new/unpublished writers each year. Weekly magazine for adults in Assemblies of God Sunday schools. Circ. 160,000. **Pays on acceptance.** Publishes ms an average of 1 year after acceptance. Not copyrighted. Submit seasonal material 12-18 months in advance of publication. "Do not mention Santa Claus, Halloween or Easter bunnies." Accepts previously published submissions. Send tearsheet of article or short story or typed ms with rights for sale noted and information about when and where the material previously appeared. Pays 60% of the amount of their fee for original material. Reports in 4-6 weeks. Free sample copy and writer's guidelines for 7½ × 10½ SAE with 2 first-class stamps. Letters without SASE will not be answered. Buys 120-150 mss/year.

Nonfiction: In the narrative mode emphasizing some phase of Christian living presented in a down-to-earth manner. Biography or missionary material using narrative techniques, but must include verification. Historical, scientific, nature, humorous material with spiritual lesson. "Be accurate in detail and factual material. Writing for Christian publications is a ministry. The spiritual emphasis must be an integral part of your material." Prefers not to see material on highly controversial subjects but would appreciate stories on contemporary issues and concerns (e.g. substance abuse, AIDS, euthanasia, cults, integrity, etc.). Length: 1,000-1,600 words. Pays 3¢/word for first serial rights; 2¢/word for second serial (reprint) rights, according to the value of the material and the amount of editorial work necessary.

Photos: Color photos or transparencies purchased with mss. Pay open.

Fiction: "Present believable characters working out their problems according to Bible principles; in other words, present Christianity in action without being preachy. The stories (fictional or true) should tell themselves without moral lessons tacked on. We want multinational, ethnic, urban and intercultural characters. Use action, suspense, humor! Stories should be true to life but not what we would feel is a sinful pattern for living. Stories should not put parents, teachers, ministers or other Christian workers in a bad light. Setting, plot and action should be realistic, with strong motivation. Characterize so that the people will live in your story. Construct your plot carefully so that each incident moves naturally and suspensefully toward crisis and conclusion. *An element of conflict is necessary in fiction.* We do not accept fiction based on incidents in the Bible." Length: 1,000-1,500 words. Pays 3¢/word for first serial rights; 2¢/word for second serial (reprint) rights.

Poetry: Traditional, free verse, blank verse. Length: 12-20 lines. "Please do not send large numbers of poems at one time." Pays $10-15/poem.

Fillers: Brief and humorous, usually containing an anecdote, and always with a strong evangelical emphasis. Length: 200-600 words.

LIVING WITH TEENAGERS, Baptist Sunday School Board, 127 Ninth Ave. N., Nashville TN 37234. (615)251-2273. Fax: (615)251-3866. Editor: Ellen Oldacre. 30% freelance written. Works with a number of new/unpublished writers each year. Monthly magazine about teenagers for parents of teenagers. Estab. 1978. Circ. 50,000. Pays within 2 months of acceptance. Publishes ms an average of 10-12 months after acceptance. Buys all rights. Accepts previously published submissions. Submit seasonal material 1 year in advance. Reports in 2 months. Sample copy for 9 × 12 SAE with 4 first-class stamps. Writer's guidelines for #10 SASE. Résumés and queries only.

THE LOOKOUT, 8121 Hamilton Ave., Cincinnati OH 45231-9981. (513)931-4050. Fax: (513)931-0904. Editor: Simon J. Dahlman. 50-60% freelance written. Often works with new/unpublished writers. Weekly magazine for Christian adults, with emphasis on spiritual growth through Sunday schools and small groups. Audience is mainly conservative Christians. Estab. 1894. **Pays on acceptance.** Publishes ms an average of 6 months after acceptance. Byline given. Buys first serial, one-time, second serial (reprint) or simultaneous rights. Accepts simultaneous and previously published submissions. Send typed ms with rights for sale noted and information about when and where the article previously appeared. Pays 60% of their fee for an original article. Reports in 4 months, sometimes longer. Sample copy and writer's guidelines for 50¢. "We now work from a theme list, which is available on request with our guidelines." Guidelines only for #10 SASE.

• Ranked as one of the best markets for fiction writers in *Writer's Digest* magazine's biannual "Fiction 50," June 1994. Now using fewer inspirational articles and more informational articles, and paying more attention to solid research when considering submissions.

Nonfiction: "Seeks stories about real people; items that are helpful in practical Christian living (how-to's); items that shed Biblical light on matters of contemporary controversy; and items that motivate, that lead the reader to ask, 'Why shouldn't I try that?' Articles should tell how real people are involved for Christ. In choosing topics, *The Lookout* considers timeliness, the church and national calendar, and the ability of the material to fit the above guidelines. Remember to aim at laymen." Submit complete ms. Length: 500-2,000 words. Pays 4-8¢/word. We also use inspirational short pieces. "About 400-700 words is a good length for these. Relate an incident that illustrates a point without preaching."

Fiction: "A short story is printed in many issues; it is usually between 1,200-2,000 words long and should be as true to life as possible while remaining inspirational and helpful. Use familiar settings and situations. Most often we use stories with a Christian slant." Pays 5-8¢/word.

Photos: Reviews b&w prints, 4 × 6 or larger. Pays $25-50. Pays $75-200 for color transparencies for covers and inside use. Needs photos of people, especially adults in a variety of settings. Send to Photo Editor, Standard Publishing, at the above address.

THE LUTHERAN, Magazine of the Evangelical Lutheran Church in America, Evangelical Lutheran Church in America, 8765 W. Higgins Rd., Chicago IL 60631-4183. (312)380-2540. Fax: (312)380-2751. Editor: Edgar R. Trexler. Managing Editor: Roger R. Kahle. 30% freelance written. Monthly magazine for "lay people in church. News and activities of the Evangelical Lutheran Church in America, news of the world of religion, ethical reflections on issues in society, personal Christian experience." Estab. 1988. Circ. 800,000.

Pays on acceptance. Publishes ms an average of 3 months after acceptance. Byline given. Offers 50% kill fee. Buys first rights. Submit seasonal/holiday material 4 months in advance. Query required. Reports in 3 weeks. Free sample copy and writer's guidelines.

Nonfiction: David L. Miller. Inspirational, interview/profile, personal experience, photo feature, religious. "No articles unrelated to the world of religion." Buys 40 mss/year. Query with published clips. Length: 300-2,000 words. Pays $400-1,000 for assigned articles; $100-500 for unsolicited articles. Pays expenses of writers on assignment.

Photos: Send photos with submission. Reviews contact sheets, transparencies, prints. Offers $50-175/photo. Captions and identification of subjects required. Buys one-time rights.

Columns/Departments: Lite Side (humor—church, religious), 25-100 words. Send complete ms. Length: 25-100 words. Pays $10.

Tips: "Writers have the best chance selling us feature articles."

LUTHERAN FORUM, P.O. Box 327, Delhi NY 13753-0327. (607)746-7511. Fax: (607)829-2158. Editor: Dr. Leonard Klein. Works with a small number of new/unpublished writers each year. Quarterly review for church leadership, clerical and lay. Estab. 1914. Circ. 3,500. Pays on publication. Publishes ms an average of 6 months after acceptance. Byline given. Rights purchased vary with author and material; buys all, first North American serial, second serial (reprint) and simultaneous rights. Will consider simultaneous submissions. Reports in 6-8 months. Sample copy and $2 for SAE with 5 first-class stamps. Writer's guidelines for #10 SASE.

Nonfiction: Articles about important issues and developments in the church's institutional life and in its cultural/social setting. No purely devotional/inspirational material. Buys 2-3 mss/year. Query or submit complete ms. Length: 1,000-3,000 words. Informational, how-to, interview, profile, think articles, exposé. Length: 500-3,000 words.

Photos: Purchased with ms and only with captions. Prefers 4×5 prints. Pays $15 minimum.

THE LUTHERAN JOURNAL, 7317 Cahill Rd., Edina MN 55439-2081. Publisher: John W. Leykom. Editor: Rev. Armin U. Deye. Quarterly family magazine for Lutheran Church members, middle age and older. Estab. 1938. Circ. 136,000. Pays on publication. Byline given. Accepts simultaneous submissions. Occasionally accepts previously published submissions. Send tearsheet or photocopy of article and information about when and where the aritcle previously appeared. Pays 50-100% of the amount paid for an original article. Reports in 3-4 months. Sample copy for 9×12 SAE with 2 first-class stamps.

Nonfiction: Inspirational, religious, human interest, historical articles. Interesting or unusual church projects. Informational, how-to, personal experience, interview, humor, think articles. Buys 25-30 mss/year. Submit complete ms. Length: 1,500 words maximum; occasionally 2,000 words. Pays 1-4¢/word.

Photos: Send b&w and color photos with accompanying ms. Captions required.

Fiction: Mainstream, religious, historical. Must be suitable for church distribution. Length: 2,000 words maximum. Pays 1-2¢/word.

MENNONITE BRETHREN HERALD, 3-169 Riverton Ave., Winnipeg, Manitoba R2L 2E5 Canada. (204)669-6575. Fax: (204)654-1865. Editor: Ron Geddert. 25% freelance written. Biweekly family publication "read mainly by people of the Mennonite faith, reaching a wide cross section of professional and occupational groups, but also including many homemakers. Readership includes people from both urban and rural communities." Estab. 1962. Circ. 14,000. Pays on publication. Publishes ms an average of 4-6 months after acceptance. Not copyrighted. Byline given. Sample copy for $1 and 9×12 SAE with 2 IRCs. Reports in 6 months. Accepts previously published submissions. Send photocopy of article or typed ms with rights for sale noted. Include information about when and where the article previously appeared.

Nonfiction: Articles with a Christian family orientation; youth directed, Christian faith and life, and current issues. Wants articles critiquing the values of a secular society, attempting to relate Christian living to the practical situations of daily living; showing how people have related their faith to their vocations. Length: 1,500 words. Pays $30-40. Pays the expenses of writers on assignment.

Photos: Photos purchased with mss. Pays $10.

THE MESSENGER OF THE SACRED HEART, Apostleship of Prayer, 661 Greenwood Ave., Toronto, Ontario M4J 4B3 Canada. (416)466-1195. Editor: Rev. F.J. Power, S.J. Monthly magazine for "Canadian and US Catholics interested in developing a life of prayer and spirituality; stresses the great value of our ordinary actions and lives." 20% freelance written. Estab. 1891. Circ. 18,000. Buys first rights only. Byline given. **Pays on acceptance.** Submit seasonal material 5 months in advance. Reports in 1 month. Sample copy for $1 and 7½×10½ SAE. Writer's guidelines for #10 SASE.

Fiction: Religious/inspirational. Stories about people, adventure, heroism, humor, drama. Buys 12 mss/year. Send complete ms with SAE and IRCs. Unsolicited mss, unaccompanied by return postage, will not be returned. Length: 750-1,500 words. Pays 4¢/word.

Tips: "Develop a story that sustains interest to the end. Do not preach, but use plot and characters to convey the message or theme. Aim to move the heart as well as the mind. Before sending, cut out unnecessary or unrelated words or sentences. If you can, add a light touch or a sense of humor to the story. Your ending should have impact, leaving a moral or faith message for the reader."

THE MIRACULOUS MEDAL, 475 E. Chelten Ave., Philadelphia PA 19144-5785. (215)848-1010. Fax: (215)848-1014. Editorial Director: Rev. John W. Gouldrick, C.M. 40% freelance written. Quarterly. Estab. 1915. **Pays on acceptance.** Publishes ms an average of 2 years after acceptance. Buys first North American serial rights. Buys articles only on special assignment. Reports in 3 months. Sample copy for 6×9 SAE with 2 first-class stamps.
Fiction: Should not be pious or sermon-like. Wants good general fiction—not necessarily religious, but if religion is basic to the story, the writer should be sure of his facts. Only restriction is that subject matter and treatment must not conflict with Catholic teaching and practice. Can use seasonal material, Christmas stories. Length: 2,000 words maximum. Occasionally uses short-shorts from 750-1,250 words. Pays 2¢/word minimum.
Poetry: Maximum of 20 lines, preferably about the Virgin Mary or at least with religious slant. Pays 50¢/line minimum.

MY DAILY VISITOR, Our Sunday Visitor, Inc., 200 Noll Plaza, Huntington IN 46750. (219)356-8400. Editors: Catherine and William Odell. 99% freelance written. Bimonthly magazine of Scripture meditations based on the day's Catholic mass readings. Circ. 30,000. **Pays on acceptance.** Publishes ms an average of 6 months after acceptance. Byline given. Not copyrighted. Buys one-time rights. Reports in 2 months. Sample copy and writer's guidelines for #10 SAE with 2 first-class stamps. "Guest editors write on assignment basis only."
Nonfiction: Inspirational, personal experience, religious. Buys 12 mss/year. Query with published clips. Length: 150-160 words times number of days in month. Pays $350 for 1 month (28-31) of meditations. Pays writers 25 gratis copies.

‡NATIONAL CHRISTIAN REPORTER, P.O. Box 222198, Dallas TX 75222. (214)630-6495. Editor: John A. Lovelace. 5% freelance written. Prefers to work with published/established writers. Weekly newspaper for an interdenominational national readership. Circ. 25,000. Pays on publication. Publishes ms an average of 1 month after acceptance. Byline given. Not copyrighted. Free sample copy and writer's guidelines.
Nonfiction: "We welcome short features, approximately 500 words. Articles need to have an explicit 'mainstream' Protestant angle. Write about a distinctly Christian response to human need or how a person's faith relates to a given situation. Include evidence of participation in a local Protestant congregation." Send complete ms. Pays 4¢/word. Sometimes pays the expenses of writers on assignment.
Photos: Purchased with accompanying ms. "We encourage the submission of good action photos (5×7 or 8×10 b&w glossy prints) of the persons or situations in the article." Pays $10.
Poetry: "Good poetry welcomed on a religious theme." Length: 4-20 lines. Pays $2.

OBLATES, Missionary Association of Mary Immaculate, 15 S. 59th St., Belleville IL 62223-4694. (618)233-2238. Managing Editor: Christine Portell. Manuscripts Editor: Mary Mohrman. 30-50% freelance written. Prefers to work with published writers. Bimonthly inspirational magazine for Christians; audience mainly older adults. Circ. 500,000. **Pays on acceptance.** Usually publishes ms within 2 years after acceptance. Byline given. Buys first North American serial rights. Submit seasonal material 8 months in advance. Reports in 6 months. Sample copy and writer's guidelines for 6×9 or larger SAE with 2 first-class stamps.
Nonfiction: Inspirational and personal experience with positive spiritual insights. No preachy, theological or research articles. Avoid current events and controversial topics. Send complete ms. Length: 500 words. Pays $80.
Poetry: Light verse—reverent, well written, perceptive, with traditional rhythm and rhyme. "Emphasis should be on inspiration, insight and relationship with God." Submit maximum 2 poems. Length: 8-16 lines. Pays $30.
Tips: "Our readership is made up mostly of mature Americans who are looking for comfort, encouragement, and a positive sense of applicable Christian direction to their lives. Focus on sharing of personal insight to problem (i.e. death or change), but must be positive, uplifting. We have well-defined needs for an established market, but are always on the lookout for exceptional work."

THE OTHER SIDE, 300 W. Apsley St., Philadelphia PA 19144-4285. (215)849-2178. Editor: Mark Olson. Managing Editor: Dee Dee Risher. Managing Editor: Doug Davidson. 50% freelance written. Prefers to work with published/established writers. Bimonthly magazine emphasizing "spiritual nurture, prophetic reflection, forgotten voices and artistic visions from a radical Christian perspective." Estab. 1965. Circ. 13,000. **Pays on acceptance.** Publishes ms an average of 6 months after acceptance. Byline given. Buys all or first serial rights. Query for electronic submissions. Reports in 3 months. Sample copy for $4.50. Writer's guidelines for #10 SASE.
Nonfiction: Doug Davidson, managing editor. Current social, political and economic issues in the US and around the world: personality profiles, interpretative essays, interviews, how-to's, personal experiences, spiritual reflections, biblical interpretation and investigative reporting. "Articles must be lively, vivid and down-to-earth, with a radical faith-based Christian perspective." Length: 500-3,500 words. Pays $25-300. Sometimes pays expenses of writers on assignment.

Photos: Cathleen Benberg, art director. Photos or photo essays illustrating current social, political, or economic reality in the US and Third World. Especially interested in creative original art offering spiritual insight and/or fresh perspectives on contemporary issues. Pays $15-75 for b&w and $50-300 for color.

Fiction: Jennifer Wilkins, fiction editor. "Short stories, humor and satire conveying insights and situations that will be helpful to Christians with a radical commitment to peace and justice." Length: 300-4,000 words. Pays $25-250.

Poetry: Rod Jellema, poetry editor. "Short, creative poetry that will be thought-provoking and appealing to radical Christians who have a strong commitment to spirituality, peace and justice." Length: 3-50 lines. No more than 4 poems may be submitted at one time by any one author. Pays $15-20.

Tips: "We're looking for tightly written pieces (1,000-1,500 words) on interesting and unusual Christians (or Christian groups) who are putting their commitment to peace and social justice into action in creative and useful ways. We're also looking for provocative analytical and reflective pieces (1,000-4,000 words) dealing with contemporary social issues in the US and abroad."

OUR FAMILY, Oblate Fathers of St. Mary's Province, P.O. Box 249, Battleford, Saskatchewan S0M 0E0 Canada. (306)937-7771. Fax: (306)937-7644. Editor: Nestor Gregoire. 60% freelance written. Prefers to work with published/established writers. Monthly magazine for average family men and women with high school and early college education. Estab. 1949. Circ. 14,265. **Pays on acceptance.** Publishes ms an average of 6 months after acceptance. Byline given. Offers 100% kill fee. Generally purchases first North American serial rights; also buys all, simultaneous, second serial (reprint) or one-time rights. Submit seasonal material 4 months in advance. Accepts simultaneous and previously published submissions. Reports in 1 month. *Writer's Market* recommends allowing 2 months for reply. Sample copy for 9 × 12 SAE with $2.50 postage. Only Canadian postage or IRC useful in Canada. Writer's guidelines 49¢.

Nonfiction: Humor (related to family life or husband/wife relations), inspirational (anything that depicts people responding to adverse conditions with courage, hope and love), personal experience (with religious dimensions), photo feature (particularly in search of photo essays on human/religious themes and on persons whose lives are an inspiration to others). Phone queries OK. Buys 72-88 unsolicited mss/year. Pays expenses of writers on assignment.

Photos: Photos purchased with or without accompanying ms. Pays $35 for 5 × 7 or larger b&w glossy prints and color photos (which are converted into b&w). Offers additional payment for photos accepted with ms (payment for these photos varies according to their quality). Free photo spec sheet for SASE.

Poetry: Avant-garde, free verse, haiku, light verse, traditional. Buys 4-10 poems/issue. Length: 3-30 lines. Pays 75¢-$1/line. Must have a religious dimension.

Fillers: Jokes, gags, anecdotes, short humor. Buys 2-10/issue.

Tips: "Writers should ask themselves whether this is the kind of an article, poem, etc. that a busy housewife would pick up and read when she has a few moments of leisure. We are particularly looking for articles on the spirituality of marriage. We will be concentrating more on recent movements and developments in the church to help make people aware of the new church of which they are a part."

OUR SUNDAY VISITOR MAGAZINE, 200 Noll Plaza, Huntington IN 46750. (219)356-8400. Publisher: Robert P. Lockwood. Editor: David Scott. 5% freelance written. Works with small number of new/unpublished writers each year. Weekly magazine for general Catholic audience. Circ. 120,000. **Pays on acceptance.** Publishes ms an average of 2 months after acceptance. Byline given. Submit seasonal material 2 months in advance. Query for electronic submissions. Reports in 1 month. Sample copy for #10 SASE.

Nonfiction: Catholic-related subjects. Should explain Catholic religious beliefs in articles of human interest, applying Catholic principles to current problems, Catholic profiles, etc. Payment varies depending on reputation of author, quality of work, and amount of research required. Buys 25 mss/year. Query. Length: 1,000-1,200 words. Minimum payment for features is $100. Pays expenses of writers on assignment.

Photos: Purchased with mss; with captions only. Reviews b&w glossy prints and transparencies. Pays minimum of $200/cover photo story; $125/b&w story; $25/color photo; $10/b&w photo.

PENTECOSTAL EVANGEL, The General Council of the Assemblies of God, 1445 Boonville, Springfield MO 65802-1894. (417)862-2781. Fax: (417)862-0416. Editor: Richard G. Champion. 33% freelance written. Works with a small number of new/unpublished writers each year. Weekly magazine emphasizing news of the Assemblies of God for members of the Assemblies and other Pentecostal and charismatic Christians. Estab. 1913. Circ. 270,000. **Pays on acceptance.** Publishes ms an average of 6 months after acceptance. Byline given. Buys first serial rights, a few second serial (reprint) or one-time rights. Submit seasonal material 6 months in advance. Reports in 3 months. Free sample copy and writer's guidelines.

Nonfiction: Informational (articles on homelife that convey Christian teachings), inspirational, personal experience. Buys 5 mss/issue. Send complete ms. Length: 500-1,200 words. Pays 8¢/word maximum. Sometimes pays the expenses of writers on assignment.

Photos: Photos purchased without accompanying ms. Pays $7.50-15 for 8 × 10 b&w glossy prints; $10-35 for 35mm or larger transparencies. Total purchase price for ms includes payment for photos.

Tips: "Break in by writing up a personal experience. We publish first-person articles concerning spiritual experiences; that is, answers to prayer for help in a particular situation, of unusual conversions or healings through faith in Christ. All articles submitted to us should be related to religious life. We are Protestant, evangelical, Pentecostal, and any doctrines or practices portrayed should be in harmony with the official position of our denomination (Assemblies of God)."

THE PENTECOSTAL MESSENGER, Messenger Publishing House, P.O. Box 850, Joplin MO 64802-0850. (417)624-7050. Fax: (417)624-7102. Editor: Don Allen. Managing Editor: Peggy Lee Allen. 25% freelance written. Works with small number of new/unpublished writers each year. Monthly (excluding July) magazine covering Pentcostal Christianity. *"The Pentecostal Messenger* is the official organ of the Pentecostal Church of God. It goes to ministers and church members." Estab. 1919. Circ. 8,000. Pays on publication. Publishes ms an average of 6 months after acceptance. Byline given. Buys second serial (reprint) or simultaneous rights. Submit seasonal material 4 months in advance. Accepts simultaneous and previously published submissions. Send tearsheet or photocopy of article or typed ms with rights for sale noted and information about when and where the article previously appeared. Pays 100% of their fee for an original article. Reports in 1 month. Sample copy for 9 × 12 SAE with 4 first-class stamps. Free writer's guidelines.
Nonfiction: Inspirational, personal experience, religious. Buys 35 mss/year. Send complete ms. Length: 1,800 words. Pays 1½¢/word.
Photos: Send photos with submission. Reviews 2¼ × 2¼ transparencies and prints. Offers $10-25/photo. Captions and model releases required. Buys one-time rights.
Tips: "Articles need to be inspirational, informative, written from a positive viewpoint, and not extremely controversial."

PIME WORLD, 17330 Quincy St., Detroit MI 48221-2765. (313)342-4066. Managing Editor: Paul Witte. 10% freelance written. Monthly (except July and August) magazine emphasizing foreign missionary activities of the Catholic Church in Burma, India, Bangladesh, the Philippines, Hong Kong, Africa, etc., for an adult audience, interested in current issues in the missions. Audience is largely high school educated, conservative in both religion and politics." Estab. 1954. Circ. 27,500. Pays on publication. Publishes ms an average of 3 months after acceptance. Buys all rights. Byline given. Submit seasonal material 4 months in advance. Accepts simultaneous submissions. Reports in 2 months.
Nonfiction: Informational and inspirational foreign missionary activities of the Catholic Church. Buys 5-10 unsolicited mss/year. Query or send complete ms. Length: 800-1,200 words. Pays 6¢/word.
Photos: Pays $10/color photo.
Tips: "Submit articles dealing with current issues of social justice, evangelization and pastoral work in Third World countries. Interviews of missionaries accepted. Good quality color photos greatly appreciated."

PRAIRIE MESSENGER, Catholic Journal, Benedictine Monks of St. Peter's Abbey, P.O. Box 190, Muenster, Saskatchewan S0K 2Y0 Canada. (306)682-1772. Fax: (306)682-5285. Editor: Rev. Andrew Britz, OSB. Associate Editor: Marian Noll. 10% freelance written. Weekly Catholic journal with strong emphasis on social justice, Third World and ecumenism. Estab. 1904. Circ. 9,000. Pays on publication. Publishes ms an average of 3-4 months after acceptance. Byline given. Offers 70% kill fee. Not copyrighted. Buys first North American serial, first, one-time, second serial (reprint) or simultaneous rights. Submit seasonal material 3 months in advance. Query for electronic submissions. Reports in 2 months. Sample copy and writers guidelines for 9 × 12 SAE with 80¢ Canadian postage or IRCs.
Nonfiction: Interview/profile, opinion, religious. "No articles on abortion or homosexuality." Buys 15 mss/year. Send complete ms. Length: 250-600 words. Pays $40-60. Sometimes pays expenses of writers on assignment.
Photos: Send photos with submission. Reviews 3 × 5 prints. Offers $10/photo. Captions required. Buys all rights.

PRESBYTERIAN RECORD, 50 Wynford Dr., North York, Ontario M3C 1J7 Canada. (416)444-1111. Fax: (416)441-2825. Editor: Rev. John Congram. 50% freelance written. Eager to work with new/unpublished writers. Monthly magazine for a church-oriented, family audience. Circ. 63,000. Pays on publication. Publishes ms an average of 4 months after acceptance. Buys first serial, one-time or simultaneous rights. Submit seasonal material 3 months in advance. Reports on ms accepted for publication in 2 months. Returns rejected material in 3 months. Sample copy and writer's guidelines for 9 × 12 SAE with $1 Canadian postage or IRCs.
Nonfiction: Material on religious themes. Check a copy of the magazine for style. Also personal experience, interview, inspirational material. No material solely or mainly American in context. When possible, photos should accompany manuscript; e.g., current events, historical events and biographies. Buys 15-20 unsolicited mss/year. Query. Length: 1,000-2,000 words. Pays $45-55 (Canadian). Sometimes pays expenses of writers on assignment.
Photos: Pays $15-20 for b&w glossy photos. Uses positive transparencies for cover. Pays $50. Captions required.
Tips: "There is a trend away from maudlin, first-person pieces redolent with tragedy and dripping with simplistic, pietistic conclusions."

PURPOSE, 616 Walnut Ave., Scottdale PA 15683-1999. (412)887-8500. Editor: James E. Horsch. 95% free-lance written. Weekly magazine "for adults, young and old, general audience with varied interests. My readership is interested in seeing how Christianity works in difficult situations." Estab. 1968. Circ. 17,000. **Pays on acceptance.** Publishes ms an average of 8 months after acceptance. Byline given, including city, state/province. Buys one-time rights. Submit seasonal material 6 months in advance. Accepts simultaneous and previously published submissions. Send tearsheet or photocopy of article or short story or typed ms with rights for sale noted and information about when and where the material previously appeared. Pays 50% of amount paid for an original article or short story. Reports in 2 months. Sample copy and writer's guidelines for 6×9 SAE with 2 first-class stamps.

• Ranked as one of the best markets for fiction writers in *Writer's Digest* magazine's biannual "Fiction 50," June 1994.

Nonfiction: Inspirational stories from a Christian perspective. "I want stories that go to the core of human problems in family, business, politics, religion, gender and any other areas—and show how the Christian faith resolves them. I want material that's upbeat. *Purpose* is a magazine which conveys truth either through quality fiction or through articles that use the best story techniques. Our magazine accents Christian disciple-ship. Christianity affects all of life, and we expect our material to demonstrate this. I would like to see story-type articles about individuals, groups and organizations who are intelligently and effectively working at some of the great human problems such as hunger, poverty, international understanding, peace, justice, etc., because of their faith." Buys 130 mss/year. Submit complete ms. Length: 900 words maximum. Pays 5¢/word maximum. Buys one-time rights only.

Photos: Photos purchased with ms. Pays $5-15 for b&w (less for color), depending on quality. Must be sharp enough for reproduction; requires prints in all cases. Captions desired.

Fiction: Humorous, religious, historical fiction related to discipleship theme. "Produce the story with specific-ity so that it appears to take place somewhere and with real people. It should not be moralistic. Essays and how-to-do-it pieces must include a lot of anecdotal, life exposure examples."

Poetry: Traditional poetry, blank verse, free verse, light verse. Buys 130 poems/year. Length: 12 lines maxi-mum. Pays $5-15/poem depending on length and quality. Buys one-time rights only.

Fillers: Anecdotal items from 200-599 words. Pays 4¢/word maximum.

Tips: "We are looking for articles which show the Christian faith working at issues where people hurt; stories need to be told and presented professionally. Good photographs help place material with us."

QUEEN OF ALL HEARTS, Montfort Missionaries, 26 S. Saxon Ave., Bay Shore NY 11706-8993. (516)665-0726. Fax: (516)665-4349. Managing Editor: Roger Charest, S.M.M. 50% freelance written. Bimonthly magazine covering Marian doctrine and devotion. "Subject: Mary, Mother of Jesus, as seen in the sacred scriptures, tradition, history of the church, the early Christian writers, lives of the saints, poetry, art, music, spiritual writers, apparitions, shrines, ecumenism, etc." Estab. 1950. Circ. 5,000. **Pays on acceptance.** Publishes ms an average of 6 months after acceptance. Byline given. Not copyrighted. Submit seasonal material 6 months in advance. Reports in 2 months. Sample copy for $2.50.

Nonfiction: Essays, inspirational, personal experience, religious. Buys 25 ms/year. Send complete ms. Length: 750-2,500 words. Pays $40-60. Sometimes pays writers in contributor copies or other premiums "by mutual agreement."

Photos: Send photos with submission. Reviews transparencies and prints. Offers variable payment per photo. Buys one-time rights.

Fiction: Religious. Buys 6 mss/year. Send complete ms. Length: 1,500-2,500 words. Pays $40-60.

Poetry: Joseph Tusiani, poetry editor. Free verse. Buys approximately 10 poems/year. Submit maximum of 2 poems at one time. Pays in contributor copies.

‡**REFORM JUDAISM**, Union of American Hebrew Congregations, 838 5th Ave., New York NY 10021. (212)249-0100. Editor: Aron Hirt-Manheimer. Managing Editor: Joy Weinberg. 20% freelance written. Quar-terly magazine of Reform Jewish issues. "*Reform Judaism* is the official voice of the Union of American Hebrew Congregations, linking the institutions and affiliates of Reform Judaism with every Reform Jew. RJ covers developments within the Movement while interpreting events and Jewish tradition from a Reform perspective." Pays on publication. Publishes ms an average of 3 months after acceptance. Byline given. Offers negotiable kill fee. Buys first North American serial rights. Submit seasonal/holiday material 3 months in advance. Accepts photocopied and previously published submissions. Send tearsheet or photocopy of article or short story or typed ms with rights for sale noted and information about when and where the material previously appeared. Reports in 2 weeks on queries; 1 month on mss. Sample copy for $3.50.

Nonfiction: Book excerpt (reviews), exposé, general interest, historical/nostalgic, inspirational, interview/profile, opinion, personal experience, photo feature, travel. Buys 60 mss/year. Submit complete ms. Length: 600-1800 words. Pays 10-30¢/word. Sometimes pays expenses of writers on assignment.

Photos: Send photos with ms. Prefers 8×10/color and b&w prints. Pays $25-75. Identification of subjects required. Buys one-time rights.

Fiction: Ethnic, humorous, mainstream, religious. Buys 4 mss/year. Send complete ms. Length: 600-1800 words. Pays 10-30¢/word. Publishes novel excerpts.

‡**THE REPORTER**, Women's American ORT, Inc., 315 Park Ave. So., New York NY 10010. (212)505-7700. Fax: (212)674-3057. Editor: Dana B. Asher. 85% freelance written. Nonprofit journal published by Jewish women's organization. Quarterly magazine covering "Jewish topics, social issues, education, Mideast and women." Estab. 1966. Circ. 104,000. Payment time varies. Publishes ms ASAP after acceptance. Byline given. Buys first North American serial rights. Submit seasonal material 6 months in advance. Reports in 3 months. Free sample copy for 9 × 12 SAE with 3 first-class stamps.

Nonfiction: Book excerpts, essays, general interest, humor, opinion. Buys approximately 40 mss/year. Send complete ms. Length: 1,800 words. Pay varies.

Photos: Send photos with submission. Reviews 5 × 7 prints. Identification of subjects required.

Columns/Departments: Books. Buys 4-10 mss/year. Send complete ms. Length: 200-1,000 words. Pay varies.

Fiction: Jewish novel excerpts. Buys 2 ms/year. Send complete ms.

Tips: "Simply send ms; do not call. Open Forum (opinion section) is most open to freelancers, although all are open. Looking for well-written essay on relevant topic that makes its point strongly—evokes response from reader."

REVIEW FOR RELIGIOUS, Room 428, 3601 Lindell Blvd., St. Louis MO 63108-3393. (314)535-3048. Fax: (314)535-0601. Editor: David L. Fleming, S.J. 100% freelance written. Bimonthly magazine for Roman Catholic priests, brothers and sisters. Estab. 1942. Pays on publication. Publishes ms an average of 9 months after acceptance. Byline given. Buys first North American serial rights; rarely buys second serial (reprint) rights. Reports in 2 months.

Nonfiction: Articles on spiritual, liturgical, canonical matters only; not for general audience. Length: 2,000-8,000 words. Pays $6/page.

Tips: "The writer must know about religious life in the Catholic Church and be familiar with prayer, vows, community life and ministry."

ST. ANTHONY MESSENGER, 1615 Republic St., Cincinnati OH 45210-1298. Fax: (513)241-0399. Editor-in-Chief: Norman Perry. 55% freelance written. "Willing to work with new/unpublished writers if their writing is of a professional caliber." Monthly magazine for a national readership of Catholic families, most of which have children in grade school, high school or college. Circ. 320,000. **Pays on acceptance.** Publishes ms an average of 9 months after acceptance. Byline given. Buys first North American serial rights. Submit seasonal material 6 months in advance. Query for electronic submissions. Reports in 2 months. Sample copy and writer's guidelines for 9 × 12 SAE with 4 first-class stamps.

● Ranked as one of the best markets for fiction writers in *Writer's Digest* magazine's biannual "Fiction 50," June 1994. According to a recent editorial in *St. Anthony Messenger*, this magazine seeks fiction about living out the Christian faith, stories in which the characters find strength and meaning in their belief and relationship with and in God.

Nonfiction: How-to (on psychological and spiritual growth, problems of parenting/better parenting, marriage problems/marriage enrichment), humor, informational, inspirational, interview, personal experience (if pertinent to our purpose), personal opinion (limited use; writer must have special qualifications for topic), profile. Buys 35-50 mss/year. Length: 1,500-3,500 words. Pays 14¢/word. Sometimes pays the expenses of writers on assignment.

Fiction: Mainstream, religious. Buys 12 mss/year. Submit complete ms. Length: 2,000-3,000 words. Pays 14¢/word.

Tips: "The freelancer should ask why his or her proposed article would be appropriate for us, rather than for *Redbook* or *Saturday Review*. We treat human problems of all kinds, but from a religious perspective. Articles should reflect Catholic theology, spirituality and employ a Catholic terminology and vocabulary. We need more articles on prayer, scripture, Catholic worship. Get authoritative information (not merely library research); we want interviews with experts. Write in popular style. Word length is an important consideration."

ST. JOSEPH'S MESSENGER & ADVOCATE OF THE BLIND, Sisters of St. Joseph of Peace, St. Joseph's Home, P.O. Box 288, Jersey City NJ 07303-0288. Editor-in-Chief: Sister Ursula Maphet. 30% freelance written. Eager to work with new/unpublished writers. Quarterly magazine. Estab. 1898. Circ. 20,000. **Pays on acceptance.** Publishes ms an average of 3 months after acceptance. Buys first serial and second serial (reprint) rights; reassigns rights back to author after publication in return for credit line in next publication. Submit seasonal material 3 months in advance (no Christmas issue). Accepts simultaneous and previously published submissions. Send photocopy of article or short story or typed ms with rights for sale noted and information about when and where the article previously appeared. Pays 100% of their fee for an original article. Reports in 1 month. Sample copy and writer's guidelines for 9 × 12 SAE with 2 first-class stamps.

● Ranked as one of the best markets for fiction writers in *Writer's Digest* magazine's biannual "Fiction 50," June 1994. Still needs contemporary short stories.

Nonfiction: Humor, inspirational, nostalgia, personal opinion, personal experience. Buys 24 mss/year. Submit complete ms. Length: 300-1,500 words. Pays $3-15.

Fiction: Romance, suspense, mainstream, religious. Buys 30 mss/year. Submit complete ms. Length: 600-1,600 words. Pays $6-25.

Poetry: Light verse, traditional. Buys 25 poems/year. Submit maximum 10 poems. Length: 50-300 words. Pays $5-20.

Tips: "It's rewarding to know that someone is waiting to see freelancers' efforts rewarded by 'print'. It's annoying, however, to receive poor copy, shallow material or inane submissions. Human interest fiction, touching on current happenings, is what is most needed. We look for social issues woven into story form. We also seek non-preaching articles that carry a message that is positive."

SCP JOURNAL AND SCP Newsletter, Spiritual Counterfeits Project, P.O. Box 4308, Berkeley CA 94704-4308. (510)540-0300. Fax: (510)540-1107. Editor: Tal Brooke. Co-editor: Brooks Alexander. 5% freelance written. Prefers to work with published/established writers. "The *SCP Journal* and *SCP Newsletter* are quarterly publications "geared to reach demanding non-believers while giving Christians authentic insight into the very latest spiritual and cultural trends." Their targeted audience is the educated lay reader. Estab. 1975. Circ. 18,000. Pays on publication. Publishes ms an average of 6 months after acceptance. Byline given. Rights negotiable. Accepts simultaneous and previously published submissions after telephone inquiry. Reports in 1-3 months. Sample copy for $5. Writer's guidelines for SASE.

Nonfiction: Book excerpts, essays, exposé, interview/profile, opinion, personal experience, religious. Query by telephone. Length: 2,500-3,500 words. Pay negotiated by phone.

• Less emphasis on book reviews and more focus on specialized "single issue" topics.

Photos: State available photos. Reviews contact sheets and prints or slides. Offers no additional payment for photos accepted with ms. Captions, model releases, identification of subjects required. Buys one-time rights.

Tips: "The area of our publication most open to freelancers is specialized topics covered by *SCP*. Send samples of work that are relevant to *SCP*'s area of interest only after telephone inquiry."

SHARING THE VICTORY, Fellowship of Christian Athletes, 8701 Leeds Rd., Kansas City MO 64129. (816)921-0909. Fax: (816)921-8755. Editor: John Dodderidge. Assistant Editor: Robyne Baker. Managing Editor: Don Hilkemeier. 60% freelance written. Prefers to work with published/established writers, but works with a growing number of new/unpublished writers each year. Monthly (September-May) magazine. "We seek to encourage and enable athletes and coaches at all levels to take their faith seriously on and off the 'field'." Estab. 1959. Circ. 50,000. Pays on publication. Publishes ms an average of 4 months after acceptance. Byline given. Buys first rights. Submit seasonal/holiday material 3 months in advance. Reports in 1 week on queries; 2 weeks on mss. *Writer's Market* recommends allowing 2 months for reply. Sample copy for $1 and 9×12 SAE with 3 first-class stamps. Free writer's guidelines for #10 SASE.

Nonfiction: Humor, inspirational, interview/profile (with "name" athletes and coaches solid in their faith), personal experience, photo feature. No "sappy articles on 'I became a Christian and now I'm a winner.'" Buys 5-20 mss/year. Query. Length: 500-1,000 words. Pays $100-200 for unsolicited articles, more for the exceptional profile.

Photos: State availability of photos with submission. Reviews contact sheets. Pay depends on quality of photo but usually a minimum $100. Model releases required for "name" individuals. Buys one-time rights.

Poetry: Free verse. Buys 3 poems/year. Pays $50.

Tips: "Profiles and interviews of particular interest to coed athlete, primarily high school and college age. Our graphics and editorial content appeal to youth. The area most open to freelancers is profiles on or interviews with well-known athletes or coaches (male, female, minorities) and offbeat but interscholastic team sports."

SIGNS OF THE TIMES, Pacific Press Publishing Association, P.O. Box 7000, Boise ID 83707. (208)465-2500. Fax: (208)465-2531. Editor: Greg Brothers. 40% freelance written. Works with a small number of new/unpublished writers each year. Monthly magazine on religion. "We are a Christian publication encouraging the general public to practice the principles of the Bible." Estab. 1874. Circ. 245,000. Pays on publication. Publishes ms an average of 8 months after acceptance. Byline given. Offers kill fee. Buys first North American serial rights. Submit seasonal material 8 months in advance. Accepts previously published submissions. Send photocopy of article or typed ms with rights for sale noted. Pays 50% of their fee for an original article. Reports in 1 month on queries; 2 months on mss. *Writer's Market* recommends allowing 2 months for reply. Sample copy and writer's guidelines for 9×12 SAE with 3 first-class stamps.

Nonfiction: General interest, how-to, inspirational, interview/profile. "We want writers with a desire to share the good news of reconciliation with God. Articles should be people-oriented, well-researched and should have a sharp focus." Buys 75 mss/year. Query with or without published clips or send complete ms. Length: 650-2,500 words. Pays $100-400. Sometimes pays the expenses of writers on assignment.

Photos: Merwin Stewart, photo editor. Send photos with query or ms. Reviews b&w contact sheets, 35mm color transparencies, 5×7 or 8×10 b&w prints. Pays $35-300 for transparencies; $20-50 for prints. Model releases and identification of subjects required (captions helpful). Buys one-time rights.

Tips: "Don't write for us unless you've read us and are familiar with SDA beliefs."

SISTERS TODAY, The Liturgical Press, St. John's Abbey, Collegeville MN 56321-2099. Editor-in-Chief: Sister Mary Anthony Wagner, O.S.B. Associate Editor: Sister Mary Elizabeth Mason, O.S.B. Review Editor: Sister Stefanie Weisgram, O.S.B. 80% freelance written. Prefers to work with published/established writers. Bimonthly magazine exploring the role of women and the Church, primarily. Circ. 8,000. Pays on publication. Publishes ms 1-2 years after acceptance. Byline given. Buys first rights. Submit seasonal material 4 months in advance. Reports in 3 months. Sample copy for $3.

Nonfiction: How-to (pray, live in a religious community, exercise faith, hope, charity etc.), informational, inspirational. Also articles concerning religious renewal, community life, worship, the role of sisters in the Church and in the world today. Buys 50-60 unsolicited mss/year. Query. Length: 500-2,500 words. Pays $5/ printed page.

Poetry: Free verse, haiku, light verse, traditional. Buys 3 poems/issue. Submit maximum 4 poems. Pays $10.

Tips: "Some of the freelance material evidences the lack of familiarity with *Sisters Today*. We would prefer submitted articles not to exceed eight or nine pages."

SOCIAL JUSTICE REVIEW, 3835 Westminister Place, St. Louis MO 63108-3472. (314)371-1653. Contact: Rev. John H. Miller, C.S.C. 25% freelance written. Works with a small number of new/unpublished writers each year. Bimonthly. Estab. 1908. Publishes ms an average of 6-12 months after acceptance. Not copyrighted; "however special articles within the magazine may be copyrighted, or an occasional special issue has been copyrighted due to author's request." Buys first serial rights. Accepts previously published submissions. Send typed ms with rights for sale noted and information about when and where the article previously appeared. Sample copy for 9 × 12 SAE with 3 first-class stamps.

Nonfiction: Wants scholarly articles on society's economic, religious, social, intellectual, political problems with the aim of bringing Catholic social thinking to bear upon these problems. Query w/SASE. Length: 2,500-3,500 words. Pays about 2¢/word.

‡SPIRIT, Lectionary-based Weekly for Catholic Teens, Editorial Development Associates, 1884 Randolph Ave., St. Paul MN 55105-1700. (612)690-7005. Editor: Joan Mitchell, CSJ. Managing Editor: Therese Sherlock, CSJ. 50% freelance written. Weekly newsletter for religious education of high schoolers. "We want realistic fiction and nonfiction that raises current ethical and religious questions and conflicts in multi-racial contexts." Estab. 1988. Circ. 26,000. Pays on publication. Publishes ms an average of 6 months after acceptance. Byline given. Buys all rights. Submit seasonal material 6 months in advance. Accepts simultaneous submissions. Reports in 2 weeks on queries; 6 weeks on mss. Free sample copy and writer's guidelines.

Nonfiction: Interview/profile, personal experience, photo feature (homelessness, illiteracy), religious, Roman Catholic leaders, human interest features, social justice leaders, projects, humanitarians. "No Christian confessional pieces." Buys 12 mss/year. Query. Length: 1,100-1,200 words. Pays $135-150 for articles; $75 for one-page articles.

Photos: State availability of photos with submission. Reviews contact sheets, transparencies, prints. Offers $25-35 per photo. Identification of subjects required. Buys one-time rights.

Fiction: Conflict vignettes. "We want realistic pieces for and about teens—non-pedantic, non-pious." We need good Christmas stories that show spirit of the season, and stories about teen relationship conflicts (boy/ girl, parent/teen). Buys 12 mss/year. Query. Length: 1,100-1,200 words. Pays $150.

Tips: "Query to receive call for stories, spec sheet, sample issues."

SPIRITUAL LIFE, 2131 Lincoln Rd. NE, Washington DC 20002-1199. (202)832-8489. Fax: (202)832-8967. Editor: Br. Edward O'Donnell, O.C.D. 80% freelance written. Prefers to work with published/established writers. Quarterly. "Largely Catholic, well-educated, serious readers. A few are non-Catholic or non-Christian." Circ. 12,000. **Pays on acceptance.** Publishes ms an average of 1 year after acceptance. Buys first North American serial rights. Reports in 2 months. Sample copy and writer's guidelines for 7 × 10 or larger SASE with 4 first-class stamps.

Nonfiction: Serious articles of contemporary spirituality. High quality articles about our encounter with God in the present day world. Language of articles should be college level. Technical terminology, if used, should be clearly explained. Material should be presented in a positive manner. Sentimental articles or those dealing with specific devotional practices not accepted. Buys inspirational and think pieces. "Brief autobiographical information (present occupation, past occupations, books and articles published, etc.) should accompany article." No fiction or poetry. Buys 20 mss/year. Length: 3,000-5,000 words. Pays $50 minimum. "Five contributor's copies are sent to author on publication of article." Book reviews should be sent to Br. Edward O'Donnell, O.C.D.

STANDARD, Nazarene International Headquarters, 6401 The Paseo, Kansas City MO 64131. (816)333-7000, ext. 2555. Editor: Everett Leadingham. 100% freelance written. Works with a small number of new/

For explanation of symbols, see the Key to Symbols and Abbreviations. For unfamiliar words, see the Glossary.

unpublished writers each year. Weekly inspirational paper with Christian reading for adults. Estab. 1938. Circ. 160,000. **Pays on acceptance.** Publishes ms an average of 15-18 months after acceptance. Byline given. Buys one-time rights and second serial (reprint) rights. Submit seasonal material 6 months in advance. Reports in 8-10 weeks. Free sample copy. Writer's guidelines for SAE with 2 first-class stamps.

• Ranked as one of the best markets for fiction writers in *Writer's Digest* magazine's biannual "Fiction 50," June 1994.

Nonfiction: How-to (grow spiritually), inspirational, social issues, personal experience (with an emphasis on spiritual growth). Buys 200 mss/year. Send complete ms. Length: 300-1,500 words. Pays 3½¢/word for first rights; 2¢/word for reprint rights.

Photos: Pays $25-45 for 8 × 10 b&w prints. Buys one-time rights. Accepts photos with ms.

Fiction: Adventure, religious, romance, suspense—all with a spiritual emphasis. Buys 600 mss/year. Send complete ms. Length: 500-1,500 words. Pays 3½¢/word for first rights; 2¢/word for reprint rights.

Poetry: Free verse, haiku, light verse, traditional. Buys 50 poems/year. Submit maximum 5 poems. Length: 50 lines maximum. Pays 25¢/line.

Fillers: Jokes, anecdotes, short humor. Buys 52/year. Length: 300 words maximum. Pays same as nonfiction and fiction.

Tips: "Articles should express Christian principles without being preachy. Setting, plot and characterization must be realistic. Fiction articles should be labeled 'Fiction' on the manuscript. True experience articles may be first person, 'as told to,' or third person."

‡STUDENT LEADERSHIP JOURNAL, InterVarsity Christian Fellowship, P.O. Box 7895, Madison WI 53707-7895. (608)274-7882. Editor: Jeff Yourison. 30% freelance written. Quarterly magazine for "college students who are leaders in their Christian fellowship groups on campus. We feature articles on Biblical leadership qualities, personal spiritual growth, and contemporary campus issues. *SLJ* is a training tool for InterVarsity's student leaders." Estab. 1988. Circ. 8,000. **Pays on acceptance.** Publishes ms an average of 3 months after acceptance. Byline sometimes given. Negotiable kill fee. Buys first rights or one-time rights. Editorial lead time 6 months. Submit seasonal material 6 months in advance. Accepts simultaneous submissions. Query for electronic submissions. Reports in 4-6 weeks on queries; 3-6 months on mss. Sample copy for $3 and 9 × 12 SAE with 4 first-class stamps. Writer's guidelines for #10 SASE.

Nonfiction: Query. Length: 800-1,700 words. Pays $25.

Photos: State availability of photos with submission. Offers $25/photo. Captions required. Buys one-time rights.

Poetry: Free verse, haiku, traditional. Buys 4 poems/year. Submit maximum 5 poems.

SUNDAY DIGEST, David C. Cook Publishing Co., 850 N. Grove Ave., Elgin IL 60120-2892. Fax: (708)741-0595. Editor: Christine Dallman. 75% freelance written. Prefers to work with established writers. Issued weekly to Christian adults in Sunday school. "*Sunday Digest* provides a combination of original articles and reprints, selected to help adult readers better understand the Christian faith, to keep them informed of issues within the Christian community, and to challenge them to a deeper personal commitment to Christ." Estab. 1886. **Pays on acceptance.** Publishes ms an average of 15 months after acceptance. Buys first or reprint rights. Accepts previously published submissions. Send tearsheet or photocopy of article or short story, or preferably typed ms with rights for sale noted and information about when and where the material previously appeared. Reports in 3 months. Sample copy and writer's guidelines for 6 × 9 SAE with 2 first-class stamps.

Nonfiction: Needs articles applying the Christian faith to personal and social problems, articles on family life and church relationships, inspirational self-help, personal experience, how-to, interview articles preferred over fiction. Length: 400-1,700 words. Pays $50-225.

Fiction: Publishes inspirational fiction.

Tips: "It is crucial that the writer is committed to quality Christian communication with a crisp, clear writing style. Christian message should be woven in, not tacked on."

TEACHERS INTERACTION, A Magazine Church School Workers Grow By, Concordia Publishing House, 3558 S. Jefferson Ave., St. Louis MO 63118-3986. Editor: Jane Haas. 20% freelance written. Quarterly magazine of practical, inspirational, theological articles for volunteer church school teachers. Material must be true to the doctrines of the Lutheran Church—Missouri Synod. Estab. 1960. Circ. 20,400. Pays on publication. Publishes ms an average of 1 year after acceptance. Byline given. Buys first rights. Submit seasonal material 1 year in advance. Query for electronic submissions. Reports in 3 months on queries; 6 months on mss. Sample copy for $1. Writer's guidelines for #10 SASE.

Nonfiction: How-to (practical help/ideas used successfully in own classroom), inspirational (to the church school worker—must be in accordance with LCMS doctrine), personal experience (of a Sunday school classroom nature—growth). No theological articles. Buys 6 mss/year. Send complete ms. Length: 750-1,500 words.

• No longer buys reprints.

Fillers: "*Teachers Interaction* buys short items—activities and ideas planned and used successfully in a church school classroom." Buys 60/year. Length: 100 words maximum. Pays $20.

Tips: "Practical, or 'it happened to me' experiences articles would have the best chance. Also short items—ideas used in classrooms; seasonal and in conjunction with our Sunday school material, Our Life in Christ.

Our format includes *all* volunteer church school teachers, Sunday school teachers, Vacation Bible School, and midweek teachers, as well as teachers of adult Bible studies."

‡**TEEN LIFE**, (formerly *Hi Call*), Gospel Publishing House, 1445 Boonville Ave., Springfield MO 65802-1894. (417)862-2781, ext. 4357. Editor: Tammy Bicket. Mostly freelance written. Eager to work with new/unpublished writers. Weekly magazine of Assemblies of God denomination of Christian fiction and articles for church-oriented teenagers, ages 12-17. Circ. 85,000. **Pays on acceptance.** Publishes ms an average of 15 months after acceptance. Byline given. Buys first North American serial, one-time, simultaneous and second serial (reprint) rights. Submit seasonal material 18 months in advance. Accepts simultaneous and previously published submissions. Send tearsheet or photocopy of article or typed ms with rights for sale noted and information about when and where the article previously appeared. Reports in 3 months. Sample copy for 9 × 12 SAE with 2 first-class stamps. Writer's guidelines for #10 SASE.
Nonfiction: Interviews with Christian athletes, musicians, missionaries, authors, or others with notable and helpful Christian testimonies or helpful experiences; transcriptions of discussion sessions where a group of teens talk about a particular issue; information on a topic or issue of interest gathered from experts in those fields (i.e. a doctor talks about teens' sexuality, a psychologist talks about dysfunctional families, a police officer talks about the dangers of gangs, etc.). Book excerpts, church history, general interest, how-to (deal with various life problems), humor, inspirational, personal experience. Buys 80-100 mss/year. Send complete ms. Length: 500-1,200 words. Pays 2-3¢/word.
Photos: Photos purchased with accompanying ms. Pays $35 for 8 × 10 b&w glossy print; $50 for 35mm slide.
Fiction: Adventure, humorous, mystery, romance, suspense. Buys 80-100 mss/year. Send complete ms. Length: 500-1,200 words. Pays 2-3¢/word.
Tips: "We need more male-oriented stories, articles, etc. Also need more stories or articles about life in the city and about people of diverse races. Avoid stereotypes. Avoid clichéd or trite situations with pat Christian answers and easy solutions. Avoid stories or articles without a Christian slant or emphasis, or those with a moral just tacked on at the end."

THIS PEOPLE MAGAZINE, Exploring LDS issues and personalities, Utah Alliance Publishing Co., Box 2250, Salt Lake City UT 84110-2250. (801)581-0881. Fax: (801)581-0881. Editors: Scot Facer Proctor and Maurine Jensen Proctor. 75% freelance written. Quarterly magazine covering Mormon issues and personalities. "This magazine is aimed at Mormon readers and examines Mormon issues and people in an upbeat, problem-solving way." Estab. 1979. Circ. 20,000. Pays on publication. Publishes ms an average of 6 months after acceptance. Byline given. Offers 15% kill fee. Buys first rights. Submit seasonal material 6 months in advance. Query for electronic submissions. Reports in 2 months. Sample copy for 9 × 12 SAE with 4 first-class stamps. Writer's guidelines for #10 SASE.
Nonfiction: Essays, historical/nostalgic, humor, inspirational, interview/profile, personal experience, photo feature, travel — all Mormon oriented. No poetry, cartoons, fiction. Buys 15-20 mss/year. Query with or without published clips, or send complete ms. Length: 1,000-3,500 words. Pays $150-400 for assigned articles; $100-400 for unsolicited articles. Sometimes pays expenses of writers on assignment.
Photos: State availability of photos with submission. Model releases and identification of subjects required. Buys all rights.
Tips: "I prefer query letters that include the first 6-8 paragraphs of an article plus an outline of the article. Clips and credits of previous publications are helpful."

‡**UNITED METHODIST REPORTER**, P.O. Box 660275, Dallas TX 75266-0275. (214)630-6495. Editor: John A. Lovelace. Weekly newspaper for a United Methodist national readership. Circ. 425,000. Pays on publication. Byline given. Not copyrighted. Free sample copy and writer's guidelines.
Nonfiction: "We accept occasional short features, approximately 500 words. Articles need not be limited to a United Methodist angle but need to have an explicit Protestant angle, preferably with evidence of participation in a local congregation. Write about a distinctly Christian response to human need or how a person's faith relates to a given situation." Send complete ms. Pays 4¢/word.
Photos: Purchased with accompanying ms. "We encourage the submission of good action photos (5 × 7 or 8 × 10 b&w glossy prints) of the persons or situations in the article." Pays $10.

THE UPPER ROOM, Daily Devotional Guide, P.O. Box 189, Nashville TN 37202-0189. (615)340-7252. Fax: (615)340-7006. Editor and Publisher: Janice T. Grana. Managing Editor: Mary Lou Redding. 95% freelance written. Eager to work with new/unpublished writers. Bimonthly magazine "offering a daily inspirational message which includes a Bible reading, text, prayer, 'Thought for the Day,' and suggestion for further prayer. Each day's meditation is written by a different person and is usually a personal witness about discover-

 A bullet introduces comments by the editor of Writer's Market indicating special information about the listing.

ing meaning and power for Christian living through scripture study which illuminates daily life." Circ. 2.2 million (US); 385,000 outside US Pays on publication. Publishes ms an average of 1 year after acceptance. Byline given. Buys first North American serial rights and translation rights. Submit seasonal material 14 months in advance. Manuscripts are not returned. If writers include a stamped, self addressed postcard, we will notify them that their writing has reached us. This does not imply acceptance or interest in purchase. Sample copy and writer's guidelines for SAE with 2 first-class stamps.

• This market does not respond unless material is accepted for publication.

Nonfiction: Inspirational, personal experience, Bible-study insights. No poetry, lengthy "spiritual journey" stories. Buys 360 unsolicited mss/year. Send complete ms. Length: 250 words maximum. Pays $12.

Tips: "The best way to break into our magazine is to send a well-written manuscript that looks at the Christian faith in a fresh way. Standard stories and sermon illustrations are immediately rejected. We very much want to find new writers and welcome good material. We are particularly interested in meditations based on Old Testament characters and stories. Good repeat meditations can lead to work on longer assignments for our other publications, which pay more. A writer who can deal concretely with everyday situations, relate them to the Bible and spiritual truths, and write clear, direct prose should be able to write for *The Upper Room*. We want material that provides for more interaction on the part of the reader—meditation suggestions, journaling suggestions, space to reflect and link personal experience with the meditation for the day."

VIRTUE, The Christian Magazine for Women, P.O. Box 850, Sisters OR 97759-0850. (503)549-8261. Fax: (503)549-0153. Editor: Marlee Alex. Managing Editor: Jeanette Thomason. 75% freelance written. Works with small number of new/unpublished writers each year. Bimonthly magazine that "shows through features and columns the depth and variety of expression that can be given to femininty and faith." Estab. 1978. Circ. 175,000. Pays on acceptance or publication. Publishes ms an average of 4 months after acceptance. Byline given. Buys first North American serial rights. Submit seasonal material 9 months in advance. Accepts previously published submissions. Send photocopy of article or short story or typed ms with rights for sale noted and information about when and where the article previously appeared. For reprints, pays 25% of the amount paid for an original article. Reports in 6 weeks on queries; 2 months on mss. Sample copy for 9 × 12 SAE with 7 first-class stamps. Writer's guidelines for #10 SASE.

Nonfiction: Book excerpts, how-to, humor, inspirational, interview/profile, opinion, personal experience, religious. Buys 60 mss/year. Query. Length: 600-1,800 words. Pays 15-25¢/word. Sometimes pays the expenses of writers on assignment.

Photos: State availability of photos with submission.

Columns/Departments: In My Opinion (reader editorial); One Woman's Journal (personal experience); Equipped for Ministry (Christian service potpourri); Romancing the Home; Real Men (women from a man's viewpoint). Buys 25 mss/year. Query. Length: 1,000-1,500. Pays 15-25¢/word.

Fiction: Humorous, religious. Buys 4-6 mss/year. Send complete ms. Length: 1,500-1,800 words. Pays 15-25¢/word.

Poetry: Free verse, haiku, traditional. Buys 7-10 poems/year. Submit maximum 3 poems. Length: 3-30 lines. Pays $15-50.

THE WESLEYAN ADVOCATE, The Wesleyan Publishing House, P.O. Box 50434, Indianapolis IN 46250-0434. (317)576-8156. Fax: (317)577-4397. Executive Editor: Dr. Norman G. Wilson. 50% freelance written. Monthly magazine of The Wesleyan Church. Estab. 1842. Circ. 20,000. Pays on publication. Publishes ms an average of 1 year after acceptance. Byline given. Buys first rights or simultaneous rights (prefers first rights). Submit seasonal material 6 months in advance. Accepts simultaneous and previously published submissions. Send typed ms with rights for sale noted and information about when and where the article previously appeared. Pays 50% of their fee for an original article. Query for electronic submissions. Reports in 2 weeks. Sample copy for $2. Writer's guidelines for #10 SASE.

Nonfiction: Humor, inspirational, religious. Buys 50 mss/year. Send complete ms. Length: 250-650 words. Pays $10-40 for assigned articles; $5-25 for unsolicited articles.

Photos: Send photos with submission. Reviews transparencies. Buys one-time rights.

Tips: "Write for a guide."

WOMAN'S TOUCH, Assemblies of God Women's Ministries Department (GPH), 1445 Boonville, Springfield MO 65802-1894. (417)862-2781. Fax: (417)862-0503. Editor: Sandra Goodwin Clopine. Associate Editor: Aleda Swartzendruber. 75-90% freelance written. Willing to work with new/unpublished writers. Bimonthly inspirational magazine for women. "Articles and contents of the magazine should be compatible with Christian teachings as well as human interests. The audience is women, both homemakers and those who are career-oriented." Estab. 1977. Circ. 21,000. **Pays on acceptance.** Byline given. Buys one-time rights. Submit seasonal/holiday material 8 months in advance. Accepts previously published submissions. Send photocopy of article or short story and information about when and where the article previously appeared. Reports in 3 months. Sample copy for 9½ × 11 SAE with 85¢ postage. Writer's guidelines for #10 SASE.

Nonfiction: General interest, how-to, inspirational, personal experience, religious, travel. Buys 75 mss/year. Send complete ms. Length: 500-1,000 words. Pays $10-35 for unsolicited articles.

Photos: State availability of photos with submission. Reviews negatives, transparencies, 4×6 prints. Offers no additional payment for photos accepted with ms. Identification of subjects required. Buys one-time rights.
Columns/Departments: A Creative Touch (special crafts, holiday decorations, family activities); 'A Final Touch' for short human interest articles—home and family or career-oriented." Buys 10 mss/year. Query with published clips. Length: 80-500 words. Pays $20-35.
Poetry: Free verse, light verse, traditional. Buys 10 poems/year. Submit maximum 4 poems. Length: 4-50 lines. Pays $5-20.
Fillers: Facts. Buys 5/year. Length: 50-200. Pays $5-15.

THE WORLD, Unitarian Universalist Association, 25 Beacon St., Boston MA 02108-2800. (617)742-2100. Fax: (617)367-3237. Editor-in-Chief: Linda Beyer. 50% freelance written. Bimonthly magazine covering religious education, spirituality, social consciousness, UUA projects and news, church communities, and personal philosophies of interesting people. "Purpose: to promote and inspire denominational self-reflection; to inform readers about the wide range of UU values, purposes, activities, aesthetics, and spiritual attitudes, and to educate readers about the history, personalities, and congregations that comprise UUism; to enhance its dual role of leadership and service to member congregations." Estab. 1987. Circ. 110,000. Pays on publication. Publishes mss an average of 1 year after acceptance. Byline given. Buys one-time rights. Editorial lead time 3 months. Submit seasonal material 3 months in advance. Accepts previously published submissions. Send tearsheet of article and information about when and where the article previously appeared. Pay varies. Query for electronic submissions. Reports in 2 months on queries; 3 months on mss. Sample copy and writer's guidelines for 9×12 SASE.
Nonfiction: Essays, historical/nostalgic (Unitarian or Universalist focus), inspirational, interview/profile (with UU individual or congregation), commentary, photo feature (of UU congregation or project), religious and travel. Buys 10 mss/year. Query with published clips. Length: 1,500-3,500 words. Pays $400 minimum for assigned feature articles. Sometimes pays expenses of writers on assignment.
Photos: State availability of photos with submission. Reviews contact sheets. Offers no additional payment for photos accepted with ms. Captions, model releases and identification of subjects required. Buys one-time rights.
Columns/Departments: Among Ourselves (news, profiles, inspirational reports), 300-700 words; Book Reviews (liberal religion, social issues, politics), 600-800 words. Buys 15 mss/year. Query (profiles, book reviews) or send complete mss (news). Pays $75-250 for assigned articles and book reviews.
Tips: "Get to know your local congregation, find its uniqueness, tell its story. We don't have enough congregational profiles."

Retirement

Retirement magazines have changed to meet the active lifestyles of their readers and editors dislike the kinds of stereotypes people have of the over-50 age group. More people are retiring in their 50s, while others are starting a business or traveling and pursuing hobbies. These publications give readers specialized information on health and fitness, medical research, finances and other topics of interest, as well as general articles on travel destinations and recreational activities.

ALIVE! A Magazine for Christian Senior Adults, Christian Seniors Fellowship, P.O. Box 46464, Cincinnati OH 45246-0464. (513)825-3681. Editor: J. David Lang. Office Editor: A. June Lang. 60% freelance written. Quarterly magazine for senior adults ages 55 and older. "We need timely articles about Christian seniors in vital, productive lifestyles, travels or ministries." Estab. 1988. Pays on publication. Byline given. Buys first or second serial (reprint) rights. Submit seasonal material 6 months in advance. Accepts previously published submissions. Send tearsheet or information about when and where the article previously appeared. Pays 60-75% of their fee for an original article. Reports in 6 weeks. Membership $10/year. Sample copy for 9×12 SAE with 3 first-class stamps. Writer's guidelines for #10 SASE.
Nonfiction: General interest, humor, inspirational, interview/profile, photo feature, religious, travel. Buys 25 mss/year. Send complete ms. Length: 600-1,200 words. Pays $18-75. Organization membership may be deducted from payment at writer's request.
Photos: State availability of photos with submission. Offers $10-25. Model releases and identification of subjects required. Buys one-time rights.
Columns/Departments: Heart Medicine (humorous personal anecdotes; prefer grandparent/grandchild stories or anecdotes re: over 55 persons), 10-100 words; Games n' Stuff (word games, puzzles, word search), 200-500 words. Buys 50 mss/year. Send complete ms. Pays $2-25.
Fiction: Adventure, humorous, religious, romance (if it fits age group), slice-of-life vignettes, motivational/inspirational. Buys 12 mss/year. Send complete ms. Length: 600-1,500 words. Pays $20-60.
Fillers: Anecdotes, facts, gags to be illustrated by cartoonist, short humor. Buys 15/year. Length: 50-500 words. Pays $2-15.

Tips: "Include SASE. If second rights, list where article has appeared and whether manuscript is to be returned or tossed."

‡FIFTY-SOMETHING MAGAZINE, For the Fifty-or-Better Mature Adult, Media Trends Publications, Unit E, 8250 Tyler Blvd., Mentor OH 44060-4219. (216)974-9594. Editor: Linda L. Lindeman. 40% freelance written. Bimonthly magazine on aging, travel, relationships, money, health, hobbies. "We are looking for a positive and upbeat attitude on aging. Proving that 50 years old is *not* over-the-hill but instead a prime time of life." Estab. 1989. Circ. 25,000. Pays on publication. Byline given. Buys all rights. Submit seasonal material 4 months in advance. Accepts simultaneous and previously published submissions. Send typed ms with rights for sale noted and information about when and where the material previously appeared. Pays 20% of fee paid for original material. Query for electronic submissions. Reports in 8 months. Sample copy for 9 × 12 SAE with 4 first-class stamps; writer's guidelines for #10 SASE.

Nonfiction: Book excerpts, essays, exposé, general interest, historical/nostalgic, how-to (sports), humor, inspirational, opinion, personal experience, photo feature, religious, travel, health, employment. Buys 6 mss/year. Query with published clips, or send complete ms. Length: 100-1,000 words. Pays $25-100. Sometimes pays expenses of writers on assignment.
   ● This magazine is overstocked with mss.

Photos: Send photos with submission. Reviews contact sheets, negatives, transparencies, 5 × 7 prints. Offers $25-100 per photo. Captions, model releases, identification of subjects required. Buys one-time or all rights.

Columns/Departments: Book Review (50 and over market); Movie/Play Review (new releases); Sports (for the mature adult); Travel (for the mature adult). Buys 50 mss/year. Send complete ms. Length: 100-1,000 words. Pays $25-100.

Fiction: Adventure, condensed novels, ethnic, experimental, fantasy, historical, humorous, mainstream, mystery, religious, romance, slice-of-life vignettes, suspense. Buys 25 mss/year. Send complete ms. Length: 100-1,000 words. Pays $25-100.

Poetry: Avant-garde, free verse, light verse, traditional. Buys 15 poems/year. Length: 25-150 lines. Pays $25-100.

Fillers: Anecdotes, facts, gags to be illustrated by cartoonist, newsbreaks, short humor. Buys 100/year. Length: 25-150 words. Pays $25-100.

Tips: "We are a regional publication in northeast Ohio. All areas are open. If you are 50 or more, write as if you are addressing your peers. If you are younger, take a generic approach to age. You don't have to be 50 to address this market."

FLORIDA RETIREMENT LIFESTYLES, Housing ● Travel ● Leisure, (formerly *Florida Retirement Living*), Gidder House Publishing, Inc., P.O. Box 161848, Altamonte Springs FL 32714-1848. Editor: Kay Fernandez. 20% freelance written. Monthly magazine directed toward Florida or Florida-bound retirees in an upbeat manner—unusual as well as typical Florida places, people, etc. Estab. 1946. Circ. 35,000. Pays on publication. Publishes ms an average of 3 months after acceptance. No kill fee. Buys first North American serial, first, one-time, second serial (reprint), simultaneous rights, all rights and/or makes work-for-hire assignments. Submit seasonal material 3 months in advance. Accepts previously published submissions. Send tearsheet or photocopy of article or typed ms with rights for sale noted and information about when and where the article previously appeared. 50% of the amount paid for an original article. Query for electronic submissions. Reports in 3 weeks on queries. Free writer's guidelines. Sample copy for $2.

Nonfiction: Hobbies, new careers, transition how to's, how-to (learn new skill as senior), humor, inspirational, interview/profile, new product, personal experience, photo feature, travel. Editorial calendar available on request. No negative or health related articles. Buys 30 mss/year. Query with or without published clips or send complete ms. Length: 750-1,250 words. Pays $100-150. Sometimes pays expenses of writers on assignment.

Photos: Send photos with submissions. Reviews transparencies and prints. Offers $5-25/photo. Model releases and identification of subjects required. Buys one-time rights or all rights.

Tips: "Look for the unusual, little known but interesting aspects of Florida living that seniors want or need to know about. Housing, finance and real estate are of primary interest."

KEY HORIZONS, The Magazine For Your Best Years, Emmis Publishing Corp., Suite 1200, 950 N. Meridian St., Indianapolis IN 46204. Editor: Deborah Paul. Managing Editor: Joan Todd. 75% freelance written. Quarterly magazine for older adults, age 55+. "*Key Horizons* takes a positive approach to life, stressing the opportunities available to older adults." Estab. 1988. Circ. 200,000 (controlled circulation—sent to certain Blue Cross/Blue Shield policy holders in several states). Pays on publication. Publishes ms an average of 1-2 months after acceptance. Byline given. Offers $50 kill fee. Buys first North American serial rights. Submit seasonal material 4 months in advance. Query for electronic submissions. Reports in 1 month on queries; 2 months on mss. Free writer's guidelines with SASE.

Nonfiction: General interest, tips for better living, health, money, travel (domestic only). Buys 25-35 mss/year. Query with published clips or send complete ms. Length: 1,500 words. Pays $250-500. SASE required for response.

Photos: State availability of photos with submission. Reviews 2¼×2¼ transparencies and 8×10 prints. Offers $25/photo. Captions and identification of subjects required. Buys one-time rights. Always looking for scenic parting shot. Payment negotiable.
Columns/Departments: Health, money, travel, food. (1,200 words). Like tips and sidebars. No nostalgia. Buys 12-16 mss/year. Query with published clips or send complete ms. Pays $300. SASE required for response.
Tips: "Take an upbeat approach. View older adults as vital, productive, active people. We appreciate detailed, well-written query letters that show some preliminary research."

MATURE LIVING, A Christian Magazine for Senior Adults, Sunday School Board of the Southern Baptist Convention, 127 Ninth Ave. N., Nashville TN 37234. (615)251-2274. Editor: Al Shackleford. 70% freelance written. Monthly leisure reading magazine for senior adults 60 and older. Estab. 1892. Circ. 350,000. **Pays on acceptance.** Byline given. Buys all rights and sometimes one-time rights. Submit seasonal material 18 months in advance. Reports in 3 months. Sample copy for 9×12 SAE with 4 first-class stamps. Writer's guidelines for #10 SASE.
Nonfiction: General interest, historical/nostalgic, how-to, humor, inspirational, interview/profile, personal experience, photo feature, crafts, travel. No pornography, profanity, occult, liquor, dancing, drugs, gambling. No book reviews. Buys 100 mss/year. Send complete ms. Length: 1,475 words maximum; prefers 950 words. Pays 5½¢/word (accepted).
Photos: State availability of photos with submission. Offers $10-15/photo. Pays on publication. Buys one-time rights.
Fiction: Humorous, mainstream, slice-of-life vignettes. No reference to liquor, dancing, drugs, gambling; no pornography, profanity or occult. Buys 12 mss/year. Send complete ms. Length: 900-1,475 words. Pays 5½¢/word.
Poetry: Light verse, traditional. Buys 50 poems/year. Submit maximum 5 poems. Length: open. Pays $5-24.
Fillers: Anecdotes, facts, short humor. Buys 15/issue. Length: 50 words maximum. Pays $5.

MATURE OUTLOOK, Meredith Corp., 1912 Grand Ave., Des Moines IA 50309-3379. Associate Editor: Peggy Person. 80% freelance written. Bimonthly magazine on travel, health, nutrition, money and garden for over-50 audience. They may or may *not* be retired. Circ. 925,000. **Pays on acceptance.** Publishes ms an average 6-7 months after acceptance. Byline given. Offers 20% kill fee. Buys all rights or makes work-for-hire assignments. Submit all material 9 months in advance. Query for electronic submissions. Reports in 2 weeks. Sample copy for $1. Writer's guidelines for #10 SASE.
Nonfiction: How-to, travel, health, fitness. No personal experience or poetry. Buys 50-60 mss/year. Query with published clips. Length: 300-1,000 words. Pays $225-750 for assigned articles. Pays telephone expenses of writers on assignment.
Photos: State availability of photos with submission.
Tips: "Please query. Please don't call."

MATURE YEARS, 201 Eighth Ave. S., Nashville TN 37202-0801. Fax: (615)749-6512. Editor: Marvin W. Cropsey. 30% freelance written. Prefers to work with published/established writers. Quarterly magazine for retired persons and those facing retirement; persons seeking help on how to handle problems and privileges of retirement. **Pays on acceptance.** Publishes ms an average of 12 months after acceptance. Rights purchased vary with author and material; usually buys one-time North American serial rights. Submit seasonal material 14 months in advance. Publishes reprints of previously published articles. Send tearsheet, photocopy or typed ms with rights for sale noted and information about when and where the article previously appeared. For reprints, pays 100% of the amount paid for an original article. Query for electronic submissions. Reports in 6-8 weeks. Sample copy for $3.50 and 9×12 SAE. Writer's guidelines for #10 SASE.
Nonfiction: "*Mature Years* is different from the secular press in that we like material with a Christian and church orientation. Usually we prefer materials that have a happy, healthy outlook regarding aging. Advocacy (for older adults) articles are at times used; some are freelance submissions. We need articles dealing with many aspects of pre-retirement and retirement living, and short stories and leisure-time hobbies related to specific seasons. Give examples of how older persons, organizations and institutions are helping others. Writing should be of interest to older adults, with Christian emphasis, though not preachy and moralizing. No poking fun or mushy, sentimental articles. We treat retirement from the religious viewpoint. How-to, humor and travel are also considered." Buys 36 unsolicited mss/year. Submit complete ms (include SASE and Social Security number with submissions). Length: 1,200-2,000 words.
Photos: 8×10 color prints or transparencies purchased with ms or on assignment.
Fiction: "We buy fiction for adults. No children's stories and no stories about depressed situations of older adults." Length: 1,000-2,000 words. Payment varies, usually 4¢/word.
Tips: "We like writing to be meaty, timely, clear and concrete."

MODERN MATURITY, American Association of Retired Persons, 3200 E. Carson St., Lakewood CA 90712. (310)496-2277. Editor: J. Henry Fenwick. 50% freelance written. Prefers to work with published/established writers. Bimonthly magazine for readership of persons 50 years of age and over. Circ. 22.6 million. **Pays on acceptance.** Publishes ms an average of 6 months after acceptance. Byline given. Buys first North American serial rights. Submit seasonal material 6 months in advance. Query for electronic submissions. Reports in 2-3 months. Free sample copy and writer's guidelines.

Nonfiction: Careers, workplace, practical information in living, financial and legal matters, personal relationships, consumerism. Query first. *No unsolicited mss.* Length: up to 2,000 words. Pays up to $3,000. Sometimes pays expenses of writers on assignment.

Photos: Photos purchased with or without accompanying ms. Pays $250 and up for color; $150 and up for b&w.

Fiction: Very occasional short fiction.

Tips: "The most frequent mistake made by writers in completing an article for us is poor follow-through with basic research. The outline is often more interesting than the finished piece. We do not accept unsolicited mss."

PARENT CARE, Newsletter for Children of Aging Parents, Parent Care Publications, Box 12624, Roanoke VA 24027-2624. (703)342-7511. Fax: (703)989-1615. Editor: Betty Robertson. 75% freelance written. Monthly newsletter covering caring for aging parents. "*Parent Care* is a monthly newsletter for children of aging parents and those involved as caregivers for the older adult." Estab. 1991. Circ. 125. **Pays on acceptance.** Publishes ms an average of 3 months after acceptance. Byline given. Buys first, one-time, second serial (reprint) or simultaneous rights. Editorial lead time 3 months. Submit seasonal material 6 months in advance. Accepts simultaneous and previously published submissions. Send typed ms with rights for sale noted. Pays 100% of the amount paid for an original article. Reports in 1 month on queries; 1-3 months on mss. Sample copy for $2.50. Writer's guidelines for #10 SASE.

Nonfiction: Book excerpts, general interest, how-to, inspirational, new product, personal experience, religious. Buys 25-30 mss/year. Send complete ms. Length: 750-1,200 words. Pays $3 minimum for assigned articles.

Columns/Departments: What's Happening In Your World (personal caregiving experience), 750 words; Pulse Check (devotion), 450 words.

Tips: "Research carefully; write about your own caregiving experiences."

SENIOR MAGAZINE, 3565 S. Higuera St., San Luis Obispo CA 93401. (805)544-8711. Fax: (805)544-4450. Editor/Publisher: Gary D. Suggs. 90% freelance written. Monthly magazine covering seniors to inform and entertain the "over-50" audience. Estab. 1981. Circ. 240,000. Pays on publication. Byline given. Publishes ms an average of 1 month after acceptance. Not copyrighted. Buys first or second rights. Submit seasonal material 2 months in advance. Reports in 1 month. *Writer's Market* recommends allowing 2 months for reply. Sample copy for 9 × 12 SAE with 6 first-class stamps. Writer's guidelines for SASE.

Nonfiction: Historical/nostalgic, humor, inspirational, personal experience, travel. Special issues: War Years (November); Christmas (December); Travel (October, March). Buys 30-75 mss/year. Query. Length: 300-900 words. Pays $1.50/inch.

Photos: Send photos with submission. Reviews 8 × 10 b&w prints only. Offers $10-25/photo. Captions and identification of subjects required. Buys one-time rights.

Columns/Departments: Finance (investment), Taxes, Auto, Health. Length: 300-900 words. Pays $1.50/inch.

SENIOR SPECTRUM, for the second half of your life, (formerly *Senior Edition USA/Colorado*), Suite 218, 1385 S. Colorado Blvd., Denver CO 80222-3312. (303)758-4040. Area Editor: Rose Beetem. 15% freelance written. Monthly tabloid. "Colorado newspaper for seniors (with national distribution) emphasizing legislation, opinion and advice columns, local and national news, features and local calendar aimed at over-55 community." Estab. 1972. Circ. 50,000. Pays on publication. Publishes ms an average of 6 months after acceptance. Byline given. Offer 25-50% kill fee for assigned stories only. Buys first North American serial rights and simultaneous rights. Submit seasonal material 3 months in advance. Reports in 3-6 months. Sample copy for $1. Writer's guidelines for SASE.

Nonfiction: Historical/nostalgic, humor, opinion, personal experience, travel. Does not want "anything aimed at less than age 50-plus market; anything patronizing or condescending to seniors." Buys 3-6 mss/year. Buys over 70 mss/year in nostalgia. Query with or without published clips or send complete ms. Length: 50-1,000 words. (Note: Nostalgia length best under 800 words.) Pays $5-30 for assigned articles; $5-25 for unsolicited articles. Sometimes pays expenses of writers on assignment.

Photos: Send photos with submission (or photocopies of available pictures). Offers $3-10/photo. Identification of subjects required. Buys one-time rights.

Columns/Departments: Senior Overlook (opinions of seniors about anything they feel strongly about: finances, grandkids, love, life, social problems, etc. May be editorial, essay, prose or poetry). Buys 3-6 mss/year. Send complete ms. Length: 150-500 words. Pays $10 maximum.

● No longer seeking fillers.

Tips: Areas most open to freelancers are "Opinion: have a good, reasonable point backed with personal experience and/or researched data. Diatribes, vague or fuzzy logic or overworked themes not appreciated. Advice: solid information and generic articles accepted. We will not promote any product or business unless it is the only one in existence. Must be applicable to senior lifestyle. Nostalgia/Old Times section always open—monthly themes. Theme list available for SASE."

SENIOR WORLD NEWSMAGAZINE, Kendell Communications, Inc., P.O. Box 1565, El Cajon CA 92022-1565. (619)593-2910. Executive Editor: Laura Impastato. Travel Editor: Jerry Goodrum. Entertainment Editor: Iris Neal. Health Editor: Doug Brunk. Feature Editor: Carolyn Pantier. 5% freelance written. Prefers to work with published/established writers. Monthly tabloid newspaper for active older adults living in San Diego, Orange, Los Angeles, Riverside and San Bernardino counties. Estab. 1973. Circ. 500,000. Pays on publication. Buys first serial rights. Accepts simultaneous submissions. Reports in 2 months. Sample copy for $3. Free writer's guidelines.
Nonfiction: "We are looking for stories on health, stressing wellness and prevention; travel—international, domestic and how-to; profiles of senior celebrities and remarkable seniors; finance and investment tips for seniors; and interesting hobbies." Send query or complete ms. Length: 500-1,000 words. Pays $50-100.
Photos: State availability of photos with submission. Needs b&w with model release.
Columns/Departments: Most of our columns are local or staff-written. We will consider a query on a column idea accompanied by a sample column.
Tips: "No pity the poor seniors material. Remember that we are primarily a news publication and that our content and style reflect that. Our readers are active, vital adults 55 years of age and older." No telephone queries.

SUCCESSFUL RETIREMENT, Grass Roots Publishing, 16th Floor, 950 Third Ave., New York NY 10022. Editor: Marcia Vickers. 90% freelance written. Bimonthly magazine covering retirement. "Fun, upbeat, a youthful approach to retirement. No fuddy-duddyness. Our audience consists of "pretirees and retirees—average age 65. (No 'little old lady from Pasadena' stories)." Estab. 1993. Circ. 20,000. Pays on publication. Publishes ms an average of 3-4 months after acceptance. Byline given. Buys all rights. Editorial lead time 3-4 months. Submit seasonal material 6 months in advance. Query for electronic submissions. Occasionally accepts previously published submissions. Send tearsheet of article and information about when and where the article previously appeared with rights for sale noted. Pays 50% of the amount paid for an original article. Reports in 2-3 months. Sample copy for $3.50 (plus postage and handling). Writer's guidelines free on request.
Nonfiction: Health, how-to, humor, motivational, interview/profile, older celebrity profiles, relationships, travel, retirement locales, second careers, profiles of retirees doing unusual, interesting things and retirement life. "No lengthy, essay-type pieces or opinion pieces. Nothing negative or drab. Must pertain to retirement or aging." Buys 60 mss/year. Query with published clips. Length: 500-1,000 words. Pays $150 minimum.
Photos: State availability of photos with submission or send photos with submission. Identification of subjects required.
Columns/Departments: "Columns are written by staff writers. Query *only* if you have new column idea." Query with published clips. Pays $150-200.

‡TODAY'S TIMES, The Elder Statesman Publishing Co., P.O. Box 1198, Station A, Nanaimo, British Columbia V9R 6E7 Canada. (604)754-2387. Fax: (604)754-2398. Managing Editor: Christopher Beddows. 40% freelance written. Monthly tabloid for people over 50. Estab. 1958. Circ. 30,000. Pays 30 days after publication. Byline given. Buys first rights. Submit seasonal material 6 months in advance. Electronic submissions on any MSDOS format (prefer Wordperfect). Reports in 2 months. Sample copy for $1. Free writer's guidelines.
Nonfiction: General interest (for 50+), historical/nostalgic, humor, personal experience, travel. Only articles that relate to 50+ readers who live in British Columbia. Buys 50 mss/year. Query with published clips. Length: 350-450 words. Pays $25-55 for assigned articles; $25 for unsolicited articles (all Canadian dollars).
● Greater emphasis on short, informational sidebar types of features.
Photos: State availability of photos with submission. Reviews prints. Offers no additional payment for photos accepted with ms. Buys one-time rights.
Tips: "Put word length on first page, and when sending SASE remember Canada has its own postal system and is not an offshoot of US. We cannot use US stamps. Best departments for freelancers are travel, nostalgia, retirement housing. Remember 50+ is a broad spectrum."

Romance and Confession

Listed here are publications that need stories of romance ranging from ethnic and adventure to romantic intrigue and confession. Each magazine has a particular slant; some are written for young adults, others to family-oriented women. Some magazines also are interested in general interest nonfiction on related subjects.

‡AFFAIRE DE COEUR,, 3976 Oak Hill Rd., Oakland CA 94605. Editor: Louise Snead. 56% freelance written. Monthly magazine of book reviews, articles and information on publishing for romance readers and writers. Circ. 115,000. Pays on publication. Publishes ms an average of 6-12 months after acceptance. Byline given.

Buys one-time rights. Submit seasonal/holiday material 3 months in advance. Accepts simultaneous and previously published submissions. Reports in 4 months. Sample copy for $5.

Nonfiction: Book excerpts, essays, general interest, historical/nostalgic, how-to, interview/profile, personal experience, photo feature. Buys 2 mss/year. Query. Length: 500-2,200 words. Pays $5-15. Sometimes pays writers with contributor copies or other premiums.

Photos: State availability of photos with submission. Review prints. Identification of subjects required. Buys one-time rights.

Columns/Departments: Reviews (book reviews), bios, articles, 2,000 word or less.

Fiction: Historical, mainstream, romance. Pays $25.

Fillers: Newsbreaks. Buys 2/year. Length: 50-100 words. Does not pay.

Tips: "Please send clean copy. Do not send material without SASE. Do not expect a return for 2-3 months. Type all information. Send some sample of your work."

BLACK SECRETS, Sterling/McFadden, 5th Floor, 233 Park Ave. S., New York NY 10003. (212)780-3500. Fax: (212)780-3555. Editor: Tonia Shakespeare. Accepts previously published submissions. Send short story or typed ms with rights for sale noted and information about when and where story previously appeared. See *Intimacy/Black Romance*.

Fiction: "This is our most romantic magazine of the five. We use one longer story between 20-24 pages for this book, and sometimes we feature it on the cover. Save your harsh, sleazy stories for another magazine. Give us your softest, dreamiest, most imaginative, most amorous story with a male love interest we can't help but fall in love with. Make sure your story has body and not just bodies. Our readers love romance, but they also require substance."

Tips: "Please request a sample and guidelines before submitting. Enclose a 9×12 SASE with 5 first-class stamps."

BRONZE THRILLS, Sterling/McFadden, 5th Floor, 233 Park Ave. S., New York NY 10003. (212)780-3500. Fax: (212)780-3522. Editor: Tonia Shakespeare. Estab. 1982. See *Intimacy/Black Romance*.

Fiction: "Stories can be a bit more extraordinary and uninhibited than in the other magazines but still they have to be romantic. For example, we might buy a story about a woman who finds out her husband is a transsexual in *Bronze Thrills*, but not for *Jive* (our younger magazine). The stories for this magazine tend to have a harder, more adult edge of reality than the others."

INTIMACY/BLACK ROMANCE, Sterling/McFadden, 5th Floor, 233 Park Ave. S., New York NY 10003. (212)780-3500. Fax: (212)780-3522. Editor: Tonia Shakespeare. 100% freelance written. Eager to work with new/unpublished writers. Bimonthly magazine of romance and love. Estab. 1982. Circ. 100,000. Pays on publication. Publishes ms an average of 2 months after acceptance. Byline given on articles only. Buys all rights. Submit seasonal material 6 months in advance. Reports in 2 months. Sample copy for 9×12 SAE with 5 first-class stamps. Writer's guidelines for #10 SASE.

Nonfiction: How-to (relating to romance and love) and feature articles on any aspect of relationships. Buys 100 mss/year. Query with published clips or send complete ms. Length: 3-5 pages. Pays $100.

Photos: Send photos with submission. Reviews contact sheets, negatives, transparencies.

Fiction: Confession and romance. "Stories that are too graphic in content and lack romance are unacceptable." Buys 300 mss/year. Accepts stories which are a bit more romantic than those written for *Jive*, *Black Confessions* or *Bronze Thrills*. Send complete ms (4,000-5,000 words). Pays $75-100.

Tips: "I still get excited when I read a ms by an unpublished writer whose use of language is magical and fresh. I'm always looking for that diamond in the fire. Send us your *best* shot. Writers who are careless, sloppy and ungrammatical are an immediate turn-off for me. Please do your homework first. Is it the type of story we buy? Is it written in ms format? Does it make one want to read it?"

JIVE, Sterling/McFadden, 5th Floor, 233 Park Ave. S., New York NY 10003. (212)780-3500. Fax: (212)780-3555. Editor: Tonia Shakespeare. 100% freelance written. Eager to work with new/unpublished writers. Bimonthly magazine of romance and love. Estab. 1982. Circ. 100,000. Pays on publication. Publishes ms an average of 2 months after acceptance. Byline given on articles only. Buys all rights. Submit seasonal material 6 months in advance. Reports in 2 months on queries; 6 months on mss. Sample copy for 9×12 SASE with 5 first-class stamps. Free writer's guidelines.

Nonfiction: How-to (relating to romance and love) and feature articles on any aspect of relationships. "We like our articles to have a down-to-earth flavor. They should be written in the spirit of sisterhood, fun and creativity. Come up with an original idea our readers may not have thought of but will be dying to try out." Buys 100 mss/year. Query with published clips or send complete ms. Length: 3-5 typed pages. Pays $100.

Columns/Departments: Fashion, health, beauty articles accepted. Length: 3-5 pages.

Fiction: Confession and romance. "Stories that are too graphic and lack romance are unacceptable. However, all stories must contain one or two love scenes. Love scenes should allude to sex—romantic, not lewd." Buys 300 mss/year. Send complete ms (4,000-5,000 words). Pays $75-100.

Tips: "We are leaning toward more romantic writing styles as opposed to the more graphic stories of the past. Our audience is largely black teenagers. The stories should reinforce Black pride and should be geared toward teenage issues. Our philosophy is to show our experiences in as positive a light as possible without promoting any of the common stereotypes that are associated with Black men, lovemaking prowess, penile size, etc. Stereotypes of any kind are totally unacceptable. The fiction section which accepts romance stories and confession stories is most open to freelancers. Also, our special features section is very open. We would also like to see stories that are set outside the US (perhaps they could be set in the Caribbean, Europe, Africa, etc.) and themes that are reflective of things happening around us in the 90s—abortion, AIDS, alienation, surrogate mothers, etc. But we also like to see stories that transcend our contemporary problems and can give us a moment of pleasure, warmth, joy and relief. The characters should be anywhere from teenage to 30s but not the typical 'country bumpkin girl who was turned out by a big city pimp' type story. Please, writers who are not Black, research your story to be sure that it depicts Black people in a positive manner. Do not make a Black character a caricature of a non-Black character. Read contemporary Black fiction to ensure that your dialogue and speech idioms are natural to the Black vernacular."

JIVE/BLACK CONFESSIONS, Sterling/McFadden, 5th Floor, 233 Park Ave. S., New York NY 10003. (212)780-3500. Fax: (212)780-3555. Editor: Tonia Shakespeare. Estab. 1982. See *Jive*.

MODERN ROMANCES, Sterling/Macfadden Partnership, 233 Park Ave. S., New York NY 10003. (212)979-4800. Editor: Cherie Clark King. 100% freelance written. Monthly magazine for family-oriented working women, ages 18-65 years old. Circ. 200,000. Pays the last week of the month of issue. Buys all rights. Submit seasonal material at least 6 months in advance. Reports in 9-11 months. Writer's guidelines for #10 SASE.
Nonfiction: Confession stories with reader identification and a strong emotional tone; a strong emphasis on characterization and well-defined plots. Should be realistic and compelling. No query letters. No third-person material. Buys 12 mss/issue. Submit complete ms. Length: 2,500-10,000 words. Pays 5¢/word.
Poetry: Light, romantic poetry and seasonal/holiday subjects. Length: 24 lines maximum. Pay depends on merit. Look at poetry published in previous issues before submitting.

TRUE CONFESSIONS, Macfadden Women's Group, 233 Park Ave. S., New York NY 10003. (212)979-4800. Editor: Pat Vitucci. 90% freelance written. Eager to work with new/unpublished writers. Monthly magazine for high-school-educated, blue-collar women, teens through maturity. Circ. 280,000. Buys all rights. Byline given on featured columns: My Man, The Feminine Side, Incredible But True, My Moment With God and You and Your Pet. Pays during the last week of month of issue. Publishes ms an average of 4 months after acceptance. Submit seasonal material 6 months in advance. Reports in 6 months.
Nonfiction and Fiction: Timely, exciting, emotional first-person stories on the problems that face today's women. The narrators should be sympathetic, and the situations they find themselves in should be intriguing, yet realistic. Many stories may have a strong romantic interest and a high moral tone; however, personal accounts or "confessions," no matter how controversial the topic, are encouraged and accepted. Careful study of a current issue is suggested. Length: 4,000-7,000 words; also book lengths of 8,000-10,000 words. Pays 5¢/word. Also publishes humor, poetry and mini-stories (3,000 words maximum). Submit complete ms. No simultaneous submissions. SASE required.
  ● Always looking for topical material.

‡TRUE EXPERIENCE, The Sterling/MacFadden Partnership, 233 Park Ave. S., New York NY 10003. (212)979-4800. Editor: Claire Cloutier LeBlanc. Contact: Alison M. Way. 90% freelance written. Monthly magazine covering women's confession stories. *"True Experience* is a women's confession magazine which publishes first-person short stories on actual occurrences. Our stories cover such topics as romantic relationships, family problems and social issues. The magazine's primary audience consists of working-class women in the South, Midwest and rural West. Our stories aim to portray the lives and problems of 'real women.' " Estab. 1928. Circ. 80,000. Pays on publication. Publishes ms an average of 4 months after acceptance. No byline. Buys all rights. Editorial lead time 2-4 months. Submit seasonal material 6 months in advance. Query for electronic submissions. Reports in 2 weeks on queries; 2-4 months on mss. Sample copy for $1.69. Writer's guidelines for #10 SASE.
Nonfiction: Confession, humorous, mystery, romance, slice-of-life vignettes. Buys 125 mss/year. Send complete ms. Length: 4,000-16,000 words. Pays 3¢/word.
Columns/Departments: Woman Talk (brief stories covering rites of passage in women's lives), 1,000-7,000 words; How We Met (anecdotes describing a couple's first meeting), 300-1,000 words. Buys 24 mss/year. Send complete ms. Pays $50-75.
Poetry: Light verse, traditional. Buys 5 poems/year. Submit maximum 10 poems. Length: 4-50 lines. Pays $2/line.
Tips: "The best way to break into our publication is to send us a well-written, interesting story with sympathetic characters. Stories focusing on topical subjects like sexual harassment, date rape, AIDS, or natural disasters are most likely to receive serious consideration. No special submission methods are called for. All stories must be written in first person."

TRUE LOVE, Macfadden Women's Group, 233 Park Ave. S., New York NY 10003. (212)979-4800. Editor: Kristina Kracht. 100% freelance written. Monthly magazine for young, blue-collar women, 22-55. Confession stories based on true happenings, with reader identification and a strong emotional tone. Circ. 200,000. Pays the last week of the month of the issue. Buys all rights. Submit seasonal material 6 months in advance. No simultaneous submissions. Reports in 2 months. Sample copy for $2 and 9 × 12 SAE. Writer's guidelines for #10 SASE.

Nonfiction and Fiction: Confessions, true love stories, problems and solutions, health problems, marital and child-rearing difficulties. Avoid graphic sex. Stories dealing with reality, current problems, everyday events, with emphasis on emotional impact. No stories written in third person. Buys 10 stories/issue. Submit complete ms; returned only with SAE and sufficient postage. Length: 2,000-10,000 words. Pays 3¢/word.

Columns/Departments: "The Life I Live," $100; "How I Know I'm In Love," 700 words or less; $75; "Pet Shop," $50; "Kids Will Be Kids," $50.

Poetry: Light romantic poetry. Length: 24 lines maximum. Pay depends on merit.

Tips: "The story must appeal to the average blue-collar woman. It must deal with her problems and interests. Characters—especially the narrator—must be sympathetic. Focus is especially on teenagers, young working (or student) women."

TRUE ROMANCE, Sterling/Macfadden Partnership, 233 Park Ave. S., New York NY 10003. (212)979-4800. Fax: (212)979-7342. Editor: Pat Byrdsong. Monthly magazine. 100% freelance written. Readership primarily young, working class women, teens through retired. Confession stories based on true happenings, with reader identification and strong emotional tone. No third-person material; no simultaneous submissions. Estab. 1923. Circ. 225,000. Pays 1 month after publication. Buys all rights. Submit seasonal/holiday material at least 6 months in advance. Reports in 5 months.

Nonfiction: Confessions, true love stories; problems and solutions; dating and marital and child-rearing difficulties. Realistic stories dealing with current problems, everyday events, with strong emotional appeal. Buys 12 stories/issue. Submit complete ms. Length 1,500-7,500 words. Pays 3¢/word; slightly higher rates for short-shorts.

Poetry: Light romantic poetry. Buys 100/year. Length: 24 lines maximum. Pay depends on merit.

Tips: "A timely, well-written story that is told by a sympathetic narrator who sees the central problem through to a satisfying resolution is *all* important to break into *True Romance*. We are always looking for good emotional, identifiable stories."

 • Editor has expressed an interest in stories with ethnic characters (i.e. Asian-Americans, Native Americans, African-Americans, etc.) as long as the story is based in the United States or Canada.

TRUE STORY, Sterling/Macfadden Partnership, 233 Park Ave. S., New York NY 10003. (212)979-4800. Editor: Susan Weiner. 80% freelance written. Monthly magazine for young married, blue-collar women, 20-35; high school education; increasingly broad interests; home-oriented, but looking beyond the home for personal fulfillment. Circ. 1.7 million. Buys all rights. Byline given "on articles only." Pays 1 month after publication. Submit seasonal material 1 year in advance. Reports in approximately 8-12 months.

Nonfiction: Pays a flat rate for columns or departments, as announced in the magazine. Query for fact articles.

Fiction: "First-person stories covering all aspects of women's interests: love, marriage, family life, careers, social problems, etc. The best direction a new writer can be given is to carefully study several issues of the magazine; then submit a fresh, exciting, well-written true story. We have no taboos. It's the handling and believability that make the difference between a rejection and an acceptance." Buys about 125 full-length mss/year. Submit only complete mss for stories. Length: 1,500-10,000 words. Pays 5¢/word; $150 minimum.

Rural

Readers may be conservative or liberal, but these publications draw them together with a focus on rural lifestyles. Surprisingly, many readers are from urban centers who dream of or plan to build a house in the country.

ALBERTA FARM AND RANCH, Alberta's Foremost Rural Magazine, North Hill Publications, 4000 19th St. NE, Calgary, Alberta T2E 6P8 Canada. (403)250-6633. Fax: (403)291-0502. Editor: Michael Dumont. 10-30% freelance written. Monthly magazine covering rural and agricultural issues in Alberta. Estab. 1983. Circ. 80,288. Pays on publication. Publishes ms an average of 4 months after acceptance. Byline given. Buys First Canadian Rights. Submit seasonal material 6 months in advance. Reports in 2 months. Sample copy for 8 × 10 SAE with 2 first class Canadian stamps or 2 IRCs. Writer's guidelines for #10 SASE with Canadian postage or #10 SAE with 1 IRC.

Nonfiction: General interest, historical/nostalgic, politics, interview/profile, technical. "September's issue always features Women in Agriculture and related issues. No non-relevant articles or articles not of interest to rural Albertans." Buys 20-30 mss/year. Query with published clips. Length: 1,000-2,000 words. Pays $50-200 for assigned articles; $50-100 for unsolicited articles.

Photos: Reviews 4×6 prints. Offers $5-10/photo. Captions and identification of subjects required.

Columns/Departments: "Columnists work on annual contracts only."

Tips: "While *AF&R* seldom accepts unsolicited manuscripts, we always encourage writers to send in queries before going to the time and expense of completing a story. The best way to break into our magazine is with a unique story idea with specific interest to rural Albertans. Stories looking at unique personalities, insightful material on age-related issues and stories of issues concerning the family tend to fill most pages. For new writers trying to solicit their material with little publishing experience, I suggest the submission of typed mss in lieu of tearsheets. Caution: the fastest way to get a rejection is to spell words incorrectly or glaring grammatical errors. Also, superficial stories that do not entice reading or leave extensive informational gaps tend to be overlooked. I would rather see penned-in corrections than errors left unchecked."

COUNTRY JOURNAL, P.O. Box 8200, Harrisburg PA 17105-8200. (717)657-9555. Fax: (717)657-9526. Editor: Peter V. Fossel. Managing Editor: Lisa Bishop. 90% freelance written. Works with a small number of new/unpublished writers each year. Bimonthly magazine "providing pragmatic, useful information that will give the reader more control over his country life." Estab. 1974. Circ. 201,000. Average issue includes 6-8 feature articles and 10 departments. **Pays on acceptance.** Rates range from 20-40¢/word. Byline given. Buys first North American serial rights. Submit seasonal material 1 year in advance. Reports in 2-4 months. Sample copy for $4. Writer's guidelines for SASE.

Nonfiction: Conservation, gardening, nature, projects, small-scale farming, how-to, issues affecting rural areas. Query with published clips and SASE. Length: 1,500-2,000 words. Pays 20-40¢/word.

Photos: David Siegfried, art director. State availability of photos. Reviews b&w contact sheets, 5×7 and 8×10 b&w glossy prints and 35mm or larger transparencies with SASE. Captions, model release, identification of subjects required. Buys one-time rights.

Columns/Departments: Sentinel (brief articles on country topics, how-tos, current events and updates). Buys 5 mss/issue. Query with published clips and SASE. Length: 200-400 words. Pays approximately $75.

Poetry: Free verse, light verse, traditional. Buys 1 poem/issue. Pays $50/poem. Include SASE.

Tips: "Be as specific in your query as possible and explain why you are qualified to write the piece (especially for how-to's and controversial subjects). The writer has a better chance of breaking in at our publication with short articles."

‡THE COUNTRYMAN, United Newspapers, Sheep St., Burford, Oxon Ox184H UK. 900382258. Editor: Christopher Hall. 75% freelance written. Bimonthly magazine covering rural life and affairs. Estab. 1927. Circ. 60,000. Pays on publication. Publishes ms an average of 6-12 months after acceptance. Byline given. Buys first rights (photos and drawings) or all rights (mss). Editorial lead time 2 months. Submit seasonal material 6 months in advance. Reports in 1-2 weeks on queries.

Nonfiction: Historical/nostalgic, personal experience, photo feature, rural. Buys 60/70 mss/year. Send complete ms. Length: 1,800 words maximum. Pays £60.

Photos: Send photos with submission. Reviews ½ plate b&w. Negotiates payment individually. Captions required. Buys one-time rights.

Poetry: Free verse, traditional. Buys 50 poems/year. Submit maximum 3 poems. Length: 4-40 lines. Pays £5-25.

Fillerss: Anecdotes. Buys 40/year. Length: 100 words maximum. Pays £5.20.

Tips: "Reading the magazine is best."

‡ELECTRIC CONSUMER, Indiana Statewide Assn. of Rural Electric Cooperatives, Inc., P.O. Box 24517, Indianapolis IN 46224. (317)248-9453. Editor: Emily Born. Associate Editor: Richard G. Biever. Monthly tabloid covering rural electric cooperatives (relevant issues affecting members). News/feature format for electric cooperative members in Indiana. "Our readers are rural/suburban, generally conservative and have the common bond of electric cooperative membership." Estab. 1951. Circ. 271,477. Pays on publication. Byline given. Buys one-time rights. Submit seasonal material 3 months in advance. Accepts simultaneous and previously published submissions. Send photocopy of article (not necessary, but helpful) or typed ms with rights for sale noted and information about when and where the article previously appeared. Reports in 2 months. Free sample copy and writer's guidelines.

Nonfiction: General interest and humor. "We are looking for upbeat, concise articles that offer tips on ways to save energy, or simply general interest articles with 'news readers can use.' Sidebars with bulleted information a big plus, as is original artwork to accompany article." Buys 12 mss/year. Send complete ms. Considers lengths up to 1,200 words. Pays $25-150. Pays expenses of writers on assignment. Accepts previously published submissions. Send typed ms with rights for sale noted and information about when and where the article previously appeared.

Photos: State availability of photos with submission. Price commensurate to quality and use. Captions, model releases, identification of subjects required. Buys one-time rights.

Columns/Departments: Humor (personal experiences usually, always "clean" family-oriented), 750-1,000 words. Buys 8 mss/year. Send complete ms. Pays $45.

Poetry: Light verse and traditional. "We don't pay for poems we publish."

Tips: "We have redesigned, downsized our publication, but upgraded our paper stock to a white newsprint. Our 10 × 12¼ publication is now stitched and trimmed. We now, though, have less space for freelance articles. They need to be concise and *useful* for our readers, tips, how-to's, etc., preferred over humor. We no longer use *fiction*."

‡**FARM & RANCH LIVING**, Reiman Publications, 5400 S. 60th St., Greendale WI 53129. (414)423-0100. Compuserve 76150,162. Editor: Nick Pabst. 80% freelance written. Eager to work with new/unpublished writers. Bimonthly lifestyle magazine aimed at families that farm or ranch full time. "*F&RL* is *not* a 'how-to' magazine—it focuses on people rather than products and profits." Estab. 1968. Circ. 380,000. **Pays on acceptance.** Publishes ms an average of 6 months after acceptance. Byline given. Buys first serial rights and one-time rights. Submit seasonal material 6 months in advance. Accepts previously published submissions. Send tearsheet of article or typed ms with rights for sale noted. Reports in 6 weeks. Sample copy for $2. Writer's guidelines for #10 SASE.

Nonfiction: Interview/profile, photo feature, nostalgia, humor, inspirational, personal experience. No how-to articles or stories about "hobby farmers" (doctors or lawyers with weekend farms); no issue-oriented stories (pollution, animal rights, etc.). Buys 30 mss/year. Submit query or finished ms. Length: 600-1,200 words. Pays $150-300 for text-and-photos package.

Photos: Scenic. State availability of photos with query. Pays $75-200 for 35mm color slides. Buys one-time rights.

Fillers: Jokes, anecdotes, short humor with farm or ranch slant. Buys 50/year. Length: 50-150 words. Pays $20.

Tips: "Our readers enjoy stories and features that are upbeat and positive. A freelancer must see *F&RL* to fully appreciate how different it is from other farm publications—ordering a sample is strongly advised (not available on newsstands). Photo features (about interesting farm or ranch families) and personality profiles are most open to freelancers. We can make separate arrangements for photography if writer is unable to provide photos."

FARM FAMILY AMERICA, Fieldhagen Publishing, Inc., Suite 121, 190 Fifth St. E., St. Paul MN 55101. (612)292-1747. Editor: George Ashfield. 75% freelance written. Quarterly magazine published by American Cyanamid and written to the lifestyle, activities and travel interests of American farm families. Circ. 350,000. **Pays on acceptance.** Publishes ms an average of 2 months after acceptance. Byline given. Offers 25% kill fee. Buys first rights or second serial (reprint) rights. Submit seasonal material 6 months in advance. Simultaneous submissions OK. Reports in 6 weeks. Writer's guidelines for #10 SASE.

Nonfiction: General interest and travel. Buys 24 mss/year. Query with published clips. Length: 1,000-1,800 words. Pays $300-650.

Photos: State availability of photos with submission. Reviews 35mm transparencies and prints. Offers $160-700/photo. Model releases and identification of subjects required. Buys one-time rights.

FARM TIMES, 707 F St., Rupert ID 83350. (208)436-1111. Assistant Managing Editor: Robyn Maxfield. 50% freelance written. Monthly tabloid for agriculture-farming/ranching. "*Farm Times* is 'dedicated to rural living.' Stories related to farming and ranching in the states of Idaho, Nevada, Utah, Wyoming and Oregon are our mainstay, but farmers and ranchers do more than just work. General, or human interest articles that appeal to rural readers, are often used." Estab. 1987. Pays on publication. Byline given. Offers 100% kill fee "if submitted in acceptable form—writer's notes won't do it." Buys first rights. Editorial lead time 1 month. Submit seasonal material 3 months in advance. Accepts previously published submissions. Send photocoy of article and information about when and where the article previously appeared. Pays 100% of the amount paid for an original article. Reports in 1-2 months on queries. Sample copy and writer's guidelines free on request.

● No longer accepts anecdotes, facts or gags; now done inhouse.

Nonfiction: Exposé, general interest, historical/nostalgic, how-to, interview/profile, new product (few), opinion, late breaking ag news. No humor, inspirational, essay, first person, personal experience or book excerpts. Buys 200 mss/year. Query with published clips. Send complete ms. Length: 600-800 words. Pays $1.25/column inch.

Photos: Send photos with submission. Reviews contact sheets with negatives, 35mm or larger transparencies and 5 × 7 or larger prints. Offers $5/b&w inside, $50/color cover. Captions, model releases, identification of subjects required. Buys one-time rights.

Column/Departments: Hoof Beats (horse care [technical]), 500-600 words; B Section Cover (winter months—travel [anywhere]), 600-1,200 words; B Section Cover (summer months—photo/essay [interesting people/places]) 600-800 words; Rural Religion (interesting churches/missions/religious activities) 600-800 words. Buys 12 mss/year. Query. Send complete ms. Pays $1.25/column inch.

Tips: "Query with a well-thought out idea that will appeal to rural readers. Of special interest is how environmental issues will affect farmers/ranchers, endangered species act, EPA, etc. We are also interested in features on specialty farming—mint, seed crops, unusual breeds of animals. All of *Farm Times* is a good market for freelancers, but Rural Religion is the best place to get started. Write tightly. Be sure of facts and names."

HARROWSMITH COUNTRY LIFE, Ferry Road, Charlotte VT 05445. (802)425-3961. Fax: (802)425-3307. Editor: John Barstow. Contact: Lisa Rathke. Bimonthly magazine covering country living, gardening, shelter, food and environmental issues. "*Harrowsmith Country Life* readers are generally college educated country dwellers, looking for good information." Estab. 1986. Circ. 215,000. Pays 45 days after acceptance. Byline given. Offers 25% kill fee. Buys first North American serial rights. Reports in 2 months. Sample copy for $4. Writer's guidelines for #10 SASE.
  ● Ranked as one of the best markets for freelance writers in *Writer's Digest* magazine's annual "Top 100 Markets," January 1994.
Nonfiction: Book excerpts, essays, exposé (environmental issues), how-to (gardening/building), humor, interview/profile, opinion. Buys 36 mss/year. Query with published clips. Length: 500-5,000 words. Pays $500-1,500. Pays expenses of writers on assignment.
Photos: State availability of photos with submission. Reviews 35mm transparencies. Offers $100-325/photo. Model releases and identification of subjects required. Buys one-time rights.
Columns/Departments: Sourcebank (ideas, tips, tools, techniques relating to gardening, the environment, food, health), 50-400 words; Gazette (brief news items). Buys 30 mss/year. Query with published clips. Length: 40-400 words. Pays $25-150.
Tips: "While main feature stories are open to freelancers, a good way for us to get to know the writer is through our Screed (essays), Sourcebank (tips and ideas) and Gazette (brief news items) departments. Articles should contain examples, quotations and anecdotes. They should be detailed and factual. Please submit material to Lisa Rathke, assistant editor."

HARROWSMITH MAGAZINE, Camden House Publishing, Ltd., Camden East, Ontario K0K 1J0 Canada. (613)378-6661. Fax: (613)378-6123. Editor: Arline Stacey. 75% freelance written. Published 6 times/year "for those interested in country life, organic gardening, energy, self-sufficiency, and owner-builder architecture. Estab. 1976. Circ. 154,000. **Pays on acceptance.** Publishes ms an average of 4 months after acceptance. Byline given. Buys first North American serial rights. Submit seasonal material 6 months in advance. Reports in 6 weeks. Sample copy for $5. Free writer's guidelines.
  ● Ranked as one of the best markets for freelance writers in *Writer's Digest* magazine's annual "Top 100 Markets," January 1994.
Nonfiction: Exposé, how-to, general interest, environmental, profile. "We are always in need of quality gardening articles geared to northern conditions. No how-to articles written by people who are not totally familiar with their subject. We feel that in this field simple research does not compensate for lack of long-time personal experience." Buys 10 mss/issue. Query. Length: 500-4,000 words. Pays $150-2,500.
Photos: State availability of photos with query. Captions required. Buys one-time rights.
Tips: "We have standards of excellence as high as any publication in the country. We welcome and give thorough consideration to all freelance submissions. Our magazine is read by Canadians who live in rural areas or who hope to make the urban to rural transition. They want to know as much about the realities of country life as the dreams."

THE MOTHER EARTH NEWS, Dept. WM, 5th Floor, 24 E. 23rd St., New York NY 10010. (212)260-7210. Editor: Owen Lipstein. Managing Editor: Sunny Edmonds. Mostly freelance written. Bimonthly magazine emphasizing "country living and country skills, for both long-time and would-be ruralites." Circ. 350,000. **Pays on acceptance.** Byline given. Submit seasonal material 5 months in advance. No handwritten mss. Reports within 3 months. Publishes ms an average of 6 months after acceptance. Sample copy for $5. Writer's guidelines for #10 SASE with 2 first-class stamps.
Nonfiction: How-to, home business, alternative energy systems, home building, home retrofit and home maintenance, energy-efficient structures, seasonal cooking, gardening, crafts. Buys 100-150 mss/year. Query. "A short, to-the-point paragraph is often enough. If it's a subject we don't need at all, we can answer immediately. If it tickles our imagination, we'll ask to take a look at the whole piece. No phone queries, please." Length: 300-3,000 words.
Photos: Purchased with accompanying ms. Send prints or transparencies. Uses 8×10 b&w glossies or any size color transparencies. Include type of film, speed and lighting used. Total purchase price for ms includes payment for photos. Captions and credits required.
Tips: "Probably the best way to break in is to study our magazine, digest our writer's guidelines, and send us a concise article illustrated with color transparencies that we can't resist. When folks query and we give a go-ahead on speculation, we often offer some suggestions. Failure to follow those suggestions can lose the sale for the author. We want articles that tell what real people are doing to take charge of their own lives. Articles should be well-documented and tightly written treatments of topics we haven't already covered. The critical thing is length, and our payment is by space, not word count. *No phone queries.*"

RURAL HERITAGE, 281 Dean Ridge Lane, Gainesboro TN 38562-5039. (615)268-0655. Editor: Gail Damerow. Publisher: Allan Damerow. 98% freelance written. Willing to work with a small number of new/

unpublished writers. Bimonthly magazine devoted to the training and care of draft animals, and other traditional country skills. Estab. 1975. Circ. 3,000. Pays on publication. Publishes ms an average of 6 months after acceptance. Byline given. Buys first English language rights. Submit seasonal material 6 months in advance. Reports in 3 months. Sample copy for $6. Writer's guidelines #10 SASE.

Nonfiction: How-to (crafting and farming); interview/profile (especially people using draft animals); photo feature. No articles on *mechanized* farming. Buys 100 mss/year. Query or send complete ms. Length: 750-1,500 words. Pays 5¢/word.

Photos: Send photos with ms. Pays $10. Captions and identification of subjects required. Buys one-time rights. Six covers/year (b&w horizontal 5×7 or larger), animals in harness $25. Photo guidelines for #10 SASE.

Columns/Departments: Self-sufficiency (modern people preserving traditional American lifestyle), 750-1,500 words; Drafter's Features (draft animals used for farming, shows and pulls—their care), 750-1,500 words; Crafting (implement designs and patterns), 750-1,500 words; Country Kids (descriptions of rural youngsters who have done [or are doing] remarkable things), 750 words; Humor, 750-900 words. Pays 5¢/word.

Poetry: Traditional. Pays $5-25.

Tips: "Always welcome are: 1) Detailed descriptions and photos of horse-drawn implements 2) Prices and other details of draft animal auctions and sales."

RURALITE, P.O. Box 558, Forest Grove OR 97116-0558. (503)357-2105. Fax: (503)357-8615. Editor-in-Chief: Curtis Condon. Associate Editor: Walt Wentz. 80% freelance written. Works with new, unpublished writers "who have mastered the basics of good writing." Monthly magazine aimed at members of consumer-owned electric utilities throughout 9 western states, including Alaska. Publishes 52 regional editions. Estab. 1954. Circ. 265,000. Buys first rights, sometimes reprint rights. Send photocopy of article or typed ms with rights for sale noted and information about when and where the article previously appeared. For reprints, pays 50% of the amount paid for an original article. Rights may be reassigned. **Pays on acceptance.** Query first; unsolicited manuscripts submitted without request rarely read by editors. Reports in 1 month. Sample copy and writer's guidelines for 10×13 SAE with 4 first-class stamps.

Nonfiction: Looking for well-written nonfiction, (occasional fiction piece) dealing primarily with human interest topics. Must have strong Northwest perspective and be sensitive to Northwest issues and attitudes. Wide range of topics possible, from energy-related subjects to little-known travel destinations to unusual businesses located in areas served by consumer-owned electric utilities. "About half of our readers are rural and small town residents; others are urban and suburban. Topics with an obvious 'big-city' focus not accepted. Family-related issues, Northwest history (no encyclopedia rewrites), people and events, unusual tidbits that tell the Northwest experience are best chances for a sale. Nostalgic, dripping sentimental pieces rejected out of hand." Buys 30-50 mss/yr. Length 800-2,000 words. Pays $140-400, quality photos may increase upper pay limit for "polished stories with impact."

Photos: "Illustrated stories are the key to a sale. Stories without art rarely make it, with the exception of humor pieces. Black and white prints, color slides, all formats, accepted with 'razor-sharp' focus. Fuzzy, low-contrast photos may lose the sale."

Tips: We need solid writers and photographers who can relate to the Northwest attitude and convey that sensibility in their stories. Magazine is repositioning as regional four-color publication and will cover a wider range of topics. Look at a recent copy. We're looking for regular contributors to whom we can assign topics from our story list after they've proven their ability to deliver quality mss."

Science

These publications are published for laymen interested in technical and scientific developments and discoveries, applied science and technical or scientific hobbies. Publications of interest to the personal computer owner/user are listed in the Personal Computers section. Journals for scientists and engineers are listed in Trade in various sections.

ARCHAEOLOGY, Archaeological Institute of America, 135 William St., New York NY 10038. (212)732-5154. Fax: (212)732-5707. Editor-in-Chief: Peter A. Young. 5% freelance written. "We generally commission articles from professional archaeologists." Bimonthly magazine on archaeology. "The only magazine of its kind to bring worldwide archaeology to the attention of the general public." Estab. 1948. Circ. 160,000. Pays on publication. Byline given. Offers 25% kill fee. Buys first North American serial rights. Submit seasonal material 6 months in advance. Accepts simultaneous submissions. Query preferred. Free sample copy and writer's guidelines.

• Ranked as one of the best markets for freelance writers in *Writer's Digest* magazine's annual "Top 100 Markets," January 1994.

Nonfiction: Essays, general interest. Buys 6 mss/year. Length: 1,000-3,000 words. Pays $750 maximum. Sometimes pays expenses of writers on assignment.

Photos: Send photos with submission.

ASTRONOMY, Kalmbach Publishing, P.O. Box 1612, Waukesha WI 53187-1612. (414)796-1142. Fax: (414)796-0126. Editor: Robert Burnham. Managing Editor: Rhoda I. Sherwood. 75% freelance written. Monthly magazine covering astronomy—the science and hobby of. "Half of our magazine is for hobbyists (who may have little interest in the heavens in a scientific way); the other half is directed toward armchair astronomers who may be intrigued by the science." Estab. 1973. Circ. 70,000. **Pays on acceptance.** "We are governed by what is happening in the space program and the heavens. It can be up to a year before we publish a manuscript." Byline given. Buys first North American serial, one-time and all rights. Query for electronic submissions. Reports in 1 month on queries; 2 months on mss. Writer's guidelines for SASE.

Nonfiction: Book excerpts, space and astronomy, how-to for astro hobbyists, humor (in the viewpoints column and about astro), new product, photo feature, technical. Buys 100-200 mss/year. Query. Length: 500-4,500 words. Pays $50-500.

Photos: Send photos with submission. Reviews transparencies and prints. Pays $25/photo. Captions, model releases and identification of subjects required.

Tips: "Submitting to *Astronomy* could be tough. (Take a look at how technical astronomy is.) But if someone is a physics teacher (or math or astronomy), he or she might want to study the magazine for a year to see the sorts of subjects and approaches we use and then submit a proposal."

THE ELECTRON, CIE Publishing, 1776 E. 17th St., Cleveland OH 44114-3679. (216)781-9400. Fax: (216)781-0331. Managing Editor: Denise M. Zakrajsek. 80% freelance written. Bimonthly tabloid on electronics and high technology. Estab. 1934. Circ. 25,000. Pays on publication. Publishes ms an average of 2 months after acceptance. Byline given. Buys all rights. Accepts previously published submissions. Reports in 2-4 months. Free sample copy and writer's guidelines.

Nonfiction: Technical (tutorial and how-to), technology news and feature, photo feature and career/educational. All submissions must be electronics/technology-related. Query with letter/proposal and published clips. Pays $50-500.

Photos: State availability of photos. Reviews 8×10 and 5×7 b&w prints. Captions and identification of subjects required.

Tips: "We would like to receive educational electronics/technical articles. They must be written in a manner understandable to the beginning-intermediate electronics student. We are also seeking news/feature-type articles covering timely developments in high technology."

OMNI, Editorial Dept: Suite 205, 324 W. Wendover Ave., Greensboro NC 27408-8439. Editor: Keith Ferrell. 75% freelance written. Prefers to work with published/established writers. Monthly magazine of the future covering science fact, fiction and fantasy for readers of all ages, backgrounds and interests. Estab. 1978. Circ. 700,000. Average issue includes 2-3 nonfiction feature articles and 1-2 fiction articles; also numerous columns. **Pays on acceptance.** Publishes ms an average of 5 months after acceptance. Offers 25% kill fee. Buys exclusive worldwide and exclusive first English rights and rights for *Omni* anthologies. Submit seasonal material 4-6 months in advance. Reports in 4 months. Free writer's guidelines with #10 SASE (request fiction or nonfiction).

● Ranked as one of the best markets for freelance writers in *Writer's Digest* magazine's annual "Top 100 Markets," January 1994 and as one of the best markets for fiction writers in its biannual "Fiction 50," June 1994.

Nonfiction: "Feature articles for *Omni* cover all branches of science with an emphasis on the future: What will this discovery or technique mean to us next year, in five years, or even by the year 2025? People want to know and understand what scientists are doing and how scientific research is affecting their lives and their future. *Omni* publishes articles about science in language that people can understand. We seek very knowledgeable science writers who are ready to work with scientists and futurists to produce articles that can inform, interest and entertain our readers with the opportunity to participate in many ground breaking studies." Send query/proposal. Length: 1,500-3,000 words. Pays $2,500-3,500, plus reasonable expenses.

Photos: Frank DeVino, graphic director. State availability of photos. Reviews 35mm slides and 4×5 transparencies.

Columns/Departments: Explorations (unusual travel or locations on Earth); Mind (psychiatry and psychology, neurology, the brain); Earth (environment); Space (technology); Arts (theatre, music, film, technology); Interview (of prominent person); Continuum (newsbreaks); Antimatter and UFO Update (unusual newsbreaks, paranormal); Stars (astronomy); Artificial Intelligence (computers, etc.); The Body (medical); Digs (anthropology, archaeology, paleontology, etc.); Books (technology, profiles); Transportation (technology); First Word (editorial commissioned, no queries); Last Word (humor, submit ms, no queries). Query with clips of previously published work. Length: 750 words. Pays $750; $175 for Continuum and Antimatter items.

Fiction: Ellen Datlow. Fantasy and science fiction. Publishes novel excerpts. Buys 2 mss/issue. Send complete ms. Length: 10,000 words maximum. Pays $1,250-2,000.

Tips: "To get an idea of the kinds of fiction we publish, check recent back issues of the magazine."

POPULAR SCIENCE, 2 Park Ave., New York NY 10016. (212)779-5000. Fax: (212)779-5468. Editor-in-Chief: Fred Abatemarco. Executive Editor: Richard Stepler. 50% freelance written. Prefers to work with published/ established writers. Monthly magazine for the well-educated adult, interested in science, technology, new products. Estab. 1872. Circ. 1.8 million. **Pays on acceptance.** Publishes ms an average of 4 months after acceptance. Byline given. Buys first North American serial rights only. Pays negotiable kill fee. Any electronic submission OK. Reports in 4 weeks. Query. Writer's guidelines for #10 SASE.
  • Ranked as one of the best markets for freelance writers in *Writer's Digest* magazine's annual "Top 100 Markets," January 1994.
Nonfiction: *"Popular Science* is devoted to exploring (and explaining) to a nontechnical but knowledgeable readership the technical world around us. We cover all of the sciences, engineering and technology, and above all, products. We are largely a 'thing'-oriented publication: things that fly or travel down a turnpike, or go on or under the sea, or cut wood, or reproduce music, or build buildings, or make pictures. We are especially focused on the new, the ingenious and the useful. Contributors should be as alert to the possibility of selling us pictures and short features as they are to major articles. Freelancers should study the magazine to see what we want and avoid irrelevant submissions." Buys several hundred mss/year. Uses mostly color photos. Pays expenses of writers on assignment.
Tips: "Probably the easiest way to break in here is by covering a news story in science and technology that we haven't heard about yet. We need people to be acting as scouts for us out there and we are willing to give the most leeway on these performances. We are interested in good, sharply focused ideas in all areas we cover. We prefer a vivid, journalistic style of writing, with the writer taking the reader along with him, showing the reader what he saw, through words. Please query first."

SCIENTIFIC AMERICAN, 415 Madison Ave., New York NY 10017. Monthly publication covering developments and topics of interest in the world of science. This magazine did not respond to our request for information. Query before submitting.

‡TECHNOLOGY REVIEW, The Association of Alumni and Alumnae of the Massachusetts Institute of Technology, W59-200, Massachusetts Institute of Technology, Cambridge MA 02139. Contact: Editor. 30% freelance written. Emphasizes technology and its implications for scientists, engineers, managers and social scientists. Magazine published 8 times/year. Estab. 1890. Circ. 92,000. Pays on publication. Publishes ms an average of 3-6 months after acceptance. Buys first rights and some exclusive rights. Phone queries OK but *much* prefer written queries. Submit seasonal material 6 months in advance. Reports in 1 month. Sample copy for $3. Writer's guidelines for #10 SASE.
Nonfiction: General interest, interview, nonfiction book excerpts, photo feature, technical. Buys 5-10 mss/ year. Query. Length: 1,000-6,000 words. Pays $200-1,500. Sometimes pays the expenses of writers on assignment. "Please send SASE for return of manuscripts. Please double-space everything!"
Columns/Departments: Book Reviews; Trends; MIT Reporter (like Trends, but only reporting MIT info). Also special reports on other appropriate subjects. Query. Length: 750-4,000 words. Pays $50-1,500.

21ST CENTURY SCIENCE & TECHNOLOGY, 21st Century Science Associates, P.O. Box 16285, Washington DC 20041. (703)777-7473. Editor: Carol White. Managing Editor: Marjorie Mazel Hecht. 10-20% freelance written. Quarterly magazine that covers frontier science and technology and science history. "We are interested in material that deals with progress." Estab. 1988. Circ. 30,000. Pays on publication. Byline given. Buys one-time rights and makes work-for-hire assignments. Accepts simultaneous and previously published submissions. Send photocopy of article and information about when and where the article previously appeared. Query for electronic submissions. Reports in 6 weeks on queries. Sample copy for 9 × 12 SAE with 5 first-class stamps.
Nonfiction: Book excerpts, exposé (environmental hoaxes), historical, interview/profile, new product, technical (new scientific research, astronomy, cold fusion, fusion, space exploration, biophysics and advanced nuclear). Buys 5-6 mss/year. Query. Length: 500-6,000 words. Pays $100 minimum. We supply copies of issue in quantity.
Photos: State availability of photos with submission. Reviews contact sheets, transparencies and prints. Offers $25 minimum/photo. Captions, model releases and identification of subjects required. Buys one-time rights.

Science Fiction, Fantasy and Horror

These publications often publish experimental fiction and many are open to new writers. More information on these markets can be found in the Contests and Awards section under the Fiction heading.

ABERRATIONS, P.O. Box 460430, San Francisco CA 94146-0430. (415)824-3622. Editor: Richard Blair. Monthly magazine of ADULT horror, science fiction and dark fantasy. "We emphasize our openness to the strange and different by the fact that even our name is an aberration. This is an 'in and out' adult publication —

in your face and out on the edge." Estab. 1992. Circ. 1,500. Pays on publication. Publishes ms an average of 1 year after acceptance. Byline given. Buys first English language serial and one-time rights. Submit seasonal material 8 months in advance. Electronic submissions only after acceptance. Reports in 4 months. Sample copy for $5 postpaid. Writer's guidelines for #10 SASE.

• This magazine changed hands recently with some editorial changes resulting. They no longer accept poetry, have done away with the $7 maximum payment for fiction, and now buy first English language serial rights.

Nonfiction: Jon L. Herron. "Interviews" with deceased madmen. "Prefer humorous, but you must pay attention to detail. Know your facts." Buys 12 mss/year. Send complete ms. Length: 1-3,000 words. Book, video, movie reviews (H/SF/F). Buys 70 mss/year. Send complete ms. Length: 350 words. Pays to $5 plus 1 copy for assigned articles; copies for unsolicited articles. Send ms with rights for sale noted.

Photos: Send photos with submission. Reviews 3 × 5 b&w prints *only*. Pays for photos in copy *only*. Model releases and subject identification required. Buys one-time rights.

Fiction: Richard Blair. Adult horror, science fiction, dark fantasy, mystery (with H/SF/F). "No formula stories. All must have science-fiction, horror, dark fantasy slant. Explicit sex, gore, profanity must be germane to the story. No work based on creation of others. We print stories other magazines are afraid to print." Buys 150 mss/year. Send complete ms. Length 500-8,000 words. Pays to $7 plus copy or copy(ies) only and discount for additional copies.

Tips: "Tell the tales that pulsate in the darkest corners of your mind, even though you believe no one would print them. Show us your aberrations. Submit original ideas. No formula stories. We cater to unpublished and underpublished writers. Writers have their best chance with nonfiction."

ABORIGINAL SCIENCE FICTION, The 2nd Renaissance Foundation, P.O. Box 2449, Woburn MA 01888-0849. Editor: Charles C. Ryan. 99% freelance written. Quarterly science fiction magazine. "We publish short, lively and entertaining science fiction short stories and poems, accompanied by b&w illustrations." Estab. 1986. Circ. 12,000. Pays on publication. Publishes ms an average of 1 year after acceptance. Byline given. Buys first North American serial rights, non-exclusive options on other rights. Electronic submissions only after acceptance. Reports in 2-3 months. Sample copy for $4.95 and 9 × 12 SAE with 4 first-class stamps. Writer's guidelines for #10 SASE.

• Ranked as one of the best markets for fiction writers in *Writer's Digest* magazine's biannual "Fiction 50," June 1994.

Fiction: Science fiction of all types. "We do not use fantasy, horror, sword and sorcery or *Twilight Zone*-type stories." Buys 40-48 mss/year. Send complete ms. Length: 2,000-6,000 words. Pays $250. Send photocopy of short story. Publishes novel excerpts only if they can stand by themselves as a short story.

Poetry: Science and science fiction. Buys 8-12 poems/year.

Tips: "Read science fiction novels and all the science fiction magazines. Do not rely on science fiction movies or TV. We are open to new fiction writers who are making a sincere effort."

AMAZING STORIES, TSR, Inc., P.O. Box 111, Lake Geneva WI 53147-0111. (414)248-3625. Fax: (414)248-0389. Editor: Mr. Kim Mohan. 95% freelance written. Quarterly magazine of science fiction, fantasy and horror short stories. "We are looking for stories and articles that truly live up to the magazine's name—imaginative, trend-setting, thought-provoking pieces of work that will hold a reader's attention and live in his or her memory long after the reading experience is over." Accepts ms submissions from new/unpublished writers as well as those with professional credentials. Circ. 13,000. **Pays on acceptance.** Publishes ms an average of 6 months after acceptance. Byline given. Buys first worldwide serial rights in the English language only; nonexclusive re-use option (with additional pay). No simultaneous or previously published submissions. Reports in 3 months. Sample copy for $5. Writer's guidelines for #10 SASE.

• Ranked as one of the best markets for fiction writers in *Writer's Digest* magazine's biannual "Fiction 50," June 1994.

Nonfiction: Science-fact articles of interest to science fiction audience; essays and opinion pieces by authorities in some area of science or speculative fiction. No true-life experiences, no "soap box" pieces about invalidated theories. Buys 2-5 mss/year. Query first, with published clips if available. Length: 1,000-5,000 words. Pays 10-12¢/word.

Fiction: Science fiction, contemporary and ethnic fantasy, horror. "We want science fiction stories to dominate the magazine's content, but will not turn away any well-written piece of speculative fiction. Horror has the best chance of selling if it has a science-fictional or fantastic setting. Stay away from predictable plot lines and rehashes of old themes—show us *new* ideas." Buys 30-40 mss/year. Send complete ms. Length: 1,000-17,500 words. Pays 6-10¢/word, with shorter stories earning higher rates.

Tips: "Although a large portion of each magazine is devoted to stories from established writers, we are also committed to finding new talent and being a place where unpublished authors can get a start. Nevertheless, we are *very* discriminating about what we purchase. Do not expect to succeed with cliché ideas, stereotypical characters or obtuse 'literary' rambling. Hard science fiction is especially in demand, but any such story must be based on a *plausible* extrapolation from real science. Be familiar with the magazine, and have a copy of our guidelines in hand, before sending us something to review."

ANALOG SCIENCE FICTION & FACT, Dell Magazines Fiction Group, 1540 Broadway, New York NY 10036. Editor: Dr. Stanley Schmidt. 100% freelance written. Eager to work with new/unpublished writers. For general future-minded audience. Monthly. Estab. 1930. Buys first North American serial and nonexclusive foreign serial rights. **Pays on acceptance.** Publishes ms an average of 10 months after acceptance. Byline given. Reports in 1 month. Sample copy for $3 and 6×9 SASE with 5 first-class stamps. Writer's guidelines for #10 SASE.

   • Ranked as one of the best markets for fiction writers in *Writer's Digest* magazine's biannual "Fiction 50," June 1994.

Nonfiction: Illustrated technical articles dealing with subjects of not only current but future interest, i.e., topics at the present frontiers of research whose likely future developments have implications of wide interest. Buys about 13 mss/year. Query. Length: 5,000 words. Pays 6¢/word.

Fiction: "Basically, we publish science fiction stories. That is, stories in which some aspect of future science or technology is so integral to the plot that, if that aspect were removed, the story would collapse. The science can be physical, sociological or psychological. The technology can be anything from electronic engineering to biogenetic engineering. But the stories must be strong and realistic, with believable people doing believable things—no matter how fantastic the background might be." Buys 60-100 unsolicited mss/year. Send complete ms of short fiction; query about serials. Length: 2,000-80,000 words. Pays 4¢/word for novels; 5-6¢/word for novelettes; 6-8¢/word for shorts under 7,500 words; $450-600 for intermediate lengths.

Tips: "In query give clear indication of central ideas and themes and general nature of story line—and what is distinctive or unusual about it. We have no hard-and-fast editorial guidelines, because science fiction is such a broad field that I don't want to inhibit a new writer's thinking by imposing 'Thou Shalt Not's.' Besides, a really good story can make an editor swallow his preconceived taboos. I want the best work I can get, regardless of who wrote it—and I need new writers. So I work closely with new writers who show definite promise, but of course it's impossible to do this with *every* new writer. No occult or fantasy."

ASIMOV'S SCIENCE FICTION, Dell Magazines Fiction Group, 1540 Broadway, New York NY 10036. (212)856-6400. Editor-in-Chief: Gardner Dozois. Managing Editor: Sheila Williams. 98% freelance written. Works with a small number of new/unpublished writers each year. Published 13 times a year, including 2 double issues. Estab. 1977. Circ. 100,000. **Pays on acceptance.** Buys first North American serial and nonexclusive foreign serial rights; reprint rights occasionally. No simultaneous submissions. Reports in 2 months. Sample copy for $3 and 6½×9½ SAE. Writer's guidelines for #10 SASE.

   • Ranked as one of the best markets for fiction writers in *Writer's Digest* magazine's biannual "Fiction 50," June 1994.

Nonfiction: Science. Query first.

Fiction: Science fiction primarily. Some fantasy and poetry. "It's best to read a great deal of material in the genre to avoid the use of some *very* old ideas." Buys 10 mss/issue. Submit complete ms. Length: 100-20,000 words. Pays 5-8¢/word except for novel serializations at 4¢/word.

Tips: "Query letters not wanted, except for nonfiction."

MARION ZIMMER BRADLEY'S FANTASY MAGAZINE, P.O. Box 249, Berkeley CA 94701-0249. Editor: Mrs. Marion Z. Bradley. 100% freelance written. Quarterly magazine of fantasy fiction. Estab. 1988. **Pays on acceptance.** Publishes ms an average of 1 year after acceptance. Byline given. Buys first North American serial rights. Reports in 3 months. Sample copy for $4.

   • Ranked as one of the best markets for fiction writers in *Writer's Digest* magazine's biannual "Fiction 50," June 1994.

Fiction: Fantasy. No science fiction, very little horror. Buys 55-60 mss/year. Send complete ms. Length: 300-7,500 words. Pays 3-10¢/word.

Tips: "Do not submit without first reading guidelines."

DEAD OF NIGHT MAGAZINE, Dead of Night Publications, Suite 228, 916 Shaker Rd., Longmeadow MA 01106-2416. Editor: Lin Stein. 90% freelance written. Semiannual April/October magazine. "Our readers enjoy horror, mystery, fantasy and sci-fi, and they also don't mind an 'old-fashioned' vampire or ghost story on occasion. Because of the genre mix in our magazine, we appeal to a wide readership." Estab. 1989. Circ. 1,000. Pays on publication. Publishes ms an average of 6-12 months after acceptance. Byline given. Offers 10% kill fee. Buys 1st North American serial rights or one-time rights. Editorial lead time 3 months. Submit seasonal material 6 months in advance. Reports in 3 weeks on queries; 1-2 months on mss. Sample copy for $5 (current issue); $2.50 (back issue subject to availability). Writer's guidelines for #10 SASE.

Nonfiction: Book excerpts, interview/profile, book/film reviews. Buys 8-10 mss/year. Send complete ms. Length: 350-1,800 words. Pays 2¢/word minimum.

Fiction: Fantasy, horror, mystery, novel excerpts, science fiction. Nothing non-genre. Buys 7-15 mss/year. Send complete ms. Length: 500-2,500 words. Pays 2-3¢/word. Publishes novel excerpts.

Tips: "We are most open to fiction. (Most of our reviews are written by our contributing editors—on a regular basis, but freelancers may query.) For tips or hints, the best, of course, is to read the magazine! The second best is to at least read our guidelines, and the last tip is to try to present us with a horror/mystery/fantasy or science fiction story that is fresh, original, and entertaining. If the story entertains the editors

here, we'll buy it so our *readers* can enjoy it and be entertained by it as well."
- Now also publishes a semiannual newsletter which uses short shorts (to 1,000 words) and poetry, reviews, etc.

‡**FURY MAGAZINE**, #740, 15445 Ventura Blvd., Sherman Oaks, CA 91403. Editor: Alex Duffy. 95% freelance written. Bimonthly magazine covering science fiction, fantasy and horror stories. "*Fury Magazine* is aimed at educated adults who enjoy stimulating literature: science fiction, fantasy, horror, literary eroticism, romance, avant-garde, etc., but who lack the time to delve into larger works. All genres are accepted." Estab. 1993. Circ. 300. Pays on acceptance. Publishes ms an average of 6-12 months after acceptance. Byline given. Buys first rights. Editorial lead time 4 months. Submit seasonal material 6 months in advance. Accepts simultaneous and previously published material. Reports in 2 months on queries; 4 months on mss. Sample copy for $3. Writer's guidelines for #10 SASE.
Fiction: Adventure, confession, erotica, ethnic, experimental, fantasy, historical, horror, humorous, mainstream, mystery, religious, romance, science fiction, slice-of-life vignettes, suspense, western. Buys 100 mss/year. Send complete ms. Length: 100-2,000 words. Pays ½-2¢/word.
Poetry: Avant-garde, free verse, haiku, light verse, traditional. Buys 35 poems/year. Submit maximum 4 poems. Length: 1-50 lines. Pays ½-2¢/word.
Fillers: Gags to be illustrated by cartoonist, short humor. Buys 2-20/year. Length: 10-200 words. Pays ½-2¢/word.
Tips: "*Fury* is a 'short short' story magazine, thus anything over 2,000 words gets sent back unread. New and established writers are encouraged to submit. Please put your word count on your manuscript. No vampire or werewolf stories. Create your own monster. Mary Shelley did. No Lovecraft pastiche. No 'I Remember Grandpa' or 'How I Hacked Grandpa to Bits' stories. We publish a varied selection of each genre per issue."

‡**HARSH MISTRESS, Science Fiction Adventures**, O.N.A. Publications, Inc., P.O. Box 13, Greenfield MA 01302. Editor: Warren Lapine. 95% freelance written. Quarterly science fiction magazine covering science fiction short stories. "We specialize in action/adventure science fiction with an emphasis on hard science. Interested in tightly-plotted, character-driven stories." Estab. 1993. Circ. 6,000. Pays on publication. Publishes ms an average of 6 months after acceptance. Byline given. Offers 25% kill fee. Buys first North American serial rights, first rights and second serial (reprint) rights. Editorial lead time 1 month. Submit seasonal material 6 months in advance. Accepts simultaneous and previously published submissions. Reports in 2 weeks on queries; 1 month on mss. Sample copy for $4. Writer's guidelines for #10 SASE.
Fiction: Science fiction. Buys 30 mss/year. Send complete ms. Length: 1,000-25,000 words. Pays 3¢/word.
Poetry: Narrative verse. Buys 2 poems/year. Submit maximum 3 poems. 1,000-25,000 words. Pays 1.5¢/word.
Tips: "We are not interested in 'drawer-cleaning' exercises. There is no point in sending less than your best effort if you are interested in a career in writing. Stories between 10,000 and 18,000 words have the best chance of selling to us as we don't buy that many short manuscripts."

HOBSON'S CHOICE, The Starwind Press, P.O. Box 98, Ripley OH 45167-0098. (513)392-4549. Editors: David F. Powell and Susannah C. West. Contact: Susannah C. West. 75% freelance written. Eager to work with new/unpublished writers. Monthly magazine "for older teenagers and adults who have an interest in science and technology, and who also enjoy reading well-crafted science fiction and fantasy." Estab. 1974. Circ. 2,500. Pays on publication. Publishes ms an average of 1 year after acceptance. Byline given. Rights vary with author and material; negotiated with author. Usually first serial rights and second serial reprint rights (nonfiction). Query for electronic submissions. "We encourage disposable submissions; easier for us and easier for the author. Just enclose SASE for our response." Accepts previously published submissions. Send photocopy of article or short story and information about when and where material previously appeared. Pays 30% of amount paid for an original article." We prefer non-simultaneous submissions." Reports in 3 months. Sample copy $2.25 for 9×12 SAE. Writer's guidelines for #10 SASE. "Tipsheet package for $1.25; contains all guidelines, tipsheets on science fiction writing, nonfiction science writing and submission etiquette."
Nonfiction: How-to (technological interest, e.g., how to build a robot eye, building your own radio receiver, etc.), interview/profile (of leaders in science and technology fields), technical ("did you know" articles dealing with development of current technology). "No speculative articles, dealing with topics such as the Abominable Snowman, Bermuda Triangle, etc. Query. Length: 1,000-7,000 words. Pays 1-4¢/word.
Photos: Send photos with accompanying query or ms. Reviews b&w contact sheets and prints. Model releases and identification of subjects required. "If photos are available, we prefer to purchase them as part of the written piece." Buys negotiable rights.
Fiction: Fantasy, science fiction. "No stories whose characters were created by others (e.g. Lovecraft, *Star Trek*, *Star Wars* characters, etc.)." Buys 15-20 mss/year. Send complete ms. Length: 2,000-10,000 words. Pays 1-4¢/word. "We prefer previously unpublished fiction. No query necessary. We don't publish horror, poetry, novel excerpts or serialized novels."
Tips: "Our need for nonfiction is greater than for fiction at present. Almost all our fiction and nonfiction is unsolicited. We rarely ask for rewrites, because we've found that rewrites are often disappointing; although the writer may have rewritten it to fix problems, he/she frequently changes parts we liked, too."

PANDORA, 2063 Belford, Holly MI 48442. Editors: Meg MacDonald, Polly Vedder (art). 99% freelance written. Works with a number of new/unpublished writers each year. Semiannual anthology covering science fiction, fantasy fiction and poetry. Estab. 1978. Circ. 500. Pays on publication. Publishes ms an average of 12-18 months after acceptance. Buys first North American serial and second serial (reprint) rights; one-time rights on some poems. Reports in 3 months. Sample copy for $6, ($10 overseas). Writer's guidelines for #10 SASE. "International contributors, please use enough IRCs to cover return of manuscript or letter."
Fiction: "Query first! We may still be overstocked with fiction. *Unsolicited mss will be returned.*" Fantasy, science fiction. "No pun stories. No Lucifer or deals with the devil stories. Nothing X-rated (no vulgar language, gratuitous violence, sex, racisim, etc.). No inaccurate science and no horror of the chainsaw variety. Scary stories, ghost stories OK. No occult material, however." Average length: under 6,000 words. Longer work must be exceptional. Pays 1-2¢/word.
Poetry: Payment starts at $5. No romance, occult or horror. "Query first."
Tips: "*Pandora* will be closed to unsolicited submissions until further notice. Please query before sending anything. The best way to get to know the editor's tastes and preferences is to READ our anthologies."

THE SCREAM FACTORY, The Magazine of Horrors, Past, Present, and Future, Deadline Press, P.O. Box 2808, Apache Junction AZ 85220. Editors: Peter Enfantino, Bob Morrish and John Scoleri. Contact: Peter Enfantino. 75% freelance written. Quarterly literary magazine about horror in films and literature. Estab. 1988. Circ. 2,500. **Pays on acceptance.** Publishes ms an average of 6 months after acceptance. Buys first North American serial rights. Submit seasonal material 6 months in advance. No simultaneous submissions or reprints. Reports in 2 weeks on queries, 1 month on ms. Sample copy for $7 (please make checks payable to *The Scream Factory*). Writer's guidelines for #10 SASE.
Nonfiction: Essays, historical/nostalgic, interview/profile, new product, personal experience. Buys 35-50 mss/year. Query or send complete ms. Pays ½¢/word.
Photos: Send photos with submission. Reviews prints. Offers no additional payment for photos accepted with ms. Captions required. Buys one-time rights.
Columns/Departments: Book reviews of horror novels/collections; Writer's Writing (what horror authors are currently working on).
Fillers: Facts, newsbreaks. Pays ½¢/word. Also small reviews (150-200 words). "Please query on these."
Tips: "Looking for reviews of horror fiction, especially the lesser known authors. News on the horror genre, interviews with horror authors and strong opinion pieces. No unsolicited fiction accepted."
● Does *not* accept fiction.

THE SILVER WEB, A Magazine of the Surreal, Buzzcity Press, P.O. Box 38190, Tallahassee FL 32315. (904)385-8948. Publisher/Editor: Ann Kennedy. 100% freelance written. Semiannual literary magazine that features science fiction, dark fantasy and horror. Estab. 1988. Circ. 1,000. **Pays on acceptance.** Byline given. Buys first North American serial, or one-time or second serial (reprint) rights. Accepts simultaneous and previously published submissions. Send information about when and where material previously appeared. Pays 100% of the amount paid for an original article or short story. Reports in 2 months. Query for electronic submissions. Sample copy for $5.75. Writer's guidelines for #10 SASE.
● Ranked as one of the best markets for fiction writers in *Writer's Digest* magazine's biannual "Fiction 50," June 1994.
Nonfiction: Essays, interview/profile, opinion. Buys 4-8 mss/year. Query. Length: 500-8,000 words. Pays 1-3¢/word.
Photos: State availability of photos with submission. Reviews prints. Offers no additional payment for photos accepted with ms. Identification of subjects required. Buys one-time rights.
Fiction: Experimental, horror, science fiction. "We do not want to see typical storylines, endings or predictable revenge stories." Buys 20-25 mss/year. Send complete ms. Length: 500-8,000 words. Pays 1-3¢/word.
Poetry: Avant-garde, free verse, haiku. Buys 10-15/year. Submit maximum 5 poems. Pays $5-15.
Fillers: Art fillers. Buys 10/year. Pays $2-5.
Tips: "Give us an unusual unpredictable story with strong, believable characters that we can care about. Surprise us with something unique. We do look for interviews with people in the field (writers, artists, filmmakers)."

STAR*LINE, Newsletter of the Science Fiction Poetry Association, 1412 NE 35th St., Ocala FL 34479. Editor: Margaret B. Simon. 95% freelance written. Eager to work with new/unpublished writers. Bimonthly newsletter covering science fiction, fantasy and horror poetry for association members. Estab. 1978. Circ. 200. Pays on publication. Byline given. Buys one-time rights. Submit seasonal material 3 months in advance. Reports in 2 months. Sample copy for $2 and 6×9 SAE with 2 first-class stamps. Writer's guidelines for #10 SASE.
Nonfiction: Articles must display familiarity with the genre. How to (write a poem), interview/profile (of science fiction, fantasy and horror poets), opinion (science fiction and poetics), essays. Buys 4-6 mss/year. Send complete ms. Length: 500-2,000 words. Pays $1-5 plus complimentary copy.

Columns/Department: Reviews: 100-500 words, ¼¢/word. Articles: 500-2,500 words, ¼¢/word. One copy to all contributors. Pays on publication for first North American serial rights with reversion of subsidiary rights on publication.

Poetry: Avant-garde, free verse, haiku, light verse, traditional. "Poetry must be related to speculative fiction subjects." Buys 60-80 poems/year. Submit maximum 3 poems. Length: 1-100 lines. Pays 5¢/line plus 2¢/word.

STARLOG MAGAZINE, The Science Fiction Universe, Starlog Group, 8th Floor, 475 Park Ave. S., New York NY 10016-1689. (212)689-2830. Editor: David McDonnell. 85% freelance written. Eager to work with new/unpublished writers. Monthly magazine covering "the science fiction-fantasy genre: its films, TV, books, art and personalities." Estab. 1976. "We concentrate on interviews with actors, directors, screenwriters, producers, special effects technicians and others. Be aware that 'sci-fi' and 'Trekkie' are seen as derogatory terms by our readers and by us." Pays on publication. Publishes ms an average of 4 months after acceptance. Byline given. Offers kill fee "only to manuscripts *written* or interviews *done.*" Buys all rights and occasionally, second serial (reprint) rights to other material. Submit seasonal material 6 months in advance. No simultaneous submissions. Reports in 6 weeks. "We provide an assignment sheet and contract to *all* writers with deadline and other info, authorizing a queried piece." Sample copy for $5. Writer's guidelines for #10 SASE.

Nonfiction: Interview/profile (actors, directors, screenwriters who've made science fiction films and science fiction novelists); photo features; retrospectives of famous SF films and TV series; coverage of science fiction fandom, etc. "We also sometimes cover SF/fantasy animation and comics." No personal opinion think pieces/essays. *No* first person. Avoids articles on horror films/creators. "We prefer article format as opposed to Q&A interviews." Buys 150 mss/year. Query first with published clips. "We prefer queries by mail. No phone calls. Ever!" Length: 500-3,000 words. Pays $35 (500-word pieces); $50-75 (sidebars); $125-250 (1,000-word plus pieces).

Photos: State availability of photos. Pays $10-25 for slide transparencies and 8 × 10 b&w prints depending on quality. "No separate payment for photos provided by film studios." Captions, model releases, identification of subjects and credit line on photos required. Photo credit given. Buys all rights.

Columns/Departments: Fan Network (articles on fandom and its aspects—mostly staff-written); Booklog (book reviews, $15 each, by assignment only); Medialog (news of upcoming science fiction films and TV projects); Videolog (videocassette and disk releases of genre interest, staff-written); Gamelog (video, computer, role-playing games). Buys 80-100 reviews/year. Query with published clips. Length: 300-500 words. No kill fee.

Tips: "Absolutely *no fiction.* We do *not* publish it. We reject *ALL* fiction. And we throw away the fiction manuscripts from writers who also *can't* be bothered to include SASES. Please do *NOT* send fiction! Nonfiction only please! A writer can best break in to *Starlog* by getting an unusual interview or by *out-thinking* us and coming up with something *new* on a current film or book. We are always looking for *new* angles on *Star Trek: The Next Generation, Deep Space Nine, Star Wars,* the original *Star Trek, Doctor Who* and seeking features on such series as *Starman, Beauty & the Beast, Lost in Space, Space 1999, Battlestar Galactica, The Twilight Zone, The Outer Limits.* Know your subject before you try us. Most full-length major assignments go to freelancers with whom we're already dealing. But if we like your clips and ideas, we'll be happy to give *you* a chance."

A THEATER OF BLOOD, Pyx Press, P.O. Box 620, Orem, UT 84059-0620. Editor: C. Darren Butler. Associate Editor: Lisa S. Laurencot. 50% freelance written. Annual serial anthology of dark fantasy and literary horror. "We try to publish intelligent horror." Estab. 1990. Circ. 500. Pays on publication. Publishes ms an average of 12 months after acceptance. Byline given. Buys first rights. Editorial lead time 6 months. Accepts simultaneous submissions. Reports in 1 month on queries; 2-6 months on mss (occasionally larger). Sample copy for $6. Writer's guidelines available for #10 SASE.

Fiction: Horror, dark fantasy. Buys 10-15 mss/year. Send complete ms. Length: 2,500-20,000 words (query for works over 8,000 words). Pays $2-30.

Tips: "*A Theater of Blood* has been published for several years as a little magazine of horrific short-short fiction and poetry. Beginning in 1996 it will be published as a serial book anthology of fiction. All types of literary horror and dark fantasy are needed, including cosmic, supernatural and quiet horror. All stories should contain a fantasy element. We no longer consider poetry."

2 AM MAGAZINE, P.O. Box 6754, Rockford IL 61125-1754. Editor: Gretta M. Anderson. 95% freelance written. Quarterly magazine of fiction, poetry, articles and art for readers of fantasy, horror and science fiction. Estab. 1986. Circ. 2,000. **Pays on acceptance.** Publishes an average of 9 months after acceptance. Byline given. Buys first North American serial rights. Submit seasonal material 1 year in advance. Reports in 1 month on queries; 3 months on mss. Sample copy for $5.95. Writer's guidelines for #10 SASE.

• Ranked as one of the best markets for fiction writers in *Writer's Digest* magazine's biannual "Fiction 50," June 1994.

Nonfiction: How-to, interview/profile, opinion, also book reviews of horror, fantasy or SF recent releases. "No essays originally written for high school or college courses." Buys 5 mss/year. Query with or without published clips or send complete ms. Length: 500-2,000 words. Pay ½-1¢/word.

Photos: State availability of photos with submission. Offers no additional payment for photos accepted with ms. Identification of subjects required. Buys one-time rights.

Fiction: Fantasy, horror, mystery, science fiction, suspense. Buys 50 mss/year. Send complete ms. Length: 500-5,000 words. Pays ½-1¢/word.

Poetry: Free verse, traditional. "No haiku/zen or short poems without imagery." Buys 20 poems/year. Submit up to 5 poems at one time. Length: 5-100 lines. Pays $1-5.

Tips: "We are looking for taut, imaginative fiction. We need more reviews of horror novels. Please use proper manuscript format; all manuscripts must include a SASE to be considered. We suggest to Canadian and foreign writers that they send disposable manuscripts with one IRC and #10 SAE for response, if US postage stamps are unavailable to them."

Sports

A variety of sports magazines, from general interest to sports medicine, are covered in this section. For the convenience of writers who specialize in one or two areas of sport and outdoor writing, the publications are subcategorized by the sport or subject matter they emphasize. Publications in related categories (for example, Hunting and Fishing; Archery and Bowhunting) often buy similar material. Writers should read through this entire section to become familiar with the subcategories. Publications on horse breeding and hunting dogs are classified in the Animal section, while horse racing is listed here. Publications dealing with automobile or motorcycle racing can be found in the Automotive and Motorcycle category. Markets interested in articles on exercise and fitness are listed in the Health and Fitness section. Outdoor publications that promote the preservation of nature, placing only secondary emphasis on nature as a setting for sport, are in the Nature, Conservation and Ecology category. Regional magazines are frequently interested in sports material with a local angle. Camping publications are classified in the Travel, Camping and Trailer category.

Archery and Bowhunting

BOW AND ARROW HUNTING, Box 2429, 34249 Camino Capistrano, Capistrano Beach CA 92624. Editorial Director: Roger Combs. 80% freelance written. Bimonthly magazine for bowhunters. **Pays on acceptance.** Publishes ms an average of 6 months after acceptance. Buys first serial rights. Byline given. Reports in 2 months. Query for electronic submissions—preferred. Author must have some knowledge of archery terms.
Nonfiction: Articles: bowhunting, techniques used by champs, how to make your own tackle and off-trail hunting tales. Likes a touch of humor in articles. "No dead animals or 'my first hunt.'" Also uses one technical and how-to article per issue. Submit complete ms. Length: 1,500-2,500 words. Pays $150-300.
Photos: Purchased as package with ms; 5×7 minimum. Pays $100 for cover chromes, 35mm or larger.
Tips: "Subject matter is more important than style—that's why we have editors and copy pencils. Good b&w photos are of primary importance. We staff-write our shorter pieces."

BOWHUNTER, The Number One Bowhunting Magazine, Cowles Magazines, 6405 Flank Dr., Harrisburg PA 17112-8200. (717)657-9555. Fax: (717)657-9552. Editor/Publisher: M.R. James. Editorial Director: Dave Canfield. Contact: Richard Cochran, Managing Editor. 85% freelance written. Bimonthly magazine (with two special issues) on hunting big and small game with bow and arrow. "We are a special interest publication, produced by bowhunters for bowhunters, covering all aspects of the sport. Material included in each issue is designed to entertain and inform readers, making them better bowhunters." Estab. 1971. Circ. 180,000. **Pays on acceptance.** Publishes ms an average of 10-12 months after acceptance. Byline given. Kill fee varies. Buys first North American serial and one-time rights. Submit seasonal material 8 months in advance. Reports in 1 month on queries; 5 weeks on mss. *Writer's Market* recommends allowing 2 months for reply. Sample copy for $2. Free writer's guidelines.
Nonfiction: General interest, how-to, interview/profile, opinion, personal experience, photo feature. "We publish a special 'Big Game' issue each Fall (September) but need all material by mid-March. Our other annual publication, *Whitetail Bowhunter*, is staff written or by assignment only. We don't want articles that graphically deal with an animal's death. And, please, no articles written from the animal's viewpoint." Buys 100 plus mss/year. Query. Length: 250-2,000 words. Pays $500 maximum for assigned articles; $75-500 for unsolicited articles. Sometimes pays expenses of writers on assignment.
Photos: Send photos with submission. Reviews 35mm and 2¼×2¼ transparencies and 5×7 and 8×10 prints. Offers $50-250/photo. Captions required. Buys one-time rights.

Columns/Departments: Would You Believe (unusual or offbeat hunting experiences), 250-1,000 words. Buys 6-8 mss/year. Send complete ms. Pays $100-200.

Tips: "A writer must know bowhunting and be willing to share that knowledge. Writers should anticipate *all* questions a reader might ask, then answer them in the article itself or in an appropriate sidebar. Articles should be written with the reader foremost in mind; we won't be impressed by writers seeking to prove how good they are—either as writers or bowhunters. We care about the reader and don't need writers with 'I' trouble. Features are a good bet because most of our material comes from freelancers. The best advice is: Be yourself. Tell your story the same as if sharing the experience around a campfire. Don't try to write like you think a writer writes."

BOWHUNTING WORLD, Ehlert Publishing Group, Suite 600, 601 Lakeshort Parkway, Minnetonka MN 55305-5215. (612)476-2200. Fax: (612)476-8065. Editor: Mike Stroudlaud. Managing Editor: Tom Kacheroski. 70% freelance written. Monthly magazine for bowhunting and archery enthusiasts who participate in the sport year-round. Estab. 1951. Circ. 130,000. **Pays on acceptance.** Publishes mss an average of 5 months after acceptance. Byline given. Buys first rights. Reports in 3 weeks on queries, 6 weeks on mss. Sample copy for $3 and 9×12 SAE with 10 first-class stamps. Free writer's and photographers guidelines.

Nonfiction: Hunting adventure, scouting and hunting how-to features (primarily from a first-person point of view), interview/profile pieces, historical articles, humor, do-it-yourself pieces. Buys 60 mss/year. Query or send complete ms. Length: 1,500-3,000 words. Pays from under $200 to over $500.

Photos: Send photos with submission. Reviews 35mm transparencies and b&w or color prints. Captions required. Buys one-time rights as part of package with ms. Send for separate photo guidelines. "We will also accept proof sheets and negs, returning any photos we do print and use to the author."

Tips: "We look for a combination of good writing and good information. Although we've expanded our focus in recent years to include all North American big and small game typically hunted with bow and arrow, nearly half the articles we buy are about bowhunting for deer. Many freelancers are submitting slides only because that allows magazines to reproduce photos in either b&w or color. Our experience shows that detail is lost converting the slides and that we typically buy additional freelance color to support the article. For that reason, we now encourage authors with access to high quality, b&w print developing services to send b&w illustrations with their packages."

‡PETERSEN'S BOWHUNTING, Petersen Publishing Company, 6420 Wilshire Blvd., Los Angeles CA 90048-5515. Editor: Greg Tinsley. 70% freelance written. Magazine published 8 times/year covering bowhunting. "Very equipment oriented. Our readers are "superenthusiasts," therefore our writers must have an advanced knowledge of hunting archery." Circ. 115,000. **Pays on acceptance.** Byline given. Buys all rights. Editorial lead time 6 months. Submit seasonal material 6 months in advance. Query for electronic submissions. Reports in 1 month. Sample copy for #10 SASE. Writer's guidelines free on request.

Nonfiction: How-to, humor, interview/profile, new product, opinion, personal experience, photo feature. Buys 40 mss/year. Send complete ms. Length: 2,000-2,500 words. Pays $300. Sometimes pays expenses of writers on assignment.

Photos: Send photos with submission. Reviews contact sheets, 35mm transparencies, 5×7 prings. Offers. $35-250/photo. Captions and model releases required. Buys one-time rights.

Columns/Departments: Query. Pays $200-300.

Fillers: Facts, newsbreaks. Buys 12/year. Length: 150-400 words. Pays $25-75.

Tips: Feature articles must be supplied to *Petersen's Bowhunting* in either 5.25 IBM (or compatible) or 3.5 MacIntosh floppy disks.

Baseball and Softball

BALLS AND STRIKES, Amateur Softball Association, 2801 NE 50th St., Oklahoma City OK 73111. (405)424-5266. Fax: (405)424-3855. 20% freelance written. Works with a small number of new/unpublished writers each year. "Only national monthly magazine covering amateur softball." Circ. 300,000. Pays on publication. Publishes mss an average of 2 months after acceptance. Buys first rights. Byline given. Reports in 3 weeks. Sample copy for SASE.

Nonfiction: General interest, historical/nostalgic, interview/profile, technical. Query. Length: 2-3 pages. Pays $50-75.

Tips: "We generally like shorter features because we try to get as many different features as possible in each issue."

Market conditions are constantly changing! If this is 1996 or later, buy the newest edition of Writer's Market *at your favorite bookstore or order directly from* Writer's Digest Books.

‡THE DIAMOND, The Official Chronicle of Major League Baseball, Fans, Inc., 6991 E. Camelback Rd., Scottsdale AZ 85251. (602)949-0100. Editor: Bill Gilbert. Contact: Douglas McDaniel, managing editor. 80% freelance written. Monthly magazine. "*The Diamond* is the official history magazine for major league baseball, specializing in nostalgia, memorabilia and major league alumni." Estab. 1993. Circ. 300,000. Pays on publication. Offers 25% kill fee. Buys first North American serial rights. Editorial lead time 4 months. Submit seasonal material 6 months in advance. Query for electronic submissions. Reports in 3 weeks on queries. Sample copy for $3.75 and SASE with 5 first-class stamps. Writer's guidelines for 8½ × 11 SASE with 2 first class stamps.

Nonfiction: Book excerpts, essays, historical/nostalgic, humor, inspirational. "Nothing on current players or current season." Buys 60 mss/year. Query with published clips. Length: 500-3,000 words. Pays $500. Sometimes pays expenses of writers on assignment.

Photos: State availability of photos with submission. Reviews transparencies and prints. Negotiates payment individually. Captions and identification of subjects required. Buys one-time rights.

Columns/Departments: On the Fly (quirky shorts, humor on baseball), 50-200 words; The Moment (short description of great moment in baseball history, accompanied by photo/art). Buys 30 mss/year. Query with published clips or send complete ms. Pays $50-100.

Fiction: Ron Bianchi, editorial director. Historical, humorous. Query. Length: 1,000-6,000 words.

Poetry: No limitations. Buys 3 poems/year. Submit maximum 3 poems. Length: 10-50 lines. Pays $50-150.

Tips: "New writers can break in writing shorts for On the Fly. We prefer writers with baseball writing experience, or, at least, a penchant for writing about the game in a literary way. Unpublished writers are rare."

SLO-PITCH NEWS, Varsity Publications, Inc., Suite 3, 13540 Lake City Way NE, Seattle WA 98125-3665. (206)367-2420. Fax: (206)367-2636. Editor: Dick Stephens. 10-25% freelance written. Monthly tabloid newspaper for slo-pitch softball. *Slo-Pitch News* focuses on slo-pitch softball tournaments, teams, players and products/services for a national and western audience. Estab. 1985. Circ. 25,000. Pays on publication. Byline given. Buys first North American serial and second serial (reprint) rights. Editorial lead time 3 months. Submit seasonal material 2 months in advance. Accepts simultaneous and previously published submissions. Query for electronic submissions. Reports in 2 months on queries. Sample copy and writer's guidelines for #10 SASE.

Nonfiction: Book excerpts, essays, exposé, general interest, historical/nostalgic, how-to, humor, inspirational, interview/profile, new product, opinion, personal experience, photo feature, travel, how-to (softball instructional). Special issues: Buyer's Guide (December); All-Star Edition (January). Buys 10 mss/year. Send complete ms. Length: 400-700 words. Pays $20 minimum. Pays contributor's copies "if piece is small enough, where payment wasn't expected."

Photos: Send photos with submission. Reviews 4×6 or 3×5 or larger prints. Offers $5-20/photo. Negotiates payment individually. Model releases and identification of subjects required. "depends on subject and focus."

Columns/Departments: Power Hitting (instructional softball), 500-600 words; numerous others on tournament coverage and administrative news. Buys 30 mss/year. Query with published clips. Send complete ms. Pays $10-30.

Fiction: "We don't solicit fiction often. No fluffy articles on sports." Buys 10 mss/year. Send complete ms. Length: 300-1,000 words. Pays $15-30.

Fillers: Anecdotes, facts, gags to be illustrated by cartoonist, newsbreaks and short humor. Buys 30/year. Length: 100-200 words. Pay negotiable.

Tips: "Send résumé with clips and refs. Contact editor for further info. Background experience in softball is appreciated. We are most open to tournament/team profiles and reports. Stay within AP style and write to an adult softball audience."

Bicycling

ADVENTURE CYCLIST, (formerly *Bikereport*), Adventure Cycling Assn., Box 8308, Missoula MT 59807. (406)721-1776. Fax: (406)721-8754. Editor: Daniel D'Ambrosio. 75% freelance written. Works with a small number of new/unpublished writers each year. Bicycle touring magazine for Adventure Cycling members published 9 times yearly. Circ. 30,000. Pays on publication. Publishes ms an average of 8 months after acceptance. Byline given. Include short bio with manuscript. Buys first serial rights. Submit seasonal/holiday material 3 months in advance. Simultaneous queries OK. Query for electronic submissions. Reports in 3 weeks on queries; 6 weeks on mss. Sample copy and guidelines for 9 × 12 SAE with 4 first-class stamps.

Nonfiction: Historical/nostalgic (interesting spots along bike trails); how-to (bicycle); humor (touring); interview/profile (bicycle industry people); personal experience ("my favorite tour"); photo feature (bicycle); technical (bicycle); and travel ("my favorite tour"). Buys 20-25 mss/year. Query with published clips or send complete ms. Length: 800-2,500 words. Pay negotiable.

Photos: Bicycle, scenery and portraits. State availability of photos. Model releases and identification of subjects required.

Fiction: Adventure, experimental, historical and humorous. Not interested in anything that doesn't involve bicycles. Query with published clips or send complete ms. Length: 800-2,500 words. Pay negotiable.

BICYCLING, Rodale Press, Inc., 33 E. Minor St., Emmaus PA 18098. (610)967-5171. Fax: (610)967-8960. Editor and Publisher: James C. McCullagh. Contact: Bill Strickland, managing editor. 20-25% freelance written. Prefers to work with published/established writers. Publishes 11 issues/year (10 monthly, 1 bi-monthly); 96-188 pages. Estab. 1961. Circ. 360,000. **Pays on acceptance**. Byline given. Buys all rights. Submit seasonal/holiday material 6 months in advance. Query for electronic submissions. Reports in 2 months. Sample copy for $2.50. Writer's guidelines for #10 SASE.

Nonfiction: How-to (on all phases of bicycle touring, repair, maintenance, commuting, new products, clothing, riding technique, nutrition for cyclists, conditioning); fitness is more important than ever; also travel (bicycling must be central here); photo feature (on cycling events of national significance); and technical (component review – query). "We are strictly a bicycling magazine. We seek readable, clear, well-informed pieces. We rarely run articles that are pure humor or inspiration but a little of either might flavor even our most technical pieces. No poetry or fiction." Buys 1-2 unsolicited mss/issue. Send complete ms. Length: 1,500 words average. Pays $25-1,200. Sometimes pays expenses of writers on assignment.

Photos: State availability of photos with query letter or send photo material with ms. Pays $15-50 for b&w prints and $35-250 for transparencies. Captions preferred; model release required.

Fillers: Anecdotes and news items for Paceline section.

Tips: "We're alway seeking interesting accounts of cycling as a lifestyle."

‡CALIFORNIA BICYCLIST, (2 editions: Northern California; Southern California), Yellow Jersey Group, Suite 304, 490 Second St., San Francisco CA 94107. E-mail: hkingman@well.sf.ca.usa. Editor: Henry Kingman. 30% freelance written. "Monthly tabloid covering bicycling, both road and mountain. We are a literate, sophisticated bike magazine with a sense of humor. We strive to entertain while educating readers about riding and bicycle care." Estab. 1983. Circ. 60,000 North/70,000 South. Pays on publication. Publishes ms an average of 1 month after acceptance. Byline given. Offers 50% kill fee. Buys first North American serial rights. Editorial lead time 1-2 months. Submit seasonal material 1-2 months in advance. Accepts simultaneous and previously published submissions. Query for electronic submissions. Sample copy for 6×9 SAE with 98¢ postage. Writer's guidelines free on request.

Nonfiction: Historical/nostalgic, humor, interview/profile, personal experience, technical, travel. "Nothing about helmets or political meetings." Buys 30 mss/year. Send complete ms. Length: 200-1,500 words. Pays $20.

Photos: State availability of photos or send photos with submission. Reviews transparencies and prints. Offers $10-50/photo. Buys one-time rights.

Columns/Departments: Guest editorials, 500 words; Pacelines (news, events, people, etc.), 200-400 words. Buys 80 mss/year. Send complete ms. Pays $20-100.

Fiction: Adventure, historical, humorous, novel excerpts. Buys 1 ms/year. Send complete ms. Length: 500-2,000 words. Pays $50-200.

Poetry: Avant-garde, free verse, haiku, light verse, traditional. Buys 50 poems/year. Submit maximum 54 poems. Length: 1-923 lines. Pays $20-200.

Fillers: Anecdotes, facts, gags to be illustrated by cartoonist, newsbreaks, short humor.

Tips: "We like weird, funny, offbeat, yet informative, witty and original cyclojournalism. Different angles on the same old bike magazine articles and most of all humor. Pacelines is most open to freelancers. We always need writers in our regions to cover local happenings and write guest editorials."

CRANKMAIL, Cycling in Northern Ohio, P.O. Box 110236, Cleveland OH 44111-0236. Editor: James Guilford. Magazine published 10 times/year covering bicycling in all aspects. "Our publication serves the interests of bicycle enthusiasts . . . established, accomplished adult cyclists. These individuals are interested in reading about the sport of cycling, bicycles as transportation, ecological tie-ins, sports nutrition, the history and future of bicycles and bicycling." Estab. 1977. Circ. 1,000. Pays on publication. Byline given. Publication not copyrighted. Buys one-time or second serial (reprint) rights. Editorial lead time 1 month. Submit seasonal material 3 months in advance. Accepts previously published submissions. Sample copy for $1. Writer's guidelines for #10 SASE.

Nonfiction: Essays, historical/nostalgic, how-to, humor, interview/profile, new product, personal experience, technical. "No articles encouraging folks to start or get involved in bicycling – our readers are already cyclists." Send complete ms. "Don't query." Length: 2,500 words maximum. Pays $10 minimum for unsolicited articles.

Fillers: Cartoons. Pays $5-10.

Tips: "Know what you're talking about. Our readers are intelligent, mostly established *adult* cyclists who subscribe to national bicycling publications."

CYCLING USA, The Official Publication of the U.S. Cycling Federation, One Olympic Plaza, Colorado Springs CO 80909. (719)578-4581. Fax: (719)578-4596. Editor: Steve Penny. Media and public relations assistant: Jason Anderson. 50% freelance written. Monthly magazine covering reportage and commentary on American bicycle racing, personalities and sports physiology, for USCF licensed cyclists. Circ. 32,000. Pays on publication. Publishes ms an average of 2 months after acceptance. Byline given. Accepts simultaneous queries and previously published submissions. Reports in 2 weeks. Sample copy for 10 × 12 SAE with 2 first-class stamps.

Nonfiction: How-to (train, prepare for a bike race), interview/profile, opinion, personal experience, photo feature, technical and race commentary on major cycling events. No comparative product evaluations. Buys 15 mss/year. Query with published clips. Length: 500-800 words. Pays 13¢/word.

Photos: State availability of photos. Pays $10-25 for 5 × 7 b&w prints; $100 for transparencies used as cover. Captions required. Buys one-time rights.

Tips: "A background in bicycle racing is important because the sport is somewhat insular, technical and complex. Most major articles are generated inhouse. Race reports are most open to freelancers. Be concise, informative and anecdotal. The most frequent mistake made by writers in completing an article for us is that it is too lengthy; our format is more compatible with shorter (500-800-word) articles than longer features."

DIRT RAG, A.K.A. Productions, 5732 3rd St., Verona PA 15147-2446. (412)795-7495. Fax: (412)795-7439. Publisher: Maurice Tierney. Contact: Elaine Tierney, editor. 75% freelance written. Mountain biking magazine published 7 times/year. "Dirt Rag's style is much looser, fun and down to earth than mainstream (glossy) magazines on the same subject. We appeal to hard-core (serious) mountain bikers, and these people make our finest contributions. Avant-garde, humorous, off-beat, alternative." Estab. 1989. Circ. 15,000. Pays on publication. Byline given. No kill fee. Buys one-time rights. Accepts simultaneous and previously published submissions. Send typed ms with rights for sale noted and information about when and where the material previously appeared. Pays 75% of the amount paid for original material. Reports in 3 months. Query for electronic submissions. Sample copy for 5 first-class stamps. Writer's guidelines for SASE.

Nonfiction: Book excerpts, essays, exposé, general interest, historical/nostalgic, how-to (bike maintenance, bike technique), humor, interview/profile, new product, opinion, personal experience, photo feature, technical, travel (places to ride). Anything with mountain biking. Buys 24 mss/year. Query. Pays $25-100. Sometimes pays expenses of writers on assignment.

Photos: Send art or photos with or without submission. Reviews contact sheets and/or prints. Offers additional payment for photos accepted with ms. $125 for color cover. $20 inside (b&w preferred, color OK). Captions preferred. Buys one-time rights. Always looking for good photography and art regardless of subject.

Columns/Departments: Place to Ride (must have map!), 500-2,000 words; Trialsin (coverage of the sport), 50-500 words; and Race Reports (coverage of race events), 50-250 words. Buys 14 mss/year. Query. Pays $10-50.

Fiction: Adventure, fantasy, historical, humorous, mainstream, slice-of-life vignettes. Buys 1-5 mss/year. Query. Pays $25-50. Publishes novel excerpts.

Poetry: Avant-garde, free verse, light verse, traditional. Pays $10-25.

Fillers: Anecdotes, facts, gags, newsbreaks, short humor. Buys 20/year. Pays $0-50.

‡TEXAS BICYCLIST, Yellow Jersey Group, Suite 304, 490 Selona St., San Francisco CA 94107. E-mail: hkingman@well.sf.ca.usa. Editor: Henry Kingman. 30% freelance written. Monthly tabloid covering bicycling—both road and mountain. "We are a literate, sophisticated bike magazine with a sense of humor. We strive to entertain while educating readers about riding and bicycle care." Estab. 1983. Circ. 40,000. Pays on publication. Byline given. Offers 50% kill fee. Buys first North American serial rights. Editorial lead time 1-2 months. Submit seasonal material 1-2 months in advance. Accepts simultaneous and previously published submissions. Query for electronic submissions. Sample copy for 6 × 9 SAE with 98¢ postage. Writer's guidelines free on request.

Nonfiction: Historical/nostalgic, humor, interview/profile, personal experience, technical and travel. "Nothing about helmets or political meetings." Buys 30 mss/year. Send complete ms. Length: 200-1,500 words. Pays $20 minimum.

Photos: State availability of photos or send photos with submission. Reviews transparencies. Offers $10-50/photo. Buys one-time rights.

Columns/Departments: Guest Editorials, 500 words; Pacelines(news, events, people), 200-400 words. Buys 40 mss/year. Send complete ms. Pays $20-100.

Fiction: Adventure, historical, humorous and novel excerpts. Buys 1 ms/year. Send complete ms. Length: 500-2,000 words. Pays $50-200.

Poetry: Avant-garde, free verse, haiku, light verse, traditional. Buys 50 poems/year. Submit maximum 54 poems. Length: 1-923 lines. Pays $20-200.

Tips: "We like weird, funny, offbeat, yet informative, witty and original cyclojournalism. Different angles on the same old bike magazine articles and most of all humor. Pacelines is most open to freelancers. We always need writers in our regions to cover local happenings: and write guest editorials."

VELONEWS, The Journal of Competitive Cycling, 1830 55th St., Boulder CO 80301-2700. (303)440-0601. Fax: (303)444-6788. Managing Editor: Tim Johnson. 60% freelance written. Monthly tabloid September-February, biweekly March-August covering bicycle racing. Estab. 1972. Circ. 48,000. Pays on publication. Publishes ms an average of 1 month after acceptance. Byline given. Buys one-time rights. Accepts simultaneous queries and submissions. Electronic submissions OK; call first. Reports in 3 weeks. Sample copy for 9 × 12 SAE with 7 first-class stamps.

Nonfiction: In addition to race coverage, opportunities for freelancers include reviews (book and videos) and health-and-fitness departments. Buys 100 mss/year. Query. Length: 300-1,200 words. Pays 10¢/word minimum.

Photos: State availability of photos. Pays $16.50-50 for b&w prints. Pays $150 for color used on cover. Captions and identification of subjects required. Buys one-time rights.

Boating

BOAT PENNSYLVANIA, Pennsylvania Fish and Boat Commission, P.O. Box 67000, Harrisburg PA 17106-7000. (717)657-4518. Editor: Art Michaels. 80% freelance written. Quarterly magazine covering motorboating, sailing, canoeing, water skiing, kayaking and rafting in Pennsylvania. Prefers to work with published/established contributors, but works with a few unpublished writers and photographers every year. Pays 2 months after acceptance. Publishes ms an average of 8 months after acceptance. Byline given. Buys variable rights. Submit seasonal/holiday material 8 months in advance. Prefers electronic or diskette submission. Reports in 2 weeks on queries; 2 months on mss. Sample copy for 9×12 SAE with 4 first-class stamps. Writer's guidelines for #10 SASE.

Nonfiction: How-to, technical, historical/nostalgic, all related to water sports in Pennsylvania. No saltwater fishing material. Buys 40 mss/year. Query. Length: 300-3,000 words. Pays $25-300.

Photos: Send photos with submission. Also reviews photos separately. Rights purchased and rates vary. Reviews 35mm and larger color transparencies and 8×10 b&w prints. Captions, model releases, identification of subjects required.

CANOE MAGAZINE, Canoe Associates, P.O. Box 3146, Kirkland WA 98083. (206)827-6363. Fax: (206)827-1893. Managing Editor: Nancy Harrison. Editor: Dennis Stuhaug. 80-90% freelance written. Bimonthly magazine on canoeing, whitewater kayaking and sea kayaking. Estab. 1972. Circ. 60,000. Pays on publication. Publishes ms an average of 9-12 months after acceptance. Byline given. Buys right to reprint in annuals; author retains copyright. Submit seasonal/holiday material 4 months in advance. Accepts previously published submissions. Send tearsheet or photocopy of article and information about where and when it previously appeared. Pays same for reprints as originals. Query for electronic submissions. Reports in 1 month. Sample copy and writer's guidelines for 9×12 SASE with 5 first-class stamps.

Nonfiction: Essays, general interest, historical/nostalgic, how-to, humor, interview/profile, new product, opinion, personal experience, photo feature, technical, travel. Plans a special entry-level guide to canoeing and kayaking. No "trip diaries." Buys 60 mss/year. Query with or without published clips or send complete ms. Length: 500-2,200 words. Pays $5/column inch. Pays the expenses of writers on assignment.

Photos: State availability of or send photos with submission. "Good photos help sell a story." Reviews contact sheets, negatives, transparencies and prints. "Some activities we cover are canoeing, kayaking, canoe fishing, camping, canoe sailing or poling, backpacking (when compatible with the main activity) and occasionally inflatable boats. We are not interested in groups of people in rafts, photos showing disregard for the environment, gasoline-powered, multi-horsepower engines unless appropriate to the discussion, or unskilled persons taking extraordinary risks." Offers $50-150/photo. Model releases and identification of subjects occasionally required. Buys one-time rights.

Columns/Departments: Continuum (essay); Counter Currents (environmental) both 1,500 words; Put-In (short interesting articles); Short Strokes (destinations), 1,000-1,500 words. Buys 60 mss/year. Pays $5/column inch.

Fiction: Uses very little fiction.

Fillers: Anecdotes, facts, newsbreaks. Buys 20/year. Length: 500-1,000 words. Pays $5/column inch.

Tips: "Start with Put-In articles (short featurettes) of approximately 500 words, book reviews, or short, unique equipment reviews. Or give us the best, most exciting article we've ever seen—with great photos. Short Strokes is also a good entry forum focusing on short trips on good waterways accessible to lots of people. Focusing more on technique and how-to articles."

‡CRUISING WORLD, Cruising World Publications, Inc., Box 3400, Newport RI 02840-0992. (401)847-1588. Editor: Bernadette Bernon. 70% freelance written. Monthly magazine for all those who cruise under sail. Circ. 146,000. **Pays on acceptance.** Publishes ms an average of 8 months after acceptance. Offers variable kill fee, $50-150. Buys first North American periodical rights or first world periodical rights. Reports in about 2 months. Query for electronic submissions. Free writer's guidelines.

Nonfiction: Book excerpts, how-to, humor, inspirational, opinion, personal experience. "We are interested in seeing informative articles on the technical and enjoyable aspects of cruising under sail, especially seamanship, navigation and how-to." Buys 135-140 unsolicited mss/year. Submit complete ms. Length: 500-3,500 words. Pays $150-800.

Photos: 35mm slides purchased with accompanying ms. Captions and identification of subjects required. Buys one-time rights.

Columns/Departments: People & Food (recipes for preparation aboard sailboats); Shoreline (sailing news, vignettes); Workbench (projects for upgrading your boat). Send complete ms. Length: 150-500 words. Pays $25-150.

Tips: "Cruising stories should be first-person narratives. In general, authors must be sailors who read the magazine. Color slides always improve a ms's chances of acceptance. Technical articles should be well-illustrated."

CURRENTS, Voice of the National Organization for River Sports, 212 W. Cheyenne Mountain Blvd., Colorado Springs CO 80906. (719)579-8759. Fax: (719)576-6238. Editor: Greg Moore. 25% freelance written. Quarterly magazine covering whitewater river running (kayaking, rafting, river canoeing). Estab. 1979. Circ. 5,000. Pays on publication. Publishes ms an average of 6 months after acceptance. Byline given. Offers 25% kill fee. Buys first North American serial, first and one-time rights. Submit seasonal/holiday material 2 months in advance. Accepts simultaneous and previously published submissions. "Please let us know if this is a simultaneous submission or if the article has been previously published." Reports in 2 weeks on queries; 1 month on mss. *Writer's Market* recommends allowing 2 months for reply. Sample copy for $1 and 9×12 SAE with 3 first-class stamps. Writer's guidelines for #10 SASE.
Nonfiction: How-to (run rivers and fix equipment), in-depth reporting on river conservation and access issues and problems, humor (related to rivers), interview/profile (any interesting river runner), opinion, personal experience, technical, travel (rivers in other countries). "We tell river runners about river conservation, river access, river equipment, how to do it, when, where, etc." No trip accounts without originality; no stories about "my first river trip." Buys 20 mss/year. Query with or without clips of published work. Length: 500-2,500 words. Pays $35-150.
Photos: State availability of photos. Pays $35-50. Reviews b&w or color prints or slides; b&w preferred. Captions and identification of subjects (if racing) required. Buys one-time rights. Captions must include names of the river and rapid.
Columns/Departments: Book and film reviews (river-related). Buys 5 mss/year. Query with or without clips of published work or send complete ms. Length: 100-500 words. Pays $25.
Fiction: Adventure (river). Buys 2 mss/year. Query. Length: 1,000-2,500 words. Pays $35-75. "Must be well-written, on well-known river and beyond the realm of possibility."
Fillers: Clippings, jokes, gags, anecdotes, short humor, newsbreaks. Buys 5/year. Length: 25-100 words. Pays $5-10.
Tips: "We need more material on river news—proposed dams, wild and scenic river studies, accidents, etc. If you can provide brief (300-500 words) on these subjects, you will have a good chance of being published. Material must be on whitewater rivers. Go to a famous river and investigate it; find out something we don't know—especially about rivers that are *not* in Colorado or adjacent states—we already know about the ones near us."

HEARTLAND BOATING, Inland Publications, Inc., P.O. Box 1067, Martin TN 38237-1067. (901)587-6791. Fax: (901)586-6893. Editor: Molly Lightfoot Blom. Estab. 1988. 50% freelance written. Bimonthly magazine on boating "devoted to both power and sail boating enthusiasts throughout middle America; houseboats are included. The focus is on the freshwater inland rivers and lakes of the Heartland; primarily the Tennessee, Cumberland, Ohio and Mississippi rivers and the Tennessee-Tombigbee Waterway. No Great Lakes or salt water material wil be considered unless it applies to our area." Estab. 1988. Circ. 14,000. Pays on publication. Publishes ms an average of 3 months after acceptance. Byline given. Buys first North American serial and sometimes second serial (reprint) rights. Submit seasonal/holiday material 6 months in advance. Accepts simultaneous and previously published submissions. Send tearsheet or photocopy of article and information about where and when it previously appeared. Pays 50% of the amount paid for an original article. Query for electronic submissions. Reports in 3-4 months. Sample copy for $5. Free writer's guidelines.
Nonfiction: General interest, historical/nostalgic, how-to, humor, interview/profile, new product, personal experience, photo feature, technical, travel. Buys 20-40 mss/year. Prefers queries to unsolicited mss with or without published clips. Length: 800-2,000 words. Negotiates payment.
Photos: Send photos with query. Reviews contact sheets, transparencies. Buys one-time rights.
Columns/Departments: Buys 50 mss/year. Query. Negotiates payment.

‡**HOT BOAT,** LFP Publishing, Suite 300, 9171 Wilshire Blvd., Beverly Hills CA 90210. (213)858-7155. Fax: (213)274-7985. Editor: Kevin Spaise. 50% freelance written. A monthly magazine on performance boating (16-35 feet), water skiing and water sports in general. "We're looking for concise, technically oriented 'how-to' articles on performance modifications; personality features on interesting boating-oriented personalities, and occasional event coverage." Circ. 90,000. Pays 1 month after acceptance. Publishes ms an average of 2 months after acceptance. Byline given. Offers 40% kill fee. Buys all rights; also reprint rights occasionally. Submit seasonal/holiday material 3 months in advance. Reports in 3 weeks on queries; 1 month on mss. Sample copy for $3 and 9×12 SAE with $1.35 postage.
Nonfiction: How-to (increase horsepower, perform simple boat related maintenance), humor, interview/profile (racers and manufacturers), new product, personal experience, photo feature, technical. "Absolutely no sailing—we deal strictly in powerboating." Buys 30 mss/year. Query with published clips. Length: 500-2,000 words. Pays $75-450. Sometimes pays expenses of writers on assignment.
Photos: Send photos with submission. Reviews transparencies. Captions, model releases, identification of subjects required. Buys all rights.

Tips: "We're always open to new writers. If you query with published clips and we like your writing, we can keep you on file even if we reject the particular query. It may be more important to simply establish contact. Once we work together there will be much more work to follow."

JET SPORTS, The Official Publication of the International Jet Sports Boating Association, Pfanner Communications, Inc., Suite E, 1371 E. Warner Ave., Tustin CA 92680. (714)259-8240. Fax: (714)259-1502. Editor: Elyse M. Barrett. Estab. 1981. 25% freelance written. Monthly magazine for "members of IJSBA, new buyers of Kawasaki personal watercraft, selected newsstands nationwide and watercraft dealers. Slant is toward *active* sports enthusiasts, racing, performance-enhancement, adventure, home mechanic subjects." Circ. 42,000. Pays on publication. Publishes ms an average of 3 months after acceptance. Byline given. Offers 50% kill fee for assigned material *only*.. Buys first North American serial or one-time rights. Submit seasonal material 4 months in advance. Accepts previously published submissions. Send tearsheet of article or typed ms with rights for sale noted and information about when and where the article previously appeared. For reprints, pays 50% of the amount paid for an original article. Query for electronic submissions. Reports in 6 weeks. Sample copy for 9×12 SAE with 7 first-class stamps. Writer's guidelines for #10 SASE.
Nonfiction: Interview/profile, personal experience, photo feature, technical, travel. Special issues: Holiday Buyers' Guide, expanded new product section (winter); Catalog special (advertorial) and World Finals report (spring). Buys 12 mss/year. Query with or without published clips or send complete ms. Length: 100-2,000 words. Pays $25-500. Sometimes pays expenses of writers on assignment.
Photos: Send photos with submission. Reviews contact sheets, 35mm transparencies and 5×7 prints. Offers $10-250/photo. Identification of subjects required. Buys one-time rights.
Columns/Departments: Starting Line (industry/business briefs, racer info); Legislative Lookout (state-by-state analysis of laws affecting personal watercraft); Club Scene (news of club activities nationwide); Regional Racing (race announcements and results). Buys 40 mss/year. Send complete ms. Length: 50-150 words. Pays $25-100.
Fillers: Anecdotes, facts. Buys 3/year. Length: 150-500 words. Pays $15-55.
Tips: "Be a skilled personal watercraft rider, understand the industry, which is much like the motocross/motorcycle world, and query first! Write simply—some slang and jargon is OK. Departments most open to freelancers: Starting Line (inside scoop, latest rumors, good photos, hero/helper stories); Club Scene (timely notice of coming events or activities; detailed follow-ups); Legislative Lookout (local and state-wide happenings (closures of waterways to PWCs, laws proposed, actions by individuals and clubs to affect new regulations)."

LAKELAND BOATING, The magazine for Great Lakes boaters, O'Meara-Brown Publications, Suite 1220, 1560 Sherman Ave., Evanston IL 60201-4802. (708)869-5400. Fax: (708)869-5989. Editor: John Wooldridge. 50% freelance written. Monthly magazine covering Great Lakes boating. Estab. 1945. Circ. 60,000. Pays on publication. Byline given. Buys first North American serial rights. Query for electronic submissions. Reports in 4 months. Sample copy for $5.50 and 9×12 SAE with 6 first-class stamps. Writer's guidelines for #10 SASE.
Nonfiction: Book excerpts, historical/nostalgic, how-to, interview/profile, personal experience, photo feature, technical, travel. No inspirational, religious, expose or poetry. Must relate to boating in Great Lakes. Buys 20-30 mss/year. Query. Length: 800-3,500 words. Pays $100-600 for assigned articles.
Photos: State availability of photos. Reviews transparencies; prefers 35mm. Captions required. Buys one-time rights.
Columns/Departments: Bosun's Locker (technical or how-to pieces on boating), 100-1,000 words. Buys 40 mss/year. Query. Pays $30-100.

‡**MOTOR BOATING & SAILING**, 250 W. 55th St., New York NY 10019. (212)649-4099. Fax: (212)489-9258. Editor and Publisher: Peter A. Janssen. Monthly magazine covering powerboats and sailboats for people who own their own boats and are active in a yachting lifestyle. Estab. 1907. Circ. 135,056. **Pays on acceptance.** Byline given. Buys one-time rights. Reports in 2 months.
Nonfiction: General interest (navigation, adventure, cruising), how-to (maintenance). Buys 5-6 mss/issue. Average issue includes 8-10 feature articles. Query. Length: 2,000 words.
Photos: Reviews 5×7 b&w glossy prints and 35mm or larger color transparencies. Offers no additional payment for photos accepted with ms. Captions and model releases required.

‡**NOR'WESTING**, Nor'westing Publications, Inc., 6044 Seaview Ave. NW, Seattle WA 98107. (206)783-8939. Managing Editor: Gloria Kruzner. 95% freelance written. Monthly magazine covering Pacific Northwest boating, cruising destinations. "We want to pack our pages with cruising articles, special Northwest destinations, local boating personalities. How to get to a destination, what's there when you arrive, etc." Estab. 1964. Circ. 18,500. Pays approximately 2 months after publication. Publishes ms an average of 2 months after acceptance. Byline given. Buys first North American serial rights and makes work-for-hire assignments. Editorial lead time 3 months. Submit seasonal material 3 months in advance. Accepts simultaneous submissions (Please note where else it's being submitted). Reports in 2 months. Sample copy and writer's guidelines for #10 SASE.

Nonfiction: How-to (boat outfitting, electronics, fish, galley), interview/profile (boat personalities), new product, personal experience (cruising), photo feature, technical, travel (local destinations). Special issues: Boat shows (Seattle) (January); Spring outfitting (March/April); Cruising destinations (June/August); Rough water boating (November/December). Buys 35-40 mss/year. Send complete ms. Length: 900-2,000 words. Pays $100-150. Sometimes pays expenses of writers on assignment.

Photos: Send photos with submission. Reviews transparencies, 3×5 prints. Negotiates payment individually. Identification of subjects required. Normally buys one-time rights.

Columns/Departments: Trailerboating (small craft boating—tech/destination), 900; Galley Ideas (cooking afloat—recipes/ideas), 900; Hardwired (Boating Electronics), 1,000; Cruising Fisherman (Fishing tips, destinations), 1,000. Buys 36-40 mss/year. Query with published clips. Pays $50-100.

Fillers: Anecdotes, gags to be illustrated by cartoonist. Buys 5-10/year. Length: 100-500 words. Pays $25-75.

Tips: "Include specific information on destination—how many moorage buoys, cost for showers, best time to visit. Any hazards to watch for while approaching? Why bother going if excitement for area/boating doesn't shine through in piece?"

OFFSHORE, Boating Magazine of the Northeast, Offshore Publications, Inc., 220-9 Reservoir St., Needham MA 02194. (617)449-6204. Editor: Herbert Gliick. Estab. 1976. 90% freelance written. Eager to work with new/unpublished writers. Monthly magazine covering boating and the coast from Maine to New Jersey. Circ. 35,000. **Pays on acceptance.** Publishes ms an average of 2 months after acceptance. Byline given. Offers negotiable kill fee. Buys first North American serial rights. Submit seasonal/holiday material 3 months in advance. Accepts simultaneous and previously published submissions. Send tearsheet of article or short story and information about when and where the article previously appeared. Pays $100 for reprints. Query for electronic submissions. Reports in 2 weeks. *Writer's Market* recommends allowing 2 months for reply. Sample copy for 10×13 SAE with 6 first-class stamps. Writer's guidelines for #10 SASE.

Nonfiction: Articles on boats, boating, New York, New Jersey and New England coastal places and people. Coastal history of NJ, NY, CT, RI, MA, NH and ME. Thumbnail and/or outline of topic will elicit immediate response. Buys 90 mss/year. Query with writing sample or send complete ms. Length: 1,000-3,000 words. Pays 15¢/word and up.

Fiction: Boat related fiction.

Photos: Reviews 35mm slides only. For covers, pays $200 and up. Identification of subjects required. Buys one-time rights.

Tips: "Demonstrate familiarity with boats or region and ability to recognize subjects of interest to regional boat owners. Those subjects need not be boats. *Offshore* is serious but does not take itself as seriously as most national boating magazines. The most frequent mistake made by writers in completing an article for us is failing to build on a theme (what is the point of the story?)."

POWER BOATING CANADA, Unit 306, 2585 Skymark Ave., Mississauga, Ontario L4W 4L5 Canada. (416)624-8218. Fax: (905)624-6764. Editor: Pam Cottrell. 40% freelance written. Bimonthly magazine covering power boating. Estab. 1984. Circ. 50,000. Pays on publication. Publishes ms an average of 3 months after acceptance. Byline given. Not copyrighted. Buys first North American serial rights in English and French or second serial (reprint) rights. Accepts simultaneous and previously published submissions. Query for electronic submissions.

Nonfiction: "Any articles related to the sport of power boating, especially boat tests." Travel (boating destinations). No personal anecdotes. Buys 20 mss/year. Query. Length: 1,000-2,500 words. Pays $150-300.

Photos: State availability of photos with submission. Send photos with submission. Reviews contact sheets, negatives, transparencies, prints. Offers no additional payment for photos accepted with ms. Identification of subjects required. Buys one-time rights.

SAIL, 275 Washington St., Newton MA 02158-1630. (617)964-3030. Fax: (617)964-8948. Editor: Patience Wales. Managing Editor: Amy Ullrich. 50% freelance written. Works with a small number of new/unpublished writers each year. Monthly magazine for audience that is "strictly sailors, average age 42, above average education." Estab. 1970. **Pays on acceptance.** Publishes ms an average of 10 months after acceptance. Buys first North American rights. Submit seasonal or special material at least 6 months in advance. Accepts previously published submissions. Send tearsheet or photocopy of article or short story with information about when and where it previously appeared. Pays 50-75% of amount paid for an original article. Reports in 10 weeks. Writer's guidelines for 1 first-class stamp.

• Ranked as one of the best markets for freelance writers in *Writer's Digest* magazine's annual "Top 100 Markets," January 1994.

Nonfiction: Amy Ullrich, managing editor. Wants "articles on sailing: technical, techniques and feature stories." Interested in how-to, personal experience, distance cruising, destinations, technical aspects of boat construction, systems. "Generally emphasize the excitement of sail and the human, personal aspect. No logs." Special issues: "Cruising, chartering, fitting-out, special race (e.g., America's Cup), boat show." Buys 100 mss/year (freelance and commissioned). Length: 1,000-2,800 words. Pays $200-800. Sometimes pays the expenses of writers on assignment.

Photos: Offers additional payment for photos. Uses b&w glossy prints or Fujichrome transparencies. Pays $600 if photo is used on the cover.
Tips: "Request an articles specification sheet."

‡**SAILING MAGAZINE**, 125 E. Main St., Port Washington WI 53074-0249. (414)284-3494. Fax: (414)284-0067. Editor: Micca Hotchins. Publisher: William F. Schanen, III. Monthly magazine. For readers ages 25-44, majority professionals. About 75% of them own their own sailboat. Estab. 1966. Circ. 35,000. Pays on publication. Accepts simultaneous and previously published submissions. Send typed ms with rights for sale noted. Reports in 2 months. Sample copy for 12 × 15 SAE with 4 first-class stamps. Writer's guidelines for #10 SASE.
Nonfiction: "Experiences of sailing, whether cruising, racing or learning. We require no special style. We're devoted exclusively to sailing and sailboat enthusiasts, and particularly interested in articles about the trend toward cruising in the sailing world." Informational, personal experience, profile, historical, travel, book reviews. Buys 24 mss/year. Query or submit complete ms. Length: open. Pays flat fee for article. Must be accompanied by photos.
Photos: B&w and color photos purchased with or without accompanying ms. Captions required.

SAILING WORLD, N.Y. Times Magazine Group, 5 John Clarke Rd., Box 3400, Newport RI 02840-0992. Fax: (401)848-5048. Editor: John Burnham. 40% freelance written. Monthly magazine. Estab. 1962. Circ. 61,000. Pays on publication. Publishes ms an average of 4 months after acceptance. Buys first North American and world serial rights. Byline given. Query for electronic submissions. Reports in 3 months. Sample copy for $5.
Nonfiction: How-to for racing and performance-oriented sailors, photo feature, profile, regatta reports and charter. No travelogs. Buys 5-10 unsolicited mss/year. Query. Length: 500-1,500 words. Pays $150-200/page text.
Tips: "Send query with outline and include your experience. The writer may have a better chance of breaking in with short articles and fillers such as regatta news reports from his or her own area."

‡**SEA, Best of Boating in the West**, Duncan McIntosh Co., Inc., Suite C, 17782 Cowan, Irvine CA 92714. Fax: (714)660-6172. Editor and Publisher: Duncan McIntosh Jr. Senior Editor: Eston Ellis. 70% freelance written. A monthly magazine covering recreational power boating, offshore fishing and coastal news of the West Coast, from Alaska to Baja California, Mexico. Estab. 1908. Circ. 70,000. Pays on publication. Publishes ms an average of 4 months after acceptance. Byline given. Buys first North American serial rights or second serial (reprint) rights. Reports in 1 month on queries; 2 months on mss. Writer's guidelines, deadline schedule and sample copy for 10 × 13 SASE.
Nonfiction: General interest (on boating and coastal topics), how-to (tips on maintaining a boat, engine, and gear), interview/profile (of a prominent boating personality), travel (West Coast cruising or fishing destination). Buys 150 mss/year. Query with published clips, or send complete ms. Length: 250 (news items) to 2,500 (features) words. Pays $35 (news items) to $350 (features). Some assignment expenses covered if requested in advance.
Photos: Stories accompanied by photos are preferred. Transparencies only; no color negatives or prints. Pays $35 (inside b&w) to $250 (color cover) for photos. Identification of photo subjects required. Buys one-time rights.
Columns/Departments: West Coast Focus (boating and fishing news with color photos); The Hands-On Boater (do-it-yourself tips with b&w photos); Sportfishing (sportfishing tips); Mexico Report (short features on boating and fishing destinations in Mexico).
Tips: "*Sea*'s editorial focus is on West Coast boating and sportfishing. We are not interested in stories about the East Coast, Midwest or foreign countries. First-time contributors should include résumé or information about themselves that identifies their knowledge of subject. Written queries required. No first-person 'what happened on our first cruise' stories. No poetry, fiction or cartoons."

SEA KAYAKER, Sea Kayaker, Inc., P.O. Box 17170, Seattle WA 98107-7170. (206)789-1326. Fax: (206)781-1141. Managing Editor: Christopher Cunningham. 80% freelance written. Works frequently with new/unpublished writers each year. Quarterly magazine on the sport of sea kayaking. Estab. 1984. Circ. 18,000. Pays on publication. Publishes ms an average of 6 months after acceptance. Byline given. Offers 10% kill fee. Buys first North American serial or second serial (reprint) rights. Submit seasonal material 6 months in advance. Reports in 2 months. Sample copy for $5.30. Free writer's guidelines with SASE.
Nonfiction: Essays, historical, how-to (on making equipment), humor, profile, opinion, personal experience, technical, travel. Buys 40 mss/year. Query with or without published clips or send complete ms. Length: 750-4,000 words. Pays about 10¢/word. Sometimes pays the expenses of writers on assignment.
Photos: Send photos with submission. Reviews contact sheets. Offers $25-50/photo. Captions requested. Buys one-time rights.
Columns/Departments: History, Safety, Environment, Journey. Length: 750-4,000 words. Pays about 10¢/word.
Fiction: Kayak related adventure, fantasy, historical, humorous, mainstream, slice-of-life vignettes. Send complete ms. Length: 750-4,000 words. Pays about 10¢/word.

Tips: "We consider unsolicited mss that include a SASE, but we give greater priority to brief (several paragraphs) descriptions of proposed articles accompanied by at least two samples — published or unpublished — of your writing. Enclose a statement as to why you're qualified to write the piece and indicate whether photographs or illustrations are available to accompany the piece."

‡SEA'S WATERFRONT NORTHWEST NEWS, Your Local Boating News, Northwest, 7500 Mercer Terrace Dr., Mercer Island, WA 98040. (206)236-1693. Fax: (206)236-1693. published by Duncan McIntosh Co. Inc., Suite C, 17782 Cowan, Irvine, CA 92714. Editor: Liz Schensted. 20% freelance written. Monthly magazine covering recreational boating from Alaska to Oregon's southern border, including British Columbia. Articles include boating news and features, with an emphasis on saltwater cruising and sportfishing. Estab. 1993. Circ. 40,000.
Nonfiction: Pays on publication. Query editor before submitting photos or mss. Publishes articles an average 2 months after acceptance. Byline given. Sample copy provided for SASE. Buys 50-60 mss/year. Length: 250-1,200 words. Pays 15¢/word.
Photos: Pays $15 for inside photos, b&w preferred; $100 for color cover photo, vertical format, 35mm Kodachrome slides preferred. Identification of subjects required. Buys one-time rights.
Columns/Departments: news Currents (News items about matters that affect PNW recreational boaters); Lifelines (news items about boating lifestyle); Venturing Out (short items about favorite PNW boating destinations); Sportfishing (where and how to fish from a boat, emphasis on saltwater); Business of Boating (news about PNW recreational boating industry). Length: 250 words. Pays 15¢/word.

‡WATERFRONT NEWS, SOUTHERN CALIFORNIA, Your Local Boating News, Duncan McIntosh Co., Inc., Suite C, 2nd Floor, 17782 Cowan, Irvine CA 92714. (714)660-6150. Fax: (714)660-6172. Associate Editor: Roger Tefft. 10% freelance written. Monthly news magazine covering recreational boating, sailing, sportfishing and lifestyles in Southern California. Articles are aimed at owners of pleasureboats with an emphasis on where to go, what to do with their vessel, locally. Estab. 1993. Circ. 40,000. Pays on publication. Publishes ms an average of 1 month after submission. Byline given. Buys first North American rights. Query for all submissions. Reports in 1 month on queries. Sample copy and writer's guidelines for SASE.
Nonfiction: Sportfishing how-to, cruising destinations, spot news of interest to boaters. Length: 150-1,000 words. Pays $25-150. No fiction. Some shipping expenses covered if requested in advance, in writing.
Photos: State availability of photos with query or send photos with submission. Reviews any size prints and transparencies, color or b&w. Offers $15-50/photo. Identification of subjects required. Buys one-time rights.
Columns/Departments: News (including changes, developments in state and federal law that affect local boaters, personality profile on a local boater who cruises somewhere outside Southern California, or a how-to piece on a Southern California port of call, or an interview/profile about a unique cruiser who is visiting Southern California during a long-range voyage aboard his own boat); Racing (covers major regattas in Southern California, both power and sail, and local racers who travel to compete at the highest levels around the world); Sportfishing (short how-to articles for catching fish in Southern California with your own boat); Business (new developments in boating accessories and services of interest to Southern California boat owners.) Query with published clips.

WATERWAY GUIDE, Argus Business, Inc., 6151 Powers Ferry Rd., NW, Atlanta GA 30339-2941. (404)618-0313. Fax: (404)618-0347. Associate Publisher: Judith Powers. 90% freelance written. Quarterly magazine on intracoastal waterway travel for recreational boats. "Writer must be knowledgable about navigation and the areas covered by the guide." Estab. 1947. Circ. 45,000. Pays on publication. Publishes ms an average of 3 months after acceptance. Byline given sometimes. Kill fee varies. Buys all rights. Reports in 3 months on queries; 4 months on mss. Sample copy for $33.95 with $3 postage.
Nonfiction: Historical/nostalgic, how-to, photo feature, technical, travel. "No personal boating experiences." Buys 25 mss/year. Query with or without published clips or send complete ms. Length: 200 words minimum. Pays $50-3,000 for assigned articles. Pays in contributor copies or other premiums for helpful tips and useful information.
Photos: Send photos with submission. Reviews 3×5 prints. Offers $25/b&w photo, $600/color photos used on the cover. Identification of subjects required. Buys one-time rights.
Fillers: Facts. Buys 6/year. Length: 250-1,000 words. Pays $50-150.
Tips: "Must have on-the-water experience and be able to provide new and accurate information on geographic areas covered by *Waterway Guide*."

WOODENBOAT MAGAZINE, The Magazine for Wooden Boat Owners, Builders, and Designers, WoodenBoat Publications, Inc., P.O. Box 78, Brooklin ME 04616. (207)359-4651. Fax: (207)359-8920. Editor: Jon Wilson. Executive Editor: Jennifer Elliott. Senior Editor: Mike O'Brien. 50% freelance written. Works with a small number of new/unpublished writers each year. Bimonthly magazine for wooden boat owners, builders and designers. "We are devoted exclusively to the design, building, care, preservation, and use of wooden boats, both commercial and pleasure, old and new, sail and power. We work to convey quality, integrity and involvement in the creation and care of these craft, to entertain, inform, inspire, and to provide our varied readers with access to individuals who are deeply experienced in the world of wooden boats."

Estab. 1974. Circ. 106,000. Pays on publication. Publishes ms an average of 1 year after acceptance. Byline given. Offers variable kill fee. Buys first North American serial rights. Accepts simultaneous and previously published submissions (with notification). Send tearsheet or photocopy of article or typed wms with rights for sale noted with information about when and where the article previously appeared. Query for electronic submissions. Reports in 3 weeks on queries; 2 months on mss. Sample copy for $4.50. Writer's guidelines for SASE.

Nonfiction: Technical (repair, restoration, maintenance, use, design and building wooden boats). No poetry, fiction. Buys 50 mss/year. Query with published clips. Length: 1,500-5,000 words. Pays $150-200/1,000 words. Sometimes pays expenses of writers on assignment.

Photos: Send photos with query. Negatives must be available. Pays $15-75 for b&w; $25-350 for color. Identification of subjects required. Buys one-time rights.

Columns/Departments: On the Waterfront pays for information on wooden boat-related events, projects, boatshop activities, etc. Buys 25/year. "We use the same columnists for each issue." Send complete information. Length: 250-1,000 words. Pays $5-50 for information.

Tips: "We appreciate a detailed, articulate query letter, accompanied by photos, that will give us a clear idea of what the author is proposing. We appreciate samples of previously published work. It is important for a prospective author to become familiar with our magazine first. It is extremely rare for us to make an assignment with a writer with whom we have not worked before. Most work is submitted on speculation. The most common failure is not exploring the subject material in enough depth."

YACHTING, Times Mirror Magazines Inc., 5th Floor, 2 Park Ave., New York NY 10016-5695. (212)779-5300. Fax: (212)725-1035. Publishing Director: Oliver S. Moore III. Executive Editor: Charles Barthold. 50% freelance written. "The magazine is written and edited for experienced, knowledgeable yachtsmen." Estab. 1907. Circ. 32,000. Pays on publication. Byline given. Buys first rights. Submit seasonal/holiday material 6 months in advance. Reports in 1 month.

• Ranked as one of the best markets for freelance writers in *Writer's Digest* magazine's annual "Top 100 Markets," January 1994.

Nonfiction: Book excerpts, personal experience, photo feature, travel. No cartoons, fiction, poetry. Query with published clips. Length: 250-2,000 words. Pays $250-1,000 for assigned articles. Pays expenses of writers on assignment.

Photos: Send photos with submission. Reviews 35mm transparencies. Offers some additional payment for photos accepted with ms. Captions, model releases and identification of subjects required.

Columns/Departments: Cruising Yachtsman (stories on cruising; contact Cynthia Taylor, senior editor); Racing Yachtsman (stories about sail or power racing; contact Lisa Ken Wooten); Yacht Yard (how-to and technical pieces on yachts and their systems; contact Dennis Caprio, Senior editor). Buys 30 mss/year. Send complete ms. Length: 750 words maximum. Pays $250-500.

Tips: "We require considerable expertise in our writing because our audience is experienced and knowledgeable. Vivid descriptions of quaint anchorages and quainter natives are fine, but our readers want to know how the yachtsmen got there, too. They also want to know how their boats work."

Bowling

BOWLERS JOURNAL, Dept. WM, 200 S. Michigan Ave., Chicago IL 60604. (312)341-1110. Publisher: Mort Luby. Editor: Jim Dressel. 30% freelance written. Prefers to work with published/established writers; works with a small number of new/unpublished writers each year. Monthly magazine covering bowling. Circ. 22,000. **Pays on acceptance.** Publishes ms an average of 2 months after acceptance. Buys all rights. Submit seasonal/holiday material 3 months in advance of issue date. Reports in 6 weeks. Sample copy for $2.

Nonfiction: General interest (stories on top pros); historical (stories of old-time bowlers or bowling alleys); interview (top pros, men and women); profile (top pros). "We publish some controversial matter, seek outspoken personalities. We reject material that is too general; that is, not written for high average bowlers and bowling proprietors who already know basics of playing the game and basics of operating a bowling alley." Buys 15-20 unsolicited mss/year. Query, phone queries OK. Length: 1,200-3,500 words. Pays $75-225.

Photos: State availability of photos with query. Pays $5-15 for 8 × 10 b&w prints; and $15-25 for 35mm or 2¼ × 2¼ color transparencies. Buys one-time rights.

BOWLING, Dept. WM, 5301 S. 76th St., Greendale WI 53129. (414)421-6400, ext. 230. Editor: Bill Vint. 15% freelance written. Bimonthly, official publication of the American Bowling Congress. Estab. 1934. Circ. 135,000. **Pays on acceptance.** Publishes ms an average of 2 months after acceptance. Byline given. Rights purchased vary with author and material; usually buys all rights. Reports in 1 month. Sample copy for $2.50.

Nonfiction: "This is a specialized field and the average writer attempting the subject of bowling should be well-informed. However, anyone is free to submit material for approval." Wants articles about unusual ABC sanctioned leagues and tournaments, personalities, etc., featuring male bowlers. Nostalgia articles also considered. No first-person articles or material on history of bowling. Length: 500-1,200 words. Pays $100-300 per article. No poems, songs or fiction.

Photos: Pays $10-15/photo.

Tips: "Submit feature material on bowlers, generally amateurs competing in local leagues, or special events involving the game of bowling. Should have connection with ABC membership. Queries should be as detailed as possible so that we may get a clear idea of what the proposed story would be all about. It saves us time and the writer time. Samples of previously published material in the bowling or general sports field would help. Once we find a talented writer in a given area, we're likely to go back to him in the future. We're looking for good writers who can handle assignments professionally and promptly." No articles on professionals.

Football

‡**NFL EXCLUSIVE, The Official Magazine of the NFL Season Ticket holder**, SportsImage, Inc., Suite 302, 2107 Elliott Ave., Seattle WA 98121. Editor: Mike Olson. 100% freelance written. Annual magazine covering NFL football. Estab. 1991. Circ. 427,350. Pays on publications. Byline given. Offers 100% kill fee. Buys all rights. Editorial lead time 3 months. Submit seasonal material 2 months in advance. Accepts previously published submissions. Sample copy for 8½ × 11 SAE with 5 first-class stamps.

Nonfiction: Historical/nostalgic, interview/profile. Buys 15 mss/year. Query with published clips. Length: 1,000 words. Pays $200. Sometimes pays expenses of writers on assignment.

Photos: Send photos with submission. Reviews transparencies. Negotiates payment individually. Identification of subjects required. Buys one-time rights.

Tips: "Come up with ideas, trends or concepts that revolve around a historical look at the NFL. Not so much the famous moments (i.e. Super Bowl), rather, the hidden, yet significant, events that shaped the league."

Gambling

‡**BLACKJACK FORUM**, RGE Publishing, 414 Santa Clara Ave., Oakland CA 94610. (510)465-6452. Editor: Arnold Synder. Contact: AlisonFinlay. 40% freelance written. Quarterly magazine covering Casino Blackjack. "This is a fairly technical journal for serious blackjack players. Many of our writers/readers are mathematicians and computer programmers. This is *not* a get-rich-quick type mag." Estab. 1981. Circ. 2,000. Pays on publication. Publishes ms an average of 3-6 months after acceptance. Byline given. Buys one-time rights. Editorial lead time 3 months. Submit seasonal material 2-3 months in advance. Query for electronic submissions. Reports in 1-3 months on queries. Sample copy for $5.

Nonfiction: Exposé, how-to, humor, personal experience, technical, travel. Buys 10-12 mss/year. Send complete ms. Length: 250-3,000 words. Pays $25 minimum for unsolicited articles. Sometimes pays expenses of writers on assignment.

Photos: State availability of photos with submission. Negotiates payment individually. Buys one-time rights.

Columns/Departments: Around The States (reports on BJ conditions in U.S. casinos especially penetration, heat, stakes, spread), 100-500; Around The World (ditto for foreign casinos), 100-500. Buys 25-30 mss/year. Send complete ms. Pays $10-150.

Tips: "Writers must be able to rate games via criteria of card counters. Knowledge of counting systems a prerequisite. Many pros read *BJF* to locate games. Writers must understand the importance of deck penetration, rule variations, heat, etc. "Around The States" & "Around The World" If you visit casinos, and you know what card counters look for, you can provide valuable information for our readers."

CASINO PLAYER, America's Premier Gaming Magazine, ACE Marketing, 2524 Arctic Ave., Atlantic City NJ 08401. (609)344-9000. Fax: (609)345-3469. Publisher: Glenn Fine. Editor: Roger Gros. 15% freelance written. Monthly magazine on casino gambling. "We cover any issue that would interest the gambler, from table games to sports betting, to slot machines. Articles should be light, entertaining and give tips on how to win." Estab. 1985. Circ. 210,000. Pays on publication. Byline not always given. Buys all rights. Submit seasonal/holiday material 3 months in advance. Accepts previously published submissions. Send photocopy of article. Reports in 3 months. Sample copy for $2 and 9 × 12 SAE with 5 first-class stamps.

Nonfiction: How-to (win!), new product (gaming equipment). "No articles dependent on statistics; no travelogues. First person gambling stories OK." Query with published clips. Length: 500-1,000 words. Pays $50-250 for assigned articles; $50-100 for unsolicited articles. Sometimes pays expenses of writers on assignment.

Photos: Send photos with submission. Reviews contact sheets and 5 × 7 prints. Offers $10/photo. Captions and identification of subjects required. Buys all rights.

Columns/Departments: Table Games (best ways to play, ratings); Slots (new machines, methods, casino policies); Nevada (what's new in state, properties); Tournaments (reports on gaming, tournaments); and Caribbean (gaming in the islands), all 500 words. Buys 10 mss/year. Query with published clips. Pays $50-100.

Fillers: Facts and gags to be illustrated by cartoonist. Buys 5/year. Length: 25-100 words. Pays $25-100.

Tips: "Writer must understand the gambler: why he gambles, what his motivations are. The spread of legalized gaming will be an increasingly important topic in the next year. Write as much to entertain as to inform. We try to give the reader information they will not find elsewhere."

‡**LOTTOWORLD MAGAZINE**, Dynamic World Distributors, Inc., Suite 200, 2150 Goodlette Rd., Naples FL 33940. (813)643-1677. Editor-in-Chief: Rich Holman. Managing Editor: Barry Miller. 60% freelance written. Biweekly magazine covering lottery-related news. "LottoWorld Magazine is a national lottery news magazine aimed at the 100 million US lottery players. Each issue is devoted to systems, tips, strategies, techniques and research 40%; human interest stories 30%; winning pick forecasting 20%; software, astrology, miscellaneous 10%." Estab. 1993. Pays 30 days after publication. Byline given. Buys first North American serial rights. Editorial lead time 2 months. Sample copy or writers guidelines for 8×11 SAE with 87¢ postage.
Nonfiction: General interest, how-to, humor, interview/profile and photo feature. Buys 36-72 mss/year. Query. Length: 400-800 words. Pay negotiated. Sometimes pays expenses of writers on assignment.
Photos: Freelancers should send photos with submission. Reviews prints. Additional payment for photos accepted with ms.

WIN, Gambling Times Incorporated, Suite 213, 16760 Stagg St., Van Nuys CA 91406. (818)781-9355. Editor: Cecil Suzuki. Managing Editor: Dwight Chuman. Contact: C. Suzuki. 12% freelance written. Monthly magazine for gambling, entertainment, computers. Estab. 1979. Circ. 54,200. Pays on publication. Publishes ms an average of 3 months after acceptance. Byline given. Buys first North American serial rights. Editorial lead time 3 months. Submit seasonal material 3 months in advance. Accepts simultaneous submissions. Query for electronic submissions. Reports in 6 weeks on queries; 2 months on mss. Sample copy and writer's guidelines with SASE.
Nonfiction: Book excerpts, essays, historical/nostalgic, how-to (casino games), interview/profile, new product, photo feature, technical. Buys 6 mss/year. Send complete ms. Length: 1,600-2,000 words. Pays $75 minimum for assigned articles. Sometimes "pays" contributors with travel, hotel rooms.
Photos: Send photos with submission. Reviews 4×5 transparencies and prints. Negotiates payment individually. Captions, model releases and identification of subjects required. Buys all rights.
Fiction: Fantasy, historical, science fiction, gambling subplots. No previously published fiction. Buys 12 mss/year. Send complete ms. Length: 1,200-2,500 words. Pay negotiable.
Fillers: Facts, newsbreaks. Buys 30/year. Length: 250-600 words. Pays $25 minimum.

WINNING!, NatCom, Inc., 15115 S. 76th East Ave., Bixby OK 74008-4147. (918)366-4441. Fax: (918)366-4439. Managing Editor: Lawrence Taylor. 30% freelance written. Monthly newsletter covering contests, gaming/travel. "How-to-win articles addressing all aspects of legal gaming-casinos, high-stakes bingo, contests and sweepstakes and so on." Estab. 1976. Circ. 150,000. Pays 30 days after acceptance. Byline given. Buys first rights. No simultaneous submissions. Query for electronic submissions. Reports in 4-6 weeks on queries; 2 months on mss. Free sample copy for 9½×12 SAE with 3 first-class stamps. Writer's guidelines for #10 SASE.
Nonfiction: How-to (gaming-casino, etc. bingo, sweepstakes and contests), winning tips, interview/profile, new product, travel. "No negative profiles of casino performers/how-to-cheat gaming articles"; no fiction or poetry. Buys 8-10 mss/year. Query. Length: 400-1,000 words. Pays $50-75 for articles; $5-25 for short items and fillers.

General Interest

CARIBBEAN SPORTS & TRAVEL, (formerly *Pleasure Boating Magazine*), Graphcom Publishing, Inc., Suite 107, 1995 NE 150th St., N. Miami FL 33181. (305)945-7403. Fax: (305)947-6410. Publisher/Owner: Robert Ulrich. 60% freelance written. Monthly magazine covering sports around The Bahamas and Caribbean. Estab. 1971. Circ. 25,000. Pays on publication. Publishes ms an average of 2 months after acceptance. Byline given. Kill fee varies. Buys first rights. Reports in 3 months on queries.
Nonfiction: General interest sports, especially diving, fishing, golf and chartering. Buys 35-40 mss/year. Query with published clips. Length: 1,200-2,000 words. Pays $200 minimum; maximum varies. Sometimes pays the expenses of writers on assignment.
Photos: Send photos with submission. Reviews transparencies. Offers no additional payment for photos accepted with ms. Identification of subjects required. Buys one-time rights.
Tips: "Know the region we cover, offer fresh perspectives and be flexible with editors."

‡**EXPLORE, Canada's Outdoor Adventure Magazine**, Thompson & Gordon Publishing Co. Ltd., Suite 420, 301-14 St. NW, Calgary Alberta T2n 2A1 Canada. (403);270-8890. Editor: Marion Harrison. 30% freelance written. Bimonthly magazine covering Outdoor Recreation "for those who seek some form of adventure in their travels. The magazine covers popular activities such as backpacking, bicycling, canoeing, and backcountry skiing featuring Canadian and international destinations. Other topics covered include ecotourism, the environment, outdoor photography, sports medicine, equipment, and new products for the outdoor recreationist." Estab. 1981. Circ. 25,000. Pays on publication. Byline given. Offers 50% kill fee. Buys first North American serial rights. Editorial lead time 6-12 months. Submit seasonal material 6 months in advance. Accepts simultaneous submissions. Query for electronic submissions. Reports in 1-2 months. Sample copy for $5. Writer's guidelines for #10 SASE—IRCs required from outside Canada.

Nonfiction: Personal experience, travel. Query with published clips. Length: 1,500-2,500 words. Pays $275.
Photos: Send photos with submission. Reviews contact sheets, transparencies and prints. Offers no additional payment for photos accepted with ms. Captions required. Buys one-time rights.
Columns/Departments: Earthwatch (environmental issues which have an impact on outdoor recreation), 1,500-1,800; Gearing Up (clothing, equipment for outdoor recreation). 1,800; Photography (outdoor photography tips), 1,200. Buys 15 mss/year. Query. Pays $275.
Tips: "Remember Explore is a *Canadian* magazine with 95% Canadian readership that wants to read about Canada! We buy three articles *per year* which feature US destinations. Submit manuscript and photos for fastest response. Feature articles are required more often than departments. Features are first-person narratives that are exciting and interesting. Quality photos are a must."

‡METRO SPORTS MAGAZINE, 695 Washington St., New York NY 10014. (212)627-7040. Editor: Miles Jaffe. 50% freelance written. Monthly magazine covers participation sports. Estab. 1987. Circ. 130,000. Pays on publication. Publishes ms an average of 2 months after acceptance. Byline given. Buys all rights. Editorial lead time 2 months. Submit seasonal material 2 months in advance. Accepts simultaneous submissions. Query for electronic submissions. Reports in 1 week on queries; 1 month on mss. Sample copy for $2. Writer's guidelines free on request.
Nonfiction: Book excerpts, essays, general interest, how-to, humor, inspirational, interview/profile, new product, opinion, personal experience, photo feature, travel. Special issues: aerobics (January/February); Triathlons (March); Running (April-October), Skiing (November/December); Cycling (May); Outdoor (June); Volleyball (July). Buys 40 mss/year. Query. Length: 600-2,000 words. Pays 15¢/word.
Photos: State availability or send photos with submission. Offers no additional payment for photos accepted with ms. Buys one-time rights.
Columns/Departments: My Two Sense, 800 words.
Tips: "Work with us relative to a particular industry. We need equipment—focused editorial on bikes, wheels, clothes, skis etc."

OUTDOOR CANADA MAGAZINE, Suite 202, 703 Evans Ave., Toronto Ontario M9C 5E9 Canada. (416)695-0311. Fax: (416)695-0382. Editor-in-Chief: Teddi Brown. 90% freelance written. Works with a small number of new/unpublished writers each year. Magazine published 9 times/year emphasizing noncompetitive outdoor recreation in Canada *only*. Estab. 1972. Circ. 102,000. Pays on publication. Publishes ms an average of 6-8 months after acceptance. Buys first rights. Submit seasonal/holiday material 1 year in advance of issue date. Byline given. *Enclose SASE or IRCs or material will not be returned.* Reports in 1 month. *Writer's Market* recommends allowing 2 months for reply. Mention *Writer's Market* in request for editorial guidelines.
Nonfiction: Fishing, hiking, canoeing, hunting, adventure, outdoor issues, exploring, outdoor destinations in Canada, some how-to. Buys 35-40 mss/year, usually with photos. Length: 1,000-2,500 words. Pays $100 and up.
Photos: Emphasize people in the outdoors. Pays $35-225 for 35mm transparencies; and $400/cover. Captions and model releases required.
Fillers: Short news pieces. Buys 70-80/year. Length: 200-500 words. Pays $6/printed inch.

OUTSIDE, Mariah Publications Corp., Dept. WM, 1165 N. Clark St., Chicago IL 60610. (312)951-0990. Editor: Mark Bryant. Managing Editor: Kathy Martin. 90% freelance written. Monthly magazine on outdoor recreation and travel. "*Outside* is a monthly national magazine for active, educated, upscale adults who love the outdoors and are concerned about its preservation." Estab. 1977. Circ. 400,000. **Pays on acceptance.** Publishes ms an average of 3 months after acceptance. Byline given. Offers 25% kill fee. Buys first North American serial rights. Submit seasonal/holiday material 4-5 months in advance. Electronic submission OK for solicited materials; not for unsolicited. Reports in 6 weeks on queries; 2 months on mss. Sample copy for $4 for 9×12 SAE with 9 first-class stamps. Writer's guidelines for SASE.
Nonfiction: Book excerpts; essays; reports on the environment; outdoor sports and expeditions; general interest; how-to; humor; inspirational; interview/profile (major figures associated with sports, travel, environment, outdoor); opinion, personal experience (expeditions; trying out new sports); photo feature (outdoor photography); technical (reviews of equipment, how-to); travel (adventure, sports-oriented travel). All should pertain to the outdoors: Bike section; Downhill Skiing; Cross-country Skiing; Adventure Travel. Do not want to see articles about sports that we don't cover (basketball, tennis, golf, etc.). Buys 40 mss/year. Query with published clips and SASE. Length: 1,500-4,000 words. Negotiates payment. Pays expenses of writers on assignment.
Photos: "Do not send photos; if we decide to use a freelancer's story, we may request to see the writer's photos." Reviews transparencies. Offers $180/photo minimum. Captions and identification of subjects required. Buys one-time rights.
Columns/Departments: Dispatches, contact Alex Heard (news, events, short profiles relevant to outdoors), 200-1,000 words; Destinations, contact Leslie Weeden, (places to explore, news, and tips for adventure travelers), 250-400 words; Review, contact Andrew Tilin, (evaluations of products), 200-1,500 words. Buys 180 mss/year. Query with published clips. Length: 200-2,000 words. Payment varies.

Tips: "Prospective writers should study the magazine before querying. Look at the magazine for our style, subject matter and standards." The departments are the best areas for freelancers to break in.

ROCKY MOUNTAIN SPORTS MAGAZINE, Sports & Fitness Publishing, 2025 Pearl St., Boulder CO 80302. (303)440-5111. Editor: Will Gadd. 50% freelance written. Monthly magazine of sports in the Rocky Mountain States and Canada. "*Rocky* is a magazine for sports-related lifestyles and activities. Our mission is to reflect and inspire the active lifestyle of Rocky Mountain residents." Estab. 1987. Circ. 45,000. Pays on publication. Publishes ms an average of 2 months after acceptance. Byline given. Offers 25% kill fee. Buys second serial (reprint) rights. Editorial lead time 1½ months. Submit seasonal material 2 months in advance. Accepts previously published submissions. Query for electronic submissions. Reports in 3 weeks on queries; 2 months on mss. Sample copy and writer's guidelines for #10 SASE.
Nonfiction: Book excerpts, essays, exposé, how-to: (no specific sports, trips, adventures), humor, inspirational, interview/profile, new product, opinion, personal experience, photo feature, travel. Special issues: Photo Annual (August); snowboarding (December); Alpine and Nordic (January and February); Mountain biking (Aapril). No articles on football, baseball, basketball or other sports covered in-depth by newspapers. Buys 24 mss/year. Query with published clips. Length: 2,500 maximum words. Pays $150 minimum for assigned articles. Sometimes pays expenses of writers on assignment.
   • The editor of this publication has expressed an interest in seeing more from freelancers on mountain biking and mountain sports coverage.
Photos: State availability of photos with submission. Reviews transparencies and prints. Offers $25-250/photo. Captions and identification of subjects required. Buys one-time rights.
Columns/Departments: Scree (short newsy items), 50-800 words; Photo Gallery (photos depicting nature and the spirit of sport); and High Altitude (essay on quirky topics related to Rockies). Buys 20 mss/year. Query. Pays $25-200.
Fiction: Adventure, experimental, humorous. "Nothing that isn't sport-related." Buys 5 mss/year. Query. Length: 250-1,500 words. Pays $50-200.
Fillers: Anecdotes, facts, gags to be illustrated by cartoonist, newsbreaks, short humor. Buys 20/year. Length: 10-200 words. Pays $25-75.
Tips: "Submit stories for the Scree section first."

SPORT, Petersen Publishing Co., 6420 Wilshire Blvd., Los Angeles CA 90048-5515. (213)782-2828. Editor: Cam Benty. 80% freelance written. Monthly magazine. **Pays on acceptance.** Publishes ms an average of 3 months after acceptance. Offers 25% kill fee. Buys first North American serial or all rights. Reports in 2 months.
Nonfiction: "Prefers to see articles on professional, big-time sports: basketball, football, baseball, with some boxing. The articles we buy must be contemporary pieces, not a history of sports or a particular sport." Query with published clips. Length: News briefs, 200-300 words; Departments, 1,400 words; Features, 1,500-3,000 words. Averages 50¢/word for articles.

THE SPORTING NEWS, Times Mirror Co., Dept. WM, 1212 N. Lindbergh Blvd., St. Louis MO 63132. (314)997-7111. Editor: John Rawlings. 50-60% freelance written. Weekly tabloid. Pays on publication. Publishes ms an average of 2-3 months after acceptance. Offers 50% kill fee. Buys first or one-time and second serial rights. Reports in 3 weeks.
Nonfiction: "Prefers to see trend stories, perspective stories, trend analysis of major spectator sports." Prefers to see complete ms, but may query with published clips. Length: 100-2,000 words. Pays $50-1,500.

SPORTS ILLUSTRATED, Time & Life Bld., Rockefeller Center, New York NY 10020-1393. Weekly publication covering sports of all kinds. This magazine did not respond to our request for information. Query before submitting.

SPORTS INTERNATIONAL, (formerly *Sports Parade*), Meridian International, Inc., P.O. Box 10010, Odgen UT 84409. (801)394-9446. 65% freelance written. Works with a small number of new/unpublished writers each year. Monthly general interest sports magazine distributed by business and professional firms to employees, customers, clients, etc. Readers are predominantly upscale, mainstream, family oriented. **Pays on acceptance.** Publishes ms an average of 3 months after acceptance. Byline given. Buys first, second serial (reprint) and nonexclusive reprint rights. Accepts simultaneous and previously published submissions. Reports in 2 months with SASE. Sample copy for $1 and 9×12 SAE. Writer's guidelines for #10 SASE, Attn: Editorial Staff.
Nonfiction: General interest and interview/profile. "General interest articles covering the entire sports spectrum, personality profiles on top flight professional and amateur sports figures. We are looking for articles on well-known athletes in the top 10% of their field. We are still looking at articles and profiles of well-known celebrities. These are cover features; photogenic appeal is important." Buys 20 mss/year. Written query. Length: 1,000 words. Pays 15¢/word. Pays 10¢/word for second rights.
Photos: Send with query or ms. Reviews 35mm or larger transparencies and 5×7 or 8×10 prints. Pays $35 for transparencies; $50 for cover. Captions and model releases required.

Tips: "I will be purchasing more articles based on personalities — today's stars. Celebrities must have positive values and be making a contribution to society. No nostalgic material."

‡**WINDY CITY SPORTS MAGAZINE,** Chicago Sports Resources, 1450 W. Randolph, Chicago IL 60607. (312)421-1551. Editor: Shelley Hill. 75% freelance written. Monthly magazine covering amateur, participatory sports. Estab. 1987. Circ. 100,000 (Chicago and suburbs). **Pays on acceptance;** pays on publication for blind submissions. Offers 25% kill fee. Buys one-time rights. Editorial lead time 2 months. Submit seasonal material 2-12 months in advance. Accepts simultaneous and previously published submissions. Reports in 2-4 weeks on queries. Sample copy for $2 or SASE. Writer's guidelines free on request.
Nonfiction: Essays (re: sports controversial issues), how-to (do sports), inspirational (profiles of accomplished athletes), interview/profile, new product, opinion, personal experience, photo feature (in Chicago), travel. No articles on professional sports. Buys 120 mss/year. Query with clips. Length: 500-1,200 words. Pays 10¢/word. Sometimes pays expenses of writers on assignment.
Photos: State availability or send photos with submission. Reviews contact sheets and prints. Negotiates payment individually. Captions and identification of subjects required. Buys one-time rights.
Columns/Departments: "We run the following columns (750-900 words) every month: running, cycling, fitness centers, nutrition, sports medicine, women's, road trip (adventure tarvel)." Buys 70 mss/year. Query with published clips. Send complete ms. Pays $75-125.
Fillers: Anecdotes, facts, gags to be illustrated by cartoonist, short humor. Buys 20/year. Length: 20-500 words. Pays $25-100. "I love cartoons!"
Tips: "Best way to get assignment: ask for writer's guidelines, editor's schedule and sample copy ($2 SASE). *Read Magazine!* Query me with story ideas for a column (I run columns every nonth and am always desperate for ideas) or query on features using editorial schedule. Always try to target Chicago/Midwest."

WOMEN'S SPORTS & FITNESS MAGAZINE, Women's Sports & Fitness, Inc., 2025 Pearl St., Boulder CO 80302-5323. (303)440-5111. Senior Editor: Allison Glock. Contact: Janet Lee, assistant editor. 90% freelance written. Works with a small number of new/unpublished writers each year. Magazine published 8 times/year emphasizing women's sports, fitness and health. Estab. 1974. Circ. 155,000. Pays on publication. Publishes ms an average of 3 months after acceptance. Buys first North American serial rights. Submit seasonal/holiday material 3 months in advance. Reports in 2-3 months. Sample copy for $5 and 9 × 12 SAE. Writer's guidelines for #10 SASE.
• Ranked as one of the best markets for freelance writers in *Writer's Digest* magazine's annual "Top 100 Markets," January 1994.
Nonfiction: Profile, service piece, interview, how-to, historical, personal experience, new product. "All articles should have the latest information from knowledgable sources. All must be of national interest to athletic women." Buys 5 mss/issue. Length: 500-1,500 words. Query with published clips. Pays $600-1,200 for features, including expenses.
Photos: State availability of photos. Pays about $50-300 for b&w prints; $50-500 for 35mm color transparencies. Buys one-time rights.
Columns/Departments: Buys 8-10/issue. Query with published clips. Length: 200-750 words. Pays $100-400.
Tips: "If the writer doesn't have published clips, best advice for breaking in is to concentrate on columns and departments (the Beat and Source) first. Query letters should tell why our readers — active women (with an average age in the mid-thirties) who partake in sports or fitness activities six times a week — would want to read the article. We're especially attracted to articles with a new angle, fresh or difficult-to-get information. We go after the latest in health, nutrition and fitness research, or reports about lesser-known women in sports who are on the threshold of greatness. We also present profiles of the best athletes and teams. We want the profiles to give insight into the person as well as the athlete. We have a cadre of writers whom we've worked with regularly, but we are always looking for new writers."

Golf

GOLF DIGEST, Dept. WM, 5520 Park Ave., Trumbull CT 06611. (203)373-7000. Editor: Jerry Tarde. 30% freelance written. Monthly magazine covering golf. Circ. 1.45 million. **Pays on acceptance.** Publishes ms an average of 6 weeks after acceptance. Buys all rights. Byline given. Submit seasonal/holiday material 4 months in advance. Reports in 6 weeks.
• Ranked as one of the best markets for freelance writers in *Writer's Digest* magazine's annual "Top 100 Markets," January 1994.
Nonfiction: Melissa Lausten, editorial assistant. How-to, informational, historical, humor, inspirational, interview, nostalgia, opinion, profile, travel, new product, personal experience, photo feature, technical; "all on playing and otherwise enjoying the game of golf." Query. Length: 1,000-2,500 words.
Photos: Nick DiDio, art director. Purchased without accompanying ms. Pays $75-150 for 5 × 7 or 8 × 10 b&w prints; $100-300/35mm transparency. Model release required.

Poetry: Lois Hains, assistant editor. Light verse. Buys 1-2/issue. Length: 4-8 lines. Pays $50.
Fillers: Lois Hains, assistant editor. Jokes, gags, anecdotes, cutlines for cartoons. Buys 1-2/issue. Length: 2-6 lines. Pays $25-50.

GOLF MAGAZINE, Times Mirror Magazines, 2 Park Ave., New York NY 10016-5695. (212)779-5000. Fax: (212)779-5522. Editor: James A. Frank. Senior Editors: David Barrett and Mike Purkey. 40% freelance written. Monthly magazine on golf, professional and amateur. Circ. 1.25 million. **Pays on acceptance.** Publishes ms an average of 4 months after acceptance. Byline sometimes given. Offers 20% kill fee. Buys first North American serial rights. Submit seasonal/holiday material 4 months in advance. Query for electronic submissions. Reports in 1 month on queries. *Writer's Market* recommends allowing 2 months for reply. Free writer's guidelines.
● Ranked as one of the best markets for freelance writers in *Writer's Digest* magazine's annual "Top 100 Markets," January 1994.
Nonfiction: General interest, historical/nostalgic, how-to, humor, interview/profile. Buys 10-20 mss/year. Query or query with published clips. Length: 100-2,500 words. Pays $100-2,500. Sometimes pays expenses of writers on assignment.
Photos: State availability of photos with submission or send photos with submission. Offers standard page rate. Captions, model releases, identification of subjects required. Buys one-time rights.
Columns/Departments: Buys 5-10 mss/year. Query with or without published clips or send complete ms. Length: 100-1,200 words. Pays $100-1,000.
Fillers: Newsbreaks, short humor. Buys 5-10/year. Length: 50-100 words. Pays $50-150.
Tips: "Be familiar with the magazine and with the game of golf."

GULF COAST GOLFER, Golfer Magazines, Inc., Suite 212. 9182 Old Katy Rd., Houston TX 77055. (713)464-0308. Fax: (713)464-0129. Editor: Steve Hunter. 30% freelance written. Prefers to work with published/established writers. Monthly magazine covering results of major area competition, data on upcoming tournaments, reports of new and improved golf courses, and how-to tips for active, competitive golfers in Texas Gulf Coast area. Estab. 1984. Circ. 30,000. Pays on publication. Publishes ms an average of 1 month after acceptance. Byline given. Buys one-time rights. Submit seasonal/holiday material 3 months in advance. Reports in 3 weeks. Sample copy for 10 × 13 SAE with 4 first-class stamps. Free writer's guidelines.
Nonfiction: How-to, humor, interview/profile, personal experience, travel. Nothing outside of Gulf Coast area. Buys 20 mss/year. Query. Length: 500-1,500 words. Pays $50-250 for assigned articles.
Photos: Send photos with submission. Offers no additional payment for photos accepted with ms. Identification of subjects required.
Tips: We publish mostly how-to, where-to articles. They're about people and events. We could use profiles of successful amateur and professional golfers—but only on a specific assignment basis. Most of the tour players already have been assigned to the staff or to freelancers. Do *not* approach people, schedule interviews, then tell us about it."

NORTH TEXAS GOLFER, Golfer Magazines, Inc., Suite 212, 9182 Old Katy Rd., Houston TX 77055. (713)464-0308. Fax: (713)464-0129. Editor: Steve Hunter. 30% freelance written. Monthly tabloid covering golf in North Texas. Emphasizes "grass roots coverage of regional golf course activities" and detailed, localized information on tournaments and competition in North Texas. Estab. 1986. Circ. 28,000. Pays on publication. Byline given. Buys one-time rights. Submit seasonal/holiday material 3 months in advance. Reports in 3 weeks. Sample copy for 9 × 12 SAE with 4 first-class stamps.
Nonfiction: How-to, humor, interview/profile, personal experience, travel. Nothing outside of Texas. Buys 20 mss/year. Query. Length: 500-1,500 words. Pays $50-250 for assigned articles.
Photos: Send photos with submission. Offers no additional payment for photos accepted with ms. Identification of subjects required.
Tips: "We publish mostly how-to, where-to articles. They're about people and events in Texas only. We could use profiles of successful amateur and professional golfers in Texas—but only on a specific assignment basis. Most of the tour players already have been assigned to the staff or to freelancers. Do *not* approach people, schedule interviews, then tell us about it."

SCORE, Canada's Golf Magazine, Canadian Controlled Media Communications, 287 MacPherson Ave., Toronto, Ontario M4V 1A4 Canada. (416)928-2909. Fax: (416)928-1357. Managing Editor: Bob Weeks. 70% freelance written. Works with a small number of new/unpublished writers each year. Magazine published 7 times/year covering golf. "*Score* magazine provides seasonal coverage of the Canadian golf scene, professional, amateur, senior and junior golf for men and women golfers in Canada, the US and Europe through profiles, history, travel, editorial comment and instruction." Estab. 1982. Circ. 140,000 audited. **Pays on acceptance.** Byline given. Offers negotiable kill fee. Buys all rights and second serial (reprint) rights. Submit seasonal/holiday material 8 months in advance. Reports in 8 months. Sample copy for $2.50 (Canadian) and 9 × 12 SAE with IRCs. Writer's guidelines for #10 SAE and IRC.
Nonfiction: Book excerpts (golf); historical/nostalgic (golf and golf characters); interview/profile (prominent golf professionals); photo feature (golf); travel (golf destinations only). The yearly April/May issue includes

tournament results from Canada, the US, Europe, Asia, Australia, etc., history, profile, and regular features. "No personal experience, technical, opinion or general-interest material. Most articles are by assignment only." Buys 25-30 mss/year. Query with published clips. Length: 700-3,500 words. Pays $200-1,500.

Photos: Send photos with query or ms. Pays $50-100 for 35mm color transparencies (positives) or $30 for 8×10 or 5×7 b&w prints. Captions, model release (if necessary), and identification of subjects required. Buys all rights.

Columns/Departments: Profile (historical or current golf personalities or characters); Great Moments ("Great Moments in Canadian Golf"—description of great single moments, usually game triumphs); New Equipment (Canadian availability only); Travel (golf destinations, including "hard" information such as greens fees, hotel accommodations, etc.); Instruction (by special assignment only; usually from teaching golf professionals); The Mental Game (psychology of the game, by special assignment only); History (golf equipment collections and collectors, development of the game, legendary figures and events). Buys 17-20 mss/year. Query with published clips or send complete ms. Length: 700-1,700 words. Pays $140-400.

Tips: "Only writers with an extensive knowledge of golf and familiarity with the Canadian golf scene should query or submit in-depth work to *Score*. Many of our features are written by professional people who play the game for a living or work in the industry. All areas mentioned under Columns/Departments are open to freelancers. Most of our *major* features are done on assignment only."

Guns

GUN DIGEST, DBI Books, Inc., 4092 Commercial Ave., Northbrook IL 60062. (312)272-6310. Editor-in-Chief: Ken Warner. 50% freelance written. Prefers to work with published/established writers but works with a small number of new/unpublished writers each year. Annual journal covering guns and shooting. Estab. 1944. **Pays on acceptance.** Publishes ms an average of 20 months after acceptance. Byline given. Buys all rights. Reports in 1 month.

Nonfiction: Buys 50 mss/issue. Query. Length: 500-5,000 words. Pays $100-600; includes photos or illustration package from author.

Photos: State availability of photos with query letter. Reviews 8×10 b&w prints. Payment for photos included in payment for ms. Captions required.

Tips: Award of $1,000 to author of best article (juried) in each issue.

GUN WORLD, 34249 Camino Capistrano, Box HH, Capistrano Beach CA 92624. Editorial Director: Jack Lewis. 50% freelance written. Monthly magazine for ages that "range from mid-teens to mid-60s; many professional types who are interested in relaxation of hunting and shooting." Estab. 1960. Circ. 128,000. Buys 80-100 unsolicited mss/year. **Pays on acceptance.** Publishes ms an average of 6 months after acceptance. Buys first rights and sometimes all rights, but rights reassigned on request. Byline given. Submit seasonal material 5 months in advance. Query for electronic submissions. Reports in 6 weeks. Editorial requirements for #10 SASE.

Nonfiction: General subject matter consists of "well-rounded articles—not by amateurs—on shooting techniques, with anecdotes; hunting stories with tips and knowledge integrated. No poems or fiction. We like broad humor in our articles, so long as it does not reflect upon firearms safety. Most arms magazines are pretty deadly, and we feel shooting can be fun. Too much material aimed at pro-gun people. Most of this is staff-written and most shooters don't have to be told of their rights under the Constitution. We want articles on new developments; off-track inventions, novel military uses of arms; police armament and training techniques; do-it-yourself projects in this field." Buys informational, how-to, personal experience, nostalgia articles. Pays up to $300, sometimes more. Prefers electronic submissions.

Photos: Purchases photos with mss. Captions required. Wants 5×7 b&w photos. Sometimes pays the expenses of writers on assignment.

Tips: "The most frequent mistake made by writers in completing an article for us is surface writing with no real knowledge of the subject. To break in, offer an anecdote having to do with proposed copy."

GUNS & AMMO, Petersen Publishing Co., 6420 Wilshire Blvd., Los Angeles CA 90048. (213)782-2160. Editor: Kevin E. Steele. Managing Editor: Christine Potvin. 10% freelance written. Monthly magazine covering firearms. "Our readers are enthusiasts of handguns, rifles, shotguns and accessories." Circ. 600,000. **Pays on acceptance.** Publishes ms 6 months after acceptance. Byline given. Buys all rights. Submit seasonal material 6 months in advance. Query for electronic submissions. Writer's guidelines for #10 SASE.

Nonfiction: Opinion. Buys 24 mss/year. Send complete ms. Length: 800-2,500 words. Pays $125-500.

Photos: Send photos with submissions. Review 7×9 prints. Offers no additional payment for photos accepted with ms. Captions, model releases, identification of subjects required. Buys all rights.

Columns/Departments: RKBA (opinion column on right to keep and bear arms). Send complete ms. Length: 800-1,200 words. Pays $125-500.

‡GUNS & AMMO ANNUAL, Petersen Publishing Co., 6420 Wilshire Blvd., Los Angeles CA 90048. (213)782-2160. Editor: Bill O'Brien. Managing Editor: Christine Skaglund. 20% freelance written. Annual magazine covering firearms. "Our audience consists of enthusiasts of firearms, shooting sports and accessories." **Pays**

on acceptance. Publishes ms an average of 9-12 months after acceptance. Byline given. Buys all rights. Reports in 1 month.

Nonfiction: Buys 10 mss/year. Send complete ms. Length: 2,000-4,000 words. Pays $250-350.

Photos: Send photos with submission. Reviews 8×10 prints. Offers no additional payment for photos accepted with ms. Captions, model releases, identification of subjects required. Buys all rights.

Tips: "We need feature articles on firearms and accessories. See current issue for examples."

GUNS MAGAZINE, Suite 200, 591 Camino de la Reina, San Diego CA 92108. (619)297-5352. Editor: Scott Ferrell. 20% freelance written. Monthly magazine for firearms enthusiasts. Circ. 200,000. Pays on publication for first North American rights. Publishes manuscripts 4-6 months after acceptance. Writer's guidelines for SASE.

Nonfiction: Test reports on new firearms; round-up articles on firearms types; guns for specific purposes (hunting, target shooting, self-defense); custom gunmakers; and history of modern guns. Buys approximately 10 ms/year. Length: 1,000-2,500 words. Pays $100-350.

Photos: Major emphasis on quality photography. Additional payment of $50-200 for color, 4×5 or 2¼×2¼ preferred.

‡MUZZLE BLASTS, National Muzzle Loading Rifle Association, P.O. Box 67, Friendship IN 47021. (812)667-5131. Editor: Mr. Robert H. Wallace. 65% freelance written. Monthly association magazine covering muzzleloading. "Articles must relate to muzzleloading or the muzzle loading era of American history." Estab. 1939. Circ. 25,000. Pays on publication. Publishes ms an average of 6 months after acceptance. Byline given. Offers $50 kill fee. Buys first North American serial rights, one-time rights and second serial (reprint) rights. Editorial lead time 4 months. Submit seasonal material 6 months in advance. Reports in 1 month on mss. Sample copy and writer's guidelines free on request.

Nonfiction: Book excerpts, general interest, historical/nostalgic, how-to, humor, interview/profile, new product, personal experience, photo feature, technical, travel. "No subject matter that does not pertain to muzzleloading." Buys 80 mss/year. Query. Length: 2,500 words. Pays $300 minimum for assigned articles; $50 minimum for unsolicited articles.

Photos: Send photos with submission. Reviews 5×7 prints. Negotiates payment individually. Captions and model releases required. Buys one-time rights.

Columns/Departments: Buys 96 mss/year. Query. Pays $50-200.

Fiction: Adventure, historical, humorous. Must pertain to muzzleloading. Buys 6 mss/year. Query. Length: 2,500 words. Pays $50-300.

Fillers: Facts. Pays $50.

Tips: Please contact the NMLRA for writer's guidelines.

MUZZLELOADER, The Publication for Black Powder Shooters, Rebel Publishing Co., Inc., Rt. 5 Box 347-M, Texarkana TX 75501. Editor: Bill Scurlock. Managing Editor: Linda Scurlock. Associate Editor: Cherry Lloyd. 50% freelance written. Bimonthly consumer magazine covering black powder shooting, hunting and history. "Devoted exclusively to black powder guns. How to load, shoot and clean them. Reviews of gun makers, specific guns and related products, American history oriented. Emphasis on frontiersmen and Indians of 18th and 19th centures. Living history reenactments and the study of the material culture of early American. Estab. 1974. Circ. 20,000. Pays on publication. Publishes ms an average of 14 months after acceptance. Byline given. Buys first North AMerican serial rights. Submit seasonal material 8-12 months in advance. Query for electronic submissions. Reports in 1 month on queries; 3 months on mss. Sample copy for $3.50. Write's guidelines free on request.

Nonfiction: Historical/nostalgic, how-to (shooting, hunting, making gear), interview/profile (craftsmen in field), new product (guns, etc.) opinion, personal experience, technical (reenacting American History). Buys 30 mss/year. Send complete ms. Length: 1,000-4,000 words. Pays $140 minimum for assigned articles; $100 minimum for unsolicited articles.

Photos: Send photos with submission. Reviews contact sheets and 35mm transparencies. Negotiates payment individually. Captions, model releases and identification of subjects required. Buys one-time rights.

WOMEN & GUNS, SAF Periodicals Group, P.O. Box 488, Buffalo NY 14209-0488. (716)885-6408. Fax: (716)884-4471. Editor: Peggy Tartaro. 30% freelance written. Monthly magazine covering "all aspects of women's involvement with firearms, including self-defense, competition, hunting, and target shooting, as well as related legal and legislative issues." Estab. 1989. Circ. 10,000. Pays within 60 days of publication. Publishes ms an average of 3 months after acceptance. Byline given. Buys first North American serial rights or second serial (reprint) rights. Submit seasonal/holiday material 3 months in advance. Accepts previously published submissions. Send tearsheet of article or typed ms with rights for sale noted and information about when and where the article previously appeared. Pays 30% of their fee for an original article. Query for electronic submissions. Reports in 1 month on queries; 3 months on mss. Free sample copy and writer's guidelines.

Nonfiction: How-to, interview/profile, new product, photo feature, technical. All stories must have photos or illustrations. Buys 20-30 mss/year. Query with or without published clips, or send complete ms. Length:

500-2,500 words. Pays $50-100 for assigned articles; $25-50 for unsolicited articles.

Photos: Send photos with submission. Reviews transparencies and 5×7 color and b&w prints. Offers no additional payment for photos accepted with ms. Captions, model releases, identification of subjects required. Buys one-time rights.

Columns/Departments: Query. Length: 250-500 words. Pays $10-50.

Tips: "Writers must possess superior working knowledge of firearms and insight into related issues."

Horse Racing

THE BACKSTRETCH, 19899 W. Nine Mile Rd., Southfield MI 48075-3960. (810)354-3232. Fax: (810)354-3157. Editor-in-Chief/Publisher: Harriet Dalley. 50% freelance written. Works with a small number of new/unpublished writers each year. Bimonthly magazine for thoroughbred horse trainers, owners, breeders, farm managers, track personnel, jockeys, grooms and racing fans who span the age range from very young to very old. Publication of United Thoroughbred Trainers of America, Inc. Estab. 1962. Circ. 12,000. Publishes ms an average of 3 months after acceptance. Accepts previously published material. Send tearsheet of article. Article fee for reprints negotiated. Reports in 3 months. Sample copy $3 for 9×12 SAE with 7 first-class stamps.

Nonfiction: "*Backstretch* contains mostly general information. Articles deal with biographical material on trainers, owners, jockeys, horses, issues and trends within the industry, historical track articles, etc. Unless writer's material is related to Thoroughbreds and Thoroughbred racing, it should not be submitted. Opinion on Thoroughbreds should be qualified with expertise on the subject. Articles accepted on speculation basis—payment made after material is used. If not suitable, articles are returned if SASE is included. Articles that do not require printing by a specified date are preferred. There is no special length requirement and amount paid depends on material. It is advisable to include photos, if possible. Articles should be original copies and should state whether presented to any other magazine, or whether previously printed in any other magazine. Submit complete ms. We do not buy crossword puzzles, cartoons, newspaper clippings, poetry."

THE QUARTER RACING JOURNAL, American Quarter Horse Association, P.O. Box 32470, Amarillo TX 79120. (806)376-4811. Fax: (806)376-8364. Editor-in-Chief: Jim Jennings. Executive Editor: Audie Rackley. 10% freelance written. Monthly magazine. "The official racing voice of The American Quarter Horse Association. We promote quarter horse racing. Articles include training, breeding, nutrition, sports medicine, health, history, etc." Estab. 1988. Circ. 12,000. **Pays on acceptance.** Publishes ms an average of 3 months after acceptance. Buys first North American serial rights. Submit seasonal/holiday material 3 months in advance. Reports in 1 month on queries. Free sample copy and writer's guidelines.

Nonfiction: Historical (must be on quarter horses or people associated with them), how-to (training), nutrition, health, breeding and opinion. "We welcome submissions year-round. No fiction." Query. Length: 700-2,500 words. Pays $150-300.

Photos: Send photos with submission. Offers no additional payment for photos accepted with ms. Captions and identification of subjects required.

Tips: "Query first—must be familiar with quarter horse racing and be knowledgeable of the sport. If writing on nutrition, it must be applicable. Most open to features covering nutrition, health care. Use a knowledgable source with credentials."

SPUR, 725 Broad St., Augusta GA 30901. (706)722-6060. Fax: (706)724-3873. Editor: Cathy Laws. 80% freelance written. Prefers to work with published/established writers but works with a small number of new/unpublished writers each year. Bimonthly magazine covering thoroughbred horses and the people who are involved in the business and sports of flat racing, steeplechasing, hunter/jumper showing, dressage, driving, foxhunting and polo. Estab. 1964. Circ. 75,000. Pays on publication. Publishes ms an average of 3 months after acceptance. Byline given. Buys first North American rights. Reports in 1 month. Sample copy for $5. Writer's guidelines for #10 SASE.

Nonfiction: Historical/nostalgic, personality profile, farm, special feature, travel and international stories. Buys 50 mss/year. Query with clips of published work, "or we will consider complete manuscripts." Length: 300-4,000 words. Payment negotiable. Sometimes pays the expenses of writers on assignment.

Photos: State availability of photos. Reviews color and b&w contact sheets. Captions, model releases and identification of subjects required.

Tips: "Writers must have a knowledge of horses, horse owners, breeding, training, racing, and riding—or the ability to obtain this knowledge from a subject."

‡**TEAM PENNING USA,** Bryler Publishing Inc. P.O. Box 161848, Ft. Worth TX 76161-1848. (800)848-3882. Editor: Patrick A. Henderson. 100% freelance written. Monthly magazine covering team penning and other equine events. "TPUSA is geared to the dedicated weekend horse-owner, connecting their love of equine sports to the traditional and professional livestock worker. The audience is primarily affluent professionals, business owners, and members of livestock-related professions." Estab. 1989. Circ. 3,000. **Pays on acceptance.** Byline given. Offers 10% kill fee. Buys one-time, second serial (reprint) or simultaneous rights. Editorial lead time 2 months. Submit seasonal material 3 months in advance. Accepts simultaneous and previously

published submissions. Query for electronic submissions. Reports in 1 month on queries; 2 months on mss. Sample copy for 9×12 SAE with 8 first-class stamps. Writer's guidelines for #10 SASE.

Nonfiction: Book excerpts, essays, exposé, general interest, historical/nostalgic, how-to (related to horses and horse handling), humor, interview/profile, new product, opinion, personal experience, photo feature, technical, travel — "just about anything related to recreational horse industry. No religious or inspirational." Buys 25-30 mss/year. Query. Length 750-3,000 words. Pays $200 for assigned articles; $50 for unsolicited articles. Sometimes pays expenses of writers on assignment.

Photos: State availability of photos with submission. Reviews 3×5 prints. Offers $50-100/photo. Negotiates payment individually. Identification of subjects required. Buys one-time rights.

Columns/Departments: Reader's Pen (opinion regarding horses and horse sports).

Fiction: Historical, humorous, mainstream, slice-of-life vignettes, western. Send complete ms. Length: 1,000-3,000 words. Pays $25 minimum.

Poetry: Light verse, traditional, cowboy. "No schmaltz, sentimental, religious or inspirational." Length: 4-48 lines. Pays $10-25.

Fillers: Anecdotes, facts, short humor. Length: 100-500 words. Pays $5-10.

Tips: "Much of our publication is reader-contributed, specifically event news. We are interested in expanding to a wider how-to profile, and news market. We are open to any long-term news events in the horse or horse-related industries. How-tos should cover care and maintenance of horses, facilities, etc., riding tips, tack, etc. especially for Western riding. General interest, how-to and long-term equine news are most open to freelancers."

Hunting and Fishing

ALABAMA GAME & FISH, Game & Fish Publications, Inc., P.O. Box 741, Marietta GA 30061. Editor: Jimmy Jacobs. See *Game & Fish Publications*.

AMERICAN HUNTER, 11250 Waples Mill Rd., Fairfax VA 22030-7400. Editor: Tom Fulgham. 90% freelance written. For hunters who are members of the National Rifle Association. Circ. 1.3 million. Buys first North American serial rights. Byline given. Free sample copy for 9×12 SAE with 5 first-class stamps. Writer's guidelines for #10 SASE.

Nonfiction: Factual material on all phases of hunting. Not interested in material on fishing or camping. Prefers queries. Length: 2,000-2,500 words. Pays $250-450.

Photos: No additional payment made for photos used with mss. Pays $25 for b&w photos purchased without accompanying mss. Pays $50-300 for color.

ARKANSAS SPORTSMAN, Game & Fish Publications, Inc., P.O. Box 741, Marietta GA 30061. (404)953-9222. Editor: Bob Borgwat. See *Game & Fish Publications*.

‡BASSIN', 15115 S. 76th E. Ave., Bixby OK 74008. (918)366-4441. Fax: (918)366-4439. Managing Editor: Simon McCaffery. 90% freelance written. Magazine published 8 times/year covering freshwater fishing with emphasis on black bass. Estab. 1985. Circ. 220,000. Publishes ms an average of 8 months after acceptance. Pays within 30 days of acceptance. Byline given. Buys first North American rights. Submit seasonal material 8 months in advance. Prefers queries. Query for electronic submissions. Reports in 4-5 weeks. Sample copy for $3. Writer's guidelines for #10 SASE.

Nonfiction: How-to and where-to stories on bass fishing. Prefers completed ms. Length: up to 1,200 words. Pays $300-500 on acceptance.

Photos: Send photos with ms. Pays $500 for color cover. Send b&w prints or transparencies. Buys one-time rights. Photo payment on publication.

Tips: "Reduce the common fishing slang terminology when writing for *Bassin'*. This slang is usually regional and confuses anglers in other areas of the country. Good strong features will win me over more quickly than short articles or fillers. Absolutely no poetry. We also need stories on fishing tackle and techniques for catching all species of freshwater bass."

BASSMASTER MAGAZINE, B.A.S.S. Publications, 5845 Carmichael Pkwy., Montgomery AL 36141-0900. (205)272-9530. Fax: (205)279-9530. Editor: Dave Precht. 80% freelance written. Prefers to work with published/established writers. Magazine published 10 issues/year about largemouth, smallmouth and spotted bass for dedicated beginning and advanced bass fishermen. Circ. 550,000. **Pays on acceptance.** Publication date of ms after acceptance "varies — seasonal material could take years"; average time is 8 months. Byline given. Buys all rights. Submit seasonal material 6 months in advance. Reports in 2 months. Sample copy for $2. Writer's guidelines for #10 SASE.

Nonfiction: Historical, interview (of knowledgeable people in the sport), profile (outstanding fishermen), travel (where to go to fish for bass), how-to (catch bass and enjoy the outdoors), new product (reels, rods and bass boats), conservation related to bass fishing. "No 'Me and Joe go fishing' type articles." Query. Length: 400-2,100 words. Pays 20¢/word.

• Needs destination stories (how to fish a certain area) for the Northwest and Northeast.

Columns/Departments: Short Cast/News & Views (upfront regular feature covering news-related events such as new state bass records, unusual bass fishing happenings, conservation, new products and editorial viewpoints); 250-400 words.

Photos: "We want a mixture of b&w and color photos." Pays $50 minimum for b&w prints. Pays $300-350 for color cover transparencies. Captions required; model releases preferred. Buys all rights.

Fillers: Anecdotes, short humor, newsbreaks. Buys 4-5 mss/issue. Length: 250-500 words. Pays $50-100.

Tips: "Editorial direction continues in the short, more direct how-to article. Compact, easy-to-read information is our objective. Shorter articles with good graphics, such as how-to diagrams, step-by-step instruction, etc., will enhance a writer's articles submitted to *Bassmaster Magazine*. The most frequent mistakes made by writers in completing an article for us are poor grammar, poor writing, poor organization and superficial research."

BC OUTDOORS, OP Publishing, 202-1132 Hamilton St., Vancouver, British Columbia V6B 2S2 Canada. (604)687-1581. Fax: (604)687-1925. Editor: Karl Bruhn. 80% freelance written. Works with a small number of new/unpublished writers each year. Magazine published 8 times/year covering fishing, camping, hunting and the environment of outdoor recreation. Estab. 1946. Circ. 42,000. Pays on publication. Publishes ms an average of 3 months after acceptance. Byline given. Offers negotiable kill fee. Buys first North American serial rights. Query for electronic submissions. Reports in 1 month. Sample copy and writer's guidelines for 8 × 10 SAE with $2 postage.

Nonfiction: How-to (new or innovative articles on outdoor subjects), personal experience (outdoor adventure), outdoor topics specific to British Columbia. "We would like to receive how-to, where-to features dealing with hunting and fishing in British Columbia and the Yukon." Buys 80-90 mss/year. Query. Length: 1,500-2,000 words. Pays $300-500. Sometimes pays the expenses of writers on assignment.
  • Wants in-depth, informative, professional writing only.

Photos: State availability of photos with query. Pays $25-75 on publication for 5 × 7 b&w prints; $35-150 for color contact sheets and 35mm transparencies. Captions and identification of subjects required. Buys one-time rights.

Tips: "Emphasis on environmental issues. Those pieces with a conservation component have a better chance of being published. Subject must be specific to British Columbia. We receive many manuscripts written by people who obviously do not know the magazine or market. The writer has a better chance of breaking in at our publication with short, lesser-paying articles and fillers, because we have a stable of regular writers in constant touch who produce most main features."

CALIFORNIA GAME & FISH, Game & Fish Publications, Inc., Box 741, Marietta GA 30061. Editor: Burt Carey. See *Game & Fish Publications*.

FIELD & STREAM, 2 Park Ave., New York NY 10016-5695. Editor: Duncan Barnes. 50% freelance written. Eager to work with new/unpublished writers. Monthly. "Broad-based service magazine for the hunter and fisherman. Editorial content ranges from very basic how-to stories detailing a useful technique or a device that sportsmen can make, to articles of penetrating depth about national hunting, fishing, and related activities. Also humor and personal essays, nostalgia and 'mood pieces' on the hunting or fishing experience." Estab. 1895. **Pays on acceptance.** Buys first rights. Byline given. Occasionally accepts previously published submissions. Send photocopy of article and information about when and where it previously appeared. Reports in 2 months. Query. Writer's guidelines for #10 SASE.
  • Ranked as one of the best markets for freelance writers in *Writer's Digest* magazine's annual "Top 100 Markets," January 1994.

Nonfiction: Length: 1,500-2,000 words for features. Payment varies depending on the quality of work, importance of the article. Pays $800 and up for major features. *Field & Stream* also publishes regional sections with feature articles on hunting and fishing in specific areas of the country. The sections are geographically divided into East, Midwest, West and South, and appear 12 months/year.

Photos: Prefers color slides to b&w. Query first with photos. When photos purchased separately, pays $450 minimum for color. Buys first rights to photos.

Fillers: Buys short "how it's done" fillers for "By the Way." Must be unusual or helpful subjects. Also buys "Field Guide" pieces, short articles on natural phenomena as specifically related to hunting and fishing; "Myths and Misconceptions," short pieces debunking a commonly held belief about hunting and fishing, and short "Outdoor Basics" of "Sportsmen's Project" articles.

‡THE FISHERMAN, LIF Publishing Corp., 14 Ramsey Rd., Shirley NY 11967-4704. (516)345-5200. Fax: (516)345-5304. Editor: Fred Golofaro. Senior Editor: Tim Coleman. 5 regional editions: *Long Island, Metropolitan New York*, Fred Golofaro, editor; *New England*, Tim Coleman, editor; *New Jersey*, Dusty Rhodes, editor; *Delaware-Maryland-Virginia*, Bruce Williams, editor; and *Florida*, Andy Dear, editor. 75% freelance written. A weekly magazine covering fishing with an emphasis on saltwater. Combined circ. 110,000. Pays on publication. Byline given. Offers variable kill fee. Buys all rights. Articles may be run in one or more regional editions by choice of the editors. Submit seasonal/holiday material 2 months in advance. Reports in 4-6 weeks. Free sample copy and writer's guidelines.

Nonfiction: Send submission to editor of regional edition. General interest, historical/nostalgic, how-to, interview/profile, personal experience, photo feature, technical, travel. Special issues: Trout Fishing (April); Bass Fishing (June); Offshore Fishing (July); Surf Fishing (September); Tackle (October); Electronics (November). "No 'me and Joe' tales. We stress how, where, when, why." Buys approx. 300 mss/year, each edition. Length: 1,200-1,500 words. Pays $100-150 for unsolicited feature articles.

Photos: Send photos with submission; also buys single photos for cover use (b&w pays $50; color pays $100). Offers no additional payment for photos accepted with ms. Identification of subjects required.

Tips: "Focus on specific how-to and where-to subjects within each region."

FISHING WORLD, KC Publishing, Suite 310, 700 47th St., Kansas City MO 64112. (816)531-5730. Fax: (816)531-3873. Editor: David Richey. 100% freelance written. Bimonthly. Estab. 1955. Circ. 250,000. **Pays on acceptance.** Buys first North American serial rights. Publishes ms an average of 6 months after acceptance. Reports in 3 weeks. Writer's guidelines for #10 SASE.

Nonfiction: "Destination-oriented fishing feature articles should range from 1,200-1,500 words with the shorter preferred. A good selection of transparencies must accompany each submission. Subject matter should be a hot fishing site, either freshwater or salt. Where-to articles should be accompanied by sidebars covering how to make reservations and arrange transportation, how to get there, where to stay. Angling methods should be developed in clear detail, with accurate and useful information about tackle and boats." Pays $350. Brief queries accompanied by photos are preferred.

Photos: "Cover shots are purchased separately, rather than selected from those accompanying mss. The editor favors boat-fishing drama rather than serenity in selecting cover shots. Transparencies selected for cover use pay an additional $300."

Tips: Looking for "quality photography and more West Coast fishing. Send laundry list (5-10 ideas) of query ideas and recent samples of published works."

FLORIDA GAME & FISH, Game & Fish Publications, Inc., Box 741, Marietta GA 30061. (404)953-9222. Editor: Jimmy Jacobs. See *Game & Fish Publications*.

FLORIDA SPORTSMAN, Wickstrom Publishers Inc., 5901 SW 74 St., Miami FL 33143. (305)661-4222. Fax: (305)284-0277. Editor: Biff Lampton. 30% freelance written. Works with new/unpublished writers. Monthly magazine covering fishing, boating and related sports—Florida and Caribbean only. Circ. 100,000. **Pays on acceptance.** Publishes ms an average of 6 months after acceptance. Byline given. Offers 50% kill fee. Buys first North American serial rights. Submit seasonal/holiday material 6 months in advance. Reports in 1 week on queries; 1 month on mss. *Writer's Market* recommends allowing 2 months for reply. Free sample copy. Writer's guidelines for #10 SASE.

Nonfiction: Essays (environment or nature), how-to (fishing, hunting, boating), humor (outdoors angle), personal experience (in fishing, etc.), technical (boats, tackle, etc., as particularly suitable for Florida specialties). "We use reader service pieces almost entirely—how-to, where-to, etc. One or two environmental pieces per issue as well. Writers *must* be Florida based, or have lengthy experience in Florida outdoors. All articles must have strong Florida emphasis. We do not want to see general how-to-fish-or-boat pieces which might well appear in a national or wide-regional magazine." Buys 40-60 mss/year. Query. Length: 2,000-3,000 words. Pays $300-400. Sometimes pays expenses of writers on assignment.

Photos: Send photos with submission. Reviews 35mm transparencies and 4×5 and larger prints. Offers no additional payment for photos accepted with ms. Buys one-time rights.

Tips: "Feature articles are most open to freelancers; however there is little chance of acceptance unless contributor is an accomplished and avid outdoorsman *and* a competent writer-photographer with considerable experience in Florida."

FLORIDA WILDLIFE, Florida Game & Fresh Water Fish Commission, 620 S. Meridian St., Tallahassee FL 32399-1600. (904)488-5563. Fax: (904)488-6988. Editor: Dick Sublette. About 30% freelance written. Bimonthly 4-color state magazine covering hunting, natural history, fishing, endangered species and wildlife conservation. "In outdoor sporting articles we seek themes of wholesome recreation. In nature articles we seek accuracy and conservation purpose." Estab. 1947. Circ. 25,000. Pays on publication. Byline given. Buys first North American serial and occasionally second serial (reprint) rights. Submit seasonal/holiday material 6 months in advance. Accepts simultaneous and previously published submissions. "Inform us if it is previously published work." Reports in 2 months (acknowledgement of receipt of materials); up to 2 years for acceptance, usually less for rejections. Prefers photo/ms packages. Sample copy for $2. Writer's/photographer's guidelines for SASE.

Nonfiction: General interest (bird watching, hiking, camping, boating), how-to (hunting and fishing), humor (wildlife related; no anthropomorphism), inspirational (conservation oriented), personal experience (wildlife, hunting, fishing, outdoors), photo feature (Florida species: game, nongame, botany), technical (rarely purchased, but open to experts). "We buy general interest hunting, fishing and nature stories. No stories that humanize animals, or opinionated stories not based on confirmable facts." Buys 30-40 mss/year. Send slides/ms. Length: 500-1,500 words. Generally pays $50/published page.

Photos: State availability of photos with story query. Prefer 35mm color slides of hunting, fishing, and natural science series of Florida wildlife species. Pays $20-50 for inside photos; $100 for front cover photos, $50 for back cover. "We like short, specific captions." Buys one-time rights.

Fiction: "We rarely buy fiction, and then only if it is true to life and directly related to good sportsmanship and conservation. No fairy tales, erotica, profanity or obscenity." Buys 2-3 mss/year. Send complete mss and label "fiction." Length: 500-1,200 words. Generally pays $50/published page.

Tips: "Read and study recent issues for subject matter, style and examples of our viewpoint, philosophy and treatment. We look for wholesome recreation, ethics, safety, and good outdoor experience more than bagging the game in our stories. We usually need well-written hunting and freshwater fishing articles that are entertaining and informative and that describe places to hunt and fish in Florida."

FLY FISHERMAN, Cowles Magazines Inc., P.O. Box 8200, Harrisburg PA 17105-8200. (717)657-9555. Fax: (717)657-9526. Editor and Publisher: John Randolph. Managing Editor: Philip Hanyok. 85-90% freelance written. Bimonthly magazine on fly fishing. Estab. 1969. Circ. 130,000. Reports in 2 months. Sample copy for 9 × 12 SAE with 7 first-class stamps.

FUR-FISH-GAME, 2878 E. Main, Columbus OH 43209-9947. Editor: Mitch Cox. 65% freelance written. Works with a small number of new/unpublished writers each year. Monthly magazine for outdoorsmen of all ages who are interested in hunting, fishing, trapping, dogs, camping, conservation and related topics. Estab. 1900. Circ. 105,000. **Pays on acceptance.** Publishes ms an average of 7 months after acceptance. Byline given. Buys first serial rights or all rights. Reports in 2 months. Query. Sample copy for $1 and 9 × 12 with SAE. Writer's guidelines for #10 SASE.

Nonfiction: "We are looking for informative, down-to-earth stories about hunting, fishing, trapping, dogs, camping, boating, conservation and related subjects. Nostalgic articles are also used. Many of our stories are 'how-to' and should appeal to small-town and rural readers who are true outdoorsmen. Some recent articles have told how to train a gun dog, catch big-water catfish, outfit a bowhunter and trap late-season muskrat. We also use personal experience stories and an occasional profile, such as an article about an old-time trapper. 'Where-to' stories are used occasionally if they have broad appeal." Length: 1,500-3,000 words. Pays $75-150 depending upon quality, photo support, and importance to magazine. Short filler stories pay $35-80.

Photos: Send photos with ms. Photos are part of ms package and receive no additional payment. Prefer b&w but color prints or transparencies OK. Prints can be 5 × 7 or 8 × 10. Captions required.

Tips: "We are always looking for quality articles that tell how to hunt or fish for game animals or birds that are popular with everyday outdoorsmen but often overlooked in other publications, such as catfish, bluegill, crappie, squirrel, rabbit, crows, etc. We also use articles on standard seasonal subjects such as deer and pheasant, but like to see a fresh approach or new technique. Trapping articles, especially instructional ones based on personal experience, are useful all year. Articles on gun dogs, ginseng and do-it-yourself projects are also popular with our readers. An assortment of photos and/or sketches greatly enhances any manuscript, and sidebars, where applicable, can also help."

GAME & FISH PUBLICATIONS, INC., Suite 110, 2250 Newmarket Parkway, Marietta GA 30067. (404)953-9222. Fax: (404)933-9510. Editorial Director: Ken Dunwoody. Publishes 30 different monthly outdoor magazines, each one covering the fishing and hunting opportunities in a particular state or region (see individual titles and editors). 90% freelance written. Estab. 1975. Total circ. 500,000. Pays 75 days prior to cover date of issue. Publishes ms an average of 6 months after acceptance. Byline given. Offers negotiable kill fee. Buys first North American serial rights. Submit seasonal material at least 8 months in advance. Editors prefer to hold queries until that season's material is assigned. Accepts previously published submissions. Send typed ms with rights for sale noted and information about when and where the article previously appeared. Pays 100% of their fee for an original article. Reports in 3 months on mss. Sample copy for $2.50 and 9 × 12 SASE. Writer's guidelines for #10 SASE.

Nonfiction: Prefer queries over unsolicited ms. Article lengths either 1,500 or 2,500 words. Pays separately for articles and accompanying photos. Manuscripts pay $125-300, cover photos $250, inside color $75 and b&w $25. Reviews transparencies and b&w prints. Prefers captions and identification of species/subjects. Buys one-time rights to photos.

Fiction: Buys some humor and nostalgia stories pertaining to hunting and fishing. Pays $125-250. Length 1,500-2,500 words.

Tips: "Our readers are experienced anglers and hunters, and we try to provide them with useful, entertaining articles about where, when and how to enjoy the best hunting and fishing in their state or region. We also cover topics concerning game and fish management, conservation and environmental issues. Most articles should be aimed at outdoorsmen in one particular state. After familiarizing themselves with our magazine(s), writers should query the appropriate state editor (see individual listings) or send to Ken Dunwoody."

GEORGIA SPORTSMAN, Game & Fish Publications, Box 741, Marietta GA 30061. (404)953-9222. Editor: Jimmy Jacobs. See *Game & Fish Publications.*

‡**GRAY'S SPORTY JOURNAL,** P.O. Box 1207, Augusta CA 30903-1207. Editor: David C. Foster. Contact: John Hewitt. 100% freelance written. Bimonthly magazine covering hunting and fishing. "Engage discerning audience with high quality literature (fiction and nonfiction), poetry, beautiful photography and original art." Estab. 1976. Circ. 30,000. Pays on publication. Publishes ms an average of 1 year after acceptance. Byline given. Buys first North American serial rights. Editorial lead time 2 months. Submit seasonal material 1 year in advance. Accepts simultaneous submissions. Query for electronic submissions. Sample copy for $3. Writer's guidelines free on request.
Nonfiction: Historical/nostalgic, humor, personal experience, photo feature, travel. Special issues: Expeditions & Guides Book (December), travel-related book for hunters and anglers). Buys 70 mss/year. Send complete ms. Pays $125-1,500. Sometimes pays expenses of writers on assignment.
Photos: Freelancers should state availability of photos with submission. Reviews transparencies. Offers $75-250/photo. Identification of subjects required. Buys one-time rights.
Fiction: Adventure, sporting life. Buys 30 mss/year. Send complete ms. Pays $500-2500.
Poetry: Contact: John Hewitt. Free verse, light verse, traditional. Buys 6 poems/year. Submit maximum 3 poems. Pays $250.

GREAT PLAINS GAME & FISH, Game & Fish Publications, Box 741, Marietta GA 30061. (404)953-9222. Editor: Nick Gilmore. See *Game & Fish Publications*.

GULF COAST FISHERMAN, Harold Wells Gulf Coast Fisherman, Inc., P.O. Drawer P, 401 W. Main St., Port Lavaca TX 77979. (512)552-8864. Publisher/Editor: Gary M. Ralston. 95% freelance written. Quarterly magazine covering Gulf Coast saltwater fishing. "All editorial material is designed to expand the knowledge of the Gulf Coast angler and promote saltwater fishing in general." Estab. 1979. Circ 15,000. Pays on publication. Publishes ms an average of 2 months after acceptance. Byline given. Buys first North American serial rights. Submit seasonal/holiday material 2 months in advance. Query for electronic submissions. Reports in 1 month. *Writer's Market* recommends allowing 2 months for reply. Sample copy and writer's guidelines for 9 × 12 SAE with 5 first-class stamps.
Nonfiction: How-to (any aspect relating to saltwater fishing that provides the reader specifics on use of tackle, boats, finding fish, etc.), interview/profile, new product, personal experience, technical. Buys 25 mss/year. Query with or without published clips or send complete ms. Length: 900-1,800 words. Pays $100-275.
Photos: State availability of photos with submission. Offers no additional payment for photos accepted with ms. Captions and identification of subjects required. Buys one-time rights.
Tips: "Features are the area of our publication most open to freelancers. Subject matter should concern some aspect of or be in relation to saltwater fishing in coastal bays or offshore. Prefers electronic submissions – 3.5 Mac-compatible, or 5.25 DOS."

ILLINOIS GAME & FISH, Game & Fish Publications, Inc., Box 741, Marietta GA 30061. (404)953-9222. Editor: Bill Hartlage. See *Game & Fish Publications*.

INDIANA GAME & FISH, Game & Fish Publications, Inc., Box 741, Marietta GA 30061. (404)953-9222. Editor: Ken Freel. See *Game & Fish Publications*.

IOWA GAME & FISH, Game & Fish Publications, Inc., Box 741, Marietta GA 30061. (404)953-9222. Editor: Bill Hartlage. See *Game & Fish Publications*.

KENTUCKY GAME & FISH, Game & Fish Publications, Inc., Box 741, Marietta GA 30061. (404)953-9222. Editor: Bill Hartlage. See *Game & Fish Publications*.

LOUISIANA GAME & FISH, Game & Fish Publications, Inc., Box 741, Marietta GA 30061. (404)953-9222. Editor: Bob Borgwat. See *Game & Fish Publications*.

MARLIN, The International Sportfishing Magazine, Marlin Magazine, a division of World Publications, Inc., P.O. Box 2456, Winter Park FL 32790. (407)628-4802. Editor: David Ritchie. 90% freelance written. Bimonthly magazine on big game fishing. "*Marlin* covers the sport of big game fishing (billfish, tuna, sharks, dorado and wahoo). Our readers are sophisticated, affluent and serious about their sport—they expect a high-class, well-written magazine that provides information and practical advice." Estab. 1982. Circ. 30,000. **Pays on acceptance for text,** on publication for photos. Publishes ms an average of 3 months after acceptance. Byline given. Buys first North American serial rights. Submit seasonal/holiday material 2-3 months in advance. Query for electronic submissions. Sample copy and writer's guidelines for $2.50 and SAE.

Always check the most recent copy of a magazine for the address and editor's name before you send in a query or manuscript.

Nonfiction: General interest, how-to (bait-rigging, tackle maintenance, etc.), new product, personal experience, photo feature, technical, travel. "No freshwater fishing stories. No 'me & Joe went fishing' stories, unless top quality writing." Buys 30-50 mss/year. Query with published clips. Length: 800-2,200 words. Pays $250-500.

Photos: State availability of photos with submission. Original slides, please. Offers $25-300/photo. $500 for a cover. Buys one-time rights.

Columns/Departments: Tournament Reports (reports on winners of major big game fishing tournaments), 300-600 words; Blue Water Currents (news features), 300-900 words. Buys 25 mss/year. Query. Pays $100-250. Accepts previously published articles in news section only. Send photocopy of article, including information about when and where the article previously appeared. For reprints, pays 50-75% of the amount paid for an original article.

Tips: "Tournament reports are a good way to break in to *Marlin*. Make them short but accurate, and provide photos of fishing action (*not* dead fish hanging up at the docks!). We always need how-tos and news items. Our destination pieces (travel stories) emphasize where and when to fish, but include information on where to stay also. For features: crisp, high action stories—nothing flowery or academic. Technical/how-to: concise and informational—specific details. News: Again, concise with good details—watch for legislation affecting big game fishing, outstanding catches, new clubs and organizations, new trends and conservation issues."

MICHIGAN OUT-OF-DOORS, P.O. Box 30235, Lansing MI 48909. (517)371-1041. Fax: (517)371-1505. Editor: Kenneth S. Lowe. 50% freelance written. Works with a small number of new/unpublished writers each year. Monthly magazine emphasizing outdoor recreation, especially hunting and fishing, conservation and environmental affairs. Estab. 1947. Circ. 130,000. **Pays on acceptance.** Publishes ms an average of 6 months after acceptance. Byline given. Buys first North American serial rights. Phone queries OK. Submit seasonal/holiday material 6 months in advance. Reports in 1 month. *Writer's Market* recommends allowing 2 months for reply. Sample copy for $2. Free writer's guidelines.

Nonfiction: Exposé, historical, how-to, informational, interview, nostalgia, personal experience, personal opinion, photo feature, profile. No humor or poetry. "Stories *must* have a Michigan slant unless they treat a subject of universal interest to our readers." Buys 8 mss/issue. Send complete ms. Length: 1,000-3,000 words. Pays $75 minimum for feature stories. Pays expenses of writers on assignment.

Photos: Purchased with or without accompanying ms. Pays $15 minimum for any size b&w glossy prints; $100 maximum for color (for cover). Offers no additional payment for photos accepted with accompanying ms. Buys one-time rights. Captions preferred.

Tips: "Top priority is placed on true accounts of personal adventures in the out-of-doors—well-written tales of very unusual incidents encountered while hunting, fishing, camping, hiking, etc. The most rewarding aspect of working with freelancers is realizing we had a part in their development. But it's annoying to respond to queries that never produce a manuscript."

MICHIGAN SPORTSMAN, Game & Fish Publications, Inc., Box 741, Marietta GA 30061. (404)953-9222. Editor: Dennis Schmidt. See *Game & Fish Publications*.

MID WEST OUTDOORS, Mid West Outdoors, Ltd., 111 Shore Drive, Hinsdale (Burr Ridge) IL 60521-5885. (708)887-7722. Fax: (708)887-1958. Editor: Gene Laulunen. Monthly tabloid emphasizing fishing, hunting, camping and boating. 100% freelance written. Estab. 1967. Circ. 50,000. Pays on publication. Buys simultaneous rights. Byline given. Submit seasonal material 2 months in advance. Accepts simultaneous and previously published submissions. Send tearsheet of article. Reports in 3 weeks. Publishes ms an average of 3 months after acceptance. Sample copy for $1. Writer's guidelines for #10 SASE.

Nonfiction: How-to (fishing, hunting, camping in the Midwest) and where-to-go (fishing, hunting, camping within 500 miles of Chicago). "We do not want to see any articles on 'my first fishing, hunting or camping experiences,' 'cleaning my tackle box,' 'tackle tune-up,' or 'catch and release.'" Buys 1,800 unsolicited mss/year. Send complete ms or story on 3.5" diskette with ms included. Length: 1,000-1,500 words. Pays $15-30. Pays $25 for reprints.

Photos: Offers no additional payment for photos accompanying ms unless used as covers; uses b&w prints. Buys all rights. Captions required.

Columns/Departments: Fishing, Hunting. Open to suggestions for columns/departments. Send complete ms. Pays $25.

Tips: "Break in with a great unknown fishing hole or new technique within 500 miles of Chicago. Where, how, when and why. Know the type of publication you are sending material to."

MID-ATLANTIC GAME & FISH, Game & Fish Publications, Inc., Box 741, Marietta GA 30061. (404)953-9222. Editor: Ken Freel. See *Game & Fish Publications*.

MINNESOTA SPORTSMAN, Game & Fish Publications, Inc., Box 741, Marietta GA 30061. (404)953-9222. Editor: Dennis Schmidt. See *Game & Fish Publications*.

MISSISSIPPI GAME & FISH, Game & Fish Publications, Inc., Box 741, Marietta GA 30061. (404)953-9222. Editor: Bob Borgwat. See *Game & Fish Publications*.

MISSOURI GAME & FISH, Game & Fish Publications, Inc., Box 741, Marietta GA 30061. (404)953-9222. Editor: Bob Borgwat. See *Game & Fish Publications*.

MUSKY HUNTER MAGAZINE, Esox Publishing, Inc., #10, 2632 S. Packerland, Green Bay WI 54313-1796. (414)496-0334. Fax: (414)496-0332. Editor: Jim Saric. 90% freelance written. Bimonthly magazine on Musky fishing. "Serves the vertical market of Musky fishing enthusiasts. We're interested in how-to where-to articles." Estab. 1988. Circ. 18,000. Pays on publication. Publishes ms an average of 4 months after acceptance. Byline given. Buys first or one-time rights. Submit seasonal/holiday material 4 months in advance. Accepts previously published submissions. Send photocopy of article or typed ms with rights for sale noted and information about when and where the article previously appeared. For reprints pays 75-100% of the amount paid for an original article. Reports in 2 months. Sample copy for 9×12 SAE with 5 first-class stamps. Writer's guidelines for #10 SASE.
Nonfiction: Historical/nostalgic (related only to Musky fishing), how-to (modify lures, boats and tackle for Musky fishing), personal experience (must be Musky fishing experience), technical (fishing equipment), travel (to lakes and areas for Musky fishing). Buys 50 mss/year. Send complete ms. Length: 1,000-2,000 words. Pays $100-200 for assigned articles; $50-200 for unsolicited articles. Payment of contributor copies or other premiums negotiable.
Photos: Send photos with submission. Reviews 35mm transparencies and 3×5 prints. Offers no additional payment for photos accepted with ms. Identification of subjects required. Buys one-time rights.

NEW ENGLAND GAME & FISH, Game & Fish Publications, Inc., Box 741, Marietta GA 30061. (404)953-9222. Editor: Steve Carpenteri. See *Game & Fish Publications*.

NEW YORK GAME & FISH, Game & Fish Publications, Inc., Box 741, Marietta GA 30061. (404)953-9222. Editor: Steve Carpenteri. See *Game & Fish Publications*.

NORTH AMERICAN FISHERMAN, Official Publication of North American Fishing Club, Suite 260, 12301 Whitewater Dr., Minnetonka MN 55343. (612)936-0555. Publisher: Mark LaBarbera. Editor: Steve Pennaz. 75% freelance written. Bimonthly magazine on fresh- and saltwater fishing across North America. Estab. 1987. Circ. 430,000. **Pays on acceptance.** Publishes ms an average of 4 months after acceptance. Offers $150 kill fee. Buys first North American serial, one-time and all rights. Submit seasonal/holiday material 6 months in advance. Reports in 1 month. Sample copy for $5 and 9×12 SAE with 6 first-class stamps. Prefers written queries.
 • No longer accepts phone queries.
Nonfiction: How-to (species-specific information on how-to catch fish), news briefs on fishing from various state agencies, travel (where to information on first class fishing lodges). Buys 35-40 mss/year. Query by mail. Length: 700-2,100. Pays $100-500.
Photos: Send photos with submission. Additional payment made for photos accepted with ms. Captions and identification of subjects required. Buys one-time rights. Pays up to $200 for inside art, $500 for cover.
Fillers: Facts, newsbreaks. Buys 60/year. Length: 50-100. Pays $35-50.
Tips: "We are looking for news briefs on important law changes, new lakes, etc. Areas most open for freelancers are: full-length features, cover photos and news briefs. Know what subject you are writing about. Our audience of avid fresh and saltwater anglers know how to fish and will see through weak or dated fishing information. Must be on cutting edge for material to be considered."

NORTH AMERICAN WHITETAIL, The Magazine Devoted to the Serious Trophy Deer Hunter, Game & Fish Publications, Inc., Suite 110, 2250 Newmarket Parkway, Marietta GA 30067. (404)953-9222. Fax: (404)933-9510. Editor: Gordon Whittington. 70% freelance written. Magazine published 8 times/year about hunting trophy-class white-tailed deer in North America, primarily the US. "We provide the serious hunter with highly sophisticated information about trophy-class whitetails and how, when and where to hunt them. We are not a general hunting magazine or a magazine for the very occasional deer hunter." Estab. 1982. Circ. 170,000. Pays 75 days prior to cover date of issue. Publishes ms an average of 6 months after acceptance. Byline given. Offers negotiable kill fee. Buys first North American serial rights. Submit seasonal/holiday material 10 months in advance. Reports in 3 months on mss. Editor prefers to keep queries on file, without notification, until the article can be assigned or author informs of prior sale. Sample copy for $3 and 9×12 SAE with 7 first-class stamps. Writer's guidelines for #10 SASE.
Nonfiction: How-to interview/profile. Buys 50 mss/year. Query. Length: 1,000-3,000 words. Pays $150-400.
Photos: Send photos with submission. Reviews 2×2 transparencies and 8×10 prints. Offers no additional payment for photos accepted with ms. Captions and identification of subjects required. Buys one-time rights.
Columns/Departments: Trails and Tails (nostalgic, humorous or other entertaining styles of deer-hunting material, fictional or nonfictional), 1,400 words. Buys 8 mss/year. Send complete ms. Pays $150.

Tips: "Our articles are written by persons who are deer hunters first, writers second. Our hard-core hunting audience can see through material produced by non-hunters or those with only marginal deer-hunting expertise. We have a continual need for expert profiles/interviews. Study the magazine to see what type of hunting expert it takes to qualify for our use, and look at how those articles have been directed by the writers. Good photography of the interviewee and his hunting results must accompany such pieces."

NORTH CAROLINA GAME & FISH, Game & Fish Publications, Inc., Box 741, Marietta GA 30061. (404)953-9222. Editor: Jeff Samsel. See *Game & Fish Publications*.

OHIO GAME & FISH, Game & Fish Publications, Inc., Box 741, Marietta GA 30061. (404)953-9222. Editor: Steve Carpenteri. See *Game & Fish Publications*.

OHIO OUT-OF-DOORS, Redbird Publications, P.O. Box 117, St. Marys OH 45885. (419)394-3226. Publisher/Managing Editor: John Andreoni. 40-50% freelance written. Monthly magazine that covers outdoor activities and conservation issues. "We cover outdoors-related topics; the wise use of game and fish management; appreciation of the outdoors. Our readers are hunters, fishermen and conservationists." Estab. 1991. Circ. 4,000. Pays on publication. Byline given. Not copyrighted. Buys first North American serial rights. Submit seasonal/holiday material 4 months in advance. Accepts previously published submissions. Send typed ms with rights for sale noted and information about when and where the article previously appeared. Pays 100% of the amount paid for an original article. Query for electronic submissions. Reports in 2 weeks on queries. Sample copy for 11 × 13 SAE with 4 first-class stamps.
Nonfiction: Essays, general interest, historical/nostalgic, how-to (catch fish, make rods, learn to shoot or do anything outdoor oriented), humor, interview/profile, new product, opinion, photo feature, technical, travel. "We are looking for material on spring fishing, upland game, wildlife hunting, fishing for specifics, turkey hunting, deer hunting, boats, mushroom hunting, ice fishing and black powder guns. No 'Bob and me' or 'me and Joe' articles focusing on kill or catch." Buys 20 mss/year. *Query* only. Length: 500-2,000 words. Pays $25-50 for assigned articles.
Photos: State availability of photos or send photos with submission. Reviews 35mm vertical transparencies, 5×7 prints. Offers $5 for b&w, $10 for color and $25 for cover (one-time use vertical shot).
Columns/Departments: Buys 36 mss/year. *Query.* Length: 500-800 words. Pays $25 minimum.
Fiction: Adventure (outdoor slant), historical (outdoor slant), humorous. Buys few mss/year. Query. Length: 500-2,000 words.
Tips: "Writers must sell publisher/editor with a query. Query should reflect writing style. Writers will have the best luck submitting material for features. Pick a specific topic, research well, quote authorities when possible and include a powerful, well-written lead."

OKLAHOMA GAME & FISH, Game & Fish Publications, Box 741, Marietta GA 30061. (404)953-9222. Fax: (404)933-9510. Editor: Nick Gilmore. See *Game & Fish Publications*.

OUTDOOR LIFE, Times Mirror Magazines, Inc., 2 Park Ave., New York NY 10016. (212)779-5000. Editor: Vin T. Sparano. Executive Editor: Gerald Bethge. 95% freelance written. Monthly magazine covering hunting and fishing. Estab. 1890. Circ. 1.5 million. **Pays on acceptance.** Publishes ms an average of 6-12 months after acceptance. Byline given. Buys first North American serial rights. Submit seasonal/holiday material 1 year in advance. Accepts previously published submissions on occasion. Reports in 1 month on queries; 2 months on mss. Writer's guidelines for #10 SASE.
Nonfiction: Book excerpts, essays, how-to (must cover hunting, fishing or related outdoor activities), interview/profile, new product, personal experience, photo feature, technical, travel. No articles that are too general in scope—need to write specifically. Buys 400 mss/year. Query first; photos are *very important.*" Length: 800-3,000 words. Pays $350-600 for 1,000-word features and regionals; $900-1,200 for 2,000-word or longer national features.
Photos: Send photos with submission. Reviews 35mm transparencies and 8 × 10 b&w prints. Offers variable payment. Captions and identification of subjects required. Buys one-time rights. "May offer to buy photos after first use if considered good and have potential to be used with other articles in the future (file photos)." Pays $100 for ¼ page color to $800 for 2-page spread in color; $1,000 for covers. All photos must be stamped with name and address.
Columns/Departments: This Happened to Me (true-to-life, personal outdoor adventure, harrowing experience), approximately 300 words. Buys 12 mss/year. Pays $50. Only those published will be notified.
Fillers: National and International newsbreaks (200 words maximum). Newsbreaks and do-it-yourself for hunters and fishermen. Buys unlimited number/year. Length: 1,000 words maximum. Payment varies.
Tips: "It is best for freelancers to break in by writing features for one of the regional sections—East, Midwest, South, West. These are where-to-go oriented and run from 800-1,500 words. Writers must send one-page query with photos."

PENNSYLVANIA ANGLER, Pennsylvania Fish and Boat Commission, P.O. Box 67000, Harrisburg PA 17106-7000. (717)657-4518. CompuServe 76247, 624. Editor: Art Michaels. 80% freelance written. Prefers to work with published/established writers but works with a few unpublished writers every year. Monthly magazine covering fishing and related conservation topics in Pennsylvania. Circ. 50,000. Pays 2 months after acceptance. Publishes ms an average of 6 months after acceptance. Byline given. Rights purchased vary. Submit seasonal/holiday material 8 months in advance. Query for electronic submission preferred. Reports in 2 weeks on queries; 2 months on mss. Sample copy for 9 × 12 SAE with 4 first-class stamps. Writer's guidelines for #10 SASE.

Nonfiction: How-to, where-to, technical. No saltwater or hunting material. Buys 120 mss/year. Query. Length: 500-3,000 words. Pays $25-300.

Photos: Send photos with submission. Reviews 35mm and larger transparencies and 8 × 10 b&w prints. Offers no additional payment for photos accepted with ms. Captions, model releases and identification of subjects required. Also reviews photos separately. Rights purchased and rates vary.

Tips: "Our mainstays are how-tos, where-tos and conservation pieces."

PENNSYLVANIA GAME & FISH, Game & Fish Publications, Inc., Box 741, Marietta GA 30061. (404)953-9222. Editor: Steve Carpenteri. See *Game & Fish Publications*.

PETERSEN'S HUNTING, Petersen's Publishing Co., 8490 Sunset Blvd., Los Angeles CA 90069. (310)854-2184. Editor: Todd Smith. Managing Editor: Denise LaSalle. 40% freelance written. Works with a small number of new/unpublished writers each year. Monthly magazine covering sport hunting. "We are a 'how-to' magazine devoted to all facets of sport hunting, with the intent to make our readers more knowledgeable, more successful and safer hunters." Circ. 325,000. **Pays on acceptance.** Publishes ms an average of 9 months after acceptance. Byline given. Offers $50 kill fee. Buys all rights. Submit seasonal/holiday material 9 months in advance. Reports in 2 weeks. Free sample copy and writer's guidelines covering format, sidebars and computer disks available on request.

Nonfiction: General interest, historical/nostalgic, how-to (on hunting techniques), humor, travel. Special issues: Hunting Annual (August). Buys 50 mss/year. Query. Length: 2,000 words. Pays $350 minimum.

Photos: Send photos with submission. Reviews 35mm transparencies and 8 × 10 b&w prints. Offers no additional payment for b&w photos accepted with ms; offers $50-250/color photo. Captions, model releases, identification of subjects required. Buys one-time rights.

ROCKY MOUNTAIN GAME & FISH, Game & Fish Publications, Inc., Box 741, Marietta GA 30061. Editor: Burt Carey. See *Game & Fish Publications*.

SAFARI MAGAZINE, The Journal of Big Game Hunting, Safari Club International, 4800 W. Gates Pass Rd., Tucson AZ 85745. (602)620-1220. Fax: (602)622-1205. Director of Publications/Editor: William R. Quimby. 90% freelance written. Bimonthly club journal covering international big game hunting and wildlife conservation. Circ. 18,000. Pays on publication. Publishes ms an average of 12-18 months after acceptance. Byline given. Offers $100 kill fee. Buys all rights. Submit seasonal/holiday material 1 year in advance. Reports in 2 weeks on queries; up to 6 weeks on mss. Sample copy for $4. Writer's guidelines for SAE.

Nonfiction: Photo feature (wildlife), technical (firearms, hunting techniques, etc.). Buys 48 mss/year. Query or send complete ms. Length: 1,500-2,500 words. Pays $200 for professional writers, lower rates if not professional.

Photos: State availability of photos with query or ms, or send photos with query or ms. Payment depends on size in magazine. Pays $45 for b&w; $50-150 color. Captions, model releases, identification of subjects required. Buys one-time rights.

Tips: "Study the magazine. Send manuscripts and photo packages with query. Make it appeal to knowledgeable, world-travelled big game hunters. Features on conservation contributions from big game hunters around the world are open to freelancers. We have enough stories on first-time African safaris and North American hunting. We need South American and Asian hunting stories, plus stories dealing with hunting and conservation."

SALT WATER SPORTSMAN MAGAZINE, 280 Summer St., Boston MA 02210. (617)439-9977. Fax: (617)439-9357. Editor: Barry Gibson. Emphasizes saltwater fishing. 85% freelance written. Works with a small number of new/unpublished writers each year. Monthly magazine. Circ. 150,000. **Pays on acceptance.** Publishes ms an average of 5 months after acceptance. Byline given. Buys first North American serial rights. Offers 100% kill fee. Submit seasonal material 8 months in advance. Accepts previously published submissions. Send tearsheet of article and information about when and where the article previously appeared. Pays negotiable. Reports in 1 month. Sample copy and writer's guidelines for 9 × 12 SAE with $2.90 postage.

Nonfiction: How-to, personal experience, technical, travel (to fishing areas). "Readers want solid how-to, where-to information written in an enjoyable, easy-to-read style. Personal anecdotes help the reader identify with the writer." Prefers new slants and specific information. Query. "It is helpful if the writer states experience in salt water fishing and any previous related articles. We want one, possibly two well-explained ideas per query letter — not merely a listing. Good pictures with query often help sell the idea." Buys 100 mss/year. Length: 1,200-1,500 words. Pays $350 and up. Sometimes pays the expenses of writers on assignment. "A good way to break in with us is to submit short (800-1,000 words) where-to/how-to pieces for one of our three regional editions (Atlantic, Southern and Pacific) with a couple of b&w photos. Write Whit Griswold for regional guidelines."

Photos: Purchased with or without accompanying ms. Captions required. Uses 5×7 or 8×10 b&w prints and color slides. Pays $1,000 minimum for 35mm, 2¼×2¼ or 8×10 transparencies for cover. Offers additional payment for photos accepted with accompanying ms.

Columns/Departments: Sportsman's Workbench (how to make fishing or fishing-related boating equipment), 100 or more words.

Tips: "There are a lot of knowledgeable fishermen/budding writers out there who could be valuable to us with a little coaching. Many don't think they can write a story for us, but they'd be surprised. We work with writers. Shorter articles that get to the point which are accompanied by good, sharp photos are hard for us to turn down. Having to delete unnecessary wordage—conversation, clichés, etc.—that writers feel is mandatory is annoying. Often they don't devote enough attention to specific fishing information."

SOUTH CAROLINA GAME & FISH, Game & Fish Publications, Inc., Box 741, Marietta GA 30061. (404)953-9222. Editor: Jeff Samsel. See *Game & Fish Publications.*

SOUTH CAROLINA WILDLIFE, P.O. Box 167, Rembert Dennis Bldg., Columbia SC 29202-0167. (803)734-3972. Editor: John Davis. Managing Editor: Linda Renshaw. Bimonthly magazine for South Carolinians interested in wildlife and outdoor activities. 75% freelance written. Estab. 1954. Circ. 69,000. Byline given. **Pays on acceptance.** Publishes ms an average of 6 months after acceptance. Buys first rights. Free sample copy. Reports in 2 months.

Nonfiction: Articles on outdoor South Carolina with an emphasis on preserving and protecting our natural resources. "Realize that the topic must be of interest to South Carolinians and that we must be able to justify using it in a publication published by the state department of natural resources—so if it isn't directly about outdoor recreation, a certain plant or animal, it must be somehow related to the environment and conservation. Readers prefer a broad mix of outdoor related topics (articles that illustrate the beauty of South Carolina's outdoors and those that help the reader get more for his/her time, effort, and money spent in outdoor recreation). These two general areas are the ones we most need. Subjects vary a great deal in topic, area and style, but must all have a common ground in the outdoor resources and heritage of South Carolina. Review back issues and query with a one-page outline citing sources, giving ideas for photographs, explaining justification and giving an example of the first two paragraphs." Does not need any column material. Generally does not seek photographs. The publisher assumes no responsibility for unsolicited material. Buys 25-30 mss/year. Length: 1,000-3,000 words. Pays an average of $200-400/article depending upon length and subject matter.

Tips: "We need more writers in the outdoor field who take pride in the craft of writing and put a real effort toward originality and preciseness in their work. Query on a topic we haven't recently done. The most frequent mistakes made by writers in completing an article are failure to check details and go in-depth on a subject."

SOUTHERN OUTDOORS MAGAZINE, B.A.S.S. Publications, 5845 Carmichael Rd., Montgomery AL 36117. (205)277-3940. Editor: Larry Teague. Magazine published 9 times/year covering Southern outdoor activities, including hunting, fishing, boating, shooting and camping. 90% freelance written. Prefers to work with published/established writers. Estab. 1952. Circ. 257,000. **Pays on acceptance.** Publishes ms an average of 6 months to 1 year after acceptance. Buys all rights. Reports in 1-2 months. Sample copy for $2.50 and 9×12 SAE with 5 first-class stamps.

Nonfiction: Articles should be service-oriented, helping the reader excel in outdoor sports. Emphasis is on techniques, trends and conservation. Some "where-to" features purchased on Southern hunting and fishing destinations. Buys 120 mss/year. Length: 2,500 words maximum. Sidebars are a selling point. Pays 15-20¢/word.

Photos: Usually purchased with mss. Pays $75 for 35mm transparencies without ms, $400 for covers.

Fillers: Humorous or thought-provoking pieces (1,500 words) appear in each issue's S.O. Essay department.

Tips: "It's easiest to break in with short articles. We buy very little first-person. Stories most likely to sell: outdoor medicine, bass fishing, deer hunting, other freshwater fishing, inshore saltwater fishing, bird and small-game hunting, shooting, camping and boating."

SPORT FISHING, The Magazine of Offshore Fishing, 330 W. Canton Ave., Winter Park FL 32789-7061. (407)628-4802. Fax: (407)628-7061. Editor: Albia Dugger. Managing Editor: Dave Ferrell. 60% freelance written. Magazine covering offshore sport fishing. Estab. 1986. Circ. 110,000. Pays within 6 weeks of acceptance. Byline given. Offers $100 kill fee. Buys first North American serial or one-time rights. Submit seasonal/holiday material 3 months in advance. Accepts simultaneous submission. Query for electronic submissions. Reports in 2 months. Free sample copy and writer's guidelines.

Nonfiction: How-to, all humor, new product, personal experience, photo feature, technical, travel, (all on sport fishing). Buys 32-40 mss/year. Query with or without published clips or send complete ms. Length: 1,500-4,500 words. Pays $150-600 for assigned articles.

Photos: Send photos with submission. Reviews transparencies. Offers $50-500/photo. Identification of subjects required. Buys one-time rights.

Columns/Departments: Fish Tales (humorous sport fishing anecdotes), 800-1,500 words; Rigging (how-to rigging for sport fishing), 800-1,500 words; Technique (how-to technique for sport fishing), 800-1,500 words. Buys 8-24 mss/year. Send complete ms. Pays $200.

SPORTS AFIELD, 250 W. 55th St., New York NY 10019-5201. (212)649-4000. Editor-in-Chief: Terry McDonnell. Executive Editor: Fred Kesting. 20% freelance written. Monthly magazine for people of all ages whose interests are centered around the out-of-doors (hunting and fishing) and related subjects. Estab. 1887. Circ. 506,011. Buys first North American serial rights for features. **Pays on acceptance.** Publishes ms an average of 6 months after acceptance. Byline given. "Our magazine is seasonal and material submitted should be in accordance. Fishing in spring and summer; hunting in the fall." Submit seasonal material 9 months in advance. Reports in 2 months. Query or submit complete ms. Writer's guidelines for 1 first-class stamp.

• Ranked as one of the best markets for freelance writers in *Writer's Digest* magazine's annual "Top 100 Markets," January 1994.

Nonfiction: "Informative how-to articles with emphasis on product and service and personal experiences with good photos on hunting, fishing, camping, conservation, and environmental issues (limited where-to-go) related to hunting and fishing. We want first-class writing and reporting." Buys 15-17 unsolicited mss/year. Length: 500-2,500 words. "Pay scale: Self-contained 1-pager $500; a spread $800; 3-pagers $1,000; 2 spreads $1,200. Backcountry $800."

Photos: Buys photos with ms. "For photos without ms, duplicates of 35mm color transparencies preferred."

Fiction: Adventure, humor, nostalgia (if related to hunting and fishing).

Fillers: Send to *Almanac* editor. *Almanac* pays $10/column inch, with a minimum $25/item. For outdoor tips specifically for hunters, fishermen and campers, unusual, how-to and nature items. Payment on publication. Buys all rights.

Tips: "We seldom give assignments to other than staff. Top-quality 35mm slides to illustrate articles a must. Read a recent copy of *Sports Afield* so you know the market you're writing for. Ms *must* be available on disk."

TENNESSEE SPORTSMAN, Game & Fish Publications, Box 741, Marietta GA 30061. (404)953-9222. Editor: Jeff Samsel. See *Game & Fish Publications*.

TEXAS SPORTSMAN, Game & Fish Publications, Inc., Box 741, Marietta GA 30061. (404)953-9222. Editor: Nick Gilmore. See *Game & Fish Publications*.

‡TURKEY & TURKEY HUNTING, Krause Publications, 800 E. State St., Iola WI 54900. Editors: Jim Casada and Gerry Blair. Managing Editor: Gordy Krahn. 80% freelance written. Covers turkey hunting and other issues related to wild turkeys. Published February, March, April, Spring, Fall, Winter. "It is imperative that contributors be well versed in the lure and lore of hunting wild turkeys." Estab. 1991. **Pays on acceptance.** Publishes ms an average of 4 months after acceptance. Byline given. Buys first North American serial rights. Editorial lead time 4 months. Query for electronic submissions. Reports in 4-6 weeks on queries; 2 months on mss. Prefer queries first. Writer's guidelines for #10 SASE.

Nonfiction: Books excerpts (rarely), historical/nostalgic, how-to, humor (rarely), interview/profile, new product, personal experience, photo feature, travel. "We normally do one or two theme issues a year. Examples from the past include calling tactics, destinations and A Turkey Hunter's Christmas. No advertorials or poetry. Buys 40-50 mss/year. Query with or without published clips. Length: 1,500-3,000. Pays $150-300.

Photos: Send photos with submission. Reviews contact sheets, negatives, transparencies. Offers $40-250/cover photo. Captions required. Buys one-time rights.

Tips: "We have the most trouble in getting good submissions on turkey biology and behavior, along with management principles and practices. These subjects *must* be covered in a fashion which is interesting and informative for the average reader. Feature articles are your best bet. Tight, bright pieces which are well-written and well-researched are most likely to be accepted. Queries with an unusual slant or touching on a subject we have not recently covered in detail are good opportunities for first-time writers. We tend to work regularly with a stable of 20 or so writers but are always looking for new talent."

TURKEY CALL, Wild Turkey Center, P.O. Box 530, Edgefield SC 29824-0530. (803)637-3106. Fax: (803)637-0034. Editor: Gene Smith. 50-60% freelance written. Eager to work with new/unpublished writers and photographers. Bimonthly educational magazine for members of the National Wild Turkey Federation. Estab. 1973. Circ. 68,000. Buys one-time rights. Byline given. **Pays on acceptance.** Publishes ms an average of 6 months after acceptance. Reports in 1 month. No queries necessary. Submit complete package. Wants original mss only. Sample copy for $3 and 9×12 SAE. Writer's guidelines for #10 SASE.

Nonfiction: Feature articles dealing with the hunting and management of the American wild turkey. Must be accurate information and must appeal to national readership of turkey hunters and wildlife management experts. No poetry or first-person accounts of unremarkable hunting trips. May use some fiction that educates or entertains in a special way. Length: up to 3,000 words. Pays $35 for items, $65 for short fillers of 600-700 words, $200-350 for illustrated features.

Photos: "We want quality photos submitted with features." Art illustrations also acceptable. "We are using more and more inside color illustrations." For b&w, prefer 8×10 glossies, but 5×7 OK. Transparencies of any size are acceptable. No typical hunter-holding-dead-turkey photos or setups using mounted birds or domestic turkeys. Photos with how-to stories must make the techniques clear (example: how to make a turkey call; how to sculpt or carve a bird in wood). Pays $20 minimum for one-time rights on b&w photos and simple art illustrations; up to $75 for inside color, reproduced any size. Covers are negotiated.

Tips: "The writer should simply keep in mind that the audience is 'expert' on wild turkey management, hunting, life history and restoration/conservation history. He/she *must know the subject*. We are buying more third-person, more fiction, more humor—in an attempt to avoid the 'predictability trap' of a single subject magazine."

VIRGINIA GAME & FISH, Game & Fish Publications, Inc., Box 741, Marietta GA 30061. (404)953-9222. Editor: Jeff Samsel. See *Game & Fish Publications*.

WASHINGTON-OREGON GAME & FISH, Game & Fish Publications, Inc., Box 741, Marietta GA 30061. Editor: Burt Carey. See *Game & Fish Publications*.

WEST VIRGINIA GAME & FISH, Game & Fish Publications, Inc., Box 741, Marietta GA 30061. (404)953-9222. Editor: Ken Freel. See *Game & Fish Publications*.

‡WESTERN OUTDOORS, 3197-E Airport Loop, Costa Mesa CA 92626. (714)546-4370. Editor: Jack Brown. 60% freelance written. Works with a small number of new/unpublished writers each year. Emphasizes hunting, fishing, camping, boating for 11 Western states only, Baja California, Canada, Hawaii and Alaska. Publishes 9 issues/year. Estab. 1961. Circ. 128,000. **Pays on acceptance.** Publishes ms an average of 6 months after acceptance. Buys first North American serial rights. Submit seasonal material 6 months in advance. Reports in 1 month. Sample copy for $2. Writer's guidelines for #10 SASE.

Nonfiction: Where-to (catch more fish, bag more game, improve equipment, etc.), how-to informational, photo feature. "We do not accept fiction, poetry." Buys 45-55 assigned mss/year. Query in writing. Length: 1,000-1,500 words. Pays average $450.

Photos: Purchased with accompanying ms. Captions required. Prefers professional quality 35mm slides. Offers no additional payment for photos accepted with accompanying ms. Pays $250 for covers.

Tips: "Provide a complete package of photos, map, trip facts and manuscript written according to our news feature format. Excellence of color photo selections make a sale more likely. The most frequent mistake made by writers in completing an article for us is that they don't follow our style. Our guidelines are quite clear."

WESTERN SPORTSMAN, P.O. Box 737, Regina, Saskatchewan S4P 3A8 Canada. (306)352-2773. Fax: (306)565-2440. Editor: Brian Bowman. 90% freelance written. Bimonthly magazine for fishermen, hunters, campers and others interested in outdoor recreation. "Note that our coverage area is Alberta, Saskatchewan and Manitoba." Estab. 1968. Circ. 29,000. Rights purchased vary with author and material. Usually buys first North American serial or second serial (reprint) rights. Accepts previously published submissions. Send tearsheet of article or typed ms with rights for sale noted and information about when and where the article previously appeared. For reprints, pays 100% of the amount paid for an original article. Byline given. Pays on publication. Publishes ms an average of 6 months after acceptance. "We try to include as much information as possible on all subjects in each edition. Therefore, we often publish fishing articles in our winter issues along with a variety of winter stories. If material is dated, we would like to receive articles 4 months in advance of our publication date." Reports in 1 month. Sample copy for $4 and 9×12 SAE with 4 IRCs (US). Free writer's guidelines with SASE.

Nonfiction: "It is necessary that all articles can identify with our coverage area. We are interested in manuscripts from writers who have experienced an interesting fishing or hunting experience. We also publish other informational pieces as long as they relate to our coverage area. We are more interested in articles which tell about the average guy living on beans, guiding his own boat, stalking his game and generally doing his own thing in our part of Western Canada than a story describing a well-to-do outdoorsman traveling by motorhome, staying at an expensive lodge with guides doing everything for him except catching the fish or shooting the big game animal. The articles that are submitted to us need to be prepared in a knowledgeable way and include more information than the actual fish catch or animal or bird kill. Discuss the terrain, the people involved on the trip, the water or weather conditions, the costs, the planning that went into the trip, the equipment and other data closely associated with the particular event. We're always looking for new writers." Buys 60 mss/year. Submit complete ms and SASE or IRCs. Length: 1,500-2,000 words. Pays up to $300 (Canadian). Sometimes pays the expenses of writers on assignment.

Photos: Photos purchased with ms with no additional payment. Also purchased without ms. Pays $30-50 for 5×7 or 8×10 b&w print; $175-250 for 35mm or larger transparency for front cover.

WISCONSIN SPORTSMAN, Game & Fish Publications, Inc., Box 741, Marietta GA 30061. Editor: Dennis Schmidt. See *Game & Fish Publications*.

Martial Arts

BLACK BELT, Rainbow Publications, Inc., 24715 Ave. Rockefeller, Valencia CA 91355. (805)257-4066. Fax: (805)257-3028. Executive Editor: Jim Coleman. 80-90% freelance written. Works with a small number of new/unpublished writers each year. Monthly magazine emphasizing martial arts for both practioner and layman. Estab. 1961. Circ. 100,000. Pays on publication. Publishes ms an average of 5 months after acceptance. Buys first North American serial rights, retains right to republish. Submit seasonal/holiday material 6 months in advance. Reports in 3 weeks.

Nonfiction: Exposé, how-to, informational, interview, new product, personal experience, profile, technical, travel. Buys 8-9 mss/issue. Query or send complete ms. Length: 1,200 words minimum. Pays $100-300.

Photos: Very seldom buys photos without accompanying mss. Captions required. Total purchase price for ms includes payment for photos. Model releases required.

Fiction: Historical, modern day. Buys 1-2 mss/year. Query. Pays $100-150.

Tips: "We also publish an annual yearbook and special issues periodically. The yearbook includes our annual 'Black Belt Hall of Fame' inductees."

INSIDE KUNG-FU, The Ultimate In Martial Arts Coverage!, Unique Publications, 4201 Vanowen Pl., Burbank CA 91505. (818)845-2656. Fax: (818)845-7761. Editor: Dave Cater. 75% freelance written. Monthly magazine covering martial arts for those with "traditional, modern, athletic and intellectual tastes. The magazine slants toward little-known martial arts, and little-known aspects of established martial arts." Estab. 1973. Circ. 100,000. Pays on publication. Publishes ms an average of 6 months after acceptance. Byline given. Buys first North American serial rights. Submit seasonal/holiday material 4 months in advance. Accepts simultaneous and previously published submissions. Send tearsheet of article or short story or typed ms with rights for sale noted and information about when and where the article previously appeared. No payment for reprints. Reports in 1 month on queries; 2 months on mss. Sample copy for $2.95 and 9 × 12 SAE with 5 first-class stamps. Writer's guidelines for #10 SASE.

Nonfiction: Exposé (topics relating to the martial arts), historical/nostalgic, how-to (primarily technical materials), cultural/philosophical, interview/profile, personal experience, photo feature, technical. "Articles must be technically or historically accurate." No "sports coverage, first-person articles or articles which constitute personal aggrandizement." Buys 120 mss/year. Query or send complete ms. Length: 8-10 pages, typewritten and double-spaced.

• Needs external, fighting and weapons articles.

Photos: Send photos with accompanying ms. Reviews b&w contact sheets, b&w negatives, 5 × 7 or 8 × 10 b&w prints. Offers no additional payment for photos. Captions and model release required.

Fiction: Adventure, historical, humorous, mystery, suspense. "Fiction must be short (1,000-2,000 words) and relate to the martial arts. We buy very few fiction pieces." Publishes novel excerpts. Buys 2-3 mss/year.

Tips: "The writer may have a better chance of breaking in at our publication with short articles and fillers since smaller pieces allow us to gauge individual ability, but we're flexible – quality writers get published, period. The most frequent mistakes made by writers in completing an article for us are ignoring photo requirements and model releases (always number one – and who knows why? All requirements are spelled out in writer's guidelines)."

JOURNAL OF ASIAN MARTIAL ARTS, Via Media Publishing Co., 821 W. 24th St., Erie PA 16502-2523. (814)455-9517. Fax: (814)838-7811. Editor: Michael A. DeMarco. 90% freelance written. Quarterly magazine covering "all historical and cultural aspects related to Asian martial arts, offering a mature, well-rounded view of this uniquely fascinating subject. Although the journal treats the subject with academic accuracy (references at end), writing need not lose the reader!" Estab. 1991. Pays on publication. Publishes ms an average of 1 year after acceptance. Byline given. Buys first rights and second serial (reprint) rights. Submit seasonal/holiday material 6 months in advance. Query for electronic submissions. Reports in 1 month on queries; 2 months on mss. Sample copy for $10. Writer's guidelines for #10 SASE.

Nonfiction: Essays, exposé, historical/nostalgic, how-to (martial art techniques and materials, e.g., weapons, symbols), interview/profile, personal experience, photo feature (place or person), religious, technical, travel. "All articles should be backed with solid, reliable reference material. No articles overburdened with technical/foreign/scholarly vocabulary, or material slanted as indirect advertising or for personal aggrandizement." Buys 30 mss/year. Query. Length: 2,000-10,000 words. Pays $150-500 for unsolicited articles.

Photos: State availability of photos with submission. Reviews contact sheets, negatives, transparencies, prints. Offers no additional payment for photos accepted with ms. Model releases and identification of subjects required. Buys one-time and reprint rights.

Columns/Departments: Location (city, area, specific site, Asian or Non-Asian, showing value for martial arts, researchers, history); Media Review (film, book, stamps, music for aspects of academic and artistic interest). Buys 16 mss/year. Query. Length: 1,000-2,500 words. Pays $50-200.

Fiction: Adventure, historical, humorous, slice-of-life vignettes, translation. "We are not interested in material that does not focus on martial arts culture." Buys 2 mss/year. Query. Length: 2,000-10,000 words. Pays $100-500.

Poetry: Avant-garde, free verse, Haiku, light verse, traditional, translation. "No poetry that does not focus on martial art culture." Buys 4 poems/year. Submit maximum 10 poems. Pays $10-100.

Fillers: Anecdotes, facts, gags to be illustrated by cartoonist, newsbreaks, short humor. Buys 10/year. Length: 25-500 words. Pays $1-50.

Tips: "Always query before sending a manuscript. We are open to varied types of articles; most however require a strong academic grasp of Asian culture. For those not having this background, we suggest trying a museum review, or interview, where authorities can be questioned, quoted and provide supportive illustrations. We especially desire articles/reports from Asia, with photo illustrations, particularly of a martial art style, so readers can visually understand the unique attributes of that style, its applications, evolution, etc. 'Location' and media reports are special areas that writers may consider, especially if they live in a location of martial art significance."

‡**KARATE/KUNG FU ILLUSTRATED,** Rainbow Publications, Inc., P.O. Box 918, Santa Clarita CA 91380. (805)257-4066. Editor: Robert Young. 70% freelance written. Bimonthly consumer magazine covering martial arts. "KKI presents factual historical accounts of the development of the martial arts, along with technical pieces on self-defense. We use only material from which readers can learn." Estab. 1969. Circ. 35,000. Pays on publication. Publishes ms an average of 6 months after acceptance. Byline given. Buys first North American serial rights. Editorial lead time 3 months. Submit seasonal material 4 months in advance.Accepts simultaneous submissions. Reports in 2 weeks on queries; 1 month on mss. Sample coy for 9 × 12 SAE and 5 first-class stamps. Writer's guidelines free on request.

Nonfiction: Book excerpts, general interest (martial arts), historical/nostalgic (martial arts development), how-to (technical articles on specific kicks, punches, etc.), interview/profile (only with *major* martial artist), new products (for annual product review), travel (to Asian countries for martial arts training/research), comparisons of various styles and techniques. "No fiction or self-promotional pieces." Buys 30 mss/year. Query. Length: 1,000-3,000 words. Pays $100.

Photos: Freelancers should send photos with submission. Reviews contact sheets, negatives and 5 × 7 prints. Offers no additional payment for photos accepted with ms. Captions, model releases and identification of subjects required.

Columns/Departments: Bushido Book (except explaining martial arts philosophy), 1,000-1,500 words; Martial Spirit (personal experience that must apply to all readers) 1,000 words. Buys 12 mss/year. Query. Pays $0-75.

Tips: "You need not be an expert in a specific martial art to write about it. But if you are not an expert, find one and use his knowledge to support your statements. Also, references to well-known books can help lend credence to the work of unknown writers. Inexperienced writers should begin by writing about a subject they know well. For example, if you study karate, start by writing about karate. Don't study karate for one year, then try to break in to a martial arts magazine by writing about Kung fu, because we already have Kung fu practitioners who write about that."

MARTIAL ARTS TRAINING, Rainbow Publications, P.O. Box 918, Santa Clarita CA 91380-9018. (805)257-4066. Fax: (805)257-3028. Executive Editor: Douglas Jeffrey. 75% freelance written. Works with many new/ unpublished writers each year. Bimonthly magazine about martial arts training. Estab. 1961. Circ. 60,000. Pays on publication. Publishes ms an average of 6 months after acceptance. Buys all rights. Submit seasonal material 4 months in advance, but best to send query letter first. Reports in 2 months. Writer's guidelines for #10 SASE.

Nonfiction: How-to (training related features). Buys 30-40 unsolicited mss/year. Send query or complete ms. Length: 1,500-2,500 words. Pays $100.

Photos: State availability of photos. Most ms should be accompanied by photos. Reviews 5 × 7 and 8 × 10 b&w glossy prints. Can reproduce prints from negatives. Offers no additional payment for photos accepted with ms. Model releases required. Buys all rights. Photos not purchased without accompanying mss.

Tips: "I'm looking for how-to, nuts-and-bolts training stories that are martial arts related. Our magazine covers fitness and conditioning, not the martial arts techniques themselves."

‡**T'AI CHI, Leading International Magazine of T'ai Chi Ch'uan,** Wayfarer Publications, P.O. Box 26156, Los Angeles CA 90026. (213)665-7773. Fax: (213)665-1627. Editor: Marvin Smalheiser. 90% freelance written. Bimonthly consumer magazine covering T'ai Chi Ch'uan as a martial art and for Health & Fitness. "Covers T'ai Chi Ch'uan and other internal martials, plus qigong and Chinese health, nutrition and philosophical disciplines. Readers are practitioners or laymen interested in developing skills and insight for self-defense, health and self-improvement." Estab. 1977. Circ. 30,000. Pays on publication. Publishes ms an average of 3-5 months after acceptance. Byline given. Buys first North American serial rights. Editorial lead time 3 months. Submit seasonal material 6 months in advance. Reports in 1-3 weeks on queries; 1-3 months on mss. Sample copy for $3.50. Writer's guidelines for #10 SASE.

Nonfiction: Book excerpts, essays, how-to (on T'ai Chi Ch'uan, gigong and related Chinese disciplines), interview/profile, personal experience. "Do not want articles promoting an individual, system or school." Buys 50-60 mss/year. Query or send complete ms. Length: 1,200-4,500 words. Pays $60-350 for assigned articles; $60-350 for unsolicited articles. Sometimes pays expenses of writers on assignment.

Photos: Send photos with submission. Reviews transparencies and 3×5 prints. Offers no additional payment for photos accepted with ms. Captions, model releases and identification of subjects required. Buys one-time rights and reprint.

Poetry: Free verse, light verse, traditional. "No poetry unrelated to our content." Buys 6 poems/year. Submit maximum 3 poems. Length: 12-30 lines. **Pays** $25-50.

Tips: "Think and write for practitioners and laymen who want information and insight and who are trying to work through problems to improve skills and their health. No promotional material."

Miscellaneous

NEW YORK OUTDOORS, 51 Atlantic Ave., Floral Park NY 11001. Fax: (516)437-6841. Editor: Gary P. Joyce. Associate Editor: John Tsaousis. 100% freelance written. Estab. 1992. Buys first North American serial rights. Publishes ms an average of 6 months after acceptance. Reports in 2 weeks on queries. Writer's guidelines for #10 SASE.

Nonfiction: *"New York Outdoors* is dedicated to providing information to its readers about all outdoor participatory activities in New York and its surrounding states. Fishing, shooting, sports, paddlesports, camping, hiking, cycling, 'adventure' sports, etc." Query. Length: 1,500-2,000 words. A good selection of transparencies must accompany submissions. Pays $250. Lead time 4 months. "Aside from accurate and interesting writing, provide source material for our readers who may wish to try the activity. We also have use for shorter pieces (to 500 words) on the same type of topics, but focusing on a single event, person, place or occurrence. Query. These pay $50."

Tips: Would like to see more queries on "non-fishing/shooting sport" topic areas.

POLO, Polo Publications, Inc., 656 Quince Orchard Rd., Gaithersburg MD 20878-1472. (301)977-0200. Fax: (301)990-9015. Editor: Martha LeGrand. Contact Shelby Sadler, senior editor. Magazine published 10 times/year on polo—the sport and lifestyle. "Our readers are an affluent group. Most are well-educated, well-read and highly sophisticated." Circ. 6,500. **Pays on acceptance.** Publishes ms an average 4 months after acceptance. Kill fee varies. Buys first North American serial rights and makes work-for-hire assignments. Submit seasonal/holiday material 3 months in advance. Accepts simultaneous and previously published submissions. Send tearsheet of article and information about when and where the article previously appeared. For reprints, pays 50% of the amount paid for an original article. Reports in 3 months. Writer's guidelines for #10 SAE with 2 first-class stamps.

Nonfiction: Shelby Sadler, senior editor. Historical/nostalgic, interview/profile, personal experience, photo feature, technical, travel. Buys 20 mss/year. Query with published clips or send complete ms. Length: 800-3,000 words. Pays $150-400 for assigned articles; $100-300 for unsolicited articles. Sometimes pays expenses of writers on assignment.

Photos: State availability of photos or send photos with submission. Reviews contact sheets, transparencies, prints. Offers $20-150/photo. Captions required. Buys one-time rights.

Columns/Departments: Yesteryears (historical pieces), 500 words; Profiles (clubs and players), 800-1,000 words. Buys 15 mss/year. Query with published clips. Pays $100-300.

Tips: "Query us on a personality or club profile or historic piece or, if you know the game, state availability to cover a tournament. Keep in mind that ours is a sophisticated, well-educated audience."

PRIME TIME SPORTS & FITNESS, GND Prime Time Publishing, P.O. Box 6097, Evanston IL 60204. (312)869-6434. Fax: (708)864-1206. Editor: Dennis A. Dorner. Managing Editor: Steven Ury. 80% freelance written. Eager to work with new/unpublished writers. Monthly magazine covering seasonal pro sports and racquet and health club sports and fitness. Estab. 1974. Circ. 35,000. Pays on publication. Publishes ms an average of 6 months after acceptance. Byline given. Buys all rights; will assign back to author in 85% of cases. Submit seasonal/holiday material 6 months in advance. Accepts simultaneous and previously published submissions. Send photocopy of article or short story or typed ms with rights for sale noted and information about when and where the article previously appeared. Pays 30-100% of their fee for an original article. Reports in 2-6 months. Sample copy for 10×12 SAE with 7 first-class stamps.

Nonfiction: Book excerpts (fitness and health), exposé (in tennis, fitness, racquetball, health clubs, diets), adult (slightly risqué and racy fitness), how-to (expert instructional pieces on any area of coverage), humor (large market for funny pieces on health clubs and fitness), inspirational (on how diet and exercise combine to bring you a better body, self), interview/profile, new product, opinion (only from recognized sources who know what they are talking about), personal experience (definitely—humor), photo feature (on related subjects), technical (on exercise and sport), travel (related to fitness, tennis camps, etc.), news reports (on racquetball, handball, tennis, running events). Special issues: Swimsuit and Resort Issue (March); Baseball Preview (April); Summer Fashion (July); Pro Football Preview (August); Fall Fashion (October); Ski Issue (November); Christmas Gifts and related articles (December). "We love short articles that get to the point. Nationally oriented big events and national championships. No articles on local only tennis and racquetball tournaments without national appeal." Buys 150 mss/year. Length: 2,000 words maximum. Pays $20-150. Sometimes pays the expenses of writers on assignment.

Photos: Nancy Thomas, photo editor. Specifically looking for fashion photo features. Send photos with ms. Pays $5-75 for b&w prints. Captions, model releases, identification of subjects required. Buys all rights, "but returns 75% of photos to submitter."

Columns/Departments: George Thomas, column/department editor. New Products; Fitness Newsletter; Handball Newsletter; Racquetball Newsletter; Tennis Newsletter; News & Capsule Summaries; Fashion Spot (photos of new fitness and bathing suits and ski equipment); related subjects. Buys 100 mss/year. Send complete ms. Length: 50-250 words ("more if author has good handle to cover complete columns"). Pays $5-25.

Fiction: Judy Johnson, fiction editor. Erotica (if related to fitness club), fantasy (related to subjects), humorous (definite market), religious ("no God-is-my shepherd, but Body-is-God's-temple OK"), romance (related subjects). "Upbeat stories are needed." Buys 20 mss/year. Send complete ms. Length: 500-2,500 words maximum. Pays $20-150.

Poetry: Free verse, Haiku, light verse, traditional on related subjects. Length: up to 150 words. Pays $10-25.

Tips: "Send us articles dealing with court club sports, exercise and nutrition that exemplify an upbeat 'you can do it' attitude. Pro sports previews 3-4 months ahead of their seasons are also needed. Good short fiction or humorous articles can break in. Expert knowledge of any related subject can bring assignments; any area is open. We consider everything as a potential article, but are turned off by credits, past work and degrees. We have a constant demand for well-written articles on instruction, health and trends in both. Other articles needed are professional sports training techniques, fad diets, tennis and fitness resorts, photo features with aerobic routines. A frequent mistake made by writers is length—articles are too long. When we assign an article, we want it newsy if it's news and opinion if opinion."

‡**RACQUETBALL MAGAZINE**, American Amateur Racquetball Association, 1685 W. Uintah, Colorado Springs CO 80904. (719)635-5396. Editor: Linda Mojer. 20-30% freelance written. Bimonthly magazine "geared toward a readership of informed, active enthusiasts who seek entertainment, instruction and accurate reporting of events." Estab. 1990. Circ. 45,000. Pays on publication. Publishes ms an average of 1-2 months after acceptance. Buys one-time rights. Editorial lead time 2-3 months. Submit seasonal material 3 months in advance. Accepts simultaneous submissions. Query for electronic submissions. Reports in 1-2 months. Sample copy for $4. Writer's guidelines free on request.

Nonfiction: How-to (instructional racquetball tips), humor, interview/profile (personalities who play racquetball). Buys 2-3 mss/year. Send complete ms. Length: 1,500-3,000 words. Pays $100. Sometimes pays expenses of writers on assignment.

Photos: Send photos with submission. Reviews 3×5 prints. Negotiates payment individually. Model releases, identification of subjects required. Buys one-time rights.

Fiction: Humorous (racquetball related). Buys 1-2 mss/year. Send complete ms. Length: 1,500-3,000 words. Pays $100-250.

REFEREE, Referee Enterprises, Inc., P.O. Box 161, Franksville WI 53126-9987. (414)632-8855. Fax: (414)632-5460. Editor: Tom Hammill. 20-25% freelance written. Works with a small number of new/unpublished writers each year. Monthly magazine for well-educated, mostly 26- to 50-year-old male sports officials. Estab. 1975. Circ. 35,000. Pays on acceptance of completed ms. Publishes ms an average of 4 months after acceptance. Rights purchased varies. Submit seasonal/holiday material 4-6 months in advance. Accepts previously published submissions. Send tearsheet or photocopy of article or typed ms with rights for sale noted and information about when and where it previously appeared. Pays 50% of their fee for an original article. Reports in 2 weeks. Sample copy for 10×13 SAE with 7 first-class stamps. Writer's guidelines for #10 SASE.

Nonfiction: How-to, informational, humor, interview, profile, personal experience, photo feature, technical. Buys 54 mss/year. Query. Length: 700-3,000 words. Pays 4-10¢/word. "No general sports articles."

Photos: Purchased with or without accompanying ms or on assignment. Captions preferred. Send contact sheet, prints, negatives or transparencies. Pays $20 for each b&w used; $35 for each color used; $100 for color cover, $75 for b&w cover.

Columns/Departments: Law (legal aspects); Take Care (fitness, medical); Between the Lines (anecdotes); Heads Up (psychology). Buys 24 mss/year. Query. Length: 200-800 words. Pays 4¢/word up to $100 maximum for regular columns.

Fillers: Jokes, gags, anecdotes, puzzles, referee shorts. Query. Length: 50-200 words. Pays 4¢/word in some cases; others offer only author credit lines.

Tips: "Queries with a specific idea appeal most to readers. Generally, we are looking more for feature writers, as we usually do our own shorter/filler-type material. It is helpful to obtain suitable photos to augment a story. Don't send fluff—we need hard-hitting, incisive material tailored just for our audience. Anything smacking of public relations is a no sale. Don't gloss over the material too lightly or fail to go in-depth looking for a quick sale (taking the avenue of least resistance)."

‡**RUGBY MAGAZINE**, Rugby Press Ltd., 2350 Broadway, New York NY 10024. (212)787-1160. Editor: Ed Hagerty. Managing Editor: Michael Malone. Contact: Ed Hagerty, Publisher. 80% freelance written. Monthly consumer tabloid covering the sport of rugby. Estab. 1974. Circ. 10,000. Pays on publication. Publishes ms

an average of 1 month after acceptance. Byline given. Buys first rights. Submit seasonal material 1 month in advance. Accepts simultaneous and previously published submissions. Query for electronic submissions. Reports in 1 month on queries. Sample copy for $3. Writer's guidelines free on request.

Nonfiction: Book excerpts, essays, general interest, historical/nostalgic, humor, interview/profile. Buys 10 mss/year. Query. Length: 500-2,000 words. Pay is negotiable. Sometimes pays expenses of writers on assignment.

SIGNPOST FOR NORTHWEST TRAILS MAGAZINE, Suite 512, 1305 Fourth Ave., Seattle WA 98101-2401. Publisher: Washington Trails Association. Executive Editor: Dan A. Nelson. 10% freelance written. "We will consider working with both previously published and unpublished freelancers." Monthly magazine about hiking, backpacking and similar trail-related activities, strictly from a Pacific Northwest viewpoint. Estab. 1966. Will consider any rights offered by author. Publishes ms an average of 6 months after acceptance. Reports in 2 months. Accepts previously published submissions. Include information about when and where the article previously appeared. Query or submit complete ms. Writer's guidelines for #10 SASE.

Nonfiction and Photos: "Most material is donated by subscribers or is staff-written. Payment for purchased material is low, but a good way to break in to print and share your outdoor experiences."

Tips: "We cover only *self-propelled* backcountry sports and won't consider manuscripts about trail bikes, snowmobiles or power boats. We *are* interested in articles about modified and customized equipment, food and nutrition, and personal experiences in the Pacific NW backcountry."

SILENT SPORTS, Waupaca Publishing Co., P.O. Box 152, Waupaca WI 54981-9990. (715)258-5546. Fax: (715)258-8162. Editor: Greg Marr. 75% freelance written. Eager to work with new/unpublished writers. Monthly magazine on running, cycling, cross-country skiing, canoeing, camping, backpacking and hiking aimed at people in Wisconsin, Minnesota, northern Illinois and portions of Michigan and Iowa. "Not a coffee table magazine. Our readers are participants from rank amateur weekend athletes to highly competitive racers." Estab. 1984. Circ. 10,000. Pays on publication. Publishes ms an average of 3 months after acceptance. Byline given. Offers 20% kill fee. Buys one-time rights. Submit seasonal/holiday material 4 months in advance. Accepts previously published submissions. Send photocopy of article and/or typed ms with rights for sale noted plus information about when and where the article previously appeared. Pay negotiated. Reports in 3 months. Sample copy and writer's guidelines for 10×13 SAE with 6 first-class stamps.

Nonfiction: General interest, how-to, interview/profile, opinion, technical, travel. All stories/articles focus on the Upper Midwest. First-person articles discouraged. Buys 25 mss/year. Query. Length: 2,500 words maximum. Pays $15-100. Sometimes pays expenses of writers on assignment.

Tips: "Where-to-go, how-to and personality profiles are areas most open to freelancers. Writers should keep in mind that this is a regional, Midwest-based publication."

SKYDIVING, 1725 N. Lexington Ave., DeLand FL 32724. (904)736-4793. Fax: (904)736-9786. Editor: Michael Truffer. 25% freelance written. Works with a small number of new/unpublished writers each year. Monthly tabloid featuring skydiving for sport parachutists, worldwide dealers and equipment manufacturers. Circ. 9,450. Average issue includes 3 feature articles and 3 columns of technical information. Pays on publication. Publishes ms an average of 3 months after acceptance. Byline given. Buys one-time rights. Accepts simultaneous and previously published submissions, if so indicated. Query for electronic submissions. Reports in 1 month. *Writer's Market* recommends allowing 2 months for reply. Sample copy for $2. Writer's guidelines for 9×12 SAE with 4 first-class stamps.

Nonfiction: "Send us news and information on equipment, techniques, events and outstanding personalities who skydive. We want articles written by people who have a solid knowledge of parachuting." No personal experience or human-interest articles. Query. Length: 500-1,000 words. Pays $25-100. Sometimes pays the expenses of writers on assignment.

Photos: State availability of photos. Reviews 5×7 and larger b&w glossy prints. Offers no additional payment for photos accepted with ms. Captions required.

Fillers: Newsbreaks. Length: 100-200 words. Pays $25 minimum.

Tips: "The most frequent mistake made by writers in completing articles for us is that the writer isn't knowledgable about the sport of parachuting."

‡TRUCKIN', World's Leading Sport Truck Publication, McMullen & Yee Publishing, 774 S. Placentia Ave., Placentia CA 92670. (714)572-2255. Editor: Steve Stillwell. 15% freelance written. Monthly magazine covering customized sport trucks. "Materials we purchase are events coverage, technical articles and truck features, all having to be associated with customized $-\frac{1}{2}$-ton pickups and mini-trucks." Estab. 1975. Circ. 200,000. Pays on publication. Buys all rights unless previously agreed upon. Editorial lead time 3 months. Submit seasonal material 6 months in advance. Query for electronic submissions. Reports in 2 weeks on queries; 1 month on mss. Sample copy for $4.50.Writer's guidelines free on request.

Nonfiction: How-to, new product, photo feature, technical, events coverage. Buys 50 mss/year. Query. Length: 1,000 words minimum. Pay negotiable. Sometimes pays expenses of writers on assignment.

Photos: Send photos with submission. Reviews contact sheets and transparencies. Captions, model releases and identification of subjects required. Buys all rights unless previously agreed upon.

Columns/Departments: Bill Blankenship. Insider (latest automotive/truck news), 2,000 words. Buys 70 mss/year. Send complete ms. Pays $25 minimum.

Fillers: Bill Blankenship. Anecdotes, facts, newsbreaks. Buys 50/year. Length: 600-1,000 words. Pay negotiable.

Tips: "Send all queries and submissions in envelopes larger than letter size to avoid being detained with a mass of reader mail. Send complete packages with transparencies and contact sheets (with negatives). Submit hard copy and a computer disc when possible. Editors purchase the materials that are the least complicated to turn into magazine pages! All materials have to be fresh/new and primarily outside of California."

‡**VOLLEYBALL MAGAZINE**, Avcom Publishing, Ltd., Suite 1600, 21700 Oxnard St., Woodland Hills CA 91367. (818)593-3900. Editor: Rick Hazeltine. Managing Editor: Don Patterson. 50% freelance written. Monthly magazine covering the sport of volleyball. Estab. 1990. Circ. 60,000. Pays on publication. Publishes ms an average of 3 months after acceptance. Byline given. Offers 50% kill fee. Buys first North American serial rights. Editorial lead time 3 months. Submit seasonal material 3 months in advance. Query for electronic submissions.

Nonfiction: Historical/nostalgic, how-to (skills instruction, nutrition strategy, fitness), humor, interview/profile, technical. No event coverage. Buys 72 mss/year. Query with published clips. Length: 250-3,000 words. Pays $100. Sometimes pays expenses of writers on assignment.

Photos: Send photos with submission. Reviews transparencies—no duplicates. Offers $40-225/photo. Captions, model releases and identification of subjects requried. Buys one-time rights.

Columns/Departments: Fitness (must relate specifically to volleyball); Nutrition (for athletes); Mental (mental side of sports). Length: 1,000-1,200 words. Buys 36 mss/year. Query with published clips. Pays $200-250.

Olympic Sports

‡**INSIDE TRIATHLON**, Inside Communications, 1830 N. 55th St., Boulder CO 80301. (303)440-0601. Editor: Bill Natovsh. 70% freelance written. Monthly tabloid covering triathlon/duathlon. Estab. 1993. Circ. 20,000. Pays on publication. Byline given. Offers 33% kill fee. Editorial lead time 2 months. Submit seasonal material 2 months in advance. Accepts simultaneous submissions. Query for electronic submissions. Reports in 1 month on queries. Sample copy and writer's guidelines free on request.

Nonfiction: Query with published clips. Length: 1,000-2,500 words. Pays $300-400.

Columns/Departments: Body Shop (training articles), 750-1,000 words; At the Races (Race Reports), 500 words. Query with published clips.

Tips: "Query with clips. Know the magazine. Suggest useful articles our readers would be interested in. Transition area/At the Races/Body Shop most open to freelancers.

INTERNATIONAL GYMNAST, Paul Ziert & Assoc., 225 Brooks St., Box 2450, Oceanside CA 92051-2450. (619)722-0030. Fax: (619)722-6208. Editor: Dwight Normile. 50% freelance written. Monthly magazine on gymnastics. "*IG* is dedicated to serving the gymnastics community with competition reports, personality profiles, training and coaching tips and innovations in the sport." Circ. 25,000. Pays on publication. Publishes ms an average of 3 months after acceptance. Byline given. Buys one-time rights. Submit seasonal/holiday material 3 months in advance. Sample copy for $4.25. Writer's guidelines for #10 SASE.

Nonfiction: How-to (coaching/training/ business, i.e. running a club), interview/profile, opinion, photo feature (meets or training sites of interest, etc.), competition reports, technical. "Nothing unsuitable for young readers." Buys 25 mss/year. Send complete ms. Length: 500-2,250 words. Pays $15-25. Pays in contributor copies or other premiums when currency exchange is not feasible i.e., foreign residents.

Photos: Send photos with submission. Reviews transparencies and prints. Offers $5-40/photo published. Identification of subjects required. Buys one-time rights.

Columns/Departments: Innovations (new moves, new approaches, coaching tips); Nutrition (hints for the competitive gymnast); Dance (ways to improve gymnasts through dance, all types); Club Corner (business hints for club owners/new programs, etc.); Book Reviews (reviews of new books pertaining to gymnastics). Buys 10 mss/year. Send complete ms. Length: 750-1,000. Pays $15-25.

Fiction: Humorous, anything pertaining to gymnastics, nothing inappropriate for young readers. Buys 1-2 ms/year. Send complete ms. Length: 1,500 words maximum. Pays $15-25.

Tips: "To *IG* readers, a lack of knowledge sticks out like a sore thumb. Writers are generally coaches, ex-gymnasts and 'hardcore' enthusiasts. Most open area would generally be competition reports. Be concise, but details are necessary when covering gymnastics. Again, thorough knowledge of the sport is indispensable."

INTERNATIONAL OLYMPIC LIFTER, IOL Publications, 3602 Eagle Rock, P.O. Box 65855, Los Angeles CA 90065. (213)257-8762. Editor: Bob Hise. 20% freelance written. Bimonthly magazine covering the Olympic sport of weightlifting. Estab. 1973. Circ. 10,000. Pays on publication. Publishes ms an average of 3 months after acceptance. Byline given. Offers $25 kill fee. Buys one-time rights or negotiable rights. Submit seasonal/holiday material 5 months in advance. Reports in 3 months. Sample copy for $4. Writer's guidelines for 9×12 SAE with 5 first-class stamps.

Nonfiction: Training articles, contest reports, diet—all related to Olympic weight lifting. Buys 4 mss/year. Query. Length: 250-2,000 words. Pays $25-100.

Photos: Action (competition and training). State availability of photos. Pays $1-5 for 5×7 b&w prints. Identification of subjects required.

Poetry: Dale Rhoades, poetry editor. Light verse, traditional—related to Olympic lifting. Buys 6-10 poems/year. Submit maximum 3 poems. Length: 12-24 lines. Pays $10-20.

Tips: "A writer must be acquainted with Olympic-style weight lifting. Since we are an international publication we do not tolerate ethnic, cultural, religious or political inclusions. Articles relating to AWA are readily accepted."

USA GYMNASTICS, United States Gymnastics Federation, Suite 300, 201 S. Capitol Ave., Pan American Plaza, Indianapolis IN 46225. (317)237-5050. Fax: (317)237-5069. Editor: Luan Peszek. 20% freelance written. Bimonthly magazine covering gymnastics—national and international competitions. Designed to educate readers on fitness, health, safety, technique, current topics, trends and personalities related to the gymnastics/fitness field. Readers are ages 7-18, parents and coaches. Estab. 1981. Circ. 63,000. Pays on publication. Publishes ms an average of 3-4 months after acceptance. Byline given. Buys all rights. Submit seasonal/holiday material 4 months in advance. Accepts simultaneous and previously published submissions. Reports in 2 months. Sample copy for $5.

Nonfiction: General interest, how-to (related to fitness, health, gymnastics), inspirational, interview/profile, new product, opinion (Open Floor section), photo feature. Buys 5 mss/year. Query. Length: 2,000 words maximum. Payment negotiated.

Photos: Send photos with submission. Offers no additional payment for photos accepted with ms. Identification of subjects required. Buys all rights.

Columns/Departments: Open Floor (opinions—regarding gymnastics/nutrition related topic), up to 1,000 words. Buys 2 mss/year. Query or send complete ms. No payment (articles donated—nonprofit organization).

Tips: "Any articles of interest to gymnasts (men, women and rhythmic gymnastics) coaches, judges and parents, are what we're looking for. This includes nutrition, toning, health, safety, current trends, gymnastics techniques, timing techniques etc. The sections most open to freelancers are Open Floor—opinions on topics related to gymnasts, and features on one of the above mentioned items."

Running

INSIDE TEXAS RUNNING, 9514 Bristlebrook Dr., Houston TX 77083. (713)498-3208. Fax: (713)879-9980. Editor: Joanne Schmidt. 70% freelance written. Monthly (except June and August) tabloid covering running, cycling and triathloning. "Our audience is made up of Texas runners and triathletes who may also be interested in cross training with biking and swimming." Estab. 1977. Circ. 10,000. **Pays on acceptance.** Publishes ms an average of 1-2 months after acceptance. Byline given. Buys first rights, one-time rights, second serial (reprint) rights, exclusive Texas and all rights. Submit seasonal/holiday material 2 months in advance. Accepts previously published submissions. Send photocopy of article. Pays 100% of their fee for an original article. Reports in 1 month on mss. Sample copy for $1.50. Writer's guidelines for #10 SASE.

Nonfiction: Exposé, historical/nostalgic, humor, interview/profile, opinion, photo feature, technical, travel. "We would like to receive controversial and detailed news pieces that cover both sides of an issue: for example, how a race director must deal with city government to put on an event. Problems seen by both sides including cost, traffic congestion, red tape, etc. No personal experience such as 'Why I Love to Run,' 'How I Ran My First Marathon.' Buys 20 mss/year. Send complete ms. Length: 500-1,500 words. Pays $100 maximum for assigned articles; $50 maximum for unsolicited articles.

Photos: Send photos with submission. Offers $25 maximum/photo. Captions required. Buys one-time rights.

Tips: "Writers should be familiar with the sport and the publication. The best way to break in to our publication is to submit brief (three or four paragraphs) write-ups on road races to be used in the Results section or submit fillers for our 'Texas Roundup' section."

NEW YORK RUNNING NEWS, New York Road Runners Club, 9 E. 89th St., New York NY 10128. (212)860-2280. Fax: (212)860-9754. Editor: Raleigh Mayer. Managing Editor: Don Mogelefsky. 75% freelance written. Bimonthly regional sports magazine covering running, racewalking, nutrition and fitness. Material should be of interest to members of the New York Road Runners Club. Estab. 1958. Circ. 45,000. Pays on publication. Time to publication varies. Byline given. Offers 33% kill fee. Buys first North American serial rights. Submit seasonal/holiday material 4 months in advance. Accepts simultaneous and previously published submissions. Send photocopy of article with information about when and where it previously appeared. Pays 25-50% of their fee for an original article. Reports in 2 months. Sample copy for $3. Writer's guidelines for #10 SASE.

Nonfiction: Running and marathon articles. Special issues: N.Y.C. Marathon (submissions in by August 1). No non-running stories. Buys 25 mss/year. Query. Length: 750-1,750 words. Pays $50-250. Pays documented expenses of writers on assignment.

Photos: Send photos with submission. Reviews 8×10 b&w prints. Offers $35-300/photo. Captions, model releases, identification of subjects required. Buys one-time rights.

Columns/Departments: Essay (running-related topics). Query. Length: 750 words. Pays $50-125.
  ● No longer accepts fiction.
Tips: "Be knowledgeable about the sport of running. Write like a runner."

RUNNER'S WORLD, Rodale Press, 33 E. Minor St., Emmaus PA 18098. (215)967-5171. Senior Editor: Bob Wischnia. 10% freelance written. Monthly magazine on running, mainly long-distance running. "The maga-zine for and about distance running, training, health and fitness, injury precaution, race coverage, personalties of the sport." Estab. 1966. Circ. 450,000. Pays on publication. Publishes ms an average of 5-6 months after acceptance. Byline given. Buys one-time rights. Submit seasonal/holiday material 6 months in advance. Query for electronic submissions. Reports in 2 months. Writer's guideline requests to Pat Erickson for #10 SASE.
Nonfiction: How-to (train, prevent injuries), interview/profile, personal experience. No "my first marathon" stories. No poetry. Buys 10 mss/year. Query. Pays the expenses of writers on assignment.
Photos: State availability of photos with submission. Identification of subjects required. Buys one-time rights.
Columns/Departments: Christina Negron. Finish Line (personal experience – humor); Training Log (train-ing of well-known runner). Buys 15 mss/year. Query.

Skiing and Snow Sports

AMERICAN SKATING WORLD, Independent Publication of the American Ice Skating Community, Business Communications Inc., 1816 Brownsville Rd., Pittsburgh PA 15210-3908. (412)885-7600. Fax: (412)885-7617. Editor: Robert A. Mock. Managing Editor: H. Kermit Jackson. 70% freelance written. Eager to work with new/unpublished writers. Monthly tabloid on figure skating. Estab. 1979. Circ. 15,000. Pays following publication. Publishes ms an average of 2-3 months after acceptance. Byline given. Buys first North American serial rights and occasionally second serial (reprint) rights. Submit seasonal/holiday material 3 months in advance. Reports in 3 months. Sample copy and writer's guidelines for $3.50.
Nonfiction: Exposé, historical/nostalgic, how-to (technique in figure skating), humor, inspirational, inter-view/profile, new product, opinion, personal experience, photo feature, technical, travel. Special issues: recre-ational (July); classic skaters (August); annual fashion issue (September); Industry (May). No fiction. AP Style Guidelines are the basic style source, but we are not bound by that convention. Short, snappy paragraphs desired. Buys 150 mss/year. Send complete ms. "Include phone number; response time longer without it." Length: 600-1,000 words. Pays $25-100.
Photos: Send photos with query or ms. Reviews transparencies and b&w prints. Pays $5 for b&w; $15 for color. Identification of subjects required. Buys all rights for b&w; one-time rights for color.
Columns/Departments: Buys 30 mss/year. Send complete ms. Length: 500-750 words. Pays $25-50.
Fillers: Clippings, anecdotes. No payment for fillers.
Tips: "Event coverage is most open to freelancers; confirm with managing editor to ensure event has not been assigned. We are drawing more extensively from non-US based writers. Questions are welcome; call managing editor EST, 10-4, Monday-Friday."

SKATING, United States Figure Skating Association, 20 1st St., Colorado Springs CO 80906-3697. (719)635-5200. Fax: (719)635-9548. Editor: Jay Miller. Monthly magazine official publication of the USFSA. Estab. 1923. Circ. 40,000. Pays on publication. Publishes ms an average of 3 months after acceptance. Buys all rights. Byline given.
Nonfiction: Historical, informational, interview, photo feature, historical biographies, profile (background and interests of national-caliber amateur skaters), technical and competition reports. Buys 4 mss/issue. All work by assignment. Length: 400-800 words. Pay varies.
Photos: Photos purchased with or without accompanying ms. Pays $15 for 8 × 10 or 5 × 7 b&w glossy prints and $35 for color prints or transparencies. Query.
Columns/Departments: Ice Breaker (news briefs), Foreign National Reports, Center Ice (guest), Letters to Editor, People. Buys 4 mss/issue. All work by assignment. Length: 500-2,000 words.
Tips: "We want writing by experienced persons knowledgeable in the technical and artistic aspects of figure skating with a new outlook on the development of the sport. Knowledge and background in technical aspects of figure skating are essential to the quality of writing expected. We would also like to receive articles on former competitive skaters. No professional skater material."

SKIING, Times Mirror Magazines, Inc., 2 Park Ave., New York NY 10016. Covers skiing equipment, fashion and news. This magazine did not respond to our request for information. Query before submitting.

‡SKI TRIPPER, P.O. Box 2035, Roanoke VA 24018. (703)772-7644. 50% freelance written. Consumer newslet-ter published November, December, January, February, March and April covering snow skiing in mid-Atlan-tic region. "Need reports on trips taken to regional ski resorts and to long-distance resorts (western US/Canada, Europe, New Zealand, South America) from the region. Trip reports are written from an unbiased viewpoint and tell good and bad things other people making the trip in the future should look out for. Also need informational pieces on resorts, skiers and skiing-related activities. Estab. 1993. Circ. 1,000. **Pays on acceptance.** Publishes ms an average of 3 months after acceptance. Buys first North American serial rights.

Editorial lead time 1 months. Submit seasonal material 2 months in advance. Query for electronic submissions. Reports in 3 weeks on queries; 1 month on mss. Sample copy and writer's guidelines free on request.
Nonfiction: Personal experience, travel. "No articles on ski shops and ski equipment." Buys 12 mss/year. Query. Length: 750-2,000 words. Pays $30-90.
Tips: "If you're going on a ski trip to or from the mid-Atlantic region, let us know—it may be one we'd like to cover."

‡**SNOW COUNTRY, The Year-Round Magazine of Mountain Sports & Living,** New York Times Magazine Group, 5520 Park Ave., Trumbull CT 06611. (203)323-7038. Editor: John Fry. Managing Editor: Robert LaMarche. 85% freelance written. Monthly (September-December) and Bimonthly (January-August). Focuses on mountain lifestyles and recreation at and around ski resorts. "Because we publish year-round, we cover a broader range of subjects than ski-only publications. Besides skiing, topics include scenic drives, mountain biking, hiking, rollerblading, real estate, etc." Estab. 1988. Circ. 460,000. **Pays on acceptance.** Publishes ms an average of 6 months after acceptance. Byline given. Kill fee varies. Buys first North American serial rights and foreign affiliates. Submit seasonal material 6 months in advance. Reports in 1 month. Free writer's guidelines.
   • Ranked as one of the best markets for freelance writers in *Writer's Digest* magazine's annual "Top 100 Markets," January 1994.
Nonfiction: General interest, historical/nostalgic, how-to, humor, interview/profile, new product, photo feature, technical and travel. Buys 45 mss/year. Query with published clips. Length: 250-1,200 words. Pays $200-1,000. Pays expenses of writers on assignment.
Photos: State availability of photos with submission. Reviews transparencies. Identification of subjects required. Buys one-time rights.
Columns/Departments: Follow Me (instructional items on skiing, mountain biking, photography, hiking), 200 words; Snow Country Store (items on mountain artisans, craftsmen and their products), 250 words. Buys 35 mss/year. Query with published clips. Pays $200-300.
Tips: "Area most open to freelancers: Snow Country Store column and short articles on people who've moved to snow country and are making a living there."

SNOWBOARDER, The Magazine, For Better Living Communications, P.O. Box 1028, Dana Point CA 92629. (714)496-5922. Editor: Douglas C. Palladini. Managing Editor: Steve Casimiro. 50% freelance written. Magazine published monthly September-February covering snowboarding. Estab. 1987. Circ. 120,000. Pays on publication. Publishes ms an average of 4 months after acceptance. Byline given. 20% kill fee. Buys first North American serial rights. Query for electronic submissions. Reports in 1 month on queries. Sample copy for $1 with 1 first class stamp. Writer's guidelines for SASE.
Nonfiction: How-to, personal experience, photo feature, technical, travel. No fiction. Buys 7-10 mss/year. Query with published clips. Length: 100-1,200 words. Pays $50-750. Sometimes pays expenses of writers on assignment.
Photos: State availability of photos with submissions. Reviews transparencies. Offers $50-600. Identification of subjects required. Buys one-time rights.

Soccer

SOCCER AMERICA, P.O. Box 23704, Oakland CA 94623-0704. (510)528-5000. Fax: (510)528-5177. Managing Editor: Paul Kennedy. 10% freelance written. Works with a small number of new writers each year. Weekly tabloid for a wide range of soccer enthusiasts. Estab. 1971. Circ. 30,000. Pays on publication. Publishes ms an average of 2 months after acceptance. Buys all rights. Byline given. Submit seasonal/holiday material 30 days in advance. Query for electronic submissions. Reports in 3 months. Sample copy and writer's guidelines for $1.
Nonfiction: Informational (news features), inspirational, interview, photo feature, profile, technical. "No 'Why I like soccer' articles in 1,000 words or less. It's been done." Buys 1-2 mss/issue. Query. Length: 200-1,500 words. Pays $30-50.
Photos: Photos purchased with or without accompanying ms or on assignment. Captions required. Pays $12 for 5×7 or larger b&w glossy prints. Query.
Tips: "Freelancers mean the addition of editorial vitality. New approaches and new minds can make a world of difference. But if they haven't familiarized themselves with the publication it is a total waste of my time and theirs."

YOUTH SOCCER NEWS, Varsity Publications, Inc., Suite 3, 13540 Lake City Way NE, Seattle WA 98125. (206)367-2420. Fax: (206)367-2636. Editor: Dick Stephens. 10-25% freelance written. Monthly tabloid newspaper for US soccer with focus on youth. *Youth Soccer News*—focus on news tied to USYSA Youth Soccer, i.e. teams, tournaments, products in western states. Estab. 1985. Circ. 60,000. Pays on publication. Byline given. Buys first North American serial and second serial (reprint) rights. Editorial lead time 3 months. Submit seasonal material 2 months in advance. Accepts simultaneous and previously published submissions.

Query for electronic submissions. Reports in 2 months on queries. Sample copy and writer's guidelines for #10 SASE.

Nonfiction: Book excerpts, essays, exposé, general interest, historical/nostalgic, how-to, humor, inspirational, interview/profile, new product, opinion, personal experience, photo feature, travel, how-to (soccer instruction). Buys 10 mss/year. Send complete ms. Length: 400-700 words. Pays $20 minimum. Pays contributor's copies "if piece was small enough, where payment wasn't expected."

Photos: Send photos with submission. Reviews 4×6 or 3×5 or larger prints. Offers $5-20/photo. Negotiates payment individually. Model releases and identification of subjects required. "depends on subject and focus."

Columns/Departments: Coaching Corner (instructional soccer), 500-600 words; numerous others on tournament coverage and administrative news. Buys 30 mss/year. Query with published clips. Send complete ms. Pays $10-30.

Fiction: "We don't solicit fiction often. No fluffy articles on sports." Buys 10 mss/year. Send complete ms. Length: 300-1,000 words. Pays $15-30.

Fillers: Anecdotes, facts, gags to be illustrated by cartoonist, newsbreaks, short humor. Buys 30/year. Length: 100-200 words. Pay negotiable.

Tips: "Send résumé with clips and refs. Contact editor for further info. Background experience in soccer is appreciated. We are most open to tournament/team profiles and reports. Stay within AP style and write to an adult softball audience."

Tennis

RACQUET, Heather & Pine, Inc. #1202, 42 W. 38th, New York NY 10018. (212)768-8360. Fax: (212)768-8365. Senior Editor: Matthew Tolan. 30% freelance written. Bimonthly tennis/lifestyle magazine. "*Racquet* celebrates the lifestyle of tennis." Estab. 1978. Circ. 145,000. Pays on publication. Publishes ms an average of 2-3 months after acceptance. Byline given. Offers negotiable kill fee. Rights purchased negotiable. Submit seasonal/holiday material 4-5 months in advance. Accepts simultaneous and previously published submissions. Send tearsheet or photocopy of article. Query for electronic submissions. Reports in 1 month. *Writer's Market* recommends allowing 2 months for reply. Sample copy for $4.

Nonfiction: Essays, exposé, historical/nostalgic, humor, interview/profile, opinion, personal experience, travel. "No instruction or poetry." Buys 15-20 mss/year. Query. Length: 1,000-4,000 words. Pays $200-750 for assigned articles; $100-300 for unsolicited articles. Pays in contributor copies or other negotiable premiums. Sometime pays expenses of writers on assignment.

Photos: State availability of photos with submission. Offers no additional payment for photos accepted with ms. Rights negotiable.

Columns/Departments: "Courtside" (personal experience—fun facts), 500-2,000 words; "Business of Tennis" (financial side of tennis and related industries), 2,000-2,500 words. Buys 5-10 mss/year. Query. Pays $100-300.

Fillers: Anecdotes, short humor. Buys 5/year. Length: 250-750 words. Pays $50-150.

Tips: "Get a copy, understand how we approach tennis, submit article written to style and follow-up. We are always looking for innovative or humorous ideas."

‡**TENNIS WEEK**, Tennis News, Inc., 124 E. 40th St., New York NY 10016. (212)808-4750. Editor: Julie Tupper. Contact: Nina Talbot. 10% freelance written. Biweekly magazine covering tennis. "For readers who are either tennis fanatics or involved in the business of tennis." Estab. 1974. Circ. 80,000. Pays on publication. Byline given. Buys all rights. Editorial lead time 1 month. Submit seasonal material 1 month in advance. Query for electronic submissions. Reports in 1 month on queries. Sample copy for $3.

Nonfiction: Buys 15 mss/year. Query with or without published clips. Length: 1,000-2,000 words. Pays $300.

Water Sports

DIVER, Seagraphic Publications, Ltd., Suite 295, 10991 Shellbridge Way, Richmond, British Columbia V6X 3C6 Canada. (604)273-4333. Fax: (604)273-0813. Editor/Publisher: Peter Vassilopoulos. Contact: Stephanie Bold, assistant editor. Magazine published 9 times/year emphasizing scuba diving, ocean science and technology (commercial and military diving) for a well-educated, outdoor-oriented readership. Circ. 17,500. Payment "follows publication." Buys first North American serial rights. Byline given. Submit seasonal/holiday material July-September for consideration for following year. Send SAE with IRCs. Reports in up to 3 months. Publishes ms up to 1 year after acceptance. "Articles are subject to being accepted for use in supplement issues on tabloid." Travel features considered only in September/October for use following year. Buys only 6 freelance travel items a year.

Nonfiction: How-to (underwater activities such as photography, etc.), general interest (underwater oriented), humor, historical (shipwrecks, treasure artifacts, archeological), interview (underwater personalities in all spheres—military, sports, scientific or commercial), personal experience (related to diving), photo feature (marine life), technical (related to oceanography, commercial/military diving, etc.), travel (dive resorts). No subjective product reports. Buys 25 mss/year. Submit complete ms. Length: 800-1,500 words. Pays $2.50/column inch.

Photos: "Features are mostly those describing dive sites, experiences, etc. Photo features are reserved more as specials, while almost all articles must be well illustrated with color or b&w prints supplemented by color transparencies." Submit original photo material with accompanying ms. Pays $7 minimum for 5×7 or 8×10 b&w glossy prints; $15 minimum for 35mm color transparencies. Captions and model releases required. Buys one-time rights.
Columns/Departments: Book reviews. Submit complete ms. Length: 200 words maximum. No payment.
Fillers: Anecdotes, newsbreaks, short humor. Buys 8-10/year. Length: 50-150 words. No payment for news items.
Tips: "No phone calls inquiring about status of manuscript. Write if no response within reasonable time. Only brief, to-the-point correspondence will be answered. Lengthy communications will probably result in return of work unused. Publisher assumes no liability to use material even after lengthy waiting period. Acceptances only subject to final and actual use."

‡**THE DIVER**, Diversified Periodicals, P.O. Box 313, Portland CT 06480. (203)342-4730. Editor: Bob Taylor. 50% freelance written. Magazine published 6 times/year for divers, coaches and officials. Estab. 1978. Circ. 1,500. Pays on publication. Byline given. Submit material at least 2 months in advance. Accepts simultaneous and previously published submissions. Reports in 2 weeks on queries; 1 month on mss. Sample copy for 9×12 SAE with 3 first-class stamps.
Nonfiction: Interview/profile (of divers, coaches, officials), results, tournament coverage, any stories connected with platform and springboard diving, photo features, technical. Buys 35 mss/year. Query. Length: 500-2,500 words. Pays $25.
Photos: Pays $5-10 for b&w prints. Captions and identification of subjects required. Buys one-time rights.
Tips: "We're very receptive to new writers."

SCUBA TIMES, The Active Diver's Magazine, GBP, Inc., 14110 Perdido Key Dr., Pensacola FL 32507. (904)492-7805. Fax: (904)492-7805. Managing Editor: Fred D. Garth. Editor: Gary Nichols. 90% freelance written. Bimonthly magazine on scuba diving. Estab. 1979. Circ. 43,000. Pays on publication. Publishes ms an average of 6 months after acceptance. Byline given. Buys first North American serial rights. Accepts previously published articles. Send information about when and where the article previously appeared. For reprints, pays 100% of the amount paid for an original article. Submit seasonal material 1 year in advance. Query for electronic submissions. Reports in 6 weeks. Sample copy for $3. Writer's guidelines for #10 SASE.
Nonfiction: How-to (advanced diving techniques such as technical, very deep, mixed gases, cave diving, wreck diving); humor; interview/profile (colorful characters in diving); personal experience (only if it is astounding); photo feature (creatures, places to dive); technical (physics, biology, medicine as it relates to diving); travel (dive destinations). No beginner-level dive material. Buys 75 mss/year. Query with published clips or send complete ms. Length: 150 words for sidebars, 1,500 for major destination features. Pays $75/ published page. Sometimes pays expenses of writers on assignment.
Photos: Send photos with submission. Reviews transparencies. Offers $25-75/page; $150/front cover photo. Captions and identification of subjects required. Buys one-time rights.
Columns/Departments: What a Wreck (informative guide to any wreck, old or new), 750 words; Creature Feature (one knock-out photo of a mysterious sea creature plus story of life cycle and circumstances that led to photo), 500 words; Last Watering Hole, (great photos, usually topside, and story about a dive site so remote most divers will never go), 500 words; Advanced Diving (how-to and advanced techniques for expanding dive adventure), 750 words. Buys 60 mss/year. Query with published clips. Length; 500-1,000 words. Pays $25-75/page.
Fillers: " 'Free Flowing' sections allows writers to be creative, thought provoking as they contemplate diver's relationship to the marine world." Anecdotes, short humor. Buys 10/year. Length: 300-900 words. Pays $25-75/page.
Tips: "Be a diver. Everyone tries for the glamorous destination assignments, but it is easier to break into the columns, especially, 'Last Watering Hole,' 'What a Wreck' and 'Creature Feature.' Outstanding photos are a must. We will coax a good article out of a great photographer whose writing skills are not developed. Very little is written in-house. Diving freelancers are the heart and soul of *STM*. Unknowns receive as much consideration as the big names. Know what you are talking about and present it with a creative flair. Divers are often technical or scientific by profession or disposition and their writing lacks flow, power and grace. Make us *feel* those currents and *smell* the diesel from the yacht."

SURFER, Surfer Publications, P.O. Box 1028, Dana Point CA 92629. (714)496-5922. Fax: (714)496-7849. Editor: Steve Hawk. Assistant Editor: Lisa Boelter. 75% freelance written. Monthly magazine "aimed at experts and beginners with strong emphasis on action surf photography." Estab. 1960. Circ. 110,000. Pays on publication. Byline given. Buys first North American serial rights. Submit seasonal/holiday material 6 months in advance. Accepts simultaneous submissions. Query for electronic submissions. Reports in 2 months. Sample copy for $3.95 with 9×12 SASE. Writer's guidelines for #10 SASE.
Nonfiction: How-to (technique in surfing), humor, inspirational, interview/profile, opinion, personal experience (all surf-related), photo feature (action surf and surf travel), technical (surfboard design), travel (surf exploration and discovery—photos required). Buys 30-50 mss/year. Query with or without published clips or

send complete ms. Length: 500-2,500 words. Pays 15-20¢/word. Sometimes pays the expenses of writers on assignment.

Photos: Send photos with submission. Reviews 35mm negatives and transparencies. Buys 12-24 illustrations/year. Prices vary. Used for columns: Environment, Surf Docs and sometimes features. Send samples with SASE to Art Director. Offers $10-250/photo. Identification of subjects required. Buys one-time and reprint rights.

Columns/Departments: Environment (environmental concerns to surfers), 1,000-1,500 words; Surf Stories (personal experiences of surfing), 1,000-1,500 words; Reviews (surf-related movies, books), 500-1,000 words; Sections (humorous surf-related items with b&w photos), 100-500 words. Buys 25-50 mss/year. Send complete ms. Pays 15-20¢/word.

Fiction: Surf-related adventure, fantasy, horror, humorous, science fiction. Buys 10 mss/year. Send complete ms. Length: 750-2,000 words. Pays 15-20¢/word.

Tips: "All sections are open to freelancers but interview/profiles are usually assigned. Try 'People Who Surf'—a good way to get a foot in the door. Stories must be authoritative and oriented to the hardcore surfer."

‡SWIM MAGAZINE, Sports Publications, Inc., #101, 155 S. El Molino, Pasadena CA 91101. (310)674-2120. Fax: (818)304-7759. Editor: Dr. Phillip Whitten. 50% freelance written. Prefers to work with published/selected writers. Bimonthly magazine. "*Swim Magazine* is for adults interested in swimming for fun, fitness and competition. Readers are fitness-oriented adults from varied social and professional backgrounds who share swimming as part of their lifestyle. Readers are well-educated, affluent and range in age from 20-100 with most in the 30-49 age group; about 50% female, 50% male." Estab. 1984. Circ. 39,100. Pays approximately 1 month after publication. Publishes ms an average of 4 months after acceptance. Byline given. Submit seasonal/holiday material 4 months in advance. Simultaneous queries OK. Reports in 1 month on queries; 3 months on mss. Sample copy for $3 (prepaid) and 9 × 12 SAE with $1.40 in first-class stamps. Free writer's guidelines.

Nonfiction: How-to (training plans and techniques), interview/profile (people associated with fitness and competitive swimming), inspirational, general health, new product (articles describing new products for fitness and competitive training). "Articles need to be informative as well as interesting. In addition to fitness and health articles, we are interested in exploring fascinating topics dealing with swimming for the adult reader." Send complete ms. Length: 1,000-3,500 words. Pays $3/published column inch. "No payment for articles about personal experiences."

● Using shorter articles.

Photos: Send photos with ms. Offers no additional payment for photos accepted with ms. Captions, model releases, identification of subjects required.

Tips: "Our how-to articles and physiology articles best typify *Swim Magazine*'s projected style for fitness and competitive swimmers. *Swim Magazine* will accept medical guidelines and exercise physiology articles only by M.D.s and Ph.Ds."

THE WATER SKIER, American Water Ski Association, 799 Overlook Dr., Winter Haven FL 33884. (813)324-4341. Editor: Greg Nixon. 60-70% freelance written. Magazine published 7 times/year for water skiing—all aspects of the sport. "*The Water Skier* is the official publication of the American Water Ski Association (AWSA), the national governing body for organized water skiing in the United States. The magazine has a controlled circulation and is available only to AWSA's membership, which is made up of 10,000 active competitive water skiers and 20,000 members who are supporting the sport. These supporting members may participate in the sport but they don't compete. The editorial content of the magazine features distinctive and informative writing about the sport of water skiing only." Estab. 1951. Circ. 30,000. Byline given. Offers 30% kill fee. Buys all rights (no exceptions). Editorial lead time 3-4 months. Submit seasonal material 6 months in advance. Reports in 2 weeks on queries. Sample copy for $1.25. Writer's guidelines for #10 SASE.

Nonfiction: Historical/nostalgic (has to pertain to water skiing), interview/profile (call for assignment), new product (boating and water ski equipment), travel (water ski vacation destinations). Buys 10-15 mss/year. Query. Length: 1,500-3,000 words. Pays $125 minimum for assigned articles; $150 minimum for unsolicited articles.

Photos: State availability of photos with submission. Reviews contact sheets. Negotiates payment individually. Captions and identification of subjects required. Buys all rights.

Columns/Departments: Sports Science/Medicine (athlete conditioning, physical/mental training), 1,000-1,500 words; The Starting Dock (small news items about people and events in the sport), 400-500 words; Waterways Issues (water skier's rights of access to waterways, environmental issues), 1,000-1,500 words. Query. Pays $75-125. Pay for columns negotiated individually with each writer.

Tips: "Contact the editor through a query letter (please no phone calls) with an idea. Avoid instruction, these articles are written by professionals. Concentrate on articles about the people of the sport. We are always looking for the interesting storys about people in the sport. Also, short news features which will make a reader say to himself, 'Hey, I didn't know that.' Keep in mind that the publication is highly specialized about the sport of water skiing." Most open to material for: feature articles (query editor with your idea), Sports/Science Medicine columns (query editor with ideas, looking for unique training or conditioning and method or sports rehabilitation), and The Starting Dock (interesting and unique news slants that are about the people and events in sport of water skiing).

WATERSKI MAGAZINE, The World's Leading Water Skiing Magazine, World Publications, 330 W. Canton Ave., Winter Park FL 32789. (407)628-4082. Fax: (407)628-7061. Editor: Rob May. Managing Editor: Barb McCarter. Contact: Rob May. 25% freelance written. Magazine published 10 times/year for water skiing and related watersports. "*WaterSki* instructs, advises, enlightens, informs *and* creates an open forum for skiers around the world. It provides definitive information on instruction, products, people and travel destinations." Estab. 1978. Circ. 105,000. **Pays on acceptance.** Publishes ms an average of 4 months after acceptance. Offers 25% kill fee. Buys first North American serial and second serial (reprint) rights. Editorial lead time 2 months. Submit seasonal material 2 months in advance. Query for electronic submissions. Reports in 1 month on queries; 2 months on mss. Sample copy for 8½×11 SAE with 4 first-class stamps. Writer's guidelines for #10 SASE.

Nonfiction: General interest, historical/nostalgic, how-to (water ski instruction boating-related), interview/profile, new product, photo feature, technical, travel. Does not want to see anything not directly related to the sport of water skiing. Buys 10 mss/year. Query with published clips. Length: 1,750-3,000 words. Pays $200 minimum for assigned articles. Pays other upon inability to meet author's pay request. Sometimes pays expenses of writers on assignment.

• Accepting more stories that are not necessarily hard-core water skiing. More travel, human interest.

Photos: Send photos with submission. Reviews 2¼×2¼ transparencies, all slides. Negotiates payment individually. Identification of subjects required. Buys one-time rights on color, all rights on b&w.

Columns/Departments: Shortline (interesting news of the sport), 300 words; Quick Tips (short instruction on water skiing and 500 words. Buys 10 mss/year. Query with published clips. Pays $75-125.

Fiction: Adventure, experimental, historical, humorous. Does not want to see anything not directly related to water skiing. Buys 10 mss/year. Query with published clips. Length: 1,750-4,000 words. Pays $200-300.

Fillers: Anecdotes, facts, gags to be illustrated by cartoonist, newsbreaks, short humor. Buys 15/year. Length: 200-500 words. Pays $75-125.

Tips: "I recommend a query call to see if there are any immediate openings in the calendar. Follow-up with a published submission (if applicable). Writers should have some interest in the sport, and understand its people, products and lifestyle. The features sections offer the most opportunity for freelancers. One requirement: It must have a positive, strong water skiing slant, whether it be personality, human interest, or travel."

Teen and Young Adult

The publications in this category are for young people ages 13-19. Publications for college students are listed in Career, College and Alumni. Those for younger children are listed in the Juvenile category.

BK NEWS, The Official Business Kids Newsletter, Busines$ Kids, Suite 1400, One Alhambra Plaza, Coral Gables FL 33134. Editor: Michael J. Holmes. 50% freelance written. Quarterly consumer magazine covering teenage entrepreneurship. "Best chance for publication is stories written about actual teen entrepreneurs—how they got started, how they market the business, etc. Pictures would be a real plus. And, any submissions that could educate teens as to how they can become a successful entrepreneur." Estab. 1988. Circ. 75,000. Pays on publication. Publishes ms an average of 3 months after acceptance. Buys all rights. Editorial lead time 3 months. Submit seasonal material 3 months in advance. No queries. Send complete ms. Sample copy for 10×12 SAE with 2 first-class stamps.

Nonfiction: How-to, humor, interview/profile, personal experience. "No articles that refer to teen employees who work for someone else. If he or she is not the top boss of the business, we will not accept the submission." Buys 5 mss/year. Send complete ms. Length: 200-600 words. Pays 15¢/word.

Photos: Freelancers should send photos with submission. Reviews prints. Offers $10/photo. Identification of subjects required. Buys all rights.

Columns/Departments: Teen Entrepreneur Profile (profile of a teenager who has his/her own business), 600 words. Buys 10 mss/year. Send complete ms. Pays 15¢/word.

Tips: "Profile a teen entrepreneur who has his/her own business. Attach a color or b&w print of any size."

CAREERS & COLLEGES, The Magazine for Today's Young Achievers, (formerly *Careers*), E.M. Guild, Inc., 6th Floor, 989 Sixth Ave., New York NY 10018. (212)563-4688. Editor: June Rogoznica. Estab. 1980. 75% freelance written. Works with a small number of new/unpublished writers each year. Quarterly magazine covering life-coping skills, career choices and educational opportunities for high school juniors and seniors. "*Careers & Colleges* is designed to offer a taste of the working world, new career opportunities, and stories covering the best ways to reach those opportunities—through education, etc." Circ. 500,000. Pays 30 days after acceptance. Publishes ms an average of 2-3 months after acceptance. Byline given. Offers 25% kill fee. Buys first North American serial rights. Submit seasonal/holiday material 6 months in advance. Sometimes accepts previously published submissions. Reports in 2 months on queries. Sample copy for $2.50. Writer's guidelines for #10 SAE with 1 first-class stamp.

Nonfiction: Book excerpts, how-to, interview/profile, humor. Buys 25 mss/year. Query with published clips. Length: 1,000-1,500 words. Pays $250-450. Sometimes pays the expenses of writers on assignment.

Photos: State availability of photos with submission. Reviews contact sheets and transparencies. Offers $100 minimum/photo. Captions, model releases, identification of subjects required. Buys one-time rights.

Columns/Departments: Money Wise, College Hotline, Career Watch, Tech Talk, Get Involved. Buys 15 mss/year. Length: 1,000-1,500 words. Pays $250.

CHALLENGE, Baptist Brotherhood Commission, 1548 Poplar Ave., Memphis TN 38104-2493. (901)272-2461. Editor: Jene Smith. Contact: Shelley Smith, Assistant Editor. 5% freelance written. Monthly magazine for "boys age 12-18 who are members of a missions organization in Southern Baptist churches." Circ. 35,000. Byline given. Pays on publication. Publishes ms an average of 6-8 months after acceptance. Buys simultaneous rights. Submit seasonal/holiday material 8 months in advance. Accepts simultaneous and previously published submissions. Send tearsheet or photocopy of article. Pays 75% of the amount paid for an original article. Reports in 1 month. *Writer's Market* recommends allowing 2 months for reply. Sample copy and writer's guidelines for 9×12 SAE with $1.20 postage. Writer's guidelines only for #10 SASE.

Nonfiction: How-to (crafts, hobbies), informational (youth), inspirational (sports/entertainment personalities); photo feature (sports, teen subjects). No "preachy" articles, fiction or excessive dialogue. Submit complete ms. Length: 500-800 words. Pays $20-50.

Photos: Purchased with accompanying ms or on assignment. Captions required. Query. Pays $10 for 8×10 b&w glossy prints.

Tips: "The writer has a better chance of breaking in at our publication with youth related articles (youth issues, and sports figures). Most topics are set years in advance. The most frequent mistake made by writers is sending us preachy articles. Aim for the mid- to older-teen instead of younger teen."

CROSSWALK, (formerly *Teens Today*), Church of the Nazarene, 6401 The Paseo, Kansas City MO 64131. (816)333-7000. Contact: Carol Gritton, Editor. 25% freelance written. Eager to work with new/unpublished writers. Weekly magazine for junior and senior high teens, to age 18, attending Church of the Nazarene Sunday School. Circ. 55,000. **Pays on acceptance.** Publishes an average of 14 months after acceptance. Byline given. Buys first and reprint rights. Submit seasonal/holiday material 10 months in advance. Accepts simultaneous and previously published submissions. Submissions not returned without SASE. Reports in 2 months. Sample copy and writer's guidelines for 50¢ and SAE with 2 first-class stamps.

Photos: Pays $10-30 for 8×10 b&w glossy prints.

• This magazine no longer takes fiction.

Tips: "We deal with teen issues: peers, self, parents, vocation, Christian truths related to life, etc. We do not condone dancing, drinking, drugs or premarital sex. Avoid overused themes."

EXPLORING MAGAZINE, Boy Scouts of America, P.O. Box 152079, Irving TX 75015-2079. (214)580-2365. Fax: (214)580-2079. Executive Editor: Scott Daniels. 85% freelance written. Prefers to work with published/ established writers. Magazine published 4 times/year—Winter (January), Spring (April), Summer (June), Fall (November)—covering the co-ed teen-age Exploring program of the BSA. Estab. 1970. Circ. 350,000. **Pays on acceptance.** Publishes ms an average of 8 months after acceptance. Byline given. Buys first rights. Submit seasonal/holiday material 6 months in advance. Reports in 1 month. *Writer's Market* recommends allowing 2 months for reply. Sample copy for 9×12 SAE with 5 first-class stamps. Writer's guidelines for #10 SASE. Write for guidelines and "What is Exploring?" fact sheet.

Nonfiction: General interest: teenage popular culture, music, films, health, fitness, fashion, cars, computers, how-to (organize trips, meetings, etc.); interview/profile (of outstanding Explorer), travel (backpacking or canoeing with Explorers). Buys 15-20 mss/year. Query with clips. Length: 800-1,600 words. Pays $350-500. Pays expenses of writers on assignment.

Photos: Brian Payne, photo editor. State availability of photos with query letter or ms. Reviews b&w contact sheets and 35mm transparencies. Captions required. Buys one-time rights.

Tips: "Contact the local Exploring Director in your area (listed in phone book white pages under Boy Scouts of America). Find out if there are some outstanding post activities going on and then query magazine editor in Irving, Texas. Strive for shorter texts, faster starts and stories that lend themselves to dramatic photographs."

FLORIDA LEADER (for high school students), Oxendine Publishing, Inc., P.O. Box 14081, Gainesville FL 32604-2081. (904)373-6907. Editor: W.H. "Butch" Oxendine Jr. Managing Editor: Kay Quinn. Quarterly magazine covering high school and pre-college youth. Estab. 1983. Circ. 50,000. Pays on publication. Publishes ms an average of 2-3 months after acceptance. Buys all rights. Submit seasonal material 4 months in advance. Accepts simultaneous and previously published submissions. Query for electronic submissions. Reports in 1-2 months on queries. Sample copy for 8×11 with 3 first-class stamps. For query response and/or writer's guidelines send #10 SASE.

Nonfiction: How-to, humor, new product, opinion. "No lengthy individual profiles or articles without primary and secondary sources of attribution." Length: 250-1,000 words. Pays $35 maximum. Pays students or first-time writers with contributor's copies.

Photos: Send photos with submission. Reviews contact sheets, negatives, transparencies. Offers $50/photo maximum. Captions, model releases, identification of subjects required. Buys all rights.

Columns/Departments: College Living (various aspects of college life, general short humor oriented to high school or college students), 250-1,000 words. Buys 10 mss/year. Query. Length: 250-1,000 words. Pays $35 maximum.

Fillers: Facts, newsbreaks, short humor. Buys 10/year. Length: 100-500 words. Pays $35 maximum.

Tips: "Read other high school and college publications for current issues, interests. Send manuscripts or outlines for review. All sections open to freelance work. Always looking for lighter, humorous articles as well as features on Florida colleges and universities, careers, jobs. Multi-sourced (5-10) articles are best."

FREEWAY, P.O. Box 632, Glen Ellyn IL 60138-0632. Editor: Amy J. Cox. 80% freelance written. Eager to work with new/unpublished writers. Weekly magazine. Estab. 1973. Prefers one-time rights but buys some reprints. Purchases 100 mss/year. Byline given. Accepts previously published submissions. Send typed ms with rights for sale noted. Reports on material accepted for publication in 2-3 months. Publishes ms an average of 1 year after acceptance. Returns rejected material in 2 months. Free sample copy and writer's guidelines with SASE.

Nonfiction: *"FreeWay's* greatest need is for personal experience stories showing how God has worked in teens' lives. Stories are best written in first-person, 'as told to' author. Incorporate specific details, anecdotes, and dialogue. Show, don't tell, how the subject thought and felt. Weave spiritual conflicts and prayers into entire manuscript; avoid tacked-on sermons and morals. Stories should show how God has helped the person resolve a problem or how God helped save a person from trying circumstances (1,000 words or less). Avoid stories about accident and illness; focus on events and emotions of everyday life. Short-short stories are needed as fillers. We also need self-help or how-to articles with practical Christian advice on daily living, and trend articles addressing secular fads from a Christian perspective. We do not use devotional material, or fictionalized Bible stories." Pays 6-10¢/word. Some poetry ($20-50).

Photos: Whenever possible, provide clear 8×10 or 5×7 b&w photos to accompany mss (or any other available photos). Payment is $5-30.

Fiction: "We use true-to-life and humorous fiction."

Tips: "Study our 'Tips to Writers' pamphlet and sample copy, then send complete ms. In your cover letter, include information about who you are, writing qualifications, and experience working with teens. Include SASE."

GUIDE, 55 W. Oak Ridge Dr., Hagerstown MD 21740. Fax: (301)790-9734. Editor: Jeannette Johnson. 50% freelance written. Works with a small number of new/unpublished writers each year. Weekly magazine journal for junior youth and early teens. "Its content reflects Christian beliefs and standards." Weekly magazine. Estab. 1953. Circ. 40,000. Buys first serial, simultaneous and second serial (reprint) rights. **Pays on acceptance.** Publishes ms an average of 6-9 months after acceptance. Byline given. Submit seasonal/holiday material 6 months in advance. Accepts previously published submissions. Send typed ms with rights for sale noted and information about when and where the material previously appeared. Pays 50% of their fee for reprints. Reports in 3 weeks. Free sample copy.

Fiction: Wants stories of character-building and spiritual value. Should emphasize the positive aspects of living, obedience to parents, perseverance, kindness, etc. "We can always use Christian humor and 'drama in real life' stories that show God's protection, and seasonal stories—Christmas, Thanksgiving, special holidays. We do not use stories of hunting, fishing, trapping or spiritualism." Buys about 300 mss/year. Send complete ms (include word count and Social Security number). Length: up to 1,200 words. Pays 3-4¢/word. Publishes novel excerpts. Length: 1,200 words maximum.

• Still looking for sparkling humor and adventure stories, filled with mystery, action, discovery, dialogue.

Tips: "Typical topics we cover in a yearly cycle include choices (music, clothes, friends, diet); friend-making skills; school problems (cheating, peer pressure, new school); self-esteem; changes; sibling relationships; divorce; step-families; drugs; and communication. We often buy short fillers, and an author who does not fully understand our needs is more likely to sell with a short-short. Our target age is 10-14. Our most successful writers are those who present stories from the viewpoint of a young teen-ager, written in the active voice. Stories that sound like an adult's sentiments passing through a young person's lips are *not* what we're looking for. Use believable dialogue."

KEYNOTER, Key Club International, 3636 Woodview Trace, Indianapolis IN 46268-3196. Executive Editor: Julie A. Carson. 65% freelance written. Works with a small number of new writers each year, but is eager to work with new/unpublished writers willing to adjust their writing styles to *Keynoter's* needs. Monthly youth magazine (December/January combined issue), distributed to members of Key Club International, a high school service organization for young men and women. Estab. 1946. Circ. 137,000. **Pays on acceptance.** Publishes ms an average of 5 months after acceptance. Byline given. Buys first North American serial rights.

Submit seasonal/holiday material 7 months in advance. Accepts simultaneous and previously published submissions. Reports in 1-2 months. Sample copy for 9×12 SAE with 3 first-class stamps. Writer's guidelines for #10 SASE.

Nonfiction: Book excerpts (included in articles), general interest (for intelligent teen audience), historical/nostalgic (generally not accepted), how-to (advice on how teens can enhance the quality of lives or communities), humor (accepted if adds to story), interview/profile (rarely purchased, "would have to be on/with an irresistible subject"), new product (affecting teens), photo feature (if subject is right), technical (understandable and interesting to teen audience), travel (must apply to club travel schedule), subjects that entertain and inform teens on topics that relate directly to their lives. "We would also like to receive self-help and school-related nonfiction on leadership, community service, and teen issues. *Please, no first-person confessions, fiction or articles that are written down to our teen readers.*" Buys 10-15 mss/year. Query. Length: 1,500-1,800 words. Pays $150-350. Sometimes pays the expenses of writers on assignment.

Photos: State availability of photos. Reviews color/b&w contact sheets and negatives. Identification of subjects required. Buys one-time rights. Payment for photos included in payment for ms.

Tips: "We want to see articles written with attention to style and detail that will enrich the world of teens. Articles must be thoroughly researched and must draw on interviews with nationally and internationally respected sources. Our readers are 13-18, mature and dedicated to community service. We are very committed to working with good writers, and if we see something we like in a well-written query, we'll try to work it through to publication."

THE MAGAZINE FOR CHRISTIAN YOUTH! The United Methodist Publishing House, 201 Eighth Ave. S., Box 801, Nashville TN 37202. (615)749-6319. Fax: (615)749-6078 or 749-6079. Editor: Anthony E. Peterson. Monthly magazine. Circ. 30,000. **Pays on acceptance.** Byline given. Buys one-time and all rights. Submit seasonal/holiday material 8-10 months in advance. Accepts previously published submissions. Writer's guidelines for #10 SASE. Sample copy for 9×12 SAE with 5 first-class stamps.

● Publisher is interested in hearing from teen writers.

Nonfiction: Book excerpts; general interest; how-to (deal with problems teens have); humor (on issues that touch teens' lives); inspirational; interview/profile (well-known singers, musicians, actors, sports); personal experience; religious, travel (include teen culture of another country). Buys 5 mss/year. Queries welcome. Length: 700-2,000 words. Pays $20-150 for assigned articles; 5¢/word for unsolicited articles.

Photos: State availability of photos with submission. Reviews transparencies and 8×10 prints. Offers $25-150/photo. Captions and model releases required. Buys one-time rights.

Fiction: From teens only: adventure, ethnic, fantasy, historical, humorous, mainstream, mystery, religious, romance, science fiction, suspense, western. No stories where the plot is too trite and predictable—or too preachy. Send complete ms. Length: 700-2,000 words. Pays 5¢/word.

Fillers: Cartoons, ideas newsbreaks, quizzes, short humor. Buys 6/year. Length: 50-200 words. Pays 5¢/word.

Tips: "Write to teens friend to friend. Treat instructional pieces with humor and grace, not judgementally. Keep tone personal. Appreciate the wonders and joys of adolescent life."

THE NEW ERA, 50 E. North Temple, Salt Lake City UT 84150. (801)240-2951. Fax: (801)240-1727. Managing Editor: Richard M. Romney. 60% freelance written. "We work with both established writers and newcomers." Monthly magazine for young people of the Church of Jesus Christ of Latter-day Saints (Mormon), their church leaders and teachers. Estab. 1971. Circ. 200,000. **Pays on acceptance.** Publishes ms an average of 1 year after acceptance. Byline given. Buys all rights. Submit seasonal material 1 year in advance. Query for electronic submissions. Reports in 2 months. Sample copy for $1 and 9×12 SAE with 2 first-class stamps. Writer's guidelines for SASE.

Nonfiction: Material that shows how the Church of Jesus Christ of Latter-day Saints is relevant in the lives of young people today. Must capture the excitement of being a young Latter-day Saint. Special interest in the experiences of young Mormons in other countries. No general library research or formula pieces without the *New Era* slant and feel. Uses informational, how-to, personal experience, interview, profile, inspirational, humor, historical, think pieces, travel, spot news. Query preferred. Length: 150-2,000 words. Pays 3-12¢/word. *For Your Information* (news of young Mormons around the world). Pays expenses of writers on assignment.

Photos: Uses b&w photos and transparencies with mss. Payment depends on use, $10-125 per photo. Individual photos used for *Photo of the Month*.

Fiction: Adventure, science fiction, humorous. Must relate to young Mormon audience. Pays minimum 3¢/word.

Poetry: Traditional forms, blank verse, free verse, light verse, all other forms. Must relate to editorial viewpoint. Pays minimum 25¢/line.

Tips: "The writer must be able to write from a Mormon point of view. We're especially looking for stories about successful family relationships. We anticipate using more staff-produced material. This means freelance quality will have to improve."

SEVENTEEN, 850 Third Ave., New York NY 10022. Editor-in-Chief: Caroline Miller. Managing Editor: Roberta Anne Myers. 80% freelance written. Works with a small number of new/unpublished writers each year. Monthly. Circ. 1.9 million. Buys one-time rights for nonfiction and fiction by adult writers and work by teenagers. Pays 25% kill fee. **Pays on acceptance.** Publishes ms an average of 6 months after acceptance. Byline given. Reports in up to 3 months.

• Ranked as one of the best markets for freelance writers in *Writer's Digest* magazine's annual "Top 100 Markets," January 1994.

Nonfiction: Articles and features of general interest to young women who are concerned with the development of their lives and the problems of the world around them; strong emphasis on topicality and helpfulness. Send brief outline and query, including a typical lead paragraph, summing up basic idea of article. Also likes to receive articles and features on speculation. Query with tearsheets or copies of published articles. Length: 1,200-2,000 words. Pays $50-150 for articles written by teenagers but more to established adult freelancers. Articles are commissioned after outlines are submitted and approved. Fees for commissioned articles $650-1,500. Sometimes pays the expenses of writers on assignment.

Photos: Margaret Kemp, art director. Photos usually by assignment only.

Fiction: Joe Bargmann, fiction editor. Thoughtful, well-written stories on subjects of interest to young women between the ages of 12 and 20. Avoid formula stories — "My sainted Granny," "My crush on Brad," etc. — no heavy moralizing or condescension of any sort. Humorous stories and mysteries are welcomed. Best lengths are 1,000-3,000 words. Pays $500-1,500.

Poetry: Contact Voice editor. By teenagers only. Pays $50. Submissions are nonreturnable unless accompanied by SASE.

Tips: "Writers have to ask themselves whether or not they feel they can find the right tone for a *Seventeen* article — a tone which is empathetic yet never patronizing; lively yet not superficial. Not all writers feel comfortable with, understand or like teenagers. If you don't like them, *Seventeen* is the wrong market for you. The best way for beginning teenage writers to crack the *Seventeen* lineup is for them to contribute suggestions and short pieces to the Voices section, a literary format which lends itself to just about every kind of writing: profiles, essays, exposes, reportage and book reviews."

STRAIGHT, Standard Publishing Co., 8121 Hamilton Ave., Cincinnati OH 45231-2323. (513)931-4050. Fax: (513)931-0904. Editor: Carla J. Crane. 90% freelance written. Estab. 1950. Weekly magazine (published quarterly) for "teens, age 13-19, from Christian backgrounds who generally receive this publication in their Sunday School classes or through subscriptions." **Pays on acceptance.** Publishes ms an average of 1 year after acceptance. Buys first rights, second serial (reprint) rights or simultaneous rights. Byline given. Submit seasonal/holiday material 9-12 months in advance. Accepts previously published submissions. Send tearsheet of article or story. Reports in 2 months. Free sample copy. Writer's guidelines for #10 SAE with 2 first-class stamps.

• Ranked as one of the best markets for fiction writers in *Writer's Digest* magazine's biannual "Fiction 50," June 1994.

Nonfiction: Religious-oriented topics, teen interest (school, church, family, dating, sports, part-time jobs), humor, inspirational, personal experience. "We want articles that promote Christian values and ideals." No puzzles. Query or submit complete ms. Include Social Security number on ms. "We're buying more short pieces these days; 12 pages fill up much too quickly." Length: 800-1,500 words.

Fiction: Adventure, humorous, religious, suspense. "All fiction should have some message for the modern Christian teen. Fiction should deal with all subjects in a forthright manner, without being preachy and without talking down to teens. No tasteless manuscripts that promote anything adverse to the Bible's teachings." Submit complete ms. Length: 1,000-1,500 words. Pays 3-7¢/word.

Photos: May submit photos with ms. Pays $25-50 for 8 × 10 b&w glossy prints and $75-125 for color slides. Model releases should be available. Buys one-time rights.

Tips: "Don't be trite. Use unusual settings or problems. Use a lot of illustrations, a good balance of conversation, narration, and action. Style must be clear, fresh — no sermonettes or sickly-sweet fiction. Take a realistic approach to problems. Be willing to submit to editorial policies on doctrine; knowledge of the *Bible* a must. Also, be aware of teens today, and what they do. Language, clothing, and activities included in mss should be contemporary. We need more fillers and stories on real teens doing something positive in their school/community, standing up for their faith. These pieces should be no longer than 800 words."

STUDENT LEADER (for college students), Oxendine Publishing Inc., P.O. Box 14081, Gainesville FL 32604-2081. (904)373-6907. Editor: W.H. "Butch" Oxendine Jr.. Managing Editor: Kay Quinn. 30% freelance written. Semiannual magazine covering student government, leadership. Estab. 1993. Circ. 200,000. Pays on publication. Byline given. Buys all rights. Submit seasonal material 4 months in advance. Query for electronic submissions. Reports in 1 month on queries. Sample copy for #10 SAE with 3 first-class stamps. For query response and/or writer's guidelines send #10 SASE.

Nonfiction: How-to, humor, new product, opinion. "No lengthy individual profiles or articles without primary or secondary sources of attribution." Buys 10 mss/year. Query. Length: 250-1,000 words. Pays $35 maximum. Pays contributor copies to students or first-time writers.

Photos: State availability of or send photos with submission. Reviews contact sheets, negatives, transparencies. Offers $50 photo/maximum. Captions, model releases, identification of subjects required. Buys all rights.

Columns/Departments: Buys 10 mss/year. Query. Length: 250-1,000 words. Pays $35 maximum.
Fillers: Facts, newsbreaks, short humor. Buys 10/year. Length: 100 words minimum. Pays $35 maximum.
Tips: "Read other high school and college publications for current ideas, interests. Send outlines or manuscripts for review. All sections open to freelance work. Always looking for lighter, humorous articles, as well as features on colleges and universities, careers, jobs. Multi-sourced (5-10) articles are best."

‡'**TEEN**, Petersen Publishing Co., 6420 Wilshire Blvd., Los Angeles CA 90048. (213)782-2950. Editor: Roxanne Camron. 40% freelance written. Monthly magazine covering teenage girls ages 12-19." 'Teen is edited for high school girls. We include all topics that are of interest to females aged 12-19. Our readers want articles on heavy hitting subjects like drugs, sex teen pregnancy, etc., and we also devote a significant number of pages each month to health, beauty and fashion." Estab. 1957. Circ. 1,143,653. **Pays on acceptance.** Byline sometimes given. Buys all rights. Editorial lead time 6 months. Submit seasonal material 6 months in advance. Accepts simultaneous submissions. Reports in 10 weeks. Sample copy for $2.50. Writer's guidelines for #10 SASE.
Nonfiction: General interest, how-to (geared for teen market), humor, inspirational, personal experience. Buys 35 mss/year. Query with or without published clips. Length: 250-750 words. Pays $175.
Fiction: Karle Dickerson. Adventure, condensed novels, fantasy, horror, mainstream, mystery, romance. Buys 12 mss/year. Send complete ms. Length: 2,500-3,500 words. Pays $200.

TEEN DREAM, Starline Publications, Suite 401, 210 Route 4 E., Paramus NJ 07652. (201)843-4004. Fax: (201)843-8636. Editor: Anne Raso. 20% freelance written. Bimonthly magazine of teen entertainment. Estab. 1988. Circ. 180,000. Pays on publication. Byline given. Offers 50% kill fee. Buys all rights. Submit seasonal/holiday material 3 months in advance. Reports in 2 months. Sample copy for $3.
Nonfiction: Photo feature. No fiction or poetry; celebrity interviews exclusively. Buys 50 mss/year. "Call editor about ms." Length: 500-1,000 words. Pays $50-100 for assigned articles. Sometimes pays expenses of writers on assignment.
Photos: State availability of or send photos with submission. Reviews color slides and 8×10 b&w prints. Offers $25-125/photo. Captions required. Buys one-time rights.

'**TEEN MAGAZINE**, 8490 Sunset Blvd., Hollywood CA 90069. (212)854-2222. Editor: Roxanne Camron. 20-30% freelance written. Prefers to work with published/established writers. Monthly magazine for teenage girls. Circ. 1.1 million. Publishes ms an average of 6 months after acceptance. Buys all rights. Reports in 6 months. Sample copy and writer's guidelines for 9×12 SAE with $2.50.
Fiction: Dealing specifically with teenage girls and contemporary teen issues. Suspense, humorous, romance. "Young love is all right, but teens want to read about it in more relevant settings." Length: 2,500-4,000 words. Pays $200. Sometimes pays the expenses of writers on assignment.
Tips: "No fiction with explicit language, casual references to drugs, alcohol, sex, or smoking; no fiction with too depressing outcome."

WITH MAGAZINE, Faith and Life Press and Mennonite Publishing House, 722 Main St., P.O. Box 347, Newton KS 67114-0347. (316)283-5100. Coeditors: Eddy Hall, Carol Duerksen. 60% freelance written. Magazine for teenagers published 8 times/year. "We approach Christianity from an Anabaptist-Mennonite perspective. Our purpose is to disciple youth within congregations." Circ. 6,100. **Pays on acceptance.** Byline given. Buys one-time rights. Submit seasonal/holiday material 6 months in advance. Accepts simultaneous and previously published submissions. Send typed ms with rights for sale noted, including information about when and where the material previously appeared. Pays 60% of the amount paid for original material. Reports in 1 month on queries; 2 months on mss. Sample copy for 9×12 SAE with 4 first-class stamps. Writer's guidelines and theme list for #10 SASE. Additional detailed guidelines for first person stories and/or how-to articles available for #10 SASE.
Nonfiction: Humor, personal experience, religious, how-to, youth. Buys 15 mss/year. Send complete ms. Length: 400-1,800 words. Pays 5¢/word for simultaneous rights; 3¢/word for reprint rights for unsolicited articles. Higher rates for first person stories and how-to articles written on assignment. (Query on these.)
Photos: Sometimes pays the expenses of writers on assignment. Send photos with submission. Reviews 8×10 b&w prints. Offers $10-50/photo. Identification of subjects required. Buys one-time rights.
Fiction: Humorous, religious, youth, parables. Buys 15 mss/year. Send complete ms. Length: 500-2,000 words. Payment same as nonfiction.
Poetry: Avant-garde, free verse, Haiku, light verse, traditional. Buys 4-6 poems. Pays $10-25.
Tips: "We're looking for more wholesome humor, not necessarily religious—fiction, nonfiction, cartoons, light verse. Christmas and Easter material has a good chance with us because we receive so little of it."

‡**YM**, Gruner & Jahr, 685 Third Ave., New York NY 10017. (212)878-8644. Editor: Bonnie Fuller. Contact: Catherine Romano. 25% freelance written. Magazine covering teenage girls/dating. "We are a national magazine for younger women ages 15-24. They're bright, enthusiastic and inquisitive. Our goal is to guide them—in effect, to be a second 'best friend' through the many exciting, yet often rough, aspects of young adulthood." Estab. 1940s. Circ. 1.8 million. **Pays on acceptance.** Byline given. Offers 25% kill fee. Buys first

North American serial rights. Editorial lead time 4 months. Submit seasonal material 5 months in advance. Accepts simultaneous submissions. Sample copy for $2.50. Writer's guidelines free on request.

Nonfiction: How-to, interview/profile, personal experience, first-person stories. "YM publishes two special issues a year. One is a self-discovery issue, the one is a love issue filled with articles on relationships." Buys 20 mss/year. Query with published clips. Length: 2,000 maximum words. Pays 75¢/word for assigned articles; 50-75¢/word for unsolicited articles. Pays expenses of writers on assignment.

Tips: "Our relationship articles are loaded with advice from psychologists and real teenagers. Areas most open to freelancers are: 2,000 word first-person stories covering a personal triumph over adversity — incorporating a topical social/political problem; 2,000 word relationship stories; 1,200 word relationship articles.

YOU! MAGAZINE, The Alternative Youth Magazine, Veritas Communications Inc., #102, 29800 Agoura Rd., Agoura Hills CA 91301. (818)991-1813. Editor: Paul Lauer. 50% freelance written. Monthly religious (Catholic) teen tabloid covering pop culture through the eyes of faith. Estab. 1987. Circ. 35,000 paid; 100,000 readership. Pays on publication. Publishes ms an average of 2 months after acceptance. Byline given. Buys one-time rights and second serial (reprint) rights. Editorial lead time 2 months. Submit seasonal material 4 months in advance. Accepts simultaneous and previously published submissions. Query for electronic submissions. Reports in 2 months on queries. Sample copy for 10 × 15 SAE with 5 first-class stamps. Writer's guidelines free on request.

● Ranked as one of the best markets for freelance writers in *Writer's Digest* magazine's annual "Top 100 Markets," January 1994.

Nonfiction: Humor, inspirational, interview/profile, personal experience, religious, teen related social. "No adult material." Buys 25-50 mss/year. Query with published clips. Length: 100-1,600 words. Pays $10 minimum. Sometimes pays expenses of writers on assignment.

Photos: Send photos with submission. Reviews transparencies and 4 × 6 or 5 × 7 prints. Negotiates payment individually. Captions and identification of subjects required.

Columns/Departments: School (school issues facing teens), 350 words; Family (family issues facint teens), 350 words; Friends (friends issues facing teens), 350 words. Buys 30 mss/year. Query with published clips. Pays $20-35.

Tips: "School, Family, Friends and Issues are open to freelancers. Give the problem with both positives and negatives and then offer solutions or ways in which Christian teens can deal with the situation from a faith perspective. Written in the language of teens!"

YOUNG SALVATIONIST, The Salvation Army, P.O. Box 269, Alexandria VA 22313-0269. (703)684-5500. Fax: (703)684-5539. Address all correspondence to Youth Editor. 75% freelance written. Works with a small number of new/unpublished writers each year. Monthly Christian magazine for high school teens. "Only material with a definite Christian emphasis or from a Christian perspective will be considered." Circ. 50,000. **Pays on acceptance.** Publishes ms an average of 10 months after acceptance. Byline given. Buys first North American serial, first, one-time or second serial (reprint) rights. Accepts previously published submissions. Send tearsheet or photocopy of article or typed ms with rights for sale noted and information about when and where the article previously appeared. For reprints, pays 100% of the amount paid for an original article. Submit seasonal/holiday material 6 months in advance. Reports in 2 months. Sample copy for 9 × 12 SAE with 3 first-class stamps. Writer's guidelines for #10 SASE.

Nonfiction: Inspirational, how-to, humor, interview/profile, personal experience, photo feature, religious. "Articles should deal with issues of relevance to teens today; avoid 'preachiness' or moralizing." Buys 60 mss/year. Send complete ms. Length: 500-1,200 words. Pays 10¢/word.

Fiction: Adventure, fantasy, humorous, religious, romance, science fiction — all from a Christian perspective. Length: 500-1,200 words. Pays 10¢/word. Publishes novel excerpts.

Tips: "Study magazine, familiarize yourself with the unique 'Salvationist' perspective of *Young Salvationist*; learn a little about the Salvation Army; media, sports, sex and dating are strongest appeal."

‡YOUNG SCHOLAR, The magazine for high performance students, Scholar Communications, Inc., Suite 1, 4905 Pine Cone Dr., Durham NC 27707. (919)493-9160. Managing Editor: Greg M. Sanders. 75% freelance written. Bimonthly consumer magazine covering high performance teenagers. "Young Scholar is about ideas for teenagers — eye-opening, mind-expanding ideas that help teenagers think about what they can do with their high school years (which is a lot more than most people realize)." Estab. 1993. Circ. 50,000. **Pays on acceptance.** Publishes ms an average of 3 months after acceptance. Byline given. Offers 25% kill fee. Buys all rights. Editorial lead time 6 months. Submit seasonal material 6 months in advance. Query for electronic submissions. Reports "as soon as we can — anywhere from 1 day to six weeks." Sample copy for 6 × 9 or larger SAE with 4 first-class stamps. Writer's guidelines for #10 SASE.

Nonfiction: Book excerpts, essays, exposé, general interest, how-to, humor, interview/profile, personal experience, travel. "We'll consider any article that can affect the lives of high performance teenagers. That kind of article isn't always predictable. August is our back-to-school issue. We're not interested in anything that traps learning in the classroom; anything that preaches or reads like a textbook, anything that's unorganized and doesn't come to a point. Buys 30 mss/year. Query with published clips. Length: 1,200-1,500 words. Pays

$300 minimum for assigned articles; $150 minimum for unsolicited articles. Sometimes pays expenses of writers on assignment.

Photos: State availability of photos with submission. Reviews 35mm transparencies and prints. Negotiates payment individually. Captions required. Buys one-time rights.

Columns/Departments: News to Use (news stories that affect teenagers and also leave them with an idea of what they can do about it), 350 words; Performance (issues relating to teenagers' performance), 750 words; Mindstuff (reviews of older, less well-known books), 350 words; What's Hot Now (products and services of interest to bright teenagers), 150-200 words. Study our departments carefully—they have a distinct style. Buys 50 mss/year. Send complete ms. Pays $15-200.

Tips: "Send published clips that show your ability to write with the style we prefer—alive, with plenty of action, dialogue (from good interviews), germane examples, and anecdotes. In a query or cover letter, show us you understand our audience of bright teenagers."News to Use" and "Performance" are our most-freelanced columns, but we encourage submissions for all departments—they're the best way to break in and get future feature assignments. For teenage writers only: "Full Court Pressure" is a 400 word, well thought-out, balanced essay on a pressing issue for teenagers."

YOUTH UPDATE, St. Anthony Messenger Press, 1615 Republic St., Cincinnati OH 45210-1298. (513)241-5615. Editor: Carol Ann Morrow. 90% freelance written. Monthly newsletter of faith life for teenagers, "designed to attract, instruct, guide and challenge Catholics of high school age by applying the Gospel to modern problems/situations." Circ. 30,000. **Pays on acceptance.** Publishes ms an average of 6 months after acceptance. Byline given. Reports in 2-3 months. Sample copy and writer's guidelines for #10 SASE.

Nonfiction: Inspirational, practical self-help, spiritual. "Adults who pay for teen subs want more church-related and curriculum-related topics." Buys 12 mss/year. Query. Length: 2,200-2,300 words. Pays $350-400. Sometimes pays expenses of writers on assignment. No reprints.

Tips: "Query first!"

Travel, Camping and Trailer

Travel magazines give travelers indepth information about destinations, detailing the best places to go, attractions in the area and sites to see—but they also keep them up-to-date about potential negative aspects of these destinations. Publications in this category tell tourists and campers the where-tos and how-tos of travel. This category is extremely competitive, demanding quality writing, background information and professional photography. Each has its own slant and should be studied carefully before sending submissions.

ACCENT, Meridian International Inc., 1720 Washington, P.O. Box 10010, Ogden UT 84409. (801)394-9446. 60-70% freelance written. Works with a small number of new/unpublished writers each year. Monthly inhouse travel magazine distributed by various companies to employees, customers, stockholders, etc. "Readers are predominantly upscale, mainstream, family oriented." Circ. 110,000. **Pays on acceptance.** Publishes ms an average of 3 months after acceptance. Byline given. Buys first rights, second serial (reprint) and nonexclusive reprint rights. Accepts simultaneous and previously published submissions. Written query first. Reports in 2 months with SASE. Sample copy for $1 and 9×12 SAE. Writer's guidelines for #10 SASE. Requests should be addressed Attn: Editorial Staff.

Nonfiction: "We want upbeat pieces slanted toward the average traveler, but we use some exotic travel. Resorts, cruises, hiking, camping, health retreats, historic sites, sports vacations, national or state forests and parks are all featured. No articles without original color photos." Buys 40 mss/year. Query. Length: 1,000 words. Pays 15¢/word.

Photos: Send color photos with ms. Pays $35 for color transparencies; $50 for cover. Captions and model releases required. Buys one-time rights. Review 35mm or larger transparencies and 5×7 or 8×10 color prints.

Tips: "Write about interesting places. We are inundated with queries for stories on California and the southeastern coast. Excellent color transparencies are essential. Most rejections are because of poor quality photography or the writer didn't study the market. We are using three times as many domestic pieces as foreign because of our readership. Avoid budget approaches and emphasize professionals who will take the worry out of your travel."

ADVENTURE WEST, America's Guide to Discovering the West, Ski West Publications, Inc., P.O. Box 3210, Incline Village NV 89450. (702)832-3700,. Editor: Marianne Porter. Contact: Katrina Veit, managing editor. 80% freelance written. Quarterly magazine covering adventure travel in the West. Estab. 1992. Circ. 121,000. Pays on publication. Publishes ms an average of 4-6 months after acceptance. Byline given. Offers 15% kill fee. Buys first North American serial rights. Editorial lead time 4 months. Submit seasonal material 5-6 months in advance. Accepts simultaneous submissions. Reports in 6-8 weeks on queries; 2 months on mss. Sample copy for $2.95 and 10×13 SASE with $1.44 postage, third class. Writer's guidelines free on request with SASE.

Nonfiction: Historical/nostalgic, humor, interview/profile, personal experience, photo feature, travel. "We only publish adventure travel done in the West, including Alaska, Hawaii, western Canada and western Mexico." Buys 40 mss/year. Query with published clips. Length: 1,000-2,500 words. Pays $150-500. Sometimes pays expenses of writers on assignment.

Photos: Send photos with submission. Reviews transparencies and slides. Negotiates payment individually. Captions and identification of subjects required. "We need itemized list of photos submitted." Buys one-time rights.

Columns/Departments: Buys 40-48 mss/year. Query with published clips. Pays $150-450.

Fiction: Humorous, western. "We publish humorous experiences in the West; that is the only fiction we accept." Buys 4 mss/year. Query with published clips. Length: 1,000-1,500 words. Pays $270-450.

Tips: "We like exciting, inspirational first-person stories on adventure. If the query or the unsolicited ms grabs us, we will use it. Our writer's guidelines are comprehensive. Follow them."

AMOCO TRAVELER, K.L. Publications, Suite 105, 2001 Killebrew Dr., Bloomington MN 55425-1879. Editor: Mary Lou Brooks. 80% freelance written. Quarterly magazine published for the Amoco Traveler Club. Circ. 55,000. Pays on acceptance by client. Byline given. Buys various rights. "This publication is a mix of original and reprinted material." Accepts simultaneous and previously published submissions. Include information about when and where the article previously appeared. Submit seasonal/holiday material 8 months in advance. Reports in 1 month. *Writer's Market* recommends allowing 2 months for reply. Sample copy for 9×12 SAE with 3 first-class stamps. Writer's guidelines for #10 SASE.

Nonfiction: Focus is on US destinations by car, although occasionally will use a foreign destination. Traveler Roads showcases a North American city or area, its attractions, history and accomodations; Traveler Focus features a romantic, getaway destination for the armchair traveler; Traveler Weekends focuses on an activity-oriented destination. Length: 1,200-1,500 words. Pays $325-425 for originals; $100-150 for reprints.

Columns/Departments: Healthwise (travel-related health tips). Length: 500-600 words. Pays $175.

Photos: Reviews 35mm transparencies. No b&w. Pay varies.

ARUBA NIGHTS, Nights Publications, 1831 Rene Levesque Blvd. West, Montreal, Quebec H3H 1R4 Canada. Fax: (514)931-6273. Editor: Stephen Trotter. Managing Editor: Zelly Zuskin. Contact: Stephen Trotter, Editor. 80% freelance written. Destination lifestyle magazine. Annual magazine covering the Aruban vacation lifestyle experience. Estab. 1988. Circ. 185,000. **Pays on acceptance.** Publishes ms an average of 6-10 months after acceptance. Offers 15% kill fee. Buys first North American serial and first Caribbean rights. Editorial lead time 2 months. Query for electronic submissions. Reports in 2 weeks on queries; 1 months on mss. *Writer's Market* recommends allowing 2 months for reply. Sample copy for $5. Writer's guidelines free on request.

Nonfiction: General interest, historical/nostalgic, how-to features relative to Aruba vacationers, humor, inspirational, interview/profile, eco-tourism, opinion, personal experience, photo feature, travel, Aruban culture, art, activities, entertainment, topics relative to vacationers in Aruba. "No negative pieces or stale rewrites." Buys 5-10 mss/year. Query with published clips. Length: 250-750 words. Pays $125-350 for assigned articles; $100-250 for unsolicited articles.

Photos: State availability with submission. Offers $25-100/photo. Captions, model releases, identification of subjects required. Buys one-time rights.

Tips: "Demonstrate your voice in your query letter. Focus on individual aspects of the Aruban lifestyle and vacation experience (e.g., art, gambling tips, windsurfing, a colorful local character, a personal experience, etc.), rather than generalized overviews. Provide an angle that will be entertaining to both vacationers and Arubans."

BACKPACKER, Rodale Press, Inc., 33 E. Minor St., Emmaus PA 18098-0099. (215)967-8296. Fax: (215)967-8181. Editor: John Viehman. Contact: Tom Shealey, managing editor. 50% freelance written. Magazine published 9 times/year covering wilderness travel. Estab. 1973. Circ. 210,000. **Pays on acceptance.** Byline given. Offers 25% kill fee. Buys one-time rights or all rights. Sometimes accepts previously published submissions. Send tearsheet of article including information about when and where the article previously appeared. Reports in 2 months. Writer's guidelines for #10 SASE.

• Prior to January 8, 1995 the area code is (215); effective that date the area code is (610).

Nonfiction: Essays, exposé, historical/nostalgic, how-to (expedition planner), humor, inspirational, interview/profile, new product, opinion, personal experience, technical, travel. No step-by-step accounts of what you did on your summer vacation—stories that chronicle every rest stop and gulp of water. Query with published clips and SASE. Length: 750-3,000 words. Pays $400-2,000. Sometimes pays (pre-determined) expenses of writers on assignment. "What we want are features that let us and the readers 'feel' the place, and experience your wonderment, excitement, disappointment or other emotions encountered 'out there.' If we feel like we've been there after reading your story, you've succeeded."

Photos: State availability of photos with submission. Amount varies—depends on size of photo used. Buys one-time rights.

Columns/Departments: Footnotes "News From All Over" (adventure, environment, wildlife, trails, techniques, organizations, special interests—well-written, entertaining, short, newsy item), 50-500 words; Body Language (in-the-field column), 750-1,200 words; Moveable Feast (food-related aspects of wilderness: nutrition, cooking techniques, recipes, products and gear), 500-750 words; Weekend Wilderness (brief but detailed guides to wilderness areas, providing thorough trip-planning information, only enough anecdote to give a hint, then the where/when/hows), 500-750 words; Technique (ranging from beginner to expert focus, written by people with solid expertise, details ways to improve performance, how-to-do-it instructions, information on equipment manufacturers and places readers can go), 750-1,500 words; and Backcountry (personal perspectives, quirky and idiosyncratic, humorous critiques, manifestos and misadventures, interesting angle, lesson, revelation or moral), 750-1,200 words. Buys 25-50 mss/year. Query with published clips. Pays $200-600. No phone calls regarding story ideas. Written queries only.

Tips: "Our best advice is to read the publication—most freelancers don't know the magazine at all. The best way to break in is with an article for the Backcountry, Weekend Wilderness or Footnotes Department."

BAJA TIMES, Editorial Playas De Rosarito, S.A., P.O. Box 5577, Chula Vista CA 91912-5577. Fax: 01152-661-22366. Editor: John W. Utley. 90% freelance written. Monthly tourist and travel publication on Baja California, Mexico. "Oriented to the Baja California, Mexico aficionado—the tourist and those Americans who are living in Baja California or have their vacation homes there. Articles should be slanted to Baja." Estab. 1978. Pays on publication. Publishes ms an average of 8 months after acceptance. Byline given. Buys first rights. Submit seasonal/holiday material 4 months in advance. Accepts previously published submissions. Send typed ms with rights for sale noted and information about when and where the article previously appeared. For reprints, pays 100% of the amount paid for an original article. Reports in 3 months. Sample copy for 9 × 12 SAE with 5 first-class stamps. Free writer's guidelines.

Nonfiction: General interest, historical/nostalgic, humor, personal experience, photo feature, travel. All with Baja California slant. "Nothing that describes any negative aspects of Mexico (bribes, bad police, etc.). We are a positive publication." Query with or without published clips or submit complete ms. Length: 750-1,600 words. Pays $50-100 for assigned articles; $35-50 for unsolicited articles. Sometimes pays expenses of writers on assignment.

Photos: Send photos with submission. Reviews 5 × 7 prints. Captions and identification of subjects required. Buys one-time rights.

Tips: "Take a chance—send in that Baja California related article. We guarantee to read them all. Over the years we have turned up some real winners from our writers—many who do not have substantial experience. The entire publication is open. We buy an average of 6 freelance each issue. Virtually any subject is acceptable as long as it has a Baja California slant. Remember Tijuana, Mexico (on the border with San Diego, CA) is the busiest border crossing in the world. We are always interested in material relating to Tijuana, Rosarito, Ensenada, San Felipe, LaPaz."

‡BLOCK ISLAND MAGAZINE & TRAVEL GUIDE, McHugh Design, Advertising & Publishing, 62 La Salle Rd., West Hartford CT 06107. (203)523-7518. Managing Editor: Tom Jakup. Annual travel magazine covering Block Island/Newport. "Any information/articles that would be helpful to people planning a trip to Block Island or its surrounding areas." Estab. 1993. Circ. over 100,000. Pays on publication. Byline given. Buys one-time rights. Editorial lead time 8 months. Submit seasonal material 8 months in advance. Accepts simultaneous and previously published submissions. Query for electronic submissions.

Nonfiction: Essays, historical/nostalgic, personal experience, photo feature, travel. Query. "We negotiate payment individually." Pays expenses of writers on assignment.

Photos: State availability of photos with submission. Reviews contact sheets. Negotiates payment individually. Captions and identification of subjects required. Buys one-time rights.

Columns/Departments: "We negotiate payment individually."

Tips: "Send query letters to either Tom Jakup, Senior Editor or Tracy McHugh, Publisher. Do not send photos. Explain how your article would benefit vacationers on Block Island."

‡BONAIRE NIGHTS, Nights Publications, 1831 René Lévesque Blvd. W., Montreal, Quebec H3H 1R4 Canada. Fax: (514)931-6273. Editor: Stephen Trotter. 80% freelance written. Annual magazine covering Bonaire vacation experience. "Upbeat entertaining lifestyle articles: colorful profiles of locals, eco-tourism; lively features on culture, activities (particularly scuba and snorkeling), special events, historical attractions, how-to features. Audience is North American tourist." Estab. 1993. Circ. 60,000. **Pays on acceptance.** Publishes ms an average of 6-10 months after acceptance. Byline given. Offers 15% kill fee. Buys first North American serial rights and first Caribbean rights. Editorial lead time 2 months. Query for electronic submissions. Reports in 2 weeks on queries; 1 month on mss. Sample copy for $5. Writer's guidelines for #10 SASE.

Nonfiction: General interest, historical/nostalgic, how-to, humor, inspirational, interview/profile, opinion, personal experience, photo feature, travel, local culture, art, activities, especially scuba diving, snorkeling, eco-tourism. Buys 6-9 mss/year. Query with published clips. Length: 250-750 words. Pays $125-350 for assigned articles; $100-250 for unsolicited articles.

Photos: State availability of photos with submission. Reviews transparencies. Offers $25-100/slide. Captions, model releases, identification of subjects required. Buys one-time or first rights.

Tips: "Demonstrate your voice in your query letter. Focus on the Bonaire lifestyle, what sets it apart from other islands. We want personal experience, not generalized overviews. Be positive and provide an angle that will appeal to residents as well as visitors."

‡CAMPERS MONTHLY, Northeast Edition–Maine to New York and Mid Atlantic Edition—New York to Virginia, P.O. Box 260, Quakertown PA 18951. (215)536-6420. Editor: Paula Finkbeiner. 50% freelance written. Monthly (except December) tabloid covering tenting and recreational vehicle camping and travel. "With the above emphasis, we want to encourage our readers to explore all forms of outdoor recreation using a tent or recreational vehicle as a 'home away from home.' Travel-places to go, things to do and see." Estab. 1991 (Mid-Atlantic), 1993 (Northeast). Circ. 35,000 (Mid-Atlantic), 25,000 (Northeast). Pays on publication. Publishes ms an average of 2 months after acceptance. Byline given. Buys simultaneous rights. Editorial lead time 2 months. Submit seasonal material 3-4 months in advance. Accepts simultaneous and previously published submissions. Query for electronic submissions. Reports in 1 month. Sample copy and writer's guidelines free on request.

Nonfiction: Historical/nostalgic (tied into a camping trip), how-to (selection, care, maintenance of RV's, tents, accessories, etc.) humor, personal experience, travel (camping in the Mid-Atlantic or Northeast region). Special issue: Snowbird Issue (October)—geared towards campers heading South. This is generally the only time we accept articles on areas outside our coverage area. Buys 15-20 mss/year. Send complete ms. Length: 800-1,500 words. Pays $60 for assigned articles; $50 for unsolicited articles. Sometimes pays expenses of writers on assignment.

Photos: Send photos with submission. Reviews 5×7 or 8×10 glossy b&w prints. Offers $5-10/photo. Don't send snapshots or polaroids. Avoid slides.

Columns/Departments: Campground Cook (Ideas for cooking in RV's, tents and over campfires, should include recipes), 500-1,000 words; Tales From The Road (humorous stories of "on-the-road" travel), 350-800 words; Tech Tips (technical pieces on maintenance and enhanced usage of RV-related equipment), 350-1,000 words. Buys 15 mss/year. Send complete ms. Pays $40-60.

Fiction: Humorous, slice-of-life vignettes. Buys 10 mss/year. Query. Length: 300-1,000 words. Pays $60-75.

Fillers: Facts, short humor. Buys 8/year. Length: 30-350. Pays $20-45.

Tips: Most open to freelancers are "destination pieces focusing on a single attraction or activity or closely clustered attractions are always needed. General interest material, technical or safety ideas (for RVs and tents) is an area we're always looking for pieces on. Off the beaten track destinations always get priority."

CAMPING TODAY, Official Publication of the Family Campers & RVers, 126 Hermitage Rd., Butler PA 16001-8509. (412)283-7401. Editors: DeWayne Johnston and June Johnston. 30% freelance written. Prefers to work with published/established writers. Monthly official membership publication of the FCRV, "the largest nonprofit family camping and RV organization in the United States and Canada. Members are heavily oriented toward RV travel, both weekend and extended vacations. Concentration is on member activities in chapters. Group is also interested in conservation and wildlife. The majority of members are retired." Estab. 1983. Circ. 25,000. Pays on publication. Publishes ms an average of 6 months after acceptance. Byline given. Buys one-time rights. Submit seasonal/holiday material 3 months in advance. Accepts simultaneous and previously published submissions. Send typed ms with rights for sale noted and information about when and where the article previously appeared. Pays 50% of their fee for an original article. Reports in 60 days. Sample copy and guidelines for 4 first-class stamps. Writer's guidelines only for #10 SASE.

Nonfiction: Travel (interesting places to visit by RV, camping), humor (camping or travel related, please, no "our first campout stories"), interview/profile (interesting campers), new products, technical (RVs related). Buys 10-15 mss/year. Send complete ms with photos. Length: 750-2,000 words. Pays $50-150.

Photos: Send photos with ms. Need b&w or sharp color prints inside (we can make prints from slides) and vertical transparencies for cover. Captions required.

Tips: "Freelance material on RV travel, RV maintenance/safety, and items of general camping interest throughout the United States and Canada will receive special attention."

CANCÚN NIGHTS, Nights Publications, 1831 Rene Levesque Blvd. West, Montreal, Quebec H3H 1R4 Canada. Fax: (514)931-6273. Editor: Stephen Trotter. Managing Editor: Zelly Zuskin. Contact: Stephen Trotter, Editor. 80% freelance written. Destination lifestyle magazine. Semiannual magazine covering the Cancún vacation experience. Seeking "upbeat, entertaining lifestyle articles: colorful profiles of locals; lively features on culture, activities, night life, special events, historical attractions, Mayan achievements; how-to features; humor. Our audience is the North American vacationer." Estab. 1991. Circ. 500,000. **Pays on acceptance.** Publishes ms an average of 6-10 months after acceptance. Offers 15% kill fee. Buys first North American serial rights and first Mexican rights. Editorial lead time 2 months. Query for electronic submissions. Reports 2 weeks on queries; 1 month on mss. *Writer's Market* recommends allowing 2 months for reply. Sample copy for $5. Writer's guidelines free on request.

Nonfiction: General interest, historical/nostalgic, how-to let vacationers get the most from their holiday, humor, inspirational, eco-tourism, interview/profile, opinion, personal experience, photo feature, travel, local culture, art, activities, night life, topics relative to vacationers in Cancún. Does not want to see negative pieces, stale rewrites. Buys 8-12 mss/year. Query with published clips. Length: 250-750 words. Pays $125-350 for assigned articles; $100-250 for unsolicited articles.

Photos: State availability of photos with submission. Reviews transparencies. Offers $25-100/photo. Captions, model releases, identification of subjects required. Buys one-time rights.

Tips: "Demonstrate your voice in your query letter. Focus on individual aspects of the Cancún lifestyle and vacation experience (e.g., art, history, snorkeling, fishing, a colorful local character, a personal experience, etc.), entertaining to both vacationers and residents."

‡CARIBBEAN DIGEST, The #1 Caribbean Magazine, Caribbean Media Group, Box 680608, Miami FL 33168. (305)372-1157. Editor: Aubrey Duncan. 70% freelance written. Quarterly consumer magazine covering Caribbean—all areas. Estab. 1992. Circ. 20,000. Pays on publication. Byline given. Buys first rights. Editorial lead time 3 months. Submit seasonal material 3 months. Accepts simultaneous and previously published submissions. Sample copy free on request.

Nonfiction: Book excerpts, essays, exposé, general interest, historical/nostalgic, how-to, humor, inspirational, interview/profile, new product, opinion, personsl experience, photo feature, religious, technical, travel. Planning a special on Jamaica. Buys 90 mss/year. Send complete ms. Length: 500-1,000 words. Pays contributor copies "if writer agrees."

Photos: Freelancers should send photos with submission. Reviews 3×5 prints. Offers no additional payment for photos accepted with ms. Negotiates payment individually. Captions, model release, identification of subjects required. Buys one-time rights.

Columns/Departments: Caribbean 500-1,000 words. Buys 40 mss/year. Send complete ms. Pays $100-200.

Fiction: Adventure, ethnic, historical, religious, romance. Buys 20 mss/year. Send complete ms. Length: 500-1,000 words. Pays $100-200.

Poetry: Uses avant-garde, free verse, Haiku, light verse, traditional. Buys 15 poems/year. Pays $100-200.

Fillers: Uses anecdotes, facts, gags to be illustrated by cartoonist, newsbreaks, Buys 50/year. Length: 150-300 words. Pays $50-150.

Tips: "Submit any material or photo related to any aspect of Caribbean life in US, Canada, Europe and throughout the Caribbean."

CARIBBEAN TRAVEL AND LIFE, Suite 830, 8403 Colesville Rd., Silver Spring MD 20910. (301)588-2300. Editor-in-Chief: Veronica Gould Stoddart. 90% freelance written. Prefers to work with published/established writers. Bimonthly magazine covering travel to the Caribbean, Bahamas and Bermuda. Estab. 1985. Circ. 115,000. Pays on publication. Publishes ms an average of 3 months after acceptance. Byline given. Offers 25% kill fee. Buys first North American serial rights. Submit seasonal/holiday material 6 months in advance. Reports in 2 months. Sample copy for 9×12 SAE with 6 first-class stamps. Writer's guidelines for #10 SASE.

Nonfiction: General interest, how-to, interview/profile, culture, personal experience, travel. No "guidebook rehashing; superficial destination pieces or critical exposes." Buys 30 mss/year. Query with published clips. Length: 2,000-2,500 words. Pays $550.

Photos: Send photos with submission. Reviews 35mm transparencies. Offers $75-400/photo. Captions and identification of subjects required. Buys one-time rights.

Columns/Departments: Resort Spotlight (in-depth review of luxury resort); Tradewinds (focus on one particular kind of water sport or sailing/cruising); Island Buys (best shopping for luxury goods, crafts, duty-free); Island Spice (best cuisine and/or restaurant reviews with recipes); all 1,000-1,500 words; Caribbeana (short items on great finds in travel, culture, and special attractions), 500 words. Buys 36 mss/year. Query with published clips or send complete ms. Length: 500-1,250 words. Pays $75-200.

Tips: "We are especially looking for stories with a personal touch and lively, entertaining anecdotes, as well as strong insight into people and places being covered. Writer should demonstrate why he/she is the best person to do that story based on extensive knowledge of the subject, frequent visits to destination, residence in destination, specialty in field."

CHEVY OUTDOORS, A Celebration of American Recreation and Leisure, The Aegis Group: Publishers, 30400 Van Dyke, Warren MI 48093. (810)574-9100. Fax: (810)558-5897. Editor: Michael Brudenell. 85% freelance written. Works with a small number of new/unpublished writers each year. Quarterly magazine covering outdoor recreation and adventure. Circ. 1 million. Pays on publication. Publishes ms an average of 3-6 months after acceptance. Offers 25% kill fee. Byline given. Buys first, one-time or second serial (reprint) rights. Submit seasonal/holiday material 6 months in advance. Accepts simultaneous and previously published submissions. Send tearsheet of article. Pays 25% of the amount paid for an original article. Reports in 6-8 weeks. Sample copy for 9×12 SAE with 5 first-class stamps.

• Prior to December 1, 1994 the area code is (313). Effective that date the area code is (810).

Nonfiction: Book excerpts, historical/nostalgic, how-to (on outdoor topics—camping, fishing, etc.), humor, interview/profile (on outdoors people, such as authorities in their fields), personal experience (must be outdoor or wilderness related), photo feature, technical (new technologies for campers, anglers, hunters, etc.), travel, stories on new trends in outdoor recreation. "No exposés or negative articles; we like an upbeat, positive approach." Buys 50 mss/year. Query with published clips. Length: 200-1,500 words. Pays $100-750 for assigned articles; $100-500 for unsolicited articles. Sometimes pays the expenses of writers on assignment.

Photos: Send photos with submission. Reviews 35mm or larger transparencies. Offers $25-100/photo. Model releases and identification of subjects required. Buys one-time rights; sometimes all rights.

Columns/Departments: Outdoor Photography (how-tos by established photographers with national reputation in outdoor photography); Outdoors People (profiles of notable outdoors enthusiasts or exceptional people who do work related to outdoor recreation). Buys 8-12 mss/year. Query with published clips. Length: 800-1,500 words. Pays $400-750.

Fillers: Anecdotes, facts, newsbreaks. Buys 25-30/year. Length: 25-200 words.

Tips: "Stories that are dynamic and active, and stories that focus on people will have a better chance of getting in. Focus queries tightly and look beyond the obvious. Use this as a touchstone—Is this a story that I would be compelled to read if I found it on a coffee table or in a waiting room? If the answer is 'yes,' we want to hear from you. Our features well is the best freelance target. Travel, personality profiles or activity features are probably the best ticket in. But the idea has to be fresh and original, and the copy has to sing. New or unpublished writers should write on topics with which they are *very* familiar; expertise can compensate for a lack of experience."

CHICAGO TRIBUNE, Travel Section, 435 N. Michigan Ave., Chicago IL 60611. (312)222-3999. Travel Editor: Randy Curwen. Weekly Sunday newspaper leisure travel section averaging 24 pages aimed at vacation travelers. Circ. 1.1 million. Pays on publication. Publishes ms an average of 1½ months after acceptance. Byline given. Buys one-time rights. Submit seasonal/holiday material 2 months in advance. Accepts simultaneous submissions. Query for electronic submissions. Reports in 2 weeks. Sample copy for large SAE with $1.50 postage. Writer's guidelines for #10 SASE.

Nonfiction: Essays, general interest, historical/nostalgic, how-to (travel, pack), humor, opinion, personal experience, photo feature, travel. "There will be 16 special issues in the next 18 months." Buys 500 mss/year. Send complete ms. Length: 500-2,000 words. Pays $100-350.

Photos: State availability of photos with submission. Reviews 35mm transparencies and 8×10 or 5×7 prints. Offers $100/color photo; $25/b&w photo. $100 for cover photo. Captions required. Buys one-time rights.

Tips: "Be professional. Use a word processor. Make the reader want to go to the area being written about. Our Page 3 Reader is a travel essay, hopefully with humor, insight, tear jerking. A great read. Only 1% of manuscripts make it."

CLUBMEX, (formerly *Mexico West*), Suite 101, 3450 Bonita Rd., Chula Vista CA 91910-3249. (619)585-3033. Fax: (619)420-8133. Publisher/Editor: Chuck Stein. 75% freelance written. Bimonthly newsletter on Baja California and Mexico as a travel destination. "Our readers are travelers to Mexico, and are interested in retirement, RV news and tours. They are knowledgeable but are always looking for new places to see." Estab. 1975. Circ. 5,000. Pays on publication. Publishes an average of 2 months after acceptance. Byline given. Buys first North American serial rights. Submit seasonal/holiday material 3 months in advance. Accepts previously published submissions. Send photocopy of article. Pays 100% of the amount paid for an original article. Reports in 1 month. Free sample copy. Writer's guidelines for #10 SAE with 2 first-class stamps.

Nonfiction: Historical, humor, interview, personal experience, travel. Buys 36-50 mss/year. Send complete ms. Length: 900-1,500 words. Pays $65 for the cover story and $50 for other articles used.

● They now accept articles dealing with all of Mexico as well as just Baja.

Photos: State availability of photos with submission. Reviews 3×5 prints. Offers no additional payment for photos accepted with ms. Captions required. Buys one-time rights.

COAST TO COAST MAGAZINE, A Publication for the Members of Coast to Coast Magazine, 3601 Calle Tecate, Camarillo CA 93012. Editor: Valerie Rogers. Associate Editor: Kathleen McLaughlin. 80% freelance written. magazine published 8 times/year for members of Coast to Coast Resorts. Estab. 1972. Circ. 300,000. **Pays on acceptance.** Publishes ms an average of 3 months after acceptance. Byline given. Offers 33% kill fee. Buys first North American serial rights. Submit seasonal/holiday material 5 months in advance. Query for electronic submissions. Accepts previously published submissions. Send photocopy of article, information about when and where the article previously appeared. Pays 50% of the amount paid for an original article. Reports in 1 month on queries; 2 months on mss. Sample copy for $2 and 9×12 SASE.

Nonfiction: Book excerpts, essays, general interest, historical/nostalgic, how-to, humor, inspirational, interview/profile, new product, opinion, personal experience, photo feature, technical, travel. Buys 35 mss/year. Query with published clips or send complete ms. Length: 500-2,500 words. Pays $75-500.

Photos: Send photos with submission. Reviews transparencies. Offers $50-600/photo. Identification of subjects required. Buys one-time rights.

Tips: "Send published clips along with queries, or story ideas will not be considered."

‡**CONDÉ NAST TRAVELER**, The Condé Nast Publications, 360 Madison Ave., New York NY 10017. Editor: Thomas J. Wallace. Managing Editor: Richard Levine. 75% freelance written. Monthly magazine covering travel. "Our motto, Truth in Travel, sums up our editorial philosophy: to present travel destinations, news and features in a candid, journalistic style. Our writers do not accept complimentary tickets, hotel rooms, gifts, or the like. While our departments present service information in a tipsheet or newsletter manner, our destination stories are literary in tone. Our readers are affluent, well-educated, and sophisticated about

travel." Estab. 1987. Circ. 1 million. **Pays on acceptance.** Publishes ms 3-6 months after acceptance. Byline given. Offers 25% kill fee. Buys all rights. Editorial lead time 3 months. Submit seasonal material 4-6 months in advance. Reports in 2 months on queries.

Nonfiction: Alison Humes, features editor. Travel. No humor. Query. Length: 500-5,000 words. Pays $1/word. Pays expenses of writers on assignment.

Columns/Departments: Stop Press, edited by Cliff Hopkinson, executive editor/news (travel news items—keep in mind that we are a monthly magazine with a long lead time), 500 words; Word of Mouth, edited by Catherine Kelley, arts editor (timely and hip items on new, trendy restaurants, shops, bars, exhibits around the world—will not consider annual events or subjects that receive much publicity elsewhere), 25-50 words (no byline). Following departments "tend not to use unsolicited ideas, but those who insist should be careful to contact the correct editor: Great Drives, As Others See Us: Peter Frank; Food in Review: Gully Wells; Gear in Review: Jason Nixon; Shopping: Catherine Kelley. Other departments are staff-generated and do not accept freelance submissions." Buys 10-20 mss/year. Query. Pays $1/word.

Tips: "Please keep in mind that we very rarely assign stories based on unsolicited queries because (1) our inventory of unused stories (features and departments) is very large, and (2) most story ideas are generated inhouse by the editors, as it is very difficult for outsiders to anticipate the needs of our inventory. To submit story ideas, send a brief (one paragraph) description of the idea(s) to the appropriate editor. Please do not send clips, resumes, photographs, itineraries, or abridged or full-length manuscripts. Due to our editorial policy, we *do not* purchase completed manuscripts. Telephone calls are not accepted."

THE COOL TRAVELER, The Rome Cappucino Review, P.O. Box 273, Selins Grove PA 17870-1813. Editor: Bob Moore. Managing Editor: MaryBeth Feeney. 100% freelance written. Bimonthly publication covering travel. "We do not emphasize affluence but rather the experiences one has while travelling: romance, adventure, thrills, chills, etc. We have even published excerpts from diaries!" Estab. 1988. Circ. 750-1,250. Pays on publication. Publishes ms an average of 2-3 months after acceptance. Byline given. Send bio. Buys one-time rights. Submit seasonal/holiday material 4 months in advance. Accepts simultaneous and previously published submissions. Query for electronic submissions. Reports in 6 weeks "unless we like it—then it could be 4-6 months." Sample copy for $3. Free writer's guidelines with SASE.

• *The Cool Traveler* now has a new feature article need: "What is a cool traveler?" The article should use the word "cool" often and feature unique, funny, bizarre experiences. No experience is too bizarre.

Nonfiction: Personal experience, travel, art history. Special issues: Christmas and International Festival. "We don't want a listing of names and prices but personal experiences and unusual experiences." Buys 15 mss/year. Send complete ms. Length: 1,000 words maximum. Pays $5-20 for unsolicited articles.

Columns/Departments: News items pertaining to particular countries. ("Really need these!") Seasonal (material pertaining to a certain time of year: like a winter festival or summer carnival), 1,500 words maximum. Women travel. Pays $5-20. Big need for tidbits.

Poetry: Free verse, light verse, traditional. No poetry that is too sentimental. Buys 3 poems/year. Submit maximum 3 poems. Length: 5-75 lines. Pays $5-20.

Tips: "Writers should have a sense of humor. We have changed our needs. We now desire material, in addition to an emphasis on experience, a strong emphasis on facts. In fact we would strongly like some strictly news-oriented material."

CRUISE TRAVEL MAGAZINE, World Publishing Co., 990 Grove St., Evanston IL 60201-4370. (708)491-6440. Editor: Robert Meyers. Contact: Charles Doherty, managing editor. 95% freelance written. Bimonthly magazine on cruise travel. "This is a consumer-oriented travel publication covering the world of pleasure cruising on large cruise ships (with some coverage of smaller ships), including ports, travel tips, roundups." Estab. 1979. **Pays on acceptance.** Publishes ms an average of 5 months after acceptance. Byline given. Offers 50% kill fee. Buys first North American serial, one-time or second serial (reprint) rights. Accepts simultaneous and previously published submissions. Send tearsheet or photocopy of article and typed ms with rights for sale noted. Pays 50% of their fee for an original article. Reports in 1 month. *Writer's Market* recommends allowing 2 months for reply. Sample copy for $3 and 9×12 SAE with 6 first-class stamps. Writer's guidelines for #10 SASE.

Nonfiction: General interest, historical/nostalgic, interview/profile, personal experience, photo feature, travel. "No daily cruise 'diary', My First Cruise, etc." Buys 72 mss/year. Query with or without published clips or send complete ms. Length: 500-2,000 words. Pays $100-400.

Photos: Send photos with submission. Reviews transparencies and prints. "Must be color, 35m preferred (other format OK); color prints second choice." Offers no additional payment for photos accepted with ms "but pay more for well-illustrated ms." Captions and identification of subjects required. Buys one-time rights.

Fillers: Anecdotes, facts. Buys 3 mss/year. Length: 300-700 words. Pays $75-200.

Tips: "Do your homework. Know what we do and what sorts of things we publish. Know the cruise industry—we can't use novices. Good, sharp, bright color photography opens the door fast. We still need good pictures—we are not interested in developing any new contributors who cannot provide color support to manuscripts."

CURAÇAO NIGHTS, Nights Publications, 1831 Rene Levesque Blvd. West, Montreal, Quebec H3H 1R4 Canada. Fax: (514)931-6273. Editor: Stephen Trotter. Managing Editor: Zelly Zuskin. Contact: Stephen Trotter. 80% freelance written. Annual magazine covering the Curaçao vacation experience. "We are seeking upbeat, entertaining lifestyle articles; colorful profiles of locals; lively features on culture, activities, night life, eco-tourism, special events, gambling; how-to features; humor. Our audience is the North American vacationer." Estab. 1989. Circ. 155,000. **Pays on acceptance.** Publishes ms an average of 6-10 months after acceptance. Byline given. Offers 15% kill fee. Buys first North American serial and first Caribbean rights. Editorial lead time 2 months. Query for electronic submissions. Reports in 2 weeks on queries; 1 month on mss. *Writer's Market* recommends allowing 2 months for reply. Sample copy for $5. Writer's guidelines free on request.

Nonfiction: General interest, historical/nostalgic, how-to help a vacationer get the most from their vacation, eco-tourism, humor, inspirational, interview/profile, opinion, personal experience, photo feature, travel, local culture, art, activities, night life, topics relative to vacationers in Curaçao. "No negative pieces or stale rewrites." Buys 5-10 mss/year. Query with published clips. Length: 250-750 words. Pays $125 minimum, $350 maximum for assigned articles; $100 minimum, $250 maximum for unsolicited articles.

Photos: State availability of photos with submission. Reviews transparencies. Offers $25-100/photo. Captions, model releases, identification of subjects required. Buys one-time rights.

Tips: "Demonstrate your voice in your query letter. Focus on individual aspects of the island lifestyle and vacation experience (e.g., art, gambling tips, windsurfing, a colorful local character, a personal experience, etc.), rather than generalized overviews. Provide an angle that will be entertaining to both vacationers and Curaçaoans."

ENDLESS VACATION, Endless Vacation, P.O. 80260, Indianapolis IN 46280-0260. (317)871-9504. Fax: (317)871-9507. Editor: Helen W. O'Guinn. Contact: Jackson Mahaney, associate editor. Prefers to work with published/established writers. Bimonthly magazine covering travel destinations, activities and issues that enhance the lives of vacationers. Estab. 1974. Circ. 907,609. **Pays on acceptance.** Publishes ms an average of 6 months after acceptance. Byline given. Buys first North American serial rights. Accepts simultaneous and previously published submissions. Send tearsheet of article and typed ms with rights for sale noted and information about when and where the article previously appeared. For reprints, pays 25% of the amount paid for an original article. Reports in 1 month. *Writer's Market* recommends allowing 2 months for reply. Sample copy for $5 and 9×12 SAE with 3 first-class stamps. Writer's guidelines for #10 SASE.

• Ranked as one of the best markets for freelance writers in *Writer's Digest* magazine's annual "Top 100 Markets," January 1994.

Nonfiction: Contact: Manuscript Editor. Buys 24 mss/year (approximately). Most are from established writers already published in *Endless Vacation. Accepts very few unsolicited pieces.* Query with published clips. Length: 1,000-2,000 words. Pays $500-1,000 for assigned articles; $250-800 for unsolicited articles. Sometimes pays the expenses of writers on assignment.

Photos: Reviews 4×5 transparencies and 35mm slides. Offers $100-500/photo. Model releases and identification of subjects required. Buys one-time rights.

Columns/Departments: Compleat Traveler (on travel news and service-related information); Weekender (on domestic weekend vacation travel). Query with published clips. Length: 800-1,000 words. Pays $150-600. Sometimes pays the expenses of writers on assignment. Also news items for Facts, Fads and Fun Stuff column on travel news, products or problems. Length: 100-200 words. Pays $100/item.

Tips: "We will continue to focus on travel trends and resort destinations. Articles must be packed with pertinent facts and applicable how-tos. Information—addresses, phone numbers, dates of events, costs—must be current and accurate. We like to see a variety of stylistic approaches, but in all cases the lead must be strong. A writer should realize that we require first-hand knowledge of the subject and plenty of practical information. For further understanding of *Endless Vacation*'s direction, the writer should study the magazine and guidelines for writers."

FAMILY MOTOR COACHING, Official Publication of the Family Motor Coach Association, 8291 Clough Pike, Cincinnati OH 45244-2796. (513)474-3622. Fax: (513)474-2332. Editor: Pamela Wisby Kay. Associate Editor: Robbin Maue. 80% freelance written. "We prefer that writers be experienced RVers." Monthly magazine emphasizing travel by motorhome, motorhome mechanics, maintenance and other technical information. Estab. 1963. Circ. 95,000. **Pays on acceptance.** Publishes ms an average of 8 months after acceptance. Buys first North American serial rights. Byline given. Submit seasonal/holiday material 4 months in advance. Reports in 2 months. Sample copy for $2.50. Writer's guidelines for #10 SASE.

Nonfiction: Motorhome travel (various areas of country accessible by motor coach), how-to (do it yourself motor home projects and modifications), bus conversions, humor, interview/profile, new product, technical, nostalgia. Buys 15-20 mss/issue. Query with published clips . Length: 1,000-2,000 words. Pays $100-500.

Photos: State availability of photos with query. Offers no additional payment for b&w contact sheets, 35mm or 2¼×2¼ color transparencies. Captions and model releases required. Prefers first North American serial rights but will consider one-hire rights on photos only.

Tips: "The greatest number of contributions we receive are travel; therefore, that area is the most competitive. However, it also represents the easiest way to break in to our publication. Articles should be written for those traveling by self-contained motor home. The destinations must be accessible to motor home travelers and any peculiar road conditions should be mentioned."

‡**FLORIDA TRAVEL & LIFE**, International Publishing Group, Suite 200, 6719 Winkler Rd., Ft. Myers FL 33919. Editor: Jack McCarthy. Managing Editor: Deborah Liftig. Associate Editor: John D. Adams. 90% freelance written. Bimonthly consumer magazine covering travel within Florida. "*Florida Travel & Life* is the only consumer magazine to exclusively showcase the diverse cultural, environmental, historical and recreational opportunities in Florida. Each bimonthly issue features exciting destinations, wilderness expeditions, scenic road trips, sporting and recreational adventures, as well as vacations for learning, browsing or just laying back." Estab. 1993. Circ. 100,000. Pays on publication. Publishes ms an average of 3 months after acceptance. Byline given. Offers 25% kill fee. Buys first rights and second serial (reprint) rights. Editorial lead time 4 months. Submit seasonal material 4 months in advance. Accepts simultaneous submissions. Query for electronic submissions. Reports in 3 months. Sample copy for $3. Writer's guidelines free on request.
Nonfiction: Book excerpts, historical/nostalgic, interview/profile, personal experience, photo feature, travel. Buys 10 mss/year. Query with published clips. Length: 150-1,200. Pays $50. Sometimes pays expenses of writers on assignment.
Photos: Freelancers should state availability of photos with submission. Reviews transparencies. Negotiates payment individually. Model releases and identification of subjects required. Buys all rights.
Columns/Departments: Off Ramp (interesting places to visit off of Interstates), 250 words. Buys 10 mss/year. Query with published clips. Pays $35-225.
Tips: "If you query, please do so by mail. Send clippings of previous articles and 3 or 4 interesting ideas for stories. Stay away from the usual topics of Disney World or the Keys. Put an unusual slant in your stories: for example, walking around for the day with some character inside a Disney costume or lobstering the Upper Keys. These are common destinations, but a unique slant. Don't send more than four ideas at once. There isn't time to look through pages and pages of query material."

GIBBONS-HUMMS GUIDE, Florida Keys-Key West, Gibbons Publishing, Inc., P.O. Box 2921, Key Largo FL 33037-7921. (800)273-1026. Fax: (305)451-5201. Editor: Gibbons D. Cline. Contact: Diane Thompson, associate editor. Key West Office: P.O. Box 6524, Key West FL 33040-6524. (305)296-7300. Fax: (305)296-7414. 15% freelance written. Quarterly magazine covering travel, tourism. Targeted to tourists and frequent visitors to Florida Keys (Monroe County, FL, from Key Largo to Key West). Estab. 1972. Circ. 55,000. Pays on publication. Publishes ms an average of 3-6 months after acceptance. Byline given. Buys all rights. Editorial lead time 4-6 months. Submit seasonal material at least 6 months in advance. Query for electronic submissions. Reports in 2-6 months on queries; 1-3 months on mss. Sample copy free on request. Writer's guidelines free on request.
Nonfiction: General interest, historical/nostalgic, how-to (water sports), humor, new product (marine related), technical (water sports), travel. Special issues: Reefs and wrecks—highlighting artificial and natural reefs offshore for fishing diving and snorkeling enthusiasts; Vacation accommodations—condos, bed and breakfast inns, resorts, hotels, hostels, etc. "We need accurate tourist tips—tell us about the best attractions and dining spots. No more vacation stories, quizzes, trivia. Would like to see more fishing, diving and boating. No religious or erotic material." Buys 5-10 mss/year. Query with published clips. Length: 500-1,500 words. Pays $2/column inch.
Photos: State availability of photos with submission. No additional payment offered for photos with ms. Reviews any size transparencies, prints, slides. Model releases and identification of subjects required. Buys all rights.
Columns/Departments: Fishing Digest (fishing hotspots, how-to, new equipment), 1,000 words; Keys Under the Seas (diving how-to, new equipment), 1,000 words; Touring Highlights (attractions: Key West, Lower Keys, Marathon, Islamorada, Key Largo), 1,000 words. Buys 5 mss/year. Query with published clips. Pays $2/column inch to $100.
Fillers: Facts, trivia, puzzles—crossword or otherwise. Buys 3-5/year. Length: 100-800 words. Pays $2/column inch to $100.
Tips: Please send résumé with query and/or mss. It is helpful to visit Keys before trying to write about them. Get a feel for unique attitude, atmosphere and lifestyle in the Keys. Focus on things to do, like water sports. Try it, then write about it—but not from a personal experience angle. Find unique angles: strange characters, humorous anecdotes, etc. What makes *your* experience in the Keys different from everyone else's? Find a special bargain? Use new, state-of-the-art equipment? Meet a 90-year-old grandmother who windsurfs? We're looking for the unusual."

GREAT EXPEDITIONS, P.O. Box 18036, Raleigh NC 27619; or P.O. Box 8000-411, Abbotsford, British Columbia V2S 6H1 Canada. Fax: (919)847-0780. Editor: George Kane. 90% freelance written. Eager to work with new/unpublished writers. Quarterly magazine covering "off-the-beaten-path" destinations, outdoor recreation, cultural discovery, budget travel, socially-responsible tourism and working abroad. Estab. 1978. Circ. 30,000. Pays on publication. Buys first and second (reprint) rights. Accepts simultaneous and previously published submissions. Send photocopy of article or typed ms with rights for sale noted and information about when and where the article previously appeared. Pays 100% of the amount paid for an original article.

Send SASE for return of article and photos. Reports in 2 months. Sample copy for $4. Free writer's guidelines.
Nonfiction: Articles range from very adventurous (living with an isolated tribe in the Philippines) to mildly adventurous (Spanish language school vacations in Guatemala and Mexico). We also like to see "how-to" pieces for adventurous travelers (i.e., How to Sail Around the World for Free, Swapping Homes with Residents of Other Countries, How to Get in on an Archaeological Dig). Buys 30 mss/year. Pays $100 maximum. Length 1,000-2,000 words, average length 1,500 words; prefer sidebar with all information and tips for persons to do an activity themselves.
  ● Need more practical information and more US and Canadian destinations.
Photos: B&w photos, color prints or slides should be sent with article. Captions required.
Tips: "It's best to send for a sample copy for a first-hand look at the style of articles we are looking for. If possible, we appreciate practical information for travelers, either in the form of a sidebar or incorporated into the article, detailing how to get there, where to stay, specific costs, where to write for visas or travel information."

‡THE INTERNATIONAL RAILWAY TRAVELER, Hardy Publishing Co., Inc., Editorial offices: P.O. Box 3747, San Diego CA 92163. (619)260-1332. Fax: (619)296-4220. 100% freelance written. Bimonthly magazine covering rail travel. Estab. 1983. Circ. 3,500. Pays on publication. Byline given. Offers 25% kill fee. Buys first North American serial rights. Editorial lead time 4 months. Submit seasonal material 6 months in advance. Query for electronic submissions. Reports in 2-4 weeks on queries; 1-2 months on mss. Sample copy for $6. Writer's guidelines for #10 SASE.
Nonfiction: Book excerpts, essays, general interest, how-to, interview/profile, new product, opinion, personal experience, photo feature, travel. Buys 12 mss/year. Query with published clips or send complete ms. Include SASE for return of ms. Length: 800-1,200 words. Pays $90.
Photos: Send photos with submission. Include SASE for return of photos. Reviews contact sheets, negatives, transparencies, prints (8 × 10 preferred; will accept 5 × 7). Offers $22.50-45/photo. Captions and identification of subjects required. Buys one-time rights.
Tips: "We want factual articles concerning world rail travel which would not appear in the mass-market travel magazines. IRT readers and editors love stories and photos on off-beat train trips as well as more conventional train trips covered in unconventional ways. With IRT, the focus is on the train travel experience, not the description. Be sure to include details (prices, passes, schedule info, etc.) for readers who might want to take the trip."

‡ISLAND HOME MAGAZINE, The Showcase of Island Architecture, Design & Lifestyle, Pacific Publishing, Penthouse 40, 1221 Kapiolani Blvd., Honolulu HI 96814. Executive Editor: Michael Latham. Contact: Kerry Tessaro, Editor. 50% freelance written. Bimonthly magazine. "We write about the uniqueness of island living, both in Hawaii and throughout the world. Our sections include Private Places (luxury homes on islands), Interiors (outstanding interior design in island residences), Travel (international island destinations and resorts), Dining (island restaurants), and Art/Collectibles (island artists/handicrafts). About half our readers are in Hawaii. Readers are either island dwellers, island travelers . . . or wish they were." Estab. 1990. Circ. 30,000. Pays within 30 days after publication. Byline given. Kill fee negotiable. Buys one-time rights. Editorial lead time 5-6 months. Submit seasonal material 6 months in advance. Accepts previously published submissions. Query for electronic submissions. Reports in 2 months. Sample copy for 10 × 13 SAE with 10 first-class stamps. Writer's guidelines for #10 SASE.
Nonfiction: Travel, island dining features, island home features (focus on architecture and design as well as location), island artist features. "Our annual golf issue is every March/April, in which we feature homes, restaurants and travel destinations with a golf or golf course focus. No articles that do not fall into our categories, which are Private Places, Interiors, Dining, Travel and Art/Collectibles. Nothing else will be considered as our categories do not change." Buys 3-4 mss/year from new freelancers; the rest are from existing pool of Hawaii freelance writers. Query with published clips. Length: 1,200-1,700 words. Pays 20¢/word.
Photos: State availability of photos or send photos with submission—preferable. Reviews contact sheets, 2¼ × 2¼ and 4 × 5 transparencies and 8 × 10 prints. Negotiates payment individually. Captions required—after acceptance only. Buys one-time rights.

ISLANDS, An International Magazine, Islands Publishing Company, 3886 State St., Santa Barbara CA 93105-3112. Fax: (805)569-0349. Editor: Joan Tapper. 95% freelance written. Works with established writers. Bimonthly magazine covering islands throughout the world. "We cover accessible and once-in-a-lifetime islands from many different perspectives: travel, culture, lifestyle. We ask our authors to give us the essence of the island and do it with literary flair." Estab. 1981. Circ. 170,000. **Pays on acceptance.** Publishes ms an average of 8 months after acceptance. Byline given. Buys all rights. Query for electronic submissions. Reports in 1 month on queries; 6 weeks on ms. Sample copy for $5.50. Writer's guidelines for #10 SASE.
  ● Ranked as one of the best markets for freelance writers in *Writer's Digest* magazine's annual "Top 100 Markets," January 1994.
Nonfiction: General interest, personal experience, photo feature, any island-related material. No service stories. "Each issue contains 3-4 feature articles of roughly 2,000-4,000 words, and 4-5 departments, each

of which runs approximately 750-1,500 words. Any authors who wish to be commissioned should send a detailed proposal for an article, an estimate of costs (if applicable) and samples of previously published work." Buys 25 feature mss/year. "The majority of our manuscripts are commissioned." Query with published clips or send complete ms. Feature length: 2,000-4,000 words. Pays $800-3,000. Pays expenses of writers on assignment.

Photos: State availability or send photos with query or ms. Pays $75-300 for 35mm transparencies. "Fine color photography is a special attraction of *Islands*, and we look for superb composition, technical quality and editorial applicability." Label slides with name and address, include captions, and submit in protective plastic sleeves. Identification of subjects required. Buys one-time rights.

Columns/Departments: "Arts, Profiles, Nature, Sports, Lifestyle, Encounters, Island Hopping featurettes—all island related. Brief Logbook items should be highly focused on some specific aspect of islands." Buys 50 mss/year. Query with published clips. Length: 500-1,500 words. Pays $100-700.

Tips: "A freelancer can best break in to our publication with short (500-1,000 word) departments or Logbooks that are highly focused on some aspect of island life, history, people, etc. Stay away from general, sweeping articles. We are always looking for topics for our Islanders and Logbook pieces. We will be using big name writers for major features; will continue to use newcomers and regulars for columns and departments."

LEISUREWAYS, Canada Wide Magazines Ltd., Suite 801, 2 Carlton St., Toronto, Ontario M5B 1J3 Canada. (416)595-5007. Fax: (416)942-6308. Editor: Deborah Milton. 80% freelance written. Bimonthly member magazine for CAA covering travel and leisure. "*Leisureways* goes to 580,000 members of Canadian Automobile Association in Ontario. Primarily travel articles plus auto-related material." Circ. 580,000. **Pays on acceptance.** Byline given. Offers 50% kill fee. Buys first North American rights. Query for electronic submission. Free sample copy. Writer's guidelines for #10 SASE (remember to use Canadian stamps or IRCs).

• Ranked as one of the best markets for freelance writers in *Writer's Digest* magazine's annual "Top 100 Markets," January 1994.

Nonfiction: Interview/profile, photo feature, travel. Buys 70 mss/year. Query with published clips or send complete ms. Length: 300-1,800 words. Pays 50¢/word (Canadian).

Photos: State availability of photos with submission. Reviews 35mm or any transparencies. Offers no additional payment for photos accepted with ms. Captions and identification of subjects required. Buys first North American serial rights.

Columns/Departments: Great Cities (profile of major cities), 1,000 words; Automotive (general interest), 500-1,500 words. Buys 25 mss/year. Query with published clips or send complete ms.

Tips: "We look for stories with interesting angles—a bit out of the ordinary. Travel pieces aimed at the mature traveler are particularly good for our readership. We have enough material for the next 6 issues."

THE MATURE TRAVELER, Travel Bonanzas for 49ers-Plus, GEM Publishing Group, Box 50820, Reno NV 89513-0820. (702)786-7419. Editor: Gene E. Malott. 30% freelance written. Monthly newsletter on senior citizen travel. Estab. 1984. Circ. 2,500. **Pays on acceptance.** Publishes ms an average of 3 months after acceptance. Byline given. Offers 25% kill fee. Buys one-time rights. Submit seasonal/holiday material 3 months in advance. Accepts simultaneous and previously published submissions, if so noted. Send tearsheet or photocopy of article and information about when and where the article previously appeared. Pays 50% of their fee for an original article. Reports in 1 month. Sample copy and guidelines for $1 and #10 SAE with 52¢ postage. Writer's guidelines only for #10 SASE.

Nonfiction: Travel for seniors. "General travel and destination pieces should be senior-specific, aimed at 49ers+." Query. Length: 600-1,200 words. Pays $50-100.

Photos: State availability of photos with submission. Reviews contact sheets and b&w (only) prints. Captions required. Buys one-time rights.

Tips: "Read the guidelines and write stories to our readers' needs—not to the general public."

MEXICO EVENTS & DESTINATIONS, A traveler's guide, Travel Mexico Magazine Group, P.O. Box 188037, Carlsbad CA 92009-0801, (619)929-0707. Group Editor: Katharine A. Diáz. Bimonthly magazine covering tourism and travel to Mexico. "*MEXICO Events & Destinations* focuses on promoting Mexico as a travel destination to readers in the United States and Canada. Our interest is in the many worlds of Mexico. We cover the people and cultures of Mexico with regular sections on food, history, ecotourism, language, walking tours, shopping guides, outdoor recreation and driving." Estab. 1992. Circ. 201,000. Pays on publication. Publishes ms an average of 1-2 months after acceptance. Byline given. Buys first rights. Editorial lead time 2-3 months. Submit seasonal material 4-5 months in advance. Query for electronic submissions. Reports in 1-2 months on queries; 1 month on mss. Sample copy for 10×13 SAE with 6 first-class stamps. Writer's guidelines for #10 SASE.

Nonfiction: Travel—Mexico only. "We do not want articles that focus on other countries. We cover Mexico exclusively." Buys 75 mss/year. Query with published clips. Length: 400-1,200 words. Pays 25¢/word.

Photos: Send photos with submission. Reviews transparencies, slides. Offers $20-200/photo. Captions and identification of subjects required. Buys one-time rights.

Tips: "We are looking for writers who know Mexico and who have experience writing about that country. A positive attitude about Mexico is a plus. We do not recommend sending mss, but rather prefer that writers send query with published clips (that will be kept on file unless SASE enclosed) along with list of their area(s) of expertise with regard to Mexico. Our features and columns are all open to freelancers. We are most interested in new discoveries or new twists on familiar destinations in Mexico. But keep in mind that most of our articles are on assignment basis."

‡**MICHIGAN LIVING**, AAA Michigan, 1 Auto Club Dr., Dearborn MI 48126-2963. (313)336-1211. Fax: (313)336-1344. Editor: Len Barnes. 50% freelance written. Emphasizes travel and auto use. Monthly magazine. Estab. 1922. Circ. 1 million. **Pays on acceptance.** Publishes ms an average of 6 months after acceptance. Buys first North American serial rights. Offers 20% kill fee. Byline given. Submit seasonal/holiday material 3 months in advance. Reports in 6 weeks. Free sample copy and writer's guidelines.
Nonfiction: Travel articles on US and Canadian topics. Buys 50-60 unsolicited mss/year. Send complete ms. Length: 200-1,000 words. Pays $88-315.
Photos: Photos purchased with accompanying ms. Captions required. Pays $350 for cover photos; $50-220 for color transparencies; total purchase price for ms includes payment for b&w photos.
Tips: "In addition to descriptions of things to see and do, articles should contain accurate, current information on costs the traveler would encounter on his trip. Items such as lodging, meal and entertainment expenses should be included, not in the form of a balance sheet but as an integral part of the piece. We want the sounds, sights, tastes, smells of a place or experience so one will feel he has been there and knows if he wants to go back."

‡**THE MIDWEST MOTORIST, AAA Auto Club of Missouri**, 12901 N. 40 Dr., St. Louis MO 63141. (314)523-7350. Editor: Michael J. Right. Managing Editor: Deborah M. Klein. 80% freelance written. Bimonthly magazine focusing on travel and auto-related topics. "We feature articles on regional and world travel, area history, auto safety, highway and transportation news." Estab. 1971. Circ. 371,083. **Pays on acceptance.** Byline given. Not copyrighted. Buys first North American serial rights, second serial (reprint) rights. Editorial lead time 8 months. Submit seasonal material 1 year in advance. Accepts simultaneous and previously published submissions. Query for electronic submissions. Reports in 1 month with SASE enclosed. Sample copy for 12½ × 9½ SAE with 3 first-class stamps. Writer's guidelines for #10 SASE.
Nonfiction: Historical/nostalgic, travel, automotive (tips, reviews). No religious, opinion or philosophical pieces. Buys 40 mss/year. Query. Length: 2,000 words maximum. Pays $200.
Photos: State availability of photos with submission. Reviews transparencies. Offers no additional payment for photos accepted with ms. Captions required. Buys one-time rights.
Tips: "Editorial schedule set a year in advance. Request a copy. Some stories available throughout the year. Travel destinations and tips are most open to freelancers. Make the story bright and quick to read. We see too many 'Here's a recount of our family vacation' manuscripts."

‡**MOTORHOME**, TL Enterprises, Inc., 3601 Calle Tecate, Camarillo CA 93012. (805)389-0300. Fax: (805)389-0484. Editor: Barbara Leonard. Managing Editor: Jim Brightly. 50% freelance written. A monthly magazine covering motorhomes. "*MotorHome* is exclusively for motorhome enthusiasts. We feature road tests on new motorhomes, travel locations, controversy concerning motorhomes, how-to and technical articles relating to motorhomes." Estab. 1968. Circ. 150,000. **Pays on acceptance.** Publishes ms an average of 6 months after acceptance. Byline given. Buys first North American serial rights. Submit seasonal/holiday material 8 months in advance. Query for electronic submissions. Reports in 3-6 weeks on queries; up to 2 months on mss depending on work load. Free sample copy and writer's guidelines.
Nonfiction: General interest, historical/nostalgic, how-to (do it yourself for motorhomes), humor, new product, photo feature, technical. Buys 80 mss/year. Query with published clips. Length: 1,000-2,000 words. Pays $250-600 for assigned articles; pays $200-500 for unsolicited articles. Sometimes pays expenses of writers and/or photographers on assignment.
Photos: Send photos with submission. Reviews contact sheets and 35mm/120/4 × 5 transparencies. Offers no additional payment for photos accepted with ms except for use on cover. Captions, model releases, identification of subjects required. Buys first North American serial rights.
Tips: "If a freelancer has an idea for a good article it's best to send a query and include possible photo locations to illustrate the article. We prefer to assign articles and work with the author in developing a piece suitable to our audience. We are in a specialized field with very enthusiastic readers who appreciate articles by authors who actually enjoy motorhomes. The following areas are most open: Travel—places to go with a motorhome, where to stay, what to see etc.; we prefer not to use travel articles where the motorhome is secondary; and How-to—personal projects on author's motorhomes to make travel easier, etc., unique projects, accessories. Also articles on unique personalities, motorhomes, humorous experiences."

MOTORLAND, Travel and news magazine of the West, California State Automobile Assn., 150 Van Ness Ave., San Francisco CA 94102. (415)565-2451. Editor: Lynn Ferrin. 25% freelance written. Bimonthly magazine covering world-wide travel, specializing in northern California and the West. Also, traffic safety and motorists' consumer issues. "Our magazine goes to members of the AAA in northern California and Nevada. Our surveys show they are an upscale audience, well educated and widely traveled. We like our travel stories to be finely crafted, evocative and personal, but we also include nitty gritty details in arranging travel to the destinations covered." Estab. 1917. Circ. 2.2 million. **Pays on acceptance.** Byline usually given. Offers 25% kill fee. Buys first rights or makes work-for-hire assignments. Editorial lead time 2 months. Submit seasonal material 6 months in advance. Query for electronic submissions. Usually reports in 2-4 weeks on queries. Writer's guidelines for #10 SASE.

Nonfiction: Travel. Cruise issue (September/October). Buys 15 mss/year. Send complete ms. Length: 500-2,000 words. Pays $150-500. Sometimes pays expenses of writers on assignment.

Photos: State availability of photos with submission. Reviews 35mm and 4×5 transparencies. Offers $50-400/photo. Model releases and identificatin of subjects required. Buys one-time rights.

Tips: "We are looking for beautifilly written pieces that evoke a destination. We purchase less than 1% of the material submitted."

‡**MYSTIC TRAVELER**, Traveler Publications Inc., Suite 207, 174 Bellevue Ave., Newport RI 02840. (401)847-0226. Managing Editor: Susan Ozirsky. 100% freelance written. Monthly tabloid covering places of interest. "Stories that get the reader to "do, see, or act upon." Estab. 1992. Circ. 120,000 winter, 240,000 summer. Pays on publication. Byline given. Buys all rights. Editorial lead time 2 months. Submit seasonal material 2 months in advance. Accepts simultaneous and previously published submissions. Query for electronic submissions. Reports in 2 months on mss. Sample copy and writer's guidelines free on request.

Nonfiction: Essays, general interest, historical/nostalgic, photo feature (travel). Buys 60 mss/year. Send complete ms. Length: 700-1,200 words. Pays 5¢/word. Sometimes pays expenses of writers on assignment.

Photos: Send photos with submission. Reviews prints. Negotiates payment individually. Buys one-time rights.

Fillers: Facts. Buys 30/year. Length: 50-200 words. Pays 5¢/word.

Tips: "We are very interested in tours that cover an entire area. It could be a tour of wineries, a certain kind of shop, golf courses, etc. Always include address, phone, hours, admission prices. Get reader to act upon an editorial."

NEW YORK DAILY NEWS, Travel Section, 220 E. 42 St., New York NY 10017. (212)210-1699. Fax: (212)210-2203. Travel Editor: Gunna Biteé Dickson. 30% freelance written. Prefers to work with published/established writers. Weekly tabloid. Circ. 1.8 million. "We are the largest circulating newspaper travel section in the country and take all types of articles ranging from experiences to service oriented pieces that tell readers how to make a certain trip." Pays on publication. Publishes ms an average of 3 months after acceptance. Byline given. Submit seasonal/holiday material 4 months in advance. Query for electronic submissions. Reports "as soon as possible." Writer's guidelines for #10 SASE.

Nonfiction: General interest, historical/nostalgic, humor, inspirational, personal experience, travel. "Most of our articles involve practical trips that the average family can afford—even if it's one you can't afford every year. We put heavy emphasis on budget saving tips for all trips. We also run stories now and then for the Armchair Traveler, an exotic and usually expensive trip. We are looking for professional quality work from professional writers who know what they are doing. The pieces have to give information and be entertaining at the same time. No 'How I Spent My Summer Vacation' type articles. No PR hype." Buys 60 mss/year. Query with SASE. Length: 1,000 words maximum. Pays $75-200.

Photos: "Good pictures always help sell good stories." State availability of photos with ms. Reviews contact sheets and negatives. Captions and identification of subjects required. Buys all rights.

Columns/Departments: Short Hops is based on trips to places within a 300-mile radius of New York City. Length: 700-800 words. Travel Watch gives practical travel advice.

Tips: "A writer might have some luck gearing a specific destination to a news event or date: In Search of Irish Crafts in March, for example, but do it well in advance."

‡**NEWSDAY**, *New York Newsday*, 235 Pinelawn Rd., Melville NY 11747. (516)843-2980. Travel Editor: Marjorie K. Robins. 20% freelance written. For general readership of Sunday newspaper travel section. Estab. 1940. Circ. 700,000. Buys all rights for New York area only. Buys 45-60 mss/year. Pays on publication. Prefer typewritten manuscripts. Simultaneous submissions considered if others are being made outside the New York area.

Nonfiction: No assignments to freelancers. No query letters. Only completed mss accepted on spec. All trips must be paid for in full by writer. Proof required. Service stories preferred. Destination pieces must be for the current year. Length: 1,200 words maximum. Pays $75-350, depending on space allotment. Fax submissions not encouraged.

Photos: Color slides and b&w photos accepted: $50-250, depending on size of photo used.

NORTHEAST OUTDOORS, Northeast Outdoors, Inc., P.O. Box 2180, Waterbury CT 06722-2180. (203)755-0158. Fax: (203)755-3480. Editorial Director: John Florian. 80% freelance written. Works with a small number of new/unpublished writers each year. Monthly tabloid covering family camping in the Northeastern US

ALWAYS enclose a self-addressed, stamped envelope (SASE) with all your queries and correspondence.

Estab. 1968. Circ. 14,000. Pays on publication. Publishes ms an average of 8 months after acceptance. Byline given. Buys first rights and regional rights. Submit seasonal/holiday material 5 months in advance. Accepts previously published submissions. Send typed ms with rights for sale noted and information about when and where the article previously appeared. Pays 50% of their fee for an original article. Query for electronic submissions. Reports in 2 weeks. Sample copy for 9×12 SAE with 6 first-class stamps. Writer's guidelines for #10 SASE.

Nonfiction: How-to (camping), humor, new product (company and RV releases only), recreation vehicle and camping experiences in the Northeast, features about private (only) campgrounds and places to visit in the Northeast while RVing, personal experience, photo feature, travel. "No diaries of trips, dog stories, or anything not camping and RV related." Length: 300-1,500 words. Pays $40-80 for articles with b&w photos; pays $30-75 for articles without art.

Photos: Send photos with submission. Reviews contact sheets and 5×7 prints or larger. Captions and identification of subjects required. Buys one-time rights.

Columns/Departments: Mealtime (campground cooking), 300-900 words. Buys 12 mss/year. Query or send complete ms. Length: 750-1,000 words. Pays $25-50.

Tips: "We most often need material on private campgrounds and attractions in New England. We are looking for upbeat, first-person stories about where to camp, what to do or see, and how to enjoy camping."

‡NORTHWEST TRAVEL, Northwest Regional Magazines, 1525 12th St., P.O. Box 18000, Florence OR 97439-0130. (800)348-8401. Editor: Dave Peden. Managing Editor: Judy Fleagle. 75% freelance written. Bimonthly magazine of Northwest living. Estab. 1991. Circ. 50,000. Pays on publication. Publishes ms an average of 6-12 months after acceptance. Byline given. Offers 33% kill fee. Buys first North American serial rights. Submit seasonal/holiday material 6 months in advance. Query for electronic submissions. Occasionally accepts previously published submissions. Send tearsheet or photocopy of article or typed ms with rights for sale noted and information about when and where the article previously appeared. Pays approximately 65% of the amount paid for an original article. Reports in 1 month on queries; 3 months on mss. Sample copy for $4.50. Writer's guidelines for #10 SASE.

Nonfiction: Travel as pertains to Pacific Northwest. "Any article not related to the Pacific Northwest will be returned." Query with published clips. Length: 500-2,000 words. Pays $50-350. "Along with payment comes 2-5 copies."

Photos: Send photos with submission. Preferred 35mm or larger transparencies, 3×5 or larger prints. Captions and identification of subjects required. Buys one-time rights.

Fillers: Newsbreaks (no-fee basis), short articles. Buys 30/year. Byline given. Length: 300-500 words. Pays $35-65.

Tips: "Slant article for readers who do not live in the Pacific Northwest. At least one historical article and at least two travel articles will be used in each issue. City and town profiles, special out-of-the-way places to visit, will also be used in each issue. An occasional restaurant review will be used. Short articles with photos (transparencies preferred) will be easiest to fit in. Query first. After go-ahead, send cover letter with manuscript/photo package. Photos often make the difference in deciding which article gets published."

‡NORWAY AT YOUR SERVICE, Magazine of Norwegian Business, Culture & Tourism, Norwegian Trade Council, in cooperation with the Norwegian Tourist Board, the Ministry of Foreign Affairs and other organizations, N-0243, Oslo, Norway. (+47)22 92 63 00. Editor: Peggy Schoen. 60-70% freelance written. Semiannual magazine covering Norwegian business, culture and tourism. "*Norway At Your Service* markets contemporary Norway, so freelance submissions should have a contemporary rather than a historical focus. We are looking for articles/photos on Norwegian travel and destinations; Norwegian modern culture and lifestyles; Norwegian companies, products and research projects; Norwegian personalities living in or outside the country." Estab. 1984. Circ. 35,000. **Pays on acceptance.** Byline given. Buys first rights, one-time rights, second serial (reprint) rights and simultaneous rights and makes work-for-hire assignments. Editorial lead time 4-6 months. Submit seasonal material 6 months in advance. Accepts simultaneous and previously published submissions. Query for electronic submissions. Reports in 1 month. Sample copy free with European C4 SAE and IRC. Writer's guidelines free with European C4 SAE and IRC.

Nonfiction: Interview/profile, new product (research), personal experience (travel), photo feature, travel. "For the most part, we are not usually looking for articles with a 'Norwegian-American' angle, such as ancestry, 19th century emigration from Norway, etc." Buys 10-12 mss/year. Query with published clips. Length: 1,000-2,500 words. Pays $200 minimum for assigned articles; $150 minimum for unsolicited articles. Sometimes pays expenses of writers on assignment.

Photos: State availability of photos with submission. Reviews contact sheets, transparencies (any size), and 5×7 prints. Negotiates payment individually. Captions and identification of subjects required. Buys one-time rights.

Tips: "We usually cannot justify paying a travel writer to come to Norway to do an article specifically for us, as it is more cost-effective to use an English-language writer living here. But we are very interested in offering foreign travel writers an 'add-on' assignment while they are here or a 'second run' on an article they have published in the UK/US Foreign-based writers have a definite advantage with respect to covering the foreign-based operations of Norwegian companies or Norwegian personalities (actors, artists, musicians, statesmen, etc.) living abroad. Queries are welcome, but preferably not by phone. Send a short idea summary with information about your background and work samples."

‡**OCEAN STATE TRAVELER,** Traveler Publications Inc., Suite 207, 174 Bellevue Ave., Newport RI 02840. (401)847-0226. Managing Editor: Susan Ozirsky. 100% freelance written. Monthly tabloid covering places of interest. "Stories that get the reader to "do, see, or act upon." Estab. 1992. Circ. 120,000 winter 240,000 summer. Pays on publication. Byline given. Buys all rights. Editorial lead time 2 months. Submit seasonal material 2 months in advance. Accepts simultaneous and previously published submissions. Query for electronic submissions. Reports in 2 months on mss. Sample copy and writer's guidelines free on request.
Nonfiction: Essays, general interest, historical/nostalgic, photo feature (travel). Buys 60 mss/year. Send complete ms. Length: 700-1,200 words. Pays 5¢/word. Sometimes pays expenses of writers on assignment.
Photos: Send photos with submission. Reviews prints. Negotiates payment individually. Buys one-time rights.
Fillers: Facts. Buys 30/year. Length: 50-200 words. Pays 5¢/word.
Tips: "We are very interested in tours that cover an entire area. It could be a tour of wineries, a certain kind of shop, golf courses, etc. Always include address, phone, hour, admissions prices. Get reader to act upon an editorial."

ONTARIO MOTOR COACH REVIEW, Naylor Communications Ltd., 6th Floor, 920 Yonge St., Toronto, Ontario M4W 3C7 Canada. (416)961-1028. Fax: (416)924-4408. Editor: Lori Knowles. 50% freelance written. Annual magazine on travel and tourist destinations. Estab 1970. Circ. 3,000. Pays 30 days from deadline. Byline given. Offers 33% kill fee. Buys first North American serial rights and all rights. Submit seasonal/ holiday material 2 months in advance. Accepts simultaneous submissions. Send photocopy of article and information about when and where the article previously appeared. Pays 80% of their fee for an original article. Query for electronic submissions. Reports in 6 weeks. *Writer's Market* recommends allowing 2 months for reply. Free sample copy and writer's guidelines.
Nonfiction: General interest, historical, interview/profile, new product, personal experience (related to motor coach travel), photo feature, technical, travel. Buys 5-10 mss/year. Query with published clips. Length: 500-3,000 words. Pays 20-25¢/word. Pays expenses of writers on assignment.
Photos: State availability of photos with submission. Reviews transparencies and prints. Offers $25-200/ photo. Identification of subjects required.

‡**OUTDOOR TRAVELER,** Suite 102, WMS Publications, P.O. Box 2748, Charlottesville VA 22902. (804)984-0655. Editor: Marianne Marks. Contact: Scott Clark, Associate Editor. 85% freelance written. Quarterly magazine. "*Outdoor Traveler* is designed to help readers (well-educated, active adults) enjoy the mid-Atlantic outdoors through year-round seasonal coverage of outdoor recreation, travel, adventure and nature." Estab. 1993. Circ. 30,000. Pays on publication. Byline given. Offers 25% kill fee. Buys first North American serial rights. Editorial lead time 6 months. Submit seasonal material 6-8 months in advance. Accepts simultaneous submissions. Query for electronic submissions. Reports in 2 months. Sample copy for $3. Writer's guidelines for #10 SASE.
Nonfiction: Book excerpts, essays, general interest, historical/nostalgic (related to outdoor sports or travel), how-to (outdoor sports technique), humor, interview/profile, new product, personal experience, photo feature, travel, nature. No "What I did on my vacation" articles; no golf or tennis. Buys 35 mss/year. Query with published clips. Length: 300-3,500 words. Pays $100. Sometimes pays expenses of writers on assignment.
Photos: Send photos with submission. Reviews transparencies. Offers $50/photo. Captions, model releases and identification of subjects required. Buys one-time rights.
Columns/Departments: Getaways (seasonal pieces on B&Bs, with outdoor slant), 300 words; Destinations (brief but detailed guides to outdoor sports destinations), 500-600 words; Book Reviews (reviews of interest to readers), 200 words. Buys 35 mss/year. Query with published clips. Pays $50-150.
Fillers: Anecdotes, facts, newsbreaks, short humor. Length: 300 words.
Tips: "Freelancers should query with clips that reveal strong writing skills, a professional style, and knowledge of our region and subject matter."

‡**OUTSIDE KIDS,** Mariah Publications Corp., 1165 N. Clark St., Chicago IL 60610. (312)951-0990. Editor: Lisa Twyman Bessone. Contact: John Alderman. 100% freelance written. Quarterly magazine covering the outdoors for kids 15 and under. "*Outside Kids* is targeted to readers 8-15. We cover adventure travel, outdoor sports, wildlife, the environment, etc. Most of our subjects are kids. Quite a few of our pieces are written by kids." Estab. 1993. Circ. 150,000. Pays on publication. Publishes ms an average of 2 months after acceptance. Byline given. Offers 20% kill fee. Buys first North American serial rights, electronic rights. Editorial lead time 6 months. Submit seasonal material 8 months in advance. Query for electronic submissions. Writer's guidelines for #10 SASE.
Nonfiction: Buys 30 mss/year. Query with published clips. Length: 1,000-1,500 words.
Photos: State availability of photos with submission. Reviews transparencies. Negotiates payment individually. Buys one-time rights.

‡**PASSENGER TRAIN JOURNAL**, Pentrex, P.O. Box 379, Waukesha WI 53187. (414)542-4900. Editor: Carl Swanson. 90% freelance written. Monthly magazine covering passenger railroading news and info. *"Passenger Train Journal* covers news and travel topics related to rail travel. Readers tend to be relatively affluent, well-educated and well-traveled." Estab. 1968. Circ. 14,000. Pays on publication. Publishes ms an average of 6 months after acceptance. Byline given. Buys all rights. Editorial lead time 2 months. Submit seasonal material 6 months in advance. Accepts previously published submissions. Query for electronic submissions. Reports in 2 months. Sample copy for $3.50. Writer's guidelines free on request.
Nonfiction: Historical/nostalgic (rail travel), travel (rail). Buys 40 mss/year. Send complete ms. Length: 1,500-3,500 words. Pays 5¢/word.
Photos: Send photos with submission. Reviews prints and transparencies. Offers $6-25/photo. Captions required. Buys one-time rights.
Columns/Departments: Rail Travel (descriptions of rail travel and destinations), 2,000 words. Buys 12 mss/year. Send complete ms. Pays 5¢/word.
Tips: "The majority of *Passenger Train Journal* is produced by freelancers and we pride ourselves on being open to new authors. Our job is easier if freelancers send complete stories and photo illustrations with their package. We particularly need stories for our 'Rail Travel' section. Stories should be slanted toward describing one train trip with the emphasis on helping readers plan a similar journey. Photo illustrations and a map of the route often tip the balance in favor of a submissions."

RV TIMES MAGAZINE, Royal Productions, Inc., P.O. Box 6294, Richmond VA 23230-0294. (804)288-5653. Editor: Alice P. Supple. 75% freelance written. Prefers to work with published/established writers; works with a small number of new/unpublished writers each year. Monthly except December. "We supply the camping public with articles and information on outdoor activities related to camping. Our audience is primarily families that own recreational vehicles." Estab. 1973. Circ. 35,000. Pays on publication. Publishes ms an average of 4-6 months after acceptance. Byline given. Buys one-time, second serial (reprint) or simultaneous rights. Submit seasonal/holiday material 2 months in advance. Accepts simultaneous and previously published submissions. Send typed ms with rights for sale noted and information about when and where the article previously appeared. Pays 100% of the amount paid for an original article. Query for electronic submissions. Sample copy and writer's guidelines for 9 × 12 SAE with 7 first-class stamps. Reports only on acceptance. Allow 2 months for reply, if one is to come.
Nonfiction: How-to, travel, information on places to camp, "tourist related articles, places to go, things to see. Does not have to be camping related." Buys 80 mss/year. Query with or without published clips or send complete ms. Length: 500-2,000 words.
Photos: Always prefers "people" pictures as opposed to scenic. Buys one-time rights. Black and white, color prints, slides; prefer vertical format.
  • Looking for more *quality* color slides, preferably with people in active pursuit of outdoor activities (verticle format).
Tips: "All areas of *RV Times* are open to freelancers. We will look at all articles and consider for publication. Return of unsolicited mss is not guaranteed; however, every effort is made to return photos."

RV WEST MAGAZINE, Prescomm Media Inc., Suite I, 4133 Mohr Ave., Pleasanton CA 94566-4750. (510)426-3200. Fax: (510)426-1422. Publisher: Dave Preston. 85% freelance written. Works with a small number of new/unpublished writers each year. Monthly magazine for Western recreational vehicle owners. Estab. 1977. Circ. 75,000. Pays on publication. Publishes ms an average of 10 months after acceptance. Byline given. Buys one-time rights. Submit seasonal/holiday material 10 months in advance. Accepts simultaneous and previously published submissions. Send typed ms with rights for sale noted. Pays 100% of their fee for an original article. Query for electronic submissions. Reports in 3 months on queries; several months on mss. Free writer's guidelines.
Nonfiction: Historical/nostalgic, new product, personal experience (particularly travel), travel (destinations for RVs). No non-RV travel articles. Buys 36 mss/year. Query with or without published clips. Length: 750-1,500 words. Pays $1.50/inch.
  • No longer accepting how-to articles.
Photos: Send photos with submissions. Color or b&w prints only please. Offers $5 minimum/photo. Identification of subjects required.
Tips: "RV travel/destination stories are most open to freelancers. Include all information of value to RVers, and reasons why they would want to visit the location (13 Western states). Indicate best time frame for publication."

ST. MAARTEN NIGHTS, Nights Publications, 1831 Rene Levesque Blvd. West, Montreal, Quebec H3H 1R4 Canada. Fax: (514)931-6273. Editor: Stephen Trotter. Managing Editor: Zelly Zuskin. Contact: Stephen Trotter. 80% freelance written. Annual magazine covering the St. Maarten/St. Martin vacation experience seeking "upbeat entertaining lifestyle articles: colorful profiles of islanders; lively features on culture, activities, night life, eco-tourism, special events, gambling; how-to features; humor. Our audience is the North American vacationer." Estab. 1981. Circ. 200,000. **Pays on acceptance.** Publishes ms an average of 6-10 months after acceptance. Byline given. Offers 15% kill fee. Buys first North American serial and first Caribbean rights. Editorial lead time 2 month. Query for electronic submissions. Reports in 2 weeks on queries; 1 month on mss. *Writer's Market* recommends allowing 2 months for reply. Sample copy for $5. Writer's guidelines free on request.

Nonfiction: General interest, historical/nostalgia, how-to (gamble), sail, etc., humor, inspirational, interview/ profile, opinion, ecological (eco-tourism), personal experience, photo feature, travel, local culture, art, activities, entertainment, topics relative to vacationers in St. Maarten/St. Martin. "No negative pieces or stale rewrites." Buys 5-10 mss/year. Query with published clips. Length: 250-750 words. Pays $125-350 for assigned articles; $100-250 for unsolicited articles.

Photos: State availability of photos with submission. Reviews transparencies. Offers $25-100/photo. Captions, model releases, identification of subjects required. Buys one-time rights.

‡SEA MASS TRAVELER, Suite 207, 174 Bellevue Ave., Newport RI 02840. (401)847-0226. Managing Editor: Susan Ozirsky. 100% freelance written. Monthly tabloid covering places of interest. "Stories that get the reader to "do, see, or act upon." Estab. 1992. Circ. 120,000 winter 240,000 summer. Pays on publication. Byline given. Buys all rights. Editorial lead time 2 months. Submit seasonal material 2 months in advance. Accepts simultaneous and previously published submissions. Query for electronic submissions. Reports in 2 months on mss. Sample copy and writer's guidelines free on request.

Nonfiction: Essays, general interest, historical/nostalgic, photo feature (travel). Buys 60 mss/year. Send complete ms. Length: 700-1,200 words. Pays 5¢/word. Sometimes pays expenses of writers on assignment.

Photos: Send photos with submission. Reviews prints. Negotiates payment individually. Buys one-time rights.

Fillers: Facts. Buys 30/year. Length: 50-200 words. Pays 5¢/word.

Tips: "We are very interested in tours that cover an entire area. It could be a tour of wineries, a certain kind of shop, golf courses, etc. Always include address, phone, hour, admissions prices. Get reader to act upon an editorial."

‡TIMES OF THE ISLANDS, The International Magazine of the Turks & Caicos Islands, Times Publications Ltd., P.O. Box 234, Caribbean Place, Providenciales Turks & Caicos Islands, British West Indies. (809)946-4788. Fax: (809)946-4703. Editor: Kathy Matusik. 80% freelance written. Quarterly magazine covering The Turks & Caicos Islands. "*Times of the Islands* is used by the public and private sector to attract visitors and potential investors/developers to the Islands. It strives to portray the advantages of the Islands and their friendly people. It is also used by tourists, once on-island, to learn about services, activities and accommodations available." Estab. 1988. Circ. 5,500-8,000. Pays on publication. Publishes ms an average of 6 months after acceptance. Byline given. Buys second serial (reprint) rights and publication rights for 6 months with respect to other publications distributed in Caribbean. Editorial lead time 4 months. Submit seasonal material 4 months in advance. Accepts simultaneous and previously published submissions. Query for electronic submissions. Reports in 6 weeks on queries; 2 months on mss. "Keep in mind, mail to Islands is SLOW. Faxing can speed response time." Sample copy for $4 and postage between Miami and your destination. Writer's guidelines for #10 SASE.

Nonfiction: Book excerpts or reviews, essays, general interest (Caribbean art, culture, cooking, crafts), historical/nostalgic, humor, interview/profile (locals), personal experience (trips to the Islands), photo feature, technical (island businesses), travel, nature, ecology, business (offshore finance), watersports. Special issues: Diving Guide to the Turks & Caicos Islands (1995). Buys 30 mss/year. Query. Length: 500-3,000 words. Pays $50-150.

Photos: Send photos with submission—slides preferred. Reviews 3×5 prints. Offers no additional payment for photos accepted with ms. Pays $15-100/photo. Identification of subjects required.

Columns/Departments: Profiles from Abroad (profiles of T&C Islanders who are doing something outstanding internationally), 500 words. Buys 4 mss/year. Query. Pays $50-100. "Also, please query with new column ideas!"

Fiction: Adventure (sailing, diving), ethnic (Caribbean), historical (Caribbean), humorous (travel-related), mystery, novel excerpts. Buys 1 ms/year. "Would buy three to four if available." Query. Length: 1,000-2,000 words. Pays $100-200.

Tips: "Make sure that the query/article specifically relates to the Turks and Caicos Islands. The theme can be general (ecotourism, for instance), but the manuscript should contain specific and current references to the Islands. We're a high-quality magazine, with a small budget and staff and are very open-minded to ideas (and manuscripts). Writers who have visited the Islands at least once would probably have a better perspective from which to write. Query well ahead of time and let me know when you plan to visit."

TOURING AMERICA, Travel in the USA, Canada and Mexico, Fancy Publications, Inc., Box 6050, Mission Viejo CA 92690. (714)855-8822, ext. 410. Editor: Bob Carpenter. Contact: Gene Booth, managing editor. 95% freelance written. Bimonthly magazine covering travel in North America. "Our niche is the trip story— from somewhere to somewhere—rather than destination pieces. We try to help the reader in planning the trip and while it is underway. The ideal piece would be on the seat beside the driver as the trip progresses. We aim for a family audience, professionals between 35-55 years." Estab. 1991. Pays on receipt of contract signed by author. Publishes ms an average of 3 months after acceptance. Byline given. Buys first North American serial and anthology rights. Editorial lead time 4 months. Submit seasonal material 6 months in advance ("after receiving go-ahead to write it.") Query for electronic submissions. Reports in 1 month on queries. Does not consider unsolicited mss. Sample copy for $5.50 from Back Issue Dept. Writer's guidelines free on request for #10 SASE. NOTE: 1994-Spring 1995 editorial calendar is filled. Query on future projects.

Nonfiction: General interest, historical/nostalgic, how-to travel successfully, humor, photo feature, technical, travel. "No 'My Last Vacation' pieces; no first person; no stories about resorts, specific hotels, restaurants, etc.; nothing with the first word 'Picture' or 'Imagine. . .'; no manuscripts without professional quality photography; no formula writing." Buys 60 mss/year. Query. Query with published clips the first time. "Study our guidelines carefully before querying." Length 1,000-1,800 words. Pays up to $750 "for accepted articles with photos and sidebars. Do not send unsolicited material!"

Photos: Send photos with submission. "We buy word-picture packages." Offers no additional payment for photos accepted with ms. Offers $25-125/photo (purchased separately.) "Cover photos $250-up." Captions, model releases (cover only) and identification of subjects required. "We always look at photos first to determine acceptance of article."

Columns/Departments: Picturing America (travel photography), 1,000-1,200 words plus sidebars; Alternative Travel (adventure, ecology, offbeat, 1,000-1,200 words plus sidebars. Buys 12 mss/year. Query. Pays $400 maximum.

Fillers: Facts. Buys 50-100/year. Length: 75-150 words with a selection of photos. Pays $25-75 for Travelers' Advisory items, One Last Snapshot.

Tips: "Have a dynamite lead—yank the reader right into the guts of the story. Tell a story—remember, a place description is not a travel story. Never have fewer than 12 tips or hints that will help the reader make the same trip easier and/or cheaper. Double check every name, address, phone number, admission charge, hour of operation before mailing in article. Always have two to four sidebars with the story. Do not write something for which you do not have professional color photography. Never ever submit a story to us that is going to another publisher at the time. Always write and send the article only after we respond to your query. Travelers' Advisory—a potpourri of short, interesting and engaging travel items—is the best place to start. Keep to 150 words or less with a couple of slides. All parts of the magazine are open, however. Just be sure you 1)create excitement and 2)deliver maximum information in your manuscript."

● More emphasis on quality of writing and photography. Virtual elimination of "farm" trips accounts.

TRANSITIONS ABROAD, P.O. Box 1300, Amherst MA 01004-1300. (413)256-3414. Editor/Publisher: Clay Hubbs. 80-90% freelance written. Eager to work with new/unpublished writers. Magazine resource for low-budget international travel with an educational or work component. Estab. 1977. Circ. 15,000. Pays on publication. Buys first rights and second (reprint) rights. Byline given. Written queries only. Accepts previously published submissions. Send typed ms with rights for sale noted including information about when and where the article previously appeared. For reprints, pays 100% of the amount paid for an original article. Reports in 2 months. Sample copy for $3.50 and 9 × 12 SASE. Writer's guidelines and topics schedule for #10 SASE. Manuscript returned only with SASE.

Nonfiction: How-to (find educational and specialty travel opportunities), practical information (evaluation of courses, special interest and study tours, economy travel), travel (new learning and cultural travel ideas). Foreign travel only. Few destination ("tourist") pieces. *Transitions Abroad* is a resource magazine for educated and adventurous travelers, not for travel novices or armchair travelers. Emphasis on information—which must be usable by readers—and on interaction with people in host country. Buys 20 unsolicited mss/issue. Query with credentials. Length: 500-2,000 words. Pays $25-150. Include author's bio with submissions.

Photos: Send photos with ms. Pays $10-45 for prints (color acceptable, b&w preferred), $125 for covers (b&w only). Photos increase likelihood of acceptance. Buys one-time rights. Captions and ID on photos required.

Columns/Departments: Worldwide Travel Bargains (destinations, activities and accomodations for budget travelers—featured in every issue); Study/Travel Program Notes (new courses or travel programs); Resources (new information and ideas for independent travel); Working Traveler (how to find jobs and what to expect). Buys 8/issue. Send complete ms. Length: 1,000 words maximum. Pays $20-50.

Fillers: Info Exchange (information, preferably first-hand—having to do with travel, particularly offbeat educational travel and work or study abroad). Buys 10/issue. Length: 1,000 words maximum. Pays $20-50.

Tips: "We like nuts and bolts stuff, practical information, especially on how to work, live and cut costs abroad. Our readers want usable information on planning their own travel itinerary. Be specific: names, addresses, current costs. We are particularly interested in educational and long-stay travel and study abroad for adults and senior citizens. More and more readers want information not only on work but retirement possibilities. *Educational Travel Resource Guide* published each year in July provides best information sources on work, study, and independent travel abroad. Each bimonthly issue contains a directory of educational and specialty travel programs. (Topics schedule included with writers' guidelines.)

TRAVEL À LA CARTE, 136 Walton St., Port Hope, Ontario L1A 1N5 Canada. (905)885-7948. Fax: (905)885-7202. Editor: Donna Carter. 70% freelance written. Bimonthly travel magazine. "Lighthearted entertaining articles on travel destinations worldwide, with a focus on the places and people visited. Our audience is travellers, airline, train and car." Pays on publication. Byline given. Offers no kill fee. Not copyrighted. Buys first North American and one-time rights. Submit seasonal/holiday material 4 months in advance. Accepts simultaneous submissions. Reports in 1 month. Free sample copy and writer's guidelines with SASE.

Nonfiction: Travel. Buys 12-15 mss/year. Query with published clips. Length: 1,500-2,000 words. Pays $125-275.

Photos: Send transparencies or slides with submission. Offers no additional payment for photos accepted with ms. Identification of subjects required. Buys one-time rights.

Tips: "Send a list of travel destinations and samples of writing and photography. Do not send off-the-beaten path articles for destinations that require flight changes followed by train, canoe and treks to remote areas."

TRAVEL AMERICA, The U.S. Vacation Magazine, World Publishing Co., 990 Grove St., Evanston IL 60201-4370. (708)491-6440. Editor-in-Chief/Associate Publisher: Bob Meyers. Contact: Randy Mink, managing editor. 80% freelance written. Bimonthly magazine covering US vacation travel. Circ. 350,000. Byline given. Buys first North American serial rights. Submit seasonal/holiday material 6 months in advance. Accepts previously published submissions, dependent upon publication—local or regional OK. Send tearsheet or photocopy of article or typed ms with rights for sale noted and information about when and where the article previously appeared. Pays 50% of their fee for an original article. Reports in 3 weeks on queries; 6-8 weeks on mss. Sample copy for $3.50 and 9×12 SASE with 5 first-class stamps.

Nonfiction: Primarily destination-oriented travel articles and resort/hotel profiles and roundups, but will consider essays, how-to, humor, nostalgia, Americana. "It is best to study current contents and query first." Buys 50 mss/year. Average length: 1,000 words. Pays $150-300.

• Could use more stories on Americana and nostalgia—collectibles or roundups of old movie palaces, diners, etc.

Photos: Top-quality original color slides preferred. Captions required. Buys one-time rights. Prefers photo feature package (ms plus slides), but will purchase slides only to support a work in progress.

Columns/Departments: Travel Views (travel tips; service articles). Buys 6 mss/year. Query or send complete ms. Length: 800 words. Pays $125-150.

Tips: "Because we are heavily photo-oriented, superb slides are our foremost concern. The most successful approach is to send 2-3 sheets of slides with the query or complete ms. Include a list of other subjects you can provide as a photo feature package."

TRAVEL & LEISURE, American Express Publishing Corp., 1120 Ave. of the Americas, New York NY 10036. (212)382-5600. Editor-in-Chief: Nancy Novogrod. Executive Editor: Douglas Brenner. Managing Editor: Maria Shaw. 80% freelance written. Monthly magazine. Circ. 900,000. **Pays on acceptance.** Byline given. Offers 25% kill fee. Buys first world and foreign edition rights. Reports in 4-6 weeks. *Writer's Market* recommends allowing 2 months for reply. Sample copy for $5. Writer's guidelines for #10 SASE.

Nonfiction: Travel. Buys 200 mss/year. Query. Length open. Payment varies. Pays the expenses of writers on assignment.

Photos: Discourages submission of unsolicited transparencies. Payment varies. Captions required. Buys one-time rights.

Tips: "Read the magazine. Regional sections are best places to start."

• *Travel and Leisure* undertook a redesign in January 1994. Departments are in front and back, there are no short features, and there are 3 regional editions: East, Heartland and West.

TRAVEL NEWS, Travel Agents International, Inc., 15th Floor, 111 2nd Ave. NE, St. Petersburg FL 33701-3434. (813)895-8241. Fax: (813)894-6318. Editor: Matthew Wiseman. 40% freelance written. Monthly travel tabloid. "Travel stories written to praise a particular trip. We want readers to consider taking a trip themselves." Estab. 1982. Circ. 250,000. Pays on publication. Publishes ms an average of 2 months after acceptance. Byline given. Not copyrighted. Buys simultaneous rights. Submit seasonal/holiday material 6 months in advance. Accepts simultaneous and previously published submissions. Send photocopy of article or typed ms with rights for sale noted. Pays 100% of the amount paid for an original article. Reports in 2 months. Sample copy and writer's guidelines for 9×12 SAE with 4 first-class stamps. No phone calls, please.

Nonfiction: General interest, new product, photo feature, travel. "Each issue focuses on one travel category. We will accept submissions anytime but prefer SASE for publication calendar. No negative articles that would discourage travel. Make sure stories you submit are geared toward the traveler using a travel agent." Buys 30 mss/year. Query with or without published clips or send complete ms. Length: 500-1,500 words. Pays $20-200 for assigned articles; $10-125 for unsolicited articles.

Photos: State availability of photos with submission. Buys one-time rights.

Tips: "Send SASE for publication calendar, sample copy and submission requirements. Write well in advance of a trip to see what angle we would like the story to take. We will also review outlines."

TRAVEL SMART, Communications House, Inc., Dobbs Ferry NY 10522. (914)693-4208. Editor/Publisher: H.J. Teison. Managing Editor: Nancy Dunnan. Covers information on "good-value travel." Monthly newsletter. Estab. 1976. Pays on publication. Buys all rights. Reports in 6 weeks. *Writer's Market* recommends allowing 2 months for reply. Sample copy and writer's guidelines for #10 SAE with 3 first-class stamps.

Nonfiction: "Interested primarily in bargains or little-known deals on transportation, lodging, food, unusual destinations that are really good values. No destination stories on major Caribbean islands, London, New

York, no travelogs, 'my vacation,' poetry, fillers. No photos or illustrations. Just hard facts. We are not part of 'Rosy fingers of dawn . . .' school." Write for guidelines, then query. Length: 100-1,500 words. Pays $150 maximum."

Tips: "When you travel, check out small hotels offering good prices, little known restaurants, and send us brief rundown (with prices, phone numbers, addresses). Information must be current. Include your phone number with submission, because we sometimes make immediate assignments."

WESTERN RV NEWS, Suite B, 1350 SW Upland Dr., Portland OR 97221-2647. (503)222-1255. Fax: (503)222-1255. Editor: Elsie Hathaway. 75% freelance written. Monthly magazine for owners of recreational vehicles. Estab. 1966. Pays on publication. Publishes ms an average of 3-6 months after acceptance. Byline given. Buys first rights and second serial (reprint) rights. Accepts simultaneous and previously published submissions. Send photocopy or typed ms with rights for sale noted and information about when and where the article previously appeared and photocopy of article if available. Pays 60% of their fee for an original article. Reports in 1 month. *Writer's Market* recommends allowing 2 months for reply. Sample copy and writer's guidelines for 9×12 SAE with 5 first-class stamps. Guidelines for #10 SASE. Request to be put on free temporary mailing list for publication.

Nonfiction: How-to (RV oriented, purchasing considerations, maintenance), humor (RV experiences), new product (with ancillary interest to RV lifestyle), personal experiences (varying or unique RV lifestyles), technical (RV systems or hardware), travel. "No articles without an RV slant." Buys 100 mss/year. Submit complete ms. Length: 250-1,200 words. Pays $15-100.

Photos: Send photos with submission. Prefer b&w. Offers $5-10/photo. Captions, model releases, identification of subjects required. Buys one-time rights.

Fillers: Encourage anecdotes, RV related tips and short humor. Length: 50-250 words. Pays $5-25.

Tips: "Highlight the RV lifestyle! Western travel (primarily NW destinations) articles should include information about the availability of RV sites, dump stations, RV parking and accessibility. Thorough research and a pleasant, informative writing style are paramount. Technical, how-to, and new product writing is also of great interest to us. Photos definitely enhance the possibility of article acceptance."

Women's

Women have an incredible variety of publications available to them — about 50 appear on newsstands in an array of specialties. A number of titles in this area have been redesigned during the past year to compete in the crowded marketplace. Many have stopped publishing fiction and are focusing more on short, human interest nonfiction articles. Magazines that also use material slanted to women's interests can be found in the following categories: Business and Finance; Child Care and Parental Guidance; Contemporary Culture; Food and Drink; Health and Fitness; Hobby and Craft; Home and Garden; Relationships; Religious; Romance and Confession; and Sports.

ALLURE, Condé Nast, 350 Madison Ave., New York NY 10017. Monthly publication covering beauty, lifestyle and culture. This magazine did not respond to our request for information. Query before submitting.

AMERICAN WOMAN, GCR Publishing, 34th Floor, 1700 Broadway, New York NY 10019-5905. (212)541-7100. Fax: (212)245-1241. Editor: Lynn Varacalli. Managing Editor: Sandy Kosherick. 50% freelance written. Bimonthly magazine for "thirty-something women, mostly single, dealing with relationships and self-help." Estab. 1990. Circ. 200,000. Pays on publication. Publishes ms an average of 2 months after acceptance. Byline given. Offers 25% kill fee. Buys one-time and second serial (reprint) rights. Submit seasonal/holiday material 5 months in advance. Accepts simultaneous and previously published submissions. Send information about when and where the article previously appeared. For reprints, pays 50% of the amount paid for an original article. Reports in 1 month. Sample copy for $2.50. Writer's guidelines for #10 SASE.

Nonfiction: Book excerpts, self-help, inspirational, interview/profile, personal experience. "No poetry, recipes or fiction." Buys 40 mss/year. Query with published clips. Length: 700-1,500 words. Pays $250-800 for assigned articles; $200-700 for unsolicited articles. Pays for phone, mailings, faxes, transportation costs of writers on assignment.

Photos: State availability of photos with submission. Reviews contact sheets, transparencies, prints. Offers $75-150/photo. Captions, model releases, identification of subjects required. Buys one-time rights.

Tips: "We are interested in true-life stories and stories of inspiration — women who have overcome obstacles in their lives, trends (new ideas in dating, relationships, places to go, new hot spots for meeting men), articles about women starting businesses on a shoestring and money-saving articles (on clothes, beauty, vacations, mail order, entertainment)."

‡BRIDAL GUIDE, Globe Communications Corp., 441 Lexington Ave., New York NY 10017. (212)949-4040. Fax: (212)286-0072. Editor-in-Chief: Stephanie Wood. Travel Editor: Lisa Leffler Gabor. Assistant Editor:

Monica Bernstein. 50% freelance written. Prefer to work with experienced/published writers. A bimonthly magazine covering relationships, sexuality, health and nutrition, psychology, finance, travel. Please do not send queries concerning wedding planning articles, beauty, and fashion, since we produce them in-house. We do not accept personal wedding essays, fiction, or poetry. Reports in 3 months. Sample copy for $4.95 and SASE with $1 postage; writer's guidelines available.

Nonfiction: We prefer queries rather than actual manuscript submissions. All correspondence accompanied by an SASE will be answered (response time is within 6 weeks). Length: 1,500-3,000 words. Pays on acceptance. Buys 100 mss/year.

Photos: Ed Melnitsky, art director. Photography and illustration submissions should be sent to the art department.

Columns/Departments: Regular columns include finance, sex and health, new products, etiquette, relationships, travel.

BRIDAL TRENDS, Meridian International, Inc., Box 10010, Ogden UT 84409-0010. (801)394-9446. 65% freelance written. Monthly magazine with useful articles for today's bride. Circ. 60,000. **Pays on acceptance.** Publishes ms an average of 10 months after acceptance. Byline given. Buys first, second serial (reprint) and nonexclusive reprint rights. Accepts simultaneous and previously published submissions. Reports in 2 months with SASE. Sample copy for $1 and 9×12 SAE. Writer's guidelines for #10 SASE. All requests for sample copies, guidelines and queries should be addressed Attn: Editorial Staff.

Nonfiction: "General interest articles about traditional and modern approaches to weddings. Topics include all aspects of ceremony and reception planning: flowers, invitations, catering, wedding apparel and fashion trends for the bride, groom, and other members of the wedding party, etc. Also featured are honeymoon destinations, how to build a relationship and keep romance alive, and adjusting to married life." Buys approximately 15 mss/year. Written query. Length: 1,200 words. Pays 15¢/word for first rights plus nonexclusive reprint rights. Pays 10¢/word for second rights.

Photos: Send photos with ms. Reviews 35mm or larger transparencies and 5×7 or 8×10 color prints. Pays $35 for inside photo. Captions, model release, identification of subjects required.

Tips: "We publish articles that detail each aspect of wedding planning: invitations, choosing your flowers, deciding on the style of your wedding, and choosing a photographer and caterer. Emphasis is on the use of wedding consultants, gift registries, floral designers, caterers, travel agents, hotel and spa coordinators."

BRIDE'S, Condé Nast, 350 Madison Ave., New York NY 10017. (212)880-8535. Managing Editor: Andrea Feld. Editor-in-Chief: Barbara D. Tober. 40% freelance written. Eager to work with new/unpublished writers. Bimonthly magazine for the first- or second-time bride, her family and friends, the groom and his family and friends. Circ. 400,000. **Pays on acceptance.** Publishes ms an average of 2 months after acceptance. Buys all rights. Also buys first and second serial rights for book excerpts on marriage, communication, finances. Offers 20% kill fee, depending on circumstances. Buys 40 unsolicited mss/year. Byline given. Reports in 2 months. Address mss to Features Department. Writer's guidelines for #10 SASE.

● Ranked as one of the best markets for freelance writers in *Writer's Digest* magazine's annual "Top 100 Markets," January 1994.

Nonfiction: "We want warm, personal articles, optimistic in tone, with help offered in a clear, specific way. All issues should be handled within the context of marriage. How-to features on all aspects of marriage: communications, in-laws, careers, money, sex, housing, housework, family planning, marriage after having a baby, religion, interfaith marriage, step-parenting, second marriage, reaffirmation of vows; informational articles on the realities of marriage, the changing roles of men and women, the kind of troubles in engagement that are likely to become big issues in marriage; stories from couples or marriage authorities that illustrate marital problems and solutions to men and women; book excerpts on marriage, communication, finances, sex; and how-to features on wedding planning that offer expert advice. Also success stories of marriages of long duration. We use first-person pieces and articles that are well researched, relying on quotes from authorities in the field, and anecdotes and dialogues from real couples. We publish first-person essays on provocative topics unique to marriage." Query or submit complete ms. Article outline preferred. Length: 800-1,000 words. Pays $300-800.

Columns/Departments: The Love column accepts reader love poems, for $25 each. The Something New section accepts reader wedding planning and craft ideas, pays $25.

Tips: "Since marriage rates are up, large, traditional weddings, personalized to reflect the couples' lifestyles, are back in style, and more women work than ever before, do *not* query us on just living together or becoming a stay-at-home wife after marriage. Send us a query or a well-written article that is both easy to read and offers real help for the bride or groom as she/he adjusts to her/his new role. No first-person narratives on wedding and reception planning, home furnishings, cooking, fashion, beauty, travel. We're interested in

A bullet introduces comments by the editor of Writer's Market *indicating special information about the listing.*

unusual ideas, experiences, and lifestyles. No 'I used baby pink rose buds' articles."

COLABORER MAGAZINE, Woman's National Auxiliary Convention, Free Will Baptists, P.O. Box 5002, Antioch TN 37011-5002. Contact: Melissa Riddle. Estab. 1961. Unpublished articles, plays, poetry, programs, art related to Christian growth and evangelism for today's woman. Publishes reprints of previously published articles. Send typed ms with rights for sale noted and information about when and where the article previously appeared.

COMPLETE WOMAN, For All The Women You Are, Associated Publications, Inc., 1165 N. Clark, Chicago IL 60610. (312)266-8680. Editor: Bonnie L. Krueger. Assistant Editor: Jean Iversen. 90% freelance written. Bimonthly magazine of general interest for women. Areas of concern are love life, health, fitness, emotions, etc. Estab. 1980. Circ. 150,000. Pays on publication. Publishes ms an average of 5 months after acceptance. Byline given. Buys first North American serial, second serial (reprint) and simultaneous rights. Submit seasonal/holiday material 5 months in advance. Accepts simultaneous and previously published submissions. Send tearsheet or photocopy of article or short story or send typed ms with rights for sale noted and information about when and where the article previously appeared. Reports in 2 months. Writer's guidelines for #10 SASE.
Nonfiction: Book excerpts, general interest, how-to, humor, inspirational, interview/profile, new product, personal experience, photo feature. "We like roundups, celebrity interviews and articles on what men want and need. Other topics should be centered on today's woman and her love life." Buys 60-100 mss/year. Query with published clips, or send complete ms. Length: 800-2,000 words. Pays $80-400. Sometimes pays expenses of writers on assignment.
Photos: Send photos with submission. Reviews 2¼ or 35mm transparencies and 5×7 prints. Offers $35-75/photo. Captions, model releases, identification of subjects required. Buys one-time rights.
Poetry: Avant-garde, free verse, light verse, traditional. Nothing over 30 lines. Buys 50 poems/year. Submit maximum 5 poems. Pays $10.

COSMOPOLITAN, The Hearst Corp., 224 W. 57th St., New York NY 10019. (212)649-2000. Exec. Editor: Roberta Ashley. 90% freelance written. Monthly magazine for 18- to 35-year-old single, married, divorced women – all working. **Pays on acceptance.** Byline given. Offers 10-15% kill fee. Buys all magazine rights and occasionally negotiates first North American rights. Submit seasonal/holiday material 6 months in advance. Accepts previously published submissions appearing in minor publications. Reports in 1 week on queries; 3 weeks on mss. *Writer's Market* recommends allowing 2 months for reply. Sample copy for $2.50. Writer's guidelines for #10 SASE.
  • Ranked as one of the best markets for fiction writers in *Writer's Digest* magazine's biannual "Fiction 50," June 1994.
Nonfiction: Book excerpts, how-to, humor, opinion, personal experience and anything of interest to young women. Buys 350 mss/year. Query with published clips or send complete ms. Length: 500-3,500 words. Pays expenses of writers on assignment.
Fiction: Betty Kelly. Condensed novels, humorous, novel excerpts, romance and original short stories with romantic plots. Buys 18 mss/year. Query. Length: 750-3,000 words.
Poetry: Free verse, light verse. Buys 30 poems/year. No maximum number. Length: 4-30 lines.
Fillers: Irene Copeland. Facts. Buys 240/year. Length: 300-1,000 words.

COUNTRY WOMAN, Reiman Publications, P.O. Box 643, Milwaukee WI 53201. (414)423-0100. Managing Editor: Kathy Pohl. 75-85% written by readers. Willing to work with new/unpublished writers. Bimonthly magazine on the interests of country women. *"Country Woman* is for contemporary rural women of all ages and backgrounds and from all over the US and Canada. It includes a sampling of the diversity that makes up rural women's lives – love of home, family, farm, ranch, community, hobbies, enduring values, humor, attaining new skills and appreciating present, past and future all within the context of the lifestyle that surrounds country living." Estab. 1970. **Pays on acceptance.** Byline given. Buys first North American serial, one-time and second serial (reprint) rights. Submit seasonal/holiday material 4-5 months in advance. Accepts previously published submissions (on occasion). Send tearsheet of article or short story and information about when and where the material previously appeared. Reports in 2 months on queries; 2-3 months on mss. Sample copy for $2. Writer's guidelines for #10 SASE.
Nonfiction: General interest, historical/nostalgic, how-to (crafts, community projects, decorative, antiquing, etc.), humor, inspirational, interview/profile, personal experience, photo/feature packages profiling interesting country women – all pertaining to a rural woman's interest. Articles must be written in a positive, light and entertaining manner. Query. Length: 1,000 words maximum.
Photos: Send color photos with query or ms. Reviews 35mm or 2¼ transparencies or excellent-quality color prints. Uses only excellent quality color photos. No b&w. "We pay for photo/feature packages." Captions, model releases and identification of subjects required. Buys one-time rights.
Columns/Departments: Why Farm Wives Age Fast (humor), I Remember When (nostalgia) and Country Decorating. Buys 10-12 mss/year (maximum). Query or send complete ms. Length: 500-1,000 words. Pays $75-125.

Fiction: Main character *must* be a country woman. All fiction must have a country setting. Fiction must have a positive, upbeat message. Includes fiction in every issue. Would buy more fiction if stories suitable for our audience were sent our way. Query or send complete ms. Length: 750-1,000 words. Pays $90-125.

Poetry: Traditional, light verse. "Poetry must have rhythm and rhyme! It must be country-related. Always looking for seasonal poetry." Buys 30 poems/year. Submit maximum 6 poems. Length: 5-24 lines. Pays $10-25.

Tips: "We have recently broadened our focus to include 'country' women, not just women on farms and ranches. This allows freelancers a wider scope in material. Write as clearly and with as much zest and enthusiasm as possible. We love good quotes, supporting materials (names, places, etc.) and strong leads and closings. Readers relate strongly to where they live and the lifestyle they've chosen. They want to be informed and entertained, and that's just exactly why they subscribe. Readers are busy—not too busy to read—but when they do sit down, they want good writing, reliable information and something that feels like a reward. How-to, humor, personal experience and nostalgia are areas most open to freelancers. Profiles, to a certain degree, are also open. Be accurate and fresh in approach."

DAUGHTERS OF SARAH, The Magazine for Christian Feminists, Daughters of Sarah, 2121 Sheridan Rd., Evanston IL 60201. (708)866-3882. Editor: Reta Finger. Managing Editor: Sandra Volentine. Contact: Cathi Falsani, assistant editor. 85% freelance written. Quarterly Christian feminist magazine published by women calling for justice, mutuality, and reconciliation in the church and the world. We are a forum for a wide variety of viewpoints that are both Christian and feminist." Estab. 1974. Circ. 5,000. Pays on publication. Publishes ms an average of 3-4 months after acceptance. Byline given. Buys first North American serial and one-time rights. Editorial lead time 3 months. Submit seasonal material 3 months in advance. Accepts simultaneous and previously published submissions. Reports in 2-4 months. Sample copy for $4. Writer's guidelines for #10 SASE.

Nonfiction: Book excerpts, essays, exposé, general interest, historical/nostalgic, humor, inspirational, interview/profile, opinion, personal experience, religious. "We are a thematic magazine. Each issue focuses on a specific theme. It is best to send for a theme list. We don't want to see anything *not* relating to women or women's issues and anything without Biblical or feminist perspective." Query. Length: 500-2,100 words. Pays $15/printed page minimum plus 2 copies.

Photos: Send photos with submission. Reviews 8 × 10 prints. Negotiates payment individually. Identification of subjects required. Buys one-time rights.

Columns/Departments: Reta Finger, editor. Segue (feminist women in conservative/mainline churches), 800 words; Bible as Feminist Pilgrim (Biblical exegesis/theological discourse), 1,000 words; Women in Ministry (clergy women and lay women in ministry tell personal stories), 1,000 words. Buys 6 mss/year. Query. Pays $15-80.

Fiction: Confession, historical, humorous, religious. Buys 2 mss/year. Query. Length: 600-2,000 words. Pays $15-80.

Poetry: Free verse, light verse. Buys 12/year. Submit maximum 4 poems. Length: 4-100 lines. Pays $15-45.

Tips: "Query, query, query! Our writer's guidelines are very helpful and speak to specific areas (and pet peeves) that will help you get published in *Daughters of Sarah*. Use inclusive language. Use a personal approach and avoid 'preachy' academic-ese, and issues not relating to women, feminism and Christianity. Our nonfiction area is most open. My greatest advice is to send for our guidelines and themes and then please query first before sending a manuscript. Stick to issues relating to a specific theme."

ESSENCE, 1500 Broadway, New York NY 10036. Editor-in-Chief: Susan L. Taylor. Editor: Stephanie Stokes Oliver. Executive Editor: Valerie Wilson Wesley. Monthly magazine. Estab. 1970. Circ. 950,000. **Pays on acceptance.** Makes assignments on one-time serial rights basis. 3 month lead time. Pays 25% kill fee. Byline given. Submit seasonal/holiday material 6 months in advance. Accepts previously published submissions. Send tearsheet of article, information about when and where the article previously appeared. Pays 50% of the amount paid for an original article. Reports in 2 months. Sample copy for $2. Free writer's guidelines.

● Ranked as one of the best markets for freelance writers in *Writer's Digest* magazine's annual "Top 100 Markets," January 1994.

Nonfiction: Valerie Wilson Wesley, executive editor. "We're looking for articles that inspire and inform Black women. The topics we include in each issue are provocative. Every article should move the *Essence* woman emotionally and intellectually. We welcome queries from good writers on a wide range of topics; general interest, health and fitness, historical, how-to, humor, self-help, relationships, work, personality interview, personal experience, political issues, business and finances, personal opinion." Buys 200 mss/year. Query only; word length will be given upon assignment. Pays $500 minimum. Also publishes novel and nonfiction book excerpts.

Photos: Marlowe Goodson, art director. State availability of photos with query. Pays $100 for b&w page; $300 for color page. Captions and model release required. "We particularly would like to see photographs for our travel section that feature Black travelers."

Columns/Departments: Query department editors: Contemporary Living (home, food, lifestyle, travel, consumer information): Pamela Johnson; Arts: Gordon Chambers; Health & Fitness: Linda Villarosa; Travel: Valerie Vaz. Query only; word length will be given upon assignment. Pays $100 minimum.

Tips: "Please note that *Essence* no longer accepts unsolicited mss for fiction, poetry or nonfiction, except for the Brothers, Windows, Back Talk and Interiors columns. So please only send query letters for nonfiction story ideas."

‡**FAIRFIELD COUNTY WOMAN**, FCW, Inc., 15 Bank St., Stamford CT 06901. (203)323-3105-3010. Editor: Joan Honig. 75% freelance written. A women's regional monthly tabloid focusing on careers, education, health, relationships and family life. Connecticut writers and Connecticut stories of interest to women only. Intern opportunities available. Estab. 1982. Circ. 65,000. Pays 60 days after publications. Byline given. Buys first rights. Submit seasonal/holiday material 3 months in advance. Accepts previously published submissions. Send photocopy of article and information about when and where the article previously appeared. Pays $25 for reprints. Query for electronic submissions. Reports in 6 months. Sample copy for 10 × 13 SAE with $1.50 postage.
Nonfiction: Essays, how-to, humor, local interview/profile. Buys 50 mss/year. Query with published clips. Length: 800-2,000 words. Pays $35-100 for assigned articles; $25-75 for unsolicited articles. Sometimes pays expenses of writers on assignment.
Photos: State availability of photos with submission. Reviews 5 × 7 prints. Offers no additional payment with ms. Buys one-time rights.

FAMILY CIRCLE MAGAZINE, 110 Fifth Ave., New York NY 10011. (212)463-1000. Editor-in-Chief: Susan Ungaro. 70% freelance written. Magazine published 17 times/year. Usually buys all print rights. Offers 20% kill fee. Byline given. **Pays on acceptance.** "We are a national women's magazine which offers advice, fresh information and entertainment to women. Query should stress the unique aspects of an article and expert sources; we want articles that will help our readers or make a difference in how they live." Reports in 1 month.
● Ranked as one of the best markets for freelance writers in *Writer's Digest* magazine's annual "Top 100 Markets," January 1994.
Nonfiction: Susan Ungaro, deputy editor. Women's interest subjects such as family and personal relationships, children, physical and mental health, nutrition, self-improvement and profiles of ordinary women doing extraordinary things for her community or the nation from 'Women Who Make a Difference' series. "We look for well-written, well-reported stories told through interesting anecdotes and insightful writing. We want well-researched service journalism on all subjects." Query. Length: 1,000-2,500 words. Pays $1/word.
Tips: "Query letters should be concise and to the point. Also, writers should keep close tabs on *Family Circle* and other women's magazines to avoid submitting recently run subject matter."

FIRST FOR WOMEN, Bauer Publishing Co., P.O. Box 1648, 270 Sylvan Ave., Englewood Cliffs NJ 07632. This publication did not respond to our request for information. Query before submitting.

GLAMOUR, Conde Nast, 350 Madison Ave., New York NY 10017. (212)880-8800. Editor-in-Chief: Ruth Whitney. 75% freelance written. Works with a small number of new/unpublished writers each year. Monthly magazine for college-educated women, 18-35 years old. Estab. 1939. Circ. 2.3 million. **Pays on acceptance.** Offers 20% kill fee. Publishes ms an average of 1 year after acceptance. Byline given. Reports in 3 months. Writer's guidelines for #10 SASE.
● Ranked as one of the best markets for freelance writers in *Writer's Digest* magazine's annual "Top 100 Markets," January 1994.
Nonfiction: Pamela Erens, articles editor. "Editorial approach is 'how-to' with articles that are relevant in the areas of careers, health, psychology, interpersonal relationships, etc. We look for queries that are fresh and include a contemporary, timely angle. Fashion, beauty, travel, food and entertainment are all staff-written. We use 1,000-word opinion essays for our Viewpoint section. Our His/Hers column features generally stylish essays on relationships or comments on current mores by male and female writers in alternate months." Pays $1,000 for His/Hers mss; $500 for Viewpoint mss. Buys first North American serial rights. Buys 10-12 mss/issue. Query "with letter that is detailed, well-focused, well-organized, and documented with surveys, statistics and research; personal essays excepted." Short articles and essays (1,500-2,000 words) pay $1,000 and up; longer mss (2,500-3,000 words) pay $1,500 minimum. Sometimes pays the expenses of writers on assignment.
Tips: "We're looking for sharply focused ideas by strong writers and are constantly raising our standards. We are interested in getting new writers, and we are approachable, mainly because our range of topics is so broad. We've increased our focus on male-female relationships."

GOOD HOUSEKEEPING, Hearst Corp., 959 Eighth Ave., New York NY 10019. (212)649-2000. Editor-in-Chief: John Mack Carter. Executive Editor: Mina Mulvey. Managing Editor: Mary Fiore. Prefers to work with published/established writers. Monthly magazine. Circ. 5 million. **Pays on acceptance.** Buys all rights. Pays 25% kill fee. Byline given. Submit seasonal/holiday material 6 months in advance. Reports in 6 weeks. *Writer's Market* recommends allowing 2 months for reply. Sample copy for $2. Writer's guidelines for #10 SASE.
● Ranked as one of the best markets for freelance writers in *Writer's Digest* magazine's annual "Top

100 Markets," January 1994 and as one of the best markets for fiction writers in its magazine's biannual "Fiction 50," June 1994.

Nonfiction: Joan Thursh, articles editor. Phyllis Levy, book editor. Shirley Howard, regional editor. Medical, informational, investigative, inspirational, interview, nostalgia, personal experience, profile. Buys 4-6 mss/issue. Query. Length: 1,500-2,500 words. Pays $1,500+ on acceptance for full articles from new writers. Pays $250-350 for local interest and travel pieces of 2,000 words. Pays the expenses of writers on assignment.

Photos: Herbert Bleiweiss, art director. Photos purchased on assignment mostly. Some short photo features with captions. Pays $100-350 for b&w; $200-400 for color photos. Query. Model releases required.

Columns/Departments: Light Housekeeping & Fillers, edited by Rosemary Leonard. Humorous short-short prose and verse. Jokes, gags, anecdotes. Pays $25-50. The Better Way, edited by Erika Mark. Ideas and in-depth research. Query. Pays $250-500. "Mostly staff written; only outstanding ideas have a chance here."

Fiction: Lee Quarfoot, fiction editor. Uses romance fiction and condensations of novels that can appear in one issue. Looks for reader identification. "We get 1,500 unsolicited mss/month—includes poetry; a freelancer's odds are overwhelming—but we do look at all submissions." Send complete mss. Manuscripts will not be returned. Only responds on acceptance. Length: 1,500 words (short-shorts); novel according to merit of material; average 5,000-word short stories. Pays $1,000 minimum for fiction short-shorts; $1,250 for short stories.

Poetry: Arleen Quarfoot, poetry editor. Light verse and traditional. "Presently overstocked." Poems used as fillers. Pays $5/line for poetry on acceptance.

Tips: "Always send an SASE. We prefer to see a query first. Do not send material on subjects already covered in-house by the Good Housekeeping Institute—these include food, beauty, needlework and crafts."

LADIES' HOME JOURNAL, Meredith Corporation, 100 Park Ave., New York NY 10017-5516. (212)953-7070. Publishing Director and Editor-in-Chief: Myrna Blyth. 50% freelance written. Monthly magazine focusing on issues of concern to women. Circ. 5 million. **Pays on acceptance.** Offers 25% kill fee. Rights bought vary with submission. Reports on queries within 3 months with SASE. Writer's guidelines for #10 SASE, attention: writer's guidelines.

- Ranked as one of the best markets for freelance writers in *Writer's Digest* magazine's annual "Top 100 Markets," January 1994 and as one of the best markets for fiction writers in its biannual "Fiction 50," June 1994.

Nonfiction: Submissions on the following subjects should be directed to the editor listed for each: investigative reports, news-related features, psychology/relationships/sex (Pam O'Brien, features editor); medical/health (Mary Hickey, health editor); celebrities/entertainment (Melanie Berger, entertainment editor); travel stories (Sharlene Johnson, associate editor). Query with published clips. Length: 1,500-3,000 words. Fees vary. Pays expenses of writers on assignment.

Photos: State availability of photos with submission. Offers variable payment for photos accepted with ms. Captions, model releases and identification of subjects required. Rights bought vary with submission. (*LHJ* arranges for its own photography almost all the time.)

Columns/Departments: Query the following editor or box for column ideas. A Woman Today (Box WT); Woman to Woman (Box WW); Parents' Journal (Mary Mohler, senior editor); Pet News (Shana Aborn, associate features editor).

Fiction: Submit to Kelly Matthews, editor, books and fiction. Only short stories and novels submitted by an agent or publisher will be considered. Buys 12 mss/year. Does not accept poetry of any kind.

McCALL'S, 110 Fifth Ave., New York NY 10011-5603. (212)463-1000. Editor: Kate White. Executive Editor: Lynne Cusack. 90% freelance written. "Study recent issues. Our publication carefully and conscientiously serves the needs of the woman reader—concentrating on matters that directly affect her life and offering information and understanding on subjects of personal importance to her." Monthly. Circ. 5 million. **Pays on acceptance.** Publishes ms an average of 6 months after acceptance. Offers 20% kill fee. Byline given. Buys exclusive or First North American rights. Reports in 2 months. Writer's guidelines for #10 SASE.

Nonfiction: The editors are seeking meaningful stories of personal experience, fresh slants for self-help and relationship pieces, and well-researched action-oriented articles and narratives dealing with social problems concerning readers. Topics must have broad appeal, but they must be approached in a fresh, new, you-haven't-read-this-elsewhere way. *McCall's* buys 200-300 articles/year, many in the 1,500-2,000-word length. Pays variable rates for nonfiction. Deputy Editor Lisel Eisenheimer is editor of nonfiction books, from which *McCall's* frequently publishes excerpts. These are on subjects of interest to women: health, personal narratives, celebrity biographies and autobiographies, etc. Almost all features on food, fashion, beauty and decorating are staff-written. Sometimes pays the expenses of writers on assignment.

Tips: Query first. Use the tone and format of our most recent issues as your guide. Preferred length: 1,500-2,000 words. Address submissions to executive editor unless otherwise specified.

- No longer publishes fiction.

MADEMOISELLE, Conde Nast, 350 Madison Ave., New York NY 10017. Managing Editor: Dana Corwin. 95% freelance written. Prefers to work with published/established writers. Columns are written by columnists; "sometimes we give new writers a 'chance' on shorter, less complex assignments." Monthly magazine for women age 21-31. Circ 1.2 million. Buys first North American serial rights. **Pays on acceptance**; rates vary.
- *Mademoiselle* no longer publishes fiction. They offer no scholarships or internships.

Nonfiction: Particular concentration on articles of interest to the intelligent young woman, including personal relationships, health, careers, trends, and current social problems. Send health queries to Jennifer Rapaport, associate editor. Send entertainment queries to Tara McKelvey entertainment editor. Query with published clips and SAE. Length: 1,000 words.

Photos: Cindy Searight, art director. Commissioned work assigned according to needs. Photos of fashion, beauty, travel. Payment ranges from no-charge to an agreed rate of payment per shot, job series or page rate. Buys all rights. Pays on publication for photos.

Tips: "We are looking for timely, well-researched manuscripts."

MIRABELLA, 200 Madison Ave., 8th Floor, New York NY 10016. Monthly publication covering fashion and culture. This magazine did not respond to our request for information. Query before submitting.

MODERN BRIDE, 249 W. 17th St., New York NY 10011. (212)337-7096. Editor: Cele Lalli. Managing Editor: Mary Ann Cavlin. **Pays on acceptance**. Offers 25% kill fee. Buys first periodical rights. Accepts previously published submissions. Reports in 1 month.
- Ranked as one of the best markets for freelance writers in *Writer's Digest* magazine's annual "Top 100 Markets," January 1994.

Nonfiction: Book excerpts, general interest, how-to, personal experience. Buys 60 mss/year. Query with published clips. Length: 500-2,000 words. Pays $600-1,200.

Columns/Departments: Geri Bain, editor. Travel.

Poetry: Free verse, light verse and traditional. Buys very few. Submit maximum 6 poems.

MS. MAGAZINE, Lang Communications, Inc., 7th Floor, 230 Park Ave., New York NY 10169-0799. (212)551-9595. Editor-in-Chief: Marcia Gillespie. Managing Editor: Barbara Findlen. 75% freelance written. Bimonthly magazine on women's issues and news. Estab. 1972. Circ. 200,000. Pays on publication. Byline given. Offers 20% kill fee. Buys all rights. Submit seasonal material 6 months in advance. Reports in 2 months. Sample copy for $5. Writer's guidelines for #10 SASE.
- Ranked as one of the best markets for freelance writers in *Writer's Digest* magazine's annual "Top 100 Markets," January 1994.

Nonfiction: International and national (US) news, the arts, books, popular culture, feminist theory and scholarship, ecofeminism, women's health, spirituality, political and economic affairs. Photo essays. Runs fiction and poetry but does not accept, acknowledge, or return unsolicited fiction or poetry. Does not discuss queries on the phone. Query with published clips. Length: 300-3,000 words. Pays expenses of writers on assignment.

Photos: State availability of photos with submission. Model releases and identification of subjects required. Buys one-time rights.

NEW WOMAN MAGAZINE, A New Woman Is An Attitude, Not An Age, K-III Magazine Corporation, 215 Lexington Ave., New York NY 10016. (212)251-1500. Editor-in-Chief: Karen Walden. Managing Editor: Kathy L. Green. Executive Editor: Susan Kane. 85% freelance written. Monthly women's general interest magazine. "*New Woman* is edited for employed women who are eager to reach for new goals and to balance their personal and professional lives. The magazine's prime focus is on self-discovery, self-development and self-esteem." Estab. 1970. Circ. 1,390,630. **Pays on acceptance**. Byline given. Offers 20% kill fee. Buys first North American serial, first or one-time rights. Submit seasonal material 5 months in advance. Reports in 1 month. Writer's guidelines for #10 SASE.
- Ranked as one of the best markets for freelance writers in *Writer's Digest* magazine's annual "Top 100 Markets," January 1994.

Nonfiction: Essays, general interest, humor (from woman's experience viewpoint), inspirational, food, fitness, finance, careers, relationship, women's issues, opinion, personal experience. "No fiction, poetry or straight travel pieces . . . travel must encompass a personal experience which leads to or adds to discovery, development and/or empowerment of a woman." Query with published clips. Length: 1,000-3,500 words. Pays $700-3,500. Sometimes pays expenses of writers on assignment.

Photos: State availability of photos with submission. Reviews contact sheets. Negotiates payment for photos. Model release and identification of subjects required. Buys one-time rights.
- No longer accepts fiction or poetry submissions.

Fillers: Cartoons. Pays $225 on acceptance.

Tips: "Send a personal letter, with clippings of published work, telling us what you are interested in and want to write about, and your perceptions of *New Woman*. It counts when a writer loves the magazine and responds to it on a personal level. We look for originality, solid research, depth and a friendly, accessible style. Freelancers will have the best chances with feature articles on relationships or inspirational essays.

Study and understand the 'voice' of *New Woman*: the magazine is friendly, helpful and accessible to its readership in all respects."

‡**PLAYGIRL**, 801 Second Ave., New York NY 10017. (212)986-5100. Editor-in-Chief: Charmian Carl. Contact: Charlene Keel, managing editor. 75% freelance written. Prefers to work with published/established writers. Monthly entertainment magazine for 18- to 55-year-old females. Circ. 500,000. Average issue 3 articles; 1 celebrity interview. Pays within 6 weeks of acceptance. Publishes ms an average of 3 months after acceptance. Byline given. Offers 20% kill fee. Buys all rights. Submit seasonal material 6 months in advance. Accepts simultaneous submissions, if so indicated. Reports in 1 month on queries; 3 months on mss. Writer's guidelines for #10 SASE.

Nonfiction: Humor for the modern woman/man, exposés (related to women's issues), interview (Q&A format with major show business celebrities), articles on sexuality, medical breakthroughs, relationships, coping, careers, insightful, lively articles on current issues, investigative pieces particularly geared to *Playgirl*. Buys 6 mss/issue. Query with clips of previously published work. Length: 1,000-2,500 words. Pays $300-1,000. Sometimes pays the expenses of writers on assignment.

Tips: "Best bets for first-time writers: Men's Room/Women's Room (humor) and Fantasy Forum. No phone calls please."

RADIANCE, The Magazine for Large Women, Box 30246, Oakland CA 94604. (510)482-0680. Editor: Alice Ansfield. 95% freelance written. Quarterly magazine "that encourages and supports women *all* sizes of large to live fully now, to stop putting their lives on hold until they lose weight." Estab. 1984. Circ. 10,000. Pays on publication. Publishes ms an average of 10 months after acceptance. Byline given. Offers $25 kill fee. Buys one-time and second serial (reprint) rights. Submit seasonal/holiday material at least 8-10 months in advance. Accepts previously published submissions. Query for electronic submissions. Reports in 2½-3 months. Sample copy for $3.50. Writer's guidelines for #10 SASE.

Nonfiction: Book excerpts (related to large women), essays, exposé, general interest, historical/nostalgic, how-to (on health/well-being/fashion/fitness, etc.), humor, inspirational, interview/profile, opinion, personal experience, photo feature, travel. "No diet successes or articles condemning people for being fat." Query with published clips. Length: 1,000-2,500 words. Pays $35-100. Sometimes pays writers with contributor copies or other premiums.

Photos: State availability of photos with submission. Offers $15-50/photo. Captions and identification of subjects preferred. Buys one-time rights.

Columns/Departments: Up Front and Personal (personal profiles of women from all areas of life); Health and Well-Being (physical/emotional well-being, self care, research); Expressions (features on artists who celebrate the full female figure); Images (designer interviews, color/style/fashion, features); Inner Journeys (spirituality, personal experiences, interviews); Perspectives (cultural and political aspects of being in a larger body); and On the Move (women active in all kinds of sports, physical activities). Buys 60 mss/year. Query with published clips. Length: 1,000-2,500 words. Pays $50-100.

Fiction: Condensed novels, ethnic, fantasy, historical, humorous, mainstream, novel excerpts, romance, science fiction, serialized novels, slice-of-life vignettes relating somehow to large women. "No woman-hates-self-till-meets-man'-type fiction!" Buys 15 mss/year. Query with published clips. Length: 800-1,500 words. Pays $35-100.

Poetry: Reflective, empowering, experiential. Related to women's feelings and experience, re: their bodies, self-esteem, acceptance. Buys 30 poems/year. Length: 4-45 lines. Pays $10-30.

Tips: "We welcome talented, sensitive, responsible, open-minded writers. We profile women from all walks of life who are all sizes of large, of all ages and from all ethnic groups and lifestyles. We welcome writers' ideas on interesting large women from across the US and abroad. We're an open, light-hearted magazine that's working to help women feel good about themselves now, whatever their body size. *Radiance* is one of the major forces working for size acceptance. We want articles to address all areas of vital importance in women's lives. Please read a copy of *Radiance* before writing for us."

REDBOOK MAGAZINE, 224 W. 57th St., New York NY 10019. Senior Editors: Diane Salvatore, Sally Lee. Health Editor: Toni Hope. Fiction Editor: Dawn Raffel. Contact: Any of editorial assistants listed on masthead. 90% freelance written. Monthly magazine. Estab. 1903. Circ. 3.2 million. **Pays on acceptance.** Publishes ms an average of 4-6 months after acceptance. Rights purchased vary with author and material. Reports in 3 months. Writer's guidelines for #10 SASE.

• Ranked as one of the best markets for freelance writers in *Writer's Digest* magazine's annual "Top 100 Markets," January 1994 and as one of the best markets for fiction writers in its biannual "Fiction 50," June 1994.

Nonfiction: "*Redbook* addresses young mothers between the ages of 25 and 44. Most of our readers are married with children 12 and under; over 60 percent work outside the home. The articles entertain, educate and inspire our readers to confront challenging issues. Each article must be timely and relevant to *Redbook* readers' lives. Article subjects of interest: social issues, parenting, sex, marriage, news profiles, true crime, dramatic narratives, money, psychology, health. Please enclose sample of previously published work with articles or unsolicited manuscripts. Length: articles, 2,500-3,000 words; short articles, 1,000-1,500 words.

Columns/Departments: "We are interested in stories for the 'A Mother's Story' series offering the dramatic retelling of an experience involving you, your husband or child. (Also done "as told to.") For each 1,500-2,000 words accepted for publication as A Mother's Story, we pay $750. Manuscripts accompanied by a 9 × 12 SASE, must be signed, and mailed to: A Mother's Story, c/o *Redbook Magazine*. Reports in 6 months. We also need stories for the back page 'Happy Endings' column, stories of about 800 words that, just as the title suggests, end happily. See past issues for samples."

Fiction: "Of the 20,000 unsolicited manuscripts that we receive annually, we buy about 10 or more stories/year. We also find many more stories that are not necessarily suited to our needs but are good enough to warrant our encouraging the author to send others. *Redbook* looks for fresh, well-crafted stories that reflect some aspect of the experiences and interests of our readers; it's a good idea to read several issues to get a feel for what we buy. No unsolicited novels or novellas, please. Payment begins at $1,000 for short stories.

Tips: "Shorter, front-of-the-book features are usually easier to develop with first-time contributors, especially A Mother's Story and Happy Endings. We also buy short takes (250 words) for our You & Your Child opening page—succinct, charming advice-driven items. Most *Redbook* articles require solid research, well-developed anecdotes from on-the-record sources, and fresh, insightful quotes from established experts in a field that pass our 'reality check' test."

‡SAGEWOMAN, Celebrating the Goddess in Every Woman, P.O. Box 641, Point Arena CA 95468. (707)882-2052. Editor: Anne Newkirk Niven. 60% freelance written. Quarterly consumer magazine covering Goddess spirituality. "SageWoman is a quarterly magazine of women's spirituality. Our readers are people (primarily but not exclusively women) who identify positively with the term 'Goddess'. This does not mean that they are necessarily self-identified Goddess worshippers, Pagans, or Wiccans, although a majority of our readers would probably be comfortable with those terms. Our readers include women of a variety of religious faiths, ranging from Roman Catholic to Lesbian Separatist Witch and everywhere in between. The majority of every issue is created from the contributions of our readers, so your creativity and willingness to share is vital to SageWoman's existence! Estab. 1988. Circ. 10,000. Pays on publication. Publishes ms an average of 3 months after acceptance. Byline given. Offers 100% kill fee. Buys first North American serial rights and second serial (reprint) rights. Editorial lead time 5 months. Submit seasonal material 5 months in advance. Query for electronic submissions. Reports in 2 weeks on queries; 1 month on mss. Sample copy for $6. Writer's guidelines free on request.

Nonfiction: Book excerpts, essays, personal experience, religious. "No material not related to our subject matter. We do not publish fiction, or poetry." Buys 50 mss/year. Query with published clips. Length: 200-6,000 words. Pays $20 minimum for assigned articles, $5 minimum for unsolicited articles. Sometimes pays expenses of writers on assignment.

Photos: State availability of photos with submission. Reviews contact sheets and any size prints. Offers $5-20/photo. Model releases required. Buys one-time rights.

Tips: "Send for a sample copy first—our subject matter is very specific and if we are not on the same path, submitting material will be a waste of energy and time. Writers should ask about upcoming themes."

TODAY'S CHRISTIAN WOMAN, 465 Gundersen Dr., Carol Stream IL 60188-2498. (708)260-6200. Fax: (708)260-0114. Editor: Julie A. Talerico. 25% freelance written. Works with a small number of new/unpublished writers each year. Bimonthly magazine for Christian women of all ages, single and married, homemakers and career women. Estab. 1979. Circ. 190,000. **Pays on acceptance.** Publishes ms an average of 3 months after acceptance. Byline given. Buys first rights only. Submit seasonal/holiday material 9 months in advance. Accepts previously published submissions. Send tearsheet of article and information about when and where the article previously appeared. Pays 50% of the amount paid for an original article. Reports in 2 months. Sample copy for $3.50. Writer's guidelines for #10 SASE.

Nonfiction: How-to, narrative, inspirational. Query only; no unsolicited mss. "The query should include article summary, purpose and reader value, author's qualifications, suggested length and date to send. Pays 15¢/word.

Tips: "Articles focus on the following relationships: marriage, parenting, self, spiritual life and friendship. All articles should be highly anecdotal, personal in tone, and universal in appeal."

VANITY FAIR, Conde Nast, 350 Madison Ave., New York NY 10017. Monthly publication covering contemporary culture. This magazine did not respond to our request for information. Query before submitting.

‡VICTORIA, Hearst Corp., 224 W. 57th St., New York NY 10019. "Specialized copywriting needs and visual nature of this magazine make it an unsuitable candidate for freelance submissions."

‡VOGUE, Conde Nast, 350 Madison Ave., New York NY 10017. Monthly publication covering style, fashion and current culture. This magazine did not respond to our request for information. Query before submitting.

‡WEDDING DAY, P.S. Communications, 3 Rockpoint Rd. S., Southborough MA 01772. Editor: Patricia Burns Fiore. 30% freelance written. Bimonthly magazine covering Wedding Planning. "Most readers are under the age of 35 and planning a wedding in the next 18 months in the New England area." Estab. 1985.

Circ. 18,000. Pays on publication. Publishes ms an average of 3 months after acceptance. Byline given. Offers 25% kill fee. Buys first North American serial rights, one-time rights or makes work-for-hire assignments. Editorial lead time 3 months. Query for electronic submissions. Reports in 1 month on queries. Sample copy for 9×12 SAE with 5 first-class stamps.

Nonfiction: How-to (plan a wedding), travel, financial planning, decorating, relationships, fashion. Buys 10 mss/year. Query with published clips. Length: 750-1,500 words. Pays $75.

Photos: State availability of photos with submission. Reviews contact sheets, prints. Negotiates payment individually. Captions, model releases, identification of subjects required. Buys one-time rights.

Tips: "Articles are geared toward weddings and the first months after. New angles and innovative ideas for couples starting out are welcome. Looking for innovative ideas for wedding planning: receptions, ceremonies, dresses, transportation, rings, cakes, flowers, honeymoons, showers/parties, invitations, music."

WEST COAST WOMAN, LMB Media, Inc., P.O. Box 819, Sarasota FL 34230-0819. (813)954-3300. Fax: (813)954-3300. Editor: Louise Bruderle. 50% freelance written. Monthly tabloid for women on the west coast of Florida. *"West Coast Woman* is a lifestyle publication with less focus on fashion, beauty." Estab. 1988. Circ. 30,000. Pays on publication. Byline given. Offers 50% kill fee. Buys first or one-time rights. Submit seasonal/holiday material 2 months in advance. Sample copy for $3.50. Writer's guidelines for #10 SASE.

Nonfiction: Real estate, gardening, how-to, health, beauty, book reviews, seniors, car care, home design, fitness, photo feature, technical, travel, sports, fashion, money/finance, nutrition, cooking, food/wine. No humor, slice-of-life, essays, poems, poetry or comics/cartoons. Buys 130 mss/year. Query with published clips. Length: 750-3,000 words. Pays $35-65 for 750 words. Also makes ad trades for promotional tie-ins.

Photos: State availability of photos with submission. Reviews contact sheets, 35mm transparencies. Model releases required. Buys one-time rights.

Columns/Departments: Money/Finance. Buys 130 mss/year. Query with published clips. Length: 750-3,000 words. Pays $35-65 for 750 words.

WOMAN'S DAY, 1633 Broadway, New York NY 10019. (212)767-6000. Senior Articles Editor: Rebecca Greer. 75% or more of articles freelance written. 17 issues/year. Circ. 6 million. Pays negotiable kill fee. Byline given. **Pays on acceptance.** Reports in 1 month or less on queries. Submit detailed queries.

• Ranked as one of the best markets for freelance writers in *Writer's Digest* magazine's annual "Top 100 Markets," January 1994. Fiction is no longer considered.

Nonfiction: Uses articles on all subjects of interest to women—marriage, family life, childrearing, education, homemaking, money management, careers, family health, work and leisure activities. Also interested in fresh, dramatic narratives of women's lives and concerns. "These must be lively and fascinating to read." Length: 500-2,500 words, depending on material. Payment varies depending on length, type, writer, and whether it's for regional or national use, but rates are high. Pays the expenses of writers on confirmed assignment. "We no longer accept unsolicited manuscripts—and cannot return or be responsible for those that are sent."

Fillers: Neighbors columns also pay $75/each for brief practical suggestions on homemaking, childrearing and relationships. Address to the editor of the section.

Tips: "Our primary need is for ideas with broad appeal that can be featured on the cover. We're buying more short pieces. Writers should consider Quick section which uses factual pieces of 100-300 words."

‡THE WOMAN'S JOURNAL, 3 Sisters' Press, #304, 8835 SW Canyon Lane, Portland OR 97225. Editor: Wendy Waller. 90% freelance written. Monthly tabloid covering professional women's issues. "We are a regional publication for professional women who are seeking career advancement, sideline money-making opportunities and/or are in business for themselves. We focus on success stories. Other topics include health and fitness, home and garden, book reviews, family issues." Estab. 1986. Circ. 10,000. Pays on publication. Publishes ms an average of 2 months after acceptance. Byline given. Buys first North American serial rights. Editorial lead time 2 months. Submit seasonal material 3 months in advance. Accepts simultaneous submissions. Reports in 1 month on queries. Sample copy for 11×17 SAE with 3 first-class stamps. Writer's guidelines for #10 SASE.

Nonfiction: Humor, interview/profile, opinion (on women's issues), photo feature, travel. Buys 120 mss/year. Query with published clips or send complete ms. Length: 250-500 words. Pays 3-4¢/word for assigned articles; 2-3¢/word for unsolicited articles. Sometimes pays expenses of writers on assignment.

Photos: Send photos with submission. Reviews 4×5 prints. Negotiates payment individually. Captions, model releases, identification of subjects required. Buys one-time rights or all rights.

Columns/Departments: Contact: Dianne Perry. "Women's Eye View" (short personal opinion piece on any topic of interest to women), 500 words; Guest editorial (discuss policies, issues or recent news developments that affect women), 500 words; Book Reviews (books that touch on topics ranging from health, wealth, relationships to travel), 500 words. Buys 40 mss/year. Send complete ms. Pays $15-25.

Tips: "We are looking for crisp, professional stories with heart. Our publication strives to enrich thought, show new possibilities and remove self-imposed limitations, without being sentimental or dipping into pop-psychology. Submit stories which support our approach. Send clips or manuscript and SASE. No telephone calls, please. We need material on career and finance, success stories of side-line businesses and at-home businesses and contributors for our 'Woman's Eye View' column. We welcome and encourage new writers."

WOMAN'S WORLD, The Woman's Weekly, Heinrich Bauer North American, Inc., 270 Sylvan Ave., Englewood Cliffs NJ 07632. (201)569-0006. Editor-in-Chief: Stephanie Saible. 95% freelance written. Weekly magazine covering "controversial, dramatic, and human interest women's issues" for women across the nation. **Pays on acceptance.** Publishes ms an average of 4 months after acceptance. Byline given. Offers kill fee. Buys first North American serial rights. Submit seasonal/holiday material 4 months in advance. Accepts simultaneous or previously published submissions. Reports in 6 weeks on queries; 2 months on mss. Writer's guidelines for #10 SASE.

Nonfiction: Well-researched material with "a hard-news edge and topics of national scope." Reports of 1,000-1,200 words, 200 word sidebar on vital trends and major issues such as women and alcohol or teen suicide; dramatic, personal women's stories; articles on self-improvement, medicine and health topics; and the economics of home, career and daily life, pays $550. Features include In Real Life (true stories); Turning Point (in a woman's life); Families (highlighting strength of family or how unusual families deal with problems); True Love (tender, beautiful, touching and unusual love stories with happy endings). Other regular features are "Topic of the Week" (investigative news features with national scope, statistics, etc.); Scales of Justice (true stories of women and crime "if possible, presented with sympathetic attitude"); Relationships (pop psychology or coping). Queries to Johnene Granger. Pays telephone interview expenses.

Fiction: Jeanne Muchnick, fiction editor. Short story, romance and mainstream of 1,900 words and mini-mysteries of 1,000 words. "Each of our stories has a light romantic theme with a protagonist no older than 40. Each can be written from either a masculine or feminine point of view. Women characters may be single, married or divorced. Plots must be fast moving with vivid dialogue and action. The problems and dilemmas inherent in them should be contemporary and realistic, handled with warmth and feeling. The stories must have a positive resolution." Not interested in science fiction, fantasy, historical romance or foreign locales. No explicit sex, graphic language or seamy settings. Specify "short story" on envelope. Always enclose SASE. Reports in 2 months. No phone queries. Pays $1,000 on acceptance for North American serial rights for 6 months. "The 1,000 word mini-mysteries may feature either a 'whodunnit' or 'howdunnit' theme. The mystery may revolve around anything from a theft to murder. However, we are not interested in sordid or grotesque crimes. Emphasis should be on intricacies of plot rather than gratuitous violence. The story must include a resolution that clearly states the villain is getting his or her come-uppance." Submit complete mss. Specify "mini mystery" on envelope. Enclose SASE. Stories slanted for a particular holiday should be sent at least 6 months in advance. No phone queries.

Photos: State availability of photos. "State photo leads. Photos are assigned to freelance photographers." Buys one-time rights.

Tips: "Come up with good queries. Short queries are best. We have a strong emphasis on well-researched material. Writers must send research with ms including book references and phone numbers for double checking. The most frequent mistakes made by writers in completing an article for us are sloppy, incomplete research, not writing to the format, and not studying the magazine carefully enough beforehand."

WOMEN'S CIRCLE, P.O. Box 299, Lynnfield MA 01940-0299. Editor: Marjorie Pearl. 100% freelance written. Bimonthly magazine for women of all ages. Usually buys first rights for ms. Buys all rights for craft and needlework projects. **Pays on acceptance.** Byline given. Publishes ms an average of 6 months to 1 year after acceptance. Submit seasonal material 8 months in advance. Reports in 3 months. Sample copy for $2. Writer's guidelines for #10 SASE.

Nonfiction: Especially interested in stories about successful, home-based female entrepreneurs with b&w photos or transparencies. Length: 1,000-2,000 words. Also interesting and unusual money-making ideas. Welcomes good quality crafts, needlework, how-to directions in any media—crochet, fabric, etc.

Consumer Magazines/Changes '94-'95

The following consumer publications were listed in the 1994 edition but do not have listings in this edition. The majority did not respond to our request to update their listings. If a reason was given for their exclusion, we have included it in parentheses after the listing.

Ad Astra
Advanced Warning!
Adventure Florida
Airbrush Action
Alert Texan
America's Equestrian
American Atheist
American Baby Magazine
American Dane (removed by request)
The American Voice
Antaeus
The Antique Trader Weekly

Applause (no freelance)
Aquarium Fish Magazine
Arabian Horse Times (removed by request)
Architectural Digest
Areopagus (unable to contact)
The Arizona Unconservative (unable to contact)
Armenian International Magazine
Art of California
The Association Executive
ASU Travel Guide

The Atlantic Salmon Journal
The Barrelhouse (unable to contact)
Bike Midwest Magazine (unable to contact)
Black Mountain Review
Boing-Boing
Boston Review
British Heritage (removed by request)
Business Atlanta (ceased publication)
Buxom

Buzzwork (declared bankruptcy)
CAA's Autopinion Annual
California Angler
California Business
Camping & RV Magazine (unable to contact)
Campus Life
Canadian Workshop
Celebrate Life
Chatelaine
Chorale (ceased publication)
Christianity & Crisis
Christmas (using less freelance)
The City
Climax
Clockwise (ceased publication)
Closing the Gap, Inc.
Colonial Homes
Colorado Review
Columbus Monthly
Coming Attractions
Commonweal (unable to contact)
Consumer Sense (no freelance)
Country Music
Cowboy Magazine
Crain's Detroit Business (using less freelance)
Creative Loafing/Tampa
Cross-Stitch Plus
Cycle World
D&B Reports (ceased publication)
Decision
Decorating Remodeling
The Detroit Free Press Magazine
Diversion
Down Memory Lane (ceased publication)
Dungeon Master
The Elks Magazine
ETC. Magazine
Expecting
Fighting Woman News (no pay)
Figment (unable to contact)
Financial World
Formula (ceased publication)
Fourth Season
The Freeman
Golf Illustrated (unable to contact)
Good Old Days
Graham House Review
Growing Churches (ceased publication)
Handwoven
Haunts (unable to contact)
Hawai'i Review
Healing Journal (no pay)
Heartland Magazine
High Adventure
High School I.D.
Hockey Illustrated (unable to contact)
Horsemen's Yankee Pedlar Newspaper
Horses All
Hyphen Magazine (no pay)

Incider/A+
Individual Investor
Inside Karate
Inside Sports
International Bowhunter Magazine
Jet
Journal of Christian Camping
Journal of Italina Food & Wine
The Joyful Woman
Kid City
Kid Sports (no unsolicited articles)
La Red/The Net
Lady's Circle
Lear's (ceased publication)
Lector
Life in the Times
Life Today
Listen Magazine
Lotus (overwhelmed by submissions)
The Magazine of Fantasy & Science Fiction
Mature Lifestyles (removed by request)
Men's Health (removed by request)
Metro Toronto Business Journal (no freelance)
Midnight Zoo (no pay)
Military Review
Miniatures Showcase (ceased publication)
Moody Magazine
Muscle & Fitness
National Forum: The Phi Kappa Phi Journal (no pay)
National Lampoon
Needlepoint Plus
Neil Sperry's Gardens
New Body
Northern California Home and Garden
Olympian Magazine
Ontario Out of Doors
Paraplegia (removed by request due to inappropriate submissions)
Parents Care, Parents Count Newsletter (ceased publication)
PC
PC World Lotus Edition (unable to contact)
Pennsylvania Game News (unable to contact)
Perspectives (ceased publication)
Petersen's Handguns
Philadelphia Magazine
Picture Perfect
Pig Iron Magazine
The Pilot Log (no freelance)
PJG Magazine
Playbill
Players Magazine
Popular Photograph (no freelance)
Portfolio (unable to contact)
Presbyterian Survey

Queen's Quarterly
Rainbow City Express (ceased publication)
Reason Magazine (removed by request due to inappropriate submissions)
Road King (changed ownership)
Rutgers Magazine
San Francisco Focus
Seattle's Child
Seek
Self (removed by request)
Senior Spotlite
Shareware Magazine
Short Fiction By Women (unable to contact)
The Single Parent
Ski Magazine
Skies America Publishing
Skin Diver
Southern Boating Magazine
Southern Living
Spark! (ceased publication)
Special Reports
Spectrum
Sports 'n Spokes (removed by request due to inappropriate submissions)
Sports Illustrated
Spy (ceased publication; changed ownership)
St. Louis Magazine
Storm Magazine
Storytelling Magazine
Sunset
Super Ford
Teen Beat
Texas Highways
The Yoga Journal
Thigh High
Timberlines (no pay)
The Toastmaster
Top Secret (unable to contact)
Traditional Quilter
Transformation Times (ceased publication)
Travel Papers (no freelance)
Treasure Diver (ceased publication)
Trilogy
Tuff Stuff
The United Church Observer
Unity Magazine
USAir Magazine
Utah Holiday Magazine (unable to contact)
Utne Reader
Valley Magazine
Vermont Business Magazine
Victoria's Business Report
Vista/USA (unable to contact)
Volleyball Monthly
Woman Bowler
Women & Performance
World Monitor (ceased publication)
Wrestling World (unable to contact)
The Yukon Reader

Trade, Technical and Professional Journals........ 670

Trade, Technical and Professional Journals

Many writers who pick up a *Writer's Market* for the first time do so with the hope of selling an article or story to one of the popular, high-profile consumer magazines likely to be found on newsstands and in bookstores. Many of those writers are surprised to find an entire world of magazine publishing that exists outside the realm of commercial magazines and that they may have never known about—trade journals. Writers who *have* discovered trade journals have found a market that offers the chance to publish regularly in subject areas they find interesting, editors who are typically more accessible than their commercial counterparts and pay rates that rival those of the big-name magazines.

Trade journal is the general term for all publications focusing on a particular occupation or industry. Other terms used to describe the different types of trade publications are business, technical and professional journals. They are read by truck drivers, brick layers, farmers, commercial fishermen, heart surgeons—let's not forget butchers, bakers, and candlestick makers—and just about everyone else working in a trade or profession. Trade periodicals are sharply angled to the specifics of the professions they report on. They offer business-related news, features and service articles that will foster their readers' professional development. A surgeon reads *Cardiology World News* to keep up with developments in cardiac disease and treatment. Readers of *Professional Mariner* are looking for the latest news and information about the shipping trade.

Trade magazine editors tell us their readers are a knowledgeable and highly interested audience. Writers for trade magazines have to either possess knowledge about the field in question or be able to report it accurately from interviews with those who do. Writers who have or can develop a good grasp of a specialized body of knowledge will find trade magazine editors who are eager to hear from them. And since good writers with specialized knowledge are a somewhat rare commodity, trade editors tend, more than typical consumer magazine editors, to cultivate ongoing relationships with writers. If you can prove yourself as a writer who "delivers," you will be paid back with frequent assignments and regular paychecks.

An ideal way to begin your foray into trade journals is to write for those that report on your present profession. Whether you've been selling real estate, managing a grocery store or performing bypass surgery, begin by familiarizing yourself with the magazines that serve your occupation. After you've read enough issues to have a feel for the kinds of pieces they run, approach the editors with your own article ideas. If you don't have experience in a profession but can demonstrate an ability to understand (and write about) the intricacies and issues of a particular trade that interests you, editors will still be willing to hear from you.

Photographs help increase the value of most stories for trade journals. If you can provide photos, mention that in your query or send copies. Since selling photos with a story usually means a bigger paycheck, it is worth any freelancer's while to spend some time developing basic camera skills.

Query a trade journal as you would a consumer magazine. Most trade editors like

INSIDER REPORT

Building a career as a trade magazine freelancer

Linda Leake majored in dairy science at the University of Wisconsin. Along with that major she took a number of journalism classes, thinking at the time that they might provide her with a skill to fall back on. As it turns out, that training, along with generous doses of self-confidence, talent and drive have provided much more than something to simply "fall back on." They have led to Leake's rewarding and much-loved career as a journalist reporting on the agriculture industry.

Immediately after college, Leake was hired on a short-term basis by the World Dairy Expo to put together a souvenir program for their prestigious, international dairy cattle exposition. But after that first experience with writing for publication, Leake's career took a different turn. She became

Linda Leake

a certified animal technician and worked for six years as an instructional specialist in a veterinary school in Madison, Wisconsin. An eventual relocation to North Carolina left her unemployed and considering her options. In 1990 she returned to Madison for that year's World Dairy Expo and passed out resumes.

She was not thinking about writing for a living until she met the editor of a dairy industry publication at the Expo who expressed an interest in seeing a freelance submission from Leake.

Leake returned to North Carolina and worked up several pieces about women farmers in her area. She sent one off to the editor of the dairy magazine. "About two days before Christmas, I got a letter in the mail from the magazine," says Leake. "My heart was pounding. I opened the envelope and a big check fell out. 'Dear Linda:' the letter said, 'Thank you so much for the excellent article and pictures. We all enjoyed them so much. Enclosed is a check for the article and your expenses.' The last thing they said was, 'We'll be happy to have any more work that you care to send us.'"

It didn't take Leake long to realize that there were many more agricultural magazines out there—many that she was already familiar with. "I knew what they were, and I knew some of the people, and I just started making phone calls." Since she began, Leake has written for over 20 different periodicals. Her success is due in large part to the professionalism with which she approaches her writing. "I've just made an effort to develop the business and contact as many agriculture publications as I can, to develop a large clientele so I'm not dependent on any one—and so that every time I come up with a good story idea I'll have a market for it."

How does Leake keep the business rolling in? "I try to get out one major piece a week, so I'm constantly on the lookout for story ideas, and when I find something that I think is suitable for a particular publication, I immediately call the editor. I have a good success rate with selling stories that way." Leake will occasionally schedule trips back to Wisconsin or elsewhere and set up interviews with various farmers along the way. Before she takes the trip, she pre-sells the articles. "I plot out my route and then I call the magazines that I think might be suitable, starting with the ones that pay the most," she says. "I tell the editors I'm going to be traveling through a particular area and I've got *this* and *this* and *this* story, then I ask which ones they would like. They take what they like, and if they don't take all of them, I call the next magazine on my list and so on until everything is sold." She splits the trip expenses among all of the magazines that agree to publish the articles.

In freelance journalism, Leake feels she has found her life's work. "I'm definitely going to stick with this," she says. "I like the self-employed lifestyle; I like coming and going as I please; I like doing my own scheduling. I feel this is something that I'll be able to do my whole life. I don't have to do certain types of work that I might not want to do because, God willing, I'll always be able to write. I love my work."

---

to discuss an article with a writer first and will sometimes offer names of helpful sources. Mention any direct experience you may have in the industry in your cover letter. Send a resume and clips if they show you have some background or related experience in the subject area. Read each listing carefully for additional submission guidelines.

To stay abreast of new trade magazines starting up, watch for news in *Folio* and *Advertising Age* magazines. Another source for information about trade publications is the *Business Publication Advertising Source*, published by Standard Rate and Data Service (SRDS) and available in most libraries. Designed primarily for people who buy ad space, the volume provides names and addresses of thousands of trade journals, listed by subject matter.

For information on additional trade publications not listed in *Writer's Market*, see Trade, Technical and Professional Journals/Changes '94-'95 at the end of this section.

Advertising, Marketing and PR

Trade journals for advertising executives, copywriters and marketing and public relations professionals are listed in this category. Those whose main focus is the advertising and marketing of specific products, such as home furnishings, are classified under individual product categories. Journals for sales personnel and general merchandisers can be found in the Selling and Merchandising category.

ADVERTISING AGE, Dept. WM, 740 N. Rush, Chicago IL 60611-2590. (312)649-5200. Managing Editor/News: Melanie Rigney. Executive Editor/Features: Larry Edwards. Executive Editor: Steve Yahn. Deputy Editor: Larry Doherty. New York office: 220 E. 42 St., New York NY 10017. (212)210-0100. Editor: Fred Danzig. Currently staff-produced. Includes weekly sections devoted to one topic (i.e., marketing in Southern California, advertising, TV syndication trends). Little of this material is done freelance—on assignment only. Pays kill fee "based on hours spent plus expenses." Byline given "except short articles or contributions to a roundup."

‡AMERICAN ADVERTISING, The American Advertising Federation, Suite 500, 1101 Vermont Ave. NW, Washington DC 20005. Editor: Jenny Pfalzgraf. 50% freelance written. Quarterly magazine covering advertising and marketing communications. *"American Advertising* is a nonprofit publication of the American Advertising Federation, covering trends in marketing, advertising and media, unique business partnerships, professional development and AAF news." Estab. 1984. Circ. 50,000. **Pays on acceptance.** Publishes ms an average of 1 month after acceptance. Byline given. Buys first rights or second serial (reprint) rights. Editorial lead time 3 months. Accepts simultaneous and previously published submissions. Query for electronic submissions. Reports in 3 weeks on queries. "Do not send manuscripts cold." Sample copy for 9×12 SAE with 4 first-class stamps.

Nonfiction: Book excerpts, general interest, how-to (marketing/advertising strategies), humor, interview/profile (leaders in ad business). "Not interested in stories slamming the ad business." Buys 4 mss/year. Query with published clips. Length: 500-2,000 words. Pays 25¢/word. All articles are assigned.

Photos: State availability of photos with submission. Reviews contact sheets. Negotiates payment individually. Captions required. Buys one-time rights.

Columns/Departments: Ad Club Spotlight (features unique programs of AAF-member ad clubs), 500 words; Legislative Watch (focuses on legislative developments affecting ad business), 500 words; People (profiles top dogs in advertising and media), 500 words. Buys 1 mss/year (other stories are contributed pro bono). Query with published clips. Pays 25¢/word.

AMERICAN DEMOGRAPHICS, American Demographics, Inc., P.O. Box 68, Ithaca NY 14851-0068. (607)273-6343. Fax: (607)273-3196. Editor-in-Chief: Brad Edmondson. Managing Editor: Nancy Ten Kate. Contact: Judith Waldrop, research editor. 25% freelance written. Works with a small number of new/unpublished writers each year. Monthly magazine for business executives, market researchers, media and communications people, public policymakers. Estab. 1978. Circ. 35,000. Pays on publication. Publishes ms an average of 6 months after acceptance. Buys all rights. Submit seasonal material 6 months in advance. Query for electronic submissions. Reports in 6 months. Include self-addressed stamped postcard for return word that ms arrived safely. Sample copy for $5 and 9×11 SAE. Writer's guidelines for #10 SASE.

Nonfiction: General interest (on demographic trends, implications of changing demographics, profile of business using demographic data); and how-to (on the use of demographic techniques, psychographics, understand projections, data, apply demography to business and planning). No anecdotal material. Sometimes pays the expenses of writers on assignment.

Tips: "Writer should have clear understanding of specific population trends and their implications for business and planning. The most important thing a freelancer can do is to read the magazine and be familiar with its style and focus."

ART DIRECTION, Advertising Trade Publications, Inc., 6th Floor, 10 E. 39th St., New York NY 10016. (212)889-6500. Fax: (212)889-6104. Editor: Dan Barron. 10% freelance written. Prefers to work with published/established writers. Monthly magazine emphasizing advertising design for art directors of ad agencies (corporate, in-plant, editorial, freelance, etc.). Circ. 10,250. Pays on publication. Buys one-time rights. Reports in 3 months. Sample copy for $4.50.

Nonfiction: How-to articles on advertising campaigns. Pays $100 minimum.

‡DECA DIMENSIONS, 1908 Association Dr., Reston VA 22091. (703)860-5000. Editor: Carol Lund. 30% freelance written. Bimonthly magazine covering professional development, business, vocational training. *"Deca Dimensions* is the membership magazine for the Association of Marketing Students—primarily ages 16-20 in all 50 states. The magazine is delivered through the classroom. These students are interested in developing their professional, leadership and career skills." Estab. 1947. Circ. 145,000. Pays on publication. Byline given. Buys first rights and second serial (reprint) rights. Editorial lead time 4 months. Submit seasonal material 5 months in advance. Accepts simultaneous and previously published submissions. Sample copy free on request.

Nonfiction: Essays, general interest, how-to (get jobs, start business, plan for college, etc.), interview/profile (business leads), personal experience (working). Buys 4 mss/year. Send complete ms. Length: 800-1,000 words. Pays $125 for assigned articles; $100 for unsolicited articles.

Photos: State availability of photos with submission. Reviews negatives, transparencies, prints. Offers $15-25/photo. Captions required. Buys one-time rights.

Columns/Departments: Professional Development leadership. Buys 4 mss/year. Send complete ms. Pays $75-100. Length: 200-500 words.

Fillers: Anecdotes, facts, short humor. Length: 400-600 words. Pays $25-50.

IDENTITY, For Specifiers and Customers of Sign and Corporate Graphics, ST Publications, Dept. WM, 407 Gilbert Ave., Cincinnati OH 45202. (513)421-2050. Fax: (513)421-5144. Editor: Lynn Baxter. 10% freelance written. Quarterly trade magazine on corporate identity. "We cover the design and implementation of corporate identity, sign programs and architectural graphics for environmental graphics designers, architects and their clients. We stress signage as a part of the total corporate identity program." Estab. 1988. Circ. 15,000. **Pays on acceptance.** Byline given. Offers 30% kill fee. Buys all rights. Query for electronic submissions. Reports in 2 weeks. Free sample copy and writer's guidelines for SASE.

Nonfiction: How-to, interview/profile, opinion, technical. "No histories or profiles of design firms or manufacturers." Buys 4-10 mss/year. Query with or without published clips or send complete ms. Length: 1,000-3,000 words. Pays $250-400. Sometimes pays expenses of writers on assignment.

Photos: Send photos with submission. Reviews 35mm to 4×5 transparencies. "We *sometimes* pay for photo rights from professional photographers." Identification of subjects required. Buys one-time rights.

Tips: "The best approach is a telephone or written query. Ours is a completely 4-color publication geared to a graphically sophisticated audience, with professional photography and specific information about design solutions, fabrication and management of corporate identity programs. We prefer a case-history approach, but may accept some theoretical articles on the use of corporate identity, the value of signs, etc. Most open are feature stories written for designers (design, fabrication details) or buyers (value, costs, management of national programs). The more specific, the better. The more 'advertorial,' the less likely to be accepted. Unusual design solutions, unusual use of materials and breadth of design scope make stories more of interest."

IMPRINT, The Magazine of Specialty Advertising Ideas, Advertising Specialty Institute, Dept. WM, 1120 Wheeler Way, Langhorne PA 19047-1785. (215)752-4200. Managing Editor: Arn Bernstein. Editor: Catherine Sigmund-Holnick. 25% freelance written. Works with a small number of new/unpublished writers each year. Quarterly magazine covering promotional products. Estab. 1967. Circ. 60,000. Pays on final acceptance. Publishes ms an average of 6 months after acceptance. Byline given. Buys one-time rights. Submit seasonal material 6 months in advance. Query for electronic submissions. Reports in 3 months. Sample copy for 9×12 SAE with 3 first-class stamps.

Nonfiction: How-to (case histories of specialty advertising campaigns); features (how ad specialties are distributed in promotions). "Emphasize effective use of promotional products. Avoid direct-buy situations. Stress the distributor's role in promotions. No generalized pieces on print, broadcast or outdoor advertising." Buys 10-12 mss/year. Query with published clips. Payment based on assigned length. "We pay authorized phone, postage, etc."

Photos: State availability of 5×7 b&w photos. Pays "some extra for *original* photos *only*." Captions, model releases and identification of subjects required.

Tips: "The predominant cause of misdirected articles is the fact that many new writers simply don't understand the medium of promotional products, or our target audience—end-users. Writers are urged to investigate the medium a bit before attempting an article or suggesting an idea for one. We can also provide additional leads and suggestions. All articles, however, are specifically geared to promotional products (or premium) use. We need writers who can clearly and closely follow directions."

MEDIA INC., Pacific Northwest media, marketing and creative services news, P.O. Box 24365, Seattle WA 98124-0365. (206)382-9220. Fax: (206)382-9437. Managing Editor: Paul Gargaro. 10% freelance written. Monthly tabloid covering Northwest US media, advertising, marketing and creative-service industries. "Audience is Northwest ad agencies, marketing professionals, media and creative-service professionals." Estab. 1987. Circ. 14,000. Byline given. Reports in 1 month. Sample copy for 9×12 SAE with 6 first-class stamps.

Tips: "It is best if writers live in the Pacific Northwest and can report on local news and events in Media Inc.'s areas of business coverage."

‡QUIRK'S MARKETING RESEARCH REVIEW, P.O. Box 23536, Minneapolis MN 55423. (612)861-8051. Editor: Joseph Rydholm. 25% freelance written. Monthly magazine covering market research. "Our readers are marketing researchers in a variety of industries, from consumer products to financial services. Unlike the academic marketing research journals, we focus on the practical, hands-on experiences of researchers through case histories of research projects and articles on specific research techniques." Estab. 1986. Circ. 16,000. Pays on publication. Byline given. Buys one-time rights. Editorial lead time 3 months. Accepts simultaneous and previously published submissions. Query for electronic submissions. Prefers PC: ASCII/Macintosh: Microsoft Word. Reports in 3 months on queries; 1 month on mss. Sample copy and writer's guidelines free on request.

Nonfiction: Interview/profile, technical. "Writers assume we want marketing-related articles. We do, but only if *marketing research* is part of it. Articles on direct marketing or telemarketing aren't of interest." Buys 10 mss/year. Query with published clips. Length: 1,500-2,500 words. Pays $200 minimum. Sometimes pays expenses of writers on assignment.

Photos: State availability of photos with submission. Reviews contact sheets and 35mm transparencies. Offers $25-75/photo. Identification of subjects required. Buys one-time rights.

Tips: "The key is to focus on *research*—telephone surveys, focus groups, mall intercepts, etc. We don't want telemarketing/direct mail, etc. articles. Make sure you know how to use research terms. We write for a broad audience because people come to the marketing research field from so many backgrounds—some know a lot, some know a little about the techniques. We're most interested in 'research in action,' application-based articles that show readers how others are using research. Our greatest need is for case history-style articles on successful marketing research projects. In these stories, the writer interviews a research user and their supplier—usually a research company—to profile the project and explain how marketing research was used, what the goals were for the research, and why certain research techniques were used. I would also like to retain stringers to attend various research conventions/gatherings and write reports on them for our magazine."

‡**RESPONSE TV, The First Magazine of Direct Response Television**, Advanstar Communications, Suite 600, 201 E. Sandpointe, Santa Ana CA 92707. (714)513-8400. Editor: Jack Schember. 30% freelance written. Monthly magazine covering direct response television. "We look for business writers with experience in advertising, marketing, direct marketing, telemarketing, TV production, cable TV industry and home shopping." Estab. 1992. Circ. 16,000. **Pays on acceptance.** Byline given. Offers 50% kill fee. Buys all rights. Editorial lead time 2 months. Accepts previously published submissions. Reports in 2 weeks on queries; 1 month on mss. Sample copy for $6.
Nonfiction: General interest, interview/profile, opinion, technical, case studies. Buys 25 mss/year. Query with published clips. Length: 1,200-2,000 words. Pays $300-500. Sometimes pays expenses of writers on assignment.
Photos: State availability of photos with submission. Reviews contact sheets, negatives, transparencies. Negotiates payment individually. Model releases, identification of subjects required. Buys one-time rights.
Columns/Departments: New TV (interactive advertising and merchandising), 200 words; Support Services (telemarketing, fulfillment), 200 words; Legal (advertising and marketing law), 800 words. Buys 12 mss/year. Query with published clips. Pays $300.
Tips: "Familiarity with topics such as home shopping, direct response TV, interactive TV and infomercials. General interest in advertising and marketing."

SIGNCRAFT, The Magazine for the Commercial Sign Shop, SignCraft Publishing Co., Inc., P.O. Box 06031, Fort Myers FL 33906. (813)939-4644. Editor: Tom McIltrot. 10% freelance written. Bimonthly magazine of the sign industry. "Like any trade magazine, we need material of direct benefit to our readers. We can't afford space for material of marginal interest." Estab. 1980. Circ. 20,500. Pays on publication. Publishes ms an average of 9 months after acceptance. Byline given. Offers negotiable kill fee. Buys first North American serial or all rights. Accepts previously published submissions. Reports in 1 month. Sample copy and writer's guidelines for $3.
Nonfiction: Interviews and profiles. "All articles should be directly related to quality commercial signs. If you are familiar with the sign trade, we'd like to hear from you." Buys 20 mss/year. Query with or without published clips. Length: 500-2,000 words. Pays up to $250.

SIGNS OF THE TIMES, The Industry Journal Since 1906, ST Publications, Dept. WM, 407 Gilbert Ave., Cincinnati OH 45202-2285. (513)421-2050. Fax: (513)421-5144. Editor: Wade Swormstedt. 15-30% freelance written. "We are willing to use more freelancers." Monthly magazine special buyer's guide between November and December issues. Estab. 1906. Circ. 16,000. Pays on publication. Publishes ms an average of 3 months after acceptance. Byline given. Buys variable rights. Accepts simultaneous and previously published submissions. Reports in 3 months. Free sample copy and writer's guidelines for 9×12 SAE with 10 first-class stamps.
  • This publication is looking for more business-related articles and short profiles.
Nonfiction: Historical/nostalgic (regarding the sign industry); how-to (carved signs, goldleaf, etc.); interview/profile (focusing on either a signshop or a specific project); photo feature (query first); and technical (sign engineering, etc.). Nothing "nonspecific on signs, an example being a photo essay on 'signs I've seen.' We are a trade journal with specific audience interests." Buys 15-20 mss/year. Query with clips. Pays $150-500. Sometimes pays the expenses of writers on assignment.
Photos: Send photos with ms. "Sign industry-related photos only. We sometimes accept photos with funny twists or misspellings."
Fillers: Open to queries; request rates.

Art, Design and Collectibles

The businesses of art, art administration, architecture, environmental/package design and antiques/collectibles are covered in these listings. Art-related topics for the general public are located in the Consumer Art and Architecture category. Antiques and collectibles magazines for enthusiasts are listed in Consumer Hobby and Craft. (Listings of markets looking for freelance artists to do artwork can be found in *Artist's and Graphic Designer's Market*—see Other Books of Interest).

APPLIED ARTS, Suite 324, 885 Don Mills Rd., Toronto, Ontario M3C 1V9 Canada. (416)510-0909. Fax: (416)510-0913. Editor: Peter Giffen. 70% freelance written. Magazine published 5 times/year covering graphic design, advertising, photography and illustration. Estab. 1986. Circ. 12,000. **Pays on acceptance.** Byline given. Buys first North American serial rights. Query for electronic submissions. Reports in 2 months on queries. Sample copy for 10×13 SAE with $1.70 Canadian postage or 4 IRCs.
Nonfiction: Interview/profile, opinion, photo feature, technical (computers and the applied arts) and trade articles about graphic design, advertising, photography and illustration. Buys 20-30 mss/year. Query with published clips. Length: 500-2,500 words. Pays 60¢ (Canadian)/word.
Photos: Offers no additional payment for photos accepted with ms. Buys one-time rights.
Tips: "It helps if writers have some familiarity with the communication arts field. Writers should include a solid selection of published articles. Writers have the best chance selling articles on graphic design and advertising. Take time to read back issues of the magazine before querying."

‡THE APPRAISERS STANDARD, New England Appraisers Assocation, 5 Gill Terrace, Ludlow VT 05149-1003. (802)228-7444. Publisher/Editor: Linda L. Tucker. 50% freelance written. Works with a small number of new/unpublished writers each year. Bimonthly publication on the appraisals of antiques, art, collectibles, jewelry, coins, stamps and real estate. "The writer should be extremely knowledgeable on the subject, and the article should be written with appraisers in mind, with prices quoted for objects, good pictures and descriptions of articles being written about." Estab. 1980. Circ. 1,300. Pays on publication. Publishes ms an average of 4-6 months after acceptance. Byline given, with short bio to establish writer's credibility. Buys first and simultaneous rights. Accepts simultaneous and previously published submissions. Send photocopy of article, typed ms with rights for sale noted and information about when and where the article previously appeared. For reprints pays 70% of the amount paid for an original article. Submit seasonal material 2 months in advance. Reports in 1 month on queries; 2 months on mss. Sample copy for 9×12 SAE with 2 first-class stamps. Writer's guidelines for #10 SASE.
Nonfiction: Interview/profile, personal experience, technical, travel. "All articles must be geared toward professional appraisers." Query with or without published clips, or send complete ms. Length: 700 words. Pays $50.
Photos: Send photos with submission. Reviews negatives and prints. Offers no additional payment for photos accepted with ms. Identification of subjects required. Buys one-time rights.
Tips: "Interviewing members of the association for articles, reviewing, shows and large auctions are all ways for writers who are not in the field to write articles for us."

ART BUSINESS NEWS, Advanstar Communications Inc., 19 Old Kings Hwy. S., Darien CT 06820. (203)656-3402. Editor: Sarah Seamark. 25% freelance written. Prefers to work with published/established writers. Monthly trade tabloid covering news relating to the art and picture framing industry. Circ. 31,000. Pays on publication. Publishes ms an average of 3 months after acceptance. Byline given. Buys first-time rights. Submit seasonal material 2 months in advance. Accepts simultaneous submissions. Reports in 3 months. Sample copy for $5 and 12×16 SAE.
Nonfiction: News in art and framing field; interview/marketing profiles (of dealers, publishers and suppliers in the art industry); new products; articles focusing on small business people—framers, art gallery management, art trends; how-to (occasional article on "how-to frame" accepted). Buys 8-20 mss/year. Length: 1,000 words maximum. Query first. Pays $75-300. Sometimes pays the expenses of writers on assignment. Photography useful.
Tips: "We have more opportunity for shorter, hard news items and news features."

ARTS MANAGEMENT, 408 W. 57th St., New York NY 10019. (212)245-3850. Editor: A.H. Reiss. Magazine published 5 times/year for cultural institutions. 2% freelance written. Estab. 1962. Circ. 6,000. Pays on publication. Byline given. Buys all rights. Query. Reports in 2 months. Writer's guidelines for #10 SASE.
Nonfiction: Short articles, 400-900 words, tightly written, expository, explaining how art administrators solved problems in publicity, fund raising and general administration; actual case histories emphasizing the how-to. Also short articles on the economics and sociology of the arts and important trends in the nonprofit cultural field. Must be fact-filled, well-organized and without rhetoric. Pays 2-4¢/word. No photographs or pictures.
  • Mostly staff-written; uses very little outside material.

THE CRAFTS REPORT, The Business Journal for the Crafts Industry, The Crafts Report Publishing Company, P.O. Box 1992, Wilmington DE 19899-1992. (302)656-2209. Fax: (302)656-4894. Editor: Marilyn Stevens. 50% freelance written. Monthly tabloid covering crafts industry. Estab. 1975. Circ. 20,000. Pays on publication. Publishes ms an average of 4 months after acceptance. Byline given. Offers $50 kill fee. Buys first rights, first North American serial, second serial (reprint) rights or makes work-for-hire assignments. Accepts previously published articles. Send tearsheet or photocopy of article or typed ms with rights for sale noted and information about when and where the article previously appeared. For reprints pays $50. Editorial lead time 3 months. Submit seasonal material 6 months in advance. Reports in 8-10 weeks. Sample copy for $3. Writer's guidelines for #10 SASE.

Nonfiction: Interview/profile, opinion, personal experience, small business tips. "No how-to (e.g. craft techniques) articles or anything general toward the hobbyist." Buys 80 mss/year. Query with published clips. Length: 400-2,000 words. Pays 12½¢/word minimum for assigned articles; 3½¢/word minimum for unsolicited articles. Sometimes pays expenses of writers on assignment (limit agreed upon in advance). "Looking for much more customized business advice, i.e. incorporating interviews/advice from crafts producers and/or retailers."

Photos: Send photos with submission. Reviews transparencies and prints. Negotiates payment individually. Identification of subjects required. Buys one-time rights.

Columns/Departments: Money (small business advice for crafts professionals), 600-800 words; Craft and Trade Show Reviews (writers work from prepared questions), 300-700 words; Back-to-Basics (everything the new entrepreneur needs to know to start or grow a business), 600-800 words. Buys 20 mss/year. Query with published clips. Pays 3½-12½¢/published word.

‡DEALER COMMUNICATOR, Fichera Publications, 777 S. State Road 7, Margate FL 33068-2823. (305)971-4360. Fax: (305)971-4362. Editor: Paul McElroy. Publisher: Mike Fichera. 20% freelance written. Works with a small number of new/unpublished writers each year. Monthly magazine covering personnel and news developments for the graphic arts industry. Circ. 13,000. Pays on publication. Publishes ms an average of 1 month after acceptance. Byline given. Not copyrighted. Buys one-time rights. Accepts simultaneous and previously published submissions. Send tearsheet or photocopy of article. Reports in 2 months on queries.

Nonfiction: Interview/profile. Buys a varying number of mss/year. Query with published clips. Length: 500-1,500 words. Pays 3-7¢/word. Pays the expenses of writers on assignment.

Photos: State availability of photos with submissions. Offers $5-10/photo. Captions required.

Fillers: Facts, newsbreaks. Buys a varying number/year. Length: 10-50 words. Pays $1-1.50.

Tips: "We cover a national market. Find out what local printing/graphic arts dealers are doing and what is news in the area."

HOW, The Bottomline Design Magazine, F&W Publications, Inc., 1507 Dana Ave., Cincinnati OH 45207-1005. (513)531-2222. Contact: Editor. 75% freelance written. Bimonthly graphic design and illustration business journal. "*HOW* gives a behind-the-scenes look at not only *how* the world's best graphic artists and illustrators conceive and create their work, but *why* they did it that way. We also focus on the *business* side of design—how to run a profitable studio." Estab. 1985. Circ. 35,000. **Pays on acceptance.** Byline given. Buys first North American serial rights. Query for electronic submissions. Reports in 6 weeks. Sample copy for $8.50. Writer's guidelines for #10 SASE.

Nonfiction: Interview/profile, business tips, new products. Special issues: Self-Promotion Annual (September/October); Business Annual (November/December). No how-to articles for beginning artists or fine-art-oriented articles. Buys 40 mss/year. Query with published clips and samples of subject's work (artwork or design). Length: 1,200-1,500 words. Pays $250-600. Sometimes pays expenses of writers on assignment.

Photos: State availability of artwork with submission. Reviews 35mm or larger transparencies. May reimburse mechanical photo expenses. Captions are required. Buys one-time rights.

Columns/Departments: Marketplace (focuses on lucrative fields for designers/illustrators); and Production (ins, outs and tips on production). Buys 20 mss/year. Query with published clips. Length: 1,000-2,000 words. Pays $150-400.

Tips: "We look for writers who can recognize graphic designers on the cutting-edge of their industry, both creatively and business-wise. Writers must have an eye for detail, and be able to relay *HOW*'s step-by-step approach in an interesting, concise manner—without omitting any details. Showing you've done your homework on a subject—and that you can go beyond asking 'those same old questions'—will give you a big advantage."

LETTERING ARTS REVIEW, (formerly *Calligraphy Review*), 1624 24th Ave. SW, Norman OK 73072. (405)364-8794. Fax: (405)364-8914. Publisher/Editor: Karyn L. Gilman. 98% freelance written. Eager to work with new/unpublished writers with calligraphic expertise and language skills. Quarterly magazine on lettering and related book arts, both historical and contemporary in nature. Estab. 1982. Circ. 5,500. Pays on publication. Publishes ms an average of 9 months after acceptance. Byline given. Offers 20% kill fee. Buys first rights. Query for electronic submissons. Reports in 3 months. Sample copy for 9 × 12 SAE with 7 first-class stamps. Free writer's guidelines.

Nonfiction: Interview/profile, opinion, contemporary, historical. Buys 50 mss/year. Query with or without published clips or send complete ms. Length: 1,000-2,000 words. Pays $50-200 for assigned articles; $25-200 for unsolicited articles. Sometimes pays the expenses of writers on assignment.

Photos: State availability of photos with submission. Reviews contact sheets, negatives, transparencies and prints. Pays agreed upon cost. Captions and identification of subjects required. Buys one-time rights.

Columns/Departments: Book Reviews, Viewpoint (critical), 500-1,500 words; Ms. (discussion of manuscripts in collections), 1,000-2,000 words; and Profile (contemporary calligraphic figure), 1,000-2,000 words. Query. Pays $50-200.

Tips: "*Lettering Arts Review*'s primary objective is to encourage the exchange of ideas on lettering, its past and present as well as trends for the future. Practical and conceptual treatments are welcomed, as are

learning and teaching experiences. Third person is preferred, however first person will be considered if appropriate. Writer should realize that this is a specialized audience."
- The emphasis here is on articles of a critical nature specifically for this audience.

MANHATTAN ARTS INTERNATIONAL MAGAZINE, Renée Phillips Associates, Suite 26L, 200 E. 72nd St., New York NY 10021. (212)472-1660. Fax: (212)794-0343. Editor-in-Chief: Renée Phillips. Managing Editor: Michael Jason. 100% freelance written. Monthly magazine covering fine art. Audience is comprised of art professionals, artists and collectors. Educational, informative, easy-to-read style, making art more accessible. Highly promotional of new artists. Estab. 1983. Circ. 50,000. Pays on publication. Publishes ms an average of 1 month after acceptance. Byline given. Makes work for hire assignments. Submit seasonal material 3 months in advance. Accepts simultaneous submissions. Reports in 3 months. Sample copy for $4, payable to Renée Phillips Associates (no postage or envelope required).
Nonfiction: Book excerpts (art), essays (art world), general interest (collecting art), inspirational (artists success stories), interview/profile (major art leaders), new product (art supplies), technical (art business). Buys 100 mss/year. Query with published clips; all articles are assigned. Length: 150-500 words. Pays $25-50. New writers receive byline and promotion, art books. Sometimes pays expenses of writers on assignment.
Photos: Send photos with submission. Offers no additional payment for photos accepted with ms. Captions, model releases and identification of subjects required.
Columns/Departments: Reviews/Previews (art critiques of exhibitions in galleries and museums), 150-250 words; Artists/Profiles (features on major art leaders), 250-500 words; The New Collector (collectibles, interviews with dealers, collectors), 250-500 words; Artopia (inspirational features, success stories), 250-500 words; Art Books, Art Services, 150-500 words. Buys 100 mss/year. Query with published clips. Pays $25-50.
Tips: "A knowledge of the current, contemporary art scene is a must. An eye for emerging talent is an asset."

THE MIDATLANTIC ANTIQUES MAGAZINE, Monthly Guide to Antiques, Art, Auctions & Collectibles, Henderson Newspapers, Inc., P.O. Box 908, Henderson NC 27536-0908. (919)492-4001. Fax: (919)430-0125. Editor: Lydia Stainback. 65% freelance written. Monthly tabloid covering antiques, art, auctions and collectibles. "The *MidAtlantic* reaches dealers, collectors, antique shows and auction houses primarily on the East Coast, but circulation includes 48 states and Europe." Estab. 1984. Circ. 14,000. Pays on publication. Byline given. Buys first rights. Submit seasonal material 6 months in advance. Reports in 1 month on queries; 2 months on mss. Sample copy and writer's guidelines for 10×13 SAE with 10 first-class stamps.
Nonfiction: Book excerpts, historical/nostalgic, how-to (choose an antique to collect; how to sell your collection; how to identify market trends), interview/profile, personal experience, photo feature, technical. Buys 60-75 mss/year. Query. Length: 800-2,000 words. Pays $50-125. Trade for advertising space. Rarely pays expenses of writers on assignment.
- The publisher needs writers to cover show and auction events.
Photos: Send photos with submission. Offers no additional payment for photos accepted with ms. Identification of subjects required. Buys one-time rights.
Tips: "Please contact by mail first, but a writer may call with specific ideas after initial contact. Looking for writers who have extensive knowledge in specific areas of antiques. Articles should be educational in nature. We are also interested in how-to articles, i.e., how to choose antiques to collect; how to sell your collection and get the most for it; looking for articles that focus on future market trends. We want writers who are active in the antiques business and can predict good investments. (Articles with photographs are given preference.) We are looking for people who are not only knowledgeable, but can write well."

PROGRESSIVE ARCHITECTURE, Dept. WM, P.O. Box 1361, Stamford CT 06904. Fax: (203)348-4023. Editor: John M. Dixon. Editorial Director: Thomas Fisher. 5-10% freelance written. Prefers to work with published/established writers. Monthly. Estab. 1920. **Pays on acceptance.** Publishes ms an average of 4 months after acceptance. Buys all rights for use in architectural press. Query for electronic submissions. Reports in 4 months.
Nonfiction: "Articles of technical, professional interest devoted to architecture, interior design, and urban design and planning, and illustrated by photographs and architectural drawings. We also use technical articles which are prepared by technical authorities and would be beyond the scope of the lay writer. Practically all the material is professional, and most of it is prepared by writers in the field who are approached by the magazine for material." Pays $150-400. Sometimes pays the expenses of writers on assignment.
Photos: Buys one-time reproduction rights to b&w and color photos.

SUCCESS NOW! FOR ARTISTS, The Fine Artists Monthly Guide To Success and Self-Empowerment, Renée Phillips Associates, #26L, 200 E. 72nd St., New York NY 10021. (212)472-1660. Contact: Michael Jason, executive editor. Monthly magazine for fine artists. "Practical solutions for today's challenges faced by fine artists. Motivational style wanted. Special opportunities for artists wanted." Estab. 1992. Circ. 2,000. **Pays on acceptance.** Publishes ms an average of 2 months after acceptance. Byline given. Offers 100% kill fee or $25-50. Buys one-time rights or makes work-for-hire assignments. Editorial lead time 1-2 months. Submit seasonal material 3 months in advance. Sample copy for $4.

Nonfiction: Book excerpts, how-to (career advice), new product, personal experience (success story). Send complete ms. Length: 150-300 words. Pays $25. Pays in copies for short articles under 150 words. Sometimes pays expenses of writers on assignment.
Columns/Departments: What's New (new products, organizations, services, books), 50-150 words. Buys 10 mss/year. Send complete ms. Pays $25-50.
Tips: "We seek advice from professionals in the field or interviews and observations about critical aspects concerning fine artists' careers. Artists themselves are welcome to submit success stories. We require concise, factual and comprehensive articles."

‡**TEXAS ARCHITECT**, Texas Society of Architects, Suite 1400, 114 W. Seventh St., Austin TX 78701. (512)478-7386, Editor: Joel Warren Barna. Associate Editor: Susan Williamson. Publications Director: Ray Don Tilley. 30% freelance written. Bimonthly trade journal of architecture and architects of Texas. "*Texas Architect* is a highly visually oriented look at Texas architecture, design and urban planning. Articles cover varied subtopics within architecture. Readers are mostly architects and related building professionals." Estab. 1951. Circ. 10,000. Pays on publication. Publishes ms an average of 2 months after acceptance. Byline given. Buys one-time rights, all rights or makes work-for-hire assignments. Submit seasonal material 4 months in advance. Query for electronic submissions. Reports in 2 weeks. Free sample copy and writer's guidelines.
Nonfiction: Book excerpts, essays, interview/profile, opinion, photo feature, technical. Buys 15 mss/year. Query with or without published clips, or send complete ms. Length: 100-2,000 words. Pays $50-500 for assigned articles; $25-300 for unsolicited articles.
Photos: Send photos with submission. Reviews contact sheets, 35mm or 4×5 transparencies and 4×5 prints. Offers no additional payment for photos accepted with ms. Identification of subjects required. Buys one-time rights.
Columns/Departments: Contact: Susan Williamson. News (timely reports on architectural issues, projects and people); 100-500 words. Buys 10 mss/year. Query with published clips. Pays $50-100.

Auto and Truck

These publications are geared to automobile, motorcycle and truck dealers; professional truck drivers; service department personnel; or fleet operators. Publications for highway planners and traffic control experts are listed in the Government and Public Service category.

AFTERMARKET BUSINESS, Advanstar Communications, 7500 Old Oak Blvd., Cleveland OH 44130-3343. (216)243-8100. Fax: (216)891-2675. Editor-in-Chief: Sandie Stambaugh-Cannon. 10% freelance written. Monthly tabloid for automotive aftermarket. Feature articles devoted to the retail aftermarket: merchandising practices, business techniques, sales techniques, customer service. Estab. 1936. Circ. 23,526. Pays on publication. Byline given. Buys all rights and/or makes work-for-hire assignments. Editorial lead time 2 months. Accepts previously published submissions. Reports in 6-9 months.
Nonfiction: Interview/profile and photo feature. Special issue: November (publish Show Dailies at major trade show). Buys 3 mss/year. Query with published clips. Length: 2,000-4,000 words. Pays $300 minimum for assigned articles. Sometimes pays expenses of writers on assignment.
Photos: State availability of photos with submission. Reviews prints. Offers no additional payment for photos accepted with ms. Identification of subjects required. Buys all rights.

AUTO GLASS JOURNAL, Grawin Publications, Inc., Suite 101, 303 Harvard E., P.O. Box 12099, Seattle WA 98102-0099. (206)322-5120. Editor: Mary Zabawa. 10% freelance written. Prefers to work with published/established writers. Monthly magazine on auto glass replacement. International publication for the auto glass replacement industry. Includes step-by-step glass replacement procedures for current model cars and business management, industry news and trends. Estab. 1953. Circ. 5,700. **Pays on acceptance.** Publishes ms an average of 5 months after acceptance. No byline given. Buys all rights. Query for electronic submissions. Reports in 5 months. Sample copy for 6×9 SAE with 3 first-class stamps. Writer's guidelines for #10 SASE.
Nonfiction: Articles relating to auto glass and general business management. Buys 12-20 mss/year. Query with published clips. Length: 1,000-3,000 words. Pays $50-200, with photos.
Photos: State availability of photos. Reviews b&w contact sheets and negatives. Payment included with ms. Captions required. Buys all rights.

THE BATTERY MAN, Independent Battery Manufacturers Association, Inc., 100 Larchwood Dr., Largo FL 34640-2811. (813)586-1409. Fax: (813)586-1400. Editor: Celwyn E. Hopkins. 20% freelance written. Monthly magazine emphasizing SLI battery manufacture, applications and new developments. Target audience: The entire, international industry that is involved in manufacturing, distributing and selling of batteries and battery-related products and technologies. Estab. 1959. Circ. 5,200. **Pays on acceptance.** Publishes ms an average of 4 months after acceptance. Submit seasonal material 2 months in advance. Accepts simultaneous and previously published submissions. Query for electronic submissions. Reports in 2 months. Send SASE for return of ms.

Nonfiction: Technical articles on secondary, storage and industrial batteries; new developments in battery manufacturing; energy topics, such as Electric Vehicles, UPS, etc. are acceptable. Also publishes articles on alloys, metals, plastics, etc. and governmental and legislative concerns of the industry. Submit complete ms. Buys 15-20 unsolicited mss/year. Length: 750-2,000 words preferred. Pays 10¢/word. Photos accepted with article also, pays $10/photo.

Tips: "Most writers are not familiar enough with this industry to be able to furnish a feature article. They try to palm off something that they wrote for a hardware store, or a dry cleaner, by calling everything a 'battery store.' We receive a lot of manuscripts on taxes and tax information (such as US income tax) and on business management in general and managing a family-owned business. Since this is an international publication, we try to stay away from such subjects. US tax information is of no use or interest to overseas readers."

EASTERN AFTERMARKET JOURNAL, Stan Hubsher Inc., Dept. WM, P.O. Box 373, Cedarhurst NY 11516. (516)295-3680. Editor: Stan Hubsher. 100% freelance written. Bimonthly magazine for automotive parts wholesaler buyers at the warehouse and jobber level, on the Eastern seaboard. "Audience operates stores and warehouses that handle replacement parts for automobiles. No technical knowledge necessary. Profiles of owners/buyers, how they operate in highly competitive market that accounts for 40% of the entire country's aftermarket business." Estab. 1956. Circ. 9,500. Pays on publication. Buys all rights. Submit material 2 months in advance. Reports in 1 month. Sample copy and writer's guidelines for 9 × 12 SAE with 8 first-class stamps.
- This magazine has increased its geographical coverage and now covers territory from Maryland to Florida.

Nonfiction: Buys 6-8 mss/year. Query. Length: 2,000 words. Pays $150 minimum to negotiable maximum. Sometimes pays expenses of writers on assignment.

Photos: Send photos with submission. Offers no additional payments for photos accepted with ms. Captions and identification of subjects required. Buys one-time rights.

OVERDRIVE, The Magazine for the American Trucker, Randall Publishing Co./Overdrive, Inc., P.O. Box 3187, Tuscaloosa AL 35403-3187. (205)349-2990. Fax: (205)750-8070. Editor: G.C. Skipper. Managing Editor: Deborah Lockridge. 25% freelance written. Monthly magazine for independent truckers. Estab. 1961. Circ. 95,000. Pays on publication. Publishes ms an average of 2 months after acceptance. Byline given. 10% kill fee. Buys all North American rights. Reports in 2 months. Sample copy and writers' guidelines for 9 × 12 SASE.

Nonfiction: Essays, exposé, how-to (truck maintainance and operation), interview/profile (successful independent truckers), personal experience, photo feature, technical. All must be related to independent trucker interest. Query with or without published clips or send complete ms. Length: 500-2,000 words. Pays $100-600 for assigned articles; $50-500 for unsolicited articles.

Photos: Send photos with submission. Reviews transparencies and 5 × 7 prints. Offers $25-50/photo. Identification of subjects required. Buys all rights.

Tips: "Talk to independent truckers. Develop a good knowledge of their concerns as small business owners, truck drivers and individuals. We prefer articles that quote experts, people in the industry and truckers to first-person expositions on a subject. Get straight facts. Look for good material on truck safety, on effects of government regulations, and on rates and business relationships between independent truckers, brokers, carriers and shippers."
- This magazine is buying fewer freelance mss – down from 30-25%.

SUCCESSFUL DEALER, Kona-Cal, Inc., Suite 300, 707 Lake Cook Rd., Deerfeld IL 60015-4933. (708)498-3180. Editor: David Zaritz. Contact: Denise L. Rondini, Editorial Director. 10% freelance written. Bimonthly magazine for heavy-duty truck dealers. "*Successful Dealer*'s primary readers are the principal owners of medium- and heavy-duty truck dealerships. Additional readers are the executives, managers and sales personnel employed by these dealerships." Estab. 1978. Circ. 17,500. **Pays on acceptance.** Publishes ms an average of 4 months after acceptance. Byline given. Buys first North American serial or second (reprint) rights. Editorial lead time 3 months. Reports in 2-3 weeks on queries. Sample copy and writer's guidelines free on request.

Nonfiction: General interest (industry trends/developments), how-to (operate more profitably), interview/profile (industry leaders), technical (new developments in truck componentry). "We do not want single new product features; no opinion pieces." Buys 8 mss/year. Query. Length: 1,000-1,500 words. Pays $400 minimum for assigned articles or departments, $350 minimum for unsolicited articles. Sometimes pays expenses of writers on assignment.

Photos: Send photos with submission. Reviews contact sheets, negatives, transparencies and prints. Offers no additional payment for photos accepted with ms. Captions, model releases and identification of subjects required.

Tips: "It helps for the writer to be familiar with the industry."

TOW-AGE, Kruza Kaleidoscopix, Inc., P.O. Box 389, Franklin MA 02038-0389. Editor: J. Kruza. For readers who run their own towing service business. 5% freelance written. Prefers to work with published/established writers. Published every 6 weeks. Estab. 1960. Circ. 18,000. Buys all rights; usually reassigns rights. **Pays on acceptance.** Accepts simultaneous submissions. Reports in 1 month. Sample copy for $3. Writer's guidelines for #10 SASE.
Nonfiction: Articles on business, legal and technical information for the towing industry. "Light reading material; short, with punch." Informational, how-to, personal, interview, profile. Buys about 18 mss/year. Query or submit complete ms. Length: 600-800 words. Pays $50-150. Spot news and successful business operations. Length: 300-800 words. Technical articles. Length: 400-1,000 words. Pays expenses of writers on assignment.
Photos: Black and white 8×10 photos purchased with or without mss, or on assignment. Pays $25 for first photo; $10 for each additional photo in series. Captions required.

TRUCK PARTS AND SERVICE, Kona Communications, Inc., Suite 300, 707 Lake Cook Rd., Deerfield IL 60015-4909. Editor: David Zaritz. Managing Editor: Denise L. Rondini. Contact: David Zaritz. 10% freelance written. Monthly magazine for repair shops and distributors in heavy-duty trucking. "Truck Parts and Service's primary readers are owners of truck parts distributorships and independent repair shops. Both types of businesses sell parts and repair service to fleet and individual owners of medium- to heavy-duty trucks, buses and trailers. Other readers include the executives, managers and sales personnel employed by the parts distributors and repair shops." Estab. 1966. Circ. 17,500. **Pays on acceptance.** Publishes ms an average of 4 months after acceptance. Byline given. Buys first North American serial or second serial (reprint) rights. Editorial lead time 3 months. Reports in 2-3 weeks on queries. Sample copy and writer's guidelines free on request.
Nonfiction: General interest (industry trends or developments); how-to (operate more profitably); interview/profile (industry leaders); and technical (new developments in truck components or repair and maintenance procedures). "We do not want single new product features; no opinion pieces." Buys 12 mss/year. Query. Length: 1,000-1,500 words. Pays $400 minimum for assigned articles, $350 for unsolicited articles. Sometimes pays expenses of writers on assignment.
Photos: Send photos with submission. Reviews contact sheets, negatives, transparencies and prints. Captions, model releases and identification of subjects required.
Tips: "It helps for the writer to be very familiar with the industry."

UTILITY FLEET MANAGEMENT, The Equipment Magazine, Public Utilities Reports, Dept. WM, #200, 2111 Wilson Blvd., Arlington VA 22201-3060. (703)243-7000. Editor: Nancy Coe Bailey. 10% freelance written. Magazine published 9 times/year covering "investor-owned utilities, trucks and equipment fleets. *UFM* reaches utility fleet managers and their staffs, and the construction and maintenance employees who use the equipment. 80% of published material is about equipment: purchasing and maintaining." Estab. 1981. Circ. 13,000. **Pays on acceptance.** Publishes ms an average of 3 months after acceptance. Byline given. Buys all rights. Submit seasonal material 6 months in advance. Reports in 1 month on queries. Sample copy for 9×12 SAE with 5 first-class stamps.
Nonfiction: How-to (i.e., new methods for recycling antifreeze, troubleshooting hydraulic systems, maintaining alternative fuel engines), interview/profile (leaders of large or innovative fleets), new product (if it's *really* new and intriguing), photo feature (want good photos of equipment in action). "No generic material. This is a technical publication and our readers want details. Not 'clean air engines are good' articles, but rather 'exactly how do they work?'" Buys 9 mss/year. Query. Length: 750-2,000 words. Pays $75 minimum for assigned articles; $75-200 for unsolicited articles. Technical/vendor "guest" writers are paid in contributor copies.
Photos: Reviews contact sheets, transparencies and prints. Offers no additional payment for photos accepted with ms. Identification of subjects required. Buys one-time rights.
Columns/Departments: Alternative Fuels/Vehicles (news, developments of alternative fuel vehicles—natural gas, electric, methanol, propane, etc.), 1,000 words; Management Forum (management techniques), 1,000 words; and Technology Report (technical tips on taking care of trucks and heavy equipment), 1,000 words. Buys 9 mss/year. Query. Pays $75-100.
Tips: "We need articles on equipment/truck selection and maintenance—things that will make a veteran fleet manager say, 'Wow, what a great idea!' Examples: A super truck big enough to hold another good-sized vehicle, with a complete rolling shop inside; an overhead crane that moves on tracks to 12 locations in a garage; tracked vehicles for emergency work that don't damage the environment."

VEHICLE LEASING TODAY, National Vehicle Leasing Association, Dept. Wm, Suite 220, 3710 S. Robertson, P.O. Box 34579, Los Angeles CA 90034-0579. (310)838-3170. Editor: Rodney Couts. 15% freelance written. Bimonthly magazine on vehicle leasing. "We cover critical issues for vehicle lessors, financial lending institutions, and computer software vendors with lessor programs." Estab. 1985. Circ. 6,000. Pays on publication. Publishes ms an average of 2 months after acceptance. Byline given. Negotiable kill fee. Buys one-time rights. Submit seasonal material 3 months in advance. Accepts previously published submissions. Sample copy for $5. Free writer's guidelines.

Nonfiction: How-to (anything relating to a vehicle lessor business), interview/profile, new product, technical. Buys 5 mss/year. Query. Length: 1,000-2,000 words. Pays $50-250 for assigned articles; $50-200 for unsolicited articles. Sometimes pays expenses of writers on assignment.

Photos: State availability of photos with submission. Reviews 5 × 7 prints. Offers no additional payment for photos accepted with ms. Model releases required. Buys one-time rights.

Columns/Departments: Financial Institutions, Lessor Issues, 500-1,000 words; New Products and Services, 500 words. Buys 3 mss/year. Send complete ms. Length: 300-1,000 words. Pays $25-100.

Aviation and Space

In this section are journals for aviation business executives, airport operators and aviation technicians. Publications for professional and private pilots can be found in the Consumer Aviation section.

AG-PILOT INTERNATIONAL MAGAZINE, Graphics Plus, P.O. Box 1607, Mt. Vernon WA 98273-1607. (206)336-9737. Fax: (206)336-2506. Editor Publisher: Tom J. Wood. Monthly magazine emphasizing agricultural aerial application (crop dusting). "This is intended to be a fun-to-read, technical, as well as humorous, and serious publication for the ag pilot and operator. They are our primary target." 20% freelance written. Estab. 1978. Circ. 7,200. Pays on publication. Publishes ms an average of 3 months after acceptance. Buys all rights. Byline given unless writer requests name held. Reports in 1 month. Sample copy for 9 × 12 SAE with 7 first-class stamps. Writer's guidelines for #10 SASE.

Nonfiction: Exposé (of EPA, OSHA, FAA or any government function concerned with this industry), general interest, historical, interview (of well-known ag/aviation person); nostalgia, personal opinion, new product, personal experience, photo feature. "If we receive an article, in any area we have solicited, it is quite possible this person could contribute intermittently. The international input is what we desire. Industry-related material is a must. *No newspaper clippings.*" Send complete ms. Length: 800-1,500 words. Pays $50-200.

Photos: "We would like one color or b&w (5 × 7 preferred) with the manuscript, if applicable — it will help increase your chance of publication." Offers no additional payment for photos accepted with ms. Captions preferred, model release required.

Columns/Departments: International (of prime interest, crop dusting-related); Embryo Birdman (should be written, or appear to be written, by a beginner spray pilot); The Chopper Hopper (by anyone in the helicopter industry); Trouble Shooter (ag aircraft maintenance tips); Catchin' The Corner (written by a person obviously skilled in the crop dusting field of experience or other interest-capturing material related to the industry) and Old Pro's Nest. Send complete ms. Length: 800-1,500 words. Pays $25-100.

Poetry: Interested in all ag-aviation related poetry. Buys 1 poem/issue. Submit no more than 2 at one time. Maximum length: 20 inch × 48 picas each maximum. Pays $10-50.

Fillers: Short jokes, short humor and industry-related newsbreaks. Length: 10-100 words. Pays $5-20.

Tips: "Writers should be witty and knowledgeable about the crop dusting aviation world. Material *must* be agricultural/aviation-oriented. *Crop dusting or nothing!*"

‡GSE TODAY, P.O. Box 480, Hatch NM 87937. Editor: G.C. Prill. Contact: Dixie Binning. 70% freelance written. Bimonthly magazine covering aviation ground support world wide. "Our readers are those aviation professionals who are involved in ground support – the equipment manufacturers, the suppliers, the ramp operators, ground handlers, airport and airline manager. We cover issues of interest to this community – deicing, ramp safety, equipment technology, pollution, etc." Estab. 1993. Circ. 14,000. Pays on publication. Publishes ms an average of 4 months after acceptance. Buys all rights. Editorial lead time 2 months. Accepts unsolicited mss. Query for electronic submissions. Reports in 3 weeks on queries; 3 months on mss. Sample copy for 9 × 11 SAE with 5 first-class stamps.

Nonfiction: How-to (use or maintain certain equipment), interview/profile, new products, personal experience (from ramp operators), technical aspects of ground support equipment and issues, industry events, meetings, new rules and regulations. Buys 12-20 mss/year. Send complete ms. Length: 400-3,000 words. Pays 20¢/published word.

Photos: Send photos with submissions. Reviews 5 × 7 prints. Offers no additional payment for photos accepted with ms. Identification of subjects required. Buys all rights.

Tips: "Write about subjects that relate to ground services. Write in clear and simple terms – personal experience is always welcome. If you have an aviation background or ground support experience, let us know."

‡WINGS WEST, 7009 S. Potomac St., Englewood CO 80112-4209. (303)397-7600. Fax: (303)397-7619. Editor: Sparky J. Imeson. 50% freelance written. Bimonthly magazine on aviation and aerospace in the West. Estab. 1985. Circ. 20,000. Pays on publication. Publishes ms an average of 12 months after acceptance. Byline given. Offers $25 kill fee. Buys all rights. Submit seasonal/holiday material 6 months in advance. Accepts previously published articles. Send tearsheet or photocopy of article or short story and information about when and where the article previously appeared. For reprints, pays 100% of the amount paid for an original article.

Query for electronic submissions. Sample copy available. Send cover letter with one copy of ms, Mac or DOS file saved as text only, unformed ASCII, or in QuarkXPress (Mac) on 3½-inch floppy diskette (telephonic submissions (303)397-6987), author's bio and photo. Writing and photographic guidelines available.

Nonfiction: General interest illustrative of people, how to fly, flying experiences, mountain flying, humor, new products, opinion, opportunities, challenges, cultures, and special places. Buys 18-35 mss/year. Length: 800-2,500 words. Pay starts at $50 per published page (includes text and photos).

Fiction: Interested in new ideas. Query.

Photos: Send photos with submission (copies acceptable for evaluation). Pays $10-35/b&w; $35-75/color. Credit line given.

Columns/Departments: Medical (aeromedical factors), legal (FARs, enforcement, legal problems), mountain flying, travel, safety, product news and reviews, industry news. *Wings West* purchases first serial rights. May consider second serial reprint rights, query.

Beauty and Salon

‡**NAILPRO, The Magazine for Nail Professionals,** Creative Age Publications, 7628 Densmore Ave., Van Nuys CA 91406. Editor: Linda Lewis. Managing Editor: Barbara Owens. 50% freelance written. Monthly magazine "written for manicurists and nail technicians working in full-service salons or nails-only salons. It covers technical and business aspects of working in and operating a nail-care service, as well as the nail-care industry in general." Estab. 1989. Circ. 44,000. **Pays on acceptance.** Publishes ms 4-6 months after acceptance. Byline given. Offers 50% kill fee. Buys one-time, second serial (reprint), simultaneous or all rights. Editorial lead time 3 months. Submit seasonal material 3 months in advance. Accepts simultaneous and previously published submissions. Query for electronic submissions. Reports in 6 weeks. Sample copy for $2 and 8½ × 11 SASE.

Nonfiction Book excerpts, how-to, humor, inspirational, interview/profile, personal experience, photo feature, technical. No general interest articles or business articles not geared to the nail-care industry. Buys 50 mss/year. Query. Length: 1,000-3,000 words. Pays $150. Sometimes pays expenses of writers on assignment.

Photos: Send photos with submission. Reviews transparencies and prints. Negotiates payment individually. Model releases and identification of subjects required. Buys one-time rights.

Columns/Departments: Building Business (articles on marketing nail services/products), 1,500-3,000 words; Shop Talk (aspects of operating a nail salon), 1,500-3,000 words; Hollywood File (nails in the news, movies or TV), 1,000-1,500 words. Buys 50 mss/year. Query. Pays $150-250.

NAILS, Bobit Publishing, 2512 Artesia Blvd., Redondo Beach CA 90278-3296. (310)376-8788. Fax: (310)376-9043. Editor: Cyndy Drummey. Executive Editor: Peggy Haynes. 10% freelance written. Monthly magazine for the nail care industry. "*NAILS* seeks to educate its readers on new techniques and products, nail anatomy and health, customer relations, working safely with chemicals, salon sanitation, and the business aspects of working in or running a salon." Estab. 1983. Circ. 48,000. **Pays on acceptance.** Byline given. Buys all rights. Submit seasonal material 4 months in advance. Query for electronic submissions. Reports in 3 months on queries. Free sample copy. No writer's guidelines available.

Nonfiction: Historical/nostalgic, how-to, inspirational, interview/profile, personal experience, photo feature, technical. "No articles on one particular product, company profiles or articles slanted towards a particular company or manufacturer." Buys 20 mss/year. Query with published clips. Length: 1,200-3,000 words. Pays $100-400. Sometimes pays expenses of writers on assignment.

Photos: State availability of photos with submission. Reviews contact sheets, transparencies and prints (any standard size acceptable). Offers $50-200/photo. Captions, model releases and identification of subjects required. Buys all rights.

Tips: "Send clips and query; *do not send unsolicited manscript*. We would like to see ideas for articles on a unique salon or a business article that focuses on a specific aspect or problem encountered when working in a salon. The Modern Nail Salon section, which profiles nail salons and full-service salons, is most open to freelancers. Focus on an innovative business idea or unique point of view. Articles from experts on specific business issues — insurance, handling difficult employees, cultivating clients — are encouraged."

Beverages and Bottling

Manufacturers, distributors and retailers of soft drinks and alcoholic beverages read these publications. Publications for bar and tavern operators and managers of restaurants are classified in the Hotels, Motels, Clubs, Resorts and Restaurants category.

AMERICAN BREWER, P.O. Box 510, Hayward CA 94543-0510. (415)538-9500 (a.m. only). Fax: (510)538-9500. Publisher: Bill Owens. 100% freelance written. Quarterly magazine covering micro-breweries. Estab. 1986. Circ. 10,000. Pays on publication. Publishes ms an average of 4 months after acceptance. Byline given. Buys one-time rights. Accepts previously published submissions. Send tearsheet or photocopy of article. For reprints pays 30% of the amount paid for an original article. Reports in 2 weeks on queries. Sample copy for $5.

Nonfiction: Humor, opinion, travel. Query. Length: 1,500-2,500 words. Pays $50-250 for assigned articles.

BEVERAGE WORLD, Keller International Publishing Corp., Dept. WM, 150 Great Neck Rd., Great Neck NY 11021. (516)829-9210. Editor: Larry Jabbonsky. Monthly magazine on the beverage industry. Estab. 1882. Circ. 35,000. **Pays on acceptance.** Publishes ms an average of 2 months after acceptance. Byline given. Buys all rights. Submit seasonal material 2 months in advance. Accepts simultaneous submissions. Free sample copy and writer's guidelines.
Nonfiction: How-to (increase profit/sales), interview/profile, technical. Buys 15 mss/year. Query with published clips. Length: 1,000-2,500 words. Pays $200/listed page. Sometimes pays expenses of writers on assignment.
Photos: State availability of photos with submission. Reviews contact sheets. Captions required. Buys one-time rights.
Columns/Departments: Buys 5 mss/year. Query with published clips. Length: 750-1,000 words. Pay varies $150/minimum.
Tips: "Requires background in beverage production and marketing. Business and/or technical writing experience *a must.* Do not call. This is a small staff that does not have much time for phone queries. Proof your queries carefully. Poor spelling/grammar is a turn-off."

MID-CONTINENT BOTTLER, Suite 218, 8575 W 110, Overland Park KS 66210. (913)469-8611. Fax: (913)469-8626. Publisher: Floyd E. Sageser. 5% freelance written. Prefers to work with published/established writers. Bimonthly magazine for "soft drink bottlers in the 20-state Midwestern area." Estab. 1970. Not copyrighted. **Pays on acceptance.** Publishes ms an average of 2 months after acceptance. Buys first rights only. Reports "immediately." Sample copy for 9 × 12 SAE with 10 first-class stamps. Guidelines for #10 SASE.
Nonfiction: "Items of specific soft drink bottler interest with special emphasis on sales and merchandising techniques. Feature style desired." Buys 2-3 mss/year. Length: 2,000 words. Pays $15-100. Sometimes pays the expenses of writers on assignment.
Photos: Photos purchased with mss.

SOUTHERN BEVERAGE JOURNAL, 13225 SW 88th Ave., Miami FL 33176. (305)233-7230. Fax: (305)252-2580. Editor: Jackie Preston. 60% freelance written. Works with a small number of new/unpublished writers each year. Monthly magazine for the alcohol beverage industry. Readers are personnel of bars, restaurants, package stores, night clubs, lounges and hotels—owners, managers and salespersons. Estab. 1945. Circ. 30,000. **Pays on acceptance.** Publishes ms an average of 4 months after acceptance. Byline given. Buys first rights. Submit seasonal material 4 months in advance. Query for electronic submissions. Reports in 3 months.
Nonfiction: General interest, historical, personal experience, interview/profile, success stories. Information on legislation (state) affecting alcohol beverage industry. No canned material. Buys 6 mss/year. Send complete ms. Length: 1,000-2,000 words. Pays 10¢/word for assigned articles.
Photos: State availability of photos with submission. Reviews 7 × 8 or 4 × 5 transparencies and 3 × 5 prints. Offers $15 maximum/photo. Identification of subjects required. Buys one-time rights.
Tips: "We are interested in legislation having to do with our industry and also views on trends, drinking and different beverages."

‡TEA & COFFEE TRADE JOURNAL, Lockwood Book Publishing Co., 130 W. 42nd St., New York NY 10036. (212)661-5980. Fax: (212)827-0945. Editor: Jane Phillips McCabe. 50% freelance written. Prefers to work with published/established writers. Monthly magazine covering the international coffee and tea market. "Tea and coffee trends are analyzed; transportation problems, new equipment for plants and packaging are featured." Estab. 1901. Circ. 10,000. Pays on publication. Publishes ms an average of 2 months after acceptance. Byline given. Makes work-for-hire assignments. Submit seasonal material 1 month in advance. Accepts simultaneous submissions. Reports in 4 months. Free sample copy.
Nonfiction: Exposé, historical/nostalgic, interview/profile, new product, photo feature, technical. Special issue includes the Coffee Market Forecast and Review (January). "No consumer related submissions. I'm only interested in the trade." Buys 60 mss/year. Query. Length: 750-1,500 words. Pays $5.50/published inch 4 months after publication.
Photos: State availability of photos with submission. Reviews contact sheets, negatives, transparencies and prints. Pays $5.50/published inch. Captions and identification of subjects required. Buys one-time rights.
Columns/Departments: Specialties (gourmet trends); and Transportation (shipping lines). Buys 36 mss/year. Query. Pays $5.50/published inch.

VINEYARD & WINERY MANAGEMENT, P.O. Box 231, Watkins Glen NY 14891-0231. (607)535-7133. Fax: (607)535-2998. Editor: J. William Moffett. 80% freelance written. Bimonthly trade magazine of professional importance to grape growers, winemakers and winery sales and business people. Estab. 1975. Circ. 4,500. Pays on publication. Byline given. Buys first North American serial rights and occasionally simultaneous rights. Query for electronic submissions. Reports in 3 weeks on queries; 1 month on mss. *Writer's Market* recommends allowing 2 months for reply. Free sample copy. Writer's guidelines for #10 SASE.

Nonfiction: How-to, interview/profile, technical. Subjects are technical in nature and explore the various methods people in these career paths use to succeed, and also the equipment and techniques they use successfully. Business articles and management topics are also featured. The audience is national with western dominance. Buys 30 mss/year. Query. Length: 300-5,000 words. Pays $30-1,000. Pays some expenses of writers on some assignments.

Photos: State availability of photos with submission. Reviews contact sheets, negatives and transparencies. Identification of subjects required. "Black and white often purchased for $20 each to accompany story material; 35mm and/or 4×5 transparencies for $50 and up; 6/year of vineyard and/or winery scene related to story. Query."

Tips: "We're looking for long-term relationships with authors who know the business and write well. Electronic submissions preferred; query for formats."

● This publication no longer considers short fiction.

WINES & VINES, 1800 Lincoln Ave., San Rafael CA 94901-1298. Fax: (415)453-2517. Editor: Philip E. Hiaring. 10-20% freelance written. Works with a small number of new/unpublished writers each year. Monthly magazine for everyone concerned with the grape and wine industry including winemakers, wine merchants, growers, suppliers, consumers, etc. Estab. 1919. Circ. 4,500. Buy first North American serial or simultaneous rights. Accepts previously published articles. Send typed ms with rights for sale noted and information about when and where the article previously appeared. **Pays on acceptance.** Publishes ms an average of 3 months after acceptance. Special issues: Winetech (January); vineyard (February); State-of-the-Art (March); Brandy/specialty wines, (April); export-import (May); enological (June); statistical (July); merchandising (August); marketing (September); equipment and supplies (November); champagne (December). Submit special issue material 3 months in advance. Reports in 2 months. Sample copy for 11 × 14 SAE with 7 first-class stamps. Free writer's guidelines.

Nonfiction: Articles of interest to the trade. "These could be on grape growing in unusual areas; new winemaking techniques; wine marketing, retailing, etc." Interview, historical, spot news, merchandising techniques and technical. No stories with a strong consumer orientation as against trade orientation. Author should know the subject matter, i.e., know proper grape growing/winemaking terminology. Buys 3-4 ms/year. Query. Length: 1,000-2,500 words. Pays 5¢/word. Sometimes pays the expenses of writers on assignment.

Photos: Pays $10 for 4×5 or 8×10 b&w photos purchased with mss. Captions required.

Tips: "Ours is a trade magazine for professionals. Therefore, we do not use 'gee-whiz' wine articles."

Book and Bookstore

Publications for book trade professionals from publishers to bookstore operators are found in this section. Journals for professional writers are classified in the Journalism and Writing category.

BLOOMSBURY REVIEW, A Book Magazine, Dept. WM, Owaissa Communications Co., Inc., 1028 Bannock, Denver CO 80204-4037. (303)892-0620. Fax: (303)892-5620. Publisher/Editor-in-chief: Tom Auer. Editor/Associate Publisher: Marilyn Auer. 75% freelance written. Tabloid published 6 times/year covering books and book-related matters. "We publish book reviews, interviews with writers and poets, literary essays and original poetry. Our audience consists of educated, literate, *non-specialized* readers." Estab. 1980. Circ. 50,000. Pays on publication. Publishes ms an average of 4 months after acceptance. Byline given. Buys first or one-time rights. Reports in 4 months. Reprints considered but not encouraged. Send photocopy of article and information about when and where the article previously appeared. Pays 100% of their fee for an original article. Sample copy for $4 and 9 × 12 SASE. Writer's guidelines for #10 SASE.

Nonfiction: Essays, interview/profile, book reviews. "Summer issue features reviews, etc. about the American West." *"We do not publish fiction."* Buys 60 mss/year. Query with published clips or send complete ms. Length 800-1,500 words. Pays $10-20. Sometimes pays writers with contributor copies or other premiums "if writer agrees."

Photos: State availability of photos with submissions. Reviews prints. Offers no additional payment for photos accepted with ms. Buys one-time rights.

Columns/Departments: Book reviews and essays. Buys 6 mss/year. Query with published clips or send complete ms. Length: 500-1,500 words. Pays $10-20.

Poetry: Ray Gonzalez, poetry editor. Avant-garde, free verse, haiku, light verse and traditional. Buys 20 poems/year. Submit up to 5 poems at one time. Pays $5-10.

Tips: "We appreciate receiving published clips and/or completed manuscripts. Please — no rough drafts. Book reviews should be of new books (within 6 months of publication)."

THE FEMINIST BOOKSTORE NEWS, P.O. Box 882554, San Francisco CA 94188-2554. (415)626-1556. Editor: Carol Seajay. Managing Editor: Christine Chia. 10% freelance written. Works with a small number of new/unpublished writers each year. Bimonthly magazine covering feminist books and the women-in-print industry.

"*Feminist Bookstore News* covers 'everything of interest' to the feminist bookstores, publishers and periodicals, books of interest and provides an overview of feminist publishing by mainstream publishers." Estab. 1976. Circ. 700. Pays on publication. Publishes ms an average of 2 months after acceptance. Byline sometimes given. Buys one-time rights. Accepts simultaneous submissions. Reports in 3 weeks. Sample copy for $6.
Nonfiction: Essays, exposé, how-to (run a bookstore), new product, opinion, personal experience (in feminist book trade only). Special issues: Sidelines (July); University Press (fall). No submissions that do not directly apply to the feminist book trade. Query with or without published clips or send complete ms. Length: 250-2,000 words. Pays in copies when appropriate.
Photos: State availability of photos with submission. Model release and identification of subjects required. Buys one-time rights.
Fillers: Anecdotes, facts, newsbreaks, short humor. Length: 100-400 words.
Tips: "The writer must have several years experience in the feminist book industry. We publish very little by anyone else."

THE HORN BOOK MAGAZINE, The Horn Book, Inc., Dept. WM, Suite 1000, 11 Beacon St., Boston MA 02108. (617)227-1555. Editor: Anita Silvey. 10% freelance written. Prefers to work with published/established writers. Bimonthly magazine covering children's literature for librarians, booksellers, professors, and students of children's literature. Estab. 1924. Circ. 22,000. Pays on publication. Publishes ms an average of 4 months after acceptance. Byline given. Buys one-time rights. Submit seasonal material 6 months in advance. Accepts simultaneous queries and submissions. Reports in 2 weeks on queries; 1 month on mss. Writer's guidelines available upon request.
Nonfiction: Interview/profile (children's book authors and illustrators). Buys 20 mss/year. Query or send complete ms. Length: 1,000-2,800 words. Pays $25-250.
Tips: "Writers have a better chance of breaking in to our publication with a query letter on a specific article they want to write."

LOS ANGELES TIMES BOOK REVIEW, Times Mirror, Times Mirror Square, Los Angeles CA 90053. (213)237-7778. Editor: Sonja Bolle. 90% freelance written. Weekly tabloid reviewing current books. Estab. 1881. Circ. 1.5 million. Pays on publication. Publishes ms an average of 3 weeks after acceptance. Byline given. Offers variable kill fee. Buys first North American serial rights. Accepts no unsolicited book reviews or requests for specific titles to review. "Query with published samples—book reviews or literary features." Buys 500 mss/year. Length: 200-1,500 words. Pay varies; approximately 35¢/word.

THE WOMEN'S REVIEW OF BOOKS, The Women's Review, Inc., Wellesley College, Wellesley MA 02181-8259. (617)283-2500. Editor: Linda Gardiner. Monthly newspaper. "Feminist review of recent trade and academic writing by and about women. Reviews recent nonfiction books, primarily." Estab. 1983. Circ. 16,000. Pays on publication. Publishes ms an average of 2 months after acceptance. Byline given. Offers $50 kill fee. Buys first North American serial rights. Editorial lead time 2 months. Query for electronic submissions. Reports in 2 months. Sample copy free on request.
Nonfiction: Book reviews only. No articles considered; no unsolicited mss. Only book review queries. Buys 200 mss/year. Query with published clips. Pays 10¢/word. Sometimes pays expenses of writers on assignment.
Tips: "Only experienced reviewers for national media are considered. Reviewers must have expertise in subject of book under review. Never send unsolicited manuscripts."

Brick, Glass and Ceramics

These publications are read by manufacturers, dealers and managers of brick, glass and ceramic retail businesses. Other publications related to glass and ceramics are listed in the Consumer Art and Architecture and Consumer Hobby and Craft sections.

AMERICAN GLASS REVIEW, P.O. Box 2147, Clifton NJ 07015-3517. (201)779-1600. Fax: (201)779-3242. Editor-in-Chief/Publisher: Jonathan Doctorow. Managing Editor: Susan Grisham. 10% freelance written. Monthly magazine. Pays on publication. Estab. 1888. Byline given. Phone queries OK. Buys first rights. Accepts previously published articles. Send tearsheet of article. For reprints, pays 10% of the amount paid for an original article. Submit seasonal material 2 months in advance of issue date. Reports in 2 months. Free sample copy and writer's guidelines; mention *Writer's Market* in request.
Nonfiction: Glass plant and glass manufacturing articles. Buys 3-4 mss/year. Query. Length: 1,500-3,000 words. Pays $200/printed page.
Photos: State availability of photos with query. No additional payment for b&w contact sheets. Captions preferred. Buys one-time rights.

GLASS MAGAZINE, For the Architectural Glass Industry, National Glass Association, Dept. WM, Suite 302, 8200 Greensboro Dr., McLean VA 22102-3881. (703)442-4890. Fax: (703)442-0630. Managing Editor-in-Chief: Caroline Wilson. 25% freelance written. Prefers to work with published/established writers. Monthly magazine covering the architectural glass industry. Circ. 16,500. **Pays on acceptance.** Publishes ms an average of 3-6 months after acceptance. Byline given. Kill fee varies. Buys first rights only. Reports in 2 months. Sample copy for $5 and 9×12 SAE with 10 first-class stamps. Free writer's guidelines.

Nonfiction: Interview/profile (of various glass businesses; profiles of industry people or glass business owners); and technical (about glazing processes). Buys 15 mss/year. Query with published clips. Length: 1,000 words minimum. Pays $150-300.
- They are doing more inhouse writing; freelance cut by half.

Photos: State availability of photos.

Tips: "Do *not* send in general glass use stories. Research the industry first, then query."

‡**STAINED GLASS**, Stained Glass Association of America, #7, 6 SW Second St., Lee's Summit MO 64063. Contact: Katei Gross. 70% freelance written. Quarterly magazine covering stained glass and glass art. "Since 1906, *Stained Glass* has been the official voice of the stained glass Association of America. As the oldest, most respected stained glass publication in North America, *Stained Glass* preserves the techniques of the past as well as illustrates the trends of the future. This vital information, of significant value to the professional stained glass studio, is also of interest to those for whom stained glass is an avocation or hobby." Estab. 1906. Circ. 5,000. Pays on publication. Publishes ms an average of 6 months after acceptance. Byline given. Buys one-time rights. Editorial lead time 3 months. Submit seasonal material 6 months in advance. Accepts simultaneous and previously published submissions. Reports in 3 months. Sample copy and writer's guidelines free on request.

Nonfiction: How-to, humor, interview/profile, new product, opinion, photo feature, technical. Strong need for technical and how to create architectural type stained glass. Glass etching, use of etched glass in stained glass compositions, framing. Buys 9 mss/year. Query or send complete ms but must include photos or slides — very heavy on photos. Pays $25/page. Sometimes pays expenses of writers on assignment.

Photos: Send photos with submission. Reviews 4×5 transparencies. Negotiates payment individually. Identification of subjects required. Buys one-time rights.

Columns/Departments: Teknixs (technical, how-to, stained and glass art), word length varies by subject. Buys 4 mss/year. Query or send complete ms, but must be illustrated.

Tips: "Writers should be extremely well versed in the glass arts. Photographs are extremely important and must be of very high quality. Very sight oriented magazine. Submissions without photographs or illustrations are seldom considered unless something special and writer states that photos are available. However, prefer to see with submission."

‡**TILE DESIGN & INSTALLATION**, (formerly *Tile World*), Business News Publishing Co., Suite 205, 1 Kalisa Way, Paramus NJ 07652. (201)599-0136. Fax: (201)599-2378. Contact: Michael Reis, assistant editor. 15% freelance written. Monthly magazine covering tile industry. "International trade magazine for buyers and sellers of ceramic, stone and all varieties of tile products, tile manufacturing equipment, installation tools and supplies and maintenance products. Readers include architects, installers, developers, importers/exporters, manufacturers, and distributors." Estab. 1987. Circ. 16,500. Pays on typesetting. Byline given. Buys first rights and second serial (reprint) rights. Editorial lead time 2 months. Submit seasonal material 4 months in advance. Accepts simultaneous and previously published submissions. Query for electronic submissions. Reports in 2 months. Sample copy for $10. Writer's guidelines for #10 SASE.

Nonfiction: How-to (install, maintain or manufacture tile), interview/profile, photo feature, architectural design, company profiles, equipment, trade show review. Buys 4 mss/year. Query with published clips. Length: 600-3,000 words. Pays $150.

Photos: State availability of photos with submission. Reviews contact sheets, slides, 4×5 transparencies or 3×5 or larger prints. Offers $10/photo. Identification of subjects required. Buys one-time rights.

Tips: "Reports on architectural tile design are most open to freelancers. Architects are very willing to be quoted and provide good photos and drawings. Be sure to include all parties involved, including the designer, tile manufacturer, supplier and installer. For architectural projects, focus on the aspect that makes the project unique. Look for innovative design, installation or application of tile."

Building Interiors

Owners, managers and sales personnel of floor covering, wall covering and remodeling businesses read the journals listed in this category. Interior design and architecture publications may be found in the Consumer Art, Design and Collectibles category. For journals aimed at other construction trades see the Construction and Contracting section.

ALUMI-NEWS, Work-4 Projects Ltd., Box 400, Victoria Station, Westmount, Quebec H3Z 2V8 Canada. (514)489-4941. Fax: (514)489-5505. Publisher: Nachmi Artzy. 75% freelance written. Home renovation — exterior building products trade journal published 6 times/year. "We are dedicated to the grass roots of the industry: installers, dealers, contractors. We do not play up to our advertisers nor government." Estab. 1977.

Circ. 18,000. Pays on publication. Byline usually given. Buys all rights. Accepts simultaneous and previously published submissions. Free sample copy.

Nonfiction: Exposé; how-to (pertaining to dealers—profit, production, or management); new product (exterior building products); technical; survey results (trends or products in our industry). Buys 12-24 mss/year. Query with published clips. Length: 200-2,000 words. Pays 10-20¢/word. Pays in contributor copies or other premiums if mutually suitable. Sometimes pays expenses of writers on assignment.

Photos: State availability of photos with submission. Reviews negatives, transparencies and prints. Pays $300/photo maximum. Captions and identification of subjects required. Buys all rights.

Columns/Departments: Industry News (company profile: new location, product, personnel), 100-250 words; Profiles (interviews), 1,000-2,500 words. Query with published clips. Length: 75-300 words. Pays 10-20¢/word.

Fillers: Facts, short humor. Length 5-50 words. Pays 10-20¢/word.

Tips: "Submit articles not found in *every* similar publication. Find a new angle; Canadian content."

PWC, Painting & Wallcovering Contractor, Finan Publishing Co. Inc., 8730 Big Bend Blvd., St. Louis MO 63119-3730. Phone/Fax: (314)961-6644. Editor: Jeffery Beckner. 90% freelance written. Bimonthly magazine for painting and wallcovering contracting. "*PWC* provides news you can use: information helpful to the painting and wallcovering contractor in the here and now." Estab. 1928. Circ. 30,000. Pays 30 days after acceptance. Publishes ms an average of 1 month after acceptance. Byline given. Kill fee "to be determined on individual basis." Buys first North American serial rights. Editorial lead time 2 months. Submit seasonal material 2 months in advance. Accepts simultaneous and previously published submissions. Send tearsheet or photocopy of article, typed ms with rights for sale noted and information about when and where the article previously appeared. Query for electronic submissions; hard copy required. Reports in 2 weeks. Sample copy free on request.

Nonfiction: Essays, exposé, how-to (painting and wallcovering), interview/profile, new product, opinion, personal experience. Buys 40 mss/year. Query with published clips. Length: 1,500-2,500 words. Pays $300 minimum. Pays expenses of writers on assignment.

Photos: State availability of photos with submission. Send photos with submission. Reviews contact sheets, negatives, transparencies and prints. Offers no additional payment for photos accepted with ms. Identification of subjects required. Buys one-time and all rights.

Columns/Departments: Anything of interest to the small businessman, 1,250 words. Buys 2 mss/year. Query with published clips. Pays $50-100.

Tips: "We almost always buy on an assignment basis. The way to break in is to send good clips, and I'll try and give you work."

REMODELING, Hanley-Wood, Inc., Suite 600, One Thomas Circle NW, Washington DC 20005. (202)452-0800. Editor: Wendy Jordan. 5% freelance written. Monthly magazine covering residential and light commercial remodeling. "We cover the best new ideas in remodeling design, business, construction and products." Estab. 1985. Circ. 98,000. Pays on publication. Publishes ms an average of 3 months after acceptance. Byline given. Offers 5¢/word kill fee. Buys first North American serial rights. Query for electronic submissions. Reports in 1 month. Free sample copy and writer's guidelines.

Nonfiction: Interview/profile, new product, technical. Buys 4 mss/year. Query with published clips. Length: 250-1,000 words. Pays 20¢/word. Sometimes pays the expenses of writers on assignment.

Photos: State availability of photos with submission. Reviews slides, 4 × 5 transparencies and 8 × 10 prints. Offers $25-100/photo. Captions, model releases and identification of subjects required. Buys one-time rights.

Tips: "The areas of our publication most open to freelancers are news and new product news."

REMODELING NEWS, SR Sound, Inc., 600C Lakde St., Ramsey NJ 07446-1245. (201)327-1600. Fax: (201)327-3185. 80% freelance written. Monthly magazine covering professionally installed home remodeling and light construction. Estab. 1987. Circ. 82,000. Pays within 30 days of publication. Publishes ms an average of 3 months after acceptance. Byline given. Negotiates rights. Submit seasonal material 6 months in advance. Query for electronic submissions. Reports in 2 months. Free sample copy and writer's guidelines.

Nonfiction: How-to for professional remodelers, running a contracting business, remodeling products and materials. "Do not submit article for consumers or do-it-yourselfers." Query with published clips. Length: 600-3,000 words. Pays 20¢/word for assigned articles; $50 for reprints.

Photos: State availability of photos with submission. Reviews transparencies, slides or photos. Captions, model releases and identification of subjects required. Buys all rights.

Tips: "Articles must be geared toward professional contractors/remodelers, not do-it-yourselfers."

Market conditions are constantly changing! If this is 1996 or later, buy the newest edition of Writer's Market *at your favorite bookstore or order directly from* Writer's Digest Books.

WALLS & CEILINGS, Dept. WM, 8602 N. 40th St., Tampa FL 33604. (813)989-9300. Fax: (813)980-3982. Editor: Greg Campbell. 20% freelance written. Monthly magazine for contractors involved in lathing and plastering, drywall, acoustics, fireproofing, curtain walls, movable partitions together with manufacturers, dealers, and architects. Estab. 1938. Circ. 20,000. Pays on publication. Byline given. Publishes ms an average of 4-6 months after acceptance. Buys all rights within trade. Submit seasonal material 4 months in advance. Accepts simultaneous and previously published submissions. Send tearsheet or photocopy of article or typed ms with rights for sale noted and information about when and where the article previously appeared. For reprints pays 50% of the amount paid for an original article. Query for electronic submissions. Reports in 6 months. Sample copy for 9 × 12 SAE with $2 postage. Writer's guidelines for #10 SASE.

Nonfiction: How-to (drywall and plaster construction and business management), technical. Buys 20 mss/year. Query or send complete ms. Length: 1,000-1,500 words. Pays $50-200. Sometimes pays the expenses of writers on assignment.

Photos: Send photos with submission. Reviews contact sheets, negatives, transparencies and prints. Photos required for ms acceptance, with captions and identification of subjects. Buys one-time rights.

Business Management

These publications cover trends, general theory and management practices for business owners and top-level business executives. Publications that use similar material but have a less technical slant are listed in the Consumer Business and Finance section. Journals for middle management, including supervisors and office managers, appear in the Management and Supervision section. Those for industrial plant managers are listed under Industrial Operations and under sections for specific industries, such as Machinery and Metal. Publications for office supply store operators are included in the Office Environment and Equipment section.

CHIEF EXECUTIVE, Dept. WM, 21st Floor, 733 Third Ave., New York NY 10017. (212)687-8288. Fax: (212)687-8456. Editor: J.P. Donlon. Written by and for CEOs. Limited freelance opportunity. Published 9 times/year. Circ. 40,000. **Pays on acceptance.** Publishes ms an average of 2-3 months after acceptance. Byline given. Offers kill fee. Buys world serial rights. Free writer's guidelines.

Nonfiction: Query required for all departments. Unsolicited mss will not be returned. Pays $300-800. Pays previously agreed upon expenses of writers on assignment.

Photos: State availability of photos with submission. Reviews 4-color transparencies and slides. Offers $100/photo maximum. Captions required. Buys one-time rights.

Column/Departments: N.B. (profile of CEO/Chairman/President of mid- to large-size company), 400-500 words; Amenities, 1,000-1,500 words; CEO-At-Leisure, 1,000-1,500 words; Business Travel (provides CEOs with *key names* and information on business/government inner network for city/area being visited—who to know to get things done), 1,000-1,500 words. Payment varies.

‡CHINA BUSINESS & ECONOMIC UPDATE, The Monthly Intelligence Resource on Commerce and Finance in China, Golden Eagle Press, 9700 Topanga Canyon Blvd., Chatsworth CA 91311. Editor: David Wolf. 20% freelance written. Monthly newsletter covering US firms doing or seeking to do business in China. Pays on publication. Publishes ms an average of 1 month after acceptance. Byline given. Offers 50% or $50 kill fee. Buys first rights. Editorial lead time 1 month. Submit seasonal material 2 months in advance. Accepts simultaneous and previously published submissions. Query for electronic submissions. Reports in 2 weeks on queries; 1 month on mss. Sample copy for 9 × 12 SAE with 3 first-class stamps. Writer's guidelines for #10 SASE.

Nonfiction: How-to, interview/profile, opinion, personal experience. No articles on language, culture or politics. Buys 12 mss/year. Send complete ms. Length: 250-750 words. Pays $100 for assigned articles; $25 for unsolicited articles. Sometimes pays expenses of writers on assignment.

Photos: State availability of photos with submission. Reviews contact sheets. Offers $10-20/photo. Captions, model releases and identification of subjects required. Buys one-time rights.

Columns/Departments: Business Outlook (essay on current China economic situation), 1,100 words; Industry Spotlight (industry-specific spotlight-situation in China), 500 words; China Hand (experience-based advice on working in China), 750 words. Buys 12 mss/year. Send complete ms. Pays $25-50.

Fillers: Anecdotes, facts, newsbreaks. Buys 12/year. Length: 25-100 words. Pays $10-50.

COMMUNICATION BRIEFINGS, Encoders, Inc., Dept. WM, Suite 110, 700 Black Horse Pike, Blackwood NJ 08012-1455. (609)232-6380. Fax: (609)232-8229. Executive Editor: Frank Grazian. 15% freelance written. Prefers to work with published/established writers. Monthly newsletter covering business communication and business management. "Most readers are in middle and upper management. They comprise public relations professionals, editors of company publications, marketing and advertising managers, fund raisers, directors of associations and foundations, school and college administrators, human resources professionals, and other middle managers who want to communicate better on the job." Estab. 1980. Circ. 46,000. **Pays on acceptance.** Publishes ms an average of 3 months after acceptance. Byline given sometimes on Bonus Items and on other items if idea originates with the writer. Buys one-time rights. Submit seasonal material 2 months in advance. Accepts previously published submissions, "but must be rewritten to conform to our style." Reports in 1 month. Sample copy and writer's guidelines for #10 SAE and 2 first-class stamps.

Nonfiction: "Most articles we buy are of the 'how-to' type. They consist of practical ideas, techniques and advice that readers can use to improve business communication and management. Areas covered: writing, speaking, listening, employee communication, human relations, public relations, interpersonal communication, persuasion, conducting meetings, advertising, marketing, fund raising, telephone techniques, teleconferencing, selling, improving publications, handling conflicts, negotiating, etc. Because half of our subscribers are in the nonprofit sector, articles that appeal to both profit and nonprofit organizations are given top priority." *Short Items:* Articles consisting of one or two brief tips that can stand alone. Length: 40-70 words. *Articles:* A collection of tips or ideas that offer a solution to a communication or management problem or that show a better way to communicate or manage. Examples: "How to produce slogans that work," "The wrong way to criticize employees," "Mistakes to avoid when leading a group discussion," and "5 ways to overcome writer's block." Length: 125-150 words. *Bonus Items:* In-depth pieces that probe one area of communication or management and cover it as thoroughly as possible. Examples: "Producing successful special events," "How to evaluate your newsletter," and "How to write to be understood." Length: 1,300 words. Buys 30-50 mss/year. Pays $15-35 for 40- to 150-word pieces; Bonus Items, $200. Pays the expenses of writers on assignment.

Tips: "Our readers are looking for specific, practical ideas and tips that will help them communicate better both within their organizations and with outside publics. Most ideas are rejected because they are too general or too elementary for our audience. Our style is down-to-earth and terse. We pack a lot of useful information into short articles. Our readers are busy executives and managers who want information dispatched quickly and without embroidery. We omit anecdotes, lengthy quotes and long-winded exposition. The writer has a better chance of breaking in at our publication with short articles and fillers since we buy only six major features (bonus items) a year. We require queries on longer items and bonus items. Writers may submit short tips (40-70 words) without querying. The most frequent mistakes made by writers completing an article for us are failure to master the style of our publication and to understand our readers' needs."

CONVENE, Professional Convention Mgt. Assn., Suite 220, 100 Vestavia Office Park, Birmingham AL 35216. (205)823-7262. Editor: Peter Shure. Managing Editor: Amy Cates Lyle. 50-60% freelance written. Monthly magazine on convention and meeting management. "Covers primarily how-to of all aspects of meeting/convention planning and management." Estab. 1986. Circ. 35,000. **Pays on acceptance.** Publishes ms an average of 3 months after acceptance. Byline given. Offers 50% kill fee. Publication not copyrighted. Buys all rights. Editorial lead time 2 months. Submit seasonal material 4 months in advance. Accepts simultaneous and previously published submissions. Query for electronic submissions. Reports in 1 month. Sample copy for $1 and SAE with 4 first-class stamps.

Nonfiction: Book excerpts, essays, general interest, how-to, humor, interview/profile, opinion, personal experience, photo feature, technical, travel. Does not want to see anything product-related. Buys 25 mss/year. Send complete ms. Length: 1,000-1,500 words. Pays $200 minimum for assigned articles. Pays expenses of writers on assignment.

Photos: State availability of photos with submission. Reviews contact sheets, transparencies and prints. Offers no additional payment for photos accepted with ms. Identification of subjects required. Buys one-time rights.

Columns/Departments: Food & Beverage (for group functions), 750 words; Hotel Industry (for group functions), 750 words; Travel Industry (for group functions), 750 words. Buys 50 mss/year. Send complete ms. Pays $200-400.

Tips: "Acquire an understanding of the industry."

‡CONVENTION SOUTH, Covey Communications Corp., 2001 W. First St., P.O. Box 2267, Gulf Shores AL 36547-2267. (205)968-5300. Fax: (205)968-4532. Editor: J.Talty O'Connor. 50% freelance written. Trade journal on planning meetings and conventions in the South. Estab. 1983. Circ. 10,000. Pays on publication. Byline given. Buys first rights or second serial (reprint) rights. Submit seasonal/holiday material 2 months in advance. Accepts simultaneous and previously published submissions. Query for electronic submissions. Reports in 2 months on queries. Free sample copy.

Nonfiction: How-to (relative to meeting planning/travel), photo feature, travel. Buys 20 mss/year. Query. Length: 1,250-3,000 words. Pays $75-150. Pays in contributor copies or other premiums if arranged in advance. Sometime pays expenses of writers on assignment.

Photos: Send photos with submission. Reviews 5 × 7 prints. Offers no additional payment for photos accepted with ms. Captions and identification of subjects required. Buys one-time rights.

EARLY CHILDHOOD NEWS, Peter Li, Inc., 1100 Superior Ave., Cleveland OH 44114. (216)696-1777. Editor: Tom Kerr. 75% freelance written. Bimonthly trade journal on child care centers. "Our publication is a news and service magazine for owners, directors and administrators of child care centers serving children from

age 6 weeks to 2nd grade." Estab. 1988. Circ. 30,000. Pays on publication. Publishes ms an average of 3-4 months after acceptance. Copyright pending. Buys first rights. Submit seasonal/holiday material 5-6 months in advance. Query for electronic submissions. Sample copy for $4 and 9 × 12 SAE with 2 first-class stamps.
Nonfiction: How-to (how I solved a problem other center directors may face), interview/profile personal experience, business aspects of child care centers. "No articles directed at early childhood teachers or lesson plans." Buys 15 mss/year. Query with or without published clips or send complete ms. Length: 500-1,500 words. Pays $50-150.
Photos: Send photos with submission if available. Reviews 35mm and 4 × 5 transparencies and 5 × 7 prints. Captions, model releases and identification of subjects required. Buys one-time rights.
Fillers: Facts, newsbreaks. Length: 100-250 words. Pays $10-25.
Tips: "Send double-spaced typed manuscripts and pay attention to grammar and punctuation. Enclose SASE for reply. No scholarly pieces with footnotes and bibliography. No activities/lesson plans for use with kids. We need short, easy-to-read articles written in popular style that give child care center owners information they can use right away to make their centers better, more effective, more efficient, etc. Feature stories and fillers are most open to freelancers. Be specific and concrete; use examples. Tightly focused topics are better than general 'The Day Care Dilemma' types."

FINANCIAL EXECUTIVE, Financial Executives Institute, 10 Madison Ave., Morristown NJ 07962-1938. Fax: (201)267-4031. Editor: Robin Couch Cardillo. 2% freelance written. Bimonthly magazine for corporate financial management. "*Financial Executive* is published for senior financial executives of major corporations and explores corporate accounting and treasury related issues without being anti-business." Circ. 16,000. Pays on publication. Byline given. Buys all rights. Sample copy for $5 and 9 × 12 SAE with 6 first-class stamps. Writer's guidelines for #10 SASE.
Nonfiction: Interviews of senior financial executives involved in issues listed above. Also, pieces ghostwritten for financial executives. Query with published clips. Length: 1,500-2,500 words. Pays $500-1,000.
Tips: "The query approach is best. (Address correspondence to Robin Couch Cardillo.) We use business or financial articles that follow a *Wall Street Journal* approach—a fresh idea, with its significance (to financial executives), quotes, anecdotes and an interpretation or evaluation. Our content will follow developments in treasury management, information management, regulatory changes, tax legislation, Congressional hearings/legislation, business and financial reporting. There is also interest in employee benefits, international business and impact of technology. We have very high journalistic standards."

‡HR MAGAZINE, Society for Human Resource Management, 606 N. Washington St., Alexandria VA 22314. (703)548-3440. Editor: Ceel Pasternak. Monthly magazine covering human resource profession "with special focus on business news that affects the workplace including court decisions, legislative actions and government regulations." Estab. 1950. Circ. 56,000. **Pays on acceptance.** Publishes ms an average of 6 months after acceptance. Byline given. Offers $200 kill fee. Buys first North American, first, one-time, all or world rights or makes work-for-hire assignments. Query for electronic submissions. Prefers IBM compatible 3.5" or 5.25" disk. Sample copy for $7.50. Writer's guidelines free on request.
Nonfiction: Interview/profile, new product, opinion, personal experience, technical. Buys 6 mss/year. Query. Length: 700-2,200 words. Pays $200 minimum. Pays expenses of writers on assignment.
Photos: State availability of photos with submission. Reviews contact sheets. Offers no additional payment for photos accepted with ms. Model releases and identification of subjects required.

‡HR NEWS, Society for Human Resource Management, 606 N. Washington St., Alexandria VA 22314. (703)548-3440. Editor: Ceel Pasternak. Monthly tabloid covering human resource profession "with special focus on business news that affects the workplace including court decisions, legislative actions and government regulations." Estab. 1982. Circ. 52,000. Pays on publication. Publishes ms an average of 1 month after acceptance. Byline given. Buys first or one-time rights or makes work-for-hire assignments. Editorial lead time 1-2 months. Query for electronic submissions. Prefers most DOS or Windows software or ASCII. Reports in 1 month on queries. Sample copy and writer's guidelines free.
Nonfiction: Interview/profile, personal experience. Buys 6 mss/year. Query with published clips. Length: 300-1,000 words. Pays 40¢/word. Sometimes pays expenses of writers on assignment.
Photos: State availability of photos with submission. Reviews contact sheets, any prints. Negotiates payment individually. Captions and identification of subjects required. Buys one-time rights.
Tips: "Experienced business/news writers should send some clips and story ideas for our file of potential writers in various regions and for various subjects. Local/state business news or government actions affecting HR management of potentially national interest is an area open to freelancers."

MAY TRENDS, George S. May International Company, 303 S. Northwest Hwy., Park Ridge IL 60068-4255. (708)825-8806. Fax: (708)825-7937. Editor: John E. McArdle. 20% freelance written. Works with a small number of new/unpublished writers each year. Triannual free magazine for owners and managers of small and medium-sized businesses, hospitals and nursing homes, trade associations, Better Business Bureaus, educational institutions and newspapers. Estab. 1966. Circ. 30,000. Buys all rights. Byline given. Buys 10-15 mss/year. Pays on publication. Publishes ms an average of 6 months after acceptance. Returns rejected material immediately. Reports in 2 months. Sample copy for 9×12 SAE with 4 first-class stamps.

Nonfiction: "We prefer articles dealing with how to solve problems of specific industries (manufacturers, wholesalers, retailers, service businesses, small hospitals and nursing homes) where contact has been made with key executives whose comments regarding their problems may be quoted. We want problem solving articles, *not* success stories that laud an individual company. We like articles that give the business manager concrete suggestions on how to deal with specific problems—i.e., 'five steps to solve . . .,' 'six key questions to ask when . . .,' and 'four tell-tale signs indicating . . .' Focus is on marketing, economic and technological trends that have an impact on medium- and small-sized businesses, not on the 'giants'; automobile dealers coping with existing dull markets; and contractors solving cost-inventory problems. Will consider material on successful business operations and merchandising techniques." Query or submit complete ms. Length: 2,000-3,000 words. Pays $150-250.

Tips: Query letter should tell "type of business and problems the article will deal with. We specialize in the problems of small (20-100 employees, $800,000-10,000,000 volume) businesses (manufacturing, wholesale, retail and service), plus medium and small healthcare facilities. We are now including nationally known writers in each issue—writers like the Vice Chairman of the Federal Reserve Bank, the US Secretary of the Treasury; names like George Bush and Malcolm Baldridge; titles like the Chairman of the Joint Committee on Accreditation of Hospitals; and Canadian Minister of Export. This places extra pressure on freelance writers to submit very good articles. Frequent mistakes: 1) writing for big business, rather than small, and 2) using language that is too academic."

PARTY & PAPER RETAILER, 4Ward Corp, 70 New Canaan Ave., Norwalk CT 06850. (203)845-8020. Editor: Trisha McMahon Drain. 90% freelance written. Monthly magazine for party goods and fine stationery industry. Covers "every aspect of how to do business better for owners of party and fine stationery shops. Tips and how-tos on display, marketing, success stories, advertising, operating costs, etc." Estab. 1985. Circ. 25,000. Pays on publication. Offers 10% kill fee. Buys first North American serial rights. Editorial lead time 6 months. Submit seasonal material 6 months in advance. Accepts previously published materials. Send tearsheet or photocopy of article and information about when and where the article previously appeared. Query for electronic submissions. Reports in 2 months. Sample copy for $4.50

Nonfiction: Book excerpts, how-to (retailing related). No articles written in the first person. Buys 100 mss/ year. Query with published clips. Length: 800-1,800 words. Pay "depends on topic, word count expertise, deadline." Pays telephone expenses of writers on assignment.

Photos: State availability of photos with submission. Reviews transparencies. Negotiates payment individually. Captions and identification of subjects required. Buys one-time rights.

Columns/Departments: Shop Talk (successful party/stationery store profile), 1,800 words; Storekeeping (selling, employees, market, running store), 800 words; Cash Flow (anything finance related), 800 words. Buys 30 mss/year. Query with published clips. Pay varies.

RECORDS MANAGEMENT QUARTERLY, Association of Records Managers and Administrators, Inc., P.O. Box 4580, Silver Spring MD 20914-4580. Editor: Ira A. Penn, CRM, CSP. 10% freelance written. Eager to work with new/unpublished writers. Quarterly professional journal covering records and information management. Estab. 1967. Circ. 12,000. Pays on publication. Publishes ms an average of 6 months after acceptance. Byline given. Buys all rights. Accepts simultaneous submissions. Reports in 1 month on mss. *Writer's Market* recommends allowing 2 months for reply. Sample copy for $14. Free writer's guidelines.

Nonfiction: Professional articles covering theory, case studies, surveys, etc., on any aspect of records and information management. Buys 20-24 mss/year. Send complete ms. Length: 2,500 words minimum. Pays $50-200 "stipend"; no contract.

Photos: Send photos with ms. Offers no additional payment for photos accepted with ms. Prefers b&w prints. Captions required.

Tips: "A writer *must* know our magazine. Most work is written by practitioners in the field. We use very little freelance writing, but we have had some and it's been good. A writer must have detailed knowledge of the subject he/she is writing about. Superficiality is not acceptable."

SECURITY DEALER, PTN Publishing Co., 445 Broad Hollow Rd., Melville NY 11747. (516)845-2700. Fax: (516)845-7109. Editor: Susan A. Brady. 25% freelance written. Monthly magazine for electronic alarm dealers, burglary and fire installers, with technical, business, sales and marketing information. Circ. 25,000. Pays 3 weeks after publication. Publishes ms an average of 4 months after acceptance. Byline sometimes given. Buys first North American serial rights. Accepts simultaneous and previously published submissions. Prefer computer disk to accompany ms.

Nonfiction: How-to, interview/profile, technical. No consumer pieces. Query or send complete ms. Length: 1,000-3,000 words. Pays $300 for assigned articles; pays $100-200 for unsolicited articles. Sometimes pays the expenses of writers on assignment.

Photos: State availability of photos with submission. Reviews contact sheets and transparencies. Offers $25 additional payment for photos accepted with ms. Captions and identification of subjects required.

Columns/Departments: Closed Circuit TV, and Access Control (both on application, installation, new products), 500-1,000 words. Buys 25 mss/year. Query. Pays $100-150.

Tips: "The areas of our publication most open to freelancers are technical innovations, trends in the alarm industry and crime patterns as related to the business as well as business finance and management pieces."

SELF-EMPLOYED AMERICA, The News Publication for Your Small Business, National Association for the Self-Employed, P.O. Box 612067, DFW Airport TX 75261-2067. Editor: Karen C. Jones. 90% freelance written. Prefers to work with published/established writers. Bimonthly tabloid for association members. "Keep in mind that the self-employed don't need business news tailored to meet needs of what government considers 'small business'. We reach those with few, if any, employees. Our readers are independent business owners going it alone—and in need of information." Estab. 1981. Circ. 300,000. Pays on publication. Byline given. Offers 10% kill fee. Buys full rights only; works primarily from query letters. Accepts previously published articles. Send photocopy of article and information about when and where the article previously appeared. For reprints, pays 50% of the amount paid for an original article. Submit seasonal material 6 months in advance. Query for electronic submissions. Reports in 2 months on queries; 6 months on mss. Sample copy and writer's guidelines for 9×12 SAE with 3 first-class stamps.

Nonfiction: Book excerpts, how-to, travel (how to save money on business travel or how to combine business and personal travel). "No big-business or how-to-claw-your-way-to-the-top stuff. Generally my readers are happy as small businesses. No legislative stories please. Staff members handle this." Buys 15-20 mss/year. Query with published clips. First article accepted many times on spec only. Length: 1500 words. Pays $500-700 for assigned articles; $250-350 for unsolicited articles. Sometimes pays expenses of writers on assignment.

Photos: State availability of photos with submission. Reviews 3×5 prints. Offers $25-50/photo. Captions, model releases and identification required. Buys one-time rights.

Columns/Departments: Tax Tips. Send complete ms. Length: 200-300 words. Pays $50-100. Touch of Success profiles. Pays $70 for 125 words. Tight writing, concise.

Tips: "Keep in mind reader demographics show 300,000 people with nothing in common except the desire to be independent. Be inventive with your subject matter proposed. We've covered the basics of small business already. Must quote knowledgable sources in copy—these are not opinion pieces."

SIGN BUSINESS, National Business Media Inc., 1008 Depot Hill Rd., P.O. Box 1416, Broomfield CO 80038-1416. (303)469-0424. Fax: (303)469-5730. Editor: Terence Wike. 25% freelance written. Trade journal on the sign industry—electric, commercial, architectural. "This is business-to-business writing; we try to produce news you can use, rather than human interest." Estab. 1985. Circ. 20,500. Pays on publication. Publishes ms an average of 2 months after acceptance. Byline given. Buys first North American serial rights. Accepts previously published articles. Send photocopy of article. For reprints pays 50% of the amount paid for an original article. Submit seasonal material 4 months in advance. Query for electronic submissions. Reports in 1 month. Sample copy for $5. Writer's guidelines for #10 SASE.

Nonfiction: How-to (sign-painting techniques, new uses for computer cutters, plotters lettering styles); interview/profile (sign company execs, shop owners with *unusual* work etc.), other (news on sign codes, legislation, unusual signs, etc.). "No humor, human interest, generic articles with sign replacing another industry, no first-person writing, no profiles of a sign shop just because someone nice runs the business." Buys 20 mss/year. Query with published clips. Length: 500-3,000 words. Pays $85-150.

Photos: Send photos with submission. Reviews 3×5 transparencies and 3×5 prints. Offers $5-10/photo. Identification of subjects required. Buys one-time rights and/or reprint rights.

Tips: "Find a sign shop, or sign company, and take some time to learn the business. The sign business is easily a $5 billion-plus industry every year in the US, and we treat it like a business, not a hobby. If you see a sign that stops you in your tracks, find out who made it; if it's a one-in-10,000 kind of sign, chances are good we'll want to know more. Writing should be factual and avoid polysyllabic words that waste a reader's time. I'll work with writers who may not know the trade, but can write well."

‡THE SMALL BUSINESS GAZETTE, America's Small Business Newspaper, Bovan Associates, 3666 Richmond Ave., Staten Island NY 10312. (718)967-3064. Managing Editor: Jim Donovan. 80% freelance written. Monthly newspaper covering small business. "Easy to implement, useful techniques and how to articles pertaining to running a successful small business." Estab. 1993. Circ. 50,000. Pays on publication. Publishes ms an average of 2 months after acceptance. Byline given. Buys first North American serial, one-time or simultaneous rights. Editorial lead time 2 months. Submit seasonal material 4 months in advance.Accepts simultaneous and previously published submissions. Reports in 2 months on queries. Sample copy for $2. Writer's guidelines free on request.

Nonfiction: Book excerpts, how-to (business), humor, inspirational, interview/profile, new product, photo feature. Length: 700-1,200 words. Pays $50 and up. Sometimes pays expenses of writers on assignment.

Photos: State availability of photos with submission. Reviews 4×5 prints. Negotiates payment individually. Captions, model releases and identification of subjects required. Buys one-time rights.

Columns/Departments: Computers (small business computing), 1,000 words; Sales/Mktg. (selling & marketing your business), 1,000 words. Buys 60 mss/year. Query with published clips. Pays $50.
Tips: "Submission on Compuserve—71141, 1331 or America Online—AOL*JimD34* preferred. Reader should learn something that will help them grow their business. No fluff!"

‡**SMALL BUSINESS NEWS, Our Business Is Small Business,** #315, 20800 Center Ridge Rd., Cleveland OH 44116. (216)331-6397. Editor: Jeff Fruit. Contact: Robin S. Martin. Monthly tabloid covering small business (local, state and national). "We provide small-business owners and managers with the information they need to gain a competitive edge. We believe small-business issues go largely unreported, and we seek to give this growing sector of the business community a voice." Estab. 1989. Pays on publication. Publishes ms an average of 2 months after acceptance. Byline sometimes given. Buys first rights. Editorial lead time 3-4 months. Submit seasonal material 3 months in advance. Accepts simultaneous submissions. Sample copy free on request.
Nonfiction: How-to (business topics), interview/profile, new product (biz related), opinion, technical (biz related). Buys 12-24 mss/year. Query with published clips. Length: 450-1,000 words. Pays $150. Sometimes pays expenses of writers on assignment.
Photos: State availability of photos with submission. Reviews contact sheets. Negotiates payment individually. Identification of subjects required. Buys one-time rights.
Columns/Departments: Government (pro small business), 500 words; Management (pro small business), 500 words. Query with published clips. Pays $150-350.
Tips: "Gear copy toward busy, no-nonsense small-business decision makers. Paper is very aggressive—all information must be innovative or analytical."

‡**VIDEO BUSINESS,** 825 Seventh Ave., New York NY 10019-6001. Fax: (212)887-8484. 35% freelance written. Monthly magazine on video software retailing. "*Video Business* covers trends in marketing and videocassette programming for 40,000 retailers of all sizes. All articles should be written with the intent of providing information that a retailer can apply to his/her business immediately." Estab. 1981. Byline given. Buys first rights. Submit seasonal/holiday material 2 months in advance. Query for electronic submissions. Reports in 2 weeks. Free sample copy.
Nonfiction: Historical/nostalgic (movie genres), interview/profile, new product, technical. Query with published clips. Pays 25-35¢/word. Sometimes pays the expenses of writers on assignment.
Photos: State availability of photos with submission. Reviews negatives. Offers additional payment for photos accepted with ms. Buys one-time rights.

WOMEN IN BUSINESS, The ABWA Co., Inc. 9100 Ward Parkway, Kansas City MO 64114-0728. (816)361-6621. Editor: Wendy Myers. 10% freelance written. Bimonthly magazine for members of the American Business Women's Association. Estab. 1949. Circ. 90,000. **Pays on acceptance.** Publishes ms an average of 2 months after acceptance. Byline given. Kill fee negotiable. Buys all rights. Submit seasonal material 4 months in advance. Reports in 1 week. *Writer's Market* recommends allowing 1 month for reply. Sample copy for 9 × 12 SAE with 4 first-class stamps. Writer's guidelines for #10 SASE.
Nonfiction: Buys 10 mss/year. Query with published clips or send complete ms. Length: 1,000-1,500 words. Pays 15¢/word.
Photos: State availability of photos with submission. Offers no additional payment for photos accepted with ms. Identification of subjects required.
Columns/Departments: Dawn J. Grubb, column/department editor. Money Wise (personal finance for women), 1,000 words; Health Scope (health topics for women); Career Smarts (career advice); and It's Your Business (for women small-business owners). Buys 10 mss/year. Query with published clips or send complete ms. Length: 1,000 words. Pays 15¢/word.

Church Administration and Ministry

Publications in this section are written for clergy members, church leaders and teachers. Magazines for lay members and the general public are listed in the Consumer Religious section.

THE CHRISTIAN MINISTRY, The Christian Century Foundation, Suite 1405, 407 S. Dearborn St., Chicago IL 60605-1150. (312)427-5380. Editor: James M. Wall. Managing Editor: Victoria Rebeck. 80% freelance written. Bimonthly magazine for parish clergy. "Most of our articles are written by parish clergy, describing parish situations. Our audience is comprised of mainline church ministers who are looking for practical ideas and insights concerning the ministry." Estab. 1969. Circ. 9,000. Pays on publication. Publishes ms an average of 6 months after acceptance. Byline given. Offers $20 kill fee. Buys all rights. Submit seasonal material 4 months in advance. Accepts simultaneous submissions. Reports in 2 months. Sample copy for $2.50 and 9 × 12 SAE with 4 first-class stamps. Writer's guidelines for #10 SASE.

Nonfiction: Book excerpts (forthcoming books), essays, how-to (parish subjects), religious, preached sermons. No articles with footnotes or inspirational poetry. Buys 60 mss/year. Send complete ms. Length: 1,000-3,000 words. Pays $50-100 for assigned articles; $40-75 for unsolicited articles. Pays in contributor copies for book reviews.

Photos: State availability of photos with submission. Reviews 8×10 b&w prints. Offers $20-50/photo. Model releases preferred. Buys one-time rights.

Columns/Departments: Reflection on ministry (discusses an instance in which the author reflects on his or her practice of ministry), 2,500 words; From the Pulpit (preached sermons), 2,500 words. Buys 18 mss/year. Send complete ms. Length: 2,000-2,500 words. Pays $50-75.

Fillers: Newsbreaks and short humor. Buys 30/year. Length: 150-300 words. Pays $10.

Tips: "Send us finished manuscripts—not rough drafts. Freelancers have the best chance selling us articles on spec about issues affecting parish clergy."

CHURCH EDUCATOR, Creative Resources for Christian Educators, Educational Ministries, Inc., 165 Plaza Dr., Prescott AZ 86303-5549. (602)771-8601. Fax: (602)771-8621. Editor: Robert G. Davidson. Managing Editor: Linda S. Davidson. 80% freelance written. Works with a small number of new/unpublished writers each year. Monthly magazine covering religious education. Estab. 1976. Circ. 7,000. Pays on publication. Publishes ms an average of 4 months after acceptance. Byline given. Buys first rights. Submit seasonal material 4 months in advance. Accepts simultaneous submissions. Publishes reprints of previously published articles. Send tearsheet, including information about when and where the article previously appeared. Reports in 3 months. Sample copy for 9×12 SAE with 3 first-class stamps. Free writer's guidelines.

Nonfiction: General interest, how-to (crafts for church school) programs for church school, adult education study classes. "Our editorial lines are very middle of the road—mainline Protestant. We are not seeking extreme conservative or liberal theology pieces." No testimonials. Buys 100 mss/year. Send complete ms. Length: 100-2,000 words. Pays 3¢/word.

Fiction: Mainstream, religious and slice-of-life vignettes. Buys 15 mss/year. Send complete ms. Length: 100-2,000 words. Pays 3¢/word.

Tips: "Send the complete manuscript with a cover letter which gives a concise summary. We are looking for how-to articles related to Christian education. That would include most any program held in a church. Be straightforward and to the point—not flowery and wordy. We're especially interested in youth programs. Give steps needed to carry out the program: preparation, starting the program, continuing the program, conclusion. List several discussion questions for each program."

LEADER, Board of Christian Education of the Church of God, P.O. Box 2458, Anderson IN 46018-2458. (317)642-0257. Fax: (317)642-0255 ext. 299. Editor: Joseph L. Cookston. 70% freelance written. Works with a small number of new/unpublished writers each year. Bimonthly magazine covering local Sunday school teaching and administrating, youth and children's work, worship, family life and other local church ministries. Estab. 1923. Circ. 4,000. Pays on publication. Publishes ms an average of 10 months after acceptance. Byline given. Buys first rights and second serial (reprint) rights. Submit seasonal material 6 months in advance. Reports in 4 months. Sample copy and writer's guidelines for 9×12 SAE with 3 first-class stamps.

Nonfiction: How-to, inspirational, personal experience, guidance for carrying out programs for special days, continuing ministries, short ministry ideas. No articles that are not specifically related to local church leadership. Buys 60 mss/year. Send complete ms, brief description of present interest in writing for church leaders, background and experience. Length: 300-800 words. Pays $10-30.

Tips: "How-to articles related to teaching, program development and personal teacher enrichment or growth, and program and teaching ideas are most open to freelancers."

LEADERSHIP, A Practical Journal for Church Leaders, Christianity Today, Inc., 465 Gundersen Dr., Carol Stream IL 60188. (708)260-6200. Editor: Kevin A. Miller. 75% freelance written. Works with a small number of new/unpublished writers each year. Quarterly magazine covering church leadership. Writers must have a "knowledge of and sympathy for the unique expectations placed on pastors and local church leaders. Each article must support points by illustrating from real life experiences in local churches." Estab. 1980. Circ. 90,000. **Pays on acceptance.** Publishes ms an average of 6 months after acceptance. Byline given. Buys first North American serial rights. Submit seasonal material 6 months in advance. Accepts previously published submissions. Reports in 6 weeks on queries; 2 months on mss. Sample copy for $3. Free writer's guidelines.

Nonfiction: How-to, humor, personal experience. "No articles from writers who have never read our journal." Buys 50 mss/year. Send complete ms. Length: 100-5,000 words. Pays $30-300. Sometimes pays the expenses of writers on assignment.

Photos: State availability of photos with submission. Offers no additional payment for photos accepted with ms. Identification of subjects required. Buys one-time rights.

Columns/Departments: People in Print (book reviews with interview of author), 1,500 words. To Illustrate (short stories or analogies that illustrate a biblical principle), 100 words. Buys 25 mss/year. Send complete ms. Pays $25-100.

PASTORAL LIFE, Society of St. Paul, P.O. Box 595, Route 224, Canfield OH 44406-0595. Fax: (216)533-1076. Editor: Anthony Chenevey, SSP. 66% freelance written. Works with new/unpublished writers. Monthly magazine emphasizing priests and those interested in pastoral ministry. Estab. 1953. Circ. 2,800. Buys first rights only. Byline given. Pays on publication. Publishes ms an average of 6 months after acceptance. Query with outline before submitting ms. "New contributors are expected to include, in addition, a few lines of personal data that indicate academic and professional background." Reports in 1 month. Sample copy and writer's guidelines for 6×9 SAE with 4 first-class stamps.
Nonfiction: "*Pastoral Life* is a professional review, principally designed to focus attention on current problems, needs, issues and important activities related to all phases of pastoral work and life." Buys 30 unsolicited mss/year. Length: 2,000-3,400 words. Pays 4¢/word minimum.

THE PREACHER'S MAGAZINE, Nazarene Publishing House, E. 10814 Broadway, Spokane WA 99206-5003. Editor: Randal E. Denny. Assistant Editor: Cindy Osso. 15% freelance written. Works with a small number of new/unpublished writers each year. Quarterly magazine of seasonal/miscellaneous articles. "A resource for ministers; Wesleyan-Arminian in theological persuasion." Circ. 18,000. Pays on publication. Publishes ms an average of 9 months after acceptance. Byline given. Buys first serial, second serial (reprint) and simultaneous rights. Accepts previously published articles. Send photocopy of article or typed ms with rights for sale noted and information about when and where the article previously appeared. For reprints, pays 100% of the amount paid for an original article (3½¢/word). Submit seasonal material 9 months in advance. Writer's guidelines for #10 SASE.
Nonfiction: How-to, humor, inspirational, opinion, personal experience, all relating to aspects of ministry. No articles that present problems without also presenting answers to them; things not relating to pastoral ministry. Buys 48 mss/year. Send complete ms. Length: 700-2,500 words. Pays 3½¢/word.
Photos: Send photos with ms. Reviews 35mm transparencies and b&w prints. Model release and identification of subjects required. Buys one-time rights.
Columns/Departments: Stories Preachers Tell Each Other (humorous).
Fiction: Publishes novel excerpts.
Fillers: Anecdotes, short humor. Buys 10/year. Length: 400 words maximum. Pays 3½¢/word.
Tips: "Writers for the *Preacher's Magazine* should have insight into the pastoral ministry, or expertise in a specialized area of ministry. Our magazine is a highly specialized publication aimed at the minister. Our goal is to assist, by both scholarly and practical articles, the modern-day minister in applying Biblical theological truths."

PREACHING, Preaching Resources, Inc., Dept. WM, P.O. Box 7728, Louisville KY 40257. (502)899-3119. Editor: Dr. Michael Duduit. 75% freelance written. Bimonthly magazine for the preaching ministry. "All articles must deal with preaching. Most articles used offer practical assistance in preparation and delivery of sermons, generally from an evangelical stance." Estab. 1985. Circ. 10,000. Pays on publication. Publishes ms an average of 1 year after acceptance. Byline given. Buys first rights. Submit seasonal material 1 year in advance. Query for electronic submissions. Reports in 4 months. Sample copy for $3.50. Writer's guidelines for SASE.
Nonfiction: How-to (preparation and delivery of sermon, worship leadership). Special issues: Personal Computing in Preaching (September-October); materials/resources to assist in preparation of seasonal preaching (November-December, March-April). Buys 18-24 mss/year. Query. Length: 1,000-2,000 words. Pays $35-50.
Photos: Send photos with submission. Reviews prints. Offers no additional payment for photos accepted with ms. Captions, model releases and identification of subjects required. Buys one-time rights.
Fillers: Buys 10-15/year. "Buys only completed cartoons." Art must be related to preaching. Pays $25.
Tips: "Most desirable are practical, 'how-to' articles on preparation and delivery of sermons."

THE PRIEST, Our Sunday Visitor, Inc., 200 Noll Plaza, Huntington IN 46750-4304. (219)356-8400. Fax: (219)356-8472. Editor: Father Owen F. Campion. Associate Editor: Robert A. Willems. 80% freelance written. Monthly magazine for the priesthood. "We run articles that will aid priests in their day-to-day ministry. Includes items on spirituality, counseling, administration, theology, personalities, the saints, etc." **Pays on acceptance.** Byline given. Publication not copyrighted. Buys first North American serial rights. Editorial lead time 3 months. Submit seasonal material at least 4 months in advance. Query for electronic submissions. Reports in 2 weeks on queries; 1 month on mss. Sample copy and writer's guidelines free on request.
Nonfiction: Essays, historical/nostalgic, humor, inspirational, interview/profile, opinion, personal experience, photo feature, religious. Buys 96 mss/year. Send complete ms. Length: 1,500-5,000 words. Pays $300 minimum for assigned articles; $50 minimum for unsolicited articles.
Photos: Send photos with submission. Reviews transparencies and prints. Negotiates payment individually. Captions and identification of subjects required. Buys one-time rights.
Columns/Departments: Viewpoint (whatever applies to priests and the Church), 1,000 words. Buys 36 mss/year. Send complete ms. Pays $50-100.
Tips: "Say what you have to say in an interesting and informative manner and stop. Freelancers are most often published in 'Viewpoints.' Please do not stray from the magisterium of the Catholic Church."

YOUR CHURCH, Helping You With the Business of Ministry, Christianity Today, Inc., 465 Gundersen Dr., Carol Stream IL 60188. (708)260-6200. Editor: James Berkley. 70% freelance written. Bimonthly magazine for the business of today's church. "Articles pertain to the business aspects of ministry pastors are called upon to perform: administration, purchasing, management, technology, building, etc." Estab. 1955. Circ. 200,000. **Pays on acceptance.** Publishes ms an average of 4 months after acceptance. Byline given. Buys one-time rights. Submit seasonal material 5 months in advance. Accepts simultaneous and previously published submissions. Send photocopy of article and information about when and where the article previously appeared. Reports in 1 month on queries; 2 months on mss. Sample copy and writer's guidelines for 9×12 SAE with 5 first-class stamps.
Nonfiction: How-to, new product, technical. Buys 12 mss/year. Send complete ms. Length: 900-1,500 words. Pays about 10¢/word. Pays 30% of amount paid for an original article.
Photos: State availability of photos with submission. Reviews 4×5 transparencies and 5×7 or 8×10 prints. Offers no additional payment for photos accepted with ms. Captions, model releases and identification of subjects required. Buys one-time rights.
Tips: "The editorial is generally geared toward brief and helpful articles dealing with some form of church business. Concise, bulletted points from experts in the field are typical for our articles."

Clothing

APPAREL INDUSTRY MAGAZINE, Shore Communications, Dept. WM, Suite 200, 6255 Barfield Rd., Atlanta GA 30328-4300. Fax: (404)252-8831. Editor: Susan Hasty. Managing Editor: Colleen Moynahan. 30% freelance written. Monthly magazine for executive management in apparel companies with interests in new developments in apparel manufacturing, equipment, distribution and management. Estab. 1946. Circ. 18,700. Pays on publication. Publishes ms an average of 4 months after acceptance. Byline given. Buys first serial rights. Query for electronic submissions. Reports in 1 month. Sample copy for $3. Writer's guidelines for #10 SASE.
• This magazine is only interested in freelance work from those with experience covering the apparel manufacturing industry.
Nonfiction: Articles dealing with equipment, manufacturing techniques, quality control, etc., related to the industry. "Use concise, precise language that is easy to read and understand. In other words, because the subjects are often technical, keep the language comprehensible. Material must be precisely related to the apparel industry. We are not a retail or fashion magazine." Buys 20 mss/year. Query. Length: 3,000 words maximum. Payment negotiated as part of assignment. Sometimes pays expenses of writers on assignment.
Photos: Pays $5/photo published with ms.
Tips: "Frequently articles are too general due to lack of industry-specific knowledge by the writer."

ATI, America's Textiles International, Billian Publishing Co., 2100 Powers Ferry Rd., Atlanta GA 30339. (404)955-5656. Fax: (404)952-0669. Editor: Monte G. Plott. Associate Editor: Rolf Viertel. 10% freelance written. Monthly magazine covering "the business of textile, apparel and fiber industries with considerable technical focus on products and processes. No puff pieces pushing a particular product." Estab. 1887. Pays on publication. Byline sometimes given. Buys first North American serial rights. Query for electronic submissions.
Nonfiction: Technical, business. "No PR, just straight technical reports." Buys 10 mss/year. Query. Length: 500 words minimum. Pays $100/published page. Sometimes pays expenses of writers on assignment.
Photos: Send photos with submission. Reviews prints. Offers no additional payment for photos accepted with ms. Captions required. Buys one-time rights.

BOBBIN, Bobbin Blenheim Media, 1110 Shop Rd., P.O. Box 1986, Columbia SC 29202-1986. (803)771-7500. Fax: (803)799-1461. Editor-in-Chief: Susan Black. 25% freelance written. Monthly magazine for CEO's and top management in apparel and sewn products manufacturing companies. Circ. 9,788. Pays on publication. Byline given. Buys all rights. Reports in 6 weeks. Free sample copy and writer's guidelines.
Columns/Departments: Trade View, R&D, Network News, Partnerships, Personnel Management, Labor Forum, NON-Apparel Highlights, Fabric Notables.
Tips: "Articles should be written in a style appealing to busy top managers and should in some way foster thought or new ideas, or present solutions/alternatives to common industry problems/concerns. CEOs are most interested in quick read pieces that are also informative and substantive. Articles should not be based on opinions but should be developed through interviews with industry manufacturers, retailers or other experts, etc. Sidebars may be included to expand upon certain aspects within the article. If available, illustrations, graphs/charts, or photographs should accompany the article."

‡IMPRINTING BUSINESS, WFC, Inc., (formerly T-Shirt Retailer and Screen Printer), 3000 Hadley Rd., S. Plainfield NJ 07080. (908)769-1160. Fax: (908)769-1171. Editor: Bruce Sachenski. 10% freelance written. A monthly magazine for persons in imprinted garment industry and screen printing. Circ. 27,000. Pays on publication. Publishes ms an average of 3 months after acceptance. Byline given. Buys one-time rights. Submit

seasonal/holiday material 3 months in advance. Accepts photocopied and previously published submissions. Reports in 1 month. Sample copy for $7.
Nonfiction: How-to, new product, photo feature, technical, business. Buys 6 mss/year. Send complete ms. Length: 1,500-3,500 words. Pays $200-500 for assigned articles.
Photos: Send photos with submission. Reviews contact sheets. Offers no additional payment for photos accepted with ms. Identification of subjects required.
Columns/Departments: Query. Length: 1,000-2,000 words. Pays $50-150.
Tips: "We need general business stories, advertising, store management, etc."

‡**TEXTILE WORLD**, Suite 420, 4170 Ashford-Dunwoody Rd. NE, Atlanta GA 30319. Fax: (404)252-6150. Editor: McAllister Isaacs III. Monthly. Estab. 1868. **Pays on acceptance.** Buys all rights. Reports in 2 months.
Nonfiction: Uses articles covering textile management methods, manufacturing and marketing techniques, new equipment, details about new and modernized mills, etc., but avoids elementary, historical or generally well-known material.
Photos: Photos purchased with accompanying ms with no additional payment, or purchased on assignment.

Coin-Operated Machines

AMERICAN COIN-OP, 500 N. Dearborn St., Chicago IL 60610-9988. (312)337-7700. Fax: (312)337-8654. Editor: Laurance Cohen. 30% freelance written. Monthly magazine for owners of coin-operated laundry and dry cleaning stores. Estab. 1960. Circ. 20,100. Rights purchased vary with author and material, but are exclusive to the field. Pays 2 weeks prior to publication. Publishes ms an average of 2 months after acceptance. Byline given. Reports as soon as possible; usually in 2 weeks. Free sample copy.
Nonfiction: "We emphasize store operation and use features on industry topics: utility use and conservation, maintenance, store management, customer service and advertising. A case study should emphasize how the store operator accomplished whatever he did — in a way that the reader can apply to his own operation. Manuscript should have a no-nonsense, business-like approach." Uses informational, how-to, interview, profile, think pieces and successful business operations articles. Length: 500-3,000 words. Pays 8¢/word minimum.
Photos: Pays $8 minimum for 5 × 7 b&w glossy photos purchased with mss. (Contact sheets with negatives preferred.)
Fillers: Newsbreaks, clippings. Pays $10 minimum.
Tips: "Query about subjects of current interest. Be observant of coin-operated laundries — how they are designed and equipped, how they serve customers and how (if) they advertise and promote their services. Most general articles are turned down because they are not aimed well enough at our audience. Most case histories are turned down because they lack practical purpose (nothing new or worth reporting). A frequent mistake is failure to follow up on an interesting point made by the interviewee — probably due to lack of knowledge about the industry."

PLAY METER MAGAZINE, Skybird Publishing Co., Inc., P.O. Box 24970, New Orleans LA 70184-9988. (504)488-7003. Fax: (504)488-7083. Publisher: Carol Lally. Editor: Valerie Cognevich. 25% freelance written. "We will work with new writers who are familiar with the amusement industry." Monthly trade magazine for owners/operators of coin-operated amusement machine companies, e.g., pinball machines, video games, arcade pieces, jukeboxes, etc. Estab. 1974. Circ. 6,000. Pays on publication. Publishes ms an average of 2 months after acceptance. Byline given. Buys all rights. Submit seasonal material 2 months in advance. Accepts previously published submissions. Reports in 2 months on queries. Sample copy for $5 and 10 × 12 SAE with 10 first-class stamps. Free writer's guidelines.
Nonfiction: How-to (get better locations for machines, promote tournaments, evaluate profitability of route, etc.); interview (with industry leaders); new product. "Our readers want to read about how they can make more money from their machines, how they can get better tax breaks, commissions, etc. Also no stories about *playing* pinball or video games. Also, submissions on video-game technology advances; technical pieces on troubleshooting videos, pinballs and novelty machines (all coin-operated); trade-show coverage (query); submissions on the pay-telephone industry. Our readers don't play the games per se; they buy the machines and make money from them." Buys 48 mss/year. Query or submit complete ms. Length: 250-3,000 words. Pays $30-215. Sometimes pays expenses of writers on assignment.
Photos: "The photography should have news value. We don't want 'stand 'em up-shoot 'em down' group shots." Pays $15 minimum for 5 × 7 or 8 × 10 b&w prints. Captions preferred. Buys all rights. Art returned on request.
Tips: "We need feature articles more than small news items or featurettes. Query first. We're interested in writers who either have a few years of reporting/feature-writing experience or who know the coin-operated amusement industry well but are relatively inexperienced writers."

VENDING TIMES, 545 Eighth Ave., New York NY 10018. Fax: (212)564-0196. Editor: Arthur E. Yohalem. Monthly magazine for operators of vending machines. Estab. 1960. Circ. 15,450. Pays on publication. Buys all rights. "We will discuss in detail the story requirements with the writer." Sample copy for $4.

Nonfiction: Feature articles and news stories about vending operations; practical and important aspects of the business. "We are always willing to pay for good material." Query.

Confectionery and Snack Foods

These publications focus on the bakery, snack and candy industries. Journals for grocers, wholesalers and other food industry personnel are listed in Groceries and Food Products.

CANDY INDUSTRY, Advanstar Communications, Inc., Dept. WM, 7500 Old Oak Blvd., Cleveland OH 44130. (216)891-2612. Fax: (216)891-2733. Editor: Susan Tiffany. 5% freelance written. Prefers to work with published/established writers. Monthly magazine for confectionery manufacturers. Publishes ms an average of 4 months after acceptance. Buys all rights. Reports in 1 month. Writer's guidelines for #10 SASE.

Nonfiction: "Feature articles of interest to large scale candy manufacturers that deal with activities in the fields of production, packaging (including package design), merchandising, financial news (sales figures, profits, earnings); advertising campaigns in all media; and promotional methods used to increase the sale or distribution of candy." Length: 1,000-1,250 words. Pays "special rates on assignments."

Photos: "Good quality glossies with complete and accurate captions, in sizes not smaller than 5×7."

Fillers: "Short news stories about the trade and anything related to candy." $1 for clippings.

PACIFIC BAKERS NEWS, 180 Mendell St., San Francisco CA 94124-1740. (415)826-2664. Publisher: C.W. Soward. 30% freelance written. Eager to work with new/unpublished writers. Monthly business newsletter for commercial bakeries in the western states. Estab. 1961. Pays on publication. No byline given; uses only 1-paragraph news items.

Nonfiction: Uses bakery business reports and news about bakers. Buys only brief "boiled-down news items about bakers and bakeries operating only in Alaska, Hawaii, Pacific Coast and Rocky Mountain states. We welcome clippings. We need monthly news reports and clippings about the baking industry and the donut business. No pictures, jokes, poetry or cartoons." Length: 10-200 words. Pays 10¢/word for news and 6¢ for clips (words used).

Construction and Contracting

Builders, architects and contractors learn the latest industry news in these publications. Journals targeted to architects are also included in the Consumer Art and Architecture category. Those for specialists in the interior aspects of construction are listed under Building Interiors.

AUTOMATED BUILDER, CMN Associates, Inc., P.O. Box 120, Cartinteria CA 93014-0120. (805)684-7659. Fax: (805)684-1765. Editor-in-Chief: Don Carlson. 15% freelance written. Monthly magazine specializing in management for industrialized (manufactured) housing and volume home builders. Estab. 1964. Circ. 25,000. **Pays on acceptance.** Publishes ms an average of 3 months after acceptance. Buys first North American serial rights. Phone queries OK. Reports in 2 weeks. Free sample copy and writer's guidelines.

Nonfiction: Case history articles on successful home building companies which may be 1) production (big volume) home builders; 2) mobile home manufacturers; 3) modular home manufacturers; 4) prefabricated (panelized) home manufacturers; 5) house component manufacturers; or 6) special unit (in-plant commercial building) manufacturers. Also uses interviews, photo features and technical articles. "No architect or plan 'dreams'. Housing projects must be built or under construction." Buys 15 mss/year. Query. Length: 500-1,000 words maximum. Pays $300 minimum.

Photos: Purchased with accompanying ms. Query. No additional payment. Wants 4×5, 5×7 or 8×10 b&w glossies or 35mm or larger color transparencies (35mm preferred). Captions required.

Tips: "Stories often are too long, too loose; we prefer 500 to 750 words. We prefer a phone query on feature articles. If accepted on query, article usually will not be rejected later."

‡CAM MAGAZINE, Construction Association of Michigan, Suite 400, 500 Stephenson Hwy., Troy MI 48083. (810)585-1000. Editor: Marla S. Janness. 5% freelance written. Monthly magazine covering all facets of the construction industry. "*CAM Magazine* is devoted to the growth and progress of individuals and companies serving and servicing the construction industry. It provides a forum on new construction industry technology and practices, current information on new construction projects, products and services, and publishes information on industry personnel changes and advancements." Estab. 1978. Circ. 4,000. Pays on publication. Byline given. Buys all rights. Editorial lead time 2 months. Submit seasonal material 3 months in advance. Query for electronic submissions. Sample copy free on request.

Nonfiction: Construction-related only. Buys 3 mss/year. Query with published clips. Length: 1,000-5,000 words. Pays $50.

Photos: Send photos with submission. Reviews contact sheets, negatives, transparencies and prints. Offers no additional payment for photos accepted with ms. Buys one-time rights.

Tips: "Anyone having *current* knowledge or expertise on some of our featured topics is welcomed to submit articles. Recent experience or information on a construction-related issue or new trends and innovations, is also helpful."

CONSTRUCTION COMMENT, Naylor Communications Ltd., 6th Floor, 920 Yonge St., Toronto, Ontario M4W 3C7 Canada. (416)961-1028. Fax: (416)924-4408. Editor: Lori Knowles. 80% freelance written. Semiannual magazine on construction industry in Ottawa. *"Construction Comment* reaches all members of the Ottawa Construction Association and most senior management of firms relating to the industry." Estab. 1970. Circ. 3,000. Pays 30 days after deadline. Byline given. Offers 33% kill fee. Buys first North American serial rights. Submit seasonal material 2 months in advance. Accepts simultaneous and previously published submissions. Send tearsheet or photocopy of article and information about when and where the article previously appeared. For reprints pays 80% of amount paid for an original article. Query for electronic submissions. Reports in 6 weeks.

Nonfiction: General interest, historical, interview/profile, new product, photo feature, technical. "We publish a spring/summer issue and a fall/winter issue. Submit correspondingly or inquire two months ahead of these times." Buys 10 mss/year. Query with published clips. Length: 500-2,500 words. Pays 25¢/word. Pays expenses of writers on assignment.

Photos: State availability of photos with submission. Reviews transparencies and prints. Offers $25-200/photo. Identification of subjects required.

Tips: "Please send copies of work and a general query. I will respond as promptly as my deadlines allow."

‡**CONSTRUCTION MARKETING TODAY, The Aberdeen Group**, 426 S. Westgate St., Addison IL 60101. (708)543-0870. Editor: Diana Granitto. Contact: Terry Noland, senior editor. 25% freelance written. Monthly tabloid covering marketing equipment or materials to the construction industry. "Our readers are manufacturers of construction equipment and building materials. Specifically, our readers are marketing people and top execs at those companies. The magazine carries business news, marketing case studies and marketing how-to articles. The magazine does not have heavily technical content, so writers need not be knowledgeable of the industry. Business writing and company profile writing experience is a plus." Estab. 1990. Circ. 4,000. **Pays on acceptance of final draft.** Byline given. Buys first rights and simultaneous rights. Editorial lead time 2 months. Query for electronic submissions. Reports in 5 weeks on queries; 2 months on mss. Sample copy free on request.

Nonfiction: Exposé, how-to (marketing), interview/profile, opinion, personal experience, business news, marketing trends. "No stories aimed at contractors or stories that show no relevancy to the industry." Buys 15 mss/year. Query with published clips. Length: 800-3,000 words. Pays $200. Pays contributor's copies if "author is an industry consultant or has a service he is trying to sell to our readers, or he works for a manufacturing company." Sometimes pays expenses of writers on assignment.

Photos: State availability of photos with submission. Reviews contact sheets. Negotiates payment individually. Captions and identification of subjects required. Buys all rights.

Tips: "Show that you have a grasp on what the magazine is about. We are not a technical how-to magazine geared to contractors, as most construction publications are. We have a unique niche. We are targeted to manufacturers marketing to contractors. We are looking for stories that have a fresh and intriguing look, that are entertaining to read, that are relevant to our readers, that are informative and that show an attention to detail in the reporting. Page 1 news, inside features, company profiles, industry marketing trends and marketing how-to stories are most open to freelancers. Stories should be tailored to our industry."

‡**CONSTRUCTION SPECIFIER**, 601 Madison St., Alexandria VA 22314-1791. (703)684-0300. Fax: (703)684-0465. Publisher: Jack Reeder. 50% freelance written. Works with a small number of new/unpublished writers each year. Monthly professional society magazine for architects, engineers, specification writers and project managers. Monthly. Estab. 1949. Circ. 19,000. Pays on publication. Publishes ms an average of 4 months after acceptance. Deadline: 60 days preceding publication on the 1st of each month. Buys World serial rights. Publishes reprints of previously published articles. Send information about when and where the article previously appeared. Query for electronic submissions. "Call or write first." Model release, author copyright transferral requested. Reports in 3 weeks. Sample copy for 9 × 12 SAE with 6 first-class stamps. Writer's guidelines for #10 SASE.

Nonfiction: Articles on selection and specification of products, materials, practices and methods used in commercial (non-residential) construction projects, specifications as related to construction design, plus legal and management subjects. Query. Length: 3,000-5,000 words maximum. Pays up to 15¢/published word (negotiable), plus art. Pays minor expenses of writers on assignment, to an agreed upon limit.

Photos: Photos desirable in consideration for publication; line art, sketches, diagrams, charts and graphs also desired. Full color transparencies may be used; 8 × 10 glossies, 3¼ slides preferred. Payment negotiable.

Tips: "We need more good technical articles."

COST CUTS, The Enterprise Foundation, American City Bldg., Suite 500, 10227 Wincopin Circle, Columbia MD 21044-3400. (410)964-1230. Fax: (410)964-1918. Editor: Peggy Armstrong. 25% freelance written. Bimonthly newsletter on rehabilitation of low-income housing. "As the construction arm of The Enterprise Foundation, the Rehab Work Group, which publishes *Cost Cuts*, seeks ways to reduce the cost of rehabbing and constructing low-income housing. *Cost Cuts* also informs of changes in federal policy, local and state efforts in low-income housing and pro bono work in this area. *Cost Cuts* is distributed nationally to rehab specialists, agencies and others involved in the production of low-income housing." Estab. 1983. Circ. 6,000. Pays on publication. Byline given. Buys one-time rights. Submit seasonal material 3 months in advance. Accepts previously published submissions. Send tearsheet of article, typed ms with rights for sale noted and information about when and where the article previously appeared. Query for electronic submissions. Reports in 1 month. Sample copy for 9 × 12 SAE with 2 first-class stamps. Writer's guidelines for #10 SASE.

Nonfiction: How-to, interview/profile, technical, international. "No personal experience of do-it-yourselfers in single-family homes. We want articles concerning high production of low-income housing." Buys 10-15 mss/year. Query with published clips. Length: 100-1,500 words. Pays $50-200 for assigned articles; $200 maximum for unsolicited articles. Sometimes pays expenses of writers on assignment.

Photos: Send photos with submission. Reviews contact sheets and 3 × 5 and 5 × 7 prints. Captions and identification of subjects required. Buys one-time rights.

Fillers: Facts and newsbreaks. Buys 20/year. Length: 100-500 words. Pays $25-50.

Tips: "The Foundation's mission is to see that all low-income people in the United States have the opportunity for fit and affordable housing within a generation and to move up and out of poverty into the mainstream of American life. Freelancers must be conscious of this context. Articles must include case studies of specific projects where costs have been cut. Charts of cost comparisons to show exactly where cuts were made are most helpful."

FINE HOMEBUILDING, The Taunton Press, Inc., Dept. WM, P.O. Box 5506, Newtown CT 06470. (203)426-8171. Editor: Kevin Ireton. Less than 5% freelance written. Bimonthly magazine covering house building, construction, design for builders, architects and serious amateurs. Estab. 1976. Circ. 245,000. Pays advance, balance on publication. Publishes ms an average of 6-12 months after acceptance. Byline given. Offers negotiable kill fee. Buys first rights and "use in books to be published." Query for electronic submissions. Reports "as soon as possible." Free writer's guidelines.

Nonfiction: Technical (techniques in design or construction process). Query. Length: 2,000-3,000 words. Pays $150-1,200.

Columns/Departments: Tools and Materials (products or techniques that are new or unusual); Great Moments in Building History (humorous, embarrassing, or otherwise noteworthy anecdotes); Reviews (short reviews of books on building or design); Reports and Comment (essays, short reports on construction and architecture trends and developments). Query. Length: 300-1,000 words. Pays $50-250.

‡INDIANA BUILDER, Pro Tec Publishing & Printing, 500 S. Cory Lane, Bloomington IN 47403. (812)332-1639. Editor: C. Dale Risch. 40% freelance written. Monthly magazine covering residential construction. "Our readers are professional builders and remodelers." Estab. 1989. Circ. 12,500. **Pays on acceptance.** Byline given. Buys one-time rights. Editorial lead time 1 month. Submit seasonal material 3 months in advance. Accepts simultaneous and previously published submissions. Query for electronic submissions. Sample copy free on request.

Nonfiction: How-to (construction). Buys 60 mss/year. Query with published clips. Length: 500-2,000 words. Pays 5¢/word. Sometimes pays expenses of writers on assignment.

Photos: State availability of photos or send photos with submission. Reviews contact sheets. Negotiates payment individually. Captions required. Buys one-time rights.

INLAND ARCHITECT, The Midwestern Building Arts Magazine, Inland Architect Press, Suite 103, 3525 W. Peterson Ave., Chicago IL 60659. (312)465-5151. Editor: Steve Klebba. 80% freelance written. Bimonthly magazine covering architecture and urban planning. "*Inland Architect* is a critical journal covering architecture and design in the Midwest for an audience primarily of architects. *Inland* is open to all points of view, providing they are intelligently expressed and of relevance to architecture." Estab. 1957. Circ. 8,000. Pays on publication. Publishes ms an average of 2 months after acceptance. Byline given. Offers 50% kill fee. Buys first rights. Reports in 2 months. Sample copy for $10 (includes shipping and handling).

Nonfiction: Book excerpts, essays, historical/nostalgic, interview/profile, criticism, photo feature of architecture. Every summer *Inland* focuses on a Midwestern city, its architecture and urban design. Call to find out 1995 city. No new products, "how to run your office," or technical pieces. Buys 40 mss/year. Query with published clips or send complete ms. Length: 750-3,500 words. Pay varies for assigned articles. Sometimes pays the expenses of writers on assignment.

Photos: Send photos with submission. Reviews 4 × 5 transparencies, slides and 8 × 10 prints. Offers no additional payment for photos accepted with ms. Identification of subjects required. Buys one-time rights.

Columns/Departments: Books (reviews of new publications on architecture, design, and occasionally, art), 250-1,000 words. Buys 10 mss/year. Query. Length: 250-1,000 words. Pays $50. Space (interiors), pay varies;

Inlandscape (news of new/under construction projects), pay varies; Earth (design projects with an emphasis on their environmental implications), pay varies.

Tips: "Propose to cover a lecture, to interview a certain architect, etc. Articles must be written for an audience primarily consisting of well-educated architects. If an author feels he has a 'hot' timely idea, a phone call is appreciated."

THE JOURNAL OF LIGHT CONSTRUCTION, Builderburg Group, Inc., RR2, Box 146, Richmond VT 05477. (802)434-4747. Fax: (802)434-4467. Editor: Steven Bliss. Managing Editor: Don Jackson. 50% freelance written. Monthly tabloid on residential and light-commercial construction/remodeling. "Most of our articles offer practical solutions to problems that small contractors face on the job site or in the office. For that reason, most of our authors have practical experience in construction. In fact, the accuracy of the information is more important to us than the quality of the writing." Estab. 1982. Pays on publication. Publishes ms an average of 4 months after acceptance. Byline given. Offers negotiable kill fee. Buys first North American serial and non-exclusive reprint rights. Query for electronic submissions. Sample copy for $3.95. Writer's guidelines for SASE.

Nonfiction: How-to, new product, technical. Buys 40 mss/year. Query. Length: 1,300-2,500 words. Pays $150-400. Sometimes pays expenses of writers on assignment.

Photos: Send photos with submission. Reviews contact sheets, transparencies and prints. Offers additional payment for photos accepted with ms. Captions required. Buys first and non-exclusive reprint rights.

Columns/Departments: Eight-Penny News (news shorts in areas of business, technology, codes, human interest related to home construction), 300-1,000 words. Buys 12 mss/year. Send complete ms. Pays $50-200.

‡**MASONRY**, 1550 Spring Rd., Oak Brook IL 60521. (708)782-6767. Editor: Gene Adams. 20% freelance written. Bimonthly magazine covering masonry contracting. "*Masonry Magazine* for masonry contractors and other members of the masonry industry, who are engaged in commercial, residential, institutional, governmental, industrial and renovation building projects. Readers include architects, engineers, specifiers, project manufacturers and others." Estab. 1961. Circ. 12,000. **Pays on acceptance.** Byline given. Buys first North American serial, first, one-time, second serial (reprint), simultaneous or all rights or makes work-for-hire assignments. Editorial lead time 2 months. Submit seasonal material 3 months in advance. Accepts simultaneous and previously published submissions. Reports in 3 weeks on queries; 8 months on mss. Sample copy and writer's guidelines free on request.

Nonfiction: Book excerpts, historical/nostalgic, how-to (contracting problems), interview/profile, new product, personal experience, photo feature, technical. Buys 12-18 mss/year. Query. Length: 500-4,000 words. Pays $200 for assigned articles; $50 for unsolicited articles.

Photos: Send photos with submission. Reviews contact sheets. Offers $10-50/photo or negotiates payment individually. Captions and identification of subjects required. Buys one-time and/or all rights.

PACIFIC BUILDER & ENGINEER, Vernon Publications Inc., Suite 200, 3000 Northup Way, Bellevue WA 98004. (206)827-9900. Editor: Richard C. Bachus. Editorial Director: Michele Andrus Dill. 44% freelance written. Biweekly magazine covering non-residential construction in the Northwest and Alaska. "Our readers are construction contractors in Washington, Oregon, Idaho, Montana and Alaska. The feature stories in *PB&E* focus on ongoing construction projects in our coverage area. They address these questions: what is the most significant challenge to the general contractor? What innovative construction techniques or equipment are being used to overcome the challenges?" Estab. 1902. Circ. 14,500. Pays on publication. Publishes ms an average of 2 months after acceptance. Byline given. Buys first North American serial and second serial (reprint) rights. Editorial lead time 1½ months. Submit seasonal material 2 months in advance. Query for electronic submissions. Reports in 2 months on queries; 6 weeks on mss. Sample copy for $7. Writer's guidelines for #10 SASE.

Nonfiction: How-to, new product, photo feature. "No non-construction stories; residential construction articles; construction stories without a Northwest or Alaska angle." Buys 18 mss/year. Query with published clips. Length: 750-2,000 words. Pays $100. Sometimes pays expenses of writers on assignment.

Photos: State availability of photos with submission. Reviews contact sheets, transparencies. Offers $15-125/photo. Captions and identification of subjects and equipment required. Buys one-time rights.

Tips: "Find an intriguing, ongoing construction project in our five-state region. Talk to the general contractor's project manager to see what he/she thinks is unusual, innovative or exciting about the project to builders. Then go ahead and query us. If we haven't already covered the project, there's a possibility that we may assign a feature. Be prepared to tour the site, put on a hard hat and get your boots dirty."

‡**PIPELINE & UTILITIES CONSTRUCTION**, Oildom Publishing, P.O. Box 219368, Houston TX 77218-9368. Editor: Robert Carpenter. 5% freelance written. Monthly magazine covering underground construction. "Magazine is edited for contractors involved in all types of underground construction transmission (gas & oil) pipelines, gas distribution pipelines, sewer and water lines, cable." Estab. 1946. Circ. 28,000. Pays on publication. Publishes ms an average of 4 months after acceptance. Byline given. Buys first rights. Editorial lead time 2 months. Accepts previously published submissions. Query for electronic submissions. Reports in 1 month. Sample copy for 10×12 SAE with 10 first-class stamps.

Nonfiction: How-to, interview/profile, new product, photo feature, technical. Buys 3 mss/year. Query. Length: 1,000-2,000 words. Pays $100. Sometimes pays expenses of writers on assignment.

Photos: State availability of photos with submission. Reviews transparencies, prints. Offers no additional payment for photos accepted with ms. Captions, model releases, identification of subjects required. Buys one-time rights.

Tips: "Understand the specific contracting job. Make sure there is something unique, challenging, complicated or even massive about the project or theme. Our readers are interested in equipment uses, applications, and benefits (both in time and money)."

ROOFER MAGAZINE, D&H Publications, Inc., Suite 214, 6719 Windler Rd., Ft. Myers FL 33919. (813)489-2929. Editor: Jack Klein. 10% freelance written. Eager to work with new/unpublished writers. Monthly magazine covering the roofing industry for roofing contractors. Estab. 1981. Circ. 19,400. Pays on publication. Publishes ms an average of 5 months after acceptance. Byline given. Buys first and second serial (reprint) rights. Submission must be exclusive to our field. Submit seasonal material 4 months in advance. Reports in 2 months. Sample copy and writer's guidelines for SAE with 6 first-class stamps.

• With an influx of material and reduction in staff, reporting times may run longer than stated.

Nonfiction: Profiles of roofing contractors (explicit guidelines available), humorous pieces; other ideas welcome. Buys 5-10 mss/year. Query in writing. Length: approximately 1,500 words. Pays $125-250 (average: $175).

Photos: Send photos with completed mss; color slides are preferred. Identification of subjects required. "We purchase photographs for specific needs, but those that accompany an article are not purchased separately. The price we pay in the article includes the use of the photos. Always searching for photos of unusual roofs or those with a humorous slant."

Tips: "Contractor profiles are our most frequent purchase from freelance writers and a favorite to our readers. Our guidelines explain exactly what we are looking for and should help freelancers select the right person to interview. We provide sample questions to ask about the topics we would like discussed the most. For those submitting queries about other articles, we prefer substantial articles (no fillers please). Slant articles toward roofing contractors. We have little use for generic articles that can appear in any business publication and give little consideration to such material submitted."

SHOPPING CENTER WORLD, Argus Business, 6151 Powers Ferry Rd., Atlanta GA 30339-2941. (404)955-2500. Fax: (404)955-0400. Editor: Teresa DeFranks. 75% freelance written. Prefers to work with published/ established writers. Monthly magazine covering the shopping center industry. "Material is written with the shopping center developer, owner, manager and shopping center tenant in mind." Estab. 1972. Pays on publication. Publishes ms an average of 3 months after acceptance. Byline given. Buys all rights. Query for electronic submissions. Reports in 2 months. Sample copy for $6.50.

Nonfiction: Interview/profile, new product, opinion, photo feature, technical. Buys 50 mss/year. Query with published clips or send complete ms. Length: 750-3,000 words. Pays $75-500. Sometimes pays expenses of writers on assignment.

Photos: State availability of photos with submission. Reviews 4×5 transparencies and 35mm slides. Offers no additional payment for photos accepted with ms. Model releases and identification of subjects required. Buys one-time rights.

Tips: "We are always looking for talented writers to work on assignment. Send résumé and published clips. Writers with real estate writing and business backgrounds have a better chance. Industry trends and state reviews are all freelance written on an assignment basis. Most assignments are made to those writers who are familiar with the magazine's subject matter and have already reviewed our editorial calendar of future topics."

‡TRANSPORTATION BUILDER, American Road & Transportation Builders Association, 1010 Massachusetts Ave. NW, Washington DC 20001. (202)289-4434. Editor: Gail M. Schell. 50% freelance written. Monthly magazine covering transportation construction. "*TB* focuses on the information and marketing needs of transportation construction professionals with particular focus on legislative and regulatory issues that will impact the market." Estab. 1923. Circ. 10,000. Pays on publication. Publishes ms an average of 3-9 months after acceptance. Byline sometimes given. Buys one-time rights or makes work-for-hire assignments. Editorial lead time 1-2 months. Submit seasonal material 2-3 months in advance. Accepts simultaneous submissions. Query for electronic submissions. Sample copy and writer's guidelines free on request.

Nonfiction: Essays, general interest, interview/profile. Special issues: environmental issues (Clean Air & Clean Water Acts); new products, technology, heavy construction equipment, safety, public-private ventures in transportation, construction materials, services, planning and design firms and issues, market forecasts, international construction markets, computers. Buys 12 mss/year. Query with published clips or send complete ms. Length: 1,500-3,000 words. Pay negotiable. Sometimes pays expenses of writers on assignment.

Photos: State availability of photos with submission. Reviews 3×5 prints. Offers no additional payment for photos accepted with ms. Captions required. Buys one-time rights.

Columns/Departments: Computers (use of software and hardware for contractors and designers) 750-1,000 words; Safety (OSHA rules, common sense construction know-how) 750-1,000 words; Business (small business issues, especially government rules) 750-1,000 words. Buys 12 mss/year. Query with published clips or send complete ms. Pays $50.

Tips: "Know audience and issues; have good sense of 'hot-buttons'; have association-writing experience; put a different slant to pieces; include photographs; *fast* turnaround, working on tight schedule; mail submission or request editorial calendar; focus on our members if possible. Features are most needed by writers experienced in transportation-related issues and government rules and regulations affecting transportation construction."

Dental

DENTAL ECONOMICS, PennWell Publishing Co., P.O. Box 3408, Tulsa OK 74101-3400. (918)835-3161. Fax: (918)831-9804. Publisher: Dick Hale. Senior Editor: Penny Anderson. Associate Editor: Ron Combs. Assistant Editor: Melba Koch. 50% freelance written. Monthly dental-trade journal. "Our readers are actively practicing dentists who look to us for current practice-building, practice-administrative and personal finance assistance." Estab. 1911. Circ. 110,000. **Pays on acceptance.** Publishes ms an average of 3-4 months after acceptance. Byline given. Buys first rights. Submit seasonal material 6 months in advance. Reports in 2 months. Free sample copy and writer's guidelines.
 • This magazine reports it is buying fewer articles. They have a backlog of accepted pieces.
Nonfiction: General interest, how-to, new products. "No human interest and consumer-related stories." Buys 40 mss/year. Query. Length: 750-3,500 words. Pays $150-500 for assigned articles; pays $75-350 for unsolicited articles. Sometimes pays the expenses of writers on assignment.
Photos: State availability of photos with submission. Reviews contact sheets. Offers no additional payment for photos accepted with ms. Model releases and identification of subjects required. Buys one-time rights.
Columns/Departments: Ron Combs, associate editor: Tax Q&A (tax tips for dentists), 1,500 words; Office Of the Month (office design); Penny Anderson, senior editor: Capitol Gram (late legislative news—dentistry), 750 words; Dental Insurance, 750 words. Buys 36 mss/year. Pays $50-300. Other monthly columns/departments are: News Digest, RX for Success, Viewpoint, Letters from Readers, Practice Productivity, Clinical Excellence, Focus on Financing, Product-Profiles.
Tips: "How-to articles on specific subjects such as practice-building, newsletters and collections should be relevant to a busy, solo-practice dentist."

PROOFS, The Magazine of Dental Sales and Marketing, PennWell Publishing Co., P.O. Box 3408, Tulsa OK 74101-3400. (918)835-3161. Fax: (918)831-9804. Editor: Mary Elizabeth Good. 5% freelance written. Magazine published 10 times/year covering dental trade. "*Proofs* is the only publication of the dental trade. It reaches dental dealers, their respective sales forces and key marketing personnel of manufacturers. It publishes news of the industry (not the profession), personnel changes and articles on how to sell dental equipment and merchandise and services that can be provided to the dentist-customer." Estab. 1917. Circ. 7,000. Pays on publication. Byline given. Buys first North American serial rights. Editorial lead time 1 month. Query for electronic submissions. Reports in 2 weeks on queries. Sample copy and writer's guidelines free on request.
Nonfiction: General interest, historical/nostalgic, how-to, interview/profile, opinion, personal experience. "No articles written for dentist-readers." Buys 15 mss/year. Query or send complete ms. Length: 400-1,250. Pays $100-200.
Photos: Either state availability of photos with submission or send photos with submission. Reviews minimum size 3½×5 prints. Offers no additional payment for photos accepted with ms. Identification of subjects required. Buys one-time rights.
Tips: "Learn something about the dental industry and how it operates. We have no interest in manufacturers who sell only direct. We do not want information on products and how they work, but will take news items on manufacturers' promotions involving products. Most interested in stories on how to sell *in the dental industry*; industry personnel feel they are 'unique' and not like other industries. In many cases, this is true, but not entirely. We are most open to feature articles on selling, supply-house operations, providing service."

RDH, The National Magazine for Dental Hygiene Professionals, Stevens Publishing Corp., 3630 J.H. Kultgen Freeway, Waco TX 76706. (817)776-9000. Editor: Kathleen Witherspoon. Assistant Editor: Terri Rayer. 65% freelance written. Monthly magazine covering information relevant to dental hygiene professionals as business-career oriented individuals. "Dental hygienists are highly trained, licensed professionals; most are women. They are concerned with ways to develop rewarding careers, give optimum service to patients and to grow both professionally and personally." Circ. 68,000. Usually pays 30 days after publication. Publishes ms an average of 8 months after acceptance. Byline given. Buys first serial rights. Reports in 2 weeks on queries; 2 months on mss. Sample copies and writer's guidelines available.
Nonfiction: Essays, general interest, interview/profile, personal experience, photo feature, technical. "We are interested in any topic that offers broad reader appeal, especially in the area of personal growth (communication, managing time, balancing career and personal life). No undocumented clinical or technical articles; how-it-feels-to-be-a-patient articles; product-oriented articles (unless in generic terms); anything cutesy-

unprofessional." Length: 1,500-3,000 words. Pays $100-350 for assigned articles; $50-200 for unsolicited articles. Sometimes pays expenses of writers on assignment.

Photos: Covers are shot on location across US.

Tips: "Freelancers should have a feel for the concerns of today's business-career woman—and address those interests and concerns with practical, meaningful and even motivational messages. We want to see good-quality manuscripts on both personal growth and lifestyle topics. For clinical and/or technical topics, we prefer the writers be members of the dental profession. New approaches to old problems and dilemmas will always get a close look from our editors. *RDH* is also interested in manuscripts for our feature section. Other than clinical information, dental hygienists are interested in all sorts of topics—finances, personal growth, educational opportunities, business management, staff/employer relations, communication and motivation, office rapport and career options. Other than clinical/technical articles, *RDH* maintains an informal tone. Writing style can easily be accommodated to our format."

Drugs, Health Care and Medical Products

THE APOTHECARY, Health Care Marketing Services, P.O. Box AP, Los Altos CA 94023. (415)941-3955. Fax: (415)941-2303. Editor: Jerold Karabensh. Publication Director: Janet Goodman. Managing Editor: Eli Traub. 100% freelance written. Prefers to work with published/established writers who possess some knowledge of pharmacy and business/management topics. Quarterly magazine. providing practical information to community retail pharmacists." Estab. 1888. Circ. 60,000. **Pays on acceptance.** Publishes ms an average of 5 months after acceptance. Byline given. Buys all rights. Submit seasonal material 8 months in advance. Reports in up to 6 months. Sample copy for 9×12 SAE with 4 first-class stamps. Writer's guidelines for #10 SASE.

Nonfiction: How-to (e.g., manage a pharmacy), opinion (of registered pharmacists), health-related feature stories. "We publish only those general health articles with some practical application for the pharmacist as business person. No general articles not geared to our pharmacy readership; no fiction." Buys 4 mss/year. Query with published clips. Length: 750-3,000 words. Pays $100-300.

Columns/Departments: Commentary (views or issues relevant to the subject of pharmacy or to pharmacists). Send complete ms. Length: 750-1,000 words. "This section is unpaid; we will take submissions with byline."

Tips: "Submit material geared to the *pharmacist* as *business person*. Write according to our policy, i.e., business articles with emphasis on practical information for a community pharmacist. We suggest reading several back issues and following general feature story tone, depth, etc. Stay away from condescending use of language. Though our articles are written in simple style, they must reflect knowledge of the subject and reasonable respect for the readers' professionalism and intelligence."

CALIFORNIA PHARMACIST, California Pharmacists Association, Suite 300, 1112 I St., Sacramento CA 95814. (916)444-7811 ext. 302. Managing Editor: Michael Ishii. 5% freelance written. Monthly magazine covering pharmacy. Readers are mostly practicing pharmacists in California in various pharmacy settings. Strong, accurate and timely clinical articles, legal articles relating cases relative to pharmacy and legislative and administrative articles pertaining to California pharmacy. Estab. 1954. Circ. 7,000. Pays on publication. Publishes ms an average of 2 months after acceptance. Byline given. Offers 100% kill fee. Buys first rights. Editorial lead time 3 months. Submit seasonal material 3 months in advance. Reports in 3 weeks on queries. Sample copy and writer's guidelines free on request.

Nonfiction: Interview/profile, photo feature, technical. Buys 15 mss/year. Send complete ms. Length: 1,500-5,000 words. Pays $150.

Tips: "Pharmacy is dynamic and writers must be ahead of the news in order to produce timely and pertinent articles. Look at how today's news will create tomorrow's headlines. Strong clinical articles are most sought after. Other articles such as HIV/AIDS research and development, managed care and Medi-Cal are important to us."

CANADIAN PHARMACEUTICAL JOURNAL, 1785 Alta Vista Dr., Ottawa, Ontario K1G 3Y6 Canada. (613)523-7877. Fax: (613)523-0445. Editor: Jane Dewar. Staff Writer: Andrew Reinboldt. Works with a small number of new/unpublished writers each year. Monthly journal for pharmacists. Estab. 1868. Circ. 13,038. Pays after editing. Publishes ms an average of 3-6 months after acceptance. Buys first serial rights. Reports in 2 months. Free sample copy and writer's guidelines.

Nonfiction: Relevant to Canadian pharmacy. Publishes continuing education, pharmacy practice, education and legislation, how-to; historical. Length: 200-400 words (for news notices); 800-1,500 words (for articles). Query. Payment is contingent on value. Sometimes pays expenses of writers on assignment.

Photos: Color and b&w (5×7) glossies purchased with mss. Captions and model releases required.

Tips: "Query with complete description of proposed article, including topic, sources (in general), length, payment requested, suggested submission date, and whether photographs will be included. It is helpful if the writer has read a *recent* copy of the journal; we are glad to send one if required. References should be included where appropriate (this is vital where medical and scientific information is included). Send 3 copies of each manuscript. Author's degree and affiliations (if any) and writing background should be listed."

CONSULTANT PHARMACIST, American Society of Consultant Pharmacists, 1321 Duke St., Alexandria VA 22314-3563. (703)739-1300. Fax: (703)739-1500. Editor: L. Michael Posey. Production Manager: Billy Stroemer. 10% freelance written. Monthly journal on consultant pharmacy. "We do not promote drugs or companies but rather ideas and information." Circ. 11,200. **Pays on acceptance**. Publishes ms an average of 4 months after acceptance. Byline given. Buys first North American serial rights. Send disk with accepted article. Reports in 2 weeks. Sample copy for 9 × 12 SAE with 6 first-class stamps. Writer's guidelines for #10 SASE.
Nonfiction: How-to (related to consultant pharmacy), interview/profile, technical. Buys 10 mss/year. Query with published clips. Length: 750-2,000 words. Pays $300-1,200. Sometimes pays expenses of writers on assignment.
Photos: Send photos with submission. Offers $100/photo session. Captions, model releases and identification of subjects required. Buys one-time rights.
Tips: "This journal is devoted to consultant pharmacy, so articles must relate to this field."

PHARMACY TIMES, Romaine Pierson Publishers, 80 Shore Rd., Port Washington NY 11050. (516)883-6350. Fax: (516)883-6609. Publisher: William J. Reynolds. Editor-in-Chief: Bruce Buckley. 15% freelance written. Monthly magazine providing clinical, educational and economic information to pharmacists. Estab. 1897. Circ. 97,000. Pays on publication. Publishes ms an average of 4 months after acceptance. Byline given. Buys one-time rights. Submit seasonal material 6 months in advance. Query for electronic submissions. Reports in 1 month on queries; 6 weeks on mss. Free sample copy and writer's guidelines.
Nonfiction: Interview/profile, new product, opinion, personal experience, photo feature, technical, travel. Buys 12-15 mss/year. Send complete ms. Length: 800-1,500 words. Pays $250-400 for assigned articles; $100-250 for unsolicited articles. Pays in contributor copies or other premiums "per author request or for reprinted material."
Photos: State availability of photos with submission. Reviews negatives and 3 × 5 prints. Offers no additional payment for photos accepted with ms. Captions, model releases and identification of subjects required. Buys one-time rights.

Education and Counseling

Professional educators, teachers, coaches and counselors—as well as other people involved in training and education—read the journals classified here. Many journals for educators are nonprofit forums for professional advancement; writers contribute articles in return for a byline and contributor's copies. *Writer's Market* includes only educational journals that pay freelancers for articles. Education-related publications for students are included in the Consumer Career, College and Alumni and Teen and Young Adult sections.

ARTS & ACTIVITIES, Publishers' Development Corporation, Dept. WM, Suite 200, 591 Camino de la Reina, San Diego CA 92108-3104. (619)297-5352. Fax: (619)297-5353. Editor: Maryellen Bridge. 95% freelance written. Eager to work with new/unpublished writers. Monthly (except July and August) art education magazine covering art education at levels from preschool through college for educators and therapists engaged in arts and crafts education and training. Estab. 1932. Circ. 24,000. Pays on publication. Publishes ms an average of 6 months after acceptance. Byline given. Buys first North American serial rights. Submit seasonal material 4 months in advance. Reports in 3 months. Sample copy for 9 × 12 SAE with 8 first-class stamps. Writer's guidelines for #10 SASE.
Nonfiction: Historical/nostalgic (arts, activities, history); how-to (classroom art experiences, artists' techniques); interview/profile (of artists); opinion (on arts activities curriculum, ideas on how to do things better); personal experience in the art classroom ("this ties in with the how-to, we like it to be *personal*, no recipe style"); articles on exceptional art programs. Buys 80-100 mss/year. Length: 200-2,000 words. Pays $35-150.
   • Editors here are seeking more materials for upper elementary and secondary levels on printmaking, ceramics, 3-dimensional design, weaving, fiber arts (stitchery, tie-dye, batik, etc.), crafts, and multicultural art.
Tips: "Frequently in unsolicited manuscripts, writers obviously have not studied the magazine to see what style of articles we publish. Send for a sample copy to familiarize yourself with our style and needs. The best way to find out if his/her writing style suits our needs is for the author to submit a manuscript on speculation."

 A bullet introduces comments by the editor of Writer's Market *indicating special information about the listing.*

‡**CLASS ACT,** Class Act, Inc., (formerly *Cottonwood Monthly*), P.O. Box 802, Henderson KY 42420. Editor: Susan Thurman. 50% freelance written. Educational newsletter published 9 times/year covering English/ language arts education. "Our writers must know English as a classroom subject and should be familiar with writing for teens. If you can't make your manuscript interesting to teenagers, we're not interested." Estab. 1993. Circ. 300. **Pays on acceptance.** Publishes ms an average of 3 months after acceptance. Byline given. Offers 100% kill fee. Buys all rights. Editorial lead time 2 months. Submit seasonal material 3 months in advance. Accepts simultaneous submissions. Reports in 1 month. Sample copy for $3. Writer's guidelines for #10 SASE.

Nonfiction: How-to (games, puzzles, assignments relating to English education). "NO Master's thesis; no esoteric articles; no poetry; no educational theory or jargon." Buys 15 mss/year. Send complete ms. Length: 100-2,000 words. Pays $10.

Columns/Departments: Writing assignments (innovative, thought-provoking for teens) 500 words; Puzzles, games (English education oriented) 200 words; Teacher tips (bulletin boards, time-saving devices), 100 words. Send complete ms. Pays $10-40.

Fillers: Teacher tips. Pays $10.

Tips: "Please know the kind of language used by junior/senior high students. Don't speak above them. Also, it helps to know what these students *don't* know, in order to explain or emphasize the concepts. Clip art is sometimes used but is not paid extra for. We like material that's slightly humorous while still being educational. Especially open to innovative writing assignments; educational puzzles and games and instructions on basics. Again, be familiar with this age group."

‡**DANCE TEACHER NOW, The Practical Magazine of Dance,** SMW Communications, Inc., #310, 3101 Poplarwood Court, Raleigh NC 27604. Editor: K.C. Patrick. 80% freelance written. Our readers are professional dance educators, business persons and related professionals. Estab. 1979. Circ. 7,000. **Pays on acceptance.** Publishes ms an average of 2-3 months after acceptance. Byline given. Negotiates rights and permission to reprint on request. Submit seasonal/holiday material 6 months in advance. Query. Prefer WP disks. Accepts previously published articles. Send tearsheet of article, information about when and where the article previously appeared and who now owns copyright. Reports in 2 months. Sample copy for 9×12 SAE with 6 first-class stamps. Free writer's guidelines.

Nonfiction: Book excerpts, how-to (teach, business), interview/profile, new product, personal experience, photo feature. Special issues: summer programs (February); music & more; (July/August); costumes and production preview (November/December). No PR or puff pieces. All articles must be well researched. Buys 50 mss/year. Query. Length: 1,000-3,500 words. Pays $100-350 for unsolicited articles.

Photos: Send photos with submission. Reviews contact sheets, negatives transparencies and prints. Limited photo budget.

Columns/Departments: Practical Tips (how-tos or updates, 100-350 words. Pays $25/published tip. Free Calendar Listings (auditions/competitions/workshops), 50 words.

Tips: Read several issues—particularly seasonal. Stay within writers guidelines.

THE EDUCATION CENTER, INC., The Mailbox (3 editions)—Magazines Division, 1607 Battleground Ave., Greensboro NC 27499-0123. Magazines Manager: Diane George. Senior Editors: Diane Badden, Primary edition (grades 1-3); Becky Andrews, Intermediate edition (grades 4-6); Karen Shelton, preschool/Kindergarten edition. "Our audience is elementary (preschool to grade 6) teachers. We are looking for practical, creative, hands-on teaching ideas and tips as opposed to articles about education. Must be educationally sound." Estab. 1973. **Pays on acceptance.** Editorial lead time varies up to one year. Reports in 2 months on queries. Query with résumé showing teaching experience. Sample copy and writer's guidelines to qualified applicants.

Nonfiction: Educational-teacher directed. "We *absolutely* require that all writers have *at least* three years of *self-contained* classroom teaching experience, preferably recent, at the same grade level. Applicants may be excellent writers, but without the teaching experience, **will be** rejected." Pays $35-50/worksheet; $165-200/8-10 idea unit.

EDUCATION IN FOCUS, Books for All Times, Inc., Box 2, Alexandria VA 22313. (703)548-0457. Editor: Joe David. Semiannual newsletter that covers educational issues. Pays on publication. Buys first, one-time and second serial (reprint) rights. Will negotiate rights to include articles in books. Accepts simultaneous submissions. Reports in 1 month. *Writer's Market* recommends allowing 2 months for reply. Please include SASE with all submissions.

Nonfiction: "We are looking for articles that expose the failures and discuss the successes of education."

INSTRUCTOR MAGAZINE, Scholastic, Inc., 555 Broadway, New York NY 10012-3199. Executive Editor: Mickey Revenaugh. Publishing Coordinator: Ellen Ongaro. Eager to work with new/unpublished writers, "especially teachers." Monthly magazine emphasizing elementary education. Estab. 1891. Circ. 275,000. **Pays on acceptance.** Publishes ms an average of 1 year after acceptance. Byline given. Buys all rights. Submit seasonal material 6 months in advance. Query for electronic submissions. Reports in 1 month on queries; 2 months on mss. Sample copy for $3. Writer's guidelines for SASE; mention *Writer's Market* in request.

Nonfiction: How-to articles on elementary classroom practice—practical suggestions and project reports. Occasionally publishes first-person accounts of classroom experiences. Buys 100 mss/year. Query. Length: 400-2,000 words. Pays $15-75 for short items; $125-400 for articles and features. Send all queries Attention: manuscripts editor.

Photos: Send photos with submission. Reviews 4×5 transparencies and prints. Offers no additional payment for photos accepted with ms. Model releases and identification of subjects required. Buys all rights.

Columns/Departments: Idea Notebook (quick teacher tips and ideas); Planner (seasonal activities, bulletin boards and crafts); Primary Place (teaching ideas for primary grades). Buys 100 mss/year. Query with SASE. Length: 50-1,000 words. Pays $30-100.

Fiction: Occasionally buys plays and read-aloud stories for children. Length: 500-2,500 words. Pays $75-200.

Tips: "How-to articles should be kept practical, with concrete examples whenever possible. Writers should keep in mind that our audience is elementary teachers."

JOURNAL OF CAREER PLANNING & EMPLOYMENT, College Placement Council, Inc., Dept. WM, 62 Highland Ave., Bethlehem PA 18017. (215)868-1421. Fax: (215)868-0208. Associate Editor: Bill Beebe. 25% freelance written. Magazine published November, January, March and May. Magazine for career development professionals who counsel and/or hire college students, graduates, and other college-educated job candidates. Estab. 1940. Circ. 4,200. **Pays on acceptance.** Publishes ms an average of 4 months after acceptance. Byline given. Buys first rights. Reports in 1 month on queries; 2 months on mss. Writer's guidelines for #10 SASE.

Nonfiction: How-to, interview/profile, new techniques/innovative practices, current issues in the field. *No articles that speak directly to job candidates.* Buys 2-5 mss/year. Query with published clips, or send complete ms or hard copy plus floppy disk. Length: 3,000-4,000 words. Pays up to $200.

Tips: "A freelancer can best break into our publication by sending query with clips of published work, by writing on topics that aim directly at the journal's audience—professionals in the college career planning, placement and recruitment field—and by using an easy-to-read, narrative style rather than a formal, thesis style. The area of our publication most open to freelancers is nonfiction feature articles only. Topics should directly relate to the career planning and employment of the college educated and should go beyond the basics of career planning, job hunting and hiring issues, since readers are well-versed in those basics."

LEARNING 95, 1111 Bethlehem Pike, Springhouse PA 19477-0908. Fax: (215)646-4399. Editor/Publisher: Charlene F. Gaynor. Executive Editor: Jeanette Moss. 45% freelance written. Magazine published monthly during school year covering elementary and junior high school education topics. Estab. 1972. Circ. 275,000. **Pays on acceptance.** Buys all rights. Submit seasonal material 9 months in advance. Reports in up to 4 months. Sample copy for $3. Free writer's guidelines.

Nonfiction: "We publish manuscripts that describe innovative, practical teaching strategies." How-to (classroom management, specific lessons or units or activities for children—all at the elementary and junior high level—and hints for teaching in all curriculum areas); personal experience (from teachers in elementary and junior high schools); profile (with teachers who are in unusual or innovative teaching situations). Strong interest in articles that deal with discipline, teaching strategy, motivation and working with parents. Buys 250 mss/year. Query. Length: 1,000-3,500 words. Pays $50-350.

• This magazine has become more selective; submissions must meet their format.

Tips: "We're looking for practical, teacher-tested ideas and strategies as well as first-hand personal accounts of dramatic successes—or failures—with a lesson to be drawn. No theoretical or academic papers. We're also interested in examples of especially creative classrooms and teachers. Emphasis on professionalism will increase: top teachers telling what they do best and others can also."

MEDIA & METHODS, American Society of Educators, 1429 Walnut St., Philadelphia PA 19102. (215)563-3501. Editorial Director: Michele Sokoloff. Bimonthly trade journal published during the school year about educational products, media technologies and programs for schools and universities. Readership: Librarians and media specialists. Estab. 1963. Circ. 42,000. Pays on publication. Publishes ms an average of 3 months after acceptance. Byline given. Buys first North American serial rights. Free sample copy and writer's guidelines.

Nonfiction: How-to, practical, new product, personal experience, technical. Must send query letter, outline or call editor. Do not send ms. Length: 600-1,200 words. Pays $75-200.

Photos: State availability of photos with submission. Reviews 3×5 prints. Offers no additional payment for photos accepted with ms. Captions and identification of subjects required. Buys one-time rights.

MEDIA PROFILES: The Health Sciences Edition, Olympic Media Information, P.O. Box 190, West Park NY 12493-0190. (914)384-6563. Publisher: Walt Carroll. 100% freelance written. Consists entirely of signed reviews of videos and films for healthcare education (no editorials or "articles"). Subscribers are medical and nursing libraries, colleges and universities where health sciences are taught. Journal magazine format, published quarterly. Estab. 1967. Circ. 1,000. Pays on publication. Publishes ms an average of 4 months after acceptance. Buys all rights. Buys 160 mss/year. Word processing (IBM or Mac) disk submissions preferred. "Sample copies and writer's guidelines sent on receipt of résumé, background, and mention of subject areas you are interested (most qualified) in reviewing. Enclose $5 for writer's guidelines and sample issue. (Refunded with first payment upon publication)." Reports in 1 month. Query.

Nonfiction: "We are the only review publication devoted exclusively to evaluation of films and videos for medical and health training. We have a highly specialized, definite format that must be followed in all cases. Samples should be seen by all means. Our writers should first have a background in health sciences; second, have some experience with audiovisuals; and third, follow our format precisely. Writers with advanced degrees and teaching affiliations with colleges and hospital education departments given preference. We are interested in reviews of media materials for nursing education, in-service education, continuing education, personnel training, patient education, patient care and medical problems. Currently seeking MDs, RNs, PhDs with clinical and technical expertise. Unsolicited mss not welcome. We will have videos sent directly to reviewers who accept the assignments." Pays $15/review.

MOMENTUM, National Catholic Educational Association, 1077 30th St. NW, Washington DC 20007-3852. Fax: (202)333-6706. Editor: Patricia Feistritzer. 10% freelance written. Quarterly magazine for Catholic administrators and teachers, some parents and students, in all levels of education (preschool, elementary, secondary, higher). Estab. 1970. Circ. 25,000. Pays on publication. Buys first serial rights. Reports in 3 months. Sample copy for 9 × 12 SASE.

Nonfiction: Articles concerned with educational philosophy, psychology, methodology, innovative programs, teacher training, research, financial and public relations programs and management systems—all applicable to nonpublic schools. Book reviews on educational/religious topics. Avoid general topics or topics applicable *only* to public education. "We look for a straightforward, journalistic style with emphasis on practical examples, as well as scholarly writing and statistics. All references must be footnoted, fully documented. Emphasis is on professionalism." Buys 28-36 mss/year. Length: 1,500-2,000 words. Pays 2¢/word.

SCHOOL ARTS MAGAZINE, 50 Portland St., Worcester MA 01608-9959. Fax: (508)753-3834. Editor: Eldon Katter. 85% freelance written. Magazine published monthly, September-May, serving arts and craft education profession, K-12, higher education and museum education programs. Written by and for art teachers. Estab. 1901. Pays on publication. Publishes ms an average of 3 months "if timely; if less pressing, can be 1 year or more" after acceptance. Buys first serial and second serial (reprint) rights. Reports in 3 months. Free sample copy and writer's guidelines.

Nonfiction: Articles on art and craft activities in schools. Should include description and photos of activity in progress, as well as examples of finished artwork. Query or send complete ms. Length: 600-1,400 words. Pays $20-100.

Tips: "We prefer articles on actual art projects or techniques done by students in actual classroom situations. Philosophical and theoretical aspects of art and art education are usually handled by our contributing editors. Our articles are reviewed and accepted on merit and each is tailored to meet our needs. Keep in mind that art teachers want practical tips, above all—more hands-on information than academic theory. Write your article with the accompanying photographs in hand." The most frequent mistakes made by writers are "bad visual material (photographs, drawings) submitted with articles, or a lack of complete descriptions of art processes; and no rationale behind programs or activities. Familiarity with the field of art education is essential."

TEACHING THEATRE, Educational Theatre Association, 3368 Central Pkwy., Cincinnati OH 45225. (513)559-1996. Editor: James Palmarini. 75% freelance written. Membership benefit of Teachers Education Association (part of ETA). Quarterly magazine covering education theater K-12, primary emphasis on secondary. *"Teaching Theatre* emphasizes the teaching, theory, philosophy issues that are of concern to teachers at the elementary, secondary, and—as they relate to teaching K-12 theater—college levels. We publish work that explains specific approaches to teaching (directing, acting, curriculum development and management, etc.); advocates curriculum reform; or offers theories of theater education." Estab. 1989. Circ. 2,000. **Pays on acceptance.** Publishes ms an average of 1-3 months after acceptance. Byline given. Buys one-time rights. Editorial lead time 2 months. Submit seasonal material 3 months in advance. Accepts simultaneous and previously published submissions. Query for electronic submissions. Reports in 1 month on queries; 3 months on mss. Sample copy for $2. Writer's guidelines for #10 SASE.

Nonfiction: Book excerpts, essays, how-to, interview/profile, opinion, technical theater. *"Teaching Theatre's* audience is well-educated and most have considerable experience in their field; while *generalist* articles are not discouraged, it should be assumed that readers already *possess* basic skills." Buys 15 mss/year. Query. Pays $100-200 for published articles. "We generally pay cash and 5 copies of issue."

Photos: State availability of photos with submission. Reviews contact sheets, 5 × 7 and 8 × 10 transparencies, 5 × 7 and 8 × 10 prints. Offers no additional payment for photos accepted with ms.

TEACHING TODAY, 9210-95 Ave., Edmonton, Alberta T6C 4N6 Canada. (403)462-0585. Fax: (403)468-0099. Co-publisher/ Editor-in-Chief: Margaret Barry. 90% freelance written. Educational magazine published 5 times/year. Estab. 1983. Circ. 10,000. Pays on publication. Publishes ms an average of 1 year after acceptance. Manuscript must be accompanied by SAE with IRCs for return. Byline given. Buys first, one-time or all rights. Accepts simultaneous and previously published submissions if so informed. Query for electronic submissions.

Reports in 3 months. Sample copy for $3 (includes postage for US destinations, in Canada 84¢ postage); check or money order addressed to *Teaching Today*.

Nonfiction: How-to (related to teaching), humor (related to education), inspiration, personal experience (if related to teaching), communication skills and professional development (teacher). Buys 50-60 mss/year. Query letters encouraged. Length: 150-1,200 words. Pays 10¢/word.

Photos: Send photos with submission. Reviews b&w or color 4×5, 3×5, or 4×6 prints; or 8×10 color (for cover only). Offers $25/photo. Model releases and identification of subjects required. Buys one-time rights.

Fillers: Anecdotes and gags to be illustrated by cartoonist. Buys 20/year. Length: 20-100 words. Pays $5-25.

Tips: "A freelancer can best break into our magazine with well-written articles related to education. Articles primarily that will *help* educators personally or professionally."

‡**TEACHING TOLERANCE**, The Southern Poverty Law Center, 400 Washington Ave., Montgomery AL 36104. (205)264-0286. Fax: (205)264-3121. Assistant Editor: David Aronson. 50% freelance written. Semiannual trade magazine covering education for diversity. "*Teaching Tolerance* is dedicated to helping K-12 teachers promote tolerance and understanding between widely diverse groups of students. Includes articles, teaching ideas, and reviews of other resources available to educators." Estab. 1991. Circ. 225,000. **Pays on acceptance.** Byline given. Buys first North American serial rights. Editorial lead time 6 months. Submit seasonal material 6 months in advance. Query for electronic submissions. Sample copy and writer's guidelines free on request.

Nonfiction: Essays, how-to (classroom techniques), interview/profile, personal experience, photo feature, multicultural education. "No jargon, rhetoric or academic analysis. No theoretical discussions on the pros/cons of multicultural education." Buys 6-8 mss/year. Query with published clips. Length: 1,000-3,000 words. Pays $500-3,000 maximum. Sometimes pays expenses of writers on assignment.

Photos: State availability of photos with submission. Reviews contact sheets and transparencies. Offers no additional payment for photos accepted with ms. Captions and identification of subjects required. Buys one-time rights.

Columns/Departments: Essays (personal reflection, how-to, school program) 400-800 words; Idea Exchange (special projects, other school activities) 100 words; Interview/profile (usually features nationally known figure) 1,000-2,500 words; Student Writings (Short essays dealing with diversity, tolerance & justice) 300-500 words. Buys 8-12 mss/year. Pays $100-1,000. Query with published clips.

Fillers: Contact: Elsie Williams, editorial assistant. Anecdotes, facts, gags to be illustrated by cartoonist, newsbreaks, short humor. Buys 10/year. Length: 25-250 words. Pays $10-25.

Tips: "We want lively, simple, concise writing. The writing style should be descriptive and reflective, showing the strength of programs dealing successfully with diversity by employing clear descriptions of real scenes and interactions, and by using quotes from teachers and students. We ask that prospective writers study previous issues of the magazine and writer's guidelines before sending a query with ideas. Most open to articles that have a strong classroom focus. We are interested in approaches to teaching tolerance and promoting understanding that really work—approaches we might not have heard of. We want to inform our readers; we also want to inspire and encourage them. We know what's happening nationally; we want to know what's happening in your neighborhood classroom."

TEACHING/K-8, The Professional Magazine, Early Years, Inc., 7th Floor, 40 Richards Ave., Norwalk CT 06854-2319. (203)855-2650. Fax: (203)855-2656. Editor: Allen Raymond. Editorial Director: Patricia Broderick. 90% freelance written. "We prefer material from classroom teachers." Monthly magazine covering teaching of K-8. Estab. 1970. Pays on publication. Publishes ms an average of 7 months after acceptance. Byline given. Buys all rights. Submit seasonal material 6 months in advance. Reports in 2 months. Sample copy for $3 and 9×12 SAE with 10 first-class stamps. Writer's guidelines for #10 SASE.

Nonfiction: Classroom curriculum material. Send complete ms. Length: 1,200-1,500 words. Pays $35 maximum.

• This magazine has substantially increased freelance needs.

Photos: Offers no additional payment for photos accepted with ms. Model releases and identification of subjects required.

Tips: "Manuscripts should be specifically oriented to a successful teaching strategy, idea, project or program. Broad overviews of programs or general theory manuscripts are not usually the type of material we select for publication. Because of the definitive learning level we cover (pre-school through grade eight) we try to avoid presenting general groups of unstructured ideas. We prefer classroom tested ideas and techniques."

TECH DIRECTIONS, (formerly *School Shop/Tech Directions*), Prakken Publications, Inc., P.O. Box 8623, Ann Arbor MI 48107-8623. (313)769-1211. Fax: (313)769-8383. Managing Editor: Paul J. Bamford. 100% freelance written. Eager to work with new/unpublished writers. Monthly magazine (except June and July) covering issues, trends and projects of interest to industrial, vocational, technical and technology educators at the secondary and postsecondary school levels. Estab. 1934. Circ. 45,000. Buys all rights. Pays on publication. Publishes ms an average of 8-12 months after acceptance. Byline given. Prefers authors who have direct connection with the field of industrial and/or technical education. Accepts simultaneous and previously published submissions. Send photocopy of article and information about when and where the article previously appeared. Pays 100% of their fee for an original article. Reports in 2 months. Sample copy and writer's guidelines for 9×12 SAE with 3 first-class stamps.

Nonfiction: Uses articles pertinent to the various teaching areas in industrial and technology education (woodwork, electronics, drafting, machine shop, graphic arts, computer training, etc.). "The outlook should be on innovation in educational programs, processes or projects that directly apply to the industrial/technical education area." Buys general interest, how-to, opinion, personal experience, technical and think pieces, interviews, humor, and coverage of new products. Buys 135 unsolicited mss/year. Length: 200-2,000 words. Pays $25-150.

Photos: Send photos with accompanying query or ms. Reviews b&w and color prints. Payment for photos included in payment for ms.

Columns/Departments: Tech-Niques (brief items which describe short-cuts or special procedures relevant to the technology or vocational education). Buys 30 mss/year. Send complete ms. Length: 20-100 words. Pays $15 minimum.

Tips: "We are most interested in articles written by industrial, vocational and technical educators about their class projects and their ideas about the field. We need more and more technology-related articles, especially written for the community college level."

TECHNOLOGY & LEARNING, Suite A4, 2169 Francisco Blvd. E., San Rafael CA 94901. Fax: (415)457-4379. Editor-in-Chief: Holly Brady. 50% freelance written. Works with a small number of new/unpublished writers each year. Monthly magazine published during school year emphasizing elementary through high school educational technology topics. Estab. 1980. Circ. 83,000. Pays on publication. Publishes ms an average of 8 months after acceptance. Buys all or first serial rights. Submit seasonal material 6 months in advance. Reports in 3-5 months. Sample copy for 8×10 SAE with 6 first-class stamps. Writer's guidelines for #10 SASE.

Nonfiction: "We publish manuscripts that describe innovative ways of using technology in the classroom as well as articles that discuss controversial issues in computer education." Interviews, brief technology-related activity ideas and longer featurettes describing fully-developed and tested classroom ideas. Buys 20 mss/year. Query. Length: 800 words for software reviews; 1,500-2,500 words for major articles. Pays $150 for reviews; $200 or more for articles. Educational Software Reviews are assigned through editorial offices. "If interested, send a letter telling us of your areas of interest and expertise as well as the microcomputer(s) and other equipment you have available to you." Pays expenses of writers on assignment.

Photos: State availability of photos with query.

Tips: "The talent that goes into writing our shorter hands-on pieces is different from that required for features (e.g., interviews, issues pieces, etc.) Write whatever taps your talent best. A frequent mistake is taking too 'novice' or too 'expert' an approach. You need to know our audience well and to understand how much they know about computers. Also, too many manuscripts lack a definite point of view or focus or opinion. We like pieces with clear, strong, well thought-out opinions."

TODAY'S CATHOLIC TEACHER, 330 Progress Rd., Dayton OH 45449-2386. (513)847-5900. Fax: (513)847-5910. Editor: Stephen Brittan. 40% freelance written. Works with a small number of new/unpublished writers each year. For administrators, teachers and parents concerned with Catholic schools and education in general. Estab. 1967. Circ. 60,000. Pays after publication. Publishes ms an average of 3 months after acceptance. Byline given. Buys all rights. Phone queries OK. Submit seasonal material 3 months in advance. Reports in 4 months. Sample copy for $3. Writer's guidelines for #10 SASE; mention *Writer's Market* in request.

Nonfiction: How-to (based on experience, particularly for teachers to use in the classroom to supplement curriculum, philosophy with practical applications); interview (of practicing educators, educational leaders); personal experience (classroom happenings other educators can learn from); and a few profiles (of educational leaders). Buys 40-50 mss/year. Submit complete ms. Length: 800-2,000 words. Pays $15-250.

Photos: State availability of photos with ms. Offers no additional payment for 8×10 b&w glossy prints. Buys one-time rights. Captions preferred; model releases required.

Tips: "We prefer articles that are of interest or practical help to educators—teaching ideas, curriculum-related material, administration suggestions, resource guides, articles teachers can use in classroom to teach current topics, etc. We use many one-page features."

‡UNIVERSITY AFFAIRS, Association of Universities and Colleges of Canada, 600-350 Albert St., Ontario K1R 1B1 Canada. (613)563-1236. Editor: Christine Tausig Ford. 50% freelance written. Tabloid published 10 times/year covering Canadian higher education. "Targeted to university faculty and administrators across Canada, *University Affairs* contains news, issues and commentary about higher education and research." Estab. 1959. Circ. 27,000. **Pays on acceptance.** Byline given. Buys first or all rights. Editorial lead time 3 months. Submit seasonal material 3 months in advance. Query for electronic submissions. Reports in 6 weeks on queries; 2 months on mss. Sample copy free on request.

Nonfiction: Essays, general interest, interview/profile, opinion, photo feature. Buys 25 mss/year. Query with published clips. Length: 1,000-1,800 words. Pays $125 (Canadian).

Photos: State availability of photos with submission. Reviews contact sheets, negatives, transparencies, prints. Negotiates payment individually. Captions, model releases, identification of subjects required. Buys all rights.

Columns/Departments: Around the Universities (short, feature articles about research or teaching achievements or "firsts"), 200 words. Buys 10 mss/year. Query with published clips. Pay $125-200 (Canadian).
Tips: "Read the publication before contacting me. Have a solid understanding of both my needs and the subject matter involved. Be accurate, check facts, and make sure your writing is high quality. Look for the human interest angle. Put yourself in place of the readers—what makes your story meaningful for them."

Electronics and Communication

These publications are edited for broadcast and telecommunications technicians and engineers, electrical engineers and electrical contractors. Included are journals for electronic equipment designers and operators who maintain electronic and telecommunication systems. Publications for appliance dealers can be found in Home Furnishings and Household Goods.

BROADCAST TECHNOLOGY, P.O. Box 420, Bolton, Ontario L7E 5T3 Canada. (905)857-6076. Fax: (905)857-6045. Editor-in-Chief: Doug Loney. 50% freelance written. Monthly (except August, December) magazine covering Canadian broadcasting industry. Estab. 1975. Circ. 8,000. Pays on publication. Byline given. Buys all rights. Phone queries OK.
Nonfiction: Technical articles on developments in broadcast engineering, especially pertaining to Canada. Query. Length: 500-1,500 words. Pays $100-300.
Photos: Purchased with accompanying ms. Black and white or color. Captions required.
Tips: "Most of our outside writing is by regular contributors, usually employed fulltime in broadcasting. The specialized nature of our magazine requires a specialized knowledge on the part of a writer."

BUSINESS RADIO, National Association of Business and Educational Radio, 1501 Duke St., Alexandria VA 22314-3450. (703)739-0300. Fax: (703)836-1608. Editor: A.E. Goetz. Managing Editor: Terry Banks. 25% freelance written. Magazine published 10 times/year on mobile communications for land mobile equipment users, dealers, service shop operators, manufacturers, communications technicians, paging and SMR system owners and operators. To acquaint members with the diversity of uses to which land mobile radio can be applied and to identify and discuss new and developing areas of RF technology and their application." Estab. 1965. Circ. 3,500. **Pays on acceptance.** Publishes ms an average of 3 months after acceptance. Byline given. Buys first rights. Query for electronic submissions. Reports in 3 months. Sample copy for 9 × 12 SAE with 5 first-class stamps. Writer's guidelines for #10 SASE.
Nonfiction: General interest, interview/profile, new product, technical, general small business or management articles all related to land mobile communications. Buys 5 mss/year. Query with or without published clips or send complete ms. Length: 1,500-2,200 words. Pays $100-300 for unsolicited articles. Sometimes pays expenses of writers on assignment.
Photos: Send photos with submission. Reviews contact sheets, negatives, transparencies and prints. Offers no additional payment for b&w photos accepted with ms. Captions, model releases and identification of subjects required. Buys one-time rights.
Columns/Departments: ShopTalk (small business, general management), 1,500-2,500 words. Buys 8 mss/ year. Query or send complete ms. Pays $150-250.
Tips: "We are seeking writers who are knowledgeable in mobile communications and telecommunications to write in-depth user profiles and new technology pieces."

CABLE COMMUNICATIONS MAGAZINE, Canada's Authoritative International Cable Television Publication, Ter-Sat Media Publications Ltd., Dept. WM, 1421 Victoria St. N., Kitchener, Ontario N2B 3E4 Canada. (519)744-4111. Fax: (519)744-1261. Editor: Udo Salewsky. 33% freelance written. Prefers to work with published/established writers. Monthly magazine covering the cable television industry. Estab. 1934. Circ. 7,200. **Pays on acceptance.** Publishes ms an average of 2 months after acceptance. Byline given. Buys all rights. Submit seasonal material 1 month in advance. Query for electronic submissions. Reports in 2 weeks on queries; 1 month on mss. Sample copy for 9 × 12 SAE with $3.50 in IRCs. Free writer's guidelines.
Nonfiction: Exposé, how-to, interview/profile, opinion, technical articles, informed views and comments on topical, industry-related issues. Also, problem solving-related articles, new marketing and operating efficiency ideas. No fiction. Buys 50 mss/year. Query with published clips or send complete ms. Length: 1,000-4,000 words. Pays $250-1,000. Pays expenses of writers on assignment.
Columns/Departments: Buys 48 items/year. Query with published clips or send complete ms. Length: 1,000-1,500 words. Pays $250-375.
Tips: "Forward manuscript and personal résumé. We don't need freelance writers for short articles and fillers. Break in with articles related to industry issues, events and new developments; analysis of current issues and events. Be able to interpret the meaning of new developments relative to the cable television industry and their potential impact on the industry from a growth opportunity as well as a competitive point of view. Material should be well supported by facts and data. Insufficient research and understanding of underlying issues are frequent mistakes."

COMMUNICATIONS QUARTERLY, P.O. Box 465, Barrington NH 03825-0465. Phone/Fax: (603)664-2515. Publisher: Richard Ross. Editor: Terry Littlefield. 80% freelance written. Quarterly publication on theoretical and technical aspects of amateur radio and communication industry technology. Estab. 1990. Circ. 10,000. Pays on publication. Reports in 1 month. Publishes ms an average of 6 months after acceptance. Byline given. Buys first rights. Query for electronic submissions. Reports in 1 month. Writer's guidelines for #10 SASE.
Nonfiction: "Interested in technical and theory pieces on all aspects of amateur radio and the communications industry. State-of-the-art developments are of particular interest to our readers. No human interest stories." Query or send complete ms. Pays $40/published page.
Photos: Send photos with submission. Reviews 5×7 b&w prints. Offers no additional payment for photos accepted with ms. Captions and identification of subjects required. Buys one-time rights.
Tips: "We are looking for writers with knowledge of the technical or theoretical aspects of the amateur radio and communication industries. Our readers are interested in state-of-the-art developments, high-tech construction projects and the theory behind the latest technologies."

ELECTRONIC SERVICING & TECHNOLOGY, CQ Communications, 76 N. Broadway, Hicksville NY 11801. (516)681-2922. Fax: (516)681-2926. Editorial Office: P.O. Box 12487, Overland Park KS 66282-2487. Phone/Fax: (913)492-4857. Editor: Conrad Persson. Associate Editor: Linda Romanello. 90% freelance written. Eager to work with new/unpublished writers. Monthly magazine for professional servicers and electronic enthusiasts who are interested in buying, building, installing and repairing consumer electronic equipment (audio, TV, video, microcomputers, electronic games, etc.). Estab. 1950. Circ. 38,000. **Pays on acceptance.** Publishes ms an average of 6 months after acceptance. Byline given. Buys all rights. Accepts previously published articles. Send typed ms with rights for sale noted and information about when and where the article previously appeared. Reports in 2 weeks on queries; 1 month on mss. Sample copy and writer's guidelines for 9×12 SAE with 5 first-class stamps.
Nonfiction: How-to (service, build, install and repair home entertainment; electronic testing and servicing equipment). "Explain the techniques used carefully so that even hobbyists can understand a how-to article." Buys 36 mss/year. Send complete ms. Length: 1,500 words minimum. Pays $100-300.
Photos: Send photos with ms. Reviews color and b&w transparencies and b&w prints. Captions and identification of subjects required. Buys all rights. Payment included in total ms package.
Columns/Departments: Linda Romanello, associate editor. Troubleshooting Tips: Buys 12 mss/year. Send complete ms. Pays $25.
Tips: "In order to write for *ES&T* it is almost essential that a writer have an electronics background: technician, engineer or serious hobbyist. Our readers want nuts-and-bolts information on electronics."

‡THE FUTURE, NOW, Innovative Video, Blue Feather Company, P.O. Box 669, N8494 Poplar Grove Rd., New Glarus WI 53574-0669. (608)527-5077. Fax: (608)527-5078. Editor: Jennifer M. Jarik. Managing Editor: Becky J. Hustad. 10% freelance written. Bimonthly tabloid that covers video industry. "Generally articles have a 'Third Wave/Information Age' slant to them." Estab. 1990. Circ. 25,000. Pays 30 days after publication. Publishes ms an average of 2 months after acceptance. Byline given. Buys first rights or second serial (reprint) rights. Submit seasonal material 3 months in advance. Accepts simultaneous and previously published submissions. Send information about when and where the article previously appeared. Query for electronic submissions. Reports in 3 weeks on queries; 1 month on mss. Sample copy for 9×12 SAE with 2 first-class stamps. Writer's guidelines for #10 SASE.
Nonfiction: How-to, humor (pertaining to business and video), new product and technical (pertaining to video). "We are looking for unique ideas presented in a light manner. Please, nothing dry or humorless. Material must pertain to video." Buys 20 mss/year. Query with or without published clips, or send complete ms. Length: 600-1,500 words. Pays $50-100 for unsolicited articles.
Photos: State availability of photos with submission. Reviews prints. Offers no additional payment for photos accepted with ms. Buys one-time rights.
Columns/Departments: Management (new ideas for managing in an information society); Technical Tips (low cost tips for fixing video emergencies); Stress Management; Video Production; Environment (generally tips about "living lightly on the earth"). Buys 20 mss/year. Send complete ms. Length: 600-1,500 words. Pays $50-100.
Fillers: Facts, gags to be illustrated by cartoonist, newsbreaks and short humor. Length: 50-150 words. Payment negotiable.
Tips: "We are looking for unique ideas which will appeal to the video industry. *The Future Now* is a new 'new wave' publication which, in addition to keeping people updated on video happenings, attempts to help people cope with a rapidly changing society. We specifically need people with good stress management techniques and 'technical video info.' However, we are open to working with new writers who have interesting perspectives."

THE INDEPENDENT Film & Video Monthly, Foundation for Independent Video & Film, 9th Floor, 625 Broadway, New York NY 10012-2611. (212)473-3400. Fax: (212)677-8732. Editor: Patricia Thomson. 60% freelance written. Works with a small number of new/unpublished writers each year. Monthly magazine of practical information for producers of independent film and video with focus on low budget, art and documentary work. Estab. 1979. Circ. 18,000. Pays on publication. Publishes ms an average of 4 months after acceptance. Byline given. Buys first serial rights. Submit seasonal material 4 months in advance. Accepts previously published submissions. Send tearsheet or photocopy of article or typed ms with rights for sale noted, and information about when and where the article previously appeared. Query for electronic submissions. Reports in 3 months. Pay varies. Sample copy for 9 × 12 SASE with 5 first-class stamps.

Nonfiction: Book excerpts ("in our area"), how-to, technical (low-tech only), theoretical/critical articles. No reviews. Buys 60 mss/year. Query with published clips. Length: 1,200-3,500 words. Pays $50-200.

Tips: "Since this is a specialized publication, we prefer to work with writers on short pieces first. Writers should be familiar with specific practical and theoretical issues concerning independent film and video."

OUTSIDE PLANT, P.O. Box 183, Cary IL 60013-0183. (312)639-2200. Fax: (312)639-9542. Editor: John H. Saxtan. 50% freelance written. Prefers to work with published/established writers. Trade publication focusing exclusively on the outside plant segment of the telephone industry. Readers are end users and/or specifiers at Bell and independent operating companies, as well as long distance firms whose chief responsibilities are construction, maintenance, OSP planning and engineering. Readership also includes telephone contracting firms. Publishes an average of 12 issues/year. Estab. 1982. Circ. 18,000. Buys first rights. Pays on publication. Accepts previously published articles. Send photocopy of article. For reprints pays 50% of the amount paid for an original article. Publishes ms an average of 3 months after acceptance. Reports in 2 months.

Nonfiction: Must deal specifically with outside plant construction, maintenance, planning and fleet vehicle subjects for the telephone industry. "Case history application articles profiling specific telephone projects are best. Also accepts trend features, tutorials, industry research and seminar presentations. Preferably, features should be bylined by someone at the telephone company profiled." Pays $35-50/published page, including photographs; pays $35 for cover photos.

Columns/Departments: OSP Tips & Advice (short nuts-and-bolts items on new or unusual work methods) and OSP Tommorrow (significant trends in outside plant), 300-600 words. Pays $5-50. Other departments include new products, literature, vehicles and fiber optics.

Tips: "Submissions should include author bio demonstrating expertise in the subject area."

PRO SOUND NEWS, International News Magazine for the Professional Sound Production Industry, 2 Park Ave., New York NY 10016. (212)213-3444. Fax: (212)213-3484. Editor: Debra A. Pagan. Managing Editor: Andrea Rotondo. 30% freelance written. Works with a small number of new/unpublished writers each year. Monthly tabloid covering the music recording, concert sound reinforcement, TV and film sound industry. Circ. 21,000. Pays on publication. Publishes ms an average of 1 month after acceptance. Byline given. Buys first serial rights. Accepts previously published submissions. Query for electronic submissions. Reports in 2 weeks.

Nonfiction: Query with published clips. Pays $200-300 for assigned articles (approximately 1,000 words). Sometimes pays the expenses of writers on assignment.

RADIO WORLD INTERNATIONAL, Industrial Marketing Advisory Services, 3rd Floor, 5827 Columbia Pike, Falls Church VA 22041-9811. (703)998-7600. Fax: (703)998-2966. Editor: Alan Carter. Managing Editor: Charles Taylor. 50% freelance written. Monthly trade newspaper for radio broadcasting "covering radio station technology, regulatory news, business and management developments outside the US. Articles should be geared toward engineers, producers and managers." Estab. 1990. Circ. 20,000. Pays on publication. Byline given. Offers 50% kill fee. Buys worldwide serial rights. Query for electronic submissions. Reports in 3 weeks. Free sample copy and writer's guidelines.

Nonfiction: New products, technical, regulatory and management news, programming trend pieces. Buys 100 mss/year. Query with published clips. Length: 750-1,000 words. Pays 20¢/word. Sometimes pays expenses of writers on assignment.

Photos: Send photos with submission. Captions and identification of subjects required. Buys all rights.

Columns/Departments: User reports (field reports from engineers on specific equipment); radio management; and studio/audio issues, 750-1,000 words. Buys 50/year. Query. Pays 20¢/word.

Fillers: Newsbreaks. Buys 50/year. Length: 100-500 words.

Tips: "Our news and feature sections are the best bets for freelancers. Focus on radio station operations and the state of the industry worldwide."

SATELLITE RETAILER, Triple D Publishing, Inc., Dept. WM, P.O. Box 2384, Shelby NC 28151-2384. (704)482-9673. Fax: (704)484-8558. Editor: David B. Melton. 75% freelance written. Monthly magazine covering home satellite TV. "We look for technical, how-to, marketing, sales, new products, product testing, and news for the satellite television dealer." Estab. 1981. Circ. 12,000. Pays on publication. Byline given. Offers 30% kill fee. Buys all rights. Submit seasonal material 3 months in advance. Accepts simultaneous submissions. Query for electronic submissions. Reports in 2 months. Free sample copy and writer's guidelines.

Nonfiction: How-to, new product, personal experience, photo feature, technical. Buys 24 mss/year. Query with or without published clips or send complete ms. Length: 1,800-3,600 words. Pays $150-400. Sometimes pays expenses of writers on assignment.

Photos: Send photos with submission. Reviews contact sheets, transparencies (35mm or 4×5). Captions, model releases and identification of subjects required. Buys all rights.
Tips: "Familiarity with electronics and television delivery systems is a definite plus."

Energy and Utilities

People who supply power to homes, businesses and industry read the publications in this section. This category includes journals covering the electric power, natural gas, petroleum, solar and alternative energy industries.

ALTERNATIVE ENERGY RETAILER, Zackin Publications, Inc., P.O. Box 2180, Waterbury CT 06722-2180. (203)755-0158. Fax: (203)755-3480. Editorial Director: John Florian. 5% freelance written. Prefers to work with published/established writers. Monthly magazine on selling alternative energy products—chiefly solid fuel and gas-burning appliances. "We seek detailed how-to tips for retailers to improve business. Most freelance material purchased is about retailers and how they succeed." Estab. 1980. Circ. 10,000. Pays on publication. Publishes ms an average of 2 months after acceptance. Buys first North American serial rights. Submit seasonal material 4 months in advance. Reports in 2 weeks on queries. Sample copy for 9×12 SAE with 4 first-class stamps. Writer's guidelines for #10 SASE.
Nonfiction: How-to (improve retail profits and business know-how), interview/profile (of successful retailers in this field). No "general business articles not adapted to this industry." Buys 10 mss/year. Query. Length: 1,000 words. Pays $200.
Photos: State availability of photos. Pays $25-125 maximum for 5×7 b&w prints. Reviews color transparencies. Identification of subject required. Buys one-time rights.
Tips: "A freelancer can best break into our publication with features about readers (retailers). Stick to details about what has made this person a success."
• Submit articles that focus on health market trends and successful sales techniques.

ELECTRICAL APPARATUS, The Magazine of the Electromechanical & Electronic Application & Maintenance, Barks Publications, Inc., 400 N. Michigan Ave., Chicago IL 60611-4198. (312)321-9440. Editorial Director: Elsie Dickson. Managing Editor: Kevin N. Jones. Monthly magazine for persons working in electrical and electronic maintenance, chiefly in industrial plants, who install and service electrical motors, transformers, generators, controls and related equipment. Estab. 1967. Circ. 17,000. **Pays on acceptance.** Publishes ms an average of 3 months after acceptance. Byline given. Buys all rights unless other arrangements made. Reports in 1 week on queries; 1 month on mss. *Writer's Market* recommends allowing 2 months for reply. Query for electronic submissions. Sample copy for $4.
Nonfiction: Technical. Length: 1,500-2,500. Pays $250-500 for assigned articles plus authorized expenses.
• Columns are now all staff-written.
Tips: "All feature articles are assigned to staff and contributing editors and correspondents. Professionals interested in appointments as contributing editors and correspondents should submit résumé and article outlines, including illustration suggestions. Writers should be competent with a camera, which should be described in résumé. Technical expertise is absolutely necessary, preferably an E.E. degree, or practical experience. We are also book publishers and some of the material in *EA* is now in book form, bringing the authors royalties. Also publishes an annual directory, subtitled *ElectroMechanical Bench Reference.*"

NATIONAL PETROLEUM NEWS, Suite 800, 25 Northwest Point Blvd., Elk Grove Village IL 60007. (708)427-9512. Fax: (708)427-2041. Editor: Don Smith. 3% freelance written. Prefers to work with published/established writers. For businessmen who make their living in the oil marketing and convenience store industry, either as company employees or through their own business operations. Monthly magazine. Estab. 1909. Circ. 14,000. Rights purchased vary with author and material. Usually buys all rights. Pays on acceptance if done on assignment. Publishes ms an average of 2 months after acceptance. "The occasional freelance copy we use is done on assignment." Query. Accepts previously published material. Send typed ms with rights for sale noted (on disk) and information about when and where the article previously appeared.
• This magazine is particularly interested in articles on international industry-related material.
Nonfiction: Material related directly to developments and issues in the oil marketing and convenience store industry and "how-to" and "what-with" case studies. "No unsolicited copy, especially with limited attribution regarding information in story." Buys 3-4 mss/year. Length: 2,000 words maximum. Pays $50-150/printed page. Sometimes pays the expenses of writers on assignment.
Photos: Pays $150/printed page. Payment for b&w photos "depends upon advance understanding."

PUBLIC POWER, Dept. WM, 2301 M St. NW, Washington DC 20037-1484. (202)467-2948. Fax: (202)467-2910. Editor/Publisher: Jeanne Wickline LaBella. 60% freelance written. Prefers to work with published/established writers. Bimonthly. Estab. 1942. **Pays on acceptance.** Publishes ms an average of 3 months after acceptance. Byline given. Query for electronic submissions. Reports in 6 months. Free sample copy and writer's guidelines.

Nonfiction: Features on municipal and other local publicly owned electric systems. Pays 20¢/word on edited ms.

Photos: Uses b&w glossy and color slides.

RELAY MAGAZINE, Florida Municipal Electric Association, P.O. Box 10114, Tallahassee FL 32302-2114. (904)224-3314. Editor: Stephanie Wolanski. 5% freelance written. Monthly trade journal. "Must be electric utility-oriented, or must address legislative issues of interest to us." Estab. 1942. Circ. 1,900. Pays on publication. Byline given. Publication not copyrighted. Buys first North American serial, one-time and second serial (reprint) rights. Accepts simultaneous and previously published submissions. Send photocopy of article or typed ms with rights for sale noted and information about when and where article previously appeared. Query for electronic submissions. Reports in 3 months. Free sample copy.

Nonfiction: Interview/profile, technical and electric innovations. No articles that haven't been pre-approved by query. Length: 3-6 pages double spaced. Pays $50.

Photos: State availability of photos with submission. Pay and rights purchased vary. Captions and identification of subjects required.

UTILITY AND TELEPHONE FLEETS, Practical Communications, Inc., 321 Cary Point Dr., P.O. Box 183, Cary IL 60013-0183. (708)639-2200. Fax: (708)639-9542. Editor/Associate Publisher: Alan Richter. 10% freelance written. Magazine published 8 times/year for fleet managers and maintenance supervisors for electric gas and water utilities, telephone, interconnect and cable TV companies, public works departments and related contractors. "We seek case history/application features are also welcome." Estab. 1987. Circ. 18,000. Pays on publication. Publishes ms an average of 1 month after acceptance. Byline given. Offers 20% kill fee. Buys all rights. Submit seasonal material 2 months in advance. Accepts previously published material. Send photocopy of article or typed ms with rights for sale noted and information about when and where the article previously appeared. For reprints pays 50% of the amount paid for an original article. Reports in 2 months. Free sample copy and writer's guidelines.

Nonfiction: How-to (ways for performing fleet maintenance/improving management skills/vehicle tutorials), technical, case history/application features. No advertorials in which specific product or company is promoted. Buys 2-3 mss/year. Query with published clips. Length: 1,000-2,800 words. Pays $50/page.

Photos: Send photos with submission. Reviews contact sheets, negatives, transparencies (3×5) and prints (3×5). Offers no additional payment for photos accepted with ms. Captions required. Buys one-time rights.

Columns/Departments: Vehicle Management and Maintenance Tips (nuts-and-bolts items dealing with new or unusual methods for fleet management, maintenance and safety). Buys 2 mss/year. Query with published clips. Length: 100-400 words. Pays $25.

Tips: "Working with a utility or telephone company and gathering information about a construction, safety or fleet project is the best approach for a freelancer."

Engineering and Technology

Engineers and professionals with various specialties read the publications in this section. Publications for electrical, electronics and telecommunications engineers are classified separately under Electronics and Communication. Magazines for computer professionals are in the Information Systems section.

GRADUATING ENGINEER, Peterson's/COG Publishing, Suite 560, 16030 Ventura Blvd., Encino CA 91436. (818)789-5371. Editor-in-Chief: Charlotte Chandler Thomas. 40% freelance written. Prefers to work with published/established writers. Magazine published September-March "to help graduating engineers make the transition from campus to the working world." Estab. 1979. Circ. 83,000. Pays 30 days after acceptance. Publishes ms an average of 2 months after acceptance. Byline given. Buys first North American serial rights. Accepts previously published articles. Send tearsheet or photocopy of article, or typed ms with rights for sale noted and information about when and where the article previously appeared. For reprints pays 25% of the amount paid for an original article. Writer's guidelines available.

Nonfiction: General interest (on management, human resources), career entry, interpersonal skills, job markets, careers, career trends. Special issues: Minority, Women and Engineers and scientists with disabilities. Buys 30 mss/year. Query. Length: 2,000-3,000 words. Pays $300-700.

• *Graduating Engineer* is using fewer freelance writers, and more inhouse and reprints.

Photos: State availability of photos, illustrations or charts. Reviews 35mm color transparencies, 8×10 b&w glossy prints. Captions and model release required.

Tips: "We're generating new types of editorial. We closely monitor economy here and abroad so that our editorial reflects economic, social and global trends."

HIGH TECHNOLOGY CAREERS, %Writers Connection, P.O. Box 24770, San Jose CA 95154-4770. (408)445-3600. Managing Editor: Meera Lester. 100% freelance written. Magazine published every six weeks focusing on high technology industries. "Articles must have a high technology tie-in and should be written in a positive and lively manner. The audience includes managers, engineers and other professionals working in the high technology industries." Circ. 348,000. Pays on publication. Publishes ms an average of 3 months after acceptance. Byline given. Offers 25% kill fee. Buys all rights. Query for electronic submissions. Reports in 2 months. Accepts previously published submissions. Send tearsheet of article and information about when and where the article previously appeared. Payment individually negotiated. Sample copy for 9×12 SAE with $4 in postage. Writer's guidelines for #10 SASE.

Nonfiction: General interest (with high-tech tie-in), technical. Publishes 5 regular 800-word columns (career-oriented) and 2 1,200-word features each issue. Buys 50-60 mss/year. Query with or without published clips or send complete ms. Length: 1,000-1,200 words. Pays 17½¢/word. Sometimes pays expenses of writers on assignment.

Photos: State availability of photos with submission.

MECHANICAL ENGINEERING, American Society of Mechanical Engineers, Dept. WM, 345 E. 47th St., New York NY 10017. (212)705-7782. Editor: John Falcioni. 20% freelance written. Monthly magazine on mechanical process and design. "We publish general interest articles for graduate mechanical engineers on high-tech topics." Circ. 135,000. **Pays on acceptance.** Sometimes byline given. Kill fee varies. Buys first rights. Submit seasonal material 4 months in advance. Reports in 6 weeks. Writer's guidelines for SASE.

Nonfiction: Historical, interview/profile, new product, photo feature, technical. Buys 25 mss/year. Query with or without published clips or send complete ms. Length: 1,500-3,500 words. Pays $500-1,500.

Photos: Send photos with submission. Reviews transparencies and prints. Offers no additional payment for photos accepted with ms. Captions and identification of subjects required. Buys one-time rights.

MINORITY ENGINEER, An Equal Opportunity Career Publication for Professional and Graduating Minority Engineers, Equal Opportunity Publications, Inc., Suite 420, 150 Motor Pkwy., Hauppauge NY 11788-5145. (516)273-0066. Fax: (516)273-8936. Editor: James Schneider. 60% freelance written. Prefers to work with published/established writers. Triannual magazine covering career guidance for minority engineering students and minority professional engineers. Estab. 1969. Circ. 16,000. Pays on publication. Publishes ms an average of 6 months after acceptance. Byline given. Buys first rights. "Deadline dates: Fall (June 1); Winter (September 15); Spring (January 15)." Accepts simultaneous and previously published submissions. Sample copy and writer's guidelines for 9×12 SAE with 5 first-class stamps.

Nonfiction: Book excerpts; articles (on job search techniques, role models); general interest (on specific minority engineering concerns); how-to (land a job, keep a job, etc.); interview/profile (minority engineer role models); new product (new career opportunities); opinion (problems of ethnic minorities); personal experience (student and career experiences); technical (on career fields offering opportunities for minority engineers). "We're interested in articles dealing with career guidance and job opportunities for minority engineers." Query or send complete ms. Length: 1,000-1,500 words. Sometimes pays the expenses of writers on assignment. Pays 10¢/word.

Photos: Prefers 35mm color slides but will accept b&w. Captions and identification of subjects required. Buys all rights. Pays $15. Cartoons accepted. Pays $25.

Tips: "Articles should focus on career guidance, role model and industry prospects for minority engineers. Prefer articles related to careers, not politically or socially sensitive."

NATIONAL DEFENSE, American Defense Preparedness Association, Dept. WM, 2101 Wilson Blvd., Arlington VA 22201-3061. (703)522-1820. Fax: (703)522-1885. Editor: Robert Williams. Managing Editor: Vincent P. Grimes. Magazine published 10 times/year covering all facets of the North American defense industrial base. "Interest is on articles offering a sound analysis of new and ongoing patterns in procurement, research and development of new technology, and budgeting trends." Estab. 1920. Circ. 40,000. Pays on publication. Byline given. Buys all rights. Requires electronic submission. Reports in 1 month on queries. Free sample copy and writer's guidelines for SASE.

Nonfiction: Feature and photos. Buys 12-15 mss/year. Query first. Length: 1,500-2,000 words. Pays negotiated fees, up to $1,000. Pays expenses of writers on assignment "with prior arrangement."

Photos: Send photos with submission. Reviews contact sheets, negatives, transparencies and prints. Offers no additional payment for photos accepted with ms. Captions required. Buys all rights.

‡SENSORS, The Journal of Applied Sensor Technology, Helmers Publishing, Inc., 174 Concord St., Peterborough NH 03458. (603)924-9631. Editor: Dorothy Rosa. 5% freelance written. Monthly magazine covering engineering—electrical and mechanical. "To provide timely, authoritative technical information on the integration of sensors—via data acquisition hardware and software—into subassemblies, manufacturing and process control systems, and products." Estab. 1984. Circ. 63,000. **Pays on acceptance.** Publishes ms an average of 6 months after acceptance. Byline given. Buys first North American serial rights, all rights or makes work-for-hire assignments. Editorial lead time 6 months. Query for electronic submissions. Reports in 1 month on queries; 2 months on mss. Sample copy and writer's guidelines free on request.

Nonfiction: New product, opinion, technical. Special issues: data acquisition (June). Buys 3 mss/year. Query. Length: 800-2,400 words. Pay negotiable. Sometimes pays expenses of writers on assignment.

Photos: Send photos with submission. Reviews prints. Offers no additional payment for photos accepted with ms. Caption, model releases and identification of subjects required. Buys one-time rights.

WOMAN ENGINEER, An Equal Opportunity Career Publication for Graduating Women and Experienced Professionals, Equal Opportunity Publications, Inc., Suite 420, 150 Motor Pkwy., Hauppauge NY 11788-5145. (516)273-8743. Fax: (516)273-8936. Editor: Anne Kelly. 60% freelance written. Works with a small number of new/unpublished writers each year. Triannual magazine covering career guidance for women engineering students and professional women engineers. Estab. 1968. Circ. 16,000. Pays on publication. Publishes ms an average of 3-12 months after acceptance. Byline given. Buys First North American serial rights. Reports in 3 months. Free sample copy and writer's guidelines.
Nonfiction: "Interested in articles dealing with career guidance and job opportunities for women engineers. Looking for manuscripts showing how to land an engineering position and advance professionally. Wants features on job-search techniques, engineering disciplines offering career opportunities to women; companies with career advancement opportunities for women; problems facing women engineers and how to cope with such problems; and role-model profiles of successful women engineers, especially in government, military and defense-related industries." Query. Length: 1,000-2,500 words. Pays 10¢/word.
Photos: Prefers color slides but will accept b&w. Captions and identification of subjects required. Buys all rights. Pays $15.
Tips: "We will be looking for shorter manuscripts (800-1,000 words) on job-search techniques and first-person 'Personal Perspective.'"

Entertainment and the Arts

The business of the entertainment/amusement industry in arts, film, dance, theater, etc. is covered by these publications. Journals that focus on the people and equipment of various music specialties are listed in the Music section, while art and design business publications can be found in Art, Design and Collectibles. Entertainment publications for the general public can be found in the Consumer Entertainment section.

AMUSEMENT BUSINESS, Billboard Publications, Inc., P.O. Box 24970, Nashville TN 37202. (615)321-4269. Fax: (615)327-1575. Managing Editor: Lisa Zhito. 25% freelance written. Works with a small number of new/unpublished writers each year. Weekly tabloid emphasizing hard news of the amusement, sports business, and mass entertainment industry for top management. Circ. 15,000. Pays on publication. Publishes ms an average of 3 weeks after acceptance. Byline sometimes given; "it depends on the quality of the individual piece." Buys all rights. Submit seasonal/holiday material 3 weeks in advance. Phone queries OK. Sample copy for 11 × 14 SAE with 5 first-class stamps.
Nonfiction: How-to (case history of successful advertising campaigns and promotions); interviews (with leaders in the areas we cover highlighting appropriate problems and issues of today, i.e. insurance, alcohol control, etc.). Likes lots of financial support data: grosses, profits, operating budgets and per-cap spending. Also needs lots of quotes. No personality pieces or interviews with stage stars. Publishes profiles of key industry leaders, but must be well-known within the entertainment industry. Buys 500-1,000 mss/year. Query. Length: 400-700 words.
Photos: State availability of photos with query. Captions and model release required. Buys all rights.
Columns/Departments: Auditorium Arenas; Fairs, Parks & Attractions; Food Concessions; Merchandise; Promotion; Shows (carnival and circus); Talent & Touring; Management Changes; Sports; Profile; Eye On Legislation; Commentary and International News.
Tips: There will be more and more emphasis on financial reporting of areas covered. "Submission must contain the whys and whos, etc. and be strong enough that others in the same field will learn from it and not find it naive. We will be increasing story count while decreasing story length."

BILLBOARD, The International News Weekly of Music and Home Entertainment, Dept. WM, 1515 Broadway, New York NY 10036. (212)764-7300; or 5055 Wilshire Blvd., Beverly Hills CA 90036. (213)273-7040. Editor-in-Chief: Timothy White. L.A. Bureau Chief: Craig Rosen. Weekly music magazine. Pays on publication. Buys all rights.
Nonfiction: "Correspondents are appointed to send in spot amusement news covering phonograph record programming by broadcasters and record merchandising by retail dealers." Concert reviews, interviews with artists, and stories on video software (both rental and merchandising).

BOXOFFICE MAGAZINE, RLD Publishing Corp., Suite 100, 6640 Sunset Blvd., Hollywood CA 90028-7159. (213)465-1186. Fax: (213)465-5049. Editor-in-Chief: Ray Greene. 5% freelance written. Monthly business magazine about the motion picture industry for members of the film industry: theater owners, film producers, directors, financiers and allied industries. Estab. 1920. Circ. 10,000. Pays on publication. Publishes ms an average of 2-4 months after acceptance. Byline given. Buys one-time rights. Submit seasonal material 2 months in advance. Accepts simultaneous and previously published submissions. Send tearsheet or photocopy of article and typed ms with rights for sale noted and information about when and where the article previously appeared. Pays 100% of their fee for original article. Reports in 3 months. Send typed ms with rights for sale noted and information about when and where the article previously appeared. For reprints pays 100% of the amount paid for an original article. Sample copy for 9 × 12 SAE with 6 first-class stamps.

Nonfiction: Investigative, interview, profile, new product, photo feature, technical. "We are a general news magazine about the motion picture industry and are looking for stories about trends, developments, problems or opportunities facing the industry. Almost any story will be considered, including corporate profiles, but we don't want gossip or celebrity stuff." Query with published clips. Length: 1,500-2,500 words. Pays $100-150.

Photos: State availability of photos. Pays $10 maximum for 8 × 10 b&w prints. Captions required.

Tips: "Request a sample copy, indicating you read about *Boxoffice* in *Writer's Market*. Write a clear, comprehensive outline of the proposed story and enclose a résumé and clip samples. We welcome new writers but don't want to be a classroom. Know how to write. We look for 'investigative' articles."

CALLBOARD, Monthly Theatre Trade Magazine, Theatre Bay Area, #402, 657 Mission St., San Francisco CA 94105. (415)957-1557. Fax: (415)957-1556. Editor: Belinda Taylor. 50% freelance written. Monthly magazine for theater. "We publish news, views, essays and features on the Northern California theater industry. We also include listings, audition notices and job resources." Estab. 1976. Circ. 10,000. Pays on publication. Publishes ms an average of 3-4 months after acceptance. Byline given. Offers 50% kill fee. Buys first rights. Editorial lead time 1 month. Submit seasonal material 2 months in advance. Accepts simultaneous and previously published submissions. Send tearsheet of article or typed ms with rights for sale noted and information about when and where the article previously appeared. For reprints pays 50% of amount paid for an original article. Query for electronic submissions. Reports in 1 month on queries. Sample copy for $4.75.

Nonfiction: Book excerpts, essays, opinion, personal experience, technical (theater topics only). *No profiles of actors.* Buys 12-15 mss/year. Query with published clips. Length: 800-2,000 words. Pays $100 minimum for assigned articles. Pays other for unsolicited articles. Sometimes pays expenses of writers on assignment (phone calls and some travel).

Photos: State availability of photos with submission. Reviews contact sheets or 5 × 7 prints. Offers no additional payment for photos accepted with ms. Identification of subjects required. Buys one-time rights.

FUNWORLD, International Association of Amusement Parks & Attractions, 1448 Duke St., Alexandria VA 22314-3464. (703)836-4800. Fax: (703)836-4801. Editor: William G. Phillips. 50% freelance written. Monthly trade journal covering the amusement park industry. "Articles should be written for amusement park executives, not the public." Estab. 1985. Circ. 7,500. Pays on publication. Publishes ms an average of 2 months after acceptance. Byline given. Offers 30% kill fee. Buys first serial rights. Submit seasonal material 4 months in advance. Accepts previously published articles. Send tearsheet or photocopy of article or typed ms with rights for sale noted and information about when and where the article previously appeared. Query for electronic submissions. Reports in 2 months on queries. Write for free sample copy and writer's guidelines.

Nonfiction: How-to, interview/profile, photo feature, technical. "No articles about industry suppliers." Buys 48 mss/year. Query with published clips. Length: 1,000-3,000 words. Pays $200-600 for assigned articles; $150-450 for unsolicited articles. Sometimes pays expenses of writers on assignment.

Photos: State availability of photos with query or send photos with submission. Reviews color; 3 × 5 prints, slides. Captions, model releases and identification of subjects required. Buys one-time rights.

Tips: "Writers should visit a small- to medium-sized park in their area and look for unique features or management styles that other park managers might like to read about. We want less fluff, more substance."

THE HOLLYWOOD REPORTER, 5055 Wilshire Blvd., Los Angeles CA 90036-4396. (213)525-2000. Fax: (213)525-2377. Publisher and Editor-in-Chief: Robert J. Dowling. Editor: Alex Ben Block. Editorial Director of Special Issues: Randall Tierney. Daily is 25% freelance written. Specials are 90% freelance written. Daily entertainment trade publication emphasizing in-depth analysis and news coverage of creative and business aspects of film, TV, theater and music production. Estab. 1930. Circ. 23,000. Publishes ms an average of 1 week after acceptance for daily; 1 month for special issues. Send queries first.

Tips: "Short articles fit our format best. The most frequent mistake made by writers in completing an article for us is that they are not familiar with our publication. We are a business publication; we don't want celebrity gossip."

LOCATION UPDATE, 2301 Bellevue Ave., Los Angeles CA 90026-4017. (213)483-9889. Fax: (213)483-0699. Editor: Manley Witten. Monthly entertainment industry magazine covering all aspects of filming on location. "*Location Update* communicates the issues, trends, problems, solutions and business matters that affect productions working on location. Features include interviews with industry professionals, controversial issues, regional spotlights, hard-to-find or difficult locations, etc. Audience is made up of producers, directors, production managers, location managers — any person who works on location for film, TV, commercials and videos." Estab. 1985. Circ. 30,000. Pays on publication. Publishes ms an average of 2 months after acceptance. Byline given. Offers 25% kill fee.

Photos: State availability of photos with submission. Reviews contact sheets, 35mm, 2¼ × 2¼ transparencies and 8 × 10 prints. Offers no additional payment for photos accepted with ms. Identification of subjects required. Buys one-time rights.

Columns/Departments: Locations (hard to find or difficult locations and how to use them), 500-1,000 words; Supporting Roles (support services used on location: security companies, catering, etc.), 500-1,000 words; Newsreel (short news briefs on location-related issues), 250 words. Buys 25-30 mss/year. Query with published clips. Pays $50-200.

Tips: "The best way to break in is to query with story ideas and to be familiar with film, TV, video and commercials. Know the workings of the entertainment industry and the roles of producers, directors and location managers. Articles about locations are most open to freelance writers. Everything is a possible location for productions. Every state has a film commission that can help with who is where and how to go about using particular locations."

MODEL & PERFORMER, Aquino Productions, P.O. Box 15760, Stamford CT 06901. (203)967-9952. Fax: (203)359-1546. Editor: Andres Aquino. 40% freelance written. Monthly magazine on fashion modeling, entertainment (video, film). "*Model & Performer* covers the business of entertainment and fashion, including: performers, entertainers, dancers, actors, models, celebrities, agents, producers and managers, photographers; casting, TV, film, video, theater and show productions; plus creative support, stage facilities, services and products to the entertainment and fashion industries, trade shows and exhibits." Estab. 1991. Circ. 100,000. Pays on publication. Publishes ms an average of 2 months after acceptance. Byline given sometimes. Offers 50% kill fee. Buys first North American serial rights or all rights. Editorial lead time 3 months. Submit seasonal material 3 months in advance. Accepts simultaneous submissions. Reports in 6 weeks on queries; 2 months on mss. Sample copy for $4. Writer's guidelines for 9 × 12 SAE with 6 first-class stamps.

Nonfiction: General interest, how-to, interview/profile, photo feature and travel. Buys 24 mss/year. Send complete ms. Length:300-1,500 words. Pays 10¢/word minimum for unsolicited articles.

Photos: Send photos with submission. Reviews 2 × 2 transparencies and 8 × 10 prints. Offers $10-25/photo. Captions, model release and identification of subjects required. Buys one-time rights or all rights.

Columns/Departments: Pays $25-50.

Tips: "Covers how-to articles: how to succeed in film, video, modeling. How to break into any aspect of the fashion and entertainment industries. Be specific. Send $4 for a sample and specific guidelines. Know the content of *Model & Performer*. We are most open to interviews with celebrities (with photos), and how-to articles."

‡OPPORTUNITIES FOR ACTORS & MODELS, A Guide to Working in Cable TV-Radio-Print Advertising, Copy Group, Suite 315, 1900 N. Vine St., Hollywood CA 90068-3980. Fax: (213)465-5161. Editor: Len Miller. 50% freelance written. Works with a small number of new/unpublished writers each year. A monthly newsletter "serving the interests of those people who are (or would like to be) a part of the cable-TV, radio, and print advertising industries." Estab. 1969. Circ. 10,000. **Pays on acceptance.** Publishes ms an average of 3 months after acceptance. Byline given. Buys all rights. Reports in 1 month. Free sample copy and writer's guidelines for #10 SASE.

Nonfiction: How-to, humor, inspirational, interview/profile, local news, personal experience, photo feature, technical (within cable TV). Coverage should include the model scene, little theatre, drama groups, comedy workshops and other related events and places. "Detailed information about your local cable TV station should be an important part of your coverage. Get to know the station and its creative personnel." Buys 120 mss/year. Query. Length: 100-950 words. Pays $50 maximum.

Photos: State availability of photos. Model release and identification of subjects required. Buys one-time or all rights.

Columns/Departments: "We will consider using your material in a column format with your byline." Buys 60 mss/year. Query. Length: 150-450 words. Pays $50 maximum.

Tips: "Good first person experiences, interviews and articles, all related to modeling, acting, little theater, photography (model shots) and other interesting items are needed."

‡STAGE DIRECTIONS, For and about regional community and academic theater, *SMW* Communications, Inc., Suite 310, 3101 Poplarwood, Raleigh NC 27604. Editor: Stephen Peithman. 25% freelance written. Magazine published 10 times/year covering theater: community, regional and academic. "*Stage Directions* covers a full range of theater-productions, design, management and marketing. Articles are based on problem-solving." Estab. 1988. Circ. 4,500. Pays on publication. Publishes ms an average of 2-3 months after acceptance. Byline given. Buys all rights. Editorial lead time 4-6 months. Submit seasonal material 6 months in advance. Accepts simultaneous submissions if noted on ms. Query for electronic submissions. Reports in 2-3 weeks on queries. Sample copy for 9 × 12 SAE with 2 first-class stamps. Writer's guidelines free on request.

Nonfiction: Stephen Perthman. How-to, new product, personal experience, photo feature, technical. Buys 24 mss/year. Prefers query or send complete ms. Length: 350-1,000 words. Pays $100. Sometimes pays expenses of writers on assignment.

Photos: State availability of photos with submission and describe. Reviews contact sheets, 2×2 transparencies and 5×7 prints. Offers $20/photo. Captions, model releases and identification of subjects required. Buys one-time rights.
Tips: "We are very receptive to new writers, but they must give evidence of quality writing and ability to follow through. Keep story focused and upbeat as you describe a theatrical problem-solving experience or situation. Use quotes from participants/experts."

WORLD'S FAIR, World's Fair, Inc., P.O. Box 339, Corte Madera CA 94976-0339. (415)924-6035. Editor: Alfred Heller. Less than 50% freelance written. Quarterly magazine exploring the people, politics, pageantry and planning of world's fairs and thematic exhibitions, with emphasis on current and upcoming events. Also looks at science museums and theme parks; investigates high-tech exhibit techniques. Mostly slanted toward exposition and amusement industry professionals. Estab. 1981. Circ. 5,000. **Pays on acceptance.** Publishes ms an average of 3 months after acceptance. Byline given. Offers 50% kill fee. Buys all rights. Reports in 1 month. Sample copy and writer's guidelines for 9×12 SAE with 3 first-class stamps.
Nonfiction: Informative articles, interview/profiles, photo features related to international fairs and world's-fair-caliber exhibits and exhibit technology. Buys 8-10 mss/year. Query with published clips. Length: 500-2,500 words. Pays $50-350. Sometimes pays expenses of writers on assignment.
Photos: State availability of photos or line drawings with submission. Reviews contact sheets and 8×10 b&w prints. Identification of subjects required. Buys one-time rights.
Tips: Looking for "correspondents in cities planning major expositions, in the US and abroad."

Farm

The successful farm writer focuses on the business side of farming. For technical articles, editors feel writers should have a farm background or agricultural training, but there are opportunities for the general freelancer too. The following farm publications are divided into seven categories, each specializing in a different aspect of farming: agricultural equipment; crops and soil management; dairy farming; livestock; management; miscellaneous and regional.

Agricultural Equipment

CUSTOM APPLICATOR, Little Publications, Suite 540, 6263 Poplar Ave., Memphis TN 38119. (901)767-4020. Fax: (901)767-4026. Managing Editor: Horace Tipton. 50% freelance written. Works with a small number of new/unpublished writers each year. For "firms that sell and custom apply agricultural fertilizer and chemicals." Estab. 1957. Circ. 16,100. **Pays on acceptance.** Publishes ms an average of 2 months after acceptance. Buys all rights. Free sample copy and writer's guidelines.
Nonfiction: "We need articles on spray/dry chemical delivery technology related to the agriculture industry. We are seeing an incredible jump in computer-related technology and software packages for farm and custom application management that need reviewing. And we always need 'people' stories, interviews of actual dealers & applicators." Publishes reprints of previously published material. Send typed ms with rights for sale noted and information about when and where the article previously appeared. Query for electronic submissions. Length: 750-1500 words. Must have photos (b&w). Pays 20¢/word.
Photos: Accepts b&w glossy prints. Color slides accepted for cover photos. Pays extra for cover shots.
Tips: "Our audience doesn't need to decipher 'computerese' or 'tech lingo' so make it readable; for a general audience. Conciseness sells here. A story without photos will not be published, so plan that into your work. Our readers are looking for methods to increase efficiency and stay abreast of new government regulations, so accuracy is important."

Crops and Soil Management

‡GRAIN JOURNAL, Grain Publications, Inc., 2490 N. Water St., Decatur IL 62526. (217)877-8660. Editor: Ed Zdrojewski. 10% freelance written. Bimonthly magazine covering grain handling and merchandising. "*Grain Journal* serves the North American grain industry, from the smallest country grain elevators and feed mills to major export terminals." Estab. 1972. Circ. 11,444. Pays on publication. Publishes ms an average of 2 months after acceptance. Byline sometimes given. Buys first rights. Editorial lead time 2 months. Submit seasonal material 2 months in advance. Accepts simultaneous submissions. Query for electronic submissions. Sample copy free on request.
Nonfiction: How-to, interview/profile, new product, technical. Query. Length: 750 words maximum. Pays $100.

Photos: Send photos with submission. Reviews contact sheets, negatives, transparencies and 3×5 prints. Offers $50-100/photo. Captions and identification of subjects required. Buys one-time rights.
Tips: "Call with your idea. We'll let you know if it is suitable for our publication."

ONION WORLD, Columbia Publishing, 2809A Fruitvale Blvd., P.O. Box 1467, Yakima WA 98907-1497. (509)248-2452. Fax: (509)248-4056. Editor: D. Brent Clement. 90% freelance written. Monthly magazine covering "the world of onion production and marketing" for onion growers and shippers. Estab. 1985. Circ. 5,500. Pays on publication. Publishes ms an average of 1 month after acceptance. Byline given. Not copyrighted. Buys first North American serial rights. Submit seasonal material 1 month in advance. Accepts simultaneous and previously published submissions. Send photocopy of article and information about when and where the article previously appeared. Pays 50% of their fee for an original article. Reports in 1 month. Sample copy for 9×12 SAE with 5 first-class stamps.
Nonfiction: General interest, historical/nostalgic, interview/profile. Buys 60 mss/year. Query. Length: 1,200-1,500 words. Pays $75-150 for assigned articles.
Photos: Send photos with submission. Offers no additional payment for photos accepted with ms unless it's a cover shot. Captions and identification of subjects required. Buys all rights.
Tips: "Writers should be familiar with growing and marketing onions. We use a lot of feature stories on growers, shippers and others in the onion trade—what they are doing, their problems, solutions, marketing plans, etc."
 • Columbia Publishing also produces *Fresh Cut, Packer/Shipper, Potato Country* and *Carrot Country.*

‡WESTERN HAY MAGAZINE, Idea Productions, P.O. Box 516, Royal City WA 99357. (509)346-9456. Editor: John Yearout. 30-50% freelance written. Bimonthly magazine covering Western Hay Production, Processing and Marketing. "Writers must be knowledgeable of hay production and agriculture practices. Stories are to be educational while also being entertaining." Estab. 1993. Circ. 4,000. Pays on publication. Publishes ms an average of 1-3 months after acceptance. Byline given. Buys simultaneous rights. Editorial lead time 2 months. Submit seasonal material 2-4 months in advance. Accepts simultaneous and previously published submissions (by arrangement). Query for electronic submissions. Sample copy for $2.75 and postage. Writer's guidelines free on request.
Nonfiction: How-to (how hay is grown, processed and marketed), interview/profile, new product, personal experience, photo feature, technical. Buys 6-12 mss/year. Query with published clips. Length: 1,000-2,000 words. Sometimes pays expenses of writers on assignment.
Photos: Send photos with submission. Reviews 4×5 prints. Offers $15/photo. Captions and identification of subjects required. Buys all rights.
Columns/Departments: Hay Hauler (stories/experiences of truckers hauling hay), 1,000 words (maximum); Barns of the West (photos & descriptive history of old barns), 1,000 words (maximum); A Look Back (historical photos & narrative of old hay scenes), 1,000 words (maximum). Buys 6 mss/year. Query with published clips. Pays $100-150 plus photo payments.
Tips: "Sample material should be ag-oriented if possible. Must demonstrate capability to produce well composed, reproducible photos. Writer needs to be living in the western states or provinces of Canada so story material can be of local nature. All stories are about hay production in Western US and Canada."

Dairy Farming

‡DAIRY GOAT JOURNAL, W. 2997 Markert Rd., Helenville WI 53137. (414)593-8385. Fax: (414)593-8384. Editor: Dave Thompson. 50% freelance written. Monthly. "We are looking for clear and accurate articles about dairy goat owners, their herds, cheesemaking, and other ways of marketing products. Some readers own two goats; others own 1,500 and are large commercial operations." Estab. 1917. Circ. 8,000, including copies to more than 70 foreign countries. Pays on publication. Makes assignments. Query first.
Nonfiction: Information on personalities and on public issues affecting dairy goats and their owners. How-to articles with plenty of practical information. Health and husbandry articles should be written with appropriate experience or academic credentials. Buys 100 mss/year. Query with published clips or send complete ms. Length: 750-2,500 words. Pays $50 to $200. Pays expenses of writers on assignment.
Photos: Black and white or color. Vertical or horizontal for cover. Goats and/or people. Pays $100 max for 35mm slides for covers; $20 to $70 for inside use or for b&w. Accurate identification of all subjects required.
Tips: "We love good articles about dairy goats and will work with beginners, if you are cooperative."

THE DAIRYMAN, Dept. WM, P.O. Box 819, Corona CA 91718-0819. (909)735-2730. Fax: (909)735-2460. Editor: Dennis Halladay. 10% freelance written. Prefers to work with published/established writers. Monthly magazine dealing with large herd commercial dairy industry. Estab. 1922. Circ. 19,000. Pays on acceptance or publication. Publishes ms an average of 2-3 months after acceptance. Byline given. Buys first North American serial rights. Submit seasonal material 3 months in advance. Accepts previously published material. Send information about when and where the article previously appeared. Pays 50% of their fee for an original article. Reports in 1 month. Sample copy for 9×12 SAE with 4 first-class stamps.

Nonfiction: Interview/profile, new product, opinion, industry analysis. Special issues: Computers (February); Herd Health (August); Feeds and Feeding (May); and Barns and Equipment (November). "No religion, nostalgia, politics or 'mom and pop' dairies." Query or send complete ms. Length: 300-5,000 words. Pays $100-300.

Photos: Send photos with query or ms. Reviews b&w contact sheets and 35mm or 2¼×2¼ transparencies. Pays $25 for b&w; $50-100 for color. Captions and identification of subjects required. Buys one-time rights.

● Photos are now a more critical part of story packages.

Tips: "Pretend you're an editor for a moment; would you want to buy a story without any artwork? Neither would I. Writers often don't know modern commercial dairying and they forget they're writing for an audience of *dairymen*. Publications are becoming more and more specialized. You've really got to know who you're writing for and why they're different."

Livestock

BEEF, The Webb Division, Intertec Publishing Corporation, Suite 300, 7900 International Dr., Minneapolis MN 55425-1563. (612)851-4668. Fax: (612)851-4600. Editor-in-Chief: Joe Roybal. 5% freelance written. Prefers to work with published/established writers. Monthly magazine for readers who have the same basic interest—making a living feeding cattle or running a cow herd. Estab. 1964. Circ. 107,000. **Pays on acceptance.** Publishes ms an average of 4 months after acceptance. Buys all rights. Byline given. Submit seasonal material 3 months in advance. Reports in 2 months.

Nonfiction: How-to and informational articles on doing a better job of producing, feeding cattle, market building, managing and animal health practices. Material must deal with beef cattle only. Buys 8-10 mss/ year. Query. Length: 500-2,000 words. Pays $25-300. Sometimes pays the expenses of writers on assignment. Articles and photos returned only if accompanied by SASE.

Photos: Black and white glossies (8×10) and color transparencies (35mm or 2¼×2¼) purchased with or without mss. Query or send contact sheet, captions and/or transparencies. Pays $10-50 for b&w; $25-100 for color. Model release required.

Tips: "Be completely knowledgeable about cattle feeding and cowherd operations. Know what makes a story. We want specifics, not a general roundup of an operation. Pick one angle and develop it fully. The most frequent mistake is not following instructions on an angle (or angles) to be developed."

THE BRAHMAN JOURNAL, Sagebrush Publishing Co., Inc., P.O. Box 220, Eddy TX 76524-0220. (817)859-5451. Editor: Joe Ed Brockett. 10% freelance written. Monthly magazine covering Brahman cattle. Estab. 1971. Circ. 6,000. Pays on publication. Publishes ms an average of 2 months after acceptance. Byline given. Not copyrighted. Buys first North American serial, one-time and second serial (reprint) rights or makes work-for-hire assignments. Submit seasonal/holiday material 3 months in advance. Accepts previously published submissions. Send typed ms with rights for sale noted. For reprints, pays 50% of the amount paid for an original article. Sample copy for 9×12 SAE with 5 first-class stamps.

Nonfiction: General interest, historical/nostalgic and interview/profile. Special issues: Herd Bull (July); Texas (October). Buys 3-4 mss/year. Query with published clips. Length: 1,200-3,000 words. Pays $100-250 for assigned articles.

Photos: Photos needed for article purchase. Send photos with submission. Reviews 4×5 prints. Offers no additional payment for photos accepted with ms. Captions required. Buys one-time rights.

FARM POND HARVEST, Dedicated to successful farm pond planning, construction, management and harvesting, Professional Sportsman's Publishing Company, 1390 N. 14500E Rd., Momence IL 60954-9420. (815)472-2686. Editor: Vic Johnson. Managing Editor: Joan Munyon. 75% freelance written. Quarterly magazine for fisheries. "Mainly informational for pond owners—we have many biologists, university libraries and government agencies on our subscription list." Estab. 1967. Pays on publication. Publishes ms an average of 1-3 months after acceptance. Byline given. Not copyrighted. Buys first rights or second serial (reprint) rights. Submit seasonal material 2 months in advance. Accepts simultaneous and previously published submissions. Send tearsheet, photocopy of article or typed ms with rights for sale noted and information about when and where the article previously appeared. Reports in 1 month. Sample copy for 9×12 SAE with 3 first-class stamps.

Nonfiction: How-to (fisheries), personal experience, photo feature and technical. Buys 25 mss/year. Query with or without published clips, or send complete ms. Length: 1,300-2,500 words. Pays $50-125 for assigned articles. Sometimes pays in free advertisement.

Photos: State availability of photos with submission. Reviews negatives and 5×7 prints. Usually offers no additional payment for photos accepted with ms, but sometimes pays $5 per photo. Buys one-time rights.

Columns/Departments: What's New (products, news bulletins, magazines, fishery field); Media Net (information pertaining to products/conventions, etc.); Ask Al (answers to questions from readers); and Cutting Bait (subscriber information). Buys 12 mss/year. Send complete ms.

Tips: Most open to freelancers are "how-to on planning, construction, management, fishing in farm ponds or small lakes. Personal experiences — some light-humorous articles accepted; also seasonal stories, winter, spring, summer or fall."

LLAMAS MAGAZINE, The International Camelid Journal, Clay Press, Inc., P.O. Box 100, Herald CA 95638. (209)223-0469. Fax: (209)223-0466. Editor: Cheryl Dal Porto. Magazine published 7 times per year covering llamas, alpacas, camels, vicunas and guanacos. Estab. 1979. Circ. 5,500. Pays on publication. Publishes ms an average of 4 months after acceptance. Byline given. Buys first rights, second serial (reprint) rights and makes work-for-hire assignments. Submit seasonal material 6 months in advance. Accepts previously published submissions. Send tearsheet of article and information about when and where the article previously appeared. Reports in 1 month. Free sample copy. Writer's guidelines for 8½ × 11 SAE with $2.90 postage.
Nonfiction: How-to (on anything related to raising llamas), humor, interview/profile, opinion, personal experience, photo feature, travel (to countries where there are camelids). "All articles must have a tie-in to one of the camelid species." Buys 30 mss/year. Query with published clips. Length: 1,000-5,000 words. Pays $50-300 for assigned articles; $50-250 for unsolicited articles. May pay new writers with contributor copies. Sometimes pays the expenses of writers on assignment.
Photos: State availability of photos or send duplicate photos with submission. Reviews transparencies and 5 × 7 prints. Offers $25-100/photo. Captions, model releases and identification of subjects required. Buys one-time rights.
Fillers: Anecdotes, gags and short humor. Buys 25/year. Length: 100-500 words. Pays $25-50.
Tips: "Get to know the llama folk in your area and query us with an idea. We are open to any and all ideas involving llamas, alpacas and the rest of the camelids. We are always looking for good photos. You must know about camelids to write for us."

NATIONAL CATTLEMEN, National Cattlemen's Association, 5420 S. Quebec St., Englewood CO 80111-1904. (303)694-0305. Editor: Kendal Frazier. 15% freelance written. Monthly trade journal on the beef-cattle industry. "We deal extensively with animal health, price outlook, consumer demand for beef, costs of production, emerging technologies, developing export markets, marketing and risk management." Estab. 1898. Circ. 35,000. Pays on publication. Byline given. "Buys one-time rights but requires non-compete agreements." Sample copy for 9 × 12 SAE.
Nonfiction: How-to (cut costs of production, risk management strategies), new product (emerging technologies), opinion, technical (emerging technologies, animal health, price outlook). Buys 20 mss/year. Query with published clips. Length: 1,300-1,500 words. Sidebars encouraged. Pays $300-400 for assigned articles.
  • Buying more articles than last year.
Photos: Send photos with submission. Reviews negatives and transparencies. Identification of subjects required.

NATIONAL WOOL GROWER, American Sheep Industry Association, Inc., 6911 S. Yosemite St., Englewood CO 80112-1414. (303)771-3500. Editor: Janice Grauberger. 20% freelance written. Monthly trade journal covering sheep industry news. Estab. 1911. Circ. 21,500. Pays on publication. Byline sometimes given. Buys first rights and makes work-for-hire assignments. Submit seasonal material 3 months in advance. Free sample copy.
Nonfiction: How-to, interview/profile. Buys 15 mss/year. Query with or without published clips or send complete ms. Length: 1,000-5,000 words. Pays $150-200 for unsolicited articles.
Photos: Send photos with submission. Reviews transparencies and prints. Offers no additional payment for photos accepted with ms. Captions required. Buys one-time rights.

POLLED HEREFORD WORLD, 11020 NW Ambassador Dr., Kansas City MO 64153-2034. (816)891-8400. Fax: (816)891-8811. Editor: Ed Bible. 1% freelance written. Monthly magazine for "breeders of Polled Hereford cattle — about 80% registered breeders, 5% commercial cattle breeders; remainder are agribusinessmen in related fields." Estab. 1947. Circ. 10,000. Not copyrighted. Buys "no unsolicited mss at present." Pays on publication. Publishes ms an average of 2 months after acceptance. Submit seasonal material "as early as possible: 2 months preferred." Reports in 1 month. Accepts previously published articles. Send tearsheet of article. Query first for reports of events, activities and features. Free sample copy.
Nonfiction: "Features on registered or commercial Polled Hereford breeders. Some on related agricultural subjects (pastures, fences, feeds, buildings, etc.). Mostly technical in nature, some human interest. Our readers make their living with cattle, so write for an informed, mature audience." Buys informational articles, how-tos, personal experience articles, interviews, photo features, coverage of successful business operations, articles on merchandising techniques and technical articles. Length: "varies with subject and content of feature." Pays about 5¢/word ("usually about 50¢/column inch, but can vary with the value of material").
Photos: Purchased with mss, sometimes purchased without mss, or on assignment; captions required. "Only good quality b&w glossies accepted, any size; good color prints or transparencies." Pays $2 for b&w, $2-25 for color. Pays $50 for color covers.

SHEEP! MAGAZINE, W2997 Markert Rd., Helenville WI 53137. (414)593-8385. Fax: (414)593-8384. Editor: Dave Thompson. 50% freelance written. Prefers to work with published/established writers. Monthly magazine. "We're looking for clear, concise, useful information for sheep raisers who have a few sheep to a 1,000 ewe flock." Estab. 1980. Circ. 15,000. Pays on publication. Byline given. Offers $30 kill fee. Buys all rights. Makes work-for-hire assignments. Submit seasonal material 3 months in advance. Accepts previously published material. Send tearsheet or photocopy of article. For reprints pays 40% of the amount paid for an original article. Free sample copy and writer's guidelines.

Nonfiction: Book excerpts; information (on personalities and/or political, legal or environmental issues affecting the sheep industry); how-to (on innovative lamb and wool marketing and promotion techniques, efficient record-keeping systems or specific aspects of health and husbandry). Health and husbandry articles should be written by someone with extensive experience or appropriate credentials (i.e., a veterinarian or animal scientist); profiles (on experienced sheep producers who detail the economics and management of their operation); features (on small businesses that promote wool products and stories about local and regional sheep producer's groups and their activities); new products (of value to sheep producers; should be written by someone who has used them); technical (on genetics, health and nutrition). First person narratives. Buys 80 mss/year. Query with published clips or send complete ms. Length: 750-2,500 words. Pays $45-250. Pays the expenses of writers on assignment.

Photos: "Color—vertical compositions of sheep and/or people—for our cover. Use only b&w inside magazine. Black and white, 35mm photos or other visuals improve your chances of a sale." Pays $100 maximum for 35mm color transparencies; $20-50 for 5×7 b&w prints. Identification of subjects required. Buys all rights.

Tips: "Send us your best ideas and photos! We love good writing!"

Management

‡AGRI-NEWS, Western Livestock Reporter Inc., P.O. Box 30755, Billings MT 59107. (406)259-5406. Editor: Chuck Rightmire. 5% freelance written. Weekly newspaper covering agriculture. "*Agri-News* follows a generally conservative slant on news and features for agricultural producers and businesses in Montana and northern Wyoming. We focus on general agricultural interests—farming and ranching—in those areas." Estab. 1968. Circ. 17,000. Pays on 1st of month after publication. Publishes ms an average of 1 month after acceptance. Byline given. Buys first rights. Editorial lead time 1 month. Submit seasonal material 1 month in advance. Accepts simultaneous and previously published submissions. Reports in 1 week on queries; 1 month on mss. Sample copy free on request.

Nonfiction: Exposé, general interest, historical/nostalgic, how-to, humor, inspirational, interview/profile, new product, personal experience, (all from agricultural and area viewpoint), photo feature. Buys 24 mss/year. Send complete ms. Length: 1,000 words maximum. Pays $50 for assigned articles; $35 for unsolicited articles. Sometimes pays expenses of writers on assignment.

Photos: Send photos with submission. Reviews prints. Offers $7.50/photo. Identification of subjects required. Buys one-time rights.

Tips: "Contact the editor with an idea, submit a final piece, or send a resume with clips to set up a freelance relationship. Unless assigned, all articles, etc., must be submitted on speculation."

AGWAY COOPERATOR, P.O. Box 4933, Syracuse NY 13221-4933. (315)449-6117. Editor: Sue Zarins. 2% freelance written. Bimonthly magazine for farmers. Estab. 1964. **Pays on acceptance.** Publishes ms an average of 6 months after acceptance. Time between acceptance and publication varies considerably. Usually reports in 1 month. Free sample copy.

Nonfiction: Should deal with topics of farm or rural interest in the Northeastern US. Length: 1,200 words maximum. Pays $100-150, depending on length, illustrations.

Tips: "We prefer an Agway tie-in, if possible. Fillers don't fit into our format. Occasionally assigns freelance articles. We will be acquiring more outside articles on topics of importance to progressive commercial farmers."

FARM FUTURES, 191 S. Gary Ave., Carol Stream IL 60188. (708)690-5600. Fax: (708)462-2869. Editor: Stewart Reeve. 40% freelance written. Estab. 1973. Circ. 225,000. **Pays on acceptance.** Publishes ms an average of 2 months after acceptance. Byline given. Buys first rights only. Accepts simultaneous submissions. Query for electronic submissions. Reports in 1 month. Free sample copy and writer's guidelines.

Nonfiction: Practical advice and insights into managing commercial farms, farm marketing how-to's, financial management, use of computers in agriculture, farmer profiles. Buys 30 mss/year. Query first; do not send unsolicited mss. Length: 750-2,000 words. Pays $200-400. Sometimes pays the expenses of writers on assignment.

Tips: "The writer has a better chance of breaking in at our publication with short articles. Our stories are written directly to farmers and must be extremely practical. The most frequent mistakes made by writers in completing an article for us are lack of thoroughness and good examples; language too lofty or convoluted; and lack of precision—inaccuracies."

FARM JOURNAL, Dept. WM, 230 W. Washington Square, Philadelphia PA 19105. (215)829-4700. Editor: Earl Ainsworth. Published 13 times/year with many regional editions. Material bought for one or more editions depending upon where it fits. Buys all rights. Byline given "except when article is too short or too heavily rewritten to justify one." **Pays on acceptance.** Payment is the same regardless of editions in which the piece is used.
Nonfiction: Timeliness and seasonableness are very important. Material must be highly practical and should be helpful to as many farmers as possible. Farmers' experiences should apply to one or more of these 8 basic commodities: corn, wheat, milo, soybeans, cotton, dairy, beef and hogs. Technical material must be accurate. No farm nostalgia. Query to describe a new idea that farmers can use. Length: 500-1,500 words. Pays 10-20¢/published word.
Photos: Much in demand either separately or with short how-to material in picture stories and as illustrations for articles. Warm human-interest-pix for covers—activities on modern farms. For inside use, shots of home-made and handy ideas to get work done easier and faster, farm news photos, and pictures of farm people with interesting sidelines. In b&w, 8×10 glossies are preferred; color submissions should be 2¼×2¼ for the cover and 35mm for inside use. Pays $50 and up for b&w shot; $75 and up for color.
Tips: "*Farm Journal* now publishes in hundreds of editions reflecting geographic, demographic and economic sectors of the farm market."

FARM SUPPLY RETAILING, Quirk Enterprises, Inc., P.O. Box 23536, 6607 18th Ave. S., Minneapolis MN 55423-0536. (612)861-8051. Fax: (612)861-1836. Editor: Joseph Rydholm. 30% freelance written. Monthly magazine for owners and managers of stores that sell farm hardware and supplies. "Our readers are the owners and managers of stores that sell feed, seed, fertilizer, farm supplies and hardware and related items. Our editorial goal is to give them practical information they can use to make their stores better and more profitable. The main stories are case history profiles of successful dealers and marketing-related articles tailored to farm store owners." Estab. 1993. Circ. 22,000. Pays on publication. Publishes ms an average of 3 months after acceptance. Byline given. Buys one-time rights. Editorial lead time 3 months. Submit seasonal material 4 months in advance. Accepts simultaneous and previously published submissions. Send typed ms with rights for sale noted and information about when and where the article previously appeared. Query for electronic submissions. Reports in 1 month on queries; 2 months on mss. Sample copy and writer's guidelines free on request.
Nonfiction: How-to, interview/profile (with successful agribusiness dealers), opinion (on controversial industry issues). Subjects must be business-oriented (taxes, credit, inventory, employee relations, etc.). "No self-serving pieces by motivational speakers/consultants or articles that don't pertain to our editorial focus." Buys 25 mss/year. Query with published clips. Length: 1,000-2,500 words. Pays $200 minimum for assigned articles, $150 minimum for unsolicited articles. Sometimes pays expenses of writers on assignment.
Photos: State availability of photos with submission. Reviews contact sheets, any size transparencies and prints. Offers $25-75/photo. Identification of subjects required. Buys one-time rights.
Tips: "We welcome articles from freelancers. Our greatest need is for profiles of successful dealers. Submit several color slides with the article. Length between 1,500-2,000 words. Our readers are curious about how other dealers run their operations. Articles should discuss the dealer's selling philosophies, the farming sectors (hog farming, soybean, corn, etc.) his or her customers work in, any companies or product lines he or she has had success with, and any promotional or marketing efforts (advertising, direct mail) that have been successful. We also need articles on various business-related topics such as store layout, displays, store appearance, customer relations, employee management. We will consider articles of a general business nature but the most desirable are those tailored to farm supply dealers."

FFA NEW HORIZONS, 5632 Mt. Vernon Memorial Highway, Alexandria VA 22309-0160. (703)360-3600. Fax: (703)360-5524. Associate Editor: Lawinna McGary. 20% freelance written. Prefers to work with published/established writers. Bimonthly magazine for members of the National FFA Organization who are students of agriculture in high school, ranging in age from 14-21 years; major interest in leadership, outdoor activities and careers in agriculture/agribusiness and other youth interest subjects. Estab. 1928. Circ. 400,000. **Pays on acceptance.** Publishes ms an average of 4 months after acceptance. Buys all rights. Byline given. Submit seasonal material 4 months in advance. Query for electronic submissions. Reports in 2 months. Free sample copy and writer's guidelines.
Nonfiction: How-to for youth (outdoor-type such as camping, hunting, fishing); informational (getting money for college, farming, and other help for youth). Informational, personal experience and interviews are used only if FFA members or former members are involved. "Science-oriented material is being used more extensively as we broaden people's understanding of agriculture." Buys 15 unsolicited mss/year. Query or send complete ms. Length: 1,000 words maximum. Pays 10-15¢/word. Sometimes pays the expenses of writers on assignment.
Photos: Purchased with mss. Reviews 5×7 or 8×10 b&w glossies; 35mm or larger color transparencies. Pays $15 for b&w; $30-40 for inside color; $100 for cover.

Tips: "Find an FFA member who has done something truly outstanding that will motivate and inspire others, or provide helpful information for a career in farming, ranching or agribusiness. We've increased emphasis on agriscience and marketing. We're accepting manuscripts now that are tighter and more concise. Get straight to the point."

FORD NEW HOLLAND NEWS, P.O. Box 1895, New Holland PA 17557-0903. Fax: (717)355-3600. Editor: Gary Martin. 50% freelance written. Works with a small number of new/unpublished writers each year. Magazine on agriculture; published 8 times/year; designed to entertain and inform farm families. Estab. 1960. **Pays on acceptance.** Publishes ms an average of 9 months after acceptance. Byline given. Offers negotiable kill fee. Buys first North American serial, one-time and second serial (reprint) rights. Submit seasonal material 6 months in advance. Accepts simultaneous queries and previously published submissions. Reports in 2 months. Sample copy and writer's guidelines for 9 × 12 SAE with 2 first-class stamps.
Nonfiction: "We need strong photo support for articles of 1,200-1,700 words on farm management and farm human interest." Buys 40 mss/year. Query. Pays $400-600. Sometimes pays the expenses of writers on assignment.
Photos: Send photos with query when possible. Reviews color transparencies. Pays $50-300. Captions, model release and identification of subjects required. Buys one-time rights.
Tips: "We thrive on good article ideas from knowledgeable farm writers. The writer must have an emotional understanding of agriculture and the farm family and must demonstrate in the article an understanding of the unique economics that affect farming in North America. We want to know about the exceptional farm managers, those leading the way in agriculture. We want new efficiencies and technologies presented through the real-life experiences of farmers themselves. Use anecdotes freely. Successful writers keep in touch with the editor as they develop the article."

PROGRESSIVE FARMER, Southern Progress Corp., Dept. WM, 2100 Lakeshore Dr., Birmingham AL 35209. (205)877-6419. Editor-in-Chief: Tom Curl. Editor: Jack Odle. 3% freelance written. Monthly agriculture trade journal. "Country people, farmers, ranchers are our audience." Estab. 1886. Circ. 865,000. **Pays on acceptance.** Publishes ms an average of 4 months after acceptance. Byline sometimes given. Buys all rights. Reports in 3 weeks. Free sample copy and writer's guidelines.
Nonfiction: How-to (agriculture and country related), humor (farm related), technical (agriculture). Buys 30-50 mss/year. Query with published clips. Length: 2,000 words maximum. Pays $100 minimum. Sometimes pays expenses of writers on assignment.
Photos: Send photos with submission. Reviews negatives and transparencies. Payment negotiable. Captions and identification of subjects required. Rights depend on assignment.
Columns/Departments: Handy Devices (need photos and short text on the little shop ideas that make farm work easier and rural living more enjoyable). Buys 70 mss/year. Send complete ms. Length: 20-75 words. Pays $50.
Tips: Query with ideas compatible with basic tone of magazine.

SMALL FARM TODAY, The how-to magazine of alternative crops, livestock, and direct marketing, Missouri Farm Publishing, Inc., Ridge Top Ranch, 3903 W. Ridge Trail Rd., Clark MO 65243-9900. (314)687-3525. Fax: (314)687-3148. Editor: Ron Macher. Bimonthly magazine "for small farmers and small-acreage landowners interested in diversification, direct marketing, alternative crops, horses, draft animals, small livestock, exotic and minor breeds, home-based businesses, gardening, vegetable and small fruit crops." Estab. 1984 as *Missouri Farm Magazine*. Circ. 12,000. Pays on publication. Publishes ms an average of 3 months after acceptance. Byline given. Buys first serial and nonexclusive reprint rights (right to reprint article in an anthology). Rarely buys reprints. Send typed ms, information about when and where article previously appeared. For reprints pays 58% of the amount paid for an original article. Submit seasonal/holiday material 3 months in advance. Reports in 3 months. Sample copy for $3. Writer's guidelines available.
• In the past this magazine concentrated on articles that applied to Missouri farms. Now they have
  a national audience and need articles from all over the US.
Nonfiction: Practical and how-to (small farming, gardening, alternative crops/livestock). Query letters recommended. Length: 500-2,000 words. Pays 3½¢/word.
Photos: Send photos with submission. Offers $6 for inside photos and $10 for cover photos. Captions required. Pays $4 for negatives or slides. Buys one-time rights and nonexclusive reprint rights (for anthologies).
Tips: "Topic must apply to the small farm or acreage. It helps to provide more practical and helpful information without the fluff."

TODAY'S FARMER, MFA Incorporated, 615 Locust, Columbia MO 65201. (314)876-5252. Editor: Chuck Lay. Managing Editor: Tom Montgomery. Contact: Chuck Lay. 50% freelance written. Company publication. Magazine published 10 times/year covering agriculture. "We are owned and published by MFA Incorporated, an agricultural cooperative. We examine techniques and issues that help farmers and ranchers better meet the challenges of the present and future." Estab. 1908. Circ. 46,000. **Pays on acceptance.** Publishes ms an average of 2 months after acceptance. Byline given. Offers 100% kill fee. Publication not copyrighted. Buys first North American serial rights. Editorial lead time 2 months. Submit seasonal material at least 3 months in advance. Query for electronic submissions. Sample copy for $1. Writer's guidelines "available by phone."

Nonfiction: How-to (ag technical), interview/profile, photo feature, technical. "No fiction, articles on MFA competitors, or subjects outside our trade territory (Missouri, Iowa, Arkansas)." Buys 30 mss/year. Query with published clips. Length: 1,000-2,000 words. Pays $200 minimum (features). Sometimes pays expenses of writers on assignment.

Photos: Send photos with submission. Reviews contact sheets. Negotiates payment individually. Identification of subjects required. Buys one-time rights.

Tips: "Freelancers can best approach us by knowing our audience (farmers/ranchers who are customers of MFA) and knowing their needs. We publish traditional agribusiness information that helps farmers do their jobs more effectively. Know the audience. We edit for length, AP style."

Miscellaneous

BEE CULTURE, P.O. Box 706, Medina OH 44256-0706. Fax: (216)725-5624. Editor: Mr. Kim Flottum. 50% freelance written. Monthly magazine for beekeepers and those interested in the natural science of honey bees. Publishes environmentally-oriented articles relating to honey bees or pollination. Estab. 1843. Buys first North American serial rights. Pays on both publication and acceptance. Publishes ms an average of 4 months after acceptance. Reports in 1 month. Accepts previously published articles. Send tearsheet or photocopy of article. Pays 100% of their fee for an original article. Sample copy for 9×12 SAE with 5 first-class stamps. Free writer's guidelines.

Nonfiction: Interested in articles giving new ideas on managing bees. Also looking for articles on honey bee/environment connections or relationships. Also uses success stories about commercial beekeepers. No "how I began beekeeping" articles. No highly advanced, technical and scientific abstracts or impractical advice. Length: 2,000 word average. Pays $30-50/published page—on negotiation.

Photos: Sharp b&w photos (pertaining to honey bees, honey plants or related to story) purchased with mss. Can be any size, prints or enlargements, but 4×5 or larger preferred. Pays $7-10/picture.

Tips: "Do an interview story on commercial beekeepers who are cooperative enough to furnish accurate, factual information on their operations. Frequent mistakes made by writers in completing articles are that they are too general in nature and lack management knowledge."

Regional

AGRI-TIMES NORTHWEST, J/A Publishing Co., 206 SE Court, P.O. Box 189, Pendleton OR 97801. (503)276-7845. Fax: (503)276-7964. Editor: Virgil Rupp. Managing Editor: Jim Eardley. 50% freelance written. Weekly newspaper on agriculture in western Idaho, eastern Oregon and eastern Washington. "News, features about regional farmers/agribusiness *only*." Estab. 1983. Circ. 5,200. Pays on 15th of month after publication. Publishes ms an average of 1 month after acceptance. Byline given. Buys one-time rights. Submit seasonal material 1 month in advance. Accepts simultaneous and previously published submissions. Send typed ms with rights for sale noted and information about when and where the article previously appeared. For reprints, pays 100% of the amount paid for an original article. Reports in 1 month. Sample copy 50¢ for 8×10 SAE with 4 first-class stamps. Writer's guidelines for #10 SASE.

Nonfiction: How-to (farming and ranching *regional*), humor (regional farming and ranching), interview/profile (regional farmers/ranchers), photo feature (regional agriculture), technical (regional farming and ranching). Buys 100 mss/year. Query with or without published clips or send complete ms. Length: 750 words maximum. Pays 75¢/column inch.

Photos: Send photos with submission. Reviews contact sheets, negatives and prints. Offers $5-10/photo. Captions and identification of subjects required. Buys one-time rights.

Columns/Departments: Agri-Talk (quips, comments of farmers/ranchers). Buys 50 mss/year. Send complete ms. Length: 100 words maximum. Pays 75¢ per column inch.

Tips: "Focus on our region's agriculture. Be accurate."

FARMWEEK, Mayhill Publications, Inc., P.O. Box 90, Knightstown IN 46148-1242. (317)345-5133. Fax: 1(800)695-8153. Editor: Nancy Searfoss. Associate Editor: Amy Butt. 5% freelance written. Weekly newspaper that covers agriculture in Indiana, Ohio and Kentucky. Estab. 1955. Circ. 30,000. Pays on publication. Byline given. Buys first rights. Submit seasonal material 1 month in advance. Reporting time varies; up to 1 year. Free sample copy and writer's guidelines.

Nonfiction: General interest (agriculture), interview/profile (ag leaders), new product, photo feature (Indiana, Ohio, Kentucky agriculture). "We don't want first-person accounts or articles from states outside Indiana, Kentucky, Ohio (unless of general interest to all farmers and agribusiness)." Query with published clips.

Length: 500-1,500 words. Pays $50 maximum. Sometimes pays expenses of writers on assignment.
  • This magazine reports receiving many queries about writing a regular column; however, they are not in need of another columnist at this time.
Photos: State availability of photos with submission. Reviews contact sheets and 4×5 and 5×7 prints. Offers $10 maximum/photo. Identification of subjects required. Buys one-time rights.
Tips: "We want feature stories about farmers and agribusiness operators in Indiana, Ohio and Kentucky. How do they operate their business? Keys to success, etc.? Best thing to do is call us first with idea, or write. Could also be a story about some pressing issue in agriculture nationally that affects farmers everywhere."

IOWA REC NEWS, Suite 48, 8525 Douglas, Urbandale IA 50322-2992. (515)276-5350. Editor: Jody Garlock. 15% freelance written. Monthly magazine emphasizing energy issues and human interest features for residents of rural Iowa. Estab. 1946. Circ. 116,000. Pays on publication. Publishes ms an average of 3 months after acceptance. Buys first serial and second serial (reprint) rights. Accepts simultaneous and previously published submissions. Send tearsheet of article and information about when and where the article previously appeared. Reports in 2 months.
Nonfiction: General interest, historical, humor, rural lifestyle trends, energy awareness features, photo feature. Send complete ms.
Tips: "The easiest way to break into our magazine is: research a particular subject well, include appropriate attributions to establish credibility, authority and include a couple paragraphs about the author. Reading and knowing about rural people is important. Stories that touch the senses or can improve the lives of the readers are highly considered, as are those with a strong Iowa angle. We're also looking for good humor articles. Freelancers have the advantage of offering subject matter that existing staff may not be able to cover. Inclusion of nice photos is also a plus. The most frequent mistakes made by writers are: story too long, story too biased; no attribution to any source of info; and not relevant to electric consumers, rural living."

THE LAND, Minnesota's Ag Publication, Free Press Co., P.O. Box 3169, Mankato MN 56002-3169. Editor: Randy Frahm. 50% freelance written. Weekly tabloid covering Minnesota agriculture. "We are interested in articles on farming in Minnesota. Although we're not tightly focused on any one type of farming, our articles must be of interest to farmers. In other words, will your article topic have an impact on people who live and work in rural areas?" Estab. 1976. Circ. 40,000. **Pays on acceptance.** Publishes ms an average of 3 months after acceptance. Byline given. Buys first North American serial rights. Editorial lead time 1 month. Submit seasonal material 2 months in advance. Reports in 3 weeks on queries; 2 months on mss. Sample copy free on request. Writer's guidelines for #10 SASE.
Nonfiction: General interest (ag), how-to, interview/profile, personal experience and technical. Buys 15-40 mss/year. Query. Length: 500-1,500 words. Pays $25 minimum for assigned articles. Pays expenses of writers on assignment.
Photos: State availability of photos with submission. Reviews contact sheets. Negotiates payment individually. Buys one-time rights.
Tips: "Be enthused about rural Minnesota life and agriculture and be willing to work with our editors. We try to stress relevance." Most open to feature articles.

MAINE ORGANIC FARMER & GARDENER, Maine Organic Farmers & Gardeners Association, RR 2, Box 594, Lincolnville ME 04849. (207)763-3043. Editor: Jean English. 40% freelance written. Prefers to work with published/established local writers. Bimonthly magazine covering organic farming and gardening for urban and rural farmers and gardeners and nutrition-oriented, environmentally concerned readers. "*MOF&G* promotes and encourages sustainable agriculture and environmentally sound living. Our primary focus is organic farming, gardening and forestry, but we also deal with local, national and international agriculture, food and environmental issues." Estab. 1976. Circ. 10,000. Pays on publication. Publishes ms an average of 8 months after acceptance. Byline and bio given. Buys first North American serial, one-time, first serial or second serial (reprint) rights. Submit seasonal material 1 year in advance. Accepts simultaneous and previously published submissions. Send typed ms with rights for sale noted and information about when and where the article previously appeared. Pays 50% of amount paid for an original article. Reports in 2 months. Sample copy for $2 and SAE with 7 first-class stamps. Free writer's guidelines.
Nonfiction: Book reviews; how-to based on personal experience, research reports, interviews. Profiles of farmers, gardeners, plants, weeds, insects. Information on renewable energy, recycling, nutrition, health, non-toxic pest control, organic farm management and marketing. "We use profiles of New England organic farmers and gardeners and news reports (500-1,000 words) dealing with US/international sustainable ag research and development, rural development, recycling projects, environmental and agricultural problems and solutions, organic farms with broad impact, cooperatives and community projects." Buys 30 mss/year. Query with published clips or send complete ms. Length: 1,000-3,000 words. Pays $20-150.
Photos: State availability of b&w photos with query; send 3×5 b&w photos with ms. Captions, model releases and identification of subjects required. Buys one-time rights.
Tips: "We are a nonprofit organization. Our publication's primary mission is to inform and educate, but we also want readers to enjoy the articles."

N.D. REC/RTC MAGAZINE, N.D. Association of RECs, P.O. Box 727, Mandan ND 58554-0727. (701)663-6501. Fax: (701)663-3745. Editor: Kent Brick. 10% freelance written. Prefers to work with published/established writers. Monthly magazine covering rural electric program and rural North Dakota lifestyle. "Our magazine goes to the 70,000 North Dakota families who get their electricity from rural electric cooperatives. We cover rural lifestyle, energy conservation, agriculture, farm family news and other features of importance to this predominantly agrarian state. Of course, we represent the views of our statewide association." Estab. 1954. Circ. 74,000. Pays on publication; **pays on acceptance for assigned features.** Publishes ms average of 6 months after acceptance. Byline given. Buys first North American serial rights. Accepts previously published articles or short stories. Send photocopy of article or short story, or typed ms with rights for sale noted. For reprints, pays 25% of the amount paid for an original article. Submit seasonal material 6 months in advance. Reports in 2 months. Sample copy for 9×12 SAE with 6 first-class stamps.

Nonfiction: Exposé (subjects of ND interest dealing with rural electric, agriculture, rural lifestyle); historical/nostalgic (ND events or people only); how-to (save energy, weatherize homes, etc.); interview/profile (on great leaders of the rural electric program, agriculture); opinion (why family farms should be saved, etc.). Buys 10-12 mss/year. Pays $100-500. Pays expenses of writers on assignment.

Photos: "Good quality photos accompanying ms improve chances for sale."

Fiction: Historical. "No fiction that does not relate to our editorial goals." Buys 2-3 mss/year. Length: 400-1,200 words. Pays $35-150. Reprints novel excerpts.

Poetry: Jo Ann Winistorfer, managing editor. Buys 2-4 poems/year. Submit maximum 8 poems. Pays $5-50.

Tips: "Write about a North Dakotan—one of our members who has done something notable in the ag/energy/rural electric/rural lifestyle areas."

OHIO FARMER, 1350 W. Fifth Ave., Columbus OH 43212. (614)486-9637. Editor: Tim White. 10% freelance written. Magazine for Ohio farmers and their families published 15 issues/year (monthly April-December; biweekly January-March). Estab. 1848. Circ. 77,000. Usually buys all rights. Pays on publication. Publishes ms an average of 2 months after acceptance. Reports in 2 months. Query for electronic submissions. Sample copy for $1 and SAE with 4 first-class stamps. Free writer's guidelines.

Nonfiction: Technical and on-the-farm stories. Buys informational, how-to and personal experience. Buys 10 mss/year. Submit complete ms. Length: 600-700 words. Pays $200.

Photos: Offers no additional payment for photos purchased with ms. Pays $5-25 for b&w; $35-100 for color; send 4×5 b&w glossies and transparencies; or 8×10 color prints.

Tips: "Freelance submissions must be of a technical agricultural nature."

• This magazine is part of Farm Progress Co. State Farm magazine group.

PENNSYLVANIA FARMER, Farm Progress Publications, 704 Lisburn Rd., Camp Hill PA 17011-0704. (717)761-6050. Editor: John Vogel. 20% freelance written. Monthly farm business magazine "oriented to providing readers with ideas to help their businesses and personal lives." Estab. 1877. Circ. 57,000. Pays on publication. Publishes ms an average of 3 months after acceptance. Buys first-time rights. Submit seasonal material 3 months in advance. Accepts simultaneous submissions. Reports in 1 month. Writer's guidelines for #10 SASE.

Nonfiction: Humor, inspirational, technical. No stories without a strong tie to Mid-Atlantic farming. Buys 15 mss/year. Query. Length: 500-1,000 words. Pays $50-150. Sometimes pays the expenses of writers on assignment.

Photos: Send photos with submission. Reviews 35mm transparencies. Pays $25-50 for each color photo accepted with ms. Captions and identification of subjects required.

WYOMING RURAL ELECTRIC NEWS, P.O. Box 380, Casper WY 82602-0380. (307)234-6152. Editor: Patty Bratton. 25% freelance written. Monthly magazine for audience of small town residents, vacation-home owners, farmers and ranchers. Estab. 1950. Circ. 30,000. Not copyrighted. Byline given. Pays on publication. Publishes ms an average of 3 months after acceptance. Buys first serial rights. Submit seasonal material 2 months in advance. "Sometimes" buys reprints; pays 80-100% of their fee for an original article. Reports in up to 3 months. Sample copy for SAE with 3 first-class stamps.

Nonfiction and Fiction: Wants energy-related material, "people" features, historical pieces about Wyoming and the West, and things of interest to Wyoming's rural people. Buys informational, humor, historical, nostalgia, photo mss. Submit complete ms. Buys 7 mss/year. Length for nonfiction and fiction: 800-1,500 words. Pays $15-45. Buys some western, humorous and historical fiction.

Photos: Photos purchased with accompanying ms with additional payment, or purchased without ms. Captions required. Pays up to $40 for cover photos. Color only.

Tips: "Study an issue or two of the magazine to become familiar with our focus and the type of freelance material we're using. We're always looking for *good* humor. Always looking for fresh, new writers, original perspectives. Submit entire manuscript. Don't submit a regionally set story from some other part of the country. Photos and illustrations (if appropriate) are always welcomed."

Finance

These magazines deal with banking, investment and financial management. Publications that use similar material but have a less technical slant are listed under the Consumer Business and Finance section.

THE BOTTOM LINE, The News and Information Publication for Canada's Financial Professionals, Bottom Line Publications Inc., Dept. WM, Suite 300, 204 Richmond St. W., Toronto, Ontario M5V 1V6 Canada. (416)598-5211. Fax: (416)598-5659. Editor: Mike Lewis. 35% freelance written. Monthly tabloid on accounting/finance/business. "Reaches 80% of all Canadian accountants. Information should be news/commentary/analysis of issues or issues of interest to or about accountants." Estab. 1985. Circ. 48,000. Pays on publication. Publishes ms an average of 2 weeks-4 months after acceptance. Byline given. Buys first rights. Query for electronic submissions. Reports in 2 months. Free sample copy for SASE.
Photos: State availability of photos with submission. Offers $50/photo maximum. Buys one-time rights.
• This magazine has reduced its freelance use during the past year.

CA MAGAZINE, 277 Wellington St., W., Toronto, Ontario M5V 3H2 Canada. Fax: (416)204-3409. Editor: Nelson Luscombe. Managing Editor: Jane Litchfield. 10% freelance written. Works with a small number of new/unpublished writers each year. Monthly magazine for accountants and financial managers published 10 times/year. Estab. 1911. Circ. 67,000. Pays on publication for the article's copyright. Buys all rights. Publishes ms an average of 4 months after acceptance. Reports in 1 month. Free sample copy.
Nonfiction: Accounting, business, finance, management, taxation. Also, subject-related humor pieces and cartoons. "We accept whatever is relevant to our readership, no matter the origin as long as it meets our standards." Length: 1,500-3,000 words. Payment varies with qualification of writers. Sometimes pays the expenses of writers on assignment.

EQUITIES MAGAZINE INC., Suites 5B and 5C, 145 E. 49th St., New York NY 10017. (212)832-7800. Editor: Robert J. Flaherty. 50% freelance written. Monthly magazine covering publicly owned middle market and emerging growth companies. "We are a financial magazine covering the fastest-growing companies in the world. We study the management of companies and act as critics reviewing their performances. We aspire to be 'The Shareholder's Friend'. We want to be a bridge between quality public companies and sophisticated investors." Estab. 1951. Circ. 15,000. Pays on publication. Publishes ms an average of 2 months after acceptance. Byline given. Buys first and reprint rights. Sample copy for 9 × 12 SAE with 5 first-class stamps.
Nonfiction: New product, technical. Buys 30 mss/year. "We must know the writer first as we are careful about whom we publish. A letter of introduction with résumé and clips is the best way to introduce yourself. Financial writing requires specialized knowledge and a feel for people as well, which can be a tough combination to find." Query with published clips. Length: 300-1,500 words. Pays $150-750 for assigned articles, more for very difficult or investigative pieces. Carries guest columns by famous money managers who are not writing for cash payments, but to showcase their ideas and approach. Pays expenses of writers on assignment.
Photos: Send photos with submission. Reviews contact sheets, negatives, transparencies and prints. Offers no additional payment for photos accepted with ms. Identification of subjects required.
Columns/Departments: Pays $25-75 for assigned items only.
Tips: "Anyone who enjoys analyzing a business and telling the story of the people who started it, or run it today, is a potential *Equities* contributor. But to protect our readers and ourselves, we are careful about who writes for us. Business writing is an exciting area and our stories reflect that. If a writer relies on numbers and percentages to tell his story, rather than the individuals involved, the result will be numbingly dull."

THE FEDERAL CREDIT UNION, National Association of Federal Credit Unions, P.O. Box 3769, Washington DC 20007-0269. (703)522-4770. Fax: (703)524-1082. Editor: Patrick M. Keefe. Managing Editor: Robin Johnston. 25% freelance written. "Looking for writer with financial, banking or credit union experience, but will work with inexperienced (unpublished) writers based on writing skill." Bimonthly magazine covering credit unions. Estab. 1967. Circ. 8,200. Pays on publication. Publishes ms an average of 3 months after acceptance. Byline given. Buys first North American serial rights. Submit seasonal material 5 months in advance. Accepts simultaneous submissions. Query for electronic submissions. Reports in 2 months; must include SASE and correct postage. Sample copy for 10 × 13 SAE with 5 first-class stamps. Writer's guidelines for #10 SASE.
Nonfiction: Query with published clips. Length: 1,200-2,000 words. Pays $200-800 for assigned articles.
Photos: Send photos with submission. Reviews 35mm transparencies and 5 × 7 prints. Offers no additional payment for photos accepted with ms. Model releases and identification of subjects required. Buys all rights.
Tips: "Provide résumé or listing of experience pertinent to subject. Looking only for articles that focus on events in Congress and regulatory agencies."

FUTURES MAGAZINE, 219 Parkade, Cedar Falls IA 50613. (319)277-6341. Publisher: Merrill Oster. Editor-in-Chief: Ginger Sczala. 20% freelance written. Monthly magazine for private, individual traders, brokers, exchange members, agribusinessmen, bankers, anyone with an interest in futures or options. Estab. 1972.

Circ. 65,000. Buys all rights. Byline given. Pays on publication. Publishes ms an average of 6 months after acceptance. Reports in 1 month. Sample copy for 9×12 SAE with 8 first-class stamps.

Nonfiction: Articles analyzing specific commodity futures and options trading strategies; fundamental and technical analysis of individual commodities and markets; interviews, book reviews, "success" stories; news items. Material on new legislation affecting commodities, trading, any new trading strategy ("results must be able to be substantiated") and personalities. No "homespun" rules for trading and simplistic approaches to the commodities market. Treatment is always in-depth and broad. Informational, how-to, interview, profile, technical. "Articles should be written for a reader who has traded commodities for one year or more; should not talk down or hypothesize. Relatively complex material is acceptable." No get-rich-quick gimmicks, astrology articles or general, broad topics. "Writers must have solid knowledge of the magazine's specific emphasis and be able to communicate well." Buys 30-40 mss/year. Query or submit complete ms. Length: 1,500 words optimum. Pays $50-1,000, depending upon author's research and writing quality. "Rarely" pays the expenses of writers on assignment.

Tips: "Writers must have a solid understanding and appreciation for futures or options trading. We will have more financial and stock index features as well as new options contracts that will require special knowledge and experience. Trading techniques and corporate strategies involving futures/options will get more emphasis in the coming year."

ILLINOIS BANKER, Illinois Bankers Association, Suite 1111, 111 N. Canal St., Chicago IL 60606-7204. (312)876-9900. Fax: (312)876-3826. Editor: Meg Bullock. Monthly magazine covering commercial banking. "*Illinois Banker* publishes articles that directly relate to commercial banking. Our audience is approximately 3,000 bankers and vendors related to the banking industry. The purpose of the publication is to educate and inform readers on major public policy issues affecting banking today, as well as provide new ideas that can be applied to day-to-day operations and management. Writers may not sell or promote a product or service." Estab. 1891. Circ. approx. 2,500. **Pays on acceptance.** Publishes ms an average of 3 months after acceptance. Reports in 3 months. Byline given. Buys first North American serial rights. Editorial lead time 1½ months. Accepts simultaneous and previously published submissions. Send tearsheet of article or short story or typed ms with rights for sale noted and information about when and where the article previously appeared. Query for electronic submissions. Reports in 3 months. Sample copy and writer's guidelines free on request.

Nonfiction: Essays, historical/nostalgic, humor, inspirational, interview/profile, new product, opinion, personal experience, financially related. "It is *IBA* policy that writers do not sell or promote a particular product, service or organization within the content of an article written for publication." Buys 3-5 mss/year. Query. Length: 500-1,000 words. Pays $50 minimum for unsolicited articles.

Photos: State availability of photos with submission. Reviews contact sheets, negatives, transparencies and prints. Offers $25-50/photo. Negotiates payment individually. Captions and identification of subjects required. Buys one-time rights.

Fiction: Historical, humorous, mainstream, slife-of-life vignettes (financial). Buys 3 mss/year. Query. Length: 500-1,000 words. Pays $50-100.

Tips: "We appreciate that authors contact the editor before submitting articles to discuss topics. Articles published in *Illinois Banker* address current issues of key importance to the banking industry in Illinois. Our intention is to keep readers informed of the latest industry news, developments and trends, as well as provide necessary technical information. We publish articles on any topic that affects the banking industry, provided the content is in agreement with Association policy and position. Because we are a trade association, most articles need to be reviewed by an advisory committee before publication; therefore, the earlier they are submitted the better. Some recent topics include: agriculture, bank architecture, commercial and consumer credit, marketing, operations/cost control, security and technology. In addition, articles are also considered on the topics of economic development and business/banking trends in Illinois and the Midwest region."

INDEPENDENT BANKER, Independent Bankers Association of America, P.O. Box 267, Sauk Centre MN 56378-0267. (612)352-6546. Editor: David C. Bordewyk. 25% freelance written. Works with a number of new/unpublished writers each year. Monthly magazine targeting the CEOs of the nation's community banks. Estab. 1950. Circ. 10,000. Pays on publication. Publishes ms an average of 4 months after acceptance. Byline given. Not copyrighted. Buys all rights. Reports in 6 weeks. Sample copy and writer's guidelines for 9×12 SAE with 6 first-class stamps.

Nonfiction: Features: interview/profile (example: a community bank's innovative economic development program), banking trends, how-to articles on bank operation and marketing issues. "Our editorial approach is predicated on two things: quality writing and an ability to give readers a sense of the people interviewed for a particular story. People enjoy reading about other people." Buys first-time rights; usually 15 mss/year. Accepts previously published articles. Send photocopy of article and information about when and where the article previously appeared. Sidebars welcome. No fiction. Query. Length: 1,500-2,500 words. Pays $250 maximum.

Photos: State availability of photos with submission. Uses color transparencies, color prints or b&w prints. Pays $5/photo. Identification of subjects required. Buys one-time rights.

Columns/Departments: "Newslines," short general-interest items about banking and finance; "Update," short pieces about community banks and bankers, such as a bank's unique home mortgage marketing program or an interesting personality in community banking. Items are 75-175 words in length. Byline given. Pays $50.

Tips: "The best way to get acquainted with us is by writing a short piece (75-175 words) for either our 'Newslines' or 'Update' departments. Since they are often read first, the accent is on crisp, clean writing that packs a punch. Our editorial content seeks to convey the strength of locally owned, locally managed community banks, and the need to protect America's diversified financial system. We are working to position *Independent Banker* as a writer's magazine that provides solid information for community bank CEOs in a creative, entertaining manner."

‡NAPFA NEWS, The Newsletter for fee-only financial advisors, National Association of Personal Financial Advisors, Suite 150, 1130 W. Lake Cook Rd., Buffalo Grove IL 60089. (708)537-7723. Editor: Margery Wasserman. 60% freelance written. Monthly newsletter covering financial planning. "*NAPFA News* publishes practice management and investment strategy articles targeted to fee-only financial advisors. Topics that relate to comprehensive financial planning geared to the practitioner are desired. Readers range from sole practitioners to members of larger firms." Estab. 1985. Circ. 1,000. Pays on publication. Publishes ms an average of 3 months after acceptance. Byline given. Buys first North American serial, first, one-time or second serial (reprint) rights. Editorial lead time 2 months. Submit seasonal material 3 months in advance. Accepts simultaneous and previously published submissions. Query for electronic submissions. Reports in 2-3 months on queries. Sample copy for 9×12 SAE with 4 first-class stamps. Writer's guidelines free on request.

Nonfiction: Reviews of financial planning books and software programs, financial planning issues, practice management tips. Buys 50 mss/year. Query. Length: 750-2,000 words. Pays 20¢/word up to $300.

Photos: State availability of photos with submission. Reviews 5×7 prints. Offers no additional payment for photos accepted with ms. Captions, model releases, identification of subjects required. Buys one-time rights.

Columns/Departments: Practice Profile (assigned), 1,700-2,000 words; Book Reviews (fee-only planning perspective), 750-1,500 words; Software Reviews (fee-only planning perspective), 750-1,500 words. Pays 20¢/word up to $300.

Tips: "All writing must be directed to the financial practitioner, not the consumer. Freelancers who are interested in writing for *NAPFA News* will have a strong background in financial planning investment, and practice management issues and will understand the differences between fee-only, fee-based, fee and commission and commission-based financial planning."

PENSION WORLD, Argus Business Inc., #200, 6151 Powers Ferry Rd. NW, Atlanta GA 30339-2941. (404)955-2500. Fax: (404)618-0348. Editor: Laurie Heavey. 50% freelance written. Monthly magazine on pension investment and employee benefits. Estab. 1964. Circ. 28,146. Pays on pasteup. Byline given. Buys all rights. Submit seasonal/holiday material 4 months in advance. Reports in 2 weeks on queries; 3 weeks on mss. *Writer's Market* recommends allowing 2 months for reply. Free writer's guidelines.

Nonfiction: General interest, interview/profile, new product, opinion. Query with published clips. Length: 1,500-2,500 words.

RESEARCH MAGAZINE, Ideas for Today's Investors, Research Services, 2201 Third St., San Francisco CA 94107. (415)621-0220. Editor: Rebecca McReynolds. 50% freelance written. Monthly business magazine of corporate profiles and subjects of interest to stockbrokers. Estab. 1977. Circ. 80,000. Pays on publication. Publishes ms an average of 2 months after acceptance. Byline given. Offers 20% kill fee. Buys first North American serial or second serial (reprint) rights. Query for electronic submissions. Reports in 1 month. Sample copy for 9×12 SAE with 4 first-class stamps. Writer's guidelines for #10 SASE.

Nonfiction: How-to (sales tips), interview/profile, new product, financial products. Buys approximately 50 mss/year. Query with published clips. Length: 1,000-3,000 words. Pays $300-900. Sometimes pays expenses of writers on assignment.

Tips: "Only submit articles that fit our editorial policy and are appropriate for our audience. *Only the non-corporate profile section is open to freelancers.* We use local freelancers on a regular basis for corporate profiles."

‡SAVINGS & COMMUNITY BANKER, Savings & Community Bankers of America, Suite 400, 900 19th St. NW, Washington DC 20006. (202)857-3100. Editor: Brian Nixon. 25% freelance written. Monthly magazine covering banking and finance. "*Savings & Community Banker* is written for senior managers and executives of community financial institutions. The magazine covers all aspects of financial institution management, with an emphasis on strategic business issues and trends. Recent features have included check imaging, fair lending, trends in mortgage finance and developing an investor regulations program." Circ. 14,000. **Pays on acceptance.** Publishes ms an average of 2 months after acceptance. Byline given. Offers 20% kill fee. Buys first North American serial rights. Editorial lead time 2-3 months. Submit seasonal material 6 months in advance. Query for electronic submissions. Reports in 1 month on queries. Sample copy and writer's guidelines free on request.

Nonfiction: How-to (articles on various aspects of a financial institution's operations). "Articles must be well-researched and backed up by a variety of sources, preferably senior managers of financial institutions or experts associated with the banking industry." Buys 12-15 mss/year. Query with published clips. Length: 1,500 words. Pays $500. Sometimes pays expenses of writers on assignment.

Photos: Send photos with submission. Reviews contact sheets, transparencies and prints. Negotiates payment individually. Identification of subjects required. Buys one-time rights.

Columns/Departments: Nationwide News (news items on banking and finance), 50-100 words; Operations Update (items on particular operational issues for financial institutions, such as marketing, retail banking or data processing), 50-200 words. Buys 30 mss/year. Query with published clips. Pays $50.

Tips: "The best way to develop a relationship with *Savings & Community Banker* is through our two departments, Nationwide News and Operations Update. If writers can prove themselves reliable there first, major feature assignments may follow."

‡**SECONDARY MARKETING EXECUTIVE,** LDJ Corporation, P.O. Box 2330, Waterbury CT 06722. (203)755-0158. Fax: (203)755-3480. Editorial Director: John Florian. 20% freelance written. Monthly tabloid on secondary marketing. "The magazine is read monthly by executives in financial institutions who are involved with secondary marketing, which is the buying and selling of mortgage loans and servicing rights. The editorial slant is toward how-to and analysis of trends, rather than spot news." Estab. 1986. Circ. 22,000. **Pays on acceptance.** Publishes ms an average of 1 month after acceptance. Byline given. Offers 30% kill fee. Buys first rights. Submit seasonal material 4 months in advance. Query for electronic submissions. Reports in 2 weeks. *Writer's Market* recommends allowing 1 month for reply. Sample copy and writer's guidelines for 9 × 12 SAE with 6 first-class stamps.

Nonfiction: How-to (how to improve secondary marketing operations and profits), opinion. Buys 20 mss/year. Query. Length: 800-1,200 words. Pays $200-400.

Photos: State availability of photos with submission. Reviews contact sheets. Offers $25/photo. Captions, model releases and identification of subjects required. Buys one-time rights.

Fishing

PACIFIC FISHING, Salmon Bay Communications, 1515 NW 51st St., Seattle WA 98107. (206)789-5333. Fax: (206)784-5545. Editor: Steve Shapiro. 75% freelance written. Eager to work with new/unpublished writers. Monthly business magazine for commercial fishermen and others in the West Coast commercial fishing industry. "*Pacific Fishing* views the fisherman as a small businessman and covers all aspects of the industry, including harvesting, processing and marketing." Estab. 1979. Circ. 11,000. Pays on publication. Publishes ms an average of 2 months after acceptance. Byline given. Offers 10-15% kill fee on assigned articles deemed unsuitable. Buys one-time rights. Accepts previously published articles. Send photocopy of article and information about when and where the article previously appeared. For reprints pays 100% of the amount paid for an original article. Reports in 2 months. Sample copy and writer's guidelines for 9 × 12 SAE with 10 first-class stamps.

Nonfiction: Interview/profile, technical (usually with a business hook or slant). "Articles must be concerned specifically with *commercial* fishing. We view fishermen as small businessmen and professionals who are innovative and success-oriented. To appeal to this reader, *Pacific Fishing* offers 4 basic features: technical, how-to articles that give fisherman hands-on tips that will make their operation more efficient and profitable; practical, well-researched business articles discussing the dollars and cents of fishing, processing and marketing; profiles of a fisherman, processor or company with emphasis on practical business and technical areas; and in-depth analysis of political, social, fisheries management and resource issues that have a direct bearing on West Coast commercial fishermen." Buys 20 mss/year. Query noting whether photos are available, and enclosing samples of previous work. Length: 1,500-2,500 words. Pays 15¢/word. Sometimes pays the expenses of writers on assignment.

● Editors here are putting more focus on local and international seafood marketing.

Photos: "We need good, high-quality photography, especially color, of West Coast commercial fishing. We prefer 35mm color slides. Our rates are $150 for cover; $50-100 for inside color; $25-50 for b&w and $10 for table of contents."

Tips: "Because of the specialized nature of our audience, the editor strongly recommends that freelance writers query the magazine in writing with a proposal. We enjoy finding a writer who understands our editorial needs and satisfies those needs, a writer willing to work with an editor to make the article just right. Most of our shorter items are staff written. Our freelance budget is such that we get the most benefit by using it for feature material."

WESTCOAST FISHERMAN, Westcoast Publishing Ltd., 1496 West 72 Ave., Vancouver, British Columbia V6P 4J4 Canada. (604)266-8611. Fax: (604)266-6437. Editor: Peter A. Robson. 40% freelance written. Monthly trade journal covering commercial fishing in British Columbia. "We're a non-aligned magazine dedicated to the people in the B.C. commercial fishing industry. Our publication reflects and celebrates the individuals and communities that collectively constitute B.C. fishermen." Estab. 1986. Pays on publication. Publishes ms an average of 2-3 months after acceptance. Byline given. Buys first and one-time rights. Accepts previously published articles. Send tearsheet or photocopy of article and information about when and where the article previously appeared. For reprints, pays 100% of their fee for an original article. Reports in 2 months.

Nonfiction: Interview/profile, photo feature, technical. Buys 30-40 mss/year. Query with or without published clips or send complete ms. Length: 250-2,500 words. Pays $25-450.

Photos: Send photos with submission. Reviews contact sheets, negatives, transparencies and 5×7 prints. Offers $5-100/photo. Identification of subjects required. Buys one-time rights.

Poetry: Avant-garde, free verse, haiku, light verse, traditional. "We use poetry written by or for West Coast fishermen." Buys 6 poems/year. Length: 1 page. Pay is $25.

Florists, Nurseries and Landscaping

Readers of these publications are involved in growing, selling or caring for plants, flowers and trees. Magazines geared to consumers interested in gardening are listed in the Consumer Home and Garden section.

FLORIST, Florists' Transworld Delivery Association, 29200 Northwestern Hwy., P.O. Box 2227, Southfield MI 48037-2227. (313)355-9300. Editor-in-Chief: William P. Golden. Managing Editor: Barbara Koch. 5% freelance written. Monthly magazine for retail flower shop owners, managers and floral designers. Other readers include floriculture growers, wholesalers, researchers and teachers. Circ. 28,000. **Pays on acceptance.** Publishes ms an average of 2 months after acceptance. Buys one-time rights. Pays 10-25% kill fee. Byline given "unless the story needs a substantial rewrite." Submit seasonal material 4 months in advance. Accepts simultaneous and previously published submissions. Reports in 1 month.

Nonfiction: Articles should pertain to marketing, merchandising, financial management or personnel management in a retail flower shop. Also, giftware, floral and interior design trends. No general interest, fiction or personal experience. Buys 5 unsolicited mss/year. Query with published clips. Length: 1,200-2,500 words. Pays $200-500.

Photos: State availability of photos with query. Pays $10-25 for 5×7 b&w photos or color transparencies. Buys one-time rights.

Tips: "Business management articles must deal specifically with retail flower shops and their unique merchandise and concerns. Send samples of published work with query. Suggest several ideas in query letter."

‡**FLOWERS, The Beautiful Magazine About the Business of Flowers,** Teleflora, Suite 118, 12233 W. Olympic, Los Angeles CA 90064. Editor: Marie Moneysmith. Contact: Bruce Wright. 20% freelance written. Monthly magazine covering retail floristry. "We are primarily a small business publication, aimed at flower shop owners and managers." Estab. 1980. Circ. 30,000. **Pays on acceptance.** Publishes ms an average of 3 months after acceptance. Byline given. Offers 20% kill fee. Buys one-time rights. Editorial lead time 2 months. Submit seasonal material 4 months in advance. Accepts simultaneous and previously published submissions. Reports in 1 month. Sample copy for $8\frac{1}{2} \times 11$ SAE with 4 first-class stamps. Writer's guidelines for #10 SASE.

Nonfiction: Book excerpts, interview/profile. Buys 12-15 mss/year. Query with published clips. Length: 1,000-3,000 words. Pays $200 for assigned articles; $750 for unsolicited articles. Sometimes pays expenses of writers on assignment.

Photos: State availability of photos with submission. Reviews $2\frac{1}{4}$ or 3×5 transparencies. Negotiates payment individually. Identification of subjects required. Buys one-time rights.

Tips: "Talk to local florists about types of articles they would like to read. That will give you insight into the issues in retail floristry. We are open to any aspect of small business operations, from creating a newsletter for customers to dealing with the IRS."

GROWERTALKS, Ball Publishing, 335 N. River St., P.O Box 9, Batavia IL 60510. (708)208-9080. Managing Editor: Chris Beytes. 50% freelance written. Monthly magazine covering ornamental horticulture—primarily greenhouse flower growers. "*GrowerTalks* serves the commercial greenhouse grower. Editorial emphasis is on floricultural crops: bedding plants, potted floral crops, foliage and fresh cut flowers. Our readers are growers, managers and owners." Estab. 1937. Circ. 10,500. Pays on publication. Publishes ms an average of 6 months after acceptance. Byline given. Buys first North American serial rights. Editorial lead time 4 months. Submit seasonal material 6 months in advance. Query for electronic submissions. Reports in 1 month. Sample copy and writer's guidelines free on request.

Nonfiction: How-to (time- or money-saving projects for professional flower/plant growers); interview/profile (ornamental horticulture growers); personal experience (of a grower); technical (about growing process in greenhouse setting). "No articles that promote only one product." Buys 36 mss/year. Query. Length: 1,200-1,600 words. Pays $125 minimum for assigned articles; $75 minimum for unsolicited articles. Sometimes pays in other premiums or contributor copies.

Photos: State availability of photos with submission. Reviews $2\frac{1}{2} \times 2\frac{1}{2}$ transparencies slides and 3×5 prints. Negotiates payment individually. Captions, model releases and identification of subjects required. Buys one-time rights.

Tips: "Discuss magazine with ornamental horticulture growers to find out what topics that have or haven't appeared in the magazine interest them."

THE GROWING EDGE, New Moon Publishing Inc., Suite 201, 215 SW Second, P.O. Box 1027, Corvallis OR 97339-1027. (503)757-2511. Fax: (503)757-0028. Editor: Don Parker. 60% freelance written. Eager to work with new or unpublished writers. Quarterly magazine signature covering indoor and outdoor high-tech gardening techniques and tips. Estab. 1980. Circ. 40,000. Pays on publication. Publishes ms an average of 3 months after acceptance. Byline given. Buys first serial and reprint rights. Submit seasonal material at least 6 months in advance. Query for electronic submissions. Reports in 3 months. Sample copy for $6.50. Writer's guidelines for #10 SASE.
Nonfiction: Book excerpts and reviews relating to high-tech gardening, general interest, how-to, interview/profile, personal experience, technical. Query first. Length: 500-2,500 words. Pays 10¢/word.
Photos: Pays $175/color cover photos; $25-50/inside photo. Pays on publication. Credit line given. Buys first and reprint rights.
Tips: Looking for information which will give the reader/gardener/farmer the "growing edge" in high-tech gardening and farming on topics such as hydroponics, high intensity grow lights, water conservation, drip irrigation, advanced organic fertilizers, new seed varieties and greenhouse cultivation.

‡**LINK MAGAZINE**, Wholesale Florists and Florist Suppliers of America, P.O. Box 7308, Arlington VA 22207. (703)241-1100. Editor: Lisa Mickey. 1% freelance written. Monthly magazine covering wholesale floristry. "*Link Magazine* covers floral and business issues that help WF & FSA members run their companies more effectively." Estab. 1978. Circ. 1,800. **Pays on acceptance.** Publishes ms an average of 1-2 months after acceptance. Byline given. Buys first North American serial rights. Editorial lead time 1-2 months. Submit seasonal material 4 months in advance. Accepts simultaneous and previously published submissions. Query for electronic submissions. Reports in 1 month. Sample copy for 8½ × 11 SAE with 7 first-class stamps.
Nonfiction: General interest (business, economics), technical (floriculture). Buys 5-10 mss/year. Query. Length: 1,500-2,500 words. Pays $200.
Photos: State availability of photos with submission. Offers no additional payment for photos accepted with ms. Captions, model releases and identification of subjects required. Buys one-time rights.
Tips: Looking for "business articles centering on new laws, new management techniques, new technology or family business issues are most desirable. Learn something about *Link*'s audience. Articles that are too broad aren't accepted."

ORNAMENTAL OUTLOOK, The Professional Magazine for the Professional Grower, FGR, Inc., 1331 N. Mills Ave., Orlando FL 32803-2598. (407)894-6522. Editor: Rhonda Hunsinger. 50% freelance written. Magazine published 10 times/year covering ornamental horticulture. "*Ornamental Outlook* is written for commercial growers of ornamental plants in Florida. Our goal is to provide interesting and informative articles on such topics as production, legislation, safety, technology, pest control, water management and new varieties as they apply to Florida growers." Estab. 1991. Circ. 25,000. Pays 30 days after publication. Publishes ms an average of 4 months after acceptance. Byline given. Buys all rights. Editorial lead time 2 months. Submit seasonal material 3 months in advance. Query for electronic submissions. Reports in 1-3 months. Sample copy for 9 × 12 SAE with 5 first-class stamps. Writer's guidelines free on request.
Nonfiction: Interview/profile, photo feature, technical. "No first-person articles. No word-for-word meeting transcripts or all-quote articles." Buys 50 mss/year. Query with published clips. Length: 750-1,000 words. Pays 12¢/word.
Photos: Send photos with submission. Reviews contact sheets, transparencies and prints. Offers $10-30/photo. Captions and identification of subjects required. Buys one-time rights.
Columns/Departments: Management (news that helps wholesale growers manage nursery), 750 words. Buys 10 mss/year. Query with published clips. Pays 12¢/word.
Tips: "I am most impressed by written queries that address specific subjects of interest to our audience, which is the *Florida* grower of *commercial* horticulture. Our biggest demand is for features, about 1,000 words, that follow subjects listed on our editorial calendar (which is sent with guidelines). Please do not send articles of national or consumer interest."

TURF MAGAZINE, P.O. Box 391, 50 Bay St., St. Johnsbury VT 05819. (802)748-8908. Fax: (802)748-1866. Editors and Publishers: Francis Carlet and Dan Hurley. Managing Editor: Bob Hookway. 60% freelance written. "Our readers are professional turf grass managers: superintendents of grounds for golf courses, cemeteries, athletic fields, parks, recreation fields, lawn care companies, landscape contractors/architects." Estab. 1977. Four regional editions: North, South, Central and West; with a combined national circulation of 56,000. Pays on publication. Byline given. Buys all rights or makes work-for-hire assignments. Submit seasonal material 2 months in advance. Reports in 3 months. Sample copy for 10 × 13 SAE with 8 first-class stamps.
Nonfiction: How-to, interview/profile, opinion, technical. "We use on-the-job type interviews with good b&w photos that combine technical information with human interest." Buys 150 mss/year. Query with clips

or send complete ms. Submissions on IBM disk preferred. Pays $100 for columns; $200 minimum for feature stories. Often pays the expenses of writers on assignment.

Photos: Send photos with ms. Payment for photos is included in payment for articles. Reviews b&w contact sheets and 8 × 10 b&w prints. Needs a variety of photos with the story. Also seeking color transparencies for cover.

Tips: "Good, accurate stories needing minimal editing, with art, are welcomed."

Government and Public Service

Listed here are journals for people who provide governmental services at the local, state or federal level or for those who work in franchised utilities. Journals for city managers, politicians, bureaucratic decision makers, civil servants, firefighters, police officers, public administrators, urban transit managers and utilities managers are listed in this section.

THE CALIFORNIA HIGHWAY PATROLMAN, California Association of Highway Patrolmen, 2030 V Street, Sacramento CA 95818-1730. (916)452-6751. Editor: Carol Perri. 70% freelance written. Monthly magazine covering CHP info; California history; history of vehicles and/or transportation. "Our readers are either uniformed officers or pro-police oriented." Estab. 1937. Circ. 20,000. Pays on publication. Publishes ms an average of 6-9 months after acceptance. No kill fee. Byline given. Buys one-time rights. Submit seasonal material 3-6 months in advance. Accepts simultaneous and previously published submissions. Send tearsheet or photocopy of article or typed ms and information on when and where the article previously appeared. Query for electronic submissions. Reports in 1 month on queries; up to 3 months on mss. Sample copy for 9 × 12 SAE with 5 first-class stamps. Writer's guidelines for #10 SASE.

Nonfiction: General interest, historical/nostalgic, humor, interview/profile, photo feature, technical, travel. "No 'how you felt when you received a ticket (or survived an accident)!' No fiction." Buys 80-100 mss/year. Query with or without published clips or send complete ms. Length: 750-3,000 words. Pays 5¢/word or $50 minimum.

Photos: State availability of photos with submission. Send photos (or photocopies of available photos) with submission. Reviews prints. Offers $5/photo. Captions and identification of subjects required. Returns all photos. Buys one-time rights.

 • Articles with accompanying photos receive preference.

CANADIAN DEFENCE QUARTERLY, Revue Canadienne de Défense, Baxter Publications Inc., 310 Dupont St., Toronto, Ontario M5R 1V9 Canada. (416)968-7252. Fax: (416)968-2377. Editor: John Marteinson. 90% freelance written. Quarterly professional journal on strategy, defense policy, military technology and history. "A professional journal for officers of the Canadian Forces and for the academic community working in Canadian foreign and defense affairs. Articles should have Canadian or NATO applicability." Estab. 1971. Pays on publication. Byline given. Offers $150 kill fee. Buys all rights. Accepts simultaneous submissions. Reports in 2 months. Free sample copy and writer's guidelines.

Nonfiction: Historical, new product, opinion, technical, military strategy. Buys 30 mss/year. Query with or without published clips or send complete ms. Length: 2,500-4,000 words. Pays $150-300.

Photos: State availability of photos with submission. Offers no additional payment for photos accepted with ms. Buys one-time rights.

Tips: "Submit a well-written manuscript in a relevant field that demonstrates an original approach to the subject matter. Manuscripts *must* be double-spaced, with good margins."

CHIEF OF POLICE MAGAZINE, National Association of Chiefs of Police, 3801 Biscayne Blvd., Miami FL 33137. (305)573-0070. Editor-in-Chief: Jim Gordon. Bimonthly trade journal for law enforcement commanders (command ranks). Circ. 13,500. **Pays on acceptance.** Publishes ms an average of 4-6 months after acceptance. Byline given. Buys first rights. Submit seasonal material 6 months in advance. Accepts simultaneous and previously published submissions. Reports in 2 weeks. Sample copy for $3 and 9 × 12 SAE with 5 first-class stamps. Writer's guidelines for #10 SASE.

Nonfiction: General interest, historical/nostalgic, how-to, humor, inspirational, interview/profile, new product, personal experience, photo feature, religious, technical. "We want stories about interesting police cases and stories on any law enforcement subject or program that is positive in nature. No exposé types. Nothing anti-police." Buys 50 mss/year. Send complete ms. Length: 600-2,500 words. Pays $25-75 for assigned articles; $10-50 for unsolicited articles. Sometimes (when pre-requested) pays the expenses of writers on assignment.

Photos: Send photos with submission. Reviews 5 × 6 prints. Pays $5-10 for b&w; $10-25 for color. Captions required. Buys one-time rights.

Columns/Departments: New Police (police equipment shown and tests), 200-600 words. Buys 6 mss/year. Send complete ms. Pays $5-25.

Fillers: Anecdote, short humor, law-oriented cartoons. Buys 100/year. Length: 100-1,600 words. Pays $5-25.
Tips: "Writers need only contact law enforcement officers right in their own areas and we would be delighted. We want to recognize good commanding officers from sergeant and above who are involved with the community. Pictures of the subject or the department are essential and can be snapshots. We are looking for interviews with police chiefs and sheriffs on command level with photos."

FIREHOUSE MAGAZINE, PTN Publishing, Suite 21, 445 Broad Hollow Rd., Melville NY 11747. (516)845-2700. Fax: (516)845-7109. Editor-in-Chief: Barbara Dunleavy. 85% freelance written. Works with a small number of new/unpublished writers each year. Monthly magazine covering fire service. "*Firehouse* covers major fires nationwide, controversial issues and trends in the fire service, the latest firefighting equipment and methods of firefighting, historical fires, firefighting history and memorabilia. Fire-related books, fire safety education, hazardous materials incidents and the emergency medical services are also covered." Estab. 1976. Circ. 110,000. Pays on publication. Byline given. Exclusive submissions only. Query for electronic submissions. Reports in 1 month. Sample copy for 9×12 SAE with 7 first-class stamps. Free writer's guidelines.
Nonfiction: Book excerpts (of recent books on fire, EMS and hazardous materials); historical/nostalgic (great fires in history, fire collectibles, the fire service of yesteryear); how-to (fight certain kinds of fires, buy and maintain equipment, run a fire department); technical (on almost any phase of firefighting, techniques, equipment, training, administration); trends (controversies in the fire service). No profiles of people or departments that are not unusual or innovative, reports of nonmajor fires, articles not slanted toward firefighters' interests. Buys 100 mss/year. Query with or without published clips or send complete ms. Length: 500-3,000 words. Pays $50-400 for assigned articles; $50-300 for unsolicited articles. Sometimes pays the expenses of writers on assignment.
Photos: Send photos with query or ms. Pays $15-45 for b&w prints; $20-200 for transparencies and color prints. Captions and identification of subjects required.
Columns/Departments: Training (effective methods); Book Reviews; Fire Safety (how departments teach fire safety to the public); Communicating (PR, dispatching); Arson (efforts to combat it). Buys 50 mss/year. Query or send complete ms. Length: 750-1,000 words. Pays $100-300.
Tips: "Read the magazine to get a full understanding of the subject matter, the writing style and the readers before sending a query or manuscript. Send photos with manuscript or indicate sources for photos. Be sure to focus articles on firefighters."

FOREIGN SERVICE JOURNAL, Dept. WM, 2101 E St. NW, Washington DC 20037-2990. (202)338-4045. Fax: (202)338-6820. Editor: Karen Krebsbach. 80% freelance written. Monthly magazine for Foreign Service personnel and others interested in foreign affairs and related subjects. Estab. 1924. Pays on publication. Publishes ms an average of 3 months after acceptance. Byline given. Buys first North American serial rights. Reports in 1 month. Sample copy for $3.50 and 10×12 SAE with 6 first-class stamps. Writer's guidelines for SASE.
  • New columns are Foreign Vignettes and Career Issues.
Nonfiction: Uses articles on "diplomacy, professional concerns of the State Department and Foreign Service, diplomatic history and articles on Foreign Service experiences. Much of our material is contributed by those working in the profession. Informed outside contributions are welcomed, however." Query. Buys 5-10 unsolicited mss/year. Length: 1,000-4,000 words. Offers honoraria. Publishes novel excerpts.
Tips: "We're more likely to want your article if it has something to do with diplomacy or diplomats."

FOUNDATION NEWS MAGAZINE: Philanthropy and the Nonprofit Sector, Council on Foundations, Dept. WM, 1828 L St. NW, Washington DC 20036. (202)466-6512. Fax: (202)785-3926. Managing Editor: Jody Curtis. 70% freelance written. Prefers to work with published/established writers. Bimonthly magazine covering the world of philanthropy, nonprofit organizations and their relation to current events. Read by staff and executives of foundations, corporations, hospitals, colleges and universities and various nonprofit organizations. Circ. 13,000. **Pays on acceptance.** Publishes ms an average of 3 months after acceptance. Byline given. Offers negotiable kill fee. Not copyrighted. Buys all rights. Submit seasonal material 5 months in advance. Accepts previously published submissions. Reports in 6 weeks.
Nonfiction: Book excerpts, expose, general interest, historical/nostalgic, how-to, interview/profile, photo feature. Submit written query; no telephone calls. Length: 2,000 words maximum. Pays $200-2,000. Pays expenses of writers on assignment.
Photos: State availability of photos with submission. Pays negotiable rates for b&w contact sheet and prints. Captions and identification of subjects required. Buys one-time rights; "some rare requests for second use."
Columns/Departments: Buys 12 mss/year. Query. Length: 900-2,000 words. Pays $250-750.
Tips: "We have a great interest in working with writers familiar with the nonprofit sector."

For explanation of symbols, see the Key to Symbols and Abbreviations. For unfamiliar words, see the Glossary.

LAW AND ORDER, Hendon Co., 1000 Skokie Blvd., Wilmette IL 60091. (312)256-8555. Editor: Bruce W. Cameron. 90% freelance written. Prefers to work with published/established writers. Monthly magazine covering the administration and operation of law enforcement agencies, directed to police chiefs and supervisors. Estab. 1952. Circ. 30,000. Pays on publication. Publishes ms an average of 6 months after acceptance. Byline given. Buys first North American serial rights. Submit seasonal material 3 months in advance. No simultaneous queries. Query for electronic submissions. Can accept mss via CompuServe: #71171, 1344. Reports in 1 month. Sample copy for 9×12 SAE. Free writer's guidelines.
Nonfiction: General police interest; how-to (do specific police assignments); new product (how applied in police operation); technical (specific police operation). Special issues: Buyers Guide (January); Communications (February); Training (March); International (April); Administration (May); Small Departments (June); Mobile Patrol (July); Equipment (August); Weapons (September); Police Science (November); and Community Relations (December). No articles dealing with courts (legal field) or convicted prisoners. No nostalgic, financial, travel or recreational material. Buys 100 mss/year. Length: 2,000-3,000 words. Pays 10¢/word for professional writers; 5¢/word for others.
Photos: Send photos with ms. Reviews transparencies and prints. Identification of subjects required. Buys all rights.
Tips: "*L&O* is a respected magazine that provides up-to-date information that chiefs can use. Writers must know their subject as it applies to this field. Case histories are well received. We are upgrading editorial quality—stories *must* show some understanding of the law enforcement field. A frequent mistake is not getting photographs to accompany article."

NATIONAL MINORITY POLITICS, Suite 3-296, 5757 Westheimer, Houston TX 77057. (713)444-4265. Editor: Gwenevere Daye Richardson. 10-15% freelance written. Monthly opinion and news magazine taking a moderate to conservative political approach. Estab. 1988. Circ. 15,000. Pays on publication. Publishes ms an average of 1 month after acceptance. Byline given. Buys one-time rights. Editorial lead time 2 months. Submit seasonal material 2 months in advance. Accepts simultaneous submissions. No previously published material. Query for electronic submissions. Reports in 3-4 weeks on queries. Sample copy and writer's guidelines free on request.
Nonfiction: Exposé, interview/profile, commentary and features on national political topics. "These topics can be, but are not limited to, those which are considered traditionally "minority" concerns. But prefer those which give a broad view or analysis of national or regional political elections, trends, issues, and economic issues as well." Buys approximately 20 mss/year. Query with published clips. Length: 750-1,000 words. Pays standard rate of $100 for unsolicited mss, usually more for assigned articles.
Columns/Departments: The Nation (commentaries on national issues), 750-1,000 words; features, 1,000-1,500 words; "Speaking Out," personal commentary, 750-1,000 words.
Fillers: Political cartoons. Pays $25.
Tips: "Submissions must be well-written, timely, have depth and take an angle not generally available in national newspapers and magazines. Since our magazine takes a moderate to conservative approach, we prefer not to receive commentaries which do not fall in either of these categories."

9-1-1 MAGAZINE, Official Publications, Inc., 18201 Weston Place, Tustin CA 92680-2251. (714)544-7776. Fax: (714)838-9233. Editor: Alan Burton. 85% freelance written. Bimonthly magazine for knowledgeable public safety communications and response personnel and those associated with those respective professions. "*9-1-1 Magazine* is published to provide information valuable to all those interested in this dangerous, exciting and rewarding profession." Estab. 1947. Circ. 30,000. Pays on publication. Publishes ms an average of 2 months after acceptance. Byline given. Offers 20% kill fee. Buys one-time and second serial (reprint) rights. Submit seasonal material well in advance. Accepts simultaneous submissions. Query for electronic submissions. Reports in 2 months on queries; 3 months on mss. Must be accompanied by SASE if to be returned. Sample copy for 9×12 SAE with 5 first-class stamps. Writer's guidelines for #10 SASE.
Nonfiction: Incident report, new product, photo feature, technical. Buys 10 mss/year. Send complete ms. "We prefer queries, but will look at manuscripts on speculation. Most positive responses to queries are considered on spec, but occasionally we will make assignments." Length: 1,000-2,500 words. Pays $100-300 for unsolicited articles.
Photos: Send photos with submission. Reviews color transparencies and prints. Offers $25-300/photo. Captions and identification of subjects required. Buys one-time rights.
Fillers: Cartoons. Buys 10/year. Pays $25-50.
Tips: "What we don't need are 'my first call' articles, or photography of a less-than-excellent quality. We seldom use poetry or fiction. *9-1-1 Magazine* is published for a knowledgeable, up-scale audience. Our primary considerations in selecting material are: quality, appropriateness of material, brevity, knowledge of our readership, accuracy, accompanying photography, originality, wit and humor, a clear direction and vision, and proper use of the language."

PLANNING, American Planning Association, 1313 E. 60th St., Chicago IL 60637-2891. (312)955-9100. Editor: Sylvia Lewis. 25% freelance written. Monthly magazine emphasizing urban planning for adult, college-educated readers who are regional and urban planners in city, state or federal agencies or in private business or university faculty or students. Estab. 1972. Circ. 30,000. Pays on publication. Publishes ms an average of 3 months after acceptance. Buys all or first rights. Byline given. Reports in 2 months. Sample copy and writer's guidelines for 9×12 SAE with 5 first-class stamps.

Nonfiction: Exposé (on government or business, but topics related to planning, housing, land use, zoning); general interest (trend stories on cities, land use, government); how-to (successful government or citizen efforts in planning, innovations, concepts that have been applied); technical (detailed articles on the nitty-gritty of planning, zoning, transportation but no footnotes or mathematical models). Also needs news stories up to 400 words. "It's best to query with a fairly detailed, one-page letter. We'll consider any article that's well written and relevant to our audience. Articles have a better chance if they are timely and related to planning and land use and if they appeal to a national audience. All articles should be written in magazine feature style." Buys 2 features and 1 news story/issue. Length: 500-2,000 words. Pays $100-750. "We pay freelance writers and photographers only, not planners."

Photos: "We prefer that authors supply their own photos, but we sometimes take our own or arrange for them in other ways." State availability of photos. Pays $25 minimum for 8×10 matte or glossy prints and $200 for 4-color cover photos. Caption material required. Buys one-time rights.

POLICE, Hare Publications, 6300 Yarrow Dr., Carlsbad CA 92009-1597. (619)438-2511. Editor: Dan Burger. 90% freelance written. Monthly magazine covering topics related to law enforcement officers. "Our audience is primarily law enforcement personnel such as patrol officers, detectives and security police." Estab. 1968. Circ. 58,000. **Pays on acceptance.** Publishes ms an average of 6 months after acceptance. Buys all rights (returned to author 45 days after publication). Submit theme material 6 months in advance. Reports in 3 months. Sample copy for $2. Writer's guidelines for #10 SAE with 2 first-class stamps.

Nonfiction: General interest, interview/profile, new product, personal experience, technical. Buys 30 mss/year. Query only. Length: 2,000-3,000 words. Pays $250-350.

Photos: Send photos with submission. Reviews color transparencies. Captions required. Buys all rights.

Columns/Departments: The Beat (entertainment section — humor, fiction, first-person drama, professional tips); The Arsenal (weapons, ammunition and equipment used in the line of duty); Fit For Duty (fitness, nutrition, mental health life style changes); and Officer Survival (theories, skills and techniques used by officers for street survival). Buys 50 mss/year. Query only. Length: 1,000-2,500 words. Pays $75-250.

Tips: "You are writing for police officers — people who live a dangerous and stressful life. Study the editorial calendar — yours for the asking — and come up with an idea that fits into a specific issue. We are actively seeking talented writers."

POLICE AND SECURITY NEWS, Days Communications, Inc.. 15 Thatcher Rd., Quakertown PA 18951-2503. (215)538-1240. Fax: (215)538-1208. Editor: James Devery. 40% freelance written. Bimonthly tabloid on public law enforcement and private security. "Our publication is designed to provide educational and entertaining information directed toward management level. Technical information written for the expert in a manner that the non-expert can understand." Estab. 1985. Circ. 20,640. Pays on publication. Publishes ms an average of 2 months after acceptance. Byline given. Buys first North American serial rights. Submit seasonal/holiday material 2 months in advance. Accepts simultaneous and previously published submissions. Free sample copy and writer's guidelines.

Nonfiction: Al Menear, articles editor. Exposé, historical/nostalgic, how-to, humor, interview/profile, opinion, personal experience, photo feature, technical. Buys 12 mss/year. Query. Length: 200-4,000 words. Pays 10¢/word. Sometimes pays in trade-out of services.

Photos: State availability of photos with submission. Reviews prints (3×5). Offers $10-50/photo. Buys one-time rights.

Fillers: Facts, newsbreaks, short humor. Buys 6/year. Length: 200-2,000 words. Pays 10¢/word.

POLICE TIMES, American Federation of Police, 3801 Biscayne Blvd., Miami FL 33137. (305)573-0070. Fax: (305)573-9819. Editor-In-Chief: Jim Gordon. 80% freelance written. Eager to work with new/unpublished writers. Bimonthly tabloid covering "law enforcement (general topics) for men and women engaged in law enforcement and private security, and citizens who are law and order concerned." Circ. 55,000. **Pays on acceptance.** Publishes ms an average of 3-6 months after acceptance. Byline given. Buys second serial (reprint) rights. Submit seasonal material 4 months in advance. Accepts simultaneous and previously published submissions. Sample copy for $2.50 and 9×12 SAE with 3 first-class stamps. Writer's guidelines for #10 SASE.

Nonfiction: Book excerpts; essays (on police science); exposé (police corruption); general interest; historical/nostalgic; how-to; humor; interview/profile; new product; personal experience (with police); photo feature; technical — all police-related. "We produce a special edition on police killed in the line of duty. It is mailed May 15 so copy must arrive six months in advance. Photos required." No anti-police materials. Buys 50 mss/year. Send complete ms. Length: 200-4,000 words. Pays $5-50 for assigned articles; $5-25 for unsolicited articles.

Photos: Send photos with submission. Reviews 5×6 prints. Offers $5-25/photo. Identification of subjects required. Buys all rights.

Columns/Departments: Legal Cases (lawsuits involving police actions); New Products (new items related to police services); Awards (police heroism acts). Buys variable number of mss/year. Send complete ms. Length: 200-1,000 words. Pays $5-25.

Fillers: Anecdotes, facts, newsbreaks, cartoons, short humor. Buys 100/year. Length: 50-100 words. Pays $5-10. Fillers are usually humorous stories about police officer and citizen situations. Special stories on police cases, public corruptions, etc. are most open to freelancers.

SUPERINTENDENT'S PROFILE & POCKET EQUIPMENT DIRECTORY, Profile Publications, 220 Central Ave., P.O. Box 43, Dunkirk NY 14048-0043. (716)366-4774. Fax: (716)366-3626. Editor: Robert Dyment. 60% freelance written. Prefers to work with published/established writers. Monthly magazine covering "outstanding" town, village, county and city highway superintendents and Department of Public Works directors throughout New York state only. Estab. 1978. Circ. 2,600. Publishes ms an average of 4 months after acceptance. Pays within 90 days. Byline given for excellent material. Buys first rights. Accepts previously published articles. Send tearsheet of article or typed ms with right for sale noted. For reprints, pays 50% of the amount paid for an original article. Submit seasonal material 3 months in advance. Reports in 2 months. Sample copy for 9×12 SAE with 4 first-class stamps.

Nonfiction: Contact: John Powers. Interview/profile (of a highway superintendent or DPW director in NY state who has improved department operations through unique methods or equipment); and technical. Special issues include winter maintenance profiles. No fiction. Buys 20 mss/year. Query. Length: 1,500-2,000 words. Pays $150 for a full-length ms. "Pays more for excellent material. All manuscripts will be edited to fit our format and space limitations." Sometimes pays the expenses of writers on assignment.

Photos: Contact: John Powers. State availability of photos. Pays $5-10 for b&w contact sheets; also reviews 5×7 prints. Captions and identification of subjects required. Buys one-time rights.

Poetry: Buys poetry if it pertains to highway departments. Pays $5-15.

Tips: "We are a widely read and highly respected state-wide magazine, and although we can't pay high rates, we expect quality work. Too many freelance writers are going for the exposé rather than the meat-and-potato type articles that will help readers. We use more major features than fillers. Writers should read sample copies first. We will be purchasing more material because our page numbers are increasing."

TRANSACTION/SOCIETY, Bldg. 4051, Rutgers University, New Brunswick NJ 08903. (201)932-2280, ext. 83. Fax: (201)932-3138. Editor: Irving Louis Horowitz. Publisher: Mary E. Curtis. 10% freelance written. Prefers to work with published/established writers. Bimonthly magazine for social scientists (policymakers with training in sociology, political issues and economics). Estab. 1962. Circ. 45,000. Buys all rights. Byline given. Pays on publication. Publishes ms an average of 6 months after acceptance. No simultaneous submissions. Query for electronic submissions; "manual provided to authors." Reports in 3 months. Sample copy and writer's guidelines for 9×12 SAE with 5 first-class stamps.

Nonfiction: Brigitte M. Goldstein, managing editor. "Articles of wide interest in areas of specific interest to the social science community. Must have an awareness of problems and issues in education, population and urbanization that are not widely reported. Articles on overpopulation, terrorism, international organizations. No general think pieces." Query. Payment for articles is made only if done on assignment. *No payment for unsolicited articles.*

Photos: Douglas Harper, photo editor. Pays $200 for photographic essays done on assignment or accepted for publication.

Tips: "Submit an article on a thoroughly unique subject, written with good literary quality. Present new ideas and research findings in a readable and useful manner. A frequent mistake is writing to satisfy a journal, rather than the intrinsic requirements of the story itself. Avoid posturing and editorializing."

‡VICTIMOLOGY: An International Journal, 2333 N. Vernon St., Arlington VA 22207-4036. (703)528-3387. Editor-in-Chief: Emilio C. Viano. "We are the only magazine specifically focusing on the victim, on the dynamics of victimization; for social scientists, criminal justice professionals and practitioners, social workers and volunteer and professional groups engaged in prevention of victimization and in offering assistance to victims of rape, spouse abuse, child abuse, incest, abuse of the elderly, natural disasters, etc." Quarterly magazine. Circ. 2,500. Pays on publication. Buys all rights. Byline given. Reports in 2 months. Sample copy for $5. Free writer's guidelines.

Nonfiction: Exposé, historical, how-to, informational, interview, personal experience, profile, research, technical. Buys 10 mss/issue. Query. Length: 500-5,000 words. Pays $50-150.

Photos: Purchased with accompanying ms. Captions required. Send contact sheet. Pays $15-50 for 5×7 or 8×10 b&w glossy prints.

Poetry: Avant-garde, free verse, light verse, traditional. Length: 30 lines maximum. Pays $10-25.

Tips: "Focus on what is being researched and discovered on the victim, the victim/offender relationship, treatment of the offender, the bystander/witness, preventive measures, and what is being done in the areas of service to the victims of rape, spouse abuse, neglect and occupational and environmental hazards, and the elderly."

‡**VIRGINIA TOWN & CITY**, Virginia Municipal League, P.O. Box 12164, Richmond VA 23241. (804)649-8471. Editor: Christine A. Everson. Monthly magazine covering Virginia local government. "*Virginia Town & City* serves as a medium of information and ideas for local governments and carries timely articles on subjects of interest such as successful or innovative local government initiatives or programs, effects of legislation. All must reflect local government point of view." Estab. 1966. Circ. 5,000. Pays on publication. Byline given. Buys first, one-time, or second serial (reprint) rights. Editorial lead time 1 month. Submit seasonal material 3 months in advance. Accepts previously published submissions. Sample copy for $1.50. Writer's guidelines free on request.
Nonfiction: Exposé, how-to, interview/profile, technical. Buys 1 mss/year. Query. Length: 1,250-1,750 words. Pays $50.
Photos: State availability or send photos with submission. Reviews transparencies and prints. Negotiates payment individually. Captions required. Buys one-time rights.
Columns/Departments: Commentary (regarding some aspect or issue of local government), 800-1,000 words. Send complete ms.
Tips: "Follow the editorial calendar and come up with a good story idea relevant to the month's theme, and have good, really insightful information on a new or highly successful local government program."

YOUR VIRGINIA STATE TROOPER MAGAZINE, Virginia State Police Association, 6944 Forest Hill Ave., Richmond VA 23225. Editor: Rebecca V. Jackson. 60% freelance written. Triannual magazine covering police topics for troopers (state police), non-sworn members of the department and legislators. Estab. 1974. Circ. 5,000. **Pays on acceptance.** Publishes ms an average of 3 months after acceptance. Byline given. Buys first North American serial and all rights on assignments. Submit seasonal material 4 months in advance. Accepts simultaneous and previously published submissions. Send typed ms with rights for sale noted and information about when and where the article previously appeared. For reprints pays 20% of amount paid for an original article. Reports in 2 months.
Nonfiction: Exposé (consumer or police-related); general interest; fitness/health; tourist (VA sites); financial planning (tax, estate planning tips); historical/nostalgic; how-to; book excerpts/reports (law enforcement related); humor, interview/profile (notable police figures); technical (radar); other (recreation). Buys 55-60 mss/year. Query with clips or send complete ms. Length: 2,500 words. Pays $250 maximum/article (10¢/word). Sometimes pays expenses of writers on assignment. Does not send sample copies.
Photos: Send photos with ms. Pays $50 maximum for several 5×7 or 8×10 b&w glossy prints to accompany ms. Cutlines and model releases required. Buys one-time rights.
Cartoons: Send copies. Pays $20. Buys one-time rights. Buys 20 cartoons/year.
Fiction: Adventure, humorous, mystery, novel excerpts, suspense. Buys 3 mss/year. Send complete ms. Length: 2,500 words minimum. Pays $250 maximum (10¢/word) on acceptance.
Tips: In addition to items of interest to the VA State Police, general interest is stressed.

Groceries and Food Products

In this section are publications for grocers, food wholesalers, processors, warehouse owners, caterers, institutional managers and suppliers of grocery store equipment. See the section on Confectionery and Snack Foods for bakery and candy industry magazines.

CANADIAN GROCER, Maclean-Hunter Ltd., Maclean Hunter Building, 777 Bay St., Toronto, Ontario M5W 1A7 Canada. (416)596-5772. Editor: George H. Condon. Managing Editor: Simone Collier. 40% freelance written. Prefers to work with published/established writers. Monthly magazine about supermarketing and food retailing for Canadian chain and independent food store managers, owners, buyers, executives, food brokers, food processors and manufacturers. Estab. 1886. Circ 18,500. **Pays on acceptance.** Publishes an average of 2 months after acceptance. Byline given. Buys first Canadian rights. Accepts previously published articles. Send typed ms with rights for sale noted and information about when and where the article previously appeared. For reprints, pays 50% of the amount paid for an original article. Phone queries OK. Submit seasonal material 2 months in advance. Reports in 2 months. Sample copy for $5.
Nonfiction: Interview (Canadian trendsetters in marketing, finance or food distribution); technical (store operations, equipment and finance); news features on supermarkets. "Freelancers should be well versed on the supermarket industry. We don't want unsolicited material. Writers with business and/or finance expertise are preferred. Know the retail food industry and be able to write concisely and accurately on subjects relevant to our readers: food store managers, senior corporate executives, etc. A good example of an article would be 'How a dairy case realignment increased profits while reducing prices, inventory and stock-outs.' " Query with clips of previously published work. Pays 30¢/word. Pays the expenses of writers on assignment.
Photos: State availability of photos. Pays $10-25 for prints or slides. Captions preferred. Buys one-time rights.
Tips: "Suitable writers will be familiar with sales per square foot, merchandising mixes and direct product profitability."

CANDY WHOLESALER, American Wholesalers Markets Association, 1128 16th St. NW, Washington DC 20036-4808. (202)463-2124. Publisher: Shelley Estersohn. Editor: Joyce Grimley. 35% freelance written. Monthly magazine for distributors of candy, tobacco, snacks, groceries and other convenience-store items. "*Candy Wholesaler* magazine is published to assist the candy/tobacco/snack food distributor in improving his business by providing a variety of relevant operational information. Serves as the voice of the distributor in the candy/tobacco/snack industry." Circ. 11,559. **Pays on acceptance.** Publishes ms an average of 4 months after acceptance. Byline given. Offers $50 kill fee. Buys all rights. Submit seasonal/holiday material 6 months in advance. Query for electronic submissions. Reports in 1 month. Sample copy for 9 × 12 SAE with 6 first-class stamps.

Nonfiction: Historical/nostalgic, how-to (related to distribution), interview/profile, photo feature, technical (data processing) and profiles of distribution films/or manufacturers. "No simplistic pieces with consumer focus that are financial, tax-related or legal." Buys 30-35 mss/year. Query with or without published clips, or send complete ms. Length: 8-12 double-spaced typewritten pages. Pays $750-1,000 for assigned articles. Pays $250-500 for unsolicited articles. Sometimes pays copies to industry members who author articles. Pays the expenses of writers on assignment.

Photos: Send photos with submission. Reviews contact sheets, transparencies and prints. Offers $5-10/photo. Captions and identification of subjects required. Buys all rights.

Fillers: Kevin Settlage, fillers editor. Anecdotes, facts, short humor. Length: 50-200 words. Pays $10-20.

Tips: "Talk to wholesalers about their business—how it works, what their problems are, etc. We need writers who understand this industry. Company profile feature stories are open to freelancers. Get into the nitty gritty of operations and management. Talk to several key people in the company."

CITRUS & VEGETABLE MAGAZINE, and the Florida Farmer, Suite 291, 4902 Eisenhower Blvd., Tampa FL 33634-6323. Fax: (813)888-5290. Editor: Gordon Smith. Monthly magazine on the citrus and vegetable industries. Estab. 1938. Circ. 12,000. Pays on publication. Publishes ms an average of 1 month after acceptance. Byline given. Kill fee varies. Buys exclusive first rights. Query first. Reports in 2 months on queries. Free sample copy and writer's guidelines.

Nonfiction: Book excerpts (if pertinent to relevant agricultural issues); how-to (grower interest—cultivation practices, etc.); new product (of interest to Florida citrus or vegetable growers); personal experience; photo feature. Buys 20 mss/year. Query with published clips or send complete ms. Length: approx. 1,200 words. Pays about $200.

Photos: Send photos with submission. Reviews 5 × 7 prints. Prefers color slides. Offers $15 minimum/photo. Captions and identification of subjects required. Buys first rights.

Columns/Departments: Citrus Summary (news to citrus industry in Florida: market trends, new product lines), and Vegetable Vignettes (new cultivars, anything on trends or developments within vegetable industry of Florida). Send complete ms.

Tips: "Show initiative—don't be afraid to call whomever you need to get your information for story together—accurately and with style. Submit ideas and/or completed ms well in advance. Focus on areas that have not been widely written about elsewhere in the press. Looking for fresh copy. Have something to sell and be convinced of its value. Become familiar with the key issues, key players in the citrus industry in Florida. Have a specific idea in mind for a news or feature story and try to submit manuscript at least 1 month in advance of publication."

FLORIDA GROCER, Florida Grocer Publications, Inc., P.O. Box 430760, South Miami FL 33243-0760. (305)441-1138. Fax: (305)661-6720. Editor: Dennis Kane. 5% freelance written. "*Florida Grocer* is a 16,000-circulation monthly trade newspaper, serving members of the Florida food industry. Our publication is edited for chain and independent food store owners and operators as well as members of allied industries." Estab. 1956. **Pays on acceptance.** Byline given. Buys all rights. Submit seasonal material 3 months in advance. Reports in 2 months. Sample copy for 10 × 14 SAE with 10 first-class stamps.

Nonfiction: Book excerpts, exposé, general interest, humor, features on supermarkets and their owners, new product, new equipment, photo feature, video. Buys variable number of mss/year. Query with or without published clips or send complete ms. Payment varies. Sometimes pays the expenses of writers on assignment.

Photos: State availability of photos with submission. Terms for payment on photos "included in terms of payment for assignment."

Tips: "We prefer feature articles on new stores (grand openings, etc.), store owners, operators; Florida-based food manufacturers, brokers, wholesalers, distributors, etc. We also publish a section in Spanish and also welcome the above types of materials in Spanish (Cuban)."

THE FOOD CHANNEL, America's Source For Food Trends, Noble & Associates, 29th Fl., 515 N. State Chicago IL 60610. (312)644-4600. Editor: John Scroggins. 30% freelance written. Biweekly newsletter cover-

---

For information on setting your freelance fees, see How Much Should I Charge?

ing food trends. "*The Food Channel* is published by Noble & Associates, a food-focused advertising, promotional marketing and new product development company. *The Food Channel* provides insight into emerging trends in the food and beverage industries and the implications for manufacturers, suppliers and consumers." Estab. 1988. Circ. 3,000. Pays on publication. Publishes ms an average of 2 months after acceptance. Byline given. Editorial lead time 2 months. Submit seasonal material 1 month in advance. Accepts simultaneous submissions. Query for electronic submissions. Reports in 1 month. Sample copy and writer's guidelines free on request.

Nonfiction: General interest, interview/profile, new product. Length: 500-1,100 words. Pays 50¢/word.
Columns/Departments: Buys 15 mss/year. Query.
Tips: "We are most open to 500-1,100-word articles covering international trends and underground trends. Using freelancers for very focused articles on NAFTA, legislation, natural disasters, specialty foods, demographics as related to food."

‡**FOOD DISTRIBUTION MAGAZINE, The Business Magazine for the Specialty Food Trade,** National Food Distribution Network, 406 Water St., Warren RI 02885. Editor: Mark Stephen Binder. 30% freelance written. Monthly magazine covering gourmet food to the trade. "We are looking for pieces of interest to supermarket buyers, food distributors, and gourmet and specialty food stores. Quality writing, interesting and informative articles." Estab. 1958. Circ. 35,000. Pays on publication. Publishes ms an average of 2 months after acceptance. Byline given. Buys all rights. Editorial lead time 2-4 months. Submit seasonal material 4 months in advance. Accepts previously published submissions. Query for electronic submissions. Reports in 1-2 months. Sample copy for $5.

Nonfiction: Humor, new product, photo feature. Buys 3-10 mss/year. Query with published clips. Length: 1,000-3,000 words. Pay negotiable. Sometimes pays expenses of writers on assignment.
Photos: Send photos with submission. Reviews transparencies, prints. Negotiates payment individually. Buys one-time rights or all rights.
Tips: Query first.

FOODSERVICE DIRECTOR, Bill Communications, 355 Park Ave. S., New York NY 10010. (212)592-6533. Fax: (212)592-6539. Editor: Walter J. Schruntek. Managing Editor: Karen Weisberg. 20% freelance written. Monthly tabloid on non-commercial foodservice operations for operators of kitchens and dining halls in schools, colleges, hospitals/health care, office and plant cafeterias, military, airline/transportation, correctional institutions. Estab. 1988. Circ. 45,000. Pays on publication. Byline given sometimes. Offers 25% kill fee. Buys all rights. Submit seasonal material 2-3 months in advance. Accepts simultaneous submissions. Free sample copy.

Nonfiction: How-to, interview/profile. Buys 60-70 mss/year. Query with published clips. Length: 700-900 words. Pays $250-500. Sometimes pays the expenses of writers on assignment.
Photos: Send photos with submission. Reviews transparencies. Offers no additional payment for photos accepted with ms. Identification of subjects required. Buys all rights.
Columns/Departments: Equipment (case studies of kitchen/serving equipment in use), 700-900 words; Food (specific category studies per publication calendar), 750-900 words. Buys 20-30 mss/year. Query. Pays $150-250.

THE GOURMET RETAILER, #300, 3301 Ponce De Leon Blvd., Coral Gables FL 33134-7273. (305)446-3388. Fax: (305)446-2868. Executive Editor: Nancy Quinn Moore. 30% freelance written. Monthly magazine covering specialty foods and housewares. "Our readers are owners and managers of specialty food and upscale housewares retail units. Writers must know the trade exceptionally well and be research-oriented." Estab. 1979. Circ. 18,000. Pays on publication. Publishes ms an average of 3 months after acceptance. Byline sometimes given. No kill fee. Buys all rights. Submit seasonal material 6 months in advance. Query for electronic submissions. Reports in 2 months on queries. Free sample copy and writer's guidelines.

Nonfiction: Interview/profile (retail stores, manufacturers). "Do not send unsolicited manuscripts; queries only." Buys 12 mss/year. Query with published clips. Length: 1,500-2,200 words.
Photos: State availability of photos with submission. Reviews negatives, 5×7 transparencies, 8×10 prints. Offers $15-25/photo. Identification of subjects required. Buys one-time rights.
Tips: "I enjoy hearing from established business writers. I am looking for upmarket food/housewares news; and for profiles of specialty retailers. We are extremely stringent on editorial quality."

HEALTH FOODS BUSINESS, Howmark Publishing Corp., 567 Morris Ave., Elizabeth NJ 07208-9808. (908)353-7373. Fax: (908)353-8221. Editor: Gina Geslewitz. 40% freelance written. Eager to work with new/unpublished writers if competent and reliable. Monthly magazine for owners and managers of health food stores. Circ. 11,000. Pays on publication. Publishes ms an average of 4 months after acceptance. Buys first North American serial rights; "also exclusive rights in our trade field." Phone queries OK. "Query us about a good health food store in your area. We use many store profile stories." Accepts simultaneous submissions if exclusive to their field. Reports in 2 months. Sample copy for $3 and SAE with 8 first class stamps. Writer's guidelines for #10 SASE.

Nonfiction: Pays $100 and up for store profiles.

Photos: "Most articles must have photos included." Reviews negatives and contact sheets. Captions required. No additional payment.

Tips: "A writer may find that submitting a letter with a sample article he/she believes to be closely related to articles read in our publication is the most expedient way to determine the appropriateness of his/her skills and expertise."

‡**MEAT BUSINESS MAGAZINE,** 9701 Gravois Ave., St. Louis MO 63123. (314)638-4050. Fax: (314)638-3880. Editor: Mary Wolford. 10% freelance written. Prefers to work with published/established writers; works with a small number of new/unpublished writers each year. For meat processors, retailers, locker plant operators, freezer provisioners, portion control packers, meat dealers and food service (food plan) operators. Monthly. Pays on publication. Publishes ms an average of 6 months after acceptance. Reports in 2 weeks.

Nonfiction and Fillers: Buys feature-length articles and shorter subjects pertinent to the field. Length: 1,000-1,500 words for features. Pays 10¢/word. Sometimes pays the expenses of writers on assignment.

Photos: Pays $5 for photos.

MINNESOTA GROCER, Serving the Upper Midwest Retail Food Industry, Minnesota Grocers Council, Inc., 533 St. Clair Ave., St. Paul MN 55102-2859. (612)228-0973. Fax: (612)228-1949. Director of Communications: Randy Schubring. 25% freelance written. Bimonthly magazine on the retail grocery industry in Minnesota. Estab. 1951. Circ. 4,200. Pays on publication. Publishes ms an average of 1-2 months after acceptance. Byline given. Buys all rights. Submit seasonal material 3 months in advance. Accepts previously published submissions. Send tearsheet of article or typed ms with rights for sale noted. Does not pay for reprints. Reports in 2 months. Sample copy and writer's guidelines for 9 × 12 SAE with 4 first-class stamps.

Nonfiction: How-to better market, display and sell food and other items in a grocery store. How to find new markets. Interview/profile and new products. Special issue: "We do an economic forecast in January/February issue." Buys 6 mss/year. Query with published clips. Length: 300-1,500 words. Pays $100-500 for assigned articles. Sometimes pays expenses of writers on assignment.

Photos: State availability of photos with submission. Reviews contact sheets and 5 × 7 prints. Captions, model releases and identification of subjects required. Buys all rights.

Columns/Departments: Query with published clips.

Tips: "The best way to be considered for a freelance assignment is first and foremost to have a crisp, journalistic writing style on clips. Second it is very helpful to have a knowledge of the issues and trends in the grocery industry. Third, because we are a regional trade publication, it is crucial that articles be localized to Minnesota or the Upper Midwest."

PRODUCE NEWS, 2185 Lemoine Ave., Fort Lee NJ 07024-6003. Fax: (201)592-0809. Editor: Gordon Hochberg. 10-15% freelance written. Works with a small number of new/unpublished writers each year. Weekly magazine for commercial growers and shippers, receivers and distributors of fresh fruits and vegetables, including chain store produce buyers and merchandisers. Estab. 1897. Circ. 10,000. Pays on publication. Publishes ms an average of 2 weeks after acceptance. Deadline is Monday afternoon before Thursday press day. Reports in 1 month. Sample copy and writer's guidelines for 10 × 13 SAE with 4 first-class stamps.

Nonfiction: News stories (about the produce industry). Buys profiles, spot news, coverage of successful business operations and articles on merchandising techniques. Query. Pays minimum of $1/column inch for original material. Sometimes pays the expenses of writers on assignment.

Photos: Black and white glossies. Pays $8-10 for each one used.

Tips: "Stories should be trade-oriented, not consumer-oriented. As our circulation grows in the next year, we are interested in stories and news articles from all fresh fruit-growing areas of the country."

• This publication looks for stringers in specific areas of the country to cover the produce business.

QUICK FROZEN FOODS INTERNATIONAL, E.W. Williams Publishing Co., Suite 305, 2125 Center Ave., Fort Lee NJ 07024-5898. (201)592-7007. Fax: (201)592-7171. Editor: John M. Saulnier. 20% freelance written. Works with a small number of new writers each year. Quarterly magazine covering frozen foods around the world — "every phase of frozen food manufacture, retailing, food service, brokerage, transport, warehousing, merchandising. Especially interested in stories from Europe, Asia and emerging nations." Circ. 13,700. Pays on publication. Publishes ms an average of 3 months after acceptance. Byline given. Offers kill fee; "if satisfactory, we will pay promised amount. If bungled, half." Buys all rights, but will relinquish any rights requested. Submit seasonal material 6 months in advance. Sample copy for $10.

Nonfiction: Book excerpts, general interest, interview/profile, new product (from overseas), personal experience, photo feature, technical, travel. No articles peripheral to frozen food industry such as taxes, insurance, government regulation, safety, etc. Buys 20-30 mss/year. Query or send complete ms. Length: 500-4,000 words. Pays 5¢/word or by arrangement. "We will reimburse postage on articles ordered from overseas."

Photos: "We prefer photos with all articles." State availability of photos or send photos with accompanying ms. Pays $10 for 5 × 7 color or b&w prints (contact sheet if many shots). Captions and identification of subject required. Buys all rights. Release on request.

Columns/Departments: News or analysis of frozen foods abroad. Buys 20 columns/year. Query. Length: 500-1,500 words. Pays by arrangement.

Fillers: Newsbreaks. Length: 100-500 words. Pays $5-20.

Tips: "We are primarily interested in feature materials (1,000-3,000 words with pictures). We are now devoting more space to frozen food company developments in Pacific Rim and East European countries. Stories on frozen food merchandising and retailing in foreign supermarket chains in Europe, Japan and Australia/New Zealand are welcome. National frozen food production profiles are also in demand worldwide. A frequent mistake is submitting general interest material instead of specific industry-related stories."

THE WISCONSIN GROCER, Wisconsin Grocers Association, Suite 185, 2601 Crossroads Dr., Madison WI 53704. (608)244-7150. Eager to work with new/unpublished writers. Bimonthly magazine covering grocery industry of Wisconsin. Estab. 1900. Circ. 1,500. Pays on publication. Publishes ms an average of 3 months after acceptance. Byline given. Not copyrighted. Buys first North American serial, second serial (reprint) or simultaneous rights. Submit seasonal material 5 months in advance. Simultaneous submissions OK. Reprints OK; send photocopy of article with information about when and where the article previously appeared. Reports in 2 weeks on queries; 2 months on mss. Sample copy for 9 × 12 SAE with 3 first-class stamps.

Nonfiction: How-to (money management, employee training/relations, store design, promotional ideas); interview/profile (of WGA members and Wisconsin politicians only); opinion; technical (store design or equipment). No articles about grocers or companies not affiliated with the WGA. Buys 6 mss/year. Query. Length: 500-2,000 words. Pays $15 minimum. Pays in copies if the writer works for a manufacturer or distributor of goods or services relevant to the grocery industry, or if a political viewpoint is expressed.

Photos: Send photos with submission. Reviews 5 × 7 prints. Offers no additional payment for photos accepted with ms. Identification of subjects required. Buys one-time rights.

Columns/Departments: Security (anti-shoplifting, vendor thefts, employee theft, burglary); Employee Relations (screening, training, management); Customer Relations (better service, corporate-community relations, buying trends); Money Management (DPP programs, bookkeeping, grocery—specific computer applications); Merchandising (promotional or advertising ideas); all 1,000 words. Buys 6 mss/year. Query. Length: 500-1,500 words.

Fillers: Facts and newsbreaks. Buys 6/year. Length: 50-250 words.

Tips: "How-tos are especially strong with our readers. They want to know how to increase sales and cut costs. Cover new management techniques, promotional ideas, customer services and industry trends."

Hardware

Journals for general and specialized hardware wholesalers and retailers are listed in this section. Journals specializing in hardware for a certain trade, such as plumbing or automotive supplies, are classified with other publications for that trade.

HARDWARE AGE, Chilton Co., 1 Chilton Way, Radnor PA 19089. (215)964-4275. Editor-in-Chief: Terry Gallagher. Managing Editor: Rick Carter. 2% freelance written. Monthly magazine emphasizing retailing, distribution and merchandising of hardware and building materials. Circ. 71,000. Buys first North American serial rights. No guarantee of byline. Accepts simultaneous and previously published submissions, if exclusive in the field. Reports in 2 months. Sample copy for $1; mention *Writer's Market* in request.

Nonfiction: Rick Carter, managing editor. How-to more profitably run a hardware store or a department within a store. "We particularly want stories on local hardware stores and home improvement centers, with photos. Stories should concentrate on one particular aspect of how the retailer in question has been successful." Also wants technical pieces (will consider stories on retail accounting, inventory management and business management by qualified writers). Buys 1-5 unsolicited mss/year. Submit complete ms. Length: 1,500-3,000 words. Pays $75-200.

Photos: "We like store features with b&w photos. Usually use b&w for small freelance features." Send photos with ms. Pays $25 for 4 × 5 glossy b&w prints. Captions preferred. Buys one-time rights.

Columns/Departments: Retailers' Business Tips; Wholesalers' Business Tips; and Moneysaving Tips. Query or submit complete ms. Length: 1,000-1,250 words. Pays $100-150. Open to suggestions for new columns/departments.

‡MEMBERS, The Magazine of and for True Value Hardware and V&S Variety Store Members, Cotter & Company, 2740 N. Clybourn, Chicago IL 60610. Contact: Teresa Piemonte, associate editor. 10% freelance written. Monthly magazine covering hardware retailing. "We give our readers examples of successful strategies in retailing. You must talk to a selection of True Value or V&W store owners to give their side of it. We won't accept generic articles." Estab. 1991. Circ. 18,000. Pays on publication. Publishes ms an average of 6 months after acceptance. Byline given. Offers 10% kill fee. Buys first North American serial rights. Editorial lead time 3 months. Submit seasonal material 6 months in advance. Query for electronic submissions. Reports in 1 month on queries. Sample copy and writer's guidelines free on request.

Nonfiction: How-to, interview/profile. Special issue: "Twice a year, we run a preview issue of our twice yearly market. Query ideas 6-9 months in advance." Buys 5 mss/year. Query with published clips. Length: 750-2,000 words. Pays $150. Sometimes pays expenses of writers on assignment.

Photos: Send photos with submission. Reviews transparencies, 5×7 prints. Offers $20-25/photo; $150 for cover. Model releases, identification of subjects required. Buys all rights.

Columns/Departments: Bright Ideas (retail/promotional ideas), 250 words; News & Reviews (news on True Value and V&S stores), 250 words; Green Corner (environmental ideas for hardware), 300 words. Query with published clips. Pays $75-175.

Home Furnishings and Household Goods

Readers rely on these publications to learn more about new products and trends in the home furnishings and appliance trade. Magazines for consumers interested in home furnishings are listed in the Consumer Home and Garden section.

APPLIANCE SERVICE NEWS, 110 W. Saint Charles Rd., P.O. Box 789, Lombard IL 60148-0789. Editor: William Wingstedt. Monthly "newspaper style" publication for professional service people whose main interest is repairing major and/or portable household appliances. Their jobs consist of service shop owner, service manager or service technician. Estab. 1950. Circ. 51,000. Buys all rights. Byline given. Pays on publication. Will consider simultaneous submissions. Reports in about 1 month. Sample copy for $2.

Nonfiction: James Hodl, associate editor. "Our main interest is in technical articles about appliances and their repair. Material should be written in a straightforward, easy-to-understand style. It should be crisp and interesting, with high informational content. Our main interest is in the major and portable appliance repair field. We are not interested in retail sales." Query. Pays $200-300/feature.

Photos: Pays $20 for b&w photos used with ms. Captions required.

CHINA GLASS & TABLEWARE, Doctorow Communications, Inc., P.O. Box 2147, Clifton NJ 07015. (201)779-1600. Fax: (201)779-3242. Editor-in-Chief: Amy Stavis. 60% freelance written. Works with a small number of new/unpublished writers each year. Monthly magazine for buyers, merchandise managers and specialty store owners who deal in tableware, dinnerware, glassware, flatware and other tabletop accessories. Estab. 1892. Pays on publication. Publishes ms an average of 3-4 months after acceptance. Buys one-time rights. Byline given. Phone queries OK. Submit seasonal material 3 months in advance. Reports in 3 months. Sample copy and writer's guidelines for 9×12 SAE; mention *Writer's Market* in request.

Nonfiction: General interest (on store successes, reasons for a store's business track record); interview (personalities of store owners, how they cope with industry problems, why they are in tableware); technical (on the business aspects of retailing china, glassware and flatware). "Bridal registry material always welcomed." No articles on how-to or gift shops. Buys 2-3 mss/issue. Query. Length: 1,500-3,000 words. Pays $60/page. Sometimes pays the expenses of writers on assignment.

Photos: State availability of photos with query. No additional payment for b&w or color contact sheets. Captions required. Buys first serial rights.

Tips: "Show imagination in the query; have a good angle on a story that makes it unique from the competition's coverage and requires less work on the editor's part for rewriting a snappy beginning."

HAPPI, (Household and Personal Products Industry), 17 S. Franklin Turnpike, P.O. Box 555, Ramsey NJ 07446-0555. Fax: (201)825-0553. Editor: Tom Branna. 5% freelance written. Magazine for "manufacturers of soaps, detergents, cosmetics and toiletries, waxes and polishes, insecticides, and aerosols." Estab. 1964. Circ. 18,000. Not copyrighted. Pays on publication. Publishes ms an average of 2 months after acceptance. Submit seasonal material 2 months in advance. Reports in 1 month.

Nonfiction: "Technical and semi-technical articles on manufacturing, distribution, marketing, new products, plant stories, etc., of the industries served. Some knowledge of the field is essential in writing for us." Buys informational interview, photo feature, spot news, coverage of successful business operations, new product articles, coverage of merchandising techniques and technical articles. No articles slanted toward consumers. Query with published clips. Buys 3 to 4 mss a year. Length: 500-2,000 words. Pays $25-300. Sometimes pays expenses of writers on assignment.

Photos: Black and white 5×7 or 8×10 glossies purchased with mss. Pays $10.

Tips: "The most frequent mistakes made by writers are unfamiliarity with our audience and our industry; slanting articles toward consumers rather than to industry members."

‡HOME FURNISHINGS EXECUTIVE, Pace Communications, 1301 Carolina St., Greensboro NC 27401. Editor: Patricia Bowling. 50-60% freelance written. Monthly magazine covering the home furnishings industry. "We try to provide a forum for constructive dialogue between the retailers and manufacturers in the home furnishings industry." (*Furniture Retailer* magazine became *Home Furnishings Executive* in 1994.) Estab. 1989. Circ. 14,000. **Pays on acceptance.** Byline given. Buys first North American serial rights. Editorial lead time 2 months. Query for electronic submissions. Sample copy for $5. Writer's guidelines for #10 SASE.

Nonfiction: How-to, interview/profile, retail marketing and advertising, technology, retail operations. Buys 25-30 mss/year. Query with published clips. Length: 750-2,500 words. Rates begin at $250.

Photos: Send photos with submission. Negotiates payment individually. Captions required. Buys one-time rights.

Tips: "We are looking for articles that are specific to our industry. Familiarity with home furnishings industry is helpful. Understanding of retail operations is essential."

‡**WINDOW FASHIONS, Design and Education Magazine,** G&W McNamara Publishing, Inc., Suite 400, 4225 White Bear Pkwy., St. Paul MN 55110. (612)293-1544. Editor: Linnea C. Addison. 50% freelance written. Monthly magazine covering custom window fashions – interior design. "Dedicated to the advancement of the window fashions industry, *Window Fashions* magazine provides comprehensive information on design and business principles, window fashion aesthetics and product applications. The magazine serves the window treatment industry, including designers, retailers, dealers, specialty stores, workrooms, manufacturers, fabricators and others associated with the field of interior design." Estab. 1981. Circ. 20,000. Pays on publication. Publishes ms an average of 3 months after acceptance. Byline given. Offers 25% kill fee. Buys all rights. Editorial lead time 2-3 months. Submit seasonal material at least 3 months in advance. Query for electronic submissions. Reports in 2 months on queries if SASE is included. Sample copy for $5.

Nonfiction: How-to (window fashion installation), interview/profile (of designers), new product, photo feature, technical, and other specific topics within the field. "No broad topics not specific to the window fashions industry." Buys 24 mss/year. Query with published clips. Length: 800-1,500 words. Pays $150 minimum for assigned articles. Sometimes pays expenses of writers on assignment.

Photos: State availability of photos with submission. Reviews transparencies (4×6 or 8×10) and prints (at least 4×6). Offers no additional payment for photos accepted with ms. Captions required. Buys all rights and release for publication, anthology, promotional use, etc.

Columns/Departments: Buys 24-36 mss/year. Query with published clips. Pays $150-250.

Tips: "The most helpful experience is if a writer has knowledge of interior design or, specifically, window treatments. We already have a pool of generalists, although we welcome clips from writers who would like to be considered for assignments. Our style is professional business writing – no flowery prose. Articles tend to be to the point as our readers are busy professionals who read for information, not for leisure. Most of all we need creative ideas and approaches to topics in the field of window treatments and interior design. A writer needs to be knowledgeable in the field because our readers would know if information was inaccurate. We are looking mostly for features on specific topics or on installation or design."

Hospitals, Nursing and Nursing Homes

In this section are journals for medical and nonmedical nursing home personnel, clinical and hospital staffs and medical laboratory technicians and managers. Journals publishing technical material on medical research and information for physicians in private practice are listed in the Medical category.

AMERICAN JOURNAL OF NURSING, 555 W. 57th St., New York NY 10019-2961. (212)582-8820. Editorial Director: Martin Di Carlanfonio. Eager to work with new/unpublished nurse-authors. Monthly magazine covering nursing and health care. Estab. 1900. Circ. 235,000. Pays on publication. Publishes ms an average of 3-4 months after acceptance. Byline given. Simultaneous queries OK. Reports in 2 weeks on queries, 4-6 weeks on mss. Sample copy for $4. Free writer's guidelines.

Nonfiction: Practical, hands-on clinical articles of interest to hospital staff nurses; professional issues; personal experience. No material other than nursing care and nursing issues. Nurse-authors only accepted for publication.

Photos: Karliese Greiner, associate art director. Reviews b&w and color transparencies and prints. Model release and identification of subjects required. Buys variable rights.

Tips: "Everything we publish is written by nurses and edited inhouse."

HOSPITAL RISK MANAGEMENT, American Health Consultants, P.O. Box 740059, Atlanta GA 30374. (404)262-7436. Fax: (404)262-7837. Managing Editor: Cheli Brown. 10% freelance written. Monthly newsletter on health care risk management. Estab. 1977. Circ. 2,500. Pays on publication. Publishes ms an average of 2 months after acceptance. Byline given. Buys all rights. Reports in 3 months. Free sample copy.

Nonfiction: How-to (pertaining to hospitals' legal liability management). We need informative articles written by experts in the field that aren't boring, on topics concerning hospital safety, insurance for hospitals and reducing legal risk. Nothing analytical. Buys 10-12 mss/year. Query. Length: 1,500 words. Pays $50-150 or free subscription.

NURSING94, Springhouse Corporation, 1111 Bethlehem Pike, P.O. Box 908, Springhouse PA 19477-0908. (215)646-8700. Fax: (215)653-0826. Contact: Pat Wolf, Editorial Assistant. Editor: Maryanne Wagner. Managing Editor: Jane Benner. 100% freelance written by nurses. Monthly magazine on the nursing field. "Our articles are written by nurses for nurses; we look for practical advice for the working nurse that reflects the author's experience." Estab. 1971. Circ. 500,000. Pays on publication. Publishes ms an average of 12-18 months after acceptance. Byline given. Offers 50% kill fee. Buys all rights. Submit seasonal material 6-8 months in advance. Publishes reprints of previously published materials. "Any form acceptable, but focus must be nursing." Query for electronic submissions. Reports in 2 weeks on queries; 3 months on mss. Sample copy for $3 with 9 × 12 SAE. Call Pat Wolf for free writers' guidelines.

Nonfiction: Book excerpts, exposé, how-to (specifically as applies to nursing field), inspirational, new product, opinion, personal experience, photo feature. No articles from patients' point of view, humor articles, poetry, etc. Buys 100 mss/year. Query. Length: 100 words minimum. Pays $50-400.

Photos: State availability of photos with submission. Offers no additional payment for photos accepted with ms. Model releases required. Buys all rights.

Hotels, Motels, Clubs, Resorts and Restaurants

These publications offer trade tips and advice to hotel, club, resort and restaurant managers, owners and operators. Journals for manufacturers and distributors of bar and beverage supplies are listed in the Beverages and Bottling section.

BARTENDER MAGAZINE, Foley Publishing, P.O. Box 158, Liberty Corner NJ 07938. (908)766-6006. Fax: (908)766-6607. Publisher: Raymond P. Foley. Editor: Jaclyn M. Wilson. Quarterly magazine emphasizing liquor and bartending for bartenders, tavern owners and owners of restaurants with full-service liquor licenses. 100% freelance written. Prefers to work with published/established writers; eager to work with new/ unpublished writers. Circ. 140,000. Pays on publication. Publishes ms an average of 3 months after acceptance. Buys first serial, first North American serial, one-time, second serial (reprint), all and simultaneous US rights. Byline given. Submit seasonal material 3 months in advance. Accepts simultaneous and previously published submissions. Send tearsheet of article. For reprints, pays 50% of the amount paid for an original article. Reports in 2 months. Sample copies for 9 × 12 SAE with 9 first-class stamps.

Nonfiction: General interest, historical, how-to, humor, interview (with famous bartenders or ex-bartenders), new products, nostalgia, personal experience, unique bars, opinion, new techniques, new drinking trends, photo feature, profile, travel, bar sports or bar magic tricks. Send complete ms. Length: 100-1,000 words.

Photos: Send photos with ms. Pays $7.50-50 for 8 × 10 b&w glossy prints; $10-75 for 8 × 10 color glossy prints. Caption preferred and model release required.

Columns/Departments: Bar of the Month; Bartender of the Month; Drink of the Month; New Drink Ideas; Bar Sports; Quiz; Bar Art; Wine Cellar; Tips from the Top (from prominent figures in the liquor industry); One For The Road (travel); Collectors (bar or liquor-related items); Photo Essays. Query. Length: 200-1,000 words. Pays $50-200.

Fillers: Clippings, jokes, gags, anecdotes, short humor, newsbreaks, anything relating to bartending and the liquor industry. Length: 25-100 words. Pays $5-25.

Tips: "To break in, absolutely make sure that your work will be of interest to all bartenders across the country. Your style of writing should reflect the audience you are addressing. The most frequent mistake made by writers in completing an article for us is using the wrong subject."

CASINO JOURNAL, Casino Journal Publishing Group, 2524 Arctic Ave., Atlantic City NJ 08401. (609)344-9000. Fax: (609)345-3469. Editor: Roger Gros. Estab. 1984. 20% freelance written. Monthly magazine that covers specific technical aspects of the casino industry. Estab. 1984. Pays on publication. Publishes ms an average of 2 months after acceptance. Byline given. Buys all rights. Submit seasonal material 4 months in advance. Query for electronic submissions. Reports in 6 months. Sample copy for $2 and SAE with 6 first-class stamps.

Nonfiction: Interview/profile, new product, photo feature, technical. "No first-person gambling stories." Buys 25-30 mss/year. Query with or without published clips or send complete ms. Length: 500-2,500 words. Pays $75-150 for assigned articles. "If author has product to sell, we run ad."

Photos: State availability of photos with submission. Reviews contact sheets, transparencies and prints. Offers $10-25/photo. Captions, model releases and identification of subjects required. Buys one-time rights.

FLORIDA HOTEL & MOTEL JOURNAL, The Official Publication of the Florida Hotel & Motel Association, Accommodations, Inc., P.O. Box 1529, Tallahassee FL 32302-1529. (904)224-2888. Editorial Associate: Janet Litherland. Editor: Mrs. Jayleen Woods. 10% freelance written. Prefers to work with published/established writers. Monthly magazine for managers in the lodging industry (every licensed hotel, motel and resort in Florida). Estab. 1978. Circ. 7,000. Pays on publication. Publishes ms an average of 2 months after acceptance. Byline given. Offers $50 kill fee. Buys all rights and makes work-for-hire assignments. Submit seasonal material 2 months in advance. Accepts previously published material. Send tearsheet of article and information about when and where the article previously appeared. For reprints, pays flat fee of $55. Reports in 4-6 weeks. Sample copy and writer's guidelines for 9 × 12 SAE with 7 first-class stamps.

Nonfiction: General interest (business, finance, taxes); historical/nostalgic (old Florida hotel reminiscences); how-to (improve management, housekeeping procedures, guest services, security and coping with common hotel problems); humor (hotel-related anecdotes); inspirational (succeeding where others have failed); interview/profile (of unusual hotel personalities); new product (industry-related and non brand preferential); photo feature (queries only); technical (emerging patterns of hotel accounting, telephone systems, etc.); travel (transportation and tourism trends only—no scenics or site visits); property renovations and maintenance techniques. "We would like to run more humorous anecdotes on hotel happenings than we're presently receiving." Buys 10-12 mss/year. Query with proposed topic and clips of published work. Length: 750-2,500 words. Pays $75-250 "depending on type of article and amount of research." Sometimes pays the expenses of writers on assignment.
Photos: Send photos with ms. Pays $25-100 for 4×5 color transparencies; $10-15 for 5×7 b&w prints. Captions, model release and identification of subjects required.
Tips: "We prefer feature stories on properties or personalities holding current membership in the Florida Hotel and Motel Association. Membership and/or leadership brochures are available (SASE) on request. We're open to articles showing how hotel management copes with energy systems, repairs, renovations, new guest needs and expectations. The writer may have a better chance of breaking in at our publication with short articles and fillers because the better a writer is at the art of condensation, the better his/her feature articles are likely to be."

FLORIDA RESTAURATEUR, Florida Restaurant Association, 2441 Hollywood Blvd., Hollywood FL 33020-6623. (305)921-6300. Fax: (305)925-6381. Editor: Hugh P. (Mickey) McLinden. 15% freelance written. Monthly magazine for food service and restaurant owners and managers "dealing with trends, legislation, training, sanitation, new products, spot news." Estab. 1946. Circ. 27,600. Pays on publication. Publishes ms an average of 1 month after acceptance. Byline given. Buys one-time rights. Submit seasonal material 3 months in advance. Accepts simultaneous and previously published submissions. Send tearsheet or photocopy of article or typed ms with rights for sale noted and information about when and where the article previously appeared. For reprints, pays 35% of the amount paid for an original article. Reports in 1 month on queries; 2 months on mss.
Nonfiction: How-to, general interest, interview/profile, new product, personal experience, technical. Query. Length: 500-2,000 words. Pays $200-300 for assigned articles; $150-250 for unsolicited articles.
Photos: State availability of photos with submission. Reviews transparencies and 5×7 prints. Offers $50-250/photo. Model releases and identification of subjects required. Buys one-time rights.

FOOD & SERVICE, Texas Restaurant Association, P.O. Box 1429, Austin TX 78767-1429. (512)472-3666 (in Texas, 1-800-395-2872). Fax: (512)472-2777. Editor: Julie Stephen Sherrier. 50% freelance written. Magazine published 11 times/year providing business solutions to Texas restaurant owners and operators. Estab. 1941. Circ. 5,700. **Pays on acceptance.** Written queries required. Reports in 1 month. Byline given. Not copyrighted. Buys first rights. No previously published submissions. Query for electronic submissions. Sample copy and editorial calendar for 11×14 SAE with 6 first-class stamps. Free writer's guidelines.
Nonfiction: Features must provide business solutions to problems in the restaurant and food service industries. Topics vary but always have business slant; usually particular to Texas. No restaurant critiques, human interest stories or seasonal copy. Quote members of the Texas Restaurant Association; substantiate with facts and examples. Query. Length: 2,000-2,500 words, features; shorter articles sometimes used; product releases, 300-word maximum. Payment rates vary.
Photos: State availability of photos, but photos usually assigned.

INNKEEPING WORLD, P.O. Box 84108, Seattle WA 98124. Fax: (206)362-7847. Editor/Publisher: Charles Nolte. 75% freelance written. Eager to work with new/unpublished writers. Magazine published 10 times/year emphasizing the hotel industry worldwide. Estab. 1979. Circ. 2,000. **Pays on acceptance.** Publishes ms an average of 2 months after acceptance. Buys all rights. No byline. Submit seasonal material 1 month in advance. Reports in 1 month. Sample copy and writer's guidelines for 9×12 SAE with 3 first-class stamps.
Nonfiction: Managing—interviews with successful hotel managers of large and/or famous hotels/resorts (600-1,200 words); Marketing—interviews with hotel marketing executives on successful promotions/case histories (300-1,000 words); Sales Promotion—innovative programs for increasing business (100-600 words); Food Service—outstanding hotel restaurants, menus and merchandising concepts (300-1,000 words); and Guest Relations—guest service programs, management philosophies relative to guests (200-800 words). Pays $100 minimum or 20¢/word (whichever is greater) for main topics. Other topics—advertising, cutting expenses, guest comfort, hospitality, ideas, reports and trends, special guestrooms, staff relations. Length: 50-500 words. Pays 20¢/word. "If a writer asks a hotel for a complimentary room, the article will not be accepted, nor will *Innkeeping World* accept future articles from the writer."
Tips: "We need more in-depth reporting on successful sales promotions—results-oriented information."

LODGING HOSPITALITY MAGAZINE, Penton Publishing, 1100 Superior Ave., Cleveland OH 44114-2543. (216)696-7000. Fax: (216)696-7658. Editor: Edward Watkins. 5% freelance written. Prefers to work with published/established writers. Monthly magazine covering the lodging industry. "Our purpose is to inform lodging management of trends and events which will affect their properties and the way they do business. Audience: owners and managers of hotels, motels, resorts." Estab. 1949. Circ. 50,000. **Pays on acceptance.** Publishes ms an average of 2 months after acceptance. Byline given. Buys first rights. Reports in 2 months. **Nonfiction:** General interest, how-to, interview/profile, travel. Special issues: renovation (April); financing (May); technology (June); franchising (July); renovation (September); human resources (October). "We do *not* want personal reviews of hotels visited by writer, or travel pieces. All articles are geared to hotel executives to help them in their business." Buys 5 mss/year. Query. Length: 700-2,000 words. Pays $150-600. Sometimes pays the expenses of writers on assignment.

Photos: State availability of photos with submission. Reviews contact sheets and transparencies. Offers no additional payment for photos accepted with ms. Captions and identification of subjects required. Buys one-time rights.

Columns/Departments: *Strategies*, all one-page reports of 700 words. Buys 10 mss/year. Query. Pays $150-250.

‡PIZZA TODAY, The Professional Guide To Pizza Profits, ProTech Publishing and Communications, Inc., P.O. Box 1347, New Albany IN 47151. (812)949-0909. Fax: (812)941-9711. Editor: James E. Reed. 30% freelance written. Prefers to work with published/established writers. Monthly magazine for the pizza industry, covering trends, features of successful pizza operators, business and management advice, etc. Estab. 1983. Circ. 55,000. Pays on publication. Publishes ms an average of 2 months after acceptance. Byline given. Offers 10-30% kill fee. Buys all and negotiable rights. Submit seasonal/holiday material 3 months in advance. Accepts simultaneous and previously published submissions. Query for electronic submissions. "All articles must be supplied on a 3½-inch disk, as accompanied by a hard copy. Most major wordprocessor formats accepted; else submit in ASCII format." Reports in 2 months on queries; 3 weeks on mss. Sample copy and writer's guidelines for 10×13 SAE with 6 first-class stamps. No phone calls, please.

Nonfiction: Interview/profile, new product, entrepreneurial slants, time management, pizza delivery, employee training. No fillers, fiction, humor or poetry. Buys 40-60 mss/year. Query with published clips. Length: 750-2,500 words. Pays $50-125/page. Sometimes pays the expenses of writers on assignment.

Photos: Send photos with submission. Reviews contact sheets, negatives, 4×5 transparencies, color slides and 5×7 prints. Offers $5-25/photo. Captions required.

Tips: "We would like to receive nutritional information for low-cal, low-salt, low-fat, etc. pizza. Writers must have strong business and foodservice background."

RESTAURANT HOSPITALITY, Penton Publishing, 1100 Superior Ave., Cleveland OH 44114. (216)696-7000. Fax: (216)696-0836. Editor-in-Chief: Michael DeLuca. Managing Editor: Michael Sanson. 10% freelance written. Works exclusively with published/established writers. Monthly magazine covering the foodservice industry for owners and operators of independent restaurants, hotel foodservices, executives of national and regional restaurant chains. Estab. 1919. Circ. 100,000. Average issue includes 5-10 features. **Pays on acceptance.** Publishes ms an average of 3 months after acceptance. Byline given. Buys first North American serial rights. Reports in 2 months. Sample copy for 9×12 SAE with 10 first-class stamps.

• *Restaurant Hospitality* is accepting fewer stories.

Nonfiction: General interest (articles that advise operators how to run their operations profitably and efficiently), interview (with operators), profile. Stories on psychology, consumer behavior, managerial problems and solutions, design elements. No restaurant reviews. Buys 20-30 mss/year. Query with clips of previously published work and a short bio. Length: 500-1,500 words. Pays $125/published page. Pays the expenses of writers on assignment.

Photos: Send color photos with ms. Captions required.

Tips: "We would like to receive queries for articles on food and management trends. More how-to articles wanted. We need new angles on old stories, and we like to see pieces on emerging trends and technologies in the restaurant industry. Our readers don't want to read how to open a restaurant or why John Smith is so successful."

VACATION INDUSTRY REVIEW, Worldex Corp., P.O. Box 431920, South Miami FL 33243-1920. (305)666-1861, ext. 7022. Fax: (305)667-4495. Editor: George Leposky. 20% freelance written. Prefers to work with published/established writers. Quarterly magazine covering leisure lodgings (timeshare resorts, fractionals, and other types of vacation ownership properties). Estab. 1982. Circ. 15,000. Pays on publication. Publishes ms an average of 3-6 months after acceptance. Byline given. Buys all rights and makes work-for-hire assignments. Submit seasonal material 6 months in advance. Query for electronic submissions. Reports in 1 month. Writer's guidelines for #10 SASE.

Nonfiction: How-to, interview/profile, new product, opinion, personal experience, technical, travel. No consumer travel or non-vacation real-estate material. Buys 8-10 mss/year. Query with published clips. Length: 1,000-2,500 words. Pays 20¢/word. Pays the expenses of writers on assignment, if previously arranged.

Photos: Send photos with submission. Reviews contact sheets, 35mm transparencies, and 5×7 or larger prints. Offers no additional payment for photos accepted with ms. Captions and identification of subjects required. Buys one-time rights.

Tips: "We want articles about the business aspects of the vacation industry: entrepreneurship, project financing, design and construction, sales and marketing, operations, management—in short, anything that will help our readers plan, build, sell, and run a quality vacation property that satisfies the owners/guests and earns a profit for the developer and marketer. Our destination pieces are trade-oriented, reporting the status of tourism and the development of various kinds of vacation ownership facilities in a city, region, or country. You can discuss things to see and do in the context of a resort located near an attraction, but that shouldn't be the main focus or reason for the article. We're also interested in owners associations at vacation ownership resorts (not residential condos). Prefers electronic submissions. Query for details."

THE WISCONSIN RESTAURATEUR, Wisconsin Restaurant Association, #300, 31 S. Henry, Madison WI 53703. (608)251-3663. Fax: (608)251-3666. Editor: Sonya Knecht Bice. 20% freelance written. Eager to work with new/unpublished writers. Bimonthly magazine emphasizing restaurant industry, particularly Wisconsin, for restaurateurs, hospitals, institutions, food service students, etc. Estab. 1933. Circ. 4,000. **Pays on acceptance, or publication, varies.** Publishes ms an average of 6 months after acceptance. Buys all rights or first rights. Editorial lead time 2 months. Pays 10% kill fee or $10. Byline given. Phone queries OK. Submit seasonal/holiday material 3 months in advance. Accepts previously published submissions. Send tearsheet of article or short story and information about when and where it previously appeared. Reports in 3 weeks. Sample copy and writer's guidelines for 9×12 SASE.
  • This magazine no longer accepts fiction.
Nonfiction: Historical/nostalgia, how-to, humor, inspirational interview/profile, new product, opinion, personal experience, photo feature articles. "All must relate to foodservice. Need more in-depth articles. No features on nonmember restaurants." Buys 6 mss/year. Query with "copyright clearance information and a note about the writer in general." Length: 1,000-5,000 words. Pays $100 minimum for assigned articles; $25 minimum for unsolicited articles. Pays other than cash payment when requested.
Photos: Fiction and how-to mss stand a better chance for publication if photos are submitted. State availability of photos; send photocopies. Pays $5-10 for b&w 8×10 glossy prints. Model release required. Buys one-time rights; varies.
Columns/Departments: Opinion, Guest Editorial. Buys 2/year. Query. Length 500-1,500 worsd. Pays $20-100.
Poetry: Uses all types of poetry, but must have foodservice as subject. Does not want to see "anything expressing bad attitude." Buys 6/year. Submit maximum 3 poems. Length: 25 lines maximum. Pays $5-50.
Fillers: Clippings, jokes, gags to be illustrated by cartoonist, newsbreaks, facts, anecdotes and short humor. No puzzles or games. Buys 6/year. Length: 100 words maximum. Pays $5-15.
Tips: "Most open to features, stand alone articles and fillers."

Industrial Operations

Industrial plant managers, executives, distributors and buyers read these journals. Some industrial management journals are also listed under the names of specific industries. Publications for industrial supervisors are listed in Management and Supervision.

CHEMICAL BUSINESS, Schnell Publishing Company, 80 Broad St., New York NY 10004-2203. (212)248-4177. Fax: (212)248-4901. Editor: J. Robert Warren. 90% freelance written. Monthly magazine covering chemicals and related process industries such as plastics, paints, some minerals, essential oils, soaps, detergents. Publishes features on the industry, management, financial (Wall Street), marketing, shipping and storage, labor, engineering, environment, research, international and company profiles. Estab. 1979. Circ. 3,000. **Pays on acceptance.** Publishes ms an average of 3 months after acceptance. Byline given. Offers $100 kill fee. Buys all rights. Query for electronic submissions. Reports in 2 weeks-12 months. Free sample copy and writer's guidelines.
  • Starting with the April 1993 issue, *Chemical Business* converted to a report-letter format and will provide managerial-style articles on issues of interest to executives in the chemical process industries. Rates ($500 for assigned articles plus expenses and a $100 kill fee) remain unchanged, as do most other particulars, but fewer freelance pieces will be used (2 per issue or 23-36 per year). Freelance mss are, thus, being cut back by nearly half.
Nonfiction: Chemical industry-targeted ideas only; no how-to articles. Publishes only assigned articles. Call before submitting article ideas. Buys 24 mss/year. Query. Length: 1,200-1,500 words. Pays $500 for assigned articles. Pays the expenses of writers on assignment.

COMPRESSED AIR, 253 E. Washington Ave., Washington NJ 07882-2495. Editor/Publications Manager: S.M. Parkhill. 75% freelance written. Magazine published 8 times/year emphasizing applied technology and industrial management subjects for engineers and managers. Estab. 1896. Circ. 145,000. Buys all rights. Publishes ms an average of 6 months after acceptance. Reports in 2 months. Free sample copy; mention *Writer's Market* in request.

Nonfiction: "Articles must be reviewed by experts in the field." Buys 56 mss/year. Query with published clips. Pays negotiable fee. Sometimes pays expenses of writers on assignment.

Photos: State availability of photos in query. Payment for slides, transparencies and glossy prints is included in total purchase price. Captions required. Buys all rights.

Tips: "We are presently looking for freelancers with a track record in industrial/technology/management writing. Editorial schedule is developed in the summer before the publication year and relies heavily on article ideas from contributors. Résumé and samples help. Writers with access to authorities preferred; and prefer interviews over library research. The magazine's name doesn't reflect its contents. We suggest writers request sample copies."

INDUSTRIAL FABRIC PRODUCTS REVIEW, Industrial Fabrics Association International, Suite 800, 345 Cedar St., St. Paul MN 55101-1088. (612)222-2508. Fax: (612)222-8215. Senior Editor: Sue Hagen. 100% staff- and industry-written. Monthly magazine covering industrial textiles and products made from them for company owners, salespersons and researchers in a variety of industrial textile areas. Estab. 1915. Circ. 10,000. Pays on publication. Publishes ms an average of 2 months after acceptance. Byline given. Buys all rights. Reports in 1 month.

Nonfiction: Technical, marketing and other topics related to any aspect of industrial fabric industry from fiber to finished fabric product. Special issues: new products, industrial products and equipment. No historical or apparel-oriented articles. Buys 10-15 mss/year. Query with phone number. Length: 1,200-3,000 words.

Tips: "We encourage freelancers to learn our industry and make regular, solicited contributions to the magazine. We no longer buy photography."

MANUFACTURING SYSTEMS, The Management Magazine of Integrated Manufacturing, Hitchcock Publishing Co., 191 S. Gary Ave., Carol Stream IL 60188. (708)665-1000. Fax: (708)462-2225 (staff). Editor: Kevin Parker. Associate Editors: Sidney Hill, Don Davis. 10-15% freelance written. Monthly magazine covering computers/information in manufacturing for upper and middle-level management in manufacturing companies. Estab. 1982. Circ. 115,000. **Pays on acceptance.** Publishes ms an average of 4 months after acceptance. Byline given. Offers 35% kill fee on assignments. Buys all rights. Accepts simultaneous and previously published submissions. Send typed ms with rights for sale noted and information about when and where the article previously appeared. For reprints pays 60% of the amount paid for an original article. Exclusive submissions receive more consideration. Query for electronic submissions. Reports in 2 months. Free sample copy and writer's guidelines.

Nonfiction: Book excerpts, essays, general interest, interview/profile, new product, opinion, technical, case history—applications of system. "Each issue emphasizes some aspect of modern manufacturing. Editorial schedule available, usually in September, for next year." Buys 6-8 mss/year. Query with or without published clips or send complete ms. Length: 500-2,500 words. Pays $150-600 for assigned articles; $50/published page for unsolicited articles. Sometimes pays limited, pre-authorized expenses of writers on assignment.

Photos: State availability of photos with submission. Reviews contact sheets, negatives, 2×2 and larger transparencies and 5×7 and larger prints. Offers no additional payment for photos accepted with ms. Captions and identification of subjects required. Buys one-time rights.

Tips: Check out success stories of companies winning against overseas competition in international marketplace. What's new in standards for computer systems, networks, operating systems; computer trends, trade, taxes; quality regulations; employee involvement, management; shop floor technology more computer power in smaller boxes. Features are the most open area. We will be happy to provide market information, reader profile and writer's guidelines on request. We are moving to 'require' submission in electronic form—diskette, MCI-mail."

PLANT, Dept. WM, 777 Bay St., Toronto, Ontario M5W 1A7 Canada. (416)596-5776. Fax: (416)596-5552. Editor: Ron Richardson. 10% freelance written. Prefers to work with published/established writers. Bimonthly magazine for Canadian plant managers and engineers. Estab. 1940. Circ. 42,000. **Pays on acceptance.** Publishes ms an average of 2 months after acceptance. Buys first Canadian rights. Reports in 3 weeks. Free sample copy.

Nonfiction: How-to, technical and management technique articles. Must have Canadian slant. No generic articles that appear to be rewritten from textbooks. Buys fewer than 20 unsolicited mss/year. Query. Pays 28¢/word minimum. Pays the expenses of writers on assignment.

• *Plant* is seeking submissions which display greater technical knowledge about computers in industry.

Photos: State availability of photos with query. Pays $60 for b&w prints; $100 for 2¼×2¼ or 35mm transparencies. Captions required. Buys one-time rights.

Always check the most recent copy of a magazine for the address and editor's name before you send in a query or manuscript.

Tips: "Increased emphasis on the use of computers and programmable controls in manufacturing will affect the types of freelance material we buy. Read the magazine. Know the Canadian readers' special needs. Case histories and interviews only—no theoretical pieces. We have gone to tabloid-size format, and this means shorter (about 800-word) features."

QUALITY ASSURANCE BULLETIN, Bureau of Business Practice, 24 Rope Ferry Rd., Waterford CT 06386-0001. (800)243-0876. Fax: (203)434-3078. Contact: Editor. 80% freelance written. Biweekly newsletter for quality assurance supervisors and managers and general middle to top management. **Pays on acceptance.** No byline given. Buys all rights. Reports in 2 weeks on queries; 1 month on mss. *Writer's Market* recommends allowing 2 months for reply. Free sample copy and writer's guidelines.
Nonfiction: Interview and articles with a strong how-to slant that make use of direct quotes whenever possible. Query before writing your article. Length: 800-1,500 words. Pays 10-15¢/word.
Tips: "Write for freelancer guidelines and follow them closely."

QUALITY DIGEST, QCI International, P.O. Box 882, 1350 Vista Way, Red Bluff CA 96080-0802. (916)527-8875. Fax: (916)527-6983. Editor: Scott M. Paton. 75% freelance written. Monthly trade magazine covering quality improvement. Estab. 1981. Circ. 30,000. **Pays on acceptance.** Byline given. Buys all rights. Submit seasonal material 4 months in advance. Accepts simultaneous and previously published submissions. Send tearsheet of article. Query for electronic submissions. Reports in 3 months. Free sample copy and writer's guidelines.
Nonfiction: Book excerpts, how-to implement quality programs, etc., interview/profile, opinion, personal experience, technical. Buys 25 mss/year. Query with or without published clips or send complete ms. Length: 2,000-3,000 words. Pays $200-600. Pays with contributor copies or other premiums for unsolicited mss. Sometimes pays expenses of writers on assignment.
Photos: Send photos with submission. Reviews any size prints. Offers no additional payment for photos accepted with ms. Captions, model releases and identification of subjects required. Buys one-time rights.
Tips: "Please be specific in your articles. Explain what the problem was, how it was solved and what the benefits are. Tell the reader how the technique described will benefit him or her."

WEIGHING & MEASUREMENT, Key Markets Publishing Co., P.O. Box 5867, Rockford IL 61125. (815)229-1818. Fax: (815)229-4086. Editor: David M. Mathieu. Bimonthly magazine for users of industrial scales and meters. Estab. 1914. Circ. 15,000. **Pays on acceptance.** Buys all rights. Pays 20% kill fee. Byline given. Reports in 2 weeks. Sample copy for $2.
Nonfiction: Interview (with presidents of companies); personal opinion (guest editorials on government involvement in business, etc.); profile (about users of weighing and measurement equipment); technical. Buys 25 mss/year. Query on technical articles; submit complete ms for general interest material. Length: 750-1,500 words. Pays $125-200.

Information Systems

These publications give computer professionals more data about their field. Consumer computer publications are listed under Personal Computers.

‡ACCESS TO WANG, The Independent Magazine for Wang System Users, New Media Publications, Suite 305, 10711 Burnet Rd., Austin TX 78758. Editor: Patrice Sarath. 75% freelance written. Monthly magazine covering Wang computers. *Access to Wang* provides how-to articles for users of Wang computer systems, Wang office automation software and coexistence and migration applications. Estab. 1984. Circ. 9,000-10,000. Pays 30 days after publication. Publishes ms an average of 2 months after acceptance. Byline given.Offers $25 kill fee. Buys first North American serial rights. Editorial lead time 3 months. Submit seasonal material 4 months in advance. Query for electronic submissions. Sample copy and writer's guidelines free on request.
Nonfiction: How-to, new product, technical, computer reviews, computer product reviews. Buys 50 mss/year. Query. Length: 1,500-2,000 words. Pays $150 for assigned articles; $100 for unsolicited articles.
Photos: Send photos with submissions. Reviews 3×5 transparencies and prints. Offers no additional payment for photos accepted with ms. Captions, model releases and identification of subjects required. Buys all rights.
Columns/Departments: Special Report (varies from month to month), 2,000-2,500. Buys 12 mss/year. Query. Pays $150.
Tips: "Writer must have computer experience specific to Wang computers. Also must have networking, Unix, programming, or similar experience. First step: call for the editorial calendar."

‡ADVANCED SYSTEMS/SUN WORLD, Client/Server Products for Unix Professionals, IDG, 501 Second St., San Francisco CA 94107. (415)267-1727. Editor: Michael McCarthy. 20% freelance written. Monthly magazine covering Unix-on-Risc. "We are a product magazine—product news, product reviews. Our readers want reliable, knowledgeable, honest analysis of products, their capabilities and shortcomings. *Advanced Systems* is written to be accessible to a semi-technical audience. Estab. 1989. Circ. 85,000. **Pays on acceptance.** Publishes ms an average of 2 months after acceptance. Byline given. Offers 50% kill fee. Buys first North American serial rights and nonexclusive all other and international rights. Editorial lead time 3 months. Submit seasonal material 3 months in advance. Query for electronic submissions. Reports in 3-4 weeks on queries; 1 month on mss.

Nonfiction: Technical, reviews, technical features. Buys 15 mss/year. Query. Length: 600-2,000 words. Pays $250. Sometimes pays expenses of writers on assignment.

Photos: State availability of photos with submission. Negotiates payment individually. Captions required. Buys all rights.

Columns/Departments: Seek columnists with hands-on experience. Query. Pays $500-1,000.

Tips: "We need reviewers of Unix products who have Risc workstations, work experience/expertise in a particular field relevant to the products being reviewed, who can write a well organized, readable review, meet a deadline, and know what they're talking about."

‡THE C/C++ USERS JOURNAL, R&D Publications, Inc., Suite 200, 1601 W. 23rd, Lawrence KS 66046. (913)841-1631. Editor: P.J. Plauger. Contact: Marc Briand. 90% freelance written. Monthly magazine covering C and C++ programming. "*CUJ* is written for professional C and C++ programmers. Articles are practical, advanced, and code-intensive. Authors are *always* professional C and C++ programmers." Estab. 1988. Circ. 43,000. Pays on publication. Publishes ms an average of 5 months after acceptance. Byline given. Kill fee $150. Buys all rights. Editorial lead time 4 months. Query for electronic submissions. Reports in 2 weeks on queries. Sample copy and writer's guidelines free on request.

Nonfiction: Technical. Buys 90-110 mss/year. Query. Length: 500 minimum. Pay varies.

‡CIRCUIT CELLAR INK, The Computer Applications Journal, 4 Park St., Vernon CT 06066. (203)875-2199. Editor: Kenneth Davidson. 99% freelance written. Monthly magazine covering design of embedded controllers. "Most of our articles are written by engineers for engineers. They deal with the lower level details of computer hardware and software design. Most articles deal with dedicated, embedded processors rather than desktop computers." Estab. 1988. Circ. 45,000. Pays on publication. Publishes ms an average of 6 months after acceptance. Byline given. Kill fee $100. Buys first rights. Editorial lead time 2 months. Submit seasonal material 3 months in advance. Accepts simultaneous submissions. Query for electronic submissions. Reports in 1 month. Sample copy and writer's guideline free on request.

Nonfiction: New product, technical. Buys 40 mss/year. Send complete ms. Length: 1,000-5,000 words. Pays $100.

Photos: Send photos with submissions. Reviews transparencies, slides and 3×5 prints. Offers no additional payment for photos accepted with ms. Captions required. Buys one-time rights.

Tips: "Contact editor with address, phone number, fax number, E-mail address, and article subject interests. Will send an author's guide."

COMPUTER GRAPHICS WORLD, PennWell Publishing Company, 10 Tara Blvd., 5th Floor, Nashua NH 03062-2801. (603)891-9160. Fax: (603)891-0539. Editor: Stephen Porter. Managing Editor: Audrey Doyle. 60% freelance written. Monthly magazine covering computer graphics. "*Computer Graphics World* specializes in covering computer-aided 3D modeling, animation, and visualization and their uses in engineering, science, and entertainment applications." Estab. 1978. Circ. 70,000. **Pays on acceptance.** Publishes ms an average of 3-4 months after acceptance. Byline given. Offers 20% kill fee. Buys all rights. Editorial lead time 4 months. Submit seasonal material 3 months in advance. Sample copy free on request.

Nonfiction: General interest, how-to (how-to create quality models and animations), interview/profile, new product, opinion, technical, user application stories. "We do not want to run articles that are geared to computer programmers. Our focus as a magazine is on users involved in specific applications." Buys 40 mss/ year. Query with published clips. Length: 1,200-3,000 words. Pays $500 minimum. Sometimes pays expenses of writers on assignment.

Columns/Departments: Output (offers personal opinion on relevant issue), 700 words; Reviews (offers hands-on review of important new products), 750 words and Application Stories (highlights a unique use of the technology by a single user), 800 words. Buys 36-40 mss/year. Query with published clips. Pays $100-500.

Tips: "Freelance writers will be most successful if they have some familiarity with computers and know how to write from a user perspective. They do not need to be computer experts, but they do have to understand how to explain the impact of the technology and the applications in which a user is involved. Both our feature section and our application story section are quite open to freelancers. The trick to winning acceptance for your story is to have a well-developed idea that highlights a fascinating new trend or development in computer graphics technology or profiles a unique and fascinating use of the technology by a single user or a specific class of users."

‡DATABASE, The Magazine of Electronic Database Reviews, Online Inc., 10 Mountain View Dr., Somers NY 10589. Editor: Paula Hane. 40% freelance written. Bimonthly magazine covering information industry. "Authors and readers are information professionals at libraries and information centers in business, universities and government—who use databases in online, CD-ROM, disk and tape formats and resources on the Internet." Estab. 1978. Circ. 4,000. Pays on publication. Publishes ms an average of 4-6 months after acceptance. Byline given. Buys first rights, second serial (reprint) rights. Editorial lead time 4 months. Submit seasonal material 4-5 months in advance. Query for electronic submissions. Reports in 3 weeks on queries. Sample copy free on request—call 1(800)248-8466. Writer's guidelines free on request.

Nonfiction: How-to (online search techniques), interview/profile, new product, opinion, technical, product reviews. Buys 40 mss/year. Query. Length: 1,000 words. Payment varies. Sometimes pays expenses of writers on assignment.

Photos: State availability of photos with submission. Negotiates payment individually. Captions required. Buys one-time rights and reprint rights.

Tips: "We are only interested in submissions from working information professionals. Inquire with an article idea or outline proposal before submitting a completed manuscript." Database reviews and comparisons are most open to freelancers.

DBMS, Miller Freeman, Dept. WM, 411 Borel Ave., San Mateo CA 94402-32522. (415)358-9500. Managing Editor: Kathleen O'Connor. 60% freelance written. Monthly magazine covering database applications and technology. "Our readers are database developers, consultants, VARs, programmers in MIS/DP departments and serious users." Estab. 1988. Circ. 58,000. **Pays on acceptance.** Publishes ms 3 months after acceptance. Byline given. Offers 33% kill fee. Buys all rights. Query for electronic submissions. Reports in 6 weeks on queries. Samply copy for 9 × 12 SAE with 8 first-class stamps.

Nonfiction: Technical. Buys 40-50 mss/year. Query with published clips. Length: 750-6,000 words. Pays $300-1,000.

Photos: Send photos with submission. Offers no additional payment for photos accepted with ms. Captions, model releases and identification of subjects required. Buys all rights.

Tips: "New writers should submit clear, concise queries of specific article subjects and ideas. *Read the magazine* to get a feel for the kind of articles we publish. This magazine is written for a highly technical computer database developer, consultant and user readership. We need technical features that inform this audience of new trends, software, hardware and techniques, including source code, screen caps and procedures."

‡**DIGITAL SYSTEMS JOURNAL, for Digital Software Professionals,** Cardinal Business Media, Inc., 101 Witmer Rd., Horsham PA 19044. (215)957-4273. Editor: Karen Detwiler. 50% freelance written. Bimonthly trade magazine covering programming for Digital Equipment Corporation computers. "Digital Systems Journal is a programming journal directed to Digital software professionals. It contains contributed articles, written by subscribers, describing helpful techniques, solutions to problems of general interest, and methods to extract the best possible performance from the operating systems in use on your system. Circ. 7,500. Pays on publication. Publishes ms an average of 6 months after acceptance. Byline given. Buys all rights and makes work-for-hire assignments. Editorial lead time 3 months. Query for electronic submissions. Reports in 1 week on queries. Sample copy and writer's guidelines free on request.

Nonfiction: Technical. "No articles that mention specific products." Query. Length: 1,000-3,000 words. Pays $400 minimum for assigned articles, $800 maximum for unsolicited articles.

Tips: "Become familiar with the technical level of the features in *DSJ*. Make sure your topic is generic and would appeal to the majority of our readers. Articles take the form of: 'Here's my programming problem. Here's how I solved it. Here's the code that I wrote to do what needed to be done.' Feature section is most open to freelancers."

‡**EASY APPROACH, Solutions for Lotus Approach users,** Pinnacle Publishing, Inc., P.O. Box 888, Kent WA 98035-0888. (206)251-1900 ext. 3060. Editor-in-Chief: Dian Schaffhauser. Editor: Linda L. Briggs. 95% freelance written. Monthly newsletter covering Lotus approach. "This hands-on newsletter provides helpful advice and tips for getting more use out of this Windows-based database manager." Estab. 1994. Pays on publication. Publishes ms an average of 3 months after acceptance. Byline given. Offers 25% kill fee. Buys all rights. Editorial lead time 4 months. Query for electronic submissions. Reports in 2 months on queries; 3 months on mss. Sample copy and writer's guidelines free on request.

Nonfiction: Book excerpts, how-to, new product, technical. "Please! No general interest articles about software use. Must be targeted to the product the newsletter covers." Buys 72 mss/year. Send complete ms. Length: 500-5,000 words. Pays $100 and up. Sometimes pays expenses of writers on assignment.

Tips: "Start with tips! Figure out ways to do something easier or faster and share that in a brief write-up. We pay $25 and a pound of Starbuck's coffee per tip and we use scads of them!"

‡**FOCUS, The Magazine of the North American Data General Users Group,** Turnkey Publishing, Inc., P.O. Box 200549, Austin TX 78720. (512)335-2286. Fax: (512)335-3083. Editor: Doug Johnson. 80% freelance written. Monthly trade journal covering Data General computers. Technical and practical information specific to the use of Data General computers. Estab. 1985. Circ. 8,000. Pays on publication. Publishes ms an average of 2 months after acceptance. Buys first North American serial rights. Reports in 1 month. Sample copy and writer's guidelines for 9 × 12 SAE with 6 first-class stamps.

Nonfiction: How-to (programming techniques, macros), technical. Query. Length: 1,000-3,000 words. Pays $50 minimum for assigned articles. Pays in contributor copies or other premiums if the writer works for a company that sells hardware or software to the Data General marketplace.

• Looking for more articles related to Unix, specifically Data General's DG/UX.

Photos: State availability of photos with submission. Reviews contact sheets, transparencies and prints. Offers no additional payment for photos accepted with ms. Model releases and identification of subjects required. Buys one-time rights.

‡**FOXTALK, Making Microsoft FoxPro development easier,** Pinnacle Publishing, Inc., P.O. Box 888, Kent WA 98035-0888. (206)251-1900 ext. 3060. Editor-in-Chief: Dian Schaffhauser. Editor: Bob Grommes. 95% freelance written. Monthly trade newsletter covering FoxPro development. *"FoxTalk* shows professional developers how to create more effective, more efficient software applications using FoxPro, a Microsoft development tool." Estab. 1989. Circ. 10,000. Pays on publication. Publishes ms an average of 3 months after acceptance. Byline given. Offers 25% kill fee. Buys all rights. Editorial lead time 4 months. Query for electronic submissions. Reports in 2 months on queries; 3 months on mss. Sample copy and writer's guidelines free on request.

Nonfiction: Book excerpts, how-to, new product, technical, technical tips. "Please! No general interest articles about software use. Must be targeted to the product the newsletter covers." Buys 72 mss/year. Send complete ms. Length: 500-5,000 words. Pays $25-600. Sometimes pays expenses of writers on assignment.

Tips: "Use the software product the newsletter covers. Be an expert in it! Develop a specific technique that other users would want to try out and explain it thoroughly in your article. Start with tips! Figure out ways to do something easier or faster and share that in a brief write-up. We pay $25 and a pound of Starbuck's coffee each and we use scads of them!"

HP/APOLLO WORKSTATION, Publications and Communications, Inc., 12416 Hymeadow Dr., Austin TX 78750-1896. (512)250-9023. Fax: (512)331-3900. Editor: Larry Storer. Managing Editor: John Mitchell. 40% freelance written. Monthly magazine covering news for Hewlett-Packard/Apollo Workstation computer users. "We provide detailed and useful information for engineers, scientists and technical managers on trends, products, services and market news about HP and Apollo Workstation computers." Estab. 1985. Circ. 18,000. Pays on publication. Publishes ms an average of 2-3 months after acceptance. Byline given. Buys one-time rights. Editorial lead time 2 months. Query for electronic submissions. Reports in 2 weeks on queries; 1 month on mss. *Writer's Market* recommends allowing 2 months for reply. Sample copy and writer's guidelines free on request.

Nonfiction: How-to, new product, technical. Buys 12-15 mss/year. Send complete ms. Length: 1,500 words maximum. Pays $200 minimum for assigned articles, $150 minimum for unsolicited articles.

Photos: State availability of photos with submission. Offers no additional payment for photos accepted with ms.

Tips: "This is as niche as the computer market writer can get. If you don't know H-P Workstations and the software and peripherals they require, pass by. If you do, call and let's talk. We can fit your interests into a story that will work for the readership by chatting rather than written correspondence. We accept good, balanced site profiles and technical articles most from freelancers. Site profiles should be unique (HP computers at the White House, using them to run housing projects, etc.). Technical pieces explain how aspects of the system work, or how to make new office configurations (networks, different vendor's computers) work."

‡**INFORM, The Magazine of Information and Image Management,** Association for Information and Image Management, 1100 Wayne Ave., Silver Spring MD 20910. (301)587-8202. Fax: (301)587-5129. Editor: John Harney. 30% freelance written. Prefers to work with writers with business/high tech experience. Monthly trade magazine on information and image processing. "Specifically we feature coverage of micrographics, electronic imaging and developments in storage and retrieval technology like optical disk, computer-assisted retrieval." Estab. 1943. Circ. 40,000. Pays on publication. Publishes ms an average of 3 months after acceptance. Byline given. Offers $50 kill fee. Buys first North American serial and second serial (reprint) rights. Accepts simultaneous and previously published submissions. Send tearsheet or photocopy of article or typed ms with rights for sale noted. Free sample copy and writer's guidelines.

• Interested in new subjects: networks, wireless, information highway, interactive multimedia, multimedia.

Nonfiction: Interview/profile, new product, photo feature, technical. Buys 4-12 mss/year. Query. Length: 1,500 words. Pays $750 for 1,500 words for assigned articles. Sometimes pays the expenses of writers on assignment.

Photos: State availability of photos with submission. Reviews negatives, 4×5 transparencies and prints. Offers no additional payment for photos accepted with ms. Captions and identification of subjects required. Buys all rights.

Columns/Departments: Trends (developments across industry segments); Technology (innovations of specific technology); Management (costs, strategies of managing information). Query. Length: 500-1,500 words. Pays $250.

Fillers: Facts and newsbreaks. Length: 150-500 words. Pays $50-250.

Tips: "We would encourage freelancers who have access to our editorial calendar to contact us regarding article ideas, inquiries, etc. Our feature section is the area where the need for quality freelance coverage of our industry is most desirable. The most likely candidate for acceptance is someone who has a proven background in business writing, and/or someone with demonstrated knowledge of high-tech industries as they relate to information management."

INFORMATION TODAY, Learned Information Inc., 143 Old Marlton Pike, Medford NJ 08055-8750. (609)654-6266. Fax: (609)654-4309. Publisher: Thomas H. Hogan. Editor: Patricia Lane. 30% freelance written. Tabloid published 11 times/year for the users and producers of electronic information services. Estab. 1979. Circ. 10,000. Pays on publication. Publishes ms an average of 1-3 months after acceptance. Byline given. Buys first North American serial rights. Submit seasonal material 2 months in advance. Reports in 2 weeks. Sample copy and writer's guidelines for 9×12 SAE with 6 first-class stamps.

Nonfiction: Book reviews; interview/profile and new product; technical (dealing with computerized information services); articles on library technology, artificial intelligence, online databases and services, and integrated online library systems. We also cover software and optical publishing (CD-ROM and Multi Media). Buys approximately 25 mss/year. Query with published clips or send complete ms on speculation. Length: 500-1,500 words. Pays $90-220.

Photos: State availability of photos with submission.

Tips: "We look for clearly-written, informative articles dealing with the electronic delivery of information. Writing style should not be jargon-laden or heavily technical."

‡JOURNAL OF INFORMATION ETHICS, McFarland & Co., Inc., Publishers, Box 611, Jefferson NC 28640. (910)246-4460. Editor: Robert Hauptman, LRS, 720 Fourth Ave. S., St. Cloud State University, St. Cloud MN 56301 (612)255-4822. All ms queries to editor. 90% freelance written. Semiannual magazine covering information sciences, ethics. Magazine "addresses ethical issues in all of the information sciences with a deliberately interdisciplinary approach. Topics range from electronic mail monitoring to library acquisition of controversial material. The journal's aim is to present thoughtful considerations of ethical dilemmas that arise in a rapidly evolving system of information exchange and dissemination." Estab. 1992. Circ. 500. Pays on publication. Publishes ms an average of 6-9 months after acceptance. Byline given. Buys all rights. Submit seasonal material 8 months in advance. Query for electronic submissions. Sample copy for $21. Writer's guidelines free on request.

Nonfiction: Essays, opinion, book reviews. Buys 10 mss/year. Send complete ms. Length: 500-3,500 words. Pays $25.

Tips: "Familiarize yourself with the many areas subsumed under the rubric of information ethics, e.g., privacy; scholarly communication; errors, peer review; confidentiality; e-mail; etc."

‡NADTP JOURNAL, National Association of Desktop Publishers, 462 Old Boston St., Topsfield MA 01983. (508)887-7900. Editor-in-Chief: Noel Ward. Contact: Marcia Sampson. 80% freelance written. Monthly magazine covering desktop publishing. "*NADTP Journal* educates and informs readers on all aspects of desktop publishing technology and shows them how to get the most out of the technology on their desktops." Estab. 1987. Circ. 50,000. Pays on publication. Publishes ms an average of 3-4 months after acceptance. Byline given. Negotiable kill fee. Buys first rights or second serial (reprint) rights. Editorial lead time 4 months. Query for electronic submissions. Reports in 1 month on queries. Sample copy for $4. Writer's guidelines for #10 SASE.

Nonfiction: How-to (use and apply DTP hardware, software and special techniques), interview/profile, new product, personal experience (within narrow limits), technical. Buys 75 mss/year. Query with published clips. Length: 300-5,000 words. Rates negotiated based on article and complexity of topic.

Photos: Send photos with submission. Offers no additional payment for photos accepted with ms. Captions, model releases, identification of subjects required.

Columns/Departments: Digital Images, Digital Paper, Scanning, Color, Alternative Media, Pre-Press, (all helping readers to understand and apply existing and emerging technologies in their work as desktop publishers), 500-1,500 words. Buys 30 mss/year. Query with published clips. Rates negotiated based on topic and complexity.

Tips: "Writers should have a clear understanding of the needs of desktop publishers and what they need to know to work faster, smarter and more professionally. Familiarity with the desktop publishing industry is essential, as is some technical knowledge of the ways DTP hardware and software are used. Departments are the easiest way to break in, although we're always looking for new writers for feature length articles."

‡NETWORK ADMINISTRATOR, R&D Publications, Inc., Suite 200, 1601 W. 23rd., Lawrence KS 66046. (913)841-1631. Editor: Robert Ward. Managing Editor: Martha Masinton. 90% freelance written. Bimonthly trade magazine covering PC LAN administration. "Network Administrator is written for PC LAN administrators. Articles are technical and practical. Articles are written by practicing administrators." Estab. 1994. Circ. 10,000. Pays on publication. Byline given. Kill fee $150. Buys all rights. Editorial lead time 4 months.

Query for electronic submissions. Reports in 3 weeks on queries. Sample and writer's guidelines free on request.

Nonfiction: Book excerpts, technical. "No *non*-technical articles." Buys 20-40 mss/year. Query. Length: 1,000 words.

NETWORK WORLD, Network World Publishing, Dept. WM, 161 Worcester Rd., Framingham MA 01701. (508)875-6400. Fax: (508)820-3467. Editor: John Gallant. Features Editor: Charles Bruno. 25% freelance written. Weekly tabloid covering data, voice and video communications networks (including news and features on communications management, hardware and software, services, education, technology and industry trends) for senior technical managers at large companies. Estab. 1986. Circ. 150,000. **Pays on acceptance.** Byline given. Offers negotiable kill fee. Buys all rights. Submit all material 2 months in advance. Query for electronic submissions. Reports in 5 months. Free sample copy and writer's guidelines.

Nonfiction: Exposé, general interest, how-to (build a strong communications staff, evaluate vendors, choose a value-added network service), humor, interview/profile, opinion, technical. Editorial calendar available. "Our readers are users: avoid vendor-oriented material." Buys 100-150 mss/year. Query with published clips. Length: 500-2,500 words. Pays $600 minimum—negotiable maximum for assigned or unsolicited articles.

Photos: Send photos with submission. Reviews 35mm, 2¼ and 4×5 transparencies and b&w prints (prefers 8×10 but can use 5×7). Captions, model releases and identification of subjects required. Buys one-time rights.

Tips: "We look for accessible treatments of technological, managerial or regulatory trends. It's OK to dig into technical issues as long as the article doesn't read like an engineering document. Feature section is most open to freelancers. Be informative, stimulating, controversial and technically accurate."

‡ONLINE, The Magazine of Online Information Systems, P.O. Box 17507, Fort Mitchell KY 41017. (606)331-6345. Editor: Nancy Garman. 95% freelance written. Bimonthly magazine covering online information and industry. "*Online* is edited and written for the 'information professional'—librarians or subject specialists who routinely use online services. *Online* stresses practical, how-to advice on the effective, efficient use of online databases. It emphasizes innovative tips and techniques and new technologies and products." Estab. 1977. Circ. 5,500. Pays on publication. Publishes ms 3-6 months after acceptance. Byline given. Negotiable kill fee. Buys first rights. Editorial lead time 3-6 months. Submit seasonal material 6 months in advance. Query for electronic submissions. Reports in 2 weeks on queries; 1 month on mss. Sample copy and writer's guidelines free on request.

Nonfiction: How-to, new product, opinion, personal experience, technical, software/hardware/feature reviews. Buys 35 mss/year. Query with published clips. Length: 1,500-4,000 words. Pays $150. Sometimes pays expenses of writers on assignment.

Photos: Send photos with submission. Reviews contact sheets, negatives, transparencies, prints. Negotiates payment individually. Captions required. Buys one-time rights.

Columns/Departments: Columnists are long-term authors. Buys 40 mss/year. Query. Pays $125-300.

Tips: "All areas open, but must know about online searching, online industry, the Internet—have some technical know-how or understanding of library/information professional market."

OPEN COMPUTING, McGraw-Hill's Magazine of Unix and Interoperable Solutions, (formerly *Unix World*), 1900 O'Farrell St., San Mateo CA 94403. (415)513-6800. Fax: (415)513-6986. Managing Editor: David Diamond. 30% freelance written. Monthly magazine directed to people who use, make or sell open computing products, particularly in a commercial environment. Readers are employed in management, systems administration, engineering and software development. Estab. 1984. Circ. 101,000. **Pays on acceptance.** A rewrite is usually required. Publishes ms an average of 4 months after acceptance. Byline given. Offers kill fee. Buys all rights. Electronic submissions only. Reports in 1 month. Sample copy for $3. Writer's guidelines sent. Ask for editorial calendar so query can be tailored to the magazine's need; send SASE with 2 first-class stamps.

Nonfiction: Increasingly looks for articles on how end-users are using UNIX and open computing as business solutions. Also needs vendor strategy stories, industry personality profiles and industry trend articles. Tutorials (technical articles on the UNIX system or the C language); new products; technical overviews; and product reviews. Query by phone or with cover letter and published clips. Length: 1,000-3,000 words. Pays $100-2,000. Sometimes pays the expenses of writers on assignment.

Tips: "We have shifted more toward a business and commercial focus. The best way to get an acceptance on an article is to consult our editorial calendar and tailor a pitch to a particular story."

‡THE QUICK ANSWER, The independent monthly guide to Q&A expertise, Pinnacle Publishing, Inc., P.O. Box 888, Kent WA 98035-0888. (206)251-1900 ext. 3060. Editor-in-Chief: Dian Schaffhauser. Editor: Tom Marcellus. 95% freelance written. Monthly newsletter covering working with Symantec's Q&A database manager. "This hands-on newsletter provides readers with helpful advice and tips for getting more use out of Q&A, a database manager and word processor from Symantec Corp." Estab. 1990. Circ. 7,000. Pays on publication. Publishes ms an average of 3 months after acceptance. Byline given. Offers 25% kill fee. Buys all rights. Editorial lead time 4 months. Query for electronic submissions. Reports in 2 months on queries; 3 months on mss. Sample copy and writer's guidelines free on request.

Nonfiction: Book excerpts, how-to, new product, technical. Buys 72 mss/year. Send complete ms. Length: 500-5,000 words. Pays $100 and up.

Tips: "Use the software product the newsletter covers. Be an expert in it! Develop a specific technique that other users would want to try out and explain it thoroughly in your article."

‡**REFERENCE CLIPPER, Making CA-Clipper development easier,** Pinnacle Publishing, Inc., P.O. Box 888, Kent WA 98035-0888. (206)251-1900 ext. 3060. Editor-in-Chief: Dian Schaffhauser. Editor: Savannah Brentnall. 95% freelance written. Monthly trade newsletter covering application development with CA Clipper. "*Reference Clipper* provides hands-on advice, techniques, and tips for creating more effective software applications using Clipper. Estab. 1988. Circ. 5,000. Pays on publication. Publishes ms an average of 3 months after acceptance. Byline given. Offers 25% kill fee. Buys all rights. Editorial lead time 4 months. Query for electronic submissions. Reports in 2 months on queries; 3 months on mss. Writer's guidelines free on request.

Nonfiction: Book excerpts, how-to, new product, technical. "Please! No general interest articles about software use. Must be targeted to the product the newsletter covers." Buys 72 mss/year. Send complete ms. Length: 500-5,000 words. Pays $100 and up.

Tips: "Use the software product the newsletter covers. Be an expert in it! Develop a specific technique that other users would want to try out and explain it thoroughly in your article. Start with tips! Figure out ways to do something easier or faster and share that in a brief write-up. We pay $25 and a pound of Starbuck's coffee each and we use scads of them!"

‡**SMART ACCESS, Solutions for Microsoft Access developers and power users,** Pinnacle Publishing, Inc., P.O. Box 888, Kent WA 98035-0888. (206)251-1900 ext. 3060. Editor-in-Chief: Dian Schaffhauser. Editor: Paul Litwin. 95% freelance written. Monthly trade newsletter covering software development with access. "Smart Access provides hands-on advice, techniques, and tips for creating more effective software applications—faster—using Microsoft Access." Estab. 1993. Circ. 9,000. Pays on publication. Publishes ms an average of 3 months after acceptance. Byline given. Offers 25% kill fee. Buys all rights. Editorial lead time 4 months. Query for electronic submissions. Reports in 2 months on queries; 3 months on mss. Sample copy and writer's guideline free on request.

Nonfiction: Book excerpts, how-to, new product, technical. "Please! No general interest articles about software use. Must be targeted to the product the newsletter covers." Buys 72 mss/year. Send complete ms. Length: 500-5,000 words. Pays $100 and up.

Tips: "Use the software product the newsletter covers. Be an expert in it! Develop a specific technique that other users would want to try out and explain it thoroughly in your article. Start with tips! Figure out ways to do something easier or faster and share that in a brief write-up. We pay $25 and a pound of Starbuck's coffee each and we use scads of them!"

‡**SYS ADMIN,** R&D Publications, Inc., Suite 200, 1601 W. 23rd St., Lawrence KS 66046. (913)841-1631. Editor: Robert Ward. Contact: Martha Masinton. 90% freelance written. Bimonthly magazine covering UNIX systems administration. "*Sys Admin* is written for UNIX systems administrators. Articles are practical and technical. Our authors are practicing UNIX systems administrators." Estab. 1992. Circ. 14,000. Pays on publication. Publishes ms an average of 6 months after acceptance. Byline given. Kill fee $150. Buys all rights. Editorial lead time 4 months. Query for electronic submissions. Reports in 1 month on queries. Sample copy and writer's guidelines free on request.

Nonfiction: Technical. Buys 40-60 mss/year. Query. Length: 1,000 minimum. Pay varies.

‡**3X/400 SYSTEMS MANAGEMENT,** Hunter Publishing, (formerly *Systems 3X/400*), Suite 800, 25 Northwest Point Blvd., Elk Grove Village IL 60007. (708)427-9512. Fax: (708)427-2006. Editor: Renée Robbins. 10% freelance written. Works with a small number of new/unpublished writers each year. Monthly magazine covering applications of IBM minicomputers (S/36/38/ and AS/400) in business. Estab. 1973. Circ. 55,000. Pays on publication. Publishes ms an average of 3 months after acceptance. Byline given. Buys all rights. Submit seasonal material 4 months in advance. Electronic submissions may be made via CompuServe number 71333, 730. Reports in 3 months on queries. Sample copy for 9×12 SAE with 4 first-class stamps. Writer's guidelines for #10 SASE.

Nonfiction: How-to (use the computer in business) and technical (organization of a data base or file system). "A writer who submits material to us should be an expert in computer applications. No material on large-scale computer equipment." No poetry. Buys 8 mss/year. Query. Length: 2,000-4,000 words. Sometimes pays expenses of writers on assignment.

Tips: "Frequent mistakes are not understanding the audience and not having read the magazine (past issues)."

UNIFORUM MONTHLY, Uniforum Association, 2901 Tasman Dr., Santa Clara CA 95054-1179. (408)986-8840. Fax: (408)986-1645. Publications Director: Richard Shippee. Managing Editor: Mary Margaret Peterson. 80% freelance writtten. Monthly trade journal covering UNIX and open systems. "Writers must have a sound knowledge of the UNIX operating system." Estab. 1981. Circ. 40,000. **Pays on acceptance.** Publishes ms an average of 2 months after acceptance. Byline given. Offers 30% kill fee. Buys all rights. Query for electronic submissions. Reports in 2 months. Free sample copy and writer's guidelines.

Nonfiction: Interview/profile, opinion, technical. Buys 35 mss/year. Query with or without published clips. Length: 1,000-3,500 words. Pays $0-1,200. Sometimes pays in other premiums or contributors copies "when article is written by industry member." Pays expenses of writers on assignment. International writers actively sought.

Photos: Send photos with submission. "Photos are required with manuscript but offers no additional payment." Buys one-time rights.

Columns/Departments: Career Corner (career tips), 700-800 words; UAR Update, 700-800 words. Federal Watch, 700-800 words. Buys 12 mss/year. Query. Pays $0-250.

‡**WINDOWS/DOS DEVELOPER'S JOURNAL,** R&D Publications, Inc., Suite 200, 1601 W. 23rd St., Lawrence KS 66046. (913)841-1631. Editor: Ron Burk. Contact: Martha Masinton, managing editor. 90% freelance written. Monthly magazine covering windows programming. "*W/DDJ* is written for advanced windows programmers. Articles are practical, advanced, and code-intensive. We expect our authors to be working Windows programmers." Estab. 1990. Circ. 22,000. **Pays on acceptance.** Publishes ms an average of 6 months after acceptance. Byline given. Kill fee $150. Buys all rights. Editorial lead time 3 months. Query for electronic submissions. Reports in 2 weeks on queries. Sample copy and writer's guidelines free on request.

Nonfiction: Technical. Buys 70-80 mss/year. Query. Length: varies. Pay varies.

Insurance

BUSINESS & HEALTH, Solutions in Managed Care, Medical Economics Publishing Co., 5 Paragon Dr., Montvale NJ 07645-1742. (201)358-7208. Fax: (201)573-1045. Editor: Joe Burns. Managing Editor: Cindy Cordero. 90% freelance written. Magazine published 12 times/year covering health care for employers offering benefits for workers. "*B&H* carries articles about how employers can cut their health care costs and improve the quality of care they provide to workers. We also write about health care policy at the federal, state and local levels." Estab. 1983. Circ. 40,000. **Pays on acceptance.** Publishes ms an average of 2 months after acceptance. Byline given. Offers 20% kill fee. Buys all rights. Editorial lead time 3 months. Submit seasonal material 4 months in advance. Query for electronic submissions. Reports in 2-3 months. Sample copy for 9×12 SAE with 6 first-class stamps. Writer's guidelines for #10 SASE.

Nonfiction: How-to (cut health care benefits costs). "No articles that do not include a cost-benefit analysis." Buys 150 mss/year. Query with published clips. Length: 2,000-3,500 words. Pays $800-1,200 for articles. Pays expenses of writers on assignment.

Columns/Departments: State Report (state health care reform measures), 1,000-2,000 words; Law Report (legal issues in employee health care), 1,000-2,000 words; and Coalition Report (efforts by employer coalitions to cut costs), 1,000-3,000 words. Buys 42 mss/year. Query with published clips. Pays $500-1,000.

Tips: "Please read and follow writer's guidelines, which include examples of well written articles that have been published in *B&H*. Readers approach articles from a business point of view and want to see an evaluation of the costs versus the benefits of all strategies discussed. Include plenty of charts, graphs and tables supporting the strategy discussed. Use plenty of cost-benefit analysis data. We've expanded our coverage of health reform."

FLORIDA UNDERWRITER, National Underwriter Company, Suite 213, 9887 Gandy Blvd. N., St. Petersburg FL 33702-2488. (813)576-1101. Fax: (813)577-4002. Editor: James E. Seymour. Managing Editor: Garry Baumgartner. 20% freelance written. Monthly magazine about insurance. "*Florida Underwriter* covers insurance for Florida insurance professionals: producers, executives, risk managers, employee benefit administrators. We want material about any insurance line, Life & Health or Property & Casualty, but *must* have a Florida tag—Florida authors preferred." Estab. 1984. Circ. 10,000. Pays on publication. Publishes ms an average of 2-3 months after acceptance. Byline given. Buys all rights. Submit seasonal material 3 months in advance. Accepts simultaneous and previously published submissions. Query for electronic submissions. Reports in 1 month. Free sample copy and writer's guidelines.

Nonfiction: Essay, exposé, historical/nostalgic, how-to, interview/profile, new product, opinion, technical. "We don't want articles that aren't about insurance for insurance people or those that lack Florida angle. No puff pieces. Note: Most non-inhouse pieces are contributed gratis by industry experts." Buys 6 mss/year. Query with or without published clips or send complete ms. Length: 500-1,500 words. Pays $50-150 for assigned articles; $25-100 for unsolicited articles. "Industry experts contribute in return for exposure." Sometimes pays expenses of writers on assignment.

Photos: State availability of photos with submission. Send photos with submission. Reviews 5×7 prints. Offers no additional payment for photos accepted with ms. Identification of subjects required.

GEICO DIRECT, K.L. Publications, Suite 105, 2001 Killebrew Dr., Bloomington MN 55425-1879. Editor: Patricia Burke. 60% freelance written. Semiannual magazine published for the Government Employees

Insurance Company (GEICO) policyholders. Estab. 1988. Circ. 1.5 million. Pays on acceptance by client. Byline given. Buys first North American serial rights. Query for electronic submissions. Reports in 2 months.
Nonfiction: Americana, home and auto safety, car care, financial, lifestyle, travel. Query with published clips. Length: 1,000 words. Pays $350-600.
Photos: Reviews 35mm transparencies. Payment varies.
Columns/Departments: Moneywise, 50+, Your Car. Query with published clips. Length: 500-600 words. Pays $175-350.
Tips: "We prefer work from published/established writers, especially those with specialized knowledge of the insurance industry, safety issues and automotive topics."

‡INSURANCE JOURNAL, The Property/Casualty Magazine of the West, Wells Publishing Co., Suite 550, 9191 Towne Centre Dr., San Diego CA 92122. (619)455-7717. Publisher: Mark Wells. Managing Editor: Denise A. Carabet. 20% freelance written. Biweekly trade magazine covering property/casualty insurance. "Market-insurance brokers and agents in 7 western states; articles must be need-to-knows; news/trend driven; insurance savvy a must; also political know-how." Estab. 1921. Circ. 10,248. Pays on publication. Byline given. Offers 10% kill fee. Buys other negotiated rights. Editorial lead time 2 months. Submit seasonal material 3 months in advance. Reports in 2 weeks on queries. Sample copy free on request.
Nonfiction: By assignment. "Nothing personal, inspirational or not intelligently pegged to P/C insurance. Query. Length: 600-1,500 words. Sometimes pays expenses of writers on assignment.
Photos: State availability of photos with submission. Reviews contact sheets and negatives. Negotiates payment individually. Identification of subjects required. Buys one-time rights.
Tips: "Identify trend in insurance—on sales or management sides—and be able to find right sources to intelligently discuss."

THE LEADER, Fireman's Fund Insurance Co., 777 San Marin Dr., Novato CA 94998-0000. (415)899-2109. Fax: (415)899-2126. Editor/Communications Manager: Jim Toland. 70% freelance written. Quarterly magazine on insurance. "*The Leader* contains articles and information for Fireman's Fund employees and retirees about special projects, meetings, events, employees and offices nationwide—emphasizing the business of insurance and the unique people who work for the company. Some travel and lifestyle features." Estab. 1863. **Pays on acceptance.** Publishes ms an average of 3 months after acceptance. Buys one-time rights. Accepts simultaneous and previously published submissions. Send photocopy of article and typed ms with rights for sale noted. Reports in 1 month or less on mss. Free sample copy with SASE.
Nonfiction: Interview/profile, new products, employees involved in positive activities in the insurance industry and in the communities where company offices are located. Query with published clips. Length: 200-2,500 words. Pays $100-500.
Photos: Reviews contact sheets and prints. Sometimes buys color slides. Offers $50-100/photo for b&w, up to $250 for color. Buys one-time rights.
Tips: "It helps to work in the insurance business and/or know people at Fireman's Fund. Writers with business reporting experience are usually most successful—though we've published many first-time writers. Research the local Fireman's Fund branch office (not sales agents who are independents). Look for newsworthy topics. Strong journalism and reporting skills are greatly appreciated."

PROFESSIONAL AGENT MAGAZINE, The Magazine of the National Association of Professional Insurance Agents, 400 N. Washington St., Alexandria VA 22314-9345. (703)836-9340; (703)836-9345 after 5 pm Eastern time. Fax: (703)836-1279. E-mail: 75410.655@Compuserve.com. Editor: Alan Prochoroff. 85% freelance written. Monthly magazine covering insurance/small business for independent insurance agents, legislators, regulators and others in the industry. Estab. 1936. Circ. 30,000. **Pays on acceptance.** Publishes ms an average of 2 months after acceptance. Byline given. Buys exclusive rights in the industry. Prefers electronic submissions. Reports in 3 months. Sample copy and writer's guidelines for 9×12 SAE with 5 first-class stamps.
Nonfiction: Management for independent insurance agents. Buys 36-40 mss/year. Query with published clips or send complete ms. Length: 2,000 words. Pays $950. Pays fax and long-distance telephone expenses of writers on assignment.
Tips: "All work is assigned. No writing on spec. We prefer to work with established magazine writers who have top-quality clips dealing with business and/or the insurance industry, particularly from an agent's perspective. We are very particular about the writers to whom we give assignments. We're always looking for top-quality writers, but we aren't a training ground for anyone with lesser skills. Query by phone or letter; send clips or mss and include SASE. We prefer submissions by modem or disk (Mac or 3.5″ IBM), with hard copy accompanying by mail. We can be contacted on the Internet, 75410.655@Compuserve.com."

Jewelry

THE DIAMOND REGISTRY BULLETIN, #806, 580 5th Ave., New York NY 10036. (212)575-0444. Fax: (212)575-0722. Editor-in-Chief: Joseph Schlussel. 50% freelance written. Monthly newsletter. Estab. 1969.

Pays on publication. Buys all rights. Submit seasonal material 1 month in advance. Accepts simultaneous and previously published submissions. Reports in 3 weeks. Sample copy for $5.

Nonfiction: Prevention advice (on crimes against jewelers); how-to (ways to increase sales in diamonds, improve security, etc.); interview (of interest to diamond dealers or jewelers). Submit complete ms. Length: 50-500 words. Pays $75-150.

Tips: "We seek ideas to increase sales of diamonds. We have more interest in diamond mining."

THE ENGRAVERS JOURNAL, 26 Summit St., P.O. Box 318, Brighton MI 48116. (313)229-5725. Fax: (313)229-8320. Co-Publisher: Michael J. Davis. Managing Editor: Rosemary Farrell. 15% freelance written. "We are eager to work with published/established writers as well as new/unpublished writers." Magazine published 10 times/year covering the recognition and identification industry (engraving, marking devices, awards, jewelry, and signage.) "We provide practical information for the education and advancement of our readers, mainly retail business owners." Estab. 1975. **Pays on acceptance.** Publishes ms an average of 1 year after acceptance. Byline given "only if writer is recognized authority." Buys all rights (usually). Query with published clips and résumé. Accepts previously published submissions. Query for electronic submissions. Reports in 2 weeks. Free writer's guidelines. Sample copy to "those who send writing samples with inquiry."

Nonfiction: General interest (industry-related); how-to (small business subjects, increase sales, develop new markets, use new sales techniques, etc.); interview/profile; new product; photo feature (a particularly outstanding signage system); technical. No general overviews of the industry. Buys 12 mss/year. Query with writing samples "published or not, or send samples and résumé to be considered for assignments on speculation." Length: 1,000-5,000 words. Pays $75-250, depending on writer's skill and expertise in handling subject.

Photos: Send photos with query. Reviews 8×10 prints. Pays variable rate. Captions, model release and identification of subjects required.

Tips: "Articles should always be down to earth, practical and thoroughly cover the subject with authority. We do not want the 'textbook' writing approach, vagueness, or theory—our readers look to us for sound practical information."

FASHION ACCESSORIES, S.C.M. Publications, Inc., 65 W. Main St., Bergenfield NJ 07621-1696. (201)384-3336. Fax: (201)384-6776. Managing Editor: Samuel Mendelson. Monthly newspaper covering costume or fashion jewelry. "Serves the manufacturers, manufacturers' sales reps, importers and exporters who sell exclusively through the wholesale level in ladies' fashion jewlery, men's jewelry, gifts and boutiques and related novelties." Estab. 1951. Circ. 8,000. **Pays on acceptance.** Byline given. Not copyrighted. Buys first rights. Submit seasonal material 3 months in advance. Sample copy for $2 and 9×12 SAE with 4 first-class stamps.

Nonfiction: Essays, general interest, historical/nostalgic, how-to, humor, interview/profile, new product, travel. Buys 20 mss/year. Query with published clips. Length: 1,000-2,000 words. Pays $100-300. Sometimes pays the expenses of writers on assignment.

Photos: Send photos with submission. Reviews 4×5 prints. Offers no additional payment for photos accepted with ms. Identification of subjects required. Buys one-time rights.

Columns/Departments: Fashion Report (interviews and reports of fashion news), 1,000-2,000 words.

Tips: "We are interested in anything that will be of interest to costume jewelry buyers."

Journalism and Writing

Journalism and writing magazines cover both the business and creative sides of writing. Writing publications offer inspiration and support for professional and beginning writers. Although there are many valuable writing publications that do not pay, we list only those that pay for articles.

AMERICAN JOURNALISM REVIEW, University of Maryland College of Journalism, 8701 Adelphi Rd., Adelphi MD 20783. (301)431-4771. Fax: (301)441-9495. Editor: Rem Rieder. Contact: Elliott Negin, Managing Editor. 90% freelance written. Magazine published 10 times/year covering journalism. "*AJR* reports on the business, ethics and problems of the news media." Estab. 1977. Circ. 25,000. Pays on publication. Publishes ms an average of 2 months after acceptance. Byline given. Offers 25% kill fee. Buys first North American serial rights. Editorial lead time 2-3 months. Submit seasonal material 3-4 months in advance. Query for electronic submissions. Reports in 1 month. Please read a copy before sending queries. Sample copy for $4.50.

Nonfiction: Analysis of media coverage, book excerpts, essays, exposé, humor, interview/profile. Buys 100 mss/year. Query with published clips. Length: 500-5,000 words. Pays 20¢/word minimum. Pays expenses of writers on assignment.

Photos: "We only use commissioned photos."

Fillers: Contact: Chip Rowe, Associate Editor. Buys 100/year. Length: 5-30 words. Pays $25. "*AJR*'s 'Take 2' column prints humorous headlines and short excerpts from articles."

‡**AUTHORSHIP**, National Writers Association, Suite 424, 1450 S. Havana, Aurora CO 80012. (303)751-7844. Editor: Sandy Whelchel. Bimonthly magazine covering writing articles only. "Association magazine targeted to beginning and professional writers. Covers how-to, humor, marketing issues." Estab. 1950's. Circ. 4,000. **Pays on acceptance.** Byline given. Buys first North American serial or second serial (reprint) rights. Editorial lead time 3 months. Submit seasonal material 6 months in advance. Accepts simultaneous and previously published submissions. Query for electronic submissions. Reports in 2 months on queries. Sample copy for #10 SASE.
Nonfiction: Writing only. Poetry (January/February). Buys 25 mss/year. Query or send complete ms. Length: 900 words. Pays $10 or discount on memberships and copies.
Photos: State availability of photos with submission. Reviews 5×7 prints. Offers no additional payment for photos accepted with ms. Model releases and identification of subjects required. Buys one-time rights.
Tips: "Members of National Writers Association are given preference."

BOOK DEALERS WORLD, North American Bookdealers Exchange, P.O. Box 606, Cottage Grove OR 97424. (503)942-7455. Editorial Director: Al Galasso. Senior Editor: Judy Wiggins. 50% freelance written. Quarterly magazine covering writing, self-publishing and marketing books by mail. Circ. 20,000. Pays on publication. Publishes ms an average of 3 months after acceptance. Byline given. Buys first serial and second serial (reprint) rights. Accepts simultaneous and previously published submissions. Reports in 1 month. Sample copy for $3.
Nonfiction: Book excerpts (writing, mail order, direct mail, publishing); how-to (home business by mail, advertising); interview/profile (of successful self-publishers). Positive articles on self-publishing, new writing angles, marketing, etc. Buys 10 mss/year. Send complete ms. Length: 1,000-1,500 words. Pays $25-50.
Columns/Departments: Print Perspective (about new magazines and newsletters); Small Press Scene (news about small press activities); and Self-Publisher Profile (on successful self-publishers and their marketing strategy). Buys 20 mss/year. Send complete ms. Length: 250-1,000 words. Pays $5-20.
Fillers: Fillers concerning writing, publishing or books. Buys 6/year. Length: 100-250 words. Pays $3-10.
Tips: "Query first. Get a sample copy of the magazine."

BYLINE, P.O. Box 130596, Edmond OK 73013-0001. (405)348-5591. Editor/Publisher: Marcia Preston. Managing Editor: Kathryn Fanning. 80-90% freelance written. Eager to work with new/unpublished writers. Monthly magazine for writers and poets. "We stress encouragement of beginning writers." Estab. 1981. Publishes ms an average of 3 months after acceptance. Byline given. Buys first North American serial rights. Reports in 2 months or less. Sample copy for $3.50 postpaid. Writer's guidelines for #10 SASE.
• Ranked as one of the best markets for fiction writers in *Writer's Digest* magazine's biannual "Fiction 50," June 1994.
Nonfiction: How-to, humor, inspirational, personal experience, *all* connected with writing and selling. Read magazine for special departments. Buys approximately 100 mss/year. Prefers queries; will read complete mss. Length: 1,500-1,800 words. Usual rate for features is $50; **pays on acceptance.** Needs short humor on writing (300-600 words). Pays $15-25 on acceptance.
Fiction: General fiction of high quality. Send complete ms: 2,000-3,000 words preferred. Pays $50 on acceptance.
Poetry: Any style, on a writing theme. Preferred length: 4-30 lines. Pays $5-10 on acceptance, plus free issue.
Tips: "We've expanded and will need more manuscripts!"

CANADIAN WRITER'S JOURNAL, Gordon M. Smart Publications, P.O. Box 6618, Depot 1, Victoria, British Columbia V8P 5N7 Canada. (604)477-8807. Editor: Gordon M. Smart. Accepts well-written articles by inexperienced writers. Quarterly magazine for writers. Estab. 1985. Circ. 350. 75% freelance written. Pays on publication, an average of 3-9 months after acceptance. Byline given. Accepts previously published submissions. Send typed ms with rights for sale noted and information about when and where the article previously appeared. For reprints pays 100% of amount paid for an original article. Reports in 2 months. Sample copy $3 with $1 postage. Writer's guidelines for #10 SAE and IRC.
Nonfiction: How-to articles for writers. Buys 50-55 mss/year. Query optional. Length: 500-1,200 words. Pays about $5/published magazine page.
Fiction: Requirements currently being met by annual contest.
Poetry: Short poems or extracts used as part of articles on the writing of poetry. Annual poetry contest. Wind Soup Column uses some short poems. Consult guidelines for details.
Tips: "We prefer short, tightly written, informative how-to articles. US writers note that US postage cannot be used to mail from Canada. Obtain Canadian stamps, use IRCs or send small amounts in cash."

THE COMICS JOURNAL, The Magazine of News and Criticism, Fantagraphics, Inc., 7563 Lake City Way, Seattle WA 98115. (206)524-1967. Editor: Gary Groth. 90% freelance written. Monthly magazine covering the comic book industry. "Comic books can appeal intellectually and emotionally to an adult audience, and can express ideas of which other media are inherently incapable." Estab. 1976. Circ. 15,000. Pays on publication. Publishes ms an average of 2 months after acceptance. Byline given. Buys first rights. Submit seasonal material 5 months in advance. Reports in 2 months. Sample copy for $3.50 and 9 × 12 SAE with 7 first-class stamps.

Nonfiction: Essays, news, exposé, historical, interview/profile, opinion, magazine reviews. Buys 120 mss/year. Send complete ms. Length: 500-3,000 words. Pays 1.5¢/word; writers may request trade for merchandise. Pays the expenses of writers on assignment.

Photos: Send photos with submission. Offers additional payment for photos accepted with ms. Identification of subjects required. Buys one-time rights.

Columns/Departments: Opening Shots (brief commentary, often humorous), 1,000 words; Newswatch (in-depth reporting on the industry, US and foreign news); The Comics Library (graphic review); Ethics (examining the ethics of the comic book industry), both 3,000 words. Buys 60 mss/year. Send complete ms. Pays 1.5¢/word; more for news items.

Tips: "Have an intelligent, sophisticated, critical approach to writing about comic books."

EDITOR & PUBLISHER, 11 W. 19th St., New York NY 10011-4234. Fax: (212)929-1259. Editor: Robert U. Brown. Managing Editor: John Consoli. 10% freelance written. Weekly magazine for newspaper publishers, editors, executives, employees and others in communications, marketing, advertising, etc. Estab. 1884. Circ. 25,000. Pays on publication. Publishes ms an average of 1 month after acceptance. Buys first serial rights. Reports in 2 months. Sample copy for $1.75.

Nonfiction: Uses newspaper business articles and news items; also newspaper personality features and printing technology. Query.

THE EDITORIAL EYE, Focusing on Publications Standards and Practices, EEI, Suite 200, 66 Canal Center Plaza, Alexandria VA 22314-5507. (703)683-0683. Fax: (703)683-4915. Editor: Linda B. Jorgensen. 5-15% range freelance written. Prefers to work with published, established and working professional editors and writers. Monthly professional newsletter on editorial subjects: writing, editing, graphic design, production, quality control and language usage. "Our readers are professional publications people. Use journalistic style but avoid overly general topics and facile prescriptions. Our review process is vigorous." Circ. 5,000. **Pays on acceptance.** Publishes ms an average of 3-6 months after acceptance. Byline given. Buys first North American serial rights. "We retain the right to use articles in our training division and in an anthology of collected articles." Reports in 3 months. Sample copy for #10 SAE with 2 first-class stamps. Guidelines tailored to the article following a proposal or outline.

Nonfiction: Editorial and production problems, issues, standards, practices and techniques; publication management; publishing technology; writing, style, grammar and usage, and neologisms. No word games, vocabulary building, language puzzles or poetry. Buys about 24 mss/year. "Would buy more if quality were higher. *Must* look at sample issue." Query. Length: 500-1,500. Pays $50-200.

Tips: "We seek mostly lead articles written by people in the publications field about the practice of editing or writing. Our style is journalistic with a light touch (not cute). We are interested in submissions on the craft of editing, levels of editing, writing and editing aided by computer, publications management, lexicography, usages, quality control, resources, and interviews with nonfiction writers and editors. Our back issue list provides a good idea of the kinds of articles we run. Do not send articles without looking at a sample. Do not expect an extensive critique. Do not send a vilification of editors and expect me to print it. Welcome repeat work from a roster of writers I'm developing."

EDITORS' FORUM, Editors' Forum Publishing Company, P.O. Box 411806, Kansas City MO 64141-1806. (913)384-2555. Managing Editor: William R. Brinton. 50% freelance written. Prefers to work with published/established writers but works with a small number of new/unpublished writers each year. Monthly newsletter geared toward communicators, particularly those involved in the editing and publication of newsletters and company publications. Estab. 1980. Circ. 1,200. Pays on publication. Publishes ms an average of 4 months after acceptance. Byline given. Offers 25% kill fee. Buys first North American serial and second serial (reprint) rights or makes work-for-hire assignments. Accepts previously published submissions. Send tearsheet or photocopy of article or typed ms with rights for sale noted. For reprints, pays 50% of the amount paid for an original article. Reports in 1 month on queries. Sample copy for 9 × 12 SAE with 2 first-class stamps. Writer's guidelines for #10 SASE.

Nonfiction: How-to on editing and writing, etc. "With the advent of computer publishing, *EF* is running a regular high tech column on desktop publishing, software, etc. We can use articles on the latest techniques in computer publishing. Not interested in anything that does not have a direct effect on writing and editing newsletters. This is a how-to newsletter." Buys 22 mss/year. Query. Length: 250-500 words. Pays $20/page maximum.

Photos: State availability of photos/illustrations with submission. Reviews contact sheets. Offers $5/photo. Captions, model releases and identification of subjects required. Buys one-time rights.

Tips: "We are necessarily interested in articles pertaining to the newsletter business. That would include articles involving writing skills, layout and makeup, the use of pictures and other graphics to brighten up our reader's publication, and an occasional article on how to put out a good publication inexpensively."

‡**FICTION WRITER'S GUIDELINE, The Newsletter of Fiction Writer's Connection (FWC)**, P.O. Box 4065, Deerfield Beach FL 33442-4065. (305)426-4705. Editor: Blythe Camenson. 20% freelance written. Monthly newsletter covering how-to for fiction writers. *"Fiction Writer's Guideline takes an upbeat approach to encourage writers, but doesn't shy away from the sometimes harsh realities of the publishing industry."* Estab. 1993. Circ. 1,000. Pays on publication. Publishes ms an average of 3 months after acceptance. Byline given. Buys first, one-time or second serial (reprint) rights. Editorial lead time 1 month. Submit seasonal material 3 months in advance. Accepts simultaneous and previously published submissions. Reports in 2 weeks on queries; 1 month on mss. Sample copy for #10 SAE with 52¢ postage. Writer's guidelines for #10 SASE.

Nonfiction: General interest, how-to (the business and craft of writing fiction), humor, inspirational, interview/profile (of agents, editors, and authors), new product, personal experience (on getting published) and short book reviews (how-to books for writers). Buys 30 mss/year. Query. Length: 200-1,500 words. Pays $10-25. Sometimes pays expenses of writers on assignment.

Columns/Departments: Advice From An Agent/Editor (how to approach, what they're looking for, advice to fiction writers), 1,500 words; 'Writing Tips' (specific advice on style and structure), 400 words. Buys 12 mss/year. Query. Pays $10-100.

Fillers: Anecdotes, facts, newsbreaks, short humor; all to do with the business or craft of writing fiction. Buys 50/year. Length: 20-100 words. Pays $1-10.

Tips: Looking for "interviews with agents or editors. Our guidelines include specific questions to ask. Query or call first to make sure your choice has not already been interviewed. We also need a cover article each month on some aspect of writing fiction, from specific tips for different categories/genres, to handling viewpoint, characterization, or dialogue etc. Also fillers.Request a sample copy to see the newsletter's format."

‡**FREELANCE**, Saskatchewan Writers Guild, Box 3986, Regina SK S4P 3R9. Editor: April Davies. 25% freelance written. Literary magazine published 10 times/year covering writing. *"FreeLance is the membership newsmagazine of the Saskatchewan Writers Guild. It publishes literary news, news about members, a Saskatchewan literary events calendar, markets and resources information, news on new books by members, updates on SWG programs, articles on the craft or business of writing and literary issues, and comments on these."* Estab. 1969. Circ. 800. Pays on publication. Publishes ms an average of 1-2 months after acceptance. Byline given. Buys first North American serial or second serial (reprint) rights. Editorial lead time 1 month. Accepts previously published submissions. Reports in 3 weeks on queries; 2 months on mss. Sample copy and writer's guidelines free on request.

Nonfiction: Essays (on the craft of writing), how-to (craft or business of writing), interview/profile (writers), new product (writing-related), opinion (literary issues), technical (craft of writing), reports on writers' conferences, colonies, workshops, etc. Buys 25 mss/year. Send complete ms. Length: 600-1,000 words. Pays $40/published page.

Photos: Send photos with submissions. Reviews prints. Offers $10 (based on publication size). Captions required. Buys one-time rights.

FREELANCE WRITER'S REPORT, CNW Publishing, Maple Ridge Rd., North Sandwich NH 03259. (603)284-6367. Fax: (603)284-6648. Editor: Dana K. Cassell. 35% freelance written. Prefers to work with published/established writers. Monthly newsletter covering writing and marketing advice for established freelance writers. Estab. 1982. Pays on publication. Publishes ms an average of 6 months after acceptance. Byline given. Buys one-time rights. Submit seasonal material 2 months in advance. Accepts simultaneous and previously published submissions. Reports in 1 month. Sample of older copy for 9 × 12 envelope with 3 first-class stamps; current copy for $4. No writer's guidelines; refer to this listing.

Nonfiction: Book excerpts (on writing profession); how-to (market, write, research); new product (only those pertaining to writers); photojournalism; promotion and administration of a writing business. No humor, fiction or poetry. Buys 100 mss/year. Send complete ms. Length: 500 words maximum. Pays 10¢/edited word to subscribers; non-subscribers receive a trade-out subscription equal to 10¢/edited word.

Tips: "Write in terse newsletter style, eliminate flowery adjectives and edit mercilessly. Send something that will help writers increase profits from writing output—must be a proven method. We're targeting more to the established writer, less to the beginner."

‡**GOTTA WRITE NETWORK LITMAG**, Maren Publications, 612 Cobblestone Circle, Glenview IL 60025. Fax: (708)296-7631. Editor: Denise Fleischer. 60-80% freelance written. Semiannual literary magazine covering writer's techniques, markets. "Any article should be presented as if openly speaking to the reader. It should inform from the first paragraph to the last." Estab. 1988. Circ. 200. Pays before publication. Publishes ms an average of 2-6 months after acceptance. Byline given. Buys first North American serial rights or makes work-for-hire assignments. Editorial lead time 6 months. Submit seasonal material 6 months in advance. Reports in 2-4 months. Sample copy for $5. Writer's guidelines for #10 SASE.

Nonfiction: Articles (on writing), how-to (on writing techniques), interview/profile (for Behind the Scenes section), new product (books, software, computers), photo feature (on poets/writers/editors big and small press). "Don't want to see 'My First Sale,' 'When I Can't Write,' 'Dealing With Rejection,' 'Writer's Block,' a speech from a writers convention, an article published 10 times by other editors." Buys 25 mss/year. Query with published clips. Send complete ms. Length: 3-5 pages. Pays $5 and contributors copy.

Photos: Freelancers should state availability of photos with submission. Reviews contact sheets and prints (standard b&w or color). Offers $10 ($20 for cover art). Captions, model releases and identification of subjects required. Buys one-time rights.

Columns/Departments: Poetry Scene (focus on poetry groups, slams, publications), 3 pages maximum; In Print (writing books—reviews), 2 pages. Buys 50 mss/year. Pays $5-10.

Fiction: Adventure, ethnic, experimental, fantasy, historical, horror, humorous, mainstream, mystery, romance, science fiction, slice-of-life vignettes, suspense, western. No dark fantasy. Buys 15 and up mss/year. Query with published clips. Send complete ms. Page length: 5-10. Pays $10 maximum.

Poetry: Avant-garde, free verse, haiku, beat—experimental. No poetry no can understand or that has no meaning.

Fillers: Anecdotes, facts, newsbreaks, tips. Buys 100/year. Length: 100-250 words. Pays in contributor's copies. Open to editor's releases, feature ideas and product information from the manufacturer.

HOUSEWIFE-WRITER'S FORUM, P.O. Box 780, Lyman WY 82937-0780. (307)786-4513. Editor: Diane Wolverton. 90% freelance written. Bimonthly newsletter and literary magazine for women writers. "We are a support network and writer's group on paper directed to the unique needs of women who write and juggle home life." Estab. 1988. Circ. 1,500. **Pays on acceptance.** Publishes ms an average of 6-12 months after acceptance. Byline given. Buys first North American serial rights. Submit seasonal material 6 months in advance. Simultaneous and previously published submissions sometimes used. Send typed ms with rights for sale noted, information about when and where the article previously appeared. For reprints, pays 50-75% of the amount paid for an original article. Reports in 1 month on queries; 2-3 months on mss. Sample copy for $3. Writer's guidelines for #10 SASE.

Nonfiction: Essays, how-to, humor, interview/profile, opinion, personal experience. Buys 60-100 mss/year. Query with or without published clips. Length: 2,000 words maximum, 1,000-1,500 words preferred. Pays 1¢/ word.

Columns/Departments: Confessions of Housewife-Writers (essays pertaining to our lives as women and writers). Buys 30-40 mss/year. Send complete ms. Length: 250-750 words. Pays 1¢/word. Share a book, tape, video, helpful hint—anything that has made your life as a writer easier, more profitable or more fun. Length: 150-250 words. Pays $3.

Fiction: Bob Haynie, fiction editor. Experimental, fantasy, historical, humorous, mainstream, mystery, romance, science fiction, and suspense. No pornography. Buys 12-15 mss/year. Send complete ms. Length: 2,000 words maximum. Pays 1¢/word.

Poetry: Avant-garde, free verse, light verse, traditional and humorous. Buys 30-60 poems/year. Submit maximum 5 poems at one time. 45 lines maximum. Pays $2 maximum.

Tips: "Our tone is warm, nurturing and supportive to writers in all stages of their writing careers. We favor how-to articles on writing and getting published and would like to see more interviews with writers who have achieved some degree of success. Our 'Confessions' department is for all the fun, interesting, funny, tragic, unbelievable things that happen to you as a Housewife-Writer."

NEW WRITER'S MAGAZINE, Sarasota Bay Publishing, P.O. Box 5976, Sarasota FL 34277-5976. (813)953-7903. Editor: George J. Haborak. 95% freelance written. Bimonthly magazine for new writers. *"New Writer's Magazine* believes that *all* writers are *new* writers in that each of us can learn from one another. So, we reach *pro* and non-pro alike." Estab. 1986. Circ. 5,000. Pays on publication. Byline given. Buys first rights. Reports in 2 weeks on queries; 1 month on mss. *Writer's Market* recommends allowing 2 months for reply. Sample copy for $3. Writer's guidelines for #10 SASE.

Nonfiction: General interest, how-to (for new writers), humor, interview/profile, opinion, personal experience (with *pro* writer). Buys 50 mss/year. Send complete ms. Length: 700-1,000 words. Pays $10-50 for assigned and unsolicited articles.

Photos: Send photos with submission. Reviews 5 × 7 prints. Offers no additional payment for photos accepted with ms. Captions required.

Fiction: Experimental, historical, humorous, mainstream, slice-of-life vignettes. "Again, we do *not* want anything that does not have a tie-in with the writing life or writers in general." Buys 2-6 mss/year. "We offer a special fiction contest held each year with cash prizes." Send complete ms. Length: 700-800 words. Pays $20-40.

Poetry: Free verse, light verse, traditional. Does not want anything *not* for writers. Buys 10-20 poems/year. Submit maximum 3 poems. Length: 8-20 lines. Pays $5 maximum.

Fillers: Anecdotes, facts, newsbreaks, short humor. Buys 5-15/year. Length: 20-100 words. Pays $5 maximum. Cartoons, writing lifestyle slant. Buys 20-30/year. Pays $10 maximum. Buys 5-15/year. Length: 20-100 words. Pays $5 maximum.

Tips: "Any article *with photos* has a good chance, especially an *up close & personal* interview with an established professional writer offering advice, etc."

‡OHIO WRITER, Poets League of Greater Cleveland, P.O. Box 528, Willoughby OH 44094. Editor: Linda Rome. 90% freelance written. Bimonthly covering writing and Ohio writers. Estab. 1987. Pays on publication. Publishes ms an average of 4 months after acceptance. Byline given. Buys one-time rights and second serial (reprint) rights. Editorial lead time 4 months. Submit seasonal material 4 months in advance. Accepts previously published submissions. Reports in 1 month. Sample copy for $2. Writer's guidelines for SASE.

Nonfiction: Essays, how-to, humor, inspirational, interview/profile, opinion, personal experience—"all must relate to the writing life or Ohio writers, or Ohio publishing scene." Buys 24 mss/year. Send complete ms. Length: 1,000-2,000 words. Pays $25 minimum, up to $50 for lead article; other payment under arrangement with writer. Pays expenses of writers on assignment.

Columns/Departments: Subjectively Yours (opinions, controversial stance on writing life), 1,500 words; Reviews (Ohio writers, publishers or publishing), 500 words; Focus On (Ohio publishing scene, how to write/publish certain kind of writing (e.g., travel). Buys 6 mss/year. Send complete ms. Pays $25-50; $5/book review.

Tips: "Profiles and interviews of writers who live in Ohio are always needed."

‡POETS & WRITERS, 3rd Floor, 72 Spring St., New York NY 10012. (212) Contact: Jane Ludlam, managing editor. 100% freelance written. Bimonthly professional trade journal for poets and fiction writers. No original poetry or fiction. Estab. 1973. Circ. 48,000. **Pays on acceptance** of finished draft. Publishes ms an average of 4 months after acceptance. Byline given. Offers 25% kill fee. Copyright reverts to the author upon publication. Buys first North American serial and first rights or makes work-for-hire assignments. Editorial lead time 1 year. Submit seasonal material 1 year in advance. Accepts simultaneous submissions. Query for electronic submissions. Reports in 6 weeks on mss. Sample copy for $3.95 to Circulation Dept. Writer's guidelines for #10 SASE.

Nonfiction: Essays (personal essays about literature), how-to (craft of poetry or fiction writing), interview/profile with poets or fiction writers (no Q&A), regional reports of literary activity, reports on small presses, service pieces about publishing trends. Buys 35 mss/year. Query with published clips or send complete ms. Length: 1,500-3,600 words.

Photos: State availability of photos with submission. Reviews b&w prints. Offers no additional payment for photos accepted with ms.

Columns/Departments: News (literary and publishing news), 500-600 words; author profiles (of emerging and established poets and fiction writers), 2,400-3,600 words; regional reports (literary activity in US), 1,800-3,600 words. Buys 24 mss/year. Query with published clips. Send complete ms. Pays $100-300.

RISING STAR, 47 Byledge Rd., Manchester NH 03104. (603)623-9796. Editor: Scott E. Green. 50% freelance written. Bimonthly newsletter on science fiction and fantasy markets for writers and artists. Estab. 1980. Circ. 150. Pays on publication. Publishes ms an average of 3 months after acceptance. Byline given. Not copyrighted. Buys first rights. Accepts simultaneous and previously published submissions. Send tearsheet of article or typed ms with rights for sale noted and information about when and where the article previously appeared. For reprints, pays 100% of the amount paid for an original article. Reports in 1 month on queries. Sample copy for $1.50 and #10 SASE. Free writer's guidelines. Subscription $7.50 for 6 issues, payable to Scott Green.

Nonfiction: Book excerpts, essays, interview/profile, opinion. Buys 8 mss/year. Query. Length: 500-900 words. Pays $3 minimum.

ST. LOUIS JOURNALISM REVIEW, 8380 Olive Blvd., St. Louis MO 63132. (314)991-1699. Fax: (314)997-1898. Editor/Publisher: Charles L. Klotzer. 50% freelance written. Prefers to work with published/established writers. Monthly tabloid newspaper critiquing St. Louis media, print, broadcasting, TV and cable primarily by working journalists and others. Also covers issues not covered adequately by dailies. Occasionally buys articles on national media criticism. Estab. 1970. Circ. 5,500. Buys all rights. Byline given. Sample copy for $2.50.

Nonfiction: "We buy material which analyzes, critically, St. Louis metro area media and, less frequently, national media institutions, personalities or trends." No taboos. Pays the expenses of writers on assignment subject to prior approval.

SCAVENGER'S NEWSLETTER, 519 Ellinwood, Osage City KS 66523-1329. (913)528-3538. Editor: Janet Fox. 15% freelance written. Eager to work with new/unpublished writers. Monthly newsletter covering markets for science fiction/fantasy/horror/mystery materials especially with regard to the small press. Estab. 1984. Circ. 1,000. Publishes ms an average of 8 months after acceptance. Byline given. Not copyrighted. Places copyright symbol on title page; rights revert to contributor on publication. Buys one-time rights. Accepts simultaneous and previously published submissions. Send information about when and where the article previously appeared. For reprints, pays 100% of amount paid for an original article. Reports in 1 month. Sample copy for $2. Writer's guidelines for #10 SASE.

Nonfiction: Essays, general interest, how-to (write, sell, publish science fiction/fantasy/horror/mystery), humor, interview/profile (writers, artists in the field), opinion. Buys 12-15 mss/year. Send complete ms. Length: 1,000 words maximum. **Pays on acceptance**, $4.

Poetry: Avant-garde, free verse, haiku, traditional. All related to science fiction/fantasy/horror/mystery genres. Buys 36 poems/year. Submit maximum 3 poems. Length: 10 lines maximum. **Pays on acceptance**, $2.

Tips: "Because this is a small publication, it has occasional overstocks. We're especially looking for science fiction/fantasy/horror/mystery commentary as opposed to writer's how-to's."

SMALL PRESS REVIEW, P.O. Box 100, Paradise CA 95967. Editor: Len Fulton. Monthly for "people interested in small presses and magazines, current trends and data; many libraries." Circ. 3,500. Byline given. "Query if you're unsure." Reports in 2 months. Free sample copy.

Nonfiction: News, short reviews, photos, short articles on small magazines and presses. Uses how-to, personal experience, interview, profile, spot news, historical, think, photo, and coverage of merchandising techniques. Accepts 50-200 mss/year. Length: 100-200 words.

THE WRITER, 120 Boylston St., Boston MA 02116-4615. Editor-in-Chief/Publisher: Sylvia K. Burack. 20-25% freelance written. Prefers to buy work of published/established writers. Monthly. Estab. 1887. **Pays on acceptance.** Publishes ms an average of 6-8 months after acceptance. Buys first serial rights. Sample copy for $3.

Nonfiction: Practical articles for writers on how to write for publication, and how and where to market manuscripts in various fields. Will consider all submissions promptly. No assignments. Length: 2,000 words maximum.

Tips: "New types of publications and our continually updated market listings in all fields will determine changes of focus and fact."

WRITERS CONNECTION, P.O. Box 24770, San Jose CA 95154-4770. Editor: Jan Stiles. 60% freelance written. Works with new/unpublished writers each year. Monthly newsletter covering writing and publishing. Estab. 1983. Circ. 2,500. Pays in services on acceptance or in cash on publication. Publishes ms an average of 8 months after acceptance for articles; much less for column updates. Byline given on articles. Buys first serial or second serial (reprint) rights. Submit seasonal material 4 months in advance. Accepts previously published submissions. Send typed ms with rights for sale noted and information about when and where the article previously appeared. For reprints, pays 50-60% of amount paid for an original article. Prefers complete ms. Reports in 2 months. Sample copy for $5 postpaid. Writer's guidelines for #10 SASE.

Nonfiction: Book excerpts (on writing/publishing); how-to (write and publish, market your writing); interview/profile (editors, agents, writers and publishers with how-to or marketing slant); new product occasionally (books, videotapes, software etc., on writing and publishing); writing for business and technical fields. "All types of writing from technical to romance novels and article writing are treated." No personal experience without a strong how-to slant. Buys 25-32 mss/year. Length: 800-1,800 words. Pays $25-75 on publication, or in certificates, on acceptance, for $50 to $150 toward WC membership and/or conferences.

Columns/Departments: Markets, contests, events, etc., are staff-written. Send information or announcements 6 weeks in advance of issue date for free listings in our newsletter; space available basis.

Tips: "We are currently seeking how-to articles that will benefit writers working for business and high-tech companies. The focus for these articles should appeal to the working professional writer. Also, find and report on new markets where freelancers can break in. Provide new techniques, ideas or perspectives for writing fiction or nonfiction; present your ideas in a lively, but practical style. No parodies or sarcasm, please. And no why-I-have-to-write or how-I-faced-writer's-block essays. We see (and return) far too many of these."

WRITER'S DIGEST, 1507 Dana Ave., Cincinnati OH 45207. (513)531-2222. Submissions Editor: Angela Terez. 90% freelance written. Monthly magazine about writing and publishing. "Our readers write fiction, poetry, nonfiction, plays and all kinds of creative writing. They're interested in improving their writing skills, improving their sales ability, and finding new outlets for their talents." Estab. 1921. Circ. 225,000. **Pays on acceptance.** Publishes ms an average of 1 year after acceptance. Buys first North American serial rights for one-time editorial use, microfilm/microfiche use and magazine promotional use. Pays 20% kill fee. Byline given. Submit seasonal material 8 months in advance. Accepts previously published submissions from noncompeting markets. Send tearsheet or photocopy of article, noting rights for sale and when and where the article previously appeared. Query for electronic submissions. "We're able to use electronic submissions only for accepted pieces and will discuss details if we buy your work. We'll accept computer printout submissions, of course — but they *must* be readable. We strongly recommend letter-quality. If you don't want your manuscript returned, indicate that on the first page of the manuscript or in a cover letter." Reports in 3-6 weeks. Sample copy for $3. Writer's guidelines for #10 SASE.

• *Writer's Digest* was ranked as one of the best freelance markets in *Writer's Digest* magazine's annual "Top 100 Markets," January 1994.

Nonfiction: "Our mainstay is the how-to article — that is, an article telling how to write and sell more of what you write. For instance, how to write compelling leads and conclusions, how to improve your character descriptions, how to become more efficient and productive. We like plenty of examples, anecdotes and $$$ in our articles — so other writers can actually see what's been done successfully by the author of a particular piece. We like our articles to speak directly to the reader through the use of the first-person voice. Don't submit an article on what five book editors say about writing mysteries. Instead, submit an article on how you cracked the mystery market and how our readers can do the same. But don't limit the article to your experiences; include the opinions of those five editors to give your article increased depth and authority." General interest (about writing); how-to (writing and marketing techniques that work); humor (short pieces); inspirational; interview and profile (query first); new product; personal experience (marketing and freelancing experiences). "We can always use articles on fiction and nonfiction technique, and solid articles on poetry or scriptwriting are always welcome. No articles titled 'So You Want to Be a Writer,' and no first-person pieces that ramble without giving a lesson or something readers can learn from in the sharing of the story." Buys 90-100 mss/year. Queries are preferred, but complete mss OK. Length: 500-3,000 words. Pays 10¢/word minimum. Sometimes pays expenses of writers on assignment.

Photos: Used only with interviews and profiles. State availability of photos or send contact sheet with ms. Captions required.

Columns/Departments: Chronicle (first-person narratives about the writing life; length: 1,200-1,500 words); The Writing Life (length: 50-800 words); and Tip Sheet (short items that offer solutions to writing and freelance business-related problems that writers commonly face). Buys approximately 200 articles/year for Writing Life and Tip Sheet sections. Send complete ms.

Poetry: Light verse about "the writing life"—joys and frustrations of writing. "We are also considering poetry other than short light verse—but related to writing, publishing, other poets and authors, etc." Buys an average of 1 an issue. Submit poems in batches of 1-8. Length: 2-20 lines. Pays $10-50/poem.

Fillers: Anecdotes and short humor, primarily for use in The Writing Life column. Uses up to 4/issue. Length: 50-250 words.

WRITER'S FORUM, Writer's Digest School, 1507 Dana Ave., Cincinnati OH 45207. (513)531-2222. Editor: Tom Clark. 100% freelance written. Quarterly newsletter covering writing techniques, marketing and inspiration for students enrolled in fiction and nonfiction writing courses offered by Writer's Digest School. Estab. 1970. Circ. 13,000. **Pays on acceptance.** Publishes ms an average of 6 months after acceptance. Byline given. Buys first serial or second serial (reprint) rights. Submit seasonal/holiday material 4 months in advance. Accepts simultaneous and previously published submissions. Query for electronic submissions. Reports in 4-6 weeks. Free sample copy.

Nonfiction: How-to (write or market short stories, or articles, novels and nonfiction books) and inspirational articles that will motivate beginning writers. Buys 12 mss/year. Prefers complete mss to queries. "If you prefer to query, please do so by mail, not phone." Length: 500-1,000 words. Pays $10-25.

WRITER'S GUIDELINES: A Roundtable for Writers and Editors, Box 608, Pittsburg MO 65724. Fax: (417)993-5544. Editor: Susan Salaki. 97% freelance written. Bimonthly roundtable forum and market news reports for writers and editors. "We are interested in what writers on both sides of the desk have to say about the craft of writing." Estab. 1988. Circ. 1,000. Pays on publication. Byline given. Rights to the original work revert to contributors after publication. Reports in 1 week. Sample copy for $4. Writer's guidelines for #10 SASE.

Nonfiction: General interest, historical articles on writers/writing, psychological aspects of being a writer, how-to, interview/profile, personal experience, humor, fillers. Buys 20 mss/year. Prefer disposable photocopy submissions complete with SASE. May use both sides of each sheet of paper to save postage costs. Include SASE with all correspondence. Length: 800-1,000 words. Pay varies from copies to up to $25.

Fillers: Facts about writing or writers, short humor and cartoons, "wide-open to any facts of interest to writers or editors." No payment for fillers.

Tips: "If you believe what you have to say about writing or editing has needed to be said for some time now, then I'm interested. If you say it well, I'll buy it. This is a unique publication in that we offer original guidelines for over 300 magazine and book publishers and because of this service, writers and editors are linked in a new and exciting way—as correspondents. Articles that help to bridge the gap which has existed between these two professions have the best chance of being accepted. Publishing background does not matter. Include a short biography and cover letter with your submissions."

WRITER'S JOURNAL, Minnesota Ink, Inc., Suite 328, 3585 N. Lexington Ave., Arden Hills MN 55126. (612)486-7818. Publisher/Managing Editor: Valerie Hockert. Poetry Editor: Esther M. Leiper. 40% freelance written. Bimonthly. Circ. 49,000. Pays on publication. Publishes ms an average of 4 months after acceptance. Byline given. Buys first North American serial rights. Submit seasonal material 6 months in advance. Simultaneous queries OK. Query for electronic submissions. Reports in 1 month on queries; 6 weeks on mss. Sample copy for $4. Writer's guidelines for #10 SASE.

Nonfiction: How-to (on the business and approach to writing), motivational, interview/profile, opinion. "*Writer's Journal* publishes articles on style, technique, editing methods, copy writing, research, writing of news releases, writing news stories and features, creative writing, grammar reviews, marketing, the business aspects of writing, copyright law and legal advice for writers/editors, independent book publishing, interview techniques, and more." Also articles on the use of computers by writers and a book review section. Buys 30-40 mss/year. Send complete ms. Length: 700-1,000 words. Pays to $50.

Poetry: Avant-garde, free verse, haiku, light verse, traditional. "The *Writer's Journal* runs two poetry contests each year in the spring and fall: Winner, 2nd, 3rd place and 10 honorable mentions." Buys 20-30 poems/year. Submit maximum 5 poems. Length: 25 lines maximum. Pays 25¢ line.

Tips: "Articles must be *well* written and slanted toward the business (or commitment) of writing and/or being a writer. Interviews with established writers should be in-depth, particularly reporting interviewee's philosophy on writing, how he or she got started, etc." The *Writer's Journal* now incorporates Minnesota Ink. Minnesota Ink is 100% freelance written and contains fiction and poetry.

‡**THE WRITER'S NOOK NEWS**, #181, 38114 3rd St., Willoughby OH 44094-6140. (216)953-9292. Fax: (216)354-6403. E-mail submissions: comprophet@delphi.com. Editor/Publisher: Eugene Ortiz. 100% freelance written. quarterly newsletter for professional writers. "We don't print fluff, anecdotes or platitudes. Articles must be specific, terse, pithy and contain information readers can put to immediate, practical use. Every article should be the kind you want to cut out and tape to your desk somewhere." Estab. 1985. Circ. 2,000. **Pays on acceptance.** Publishes ms an average of 5 months after acceptance. Byline given. Publication is not copyrighted. Buys first North American serial rights. Reports within 6 months. Sample copy for $5. Writer's guidelines for 9×12 SAE with 2 first-class stamps.

Nonfiction: How-to and interview/profile (writing and marketing). "No essays, poetry, fiction, ruminations or anecdotes. Will accept an occasional positive, thoughtful essay." Buys 80 mss/year. Send complete ms with credits and short bio. Length: 100-400 words. Pays 6¢/word.

Photos: Send photos with submission. Reviews b&w prints. Offers $5/photo maximum. Identification of subjects required. Buys one-time rights.

Columns/Departments: Book Bench (short reviews of books related to writing), 400 words; Conferences & Klatches (listings of conferences and gatherings), 400-1,200 words; Contests & Awards (listings of contests and awards), 400 words; Writer's Rights (latest information on what's happening on Capitol Hill), 400 words; Markets (listings of information on markets for writers), 400 words. Buys 80 mss/year. Length: 400 words. Pays 6¢/word.

Fillers: Facts and newsbreaks. Buys 20/year. Length: 20-100 words. Pays 6¢/word.

Tips: "Take the writer's guidelines very seriously. 90% of the best submissions are still about 25% fluff. Don't tell me how hard or impossible it is to write anything of worth in only 400 words. This is not a market for beginners. Particularly looking for genre tips. Any genre. I need more helpful information for established writers, on alternative ways of earning money as a writer, songwriter, playwriter and screenwriter. Also looking for articles on functional illiteracy, first amendment rights, use of process theory and Internet. Nook News costs $5 for a sample copy and $18 for a one-year subscription. Now is the time to wisely invest in your career. Unfortunately, writers increasingly try to sell me articles even though they are unqualified. It would be better to subscribe and learn how to make sales elsewhere. Don't be penny wise and pound foolish."

WRITERS OPEN FORUM, Bristol Publishing, P.O. Box 516, Tracyton WA 98393-0516. Editorial Director: Sandra E. Haven. Fiction Editor: Paul Keck. 90% freelance written. Bimonthly publication designed to publish aspiring writers' stories, and to forward resulting responses from readers. Estab. 1990. Buys first rights. Byline and brief bio given. No poetry. Also offers a column of tips from readers, a markets listing, and a lesson on writing in each issue. Submit mss with SASE, cover letter, clear copies (not originals as notations may be made prior to return). No multiple or simultaneous submissions. Reports in 6 weeks. Guidelines and contest information available for SASE and details on upcoming themes or special Junior and Senior editions. Sample copy for $3; subscription $14.

• Ranked as one of the best markets for fiction writers in *Writer's Digest* magazine's biannual "Fiction 50," June 1994.

Columns/Departments: Writer to Writer: tips on writing sent in by writers (max. 300 words), pays 1 copy; Perspectives: 1 essay published per issue that offers a writer's personal, philosophic and/or humorous perspective (maximum 500 words), pays $5 and 3 contributor copies. Send complete ms; mark for intended column.

Fiction: Any genre (no slice-of-life, violence, graphic sex or experimental formats). "We also publish 2 special editions. Stories written for, about, and/or by those aged 6-18 can be submitted for our Juniors edition (mark manuscript accordingly). Stories that concern the lives of seniors as well as manuscripts written by seniors can be submitted for our Seniors edition (mark manuscript accordingly). Stories published will be open to responses by readers. Send complete ms. Book excerpts considered if they are so marked and within our fiction limits (include brief overview of book). Length: 2,000 words maximum, 600-1,200 preferred. **Pays on acceptance**, $5, plus 3 copies.

Tips: "Shorter manuscripts have greater chance of acceptance. In stories we like definite plots and resolutions resulting from the main character's action and/or decision. Always include a cover letter telling us a bit about yourself and your manuscript's intended audience (children's story, mystery, whatever). All sincere submissions (clean copy, guidelines followed, cover letter included) receive a personal reply; all subscriber submissions receive a brief critique."

‡**WRITERS' REPORT, A Monthly Review of Products & Services for Writers**, Juhl Communications, P.O. Box 27614, Lansing MI 48909. (517)394-1364. Editor: Karel Juhl. 90% freelance written. Monthly trade newsletter for writers. "We publish reviews of books, workshops, videos, software and other writing tools currently on the market to aid writers in making informed purchase decisions." Estab. 1994. **Pays on acceptance.** Publishes ms an average of 3 months after acceptance. Byline given. Buys first north American serial or second serial (reprint) rights. Editorial lead time 3 months. Submit seasonal material 5 months in advance. Accepts simultaneous and previously published submissions. Query for electronic submissions. Reports in 2 months. Sample copy for $1. Writer's guidelines for #10 SASE.

Nonfiction: Interview/profile, new product, (product reviews on books, workshops, videos, schools, services, etc. marketed to staff and freelance writers.) "Nothing on how to get published; how to write novels/stories/ articles/poems/screenplays. No reviews of one-time only workshops or seminars that readers will have no further opportunity of attending." Buys 18 mss/year. Query with published clips. Length: 500-2,500 words. Pays $10.

Photos: State availability of photos with submission. Reviews prints. Negotiates payment individually.

Columns/Departments: In A Word (short reviews on products with a narrower audience), 100-500 words. Buys 15-30 mss/year. Send complete ms. Pays $5-10.

Fillers: Anecdotes, facts, gags to be illustrated by cartoonist, newsbreaks, short humor, poems (max. 10 lines). Length: 100 words. Byline only; no payment for fillers used in our Readers' Corner.

Tips: "Our style is relaxed. We need reviews with broad and limited appeal that will help readers decide which books/equipment/software to buy; which workshops/schools/conferences to attend, etc. Workshop reviewers shouldn't tell what we missed by not attending this year's event, but what we can expect if we go next year. Reviewers must sign a statement of non-bias in a product's success/failure, and readers are encouraged to tell, through the letters column, why they agree or disagree with a review. 'In A Word' is most open to freelancers. Feel free to write first person and put feeling into why, specifically, you liked/disliked the product or service. SASE a must!"

WRITER'S YEARBOOK, 1507 Dana Ave., Cincinnati OH 45207. Submissions Editor: Angela Terez. 90% freelance written. Newsstand annual for freelance writers, journalists and teachers of creative writing. "Please note that the *Yearbook* is currently using a 'best of' format. That is, we are reprinting the best writing about writing published in the last year: articles, fiction and book excerpts. The *Yearbook* now uses little original material, so do not submit queries or original manuscripts. We will, however, consider already-published material for possible inclusion." Estab. 1929. Buys reprint rights. Accepts previously published submissions. Send tearsheet or photocopy of article, noting rights for sale and when and where the article previously appeared. Pays 20% kill fee. Byline given. **Pays on acceptance.** Publishes ms an average of 6 months after acceptance. "If you don't want your manuscript returned, indicate that on the first page of the manuscript or in a cover letter."

Nonfiction: "In reprints, we want articles that reflect the current state of writing in America: trends, inside information, and money-saving and money-making ideas for the freelance writer. We try to touch on the various facets of writing in each issue of the *Yearbook*—from fiction to poetry to playwriting, and any other endeavor a writer can pursue. How-to articles—that is, articles that explain in detail how to do something—are very important to us. For example, you could explain how to establish mood in fiction, how to improve interviewing techniques, how to write for and sell to specialty magazines, or how to construct and market a good poem. We are also interested in the writer's spare time—what she/he does to retreat occasionally from the writing wars, where and how to refuel and replenish the writing spirit. 'How Beats the Heart of a Writer' features interest us, if written warmly, in the first person, by a writer who has had considerable success. We also want interviews or profiles of well-known bestselling authors, always with good pictures. Articles on writing techniques that are effective today are always welcome. We provide how-to features and information to help our readers become more skilled at writing and successful at selling their writing." Buys 15-20 mss (reprints only)/year. Length: 750-4,500 words. Pays 2½¢/word minimum.

Photos: Interviews and profiles must be accompanied by high-quality photos. Reviews b&w photos only, depending on use. Captions required.

WRITING CONCEPTS, The Business Communications Report, Suite 720, 7481 Huntsman Blvd., Springfield VA 22153-1648. Editor/Publisher: John De Lellis. Monthly business newsletter on writing, editing, publication management and production, communications and publications technology, public relations and marketing. "Our readers are experienced staff professionals responsible for communications and publications in businesses, corporations and nonprofit organizations. They need specific, practical advice on how to do their job better." Estab. 1983. Pays within 45 days of acceptance. Publishes ms an average of 2 months after acceptance. Byline sometimes given. Buys all rights. Editorial lead time 2 months. Need submissions on 3.5" disk in both ASCII and word processing format. Reports in 6 weeks on queries. Two sample copies and writer's guidelines for $3.00 and #10 SASE with .75¢ postage.

• *Writing Concepts* does *not* use material on how to get published or on the business side of freelance writing/editing.

Nonfiction: "Practical, short, well-researched, how-to articles geared to organizational staff communications/publications managers. We need source and ordering information for each article. See sample issues for style. No humor, opinion, inspirational items. All articles must be *interviews* of leading experts in the communications field. No long articles, except special reports. We are open to ideas for 3,000 word special reports in the communications and publication production field." Buys 20 mss/year. Length: 100-600 words. Pays 15¢/word.

Photos: State availability of photos with submission. Offers no additional payment for photos accepted with ms.

Column/Departments: Publications Management, Quick Takes (useful sources, tips on publications, communications, writing and editing, PR and marketing, and communications/publications technology), Writing Techniques (*business* writing for organization staffers), Style Matters (business editing for organization staffers), PR and Marketing, and Technology Watch (technology trends/issues relating to communications and publications work in organizations).

Tips: "Read sample issues and editorial guidelines *before* you query. The Publications Management, Technology Watch, Quick Takes and PR and Marketing departments are most open to freelancers."

‡**WRITING FOR MONEY,** P.O. Box 1144, Hendersonville NC 28793. (704)696-9708. Editor: John Clausen. 25% freelance written. Trade newsletter published every 3 weeks covering freelance writing opportunities. "Our newsletter covers writing opportunities for freelance magazine writers and copywriters, authors, script writers, screenplay writers, playwrights, catalog copywriters, greeting card writers, and just about every kind of writer looking to make a buck." Estab. 1993. Circ. 3,500. **Pays on acceptance.** Publishes ms an average of 2 months after acceptance. Byline given. Buys first North American serial and non-exclusive reprint rights. Editorial lead time 2 months (sometimes shorter). Submit seasonal material 3 months in advance. Query for electronic submissions. Reports in 6 weeks on queries; 6 months on mss. Sample copy for $5. Writer's guidelines for #10 SASE.
Columns/Departments: 1st Person (personal success stories from freelancers), 500-900 words; Business Tactics (ways for freelancers to handle the "business side" of writing), 500-900 words; Other Markets (new, innovative ways for freelancers to make money writing), 500-900 words. Buys 50 mss/year. Query with published clips. Pays $50.
Tips: "Study the back issues to see what we are buying."

Law

While all of these publications deal with topics of interest to attorneys, each has a particular slant. Be sure that your subject is geared to a specific market – lawyers in a single region, law students, paralegals, etc. Publications for law enforcement personnel are listed under Government and Public Service.

ABA JOURNAL, American Bar Association, Dept. WM, 6th Floor, 750 N. Lake Shore Dr., Chicago IL 60611. (312)988-5000. Fax: (312)988-6014. Editor: Gary A. Hengstler. Managing Editor: Kerry Klumpe. 35% freelance written. Prefers to work with published/established writers. Monthly magazine covering law and lawyers. "The content of the *Journal* is designed to appeal to the association's diverse membership with emphasis on the general practitioner." Circ. 400,000. **Pays on acceptance.** Publishes ms an average of 2 months after acceptance. Byline given. "Editor works with writer until article is in acceptable form." Buys all rights. Submit seasonal material 3 months in advance. Accepts simultaneous submissions. Query for electronic submissions. Reports in 1 month. Free sample copy and writer's guidelines.
Nonfiction: Book excerpts, general interest (legal), how-to (law practice techniques), interview/profile (law firms and prominent individuals), technical (legal trends). "The emphasis of the *Journal* is on the practical problems faced by lawyers in general practice and how those problems can be overcome. Articles should emphasize the practical rather than the theoretical or esoteric. Writers should avoid the style of law reviews, academic journals or legal briefs and should write in an informal, journalistic style. Short quotations from people and specific examples of your point will improve an article." Special issues have featured women and minorities in the legal profession. Buys 30 mss/year. Send complete ms. Length: 3,000 words. Pays $350-2,000. Pays expenses of writers on assignment.
Tips: "We require more sophisticated treatment of complex topics in a narrative style. Writers must provide sidebars and breakouts. Write to us with a specific idea in mind and spell out how the subject would be covered. Full-length profiles and feature articles are always needed. We look for practical information. If *The New York Times* or *Wall Street Journal* would like your style, so will we."

THE ALTMAN WEIL PENSA REPORT TO LEGAL MANAGEMENT, Altman Weil Pensa Publications, 1100 Commerce Dr., Racine WI 53406. (414)886-1304. Fax: (414)886-1139. Editor: James Wilber. 15-20% freelance written. Works with a small number of new/unpublished writers each year. Monthly newsletter covering law office management purchases (equipment, insurance services, space, etc.) and technology. Estab. 1974. Circ. 2,200. Pays on publication. Publishes ms an average of 3-6 months after acceptance. Byline given. Buys all rights; sometimes second serial (reprint) rights. Accepts previously published material. Send photocopy of article or short story, typed ms with rights for sale noted plus diskette, and information about when and where the article previously appeared. For reprints, pays 50% of the amount paid for an original article. Query for electronic submissions. Reports in 1 month on queries; 2-3 months on mss. Sample copy for #10 SASE.
Nonfiction: How-to (buy, use, repair), interview/profile, new product. "Looking especially for practical, "how-to" articles on law office management and technology." Buys 12 mss/year. Query. Submit a sample of previous writing. Length: 500-2,500 words. Pays $125/published page.

BARRISTER, American Bar Association Press, 750 N. Lake Shore Dr., Chicago IL 60611-4403. (312)988-6068. Fax: (312)988-6281. Editor: Cie Brown-Armstead. 60% freelance written. Prefers to work with published/established writers. Quarterly magazine for young lawyers who are members of the American Bar Association concerned about practice of law, career trends, public service, social issues, personalities. Estab. 1971. Circ.

175,000. **Pays on acceptance.** Publishes ms an average of 3-6 months after acceptance. Buys first serial rights. Query for electronic submissions. Reports in 2 months. Sample copy for $5.

Nonfiction: "All areas of law are fair game, but stories should have a young lawyer tie-in. Readers interested in career stories (such as what to do when you lose your job), social issues (such as free speech and hate crimes), and personality profiles of innovative or prominent young lawyers. Rarely use humor. No political opinion pieces." Length: 2,500-3,000 words. Pays $600-750 and reasonable expenses. Must query with outline. Buys 12 mss/year. Special issue: "20 Young Lawyers Whose Work Makes a Difference" (summer), 700-1,000 words; $250 payment. Buys 15 mss/year. Query.

Photos: Gina Wilson, photo editor. Black and white photos and color transparencies purchased without accompanying ms. Pays $35-150.

Tips: "The biggest mistake writers make is to think of us as a law review journal. We are a general interest magazine with a focus on young lawyers. We want cutting-edge topics written in a crisp journalistic style."

‡BENCH & BAR OF MINNESOTA, Minnesota State Bar Association, Suite 300, 514 Nicollet Ave., Minneapolis MN 55402-1021. (612)333-1183. Fax: (612)333-4927. Editor: Judson Haverkamp. 10% freelance written. Magazine published 11 times/year covering the law/legal profession. "Audience is mostly Minnesota lawyers. *Bench & Bar* seeks reportage, analysis, and commentary on trends and issues in the law and the legal profession, especially in Minnesota. Preference to items of practical/human interest to professionals in law." Estab. 1931. Circ. 14,000. **Pays on acceptance.** Publishes ms an average of 3 months after acceptence. Byline given. Buys first North American serial rights and makes work-for-hire assignments. Reports in 1 month. Sample copy for 9×12 SAE and 4 first-class stamps. Writer's guidelines free.

Nonfiction: General interest, historical/nostalgic, how-to (how to handle particular types of legal, ethical problems in office management, representation, etc.), humor, interview/profile, technical/legal. "We do not want one-sided opinion pieces or advertorial." Buys 4-5 mss/year. Query with published clips, or send complete ms. Length: 1,500-3,000 words. Pays $300-800. Sometimes pays expenses of writers on assignment.

Photos: State availability of photos with submission. Reviews 5×7 or larger prints. Offers $25-100/photo upon publication. Model releases and identification of subjects required. Buys one-time rights.

CALIFORNIA LAWYER, Dept. WM, 1210 Fox Plaza, 1390 Market St., San Francisco CA 94102. (415)252-0500. Editor: Jane Goldman. Managing Editor: Tom Brom. 80% freelance written. Monthly magazine of law-related articles and general interest subjects of appeal to lawyers and judges. Estab. 1928. Circ. 135,000. **Pays on acceptance.** Publishes ms an average of 3 months after acceptance. Byline given. Buys first rights; publishes only original material. Accepts simultaneous submissions. Reports in 2 weeks on queries; 3 weeks on mss. *Writer's Market* recommends allowing 2 months for reply. Sample copy and writer's guidelines on request with SASE.

Nonfiction: General interest, news and feature articles on law-related topics. "We are interested in concise, well-written and well-researched articles on legal aspects of issues of current concern, as well as general interest articles of potential appeal and benefit to the state's lawyers. We would like to see a description or outline of your proposed idea, including a list of possible sources." Buys 36 mss/year. Query with published clips if available. Length: 500-3,000 words. Pays $200-1,500.

Photos: Cristina Taccone, photo editor. State availability of photos with query letter or manuscript. Reviews prints. Identification of subjects and releases required.

Columns/Departments: Legal Technology, Short News, Legal Culture, Books. Query with published clips if available. Length: 750-1,500 words. Pays $200-600.

‡CORPORATE LEGAL TIMES, Suite 1513, 222 Merchandise Mart Plaza, Chicago IL 60654. (312)644-4378. Editor: Charles H. Carman. Contact: Zan Hale. 50% freelance written. Monthly tabloid covering corporate general counsel and inhouse attorneys. "*Corporate Legal Times* is a monthly national magazine that gives general counsel and inhouse attorneys information on legal and business issues to help them better manage corporate law departments. It routinely addresses changes and trends in law departments, litigation management, legal technology, corporate governance and inhouse careers. Law areas covered monthly include: environmental, intellectual property, international, and labor and employment. All stories need to be geared toward the inhouse attorney's perspective." Estab. 1991. Circ. 45,000. Pays on publication. Publishes ms an average of 3 months after acceptance. Byline given. Buys all rights. Editorial lead time 3 months. Submit seasonal material 6 months in advance. Query for electronic submissions. Reports in 3 weeks on queries. Sample copy for 9×12 SAE with 8 first-class stamps. Writer's guidelines for #10 SASE.

Nonfiction: Interview/profile, technical, news about legal aspects of business issues and events. Buys 12-25 mss/year. Query with published clips. Length: 500-2,000 words. Pays $300-1,000. Freelancers should state availability of photos with submission.

Photos: Reviews color transparencies, b&w prints. Offers $25-150/photo. Identification of subjects required. Buys all rights.

Tips: "Our publication targets general counsel and inhouse lawyers. All stories need to speak to them—not to the general attorney population. Query with clips and a list of potential inhouse sources. Non-paid, contributed articles from law firm attorneys are accepted only if there is an inhouse attorney co-author."

THE DOCKET, National Association of Legal Secretaries, Suite 550, 2250 E. 73rd St., Tulsa OK 74103-4503. (918)493-3540. Editor: Steven Wood. 10% freelance written. Bimonthly magazine that covers continuing legal education for legal support staff. "*The Docket* is written and edited for legal secretaries, legal assistants and other non-attorney personnel. Feature articles address general trends and emerging issues in the legal field, provide practical information to achieve proficiency in the delivery of legal services, and offer techniques for career growth and fulfillment." Circ. 20,000. Pays on publication. Publishes ms an average of 3-6 months after acceptance. Byline given. Offers 25-35% kill fee. Buys first North American serial rights. Accepts simultaneous and previously published submissions. Reports in 4 months. Sample copy for 9 × 12 SAE with 2 first-class stamps.

Nonfiction: How-to (enhance the delivery of legal services or any aspect thereof), new product (must be a service or equipment used in a legal office), personal experience (legal related), technical (legal services and equipment). Buys 10-15 mss/year. Query about specific subjects/articles or send complete ms. Length: 500-2,500 words. Pays $50-250.

● Articles are shorter and material must be timely and news-oriented.

Photos: State availability of photos with submission. Reviews contact sheets, negatives, transparencies and prints. Buys one-time rights.

‡ILLINOIS LEGAL TIMES, The Independent Monthly on the Business of Law, Giant Steps Publishing, Suite 1513, 222 Merchandise Mart Plaza, Chicago IL 60654. (312)644-4378. Editor-in-Chief: Charles H. Carman. Managing Editor: Kelly A. Fox. 20% freelance written. Monthly trade tabloid covering the legal industry. "*Illinois Legal Times* is on the business of law. Monthly articles and columns deal with how to manage a law firm. Its audience includes private practice lawyers, inhouse counsel and government lawyers." Estab. 1986. Circ. 13,500. Pays on publication. Publishes ms an average of 1½ months after acceptance. Offers 25% kill fee. Buys all rights. Editorial lead time 1½ months. Submit seasonal material 2 months in advance. Query for electronic submissions. Reports in weeks on queries. Sample copy and writer's guidelines free on request.

Nonfiction: Exposé, how-to, interview/profile, photo feature. Buys 6 mss/year. Query with published clips. Length: 2,500 words. "We pay per page; we don't have a minimum." Sometimes pays expenses of writers on assignment.

Photos: State availability of photos with submission. Reviews 5 × 7 prints. Offers no additional payment for photos accepted with ms. Identification of subjects required. Rights purchased varies.

Tips: "A writer must have business writing experience. Clips of past articles are a must. A writer should familiarize themselves with the publication and the issues we cover, well before making initial contact. If a writer has business writing experience and an understanding of the paper, that's his or her foot in the door. Front page feature articles are most open to freelancers. A writer would have to develop a relationship with our organization before being assigned a cover story."

LAW PRACTICE MANAGEMENT—the Magazine of the Section of Law Practice Management of the American Bar Association, P.O. Box 11418, Columbia SC 29211-1418. Managing Editor/Art Director: Delmar L. Roberts. Editorial contact for freelance submissions: John C. Tredennick, Esq., articles editor; Holland & Hart, P.O. Box 8749, Denver CO 80201. 10% freelance written. Magazine published 8 times/year for the practicing lawyer and law practice administrator. Estab. 1975. Circ. 22,234 (BPA). Rights purchased vary with author and material. Usually buys all rights. Byline given. Pays on publication. Publishes ms an average of 8 months after acceptance. Query. Sample copy for $7 (make check payable to American Bar Association). Free writer's guidelines. Returns rejected material in 3 months, if requested.

Nonfiction: "We assist the practicing lawyer in operating and managing his or her office by providing relevant articles and departments written in a readable and informative style. Editorial content is intended to aid the lawyer by conveying management methods that will allow him or her to provide legal services to clients in a prompt and efficient manner at reasonable cost. Typical topics of articles include fees and billing; client/lawyer relations; computer hardware/software; mergers; retirement/disability; marketing; compensation of partners and associates; legal data base research; and use of paralegals." No elementary articles on a whole field of technology, such as, "why you need computers in the law office." Pays $100-400.

Photos: Pays $50-60 for b&w photos purchased with mss; $50-100 for color; $200-300 for cover transparencies.

Tips: "We have a theme for each issue with two to three articles relating to the theme. We also publish thematic issues occasionally in which an entire issue is devoted to a single topic. The March and November/December issues each year are devoted to law practice technology."

THE LAWYER'S PC, A Newsletter for Lawyers Using Personal Computers, Shepard's/McGraw-Hill, Inc., P.O. Box 1108, Lexington SC 29071-1108. (803)359-9941. Editor: Robert P. Wilkins. Managing Editor: Daniel E. Harmon. 50% freelance written. Biweekly newsletter covering computerized law firms. "Our readers are lawyers who want to be told how a particular microcomputer program or type of program is being applied to a legal office task, such as timekeeping, litigation support, etc." Estab. 1983. Circ. 4,500. Pays end of the month of publication. Publishes ms an average of 1-2 months after acceptance. Byline given. Buys first North American serial rights and the right to reprint. Submit seasonal material 5 months in advance. Query for electronic submissions. Reports in 1 month on queries; 4 months on mss. Sample copy for 9 × 12 SAE with 3 first-class stamps. Free writer's guidelines.

Nonfiction: How-to (applications articles on law office computerization) and software reviews written by lawyers who have no compromising interests. No general articles on why lawyers need computers or reviews of products written by public relations representatives or vending consultants. Buys 30-35 mss/year. Query. Length: 500-2,500 words. Pays $50-300. Sometimes pays the expenses of writers on assignment.

Tips: "Most of our writers are lawyers. If you're not a lawyer, you need to at least understand why general business software may not work well in a law firm. If you understand lawyers' specific computer problems, write an article describing how to solve one of those problems, and we'd like to see it."

THE LAWYERS WEEKLY, The Newspaper for the Legal Profession in Canada, Butterworth (Canada) Inc., Suite 300, 204 Richmond St. West, Toronto Ontario M5V 1V6 Canada. (416)598-5211. Fax: (416)598-5659. Editor: Don Brillinger. 30% freelance written. "We will work with any *talented* writer of whatever experience level." Tabloid published 48 times/year covering law and legal affairs for a "sophisticated up-market readership of lawyers." Estab. 1983. Circ. 8,000/week; 22,500 once per month. Pays on publication. Publishes ms within 1 month after acceptance. Byline given. Offers 50% kill fee. Usually buys all rights. Submit seasonal material 6 weeks in advance. Accepts simultaneous submissions. Query for electronic submissions. Reports in 1 month. Sample copy for $7 (Canadian) with 9 × 12 SAE.

Nonfiction: Exposé, general interest (law), how-to (professional), humor, interview/profile (Canadian lawyers and judges), opinion, technical, news, case comments. "We try to wrap up the week's legal events and issues in a snappy informal package. We especially like news stories with photos or illustrations. We are always interested in feature or newsfeature articles involving current legal issues, but contributors should keep in mind our audience is trained in *English/Canadian common law*—not US law. That means most US-focused stories will generally not be accepted. No routine court reporting or fake news stories about commercial products. Buys 200-300 mss/year. Query or send complete ms. Length: 700-1,500 words. Payment negotiable. Payment in Canadian dollars. Sometimes pays the expenses of writers on assignment.

Photos: State availability of photos with query letter or ms. Reviews b&w and color contact sheets, negatives and 5 × 7 prints. Identification of subjects required. Buys one-time rights.

Fillers: Clippings and newsbreaks. Length: 50-200 words. Pays $10 minimum.

Tips: "Freelancers can best break into our publication by submitting news, features, and accounts of unusual or bizarre legal events. A frequent mistake made by writers is forgetting that our audience is intelligent and learned in law. They don't need the word 'plaintiff' explained to them." No unsolicited mss returned without SASE (or IRC to US or non-Canadian destinations). "No US postage on SASEs, please!"

LAWYERS WEEKLY USA, Lawyers Weekly Publications, 41 West St., Boston MA 02111. (617)451-7300. Editor: Michelle Bates Deakin. Biweekly newspaper covering the legal profession for small-firm lawyers. Estab. 1993. **Pays on acceptance.** Publishes ms an average of 1 month after acceptance. Byline given. Buys all rights. Accepts simultaneous submissions. Query for electronic submissions. Reports in 1 month. Sample copy for 9 × 12 SAE with 2 first-class stamps. Writer's guidelines for SASE.

Nonfiction: How-to (articles about law practice and law office management), humor, interview/profile, opinion. Query with published clips. Length: 250-2,000 words. Pay negotiable. Sometimes pays expenses of writers on assignment.

Tips: "Writers should be familiar with the specific concerns of lawyers practicing in small law firms and tailor their stories to them. We are most open to news stories about local legal issues of national relevance, trends in law practice, and how-to stories about law office management, marketing, and legal technology."

THE PENNSYLVANIA LAWYER, Pennsylvania Bar Association, P.O. Box 186, 100 South St., Harrisburg PA 17108-0186. (717)238-6715. Executive Editor: Marcy Carey Mallory. Managing Editor: Donald C. Sarvey. 25% freelance written. Prefers to work with published/established writers. Magazine published 6 times/year as a service to the legal profession. Estab. 1895. Circ. 27,000. **Pays on acceptance.** Publishes ms an average of 3-6 months after acceptance. Byline given. Buys negotiable serial rights; generally first rights, occasionally one-time rights or second serial (reprint) rights. Submit seasonal material 6 months in advance. Simultaneous submissions are discouraged. Reports in 6 weeks. Free sample copy and writer's guidelines for #10 SAE with 3 first-class stamps.

Nonfiction: General interest, how-to, interview/profile, new product, law-practice management, personal experience. All features *must* relate in some way to Pennsylvania lawyers or the practice of law in Pennsylvania. Buys 10-12 mss/year. Query. Length: 600-1,500 words. Pays $75-350. Sometimes pays the expenses of writers on assignment.

THE PERFECT LAWYER, A Newsletter for Lawyers Using WordPerfect Products, Shepard's/McGraw-Hill Inc., P.O. Box 1108, Lexington SC 29071-1108. (803)359-9941. Editor: Robert P. Wilkins. Associate Editor: Daniel E. Harmon. 50% freelance written. Monthly newsletter covering the use of WordPerfect Corporation-related products in law offices. Estab. 1990. Circ. 4,500. Pays at end of the month after publication. Publishes ms an average of 2-3 months after acceptance. Byline given. Buys first North American serial rights, electronic rights and the right to reprint. Submit seasonal material 5 months in advance. Query for electronic submissions. Reports in 4 months. Sample copy for 9×12 SAE with 4 first-class stamps. Free writer's guidelines.

Nonfiction: How-to computer articles, must be law office-specific. Occasional reviews of WordPerfect-related products for law firms. Buys 25-35 mss/year. Query. Length: 500-2,500 words. Pays $25-200. Sometimes pays expenses of writers on assignment.

Tips: "Writers should understand the specific computer needs of law firms. Our readers are interested in how to solve office automation problems with computers and WordPerfect or related software products."

SHEPARD'S ELDER CARE/LAW NEWSLETTER, Shepard's/McGraw-Hill, Inc., P.O. Box 1108, Lexington SC 29071-1108. (803)359-9941. Fax: (803)857-8226. Editor: Robert P. Wilkins. Managing Editor: Daniel E. Harmon. Associate Editor: Aida Rogers. 40% freelance written. Monthly newsletter for lawyers and other professionals who work with older clients, focusing on legal and related issues of concern to the aging community. Estab. 1991. Pays end of the month of publication. Publishes ms an average of 2 months after acceptance. Byline given. Buys first North American serial rights, electronic rights and reprint rights. Accepts previously published submissions. Submit seasonal material 5 months in advance. Query for electronic submissions. Reports in 1 month on queries; 2 months on mss. Pay negotiable. Sample copy for 9×12 SAE with 3 first-class stamps. Free writer's guidelines.

Nonfiction: Informational articles about legal issues, pending and new legislation, organizations and other resources of interest to lawyers who work with aging clients and their families. Query. Pays $25-200. Does not pay phone expenses.

STUDENT LAWYER, American Bar Association, 750 N. Lake Shore Dr., Chicago IL 60611. (312)988-6048. Editor: Sarah Hoban. Managing Editor: Miriam R. Krasno. 95% freelance written. Works with a small number of new/unpublished writers each year. Monthly (September-May) magazine. Estab. 1972. Circ. 30,000. Pays on publication. Buys first serial and second serial (reprint) rights. Publishes reprints of previously published articles. Send tearsheet of article, typed ms with rights for sale noted and information about when and where the article previously appeared. For reprints, pays 25-50% of the amount paid for an original article. Pays negotiable kill fee. Byline given. Submit seasonal material 4 months in advance. Reports in 6 weeks. Publishes ms an average of 3 months after acceptance. Sample copy for $4. Free writer's guidelines.

Nonfiction: Features cover legal education and careers and social/legal subjects. The magazine also publishes profiles (prominent persons in law-related fields); opinion (on matters of current legal interest); essays (on legal affairs); interviews; and photo features. Query. Length: 3,000-5,000 words. Pays $300-900 for main features. Covers some writer's expenses.

Columns/Departments: Briefly (short stories on unusual and interesting developments in the law); Legal Aids (unusual approaches and programs connected to teaching law students and lawyers); Esq. (brief profiles of people in the law); End Note (short pieces on a variety of topics; can be humorous, educational, outrageous); Pro Se (opinion slot for authors to wax eloquent on legal issues, civil rights conflicts, the state of the union); and Et Al. (column for short features that fit none of the above categories). Buys 4-8 mss/issue. Length: 250-1,000 words. Pays $100-350.

Fiction: "We buy fiction only when it is very good and deals with issues of law in the contemporary world or offers insights into the inner workings of lawyers. No mystery, poetry or science fiction accepted."

Tips: "*Student Lawyer* actively seeks good new writers. Legal training definitely not essential; writing talent is. The writer should not think we are a law review; we are a feature magazine with the law (in the broadest sense) as the common denominator. Past articles concerned gay rights, prison reform, the media, pornography, capital punishment and drug education. Find issues of national scope and interest to write about; be aware of subjects the magazine—and other media—have already covered and propose something new. Write clearly and well."

Leather Goods

SHOE RETAILING TODAY, National Shoe Retailers Association, Suite 255, 9861 Broken Land Pkwy., Columbia MD 21046-1151. (410)381-8282. Fax: (410)381-1167. Editor: Carol Blank. 10% freelance written. Bimonthly newsletter covering footwear/accessory industry. Looks for articles that are "informative, educational, but with wit, interest and creativity. I hate dry, dusty articles." Estab. 1972. Circ. 4,000-5,000. Byline given. Buys one-time rights. Submit seasonal material 3 months in advance. Accepts previously published submissions. Send photocopy of article. For reprints, pays 50% of their fee for an original article. Reports in 3 months. Sample copy and writer's guidelines for 9×12 SAE with 2 first-class stamps.

Nonfiction: How-to, interview/profile, new product, technical. Special issues: shoe show (January, July). Buys 6 mss/year. Length: 500 words. Pays $50-100 for assigned articles. Pays up to $200 for "full-fledged research—1,000 words or more on assigned articles."

Photos: State availability of photos with submission. Offers no additional payment for photos accepted with ms. Buys one-time rights.

Columns/Departments: Query. Pays $50-125.

Tips: "We are a trade magazine/newsletter for the footwear industry. Any information pertaining to our market is helpful: advertising/display/how-tos."

SHOE SERVICE, SSIA Service Corp., 5024-R Campbell Blvd., Baltimore MD 21236-5974. (410)931-8100. Fax: (410)931-8111. Editor: Mitchell Lebovic. 25% freelance written. "We want well-written articles, whether they come from new or established writers." Monthly magazine for business people who own and operate small shoe repair shops. Estab. 1921. Circ. 8,000. Pays on publication. Publishes ms an average of 3 months after acceptance. Byline given. Buys first serial, first North American serial and one-time rights. Submit seasonal material 3 months in advance. Accepts simultaneous and previously published submissions. Reports in 6 weeks. Sample copy for $2 and 9×12 SAE.

Nonfiction: How-to (run a profitable shop); interview/profile (of an outstanding or unusual person on shoe repair); business articles (particularly about small business practices in a service/retail shop). Buys 12-24 mss/year. Query with published clips or send complete ms. Length: 500-2,000 words. Pays 5¢/word.

Photos: "Quality photos will help sell an article." State availability of photos. Pays $10-30 for 8×10 b&w prints. Uses some color photos, but mostly uses b&w glossies. Captions, model release and identification of subjects required.

Tips: "Visit some shoe repair shops to get an idea of the kind of person who reads *Shoe Service*. Profiles are the easiest to sell to us if you can find a repairer we think is unusual."

Library Science

Librarians read these journals for advice on promotion and management of libraries, library and book trade issues and information access and transfer. Be aware of current issues such as censorship, declines in funding and government information policies. For journals on the book trade see Book and Bookstore.

AMERICAN LIBRARIES, 50 E. Huron St., Chicago IL 60611. (312)280-4216. Fax: (312)440-0901. Editor: Thomas Gaughan. Senior Editor: Gordon Flagg. 10-20% freelance written. Works with a small number of new/unpublished writers each year. Magazine published 11 times/year for librarians. "A highly literate audience. They are for the most part practicing professionals with a down-to-earth interest in people and current professional trends." Estab. 1907. Circ. 56,000. Buys first North American serial rights. Publishes ms an average of 4 months after acceptance. Pays negotiable kill fee. Byline given. Submit seasonal material 6 months in advance. Reports in 10 weeks.

Nonfiction: "Material reflecting the special and current interests of the library profession. Nonlibrarians should browse recent journals in the field, available on request in medium-sized and large libraries everywhere. Topic and/or approach must be fresh, vital or highly entertaining. Library memoirs and stereotyped stories about old maids, overdue books, fines, etc., are unacceptable. Our first concern is with the American Library Association's activities and how they relate to the 55,000 reader/members. Tough for an outsider to write on this topic, but not to supplement it with short, offbeat or significant library stories and features." No fillers. Buys 2-6 freelance mss/year. Pays $15 for news tips used, and $25-300 for briefs and articles.

Photos: "Will look at color transparencies and bright color prints for inside and cover use." Pays $50-200 for photos.

Tips: "You can break in with a sparkling, 300-word report on a true, offbeat library event, use of new technology, or with an exciting color photo and caption. Though stories on public libraries are always of interest, we especially need arresting material on academic and school libraries."

CHURCH MEDIA LIBRARY MAGAZINE, 127 Ninth Ave. N., Nashville TN 37234. (615)251-2752. Editor: Floyd B. Simpson. Quarterly magazine for adult leaders in church organizations and people interested in library work (especially church library work). Estab. 1891. Circ. 30,000. Pays on publication. Buys all, first serial and second serial (reprint) rights. Byline given. Phone queries OK. Submit seasonal material 14 months in advance. Accepts previously published submissions. Reports in 1 month. Free sample copy and writer's guidelines.

Nonfiction: "We are primarily interested in articles that relate to the development of church libraries in providing media and services to support the total program of a church and in meeting individual needs. We publish how-to accounts of services provided, promotional ideas, exciting things that have happened as a result of implementing an idea or service; human interest stories that are library-related; and media training (teaching and learning with a media mix). Articles should be practical for church library staffs and for teachers and other leaders of the church." Buys 10-15 mss/issue. Query. Pays 5½¢/word.

‡EMERGENCY LIBRARIAN, Dyad Services, Box C34069, Dept. 284, Seattle WA 98124-1069. (604)925-0266. Fax: (604)925-0566. Editor: Ken Haycock. Publishes 5 issues/year. Estab. 1979. Circ. 7,500. Pays on publication. No multiple submissions. Reports in 6 weeks. Free writer's guidelines.

Nonfiction: Emphasis is on improvement of library service for children and young adults in school and public libraries. Also annotated bibliographies. Buys 3 mss/issue. Query. Length: 1,000-3,500 words. Pays $50.

Columns/Departments: Five regular columnists. Also Book Reviews (of professional materials in education, librarianship). Query. Length: 100-300 words. Payment consists of book reviewed.

THE LIBRARY IMAGINATION PAPER, Carol Bryan Imagines, 1000 Byus Dr., Charleston WV 25311-1310. (304)345-2378. 30% freelance written. Quarterly newspaper covering public relations education for librarians. Clip art included in each issue. Estab. 1978. Circ. 3,000. Pays on publication. Publishes ms an average of 6 months after acceptance. Byline given. Buys one-time rights. Submit seasonal material 3 months in advance. Accepts simultaneous and previously published submissions. Send tearsheet or photocopy of article and information about when and where the article previously appeared. Reports in 2 months. Sample copy for $5. Writer's guidelines for SASE.

Nonfiction: How-to (on "all aspects of good library public relations—both mental tips and hands-on methods. We need how-to and tips pieces on all aspects of PR, for library subscribers—both school and public libraries. In the past we've featured pieces on taking good photos, promoting an anniversary celebration, working with printers, and producing a slide show.") No articles on "what the library means to me." Buys 4-6 mss/year. Query with or without published clips, or send complete ms. Length: 600 or 2,200 words. Pays $25 or $50.

Photos: Send photos with submission. Reviews 3×5, 5×7 or 8×10 prints. Offers $5/photo. Captions required. Buys one-time rights.

Tips: "Someone who has worked in the library field and has first-hand knowledge of library PR needs, methods and processes will do far better with us. Our readers are people who cannot be written down to—but their library training has not always incorporated enough preparation for handling promotion, publicity and the public."

LIBRARY JOURNAL, Dept. WM, 249 W. 17th St., New York NY 10011. (212)463-6819. Editor-in-Chief: John N. Berry III. 60% freelance written by librarians. Eager to work with new/unpublished writers. Magazine published 20 times/year for librarians (academic, public, special). Circ. 30,000. Buys all rights. Pays on publication. Publishes ms an average of 12-18 months after acceptance. "Our response time is slow, but improving."

Nonfiction: *"Library Journal* is a professional magazine for librarians. We need material of greater sophistication, government information, dealing with issues related to the transfer of information, access to it, or related phenomena." Professional articles on criticism, censorship, professional concerns, library activities, historical articles, information technology, automation and management, internet and spot news. Outlook should be from librarian's point of view. Buys 50-65 unsolicited mss/year. Submit complete ms. Length: 1,500-2,000 words. Pays $50-350. Sometimes pays the expenses of writers on assignment.

Photos: Payment for b&w or color glossy photos purchased without accompanying mss is $35. Must be at least 5×7. Captions required.

Tips: "We're increasingly interested in material on library management, public sector fundraising, and information policy."

WILSON LIBRARY BULLETIN, Dept. WM, 950 University Ave., Bronx NY 10452-4221. (718)588-8400 ext. 2245. Fax: (718)681-1511. E-mail: graceann@wlb.hwwilson.com. Editor: GraceAnne A. DeCandido. 75% freelance written. Monthly (September-June) for professional librarians and those interested in the book and library worlds. Estab. 1914. Circ. 13,000. Pays on publication. Publishes ms an average of 3 months after acceptance. Buys first North American serial rights, electronic rights. Sample copies may be seen on request in most libraries. "Manuscript must be original copy, double-spaced." Deadlines are a minimum 2 months before publication. Reports in 3 months. Free sample copy and writer's guidelines.

Nonfiction: Uses articles "of interest to librarians and information professionals throughout the nation and around the world. Style must be lively, readable and sophisticated, with appeal to modern professionals; facts must be thoroughly researched. Subjects range from the political to the comic in the world of media and libraries, with an emphasis on the human as well as the technical aspects of any story. No condescension: no library stereotypes." Prefers material from practicing librarians; "we rarely accept submissions from freelancers who are not librarians." Buys 20-30 mss/year. Send complete ms. Length: 1,000-3,500 words. Pays about $100-400. Sometimes pays the expenses of writers on assignment.

Tips: "Libraries have changed. You'd better first discover how."

Lumber

NORTHERN LOGGER AND TIMBER PROCESSOR, Northeastern Loggers' Association, Dept WM, P.O. Box 69, Old Forge NY 13420. (315)369-3078. Fax: (315)369-3736. Editor: Eric A. Johnson. 40% freelance written. Monthly magazine of the forest industry in the northern US (Maine to Minnesota and south to Virginia and Missouri). "We are not a purely technical journal, but are more information oriented." Estab. 1952. Circ. 13,600. Pays on publication. Publishes ms an average of 3 months after acceptance. Byline given. Buys all rights. Submit seasonal material 3 months in advance. Accepts previously published submissions. Reports in 2 weeks. Free sample copy and writer's guidelines.

Nonfiction: Exposé, general interest, historical/nostalgic, how-to, interview/profile, new product, opinion. "We only buy feature articles, and those should contain some technical or historical material relating to the forest products industry." Buys 12-15 mss/year. Query. Length: 500-2,500 words. Pays $50-250.

Photos: Send photos with ms. Pays $35 for 35mm color transparencies; $15 for 5×7 b&w prints. Captions and identification of subjects required.

Tips: "We accept most any subject dealing with this part of the country's forest industry, from historical to logging, firewood and timber processing."

SOUTHERN LUMBERMAN, Greysmith Publishing, Inc., P.O. Box 681629, Franklin TN 37068-1629. (615)791-1961. Fax: (615)790-6188. Editor: Nanci P. Gregg. 20-30% freelance written. Works with a small number of new/unpublished writers each year. Monthly trade journal for the sawmill industry. Estab. 1881. Circ. 12,000. Pays on publication. Publishes ms an average of 3 months after acceptance. Byline given. Not copyrighted. Buys first North American rights. Submit seasonal material 6 months in advance. Query for electonic submissions. Accepts previously published material. Send tearsheet or photocopy of article and information about when and where the article previously appeared. For reprints, pays 25-50% of fee paid for an original article. Reports in 1 month on queries; 2 months on mss. Sample copy for $2 and 9×12 SAE with 5 first-class stamps. Writer's guidelines for #10 SASE.

Nonfiction: How to sawmill better, interview/profile, equipment analysis, technical. Sawmill features. Buys 10-15 mss/year. Query with or without published clips, or send complete ms. Length: 500-2,000 words. Pays $150-350 for assigned articles; pays $100-250 for unsolicited articles. Sometimes pays the expenses of writers on assignment.

Photos: Send photos with submission. Reviews transparencies and 4×5 b&w prints. Offers $10-25/photo. Captions and identification of subjects required.

Tips: "Like most, we appreciate a clearly-worded query listing merits of suggested story—what it will tell our readers they need/want to know. We want quotes, we want opinions to make others discuss the article. Best hint? Find an interesting sawmill operation owner and start asking questions—I bet a story idea develops. We need b&w photos too. Most open is what we call the Sweethart Mill stories. We publish at least one per month, and hope to be printing two or more monthly in the immediate future. Find a sawmill operator and ask questions—what's he doing bigger, better, different. We're interested in new facilities, better marketing, improved production."

Machinery and Metal

‡AMERICAN METAL MARKET, Chilton Publications, A Unit of Capital Cities/ABC, Inc., 825 Seventh Ave., New York NY 10019. (212)887-8550. Editor: Michael G. Botta. Contact: Peter Kelton, international news editor. 5% freelance written. Daily newspaper covering metals production and trade. "Bible of the metals industry. Covers production and trade of ferrous, nonferrous, and scrap metals. Read by senior executives. Focus on *breaking* news and price information." Estab. 1882. Circ. 11,000. Pays on publication per inch used in publication. Publishes ms an average of 0-1 months after acceptance. Byline given. Buys all rights and electronic rights. Editorial lead time 0-1 months. Query for electronic submissions. Reports in 0-1 weeks on queries. Sample copy and writer's guidelines free on request.

Nonfiction: We publish roughly 45 special issues per year. Query. Pays $7/in.

Photos: Send photos with submission. Reviews 5×7 prints. Negotiates payment individually. Identification of subjects required. Buys all rights.

Tips: "Contact Peter Kelton, or Christopher Munford, managing editor, directly with story ideas. Primarily we are interested in purchasing *breaking* news items. Clear all stories with news desk (Kelton or Munford) in advance. Unsolicited articles submitted at writer's risk. Contact Bob Manas, Senior Editor, special issues, to discuss upcoming topics."

AUTOMATIC MACHINING, 100 Seneca Ave., Rochester NY 14621. (716)338-1522. Editor: Donald E. Wood. For metalworking technical management. Buys all rights. Byline given.

Nonfiction: "This is not a market for the average freelancer. A personal knowledge of the trade is essential. Articles deal in depth with specific job operations on automatic screw machines, chucking machines, high production metal turning lathes and cold heading machines. Part prints, tooling layouts always required, plus written agreement of source to publish the material. Without personal background in operation of this type of equipment, freelancers are wasting time. No material researched from library sources." Query. Length: 4 double-spaced pages."

FABRICATOR, Ornamental & Miscellaneous Metal, National Ornamental & Miscellaneous Metals Assoc., #E, 804-10 Main St., Forest Park GA 30050. Editor: Todd Daniel. 20% freelance written. Bimonthly magazine covering ornamental metalwork. "Any 'business' stories published must contain an angle specific to this industry." Estab. 1959. Circ. 8,000. **Pays on acceptance.** Byline given. Publication not copyrighted. Buys one-time rights. Editorial lead time 2 months. Accepts simultaneous and previously published submissions. Send typed ms with rights for sale noted. For reprints pays 100% of the amount paid for an original article. Query for electronic submissions. Reports in 6 weeks on queries. Sample copy for #10 SASE. Writer's guidelines for $1.

Nonfiction: How-to, humor, interview/profile, personal experience, photo feature, technical. "Nothing in a Q&A format." Buys 3-6 mss/year. Query. Length: 1,200-2,000 words. Pays $150 minumum for assigned articles, $125 minimum for unsolicited articles. "Many write for publicity." Sometimes pays expenses of writers on assignment.

Photos: State availability of photos with submission. Reviews contact sheets, negatives, transparencies and prints. Offers no additional payment for photos acepted with ms. Model releases required. Buys one-time rights.

Tips: "Don't write articles in passive voice."

MODERN MACHINE SHOP, 6600 Clough Pike, Cincinnati OH 45244-4090. (513)231-8020. Fax: (513)231-2818. Executive Editor: Mark Albert. 25% freelance written. Monthly. Estab. 1928. Pays 1 month following acceptance. Publishes ms an average of 6 months after acceptance. Byline given. Query for electronic submissions. Reports in 1 month. Call for sample copy. Writer's guidelines for #10 SASE.

Nonfiction: Uses articles dealing with all phases of metalworking, manufacturing and machine shop work, with photos. No general articles. "Ours is an industrial publication, and contributing authors should have a working knowledge of the metalworking industry. "We regularly use contributions from machine shop owners, engineers, other technical experts, and suppliers to the metalworking industry. Almost all of these contributors pursue these projects to promote their own commercial interests. " Buys 10 unsolicited mss/year. Query. Length: 1,000-3,500 words. Pays current market rate.

Tips: "The use of articles relating to computers in manufacturing is growing."

NICKEL, The magazine devoted to nickel and its applications, Nickel Development Institute, Suite 510, 214 King St. W., Toronto, Ontario M5H 3S6 Canada. (416)591-7999. Fax: (416)591-7987. Editor: James S. Borland. 30% freelance written. Quarterly magazine covering the metal nickel and all of its applications. Estab. 1985. Circ. 34,000. **Pays on acceptance.** Publishes ms an average of 3 months after acceptance. Byline given. Buys first rights. Accepts previously published articles. Send tearsheet of article, or send typed ms with rights for sale noted. Include information about when and where the article previously appeared. For reprints, pays 50% of the amount paid for an original article. Reports in 1 month. Free sample copies and writer's guidelines from Nickel Development Institute Librarian.

Nonfiction: Semi-technical. Buys 20 mss/year. Query. Length: 50-1,000 words. Pays competitive rates, by negotiation. Sometimes pays expenses of writers on assignment.

Photos: State availability of photos (uses color transparencies only) with submission. Offers competitive rates by negotiation. Captions, model releases and identification of subjects required.

Tips: "Write to Librarian, Nickel Development Institute, for two free copies of *Nickel* and study them. Know something about nickel's 300,000 end uses. Be at home in writing semitechnical material. Then query the editor with a story idea in a one-page letter—no fax queries or phone calls. Complete magazine is open, except Technical Literature column."

‡ORNAMENTAL AND MISCELLANEOUS METAL FABRICATOR, National Ornamental And Miscellaneous Metals Association, Suite E, 804-10 Main St., Forest Park GA 30050. Editor: Todd Daniel. 20% freelance written. Bimonthly trade magazine covering ornamental metalworking. "To inform, educate and inspire members of the ornamental and miscellaneous metalworking industry." Estab. 1959. Circ. 8,000. Pays when article actually received. Byline given. Buys one-time rights. Editorial lead time 2 months. Submit seasonal material 2 months in advance. Query for electronic submissions. Reports in 1 month on queries. Sample copy for 9×12 SAE and 6 first-class stamps. Writer's guidelines for $1.

Nonfiction: Book excerpts, essays, exposé, general interest, historical/nostalgic, how-to, humor, inspirational, interview/profile, new product, opinion, personal experience, photo feature, technical. Buys 3-4 mss/year. Query. Length: 1,200-2,000 words. Pays $150 minimum for assigned articles; $50 miminum for unsolicited articles. Sometimes pays expenses of writers on assignment.

Photos: State availability of photos with submission. Reviews contact sheets, negatives, transparencies, prints.Offers no additional payment for photos accepted with ms. Model releases required.

Tips: "Make article relevant to our industry. Don't write in passive voice."

Maintenance and Safety

CLEANING BUSINESS, 1512 Western Ave., P.O. Box 1273, Seattle WA 98111. (206)622-4241. Fax: (206)622-6876. Publisher: William R. Griffin. Associate Editor: Jim Saunders. 80% freelance written. Quarterly magazine covering technical and management information relating to cleaning and self-employment. "We cater to those who are self-employed in any facet of the cleaning and maintenance industry and seek to be top professionals in their field. *Cleaning Business* is published for self-employed cleaning professionals, specifically carpet, upholstery and drapery cleaners; janitorial and maid services; window washers; odor, water and fire damage restoration contractors. Our readership is small but select. We seek concise, factual articles, realistic but definitely upbeat." Circ. 6,000. Pays 1 month after publication. Publishes ms an average of 3 months after acceptance. Byline given. Buys first serial, second serial (reprint) and all rights or makes work-for-hire assignments. Submit seasonal material 6 months in advance. Reports in 3 months. Sample copy for $3 and 8×10 SAE with 3 first-class stamps. Writer's guidelines for #10 SASE.

Nonfiction: Exposé (safety/health business practices); how-to (on cleaning, maintenance, small business management); humor (clean jokes, cartoons); interview/profile; new product (must be unusual to rate full article — mostly obtained from manufacturers); opinion; personal experience; technical. Special issues: "What's New?" (February). No "wordy articles written off the top of the head, obviously without research, and needing more editing time than was spent on writing." Buys 40 mss/year. Query with or without published clips. Length: 500-3,000 words. Pays $5-80. ("Pay depends on amount of work, research and polishing put into article much more than on length.") Pays expenses of writers on assignment with prior approval only.

Photos: State availability of photos or send photos with ms. Pays $5-25 for "smallish" b&w prints. Captions, model release and identification of subjects required. Buys one-time rights and reprint rights. "Magazine size is 8½×11 — photos need to be proportionate. Also seeks full-color photos of relevant subjects for cover."

Columns/Departments: "Ten regular columnists now sell four columns per year to us. We are interested in adding Safety & Health and Fire Restoration columns (related to cleaning and maintenance industry). We are also open to other suggestions — send query." Buys 36 columns/year; department information obtained at no cost. Query with or without published clips. Length: 500-1,500 words. Pays $15-85.

Fillers: Jokes, gags, anecdotes, short humor, newsbreaks, cartoons. Buys 40/year. Length: 3-200 words. Pays $1-20.

Tips: "We are constantly seeking quality freelancers from all parts of the country. A freelancer can best break in to our publication with fairly technical articles on how to do specific cleaning/maintenance jobs; interviews with top professionals covering this and how they manage their business; and personal experience. Our readers demand concise, accurate information. Don't ramble. Write only about what you know and/or have researched. Editors don't have time to rewrite your rough draft. Organize and polish before submitting."

CLEANING MANAGEMENT, The Magazine for Today's Building Cleaning Maintenance/Housekeeping Executive, National Trade Publications, Inc., 13 Century Hill Dr., Latham NY 12110-2197. (518)783-1281. Fax: (518)783-1386. Editor: Thomas H. Williams. Monthly national trade magazine covering building cleaning maintenance/housekeeping operations in larger institutions such as hotels, schools, hospitals, office buildings, industrial plants, recreational and religious buildings, shopping centers, airports, etc. Articles must be aimed at managers of on-site building/facility cleaning staffs or owners/managers of contract cleaning companies. Estab. 1963. Circ. 40,000. Pays on publication, with invoice. Byline given. Buys all rights. Reports in 2 weeks. Sample copy and writer's guidelines for 9×12 SAE with 8 first-class stamps.

Nonfiction: Articles on: discussions of facility-wide systems for custodial operations/cleaning tasks; system-wide analysis of custodial task cost-effectiveness and staffing levels; the organization of cleaning tasks on an institution-wide basis; recruitment, training, motivation and supervision of building cleaning employees; the cleaning of buildings or facilities of unusual size, type, design, construction or notoriety; interesting case studies; or advice for the successful operation of a contract cleaning business. Buys 6-12 mss/year. Length: 500-1,500 words. Pays $50-250. Please query.

Photos: State availability of photos. Prefer color or b&w prints, rates negotiable. Captions, model releases and identification of subjects required.

Tips: Chances of acceptance are directly proportional to the article's relevance to the professional, on-the-job needs and interests of facility/custodial managers or contract building cleaners.

OCCUPATIONAL HEALTH & SAFETY, Stevens Publishing Corporation, P.O. Box 2573, Waco TX 76702-2573. Editor: Mark Hartley. Associate Editor: Teri Lynn Eisma. 30% freelance written. Monthly magazine covering workplace safety and health issues. "*Occupational Health & Safety* is a business magazine whose editorial promotes the understanding and control of occupational illness, injury and hazardous exposure in the workplace. The mission of *Occupational Health & Safety*, as a professional publication, is to serve the market's editorial and advertising needs by consistently providing the industrial and corporate workplace with this field's definitive source of reliable information, which is useful in decreasing worker risk while increasing job productivity." Estab. 1932. Circ. 83,000. Pays on publication. Publishes ms an average of 3 months after acceptance. Byline given. Offers 25% kill fee. Buys first North American serial rights. Editorial lead time 3 months. Query for electronic submissions. Reports in 2 months on mss; 1 month on queries; "manuscripts are reviewed by editorial board 50-75% of time." Sample copy free on request "by calling Customer Service Department or fax request to (817)776-9018 attn: Customer Service." Writer's guidelines and editorial calendar free on request.

Nonfiction: How-to (implement safety programs in a company, for example); interview/profile (of innovative people in safety field); and technical. "No humor (particularly cartoons) or personal experience." Buys 20-30 mss/year. Query. Length: 1,000-3,000 words. Pays $300 minimum for assigned articles, $100 minimum for unsolicited articles. Seldom pays in other premiums or contributor copies, "but it's negotiable." Sometimes pays expenses of writers on assignment.

Photos: State availability of photos with submission. Reviews negatives. Negotiates payment individually. Model releases and identification of subjects required. Buys one-time rights.

Tips: "The magazine's readers are typically mid-level management, engineers or professional safety consultants. They all face increasing pressure to comply with a myriad of federal regulations. Any information that helps them perform their jobs more easily will be bought. We are most open to feature articles. If you have good contacts with local industry, keep an eye out for innovative programs that minimize the risk of injury or illness to workers."

PEST CONTROL MAGAZINE, 7500 Old Oak Blvd., Cleveland OH 44130. (216)243-8100. Fax: (216)891-2675. Editor: Tom Johnson. Monthly magazine for professional pest control operators and sanitarians. Estab. 1933. Circ. 15,000. Buys all rights. Buys 12 mss/year. Pays on publication. Submit seasonal material 2 months in advance. Reports in 1 month. Query or submit complete ms.
Nonfiction: Business tips, unique control situations, personal experience (stories about 1-man operations and their problems). Must have trade or business orientation. No general information type of articles desired. Buys 3 unsolicited mss/year. Length: 1,000 words. Pays $150-500 minimum. Regular columns use material oriented to this profession. Length: 2,000 words.
Photos: No additional payment for photos used with mss. Pays $50-150 for 8×10 color or transparencies.

‡PEST MANAGEMENT, National Pest Control Association, Inc., 8100 Oak St., Dunn Loring VA 22027-1000. (703)573-8330. Fax: (703)573-4116. Editor: Kathleen H. Bova. Assistant Editor: Eileen C. Smith. 30% freelance written. Monthly, except combined November/December issue trade journal. "Our readers are members of the structural pest control industry. They include owners/operators of large corporations and one-man operations, and professional entomologists. Our style is in between Barry and Buckley—not informal, but not high-brow." Estab. 1981. Circ. 5,500. Pays on publication. Publishes ms an average of 2 months after acceptance. Byline given. Buys all rights. Submit seasonal material 3 months in advance. Accepts simultaneous and previously published submissions. Send photocopy of article or typed ms with rights for sale noted and information about when and where the article previously appeared. Query for electronic submissions. Reports in 2 months. Free sample copy and writer's guidelines.
Nonfiction: Book excerpts, how-to, interview/profile, opinion, personal experience, photo feature, technical, travel. Special issues planned on public relations, office equipment and office automation, safety, add-on business opportunities, ant, fleas, rodents, spiders and termites. No articles about specific products, general information articles. Buys 12 mss/year. Query with or without published clips, or send complete ms. Length: 1,500-5,000 words. Pays $150-500.
Photos: State availability of photos with submission. Reviews any size prints. Offers no additional payment for photos accepted with ms. Identification of subjects required.
Tips: "Tailor articles to our readership; leave technical articles to staff; concentrate on special issues; don't be afraid to contact us with innovative ideas."

SAFETY COMPLIANCE LETTER, with OSHA Highlights, Bureau of Business Practice, 24 Rope Ferry Rd., Waterford CT 06386. (203)442-4365. Fax: (203)434-3078. Editor: Michele Rubin. Managing Editor: Many Schantz. 80% freelance written. Bimonthly newsletter covering occupational safety and health. Publishes interview-based how-to and success stories for personnel in charge of safety and health in manufacturing/industrial environments. Circ. 15,000. Pays on acceptance after editing. Publishes ms an average of 3-6 months after acceptance. No byline given. Buys all rights. Submit seasonal material 4 months in advance. Reports in 1 month. Free sample copy and writer's guidelines.
Nonfiction: How-to implement a particular occupational safety/health program, changes in OSHA regulations, and examples of exceptional safety/health programs. Only accepts articles that are based on an interview with a safety manager, safety consultant, occupational physician, or OSHA expert. Buys 48 mss/year. Query. Length: 750-1,200 words. Pays 10-15¢/word.

SANITARY MAINTENANCE, Trade Press Publishing Co., Dept. WM, 2100 W. Florist Ave., Milwaukee WI 53209-3799. (414)228-7701. Fax: (414)228-1134. Managing Editor: Austin Weber. Associate Editor: Susan M. Netz. 15-20% freelance written. Prefers to work with published/established writers, although all will be considered. Monthly magazine for the sanitary supply and paper industry covering "trends; offering information concerning the operations of janitor supply distributors and paper merchants; and helping distributors in the development of sales personnel." Estab. 1943. Circ. 18,000. Pays on publication. Publishes ms an average of 2 months after acceptance. Byline given. Buys first North American serial rights. Query for electronic submissions. Reports in 1 month. Free sample copy and writer's guidelines.
Nonfiction: How-to (improve sales, profitability as it applies to distributors), technical. No product application stories. Buys 12-15 mss/year. Query with published clips. Length: 2,000 words. Pays $300-400.
Photos: State availability of photos with query letter or ms. Reviews 5×7 prints. Payment for photos included in payment for ms. Identification of subjects required.
Tips: Articles on wholesaling/distribution management issues are open to freelancers.

SECURITY SALES, Management Resource for the Professional Installing Dealer, Bobit Publishing, 2512 Artesia Blvd., Redondo Beach CA 90278-3296. (310)376-8788. Editor: Jason Knott. Associate Editor: Amy K. Jones. 5% freelance written. Monthly magazine that covers the security industry. "Editorial covers technology, management and marketing designed to help installing security dealers improve their businesses. Closed-circuit TV, burglary and fire equipment, and access control systems are main topics." Estab. 1979. Circ.

22,000. Pays on publication. Publishes ms an average of 3-6 months after acceptance. Byline sometimes given. Buys all rights. Editorial lead time 2 months. Submit seasonal material 4 months in advance. Query for electronic submissions. Accepts simultaneous submissions. Sample copy free on request.

Nonfiction: How-to, technical. "No generic business operations articles. Submissions must be specific to security and contain interviews with installing dealers." Buys 3-6 mss/year. Send complete ms. Length: 800-1,500 words. Pays $50 minimum.

Photos: Send photos with submission. Reviews prints. Offers no additional payment for photos accepted with ms. Captions, model releases and identification of subjects required.

Tips: "Case studies of specific security installations with photos and diagrams are needed. Interview dealers who installed system and ask how they solved specific problems, why they chose certain equipment, cost of job, etc."

UTILITY CONSTRUCTION AND MAINTENANCE, Practical Communications, Inc., 321 Cary Point Dr., P.O. Box 183, Cary IL 60013-0183. (708)639-2200. Fax: (708)639-9542. Editor: Alan Richter. 5% freelance written. Quarterly magazine for equipment managers and maintenance supervisors for electric, gas and water utilities; interconnect and cable TV companies, public works departments and related contractors. "We seek case history/application features covering specific equipment management and maintenance projects/installations. Instructional/tutorial features are also welcome." Circ. 25,000. Pays on publication. Publishes ms an average of 1 month after acceptance. Byline given. 20% kill fee. Buys all rights. Accepts previously published articles. Send tearsheet or photocopy of article and information about when and where the article previously appeared. For reprints pays 50% of the amount paid for an original article. Submit seasonal material 2 months in advance. Reports in 2 weeks. Free sample copy and writer's guidelines.

Nonfiction: How-to (ways for performing fleet maintenance/improving management skills/vehicle tutorials), technical, case history/application features. No advertorials in which specific product or company is promoted. Buys 2-3 ms/year. Query with published clips. Length: 1,000-2,800 words. Pays $50/page.

Photos: Send photos with submission. Reviews contact sheets, negatives, 3×5 tranparencies and 3×5 prints. Offers no additional payment for photos accepted with ms. Captions required. Buys one-time rights.

Management and Supervision

This category includes trade journals for middle management business and industrial managers, including supervisors and office managers. Journals for business executives and owners are classified under Business Management. Those for industrial plant managers are listed in Industrial Operations.

EMPLOYEE RELATIONS AND HUMAN RESOURCES BULLETIN, Bureau of Business Practice, 24 Rope Ferry Rd., Waterford CT 06386. Fax: (203)434-3078, CompuServe E-mail 70303, 2324. Senior Editor: Barbara Kelsey. 40% freelance written. Works with a small number of new/unpublished writers each year. Semimonthly newsletter for personnel, human resources and employee relations managers on the executive level. Estab. 1940. Circ. 8,000. **Pays on acceptance.** Publishes ms an average of 3 months after acceptance. Buys all rights. No byline. Phone queries OK. Submit seasonal material 6 months in advance. Reports in 1 month. Free sample copy and writer's guidelines.

Nonfiction: Interviews about all types of business and industry such as banks, insurance companies, public utilities, airlines, consulting firms, etc. Interviewee should be a high level company officer—human resources executive, president, industrial relations manager, etc. Writer must get signed release from person interviewed showing that article has been read and approved by him/her, before submission. Some subjects for interviews might be productivity improvement, communications, compensation, labor relations, safety and health, grievance handling, human relations techniques and problems, etc. No general opinions and/or philosophy of good employee relations or general good motivation/morale material. Buys 2 mss/issue. Query is mandatory. Length: 2,000-2,500 words. Pays 8-18¢/word after editing. Sometimes pays the telephone expenses of writers on assignment. Modem transmission available by prior arrangement with editor.

Tips: "We are outsourcing more, which means we're looking for a wider variety of freelancers with solid knowledge of various business fields."

INDUSTRY WEEK, The Management Magazine for Industry, Penton Publishing Inc., Dept. WM, 1100 Superior Ave., Cleveland OH 44114-2543. (216)696-7000. Fax: (216)696-7670. Managing Editor: David Altany. 15% freelance written. Biweekly industrial management magazine. "*Industry Week* is designed to help its audience—mid- and upper-level managers in industry—manage and lead their organizations better. Every article should address this editorial mission." Estab. 1921. Circ. 288,000. **Pays on acceptance.** Publishes ms an average of 2-4 months after acceptance. Byline given. Buys first North American serial rights. Reports in 1 month. Free sample copy and writer's guidelines. "An SAE speeds replies."

Nonfiction: Interview/profile. "Any article submitted to *Industry Week* should be consistent with its mission. We suggest authors contact us before submitting anything." Buys 15-20 mss/year. Query with or without published clips or send complete ms. Length: 750-2,500 words. Pays $350 minimum. "We pay *routine* expenses; we do *not* pay for travel unless arranged in advance."

Photos: State availability of photos with submission or send photo with submission. Reviews contact sheets, transparencies and prints. Payment arranged individually. Captions and identification of subjects required. Buys one-time rights.

Tips: "Become familiar with *Industry Week*. We're after articles about managing in industry, period. While we do not use freelancers too often, we do use some. The stories we accept are written with an understanding of our audience, and mission. We prefer multi-source stories that offer lessons for all managers in industry."

MANAGE, 2210 Arbor Blvd., Dayton OH 45439. (513)294-0421. Fax: (513)294-2374. Editor-in-Chief: Douglas E. Shaw. 60% freelance written. Works with a small number of new/unpublished writers each year. Quarterly magazine for first-line and middle management and scientific/technical managers. Estab. 1925. Circ. 65,000. **Pays on acceptance.** Publishes ms an average of 6 months after acceptance. Buys North American magazine rights with reprint privileges; book rights remain with the author. Reports in 3 months. Sample copy and writer's guidelines for 9×12 SAE with 3 first-class stamps.

Nonfiction: "All material published by *Manage* is in some way management oriented. Most articles concern one or more of the following categories: communications, executive abilities, human relations, job status, leadership, motivation and productivity and professionalism. Articles should be specific and tell the manager how to apply the information to his job immediately. Be sure to include pertinent examples, and back up statements with facts. *Manage* does not want essays or academic reports, but interesting, well-written and practical articles for and about management." Buys 6 mss/issue. Phone queries OK. Submit complete ms. Length: 600-1,200 words. Pays 5¢/word.

Tips: "Keep current on management subjects; submit timely work. Include word count on first page of ms."

‡MANAGEMENT REVIEW, The American Management Association Magazine, American Management Association, 135 W. 50th St., New York NY 10020-1201. Editor: Martha H. Peak. Monthly magazine covering "Hands On" management issues for top/middle managers. "*Management Review* is the global membership magazine of the American Management Association, dedicated to broadening managers' know-how through insightful reporting of management trends and tips on how to manage more effectively." Estab. 1923. Circ. 75,000. Pays on publication. Publishes ms an average of 5 months after acceptance. Byline given. Buys first worldwide rights. Editorial lead time 3-4 months. Submit seasonal material 3-4 months in advance. Reports in 4-5 weeks on queries. Sample copy for $5. Writer's guidelines free on request.

Nonfiction: Business stories only. Buys 24 mss/year. Query. Length: 1,200-2,000 words.

Photos: State availability of photos with submission. Captions and identification of subjects required.

Tips: "Submissions in writing ONLY. No fax. No cold calls."

SALES MANAGER'S BULLETIN, The Bureau of Business Practice, 24 Rope Ferry Rd., Waterford CT 06386-0001. Fax: (203)434-3078. Editor: Paulette S. Kitchens. 33% freelance written. Prefers to work with published/established writers. Semimonthly newsletter for sales managers and salespeople interested in getting into sales management. Estab. 1917. **Pays on acceptance.** Publishes ms an average of 3-6 months after acceptance. Written queries only except from regulars. Submit seasonal material 6 months in advance. Original interview-based material only. Buys all rights. Reports in 1 month. Sample copy and writer's guidelines only when request is accompanied by SAE with 2 first-class stamps.

Nonfiction: How-to (motivate salespeople, cut costs, create territories, etc.); interview (with working sales managers who use innovative techniques); technical (marketing stories based on interviews with experts). No articles on territory management, saving fuel in the field, or public speaking skills. Break into this publication by reading the guidelines and sample issue. Follow the directions closely and chances for acceptance go up dramatically. One easy way to start is with an interview article ("Here's what sales executives have to say about . . ."). Query is vital to acceptance: "Send a simple note explaining briefly the subject matter, the interviewees, slant, length, and date of expected completion, accompanied by a SASE. Does not accept unqueried mss. Length: 800-1,200 words. Pays 10-15¢/word.

Tips: "Freelancers should always request samples and writer's guidelines, accompanied by SASE. Requests without SASE are discarded immediately. Examine the sample, and don't try to improve on our style. Write as we write. Don't 'jump around' from point to point and don't submit articles that are too chatty and with not enough real information. The more time a writer can save the editors, the greater his or her chance of a sale and repeated sales, when queries may no longer be necessary. We will focus more on selling more product, meeting intense competition, customer relations/partnerships, and sales forecasting."

SECURITY MANAGEMENT BULLETIN: Protecting Property, People & Assets, Bureau of Business Practice, 24 Rope Ferry Rd., Waterford CT 06386. Editor: Alex Vaughn. 75% freelance written. Eager to work

with new/unpublished writers. Semimonthly newsletter emphasizing security for industry. "All material should be slanted toward security directors, primarily industrial, retail and service businesses, but others as well." Circ. 3,000. **Pays on acceptance.** Buys all rights. Phone queries OK. Reports in 2 weeks. Free sample copy and writer's guidelines.
Nonfiction: Interview (with security professionals only). "Articles should be tight and specific. They should deal with new security techniques or new twists on old ones." Buys 2-5 mss/issue. Query. Length: 750-1,000 words. Pays 15¢/word.

SUPERVISION, P.O. Box 1, Burlington IA 52601-0001. Fax: (319)752-3421. Publisher: Michael S. Darnall. Editor: Barbara Boeding. 95% freelance written. Monthly magazine for first-line foremen, supervisors and office managers. Estab. 1939. Circ. 3,600. Pays on publication. Publishes ms an average of 6 months after acceptance. Buys all rights. Reports in 1 month. Sample copy and writer's guidelines for 9×12 SAE with 4 first-class stamps; mention *Writer's Market* in request.
Nonfiction: How-to (cope with supervisory problems, discipline, absenteeism, safety, productivity, goal setting, etc.); personal experience (unusual success story of foreman or supervisor). No sexist material written from only a male viewpoint. Include biography and/or byline with ms submissions. Author photos requested. Buys 12 mss/issue. Query. Length: 1,500-1,800 words. Pays 4¢/word.
Tips: "Following AP stylebook would be helpful." Uses no advertising. Send correspondence to Editor.

SUPERVISOR'S BULLETIN, Bureau of Business Practice, 24 Rope Ferry Rd., Waterford CT 06386-0001. (203)442-4365. Fax: (203)434-3078. Editor: Carl Thunberg. 50-75% freelance written. "We work with both new and established writers, and are always looking for fresh talent." Bimonthly newsletter for manufacturing supervisors wishing to improve their managerial skills. Estab. 1915. **Pays on acceptance.** Publishes ms an average of 3 months after acceptance. No byline given. Buys all rights. Reports in 2 weeks on queries; 6 weeks on mss. Free sample copy and writer's guidelines.
Nonfiction: How-to (solve a supervisory problem on the job or avoid litigation); interview (of top-notch supervisors or experts who can give advice on supervisory issues). Sample topics could include: how to increase productivity, cut costs, achieve better teamwork, and step-by-step approaches to problem-solving. No filler or non-interview based copy. Buys 72 mss/year. Query first. "Strongly urge writers to study guidelines and samples." Length: 750-1,000 words. Pays 12-18¢/word.
Tips: "We need interview-based articles that emphasize direct quotes. Define a problem and show how the supervisor solved it. Write in a light, conversational style, talking directly to supervisors who can benefit from putting the interviewee's tips into practice."

‡TRAINING MAGAZINE, Lakewood Publications, 50 S. 9th St., Minneapolis MN 55402. (612)333-0471. Editor: Jack Gordon. Managing Editor: Chris Lee. 10% freelance written. A monthly magazine covering training and employee development in the business world. "Our core readers are managers and professionals who specialize in employee training and development (e.g., corporate training directors, VP-human resource development, etc.). We have a large secondary readership among managers of all sorts who are concerned with improving human performance in their organizations. We take a businesslike approach to training and employee education." Estab. 1964. Circ. 56,000. **Pays on acceptance.** Publishes ms an average of 3 months after acceptance. Byline given. Buys first North American serial and second serial (reprint) rights. Accepts simultaneous submissions. Reports in 2 weeks on queries; 6 weeks on mss. Sample copy for 9×12 SAE with 4 first-class stamps. Writer's guidelines for #10 SASE.
Nonfiction: Essay; exposé; how-to (on training, management, sales, productivity improvement, etc.); humor; interview/profile; new product; opinion; photo feature; technical (use of audiovisual aids, computers, etc.). "No puff, no 'testimonials' or disguised ads in any form, no 'gee-whiz' approaches to the subjects." Buys 10-12 mss/year. Query with or without published clips, or send complete ms. Length: 200-3,000 words. Pays $50-750.
Photos: State availability of photos or send with submission. Reviews contact sheets and prints. Offers no additional payment for photos accepted with ms. Identification of subjects required. Buys one-time rights and reprint rights.
Columns/Departments: Training Today (news briefs, how-to tips, reports on pertinent research, trend analysis, etc.), 200-800 words. Buys 6 mss/year. Query or send complete ms. Pays $50-125.
Tips: "We almost never give firm assignments to unfamiliar writers, so you have to be willing to hit us with one or two on spec to break in. Short pieces for our Training Today section involve least investment on your part, but also are less likely to convince us to assign you a feature. When studying the magazine, freelancers should look at our staff-written articles for style, approach and tone. Do not concentrate on articles written by people identified as consultants, training directors, etc."

WAREHOUSING SUPERVISOR'S BULLETIN, Bureau of Business Practice, 24 Rope Ferry Rd., Waterford CT 06386-0001. (203)442-4365. Fax: (203)434-2546. Editor: Peter Hawkins. 75-90% freelance written. "We work with a wide variety of writers, and are always looking for fresh talent." Biweekly newsletter covering traffic, materials handling and distribution for warehouse supervisors "interested in becoming more effective on the job." **Pays on acceptance.** Publishes ms an average of 3 months after acceptance. No byline given.

Buys all rights. Reports in 2 weeks on queries; 6 weeks on mss. Free sample copy and writer's guidelines.
Nonfiction: How-to (increase efficiency, control or cut costs, cut absenteeism or tardiness, increase productivity, raise morale); interview (of warehouse supervisors or managers who have solved problems on the job). No noninterview articles, textbook-like descriptions, union references or advertising of products. Buys 50 mss/year. Query. "A résumé and sample of work are helpful." Length: 1,580-2,900 words. Pays 10-15¢/word. Sometimes pays the expenses of writers on assignment.
Tips: "All articles must be interview-based and emphasize how-to information. They should also include a reference to the interviewee's company (location, size, products, function of the interviewee's department and number of employees under his control). Focus articles on one problem, and get the interviewee to pinpoint the best way to solve it. Appropriate artwork (charts, forms, photos) is helpful. Write in a light, conversational style, talking directly to warehouse supervisors who can benefit from putting the interviewee's tips into practice."

Marine and Maritime Industries

CHARTER INDUSTRY, The Management Magazine for the Charter Industry, Charter Industry Services, Inc., 43 Kindred St., P.O. Box 375, Stuart FL 34995-0375. (407)288-1066. Editor: Paul McElroy. 50% freelance written. Bimonthly trade journal that covers legislative and industry issues. "*CI* is not a consumer 'Let's go on a fishing trip' publication, but is a business publication for people in the charter business, including sportfishing, diving, excursion and sailing charters." Estab. 1985. Circ. 10,750. Pays on publication. Byline given. No kill fee. Buys all rights and makes work-for-hire assignments. Accepts previously published submissions. Send tearsheet or photocopy of article or typed ms with rights for sale noted and information about when and where the article previously appeared. For reprints pays 25% of the amount paid for an original article. Reports in 2 weeks on queries. Sample copy for 9 × 12 SAE with 6 first-class stamps. Writer's guidelines for #10 SAE with 2 first-class stamps.
Nonfiction: Historical/nostalgic, how-to, humor, inspirational, interview/profile, opinion. No fishing stories. Buys 24 mss/year. Query with published clips. Length: 800-2,000 words. Pays $75-150. Sometimes pays expenses of writers on assignment.
Photos: State availability of photos with submission or send photos with submission. Reviews 5 × 7 prints. Offers no additional payment for photos accepted with ms. Captions, model releases and identification of subjects required. Buys one-time rights.
Columns/Departments: Taxes, Legal and Photography. Buys 12 mss/year. Query. Length: 600 words.
Tips: "Writers should know that the readers are professional captains who depend upon their boats and the sea to make their living. They demand the writer know the subject and the application to the industry. Those without knowledge of the industry should save their postage." Areas most open to freelancers are "personal profiles of sucessful charter captains and charter ports. We have guidelines for articles on both subjects. Most freelancer submissions are rejected because they don't do their homework properly. Our readers are tough taskmasters. Don't try to fool them!"

MARINE BUSINESS JOURNAL, The Voice of the Marine Industries Nationwide, 1766 Bay Rd., Miami Beach FL 33139. (305)538-0700. Editorial Director: Andree Conrad. 25% freelance written. Bimonthly tabloid that covers the recreational boating industry. "*The Marine Business Journal* is aimed at boating dealers, distributors and manufacturers, naval architects, yacht brokers, marina owners and builders, marine electronics dealers, distributors and manufacturers, and anyone involved in the US marine industry. Articles cover news, new product technology and public affairs affecting the industry." Estab. 1986. Circ. 26,000. Pays on publication. Publishes ms an average of 1 month after acceptance. Byline given. Buys first North American serial, one-time or second serial (reprint rights). Query for electronic submissions. Reports in 2 weeks on queries. Sample copy for $2.50 and 9 × 12 SAE with 7 first-class stamps. Writer's guidelines for #10 SASE.
Nonfiction: "Send query before sending ms." Buys 20 mss/year. Query with published clips. Length: 500-2,000 words. Pays $100-200 for assigned articles. Sometimes pays expenses of writers on assignment.
Photos: State availability of photos with submission. Reviews 35mm or larger transparencies and 5 × 7 prints. Offers $25-50/photo. Captions, model releases and identification of subjects required. Buys one-time rights.
Tips: "Query with clips. It's a highly specialized field, written for professionals by professionals, almost all on assignment or by staff."

NORTHERN AQUACULTURE, Harrison House Publishers, 4611 William Head Rd., Victoria, British Columbia V9B 5T7 Canada. (604)478-9209. Fax: (604)478-1184. Editor: Peter Chettleburgh. 50% freelance written. Works with a small number of new/unpublished writers each year. Bimonthly magazine covering aquaculture in Canada and the northern US. Estab. 1985. Circ. 4,000. Pays on publication. Publishes ms an average of 3 months after acceptance. Byline given. Buys first North American serial rights. Submit seasonal material 5 months in advance. Reports in 3 weeks. Free sample copy for 9 × 12 SAE with $2 IRCs. Free writer's guidelines.
Nonfiction: How-to, interview/profile, new product, opinion, photo feature. Buys 20-24 mss/year. Query. Length: 200-1,500 words. Pays 10-20¢/word for assigned articles; 10-15¢/word for unsolicited articles. May

pay writers with contributor copies if writer requests. Sometimes pays the expenses of writers on assignment.
Photos: Send photos with submission. Reviews 5×7 prints. Captions required. Buys one-time rights.

‡OCEAN NAVIGATOR, Marine Navigation & Ocean Voyaging, Navigator Publishing Corp., 18 Danforth St., Portland ME 04101. (207)772-2466. Editor: Tim Queeney. Bimonthly magazine covering marine navigation and ocean voyaging. Estab. 1985. Circ. 40,600. Pays on publication. Byline given. Accepts simultaneous and previously published submissions. Query for electronic submissions. Sample copy and writer's guidelines free on request.
Nonfiction: How-to, personal experience, technical. No racing (except navigational challenges); no travel logs/diaries. Query or send complete ms. Pays 15¢/word up to $500.
Photos: Send photos with submission. Offers $50-75/photo; $400 for cover photo.

PROCEEDINGS, Dept. WM, U.S. Naval Institute, Annapolis MD 21402. (410)268-6110. Fax: (410)269-7940. Editor: Fred H. Rainbow. Managing Editor: John G. Miller. 95% freelance written. Eager to work with new/published writers. Monthly magazine covering general military, naval and maritime subjects. Circ. 100,000. **Pays on acceptance.** Publishes ms an average of 5 months after acceptance. Byline given. Buys all rights. Submit seasonal material 3 months in advance. Reports in 2 weeks on queries; 1 month on mss. *Writer's Market* recommends allowing 2 months for reply. Free sample copy and writer's guidelines.
Nonfiction: Essays, exposé, general interest, historical/nostalgic, how-to (related to sea service professional subjects), humor, interview/profile, new product, opinion, personal experience, photo feature, technical. "*Proceedings* is an unofficial, open forum for the discussion of naval and maritime topics." Special issues: International Navies (March); Naval Review (May). Buys 250 mss/year. Query or send complete ms. Length: up to 3,500 words. Pays $50-600. Sometimes pays writers with contributor copies or other premiums "if author desires." Sometimes pays the expenses of writers on assignment.
Photos: Send photos with submission. Reviews contact sheets, negatives, transparencies and prints. Offers $10-100/photo. Buys one-time rights.
Columns/Departments: Book Reviews, Nobody Asked Me But . . .(all with general military, naval or maritime slants, all 500-2,000 words. Buys 90 mss/year. Query. Pays $50-200.
Fiction: Adventure, historical, humorous. Buys 6 mss/year. Query. Length: 500-3,000 words. Pays $50-600.
Fillers: Anecdotes. Buys 50/year. Length: 1,000 words maximum. Pays $25-150.
Tips: "Write about something you know about, either from first-hand experience or based on primary source material. Our letters to the editor column is most open to freelancers."

‡PROFESSIONAL MARINER, Journal of Professional Seamanship, Navigator Publishing, 18 Danforth St., Portland ME 04101. (207)772-2466. Editor: Gregory Walsh. 50% freelance written. Bimonthly magazine covering professional and government seamanship and news. Estab. 1993. Circ. 14,000. Pays on publication. Byline given. Buys all rights. Editorial lead time 3 months. Accepts simultaneous submissions. Query for electronic submissions. Sample copy and writer's guidelines free on request.
Nonfiction: Inspirational, interview/profile, technical. No business news. Buys 15 mss/year. Query. Length varies: short clips to long profiles/features. Pays 15¢/word. Sometimes pays expenses of writers on assignment.
Photos: Send photos with submission. Reviews contact sheets, negatives, transparencies and prints. Negotiates payment individually. Identification of subjects required. Buys one-time rights.

Medical

Through these journals physicians, therapists and mental health professionals learn how other professionals help their patients and manage their medical practices. Publications for nurses, laboratory technicians and other medical personnel are listed in the Hospitals, Nursing and Nursing Home section. Publications for drug store managers and drug wholesalers and retailers, as well as hospital equipment suppliers, are listed with Drugs, Health Care and Medical Products. Publications for consumers that report trends in the medical field are found in the Consumer Health and Fitness categories.

AMERICAN MEDICAL NEWS, American Medical Association, Dept. WM, 515 N. State St., Chicago IL 60610. (312)464-4429. Fax: (312)464-4445. Editor: Barbara Bolsen. Contact Topic Editor: Ronnie Scheier, Public Health and Physician Well-Being; Howard Larkin, Health Systems Finance & Delivery (edits business section, which publishes service features intended to help doctors run their medical practices more effectively); Bill Silberg, Professional Issues; Mary O'Connell, Health Systems Trends/Health System Reform. 5-10% freelance written. "Prefers writers experienced at covering health policy and public health issues—not clinical medicine." Weekly tabloid "providing physician readers with news, information and analysis of issues and trends affecting the practice of medicine.The aim is to help them understand and react effectively to events and trends." This is a well-educated, highly sophisticated physician audience." Circ. 375,000 physi-

cians. **Pays on acceptance.** Publishes ms an average of 2 months after acceptance. Byline given. Offers variable kill fee. Buys first North American rights. Simultaneous queries OK. Reports in 1 month. Sample copy for 9 × 12 SAE with 2 first-class stamps. Free writer's guidelines.
Tips: "An understanding of our publication and its needs is crucial for the successful query."

CARDIOLOGY WORLD NEWS, Medical Publishing Enterprises, P.O. Box 1548, Marco Island FL 33969. (813)394-0400. Editor: John H. Lavin. 75% freelance written. Prefers to work with published/established writers. Monthly magazine covering cardiology and the cardiovascular system. "We need short news articles *for doctors* on any aspect of our field — diagnosis, treatment, risk factors, etc." Estab. 1985. **Pays on acceptance.** Publishes ms an average of 2 months after acceptance. Byline given "for special reports and feature-length articles." Offers 20% kill fee. Buys first North American serial rights. Query for electronic submissions. Reports in 2 months. Sample copy for $1. Free writer's guidelines with #10 SASE.
Nonfiction: New product and technical (clinical). No fiction, fillers, profiles of doctors or poetry. Query with published clips. Length: 250-1,200 words. Pays $50-300; $50/column for news articles. Pays expenses of writers on assignment.
Photos: State availability of photos with query. Pays $50/published photo. Rough captions, model release and identification of subjects required. Buys one-time rights.
Tips: "Submit written news articles of 250-500 words on speculation with basic source material (not interview notes) for fact-checking. We demand clinical or writing expertise for full-length feature. Clinical cardiology conventions/symposia are the best source of news and feature articles."

EMERGENCY, The Journal of Emergency Services, 6300 Yarrow Dr., Carlsbad CA 92009-1597. (619)438-2511. Fax: (619)931-5809. Editor: Doug Fiske. 100% freelance written. Works with a small number of new/ unpublished writers each year. Monthly magazine covering prehospital emergency care. "Our readership is primarily composed of EMTs, paramedics and other EMS personnel. We prefer a professional, semi-technical approach to prehospital subjects." Estab. 1969. Circ. 30,000. **Pays on acceptance.** Publishes ms an average of 4 months after acceptance. Byline given. Buys all rights (revert back to author after 3 months). Submit seasonal material 6 months in advance. Reports in 2-3 months. Sample copy for $3. Writer's guidelines for #10 SASE.
Nonfiction: Semi-technical exposé, how-to (on treating prehospital emergency patients), interview/profile, new techniques, opinion, photo feature. "We do not publish cartoons, term papers, product promotions disguised as articles or overly technical manuscripts." Buys 60 mss/year. Query with published clips. Length 1,500-3,000 words. Pays $100-300.
Photos: Send photos with submission. Reviews color transparencies and b&w prints. Photos accepted with mss increase payment. Offers $30/photo without ms; $100 for cover photos. Captions and identification of subjects required. All medics pictured must be using universal precautions (gloves, etc.).
Columns/Departments: Open Forum (opinion page for EMS professionals), 500 words; Skills Primer (basic skills, how-to with photos), 1,000-2,000 words; Rescue Call (cover a specific rescue or technique); Drug Watch (focus on one particular drug a month). Buys 10 mss/year. Query first. Pays $50-250.
Fillers: Facts, newsbreaks. Buys 10/year. Length: no more than 500 words. Pays $0-75.
Tips: "Writing style for features and departments should be knowledgeable and lively with a clear theme or story line to maintain reader interest and enhance comprehension. The biggest problem we encounter is dull, lifeless term-paper-style writing with nothing to pique reader interest. Keep in mind we are not a textbook, but all technical articles must be well referenced with footnotes within the text. We follow AP style. Accompanying photos are a plus.We appreciate a short, one paragraph biography on the author."

FACETS, American Medical Association Auxiliary, Inc., 515 N. State St., Chicago IL 60610. (312)464-4470. Fax: (312)464-4184. Editor: Kathleen T. Jordan. 25% freelance written. Work with both established and new writers. Bimonthly magazine for physicians' spouses. Estab. 1965. Circ. 65,000. **Pays on acceptance.** Publishes ms an average of 6 months after acceptance. Buys first rights. Accepts simultaneous and previously published submissions. Reports in 2 months. Sample copy and writer's guidelines for 9 × 12 SAE with 2 first-class stamps.
Nonfiction: All articles must be related to the experiences of physicians' spouses. Current health issues; financial topics, physicians' family circumstances, business management and volunteer leadership how-to's. Buys 10 mss/year. Query with clear outline of article — what points will be made, what conclusions drawn, what sources will be used. No personal experience or personality stories. Length: 1,000-2,500 words. Pays $300-800. Pays expenses of writers on assignment.
Photos: State availability of photos with query. Uses 8 × 10 glossy b&w prints and 2¼ × 2¼ transparencies.
Tips: Uses "articles only on specified topical matter with good sources, not hearsay or personal opinion. Since we use only nonfiction and have a limited readership, we must relate factual material."

FITNESS MANAGEMENT, Issues and solutions for fitness services, Leisure Publications, Inc., Suite 110, 215 S. Highway 101, P.O. Box 1198, Solana Beach CA 92075-0910. (619)481-4155. Fax: (619)481-4228. Editor: Edward H. Pitts. 50% freelance written. Monthly magazine covering commercial, corporate and community fitness centers. "Readers are owners, managers and program directors of physical fitness facilities. *FM* helps them run their enterprises safely, efficiently and profitably. Ethical and professional positions in health, nutrition, sports medicine, management, etc., are consistent with those of established national bodies." Estab. 1985. Circ. 25,000. Pays on publication. Publishes ms an average of 5 months after acceptance. Byline given. Pays 50% kill fee. Buys all rights. Submit seasonal material 6 months in advance. Query for electronic submissions. Reports in 3 months. Sample copy for $5. Writer's guidelines for #10 SASE.

Nonfiction: Book excerpts (prepublication), how-to (manage fitness center and program), new product (no pay), photo feature (facilities/programs), technical and other (news of fitness research and major happenings in fitness industry). No exercise instructions or general ideas without examples of fitness businesses that have used them successfully. Buys 50 mss/year. Query. Length: 750-2,000 words. Pays $60-300 for assigned articles; up to $300 for unsolicited articles. Pays expenses of writers on assignment.

Photos: Send photos with submission. Reviews contact sheets, 2×2 and 4×5 transparencies; prefers glossy prints, 5×7 to 8×10. Offers $10-25/photo. Captions and model releases required.

Tips: "We seek writers who are expert in a business or science field related to the fitness-service industry or who are experienced in the industry. Be current with the state of the art/science in business and fitness and communicate it in human terms (avoid intimidating academic language; tell the story of how this was learned and/or cite examples of quotes of people who have applied the knowledge successfully)."

HEALTH SYSTEMS REVIEW, P.O. Box 8708, Little Rock AR 72217-8708. (501)661-9555. Fax: (501)663-4903. Executive Editor: John Herrmann. 5% freelance written. Bimonthly trade journal on health care issues and health care politics (federal and state). *"Health Systems Review* publishes articles concerning the politics of health care, covers legislative activities and broad grass roots stories involving particular hospitals or organizations and their problems/solutions. Goes to health care managers, executives, to all members of the Congress, its staffs, the Administration and staff." Estab. 1967. Circ. 30,000. **Pays on acceptance.** Byline given. Buys first North American serial and second serial (reprint) rights. Accepts simultaneous and previously published articles. Send tearsheet of article. Submit seasonal material 6 months in advance. Query for electronic submissions. Reports in 1 week on queries; 1 month on mss. *Writer's Market* recommends allowing 2 months for reply. Sample copy for 9×12 SAE with 5 first-class stamps.

Nonfiction: Essays, interview/profile, opinion, personal experience. "No articles about health care or medical procedures. No new products pieces. No articles about health care and the stock market." Buys 2-4 mss/year. Query with published clips. Length: 1,500-3,500 words. Pays $200. "Articles by health care leaders, members of Congress and staff and legal columns generally not paid." Pays expenses of writers on assignment.

Photos: Send photos with submission. Reviews contact sheets, transparencies and prints. Offers no additional payment for photos accepted with ms. Captions and identification of subjects required. Buys one-time rights.

Columns/Departments: Jennifer L. Smith. Health Care Financing (business issues in health care), 1,500-3,500 words; Health Law Perspectives (written in-house); and Supply Side (health care suppliers news update), 1,500-3,500 words. Buys 2 mss/year. Query with published clips. Pays $100-200.

Tips: "Health care reform measures; a good large multi-hospital group business story (failure or success); good contacts with state or federal senators and representatives and/or their staff members for close-ups, profiles. No writing in supply side that sells the supplier or its products but, rather, how it sees current issues from its perspective."

HMO MAGAZINE, Directions in Managed Health Care, Group Health Association of America, Suite 600, 1129 20th St. NW, Washington DC 20036. (202)778-3250. Editor: Susan Pisano. Contact: Lisa Lopez, Managing Editor. 35% freelance written. Bimonthly magazine for news and analysis of the health maintenance organization (HMO) industry. *"HMO Magazine* is geared toward senior administrative and medical managers in HMOs. Articles must succinctly and clearly define issues of concern or news to the HMO industry. Articles must ask 'why' and 'how' and answer with examples. Articles should inform and generate interest and discussion about topics on anything from medical management to regulatory issues." Estab. 1990. Circ. 6,000. Pays 30 days within acceptance of article in final form. Publishes ms an average of 2 months after acceptance. Byline given. Offers 30% kill fee. Buys all rights. Editorial lead time 2 months. Submit seasonal material 2 months in advance. Accepts simultaneous submissions. Query for electronic submissions. Reports in 1 month on queries. Sample copy and writer's guidelnes free on request.

Nonfiction: How-to (how industry professionals can better operate their health plans), opinion. "We do not accept any articles relating to clinical health issues, such as nutrition or any general health topics that do not address issues of concern to HMO administrators; nor do we accept stories that promote products." Buys 20 mss/year. Query. Length: 1,800-2,500 words. Pays 40¢/word minimum for assigned articles; 35¢/word minimum for unsolicited articles. Pays phone expenses of writers on assignment.

Photos: State availability of photos with submission. Reviews contact sheets. Offers no additional payment for photos accepted with ms. Buys all rights.

Columns/Departments: Washington File (health policy issues relating to HMOs and managed health care), 1,800 words; Preventive Care (case study or discussion of public health HMOs), 1,800 words; The Market (market niches for HMOs—with examples), 1,800 words. Buys 6 mss/year. Query with published clips. Pays 35-50¢/word.

Tips: "Follow the current health care debate. Much of what the Clinton Administration proposes will definitely impact the HMO industry. Look for HMO success stories in your community; we like to include case studies on everything from medical management to regulatory issues so that our readers can learn from their colleagues. Our readers are members of our trade association and look for advice and news. Topics relating to the quality and cost benefits of HMOs are the ones most frequently assigned to writers, whether a feature or department. For example, a recent story on 'The High Price of Compliance' relating to costs associated with not complying with prescription advice, got a lot of reader interest. The writer interviewed a number of experts inside and outside the HMO field."

JEMS, The Journal of Emergency Medical Services, Jems Communications, Suite 200, 1947 Camino Vida Roble, Carlsbad CA 92008-2789. (619)431-9797. Fax: (619)431-8176. Executive Editor: Keith Griffiths. Managing Editor: Tara Regan. 25% freelance written. Monthly magazine for emergency medical services— all phases. The journal is directed to the personnel who serve the emergency medicine industry: paramedics, EMTs, emergency physicians and nurses, administrators, EMS consultants, etc. Estab. 1980. Circ. 35,000. Pays on publication. Publishes ms an average of 3-6 months after acceptance. Byline given. Buys all North American serial rights. Submit seasonal material 6 months in advance. Query for electronic submissions. Reports in 2 months. Free sample copy and writer's guidelines.
Nonfiction: Essays, general interest, how-to (prehospital care), continuing education, humor, interview/profile, new product, opinion, photo feature, technical. Buys 18 mss/year. Query. Length: 900-3,600 words. Pays $150-400.
 • *JEMS* has an increased need for investigative reporters who can cover system politics, trends and product concerns and have a strong ENS knowledge base.
Photos: State availability of photos with submission. Offers no additional payment for photos accepted with ms. Buys one-time rights.
Columns/Departments: Teacher Talk (directed toward EMS instructors), 2,400 words; Manager's Forum (EMS administrators), 1,500-2,000 words; and First Person (personal accounts of life in EMS); Law and Policy (legislative reports).
Tips: "Feature articles are most open to freelancers. We have guidelines available upon request and, of course, manuscripts must be geared toward our specific EMS audience."

‡**JOURNAL OF NURSING JOCULARITY, The Humor Magazine for Nurses**, JNJ Publishing, Inc., P.O. Box 40416, Mesa AZ 85274. (602)835-6165. Editor: Fran London, RN, MS. 75% freelance written. Quarterly magazine covering nursing and medical humor. *"Journal of Nursing Jocularity* is read by health care professionals. Published manuscripts pertain to the lighter side of health care, predominantly from the perspective of the health care provider." Estab. 1990. Circ. 20,000. Pays on publication. Publishes ms an average of 1 year after acceptance. Offers 100% kill fee. Buys one-time rights. Editorial lead time 6-12 months. Submit seasonal material 9-12 months in advance. Accepts simultaneous submissions. Query for electronic submissions. Reports in 2 months on queries; 3 months on mss. Sample copy for $2. Writer's guidelines for 9×10 SAE with 2 first-class stamps.
Nonfiction: Essays, historical/nostalgic, humor, interview/profile, opinion, personal experience, *current* research on therapeutic use of humor. "Our readers are primarily active nurses. Our focus is *insider humor*." Buys 4-8 mss/year. Length: 500-1,500 words. Pays $5. Sometimes pays expenses of writers on assignment.
Photos: State availability of photos with submission. Model releases required. Buys one-time rights.
Columns/Departments: Stories from the Floor (anecdotes—true nursing experiences), 16-200 words; Call Lites (health care jokes with insider edge), 16-200 words; Student Nurse Cut-Ups (anecdotes—true student nurse experiences), 16-150 words. Pays *JNJ* T-shirt.
Fiction: Humorous, slice-of-life vignettes. Buys 30 mss/year. Query or send complete ms. Length: 500-1,500 words. Pays $5.
Poetry: Avant-garde, free verse, haiku, light verse, traditional, songs and cheers. Buys 4-6 poems/year. Submit maximum 3 poems. Pays $5.
Fillers: Anecdotes, gags to be illustrated by cartoonist, short humor. Length: 16-200 words. Pays T-shirt.
Tips: "Our readers are primarily working nurses. *JNJ*'s focus is insider humor—the kind only a health care provider understands. *Very few* non-health care providers have been able to submit material that rings true. We do not publish material written from a patient's point of view."

‡**MANAGED HEALTHCARE**, Advanstar Communications, 7500 Old Oak Blvd., Cleveland OH 44130. (216)891-3104. Editor: Joseph F. McKenna. Managing Editor: Susan Hirschman. 65% freelance written. Monthly trade magazine covering managed health care industry. "We cover the spectrum of managed health care, including news, finance and in-depth analysis of buyer and provider issues." Estab. 1991. Circ. 36,000. **Pays on acceptance.** Publishes ms an average of 1 month after acceptance. Byline given. Editorial lead time 1-2 months. Query for electronic submissions. Sample copy not available.
Nonfiction: Buys 85 mss/year. Query. Length: 750-3,000 words. Pays $100 minimum for assigned articles; $700 minimum for unsolicited articles. Sometimes pays expenses of writers on assignment.
Photos: State availability of photos or send photos with submission. Reviews prints. Negotiates payment individually. Identification of subjects required. Buys one-time rights.

Columns/Departments: Contact: Joseph F. McKenna, Editor. Commentary (expert opinion on managed care issues), 750-1,000 words. Query.
Tips: News section is most open to freelancers.

MD MAGAZINE, MD Publications, 14th Floor, 55 5th Ave., New York NY 10003-4301. (212)989-2100. Editor: Helen Smith. 40% freelance written. Monthly magazine that is distributed nationally to physicians. *"MD* is a cultural/general-interest magazine for physicians. It covers medicine, science, art, travel, food, social issues, books, technology, history, theater, biography, music and sports—the world outside the doctor's office. It does not cover clinical subjects." Estab. 1957. Circ. 120,000. Pays on publication. Publishes ms 3 months after acceptance. Byline given. Offers 33% kill fee. Buys first North American serial rights. Submit seasonal material 4 months in advance. Accepts previously published material. Send photocopy of article or short story, information about when and where the article previously appeared. Query for electronic submissions. Reports in 2 months. Sample copy for 9×12 SASE with 5 first-class stamps. Writer's guidelines for #10 SASE.
Nonfiction: General interest, historical, interview/profile, photo feature, food, travel. "No articles on clinical medicine or problems of running a medical practice." Buys 45 mss/year. Query only or query with published clips. Length: 750-3,000 words. Pays $250-3,000. Sometimes pays expenses of writers on assignment.
Photos: State availability of photos with submission. Offers no additional payment for photos accepted with ms. Captions, model releases and identification of subjects required. Buys one-time rights.
Tips: "Our purview is broad, but our approach is particular: we seek to portray the world the way a doctor sees it. We focus particularly on the doctor-reader's concerns. We look *through* the physicians' eyes—from their perspective—we don't just present material *for* them. All nonfiction areas are open to freelancers. The level of information should not be elementary—articles should be written with a sophisticated, demanding audience in mind. We are looking for short, well-written food articles. We also publish short stories and essays by physicians *only.* Any fiction submitted by a nonphysician will be returned unread."

MEDICAL ECONOMICS, Medical Economics Publishing, 5 Paragon Dr., Montvale NJ 07645-1742. (201)358-7200. Fax: (201)476-1734. Editor: Stephen K. Murata. Managing Editor: Larry Frederick. Less than 10% freelance written. Biweekly magazine covering topics of nonclinical interest to office-based private physicians (MDs and DOs only). "We publish practice/management and personal/finance advice for office-based MDs and osteopaths." Circ. 175,000. **Pays on acceptance.** Publishes ms an average of 3 months after acceptance. Byline given. Offers 25% of full article fee as kill fee. Buys all rights and first serial rights. Reports in 2 months on queries; 3 weeks on mss. *Writer's Market* recommends allowing 2 months for reply. Sample copy for $10 and 9×12 SASE.
Nonfiction: Contact Lilian Fine, chief of Outside Copy Division. How-to (office and personnel management, personal-money management); personal experience (only involving MDs or DOs in private practice); travel (how-to articles). No clinical articles, hobby articles, personality profiles or office design articles. Query with published clips. Length: 1,500-3,000 words. Pays $750-1,800. "The payment level is decided at the time go-ahead is given after query."
Tips: "How-to articles should fully describe techniques, goals, options and caveats—in terms that are clear and *realistic* for the average physician. Use of anecdotal examples to support major points is crucial. Our full-time staff is quite large, and therefore we buy only freelance articles that are not already assigned to staff writers. This puts a premium on unusual and appealing subjects."

‡MEDICAL IMAGING, The Business Magazine for Technology Management, (formerly *Second Source Imaging*), P.O. Box 930, 207 High Point Ave., Portsmouth RI 02871-0947. (401)633-7470. Editor: Jack Spears. Contact: Michael Buller, managing editor. 5% freelance written. Monthly magazine covering diagnostic imaging equipment. "Our editorial statement is to provide cost-effective solutions to the maintenance and management of diagnostic imaging equipment. Articles should address this." Estab. 1986. Circ. 14,000. **Pays on acceptance.** Publishes ms an average of 2 months after acceptance. Byline given. Offers 50% kill fee. Buys all rights. Editorial lead time two 2 months. Responds to query letters, "as soon as possible." Sample copy for $10 prepaid. Writer's guidelines for #10 SASE.
Nonfiction: Interview/profile, technical. "No general interest/human interest stories about healthcare. Articles *must* deal with our industry-diagnostic imaging." Buys 6 mss/year. Query with published clips. Length: 1,500-2,500 words. Pays approximately 25¢/word. Sometimes pays expenses of writers on assignment.
Photos: State availability of photos with submission. Reviews negatives. Offers no additional payment for photos accepted with ms "unless assigned separately." Model releases and identification of subjects required. Buys all rights.
Tips: "Send a letter with an interesting story idea that is applicable to our industry, diagnostic imaging. Then follow up with a phone call. Areas most open to freelancers are feature and technology. You don't have to be an engineer or doctor but you have to know how to talk and listen to them."

THE NEW PHYSICIAN, 1890 Preston White Dr., Reston VA 22091-4325. Contact: Editor. 40% freelance written. Magazine published 9 times/year for medical students, interns, residents and educators. Circ. 30,000. Buys first serial rights. **Pays on acceptance.** Publishes an average of 2 months after acceptance. Will consider simultaneous submissions. Accepts previously published articles. Send photocopy of article and information about when and where the article previously appeared. Publishes novel excerpts. Reports in 2 months. Sample copy for 10×13 SAE with 5 first-class stamps. Writer's guidelines for SASE.

Nonfiction: Articles on social, political, economic issues in medicine/medical education. Buys about 12 features/year. Query or send complete ms. Length: 800-3,500 words. Pays 25¢-50¢/word with higher fees for selected pieces. Pays expenses of writers on assignment.

Tips: "Although we are published by an association (the American Medical Student Association), we are not a 'house organ.' We are a professional magazine for readers with a progressive view on health care issues and a particular interest in improving the health care system. Our readers demand sophistication on the issues we cover. Freelancers should be willing to look deeply into the issues in question and not be satisfied with a cursory review of those issues."

PHYSICIAN'S MANAGEMENT, Advanstar Communications, 7500 Old Oak Blvd., Cleveland OH 44130. (216)243-8100. Fax: (216)891-2683. Editor-in-Chief: Bob Feigenbaum. Prefers to work with published/established writers. Monthly magazine emphasizing finances, investments, malpractice, socioeconomic issues, estate and retirement planning, small office administration, practice management, computers and taxes for primary care physicians in private practice. Estab. 1960. Circ. 120,000. **Pays on acceptance.** Publishes ms an average of 2-6 months after acceptance. Submit seasonal material 5 months in advance. Query for electronic submissions. Reports in 1 month. Sample copy for $5. Writer's guidelines for #10 SASE.

Nonfiction: *"Physician's Management* is a practice management/economic publication, not a clinical one." Publishes how-to articles (limited to medical practice management); informational (when relevant to audience); and personal experience articles (if written by a physician). No fiction, clinical material or satire that portrays MD in an unfavorable light; or soap opera, "real-life" articles. Length: 2,000-2,500 words. Query with SASE. Pays $125/3-column printed page. Use of charts, tables, graphs, sidebars and photos strongly encouraged. Sometimes pays expenses of writers on assignment.

Tips: "Talk to doctors first about their practices, financial interests, and day-to-day nonclinical problems and then query us. Also, the ability to write a concise, well-structured and well-researched magazine article is essential. Freelancers who think like patients fail with us. Those who can think like MDs are successful."

‡PHYSICIAN'S PRACTICE DIGEST, 13th Floor, 100 S. Charles St., Baltimore MD 21201. (410)539-3100. Editor: Bruce Goldfarb. 75% freelance written. Quarterly trade magazine covering the business side of medical practice. "Magazine is about physician practice management, the business of medicine and health care. Readers are primarily in solo practice or small groups. Not a clinical publication." Estab. 1990. Circ. 30,000. **Pays on acceptance.** Publishes ms an average of 2 months after acceptance. Byline given. Offers 25% kill fee. Buys one-time rights. Editorial lead time 3 months. Submit seasonal material 6 months in advance. Accepts previously published submissions. Query for electronic submissions. Sample copy and writer's guidelines free on request.

Nonfiction: How-to, interview/profile, opinion. "Anything related to health reform is hot now—managed care, reimbursement. No clinical articles." Buys 40 mss/year. Query with published clips. Length: 500-2,500 words. Pays 25¢/word minimum for assigned articles. Sometimes pays expenses of writers on assignment.

Photos: State availability of photos with submission. Reviews transparencies. Negotiates payment individually. Captions, model releases and identification of subjects required. Buys one-time rights.

Columns/Departments: Office Technology (computers, software, simulators, etc.), 500 words; Malpractice (reform, arbitration, etc.), 500 words; Managed Care (contracting, UR, guidelines, etc.), 500 words. Query with published clips. Pays 25-50¢/word.

Tips: "It's absolutely essential to read the magazine. We *do not* run clinical articles. We're trying to help our readers cope while the health care industry undergoes radical transformation. We welcome ideas and information that will help the physician better manage the practice. Read the magazine! Think about what the reader *needs to know.* Look for health care trends and find the angle that affects physicians."

PODIATRY MANAGEMENT, P.O. Box 50, Island Station NY 10044. (212)355-5216. Fax: (212)486-7706. Publisher: Scott C. Borowsky. Editor: Barry Block, DPM, J.D. Managing Editor: Martin Kruth. Magazine published 9 times/year for practicing podiatrists. "Aims to help the doctor of podiatric medicine to build a bigger, more successful practice, to conserve and invest his money, to keep him posted on the economic, legal and sociological changes that affect him." Estab. 1982. Circ. 13,000. Pays on publication. Byline given. Buys first North American serial and second serial (reprint) rights. Submit seasonal material 4 months in advance. Accepts simultaneous and previously published submissions. Send photocopy of article. For reprints, pays 20-50% of their fee for an original article. Reports in 2 weeks. Sample copy for $3 and 9×12 SAE. Writer's guidelines for #10 SASE.

Nonfiction: General interest (taxes, investments, estate planning, recreation, hobbies); how-to (establish and collect fees, practice management, organize office routines, supervise office assistants, handle patient relations); interview/profile about interesting or well-known podiatrists; and personal experience. "These subjects are the mainstay of the magazine, but offbeat articles and humor are always welcome." Send tax

and financial articles to Martin Kruth, 5 Wagon Hill Lane, Avon, CT 06001. Buys 25 mss/year. Query. Length: 1,000-2,500 words. Pays $150-600.
Photos: State availability of photos. Pays $15 for b&w contact sheet. Buys one-time rights.

RESCUE, Jems Communications, P.O. Box 2789, Carlsbad CA 92018-2789. (619)431-9797. Fax: (619)431-8176. Managing Editor: Jeff Berend. 60% freelance written. Bimonthly magazine covering both the technical side and excitement of being a rescuer. Estab. 1988. Circ. 25,000. Pays on publication. Byline given. Buys first North American and one-time rights. Submit seasonal material 6 months in advance. Query for electronic submissions (prefers diskette to accompany ms). Reports in 3 weeks on queries; 2 months on mss. Sample copy and writer's guidelines for 9 × 12 SAE with 5 first-class stamps.
Nonfiction: Book excerpts, how-to, humor, new product, opinion, photo feature, technical. Special issues: Vehicle extrication, rescue training, mass-casualty incidents, water rescue and wilderness rescue. No hazardous material incidents or "I was saved by a ranger" articles. Buys 15-20 mss/year. Query first with published clips or send complete ms. Length: 1,000-3,000 words. Pays $125-250. Sometimes pays the expenses of writers on assignment.
Photos: Send photos with submission. Reviews contact sheets, negatives, 2 × 2 and 35mm transparencies and 5 × 7 prints. Offers $50-125/photo. Buys one-time rights.
Tips: "Read our magazine, spend some time with a rescue team. We focus on all aspects of rescue, including vehicle extrication, rope rescue, disaster training, search and rescue, collapse rescue, and mountain rescue in addition to specialized rescue. Emphasis on techniques and new technology, with color photos as support."

STRATEGIC HEALTH CARE MARKETING, Health Care Communications, 11 Heritage Ln., P.O. Box 594, Rye NY 10580. (914)967-6741. Editor: Michele von Dambrowski. 75% freelance written. Prefers to work with published/established writers. "Will only work with unpublished writer on a 'stringer' basis initially." Monthly newsletter covering health care services marketing in a wide range of settings including hospitals and medical group practices, home health services and ambulatory care centers, Emphasizing strategies and techniques employed within the health care field and relevant applications from other service industries. Estab. 1984. Pays on publication. Publishes ms an average of 2 months after acceptance. Byline given. Offers 25% kill fee. Buys first North American serial rights. Reports in 1 month. Sample copy for 9 × 12 SAE with 3 first-class stamps. Guidelines sent with sample copy only.
Nonfiction: How-to, interview/profile, new product, technical. Buys 45 mss/year. Query with published clips. No unsolicited mss accepted. Length: 700-3,000 words. Pays $100-450. Sometimes pays the expenses of writers on assignment with prior authorization.
Photos: State availability of photos with submissions. (Photos, unless necessary for subject explanation, are rarely used.) Reviews contact sheets. Offers $10-30/photo. Captions and model releases required. Buys one-time rights.
Tips: "Writers with prior experience on business beat for newspaper or newsletter will do well. We require more sophisticated, indepth knowledge of health care reform issues and impact. This is not a consumer publication — the writer with knowledge of both health care and marketing will excel. Interviews or profiles are most open to freelancers. Absolutely no unsolicited manuscripts; any received will be returned or discarded unread."

‡UNIQUE OPPORTUNITIES, The Physician's Resource, U O Inc., Suite 817, 455 S. Fourth Ave., Louisville KY 40202. Editor: Mollie Vento Hudson. Contact: Bett Coffman, assistant editor. 45% freelance written. Bimonthly magazine covering physician relocation. "Published for physicians interested in a new career opportunity. It offers physicians useful information and first-hand experiences to guide them in making informed decisions concerning their first or next career opportunity. It provides regular features and columns about specific aspects of the search process." Estab. 1991. Circ. 80,000 physicians. **Pays on acceptance.** Publishes ms an average of 2 months after acceptance. Byline given. Offers 33% kill fee. Buys first North American serial rights. Editorial lead time 3 months. Submit seasonal material 6 months in advance. Query for electronic submissions. Reports in 2 months on queries. Sample copy for 9 × 12 SAE and 6 first-class stamps. Writer's guidelines for #10 SASE.
Nonfiction: Opinion (on issues relating to physician recruitment), practice options and information of interest to relocating physicians. Buys 12 mss/year. Query with published clips. Length: 1,500-3,500 words. Pays $750-1,500. Sometimes pays expenses of writers on assignment.
Photos: State availability of photos with submission. Negotiates payment individually. Model releases and identification of subjects required. Buys one-time rights.
Columns/Departments: Remarks (opinion from industry experts on physician relocation), 500 words. Buys 6 mss/year. Query with published clips. Pays $250-500.
Tips: "Submit queries via letter with ideas for articles that directly pertain to physician career issues, such as specific or unusual practice opportunities, relocation or practice establishment subjects, etc. Feature articles are most open to freelancers. Physician sources are most important, with tips and advice from both the physicians and business experts. Physicians like to know what other physicians think and are doing, but also appreciate the suggestions of other business people."

Music

Publications for musicians and for the recording industry are listed in this section. Other professional performing arts publications are classified under Entertainment and the Arts. Magazines featuring music industry news for the general public are listed in the Consumer Entertainment and Music sections. (Markets for songwriters can be found in *Songwriter's Market*—see Other Books of Interest).

‡**EARSHOT JAZZ,** #309, 3429 Fremont Place, Seattle WA 98103. (206)547-6763. Editor: John Hillmer. 30% freelance written. Monthly newsletter covering Northwest jazz. *"Earshot Jazz* is a 'mirror and focus' for the jazz community" in the Pacific Northwest. Estab. 1986. Circ. 5,000. Pays on publication. Byline given. Buys one-time rights. Editorial lead time 2 months. Submit seasonal material 3 months in advance. Accepts simultaneous and previously published submissions. Query for electronic submissions. Sample copy and writer's guideline for #10 SASE.
Nonfiction: Book excerpts, essays, how-to, humor, interview/profile, personal experience, technical. Query with published clips. Length: 200-1,500 words. Pays $30 minimum for assigned articles; $15 minimum for unsolicited articles. Sometimes pays expenses of writers on assignment.
Photos: Send photos with submission. Reviews 5×7 prints. Offers $15/photo.
Columns/Departments: Buys 30 mss/year. Query with published clips. Pays $20.
Fiction: Jazz music. Buys 2 mss/year. Query with published clips. Length: 200-2,000 words. Pays $20-60.
Poetry: Avant-garde, free verse, light verse, traditional, haiku. Buys 2 poems/year. Submit 1 poem at a time.

OPERA NEWS, Metropolitan Opera Guild, Inc., 70 Lincoln Center Plaza, New York NY 10023-6593. (212)769-7080. Fax: (212)769-7007. Editor: Patrick J. Smith. Managing Editor: Brian Kellow. 75% freelance written. Monthly magazine (May-November, biweekly December-April), for people interested in opera; the opera professional as well as the opera audience. Estab. 1936. Circ. 120,000. Pays on publication. Publishes ms an average of 4 months after acceptance. Byline given. Buys first serial rights only. Query for electronic submissions. Sample copy for $4.
Nonfiction: Most articles are commissioned in advance. Monthly issues feature articles on various aspects of opera worldwide; biweekly issues contain articles related to the broadcasts from the Metropolitan Opera. Emphasis is on high quality writing and an intellectual interest to the opera-oriented public. Informational, personal experience, interview, profile, historical, think pieces, personal opinion, opera reviews. "Also willing to consider quality fiction and poetry on opera-related themes though acceptance is rare." Query; no telephone inquiries. Length: 1,500-2,800 words. Pays $450-1,000. Sometimes pays the expenses of writers on assignment.
Photos: State availability of photos with submission. Buys one-time rights.
Columns/Departments: Buys 24 mss/year.

STUDIO SOUND, and Broadcast Engineering, Spotlight Publications, Ludgate House, 245 Blackfriars Rd., London SE1 9UR United Kingdom. (+)71-620-3636. Fax: (+)44 71-401-8036. Editor: Tim Goodyer. Assistant Editor: Julian Mitchell. 80% freelance written. Monthly magazine covering professional audio and recording. Covers "all matters relating to pro audio—music recording, music for picture, post production—reviews and feature articles." Estab. 1959. Circ. 20,000 worldwide. Pays on publication. Byline given. Offers 20% kill fee. Buys first rights. Editorial lead time 3 months. Accepts simultaneous submissions. Query for electronic submissions.
Nonfiction: Historical/nostalgic, how-to, interview/profile, new product, opinion, personal experience, photo feature. No company profiles. Buys 80 mss/year. Send complete ms. Length: 850-4,000 words. Pays $150 minimum. Sometimes pays expenses of writers on assignment.
Photos: State availability of photos with submission. Reviews 35mm transparencies and 5×7 prints. Negotiates payment individually. Identification of subjects required. Buys one-time rights.

‡**THE WOODWIND QUARTERLY,** 1513 Old CC Rd., Colville WA 99114-9526. (509)935-4875. Editor: Scott Hirsch. 90% freelance written. Quarterly journal covering making and repairing woodwind instruments. "A 124-page soft-bound journal covering a wide variety of topics directed at repair technicians and makers of woodwind instruments, both historical instruments and modern. Articles can be about the tools used, or other how-to articles on construction methods and repair techniques." Estab. 1993. Circ. 1,500. **Pays on acceptance.** Publishes ms an average of 3 months after acceptance. Byline given. Offers 100% kill fee. Buys all rights. Editorial lead time 3 months. Accepts simultaneous and previously published submissions. Query for electronic submissions. Reports in 1 week on queries. Sample copy for $4. Writer's guidelines free on request.
Nonfiction: Book excerpts, essays, exposé, general interest, historical/nostalgic, how-to, humor, inspirational, interview/profile, new product, opinion, personal experience, photo feature, technical. Special issues: How successful is the ivory ban and what substitute materials are being used? Articles should not be directed

to players but makers and repair technicians. Buys 75-100 mss/year. Query. Length: 1,000 words minimum. Pays $150 for assigned articles; $100 for unsolicited articles. Pays expenses of writers on assignment.

Photos: State availability of photos with submission. Reviews 5×3½ prints. Negotiates payment individually. Buys all rights.

Columns/Departments: Laws Column (how to make a small business succeed), 4,000-6,000 words. Buys 12 mss/year. Query. Pays $100-150.

Fillers: Anecdotes, facts, gags to be illustrated by cartoonist, newsbreaks, short humor. Buys 25/year. Length: 50-500 words. Pays $20-100.

Tips: "Freelancers are invited to speak to the editor and discuss ideas for how to tailor articles to the readership."

Office Environment and Equipment

MODERN OFFICE TECHNOLOGY, Penton Publishing, Dept. WM, 1100 Superior Ave., Cleveland OH 44114-2501. (216)696-7000. Fax: (216)696-7648. Editor: Lura K. Romei. Production Manager: Gina Runyon. 5-10% freelance written. Monthly magazine covering office automation for corporate management and personnel, financial management, administrative and operating management, systems and information management, managers and supervisors of support personnel and purchasing. Estab. 1956. Circ. 130,000. Pays on publication. Publishes ms an average of 6 months after acceptance. Byline given. Buys first and one-time rights. Query for electronic submissions. Reports in 3 months. Accepts previously published material. Send photocopy of article, information about when and where the article previously appeared. Sample copy and writer's guidelines for 9×12 SAE with 4 first-class stamps.

Nonfiction: New product, opinion, technical. Query with or without published clips or send complete ms. Length: open. Pays $300-600 for assigned articles; $250-400 for unsolicited articles. Pays expenses of writers on assignment.

Photos: Send photos with submission. Reviews contact sheets, 4×5 transparencies and prints. Additional payment for photos accepted with ms. Consult editor. Captions and identification of subjects required. Buys one-time rights.

Tips: "Submitted material should alway present topics and ideas, on issues that are clearly and concisely defined. Material should describe problems and solution. Writer should describe benefits to reader in tangible results whenever possible."

THE SECRETARY®, Stratton Publishing & Marketing, Inc., Suite 706, 2800 Shirlington Rd., Arlington VA 22206. Publisher: Debra J. Stratton. Managing Editor: Robin Perry Allen; Editor: Tracy Fellin Savidge. 90% freelance written. Magazine published 9 times/year covering the secretarial profession. Estab. 1946. Circ. 44,000. Pays on publication or "mostly unpaid." Publishes ms an average of 6-18 months after acceptance. Byline given. Kill fee negotiable. Buys first rights. Editorial lead time 3 months. Submit seasonal material 5 months in advance. Accepts simultaneous and previously published submissions. Send tearsheet of article, typed ms with rights for sale noted (on disk, preferred) and information about when and where the article previously appeared. Query for electronic submissions. For electronic (IBM) PC-compatible, Word Perfect or ASCII on disk. Reports in 1 month. Sample copy $3 through (816)891-6600 ext. 235. Writer's guidelines free on request through publishing office.

Nonfiction: Book excerpts, general interest, how-to (buy and use office equipment, advance career, etc.), interview/profile, new product, personal experience. Buys 6-10 mss/year. Query. Length: 2,000 words. Pays $250 minimum for assigned articles; $0-75 minimum for unsolicited articles. Pays expenses of writers on assignment.

Photos: Send photos with submission. Reviews transparencies and prints. Offers no additional payment for photos accepted with ms. Identification of subjects required. Buys one-time rights.

Columns/Departments: Product News (new office products, non promotional), 500 words maximum; Random Input (general interest—career, woman's, workplace issues), 500 words maximum; First Person (first-hand experiences from secretaries), 800 words. Send complete ms.

Tips: "We're in search of articles addressing travel; meeting and event-planning; office recycling programs; computer hardware and software; workplace issues; international business topics. Must be appropriate to secretaries."

Paper

BOXBOARD CONTAINERS, Maclean Hunter Publishing Co., Dept. WM, 29 N. Wacker Dr., Chicago IL 60606-3298. (312)726-2802. Fax: (312)726-2574. Editor: Greg Kishbaugh. Managing Editor: Rick Pedraza. Monthly magazine covering box and carton manufacturing for corrugated box, folding carton, setup box manufacturers internationally emphasizing technology and management. Circ. 14,000. Pays on publication. Byline given. Buys first North American serial rights. Submit seasonal material 2 months in advance. Query for electronic submissions. Reports in 1 month. Free sample copy.

Nonfiction: How-to, interview/profile, new product, opinion, personal experience, photo feature, technical. Buys 10 mss/year. Query. Length: 2,000-6,000 words. Pays $75-350 for assigned articles; $50-200 for unsolicited articles. Sometimes pays the expenses of writers on assignment.
Photos: Send photos with submission. Reviews 35mm, 4×5 and 6×6 transparencies and 8×10 prints. Offers no additional payment for photos accepted with ms. Captions, model releases and identification of subjects required. Buys one-time rights.
Tips: Features are most open to freelancers.

PULP & PAPER CANADA, Southam Business Communications Inc., Suite 410, 3300 Côte Vertu, St. Laurent, Quebec H4R 2B7 Canada. (514)339-1399. Fax: (514)339-1396. Publisher: Guy Tortolano. Editor: Graeme Rodden. 5% freelance written. Prefers to work with published/established writers. Monthly magazine. Estab. 1903. Circ. 9,309. **Pays on acceptance.** Publishes ms "as soon as possible" after acceptance. Byline given. Offers kill fee according to prior agreement. Buys first North American serial rights. Reports in 1 month. Free sample copy and writer's guidelines.
Nonfiction: How-to (related to processes and procedures in the industry); interview/profile (of Canadian leaders in pulp and paper industry); technical (relevant to modern pulp and/or paper industry). No fillers, short industry news items, or product news items. Buys 10 mss/year. Query first with published clips or send complete ms. Articles with photographs (b&w glossy) or other good quality illustrations will get priority review. Length: maximum 1,500 words (with photos). Pays $160/published page (Canadian funds), including photos, graphics, charts, etc.
Tips: "Any return postage must be in either Canadian stamps or International Reply Coupons *only.*"

Pets

Listed here are publications for professionals in the pet industry—pet product wholesalers, manufacturers, suppliers, and retailers, and owners of pet specialty stores, grooming businesses, aquarium retailers and those interested in the pet fish industry. The Veterinary section lists journals for animal health professionals. Publications for pet owners are listed in the Consumer Animal section.

GROOM & BOARD, Incorporating "Groomers Gazette Kennel News," H.H. Backer Associates Inc., Suite 200, 20 E. Jackson Blvd., Chicago IL 60604-2383. (312)663-4040. Fax: (312)663-5676. Editor: Karen Long MacLeod. 30-50% freelance written. Magazine published 9 times/year about grooming and boarding pets. "*Groom & Board* is the only national trade publication for pet-care professionals, including pet groomers, boarding kennel operators and service-oriented veterinarians. It provides news, technical articles and features to help them operate their businesses more successfully." Estab. 1980. Circ. 17,968. **Pays on acceptance.** Publishes ms an average of 6 months after acceptance. Byline given. Buys first North American serial, one-time, all rights or exclusive to industry. Query for electronic submissions. Accepts previously published material. Send tearsheet or photocoy of article or typed ms with rights for sale noted information about when and where the article previously appeared. Reports in 6 months. Sample copy for $6 ($2.50 plus $3.50 shipping and handling). Writer's guidelines for #10 SASE.
Nonfiction: How-to (groom specific breeds of pets, run business, etc.), interview/profile (successful grooming and/or kennel operations), technical. "No consumer-oriented articles or stories about a single animal (animal heroes, grief, etc.)." Buys 10-20 mss/year. Query with published clips, or send complete ms. Length: 1,000-3,000 words. Pays $90-500 for assigned articles; $65-150 for unsolicited articles. Sometimes pays expenses of writers on assignment.
Photos: Reviews slides, transparencies and 5×7 b&w glossy prints. Offers $8 (negotiable)/photo. Captions and identification of subjects required. Buys one-time rights.

PET AGE, The Magazine for the Professional Retailer, H.H. Backer Associates, Inc., Suite 200, 20 E. Jackson Blvd., Chicago IL 60604-2383. (312)663-4040. Fax: (312)663-5676. Editor: Karen Long MacLeod. 30-50% freelance written. Prefers to work with published/established writers. Monthly magazine for pet/pet supplies retailers, covering the complete pet industry. Estab. 1971. Circ. 18,121. **Pays on acceptance.** Publishes ms an average of 6 months after acceptance. Byline given. Buys first North American serial, one-time, all or exclusive industry rights. Submit seasonal material 6 months in advance. Query for electronic submissions. Accepts previously published material. Send tearsheet of article, photocopy of article typed ms with rights for sale noted and information about when and where the article previously appeared. Reports in 6 months on queries; 2 months on mss. Sample copy for $6 ($2.50 plus $3.50 shipping and handling). Writer's guidelines for #10 SASE.
Nonfiction: Book excerpts, profile (of a successful, well-run pet retail operation), how-to, business management, technical—all trade-related. Query first with published clips. Buys 10-30 mss/year. "Query as to the name and location of a pet operation you wish to profile and why it would make a good feature. No general retailing articles or consumer-oriented pet articles." Length: 1,000-3,000 words. Pays $100-500 for assigned articles; $65-150 for unsolicited articles. Sometimes pays the expenses of writers on assignment.

Photos: Reviews slides, transparencies and 5×7 b&w glossy prints and color transparencies. Captions and identification of subjects required. Offers $8 (negotiable)/photo. Buys one-time rights.
Tips: "This is a business publication for busy people, and must be very informative in easy-to-read, concise style. Articles about animal care or business practices should have the pet-retail angle or cover issues specific to this industry."

‡**PET BUSINESS**, 5400 NW 84th Ave., Miami FL 33166-3333. (305)592-9890. Editorial Director: Elizabeth McKey. 30% freelance written. "Our monthly news magazine reaches retailers, distributors and manufacturers of pet products. Groomers, veterinarians and serious hobbyists are also represented." Estab. 1973. Circ. 18,000. Pays on publication. Publishes ms an average of 2 months after acceptance. Byline given. Buys first rights. Submit seasonal/holiday material 3 months in advance. Reports in 3-4 months. Sample copy for $3. Writer's guidelines for SASE.
Nonfiction: "Articles must be well-researched and pertain to major business trends in the pet industry. Research, legislative and animal behavior reports are of interest. All data must be attributed. Articles should be business-oriented, not intended for the pet owner market. Send query or complete ms. Length: 250-2,000 words. Pays 14¢/word.
Photos: Send color slides, transparencies or prints with submission. Offers $20/photo. Buys one-time rights.
Tips: "We are open to national and international news of the pet industry written in standard news format, or well-researched, business- or trend-oriented feature articles."

THE PET DEALER, Howmark Publishing Corp., 567 Morris Ave., Elizabeth NJ 07208-1995. (908)353-7373. Fax: (908)353-8221. Editor: Gina Geslewitz. 70% freelance written. Prefers to work with published/established writers, but is eager to work with new/published writers. "We want writers who are good reporters and clear communicators with a fine command of the English language." Monthly magazine emphasizing merchandising, marketing and management for owners and managers of pet specialty stores, departments, and pet groomers and their suppliers. Estab. 1949. Circ. 17,500. Pays on publication. "May be many months between acceptance of a manuscript and publication." Byline given. Submit seasonal material 4 months in advance. Accepts previously published submissions. Send typed ms with rights for sale noted and information about when and where the article previously appeared. For reprints, pays 1-10% of their fee for an original article. Reports in 3 months. Sample copy for $5 and 8×10 SAE with 10 first-class stamps. Queries without SASE will not be answered.
Nonfiction: How-to (store operations, administration, merchandising, marketing, management, promotion and purchasing). Consumer pet articles—lost pets, best pets, humane themes—*not* welcome. "We *are* interested in helping—dog, cat, monkey, whatever stories tie in with the human/animal bond. Emphasis is on *trade* merchandising and marketing of pets and supplies." Buys 2-4 unsolicited mss/year. Length: 800-1,500 words. Pays $40-100.
Photos: Submit undeveloped photo material with ms. No additional payment for 5×7 b&w glossy prints. Buys one-time rights. Will give photo credit for photography students. Also seeking cover art: original illustrated animal portraits (paid).
Fillers: "Will publish poetry and cartoons (unpaid) as fillers."
Tips: "We're interested in store profiles outside the New York, New Jersey, Connecticut and Pennsylvania metro areas. Photos are of key importance and should include a storefront shot. Articles focus on new techniques in merchandising or promotion, and overall trends in the Pet Industry. Want to see more articles from retailers and veterinarians with retail operations. Submit query letter first, with writing background summarized; include samples. We seek one-to-one, interview-type features on retail pet store merchandising. Indicate the availability of the proposed article, and your willingness to submit on exclusive or first-in-the-trade-field basis."

PET PRODUCT NEWS, Fancy Publications, P.O. Box 6050, Mission Viejo CA 92690. (714)855-8822. Fax: (714)855-3045. Editor: Scott McElhaney. 90% freelance written. Monthly magazine for retail pet stores. "*Pet Product News* covers business/legal and economic issues of importance to small business owners of pet retail stores, as well as product information and animal care issues. We're looking for straightforward articles on the proper care of dogs, cats, birds, fish and exotics (reptiles, hamsters, etc.) as information the retailers can pass on to new pet owners." Estab. 1947. Circ. 25,000. Pays on publication. Byline given. Offers 50% kill fee or $100. Buys first North American serial rights. Editorial lead time 3 months. Submit seasonal material 4 months in advance. Query for electronic submissions. Reports in 2 weeks on queries. Sample copy for $4.50. Writer's guidelines free on request.
Nonfiction: General interest, how-to, interview/profile, new product, photo feature, technical. "No cute animal stories or those directed at the pet owner." Buys 150 mss/year. Query. Length: 500-1,500 words. Pays $175-350.
Columns/Departments: Dog & Cat (products and care of), 1,000-1,500 words; Fish & Bird (products and care of), 1,800-1,500 words; Exotics (products and care of), 1,500-2,000 words. Buys 120 mss/year. Query. Send complete ms. Pays $175-350.
Tips: "Be more than just an animal lover. You have to know about health, nutrition and care. Product articles are told in both an informative and entertaining style. Go into pet stores, talk to the owners and see what

they need to know to be better business people in general, who have to deal with everything from balancing the books, free trade agreements and animal right activists. All sections are open, but you have to be extremely knowledgeable on the topic, be it taxes, management, profit building, products, nutrition, animal care or marketing."

Photography Trade

Journals for professional photographers are listed in this section. Magazines for the general public interested in photography techniques are in the Consumer Photography section. (For listings of markets for freelance photography use *Photographer's Market* — see Other Books of Interest).

AMERICAN CINEMATOGRAPHER, A.S.C. Holding Corp., P.O. Box 2230, Hollywood CA 90078-2230. (213)969-4333. Fax: (213)876-4973. Editor: David Heuring. 50% freelance written. Monthly international journal of film and video production techniques "addressed to creative, managerial and technical people in all aspects of production. Its function is to disseminate practical information about the creative use of film and video equipment, and it strives to maintain a balance between technical sophistication and accessibility." Estab. 1919. Circ. 30,000. Pays on publication. Buys all rights. Submit one-page proposal. Writer's guidelines for #10 SASE.
Nonfiction: Stephen Pizzello, associate editor. Descriptions of new equipment and techniques or accounts of specific productions involving unique problems or techniques; historical articles detailing the production of a classic film, the work of a pioneer or legendary cinematographer or the development of a significant technique or type of equipment. Also discussions of the aesthetic principles involved in production techniques. Pays according to position and worth. Negotiable.
Photos: Black and white and color purchased with mss. No additional payment.
Tips: "No unsolicited articles. Do not call. Doesn't matter whether you are published or new. Queries must describe writer's qualifications and include writing samples."

PHOTO LAB MANAGEMENT, PLM Publishing, Inc., 1312 Lincoln Blvd., Santa Monica CA 90401. (310)451-1344. Fax: (310)395-9058. Editor: Carolyn Ryan. Associate Editor: Arthur Stern. 75% freelance written. Monthly magazine covering process chemistries and equipment, digital imaging, and marketing/administration for photo lab owners, managers and management personnel. Estab. 1979. Circ. 23,000. Pays on publication. Publishes ms an average of 3 months after acceptance. Byline and brief bio given. Buys first North American serial rights. Query for electronic submissions. Reports on queries in 6 weeks. Sample copy and writer's guidelines for #10 SAE with 3 first-class stamps.
Nonfiction: Personal experience (lab manager); technical; management or administration. Buys 40-50 mss/year. Query with brief biography. Length: 1,200-1,800 words. Payment negotiable.
Photos: Reviews 35mm color transparencies and 4-color prints suitable for cover. "We're looking for outstanding cover shots of photofinishing images."
Tips: "Our departments are written inhouse and we don't use 'fillers'. Send a query if you have some background in the industry or have a specific news story relating to photo processing or digital imaging. This industry is changing quickly due to computer technology, so articles must be cutting edge. Business management articles must focus on a photo lab approach and not be generic. Writers must have photofinishing knowledge."

PHOTO MARKETING, Photo Marketing Assocation Intl., 3000 Picture Place, Jackson MI 49201-8853. (517)788-8100. Fax: (517)788-8371. Director, Publications: Margaret Hooks. 2% freelance written. Monthly magazine for photo industry retailers, finishers and suppliers. "Articles must be specific to the photo industry and cannot be authored by anyone who writes for other magazines in the photo industry. We provide management information on a variety of topics as well as profiles of successful photo businesses and analyses of current issues in the industry." Estab. 1925. Circ. 22,000. **Pays on acceptance.** Publishes ms an average of 2 months after acceptance. Byline given. Buys one-time rights and exclusive photo magazine rights. Accepts simultaneous submissions. Reports in 2 months. Free sample copy. Writer's guidelines for #10 SASE.
Nonfiction: Interview/profile (anonymous consumer shops for equipment); personal experience (interviews with photo retailers); technical (photofinishing lab equipment); new technology (still electronic video). Buys 5 mss/year. Send complete ms. Length: 1,000-2,300 words. Pays $150-350.
Photos: State availability of photos with submission. Reviews negatives, 5×7 transparencies and prints. Offers $25-35/photo. Buys one-time rights.
Columns/Departments: Anonymous Consumer (anonymous shopper shops for equipment at photo stores), 1,800 words. Buys 5 mss/year. Query with published clips. Length: 1,800 words. Pays up to $200.
Tips: "All main sections use freelance material: business tips, promotion ideas, employee concerns, advertising, co-op, marketing. But they must be geared to and have direct quotes from members of the association."
  • *Photo Marketing* has less need for freelancers this year.

THE PHOTO REVIEW, 301 Hill Ave., Langhorne PA 19047-2819. (215)757-8921. Editor: Stephen Perloff. 50% freelance written. Quarterly magazine on photography with reviews, interviews and articles on art photography. Estab. 1976. Circ. 2,500. Pays on publication. Publishes ms an average of 3 months after acceptance. Byline given. Buys one-time rights. Accepts simultaneous and previously published submissions. Reports in 1 month on queries; 2 months on mss. Sample copy for 9 × 12 SAE with 6 first-class stamps. Writer's guidelines for #10 SASE.
Nonfiction: Essays, historical/nostalgic, interview/profile, opinion. No how-to articles. Buys 10-15 mss/year. Query. Pays $25-200.
Photos: Send photos with submission. Reviews 8 × 10 prints. Offers no additional payment for photos accepted with ms. Captions and identification of subjects required. Buys one-time rights.

PHOTOSTOCKNOTES, PhotoSource International, (formerly *Photoletter*), Pine Lake Farm, Osceola WI 54020. (715)248-3800. Fax: (715)248-7394. Editor: Lori Johnson. Managing Editor: H.T. White. 10% freelance written. Monthly newsletter on marketing photographs. "*PhotoStockNotes* reports on the changing stock photography industry." Estab. 1976. Circ. 780. **Pays on acceptance.** Publishes ms an average of 6 months after acceptance. Byline given. Buys one-time and simultaneous rights. Submit seasonal material 3 months in advance. Accepts simultaneous and previously published submissions. Query for electronic submissions. Reports in 2 weeks on queries. Sample copy free. Writer's guidelines for #10 SASE.
Nonfiction: How-to market photos and personal experience in marketing photos. "Our readers expect advice in how-to articles." No submissions that do not deal with selling photos or keeping up with the technological advances in the stock photography industry. Buys 6 mss/year. Query. Length: 150-300 words. Pays $50-100 for unsolicited articles.
Columns/Departments: Jeri Engh, columns department editor. "We welcome column ideas." Length: 150-300 words. Pays $45-75.
Fillers: Facts. Buys 20/year. Length: 50-75 words. Pays $10.
Tips: "Columns are most open to freelancers. Bring an *expertise* on marketing photos or some other aspect of aid to small business persons."

PROFESSIONAL PHOTOGRAPHER, The Business Magazine of Professional Photography, #1600, 57 Forsyth St. NW, Atlanta GA 30303-2206. (404)522-8600. Fax: (404)614-6405. Editor: Kim Brady. 80% freelance written. Monthly magazine of professional portrait, wedding, commercial, corporate and industrial photography. Describes the technical and business sides of professional photography—successful photo techniques, money-making business tips, legal considerations, selling to new markets, and descriptions of tough assignments and how completed. Estab. 1907. Circ. 32,000. Publishes ms an average of 6-9 months after acceptance. Byline given. Buys one-time rights. Submit seasonal material 6 months in advance. Accepts simultaneous queries and previously published submissions. Reports in 2 months. Sample copy for $5. Free writer's guidelines.
Nonfiction: How-to. Professional photographic techniques: How I solved this difficult assignment, How I increased my photo sales, How to buy a studio, run a photo business, etc. Special issues: Wedding Photography (February); Portrait Photography (April); Commercial Photography (May); and Corporate Photography (August). Buys 8-10 ms/issue. Query. Length: 1,000-3,000 words. "We seldom pay, as most writers are PP of A members and pro photographers who want recognition for their professional skills, publicity, etc."
Photos: State availability of photos. Reviews color transparencies and 8 × 10 unmounted prints. Captions and model release required. Buys one-time rights.
Tips: "We have an increased interest in electronic imaging and computer manipulation of images in professional photography."

THE RANGEFINDER, 1312 Lincoln Blvd., Santa Monica CA 90406-1703. (310)451-8506. Fax: (310)395-9058. Editor: Arthur C. Stern. Associate Editor: Sandi Messana. Monthly magazine emphasizing professional photography. Circ. 50,000. Pays on publication. Publishes ms an average of 6-9 months after acceptance. Byline given. Buys first North American serial rights. Phone queries OK. Submit seasonal material 4 months in advance. Reports in 6 weeks. Sample copy for $3.50. Writer's guidelines for SASE.
Nonfiction: How-to (solve a photographic problem, such as new techniques in lighting, new poses or setups), profile, technical. "Articles should contain practical, solid information. Issues should be covered in-depth. Look thoroughly into the topic." Buys 5-7 mss/issue. Query with outline. Length: 800-1,200 words. Pays $60/published page.
Photos: State availability of photos with query. Captions preferred; model release required.
Tips: "Exhibit knowledge of photography. Introduce yourself with a well-written letter and a great story idea."

SHOOTER'S RAG, The Practical Photographic Gazette, Havelin Communications, P.O. Box 8509, Asheville NC 28814. (704)254-6700. Editor: Michael Havelin. 50-70% freelance written. Quarterly magazine covering photography and electronic imaging. "*Shooter's Rag* is a magazine for the productive photographer, whether amateur, semi-pro or fulltime professional. Our magazine is designed to provide information on shooting techniques, electronic imaging, photographer's legal issues and ethics, marketing, interviews, reviews and photographic adventures." Estab. 1992. Circ. 2,500. Pays on publication. Publishes ms an average of 2-6 months after acceptance. Byline given. Buys one-time rights. Submit seasonal material 6 months in advance. Accepts simultaneous submissions. Query for electronic submissions. Reports in 1 month. Sample copy for $3. Writer's guidelines for #10 SASE.

Nonfiction: Book excerpts, essays, historical/nostalgic, how-to (varied photographic techniques), humor (in photographic experience), interview/profile, new product, opinion, personal experience, photo feature, technical, travel and investigative. "We are open to all photo-related material." Buys 6-14 mss/year. Query with or without clips. Length: 500-2,000 words. Pays 5¢/word minimum. Sometimes pays expenses of writers on assignment.

Photos: State availability of photos with submission. Reviews contact sheets, all size transparencies, 8×10 b&w prints. Package price for text and photos. Captions, model releases and identification of subjects required. Buys one-time rights.

Columns/Departments: Columns are written on a contract basis. Buys 8-16 mss/year. Query with published clips. Length: 500-2,000 words. Pays 5¢/word minimum.

Fiction: Photo related stories. Query with published clips. Length: 500-2,000 words. Pays 5¢/word minimum.

Fillers: Anecdotes, facts, cartoons, newsbreaks, short humor. Length: 25-150 words. Pays 5¢/word minimum.

Tips: "We are open to all sorts of well-written, articulate, factually accurate and concise articles on photography-related subjects. Strong material on photographic subjects will always be considered. The photographer who writes, or the writer who shoots well, stands a far better chance of publication than someone who submits a story without pictures or pictures without text."

Plumbing, Heating, Air Conditioning and Refrigeration

‡**CONTRACTOR, The Newsmagazine of Mechanical Contracting,** Cahners Publishing, P.O. Box 5080, Des Plaines IL 60017-5080. Editor: Bob Miodonski. Contact: Bob Mader. 5% freelance written. Monthly tabloid covering plumbing, heating, cooling, piping. "*Contractor* is a monthly tabloid newsmagazine that is directed towards owners, presidents and top management of plumbing, heating, air conditioning and mechanical contracting firms." Estab. 1954. Circ. 50,000. **Pays on acceptance.** Publishes ms an average of 1 month after acceptance. Byline sometimes given. Buys all rights. Editorial lead time 1 month. Submit seasonal material 2 months in advance. Query for electronic submissions. Reports in 1 month on queries. Sample copy free on request.

Nonfiction: Exposé, news. Special issue: Your Healthy Home annual (Spring—focusing on residential indoor air quality). Queries by December. Buys 6 mss/year. Query with published clips. Length: 100-750 words. Pays $100 for assigned articles; $25 for unsolicited articles. Sometimes pays expenses of writers on assignment.

Photos: State availability of or send photos with submission. Reviews contact sheets, 2×2 transparencies, 5×7 prints. Negotiates payment individually. Captions, identification of subjects required. Buys all rights.

Fillers: Newsbreaks. Buys 6/year. Length: 10-50 words. Pays $10-25.

Tips: "Find out what the news is in your area. Locate plumbing, heating, air conditioning trade associations in your phone book. Talk to them. Get on their mailing lists. Find out what the big problems and hot topics are for them. Talk to contractors. Some big mechanicals publish their own newsletters. Get on their mailing lists. We need good news stringers in new England, Texas, and the West Coast."

‡**HEATING, PLUMBING, AIR CONDITIONING,** Suite 300, 1370 Don Mills Rd., Don Mills, Ontario M3B 3N7 Canada. (416)759-2500. Fax: (416)759-6979. Publisher: Bruce Meacock. Editor: Bruce Cole. 20% freelance written. Monthly magazine for mechanical contractors; plumbers; warm air and hydronic heating, refrigeration, ventilation, air conditioning and insulation contractors; wholesalers; architects; consulting and mechanical engineers who are in key management or specifying positions in the plumbing, heating, air conditioning and refrigeration industries in Canada. Estab. 1923. Circ. 16,500. Pays on publication. Publishes ms an average of 3 months after acceptance. Accepts previously published articles. Send tearsheet of article, photocopy of article or typed ms with rights for sale noted. Reports in 2 months. For a prompt reply, "enclose a sheet on which is typed a statement either approving or rejecting the suggested article which can either be checked off, or a quick answer written in and signed and returned." Free sample copy.

Nonfiction: News, technical, business management and "how-to" articles that will inform, educate, motivate and help readers to be more efficient and profitable who design, manufacture, install, sell, service, maintain or supply all mechanical components and systems in residential, commercial, institutional and industrial installations across Canada. Length: 1,000-1,500 words. Pays 25¢/word. Sometimes pays expenses of writers on assignment.

Photos: Photos purchased with ms. Prefers 4×5 or 5×7 glossies.

Tips: "Topics must relate directly to the day-to-day activities of *HPAC* readers in Canada. Must be detailed, with specific examples, quotes from specific people or authorities—show depth. We specifically want material from other parts of Canada besides southern Ontario. Not really interested in material from US unless specifically related to Canadian readers' concerns. We primarily want articles that show *HPAC* readers how they can increase their sales and business step-by-step based on specific examples of what others have done."

SNIPS MAGAZINE, 1949 N. Cornell Ave., Melrose Park IL 60160. (708)544-3870. Fax: (708)544-3884. Editor: Nick Carter. 2% freelance written. Monthly magazine for sheet metal, warm air heating, ventilating, air conditioning and roofing contractors. Estab. 1932. Publishes ms an average of 3 months after acceptance. Buys all rights. "Write for detailed list of requirements before submitting any work."
Nonfiction: Material should deal with information about contractors who do sheet metal, warm air heating, air conditioning, ventilation and roofing work; also about successful advertising campaigns conducted by these contractors and the results. Length: "prefers stories to run less than 1,000 words unless on special assignment." Pays 5¢/word for first 500 words, 2¢/word thereafter.
Photos: Pays $5 each for small snapshot pictures, $10 each for usable 8 × 10 pictures.

Printing

CANADIAN PRINTER, Maclean Hunter Ltd., 777 Bay St., Toronto, Ontario M5W 1A7 Canada. (416)596-5781. Fax: (416)596-5965. Editor: Nick Hancock. Assistant Editor: Stephen Forbes. 20% freelance written. Monthly magazine for printing and the allied industries. "*Canadian Printer* wants technical matter on graphic arts, printing, binding, typesetting, packaging, specialty production and trends in technology." Circ. 13,000. Pays on publication. Publishes ms an average of 1-3 months after acceptance. Byline given. Buys first North American serial rights. Reports in 6 months. Sample copy for 9 × 12 SAE and 2 IRCs.
Nonfiction: Technical. "We do not want US plant articles—this is a Canadian magazine." Buys 5-10 mss/ year. Query or send complete ms. Length: 400-1,600 words. Pays 30¢/word Canadian. Pays expenses of writers on assignment "on prior arrangement."
Photos: Send photos with submission. Reviews 4 × 5 prints. Offers $50/photo. Captions and identification of subjects required. Buys one-time rights.

HIGH VOLUME PRINTING, Innes Publishing Co., P.O. Box 368, Northbrook IL 60062-2319. (708)564-5940. Fax: (708)564-8361. Editor: Catherine M. Stanulis. Estab. 1982. 35% freelance written. Eager to work with new/unpublished writers. Bimonthly magazine for book, magazine printers, large commercial printing plants with 20 or more employees. Aimed at telling the reader what he needs to know to print more efficiently and more profitably. Circ. 41,000. Pays on publication. Publishes ms an average of 9 months after acceptance. Byline given. Buys first and second serial rights. Accepts previously published articles from noncompetitive or regional publications only. Send photocopy of article along with information about when and where the article previously appeared. Pays 50% of their fee for an original article. Query for electronic submissions. Reports in 2 months. Writer's guidelines, sample articles provided.
• Printing industry/technology knowledge is a *must!*
Nonfiction: How-to (printing production techniques); new product (printing, auxiliary equipment, plant equipment); photo feature (case histories featuring unique equipment); technical (printing product research and development); shipping; publishing distribution methods. No product puff. Buys 12 mss/year. Query. Length: 700-3,000 words. Pays $50-300.
Photos: Send photos with ms. Pays $25-150 for any size color transparencies and prints. Captions, model release, and identification of subjects required.
Tips: "Feature articles covering actual installations and industry trends are most open to freelancers. Be familiar with the industry, spend time in the field, and attend industry meetings and trade shows where equipment is displayed. We would also like to receive clips and shorts about printing mergers."

‡MODERN REPROGRAPHICS, Marion Street Press, Inc., P.O. Box 577339, Chicago IL 60657. (312)868-1238. Editor: Ed Avis. 60% freelance written. Bimonthly magazine covering large-format reproduction (blueprints, etc.). "Modern Reprographics is for people who do large-format reproduction, such as blueprints, color posters, etc. Articles are geared towards blueprint shops, service bureaus, and in-plant repro departments and help them find new markets and do their work better." Estab. 1993. Circ. 6,000. Pays on publication. Publishes ms an average of 1 month after acceptance. Byline given. Offers 25% kill fee. Buys first North American serial rights. Editorial lead time 2 months. Accepts previously published submissions. Query for electronic submissions. Reports in 3 weeks on queries; 1 month on mss. Sample copy for 11 × 14 SAE and 5 first-class stamps.
Nonfiction: How-to, interview/profile (blueprint shop owner, e.g.), new product, personal experience, technical, new markets. Buys 15 mss/year. Query with published clips. Length: 800-2,000 words.Pays $100. Sometimes pays expenses of writers on assignment.

Market conditions are constantly changing! If this is 1996 or later, buy the newest edition of Writer's Market *at your favorite bookstore or order directly from* Writer's Digest Books.

Photos: State availability of photos with submission. Captions and identification of subjects required. Buys one-time rigths.

Tips: "Writers can best break in with a profile of an interesting, innovative reprographics shop or department. Profiles should have a 'hook,' and some historical background on the shop or department. We are picky about technical articles, so please query first. All articles are written in language that non-reprographers can understand."

‡**PERSPECTIVES**, In-Plant Management Association (IPMA), 1205 W. College St., Liberty MO 64068-3733. (816)781-1111. Editor: Barbara Schaaf Petty. 25% freelance written. Monthly trade newsletter covering in-house print and mail operations. "In-house print/mail departments are faced with competition from commercial printers and facilities management companies. Writers must be pro-insourcing and reflect that this industry is a profitable profession." Estab. 1986. Circ. 2,500; twice a year it reaches 8,000. Pays on publication. Publishes ms an average of 2 months after acceptance. Byline given. Buys all rights. Editorial lead time 2 months. Accepts previously published submissions. Reports in 1 month. Sample copy for 9 × 12 SAE.

Nonfiction: Interview/profile, new product, technical, general management. Payment negotiated individually. Sometimes pays expenses of writers on assignment.

Photos: State availability of photos with submission. Reviews contact sheets and 5 × 7 prints. Offers no additional payment for photos accepted with ms. Captions required. Buys one-time rights.

Columns/Departments: Executive Insight (management, personnel how-tos, employment law), 650-1,500 words. Buys 12 mss/year. Query with published clips.

Tips: "A knowledge of the printing industry is helpful. Articles with concrete examples or company/individual profiles work best."

PRINT & GRAPHICS, 1432 Duke St., Alexandria VA 22314-3436. (703)683-8800. Fax: (703)683-8801. Editor: Carole Anne Turner. Publisher: Geoff Lindsay. 10% freelance written. Eager to work with new/unpublished writers. Monthly tabloid of the commercial printing industry for owners and executives of graphic arts firms. Estab. 1980. Circ. 20,000. **Pays on acceptance.** Publishes ms an average of 2 months after acceptance. Byline given. Buys one-time rights. Accepts simultaneous and previously published submissions. Send photocopy of article, information about when and where the article previously appeared. Publishes trade book excerpts. Electronic submissions OK via standard protocols, but requires hard copy also. Reports in 2 months. Sample copy for $2.

Nonfiction: Book excerpts, historical/nostalgic, how-to, interview/profile, new product, opinion, personal experience, photo feature, technical. "All articles should relate to graphic arts management or production." Buys 20 mss/year. Query with published clips. Length: 750-2,000 words. Pays $100-250.

Photos: State availability of photos. Pays $25-75 for 5 × 7 b&w prints. Captions and identification of subjects required.

QUICK PRINTING, The Information Source for Commercial Copyshops and Printshops, Coast Publishing, 1680 SW Bayshore Blvd., Port St. Lucie FL 34984-3598. (407)879-6666. Fax: (407)879-7388. Publisher: K.J. Moran. Managing Editor: Tara Marini. 50% freelance written. Monthly magazine covering the quick printing industry. "Our articles tell quick printers how they can be more profitable. We want figures to illustrate points made." Estab. 1977. Circ. 69,000. **Pays on acceptance.** Publishes ms an average of 4 months after acceptance. Byline given. Buys first North American serial or all rights. Submit seasonal material 6 months in advance. Rarely uses previously published submissions. Query for electronic submissions. Reports in 1 month. Sample copy for $3 and 9 × 12 SAE with 7 first-class stamps. Writer's guidelines for #10 SASE.

Nonfiction: How-to (on marketing products better or accomplishing more with equipment); new product; opinion (on the quick printing industry); personal experience (from which others can learn); technical (on printing). No generic business articles, or articles on larger printing applications. Buys 75 mss/year. Send complete ms. Length: 1,500-3,000 words. Pays $150 and up.

Photos: State availability of photos with submission. Reviews transparencies and prints. Offers no payment for photos. Captions and identification of subjects required.

Columns/Departments: Viewpoint/Counterpoint (opinion on the industry); QP Profile (shop profiles with a marketing slant); Management (how to handle employees and/or business strategies); and Marketing Impressions, all 500-1,500 words. Buys 10 mss/year. Send complete ms. Pays $75.

Tips: "The use of electronic publishing systems by quick printers is of increasing interest. Show a knowledge of the industry. Try visiting your local quick printer for an afternoon to get to know about us. When your articles make a point, back it up with examples, statistics, and dollar figures. We need good material in all areas, but avoid the shop profile. Technical articles are most needed, but they must be accurate. No puff pieces for a certain industry supplier."

SCREEN PRINTING, 407 Gilbert Ave., Cincinnati OH 45202-2285. (513)421-2050. Fax: (513)421-5144. Editor: Steve Duccilli. 30% freelance written. Works with a small number of new/unpublished writers each year. Monthly magazine for the screen printing industry, including screen printers (commercial, industrial and captive shops), suppliers and manufacturers, ad agencies and allied professions. Estab. 1953. Circ. 15,000. Pays on publication. Publishes ms an average of 3-4 months after acceptance. Byline given. Buys all rights.

Reporting time varies. Sample copies available for sale through circulation department. Writer's guidelines for SAE.

• There's an increasing emphasis here on personality features and coverage of fine art screen printers.

Nonfiction: "Because the screen printing industry is a specialized but diverse trade, we do not publish general interest articles with no pertinence to our readers. Subject matter is open, but should fall into one of four categories—technology, management, profile, or news. Features in all categories must identify the relevance of the subject matter to our readership. Technology articles must be informative, thorough, and objective—no promotional or 'advertorial' pieces accepted. Management articles may cover broader business or industry specific issues, but they must address the screen printer's unique needs. Profiles may cover serigraphers, outstanding shops, unique jobs and projects, or industry personalities; they should be in-depth features, not PR puff pieces, that clearly show the human interest or business relevance of the subject. News pieces should be timely (reprints from non-industry publications will be considered) and must cover an event or topic of industry concern." Buys 6-10 mss/year. Query. Unsolicited mss not returned. Length: 1,500-3,500 words. Pays minimum of $200 for major features. Sometimes pays the expenses of writers on assignment.

Photos: Cover photos negotiable; b&w or color. Published material becomes the property of the magazine.

Tips: "If the author has a working knowledge of screen printing, assignments are more readily available. General management articles are rarely used."

Real Estate

AREA DEVELOPMENT MAGAZINE, 400 Post Ave., Westbury NY 11590. (516)338-0900. Fax: (516)338-0100. Editor-in-Chief: Tom Bergeron. 50% freelance written. Prefers to work with published/established writers. Monthly magazine emphasizing corporate facility planning and site selection for industrial chief executives worldwide. Estab. 1964. Circ. 42,000. Pays following publication. Publishes ms an average of 2 months after acceptance. Buys first rights only. Byline given. Reports in 1 month. Free sample copy. Writer's guidelines for #10 SASE.

Nonfiction: How-to (experiences in site selection and all other aspects of corporate facility planning); historical (if it deals with corporate facility planning); interview (corporate executives and industrial developers); and related areas of site selection and facility planning such as taxes, labor, government, energy, architecture and finance. Buys 100 mss/year. Query. Pays $60/ms page; rates for illustrations depend on quality and printed size. Sometimes pays the expenses of writers on assignment.

Photos: State availability of photos with query. Prefer color transparencies—35mm OK. Captions preferred.

Tips: "Articles must be accurate, objective (no puffery) and useful to our industrial executive readers. Avoid any discussion of the merits or disadvantages of any particular areas or communities. Writers should realize we serve an intelligent and busy readership—they should avoid 'cute' allegories and get right to the point."

BUSINESS FACILITIES, Group C Communications, Inc., 121 Monmouth St., P.O. Box 2060, Red Bank NJ 07701. (908)842-7433. Fax: (908)758-6634. Editor: Eric Peterson. Managing Editor: Mary Ellen McCandless. 20% freelance written. Prefers to work with published/established writers. Monthly magazine covering corporate expansion, economic development and commercial and industrial real estate. "Our audience consists of corporate site selectors and real estate people; our editorial coverage is aimed at providing news and trends on the plant location and corporate expansion field." Estab. 1967. Circ. 40,000. Pays on publication. Publishes ms an average of 2 months after acceptance. Byline given. Buys all rights. Reports in 2 weeks. Sample copy and writer's guidelines for SASE.

• Magazine is currently overstocked, and will be accepting fewer pieces for the near future.

Nonfiction: General interest, how-to, interview/profile, personal experience. No news shorts or clippings; feature material only. Buys 12-15 mss/year. Query. Length: 1,000-3,000 words. Pays $200-1,000 for assigned articles; $200-600 for unsolicited articles. Sometimes pays the expenses of writers on assignment.

Photos: State availability of photos with submission. Reviews contact sheets, transparencies and 8 × 10 prints. Payment negotiable. Captions and identification of subjects required. Buys one-time rights.

Tips: "First, remember that our reader is a corporate executive responsible for his company's expansion and/or relocation decisions and our writers have to get inside that person's head in order to provide him with something that's helpful in his decision-making process. And second, the biggest turnoff is a telephone query. We're too busy to accept them and must require that all queries be put in writing. Submit major feature articles only; all news departments, fillers, etc., are staff prepared. A writer should be aware that our style is not necessarily dry and business-like. We tend to be more casual and a writer should look for that aspect of our approach."

FINANCIAL FREEDOM REPORT QUARTERLY, 4505 S. Wasatch Blvd., Salt Lake City UT 84124. (801)272-3500. Fax: (801)273-5425. Chairman of the Board: Mark O. Haroldsen. Managing Editor: Carolyn Tice. 25% freelance written. Eager to work with new/unpublished writers. Quarterly magazine for "professional and nonprofessional investors and would-be investors in real estate—real estate brokers, insurance companies, investment planners, truck drivers, housewives, doctors, architects, contractors, etc. The magazine's content is presently expanding to interest and inform the readers about other ways to put their money to work for them." Estab. 1976. Circ. 50,000. Pays on publication. Publishes ms an average of 3 months after acceptance. Buys all rights. Phone queries OK. Accepts simultaneous submissions. Query for electronic submissions. Reports in 3 months. Sample copy for $5.

Nonfiction: How-to (find real estate bargains, finance property, use of leverage, managing property, developing market trends, goal setting, motivational); interviews (success stories of those who have relied on own initiative and determination in real estate market or related fields). Buys 10 unsolicited mss/year. Query with clips of published work or submit complete ms. Length: 1,500-3,000 words. Pays 5-10¢/word. Sometimes pays the expenses of writers on assignment.

Photos: Send photos with ms. Uses 8×10 b&w or color matte prints. Captions required.

Tips: "We would like to find several specialized writers in our field of real estate investments. A writer must have had some hands-on experience in the real estate field."

JOURNAL OF PROPERTY MANAGEMENT, Institute of Real Estate Management, P.O. Box 109025, Chicago IL 60610-9025. (312)329-6058. Fax: (312)661-0217. Executive Editor: Mariwyn Evans. 30% freelance written. Bimonthly magazine covering real estate management and development. "The *Journal* has a feature/information slant designed to educate readers in the application of new techniques and to keep them abreast of current industry trends." Circ. 20,300. **Pays on acceptance.** Publishes ms an average of 3 months after acceptance. Byline given. Buys all rights. Query for electronic submissions. Accepts simultaneous and previously published submissions. Send photocopy of article and information about when and where the article previously appeared. Reports in 6 weeks on queries; 1 month on mss. *Writer's Market* recommends allowing 2 months for reply. Free sample copy and writer's guidelines.

• This journal wants more "nuts-and-bolts" articles.

Nonfiction: How-to, interview, technical (building systems/computers), demographic shifts in business employment and buying patterns, marketing. "No non-real estate subjects, personality or company, humor." Buys 8-12 mss/year. Query with published clips. Length: 1,500-4,000 words. Sometimes pays the expenses of writers on assignment.

Photos: State availability of photos with submission. Reviews contact sheets. May offer additional payment for photos accepted with ms. Model releases and identification of subjects required. Buys one-time rights.

Columns/Departments: Katherine Anderson, associate editor. Insurance Insights, Tax Issues, Investment and Finance Insights and Legal Issues. Buys 6-8 mss/year. Query. Length: 750-1,500 words.

‡MANAGERS REPORT: The Only National Trade Journal Serving Condominiums and Property Management, Ivor Thomas and Associates, 1700 Southern Blvd., West Palm Beach FL 33406. (407)687-4700. Editor: Ivor Thomas. Managing Editor: Marcia Thomas. 40% freelance written. Monthly magazine covering condominiums and property management. Estab. 1987. Circ. 10,000. **Pays on acceptance.** Buys second serial (reprint) rights. Editorial lead time 3 months. Submit seasonal material 3-4 months in advance. Accepts simultaneous and previously published submissions. Query for electronic submissions. Prefers IBM compatible disk of any size. Sample copy and writers guidelines free on request.

Nonfiction: How-to, interview/profile, new product, opinion, personal experience, photo feature, technical. Buys 120 mss/year. Query. Length: 50-3,000 words. Pays 5¢/word.

Photos: Send photos with submission. Reviews contact sheets, negatives, prints. Offers $5-50/photo. Identification of subjects required. Buys all rights.

Poetry: Light verse, humorous relating to condominiums. Buys 12 poems/year. Submit maximum 12 poems at one time. Pays $10-50.

Fillers: Anecdotes, facts, gags to be illustrated by cartoonist, newsbreaks, short humor. Buys 60/year. Length: 6-50 words. Pays $10-50.

Tips: "We want to get more technical information. We need a layman's description of: e.g., how an air conditioner really cools air. We would like maintenance remedies: e.g., what is the best thing to be done for cracked pavement in a parking lot. Consult the reader response in the magazine for maintenance categories. We ask that our advertisers be used exclusively for research. Our readers are extremmly interested in knowing such things as the difference between latex and acrylic paint and when you use one or the other. We find that the more specific and technical the better. This also applies to interviews. Interviews are to gather good technical information. Legal, administrative maintenance. See our guidelines for primer questions. We would like interviews with pictures of individuals and/or associations. 95% of our interviews are done by phone. We would like to have regular correspondents in different areas of the country."

PLANTS SITES & PARKS, The Corporate Advisor for Relocation Strategies, BPI Communications Inc., Suite 201, 10100 West Sample Rd., Coral Springs FL 33065. (800)753-2660. Fax: (305)752-2995. Editor: Ken Ibold. 35% freelance written. Bimonthly magazine covering business, especially as it involves site locations. Estab. 1974. Circ. 40,500. **Pays on acceptance.** Publishes ms an average of 1 month after acceptance. Byline given. Negotiable kill fee. Buys all rights. Editorial lead time 3-4 months. Reports in 1 month on queries. Sample copy and writer's guidelines free on request.

Nonfiction: Book excerpts, real estate, labor, industry, finance topics geared toward manufacturing executives. Buys 25-30 mss/year (total for features *and* columns/departments). Query with published clips. Length: 1,000-7,000 words. Pays $300 minimum for assigned articles. Pays expenses of writers on assignment.

Photos: State availability of photos with submission. Negotiates payment individually. Captions required. Rights negotiable.

Columns/Departments: Regional Review (profile business climate of each state), 3,000-5,000 words; Industry Outlook (trend stories on specific industries), 5,000-7,500 words; Global Market (business outlook for specific overseas areas), 2,000-5,000 words. Buys 25-30 mss/year (total for columns/departments and features). Query with published clips. Pays $300-2,000.

REALTOR® MAGAZINE, Network Publications, Suite 330, 4940 Peachtree Industrial Blvd., Norcross GA 30071. (404)242-1800. Fax: (404)242-0746. Editor: Tim Darnell. 40% freelance written. Monthly magazine covering Atlanta residential real estate. "Our goal is to provide information to real estate agents enabling them to become more profitable in their businesses. We are issues-oriented, and we are particularly interested in real estate market trends." Estab. 1989. Circ. 18,000. Pays on publication. Publishes ms an average of 2 months after acceptance. Byline given. Buys all rights. Editorial lead time 3 months. Submit seasonal material 4 months in advance. Reports in 3 months. Sample copy and writer's guidelines free on request.

Nonfiction: How-to, inspirational, interview/profile, personal experience, photo feature, technical. No humor or historical/nostalgic pieces. Buys 16 mss/year. Query. Query with published clips. Length: 1,000-3,000 words. Pays $100 minimum for assigned articles. Sometimes pays expenses of writers on assignment (limit agreed upon in advance).

Photos: State availability of photos with submission. Reviews 4×6 transparencies, 4 color slides and 3×5 prints. Offers no additional payment for photos accepted with ms. Captions and identification of subjects required. Buys all rights.

Columns/Departments: Countdown to 96 (Olympics coverage), 750 words. Buys 12 mss/year. Query with published clips. Pays $75.

Resources and Waste Reduction

‡EROSION CONTROL, The Journal for Erosion and Sediment Control Professionals, Forester Communications, Inc., 216 E. Gutierrez St., Santa Barbara CA 93101. (805)899-3355. Editor: John Trotti. 70% freelance written. Bimonthly magazine covering all aspects of erosion prevention and sediment control. "*Erosion Control* is a practical, hands-on, 'how-to' professional journal, and is the 'official journal of the International Erosion Control Association.' Our readers are civil engineers, landscape architects, builders, developers, public works officials, road and highway construction officials and engineers, soils specialists, farmers, landscape contractors and others involved with any activity that disturbs significant areas of surface vegetation. We ask all writers to tailor what they submit to this audience." Estab. 1994. Circ. 17,000. Pays on publication. Publishes ms an average of 3 months after acceptance. Byline given. Offers 10% or $10 kill fee. Buys all rights. Editorial lead time 3 months. Submit seasonal material 4 months in advance. Query for electronic submissions. Reports in 6 weeks on queries; 2 months on mss. Sample copy and writer's guidelines free on request.

Nonfiction: Book excerpts, interview/profile, personal experience, photo feature, technical. "No rudimentary, basic articles written for the average layperson. Our readers are experienced professionals with years of technical, practical experience in the field. Anything submitted that is judged by us to be speaking beneath the readers will be rejected." Buys 20 mss/year. Query with published clips. Length: 1,800-3,200 words. Pays $400. Sometimes pays expenses of writers on assignment.

Photos: Send photos with submission. Reviews transparencies and 5×7 or 8×10 prints. Negotiates payment individually. Captions, model releases and identification of subjects required. Buys all rights.

Columns/Departments: Field Report (news from the readers), 500-2,000 words. Buys 12 mss/year. Query. Pays $50-150.

Fillers: Anecdotes, facts, gags to be illustrated by cartoonist. Buys 30/year. Pays $25-250.

Tips: "We're a small company and easy to reach. We're open to any and all ideas as to editorial topics to cover. We strive to provide the reader with usable material, and present it in full color with graphic embellishment whenever possible. Dry, highly technical material is edited to make it more palatable and concise for the reader. Most of our feature articles come from freelancers. Interviews and quotes should be from the readers—the professionals working in the field—*not* manufacturers, *not* professional PR firms. Strive to write material that is 'over the heads' of our readers. If anything, attempt to make them 'reach.' Anything submitted that is too rudimentary, fundamental, elementary, etc., cannot be accepted for publication."

GROUND WATER AGE, National Trade Publications, 13 Century Hill Dr., Latham NY 12110-2197. (518)783-1281. Managing Editor: Stephen Smith. Monthly magazine covering water well drilling and pump installation. Estab. 1981. Circ. 14,000. **Pays on acceptance.** Publishes ms an average of 3-4 months after acceptance. Byline given. Buys first North American serial rights. Submit seasonal material 6 months in advance. Reports in 1 month on queries; 2 months on mss. Sample copy for 9×12 SAE with 10 first-class stamps.

Nonfiction: Historical/nostalgic, interview/profile, new product, photo feature, technical. Buys 1-5 mss/year. Query with published clips. Length: 750-3,000 words. Pays $50-350 for assigned articles; $50-250 for unsolicited articles. "Trades articles for advertising, on occasion and when desirable."

Photos: State availability of photos with submission. "We need quality photos of water well drillers, monitoring well contractors or pump installers in action, on the job." Reviews contact sheets, negatives, transparencies and prints. Offers no additional payment for photos accepted with ms. Identification of subjects required. Buys one-time rights.

Columns/Departments: Technically Speaking (technical, how-to aspects of water well or monitoring well drilling and technical aspects of water well pumps, tanks, valves and piping for domestic well systems); Business Strategies (business topics for improving productivity, marketing, etc.), 300-1,000 words. Buys 1-5 mss/year. Query first by phone or mail. Pays $50-150.

‡MSW MANAGEMENT, The Journal for Municipal Solid Waste Professionals, Forester Communications, Inc., 216 Gutierrez St., Santa Barbara CA 93101. (805)899-3355. Editor: John Trotti. 70% freelance written. Bimonthly magazine covering solid waste management—landfilling, composting, recycling, incineration. "*MSW Management* is written for *public sector* solid waste professionals—the people working for the local counties, cities, towns, boroughs and provinces. They run the landfills, recycling programs, composting, incineration. They are responsible for all aspects of garbage collection and disposal; buying and maintaining the associated equipment; and designing, engineering and building the waste processing facilities, transfer stations and landfills." Estab. 1991. Circ. 24,000. Pays on publication. Byline given. Offers 10% or $100 kill fee. Buys all rights. Editorial lead time 3 months. Submit seasonal material 4 months in advance. Query for electronic submissions. Reports in 6 weeks on queries; 2 months on mss. Sample copy free on request.

Nonfiction: Book excerpts, interview/profile, personal experience, photo feature, technical. *Elements of Integral Solid Waste Management*, published every October, includes articles and essays on *all* aspects of solid waste management. "No rudimentary, basic articles written for the average person on the street. Our readers are experienced professionals with years of practical, in-the-field experience. Any material submitted that we judge as too fundamental will be rejected." Buys 27 mss/year. Query. Length: 1,800-3,500 words. Pays $400. Sometimes pays expenses of writers on assignment.

Photos: Send photos with submission. Reviews transparencies and 5×7 or 8×10 prints. Negotiates payment individually. Captions, model releases and identification of subjects required. Buys all rights.

Columns/Departments: Field Report (news from the readers), 2,000 words; Washington Watch (news from DC), 1,500 words; Contracting (negotiating with the private sector). Buys 18 mss/year. Query. Pays $50-250.

Fillers: Anecdotes, facts, gags to be illustrated by cartoonist. Buys 30/year. Pays $25-250.

Tips: "We're a small company, easy to reach. We're open to any and all ideas as to possible editorial topics. We endeavor to provide the reader with usable material, and present it in full color with graphic embellishment whenever possible. Dry, highly technical material is edited to make it more palatable and concise. Most of our feature articles come from freelancers. Interviews and quotes should be from public sector solid waste managers and engineers—*not* PR people, *not* manufacturers. Strive to write material that is 'over the heads' of our readers. If anything, attempt to make them 'reach.' Anything submitted that is too basic, elementary, fundamental, rudimentary, etc. cannot be accepted for publication."

RECYCLING TODAY, Municipal Market Edition, GIE Inc., Dept. WM, 4012 Bridge Ave., Cleveland OH 44113. (216)961-4130. Editor: John Bruening. 25% freelance written. Monthly trade magazine covering recycling programs for municipalities. *Recycling Today* serves recycling coordinators at the state, county and municipal levels, as well as private companies providing information and services to government. Estab. 1990. Circ. 15,000. Pays on publication. Publishes ms an average of 2 months after acceptance. Byline given. No kill fee. Buys all rights (will reassign). Submit seasonal material 3 months in advance. Accepts simultaneous submissions. Sample copy for 9×12 SAE with 6 first-class stamps.

Nonfiction: Profiles of innovative recycling programs, solutions to current recycling challenges. Buys 40 mss/year. Query with published clips. Length: 2,000-3,000 words. Pays $200-300. Sometimes pays expenses of writers on assignment.

Photos: Send photos with submission. Reviews contact sheets, 2×3 slide or transparencies or 3×5 prints. Offers no additional payment for photos accepted with ms. Captions and identification of subjects required. Buys all rights (will reassign).

RESOURCE RECYCLING, North America's Recycling Journal, Resource Recycling, Inc., Dept. WM, P.O. Box 10540, Portland OR 97210-0540. (503)227-1319. Fax: (503)227-6135. Editor-in-Chief: Jerry Powell. Editor: Meg Lynch. 5% freelance written. Eager to work with new/unpublished writers. Monthly trade journal covering post-consumer recycling of paper, plastics, metals, glass and other materials. Estab. 1982. Circ. 15,000. Pays on publication. Publishes ms an average of 3-9 months after acceptance. Byline given. Buys first rights. Accepts simultaneous and previously published material. Send photocopy of article and information about when and where the article previously appeared. For reprints, pays 100% of their fee for an original article. Query for electronic submissions. Reports in 2-3 months on queries. Sample copy and writer's guidelines for 9×12 SAE with 7 first-class stamps.

Nonfiction: "No non-technical or opinion pieces." Buys 5-10 mss/year. Query with published clips. Length: 1,200-1,800 words. Pays $300-350. Pays with contributor copies "if writers are more interested in professional recognition than financial compensation." Sometimes pays the expenses of writers on assignment.

Photos: State availability of photos with submission. Reviews contact sheets, negatives and prints. Offers $5-50. Identification of subjects required. Buys one-time rights.

Tips: "Overviews of one recycling aspect in one state (e.g., oil recycling in Alabama) will receive attention. We will increase coverage of source reduction and yard waste composting."

Selling and Merchandising

Sales personnel and merchandisers interested in how to sell and market products successfully consult these journals. Publications in nearly every category of Trade also buy sales-related materials if they are slanted to the product or industry with which they deal.

THE AMERICAN SALESMAN, P.O. Box 1, Burlington IA 52601-0001. Fax: (319)752-3421. Publisher: Michael S. Darnall. Editor: Barbara Boeding. 95% freelance written. Prefers to work with published/established writers, but works with a small number of new/unpublished writers each year. Monthly magazine for distribution through company sales representatives. Estab. 1955. Circ. 1,500. Pays on publication. Publishes ms an average of 4 months after acceptance. Buys all rights. Reports in 3 months. Sample copy and writer's guidelines for 6 × 9 SAE with 3 first-class stamps; mention *Writer's Market* in request.

Nonfiction: Sales seminars, customer service and follow-up, closing sales, sales presentations, handling objections, competition, telephone usage and correspondence, managing territory, new innovative sales concepts. No sexist material, illustration written from a salesperson's viewpoint. No ms dealing with supervisory problems. Length: 900-1,200 words. Pays 3¢/word. Uses no advertising. Follow AP Stylebook. Include biography and/or byline with ms submissions. Author photos used. Send correspondence to Editor.

ASD/AMD TRADE NEWS, Associated Surplus Dealers/Associated Merchandise Dealers, 2525 Ocean Park Blvd., Santa Monica CA 90405-5201. (310)396-6006. Fax: (310)399-2662. Editor: Jay Hammeran. 75% freelance written. Monthly trade newspaper on trade shows and areas of interest to surplus/merchandise dealers. "Many of our readers have small, family-owned businesses." Estab. 1967. Circ. 80,000. Pays on publication. Publishes ms an average of 1-2 months after acceptance. Byline given. Negotiable kill fee. Buys all rights. Submit seasonal material 3 months in advance. Accepts simultaneous and previously published submissions. Send photocopy of article or typed ms with rights for sale noted and information about when and where the article previously appeared. For reprints pays 100% of the amount paid for an original article. Query for electronic submissions. Reports in 2 weeks on queries; 2 months on mss. Free sample copy and writer's guidelines.

Nonfiction: How-to (merchandise a store more effectively, buy and sell products), interview/profile (dealers/owners), personal experience (of dealers and merchandisers), photo feature (ASD/AMD trade shows), general business articles of interest. "February and August are the largest issues of the year. We generally need more freelance material for those two issues. No articles that are solely self-promotion pieces or straight editorials. We also need articles that tell a small business owner/manager how to handle legal issues, personnel questions and business matters, such as accounting." Buys 100 mss/year. Query with or without published clips, or send complete ms. Length: 500-1,250 words. Pays $50-100. Pays expenses of writers on assignment.

Photos: State availability of photos with submission. Reviews 3½ × 5 prints. Payment depends on whether photos were assigned or not. Identification of subjects required. Buys all rights.

Columns/Departments: Business & News Briefs (summarizes important news/business news affecting small businesses/dealers/merchandisers), 500 words; ASD Profile (interview with successful dealer), 1,000-1,250 words; Merchandising Tips (how to better merchandise a business), 750-1,000 words. Legal, Finance, Marketing, Advertising, Personnel sections: 1,000 words. Buys 70 mss/year. Query or send complete ms. Pays $50-100.

Fillers: Facts and newsbreaks. Buys 10/year. Length: 50-300 words. Pays $25-45.

Tips: "Talk to retailers. Find out what their concerns are, and the types of wholesalers/merchandisers they deal with. Write articles to meet those needs. It's as simple as that. The entire publication is open to freelance writers who can write good articles. We're now more sectionalized. We especially need articles that are of use or interest to very small businesses (1-10 employees). We need new looks at the cities in which we hold trade shows (Las Vegas, Atlantic City, Reno and New York.)"

BALLOONS AND PARTIES TODAY MAGAZINE, The Original Balloon Magazine of New-Fashioned Ideas, Festivities Publications, 1205 W. Forsyth St., Jacksonville FL 32204. (904)634-1902. Fax: (904)633-8764. Publisher: Debra Paulk. Editor: April Anderson. 10% freelance written. Monthly international trade journal for professional party decorators and for gift delivery businesses. Estab. 1986. Circ. 15,000. Pays on publication. Publishes ms an average of 3 months after acceptance. Byline given. Buys one-time rights. Submit seasonal material 6 months in advance. Query for electronic submissions. Reports in 6 weeks. Sample copy for 9 × 12 SAE with $2.40 in postage.

Nonfiction: Interview/profile, photo feature, technical, craft. Buys 24 mss/year. Query with or without published clips or send complete ms. Length: 500-1,500 words. Pays $100-300 for assigned articles; $50-200 for unsolicited articles. Sometimes pays expenses of writers on assignment.

Photos: Send photos with submission. Reviews 2×2 transparencies and 3×5 prints. Pays $10/photo accepted with ms (designs, arrangements, decorations only—no payment for new products). Captions, model releases and identification of subjects required. Buys one-time rights.

Columns/Departments: Great Ideas (craft projects using balloons, large scale decorations), 200-500 words. Send full manuscript with photos. Pays $10/photo.

Tips: "Show unusual, lavish, and outstanding examples of balloon sculpture, design and decorating. Offer specific how-to information. Be positive and motivational in style."

CHRISTIAN RETAILING, Strang Communications, 600 Rinehart Road, Lake Mary FL 32746. (407)333-0600. Fax: (407)333-9753. Managing Editor: Carol Chapman Stertzer. 60% freelance written. Trade journal featuring 18 issues/year covering issues and products of interest to Christian vendors and retail stores. "Our editorial is geared to help retailers run a successful business. We do this with product information, industry news and feature articles." Estab. 1958. Circ. 9,500. Pays on publication. Publishes ms an average of 5 months after acceptance. Bylines sometimes given. Kill fee varies with writer, length of article. Buys all rights. Submit seasonal material 5 months in advance. Accepts previously published submissions. Reports in 2 months. Sample copy for $3. Writer's guidelines for #10 SASE.

Nonfiction: How-to (any articles on running a retail business—books, gifts, music, video, clothing of interest to Christians), new product, religious, technical. Buys 36 mss/year. Send complete ms. Length: 700-2,000 words. Pays $200-340. Sometimes pays expenses of writers on assignment.

Photos: State availability of photos with submission. Reviews contact sheets, transparencies and prints. Usually offers no additional payment for photos accepted with ms. Captions required. Buys one-time rights.

Columns/Departments: Industry News; Book News; Music News; Video Talk; Product Spectrum.

Fillers: Cartoon; illustrations; graphs/charts.

Tips: "Visit Christian bookstores and see what they're doing—the products they carry, the issues that concern them. Then write about it!"

‡COLLEGE STORE JOURNAL, National Association of College Stores, 500 E. Lorain, Oberlin OH 44074. (216)775-7777. Editor: Ronald D. Stevens. 50% freelance written. Bimonthly association magazine covering college bookstore operations (retailing). "The *College Store Journal* is the journal of record for the National Association of College Stores and serves its members by publishing information and expert opinion on all phases of college store retailing." Estab. 1928. Circ. 7,200. Pays on publication or special arrangement. Byline given. Buys first rights. Editorial lead time 2 months. Submit seasonal material 6 months in advance. Accepts simultaneous submissions. Query for electronic submissions. Reports in 1 month. Sample copy free on request. Writer's guidelines not available.

Nonfiction: Historical/nostalgic, how-to, interview/profile, personal experience, technical (unique attributes of college stores/personnel). "Articles must have clearly defined connection to college stores and collegiate retailing." Buys 24 mss/year. Query with published clips. Length: 1,500-3,000 words. Pays $400 minimum for assigned articles; $200 minimum for unsolicited articles. Sometimes pays expenses of writers on assignment.

Photos: Send photos with submission. Reviews 2¼×2¼ transparencies and 5×7 prints. Negotiates payment individually. Captions and identification of subjects required. Buys one-time rights.

Columns/Departments: Buys 12 mss/year. Query with published clips. Pays $200-400.

Tips: "It's best if writers work (or have worked) in a college store. Articles on specific retailing successes are most open to freelancers—they should include information on how well an approach worked and the reasons for it, whether they are specific to a campus or region, etc."

‡EDUCATIONAL DEALER, Fahy-Williams Publishing, Inc., 171 Reed St., P.O. Box 1080, Geneva NY 14456-8080. (315)789-0458. Editor: J. Kevin Fahy. 3% freelance written. Magazine covering the educational supply industry, published 5 times/year—January, March, May, August and October. "Slant should be toward educational supply *dealers*, *not* teachers or educators, as most commonly happens." Estab. 1973. Circ. 12,500. Pays on publication. Byline given. Buys one-time rights. Accepts simultaneous and previously published submissions. Send photocopy of article. Reports in 3 weeks on queries; 3 months on mss. Sample copy for $3.

Nonfiction: New product, technical. Buys 3 mss/year. Query. Length: 1,500 words minimum. Pays $50 minimum.

Photos: Send photos with submission. Reviews contact sheets. Offers no additional payment for photos accepted with ms. Identification of subjects required. Buys one-time rights.

Tips: "Our special features section is most open to freelancers. Become familiar with the educational supply industry, which is growing quickly. While the industry is a large one in terms of dollars spent on school supply products, it's a 'small' one in terms of its players and what they're doing. Everyone knows everyone else; they belong to the same organizations: NSSEA and EDSA."

FOREIGN TRADE, A Survival Tool For World Traders, Defense & Diplomacy Inc., Suite 200, 6849 Old Dominion Dr., McLean VA 22101-3705. (703)448-1338. Editor: Russell W. Goodman. 50% freelance written. Magazine published 10 times/year covering international trade. *"Foreign Trade* publishes practical, 'News You Can Use' articles on international trade for readers worldwide who specialize in importing, exporting and manufacturing." Estab. 1991. Circ. 15,000. Pays on publication. Publishes ms an average of 1 month after acceptance. Byline given. Buys all rights. Editorial lead time 2 months. Reports in 1 week on queries.
Nonfiction: How-to (break into certain markets), travel. Buys 200 mss/year. Query with published clips. Length: 300-800 words. Pays $150 minimum.
Columns/Departments: Trade Briefs (articles on trading with certain countries), 300-800 words; Financing Deals (financial aspects of importing/exporting), 300-800 words. Buys 200 mss/year. Query with published clips. Pays $150-400.
Tips: "Writers approaching us should have practical experience in trading, banking, government regulations *or* experience in business writing. We are most open to trade briefs – articles should be short, precise, practical about specific trading opportunities."

GIFT BASKET REVIEW, Festivities Publications, 1205 W. Forsyth St., Jacksonville FL 32204. (904)634-1902. Fax: (904)633-8764. Publisher: Debra Paulk. Editor: Elizabeth Skelton. 25% freelance written. Monthly magazine for gourmet food and gift basket retailers. "Our readers are creative small business entrepreneurs. Many are women who start their business out of their homes and eventually branch into retail." Estab. 1990. Circ. 19,000. Pays on publication. Publishes ms an average of 3 months after acceptance. Byline given. Buys one-time rights. Submit seasonal material 9 months in advance. Accepts simultaneous and previously published submissions. Reports in 2 months.
Nonfiction: How-to (how to give a corporate presentation, negotiate a lease, etc.), photo feature, technical. "No personal profiles or general experience." Buys 6-8 mss/year. Send complete ms. Length: 500-2,000 words. Pays 10¢/word. Sometimes pays expenses of writers on assignment.
Photos: Send photos with submission. Reviews contact sheets, negatives, 2×2 transparencies and 3×5 prints. Offers $10/photo minimum. Model releases and identification of subjects required. Buys one-time rights.
Columns/Departments: Corporate Talk (deals with obtaining corporate clients), 1,500 words; In the Storefront (emphasis on small business owners with a retail storefront), 1,500 words; and On the Homefront (specifically for home-based entrepreneurs), 1,500 words. Buys 12 mss/year. Send complete ms. Pays 10¢/word.
Fillers: Anecdotes, facts, gags to be illustrated by cartoonist, newsbreaks, short humor. Length: 300 words maximum. Pays 10¢/word.
Tips: "Freelancers can best approach us by attending the various conventions (including our annual Jubilee convention) involving gift basket, floral and gourmet foods. Become involved with these businesses. All departments are open to freelancers. Be very specific with concrete tips and creative marketing ideas. Don't generalize. Don't tell us to take an ad in the yellow pages, tell us how to write an ad to promote a small creative business."

‡GIFTWARE NEWS, Talcott Corp., 112 Adrossan, P.O. Box 5398, Deptford NJ 08096. (609)227-0798. Editor: Anthony DeMasi. 30% freelance written. Monthly magazine covering gifts, collectibles, and tabletops for giftware retailers. Estab. 1976. Circ. 45,000. Pays on publication. Publishes ms an average of 2 months after acceptance. Byline given. Buys all rights. Submit seasonal/holiday material 4 months in advance. Reports in 2 months on mss. Sample copy for $3.
Nonfiction: How-to (sell, display), new product. Buys 50 mss/year. Send complete ms. Length: 1,500-2,500 words. Pays $150-250 for assigned articles; $75-100 for unsolicited articles.
Photos: Send photos with submission. Reviews 4×5 transparencies and 5×7 prints. Offers no additional payment for photos accepted with ms. Identification of subjects required.
Columns/Departments: Stationery, giftbaskets, collectibles, holiday merchandise, tabletop, wedding market and display – all for the gift retailer. Buys 36 mss/year. Send complete ms. Length: 1,500-2,500 words. Pays $75-200.
Tips: "We are not looking so much for general journalists but rather experts in particular fields who can also write."

‡INCENTIVE, Bill Communications, Dept. WM, 355 Park Ave., New York NY 10010. (212)986-4800. Fax: (212)867-4395. Editor: Jennifer Juergens. Executive Editor: Judy Quinn. Monthly magazine covering sales promotion and employee motivation: managing and marketing through motivation. Estab. 1905. Circ. 41,000. **Pays on acceptance.** Publishes ms an average of 3 months after acceptance. Byline always given. Buys all rights. Accepts previously published articles. Send tearsheet and information about when and where the article previously appeared. For reprints pays 50% of the amount paid for an original article. Query for electronic submissions. Reports in 1 month on queries; 2 months on mss. Sample copy for 9×12 SAE.
Nonfiction: General interest (motivation, demographics), how-to (types of sales promotion, buying product categories, using destinations), interview/profile (sales promotion executives); corporate case studies; travel (incentive-oriented). Buys up to 48 mss/year. Query with 2 published clips. Length: 1,000-2,000 words. Pays

$250-700 for assigned articles; pays $0 for unsolicited articles. Pays expenses of writers on assignment.

Photos: Send photos with submission. Reviews contact sheets and transparencies. Offers no additional payment for photos accepted with ms. Identification of subjects required.

Tips: "Read the publication, then query."

‡**NICHE, The Magazine For Progressive Retailers,** The Rosen Group, Suite 300, 3000 Chestnut Ave., Baltimore MD 21211. (410)889-2933. Editor: Laura Rosen. 10% freelance written. Quarterly magazine covering contemporary art and craft retailers. "*NICHE* centers on creative answers to the various problems and dilemmas retailers face daily. Minimal coverage of product. Audience is 80% independent retailers of contemporary craft and unique products designed and made in the US, other 20% are professional craftspeople." Estab. 1988. Circ. 20,000. Pays on publication. Publishes ms an average of 4 months after acceptance. Byline given. Buys second serial (reprint) or all rights. Editorial lead time 2 months. Submit seasonal material 6 months in advance. Accepts previously published submissions. Query for electronic submissions. Reports in 1 month on queries; 6 weeks on mss. Sample copy for $3. Writer's guidelines for #10 SASE.

Nonfiction: Interview/profile, opinion, photo feature, and articles targeted to independent retailers and small business owners. Buys 6-10 mss/year. Query with published clips. Length: 500-3,000 words. Pays $100. Sometimes pays expenses of writers on assignment.

Photos: Freelancers should send photos with submission. Reviews 4×5 transparencies or slides. Negotiates payment individually. Identification of subjects required. Buys all rights.

Columns/Departments: Retail Details (general retail information), 350 words; Artist Profiles (biographies of American Craft Artists), 450 words; Resources (book/video/seminar reviews pertaining to retailers), 200 words. Buys 6 mss/year. Query with published clips. Pays $40-300.

PROFESSIONAL SELLING, 24 Rope Ferry Rd., Waterford CT 06386-0001. (203)442-4365. Fax: (203)434-3078. Editor: Paulette S. Kitchens. 33% freelance written. Prefers to work with published/established writers. Bimonthly newsletter in two sections for sales professionals covering industrial, wholesale, high-tech and financial services sales. "*Professional Selling* provides field sales personnel with both the basics and current information that can help them better perform the sales function." Estab. 1917. **Pays on acceptance.** Publishes ms an average of 4-6 months after acceptance. No byline given. Buys all rights. Submit seasonal material 6 months in advance. Reports in 1 month. Sample copy and writer's guidelines for #10 SAE with 2 first-class stamps.

Nonfiction: How-to (successful sales techniques); interview/profile (interview-based articles). "We buy only interview-based material." Buys 12-15 mss/year. No unsolicited mss; written queries only. Length: 1,000-1,200 words.

Tips: "*Professional Selling* includes a 4-page clinic devoted to a single topic of major importance to sales professionals. Only the lead article for each section is open to freelancers. Lead article must be based on an interview with an actual sales professional. Freelancers may occasionally interview sales managers, but the slant must be toward field sales, *not* management."

SPECIAL EVENTS BUSINESS NEWS, ST Century Marketing, 7250C Westfield Ave., Pennsauken NJ 08110. (609)488-5255. Contact: Maria King. 20% freelance written. Monthly tabloid covering special events across North America, including festivals, fairs, auto shows, home shows, trade shows, etc. There are 21 categories of shows/events that are covered. Byline given. Buys first rights. Submit seasonal material 3 months in advance. Accepts previously published submissions. Free sample copy and writers guidelines.

Nonfiction: How-to, interview/profile, event review, new product. Special issues: annual event directory, semiannual flea market directory. No submissions unrelated to selling at events. Query. Length: 400-750 words. Pays $2.50/column inch.

Photos: Send photos with submission. Reviews contact sheets. Offers $10/photo. Captions required. Buys one-time rights.

Columns/Departments: 5 columns monthly (must deal with background of event, vendors or unique facets of industry in North America). Query with published clips. Length: 400-700 words. Pays $3/column inch.

Sport Trade

Retailers and wholesalers of sports equipment and operators of recreation programs read these journals. Magazines about general and specific sports are classified in the Consumer Sports section.

ACTION SPORTS RETAILER MAGAZINE, A Miller Freeman, Inc. publication, Box 9348, South Laguna CA 92677-0348. (714)499-5374. Editor: Pat Cochran. 75% freelance written. Magazine published 12 times/year covering surf, volleyball, in-line, sailboard swim, snowboard, apparel and hard goods retailers. "We publish in the interests of the growth and development of specialty sport retailers and related lifestyles and apparel." Estab. 1979. Circ. 15,000. **Pays on acceptance.** Publishes ms an average of 2 months after acceptance. Byline given. Offers 25% kill fee. Buys all rights and other rights (negotiable). Editorial lead time 3-4 months.

Accepts simultaneous submissions. Query for electronic submissions. Reports in 2 weeks on queries; 1 month on mss. *Writer's Market* recommends allowing 2 months for reply. Sample copy free on request.

Nonfiction: "This is a trade publication for the action sports industry. We are interested primarily in business articles," also how-tos, interview/profiles, new products (all related to industry) and technical (related to sports covered). How-to related to business management for specialty store employers/owners. Also needs articles on visual merchandising and display ideas; men's and junior's fashion trends in casual/active sportswear. "No general interest not related to our specific sports, which include surfing, snowboarding, volleyball, in-line, sailboard." Buys 120 mss/year. Query with published clips. Length: 100-2,000 words. Pays $75 minimum (dependent upon length). Sometimes pays expenses of writers on assignment.

Photos: State availability of photos with submission. Reviews transparencies. Negotiates payment individually. Buys one-time rights.

Columns/Departments: Snowboarding (new product information, etc.), 500-750 words; Swimwear (trend reports, profiles, etc.), 500-750 words; Surfing (manufacture related stories), 500-750 words. Buys 40 mss/year. Query with published clips. Pays $100-300.

Fillers: Facts, Buys 5/year. Length: 50 maximum words. Pays $25-100.

Tips: "Our magazine is edited for small, specialty retailer—and tries to provide information that will help them with their daily business needs. It's best if potential writers first send in a resumé and writing samples. Follow-up with a phone call, and the editors can make an evaluation of their abilities. We are using more profiles of business people in our industry. We need more statistical analysis and trend reporting. We especially need writers in areas outside California, particularly Florida, Texas, the Northeast and Hawaii."

AMERICAN FIREARMS INDUSTRY, AFI Communications Group, Inc., 9th Floor, 2455 E. Sunrise Blvd., Ft. Lauderdale FL 33304-3118. Fax: (305)561-4129. 10% freelance written. "Work with writers specifically in the firearms trade." Monthly magazine specializing in the sporting arms trade. Estab. 1973. Circ. 30,000. Pays on publication. Publishes ms an average of 1 month after acceptance. Buys all rights. Reports in 2 weeks.

Nonfiction: R.A. Lesmeister, articles editor. Publishes informational, technical and new product articles. No general firearms subjects. Query. Length: 900-1,500 words. Pays $150-300. Sometimes pays the expenses of writers on assignment.

Photos: Reviews 8×10 b&w glossy prints. Manuscript price includes payment for photos.

AMERICAN FITNESS, Suite 200, 15250 Ventura Blvd., Sherman Oaks CA 91403. (818)905-0040. Fax: (818)990-5468. Editor-at-Large: Peg Jordan, R.N. Managing Editor: Rhonda J. Wilson. 75% freelance written. Eager to work with new/unpublished writers. Bimonthly magazine covering exercise and fitness, health and nutrition. "We need timely, in-depth, informative articles on health, fitness, aerobic exercise, sports nutrition, age-specific fitness and outdoor activity." Circ. 25,100. Pays 4-6 weeks after publication. Publishes ms an average of 6 months after acceptance. Byline given. Buys all rights. Submit seasonal material 4 months in advance. Accepts simultaneous and previously published submissions. Query for electronic submissions. Reports in 6 weeks. Sample copy for $1 and SAE with 6 first-class stamps. Writer's guidelines for SAE.

Nonfiction: Women's health and fitness issues (pregnancy, family, pre- and post-natal, menopause and eating disorders); exposé (on nutritional gimmickry); historical/nostalgic (history of various athletic events); inspirational (sports leader's motivational pieces); interview/profile (fitness figures); new product (plus equipment review); personal experience (successful fitness story); photo feature (on exercise, fitness, new sport); youth and senior fitness and travel (spas that cater to fitness industry). No articles on unsound nutritional practices, popular trends or unsafe exercise gimmicks. Buys 18-25 mss/year. Query. Length: 800-1,500 words. Pays $80-140. Sometimes pays expenses of writers on assignment.

Photos: Sports, action, fitness, aquatic aerobics, aerobic competitions and exercise classes. "We are especially interested in photos of high-adrenalin sports like rock climbing and mountain biking." Pays $10 for b&w prints; $35 for transparencies. Captions, model release, and identification of subjects required. Usually buys all rights; other rights purchased depend on use of photo.

Columns/Departments: Adventure (treks, trails and global challenges); strength (the latest breakthroughs in weight training) and clubscene (profiles and highlights of the fitness club industry). Query with published clips or send complete ms. Length: 800-1,000 words. Pays $80-100.

Fillers: Cartoons, clippings, jokes, short humor, newsbreaks. Buys 12/year. Length: 75-200 words. Pays $35.

Tips: "Cover a unique aerobics or fitness angle, provide accurate and interesting findings, and write in a lively, intelligent manner. We are looking for new health and fitness reporters and writers. *AF* is a good place for first-time authors or for regularly published authors who want to sell spin-offs or reprints."

AQUA, The Business Magazine for Spa and Pool Professionals, AB Publications, 1846 Hoffman St., Madison WI 53704. (608)836-9470. Fax: (608)249-1153. Editor: Alan E. Sanderfoot. Managing Editor: Elissa Sard Pollack. Contact: Alan E. Sanderfoot. 20% freelance written. Monthly magazine covering swimming pools and spas. "*AQUA* is written for spa and pool dealers to help them improve their retail operations and increase their profitability." Estab. 1973. Circ. 15,000. Pays on publication. Byline given. Offers 25% kill fee. Buys first North American serial rights. Editorial lead time 2½ months. Submit seasonal material 2½ months in advance. Accepts simultaneous and previously published submissions. Send photocopy of article or typed ms with rights for sale noted and information about when and where the article previously appeared. For reprints, pays 25% of the amount paid for an original article. Query for electronic submissions. Reports in 1 month on queries; 2 month on mss. Sample copy free on request.

Nonfiction: Book excerpts, how-to, interview/profile, new product, opinion, photo feature, technical. No consumer-oriented lifestyle pieces. Buys 36 mss/year. Query with published clips. Length:1,500-2,500 words. Pays $300 minimum for assigned articles, $150 minimum for unsolicited articles. Sometimes pays expenses of writers on assignment (limit agreed upon in advance).

Photos: Send photos with submission. Reviews 3×5 prints. Negotiates payment individually. Captions and identification of subjects required. Buys one-time rights.

Columns/Departments: Sales (retail sales suggestions for spa and pool dealers), 1,000 words; Management (management tips for small retail businesses), 1,000 words; Finance (business column on some aspect of small business finance management), 1,000 words. Buys 36 mss/year. Send complete ms. Pays $50 minimum.

Tips: "Read the magazine, learn about pool and spa construction, and understand retailing. We are most open to profiles—find pool/spa dealers with a unique approach to retailing and highlight that in a query."

BICYCLE BUSINESS JOURNAL, 1904 Wenneca, P.O. Box 1570, Fort Worth TX 76101. (817)870-0341. Fax: (817)332-1619. Editor: Rix Quinn. Works with a small number of new/unpublished writers each year. 10% freelance written. Monthly. Circ. 10,000. **Pays on acceptance.** Publishes ms an average of 3 months after acceptance. Buys all rights. Reports in 2 months. Sample copy for 9×12 SAE with 6 first-class stamps.

Nonfiction: Stories about dealers who service what they sell, emphasizing progressive, successful sales ideas in the face of rising costs and increased competition. Length: 500 words.

Photos: Black and white or color glossy photo a must; vertical photo preferred. Query.

BOWLING PROPRIETOR, Bowling Proprietors' Association of America, P.O. Box 5802, Arlington TX 76017. (817)649-5105. Editor: Daniel W. Burgess. 5% freelance written. Monthly magazine covering bowling industry. "We cover the business of bowling, from the perspective of the owners and operators of bowling *centers* (not alleys)." Estab. 1954. Circ. 5,000. Pays on publication. Publishes ms an average of 2 months after acceptance. Byline sometimes given. Offers 50% kill fee. Buys first North American serial rights. Editorial lead time 2 months. Submit seasonal material 4 months in advance. Accepts simultaneous and previously published submissions. Send photocopy of article and information about when and where the article previously appeared. For reprints pays 25% of the amount paid for an original article. Query for electronic submissions. Reports in 6 weeks on queries. Sample copy free on request.

Nonfiction: Book excerpts, how-to, interview/profile, new product, opinion, technical and business angles, i.e.: marketing, customer service. "No 50s, 60s nostalgia pieces." Buys 2 mss/year. Query with published clips. Length: 500-1,200 words. Pays $300 minimum for assigned articles, $100 minimum for unsolicited articles. Sometimes pays in contributor copies or other premiums for "unsolicited, mutually beneficial articles." Sometimes pays expenses of writers on assignment (limit agreed upon in advance).

Photos: State availability of photos with submission. Reviews contact sheets, 35mm transparencies, 5×7 or 8×10 prints. Negotiates payment individually. Captions and identification of subjects required. Buys one-time rights.

Columns/Departments: News Notes (regular news items of the industry), 250 words. Buys 1 ms/year. Send complete ms. Pays $10-50.

‡GOLF COURSE NEWS, The Newspaper for the Golf Course Industry, United Publications Inc., P.O. Box 997, 38 Lafayette St., Yarmouth ME 04096. (207)846-0600. Fax: (207)846-0657. Managing Editor: Mark Leslie. 15% freelance written. Monthly tabloid that covers golf course maintenance, design, construction and management. "Articles should be written with the golf course superintendent in mind. Our readers are superintendents, course architects and builders, owners and general managers." Estab. 1989. Circ. 22,000. **Pays on acceptance.** Publishes ms an average of 2 months after acceptance. Byline given. Buys first North American serial rights. Editorial lead time 1 month. Submit seasonal material 2 months in advance. Accepts simultaneous submissions. Query for electronic submissions. Reports in 2 weeks on queries; 2 months on mss. Free sample copy and writer's guidelines.

Nonfiction: Book excerpts, general interest, interview/profile, new product, opinion, photo feature. "No how-to articles." Buys 24 mss/year. Query with published clips. Length: 500-1,500 words. Pays $200. Sometimes pays expenses of writers on assignment.

Photos: Send photos with submission. Reviews negatives, transparencies and prints. Offers no additional payment for photos accepted with ms. Identification of subjects required. Buys one-time rights.

Columns/Departments: On the Green (innovative ideas in the industry), 1,000 words. Buys 4 mss/year. Query with published clips. Pays $200-500.

Tips: "Keep your eye out for news affecting the golf industry. Then contact us with your story ideas. We are a national paper and accept both national and regional interest articles. We are interested in receiving features on development of golf projects."

‡INLINE RETAILER & INDUSTRY NEWS, Sports & Fitness Publishing, 2025 Pearl St., Boulder CO 80302. (303)440-5111. Editor: Michael W. Shafran. 15% freelance written. Tabloid published every 6 weeks covering the inline skating industry. "*InLine Retailer* is a business magazine dedicated to spotting new trends, products and procedures that will help inline retailers and manufacturers keep a competitive edge." Estab. 1992. Circ. 6,000. Pays on publication. Publishes ms an average of 1 month after acceptance. Byline given. Offers 30% kill fee. Buys first North American serial rights. Editorial lead time 2 months. Submit seasonal material 3-4 months in advance. Query for electronic submissions. Prefers Macintosh compatible. Reports in 2 weeks on queries. Sample copy for $5.

Nonfiction: How-to, interview/profile, new product, technical. Buys 10 mss/year. Query with published clips. Length: 500-2,000 words. Pays 15¢/word minimum for assigned articles; 10¢/word for unsolicited articles. Sometimes pays expenses of writers on assignment.

Columns/Departments: Shop Talk (tips for running an inline retail store), 1,000-1,200 words; Industry Interview (insights from high-level industry figures), 1,200-1,500 words. Buys 10 mss/year. Query with published clips or send complete ms. Pays 10-15¢/word.

Tips: "It's best to write us and explain your background in either the sporting goods business or inline skating. Mail several clips and also send some ideas that you think would be suitable for our readers. The features and Shop Talk sections are the ones we typically assign to freelancers. Writers should have solid reporting skills, particularly when it comes to getting subjects to disclose technology, news or tips that they may be willing to do without some prodding."

THE INTERNATIONAL SADDLERY AND APPAREL JOURNAL, EEMG, Inc., P.O. Box 3039, Berea KY 40403-3039. (606)986-4644. Fax: (606)986-1770. Editor: Pamela R. Harrell. 25% freelance written. Monthly magazine on the US equine trade "serving the business and marketing needs of the equine trade industry. Feature departments present articles which address the current business and marketing issues, trends, and practices in the equestrian and equine goods industries. Monthly news and products sections are also included." Estab. 1987. Circ. 8,000. Pays on publication. Byline given. Offers negotiable kill fee. Buys first North American serial rights. Accepts previously published submissions. Send photocopy of article, typed ms with rights for sale noted and information about when and where the article previously appeared. Reports in 1 month on queries. Sample copy and writer's guidelines for $4.

Nonfiction: Exposé (business-oriented), how-to (should be useable business information), interview/profile (with industry people). We are not a "backyard," casual interest horse magazine. No fiction. Buys 60 mss/year. Query with published clips. Length: 1,000-2,500 words. Payment based on piece and the information and value of the article. Rarely pays expenses of writers on assignment.

Photos: State availability or send photos with submissions. Reviews 3½×5 prints. Offers $5-15/photo (negotiable). Captions or model releases required. Buys one-time rights.

Columns/Departments: International (overseas, business interest pieces), 1,000 words; Retail Marketing (articles that give tack shop retailers information about marketing products), 1,000 words. Buys 10 mss/year. Query with published clips.

Tips: "Read *SAJ* and other trade publications. Understand that we serve the professional business community, including: tack shops, feed stores, gift shops, and manufacturers. People in the equine trade are like other business-people; they have employees, need insurance, travel, own computers, advertise and want pertinent business information."

‡ISIA, Ice Skating Institute of America, 355 W. Dundee Rd., Buffalo Grove IL 60089. Managing Editor: Lara Dailey. 20% freelance written. Bimonthly newsletter covering ice skating industry. "News-oriented articles on rink/facility management, coaching issues, health, industry business news." Estab. 1961. Circ. 3,800. Pays on publication. Publishes ms an average of 2 months after acceptance. Byline given. Buys one-time rights, second serial (reprint) rights or makes work-for-hire assignments. Editorial lead time 2 months. Submit seasonal material 6 months in advance. Accepts simultaneous and previously published submissions. Query for electronic submissions. Reports in 1 month on queries; 2 months on mss. Sample copy free on request.

Nonfiction: Book excerpts, how-to, interview/profile, new product, technical, ice skating industry issues and news. Query with published clips. Length: 250-500 words. Pays $75. Sometimes pays expenses of writers on assignment.

Photos: State availability of photos or send photos with submission. Reviews contact sheets, 5×7 prints. Offers $10-35/photo. Captions, model releases and identification of subjects required. Buys one-time rights or all rights if work-for-hire assignment.

Columns/Departments: WORD (What Other Rinks Are Doing—marketing their program/facility), 250 words or less; Safety (product/air quality/facility safety), 250-500 words; News (industry issues/news), 250-500 words. Buys 6-8 mss/year. Query with published clips. Pays $75-150 depending on extent of research needed for work.

‡NSGA RETAIL FOCUS, National Sporting Goods Association, Suite 700, 1699 Wall St., Mt. Prospect IL 60056-5780. (708)439-4000. Fax: (708)439-0111. Publisher: Thomas G. Drake. Associate Publisher: Larry Weindruch. Editor: Bob Nieman. 75% freelance written. Works with a small number of new/unpublished writers each year. *NSGA Retail Focus* serves as a monthly trade journal for presidents, CEOs and owners of more than 22,000 retail sporting goods firms. Estab. 1948. Circ. 9,000. Pays on publication. Publishes ms an average of 1 month after acceptance. Byline given. Offers 50% kill fee. Buys first and second serial (reprint) rights. Submit seasonal material 3 months in advance. Query for electronic submissions. Sample copy for 9×12 SAE with 5 first-class stamps.

Nonfiction: Essays, interview/profile, photo feature. "No articles written without sporting goods retail businesspeople in mind as the audience. In other words, no generic articles sent to several industries." Buys 50 mss/year. Query with published clips. Pays $75-500. Sometimes pays the expenses of writers on assignment.

Photos: State availability of photos with submission. Reviews contact sheets, negatives, transparencies and 5×7 prints. Payment negotiable. Buys one-time rights.

Columns/Departments: Personnel Management (succinct tips on hiring, motivating, firing, etc.); Tax Advisor (simplified explanation of how tax laws affect retailer); Sales Management (in-depth tips to improve sales force performance); Retail Management (detailed explanation of merchandising/inventory control); Advertising (case histories of successful ad campaigns/ad critiques); Legal Advisor; Computers; Store Design; Visual Merchandising; all 1,500 words. Buys 50 mss/year. Query. Length: 1,000-1,500 words. Pays $75-300.

POOL & SPA NEWS, Leisure Publications, 3923 W. Sixth St., Los Angeles CA 90020-4290. (213)385-3926. Fax: (213)383-1152. Editor-in-Chief: Jim McCloskey. 15-20% freelance written. Semimonthly magazine emphasizing news of the swimming pool and spa industry for pool builders, pool retail stores and pool service firms. Estab. 1960. Circ. 17,000. Pays on publication. Publishes ms an average of 1-2 months after acceptance. Buys all rights. Query for electronic submissions. Reports in 2 weeks. Sample copy for $5 and 9×12 SAE with 10 first-class stamps.

Nonfiction: Interview, new product, profile, technical. Phone queries OK. Length: 500-2,000 words. Pays 5-14¢/word. Pays expenses of writers on assignment.

Photos: Pays $10 per b&w photo used.

PROFESSIONAL BOATBUILDER MAGAZINE, WoodenBoat Publications Inc., P.O. Box 78, Naskeag Rd., Brooklin ME 04616-0078. (207)359-4651. Fax: (207)359-8920. Editor: Chris Cornell. 75% freelance written. Bimonthly magazine for boat building companies, repair yards, naval architects, and marine surveyors. Estab. 1989. Circ. 21,000 (BPA audited). Pays 45 days after acceptance. Byline given. Buys first North American serial rights. Considers previously published articles. Send tearsheet of article, or send typed ms with rights for sale noted. Include information about when and where article previously appeared. Reports in 2 months. Free sample copy and writer's guidelines.

Nonfiction: How-to, new product, opinion, technical. "We are now looking for more articles on marine systems (electrical, hydraulic, propulsion, etc.) and accessory equipment (deck hardware, engine controls, etc.)" No information better directed to boating consumers. Buys 30 mss/year. Query with or without published clips or send complete ms. Length: 1,000-4,000 words. Pays 20¢/word. Sometimes pays expenses of writers on assignment.

Photos: State availability of photos with submission. Reviews transparencies and 8×10 b&w prints. Offers $15-200/photo; $350 for color cover. Identification of subjects and full captions required. Buys one-time rights.

Columns/Departments: Judy Robbins, managing editor. Tools of the Trade (new tools/materials/machinery of interest to boatbuilders), 100-500 words. Buys 10 mss/year. Query with published clips. Pays $25-100.

PRORODEO SPORTS NEWS, Professional Rodeo Cowboys Association, 101 Pro Rodeo Dr., Colorado Springs CO 80919-9989. (719)593-8840. Fax: (719)593-8235. Editor: Kendra Santos. Biweekly tabloid that covers PRCA Rodeo. "The *Prorodeo Sports News* is the official publication of the PRCA, covering cowboys, stock contractors, contract members and general rodeo-related news about the PRCA membership and PRCA sponsors. We do not print material about any non-sanctioned rodeo event, or other rodeo associations." Estab. 1952. Circ. 35,000. Pays on publication. Publishes ms 1 month after acceptance. Byline given. Submit seasonal material 2 months in advance. Sample copy for 8×10 SAE with 4 first-class stamps. Free writer's guidelines.

Nonfiction: Interview/profile, photo feature. Buys 15 mss/year. Query. Length: 1,500 words maximum. Pays $50-100. Sometimes pays expenses of writers on assignment.

Photos: Send photos with submission. Reviews negatives and 5×7 or 8×10 prints. Offers $15-85/photo. Identification of subjects required.

Tips: "Feature stories written about PRCA cowboys will always be considered for publication. Along with feature stories on PRCA members, I foresee the *Prorodeo Sports News* printing more articles about rodeo sponsorship and creative rodeo promotions. Like all professional sports, PRCA rodeo is a business. The

The double dagger before a listing indicates that the listing is new in this edition. New markets are often more receptive to freelance submissions.

Prorodeo Sports News will reflect the business aspect of professional rodeo, as well as cover the people who make it all happen."

SWIMMING POOL/SPA AGE, Communication Channels, Inc., Suite 200, 6151 Powers Ferry Rd., Atlanta GA 30339-2941. (404)955-2500. Fax: (404)955-0400. Editor: Terri Simmons. 30% freelance written. Works with a small number of new/unpublished writers each year. Monthly tabloid emphasizing pool, spa and hot tub industry. Estab. 1926. Circ. 17,500. Pays on publication. Publishes ms an average of 3 months after acceptance. Buys all rights. Submit seasonal material 3 months in advance. Accepts previously published submissions. Send typed ms with rights for sale noted, disk and information about when and where the article previously appeared. For reprints pays 50% of the amount paid for an original article. Query for electronic submissions. Reports in 3-6 months.
Nonfiction: How-to (installation techniques, service and repairs, tips, etc.); interview (with people and groups within the industry); photo feature (pool/spa/tub construction or special use); technical (should be prepared with expert within the industry); industry news; market research reports. Also, comparison articles exploring the same type of products produced by numerous manufacturers. Buys 1-3 unsolicited mss/year. Query. Length: 250-1,500 words. Pays 10¢/word. Sometimes pays the expenses of writers on assignment.
Photos: Purchased with accompanying ms or on assignment. Query or send contact sheet. Will accept 35mm transparencies of good quality. Captions required.
Tips: "If a writer can produce easily understood technical articles containing unbiased, hard facts, we are definitely interested. We will be concentrating on technical and how-to articles because that's what our readers want."

THOROUGHBRED TIMES, Thoroughbred Publications, Inc., Suite 101, 801 Corporate Dr., P.O. Box 8237, Lexington KY 40533. (606)223-9800. Editor: Mark Simon. 10% freelance written. Weekly tabloid that covers thoroughbred racing and breeding. "Articles are written for professionals who breed and/or race thoroughbreds at tracks in the US. Articles must help owners and breeders understand racing to help them realize a profit." Estab. 1985. Circ. 15,000. Pays on publication. Publishes ms an average of 1 month after acceptance. Byline given. Offers 50% kill fee. Buys all rights. Submit seasonal material 2 months in advance. Query for electronic submissions. Reports in 2 weeks.
Nonfiction: General interest, historical/nostalgic, interview/profile, technical. Buys 52 mss/year. Query. Length: 500-2,500 words. Pays 10-20¢/word. Sometimes pays expenses of writers on assignment.
Photos: State availability of photos with submission. Reviews prints. Offers $25/photo. Identification of subjects required. Buys one-time rights.
Tips: "We are looking for farm stories and profiles of owners, breeders, jockeys and trainers."

WOODALL'S CAMPGROUND MANAGEMENT, Woodall Publishing Co., 28167 N. Keith Dr., Lake Forest IL 60045-4528. (708)362-6700. Editor: Mike Byrnes. 10% freelance written. Monthly tabloid covering campground management and operation for managers of private and public campgrounds throughout the US. Estab. 1970. Circ. 10,000. Pays after publication. Publishes ms an average of 8 months after acceptance. Byline given. Buys all rights. Will reassign rights to author upon written request. Submit seasonal material 4 months in advance. Reports in 1 month on queries; 2 months on mss. Free sample copy and writer's guidelines.
Nonfiction: How-to, interview/profile, technical. "Our articles tell our readers how to maintain their resources, manage personnel and guests, market, develop new campground areas and activities, and interrelate with the major tourism organizations within their areas. 'Improvement' and 'profit' are the two key words." Buys 14 mss/year. Query. Length: 500 words minimum. Pays $50-200.
Photos: Send contact sheets and negatives. "We pay for each photo used."
Tips: "The best type of story to break in with is a case history approach about how a campground improved its maintenance, physical plant or profitability."

Stone, Quarry and Mining

COAL PEOPLE MAGAZINE, Al Skinner Productions, Dept. WM, 629 Virginia St. W., P.O. Box 6247, Charleston WV 25362. (304)342-4129. Fax: (304)343-3124. Editor/Publisher: Al Skinner. 50% freelance written. Monthly magazine with stories about coal people, towns and history. "Most stories are about people or historical—either narrative or biographical on all levels of coal people, past and present—from coal execs down to grass roots miners. Most stories are upbeat—showing warmth of family or success from underground up!" Estab. 1976. Circ. 11,000. Pays on publication. Publishes ms an average of 3 months after acceptance. Byline given. Buys first rights, second serial (reprint) rights and makes work-for-hire assignments. Accepts previously published submissions. Submit seasonal material 2 months in advance. Reports in 3 months. Sample copy for 9×12 SAE with 10 first-class stamps.
Nonfiction: Book excerpts (and film if related to coal), historical/nostalgic (coal towns, people, lifestyles), humor (including anecdotes and cartoons), interview/profile (for coal personalities), personal experience (as relates to coal mining), photo feature (on old coal towns, people, past and present). Special issues: calendar

issue for more than 300 annual coal shows, association meetings, etc. (January); surface mining/reclamation award (July); Christmas in Coal Country (December). No poetry, no fiction or environmental attacks on the coal industry. Buys 32 mss/year. Query with published clips. Length: 5,000 words. Pays $50.

Photos: Send photos with submission. Reviews contact sheets, transparencies, and 5×7 prints. Captions and identification of subjects required. Buys one-time rights and one-time reprint rights.

Columns/Departments: Editorials — anything to do with current coal issues (non-paid); Mine'ing Our Business (bull pen column — gossip — humorous anecdotes), Coal Show Coverage (freelance photojournalist coverage of any coal function across the US). Buys 10 mss/year. Query. Length: 300-500 words. Pays $5.

Fillers: Anecdotes. Buys 10/year. Length: 300 words. Pays $5.

Tips: "We are looking for good feature articles on coal people, towns, companies — past and present, color slides (for possible cover use) and b&w photos to complement stories. Could also use a few news writers to take photos and do journalistic coverage on coal events across the country. Slant stories more toward people and less on historical. More faces and names than old town, company store photos. Include more quotes from people who lived these moments!" The following geographical areas are covered: Eastern Canada; Mexico; Europe; China; Russia; Poland; Australia; as well as US states Alabama, Tennessee, Virginia, Washington, Oregon, North and South Dakota, Arizona, Colorado, Alaska and Wyoming.

DIMENSIONAL STONE, Dimensional Stone Institute, Inc., Suite I, 6300 Variel Ave., Woodland Hills CA 91367. Editor: Marc Birenbaum. 25% freelance written. Monthly international magazine covering dimensional stone use for managers of producers, importers, contractors, fabricators and specifiers of dimensional stone. Estab. 1985. Circ. 15,849. Pays on publication. Publishes ms an average of 2 months after acceptance. Byline given. Buys first rights or second serial (reprint) rights. Reports in 1 month. Accepts previously published submissions. Send tearsheet of article and information about when and where the article previously appeared. Sample copy for 9×12 SAE with 11 first-class stamps.

Nonfiction: Interview/profile, technical, only on users of dimensional stone. Buys 6-7 mss/year. Send complete ms. Length: 1,000-3,000 words. Pays $100 maximum. Sometimes pays the expenses of writers on assignment.

Photos: Send photos with submission. Reviews transparencies, slides and prints. Publication produced using desktop publishing with scanning capabilities. Offers no additional payment for photos accepted with ms. Identification of subjects required.

Tips: "Articles on outstanding commercial and residential uses of dimensional stone are most open to freelancers. For queries, fax editor. Editors work in Microsoft Word on Macintosh system, so copy delivered on disk is appreciated."

MINE REGULATION REPORTER, Pasha Publications, #1000, 1616 N. Fort Myer Dr., Arlington VA 22209. (703)528-1244. Editor: Wayne Barber. 30% freelance written. Biweekly newsletter covering health, safety and environmental issues that relate to mine operations. Estab. 1989. Pays on publication. Publishes ms an average of 1 week after acceptance. Offers $25 kill fee. Buys all rights. Accepts simultaneous submissions. Query for electronic submissions, which are preferred. Free sample copy.

Nonfiction: Interview/profile, new product, technical. Buys 2 mss/year. Query. Pays $12.50/published inch — minimum 5 inches. Sometimes pays expenses of writers on assignment.

Tips: "Just give us the facts." Stories wanted on safety, health or environmental issues, such as in the mining industry.

STONE REVIEW, National Stone Association, 1415 Elliot Place NW, Washington DC 20007. (202)342-1100. Fax: (202)342-0702. Editor: Frank Atlee. Bimonthly magazine covering quarrying and supplying of crushed stone, "designed to be a communications forum for the crushed stone industry. Publishes information on industry technology, trends, developments and concerns. Audience are quarry operations/management, and manufacturers of equipment, suppliers of services to the industry." Estab. 1985. Circ. 4,000. Pays on publication. Publishes ms an average of 3 months after acceptance. Byline given. Negotiable kill fee. Buys one-time rights. Accepts simultaneous and previously published submissions. Send tearsheet, photocopy or typed ms with information about when and where the article previously appeared. Payment negotiable. Reports in 1 month. Sample copy for 9×12 SAE with 3 first-class stamps.

Nonfiction: Technical. Query with or without published clips or send complete ms. Length: 1,000-2,500 words. "Note: We have no budget for freelance material, but I'm willing to secure payment for right material."

Photos: State availability of photos with query, then send photos with submission. Reviews contact sheets, negatives, transparencies and prints. Offers no additional payment for photos accepted with ms. Identification of subjects required. Buys one-time rights.

Tips: "At this point, most features are written by contributors in the industry, but I'd like to open it up. Articles on unique equipment, applications, etc. are good, as are those reporting on trends (e.g., there is a strong push on now for environmentally sound operations). Also interested in stories on family-run operations involving three or more generations."

STONE WORLD, Business News Publishing Company, Suite 205, 1 Kalisa Way, Paramus NJ 07652. (201)599-0136. Fax: (201)599-2378. Editor: John Sailer. Associate Editor: Susan Springstead. Assistant Editor: Michael

Reis. Monthly magazine on natural building stone for producers and users of granite, marble, limestone, slate, sandstone, onyx and other natural stone products. Estab. 1984. Circ. 16,000. Pays on publication. Publishes ms an average of 6 months after acceptance. Byline given. Buys first rights or second serial (reprint) rights. Submit seasonal material 6 months in advance. Accepts previously published articles. Send photocopy of article. Reports in 2 months. Sample copy for $10.

Nonfiction: How-to (fabricate and/or install natural building stone), interview/profile, photo feature, technical, architectural design, artistic stone uses, statistics, factory profile, equipment profile, trade show review. Buys 25 mss/year. Query with or without published clips or send complete ms. Length: 600-3,000 words. Pays $115/page. Pays the expenses of writers on assignment.

Photos: State availability of photos with submission. Reviews transparencies and prints. Pays $10/photo accepted with ms. Captions and identification of subjects required. Buys one-time rights.

Columns/Departments: News (pertaining to stone or design community); New Literature (brochures, catalogs, books, videos, etc. about stone); New Products (stone products); New Equipment (equipment and machinery for working with stone); Calendar (dates and locations of events in stone and design communities). Query or send complete ms. Length: 300-600 words. Pays $4/inch.

Tips: "Articles about architectural stone design accompanied by professional color photographs and quotes from designing firms are often published, especially when one unique aspect of the stone selection or installation is highlighted. We are also interested in articles about new techniques of quarrying and/or fabricating natural building stone."

Toy, Novelty and Hobby

Publications focusing on the toy and hobby industry are listed in this section. For magazines for hobbyists see the Consumer Hobby and Craft section.

PLAYTHINGS, Geyer-McAllister, 51 Madison Ave., New York NY 10010-1675. (212)689-4411. Fax: (212)683-7929. Editor: Frank Reysen, Jr. Executive Editor: Eugene Gilligan. 20-30% freelance written. Monthly merchandising magazine covering toys and hobbies aimed mainly at mass market toy retailers. Estab. 1903. Circ. 15,000. **Pays on acceptance.** Publishes ms an average of 3 months after acceptance. Byline sometimes given. Buys one-time rights. Submit seasonal material 3 months in advance. Accepts simultaneous submissions. Reports in 1 month. Free sample copy and writer's guidelines.

Nonfiction: Interview/profile, photo feature, retail profiles of toy and hobby stores and chains. Annual directory published in May. Buys 10 mss/year. Query. Length: 900-2,500 words. Pays $100-350. Sometimes pays the expenses of writers on assignment.

Photos: Send photos with submission. Captions and identification of subjects required. Buys one-time rights.

Columns/Departments: Buys 5 mss/year. Query. Pays $100-200.

SOUVENIRS & NOVELTIES MAGAZINE, Kane Communications, Inc., Suite 210, 7000 Terminal Square, Upper Darby PA 19082. President: Scott Borowsky. Editor: Sandy Meschkow. Magazine published 7 times/year for resort and gift industry. Circ. 27,000. Pays on publication. Byline given. Buys all rights. Reports in 3 weeks. Sample copy for 6×9 SAE with 5 first-class stamps.

Nonfiction: Interview/profile, new product. Buys 6 mss/year. Query. Length: 700-1,500 words. Pays $25-175 for assigned articles. Sometimes pays the expenses of writers on assignment.

Photos: State availability of photos with submission. Captions, model releases and identification of subjects required.

THE STAMP WHOLESALER, P.O. Box 706, Albany OR 97321-0006. (503)928-4484. Fax: (503)967-7262. Managing Editor: Carol Ann Lysek. 80% freelance written. Newspaper published 28 times/year for philatelic businesspeople; many are part-time and/or retired from other work. Estab. 1937. Circ. 4,700. Pays on publication. Byline given. Buys all rights. Reports in 1 month. Free sample copy and writer's guidelines.

Nonfiction: "Focus on how-to, general business techniques, computer how-to for business, stamp business trends and history, specialty aspects of the stamp business i.e., auctions, catalogs, postal history, cinderellas, approvals, mail order, opinion pieces. The articles must be directed specifically to stamp dealers. Most of our writers are stamp dealers themselves. We are beginning to cover phone cards as well as stamps." Buys 120 ms/year. Submit complete ms. Length: 1,000-2,000 words. Pays $35 and up/article.

Tips: "Send queries on business stories or stamp dealer profiles. We need stories to help dealers make and save money. We also buy cartoons on stamp dealer topics. We especially need business profiles of stamp dealers located in various parts of the country. We pay $250 for these, but we expect an in-depth, facts and figures business article with color pictures in return. We are also looking for writers who can write about computers in a way that is relevant to small business stamp dealers."

Transportation

These publications are for professional movers and people involved in transportation of goods. For magazines focusing on trucking see also Auto and Truck.

BUS WORLD, Magazine of Buses and Bus Systems, Stauss Publications, P.O. Box 39, Woodland Hills CA 91365-0039. (818)710-0208. Editor: Ed Stauss. 25% freelance written. Quarterly trade journal covering the transit and intercity bus industries. Estab. 1978. Circ. 5,000. Pays on publication. Reports in 1 month. Sample copy with writer's guidelines for $2.
Photos: "We buy photos with manuscripts under one payment."
Fillers: Cartoons. Buys 4-6/year. Pays $10.
Tips: "No tourist or travelog viewpoints. Be employed in or have a good understanding of the bus industry. Be enthusiastic about buses—their history and future. Acceptable material will be held until used and will not be returned unless requested by sender. Unacceptable and excess material will be returned only if accompanied by suitable SASE."

INBOUND LOGISTICS, Thomas Publishing Co., Dept. WM, 8th Floor, 5 Penn Plaza, New York NY 10001. (212)629-1560. Fax: (212)629-1565. Publisher: Keith Biondo. Editor: Felecia Stratton. 50% freelance written. Prefers to work with published/established writers. Monthly magazine covering the transportation industry. "*Inbound Logistics* is distributed to people who buy, specify, or recommend inbound freight transportation services and equipment. The editorial matter provides basic explanations of inbound freight transportation, directory listings, how-to technical information, trends and developments affecting inbound freight movements, and expository, case history feature stories." Estab. 1980. Circ. 50,000. Pays on publication. Publishes ms an average of 3 months after acceptance. Byline given. Buys all rights. Accepts simultaneous and previously published submissions. Send tearsheet of article and information about when and where the article previously appeared. Pays 20% of amount paid for an original article. Reports in 2 months. Sample copy and writer's guidelines for 9×12 SAE with 5 first-class stamps.
Nonfiction: How-to (basic help for purchasing agents and traffic managers), interview/profile (purchasing and transportation professionals). Buys 20 mss/year. Query with published clips. Length: 750-1,000 words. Pays $100-400. Pays expenses of writers on assignment.
Photos: Chelsea Michaels, photo editor. State availability of photos with query. Pays $100-500 for b&w contact sheets, negatives, transparencies and prints; $250-500 for color contact sheets, negative transparencies and prints. Captions and identification of subjects required.
Columns/Departments: Viewpoint (discusses current opinions on transportation topics). Query with published clips.
Tips: "Have a sound knowledge of the transportation industry; educational how-to articles get our attention."

NATIONAL BUS TRADER, The Magazine of Bus Equipment for the United States and Canada, 9698 W. Judson Rd., Polo IL 61064-9015. (815)946-2341. Fax: (815)946-2347. Editor: Larry Plachno. 25% freelance written. Eager to work with new/unpublished writers. Monthly magazine for manufacturers, dealers and owners of buses and motor coaches. Estab. 1977. Circ. 7,354. Pays on either acceptance or publication. Publishes ms an average of 3 months after acceptance. Byline given. Not copyrighted. Buys rights "as required by writer." Accepts simultaneous and previously published submissions. Reports in 1 month. Sample copy for 9×12 SAE.
Nonfiction: Historical/nostalgic (on old buses); how-to (maintenance repair); new products; photo feature; technical (aspects of mechanical operation of buses). "We are finding that more and more firms and agencies are hiring freelancers to write articles to our specifications. We are more likely to run them if someone else pays." No material that does *not* pertain to bus tours or bus equipment. Buys 3-5 unsolicited mss/year. Query. Length varies. Pays variable rate. Sometimes pays the expenses of writers on assignment.
Photos: State availability of photos. Reviews 5×7 or 8×10 prints and 35mm transparencies. Captions, model release and identification of subjects required.
Columns/Departments: Bus Maintenance; Buses and the Law; Regulations; Bus of the Month. Buys 20-30 mss/year. Query. Length: 250-400 words. Pays variable rate.
Tips: "We are a very technical publication. Writers should submit qualifications showing extensive background in bus vehicles. We're very interested in well-researched articles on older bus models and manufacturers, or current converted coaches. We would like to receive history of individual bus models prior to 1953 and history of GMC 'new look' models. Write or phone editors with article concept or outline for comments and approval."

SHIPPING DIGEST, The National Shipping Weekly of Export Transportation, Geyer McAllister Publications Inc., 51 Madison Ave., New York NY 10010. (212)689-4411. Fax: (212)683-7929. Editor: Maria Reines. 20% freelance written. Weekly magazine that covers ocean, surface, air transportation, ports, intermodal and EDI. "Read by executives responsible for exporting US goods to foreign markets. Emphasis is on services offered by ocean, surface and air carriers, their development and trends; port developments; trade agreements; government regulation; electronic data interchange." Pays on publication. Publishes ms an average of 1 month after acceptance. Byline given. Buys first rights. Reports in 2 months. Free sample copy and writers guidelines.
Nonfiction: Interview/profile. Query. Length: 800-1,500 words. Pays $125-300.
Photos: State availability of photos with submission. Reviews contact sheets and 5×7 prints. Offers no payment for photos accepted with ms. Identification of subjects required. Buys one-time rights.

Travel

Travel professionals read these publications to keep up with trends, tours and changes in transportation. Magazines about vacations and travel for the general public are listed in the Consumer Travel section.

BUS TOURS MAGAZINE, The Magazine of Bus Tours and Long Distance Charters, National Bus Trader, Inc., 9698 W. Judson Rd., Polo IL 61064-9015. (815)946-2341. Fax: (815)946-2347. Editor: Larry Plachno. Editorial Assistant: Karen Ball. 80% freelance written. Eager to work with new/unpublished writers. Bimonthly magazine for bus companies and tour brokers who design or sell bus tours. Estab. 1979. Circ. 9,306. Pays as arranged. Publishes ms an average of 6 months after acceptance. Byline given. Not copyrighted. Buys rights as arranged. Submit seasonal material 9 months in advance. Reports in 1 month. Sample copy and writer's guidelines for 9 × 12 SAE.
Nonfiction: Historical/nostalgic, how-to, humor, interview/profile, new product, professional, personal experience, travel; all on bus tours. Buys 10 mss/year. Query. Length: open. Pays negotiable fee.
Photos: State availability of photos. Reviews 35mm transparencies and 6 × 9 or 8 × 10 prints. Caption, model release and identification of subjects required.
Columns/Departments: Bus Tour Marketing; Buses and the Law. Buys 15-20 mss/year. Query. Length: 1-1½ pages.
Tips: "Most of our feature articles are written by freelancers under contract from local convention and tourism bureaus. Specifications sent on request. Writers should query local bureaus regarding their interest. Writer need not have extensive background and knowledge of bus tours."

MEXICO UPDATE, For the North American travel industry, Travel Mexico Magazine Group, P.O. Box 188037, Carlsbad CA 92009-0801. (619)929-0707. Group Editor: Katharine A. Diáz. 50% freelance written. Bimonthly magazine covering tourism and travel to Mexico. "*Mexico Update* focuses on keeping travel professionals in the Annual US and Canada up to date on the travel industry in Mexico. Our goal is to help them better sell Mexico as a travel destination to their clients. Target: travel agents; wholesalers; tour operators; incentive, meeting and convention planners; etc." Estab. 1992. Circ. 41,000. Pays on publication. Publishes ms an average of 1-2 months after acceptance. Byline given. Buys first rights. Editorial lead time 2-3 months. Submit seasonal material 4-5 months in advance. Query for electronic submissions. Reports in 1 to 2 months. Sample copy for 10 × 13 SAE with 6 first-class stamps. Writer's guidelines for #10 SASE.
Nonfiction: Travel and Mexico – only from trade angle. "We do not want articles that focus on any other topic than Mexico." Buys 35 mss/year. Query with published clips. Length: 400-1,200 words. Pays 25¢/word.
Photos: Send photos with submission. Reviews transparencies and slides. Offers $20-200/photo. Captions and identification of subjects required. Buys one-time rights.
Tips: "We are looking for writers who have had experience writing about the travel trade – specifically Mexico. Freelancers should have intimate knowledge of Mexico's travel industry infrastructure, key players within the industry, organizations and associations, hotels and other travel service providers. Because we work only on assignment it's best to send query with published clips (that will be kept on file unless SASE enclosed) that establish writer's expertise."

RV BUSINESS, TL Enterprises, Inc., 3601 Calle Tecate, Camarillo CA 93012. (805)389-0300. Fax: (805)389-0484. Senior Managing Editor: Stephen Boilon. 60% freelance written. Prefers to work with published/established writers. Monthly magazine covering the recreational vehicle and allied industries for people in the RV industry – dealers, manufacturers, suppliers and finance experts. Estab. 1950. Circ. 19,000. **Pays on acceptance.** Publishes ms an average of 2 months after acceptance. Byline given. Offers 50% kill fee. Buys first North American serial rights. Submit seasonal material 6 months in advance. Query for electronic submissions. Reports in 2 months. Sample copy for 9 × 12 SAE with 5 first-class stamps.
Nonfiction: Technical, financial, legal or marketing issues; how-to (deal with any specific aspect of the RV business); specifics and verification of statistics required – must be factual; and technical (photos required, 4-color preferred). General business articles may be considered. Buys 50 mss/year. Query with published clips. Send complete ms – "but only read on speculation." Length: 1,000-1,500 words. Pays variable rate up to $500. Sometimes pays expenses of writers on assignment.
Photos: State availability of photos with query or send photos with ms. Reviews 35mm transparencies and 8 × 10 b&w prints. Captions, model release, and identification of subjects required. Buys one-time or all rights; unused photos returned.
Columns/Departments: Guest editorial; News (50-500 words maximum, b&w photos appreciated); and RV People (color photos/4-color transparencies; this section lends itself to fun, upbeat copy). Buys 100-120 mss/year. Query or send complete ms. Pays $25-200 "depending on where used and importance."
Tips: "Query. Phone OK; letter preferable. Send one or several ideas and a few lines letting us know how you plan to treat it/them. We are always looking for good authors knowledgable in the RV industry or related industries. Change of editorial focus requires more articles that are brief, factual, hard hitting, business oriented and in-depth. Will work with promising writers, published or unpublished."

SPECIALTY TRAVEL INDEX, Alpine Hansen, #313, 305 San Anselmo Ave., San Anselmo CA 94960. (415)459-4900. Editor: C. Steen Hansen. Managing Editor: Barbara Bell. Contact: C. Steen Hansen. 90% freelance written. Semiannual magazine covering adventure and special interest travel. Estab. 1980. Circ. 45,000. Pays on publication. Byline given. Buys one-time rights. Editorial lead time 3 months. Submit seasonal material 3 months in advance. Accepts previously published submissions. Query for electronic submissions. Sample copy and writer's guidelines free on request.

Nonfiction: How-to, new product, personal experience, photo feature, travel. Buys 15 mss/year. Query. Length: 1,000 words. Pays $200 minimum.

Photos: State availability of photos with submission. Reviews 35mm transparencies and 5×7 prints. Negotiates payment individually. Captions and identification of subjects required.

STAR SERVICE, Reed Travel Group, 500 Plaza Dr., Secaucus NJ 07096-3602. (201)902-2000. Fax: (201)319-1797. Publisher: Steven R. Gordon. "Eager to work with new/unpublished writers as well as those working from a home base abroad, planning trips that would allow time for hotel reporting, or living in major ports for cruise ships." Worldwide guide to accommodations and cruise ships founded in 1960 (as *Sloane Travel Agency Reports*) and sold to travel agencies on subscription basis. Pays 15 days after publication. Buys all rights. Query should include details on writer's experience in travel and writing, clips, specific forthcoming travel plans, and how much time would be available for hotel or ship inspections. Buys 5,000 reports/year. Pays $18/report used. Sponsored trips are acceptable. General query statement should precede electronic submission. Reports in 3 months. Writer's guidelines and list of available assignments for #10 SASE.

Nonfiction: Objective, critical evaluations of hotels and cruise ships suitable for international travelers, based on personal inspections. Freelance correspondents ordinarily are assigned to update an entire state or country. "Assignment involves on-site inspections of all hotels and cruise ships we review; revising and updating published reports; and reviewing new properties. Qualities needed are thoroughness, precision, perseverance and keen judgment. Solid research skills and powers of observation are crucial. Travel and travel writing experience are highly desirable. Reviews must be colorful, clear, and documented with hotel's brochure, rate sheet, etc. We accept no advertising or payment for listings, so reviews should dispense praise and criticism where deserved."

Tips: "We may require sample hotel or cruise reports on facilities near freelancer's hometown before giving the first assignment. No byline because of sensitive nature of reviews."

TRAVELAGE WEST, Official Airline Guides, Inc., # 460, 49 Stevenson St., San Francisco CA 94105. Managing Editor: Robert Carlsen. 5% freelance written. Prefers to work with published/established writers. Weekly magazine for travel agency sales counselors in the western US and Canada. Estab. 1969. Circ. 35,000. Pays on publication. Publishes ms an average of 1 month after acceptance. Byline given. Buys all rights. Offers kill fee. Submit seasonal/holiday material 2 months in advance. Query for electronic submissions. Reports in 6 months. Free writer's guidelines.

Nonfiction: Travel. "No promotional approach or any hint of do-it-yourself travel. Emphasis is on news, not description. No static descriptions of places, particularly resort hotels." Buys 40 mss/year. Query. Length: 1,000 words maximum. Pays $2/column inch.

Tips: "Query should be a straightforward description of the proposed story, including (1) an indication of the news angle, no matter how tenuous, and (2) a recognition by the author that we run a trade magazine for travel agents, not a consumer book. I am particularly turned off by letters that try to get me all worked up about the 'beauty' or excitement of some place. Authors planning to travel might discuss with us a proposed angle before they go; otherwise their chances of gathering the right information are slim."

Veterinary

VETERINARY ECONOMICS MAGAZINE, 9073 Lenexa Dr., Lenexa KS 66215. (913)492-4300. Fax: (913)492-4157. Editor: Rebecca R. Turner. Managing Editor: Renée Anderson. 25% freelance written. Prefers to work with published/established writers but will work with several new/unpublished writers each year. Monthly business magazine for all practicing veterinarians in the US. Estab. 1960. Buys exclusive rights in the field. Pays on publication. Publishes ms 3-6 months after acceptance. Reports in 4 months. Free sample copy and writer's guidelines.

Nonfiction: Publishes non-clinical articles on business and management techniques that will strengthen a veterinarian's private practice. Also interested in articles on financial problems, employee relations, marketing and similar subjects of particular interest to business owners. "We look for carefully researched articles that are specifically directed to our field." Pays negotiable rates. Pays expenses of writers on assignment.

Tips: "Our articles focus on nuts-and-bolts practice management techniques prescribed by experts in the practice management field and applied by successful veterinarians. Articles must be useful and appeal to a broad section of our readers."

822   *Writer's Market '95*

Trade, Technical and Professional Journals/ Changes '94-'95

The following trade publications were listed in the 1994 edition but do not have listings in this edition of *Writer's Market*. The majority did not respond to our request to update their listings or return a questionnaire for a new listing. If a reason was given for their exclusion, we have included it in parentheses after the listing.

Access Control
American Machinist
AntiqueWeek
Arts & Craft Retailer (ceased publication)
Automatic Machining (no freelance)
Barter Communique (ceased publication)
Bedroom Magazine (ceased publication)
Book Writers Market Letter
Butter-Fat (ceaseed publication)
Cadalyst
Campaigns and Elections
Canadian Author
Canadian Computer Dealer News
Casual Living
Checklist (removed by request due to inappropriate submissions)
Church Administration (unable to contact)
Cincinnati Medicine
Circuit Rider
Columbia Journalism Review
Communications Manager (no freelance)
Compass
Confetti (ceased publication)
Construction Supervision & Safety Letter
The Counselor Magazine
Credit Union News (removed by request due to inappropriate submissions)
Cross & Quill (no pay)
Cutting Tool Engineering
Distributor
Doctors Shopper

Dr. Dobb's Journal
The Electric Weenie (no freelance)
EQ Retailer (removed by request)
Flexlines
Flooring Magazine
Florida Architect
Florida Grower and Rancher
Flower News (removed by request)
Geriatric Consultant (ceased publication)
Gold Prospector
High Plains Journal (removed by request due to inappropriate submissions)
Home Builder
Home Lighting & Accessories
Human Resource Executive
ID Systems
Idea Today
The Illinois Publisher (ceased publication)
Info Franchise Newsletter
The Instrumentalist (no freelance)
The Journal (no freelance)
La Barrique (no freelance)
Legal Assistant Today
Looking Fit
Machine Design
Mari/Board Converting News
The Meeting Manager (no freelance)
Microwaves & RF (no pay)
Mini-Storage Messenger
More Business
The National Law Journal
New Methods (no pay)
The New York Doctor (ceased publication)

Nurseweek
Personnel Manager's Letter
Physicians' Travel & Meeting Guide
The Private Carrier
Private Practice
Pro
Production Management Bulletin
The Pumper
Radio World Newspaper
Refrigerated Transporter
Science Fiction Chronicle (removed by request)
Sea's Industry West (ceased publication)
The Servicing Dealer (ceased publication)
Small Press
Software Management News
Southwest Contractor
Soybean Digest
Stripper Magazine
Successful Farmer (removed by request)
The Successful Hotel Marketer
Tennis Buyer's Guide (no freelance)
Tourist Attractions & Parks Magazine
Truck World
USAgriculture (ceased publication)
Utility Supervision
VM & SD (removed by request)
Ward's Auto World
Workboat
Writer's Info (unable to contact)

Scriptwriting

Everyone has a story to tell, something to say. In telling that story as a play, movie, TV show or educational video you have selected that form over other possibilities. Scriptwriting makes some particular demands, but one thing remains the same for authors of novels, nonfiction books and scripts: you'll learn to write by rewriting. Draft after draft your skills improve until, hopefully, someone likes your work enough to hire you.

Whether you are writing a video to train doctors in a new surgical technique, alternative theater for an Off-Broadway company or you want to see your name on the credits of the next Arnold Schwarzenegger movie, you must perfect both writing and marketing skills. A successful scriptwriter is a talented artist and a savvy business-person. But marketing must always be secondary to writing. A mediocre pitch for a great script will still get you farther than a brilliant pitch for a mediocre script. The art and craft of scriptwriting lies in successfully executing inspiration.

Writing a script is a private act. Polishing it may involve more people as you ask friends and fellow writers to take a look at it. Marketing takes your script public in an effort to find the person willing to give the most of what you want, whether it's money, exposure or control, in return for your work.

There are accepted ground rules to presenting and marketing scripts. Following those guidelines will maximize your chances of getting your work before an audience.

Presenting your script professionally earns a serious consideration of its content. Certain types of scripts have a definite format and structure. An educational video written in a one-column format, a feature film much longer than 120 pages or an hour-long TV show that peaks during the first 20 minutes indicates an amateur writer. There are several sources for correct formats, including *The Writer's Digest Book of Manuscript Formats*, by Buchman and Groves and *The Complete Guide to Script Formats*, by Cole and Haig.

Submission guidelines are similar to those for other types of writing. The initial contact is a one-page query letter, with a brief synopsis and a few lines as to your credits or experience relevant to the subject of your script. Never send a complete manuscript until it is requested. Almost every script sent to a producer, studio, or agent must be accompanied by a release form. Ask the producer or agent for his form when invited to submit the complete script. Always include a self-addressed stamped envelope if you want your work returned; a self-addressed stamped postcard will do for acknowledgement or reply if you do not need your script returned.

Most writers break in with spec scripts, written "for free," which serve as calling cards to show what they can do. These scripts plant the seeds of your professional reputation by making the rounds of influential people looking to hire writers, from advertising executives to movie moguls. Good writing is more important than a specific plot. Make sure you are sending out your best work; a first draft is not a finished product. Have several spec scripts completed, as a producer will often decide that a story is not right for him, or a similar work is already in production, but want to know what else you have. Be ready for that invitation.

Writing a script is a matter of learning how to refine your writing so that the work reads as a journey, not a technical manual. The best scripts have concise, visceral scenes that demand to be presented in a specific order and accomplish definite goals.

Educational videos have a message that must be expressed economically and directly, engaging the audience in an entertaining way while maintaining interest in the topic. Theatrical plays are driven by character and dialogue that expose a thematic core and engender enthusiasm or involvement in the conflict. Cinematic screenplays, while more visually-oriented, are a series of discontinuous scenes stacked to illuminate the characters, the obstacles confronting them and the resolution they reach.

A script is a difficult medium—written words that sound natural when spoken, characters that are original yet resonate with the audience, believable conflicts and obstacles in tune with the end result. One theater added to their listing the following tip: "Don't write plays. Write novels, short stories, anything but plays. But if you *must* write plays. . . . " If you are compelled to present your story visually, be aware of the intense competition it will face. Hone it, refine it, keep working on it until it can be no better, then look for the best home you can find. That's success.

Business and Educational Writing

"It's no longer the plankton of the filmmaking food chain," says Kirby Timmons, creative director of the video production company CRM Films. Scripts for corporate training, business management and education videos have become as sophisticated as those designed for TV and film, and they carry the additional requirement of conveying specific content. With an audience that is increasingly media literate, anything that looks and feels like a "training film" will be dead in the water. The trick is to produce a script that engages, compels *and* informs about the topic, whether it's customer relations, listening skills or effective employee management, while staying on a tight budget.

This can create its own challenges, but is an excellent way to increase your skills and exercise your craft. Good scriptwriters are in demand in this field. There is a strong emphasis on producing a polished complete script before filming begins, and a writer's involvement doesn't end until the film is "in the can."

A remarkably diverse industry, educational and corporate video is a $18-25 billion business, compared to theatrical films and TV, estimated at $5 billion. And there is the added advantage that opportunities are widespread, from large local corporations to small video production houses in your area. Larger companies often have inhouse video production companies, but others rely on freelance writers. Your best bet would be to find work with companies that specialize in making educational and corporate video while at the same time making yourself known to the creative directors of inhouse video staffs in large corporations. Advertising agencies are also a good source of work, as they often are asked by their clients for help in creating films and use freelance writers and producers.

Business and educational video is a market-driven industry, with material created either in response to a general need or a specific demand. The production company usually identifies a subject and finds the writer. As such, there is a perception that a spec script will not work in this media. While it is true that, as in TV and theatrical films, a writer's spec script is rarely produced, it is a good résumé of qualifications and sample of skills. It can get you other work even though it isn't produced. Your spec script should demonstrate a knowledge of this industry's specific format. For the most part video scripts are written in two-columns, video on the left, audio on the right. Computer software is available to format the action and dialogue; *The Writer's Digest Guide to Manuscript Formats* also covers the basics of video script format.

Aside from the original script, another opportunity for the writer is the user's guide that often accompanies a video. If you are hired to create the auxiliary material you'll receive a copy of the finished video and write a concurrent text for the teacher or implementor to use.

Networking is very important. There is no substitute for calling companies and finding out what is in your area. Contact local training and development companies and find out who they serve and what they need. It pays to join professional organizations such as the Association of Visual Communicators and the Association for Training and Development, which offers seminars and conventions. Making the rounds at a business convention of video producers with your business card could earn you a few calls and invitations to submit writing samples.

Budgets are tighter for educational or corporate videos than for theatrical films. You'll want to work closely with the producer to make sure your ideas can be realized within the budget. Your fee will vary with each job, but generally a script written for a production house such as CRM or McGraw-Hill in a subject area with broad marketability will pay $5,000-7,000. A custom-produced video for a specific company will usually pay less. The pay does not increase exponentially with your experience; large increases come if you choose to direct and produce as well as write.

The future of business and educational video lies in interactive media or multimedia. Interactive media combines computer and video technology to create a product that doesn't have to progress along a linear path. Videos that offer the viewer the opportunity to direct the course of events hold exciting possibilities for corporate training and educational applications. Writers will be in high demand as stories offer dozens of choices in storylines. Interactive video will literally eat up pages of script as quickly as a good writer produces them. A training session may last only 20 minutes, but the potential untapped story lines could add up to hours worth of script that must be written, realized and made available. From training salespeople to doctors, or teaching traffic rules to issues in urbanization, corporate and educational video is about to undergo a tremendous revolution.

For information on more business and educational scriptwriting markets, see Scriptwriting Markets/Changes '94-'95 at the end of the Screenwriting section.

☐**ABS ENTERPRISES,** P.O. Box 5127, Evanston IL 60204-5127. (708)982-1414. Fax: (708)982-1418. President: Alan Soell. "We produce material for all levels of corporate, medical, cable and educational institutions for the purposes of training and development, marketing and meeting presentations. We also are developing programming for the broadcast areas." 75% freelance written. "We work with a core of three to five freelance writers from development to final drafts." All scripts published are unagented submissions. Buys all rights. Accepts previously produced material. Reports in 2 weeks on queries.
Needs: Videotape, multimedia, realia, slides, tapes and cassettes, television shows/series. Currently interested in "sports instructional series that could be produced for the consumer market on tennis, gymnastics, bowling, golf, aerobics, health and fitness, cross-country skiing and cycling. Also motivational and self-improvement type videos and film ideas to be produced. These could cover all ages '6-60'; and from professional to blue collar jobs. These two areas should be 30 minutes and be timeless in approach for long shelf life. Sports audience, age 25-45; home improvement, 25-65. Cable TV needs include the two groups of programming detailed here. We are also looking for documentary work on current issues, nuclear power, solar power, urban development, senior citizens—but with a new approach." Query or submit synopsis/outline and résumé. Pays by contractual agreement.
Tips: "I am looking for innovative approaches to old problems that just don't go away. The approach should be simple and direct so there is immediate audience identification with the presentation. I also like to see a sense of humor used. Trends in the audiovisual field include interactive video with disk—for training purposes."

ADVANTAGE MEDIA INC., Suite 102, 21356 Nordhoff St., Chatsworth CA 91311. (818)700-0504. Vice President: Susan Cherno. Estab. 1983. Audience is "all employees, including supervisory and management staff; generic audiences; medium-large companies, educational institutions, government, healthcare, insurance, financial." Works with 1-2 writers/year. Buys exclusive rights for distribution. Accepts previously produced material (exclusive distribution only). Reports in 1 month on queries. Free catalog. Submit synopsis/outline,

INSIDER REPORT

Interactive media is the writer's next frontier

"Interactive media is like the Oklahoma Land Rush," says Kirby Timmons, Creative Director of CRM Films, one of the largest producers of educational and business management videos. "We're standing at the line and the shot hasn't gone off yet. But it could come at any minute."

Interactive media or multimedia is the hot new topic in the communications industry, from filmmakers to book publishing. "The distinction between entertainment and information has become blurred, and interactive finally erases the line," asserts Timmons, a former TV writer and USC film school grad who has worked in corporate and educational films for 15 years. "Interactive media is the marriage of computer technology and video technology. Computers control the video to extend

Kirby Timmons

the possibilities of both. It's not limited to a linear concept, but can branch out in different directions, the way people think. It's a medium that mimics the way your brain works," explains Timmons.

Timmons encourages writers to take the initiative in this emerging area. "Interactive doesn't know yet what it wants to be. Writers can have a hand in developing the future." He feels that writers, especially screenwriters, have been at the forefront of recognizing the potential of computers. This computer literacy particularly enables them to take part in these early stages. "It's our chance to leave our fingerprints on a brand new medium." He notes that interactive scriptwriting programs are available for as little as $125, and offer not only linear scene-by-scene scripts but also link-by-link flow charts to track the burgeoning possibilities as the story branches out. As the software becomes simpler, writers can produce interactive prototypes themselves, taking on the roles of creator and designer.

Learning the technology is crucial to survival in this coming revolution. While computer classes in university telecommunications or film departments are helpful, writers can learn much simply by using the software, working through the tutorials and exploring the program. "Don't assume that there is a training program out there," says Timmons. "Jump off into the unknown."

Timmons feels that the industry is waiting to see which platform will form the basis of most interactive media, a process called "platform shakeout" much like the battle between Apple and IBM for the business computer market. The primary capability that everyone is waiting for is full-motion video. "That's what everyone from MGM to CRM is interested in—accessing libraries of films to put on interactive." He feels that this is very feasible – and very close. The technology has moved quickly from single speed CD-ROM disc drives to double speed and is approaching quad speed. "It's estimated that less than 30% of homes have computers, and the percentage of those with CD-ROM capabilities is even smaller. Compared to TV penetration the numbers are paltry. But more computers are shipping with CD-ROM built in." Timmons believes it is likely that no one platform will dominate to the exclusion of the others, and that each application may demand its own platform.

A former chair of the Writers Guild of America west's Creative Media and Technologies Committee, Timmons feels that the WGA has been at the forefront in exploring this new media. Traditionally when a new media form arrives writers have been exploited as networks and studios control the power and capital. But with interactive, writers have the opportunity to become the producers. "Writers aren't waiting to be exploited." Although the WGA has set no strict minimums for compensation to writers in the area of interactive programming, Timmons notes that few writers are aware that interactive media production can qualify a writer towards WGA membership and count towards pension and health coverage qualification.

Timmons senses that the surge forward will be sudden and unexpected. "Things are happening so quickly. Interactive is coming, and when it does, you don't want to be behind the eight ball on the learning curve."

completed script or résumé. Usually pays flat fee for writing. Negotiable by project.
Needs: Videotapes. "Generic settings, rainbow mix of characters. Topics: change, motivation, diversity, quality, safety, customer service. 20 minutes max. Documentary if points are clear or skill-building 'how to'. Must make a point for teaching purposes."
Tips: "Training programs must appeal to a diverse audience but be 'TV quality'. They must teach, as well as be somewhat entertaining. Must hold interest. Should present the problem, but solve it and not leave the audience hanging or to solve it themsvles. Must stay realistic, believable and be fast-paced. I think there will be a need for even more types of video-based materials for a growing need for training within organizations."

ARNOLD AND ASSOCIATES PRODUCTIONS, INC., 1204 16th Ave. S., Nashville TN 37212. (615)329-2800. President: John Arnold. Executive Producers: Deirdre Say, James W. Morris and Peter Dutton. Produces material for the general public (entertainment/motion pictures) and for corporate clients (employees/customers/consumers). Buys 10-15 scripts/year. Works with 3 writers/year. Buys all rights. Accepts previously produced material. Reports in 1 month.
Needs: Films (35mm), videotape. Looking for "upscale image and marketing programs." Dramatic writing for "name narrators and post scored original music; and motion picture. $5-6 million dollar budget. Dramatic or horror." Query with samples or submit completed script. Makes outright purchase of $1,000.
Tips: Looking for "upscale writers who understand corporate image production, and motion picture writers who understand story and dialogue."

A/V CONCEPTS CORP., 30 Montauk Blvd., Oakdale NY 11769-1399. (516)567-7227. Fax: (516)567-8745. Contact: P. Solimene or L. Solimene. Produces material for elementary-high school students, either on grade level or in remedial situations. Estab. 1971. 100% freelance written. Buys 25 scripts/year from unpublished/unproduced writers. Employs video, book and personal computer media. Reports in 1 month on outline, 6 weeks on final scripts. Buys all rights. Sample copy for 9×12 SAE with 5 first-class stamps.
Needs: Interested in original educational computer (disk-based) software programs for Apple +, 48k. Main concentration in language arts, mathematics and reading. "Manuscripts must be written using our lists of vocabulary words and meet our readability formula requirements. Specific guidelines are devised for each level. Length of manuscript and subjects will vary according to grade level for which material is prepared. Basically, we want material that will motivate people to read." Pays $300 and up.
Tips: "Writers must be highly creative and highly disciplined. We are interested in high interest/low readability materials."

SAMUEL R. BLATE ASSOCIATES, 10331 Watkins Mill Dr., Gaithersburg MD 20879-2935. (301)840-2248. Fax: (301)840-2248. President: Samuel R. Blate. Produces audiovisual and educational material for business, education, institutions, state and federal governments. "We work with 2 *local* writers per year on a per project basis—it varies as to business conditions and demand." Buys first rights when possible. Query for electronic submissions. Reports in 1 month. SASE for return.
Needs: Scripts on technical subjects. Query with samples. SASE for return. Payment "depends on type of contract with principal client." Pays some expenses of writers on assignment.
Tips: "Writers must have a strong track record of technical and aesthetic excellence. Clarity is not next to divinity—it is above it."

‡BOLDER MULTIMEDIA, 64 Meadow Lake Dr., Golden CO 80403. E-Mail: thibault@CSN.ORG. (303)642-3087. Fax: (303)440-9515. Contact: John Thibault. Estab. 1993. Audience is CD-ROM users, age 3-10, 100% Mac and MPC/Windows™ compatible. Buys 3-5 scripts/year. Works with 3-5 writers/year. Buys all rights including digital rights. Accepts previously produced material. Reports in 1 week on queries; 1 month on submissions. Query only. Pays 3-5% royalty.
Needs: Multimedia and interactive multimedia CD-ROM and other platforms. "Animated illustrated children's books with multiple characters, dialogue and simple contemporary, violence-free story lines using bold, bright colors, 12-20 pages long. Caldecott Award winners and character series books preferred."
Tips: "Call if you have a cool, illustrated children's book with interactive potential."

BOSUSTOW MEDIA GROUP, Suite 114, 7655 Sunset Blvd., Hollywood CA 90046-2700. (213)874-7613. Owner: Tee Bosustow. Estab. 1983. Produces material for corporate, TV and home video clients. Reports in 2 weeks on queries.
Needs: Tapes, cassettes, videotapes. "Unfortunately, no one style, etc. exists. We produce a variety of products, a good deal of it children's programming." Submit synopsis/outline and résumé only. Pays agreed upon fee.

CAMBRIDGE EDUCATIONAL, 90 MacCorkle Ave. SW, South Charleston WV 25303. Production Staff: Charlotte Angel. Estab. 1983. Audience is junior high/high schools, vocational schools, libraries, guidance centers. Buys 18-24 scripts/year. Works with 12-18 writers/year. Buys all rights. "Samples are kept for file reference." Reports only if interested. Free catalog. Query with synopsis, résumé or writing sample ("excerpt from a previous script, preferably"). Makes outright purchase of $2,000-4,000.
Needs: Videotapes. Educational programming suitable for junior high and high school age groups (classroom viewing and library reference). "Programs range from 20-35-minutes in length. Each should have a fresh approach for how-to's, awareness, and introductions to various subject matters. Subjects range from guidance, home economics, parenting, health, and vocational to social studies, fine arts, music, and business."
Tips: "We are looking for a new slant on some standard educational topics, as well as more contemporary issues. Currently focusing on job search and parenting issues."

‡THE CARRONADE GROUP, (fomerly Samsel/Fort), P.O. Box 36157, Los Angeles CA 90036. Editor/Publisher: Jon Samsel. Estab. 1993. Produces books and CD-ROMs in the fields of interactive multimedia, entertainment industry, digital media, telecommunications, computer software. Works with 5-10 writers/year. Buys first rights, all rights, book rights and interactive rights. Accepts previously produced material. Reports in 1 month on queries; 1-2 months on submissions. Catalog for #10 SASE. Query with résumé. Royalty varies on project-to-project basis.
Needs: "Looking for unpublished manuscripts profiling the interactive multimedia field, educational subjects, erotic subjects, entertainment industry (CD-ROM rights). Also 'How-To' books on same subject. Wish to acquire interactive (CD-ROM) rights to completed short subject films or full-length independent films."

‡CLEARVUE, INC., Dept. WM, 6465 N. Avondale Ave., Chicago IL 60631-1909. (312)775-9433. President: Mark Ventling. Contact: Mary Watanabe. Produces material for educational markets—grades k-12. 90% freelance written. Prefers to work with published/established writers. Buys 5-10 scripts/year. Buys all rights. Accepts previously produced material. Query for electronic submissions. Reports in 2 weeks on queries; 3 weeks on submissions. Free catalog.
Needs: Videos, multimedia kits, CD-ROM. "Our videos are 8-30 minutes for all curriculum areas." Query. Makes outright purchase, $500-1,000. Sometimes pays the expenses of writers on assignment.
Tips: "Our interests are in video for the elementary and high school markets on all subjects."

COMPRO PRODUCTIONS, Suite 114, 2080 Peachtree Ind. Court, Atlanta GA 30341-2281. (404)455-1943. Fax: (404)455-3356. Producers: Nels Anderson and Steve Brinson. Estab. 1977. Audience is general public and specific business audience. Buys 10-25 scripts/year. Buys all rights. No previously produced material. No unsolicited material; submissions will not be returned because "all work is contracted."
Needs: "We solicit writers for corporate films/video in the areas of training, point purchase, sales, how-to, benefit programs, resorts and colleges." Produces 16-35mm films and videotapes. Query with samples. Makes outright purchase or pays cost/minute.

‡**CRM FILMS,** 6399 Wilshire Blvd., Los Angeles CA 90048. (213)852-6053. Creative Director: Kirby Timmons. Estab. 1960. Material for business and organizational training departments. Buys 2-4 scripts/year. Works with 6-8 writers/year. Buys all rights and interactive training rights. No previously produced material. Reports in 1 month. Catalog for 10 × 13 SAE with 4 first-class stamps. Query with résumé and script sample of writer's work in informational or training media. Makes outright purchase of $4,000-7,000, or in accordance with Writers Guild standard. "We accept WGA standard one-page informational/interactive agreement which stipulates *no* minimum but qualifies writer for pension and health coverage."
Needs: Videotapes, multimedia kits. "CRM is looking for short (10-20 minute) scripts on management topics such as communication, decision making, team building and customer service. No 'talking heads,' prefer drama-based, awareness approach as opposed to 'how-to' style, but will on occasion produce either."
Tips: "Know the *specific* training need which your idea or script fulfills! Total quality management will influence product line for forseeable future – learn about 'TQM' before submitting."

‡**DELTA MAX PRODUCTIONS,** P.O. Box 7188, Newport Beach CA 92660. (714)760-9638. President: Robert Swanson. Estab. 1983. Produces material for feature film audience. Buys 1-5 scripts/year. Works with 10-20 writers/year. Buys all rights or other rights depending on material. Accepts previously produced material. Reports in 1 month.
Needs: Film loops (35mm), films (35/70mm), tapes and cassettes, videotapes. "We are seeking feature film scripts; proper format, two hour length. All subjects, particularly comedy, action-adventure, drama, sci/fi." Submit complete script. Makes outright purchase, in accordance with Writers Guild standards; a varied amount of options, with money.
Tips: "Get the script in as complete a form as possible before submitting; submit with release form, agent's letter or attorney letter; include a SASE if you want it returned; include *where* you have sent the project and *to whom* it was sent; do not ask for constructive criticism – it will be given if appropriate."

EDUCATIONAL IMAGES LTD., P.O. Box 3456, Elmira NY 14905. (607)732-1090. Executive Director: Dr. Charles R. Belinky. Produces material (videos, sound filmstrips, multimedia kits and slide sets) for schools, kindergarten through college and graduate school, public libraries, parks, nature centers, etc. Also produces science-related software material. Buys 50 scripts/year. Buys all AV rights. Free catalog.
Needs: Videos, slide sets, filmstrips on science, natural history, anthropology and social studies. "We are looking primarily for complete AV programs; we will consider slide collections to add to our files. This requires high quality, factual text and pictures." Query with a meaningful sample of proposed program. Pays $150 minimum.
Tips: The writer/photographer is given high consideration. "Once we express interest, follow up. Potential contributors lose many sales to us by not following up on initial query. Don't waste our time and yours if you can't deliver. The market seems to be shifting to greater popularity of video and computer software formats."

‡**EDUCATIONAL INSIGHTS,** Editorial Dept., 19560 S. Rancho Way, Dominguez Hills CA 90220. (310)637-2131. Fax: (310)605-5048. Editorial Director: Debra Hayes. Estab. 1962. Produces material for elementary schools and retail "home-learning" markets. Works with 10 writers/year. Buys all rights or exclusive licensing agreements. Accepts previously produced material. Reports in 2-4 weeks. Catalog for 9 × 12 SAE with 2 first-class stamps.
Needs: Charts, models, multimedia kits, study prints, tapes and cassettes, teaching machine programs. Query with samples. Pays varied royalties or makes outright purchase.
Tips: "Keep up-to-date information on educational trends in mind. Study the market before starting to work. We receive 20 manuscripts per week – all reviewed and returned, if rejected."

EDUCATIONAL VIDEO NETWORK, 1401 19th St., Huntsville TX 77340. (409)295-5767. President: Dr. Kenneth L. Russell. Executive Editor: Gary Edmondson. Estab. 1953. Produces material for junior high, senior high, college and university audiences. Buys "perhaps 20 scripts/year." Buys all rights or pays royalty on gross retail and wholesale. Accepts previously produced material. Reports in 1-2 months. Free catalog and writer's guidelines.
Needs: Video for educational purposes. Query. Royalty varies.
Tips: Looks for writers with the "ability to write and illustrate for educational purposes. Schools are asking for more curriculum-oriented live-action video."

EFFECTIVE COMMUNICATION ARTS, INC., P.O. Box 250, Wilton CT 06897-0250. (203)761-8787. President: David Jacobson. Estab. 1965. Produces films, videotapes and interactive multimedia for physicians, nurses and medical personnel. Prefers to work with published/established writers. 80% freelance written. Buys approximately 20 scripts/year. Query for electronic submissions. Buys all rights. Reports in 1 month.
Needs: Multimedia kits, television shows/series, videotape presentations, interactive videodisks, CD-ROM multimedia. Currently producing about 15 videotapes for medical audiences; 6 interactive disks for medical audience; 3 interactive disks for point-of-purchase. Submit complete script and résumé. Makes outright purchase. Pays expenses of writers on assignment.

Tips: "Interactive design skills are increasingly important."

‡GESSLER PUBLISHING CO., INC., Gessler Educational Software, 55 W. 13th St., New York NY 10011. (212)627-0099. Fax: (212)627-5948. President: Seth C. Levin. Produces material for students learning ESL and foreign languages. 50% freelance written; eager to work with new/unpublished writers. Buys about 60-75 scripts/year. 100% of scripts unagented submissions. Prefers to buy all rights, but will work on royalty basis. Do not send disk submission without documentation. Query for electronic submissions. Reports in 3 weeks on queries; 2 months on submissions.
Needs: Books, video and filmstrips "to create an interest in learning a foreign language and its usefulness in career objectives; also culturally insightful video/filmstrips on French, German, Italian and Spanish speaking countries." Produces sound filmstrips, multimedia kits, overhead transparencies, games, realia, tapes and cassettes, computer software, books. Also produces scripts for videos. Submit synopsis/outline or software with complete documentation, introduction, objectives. Makes outright purchase and pays royalties.
Tips: "Be organized in your presentation; be creative but keep in mind that your audience is primarily junior/senior high school teachers. We will be looking for new filmstrips, videotapes, software and videodisks which can be used in foreign language and ESL classes. Also, more of a concentration on hypercard and interactive video projects."

HAYES SCHOOL PUBLISHING CO., INC., 321 Pennwood Ave., Wilkinsburg PA 15221-3398. (412)371-2373. Fax: (412)371-6408. President: Clair N. Hayes, III. Estab. 1940. Produces material for school teachers and principals, elementary through high school. Also produces charts, workbooks, teacher's handbooks, posters, bulletin board material and reproducible blackline masters (grades K-12). 25% freelance written. Prefers to work with published/established writers. Buys 5-10 scripts/year from unpublished/unproduced writers. 100% of scripts produced are unagented submissions. Buys all rights. Query for electronic submissions. Reports in 3 months. Catalog for SAE with 3 first-class stamps. Writer's guidelines for #10 SAE with 2 first-class stamps.
Needs: Educational material only. Particularly interested in educational material for elementary school level. Query. Pays $25 minimum.

‡HOKUS POKUS PRODUCTIONS, INC., Suite 265, 22900 Ventura Blvd., Woodland Hills CA 91364. Estab. 1989. Produces commercial, home video and industrial material. Buys 3 scripts/year. Works with 2-3 writers/year. Does not read or return unsolicited submissions. Query with résumé. Makes outright purchase.

IMAGE INNOVATIONS, INC., Suite 201, 29 Clyde Rd., Somerset NJ 08873. (908)873-0700. President: Mark A. Else. Estab. 1974. Produces material for business, education and general audiences. 50% freelance written. "Credentials and reputation important." Commissions 5-10 scripts/year for clients. All scripts produced are unagented submissions. Reports in 2 weeks. Buys all rights.
Needs: Subject topics include education, sales, public relations and technical. Produces hi-image 1" and ½" Betacam video and tapes and cassettes. Query with samples. Pays in outright purchase of $1,000-5,000. Sometimes pays the expenses of writers on assignment.

JACOBY/STORM PRODUCTIONS INC., 22 Crescent Rd., Westport CT 06880. (203)227-2220. Contact: Doris Storm. Produces material for corporations, schools, TV. Works with 4-6 writers annually. Buys all rights. No previously produced material. Reports in 2 weeks.
Needs: "Short dramatic films on business subjects, educational films at all levels, sales and corporate image films." Produces 16mm films, slides, tapes and cassettes, videotapes and videodisks. Query. Usually makes outright purchase.
Tips: "Prefers local people. Looks for experience, creativity, dependability, attention to detail, enthusiasm for project, ability to interface with client. Wants creative approaches to material."

‡JIST WORKS, INC., 720 N. Park Ave., Indianapolis IN 46202. (317)264-3767. Video Production Manager: Jeff Heck. Estab. 1981. Produces career counseling, motivational materials (youth to adult) that encourage good planning and decision making for a successful future. Buys 7-10 scripts/year. Works with 2-3 writers/year. Buys all rights. Accepts previously produced material. Reports in 2 months. Catalog free. Query with synopsis. Makes outright purchase of $500 minimum.
Needs: Videotapes, multimedia kits. 15-30 minute video VHS tapes on job search materials and related markets.

KOLMOR VISIONS (KMV), 1 Bank St., Stamford CT 06901. (203)325-2978. Executive Producer: Tom Moore. Estab. 1982. Corporate audience. Buys 2-4 scripts/year. Works with 10-12 writers/year. Buys all rights. Accepts previously produced material. Reports in 2 months on queries; 6 months on scripts. Query with synopsis. Pays 10% royalty.
Needs: Videotapes. "We are developing 'how to' and educational programs for cable and sale. 'Over 60' and children programming ideas usually receive the most attention. Next area of interest—environmental safety."

LOCKWOOD FILMS, 365 Ontario St., London, Ontario N5W 3W6 Canada. (519)434-6006. Fax: (519)645-0507. President: Nancy Johnson. Estab. 1974. Audience is corporate, education, general broadcast. Works with 5-6 writers/year. Buys all rights. No previously produced material. Reports in 2 months on queries. Submit query with synopsis, résumé or sample scripts. Negotiated fee.
Needs: Videotapes, multimedia kits. Seeking education programs for elementary and high school students; corporate videos for training, orientation, sales promotion (length from 10-30 minutes); television documentary/general interest/entertainment.
Tips: "Potential contributors should have a fax machine."

☐**MEDIACOM DEVELOPMENT CORP.**, P.O. Box 6331, Burbank CA 91510-6331. (818)594-4089. Director/Program Development: Felix Girard. Estab. 1978. 80% freelance written. Buys 8-12 scripts annually from unpublished/unproduced writers. 50% of scripts produced are unagented submissions. Query with samples. Reports in 1 month. Buys all rights or first rights.
Needs: Produces films, multimedia kits, tapes and cassettes, slides and videotape with programmed instructional print materials, broadcast and cable television programs. Publishes software ("programmed instruction training courses"). Negotiates payment depending on project. Looking for new ideas for CD-ROM titles.
Tips: "Send short samples of work. Especially interested in flexibility to meet clients' demands, creativity in treatment of precise subject matter. We are looking for good, fresh projects (both special and series) for cable and pay television markets. A trend in the audiovisual field that freelance writers should be aware of is the move toward more interactive video disc/computer CRT delivery of training materials for corporate markets."

‡**MIRIMAR ENTERPRISES**, P.O. Box 4621, North Hollywood CA 91617-4621. (818)784-4177. Fax: (818)990-3439. CEO: Mirk Mirkin. Estab. 1967. "Audience is varied, sophisticated and intelligent." Buys 2-3 scripts/year. Buys all rights or first rights (in some cases). Accepts previously published material (in rare cases). Reports in 1 month on queries; 2 months on submissions.
Needs: Slides, tapes and cassettes, videotapes. "We are seeking travel topics—particularly exotic, rarely visited places. First person, indepth experiences, with some visuals to show them *in situ*." Query with synopsis and résumé. Pays in accordance with Writers Guild standards.
Tips: "Be honest in your approach. Don't be over-flowery in language unless you can back it up. Writers should express themselves in a down-to-earth manner. Not raw or crude, but in graphic terms that are real."

OMNI PRODUCTIONS, 655 West Carmel Dr., Carmel IN 46032-2500. (317)844-6664. Vice President: Dr. Sandra M. Long. Estab. 1976. Produces commercial, training, educational and documentary material. Buys all rights.
Needs: "Educational, documentary, commercial, training, motivational." Produces slides, video shows, multi-image, videotapes. Query. Makes outright purchase.
Tips: "Must have experience as writer and have examples of work. Examples need to include print copy and finished copy of videotape if possible. A résumé with educational background, general work experience and experience as a writer must be included. Especially interested in documentary-style writing. Writers' payment varies, depending on amount of research needed, complexity of project, length of production and other factors."

ONE ON ONE COMPUTER TRAINING, Division of Mosaic Media, Inc., Suite 100, 2055 Army Trail Rd., Addison IL 60101-9961. (708)628-0500. Fax: (708)628-0550. Publisher: F. Lee McFadden. Contact: Natalie Young. Estab. 1976. Produces training courses for microcomputers and business software. Works with a small number of new/unpublished writers each year. 90% freelance written. Buys 3-5 courses/year; 1-2 from unpublished/unproduced writers. 100% of courses published are unagented submissions. Works with 3-5 writers/year. Buys all rights. Query for electronic submissions. Reports in 3 weeks. Free product literature. Sample copy for 9×12 SAE.
Needs: Training courses on how to use personal computers/software, primarily audio geared to the adult student in a business setting and usually to the beginning/intermediate user; also some courses at advanced levels. Primarily audio, also some reference manuals, other training formats for personal computers considered. Query with résumé and samples if available. Pays negotiable royalty or makes outright purchase.
Tips: "We prefer to work with Chicago-area writers with strong teaching/training backgrounds and experience with microcomputers. Writers from other regions are also welcome."

PALARDO PRODUCTIONS, Suite 4, 1807 Taft Ave., Hollywood CA 90028. (213)469-8991. Director: Paul Ardolino. Estab. 1971. Produces material for youth ages 13-35. Buys 3-4 scripts/year. Buys all rights. Reports in 2 weeks on queries; 1 month on scripts.
Needs: Multimedia kits, tapes and cassettes, videotapes. "We are seeking ideas relating to virtual reality, comedy scripts involving technology and coming of age; rock'n'roll bios." Submit synopsis/outline and résumé. Pays in accordance with Writers Guild standards.
Tips: "Do not send a complete script—only synopsis of four pages or less *first*."

PHOTO COMMUNICATION SERVICES, INC., P.O. Box 508, Acme MI 49610. (616)922-3050. President: Lynn Hartwell. Produces commercial, industrial, sales, training material etc. 95% freelance written. No scripts from unpublished/unproduced writers. 100% of scripts produced are unagented submissions. Buys all rights and first serial rights. Query for electronic submissions. Reports in 1 month.
Needs: Multimedia kits, slides, tapes and cassettes, video presentations. Primarily interested in 35mm multimedia and video. Query with samples or submit completed script and résumé. Pays by agreement.

PICTURE ENTERTAINMENT CORPORATION, Suite 505, 9595 Wilshire Blvd., Beverly Hills CA 90212. (310)858-8300. President/CEO: Lee Caplin. Vice President Development: Sonia Mintz. Produces feature films for theatrical audience and TV audience. Buys 2 scripts/year, works with 10 writers/year. Buys all rights. Reports on submissions in 2 months.
Needs: Films (35mm); videotapes. Feature scripts 100-120 pages. Submit completed script. "Pays on a deal by deal basis; some WGA, some not."
Tips: "Don't send derivitive standard material. Emphasis on unique plot and characters, realistic dialogue. *Discourage* period pieces, over-the-top comedy, graphic sex/violence, SciFi. *Encourage* action, action/comedy, thriller, thriller/comedy."

CHARLES RAPP ENTERPRISES, INC., 1650 Broadway, New York NY 10019. (212)247-6646. President: Howard Rapp. Estab. 1954. Produces materials for firms and buyers. Works with 5 writers/year. "Work as personal manager/agent in sales." Accepts previously produced material. Reports in 1 month on queries; 2 months on submissions. Submit résumé or sample of writing. Pays in accordance with Writers Guild standards.
Needs: Videotapes, treatments, scripts.

‡**RHYTHMS PRODUCTIONS**, P.O. Box 34485, Los Angeles CA 90034-0485. President: Ruth White. Estab. 1955. Produces children's musically-oriented educational cassettes/books. Buys all rights. Accepts previously published material "if it is suitable for our market and is not now currently on the market. We look for tapes that have been produced and are ready for publication." Reports on mss in 2 months. Catalog for 9 × 12 SAE with 3 first-class stamps.
Needs: Audio or video cassettes. "Looking for children's stories or ideas with musical treatments. Must have educational content or values and must be ready for publication (complete with musical and/or video treatments as per above)." Query with samples. Payment is negotiable.
Tips: "SASE required for return of materials."

‡**PATRICIA RUST PRODUCTIONS**, Suite 924, 12021 Wilshire Blvd., Los Angeles CA 90025. President: Patricia Rust. Estab. 1984. "Company spans poetry publication to childrens to humor. While it encompasses a wide range, it is highly selective and tries to be visionary and ahead of the pack in scope, originality and execution." Buys variable rights depending on the situation and goals. Reports in 2 months on queries. Query. "Our production includes publishing, audio-video and theatrical and each project is carefully conceived and executed to influence and entertain in a meaningful way. Our standards are extremely high with regard to quality, message and meaning."
Needs: Film loops, films, videotapes, tapes and cassettes.
Tips: "While we are in the business of entertainment, we look for projects that provide answers and elevate thinking. We work with only top industry professionals and strive to represent quality and commerciality."

SPENCER PRODUCTIONS, INC., 234 Fifth Ave., New York NY 10001. (212)697-5895. General Manager: Bruce Spencer. Executive Producer: Alan Abel. Produces material for high school students, college students and adults. Occasionally uses freelance writers with considerable talent. Reports in 1 month. Catalog for #10 SASE.
Needs: 16mm films, prerecorded tapes and cassettes. Satirical material only. Query. Pay is negotiable.

TALCO PRODUCTIONS, 279 E. 44th St., New York NY 10017-4354. (212)697-4015. President: Alan Lawrence. Vice President: Marty Holberton. Estab. 1968. Produces variety of material for TV, radio, business, trade associations, nonprofit organizations, etc. Audiences range from young children to senior citizens. 20-40% freelance written. Buys scripts from published/produced writers only. Buys all rights. No previously published material. Reports in 3 weeks on queries. *Does not accept unsolicited mss.*
Needs: Films (16, 35mm), slides, radio tapes and cassettes, videotape. "We maintain a file of writers and call on those with experience in the same general category as the project in production. We do not accept unsolicited manuscripts. We prefer to receive a writer's résumé listing credits. If his/her background merits, we will be in touch when a project seems right." Makes outright purchase/project and in accordance with Writers Guild standards (when appropriate). Sometimes pays the expenses of writers on assignment.

ALWAYS enclose a self-addressed, stamped envelope (SASE) with all your queries and correspondence.

Tips: "Concentration is now in TV productions. Production budgets will be tighter."

ED TAR ASSOCIATES, INC., 230 Venice Way, Venice CA 90291. (310)306-2195. Fax: (310)306-0654. Estab. 1972. Audience is dealers, salespeople, public. Buys all rights. No previously produced material. Makes outright purchase.
Needs: Films (16, 35mm), videotapes, slides, tapes, business theater and live shows. "We are constantly looking for *experienced* writers of corporate, product and live show scripts. (We do not consider writers of 30 second commercials or PR press releases for our work.) Send a résumé and samples. Track record of proven writing for a variety of corporate clients a must."

‡TARGET CANADA PRODUCTIONS, W. Second Ave., Vancouver, British Columbia V6J 1H6 Canada. (604)734-9122. Fax: (604)669-6446. VP Marketing: Ed Kolic. VP Production: Cliff Craven. Estab. 1976. Audience is government, corporate and educational market. Buys 25 scripts/year. Works with 6 writers/year. Buys all rights. Accepts previously produced material. Submit synopsis/outline. Pays in accordance with Writers Guild standards.
Needs: Videotapes, slides. "Currently looking for 10-60 minute films or videos covering the Pacific Rim (economics, social issues, history), educational material for grades 8-12, preventive health care, native relations, immigration."

TEL-AIR INTERESTS, INC., 1755 NE 149th St., Miami FL 33181. (305)944-3268. President: Grant H. Gravitt. Produces material for groups and theatrical and TV audiences. Buys all rights. Submit résumé.
Needs: Documentary films on education, travel and sports. Produces films and videotape. Makes outright purchase.

TROLL ASSOCIATES, 100 Corporate Dr., Mahwah NJ 07430. (201)529-4000. Contact: M. Schecter. Produces material for elementary and high school students. Buys approximately 200 scripts/year. Buys all rights. Reports in 3 weeks. Free catalog.
Needs: Produces multimedia kits, tapes and cassettes, and (mainly) books. Query or submit outline/synopsis. Pays royalty or makes outright purchase.

‡ULTITECH, INC., Foot of Broad St., Stratford CT 06497. (203)375-7300. Fax/BBS: (203)375-6699. Estab. 1993. Designs, develops and produces interactive communications programs including video, multimedia, expert systems, software tools, computer-based training and audience response meetings. Specializes in medicine, science and technology. Prefers to work with published/established writers with video, multimedia and medical experience. 90% freelance written. Buys writing for approximately 15-20 programs/year. Electronic submissions onto BBS. Buys all rights. Reports in 1 month.
Needs: Currently producing about 10 interactive programs for medical audiences. Submit résumé and complete script. Makes outright purchase. Pays expenses of writers on assignment.
Tips: Interactive media for learning and entertainment is a growing outlet for writers—acquiring skills for interactive design and development will pay back in assignments.

VISUAL HORIZONS, 180 Metro Park, Rochester NY 14623. (716)424-5300. Fax: (716)424-5313. President: Stanley Feingold. Produces material for general audiences. Buys 5 programs/year. Reports in 5 months. Free 64 page catalog.
Needs: Business, medical and general subjects. Produces silent and sound filmstrips, multimedia kits, slide sets, videotapes. Query with samples. Payment negotiable.

Playwriting

TV and movies are visual media where the words are often less important than the images. Writing plays uses different muscles, different techniques. Plays are built on character and dialog—words put together to explore and examine characters.

The written word is respected in the theater by producer, cast, director and even audience, to a degree unparalleled in other formats. While any work involving so many people to reach its final form is in essence a collaboration, it is presided over by the playwright and changes can be made only with her approval, a power many screenwriters can only envy. If a play is worth producing, it will be produced "as is."

Counterbalancing the greater freedom of expression are the physical limitations inherent in live performance: a single stage, smaller cast, limited sets and lighting and, most importantly, a strict, smaller budget. These conditions affect not only what but also how you write.

Start writing your play by reading. Your local library has play anthologies. Check the listings in this section for play publishers such as Aran Press, Baker's Plays and Samuel French. Reading gives you a feel for how characters are built, layer by layer, word by word, how each interaction presents another facet of a character. Exposition must mean something to the character, and the story must be worth telling for a play to be successful.

There are plenty of books, seminars and workshops to help you with the writing of your play. The development of character, setting, dialog and plot are skills that will improve with each draft. The specific play format is demonstrated in *The Complete Book of Script Formats*, by Cole and Haig and *The Writer's Digest Book of Manuscript Formats*, by Buchman and Groves.

Once the final draft of your play is finished you begin marketing it, which can take as long (or longer) than writing it. Before you begin you must have your script bound (three brads and a cover are fine) and copyrighted at the Copyright Office of the Library of Congress or registered with the Writers Guild of America. Write either agency and ask for information and an application.

Your first goal will be to get at least a reading of your play. You might be lucky and get a small production. Community theaters or smaller regional houses are good places to start. Volunteer at a local theater. As prop mistress or spotlight operator you will get a sense of how a theater operates, the various elements of presenting a play and what can and cannot be done, physically as well as dramatically. Personal contacts are important. Get to know the literary manager or artistic director of local theaters, which is the best way to get your script considered for production. Find out about any playwrights' groups in your area through local theaters or the drama departments of nearby colleges and universities. Use your creativity to connect with people that might be able to push your work higher.

Contests can be a good way to get noticed. Many playwriting contests offer as a prize at least a staged reading and often a full production. Once you've had a reading or workshop production, set your sights on a small production. Use this as a learning experience. Seeing your play on stage can help you view it more objectively and give you the chance to correct any flaws or inconsistencies. Incorporate any comments and ideas from the actors, director or even audience that you feel are on the mark into revisions of your script.

Use a small production also as a marketing tool. Keep track of all the press reviews, any interviews with you, members of the cast or production and put together a "press kit" for your play that can make the rounds with the script.

After you've been produced you have several directions to take your play. You can aim for a larger commercial production; you can try to get it published; you can seek artistic grants. After you have successfully pursued at least one of those avenues you can look for an agent. Choosing one direction does not rule out pursuing others at the same time. *The Dramatists Sourcebook*, published annually by Theatre Communications Group (355 Lexington Ave., New York NY 10017) lists opportunities in all these areas. The Dramatists Guild (234 W. 45th St., New York NY 10036) has three helpful publications: a bimonthly newsletter with articles, news and up-to-date information and opportunities, a quarterly journal, and an annual directory, a resource book for playwrights listing theaters, agents, workshops, grants, contests, etc.

Good reviews in a smaller production can get you noticed by larger theaters paying higher royalties and doing more ambitious productions. To submit your play to larger theaters you'll put together a submission package. This will include a one-page query letter to the literary manager or dramaturg briefly describing the play. Mention any reviews and give the number of cast members and sets. You will also send a two- to three-page synopsis, a ten-page sample of the most interesting section of your play, your résumé and the press kit you've assembled. Do not send your complete manuscript until it is requested.

You can also explore publishing your play. *Writer's Market* lists many play publishers. When your script is published your play will make money while someone else does the marketing. You'll be listed in a catalog that is sent out to hundreds or thousands of potential performance spaces—high schools, experimental companies, regional and community theaters—for possible production. You'll receive royalty checks for both performance fees and book sales. In contacting publishers you'll want to send your query letter with the synopsis and reviews.

There are several sources for grants. Some are federal or state, but don't overlook sources closer to home. The category "Arts Councils and Foundations" in Contests and Awards in this book lists a number of sources. On the national level contact the NEA Theater Program Fellowship for Playwrights (1100 Pennsylvania Ave. NW, Washington DC 20506). State arts commissions are another possible source, and also offer opportunities for involvement in programs where you can meet fellow playwrights. Some cities have arts and cultural commissions that offer grants for local artists. PEN publishes a comprehensive annual book, *Grants and Awards Available to American Writers* that also includes a section for Canadian writers. The eighteenth edition is available from the PEN American Center (568 Broadway, New York NY 10012).

Once you have been produced on a commercial level, your play has been published or you have won an important grant, you can start pursuing an agent. This is not always easy. Fewer agents represent playwrights alone—there's more money in movies and TV. No agent will represent an unknown playwright. Having an agent does *not* mean you can sit back and enjoy the ride. You will still need to get out there and network, establishing ties with theaters, directors, literary managers, other writers, producers, state art agencies and publishers, trying to get your work noticed. What it does mean is that you'll have some help. A good agent will have personal contacts that can place your work for consideration at a higher level than your efforts alone might.

There is always the possibility of moving from plays to TV and movies. There is a certain cachet in Hollywood surrounding successful playwrights. The writing style will be different—more visually oriented, less dependent on your words. The money is better, but you will have less command over the work once you've sold that copyright. It seems to be easier for a playwright to cross over to movies than for a screenwriter to cross over to plays.

Writing a script can make you feel isolated, even when your characters are so real to you they seem to be in the room as you write. Sometimes the experience and companionship of other playwrights is what you need to get you over a particular hurdle in your play. Membership and service organizations such as The Dramatists Guild, The International Women's Writing Guild and local groups such as the Playwright's Center in Minneapolis and the Northwest Playwright's Guild in Seattle can help you feel still a part of this world as you are off creating your own.

For information on more playwriting markets, see Scriptwriting Markets/Changes '94-'95 at the end of the Screenwriting section.

A.D. PLAYERS, 2710 W. Alabama, Houston TX 77098-2106. (713)526-2721. Artistic Director: Jeannette Clift George. Estab. 1967. Produces 4-6 plays/year. Professional Christian theater company. "Productions include 4-6 Grace Theater Series shows and 4 Nancy Calhoun Paulson Children's Theatre Series shows, 2-3 staged readings and 10-12 Repertory Series shows on tour. The mainstage performance area is a proscenium stage with minimal wing space and no fly space; the children's theater space is in the round. Tour performance arenas vary from auditoriums and theaters to gymnasiums/cafetoriums and churches. Audiences for each series include adults and children, some with church affiliation." Query with synopsis only. Send materials to Martha Doolittle, Dramaturg/literary manager. Reports in 2-12 months. Payment terms negotiable.

Needs: "One-act and full-length plays, any style, reflecting God's reality in everyday life. Seasonal plays, any length, and short pieces (up to one hour) especially needed." Write to the Literary Manager for specific script submittal guidelines. No unsolicited scripts.

● A.D. Players is interested in seeing more children's material.

Tips: "Because of our specific signature as a Christian repertory company we would not be interested in plays that have no reference to the reality of God or man's search for spiritual significance in his world."

ACTORS' STOCK COMPANY, 3884 Van Ness Lane, Dallas TX 75220. (214)353-9916. Artistic Director: Keith Oncale. Estab. 1988. Produces 3-4 plays/year. "We stage semi-professional productions to a young adult to middle-aged general audience." Query with synopsis. Reports in 3 months. Purchases reading privileges. Pays royalty.

Needs: Two-and three-act plays, covering a wide variety of styles, but with fewer than 12 cast members. Our average staging facilities are 100 seat houses or smaller.

Tips: "Trends today reflect a return to comic realism that comments on our society without commenting on the play itself."

ACTORS THEATRE OF LOUISVILLE, 316 W. Main St., Louisville KY 40202-4218. (502)584-1265. Producing Director: Jon Jory. Estab. 1964. Produces approximately 20 new plays of varying lengths/year. Professional productions are performed for subscription audience from diverse backgrounds. Agented submissions only for full-length plays; open submissions to National Ten-Minute Play Contest (plays 10 pages or less). Reports in 6-9 months on submissions, mostly in the fall. Buys variable rights. Offers variable royalty.

Needs: "We are interested in full-length, one-act and ten-minute plays and in plays of ideas, language, humor, experiment and passion."

‡ALABAMA SHAKESPEARE FESTIVAL, 1 Festival Dr., Montgomery AL 36117-4605. Artistic Director: Kent Thompson. Produces 14 plays/year. Inhouse productions, tours, general audience, children audience. Query with synopsis. Reports in 4-6 months. Pays royalty.

Needs: "ASF develops works by Southern writers, works that deal with the South and/or African-American themes, works that deal with Southern and/or African-American history, works that illuminate the classics."

AMELIA MAGAZINE, 329 "E" St., Bakersfield CA 93304. (805)323-4064. Editor: Frederick A. Raborg, Jr. Estab. 1983. Publishes 1 play/year. Submit complete ms. Reports in 2 months. Buys first North American serial rights only. Pays $150 plus publication as winner of annual Frank McClure One-Act Play Award.

Needs: "Plays with virtually any theme or concept. We look for excellence within the one-act, 45 minutes running time format. We welcome the avant-garde and experimental. We do not object to the erotic, though not pornographic. Fewer plays are being produced on Broadway, but the regionals seem to be picking up the slack. That means fewer equity stages and more equity waivers."

‡AMERICAN INSIDE THEATRE, P.O. Box 217, Genesee Depot WI 53127. (414)968-4770. Artistic Director: Morrigan Hurt. Produces 5 plays/year. Query with synopsis. Reports in 3 months. Pays 3-6% royalty.

Needs: "American Inside Theatre produces works by American playwrights, and is particularly interested in scripts by and about the experiences of women and minorities." Scripts with single unit sets preferred and smaller casts (minimum 6 actors).

AMERICAN STAGE FESTIVAL, P.O. Box 225, Milford NH 03055-0225. Fax: (603)673-4792. Producing Director: Matthew Parent. Estab. 1975. "The ASF is a central New England professional theater (professional equity company) with a 3-month summer season (June-August)" for audience of all ages, interests, education and sophistication levels. Query with synopsis. Produces 20% musicals, 80% nonmusicals. Five are mainstage and ten are children's productions; 40% are originals. Royalty option and subsequent amount of gross: optional. Reports in 6 months.

● This theater is looking for more comedies and musicals—works with broad appeal.

Needs: "The Festival can do comedies, musicals and dramas. However, the most frequent problems are bolder language and action than a general mixed audience will accept. Prefer not to produce plays with strictly urban themes. We have a 40-foot proscenium stage with 30-foot wings, but no fly system. Festival plays are chosen to present scale and opportunities for scenic and costume projects far beyond the 'summer theater' type of play." Length: mainstage: 2-3 acts; children's productions: 50 minutes.

Tips: "Our audiences prefer plays that deal with human problems presented in a conventional manner."

AN CLAIDHEAMH SOLUIS/CELTIC ARTS CENTER, P.O. Box 20630, Los Angeles CA 90006-0630. (213)462-6844. Fax: (213)383-0772. Artistic Director: Sean Walsh. Estab. 1985. Produces 6 plays/year. Equity 99-seat plan. Query with synopsis. Reports in 6 months. Rights acquired vary. Pays $25-50.

Needs: Scripts of Celtic interest (Scottish, Welsh, Irish, Cornish, Manx, Breton). "This can apply to writer's background or subject matter. We are particularly concerned with works that relate to the survival of ethnic cultures and traditions, especially those in danger of extinction."

ARAN PRESS, 1320 S. Third St., Louisville KY 40208-2306. (502)636-0115. Editor/Publisher: Tom Eagan. Estab. 1983. Audience is professional, community, college, university, summer stock and dinner theaters. Query. Reports in 1-2 weeks on submissions. Contracts for publication and play production. Pays 10% book royalty and 50% production royalty.
• Aran Press would like to see more comedies.
Tips: No children's plays. "Tip to writers of plays: don't. Write novels, nonfiction, whatever, but don't write plays. If you *must* write plays, and you can't get published by one of the other publishers, send us an inquiry. If you care for what we have to offer, welcome aboard."

‡ARDEN THEATRE COMPANY, P.O. Box 779, Philadelphia PA 19105. (215)829-8900. Artistic Directors: Terrence J. Arden, Aaron Pogner. Estab. 1988. Produces 5 plays/year. Query with synopsis. Reports in 6 months. Pays 5% royalty.
Needs: Full-length, adaptations and musicals. Flexible in terms of cast size.

ARKANSAS REPERTORY THEATRE, P.O. Box 110, Little Rock AR 72203-0110. (501)378-0445. Fax: (501)378-0012. Literary Manager: Brad Mooy. Estab. 1976. Produces 11 full productions each season (7 on the Main-Stage, 3 on the SecondStage and 1 Educational Tour). We also produce staged readings and Celebrity Playreadings plus workshop productions. One MainStage show tours the country and the Educational Tour is regional. Query with synopsis. Reports in up to 3 months. Rights purchased vary. Pays royalty or per performance; "this also varies per show."
Needs: "We produce an ecclectic season, with musicals, comedies, dramas and at least one original premiere per season."

ART CRAFT PUBLISHING CO., 233 Dows Bldg., Box 1058, Cedar Rapids IA 52406-1058. (319)364-6311. Fax: (319)364-1771. Publisher: C. McMullen. Estab. 1928. Publishes plays and musicals for the junior and senior high school market. Query with synopsis or submit complete script. Reports in 2 months. Purchases amateur rights only. Makes outright purchase or pays royalty.
Needs: "Our current need is for full length productions, two and three act plays and musicals preferably comedy or mystery-comedy with a large number of characters. We sell almost exclusively to junior and smaller senior high school groups, thus we are unable to publish material that may contain controversial or offensive subject matter."

ASOLO THEATRE COMPANY, 5555 N. Tamiami Tr., Sarasota FL 34243-2141. (813)351-9010. Contact: Literary Manager. Estab. 1960. Produces 8 plays/year. 20% freelance written. A LORT theater with an intimate performing space. Works with 2-4 unpublished/unproduced writers annually. "We do not accept unsolicited scripts. Writers must send us a letter with 1 page synopsis and 1 page of dialogue with SAE." Reports in 8 months. Negotiates rights and payment.
Needs: Play must be *full length*. "We do not restrict ourselves to any particular genre or style—generally we do a good mix of classical and modern works."

BAKER'S PLAYS PUBLISHING CO., Dept. WM, 100 Chauncy St., Boston MA 02111-1783. (617)482-1280. Fax: (617)482-7613. Editor: John B. Welch. Estab. 1845. 80% freelance written. Plays performed by amateur groups, high schools, children's theater, churches and community theater groups. 75% of scripts unagented submissions. Works with 2-3 unpublished/unproduced writers annually. Submit complete script with news clippings, résumé. Submit complete cassette of music with musical submissions. Publishes 18-25 straight plays and musicals, all originals. Pay varies; makes outright purchase price to split in production fees; 10% book royalty. Reports in 2-6 months.
Needs: "We are finding strong support in our new division—plays from young authors featuring contemporary pieces for high school production."
• Send SASE for information on Baker's Plays High School Playwriting Contest.

BARTER THEATRE, P.O. Box 867, Abingdon VA 24210-0867. (703)628-2281. Fax: (703)628-4551. Artistic Director: Richard Rose. Estab. 1933. Produces 11 plays/year. Play performed in residency at 2 facilities, a 400-seat proscenium theater and a smaller 150-seat thrust theater. "Our plays are intended for diversified audiences of all ages." Submit synopsis and dialogue sample only to: Richard Rowe, Artistic Director. Reports in 3-6 months. Royalty negotiable.
Needs: "We are looking for good plays, comedies and dramas, that entertain and are relevant; plays that comment on the times and mankind; plays that are universal. We prefer casts of 4-12, single or unit set. Hard language can be a factor."

BILINGUAL FOUNDATION OF THE ARTS, #19, 421 North Ave., Los Angeles CA 90031. (213)225-4044. Fax: (213)225-1250. Artistic Director: Margarita Galban. Dramaturg/Literary Manager: Guillermo Reyes. Estab. 1973. Produces 3-5 plays plus 9-10 staged readings/year. "Productions are presented at home theater in Los Angeles, California. Our audiences are largely Hispanic and all productions are performed in English and Spanish. The Bilingual Foundation of the Arts produces plays in order to promote the rich heritage of Hispanic history and culture. Though our plays must be Hispanic in theme, we reach out to the entire community." Submit complete script. Reports in 3-6 months. Rights negotiable. Pays royalty.
Needs: "Plays must be Hispanic in theme. Comedy, drama, light musical, children's theater, etc. are accepted for consideration. Theater is 99-seater, no flies."
 • More plays in Spanish are needed.

BOARSHEAD THEATER, 425 S. Grand Ave., Lansing MI 48933. (517)484-7800. Artistic Director: John Peakes. Estab. 1966. Produces 7-9 plays/year. Mainstage Actors' Equity Association company; also Youth Theater—touring to schools by our intern company. Query with synopsis, cast list (with descriptions), 5-10 pages of representative dialogue, SASE postcard. "Reports on query and synopsis in 1 week. Full scripts (when requested by us) in 4-8 months." Pays royalty.
Needs: Thrust stage. Cast usually 8 or less; ocassionally up to 12-14. Prefer staging which depends on theatricality rather than multiple sets.

‡**BRISTOL RIVERSIDE THEATRE,** P.O. Box 1250, Bristol PA 19007. (215)785-6664. Producing Artistic Director: Susan D. Atkinson. Estab. 1986. "Due to a backlog of submitted scripts, we will not be accepting any new scripts until June, 1995."

CALIFORNIA THEATER CENTER, P.O. Box 2007, Sunnyvale CA 94087. (408)245-2978. Literary Manager: Will Huddleston. Estab. 1976. Produces 15 plays/year. Plays are for young audiences in both our home theater and for tour. Query with synopsis. Reports in 6 months. "We negotiate a set fee."
Needs: All plays must be suitable for young audiences, must be under 1 hour in length. Cast sizes vary. Sets must be able to tour easily.

CENTER STAGE, 700 N. Calvert St., Baltimore MD 21202-3686. (410)685-3200. Resident Dramaturg: James Magruder. Estab. 1963. Produces 6-8 plays/year. "LORT 'B' and LORT 'C' theaters; audience is both subscription and single-ticket. Wide-ranging audience profile." Query with synopsis, 10 sample pages and résumé, or submit through agent. Reports in 3 months. Rights and payment negotiated.
Needs: Produces "dramas and comedies, musical theater works. No restrictions on topics or styles, though experimental work is encouraged. No one-act plays. Casts over 12 would give us pause. Be inventive, theatrical, not precious; we like plays with vigorous language and stage image. Domestic naturalism is discouraged; strong thematic, political, or social interests are encouraged."
Tips: "We are interested in reading adaptations and translations as well as original work."

CENTER THEATER, 1346 W. Devon Ave., Chicago IL 60660. (312)508-0200. Artistic Director: Daniel S. LaMorte. Estab. 1984. Produces approximately 13 plays/year. "We run professional productions in our Chicago 'off-Loop' theaters for a diverse audience. We also hold an international play contest annually. For more info send SASE to Dale Calandra, Literary Manager." *Agented submissions only.* Reports in 3 months.
 • This theater has recently established a playwright-in-residence program and professional seminars in playwriting and screenwriting.

THE CHANGING SCENE THEATER, 1527½ Champa St., Denver CO 80202. Director: Alfred Brooks. Contact: Maxine Munt. Year-round productions in theater space. Cast may be made up of both professional and amateur actors. For public audience; age varies, but mostly youthful and interested in taking a chance on new and/or experimental works. No limit to subject matter or story themes. Emphasis is on the innovative. "Also, we require that the playwright be present for at least one performance of his work, if not for the entire rehearsal period. We have a small stage area, but are able to convert to round, semi-round or environmental. Prefer to do plays with limited sets and props." Two and three act.
Needs: Produces 8-10 nonmusicals a year; all are originals. 90% freelance written. 65% of scripts produced are unagented submissions. Works with 3-4 unpublished/unproduced writers annually. "We do not pay royalties or sign contracts with playwrights. We function on a performance-share basis of payment. Our theater seats 76; the first 50 seats go to the theater; the balance is divided among the participants in the production. The performance-share process is based on the entire production run and not determined by individual performances. We do not copyright our plays." Send complete script. Reporting time varies; usually several months.
Recent Production: *Plague Song* by David Nuss.
Tips: "We are experimental: open to young artists who want to test their talents and open to experienced artists who want to test new ideas/explore new techniques. Dare to write 'strange and wonderful' well-thought-out scripts. We want upbeat ones. Consider that we have a small performance area (24' × 31') when submitting."

CHARLOTTE REPERTORY THEATRE, 2040 Charlotte Plaza, Charlotte NC 28244. (704)375-4796. Fax: (704)375-9462. Literary Manager: Claudia Carter Covington. Literary Associate: Carol Bellamy. Estab. 1976. Produces 13 plays/year. "We are a not-for-profit regional theater." Submit complete script. Reports in 2-3 months. Writers receive free plane fare and housing for festival. Send SASE.
Needs: "Need full-length, not previously produced professionally, non-musical scripts. No limitations in cast, props, staging, etc."

CHILDREN'S STORY SCRIPTS, Baymax Productions, Suite 130, 2219 W. Olive Ave., Burbank CA 91506-2648. (818)563-6105. Fax: (818)563-2968. Editor: Deedra Bebout. Estab. 1990. "Our audience consists of children, grades K-8 (5-13-year-olds)." Send complete script with SASE. Reports in 1 month. Licenses all rights to story; author retains copyright. Pays graduated royalty based on sales.
Needs: "We are not publishing new titles until we have a firm foothold in the market. However, I still read submissions. If I find something that would work for us, I contact author, tell him/her of our interest. If it's still available when we resume publishing new titles, great."
Tips: "The scripts are not like theatrical scripts. They read like prose. If a writer shows promise, we'll work with him. Our most important goal is to benefit children. Send #10 SASE for guidelines with samples."

CHILDSPLAY, INC., P.O. Box 517, Tempe AZ 85280. (602)350-8101. Fax: (602)350-8584. Artistic Director: David P. Saar. Estab. 1978. Produces 5-6 plays/year. "Professional: Touring and in-house productions for youth and family audiences." Submit complete script. Reports in 6 months. "On commissioned work we hold a small percentage of royalties for 3-5 years." Pays royalty of $20-35/performance (touring) or pays $3,000-8,000 commission.
Needs: Seeking "*theatrical* plays on a wide range of comtemporary topics. Touring shows: 5-6 actors; van-size. In-house: 6-10 actors; no technical limitations."
Tips: No traditionally handled fairy tales. "Theater for young people is growing up and is able to speak to youth and adults. The material *must* respect the artistry of the theater and the intelligence of our audience. Our most important goal is to benefit children. If you wish your manuscript returned send #10 SASE."

CIRCUIT PLAYHOUSE/PLAYHOUSE ON THE SQUARE, 51 S. Cooper, Memphis TN 38104. (901)725-0776. Artistic Director: Jackie Nichols. Produces 16 plays/year. 100% freelance written. Professional plays performed for the Memphis/Mid-South area. Member of the Theatre Communications Group. 100% of scripts unagented submissions. Works with 1 unpublished/unproduced writer annually. Play contest held each fall. Submit complete script. Reports in 6 months. Buys percentage of royalty rights for 2 years. Pays $500.
Needs: All types; limited to single or unit sets. Cast of 20 or fewer.
Tips: "Each play is read by three readers through the extended length of time a script is kept. Preference is given to scripts for the southeastern region of the US."

I.E. CLARK, PUBLISHER, Saint John's Rd., P.O. Box 246, Schulenburg TX 78956-0246. (409)743-3232. Contact: Carol Drabek. Estab. 1956. Publishes 15 plays/year for educational theater, children's theater, religious theater, regional professional theater and amateur community theater. 20% freelance written. 3-4 scripts/year unagented submissions. Works with 2-3 unpublished writers annually. Submit complete script, one at a time. Script will not be returned without SASE. Reports in 3-6 months. Buys all available rights; "we serve as an agency as well as a publisher." Pays standard book and performance royalty, "the amount and percentages dependent upon type and marketability of play." Catalog $2. Writer's guidelines for #10 SASE.
Needs: "We are interested in plays of all types—short or long. Audiotapes of music or videotapes of a performance are requested with submissions of musicals. We require that a play has been produced (directed by someone other than the author); photos, videos, and reviews of the production are helpful. No limitations in cast, props, staging, etc. Plays with only one or two characters are difficult to sell. We insist on literary quality. We like plays that give new interpretations and understanding of human nature. Correct spelling, punctuation and grammar (befitting the characters, of course) impress our editors."
Tips: "Entertainment value and a sense of moral responsibility seem to be returning as essential qualities of a good play script. The era of glorifying the negative elements of society seems to be fading rapidly. Literary quality, entertainment value and good craftsmanship rank in that order as the characteristics of a good script in our opinion. 'Literary quality' means that the play must—in beautiful, distinctive, and un-trite language—say something; preferably something new and important concerning man's relations with his fellow man or God; and these 'lessons in living' must be presented in an intelligent, believable and creative manner. Plays for children's theater are tending more toward realism and childhood problems rather than fantasy or dramatization of fairy tales."

‡COAST TO COAST THEATER COMPANY, P.O. Box 3855, Hollywood CA 90078. (818)782-1212. Artistic Director: Bryan W. Simon. Estab. 1989. Produces 2-3 plays/year. Equity and equity waiver theater. Query and synopsis. Reports in up to 1 year. Buys West Coast, Midwest or East Coast rights, depending on location of production. Pays 5% royalty or makes outright purchase $100-250 or pays per performance.
Needs: Full-length off-beat comedies or dramas with small cast, simple sets.

COLONY STUDIO THEATRE, 1944 Riverside Dr., Los Angeles CA 90039. New play selection committee: Judith Goldstein. Produces 4 mainstage productions and 4 workshop productions/year. Professional 99-seat theater with thrust stage. Casts from a resident company of professional actors. No unsolicited scripts. Submission guidelines for #10 SASE. Reports in up to 1 year. Negotiated rights. Pays royalties for each performance.
Needs: Full length (90-120 minutes) with a cast of 2-10. No musicals or experimental works.
Tips: "A polished script is the mark of a skilled writer. Submissions should be in professional (centered) format."

CONTEMPORARY DRAMA SERVICE, Meriwether Publishing Ltd., P.O. Box 7710, Colorado Springs CO 80933. (303)594-4422. Fax: (719)594-9916. Editor-in-Chief: Arthur Zapel. Associate Editors: Theodore Zapel and Rhonda Wray. Estab. 1969. Publishes 50-60 plays/year. "We publish for the secondary school market and colleges. We also publish for mainline liturgical churches—drama activities for church holidays, youth activities and fundraising entertainments. These may be plays or drama-related books." Query with synopsis or submit complete script. Reports in 6 weeks or less. Obtains either amateur or all rights. Pays 10% royalty or makes outright negotiated purchase.
Needs: "Most of the plays we publish are one-acts, 15-45 minutes in length. We occasionally publish full-length three-act plays. We prefer comedies in the longer plays. Musical plays must have name appeal either by prestige author, prestige title adaptation or performance on Broadway or TV. Comedy sketches, monologues and 2-character plays are welcomed. We prefer simple staging appropriate to high school, college or church performance. We like playwrights who see the world positively and with a sense of humor. Offbeat themes and treatments are accepted if the playwright can sustain a light touch and not take himself or herself too seriously. In documentary or religious plays we look for good research and authenticity. We are publishing many textbooks on the theatrical arts and scenebooks. We are especially interested in authority-books on costuming, acting, set design and lighting."

THE COTERIE, 2450 Grand Ave., Kansas City MO 64108-2520. (816)474-6785. Fax: (816)474-6785. Artistic Director: Jeff Church. Estab. 1979. Produces 7-8 plays/year. "Plays produced at Hallmark's Crown Center in downtown Kansas City in the Coterie's resident theater (capacity 240). A typical performance run is one month in length." Query with synopsis; submit complete script only if an established playwright in youth theater field. Reports in 2-4 months. "We retain some rights on commissioned plays." Pays royalty per performance and flat fee.
Needs: "We produce plays which are universal in appeal; they may be original or adaptations of classic or contemporary literature. Typically, not more than 12 in a cast—prefer 5-9 in size. No fly space or wing space."
Tips: "No couch plays. Prefer plays by seasoned writers who have established reputations. Groundbreaking and exciting scripts from the youth theater field welcome. It's prefectly fine if your play is a little off-center." Trends in the field that writers should be mindful of: "Make certain your submitted play to us is *very* theatrical and not cinematic. Writers need to see how far the field of youth and family theater has come—the interesting new areas we're going—before sending us your query or manuscript."

CREATIVE PRODUCTIONS, INC., 2 Beaver Place, Aberdeen NJ 07747. (908)566-6985. Artistic Director: Walter L. Born. Produces 2 musicals/year. Non-equity, year-round productions. "We use musicals with folks with disabilities and older performers in addition to 'normal' performers, for the broad spectrum of viewers." Query with synopsis. Reports in 2 weeks. Buys rights to perform play for specified number of performances. Pay negotiable.
Needs: Original musicals with upbeat themes adaptable to integrated company of traditional and non-traditional performers. Limitations: maximum cast of 12, sets can't "fly," facilities are schools, no mammoth sets and multiple scene changes, 90 minutes maximum run time.
Tips: No blue material, pornographic, obscene language. Submit info on any performances. Demo tape (musicals) plus vocal/piano score list of references on users of their material to confirm bio info.

CREEDE REPERTORY THEATRE, P.O. Box 269, Creede CO 81130-0269. (719)658-2541. Artistic Director: Richard Baxter. Estab. 1966. Produces 6 plays/year. Plays performed for a summer audience. Query with synopsis. Reports in 1 year. Royalties negotiated with each author—paid on a per performance basis.
Needs: One-act children's scripts. Special consideration given to plays focusing on the cultures and history of the American West and Southwest.
Tips: "No avant-garde or experimental work. We seek new adaptations of classical or older works as well as original scripts."

DELAWARE THEATRE COMPANY, 200 Water St., Wilmington DE 19801-5030. (302)594-1104. Artistic Director: Cleveland Morris. Estab. 1978. Produces 5 plays/year. 10% freelance written. "Plays are performed as part of a five-play subscription season in a 300-seat auditorium. Professional actors, directors and designers are engaged. The season is intended for a general audience." 10% of scripts are unagented submissions. Works with 1 unpublished/unproduced writer every 2 years. Query with synopsis and an excerpt of 5-10 pages. Reports in 6 months. Buys variable rights. Pays 5% (variable) royalty.

Needs: "We present comedies, dramas, tragedies and musicals. All works must be full length and fit in with a season composed of standards and classics. All works have a strong literary element. Plays showing a flair for language and a strong involvement with the interests of classical humanism are of greatest interest. Single-set, small-cast works are likeliest for consideration." Recent trend toward "more economical productions."

‡DINER THEATRE, 2015 S. 60th St., Omaha NE 68106. (402)553-4715. Artistic Director: Doug Marr. Estab. 1983. Produces 5 plays/year. Professional productions, general audience. Query with synopsis. Reports in 2 months on submissions. Pays $15-30/performance.

Needs: Comedies, dramas, musicals—original unproduced works. Full length, all styles/topics.

DISCOVERY '95, Paul Mellon Arts Center, P.O. Box 788, Wallingford CT 06492. (203)284-5398. Fax: (203)284-5396. Artistic Director: Terrence Ortwein. Estab. 1984. Produces 3 plays/year. "Choate Rosemary Hall in Wallingford, Connecticut, will host its 11th summer theater program committed to the discovery and development of new scripts written specifically for secondary school production. Students with an interest in theater from around the country will join directors and writers-in-residence in order to rehearse and perform new works in July. Playwrights will have the opportunity to hear, see and rewrite their scripts during three-week residencies. Public workshop performances will provide audience reactions to the works-in-progress and will enable the playwrights to further develop their scripts for future productions." Submit complete ms. Playwrights selected must agree to be in residence at Choate Rosemary Hall the last 3½ weeks in July. Room, board and a $700 stipend will be given each playwright selected. "The workshop productions, script-in-hand so that the playwright will have every opportunity to rewrite during every step of his or her *discovery*, will be the responsibility of Choate Rosemary Hall."

Tips: "The content should appeal strongly and directly to teenagers. Although all the characters don't have to be teenagers, the actors will be. In most high schools, more girls than boys participate in drama. Most high schools have limited technical resources and limited budgets. Although we will look at full-length scripts, the real need and interest is in the one-act and hour-length play. This program is established to help playwrights develop scripts, not to produce already finished scripts. *Only unproduced and unpublished scripts may be submitted.*" Submission date: March 1, 1995. Notification: May 1, 1995. Include SASE for returns.

DORSET THEATRE FESTIVAL, Box 519, Dorset VT 05251-0519. (802)867-2223. Fax: (802)867-0144. Artistic Director: Jill Charles. Estab. 1976. Produces 5 plays/year, 1 a new work. "Our plays will be performed in our Equity summer stock theatre and are intended for a sophisticated community." Agented submissions only. Reports in 3-6 months. Rights and compensation arranged on an individual basis.

Needs: "We are looking for full-length contemporary American comedy or drama. We are limited to a cast of six."

Tips: "Language and subject matter appropriate to general audience."

DRAMATICS MAGAZINE, Dept. WM, 3368 Central Pkwy., Cincinnati OH 45225. (513)559-1996. Editor: Don Corathers. Estab. 1929. Publishes 5 plays/year. For high school theater students and teachers. Submit complete ms. Reports in 3 months. Buys first North American serial rights only. Purchases one-time publication rights only for $100-400.

Needs: "We are seeking one-acts to full-lengths that can be produced in an educational theater setting. We don't publish musicals."

Tips: "No melodrama, farce, children's theater, or cheap knock-offs of TV sitcoms or movies. Fewer writers are taking the time to learn the conventions of theater—what makes a piece work on stage, as opposed to film and television—and their scripts show it."

‡EAST WEST PLAYERS, 4424 Santa Monica Blvd., Los Angeles CA 90029. (213)666-1929. Artistic Director: Tim Dang. Estab. 1965. Produces 5 plays/year. Professional theater performing under Equity 99-seat contract, presenting plays which explore the Asian or Asian-American experience. Query with synopsis. Reports in 3 months on submissions. Pays royalty against percentage of box office.

Needs: "Whether dramas, comedies or performance art or musicals, all plays must either address the Asian-American experience or have a special resonance when cast with Asian-American actors."

ELDRIDGE PUBLISHING CO., P.O. Box 1595, Venice FL 34284. (813)496-4679. Editor: Nancy Vorhis. Estab. 1906. Publishes 35-40 new plays/year for middle school, junior high, senior high, church and community audience. Query with synopsis (acceptable) or submit complete ms (preferred). Please send cassette tapes

The double dagger before a listing indicates that the listing is new in this edition. New markets are often more receptive to freelance submissions.

with any operettas. Reports in 2 months. Buys all rights. Pays 50% royalties and 10% copy sales. Makes outright purchase from $200-500. Writer's guidelines for #10 SASE.

Needs: "We are most interested in full-length plays and musicals for our school and community theater market. Prefer large, flexible casts, if possible. Nothing lower than junior high level, please. We always love comedies but also look for serious, high caliber plays reflective of today's sophisticated students. We also need one-acts and plays for children's theater. In addition, in our religious market we're always searching for Christmas and Easter plays."

Tips: "Submissions are welcomed at any time but during our fall season; response will definitely take 2 months. Authors are paid royalties twice a year. They receive complimentary copies of their published plays, the annual catalog and 50% discount if buying additional copies."

ENCORE PERFORMANCE PUBLISHING, P.O. Box 692, Orem UT 84059-4554. (801)225-0605. Editor: Michael C. Perry. Estab. 1979. Publishes 20-50 plays/year. "Our audience consists of all ages with emphasis on the family; educational institutions from elementary through college/university, community theaters and professional theaters." Query with synopsis. Reports in 1 month on queries; 3 months on scripts. Pays 50% performance royalty; 10% book royalty.

Needs: "We are looking for plays with strong message about or for families, plays with young actors among cast, any length, all genres. We prefer scripts with at least close or equal male/female roles, could lean to more female roles." Plays must have had at least 2 fully staged productions. Unproduced plays can be read with letter of recomendation accompanying the query.

Tips: "No performance art pieces or plays with overtly sexual themes or language. Looking for adaptations of Twain and other American authors."

‡ENCORE THEATRE CO., 6th Floor, 30 Grant, San Francisco CA 94108. (415)346-7671. Artistic Director: Andrew Dolan. Estab. 1986. Professional productions in 70-seat black box theater for San Francisco and Bay Area audience, some tourists. Query with synopsis. Reports in 3 months. Buys variable rights. Pays variable royalty.

Needs: Full-length, contemporary, strong actor roles. Limitations in cost.

Tips: Wants to see contemporary issues but not polemic; strong acting ensemble required. No light material, musicals, "fluff."

‡THE FOOTHILL THEATRE COMPANY, P.O. Box 1812, Nevada City CA 95959. (916)265-9320. Artistic Director: Philip Charles Sneed. Estab. 1977. Produces 10 plays/year. "We are a professional theater company operating under an Actor's Equity Association contract, and performing in the historic 247-seat Nevada Theatre (built in 1865) and in a converted space in a nearby cultural center (70-seat black box). The audience is a mix of locals and tourists." Query with synopsis or submit complete script. Reports in 6 months. Buys negotiable rights. Pay varies.

Needs: "We are most interested in plays which speak to the region and its history, as well as to its current concerns. No melodramas. Theatrical, above all." No limitations.

Tips: "Avoid the cliché at all costs, and don't be derivative; we're interested in a unique and unassailable vision."

‡FOUNTAIN THEATRE, 5060 Fountain Ave., Los Angeles CA 90029. (213)663-2235. Artistic Directors: Deborah Lawlor, Stephen Sachs. Estab. 1990. Produces 6 plays/year. Produced at Fountain Theatre (99-seat equity plan). Query and synopsis to: Jay Alan Quantrill, Dramaturg. Reports in 3 months. Rights acquired vary. Pays 6% royalty.

Needs: Original plays, adaptations of American literature, "material that incorporates dance of language into text with unique use and vision."

SAMUEL FRENCH, INC., 45 W. 25th St., New York NY 10010-2751. Fax: (212)206-1429. Editor: Lawrence Harbison. "We publish about 50-60 new titles/year. We are the world's largest publisher of plays. 10-20% unagented submissions. Pays on royalty basis. Submit complete script (bound). Always type your play in the standard, accepted stageplay format used by all professional playwrights in the US. If in doubt, send $4 to the attention of Lawrence Harbison for a copy of 'Guidelines.' We require a minimum of 2 months to report."

Needs: "We are willing at all times to read the work of freelancers. Our markets prefer simple-to-stage, light, happy romantic comedies or mysteries with a good complement of female roles. No puppet plays; no adaptations of public domain children's stories; no verse plays; no large-cast historical (costume) plays; no seasonal plays; no television, film or radio scripts."

GEORGE STREET PLAYHOUSE, 9 Livingston Ave., New Brunswick NJ 08901. (908)846-2895. Producing Director: Gregory Hurst. Literary Manager: Wendy Liscow. Produces 7 plays/year. Professional regional theater (LORT C). No unsolicited scripts. Professional recommendation only. Reports on scripts in 4-8 months.

Needs: Full-length dramas, comedies and musicals that present a fresh perspective on society and challenge expectations of theatricality. Prefers cast size under 9. Also presents 40-minute social issue-plays appropriate for touring to school-age children; cast size limited to 4 actors.

Tips: "We present a series of six staged readings each year. We produce up to four new plays and one new musical each season. We have a strong interest in receiving work from minority writers whose voices are not traditionally heard on America's main stages."

THE GOODMAN THEATRE, 200 S. Columbus Ave., Chicago IL 60603. (312)443-3811. Artistic Director: Robert Falls. Literary Manager: Susan V. Booth. Estab. 1925. Produces 9 plays/year. "The Goodman is a professional, not-for-profit theater producing both a mainstage and studio series for its subscription-based audience. The Goodman does not accept unsolicited scripts from playwrights or agents, nor will it respond to synopses of plays submitted by playwrights, unless accompanied by a stamped, self-addressed postcard. The Goodman may request plays to be submitted for production consideration after receiving a letter of inquiry or telephone call from recognized literary agents or producing organizations." Reports in 6 months. Buys variable rights. Pay is variable.

Needs: Full-length plays, translations, musicals; special interest in social or political themes.

‡GREAT AMERICAN HISTORY THEATRE, 30 E. Tenth St., St. Paul MN 55101. (612)292-4323. Artistic Director: Lance Belville. Estab. 1978. Produces 6-7 plays/year. "We have two spaces in which to do professional productions. Our main house theater seats 600 while our cabaret has 200 seats. Our performances are intended for mainstream audiences." Query with synopsis. Reports in 2 weeks on synopsis; 2 months on scripts. Buys production rights. Pays variable royalty. "We commission new works, amount to be negotiated."

Needs: We try to provide audiences with a mirror to the lives of the people of Minnesota and the Midwest, and a window to other people and times. We do this by commissioning, producing and touring plays that dramatize the history, folklore and social issues of its own region and other locales. We limit our cast sizes to no larger than ten and we prefer pieces that can be staged simply."

GRETNA THEATRE, P.O. Box 578, Mt. Gretna PA 17064. (717)964-3322. Producing Director: Al Franklin. Estab. 1977. Produces 1 new play/year. "Plays are performed at a professional equity theater during summer for a conservative audience." Query with synopsis. "Include character breakdown with script's production history, plus five pages." Reports in 4-6 weeks. Rights negotiated. Royalty negotiated (6-12%).

Needs: "We produce full-length plays for a conservative, summer audience—subject, language, content important; comedy is popular." Cast of 10 limit—simple settings best.

Tips: "No one-acts, musicals, *heavy* drama or poorly written work."

THE GROUP (Seattle Group Theatre), 305 Harrison St., Seattle WA 98109. (206)441-9480. Artistic Director: Tim Bond. (Submit to Nancy Griffiths, Dramaturg/Literary Manager). Estab. 1978. Produces 6 plays and 1-3 workshop productions/year. "Plays are performed in our 197-seat theater—The Carlton Playhouse. Intended for a multiethnic audience. Professional, year-round theater." Query with synopsis, sample pages of dialogue and SASE for reply. Reports in 6-8 weeks. Rights obtained varies per production. Royalty varies.

Needs: "We look for scripts suitable for multiethnic casting that deal with social, cultural and political issues relevant to the world today."

Tips: *No phone calls.*

HEUER PUBLISHING CO., 233 Dows Bldg., Box 248, Cedar Rapids IA 52406-0248. (319)364-6311. Fax: (319)364-1771. Owner/Editor: C. Emmett McMullen. Estab. 1928. Publishes plays and musicals for junior and senior high school and church groups. Query with synopsis or submit complete script. Reports in 2 months. Purchases amateur rights only. Pays royalty or makes outright purchase.

Needs: "One- and three-act plays suitable for school production. Preferably comedy or mystery/comedy. All material should be of the capabilities of high school actors. We prefer material with one set. No special day material or material with controversial subject matter."

HONOLULU THEATRE FOR YOUTH, 2846 Ualena St., Honolulu HI 96819-1910. (808)839-9885. Fax: (808)839-7018. Artistic Director: Pam Sterling. Produces 6 plays/year. 50% freelance written. Plays are professional productions in Hawaii, primarily for young audiences (ages 2-20). 80% of scripts unagented submissions. Works with 2 unpublished/unproduced writers annually. Reports in 4 months. Buys negotiable rights.

Needs: Contemporary subjects of concern/interest to young people; adaptations of literary classics; fantasy including space, fairy tales, myth and legend. "HTY wants well-written plays, 60-90 minutes in length, that have something worthwhile to say and that will stretch the talents of professional adult actors." Cast not exceeding 8; *no* technical extravaganzas; *no* full-orchestra musicals; simple sets and props, costumes can be elaborate. No plays to be enacted by children or camp versions of popular fairytales. Query with synopsis. Pays $1,000-2,500.

Tips: "Young people are intelligent and perceptive; if anything, more so than lots of adults, and if they are to become fans and eventual supporters of good theater, they must see good theater while they are young. Trends on the American stage that freelance writers should be aware of include a growing awareness that we are living in a world community. We must learn to share and understand other people and other cultures."

HORIZON THEATRE COMPANY, P.O. Box 5376, Station E, Atlanta GA 31107. (404)584-7450. Artistic Director: Lisa Adler. Estab. 1983. Produces 4 plays/year. Professional productions. Query with synopsis and résumé. Reports in 1-2 years. Buys rights to produce in Atlanta area. Pays 6-8% royalty or $50-75/performance.
Needs: "We produce contemporary plays with realistic base, but which utilize heightened visual or language elements. Interested in comedy, satire, plays that are entertaining and topical, but also thought provoking. Also particular interest in plays by women or with Southern themes." No more than 10 in cast.
Tips: "No plays about being in theater or film; no plays without hope; no plays that include playwrights as leading characters; no all-male casts; no plays with all older (50 plus) characters."

WILLIAM E. HUNT, 801 West End Ave., New York NY 10025. Estab. 1947. Producer/Director: William E. Hunt. Interested in reading scripts for stock production, off-Broadway and even Broadway production. "Small cast, youth-oriented, meaningful, technically adventuresome; serious, funny, far-out. Must be about people first, ideas second. No political or social tracts." No one-act, anti-Black, anti-Semitic or anti-gay plays. "I do not want 1920, 1930 or 1940s plays disguised as modern by 'modern' language. I do not want plays with 24 characters or 150 costumes, plays about symbols instead of people. I do not want plays that are really movie or TV scripts." Works with 2-3 unpublished/unproduced writers annually. Pays royalties on production. Off-Broadway, 5%; on Broadway, 5%, 7½% and 10%, based on gross. No royalty paid if play is selected for a showcase production. Reports in "a few weeks." Must have SASE or script will not be returned.
Tips: "Production costs and weekly running costs in the legitimate theater are so high today that no play (or it is the very rare play) with more than six characters and more than one set, by a novice playwright, is likely to be produced unless that playwright will either put up or raise the money him or herself for the production."

JEWEL BOX THEATRE, 3700 N. Walker, Oklahoma City OK 73118-7099. (405)521-1786. Artistic Director: Charles Tweed. Estab. 1986. Produces 6 plays/year. Amateur productions. For 3,000 season subscribers and general public. Submit complete script. Reports in 4 months. Pays $500 contest prize.
Needs: "Write theater for entry form during September-October. We produce dramas, comedies and musicals. Only two- or three-act plays can be accepted. Our theater is in-the-round, so we adapt plays accordingly." Deadline: middle of January.

JEWISH REPERTORY THEATRE, 1395 Lexington Ave., New York NY 10128. (212)415-5550. Artistic Director: Ran Avni. Associate Director: Edward M. Cohen. Estab. 1974. Produces 4 plays, 15 readings/year. New York City professional off-Broadway production. Submit complete script and SASE. Reports in 1 month. First production/option to move to Broadway or off-Broadway. Pays royalty.
Needs: Full-length only. Straight plays and musicals. Must have some connection to Jewish life, characters, history. Maximum 7 characters. Limited technical facilities.
Tips: No biblical plays.

KUMU KAHUA, 46 Merchant St., Honolulu HI 96813. (808)737-4161. Managing Director: Dennis Carroll. Estab. 1971. Produces 5 productions, 3-4 public readings/year. "Plays performed at new Kumu Kahua Theatre, flexible 120 seat theater, for community audiences." Submit complete script. Reports in 4 months. Royalty $35/performance; usually 10 performances of each production.
Needs: "Plays must have some interest for local audiences, preferably by being set in Hawaii or dealing with some aspect of the Hawaiian experience. Prefer small cast, with simple staging demands."
Tips: "We need time to evaluate scripts (our response time is four months)."

LAGUNA PLAYHOUSE, P.O. Box 1747, Laguna Beach CA 92652-1747. (714)497-5900, ext. 206. Fax: (714)497-6948. Artistic Director: Andrew Barnicle. Estab. 1920. Produces 10 plays/year. Amateur with Equity Guest Artists: 5 mainstage (9,000 subscribers); Amateur: 5 youth theater (1,500 subscribers). Submit complete script. Reports in 2-12 months. Royalty negotiable.
Needs: Seeking full-length plays: comedy, drama, classical, musical, youth theater.
Recent Production: *Teachers' Lounge*, by John Twomey.
Tips: "We are committed to one full production of an original play every other season."
   • Laguna Playhouse has opened a second theater venue and expects to mount full productions of original works more regularly than in the past. However, limited staff to read and process original works can mean a long response time.

LILLENAS PUBLISHING CO., P.O. Box 419527, Kansas City MO 64141-6527. (816)931-1900. Fax: (816)753-4071. Editor: Paul M. Miller. Estab. 1926. "We publish on two levels: (1) Program Builders—seasonal and topical collections of recitations, sketches, dialogues and short plays; (2) Drama Resources. These assume more than one format: (a) full-length scripts, (b) one-acts, shorter plays and sketches all by one author, (c) collection of short plays and sketches by various authors. All program and play resources are produced with local church and Christian school in mind. Therefore there are taboos." Queries are encouraged, but synopses and complete scripts are read. "First rights are purchased for Program Builder scripts. For our line of Drama

Resources, we purchase all print rights, but this is negotiable." Writer's guidelines for #10 SASE. Reports in 3 months

● This publisher has added a line of full-length plays for school and dinner theater use; wholesome entertainment—not religious.

Needs: 98% of Program Builder materials are freelance written. Scripts selected for these publications are outright purchases; verse is 25 cents/line, prose (play scripts) are $5/double-spaced page. "Lillenas Drama Resources is a line of play scripts that are, for the most part, written by professionals with experience in production as well as writing. However, while we do read unsolicited scripts, more than half of what we publish is written by experienced authors whom we have already published." Drama Resources (whether full-length scripts, one-acts, or sketches) are paid on a 10% royalty. There are no advances.

Tips: "All plays need to be presented in standard play script format. We welcome a summary statement of each play. Purpose statements are always desirable. Approximate playing time, cast and prop lists, etc. are important to include. We are interested in fully scripted traditional plays, reader's theater scripts, choral speaking pieces. Contemporary settings generally have it over Biblical settings. Christmas and Easter scripts must have a bit of a twist. Secular approaches to these seasons (Santas, Easter bunnies, and so on), are not considered. We sell our product in 10,000 Christian bookstores and by catalog. We are probably in the forefront as a publisher of religious drama resources."

LIVE OAK THEATRE, 311 Nueces St., Austin TX 78701. (512)472-5143. Artistic Director: Don Toner. Literary Manager: Amparo Garcia. Estab. 1982. Professional theater produces 6 plays/season. "Live Oak has a history of producing works of Texan and Southern topics. Well-crafted, new American plays that are strongly theatrical." Reports in 1 month on queries; 6 months on scripts. Pays royalty.

Needs: Full-length, translations, adaptations, musicals. Guidelines for #10 SASE.

Tips: Also sponsors annual new play awards. Guidelines for #10 SASE after July 1.

● Playwrights are provided airfare and stipend during reading of new plays at the Harvest Festival of new plays in October.

MAD RIVER THEATER WORKS, P.O. Box 248, West Liberty OH 43357-0248. (513)465-6751. Fax: (513)465-3914. Artistic Director: Jeff Hooper. Estab. 1978. Produces 3 plays/year. "Mad River is a professional company. We present over 150 performances each year at colleges, universities and in small towns, for a broad, multigenerational audience. Our intended audience is primarily rural." Query with synopsis. Reports in 2 months. Buys exclusive production rights for a limited time. Pays negotiable royalty.

Needs: "We primarily produce works that deal with rural themes and/or issues. A small cast is most likely to be accepted. As a touring company, simple technical requirements are also a factor."

Tips: "We reach out to many different kinds of people, particularly audiences in rural areas without other access to professional theater. We seek to challenge, as well as entertain, and present works which can speak to conservative individuals as well as seasoned theatergoers."

MODERN INTERNATIONAL DRAMA, Theater Dept., SUNY, P.O. Box 6000, Binghamton NY 13902-6000. (607)777-2704. Managing Editor: George E. Wellwarth. Estab. 1967. Publishes 5-6 plays/year. "Audience is academic and professional." Query with synopsis or submit complete script. Reports in 3 months. "Rights remain with author and translator." Pays 3 complimentary copies.

Needs: Publishes plays of ideas; 20th century; any style and any length; *translations from any language of previously untranslated plays only.*

Tips: "No popular theater."

MUSICAL THEATRE WORKS, INC., Dept. WM, 4th Floor, 440 Lafayette St., New York NY 10003-6919. (212)677-0040. Artistic Director: Anthony Stimac. Estab. 1983. "MTW develops scripts from informal to staged readings. When the project is deemed ready for the public, a showcase is set up for commercial interest. MTW musicals are professionally produced and presented in an off-Broadway New York City theater and intended for a well-rounded, sophisticated, theater-going audience. Additionally, 50% of all MTW MainStage productions have gone on to engagements on Broadway and in 12 states across the country." Submit complete script with audiotape. Reports in 2-4 months. Buys 1% future gross; on fully-produced works. Pays negotiable royalty. SASE required to return script and tape.

Needs: "MTW only produces full-length works of musical theater and is interested not only in those classically written, but has a keen interest in works which expand the boundaries and subject matter of the artform. MTW is a small, but prolific, organization with a limited budget. It is, therefore, necessary to limit production costs."

Tips: "The dramatic stage of recent years has successfully interpreted societal problems of the day, while the musical theater has grown in spectacle and foregone substance. Since the musical theater traditionally incorporated large themes and issues it is imperative that we now marry these two ideas—large themes and current issues—to the form. Send a neat, clean, typewritten script with a well marked, clear audiotape, produced as professionally as possible, to the attention of the Literary Manager."

NATIONAL MUSIC THEATER CONFERENCE, EUGENE O'NEILL THEATER CENTER, Suite 901, 234 W. 44th St., New York NY 10036. (212)382-2790. Fax: (212)921-5538. Artistic Director: Paulette Haupt. Estab. 1978. Paying audiences drawn from local residents, New York and regional theater professionals and others. Conference takes place each August at center in Waterford, Connecticut. Application guidelines for #10 SASE after September 15. Application deadline: February 1 (subject to change). Pays stipend plus room and board during conference.

Needs: "We develop new music theater works of all forms, traditional and non-traditional. Singing must play a dominant role. Works are given minimally staged readings, script in hand, no props or lighting, piano only."

Tips: Works not considered eligible are those that have been fully produced by a professional company and adapted works for which rights have not been obtained. Writers and composers must be US citizens or permanent residents.

NECESSARY ANGEL THEATRE, Suite #201, 490 Adelaide St. W., Toronto, Ontario M5V 1T2 Canada. (416)365-0406. Fax: (416)363-8702. Artistic Director: Richard Rose. Estab. 1978. Produces 2 plays/year. Plays are Equity productions in various Toronto theaters and performance spaces for an urban audience between 20-55 years of age. Submit synopsis only. Does not return submissions. Reports in 6 months. Pays 10% royalty.

Needs: "We are open to new theatrical ideas, environmental pieces, unusual acting styles and large casts. The usual financial constraints exist, but they have never eliminated a work to which we felt a strong commitment." No "TV-influenced sitcoms or melodramas."

THE NEW CONSERVATORY CHILDREN'S THEATRE COMPANY AND SCHOOL, New Conservatory Theatre Center, 25 Van Ness, Lower Level, San Francisco CA 94102. (415)861-4814. Fax: (415)861-6988. Artistic Director: Ed Decker. Produces 4-5 plays/year. "The New Conservatory is a children's theater school (ages 4-19) and operates year-round. Each year we produce several plays, for which the older students (usually 10 and up) audition. These are presented to the general public at the New Conservatory Theatre Center in San Francisco (50-150 seats). Our audience is approximately age 5-adult." Query with synopsis. Reports in 3 months. Royalty negotiable.

Needs: "We emphasize works in which children play *children*, and prefer relevant and controversial subjects, although we also do musicals. We have a commitment to new plays. Examples of our shows are: Mary Gail's *Nobody Home* (world premiere; about latchkey kids); Brian Kral's *Special Class* (about disabled kids); and *The Inner Circle*, by Patricia Loughrey (commissioned scripts about AIDS prevention for kids). As we are a nonprofit group on limited budget, we tend not to have elaborate staging; however, our staff is inventive — includes choreographer and composer. Write innovative theater that explores topics of concern/interest to young people, that takes risks. We concentrate more on ensemble than individual roles, too. We do *not* want to see fairy tales or trite rehashings of things children have seen/heard since the age of two. See theater as education, rather than 'children being cute'."

Tips: "It is important for young people and their families to explore and confront issues relevant to growing up in the 90s. Theater is a marvelous teaching tool that can educate while it entertains."

NEW PLAYS INCORPORATED, Dept. WM, P.O. Box 5074, Charlottesville VA 22905-5074. (804)979-2777. Publisher: Patricia Whitton. Estab. 1964. Publishes an average of 4 plays/year. Publishes for producers of plays for young audiences and teachers in college courses on child drama. Query with synopsis. Reports in 2 months. Agent for amateur and semi-professional productions, exclusive agency for script sales. Pays 50% royalty on productions; 10% on script sales. Free catalog.

Needs: Plays for young audiences with something innovative in form and content. Length: usually 45-90 minutes. "Should be suitable for performance by adults for young audiences." No skits, assembly programs, improvisations or unproduced scripts.

NEW PLAYWRIGHTS' PROGRAM, The University of Alabama, P.O. Box 870239, Tuscaloosa AL 35487-0239. (205)348-9032. Fax: (205)348-9098. Director/Dramaturg: Dr. Paul C. Castagno. Endowed by Gallaway Fund, estab. 1982. Produces at least 1 new play/year. Mainstage and second stage. Collaborations with Stillman College and Theatre Tuscaloosa, University Theatre, The University of Alabama. Submit complete ms. Playwrights may submit potential workshop ideas for consideration. Reports in 3-6 months. Accepts scripts in various forms: new dramaturgy to traditional. If you are a recent MFA playwriting graduate (within 1 year) you may be given consideration for ACTF productions. Send SASE. Stipends competitive with or exceed most contests.

‡THE NEW THEATRE GUILD, #303, 570 N. Rossmore Ave., Los Angeles CA 90004. Artistic Director: George Hale. Estab. 1987. Produces 2-3 plays/year. USA (Los Angeles/New York) and Western Europe. Query with synopsis; submit complete script or agented submissions. Reports in 2 months. Negotiable.

Needs: Full length plays—comedies and dramas. Lead characters mid-thirties and political/social issues. Especially interested in female lead, mid-thirties or aging (20-45) at this time.

NEW TUNERS THEATRE, 1225 W. Belmont Ave., Chicago IL 60657. (312)929-7287. Literary Manager: Allan Chambers. Produces 1-3 new musicals/year. 66% developed in our New Tuners workshop. "Some scripts produced are unagented submissions. Plays performed in a small off-Loop theater seating 148 for a general theater audience, urban/suburban mix. Submit synopsis, cover letter and cassette selections of the score, if available. Reports in 3 months. Next step is script and score (reports in 6 months). "Submit first, we'll negotiate later." Pays 5-10% of gross. "Authors are given a stipend to cover a residency of at least two weeks."
Needs: "We're interested in all forms of musical theater including more innovative styles. Our production capabilities are limited by the lack of space, but we're very creative and authors should submit anyway. The smaller the cast, the better. We are especially interested in scripts using a younger (35 and under) ensemble of actors. We mostly look for authors who are interested in developing their script through workshops, rehearsals and production. No casts over 12. No one-man shows."
Tips: "We would like to see the musical theater articulating something about the world around us, rather than merely diverting an audience's attention from that world."

‡NINE O'CLOCK PLAYERS, 1367 N. St. Andrews Place, Los Angeles CA 90028. (213)469-1973. Artistic Director: Arien O'Hara. Estab. 1928. Produces 2 plays/year. "Plays produced at Assistance League Playhouse by resident amateur and semi-professional company. All plays are musical adaptations of classical children's literature. Plays must be appropriate for children ages 4-12." Query and synopsis. Reports in 1 month. Pays negotiable royalty or per performance.
Needs: "Plays must have at least 15 characters and be 1 hour 15 minutes long. Productions are done on a proscenium stage in classical theater style. All plays must have humor, music and good moral values. No audience participation improvisational plays."

NORTHLIGHT THEATRE, 2840 Sheridan Rd.., Evanston IL 60201. (708)869-7732. Artistic Director: Russell Vandenbroucke. Estab. 1975. Produces 5 plays/year. "We are a professional, Equity theater, LORT D. We perform in a 630-seat house. We have a subscription base of 5,800, and have a significant number of single ticket buyers." Query with synopsis. Reports in 3 months. Buys production rights plus royalty on future mountings. Pays royalty and fee to playwright that is a guarantee against royalties.
Needs: "Full-length plays, translations, adaptations, musicals. Interested in plays of 'ideas,' plays that are passionate and/or hilarious, stylistic exploration and complexity. Generally looking for cast size of eight or less, but there are always exceptions made for the right play."
Tips: "Please, do not try to do what television and film do better! Also, no domestic realism."

ODYSSEY THEATRE ENSEMBLE, 2055 S. Sepulveda Blvd., Los Angeles CA 90025. (310)477-2055. Literary Manager: Jan Lewis. Estab. 1965. Produces 9 plays/year. Plays performed in a 3-theater facility. "All three theaters are Equity 99-seat theater plan. We have a subscription audience of 3,000 for a nine-play main season, and they are offered a discount on our rentals and co-productions. Remaining seats are sold to the general public." Query with résumé, synopsis, cast breakdown and 8-10 pages of sample dialogue. Scripts must be securely bound. Reports in 1 month on queries; 6 months on scripts. Buys negotiable rights. Pays 5-7% royalty. "We will *not* return scripts without SASE."
Needs: "Full-length plays only with either an innovative form and/or provocative subject matter. We desire highly theatrical pieces that explore possibilities of the live theater experience. We are seeking full-length musicals and some plays with smaller casts (2-4). We are not reading one-act plays or light situation comedies. We are seeking Hispanic material for our resident Hispanic unit as well as plays from all cultures and ethnicities."

OLD GLOBE THEATRE, P.O. Box 2171, San Diego CA 92112-2171. (619)231-1941. Literary Manager: Raúl Moncada. Produces 12 plays/year. "We are a LORT B+ institution with three theaters: 581-seat mainstage, 225-seat arena, 621-seat outdoor. Our plays are produced for a single-ticket and subscription audience of 250,000 patrons from a large cross-section of southern California, including visitors from throughout the US." Submit complete script through agent only. One-page query or synopsis if not represented. Reports in 3-10 months. Buys negotiable rights. Royalty varies.
Needs: "We are looking for plays of strong literary and theatrical merit, works that display an accomplished sense of craft, and pieces that present a detailed cultural vision. All submissions must be full-length plays or musicals."

EUGENE O'NEILL THEATER CENTER'S NATIONAL PLAYWRIGHTS CONFERENCE and NEW DRAMA FOR MEDIA PROJECT, Suite 901, 234 W. 44th St., New York NY 10036-3909. (212)382-2790. Fax: (212)921-5538. Artistic Director: Lloyd Richards. Administrator: Lori Robishaw. Estab. 1965. Develops staged readings of 9-12 stage plays, 2-3 screenplays or teleplays/year. "We accept unsolicited scripts with no prejudice toward either represented or unrepresented writers. Our theater is located in Waterford, Connecticut, and we operate under an Equity LORT contract. We have three theaters: Barn—250 seats, Amphitheater—300 seats, Instant Theater—150 seats. Submission guidelines for #10 SASE in the fall. Complete bound, unproduced, original plays are eligible (no adaptations). Decision by late April. Pays stipend plus room, board and transportation. We accept script submissions from September 15-December 1 of each year. Conference takes place during July each summer."

● Scripts are selected on the basis of talent, not commercial potential.

Needs: "We use modular sets for all plays, minimal lighting, minimal props and no costumes. We do script-in-hand readings with professional actors and directors. Our focus is on new play/playwright development."

THE OPEN EYE: NEW STAGINGS, 270 W. 89th St., New York NY 10024-1705. (212)769-4143. Fax: (212)595-0336. Artistic Director: Amie Brockway. Estab. 1972. Produces 3 full-length plays/year plus a Lab series. "The Open Eye is a professional, Equity LOA and TYA 115-seat, off-off Broadway theater. Our audience includes a broad spectrum of ages and backgrounds." Submit letter of inquiry only. Playwright fee for mainstage varies.

Needs: "New Stagings is particularly interested in one-act and full-length plays that take full advantage of the live performance situation. We especially like plays that appeal to young people and adults alike."

OREGON SHAKESPEARE FESTIVAL ASSOCIATION, P.O. Box 158, Ashland OR 97520. (503)482-2111. Fax: (503)482-0446. Associate Director/Play Development: Cynthia White. Estab. 1935. Produces 12 plays/year. The Angus Bowmer Theater has a thrust stage and seats 600. The Black Swan is an experimental space and seats 150. The Elizabethan Outdoor Theatre seats 1,200 (stages almost exclusively Shakespearean productions there, mid-June through September). Query with synopsis, résumé and 10 pages of dialogue from unsolicited sources. Complete scripts from agents only. Reports in 6-18 months. Negotiates individually for rights with the playwright's agent. "Most plays run within our ten-month season for 6-10 months, so royalties are paid accordingly."

Needs: "A broad range of classic and contemporary scripts. One or two fairly new scripts/season. Also a play readings series which focuses on new work. Plays must fit into our ten month rotating repertory season. Black Swan shows usually limited to ten actors." No one-acts or musicals. Submissions from women and minority writers are strongly encouraged.

Tips: "Send your work through an agent if possible. Send the best examples of your work rather than all of it. Don't become impatient or discouraged if it takes six months or more for a response. Don't expect detailed critiques with rejections. I want to see plays with heart and soul, intelligence, humor and wit. We're seeking plays with characters that *live* – that exist as living beings, not simply mouthpieces for particular positions. Try to avoid TV writing (i.e., cliché situations, dialogue, characters), unless it's specifically for broad comic purposes. I also think theater is a place for the *word*. So, the word first, then spectacle and high-tech effects."

ORGANIC THEATER COMPANY, 3319 N. Clark, Chicago IL 60657. (312)327-2427. Estab. 1969. AEA, CAT and non-equity productions and workshops. Query with synopsis and 10 page sample. Reports in 1-3 weeks on queries. Negotiable royalty. Send inquiries to Literary Manager.

Needs: "We are seeking full-length or long one-acts – challenging plays that fully explore the theatrical medium; strong visual and physical potential (unproduced works only)."

‡PEOPLE'S LIGHT & THEATRE COMPANY, 39 Conestoga Rd., Malvern PA 19355. (610)647-1900. Co-Artistic Directors: Abigail Adams, Stephen Novelli. Estab. 1974. Produces 5-6 plays/year. LORT theater, general audience. Query with synopsis with 10 page dialogue sample. Reports in 6 months. Pays negotiable royalty.

Needs: Full-length, sometime one-acts, no musicals. Cast of 8-10 maximum. Prefers single set.

PERSEVERANCE THEATRE, 914 Third St., Douglas AK 99801. (907)364-2421. Artistic Director: Molly Smith. Produces 5 mainstage, 2-3 second stage plays/year. Professional productions, Southeast Alaska. Primarily Juneau audiences; occasional tours to other places. Query with synopsis, no unsolicited scripts. Reports in 6-8 months. Pays $25-50/performance.

Tips: "We are producing very few original pieces from writers outside of Alaska. Because of that, we are reading few new plays."

PIER ONE THEATRE, P.O. Box 894, Homer AK 99603. (907)235-7333. Artistic Director: Lance Petersen. Estab. 1973. Produces 5-8 plays/year. "Plays to various audiences for various plays – e.g. children's, senior citizens, adult, family, etc. Plays are produced on Kemai Peninsula." Submit complete script. Reports in 3 months. Pays $25-125/performance.

Needs: "No restrictions – willing to read *all* genres." No stock reviews, hillbilly or sitcoms.

Tips: "There are slightly increased opportunities for new works. Don't start your play with a telephone conversation. New plays ought to be risky business; they ought to be something the playwright feels is terribly important."

PIONEER DRAMA SERVICE, INC., P.O. Box 4267, Englewood CO 80155-4267. (303)779-4035. Fax: (303)779-4315. Publisher: Steven Fendrich. Estab. 1963. 10% freelance written. Plays are performed by high school, junior high and adult groups, colleges, churches and recreation programs for audiences of all ages. "We are one of the largest full-service play publishers in the country in that we handle straight plays, musicals, children's theater and melodrama." Publishes 15 plays/year; 20% musicals and 80% straight plays. Query only; no unsolicited scripts. Buys all rights. Reports in 2 months. Pays on royalty basis with some outright purchase. All submissions automatically entered in Shubert Fendrich Memorial Playwriting Contest. Contest guidelines for SASE.

Needs: "We use the standard two-act format, two-act musicals, religious drama, comedies, mysteries, drama, melodrama and plays for children's theater (plays to be done by adult actors for children). We are looking for more plays dealing with the problems of teens." Length: two-act musicals and comedies, up to 90 minutes; children's theater, 1 hour. Prefer many female roles, 1 simple set. Currently overstocked on one-act plays.

‡**PITTSBURGH PUBLIC THEATER,** Allegheny Square, Pittsburgh PA 15212. (412)323-8200. Artistic Director: Edward Gilbert. Estab. 1974. Produces 6 plays/year. Theodore L. Hazelett Theatre, 457 seats, thrust or arena seating. Query with synopsis or agented submissions. Reports in 3 months.
Needs: Full-length plays, adaptations, musicals.

□**PLAYERS PRESS, INC.,** P.O. Box 1132, Studio City CA 91614-0132. Senior Editor: Robert W. Gordon. "We deal in all entertainment areas and handle publishable works for film and television as well as theater. Performing arts books, plays and musicals. All plays must be in stage format for publication." Also produces scripts for video and material for cable television. 80% freelance written. 20-30 scripts/year unagented submissions; 5-15 books also unagented. Works with 1-10 unpublished/unproduced writers annually. Query. "Include #10 SASE, reviews and proof of production. All play submissions must have been produced and should include a flier and/or program with dates of performance." Reports in 1 month on queries; 1 year on mss. Buys negotiable rights. "We prefer all area rights." Pays variable royalty "according to area; approximately 10-75% of gross receipts." Also makes outright purchase of $100-25,000 or $5-5,000/performance.
Needs: "We prefer comedies, musicals and children's theater, but are open to all genres. We will rework the script after acceptance. We are interested in the quality, not the format. Performing Arts Books that deal with theater how-to are of strong interest."
Tips: "Send only material requested. Do not telephone."

PLAYS, The Drama Magazine for Young People, 120 Boylston St., Boston MA 02116-4615. Editor: Sylvia K. Burack. Estab. 1941. Publishes approximately 75 one-act plays and dramatic program material each school year to be performed by junior and senior high, middle grades, lower grades. "Scripts should follow the general style of *Plays*. Stage directions should not be typed in capital letters or underlined. No incorrect grammar or dialect." Desired lengths are: junior and senior high—15-20 double-spaced pages (20-30 minutes playing time); middle grades—10-15 pages (15-20 minutes playing time); lower grades—6-10 pages (8-15 minutes playing time). Pays "good rates on acceptance." Query first for adaptations. Reports in 2-3 weeks. Sample copy $3.50. Send SASE for specification sheet.
Needs: "Can use comedies, farces, melodramas, skits, mysteries and dramas, plays for holidays and other special occasions, such as Book Week; adaptations of classic stories and fables; historical plays; plays about black history and heroes; puppet plays; folk and fairy tales; creative dramatics; and plays for conservation, ecology or human rights programs."

PLAYWRIGHTS PREVIEW PRODUCTIONS, Lenox Hill Station, P.O. Box 1019, New York NY 10021-0036. Fax: (212)289-2168. Artistic Director: Frances Hill. Literary Manager: David Sheppard. Estab. 1983. Produces 2-3 plays/year. Professional productions off or off off-Broadway—throughout the year. General audience. Submit complete script. Reports in 4 months. If produced, option for 6 months. Pays royalty.
Needs: Both one-act and full-length; generally 1 set or styled playing dual. Good imaginative, creative writing. Cast limited to 3-7.
Tips: "We tend to reject 'living-room' plays. We look for imaginative settings. Be creative and interesting with intellectual content. All submissions should be bound. We are looking for plays with ethnic backgrounds."

‡**POPE THEATRE COMPANY,** 262 S. Ocean Blvd., Manalapan FL 33462. (407)585-3404. Producing Artistic Director: Louis Tyrrell. Estab. 1987. Produces 7 plays/year (5 during the regular season, 2 in the summer). "We are a fully professional (LOA) theater. We attract an audience comprised of both local residents and seasonal visitors. Many, but by no means all, of our subscribers are retirees." Agented submissions only. Reports in 6 months. Buys production rights only. Pays 6-10% royalty. "A reminder phone call is helpful if a playwright wants a script returned."
Needs: "We produce new American plays. We prefer to do Florida premieres of thought-provoking, socially-conscious, challenging plays. Our stage is relatively small, which prevents us from producing works with a large cast."

PORTLAND REPERTORY THEATER, 815 NW 12th, Portland OR 97209. (503)224-2403. Producing Artistic Director: Geoffrey Sherman. Literary Manager: Kit Koenig. Estab. 1980. Produces 9 plays/year. "Small, professional, not-for-profit, regional theater. Two stages: Mainstage—230 seat, proscenium with long-time subscriber base (age 30-70s); Stage II—160 seat thrust, new, for new plays/experimental works and a staged reading series." Query, synopsis, first 10-15 pages, character breakdown, set description and SASE. Agented submissions. Reports in 2-6 months. Pays percentage of gross.

Needs: Comedies, thriller, drama, small musicals; with smaller casts, no more than 2 sets to run approximately 2 hours. Cast not to exceed 8; no more than 2 sets.

Tips: "No puppet shows, mime, melodrama or children's shows."

PRIMARY STAGES COMPANY, INC., 584 Ninth Ave., New York NY 10036. (212)333-7471. Artistic Director: Casey Childs. Estab. 1983. Produces 4 plays, 3 workshops, over 100 readings/year. All plays are produced professionally off-Broadway at the 45th Street Theatre, 354 West 45th St. Query with synopsis. Reports in 3 months. "If Primary Stages produces the play, we ask for the right to move it for up to six months after the closing performance." Writers paid "same as the actors."

Needs: "We are looking for highly theatrical works that were written exclusively with the stage in mind. We do not want TV scripts or strictly realistic plays."

Tips: No "living room plays, disease-of-the-week plays, back-porch plays, father/son work-it-all-out-plays, etc."

QUAIGH THEATRE, 205 W. 89th St., New York NY 10024-1868. (212)787-0862. Artistic Director: Will Lieberson. Estab. 1973. Produces 4 major productions/year. Off off-Broadway. Query with synopsis. Reports in 1 month on queries; 6 months on scripts. Rights differ on each script. Pays variable royalty.

Tips: "No plays on familiar subjects done in a familiar way. Plays need action as well as words. Plays are not meant for public reading. If they work as readings they really are rotten plays."

THE QUARTZ THEATRE, 392 Taylor, Ashland OR 97520-3058. (503)482-8119. Artistic Director: Dr. Robert Spira. Estab. 1973. Produces several video films/year. Send 3 pages of dialogue and personal bio. Reports in 2 weeks. Pays 5% royalty after expenses.

Needs: "Any length, any subject, with or without music. We seek playwrights with a flair for language and theatrical imagination."

Tips: "We look at anything. We do not do second productions unless substantial rewriting is involved. Our theater is a stepping stone to further production. Our playwrights are usually well-read in comparative religion, philosophy, psychology, and have a comprehensive grasp of human problems. We seek the 'self-indulgent' playwright who pleases him/herself first of all."

‡RIVERSIDE THEATRE, INC., P.O. Box 3788, Vero Beach FL 32964. (407)231-5860. Artistic Director: Allen D. Cornell. Estab. 1985. Produces 6 plays/year. Professional Equity company. Audience is primarily affluent, older, retirees. Query with synopsis. Reports in 2-4 months. Pays commission for readings, royalty if fully staged.

Needs: For new play series, seeking works on timely issues, "alternative" theater; dramas or comedies of substance. No fluff or musicals. Prefer smallish cast—2-8 actors.

Tips: "No children's theater; no previously produced plays; no fluffy comedy or drama; no musicals—unless they are socially significant. Always send SASE—we will not respond otherwise."

THE ROAD COMPANY, P.O. Box 5278 EKS, Johnson City TN 37603-5278. (615)926-7726. Literary Manager: Christine Murdock. Estab. 1975. Produces 3 plays/year. "Our professional productions are intended for a general adult audience." Query with synopsis. Reports in 4 months. Pays royalty. "When we do new plays we generally try to have the playwright in residence during rehearsal for 3-4 weeks for about $1,000 plus room and board."

Needs: "We like plays that experiment with form, that challenge, inform and entertain. We are a small ensemble based company. We look for smaller cast shows of 4-6."

Tips: "We are always looking for 2-character (male/female) plays. We are interested in plays set in the South. We are most interested in new work that deals with new forms. We write our own plays using improvisational techniques which we then tour throughout the Southeast. When funding permits, we include one of our own new plays in our home season."

‡RUBBERTREE PRODUCTIONS, #511, 11301 W. Olympic Blvd., Los Angeles CA 90064. (213)939-6747. Estab. 1992. Produces 1 play/year. Equity-waiver/Los Angeles smaller (99 seat) theaters—audience: twenty something crowd. Query letter only—no phone calls. Reports in 2 weeks. Pay varies according to arrangement with writers.

Needs: Full length only—prefer plays targeted to "Generation X" audience.

‡SECOND STAGE THEATRE, P.O. Box 1807, Ansonia Station, New York NY 10023. (212)966-2465. Artistic Director: Carole Rothman. Estab. 1979. Produces 4 plays/year. Off-Broadway professional, 108 seat McGinn/Cazale Theatre; AEA; subscription audience. Query with synopsis, résumé and 5 pages sample dialogue to (Mr.) Erin Sanders Literary Manager/Dramaturg. Reports in 1 month. Buys variable rights. Pay varies. No unsolicited scripts.

Needs: New and previously produced American plays; "heightened" realism; sociopolitical issues; plays by women and minority writers.

‡**SHENANDOAH PLAYWRIGHTS RETREAT**, Rt. 5, Box 167F, Staunton VA 24401. (703)248-1868. Program Director: Robert Graham Small. Estab. 1976. Produces in workshop 11 plays/year. Submit complete script. Obtains no rights. Writers are provided fellowships, room and board to Shenandoah.

Tips: "We are looking for *good* material, not derivative; from writers who enjoy exploration with dedicated theater professionals. Kitchen-sink dramas and sitcoms are self-limiting. Live theater *must* be theatrical! Consider global issues. Look beyond your personal life-experience and explore connections that will lift your characters/conflicts to a more universal plane."

‡**SILVERHAWK L.L.C.**, P.O. Box 1640, Escondido CA 92033. Publishes 25-30 plays/year. Professional, community and college theaters. Submit complete script that can be written on. Reports in 2 months. Buys all rights. Pays 50% production royalty and 10% of script sales.

Needs: "We will look at all plays, but would particularly like to see one-act plays of literary and artistic merit that are suitable for one-act competitions. Also we'd like groups of three one acts that can use the same stage set, and groups of one-acts with a common theme, including seasonal. We have a youth and children's editor looking for children's plays of real merit. We will also consider unusual works and literary works that some publishers would consider to be not sufficiently commercial."

Tips: "Please don't send us children's plays that assume children are real morons. The same for amateur plays. Please be sure your story line is original. Mark children's plays Attn: Mary Jo Leap."

AUDREY SKIRBALL-KENIS THEATRE, Suite 304, 9478 W. Olympic Blvd., Beverly Hills CA 90212. (310)284-8965. Literary Manager: Mead Hunter. Estab. 1989. Produces 18-22 stage readings and 3-4 workshop productions/year. "We utilize three theater facilities in the Los Angeles area with professional director and casts. Our rehearsal readings and workshop productions are offered year-round. Our audience is the general public *and* theater professionals." Query with synopsis. Reports in 3-4 months. Obtains no rights. Pays $100 for stage readings; $500 for workshop productions.

Needs: "We need full-length original plays that have not yet had full productions which would benefit from a rehearsal reading as a means of further developing the play."

Tips: "We are a nonprofit organization dedicated to new plays and playwrights. We do not produce plays for commercial runs, nor do we request any future commitment from the playwright should their play find a production by virtue of our reading or workshop programs."

SOUTH COAST REPERTORY, P.O. Box 2197, Costa Mesa CA 92628-1197. (714)957-2602. Fax: (714)545-0391. Dramaturg: Jerry Patch. Literary Manager: John Glore. Estab. 1964. Produces 6 plays/year on mainstage, 5 on second stage. Professional nonprofit theater; a member of LORT and TCG. "We operate in our own facility which houses a 507-seat mainstage theater and a 161-seat second stage theater. We have a combined subscription audience of 21,000." Query with synopsis; scripts considered if submitted by agent. Reports in 4 months. Acquires negotiable rights. Pays negotiable royalty.

Needs: "We produce full-lengths. We prefer well-written plays that address contemporary concerns and are dramaturgically innovative. A play whose cast is larger than 15-20 will need to be extremely compelling and its cast size must be justifiable."

Tips: "We don't look for a writer to write for us—he or she should write for him or herself. We look for honesty and a fresh voice. We're not likely to be interested in writers who are mindful of *any* trends. Originality and craftsmanship are the most important qualities we look for."

SOUTHERN APPALACHIAN REPERTORY THEATRE (SART), Mars Hill College, P.O. Box 620, Mars Hill NC 28754-0620. (704)689-1384. Artistic Director: James W. Thomas. Asst. Managing Director: Gaynelle Caldwell. Estab. 1975. Produces 5 plays/year. "Since 1975 the Southern Appalachian Repertory Theatre has produced 866 performances of 94 plays and played to over 116,000 patrons in the 152-seat Owen Theatre on the Mars Hill College campus. The theater's goals are quality, adventurous programming and integrity, both in artistic form and in the treatment of various aspects of the human condition. SART is a professional summer theater company whose audiences range from students to senior citizens." Reports in 6-12 months. Also conducts an annual Southern Appalachian Playwrights' Conference in which 5 playwrights are invited for informal readings of their new scripts. Deadline for submission is October 1 and conference is held the last weekend in January. If script is selected for production during the summer season, an honorarium is paid to the playwright in the amount of $500. Please enclose SASE for return of script.

Needs: "Since 1975, one of SART's goals has been to produce at least one original play each summer season. To date, 31 original scripts have been produced. Plays by southern Appalachian playwrights or about southern Appalachia are preferred, but by no means exclusively. Complete new scripts welcomed."

STAGE ONE: The Louisville Children's Theatre, 425 W. Market St., Louisville KY 40202-3300. (502)589-5946. Fax: (502)589-5779. Producing Director: Moses Goldberg. Estab. 1946. Produces 6-7 plays/year. 20% freelance written; 15-20% unagented submissions (excluding work of playwright-in-residence). Plays performed by an Equity company for young audiences ages 4-18; usually does different plays for different age groups within that range. Submit complete script. Reports in 4 months. Pays negotiable royalty or $25-50/performance.

Needs: "Good plays for young audiences of all types: adventure, fantasy, realism, serious problem plays about growing up or family entertainment. Cast: ideally, ten or less. Honest, visual potentiality, worthwhile story and characters are necessary. An awareness of children and their schooling is a plus. No campy material or anything condescending to children. No musicals unless they are fairly limited in orchestration."

STAGE WEST, P.O. Box 2587, Fort Worth TX 76113. (817)924-9454. Artistic Director: Jerry Russell. Estab. 1979. Produces 8 plays/year. "We stage professional productions at our own theater for a mixed general audience." Query with synopsis. Reports in 3-6 months. Rights are negotiable. Pays 7% royalty.
Needs: "We want full-length plays that are accessible to a mainstream audience but possess traits that are highly theatrical. Cast size of ten or less and single or unit set are desired."

CHARLES STILWILL, Managing Artistic Director, Community Playhouse, P.O. Box 433, Waterloo IA 50704-0433. (319)235-0367. Estab. 1917. Plays performed by Waterloo Community Playhouse with a volunteer cast. Produces 11 plays (6 adult, 5 children's); 1-2 musicals and 9-10 nonmusicals/year; 1-3 originals. 17% freelance written; most unagented submissions. Works with 1-3 unpublished/unproduced writers annually. "We are one of few community theaters with a commitment to new scripts. We do at least one and have done as many as four a year. We have 4,300 season members. Average attendance is 3,000. We do a wide variety of plays. Our public isn't going to accept nudity, too much sex, too much strong language. We don't have enough Black actors to do all-Black shows. Theater has done plays with as few as 2 characters, and as many as 98. On the main stage, we usually pay between $400 and $500. We also produce children's theater. Submit complete script. Please, no loose pages. Reports negatively within 1 year, but acceptance sometimes takes longer because we try to fit a wanted script into the balanced season. We sometimes hold a script longer than a year if we like it but cannot immediately find the right slot for it. We just did the world premiere of *The Ninth Step* which was written in 1989 and last year we did the midwest premiere of *Grace Under Pressure* which was written in 1984. January 1995 we will do the World Premiere of *First Child*."
Needs: "For our Children's Theater and our Adult Biannual Holiday (Christmas) show, we are looking for good adaptations of name children's stories or very good shows that don't necessarily have a name. We produce children's theater with both adult and child actors."

TACOMA ACTORS GUILD, 6th Floor, 901 Broadway, Tacoma WA 98402-4404. (206)272-3107. Fax: (206)272-3358. Artistic Director: Bruce K. Sevy. Estab. 1978. Produces 6-7 plays/year. Plays perfomed at Theatre On The Square. Audience consists of playgoers in the south Puget Sound region. Query with synopsis. Reports in 2-4 months on queries; 1 year on scripts. Rights negotiable. Pays negotiable royalty or makes outright purchase of $500 minimum.
Needs: "Full length. Single or simple set. Modest cast (two-seven). Comedy, drama, musical. Our budgets are modest."
Tips: "No extreme language, violence, nudity, sexual situations. We don't do a *lot* of new work so opportunities are limited."

TADA!, 120 W. 28th St., New York NY 10001. (212)627-1732. Artistic Director: Janine Nina Trevens. Estab. 1984. Produces 2-4 plays/year. "TADA! produces original musicals and plays performed by children at our 95-seat theater. Productions are for family audiences." Submit complete script and tape, if musical. Reports in 6 months. Pays 5% royalty or commission fee (varies).
Needs: "Generally pieces run from 45-70 minutes. Must be enjoyed by children and adults and performed by a cast of children ages 6-17."
Tips: "No redone fairy tales or pieces where children are expected to play adults. Be careful not to condescend when writing for children's theater."

THE TEN-MINUTE MUSICALS PROJECT, P.O. Box 461194, West Hollywood CA 90046. (213)656-8751. Producer: Michael Koppy. Estab. 1987. Produces 1-10 plays/year. "Plays performed in Equity regional theaters in the US and Canada." Submit complete script, lead sheets and cassette. Deadline August 31; notification by December 15 annually. Buys performance rights. Pays $250 royalty advance upon selection, against equal share of performance royalties when produced. Submission guidelines for #10 SASE.
Needs: "We are looking for complete short stage musicals playing between 7-14 minutes. Limit cast to ten (five women, five men). No fairy tales or works based on contemporary news events."
 • See the Insider Report interview with Michael Koppy in the 1995 *Songwriter's Market*.

THEATER ARTISTS OF MARIN, P.O. Box 150473, San Rafael CA 94915. (415)454-2380. Artistic Director: Charles Brousse. Estab. 1980. Produces 3 plays/year. Professional showcase productions for a general adult audience. Submit complete script. Reports in 6 months. Assists in marketing to other theaters and offers script development assistance.
Needs: "All types of scripts: comedy, drama, farce. Prefers contemporary setting, with some relevance to current issues in American society. Will also consider 'small musicals,' reviews or plays with music." No children's shows, domestic sitcoms, one-man shows or commercial thrillers.

THE THEATER OF NECESSITY, 11702 Webercrest, Houston TX 77048. (713)733-6042. Artistic Director: Philbert Plumb. Estab. 1981. Produces 4 plays/year. Plays are produced in a small professional theater. Submit complete script. Reports in 1 year. Buys performance rights. Pays standard royalties based on size of house for small productions or individual contracts for large productions (average $500/run). "We usually keep script on file unless we are certain we will never use it." Send SASE for script and #10 SASE for response.
Needs: "Any play in a recognizable genre must be superlative in form and intensity. Experimental plays are given an easier read. We move to larger venue if the play warrants the expense."

THEATRE & COMPANY, 20 Queen St. N., Kitchener, Ontario N2H 2G8 Canada. Artistic Director: Stuart Scadron-Wattles. Literary Manager: Wes Wikkerink. Estab. 1988. Produces 4 plays/year. Semi-professional productions for a general audience. Query with synopsis and SAE with IRCs. Reports in 3 months. Pays $50-100/performance.
Needs: "One-act or full-length; comedy or drama; musical or straight; written from or compatible with a biblical world view." No cast above 10; prefers unit staging. Looking for small cast (less than 5) ensemble comedies.
Tips: Looks for "non-religious writing from a biblical world view for an audience which loves the theater. Avoid current trends toward shorter scenes. Playwrights should be aware that they are writing for the stage — not television. We encourage audience interaction, using an acting ensemble trained in improvisation."

THEATRE DE LA JEUNE LUNE, 105 N. First St., Minneapolis MN 55401-1411. (612)332-3968. Artistic Directors: Barbra Berlovitz Desbois, Vincent Garcieux, Robert Rosen, Dominique Serrand. Estab. 1979. Produces 2-3 plays/year. Professional nonprofit company producing September-May for general audience. Query with synopsis. Reports in 3 months. Pays royalty or per performance. No unsolicited scripts, please.
Needs: "All subject matter considered, although plays with universal themes are desired; plays that concern people of today. We are constantly looking for plays with large casts. Generally *not* interested in plays with 1-4 characters. No psychological drama or plays that are written alone in a room without the input of outside vitality and life."
Tips: "We are an acting company that takes plays and makes them ours; this could mean cutting a script or not heeding a writer's stage directions. We are committed to the performance in front of the audience as the goal of all the contributing factors; therefore, the actors' voice is extremely important."

THEATRE VIRGINIA, 2800 Grove Ave., Richmond VA 23221-2466. Artistic Director: George Black. Estab. 1955. Produces 5-8, publishes 0-1 new play/year. Query with synopsis and 15 page sample. Accepts agented submissions. Solicitations in 1 month for initial query, 3-8 months for script. Rights negotiated. Payment negotiated.
Needs: No one-acts; no children's theater.

THEATRE WEST, 3333 Cahuenga W., Los Angeles CA 90068-1365. Contact: Jan Harris. Estab. 1962. Produces 6 plays/year. "99-seat waiver productions in our theater. Audiences are primarily young urban professionals." Submit script, résumé and letter requesting membership. Reports in 2 months. Buys 5% of writer's share of sale to another media. Pays royalty "based on gross box office — equal to all other participants."
Needs: Uses minimalistic scenery.
Tips: "TW is a dues-paying membership company. Only members can submit plays for production. So you must seek membership prior to action for a production."

THEATREWORKS, University of Colorado, P.O. Box 7150, Colorado Springs CO 80933-7150. (719)593-3232. Fax: (719)593-3582. Producing Director: Ronnie Storey. Estab. 1975. Produces 4 full-length plays/year and 2 new one-acts. "New full-length plays produced on an irregular basis. Casts are semi-professional and plays are produced at the university." Query with synopsis. No unsolicited scripts. One-act plays are accepted as Playwrights' Forum competition entries. Submit complete script. Deadline: December 1; winners announced March 1. Two one-act competition winners receive full production, cash awards and travel allowances. Acquires exclusive regional option for duration of production. Full rights revert to author upon closing. Pays $200 prize plus travel and accommodations.
Needs: Full-lengths and one-acts — no restrictions on subject. "Cast size should not exceed 20; stage area is small with limited wing and fly space. Theatreworks is interested in the exploration of new and inventive theatrical work. Points are scored by imaginative use of visual image and bold approach to subject." No melodrama or children's plays.

For information on setting your freelance fees, see How Much Should I Charge?

Tips: "Too often, new plays seem far too derivative of television and film writing. We think theater is a medium which an author must specifically attack. The standard three-act form would appear to be obsolete. Economy, brevity and innovation are favorably received."

THEATREWORKS/USA, 890 Broadway, New York NY 10003. (212)677-5959. Artistic Director: Jay Harnick. Literary Manager: Barbara Pasternack. Produces 3 new musical plays/season. Produces professional musicals and plays that primarily tour (TYA contract) but also play at an off-Broadway theater for a young audience. Query with synopsis or sample song. Reports in 8 months. Buys all rights. Pays 6% royalty. Offers $1,500 advance against future royalties for new, commissioned plays.
Needs: Musicals and plays with music for children. Historical/biographical themes (ages 8-15), classic litera-ture, fairy tales, and issue-oriented themes and material suitable for young people ages 5-12. Five person cast, minimal lighting. "We like well-crafted shows with good dramatic structure—a protagonist who wants something specific, an antagonist, a problem to be solved—character development, tension, climax, etc. No Saturday Afternoon Special-type shows, shows with nothing to say or 'kiddie' theater shows or fractured fairy tales. We do not address high school audiences."
Tips: "Writing for kids is just like writing for adults—only better (clearer, cleaner). Kids will not sit still for unnecessary exposition and overblown prose. Long monologues, soliloquies and 'I Am' songs and ballads should be avoided. Television, movies and video make the world of entertainment highly competitive. We've noticed lately how well popular children's titles, contemporary and in public domain, sell. We are very interested in acquiring adaptations of this type of material."

‡**STEVE TYLER**, 6915 Fantain Ave., Los Angeles CA 90028. Estab. 1991. Produces 4 plays/year. "Mostly 99 AEA seat plan theater—with hopes to move to a larger venue." Query with synopsis. Reports in months. Royalty varies.
Needs: Full-length plays that are political, topical, controversial and/or a great comedy. Prefers smaller casts (less than 8).

‡**UNICORN THEATRE**, 3820 Main St., Kansas City MO 64111. (816)531-PLAY. Producing Artistic Director: Cynthia Levin. Produces 6-8 plays/year. "We are a professional Equity Theatre. Typically, we produce plays dealing with contemporary issues." Query with synopsis and sample dialogue. Will not consider unsolicited scripts. Reports in 2 months.
Needs: Prefers contemporary (post-1950) scripts. Does not accept musicals, one-acts, or historical plays. When a script is requested, include a brief synopsis, a bio, a character breakdown, SASE if script is to be returned, a self-addressed, stamped post card for acknowledgement of receipt is desired. A royalty/prize of $1,000 will be awarded the playwright of any play selected through this process, The National Playwright Award. This script receives production as part of the Unicorn's regular season.

THE UNUSUAL CABARET, 14½ Mt. Desert St., Bar Harbor ME 04609. (207)288-3306. (Phone *only* June through mid-October). Owner: Christopher Mitchell. Estab. 1990. "Our audience tends to be youthful (25-50) and educated. They are tourists from all over the world, as well as dedicated, local regulars." Produces 3 plays/year. Reports on submissions in 1 month. "We produce two musical scripts and one non-musical script every season. Scripts must be 45-75 minutes in length and require no more than eight actors. Our space is intimate, with minimal technical capacity. We always strive for the unusual in format and subject matter, without sacrificing accessibility." Submit completed script (with tape, if applicable). Pays 10-12% royalty.
Tips: "As a true cabaret in the tradition of the Chat Noir and Cabaret Voltaire, we attempt to narrow or even eliminate the distance between spectator and performer, so pervasive in elitist or high art. We look for non-naturalistic scripts which are simultaneously challenging and playful. We encourage writers to be in-volved in the actual production process."

‡**VIGILANTE THEATRE CO.**, P.O. Box 507, Bozeman MT 59771-0507. (406)586-3897. Artistic Director: John M. Hosking. Estab. 1982. Produces 3-4 plays/year. Plays by professional touring company that does produc-tions by or about people and themes of the Northwest. "Past productions were concerned with homeless people, agriculture, literature by Northwest writers, one-company towns and spouse abuse in rural areas." Submit complete ms. Reports in 6 months. Pays $10-50/performance.
Needs: Produces full-length plays and some one-acts. "Staging suitable for a small touring company and cast limited to four actors (two men, two women). Double casting actors for more play characters is also an option."
Tips: "No musicals requiring orchestras and a chorus line. Although we prefer a script of some thematic substance, the company is very adept at comedy and would prefer the topic to include humor."

VIRGINIA STAGE COMPANY, P.O. Box 3770, Norfolk VA 23514-3770. (804)627-6988. Fax: (804)628-5958. Literary Manager: Jefferson H. Lindquist. Estab. 1979. VSC is a LORT C-1 theatre serving southeastern Virginia audiences. Performing spaces are mainstage (700-seat) theatre with proscenium stage and a 99-seat second stage. Produces 4-6 plays/year. Accepts and encourages unsolicited scripts—especially from playwrights residing in Virginia. Submission time: January-April. Responds in 6 months. Scripts returned to author or agent only if postage is included.

Needs: Full-length plays, and musicals with tapes only.

WALNUT STREET THEATRE, 9th and Walnut Streets, Philadelphia PA 19107. (215)574-3550. Executive Director: Bernard Havard. Literary Manager: Alexa Kelly. Estab. 1809. Produces 5 mainstage and 4 studio plays/year. "Our plays are performed in our own space. WST has 3 theaters—a proscenium (mainstage), 1,052 seats; 2 studios, 79-99 seats. We have a subscription audience, second largest in the nation." Query with synopsis and 10 pages. Reports in 5 months. Rights negotiated per project. Pays royalty (negotiated per project) or outright purchase.

Needs: "Full-length dramas and comedies, musicals, translations, adaptations and revues. The studio plays must be small cast, simple sets."

Tips: "We will consider anything. Bear in mind that on the mainstage we look for plays with mass appeal, Broadway-style. The studio spaces are our off-Broadway. No children's plays. Our mainstage audience goes for work that is entertaining and light. Our studio season is when we look for plays that have bite and are more provocative."

WEST COAST ENSEMBLE, P.O. Box 38728, Los Angeles CA 90038. (213)871-8673. Artistic Director: Les Hanson. Estab. 1982. Produces 6 plays/year. Plays performed in 1 of 2 theaters in Hollywood. Submit complete script. Reports in 6-9 months. Obtains exclusive rights in southern California to present the play for the period specified. All ownership and rights remain with the playwright. Pays $25-45/performance. Writers guidelines for #10 SASE.

Needs: Prefers a cast of 6-12.

Tips: "Submit the script in acceptable dramatic script format."

WESTBETH THEATRE CENTER, INC., 151 Bank St., New York NY 10014-2049. (212)691-2272. Fax: (212)924-7185. Producing Director: Arnold Engelman. Literary Manager: Steven Bloom. Estab. 1977. Produces 10 readings and 6 productions/year. Professional off-Broadway theater. Submit complete ms with SASE. Responds in 4 months. Obtains rights to produce as showcase with option to enter into full option agreement.

Needs: "Contemporary full-length plays. Production values (i.e., set, costumes, etc.) should be kept to a minimum." No period pieces. Limit 10 actors; doubling explained.

THE WHITE-WILLIS THEATRE, (formerly The Ann White Theatre), 5266 Gate Lake Rd., Fort Lauderdale FL 33319. (305)772-4371. Artistic Director: Ann White. Estab. 1984. Produces 6 plays/year. "Alternative theater, professional productions for mature audiences. Plays performed in various settings: libraries, theaters, colleges and universities, hotels and dinner theaters." Conducts annual playwrights' competition and festival. Submit scripts June 1-August 1 for productions in spring. SASE for guidelines. Winning playwright receives $500 and production by The White-Willis Theatre.

Tips: "We are always interested in plays that focus on contemporary issues."

‡THE WILMA THEATER, 2030 Sansom St., Philadelphia PA 19103-4417. (215)963-0249. Artistic Directors: Ms. Blanka Zizka, Mr. Jiri Zizka. Estab. 1973. Produces 4 plays/year. Leading regional theater; professional Equity productions (A.E.A. Letter of Agreement) in city of Philadelphia. Some co-productions with other regional and New York theaters. The Wilma has a subscription audience of 4,000 and a reputation as the "Philadelphia equivalent of off-Broadway." Query with synopsis. Pays royalty.

Needs: "Innovative, artistic theater; full-length productions of a variety of genres and topics. Special interest in works from the international repertoire, new plays, plays with music, and plays with passionate, universal sensibility. Stage is small, requires unit or relatively simple sets; cast sizes of 12 are difficult."

Tips: "Please be patient in waiting for a response; please be sure to enclose an SAS postcard with synopsis submission; send an up to 10-page dialogue sample with synopsis."

THE WOMEN'S PROJECT AND PRODUCTIONS, 7 W. 63rd St., New York NY 10023-7102. (212)873-3040. Artistic Director: Julia Miles. Estab. 1978. Produces 3 plays/year. Professional Off-Broadway productions. Query with synopsis and 10 sample pages of dialogue. Reports in 1 month on queries.

Needs: "We are looking for full-length plays, written by women."

WOOLLY MAMMOTH THEATRE COMPANY, Dept. WM, 1401 Church St. NW, Washington DC 20005-1903. (202)393-3939. Artistic Director: Howard Shalwitz. Literary Manager: Jim Byrnes. Produces 5 plays/year. 50% freelance written. Produces professional productions for the general public in Washington, DC. 2-3 scripts/year unagented submissions. Works with 1-2 unpublished/unproduced writers annually. Accepts unsolicited scripts. Reports in 3 months on scripts; very interesting scripts often take much longer. Buys first- and second- class production rights. Pays 5% royalty.

• Writer John Rolfe Gardner received a Lila Wallace-Reader's Digest Fund Award to present a series of programs of dramatized short fiction with the Wooly Mammoth Theater.

Needs: "We look only for plays that are highly unusual in some way. Also interested in multicultural projects. Apart from an innovative approach, there is no formula. One-acts are not used." Cast limit of 8.

Screenwriting

Practically everyone you meet in Los Angeles, from your airport cabbie on, is writing a script. It might be a feature film, movie of the week, TV series or documentary, but the sheer amount of competition can seem overwhelming. Some will never make a sale, while others make a decent living on sales and options without ever having any of their work produced. But there are those writers who make a living doing what they love and see their names roll by on the credits. How do they get there? How do *you* get there?

First, work on your writing. You'll improve with each script, so there is no way of getting around the need to write and write some more. It's a good idea to read as many scripts as you can get your hands on. Check your local bookstores and libraries. Script City (Suite 1500, 8033 Sunset Blvd., Hollywood CA 90046, (800)676-2522) carries thousands of movie and TV scripts, classics to current releases, as well as books, audio/video seminars and software in their $2 catalog. Book City (Dept. 101, 308 N. San Fernando Blvd., Burbank CA 91502, (800)4-CINEMA) has film and TV scripts in all genres and a large selection of movie books in their $2.50 catalog.

There are lots of books that will give you the "rules" of format and structure for writing for TV or film. Samuel French (7623 Sunset Blvd., Hollywood CA 90046 (213)876-0570) carries a number of how-to books and reference materials on these subjects. The correct format marks your script as a professional submission. Most successful scriptwriters will tell you to learn the correct structure, internalize those rules—and then throw them away and write intuitively.

Writing for TV

To break into TV you must have spec scripts—work written for free that serves as a calling card and gets you in the door. A spec script showcases your writing abilities and gets your name in front of influential people. Whether a network has invited you in to pitch some ideas, or a movie producer has contacted you to write a first draft for a feature film, the quality of writing in your spec script got their attention and that may get you the job.

It's a good idea to have several spec scripts, perhaps one each for three of the top five shows in the format you prefer to work in, whether it's sitcom (half-hour comedies), episodic (one hour series) or movie of the week (two hour dramatic movies). Perhaps you want to showcase the breadth of your writing ability; some writers have a portfolio of a few eight o'clock type shows (i.e., *Mad About You, Home Improvement*), a few nine-o'clock shows (i.e., *Murphy Brown, Seinfeld*) and one or two episodics (i.e., *Northern Exposure, Law and Order, NYPD Blue*). These are all "hot" shows for writers and can demonstrate your abilities to create believable dialogue for characters already familiar to your intended readers. For TV and cable movies you should have completed original scripts (not sequels to existing movies) and you might also have a few for episodic TV shows.

In choosing the shows you write spec scripts for you must remember one thing: don't write a script for a show you want to work on. If you want to work on *Northern Exposure*, you'll send a *Law and Order* script and vice versa. It may seem contradictory, but it is standard practice. Writers and producers can feel very proprietary about their show and their stories. They may not be objective enough to fairly evaluate your writing. In submitting another similar type of show you'll avoid that problem while demonstrating comparable skills.

In writing your TV script you must get *inside* the show and understand the characters' internal motivations. You must immerse yourself in how the characters speak, think and interact. Don't introduce new characters in a spec script for an existing show—write believable dialogue for the characters as they are portrayed. Be sure to choose a show that you like—you'll be better able to demonstrate your writing ability through characters you respond to.

You must also understand the external factors. How the show is filmed bears on how you write. Most sitcoms are shot on videotape with three cameras, on a sound stage with a studio audience. Episodics are often shot on film with one camera and include on-location shots. *Mad About You* has a flat, evenly-lit look and takes place in the Buckman's apartment, the restaurant and Paul's studio. *Law and Order* has a gritty realism with varying lighting and a variety of settings from Stone's office to a bodega on East 135th.

Another important external influence in writing for TV is the timing of commercials in conjunction with the act structure. There are lots of sources detailing the suggested content and length of acts, but generally a sitcom has a teaser (short opening scene), two acts and a tag (short closing scene), and an episodic has a teaser, four acts and a tag. Each act closes with a turning point. Watching TV analytically and keeping a log of events will reveal some elements of basic structure. *Successful Scriptwriting*, by Wolff & Cox, offers detailed discussions of various types of shows.

Writing for the movies

With feature films you may feel at once more liberated and more bound by structure. An original movie script contains characters you have created, with storylines you design, allowing you more freedom than you have in TV. However, your writing must still convey believable dialogue and realistic characters, with a plausible plot and high-quality writing carried through the roughly 120 pages. The characters must have a problem that involves the audience. When you go to a movie you don't want to spend time watching the *second* worst night of a character's life. You're looking for the big issue that crystallizes a character, that portrays a journey with important consequences.

At the same time you are creating, you should also be constructing. Be aware of the basic three act structure for feature films. Scenes can be of varying lengths, but are usually no longer than three to three and a half pages. Some writers list scenes that must occur, then flesh them out from beginning to end, writing with the structure of events in mind. The beginning and climactic scenes are the easiest; it's how they get there from here that's difficult.

Many novice screenwriters tend to write too many visual cues and camera directions into their scripts. Your goal should be to write something readable, like a "compressed novella." Write succinct resonant scenes and leave the camera technique to the director and producer. In action/adventure movies, however, there needs to be a balance since the script demands more visual direction.

It seems to be easier for TV writers to cross over to movies. Cable movies bridge the two, and are generally less derivative and more willing to take chances with a higher quality show designed to attract an audience not interested in network offerings. Cable is also less susceptible to advertiser pullout, which means it can tackle more controversial topics.

Feature films and TV are very different and writers occupy different positions. TV is a medium for writers and producers; directors work for them. Many TV writers are also producers. In feature films the writers and producers work for the director and often have little or no say about what happens to the work once the script has been sold. For TV the writer pitches the idea; for feature films generally the producer pitches the idea and then finds a writer.

Marketing your scripts

If you intend to make writing your profession you must act professionally. Accepted submission practices should become second nature.

- The initial pitch is made through a query letter, which is no longer than one page with a one paragraph synopsis and brief summary of your credits if they are relevant to the subject of your script.
- Never send a complete manuscript until it is requested.
- Almost every script sent to a producer, studio or agent must be accompanied by a release form. Ask for that company's form when you receive an invitation to submit the whole script. Mark your envelope "release form enclosed" to prevent it being returned unread.
- Always include a self-addressed stamped envelope if you want your work returned; a disposable copy may be accompanied by a self-addressed stamped postcard for reply.
- Allow four to six weeks from receipt of your manuscript before writing a follow-up letter.

When your script is requested, be sure it's written in the appropriate format. Unusual binding, fancy covers or illustrations mark an amateur. Three brass brads with a plain or black cover indicate a pro.

There are a limited number of ideas in the world, so it's inevitable that similar ideas occur to more than one person. Hollywood is a buyers' market and a release form states that pretty clearly. An idea is not copyrightable, so be careful about sharing premises. The written expression of that idea, however, can be protected and it's a good idea to do so. The Writers Guild of America can register scripts for television and theatrical motion pictures, series formats, storylines and step outlines. You need not be a member of the WGA to use this service. Copyrighting your work with the Copyright Office of the Library of Congress also protects your work from infringement. Contact either agency for more information and an application form.

If you are a writer, you should write—all the time. When you're not writing, read. There are numerous books on the art, craft and business of screenwriting. See the Publications of Interest at the end of *Writer's Market* for a few or check the catalogs of companies previously mentioned. The different trade papers of the industry such as *Daily Variety* and *Hollywood Reporter* can keep you in touch with the day to day doings and upcoming events. Specialty newsletters such as *Hollywood Scriptwriter*, *Creative Screenwriting* and *New York Scriptwriter* offer tips from successful scriptwriters and agents. The *Hollywood Creative Directory* is an extensive list of production companies, studios and networks that also lists companies and talent with studio deals.

Computer services, such as America Online, have various bulletin boards and chat hours for scriptwriters that provide contact with other writers and a chance to share information and encouragement.

It may take years of work before you come up with a script someone is willing to take a chance on. Those years need to be spent learning your craft and understanding the business. Polishing scripts, writing new material, keeping current with the industry and networking constantly will keep you busy. When you do get that call you'll be confident in your abilities and know that your hard work is beginning to pay off.

For information on more screenwriting markets, see Scriptwriting Markets/ Changes '94-'95 at the end of the Screenwriting section.

‡□**ALL AMERICAN COMMUNICATIONS**, #224, 5301 Beethoven St., Los Angeles CA 90066. (310)301-1721. Contact: Dan Watanabe. Estab. 1974. Produces *Baywatch*, *Acapulco Heat* and *Sirens*. Looking for television

programs—syndicated, network, cable original. Works with 10 writers/year. Buys all rights. Reports in 1 month. Query with synopsis. Pay varies depending on project.
Needs: Looking for one-hour dramatic TV series proposals or movies of the week.

ALLIED ARTISTS, INC., Suite 377, 859 N. Hollywood Way, Burbank CA 91505. (818)594-4089. Vice President, Development: John Nichols. Estab. 1990. Produces material for broadcast and cable television, home video and theater. Buys 3-5 scripts/year. Works with 10-20 writers/year. Buys first rights or all rights. Accepts previously produced material. Reports in 2 months on queries; 3 months on scripts. Submit synopsis/outline. Pays in accordance with Writers Guild standards (amount and method negotiable).
Needs: Films (16, 35mm), videotapes. Social issue TV special (30-60 minutes); special interest home video topics; instruction and entertainment; positive values feature screenplays.
Tips: "We are looking for positive, up-lifting dramatic stories involving real people situations. Future trend is for more reality-based programming, as well as interactive television programs for viewer participation."

ANGEL FILMS, 967 Hwy. 40, New Franklin MO 65274-9778. (314)698-3900. Fax: (314)698-3900. Vice President Production: Matthew Eastman. Estab. 1980. Produces material for feature films, television. Buys 10 scripts/year. Works with 20 writers/year. Buys all rights. Accepts previously published material (if rights available). Reports in 1 months on queries; 1-2 months on scripts. Query with synopsis. Makes outright purchase "depending upon budget for project. Our company is a low-budget producer which means people get paid fairly, but don't get rich."
Needs: Films (35mm), videotapes. "We are looking for projects that can be used to produce feature film and television feature film and series work. These would be in the areas of action adventure, comedy, horror, thriller, science fiction, animation for children."
Tips: "Don't copy others. Try to be original. Don't overwork your idea. As far as trends are concerned, don't pay attention to what is 'in'. By the time it gets to us it will most likely be on the way 'out.' And if you can't let your own grandmother read it, don't send it. If you wish material returned, enclose proper postage with all submissions. Send SASE for response to queries and return of scripts."

ANGEL'S TOUCH PRODUCTIONS, Suite B, 1055 Allen Ave., Glendale CA 91201-1654. Director of Development: Phil Nemy. Estab. 1986. Professional screenplays and teleplays. Send synopsis. Reports in 6 months. Rights negotiated between production company and author. Payment negotiated.
Needs: All types, all genres, only full-length teleplays and screenplays—no one-acts.
Tips: "We are now only seeking feature film screenplays, television screenplays, and episodic teleplays."

ASKA FILM PRODUCTIONS, Suite 211, 1600 De Lorimier, Montreal, Quebec H2K 3W5 Canada. Fax: (514)521-7103. Story Editor: Natalya Rybina. Estab. 1979. Buys 2 scripts/year. Works with 2 writers/year. Buys all rights. Accepts previously produced material. Reports in 3 months. Submit completed script. Pays in accordance with Writers Guild standards.
Needs: Films (35mm).

BARNSTORM FILMS, (formerly Tony Bill Productions), 73 Market St., Venice CA 90291. (310)396-5937. Contact: Denise Stewart. Estab. 1969. Produces feature films. Has an overall deal with MGM Studios. Buys 2-3 scripts/year. Works with 4-5 writers/year. Reports in 2 months. Submit synopsis and SASE. Pays in accordance with Writers Guild standards or option.
Needs: 35mm films.

☐**BIG STAR MOTION PICTURES LTD.,** #201, 13025 Yonge St., Richmond Hill, Ontario L4E 1Z5 Canada. (416)720-9825. Contact: Frank A. Deluca. Estab. 1991. Buys 5 scripts/year. Works with 5-10 writers/year. Reports in 1 month on queries; 2 months on scripts. Submit synopsis. "We deal with each situation differently and work on a project-by-project basis.
Needs: Films (35mm). "We are very active in all medias, but are primarily looking for television projects, cable, network, etc. True life situations are of special interest for M.O.W."

‡**BLACKTAIL PRODUCTIONS,** P.O. Box 462061, Los Angeles CA 90046. President: Michael Valdes. Estab. 1993. Audience concentration is low-budget action films. Buys 5 scripts/year. Works with 10-15 writers/year. Buys all rights. No previously produced material. Reports in 2-3 months on queries; 3-5 months on scripts. Catalog for #10 SASE. Query with synopsis, complete script, résumé, SASE and contact numbers. Pay varies.
Needs: Films (16, 35mm), videotapes. Looking for "action films—well-written, character driven—overall budget $200,000-300,000; script $ accordingly."

‡**BLUE RIDER PICTURES,** 2800 28th St., Santa Monica CA 90404. (310)314-8246. Contact: Henry Seggerman. Estab. 1991. Theatrical, home video material. Buys 15 scripts/year. Works with 30 writers/year. Buys film and TV rights. No previously produced material. Reports in 1 month. Query with synopsis and résumé. Pays option against purchase price.

Needs: Films (35mm). Will need 25 completed screenplays suitable for independent production and distribution in the next 18 months.

‡**BOZ PRODUCTIONS,** 7612 Fountain Ave., Los Angeles CA 90046. (213)876-3232. Estab. 1987. All audiences. Buys 3-5 scripts/year. Works with several writers/year. Buys all rights. Accepts previously produced material. Reports in 1 month on queries; 1-2 months on scripts. Query with synopsis and résumé. Pay varies.
Needs: Films (35mm). Feature-length film scripts or rights to real stories for MOW's.

‡**BREAKNECK FEATURES,** 739 N. Occidental Blvd., Los Angeles CA 90026. (213)413-7091. Producer: Charles Doane. Estab. 1991. Feature film and television. Buys 5-10 scripts/year. Works with 5-6 writers/year. Buys all rights. Accepts previously produced material. Reports in 1 month on queries; 1 month on scripts. Query with synopsis and résumé. Pays royalty or makes outright purchases in accordance with Writers Guild standards.
Needs: Films (16, 35mm). "Looking for feature films and television film scripts in all genres including films to be produced in America, Canada, South Africa, England, Ireland and Australia."

THE BROOKLYN BRIDGE PEOPLE, 5460 White Oak, Encino CA 91316. (818)986-3813. Producer: Bert Steinberger. Estab. 1991. Produces material for all audiences. Buys/options 2-3 scripts/year. Works with 4-6 writers/year. "The company puts it's effort in committing financeable actors and directors to scripts before presenting to Majors and private investors." Reports in 1 month. Query. Pays in accordance with Writers Guild standards.
Needs: Films (35mm). Highly original concepts and great execution. Feature material only.
Tips: "We are predominantly interested in finding and developing new writers."

‡**CAREY-IT-OFF PRODUCTIONS,** 5215 Saloma Ave., Van Nuys CA 91411-3949. (818)789-0954. Fax: (818)789-5967. President: Kathi Carey. Estab. 1984. Works with 1-2 writers/year. Buys all rights. No previously produced material. Reports in 6 months on queries; 6 months on scripts.
Needs: Looking for true stories to develop for MOWs—stories can be written as teleplays or not. Please do *not* send unsolicited scripts; all unsolicited scripts will be returned. Query with synopsis or treatment. Always enclose SASE. Makes outright purchase in accordance with Writers Guild standards.
Tips: "Please do not send articles by registered or certified mail. Do *not* call. You will be notified of any interest in your work."

‡**CINE/DESIGN FILMS, INC.,** P.O. Box 6495, Denver CO 80206. (303)777-4222. Producer/Director: Jon Husband. Produces educational material for general, sales-training and theatrical audiences. 75% freelance written; 90% unagented submissions. "Original, solid ideas are encouraged." Rights purchased vary.
Needs: Films (16, 35mm). "Motion picture outlines in the theatrical and documentary areas. We are seeking theatrical scripts in the low-budget area that are possible to produce for under $1 million. We seek flexibility and personalities who can work well with our clients." Send 8-10-page outline before submitting ms. Pays $100-200/screen minute on 16mm productions. Theatrical scripts negotiable.
Tips: "Understand the marketing needs of film production today. Materials will not be returned."

‡**CINE QUA NON PICTURES,** 8489 W. Third St., Los Angeles CA 90048. Director, Development and Acquisitions: Alicia Hollinger. Estab. 1993. Produces material for all audiences. Works with 20 writers/year. Buys option rights. No previously produced material. Reports in 1 month on queries; 2 months on submissions. Query with synopsis. All terms and conditions are negotiable.
Needs: Films (35mm). " 'A' quality movies, feature-length, WGA protected."
Tips: "Make sure script looks professional. Science fiction, high-tech, action, hip youth-oriented. Erotic thrillers are losing steam."

CLARK PRODUCTIONS, INC., P.O. Box 773, Balboa CA 92661. President: Mr. Clark. Estab. 1987. General audience. Buys 1 script/year. Works with 4 writers/year. Buys first rights. No previously produced material. Reports in 6 months. Submit synopsis/outline. Pays in accordance with Writers Guild standards.
Needs: "We will rewrite existing screenplay (owned). Full-length motion picture, *The Ralph DePalma Story*."

□**CORNERSTONE PRODUCTIONS,** #600, 6290 Sunset Blvd., Hollywood CA 90028-8710. (213)871-2255. Fax: (213)871-1627. Development Executive: John Burlein. Estab. 1969. Produces material for the Disney Channel, After School Specials, network TV movies and cable movies (USA, HBO, etc.). Buys 2 scripts/year. Works with 4 writers/year. Buys all rights. Reports in 2 months. Query with SASE. Pays in accordance with Writers Guild standards. Payment negotiable.
Needs: "We are currently seeking completed screenplays or treatments."

‡**CREATIVE EDGE FILMS,** #1070, 100 Wilshire Blvd., Santa Monica CA 90401. Partner: Martin Wiley. Estab. 1982. Feature films. Buys 1-2 scripts/year. Options more. Works with 5-6 writers/year. Buys first or all rights

and standard film options. Reports in 1 month. Query with synopsis or complete script. Pays option to purchase at fixed price with some percentage and/or escalators possible.

Needs: Films (35mm). Feature film screenplays or adaptable other material for major and independent features. All genres.

Tips: "Story structure, a well-constructed screenplay and readability are key."

‡□**CRONUS INTERNATIONAL ENTERTAINMENT, INC.,** #4, 5110 Tujunga Ave., North Hollywood CA 91601-4925. (818)763-1977. Producing Director: Herb Rodgers. "The company was formed in 1990 for the purpose of selecting screenplays and developing them for production, either as movies of the week for network/cable, or for production for feature length films for distribution internationally. All scripts should follow professional format and be 100-120 pages in length. Authors of selected scripts will be contacted about options to produce. Only scripts with SASE will be returned."

‡**DAKOTA NORTH ENTERTAINMENT,** Hollywood TV Studios, Bldg. 11, 5800 Sunset Blvd., Los Angeles CA 90028. Producer/Director: Troy Miller. Estab. 1987. Works with 4-8 writers/year. No previously produced material. Reports in 1 month. Query with synopsis. Pay varies.

Needs: Films (16, 35mm), videotapes, multimedia kits. Looking for "theatrical: original screenplays for production (broad comedy, action, adventure); multimedia: event-oriented or self-contained properties for CD-ROM."

EARTH TRACKS PRODUCTIONS, Suite 286, 4809 Avenue N., Brooklyn NY 11234. Contact: David Krinsky. Estab. 1985. Produces material for "major and independent studios." Buys 1-3 scripts/year. Buys all rights. No books, no treatments, no articles. *Only* completed movie and TV movie scripts. Reports in 6 weeks on queries.

Needs: Commercial, well-written, high concept scripts in the drama, comedy, action and thriller genres. No other scripts. Query with 1-page synopsis. No treatments. Include SASE. *Do not send any scripts unless requested.*

Tips: "Can always use a *good* comedy. Writers should be flexible and open to suggestions. Material with interest (in writing) from a known actor/director is a *major plus* in the consideration of the material. We also need sexy thrillers. Any submissions of more than two pages will *not* be read or returned."

● This producer notes a high rate of inappropriate submissions. Please read and follow his guidelines carefully.

‡**EAST EL LAY FILMS,** 12041 Hoffman St., Studio City CA 91604. (818)769-4565. President: Daniel Kuhn. Estab. 1992. Audience is low-budget feature films for television markets. Buys 2 scripts/year. Works with many writers/year. Buys first rights and options for at least 1 year with refusal rights. Accepts previously produced material. Reports in 3-4 weeks on queries. Query with synopsis and résumé. Pays royalty, makes outright purchase or option fee.

Needs: Film loops (35mm), videotapes.

‡**ECLECTIC FILMS, INC.,** Suite 200, 650 N. Bronson Ave., Los Angeles CA 90004. Principals: Robert Schaffel, Youssef Vahabzadeh. Vice President, Creative Affairs: Sharon Roesler. Feature film audience—worldwide. Reports in 1-2 months on script. Call or write to request permission to submit completed screenplays.

ENTERTAINMENT PRODUCTIONS, INC., Suite 744, 2210 Wilshire Blvd., Santa Monica CA 90403. (310)456-3143. Producer: Edward Coe. Contact: Story Editor. Estab. 1971. Produces films for theatrical and television (worldwide) distribution. Reports in 1 month (only if SASE is enclosed for reply and/or return of material).

Needs: Screenplays. Only unencumbered originals. Query with synopsis. Makes outright purchase for all rights. Price negotiated on a project-by-project basis. Writer's release in any form will be acceptable.

Tips: "State why script has great potential."

FINE ART PRODUCTIONS, 67 Maple St., Newburgh NY 12550. (914)561-5866. Contact: Richie Suraci. Estab. 1992. Produces material for all genres. Buys variable number of scripts/year. Works with variable number of writers/year. Buys first rights, all rights, "varies with project. Negotiable." Accepts previously produced material. Reports in 3-6 months. Catalog for 8½ × 11 SAE with 52¢ postage. Query with synopsis, outline, script and résumé. "Everything is negotiable by project, varies per project."

Needs: Charts, film loops (all formats), films (all formats), kinescopes, microfilm, videotapes, multimedia kits, phonograph records, silent and sound filmstrips, teaching machine programs, overhead transparencies, slides, study prints, tapes and cassettes, models. "Looking for all genres. Submit or we won't know it exists."

‡**EDWARD D. HANSEN, INC.,** 437 Harvard Dr., Arcadia CA 91006-2639. (818)447-3168. President: Ed Hansen. Supervisor, Literary Development: Buck Flower. Estab. 1973. Theatrical, TV and home video markets comprise our audience. Optioned, purchased, marketed and/or produced 10 screenplays in 1993. Reports in 3 months.

Needs: Looking for scripts for feature films, movies of the week and home videos: all genres. Query with synopsis and SASE for release form. Pays in accordance with Writers Guild standards. Professional assistance available for novel or play adaptations, concept development and certain properties not "ready to shoot" that contain unique characters or an extremely marketable storyline.
Tips: "Don't try to tap into a trend. By the time you get it done, it's gone. What comes around goes around."

INTERNATIONAL HOME ENTERTAINMENT, Suite 650, 1440 Veteran Ave., Los Angeles CA 90024. (213)460-4545. Assistant to the President: Jed Leland, Jr. Estab. 1976. Buys first rights. Reports in 2 months. Query. Pays in accordance with Writers Guild standards. *No unsolicited scripts.*
• Looking for material that is international in scope.

JAG ENTERTAINMENT, 4508 Noeline Ave., Encino CA 91436. President/CEO: Jo-Ann Geffen. Estab. 1992. Produces material for TV/film, audience ages 18-40. Works with "many" writers/year. Buys all rights. No previously produced material. Reports in 1 month on queries; 3 months on scripts. Submit synopsis/outline, complete script and résumé.
Needs: "Features, TV movies only; reality shows and 'smart' children's series." Looking for "female character-driven pieces. True stories are particularly interesting."

KJD TELEPRODUCTIONS, 30 Whyte Dr., Voorhees NJ 08043. (609)751-3500. President: Larry Scott. Estab. 1989. Broadcast audience. Buys 6 scripts/year. Works with 3 writers/year. Buys all rights. No previously produced material. Reports in 1 month. Free catalog. Query. Makes outright purchase.
Needs: Films, videotapes, multimedia kits.

KN'K PRODUCTIONS INC., 5230 Shira Dr., Valley Village CA 91607-2300. (818)760-3106. Fax: (818)788-6606 or (818)760-3106. Creative Director: Katharine Kramer. Contact: Martin Shapiro. Estab. 1992. "Looking for film material with strong roles for mature women (ages 40-55 etc.). Also roles for young women and potential movie musicals, message movies." Buys 3 scripts/year. Works with 5 writers/year. Buys all rights. No previously produced material. Reports in 2-3 months. Catalog for #10 SASE. Submit synopsis, complete script and résumé. Pays in accordance with Writers Guild standards or partnership.
Needs: Multimedia kits. "Doing more partnerships with writers as opposed to just Writers Guild minimum. Concentration on original vehicles for the mature actress to fill the gap that's missing from mainstream cinema."
Tips: "We are seeking inspirational true/life stories such as women overcoming obstacles, human growth, movie musicals."
• Kn'K is looking particularly for female-driven vehicles for mature actresses, 45-55.

DAVID LANCASTER PRODUCTIONS, 3356 Bennett Dr, Los Angeles CA 90068-1704. Story Editor: Scott ... Estab. 1985. Feature films audience. Buys 8-10 scripts/year. Works with 18-25 writers/year. Buys film and TV rights. No previously produced material. Reports in 2-3 weeks on queries; 2 weeks on scripts. Query with synopsis.
Needs: Action oriented screenplays, dramas with an edge.
Tips: "We will accept nothing without a release on outside of envelope. Please do not call us."

‡RON LEVINSON PRODUCTIONS, #312, 1545 26th St., Santa Monica CA 90404. (310)449-3290. TV and film material. Buys first and all rights. Submissions through agents or with release.

LIGHTVIEW ENTERTAINMENT, Suite 571, 11901 Santa Monica Blvd., Los Angeles CA 90025. Producer: Laura McCorkindale. Estab. 1991. Buys 20 scripts/year. Buys all rights. Options include purchase price which incorporates all rights. Send 1-2 page detailed synopsis with SASE to the attention of Vivian Poutakoglou. "We will respond via mail within 2 months to let you know if we want to see your screenplay. If we request your screenplay after reading synopsis, please allow 3 months for a second response." Purchase price negotiable.
Needs: Mostly feature film screenplays and books (only if they would adapt well to film). Occasionally will look at teleplays intended as Movies of the Week. Feature film screenplays range from smaller budget independent films to big budget studio films. All genres.
Tips: "Take time writing your synopsis and be detailed! Synopsis should be well written as your screenplay. Be sure it is at least one page—but not more than two! Although we are looking for all types of screenplays, we are especially drawn to inspirational stories that enlighten and entertain. We do not accept unsolicited phone calls, so please correspond only through the mail."

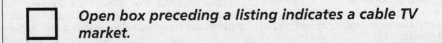

Open box preceding a listing indicates a cable TV market.

MARS PRODUCTIONS CORPORATION, 10215 Riverside Dr., Toluca Lake CA 91602. (818)980-8011. Executive Assistant: Julia Fakhouri. Estab. 1969. Produces family and action films. Buys 3 scripts/year. Works with 5 writers/year. Buys all rights, options. No previously produced material. Reports in 3 months. Query with synopsis/outline. Makes outright purchase "depending on the project."
Needs: Film (35mm).
Tips: "Follow the standard script format. I do not like too much detail of action or camera angles."

☐**MEDIACOM DEVELOPMENT CORP.**, P.O. Box 6331, Burbank CA 91510-6331. (818)594-4089. Director/Program Development: Felix Girard. Estab. 1978. 80% freelance written. Buys 8-12 scripts annually from unpublished/unproduced writers. 50% of scripts produced are unagented submissions. Query with samples. Reports in 1 month. Buys all rights or first rights.
Needs: Produces films, multimedia kits, tapes and cassettes, slides and videotape with programmed instructional print materials, broadcast and cable television programs. Publishes software ("programmed instruction training courses"). Negotiates payment depending on project. Looking for new ideas for CD-ROM titles.
Tips: "Send short samples of work. Especially interested in flexibility to meet clients' demands, creativity in treatment of precise subject matter. We are looking for good, fresh projects (both special and series) for cable and pay television markets. A trend in the audiovisual field that freelance writers should be aware of is the move toward more interactive video disc/computer CRT delivery of training materials for corporate markets."

THE MERRYWOOD STUDIO, #75, 137 E. 38th St., New York NY 10016-2650. Creative Director: Raul daSilva. Estab. 1984. Produces animated motion pictures for entertainment audiences. "We are planning to severely limit but not close out freelance input. Will be taking roughly 5-7%. However, we might be seeking a few *experienced* top writers for new children's animation business (age 10 and above/crossover to adult)."
Needs: Proprietary material only. Human potential themes woven into highly entertaining drama, high adventure, comedy. This is a new market for animation with only precedent in the illustrated novels published in France and Japan. Cannot handle unsolicited mail/scripts and will not return mail. Open to *agented* submissions of credit sheets, concepts and synopses only. Profit sharing depending upon value of concept and writer's following. Will pay at least Writers Guild levels or better, plus expenses.
Tips: "This is *not a market for beginning writers*. Established, professional work with highly unusual and original themes is sought. If you love writing, it will show and we will recognize it and reward it in every way you can imagine. We are not a 'factory' and work on a very high level of excellence."

‡**MILWAUKEE FILMWORKS**, #610, 9595 Wilshire Blvd., Beverly Hills CA 90212. Contact: Douglas. Estab. 1991. Film and television audience. Buys 2 scripts/year. Works with 6 writers/year. Buys screenplays-option. Accepts previously produced material. Will return submissions on a case to case basis. Reports in 1 month. Query with complete script. Pay varies in accordance with Writers Guild standards.
Needs: Films (35mm).

‡**MNC FILMS**, P.O. Box 16195, Beverly Hills CA 90209-2195. Contact: Mark Cohen. Estab. 1991. Feature film audience. Buys 2 scripts/year. Works with 3 writers/year. Buys all rights or purchases option on screenplay. Accepts previously produced material. Reports in 2 months. Query with synopsis. Pays in accordance with Writers Guild standards (work for hire) or variable fee for option of material.
Needs: Film (35mm). Feature length films. "I'm looking for story-driven films with well-developed characters. Screenplays or books easily adaptable for lower budget (few locations, stunts, special effects)."
Tips: "In the past I have received many submissions from writers who obviously did not pay attention to the type of material that I am looking for. I personally believe that stories with more of an emphasis on individuals and relationships are more interesting and many times more successful than stories driven by other elements."

MONAREX HOLLYWOOD CORPORATION, 9421½ W. Pico Blvd., Los Angeles CA 90035. (310)552-1069. Fax: (310)552-1724. President: Chris D. Nebe. Estab. 1978. Producers of theatrical and television motion pictures and miniseries; also international distributors. Buys 5-6 scripts/year. Buys all rights. Reports in 2 months.
Needs: Films (35mm), videotapes. "We are seeking action, adventure, comedy and character-oriented love stories, dance, horror and dramatic screenplays." Submit synopsis/outline and complete script with SASE. Pays in accordance with Writers Guild standards.
Tips: "We look for exciting visuals with strong characters and a unique plot."

‡**MONTIVAGUS PRODUCTIONS**, Suite 203, 6310 Hazeltine Ave., Van Nuys CA 91401. (818)782-1212. Executive VP, Creative Affairs: Mary Alvarado. Estab. 1990. Buys 3 scripts/year. Works with 3-4 writers/year. Buys all rights. Reports in 1-3 months on queries; 1 month on scripts. Query with synopsis only. Pays in accordance with Writers Guild standards.
Needs: Films (35mm), videotapes.

‡MOXIE PICTURES INC., 1040 N. Sycamore Ave., Hollywood CA 90038. (213)957-5420. Artistic Director: Gary Rose. Estab. 1989. Looking for films and MOWs. Query with synopsis. Reports in 2-8 weeks on submissions. Pay varies.
Tips: Does not want to see animation projects. Sees a trend for more female-driven plots.

‡NEVER A DULL MOMENT PRODUCTIONS, 1406 N. Topanga Canyon Blvd., Topanga CA 90290. (310)455-1651. Contact: Lisa Hallas Gottlieb. Estab. 1986. General audience. Buys 3 scripts/year. Works with 10 writers/year. Buys all rights. Reports in 1 month on queries; 2 months on submissions. Query with synopsis. Buys minimal option with agreement; if script is sold will pay at least WGA minimum.
Needs: Films (35mm), videotapes. Full-length scripts for TV movies and features. Prefer dramas, romantic comedies and science fiction.

NEW & UNIQUE VIDEOS, 2336 Sumac Dr., San Diego CA 92105. (619)282-6126. Creative Director: Candace Love. Estab. 1982. General TV and videotape audiences. Buys 10-15 scripts/year. Buys first rights, all rights. No previously produced material. Reports in 1-2 months. Catalog for #10 SASE. Query with synopsis. Makes outright purchase, negotiable.
Needs: Videotapes.
Tips: "We are seeking unique slants on interesting topics in 60-90 minute special-interest videotape format. Imagination and passion, not to mention humor are pluses. Titles produced include "Massage for Relaxation"; "Ultimate Mountain Biking" and "Full Cycle: World Odyssey." "No threatical titles. Please study the genre and get an understanding of what 'special interest' means." Trends: "We are moving toward moving pictures (i.e. video, computers, CD-ROM, etc.) in a big way as book sales diminish. If writers can adapt to the changes, their work will always be in demand."

NEW LINE PRODUCTIONS, Suite 200, 116 N. Robertson Blvd., Los Angeles CA 90048. Fax: (310)854-1824. Story Editor: Brian Morewitz. "Agented submissions only. Query letter, including synopsis, must be sent first. No unsolicited submissions, even from agents." Reports in 1 month.

‡NO MAS ENTERTAINMENT, (formerly AAFTA Entertainment), Suite 211, 1222 N. Olive Dr., Los Angeles CA 90069. (213)650-7191. President: J. Jay Cohen. Estab. 1987. Produces material for 18-62 year old audience. Buys 1 script/year. Works with 2 writers/year. Buys first rights, all rights. Accepts previously produced material. Reports in 1-2 months on queries; 2-3 months on scripts. Query with synopsis and complete script. Pay varies, but minimum in accordance with Writers Guild standards.
Needs: Films (16, 35mm), videotapes. Erotic thrillers, action adventures, dramas and comedies—completed scripts for film and TV movies of the week, no longer than 110 pages, preferably. "Any slant, any subject!"
Tips: "Submit script-sized SASE with all submissions. Also, please don't submit scripts that are loose with no brads or aren't held together by a folder of some sort. Difficult to handle by reader and quite frankly, it's a lousy presentation."

‡OCEAN PARK PICTURES, 220 Main St., Venice CA 90291. (310)450-1220. Executive Producer: Tim Goldberg. Estab. 1989. All audiences. Buys 5 scripts/year. Works with 10 writers/year. Buys first or all rights. Accepts previously produced material. Reports in 1 month on queries; 2 months on scripts. Query with synopsis, complete script and résumé. Pay varies.
Needs: Film (35mm).

‡ODYSSEY INTERNATIONAL, P.O. Box 230902, Encinitas CA 92023. Contact: Gary Schmad. Estab. 1983. General, educational, mature/adult audience. Buys 2-3 scripts/year. Works with 2-3 writers/year. Buys all rights. No previously produced material. Reports in 2 months on queries. Catalog for #10 SASE. Query with synopsis. Pays 2-8% royalty or will consider outright purchase.
Needs: Films (16, 35mm), videotapes. Sitcom—"Flannigan's Last Resort"—Cheers in a topless bar (22½-28½ minutes); Feature—"R" exotic adventure (90-115 mintues); Video—Playboy style with Shakespearean ploys (58 minutes); Travelog—"On the Road"—off-beat travel series (22½ minutes).
Tips: "Our venue is sexy, but tasteful. No sleaze, please."

PACE FILMS, INC., PHC, 411 E. 53rd St., New York NY 10022. (212)755-5486. President: R. Vanderbes. Estab. 1965. Produces material for a general theatrical audience. Buys all rights. Reports in 2 months.
Needs: Theatrical motion pictures. Produces and distributes 35mm motion pictures for theatrical, TV and videocassettes. Query with synopsis/outline and writing background/credits. Submit complete script, outline and SASE. Pays in accordance with Writers Guild standards.

PARALLEL PICTURES, P.O. Box 985B, Hollywood CA 90078. New Projects Executive: Rick Tyler. Estab. 1988. "For a general audience, ages 16-45; depends on project. We produce for domestic as well as overseas audiences." Works with 3 writers/year. Buys all rights. No previously published material. Reports in 2 months on queries; 6 months on scripts.

Needs: Films (35mm). "We are looking for feature-length screenplays—action/adventure, romantic comedy. We accept all genres—very openminded. We love rare and new ideas." Submit a short synopsis of script or project with a release form. Makes outright purchase.
Tips: "Take risks. I see too many replicas and poor development. If I don't see a plan of action or direction by the first 30 pages, something is wrong. Plots make the movie. That doesn't mean having many plots. You can keep it simple. Also, 80 pages is not feature length. Please bind all material. We won't look at a script made up of loose papers. Don't call us. We will call you."

☐ **TOM PARKER MOTION PICTURES,** #285, 3941 S. Bristol, Santa Anna CA 92704. (714)545-2887. Fax: (714)545-9775. President: Tom Parker. Produces and distributes feature-length motion pictures worldwide for theatrical, home video, pay and free TV. Also produces short subject "special interest films (30, 45, 60 minutes). Works with 5-10 scripts/year. Previously produced and distributed "Amazing Love Secret" (R), "Amorous Adventures of Ricky D." (R), and "The Sturgis Story" (R). Reports in 3-6 months. "Follow the instructions herein and do not phone for info or to inquire about your script."
Needs: "Complete script *only* for low budget (under $1 million) "R" or "PG" rated action/thriller, action/ adventure, comedy, adult romance (R), sex comedy (R), family action/adventure to be filmed in 35mm film for the theatrical and home video market (do not send TV movie scripts, series, teleplays, stage plays). *Very limited dialogue.* Scripts should be action-oriented and fully described. Screen stories or scripts OK, but no camera angles please. No heavy drama, documentaries, social commentaries, dope stories, weird or horror. Violence or sex OK, but must be well motivated with strong story line." Submit synopsis and description of characters with finished scripts. Makes outright purchase: $5,000-25,000. Will consider participation, co-production.
Tips: "Absolutely will not return scripts or report on rejected scripts unless accompanied by SASE."

‡**PLOTPOINT INC.,** Suite 301, 723 Westmount Dr., Los Angeles CA 90069. Contact: Rick Gitelson. Estab. 1987. Feature film and television audience. Buys 3 scripts/year. Works with 6-10 writers/year. Buys all rights. Accepts previously produced material. Reports in 1 month. Query with synopsis. Pay varies.

THE PUPPETOON STUDIOS, P.O. Box 2019, Beverly Hills CA 90213. Producer/Director: Arnold Leibovit. Estab. 1987. "Broad audience." Works with 5 writers/year. Buys all rights. Reports in 1 month on queries; 2 months on scripts. Query with synopsis. Submit complete script. A Submission Release *must* be included with all queries. Produced and directed "The Puppetoon Movie." SASE required for return of all materials— otherwise they will not be returned." Pays in accordance with Writers Guild standards. No novels, plays, poems, treatments; no submissions on computer disk.
Needs: Films (35mm). "We are seeking animation properties including presentation drawings and character designs. The more detailed drawings with animation scripts the better."

‡**RAINMAKER PRODUCTIONS,** 433 K St., Davis CA 95616. Producer/Publisher: Anastasia Ashman. Estab. 1992. Intelligent well rounded urban audience. Buys 1 ms/year. Works with 5 writers/year. Buys options, adaptations, screenplay rights, depends on the material's prospects. No previously produced material. Reports in 1 month. Query with synopsis of unpublished novels suitable for adaptation or publication. Pay varies. Options or makes outright purchase.
Needs: "Looking for fiction and nonfiction: clever suspense; women's back-to-nature issues; ecology and preservation; alternative health and fitness; feature length novels, progressive, positive; new family rearing techniques—post-self help."
Tips: "Give small companies a chance if you're a first-time writer; although their network may be small, the attention and understanding a new writer gets is far superior. A lot less heartache, more communication and opportunity to participate."

‡**ROCKET PICTURES,** #300, 9560 Wilshire Blvd., Beverly Hills CA 90212. (310)550-3300. Director of Development: Rod Park. Audience encompasses all ages, emphasis on teenage themes. Buys 20-25 scripts/year. Buys first or all rights. No previously produced material. Reports in 1-2 months. Query with synopsis. Pays in accordance with Writers Guild standards.
Needs: Films (35mm), videotapes, multimedia kits.

‡**ROSSHEIM PRODUCTIONS,** #15, 2441 Beverly Ave., Santa Monica CA 90405. President: Phyllis Caroll. Estab. 1991. TV and feature film audience. Buys several scripts/year. Works with several writers/year. Buys TV and movie/feature rights. Produced 1993 ABC TV movie "For Their Own Good." Reports in 3 months. Query with synopsis of story and complete script. "I am also looking for true stories for TV MOWs. I prefer news articles or some documentation to accompany material." Pay varies in accordance with Writers Guild standards. Must include SASE for return of materials.

‡**RUSH STREET PRODUCTIONS,** Suite 200, 8881 W. Pico Blvd., Los Angeles CA 90035. (310)550-0824. Producer/Writer: Jordan Rush. Head of Development: Suzanne Fenton. Estab. 1990. Film and TV audience.

Works with unlimited writers/year. Buys all rights. Produced "Clubfed" (feature) and "Coach" (TV). Reports in 2 weeks on queries. Send résumé.

‡**SCENENES PRODUCTIONS,** (formerly Papillon Productions), 1712 Anacapa St., Santa Barbara CA 93101. Phone/Fax: (805)569-0733. Los Angeles Office: 8670 Wilshire Blvd., Beverly Hills CA 90211. (310)289-6100. Head of Acquisitions: Emmanuel Itier. Estab. 1989. Produces material for any audience. Buys 5 scripts/year. Works with 4 writers/year. Buys all rights. Accepts previously produced material. Reports in 1 month. Free catalog. Submit complete script and résumé. Pays in accordance with Writers Guild standards.
Needs: Films. "We are seeking any screenplay for full-length motion pictures."
Tips: "Be patient but aggressive enough to keep people interested in your screenplay."

THE SHELDON/POST COMPANY, 1437 Rising Glen Rd., Los Angeles CA 90069. (213)467-7989. Producers: David Sheldon and Ira Post. Estab. 1989. "We produce theatrical motion pictures, movies and series for television. Have contracts with Twentieth Century-Fox and Aaron Spelling Entertainment. Options and acquires all rights. Reports in 1 month. Query with detailed synopsis and SASE. Pays in accordance with Writers Guild standards. No advance payments.
Needs: "We look for all types of material, including strong women's stories, suspense thrillers, action-adventure—scripts or treatments." True stories must include documentation.
Tips: "Write realistic stories with strong characters with whom the viewer can identify. Be original."

‡**SHORELINE PICTURES,** #1774, 1901 Avenue of the Stars, Los Angeles CA 90067. (310)551-2060. Director of Development: Peter Soby, Jr. Estab. 1993. Mass audiences. Buys 8 scripts/year. Works with 8 writers/year. Buys all rights. Reports immediately on queries; 1 week on submissions. Query. Pays in accordance with Writers Guild standards.
Needs: Films (35, 70mm). Looking for "character-driven films that are very commercial. No exploitation or horror. Comedies and dramas, yes. Want completed screenplays only. We are especially keen to find a comedy. Note, there is an audience for adult films as reflected in films like *The Piano*, *The Player*, *Crying Game*, *Joy Luck Club*, etc. Principal of our company co-produced *Glengarry Glen Ross*."

‡**SILHOUETTE PICTURES,** 12420 Albers St., North Hollywood CA 91607. Contact: Laszlo Bene or Rizelle Mendoza. Estab. 1992. Buys 3 scripts/year. Works with 6 writers/year. Buys all rights. No previously produced material. Reports in 1 month on queries. Query with synopsis/outline. Pays in accordance with Writers Guild standards.
Needs: Films (35mm). Full-length theatrical features—low budget (up to 3M). Genres: action adventure, thriller, character-driven drama.
Tips: "Focus on stories of personal convictions. Don't be afraid of controversial subject matters."

SOUTH FORK PRODUCTIONS, P.O. Box 1935, Santa Monica CA 90406-1935. Producer: Jerry Burke. Estab. 1980. Produces material for TV and film. Buys 2 scripts/year. Works with 4 writers/year. Buys all rights. No previously produced material. Send synopsis/outline and motion picture treatments, plus previous credits. Do not send complete script. Pays in accordance with Writers Guild Standards.
Needs: Films (16, 35mm), videotapes.
Tips: "Follow established formats for treatments. SASE for return."

‡**SOUTHWEST PICTURES,** P.O. Box 64428, Los Angeles CA 90064. (213)876-1163. Contact: Christopher Daniel or Andrew Crofoot. Estab. 1993. Audience is mass market (theatrical outlet). Buys 3 scripts/year. Works with 15 writers/year. Buys first rights. No previously produced material. Reports in 2 months. Catalog for #10 SASE. Send complete script. Pays in accordance with Writers Guild standards.
Needs: Films (35mm).

‡□**STONEROAD PRODUCTIONS, INC.,** #909, 11288 Ventura Blvd., Studio City CA 91604. Contact: Story Department. Estab. 1992. Produces feature films for theaters, cable TV and home video. PG, R, and G-rated films. Buys/options 15-25 scripts/year. Works with 10 writers/year. Buys all rights; if published material, subsidiary rights. Accepts previously produced material. Reports in 1 month on queries; 2 months on submissions. Query with synopsis. Pay varies greatly: option, outright purchase, wide range.
Needs: Films (35mm). All genres. Looking for good material from writers who have taken the time to learn the unique and difficult craft of scriptwriting.
Tips: "Interesting query letters intrigue us—and tell us something about the writer. Query letter should include a short 'Log Line' or 'Pitch' encapsulating 'what this story is about and the genre' in just a few sentences. We look for strong stories and strong characters. We make movies that we would like to see. Producers are known for encouraging new (e.g. unproduced) screenwriters and giving real consideration to their scripts."

TALKING RINGS ENTERTAINMENT, P.O. Box 2019, Beverly Hills CA 90213-2019. President and Artistic Director: Arnold Leibovit. Estab. 1988. "We produce material for motion pictures and television." Buys 2

scripts/year. Works with 5 writers/year. Buys first rights or all rights. Reports on submissions in 2 months. Only send complete scripts. No treatments, novels, poems or plays, no submissions on computer disk. Query with synopsis. A Submission Release must be included with all queries. Produced and directed "The Fantasy Film Worlds of George Pal," "The Puppetoon Movie." Currently producing "The Time Machine Returns" and a remake of "The Seven Faces of Dr. Lao." SASE required for return of all materials. Pays in accordance with Writers Guild Standards.
Needs: Films (35mm), videotapes.

‡**TAPESTRY FILMS,** 9328 Civic Center Dr., Beverly Hills CA 90210. (310)275-1191. Vice President, Creative Development: Tara V. Zanecki. Estab. 1982. Audience is movie-goers and home video. Buys 4-5 scripts and/or ideas/year. Works with 5-10 writers/year. Buys all rights and a variety of deals and arrangements. Reports in 1-2 weeks on queries; 1-2 months on submissions. Query with synopsis and résumé. Makes outright purchase $10,000-200,000, in accordance with Writers Guild standards or based on film budget/collaboration deals/etc.
Needs: Films (35mm), videotapes. Looking for "treatments/full-length spec scripts. All genres except comedy and romance. Budgets either $1-5 million—or big studio pictures. Story driven (events/occurences) rather than character (actor)-driven material. Foreign locale preferred—LA and NYC too overdone!"

☐ **TELEVISION PRODUCTION SERVICES CORP.,** Box 1233, Edison NJ 08818. (201)287-3626. Executive Director/Producer: R.S. Burks. Produces corporate and video music materials for major market distributor networks, etc. Buys 50-100 scripts/year. Buys all rights. Reports in 2 weeks.
Needs: "We do corporate and video music for record companies, ATT, HBO networks and commercials. We use treatments of story ideas from the groups' management. We also do commercials for over-the-air broadcast and cable. We are now doing internal inhouse video for display on disk or internally distributed channels, and need good script writers." Submit synopsis/outline or complete script and résumé; *include SASE for response or materials will not be returned.*
Tips: Looks for rewrite flexibility and availability. "We have the capability of transmission electronically over the phone modem to our printer or directly onto disk for storage. We commission or contract out all scripts."

‡☐**FRANCIS TERI, INDEPENDENT PRODUCTIONS,** 807 E. 27th St., Brooklyn NY 11210. (718)258-4276. Contact: F. Teri. Estab. 1987. Produces material for foreign and domestic theatrical, video, cable, TV. Buys 1 script/year. Works with few writers/year. Buys all rights. Accepts previously produced material. Send complete script with synopsis. Makes outright purchase with royalty.
Needs: Films (35mm), videotapes, tapes and cassettes.

UNIFILMS, INC., 22931 Sycamore Creek Dr., Valencia CA 91354-2050. (805)297-2000. Vice President, Development: Jack Adams. Estab. 1984. Buys 0-5 scripts/year. Reports in 2 weeks on queries.
Needs: Feature films *only.* Looking for feature film screenplays, current format, 100-120 pages long; commercial but not stupid, dramatic but not "artsy," funny but not puerile. Query with synopsis and SASE. "If you don't include a SASE, we won't reply. We do not accept unsolicited scripts. Save your postage; if you send us a script we'll return it unopened."
Tips: "If you've taken classes, read books, attended seminars and writers' workshops all concerned with scriptwriting and read hundreds of produced studio screenplays *prior* to seeing the film and you're still convinced you've got a wonderful script, we might want to see it. But desire and enthusiasm are not enough; you have to have independent corroboration that your work is as good as you think it is. If you've got someone else in the entertainment industry to recommend your script, we might be more interested in seeing it. But if you waste our time with a project that's not yet ready to be seen, we're not going to react well. Your first draft is not usually the draft you're going to show to the industry. *Get a professional opinion first,* then rewrite before you submit to us. Very few people care about synopses, outlines or treatments for sales consideration. THE SCRIPT is the basic blueprint, and everyone in the country is working on a script. Ideas are a dime a dozen. If you can *execute* that idea well and get people *excited* about that idea, you've got something. But most writers are wanna-bes, who submit scripts that need a lot more work just to get to the 'promising' stage. Scripts are *always* rewritten. If you can't convince us you're a *writer,* we don't care. But if you *can* write and you've got a *second* wonderful script we might talk. But don't send a 'laundry list' of your scripts; pick the best one and pitch it to us. If it's not for us, then maybe come back with project number two. More than one project at a time confuses Hollywood; make it easy for us and you'll make it easy for yourself. And if you do it in a professional manner, you'll convince us sooner. Good luck, and keep writing. (Rewriting.)"

‡**VANGUARD FILMS,** 135 E. 65th St., New York NY 10021. (212)517-4333. Artistic Director: Charles Hobson. Estab. 1983. Produces 3 PBS TV productions/year. Query with synopsis. Reports in 3 weeks on submissions. Makes outright purchase.
Needs: Scripts that will make TV drama.

‡**VANGUARD PRODUCTIONS,** 12111 Beatrice St., Culver City CA 90230. Contact: Terrence M. O'Keefe. Estab. 1985. Buys 1 script/year. Buys all rights or options rights. Accepts previously produced material.

Reports in 3 months on queries; 6 months on scripts. Query with synopsis and résumé. Pays in accordance with Writers Guild standards or negotiated option.
Needs: Films (35mm), videotapes.

‡VECCHIO ENTERTAINMENT, 3599 Beverly Glen Terrace, Sherman Oaks CA 91423. Director of Development: Eliot Winks. Estab. 1988. Buys 10 scripts/year. Works with 20 writers/year. Buys film and TV rights. Accepts previously produced plays. Reports in 1 month on queries; 2 months on scripts. Query with synopsis. Makes outright purchase in accordance with Writers Guild standards.
Needs: Feature films, MOWs. Looking for "We are looking for scripts that are commercial yet have a social issue edge to them."

VIDEO-VISIONS, #102, 10635 Wilshire Blvd., Los Angeles CA 90024-4530. Executive Producer: Christine Peres-Peña. Estab. 1986. "We produce material for children—educational as well as entertaining. I'm looking for a Spanish writer to write a Sesame Street/puppet-like show for Spanish TV with references to the Hispanic culture: its folklore, myths, music, art, architecture, food, roots etc. It must have comedic elements. It should teach morality, principles, virtues, science, math, history etc. I also need similar material in English." Buys 2-5 scripts/year. Buys all rights. Reports in 1 month on queries; 2 months on scripts. Catalog for 9 × 12 SAE.
Needs: Films (16, 35mm), videotapes. "We need children's programming for the Hispanic market and cartoons, educational programs (30 minutes)—fast action entertainment (1½ or 2 hours) and scripts that are dramatic experiences of women (and their relationships). Submit complete script. Makes outright purchase of $500-5,000 in accordance with Writers Guild standards.
Tips: "We are looking for original ideas that are entertaining, educational and meaningful with morals and principles."

☐VISION FILMS, 4626 Lemona Ave., Sherman Oaks CA 91403. (818)784-1702. President: Stephen Rocha. Estab. 1989. "Worldwide audience." Buys 1 script/year. Works with 2-3 writers/year. Buys all rights. Reports in 2 months only with SASE. Submit synopsis/outline with résumé and information about where project has been previously pitched. Makes outright purchase to $5,000 with co-production opportunities.
Needs: Films (35mm), videotapes. Seeking 1) entertaining documentary 1 hour television program specials with worldwide appeal; 2) movies with Hispanic appeal; 3) movies with special effects (under 5 million dollar budget).
Tips: "We are currently producing 18-part series for The Discovery Channel entitled *Movie Magic* about special effects. Entering into season two."

‡ZACHARY ENTERTAINMENT, 1139 S. Crest Dr., Los Angeles CA 90035. Development Associate: Lois Gore. Estab. 1981. Audience is film goers of all ages, television viewers. Buys 8-10 scripts/year. Works with 50 writers/year. Rights purchased vary. No previously produced material. Reports in 2 weeks on queries; 3 months on submissions. Query with synopsis. Pay varies.
Needs: Films.

‡ZETA ENTERTAINMENT LTD., 8315 Beverly Blvd., Los Angeles CA 90048. (213)653-4077. Director of Development: Kristen March. Estab. 1988. Buys 6 scripts/year. Works with over 12 writers/year. Buys all rights. No previously produced material. Reports in 1 month on queries; 2 months on scripts. Query with synopsis. Pays in accordance with Writers Guild standards.
Needs: Films (35mm)

‡THE ZVEJNIEKS GROUP, INC., 187 Cocohatchee St., Naples FL 33963. Contact: Ingrida Sylvia. Estab. 1983. "Emphasis is placed on quality of original written work for major motion picture production. Good writing creates its own audience." Limited to 15 projects in development at any given time. Rights negotiated on an individual basis. Accepts previously produced material. Reports in 1-2 months. Submit 1-page synopsis of story and characters. Pay negotiated on individual basis.
Needs: "As a producer of major motion pictures, our primary goal is to entertain audiences with quality movies. We are always looking for fresh, interesting, well-written stories with good character development. The script should elicit some sort of emotion from the reader/audience."
Tips: "According to Chairman Eric S. Zvejnieks, a serious problem facing the industry is a lack of genuine original creative material which would allow for greater diversity in films. Writing talent is often overlooked, an unfortunate reality partially attributable to the system within which writers work. The underlying philosophy of the company is that every great movie starts with a great story, a simple yet often forgotten concept."

Scriptwriting Markets/Changes '94-'95

The following scriptwriting markets were listed in the 1994 edition but do not have listings in this edition of *Writer's Market*. The majority did not respond to our request to update their listing or return a questionnaire for a new listing. If a reason was given for their exclusion, we have included it in parentheses after the listing name.

AFA Film Productions
Albundegus All-Stars
Alley Theatre
American Repertory Theatre (removed by request)
Arrow Rock Lyceum (removed by request for 1 year)
Art Extensions Theatre
Artreach Touring Theatre
Bailiwick Repertory
Mary Baldwin College Theatre
Berkshire Public Theatre
Bradyco Productions (removed by request for 1 year)
David Brooks Productions (removed by request)
Capital Repertory Company
Anthony Cardoza Enterprises (removed by request)
The Chicago Board of Rabbis Broadcasting Commission
Cincinnati Playhouse in the Park
Cinebar Productions Inc.
Citiarts Theatre
City Theatre Company
The Cleveland Play House
Cleveland Public Theatre
Cutting Edge Productions
Dawber & Company
Harry Deligter Productions (removed by request)
Denver Center Theatre Company

Doomsday Studios Ltd. (overwhelmed by submissions)
The Empty Space
The Ensemble Studio Theatre
The Ensemble Theatre of Cincinnati
Fairfield County
Florida Studio Theatre
The Freelance Press
Furman Films, Inc.
Georgetown Productions
Goodman Associates, Inc.
Greatworks Play Service
Hartford Stage Company
Hilberry Theatre (removed by request for 1 year)
Hippodrome State Theatre
Instructional/Communications Technology (unable to contact)
Invisible Theatre
JEF Films
Lawson Productions Ltd.
Lucasfilm, Ltd.
Magic Theatre Inc.
Lee Magid Productions
Manhattan Theatre Club
Marsh Media (removed by request)
Meriwether Publishing Ltd.
Merrimack Repertory Theatre
Merry-Go-Round Playhouse
Metro-Goldwin-Mayer Inc. Communications

Mill Mountain Theatre
Milwaukee Public Theatre
Mixed Blood Theatre Company
Motivation Media, Inc.
The MUNY Student Theatre
New York Shakespeare Festival/Public Theater
New York State Theatre Institute
New York Theatre Workshop
The North Carolina Black Repertory Company
Papillon Productions
Pennsylvania Stage Company
Philadelphia Drama Guild
The Playwrights' Center's Playlabs
Pop/Art Film Factory
Premier Film, Video & Recording Corp. (out of business)
Pulsar Film Corporation
Bill Rase Productions Inc.
Red Hots Entertainment
Shaw Festival Theatre
The Shazzam Production Company
Theatre on the Move
Tri Video Teleproduction
University of Minnesota, Duluth Theatre
Worcester Foothills Theatre Company

Syndicates

Newspaper syndicates distribute columns, cartoons and other written material to newspapers around the country—and sometimes around the world. With newspaper circulation expected to drop over the next few years, competition for syndication slots is stiff. Coveted spots in sports, humor and political commentary are held by big-name columnists such as Peter Gammons, Dave Barry and Anna Quindlen. And multitudes of aspiring writers wait in the wings, hoping one of these heavy hitters will move on to something else and leave the spotlight open.

Although this may seem discouraging, there are in fact many areas in which less-known writers are syndicated. As consumer interests and lifestyles change, new doors are being opened for innovative writers who can cover fitness; recycling/environmental issues; money-saving tips; and how-to material such as woodworking, gardening and cooking.

Most syndicates distribute a variety of columns, cartoons and features. Although the larger ones are usually only interested in running ongoing material, smaller ones often accept short features and one-shots in addition to continuous columns. Specialized syndicates—those that deal with a single area such as business—often sell to magazines, trade journals and other business publications as well as to newspapers.

The winning combination

In presenting yourself and your work, note that most syndicated columnists start out writing for local newspapers. Many begin as staff writers, develop a following in a particular area, and are then picked up by a syndicate. Before approaching a syndicate, write for a paper in your area. Be sure to develop a good collection of clips that you feel is representative of your best writing.

New ideas are paramount to syndication. Sure, you'll want to study the popular columnists to see how their pieces are structured (most are short—from 500-750 words—and really pack a punch), but don't make the mistake of imitating a well-known columnist. Syndicates are looking for original material that is timely, saleable and original. Do not submit a column to a syndicate on a subject it already covers. The more unique the topic, the greater your chances of having it picked up. Most importantly, be sure to choose a topic that interests you and one you know well.

Approaching markets

Most syndicates prefer a query letter and about six sample columns or writing samples and a SASE. You may also want to include a client list and business card if available. If you have a particular area of expertise pertinent to your submission, mention this in your letter and back it up by sending related material. For highly specialized or technical matter, provide credentials to show you are qualified to handle the topic.

In essence, syndicates act as agents or brokers for the material they handle. Writing material is usually sold as a package. The syndicate will promote and market the work to newspapers (and sometimes to magazines) and keep careful records of sales. Writers usually receive 40-60% of gross receipts. Some syndicates may also pay a small salary or flat fee for one-shot items.

Syndicates usually acquire all rights to accepted material, although a few are now offering writers and artists the option of retaining ownership. In selling all rights, writers give up ownership and future use of their creations. Consequently, sale of all rights is not the best deal for writers, and has been the reason many choose to work with syndicates that buy less restrictive rights. Before signing a contract with a syndicate, you may want to go over the terms with an attorney or with an agent who has a background in law. The best contracts will usually offer the writer a percentage of gross receipts (as opposed to net receipts) and will not bind the writer for longer than five years.

The self-syndication option

Many writers choose to self-syndicate. This route allows you to retain all rights, and gives you the freedom of a business owner. But as a self-syndicated writer, you must also act as your own manager, marketing team and sales force. You must develop mailing lists, and a pricing, billing and collections structure.

Payment is usually negotiated on a case-by-case basis. Small newspapers may offer only $10-20 per column, but larger papers may pay much more (for more information on pay rates, see How Much Should I Charge? on page 42.). The number of papers you deal with is only limited by your marketing budget and your tenacity.

If you self-syndicate, be aware that some newspapers are not copyrighted, so you should copyright your own material. It's less expensive to copyright columns as a collection than individually. For more information on copyright procedures, see Copyrighting Your Writing in the Business of Writing section.

Additional information on newspaper markets can be found in *The Gale Directory of Publications* (available in most libraries). The *Editor & Publisher Syndicate Directory* (11 W. 19th St., New York NY 10011) has a list of syndicates, contact names and features; the weekly magazine, *Editor & Publisher,* also has news articles about syndicates and can provide you with information about changes and events in the industry.

For information on syndicates not included in *Writer's Market*, see Syndicates/Changes '94-'95 at the end of this section.

‡**ADVENTURE FEATURE SYNDICATE**, 329 Harvery Dr., Glendale CA 91206. (818)247-1721. Editor: Vicky D. Letcher. Estab. 1976. Reports in 1 month. Buys all rights, first North American serial rights and second serial (reprint) rights. Free cartoonist's guidelines.
Needs: Fiction (spies), fillers (adventure/travel), action/adventure comic strips and graphic novels. Submit complete ms.

ALLIED FEATURE SYNDICATE, P.O. Drawer 48, Joplin MO 64802-0048. (417)673-2860. Fax: (800)628-1705. Editor: Robert J. Blanset. Contact: Irene Blanset. Estab. 1944. 70% written on contract; 30% freelance on a one-time basis. Works with 36 writers/year. Works with 30 previously unpublished writers/year. Syndicates to newspapers (60%); magazines (30%); inhouse organs (10%). Submissions will be returned "only on request." Reports in 6 weeks. Buys all rights.
Needs: Buys news articles, cartoon strips, panels and features. Must be directly related to business, electronics, human resources, computers or quality and test design. All other non-related materials will be rejected and returned to sender if SASE is included. Query with clips of published work. Pays 50% author's percentage "after production costs" or 5¢/word. Currently syndicates "A Little Prayer," by Mary Alice Bennett (religious filler); "Murphy's Law of Electronics," by Nic Frising (cartoon panel); "Selling in the Year 2000," by Dick Meza (marketing column).
Tips: "Allied Feature Syndicate is one of very few agencies syndicating electronics manufacturing targeted materials and information."

AMERICA INTERNATIONAL SYNDICATE, 1324 N. Third St., St. Joseph MO 64561. (816)233-8190. Fax: (816)279-9315. Executive Director: Gerald A. Bennett. Associate Director (London office): Paul Eisler. Estab. 1979. 100% freelance written by cartoonists on contract. "We sell to newspapers, trade magazines, puzzle books and comic books." Reports in 6 weeks. Buys all rights.

Needs: Short fictional crime story "You Are The Detective" for magazines, books and comics; also comic strips of adventure, western or family type. Children's features and games also needed. Scientific or unusual features with art and written text needed. Send 6-8 samples with SASE. Pays 50% of gross sales. Currently syndication features: "Alfonso," "Silent Sam," "Tex Benson," "Buccaneers," "Figment," "Adventures in Nature" (comic strips). Panel features are "Stacey," "Girls," "The Edge," "Kids & Pets," and "Odds & Ends."

Tips: "Keep the art simple and uncluttered as possible. Know your subject and strive for humor. We have a need for uncaptioned cartoon panels and strips at present time."

AMPERSAND COMMUNICATIONS, 2311 S. Bayshore Dr., Miami FL 33133-4728. (305)285-2200. Editor: George Leposky. Estab. 1982. 100% written by writers on contract. "We syndicate only our own material at present, but we will consider working with others whose material is exceptionally good. Novices need not contact us." Syndicates to magazines and newspapers. Query for electronic submissions. Reports in up to 4 months. Buys all rights. Writer's guidelines $2 for SASE.

Needs: Newspaper columns, travel, business, science and health, regional cuisine, natural foods, environment; typically 500-750 words, rarely up to 1,500 words. Material from other writers must complement, not compete with, our own travel, business, environment, health and home improvement columns. Query with clips of published work and complete ms – samples of proposal columns. Pays 50% of net after production. "Note: For columns requiring photos, the writer must supply to us the required number of images and quantity of each image at his/her expense. We are not in the photo duplication business and will not provide this service." Currently syndicates Traveling the South, by George and Rosalie Leposky (travel); Business Insights, by Lincoln Avery (business); Food for Thought (cooking) by Rosalie Leposky; HealthScan, by George Leposky (health); EnviroScan, by George Leposky (environment); House and Home, by Lynne Avery (home improvement).

Tips: "Be an *excruciatingly* good writer; good alone isn't enough. Find a niche that doesn't seem to be covered. Do research to cover your topics in-depth, but in few words. The reader's attention span is shriveling, and so are ad lineage and column inches available for syndicated features."

ARKIN MAGAZINE SYNDICATE INC., Suite A8, 300 Bayview Dr., N. Miami Beach FL 33160-4747. Editor: Joseph Arkin. Estab. 1958. 20% freelance written by writers on contract; 70% freelance written on a one-time basis. "We regularly purchase articles from several freelancers for syndication in trade and professional magazines." Accepts previously published submissions, "if all rights haven't been sold." Reports in 3 weeks. Buys all North American magazine and newspaper rights.

Needs: Magazine articles (nonfiction, 750-2,200 words), directly relating to business problems common to several different types of businesses and photos (purchased with written material). "We are in dire need of the 'how-to' business article." Will not consider article series. Submit complete ms; "SASE required with all submissions." Pays 3-10¢/word; $5-10 for photos; "actually, line drawings are preferred instead of photos." **Pays on acceptance.**

Tips: "Study a representative group of trade magazines to learn style, needs and other facets of the field."

ARTHUR'S INTERNATIONAL, Suite 28-88, 101 S. Rainbow, Las Vegas NV 89128. (702)255-7866. Editor: Marvin C. Arthur. Syndicates to newspapers and magazines. Reports in 1 week. "SASE must be enclosed." Buys all rights.

Needs: Fillers, magazine columns, magazine features, newspaper columns, newspaper features and news items. "We specialize in timely nonfiction and historical stories, and columns, preferably the unusual. We utilize humor. Travel stories utilized in 'World Traveler.' " Buys one-shot features and article series. "Since the majority of what we utilize is column or short story length, it is better to submit the article so as to expedite consideration and reply. Do not send any lengthy manuscripts." Pays 50% of net sales, salary on some contracted work and flat rate on commissioned work. Currently syndicates "Marv," by Marvin C. Arthur (informative, humorous, commentary); "Humoresque," by Don Alexander (humorous); and "World Spotlight," by Don Kampel (commentary).

Tips: "We do not use cartoons but we are open for fine illustrators."

BUDDY BASCH FEATURE SYNDICATE, 771 West End Ave., New York NY 10025-5572. (212)666-2300. Editor/Publisher: Buddy Basch. Estab. 1965. 10% written on contract; 2% freelance written on a one-time basis. Buys 10 features/year. Works with 3-4 previously unpublished writers annually. Syndicates To print media: newspapers, magazines, giveaways, house organs, etc. Reports in 3 weeks. Buys first North American serial rights.

● Most stories are done inhouse.

Needs: Magazine features, newspaper features, and one-shot ideas that are really different. "Try to make them unusual, unique, real 'stoppers,' not the usual stuff." Will consider one-shots and article series on travel, entertainment, human interest – "the latter, a wide umbrella that makes people stop and read the piece. Different, unusual and unique are the key words, not what the *writer* thinks is, but which have been done nine million times before." Query. Pays 20-50% commission. Additional payment for photos $10-50.

Currently syndicates "It Takes a Woman," by Frances Scott (woman's feature), "Travel Whirl," "Scramble Steps" (puzzle) and others.

Tips: "Never mind what your mother, fiancé or friend thinks is good. If it has been done before and is old hat, it has no chance. Do some research and see if there are a dozen similar items in the press. Don't just try a very close 'switch' on them. You don't fool anyone with this. There are fewer and fewer newspapers, with more and more people vying for the available space. But there's *always* room for a really good, *different* feature or story. Trouble is few writers (amateurs especially) know a good piece, I'm sorry to say. Read *Writer's Market*, carefully, noting which syndicate might be interested in the type of feature you are submitting. That will save you time and money."

‡BLACK PRESS SERVICE, INC., 166 Madison Ave., New York NY 10016. (212)686-6850. Editor: Roy Thompson. Estab. 1966. 10% written on contract; 10% freelance written on a one-time basis. Buys 100s of features/year. Works with 100s of writers/year. Syndicates to magazines, newspapers and radio. Reports in 2 months. Buys all rights. Submit complete ms.
Needs: Magazine and newspaper columns; news items; magazine and newspaper features; radio broadcast material. Purchases single (one shot) features and articles series (current events oriented). Pays variable flat rate. Currently syndicates *Bimonthly Report*, by staff (roundup of minority-oriented news).

CHRONICLE FEATURES, Dept. WM, Suite 1011, 870 Market St., San Francisco CA 94102. (415)777-7212. General Manager: Stuart Dodds. Contact: Jean W. Arnold. Buys 3 features/year. Syndicates to daily newspapers in the US and Canada with representation overseas. Reports in 2 months.
Needs: Newspaper columns and features. "In choosing a column subject, the writer should be guided by the concerns and aspirations of today's newspaper reader. We look for originality of expression and, in special fields of interest, exceptional expertise." Preferred length: 500-700 words. Submit complete ms. Pays 50% revenue from syndication. Offers no additional payment for photos or artwork accompanying ms. Currently syndicates Latino Spectrum, by Roberto Rodriguez and Patrisia Gonazles (op-ed colun); Bizarro, by Dan Piraro (cartoon panel); Earthweek, by Steve Newman (planetary diary); Home Entertainment, by Harry Somerfield (audiovisual equipment advice and reviews); and Streetwise, by Herb Greenberg (up-to-the-minute business column).
Tips: "We are seeking features that will be ongoing enterprises, not single articles or news releases. Examples of a proposed feature are more welcome than a query letter describing it. Please conduct all correspondence by mail rather than by telephone."

‡CLEAR CREEK FEATURES, Box 3303, Grass Valley CA 95945. Editor: M. Drummond. Estab. 1988. 50% written on contract; 0% freelance written on a one-time basis. Buys 0 features/year. Works with 5 writers/year. Works with 2 previously unpublished writers/year. Syndicates to magazines and newspapers. Query for electronic submissions. Reports in 1 month. Buys first North American serial, all and second serial (reprint) rights. Writer's guidelines for #10 SASE. Submit complete ms or query with clips of published work.
Needs: Fiction, magazine and newspaper columns, fillers, magazine features. Pays 50% author's percentage. Currently syndicates Coping in the Country, by Mike Drummond (humor); *The Voice of Experience*, by various (humor/commentary).
Tips: "Identify a niche and dig in!"

‡THE COLUMBIA COMPANY, (formerly Columbia Features, Inc.), P.O. Box 1957, New Smyrna Beach FL 32169. (904)428-3024. Estab. 1994 (1953, CFI). 40% written on contract; 5% freelance written on a one-time basis. Buys 2 columns/features/year. Works with 4-5 writers/year. Syndicates to newspapers and radio. Query for electronic submissions. Reports in 6-8 weeks. Buys first North American serial rights. Free writer's guidelines. Query.
Needs: Newspaper columns and features, radio broadcast material and article series. Pays 60% author's percentage; $100 minimum guarantee; $150 flate rate; $500 monthly salary. Pays $50-150 for photos. Currently syndicates Trivia I.Q., by Robert Ferguson and submissions (newspaper); Sportsman's Digest, by Robert Ferguson, Hal Sharp (newspaper); Antique Wise, by freelance writers (newspaper).
Tips: "Writers should research newspapers and find absolutely nothing like their submission available through other syndicates (i.e., unique columns, not versions (better or worse) than other available columns and features)."

‡COMIC ART THERAPY, P.O. Box 7981, Corpus Christi TX 78415. (512)853-5406. Art Director: Pedro Moreno. Estab. 1975. 40% written on contract; 10% freelance written on a one-time basis. Buys 25 features/year. Works with 25 writers/year. Works with 10 new previously unpublished writers/year. Syndicates to magazines, newspapers and book stores. Submissions with SASE will not be returned. Reports in 1 month. Buys first North American serial rights, all rights or second serial (reprint) rights. Guidelines for $10. Submit $10 first (check or money order) for guidelines, then material.
Needs: Fillers; magazine and newspaper columns and features; news items; comic strips and panels, single features (500 words or less with illustration, comic strip or comic panel). Pays negotiable flat rate. Pays $25-100 for photos. Currently syndicates Oh! Rats, by Jerry Cardona (comic book); Don Pedrito Jaramillo, by

Pedro Moreno (faith healing); How Great Thou Art, by James Rodriguez (song comic book).

Tips: "Always query first! Do not submit handwritten material especially; gray photocopies are a no-no!"

CONTINENTAL FEATURES/CONTINENTAL NEWS SERVICE, Suite 265, 341 W. Broadway, San Diego CA 92101-3802. (619)492-8696. Editor: Gary P. Salamone. Estab. 1981. 100% written on contract; 30% freelance written on a one-time basis. "Writers who offer the kind and quality of writing we seek stand an equal chance regardless of experience." Syndicates to the print media. Reports in 1 month. Writer's guidelines for #10 SASE.

Needs: Magazine and newspaper features. "Feature material should fit the equivalent of one-quarter to one-half standard newspaper page, and Continental News considers an ultra-liberal or ultra-conservative slant inappropriate." Query. Pays 70% author's percentage. Currently syndicates "News and Comment," by Charles Hampton Savage (general news commentary/analysis); "Continental Viewpoint," by staff; "Portfolio," (cartoon/caricature art); "Travelers Checks," by Ann Hattes; "Middle East Cable," by Mike Maggio; and "InVideo," by Harley Lond; 24 features in all.

● This syndicate is now considering submissions for children's features.

Tips: "Continental News seeks country profiles/background articles that pertain to foreign countries. Writers who possess such specific knowledge/personal experience stand an excellent chance of acceptance, provided they can focus the political, economic and social issues. We welcome them to submit their proposals. We foresee the possibility of diversifying our feature package by representing writers and feature creators through a team-marketing network nationwide. We have plans to introduce 40 new text features alone."

COPLEY NEWS SERVICE, P.O. Box 190, San Diego CA 92112. (619)293-1818. Fax: (619)293-2322. Editorial Director: Nanette Wiser. 85% written by stringers on contract; 15% freelance written on a one-time basis. Offers 200 features/week. Sells to magazines, newspapers, radio, on-line television. Reports in 1-2 months. Buys all rights or second serial (reprint) rights (sometimes).

Needs: Fillers, magazine and newspaper columns and features. Looking for video, food, travel, opinion, new ideas. Subjects include interior design, outdoor recreation, fashion, antiques, real estate, pets, gardening. Buys one-shot and articles series. Query with clips of published work. Pays $50-100 flat rate or $400 salary/month.

CREATE-A-CRAFT, P.O. Box 330008, Ft. Worth TX 76163. (817)292-1855. Contact: Editor. Estab. 1967. 5% written by writers on contract; 50% freelance written. Buys 5 features/year. Works with 3 writers/year. Works with 3 previously unpublished writers/year. Syndicates to magazines and newspapers. Reports in 4 months. Submissions will not be returned. Buys all rights. Writer's guidelines $2.50 for #10 SASE. Prefers agented submissions only (submit complete ms).

Needs: Magazine and newspaper columns and features. "Looking for material on appraising, art, decorative arts, politics (how politics affect art only); 400-2,000 words. Comics must be in strip form only." Pays $6-10 flat hourly rate (depending on project). All work is work-for-hire. Currently syndicates Appraisals by Abramson (appraisal column); Those Characters from Cowtown (cartoon); Rojo (cartoon); Golden Gourmets (cartoon); Gallant Gators (cartoon). Author is always listed as Create-A-Craft (no byline given).

Tips: "Know the market you are writing for."

CREATIVE SYNDICATION SERVICES, P.O. Box 40, Eureka MO 63025-0040. (314)938-9116. Fax: (314)343-0966. Editor: Debra Holly. Estab. 1977. 10% written on contract; 50% freelance written on a one-time basis. Syndicates to magazines, newspapers and radio. Query for electronic submissions. Reports in 1 month. Buys all rights. Currently syndicates The Weekend Workshop, by Ed Baldwin; Woodcrafting, by Ed Baldwin; and Classified Clippers, a feature exclusive for the Classified Section of newspapers.

Tips: "We are looking for writers who do crafts, woodworking, needle-crafts and sewing."

CREATORS SYNDICATE, INC., Suite 700, 5777 W. Century Blvd., Los Angeles CA 90045. (310)337-7003. Vice President/General Manager: Anita Tobias. Estab. 1987. Syndicates to newspapers. Reports in 1-2 months. Buys negotiable rights. Writer's guidelines for #10 SASE.

Needs: Newspaper columns and features. Query with clips of published work or submit complete ms. Author's percentage: approximately 50%. Currently syndicates Ann Landers (advice), Harris Poll, Walter E. Williams, Mona Charen, Percy Ross and Thomas Sowell (columns), B.C. and Wizard of Id (comic strips) and Herblock (editorial cartoon).

Tips: "Syndication is very competitive. Writing regularly for your local newspaper is a good start."

CRICKET COMMUNICATIONS, INC., P.O. Box 527, Ardmore PA 19003-0527. (215)789-2480. Editor: J.D. Krickett. Estab. 1975. 10% written on contract; 10% freelance written on a one-time basis. Works with 2-3 previously unpublished writers/year. Syndicates to trade magazines and newspapers. Reports in 1 month. Buys all rights.

Needs: Magazine and newspaper columns and features, news items—all tax and financial-oriented (700-1,500 words); also newspaper columns, features and news items directed to small business. Query with clips of published work. Pays $50-500. Currently syndicates Hobby/Business, by Mark E. Battersby (tax and financial); Farm Taxes, by various authors; and Small Business Taxes, by Mark E. Battersby.

CROWN SYNDICATE, INC., P.O. Box 99126, Seattle WA 98199. President: L.M. Boyd. Estab. 1967. Buys countless trivia items. Syndicates to newspapers, radio. Reports in 1 month. Buys first North American serial rights. Free writer's guidelines.
Needs: Filler material used weekly, items for trivia column (format guidelines sent on request). Pays $1-5/item, depending on how it's used, i.e., trivia or filler service. Offers no additional payment for photos accompanying ms. Currently syndicates columns and puzzle panels.

DANY NEWS SERVICE, 22 Lesley Dr., Syosset NY 11791. Editor: David Nydick. Estab. 1966. Buys 10% from freelancers. Buys 30 features/year (from freelancers). Syndicates to newspapers. Reports in 1 month. Buys all rights. Submit complete ms.
Needs: Newspaper columns and features, how-to (help your child). Pays $50 minimum guarantee. "You, Your Child and School," "You, Your Child and Sports," and "You, Your Child and Entertainment," (how-to help your child).

EDITORIAL CONSULTANT SERVICE, P.O. Box 524, West Hempstead NY 11552-1206. (516)565-6332. Editorial Director: Arthur A. Ingoglia. Estab. 1964. 40% written on contract; 25% freelance written on a one-time basis. "We work with 75 writers in the US and Canada." Previously published writers only. Adds about 5 new columnists/year. Syndicates material to an average of 60 newspapers, magazines, automotive trade and consumer publications, and radio stations with circulation of 50,000-575,000. Buys all rights. Writer's guidelines for #10 SASE. Reports in 1-2 months.
Needs: Magazine and newspaper columns and features, news items, radio broadcast material. Prefers carefully documented material with automotive slant. Also considers automotive trade features. Will consider article series. No horoscope, child care, lovelorn or pet care. Query. Author's percentage varies; usually averages 50%. Additional payment for 8×10 b&w and color photos accepted with ms. Submit 2-3 columns. Currently syndicates Let's Talk About Your Car, by R. Hite.
Tips: "Emphasis is placed on articles and columns with an automotive slant. We prefer consumer-oriented features, how to save money on your car, what every woman should know about her car, how to get more miles per gallon, etc."

ENTERTAINMENT NEWS SYNDICATE, 155 East 55th St., New York NY 10022. (212)223-1821. Fax: (212)223-3737. Editor: Lee Canaan. Estab. 1970. 10% written on contract. Syndicates to newspapers and magazines. Reports in 1 month. Buys all rights. Free writer's guidelines.
Needs: Fillers, magazine and newspaper features, news on travel and entertainment. No single (one-shot) features. Query. Payment negotiable. Currently syndicates Cruise Callings, Hotels & Spas and Tour Treats, by L. Canaan (column).

‡FEATURE ENTERPRISES, 33 Bellwood, Northport AL 35476. Editor: Maury M. Breecher. Estab. 1979. 10% written on contract; 90% freelance written on a one-time basis. Syndicates 100 mss/year. Works with 10-20 previously unpublished writers/year. Syndicates to magazines and newspapers. Reports in 1 month. Buys first North American serial rights and second serial (reprint) rights. Writer's guidelines for $2.
Needs: No columns or cartoons. Need one-shot features, popular psychology, medical breakthroughs and celebrity interviews. Payment on 50/50 standard syndicate split. SASE required for return of material.
Tips: "Use lots of direct, to-the-point quotes. Completely identify experts with full title and affiliation. Supply contact numbers."

FOTOPRESS, INDEPENDENT NEWS SERVICE INTERNATIONAL, Box 1268, Station Q, Toronto, Ontario M4T 2P4 Canada. (905)841-1065. Fax: (905)841-2283. Executive Editor: John Milan Kubik. Estab. 1983. 50% written on contract; 25% freelance written on a one-time basis. Works with 30% previously unpublished writers. Syndicates to domestic and international magazines, newspapers, radio, TV stations and motion picture industry. Reports in 2 months. Buys variable rights. Writer's guidelines for $3 money order, SAE with IRC.
Needs: Fillers, magazine and newspaper columns and features, news items, radio broadcast material, documentary, the environment, travel and art. Buys one-shot and article series for international politics, scientists, celebrities and religious leaders. Query or submit complete ms. Pays 50-75% author's percentage. Offers $5-150 for accompanying ms.
Tips: "We need all subjects from 500-3,000 words. Photos are purchased with or without features. All writers are regarded respectfully—their success is our success."

(GABRIEL) GRAPHICS NEWS BUREAU, P.O. Box 38, Madison Square Station, New York NY 10010. (212)254-8863. Cable: NOLNOEL, NY. Editor: J. G. Bumberg. 25% freelance written on contract; 50% freelance written on one-time basis. Custom-syndicates for clients to selected weeklies, suburbans and small dailies. Reports in 1 month. Buys all rights for clients' packages.

Needs: Magazine features, newspaper columns, fillers and features and news items for PR clients, custom packages. Pays 15% from client. Also has consulting/conceptualizing services in communications/graphics/management; developing, stylizing and upgrading desktop newsletter/publishers.

‡**GLENMOOR MEDIA GROUP**, Suite 173, 733 Main St., Willits CA 95490. (707)459-6027. Contact: R.C. Moorhead. Estab. 1989. 25% written on contract; 25% freelance written on a one-time basis. Buys 10-15 features/year. Works with 10 writers/year. Works with 0 previously unpublished writers/year. Syndicates to magazines and newspapers. Reports in 3 months. Buys first North American serial rights. Query with clips of published work.

Needs: Newspaper columns, magazine and single features. Pays 50% author's percentage. Pays $5-50 for photos. Currently syndicates On The Road With Ron Moorhead, by Ron Moorhead (automotive road tests); Women & Wheels, by G.A. Blake (automotive topics for women); Automobiles & Questions, by Ron Moorhead (automotive Q&A).

HISPANIC LINK NEWS SERVICE, 1420 N St. NW, Washington DC 20005. (202)234-0280. Fax: (202)234-4090. Publisher: Charles A. Ericksen. Editor: Jonathan Higuera. Estab. 1980. 50% freelance written on contract; 50% freelance written on a one-time basis. Buys 156 columns and features/year. Works with 50 writers/year; 5 previously unpublished writers. Syndicates to 100 newspapers and magazines with circulations ranging from 5,000 to 300,000. Reports in up to 1 month. Buys second serial (reprint) or negotiable rights. For reprints, send photocopy of article. Pays 100% of the amount paid for an original article ($25 for guest columns). Free writer's guidelines.

Needs: Newspaper columns and features. One-shot features and article series. "We prefer 650-700 word op/ed analysis or new features geared to a general national audience, but focus on issue or subject of particular interest to Hispanic Americans. Some longer pieces accepted occasionally." Query or submit complete ms. Pays $25-100. Currently syndicates Hispanic Link, by various authors (opinion and/or feature columns).

Tips: "We would especially like to get topical material and vignettes relating to Hispanic presence and progress in the United States. Provide insights on Hispanic experience geared to a general audience. Of the columns we accept, 85 to 90% are authored by Hispanics; the Link presents Hispanic viewpoints and showcases Hispanic writing talent through its subscribing newspapers and magazines. Copy should be submitted in English. We syndicate in English and Spanish."

HOLLYWOOD INSIDE SYNDICATE, P.O. Box 49957, Los Angeles CA 90049-0957. (909)678-6237. Fax: (909)678-6237. Editor: John Austin. Estab. 1968. 10% written on contract; 40% freelance written on a one-time basis. Purchases entertainment-oriented mss for syndication to newspapers in San Francisco, Philadelphia, Detroit, Montreal, London, Sydney, Manila, South Africa, etc. Accepts previously published submissions, if published in the US and Canada only. Reports in 3 months.

Needs: News items (column items concerning entertainment—motion picture—personalities and jet setters for syndicated column; 750-800 words). Also considers series of 1,500-word articles; "suggest descriptive query first. We are also looking for off-beat travel pieces (with pictures) but not on areas covered extensively in the Sunday supplements; not luxury cruise liners but lower cost cruises. We also syndicate nonfiction book subjects—sex, travel, etc., to overseas markets. No fiction. Must have b&w photos with submissions if possible." Also require 1,500-word celebrity profiles on internationally recognized celebrities. We stress *internationally*." Query or submit complete ms. Currently syndicates Books of the Week column and "Celebri-Quotes," "Movie Trivia Quiz," "Hollywood Inside."

Tips: "Study the entertainment pages of Sunday (and daily) newspapers to see the type of specialized material we deal in. Perhaps we are different from other syndicates, but we deal with celebrities. No 'I' journalism such as 'when I spoke to Cloris Leachman.' Many freelancers submit material from the 'dinner theater' and summer stock circuit of 'gossip type' items from what they have observed about the 'stars' or featured players in these productions—how they act off stage, who they romance, etc. We use this material."

‡**INTERNATIONAL PUZZLE FEATURES**, 740 Van Rensselaer Ave., Niagara Falls NY 14305. Contact: Pat Battaglia. Estab. 1990. 0% written on contract; 5-10% freelance written on a one-time basis. Buys 10 features/year. Works with 0 writers/year. Works with all new previously unpublished writers. Syndicates to newspapers. Reports in 1 month. Writer's guidelines for #10 SASE. Submit complete ms.

Needs: Concisely written, entertaining word puzzles. Pays $5 flat rate/puzzle. Currently syndicates If You're So Smart . . ., by Pat Battaglia (word puzzles).

INTERPRESS OF LONDON AND NEW YORK, 400 Madison Ave., New York NY 10017-1909. (212)832-2839. Editor: Jeffrey Blyth. Estab. 1971. 50% freelance written on contract; 50% freelance written on a one-time basis. Works with 3-6 previously unpublished writers/year. Buys British and European rights mostly, but can handle world rights. Accepts previously published submissions "for overseas." Pays on publication or agreement of sale. Reports in 3 weeks.

Needs: "Unusual nonfiction stories and photos for British and European press. Picture stories, for example, on such 'Americana' as a 5-year-old evangelist; the 800-pound 'con-man'; the nude-male calendar; tallest girl in the world; interviews with pop celebrities such as Madonna, Michael Jackson, Bill Cosby, Tom Selleck,

Cher, Priscilla Presley, Bette Midler, Eddie Murphy, Liza Minelli; also news of stars on top TV shows; cult subjects such as voodoo, college fads, anything amusing or offbeat. Extracts from books such as Earl Wilson's *Show Business Laid Bare*, inside-Hollywood type series ('Secrets of the Stuntmen'). Real life adventure dramas ('Three Months in an Open Boat,' 'The Air Crash Cannibals of the Andes'). No length limits—short or long, but not too long. Query or submit complete ms. Payment varies; depending on whether material is original, or world rights. Pays top rates, up to several thousand dollars, for exclusive material."
Photos: Purchased with or without features. Captions required. Standard size prints. Pay $50-100, but no limit on exclusive material.
Tips: "Be alert to the unusual story in your area—the sort that interests the American tabloids (and also the European press)."

INTERSTATE NEWS SERVICE, 237 S. Clark Ave., St. Louis MO 63135. (314)522-1300. Fax: (314)522-1999. Editor: Michael J. Olds. Estab. 1985. "Interstate acts as the local news bureau for newspapers that are too small to operate their own state capital bureau." Buys all rights and makes work-for-hire assignments. Call for information.
Needs: Independent news reporters on long-term contract to open new state capital bureaus. Must be experienced news reporters to write stories with hard news emphasis, concentrating on local delegations, tax money and local issues. Query with clips of published work. Negotiates with writers under contract. "Interstate News is interested in contracting with reporters in all states not now served, and all Canadian provinces."
Tips: "We do not buy unsolicited manuscripts."

JODI JILL FEATURES, Suite 321, 1705 14th St., Boulder CO 80302-1200. Art/Writer Editor: Carol Handz. Estab. 1985. 40-60% written on contract; 25% freelance written on a one-time basis. Buys 10 features/year. Works with 20 writers/year. Works with 5 new previously unpublished writers/year. Syndicates to magazines, newspapers, weekly shoppers. Reports in 2 months. Buys first North American serial rights. Free writer's guidelines. Submit complete ms with SASE.
Needs: Fillers (cartoons and 500-word articles), newspaper columns (500-750 words on general topics), puzzles. "We purchase mostly puzzles, visual and word, that can be made into quarter page inserts. These features can be for children or adults. They are placed in weekly papers." Pays 45% author's percentage of gross for columns. Pays $10 flat rate per paper for single features. Pays $17-150 for photos. Currently syndicates Brain Baffler, by Jodi Jill (puzzle); Minor Cartoon, by various artists every week (cartoons); Mirage, by Jodi Jill (puzzle).
Tips: "A writer will only succeed by promotion of his/her own work. Beating your own drum is tough, but it is better than not eating. Keep trying and you will be a success in syndication. And finally, send us your column—we are looking for some great material."

‡KING FEATURES, 235 E. 42nd St., New York NY 10017. (800)526-5464. Contact: Submissions Editor. Estab. 1915. 99% written on contract; 1% freelance written on a one-time basis. Buys 5 features/year. Works with 5 writers/year. Works with 15 new previously unpublished writers/year. Syndicates to newspapers. Query for electronic submissions. Reports in 1 month. Buys all rights. Free writer's guidelines. Submit complete ms. ✓
Needs: Newspaper columns, puzzles, games. Pays 50% author's percentage.
Tips: "Check Editor & Publisher Syndicate Guide at your local library."

LANDMARK DESIGNS, INC., P.O. Box 2307, Eugene OR 97402. (503)345-3429. President: Jim McAlexander. Estab. 1977. 99% written on contract; 1% freelance written on a one-time basis. Buys 60 features/year. Works with 3 writers/year. Works with 2 previously unpublished writers/year. Syndicates to newspapers. Query for electronic submissions. Reports in 3 months. Buys all rights. Writer's guidelines for #10 SASE. Query with clips of published work.
Needs: Newspaper features. Purchases one shot features and article series. Pays flat rate. Currently syndicates Landmark Designs, Designer Homes and Today's Homes.

LEW LITTLE ENTERPRISES, INC., P.O. Box 5318, Bisbee AZ 85603-8003. (602)432-8003. Editor: Lewis A. Little. Estab. 1986. 100% written on contract. Buys 2-3 features/year. Works with 10-20 writers/year. Works with 10-15 previously unpublished writers/year. Syndicates to newspapers. Reports in 1 month. Buys all rights. ✓ Writer's guidelines for #10 SASE. "For cartoon features, I prefer that writers, after receiving my guidelines, submit an outline and about 12 finished and rough samples."

Needs: Newspaper columns and features. "I specialize in the development of comics." No one-shot features. All contracts vary and all terms negotiable. Currently syndicates The Fusco Brothers, by J.C. Duffy (comic strip); Sibling Revelry, by Man Martin (comic strip); Brainstormers, by Mike Smith (comic strip).

LOS ANGELES TIMES SYNDICATE, Times Mirror Square, Los Angeles CA 90053. (213)237-7987. Special Articles Editor: Dan O'Toole. Syndicates to US and worldwide markets. Reports in 2 months. Usually buys first North American serial rights and world rights, but rights purchased can vary. Submit seasonal material 6 weeks in advance. Material ranges from 800-2,000 words.
Needs: Reviews continuing columns and comic strips for US and foreign markets. Send comics to Don Michel, VP Administration and Editorial Development, columns to Tim Lange, Managing Editor. Also reviews single articles, series, magazine reprints, and book serials; send these submissions to Dan O'Toole. Send complete ms. Pays 50% commission. Currently syndicates Art Buchwald, Dr. Henry Kissinger, Dr. Jeane Kirkpatrick, William Pfaff and Paul Conrad.
Tips: "We're dealing with fewer undiscovered writers but still do review material."

‡M GROUP FEATURES SYNDICATE, P.O. Box 12486, San Antonio TX 78212-2486. (210)737-1404. Contact: Randall Sherman. Estab. 1994. Syndicates to publications in lesbian, bisexual, gay and transgendered communities. Query for electronic submissions. Reports in 1 month. Buys first North American serial rights, all rights, second serial (reprint) rights. Guidelines for SASE. Submit complete ms.
Needs: Fiction (500-1,000 words); magazine columns (500-1,000 words); Newspaper columns (500-1,000 words); fillers (100-500 words); magazine features (500-1,800 words); newspaper features (500-1,800 words); cartoon strips and panels; word puzzles; trivia quizzes. Pays 35-50% authors percentage or flat rate $5-25. Pays $5-100 for photos. Currently syndicates *Ask Br. Rick*, by Brother Rick (positive religious peer counseling for lesbians, bisexuals, gays).
Tips: "Writing about the positive aspects of alternative lifestyles is most important, because raising the consciousness of the lesbian, bisexual, gay and transgendered communities will promote a higher level of self-respect. These are 'uncharted waters' that should excite new talents."

‡JERRY D. MEAD ENTERPRISES, P.O. Box 2796, Carson City NV 89702. (702)884-2648. Contact: Jerry D. Mead. Estab. 1969. 70% written on contract; 30% freelance written on a one-time basis. Syndicates to magazines and newspapers. Query for electronic submissions. Reports immediately or not at all. Buys first North American serial rights or second serial (reprint) rights. Query only.
Needs: Magazine and newspaper columns and features; single features. Pays 50% author's percentage. Currently syndicates Mead on Wine, by Jerry D. Mead (weekly/newspaper); The Travel Trader, by E. Edward Boyd (monthly/travel); The Lodging Report, by Sandra Wechsler (monthly/travel).

MEGALO MEDIA, P.O. Box 678, Syosset NY 11791. (212)535-6811. Editor: J. Baxter Newgate. Estab. 1972. 50% written on contract; 50% freelance written on a one-time basis. Works with 5 previously unpublished writers/year. Syndicates to newspapers. Query for electronic submissions. Reports in 1 month. Buys all rights. Free writer's guidelines.
Needs: Crossword puzzles. Buys one-shot features. Submit complete ms. Pays flat rate of $150 for Sunday puzzle. Currently syndicates National Challenge, by J. Baxter Newgate (crossword puzzle); Crossword Puzzle, by J. Baxter Newgate.

‡MIDWEST FEATURES INC., P.O. Box 9907, Madison WI 53715-0907. Contact: Mary Bergin. Estab. 1991. 80% written on contract; 20% freelance written on a one-time basis. Buys 2-3 features/year. Works with 10-12 writers/year. Syndicates to newspapers. Query for electronic submissions. Reports in 2 months. Buys second serial (reprint) rights. Query with clips of published work.
Needs: Newspaper columns and features. Material must have a Wisconsin emphasis (or Midwest focus at minimum); length: 500-1,000 words. Purchases single (one shot) features. Ideal length: 750 words. Series in past have been book excerpts and seasonal material (spring gardening, Milwaukee Brewer Spring Training). Pays author's percentage 50%. Currently syndicates *Cross Country*, by John Oncken (farming); *Midwest Gardening*, by Jan Riggenbagh (gardening); *Beyond Hooks & Bullets*, by Pat Durkin (outdoor sports).

NEW LIVING, P.O. Box 1519, Stony Brook NY 11790. (516)981-7232. Publisher: Christine Lynn Harvey. Estab. 1991. 20% written under contract; 5% freelance written on one-time basis. Buys 20 features/year. Works with 20 writers/year. Works with 5 previously unpublished writers/year. Syndicates to magazines, newspapers, radio, 900 phone lines. Query for electronic submissions. Reports in 6 months. Buys all rights. Query with clips of published work. Writer's guidelines for #10 SASE.
Needs: Magazine and newspaper columns and features, news items, fillers, radio broadcast material. Purchases single (one shot) features and articles series. "Looking for articles on health and fitness (nutrition, healthy recipes, sports medicine, exercise tips, running, tennis, golf, bowling, aerobics, cycling, swimming, cross-training, watersports, travel, medical advice)." Also offers to list author's business affiliation, address, and phone number in article.

Photos: Offers $25-100 for photos accepted with ms.

Tips: "Be highly qualified in the area that you are writing about. If you are going to write a medical column, you must be a doctor, or at least affiliated with a nationally recognized medical organization."

NEW YORK TIMES SYNDICATION SALES CORP., Dept. WM, 122 E. 42nd St., New York NY 10068. (212)499-3300. Fax: (212)499-3382. Executive Editor: Gloria Brown Anderson. Syndicates numerous one-shot articles. Buys second serial (reprint) rights or all rights.

Needs: Magazine and newspaper features. "On syndicated articles, payment to author is varied. We consider only articles that have been previously published." Send tearsheets of article. Pays 50% of any sales. Photos are welcome with articles.

Tips: "Topics should cover universal markets and either be by a well-known writer or have an off-beat quality. Quizzes are welcomed if well researched."

NEWS FLASH INTERNATIONAL, INC., Division of the Observer Newspapers, 2262 Centre Ave., Bellmore NY 11710-3400. (516)679-9888. Editor: Jackson B. Pokress. Estab. 1960. 25% written on contract; 25% freelance written on a one-time basis. Supplies material to Observer newspapers and overseas publications. Works with 10-20 previously unpublished writers annually. "Contact editor prior to submission to allow for space if article is newsworthy." Pays on publication. Reports in 2 months.

Nonfiction: "We have been supplying a 'ready-for-camera' sports page (tabloid size) complete with column and current sports photos on a weekly basis to many newspapers on Long Island, as well as pictures and written material to publications in England and Canada. Payment for assignments is based on the article. Payments vary from $20 for a feature of 800 words. Our sports stories feature in-depth reporting as well as book reviews on this subject. We are always in the market for good photos, sharp and clear, action photos of boxing, wrestling, football, baseball and hockey. We cover all major league ball parks during the baseball and football seasons. We are accredited to the Mets, Yanks, Jets and Giants. During the winter we cover basketball and hockey and all sports events at the Nassau Coliseum."

Photos: Purchased on assignment; captions required. Uses "good quality 8×10 b&w glossy prints; good choice of angles and lenses." Pays $7.50 minimum for b&w photos.

Tips: "Submit articles which are fresh in their approach on a regular basis with good quality black and white glossy photos if possible; include samples of work. We prefer well-researched, documented stories with quotes where possible. We are interested in profiles and bios on woman athletes. There is a big interest in this in the foreign market. Women's boxing, volleyball and basketball are major interests."

NEWSPAPER ENTERPRISE ASSOCIATION, INC., Dept. WM, 200 Park Ave., New York NY 10166-0079. (212)692-3700. Director, Syndicate: Sidney Goldberg. Editorial Director: Diana Loevy. Managing Editor, Comic Art: Amy Lago. 100% written by writers on contract. "We provide a comprehensive package of features to mostly small- and medium-sized newspapers." Reports in 6 weeks. Buys all rights.

Needs: "Any column we purchase must fill a need in our feature lineup and must have appeal for a wide variety of people in all parts of the country. We are most interested in lively writing. We are also interested in features that are not merely copies of other features already on the market. The writer must know his or her subject. Any writer who has a feature that meets all of those requirements should send a few copies of the feature to us, along with his or her plans for the column and some background material on the writer." Current columnists include Hodding Carter, III, Chuck Stone, Dr. Peter Gott, Ben Wattenberg and William Rusher. Current comics include Born Loser, Frank & Ernest, Big Nate, Kit'n' Carlyle, Berry's World, Arlo and Janis, and Snafu.

Tips: "We get enormous numbers of proposals for first person columns—slice of life material with lots of anecdotes. While many of these columns are big successes in local newspapers, it's been our experience that they are extremely difficult to sell nationally. Most papers seem to prefer to buy this sort of column from a talented local writer."

ROYAL FEATURES, P.O. Box 58174, Houston TX 77258. (713)280-0777. Executive Director: Fay W. Henry. Estab. 1984. 80% written on contract; 10% freelance written on one-time basis. Syndicates to magazines and newspapers. Reports in 2 months. Buys all rights or first North American serial rights.

Needs: Magazine and newspaper columns and features. Buys one-shot features and article series. No previously published material. Query with or without published clips. Send SASE with unsolicited queries or materials. Pays 40-60% authors percentage.

SENIOR WIRE, Clear Mountain Communications, 2377 Elm St., Denver CO 80207. (303)355-3882. Fax: (303)355-2720. Editor: Allison St. Claire. Estab. 1988. 100% freelance written. Monthly news, information and feature syndication service to various senior publications, and companies interested in senior market. Circulation nationwide, varies per article depending on which articles are bought for publication. Pays 50% of fee for each use of ms (fees range from $5-30). Pays on publication. Buys first North American serial and simultaneous rights. Submit seasonal/holiday material 3 months in advance. Prefers mss; queries only with SASE. No payment for photos but they help increase sales. Reports in up to 3 months. Writer's guidelines

$1 with SASE. Query for electronic submissions. Please indicate on top of ms if available on 3.5″ or 5.25″ floppy disk or by modem.

Needs: Does not want "anything aimed at less than age 55-plus market; anything patronizing or condescending to seniors." Manuscripts requested include: seasonal features, especially those with a nostalgic angle (750-800 words); older celebrity profiles, photos required (900-1,100 words); travel tips (no more than 500-750 words); personal travel experiences as a mature traveler, photos a must (1,000 words); poems (100-500 words); or miscellaneous other material of universal interest to seniors. Accepts 12 mss in each category/year.

Tips: "All areas open to freelancers. Sometimes give assignments to proven, reliable freelancers whose work has sold well through the syndication. Want fresh approach to senior issues; overworked themes not appreciated. Solid informational and generic articles accepted. We will not promote any product or business unless it is the only one in existence. Must be applicable to senior lifestyle."

SINGER MEDIA CORPORATION, Seaview Business Park, Unit #106, 1030 Calle Cordillera, San Clemente CA 92673-6234. (714)498-7227. Fax: (714)498-2162. Editors: Helen J. Lee and Kurt Singer. Contact: Peter Carbone. Estab. 1940. 25% written on contract; 25% freelance written on a one-time basis. Syndicates to magazines, newspapers, cassettes, book publishers. Reports in 1 month. Rights negotiable, world rights preferred. Writer's guidelines for $2 and #10 SAE.

Needs: Puzzles, quizzes, interviews, entertainment and psychology features, cartoons, books for serialization and foreign reprints. Syndicates one-shot features and article series on celebrities. Query with clips of published work. Pays 50% author's percentage. Currently syndicates Solve a Crime, by B. Gordon (mystery puzzle) and Hollywood Gossip, by June Finletter (entertainment).

Tips: "Good interviews with celebrities, men/women relations, business and job-related features have a good chance with us. Aim at world distribution and therefore have a universal approach."

‡SPECIALTY FEATURES SYNDICATE, 17255 Redford Ave., Detroit MI 48219. Managing Editor: L. E. Crandall. Estab. 1952. Buys 40-50 features/year. Syndicates to magazines (occasionally) and newspapers (currently serving 480 newspapers). Reports in 2-3 months. Buys all rights. Query with brief outlines.

Needs: Magazine and newspaper features, single features, articles series. "We specialize in 'how-to' material with emphasis on health, food, nutrition, self-improvement and book condensations of subjects with wide appeal. **Pays on acceptance** and is negotiable.

‡THE SPORTS NETWORK, 701 Masons Mill, Huntingdon Valley PA 19006. (215)947-2400. Contact: Rosalind Tucker. Estab. 1980. 30% written on contract; 10-15% freelance written on a one-time basis. Buys 200-250 features/year. Works with 50-60 writers/year. Works with 7-10 new previously unpublished writers/year. Syndicates to magazines, newspapers, radio and "we are also an international wire service." Query for electronic submissions. Reports immediately. Buys all rights. Free writer's guidelines. Query with clips of published work.

Needs: Fillers, magazine and newspaper columns and features, news items, radio broadcast material, single features (timely sports pieces, 200-300 words—more if piece is exceptional). Pays variable. Currently syndicates Sports Marketing, by Howard Schlossberg (marketing sports plus opinions on topical matters); NHL Update, by Anthony Gargano (NHL); Olympic Update, by Steve Abbott (Olympics); College Football and Basketball Analysis, by Mark Narducci; Opinion and Commentary, by Jack Whitaker.

Tips: "The competition is fast and furious so luck is as much an ingredient as talent. Making inroads to one syndicate for even one feature is an amazing door opener. Focus on the needs of that syndicate or wire (as we are) and establish a proven track record with quality work that suits specific needs. Don't give up and don't abandon the day job. No one who reads submissions really 'knows' but we are different in that we are looking for very specific items and not that magical cartoon, feature or story. Just give us your best in sports and make certain that it is in tune with what is happening right now."

SYNDICATED FICTION PROJECT, P.O. Box 15650, Washington DC 20003. Director: Caroline Marshall. Estab. 1982. 100% freelance written on a one-time basis. Buys 35-40 short stories/year (short fiction of 2,500 words or less). Syndicates to newspapers, literary magazines, etc. The quarterly *American Short Fiction*, and radio (NPR, BBC). Receives submissions in January *only* each year; replies by late May. Buys all rights for 3 years. Reports in 4 months.

Needs: Fiction (short stories of 2,500 words or fewer). Submit complete ms (January only). "Please send #10 SASE to Project for guidelines first." Pays flat rate of $500 for purchase of rights, $100/print publication thereafter, $100 if used in print or audio anthology.

Tips: "We're looking for stories of exceptional quality that have a 'high narrative profile' (principally because they work best on radio)."

SYNDICATED NEWS SERVICE, 232 Post Ave., Rochester NY 14619-1398. (716)328-2144. Fax: (716)328-7018. E-mail: SWS@rochgte.fidonet.org; also New York and Toronto bureaus. Editor/Publisher: Frank Judge. Estab. 1982. 50% written by writers on contract. Buys 10-20 features/year. Works with 5-10 previously unpublished writers/year. Syndicates to newspapers and magazines (weekly, daily and monthly). Reports in

6 months. Buys all rights. "Use *Writer's Digest* recommendations for submission format." Accepts submissions by disk, fax and e-mail.

Needs: Fiction, fillers, magazine and newspaper columns and features and news items. "Please send submissions in manuscript form with finished art if applicable." Does not purchase single (one-shot) features. Submit complete ms. Author's percentage 50% of gross sales. Currently syndicates Filmbriefs by Frank Judge (entertainment), Windows by Paul Murphy (computer), Mind & Body by Dr. Julian Whitaker (health), Fast Forward by Mike Cidoni (entertainment), Fractured Facts by John Locke (cartoons), Deliberate Tourist by Mary Whitney (travel).

‡**UNITED CARTOONIST SYNDICATE**, P.O. Box 7081, Corpus Christi TX 78415. (512)850-2930. Contact: Pedro Moreno. Estab. 1975. 40% written on contract; 10% freelance written on a one-time basis. Buys 25 features/year. Works with 25 writers/year. Works with 10 new previously unpublished writers/year. Syndicates to magazines, newspapers and book stores. Buys all rights. Writer's guidelines for $10. Submit $10 first (check or money order) for guidelines, then material.

Needs: Fiction, fillers, magazine and newspaper columns and features, news items, comic strips and panels and single features (500 words or less with brief illustration, comic strip or comic panel). Pays $25-100 for photos. Currently syndicates Ten Commandments, by James Rodriguez (comic book); Comic Guidelines, by Pedro Moreno (guidelines); Caricatures, by Pedro Moreno (caricatures).

Tips: "Do not submit handwritten material or bad copies. Send clean typewritten material."

UNITED FEATURE SYNDICATE, 200 Park Ave., New York NY 10166-0079. (212)692-3700. Syndicate Director: Sid Goldberg. Executive Editor: Diana Loevy. Director International Newspaper Operations: Edvard Kaplan. Managing Editor, Comic Art: Amy Lago. 100% contract writers. Supplies features to 1,700 US newspapers, plus Canadian and other international papers. Works with published writers. Query with 4-6 samples and SASE. Reports in 2 months.

Needs: Current columnists include Jack Anderson, Judith Martin, Donald Lambro, Martin Sloane. Comic strips include Peanuts, Nancy, Drabble, Marmaduke, Rose is Rose to Dilbert. Standard syndication contracts are offered for columns and comic strips.

Tips: "We buy the kind of writing similar to other major syndicates—varied material, well-known writers. The best way to break in to the syndicate market is for writers to latch on with a major newspaper and to develop a following. Also, cultivate new areas and try to anticipate trends."

UNIVERSAL PRESS SYNDICATE, Dept. WM, 4900 Main St., Kansas City MO 64112. (816)932-6600. Contact: Syndicate Editorial. Estab. 1970. Buys syndication rights. Reports normally in 1 month. Return postage required.

Nonfiction: Looking for features—columns for daily and weekly newspapers. Distributes one-shot articles (profiles, lifestyle pieces, etc). "Any material suitable for syndication in daily newspapers." Currently handling James J. Kilpatrick, Dear Abby, Erma Bombeck and others. Payment varies according to contract.

WASHINGTON POST WRITERS GROUP, 1150 15th St. NW, Washington DC 20071-9200. (202)334-6375. Editorial Director/General Manager: Alan Shearer. Estab. 1973. Currently syndicates 32 features (columns and cartoons). News syndicate that provides features for newspapers nationwide. Reports in 3 weeks. Buys all rights.

Needs: Newspaper columns (editorial, lifestyle, humor), and features (comic strips, political cartoons). Query with clips of published work and samples of proposed column. Currently syndicates George F. Will column (editorial), Ellen Goodman column (editorial), David Broder column (editorial), William Raspberry column (editorial) and June Bryant Quinn column (financial). Writers Group will not consider freelance single articles or stories.

Tips: "The Washington Post Writers Group will review editorial page and lifestyle page columns, as well as political cartoons and comic strips. Probably will not consider games, puzzles, or similar features. Send sample columns and cartoons or comic strips (photocopies—no original artwork, please) to the attention of Alan Shearer, editorial director. Enclose a SASE for the return and response."

WHITEGATE FEATURES SYNDICATE, 71 Faunce Dr., Providence RI 02906. (401)274-2149. Contact: Eve Green. Editor: Ed Isaac. Estab. 1987. Buys 100% of material from freelance writers. Syndicates to newspapers; planning to begin selling to magazines and radio. Query for electronic submissions. Reports in 3 months. Buys all rights.

Needs: Fiction for Sunday newspaper magazines; magazine and newspaper columns and features, cartoon strips. Buys one-shots and article series. Query with clips of published work. For cartoon strips, submit samples. Pays 50% author's percentage on columns. Additional payment for photos accepted with ms. Currently syndicates Indoor Gardening, by Jane Adler; Looking Great, by Gloria Lintermans; Strong Style, by Hope Strong; On Marriage and Divorce, by Dr. Melvyn A. Berke.

Tips: "Please aim for a topic that is fresh. Newspapers seem to want short text pieces, 400-800 words. We do *not* to return materials. We like to know a little about author's or cartoonist's background. We prefer people who have already been published. Please send material to Eve Green."

● Whitegate features is looking for more gardening, travel, medical and food text columns.

WORLD NEWS SYNDICATE, LTD., P.O. Box 419, Hollywood CA 90078-0419. (213)469-2333. Fax: (818)398-9624. Managing Editor: Laurie Williams. Estab. 1965. Syndicates to newspapers. Reports in 1 month. Buys first North American serial rights. Query with published clips. "We're looking for short columns, featurettes, home, medical, entertainment-interest, music, TV, films. Nothing over 500-600 words."
Needs: Fillers and newspaper columns. Pays 45-50% author's percentage.

Syndicates/Changes '94-'95

The following syndicates were listed in the 1994 edition but do not have listings in this edition of *Writer's Market*. The majority did not respond to our request to update their listings or return a questionnaire for a new listing. If a reason was given for their exclusion, we have included it in parentheses after the listing name.

American News Feature Syndicate (unable to contact)
Ameripress/Ameriprensa
Craft Patterns, Inc.
Europa Press News Service
FNA News (out of business)
(Gabriel) Graphics News Bureau

General News Syndicate (out of business)
GSM Features
A.D. Kahn, Inc.
National News Bureau
Newspaper Enterprise Association
Oceanic Press Service (see

Singer Media Corporation)
Pacific News Service (overwhelmed by submissions)
The Southam Syndicate
Teenage Corner, Inc.
Tribune Media Services
United Features Syndicate
United Media

Greeting Cards & Gift Ideas

How many greeting cards showed up in your mailbox last year? If you are in line with the national average, you received 31 cards, seven of them for your birthday. That's according to figures published by The Greeting Card Association, a national trade organization representing the multi-billion dollar greeting card industry.

In fact, nearly 50% of all first class mail now consists of greeting cards. And, of course, card manufacturers rely on writers to supply them with enough skillfully crafted sentiments to meet the demand. The perfect greeting card verse is one that will appeal to a large audience, yet will make each buyer feel that the card was written exclusively for him or her.

Three greeting card companies continue to dominate this industry; together, American Greetings, Hallmark and Gibson Greetings supply about 80% of all cards sold. The other 20% are published by hundreds of companies who have found success mainly by not competing head to head with the big three but by choosing instead to pursue niche markets—regional and special-interest markets that the big three either cannot or do not supply.

A professional approach to markets

As markets become more focused, it's important to keep current on specific company needs. Familiarize yourself with the differences among lines of cards by visiting card racks. Ask retailers which lines are selling best. You may also find it helpful to read trade magazines such as *Greetings* and *Party and Paper Retailer*. These publications will keep you apprised of changes and events within the field, including seminars and trade shows.

Once you find a card line that appeals to you, write to the company and request its market list, catalog or submission guidelines (usually available for a SASE or a small fee). This information will help you determine whether or not your ideas are appropriate for that market.

Submission procedures vary among greeting card publishers, depending on the size and nature of the company. Keep in mind that many companies (especially the large ones) will not review your writing samples until you've signed and returned their disclosure contract or submission agreement, assuring them that your material is original and has not been submitted elsewhere.

Some editors prefer to see individual card ideas on 3×5 cards, while others prefer to receive a number of complete ideas on $8\frac{1}{2} \times 11$ bond paper. Be sure to put your best pieces at the top of the stack. Most editors do not want to see artwork unless it is professional, but they do appreciate conceptual suggestions for design elements. If your verse depends on an illustration to make its point or if you have an idea for a unique card shape or foldout, include a dummy card with your writing samples.

The usual submission includes from 5 to 15 card ideas and an accompanying cover letter, plus mechanical dummy cards, if necessary. Some editors also like to receive a résumé, client list and business card. Some do not. Be sure to check the listings and the company's writer's guidelines for such specifications before submitting material.

Payment for greeting card verse varies, but most firms pay per card or per idea; a handful pay small royalties. Some companies prefer to test a card first and will pay a small fee for a used card idea. In some instances, a company may even purchase an idea and revise it.

Greeting card companies will also buy ideas for gift products and may plan to use card material for a number of subsequent items. Licensing—the sale of rights to a particular character for a variety of products from mugs to T-shirts—is a growing part of the greetings industry. Because of this, however, note that most card companies buy all rights. We now include in this section markets for licensed product lines such as mugs, bumper stickers, buttons, posters and the like.

Information of interest to writers wishing to know more about working with the greeting card industry is available from the Greeting Card Creative Network. Write them at Suite 760, 1200 G Street NW, Suite 760, Washington, DC 20005.

Managing your submissions

Because you will be sending out many samples, you may want to label each sample. Establish a master card for each verse idea and record where and when each was sent and whether it was rejected or purchased. Keep all cards sent to one company in a batch and give each batch a number. Write this number on the back of your return SASE to help you match up your verses as they are returned.

For more information on greeting card companies not listed in *Writer's Market*, see Greeting Card & Gift Ideas/Changes '94-'95 at the end of this section.

‡**ALLPORT EDITIONS INC.**, 532 NW 12th, Portland OR 97209. Contact: Michael Allport or Victoria Allport. Estab. 1982. 10% freelance written. Bought 25 ideas/samples last year. Submit seasonal/holiday material 6 months in advance. Reports in 3 months. Pays on publication. Writer's guidelines free. Market list available on mailing list basis.
Needs: Juvenile, conventional, inspirational, humorous. Submit no fewer than 8 ideas/batch.
Tips: Looking for "alternative cards, whimsical, humorous."

AMBERLEY GREETING CARD CO., 11510 Goldcoast Dr., Cincinnati OH 45249-1695. (513)489-2775. Editor: Ned Stern. Estab. 1966. 90% freelance written. Bought 200 freelance ideas/samples last year. Reports in 1 month. Material copyrighted. Buys all rights. **Pays on acceptance.** Writer's guidelines for #10 SASE. Market list regularly revised.
Needs: "Original, easy to understand, belly-laugh or outrageous humor. We sell to the 'masses, not the classes' so keep it simple and to the point. Humor accepted in all captions, including general birthday, family birthday, get well, anniversary, thank you, friendship, etc. No non-humorous material needed or considered this year. Pays $150/card idea."
  • This company is now accepting seasonal humor.
Tips: "Send SASE for our writer's guidelines before submitting. Amberley publishes humorous specialty lines in addition to a complete conventional line that is accented with humor. Since humor is our specialty, we are highly selective. Be sure that a SASE with the correct US postage is included with your material. Otherwise it will not be returned."

AMERICAN GREETINGS, Dept. WM, One American Rd., Cleveland OH 44144. (216)252-7300. Creative Recruitment Dept: Lynne Shlonsky. No unsolicited material. "We like to receive a letter of inquiry describing education or experience, or a résumé first. We then request samples from those that interest us." Reports in 3 months. Buys all rights. **Pays on acceptance.** Guidelines for #10 SASE.
Tips: "Our target audience is the mass-market retail crowd, so we're open to conventional verse, contemporary prose, humorous verse and off-the-wall humor styles."

ARGUS COMMUNICATIONS, 200 E. Bethany, Allen TX 75002-3804. (214)390-6300. Fax: (214)727-2175. Editorial Coordinator: Lori Potter. 90% freelance written. Primarily interested in material for posters. Reports in 2 months. Buys all rights. **Pays on acceptance.** Submission guidelines available for #10 SASE.
Needs: Posters for teachers to place in their classrooms that are positive, motivational, inspirational, thought-provoking and success oriented. Also poster editorial that reflects basic values such as honesty, integrity, kindness, trust etc. Teamwork and conflict resolution are target subjects as well. Also posters for teenagers ages 13-18 humorously captioned with brief text reflecting current trends, lifestyles and attitudes. Humor and light sarcasm are the emphasis for this age group.

Other Product Lines: Greeting cards, postcards, calendars.

Tips: "Keep in mind that poster editorial is an at-a-glance message that is succinct and memorable. Our posters capture your attention with a creative mixture of humorous, dynamic and motivational editorial. We encourage you to be funny, to be inspirational, but also to be brief. Please indicate the market your submission is for on the outside of your envelope."

BLUE MOUNTAIN ARTS, INC., Dept. WM, P.O. Box 1007, Boulder CO 80306-1007. Contact: Editorial Staff. Estab. 1971. Buys 100+ items/year. Reports in 6-8 months. Pays on publication.

Needs: "We are interested in reviewing poetry and writings that would be appropriate for greeting cards, which means that they should reflect a message, feeling, or sentiment that one person would want to share with another. We'd like to receive sensitive, original submissions about love relationships, family members, friendships, philosophies, and any other aspect of life. Poems and writings for specific holidays (Christmas, Valentine's Day, etc.) and special occasions, such as graduation, birthdays, anniversary, and get well are also considered." Submit seasonal material at least 4 months in advance. Buys worldwide, exclusive rights, $200/poem; anthology rights $25.

Other Product Lines: Calendars, gift books, prints, mugs.

Tips: "We strongly suggest that you familiarize yourself with our products before submitting material, although we caution you not to study them too hard. We do *not* need more poems that sound like something we've already published. We're looking for poetry that expresses real emotions and feelings, so we suggest that you have someone specific in mind (a friend, relative, etc.) as you write. The majority of the poetry we publish *does not rhyme*. We do not wish to receive books, unless you are interested in having portions excerpted for greeting cards; nor do we wish to receive artwork or photography. We prefer that submissions be typewritten, one poem per page. Only a small portion of the freelance material we receive is selected each year, either for publication on a notecard or in a gift anthology, and the review process can also be lengthy, but please be assured that every manuscript is given serious consideration."

THE BRANCHES, INC., (formerly New Boundary Designs, Inc.), 1389 Park Rd., Chanhassen MN 55317. (612)474-0924. Fax: (612)474-9525. President: Chuck Schneider. Estab. 1979. 5% freelance written. Receives 100 submissions/year; bought 9 freelance ideas/samples last year. Submit seasonal/holiday material 1 year in advance. Reports in 3 months. Pays on publication.

Needs: Traditional, inspirational, juvenile, sensitivity. Prefers unrhymed verse.

‡BRIGHTON PUBLICATIONS, INC., P.O. Box 120706, St. Paul MN 55112-0706. (612)636-2220. Fax: (612)636-2220. President: Sharon Dlugosch. Estab. 1977. 100% freelance written. Receives minimal submissions each year; bought minimal ideas/samples last year. Reports in 3 months. Pays royalties. Free writer's guidelines/market list. Market list issued one time only.

BRILLIANT ENTERPRISES, 117 W. Valerio St., Santa Barbara CA 93101-2927. President: Ashleigh Brilliant. Estab. 1967. Buys all rights. Submit words and art in black on 3½ × 3½ horizontal, thin white paper in batches of no more than 15. Reports "usually in 2 weeks." Catalog and sample set for $2.

Needs: Postcards. Messages should be "of a highly original nature, emphasizing subtlety, simplicity, insight, wit, profundity, beauty and felicity of expression. Accompanying art should be in the nature of oblique commentary or decoration rather than direct illustration. Messages should be of universal appeal, capable of being appreciated by all types of people and of being easily translated into other languages. Because our line of cards is highly unconventional, it is essential that freelancers study it before submitting. No topical references or subjects limited to American culture or puns." Limit of 17 words/card. Pays $50 for "complete ready-to-print word and picture design."

THE CALLIGRAPHY COLLECTION INC., 2604 NW 74th Place, Gainesville FL 32606-1237. (904)375-8530. Fax: (904)374-9957. Editor: Katy Fischer. Reports in 6 months. Buys all rights. Pays on publication.

Needs: "Ours is a line of framed prints of watercolors with calligraphy." Conventional, humorous, informal, inspirational, sensitivity, soft line. Prefers unrhymed verse, but will consider rhymed. Submit 3 ideas/batch. Pays $50-100/framed print idea.

Other Product Lines: Gift books, greeting books, plaques.

Tips: "Sayings for friendship are difficult to get. Bestsellers are humorous, sentimental and inspirational ideas—such as for wedding and family and friends. Our audience is women 20 to 50 years of age. Write something they would like to give or receive as a lasting gift."

COMSTOCK CARDS, Suite 15, 600 S. Rock, Reno NV 89502-4115. Fax: (702)856-9406. Owner: Patti P.Wolf. Art Director: David Delacroix. Estab. 1986. 35% freelance written. Receives 200 submissions/year; bought 150 freelance ideas/samples last year. Submit seasonal/holiday material 1 year in advance. Reports in 5 weeks. Buys all rights. **Pays on acceptance.** Writer's guidelines/market list for SASE. Market list issued one time only.

Needs: Humorous, informal, invitations, "puns, put-downs, put-ons, outrageous humor aimed at a sophisticated, adult female audience. Also risqué cartoon cards. No conventional, soft line or sensitivity hearts and flowers, etc." Pays $50-75/card idea, negotiable.
Other Product Lines: Notepads, cartoon cards, invitations.
Tips: "Always keep holiday occasions in mind and personal me-to-you expressions that relate to today's occurrences. Ideas must be simple and concisely delivered. A combination of strong image and strong gag line make a successful greeting card. Consumers relate to themes of work, sex and friendship combined with current social, political and economic issues."

CONTEMPORARY DESIGNS, 213 Main St., Gilbert IA 50105. (515)232-5188. Fax: (515)232-3380. Editor: Sallie Abelson. Estab. 1977. 90% freelance written. Submit seasonal/holiday material 1 year in advance. Reports in 1-2 months. Buys all rights. **Pays on acceptance.**
Needs: Short positive humorous copy for memo pads, mugs, etc.
Other Product Lines: Quote and gift books, mugs, tote bags, aprons and pillow cases.

CONTENOVA GIFTS, 1239 Adanac St. Vancouver, British Columbia V6A 2C8 Canada. (604)253-4444. Fax: (604)253-4014. Creative Director: Russ Morris. Estab. 1965. 100% freelance written. Receives an estimated 15,000 submissions/year. Submit ideas on 3×5 cards or small mock-ups in batches of 10-15. Buys world rights. **Pays on acceptance.** Current needs list for SAE and IRC.
Needs: Humorous. Both risqué and non-risqué for mugs. "Short gags with good punch work best." Birthday, belated birthday, get well, anniversary, thank you, congratulations, miss you, new job, etc. Seasonal ideas needed for Christmas, Valentine's Day, Mother's Day, Father's Day. Pays $30.
Tips: "No longer using drinking themes. Put together your best ideas and submit them. One great idea sent is much better than 20 poor ideas filling an envelope. We are always searching for new writers who can produce quality work. You need not be previously published. Our audience is 18-65 — the full mug consumers. We do *not* use poetry."

CREATE-A-CRAFT, P.O. Box 330008, Fort Worth TX 76163-0008. (817)292-1855. Estab. 1967. 5% freelance written. Receives 300 submissions/year; bought 2 freelance ideas/samples last year. Submit seasonal/holiday material 1 year in advance. "No phone calls from freelancers accepted. We deal through agents only. Submissions not returned even if accompanied by SASE — not enough staff to take time to package up returns." Buys all rights. Sample greeting cards $2.50 for #10 SASE.
Needs: Announcements, conventional, humorous, juvenile, studio. "Payment depends upon the assignment, amount of work involved, and production costs involved in project."
Tips: No unsolicited material. "Send letter of inquiry describing education and experience, or résumé with one sample first. We will screen applicants and request samples from those who interest us."

CURRENT, INC., Box 2559, Colorado Springs CO 80901-2559. (719)594-4100. Creative Writing Manager: Nan Roloff Stine. Estab. 1950. 5-10% freelance written. Receives an estimated 1,500 submissions/year; bought 180 ideas/samples last year. Submit seasonal/holiday material 18 months in advance. Reports in 2 months. Buys all rights. **Pays on acceptance.** "Flat fee only; no royalty." Writer's guidelines for #10 SASE.
Needs: Humorous. All occasion and woman-to-woman cards; short 1-2 line puns for all occasions not too risque; short children's stories. Pays $50/sentiment.
Tips: "We are primarily looking for original humor of all forms, except risqué, off-color sentiments. 99% of our customers are women and 80% of them are married and have children under the age of 18. Writers need to keep in mind that this is the audience we are trying to reach. We pick up trends and create our own. We suggest that writers keep abreast of what's selling at retail. Don't send traditional short prose sentiments or off-color humor because we *don't* buy it. Read our direct mail catalog."

DESIGN DESIGN INC., P.O. Box 2266, Grand Rapids MI 49501-2266. Fax: (616)774-4020. President: Don Kallil. Estab. 1985. 100% freelance written. Receives 450 submissions/year. Submit seasonal/holiday material 1 year in advance. Reports in 2 months. Buys all rights. Pays on publication. Free writer's guidelines on request.
Needs: Announcements, informal, juvenile, conventional, sensitivity, seasonal, humorous, invitations. Prefers unrhymed verse. Submit 12 ideas/batch. Also looking for traditional, sentimental, beautiful.
Tips: "All ages of adults is our target audience. No risqué material."

DIGRESSIONS, INC., 44 Old Pomona Rd., Suffern NY 10901. (914)354-0816. Vice President: Lenore Benowitz. Estab. 1989. 25% freelance written. Receives 500 submissions annually; bought 25 ideas/samples last

---

ALWAYS enclose a self-addressed, stamped envelope (SASE) with all your queries and correspondence.

year. Submit seasonal/holiday material 6 months in advance. Reports in 1 month. Buys all first time rights. Pays on publication. Writer's guidelines/market list for #10 SASE.
Needs: Humorous, seasonal/holidays, birthdays. Prefers unrhymed verse ideas. Submit 10 ideas/batch.
Tips: Seeking humorous material, all ages.

‡**DISKOTECH INC.**, Suite 210, 7930 State Line, Prairie Village KS 66208. (913)432-8606. Fax: (913)362-4869. CompuServe CIS: 72754, 2773. Publisher/Editor: John Slegman. Estab. 1989. Publishes PCcards™ which are multimedia greeting cards that come on computer diskettes and run on PCs. PCcards™ are for all seasons, ages and tastes. Looking for short, exciting computer animations, better if they include music or sound effects. Also looking for freelance writers with ideas/sentiments. Need all types of humor. Enclose SASE with submissions. Reprots in 6 weeks. Recent PCcards™ include 3-D, interactive 4-D and virtual reality.

EPHEMERA, INC., P.O. Box 490, Phoenix OR 97535. Contact: Editor. Estab. 1979. 90% freelance written. Receives 20,000 submissions/year; bought 200 ideas/samples last year. Reports in 2½ months. Buys all rights. Pays on publication. Writer's guidelines/market list for #10 SASE. Market list issued one time only.
Needs: Button ideas: "original, provocative, irreverent and outrageously funny slogans for buttons and magnets sold in card and gift shops, bookstores, record shops, political and gay shops, adult stores, amusement parks etc.!" Pays $25/slogan.

FLAVIA STUDIOS, (formerly Weedn Design), 3rd Floor, 740 State St., Santa Barbara CA 93101. (805)564-6905. Estab. 1986. 5% freelance written. Receives 20 submissions/year. Submit seasonal/holiday material 2 years in advance. Reports in 1 month. Buys licensing rights. Pays on royalty basis.
Needs: Inspirational, sensitivity, soft line. Prefers unrhymed verse. Submit 10-15 ideas/batch.
Other Product Lines: Calendars, gift books, greeting books, posters. "Payment is based on royalties, not bought outright."
Tips: "Most of our cards and books are written by in-house writers, mainly Flavia, our most well known property. Audience is 18-55-year-old caring women. Products marketed worldwide, strong inspirational following."

FOTOFOLIO, INC., 536 Broadway, New York NY 10012. (212)226-0923. Fax: (212)226-0072. Editors: Julie Galant and Ron Schick. Estab. 1976. Submit seasonal/holiday material one year in advance (visuals only). Reports in 1 month. Pays on publication.
Other Product Lines: Postcards, notecards, posters.
Tips: "We specialize in high quality fine art photography."

‡**THE C.R. GIBSON COMPANY**, 32 Knight St. Norwalk CT 06856. (203)847-4543. Contact: Julie Mitchell. 50% freelance written. Receives 200 submissions/year; bought 15 ideas/samples last year. Submit holiday/seasonal material 8-9 months in advance. Reports in 4-5 months. Buys book, greeting card rights. **Pays on acceptance.** Writer's guidelines free.
Needs: Conventional, inspirational, humorous. Prefers unrhymed verse. Submit 10 ideas/batch.
Other Product Lines: Gift books.

GIBSON GREETINGS, INC., 2100 Section Rd., Box 371804, Cincinnati OH 45222.
- Gibson is one of the three largest publishers in the greeting card business. They publish cards in all popular subject areas. Query for guidelines before submitting.

‡**GIFTED LINE**, 999 Canal Blvd., Point Richmond CA 94804. Contact: Julie Grovhoug. Estab. 1985. 5% freelance written. Bought 1 idea/sample last year. Submit seasonal/holiday material 6 months in advance. Reports in 1 month. Material not copyrighted. **Pays on acceptance.** Market list regularly revised.
Needs: Announcements, inspirational. Submit 6-10 ideas/batch.
Tips: "We design Victorian greeting cards only. We enjoy clever, thoughtful, sweet verses. A touch of humor is good, too."

HALLMARK CARDS, INC., P.O. Box 419580, Mail Drop 216, Kansas City MO 64141-6580. Contact Carol King for submission agreement and guidelines. Include SASE; no samples. Reports in 2 months. Work is on assignment basis, working from "needs lists" only. "Most needs are met by large writing staff; freelancers must show exceptional originality and stylings not available from inhouse employees, and must have previous sentiment writing experience."

IMAGINE, Dept. WM, 21431 Stans Lane, Laguna Beach CA 92651. (714)497-1800. Contact/Owners: John Stuhr/Nan Goin. Estab. 1982. 50% freelance written. Receives 150 submissions/year; bought 75 ideas/samples last year. Submit seasonal/holiday material 1 year in advance. Reports in 2 months. Material not copyrighted. Time of payment varies. Free writer's guidelines/market list. Market list regularly revised.

Needs: "We are open to all ideas." Submit 12 ideas/batch.
Other Product Lines: Bumper stickers, gift books, greeting books, plaques, postcards, promotions, puzzles, greeting cards, humorous slogans. Pays $25 and up.

KIMBERLEY ENTERPRISES, INC., 15029 S. Figueroa St., Gardena CA 90248-1721. (310)538-1331. Fax: (310)538-2045. Vice President: M. Hernandez. Estab. 1979. 15% freelance written. Receives less than 100 submissions/year; bought 12 ideas/samples last year. Submit seasonal material 9 months in advance. Reports in up to 3 months. Material not copyrighted. Pays on acceptance. Market list available on mailing list basis.
Needs: Announcements, conventional, inspirational, invitations. Send 12 ideas maximum.
Other Product Lines: Plaques. Pays $10-250.
Tips: "The primary future interest for the company is in the plaque line, with an emphasis on inspirational or conventional appeal."

‡KOGLE CARDS, INC., 1498 S. Lipan St., Denver CO 80223. (303)698-9007. Art Director: Patricia Koller. Estab. 1982. 40% freelance written. Receives 100 submissions/year; bought 80 ideas/samples last year. Submit seasonal/holiday material 18 months in advance. Reports in 1 month. Buys all rights. Pays on publication. No guidelines.
Needs: Humorous, business related. Rhymed or unrhymed verse ideas.
Tips: "We produce cards designed for the business community, in particular salespeople, real estate, travel, hairdresser, insurance and chiropractic."

‡LOVE GREETING CARDS, INC., 1717 Opa Loca Blvd., Opa-Locka FL 33054. (305)685-5683. Contact: Anita Drittel. Estab. 1984. 75% freelance written. Receives 200-300 submissions/year; bought 400 ideas/samples last year. Submit seasonal/holiday material 6 months in advance. Reports in 1 month. Buys all rights. **Pays on acceptance.** Market list regularly revised.
Needs: Informal, juvenile, humorous, general.
Other Product Lines: Greeting books ($100-300), posters ($200-500).
Tips: "There's a great demand for animal cards."

MAILAWAYS, P.O. Box 782, Tavares FL 32778-0782. (904)742-8196. Editor: Gene Chambers. Estab. 1992. Submit seasonal/holiday material 3 months in advance. Reports in 1 month. Material "not yet copyrighted, but will be." Rights negotiable. **Pays on acceptance.** Writer's guidelines for #10 SASE. Market list issued one time only.
Needs: Inspirational, sensitivity, experimental poetry. Prefers either rhymed or unrhymed verse. Submit 5 ideas/batch.
Other Product Lines: Gift books ($10, negotiable), greeting books ($10, negotiable).
Tips: "What sells best is the *short*, inspirational verse, rhymed or not, upbeat but with an emotional *jolt* of familiar feeling. Audience is both the average person *and* the *sensitive soul.*"

OATMEAL STUDIOS, P.O. Box 138W3, Rochester VT 05767. (802)767-3171. Creative Director: Helene Lehrer. Estab. 1979. 85% freelance written. Buys 200-300 greeting card lines/year. **Pays on acceptance.** Reports within 2 months. Current market list for #10 SASE.
Needs: Birthday, friendship, anniversary, get well cards, etc. Also Christmas, Chanukah, Mother's Day, Father's Day, Easter, Valentine's Day, etc. Will review concepts. Humorous material (clever and *very* funny) year-round. "Humor, conversational in tone and format, sells best for us." Prefers unrhymed contemporary humor. Current pay schedule available with guidelines.
Other Product Lines: Notepads, stick-on notes.
Tips: "The greeting card market has become more competitive with a greater need for creative and original ideas. We are looking for writers who can communicate situations, thoughts, and relationships in a funny way and apply them to a birthday, get well, etc., greeting and we are willing to work with them in targeting our style. We will be looking for material that says something funny about life in a new way."

‡PAPER MOON GRAPHICS, P.O. Box 34672, Los Angeles CA 90034. (310)645-8700. Contact: Angie Novak. Estab. 1978. 90% freelance written. Receives 2,000 submissions/year; bought 500 ideas/samples last year. Submit seasonal/holiday material 7 months in advance. Reports in 2 months. Buys card, stationery, advertising rights. **Pays on acceptance.** Writer's guidelines for SASE. Market list regularly revised.
Needs: Humorous, alternative humor/risqué. Prefers unrhymed verse ideas. Submit 12-18 ideas/batch.
Other Product Lines: Stationery.
Tips: "Humor cards sell best for female audience 19-45. Trends are changing daily—humor always sells."

PARAMOUNT CARDS INC., Dept. WM, P.O. Box 6546, Providence RI 02940-6546. (401)726-0800. Contact: Editorial Freelance Coordinator. Estab. 1906. Buys 200 greeting card ideas/year. Submit seasonal/material at least 6 months in advance. Reports in 1 month. Buys all rights. **Pays on acceptance.** Writer's guidelines for SASE.

Needs: All types of conventional verses. Fresh, inventive humorous verses, especially family birthday cards. Would also like to see more conversational prose, especially in family titles such as Mother, Father, Sister, Husband, Wife, etc. Submit in batches of 10-15. Does not want tired, formulaic rhymes.

Tips: "Study the market! Go to your local card shops and analyze what you see. Ask the storekeepers which cards are selling. Then apply what you've learned to your own writing. The best cards (and we buy only the best) will have mass appeal and yet, in the consumer's eyes, will read as though they were created exclusively for her. A feminine touch is important, as 90% of all greeting cards are purchased by women."

C.M. PAULA COMPANY, 7773 School Rd., Cincinnati OH 45249. Contact: Editorial Supervisor. Estab. 1958. 10% freelance written. Receives 100 submissions/year. "We purchase both per idea or set fee per project." Reports in 4-6 weeks. Buys all rights. **Pays on acceptance.** Writer's guidelines issued only to previously published social-expression writers. Send SASE.

Product Lines: Plaques, key rings, magnets, stationery pads, coffee mugs, collectible plates, dimensional statues and awards.

Tips: "Our needs range from inspirational verse and prose to cute sayings and light humor (nothing risqué). A writer can get a quick idea of the variety of copy we use by looking over our store displays. Please note—we do not publish greeting cards."

PEACOCK PAPERS INC., 273 Summer St., Boston MA 02210-1500. Fax: (617)423-3717. Contact: Mia Miranda, New Product Manager. Estab. 1982. 85% freelance written. Receives 1,000 submissions/year; bought 100 ideas/samples last year. Submit seasonal/holiday material 10 months in advance. Reports in 3 months. Buys all rights. **Pays on acceptance.** Writer's guidelines/market list for #10 SASE. Market list regularly revised.

Needs: Prefers unrhymed verse. Submit ideas on 8½×11 paper, double spaced.

Other Product Lines: Also produces soft goods (T-shirts, night shirts, boxer shorts, women's bikinis), ceramic mugs, lapel and jumbo buttons, key tags, gift bags (all sizes). Pays $50 for first product use; $25 for second; $12.50 for additional uses.

Tips: "Best-selling lines for us are ones that capture current events/themes, witty or humorous thoughts with current themes, age-related lines and series (however, they must be up-beat and must relate to a broad group of people). We do not accept risqué, off-color lines nor do we purchase greeting card copy."

PLUM GRAPHICS INC., P.O. Box 136, Prince Station, New York NY 10012. (212)966-2573. Editor: Dennis James. Estab. 1983. 100% freelance written. Bought 21 samples last year. Does not return samples unless accompanied by SASE. Reports in 3-4 months. Buys greeting card and stationery rights. Pays on publication. Guidelines sheet for SASE. "Sent out about twice a year in conjunction with the development of new cards."

Needs: Humorous. "We don't want general submissions. We want them to relate to our next line." Prefers unrhymed verse. Greeting cards pay $40.

Tips: "Sell to all ages. Humor is always appreciated. Wants short, to-the-point lines."

PORTAL PUBLICATIONS, 770 Tamalpias Dr., Corte Madera CA 94925. (415)924-5652. Attention: Editorial Department. Estab. 1954. 50% freelance written. Receives 200 submissions/year; bought 100 freelance ideas/samples last year. Reports in 3 months. Pays on publication. "Please send an example of your work so that we may keep it on file. If in the future, we have a need for writers for our greeting cards or other products we will contact you."

Needs: Conventional, humorous, informal, soft line, studio. Also copy for humorous and inspirational posters. Prefers unrhymed verse. Submit 12 ideas/batch.

Other Product Lines: Calendars, posters.

Tips: "Upscale, cute, humorous cards for bookstores and college bookstores."

QUALITY ARTWORKS, 2262 N. Penn Rd., P.O. Box 369, Hatfield PA 19440-0369. Creative Director: Linda Tomezsko Morris. Estab. 1985. 10% freelance written. Reports in 2 months. Buys all rights. **Pays on acceptance.** Writer's guidelines/market list for #10 SASE. Market list issued one time only.

Needs: Conventional, humorous, inspirational, juvenile, sensitivity, soft line. Prefers unrhymed verse.

Other Product Lines: Gift books, bookmarks, scrolls, stationery, blank books. Payment is negotiable.

Tips: "We are looking for sophisticated yet inspirational verse, as well as humor (directed towards children and women). The main emphasis of our business is bookmarks."

‡RESTAURANT GREETING CARDS, 9038 Chrysanthemum Dr., Boynton Beach FL 33937. (407)732-8297. Contact: Michael Tomasso. Estab. 1975. 75% freelance written. Receives 100 submissions/year; bought 10 ideas/samples last year. Submit seasonal/holiday material 8 months in advance. Reports in 3 months. Pays on publication. Market list is available to writer on mailing list basis.

Needs: Humorous (must be restaurant related). Prefers unrhymed verse.

Tips: "Target market is restaurants. Humorous greeting, birthday, thank you, sells well. Pizza delivery, Chinese delivery, bagel, bakery, deli. Be sure not to offend ethnicity of card."

ROCKSHOTS, INC., 632 Broadway, New York NY 10012. (212)420-1400. Fax: (212)353-8756. Editor: Bob Vesce. Estab. 1979. "We buy 75 greeting card verse (or gag) lines annually." Submit seasonal/holiday material 1 year in advance. Reports in 2 months. Buys rights for greeting-card use. Writer's guidelines for SASE.
Needs: Humorous ("should be off-the-wall, as outrageous as possible, preferably for sophisticated buyer"); soft line; combination of sexy and humorous come-on type greeting ("sentimental is not our style"); and insult cards ("looking for cute insults"). No sentimental or conventional material. "Card gag can adopt a sentimental style, then take an ironic twist and end on an off-beat note." Submit no more than 10 card ideas/samples per batch. Send to attention: Submissions. Pays $50/gagline. Prefers gag lines on 8 × 11 paper with name, address, and phone and social security numbers in right corner, or individually on 3 × 5 cards.
Tips: "Think of a concept that would normally be too outrageous to use, give it a cute and clever wording to make it drop-dead funny and you will have commercialized a non-commercial message. It's always good to mix sex and humor. Our emphasis is definitely on the erotic. Hard-core eroticism is difficult for the general public to handle on greeting cards. The trend is toward 'light' sexy humor, even cute sexy humor. 'Cute' has always sold cards, and it's a good word to think of even with the most sophisticated, crazy ideas. 80% of our audience is female. Remember that your gag line will be illustrated by a photographer. So try to think visually. If no visual is needed, the gag line *can* stand alone, but we generally prefer some visual representation. It is a very good idea to preview our cards at your local store if this is possible to give you a feeling of our style."

SANGAMON, INC., P.O. Box 410, Taylorville IL 62568. (217)824-2261. Contact: Editorial Department. Estab. 1931. 90% freelance written. Reports in 3 months. Buys all rights. **Pays on acceptance.** Writer's guidelines or market list for SASE. Market list is regularly revised.
Needs: Conventional, humorous, inspirational, juvenile, sensitivity, studio. "We offer a balance of many styles. We'd like to see more conversational prose styles for the conventional lines." Submit 15 ideas maximum/batch.
Other Product Lines: Calendars, promotions.
Tips: "We only request submissions based on background and writing experience. We work 12-18 months ahead of a season and only accept material on assignment."

‡SCANDECOR INC., 430 Pike Rd., Southampton PA 18966. (215)355-2410. Fax: (215)364-8737. Creative Director: Lauren B. Harris. Estab. 1970. 40% freelance written. Receive 700 submissions/year; bought 46 freelance ideas/samples last year. Reports in 2 months. Buys poster rights.
Needs: Humorous, inspirational, juvenile, sensitivity, soft line, studio. Rhymed or unrhymed OK.
Other Product Lines: Posters ($150-1,000).
Tips: "Our posters are our main product in the US. Our target audience is mother-child, 0-8, teen market, 8-22 and adult."

‡MARCEL SCHURMAN CO., INC., 2500 N. Watney Way, Fairfield CA 94533. Editor: Meg Schutte. Estab. 1950. 20% freelance written. Receives 500 submissions/year; bought 50 freelance ideas/samples last year. Reports in 1 month. **Pays on acceptance.** Writer's guidelines for #10 SASE.
Needs: Conventional, light humor, informal, juvenile, sensitivity, conversational, seasonal and everyday categories. Prefers unrhymed verse, but on juvenile cards rhyme is OK. Submit 10-15 cards in single batch.
Tips: "Historically, our nostalgic and art museum cards sell best. However, we are moving toward more contemporary cards and humor. Target market: upscale, professional, well-educated; average age 40; more female."

SCOTT CARDS INC., P.O. Box 906, Newbury Park CA 91319. President: Larry Templeman. Estab. 1985. 95% freelance written. Bought 75 freelance ideas/samples last year. Now looking at seasonal/holiday cards. Reports in 5 months. **Pays on acceptance.** Writer's guidelines/brochure for #10 SAE with 2 first-class stamps. "Please do not send sample work to P.O. Box 906. Our guidelines will give specific information on how to submit your work for consideration."
Needs: Conventional, humorous, sensitivity.
Tips: "New ways to say 'I love you' always sell if they aren't corny or too obvious. Humor helps, especially if there is a twist. We are looking for non-traditional sentiments that are sensitive, timely and sophisticated. Our cards have a distinct flavor, so before submitting your work, write for our guidelines and sample brochure."

SILVER VISIONS, P.O. Box 415, Newton Highlands MA 02161. (617)244-9504. Editor: B. Kaufman. Estab. 1981. Submit seasonal/holiday material 9-12 months in advance. Reports in 6 months. Pays on publication. Guidelines for SASE.
Needs: Humorous, humorous Jewish, contemporary occasion for photography line. "Copy must work with a photograph; in other words, submit copy that can be illustrated photographically." Send 10-16 card ideas/batch.

SNAFU DESIGNS, Box 16643, St. Paul MN 55116. (612)646-6118. Editor: Scott F. Austin. Estab. 1985. Reports in 6 weeks. Buys all rights. **Pays on acceptance.** "Before we send you our guidelines, please send us something that is representative of your sense of humor (include a SASE). We will send you our guidelines if we feel your humor is consistent with ours."

Needs: Humorous, informal, birthday, friendship, thank you, anniversary, congratulations, get well, new baby. Prefers unrhymed verse. Submit no more than 10 ideas/batch. Pays $75/idea.

Tips: "We use clever ideas that are simple and concisely delivered and are aimed at a sophisticated adult audience. Off-the-wall humor that pokes fun at the human condition. Please do not submit anything cute."

SUNRISE PUBLICATIONS, INC., P.O. Box 4699, Bloomington IN 47402-4699. (812)336-9900. Contact: Editorial Coordinator. Estab. 1974. 100% freelance written. Receives an estimated 1,000 submissions/year; bought 50 freelance ideas/samples last year. Reports in 2 months. Buys worldwide exclusive license in all commercial formats. **Pays on acceptance.** Free writer's guidelines. Market list regularly revised.

Needs: Contemporary, conventional, humorous, informal, soft line. No "off-color humor or lengthy poetry." Prefers unrhymed verses/ideas. "Generally, we like short one- or two-line captions, sincere or clever. Our customers prefer this to lengthy rhymed verse. Longer copy is used but should be conversational. Submit ideas for birthday, get well, friendship, wedding, baby congrats, sympathy, thinking of you, anniversary, belated birthday, thank you, fun and love. We also have strong seasonal lines that use traditional, humorous and inspirational verses. These seasons include Christmas, Valentine's Day, Easter, Mother's Day, Father's Day, Graduation, Halloween and Thanksgiving." Payment varies.

Tips: "Think always of the sending situation and both the person buying the card and its intended recipient."

TLC GREETINGS, 615 McCall Rd., Manhattan KS 66502. (913)776-4041. Fax: (913)539-2107, ext. 232. Creative Director: Michele Johnson. Estab. 1987. 80% freelance written. Bought approximately 25 ideas/samples per month. Submit seasonal/holiday material 6 months in advance. Reports in 1 month. Buys rights to the purchased idea/sentiment. **Pays on acceptance.** Writer's guidelines/market list for any size SAE with 2 first-class stamps. Market list regularly revised; available to writer on mailing list basis.

 • This company reports it is working with writers on an assignment basis instead of making individual purchases.

Needs: Studio, humorous, invitations, soft line. Prefers unrhymed verse. Submit 30 ideas/batch.

Other Product Lines: Mugs, note pads, posters, gift bags, greeting books. ("Our minimum is $35; maximum we negotiate.")

Tips: "Our target audience is women. What sells well for us are cards that are humorous. We do not use risqué, although we're beginning to use more cards that are a little biting (making fun of the recipient). Also expanding into the male audience, by looking at sports/leisure related activities. Interested also in college humor."

TRISAR, INC., 121 Old Springs Rd., Anaheim CA 92808. (714)282-2626. Editor: Randy Harris. Estab. 1979. 50% freelance written. Receives 1,000 submissions/year; bought 50 ideas/samples last year. Submit seasonal/holiday material 10 months in advance. Reports in 3 months. Buys all rights. **Pays on acceptance.** Writer guidelines for #10 SASE.

Needs: Humorous, studio, age-related feelings about turning 40, 50, 60; seasonal oriented themes including Love, Mom, Dad, Grad, Halloween, Christmas. Unrhymed verse and one-liners only. Submit ideas on 3×5 cards.

Other Product Lines: T-shirts, boxers, mugs, greeting cards, buttons. Also gift bags and paper party goods. Current pay scale available with guidelines.

Tips: "Best-selling lines capture current lifestyle, witty thoughts on growing older. We do not accept risqué statements. Up-beat statements that appeal to a broad range of people are best. Especially looking for humor about turning 50 and retirement. Fresh puns for graduation and holidays such as Halloween are important."

VAGABOND CREATIONS, INC., 2560 Lance Dr., Dayton OH 45409. (513)298-1124. Editor: George F. Stanley, Jr. 10% freelance written. Bought 10-15 ideas/samples last year. Submit seasonal/holiday material 6 months in advance. Reports in 1 week. Buys all rights. Ideas sometimes copyrighted. **Pays on acceptance.** Writer's guidelines for #10 SASE. Market list issued one time only.

Needs: Cute, humorous greeting cards (illustrations and copy) often with animated animals or objects in people-situations with short, subtle tie-in message on inside page only. No poetry. Pays $15-25/card idea.

VINTAGE IMAGES, P.O. Box 228, Lorton VA 22199. (703)550-1881. Editor: Brian Smolens. Estab. 1986. Not accepting freelance material at this time. Reports in 3 months. Buys all rights. Pays on publication. Writer's guidelines/market list for 9×12 SAE with 3 first-class stamps.

Needs: Humorous only. "We supply pictures—caption *must* be written to match." Also developing new architectural and travel series.

Other Product Lines: Postcards ($20), posters ($25-50).

WARNER PRESS, PUBLISHERS, P.O. Box 2499, 1200 E. Fifth St., Anderson IN 46018-9988. Product Editor: Robin Fogle. Estab. 1880. 50% freelance written. Reports in 2 months. Buys all rights. **Pays on acceptance.** Must send #10 SASE for guidelines before submitting.

• This company reports that they are watching their spending more closely, mainly purchasing material for immediate use only.
Needs: Religious themes; sensitive prose and inspirational verse for boxed cards, posters, calendars. Pays $20-35. Also accepts ideas for coloring and activity books.

WEST GRAPHICS, #7, 385 Oyster Point Blvd., South San Francisco CA 94080. (800)648-9378. Fax: (415)588-5552. Contact: Production Department. Estab. 1980. 60% freelance written. Receives 1,000 submissions/year; bought 200 freelance ideas/samples last year. Reports in 6 weeks. Buys greeting card rights. Pays 30 days after publication. Writer's guidelines/market list for #10 SASE.
Needs: "We are looking for outrageous contemporary humor that is on the cutting edge. Our most successful cards humorously capture the contradiction between innocence and that which surprises, shocks or insults." Prefers unrhymed verse. Submit 10-30 ideas/batch. Pays $100.
Other Product Lines: Notepads, gift bags.
Tips: "West Graphics is an alternative greeting card company committed to the production and distribution of quality products. West Graphics offers a diversity of humor from 'off the wall' to 'tastefully tasteless'. Our goal is to publish cards that challenge the limits of taste and keep people laughing. The majority of our audience is women in their 30s and 40s, ideas should be targeted to issues they care about: relationships, sex, aging, success, money, crime, etc."

CAROL WILSON FINE ARTS, INC., P.O. Box 17394, Portland OR 97217-1810. Fax: (503)287-2217. Editor: Gary Spector. Estab. 1983. 90% freelance written. Receives thousands of submissions/year; bought 100 freelance ideas/samples last year. Submit seasonal/holiday material 1 year in advance. Reports in 2 months. Buys negotiable rights. Pays on acceptance or publication depending on type of agreement. Writer's guidelines/market list for #10 SASE.
Needs: Humorous, unrhymed. Pays $50-100/card idea. "Royalties could be considered for a body of work."
Tips: "We are looking for laugh-out-loud, unusual and clever ideas for greeting cards. All occasions are needed but birthday cards are needed most of all. It's OK to be outrageous or risqué. Cards should be 'personal.' Ask yourself—is this a card that someone would buy for a specific person?"

Greeting Cards & Gift Ideas/Changes '94-'95

The following greeting card publishers were listed in the 1994 edition but do not have listings in this edition of *Writer's Market*. The majority did not respond to our request to up date their listings or return a questionnaire for a new listing. If a reason was given for their exclusion, we have included it in parentheses after the listing name.

Amcal (no freelance writing)
Blue Sky
Country Toons (unable to contact)
Create-A-Craft
N.J. Croce (no freelance writing)
Fullmoon Creations Inc. (removed by request)
Gallant Greetings
Marian Heath Greeting Cards, Inc. (no freelance writing)
Life Greetings
Malena Productions (no freelance writing)
Outreach Publications (removed by request for 1 year)
P.S. Greetings/ Fantus Paper
Products
Painted Hearts & Friends
Red Farm Studio
Rule 62 Studio (out of business)
Second Nature Inc. (removed by request for 1 year)

Resources

Contests and Awards

The contests and awards listed in this section are arranged alphabetically by subject. Nonfiction writers can turn immediately to nonfiction awards listed alphabetically by the name of the contest or award. The same is true for fiction writers, poets, playwrights and screenwriters, journalists, children's writers and translators. You'll also find general book awards, miscellaneous awards, arts council and foundation fellowships, and multiple category contests.

New contests and awards are announced in various writer's publications nearly every day. However, many lose their funding or fold—and sponsoring magazines go out of business just as often. We have contacted the organizations whose contests and awards are listed here with the understanding that they are valid through 1995. If you are using this section in 1996 or later, keep in mind that much of the contest information listed here will not be current. Requirements such as entry fees change, as do deadlines, addresses and contact names.

To make sure you have all the information you need about a particular contest, always send a self-addressed, stamped, business-sized envelope (#10 SASE) to the contact person in the listing before entering a contest. The listings in this section are brief, and many contests have lengthy, specific rules and requirements that we could not include in our limited space. And many contests have specific entry forms that must accompany your submission. A response with rules and guidelines will not only provide specific instructions, it will also confirm that the award is still being offered.

When you receive a set of guidelines, you will see that some contests are not for some writers. The writer's age, previous publication, geographic location and the length of the work are common matters of eligibility. Read the requirements carefully to ensure you don't enter a contest for which you are not qualified. You should also be aware that every year, more and more contests, especially those sponsored by "little" literary magazines, are charging entry fees.

Contest and award competition is very strong. While a literary magazine may publish 10 short stories in an issue, only one will win the prize in a contest. Give yourself the best chance of winning by sending only your best work. There is always a percentage of manuscripts a contest judge or award director casts off immediately as unpolished, amateurish or wholly unsuitable for the competition.

To avoid first-round rejection, make certain that you and your work qualify in every way for the award. Some contests are more specific than others. There are many contests and awards for a "best poem," but some award only the best lyric poem, sonnet or haiku.

Winning a contest or award can launch a successful writing career. Take a professional approach by doing a little extra research. Find out who the previous winner of the award was by investing in a sample copy of the magazine in which the prize-winning article, poem or short story appeared. Attend the staged reading of an award-winning play. Your extra effort will be to your advantage in competing with writers who simply submit blindly.

If a contest or award requires nomination by your publisher, ask your publisher to nominate you. Many welcome the opportunity to promote a work (beyond their own, conventional means) they've published. Just be sure the publisher has plenty of time before the deadline to nominate your work.

Further information on funding for writers is available at most large public libraries. See the *Annual Register of Grant Support* (National Register Publishing Co., 3004 Glenview Rd., Wilmette IL 60091); *Foundations and Grants to Individuals* (Foundation Center, 79 Fifth Ave., New York NY 10003) and *Grants and Awards Available to American Writers* (PEN American Center, 568 Broadway, New York NY 10012). For more listings of contests and awards for fiction writers, see *Novel & Short Story Writer's Market* (Writer's Digest Books). *Poet's Market* (Writer's Digest Books) lists contests and awards available to poets. *Children's Writer's & Illustrator's Market* (Writer's Digest Books) has a section of contests and awards, as well. Two more good sources for literary contests are *Poets & Writers* (72 Spring St., New York NY 10012), and the *Associated Writing Programs Newsletter* (Old Dominion University, Norfolk VA 23529). Journalists should look into the annual Journalism Awards Issue of *Editor & Publisher* magazine (11 W. 19th St., New York NY 10011), published in the last week of December. Playwrights should be aware of the newsletter put out by The Dramatists Guild, (234 W. 44th St., New York NY 10036).

For more information on contests and awards not listed in *Writer's Market*, see Contests and Awards/Changes '94-'95 at the end of this section.

General

THE ATHENAEUM OF PHILADELPHIA LITERARY AWARD, The Athenaeum of Philadelphia, 219 S. Sixth St., Philadelphia PA 19106-3794. (215)925-2688. Award Director: Lea C. Sherk. Estab. 1949. Nominated book by a Philadelphia resident. Deadline: December 31.

THE CHRISTOPHER AWARD, The Christophers, 12 E. 48th St., New York NY 10017. (212)759-4050. Award Director: Peggy Flanagan. Estab. 1949. Outstanding books published during the calendar year that "affirm the highest values of the human spirit."

COMMONWEALTH CLUB OF CALIFORNIA BOOK AWARDS, (formerly California Literature Award), 595 Market St., San Francisco CA 94105. (415)597-6700. Fax: (415)597-6729. Contest/Award Director: Annie Hayflick. Estab. 1931. Offered annually. Previously published submissions must have appeared in print between 1/1 and 12/31 of the previous year. "Purpose of award is the encouragement and production of literature in California. Categories include: fiction, nonfiction, poetry, first novel, juvenile ages up to 10, juvenile 11-16, notable contribution to publishing and California." Deadline: January 1. Guidelines for SASE. Can be nominated by publisher as well. Prize: "Medals to be awarded at publicized event." Judged by jury of 8-10 academics and peers selected by the club's Board of Governors. "Work must be authored by California resident (or must have been a resident at time of publication)."

EDITORS' BOOK AWARD, Pushcart Press, P.O. Box 380, Wainscott NY 11975. (516)324-9300. President: Bill Henderson. Unpublished books. Deadline: September 15. "All manuscripts must be nominated by an editor in a publishing house."

‡HOOSIER HORIZON WRITING CONTEST, Write-On, Hoosiers, Inc., P.O. Box 51, Crown Point IN 46307. (219)663-707. Contact: Sharon Palmieri. Offered annually for unpublished work to build an awareness of Indiana talent. Deadline: July. Guidelines for SASE. Charges $1 fee per poem or story (check or money order only). Prize: 1st-$15, publication and plaque; 2nd-$10, certificate and ribbon; 3rd-$5, certificate and ribbon. Open to all Indiana writers.

JERUSALEM PRIZE, Jerusalem International Book Fair, Municipality of Jerusalem, 1 Safra Square P.O. Box 775, Jerusalem, Israel 91007. 02-240663 or 245142. Fax: 02-243144. Estab. 1963. "Biennial competition for which authors must be nominated. Winner receives $5,000 and citation, and becomes a guest of Jerusalem Book Fair." Contest is judged by a jury of three (Israeli professors, authors, dignitaries). "Any writer can be nominated. The prize, however, is awarded to an internationally recognized author whose works express the idea of the freedom of man in society."

MINNESOTA VOICES PROJECT COMPETITION, New Rivers Press, #910, 420 N. Fifth St., Minneapolis MN 55401. (612)339-7114. Editor/Publisher: C.W. Truesdale. Annual award for new and emerging writers of poetry, prose, essays, and memoirs (as well as other forms of creative prose) from Wisconsin, Minnesota, Iowa and the Dakotas, to be published in book form for the first time. Deadline: April 1. Guidelines for SASE.

‡MODERN LANGUAGE ASSOCIATION PRIZE FOR A FIRST BOOK, Modern Language Association, 10 Astor Place, New York NY 10003-6981. (212)475-9500. Fax: (212)477-9863. Contest Director: Richard Brod. Offered annually for the first book-length publication by a current member of the association. To qualify, a book must be a literary or linguistic study, a critical edition of an important work, or a critical biography. Studies dealing with literary theory, media, cultural history and writer disciplinary topics are eligible. Deadline: May 1. Guidelines for SASE. Prize: $1,000 and certificate.

NEW WRITING AWARD, New Writing, Box 1812, Amherst NY 14226-7812. Contest/Award Director: Sam Meade. Offered annually for unpublished work. "Purpose is to award the best of *new* writing. We accept short stories, poems, plays, novels, essays, films and emergent forms. All are considered for the award based on originality. Charges $10 fee first entry; $5 additional—no limit. Prize: Monetary award and possible publication. Judged by editors of magazine. "We are looking for new, interesting and experimental work."

OHIOANA BOOK AWARDS, Ohioana Library Association, Room 1105, 65 S. Front St., Columbus OH 43215. Phone/fax: (614)466-3831. Editor: Barbara Maslekoff. Estab. 1929. Books published within the past 12 months by Ohioans or about Ohio and Ohioans. Submit 2 copies of book on publication.

PULITZER PRIZES, The Pulitzer Prize Board, 702 Journalism, Columbia University, New York NY 10027. (212)854-3841. Estab. 1917. Awards for journalism in US newspapers (published daily or weekly), and in letters, drama and music by Americans. Deadline: February 1 (journalism); March 1 (music and drama); July 1 and November 1 (letters).

‡ROCKY MOUNTAIN ARTIST'S/ECCENTRIC BOOK COMPETITION, Hemingway Western Studies Center, Boise State University, 1910 University Dr., Boise ID 83725. (208)385-1999. Fax: (208)385-4373. Contest Director: Tom Trusky. Offered annually "to publish multiple edition artist's or eccentric books of special interest to Rocky Mountain readers. Topics must be public issues (race, gender, environment, etc.). Authors may hail from Topeka or Ulan Bator, but their books must initially have regional appeal." Deadline: September 1-December 1. Guidelines for SASE. Prize: $500, publication, standard royalties. Judged by: First round: 5 regional judges; semi-finalists are evaluated by four judges from a national board. First rights to Hemingway Center. Open to any writer.

SAINT LOUIS LITERARY AWARD, Associates of Saint Louis University Libraries, 40 N. Kingshighway, St. Louis MO 63108-1392. (314)361-1616. Fax: (314)361-0812. Estab. 1967. Annual award. Works are nominated by committee.

THE CARL SANDBURG LITERARY ARTS AWARDS, The Friends of the Chicago Public Library, 400 S. State St., 9S-7, Chicago IL 60605. (312)747-4907. Estab. 1979. Chicago (and metropolitan area) writers of published fiction, nonfiction, poetry and children's literature. Deadline for submission: August 1.

SMALL PRESS PUBLISHER OF THE YEAR, Quality Books Inc., 918 Sherwood Dr., Lake Bluff IL 60044-2204. (312)295-2010. Fax: (708)295-1556. Contact: Amy Mascillino. Estab. 1964. "Each year a publisher is named that publishes titles we stock and has demonstrated ability to produce a timely and topical title, suitable for libraries. This publisher attains 'quality bestseller status and supports their distributor.' " Title must have been selected for stocking by Quality Books Inc. QBI is the principal nationwide distributor of small press titles to libraries.

SOCIETY OF MIDLAND AUTHORS AWARD, Society of Midland Authors, % Ford-Choyke, 29 E. Division St., Chicago IL 60610. (312)337-1482. President: Jim Bowman. Offered annually for work published between January 1 and December 31. "Award for best work by writers of the 12 Midwestern states: Illinois, Indiana, Iowa, Kansas, Michigan, Minnesota, Missouri, Nebraska, North Dakota, South Dakota, Wisconsin, Ohio and the stimulation of creative literary effort. Seven categories: poetry, adult fiction, adult nonfiction, biography, juvenile fiction, juvenile nonfiction, drama." Deadline: January 15. Guidelines for SASE. Money and plaque given at annual dinner in Chicago, in May.

TOWSON STATE UNIVERSITY PRIZE FOR LITERATURE, College of Liberal Arts, Towson State University, Towson MD 21204-7097. (410)830-2128. Award Director: Dean Annette Chappell. Estab. 1979. Book or book-length ms that has been accepted for publication, written by a Maryland author of no more than 40 years of age. Deadline: May 15.

SAUL VIENER PRIZE, American Jewish Historical Society, 2 Thornton Rd., Waltham MA 02154. Editor: Marc Lee Raphael. Estab. 1985. Offered every 2 years for work published within previous 2 years. "Award for outstanding scholarly work in American Jewish history." Deadline: February 15. Write/call Marc Lee Raphael. Prize: $500. Open to any writer.

WHITING WRITERS' AWARDS, Mrs. Giles Whiting Foundation, 1133 Avenue of the Americas, New York NY 10036. Director: Gerald Freund. "The Foundation gives annually $30,000 each to up to ten writers of poetry, fiction, nonfiction and plays. The awards place special emphasis on exceptionally promising emerging talent." Direct applications and informal nominations are not accepted by the Foundation.

H.W. WILSON LIBRARY PERIODICAL AWARD, donated by H.W. Wilson Company, administered by the American Library Association, Awards Committee, 50 E. Huron, Chicago IL 60611. (312)280-3217. Annual award consisting of $1,000 and certificate presented to a periodical published by a local, state or regional library, library group, or association in US or Canada which has made an outstanding contribution to librarianship. (This excludes publications of ALA, CLA and their divisions.) All issues for the calendar year prior to the presentation of the award will be judged on the basis of sustained excellence in both content and format, with consideration being given to both purpose and budget. Deadline for nominations is December 1.

WORLD FANTASY AWARDS ASSOCIATION, #1B, 5 Winding Brook Dr., Guilderland NY 12084-9719. President: Peter Dennis Pautz. Estab. 1975. Previously published work recommended by previous convention attendees in several categories, including life achievement, novel, novella, short story, anthology, collection, artist, special award-pro and special award non-pro. Deadline: July 1. Works are recommended by attendees of previous 2 years' conventions, and a panel of judges. Winners determined by vote of panel.

Nonfiction

‡**HERBERT BAXTER ADAMS PRIZE**, American Historical Association, 400 A St. SE, Washington DC 20003. Contact: Executive Assistant. Annual award for "an author's first substantial book by a US or Canadian author in the field of ancient, medieval or early modern European history (to 1815) history." Guidelines for #10 SASE. Prize: $1,000. Deadline: May 15.

ANNUAL PERSONAL ESSAY CONTEST, Belles Lettres: A Review of Books by Women, 11151 Captain's Walk Ct., North Potomac MD 20878-0441. Phone/fax: (301)294-0278. Contest Director: Renee Shea. Send entries to 1151 Captain's Walk Court, North Potomoc MD 20878. Estab. 1993. Offered annually for unpublished work "to promote excellence in personal essay writing." Entries accepted January 1-July 31 of each year. Contest rules and entry forms available for SASE. Charges $20 fee. "This entitles writer to 1 year's subscription to *Belles Lettres*. Current subscribers may enter for free." Prize: $500. "Rights revert to author after piece is published, except for anthology inclusions." Open to women only.

‡**ANTHEM ESSAY CONTEST**, Anthem Contest Information, P.O. Box 6099 Dept. DB, Inglewood CA 90312. Contest Director: Dr. Michael S. Berliner. Offered annually for unpublished essays to encourage analytical thinking and writing excellence, and to introduce students to the philosophic and psychological meaning of Ayn Rand's novelette *Anthem*. Deadline: March 30. Guidelines for SASE. Prize: 1st-$1,000; 2nd-$200 (10); 3rd-$100 each (10). All papers are first read by a national testing service; semi-finalists' and finalists' papers are read by a panel of writers, professors and high school teachers. Submissions are not returned, but entrants retain publishing rights. Entrants must be 9th and 10th graders in high school.

‡**MRS. SIMON BARUCH UNIVERSITY AWARD**, United Daughters of the Confederacy, 328 N. Boulevard, Richmond VA 23220-4057. (404)255-0549. Biennial award offered in even years for unpublished work for the purpose of encouraging research in Southern history, the United Daughters of the Confederacy offers

The double dagger before a listing indicates that the listing is new in this edition. New markets are often more receptive to freelance submissions.

as a grant-aid of publication the Mrs. Simon Baruch University Award of $2,000. Deadline: May 1. Authors and publishers interested in the Baruch Award contest should ask for a copy of these rules. All inquiries should be addressed to the Chairman of the Mrs. Simon Baruch University Award Committee at the above address. Award: $2,000 plus $500. Invitation to participate in the contest is extended (1) to anyone who has received a Master's, Doctoral, or other advanced degree within the past fifteen years, from a university in the United States: and (2) to any graduate student whose thesis or dissertation has been accepted by such an institution. Manuscripts must be accompanied by a statement from the registrar giving dates of attendance, and by full biographical data together with passport photograph of the authors.

‡**GEORGE LOUIS BEER PRIZE**, American Historical Association, 400 A St. SE, Washington DC 20003. Contact: Executive Assistant. Awarded annually for the best work on European international history since 1895. Prize: $1,000. Deadline: May 15.

‡**ALBERT J. BEVERIDGE AWARD**, American Historical Association, 400 A St. SE, Washington DC 20003. Annual award for a "distinguished book in English on the history of the US, Latin America or Canada from 1492 to the present." Guidelines for #10 SASE. Prize: $1,000. Deadline: May 15.

‡**THE PAUL BIRDSALL PRIZE IN EUROPEAN MILITARY & STRATEGIC HISTORY**, The American Historical Association, 400 A. St. SE, Washington DC 20003. Contact: Executive Assistant. Biennial award of $1,000 for "a major work in European military and strategic history." Guidelines for SASE. Deadline: May 15.

‡**JAMES HENRY BREASTED PRIZE**, American Historical Association, 400 A St. SE, Washington DC 20003. Contact: Executive Assistant. Offered annually in a four-year chronological cycle for an outstanding book in any field of history prior to 1000 A.D. Prize: $1,000. Deadline: May 15.

CLIFFORD PRIZE, American Society for 18th Century Studies, Computer Center 108, Utah State University, Logan UT 84322-3730. (801)750-4065. Fax: (801)750-4065. Executive Secretary: Dr. Jeffrey Smitten. Offered annually for previously published work, "the best nominated article, an outstanding study of some aspect of 18th-century culture, interesting to any 18th-century specialist, regardless of discipline." Guidelines for SASE. Prize: $500, certificate from ASECS. Judged by committee of distinguished members. Winners must be society members.

MORTON N. COHEN AWARD, Modern Language Association of America, 10 Astor Place, New York NY 10003-6981. (212)475-9500. Fax: (212)477-9863. Director: Richard Brod. Estab. 1989. Awarded in odd numbered years for a previously published distinguished edition of letters. At least 1 volume of the edition must have been published during the previous 2 years. Prize: $1,000. Guidelines for #10 SASE. Deadline: May 1.

DE LA TORRE BUENO PRIZE, Dance Perspectives Foundation, % 85 Ford Ave., Fords NJ 08863-1652. (908)738-7598. Fax: (908)548-2642. Contact: Barbara Palfy. Estab. 1973. Open to writers or their publishers who have published an original book of dance scholarship within the previous year. Deadline: January 15.

‡**THE PREMIO DEL REY PRIZE**, The American Historical Association, 400 A St. SE, Washington DC 20003. Contact: Executive Assistant. Biennial award of $1,000 "for a distinguished book in English in the field of early Spanish and Hispanic history and culture (prior to 1516)." Guidelines for SASE. Deadline: May 15.

DEXTER PRIZE, Society for the History of Technology, Dept. of Social Sciences, Michigan Tech Univ., 1400 Townsend Dr., Houghton MI 49931-1295. (906)487-2459. Fax: (906)487-2468. Contact: Society Secretary. Estab. 1968. For work published in the previous 3 years: for 1995–1992 to 1994. "Award given to the best book in the history of technology." Deadline: April 15. Guidelines for SASE. Prize: $2,000 and a plaque from the Dexter Chemical Company.

‡**JOHN H. DUNNING PRIZE IN AMERICAN HISTORY**, Executive Assistant, American Historical Association, 400 A St. SE, Washington DC 20003. Biennial award offered in odd years. $1,000 award for any topic in US history. Deadline: June 15.

THE RALPH WALDO EMERSON AWARD, The Phi Beta Kappa Society, 1811 Q St. NW, Washington DC 20009-1696. (202)265-3808. Contact: Administrator, Phi Beta Kappa Book Awards. Estab. 1960. Studies of the intellectual and cultural condition of man published in the US during the 12-month period preceding the entry deadline, and submitted by the publisher. Books must have been published between May 1, 1993 and April 30, 1994. Deadline: April 30. Author must be a US citizen or resident.

DAVID W. AND BEATRICE C. EVANS BIOGRAPHY AWARD, Mountain West Center for Regional Studies, Utah Sate University, University Hill, Logan UT 84322-0735. (801)750-3630. Fax: (801)750-3899. Contact: F. Ross Peterson or Shannon R. Hoskins. Estab. 1983. Offered for published or unpublished work to encour-

age the writing of biography about people who have played a role in Mormon Country. (Not the religion, the country: Intermountain West with parts of Southwestern Canada and Northwestern Mexico.) Deadline: December 31, 1994. Publishers or author may nominate book. Criteria for consideration: Work must be a biography or autobiography on "Mormon Country"; must be submitted for consideration for publication year's award; new editions or reprints are not eligible; mss are accepted. Submit 6 copies.
- The award continues to be $10,000, but this may change in the near future.

‡JOHN K. FAIRBANK PRIZE IN EAST ASIAN HISTORY, American Historical Association, 400 A St. SE, Washington DC 20003. Contact: Executive Assistant. Annual award for "an outstanding book on the history of China proper, Vietnam, Chinese central Asia, Mongolia, Manchuria, Korea or Japan since the year 1800." Guidelines for #10 SASE. Prize: $1,000. Deadline: May 15.

‡HERBERT FEIS AWARD FOR NONACADEMICALLY-AFFILIATED HISTORIANS, American Historical Association, 400 A St. SE, Washington DC 20003. Contact: Executive Assistant. Estab. 1984. Awarded annually for the best book, article/articles, or policy paper by an historian not affiliated with academe. Funded by a grant from the Rockefeller Foundation, the prize is $1,000. Deadline: May 15.

‡FOUNTAINHEAD ESSAY CONTEST, Ayn Rand Institute, Fountainhead Essay Contest Information, P.O. Box 6004 Dept. DB, Inglewood CA 90312. Contest Director: Dr. Michael S. Berliner. Offered annually for unpublished essays to encourage analytical thinking and writing excellence, and to introduce students to the philosophic and psychological meaning of Ayn Rands' novel *The Fountainhead*. Deadline: April 15. Guidelines for SASE. Prize: 1st-$5,000; 2nd-$1,000 (5); 3rd-$500 each (10). All papers are first read by a national testing service; semi-finalists' and finalists' papers are read by a panel of writers, professors and high school teachers. Submissions are not returned, but entrants retain publishing rights. Entrants must be juniors or seniors in high school.

THE CHRISTIAN GAUSS AWARD, The Phi Beta Kappa Society, 1811 Q St. NW, Washington DC 20009-1696. (202)265-3808. Contact: Administrator, Phi Beta Kappa Book Awards. Estab. 1950. Works of literary criticism or scholarship published in the US during the 12-month period preceding the entry deadline, and submitted by the publisher. Books must have been published between May 1, 1993 and April 30, 1994. Deadline: April 30. Author must be a US citizen or resident.

‡LEO GERSHOY AWARD, American Historical Association, 400 A St. SE, Washington DC 20003. Contact: Executive Assistant. Awarded annually to the author of the most outstanding work in English on any aspect of the field of 17th and 18th-century Western European history. Prize: $1,000. Deadline: May 15.
- The Leo Gershoy Award has doubled its cash prize.

CLARENCE HARING PRIZE, American Historical Association, 400 A St. SE, Washington DC 20003. Contact: Executive Assistant. Awarded quinquennially for the best work by a Latin American scholar in Latin American history. Prize: $500. Deadline: May 15. Next award year is 1996.

‡JOAN KELLY MEMORIAL PRIZE IN WOMEN'S HISTORY, American Historical Association, 400 A St. SE, Washington DC 20003. Contact: Executive Assistant. Estab. 1984. Offered annually for the best work in women's history and/or feminist theory. Prize: $1,000. Deadline: May 15.

KATHERINE SINGER KOVACS PRIZE, Modern Language Association of America, 10 Astor Place, New York NY 10003-6981. (212)475-9500. Fax: (212)477-9863. Director: Richard Brod. Estab. 1990. Annual award for book in English on Latin American or Spanish literatures and cultures published in previous year. Guidelines for #10 SASE. Prize: $1,000. Deadline: May 1.

‡THE LINCOLN PRIZE AT GETTYSBURG COLLEGE, Lincoln & Soldiers Institute, Gettysburg College, Campus Box 435, Gettysburg PA 17325. (717)337-6590. Fax: (717)337-6596. Chairman of the Board: Gabor S. Boritt. Previously published works appearing in print between January 1 and December 31 each year; prize to be awarded February of the following year. "To recognize annually the finest scholarly work on Abraham Lincoln, the Civil War soldier, or on the American Civil War. All things being equal, preference will be given to work on Lincoln, the Civil War soldier and work that addresses the literate general public. In rare instances the Prize may go to a work of fiction, poetry, drama and beyond." Deadline: December 1, July 1 (for spring publications). Guidelines for #10 SASE. Prize: $50,000 cash award and sculpture. "Ten copies of the published entry must be submitted by the appropriate deadline, accompanied by a brief letter stating the author, title of work and publication date."

JOSEPH W. LIPPINCOTT AWARD, Donated by Joseph W. Lippincott, Jr. Administered by the American Library Association Awards Committee, 50 E. Huron, Chicago IL 60611. (312)280-3217. "Annual award consisting of $1,000 and a citation of achievement presented to a librarian for distinguished service to the profession, such service to include outstanding participation in the activities of professional library associations, notable published professional writing, or other significant activity on behalf of the profession and its aim." Deadline for nominations: December 1.

‡**LITTLETON-GRISWOLD PRIZE**, American Historical Association, 400 A St. SE, Washington DC 20003. Contact: Executive Assistant. Estab. 1985. Awarded annually for the best book in any subject on the history of American law and society. Deadline: May 15.

LOFT CREATIVE NONFICTION RESIDENCY PROGRAM, The Loft, Pratt Community Center, 66 Malcolm Ave. SE, Minneapolis MN 55414-3551. Attn: Program Director. Estab. 1974. Opportunity to work in month-long seminar with resident writer and cash award to 6 creative nonfiction writers. "Must live close enough to Minneapolis to participate fully." Deadline: November (subject to change).

JAMES RUSSELL LOWELL PRIZE, Modern Language Association of America, 10 Astor Place, New York NY 10003-6981. (212)475-9500. Fax: (212)477-9863. Director: Richard Brod. Annual award for literary or linguistic study, or critical edition or biography published in previous year. Open to MLA members only. Guidelines for #10 SASE. Prize: $1,000. Deadline: March 1.

‡**HOWARD R. MARRARO PRIZE**, American Historical Association, 400 A St. SE, Washington DC 20003. Contact: Executive Assistant. Awarded annually for the best work in any epoch of Italian history, Italian cultural history, or Italian-American relations. Prize: $500. Deadline: May 15.

HOWARD R. MARRARO PRIZE, Modern Language Association of America, 10 Astor Place, New York NY 10003-6981. (212)475-9500. Fax: (212)477-9863. Director: Richard Brod. Awarded in even numbered years for books or essays on any phase of Italian literature or comparative literature involving Italian, published in previous 2 years. Open to MLA members only. Guidelines for #10 SASE. Prize: $750. Deadline: May 1.

‡**MELCHER BOOK AWARD**, Unitarian Universalist Association, 25 Beacon St., Boston MA 02108-2800. Fax: (617)367-3237. Staff Liaison: Patricia Frevert. Estab. 1964. Previously published book on religious liberalism. Deadline: December 31.

KENNETH W. MILDENBERGER PRIZE, Modern Language Association of America, 10 Astor Place, New York NY 10003-6981. (212)475-9500. Fax: (212)477-9863. Director: Richard Brod. Annual award for previously published research in the field of teaching foreign languages and literatures. Guidelines for #10 SASE. Prize: $500. Deadline: May 1.

MLA PRIZE FOR INDEPENDENT SCHOLARS, Modern Language Association of America, 10 Astor Place, New York NY 10003-6981. (212)475-9500. Fax: (212)477-9863. Director: Richard Brod. Annual award for book or article in the field of English or another modern language literature published in previous year. Authors who hold tenure or tenure-track positions in higher education are not eligible. Guidelines and application form for #10 SASE. Prize: $1,000. Deadline: May 1.

ROBERT T. MORSE WRITERS AWARD, American Psychiatric Association, 1400 K Street, NW, Washington DC 20005. (202)682-6220. Contact: Media Coordinator. Offered annually for work published between January 1 and December 31 of preceding year "to recognize the outstanding achievement and excellence in media coverage of mental illnesses and psychiatric treatment for significant contribution(s) to public understanding of these illnesses and the treatments available to those who suffer from the illnesses." Deadline: January. "Deadline is first few days of January, exact day depends on what day January 1 falls on." Contest/award rules and entry forms available on request. "Entries can be self-nominated, by organization or by a District Branch of the APA." Prize: $1,000 honorarium and an engraved plaque. "Entries are accepted from national and local news writers or groups of writers who have covered the mental health/illness field or who have written an exemplary article or special series of articles. The entry(s) must be intended for the general public and must address pertinent mental health or mental illness issues and the *role of psychiatry within these issues*."

GEORGE JEAN NATHAN AWARD FOR DRAMATIC CRITICISM, Cornell University, Dept. of English, Goldwin Smith Hall, Ithaca NY 14853. (607)255-6801. Contact: Chair, Dept. of English. "Awarded annually to the American who has written the best piece of drama criticism during the theatrical year (July 1-June 30), whether it is an article, an essay, treatise or book." Guidelines for SASE. Prize: $5,000. "Winner also receives a silver medallion and a certificate symbolic of, and attesting to, the award. Only published work may be submitted, and the author must be an American citizen."

NATIONAL JEWISH BOOK AWARD—JEWISH HISTORY, Gerrard and Ella Berman Award, Jewish Book Council, 15 E. 26th St., New York NY 10010. (212)532-4949. Director: Carolyn Starman Hessel. Book of Jewish history. Deadline: July 30.

NATIONAL WRITERS ASSOCIATION ARTICLES AND ESSAYS CONTEST, The National Writers Association, Suite 424, 1450 S. Havana, Aurora CO 80012. (303)751-7844. Fax: (303)751-8593. Director: Sandy Whelchel. Annual contest "to encourage writers in this creative form and to recognize those who excel in nonfiction writing." Charges $12 fee. Prizes: $200, $100, $50. Guidelines for #10 SASE.

THE FREDERIC W. NESS BOOK AWARD, Assn. of American Colleges and Universities, 1818 R St. NW, Washington DC 20009. (202)387-3760. Fax: (202)265-9532. Director For Membership: Peggy Neal. Offered annually for work previously published between July 1 and June 30 of the year in which it is being considered. "Each year the Frederic W. Ness Book Award Committee of the Association of American Colleges and Universities recognizes books which contribute to the understanding and improvement of liberal education." Deadline: August 15. Contest/award rules and entry forms available for SASE. "Writers may nominate their own work; however, we send letters of invitation to publishers to nominate qualified books." Prize: Presentation at the association's annual meeting and $1,000. (Transportation and one night hotel for meeting are also provided.)

ALLAN NEVINS PRIZE, Society of American Historians, 2 Butler Library, Columbia University, New York NY 10027. Secretary/Treasurer: Professor Mark Carnes. American history (nominated doctoral dissertations on arts, literature, science and American biographies). Deadline: January 15. Prize: $1,000, certificate and publication.

NEW JERSEY COUNCIL FOR THE HUMANITIES BOOK AWARD, New Jersey Council for the Humanities (NJCH), Suite 602, 390 George St., New Brunswick NJ 08901-2018. (908)932-7726. Fax: (908)932-1179. Coordinator: Erica Mosner. Offered annually for work previously published between January 1 and December 31 "to honor a New Jersey author by virtue of birth, residence, or occupation, and to bring more exposure to humanities books that stimulate curiosity and enrich the general public's understanding of their world." Deadline: "Usually February 1." Guidelines for SASE. "Publisher only must nominate the book, but author can call us and we will send the information directly to their publisher." Prize: $1,000 for the author, $2,000 pro forma marketing award to publisher, and title distributed to up to 100 libraries throughout New Jersey. Judged by NJCH's Book Award Committee.

NEW YORK STATE HISTORICAL ASSOCIATION MANUSCRIPT AWARD, P.O. Box 800, Cooperstown NY 13326-0800. (607)547-2508. Director of Publications: Dr. Wendell Tripp. Estab. 1973. Unpublished book-length monograph on New York State history. Deadline: February 20.

‡FRANK LAWRENCE AND HARRIET CHAPPELL OWSLEY AWARD, Southern Historical Association, Dept. of History, University of Georgia, Athens GA 30602-1602. (706)542-8848. Fax: (706)542-2455. Managing Editor: John B. Boles. Estab. 1934. For recognition of a distinguished book in Southern history published in even-numbered years. Awarded in odd-numbered years. Publishers usually submit the books. Deadline: March 1.

PEN/JERARD FUND, PEN American Center, 568 Broadway, New York NY 10012. (212)334-1660. Fax: (212)334-2181. Contact: John Morrone. Estab. 1986. Biennial grant of $4,000 for American woman writer of nonfiction for a booklength work in progress in odd-numbered years. Next award: 1995. Deadline: January 15.

PEN/MARTHA ALBRAND AWARD FOR NONFICTION, PEN American Center, 568 Broadway, New York NY 10012. (212)334-1660. Fax: (212)334-2181. Coordinator: John Morrone. For a first-published book of general nonfiction distinguished by qualities of literary and stylistic excellence. Eligible books must have been published in the calendar year under consideration. Authors must be American citizens or permanent residents. Although there are no restrictions on the subject matter of titles submitted, non-literary books will not be considered. Books should be of adult nonfiction for the general or academic reader. Deadline: December 31. Publishers, agents and authors themselves must submit 3 copies of each eligible title. Prize: $1,000.

PEN/SPIELVOGEL-DIAMONSTEIN AWARD, PEN American Center, 568 Broadway, New York NY 10012. (212)334-1660. Fax: (212)334-2181. Coordinator: John Morrone. "For the best previously unpublished collection of essays on any subject by an American writer. The $5,000 prize is awarded to preserve the dignity and esteem that the essay form imparts to literature. Authors must be American citizens or permanent residents. The essays included in books submitted may have been previously published in magazines, journals or anthologies, but must not have collectively appeared before in book form. Books will be judged on the basis of the literary character and distinction of the writing. *Four* copies of each eligible title may be submitted by publishers, agents, or the authors themselves." Deadline: December 31.

PHI BETA KAPPA AWARD IN SCIENCE, The Phi Beta Kappa Society, 1811 Q St. NW, Washington DC 20009-1696. (202)265-3808. Contact: Administrator, Phi Beta Kappa Book Awards. Estab. 1959. Interpretations of the physical or biological sciences or mathematics published in the US during the 12-month period preceding the entry deadline, and submitted by the publisher. Books must have been published between May 1, 1993 and April 30, 1994. Books that are exclusively histories of science are *not* eligible, nor are biographies of scientists in which a narrative emphasis predominates. Works of fiction are not eligible. Deadline: April 30. Author must be a US citizen or resident.

PHI BETA KAPPA BOOK AWARDS, The Phi Beta Kappa Society, 1811 Q St. NW, Washington DC 20009-1696. (202)265-3808. Contact: Linda Surles. Estab. 1776. "Annual award to recognize and honor outstanding scholarly books published in the United States in the fields of the humanities, the social sciences, and the natural sciences and mathematics." Books must have been published between May 1, 1993 and April 30, 1994. Deadline: April 30. "Authors may request information, however books must be submitted by the publisher." Entries must be the works of authors who are US citizens or residents.

THE BARBARA SAVAGE "MILES FROM NOWHERE" MEMORIAL AWARD, The Mountaineers Books, Suite 107, 1011 SW Klickitat Way, Seattle WA 98134. (206)223-6303. Award Director: Margaret Foster. Awarded for previously unpublished book-length nonfiction personal adventure narrative. Narrative must be based on an outdoor adventure involving hiking, mountain climbing, bicycling, paddle sports, skiing, snowshoeing, nature, conservation, ecology, or adventure travel not dependent upon motorized transport. Subjects *not* acceptable include hunting, fishing, or motorized or competitive sports. Guidelines for 9 × 12 SASE. Prize: $3,000 cash award, a $12,000 guaranteed advance against royalties and publication by The Mountaineers. Deadline for entries is October 1 of each year.
- They would like to see more regional and conservation-oriented titles.

ALDO AND JEANNE SCAGLIONE PRIZE FOR STUDIES IN SLAVIC LANGUAGES AND LITERATURES, Modern Language Association, 10 Astor Place, New York NY 10003-6981. (212)475-9500. Fax: (212)477-9863. Contest Director: Richard Brod. Contest offered every 2 years for books published in the previous 2 years. Books published in 1993 or 1994 are eligible. Membership in the MLA is not required. Works of literary history, literary criticism, philology and literary theory are eligible. Deadline: May 1. Guidelines for SASE. Prize: $1,000 and a certificate.

ALDO AND JEANNE SCAGLIONE PRIZE IN COMPARATIVE LITERARY STUDIES, Modern Language Association of America, 10 Astor Place, New York NY 10003-6981. (212)614-6406. Director of Special Projects: Richard Brod. Offered for work published in the year preceding award. Award is for outstanding scholarly work in the field of comparative literary studies that involve at least 2 literatures. Prize: $1,000 and certificate. Judged by committee of the Modern Language Association of America. "Writer must be a member of the MLA. Works of scholarship, literary history, literary criticism and literary theory are eligible. Books that are primarily translations are not."

ALDO AND JEANNE SCAGLIONE PRIZE IN FRENCH AND FRANCOPHONE STUDIES, 10 Astor Place, New York NY 10003-6981. (212)614-6406. Director of Special Projects: Richard Brod. Offered for work published in the year preceding award. Award is for an outstanding scholarly work in the field of French or francophone linguistic or literary studies. Prize: $1,000 and certificate. Judged by a committee of the Modern Language Association. Writer must be a member of the MLA. Works of scholarship, literary history, literary criticism and literary theory are eligible; books that are primarily translations are not. Deadline: May 1.

‡SCIENCE-WRITING AWARD IN PHYSICS AND ASTRONOMY, American Institute of Physics, 1 Physics Ellipse, College Park MD 20740-3843. (301)209-3090. Contact: Public Information Division. Previously published articles, booklets or books "that improve public understanding of physics and astronomy." Deadline: February 7 for professional writers; May 10 for physicists, astronomers or members of AIP member and affiliated societies; October 10 for articles or books intended for children, preschool-15 years old.

MINA P. SHAUGHNESSY PRIZE, Modern Language Association of America, 10 Astor Place, New York NY 10003-6981. (212)475-9500. Fax: (212)477-9863. Director: Richard Brod. Annual award for research publication (book or article) in the field of teaching English language and literature published during preceding year. Guidelines for #10 SASE. Prize: $500. Deadline: May 1.

‡FRANCIS B. SIMKINS AWARD, Southern Historical Association, Dept. of History, University of Georgia, Athens GA 30602-1602. (706)542-8848. Fax: (706)542-2455. Managing Editor: John B. Boles. Estab. 1934. For recognition of the best first book by an author in the field of Southern history over a 2-year period. The award is sponsored jointly with Longwood College. Awarded in odd-numbered years. Longwood College supplies the cash amount and the certificate to the author(s) for this award. The SHA furnishes a certificate to the publisher. Deadline: March 1.

THE JOHN BEN SNOW PRIZE, Syracuse University Press, 1600 Jamesville Ave., Syracuse NY 13244. (315)443-5541. Fax: (315)443-5545. Contact: Director. Offered annually for unpublished submissions. The John Ben

Snow Prize, inauguarated in 1978, is given annually by Syracuse University Press to the author of a nonfiction manuscript dealing with some aspect of New York State. The purpose of the award is to encourage the writing of books of genuine significance and literary distinction that will augment knowledge of New York State and appreciation for its unique physical, historical and cultural characteristics. A manuscript based on direct, personal experience will receive the same consideration as one relying on scholarly research. The criteria are authenticity, accuracy, readability and importance. Deadline: December 31. Prize: $1,500 to the author as advance against royalties and publication by Syracuse University Press. Guidelines for SASE.

‡C.L. SONNICHSEN BOOK AWARD, Texas Western Press of the University of Texas at El Paso, El Paso TX 79968-0633. (915)747-5688. Press Director: John Bristol. Estab. 1952. Previously unpublished nonfiction ms dealing with the history, literature or cultures of the Southwest. Deadline: March 1.

BRYANT SPANN MEMORIAL PRIZE, History Dept., Indiana State University, Terre Haute IN 47809. Estab. 1980. Social criticism in the tradition of Eugene V. Debs. Deadline: April 30. Guidelines for SASE. SASE also required with submissions. Prize: $1,000.

‡AMAURY TALBOT PRIZE FUND FOR AFRICAN ANTHROPOLOGY, Barclays Bank Trust Limited, Trust Management Office, 66 Group, Osborne Court, Gadbrook Park, Rudheath, Northwich Cheshire CW9 7UE England. Annual award for previously published nonfiction on anthropological research relating to Africa. Deadline: March 31. Guidelines for #10 SAE with 1 IRC.

THE TEN BEST "CENSORED" STORIES OF 1995, Project Censored—Sonoma State University, Rohnert Park CA 94928. (707)664-2500. Fax: (707)664-2505. Assistant Director: Mark Lowenthal. Estab. 1976. Current published, nonfiction stories of national social significance that have been overlooked or under-reported by the news media. Deadline: November 1.
• Carl Jensen and Project Censored have chosen 25 stories that have been underreported to make up *Censored: The News That Didn't Make the News and Why* published by Four Walls Eight Windows.

THE THEATRE LIBRARY ASSOCIATION AWARD, Theatre Library Association, 91 Mohr Ave., Bloomfield NJ 07003. (212)870-1640. Fax: (212)787-3852. Awards Committee Chair: Stephen M. Vallillo. Estab. 1968. Book published in the United States in the field of live theater performance, including vaudeville, puppetry, pantomime and the circus. Publication may cover biography, history, criticism, reference or related fields. Prize: $250 and certificate to the winner; $100 and certificate for Honorable Mention. Deadline: February 1.

‡UNDERGRADUATE ANNUAL PAPER COMPETITION IN CRYPTOLOGY, *Cryptologia*, Rose-Hulman Institute of Technology, Terre Haute IN 47803. Contact: Editor. Unpublished papers on cryptology from undergraduates only. Deadline: January 1.

Fiction

AIM MAGAZINE SHORT STORY CONTEST, P.O. Box 20554, Chicago IL 60620-0554. (312)874-6184. Fiction Editor: Mark Boone. Estab. 1974. Unpublished short stories (4,000 words maximum) "promoting brotherhood among people and cultures." Deadline: August 15.
• *Aim* is a nonprofit publication; its staff is volunteer.

‡ALBERTA NEW FICTION COMPETITION, Alberta Foundation for the Arts, 3rd Floor, Beaver House, 10158 103rd St., Edmonton, Alberta T5J 0X6 Canada. (403)427-6315. Contest offered every 2 years for unpublished work to encourage, recognize and develop the diversity of Alberta writers of novels. The competition is open to all Alberta writers from emerging to established authors, ages 18 and over. Deadline: December 1, 1995. Prize 1st-$5,000 (a $2,500 prize from the Alberta Foundation for the Arts, a $1,000 advance against royalties from the publisher, a $1,500 12-month option agreement for motion picture/television rights from ITV and a publishing contract from Red Deer College Press). Manuscripts must be in English.

‡ALBERTA WRITING FOR YOUTH COMPETITION, Alberta Foundation for the Arts, 3rd Floor, Beaver House, 10158 103rd St., Edmonton, Alberta T5J 0X6 Canada. (403)427-6315. Contest offered every 2 years for unpublished work to encourage, recognize and develop the diversity of Alberta writers who write fiction for young people. The competition is open to *all* Alberta writers, aged 18 and over. Deadline: December 1, 1994. Prize: 1st-$4,500 (a $2,000 prize from the Alberta Foundation for the Arts, a $1,000 advance against royalties from the publisher, a $1,500 12-month option agreement for motion picture/television rights from ITV and a publishing contract from Tree Frog Press). Manuscripts must be in English.

‡NELSON ALGREN SHORT STORY AWARDS, *Chicago Tribune*, 435 N. Michigan Ave., Chicago IL 60611. Contact: Larry Kart. Offered annually for previously unpublished work by an American. Deadline: February

1. Guidelines for SASE. Prize: 1st-$5,000; $1,000 each to 3 runners-up. Must be stories between 2,500 and 10,000 words by American writers. No phone calls please.

ANVIL PRESS INTERNATIONAL 3-DAY NOVEL WRITING CONTEST, Anvil Press, 204-A 175 E. Broadway, Vancouver, British Columbia V5T 1W2 Canada. (604)876-8710. Fax: (604)879-2667. Contact: Brian Kaufman. Estab. 1988. Best novel written in 3 days; specifically, over the Labor Day weekend. Entrants return finished novels to Anvil Press for judging. Registration deadline: Friday before Labor Day weekend. Send SASE (IRC if from the US) for details. Charges $15 fee.

RAYMOND CARVER SHORT STORY CONTEST, English Department, Humboldt State University, Arcata CA 95521. Coordinator: Kim T. Halliday. Offered annually for unpublished work. Deadline: November 1. Contest/award rules available for SASE. Charges $7.50 fee. "Prize: 1st-$500 plus publication in *Toyon*, Humboldt State University's literary magazine; 2nd-$250. Previous year's judges include Ann Beattie, Deena Metzger, James D. Houston, Gary Fisketjon." Contest open to any writer living in the US.

JAMES FENIMORE COOPER PRIZE, Society of American Historians, Box 2, Butler Library, Columbia University, New York NY 10027. (212)854-2221. Contact: Professor Mark Carnes. Historical novel on an American theme. Deadline: January 15. Prize: $1,000 and certificates to author or publisher.

‡DAVID DORNSTEIN MEMORIAL CREATIVE WRITING CONTEST FOR YOUNG ADULT WRITERS, The Coalition for the Advancement of Jewish Education, Floor 12A, 261 W. 35th St., New York NY 10001. (212)268-4210. Fax: (212)268-4214. Executive Director: Eliot Spack. Contest offered annually for unpublished short story based on a Jewish theme or topic. Deadline: December 31. Guidelines for SASE. Prize: $1,000 and publication in the *Jewish Education News*. Writer must prove age of 18-35 years old. Story must be based on Jewish theme, topic. A writer may submit only 1 story each year.

‡FIRST NOVEL SERIES AWARD, Mid-List Press, 4324 12th Ave., Minneapolis MN 55407-3218. (612)822-3733. Acquisitions Editor: Maria Ahrens. Estab. 1989. Offered annually for unpublished novel to encourage new novelists and provide a publishing outlet for those writers whose works don't fit neatly or conveniently into contemporary marketing categories, or whose works have mid-list rather than front-list potential. Deadline: February 1. Guidelines available for SASE. Charges $10 fee. Prize: publication and an advance against royalties ($1,000). Judged by Mid-List's editors and ms readers. Winners are offered contracts at the conclusion of the judging. The First Novel Series Award is open to any writer who has never published a novel.

ROBERT L. FISH MEMORIAL AWARD, Mystery Writers of America, Inc., 6th Floor, 17 E. 47th St., New York NY 10017. (212)888-8171. Contact: Priscilla Ridgway. Annual award for the best first mystery or suspense short story published during the previous year. Deadline: December 1.

‡GLIMMER TRAIN'S SHORT STORY AWARD FOR NEW WRITERS, Glimmer Train Press, Inc., Suite 1205, 812 SW Washington St., Portland OR 97205. (503)221-0836. Fax: (503)221-0837. Contest Director: Linda Davies. Contest offered 2 times/year for any writer whose fiction hasn't appeared in a nationally-distributed magazine with a circulation over 5,000. "Send original, unpublished short (1,200-8,000 words) story with $10 reading fee (covers up to two stories sent together in same envelope) during the months of February/March and August/September. Title page must include name, address, phone, and Short-Story Award for New Writers must be written on outside of envelope. No need for SASE as materials will not be returned. We cannot acknowledge receipt or provide status of any particular manuscript. Winners notified by July 1 (for February/March entrants) and January 1 (for August/September entrants). Winner receives $1,200 and publication in *Glimmer Train Stories*. First/second runners-up receive $500/$300, respectively, and honorable mention. All applicants receive a copy of the issue in which winning entry is published and runners-up announced."

HEEKIN GROUP FOUNDATION FICTION FELLOWSHIPS, The Heekin Group Foundation, P.O. Box 1534, Sisters OR 97759. (503)548-4147. Contest/Award Director: Sarah Heekin Redfield. Offered annually for unpublished works. "James J. Fellowship for the Novel in Progress, Tara Fellowship for Short Fiction; both fellowships are awarded to beginning career writers for assistance in their literary pursuits." Deadline: December 1. Guidelines for SASE. Charges $15 for short fiction, $20 for Novel in Progress. Prize: James Fellowship: $10,000; Tara Fellowship: $5,000. Roster of finalist judges include Graywolf Press, SOHO Press, Dalkey Archive Press. "Fellowship competition is open to all begining career writers, those writers who are still unpublished in the novel and those writers who have published five or fewer short stories in magazines or journals of national distribution."

DRUE HEINZ LITERATURE PRIZE, University of Pittsburgh Press, 127 N. Bellefield Ave., Pittsburgh PA 15260. (412)624-4110. Fax: (412)624-7380. Series Editor: Ed Ochester. Estab. 1936. Collection of short fiction. Award open to writers who have published a book-length collection of fiction or a minimum of three short stories or novellas in commercial magazines or literary journals of national distribution. "We are unable to return any manuscripts for this contest." Guidelines for SASE. Submit: July-August.

ERNEST HEMINGWAY FOUNDATION AWARD, PEN American Center, 568 Broadway, New York NY 10012. Contact: John Morrone. First-published novel or short story collection by an American author. Submit 3 copies. Deadline: December 31.

HEMINGWAY SHORT STORY COMPETITION, Hemingway Days Festival, P.O. Box 4045, Key West FL 33041-4045. (305)294-4440. Coordinator: Lorian Hemingway. Estab. 1981. Unpublished short stories. Deadline: July 1. Charges $10 fee. Guidelines for SASE. Prize: 1st-$1,000 cash; 2nd-$500 runner-up awards.
 • A new contest has been created for first novels. Write for guidelines.

L. RON HUBBARD'S WRITERS OF THE FUTURE CONTEST, P.O. Box 1630, Los Angeles CA 90078-1630. (213)466-3310. Estab. 1983. Contest Administrator: Rachel Denk. Unpublished science fiction and fantasy. Send #10 SASE for guidelines.

INTERNATIONAL IMITATION HEMINGWAY COMPETITION, PEN Center West, Suite 41, 672 S. Lafayette Park Place, Los Angeles CA 90057. (213)365-8500. Unpublished one-page (500 words) parody of Hemingway. Must mention Harry's Bar and must be funny. Deadline: February 15th. Winner receives round trip transportation for 2 to Florence, Italy and dinner at Harry's Bar & American Grill in Florence. Three finalists are published in *American Way* Magazine.

‡AGA KHAN PRIZE FOR FICTION, Box 5, 541 E. 72nd St., New York NY 10021. Estab. 1953. $1,000 is awarded for the best previously unpublished short story published in *The Paris Review* that year. Manuscripts must be a minimum of 1,000 words and a maximum of 10,000 words. All fiction mss submitted will be considered. Submissions should be addressed to the Fiction Editor.

LAWRENCE FOUNDATION AWARD, *Prairie Schooner*, 201 Andrews, University of Nebraska, Lincoln NE 68588-0334. (402)472-3191. Fax: (402)472-4636. Editor: Hilda Raz. Estab. 1978. Annual award for the best short story published in *Prairie Schooner*. Winner announced in the spring issue of the following year. Prize: $1,500. The Lawrence Foundation is a charitable trust located in New York City.

LINES IN THE SAND SHORT FICTION CONTEST, LeSand Publications, 1252 Terra Nova Blvd., Pacifica CA 94044. (415)355-9069. Associate Editor: Barbara J. Less. Estab. 1992. Annual contest "to encourage the writing of good, short fiction." Deadline: October 31. Guidelines for #10 SASE. Charges $5 fee. Prizes: $50-1st; $25-2nd; $10-3rd; plus publication in January/February Awards edition.

MID-LIST PRESS FIRST NOVEL SERIES AWARD, Mid-List Press, 4324-12th Ave. S., Minneapolis MN 55407-3218. (612)822-3733. Acquisitions Editor: Maria Ahrens. Offered annually for unpublished novels "to locate and publish quality manuscripts by first-time writers, particularly those mid-list titles that major publishers may be rejecting." Deadline: February 1. Guidelines for SASE. *Applicants should write, not call, for guidelines.* Charges $10 fee. Prize: $1,000 advance against royalties, plus publication. Judged by ms readers and editors of Mid-List Press; editors and publishers make final decisions." Open to any writer who has never published a *novel*.

MILITARY LIFESTYLE FICTION CONTEST, *Military Lifestyle Magazine*, Suite 710, 4800 Montgomery Lane, Bethesda MD 20814-5341. (301)718-7600. Fax: (301)718-7652. Editor-in-Chief: Hope M. Daniels. Estab. 1969. Annual award for short stories featuring US military service members and/or military families. Check the December, January and February issues for the contest announcement or write to request current year's theme and rules, usually available by January 1. Deadline: March 31.

MILKWEED NATIONAL FICTION PRIZE, Milkweed Editions, Suite 400, First Ave. N., Minneapolis MN 55401. (612)332-3192. Fax: (612)332-6248. Assistant Editor: Fiona Grant. Estab. 1986. Annual award for unpublished works. "Milkweed is looking for a novel, novella, or a collection of short stories. Manuscripts should be of high literary quality and must be double-spaced and between 150-400 pages in length." Deadline: July 15. *Must* request contest guidelines, send SASE. Prize: Publication by Milkweed Editions and a cash advance of $3,000 against royalties. "Entry must be written in English. Contest is open to writers who have previously published a book of fiction or three short stories (or novellas) in magazines/journals with national distribution." Catalog available on request for 2 first-class stamps.

MINNESOTA INK FICTION CONTEST, Minnesota Ink, Inc., Suite 328, 3585 N. Lexington Ave., Arden Hills MN 55126. (612)486-7818. Contact: Valerie Hockert. Previously unpublished fiction. Deadline: December 31. Charges $5 fee.

‡**NATIONAL WRITERS ASSOCIATION NOVEL WRITING CONTEST**, The National Writers Association, Suite 424, 1450 S. Havana, Aurora CO 80012. (303)751-7844. Fax:(303)751-8593. Director: Sandy Whelchel. Annual contest "to help develop creative skills, to recognize and reward outstanding ability and to increase the opportunity for the marketing and subsequent publication of novel manuscripts." Guidelines for #10 SASE. Charges $30 fee. Prize: 1st-$500; 2nd-$300; 3rd-$200.

‡**NATIONAL WRITERS ASSOCIATION SHORT STORY CONTEST**, The National Writers Association, Suite 620, 1450 S. Havana, Aurora CO 80012. (303)751-7844. Fax:(303)751-8593. Director: Sandy Welchel. Annual contest "to encourage writers in this creative form and to recognize those who excel in fiction writing." Guidelines for #10 SASE. Charges $11 fee. Prizes: $200, $100, $50, copy of *Writer's Market*.

‡**NEW RIVERS PRESS AMERICAN FICTION CONTEST**, (formerly Birch Lane Press American Fiction Contest), New Rivers Press, English Dept., Moorhead State University, Moorhead MN 56563-2996. Contest Director: Alan Davis. Estab. 1987. "Annual fiction contest to promote established and emerging writers. Submissions cannot be previously published. $1,000, $500, $250 awards presented by annual contest judge. (20-25 finalists published.) All finalists also receive a free copy of publication." Submit January 1-May 1. Guidelines for #10 SASE. Charges $7.50/story fee. Multiple and simultaneous submissions acceptable. Buys first North American serial rights to winning stories.

CHARLES H. AND N. MILDRED NILON EXCELLENCE IN MINORITY FICTION AWARD, University of Colorado at Boulder and Fiction Collective Two, University of Colorado, Campus Box 494, Boulder CO 80309-0494. Contact: Shawna Minion. Estab. 1989. Unpublished book-length fiction, 200 pages minimum. Only mss from protected racial and ethnic minority authors will be considered.

THE FLANNERY O'CONNOR AWARD FOR SHORT FICTION, The University of Georgia Press, 330 Research Dr., Athens GA 30602-4901. (706)369-6130. Fax: (706)369-6131. Series Editor: Charles East. Editorial Assistant: Jane Kobres. Estab. 1981. Submission period: June-July 31. Charges $10 fee. Manuscripts will not be returned. Manuscripts must be 175-250 pages long. Authors do not have to be previously published. Guidelines for SASE.

FRANK O'CONNOR PRIZE FOR FICTION, *Descant*, Texas Christian University, P.O. Box 32872, Fort Worth TX 76129-1000. (817)921-7240. Estab. 1984. Annual award for the best short story in the *Descant* volume; writer of the story receives a $500 prize given through the magazine by an anonymous donor.

‡**WILLIAM PEDEN PRIZE IN FICTION**, *Missouri Review*, 1507 Hillcrest Hall, Columbia MO 65211. (314)882-4474. Contact: Greg Michalson. Awarded annually to best piece of fiction published in *MR* in a given volume year. All work published in *MR* automatically eligible. No other guidelines available.

‡**PLAYBOY COLLEGE FICTION CONTEST**, *Playboy*, 680 N. Lake Shore Dr., Chicago IL 60611. (312)751-8000. Fiction Editor: Alice Turner. Annual award for unpublished short stories by registered students at a college or university. Deadline: January 1. Information in October issue or send SASE.

EDGAR ALLAN POE AWARD, Mystery Writers of America, Inc., 17 E. 47th St., New York NY 10017. (212)888-8171. Contact: Priscilla Ridgway. Entries must be copyrighted or produced/published in the year they are submitted. Deadline: December 1. Entries for the book categories are usually submitted by the publisher but may be submitted by the author or his agent.

‡**PRISM INTERNATIONAL FICTION CONTEST**, *Prism International*, University of British Columbia, Buch E462, 1866 Main Mall, Vancouver, British Columbia V6T 1Z1 Canada. (604)822-2514. Previously unpublished fiction. Deadline: December 1. Guidelines for #10 SASE with Canadian postage or #10 SAE with 1 IRC. Entry fee includes 1 year subscription. Prizes: 1st-$2,000; 5 honorable mentions of $200 each.

‡**PROMETHEUS AWARD/HALL OF FAME**, Libertarian Futurist Society, 89 Gebhardt Rd., Penfield NY 14526. (716)288-6137. Contact: Victoria Varga. Estab. 1979. Prometheus Award: pro-freedom, anti-authoritarian novel published during previous year. Hall of Fame: one classic libertarian novel at least 5 years old. Deadline: March 1.

‡**PURE-BRED DOGS AMERICAN KENNEL GAZETTE FICTION CONTEST**, The American Kennel Club, 51 Madison Ave., New York NY 10010. Editorial Assistant: David Savage. Estab. 1885. Cash prize to top 3 winners, 1st prize $500 and publication. Guidelines for #10 SASE.

QUARTERLY WEST NOVELLA COMPETITION, *Quarterly West*, 317 Olpin Union, University of Utah, Salt Lake City UT 84112. (801)581-3938. Estab. 1976. Award given every 2 years for 2 unpublished novellas. Guidelines for SASE. Deadline: December 31 of even-numbered years.

SIR WALTER RALEIGH AWARD, North Carolina Literary and Historical Association, 109 E. Jones St., Raleigh NC 27601-2807. (919)733-7305. Awards Coordinator: Freda Brittain. Previously published fiction by a North Carolina resident. Deadline: July 15.

HAROLD U. RIBALOW AWARD, Hadassah WZOA, 50 W. 58th St., New York NY 10019. Editor: Alan Tigay. Offered annually for an English-language book of fiction on a Jewish theme. "Books *published* between January 1 and December 31 in a calendar year will be eligible for that year's award. The award for a given year will be made the following year." Deadline: March. Prize: $1,000. Books should be submitted by the publisher.

SFWA NEBULA® AWARDS, Science-fiction and Fantasy Writers of America, Inc., #1B, 5 Winding Brook Dr., Guilderland NY 12084-9719. Estab. 1966. Science fiction or fantasy in the categories of novel, novella, novelette and short story recommended by members. Final ballot and awards decided by ballot of the active members for works professionally published during the previous calendar year.

SHORT STORY CONTEST, *Japanophile,* P.O. Box 223, Okemos MI 48864-0223. (517)669-2109. Contact: Earl Snodgrass. Estab. 1974. Annual award for unpublished short stories "that lead to a better understanding of Japanese culture. We prefer a setting in Japan and at least one Japanese and one non-Japanese character." Charges $5 fee. Deadline: December 31.

JOHN SIMMONS SHORT FICTION AWARD and IOWA SHORT FICTION AWARDS, Department of English, University of Iowa. English-Philosophy Building, Iowa City IA 52242-1408. Previously unpublished fiction. Two awards and publications. Guidelines for #10 SASE. Deadline: August 1-September 30.

THE SOUTHERN REVIEW/LOUISIANA STATE UNIVERSITY SHORT FICTION AWARD, Louisiana State University, 43 Allen Hall, Baton Rouge LA 70803. (504)388-5108. Selection Committee Chairman: Jim Bennett. First collection of short stories by an American published in the US during previous year. Deadline: January 31. A publisher or an author may submit an entry by mailing 2 copies of the collection to *The Southern Review* Short Fiction Award.

THE STAND MAGAZINE SHORT STORY COMPETITION, *Stand Magazine* and the Cheltenham Festival of Literature, 179 Wingrove Rd., Newcastle on Tyne, NE4 9DA United Kingdom. (091)-2733280. Contact: Editors of *Stand Magazine.* "This competition is an open international contest for unpublished writing in the English language intended to foster a wider interest in the short story as a literary form and to promote and encourage excellent writing in it." Deadline: March. "Please note that intending entrants enquiring from outside the UK should send International Reply Coupons, not stamps from their own countries. In lieu of an entry fee we ask for a minimum donation of £3.50 or $7 US per story entered." Editorial inquiries should be made with SASE to: Daniel Schenker and Amanda Kay, Route #2, Box 122-B, Lacey's Spring AL 35754.

EDWARD LEWIS WALLANT BOOK AWARD, Mrs. Irving Waltman, 3 Brighton Rd., West Hartford CT 06117. Estab. 1963. Published fiction with significance for the American Jew (novel or short stories) by an American writer. Book must have been published during current year. Deadline: December 31.

WASHINGTON PRIZE FOR FICTION, Larry Kaltman Literary Agency, 1301 S. Scott St., Arlington VA 22204-4656. (703)920-3771. Estab. 1989. Fiction, previously unpublished, of at least 65,000 words. Deadline: November 30. Charges $25 fee. Prize: $3,000, $2,000, $1,000.

WELLSPRING'S SHORT FICTION CONTEST, 770 Tonkawa Rd., Long Lake MN 55356-9233. (612)471-9259. Contest Director: Maureen LaJoy. Estab. 1988. Contest offered twice annually for previously unpublished short fiction. "To encourage the writing of well-crafted and plotted, meaningful short fiction." Deadlines January 1 and July 1. Guidelines for #10 SASE. Charges $10 fee. Prizes: $100, $75, $25.

WRITERS' JOURNAL ANNUAL SHORT STORY CONTEST, Minnesota Ink, Inc., Suite 328, 3585 N. Lexington Ave., Arden Hills MN 55126. (612)486-7818. Contact: Valerie Hockert. Estab. 1987. Previously unpublished short stories. Deadline: May 31. Charges $5/entry fee.

Poetry

‡AARONS ALL STAR POETRY AWARDS, P.O. Box 761, Clearfield UT 84015. (801)825-9637. Award Director: Paul Mewing. Offered twice a year for unpublished work to "award poets a cash prize for their efforts. 1st place winner will be sent to a related publisher for further review." Deadline: May 31-November 30. Guidelines for $1.00 plus SASE (deducted from first entry). Charges $5/entry fee; $12/3 entries; $20/5 entries. Prize: 20% of total entry fees divided into 1st, 2nd, 3rd and 4th place. Judged by a group of professional musicians, an English instructor (high school level) and at times students from Ogdens Weber University creative writing classes. "Most open to 18-25 year old entries. However all ages are welcome."

JOHN WILLIAMS ANDREWS NARRATIVE POETRY CONTEST, *Poet Lore,* The Writer's Center, 4508 Walsh St., Bethesda MD 20815-2009. (301)654-8664. Director: Phillip Jason. Estab. 1889. "Annual contest for unpublished narrative poems of 100 lines or more." Deadline: November 30. Prize: $350 and publication in *Poet Lore.* "*Poet Lore* has first publication rights for poems submitted. All rights revert to the author after publication in *Poet Lore.*"

ANHINGA PRIZE FOR POETRY, Anhinga Press, P.O. Box 10595, Tallahassee FL 32302. (904)575-5592. Fax: (904)224-5127. Contact: Rick Campbell. Offered annually. "We publish a book-length collection of poetry by an author who has not published more than one book of poetry. We use a well-known independent judge." Manuscripts accepted January 1-March 1. Guidelines for SASE. Charges $15 fee. Prize: $1,000 and publication. "Open to any writer writing in English."

ANNUAL INTERNATIONAL NARRATIVE POETRY CONTEST, Poets and Patrons, Inc., 8 Pembroke Ave., Oak Brook IL 60521. Contact: Pat Gangas. Unpublished poetry. Deadline: September 1. Prizes: $75, 1st prize; $25, 2nd.

ANNUAL POETRY CONTEST, National Federation of State Poetry Societies, 3520 State Rt. 56, Mechanicsburg OH 43044. (513)834-2666. Chairman: Amy Jo Zook. Estab. 1959. Previously unpublished poetry. "There are fifty categories. Entrant must have flyer to see them all." Deadline: March 15. Guidelines for #10 SASE. Charges entry fees. See guidelines for fees and prizes.

● All awards are announced in June and published in August.

GORDON BARBER MEMORIAL AWARD, Poetry Society of America, 15 Gramercy Park S., New York NY 10003. (212)254-9628. Contact: Award Director. "For a poem of exceptional merit or character." Guidelines for SASE. Deadline: December 22. Open to members only. Award: $200.

GEORGE BOGIN MEMORIAL AWARD, Poetry Society of America, 15 Gramercy Park S., New York NY 10003. (212) 254-9628. Contact: Award Director. "For a selection of four or five poems that reflects the encounter of the ordinary and the extraordinary, uses language in an original way, and takes a stand against oppression in any of its forms." Guidelines for SASE. Deadline: December 22. Charges $5 fee.

BRITTINGHAM PRIZE IN POETRY, FELIX POLLAK PRIZE IN POETRY, University of Wisconsin Press, 114 N. Murray St., Madison WI 53715. Contest Director: Ronald Wallace. Estab. 1985. Unpublished book-length mss of original poetry. Submissions must be *received* by the press *during* the month of September (postmark is irrelevant) and must be accompanied by a SASE for contest results. Prizes are $1,000 each and publication of winning mss. Guidelines for #10 SASE. Manuscripts will *not* be returned. Charges $15 fee, payable to University of Wisconsin Press. Results in February.

BUCKNELL SEMINAR FOR YOUNGER POETS, Stadler Center for Poetry, Bucknell University, Lewisburg PA 17837. (717)524-1853. Contact: John Wheatcroft. Offered annually. "The Seminar provides an extended opportunity for undergraduates to write and to be guided by established poets. It balances private time for writing, disciplined learning, and camaraderie among the ten Fellows selected." Deadline: March 1. Guidelines for SASE. Prize: 10 fellowships provide tuition, room, board, and spaces for writing during 4-week long seminar. Fellows are responsible for their own transportation. Only students from American colleges who have completed their sophomore, junior, or senior years are eligible to apply.

WITTER BYNNER FOUNDATION FOR POETRY, INC. GRANTS, P.O. Box 10169, Santa Fe NM 87504. (505)988-3251. Fax: (505)986-8222. Executive Director: Steven D. Schwartz. Estab. 1972. Grants for poetry and poetry-related projects. Deadline: February 1. Only nonprofit organizations are eligible to apply.

GERALD CABLE POETRY CHAPBOOK COMPETITION, Silverfish Review Press, P.O. Box 3541, Eugene OR 97403-0541. (503)344-5060. Editor: Rodger Moody. Previously published poems and simultaneous submissions are acceptable. All entrants will receive a copy of the winning chapbook. Purpose is to publish a poetry chapbook by a deserving author. Submit mss during August and September. Guidelines for SASE. Charges $10 fee. Prize: $500 and 50 copies (press run of 750).

‡**MELVILLE CANE AWARD,** Poetry Society of America, 15 Gramercy Park S., New York NY 10003. (212)254-9268. Contact: Award Director. Published book of poems or prose work on a poet or poetry submitted by the publisher. Deadline: December 22. Charges $10/book fee.

GERTRUDE B. CLAYTOR MEMORIAL AWARD, Poetry Society of America, 15 Gramercy Park S., New York NY 10003. (212)254-9628. Contact: Award Director. Poem in any form on the American scene or character. Guidelines for SASE. Deadline: December 22. Members only. Award: $250.

CLEVELAND STATE UNIVERSITY POETRY CENTER PRIZE, Cleveland State University Poetry Center, Cleveland OH 44115. (216)687-3986. Fax: (216)687-9366. Contact: Editor. Estab. 1962. To identify, reward and publish the best unpublished book-length poetry ms submitted. Submissions accepted only December-February. Deadline: Postmarked on or before March 1. Charges $10 fee. "Submission implies willingness to sign contract for publication if manuscript wins." $1,000 prize for best ms. Two of the other finalist mss are also published for standard royalty (no prize). Send SASE for guidelines and entry form.

COLLEGIATE POETRY CONTEST, *The Lyric,* 307 Dunton Dr. SW, Blacksburg VA 24060-5127. Editor: Leslie Mellichamp. Estab. 1921. Unpublished poems (40 lines or less) by fulltime undergraduates in US or Canadian colleges. Winners receive one-time cash awards totalling approximately $500. Deadline: June 1. Send #10 SASE for rules.

COMPUWRITE, The Writers Alliance, 12 Skylark Lane, Stony Brook NY 11790. Contest Director: Kiel Stuart. Estab. 1982. Previously unpublished poems. "We want an expressive, clever poem (up to 30 lines) on the act of writing with a personal computer." Deadline January 15. Guidelines for #10 SASE. Charges $2/poem fee. First prize: publication plus a software package with at least $100 retail value.

‡THE BERNARD F. CONNERS PRIZE FOR POETRY, *The Paris Review,* Box 5, 541 E. 72nd St., New York NY 10021. Poetry Editor: Richard Howard. Estab. 1953. Unpublished poetry over 200 lines published in *The Paris Review* that year. The winner will be awarded $1,000. Deadline: April 1-May 1. Must include SASE.

GUSTAV DAVIDSON MEMORIAL AWARD, Poetry Society of America, 15 Gramercy Park S., New York NY 10003. (212)254-9628. Contact: Award Director. Sonnet or sequence in traditional forms. Guidelines for SASE. Deadline: December 22. Members only. Award: $500.

MARY CAROLYN DAVIES MEMORIAL AWARD, Poetry Society of America, 15 Gramercy Park S., New York NY 10003. (212)254-9628. Contact: Award Director. Unpublished poem suitable for setting to music. Guidelines for SASE. Deadline: December 22. Award: $250. Members only.

BILLEE MURRAY DENNY POETRY CONTEST, Lincoln College, 300 Keokuk St., Lincoln IL 62656. Contest Administrator: Valecia Crisafulli. Estab. 1981. Unpublished poetry. Deadline: May 31. Charges $10/poem fee (limit 3). Entry form for SASE.

MARIE LOUISE D'ESTERNAUX POETRY CONTEST, Brooklyn Poetry Circle, #3U, 2550 Independence Ave. Bronx NY 10463. Contact: Ruth M. Fowler. "Annual contest for previously unpublished poetry to encourage young people to study poetry, to write poetry and to enrich themselves and others." Deadline: April 15. Guidelines for SASE. Prize: 1st-$50; 2nd-$25.

ALICE FAY DI CASTAGNOLA AWARD, Poetry Society of America, 15 Gramercy Park S., New York NY 10003. (212)254-9628. Contact: Award Director. Manuscript in progress: poetry, prose (on poetry) or verse-drama. Guidelines for SASE. Deadline: December 22. Award: $2,000. Members only.

"DISCOVERY"/THE NATION, The Joan Leiman Jacobson Poetry Prizes, The Unterberg Poetry Center of the 92nd Street YM-YWHA, 1395 Lexington Ave., New York NY 10128. (212)415-5760. Estab. 1973. Open to poets who have not published a book of poems (chapbooks, self-published books included). Deadline: early February. Write or call for competition guidelines.

‡MILTON DORFMAN POETRY PRIZE, Rome Art & Community Center, 308 W. Bloomfield St., Rome NY 13440. (315)336-1040. Contact: Leo G. Crandall. Estab. 1990. "The purpose of the Milton Dorfman Poetry Prize is to offer amateur/beginning poets an outlet for their craft. All submissions must be previously unpublished." Entries accepted: July 1-November 1, postmarked. Guidelines for #10 SASE. Charges $3 fee. Prize: 1st-$500; 2nd-$200; 3rd-$100. Open to any writer.

THE EIGHTH MOUNTAIN POETRY PRIZE, The Eighth Mountain Press, 624 SE 29th Ave., Portland OR 97214-3026. (503)233-3936. Contact: Ruth Gundle. Estab. 1987. "Biennial prize for a book-length manuscript by a woman writer. Poems may be considered if submission is termed 'collected' or 'selected'. Award is judged by a nationally recognized woman poet." Buys all rights. Entries must be postmarked in January of even-numbered years. Guidelines for #10 SASE. Charges $15 fee. Prize: $1,000 advance against royalties and publication in the prize series.

NORMA FARBER FIRST BOOK AWARD, Poetry Society of America, 15 Gramercy Park S., New York NY 10003. (212)254-9628. Contact: Award Director. Book of original poetry submitted by the publisher. Deadline: December 22. Charges $10/book fee. Award: $1,000.

‡**FIRST BOOK OF POETRY SERIES AWARD**, Mid-List Press, 4324 12th Ave. S., Minneapolis MN 55407-3218. (612)822-3733. Acquisitions Editor: Maria Ahrens. Estab. 1989. Offered annually for unpublished book of poetry to encourage new poets. Deadline: February 1. Guidelines for SASE. Charges $10 fee. Prize: publication and an advance against royalties $500. Judged by Mid-List's editors and ms readers. Winners are offered a contract at the conclusion of the judging. Contest is open to any writer who has never published a book of poetry. ("We do not consider a chapbook to be a book of poetry.")

‡**CONSUELO FORD AWARD**, Poetry Society of America, 15 Gramercy Park S., New York NY 10003. (212)254-9628. Contact: Award Director. Unpublished lyric. Guidelines for SASE. Deadline: December 22. Members only.

THE 49th PARALLEL POETRY CONTEST, The Signpost Press Inc., 1007 Queen St., Bellingham WA 98226-2139. (206)734-9781. Contest Director: Knute Skinner. Estab. 1977. Unpublished poetry. Submission period: September 15-December 1. Charges $3/poem fee. Anyone submitting 3 or more poems will receive a complimentary 1-year subscription to *The Bellingham Review*. Awards: 1st-$150; 2nd-$100; 3rd-$50.

GROLIER POETRY PRIZE, Grolier Poetry Book Shop, Inc. & Ellen LaForge Memorial Poetry Foundation, Inc., 6 Plympton St., Cambridge MA 02138. (617)547-4648. Fax: (617)547-4230. Contact: Ms. Louisa Solano. Estab. 1973. For previously unpublished work to encourage and recognize developing writers. Open to all poets who have not published with either a vanity, small press, trade, or chapbook of poetry. Deadline: May 1. Guidelines for SASE. Charges $5 fee. Prize: honorarium of $150 for two poets. Also 4 poems of each winner and 2 poems of 4 runners-up will be chosen for publication in the Grolier Poetry Prize Annual.

‡**CECIL HEMLEY MEMORIAL AWARD**, Poetry Society of America, 15 Gramercy Park S., New York NY 10003. (212)254-9628. Contact: Award Director. Unpublished lyric poem on a philosophical theme. Send #10 SASE for guidelines. Deadline: December 22. Members only.

‡**IOWA POETRY PRIZES**, (formerly The Edwin Ford Piper Poetry Award), University of Iowa Press, 119 W. Park Rd., Iowa City IA 52242. "The awards were initiated to encourage mature poets and their work." Manuscripts received in February and March. Send SASE. No reader's fee. Two $1,000 prizes are awarded annually. Final judging is performed by nationally prominent poets. Competition open to writers of English (whether citizens of US or not) who have published at least 1 previous book. No member of the faculty, staff or student body of University of Iowa is eligible.

THE CHESTER H. JONES FOUNDATION NATIONAL POETRY COMPETITION, P.O. Box 498, Chardon OH 44024-9996. Estab. 1982. Annual competition for persons in the US, Canada and US citizens living abroad. Winning poems plus others, called "commendations," are published in a chapbook available from the foundation. Deadline: March 31. Charges $2 fee for first poem, $1 for each succeeding poem up to 10. Maximum 10 entries, no more than 32 lines each; must be unpublished.

‡**RUTH LAKE MEMORIAL AWARD**, Poetry Society of America, 15 Gramercy Park S., New York NY 10003. (212)254-9628. Contact: Award Director. Unpublished poem of retrospection in any style. Guidelines for SASE. Deadline: December 22. Charges $5 fee.

LAMONT POETRY SELECTION, The Academy of American Poets, Suite 1208, 584 Broadway, New York NY 10012-3250. (212)427-5665. Award Director: Matthew Brogan. Second book of unpublished poems by an American citizen, submitted by publisher in manuscript form. Deadline: April 30. Contact the Academy office for guidelines and official entry form.

THE PETER I.B. LAVAN YOUNGER POETS AWARD, The Academy of American Poets, Suite 1208, 584 Broadway, New York NY 10012. (212)274-0343. American poets 40 years old or younger who have published at least one full-length collection of poetry. Recipients are selected by the Academy's Chancellors. No applications.

‡**LEAGUE OF CANADIAN POETS AWARDS**, National Poetry Contest, Gerald Lampert Award, and Pat Lowther Award. 3rd Floor, 54 Wolseley St., Toronto, Ontario M5T 1A5 Canada. (416)504-1657. Fax: (416)947-0159. Estab. 1966. Submissions to be published in the preceding year (awards), or previously unpublished (poetry contest). To promote new Canadian poetry/poets and also to recognize exceptional work in each category. Awards and contest deadline: January 31. Enquiries from publishers welcome. Charge: $6/poem for contest *only*. Open to Canadians living at home and abroad. The candidate must be a Canadian

citizen or landed immigrant, although publisher need not be Canadian. For complete contest and awards rules, contact Edita Petrauskaite at address above.

ELIAS LIEBERMAN STUDENT POETRY AWARD, Poetry Society of America, 15 Gramercy Park S., New York NY 10003. (212)254-9628. Contact: Award Director. Unpublished poem by student (grades 9-12). Poet must reside in the US or its territories. Guidelines for SASE. Deadline: December 22. Charges $5 fee.

THE RUTH LILLY POETRY PRIZE, The Modern Poetry Association and The American Council for the Arts, 60 W. Walton St., Chicago IL 60610-3305. Contact: Joseph Parisi. Estab. 1986. Annual prize to poet "whose accomplishments in the field of poetry warrant extraordinary recognition." No applicants or nominations are accepted. Deadline varies.

‡LOCAL 7's ANNUAL NATIONAL POETRY COMPETITION, Santa Cruz/Monterey Local 7, National Writers Union, P.O. Box 2409, Aptos CA 95001-2409. (408)728-2855. Coordinator: Don Monkerud. Previously unpublished poetry. "To encourage the writing of poetry and to showcase unpublished work of high quality. Proceeds support the work of Local 7 of the National Writers Union." Deadline varies. Guidelines for #10 SASE. Charges $3/poem fee. Prizes: 1st-$200; 2nd-$100; 3rd-$50.

LOUISIANA LITERATURE PRIZE FOR POETRY, *Louisiana Literature*, SLU—Box 792, Southeastern Louisiana University, Hammond LA 70403. Contest Director: Dr. David Hanson. Estab. 1984. Unpublished poetry. Deadline: February 15. Write for rules. Prize: $400. Entries considered for publication.

THE LENORE MARSHALL/NATION PRIZE FOR POETRY, The New Hope Foundation and *The Nation* Magazine, 72 Fifth Ave., New York NY 10011. (212)242-8400. Administrator: Peter Meyer. Book of poems published in the United States during the previous year and nominated by the publisher. Prize: $10,000. Deadline: June 1. Books must be submitted *directly* to judges. Query *The Nation* for addresses of judges.

‡JOHN MASEFIELD MEMORIAL AWARD, Poetry Society of America, 15 Gramercy Park S., New York NY 10003. (212)254-9628. Contact: Award Director. Unpublished narrative poem in English. No translations. Guidelines for SASE. Deadline: December 22. Charges $5 fee.

‡LUCILLE MEDWICK MEMORIAL AWARD, Poetry Society of America, 15 Gramercy Park S., New York NY 10003. (212)254-9628. Contact: Award Director. Original poem on a humanitarian theme. Guidelines for SASE. Deadline: December 22. Members only.

MINNESOTA INK SEMI-ANNUAL POETRY CONTEST, Minnesota Ink, Inc., Suite 328, 3585 N. Lexington Ave., Arden Hills MN 55126. (612)486-7818. Contact: Glenda Olsen. Offered winter and summer. Unpublished poets. Deadlines: February 28; August 15. Charges $2 fee for first poem; $1 each poem thereafter.

MIRRORS INTERNATIONAL TANKA AWARD, AHA Books, P.O. Box 1250, Gualala CA 95445-1250. (707)882-2226. Editor: Jane Reichhold. Estab. 1988. "The purpose of the contest is to acquaint writers with the Japanese poetry form, tanka. By choosing 31 winners for publication in a chapbook, it is hoped that standards and examples will be set, re-evaluated, changed and enlarged. The genre is one of Japan's oldest, but the newest to English." Deadline: November 30. Guidelines for #10 SASE. Maximum 10 entries. No fee. Send SASE for winners list. 31 winning entries published in *Tanka Splendor*, which is given to the winners and then goes on sale for up to 3 years by AHA Books distribution.

MISSISSIPPI VALLEY NON-PROFIT POETRY CONTEST, P.O. Box 3188, Rock Island IL 61204-3188. (309)788-8041. Director: Max Molleston. Estab. 1971. Unpublished poetry: adult general, student division, Mississippi Valley, senior citizen, religious, rhyming, humorous, haiku, history and ethnic. Deadline: September 7. Charges $5 to enter contest; $3 for students. Up to 5 poems may be submitted with a limit of 50 lines/poem.

MORSE POETRY PRIZE, Northeastern University English Deptment, 406 Holmes Hall, Boston MA 02115. (617)437-2512. Contact: Guy Rotella. Previously published poetry, book-length mss of first or second books. Charges $10/fee. Prize: Publication by Northeastern University Press and a $500 cash award.

ALWAYS submit unsolicited manuscripts or queries with a self-addressed, stamped envelope (SASE) within your country or a self-addressed envelope with International Reply Coupons (IRC) purchased from the post office for other countries.

‡**NATIONAL LOOKING GLASS AWARD FOR A SINGLE POEM**, *Pudding Magazine: The International Journal of Applied Poetry*, 60 N. Main St., Johnstown OH 43031. (614)967-6060. Contest Director: Jennifer Bosveld. Estab. 1979. Previously unpublished poems. "To identify and publish the finest work reflecting the editorial slant of *Pudding Magazine: The International Journal of Applied Poetry*. We recommend subject matter in the area of social justice, ecology and human impact, human relations, popular culture and *artistic* work from a therapuetic process." Deadline: September 30. Guidelines for #10 SASE. Charges $2/poem fee. Number of entries unlimited. Prize: $250 total in cash prizes.

NATIONAL LOOKING GLASS POETRY CHAPBOOK COMPETITION, *Pudding Magazine: The International Journal of Applied Poetry*, 60 N. Main St., Johnstown OH 43031. (614)967-6060. Contest Director: Jennifer Bosveld. "To publish a collection of poems that represents our magazine's editorial slant: popular culture, social justice, psychological, etc. Poems might be themed or not." Deadline: June 30. Guidelines for #10 SASE. Charges $9 fee. Prize: publication of the book and 20 copies to the author plus wholesale rights.

NATIONAL WRITERS ASSOCIATION POETRY CONTEST, The National Writers Association, Suite 424, 1450 S. Havana, Aurora CO 80012. (303)751-7844. Fax:(303)751-8593. Director: Sandy Whelchel. Annual contest "to encourage the writing of poetry, an important form of individual expression but with a limited commercial market." Charges $8 fee. Prizes: $100, $50, $25. Guidelines for #10 SASE.

GUY OWEN POETRY PRIZE, *Southern Poetry Review*, English Dept. UNCC, Charlotte NC 28223. (704)547-4336. Award Director: Ken McLaurin. Estab. 1985. Annual award for the best unpublished poem submitted in an open competition. Given in memory of Guy Owen, a poet, fiction writer and founder of *Southern Poetry Review*. Submit in April only. Guidelines for SASE. Charges $8 fee that includes one year subscription to *SPR* to begin with the fall issue, containing the winning poem. Prize: $500 and publication in *SPR*.

PANHANDLER POETRY CHAPBOOK COMPETITION, *The Panhandler Magazine*, English Dept., University of West Florida, Pensacola FL 32514-5751. (904)474-2923. Editor: Laurie O'Brien. Estab. 1979. Individual poems may have been published. To honor excellence in the writing of short collections of poetry. Two winning mss are published each year. Submit October 15-January 15. Charges $7 fee (includes copy of winning chapbooks).

PETERLOO POETS OPEN POETRY COMPETITION, 2 Kelly Gardens, Calstock, Cornwall PL18 9SA UK. Publication Director: Harry Chambers. Estab. 1971."Annual competition for new (unpublished) poetry." Deadline: March 1. Entry fee indicated on rules/entry form. Awards consist of cash prizes and publication. Sponsored by Marks & Spencer plc.

‡**THE RICHARD PHILLIPS POETRY PRIZE**, The Phillips Publishing Co. 719 E. Delaware, Siloam Springs AR 72761. Contact: Richard Phillips, Jr. Offered annually to give a modest financial reward to emerging poets who have not yet established themselves sufficiently to generate appropriate compensation for their work. Deadline: September 5. Guidelines for SASE. Charges $10/ms fee. Prize: $1,000 and publication. Open to all poets.

THE POETRY CENTER BOOK AWARD, The Poetry Center, San Francisco State University, 1600 Holloway Ave., San Francisco CA 94132-9901. (415)338-2227. Fax: (415)338-1498. Award Director: Melissa Black. Estab. 1980. Offered annually for previously published books of poetry and chapbooks, appearing in year of the prize. "Prize given for an extraordinary book of American poetry." Deadline December 31. Guidelines for #10 SASE. Charges $10/book fee. Prize: $500 and an invitation to read in The Poetry Center Reading Series. Please include a cover letter noting author name, book title(s), name of person issuing check, and check number.

POETRY MAGAZINE POETRY AWARDS, 60 W. Walton St., Chicago IL 60610. (312)280-4870. Editor: Joseph Parisi. Estab. 1912. All poems already published in *Poetry* during the year are automatically considered for annual prizes.

POETRY PUBLICATION, (formerly Poetry Contest), The Poet Band Co., P.O. Box 2648, Newport News VA 23609-0648. Editor: Arthur C. Ford. Estab. 1984. Send maximum of 5 poems. Enclose $1 for reading fee. Use rhyme and non-rhyming verse. Maximum lines: 40. Prose maximum: 200-300 words. Allow 1 month for response. Sample copy $3. Send SASE for more information. Quarterly newsletter (*The Pen*) issued March, June, September and December.

‡**POETS CLUB OF CHICAGO INTERNATIONAL SHAKESPEAREAN SONNET CONTEST**, 2930 Franklin St., Highland IN 46332-1636. Chairman: June Shipley. Estab. 1954. Deadline: September 1. Guidelines for SASE after March 1.

‡FELIX POLLACK PRIZE IN POETRY, University of Wisconsin Press, 114 N. Murray St., Madison WI 53715. Contest Director: Ronald Wallace. Estab. 1985. Unpublished book length ms of original poetry. Submissions must be received by the press during the month of September (postmark is irrelevant) and must be accompanied by SASE for contest results. Prize: $1,000 and publication. Guidelines for #10 SASE. Manuscripts will not be returned. Charges $15 fee, payable to University of Wisconsin Press. Notification in February.

‡PORTER'S QUARTERLY POETRY CONTEST, Porter Publishing Company, Suite 294, Dept. M, 5840 N. Orange Blossom Trail, Orlando FL 32810. (407)290-9214. Contest Director: Gail B. Porter. Offered quarterly (anthology published semiannually) for unpublished work "to encourage new poets and to keep alive the beauty and spirit of good poetry. Poetry can be any subject, any style." Deadlines: Summer (July 1); Fall (October 1); Winter (January 1); Spring (April 1). Guidelines for SASE. Charges $1/poem, $5/3 poems. Prize: 1st-$200; 2nd-$100; 3rd-$50; Honorable Mentions. Writers retain full rights to their work. Contest open to any writer, only unpublished poems will be considered.

PRAIRIE SCHOONER STROUSSE AWARD, *Prairie Schooner*, 201 Andrews, University of Nebraska, Lincoln NE 68588-0334. (402)472-3191. Fax: (402)472-4636. Editor: Hilda Raz. Estab. 1977. Annual award given for the best poem or group of poems published in *Prairie Schooner*. Winner announced in the spring issue of the following year. Prize $500.

‡QUARTERLY REVIEW OF LITERATURE POETRY SERIES, 26 Hazlet Ave., Princeton NJ 08540. (609)921-6976. "QRL Poetry Series is a book publishing series chosen from an open competition." Publishes 4-6 titles/year. Awards $1,000, publication and 100 copies to each winner for a book of miscellaneous poems, a single long poem, a poetic play or a book of translations. Guidelines for SASE. Submission May and October *only*.

THE BYRON HERBERT REECE INTERNATIONAL POETRY AWARDS, Georgia State Poetry Society, Inc., 1590 Riderwood Court, Decatur GA 30033-1531. (404)633-1647. Contest Director: Betty Lou Gore. Estab. 1987. Offered annually for previously unpublished poetry "to honor the late Georgia poet, Byron Herbert Reece." Deadline in January. Guidelines for #10 SASE. Charges $5/first poem; $1/additional poem. Prizes: 1st-$250; 2nd-$100; 3rd-$50.

ROANOKE-CHOWAN AWARD FOR POETRY, North Carolina Literary and Historical Association, 109 E. Jones St., Raleigh NC 27601-2807. (919)733-7305. Previously published poetry by a resident of North Carolina. Deadline: July 15.

NICHOLAS ROERICH POETRY PRIZE, Story Line Press, Three Oaks Farm, Brownsville OR 97327-9718. (503)466-5352. Fax: (503)466-3200. Contact: Joseph Bednarik. Estab. 1988. First full-length book of poetry. Any writer who has not published a full-length collection of poetry (48 pages or more) in English is eligible to apply. Deadline: October 15. Charges $15 fee. Prizes: $1,000, publication, a reading at the Nicholas Roerich Museum in New York.

†SHELLEY MEMORIAL AWARD, Poetry Society of America, 15 Gramercy Park S., New York NY 10003. (212)254-9628. Contact: Award Director. Deadline: December 22. By nomination only to a living American poet.

[SNA]KE NATION PRESS'S ANNUAL POETRY CONTEST, Snake Nation Press, 110 #2 W. Force St., Valdosta [GA 3]1601. (912)219-8334. Contest Director: Roberta George. Estab. 1989. Annual contest to give a wider a[udien]ce to readable, understandable poetry. Deadline: January 1. Guidelines for #10 SASE. Charges $10 fee[. Pri]ze consists of $500, 50 copies and distribution. Open to everyone.

‡THE [SO]W'S EAR CHAPBOOK PRIZE, *The Sow's Ear Poetry Review*, 19535 Pleasant View Dr., Abingdon VA 2421[1-68]27. (703)628-2651. Contest Director: Larry K. Richman. Estab. 1988. 24-26 pages of poetry. Submit March-[Ap]ril. Guidelines for #10 SASE. Charges $10 fee. Prize: $500, 50 copies and distribution to subscribers.

‡THE SO[W'S] EAR POETRY PRIZE, The Sow's Ear Poetry Review, 19535 Pleasant View Dr., Abingdon VA 24211-68[27.] (703)628-2651. Contest Director: Larry K. Richman. Estab. 1988. Previously unpublished poetry. Submit [Septe]mber-October. Guidelines for #10 SASE. Charges $2 fee/poem. Prize: $500, $100, $50 and public[ation plu]s publication for 20-25 finalists. All submissions considered for publication.

EDW[ARD STANLEY] AWARD, *Prairie Schooner*, 201 Andrews, University of Nebraska, Lincoln NE 68588-0334[. (402)472-3]191. Fax: (402)472-4636. Editor: Hilda Raz. Annual award for poems published in *Prairie Sc[hooner]*. [Winner] announced in the spring issue of the following year. Prize: $300.

[AGNES LYNCH STARRETT POETRY PRIZE, University of Pittsburgh Press, 127 N. Bellefield Ave., Pitts[burgh PA 15260. (4]12)624-4110. Fax: (412)624-7380. Series Editor: Ed Ochester. Estab. 1936. First book of poetry for poets who have not had a full-length book published. Deadline: March and April only. Guidelines for SASE.

ELIZABETH MATCHETT STOVER MEMORIAL AWARD, *Southwest Review*, 307 Fondren Library W., P.O. Box 374, Southern Methodist University, Dallas TX 75275-0374. (214)373-7440. For the best poem or group of poems that appeared in the magazine during the previous year. Prize: $150.

TROIKA COMPETITION, Thorntree Press, 547 Hawthorn Lane, Winnetka IL 60093. (708)446-8099. Contact: Eloise Bradley Fink. Estab. 1985. Imagery is important. Manuscripts considered January 1-February 14, in *odd-numbered years*. "We will be selecting three poets for our next *Troika*. Contestants are asked to submit a stapled group of ten pages of *unpublished* poetry, single or double spaced, photocopied, with a $4 reader's fee. Manuscripts will not be returned."

‡KATE TUFTS DISCOVERY AWARD FOR POETRY, The Claremont Graduate School, 160 E. Tenth St., Claremont CA 91711. (909)621-8974. Award Director: Murray M. Schwartz. Offered annually for poetry published in book form in English during the previous year. Guidelines for SASE. Deadline: December 15. Prize: $5,000. Entrants must agree to reproduction rights and to be present at award ceremony.

‡KINGSLEY TUFTS POETRY AWARD AT THE CLAREMONT GRADUATE SCHOOL, The Claremont Graduate School, 160 E. Tenth St., Claremont CA 91711. (909)621-8974. Award Director: Murray M. Schwartz. Offered annually for poetry published in book form in English during the previous year. Guidelines for SASE. Deadline: December 15. Prize: $50,000. Entrants must agree to reproduction rights and to be present at award ceremony and week's residency the Claremont Graduate School.

VERVE POETRY CONTEST, *VERVE* Magazine, P.O. Box 3205, Simi Valley CA 93093. Contest Director: Ron Reichick. Estab. 1989. Contest offered 2 times annually for previously unpublished poetry. "Fund raiser for *VERVE* Magazine which receives no grants and has no ties with any institutions." Deadlines: April 1 and October 1. Guidelines for #10 SASE. Charges $2/poem. Prize: 1st-$100; 2nd-$50; 3rd-$25.

‡CELIA B. WAGNER AWARD, Poetry Society of America, 15 Gramercy Park St. S., New York NY 10003. (212)254-9628. Contact: Award Director. Unpublished poem. "Poem worthy of the tradition of the art in any style." Guidelines for SASE. Deadline: December 22. Charges $5 fee.

WILLIAM CARLOS WILLIAMS AWARD, Poetry Society of America, 15 Gramercy Park S., New York NY 10003. (212)254-9628. Contact: Award Director. Small press, nonprofit, or university press book of poetry submitted by publisher. Deadline: December 22. Charges $10/book fee. Award: $1,250.

ROBERT H. WINNER MEMORIAL AWARD, Poetry Society of America, 15 Gramercy Park S., New York NY 10003. (212)254-9628. Contact: Award Director. "For a poet whose first book appeared when he was almost 50, recognizing and rewarding the work of someone in midlife. Open to poets over 40, still unpublished or with one book." Guidelines for SASE. Charges $5 fee. Deadline: December 22. Award: $2,750.

WINTER POETRY COMPETITION, Still Waters Press, 112 W. Duerer St., Galloway NJ 08201-9402. Contest Director: Shirley A. Warren. Estab. 1989. Guidelines for #10 SASE. Charges $10 fee. Deadline: September 30. Sample winning chapbook: $5.

‡WOMEN'S WORDS POETRY COMPETITION, Still Waters Press, 112 W. Duerer St., Galloway NJ 08201-9402. Contest Director: Shirley A. Warren. Guidelines for #10 SASE.Charges $10 fee. Deadline: February 28.

‡THE WRITER MAGAZINE/EMILY DICKINSON AWARD, Poetry Society of America, 15 Gramercy Park S., New York NY 10003. (212)254-9628. Contact: Award Director. Poem inspired by Emily Dickinson, though not necessarily in her style. Guidelines for SASE. Deadline: December 22. Members only.

‡WRITERS' JOURNAL SEMI-ANNUAL POETRY CONTEST, Minnesota Ink, Inc., Suite 328, 3585 N. Lexington Ave., Arden Hills MN 55126. (612)486-7818. Contact: Esther M. Leiper. Previously unpublished poetry. Deadlines: November 30 and April 15. Charges fee: $2 first poem; $1 each thereafter.

‡YALE SERIES OF YOUNGER POETS, Yale University Press, P.O. Box 209040, New Haven CT 06520. Contact: Jonathan Brent. Previously unpublished poetry. Submit during February. Guidelines for #10 SASE. Charges $8 fee. "Winning manuscript is published by Yale University Press. The author receives the usual royalties."

ZUZU'S PETALS POETRY CONTEST, *Zuzu's Petals Quarterly*, P.O. Box 4476, Allentown PA 18105-4476. (610)821-1324. Editor: T. Dunn. Offered 2 times/year for previously unpublished poetry. Deadlines: March

1 and September 1. Guidelines for #10 SASE. Charges $2/poem. Prize: top 3 winners share 40% of the contest's proceeds. All entries automatically considered for publication.

Playwriting and Scriptwriting

‡AMERICAN SHORTS, Florida Studio Theater, 1241 N. Palm Ave., Sarasota FL 34236. (813)366-9017. Fax: (813)955-4137. Offered annually for unpublished plays no more than 5 pages long on a theme that changes every year. 1994 theme was "men and women, not necessarily in that order." Deadline: June 15. Prize: $500.

‡ATHE PLAYWRIGHTS PRIZE, Association for Theatrical Higher Education, % Dept. of Theatre, PCAC, University of New Hampshire, Durham NJ 03824. (603)862-2078. Fax: (603)862-2030. Contact: Paul Mroszka. Offered every 2 years for unpublished works "to encourage student playwrights. Open to one-act plays, prior production is okay." Deadline: January 26, 1995. Guidelines for SASE. Prize: at least $200 and a staged reading at ATHE's national conference. Open to writers enrolled or recently enrolled at an institution of higher education.

‡THE MARGARET BARTLE PLAYWRITING AWARD, Community Children's Theatre of Kansas City, 8021 E. 129th Terrace, Grandview MO 64030-2114. (816)761-5775. Award Director: E. Blanche Sellens. Estab. 1951. Offered annually for unpublished plays for elementary school audiences. "Our purpose is two-fold: to award a deserving author of a good, well-written play, and to produce the play royalty-free by one of our trouping units." Deadline: January 31. Guidelines for SASE. Prize: $500.

THE BEVERLY HILLS THEATRE GUILD-JULIE HARRIS PLAYWRIGHT AWARD COMPETITION, 2815 N. Beachwood Drive, Los Angeles CA 90068. (213)465-2703. Playwright Award Coordinator: Marcella Meharg. Estab. 1978. Original full-length plays, unpublished, unproduced and not currently under option. Application required, available upon request with SASE. Submissions accepted with applications from August 1 through annual deadline of November 1.

CALIFORNIA PLAYWRIGHTS COMPETITION, South Coast Repertory, P.O. Box 2197, Costa Mesa CA 92628. (714)957-2602. Contact: John Glore. Estab. 1988. Previously unpublished and unproduced submissions. Deadline: TBA. Guidelines and application form available after September 1; writers must phone or write for complete guidelines and application form. Prize: 1st-$5,000; 2nd-$3,000. "Writer must maintain principal residence in California."

CALIFORNIA YOUNG PLAYWRIGHTS CONTEST, The Playwright Project, Suite 215, 1450 Frazee Rd., San Diego CA 92108. (619)298-9242. Fax: (619)298-9244. Contest Director: Deborah Salzer. Annual contest for previously unpublished plays by young writers "to stimulate young people to create dramatic works, and to nurture promising young writers (under age 19)." Deadline: April 1. Guidelines for 9×12 SASE. Award consists of "professional production of 3-5 winning plays at the Old Globe Theatre in San Diego, plus royalty. All entrants receive detailed evaluation letter." Judged by theater professionals in the Southern California area. "Scripts must be a minimum of ten standard typewritten pages. Writers must be California residents under age 19 as of the deadline date."

CEC JACKIE WHITE MEMORIAL NATIONAL CHILDREN'S PLAYWRITING CONTEST, Columbia Entertainment Company, 309 Parkade Blvd., Columbia MO 65202. (314)874-5628. Contact: Betsy Phillips. Estab. 1988. Annual award for "top notch unpublished scripts for theater school use, to challenge and expand the talents of our students, ages 10-15. The entry should be a full length play with speaking roles for 20-30 characters of all ages and with at least 10 roles developed in some detail." Deadline: May 30. Production and some travel expenses for 1st and 2nd place winners, plus cash award for 1st place. Guidelines for SASE. Entrants receive written evaluation of work. Charges $10 fee.

CELEBRATION OF ONE-ACTS, West Coast Ensemble, P.O. Box 38728, Los Angeles CA 90038-5306. Artistic Director: Les Hanson. Estab. 1984. Unpublished (in Southern California) one-act plays. Deadline: November 15. "Up to three submissions allowed for each playwright." Casts should be no more than 6 and plays no longer than 35 minutes.

JANE CHAMBERS PLAYWRITING AWARD, Women and Theatre Program of Association for Theatre in Higher Education (WTP/ATHE).% Tori Haring-Smith, English Dept., Box 1852, Brown University, Providence RI 02912. (401)247-2911. Director: Tori Haring-Smith. Estab. 1983. "Purpose is to recognize a woman playwright who has written a play with a feminist perspective, a majority of roles for women, and which experiments with the dramatic form." Deadline: February 15. Notification: May 31. Guidelines for #10 SASE. Award: $1,000, plus travel expenses, and reading at the WTP/ATHE national conference in August. Student award: $250. "Writer must be female. A recommendation from a theatre professional is helpful, but not required."

CLEVELAND PUBLIC THEATRE FESTIVAL OF NEW PLAYS, Cleveland Public Theatre, 6415 Detroit Ave., Cleveland OH 44102. (216)631-2727. Contest Director: Linda Eisenstein. Estab. 1993. Annual festival of staged readings of 10-15 alternative, experimental, poetic, political work, and plays by women, people of color, gays/lesbians. Deadline: September 1. Guidelines for SASE. Charges $10 fee.

COE COLLEGE PLAYWRITING FESTIVAL, Coe College, 1220 First Ave. NE., Cedar Rapids IA 52402-5092. (319)399-8689. Fax: (319)399-8748. Contact: Susan Wolverton. Estab. 1993. Offered every 2 years for unpublished work. Next festival: 1994-95. Purpose is "to provide a venue for new works for the stage. There is usually a theme for the festival. We are interested in full-length productions, *not* one acts or musicals." Guidelines for SASE. Prize: "$325, plus one-week residency as guest artist with airfare, room and board provided." Judges are a select committee of professionals. "There are no specific criteria although a current résumé is requested."

THE CHRISTOPHER COLUMBUS SCREENPLAY DISCOVERY AWARDS, #600, 433 N. Camden Dr., Beverly Hills CA 90210. (310)288-1988. Fax: (310)475-0193. Monthly and annual contest "to discover new screenplay writers." Deadline: December 1. Charges $45 entry fee. Prize consists of "options up to $10,000, plus professional development guidance and access to agents, producers, and studios." Judged by reputable industry professionals (producers, development executives, story analysts). Writer must give option to purchase if selected.

‡CORNERSTONE DRAMATURGY AND DEVELOPMENT PROJECT, Penumbra Theatre, 270 N. Kent, St. Paul MN 55102. (612)224-3180. Fax: (612)224-7074. Contest/Award Director: L. Bellamy. Annual project for "new plays addressing Pan-African and African-American experiences. Must be a full-length drama or comedy." Scripts accepted year-round. Guidelines for SASE. Selected script will receive support in the form of writer commissions, per diem, workshops, lodging expenses, readings and possible production in Penumbra's regular season.

CUNNINGHAM PRIZE FOR PLAYWRITING, The Theatre School, DePaul University, 2135 N. Kenmore, Chicago IL 60614. (312)362-6150. Fax: (312)362-5453. Contact: Lisa A. Quinn. Offered annually for either previously published or unpublished work "to recognize and encourage the writing of dramatic works which affirm the centrality of religion, broadly defined, and the human quest for meaning, truth and community." Deadline: December 1. Guidelines for SASE. Prize: $5,000. Judged by "a panel of distinguished citizens including members of the faculty of DePaul University, representatives of the Cunningham Prize Advisory Commitee, critics and others from the theater professions, chaired by John Ransford Watts, dean of the Theatre School." Open to writers whose usual residence or base of operations is in the Chicago area.

DAYTON PLAYHOUSE FUTURE FEST, The Dayton Playhouse, 1301 E. Siebenthaler Ave., Dayton OH 45414-5357. (513)277-0144. Fax: (513)227-9539. Managing Director: Jim Payne. Estab. 1983. "Three plays selected for full productions, three for readings at July 1995 Future Fest weekend; possible travel, room and board to attend rehearsals; judges view all productions and select winner of $1,000 1st prize." Guidelines for SASE. Deadline: September 30.

‡DFAP ONE-ACT PLAYWRITING CONTEST, Dubuque Fine Arts Players, 569 S. Grandview, Dubuque IA 52003. (319)582-5558. Contest Director: Sally T. Ryan. Offered annually for unpublished work to encourage playwrights. Deadline: January 31. Guidelines for SASE. Charges $10 fee. Prize: staged productions and money: $600, $300, $200. Acquires right to produce for our 4 performances. Must be original, unproduced; submit 2 copies plus entry fee.

‡DRAMARAMA, Playwrights' Center of San Francisco, P.O. Box 460466, San Francisco CA 94146-0466. (415)626-4603. Annual contest for unproduced, unpublished plays. No musicals or childrens' plays. Deadline: March 15. Guidelines for SASE. Charges $15 readers fee. Staged reading for all finalists. Prize: $200.

DRURY COLLEGE ONE-ACT PLAY CONTEST, Drury College, 900 N. Benton Ave., Springfield MO 65802-3344. (417)873-7430. Contact: Sandy Asher. Estab. 1986. Offered every 2 years, even years only. Plays must be unpublished and professionally unproduced. One play per playwright. Deadline: December 1. Guidelines for SASE. Winning plays receive special recommendation to The Open Eye: New Stagings, an Off-Broadway theater in New York City.

‡DUBUQUE FINE ARTS PLAYERS ANNUAL ONE-ACT PLAYWRITING CONTEST, 569 S. Grandview, Dubuque IA 52003. (319)582-5558. Contest Coordinator: Sally T. Ryan. Annual competition since 1977 for previously unpublished, unproduced plays. Adaptations must be of playwright's own work or of a work in the public domain. No children's plays or musicals. No scripts over 35 pages or 40 minutes performance time. Two copies of manuscript required. Script Readers' review sheets available. "Concentrate on character, relationships, and a good story." Deadline: January 31. Guidelines for #10 SASE. Charges $10 fee. Prizes:

$600, $300, $200, plus possible full production of play. Buys rights to first full-stage production and subsequent local video rights. Reports by June 30.

‡**SAM EDWARDS DEAF PLAYWRIGHTS COMPETITION**, New York Deaf Theatre, Ltd., 11th Floor, 305 Seventh Ave., New York NY 10001-6008. (212)924-9491 Voice. (212)924-9535 TTY. Contest Director: Jackie Roth. Offered annually for unpublished and unproduced work. "Established in 1989 to honor the memory of a founding member of the New York Deaf Theatre, the competition seeks to encourage deaf writers to create their unique stories for the stage. Keenly aware of the void which exists of plays written by deaf playwrights, the competition is the only opportunity of its kind that nurtures deaf writers in the development of their play writing skills. Unproduced scripts by deaf playwrights are accepted in two categories: full-length and one act plays." Deadline: September 1. Guidelines for SASE. Charges $10 US/Canadian and $15 foreign countries. Prize: $400 for full-length play, $200 for one-act play. "New York Deaf Theatre exercises the right to produce the winning plays, within a two-year period, as a staged reading, workshop production or full production. The competition is open to deaf writers only. It should be noted that while NYDT's mission is to create opportunities for American Sign Language Theatre for deaf theater artists and, in doing so, fosters a better understanding of Deaf Culture, the competition will accept scripts from all deaf people no matter what their primary mode of communication. However, we will only produce scripts that are in harmony with our mission."

EMERGING PLAYWRIGHT AWARD, Playwrights Preview Productions, P.O. Box 1019, Lenox Hall Station, New York NY 10021. (212)289-2168. Fax: (212)289-2168. Contact: David Sheppard. Submissions required to be unpublished. Awards are announced in the spring/fall. Estab. 1983. Submissions accepted year-round.

THE FESTIVAL OF EMERGING AMERICAN THEATRE, (formerly The RCI Festival of Emerging American Theatre), The Phoenix Theatre, 749 N. Park Ave., Indianapolis IN 46202. (317)635-7529. Contact: Bryan Fonseca. Annual playwriting competition. Deadline: February 28.

FMCT'S BIENNIAL PLAYWRIGHTS COMPETITION (MID-WEST), Fargo-Moorhead Community Theatre, P.O. Box 644, Fargo ND 58107-0644. (701)235-1901. Contact: Bruce Tinker. Estab. 1988. Biennial contest (next contest will be held 1995-96). Submissions required to be unpublished. Deadline: July 1, 1995.

‡**FORAY AWARDS, Associated Actors Agency**, 16 Sycamore Ct., Lawrenceville NJ 08648. (609)896-0293. Offered every 2 years for unpublished plays to discover new playwrights whose work is adaptable to stage or TV. Awards for 10-minute story and 30-minute story. Guidelines for SASE. Charges $20 fee. Prize: $200 and production contract. Acquires rights for 3 years. Open to any writer.

FUND FOR NEW AMERICAN PLAYS, American Express & President's Committee on Arts & Humanities, J.F. Kennedy Center, Washington DC 20566. (202)416-8024. Fax: (202)416-8026. Program Director: Sophy Burnham. Estab. 1988. Previously unproduced work. "Program objectives: to encourage playwrights to write, and nonprofit professional theaters to produce, new American plays; to ease the financial burdens of nonprofit professional theater organizations producing new plays; to provide a playwright with a better production of the play than the producing theater would normally be able to accomplish." Deadline: March 15, (date changes from year to year). "Writers or nonprofit theater organizations can mail in name and address to be placed on the mailing list." Prize: $10,000 for playwrights and grants to theaters according to need and based on scripts submitted by producing theaters. A few encouragement grants of $2,500 are given to promising playwrights. Submissions and funding proposals only through the producing theater.

JOHN GASSNER MEMORIAL PLAYWRITING AWARD, The New England Theatre Conference, Dept. of Theatre, Northeastern University, 360 Huntington Ave., Boston MA 02115. (617)424-9275. Estab. 1952. Unpublished full-length plays. Guidelines for #10 SASE. Deadline: April 15. Charges $10 fee; free for members of New England Theatre Conference.

‡**GILMAN & GONZALEZ-FALLA THEATER FOUNDATION AWARD**, 109 E. 64th St., New York NY 10021. (212)734-8011. Offered annually for previously produced work to encourage the creative elements in the American musical theater. Deadline July 30. Guidelines for SASE. Prize: $25,000. The script or lyrics must have been part of a musical theater work produced in the US in either a commercial theater, professional not-for-profit theater or an accredited university or college theater program.

GREAT PLATTE RIVER PLAYWRIGHTS FESTIVAL, University of Nebraska at Kearney, Theatre Department, 905 W. 25th St., Kearney NE 68849. (308)234-8406. Fax: (308)234-8157. Contact: Charles Davies. Estab. 1988. Unpublished submissions. "Purpose of award is to develop original dramas and encourage playwrights to work in regional settings. There are five catagories: 1) Adult; 2) Youth (Adolescent); 3) Children's; 4) Musical Theater; 5) Native American. Entries may be drama or comedy." Deadline: March 15. Awards: 1st-$500, 2nd-$300; 3rd-$200; plus free lodging and a travel stipend. "The Festival reserves the rights to development and premiere production of the winning plays without payment of royalties." Contest open to entry by any writer "provided that the writer submits playscripts to be performed on stage—works in progress also acceptable. Works involving the Great Plains will be most favored. More than one entry may be submitted." SASE required for return of scripts. Selection announcement by April 1 only to writers who provide prepaid postcard or SASE.

 • University of Nebraska Theatre Department is expanding into the professional sector and producing works off-campus.

‡HBO NEW WRITERS PROJECT, HBO and Wavy Line Productions, Suite 4200, 2049 Century Park E., Los Angeles CA 90067. Award Director: Steve Kaplan. Offered annually. "The HBO New Writers Project is designed to encourage and cultivate emerging multicultural writers and performing talent. We are seeking submissions of one-act plays, solo performance pieces or original ½ hour teleplays. Plays should be no more than 60 pages in length. We are seeking to discover a new generation of comic voices, who reflect the multicultural world in which we live." Deadline: February 15. Guidelines for SASE. "The Project will select 25 plays for participation in a Writers Workshop sponsored by HBO, in conjunction with Wavy Line Productions, Inc., with the intention that these works will be nurtured for possible stage, TV or film development."

HENRICO THEATRE COMPANY ONE-ACT PLAYWRITING COMPETITION, Henrico Theatre Company, P.O. Box 27032, Richmond VA 23273. (804)672-5100. Fax: (804)672-5284. Contest/Award Director: J. Larkin Brown. Annual competition for previously unpublished plays "to produce new dramatic works in one-act form. Award also for plays/musicals with a Christmas theme." Deadline: July 1. Guidelines for SASE. Prizes are: one-act $250; runner-up $125; Christmas show $250. All winning entries are produced; videotape sent to author. Judged by H.T.C. Playreading Committee. "Scripts with small casts and simpler sets given preference. Controversial themes should be avoided."

HIGH SCHOOL PLAYWRITING CONTEST, Baker's Plays, 100 Chauncy St., Boston MA 02111-1783. Phone/ fax: (617)482-1280. Contest Director: Raymond Pape. Annual contest for previously unpublished plays. "Open to any high school student. Plays must be accompanied by the signature of a sponsoring high school drama or English teacher, and it is recommended that the play receive a production or a public reading prior to the submission." Deadline: postmarked by January 31. Guidelines for #10 SASE. Prize: 1st-$500 and the play published by Baker's Plays; 2nd-$250 and Honorable Mention; 3rd-$100 and Honorable Mention.

INNER CITY CULTURAL CENTER'S NATIONAL SHORT PLAY COMPETITION, Inner City Cultural Center, 1605 N. Ivar St., Los Angeles CA 90028. (213)962-2102. Contact: C. Bernard Jackson. Offered annually for unpublished work. Deadline: June. Charges $35 fee. "All entries are presented live before an audience and jurors who are professionals in the arts and entertainment industry. Writer is responsible for preparation of submission for presentation."

‡INTERNATIONAL PLAY COMPETITION, Theater Department, Southern Illinois University—Carbondale, Communications Bldg., Carbondale IL 62901. (618)453-5741. Fax: (618)453-7714. Contest Director: Christian H. Moe. Offered every 2 years for unpublished work "to seek out a new play about an environmental issue (in order to stimulate the writing of plays about environmental concerns)." Deadline: December 1, 1995. Guidelines for SASE. Charges $5 fee. Prize: cash award of $500 and the option of production by the McLeod Theater at Southern Illinois University at Carbondale. Any writer may enter. Plays must be written in English; full-length, not hitherto produced professionally or published.

‡INTERNATIONAL PLAY CONTEST, Center Theater, 1346 W. Devon, Chicago IL 60660. (312)508-0200. Contest Director: Dale Calandra. Offered annually for unpublished work "to encourage the writer of new plays and to open up into the Chicago professional theater market." Deadline: February 15. Guidelines for SASE. Charges $15 fee. Prize: 1st-$300 and production, other cash prizes offered, finalist listed in letter to all all TC6 Theaters. Full length plays, all subject matter and type.

JEWEL BOX THEATRE PLAYWRIGHTING COMPETITION, Jewel Box Theatre, 3700 N. Walker, Oklahoma City OK 73118-7099. (405)521-1786. Contact: Charles Tweed. Estab. 1982. Only two or three acts accepted. Deadline: January 15. Prize: $500.

MARC A. KLEIN PLAYWRITING AWARD FOR STUDENTS, Department of Theater Arts, Case Western Reserve University, 10900 Euclid Ave., Cleveland OH 44106-7077. (216)368-2858. Chair, Reading Committee: John Orlock. Estab. 1975. Unpublished, professionally unproduced full-length play, or evening of related short plays by student in American college or university. Deadline: May 15.

LEE KORF PLAYWRITING AWARDS, The Original Theatre Works, Cerritos College, 11110 Alondra, Norwalk CA 90650. (310)860-2451, ext. 2638. Fax: (310)467-5005. Contact: Gloria Manriquez. Estab. 1984. Award for previously unproduced plays. Deadline: January 1. "All plays—special attention paid to plays with multicultural theme." Prize: $750 royalty award and full-scale production during summer theater.

LOVE CREEK ANNUAL SHORT PLAY FESTIVAL, Love Creek Productions, % Granville, 47 El Dorado Place, Weehawken NJ 07087-7004. Festival Manager: Cynthia Granville. Estab. 1985. Annual festival for unpublished plays, unproduced in New York in the previous year. "We believe that a script is incomplete as a work of art until it is performed. As an encouragement to playwrights and an enrichment opportunity for Love Creek's over 150 member artists, administrators and technicians, we have therefore established the Festival as a playwriting competition in which scripts are judged on their merits in performance." Deadline: September 30. Guidelines for #10 SASE. All entries must specify "festival" on envelope and must include letter giving permission to produce script, if chosen and stating whether equity showcase is acceptable.
  • Love Creek is now able to produce more small cast full-length plays if they require simple sets and run under 100 minutes.

LOVE CREEK MINI FESTIVALS, Love Creek Productions, % Granville, 47 El Dorado Place, Weehawken NJ 07087-7004. Festival Literary Manager: Cynthia Granville. "The Mini Festivals are an outgrowth of our annual Short Play Festival in which we produce scripts concerning a particular issue or theme which our artistic staff selects according to current needs, interests and concerns of both our members and playwrights submitting to our Short Play Festival throughout the year." Guidelines for #10 SASE. Submissions must list name of festival on envelope and must include letter giving permission to produce script, if chosen, and stating whether equity showcase is acceptable. Finalists receive a mini-showcase production in New York City. Winner receives a $200 prize. Upcoming theme are Gay and Lesbian Perspectives, deadline: May 31; Fear of God: Religion in the 90s, deadline: July 31.

DENNIS McINTYRE PLAYWRITING AWARD, Philadelphia Festival Theatre for New Plays, 7th Floor, 1515 Locust St., Philadelphia PA 19102-8710. (215)735-1500. Literary Manager: Michael Hollinger. Estab. 1981. Annual award for previously unproduced plays "to encourage emerging playwrights of conscience examining society's ills with honest scrutiny." Deadline: ongoing. No longer accepts unsolicited scripts. Submit synopsis, résumé and 10 pages of sample dialogue with query. Prize includes production or staged reading plus cash prize (determined annually), plus residency during rehearsal period.

MAXIM MAZUMDAR NEW PLAY COMPETITION, Alleyway Theatre, One Curtain Up Alley, Buffalo NY 14202-1911. (716)852-2266. Dramaturg: Joyce Stilson. Estab. 1990. Annual competition. Full Length: not less than 90 minutes, no more than 10 performers. One-Act: less than 60 minutes, no more than 6 performers. Deadline: September 1. Finalists announced January 1. "Playwrights may submit work directly. There is no entry form. Annual playwright's fee $5. Please specify if submission is to be included in competition." Prize: full length – $400, travel plus lodging, production and royalties; one-act – $100, production plus royalties. "Alleyway Theatre must receive first production credit in subsequent printings and productions."

MILL MOUNTAIN THEATRE NEW PLAY COMPETITION, Mill Mountain Theatre, Center in the Square, 2nd Floor, 1 Market Square, Roanoke VA 24011-1437. (703)342-5730. Literary Manager: Jo Weinstein. Estab. 1985. Previously unpublished and unproduced plays for up to 10 cast members. Deadline: January 1. Guidelines for SASE.

MIXED BLOOD VERSUS AMERICA, Mixed Blood Theatre Company, 1501 S. Fourth St., Minneapolis MN 55454. (612)338-0984. Contact: David B. Kunz. Estab. 1983. Theater Company. Estab. 1975. "Mixed Blood Versus America encourages and seeks out the emerging playwright. Mixed Blood is not necessarily looking for scripts that have multi-racial casts, rather good scripts that will be cast with the best actors available." Open to all playwrights who have had at least one of their works produced or workshopped (either professionally or educationally). Only unpublished, unproduced plays are eligible for contest. Limit 2 submissions per playwright. No translations or adaptations. Guidelines for SASE. Deadline: March 15.

MRTW ANNUAL RADIO SCRIPT CONTEST, Midwest Radio Theatre Workshop, 915 E. Broadway, Columbia MO 65201. (314)874-5676. Contact: Steve Donofrio. Estab. 1979. "The purpose of the award is to encourage the writing of radio scripts and to showcase both established and emerging radio playwrights. Some winning works are produced for radio and all winning works are published in the annual MRTW Scriptbook. Our scriptbook is the only one of it's kind in this country." Deadline: November 15. Guidelines for SASE. "A cash award of $800 is split among the top 2-4 entries, depending on recommendation of the jurors. Winners receive free workshop registration. Those who receive honorable mention, as well as award-winning plays, are included in the scriptbook; a total of 10-16 are published annually. We acquire the right to publish the script in the scriptbook, which is distributed at cost, and the right to produce the script for air; all other rights retained by the author."
  • A new 60-second PSA category has been added that uses Radio Theater to facilitate AIDS awareness. The winner of the PSA category receives $200 plus production and national distribution of the PSA.

MULTICULTURAL THEATRE WORKS SERIES, Seattle Group Theatre, 305 Harrison St., Seattle WA 98109. (206)441-9480. Estab. 1984. Full-length translations, adaptations and plays for young audiences. Musicals are not eligible. "New works, by culturally diverse playwrights, focusing on contemporary social, political and cultural issues relevant to the world community. Submission packet should include query, sample pages of dialogue, synopsis and an SASE for reply. Full manuscript submitted by solicitation only." Honorarium, airfare and housing. Submission period: ongoing.

‡**NANTUCKET SHORT PLAY COMPETITION AND FESTIVAL,** Nantucket Theatrical Productions, Box 2177, Nantucket MA 02584. (508)228-5002. Contest Director: Jim Patrick. Offered annually for unpublished work to "seek out quality new short plays." Deadline: April 1. Guidelines for SASE. Charges $5 fee. Prize: $200 grand prize to overall winner. Staged readings to several runners-up. Possible publishers referral. Acquires right to give staged readings at our festival. Open to any writer. No special criteria. Running time 1 hour or less.

‡**NATIONAL CANADIAN ONE-ACT PLAYWRITING COMPETITION,** Ottawa Little Theatre, 400 King Edward Ave., Ottawa, Ontario K1N 7M7 Canada. (613)233-8948. Fax: (613)233-8027. Director: George Stonyk. Estab. 1913. "To encourage literary and dramatic talent in Canada." Submit January-May. Guidelines for #10 SASE with Canadian postage or #10 SAE with 1 IRC. Prize: $1,000, $700, $500.

NATIONAL ONE-ACT PLAYWRITING COMPETITION, Little Theatre of Alexandria, 600 Wolfe St., Alexandria VA 22314. (703)683-5778. Contact: Chairman Playreading Committee. Estab. 1978. To encourage original writing for theatre. Submissions must be original, unpublished, unproduced one-act stage plays. Deadline: March 31. Guidelines for SASE. Prize: 1st-$350; 2nd-$250; 3rd-$150.

NATIONAL PLAYWRIGHTS' AWARD, Unicorn Theatre, 3820 Main St., Kansas City MO 64111. (816)531-7529. Literary Manager: Lisa J. Church. Offered annually for previously unproduced work. "We produce contemporary original scripts, preferring scripts that deal with social concerns. However, we accept (and have produced) comedies." Guidelines for SASE. Prize: $1,000 in royalty/prize fee and mainstage production at the Unicorn as part of its regular season.

NATIONAL TEN-MINUTE PLAY CONTEST, Actors Theatre of Louisville, 316 W. Main St., Louisville KY 40202-4218. (502)584-1265. Literary Manager: Michael Bigelow Dixon. Estab. 1964. Previously unproduced (professionally) ten-minute plays (10 pages or less). "Entries must *not* have had an Equity or Equity-waiver production." Deadline: December 1. Prize: $1,000.

‡**NEW ENGLAND NEW PLAY COMPETITION AND SHOWCASE,** The Vineyard Playhouse Co., Inc., Box 2452, Vineyard Haven MA 02568. (508)693-6450. Contact: M.J. Munafo. Offered annually for unpublished, unproduced full-length, non-musical works suitable for a cast of 10 or fewer. Deadline: June 1. Notification: September 1. Guidelines for SASE. Charges $5 fee. Prize: 4 finalists receive transportation to Martha's Vineyard from a New England location and up to 3 nights accommodation to attend staged reading and consideration for full stage production. Grand prize winner also receives $4,000.

NEW WORKS COMPETITION, Ferndale Repertory Theatre, P.O. Box 892, Ferndale CA 95536-0892. (707)725-4636. Artistic Director: Clinton Rebik. Estab. 1972. Annual competition for unpublished plays "to encourage the development of new theatrical scripts; and to showcase the talents of these artists in production." Deadline: October 15. Guidelines for SASE. Prize: $250 royalty for 8 performances; plus a set of all publicity and promotional materials and photos. Theater has rights for first 8 performances (and will pay $250 for privilege); all subsequent rights revert to author.

DON AND GEE NICHOLL FELLOWSHIPS IN SCREENWRITING, Academy of Motion Picture Arts & Sciences, 8949 Wilshire Blvd., Beverly Hills CA 90211-1972. (310)247-3059. Director: Greg Beal. Estab. 1985. Unproduced screenplays; up to 5 $25,000 fellowships awarded each year. Deadline: May 1. Charges $25 fee. Guidelines for SASE. Recipients announced late-October.

OFF-OFF-BROADWAY ORIGINAL SHORT PLAY FESTIVAL, 45 W. 25th St., New York NY 10010. Contact: William Talbot. Offered annually for unpublished work. "The Festival was developed in 1976 to bolster those theater companies and schools offering workshops, programs and instruction in playwriting. It proposes to encourage them by offering them and their playwrights the opportunity of having their plays seen by new audiences and critics, and of having them reviewed for publication." Deadline: January-February. Guidelines for SASE. Prize: "Presentation on NY stage before NY audiences and critics. Publication of selected plays by Samuel French Inc." Judged by members of NYC critics' circles. "No individual writer may enter on his/ her own initiative. Entries must come from theater companies, professional schools or colleges which foster playwriting by conducting classes, workshops or similar programs of assistance to playwrights."

OGLEBAY INSTITUTE TOWNGATE THEATRE PLAYWRITING CONTEST, Oglebay Institute, Stifel Fine Arts Center, 1330 National Rd., Wheeling WV 26003. (304)242-7700. Fax: (304)242-4203. Associate Director, Performing Arts Dept.: Debbie Hynes. Estab. 1976. Annual contest for unpublished works. Deadline: January

1. Guidelines for SASE. Prize: $300, limited-run production of play. "All full-length *non-musical* plays that have never been professionally produced or published are eligible." Winner announced March 1.

ROBERT J. PICKERING AWARD FOR PLAYWRIGHTING EXCELLENCE, Coldwater Community Theater, % 89 Division, Coldwater MI 49036. (517)279-7963. Committee Chairperson: J. Richard Colbeck. Estab. 1982. Previously unproduced monetarily. "To encourage playwrights to submit their work, to present a previously unproduced play in full production." Deadline: end of year. Guidelines for #10 SASE. Prize: 1st-$200; 2nd-$50; 3rd-$25. "We reserve right to produce winning script."

PLAYHOUSE ON THE SQUARE NEW PLAY COMPETITION, (formerly Mid-South Playwright Contest), Playhouse on the Square, 51 S. Cooper, Memphis TN 38104. Contact: Jackie Nichols. Submissions required to be unproduced. Deadline: April 1. Contest/award rules and entry forms for SASE. Prize: $500 plus production.

PLAYWRIGHTS PROJECT, Suite 215, 1450 Frazee Rd., San Diego CA 92108. (619)298-9242. Fax: (619)298-9244. Contact: Deborah Salzer. Estab. 1985. For Californians under 19 years of age. Every writer receives an individualized script critique if requested in cover letter; selected scripts receive professional productions. Deadline April 1. Request for poster is sufficient. For California residents under 19 years of age.

‡PLAYWRIGHTS' THEATER OF DENTON NEW PLAY COMPETITION, Playwrights' Theater of Denton, P.O. Box 732, Denton TX 76202-0732. Contact: Mark Pearce. Offered annually for stage plays of any length. Deadline: December 15. Guidelines for SASE. Charges $15 fee, payable to Sigma Corporation. Prize: $1,000, possible production. Open to any writer.

PLAYWRITING COMPETITION FOR YOUNG AUDIENCES, Indiana University-Purdue University at Indianapolis, Young Audiences Playwriting Competition, 525 N. Blackford St., Indianapolis IN 46202-3120. (317)274-2095. Fax: (317)278-1028. Assistant to the Director: W. Mark McCreary. Estab. 1983. Biennial competition held in even years for previously unpublished plays for young audiences through high school. Guidelines for SASE.

‡PROMISING PLAYWRIGHT AWARD, Colonial Players, Inc. 108 East St., Annapolis MD 21401. (410)263-0533. Coordinator: Frank B. Moorman. Offered every 2 years for unpublished plays by residents of MD, VA, WV, PA, DE and DC "to encourage aspiring playwrights." Submissions accepted September 1-December 31 of even-numbered years. Guidelines for #10 SASE. Prize: $750 plus possible production of play.

‡RADIO SCRIPT WRITERS COMPETITION, American Radio Theatre, 3035 23rd St., San Francisco CA 94110. Vice President: Frances Altvater. Offered annually for unpublished work "to encourage writers to expand their creative efforts to the American-oriented genre of radio theater. Works are judged on their use of the *audio* medium; we do not accept works in other mediums such as stage or screenplays." Deadline: August 31. Guidelines for SASE. Charge $9 fee. Prize: 1st-$250; 2nd-$100; 3 awards of $50. Finalists may be produced as part of "ART Showcase," an anthology series. This is negotiated upon acceptance. Contest open to any writer. "We request works be no more than 50 minutes in performance time (generally 50-55 pages). Scripts should be typewritten on 8 1/2×11 paper, double-spaced with lines numbered along the left hand margin. Script title and page numbers should appear on every page. We do not accept scripts on disk. Additional formatting rules available with contest guidelines."

‡RIVERFRONT PLAYHOUSE SCRIPTWRITING COMPETITION, Riverfront Playhouse, P.O. Box 105, Palo Cedro CA 96073; Playhouse: 1620 E. Cypress, Redding, CA 96002. (916)547-4108. Contest Director: Paul Robeson. "Offered annually for unpublished scripts to broaden the appreciation, awareness, and understanding of live theater by providing the environment for local talent to act, direct and creatively express themselves in the arts of the stage.The competition is designed to encourage and stimulate artistic growth among community playwrights. It provides playwrights the unique opportunity to mount and produce an original work at the *Riverfront Playhouse*." Deadline: February 2. Guidelines for SASE. Charges $25 fee. Prize: a reading, workshop and/or a full production of the winning entry. Cash prizes, as determined by the Board of Directors of the *Riverfront Playhouse*. Judged by college instructors and professional writers.

THE LOIS AND RICHARD ROSENTHAL NEW PLAY PRIZE, Cincinnati Playhouse in the Park, Box 6537, Cincinnati OH 45206. (513)345-2242. Contact: Susan Banks. Unpublished plays. Complete scripts will not be accepted. Query first for guidelines. "Scripts must not have received a full-scale professional production." Deadline: October 15-January 15.

‡MORTON R. SARETT NATIONAL PLAYWRITING COMPETITION, University of Nevada Las Vegas Theatre Arts, P.O. Box 455036, Las Vegas NV 89154-5036. (702)895-3666. Contact: Corrine A. Bonate. Offered every 2 years for unpublished, unproduced original, innovative, full-length plays in English on any subject. Deadline: mid-December, 1995. Guidelines for SASE. Prize: $3,000 and production by UNLV Theatre Arts. Open to any writer.

SHENANDOAH PLAYWRIGHTS RETREAT, ShenanArts, Inc., Rt. 5, Box 167F, Staunton VA 24401. (703)248-1868. Fax: (703)248-1868. Program Director: Robert Graham Small. Estab. 1976. Offered annually. "Shenandoah exists to provide young and established playwrights with a challenging, stimulating environment to test and develop new work." Deadline: March 1. Award application form available for SASE. "The writers, each on fellowship, work in close and intensive collaboration with dramaturgs, directors and the acting company. What occurs is a simultaneous 'on-the-feet/on-the-page' exploration of each play, culminating in a staged reading and company response."

SHUBERT FENDRICH MEMORIAL PLAYWRITING CONTEST, Pioneer Drama Service, P.O. Box 4267, Englewood CO 80155-4267. (303)779-4035. Fax: (303)779-4315. Contest Director: Steven Fendrich. Annual contest for previously produced, but unpublished plays. Deadline: March 1. Estab. 1990. Prize: publication with $1,000 advance in royalty. "All rights to work are obtained by Pioneer. All submitted work must be produced prior to submission."

‡SIENA COLLEGE PLAYWRIGHTS' COMPETITION, Siena College Theatre Program, Department of Fine Arts, Londonville NY 12211-1462. (518)783-2381. Fax: (518)783-4293. Director of Theater: Mark A. Heckler. Estab. 1985. Contest offered during even numbered years to recognize unpublished and unproduced works of playwrights, professional and amateur. Winning playwright required to participate in 6-week residency on college campus to prepare play for production. Deadline: February 1-June 30. Prize: $2,000 prize plus $1,000 in living expenses for residency. Guidelines for SASE.

SIERRA REPERTORY THEATRE, P.O. Box 3030, Sonora CA 95370-3030. (209)532-3120. Contact: Dennis Jones. Estab. 1981. Full-length plays. Deadline: August 31.

DOROTHY SILVER PLAYWRITING COMPETITION, Jewish Community Center, 3505 Mayfield Rd., Cleveland Heights OH 44118. (216)382-4000, ext. 275. Fax: (216)382-5401. Contact: Elaine Rembrandt. Estab. 1948. All entries must be original works, not previously produced, suitable for a full-length presentation; directly concerned with the Jewish experience. Deadline: December 15. Cash award plus staged reading.

‡SILVERHAWKE ONE ACT PLAY COMPETITION, P.O. Box 1640, Escondido CA 92033. Contact: Ms. Chris Watkins. Offered annually for previously unpublished plays in 4 categories: student writer, teacher, open, plays for children. Deadline: July 1. Notification: December 1. Prize: publication and inclusion in Silverhawke catalog. SASE for return of materials.

‡SILVERHAWKE PLAYWRIGHT'S COMPETITION, P.O. Box 1640, Escondido CA 92023. Contact: Ms. Chris Watkins. Offered annually for previously unpublished plays in 4 categories: student writer, teacher, open, plays for children. Deadline: July 1. Notification: December 1. Prize: publication and inclusion in Silverhawke catalog. SASE for return of materials.

SUSAN SMITH BLACKBURN PRIZE, 3239 Avalon Place, Houston TX 77019. (713)654-4484. Fax: (713)654-8184. Director: Emilie S. Kilgore. Annual awards for women playwrights for full-length plays written in English. Prize: 1st-$5,000 and signed de Kooning print; 2nd-$1,000; other finalists $500 each. Deadline: September 20. Nomination by artistic directors or theater professionals only.

‡SONOMA COUNTY PLAYWRIGHTS FESTIVAL, Actors Theatre Santa Rosa, P.O. Box 5313, Santa Rosa CA 95402. (707)523-4185. Contest Director: Douglas Stout. Offered annually for unproduced work "to provide promising Northern California playwrights theater for their plays, a developmental process in which the playwright attends rehearsals and performances." Deadline: March 30. Festival takes place first or second week in August. Guidelines for SASE. Prize: $200 for prize-winning play with full production, $50 for 2 or more staged readings. Criteria include small casts (8 or less), simple sets, technical requirements. No musicals or children's theater.

SOUTH CAROLINA PLAYWRIGHTS FESTIVAL, Trustus Theatre, P.O. Box 11721, Columbia SC 29211. (803)771-9153. Literary Manager: Jayce T. Tromsness. Estab. 1989. Offered annually for previously unpublished work. "Full-length plays accepted. No musicals, cast limit 8." Accepts plays January 1-March 1. Contact by phone between 1-6 pm. See attached guidelines. "If script is accepted as an entry, after review of application, there is a $5 reader processing fee." Prize: 1st-$500, full production, travel and housing for rehearsals; 2nd-$250 plus staged reading.

SOUTHEASTERN THEATRE CONFERENCE NEW PLAY PROJECT, P.O. Box 2250, 130 McComas Hall, Mississippi State University MS 39762. (601)325-7952. Contact: Jeff Elwell. Annual contest dedicated to the discovery, development and publicizing of worthy new unproduced plays and playwrights. Eligibility limited to members of 10 state SETC Region: AL, FL, GA, KY, MS, NC, SC, TN, VA, WV. Submit: March 15-June 1. Bound full-length or related one-acts under single cover (one submission only). SASE stapled to back cover. Guidelines available upon request. Prize: $1,000, staged reading at SETC Convention, expenses paid trip to convention and preferred consideration for National Playwrights Conference.

SOUTHERN PLAYWRIGHTS COMPETITION, Center for Southern Studies/Jacksonville State University, Pelham Rd., Jacksonville AL 36265-9982. (205)782-5411. Fax: (205)782-5689. Contact: Steven J. Whitton. Estab. 1988. Offered annually. "The Center for Southern Studies seeks to identify and encourage the best of Southern Playwrighting." Deadline: February 15. Guidelines for SASE. Prize: $1,000 and a production of the play. Playwrights must be native to or resident of AL, AR, FL, GA, KY, LA, MS, NC, SC, TN, TX, VA, or WV.

‡SPRING STAGED READING PLAY CONTEST, TADA!, 120 W. 28th St., New York NY 10001. (212)627-1732. Fax: (212)727-3611. Contest Director: Janine Nina Trevens. Offered annually for unpublished work "to introduce the playwriting process to family audiences in a staged reading series featuring the winning entries. One-act plays to be appropriate for children or teenage or family audiences, cast to be mostly children up to age 17." Deadline: January 15. Please send a cover letter and play with SASE for return, no application form necessary. Prize: $200 and a staged reading held in TADA!'s theater with TADA! cast and others hired by TADA! Contest is open. Plays must be appropriate for children or family audiences.

‡STANLEY DRAMA AWARD, Dept. of Humanities, Wagner College, Staten Island NY 10301. (212)390-3256. Estab. 1957. Award for "best original full-length play or musical which has not been professionally produced or received tradebook publication. Presented as a memorial to Mrs. Robert C. Stanley." Write for application. Reports in 6 months. Acquires right to use name of play and of writer in publicity. Prize: $2,000. Deadline: September 1.

MARVIN TAYLOR PLAYWRITING AWARD, Sierra Repertory Theatre, P.O. Box 3030, Sonora CA 95370-3030. (209)532-3120. Producing Director: Dennis Jones. Estab. 1981. Full-length plays. Deadline: August 31.

‡THEATRE IN PROCESS PLAYWRIGHTING AWARD, #4, 220 Marlborough St., Boston MA 02116. (617)267-1053. Artistic director: June Judson. Offered annually for unpublished new and promising works for the state, to develop and produce. TIP is now searching for 5-6 works celebrating the Jewish spirit. Rolling deadline. Guidelines for SASE. Prize: reading or workshop production of work. Please send synopses first; only requested mss will be read.

THEATRE MEMPHIS NEW PLAY COMPETITION, Theatre Memphis, P.O. Box 240117, Memphis TN 38124-0117. (901)682-8323. Estab. 1981. Chairman, New Play Competition: Kim Ford. Award offered every 3 years "to promote new playwrights' works and new works by established playwrights." No musicals or one-acts. Bound scripts only. Deadline: July 1, 1996. Include SASE if scripts are to be returned.
 • This competition runs in a 3-year cycle. Do not submit before January 1, 1996.

UNIVERSITY OF ALABAMA NEW PLAYWRIGHTS PROGRAM, P.O. Box 870239, Tuscaloosa AL 35487-0239. (205)348-9032. Director/Dramaturg: Dr. Paul C. Castagno. Estab. 1982. Full-length plays for mainstage; experimental plays for B stage. Workshops and small musicals can be proposed. Queries responded to quickly. Stipends competitive with, or exceed most contests. Development process includes readings, visitations, and possible complete productions with faculty director and dramaturg. Guidelines for SASE. Up to 6 months assessment time.

‡VERMONT PLAYWRIGHT'S AWARD, The Valley Players, P.O. Box 441, Waitsfield VT 05673. Award Director: Tony Egan. Offered annually for unpublished nonmusical, full-length play suitable for production by a community theater group. Purpose is "to encourage development of playwrights in Vermont, New Hampshire and Maine." Deadline: October 1. SASE. No entry fee. Prize: $1,000. Judged by resident professionals in theater, journalism, publishing or public relations or broadcasting. Must be a resident of VT, NH or ME.

VERY SPECIAL ARTS YOUNG PLAYWRIGHTS PROGRAM, Very Special Arts, Education Office, The John F. Kennedy Center for the Performing Arts, Washington DC 20566. (202)628-2800. Fax: (202)737-0725. Contact: National Programs, Young Playwrights Program. Annual contest for unpublished plays by teens. "Students between the ages of 12 and 18 may write a script that incorporates some aspect of disability." Deadline: mid-April. Write for guidelines. Winning play produced at The John F. Kennedy Center for the Performing Arts Theater Lab. "Very Special Arts retains the rights to make the script available to other organizations for educational purposes." Contestants must be 12-18 years of age.

THEODORE WARD PRIZE FOR PLAYWRITING, Columbia College Theater/Music Center, 72 E. 11th St., Chicago IL 60605-1996. Fax: (312)663-9591. Contact: Chuck Smith. Estab. 1985. "To uncover and identify new unpublished African-American plays that are promising and produceable." Deadline: August 1. All rights for music or biographies must be secured prior to submission. All entrants must be of African-American descent and residing within the US. Only 1 complete script per playwright will be accepted.

L. ARNOLD WEISSBERGER PLAYWRITING COMPETITION, New Dramatists, Inc., 424 W. 44th St., New York NY 10036-5205. (212)757-6960. Fax: (212)265-4738. Contest Director: Paul A. Slee. Estab. 1984. Offered annually for previously unproduced plays. "The L. Arnold Weissberger Award is a cash prize that recognizes a previously unproduced new play by a playwright with any level of experience. The $5,000 prize is awarded annually, and the competition is judged by professional theater critics. The selection criteria was established by L. Arnold Weissberger, a theatrical attorney, who sought to discover a 'well-made play.' " Deadline: May 31. Applications accepted between December 31 of the previous year and May 31, the deadline, for an award announcement the following May. Guidelines for SASE. Prize: $5,000 and a public staged reading of the prize-winning play. "No special criteria or nominating process required. 'The play's the thing.' "
- New Dramatists Inc. is a service organization offering playwrights time, space and tools (at no charge). Write for membership information.

WEST COAST ENSEMBLE FULL-PLAY COMPETITION, CELEBRATION OF ONE-ACTS, West Coast Ensemble, P.O. Box 38728, Los Angeles CA 90038. Artistic Director: Les Hanson. Estab. 1982. Unpublished (in Southern California) plays. No musicals or children's plays for full-play competition. No restrictions on subject matter. Deadline: November 15 for one-act plays; December 31 for full-length plays.

WICHITA STATE UNIVERSITY PLAYWRITING CONTEST, University Theatre, Wichita State University, Wichita KS 67260-0031. (316)689-3185. Contest Director: Professor Bela Kiralyfalvi. Estab. 1974. Two or three short, unpublished, unproduced plays or full-length plays of at least 90 minutes in playing time. No musicals or children's plays. Deadline: February 15. Guidelines for SASE. Award: production of winning play (ACTF) and expenses paid trip for playwright to see final rehearsals and/or performances. Contestants must be graduate or undergraduate students in a US college or university.

‡TENNESSEE WILLIAMS ONE-ACT PLAY CONTEST, Tennessee Williams/New Orleans Literary Festival, University of New Orleans, New Orleans LA 70148. Fax: (504)286-7317. Contest Director: Anne O'Heren Jakob. "A one-act play on an American subject that can be performed in one hour or less." Deadline: December 1. Charges $15 fee, payable to the University of New Orleans. Prize: $1,000. Open to New Orleans-based writers, actors and director. Festival holds the right to produce the play a year later. Play must be previously unproduced.

‡WRITER'S FILM PROJECT, The Chesterfield Film Co., Universal Studios, Building 447, 100 Universal City Plaza, Universal City CA 91608. (818)777-0998. Contest Director: Kat Williams. Offered annually. "The purpose of the Writer's Film Project is to offer fiction, theater and film writers the opportunity to begin a career in screenwriting. Workshop and mentoring lead each participant to create two original feature-length screenplays and initiates contacts for production." Deadline: May. Guidelines for SASE. Prize: 10 writers to receive $20,000 stipend for living expenses, year-long screenwriting workshops, including meetings with development executives from Universal Studio and Amblin Entertainment. Writers are paired with professional screenwriting mentors who offer critique and commentary on each screenplay. At the end of the program year writers are introduced to literary agents. Each screenplay is considered for production or sale by the Chesterfield Film Company.

‡Y.E.S. NEW PLAY FESTIVAL, Northern Kentucky University, 207FA, Department of Theatre, Highland Heights KY 41099-1007. (606)572-6303. Fax: (606)572-5566. Artistic Director: Mike King. Offered every 2 years for unproduced plays. "The purpose of the Y.E.S. festival is to encourage the development of playwrights and to bring previously unproduced works to the stage." Estab. 1981. Deadline: May 1-October 15 for scripts. Full-length plays, adaptations and musicals. Guidelines for SASE. No application fee. Prize: $400 and expense-paid visit to NKU to see their play in production.

YOUNG PLAYWRIGHTS FESTIVAL, Young Playwrights Inc., Suite 906, 321 W. 44th St., New York NY 10036. (212)307-1140. Fax: (212)307-1454. Artistic Director: Sheri M. Goldhirsch. Offered annually. Only stage plays accepted for submission (no musicals, screenplays or adaptations). "Writers age 18 and younger are invited to send scripts for consideration in the annual Young Playwrights Festival. Winning plays will be performed in professional Off-Broadway production." Deadline: October 1. Contest/award rules and entry forms available for SASE. Entrants must be 18 or younger as of the annual deadline.

ANNA ZORNIO MEMORIAL THEATRE FOR YOUTH PLAYWRITING AWARD, University of New Hampshire Theatre In Education Program /TRY, Paul Creative Arts, Durham NH 03824-3538. (603)862-3288. Contact: Peggy Rae Johnson. Estab. 1979. Purpose: To bring quality unpublished plays and musicals (45 minutes-1 hour in length) to elementary to middle school audiences. Deadline: April 15. Production guaranteed, award of $250.

Journalism

AMERICAN SPEECH-LANGUAGE-HEARING ASSOCIATION (ASHA), NATIONAL MEDIA AWARDS, 10801 Rockville Pike, Rockville MD 20852-3279. (301)897-5700. Fax: (301)571-0457. Estab. 1978. Speech-language pathology and audiology (radio, TV, newspaper, magazine). Deadline: June 30.

AMY WRITING AWARDS, The Amy Foundation, P.O. Box 16091, Lansing MI 48901. (517)323-6233. President: James Russell. Estab. 1985. Articles communicating Biblical truth in the secular media, published in the previous calendar year. Deadline: January 31. Prize: $10,000, $5,000, $4,000, $3,000, $2,000 and 10 prizes of $1,000.

HOWARD W. BLAKESLEE AWARDS, American Heart Association, 7272 Greenville Ave., Dallas TX 75231-4596. (214)706-1173. Fax: (214)706-1551. Award Director: Howard L. Lewis. Estab. 1952. Offered annually for work previously published between January 1 and December 31 of preceding calendar year "to recognize outstanding medical/science journalism in the US that has contributed to the public's knowledge and understanding of heart and blood vessel disease." Print or broadcast reports on cardiovascular diseases published during preceding calendar year. Deadline: February 1. Guidelines for SASE "or call (214)706-1173 and ask for an entry form." Prize: Plaque and $1,000 honorarium. Entry must have been published or broadcast in mass media publication/program during preceding calendar year. Advertising/PSA material not accepted."

THE HEYWOOD BROUN AWARD, The Newspaper Guild (AFL-CIO, CLC), 8611 Second Ave., Silver Spring MD 20910-3372. (301)585-2990. Contact: David J. Eisen. Estab. 1941. For work published between January 1 and December 31. Deadline: January 27. Guidelines for SASE available in November. Prize: $2,000 and a Guild citation. "Entries become the property of the award committee unless return is requested." Contest open to news writers, broadcasters, cartoonists, etc., but not to freelancers.

RUSSELL L. CECIL ARTHRITIS MEDICAL JOURNALISM AWARDS, Arthritis Foundation, 1314 Spring St. NW, Atlanta GA 30309-9901. (404)872-7100. Fax: (404)872-0457. Contact: Lisa M. Newbern. Estab. 1956. News stories, articles and radio/TV scripts on the subject of arthritis and the Arthritis Foundation published or broadcast for general circulation during the previous calendar year. Deadline: February 15.

HARRY CHAPIN MEDIA AWARDS, World Hunger Year, 21st Floor, 505 Eighth Ave., New York NY 10018-6582. (212)629-8850. Fax: (212)465-9274. Coordinator: Peter Mann. Estab. 1982. Critical issues of domestic and world hunger, poverty and development (newspaper, periodical, TV, radio, photojournalism, books). Prizes: $1,000-2,500. Deadline: February 15.

‡FOURTH ESTATE AWARD, American Legion National Headquarters, 700 N. Pennsylvania, Indianapolis IN 46206. (317)630-1253. Editor: John Greenwold. Estab. 1919. For excellence in journalism in a published or broadcast piece on an issue of national concern during the previous calendar year. Deadline: January 31 each year.

THE GREAT AMERICAN TENNIS WRITING AWARDS, *Tennis Week*, 124 E. 40th St., New York NY 10016. (212)808-4750. Fax: (212)983-6302. Publisher: Eugene L. Scott. Estab. 1986. Category 1: unpublished ms by an aspiring journalist with no previous national byline. Category 2: unpublished ms by a non-tennis journalist. Category 3: unpublished ms by a tennis journalist. Categories 4-6: published articles and one award to a book. Deadline: December 15.

SIDNEY HILLMAN PRIZE AWARD, Sidney Hillman Foundation, Inc., 15 Union Square, New York NY 10003. (212)242-0700. Executive Director: Jo-Ann Mort. Estab. 1946. Social/economic themes related to ideals of Sidney Hillman (daily or periodical journalism, nonfiction, radio and TV). Deadline: January 15.

THE ROY W. HOWARD AWARDS, Scripps Howard Foundation, P.O. Box 5380, Cincinnati OH 45201-5380. (513)977-3035. Estab. 1972. Public service reporting by a daily newspaper in the US or its territories. Fact sheet available in fall of year.

INTERNATIONAL READING ASSOCIATION PRINT MEDIA AWARD, International Reading Association, P.O. Box 8139, Newark DE 19714-8139. (302)731-1600 ext. 215. Fax: (302)731-1057. Contact: Cindy Kirkpatrick. Estab. 1956. Recognizes outstanding reporting on reading and literacy by professional journalists. Deadline: January 15.

DONALD E. KEYHOE JOURNALISM AWARD, Fund for UFO Research, P.O. Box 277, Mt. Rainier MD 20712. (703)684-6032. Fax: (703)684-6032. Chairman: Richard Hall. Estab. 1979. Annual awards for the best article or story published or broadcast in a newspaper, magazine, TV or radio news outlet during the previous calendar year. Separate awards for print and broadcast media. Also makes unscheduled cash awards for published works on UFO phenomena research or public education.

THE EDWARD J. MEEMAN AWARDS, Scripps Howard Foundation, P.O. Box 5380, Cincinnati OH 45201-5380. (513)977-3035. Estab. 1967. Environmental reporting by a daily newspaper in the US or its territories. Fact sheet available in fall of the year.

MENCKEN AWARDS, Free Press Association, P.O. Box 15548, Columbus OH 43215. FPA Executive Director: Michael Grossberg. Estab. 1981. Honoring defense of human rights and individual liberties, or exposés of governmental abuses of power. Categories: News Story or Investigative Report, Feature Story or Essay/Review, Editorial or Op-Ed Column, Editorial Cartoon, Book, and Defense of First Amendment. Entries *must* have been published or broadcast during previous calendar year. Deadline: April 1 (for work from previous year). Charges $5/entry fee. Late deadline May 1 with extra fee. *Must* send SASE for entry form.

FRANK LUTHER MOTT-KAPPA TAU ALPHA RESEARCH AWARD IN JOURNALISM, University of Missouri, School of Journalism, Columbia MO 65205. (314)882-7685. Executive Director, Central Office: Dr. Keith Sanders. For "best researched book in journalism." Requires 6 copies. No forms required. Deadline: January 15. Award: $1,000.

NATIONAL AWARDS FOR EDUCATION REPORTING, Education Writers Association, 1001 Connecticut Ave. NW, Washington DC 20036. (202)429-9680. Fax: (202)872-4016. Executive Director: Lisa Walker. Estab. 1980. Submissions to be published during the previous year. There are 17 categories; write for more information. Deadline: mid-January. Charges $30 for first entry, $20 for each additional.

‡OLGA "OLLIE" TSCHIRLEY NORDHAUS FEATURE WRITING COMPETITION, *Near West Gazette*, 1660 W. Ogden, Chicago IL 60612. (312)243-4288. Fax: (312)243-4270. Contest Director: Anne M. Nordhaus. Offered annually for work published between April 1 (of previous year) and March 31 (of current year) to "determine the best feature article published in a collegiate newspaper in Illinois." Deadline: April 30. Guidelines for SASE. Prize: $100.

ERNIE PYLE AWARD, Scripps Howard Foundation, P.O. Box 5380, Cincinnati OH 45201-5380. (513)977-3035. Estab. 1953. Human interest reporting by a newspaper man or woman for work published in a daily newspaper in the US or its territories. Fact sheet available in fall of the year.

‡WILLIAM B. RUGGLES JOURNALISM SCHOLARSHIP, National Right to Work Committee, Suite 500, 8001 Braddock Rd., Springfield VA 22160-0999. (703)321-9820. Fax: 7143. Contact: Linda Staukup. Estab. 1974. "To honor the late William B. Ruggles, editor emeritas of the Dallas Morning News, who coined the phrase 'Right to Work.'" Deadline: January 1-March 31. Prize: $2,000 scholarship. "We do reserve the right to reprint the material/excerpt from the essay in publicizing the award. Applicant must be a graduate or undergraduate student majoring in journalism in institutions of higher learning throughout the US."

THE CHARLES M. SCHULZ AWARD, Scripps Howard Foundation, P.O. Box 5380, Cincinnati OH 45201-5380. (513)977-3035. Estab. 1980. For a student cartoonist at a college newspaper or magazine. Fact sheet available in fall of the year.

SCIENCE IN SOCIETY JOURNALISM AWARDS, National Association of Science Writers, Box 294, Greenlawn NY 11740. (516)757-5664. Contact: Diane McGurgan. Newspaper, magazine and broadcast science writing. Deadline: (postmarked) July 1 for work published June 1-May 31 of previous year.

THE EDWARD WILLIS SCRIPPS AWARD, Scripps Howard Foundation, P.O. Box 5380, Cincinnati OH 45201. (513)977-3035. Estab. 1976. Service to the First Amendment by a daily newspaper in the US or its territories. Fact sheet available in fall of the year.

CHARLES E. SCRIPPS AWARDS, Scripps Howard Foundation, P.O. Box 5380, Cincinnati OH 45201-5380. (513)977-3035. Estab. 1986. Combatting illiteracy, by a daily newspaper, television, cable and/or radio station in the US or its territories. Fact sheet available in fall of the year.

SPECIAL LIBRARIES ASSOCIATION MEDIA AWARD, Special Libraries Association, 1700 18th St., NW, Washington DC 20009-2508. (202)234-4700. Fax: (202)265-9317. Manager, Communications: Lauren Emmob. Estab. 1987. SLA's Media Award is presented to a writer who develops an outstanding feature story on the special libraries profession published previous calendar year. The feature must appear in a general-circulation publication, radio or television production. Library journal magazine articles are not eligible. Deadline: December 10.

I.F. STONE AWARD FOR STUDENT JOURNALISM, The Nation Institute, 72 Fifth Ave., New York NY 10011. (212)242-8400. Fax: (212)463-9712. Director: Peter Meyer. Annual award "to recognize excellence in student journalism." Open to undergraduate students in US colleges. Award: $1,000, plus publication. Deadline: June 30.

THE WALKER STONE AWARD, Scripps Howard Foundation, P.O. Box 5380, Cincinnati OH 45201-5380. (513)977-3035. Estab. 1973. Editorial writing by a newspaper man or woman, for work published in a daily newspaper in the US or its territories. Fact sheet available in fall of the year.

TRAVEL JOURNALISM AWARDS, Hawaii Visitors Bureau, Suite 801, 2270 Kalakaua Ave., Honolulu HI 96815. (808)924-0213. Fax: (808)924-2120. Contact: Gail Ann Chew. Annual award for travel journalism. Deadline: March.

Writing for Children and Young Adults

‡**ALBERTA WRITING FOR YOUTH COMPETITION**, Alberta Foundation for the Arts, 3rd Floor, Beaver House, 10158 103rd St., Edmonton, Alberta T5J 0X6 Canada. Contest is offered every two years. Submissions required to be unpublished. To encourage, recognize and develop the diversity of Alberta writers who write fiction for young people. The competition is open to *all* Alberta writers, aged 18 and over. Deadline: December 1, even years. First prize is $4,500 (a $2,000 prize from the Alberta Foundation for the Arts, a $1,000 advance against royalties from the publisher, a $1,500 12-month option agreement for motion picture/television rights from ITV and a publishing contract from Tree Frog Press). Manuscripts must be in English.

AMERICAN ASSOCIATION OF UNIVERSITY WOMEN AWARD, NORTH CAROLINA DIVISION, North Carolina Literary and Historical Association, 109 E. Jones St., Raleigh NC 27601-2807. (919)733-7305. Awards Coordinator: Freda Brittain. Previously published juvenile literature by a North Carolina resident. Deadline: July 15.

‡**ARROZ CON LECHE**, Hispanic Books Distributors, Inc., 1665 W. Grant Rd. Tucson AZ 85745. Contact: Dr. Arnulfo D. Trejo. Offered annually for unpublished works of fiction for ages k-4 to encourage more Hispanic authors to write for children. Deadline: February 28. Guidelines for SASE. Prize: $1,000. Open to adult authors of Latino heritage, born, raised or residing permanently in this country, including Puerto Rico.

IRMA S. AND JAMES H. BLACK AWARD, Bank Street College of Education, 610 W. 112th St., New York NY 10025. (212)875-4452. Fax: (212)875-4759. Award Director: Linda Greengrass. Annual award. Estab. 1972. "The award is given each spring for a book for young children, published in the previous year, for excellence of both text and illustrations." Entries must have been published during the previous calendar year. Deadline for entries: January after book is published.

BOSTON GLOBE-HORN BOOK AWARD, *The Boston Globe*, 135 Morissey Blvd, P.O. Box 2378, Boston MA 02107. Offered annually for previously published work in children's literature. One award for each category: original fiction or poetry, picture book, and nonfiction. Publisher submits entry. Prize: $500 in each category.

MARGUERITE DE ANGELI PRIZE, Bantam Doubleday Dell Books for Young Readers, 1540 Broadway, New York NY 10036. (212)354-6500. Fax: (212)782-9698. Offered annually for unpublished work. "Submissions should consist of a fiction manuscript suitable for readers 7-10 years of age that concerns the diversity of the American experience, either contemporary or historical." Write for details. Guidelines for SASE. Prize includes a book contract with a cash advance. Judged by editors at Bantam Doubleday Dell.

DELACORTE PRESS PRIZE FOR A FIRST YOUNG ADULT NOVEL, Delacorte Press, 1540 Broadway, New York NY 10036. (212)354-6500. Estab. 1983. Previously unpublished young adult fiction. Submissions: Labor Day-December 30 only. Guidelines for SASE. Prize: $1,500 cash, publicaton and $6,000 advance against royalties. Judged by editors of Delacorte.

DON FREEMAN MEMORIAL GRANT-IN-AID, Society of Children's Book Writers and Illustrators (SCBWI), #106, 22736 Vandowen St., West Hills CA 91307. To enable picture-book artists to further their understanding, training and/or work. Members only. Deadline: February 15. Grants: $1,000 and $500 runner-up.

GOLDEN KITE AWARDS, Society of Children's Book Writers and Illustrators (SCBWI), Suite 106, 22736 Vanowen St., West Hills CA 91307. (818)888-8760. Coordinator: Sue Alexander. Estab. 1973. Calendar year published children's fiction, nonfiction and picture illustration books by a SCBWI member. Deadline: December 15.

HIGHLIGHTS FOR CHILDREN FICTION CONTEST, *Highlights for Children*, 803 Church St., Honesdale PA 18431-1824. Manuscript Coordinator: Beth Troop Estab. 1946. Stories for children ages 2-12; category varies each year. Write for guidelines. Stories should be limited to 900 words for older readers, 600 words for younger readers. No crime or violence, please. Specify that ms is a contest entry. All entries must be postmarked January 1-February 28.

INTERNATIONAL READING ASSOCIATION CHILDREN'S BOOK AWARD, International Reading Association, P.O. Box 8139, 800 Barksdale Rd., Newark DE 19714-8139. (302)731-1600 ext. 221. Given for a first or second book by an author who shows unusual promise in the children's book field. Three categories:

younger readers, ages 4-10; older readers, ages 10-16 and over, and informational book. Deadline: December 1.

MILKWEED PRIZE FOR CHILDREN'S LITERATURE, Milkweed Editions, Suite 400, First Ave. N., Minneapolis MN 55401. (612)332-3192. Fax: (612)332-6248. Annual prize for unpublished works. Estab. 1993. "Milkweed is looking for a novel or biography intended for readers aged 8-14. Manuscripts should be of high literary quality and must be double-spaced, 110-350 pages in length." Deadline: March 15. Charges $5 fee. *Must* request contest guidelines (send SASE). Editions and cash advance of $3,000 against royalties. "Entry must be written in English. Prize: Publication by Milkweed. Contest open to writers who have previously published a book of fiction or nonfiction for children or adults, or a minimum of three short stories or articles in magazines for children or adults." Catalog for 2 first-class stamps.

SCOTT O'DELL AWARD FOR HISTORICAL FICTION, 1418 E. 57th St., Chicago IL 60637. (312)752-7880. Director: Zena Sutherland. Estab. 1981. Historical fiction book for children set in the Americas. Entries must have been published during previous year. Deadline: December 31.
  • Paul Fleischman was the 1994 winner of this award for *Bull Run*, a fictional account of the Civil War battle, published by HarperCollins/Geringer.

PEN/NORMA KLEIN AWARD, PEN American Center, 568 Broadway, New York NY 10012. (212)334-1660. Fax: (212)334-2181. Contact: John Morrone. Awarded biennially to "recognize an emerging voice of literary merit among American writers of children's fiction." *Candidates may not nominate themselves.* Deadline for nominations: January 31, 1995. Guidelines for #10 SASE. Award: $3,000.

‡SILVER BAY AWARDS FOR CHILDREN'S LITERATURE, The Writer's Voice of the Silver Bay Association, Silver Bay NY 12874. (518)543-8833. Fax: (518)543-6733. Contact: Sharon Ofner. Offered annually for best unpublished children's ms set in the Adirondack Mountains, illustrated or non-illustrated. Deadline: February 1. Charges $20 fee. Prize: $500.

TEXAS BLUEBONNET AWARD, Texas Library Association's Texas Association of School Librarians and Children's Round Table, Suite 401, 3355 Bee Cave Rd., Austin TX 78746. (512)328-1518. Contact: Patricia Smith. Published books for children recommended by librarians, teachers and students.

WORK-IN-PROGRESS GRANT, Society of Children's Book Writers and Illustrators (SCBWI) and Judy Blume, #106, 22736 Vanowen St., West Hills CA 91307. Write *SCBWI* at preceding address. Two grants — one designated specifically for a contemporary novel for young people — to assist SCBWI members in the completion of a specific project. Deadline: June 1.

Translation

‡AWARD FOR GERMAN LITERARY TRANSLATION, (formerly Award for Literary Translation), American Translators Association, % Professor Breon Mitchell, Honors Division, 324 N. Jordan, Indiana University, Bloomington IN 47405. (812)855-9491. Contact: Chair, Honors & Awards. Previously published book translated from German to English. In even years, Lewis Galentière Prize awarded for translations other than German to English. Deadline: April 15.

PIERRE-FRANÇOIS CAILLÉ MEMORIAL MEDAL, Fédération Internationale des Traducteurs (FIT), Dr. H. Maierstrasse 9, Vienna A 1180 Austria. 43-1-443607. Fax: 43-1-443756. Contact: Council of FIT. "Medal is given every three years to individuals who have earned outstanding merit in promoting the standing and reputation of the translation profession on an international level. Deadline is two months before congress." Recipients receive medal and diploma.

KAREL ČAPEK TRANSLATION REWARD, Fédération International des Traducteurs (FIT), Dr. H. Maierstrasse 9, Vienna A 1180 Austria. 43-7-443607. Fax: 43-7-443756. Contact: FIT Council. "The purpose of this contest is to promote the literary translation of works written in languages of limited diffusion. Contest runs every three years. Deadline is six months prior to the opening of FIT's triannual congress, last held in 1993." Guidelines for SASE. Prize: medal and diploma. The contest is judged by an international jury of 5 members, appointed by the FIT Committee for LLD Translation and approved by the Executive Committee of FIT. Translators must be nominated by a Member Society of FIT.

LEWIS GALANTIÈRE PRIZE FOR LITERARY TRANSLATION, American Translators Association, % Professor Breon Mitchell, Honors Division, 324 N. Jordan, Indiana University, Bloomington IN 47405. (812)855-9491. Award offered in even years recognizing the "outstanding translation of a previously published work from languages other than German published in the United States." Deadline: April 15.

JOHN GLASSCO TRANSLATION PRIZE, Literary Translators' Association of Canada, Association des traducteurs et traductrices du Canada, 3492, rue Lavel, Montreal, Quebec H2X 3C8 Canada. Estab. 1981. Annual award for a translator's *first* book-length literary translation into French or English, published in Canada during the previous calendar year. The translator must be a Canadian citizen or landed immigrant. Eligible genres include fiction, creative nonfiction, poetry, published plays, children's books. Deadline: January 15. Write for application form. Award: $500.

‡NATIONAL THEATER TRANSLATION FUND COMMISSIONING GRANTS, National Theater Translation Fund, % LMDA, Box 355 CUNY/CASTA, 33 W. 42nd St., New York NY 10036. (212)642-2657. Fax: (212)642-2642. Contact: Royston Coppenger. Offered annually to "encourage and support the creation of new, stageworthy translations of foreign plays into American English." Deadline: October 15. Guidelines for SASE. Prize: Cash awards of $2,000-5,000; some additional monies may be made available for staged readings of funded translations. All rights remain with the translator, in accordance with US Copyright Law. "Each applicant must submit a *previously* translated work along with the proposed translation; language skills must be verifiable through assessment of the submitted application materials."

PEN/BOOK-OF-THE-MONTH CLUB TRANSLATION PRIZE, PEN American Center, 568 Broadway, New York NY 10012. Contact: John Morrone. One award of $3,000 to a literary book-length translation into English published in 1993. (No technical, scientific or reference.) Deadline: December 31.
 • The 1993 award went to Thomas Hoisington for his English-language translation of *The Adventures of Mr. Nicholas Wisdom*, by Ignacy Krasicki, which was acquired by the Book of the Month Club.

PEN/RALPH MANHEIM MEDAL FOR TRANSLATION, PEN American Center, (formerly Pen Medal For Translation), 568 Broadway, New York NY 10012. (212)334-1660. Fax: (212)334-2181. Contact: John Morrone. Translators nominated by the PEN Translation Committee. Given every 3 years. Next award: 1997.
 • The 1993 award went to Ann Goldstein, translator of an English-language version of *Journey to the Land of Flies* by Aldo Buzzi.

RENATO POGGIOLI TRANSLATION AWARD, PEN American Center, 568 Broadway, New York NY 10012. (212)334-1660. Fax: (212)334-2181. Contact: John Morrone. "Given to encourage a beginning and promising translator who is working on a first book-length translation from Italian into English." Deadline: January 15. Prize: $3,000.

‡STUDENT TRANSLATION PRIZE, American Translators Association, % Prof. Breon Mitchell, Honors Division, 324 N. Jordan, Indiana University, Bloomington IN 47405 (812)855-9491. Support is granted for a promising project to an unpublished student enrolled in a translation program at a US college or university. Deadline: April 15. Must be sponsored by a faculty member.

TRANSLATION COMMISSIONS, National Theater Translation Fund, Box 355 Casta, CUNY Grad Ctr., 33 W. 42nd St., New York NY 10036. (212)642-2657. Fax: (212)642-2642. Contact: Executive Director. Offered annually. "The National Theater Translation Fund encourages the translation of foreign plays into stageworthy American English." Deadline: October 15. Call or write for guidelines. Prize: $2,000-5,000. Judged by a peer panel. Requires a statement of the rights to the work proposed for translation that states if work is in public domain; if rights have been obtained from author or author's representatives, or if translator is in process of obtaining rights. "Competition is open to translators who have completed a previous translation of a full-length work."

Multiple Writing Areas

AKRON MANUSCRIPT CLUB WRITER'S CONTEST, Akron Manuscript Club & Akron University, P.O. Box 1011, Cuyahoga Falls OH 44223. (216)923-2094. Contact: M.M. Lopiccolo. Estab. 1929. "Annual contest for previously unpublished stories or poems. The purpose of the contest is to provide critique, encouragement and some financial help to authors in six categories." Deadline is always some time in April. Guidelines for #10 SASE. "Entry fee varies according to whether applicant is mail-in or conference attendant." Prizes: 1st-$100; 2nd-$50; 3rd-$25. "May vary according to funding."

AMELIA STUDENT AWARD, *Amelia Magazine*, 329 E St., Bakersfield CA 93304. (805)323-4064. Editor: Frederick A. Raborg, Jr. Previously unpublished poems, essays and short stories by high school students, 1 entry per student; each entry should be signed by parent, guardian *or* teacher to verify originality. Deadline: May 15.

‡ANNUAL FICTION AND POETRY CONTEST, Rambunctious Press, 1221 W. Pratt, Chicago IL 60626-4329. Contest Director: Mary Dellutri. Estab. 1982. Unpublished short stories and poems. Deadline varies. Charges $3/story, $2/poem.

ARIZONA AUTHORS' ASSOCIATION ANNUAL NATIONAL LITERARY CONTEST, Arizona Authors' Association, Suite 117WM, 3509 E. Shea Blvd., Phoenix AZ 85028-3339. (602)942-4240. Contact: Gerry Benninger. Previously unpublished poetry, short stories, essays. Deadline: July 29. Charges $5 for poetry; $7 for short stories and essays.

AWP ANNUAL AWARD SERIES, Associated Writing Programs, Old Dominion University, Norfolk VA 23529-0079. (804)683-3839. Fax: (804)683-5901. Contact: Beth Jarock. Estab. 1967. Annual award series for book length mss in poetry, short fiction, nonfiction and novel. Deadline: February 28. Charges $10/ms for AWP members; $15/ms for nonmembers.

‡**EMILY CLARK BALCH AWARD**, *Virginia Quarterly Review*, 1 West Range, Charlottesville VA 22903. (804)924-3124. Fax:(804)924-1397. Editor: Staige D. Blackford. Best short story/poetry accepted and published by the *Virginia Quarterly Review* during a calendar year. No deadline.

BEST OF HOUSEWIFE-WRITER'S FORUM: THE CONTESTED WILLS TO WRITE, *Housewife-Writer's Forum*, P.O. Box 780, Lyman WY 82937-0780. (307)786-4513. Contest Director: Diane Wolverton. Estab. 1988. Unpublished prose and poetry categories. Deadline: June 1. Charges $4 for prose; $2 for poetry. Also sponsors Rejection Revenge contest for most rejection slips collected in contest year. No entry fee. Contest runs June 1-May 31.

BLACK WARRIOR REVIEW LITERARY AWARDS, *Black Warrior Review*, P.O. Box 2936, Tuscaloosa AL 35486-2936. (205)348-4518. Estab. 1974. Submit work for possible publication to the appropriate genre editor. Awarded annually "to award $500 each to a poet and fiction writer for outstanding work published in the *BWR*. All poetry and fiction appearing in the *BWR* is considered for that volume's award; we treat submissions for the contest as submissions for publication in the *BWR*." Guidelines for SASE. Winners are announced in the Fall/Winter issue.

BYLINE MAGAZINE CONTESTS, P.O. Box 130596, Edmond OK 73013. (405)348-5591. Publisher: Marcia Preston. Estab. 1981. Unpublished short stories, poems and other categories. Several categories offered each month which are open to anyone. Deadline on annual award, which is for subscribers only, December 1. Send #10 SASE for information. Charges $5 for short story; $3 for poems on annual award. Similar small fees for monthly contests.

CALIFORNIA WRITERS' CLUB CONFERENCE CONTEST, 2214 Derby St., Berkeley CA 94705. (510)841-1217. Unpublished adult fiction (short stories), adult fiction (novels), adult nonfiction, juvenile fiction, poetry and scripts. "Our conference is biennial, next being in 1995." Deadline: varies in spring. Charges fee.

THE CHELSEA AWARDS FOR POETRY AND SHORT FICTION, % Richard Foerster, Associate Editor, P.O. Box 1040, York Beach ME 03910-5880. Estab. 1958. Previously unpublished submissions. "Two prizes awarded for the best work of short fiction and for the best group of 4-6 poems selected by the editors in anonymous competitions." Deadline: June 15 for fiction; December 15 for poetry. Guidelines for SASE. Charges $10 fee (includes free subscription to *Chelsea*). Checks made payable to Chelsea Associates, Inc. Prize: $500, winning entries published in *Chelsea*. Include SASE for notification of competition results. Manuscripts will not be returned. *Note:* General submissions and other business should be addressed to the editor at *Chelsea*, P.O. Box 5880, Grand Central Station, New York, NY 10163.

‡**CHICAGO SUN-TIMES/FRIENDS OF LITERATURE AWARDS**, *Chicago Sun-Times*, 401 N. Wabash Ave., Chicago IL 60611. (312)321-2158. Fax: (312)321-3679. Book Editor, *Chicago Sun-Times*: Henry Kisor. Offered annually for works published between January 1-December 31. Awards cash prizes for the best fiction, nonfiction, poetry and first book by a Chicagoan or about Chicago. Deadline: December 31. SASE. Prize: $2,000 each. A panel of 3 judges selected by Henry Kisor.

CHICANO/LATINO LITERARY CONTEST, Dept. of Spanish and Portuguese, University of California-Irvine, Irvine CA 92717. (714)856-8429. Contact: Juan Bruce-Novoa or Lucy Reguera. Estab. 1974. "To promote the dissemination of unpublished Chicano/Latino literature, and to encourage its development. The call for entries will be genre specific, rotating through four categories: drama (1994), novel (1995), short story (1996) and poetry (1997)." Deadline: April 30. "Interested parties may write for entry procedures." The contest is open to all citizens or permanent residents of the US.

‡**COLORADO VISIONS (COVISIONS) PROJECT GRANTS**, Colorado Council on the Arts, 750 Pennsylvania St., Denver CO 80203-3699. (303)894-2619. Director: Daniel Salazar. Annual grants to support innovative projects of high artistic merit in all disciplines, including literature. Colorado residents only. Deadline: June 15.

‡**COLORADO VISIONS (COVISIONS) RECOGNITION AWARDS IN LITERATURE**, Colorado Council on the Arts, 750 Pennsylvania St., Denver CO 80203-3699. (303)894-2619. Director: Daniel Salazar. Annual award to "acknowledge outstanding accomplishment among individual arts as well as encourage public accessibility to their work." Colorado residents only. Deadline: December 15.

‡**DEEP SOUTH WRITERS CONTEST**, Deep South Writers Conference, P.O. Box 44691, University of Southwestern Louisiana, Lafayette LA 70504-4691. (318)231-6908. Contact: Contest Clerk. Estab. 1960. Deadline: July 15. Guidelines for SASE. Charges $15 entry fee for novels and full-length plays; $10 for other submissions. No mss returned.

EATON LITERARY ASSOCIATES LITERARY AWARDS PROGRAM, P.O. Box 49795, Sarasota FL 34230-6795. (813)366-6589. Vice President: Richard Lawrence. Estab. 1984. Previously unpublished short stories and book-length mss. Deadline: March 31 (short story); August 31 (book length). Prizes: $500 short story; $2,500 book length.
  • This program is sponsored by a literary agency.

‡**EXCALIBUR BOOK AWARD**, Excalibur Publishing, Suite 790, 434 Avenue of the Americas, New York NY 10011. Award offered for unpublished full-length fiction and nonfiction. Guidelines for SASE. Charges $25 fee. Prize: first prize publishing contract with Excalibur Publishing; second and third cash prizes, honorable mention certificates.

EYSTER PRIZE, *New Delta Review*, % Department of English, Louisiana State University, Baton Rouge LA 70803-5001. (504)388-4079. Editors: Catherine Williamson, Randi Gray, Nicola Mason. Estab. 1983. Semiannual award for best works of poetry and fiction in each issue. Deadlines: March 1 (spring/summer issue); September 1 (fall/winter issue).

VIRGINIA FAULKNER AWARD FOR EXCELLENCE IN WRITING, *Prairie Schooner*, 201 Andrews, University of Nebraska, Lincoln NE 68588-0334. (402)472-3191. Editor: Hilda Raz. Estab. 1988. All genres eligible for consideration. The winning piece must have been published in *Prairie Schooner* during that calendar year. Prize: $1,000.

FEMINIST WRITERS' CONTEST, Dept WM, #258, 648 N. Northwest Hwy., Park Ridge IL 60068. Contact: Pamela Sims for rules; SASE required. Estab. 1990. Categories: Fiction and nonfiction (5,000 or fewer words). Work should reflect feminist perspectives (should not endorse or promote sexism, racism, ageism, anti-lesbianism, etc.) Deadline: August 31. Charge $10 fee. Cash awards.

FLORIDA STATE WRITING COMPETITION, Florida Freelance Writers Association, Contest Administrator, Maple Ridge Rd., North Sandwich NH 03259. Annual contest. Deadline: March 15. Subject areas include: adult articles, adult short stories, writing for children, poetry. Guidelines for #10 SASE. Entry fees vary, depending on subject area. *Note: Do not send entries to FFWA office.*

‡**FOSTER CITY ANNUAL WRITERS CONTEST**, Foster City Committee for the Arts, 650 Shell Blvd., Foster City CA 94404. Unpublished fiction, poetry, humor and childrens' stories. $1500 in prizes. Deadline: April 1-August 31. Guidelines for SASE.

MILES FRANKLIN LITERARY AWARD, Arts Management Pty. Ltd., 180 Goulburn St., Darlinghurst, NSW 2011 Australia. Annual award for work published for the first time the year preceding award. "The award is for a novel or play which presents Australian life in any of its phases. Biographies, collections of short stories or children's books are *not* eligible for the award." Deadline: January 31. Guidelines for #10 SAE with 1 IRC. Prize: $25,000 (Australian). "This award is open to writers of any nationality. However, the novel or play must be about Australian life."

GREAT LAKES COLLEGES ASSOCIATION NEW WRITERS AWARDS, English Department, Wabash College, Crawfordsville IN 47933. Director: Marc Hudson. (317)364-4232. Estab. 1970. Entries must have appeared between February and subsequent January of year submitted. Offered annually to the best *first* book of poetry and fiction submitted by publishers to encourage writers of previously published poetry and fiction whose publishers consider their work especially meritorious and to bring those writers together with the students and faculty of the twelve sponsoring colleges of the GLCA to their mutual benefit." Deadline: February 28/29. "Publishers must nominate the works to be considered and may do so by sending *four copies* of the nominated work together with a statement assuring the author will accept the prize under the terms stipulated in the official contest announcement."

THE GREENSBORO REVIEW LITERARY AWARD IN FICTION AND POETRY, *The Greensboro Review*, English Department, University of North Carolina-Greensboro, Greensboro NC 27412-5001. (910)334-5459. Fax: (910)334-3281. Contact: Fiction or Poetry Editor. Estab. 1984. Annual award for fiction and poetry recognizing the best work published in the winter issue of *The Greensboro Review*. Deadline: September 15. Sample copy for $4.

HACKNEY LITERARY AWARDS, *Writing Today*, Box A-3/Birmingham-Southern College, Birmingham AL 35254. (205)226-4921. Contact: Special Events Office. Estab. 1969. Annual award for unpublished novel, short story and poetry. Deadline: September 30 for novels, December 31 for short stories and poetry. Guidelines for SASE.

KANSAS QUARTERLY/KANSAS ARTS COMMISSION AWARDS, SEATON AWARDS, Department of English, Kansas State University, Manhattan KS 66506. (913)532-6716. Editor: Ben Nyberg, et al. Estab. 1968. *KQ/KAC* awards for poetry and fiction published in *KQ*; Seaton awards for Kansas writers whose poetry, fiction and prose appear in *KQ*.

JACK KEROUAC LITERARY PRIZE, Lowell Historic Preservation Commission, Suite 310, 222 Merrimack St., Lowell MA 01852. (508)458-7653. Annual award for unpublished nonfiction, fiction and poetry. Deadline: August 1. Guidelines for SASE. Prize: $500 honorarium and presentation of ms at public meeting.

ROSE LEFCOWITZ PRIZES, *Poet Lore*, The Writer's Center, 4508 Walsh St., Bethesda MD 20815-2004. (301)654-8664. Editor: Philip Jason. "Annual award for previously unpublished poetry or criticism. The prizes go to the single best poem and piece of critical prose to appear in a given volume of *Poet Lore*. Guidelines for #10 SASE. Prizes include $150 for each winner (1 winner for poetry, 1 for prose). Rights revert to the author after first publication in *Poet Lore*. "Only poems and prose that appear in a volume of *Poet Lore* are considered. A poem or piece of critical prose must first appear in the magazine before it will be considered for the prize."

HUGH J. LUKE AWARD, *Prairie Schooner*, 201 Andrews, University of Nebraska, Lincoln NE 68588-0334. (402)472-3191. Fax: (402)472-4636. Editor: Hilda Raz. Annual award for work published in *Prairie Schooner*. Winner announced in the spring issue of the following year. Prize: $250.

MASTERS LITERARY AWARDS, Center Press, P.O. Box 16452, Encino CA 91416-6452. (818)377-4301. Contact: Jana Cain. Offered annually and quarterly for work previously published within 2 years (preferred) and unpublished work (accepted). Fiction: 15 page, maximum; Poetry: 5 pages or 150 lines, maximum; Nonfiction: 10 page, maximum. Deadlines: March 15, June 15th, August 15th, December 15. Guidelines for SASE. Charges $10 reading/administration fee. Prize: one quarterly prize of $500 *and* one annual of $1,500. Judged by "three anonymous experts chosen yearly from literary and publishing field." Center Press retains "one time publishing" rights to selected winners. Open to all writers.

THE MENTOR AWARD, *Mentor Newsletter*, P.O. Box 4382, Overland Park KS 66204-0382. Award Director: Maureen Waters. Estab. 1989. Award offered annually to promote and encourage mentoring through feature articles, essays, book/movie reviews, interviews or short stories." Submissions must be mentoring related. Guidelines for #10 SASE. Charges $4 fee. Prize: $100. Writer must be 16 years old.

MIDLAND AUTHORS AWARD, Society of Midland Authors, % Ford-Choyke, 29 E. Division St., Chicago IL 60610. (312)337-1482. Estab. 1915. Annual awards for published or produced drama, fiction, nonfiction, poetry, biography, children's fiction and children's nonfiction. Authors must reside in the states of Illinois, Indiana, Iowa, Kansas, Michigan, Minnesota, Missouri, Nebraska, North Dakota, South Dakota, Wisconsin or Ohio. Guidelines for SASE. Deadline: January 15.

THE NEBRASKA REVIEW AWARDS IN FICTION AND POETRY, *The Nebraska Review*, ASH 215, University of Nebraska-Omaha, Omaha NE 68182-0324. (402)554-2771. Contact: Susan Aizenberg (poetry) and James Reed (fiction). Estab. 1973. Previously unpublished fiction and a poem or group of poems. Deadline: November 30.

NEUSTADT INTERNATIONAL PRIZE FOR LITERATURE, 110 Monnet Hall, Norman OK 73019. (405)325-4531. Estab. 1969. Previously published fiction, poetry and drama. Nominations are made only by members of the jury, which changes every 2 years.

NEW LETTERS LITERARY AWARDS, University of Missouri-Kansas City, Kansas City MO 64110-2499. Fax: (816)235-2611. Awards Coordinator: Glenda McCrary. Estab. 1986. Unpublished fiction, poetry and essays. Deadline: May 15. Finalists are notified the middle of August; winners announced the third week in September. Charges $10/entry fee. Guidelines for SASE.

NIMROD, ARTS AND HUMANITIES COUNCIL OF TULSA PRIZES, 2210 S. Main, Tulsa OK 74114. (918)584-3333. Editor: Francine Ringold. Unpublished fiction (Katherine Anne Porter prize) and poetry (Pablo Neruda Prize). Deadline: April 18. Fee $10, includes an issue of *Nimrod*. (Writers entering both fiction and poetry contest need only pay once.) Guidelines for #10 SASE. Sample copies $5 for an older issue, $7 for a recent issue.

PRAIRIE SCHOONER BERNICE SLOTE AWARD, *Prairie Schooner*, 201 Andrews, University of Nebraska, Lincoln NE 68588-0334. (402)472-3191. Fax: (402)472-4636. Editor: Hilda Raz. Estab. 1984. Annual award for the best work by a beginning writer published in *Prairie Schooner*. Winner announced in the spring issue of the following year. Prize: $500.

PRAIRIE SCHOONER READERS' CHOICE AWARDS, *Prairie Schooner*, 201 Andrews, University of Nebraska, Lincoln NE 68588-0334. (402)472-3191. Fax: (402)472-4636. Editor: Hilda Raz. Annual awards for work published in *Prairie Schooner*. Winners announced in the spring issue of the following year. Prize: $250 each. Several Readers' Choice Awards are given each year.

‡**THE PRESIDIO LA BAHIA AWARD**, Sons of the Republic of Texas, #222, 5942 Abrams Rd., Dallas TX 75231. Offered annually "to promote suitable preservation of relics, appropriate dissemination of data, and research into our Texas heritage, with particular attention to the Spanish Colonial period." Deadline: June 1-September 30. Guidelines for SASE. Prize: $2,000 total; 1st prize a minimum of $1,200, 2nd and 3rd prizes at the discretion of the judges.

QUINCY WRITER'S GUILD ANNUAL CREATIVE WRITING CONTEST, Quincy Writer's Guild, c/o Natalie Miller Rotunda, P.O. Box 112, Quincy IL 62306-0112. (217)223-3117. Categories include: poetry, short story, fiction. Opens: January 1. Deadline: April 15. Entry fees: $2 per poem; $3 for Clara; $4 for short stories and articles. "No identification should appear on manuscripts, but should be on a separate 3×5 card attached to the entry with name, address, phone number, word count, and title of work." Previously unpublished work. Cash prizes. Guidelines for SASE.

RHYME TIME CREATIVE WRITING COMPETITION, *Rhyme Time*, P.O. Box 2907, Decatur IL 62524. Award Director: Linda Hutton. Estab. 1981. Annual no-fee contest. Submit 1 typed poem, any style, any length. One winner will receive $25; one runner-up will receive a year's subscription to *Rhyme Time*. No poems will be published. Include SASE and submit before November 1.

‡**SUMMERFIELD G. ROBERTS AWARD**, Sons of the Republic of Texas, #222, 5942 Abrams Rd., Dallas TX 75231. Offered annually for previously published submissions during the calendar year "to encourage literary effort and research about historical events and personalities during the days of the Republic of Texas, 1836-1846, and to stimulate interest in the period." Deadline: January 15. Guidelines for SASE. Prize: $2,500. Judges are 3 previous winners of the award.

SOUTHWEST REVIEW AWARDS, Southern Methodist University, 307 Fondren Library West, P.O. Box 0374, Dallas TX 75275-0374. (214)768-1036. Contact: Rose Torres. Annual awards for fiction, nonfiction and poetry published in the magazine. "The $1,000 John H. McGinnis Memorial Award is given each year for fiction and nonfiction that has been published in the *Southwest Review* in the previous year. Stories or articles are not submitted directly for the award, but simply for publication in the magazine. The Elizabeth Matchett Stover Award, an annual prize of $150, is awarded to the author of the best poem or group of poems published in the magazine during the preceding year."

SUCARNOCHEE REVIEW POETRY/FICTION AWARD, *The Sucarnochee Review*, Station 22, Livingston University, Livingston AL 35470. (205)652-9661. Award Director: Joe Taylor. Annual contest for previously unpublished work. No deadlines. "We roll over entries for subsequent issues. Send work to magazine; all submissions are automatically considered for competition. Multiple submissions OK." Prize consists of publication, 3 copies of magazine and $50.

‡**FRANK WATERS SOUTHWEST WRITERS AWARD**, Martin Foundation/Frank Waters Foundation, P.O. Box 1357, Ranchos De Taos NM 87557. (505)758-9869. Award Directors: Barbara Waters, Mag Dimond. Award offered annually for unpublished works of fiction and nonfiction to give recognition and monetary grants to 3 western writers of fiction and nonfiction, from 6 western states. Top prize winner will have piece published. Theme of writings to be "The Living Land." Word limit: 10,000. Deadline: May 31. Charges $10 fee. Prize: 1st-$5,000; 2nd-$3,000; 3rd-$1,000. Judges are 3 panels of writers, editors, publishers, etc. including: Rudolfo Anaya, John Nichols, Frank Waters. Open to writers from the 6 western states of Colorado, New Mexico, Utah, Arizona, Nevada and Texas.

WESTERN MAGAZINE AWARDS, Western Magazine Awards Foundation, 3898 Hillcrest Ave., Vancouver, British Columbia V7R 4B6 Canada. (604)984-7525. Fax: (604)985-6262. Contact: Tina Baird. "Annual awards for previously published magazine work. Entries must have appeared in print between January 1 and December 31 of previous calendar year. Entry categories include business, culture and science, technology and medicine, entertainment, fiction, political issues, and much more. Write or phone for rules and entry forms.

Deadline: February 1. Entry fee: $20 for work in magazines with circulation under 20,000; $25 for work in magazines with circulation over 20,000. $500 award. Applicant must be a Canadian citizen, landed immigrant, or a fulltime resident of Canada. The work must have been published in a magazine whose main editorial office is in Western Canada, the NW Territories and Yukon.

WRITERS AT WORK FELLOWSHIP COMPETITION, Writers at Work, P.O. Box 1146, Centerville UT 84014-5146. (801)292-9285. Contact: Barry Scholl. Offered annually for unpublished short stories, novel excerpts and poetry. Deadline: February 28. Guidelines for SASE. "Call (801)292-9285." Charges $12 fee. "Only the fee is required for consideration. Short stories or novel excerpts must be no longer than 20 double-spaced pages (one story per entry only). Poetry submissions are limited to 6 poems, 20 pages maximum." Prize: $1,500, pubilcation and conference tuition; $500, conference tuition.

WRITER'S DIGEST WRITING COMPETITION, *Writer's Digest* Magazine, 1507 Dana Ave., Cincinnati OH 45207-9966. (513)531-2222. Fax: (513)531-2902. Contest Director: Rachel Johnson. Contest in 62nd year. Categories: Personal Essays, Feature Articles, Literary Short Stories, Mainstream/Genre Short Stories, Rhyming Poems, Non-Rhyming Poems, Stage Plays and Television/Movie Scripts. Submissions must be unpublished. Guidelines for #10 SASE. Deadline: May 31.

Arts Councils and Foundations

‡**ANNUAL ASSOCIATESHIP,** Rocky Mountain Women's Institute, 7150 Montview Blvd., Denver CO 80220. Contact: Executive Director. "The Rocky Mountain Women's Institute offers 1-year Associateships to selected artists, writers and independent scholars. Associates are given a modest stipend, office/studio space (based on need and use), exhibition opportunities and other services to support them in the completion of a project. Denver offices, this is not a residency program." Deadline: March 15. Send SASE for application. Prize: Stipend (currently at $1,000), office/studio space (based on need and use), exhibition opportunities and other support services.

ARTIST PROJECTS, Rhode Island State Council on the Arts, Suite 103, 95 Cedar St., Providence RI 02903. (401)277-3880. Fax: (401)521-1351. Contact: Sheila Haggerty. Previously published or unpublished submissions. "Artist Project grants enable an artist to create new work and/or complete works-in-progress by providing direct financial assistance. By encouraging significant development in the work of an individual artist, these grants recognize the central contribution artists make to the creative environment of Rhode Island." Deadline: October 1. Guidelines for 9×12 SASE. Prize: non-matching grants of $1,500-4,000. Open only to RI residents, age 18 or older. Students not eligible. Consult program director.

‡**ARTISTS FELLOWSHIP,** Japan Foundation, 39th Floor, 152 W. 57th St., New York NY 10019. (212)489-0299. Fax: (212)489-0409. Contact: Program Assistant. Offered annually. Deadline: December 1. "Contact us around September. Write or fax interest. Judged by committee in Japan Foundation headquarters in Tokyo.Keep in mind that this is an international competition. Due to the breadth of the application pool only four artists are selected for awards in the US. Applicants need not submit a writing sample, but if one is submitted it must be brief. Three letters of recommendation must be submitted from peers. One letter will double as a letter of affiliation, which must be submitted by a *Japan-based* (not necessarily an ethnic Japanese) peer artist. The applicant must present have a concise and cogent project objective and must be a professional writer/artist with accessible qualifications, i.e., a list of major works or publications."

ARTIST'S FELLOWSHIPS, New York Foundation for the Arts, 155 Avenue of the Americas, New York NY 10013-1507. (212)366-6900 ext. 217. Contact: Penelope Dannenberg. "Artists' Fellowships are cash grants of $7,000 awarded in 15 disciplines on a biannual rotation. Nonfiction Literature and Poetry will be the literature disciplines under review in 1994-1995. Awards are based upon the recommendations of peer panels and are not project support. The fellowship may be used by each recipient as she/he sees fit. All applicants must be 18 years of age and a New York resident for two years prior to the time of application. Call for application in July. Deadlines will be in October 1994. Results announced in April, 1995. The New York Foundation for the Arts supports artists at all stages of their careers and from diverse backgrounds."

ARTS RECOGNITION AND TALENT SEARCH, National Foundation for Advancement in the Arts, Suite 500, 800 Brickell Ave., Miami FL 33131. (305)573-0490. Fax: (305)573-4870. Communications Officer: Suzette L. Prude. Estab. 1981. For achievements in dance, music, theater, visual arts and writing. Students fill in and return the application, available at every public and private high school around the nation, for cash awards of up to $3,000 each and scholarship opportunities worth more than 3 million. Deadline: early-June 1, regular-October 1. Charges $25 registration fee for June; $35 for October registration.

ASSISTANCE TO ESTABLISHED WRITERS, Nova Scotia Dept. of Tourism and Culture, Cultural Affairs Division, P.O. Box 456, Halifax, Nova Scotia B3J 2R5 Canada. (902)424-6389. Fax: (902)424-2668. Offered twice annually for unpublished submissions to assist the professional writer with the costs of completing the research or manuscript preparation for a project in which a trade publisher has expressed serious interest." Deadline: April 1 and October 1. Prize: Maximum of $2,000 (Canadian). Applicant must be a Canadian citizen or landed immigrant and must have had their principal residence in Nova Scotia for 12 consecutive months at the time of application. Applicant must be an experienced writer who writes for print or broadcast media, film or stage, who has been consistently published and/or produced in the media.

GEORGE BENNETT FELLOWSHIP, Phillips Exeter Academy, Exeter NH 03833-1104. Coordinator, Selection Committee: Charles Pratt. Estab. 1968. Annual award of stipend, room and board "to provide time and freedom from material considerations to a person seriously contemplating or pursuing a career as a writer. Applicants should have a manuscript in progress which they intend to complete during the fellowship period." Guidelines for SASE. "Telephone inquiries strongly discouraged." Deadline: December 1. Charges $5 fee. Residence at the Academy during the Fellowship period required.

BRODY ARTS FUND FELLOWSHIP, California Community Foundation, Suite 2400, 606 S. Olive St., Los Angeles CA 90014-1526. (213)413-4042. Estab. 1985. "The Brody Arts Fund is designed to serve the needs of emerging artists and arts organizations, especially those rooted in the diverse, multicultural communities of Los Angeles. The fellowship program rotates annually between three main subsections of the arts. Literary artists were considered in 1994; and will be again in 1997. Applications area available and due in the first quarter of the year. Applicants must reside in Los Angeles County. Students not eligible."

BUSH ARTIST FELLOWSHIPS, The Bush Foundation, E-900 First National Bank Bldg., 332 Minnesota St., St. Paul MN 55101. (612)227-5222. Contact: Sally F. Dixon. Estab. 1976. Award for Minnesota, North Dakota, South Dakota, and western Wisconsin residents "to buy 6-18 months of time for the applicant to do his/her own work." Up to 15 fellowships annually. $26,000 stipend each plus additional $7,000 for production and travel. Deadline: mid-November.

‡COLORADO VISIONS (COVISIONS) PROJECT GRANTS, Colorado Council on the Arts, 750 Pennsylvania St., Denver CO 80203-3699. (303)894-2619. Director: Daniel Salazar. Annual grants to support innovative projects of high artistic merit in all disciplines, including literature. Colorado residents only. Deadline: June 15.

‡COLORADO VISIONS (COVISIONS) RECOGNITION AWARDS IN LITERATURE, Colorado Council on the Arts, 750 Pennsylvania St., Denver CO 80203-3699. (303)894-2619. Director: Daniel Salazar. Annual award to "acknowledge outstanding accomplishment amount individual arts as well as encourage public accessibility to their work." Colorado residents only. Deadline: December 15.

COMMONWEALTH OF PENNSYLVANIA COUNCIL ON THE ARTS LITERATURE FELLOWSHIPS, 216 Finance Bldg., Harrisburg PA 17120. (717)787-6883. Award Director: Marcia D. Salvatore. Estab. 1966. Fellowships for Pennsylvania writers of fiction and poetry. Deadline: August 1.

CREATIVE ARTISTS GRANT, Arts Foundation of Michigan, 2164 Penobscot Bldg., 645 Griswold St., Detroit MI 48226. (313)964-2244. Individual Artist Coordinator: Robert Mark Packer. Grants of up to $7,000 for Michigan creative artists. Check yearly for specific deadline.

CREATIVITY FELLOWSHIP, Northwood University Alden B. Dow Creativity Center, Midland MI 48640-2398. (517)837-4478. Award Director: Carol B. Coppage. Estab. 1979. Eight-week summer residency for individuals in any field who wish to pursue a new and different creative idea that has the potential of impact in that field. No accommodations for family/pets. Deadline: December 31.

DIVERSE VISIONS INTERDISCIPLINARY GRANTS PROGRAM, (formerly Diverse Visions Regional Grants Program), Intermedia Arts, 425 Ontario St. SE, Minneapolis MN 55414. (612)627-4444. Director of Artist Programs: Al Kosters. Estab. 1986. Regional (IA, KS, MN, NE, ND, SD, WI) interdisciplinary grants. Deadline: spring

DORLAND MOUNTAIN ARTS COLONY RESIDENCIES, Dorland Mountain Arts Colony, P.O. Box 6, Temecula CA 92593. (909)676-5039. Contact: Admissions Secretary. "Dorland Mountain Colony's Artist residencies are awarded semiannually to writers, artists, composers whose work passes review by a committee of established artists in the appropriate discipline." Deadline: March 1, September 1. Guidelines and entry forms available for SASE. Residencies 1-2 months. "Small cabin donations are asked of accepted artists."

ALWAYS enclose a self-addressed, stamped envelope (SASE) with all your queries and correspondence.

FELLOWSHIP/NEW JERSEY STATE COUNCIL ON THE ARTS, CN306, Trenton NJ 08625. (609)292-6130. Contact: Grants Office. Annual prose, poetry, playwriting in literature awards for New Jersey residents. Applications available in September. Deadline: December.

WILLIAM FLANAGAN MEMORIAL CREATIVE PERSONS CENTER, Edward F. Albee Foundation, 14 Harrison St., New York NY 10013. (212)226-2020. Foundation Secretary: David Briggs. Annual award for either previously published or unpublished work. One month residency at "The Barn" in Montauk, New York offers writers privacy and a peaceful atmosphere in which to work. Deadline: April 1. Prize: room only, writers pay for food and travel expenses. Judging by panel of qualified professionals.

FLORIDA INDIVIDUAL ARTIST FELLOWSHIPS, Florida Department of State, Bureau of Grants Services, Division of Cultural Affairs, The Capitol, Tallahassee FL 32399-0250. (904)487-2980. Director: Peyton Fearington. Fellowship for Florida writers only. Award: $5,000 each for fiction, poetry and children's literature. Deadline: mid-February.

GAP (GRANTS FOR ARTIST PROJECTS); FELLOWSHIP, Artist Trust, Suite 415, 1402 Third Ave, Seattle WA 98101-2118. (206)467-8734. Fax: (206)467-9633. Executive Director: Marschel Paul. Fellowship offered as announced for either published or unpublished work. "The GAP is awarded to 30-50 artists, including writers, per year. The award is meant to help finance a specific project, which can be in very early stages or near completion. The Fellowship is awarded to eight artists per year; the award is made on the basis of work of the past five years. It is 'no-strings-attached' funding." Guidelines for SASE. Prize: GAP: up to $1,000. Fellowship: $5,000. Fulltime students not eligible. *Only Washington state residents are eligible.*

ILLINOIS ARTS COUNCIL ARTISTS FELLOWSHIP, James R. Thompson Center, Suite 10-500, 100 W. Randolph, Chicago IL 60601. (312)814-6750. Contact: Director of Communication Arts. Offered every 2 years for previously published or unpublished work. "Submitted work must have been completed no more than four years prior to deadline. Artists fellowships are awarded to Illinois artists of exceptional talent to enable them to pursue their artistic goals; fellowships are offered in poetry and prose (fiction and creative nonfiction)." Deadline: September 1. "Interested Illinois writers should write or call for information." Prize: $500 finalist award; $5,000 or $10,000 Artist's Fellowship. "Writer must be Illinois resident and not a degree-seeking student. Applicants for Poetry Fellowship can submit up to 15 pages of work in manuscript; prose fellowship applicants can submit up to 30 pages of work in manuscript."

INDIVIDUAL ARTIST FELLOWSHIP, Oregon Arts Commission, 550 Airport Rd. SE, Salem OR 97310. (503)378-3625. Contact: Assistant Director. Offered every 2 years (even years only). "Fellowships reward achievement in the field of literature." Deadline: September 1. Guidelines for SASE. Prize: $3,000. "Writers must be Oregon residents 18 years and older. Degree candidate students not eligible."

INDIVIDUAL ARTIST PROGRAM, Wisconsin Arts Board, 1st Floor, 101 E. Wilson St., Madison WI 53703. Grant Coordinator: Elizabeth Malnon. Estab. 1990. (608)266-0190. Annual fellowships and grants for Wisconsin residents. Deadline: September 15.

INDIVIDUAL ARTISTS FELLOWSHIPS, Nebraska Arts Council, 3838 Davenport St., Omaha NE 68131-2329. (402)595-2122. Fax: (402)595-2334. Contact: Suzanne Wise. Estab. 1991. Offered every 2 years (literature alternates with performing arts). Previously unpublished work preferred, not mandated. "The Individual Artists Fellowship program recognizes exemplary achievements by originating artists in their fields of endeavor and supports the contributions made by Nebraska artists to the quality of life in this state." Deadline: November 1. "Generally, master awards are $3,000-4,000 and merit awards are $1,000-2,000. Funds available are announced in September prior to the deadline." Must be a resident of Nebraska for at least 2 years prior to submission date; 18 years of age; not enrolled in an undergraduate, graduate or certificate-granting program in English, creative writing, literature, or related field.

ISLAND LITERARY AWARDS, Prince Edward Island Council of the Arts, P.O. Box 2234, Chardottetown, Prince Edward Island C1A 8B9 Canada. (902)368-4410. Award Director: Judy K. MacDonald. Offers 6 awards for previously unpublished poetry, short fiction, playwriting feature article, children's literature and student writing. Deadline: February 15. Guidelines for #10 SAE with 1 IRC. Charges $6 fee. *Available to residents of PEI only.*

JOSEPH HENRY JACKSON/JAMES D. PHELAN LITERARY AWARDS, The San Francisco Foundation, Administered by Intersection for the Arts, 446 Valencia St., San Francisco CA 94103. (415)626-2787. Contact: Awards Coordinator. Estab. 1965. Jackson Award: unpublished, work-in-progress fiction (novel or short story), nonfiction or poetry by author age 20-35, with 3-year consecutive residency in northern California or

Nevada prior to submission. Phelan: unpublished, work-in-progress fiction, nonfiction, short story, poetry or drama by California-born author age 20-35. Deadline: January 30.

EZRA JACK KEATS MEMORIAL FELLOWSHIP, Ezra Jack Keats Foundation (funding) awarded through Kerlan Collection, University of Minnesota, 109 Walter Library, 117 Pleasant St. SE., Minneapolis MN 55455. (612)624-4576. Curator, Kerlan Collection: Karen Hoyle. "Purpose is to award a talented writer and/ or illustrator of children's books who wishes to use Kerlan Collection for the furtherance of his or her artistic development." Deadline: early May. Guidelines for SASE. Prize: $1,500 for travel to study at Kerlan Collection. Judged by a committee of 4-5 members from varying colleges at University of Minnesota and outside the University. "Special consideration will be given to someone who would find it difficult to finance the visit to the Kerlan Collection."

LITERARY ARTS PROGRAMS, Arts Branch, Dept. of Municipalities, Culture and Housing, P.O. Box 6000, Fredericton, New Brunswick E3B 5H1 Canada. (506)453-2555. Fax: (506)453-2416. Contact: Bruce Dennis, Literary Arts Officer, Arts Branch. Annual awards: Excellence Award, Creation Grant, Artist-in-Residence program, Arts Awards, Creation Grant and travel program. *Available to New Brunswick residents only. (Must have resided in NB 2 of past 4 years.)*

‡LITERATURE FELLOWSHIPS, D.C. Commission on the Arts and Humanities, 5th Floor, 410 Eighth St., NW, Washington DC 20004. (202)724-5613. Fax: (202)727-4135. TDD: (202)727-3148. Literature Staff Liaison: Diem Jones. Estab. 1977. "Annual fellowships to support individual artists (writers of creative fiction, nonfiction, poetry, prose, novels, etc.)." Deadline: spring. Guidelines for #10 SASE. Fellowship: $5,000/ year.

THE GERALD LOEB AWARDS, The John E. Anderson Graduate School of Management at UCLA, 405 Hilgard Ave., Los Angeles CA 90024-1481. (310)206-1877. Fax: (310)206-9830. Contact: Office of Communications. Consideration is limited to articles published in the previous calendar year. "To recognize writers who make significant contributions to the understanding of business, finance and the economy." Deadline: February 15 "unless it lands on a holiday." Charges $20/entry fee. Winners in each category receive $1,000. Honorable mentions, when awarded, receive $500.

LOFT-McKNIGHT WRITERS AWARD, The Loft, Pratt Community Center, 66 Malcolm Ave. SE, Minneapolis MN 55414-3551. Contact: Program Coordinator. Eight awards of $7,500 and two awards of distinction at $10,500 each for *Minnesota* writers of poetry and creative prose. Deadline: November. Guidelines for SASE.

LOFT-MENTOR SERIES, The Loft, Pratt Community Center, 66 Malcolm Ave. SE, Minneapolis MN 55414-3551. Contact: Program Coordinator. Estab. 1974. Opportunity to work with 4 nationally known writers and small stipend available to 8 winning poets and fiction writers. "Must live with close enough to Minneapolis to participate fully in the series." Deadline: May. Guidelines for SASE.

MARIN INDIVIDUAL ARTISTS GRANTS, Marin Arts Council, 251 N. San Pedro Rd., San Rafael CA 94903. (415)499-8350. Fax: (415)499-8537. Contact: Beky Carter. "Frequency of award depends on funding source. Open to Marin residents only. No students. Categories include poetry, playwriting, art for youth, fiction/ creative prose and screenwriting. Submit works completed in last 2 years only. Unrestricted fellowships based on the quality of the work submitted." Deadlines: usually end of January or March. Guidelines for SASE. Awards grants amounting between $2,000-10,000.

WALTER RUMSEY MARVIN GRANT, Ohioana Library Association, Suite 1105, 65 S. Front St., Columbus OH 43215. (614)466-3831. Director: Linda Hengst. Award given every 2 years (even years). Applicant must have been born in Ohio or have lived in Ohio for 5 years or more, must be 30 years of age or younger, and not have published a book. Deadline: January 31.

MONEY FOR WOMEN, Barbara Deming Memorial Fund, Inc., P.O. Box 40-1043, Brooklyn NY 11240-1043. Contact: Pam McAllister. "Small grants to individual feminists in the arts (musicians, artists, writers, poets, photographers) whose work addresses women's concerns and/or speaks for peace and justice from a feminist perspective." Deadline: December 31-June 30. Guidelines for SASE. Prize: grants up to $1,000: "The Fund does *not* give educational assistance, monies for personal study or loans, monies for dissertation or research projects, grants for group projects, business ventures, or emergency funds for hardships." Open to individual feminists in the arts. Applicants must be citizens of the US or Canada.

• The fund also offers two awards, the "Gerty, Gerty, Gerty in the Arts, Arts, Arts" for outstanding works by a lesbian and the "Fannie Lou Hamer Award" for work which combats racism and celebrates women of color.

‡NANTUCKET PLAYWRIGHT'S RETREAT, Nantucket Theatrical Productins, Box 2171, Nantucket MA 02584. (508)228-5002. Director: Jim Patrick. Retreat offered annually for "opportunities to have works in progress read; discussion and criticism by directors, actors, and peers; workshops and seminars; and a relatively inexpensive chance to write and visit the historic and beautiful island of Nantucket. We anticipate offering weekend seminars and weeklong increments at our retreat at an affordable price with a loosely structured program to facilitate an author's work in progress. Likely dates January through March. Write for more information."

NATIONAL ENDOWMENT FOR THE ARTS: ARTS ADMINISTRATION FELLOWS PROGRAM/FELLOWSHIP, National Endowment for the Arts, 1100 Pennsylvania Ave. NW, Washington DC 20506. (202)682-5786. Fax: (202)682-5610. Contact: Anya Nykyforiak. Estab. 1973. Offered 3 times each year: Spring, Summer and Fall. "The Arts Administration Fellowships are for arts managers and administrators including those in the nonprofit literary publishing field or writers' centers. Fellows come from all arts disciplines to the NEA for an 11-week residency to acquire an overview of this Federal agency's operations. Deadline: January, April, July. Guidelines may be requested by letter or telephone.

NEW HAMPSHIRE INDIVIDUAL ARTISTS' FELLOWSHIPS, New Hampshire State Council on the Arts, 40 N. Main St., Concord NH 03301-4974. (603)271-2789. Fax: (603)271-3584. Coordinator: Audrey V. Sylvester. Estab. 1982. "To recognize artistic excellence and professional commitment." Deadline: July 1. Guidelines for SASE or call for application. Prize: up to $3,000. Applicant must be over 18; not enrolled as fulltime student; be a New Hampshire resident and may not have been a fellow in preceding year.

NEW YORK STATE WRITER IN RESIDENCE PROGRAM, New York State Council on the Arts, 915 Broadway, New York NY 10010. (212)387-7028. Contact: Literature Program Director. Biannual residency program. "In addition to rewarding the writers' work, residencies are awarded to give writers a chance to work with a nonprofit organization in a community setting." Deadline: March 1. Award: $8,000 stipend for a 3 month residency." Applications are judged by a panel of writers, administrators, and translators. Applicant must be nominated by a New York state nonprofit organization.

PALENVILLE INTERARTS COLONY RESIDENCY PROGRAM, June-September 30: 2 Bond St., New York NY 10012, (212)254-4614; or October 1-May 30: P.O. Box 59, Palenville NY 12463 (518)678-3332. Contact: Joanna Sherman/Patrick Sciarratta. Offered annually. "Competitive residency program offers room or cabin for writers to work in a creative, unpressured environment free from distractions. Residencies, partially or fully subsidized, available between May 1 and September 30." Deadline: April 1, 1994. Guidelines for SASE. Charges $10 application fee. Prize: partially or fully subsidized residencies. Judged by panel of artists in each discipline. "Writing panel is one person, changes every other year. Writer should have three years professional experience — but acceptance is based on quality of submitted sample writing, primarily. Open to playwrights, poets, etc. etc. Emerging writers welcome to apply."

RESIDENCY, Millay Colony for the Arts, Steepletop, P.O. Box 3, Austerlitz NY 12017. (518)392-3103. Executive Director: Ann-Ellen Lesser. Offered to fiction and nonfiction writers, poets and playwrights of talent. In-office deadlines: February 1 for June-September; May 1 for October-January, September 1 for February-May. Write or call for brochure and application form. Prize: 1-month residency, room and board and studio. Open to writers, composers and visual artists.

STEGNER FELLOWSHIP, Stanford Creative Writing Program, Stanford University, Stanford CA 94305-2087. (415)723-2637. Fax: (415)725-0755. Contact: Gay Pierce. Estab. 1940. Annual fellowships (5 fiction, 5 poetry) include all tuition costs and a living stipend for writers to come to Stanford for 2 years to attend workshop to develop their particular writing. Deadline: January 1. Charges $25 fee.

UCROSS FOUNDATION RESIDENCY, 2836 US Highway 14-16E, Clearmont WY 82835. (307)737-2291. Fax: (307)737-2322. Contact: Elizabeth Guheen. Eight concurrent positions open for artists-in-residence in various disciplines (includes writers, visual artists, music, humanities) extending from 2 weeks-2 months. No charge for room, board or studio space. Deadline: March 1 for August-December program; October 1 for January-May program.

VERMONT COUNCIL ON THE ARTS, 136 State St., Drawer 33, Montpelier VT 05633-6001. (802)828-329. Fax: (802)828-3233. Grants Officer: Cornelia Carey. Offered annually for previously published or unpublished works. "Project Grants are for specific projects of writers (poetry, playwriters, fiction, nonfiction) as well as not-for-profit presses. Fellowships are awarded in recognition of artistic accomplishment." Deadline: March 2. Artist Development Grants provide technical assistance for Vermont writers. Rolling deadline. Write or call for entry information. Prize: up to $3,000 for projects; $3,500 for fellowships. "All programs are open to Vermont residents only."

WALDEN RESIDENCY FELLOWSHIPS, Northwest Writing Institute, Campus Box 100, Lewis & Clark College, Portland OR 97219-7899. (503)768-7745. Fax: (503)768-7715. Offered annually for previously published or unpublished work "to provide a quiet, remote work space for Oregon writers who are working on a project." Deadline: late November. Guidelines for SASE. Prize: 6- to 8-week residencies (3 per year) in a cabin in Southern Oregon. Utilities and partial board are included. "The sponsor and two other writers form a committee to judge the applications and select recipients." Writer must be from Oregon.

Miscellaneous

AMWA MEDICAL BOOK AWARDS COMPETITION, American Medical Writers Association, 9650 Rockville Pike, Bethesda MD 20814. (301)493-0003. Contact: Book Awards Committee. Contest to honor the best medical book published in the previous year in each of 3 categories: Books for Physicians, Books for Allied Health Professionals and Trade Books. Deadline April 1. Charges $20 fee.

ANIMAL RIGHTS WRITING AWARD, 421 S. State St., Clarks Summit PA 18411. Chairperson: Helen Jones. Offered annually for previously published works. "Awarded to the author of an exceptionally meritorious book or article which advances the cause of animal rights. Works will be judged for content and literary excellence." Prize: $500 and plaque. "Nominations may be made by anyone providing the work has been published in the English language. Suggested divisions are: novel, book length nonfiction, children's book, article. Three copies of the work shall be submitted to the ISAR, with a cover letter stating author, date of publication, and name of person or entity submitting. If no submission is considered deserving, an award will not be given in that division. Special awards may be given at the discretion of the judges."

BOWLING WRITING COMPETITION, American Bowling Congress Publications, 5301 S. 76th St., Greendale WI 53129-1127. Fax: (414)421-7977. Editor: Bill Vint. Estab. 1935. Feature, editorial and news all relating to the sport of bowling. Deadline: December 1. Prizes: $300 1st prize in each category and additional awards of $225, $200, $175, $150, $75 and $50.

GAVEL AWARDS, American Bar Association, 750 N. Lake Shore Dr., Chicago IL 60611. (312)988-6137. Fax: (312)988-5865. Contact: Peggy O'Carroll. Estab. 1957. Previously published, performed or broadcast works that promote "public understanding of the American system of law and justice." Deadline: February 1.

GOLF WRITER'S CONTEST, Golf Course Superintendents Association of America, GCSAA, 1421 Research Park Dr., Lawrence KS 66049-3859. Fax: (913)832-4466. Public Relations Manager: Scott Smith. Previously published work pertaining to golf course superintendents. Must be a member of Golf Writers Association of America.

HARVARD OAKS CAREER GUIDANCE AWARD, #1681, 208 S. LaSalle, Chicago IL 60604. Award Director: William A. Potter. "Quarterly award to writers of published articles covering relevant topics in career selection and job search strategies." Deadlines: March 31, June 30, September 30, December 31. Guidelines for #10 SASE.

STEPHEN LEACOCK MEMORIAL AWARD FOR HUMOUR, Stephen Leacock Associates, P.O. Box 854, Orillia, Ontario L3V 6K8 Canada. (705)325-6546. Contest Director: Jean Dickson. Estab. 1947. For a book of humor published in previous year by a Canadian author. Include 10 copies of each entry and a b&w photo with bio. Deadline: December 31. Charges $25 fee. Prize: Stephen Leacock Memorial Medal and Manulife Bank of Canada Award of $5,000.

1995 2ND ANNUAL LOUDEST LAF! LAUREL, (formerly *Loudest Laf! Laurel*), *Laf!* Scher Maihem Publishing Ltd., P.O. Box 313, Avilla IN 46710-0313. Contact: Fran Glass. "To encourage the writing of excellent short humor (600 words or less), and to develop great humorists in the tradition of Mark Twain." Deadline: June 1, 1995. Guidelines for #10 SASE. Charges $8—includes a one-year subscription to *Laf!*, a bimonthly humor magloid. Prize: $100 first prize. Top 6 will be published in January/February awards edition of *Laf!*

PEN WRITING AWARDS FOR PRISONERS, PEN American Center, 568 Broadway, New York NY 10012. "Awarded to the authors of the best poetry, plays, short fiction and nonfiction received from prison writers in the US." SASE. Deadline September 1.

Contests and Awards/Changes '94-95

The following contests were listed in the 1994 edition but do not have listings in this edition of *Writer's Market*. The majority did not respond to our request to update their listings or return a questionnaire for a new listing. If a reason was given for their exclusion, we have included it in parentheses after the listing name.

AAAS Prize for Behavioral Science Research
AAAS-Westinghouse Science Journalism Awards
AJL Reference Book Award
Jane Addams Children's Book Award
Ambergris Annual Fiction Award
American-Scandinavian Foundation/Translation Prize
Annual One Act Playwriting Competition
Arkansas Poetry Award
Artist Assistance Fellowship—MN
Artist Fellowships—WA (program transferred)
Artists Fellowship Grants—OR (removed by request)
Asian American Playwrights Contest
Vincent Astor Memorial Leadership Essay Contest
Best of *Housewife Writer's Forum*
Bunting Fellowship
Arleigh Burke Essay Contest
Canadian Author Student Creative Writing Awards
Career Opportunity Grants
Bill Casey Award
Chicago Foundation for Literature Awards
Gordon W. Dillon/Richard C. Peterson Memorial Essay Contest Prize
Dog Writer's Association of America Annual Writing Contest
Eve of St. Agnes Poetry Competition
Family One-Act Play Festival
FAW Literary Award
Fellowship-Literature (AL)
Fellowship in Literature (RI)
Fellowships to Assist Research and Artistic Creation
Folio
George Freedley Memorial Award
French-American Foundation Translation Prize
Friends of American Writers Young People's Literature Awards
Fulbright Scholar Program
German Prize for Literary Translation
GeVa Playwrights Award
Louis Gottschalk Prize

Governor General's Literary Awards
Hopewell Review
Darrell Bob Houston Prize
Idaho Writer-in-Residence
Individual Artist Fellowship Award
Anson Jones Award
The Juniper Prize
Juried Competition (FL)
Robert F. Kennedy Book Award
Kentudky Arts Councils Fellowships in Writing
Kumu Kahua/UHM Theatre Department Playwriting Contest
La Napoule Residency
Landmark Editions Awards for Students
Linden Lane Magazine English Language Poetry Contest
Literary Nonfiction Writers' Project Grants
Amy Lowell Poetry Traveling Scholarship
Mature Women Scholarship Award
The Mayflower Society Cup Competition
McLaren Memorial Comedy Playwriting Competition
McLemore Prize
Milweed Prize for Children's Literature
Minority Screenwriters Development and Promotional Program
National Book Awards
National Jewish Book Award—Autobiography/Memoir
National Jewish Book Award—Children's Literature
National Jewish Book Award—Children's Picture Book
National Jewish Book Award—Contemporary Jewish Life
National Jewish Book Award—Fiction
National Jewish Book Award—Holocaust
National Jewish Book Award—Israel
National Jewish Book Award—Jewish Thought
National Jewish Book Award—Scholarship
National Jewish Book Award—Visual Arts
National Play Award
National Poetry Competition

National Poetry Series
Negative Capability Short Fiction
New American Comedy Festival
New Play Competition
New Play Grant
New Playwrights Competition
North American Indian Prose Award
Eli M. Oboler Memorial Award
One-Act Family Play Festival
One-Act Playwriting Competition
Original Playwriting Award Competition
The Orvis Wildbranch Grant
Francis Parkman Prize
Alicia Patterson Journalism Fellowship
PEN Center West Literary Awards
PEN Publisher Citation
People's Voice Poetry Contest
Playwrighting Fellowship
Playwrights' Center Jerome Playwright-in-Residence Fellowship
The Playwrights' Center Play-labs
Playwrights' Forum Awards
Felix Pollak/Chris O'Malley Prizes in Poetry and Fiction
Prix Alvine-Belisle
Reader Riter Poll
Mary Roberts Rinehart Fund
Roberts Writing Awards (discontinued)
Seventeen Magazine Fiction Contest
Shiras Institute/Mildred & Albert Panowski Playwriting Award
Sonora Review Annual Literary Awards
Student Research Grant
The Translation Center Awards
Translation Commissions
US Residencies
US West Theatrefest

Daniel Varoujian Award
Western Heritage Award
White Bird Annual Playwriting Contest
Whitney-Carnegie Award
Writer-in-Residence Program
Writers Fellowships—NC
Your Writing Life Dream Contest

Organizations of Interest

As markets become more competitive, contacts are increasingly important for free-lancers. Professional organizations on both local and national levels can be very helpful in this capacity. They often provide valuable opportunities for networking, information about new developments in the industry, and guidance in business or legal matters.

The majority of organizations listed here publish newsletters and other materials that can provide you with useful information for your writing career. Some even provide such opportunities as conferences and referral services.

Keep in mind that numerous local organizations and writers' clubs also exist, and can provide occasions for networking in your own area. You can usually find information about such groups in your local library or through an area college writing program.

Some of the following national organizations have branches or chapters in different cities across the country. Write to the organization for information about their membership requirements, individual chapters and programs for writers.

American Book Producers Association
Suite 604, 160 Fifth Ave.
New York NY 10010-7000
(212)645-2368

American Medical Writers Association
9650 Rockville Pike
Bethesda MD 20814-3998
(301)493-0003

American Society of Journalists & Authors, Inc.
Suite 302, 1501 Broadway
New York NY 10036
(212)997-0947

American Translators Association
Suite 903, 1735 Jefferson Davis Highway
Arlington VA 22202-3413
(703)412-1500

Associated Writing Programs
Old Dominion University
Norfolk VA 23529-0079
(804)683-3839

Association of Authors Representatives
3rd Floor, 10 Astor Pl.
New York NY 10003
(212)353-3709

Association of Desk-Top Publishers
Suite 800, 4677 30th St.
San Diego CA 92116-3245
(619)563-9714

The Authors Resource Center
P.O. Box 64785
Tucson AZ 85728
(602)325-4733

The Authors Guild
330 W. 42nd St.
New York NY 10036
(212)563-5904

The Authors League of America, Inc.
330 W. 42nd St.
New York NY 10036
(212)564-8350

Copywriters Council of America, Freelance
Linick Bldg. 102, 7 Putter Lane
Middle Island NY 11953-0102
(516)924-8555

Council of Authors & Journalists, Inc.
% Uncle Remus Regional Library System
1131 East Ave.
Madison GA 30650
(404)432-0290

Council of Literary Magazines & Presses
Suite 3C, 154 Christopher St.
New York NY 10014
(212)741-9110

The Dramatists Guild
11th Floor, 234 W. 44th St.
New York NY 10036
(212)398-9366

Editorial Freelancers Association
Room 9R, 36 E. 23rd St.,
New York NY 10159-2050
(212)677-3357

Education Writers Association
Suite 310, 1001 Connecticut Ave. NW
Washington DC 20036
(202)429-9680

Freelance Editorial Association
P.O. Box 835
Cambridge MA 02238
(617)729-8164

International Association of Business Communicators
Suite 600, 1 Hallidie Plaza
San Francisco CA 94102
(415)433-3400

International Association of Crime Writers Inc., North American Branch
JAF Box 1500
New York NY 10116
(212)757-3915

International Television Association
Suite 230, 6311 N. O'Connor Rd.
Irving TX 75039
(214)869-1112

International Women's Writing Guild
Box 810, Gracie Station
New York NY 10028-0082
(212)737-7536

Mystery Writers of America
6th Floor, 17 E. 47th St.
New York NY 10017
(212)888-8171

National Association of Science Writers
Box 294
Greenlawn NY 11740
(516)757-5664

National Writers Club
Suite 424, 1450 S. Havana
Aurora CO 80012
(303)751-7844

National Writers Union
Suite 203, 873 Broadway
New York NY 10003
(212)254-0279

PEN American Center
568 Broadway
New York NY 10012
(212)334-1660

Poetry Society of America
15 Grammercy Park
New York NY 10003
(212)254-9628

Poets & Writers
72 Spring St.
New York NY 10012
(212)226-3586

Publication Services Guild
P.O. Box 19663
Atlanta GA 30325
(404)525-0985

Public Relations Society of America
33 Irving Place
New York NY 10003
(212)995-2230

Romance Writers of America
Suite 315, 13700 Veterans Memorial Dr.
Houston TX 77014
(713)440-6885

Science-Fiction Fantasy Writers of America
Suite 1B, 5 Winding Brook Dr.
Guilderland NY 12084
(518)869-5361

Society of American Business Editors & Writers
% Janine Latus-Musick
University of Missouri
P.O. Box 838
Columbia MO 65205
(314)882-7862

Society of American Travel Writers
Suite 500, 1155 Connecticut Ave. NW
Washington DC 20036
(202)429-6639

Society of Children's Book Writers
NW Oregon Retreat
Suite 106, 22736 Vanowen St.
West Hills CA 91307
(818)888-8760

Society of Professional Journalists
16 S. Jackson
Greencastle IN 46135
(317)653-3333

Volunteer Lawyers for the Arts
6th Floor, 1 E. 53rd St.
New York NY 10022
(212)319-2787

Women in Communications, Inc.
Suite 417, 2101 Wilson Blvd.
Arlington VA 22201
(703)528-4200

Writers Alliance
Box 2014
Setauket NY 11733
(516)751-7080

Writers Connection
Suite 103, 275 Saratoga Ave.
Santa Clara CA 95050
(408)554-2090

Writers Guild of America (East)
555 W. 57th St.
New York NY 10019
(212)767-7800

Writers Guild of America (West)
8955 Beverly Blvd.
West Hollywood CA 90048
(310)550-1000

Publications of Interest

In addition to newsletters and publications from local and national organizations, there are trade publications, books, and directories which offer valuable information about writing and about marketing your manuscripts and understanding the business side of publishing. Some also list employment agencies that specialize in placing publishing professionals, and some announce actual freelance opportunities.

Trade magazines

ADVERTISING AGE, Crain Communications Inc., 740 N. Rush St., Chicago IL 60611. (312)649-5200. *Weekly magazine covering advertising in magazines, trade journals and business.*

AMERICAN JOURNALISM REVIEW, 8701 Adelphi Rd., Adelphi MD 20783. (301)431-4771. *10 issues/year magazine for journalists and communications professionals.*

DAILY VARIETY, Daily Variety Ltd./Cahners Publishing Co., 5700 Wilshire Blvd., Los Angeles CA 90036. (213)857-6600. *Trade publication on the entertainment industry, with helpful information for screenwriters.*

EDITOR & PUBLISHER, The Editor & Publisher Co., 11 W. 19th St., New York NY 10011. (212)675-4380. *Weekly magazine covering the newspaper publishing industry.*

FOLIO, Cowles Business Media, P.O. Box 4949, 911 Hope St., Stamford CT 06907-0949. (203)358-9900. *Monthly magazine covering the magazine publishing industry.*

GREETINGS MAGAZINE, MacKay Publishing Corp., 309 5th Ave., New York NY 10016. (212)679-6677. *Monthly magazine covering the greeting card industry.*

HORN BOOK MAGAZINE, 14 Beacon St., Boston MA 02108. (617)227-1555. *Bi-monthly magazine that covers children's literature.*

PARTY & PAPER RETAILER, 4 Ward Corp., 70 New Canaan Ave., Norwalk CT 06850. (203)845-8020. *Monthly magazine covering the greeting card and gift industry.*

POETS & WRITERS INC., 72 Spring St., New York NY 10012. (212)226-3586. *Monthly magazine, primarily for literary writers and poets.*

PUBLISHERS WEEKLY, Bowker Magazine Group, Cahners Publishing Co., 249 W. 17th St., New York NY 10011. (212)645-0067. *Weekly magazine covering the book publishing industry.*

SCIENCE FICTION CHRONICLE, P.O. Box 022730, Brooklyn NY 11202-0056. (718)643-9011. *Monthly magazine for science fiction, fantasy and horror writers.*

THE WRITER, 120 Boylston St., Boston MA 02116. (617)423-3157. *Monthly writers' magazine.*

WRITER'S DIGEST, 1507 Dana Ave., Cincinnati OH 45207. (513)531-2222. *Monthly writers' magazine.*

Books and directories

AV MARKET PLACE, R.R. Bowker, A Reed Reference Publishing Co., 121 Chanlon Rd., New Providence NJ 07974. (908)464-6800.

THE COMPLETE BOOK OF SCRIPTWRITING, by J. Michael Straczynski, Writer's Digest Books, 1507 Dana Ave., Cincinnati OH 45207. (513)531-2690.

THE COMPLETE GUIDE TO SELF PUBLISHING, by Marilyn and Tom Ross, Writer's Digest Books, 1507 Dana Ave., Cincinnati OH 45207. (513)531-2222.

COPYRIGHT HANDBOOK, R.R. Bowker, A Reed Reference Publishing Co., 121 Chanlon Rd., New Providence NJ 07974. (908)464-6800.

DIRECTORY OF EDITORIAL RESOURCES, Suite 200, 66 Canal Center Plaza, Alexandria VA 22314-5507. (703)683-0683.

DRAMATISTS SOURCEBOOK, edited by Gillian Richards and Linda MacColl, Theatre Communications Group, Inc., 355 Lexington Ave., New York NY 10017. (212)697-5230.

GUIDE TO LITERARY AGENTS, edited by Kirsten Holm, Writer's Digest Books, 1507 Dana Ave., Cincinnati OH 45207. (513)531-2222.

THE GUIDE TO WRITERS CONFERENCES, ShawGuides Inc. Educational Publishers, Suite 1406, 625 Biltmore Way, Coral Gables FL 33134. (305)446-8888.

HOW TO WRITE IRRESISTIBLE QUERY LETTERS, by Lisa Collier Cool, Writer's Digest Books, 1507 Dana Ave., Cincinnati OH 45207. (513)531-2222.

THE INSIDER'S GUIDE TO BOOK EDITORS, PUBLISHERS & LITERARY AGENTS, by Jeff Herman, Prima Publishing, Box 1260, Rocklin CA 95677-1260. (916)786-0426.

INTERNATIONAL DIRECTORY OF LITTLE MAGAZINES & SMALL PRESSES, edited by Len Fulton, Dustbooks, P.O. Box 100, Paradise CA 95967. (916)877-6110.

LITERARY MARKET PLACE and INTERNATIONAL LITERARY MARKET PLACE, R.R. Bowker, A Reed Reference Publishing Co., 121 Chanlon Rd., New Providence NJ 07974. (908)464-6800.

PROFESSIONAL WRITER'S GUIDE, edited by Donald Bower and James Lee Young, National Writers Press, Suite 424, 1450 S. Havana, Aurora CO 80012. (303)751-7844.

STANDARD DIRECTORY OF ADVERTISING AGENCIES, National Register Publishing, A Reed Reference Publishing Co., 121 Chanlon Rd., New Providence NJ 07974. (908)464-6800.

THE WRITER'S GUIDE TO SELF-PROMOTION AND PUBLICITY, by Elane Feldman, Writer's Digest Books, 1507 Dana Ave., Cincinnati OH 45207. (513)531-2222.

THE WRITER'S LEGAL COMPANION, by Brad Bunnin and Peter Beren, Addison-Wesley Publishing Co., 1 Jacob Way, Reading MA 01867. (617)944-3000.

WRITING TOOLS: Essential Software for Anyone Who Writes with a PC, by Hy Bender; Random House Electronic Publishing, 201 E. 50 St., New York NY 10022. (212)572-8700.

Glossary

Key to symbols and abbreviations is on page 54.

Advance. A sum of money a publisher pays a writer prior to the publication of a book. It is usually paid in installments, such as one-half on signing the contract; one-half on delivery of a complete and satisfactory manuscript. The advance is paid against the royalty money that will be earned by the book.

Advertorial. Advertising presented in such a way as to resemble editorial material. Information may be the same as that contained in an editorial feature, but it is paid for or supplied by an advertiser and the word "advertisement" appears at the top of the page.

All rights. See Rights and the Writer in the Minding the Details article.

Anthology. A collection of selected writings by various authors or a gathering of works by one author.

Assignment. Editor asks a writer to produce a specific article for an agreed-upon fee.

Auction. Publishers sometimes bid for the acquisition of a book manuscript that has excellent sales prospects. The bids are for the amount of the author's advance, advertising and promotional expenses, royalty percentage, etc. Auctions are conducted by agents.

B&W. Abbreviation for black and white photographs.

Backlist. A publisher's list of its books that were not published during the current season, but that are still in print.

Belles lettres. A term used to describe fine or literary writing—writing more to entertain than to inform or instruct.

Bimonthly. Every two months. See also *semimonthly*.

Bionote. A sentence or brief paragraph about the writer. Also called a "bio," it can appear at the bottom of the first or last page of a writer's article or short story or on a contributor's page.

Biweekly. Every two weeks.

Boilerplate. A standardized contract. When an editor says "our standard contract," he means the boilerplate with no changes. Writers should be aware that most authors and/or agents make many changes on the boilerplate.

Book packager. Draws all elements of a book together, from the initial concept to writing and marketing strategies, then sells the book package to a book publisher and/or movie producer. Also known as book producer or book developer.

Business size envelope. Also known as a #10 envelope, it is the standard size used in sending business correspondence.

Byline. Name of the author appearing with the published piece.

Category fiction. A term used to include all various labels attached to types of fiction. See also *genre*.

Chapbook. A small booklet, usually paperback, of poetry, ballads or tales.

Clean copy. A manuscript free of errors, cross-outs, wrinkles or smudges.

Clips. Samples, usually from newspapers or magazines, of your *published* work.

Coffee table book. An oversize book, heavily illustrated..

Column inch. The amount of space contained in one inch of a typeset column.

Commercial novels. Novels designed to appeal to a broad audience. These are often broken down into categories such as western, mystery and romance. See also *genre*.

Commissioned work. See *assignment*.

Concept. A statement that summarizes a screenplay or teleplay—before the outline or treatment is written.

Contributor's copies. Copies of the issues of magazines sent to the author in which the author's work appears.

Cooperative publishing. See *co-publishing*.

Co-publishing. Arrangement where author and publisher share publication costs and profits of a book. Also known as *cooperative publishing*. See also *subsidy publisher*.

Copyediting. Editing a manuscript for grammar, punctuation and printing style, not subject content.

Copyright. A means to protect an author's work. See Copyright in the Minding the Details section.

Cover letter. A brief letter, accompanying a complete manuscript, especially useful if responding to an editor's request for a manuscript. A cover letter may also accompany a book proposal. A cover letter is *not* a query letter; see Targeting Your Ideas in the Getting Published section.

Derivative works. A work that has been translated, adapted, abridged, condensed, annotated or otherwise produced by altering a previously created work. Before producing a derivative work, it is necessary to secure the written permission of the copyright owner of the original piece.

Desktop publishing. A publishing system designed for a personal computer. The system is capable of typesetting, some illustration, layout, design and printing—so that the final piece can be distributed and/or sold.

Disk. A round, flat magnetic plate on which computer data may be stored.

Docudrama. A fictional film rendition of recent newsmaking events and people.

Dot-matrix. Printed type where individual characters are composed of a matrix or pattern of tiny dots. Near letter quality (see *NLQ*) dot-matrix submissions are generally acceptable to editors.

Electronic submission. A submission made by modem or on computer disk.

El-hi. Elementary to high school.

Epigram. A short, witty sometimes paradoxical saying.

Erotica. Fiction or art that is sexually oriented.

Fair use. A provision of the copyright law that says short passages from copyrighted material may be used without infringing on the owner's rights.

Fax (facsimile machine). A communication system used to transmit documents over telephone lines.

Feature. An article giving the reader information of human interest rather than news. Also used by magazines to indicate a lead article or distinctive department.

Filler. A short item used by an editor to "fill" out a newspaper column or magazine page. It could be a timeless news item, a joke, an anecdote, some light verse or short humor, puzzle, etc.

First North American serial rights. See Rights and the Writer in the Minding the Details article.

Formula story. Familiar theme treated in a predictable plot structure—such as boy meets girl, boy loses girl, boy gets girl.

Frontlist. A publisher's list of its books that are new to the current season.

Galleys. The first typeset version of a manuscript that has not yet been divided into pages.

Genre. Refers either to a general classification of writing, such as the novel or the poem, or to the categories within those classifications, such as the problem novel or the sonnet. Genre fiction describes commercial novels, such as mysteries, romances and science fiction. Also called category fiction.

Ghostwriter. A writer who puts into literary form an article, speech, story or book based on another person's ideas or knowledge.

Glossy. A black and white photograph with a shiny surface as opposed to one with a non-shiny matte finish.

Gothic novel. A fiction category or genre in which the central character is usually a beautiful young girl, the setting an old mansion or castle, and there is a handsome hero and a real menace, either natural or supernatural.

Graphic novel. An adaptation of a novel in graphic form, long comic strip or heavily illustrated story, of 40 pages or more, produced in paperback form.

Hard copy. The printed copy of a computer's output.

Hardware. All the mechanically-integrated components of a computer that are not software. Circuit boards, transistors and the machines that are the actual computer are the hardware.

Honorarium. Token payment—small amount of money, or a byline and copies of the publication.

Illustrations. May be photographs, old engravings, artwork. Usually paid for separately from the manuscript. See also *package sale*.

Imprint. Name applied to a publisher's specific line or lines of books (e.g., Anchor Books is an imprint of Doubleday).

Interactive fiction. Works of fiction in book or computer software format in which the reader determines the path the story will take. The reader chooses from several alternatives at the end of a "chapter," and thus determines the structure of the story. Interactive fiction features multiple plots and endings.

Invasion of privacy. Writing about persons (even though truthfully) without their consent.

Kill fee. Fee for a complete article that was assigned but which was subsequently cancelled.

Lead time. The time between the acquisition of a manuscript by an editor and its actual publication.

Letter-quality submission. Computer printout that looks typewritten.

Libel. A false accusation or any published statement or presentation that tends to expose another to public contempt, ridicule, etc. Defenses are truth; fair comment on a matter of public interest; and privileged communication — such as a report of legal proceedings or client's communication to a lawyer.

List royalty. A royalty payment based on a percentage of a book's retail (or "list") price. Compare *net royalty*.

Little magazine. Publications of limited circulation, usually on literary or political subject matter.

LORT. An acronym for League of Resident Theatres. Letters from A to D follow LORT and designate the size of the theater.

Magalog. Mail order catalog with how-to articles pertaining to the items for sale..

Mainstream fiction. Fiction that transcends popular novel categories such as mystery, romance and science fiction. Using conventional methods, this kind of fiction tells stories about people and their conflicts with greater depth of characterization, background, etc., than the more narrowly focused genre novels.

Mass market. Nonspecialized books of wide appeal directed toward a large audience. Smaller and more cheaply produced than trade paperbacks, they are found in many non-bookstore outlets, such as drug stores, supermarkets, etc.

Microcomputer. A small computer system capable of performing various specific tasks with data it receives. Personal computers are microcomputers.

Midlist. Those titles on a publisher's list that are not expected to be big sellers, but are expected to have limited sales. Midlist books are mainstream, not literary, scholarly or genre, and are usually written by new or unknown writers.

Model release. A paper signed by the subject of a photograph (or the subject's guardian, if a juvenile) giving the photographer permission to use the photograph, editorially or for advertising purposes or for some specific purpose as stated.

Modem. A device used to transmit data from one computer to another via telephone lines.

Monograph. A detailed and documented scholarly study concerning a single subject.

Multiple submissions. Sending more than one poem, gag or greeting card idea at the same time. This term is often used synonymously with simultaneous submission.

Net royalty. A royalty payment based on the amount of money a book publisher receives on the sale of a book after booksellers' discounts, special sales discounts and returns. Compare *list royalty*.

Newsbreak. A brief, late-breaking news story added to the front page of a newspaper at press time or a magazine news item of importance to readers.

NLQ. Near letter-quality print required by some editors for computer printout submissions. See also *dot-matrix*.

Novelette. A short novel, or a long short story; 7,000 to 15,000 words approximately. Also known as a novella.

Novelization. A novel created from the script of a popular movie, usually called a movie "tie-in" and published in paperback.

Offprint. Copies of an author's article taken "out of issue" before a magazine is bound and given to the author in lieu of monetary payment. An offprint could be used by the writer as a published writing sample.

On spec. An editor expresses an interest in a proposed article idea and agrees to consider the finished piece for publication "on speculation." The editor is under no obligation to buy the finished manuscript.

One-shot feature. As applies to syndicates, single feature article for syndicate to sell;

as contrasted with article series or regular columns syndicated.

One-time rights. See Rights and the Writer in the Minding the Details article.

Outline. A summary of a book's contents in five to 15 double-spaced pages; often in the form of chapter headings with a descriptive sentence or two under each one to show the scope of the book. A screenplay's or teleplay's outline is a scene-by-scene narrative description of the story (10-15 pages for a ½-hour teleplay; 15-25 pages for a 1-hour teleplay; 25-40 pages for a 90-minute teleplay; 40-60 pages for a 2-hour feature film or teleplay).

Over-the-transom. Describes the submission of unsolicited material by a freelance writer.

Package sale. The editor buys manuscript and photos as a "package" and pays for them with one check.

Page rate. Some magazines pay for material at a fixed rate per published page, rather than per word.

Parallel submission. A strategy of developing several articles from one unit of research for submission to similar magazines. This strategy differs from simultaneous or multiple submission, where the same article is marketed to several magazines at the same time.

Payment on acceptance. The editor sends you a check for your article, story or poem as soon as he decides to publish it.

Payment on publication. The editor doesn't send you a check for your material until it is published.

Pen name. The use of a name other than your legal name on articles, stories or books when you wish to remain anonymous. Simply notify your post office and bank that you are using the name so that you'll receive mail and/or checks in that name. Also called a pseudonym.

Photo feature. Feature in which the emphasis is on the photographs rather than on accompanying written material.

Plagiarism. Passing off as one's own the expression of ideas and words of another writer.

Potboiler. Refers to writing projects a freelance writer does to "keep the pot boiling" while working on major articles—quick projects to bring in money with little time or effort. These may be fillers such as anecdotes or how-to tips, but could be short articles or stories.

Proofreading. Close reading and correction of a manuscript's typographical errors.

Proscenium. The area of the stage in front of the curtain.

Prospectus. A preliminary written description of a book or article, usually one page in length.

Pseudonym. See *pen name*.

Public domain. Material that was either never copyrighted or whose copyright term has expired.

Query. A letter to an editor intended to raise interest in an article you propose to write.

Release. A statement that your idea is original, has never been sold to anyone else and that you are selling the negotiated rights to the idea upon payment.

Remainders. Copies of a book that are slow to sell and can be purchased from the publisher at a reduced price. Depending on the author's book contract, a reduced royalty or no royalty is paid on remainder books.

Reporting time. The time it takes for an editor to report to the author on his/her query or manuscript.

Reprint rights. See Rights and the Writer in the Minding the Details article.

Round-up article. Comments from, or interviews with, a number of celebrities or experts on a single theme.

Royalties, standard hardcover book. 10% of the retail price on the first 5,000 copies sold; 12½% on the next 5,000; 15% thereafter.

Royalties, standard mass paperback book. 4 to 8% of the retail price on the first 150,000 copies sold.

Royalties, standard trade paperback book. No less than 6% of list price on the first 20,000 copies; 7½% thereafter.

Scanning. A process through which letter-quality printed text (see *NLQ*) or artwork is read by a computer scanner and converted into workable data.

Screenplay. Script for a film intended to be shown in theaters.

Self-publishing. In this arrangement, the author keeps all income derived from the book, but he pays for its manufacturing, production and marketing.

Semimonthly. Twice per month.

Semiweekly. Twice per week.

Serial. Published periodically, such as a newspaper or magazine.

Sidebar. A feature presented as a companion to a straight news report (or main magazine article) giving sidelights on human-interest aspects or sometimes elucidating just one aspect of the story.

Similar submission. See *parallel submission*.

Simultaneous submissions. Sending the same article, story or poem to several publishers at the same time. Some publishers refuse to consider such submissions. No simultaneous submissions should be made without stating the fact in your letter.

Slant. The approach or style of a story or article that will appeal to readers of a specific magazine. For example, a magazine may always use stories with an upbeat ending.

Slice-of-life vignette. A short fiction piece intended to realistically depict an interesting moment of everyday living.

Slides. Usually called transparencies by editors looking for color photographs.

Slush pile. The stack of unsolicited or misdirected manuscripts received by an editor or book publisher.

Software. Computer programs and related manuals.

Speculation. The editor agrees to look at the author's manuscript with no assurance that it will be bought.

Style. The way in which something is written—for example, short, punchy sentences or flowing narrative.

Subsidiary rights. All those rights, other than book publishing rights included in a book contract—such as paperback, book club, movie rights, etc.

Subsidy publisher. A book publisher who charges the author for the cost to typeset and print his book, the jacket, etc. as opposed to a royalty publisher who pays the author. .

Synopsis. A brief summary of a story, novel or play. As part of a book proposal, it is a comprehensive summary condensed in a page or page and a half, single-spaced. See also *outline*.

Tabloid. Newspaper format publication on about half the size of the regular newspaper page, such as the *National Enquirer*.

Tagline. A caption for a photo or a comment added to a filler.

Tearsheet. Page from a magazine or newspaper containing your printed story, article, poem or ad.

Trade. Either a hardcover or paperback book; subject matter frequently concerns a special interest. Books are directed toward the layperson rather than the professional.

Transparencies. Positive color slides; not color prints.

Treatment. Synopsis of a television or film script (40-60 pages for a 2-hour feature film or teleplay).

Unsolicited manuscript. A story, article, poem or book that an editor did not specifically ask to see.

User friendly. Easy to handle and use. Refers to computer hardware and software designed with the user in mind.

Vanity publisher. See *subsidy publisher*.

Word processor. A computer program, used in lieu of a typewriter, that allows for easy, flexible manipulation and output of printed copy.

Work-for-hire. See Copyright in the Minding the Details article.

YA. Young adult books.

Book Publishers Subject Index

This index will help you find publishers that consider books on specific subjects—the subjects you choose to write about. Remember that a publisher may be listed here under a general subject category such as Art and Architecture, while the company publishes *only* art history or how-to books. Be sure to consult each company's detailed individual listing, its book catalog and several of its books before you send your query or proposal. The page number of the detailed listing is provided for your convenience.

Fiction

Adventure. Aardvark 233; Advance 64; Advocacy 64; Atheneum Books For Young Readers 74; Avanyu 75; Avon 76; Avon Flare 76; Bantam 78; Bethel 80; Black Heron 258; Black Tie 258; Blizzard 214; Book Creations 271; British American 86; Burning Gate 87; Caitlin 216; Camelot 89; Carol 91; Cave 92; Clarion 96; Council for Indian Education 101; Dan River 103; Davenport, May 104; Dial Books For Young Readers 106; Down The Shore 259; Fine, Donald I. 112; Gryphon 120; HarperCollins 121; Hendrick-Long 123; Ican 243; Jacobs 132; K.I.P. Children's Books 134; Kar-Ben Copies 135; Literary Works 140; Little, Brown, Children's Book Division 140; Lodestar 141; Mancorp 246; Mayhaven 246; Mount Olive College 246; Mountaineers 151; New Victoria 155; North Country 247; O'Donnell Literary Services 247; Paradigm 248; Permanent/Second Chance 164; Pippin 167; Players 167; Presidio 170; Purple Finch 265; QED 249; Random House 173; Rising Tide 175; Saurie Island 179; Serendipity 180; Severn House 225; Shoestring 225; Sierra Club 181; Simon & Pierre 226; Soho 184; SouthPark 185; Star Song 187; Turnstone 227; Vandamere 203; Vista 250; Walker and Co. 205; Wayfinder 207; Whitman 208; Willowisp 210; Windflower 230; Zebra And Pinnacle 212.

Confession. Aardvark 233; British American 86; Carol 91; Dan River 103; O'Donnell Literary Services 247; Players 167; Random House 173.

Erotica. Asylum Arts 234; Black Tie 258; Blue Moon 83; Caradium 90; Circlet 96; Dan River 103; Ekstasis 218; Gay Sunshine and Leyland 115; HMS 219; Jacobs 132; Masquerade 146; Merry Men 263; New Falcon 246; New Victoria 155; O'Donnell Literary Services 247; Paradigm 248; Permeable 265; Rising Tide 175; Saurie Island 179; Serendipity 180; Singer Media 182; Spectrum 185; Vandamere 203; Women's 230; Zebra And Pinnacle 212.

Ethnic. Another Chicago 257; Arcade 72; Arsenal Pulp 214; Asian Humanities 74; Atheneum Books For Young Readers 74; Avalon 75; Avon Flare 76; Branden 85; Champion 93; Charlesbridge 93; China Books & Periodicals 94; Coffee House 98; Confluence 99; Coteau 217; Council for Indian Education 101; Cuff, Harry 217; Eastern Caribbean Institute 260; Ecco 108; Faber & Faber 110; Four Walls Eight Windows 114; Gay Sunshine and Leyland 115; Guernica 219; Herald Canada 219; Ican 243; Interlink 130; K.I.P. Children's Books 134; Kar-Ben Copies 135; Lincoln Springs 262; Literary Works 140; Lodestar 141; Mayhaven 246; Northland 156; Paradigm 248; Permanent/Second Chance 164; Players 167; QED 249; Serendipity 180; Soho 184; Spectrum 185; Spinsters Ink 186; Star Song 187; Third World 193; Turnstone 227; University of Illinois 199; Vesta 229; Weigl 229; White Pine 208.

Experimental. Asylum 234; Atheneum Books For Young Readers 74; Beach Holme 214; Black Heron 258; Blizzard 214; Blue Buddha 258; British American 86; Buddha Rose 236; Cacanadadada 215; China Books & Periodicals 94; Coach House 217; Dan River 103; Ekstasis 218; Faber & Faber 110; Four Walls Eight Windows 114; Gay Sunshine and Leyland Publications 115; Goose Lane 218; Jacobs 132; Lintel 263; Literary Works 140; McClelland & Stewart 221; New Falcon 246; O'Donnell Literary Services 247; Permeable 265; Players 167; QED 249; Random House 173; Rutgers University 176; Scots Plaid 266; Serendipity 180; Shoestring 225; Smith 183; Spectrum 185; Star Song 187; Turnstone 227; University of Illinois 199; Xenos 269; York 231.

Fantasy. Ace Science Fiction 63; Atheneum Books For Young Readers 74; Avon 76; Baen 77; Bantam 78; Blizzard 214; British American 86; Camelot 89; Carol 91; Circlet 96; Crossway 102; Dan River 103; DAW 104; Del Rey 105; Delta Sales 239; Dial Books For Young Readers 106; Fine, Donald I. 112; Gryphon 120; HarperCollins 121; HMS 219; Ican 243; Jacobs 132; K.I.P. Children's Books 134; Kar-Ben Copies 135; Literary Works 140; Little, Brown, Children's Book Division 140; Lodestar 141; Merry Men 263; Naiad 152; New Falcon 246; New Victoria 155; O'Donnell Literary Services 247; Overlook 160; Pippin 167; Players 167; QED 249; Random House 173; Rising Tide 175; Saurie Island 179; Severn House 225; Singer Media 182; Smith 183; Southwest Publishing of Arizona 185; TOR 195; TSR 196; Whitman 208; Windflower 230; Zebra And Pinnacle 212.

Feminist. Advocacy 64; Arsenal Pulp 214; Bantam 78; Black Sparrow 82; Black Tie 258; Blizzard 214; British American 86; Calyx 258; Champion 93; Circlet 96; Cleis 97; Coach House 217; Coteau 217; Firebrand 112; Four Walls Eight Windows 114; Goose Lane Editions 218; HMS 219; Interlink 130; Lincoln Springs 262; Literary Works 140; Little, Brown, Children's Book Division 140; Mercury 222; Naiad 152; O'Donnell Literary Services 247; Paradigm 248; Permeable 265; Rutgers University 176; Serendipity 180; Smith 183; Soho 184; Spectrum 185; Star Song 187; Third World 193; Turnstone 227; Vista 250; Women's 230.

Gay/Lesbian. Alyson 66; Arsenal Pulp 214; Bantam 78; Black Sparrow 82; Blizzard 214; Calyx 258; Caradium 90; Champion 93; Circlet 96; Cleis 97; Coach House 217; Firebrand 112; Gay Sunshine and Leyland 115; HMS 219; Literary Works 140; Little, Brown, Children's Book Division 140; Madwoman 263; Masquerade 146; Naiad 152; New Falcon 246; O'Donnell Literary Services 247; Paradigm 248; Permeable 265; Rising Tide 175; Rutgers University 176; Serendipity 180; Spectrum 185; Spinsters Ink 186; Starbooks 250; Women's 230.

Gothic. Atheneum Books For Young Readers 74; Dan River 103; Ekstasis 218; HarperCollins 121; Ican 243; Lincoln Springs 262; Mayhaven 246; O'Donnell Literary 247; Purple Finch 265; TSR 196; Zebra And Pinnacle 212.

Hi-Lo. Afcom 65; China Books & Periodicals 94; Simon & Pierre 226; Singer Media 182.

Historical. Aardvark 233; Advocacy 64; Arcade 72; Archives 73; Atheneum Books For Young Readers 74; Augsburg 75; Avanyu 75; Avon 76; Bantam 78; Beach Holme 214; Berkley 80; Book Creations 271; Branden 85; Brassey's 85; British American 86; Caitlin 216; Capra 90; Carolrhoda 91; Cave 92; Center For Western Studies 237; Chapel Street 259; China Books & Periodicals 94; Council for Indian Education 101; Cuff, Harry 217; Dan River 103; Dial Books For Young Readers 106; Down The Shore 259; Ecco 108; Éditions La Liberté 218; Fine, Donald I. 112; Friends United 115; Gay Sunshine and Leyland 115; Goose Lane 218; HarperCollins 121; Harvest House 122; Hendrick-Long 123; Herald Canada 219; HMS 219; Horseshoe 261; Howells House 126; Ican 243; Kar-Ben Copies 135; Leisure Books 138; Lincoln Springs 262; Literary Works 140; Little, Brown, Children's Book Division 140; Lodestar 141; McClelland & Stewart 221; Markgraf 263; Mayhaven 246; Nautical & Aviation 153; New England 154; New Victoria 155; O'Donnell Literary Services 247; Pelican 163; Permanent/Second Chance 164; Permeable 265; Pineapple 167; Pippin 167; Players 167; Presidio 170; Purple Finch 265; QED 249; Random House 173; Republic of Texas 174; Rising Tide 175; Rutgers University 176; Saurie Island 179; Scots Plaid 266; Serendipity Systems 180; Servant 180; Severn House 225; Sierra Club 181; Signature 182; Soho 184; Star Song 187; Sunflower University 250; Third World 193; TOR 195; Tyndale House 196; Victory House 250; Walker and Co. 205; Wayfinder 207; Whitman 208; Wilderness Adventure 209; Windflower 230; Ye Galleon 251; Zebra And Pinnacle 212.

Horror. Aardvark 233; Atheneum Books For Young Readers 74; Bantam 78; Black Tie 258; British American 86; Carol 91; Cool Hand Communications 100; Dan River 103; Fine, Donald I. 112; Gryphon 120; HMS 219; New Falcon 246; O'Donnell Literary Services 247; Players 167; Random House 173; Rising Tide 175; Serendipity 180; Severn House 225; TOR 195; Zebra And Pinnacle 212.

Humor. Aardvark 233; Acme 256; American Atheist 68; Arcade 72; Arsenal Pulp 214; Atheneum Books For Young Readers 74; Avon Flare 76; British American 86; Caitlin 216; Camelot 89; Carol 91; Catbird 92; Center 93; Clarion 96; Coteau 217; Council for Indian Education 101; Cuff, Harry 217; Dan River 103; Delta Sales 239; E.M. 259; Fine, Donald I. 112; Herald Canada 219; HMS 219; Howells House 126; Ican 243; Jacobs 132; Key Porter 221; Literary Works 140; Little, Brown, Children's Book Division 140; Lodestar 141; McClelland & Stewart 221; Mancorp 246; Mayhaven 246; New Victoria 155; O'Donnell Literary Services 247; Paradigm 248; Pelican 163; Permanent/Second Chance 164; Piccadilly 166; Pippin 167; Players 167; Rising Tide 175; Saurie Island 179; Serendipity 180; Sevgo 249; Signature 182; SJL 182; Star Song 187; TSR 196; Turnstone 227;

Vandamere 203; Wayfinder 207; Whitman 208; Willowisp 210; Zebra And Pinnacle 212.

Juvenile. Aardvark 233; Advance 64; Advocacy 64; Afcom 65; African American Images 65; American Education 69; Archway Paperbacks/Minstrel Books 73; Atheneum Books For Young Readers 74; Augsburg 75; Bantam 78; Blizzard 214; Blue Heron 83; Boyds Mills 85; Camelot 89; Carolrhoda 91; Chapel Street 259; Christian Education 95; Christian 95; Chronicle 95; Cobblehill 98; Consortium 238; Coteau 217; Council for Indian Education 101; Crossway 102; Denison & Co., T.S. 106; Down East 107; Down The Shore 259; E.M. 259; Éditions La Liberté 218; Ekstasis 218; Farrar, Straus and Giroux 111; Friends United 115; Great Quotations 118; Grosset & Dunlap 119; Harcourt Brace 121; Hendrick-Long 123; Herald 123; Herald Canada 219; HMS 219; Houghton Mifflin 125; Ican 243; Ideals Children's Books 128; Interlink 130; Jacobs 132; Jones University, Bob 133; K.I.P. Children's Books 134; Lee & Low 262; Lerner 138; Literary Works 140; Little, Brown, Children's Book Division 140; Lodestar 141; Lorimer 221; Lothrop, Lee & Shepard 143; Lucas-Evans 274; McClanahan 274; McClelland & Stewart 221; Markowski International 274; Mayhaven 246; Mega-Books of New York 274; Morrow Junior Books 151; Northland 156; O'Donnell Literary Services 247; Orca 223; Orchard 158; Owen, Richard C. 160; Pacific Educational 223; Peachtree 163; Peel 265; Peguis 223; Pelican 163; Philomel 166; Piccadilly 166; Pippin 167; Pleasant 168; Polychrome 169; Purple Finch 265; Roussan 225; St. Paul Books & Media 177; Seacoast of New England 266; Serendipity Systems 180; Sevgo 249; Singer Media 182; SJL 182; Soundprints 184; Speech Bin, The 186; Spheric 267; Standard 186; Star Song 187; Sunbelt Media 189; Tambourine 191; Third World 193; Thistledown 226; Tidewater 194; Tundra 227; Victor 204; Walker 205; Weigl Educational 229; Weiss Associates, Daniel 276; Whitman 208; Willowisp 210; Windflower 230.

Literary. Aardvark 233; Another Chicago 257; Applezaba 72; Arcade 72; Archives 73; Arsenal Pulp 214; Asylum Arts 234; Bantam 78; Black Heron 258; Black Sparrow 82; Black Tie 258; Blizzard 214; Blue Buddha 258; British American 86; Buddha Rose 236; Burning Gate 87; Cacanadadada 215; Cadmus 258; Calyx 258; Capra 90; Carol 91; Catbird 92; Cave 92; Center 93; Champion 93; China Books & Periodicals 94; Cleis 97; Coach House 217; Coffee House 98; Confluence 99; Coteau 217; Creative Arts 238; Crossing, The 102; Dan River 103; Down The Shore 259; E.M. 259; Eastern Caribbean Institute 260; Ecco, The 108; Éditions La Liberté 218; Ekstasis 218; Eriksson, Paul S. 110; Fine, Donald I. 112; Four Walls Eight Windows 114; Goose Lane 218; Great Quotations 118; Hampton Roads 241; HarperCollins 121; Heaven Bone 261; Herald Canada 219; HMS 219; Hounslow 220; Howells House 126; Ican 243; Jackson, Hart & Leslie 262; Knopf 135; Lawrence, Seymour 137; Lincoln Springs 262; Literary Works 140; Little, Brown 140; Longstreet 142; Louisiana State University 143; McClelland & Stewart 221; Mancorp 246; Masquerade 146; Mercury, The 222; Mount Olive College 246; Netherlandic 222; New Rivers 155; NeWest 222; Nightshade 264; O'Donnell Literary Services 247; Orca 223; Overlook, The 160; Peachtree 163; Permanent/Second Chance 164; Permeable 265; Pineapple 167; Puckerbrush 265; Purple Finch 265; QED 249; Random House Of Canada 224; Rising Tide 175; Rock, Andrew 275; Rutgers University 176; Sand River 266; Saurie Island 179; Scots Plaid 266; Serendipity Systems 180; Silver Mountain 267; Simon & Pierre 226; Smith, The 183; Soho 184; Southern Methodist University 185; Spectrum 185; Star Song 187; Stone Bridge 267; Third World 193; Thistledown 226; Three Continents 194; Turnstone 227; UCLA-American Indian Studies Center 268; University of Arkansas 198; University of North Texas 201; University of Pittsburgh 201; Vesta Publications 229; White Pine 208; Willowisp 210; Zebra And Pinnacle 212; Zoland 212.

Mainstream/Contemporary. Aardvark 233; Academy Chicago 62; Arcade 72; Atheneum Books For Young Readers 74; Avon Flare 76; Bantam 78; Beach Holme 214; Berkley 80; Blizzard 214; Branden 85; British American 86; Burning Gate 87; Caitlin 216; Camelot 89; Capra 90; Citadel 96; Confluence 99; Cool Hand Communications 100; Coteau 217; Crossway 102; Cuff, Harry 217; Dan River 103; Delancey 259; Dickens 259; Down East 107; Down The Shore 259; Dutton 108; E.M. 259; Edicones Universal 239; Éditions La Liberté 218; Ekstasis 218; Faber & Faber 110; Fawcett Juniper 112; Fine, Donald I. 112; Great Quotations 118; Hampton Roads 241; HMS 219; Howells House 126; Ican 243; International 131; Jackson, Hart & Leslie 262; Key Porter 221; Lerner 138; Lincoln Springs 262; Literary Works 140; Little, Brown 140; Lodestar 141; Longstreet 142; McClelland & Stewart 221; Mancorp 246; Mayhaven 246; Mercury 222; Morrow, William 151; Norton, W.W. 157; O'Donnell Literary Services 247; Orca 223; Peachtree 163; Permanent/Second Chance 164; Perspectives 165; Pineapple 167; Players 167; QED 249; Random House 173; Rising Tide 175; Rock Andrew 275; Scots Plaid 266; Serendipity 180; Severn House 225; Sierra Club 181; Silver Mountain 267; Simon & Pierre 226; Simon & Schuster 182; Singer Media 182; Soho 184; Spectrum 185; Star Song 187; Sunbelt Media 189; Third World 193; Turnstone 227; Twin Peaks

196; University of Illinois 199; University of Iowa 199; University of Mississippi 203; Vandamere 203; Villard 204; Vista 250; Ward Hill 206; Willowisp 210; Zebra And Pinnacle 212.

Military/War. Naval Institute 154; Presidio 170; Sunflower University 250.

Multicultural. Charlesbridge 93; Guernica 219; Lee & Low 262; Lerner 138; Lodestar 141; Pippin 167; Polychrome 169; Weigl Educational 229.

Mystery. Aardvark 233; Academy Chicago 62; Accord 63; Arcade 72; Atheneum Books For Young Readers 74; Avalon 75; Avon 76; Avon Flare 76; Baker 77; Bantam 78; Berkley 80; Blizzard 214; Book Creations 271; British American 86; Camelot 89; Carol 91; Cave 92; Chapel Street 259; Clarion 96; Cool Hand Communications 100; Council for Indian Education 101; Countryman, The 101; Dan River 103; Delta Sales 239; Dial Books For Young Readers 106; Dickens 259; Doubleday 107; Earth-Love 259; Fine, Donald I. 112; Four Walls Eight Windows 114; Gay Sunshine and Leyland 115; Great Quotations 118; Gryphon 120; HarperCollins 121; Harvest House 122; Hendrick-Long 123; HMS 219; Ican 243; Jacobs 132; K.I.P. 134; Lincoln Springs 262; Little, Brown, Children's Book Division 140; Lodestar 141; McClelland & Stewart 221; Mayhaven 246; Mega 274; Mysterious, The 152; Naiad, The 152; New Victoria 155; North Country 247; Paradigm 248; Permanent/Second Chance, The 164; Pippin 167; Players 167; Pocket 168; Presidio 170; Purple Finch 265; QED 249; Random House 173; Rising Tide 175; Rock & Co., Andrew 275; Saurie Island 179; Scholastic 180; Serendipity 180; Severn House 225; Simon & Pierre 226; Singer Media 182; Soho 184; Turnstone 227; Vandamere 203; Victory House 250; Vista 250; Walker 205; Wayfinder 207; Whitman 208; Willowisp 210; Zebra And Pinnacle 212.

Occult. Archives 73; Dan River 103; Hampton Roads 241; Llewellyn 141; New Falcon 246; Rising Tide 175; Saurie Island 179; Singer Media 182; Zebra And Pinnacle 212.

Picture Books. Advocacy 64; American Education 69; Blizzard 214; Center 93; Charlesbridge 93; Chronicle 95; Cobblehill 98; Council for Indian Education 101; Down The Shore 259; Farrar, Straus and Giroux 111; Farrar, Straus and Giroux 111; Gibson, The C.R. 116; Gold'n' Honey 117; Great Quotations 118; Greey De Pencier 273; Grosset & Dunlap 119; Harcourt Brace 121; Herald Canada 219; Highsmith 125; Ideals 128; Interlink 130; Jacobs 132; Key Porter 221; Literary Works 140; Little, Brown, Children's Book Division 140; Lodestar 141; Lothrop, Lee & Shepard 143; Lucas-Evans 274; McClanahan 274; Markowski International 274; Mayhaven 246; O'Donnell Literary Services 247; Orca 223; Orchard 158; Owen, Richard C. 160; Peel Productions 265; Philomel 166; Pippin 167; Polychrome 169; Singer Media 182; Tambourine 191; Third World 193; Tundra 227; Unity 197; Warren 206; Wayfinder 207; Weiss, Daniel 276; Whitman 208; Willowisp 210.

Plays. Anchorage 71; Asylum Arts 234; Blizzard 214; Coteau 217; Dan River 103; Drama 107; Eastern Caribbean Institute 260; Ecco, The 108; Ekstasis 218; French, Samuel 114; HMS 219; Ican 243; Jacobs 132; Literary Works 140; Meriwether 148; Mount Olive College 246; Peel Productions 265; Players 167; Playwrights Canada 224; Scots Plaid 266; Serendipity 180; Simon & Pierre 226; Spectrum 185; Tambra 267; Third World 193.

Poetry. Black Sparrow 82; Acme 256; Adastra 256; Ahsahta 257; Applezaba 72; Asian Humanities 74; Asylum Arts 234; Black Bear 258; Black Hat 235; Black Tie 258; Blizzard 214; Blue Dolphin 82; Boyds Mills 85; British American 86; Buddha Rose 236; Cadmus 258; Caitlin, The 216; Calyx 258; Champion 93; Christopher House, The 237; Cleveland State University Poetry Center 97; Council for Indian Education 101; Daniel, John 103; Dante University Of America 103; Dusty Dog 259; Ecco, The 108; Ecrits Des Forges 217; Edicones 239; Ford-Brown 260; Gaff 260; Guernica 219; Heaven Bone 261; High Plains 124; Intertext 262; Inverted-A 262; Jacobs 132; James, Alice 262; Lintel 263; Louisiana State University 143; Mercury, The 222; Mid-List 263; Morrow and , William 151; Mortal 263; Mount Olive College 246; New Rivers 155; Nightshade 264; Orchises 159; Papier-Mache 264; Paragon House 248; Pennywhistle 164; Puckerbrush 265; QED 249; Scots Plaid 266; Sheep Meadow, The 181; Signature 182; Simon & Pierre 226; Smith, The 183; Sono Nis 226; Spectrum 185; Spinsters Ink 186; Star 187; Starbooks 250; Still Waters 188; Texas Tech University 192; Thistledown 226; Three Continents 194; Turnstone 227; UCLA-American Indian Studies Center 268; University of Arkansas, The 198; University of California 198; University of Iowa 199; University of Massachusetts 199; University of North Texas 201; University of Pittsburgh 201; University of Scranton 202; Vehicule 229; Vesta 229; Vista 268; Wake Forest University 205; White Pine 208; Whole Notes 269; Wolsak And Wynn 230; Xenos 269.

Regional. Beach Holme 214; Blair, John F. 82; Borealis 214; Cuff, Harry 217; Down East Books 107; Eastern Caribbean Institute 260; Faber & Faber 110; Interlink 130; Nightshade 264; Northland 156; Peachtree 163; Pelican 163; Philomel 166; Sunstone 190; Texas Christian University 192; Thistledown 226; Tidewater 194; University of New England 203; Vista 268; Windflower 230.

Religious. A.R.E. 61; ACTA 63; Archives 73; Barbour 78; Bethel 80; Bookcraft 84; Branden 85; Bridge 236; British American 86; Christian Education 95; Christian 95; Crossway 102; Friends United 115; Gibson, The C.R. 116; Gold'n' Honey 117; Harvest House 122; Hensley, Virgil W. 123; Herald 123; Herald Canada 219; HMS 219; Ican 243; Kar-Ben Copies 135; Literary Works 140; Mancorp 246; Mount Olive College 246; Nelson Publishers, Thomas 154; New Falcon 246; O'Donnell Literary Services 247; Players 167; St. Paul 177; Shaw, Harold 181; Signature 182; Southwest of Arizona 185; Standard 186; Star 187; Star Song 187; Tyndale House 196; Unity 197; Victor 204; Victory House 250; Windflower Communications 230.

Romance. Aardvark 233; Atheneum Books For Young Readers 74; Audio Entertainment 75; Avalon 75; Avon 76; Avon Flare 76; Bantam 78; Barbour 78; Berkley, The 80; Book Creations 271; Branden 85; British American 86; Dan River 103; Dial Books For Young Readers 106; Doubleday 107; Herald Canada 219; HMS 219; Ican 243; Jacobs 132; Leisure 138; Lincoln Springs 262; Mancorp 246; Mayhaven 246; Meteor 148; New Victoria 155; North Country 247; O'Donnell Literary Services 247; Paradigm 248; Players 167; Pocket Books 168; Purple Finch 265; Rising Tide 175; Saurie Island 179; Scholastic 180; Severn House 225; Silhouette 182; Singer Media 182; Walker 205; Willowisp 210; Zebra And Pinnacle 212.

Science Fiction. Aardvark 233; Ace Science Fiction 63; Atheneum Books For Young Readers 74; Avon 76; Baen 77; Bantam 78; Black Heron 258; Blizzard 214; Carol 91; Circlet 96; Crossway 102; Dan River 103; DAW 104; Del Rey 105; Delta Sales 239; Ekstasis 218; Fine, Donald I. 112; Gay Sunshine and Leyland 115; Gryphon 120; HarperCollins 121; HMS 219; Ican 243; Inverted-A 262; Jacobs 132; Little, Brown, Children's Book Division 140; Lodestar 141; Mayhaven 246; Merry Men 263; New Falcon 246; New Victoria 155; O'Donnell Literary Services 247; Paradigm 248; Permeable 265; Players 167; Pocket Books 168; Purple Finch 265; QED 249; Saurie Island 179; Serendipity Systems 180; Severn House 225; Shoestring 225; SJL 182; Smith,The 183; Swan-Raven 190; TOR 195; TSR 196; Walker 205; Willowisp 210.

Short Story Collections. Aardvark 233; Another Chicago 257; Applezaba 72; Arcade 72; Arsenal Pulp 214; Asylum Arts 234; Black Sparrow 82; Blizzard 214; Blue Buddha 258; British American 86; Cacanadadada 215; Caitlin, The 216; Calyx 258; Capra 90; Center For Western Studies, The 237; Center 93; Champion 93; Chapel Street 259; Chronicle 95; Circlet 96; Coach House 217; Coffee House 98; Confluence 99; Coteau 217; Council for Indian Education 101; Dan River 103; Daniel, John 103; Down The Shore 259; E.M. 259; Ecco, The 108; Éditions La Liberté 218; Ekstasis 218; Faber & Faber 110; Fall Creek 260; Gay Sunshine and Leyland 115; Gibson, The C.R. 116; Goose Lane 218; Herald Canada 219; HMS 219; Ican 243; Indiana Historical Society 262; Interlink Group 130; International 131; Inverted-A 262; Jacobs 132; Lincoln Springs 262; Literary Works 140; Little, Brown, Children's Book Division 140; Louisiana State University 143; McClelland & Stewart 221; Mercury, The 222; Naiad, The 152; Netherlandic 222; New Rivers 155; NeWest 222; O'Donnell Literary Services 247; Permeable 265; Purple Finch 265; QED 249; Saurie Island 179; Scots Plaid 266; Serendipity Systems 180; Severn House 225; Simon & Pierre 226; Southern Methodist University 185; Spectrum 185; Star 187; Still Waters 188; Third World 193; TSR 196; Turnstone 227; University of Arkansas, The 198; University of Illinois 199; University of Missouri 200; University of North Texas 201; Vista 250; White Pine 208; Willowisp 210; Women's 230; Zebra And Pinnacle 212; Zoland 212.

Suspense. Aardvark 233; Accord Communications 63; Arcade 72; Atheneum Books For Young Readers 74; Avon 76; Avon Flare 76; Bantam 78; Berkley 80; Bethel 80; British American 86; Camelot 89; Clarion 96; Dial Books For Young Readers 106; Doubleday 107; Fine, Donald I. 112; Gryphon 120; HarperCollins 121; HMS 219; Hounslow 220; Ican 243; Ivy League 262; Jacobs 132; Little, Brown, Children's Book Division 140; Lodestar 141; Mayhaven 246; Mysterious, The 152; North Country 247; O'Donnell Literary Services 247; Paradigm 248; Permanent/Second Chance 164; Pippin 167; Players 167; Pocket 168; Purple Finch 265; QED 249; Random House 173; Rising Tide 175; Saurie Island 179; Serendipity Systems 180; Severn House 225; Singer Media 182; Soho 184; TOR 195; Vandamere 203; Vista 250; Walker 205; Willowisp 210; Zebra And Pinnacle 212.

Western. Atheneum Books For Young Readers 74; Avalon 75; Avanyu 75; Avon 76; Bantam 78; Berkley 80; Book Creations 271; Center For Western Studies, The 237; Council for Indian Education 101; Creative Arts 238; Dan River 103; Doubleday 107; Evans 110; Fine, Donald I. 112; HarperCollins 121; Hendrick-Long 123; Ican 243; Jacobs 132; Lodestar 141; Mayhaven 246; New Victoria 155; O'Donnell Literary Services 247; Players 167; Pocket 168; Regnery 174; Republic Of Texas 174; Serendipity 180; Sunflower University 250; Walker 205; Zebra And Pinnacle 212.

Young Adult. Aardvark 233; Advocacy 64; Archway/Minstrel 73; Augsburg 75; Bantam 78; Beach

Holme 214; Bethel 80; Blizzard 214; Blue Heron 83; Book Creations 271; Boyds Mills 85; Caitlin, The 216; Chapel Street 259; Cobblehill 98; Crossway 102; Eastern Caribbean Institute 260; Éditions La Liberté 218; Farrar, Straus and Giroux 111; Fawcett Juniper 112; Great Quotations 118; Harcourt Brace 121; Herald 123; Herald Canada 219; HMS 219; Houghton Mifflin 125; Ican 243; Jones University, Bob 133; Lerner 138; Little, Brown, Children's Book Division 140; Lodestar Books 141; Lorimer 221; Lucas-Evans 274; McClelland & Stewart 221; McElderry, Margaret K. 144; Mayhaven 246; Mega-Books of New York 274; Morrow, William 151; Nelson, Thomas 154; O'Donnell Literary Services 247; Orchard 158; Pacific Educational 223; Philomel 166; Polychrome 169; Purple Finch 265; Roussan 225; Scholastic 180; Serendipity 180; Simon & Pierre 226; Singer Media 182; Spheric House 267; Star 187; Star Song 187; Tambourine 191; Texas Christian University 192; Third World 193; Thistledown 226; Tundra 227; Ward Hill 206; Weiss, Daniel 276; Willowisp 210; Women's 230; Zebra And Pinnacle 212.

Nonfiction

Agriculture/Horticulture. Agritech 257; Global Professional 116; Key Porter 221; Maupin House 246; O'Donnell Literary Services 247; Revisionist 175; University Of Idaho 199; Advance 64; American 70; Bright Mountain 258; Camden House 216; Camino 89; China Books & Periodicals 94; Godine, David R. 117; Hartley & Marks 121; Haworth, The 122; HMS 219; Hoard & Sons, W.D. 261; Interstate 243; Iowa State University 132; Kumarian 244; Lyons & Burford 144; McClelland & Stewart 221; Maupin House 263; Mayhaven 246; Michigan State University 149; Pruett 171; Purdue University 172; Ross 266; Stipes 188; Story Communications/Garden Way 189; Sunflower University 250; Timber 194; University of Alaska 198; University of Nebraska 200; University of North Texas 201; Warren 206; Weidner & Sons 207; Whitman 208; Windward 210; Woodbridge 211.

Alternative Lifestyles. Beach Holme 214; Luramedia 144; Sterling 188.

Americana. Aardvark 233; Advance 64; Agritech 257; Alaska Northwest 65; Ancestry 71; Atheneum Books For Young Readers 74; Avanyu 75; B&B 77; Bantam 78; Berwick 80; Blair, John F. 82; Boston Mills, The 215; Bowling Green State University Popular 84; Branden 85; Brevet 85; Camino 89; Capstone 90; Carol 91; Cave 92; Caxton Printers, The 92; Christopher The 237; Clarion 96; Clark, Arthur H. 238; Clear Light 97; Confluence 99; Creative 102; Denali, The 106; Down East 107; Down The Shore 259; Ecco, The 108; Éditions La Liberté 218; Elliott & Clark 109; Epicenter 109; Eriksson, Paul S. 110; Faber & Faber 110; Filter 240; Fox Chapel 114; Friedman, Michael 272; Glenbridge 116; Globe Pequot, The 117; Godine, David R. 117; Golden West Books 117; Greey De Pencier 273; Hancock House 121; HarperCollins 121; Herald 124; Heyday 124; High Plains 124; HMS 219; Hope 242; Howells House 126; International 131; Jefferson University, Thomas 262; Jordan Enterprises 244; JSA 273; Ketz Agency, Louise B. 273; Laing Communications 274; Layla 274; Lehigh University 138; Lerner 138; Lexikos 138; Library Research 245; Lincoln Springs 262; Little, Brown, Children's Book Division 140; Longstreet 142; Lorien House 263; Lyons & Burford 144; McDonald & Woodward 144; McFarland 144; Mayhaven 246; Media Publishing/Midgard 147; Meyerbooks 263; Monitor 150; Mosaic Miniature 263; Mountain 151; Mustang 152; Mystic Seaport Museum 263; New England, The 154; Nova Science 157; O'Donnell Literary Services 247; Oregon Historical Society 159; Pacific 160; Pelican 163; Peter Pauper 165; PHB 165; Picton 166; Pleasant 168; Pruett 171; Purdue University 172; Ragged Mountain 173; Reference 266; Revisionist 175; Rutgers University 176; Sachem Associates 276; Sand River 266; Sarpedon 178; Schiffer 179; Shoestring 225; Signature 182; Smith, Gibbs 183; Spectrum 185; Sunbelt Media 189; Sunflower University 250; Texas Christian University 192; Texas Tech University 192; University Of Idaho 199; University of Alaska 198; University of Arkansas, The 198; University of Illinois 199; University of Nebraska 200; University of North Carolina, The 200; University of North Texas 201; University of Oklahoma 201; University of Pennsylvania 201; University of Tennessee, The 202; University of Mississippi 203; University of New England 203; Utah State University 203; Vandamere 203; Vesta 229; Washington State University 206; Wayfinder 207; Webb Research Group 251; Wieser & Wieser 276; Wilderness Adventure 209; Ye Galleon 251.

Animals. Agritech 257; Alpine 233; American Education 69; Archway Paperbacks/Minstrel Books 73; Atheneum Books For Young Readers 74; Barron's Educational Series 79; Beaver Pond 234; Bergh 235; Blackbirch 82; Boxwood, The 236; Camden House 216; Canadian Plains Research Center 216; Capra 90; Capstone 90; Carol 91; Carolrhoda 91; Cave 92; Charles, The 237; Christopher 237; Creative Spark, The 272; Éditions La Liberté 218; Eriksson, Paul S. 110; Faber & Faber 110; Friedman, Michael 272; Half Halt 120; Harmony House 242; HarperCollins 121; Hay House

Of Canada 224; Regnery 174; Revisionist 175; Rhombus 266; Rutgers University 176; Rutledge Hill 176; St. Paul Books & Media 177; Sandlapper 178; Sarpedon 178; Schirmer 1 ; Scots Plaid 266; Sevgo 249; Shoestring 225; Signature 182; Simon & Schuster 182; Simon & Pie 226; Singer Media 182; Sky Publishing 183; Smith, Gibbs 183; Soho 184; Sono Nis 226; Spect n 185; Star 187; Star Song 187; Sunbelt Media 189; Sunflower University 250; Taylor 191; T th Avenue Editions 276; Texas State Historical 192; Thunder's Mouth 194; Times 195; Titan 7; Twayne 196; 2M 276; Umbrella 227; United Church (UCPH), The 228; University Of Idaho 19 University of Alabama 197; University of Alaska 198; University of Alberta, The 228; University c Arkansas, The 198; University of Illinois 199; University of Massachusetts 199; University of Ne ska 200; University of Nevada 200; University of New Mexico 200; University of North Texas 201; iversity of Pennsylvania 201; University of Pittsburgh 201; University of Kentucky 202; University Missis- sippi 203; University of New England 203; Utah State University 203; Vandamere 203 anwell 228; Vehicule 229; Vesta 229; Victory House 250; Virginia State Library and Archives 2 Vista 250; Walker 205; Ward Hill 206; Washington State University 206; Watts, Franklin 206; W inder 207; Weatherhill 251; Webb Research Group 251; Western Book/Journal 251; Western ager 269; Whitecap 230; Whitman 208; Wilderness Adventure 209; Wiley & Sons, John 209; Win wer 230; Women's 230; WRS 212; Ye Galleon 251; Zebra And Pinnacle 212; Zoland 212; Zon van 212; Amadeus 67.

Business/Economics. Abbott, Langer & Associates 61; Adams, Bob 64; Adams-Blake 64; gis 257; Afcom 65; Allen 66; Almar 66; Amacom Books 67; America West 67; American Hospit 0; American 234; American 70; Amherst Media 70; Amigadget 257; Ashgate 234; ASQC 74; A e- neum Books For Young Readers 74; Austin & Winfield 75; Avery 76; Avon 76; Bantam 78; B i- cade 78; Barron's Educational Series 79; Benjamin, The 271; Berkley 80; Betterway 81; BNA Bonus 84; Brevet 85; Brighton 86; British American 86; Broadview 215; Brookings Institution Burning Gate 87; Business & Legal Reports 87; Business McGraw-Hill 88; Cambridge Univers 89; Canadian Plains Research Center 216; Caradium 90; Career, The 90; Carol 91; Cato 92; Cent For Afro-American Studies 259; China Books & Periodicals 94; Christopher 237; Cleaning Consu tant Services 238; Computer Technology Research 99; Consultant, The 100; Contemporary 100 Davidson, Harlan 104; Dearborn Financial 105; Delta Sales 239; Desktop Grafx 272; Dimensions & Directions 272; Drama 107; East Coast 108; Eastern Caribbean Institute 260; Eastwind 239; Eckert, J.K. 272; Eriksson, Paul S. 110; Facts On File 111; Fairleigh Dickinson University 111; Formac 218; Forum 114; Giniger, The K S 272; Glenbridge 116; Global Professional 116; Globe Pequot, The 117; GMS 261; Golden Eagle 241; Great Quotations 118; HarperCollins 121; Harvard Common, The 121; Hastings House 122; Haworth, The 122; Hay House 122; HMS 219; Hounslow 220; Howells House 126; HRD 126; Humdinger 127; Ican 243; ILR 128; Industrial 129; Insight 130; International Foundation Of Employee Benefit Plans 130; International Information Associ- ates 130; International 131; Iowa State University 132; Jackson, Hart & Leslie 262; Jacobs 132; Jain 133; Jist Works 133; Ketz Agency, Louise B. 273; Key Porter 221; Kodansha America 136; Kumarian 244; Laing Communications 274; Lang, Peter 244; Larksdale 245; LAWCO 262; Lerner 138; Lexington 139; Library Research Associates 245; Lifetime Books 139; Locust Hill 141; Lone Pine 221; Longman 142; Lorimer, James 221; Lucent 143; McClelland & Stewart 221; McFarland 144; McGuinn & McGuire 145; Macmillan Canada 222; Mancorp 246; Markowski International 274; Menasha Ridge 275; Metamorphous 148; Michigan State University 149; Mid-List 263; Mosaic Miniature 263; National 153; National Textbook 153; Neal-Schuman 154; Nova Science 157; Noyes Data 157; NTC 157; Oceana 157; O'Donnell Literary Services 247; Oryx 160; Pace University 264; Paradigm 162; Pax 265; Pelican 163; Peterson's 165; Pfeiffer 165; Piccadilly 166; Pilot 167; PMN 248; Policy Studies Organization 169; Precept 169; Prentice-Hall Canada 224; Prima Publishing 170; Probus 170; PSI Research 172; Publicom 275; Rainbow 173; Random House 173; Regnery 174; Revisionist 175; Rock, Andrew 275; Ross 176; Ross 266; Roxbury 176; Schenkman 249; Self- Counsel 225; Singer Media 182; SJL 182; Sourcebooks 184; South End 184; Sterling 188; Stipes 188; Stone Bridge 267; Success 189; Sulzburger & Graham 189; Sunbelt Media 189; Sunflower University 250; TAB 190; Technical Analysis of Stocks & Commodities 267; Ten Speed 191; Texas A&M University 192; Times 195; Trend Book Division 196; Twin Peaks 196; University of Pennsyl- vania 201; University of Pittsburgh 201; Verso 229; VGM Career Horizons 204; Vista 250; Walch, J. Weston 205; Walker 205; Washington State University 206; Weatherhill 251; Weidner & Sons 207; Wheatley 276; Wiley & Sons, John 209; Wilshire 210; Windsor 210; Zebra And Pinnacle 212.

Child Guidance/Parenting. A.R.E. 61; Active Parenting 64; Advance Corproation 64; Avery 76; Baker 77; Bantam 78; Barricade 78; Barron's Educational Series 79; Blue Bird 82; British American

86; Cambridge Educational 88; Camino 89; Career 90; Carol 91; Child Welfare League Of America 94; Cline/Fay Institute 98; College Board, The 98; Consortium 238; Creative Spark, The 272; Deaconess 105; Discipleship Resources 107; Distinctive 107; Éditions La Liberté 218; Fisher 113; Focus on the Family 113; Free Spirit 260; Gallaudet University 115; Gardner 240; Great Quotations 118; Gylantic 120; Hampton Roads 241; Harvard Common, The 121; Harvest House 122; Hensley, Virgil W. 123; Herald Canada 219; HMS 219; Home Education 125; Hope 242; Hounslow 220; Human Services Institute 126; Insight 130; Interlink 130; Jordan Enterprises 244; Lamppost 274; Lawrence, Merloyd 137; Lexington 139; Lifetime 139; Luramedia 144; McClelland & Stewart 221; Marketscope 146; Marlor 146; Mayfield 147; Meadowbrook 147; Mills & Sanderson 149; National 153; Neal-Schuman 154; New Hope 154; O'Donnell Literary Services 247; Our Child 264; Parenting 162; Peterson's 165; Phi Delta Kappa Educational Foundation 165; Publicom 275; Purple Finch 265; Rock, Andrew 275; St. Paul Books & Media 177; Sidran, The 181; Singer Media 182; Spheric House 267; Sulzburger & Graham 189; Taylor 191; Ten Speed 191; 2M Communications 276; Vandamere 203; Victor 204; Volcano 268; Vortex Communications 268; Walker 205; Warren 206; Weidner & Sons 207; Westport 207; Wheetley 276; Wiley & Sons, John 209; Williamson 209; WRS 212.

Coffee Table Book. Aardvark 233; American Media 234; Benjamin 235; Bentley, Robert 80; Berwick 80; Blizzard 214; Bonus 84; Brassey's 85; Bridge 236; Canadian Plains Research Center 216; Caxton Printers 92; Center For Western Studies, The 237; China Books & Periodicals 94; Chronicle 95; Clear Light 97; Down The Shore 259; Dundurn 217; Ecco, The 108; Elliott & Clark 109; Epicenter 109; Formac 218; Friedman, Michael 272; Giniger, The K S 272; Godine, David R. 117; Harmony House 242; Hastings 122; Herald Canada 219; Hounslow 220; Howells House 126; Ideals 128; Imagine 128; Interlink 130; Jacobs 132; Judaica 262; Key Porter 221; Laing Communications 274; Lark 137; Larksdale 245; Layla Productions 274; Lexikos 138; Longstreet 142; McClelland & Stewart 221; McDonald & Woodward 144; Magicimage Filmbooks 246; Mayhaven 246; Minnesota Historical Society 149; Mount Olive College 246; Museum of Northern Arizona 152; North Country 247; NorthWord 156; O'Donnell Literary Services 247; Pelican 163; Pendaya 163; Pennsylvania Historical and Museum Commission 163; Schiffer 179; Singer Media 182; Star Song 187; Texas State Historical Association 192; Texas Tech University 192; 2M Communications 276; Victory House 250; Voyageur 205; Weatherhill 251; Whitecap Books 230; Wieser & Wieser 276; WRS 212; Zoland 212.

Communications. Longman 142; Paradigm 162; TAB 190; Tiare 194; Univelt 197; Vestal, The 204.

Community/Public Affairs. Madison 145; Pfeiffer 165; University of Alabama 197.

Computers/Electronic. Adams-Blake 64; Advance 64; Aegean Park 65; Afcom 65; Amacom 67; Amigadget 257; And 71; Baywood 79; Boyd & Fraser Publishing 84; Branden 85; Career 90; Carol 91; Compute 99; Computer Technology Research 99; Desktop Grafx 272; Eckert, J.K. 272; Gifted Education 116; Gleason Group 273; Global Professional 116; GMS 261; Golden Eagle 241; Grapevine 118; HMS 219; Ican 243; IEEE 243; Index 129; Industrial 129; Jacobs 132; Jain 133; Laing Communications 274; Lerner 138; Literary Works 140; Lucent 143; Mayhaven 246; MIS 150; Neal-Schuman 154; Nova Science 157; Noyes Data 157; O'Donnell Literary Services 247; One On One Computer Training 158; O'Reilly & Associates 159; Orion Research 247; Pace University 264; Paradigm 162; Peachpit 162; Policy Studies Organization 169; PSI Research 172; Revisionist 175; Ross 176; Ross 266; San Francisco 177; Serendipity Systems 180; Singer Media 182; SJL 182; Sourcebooks 184; Sterling 188; Sulzburger & Graham 189; Sybex 190; Systemsware, The 267; TAB 190; Teachers College 191; Tiare 194; University of North Texas 201; Waite Group 205; Walch, J. Weston 205; Weidner & Sons 207; Wheetley, The 276; Whitman 208; Wiley & Sons, John 209; Wordware 211.

Consumer Affairs. Almar 66; And 71; Benjamin, The 271; Consumer Reports 100; International Foundation Of Employee Benefit Plans 130.

Cooking/Foods/Nutrition. A.R.E. 61; Alaska Northwest 65; American Media 234; Arcade 72; Archives 73; Atheneum Books For Young Readers 74; Avery Group 76; Bantam 78; Barron's Educational Series 79; Benjamin, The 271; Benjamin 235; Bergh 235; Better Homes and Gardens 81; Blizzard 214; Blue Dolphin 82; Bonus 84; Book Creations 271; Border 258; Briarcliff 236; Bright Mountain 258; Bristol 86; British American 86; Bull 87; Caitlin, The 216; Cambridge Educational 88; Camden House 216; Camino 89; Carol 91; Cassandra 91; Chicago Review 94; China Books & Periodicals 94; Christopher, The 237; Chronicle 95; Chronimed 96; Clarkson Potter 97; Clear Light 97; Consumer Reports 100; Contemporary 100; Cool Hand Communications 100; Countryman, The 101; Crossing, The 102; David, Jonathan 104; Ecco, The 108; Edicones 239;

Éditions La Liberté 218; Eriksson, Paul S. 110; Evans, M. 110; Explorer's Guide 110; Facts On File 111; Filter 240; Fine, Donald I. 112; Fisher 113; Formac 218; Four Walls Eight Windows 114; Fox Chapel 114; Friedman, Michael 272; Gem Guides 116; Globe Pequot, The 117; Godine, Publisher, David R. 117; Golden West 117; Great Quotations 118; Hampton Roads 241; Harmony House 242; HarperCollins 121; Harvard Common, The 121; Hastings House 122; Hawkes 242; Haworth, The 122; Hay House 122; Herald Canada 219; HMS 219; Hounslow 220; Howell 126; Ican 243; Interlink 130; Jacobs 132; Jain 133; Jordan Enterprises 244; Key Porter 221; Kodansha America 136; Laing Communications 274; Lamppost 274; Lark 137; Larksdale 245; Layla Productions 274; Lerner 138; Lifetime 139; Literary Works 140; Little, Brown, Children's Book Division 140; Little, Brown 140; Longstreet 142; Lyons & Burford 144; McClelland & Stewart 221; Macmillan Canada 222; Mancorp 246; Maverick 147; Mayhaven 246; Menasha Ridge 275; Meyerbooks 263; Minnesota Historical Society 149; Morrow, William 151; Mosaic Miniature Books 263; Mount Olive College 246; National Books 153; Northland 156; Nova Science 157; Nucleus 264; O'Donnell Literary Services 247; Pacific 160; Peachtree 163; Pelican 163; Pennsylvania Historical and Museum Commission 163; Pocket 168; Pollard 265; Prentice-Hall Canada 224; Prima 170; Pruett 171; Purple Finch 265; QED 249; Quail Ridge 265; Ragged Mountain 173; Random House 173; Random House Of Canada 224; RedBrick 266; Republic Of Texas 174; Revisionist 175; Revisionist 175; Richboro 175; Ross 266; Rutledge Hill 176; Sand River 266; Sandlapper 178; Sasquatch 179; Sevgo 249; Shoestring 225; SJL 182; Spheric House 267; Story Communications/Garden Way 189; Sunbelt Media 189; Ten Speed 191; Tidewater 194; Times 195; Twin Peaks 196; 2M Communications 276; University of North Carolina , The 200; Victory House 250; Vortex Communications 268; Voyageur 205; Warren 206; Weatherhill 251; Westport 207; Wheetley, The 276; Whitecap Books 230; Whitman 208; Wieser & Wieser 276; Williamson 209; Wine Appreciation Guild 210; Woodbridge 211.

Counseling/Career Guidance. Accelerated Development 63; Adams, Bob 64; Almar 66; Career Publishing 90; Ferguson, J.G. 112; Garrett Park 115; Graduate Group, The 241; Harvard Common, The 121; Jist Works 133; NASW 153; National Textbook 153; Octameron Associates 157; Peterson's 165; Pilot 167; Professional 171; Teachers College 191; Ticket To Adventure 268; Vandamere 203; VGM Career Horizons 204; Williamson 209.

Crafts. Barron's Educational Series 79; Better Homes and Gardens 81; Briarcliff 236; C&T 89; Davis 104; Down East 107; Eagle's View 108; Friedman, Michael 272; Greey De Pencier 273; Hartley & Marks 121; Interweave 132; Kodansha America 136; Lark 137; Naturegraph 264; Standard 186; Tenth Avenue 276.

Educational. ABC-CLIO 62; Accelerated Development 63; Accent 63; Active Parenting 64; Advance 64; Advocacy 64; Afcom 65; African American Images 65; Amacom 67; American Catholic 257; American Education 69; American Media 234; American 70; Anchorage 71; ASQC 74; Austin & Winfield 75; Bandanna 77; B&B 258; Barricade 78; Barron's Educational Series 79; Baywood 79; Benjamin, The 271; Blue Bird 82; Blue Dolphin 82; Bosco Multimedia, Don 235; British American 86; Brookings Institution 87; Bull 87; Caddo Gap 88; Cambridge Educational 88; Canadian Institute of Ukrainian Studies 216; Career, The 90; Cato Institute 92; Cline/Fay Institute 98; College Board, The 98; Consortium 238; Corwin 101; Cottonwood 101; Council for Indian Education 101; Creative Spark, The 272; Dante University Of America 103; Davidson, Harlan 104; Davis 104; Denison, T.S. 106; Dimensions & Directions 272; Discipleship Resources 107; Discovery Enterprises 239; Distinctive 107; Duquesne University 108; Eastern Caribbean Institute 260; Éditions La Liberté 218; Education Center, The 109; EES 260; ETC 110; Fitzhenry & Whiteside 218; Front Row Experience 260; Gallaudet University 115; Gardner 240; Garrett Park 115; Gifted Education 116; Group 119; Gryphon House 261; Harmony House 242; Hay House 122; Herald Canada 219; Highsmith 125; HMS 219; Holmes & Meier 125; Home Education 125; Hope 242; Howells House 126; Ican 243; Incentive 128; Insight 130; Interstate 243; Ishiyaku Euroamerica 132; Jordan Enterprises 244; K.I.P. 134; Kent State University 135; Leadership 138; Lifetime 139; Literary Works 140; Longman 142; McClelland & Stewart 221; Mancorp 246; Masefield 263; Maupin House 246; Maupin House 263; Mega-Books of New York 274; Meriwether 148; Metamorphous 148; Milkweed Editions 149; Modern Language Association of America 150; Morehouse 150; Mount Olive College 246; Naturegraph 264; Neal-Schuman 154; New Falcon 246; New Hope 154; Noble, The 155; Nova Science 157; NTC 157; Octameron Associates 157; O'Donnell Literary Services 247; Open Court 158; Orion Research 247; Oryx 160; Owen, Richard C. 160; Pace University 264; Partners in Publishing 265; Pax 265; Peguis 223; Perfection Learning 265; Peterson's 165; Pfeiffer 165; Phi Delta Kappa Educational Foundation 165; Policy Studies Organization 169; Pollard 265; Prakken 169; Preservation, The 169; PSI Research 172; Publicom 275; Purple Finch 265; Reference Service

173; Regnery 174; Revisionist 175; Ross 266; Rutgers University 176; Schenkman 249; Scholastic Professional 180; Sevgo 249; Social Science Education Consortium 183; South End 184; Speech Bin, The 186; Spheric House 267; Standard 186; Sugar Hill, The 267; Sulzburger & Graham 189; TAB 190; Teachers College 191; Third World 193; UCLA-American Indian Studies Center 268; Umbrella 227; University of Alaska 198; University of Ottawa, The 228; Vandamere 203; Verso 229; Walch, J. Weston 205; Wall & Emerson 229; Warren 206; Weidner & Sons 207; Wheetley, The 276; Williamson 209; Women's 230; WRS 212.

Entertainment/Games. Boyds Mills 85; Broadway 87; Chess Enterprises 94; Citadel 96; Compute Books 99; Devyn 106; Drama 107; Faber & Faber 110; Facts On File 111; Fairleigh Dickinson University 111; Focal 113; Friedman, Michael 272; Love Child 143; McFarland 144; New York Zoetrope 155; Piccadilly 166; Speech Bin, The 186; Standard 186; Sterling 188; University of Nevada 200.

Ethnic. African American Images 65; Alaska Northwest 65; American Associates 67; Arsenal Pulp 214; Avanyu 75; Beacon 79; Benjamin 235; Blizzard 214; Bowling Green State University 84; Buddha Rose 236; Calyx 258; Camino 89; Canadian Institute of Ukrainian Studies 216; Carol 91; Center For Afro-American Studies 259; Center For Western Studies, The 237; China Books & Periodicals 94; Clarity 259; Clear Light 97; Confluence 99; Council for Indian Education 101; Creative Spark, The 272; Davidson, Harlan 104; Denali, The 106; Discipleship Resources 107; Eagle's View 108; Eastern Caribbean Institute 260; Facts On File 111; Fairleigh Dickinson University 111; Feminist at the City University of New York, The 112; Filter 240; Fitzhenry & Whiteside, 218; Formac 218; Garrett Park 115; Guernica 219; Herald 123; Herald Canada 219; HMS 219; Holmes & Meier 125; Hope 242; Hyperion 220; Ican 243; Indiana University 129; Inner Traditions International 130; Insight 130; Interlink 130; International 131; Italica 132; Jordan Enterprises 244; Judson 134; K.I.P. Children's Books 134; Kar-Ben Copies 135; Kodansha America 136; Lee & Low Books 262; Lerner Publications 138; Lincoln Springs 262; Literary Works Publishers 140; Little, Brown, Children's Book Division 140; Locust Hill 141; Louisiana State University 143; Love Child 143; Loyola University 143; Luramedia 144; McDonald & Woodward 144; Maverick 147; Media Forum International 147; Middle Passage 263; Millbrook, The 149; Minnesota Historical Society 149; Naturegraph 264; Netherlandic 222; NeWest 222; Noble, The 155; O'Donnell Literary Services 247; Oregon Historical Society 159; Pace University 264; Paradigm 248; Pelican 163; Policy Studies Organization 169; Polychrome 169; Pruett 171; Reference 266; Reference Service 173; Reidmore 225; Revisionist 175; Scots Plaid 266; Shoestring 225; South End 184; Spectrum 185; Sunflower University 250; Temple University 191; Texas Tech University 192; Third World 193; Three Continents 194; 2M Communications 276; UCLA-American Indian Studies Center 268; University Of Idaho 199; University of Alaska 198; University of Arizona 198; University of California Los Angeles Center for Afro-American Studies 268; University of Massachusetts 199; University of Nevada 200; University of New Mexico 200; University of North Texas 201; University of Oklahoma 201; University of Pittsburgh 201; University of Tennessee, The 202; University of Texas 202; University of Mississippi 203; Vesta 229; Warren 206; Washington State University 206; Watts, Franklin 206; Webb Research Group 251; Weigl Educational 229; White Pine 208; Whitman 208; Windflower Communications 230; Women's 230.

Feminism. Chicago Review 94; Crossing, The 102; Feminist at the City University of New York, The 112; Firebrand 112; New Victoria 155; Publishers Associates 172; Times Change 268; Vehicle 229.

Film/Cinema/Stage. Citadel 96; Dee, Ivan R. 105; Drama 107; Fairleigh Dickinson University 111; Focal 113; French, Samuel 114; Gaslight 115; Guernica Editions 219; Imagine 128; Indiana University 129; Knowledge Industry 136; Limelight Editions 140; Lone Eagle 141; Love Child 143; McFarland 144; Magicimage Filmbooks 246; Media Forum International 147; Meriwether 148; New York Zoetrope 155; Overlook, The 160; Piccadilly 166; Players 167; Scarecrow 179; Schirmer 179; Teachers College 191; Titan 227; Twayne 196; University of Texas 202; Vestal, The 204.

Gardening. Agritech 257; Better Homes and Gardens 81; Blizzard 214; Border 258; Briarcliff 236; Camden House 216; Camino Books 89; Capra 90; Chicago Review 94; China Books & Periodicals 94; Chronicle 95; Elliott & Clark 109; Fisher 113; Friedman, Michael 272; Globe Pequot, The 117; Godine, David R. 117; Graber Productions 273; Hartley & Marks 121; Hay House 122; Herbal Studies Library 261; HMS 219; Howell 126; Interlink 130; Jones University, Bob 133; Jordan Enterprises 244; Kodansha America 136; Lamppost 274; Lark 137; Layla Productions 274; Literary Works 140; Lone Pine 221; Longstreet 142; Lyons & Burford 144; McClelland & Stewart 221; Naturegraph 264; O'Donnell Literary Services 247; Ottenheimer 275; Peachtree 163; Pineapple

167; Pruett 171; Random House Of Canada 224; Revisionist 175; Richboro 175; Ross 266; Sasquatch 179; SJL 182; Stackpole 186; Sterling 188; Story Communications/Garden Way 189; Taylor 191; Ten Speed 191; Timber 194; University of North Carolina, The 200; Van Patten 268; Vandamere 203; Warren 206; Weatherhill 251; Weidner & Sons 207; Whitecap 230; Whitman 208; Wieser & Wieser 276; Williamson Publishing 209; Windward 210; Woodbridge 211.

Gay/Lesbian. Alyson 66; Amigadget 257; Bantam 78; Barricade 78; Beacon 79; Blizzard 214; Calyx 258; Carol 91; Cleis 97; Crossing, The 102; Da Capo 103; Feminist at the City University of New York, The 112; Firebrand 112; Gay Sunshine and Leyland 115; Gylantic 120; Haworth, The 122; Hay House 122; HMS 219; Ide House 127; Insight 130; Lexington 139; Liberal, The 139; Literary Works 140; Little, Brown, Children's Book Division 140; McClelland & Stewart 221; Madwoman 263; Masquerade 146; Monument 150; Neal-Schuman 154; New Falcon 246; New Victoria 155; O'Donnell Literary Services 247; Pace University 264; Paradigm 248; Publishers Associates 172; Rising Tide 175; Rutgers University 176; Signature 182; South End 184; Spectrum 185; Starbooks 250; 2M Communications 276; Volcano 268; Wiley & Sons, John 209; Women's 230.

General Nonfiction. American Atheist 68; American Psychiatric, The 70; Arcade 72; Avon Flare 76; Bandb 270; Beacon 79; Biddle 258; Brett 258; Broadview 215; Delancey 259; Dimensions & Directions 272; Evans, M. 110; Fawcett Juniper 112; Indiana University 129; Inverted-A 262; Johnson 133; Kent State University 135; Knopf, Alfred A. 135; Lang, Peter 244; Leisure Books 138; Lothrop, Lee & Shepard 143; Mills & Sanderson 149; Morrow, William 151; New England Associates 275; NewSage 264; Norton, W.W. 157; Pacific 160; Pantex International 264; Peachtree 163; Pippin 167; Pocket 168; Potential Development 265; Rainbow 173; Republic Of Texas 174; Rock, Andrew 275; Scholastic 180; Shaw, Harold 181; Silvercat 267; Taylor 191; Tiare 194; Time-Life 195; Twayne 196; Twin Peaks 196; Villard 204; Writer's Digest 211.

Gift Books. Gibson, The C.R. 116; Jain 133; LAWCO 262; McGuinn & McGuire 145; Peachtree 163; Sourcebooks 184.

Government/Politics. ABC-CLIO 62; America West 67; American Atheist 68; American Media 234; American 70; Arcade 72; Arden 73; Ashgate 234; ASQC 74; Atheneum Books For Young Readers 74; Austin & Winfield 75; Avon Books 76; Bandanna 77; Bantam 78; Barricade 78; Bergh 235; Blizzard 214; Bonus 84; Branden 85; Brassey's 85; British American 86; Broadview 215; Brookings Institution 87; Bucknell University 87; Buddha Rose 236; Business McGraw-Hill 88; CQ 88; C Q 88; Camino 89; Canadian Institute of Ukrainian Studies 216; Canadian Plains Research Center 216; Catholic University of America 92; Cato Institute 92; Center For Afro-American Studies 259; Chelsea Green 93; China Books & Periodicals 94; Christopher, The 237; Cleis 97; Creative Spark, The 272; Cross Cultural 102; Cuff, Harry 217; Da Capo 103; Davidson, Harlan 104; Dee, Ivan R. 105; Denali, The 106; Dimensions & Directions 272; Dutton 108; East Coast 108; Eastern Caribbean Institute 260; Ecco, The 108; Edicones Universal 239; Éditions La Liberté 218; Ekstasis 218; Eriksson, Publisher, Paul S. 110; Fairleigh Dickinson University 111; Feminist at the City University of New York, The 112; Formac 218; Four Walls Eight Windows 114; FPMI Communications 114; Glenbridge 116; Golden Eagle 241; Guernica 219; HarperCollins 121; HMS 219; Holmes & Meier 125; Hope 242; Horsdale & Schubart 220; Howells House 126; Huntington House 127; Ican 243; Ide House 127; ILR 128; Indiana University 129; Insight 130; Interlink 130; International 131; Jacobs 132; Jefferson University, Thomas 262; Justice Systems 134; Key Porter 221; Kumarian 244; Lake View 137; Lang, Peter 244; Lerner 138; Liberal, The 139; Library Research Associates 245; Lincoln Springs 262; Literary Works 140; Lone Pine 221; Longman 142; Loompanics Unlimited 142; Lorimer, James 221; Louisiana State University 143; Lucent 143; McClelland & Stewart 221; Mancorp 246; Markgraf 263; Masefield 263; Mercury, The 222; Michigan State University 149; Milkweed Editions 149; Millbrook, The 149; Monument 150; National 153; Neal-Schuman 154; NeWest 222; Noble, The 155; Northern Illinois University 156; Nova Science 157; O'Donnell Literary Services 247; Oregon Historical Society 159; Pace University 264; Pelican 163; Pennsylvania Historical and Museum Commission 163; Policy Studies Organization 169; Prentice-Hall Canada 224; Prima 170; Probe 265; Publishers Associates 172; Purdue University 172; Regnery 174; Reidmore 225; Republic Of Texas 174; Revisionist 175; Rhombus 266; Rutgers University 176; Sachem 276; Sarpedon 178; Shoestring 225; SJL 182; Social Science Education Consortium 183; South End 184; Spectrum 185; Stanford University 187; Sunflower University 250; Teachers College 191; Temple University 191; Third World 193; Thunder's Mouth 194; Trend Book Division 196; UCLA-American Indian Studies Center 268; University of Alabama 197; University of Alaska 198; University of Alberta, The 228; University of Arkansas, The 198; University of Illinois 199; University of Missouri 200; University of North Carolina , The 200; University of North Texas 201; University of Ottawa, The 228; University of Pittsburgh 201; University of Mississippi 203; University of New England 203; Utah State University 203; Vehicule 229; Verso 229; Vesta Publications 229; Vista 268; Walch, J. Weston 205; Washington State University 206; Watts, Franklin 206; Wayfinder 207; Weatherhill 251; Western Book/Journal 251; Wheetley , The 276; Wiley & Sons, John 209; Women's 230.

Health/Medicine. A.R.E. 61; Abelexpress 254; Accelerated Development 63; Acorn Publishing 256; Adams-Blake 64; Almar 66; America West 67; American Hospital 70; American 70; American Veterinary 257; ASQC 74; Atheneum Books For Young Readers 74; Avery 76; Avon 76; Bantam 78; Barricade 78; Barron's Educational Series 79; Barron's Educational Series 79; Baywood 79; Benjamin, The 271; Berkley 80; Blackbirch 82; Blue Dolphin 82; Blue Poppy 83; Bonus 84; Book Creations 271; Branden 85; Briarcliff 236; Broadview 215; Bull 87; Cambridge Educational 88; Cambridge University 89; Carol 91; Cassandra 91; Cato Institute 92; Charles 237; Christopher 237; Chronicle 95; Chronimed 96; Cleaning Consultant Services 238; Cline/Fay Institute 98; Consortium 238; Consumer Reports 100; Contemporary 100; Cool Hand Communications 100; Crossing, The 102; Deaconess 105; Dimensions & Directions 272; Dimi 259; Distinctive 107; Eastwind 239; Eckert, J.K. 272; EES 260; Elysium Growth 109; Eriksson, Paul S. 110; Evans, M. 110; Facts On File 111; Feminist at the City University of New York, The 112; Ferguson, J.G. 112; Fisher 113; Fitzhenry & Whiteside 218; Gallaudet University 115; Giniger, The K S 272; Global Professional 116; Government Institutes 118; Graber 273; Green, Warren H. 241; Gylantic 120; Hampton Roads 241; HarperCollins 121; Hartley & Marks 121; Harvard Common, The 121; Hastings House 122; Hawkes 242; Haworth, The 122; Hay House 122; Health 123; Herbal Studies Library 261; HMS 219; Hope 242; Hounslow 220; Hunter House 242; Ican 243; Information Resources 129; Inner Traditions International 130; Insight 130; International Foundation Of Employee Benefit Plans 130; International Information Associates 130; International Medical 131; Iowa State University 132; Ishiyaku Euroamerica 132; Ivy League 262; Jackson, Hart & Leslie 262; Jain 133; Jokes 273; Jones University, Bob 133; Jordan Enterprises 244; K.I.P. Children's Books 134; Kesend, Michael 135; Key Porter 221; Krieger 136; Laing Communications 274; Lamppost 274; Larksdale 245; Lawrence, Merloyd 137; Lerner 138; Life Survival Digest 262; Llewellyn 141; Luramedia 144; McClelland & Stewart 221; McFarland 144; McGuinn & McGuire 145; Macmillan Canada 222; Mancorp 246; Marcus 222; Marketscope 146; Markowski International 146; Markowski International 274; Maupin House 263; Mayfield 147; Medical Physics 147; Metamorphous 148; Meyerbooks 263; Mid-List 263; Millbrook, The 149; Mosaic Miniature 263; NASW 153; Naturegraph 264; Neal-Schuman 154; New Falcon 246; New Readers 155; Nova Science 157; O'Donnell Literary Services 247; Olson, C. 264; Oryx 160; Ottenheimer 275; Pace University 264; Pacific 160; Parable 161; Paradigm 248; Pax 265; Pelican 163; Perspectives 165; Plenum 168; Popular Medicine 265; Precept 169; Prentice-Hall Canada 224; Prima 170; Random House 173; Revisionist 175; Rock, Andrew 275; Rocky Top 175; Rosen, The 175; Rutgers University 176; San Francisco 177; Sidran, The 181; Sierra Club 181; Singer Media 182; Skidmore-Roth 249; Society 183; South End 184; Southern Methodist University 185; Speech Bin, The 186; Spheric House 267; Sterling 188; Stillpoint 188; Sulzburger & Graham 189; Sunflower University 250; Swan-Raven 190; Taylor 191; Temple University 191; Ten Speed 191; Texas Tech University 192; Theosophical 193; Third World 193; Times 195; Twin Peaks 196; 2M Communications 276; Ulysses 197; Unity 197; University of Alaska 198; University of Pennsylvania 201; University of Pittsburgh 201; VGM Career Horizons 204; Vista 250; Volcano 268; Vortex Communications 268; Walch, J. Weston 205; Walker 205; Wall & Emerson 229; Warren 206; Weidner & Sons 207; Weiser, Samuel 207; Westport 207; Wheetley, The 276; Whitman 208; Wieser & Wieser 276; Wiley & Sons, John 209; Williamson 209; Wingbow 269; Woodbine House 211; Woodbridge 211; WRS 212; Yes International 252; YMAA Publication Center 269; Zebra And Pinnacle 212.

Hi-Lo. Cambridge Educational 88; National Textbook 153; New Readers 155; Prolingua Associates 171; Rosen 175.

History. Aardvark 233; ABC-CLIO 62; Academy Chicago 62; Accord Communications, 63; Aegean Park 65; African American Images 65; Alaska Northwest 65; American Associates 67; American Atheist 68; American Media 234; American 70; Ancestry 71; Appalachian Mountain Club 71; Arcade 72; Architectural Book Publishing 72; Arden 73; Arsenal Pulp 214; Atheneum Books For Young Readers 74; Austin & Winfield 75; Avanyu 75; Avery 76; Aviation 258; Avon 76; Aztex 76; Bandanna 77; B&B 77; Barricade 78; Behrman House 79; Berwick 80; Biddle 258; Binford & Mort 235; Blackbirch 82; Blizzard 214; Boston Mills, The 215; Bowling Green State University Popular 84; Boxwood, The 236; Branden 85; Brassey's 85; Brevet 85; Bright Mountain 258; British American

200; University of Nevada 200; University of New Mexico 200; University of North Carolina, The 200; University of North Texas 201; University of Oklahoma 201; University of Ottawa, The 228; University of Pennsylvania 201; University of Pittsburgh 201; University of Tennessee, The 202; University of Texas 202; University of Mississippi 203; University of New England 203; Utah State University 203; Vandamere 203; Vehicule 229; Vestal, The 204; Virginia State Library and Archives 268; Vista 268; Walch, J. Weston 205; Walker and 205; Warren House 206; Washington State University 206; Watts, Franklin 206; Wayfinder 207; Weatherhill 251; Webb Research Group 251; Western Book/Journal 251; Western Tanager 269; Wheetley, The 276; Whitecap 230; Whitman 208; Wieser & Wieser 276; Wilderness Adventure 209; Wiley & Sons, John 209; Williamson 209; Windflower Communications 230; Women's 230; Ye Galleon 251; Zondervan 212.

Hobby. Accord Communications 63; Afcom 65; Almar 66; Ancestry 71; Atheneum For Young Readers 74; Bale 77; Benjamin, The 271; Betterway 81; Blizzard 214; Camden House 216; C&T 89; Capstone 90; Carstens 91; Council for Indian Education 101; Dundurn 217; E.M. 259; Eagle's View 108; Éditions La Liberté 218; Eriksson, Paul S. 110; Facts On File 111; Filter 240; Fox Chapel 114; Friedman, Michael 272; Gem Guides 116; Greey De Pencier 273; Gryphon 120; Hawkes 242; HMS 219; Index 129; Interweave 132; Jordan Enterprises 244; JSA 273; Kalmbach 134; Kesend, Michael 135; Lark 137; Lifetime 139; Literary Works 140; Little, Brown, Children's Book Division 140; Lyons & Burford 144; McClelland & Stewart 221; Markowski International 146; Markowski International 274; Maverick 147; Mayhaven 246; Millbrook, The 149; Mosaic Miniature 263; Mustang 152; O'Donnell Literary Services 247; Pollard 265; Rocky Top 175; Schiffer 179; Sky 183; Sono Nis 226; SouthPark 185; Stackpole 186; Sterling 188; Story Communications/Garden Way 189; Success 189; Sulzburger & Graham 189; Twin Peaks 196; University of North Carolina, The 200; Vestal, The 204; Warren 206; Weidner & Sons 207; Whitman 208; Wieser & Wieser 276.

Horror. Carol 91.

House and Home. Better Homes and Gardens 81; Bookworks 271; Brighton 86; Lifetime 139; Sterling 188; Taylor 191; Williamson 209.

How-To. A Capella 233; Abbott, Langer & Associates 61; Aberdeen Group, The 62; Accent On Living 63; Accent 63; Accord Communications 63; Adams-Blake 64; Advance Corproation 64; Afcom 65; Allen 66; Almar 66; Alpine 233; Amacom 67; American Association for State and Local History 68; American Correctional Association 69; Amherst Media 70; Amigadget 257; Ancestry 71; Andrews and McMeel 71; Appalachian Mountain Club 71; Archives 73; Aronson, Jason 73; Art Direction 73; ASQC 74; Atheneum Books For Young Readers 74; Auto 257; Avery 76; Avon 76; Aztex 76; Bantam 78; Barricade 78; Beaver Pond 234; Benjamin, The 271; Bentley, Robert 80; Berkley 80; Better Homes and Gardens 81; Betterway 81; Bicycle 81; Blizzard 214; Blue Bird 82; Blue Dolphin 82; Bonus 84; Bookworks 271; Briarcliff 236; Brick House 86; Bright Mountain 258; Brighton 86; British American 86; Bull 87; Burning Gate 87; McGraw-Hill 88; C.F.W. Enterprises 258; Cambridge Educational 88; Camden House 216; Camino 89; C&T 89; Capra 90; Caradium 90; Cardoza 90; Career, The 90; Carol 91; Cassandra 91; CCC 93; Center 93; Charles 237; Chicago Review 94; China Books & Periodicals 94; Chosen 95; Christian 95; Christopher, The 237; Clarkson Potter 97; Cleaning Consultant Services 238; College Board, The 98; Consultant , The 100; Consumer Reports 100; Contemporary 100; Cool Hand Communications 100; Corkscrew 259; Cornell Maritime 100; Council for Indian Education 101; Countryman, The 101; Craftsman 101; Crossing, The 102; David, Jonathan 104; Dearborn Financial 105; Delta Sales 239; Desktop Grafx 272; Devyn 106; Dickens 259; Diskotech 259; Distinctive 107; E.M. 259; Eagle's View 108; East Coast 108; Eastwind 239; EES 260; Eriksson, Paul S. 110; Filter 240; Flores, J. 113; Focal 113; Focus on the Family 113; Fox Chapel 114; Friedman, Michael 272; Gambling Times 260; Gay Sunshine and Leyland 115; Gifted Education 116; Globe Pequot, The 117; Grapevine 118; Graphic Arts 261; Great Northwest 118; Greey De Pencier 273; Group 119; Gryphon House 261; Half Halt 120; Hamilton Institute, Alexander 120; Hampton Roads 241; Hancock House 121; Harper San Francisco 121; HarperCollins 121; Hartley & Marks 121; Harvard Common, The 121; Harvest House 122; Hastings House 122; Hawkes 242; Hay House 122; Herbal Studies Library 261; Heyday 124; Home Education 125; Hope 242; Hounslow 220; Imagine 128; In Print 262; Insight 130; Interlink 130; International Information Associates 130; International Wealth Success 131; Interweave 132; Jain 133; Jelmar 262; Jist Works 133; Jordan Enterprises 244; JSA 273; Kalmbach 134; Kesend, Michael 135; Laing Communications 274; Lamppost 274; Lark 137; Larksdale 245; LAWCO 262; Layla Productions 274; Library Research Associates 245; Lifetime 139; Little, Brown 140; Llewellyn 141; Lone Eagle 141; Lone Pine 221; Loompanics Unlimited 142; Lorien House 263; Love Child 143; McClelland & Stewart 221; McDonald & Woodward 144; McGuinn & McGuire 145;

Mancorp 246; Marketscope 146; Markowski International 146; Markowski Interna¹
pin House 263; Maverick 147; Meadowbrook 147; Media/Midgard 147; Menasha
wether 148; Metamorphous 148; Mid-List 263; Morrow, William 151; Motorbo
151; Mount Olive College 246; Mountaineers, The 151; Mustang 152; Mystic Seaport ᴍ.
263; Naturegraph 264; Neal-Schuman 154; New England, The 154; New Falcon 246; North Light
156; NorthWord 156; O'Donnell Literary Services 247; Olson, C. 264; One On One Computer
Training 158; Optimus 264; Orchises 159; Orion Research 247; Ottenheimer 275; Pacific Learning
Council 264; Pacific Association 160; Paladin 161; Paradigm 248; Partners in Publishing 265; Peach-
pit 162; Peel Productions 265; Pelican 163; Pennsylvania Historical and Museum Commission 163;
Perspectives 165; Piccadilly 166; Pickering, The 166; Pineapple 167; PMN 248; Prima 170;
Princeton 170; Probus 170; ProStar 249; PSI Research 172; Publicom 275; QED 249; Ragged
Mountain 173; Rainbow 173; Rainbow 173; Revisionist 175; Richboro 175; Rocky Mountain 225;
Rocky Top 175; Ross 176; Ross 266; Saurie Island 179; Schiffer 179; Scots Plaid 266; Seaside 180;
Self-Counsel 225; Sevgo 249; Sierra Club 181; Singer Media 182; Sky 183; SouthPark 185; Speech
Bin, The 186; Spheric House 267; Sterling 188; Still Waters 188; Stoeger 188; Stoneydale 189;
Story Communications/Garden Way 189; Success 189; Sulzburger & Graham 189; Sunstone 190;
TAB 190; Tambra 267; Ten Speed 191; Tenth Avenue Editions 276; Thomas Investigative 193;
Tiare 194; Tiare 194; Titan 227; Turtle 268; Twin Peaks 196; 2M Communications 276; UCLA-
American Indian Studies Center 268; University of Alberta, The 228; Van Patten 268; Victory
House 250; Vista 250; Waite Group 205; Wasatch 268; Weatherhill 251; Weiser, Samuel 207;
Whitehorse 269; Whitford 208; Wilderness Adventure 209; Wilderness 209; Wiley & Sons, John
209; Williamson 209; Wilshire 210; Windsor 210; Windward 210; Wine Appreciation Guild 210;
Writer's Digest 211; Zebra And Pinnacle 212.

Humanities. Asian Humanities 74; Duquesne University 108; Feminist at the City University of New
York, The 112; Garland 115; Gifted Education 116; Indiana University 129; Lang Peter 244;
Roxbury 176; Southern Illinois University 185; Stanford University 187; University of Arkansas,
The 198; Whitson 208; Zondervan 212.

Humor. Aardvark 233; Acme 256; American Atheist 68; Andrews and McMeel 71; Arsenal Pulp 214;
Atheneum Books For Young Readers 74; Bale 77; Bantam 78; Barbour 78; Black Tooth 258; Blue
Dolphin 82; British American 86; Carol 91; Catbird 92; CCC 93; Citadel 96; Clarion 96; Clarkson
Potter 97; Clear Light 97; Contemporary 100; Cool Hand Communications 100; Corkscrew 259;
Council for Indian Education 101; Creative Spark, The 272; CSS 239; Cuff, Harry 217; Dawson,
W.S. 105; Delta Sales 239; Edicones 239; Epicenter 109; Eriksson, Paul S. 110; Fine, Donald I.
112; Friends United 115; Godine, David R. 117; Great Quotations 118; HarperCollins 121; Has-
tings House 122; Hay House 122; HMS 219; Hoard & Sons, W.D. 261; Horsdale & Schubart 220;
Hounslow 220; Hyperion 220; Ican 243; Jacobs 132; Jordan Enterprises 244; JSA 273; Key Porter
221; Lamppost 274; Layla 274; Limelight Editions 140; Literary Works 140; Longstreet 142;
McClelland & Stewart 221; Macmillan Canada 222; Marketscope 146; Mayhaven 246; Media Fo-
rum International 147; Meriwether 148; Mosaic Miniature 263; Mustang 152; O'Donnell Literary
Services 247; Orchises 159; Paladin 161; Paradigm 248; Pax 265; Peachtree 163; Pelican 163; Peter
Pauper 165; Piccadilly 166; Pippin 167; Pollard 265; Price Stern Sloan 170; QED 249; Ragged
Mountain 173; Random House 173; Republic Of Texas 174; Rutledge Hill 176; Sandlapper 178;
Scots Plaid 266; Signature Books 182; Star 187; Sterling 188; Still Waters 188; Success 189; Titan
227; 2M Communications 276; Weatherhill 251; Zebra And Pinnacle 212.

Illustrated Book. Aardvark 233; Advance Corproation 64; Atheneum Books For Young Readers
74; Avanyu 75; Bandanna 77; Bantam 78; Bear 79; Bergh 235; Betterway 81; Blackbirch 82; Boston
Mills, The 215; Branden 85; Burning Gate 87; Canadian Plains Research Center 216; C&T 89;
Carol 91; Charlesbridge 93; Cleaning Consultant Services 238; Coach House 217; Council for
Indian Education 101; Creative Spark, The 272; Davis 104; Dial Books For Young Readers 106;
Discovery Enterprises 239; Down The Shore 259; Elysium Growth 109; Epicenter 109; Flores, J.
113; Formac 218; Friedman, Michael 272; Giniger, The K S 272; Godine, David R. 117; Gold'n'
Honey 117; Goose Lane 218; Graphic Arts Center 118; Great Quotations 118; Group's Hands-
On™ Bible Curriculum 119; Hampton Roads 241; Harmony House 242; Harvest House 122; Herald
Canada 219; Hounslow 220; Howell 126; Howells House 126; Imagine 128; Indiana Historical
Society 262; Interlink 130; Jacobs 132; Jefferson University, Thomas 262; Jordan Enterprises 244;
Judaica 262; Kesend, Michael 135; Key Porter 221; Laing Communications 274; Lamppost 274;
Lark 137; Layla Productions 274; Lexikos 138; Limelight Editions 140; Longstreet 142; Lothrop,
Lee & Shepard 143; McClelland & Stewart 221; McDonald & Woodward 144; Mayhaven 246;

Meadowbrook 147; Metamorphous 148; Milkweed Editions 149; Minnesota Historical Society 149; Mosaic Miniature 263; Mountain Automation 263; New England, The 154; NorthWord 156; O'Donnell Literary Services 247; Orca 223; Owen, Richard C. 160; Pelican 163; Pendaya 163; Pennsylvania Historical and Museum Commission 163; Philomel 166; Pickering, The 166; Pippin 167; Pogo 168; Princeton Architectural 248; Pruett 171; Publicom 275; Random House 173; Ross 266; Sandlapper 178; Schiffer 179; Shoestring 225; Singer Media 182; Sky 183; Smith, Gibbs 183; Soundprints 184; Speech Bin, The 186; Sunbelt Media 189; Sunflower University 250; Tenth Avenue Editions 276; Texas State Historical Association 192; Texas Tech University 192; Third World 193; Tidewater Publishers 194; Titan 227; 2M Communications 276; UAHC 250; University of New Mexico 200; Warren 206; Wayfinder 207; Weatherhill 251; Wilderness Adventure 209; Willowisp 210; Windward 210.

Juvenile Books. Aardvark 233; Abingdon 62; Advance Corproation 64; Advocacy 64; African American Images 65; American Education 69; Appalachian Mountain Club 71; Archway/Minstrel 73; Atheneum Books For Young Readers 74; Augsburg 75; Baker 77; B&B 77; Barbour 78; Barron's Educational Series 79; Beacon 79; Behrman House 79; Benjamin 235; Bergh 235; Blackbirch 82; Blizzard 214; Bookcraft 84; Bosco Multimedia, Don 235; Boyds Mills 85; Branden 85; Bridge 236; Cambridge Educational 88; Camino 89; C&T 89; Capstone 90; Carolrhoda 91; Centering 93; Charlesbridge 93; Chicago Review 94; China Books & Periodicals 94; Clarion 96; Clarkson Potter 97; Cobblehill 98; Council for Indian Education 101; Creative Spark, The 272; Davenport, May 104; Denison, T.S. 106; Dial Books For Young Readers 106; Dickens 259; Discovery Enterprises 239; Down The Shore 259; Dundurn 217; Éditions La Liberté 218; Enslow 109; Explorer's Guide 110; Feminist at the City University of New York, The 112; Fitzhenry & Whiteside 218; Focus on the Family 113; Formac 218; Free Spirit 260; Friends United 115; Gibson , The C.R. 116; Godine, Publisher, David R. 117; Gold'n' Honey 117; Graber Productions 273; Great Quotations 118; Greenhaven 119; Greey De Pencier 273; Grosset & Dunlap 119; Group's Hands-On™ Bible Curriculum 119; Gryphon House 261; Harcourt Brace 121; Harvest House 122; Hastings House 122; Hay House 122; Hendrick-Long 123; Herald 123; Herald Canada 219; Highsmith 125; HMS 219; Hope House 242; Houghton Mifflin 125; Huntington House 127; Hyperion 220; Ican 243; Ideals Children's Books 128; Incentive 128; Interlink 130; Jacobs 132; Jones University, Bob 133; Jordan Enterprises 244; Judaica 262; K.I.P. Children's 134; Kar-Ben Copies 135; Key Porter 221; Laing Communications 274; Lamppost 274; Lark 137; Layla Productions 274; Lee & Low 262; Lerner 138; Ligouri 139; Literary Works 140; Little, Brown, Children's Book Division 140; Lodestar 141; Lone Pine 221; Lorimer, James 221; Lothrop, Lee & Shepard 143; Lucas-Evans 274; Lucent 143; McClanahan 274; McClelland & Stewart 221; McElderry, Margaret K. 144; Marlor 146; Mayhaven 246; Meadowbrook 147; Millbrook, The 149; Morehouse 150; Morrow, William 151; Morrow Junior 151; Mount Olive College 246; New Hope 154; NorthWord 156; O'Donnell Literary Services 247; Orca 223; Orchard 158; Oregon Historical Society 159; Ottenheimer 275; Owen, Richard C. 160; Pacific Educational 223; Pacific 160; Parenting 162; Peachtree 163; Pelican 163; Perfection Learning 265; Perspectives 165; Philomel 166; Players 167; Polychrome 169; Preservation, The 169; Price Stern Sloan 170; Publicom 275; Purple Finch 265; St. Paul 177; Sandlapper 178; Sasquatch 179; Scholastic Professional 180; Seaside 180; Shoestring 225; Sierra Club 181; Singer Media 182; SJL 182; Soundprints 184; Speech Bin, The 186; Spheric House 267; Standard 186; Star 187; Star Song 187; Sterling 188; Story Communications/Garden Way 189; Sunbelt Media 189; Tambourine 191; Tenth Avenue Editions 276; Tenth Avenue Editions 276; Texas Christian University 192; Third World 193; Tidewater 194; UAHC 250; Unity 197; Victor 204; Victory House 250; Volcano 268; Voyageur 205; Walker 205; Ward Hill 206; Warren Publishing House 206; Weiss Associates, Daniel 276; Whitecap Books 230; Whitman 208; Wiley & Sons, John 209; Williamson 209; Willowisp 210; Windflower Communications 230; Windward 210; Women's 230; Zondervan 212.

Labor/Management. Abbott, Langer & Associates 61; BNA 83; Brevet 85; CEDI 259; Drama Book 107; FPMI Communications 114; Hamilton Institute, Alexander 120; ILR 128; International 131; Larksdale 245; Pfeiffer 165; Temple University 191.

Language and Literataure. Amigadget 257; Anchorage 71; Asian Humanities 74; Austin & Winfield 75; Bandanna 77; Bantam 78; Barron's Educational Series 79; Black Sparrow 82; Blizzard 214; Bowling Green State University Popular 84; British American 86; Broadview 215; Cacanadadada 215; Calyx Books 258; Canadian Institute of Ukrainian Studies 216; Capra 90; Caratzas, Publisher, Aristide D. 236; Catholic University of America 92; Center 93; China Books & Periodicals 94; Clarion 96; Clarkson Potter 97; Coach House 217; College Board, The 98; Confluence 99;

Consortium 238; Coteau 217; Cottonwood 101; Creative Arts 238; Crossing, The 102; Daniel, John 103; Dante University Of America 103; Davidson, Harlan 104; Dee, Ivan R. 105; Dimensions & Directions 272; Dundurn 217; Ecco, The 108; Éditions La Liberté 218; Education Center, The 109; Facts On File 111; Family Album, The 111; Feminist at the City University of New York, The 112; Ford-Brown 260; Four Walls Eight Windows 114; Gallaudet University 115; Goose Lane 218; Gryphon 120; Guernica 219; Herald Canada 219; Highsmith 125; Hippocrene 125; HMS 219; Hope 242; Insight 130; Interlink 130; Italica 132; Jefferson University, Thomas 262; Jordan Enterprises 244; K.I.P. Children's Books 134; Kent State University 135; Kodansha America 136; Lake View 137; Lang, Peter 244; Langenscheidt 137; Lehigh University 138; Lerner 138; Les Editions La Lignée 221; Lincoln Springs 262; Literary Works 140; Locust Hill 141; Longman Group 142; Longstreet 142; Louisiana State University 143; McClelland & Stewart 221; Mancorp 246; Mayfield 147; Mercury, The 222; Michigan State University 149; Milkweed Editions 149; Modern Language Association of America 150; Mount Olive College 246; National Textbook 153; Neal-Schuman 154; Netherlandic 222; New England Publishing Associates 275; New Readers 155; Nightshade 264; NTC Publishing Group 157; O'Donnell Literary Services 247; Oregon State University 159; Pace University 264; Pandemic International 161; Peguis 223; Pippin 167; Prolingua Associates 171; Purdue University 172; Purple Finch 265; Revisionist 175; Roxbury 176; Rutgers University 176; Sand River 266; Schenkman 249; Scots Plaid 266; Serendipity Systems 180; Simon & Pierre 226; 16th Century Journal 267; Smith, The 183; Spectrum 185; Spheric House 267; Stanford University 187; Still Waters 188; Stone Bridge 267; Sunflower University 250; Texas Tech University 192; Third World 193; Three Continents 194; Twayne 196; UCLA-American Indian Studies Center 268; University Of Idaho 199; University of Alabama 197; University of Alaska 198; University of California 198; University of Illinois 199; University of Iowa 199; University of Nebraska 200; University of Nevada 200; University of North Carolina, The 200; University of North Texas 201; University of Oklahoma 201; University of Ottawa, The 228; University of Pennsylvania 201; University of Pennsylvania 201; University of Pittsburgh 201; University of Scranton 202; University of Texas 202; University of Kentucky 202; University of Mississippi 203; Utah State University 203; Vehicule 229; Verso 229; Vesta 229; Vista 268; Wake Forest University 205; Walch, J. Weston 205; Warren 206; Weatherhill 251; Weidner & Sons 207; Wheetley, The 276; White Pine 208; Whitman 208; Wiley & Sons, John 209; Women's 230; Writer's Digest 211; York 231; Zoland 212.

Law. Almar 66; American Bar Association, Publications Planning & Marketing 68; Banks-Baldwin Law 78; BNA 83; Catbird 92; East Coast 108; EES 260; Government Institutes 118; Hamilton Institute, Alexander 120; Justice Systems 134; Lawyers & Judges 137; Library Research Associates 245; Monitor Book 150; Oceana 157; Temple University 191; Transnational 195; Trend Book Division 196; University of North Carolina, The 200; University of Pennsylvania 201.

Literary Criticism. Accord Communications 63; Barron's Educational Series 79; Bucknell University 87; Coach House 217; Dundurn 217; ECW 218; Fairleigh Dickinson University 111; Gaslight 115; Holmes & Meier 125; Lang, Peter 244; Loyola University 143; Mysterious, The 152; Northern Illinois University 156; Purdue University 172; Stanford University 187; Texas Christian University 192; Three Continents 194; University of Alabama 197; University of Arkansas, The 198; University of Massachusetts 199; University of Missouri 200; University of Tennessee, The 202; University of Mississippi 203; York 231.

Marine Subjects. Binford & Mort 235; Cornell Maritime 100; Howell 126; International Marine 131; Maverick 147; Mystic Seaport Museum 263; ProStar 249; Sono Nis 226; TAB Books 190; Transportation Trails 195; Wescott Cove 207.

Military/War. ABC-CLIO 62; Aegean Park 65; American Media 234; Avery 76; Avon 76; B&B 77; Blair, John F. 82; Brassey's 85; Burning Gate 87; Cato Institute 92; Da Capo 103; Fairleigh Dickinson University 111; Fine, Donald I. 112; Flores, J. 113; Golden Eagle 241; Harmony House 242; Hippocrene 125; HMS 219; Hope 242; Howell 126; Howells House 126; Ican 243; Jefferson University, Thomas 262; Justice Systems 134; Ketz Agency, Louise B. 273; Key Porter 221; Larksdale 245; Lincoln Springs 262; Longstreet House 245; Louisiana State University 143; Lucent 143; McClelland & Stewart 221; Macmillan Canada 222; Monument 150; Nautical & Aviation, The 153; Naval Institute 154; O'Donnell Literary Services 247; Paladin 161; Parallax 248; Picton 166; PMN 248; Presidio 170; Publishers Syndication International 265; Random House Of Canada 224; Reference Service 173; Regnery 174; Revisionist 175; Sachem 276; Sarpedon 178; Schiffer 179; Sevgo 249; Shoestring 225; South End 184; Stackpole 186; Sterling 188; Sunbelt Media 189; Sunflower University 250; Texas A&M University 192; University of Alaska 198; University of North

Texas 201; Vandamere 203; Vanwell Limited 228; Virginia State Library and Archives 268; Webb Research Group 251; Wieser & Wieser 276; Wiley & Sons, John 209; Zebra And Pinnacle 212.

Money/Finance. Adams-Blake 64; Advance Corproation 64; Allen 66; Almar 66; American Media 234; Ashgate 234; ASQC 74; Bale 77; Better Homes and Gardens 81; Blue Horizon 235; Bonus 84; Briarcliff 236; Brick House 86; Broadview 215; Brookings Institution 87; Business McGraw-Hill 88; Cambridge Educational 88; Caradium 90; Career, The 90; Carol 91; Cato Institute 92; Center 93; Consumer Reports 100; Contemporary 100; Dearborn Financial 105; Delta Sales 239; Flores, J. 113; Focus on the Family 113; Forum 114; Golden Eagle 241; Hampton Roads 241; Hancock House 121; Harvard Common, The 121; Hay House 122; Hensley, Virgil W. 123; Herald Canada 219; HMS 219; Hounslow 220; Insight 130; International Information Associates 130; International Wealth Success 131; Jacobs 132; Jain 133; Jordan Enterprises 244; Key Porter 221; Lamppost 274; Larksdale 245; Lerner 138; Lexington 139; Lifetime 139; McClelland & Stewart 221; Macmillan Canada 222; Marketscope 146; Markowski International 274; National 153; Neal-Schuman 154; Nova Science 157; O'Donnell Literary Services 247; Pace University 264; Pax 265; Pilot 167; PMN 248; Policy Studies Organization 169; Probus 170; PSI Research 172; QED 249; Revisionist 175; Ross 266; Singer Media 182; Sourcebooks 184; Success 189; Sulzburger & Graham 189; Sunflower University 250; Technical Analysis of Stocks & Commodities 267; Ten Speed 191; ULI, The Urban Land Institute 196; Vesta 229; Wheetley, The 276; Windsor 210; Zebra And Pinnacle 212.

Multicultural. ABC-CLIO 62.

Music and Dance. A Capella 233; American Catholic 257; American 70; And 71; Atheneum Books For Young Readers 74; Betterway 81; Blizzard 214; Bold Strummer, The 83; Branden 85; Bucknell University 87; Cambridge University 89; Cambridge University 89; Carol 91; Carolrhoda 91; Center For Afro-American Studies 259; Centerstream 93; Consortium 238; Creative Arts 238; Da Capo 103; Dance Horizons 103; Davenport, May 104; Discipleship Resources 107; Distinctive 107; Drama 107; Ecco, The 108; Éditions La Liberté 218; Faber & Faber 110; Fairleigh Dickinson University 111; Fallen Leaf 260; Feminist at the City University of New York, The 112; Friedman, Michael 272; Glenbridge 116; Guernica 219; HarperCollins 121; HMS 219; Indiana University 129; Inner Traditions International 130; Jordan Enterprises 244; JSA 273; Krieger 136; Lang, Peter 244; Lerner 138; Limelight Editions 140; Locust Hill 141; Louisiana State University 143; McClelland & Stewart 221; McFarland 144; Mancorp 246; Mayfield 147; Mercury, The 222; Meriwether 148; Mosaic Miniature 263; Parable 161; Pelican 163; Pennywhistle 164; Prima 170; Princeton 170; Pro/AM Music Resources 170; Purple Finch 265; Random House 173; Revisionist 175; Rosen 175; Ross 266; San Francisco 177; Scarecrow 179; Schirmer 179; Simon & Pierre 226; South End 184; Stipes 188; Sunflower University 250; Tenth Avenue Editions 276; Texas Tech University 192; Tiare 194; Timber 194; Titan 227; University of Illinois 199; University of Pittsburgh 201; University of New England 203; Vestal, The 204; Walch, J. Weston 205; Walker 205; Warren 206; Weiser, Samuel 207; Wheetley, The 276; Writer's Digest 211.

Nature and Environment. Alaska Northwest 65; American Education 69; Appalachian Mountain Club 71; Arcade 72; Atheneum Books For Young Readers 74; Avery 76; Backcountry 76; B&B 77; Bantam 78; Barricade 78; Baywood 79; Beacon 79; Bear 79; Beaver Pond & Printing 234; Binford & Mort 235; Blackbirch 82; Blue Dolphin 82; BNA 83; Boxwood, The 236; Brick House 86; Broadview 215; Buddha Rose 236; Cacanadadada 215; Camden House 216; Canadian Plains Research Center 216; Capra 90; Carol 91; Carolrhoda 91; Cave 92; Chapel Street 259; Charlesbridge 93; Chelsea Green 93; China Books & Periodicals 94; Chronicle 95; Clarion 96; Clarkson Potter 97; Clear Light 97; Confluence 99; Council for Indian Education 101; Countryman, The 101; Discipleship Resources 107; Down East 107; Down The Shore 259; Éditions La Liberté 218; Ekstasis 218; Elliott & Clark 109; Elysium Growth 109; Epicenter 109; Eriksson, Paul S. 110; Explorer's Guide 110; Facts On File 111; Foghorn 113; Formac 218; Four Walls Eight Windows 114; Friedman, Michael 272; Gem Guides 116; Godine, David R. 117; Goose Lane 218; Government Institutes 118; Great Quotations 118; Greey De Pencier 273; Grosset & Dunlap 119; Hancock House 121; Harmony House 242; HarperCollins 121; Hartley & Marks 121; Hay House 122; Herald Canada 219; Heyday 124; High Plains 124; HMS 219; Hope 242; Horsdale & Schubart 220; Hunter House 242; Inner Traditions International 130; Insight 130; Interlink 130; Johnson 133; Jones University, Bob 133; Jordan Enterprises 244; Kesend, Michael 135; Key Porter 221; Kodansha America 136; Kumarian 244; Lark 137; Lawrence, Merloyd 137; Lawrence, Seymour 137; Lerner 138; Lexikos 138; Lifetime 139; Literary Works 140; Little, Brown, Children's Book Division 140; Llewellyn 141; Lone Pine 221; Longstreet 142; Lorien House 263; Lucent 143; Luramedia 144;

Lyons & Burford 144; McClelland & Stewart 221; McDonald & Woodward 144; McGuinn & McGuire 145; Marketscope 146; Maverick 147; Mayhaven 246; Medical Physics 147; Meyerbooks 263; Milkweed 149; Millbrook, The 149; Mosaic Miniature 263; Mountain 151; Mountaineers The 151; Museum of Northern Arizona 152; Naturegraph 264; New England, The 154; Nightshade 264; Noble, The 155; North Country 247; Northland 156; NorthWord 156; Nova Science 157; Noyes Data 157; O'Donnell Literary Services 247; Olson, C. 264; Orca 223; Oregon Historical Society 159; Oregon State University 159; Pace University 264; Pacific Publishing Association 160; Pennsylvania Historical and Museum Commission 163; Pennywhistle 164; Pineapple 167; Pippin 167; Plexus 168; Policy Studies Organization 169; Pruett 171; PSI Research 172; Ragged Mountain 173; Reference 266; Regnery 174; Revisionist 175; Rhombus 266; Rocky Mountain 225; Rocky Top 175; Rutgers University 176; Sandhill Crane 178; Sasquatch 179; Schenkman 249; Scots Plaid 266; Sierra Club 181; Sky 183; Smith, Gibbs 183; Soundprints 184; South End 184; Sterling 188; Stillpoint 188; Stipes 188; Story Communications/Garden Way 189; Sunbelt Media 189; Sunflower University 250; Taylor 191; Ten Speed 191; Texas A&M University 192; Texas Tech University 192; Timber 194; Times Change 268; University Of Idaho 199; University of Alaska 198; University of Alberta, The 228; University of Arizona 198; University of Arkansas, The 198; University of California 198; University of Nebraska 200; University of North Carolina , The 200; University of North Texas 201; University of Ottawa, The 228; University of Texas 202; University of Colorado 202; University of Mississippi 203; University of New England 203; Venture 204; Verso 229; VGM Career Horizons 204; Voyageur 205; Walker and 205; Warren House 206; Wasatch 268; Washington State University 206; Wayfinder 207; Weatherhill 251; Weidner & Sons 207; Wheetley, The 276; Whitecap 230; Whitman 208; Wieser & Wieser 276; Wilderness Adventure 209; Wilderness 209; Williamson 209; Willowisp 210; Windward 210; Zoland 212.

Philosophy. American Associates 67; American Atheist 68; Ashgate 234; Asian Humanities 74; Atheneum Books For Young Readers 74; Austin & Winfield 75; Baker 77; Bandanna 77; Bantam 78; Beacon 79; Boxwood, The 236; Broadview 215; Bucknell University 87; Bucknell University 87; Buddha Rose 236; Carol 91; Cassandra 91; Catholic University of America 92; Center 93; Christian Classics 237; Christopher, The 237; Clear Light 97; Cross Cultural 102; Davidson, Harlan 104; Eastern Caribbean Institute 260; Eastwind 239; Edicones Universal 239; Eerdmans, William B. 240; Elysium Growth 109; Epicenter 109; Facts On File 111; Fairleigh Dickinson University 111; Friedlander, Joel 260; Gifted Education 116; Glenbridge 116; Green, Warren H. 241; Guernica 219; Harper San Francisco 121; HarperCollins 121; Hay House 122; HMS 219; Hope 242; Indiana University 129; Inner Traditions International 130; Institute of Psychological Research, Inc/Institute de Recherches Psychologiques 220; International 131; Italica 132; Jefferson University, Thomas 262; Jordan Enterprises 244; Judaica 262; Kodansha America 136; Krieger 136; Lang, Peter 244; Lifetime 139; Literary Works 140; Locust Hill 141; Lone Pine 221; Louisiana State University 143; McClelland & Stewart 221; Mayfield 147; Michigan State University 149; New Falcon 246; Noble, The 155; Northern Illinois University 156; Nova Science 157; O'Donnell Literary Services 247; Open Court 158; Pace University 264; Paragon House 248; Paulist 162; Pax 265; Pennywhistle 164; Policy Studies Organization 169; Purdue University 172; Regnery 174; Revisionist 175; Rocky Top 175; St. Bede's 177; Savant Garde Workshop, The 266; Scots Plaid 266; Seaside 180; Sierra Club 181; Simon & Schuster 182; South End 184; Southwest of Arizona 185; Spectrum 185; Swan-Raven 190; Teachers College 191; Temple University 191; Theosophical, The 193; Third World 193; Turtle 268; Unity 197; University of Alberta, The 228; University of Illinois 199; University of Massachusetts 199; University of Ottawa, The 228; University of Pittsburgh 201; University of Scranton 202; Verso 229; Vesta 229; Wall & Emerson 229; Washington State University 206; Weatherhill 251; Weiser, Samuel 207; Wheetley, The 276; Wisdom. 211; Women's 230; Yes International Publishers 252.

Photography. Amherst Media 70; Atheneum Books For Young Readers 74; Avanyu Publishing 75; Beaver Pond 234; Benjamin 235; Bowling Green State University Popular 84; Branden 85; Caitlin, The 216; Camden House 216; Carstens 91; Cave 92; Center 93; Chronicle 95; Clarion 96; Clarkson Potter 97; Clear Light 97; Consultant, The 100; Cuff, Harry 217; Elliott & Clark 109; Elysium Growth 109; Focal 113; Goose Lane 218; Harmony House 242; HMS 219; Hounslow 220; Howells House 126; Hudson Hill 126; Jordan Enterprises 244; Key Porter 221; Layla Productions 274; Lone Pine 221; Longstreet 142; Louisiana State University 143; McClelland & Stewart 221; Minnesota Historical Society 149; Motorbooks International 151; Northland 156; NTC 157; O'Donnell Literary Services 247; Oregon Historical Society 159; Orion Research 247; Pendaya 163; Pennsylvania Historical and Museum Commission 163; Pennywhistle 164; PHB 165; Random House 173; Sierra

Club 181; Sunflower University 250; Temple University 191; Tenth Avenue Editions 276; University of Iowa 199; University of Nebraska 200; University of New Mexico 200; Voyageur 205; Wayfinder 207; Weatherhill 251; Whitman 208; Wieser & Wieser 276; Writer's Digest 211; Zoland 212.

Psychology. A.R.E. 61; Accelerated Development 63; Active Parenting 64; Advocacy 64; African American Images 65; American 70; And 71; Aronson, Jason 73; Asian Humanities 74; Atheneum Books For Young Readers 74; Austin & Winfield 75; Avon 76; Baker Book House 77; Bantam 78; Barricade 78; Baywood 79; Blue Dolphin Publishing 82; Boxwood, The 236; British American 86; Broadview 215; Bucknell University 87; Buddha Rose 236; Cambridge University 89; Carol 91; Cassandra 91; Center For Afro-American Studies 259; Charles, Publishers, The 237; Christopher The 237; Chronimed 96; Citadel 96; Cline/Fay Institute 98; Conari 99; Consortium 238; Contemporary 100; Da Capo 103; Deaconess 105; Delta Sales 239; Dimensions & Directions 272; Dimi 259; Distinctive 107; Dutton 108; Edicones 239; Éditions La Liberté 218; Eerdmans, William B. 240; Ekstasis 218; Elysium Growth 109; Eriksson, Publisher, Paul S. 110; Facts On File 111; Fairleigh Dickinson University 111; Free Spirit 260; Friedlander, Joel 260; Gallaudet University 115; Gardner 240; Gifted Education 116; Glenbridge 116; Green, Warren H. 241; Guernica 219; Harper San Francisco 121; HarperCollins 121; Hartley & Marks 121; Hastings House 122; Hawkes 242; Haworth, The 122; Hay House 122; Herald Canada 219; Hope 242; Human Services Institute 126; Hunter House 242; Ican 243; Inner Traditions International 130; Insight 130; Institute of Psychological Research, Inc/Institute de Recherches Psychologiques 220; International Information Associates 130; Ishiyaku Euroamerica 132; Jacobs 132; Jordan Enterprises 244; Kodansha America 136; Krieger 136; Lang, Peter 244; Lawrence, Merloyd 137; Lexington 139; Libra 245; Lifetime 139; Llewellyn 141; Locust Hill 141; Lorien House 263; Luramedia 144; McClelland & Stewart 221; Mancorp 246; Markowski International 274; Masefield 263; Mayfield 147; Metamorphous 148; National 153; New Falcon 246; Nova Science 157; O'Donnell Literary Services 247; Open Court 158; Pace University 264; Parable 161; Paradigm 162; Pax 265; Perspectives 165; Plenum 168; Prima 170; Revisionist 175; St. Paul Books & Media 177; Schenkman 249; Scots Plaid 266; Self-Counsel 225; Sidran, The 181; Singer Media 182; Society 183; Stanford University 187; Sulzburger & Graham 189; Theosophical 193; Third World 193; Twayne 196; 2M Communications 276; Unity Books 197; University of Nebraska 200; University of New England 203; Victor Books 204; Victory House 250; Vista Publishing 250; Walch, J. Weston 205; Wall & Emerson 229; Washington State University 206; Weidner & Sons, 207; Weiser, Samuel 207; Westport 207; Wheetley, The 276; Wiley & Sons, John 209; Williamson 209; Wilshire 210; Wingbow Press 269; Wisdom 211; Woodbridge 211; WRS 212; Yes International 252.

Real Estate. Contemporary 100; Dearborn Financial 105; Government Institutes 118; PMN 248; Revisionist 175; ULI, The Urban Land Institute 196.

Recreation. Accord Communications 63; Acorn 256; Afcom 65; Alaska Northwest 65; Appalachian Mountain Club 71; Atheneum Books For Young Readers 74; Backcountry 76; Beaver Pond 234; Betterway 81; Bicycle 81; Binford & Mort 235; Bonus 84; Book Creations 271; British American 86; Cambridge Educational 88; Camden House 216; Capra 90; Cardoza 90; Carol 91; Cave 92; Chicago Review 94; Chronicle 95; Council for Indian Education 101; Countryman, The 101; Denali, The 106; Discipleship Resources 107; Down East 107; Elysium Growth 109; Enslow 109; Epicenter 109; Eriksson, Paul S. 110; Explorer's Guide 110; Facts On File 111; Falcon 240; Foghorn 113; Friedman, Michael 272; Gem Guides 116; Globe Pequot, The 117; Golden West 117; Hancock House 121; Hay House 122; Herald Canada 219; Heyday 124; HMS 219; Horsdale & Schubart 220; Jacobs 132; Johnson 133; Jordan Enterprises 244; Layla Productions 274; Literary Works 140; Little, Brown, Children's Book Division 140; Lone Pine 221; McClelland & Stewart 221; McFarland 144; Macmillan Canada 222; Marketscope 146; Maverick 147; Menasha Ridge 275; Meriwether 148; Mountaineers, The 151; Publishing 152; Neal-Schuman 154; O'Donnell Literary Services 247; Optimus 264; Orca 223; Peachtree 163; Pelican 163; Pennywhistle 164; Pollard 265; ProStar 249; Pruett 171; Republic Of Texas 174; Revisionist 175; Rocky Mountain 225; Sasquatch 179; Sierra Club 181; Singer Media 182; SouthPark 185; Sterling 188; Stipes 188; Sulzburger & Graham 189; Sunflower University 250; Ten Speed 191; Twin Peaks 196; University Of Idaho 199; Vandamere 203; Venture 204; Voyageur 205; Wasatch 268; Wayfinder 207; Webb Research Group 251; Western Tanager 269; Wheetley The 276; Whitecap 230; Whitman 208; Wieser & Wieser 276; Wilderness 209; Wilshire 210; Windward 210; World Leisure 269; WRS 212.

Reference. A Capella 233; Abbott, Langer & Associates 61; ABC-CLIO 62; Accelerated Development 63; Accord Communications 63; Adams, Bob 64; Advance Corproation 64; Afcom 65; Amacom 67; Amadeus 67; American Associates 67; American Association for State and Local History

68; American Atheist 68; American Correctional Association 69; American Hospital 70; American Library Association 70; American Media 234; American Psychiatric, The 70; American Veterinary 257; Ancestry 71; Andrews and McMeel 71; Appalachian Mountain Club 71; Architectural Book 72; Archives 73; Arden 73; Aronson, Jason 73; Ashgate 234; Asian Humanities 74; Austin & Winfield 75; Avanyu 75; Avery 76; Backcountry 76; Baker Book House 77; B&B 77; Banks-Baldwin Law 78; Barricade 78; Behrman House 79; Bethel 80; Betterway 81; Binford & Mort 235; Blackbirch 82; Blue Bird 82; BNA 83; Bowling Green State University Popular 84; Branden 85; Brassey's 85; Brick House 86; Broadview 215; Broadway 87; Buddha Rose 236; Business & Legal Reports 87; Business McGraw-Hill 88; CQ 88; Cambridge University 89; Camden House 89; Camden House 216; Caradium 90; Caratzas, Aristide D. 236; Cardoza 90; Career, The 90; Catbird 92; Center For Western Studies, The 237; Christian Classics 237; Christian Media 259; Christian 95; Christopher, The 237; Clark, Arthur H. 238; Cleaning Consultant Services 238; College Board, The 98; Compute 99; Computer Technology Research 99; Confluence 99; Consultant, The 100; Consumer Reports 100; Contemporary 100; Coteau 217; Creative Spark, The 272; Cuff, Harry 217; Dante University Of America 103; David, Jonathan 104; Dearborn Financial 105; Delphi 106; Denali, The 106; Distinctive 107; Drama 107; Dundurn 217; Dustbooks 108; Earth-Love 259; East Coast Publishing 108; Eastwind 239; Eckert, J.K. 272; Edicones 239; Eerdmans, William B. 240; EES 260; Enslow 109; Evans, M. 110; Facts On File 111; Fairleigh Dickinson University 111; Fallen Leaf 260; Fathom 260; Ferguson, J.G. 112; Fire Engineering 112; Focal 113; Formac 218; Friends United 115; Gambling Times 260; Gardner 240; Garland 115; Garrett Park 115; Gaslight 115; Genealogical 241; Giniger, The K S 272; Glenbridge 116; Global Professional 116; Government Institutes 118; Graber 273; Graduate Group, The 241; Graphic Arts 261; Great Lakes 261; Gryphon 120; Harper San Francisco 121; HarperCollins 121; Harvard Common, The 121; Harvest House 122; Hastings House 122; Haworth, The 122; Hay House 122; Herald Canada 219; Herbal Studies Library 261; Heyday 124; Highsmith 125; Hippocrene 125; HMS 219; Hoard & Sons, W.D. 261; Holmes & Meier Publishers 125; Hope Publishing House 242; HRD 126; Hunter Publishing 127; IEEE 243; Imagine 128; Index 129; Indiana Historical Society 262; Indiana University 129; Industrial 129; Information Resources 129; International Foundation Of Employee Benefit Plans 130; International Information Associates 130; International Medical 131; International 131; Ishiyaku Euroamerica 132; Jackson, Hart & Leslie 262; Jain 133; Jist Works 133; Jordan Enterprises 244; JSA 273; Judaica 262; Ketz Agency, Louise B. 273; Kinseeker 135; Kregel 136; Krieger 136; Laing Communications 274; Lake View 137; Lang, Peter 244; Langenscheidt 137; Lawyers & Judges 137; Leadership 138; Lehigh University 138; Lexington 139; Libraries Unlimited 139; Library Research Associates 245; Literary Works 140; Locust Hill 141; Lone Eagle 141; Longstreet 142; Loompanics Unlimited 142; Love Child 143; McClelland & Stewart 221; McFarland 144; Macmillan Canada 222; Madison 145; Mancorp 246; Maupin House 263; Maverick 147; Mayhaven 246; Meadowbrook 147; Media Forum International 147; Media 147; Meriwether 148; Metamorphous 148; Meyerbooks 263; Michigan State University 149; Minnesota Historical Society 149; Monitor 150; Museum of Northern Arizona 152; Mysterious, The 152; Mystic Seaport Museum 263; Nautical & Aviation 153; Neal-Schuman 154; Nelson, Thomas 154; New England 275; New York Zoetrope 155; NTC 157; Oceana 157; Octameron Associates 157; O'Donnell Literary Services 247; Ohio Biological Survey 264; Orbis 158; Orchises 159; Oregon Historical Society 159; Orion Research 247; Oryx 160; Ottenheimer 275; Our Sunday Visitor 160; Pacific 160; Pandemic International 161; Pandora 223; Paragon House 248; Partners in Publishing 265; Peachpit 162; Pennsylvania Historical and Museum Commission 163; Phi Delta Kappa Educational Foundation 165; Picton 166; Pineapple 167; Plexus 168; PMN 248; Pocket 168; Policy Studies Organization 169; Precept 169; Princeton 170; Professional 171; Professional Resource 171; Prolingua Associates 171; PSI Research 172; Rainbow 173; Reference Service 173; Revisionist 175; Revisionist 175; Rocky Top 175; Rosen 175; Rutledge Hill 176; Sachem ates 276; Sandhill Crane 178; Sandlapper 178; Scarecrow 179; Schenkman 249; Schiffer 179; Schirmer 179; Serendipity Systems 180; Shoestring 225; Sidran, The 181; Simon & Pierre 226; Singer Media 182; SJL 182; Sky 183; Sono Nis 226; Sourcebooks 184; Spectrum 185; Speech Bin, The 186; Standard 186; Star Song 187; Sterling 188; Stoeger 188; Sulzburger & Graham 189; Sunflower University 250; TAB 190; Ten Speed 191; Texas State Historical Association 192; Third World 193; Thomas Investigative 193; Tidewater 194; Trend Book Division 196; Twin Peaks 196; UCLA-American Indian Studies Center 268; Umbrella 227; United Church (UCPH), The 228; Unity 197; University Of Idaho 199; University of Alaska 198; University of Alberta, The 228; University of Illinois 199; University of North Texas 201; University of Ottawa, The 228; University of Pittsburgh 201; University of Kentucky 202; University of New England 203; Utah State University 203; Vesta 229; Victor 204; Virginia State Library and Archives 268; Vista 250; Vortex Communications 268; Waite Group 205; Walker 205; Wall & Emerson 229; Wayfinder 207; Weatherhill 251; Webb Research Group 251; Weidner & Sons 207; Whitehorse 269; Whitford 208; Wiley & Sons, John 209; Wingbow 269; Wisdom 211; Woodbine House 211; Wordware 211; York 231; Zondervan 212.

Regional. Alaska Northwest 65; Alaskan Viewpoint 257; Almar 66; American Associates 67; Appalachian Mountain 71; Arsenal Pulp 214; Avanyu 75; B&B 258; Berwick 80; Binford & Mort 235; Blair, John F. 82; Border 258; Borealis 214; Boston Mills, The 215; Bowling Green State University Popular 84; Boxwood, The 236; Brick House 86; Bright Mountain 258; British American 86; Cacanadadada 215; Caddo Gap 88; Caitlin, The 216; Camino 89; Canadian Plains Research Center 216; Capra 90; Carol 91; Cave 92; Caxton Printers, The 92; Center For Western Studies, The 237; Chapel Street 259; Chicago Review 94; Chronicle 95; Clear Light 97; Confluence 99; Coteau 217; Countryman, The 101; Creative Arts 238; Creative 102; Cuff, Harry 217; Davidson, Harlan 104; Dawson, W.S. 105; Denali, The 106; Desktop Grafx 272; Distinctive 107; Down East 107; Down The Shore 259; Dundurn 217; Ecco, The 108; ECW 218; Eerdmans, William B. 240; Epicenter 109; Explorer's Guide 110; Faber & Faber 110; Family Album, The 111; Filter 240; Fitzhenry & Whiteside 218; Foghorn 113; Formac 218; Gem Guides 116; Gem Guides 116; Globe Pequot, The 117; Golden West 117; Golden West 117; Great Northwest 118; Guernica 219; Hampton Roads 241; Hancock House 121; Heart Of The Lakes 242; Hemingway Western Studies Series 261; Hendrick-Long 123; Herald 124; Heyday 124; High Plains 124; HMS 219; Hoard & Sons, W.D. 261; Horsdale & Schubart 220; Hunter 127; Indiana Historical Society 262; Indiana University 129; Johnson 133; Jordan Enterprises 244; Kent State University 135; Kinseeker 135; Lahontan Images 262; Laing Communications 274; Lerner 138; Lexikos 138; Lifetime 139; Literary Works 140; Longstreet House 245; Longstreet 142; Louisiana State University 143; Mancorp 246; Marketscope 146; Maupin House 246; Maupin House 263; Maverick 147; Mayhaven 246; Media/Midgard 147; Menasha Ridge 275; Minnesota Historical Society 149; Moon 150; Mountain 151; Museum of Northern Arizona 152; National 153; New England, The 154; Nightshade 264; North Country 247; Northern Illinois University 156; Northland 156; O'Donnell Literary Services 247; Orca 223; Oregon Historical Society 159; Oregon State University 159; Overlook, The 160; Pace University 264; Pacific 160; Pelican 163; Pennsylvania Historical and Museum Commission 163; Pennywhistle 164; Pickering, The 166; Prairie Oak 265; Prentice-Hall Canada 224; Pruett 171; Purdue University 172; Quail Ridge 265; Renaissance House 174; Republic Of Texas 174; Rhombus 266; Rutgers University 176; Sand River 266; Sandlapper 178; Sasquatch 179; Schiffer 179; Scots Plaid 266; Seacoast of New England 266; Sevgo 249; Shoestring 225; Signature 182; Smith, Gibbs 183; Sono Nis 226; Southern Methodist University 185; Southwest of Arizona 185; Sunbelt Media 189; Sunflower University 250; Sunstone 190; Syracuse University 190; Tamarack 267; Temple University 191; Texas A&M University 192; Texas Christian University 192; Texas Tech University 192; Texas Western 193; Third World 193; Tidewater 194; Timber 194; Trend Book Division 196; Umbrella 197; University Of Idaho 199; University of Alaska 198; University of Alberta, The 228; University of Arizona 198; University of Iowa 199; University of Manitoba 228; University of Missouri 200; University of Nevada 200; University of North Texas 201; University of Oklahoma 201; University of Pittsburgh 201; University of Scranton 202; University of Tennessee, The 202; University of Texas 202; University of Colorado 202; University Press of Mississippi 203; University Press of New England 203; Utah State University 203; Valiant 268; Vandamere 203; Vanwell 228; Vehicule 229; Vestal, The 204; Victory House 250; Vista 268; Voyageur 205; Wasatch 268; Washington State University 206; Wayfinder 207; Western Book/Journal 251; Western Tanager 269; Wheetley, The 276; Whitecap 230; Wilderness Adventure 209; Yes International 252; Zoland 212.

Religion. A.R.E. 61; Abingdon 62; Accent 63; ACTA 63; Alban Institute, The 66; American Atheist 68; American Catholic 257; And 71; Anima 257; Aronson, Jason 73; Asian Humanities 74; Atheneum Books For Young Readers 74; Augsburg 75; Austin & Winfield 75; Baker 77; Bantam 78; Beacon Hill of Kansas City 79; Beacon 79; Bear 79; Behrman House 79; Berkley 80; Bethel 80; Blue Dolphin 82; Bookcraft 84; Bosco Multimedia, Don 235; Bridge 236; Bucknell University 87; Buddha Rose 236; Canadian Institute of Ukrainian Studies 216; Caratzas, Aristide D. 236; Cassandra 91; Catholic University of America 92; China Books & Periodicals 94; Chosen 95; Christian Classics 237; Christian Education 95; Christian 95; Christopher, The 237; College 238; Cross Cultural 102; Crossway 102; CSS 239; David, Jonathan 104; Delphi 106; Discipleship Resources 107; Eastwind 239; Eerdmans, William B. 240; Facts On File 111; Franciscan 260; Friends United 115; Gibson, The C.R. 116; Gold'n' Honey 117; Great Quotations 118; Greenlawn 119; Group 119;

Group's Hands-On™ Bible Curriculum 119; Guernica 219; HarperCollins 121; Harvest House 122; Haworth, The 122; Hay House 122; Hendrickson 123; Hensley, Virgil W. 123; Herald 123; Herald Canada 219; Herald 124; HMS 219; Holmes & Meier 125; Hope 242; Ican 243; ICS 127; Indiana University 129; Inner Traditions International 130; Interlink 130; Italica 132; Jefferson University, Thomas 262; Jordan Enterprises 244; Judaica 262; Judson 134; Kodansha America 136; Kregel 136; Kumarian 244; Lang, Peter 244; Lifetime 139; Ligouri 139; Locust Hill 141; Loyola University 143; Luramedia 144; McClelland & Stewart 221; Marketscope 146; Mayfield 147; Meriwether 148; Michigan State University 149; Monument 150; Morehouse 150; Morrow, William 151; Mount Olive College 246; National 264; Nelson, Thomas 154; New Falcon 246; New Hope 154; New Leaf 154; O'Donnell Literary Services 247; Open Court 158; Orbis 158; Our Sunday Visitor 160; Pacific 160; P&R 161; Parable 161; Paragon House 248; Parallax 248; Paulist 162; Pelican 163; Peter Pauper 165; Picton 166; Pilgrim, The 167; PMN 248; Probe 265; Publishers Associates 172; Purdue University 172; Purple Finch 265; Rainbow 73; Random House 173; Regnery 174; Resurrection 174; Revisionist 175; Ross 266; St. Anthony Messenger 176; St. Bede's 177; St. Paul Books & Media 177; Seaside 180; Servant 180; Shaw, Harold 181; Signature 182; 16th Century Journal 267; Standard 186; Star 187; Star Song 187; Stillpoint 188; Sunflower University 250; Theosophical 193; Third World 193; Tyndale House 196; UAHC 250; United Church (UCPH), The 228; Unity 197; University of Alabama 197; University of Manitoba 228; University of North Carolina, The 200; University of Ottawa, The 228; University of Scranton 202; University of Tennessee, The 202; Vesta 229; Victor 204; Victory House 250; Webb Research Group 251; Weiser, Samuel 207; Wheatley, The 276; Whitman 208; Windflower Communications 230; Wisdom 211; Zondervan 212; Harper San Francisco 121.

Scholarly. Baywood 79; Beacon 79; BNA 83; Brookings Institution 87; Cambridge University 89; Canadian Institute of Ukrainian Studies 216; Canadian Plains Research Center 216; Cross Cultural 102; Dante University Of America 103; Fairleigh Dickinson University 111; Gallaudet University 115; Garland 115; Hemingway Western Studies Series 261; Kent State University 135; Knopf, Alfred A. 135; Lang, Peter 244; Lehigh University 138; McFarland 144; Michigan State University 149; Modern Language Association of America 150; Oregon State University 159; Pacific 160; Paragon House 248; Phi Delta Kappa Educational Foundation 165; Pilgrim, The 167; Publishers Associates 172; Purdue University 172; Scarecrow 179; Schirmer 179; Southern Illinois University 185; Stanford University 187; Temple University 191; Texas Christian University 192; Texas Tech University 192; Texas Western 193; Three Continents 194; Twayne 196; University of Alabama 197; University of Alaska 198; University of Alberta, The 228; University of Arizona 198; University of California Los Angeles Center for Afro-American Studies Publications 268; University of California 198; University of Illinois 199; University of Manitoba 228; University of Missouri 200; University of New Mexico 200; University of North Carolina, The 200; University of Ottawa, The 228; University of Pennsylvania 201; University of Pittsburgh 201; University of Scranton 202; University of Tennessee, The 202; University of Texas 202; University of Colorado 202; University of Kentucky 202; University of Mississippi 203; Utah State University 203; Venture 204; Washington State University 206; Whitson 208; York 231.

Science/Technology. Abelexpress 254; Alaska Northwest Books 65; American Astronautical Society 68; American Chemical Society 69; American 70; American Veterinary 257; Amherst Media 70; B&B 77; Bantam 78; Bear and 79; Blackbirch 82; Boxwood, The 236; Buddha Rose 236; Cambridge University 89; Capstone 90; Carol 91; Cave 92; Charlesbridge 93; Chicago Review 94; College Board, The 98; Consortium 238; Da Capo 103; Dutton 108; Eastwind 239; Éditions La Liberté 218; Enslow 109; Focal 113; Four Walls Eight Windows 114; Gifted Education 116; Global Professional 116; Graber Productions 273; Grapevine 118; Greey De Pencier 273; Grosset & Dunlap 119; HarperCollins 121; Hay House 122; Helix 261; HMS 219; Howells House 126; HRD 126; IEEE 243; Industrial 129; Insight 130; Institute of Psychological Research, Inc/Institute de Recherches Psychologiques 220; International Information Associates 130; Interstate The 243; Iowa State University 132; Jacobs 132; Johnson 133; Jordan Enterprises 244; K.I.P. Children's Books 134; Kalmbach 134; Ketz Agency, Louise B. 273; Kodansha America 136; Krieger 136; Laing Communications 274; Lehigh University 138; Lerner 138; Literary Works 140; Little, Brown, Children's Book Division 140; Little, Brown 140; Locust Hill 141; Lorien House 263; Lucent 143; Lyons & Burford 144; McClelland & Stewart 221; McDonald & Woodward 144; McGuinn & McGuire 145; Medical Physics 147; Metamorphous 148; Mid-List 263; Millbrook, The 149; Mountain 151; Museum of Northern Arizona 152; Naturegraph 264; New Readers 155; Nova Science 157; Noyes Data 157; O'Donnell Literary Services 247; Omni 275; Open Court 158; Oregon State

University 159; Pippin 167; Plenum 168; Plexus 168; Policy Studies Organization 169; Precept 169; Purdue University 172; Rainbow 173; Regnery 174; Revisionist 175; Rocky Top 175; Ross 176; Ross 266; Rutgers University 176; San Francisco 177; Schenkman 249; Shoestring 225; Sierra Club 181; Simon & Schuster 182; SJL 182; Sky 183; South End 184; Stanford University 187; Sterling 188; Stipes 188; Sulzburger & Graham 189; Sunflower University 250; TAB 190; Ten Speed 191; Texas Tech University 192; Theosophical House, The 193; Times 195; Univelt 197; University of Alaska 198; University of Arizona 198; University of Pennsylvania 201; University of Texas 202; University of New England 203; Verso 229; Walch, Publisher, J. Weston 205; Walker and 205; Wall & Emerson 229; Warren House 206; Watts, Franklin 206; Weidner & Sons 207; Western Book/Journal 251; Wheetley , The 276; Whitman 208; Wiley & Sons, John 209; Williamson 209; Willowisp 210; Windward 210; WRS 212.

Self-Help. A.R.E. 61; Accent 63; Active Parenting 64; Adams, Bob 64; Advance Corproation 64; Advocacy 64; Aegis 257; Afcom 65; Allen 66; Almar 66; Amacom 67; Atheneum Books For Young Readers 74; Augsburg 75; Avon 76; Baker 77; Bantam 78; Barricade 78; Benjamin, The 271; Betterway 81; Blue Dolphin 82; Blue Poppy 83; Book Creations 271; Bridge 236; British American 86; Broadview 215; Buddha Rose 236; Bull 87; Burning Gate 87; Business McGraw-Hill 88; Cambridge Educational 88; Capra 90; Caradium 90; Career, The 90; Carol 91; Cassandra 91; CCC 93; CEDI 259; Centering 93; Charles, The 237; China Books & Periodicals 94; Chosen 95; Christian 95; Christopher 237; Chronimed 96; Clarkson Potter 97; Cleaning Consultant Services 238; Cliffs Notes 98; Cline/Fay Institute 98; College Board, The 98; Conari 99; Consortium 238; Consumer Reports 100; Contemporary 100; Cool Hand Communications 100; Creative Spark, The 272; CSS 239; David, Jonathan 104; Deaconess 105; Delta Sales 239; Desktop Grafx 272; Devyn 106; Distinctive 107; Dutton 108; Earth-Love 259; Elliott & Clark 109; Elysium Growth 109; Eriksson, Paul S. 110; Fine, Donald I. 112; Fisher 113; Flores, J. 113; Focus on the Family 113; Free Spirit 260; Friedlander, Joel 260; Gambling Times 260; Gardner 240; Giniger, The K S 272; Graber Productions 273; Grapevine 118; Great Quotations 118; Hampton Roads 241; Hancock House 121; Harper San Francisco 121; HarperCollins 121; Hartley & Marks 121; Harvard Common, The 121; Harvest House 122; Hastings House 122; Hawkes 242; Hay House 122; Herald 123; Herald Canada 219; Herald House 124; Herbal Studies Library 261; HMS 219; Hounslow 220; Human Services Institute 126; Humdinger 127; Hunter House 242; Huntington House 127; Ican Book 243; Insight 130; International Wealth Success 131; Ivy League 262; Jacobs 132; Jain 133; Jist Works 133; Jordan Enterprises 244; Kesend, Michael 135; Lamppost 274; Larksdale 245; Lifetime 139; Ligouri 139; Limelight Editions 140; Literary Works 140; Llewellyn 141; Loompanics Unlimited 142; Luramedia 144; McClelland & Stewart 221; McDonald & Woodward 144; McGuinn & McGuire 145; Macmillan Canada 222; Mancorp 246; Marketscope 146; Markowski International 146; Markowski International 274; Maupin House 263; Metamorphous 148; Meyerbooks 263; Mid-List 263; Mills & Sanderson 149; Mustang 152; National 153; Nelson, Thomas 154; New Falcon 246; New Leaf 154; Nova Science 157; O'Donnell Literary Services 247; One On One Computer Training 158; Optimus 264; Pacific Learning Council 264; Pacific Publishing Association 160; Parable 161; Partners 265; Paulist 162; Pax 265; Peachtree 163; Pelican 163; Perspectives 165; Pickering, The 166; PMN 248; Prima 170; Princeton 170; Publicom 275; Purple Finch 265; QED 249; Rainbow Books 173; Random House 173; Resurrection 174; Revisionist 175; Rocky Top 175; Rosen 175; Rutledge Hill 176; St. Paul Books & Media 177; Saurie Island 179; Schenkman 249; Seaside 180; Self-Counsel 225; Servant 180; Shaw, Harold 181; Sidran, The 181; Singer Media 182; SJL 182; Society 183; SouthPark 185; Spinsters Ink 186; Star 187; Stillpoint 188; Success 189; Sulzburger & Graham 189; Tambra 267; Ten Speed 191; Theosophical, The 193; Third World 193; Turtle 268; Twin Peaks 196; Tyndale House 196; United Church (UCPH), The 228; Unity 197; Victor 204; Victory House 250; Vista 250; Volcano 268; Waite Group 205; Walker 205; Weiser, Samuel 207; Western Book/Journal 251; Whitford 208; Wiley & Sons, John 209; Wilshire 210; Windflower Communications 230; Wingbow Press 269; Wisdom 211; Woodbridge 211; World Leisure 269; WRS 212; Yes International 252; Zondervan 212.

Social Sciences. C Q 88; Caratzas, Aristide D. 236; Duquesne University 108; Eerdmans, William B. 240; Feminist at the City University of New York, The 112; Garland 115; Indiana Historical Society 262; Indiana University 129; Insight Books 130; International 131; Lang, Peter 244; Longman 142; New Readers 155; Northern Illinois University 156; Open Court 158; Plenum 168; Roxbury 176; Social Science Education Consortium 183; Southern Illinois University 185; Stanford University 187; Teachers College 191; University of California 198; University of Missouri 200; Verso 229; Walch, J. Weston 205; Whitson Publishing, The 208.

Sociology. American Associates 67; American 70; Arsenal Pulp 214; Ashgate Publishing 234; Atheneum Books For Young Readers 74; Austin & Winfield 75; Avanyu 75; Baker Book House 77; Bantam 78; Barricade 78; Baywood 79; Blue Bird 82; Branden 85; Bucknell University 87; Buddha Rose 236; Canadian Institute of Ukrainian Studies 216; Canadian Plains Research Center 216; Capra 90; Cato Institute 92; Center For Afro-American Studies 259; Charles, The 237; Child Welfare League Of America 94; China Books & Periodicals 94; Christopher Publishing House, The 237; Cleis 97; Cline/Fay Institute 98; Coach House 217; Creative Spark, The 272; Cross Cultural 102; Cuff, Harry 217; Davidson, Harlan 104; Deaconess 105; Distinctive 107; Edicones Universal 239; Éditions La Liberté 218; Eerdmans, William B. 240; Elysium Growth 109; Enslow 109; Eriksson, Paul S. 110; Faber & Faber 110; Fairleigh Dickinson University 111; Feminist at the City University of New York, The 112; Formac 218; Gallaudet University 115; Gardner 240; Glenbridge 116; Green, Warren H. 241; HarperCollins 121; Haworth, The 122; Hay House 122; HMS 219; Holmes & Meier 125; Hope Publishing House 242; Howells House 126; Ican 243; ILR 128; Insight 130; Jefferson University, Thomas 262; Jordan Enterprises 244; Kodansha America 136; Kumarian 244; Lake View 137; Lang, Peter 244; Lexington 139; Libra 245; Lincoln Springs 262; Longman 142; Lorimer, James 221; McClelland & Stewart 221; McFarland 144; Madison 145; Marketscope 146; Markowski International 274; Masefield 263; Mayfield 147; Mercury, The 222; Metamorphous 148; NASW 153; New Falcon 246; Noble, The 155; Nova Science Publishers 157; O'Donnell Literary Services 247; Perspectives 165; Plenum 168; Policy Studies Organization 169; Purdue University 172; Random House 173; Regnery 174; Revisionist 175; Roxbury 176; Rutgers University 176; Schenkman 249; Scots Plaid 266; South End 184; Spectrum 185; Stanford University 187; Sunflower University 250; Teachers College 191; Temple University 191; Third World 193; Thomas Investigative 193; Twayne 196; Twin Peaks 196; UCLA-American Indian Studies Center 268; United Church (UCPH), The 228; University of Alberta, The 228; University of Arkansas, The 198; University of Illinois 199; University of Massachusetts 199; University of North Carolina, The 200; University of Ottawa, The 228; University of Pittsburgh 201; University of Scranton 202; University of New England 203; Vehicule 229; Venture 204; Verso 229; Walch, J. Weston 205; Washington State University 206; Wayfinder 207; Wheetley, The 276; Wiley & Sons, John 209; Windflower Communications 230; Women's 230; Louisiana State University 143.

Software. Adams-Blake 64; Agritech 257; ASQC 74; Barron's Educational Series 79; Boyds Mills 85; Branden 85; Career 90; Compute 99; Computer Technology Research 99; Desktop Grafx 272; Eastwind 239; Eckert & , J.K. 272; Family Album, The 111; Global Professional 116; Grapevine 118; HMS 219; HRD 126; Jist Works 133; Laing Communications 274; Libraries Unlimited 139; Literary Works 140; MIS 150; National Textbook 153; Neal-Schuman 154; New York Zoetrope 155; Nova Science 157; O'Donnell Literary Services 247; One On One Computer Training 158; Paradigm 162; Revisionist 175; Richboro 175; Ross 176; SAS Institute 178; Schirmer 179; Serendipity 180; Singer Media 182; Sugar Hill, The 267; Sulzburger & Graham 189; Swan-Raven 190; Sybex 190; TAB 190; Technical Analysis of Stocks & Commodities 267; Walch, J. Weston 205; Wiley & Sons, John 209; Windsor 210; Wine Appreciation Guild 210.

Sports. Acorn 256; Afcom 65; Alaska Northwest 65; American 70; Archway Paperbacks/Minstrel Books 73; Atheneum Books For Young Readers 74; Avon 76; Backcountry 76; Bantam 78; Barron's Educational Series 79; Benjamin , The 271; Bentley, Robert 80; Betterway 81; Bicycle 81; Blackbirch 82; Bonus 84; Book Creations 271; Bowling Green State University Popular 84; Briarcliff 236; British American 86; Broadview 215; Bull 87; C.F.W. Enterprises 258; Cambridge Educational 88; Capstone 90; Cardoza 90; Carol 91; Cave 92; Contemporary 100; Creative Spark, The 272; Da Capo 103; David, Jonathan 104; Denali, The 106; Devyn 106; Diamond 259; E.M. 259; Eagle's View 108; Eriksson, Paul S. 110; Facts On File 111; Fine, Donald I. 112; Foghorn 113; Friedman, Michael 272; Gallaudet University 115; Graber Productions 273; Great Quotations 118; Hancock House 121; Harmony House 242; HarperCollins 121; HMS 219; Horsdale & Schubart 220; Howell 126; Jones University, Bob 133; Jordan Enterprises 244; JSA 273; Kesend, Michael 135; Ketz Agency, Louise B. 273; Key Porter 221; LAWCO 262; Lerner 138; Lifetime 139; Little, Brown, Children's Book Division 140; Little, Brown 140; Lone Pine 221; Longstreet 142; Lucent 143; Lyons & Burford 144; McClelland & Stewart 221; McFarland 144; Macmillan Canada 222; Marabou 263; Masters 146; Maupin House 246; Maverick 147; Menasha Ridge 275; Millbrook, The 149; Mosaic Miniature 263; Motorbooks International 151; Mountaineers, The 151; Mustang 152; National 153; Nova Science 157; O'Donnell Literary Services 247; Open Road 158; Orca 223; Pennsylvania Historical and Museum Commission 163; Pennywhistle 164; ProStar 249; Pruett 171; Ragged Mountain 173; Random House 173; Sasquatch 179; Sierra Club 181; Singer Media 182; SJL 182;

Stackpole 186; Sterling 188; Stoeger 188; Stoneydale 189; Sunbelt Media 189; Sunflower University 250; Taylor 191; Turtle 268; Twin Peaks 196; University of Illinois 199; University of Nebraska 200; Weatherhill 251; Wheetley, The 276; Whitman 208; Wieser & Wieser 276; Wilderness Adventure 209; Willowisp 210; Wilshire 210; Women's 230.

Technical. A Capella 233; Abbott, Langer & Associates 61; Aberdeen Group, The 62; Aegean Park 65; Almar 66; American Associates 67; American Correctional Association 69; American Hospital 70; American 70; American Psychiatric, The 70; American Society of Civil Engineers 70; American Veterinary 257; Amigadget 257; Aronson, Jason 73; Ashgate 234; ASQC 74; Auto Book 257; Aviation Book 258; Baywood 79; Bentley, Robert 80; Bicycle 81; Blue Poppy 83; Boxwood, The 236; Branden 85; Brevet 85; Brick House 86; Broadway 87; Burning Gate 87; Business McGraw-Hill 88; Canadian Plains Research Center 216; Caratzas, Publisher, Aristide D. 236; Cave 92; Cleaning Consultant Services 238; Computer Technology Research 99; Consortium Publishing 238; Cornell Maritime 100; Craftsman 101; Cuff, Harry 217; Desktop Grafx 272; Dickens 259; Distinctive 107; Drama Book 107; East Coast 108; Eastern Caribbean Institute 260; Eastwind 239; Eckert & , J.K. 272; EES 260; Fire Engineering Books & Videos 112; Focal 113; Fox Chapel 114; FPMI Communications 114; Gardner 240; Global Professional 116; Government Institutes 118; Grapevine 118; Graphic Arts 261; Great Lakes 261; Green, Warren H. 241; Hartley & Marks 121; Hoard & Sons, W.D. 261; Hope Publishing 242; HRD 126; Ican 243; IEEE 243; Index 129; Industrial 129; Information Resources 129; International Foundation Of Employee Benefit Plans 130; International Information Associates 130; Interweave 132; Iowa State University 132; Jacobs 132; Jelmar 262; Jordan Enterprises 244; Krieger 136; Laing Communications 274; Lake View 137; Library Research Associates 245; Lone Eagle 141; Lorien House 263; McFarland 144; McGuinn & McGuire 145; Mancorp 246; Markowski International 146; Medical Physics Publishing 147; Metamorphous 148; Michigan State University 149; MIS 150; Museum of Northern Arizona 152; Neal-Schuman 154; New York Zoetrope 155; Nova Science 157; Noyes Data 157; O'Donnell Literary Services 247; Ohio Biological Survey 264; One On One Computer Training 158; Orchises 159; O'Reilly & Associates 159; Pacific 160; Partners in Publishing 265; Peachpit 162; Pennsylvania Historical and Museum Commission 163; PMN 248; Policy Studies Organization 169; Precept 169; Probus Publishing 170; Professional 171; ProStar 249; Revisionist 175; Rocky Top 175; Ross 266; San Francisco 177; Sandhill Crane 178; SAS Institute 178; Saurie Island 179; Shoestring 225; Sidran, The 181; SJL 182; Skidmore-Roth 249; Sky 183; Sourcebooks 184; Spheric House 267; Sterling 188; Stipes 188; Sulzburger & Graham 189; Sybex 190; Systemsware, The 267; TAB 190; Texas Tech University 192; Texas Western 193; Tiare 194; ULI, The Urban Land Institute 196; Univelt 197; University Of Idaho 199; University of Alaska 198; University of Alberta, The 228; Vestal, The 204; Waite Group 205; Weidner & Sons 207; Western Book/Journal 251; Wheetley, The 276; Wiley & Sons, John 209; Windsor 210; Wordware 211.

Textbook. A Capella 233; Abingdon 62; Accelerated Development 63; Active Parenting 64; Afcom 65; Amacom 67; American Associates 67; American Association for State and Local History 68; American Correctional Association 69; American Hospital 70; American 70; American Psychiatric, The 70; American Veterinary 257; Amigadget 257; Anchorage 71; Anima 257; Arden 73; Art Direction Book 73; Ashgate 234; Asian Humanities 74; Austin & Winfield 75; Avery 76; Aviation 258; Baker Book House 77; Bandanna 77; Barron's Educational Series 79; Beacon Hill of Kansas City 79; Behrman House 79; Blue Poppy 83; Bosco Multimedia, Don 235; Bowling Green State University Popular 84; Boxwood, The 236; Boyd & Fraser 84; Branden 85; Brassey's 85; Bridge 236; Broadview 215; Buddha Rose 236; C Q 88; Cambridge University 89; Canadian Plains Research Center 216; Caratzas, Aristide D. 236; Career 90; Center For Afro-American Studies 259; Center For Western Studies, The 237; Charlesbridge 93; China Books & Periodicals 94; Christian Classics 237; Christian Education 95; Christopher Publishing House, The 237; Cleaning Consultant Services 238; Cliffs Notes 98; College 238; Consortium 238; Corwin 101; Cottonwood 101; Cuff, Harry 217; Davidson, Harlan 104; Dearborn Financial 105; Desktop Grafx 272; Dimensions & Directions 272; Discovery Enterprises 239; Distinctive 107; Drama Book 107; Eastern Caribbean Institute 260; Eastwind 239; Eckert, J.K. 272; Eerdmans, William B. 240; EES 260; Elysium Growth 109; ETC 110; Fire Engineering Books & Videos 112; Fitzhenry & Whiteside 218; Focal 113; Formac 218; Friends United 115; Gardner 240; Garland 115; Glenbridge 116; Global Professional 116; Grapevine 118; Graphic Arts 261; Group 119; Group's Hands-On™ Bible Curriculum 119; Haworth, The 122; Herald Canada 219; HMS 219; Hoard & Sons, W.D. 261; Hope Publishing House 242; Howells House 126; Ican 243; IEEE 243; Information Resources 129; Institute of Psychological Research, Inc/Institute de Recherches Psychologiques 220; International Founda-

243; Interlink 130; Italica 132; Jain 133; Jefferson University, Thomas 262; Johnson 133; Jordan Enterprises 244; Kesend, Michael 135; Kodansha America 136; Lifetime 139; Literary Works 140; Lone Pine 221; Lonely Planet 142; Lyons & Burford 144; McClelland & Stewart 221; McDonald & Woodward 144; Mancorp 246; Marlor 146; Maupin House 263; Maverick 147; Menasha Ridge 275; Moon 150; Mosaic Miniature 263; Mount Olive College 246; Mountain 151; Mountaineers, The 151; Mustang 152; Neal-Schuman 154; NTC 157; O'Donnell Literary Services 247; Open Road 158; Orca 223; Pandemic International 161; Paradise 264; Passport 162; Pelican 163; Pendaya 163; Pennsylvania Historical and Museum Commission 163; Pennywhistle 164; Pilot 167; Prairie Oak 265; Prima 170; Pruett 171; Rainbow 173; RedBrick 266; Renaissance House 174; Revisionist 175; Rockbridge 266; Rocky Mountain 225; Ross 266; Sasquatch 179; Scots Plaid 266; Shoestring 225; Sierra Club 181; Soho 184; SouthPark 185; Spectrum 185; Stone Bridge 267; Sulzburger & Graham 189; Trend 196; Twin Peaks 196; Ulysses 197; Umbrella 197; Vandamere 203; Verso 229; Vista 268; Voyageur 205; Wasatch 268; Wayfinder 207; Weatherhill 251; Webb Research Group 251; Wescott Cove 207; White Pine 208; Whitehorse 269; Whitman 208; Wieser & Wieser 276; Wilderness Adventure 209; Wine Appreciation Guild 210; World Leisure 269; Zoland 212.

Women's Issues/Studies. ABC-CLIO 62; Advocacy 64; American Associates 67; Arden 73; Astarte Shell 257; Austin & Winfield 75; Baker Book House 77; Bandanna 77; Bantam 78; Barricade 78; Baywood 79; Beacon 79; Blackbirch 82; Blue Poppy 83; Bonus 84; Bowling Green State University Popular 84; Broadview 215; Burning Gate 87; Calyx 258; C&T 89; Carol 91; Center For Afro-American Studies 259; China Books & Periodicals 94; Cleis 97; Conari 99; Contemporary 100; Creative Spark, The 272; Crossing, The 102; Davidson, Harlan 104; Delphi 106; Fairleigh Dickinson University 111; Feminist at the City University of New York, The 112; Focus on the Family 113; Formac 218; Gardner 240; Goose Lane 218; Great Quotations 118; Gylantic 120; Harvest House 122; Haworth, The 122; Hay House 122; Hensley, Virgil W. 123; Holmes & Meier 125; Hope Publishing House 242; Human Services Institute 126; Ide House 127; ILR 128; Indiana University 129; Inner Traditions International 130; Insight 130; Interlink Group 130; International 131; Jordan Enterprises 244; Key Porter 221; Kumarian 244; Lamppost 274; Lexington 139; Liberal, The 139; Lifetime 139; Lincoln Springs 262; Literary Works 140; Llewellyn 141; Locust Hill 141; Longstreet 142; Lorimer, James 221; Lucent 143; Luramedia 144; McClelland & Stewart 221; McFarland 144; McGuinn & McGuire 145; Mercury, The 222; Milkweed Editions 149; Minnesota Historical Society 149; Monument 150; New Hope 154; Noble, The 155; O'Donnell Literary Services 247; Open Court 158; Oregon Historical Society 159; Pace University 264; Pandora 223; Papier-Mache 264; Paradigm 248; Parallax 248; Pennywhistle 164; Publicom 275; Publishers Associates 172; Random House Of Canada 224; Reference Service 173; Revisionist 175; Rutgers University 176; Scarecrow 179; Schenkman 249; Sidran, The 181; Signature 182; Singer Media 182; South End 184; Spectrum 185; Spinsters Ink 186; Still Waters 188; Sulzburger & Graham 189; Sunflower University 250; Swan-Raven 190; Teachers College 191; Temple University 191; Tenth Avenue Editions 276; Texas A&M University 192; Third World 193; Times 195; Times Change 268; Transnational 195; Turtle 268; Twayne 196; 2M Communications 276; Umbrella 227; United Church (UCPH), The 228; University Of Idaho 199; University of Arizona 198; University of Arizona 198; University of Manitoba 228; University of Massachusetts 199; University of Oklahoma 201; University of Ottawa , The 228; University of Tennessee, The 202; University of Texas 202; Verso 229; Victor 204; Victory House 250; Vista 250; Volcano 268; White Pine 208; Wiley & Sons, John 209; Williamson 209; Windflower Communications 230; Wingbow 269; Women's 230; Yes International 252; Zoland 212; HMS 219; ABC-CLIO 62; Beacon 79; Clarity 259; Family Album, The 111; McFarland 144; Probe 265; Stillpoint 188; University of Kentucky 202.

Young Adult. Archway Paperbacks/Minstrel Books 73; Atheneum Books For Young Readers 74; Bale 77; Barron's Educational Series 79; Cliffs Notes 98; Cobblehill 98; College Board, The 98; Davenport, May 104; Deaconess 105; Dial Books For Young Readers 106; Enslow 109; Falcon 240; Fitzhenry & Whiteside 218; Group 119; Group's Hands-On™ Bible Curriculum 119; Hendrick-Long 123; Houghton Mifflin 125; Hunter House 242; Lucas-Evans 274; McElderry, Margaret K. 144; Partners in Publishing 265; Perfection Learning 265; Philomel 166; Rosen 175; Tyndale House 196; Walker 205; Ward Hill 206; Watts, Franklin 206.

General Index

Can't find a listing? Check the Changes '94-'95 at the end of each section: Book Publishers, page 277; Consumer Publications, page 667; Trade Journals, page 822; Scriptwriting Markets, page 869; Syndicates, page 882; Greeting Card Publishers, page 892; and Contests, page 939.

Canadian Postage by the Page

The following chart is for the convenience of Canadian writers sending domestic mail and American writers sending a SAE with International Reply Coupons (IRCs) or Canadian stamps for return of a manuscript from a Canadian publisher.

For complete postage assistance, use in conjunction with the U.S. Postage by the Page (see inside front cover). Remember that manuscripts returning from the U.S. to Canada will take a U.S. stamped envelope although the original manuscript was sent with Canadian postage. The reverse applies to return envelopes sent by American writers to Canada; they must be accompanied with IRCs or Canadian postage.

In a #10 envelope, you can have up to five pages for 43¢ (on manuscripts within Canada) or 50¢ (on manuscripts going to the U.S.). If you enclose a SASE, four pages is the limit. If you use 10×13 envelopes, send one page less than indicated on the chart.

IRC's are worth 43¢ Canadian postage and 50¢ U.S. postage but cost 95¢ to buy in the U.S. and $1.40 to buy in Canada. (Hint to U.S. writers: If you live near the border or have a friend in Canada, stock up on Canadian stamps. Not only are they more convenient than IRCs, they are cheaper.)

Canada Post designations for types of mail are:

Standard Letter Mail
Minimum size: 9cm × 14cm (3⁹⁄₁₆″ × 5½″); Maximum size: 15cm × 24.5cm (5⅞″ × 9⅝″); Maximum thickness: 5mm (³⁄₁₆″)

Oversize Letter Mail
(Exceeds any measurement for Standard)
Maximum size: 27cm ×38cm (10⅞″ ×15″); Maximum thickness: 2cm (¹³⁄₁₆″)

International Letter Mail
Minimum size: 9cm × 14cm (3⅝″ × 5½″); Maximum size: Length + width + depth 90cm (36″); Greatest dimension must not exceed 60cm (24″)

Insurance: To U.S.—45¢ for each $100 coverage to the maximum coverage of $1,000. Within Canada—$1 for first $100 coverage; 45¢ for each additional $100 coverage to a maximum coverage of $1,000. International—65¢ for each $100 coverage to the maximum coverage allowed by country of destination. (Not accepted by all countries.)
Registered Mail: $3.05 plus postage (air or surface—Canadian destination). Legal proof of mailing provided. No indemnity coverage. International destination: $5.15 plus postage. Fee includes fixed indemnity of $40.
Security Registered Mail: Within Canada—$5.30 for the first $250 indemnity; 45¢ for each additional $100 to a maximum of $5,000. (Plus appropriate postage.)* To U.S.—$5.30 for the first $100 indemnity; 45¢ for each additional $100 to a maximum of $1,000. (Plus appropriate postage.)

* Acknowledgement of receipt (Canadian or U.S. destination) 88¢ at time of mailing or $1.55 after mailing (Canadian destination only).